The Old Testament
World

• Persepolis

PERSIS

N GULF

Palestine in the Time of David

Encyclopedia
of the Bible

Encyclopedia
of the Bible

VOLUME 1 **A–I**

Walter A. Elwell

General Editor

Associate Editors
Peter C. Craigie
J. D. Douglas
Robert Guelich
R. K. Harrison
Thomas E. McComiskey

Assistant Editors

Barry J. Beitzel
H. Douglas Buckwalter
Walter R. Hearn
Virginia K. Hearn
James S. McClanahan
Robert L. Morrison
Stephen Taylor
R. Milton Winter
Ronald F. Youngblood

MARSHALL PICKERING

Marshall Morgan and Scott
Marshall Pickering
34–42 Cleveland Street, London, W1P 5FB. U.K.

ISBN: 0-551-01970-0 Volume 1
         0-551-02052-0 Volume 2

First published in the UK 1990
by Marshall Morgan and Scott Publications Ltd
Pickering and Inglis Ltd
Part of Marshall Pickering Holdings Group

Portions of the text of this volume were originally prepared by
Tyndale House Publishers, Inc., and have been used with
permission.

Printed in the United States of America

Preface

Almost fifty years ago (1941) Alfred North Whitehead lamented the crumbling moral values of his day with the observation, "There is no doubt of it. One sees it in two obvious ways: the generation now growing up does not recognize either quotations from or allusions to the Bible; and the classical tradition is equally on the wane." A Gallup survey conducted in 1978 showed that matters had not since improved. Although 84 percent of the general public thought the Ten Commandments are still valid, more than half could not name even five of them. When asked which of four listed statements Jesus made to Nicodemus, 44 percent did not know and 14 percent said, "Take up thy bed and walk." More than half the general public read the Bible less than once a month or not at all.

Why is this? No doubt the increasing secularization of our society, with the attendant loss of faith in the church, is a large part of the answer, but there is more to it than that. To many people the Bible is just too hard to understand—both the language and the concepts are out of reach for them. The problem of language has largely been solved by the many modern translations that are now available. The phenomenal success of the *Living Bible* is testimony to the hunger that people have to read a Bible in simple, everyday language. The problem of making ancient concepts understandable to moderns is a bit more difficult. To begin with, the Bible itself was not all written at the same time, but spans at least a thousand years. Add to that the passage of the last two thousand years, and one sees the difficulty. How can concepts drawn from ancient civilizations, written in obsolete languages, in the context of cultures long dead, be made vibrant and understandable for today's world?

This Bible encyclopedia is an attempt to solve that problem. It is designed to be a bridge between the past and the present, a mine, a source of information about those days long past that opens them up to us. It is not meant to replace the Bible; far from it. It is meant to be read alongside the Bible to clarify and illuminate the text of Scripture for the modern reader, so that its truths can be assimilated by the people of today. They might still choose to ignore its teaching as Whitehead lamented and Gallup observed, but it need not be any longer for the reason that the Bible cannot be understood.

There is yet another compelling reason for producing a Bible encyclopedia of this sort. To the writers of this encyclopedia the Bible is not just a collection of ancient writings, parallel to those of Hammurabi or Aristotle. It is the very word of God himself. Surprisingly, the same Gallup poll that revealed the appalling ignorance of the Bible also disclosed that only 23 percent of the general public thought the Bible is simply a collection of ancient religious writings, with 42 percent willing to say that it is the "word of God and is *not* mistaken in its statement and teachings." But whether the idea is popular or not, the fact remains that to the orthodox Christian believer the Bible is the Word of God, being our only infallible rule of faith and practice. This compels us to learn all that we can about it so that what God communicated to his people of old and through his Son Jesus Christ may be fully understood today.

The editors of this encyclopedia asked themselves what kinds of information are needed to accomplish the task of making the Bible understandable for today. Many answers were given—far more than could be incorporated into a two-volume work—so the list was narrowed to a dozen:

1. It was felt that the contents of all the books of the Bible should be discussed. Consequently, there are mini-commen-

taries on each book, dealing with the author, background, data and place of writing, purpose, theological teaching, and content. Not all the books require all of this, but the essential information is there.

2. There is a heavy emphasis on the theological content of the Bible, comprising virtually a textbook of biblical theology. Articles in the encyclopedia cover such topics as the being and attributes of God; the names of God; the life and teaching of Jesus Christ; Christology; the Holy Spirit; eschatology; the church; sin; salvation; and the doctrine of creation.

3. Comprehensive articles cover the general life and times of the biblical world, including civil law and justice; criminal law and punishment; courts and trials; coins; money and banking; trades and occupations; travel and transportation; writing and books; medicine and medical practice; music and musical instruments; arms and warfare; and homes and dwellings. In addition, there are extensive general articles on animals, birds, plants, and minerals, metals, and precious stones.

4. The nations surrounding Israel and the cities that played a significant role in biblical history are discussed: Egypt, Syria, Babylon, Assyria, and Rome. This provides the background information needed to understand what was happening in Israel or the church at any given time.

5. Persons mentioned in the Bible are discussed, from the most significant to the least important. All of this was done from scratch, using the Hebrew and Greek texts, and it turned out to be an incredibly complex undertaking. In some cases almost a week was spent trying to unravel just one relatively small family. Significant people who are not mentioned in the Bible are also discussed, but such references are kept to a minimum.

6. Extensive historical entries are also included, covering every phase of Israel's and Judah's history and chronology. In addition there are biographies of significant people, such as Paul, Peter, John, Abraham, Moses, David, Solomon, Herod and his family, and the Caesars.

7. Religious practices and groups are treated at length—feasts and festivals, priests, prophets, Sadducees, Pharisees, sacrifices, offerings, Judaism, the temple, the Law, the religion of Israel, and various pagan religious practices.

8. The Bible as a document is surveyed. This includes canon, text, languages, inspiration, writing, and hermeneutics.

9. Selective current scholarly opinion is presented. It is not possible to deal with everything, but such current theories or problems as redaction criticism, form criticism, the synoptic Gospels, the documentary hypothesis, and tradition criticism are covered.

10. The social customs of Bible times are discussed, including burial customs, family life and relations, fashion and dress, marriage customs, food and food preparation.

11. Geographical information is included, much of it to be found in the articles dealing with cities and countries, but some of it standing on its own, such as articles about Palestine, the Mount of Olives, Sinai, the Jordan River, the Sea of Galilee, and the Wilderness.

12. Archaeology, both as a subject in its own right and the results that derive from it, is treated.

Needless to say, the preceding list does not include everything that is treated in this encyclopedia, but it does give the reader a good idea of what will be found here. The editors tried to touch upon every significant thing that would be of any consequence in understanding the Bible.

A few of the additional distinctives that characterize this work could be mentioned at this point. Select bibliographies of works in the English language are included for further study, if the reader is so inclined. A system of cross-references moving from minor to major articles will aid the reader in pursuing a given topic in full. One feature that we trust will be helpful is the inclusion of more than thirty omnibus articles, where many related items are discussed in one place so the reader will not have to leaf through numerous pages to cover a specific topic. Let a single example, that of trades and occupations, suffice; every item related to this topic is to be found in one convenient place. Subjects that are secondarily related to them, such as industry, commerce, travel, transportation, and money are indicated (with cross-references) for further study. Extensive Scripture references are to be found so that the biblical testimony can be examined at length. Appropriate illustrations accompany many of the major articles to provide visual enrichment of the topic. These illustrations range from geography, archaeology, and animals to persons, religious artifacts, and documents. The entire work is written so that laypeople can understand it. For this reason technical jargon is avoided wherever possible; Greek and Hebrew words are transliterated; extensive scholarly argumentation is kept to a minimum; and unobtainable or foreign language journals and books are not cited. It was the editors' desire that what is found in this encyclopedia be accessible to the average layperson, in such a way that it can be readily assimilated. It is hoped that scholars will find the work satisfactory for their purposes as well, but the encyclopedia is not written with them primarily in mind; except insofar as the content was scrutinized for accuracy. Finally, the entire project is written from an evangelical point of view. This means that a conservative stance is taken on critical issues and that the biblical text is handled in such a way as to reflect its verbally inspired nature.

Special care was exercised in the production of this encyclopedia in order to make it as accurate as possible. The editors established a system whereby each article went through a lengthy series of both writing and editorial steps. In some instances it was no longer possible to assign only one name to an article. When this happened, any attribution was left off; the reader may assume that article is the joint product of several writers and editors. When only one or two individuals were primarily responsible, their names were retained at the end of the article. As a matter of course, brief articles are not attributed, although they are the work of a single author.

It is not possible to mention all of the people who had a hand in this project during ten years, but some names stand out and we are deeply grateful for all of the time and energy they have put into this over the years—Allan Fisher, Edythe Draper, Chandler Barnes, Dr. William Kerr, Barbara Dismeier, Martha Myers, Mary Lou McCurdy, David Hall, Donald Keeney, Maria Bulgarello, Dan Malda, Lisa Ramsey-Hershberger, and Randy Tucker.

It is with humble thanks to God that this Bible encyclopedia is now presented to the public. If it helps anyone to understand God's Word better, to love God more fervently, to serve Christ more single-mindedly, or to experience the truth of the Christian faith in a more vital way, then the prayers of the editors and writers will have been answered. We are better people for having done this work, and we trust that the reader will similarly benefit by entering into our labors.

Contributors

Alden, Robert L. Ph.D., Hebrew Union College. Professor of Old Testament, Denver Seminary, Denver, Colorado.

Alexander, Ralph H. Th.D., Dallas Theological Seminary. Professor of Hebrew Scripture, Western Conservative Baptist Seminary, Portland, Oregon.

Allen, Leslie C. Ph.D., University of London. Professor of Old Testament, Fuller Theological Seminary, Pasadena, California.

Allen, Ronald B. Th.D., Dallas Theological Seminary. Chairman, Division of Biblical Studies; Professor of Hebrew Scripture, Western Baptist Seminary, Portland, Oregon.

Archer, Gleason L. Ph.D., Harvard University. Professor Emeritus Old Testament and Semitic Languages, Trinity Evangelical Divinity School, Deerfield, Illinois.

Aune, David E. Ph.D., University of Chicago. Professor of Religious Studies, Saint Xavier College, Chicago, Illinois.

Babcock, James F. M.Div., Trinity Evangelical Divinity School. Senior Technical Training Instructor, Gould Inc., Information Systems Computer Systems Division, Greenbelt, Maryland.

Barabas, Steven. Th.D., Princeton Theological Seminary. Sometime Professor Emeritus of Theology, Wheaton College, Wheaton, Illinois.

Barber, Cyril J. D.Min., Talbot Theological Seminary. Counselor, Insight for Living, California.

Barker, Kenneth L. Ph.D., Dropsie College for Hebrew and Cognate Learning. Academic Dean and Professor of Old Testament Literature and Exegesis, Capitol Bible Seminary, Lanham, Maryland.

Bass, Clarence B. Ph.D., University of Edinburgh. Professor of Theology and Ethics, Bethel Theological Seminary, St. Paul, Minnesota.

Baylis, Albert H. Th.D., Dallas Theological Seminary. Chairman, Department of Theology, Multnomah School of the Bible, Portland, Oregon.

Beckman, L. David. Th.D., Dallas Theological Seminary. Chancellor, Professor of Biblical Studies, Colorado Christian College; Pastor, Windsor Gardens Community Church, Denver, Colorado.

Beitzel, Barry J. Ph.D., Dropsie University. Associate Dean of Education and Professor of Old Testament and Semitic Languages, Trinity Evangelical Divinity School, Deerfield, Illinois.

Benton, W. Wilson, Jr. Ph.D., University of Edinburgh. Senior Minister, The Kirk of the Hills Presbyterian Church, St. Louis, Missouri.

Bilezikian, Gilbert. Th.D., Boston University. Professor of Biblical Studies, Wheaton College, Wheaton, Illinois.

Blaiklock, E. M. Ph.D., University of Auckland. Sometime Professor Emeritus of Classics, University of Auckland, New Zealand.

Blankenbaker, George. Ph.D., Claremont Graduate School. Vice President and Academic Dean, Associate Professor of Religious Studies, Westmont College, Claremont, California.

Bodey, Richard Allen. D.Min., Trinity Evangelical Divinity School. Associate Professor of Practical Theology, Trinity Evangelical Divinity School, Deerfield, Illinois.

Borchert, Gerald L. Ph.D., Princeton Theological Seminary; LL.B., University of Alberta Law School. Professor of New Testament Interpretation, Southern Baptist Theological Seminary, Louisville, Kentucky.

Brauch, Manfred T. Ph.D., McMaster University, Ontario. Maxwell Professor of Biblical Theology, Eastern Baptist Theological Seminary, Philadelphia, Pennsylvania.

Brown, Colin. Ph.D., University of Bristol. Professor of Systematic Theology, Fuller Theological Seminary, Pasadena, California.

Bruce, F. F. M.A., Universities of Aberdeen, Cambridge, Manchester. Emeritus Professor, University of Manchester, England.

Buckwalter, H. Douglas. M.A., Wheaton College. Doctoral student, University of Aberdeen, Scotland.

Buehler, William W. D.Theol., University of Basel. Professor of Biblical and Theological Studies, Gordon College, Wenham, Massachusetts.

Burge, Gary M. Ph.D., King's College, Aberdeen University. Department of Philosophy and Religion, North Park Theological Seminary, Chicago, Illinois.

Bush, Frederic W. Ph.D., Brandeis University. Associate Professor of Old Testament, Fuller Theological Seminary, Pasadena, California.

Campbell, Donald K. Th.D., Dallas Theological Seminary. President and Professor of Bible Exposition, Dallas Theological Seminary, Dallas, Texas.

Cannon, George E. Ph.D., Fuller Theological Seminary. Professor of New Testament, Bethel Theological Seminary, St. Paul, Minnesota.

Carlson, David C. Ph.D., University of Aberdeen. Associate Professor of Philosophy and Religion, Franklin College, Franklin, Indiana.

Carr, G. Lloyd. Ph.D., Boston University. Professor of Biblical and Theological Studies; Chairman, Division of Humanities, Gordon College, Wenham, Massachusetts.

Cartledge, Samuel. Ph.D., University of Chicago. Emeritus Professor of New Testament, Columbia Theological Seminary, Decatur, Georgia.

Ceperley, Gordon G. Th.M., Dallas Theological Seminary. Professor of Bible, Philadelphia College of the Bible, Langhorne, Pennsylvania.

Chamblin, J. Knox. Th.D., Union Theological Seminary in Virginia. Professor of New Testament, Reformed Theological Seminary, Jackson, Mississippi.

Cole, R. Alan. Ph.D., Dublin University. Federal Secretary, Church Missionary Society of Australia.

Congdon, Roger Douglass. Th.D., Dallas Theological Seminary. Professor of Bible, Multnomah School of the Bible, Portland, Oregon.

Coppenger, Mark T. Ph.D., Vanderbilt University. Pastor, First Baptist Church, El Dorado, Arkansas.

Craigie, Peter C. Ph.D., McMaster University. Formerly Dean, Faculty of Humanities, Calgary, Alberta, Canada.

Culver, Robert D. Th.D., Grace Theological Seminary. Freelance Author and Visiting Professor of Theology, Winnipeg Theological Seminary, Manitoba, Canada.

Cundall, Arthur E. B.D., London University. Principal, Bible College of Victoria, Australia.

Davids, Peter H. Ph.D., University of Manchester. Adjunct Professor of New Testament, Regent College, Vancouver, British Columbia, Canada.

de Vries, Paul H. Ph.D., University of Virginia. Associate Professor of Philosophy and Coordinator of General Education, Wheaton College, Wheaton, Illinois.

DeVries, Carl E. Ph.D., University of Chicago. Retired, The Oriental Institute, University of Chicago. Research Associate, The Oriental Institute, University of Chicago. Retired.

DeYoung, James C. Th.D., Free University of Amsterdam. Professor of New Testament, Reformed Theological Seminary, Jackson, Mississippi.

Demarest, Bruce A. Ph.D., University of Manchester. Professor of Systematic Theology, Denver Seminary, Denver, Colorado.

Dillard, Raymond B. Ph.D., Dropsie University. Professor of Old Testament Language and Literature, Westminster Theological Seminary, Philadelphia, Pennsylvania.

Douglas, J. D. Ph.D., Hartford Seminary Foundation. Editor and writer.

Dunn, James D. G. Ph.D., Cambridge University. Professor of Divinity, University of Durham, England.

Dyrness, William A. D.Theol., Strasbourg University. President and Professor of Theology, New College—Berkeley, Berkeley, California.

Earle, Ralph. Th.D., Gordon Divinity School. Emeritus Professor of New Testament, Nazarene Theological Seminary, Kansas City, Missouri.

Contributors

Ecklebarger, Kermit A. M.A., Wheaton College. Associate Professor of New Testament, Denver Seminary, Denver, Colorado.

Elwell, Walter A. Ph.D., University of Edinburgh. Professor of Biblical and Theological Studies, Wheaton College Graduate School, Wheaton, Illinois.

Erickson, Millard J. Ph.D., Northwestern University. Dean, Professor of Theology, Bethel Theological Seminary, St. Paul, Minnesota.

Ericson, Norman R. Ph.D., University of Chicago. Professor of New Testament; Chairman, Biblical, Theological, and Archaeological Studies, Wheaton College, Wheaton, Illinois.

Fackler, Mark. Ph.D., University of Illinois. Assistant Professor of Communication, Wheaton College, Wheaton, Illinois.

Farrell, Hobert K. Ph.D., Boston University. Professor of Biblical Studies, LeTourneau College, Longview, Texas.

Feinberg, Charles L. Th.D., Dallas Theological Seminary; Ph.D., Johns Hopkins University. Dean Emeritus and Professor Emeritus of Old Testament, Talbot Theological Seminary, La Mirada, California.

Field, David H. B.A., University of Cambridge. Vice-Principal, Oak Hill College, London, England.

Finley, Harvey E. Ph.D., Johns Hopkins University. Professor of Old Testament, Nazarene Theological Seminary, Kansas City, Missouri.

Fisher, Milton C. Ph.D., Brandeis University. Professor of Old Testament and Academic Dean, Reformed Episcopal Seminary, Philadelphia, Pennsylvania.

Foulkes, Francis. B.D., Oxford. Warden, St. John's College, Auckland, New Zealand.

Fowler, Paul B. Ph.D., University of Edinburgh. Professor of New Testament, Columbia Graduate School of Bible and Missions, Columbia, South Carolina.

Gaffin, Richard B., Jr. Th.D., Westminster Theological Seminary. Professor of Systematic Theology, Westminster Theological Seminary, Philadelphia, Pennsylvania.

Gerig, Wesley L. Ph.D., University of Iowa. Chairperson of the Division of Biblical Studies and Professor of Bible and Theology, Fort Wayne Bible College, Fort Wayne, Indiana.

Goldberg, Louis. Th.D., Grace Theological Seminary. Professor of Theology and Jewish Studies, Moody Bible Institute, Chicago, Illinois.

Guelich, Robert. D. Theol., University of Hamburg. Professor of New Testament, Fuller Theological Seminary, Pasadena, California.

Guthrie, Donald. Ph.D., University of London. Visiting Lecturer, London Bible College, London, England.

Haik, Paul S. Th.D., Dallas Theological Seminary. Professor of Bible and Chairman, Department of Bible, Moody Bible Institute, Chicago, Illinois.

Harris, J. Gordon. Ph.D., Southern Baptist Seminary. Vice President for Academic Affairs, North American Baptist Seminary, Sioux Falls, South Dakota.

Harrison, R. K. Ph.D., University of London; D.D. (Hon.), Huron College, University of Western Ontario. Emeritus Professor of Old Testament Studies, Wycliffe College, University of Toronto, Ontario, Canada.

Hearn, Walter R. Ph.D., University of Illinois. Editor, American Scientific Affiliation Newsletter and Adjunct Professor of Science, New College for Advanced Christian Studies, Berkeley, California.

Hearn, Virginia K. B.A., Otterbein College. Editor; adjunct professor of communications, New College for Advanced Studies, Berkeley, California.

Helm, Paul. B.A., Oxford University. Senior Lecturer in Philosophy, University of Liverpool, England.

Henry, Carl F. H. Ph.D., Boston University. Lecturer-At-Large, World Division, Monrovia, California.

Hensley, C. L. V. Ph.D., University of Liverpool.

Hensley, Wayne C. Ph.D., University of Minnesota. Professor of Speech Communication, Bethel College, St. Paul, Minnesota.

Hill, Andrew E. Ph.D., University of Michigan. Assistant Professor of Old Testament, Wheaton College, Wheaton, Illinois.

Hoehner, Harold W. Ph.D., Cambridge University. Chairman and Professor of New Testament Literature and Exegesis; Director of Th.D. Studies, Dallas Theological Seminary, Dallas, Texas.

Hoffmeier, James K. Ph.D., University of Toronto. Associate Professor of Archaeology and Old Testament, Wheaton College, Wheaton, Illinois.

Holloman, Henry W. Th.D., Dallas Theological Seminary. Professor of Systematic Theology, Talbot School of Theology, La Mirada, California.

Holmes, Arthur F. Ph.D., Northwestern University. Professor of Philosophy, Wheaton College, Wheaton, Illinois.

Hopper, Mary. D.M.A., University of Iowa. Assistant Professor of Music, Wheaton College, Wheaton, Illinois.

House, H. Wayne. Th.D., Concordia Theological Seminary; J.D., O.W. Coburn School of Law. Assistant Professor of Systematic Theology, Dallas Theological Seminary, Dallas, Texas.

Houston, James H. D.Phil., Oxford University. Professor of Spiritual Theology, Regent College, Vancouver, British Columbia, Canada.

Howe, E. Margaret. Ph.D., University of Manchester. Professor of Religious Studies, Western Kentucky University, Bowling Green, Kentucky.

Huey, F. B., Jr. Ph.D., Southwestern Baptist Theological Seminary. Professor of Old Testament, Southwestern Baptist Theological Seminary, Fort Worth, Texas.

Hughes, Philip Edgcumbe. Th.D., Australian College of Theology; D.Litt., University of Cape Town. Visiting Professor, Westminster Theological Seminary, Philadelphia; Associate Rector, St. John's Episcopal Church, Huntingdon Valley, Pennsylvania.

Huttar, David K. Ph.D., Brandeis University. Professor of Bible and Greek, Nyack College, Nyack, New York.

Inch, Morris A. Ph.D., Boston University. Executive Director, Institute of Holy Land Studies, Jerusalem, Israel.

James, Edgar C. Th.D., Dallas Theological Seminary. Professor of Bible and Theology, Moody Bible Institute, Chicago, Illinois.

Jewett, Paul K. Ph.D., Harvard University. Professor of Systematic Theology, Fuller Theological Seminary, Pasadena, California.

Jocz, Jakob. Ph.D., University of Edinburgh. Sometime Professor Emeritus of Systematic Theology, Wycliffe College, University of Toronto, Toronto, Ontario, Canada.

Johnson, Alan F. Th.D., Dallas Theological Seminary. Professor of New Testament and Christian Ethics, Wheaton College, Wheaton, Illinois.

Jordan, Gregory D. Ph.D., Hebrew Union College—Jewish Institute of Religion. Assistant Professor, Department of Bible and Religion (Old Testament), King College, Bristol, Tennessee.

Kaufman, Paul L. M.A., Wheaton College. Sometime Professor of New Testament Language and Literature, Western Conservative Baptist Seminary, Portland, Oregon.

Kistemaker, Simon J. Th.D., Free University of Amsterdam. Professor of New Testament, Reformed Theological Seminary, Jackson, Mississippi.

Klooster, Fred H. Th.D., Free University of Amsterdam. Professor Emeritus of Systematic Theology, Calvin Theological Seminary, Grand Rapids, Michigan.

Klotz, John W. Ph.D., University of Pittsburgh. Director of Graduate Studies, Concordia Seminary, St. Louis, Missouri.

Klug, Eugene F. A. D.Theol., Free University of Amsterdam. Professor of Systematic Theology, Concordia Theological Seminary, Fort Wayne, Indiana.

Knight, George W., III. Th.D., Free University of Amsterdam. Chairman of New Testament Department, Covenant Theological Seminary, St. Louis, Missouri.

Ladd, George E. Ph.D., Harvard University. Sometime Professor Emeritus of New Testament Theology and Exegesis, Fuller Theological Seminary, Pasadena, California.

Lake, Donald M. Ph.D., University of Iowa. Associate Professor of Bible, Wheaton College, Wheaton, Illinois.

Lane, William L. Th.D., Harvard University. Professor of Religious Studies, Western Kentucky University, Bowling Green, Kentucky.

Larson, Gary N. M.A., Wheaton Graduate School. Assistant Professor of Communications, Wheaton College, Wheaton, Illinois.

LaSor, William Sanford. Ph.D., Dropsie College; Th.D., University of Southern California. Professor Emeritus of Old Testament, Fuller Theological Seminary, Pasadena, California.

Launstein, Donald H. Th.M., Dallas Theological Seminary. Pastor, Wortley Baptist Church, London, Ontario, Canada.

Liefeld, Walter L. Ph.D., Columbia University. Distinguished Professor of New Testament, Trinity Evangelical Divinity School, Deerfield, Illinois.

Contributors

Lindsey, F. Duane. Th.D., Dallas Theological Seminary. Assistant Professor of Systematic Theology.

Long, John E. Ph.D., Brandeis University. Associate Professor of Religion, Western Kentucky University, Bowling Green, Kentucky.

Lyon, Robert W. Ph.D., St. Andrews University. Professor of New Testament Interpretation, Asbury Theological Seminary, Wilmore, Kentucky.

McAlister, Paul K. D.Min., Bethel Theological Seminary. Professor of Theology and Social Ethics, Minnesota Bible College, Rochester, Minnesota.

McClanahan, James S. Th.D., Union Theological Seminary in Virginia.

McComiskey, Thomas E. Ph.D., Brandeis University. Professor of Old Testament and Semitic Languages, Trinity Evangelical Divinity School, Deerfield, Illinois.

McConville, J. Gordon. Ph.D., Queen's University, Belfast. Lecturer in Old Testament and Course Leader, Trinity College, Bristol, England.

McDonald, H. D. Ph.D., D.D., University of London. Formerly Vice-Principal, London Bible College, London, England.

MacDonald, William Graham. Th.D., Southern Baptist Theological Seminary. Freelance author, Front Royal, Virginia.

McNeely, Richard I. Th.D., Dallas Theological Seminary; Ph.D., University of Southern California. Writer, Educational Consultant, Missoula, Montana.

McRay, John R. Ph.D., University of Chicago. Professor of New Testament and Archaeology, Wheaton College, Wheaton, Illinois.

Mare, W. Harold. Ph.D., University of Pennsylvania. Professor of New Testament, Covenant Theological Seminary, St. Louis, Missouri.

Marshall, I. Howard. Ph.D., University of Aberdeen. Professor of New Testament Exegesis, University of Aberdeen, Scotland.

Mason, James L. Ph.D., University of Southern California. Retired Full Professor of Speech Communication, and Adjunct Professor in Greek and Homiletic Courses at Bethel College and Seminary, St. Paul, Minnesota. Semi-retired and Preaching Minister, Oakmont Community Church, Santa Rosa, California.

Mattingly, Gerald L. Ph.D., Southern Baptist Theological Seminary. Professor of Old Testament and Archaeology, Cincinnati Christian Seminary, Cincinnati, Ohio.

Merrill, Eugene H. Ph.D., Columbia University. Professor of Semitics and Old Testament Studies, Dallas Theological Seminary, Dallas, Texas.

Mickelsen, A. Berkeley. Ph.D., University of Chicago. Professor Emeritus of Biblical Interpretation, Bethel Theological Seminary, St. Paul, Minnesota.

Miller, Douglas J. Ph.D., Claremont Graduate School and University Center. Professor of Christian Social Ethics, Eastern Baptist Theological Seminary, Philadelphia, Pennsylvania.

Morris, Leon L. Ph.D., University of Cambridge. Formerly Principal, Ridley College, Melbourne, Australia.

Morrison, Robert L. M.A., Wheaton College. Ph.D. candidate, Boston University.

Motyer, Alec. B.D., University of Dublin. Minister of Christ Church, Westbourne, Bournemouth, England.

Motyer, Stephen. M.Litt., University of Bristol. Formerly New Testament Tutor, Oak Hill College, London, England.

Mounce, Robert H. Ph.D., University of Aberdeen. President, Whitworth College, Spokane, Washington.

Norman, James Garth Gifford. B.D., M.Th. Studied at Spurgeon's College, London. Minister of the following Baptist churches: Stourport-on-Severn, Worcestershire, England; George Road, Erdington, Birmingham, England; Shettleston, Glasgow, Scotland; Rosyth, Fife, Scotland.

Osborne, Grant R. Ph.D., University of Aberdeen. Professor of New Testament, Trinity Evangelical Divinity School, Deerfield, Illinois.

Patterson, Richard. Ph.D., University of California—Los Angeles. Chairman, Department of Biblical Studies, Liberty University, Lynchburg, Virginia.

Payne, J. Barton. Ph.D., Princeton Theological Seminary. Sometime Professor of Old Testament, Covenant Theological Seminary, St. Louis, Missouri.

Perkin, Hazel W. M.A., McGill. Principal, St. Clement's School, Toronto, Canada.

Piper, John. D.Theol., University of Munich. Senior Pastor, Bethlehem Baptist Church, Minneapolis, Minnesota.

Potts, Austin H. Ph.D., Dropsie College. Professor of Bible, Philadelphia College of Bible, Langhorne, Pennsylvania.

Powell, Ralph E. Th.D., Northern Baptist Theological Seminary. Distinguished Professor of Theology Emeritus, North American Baptist Seminary, Sioux Falls, South Dakota.

Price, James D. Ph.D., Dropsie College for Hebrew and Cognate Learning. Professor of Old Testament, Temple Baptist Seminary, Chattanooga, Tennessee.

Rainey, Anson F. Ph.D., Brandeis University. Professor of Ancient Near Eastern Cultures and Semitic Linguistics, Tel Aviv University, Ramat Aviv, Israel.

Ramm, Bernard L. Ph.D., University of Southern California. Professor of Christian Theology, American Baptist Seminary of the West, Berkeley, California.

Reymond, Robert L. Ph.D., Bob Jones University. Professor of Systematic Theology and Apologetics, Covenant Theological Seminary, St. Louis, Missouri.

Rupprecht, Arthur. Ph.D., University of Pennsylvania. Professor of Classical Languages, Wheaton College, Wheaton, Illinois.

Sacks, Stuart D. Th.D., Southwest Theological Seminary. Senior Pastor, Berith Presbyterian Church, Bryn Mawr, Pennsylvania.

Sailer, William S. S.T.D., Temple University. Professor of Theology, Evangelical School of Theology, Myerstown, Pennsylvania.

Scaer, David P. Th.D., Concordia Seminary, St. Louis. Academic Dean and Professor of Systematic Theology and New Testament, Concordia Theological Seminary, Fort Wayne, Indiana.

Schultz, Richard L. Ph.D., Yale University. Lecturer in Old Testament, Freie Theologische Akademie, Giessen, West Germany.

Schultz, Samuel J. Th.D., Harvard Divinity School. Samuel Robinson Professor Emeritus of Biblical Studies and Theology, Wheaton College, Wheaton, Illinois.

Scott, J. Julius, Jr. Ph.D., University of Manchester. Professor of Biblical and Historical Studies, Wheaton College Graduate School, Wheaton, Illinois.

Scott, Jack B. Ph.D., Dropsie University. Professor of Biblical Studies and Chairman of the Division of Biblical Religion and Philosophy, Belhaven College, Jackson, Mississippi.

Shepherd, Norman. Th.M., Westminster Theological Seminary. Senior Pastor, First Christian Reformed Church, Minneapolis, Minnesota.

Shipps, Kenneth W. Ph.D., Yale University. Vice President for Academic Affairs, Phillips University, Enid, Oklahoma.

Sider, John W. Ph.D., University of Notre Dame. Professor of English, Westmont College, Santa Barbara, California.

Silva, Moisés. Ph.D., University of Manchester. Professor of New Testament, Westminster Theological Seminary, Philadelphia, Pennsylvania.

Smick, Elmer B. Ph.D., Dropsie College for Hebrew and Cognate Learning. Professor of Old Testament, Gordon-Conwell Theological Seminary, South Hamilton, Massachusetts.

Smith, Albert J. Ph.D., University of Chicago. Professor of Biology, Wheaton College, Wheaton, Illinois.

Smith, Ralph L. Th.D., Southwestern Baptist Theological Seminary. Professor of Old Testament, Southwestern Baptist Theological Seminary, Fort Worth, Texas.

Snodgrass, Klyne R. Ph.D., University of St. Andrews, Scotland. Professor of Biblical Literature, North Park Theological Seminary, Chicago, Illinois.

Spender, Robert D. Ph.D., Dropsie University. Associate Professor of Biblical Studies, The King's College, Briarcliff Manor, New York.

Stein, Robert H. Ph.D., Princeton Theological Seminary. Professor of New Testament, Bethel Theological Seminary, St. Paul, Minnesota.

Taylor, Stephen. M.A., Wheaton College. Ph.D. candidate, University of Pennsylvania.

Thompson, John A. Ph.D., University of Cambridge. Former Reader and Chairman of the Department of Middle Eastern Studies, University of Melbourne.

Thomson, J. G. S. S. Ph.D., University of Edinburgh. Minister Emeritus, Church of Scotland.

Tolar, William B. Th.D., Southwestern Baptist Theological Seminary. Dean and Professor of Biblical Backgrounds.

Toon, Peter. D.Phil., Oxford University. Rector of Boxford Parish; Director of Post-Ordination Training, Diocese of St. Edmundsbury and Ipswich.

Contributors

Travis, William. Ph.D., New York University. Professor of Church History, Bethel Theological Seminary, St. Paul, Minnesota.

Turner, George A. Ph.D., Harvard University. Professor of Biblical Literature (Emeritus), Asbury Theological Seminary, Wilmore, Kentucky.

VanGemeren, Willem A. Ph.D., University of Wisconsin. Professor of Old Testament, Reformed Theological Seminary, Jackson, Mississippi.

Van Groningen, Gerard. Ph.D., University of Melbourne, Victoria. President Emeritus, Trinity Christian College, Palos Heights, Illinois.

Vannoy, J. Robert. Th.D., Free University of Amsterdam. Professor of Old Testament, Biblical Theological Seminary, Hatfield, Pennsylvania.

Van Reken, David E. M.D., University of Illinois College of Medicine. Lecturer in Pediatrics, Indiana University School of Medicine, Indianapolis, Indiana.

Vos, Arvin G. Ph.D., University of Toronto. Professor of Philosophy, Department of Philosophy of Religion, Western Kentucky University, Bowling Green, Kentucky.

Vos, Howard F. Th.D., Dallas Theological Seminary; Ph.D., Northwestern University. Professor of History and Archaeology, The King's College, Briarcliff Manor, New York.

Walker, Larry Lee. Ph.D., Dropsie College for Hebrew and Cognate Learning. Professor of Old Testament and Semitic Languages, Mid-America Baptist Theological Seminary, Memphis, Tennessee.

Waltke, Bruce K. Ph.D., Harvard University; Th.D., Dallas Theological Seminary. Professor of Old Testament, Westminster Theological Seminary, Philadelphia, Pennsylvania.

Walton, John H. Ph.D., Hebrew Union College. Assistant Professor of Bible, Moody Bible Institute, Chicago, Illinois.

Wead, David W. D.Theol., Basel University. Senior Minister, First Christian College, Nashville, Tennessee.

Webber, Robert Eugene. Th.D., Concordia. Professor of Theology, Wheaton College, Wheaton, Illinois.

Weigelt, Morris A. Ph.D., Princeton Theological Seminary. Professor of New Testament, Nazarene Theological Seminary, Kansas City, Missouri.

Wenham, Gordon J. Ph.D., King's College, University of London. Senior Lecturer in Religious Studies, The College of St. Paul and St. Mary, Cheltenham, England.

Wessel, Walter W. Ph.D., University of Edinburgh. Professor of New Testament and Greek, Bethel Theological Seminary West, San Diego, California.

Wheaton, David H. M.A., St. John's College, Oxford. Vicar and Honorary Canon of the Cathedral and Abbey Church of St. Albans, Christ Church, Ware, Herts, United Kingdom.

White, R. E. O. M.A., University of Liverpool; B.D., University of London. Formerly Principal, Baptist Theological College of Scotland, Glasgow.

White, William, Jr. Ph.D., Dropsie College for Hebrew and Cognate Learning. President, Nitech Research Corporation, Warrington, Pennsylvania.

Whitlock, Luder G., Jr. D.Min., Vanderbilt University. President, Reformed Theological Seminary, Jackson, Mississippi.

Wilcock, Michael J. B.A., University of Durham. Vicar, St. Nicholas' Church, Durham, England.

Winter, R. Milton. Th.M., Princeton Theological Seminary. Pastor, First Presbyterian Church, Holly Springs, Mississippi.

Wolf, Herbert M. Ph.D., Brandeis University. Associate Professor of Theological Studies, Wheaton College, Wheaton, Illinois.

Woudstra, Marten H. Th.D., Westminster Theological Seminary. Professor of Old Testament Emeritus, Calvin Theological Seminary, Grand Rapids, Michigan.

Yamauchi, Edwin M. Ph.D., Brandeis University. Professor of History, Miami University, Oxford, Ohio.

Yarbrough, Robert W. Ph.D., University of Aberdeen. Associate Professor of Biblical and Theological Studies, Liberty University, Lynchburg, Virginia.

Young, Warren C. Ph.D., Boston University. Distinguished Professor of Theology and Christian Philosophy Emeritus, Northern Baptist Theological Seminary, Lombard, Illinois.

Youngblood, Ronald F. Ph.D., Dropsie College for Hebrew and Cognate Learning. Professor of Old Testament and Hebrew, Bethel Theological Seminary West, San Diego, California.

Abbreviations

General Abbreviations

c.	about, approximately
cf.	compare
ch	chapter (*pl.* chs)
ed	edition, editor (*pl.* eds)
e.g.	for example
et al.	and others
etc.	and so forth
f.	and following (*pl.* ff.)
Gr.	Greek
Heb.	Hebrew
i.e.	that is
km.	kilometers
lit.	literal(ly)
LXX	Septuagint
m.	meters
mg.	margin
MS	manuscript (*pl.* MSS)
MT	Masoretic Text
N,NE	north, northeast
N,NW	north, northwest
NT	New Testament
OT	Old Testament
p	page (*pl.* pp)
S,SE	south, southeast
S,SW	south, southwest
TR	Textus Receptus
v	verse (*pl.* vv)
vol	volume (*pl.* vols)

Books of the Bible

Old Testament

Gn	Genesis
Ex	Exodus
Lv	Leviticus
Nm	Numbers
Dt	Deuteronomy
Jos	Joshua
Jgs	Judges
Ru	Ruth
1 Sm	1 Samuel
2 Sm	2 Samuel
1 Kgs	1 Kings
2 Kgs	2 Kings
1 Chr	1 Chronicles
2 Chr	2 Chronicles
Ezr	Ezra
Neh	Nehemiah
Est	Esther
Jb	Job
Ps(s)	Psalms
Prv	Proverbs
Eccl	Ecclesiastes
Sg	Song of Solomon
Is	Isaiah
Jer	Jeremiah
Lam	Lamentations
Ez	Ezekiel
Dn	Daniel
Hos	Hosea
Jl	Joel
Am	Amos
Ob	Obadiah
Jon	Jonah
Mi	Micah
Na	Nahum
Hb	Habakkuk
Zep	Zephaniah
Hg	Haggai
Zec	Zechariah
Mal	Malachi

New Testament

Mt	Matthew
Mk	Mark
Lk	Luke
Jn	John
Acts	Acts
Rom	Romans
1 Cor	1 Corinthians
2 Cor	2 Corinthians
Gal	Galatians
Eph	Ephesians

Abbreviations

Phil	Philippians
Col	Colossians
1 Thes	1 Thessalonians
2 Thes	2 Thessalonians
1 Tm	1 Timothy
2 Tm	2 Timothy
Ti	Titus
Phlm	Philemon
Heb	Hebrews
Jas	James
1 Pt	1 Peter
2 Pt	2 Peter
1 Jn	1 John
2 Jn	2 John
3 Jn	3 John
Jude	Jude
Rv	Revelation

Extracanonical Literature

Apocryphal Books

Ecclus	Ecclesiasticus
1 Esd	1 Esdras
Jth	Judith
1 Macc	1 Maccabees
2 Macc	2 Maccabees
Wisd of Sol	Wisdom of Solomon

Pseudepigraphal Books

2 Bar	Syriac Apocalypse of Baruch
1 Enoch	Ethiopic Book of Enoch
4 Ezr	4 Ezra
Life AE	Life of Adam and Eve
Pss of Sol	Psalms of Solomon

Dead Sea Scrolls

CD	Cairo (Genizah text of the) Damascus (Document)
1 QM	War Scroll
1 QS	Manual of Discipline
1 QSa	Rule of the Congregation

Early Christian Writings

1 Clem	1 Clement
2 Clem	2 Clement

Bible Versions and Other Sources

Antiq.	Josephus, Antiquities of the Jews
Dio Cassius	Dio Cassius, Roman History
Ep Fest	Athanasius, Festal Letters
HE	Eusebius, Historia Ecclesiastica
KJV	The King James Version
NASB	The New American Standard Bible
NEB	The New English Bible
NIV	The New International Version
Prol Gal	Jerome, Prologue to Galatians
RSV	The Revised Standard Version
Strabo	Strabo, Geography
Tacitus, Hist.	Tacitus, Histories
War	Josephus, The Jewish War

Aa

Aaron. Moses' brother and Israel's first high priest. In the biblical Books of Exodus, Leviticus, and Numbers, Aaron was Moses' spokesman and assistant during the Israelites' exodus from Egypt. Aaron was three years older than Moses and was 83 when they first confronted the pharaoh (Ex 7:7). Their sister Miriam (Nm 26:59) must have been the eldest child, old enough to carry messages when the infant Moses was found by the pharaoh's daughter (Ex 2:1–9). Aaron's mother was Jochebed and his father was Amram, a descendant of the Kohath family of Levi's tribe (Ex 6:18–20).

Aaron and his wife Elisheba had four sons (Ex 6:23), who were to follow him in the priesthood (Lv 1:5). Two of them, Nadab and Abihu, violated God's instructions by performing a sacrilegious act while burning incense, and were burned to death as a result (Lv 10:1–5). The priesthood was then passed on through the other two sons, Eleazar and Ithamar, who also sometimes failed to carry out God's instructions precisely (Lv 10:6–20).

Aaron's prominence in the events of the exodus arose partly from the fact that he was Moses' brother. When Moses tried to avoid becoming Israel's leader on the grounds of a speech impediment, Aaron's ability as a speaker was recognized and used by God (Ex 4:10–16).

Events of Aaron's Life. The Hebrew people were slaves in Egypt at the beginning of Aaron's life. Raised as an Egyptian by one of the pharaoh's daughters, Moses had fled into the Midian desert after killing a cruel Egyptian taskmaster (Ex 1,2). When God sent Moses back as a liberator (Ex 3,4), he also sent Aaron out to meet Moses in the desert (Ex 4:27). Moses was a stranger to his people after so many years of exile, so Aaron made contact with Israel's elders for him (Ex 4:29–31). When Moses and Aaron went to see the pharaoh, God told the Egyptian monarch through the two of them to "let my people go" (Ex 5:1). When the

The garments of a priest (left) and a high priest.

pharaoh made life even more miserable for the Hebrew slaves, God began to show his power to the Egyptian ruler through a series of miracles (Ex 5–12). God performed the first three miracles through Aaron, using a rod (probably a shepherd's staff). The pharaoh had his palace sorcerers do similar tricks with their "magic wands." After God brought a plague of lice over all Egypt, the Egyptian magicians admitted defeat and said, "This is the finger of God" (Ex 8:19). Then God brought on more plagues through Moses, culminating in the death of all the Egyptians' firstborn sons.

Aaron was with Moses (Ex 12:1–28) when God revealed how he would "pass over" the properly marked homes of the Israelites, sparing their children on the night the Egyptian children died. That event was the origin of the Passover feast still observed by Jews today (Ex 13:1–16).

After God led the Israelites to safety and destroyed the pursuing Egyptians, Aaron participated with Moses in governing the people on their long wilderness journey to the Promised Land (Ex 16:1–6). Aaron figures in many incidents recorded in Exodus and Numbers, such as the gathering of manna, the food God miraculously provided (Ex 16:6–36). Later, battling against Amalek's army, Aaron helped hold up Moses' weary arms in prayer to maintain God's blessing (Ex 17:8–16). Although always subordinate to Moses, Aaron seems to have been recognized as an important leader (Ex 18:12). God summoned him to assist when Moses received the Law on Mt Sinai (Ex 19:24). Aaron was among the representatives of the people who ratified God's statutes, the "Book of the Covenant" (Ex 24:1–8). Aaron went with those leaders partway up the holy mountain and saw the vision of the God of Israel (Ex 24:9–11). With Hur, he was left in charge when Moses was with God on the mountaintop (Ex 24:13–18).

Moses was gone for over a month, and in a moment of weakness Aaron gave in to the people's request for an idol to worship. He melted down their gold ornaments to make a golden image of a calf (Ex 32:1–4). (The Israelites had probably been influenced in Egypt by the cult of Apis, a fertility god in the form of a bull.) At first, Aaron seemed to think he might be doing something acceptable to God (Ex 32:5), but things got out of hand and a drunken sex orgy took place around the idol (Ex 32:6). God was angry enough to destroy the people, but Moses interceded, reminding God of his promise to multiply Abraham's descendants (Ex 32:7–14). Moses confronted Aaron furiously about the immorality and idolatry, which Aaron blamed on the people without admitting any guilt of his own (Ex 32:21–24). Although the adulterers were punished by death (Ex 32:25–28) and the whole camp by a plague (Ex 32:35), Aaron was evidently not punished. In a retelling of the events, Moses said that Aaron was in great danger but was spared because he had prayed for him (Dt 9:20).

In their second year of nomadic wilderness life, Aaron helped Moses carry out a census (Nm 1:1–3,17). Eventually, Aaron may have become jealous of Moses' position of leadership, for Miriam and Aaron began to slander their brother, even though the elderly Moses was by then more humble than any man on earth (Nm 12:1–4). God's anger toward the two was averted by Moses' prayer, although Miriam did suffer for her sin (Nm 12:5–15). Aaron again seems to have escaped punishment entirely. With Moses, Aaron opposed a rebellion at Kadesh (Nm 14:1–5). He stood with Moses against a later revolt (Nm 16). When God punished that uprising with a plague, Aaron performed a priestly act of running among the people with burning incense (Nm 16:46–50), and the plague was stopped. After a final incident at Meribah, where the Israelites almost revolted again, God accused Moses and Aaron of having failed to take him at his word and denied them entry into the Promised Land (Nm 20:1–13). Aaron died at the age of 123 on Mt Hor, after Moses had removed his elabo-

The traditional site of place where Aaron died.

rate priestly garments and put them on Aaron's son Eleazar (Nm 20:23–29; 33:38,39).

Aaron and the Priesthood. Because it marked the beginning of the priesthood in Israel, the consecration of Aaron to his office was both instructive and solemn. Nothing was left to human ingenuity; all was precisely commanded of God. There were three ceremonies: washing, clothing, and anointing. When the tabernacle was finished, Aaron and his sons were set apart to the priesthood by washing (to signify purification), clothing with official garments (for beauty and glory), and anointing with oil (to picture the need of empowering by the Spirit; cf. Ex 28; 40:12–15; Lv 8). Aaron thus became the first high priest, serving nearly 40 years. The sumptuous garments of Aaron as high priest underscored the sanctity of the office (Ex 39). All the priests in Israel had special garments (predominantly linen), but Aaron's were even more distinctive (Ex 28:2). He wore a girdle and a breastplate with the names of the 12 tribes of Israel inscribed on it (Ex 28:9,10, 21,29); also in a pouch in the breastplate were the Urim and Thummin, which were used to ascertain the will of God in certain matters (v 30). In addition, he had a turban with a plate of gold upon which was engraved the words "Holy to the Lord." He was the chief mediator between Israel and God. The character of his office was hereditary; this is attested to by his sons' wearing his garments when they succeeded to the office of high priest (Ex 29:29,30; Nm 20:25–28). Although all priests were anointed with oil, the anointing of Aaron and his successors was distinct from that of the ordinary priests (Ex 29:7; 40:12–15; Lv 8:12). Because the priesthood was inherited, all subsequent priests had to trace their ancestry back to Aaron (Ezr 7:1–5; Lk 1:5). Also, a sharp distinction was always drawn between the family of Aaron and the rest of the Levites (cf. Nm 3:4). Thus, the high priest was designated as the "anointed priest" in a special sense (Lv 4:3,5; 6:20,22; 21:10).

Because of Aaron's priestly role, the NT looks back upon him as prefiguring the Messiah of Israel. Jesus Christ was appointed high priest (Heb 3:1,2) in the same way that God chose Aaron (Heb 5:1–4), but he was described as a greater high priest than Aaron (Heb 7:11–28). The writer of Hebrews may have had Aaron in mind when he wrote that "the law appoints men in their weakness as high priests," in contrast with God's Son, "who has been made perfect for ever" (Heb 7:28).

CHARLES L. FEINBERG

See ISRAEL, HISTORY OF; EXODUS, THE; WILDERNESS WANDERINGS; FEASTS AND FESTIVALS OF ISRAEL; PRIESTS AND LEVITES; LEVI, TRIBE OF; AARON'S ROD.

Aaronites. Collective name for the priests who descended from Aaron through his sons Eleazar and Ithamar. The term is used twice in the KJV to refer to 3,700 men who supported David against Saul (1 Chr 12:27) and of whom Zadok later became leader (1 Chr 27:17). Both "house of Aaron" (1 Chr 12:27; Ps 115:10,12; 118:3; 135:19) and "Aaron" (1 Chr 27:17) are used to refer to the Aaronites.

See AARON.

Aaron's Rod. Staff belonging to Moses' brother, Aaron, symbolizing the two brothers' authority in Israel.

When the Israelites were wandering in the wilderness a threat against Moses' and Aaron's leadership was led by Korah, Dathan, and Abiram (Nm 16:1–40). In spite of the Lord's destruction of those rebels and their followers, the rest of the people of Israel turned against Moses and Aaron, saying that they had "killed the people of the Lord" (Nm 16:41). In order to restore respect for the divinely appointed leadership, the Lord told Moses to collect a rod from each tribe and have the leader of the tribe write his name on it. Aaron was told to write his name on the rod of Levi. The rods were placed in the inner room of the tabernacle, in front of the ark (of the covenant). In the morning Aaron's rod had sprouted blossoms and produced ripe almonds. The rod was then kept there as a continual sign to Israel that the Lord had established the authority of Moses and Aaron (Nm 17:1–11; cf Heb 9:4).

Following that incident the people of Israel entered the wilderness of Zin, where there was no water for them and their flocks. Again the people argued with Moses and Aaron. The Lord instructed Moses to get the rod and, in the presence of Aaron and the rest of the people, command a particular rock to bring forth water. Taking the rod, Moses asked dramatically, "Shall we bring forth water for you out of this rock?" and struck the rock twice. Water gushed out and the people drank. Yet Moses and Aaron were forbidden to enter the Promised Land because they did not sanctify the Lord in the people's eyes (Nm 20:12–13). An earlier event had provided evidence that the Lord was able to provide needed water in that manner (Ex 17:1–7).

This rod may have been the same one given to Moses and Aaron before the exodus from Egypt (Ex 4:1–5,17). That rod was instrumental in the events leading to the pharaoh's release of the Israelites. When it became a snake and devoured the rods of the pharaoh's magicians, the superiority of the Lord's power was demonstrated (Ex 7:8–13). It was used to turn the waters of the Nile to blood (Ex 7:14–23) and to bring about the plagues of frogs (Ex 8:1–15) and gnats or lice (Ex 8:16–19). When Moses stretched the rod out over the waters of the Red Sea the Israelites were allowed to pass through on dry land, but the army of Egypt was destroyed (Ex 14).

See AARON.

Ab. Month in the Hebrew calendar, about mid-July to mid-August.

See CALENDARS, ANCIENT AND MODERN.

Abaddon. "Place of destruction," a Hebrew word that occurs six times in the OT, generally referring to the place of the dead (Jb 26:6; 28:22; 31:12; Ps 88:11; Prv 15:11; 27:20). It serves as a synonym for Sheol and is variously translated "hell," "death," "the grave," or "destruction."

The same Hebrew word occurs once in the NT in its Greek equivalent, *Apollyon* (Rv 9:11). Here the idea of destruction is personified as the "angel of the bottomless pit," so the word is translated "destroyer." Abaddon (or Apollyon) was the angel reigning over the realm of the dead, who appeared after the fifth trumpet in John's vision (Rv 9:1).

See SHEOL.

Abagtha. One of the seven eunuchs commanded by King Ahasuerus to bring Queen Vashti to his drunken party (Est 1:10).

Abana. Syrian river (modern Barada) running through the city of Damascus. Although Naaman thought the Abana should be more effective than the Jordan River in curing leprosy, he obeyed the prophet Elisha, washed in the Jordan, and was cured (2 Kgs 5:9–14; "Amana" is alternate textual reading in v 12).

See AMANA.

Abarim. Mountainous area located east of the Jordan River and Dead Sea, and extending northward from the plains of Moab. From the highest point on Mt Nebo, called Pisgah, located in Abarim (2,643 feet), Moses looked into the Promised Land shortly before he died (Dt 32:48–50; 34:1–6).

Abba. Aramaic word for "Father" which is applied to God in Mark 14:36; Romans 8:15; and Galatians 4:6.

See GOD, NAMES OF.

Abda. 1. Adoniram's father. Adoniram was superintendent of public works under King Solomon (1 Kgs 4:6).

2. Shammua's son, who was a Levite leader in Jerusalem after the exile (Neh 11:17). The same father and son are elsewhere identified as Shemaiah and Obadiah (1 Chr 9:16).

Abdeel. Shelemiah's father. Shelemiah was an officer sent by King Jehoiakim of Judah to arrest Jeremiah and Baruch after the king had read (and burned) their prophetic scroll (Jer 36:26).

Abdi. 1. Member of the Merari clan of Levites. Abdi's grandson Ethan was a musician in King David's time (1 Chr 6:44; 15:17).

2. Levite whose son Kish served in King Hezekiah's time (2 Chr 29:12). This Abdi has sometimes been confused with Abdi #1.

3. Member of the Elam clan in Ezra's time. This Abdi is listed as one of the Israelites who

The Abarim mountains.

married a foreign wife after the exile (Ezr 10:26).

Abdi-el. Guni's son, and father of Ahi (1 Chr 5:15). Ahi was a clan leader in Gad's tribe during the reigns of King Jotham of Judah and King Jeroboam II of Israel (1 Chr 5:15–17).

Abdon (Person). 1. Hillel's son who judged Israel for eight years (Jgs 12:13–15). Abdon was a very wealthy man, as indicated by reference to the 70 donkeys he owned.
2. Shashak's son from Benjamin's tribe who lived in Jerusalem (1 Chr 8:23,28).
3. Jeiel's oldest son from Benjamin's tribe who lived in Gibeon. This Abdon is mentioned in Saul's genealogy (1 Chr 8:30; 9:36).
4. Micah's son (2 Chr 34:20), also called Achbor, son of Michah.
See ACHBOR #2.

Abdon (Place). One of four cities in Asher's territory given to the Levites after the conquest of Canaan, the Promised Land (Jos 21:30; 1 Chr 6:74). Abdon is probably the same as Ebron (Jos 19:28). Today Abdon is called Khirbet 'Abdeh.

See LEVITICAL CITIES.

Abednego. One of Daniel's three friends who was sentenced to death by Nebuchadnezzar but was protected in the fiery furnace by an angel (Dn 1:7; 3:12–30).

See SHADRACH, MESHACH, AND ABEDNEGO.

Abel (Person). Second male child of Adam and Eve (Gn 4:2). The meaning of the name in Hebrew is unknown, but *vanity*, *vapor*, and *fragility* have been suggested. More likely the name is related to Sumerian and Akkadian words meaning "son" and was thus used as a generic term for the human race.
Abel's older brother Cain was engaged in agriculture, but Abel himself was a shepherd. Domestication of animals and cultivation of cereal grains or other vegetables indicates an advanced degree of cultural development. When both brothers brought offerings, God accepted Abel's animal sacrifice but rejected Cain's vegetable offering. As a result Cain became jealous of Abel and killed him.
The narrative indicates that Abel's character was more worthy of God's blessing; hence his offering was accepted and Cain's was not (v 7). There is no scriptural evidence that cereal or vegetable offerings were less effective as either sin offerings or fellowship meals than offerings involving the shedding of blood, since in later Mosaic law both were prescribed. In the NT Abel is regarded as the first martyr (Mt 23:35; Lk 11:51) and a prototype of Christ (Heb 12:24).

Abel (Place). Fortified border city in upper Galilee to which King David's general Joab pursued the rebel Sheba. After a wise woman of the city negotiated with Joab, the citizens executed Sheba and threw his head over the wall. Joab then called off the siege (2 Sm 20:13–22). The city was later conquered by the Syrian Ben-hadad during a continuing war between King Asa of Judah and King Baasha of Israel. When Asa persuaded Ben-hadad to break a treaty with Baasha, Ben-hadad took a large amount of territory, including Abel, or Abel-beth-maacah, as it was also called (1 Kgs 15:16–20). Still later, Abel-beth-maacah (sometimes called simply Abel of Beth-maacah, or Abel of Beth-maachah) was conquered by Tiglath-pileser III and its inhabitants were taken captive to Assyria (2 Kgs 15:29). The same city is called Abel-maim ("meadow of water"), emphasizing the productivity of the region (2 Chr 16:4). The town has been identified with modern Tell Abil-el-Qamh.

Abel-beth-maacah (Maachah), Abel of Beth-maacah (Maachah). Alternate names for Abel, a fortified city in upper Galilee, in 1 Kings 15:20 and 2 Kings 15:29.

See ABEL (PLACE).

Abel-keramim. City taken by Jephthah the Israelite judge when subjugating the Ammonites (Jgs 11:33, KJV plain of the vineyards). It was located south of the Jabbok River, perhaps near the modern city of Amman.

Abel-maim. Alternate name for Abel, a fortified city in upper Galilee, in 2 Chronicles 16:4.

See ABEL (PLACE).

Abel-meholah. Birthplace of the prophet Elisha (1 Kgs 19:16). Here Elijah found Elisha plowing and threw his coat over Elisha's shoulders, symbolizing God's call to Elisha to become a prophet (1 Kgs 19:19–21). The town is earlier mentioned as one place to which the Midianites fled from Gideon's 300 warriors (Jgs 7:22). It is also mentioned in a list of administrative districts set up by King Solomon (1 Kgs 4:12). The most likely modern identification is Khirbet Tell el-Hilu.

Abel-mizraim. Alternate name for Atad, a place in Canaan, in Genesis 50:11.

See ATAD.

Abel-shittim. Alternate name for Shittim, a place on the plains of Moab, in Numbers 33:49.

See SHITTIM (PLACE).

Abez. KJV form of Ebez, a place in Issachar's territory, in Joshua 19:20.

See EBEZ.

Abi. Shortened form of Abijah, the name of the mother of Judah's King Hezekiah (2 Kgs 18:2).

See ABIJAH #4.

Abia. 1. KJV rendering of Abijam, Rehoboam's son and king of Judah, in 1 Chronicles 3:10 and Matthew 1:7.

See ABIJAM.

2. KJV rendering of Abijah in Luke 1:5.

See ABIJAH #6.

Abiah. 1. KJV translation for Abijah, Samuel's son, in 1 Samuel 8:2 and 1 Chronicles 6:28.

See ABIJAH #1.

2. KJV translation of a Hebrew word in 1 Chronicles 2:24 which renders it as a proper name referring to the wife of Hezron. Most modern translations render it "his father": "Caleb went in to Ephrathah, the wife of Hezron his father." The Hebrew is difficult, with different textual families evidently preserving variant readings and thus accounting for the divergences between the versions.

3. KJV translation for Abijah, Becher's son, in 1 Chronicles 7:8.

See ABIJAH #5.

Abi-Albon. Alternate name of Abiel in 2 Samuel 23:31.

See ABIEL #2.

Abiasaph. Alternate form of Ebiasaph, a descendant of Korah, in Exodus 6:24.

See EBIASAPH.

Abiathar. One of two high priests during the reign of King David. The other high priest was Zadok, who evidently was appointed by David after his conquest of Jerusalem.

Only Abiathar escaped when the priestly families at Nob were massacred at the instigation of King Saul. The priests of Nob had given food and Goliath's sword to David during David's escape from the wrath of Saul, thus bringing Saul's enmity on themselves (1 Sm 21–22). When Abiathar joined David he brought the ephod, which David then often used in determining the will of God (23:6,9–11; 30:7,8). Abiathar was one of the first persons from Saul's administration to support David.

His support was formidable because he represented the priesthood of the old tribal league of the line of Eli.

During the last days of David's kingship his sons struggled for the throne. The two major rivals were Adonijah and Solomon. Abiathar the high priest supported Adonijah's claim to the throne, probably because Adonijah was David's oldest living heir and because David's general Joab, one of the strongest men in the kingdom, supported Adonijah (1 Kgs 1:5–7). Zadok supported Solomon, who actually succeeded David on the throne. Having fallen out of favor with the new king, Abiathar was banished to his estate in Anathoth (1 Kgs 2:26,27), a village about four miles northeast of Jerusalem. (About 300 years later a great prophet was born among the priests of Anathoth, Jeremiah, possibly a descendant of Abiathar.)

The relationship of Abiathar to Ahimelech is confusing. Ahimelech could have been the name of both Abiathar's father (1 Sm 22:20; 23:6) and son (2 Sm 8:17; 1 Chr 18:16; 24:6). If each of the references was to the same Ahimelech, then the names were reversed in the later passages. In the NT, Abiathar is mentioned as the high priest when David came to Nob needing food and weapons (Mk 2:26). The OT account says that Ahimelech was the priest at that time (1 Sm 21:1,2). The apparent discrepancy may have resulted from scribal error or from the fact that Abiathar as high priest was more prominent than either Ahimelech.

Abib. Canaanite name of the Hebrew month Nisan, about mid-March to mid-April.

See CALENDARS, ANCIENT AND MODERN.

Abida. One of Midian's sons. Midian was Abraham's son by the concubine Keturah (Gn 25:2, 4; 1 Chr 1:33).

Abidan. Gideoni's son, and leader of Benjamin's tribe when the Israelites were wandering in the Sinai wilderness after their escape from Egypt (Nm 1:11; 2:22). As leader he presented his tribe's offering at the consecration of the tabernacle (7:60–65).

Abiel. 1. Father of Kish and Ner and grandfather of King Saul, according to 1 Samuel 9:1 and 14:51. Other genealogies in 1 Chronicles list Ner, instead of Abiel, as Kish's father and Saul's grandfather (1 Chr 8:33; 9:39). This confusion is due either to a copyist error or to the possibility that Saul had two relatives named Ner, a great-grandfather and an uncle.

2. Warrior among David's mighty men who were known as "the thirty" (1 Chr 11:32), also called Abi-albon the Arbathite (2 Sm 23:31).

Abiezer. 1. Descendant of Manasseh (Jos 17:1,2). Although Abiezer's father is not named, Abiezer is listed with the descendants of his mother's brother, Gilead (1 Chr 7:18). In Numbers 26:30 Abiezer's name is shortened to Iezer (KJV Jeezer) and the family is called Iezerites (KJV Jeezerites). Abiezer's family, to which Gideon belonged, was the first clan to respond to Gideon's call to fight the Midianites (Jgs 6:34). Abiezer's descendants were referred to as Abiezrites (Jgs 6:11, 24,34; 8:32).

2. Member of Benjamin's tribe from Anathoth and warrior among David's mighty men, known as "the thirty" (2 Sm 23:27; 1 Chr 11:28). This Abiezer was commander of the ninth division of the army in the rotation system established by David (1 Chr 27:12).

Abiezrite. Member of Abiezer's family (Jgs 6:11,24,34; 8:32).

See ABIEZER #1.

Abigail. 1. Nabal's wife, who later became the wife of David (1 Sm 25:2–42). Nabal was a wealthy sheep owner whose holdings had been protected by David's men. When David requested provisions in return for that protection, Nabal insultingly refused. Enraged, David set out with 400 armed men to destroy Nabal and his house. Abigail had been informed of her husband's behavior and met David with many provisions, taking the blame for her boorish husband. David thanked God for using Abigail to restrain his wrath.

When Nabal woke from a drunken stupor the next morning and learned what had happened, he had a stroke from which he died 10 days later. Abigail then married David and shared his adventurous life among the Philistines (1 Sm 27:3). She was captured by the Amalekites and rescued by David (1 Sm 30:1–19). Abigail went with David to Hebron when he became king of Judah (2 Sm 2:2), and she bore his second son, Chileab (2 Sm 3:3), also called Daniel (1 Chr 3:1).

2. David's sister, who married Jether and gave birth to Amasa (1 Chr 2:16,17). The paternity of this Abigail seems to be somewhat confused. In 1 Chronicles 2:13–17 she is listed as a daughter of Jesse. However, in 2 Samuel 17:25 (RSV Abigal), her father is identified as Nahash. The discrepancy could be due to scribal error, or Nahash may be another name for Jesse, or the widow of Nahash could have married Jesse.

Abigal. RSV rendering of Abigail, David's sister, in 2 Samuel 17:25.

See ABIGAIL #2.

Abihail. Name used for both men and women in the OT.

1. Zuriel's father and a leader of the Merari family of Levites in Israel's wilderness community (Nm 3:35).

2. Abishur's wife, and mother of Ahban and Molid (1 Chr 2:29).

3. Huri's son, a descendant of Gad, living in Gilead and Bashan (1 Chr 5:14).

4. Woman named in 2 Chronicles 11:18 whose relationship to King Rehoboam is not clear from the Hebrew text. In some translations, Abihail seems to be the second wife of Rehoboam. However, only one wife is mentioned at first, so Abihail was probably the mother of Rehoboam's first wife, Mahalath. This Abihail was thus a daughter of Eliab, David's eldest brother. She married her cousin Jerimoth, one of David's sons.

5. Esther's father and uncle of Mordecai (Est 2:15; 9:29).

Abihu. Second son of Aaron and Elisheba (Ex 6:23; Nm 26:60; 1 Chr 6:3). Abihu and his brother Nadab joined Moses, Aaron, and the 70 elders of Israel in worshiping the glory of God on Mt Sinai (Ex 24:1–11). The four sons of Aaron were made priests along with their father (Ex 28:1), but later Abihu and Nadab were burned to death for offering "unholy fire" before the Lord (Lv 10:1–3; Nm 3:2–4; 26:61; 1 Chr 24:1,2).

Abihud. One of Bela's nine sons (1 Chr 8:3). Abihud should not be confused with the Abiud of Matthew's genealogy of Christ in the NT.

Abijah. 1. Samuel's second son who, with his elder brother Joel, was a corrupt judge in Beersheba. Because of the corruption, Israel's leaders asked to be ruled instead by a king (1 Sm 8:2; 1 Chr 6:28, KJV Abiah).

2. Son of Jeroboam I of the northern kingdom of Israel. The boy's illness impelled his family to seek guidance from the prophet Ahijah at Shiloh. This Abijah was the only member of Jeroboam's family whose death caused Israel to mourn (1 Kgs 14:13,18).

3. Alternate name for Abijam, king of Judah, in 2 Chronicles and Matthew 1:7.

See ABIJAM.

4. Ahaz's wife, and mother of King Hezekiah (2 Kgs 18:2, short form Abi; 2 Chr 29:1). This Abijah was Zechariah's daughter.

5. Becher's son from Benjamin's tribe (1 Chr 7:8, KJV Abiah).

6. Levite who headed the eighth of 24 priestly divisions established in David's time (1 Chr 24:10; Lk 1:5; KJV Abia).

7. Head of a priestly family who signed Ez-

ra's covenant of faithfulness to God with Nehemiah and others after the exile (Neh 10:7).

8. Head of a priestly family who returned to Jerusalem with Zerubbabel after the exile (Neh 12:4). Later, a member of this family, Zichri, was a leading priest during Nehemiah's time (v 17). Perhaps of the same family as #7.

Abijam. Rehoboam's son and successor as king of Judah, 913–910 BC (1 Chr 3:10, KJV Abia; alternately called Abijah in 2 Chr 11:18–22; 12:16; 13:1–22; 14:1). A major focus of Abijam's reign was his war with King Jeroboam I of Israel (2 Chr 13:1–3). Before a decisive battle Abijam stood on Mt Zemaraim and shouted condemnation of Jeroboam's political divisiveness and religious idolatry (vv 4–12). Abijam and his army then prayed for God's help in their precarious military position. Against two-to-one odds they fought their way out of an ambush and won a stunning victory over Jeroboam (vv 13–19). Abijam's reign in the southern kingdom of Judah was summed up rather unfavorably in 1 Kings 15:1–8: "And he walked in all the sins which his father did before him; and his heart was not wholly true to the Lord his God, as the heart of David his father" (v 3). But God had promised to keep David's descendants on the throne in Jerusalem (1 Kgs 11:36), so Abijam's son Asa succeeded him. Being of David's line, Abijam was an ancestor of Jesus, the Christ (Mt 1:7, Abijah, KJV Abia).

See ISRAEL, HISTORY OF; CHRONOLOGY, OLD TESTAMENT; GENEALOGY OF JESUS CHRIST.

Abilene. Region on the east side of the Anti-Lebanon mountains in Syria. The district took its name from the capital city of Abila, located about 18 miles from Damascus. At the time of John the Baptist, Abilene was governed by the tetrarch Lysanias (Lk 3:1).

Abimael. One of the many sons or descendants of Joktan, and thus a descendant of Shem (Gn 10:28; 1 Chr 1:22).

Abimelech. Royal title for Philistine rulers, similar to the designation "pharaoh" among the Egyptians and "agag" among the Amalekites.

1. King of Gerar in Abraham's time. At Gerar, a city a few miles south of Gaza, Abraham presented his wife as his sister out of fear of the king's rights (Gn 20:1–18), as he had once done in Egypt (12:10–20). As Abraham feared, Sarah was taken into Abimelech's harem. But Abimelech was warned by God in a dream not to come near her on pain of death because she

was a married woman, so she was restored to her husband. The same Abimelech and Abraham later entered into a treaty to clarify water rights in the Negeb desert at Beersheba (21:22–34).

2. King of Gerar in Isaac's time. Isaac, too, passed off his wife Rebekah as his sister at Gerar. Abimelech, perhaps remembering the near judgment on his predecessor, acted decisively to protect Rebekah's integrity. He proclaimed a death penalty on any who touched her or her husband (Gn 26:1–11). Abimelech asked Isaac to leave Philistine territory because of overcrowding and continuing dispute over water (vv 12–22). Eventually, at Beersheba, Isaac and Abimelech ended their hostility by renewing the treaty made by Abraham and the earlier Abimelech (vv 26–33).

3. Gideon's son by a concubine in Shechem (Jgs 8:31). After his father's death, Abimelech conspired with his mother's family to assassinate his 70 half brothers. Only one of them, Jotham, escaped (9:1–5). When Abimelech was made king in Shechem, Jotham warned Abimelech's followers that they were choosing a thorn bush to be their king (vv 7–21). In Abimelech's third year of rule, he cruelly suppressed a rebellion (vv 22–49). Eventually his skull was crushed by a millstone thrown down by a woman on a tower. Abimelech ordered his armor bearer to kill him with a sword so that no one could say he had been killed by a woman (vv 53–57).

4. Achish, king of the Philistine city of Gath (1 Sm 21:10–15). Hebrew texts have an introduction to Psalm 34, saying that David wrote it when he "feigned madness before Abimelech." Since "abimelech" was used as a general title for Philistine kings, this reference was undoubtedly to Achish.

5. Abiathar's son, a priest associated with Zadok in David's time (1 Chr 18:16 KJV); un-

A sacred pillar from a temple, which is thought to be the house of Baal-berith that Abimelech destroyed (Jdg 9:3–4,46).

doubtedly a scribal error for Ahimelech (2 Sm 8:17).

See AHIMELECH #3.

Abinadab. 1. Resident of Kiriath-jearim to whose home the ark of God was brought on its return by the Philistines (1 Sm 6:21–7:2).

2. Jesse's second son, and brother of David (1 Sm 16:8; 17:13; 1 Chr 2:13). This Abinadab served in Saul's army for part of the Philistine war.

3. KJV form of Ben-abinadab, one of King Solomon's administrative officers in 1 Kings 4:11.

See BEN-ABINADAB.

4. One of Saul's sons (1 Chr 8:33; 10:2).

Abinoam. Barak's father. Barak was the companion of Deborah, an Israelite judge, in the war against the Canaanites (Jgs 4:6,12; 5:1,12).

Abiram. 1. One of Eliab's two sons. Abiram and his brother Dathan joined in an uprising against Moses and Aaron (Nm 16). At Moses' word, the ground split open beneath the two rebellious brothers and everything associated with them was swallowed up in a massive earthquake (Nm 16:31–33; 26:9,10; Dt 11:6; Ps 106:16–18).

2. Hiel's oldest son, who died prematurely when his father presumptuously rebuilt Jericho (1 Kgs 16:34). It is not clear whether the death of Abiram and later of his brother resulted from God's direct judgment or whether they died as a result of Hiel's acting in accordance with the Canaanite practice of child sacrifice. Either way, Joshua's prophetic curse was fulfilled (Jos 6:26).

Abishag. Beautiful young woman from Shunem who was appointed to care for David during his last days (1 Kgs 1:1–4). After David's death, Adonijah asked permission from his half brother, King Solomon, to marry Abishag. In the ancient Near East, to claim the concubine of a deceased king was to claim the throne. Enraged, Solomon ordered Adonijah to be killed (1 Kgs 2:13–25).

Abishai. David's nephew, son of Zeruiah (by an unnamed father), and brother of Joab and Asahel (1 Chr 2:16). Abishai volunteered to accompany David to Saul's camp one night and would have killed the sleeping Saul if David had not restrained him (1 Sm 26:6–12). He also helped Joab kill Abner, Saul's general, in revenge for the death of another brother (2 Sm 3:30). Later Abishai won a victory over the Edomites (1 Chr 18:12,13) and was second in command in a decisive battle against the Am-

monites (1 Chr 19:10–15). Often vengeful and cruel, Abishai wanted to behead the spiteful Shimei during Absalom's rebellion, but again David intervened (2 Sm 16:5–12; 19:21–23). When King David fled beyond the Jordan, Abishai was given command of one of David's three divisions, which crushed the rebellion (2 Sm 18:1–15).

In a later battle with the Philistines, Abishai saved David's life by killing the giant Ishbi-benob (2 Sm 21:15–17). He ranked among David's bravest warriors (2 Sm 23:18,19; 1 Chr 11:20,21).

Abishalom. Alternate name for Absalom, King David's son, in 1 Kings 15:2,10.

See ABSALOM.

Abishua. 1. Aaron's great-grandson, son of Phinehas, and ancestor of Ezra the scribe (1 Chr 6:4,5,50; Ezr 7:5). Abishua's name also appears in the apocryphal genealogy of Ezra (1 Esd 8:2, 2 Esd 1:2).

2. Bela's son and grandson of Benjamin (1 Chr 8:4).

Abishur. Shammai's son and the father of Ahban and Molid from Judah's tribe. Abishur's wife was Abihail (1 Chr 2:28,29).

Abital. Mother of King David's fifth son, Shephatiah (2 Sm 3:4; 1 Chr 3:3).

Abitub. Son of Shaharaim and Hushim from Benjamin's tribe (1 Chr 8:11).

Abiud. Individual listed in Matthew's genealogy of Christ in the NT as Eliakim's father (Mt 1:13). Abiud is not mentioned in the OT, but his name could have been taken from non-canonical family registers, which the Jews carefully maintained.

See GENEALOGY OF JESUS CHRIST.

Abner. Ner's son and Saul's cousin. Abner was commander of Saul's army (1 Sm 14:51; 17:55). Highly respected by Saul, he even ate at the king's table together with David and Jonathan (1 Sm 20:25).

Five years after Saul's death, Abner made Ish-bosheth, Saul's son, king over Israel (2 Sm 2:8,9). War between Ish-bosheth and David, who then was king over Judah, lasted for two years (v 10). Abner was in command of Ish-bosheth's army, Joab of David's, in a series of skirmishes (vv 11–21). David's position was generally stronger (3:1), but Abner became a powerful figure among Saul's followers (v 6).

Although only the king had a right to sexual relationships with the previous king's con-

The pool of Gibeon (2 Sm 2:12–17).

cubines, Abner slept with Saul's concubine Rizpah, perhaps planning to take over the kingdom himself at the first opportunity. When Ish-bosheth rebuked him, Abner became so angry that he broke with Ish-bosheth and came to terms with David. David showed him great respect, and in return Abner promised to bring the whole of Israel over to David. Joab, however, feared Abner's influence with the king and killed him, claiming revenge for the death of his brother at Abner's hand in a battle. Abner was honored with a public funeral and mourning, an honor given only to a ruler or great leader. King David wept aloud at the tomb, and even the people wept with him (2 Sm 3:7–34). David condemned Joab for murdering Abner, whom David called "a prince and a great man" (vv 35–39).

See DAVID; ISRAEL, HISTORY OF.

Abomination. Repugnant or detestable act, person, or thing. The idea of abomination derives from the specific demands God's holiness makes upon his people. Adjectives frequently used for abominations in the OT are "abhorrent," "loathsome," "unclean," and "rejected."

Of the four major Hebrew words translated "abomination," the one most frequently used indicates violation of an established custom or ritual which, in turn, draws the judgment of God. Examples range from defective sacrifices (Dt 17:1) to magic and divination (Dt 18:12) or idolatrous practices (2 Kgs 16:3). A second Hebrew word refers to the meat of certain kinds of animals that was ritually defiling, whether

touched or eaten (Lv 11:10–13). A third word designates three-day-old sacrificial meat (Lv 7:18). A fourth word refers almost exclusively to idolatrous objects of pagan origin (Jer 4:1; 7:30). The Greek OT, particularly in the Book of Ezekiel, associates the term "lawlessness" with abomination, thus adding ethical and moral content to the term. Apart from the specialized usage of "abomination of desolation," the Greek word for "abomination" is used only infrequently in the NT (Lk 16:15; Rom 2:22; Ti 1:16; Rv 17:4,5; 21:8,27) and is translated by many English words. The primary connotation is anything that is abhorrent to a holy God.

MORRIS A. WEIGELT

See ABOMINATION OF DESOLATION; CLEANNESS AND UNCLEANNESS, REGULATIONS CONCERNING.

Abomination of Desolation. Phrase used in Daniel, 1 Maccabees, Matthew, and Mark to designate a destestable object of pagan idolatry so loathsome to God that his people would feel desolate and devastated in its presence.

In Daniel's vision of the assault of evil, the ultimate corruption was seen as the "wing of abominations" and subsequent desolation (Dn 9:27). In another vision of coming abomination, a detestable object would be set up in the temple in Jerusalem (Dn 11:31) 1,290 days after the beginning of a period of sacrilege (Dn 12:11), thus destroying the temple's holiness and rendering it unclean by ceremonial and ethical standards.

In 1 Maccabees it is recorded that the Syrian Antiochus Epiphanes invaded Palestine (167 BC) and erected a desolating sacrilege, probably a statue of Zeus, upon the altar of burnt offering in the temple (1 Mc 1:54). The humiliation of the Jews was climaxed by sacrificing swine on the altar, and by the death penalty for circumcision or for possessing the "Book of the Covenant."

Jesus used the phrase "abomination of desolation" in answering the disciples' questions concerning the destruction of the temple and the general course of the age until his return (Mt 24:1–31; Mk 13:1–27; Lk 21:5–28). In alluding to the Daniel passages, Jesus predicted that something analogous to the destruction by Antiochus would reoccur. Jesus applied the prediction and fulfillment of Daniel's prophecy in part to the coming Roman desecration which did take place in AD 70. In Luke 21:20, the words "surrounded by armies" were perhaps an allusion to the capture and sack of Jerusalem by Nebuchadnezzar in 586 BC. Jesus' point was that in rejecting him, Israel again had chosen the road which would end in disaster. To refuse his mercy was to choose destruction.

Jesus warned that the erection of the abomination of desolation (desolating sacrilege, RSV) was a signal to flee the city of Jerusalem (Mt 24:15; Mk 13:14). The phrase "let the reader understand" shows that the enigmatic phrase symbolized an appalling and complete devastation of the sanctity of the temple.

The Greek version of the Book of Ezekiel sometimes used "lawlessness" in place of abomination, leading to association of "man of lawlessness" (man of abomination) with the detestable sacrilege of the antichrist (2 Thes 2:3). A similar theme is reflected in the Book of Revelation, where the image of the creature or beast from the sea symbolizes the power of the forces of evil demanding obedience and submission (Rv 13:1–10).

Abomination of desolation is thus a symbol for the most devastating activities through which the hostile forces of evil make their attack, whether upon the Jewish people in Maccabean times, upon Jerusalem in the first century AD, or upon the people of God in a final assault of evil at the end time.

MORRIS A. WEIGELT

See ANTICHRIST; DANIEL, BOOK OF; SEVENTY WEEKS, DANIEL'S; ABOMINATION.

Abraham. One of the Bible's most significant personalities, the "wandering Aramean" (Dt 26:5) whom God called from the city of Ur to become patriarch of God's own people. Referred to as the "friend of God" (2 Chr 20:7; Jas 2:23), Abraham played an important role in Hebrew history and in the "drama of salvation." Through Abraham's life, God revealed a program of "election" and "covenant" which culminated in the work of the Messiah Jesus Christ. God said to Abraham, "in you all the families of earth shall be blessed" (Gn 12:3; another rendering of the last two words of this quote is "bless themselves"). Centuries later, the apostle Paul explained that the full import of God's promise was seen in the preaching of the gospel to all nations and the response of faith in Christ, which signifies believers from all families of the earth as sons of Abraham (Gal 3:6–9).

Name. Abraham's name was originally Abram, meaning "(the) father is exalted." When he was given that name by his parents, they were probably participants in the moon cult of Ur, so the father deity suggested in his old name could have been the moon god or other pagan deity. God changed Abram's name to Abraham (Gn 17:5), partly no doubt to indicate a clear-cut separation from pagan roots. The new name, interpreted by the biblical text as meaning "father of a multitude," was also a statement of God's promise to Abraham that he would have many descendants, and a significant test of his faith in God—since he was 99 years old at the time and his childless wife was 90 (Gn 11:30; 17:1–4,17).

Chronological Setting. The period of Abraham's life has been estimated in various ways. Some scholars have placed him as late as 1500 BC, requiring considerable compression of biblical chronology, including a late date for the exodus (c. 1230 BC). Most place Abraham toward the beginning of the Middle Bronze Age (1900–1800 BC) or the end of the Early Bronze Age (2150–2000 BC).

Cultural Setting. Archaeological discoveries have supplemented and illuminated what we know about Abraham from the biblical text. Few periods from ancient history are as well documented by artifacts and inscriptions as is the time of Abraham, called by scholars the patriarchal age. Texts from Nuzi, Mari, Boghazköy, and Babylon shed light on his life and actions. His name, travels, manner of life, his barren wife, and his relationship with her slave—all fit the culture of the Early and Middle Bronze periods. Some indirect inscriptional evidence dates from a period later than Abraham, but the cultural procedures are age-old customs in those inscriptions, not newly introduced ones. Because of the major input from archaeological research, Abraham the patriarch has become more real and understandable and his setting in history thoroughly believable.

Abraham's Life. *Family.* The story of Abram begins in Genesis 11, where his family relationships are recorded (Gn 11:26–32). Terah, Abram's father, was named after the moon deity worshiped at Ur. Terah had three sons, Abram, Nahor, and Haran. Haran, the father of Lot, died before the family left Ur for Mesopotamia (now Iraq). Terah took Lot, Abram, and Abram's wife Sarai from Ur to go to Canaan, but settled at the city of Haran (Gn 11:31). It is stated in Acts 7:2–4 that Abraham heard the call of God to leave for a new land while he was still in Ur. It may be that Terah went along in the migration prompted by his son but never fully deserted the idolatries of his past. Terah is expressly identified as having served other gods (Jos 24:2).

A note of major importance to the course of Abram's life is found in Genesis 11:30, "Sarai was barren; she had no child." The problem of Sarai's barrenness provided the basis for great crises of faith, promise, and fulfillment in the lives of Abram and Sarai.

Arrival in Canaan. After Terah's death, God told Abram, "Go from your country and your kindred and your father's house to the land that I will show you." This command was the basis of a "covenant," in which God

A game board from Ur, the city from which God called Abraham.

promised to make Abram the founder of a new nation in that new land (Gn 12:1–3). Abram, trusting God's promise, left Haran at the age of 75. Entering Canaan, he went first to Shechem, an important Canaanite royal city between Mt Gerizim and Mt Ebal. Near the oak of Moreh, a Canaanite shrine, God appeared to him (12:7). Abram built an altar at Shechem, then moved to the vicinity of Bethel and again built an altar to the Lord (12:8). The expression, "to call on the name of the Lord" (rsv), means more than just to pray. Rather, Abram made a proclamation, declaring the reality of God to the Canaanites in their centers of false worship. From Bethel, Abram continued journeying into the arid south, the Negeb desert area.

Because of a famine in Canaan, Abram went to Egypt and while there attempted to portray his wife as merely his sister in order to preserve his life (12:10–20). In Hurrian society, the culture of Haran, special privileges were attached to a man who married his natural or adoptive sister. The wife-sister relationship suggests that Abram was high in Hurrian society and that Sarai also enjoyed superior status. Later the Scripture states that she was indeed his half sister (20:12). Yet his use of half of the truth to conceal the other half was clearly a lie. Abram resorted to a cultural expedient but found that the expedient did not work well. Without God's intervention, Sarai could have been absorbed into the royal harem, and the promise of offspring for Abram would have gone unfulfilled. Abram left Egypt and went back to his "altar-pulpit" near Bethel and to a renewal of his relationship with God.

In Canaan, family strife developed between Abram and his nephew Lot (13:2–18). Both had become so wealthy in livestock that their herds-

men were constantly quarreling. Abram's magnanimous affirmation, "we are kinsmen" (v 8), and his subsequent action in allowing Lot his choice of land demonstrate his wisdom and faith. Lot's choice of the fertile Jordan valley was viewed ominously by the writer: "Now the men of Sodom were wicked, great sinners against the Lord" (13:13). Abram's choice showed his faith in God and led to a reaffirmation of God's covenant with him, with emphasis on the guarantee of land and descendants (13:14–17). Abram then moved to Hebron by the oaks of Mamre, where again he built an altar to worship God. Here he could see the whole land stretched out before him.

Genesis 14 has received much attention from archaeologists and biblical historians, as it concerns multinational confederations and wide geographical boundaries. The names of the kings cannot be identified accurately with known rulers of the period, but the geographical dimensions are detailed and accurate. Abram rescued Lot in a daring military action, demonstrating a strong bond to his nephew as well as leadership capacity. Abram routed the armies that had plundered Sodom and Gomorrah.

On his victorious return to Canaan, Abram was met by two kings, a study in contrasts: the king of Sodom and the king of Salem. Abram refused all offers of gifts from the king of Sodom on the basis of a solemn oath that no one should attribute any part of his wealth to the Canaanite king. Abram's allies (Aner, Eshcol, and Mamre) did profit from the booty he had captured.

The encounter with Melchizedek, king of Salem, was a different matter. That priest-king met Abram not with promise of booty, but with a blessing in the name of "God Most High, maker of heaven and earth" (14:19). The word used for God had been used of other gods also, but Melchizedek used it to refer to the true God, creator of heaven and earth. Abram paid him tithes and then to the words "Most High" added the name Yahweh (14:22, "Lord").

Another blessing given in a vision (15:1) led Abram to exclaim that he was still childless and that Eliezer of Damascus was his heir (15:2). Discovery of the Nuzi documents has helped to clarify that otherwise obscure statement. According to Hurrian custom, a childless couple of station and substance would adopt an heir. Often a slave, the heir would be responsible for the burial and mourning of his adoptive parents. If a son should be born after the adoption of a slave-heir, the natural son would of course supplant him. Thus God's response to Abram's question is directly to the point: "This man shall not be your heir; your own son shall be your heir" (15:4).

God then made a covenant with Abram insuring an heir, a nation, and the land. The covenant ratification ceremony is described vividly and chillingly (15:9–17). Animals were killed, cut in two, and a path was made between the halved carcasses. Presumably in two-way covenants both contracting parties would then pass between the carcasses, as if to say, "May I be cut in two if I fail my part of the bargain." However, in this instance Abram was only a spectator, and God alone passed between the animal parts. The symbols of God's presence were a smoking fire pot and flaming torch.

Promise of a Son. The story of the birth of Ishmael to Hagar (Gn 16) is another example of a difficult text amplified by archaeological research. Barrenness was regarded as a terrible plight in the ancient Near East. A woman who had been married but who had produced no children was thought to have failed as a woman. To alleviate in part the distress of the barren, the Hurrian texts at Nuzi speak of an obligation on the wife's part to provide her husband with a slave maiden as a substitute wife. The child born would be considered a legal child of the official wife. Thus Sarai and Abram were functioning within their cultural pattern, but the intent of God's promise was that Sarai herself, even though barren, would bear Abram's child. Their action was a choice of expediency, not in line with the Lord's intent.

The child born of the union with Hagar was Ishmael, progenitor of the Arab peoples. Trouble came between Sarai and Hagar. Nuzi texts speak of the rights of wife and slave-wife when trouble arose. The impudent slave-wife was not to be expelled nor was her child to be cast off, but she could be disciplined (16:6). When Hagar and Ishmael were actually expelled (21:9–11), God intervened, stating that he would bless the child even apart from the patriarch's household (21:12,13).

Abram was 86 years old when Ishmael was born. When Abram was 99, the Lord appeared to the aged patriarch and again reaffirmed his covenant promise of a son and blessing (Gn 17). Circumcision was added as the seal of covenantal relationship (17:9–14), and at that point the names Abram and Sarai were changed to Abraham and Sarah (17:5,15). Abraham's response to the promise of another son was to laugh. "Shall a child be born to a man who is a hundred years old? Shall Sarah, who is ninety years old, bear a child?" (17:17).

Genesis 18 and 19 recount the total destruction of two cities of the Jordan plain, Sodom and Gomorrah. Chapter 18 begins with three individuals seeking comfort in the heat of the day. Abraham offered refreshment and a meal to his guests. They turned out to be no ordinary travelers, however, but the angel of the Lord along with two other angels (18:1,2; 19:1). There is reason to believe that the angel of the Lord was God himself (Gn 18:17,33). Another announcement of a promised son this time made Sarah laugh in unbelief and then deny having laughed (18:12–15).

The esteem with which God regarded Abraham is shown by his taking Abraham into his confidence about Sodom and Gomorrah (Gn 18:17–19). Abraham's bargaining for Sodom would sound humorous if the issues were not so terrible (18:22–33). The two angels proceeded to the city and were met by Lot. Sodom's wickedness was demonstrated in unmistakable terms, and its destruction was total.

Abraham's lapse at Gerar (Gn 20) parallels the earlier incident in Egypt (12:10–20). On the verge of the fulfillment of God's promise to Abraham to give him and Sarah their own son, Abraham again endangered the promise by deviously representing Sarah as his sister. That seemed to be Abraham's standard operating procedure in a new land (12:13). Neither the Egyptian Pharaoh nor the Philistine Abimelech understood what Abraham meant by the privileged status of his sister-wife. On this occasion too, Sarah was almost added to a royal harem, but God intervened by warning Abimelech in a dream of the dangerous situation.

Birth of Isaac. Genesis 21 to 23 form the climax of the story of Abraham. At long last, when Abraham was 100 years old and his wife 90, "the Lord did to Sarah as he had promised" (Gn 21:1). The joy of the aged couple on the birth of their long-promised son could not be contained. Both Abraham and Sarah had laughed in unbelief in the days of promise;

now they laughed in joy as God had "the last laugh." The baby, born at the time God promised, was named Isaac ("he laughs!"). Sarah said, "God has made laughter for me; every one who hears will laugh over me" (21:6).

However, the joy of the home was disrupted by jealousy and strife, for when Isaac was weaned Ishmael laughed mockingly at Isaac. This led to the expulsion of Hagar and Ishmael. Chapter 21 also details the relationship between Abraham and Abimelech, and Abraham's move to Beersheba, where he made proclamation of the Lord, the Eternal God (21:22–34).

The laughter over Isaac's birth subsided entirely in the test of Abraham's faith described in chapter 22, God's command to sacrifice Isaac. Only when one has experienced vicariously with Abraham the long 25 years of God's promise of a son can one imagine the trauma of such a supreme test. Just as the knife was about to fall, and only then, did the angel of God break the silence of heaven with the call, "Abraham!" (22:11). The name of promise, "father of a multitude," took on its most significant meaning when Abraham's son was spared and the test was explained: "I know that you fear God, seeing you have not withheld your son, your only son, from me" (22:12).

Those words were coupled with a promise implicit in the discovery of a ram caught in the thicket. The Lord provided an alternative sacrifice, a substitute. The place was named "the Lord will provide." Christian believers generally see the whole episode as looking ahead to God's provision of his only Son, Jesus Christ, as a sacrifice for the sins of the world.

The story of Sarah's death and burial (Gn 23) has an emotional quality despite the focus on legal maneuvering. The fact that Abraham was promised the whole land, but had to buy a burial place for his wife, is a stirring paradox of faith. The agreement for the purchase of the cave Machpelah near Mamre from Ephron the Hittite accords with contracts known from Hittite sources. Abraham apparently wished to buy only the cave but gave in to Ephron's urging that he purchase the field as well. That meant that Abraham was encumbered with the feudal responsibilities of maintaining the trees (note the wording of 23:17). The chapter illustrates the kind of legal contracts drawn up in that period of history.

Death of the Patriarch. In Genesis 24 the scene shifts from Abraham to Isaac. Chapter 25 records Abraham's marriage to Keturah (25:1–6), but the large number of sons born to Keturah could argue against her being married to Abraham after the death of Sarah, especially since Keturah is called a concubine in 1 Chronicles 1:32. It is possible that her six sons

Ruins of Mamre.

were born earlier, while Sarah was still alive. The note is appended in connection with Abraham's death in order to detail the disposition of his wealth. To the sons born of concubines, Abraham gave inheritance gifts while he was still alive and then sent them away in order that Isaac's inheritance would not be jeopardized. So at the age of 175 Abraham died and was buried with his wife Sarah (25:7–10).

Abraham's Character and Significance. Commanded by God to leave all that was near and familiar and to go to a place that was remote, unknown, and perhaps undesirable, Abraham obeyed. He had no pattern before him for guidance and encouragement. His obedience was an expression of faith, and his faith was accounted to him as righteousness by God (Gn 15:6; Rom 4:9).

God's promise to Abraham at an advanced age that he would have a son was not realized for another quarter-century. Although he and his wife were well beyond the age of producing children, "no distrust made him waver concerning the promise of God, but he grew strong in his faith as he gave glory to God, fully convinced that God was able to do what he had promised" (Rom 4:20,21).

But the supreme challenge to his faith, surpassing the call to leave his homeland and even the promise of a son so late in life, was the command some years later to sacrifice that son, Isaac, to God (Gn 22). In a chapter written with great literary skill, the narrator describes a scene of pathos, terror, and the specter of savagery. Abraham was not only about to slaughter his son (Gn 22:2), but also about to destroy the promise of heirs that God had given him. The test was passed: Abraham believed God even at the point of despair and destruction. He believed that if Isaac died God would bring him back to life again; and "figuratively speaking, he did receive him back" (Heb 11:19).

Nevertheless, Abraham is pictured as a real person with various lapses into expedience in difficult circumstances. As "the friend of God," Abraham received the promises of an eternal covenant that eventuated in the Person of Jesus Christ. Abraham is the pioneer of faith. His life is a kind of study in faith: believing God's promises even when they seem impossible. This "father of a multitude" is the father of all who have faith in God. He fathered many nations and is known particularly as the father of the nation of Israel. Nevertheless, the NT considers all Christians, irrespective of national or racial origin, as Abraham's children (Gal 3:7–9) and heirs according to promise (3:29).

RONALD B. ALLEN

See LOT; MELCHIZEDEK; CIRCUMCISION; COVENANT; PATRIARCHS, PERIOD OF THE; ISRAEL, HISTORY OF; ABRAHAM'S BOSOM; SARAH #1.

Bibliography. R.E. Clements, *Abraham and David;* C.F. Keil, *Commentary on the Pentateuch,* vol 1, pp 192–269 (Grand Rapids, 1949); A. Parrot, *Abraham and His Times;* M. Rist, "The God of Abraham, Isaac, and Jacob" *JBL* (57) 1938, pp 289–303; J.A. Van Seters, *Abraham in History and Tradition.*

Abraham's Bosom.

Figure of speech probably derived from the Roman custom of reclining on one's left side at meals with the guest of honor at the bosom of his host (cf. Jn 13:25). It was used by Jesus in the story of Lazarus as a description of paradise (Lk 16:22,23). In rabbinical writings as well as 4 Maccabees 13:17, the just were thought to be welcomed at death by Abraham, Isaac, and Jacob. Jesus, probably aware of this, was also alluding to the "messianic banquet," an image he used a number of times. Thus, in the world to come, the godly poor like Lazarus would not only be welcomed by Abraham but would occupy the place of honor next to him at the banquet. Such a picture is presented by Jesus in contrast to the torment of the rich man in Hades.

See HEAVEN; PARADISE.

Abram.

Original name of Abraham (Gn 11:26).

See ABRAHAM.

Abronah.

Place near Elath where the Israelites camped on their journey from Egypt to Canaan (Nm 33:34,35, KJV Ebronah).

See WILDERNESS WANDERINGS.

Absalom.

Son of King David and his wife Maacah (2 Sm 3:3). The name is also spelled Abishalom (1 Kgs 15:2,10). Absalom was a handsome young prince who was noted for his long, full hair (2 Sm 14:25,26). He had a beautiful sister, Tamar, who was raped by their half brother, Amnon. After dishonoring Tamar, Amnon refused to marry her (2 Sm 13:1–20).

Absalom took his dejected sister into his own house, expecting his father David to punish Amnon for his incestuous act. After two years of suppressed rage and hatred, Absalom plotted his own revenge. He gave a feast for King David and his princes at his country estate. Although David did not attend, Amnon did and was murdered by Absalom's servants after Absalom got him drunk. Then, afraid of King David's anger, Absalom fled across the Jordan River to King Talmai of Geshur, his mother's father (2 Sm 13:21–39).

After three years in exile, Absalom was called back to Jerusalem through the efforts of David's general, Joab, and a wise woman from Tekoa. After two years he was back in full favor with the king (2 Sm 14), and in that position he began to maneuver himself toward the throne. He put on an impressive public relations campaign, in the process undermining confidence in his father the king (2 Sm 15:1–6).

Eventually Absalom plotted a rebellion against David, gathering supporters in Hebron from all over Israel. After Ahithophel, one of David's wisest counselors, joined Absalom, he announced his own kingship. By the time news of Absalom's conspiracy reached him, David was unable to do anything but flee from Jerusalem (2 Sm 15; Ps 3).

Absalom arrived in Jerusalem without a struggle, and Ahithophel asked permission to attack David immediately with 12,000 troops. But Hushai, David's secret agent in Absalom's court, advised Absalom instead to take the time to mobilize the entire nation against David. He also used flattery, suggesting that Absalom himself should lead the attack. Absalom preferred Hushai's advice, and Ahithophel out of desperation committed suicide. Meanwhile, Hushai sent word of Absalom's plans to David by two priests, Zadok and Abiathar. With this information, David crossed the Jordan and camped at Mahanaim (2 Sm 16,17).

Absalom led his forces across the Jordan to do battle in the forest of Ephraim. David's loyal forces were under the able generalship of Joab, Abishai, and Ittai the Gittite, who routed Absalom's forces. Absalom himself fled on a mule, but his long hair got caught in the branches of an oak tree, and he was left dangling helplessly. Joab, leading his men in pursuit, came upon Absalom and killed him. Joab's men threw the body in a pit and piled stones on it (2 Sm 18:1–18). Absalom's death stunned David, who had given explicit orders to keep Absalom from harm. David moaned: "O my son Absalom, my son, my son Absalom! Would I had died instead of you, O Absalom,

The Mount of Olives, perhaps the burial place of Absalom.

my son, my son!'' (2 Sm 18:33). In his excessive grief, David took no notice that a serious rebellion had been crushed until Joab reminded him that David's followers had risked their lives for him (2 Sm 19:1–8).

See DAVID.

Abyss. Bottomless, immeasurable deep or underworld.

See BOTTOMLESS PIT.

Acacia. Palestinian wood used in the construction of the ark of the covenant (Ex 25:10).

See PLANTS.

Accad. One of the three cities (Babel, Erech, and Accad, RSV) in the plains between the Tigris and Euphrates rivers said to have been founded by Nimrod (Gn 10:10). ''Akkadian'' (from Accad) has become a general designation for the Semitic language of Mesopotamia from the days of Sargon (*c.* 2360 BC) through Assyrian and Babylonian times. The precise location of ancient Accad is unknown.

See AKKAD, AKKADIANS.

Acco, Accho. Major Palestinian port city from the earliest Canaanite period. The only clear OT reference to Acco is the statement that at the time of Israel's conquest of Canaan, Asher's tribe failed to drive out its inhabitants (Jgs 1:31, KJV Accho). Acco is frequently mentioned in Middle and New Kingdom Egyptian texts and in Assyrian records. Presumably Acco came under Israelite control during David's reign and was among the 20 cities given by Solomon to King Hiram of Tyre (1 Kgs 9:11–14). In later centuries Acco was captured by Alexander the Great of Macedonia. It was eventually rebuilt and renamed Ptolemais (Acts 21:7).

The Crusaders of the 13th century AD used Acco, which they called Acre, as a major base for their operations in Palestine. Today Acco is located on the northern promontory of the bay dominated by the modern Jewish city of Haifa. The bay has provided the finest harbor in both ancient and modern Palestine. Ancient Acco was located a little farther inland at a site called Tell el-Fukhar. Excavations since 1973 have uncovered remains dating to Canaanite, Israelite, and Hellenistic periods.

Aceldama. KJV form of Akeldama, meaning ''Field of Blood,'' in Acts 1:19.

See BLOOD, FIELD OF.

Achaia. Name generally used in NT times to refer to the entire Greek peninsula south of Thessalonica.

See GREECE, GREEKS.

Achaicus. Early convert in Corinth. Achaicus, Stephanas, and Fortunatus were visiting Paul in Ephesus when he wrote 1 Corinthians (1 Cor 16:17). It was probably Achaicus and his companions who brought Paul a letter from the Corinthian church (1 Cor 7:1) and returned with Paul's reply.

Achan, Achar. Member of Judah's tribe who kept some of the spoils from the Israelite victory at Jericho in violation of Joshua's order and God's command (Jos 6:1–7:1). A subsequent Israelite defeat at Ai, a weaker city than Jericho, revealed God's anger to Joshua. With God's help, Joshua determined which of the Israelites had been guilty of disobedience. Achan confessed that he had buried a robe and some gold and silver from Jericho in his tent (Jos 7:20–22). The recovered loot was taken to the valley of Achor (meaning ''trouble,'' ''calamity"), where Achan and his family were stoned. In the Hebrew, 1 Chronicles 2:7 gives Achan's name (exact meaning unknown) as Achar ("troubler") because he was "the troubler of Israel, who transgressed in the matter of the devoted thing."

WALTER R. HEARN

See CONQUEST AND ALLOTMENT OF THE LAND.

Achaz. KJV form of Ahaz, Judah's king, in Matthew 1:9.

See AHAZ #1.

Achbor. 1. Father of the Edomite king Baalhanan, before the establishment of Israel's monarchy (Gn 36:38,39; 1 Chr 1:49).

2. Michaiah's son, courtier of King Josiah of the southern kingdom of Judah. Josiah sent Achbor in a delegation to ask Huldah the prophetess about the newly found Book of the Law (2 Kgs 22:12–14). Achbor was also referred to as Abdon, son of Micah (2 Chr 34:20). He was the father of Elnathan (Jer 26:22; 36:12).

Achim. Descendant of Zerubbabel, listed in the NT as an ancestor of Jesus (Mt 1:14).

See GENEALOGY OF JESUS CHRIST.

Achish. King of the Philistine city of Gath. Although David had killed Goliath, Gath's champion (1 Sm 17), David later fled from Saul to Achish's court. Realizing his mistake, David pretended to be crazy in order to preserve his life. His feigned madness caused Achish to cast him out as unwelcome (1 Sm 21:10–15), but later when David came back to Gath with a band of 600 guerrilla fighters, Achish gave him the city of Ziklag as a base of operations (1 Sm 27:1–7). Achish thought David's men were raiding the Israelites, not realizing they were actually wiping out Philistine towns (1 Sm 27:8–12). Achish is designated by the Philistine title Abimelech in the title of Psalm 34.

Achmetha. KJV form of Ecbatana, a Persian city, in Ezra 6:2.

See ECBATANA.

Achor. Valley that received its name when Achan, the "troubler" of Israel, was stoned and burned there (Jos 7:24,26; cf. 1 Chr 2:7). Achor was on the northern boundary of Judah's tribal allotment (Jos 15:7). Later the valley is mentioned in prophecies of Israel's future blessings. A valley once known as the scene of Israel's trouble would become "a door of hope" and a place for joyful singing (Hos 2:15); a place of relative desolation would one day become "a place for herds to lie down" (Is 65:10). The Valley of Achor is commonly identified as the Buqe'ah.

Achsah, Achsa. Caleb's daughter (1 Chr 2:49, KJV Achsa). Othniel, Caleb's nephew, accepted his uncle's challenge to capture Kiriathsepher in order to marry Achsah. She persuaded Othniel to ask her father Caleb for a field, and she herself asked Caleb for two springs of water, a necessity for life in the desert (Jos 15:16–19; Jgs 1:12–15).

Achshaph. Canaanite royal city in Joshua's time. Its king joined an alliance led by Jabin, king of Hazor, against Israel in a battle at the springs of Merom (Jos 11:1). After Israel's decisive victory, Achshaph's king was one of 31 Canaanite kings conquered by Joshua (12:20), fulfilling God's promise to deliver kings into Israel's hand (Dt 7:24). The city was subsequently assigned to Asher's tribe for an inheritance (Jos 19:25). Achshaph has been tentatively identified as Khirbet Harbaj.

Achzib. 1. City in Judah's territory (Jos 15:44). The prophet Micah listed it among cities that would be destroyed with Samaria (Mi 1:14). It was probably the same as Chezib (Gn 38:5) and Cozeba (1 Chr 4:22, KJV Chozeba).

2. City in Asher's territory (Jos 19:29), one of seven from which the tribe failed to drive out the Canaanite inhabitants (Jgs 1:31). Recent excavations at Achzib (modern ez-Zib) show that the town was occupied almost continuously from the ninth to the third centuries BC. Evidence of the Canaanite town during earlier centuries has not been found. However, two cemeteries, one of the 10th through 9th centuries BC, have produced an amazing number of scarabs, ivories, pottery, and jewelry of excellent craftsmanship, which indicates early occupation.

Acra. Citadel of Jerusalem during the Seleucid and Hasmonean periods. The citadel was located on a high point near the temple. An exceptionally strong fortress, the Acra housed the garrison and controlled the city throughout the Maccabean wars. The Seleucid government considered the Acra a royal stronghold to be administered separately from the rest of Judea. At times, one armed force held the Acra and its opponent held the city itself, so that the fortress almost became an independent city. Josephus made mention of two forts called Acra. The earlier citadel was captured by Antiochus III in 198 BC. That Acra must be identical with the temple fortress of the Persian and Ptolemaic periods, the "castle" of Nehemiah 7:2. The site later became the fortress called Antonia in the Roman period.

A new citadel, the Acra proper, was later built by the Seleucids. Antiochus IV Epiphanes (ruled 175–164 BC), after a humiliating defeat in Alexandria by the Romans, decided to abolish all Jewish worship practices. In 167 BC he violated the most sacred Jewish laws by constructing an altar to the Greek god Zeus in the temple at Jerusalem and perhaps by sacrificing a pig on it (1 Mc 1:20–64; 2 Mc 6:1–6). The next year Antiochus sent a garrison to build the Acra and maintain his religious reforms, primarily to see that no aspect of the Jewish religion was practiced in the city. The Acra also served as a storehouse for food and loot plundered from the city. The Jews considered it "an ambush against the sanctuary, an evil adversary of Israel continually" (1 Mc 1:36).

Josephus reported that Simon, the second of the Maccabean brothers, captured the Acra in 142 BC and spent three years leveling both the fort and the hill on which it stood. Josephus' account is questioned, however, because other accounts mention Simon as ritually cleansing the citadel and using it to maintain the city's security (see 1 Mc 13:50; 14:37).

The Acra's exact location is unknown. Scholars formerly placed it south of the temple on the Ophel ridge. Most scholars now locate it on the western hill, just across the Tyropean valley from the temple area—either on the site of Herod the Great's palace or, more probably, in the large area surrounding the Maccabean palace.

See JERUSALEM; JUDAISM.

Acre. Measure of an area of land. Literally, the Hebrew word means "yoke" and probably refers to the amount of land a yoke of oxen could plow in a day.

See WEIGHTS AND MEASURES.

Acts of the Apostles, Book of the. NT book presenting the history of the early church and written as a sequel to the Gospel of Luke. In the arrangement of the NT books, Acts comes after the four Gospels and before the Epistles.

Authorship. The Book of Acts does not state clearly who its writer is, but the general consensus is that Luke was its author.

Early church tradition from the second century states that Acts (as well as the third Gospel) was written by a traveling companion and fellow worker of the apostle Paul. That companion is identified in Colossians 4:14 as "Luke the beloved physician," and mentioned among Paul's gentile fellow workers (Col 4:10–17; see also 2 Tm 4:11; Phlm 24).

Strong support for the tradition that the author of Acts was a companion of Paul comes from the second half of the book, which recounts Paul's ministry. There, several narratives are told in the first person plural: "And a vision appeared to Paul in the night. . . . We sought to go on into Macedonia . . ." (Acts 16:9–18); "These went on and were waiting for us at Troas, but we sailed away from Philippi . . ." (20:5–21:18); "And when it was decided that we should sail for Italy . . ." (27:1–28:16). These "we" sections sound like part of a travel narrative or diary written by an eyewitness who accompanied Paul from Troas to Philippi on his second missionary journey; from Philippi to Miletus on the third; from Miletus to Jerusalem; and from Caesarea to Rome. Since the style and vocabulary of these travel narratives resemble those of the rest of the book, it is highly probable that the diarist was also the author of the entire book.

The sophisticated literary style and polished use of the Greek language in the book, as well as the fact that it is addressed to someone called Theophilus (possibly a highly placed Roman official), provide strong support for the tradition that Luke was a gentile convert to Christianity. His consistent and frequent use of the Greek OT may indicate that he had been a gentile "God-fearer" before conversion to the new faith.

Date, Origin, Destination. The question of the date and place of the origin of Acts continues to be debated. There are no clear indications in the book itself. With regard to its destination, Luke did not leave any doubt. In the opening verse he addresses a certain Theophilus, to whom he had already written an earlier book about the life of Jesus. There can be no doubt that he was referring to the work we know as the Gospel of Luke. In the preface to that Gospel (Lk 1:1–4), Luke clearly stated his purpose for writing and addressed his account "for you, most excellent Theophilus." It is not clear who that person was. Some interpreters think that Theophilus (which means "dear to God" or "lover of God") stands for Christian readers in general rather than any specific individual. However, the designation "most excellent" argues against such an assumption. That ascription was a common title of honor, designating a person with official standing in the Roman sociopolitical order (cf. use of the title for Felix, Acts 23:26; 24:2; and for Festus, 26:25). It is thus likely that Luke intended his two-volume work for an official representative of Roman society.

When was Acts written? Scholarly opinion is divided, with some dating Acts in the last quarter of the first century. A date that late is strongly dependent on the dating of the Gospel of Luke. Since the Gospel was written first, and since Luke based his story of Jesus on eyewitness accounts and written sources (among which was possibly the Gospel of Mark, probably written in the 60s), Acts should not be dated much before AD 85. Proponents of such a late date claim support from the theology of Acts, which they see as picturing a Christian church settled into history, adjusted to the prospect of a lengthy period before the Lord's return. Since expectation of the Lord's imminent return was fanned into a living flame by the Jewish revolt and the fall of Jerusalem in AD 70, time must be allowed for that flame to have died down a bit.

Other scholars date Acts around AD 70 or shortly thereafter. The Jewish rebellion of AD 66–70, which culminated in the destruction of Jerusalem, brought the Jewish faith—legal until then—into disrepute. The Christian movement, which had been accepted as a Jewish sect, became suspect. Christians were increasingly charged with being enemies of Rome. A study of Acts shows that among a number of purposes (see below), Luke seems to have been defending the Christians against the charge of hostility toward the state. He showed how Roman officials repeatedly testified to the complete innocence of Christians and above all else of Paul (16:39; 18:14–17; 19:37; 23:29; 25:25; 26:32). Luke also made it clear that Paul was allowed to carry on his mission with full approval of Roman officials in the very heart of the imperial capital (28:16–31).

A still earlier date, closer to Paul's Roman imprisonment (early 60s), has been advocated by a number of scholars. Several considerations give weighty support to such an early date.

1. The abrupt ending of Acts, describing Paul carrying on a ministry in Rome before his trial had commenced, may indicate that Luke was writing at that point. It is possible, of course, that Luke ended his story with Paul preaching the gospel in Rome because one of his purposes had been accomplished: namely, showing how the gospel spread from Jerusalem to Rome. But it seems highly unlikely that Luke would close his history without Paul's defense of the gospel before Caesar himself, if that had already happened.

2. Acts contains much detailed information on conditions existing in Paul's time: on the geographical, historical, and political situations in Palestine and the Roman provinces. Such specific information, together with the names of many first-generation Christians, contemporary kings, and procurators, is too precise to have been available at a date much later than the 60s.

3. A third argument for an early date is the fact that Luke wrote his work without making use of Paul's letters. Luke seems to be writing his history without the benefit of that important firsthand source dealing with Paul and primitive Christianity. A collection of Paul's letters was not yet available to him, which may explain some difficulties in historical details between Luke's account and those documented in Paul's letters.

4. Finally, the most appropriate period for Luke's history, with its defense of the Christian movement against all kinds of accusations from both Jews and Gentiles, is the period when Christianity was becoming suspect but was not yet proscribed. That was the time before the start of the persecutions under Nero in AD 64.

The early date would correspond with the contention that Luke was with Paul during his Roman imprisonment and that he wrote his history in Rome while waiting for Paul's trial to begin. NT scholar J. Munck suggested the possibility that Luke's work was partially intended to influence the verdict. Luke presented a picture of Christianity and of Paul that he hoped would enable Paul to continue his work among the Gentiles.

How does the Gospel of Luke, which many scholars date in the late 70s or 80s, fit with such an early date for the writing of Acts, the second volume of a two-volume history? One solution based on literary study of the Gospel of Luke and a comparison of Luke's Gospel with Mark's is that Luke may have written an early edition of his Gospel before he became acquainted with the Gospel of Mark. Thus, Acts followed his first edition of the Gospel, which was later expanded into our present Gospel of Luke by the addition of material from Mark.

Background. Luke grounds his documentary of the rapid expansion of Christianity in the history of the Roman Empire and Palestine during the three decades from AD 30 to 60. Some brief historical and geographical considerations will aid in understanding Luke's history.

Acts 1 to 12 reports the beginnings of the Christian movement within the imperial province of Syria, which included Judea and Samaria. In the first century AD those regions were generally governed by Roman procurators or puppet kings. At the time of Jesus' death and resurrection (AD 30?), Pontius Pilate was procurator in Judea and Samaria (AD 26–36). Galilee was ruled by King Herod Antipas (4 BC–AD 39). Tiberius was emperor of the Roman Empire (AD 14–37). The account of Acts 1 to 12 took place in the period AD 30–44.

The conversion of Saul (Acts 9) is generally dated in AD 33. In the years leading up to that

Paul's window in Damascus.

crucial event, opposition to the early church, climaxing in the stoning of Stephen (Acts 7) and Saul's attempt to track down Jewish Christians even to the synagogues in Damascus (Acts 9), was guided by the Jewish religious leadership. How was that possible under Roman sovereignty? One aspect of Rome's imperial policy was to give local populations a measure of autonomy, particularly in matters of religious law and order. Religious jurisdiction in Palestine was in the hands of the high priest and leading scribes and Pharisees. Though the death penalty was not included in such jurisdiction, a procurator such as Pilate, anxious to maintain relative order, could be counted on to turn his back while an illegal action such as the stoning of Stephen was going on. Also, offenders against local religious authority who fled to areas outside that particular jurisdiction could be extradited. Thus it was possible for Saul to go to the foreign city of Damascus with arrest warrants for Jewish Christians there (9:1,2).

Persecution against the church in Jerusalem (8:1–3) under Saul's auspices led to dispersion of Jerusalem Christians into the surrounding regions of Judea and Samaria to the north. Philip's mission into Samaria is of particular significance because of a longstanding bitterness and animosity between Jews and Samaritans, going back to very early times (see the words of a Samaritan woman to Jesus: "for Jews have no dealings with Samaritans," Jn 4:9). The Jews regarded Samaritans as racial and religious half-breeds; in Samaria Jews and foreign settlers had intermingled as a result of Assyrian policy after the fall of the

northern kingdom of Israel in 722 BC. In spite of attempts to effect a reconciliation after the Babylonian exile (c. 500 BC), the split was widened when the Samaritans erected a temple on Mt Gerizim as a rival to the restored temple in Jerusalem (Jn 4:20). In light of that background, Philip's Samaritan mission was a bold action, signaling the move of the Christian faith beyond the confines of orthodox Judaism.

Not much is known about developments in early Christianity during the next decade. After Saul's conversion and departure to his native Tarsus, the church evidently enjoyed a period of tranquility, consolidating its gains and growing steadily (9:31–11:26). It can be assumed, from Galatians 1:18–21 and the existence of Christian communities which Paul and Silas visited on the second missionary tour (Acts 15:40,41), that Paul was not idle during that decade, but intensely involved in the mission to the Gentiles. (After Acts 13:9, the name "Saul" is dropped from the narrative.)

In AD 41 Claudius became emperor of Rome and installed Herod Agrippa I as king of the Jews. (The procurator Pontius Pilate had been removed several years earlier for inept administration of the region.) Agrippa I was grandson of Herod the Great and his Jewish princess Mariamne. Because of his Jewish roots, he was more popular with his subjects than the former Herods. No doubt it was his desire to increase that popularity and gain the support of the Jewish religious authorities which led to a renewed outbreak of violence against the Jerusalem church. Acts 12 recounts the execution of James (the brother of the apostle John) and the imprisonment of Peter. The story of Agrippa I's death (Acts 12:20–23) is paralleled in an account by the Jewish historian Josephus, who dates the event in AD 44.

A second event providing a time reference for the unfolding story of the early church is the collection of famine relief in Antioch for Christians in Judea (Acts 11:27–29). Luke stated that a severe famine took place (11:28) during the reign of Emperor Claudius (AD 41–54). Josephus, writing his *Antiquities* at the end of the first century, spoke of a severe famine in Palestine between the years 44 and 48. According to Acts 12:25, Barnabas and Paul finished their mission to famine-stricken Christians in Judea after the death of Agrippa I, making it possible to date their mission about AD 45.

At that point in the narrative of Acts, Paul is launched officially into his mission to the Gentiles (13:1–3), for which the history and geography of the larger Roman empire form the backdrop. The official Roman policy toward the various religions in the empire was one of toleration. That policy, plus use of the Greek language throughout the empire and a phenomenal network of roads and sea routes, paved the way for Paul's far-ranging missionary work.

The first tour (AD 46–47) took Paul and Barnabas through the island province of Cyprus in the northeastern tip of the Mediterranean Sea and into the province of Galatia, where churches were established in several cities in southern Galatia (Antioch of Pisidia, Iconium, Lystra, Derbe). Galatia is located in Asia Minor, bordered by the Black Sea, the Aegean Sea, and the Mediterranean Sea on its northern, western, and southern sides. Those cities, important colonial outposts for the Romans, contained mixed populations, including large Jewish communities. It was in the synagogues of those communities that Paul launched his missionary efforts, almost always meeting with considerable opposition (Acts 13,14).

The deliberations of the Jerusalem Council about differences between Jewish and gentile Christians (Acts 15) can be dated in the year 48. It was followed by Paul's second missionary journey, which led him through the already evangelized territory of his native Cilicia, Galatia, and through Troas on the Aegean coast to Macedonia and down into Achaia, the Greek peninsula (Acts 15:40–18:22). Churches were established in the important Macedonian cities of Philippi, Thessalonica, and Beroea.

Paul's one-and-a-half years in Corinth (Acts 18:11) can be dated with some certainty in AD 51–52. An ancient inscription among the ruins of Delphi, a city in central Greece, states that Gallio became proconsul of Achaia in 51. Acts 18:12–17 tells how Paul was accused by antagonistic Jews before Gallio. The implication is that Paul's adversaries in Corinth felt that a new proconsul could be persuaded to side with their cause. Thus, Paul's stay in Corinth can be dated around the beginning of Gallio's proconsulship.

Another significant historical detail is Paul's encounter with Priscilla and Aquila in Corinth (Acts 18:1,2). The couple had recently come from Rome as a result of Claudius's banishment of all Jews from that city. In his *Life of Claudius*, the Roman biographer Suetonius makes a statement which may indicate that the introduction of the Christian faith into synagogues in Rome caused considerable strife to erupt. Such a disturbance would have been ample cause for Claudius's edict. In that period Christians were still considered a sect within Judaism by Roman officials.

Luke's account of Paul's return to Palestine and the beginning of his third missionary tour brings up a fascinating historical question about what happened to the followers of John

Ruins in Corinth.

the Baptist (Acts 13:13–19:7). Acts 18:24–28 refers to a learned Jew, Apollos, who was actively teaching about Jesus in the synagogue at Ephesus, but who was apparently not a member of a distinctively Christian community, not having been baptized in the name of Jesus. He was acquainted only with the baptism of repentance practiced by John the Baptist. After Apollos went to Corinth to minister to the young congregation which Paul founded the previous year, Paul went to Ephesus. There he met several disciples of Jesus who, like Apollos, had experienced John's baptism of repentance, but who had not been baptized as Christians.

Luke's reference to Apollos and those disciples, as well as several passages in the Gospels, indicate that the movement begun by John the Baptist did not simply come to an end when Jesus began his ministry. Evidently John continued to baptize until his death (Jn 3:22–24), and many of his disciples maintained John's work after his death. Probably both Apollos and the disciples at Ephesus were products of the continuing ministry of John's disciples. Eventually they were introduced to "the way of the Lord" (Acts 18:25). Their lack of knowledge about a distinctive Christian baptism or about the reality of the Holy Spirit (19:2–4) shows how much diversity in both belief and practice existed in early Christianity.

Paul's third missionary tour began with a three-year ministry in Ephesus (19:1–20:1), continued with a visit to churches established on the previous journey (20:2–12), and came to a climax with his arrest in Jerusalem (Acts 21). It took place in the mid-50s (53–57). Paul's arrest in Jerusalem and arraignment before the provincial governor, Felix, in Caesarea (23:23–24:23) must be dated about 57. After Paul had spent two years in house arrest, no doubt prolonged by Felix to gain favor with Jewish subjects, Felix was replaced by Porcius Festus (AD 59–60). Josephus noted that Felix was recalled because of an outbreak of civil strife between Jewish and gentile inhabitants of Caesarea and Felix's unwise handling of the situation.

The new procurator, Festus, was uncertain about what to do with his prisoner. The Jewish leadership sought to seize that opportunity, aware of the desire of new procurators to gain popularity with their subjects (25:1–9). Realizing the threat, Paul appealed his case to the highest court of the empire, presided over by Caesar himself (25:10–12). By exercising his right as a Roman citizen, Paul insured his removal from the shadow of Jerusalem.

Festus was then left with a problem. He had to send with his prisoner a report to the emperor, clearly outlining the charges. Since he did not really comprehend the case (25:25–27), he sought the advice of Herod Agrippa II, who with his sister had come to Caesarea to pay their respects to the new imperial governor of Palestine (25:13). Agrippa II was the son of Herod Agrippa I and at least in theory a Jew. He ruled over parts of Palestine from AD 50 to 100 and had been given the right to appoint the Jewish high priests. His familiarity with Jewish religious traditions and the Law thus put him in a better position to understand Jerusalem's case against Paul. The outcome of Paul's appearance before Festus and Agrippa (26:1–29) was recognition of Paul's innocence (26:31). Yet Paul's appeal to Rome had to be honored; the law governing such cases had to be followed (26:32).

Paul's relative freedom during the next two-year period (Acts 28:30) seems unusual, but was a rather common practice in Roman judicial proceedings, especially for Roman citizens who had appealed to the emperor. There is no good reason to believe that Paul was executed at the time when Luke's narrative ends (c. AD 61–62). The great fire of Rome and Nero's subsequent persecution of Christians were still several years away (AD 64). It is likely that the case against Paul was dismissed, especially in light of the favorable verdict by Festus and King Agrippa. It is also likely that Paul was executed during the later, more general persecution of Christians. Such a sequence would correspond with the tradition cited by Eusebius, a 4th-century church historian, that Paul resumed his ministry and later suffered martyrdom under Nero.

Purpose and Theological Teaching. The purpose of any written document can be discerned in two ways: by the author's explicit statements or by an analysis of the content. An interpreter is often forced to depend entirely on the content, but Luke's two-volume work (the Gospel and Acts) permits both ways. In the preface to the Gospel, intended to cover the second volume also, Luke told Theophilus (and the audience he represented) that he had set out to write an accurate, orderly account about the beginnings of the Christian movement in the ministry of Jesus of Nazareth (Lk 1:1–4). The opening lines in Acts indicate that the narrative beginning with Jesus of Nazareth (vol 1) is continuing, and that Luke's second volume intends to trace the story from Palestine to Rome (Acts 1:1–8).

Why was Luke interested in documenting the story for Theophilus? A brief statement in Luke 1:4 points to an answer: ". . . that you may know the truth concerning the things of which you have been informed." The implication seems to be that Luke was writing an apologetic work, hoping thereby to correct misunderstandings or misconceptions, and defending Christianity against false charges brought against it. Much in the content of Luke's work, especially in Acts, supports this understanding of his purpose.

A number of misconceptions attended the birth and growth of the Christian movement. One concerned the relationship between the new faith and Judaism. Many, both within the church and among Roman officials, understood the Christian faith as no more than a particular expression of, or sect within, Judaism. Against that restricted notion, Luke–Acts strikes a universal note. The Gospel proclaims Jesus as Savior of the world (Lk 2:29–32). In Acts, Stephen's defense before the Jewish council (Acts 7), Peter's experience in Joppa with Cornelius (Acts 10), and Paul's speech at Athens (Acts 17) all demonstrate that Christianity is not merely a Jewish sect, some narrow messianic movement, but rather a universal faith. Another problem was popular identification of the new faith with the various religious cults and mystery religions in the Roman Empire. The accounts of the early church's conflict with Simon the magician (Acts 8) and of Paul and Barnabas's rejection of an attempt to worship them at Lystra (Acts 14) undermine the popular charge of superstition. Also, Christianity is not a mystery cult in which esoteric, secret rites bring a worshiper into union with the divine. The Lord worshiped by Christians, said Luke, belongs to real history; he lived his life in Palestine in the then-recent past, openly, for all to observe (see the speeches of Peter and Paul in Acts 2,10,13).

Luke's major purpose, however, was defense of Christianity against the charge that it posed a threat to the order and stability of the Roman Empire. There were, of course, grounds for such suspicions. After all, the founder of the movement had been crucified on a charge of sedition by a Roman procurator, and the movement which claimed his name seemed to evoke tumult, disorder, and riots wherever it spread. Luke's account met those problems head-on. In the Gospel he presented the trial of Jesus as a serious miscarriage of justice. Pilate had handed Jesus over for crucifixion, but he had found Jesus not guilty. Herod Antipas likewise found no substance in the charges against Jesus (Lk 23:13–16; Acts 13:28). A neutral or even friendly attitude of Roman officials toward leading Christians and the movement as a whole is documented throughout Acts. The Roman proconsul of Cyprus, Sergius Paulus, gladly received Paul and Barnabas and responded positively to their message (Acts 13:7–12). The chief magistrate in Philippi apologized for an illegal beating and imprisonment of Paul and Silas (Acts 16:37–39). The proconsul of Achaia, Gallio, found Paul guiltless in the eyes of Roman law (Acts 18:12–16). In Ephesus the magistrate intervened in a crowd's attack on Paul and his companions, rejecting the charges against them (Acts 19:35–39). A tribune of the Roman military contingent in Jerusalem arrested Paul, but it turned out that he really saved him from the wrath of a mob; in his letter to the procurator Felix, the tribune acknowledged that Paul was not guilty by Roman law (Acts 23:26–29). The same verdict was repeated after Paul's arraignment before Felix, his successor Festus, and Herod Agrippa II: "This man is doing nothing to deserve death or imprisonment" (Acts 26:31). Luke climaxed his story by telling how Paul carried on his missionary activity in Rome, the very heart of the empire, and with the permission of the imperial guards (Acts 28:30,31). It is clear throughout Luke's defense that the strife which attended the beginnings and progress of Christianity was not due primarily to anything within the movement, but rather to Jewish opposition and falsification.

Within his lengthy apology for the integrity of Christianity, Luke's specific theological perspectives can be clearly seen. The two-volume work presents a grand scheme of the history of redemption, extending from the *time of Israel* (Lk 1,2) through the *time of Jesus*, and continuing through *the time of the church*, when the good news for Israel is extended to all nations. Paralleling that emphasis is an insistence that God is present in the redemptive story through the Holy Spirit. In the Gospel, Jesus is presented as the Man of the Spirit; the reality of the Spirit empowered him for his work (Lk 3:22; 4:1,14,18). In Acts, the fellowship of Jesus' disciples is presented as the community of the Spirit (Acts 1:8; 2:1–8). What Jesus in the power of the Spirit had begun in his own ministry, the church in the power of the Spirit continues to do. The promise of John the Baptist (Lk 3:16) that Jesus would empower his people with the Spirit was reaffirmed by Jesus at the end of his own ministry (Lk 24:49; Acts 1:5). That promise found initial fulfillment at Pentecost (Acts 2) and expression through the movement of the faith from Jerusalem to Rome.

For Luke, the empowering presence of God's Spirit was a reality that gave the new faith its power, integrity, and perseverance. It enabled faithful witness (Acts 1:8) and created genuine community (2:44–47; 4:32–37), something for which the ancient world desperately longed. The Spirit in the new community produced courage and boldness (see Peter's defenses in Acts 2–5), empowered for service (Acts 6), overcame prejudice as in the mission in Samaria (Acts 8), broke down walls as in the Cornelius episode (chs 10 and 11), and sent believers out on missions (ch 13).

The entire story is also punctuated by the centrality of Jesus' resurrection. Luke, like Paul (see 1 Cor 15:12–20), must have been convinced that without the resurrection of Jesus there would be no Christian faith at all. More than that, the resurrection put God's stamp of approval on Jesus' life and ministry, authenticating the truth of his claims. Luke announced his interest in that theme at the outset: the ultimate criterion for an apostolic replacement for Judas was that he must have been, with the other disciples, a witness to Jesus' resurrection. Throughout Acts, from Peter's Pentecost sermon and defenses before the Sanhedrin to Paul's speeches before Felix and Agrippa, the church is shown bearing witness to Jesus' resurrection as the "great reversal" executed by God (2:22–24,36; 3:14,15; 5:30,31; 10:39–42).

A subsidiary theme is the idea that Christ's resurrection is the basis for the resurrection of believers and thus the foundation of Christian hope (4:2; 13:32,33; 17:18,29–32; 23:6; 24:21; 26:23).

A further theme related to the centrality of Christ's resurrection is Luke's teaching that the resurrection and ascension of Jesus were events that inaugurated his lordship over the church, and (through it) over the world. In his Gospel, Luke showed how the reign of

God broke into human history in a unique and decisive way in the ministry of Jesus. The resurrection confirmed that fact, at the same time removing the limitation of the Lord's earthly presence. "Exalted at the right hand of God" (Acts 2:32,33; 5:31) is a biblical metaphor indicating rule and authority. In the final moments of his life, Stephen saw a vision of the exalted Christ standing at God's right hand (7:56). Through the resurrection, Peter said in his Pentecost address, God made Jesus "Lord" (2:34–36). To the religious leaders in Jerusalem, Peter claimed that the power of Christ was responsible for the healing of a cripple (4:10), and that Christ was the one who, though rejected by official Judaism, had become the most important factor in God's redemptive story (4:11). Paul's vision on the road to Damascus confirmed it; his question "Who are you, Lord?" was answered by "I am Jesus, whom you are persecuting" (9:5). The good news of the kingdom which God sent to Israel came preeminently through Jesus Christ; this one, said Peter, is now Lord of all (10:36).

The reality of the forgiveness of sins is another emphasis in Luke's theology. In his Gospel, he understood as central Jesus' acceptance of those individuals who were defined in Judaism as "sinners." In Acts the reality of forgiveness is also prominent. The response to Peter's Pentecost sermon was "What shall we do?" (Acts 2:37). The answer was twofold: Repent, and be baptized in Jesus' name. Forgiveness of sins and the experience of the Spirit's presence were promised as a result. Several more times throughout Acts, forgiveness of sin is associated with repentance (3:19,26; 5:31). At other times, forgiveness of sin is associated with the act of faith (10:43; 13:38,39; 15:9).

In his defense before Agrippa, Paul brought repentance and faith together with the forgiveness of sins. Thus for Luke the act of faith (believing in Jesus) and the act of repentance were virtually synonymous. To believe was to turn toward Christ in trust and commitment. Faith created a new orientation for one's life. Similarly, to repent was to "turn about," to face in a new direction. In early Christianity the event of baptism was understood primarily as an act of initiation into the community of faith; therefore, the experience of the forgiveness of sins came in the context of that accepting and forgiving community. Thus the phrase "be baptized . . . for the forgiveness of your sins" (2:38) does not mean that something magically happens in the ritual itself. It means that on the basis of repentance and faith one is baptized into a new community in which forgiveness becomes a reality. For Luke the community of the Spirit was the vehicle

for the forgiving and re-creating presence of God.

Content. The best way to get an overview of the Book of Acts is to follow its own structure. There are several ways to understand the structure of Luke's work. Each approach focuses on the content and movement in a particular way, and each has a contribution to make.

Acts falls naturally into two parts, chapters 1 to 12, and 13 to 28. The first part, roughly speaking, contains the "acts of Peter." Part two is largely concerned with the "acts of Paul." In the first 12 chapters Peter is the central figure who initiates the choosing of a replacement for Judas Iscariot (ch 1); addresses the multitudes at Pentecost (2); interprets the significance of the healing of a lame man to a temple crowd (3); delivers a defense of the Christian proclamation before the supreme Jewish council (4); leads the apostles in a healing ministry and speaks for them (5); stands in the forefront of conflict with a Samaritan magician, "Simon the Great" (8); launches—though somewhat unwillingly—the movement of the gospel to the Gentiles through Cornelius (10,11); and draws the fire of Herod's campaign against the church, yet is miraculously delivered from prison (12).

Peter's dominance in part one of Acts is interrupted only slightly and occasionally, by accounts of: Stephen's defense before the council and his martyrdom (6,7); Philip's ministry in Samaria and with an Ethiopian official (8); and Saul's persecution of the church, and his conversion (9).

Proclamation of the gospel to the Gentiles through Paul's ministry is the theme of part two of Acts (13–28). The story primarily concerns three major missionary tours, each of which moved the gospel into yet untouched territory and expanded earlier missionary efforts. The account of Paul's life and work climaxes in his arrest in Jerusalem (21,22), a lengthy imprisonment in Caesarea (23–26), and a voyage to Rome (27,28).

Paul's dominance of this section of Acts is hardly interrupted. His coworker, Barnabas, is seen as playing only a secondary role during the first missionary tour into Asia Minor (13,14). Silas exercised a similar function on the second tour to Greece (16–18). In the only major interlude where Paul was not the focus, the council at Jerusalem (15), church leaders wrestled with questions of the relationship between Jewish and gentile Christians and of the observance of the Law. Yet even that event was occasioned by Paul's mission to the Gentiles. A minor intermission is the account of Apollos's preaching in Ephesus just before Paul's arrival on his third tour (13:24–28). It is

Ruins of the Roman amphitheater in Samaria.

clear that Luke centered his account of the expansion of Christianity on two giants of the early church.

Another way of getting at the structure and content of Acts is thematic. It has its starting point in Jesus' statement, "you shall receive power when the Holy Spirit has come upon you; and you shall be my witnesses in Jerusalem and in all Judea and Samaria and to the end of the earth" (Acts 1:8). Acts can be seen as the story of the fulfillment of that "Great Commission," unfolding essentially in three stages: (1) witness to Judaism, focused in Jerusalem but also expanding into surrounding Judea and north into Galilee (chs 1–7); (2) witness to Samaria through Philip, Peter, and John (8:1–9:31); (3) witness to the gentile world, first haltingly through Peter (9:32–12:25), and then decisively through Paul (13–28).

Whatever approach one takes, the Book of Acts stands out as a gripping story, full of action, adventure, insight, and even surprise. It can be candidly stated, for example, that Paul's final journey to Rome—in chains—was not exactly what he had in mind. Nonetheless, even in that event, and perhaps most of all in that event, Luke saw the hand of God mightily at work. Right there in Rome, Paul was "preaching the kingdom of God and teaching about the Lord Jesus Christ quite openly and unhindered" (Acts 28:31). With that powerful affirmation Luke brought his narrative to a close.

MANFRED T. BRAUCH

See APOSTOLIC AGE; JERUSALEM COUNCIL; LUKE (PERSON); PAUL, THE APOSTLE; PETER, THE APOSTLE; THEOPHILUS #1; CHRONOLOGY, NEW TESTAMENT.

Bibliography. E.M. Blaiklock, *Acts: The Birth of the Church;* F.F. Bruce, *Commentary on the Book of the Acts;* M. Hengel, *Acts and the History of Earliest Christianity;* I.H. Marshall, *Acts;* C.H. Talbert (ed.), *Prospectus on Luke-Acts;* C.S.C. Williams, *The Acts of the Apostles.*

Adadah. One of 30 cities assigned to Judah's tribe in the Negeb, or southern desert region (Jos 15:22). A Greek textual variant is Ararah, which appears as Aroer in 1 Samuel 30:28. It may be modern Khirbet Ar'arah, located 12 miles south of Beersheba.

Adah. 1. One of Lamech's two wives, and mother of two sons, Jabal and Jubal (Gn 4:19–21,23).

2. Esau's first wife, daughter of Elon the Hittite and mother of Eliphaz (Gn 36:2–16). She is perhaps also called Basemath in Genesis 26:34.

See BASEMATH #1.

Adaiah. 1. Josiah's maternal grandfather. Josiah's mother, Jedidah, was Adaiah's daughter (2 Kgs 22:1).

2. Ethan's son, a Levite of the Gershom clan and an ancestor of Asaph the psalmist (1 Chr 6:41). He is sometimes identified with the Iddo of 1 Chronicles 6:21.

See IDDO #2.

3. Shimei's son, a minor member of Benjamin's tribe (1 Chr 8:21).

4. Jeroham's son, a priest who returned to Jerusalem after the exile (1 Chr 9:12; Neh 11:12).

5. Maaseiah's father. Maaseiah was a captain under Jehoiada the priest (2 Chr 23:1).

6. Bani's son, who obeyed Ezra's exhortation to divorce his pagan wife after the exile (Ezr 10:29).

7. Son of a different Bani, who also obeyed that exhortation (Ezr 10:39).

8. Joiarib's son, descended from Perez, and an ancestor of Maaseiah (Neh 11:5).

Adalia. Fifth of Haman's 10 sons, all of whom were killed with their father when his plot to destroy the Jews was foiled (Est 9:8).

Adam (Person).   First man and father of the human race. Adam's role in biblical history is important not only in OT considerations but also in understanding the meaning of salvation and the person and work of Jesus Christ.

Adam's Story.   The creation of Adam and the first woman, Eve, is recited in two biblical accounts. The intent of the first account (Gn 1:26–31) is to present the first pair in their relationship to God and to the rest of the created order. It teaches that with regard to God the first humans were created male and female in God's image with his specific mandate to populate and rule over the earth. With regard to the rest of creation the first humans were, on one hand, part of it, being created on the same day as other land animals; on the other hand, they were distinctly above it, being the culmination of the creation process and sole bearers of God's image. Clearly the proper position and dignity of Adam and Eve before God and within creation is the focus of the first Genesis account.

The intent of the second account is much more specific (Gn 2:4–3:24); it seeks to explain the origin of the present human condition of sin and death and to set the stage for the drama of redemption. The story treats in detail aspects of Adam's creation omitted from the first story. For example, it tells of the formation of Adam from the dust of the ground and of his receiving the breath of life from God (Gn 2:7). It recounts the planting of the garden and the responsibility given to Adam to cultivate it (2:8–15). God's instruction to Adam that the fruit of every tree in the garden except one was his for food is carefully recorded, as well as the solemn warning that the fruit of the "tree of the knowledge of good and evil" was never to be eaten, under the pain of death (2:16,17). Adam's loneliness after naming the animals and not finding a suitable companion is also described, thus introducing the creation of the first woman (2:18–22). The creation of Eve from Adam's rib poignantly portrays the essential unity of spirit and purpose of the sexes intended by God. A strong desire for such unity and companionship is shown in Adam's response when he first sees Eve: "This at last is bone of my bones and flesh of my flesh" (2:23).

The story does not end on such a positive note, however. It moves on to record the great deception Satan played upon Eve through the serpent. By clever insinuations and distortion of God's original commandment (cf. Gn 3:1 with 2:16,17) the serpent tricked Eve into eating the forbidden fruit and sharing it with Adam. Eve seems to have eaten because she was deceived (1 Tm 2:14), Adam out of a willful and conscious rebellion. Ironically, the two beings originally created in God's image and likeness believed that they could become "like" God by disobeying him (Gn 3:5).

The effects of their disobedience were immediate though not at all what Adam had expected. For the first time a barrier of shame disrupted the unity of man and woman (Gn 3:7). More important, a barrier of real moral guilt was erected between the first couple and God. The story relates that when God came looking for Adam after his rebellion he was hiding among the trees, already aware of his separation from God (3:8). When God questioned him, Adam threw the blame on Eve and, by implication, back on God: "The woman whom thou gavest to be with me . . ." (3:12). Eve in turn blamed the serpent (3:13).

According to the story, God held all three responsible and informed each one of the calamitous consequences of their rebellion (Gn 3:14–19). The two great mandates, originally signs of pure blessing, became mixed with curse and pain—the earth could now be populated only through the woman's birth pangs and could be subdued only by the man's labor and perspiration (3:16–18). Further, the unity of man and woman would be strained by man's subjugation of her, or possibly by the beginning of a struggle for dominance between them (3:16b can be taken both ways). Finally, God pronounced the ultimate consequence: as he had originally warned, Adam and Eve were to die. Someday the breath of life would be taken from them, and their bodies would return to the dust from which they were made (3:19). That very day they also experienced a "spiritual" death; they were separated from God the giver of life and from the tree of life, the symbol of eternal life (3:22). God sent them out of Eden, and there was no way back. The entrance to paradise was blocked by the cherubim and flaming sword (3:23,24). Only God could restore what they had lost.

The story is not devoid of hope. God was merciful even then. He made them garments of skin to cover their bodies and promised that someday the power of Satan behind the serpent would be crushed by the woman's "seed" (Gn 3:15; cf. Rom 16:20). Many scholars consider that promise to be the first biblical mention of redemption.

After those central events Adam went on to live a full life. He had many children and died at the astounding age of 930 (Gn 4:1,2,25; 5:4,5).

Adam's Significance. Adam's significance is based upon several assumptions, the first being that he was a historical individual. That assumption was made by many OT writers (Gn 4:25; 5:1,3,4,5; 1 Chr 1:1; Jb 31:33 RSV margin; Hos 6:7, if Adam [city] is not intended). The NT writers agreed (Lk 3:38; Rom 5:14; 1 Cor 15:22,45; 1 Tm 2:13,14; Jude 14). Jesus himself justified his view of marriage by alluding to the first couple, an allusion that would be meaningless if Adam were a myth or a mere symbol (Mt 19:4–6; Mk 10:6–9). The historicity and individuality of Adam, although never defended in the Bible, is assumed in the biblical discussions of the significance of his life and actions.

Equally essential to Adam's significance is a second assumption, that he was more than an individual. To begin with, the Hebrew word *adam* (more correctly *'ādhām)* is not merely a proper name. Even in the Genesis story it is not used as a name until Genesis 4:25. The word is one of several Hebrew words meaning "man" and is the generic term for "human race." In the vast majority of cases it refers either to a male individual (Lv 1:2; Jos 14:15; Neh 9:29; Is 56:2) or to humanity in general (Ex 4:11; Nm 12:3; 16:29; Dt 4:28; 1 Kgs 4:31; Jb 7:20; 14:1). The generic, collective sense of the word *adam* is also behind the phrase "children (or sons) of men" (2 Sm 7:14; Pss 11:4; 12:1; 14:2; 53:2; 90:3; Eccl 1:13; 2:3). That phrase, literally "sons of *adam*," simply means "men" or "human beings," and when it is used the entire human race is in view. Indeed, the universalistic human connotation of the word *adam* indicates a concern in the OT going far beyond Israel's nationalistic hopes and its God—to all the earth's peoples and the Lord of all nations (Gn 9:5–7; Dt 5:24; 8:3; 1 Kgs 8:38,39; Pss 8:4; 89:48; 107:8–31; Prv 12:14; Mi 6:8).

It is no accident, then, that the first man was named "Adam" or "Man." The name intimates that to speak about Adam is somehow also to speak about the entire human race. Such usage can perhaps best be understood through the ancient concept of corporate personality and representation familiar to the Hebrews and other Near Eastern peoples. Modern thinking emphasizes the individual; existence of the social group and all social relationships has been seen as secondary to, and dependent upon, the existence and desire of the individual. Accordingly, moderns also perceive a group representative as a mere individual, related to the group in an official, formal, and temporary way, empowered to act for the group only in specific instances.

The Hebrew understanding was quite different. Though the separate personality of the individual was appreciated (Jer 31:29,30; Ez 18:4), there was a strong tendency to see the social group (family, tribe, nation) as a single organism with a corporate identity of its own (note the interesting use of the singular for groups of people in Nm 20:14–21; 21:1–3 in RSV, KJV, and NASB; 1 Sm 5:10, KJV margin, NASB margin). Likewise the group representative was seen as the embodiment or personification of the corporate personality of the group. Within the representative the essential qualities and characteristics of the social group resided in such a way that the actions and decisions of the representative were binding on the entire group. If the group was a family, the father was usually considered the corporate representative; for good or for ill his family, and sometimes his descendants, received the results of his actions (Gn 17:1–8; cf. Gn 20:1–9,18; Ex 20:5,6; Jos 7:24,25; Rom 11:28; Heb 7:1–10). Cities and entire nations, however, were also bound by the actions of their corporate representatives, whether they were recognized leaders (1 Chr 21:1–7,14; Mi 3:11,12) or insignificant individuals (Jos 7:1–5; cf. 22:20). In Daniel 7:13–22 the "one like a son of man" receives an everlasting kingdom as the corporate representative of "the saints of the Most High" (cf. vv 13,14 with vv 18,22).

As the original man and father of humankind, in whose image all succeeding generations would be born (Gn 5:3), Adam was the corporate representative of humanity. The creation accounts themselves give the impression that the mandates of Genesis 1:26–30 (cf. Gn 9:1,7; Pss 8:5–8; 104:14) as well as the curses of Genesis 3:16–19 (cf. Ps 90:3; Eccl 12:7; Is 13:8; 21:3) were meant not only for Adam (and Eve) but, through him, for the entire race.

Though Adam's corporate representativeness was not developed in the OT, it was certainly understood in intertestamental Judaism. The writer of the apocryphal 2 Esdras, bemoaning the condition of the human race, cried out, "O Adam, what have you done? For though it was you who sinned, the fall was not yours alone, but ours also who are your descendants" (2 Esd 7:48 [118]). Elsewhere the same writer stated that death was appointed to Adam's descendants because of his transgression (2 Esd 3:7; cf. 3:21,26; 4:30; 7:11; see also 2 Bar 17:3).

Later the rabbis expressed Adam's corporate significance in fanciful but ingenious speculations. Adam's body was said to have been as large as the earth and to have incorporated the entire human race. Some taught that the dust of his body had been gathered from all parts of the globe. One rabbi, Oshaiah, stated that "Adam's trunk came from Babylon, his head from the land of Israel, his limbs from other lands, and his private parts according to R. Aha, from Akra di Agma" (a city known for its moral laxity!).

Adam and Christ. For Christians, the real significance of Adam as the corporate representative of humanity could be understood only after the life and work of Jesus Christ. Although we have no evidence that Jesus saw his role as being similar to Adam's, his favorite self-designation, "Son of man," had in earlier Jewish thought often been connected with the first "man."

From the very beginning of the church, however, Christians saw similarities between Christ's role and that of Adam. Both had the function of displaying the image of God (Gn 1:26,27; cf. Phil 2:6,7; Col 1:15), and both, as corporate heads, were significant for all humanity. The Gospel writer Luke stressed the universal significance of Christ by tracing his ancestry back to Adam (Lk 3:38; cf. Mt 1:1).

Such similarities in the roles of Adam and Christ ultimately led the early church to emphasize the vast dissimilarities in their accomplishments. Adam was unfaithful and defeated; Christ was supremely faithful and victorious. Contrast of Adam and Christ probably lies behind the story of Christ's temptation as told by both Mark and Luke. Mark was evidently aware of rabbinical lore that spoke of Adam being honored by wild beasts and eating angels' food in paradise, since he includes similar details in his temptation account (Mk 1:13). Luke, on the other hand, introduced his account with a genealogy ending with the significant phrase, "Adam, the son of God" (Lk 3:38); in two of the temptations which immediately follow, Satan is pictured as taunting Christ with the challenge, "If you are the Son of God . . . " (Lk 4:3,9). Though their methods were different, Mark and Luke were both saying that, like Adam, Christ was tempted but, unlike Adam, he refused to disobey God.

The same comparison is implied in Philippians 2:6–11. There the self-arrogating attitude of Adam as the image of God is contrasted with the self-humiliating attitude of Christ, the true image of God. In other passages the apostle Paul moved beyond a comparison of individuals to a comparison of the two corporate representatives of humanity. In Romans 5:12–21 he contrasted the death and condemnation brought upon humanity by Adam's disobedience with the life and justification given to humanity through Christ's obedience. More explicitly, in 1 Corinthians 15:45–50, Paul called Christ the "last Adam," "second man," and the "man of heaven" in juxtaposition to the "first Adam," the "first man," and the "man of dust."

For Paul the human race was divided into two groups in the persons of Adam and Christ. Those who remain "incorporated" in Adam are the "old" humanity, bearing the image of the "man of dust" and partaking of his sin and alienation from God and creation (Rom 5:12–19; 8:20–22). But those who are incorporated into Christ by faith become Christ's "body" (Rom 12:4,5; 1 Cor 12:12,13,27; Eph 1:22,23; Col 1:18); they are re-created in Christ's image (Rom 8:29; 1 Cor 15:49; 2 Cor 3:18); they become one "new man" (Eph 2:15; 4:22 KJV; "nature," RSV; Col 3:9,10 KJV; "nature," RSV; cf. Gal 3:27); and partake of the new creation (2 Cor 5:17; Gal 6:15). The old barriers raised by Adam are removed by Christ (Rom 5:1; 2 Cor 5:19; Gal 3:27,28; Eph 2:14–16). For Paul, the functional similarity of Adam and Christ as representatives meant that Christ had restored what Adam had lost (see also Rv 2:7; cf. Gn 3:24).

Throughout the history of the church the person of Adam has continued to spark discussions and speculations. Why did he sin? Will he be among the redeemed humanity of Christ? Christians through the centuries, including such writers as Dante Alighieri (*The Divine Comedy*), John Milton (*Paradise Lost; Paradise Regained*), George MacDonald (*Lilith*), have given imaginative answers. Yet, apart from the biblical material, Adam remains an enigmatic figure.

STEPHEN TAYLOR

See GARDEN OF EDEN; EVE; MAN, OLD AND NEW; NEW CREATION, NEW CREATURE; SECOND ADAM, THE.

Adam (Place). City on the Jordan River. When Joshua led the Israelites across the river, the stretch of riverbed from this city to the Dead Sea dried up miraculously so the people could cross on dry land (Jos 3:16). Adam is identified with modern Tell ed-Damiyeh.

Adam, The Second. Theological term applied to Christ as head of a second race, the redeemed people of God.

See SECOND ADAM, THE.

Adamah. One of the 19 fortified cities belonging to Naphtali's tribe (Jos 19:36). It is possibly identified with Qarn Hattin.

Adami, Adami-Nekeb. Names of a city located near the southern border of Naphtali's territory (Jos 19:33), although the KJV lists it as two cities. Adami-Nekeb is usually identified as modern Khirbet ed-Damiyeh.

The site near Adam.

Adar (Month). Babylonian name for a Hebrew month (Ezr 6:15).

See CALENDARS, ANCIENT AND MODERN.

Adar (Place). KJV form of Addar in Joshua 15:3.

See ADDAR (PLACE).

Adbeel. Third of Ishmael's 12 sons (Gn 25:13; 1 Chr 1:29).

Addan. Persian city from which Israelite exiles returned with Ezra to Jerusalem (Ezr 2:59), probably named after a Babylonian god called Addu. The exiles returning from this city were unable to give evidence of their Jewish descent, having lost their genealogical credentials. Also spelled Addon (Neh 7:61).

Addar (Person). Alternate name for Ard, one of Benjamin's descendants, in 1 Chronicles 8:3.

See ARD, ARDITE.

Addar (Place). Town on Judah's southwest border, northwest of Kadesh-barnea (Jos 15:3, KJV Adar). The towns Hezron and Addar were called Hazar-addar (Nm 34:4).

Adder. Any of several kinds of poisonous and nonpoisonous snakes, especially the common viper of Europe and Asia.

See ANIMALS.

Addi. 1. One whose descendants obeyed Ezra's exhortation to divorce their pagan wives after the exile (1 Esd 9:31). The parallel list of Ezra has Pahath-moab in place of Addi (Ezr 10:30).

2. Ancestor of Jesus, mentioned in Luke's genealogy (3:28).

See GENEALOGY OF JESUS CHRIST.

Addon. Alternate form of Addan, a place in Babylonia, in Nehemiah 7:61.

See ADDAN.

Ader. KJV form of Eder, Beriah's son, in 1 Chronicles 8:15.

See EDER (PERSON) #2.

Adiel. 1. Prince of Simeon's tribe who led some Simeonites to the entrance of Gedor to find pasture for their flocks (1 Chr 4:36).

2. Ancestor of Maasai, a priest of Israel who was among the first to return to Palestine following the Babylonian captivity (1 Chr 9:12).

3. Ancestor of Azmaveth. Azmaveth was in charge of King David's treasuries (1 Chr 27:25).

Adin. 1. Ancestor of a group of people who returned to Judah with Zerubbabel after the Babylonian exile. Comparison of various lists (Ezr 2:15; 8:6; Neh 7:20; 1 Esd 5:14; 8:32) shows that groups of Adin's descendants returned at different times.

2. Political leader who signed Ezra's covenant of faithfulness to God with Nehemiah and others after the exile (Neh 10:16).

Adina. Shiza's son and a warrior among David's mighty men who were known as "the thirty" (1 Chr 11:42).

Adino. Possibly another name for Joshebbasshebeth, one of the top three of David's military heroes (2 Sm 23:8); also called Jashobeam (1 Chr 11:11). Since the Hebrew text is unclear, "Adino, the Eznite" may not be a proper name but a reference to the warrior's spear (RSV, NASB).

See JASHOBEAM #1.

Adithaim. Town in the lowlands of Judah's territory (Jos 15:36).

Adlai. Father of Shaphat, the chief herdsman of the king's flocks in the valleys during David's reign (1 Chr 27:29).

Admah. City associated with Sodom, Gomorrah, and Zeboiim (Gn 10:19; 14:2,8) and thus probably destroyed in God's judgment of Sodom and Gomorrah (Dt 29:23; not specifically mentioned in Gn 19:28,29). A recent survey of the area east and south of the Dead Sea has revealed five Early Bronze Age cities which probably correspond to the five cities of the plain spoken of in Genesis. Each city was located next to the valley of a river that flowed into the plain around the Dead Sea. These sites are Khanazir, Felfa, Safi, Numeira, and Bab edh-Dhrá. Further work will be necessary to verify this identification.

See CITIES OF THE VALLEY, CITIES OF THE PLAIN.

Admatha. One of seven counselors of King Ahasuerus (Est 1:14). The king's counselors advised him to banish Queen Vashti for refusing his summons to appear at a drunken party.

Admin. Ancestor of Jesus mentioned in Luke's genealogy (3:33).

See GENEALOGY OF JESUS CHRIST.

Adna. 1. Descendant of Pahath-moab who obeyed Ezra's exhortation to divorce his pagan wife after the exile (Ezr 10:30).
2. Priest under the high priest Joiakim who returned to Jerusalem with Zerubbabel after the exile (Neh 12:15).

Adnah. 1. Captain from Manasseh's tribe who left Saul to join David's army at Ziklag (1 Chr 12:20).
2. General under King Jehoshaphat of Judah (2 Chr 17:14).

Adonai. Divine name translated as "Lord" signifying honor, majesty, and sovereignty.

See GOD, NAMES OF.

Adonibezek. Title of the Canaanite king of Bezek, a city in northern Palestine. Soon after Joshua's death, the tribes of Judah and Simeon defeated Adonibezek and amputated his thumbs and big toes. Adonibezek himself had treated many captured kings that way, so he regarded his fate as divine retribution (Jgs 1:5–7). Some have suggested that he and Adoni-zedek (Jos 10:1) were the same person.

Adonijah. 1. David's fourth son, born to Haggith at Hebron (2 Sm 3:4). After the death of his three older brothers (Amnon, Chileab, and Absalom), Adonijah was next in line for the throne. King David, however, had promised his wife Bathsheba that their son Solomon would be the one to succeed him (1 Kgs 1:17). When his elderly father seemed to be dying, Adonijah began preparations to crown himself king (1:1–10). Before the ceremonies could take place, David appointed Solomon as his successor (1:11–40). Adonijah kept out of Solomon's way at first (1:41–53) but eventually worked up enough courage to ask King Solomon for permission to marry Abishag, the woman from Shunem who was appointed to care for David during his last days. In the ancient Near East, to claim the concubine of a deceased king was to claim the throne. Enraged, Solomon ordered Adonijah to be killed (2:13–25).
2. Levite sent out by King Jehoshaphat of the southern kingdom of Judah to teach the people the Law of the Lord (2 Chr 17:8).
3. Political leader who signed Ezra's covenant of faithfulness to God with Nehemiah and others after the exile (Neh 10:16).

Adonikam. Head of a family whose descendants returned to Jerusalem with Zerubbabel after the Babylonian exile (Ezr 2:13; Neh 7:18). Ezra states the number of Adonikam's family returning as 666; Nehemiah gives the number as 667 (as does 1 Esd 5:14), probably a scribal variation.

Adoniram. Important official in Israel during the reigns of David, Solomon, and Rehoboam (1 Kgs 4:6; 5:14). Adoniram is also referred to as Adoram, possibly a contraction of his name (2 Sm 20:24; 1 Kgs 12:18), and as Hadoram (2 Chr 10:18). While Solomon's temple was under construction, Adoniram was overseer of a labor force of 30,000 men (1 Kgs 5:13,14). Evidently David had instituted a system of forced Israelite labor that Solomon continued, not only for building the temple, but for many other projects.
When Rehoboam became king the people asked for relief, but Rehoboam announced that instead he would increase the labor re-

quirements (1 Kgs 12:1–15). When Adoniram was sent to enforce the king's orders, he was stoned to death by the rebellious people (12:16–19).

Adoni-Zedek (Zedec). Amorite king of Jerusalem at the time of the Israelite conquest of the Promised Land (Jos 10:1–5). A battle between the Amorites and Israelites for control of Gibeon was the occasion on which Joshua prayed for the sun to stand still (10:6–15). The Israelites won a decisive victory. Adoni-zedek and four other enemy kings were discovered hiding in a cave and were executed by Joshua (10:16–27).

See CONQUEST AND ALLOTMENT OF THE LAND.

Adoption. Theologically, the act of God by which believers become members of "God's family" with all the privileges and obligations of family membership. "Sons of God," a common KJV expression, includes individuals of both sexes numbered among God's children (Is 43:6; 2 Cor 6:18).

According to the NT, all persons are sinners by nature, and hence are called "children of wrath" (Eph 2:3); however, those upon whom God bestows his love, by grace become "children of God" (1 Jn 3:1). The adoption through which this happens has its origin in God's love and its foundation in Jesus Christ who is uniquely the "Son of God." Theologians regard the term *Son of God* as referring preeminently to Christ's deity (Mt 11:25–27; 16:16,17), for he is one in substance and glory with the Father. As the second person of the Trinity, Christ is distinguished from the Father as "the only begotten Son." Believers in Christ, although "adopted," are never seen as on a par with the uncreated, divine Son.

Nevertheless, in the "beloved Son," sinners have been from eternity loved and predestined by God the Father to become his children by adoption (Eph 1:4–6). That adoption is secured by Christ the Redeemer; through his death and resurrection he destroyed sin and its death penalty, restoring the righteousness and life requisite for the status of sonship.

Although the "new birth" is necessary for adoption, some theologians distinguish the act of adoption from regeneration. Regeneration is the act of God by which an initial and radical transformation of a sinner occurs so that a person once dead in sin becomes "alive in Jesus Christ." The new birth is also called a resurrection and a new creation. In contrast, adoption does not refer to the experience of transformation of a sinner. It is a legal term describing the right or power granted to a transformed believer to become God's child (Jn 1:12,13). It is analogous to the act of a modern court by which a husband and wife become adoptive parents of children who are not their natural offspring.

Theologically, adoption is closely related to justification, sometimes being viewed simply as an aspect of justification. Both terms indicate that sinners who are by themselves unworthy are nevertheless received by God and given "title" to eternal life on the basis of Christ's redeeming work. Justification focuses on the believer's legal standing as forgiven and accepted as righteous in God's sight. Adoption goes beyond legality to establish an intimate, personal relationship to God as Father. Adoption is seen as the acme of blessing and privilege enjoyed by God's people. Sanctification is the theological term for the mortification of sin and growth in holiness. In this process God empowers his adopted children to live and act more and more as children of a holy God.

Believers live in fellowship with God the Father, Son, and Holy Spirit. Quite naturally, in NT language, it is the Father in particular to whom believers are seen as having a filial relationship (Jn 20:17; Rom 1:7; 2 Thes 2:16). The Father knows the physical and spiritual needs of his children and in his providential care supplies everything necessary for their temporal and eternal welfare (Ps 103; Mt 6:8). Not even a hair can fall from their heads without his knowledge (Mt 10:30).

A hallmark of liberalism has been emphasis on the doctrine of the universal fatherhood of God. The Bible does refer to God as Father of all by virtue of creation (Gn 1,2; Lk 3:38; Acts 17:24–29). The older liberal theology, however, did not take sufficient account of the alienation caused by sin. In the Bible, adoption and the blessing of sonship are viewed almost exclusively as benefits of redemption, so that only the "saved" are God's children. The ungodly are called children of the devil (Jn 8:42,44; 1 Jn 3:10).

Although God's adopted children have the only begotten Son, Jesus Christ, as a brother, they are not equal with him. He is the head of the "new covenant" as its mediator and guarantor. His brothers and sisters, as its beneficiaries, become God's heirs and his joint heirs (Rom 8:17). God gives to them the Holy Spirit, the Spirit of his Son, as the Spirit of adoption (Rom 8:15; Gal 4:6). The indwelling Spirit gives believers assurance that they are indeed God's children and enables them to cry out to God as Father (Rom 8:15,16). Such intimacy with the Creator and Savior in prayer is one privilege of adoption.

Because Christ sanctifies his people, refashioning them in his image, he is not ashamed to call them his brothers and sisters (Heb

2:11,12). His Spirit in them frees God's children from obligation to their old sinful nature, helping them live more and more like his children (Rom 8:12–14). That spiritual leading includes discipline because God does not neglect his children as though they were illegitimate (Heb 12:7,8). Although there is no condemnation for those who are in Christ, sin provokes fatherly displeasure; therefore, disobedient children must have daily recourse to the Father for forgiveness (Mt 6:9,12).

Adoption was a privilege given to God's people under the "old covenant" (Rom 9:4). Both Israel as a whole and individual Israelites knew God as Father (Is 64:8,9; Hos 11:1). Since the NT regards adoption as ultimately possible only through Jesus Christ, Israel's adoption before the incarnation was an under-age sonship comparable to the status of servanthood (Gal 4:1–7). In Jesus the privilege of mature sonship was extended to include both Jews and Gentiles (Gal 3:25–29). Though adoption is a benefit enjoyed in the present experience of God's people (1 Jn 3:1), its full extent is seen as realized only at their resurrection from the dead in the cosmic renovation at the endtime (Rom 8:21,23).

NORMAN SHEPHERD

See JUSTIFICATION; INHERITANCE.

Adoraim. City in the southern kingdom of Judah fortified by King Rehoboam (2 Chr 11:9). Adoraim and Mareshah later became the two principal cities of Idumaea. In 1 Maccabees 13:20 it is called Adora. The modern identification is Dura, south of Hebron.

Adoram. Alternate spelling of Adoniram in 2 Samuel 20:24 and 1 Kings 12:18.

See ADONIRAM.

Adrammelech. 1. Son of the Assyrian monarch Sennacherib. This Adrammelech and his brother Sharezer killed their father in the temple of Nisroch in Nineveh (2 Kgs 19:37; Is 37:38). The nonbiblical Babylonian Chronicles also refer to this assassination but do not name the sons.

See SENNACHERIB.

2. Deity worshiped by the Syrians from Sepharvaim whom the Assyrians resettled in Samaria. Adrammelech was a god to whom children were sacrificed by the Sepharvites (2 Kgs 17:31).

See MESOPOTAMIA; SYRIA, SYRIANS.

Adramyttium. Ancient port city in Asia Minor. En route to Rome as a prisoner, Paul embarked on a ship having Adramyttium as its home port (Acts 27:2). Today Adramyttium is the Turkish city of Edremit. Coinage found in the area indicates that Adramyttium may have been a center for the worship of Castor and Pollux (twin sons of the pagan god, Zeus).

Adria. The Adriatic Sea, an arm of the Mediterranean Sea bordered by Italy on the west and by Greece, Albania, and Yugoslavia on the east. The apostle Paul was tossed about in a ship for 14 days in a violent storm on this body of water (Acts 27:27). Other ancient literature attests to the violence of the Adriatic Sea. The Jewish historian Josephus was shipwrecked in the Adriatic in AD 64, and the Greek poet Homer made several references in his writings to the great storms on this sea.

Adriel. Barzillai's son, to whom Saul gave his daughter Merab in marriage, although she had been promised to David (1 Sm 18:19). King David later handed over Adriel's five sons to the Gibeonites to execute in vengeance against Saul's family (2 Sm 21:1–9).

Adullam, Adullamite. Old Canaanite city between Lachish and Hebron, as well as a cave region nearby. The first biblical mention of the city is in the word "Adullamite" (someone from Adullam), used of Hirah, a friend of Judah. After acting as a ringleader in selling his brother Joseph into slavery, Judah left home and lived in Adullam with Hirah (Gn 38:1,12,20).

Adullam was in the lowlands of Judah's tribal territory (Jos 15:35). It was one of 31 Canaanite royal cities conquered by Joshua (Jos 12:15) and one of 15 cities later fortified by King Rehoboam of Judah (2 Chr 11:7). After the exiles' return from captivity in Babylon, Adullam was again resettled by Judah's tribe (Neh 11:30).

A cave near Adullam figured in several events in David's life. It was a refuge when he fled from King Saul (1 Sm 22:1) and a stronghold in his war against the Philistines (2 Sm 23:13–17; 1 Chr 11:15–19). The Hebrew superscriptions to Psalms 57 and 142 indicate that David wrote them at the time of his experiences in the cave. Adullam is identified as modern esh-Sheikh Madhkur.

Adultery. Biblically, adultery is a breach of the "one flesh" relationship of marriage. It describes any act of sexual intercourse between a married woman and a man other than her husband, and all sexual intercourse involving a married man and another man's wife or fiancée.

In OT times, polygamous unions were not considered adulterous (cf. Dt 21:15). Nor was a

The cave of Adullam, where David hid from Saul.

husband branded as an adulterer if he had intercourse with a slave woman (Gn 16:1–4; 30:1–5) or a prostitute (Gn 38:15–18)—though the latter was, of course, condemned as immoral (1 Cor 6:15).

Any imbalance between the sexes was dispelled by Jesus in his teaching on divorce and remarriage. While he did not rule out the possibility of divorce in cases of sexual unfaithfulness (Mt 5:32; 19:9), he warned that in all other circumstances remarriage involves both (ex-)husband and (ex-)wife in adultery. Paul added that the charge of adultery only applies if the remarried person's original partner is still alive (Rom 7:2,3).

Jesus also sharpened the OT's definition of adultery by applying it to a man's thought life. Any man who fantasizes in lust (as distinct from just being tempted) has committed adultery in mind and intention, he taught, even though there is no physical contact (Mt 5:27,28; cf. Jb 31:1,9).

The Bible's condemnation of adultery is written into the heart of the OT law, prophecy, and wisdom literature. The Ten Commandments ban it unequivocally (Ex 20:14; Dt 5:18). The prophets list it among offenses which attract God's anger and judgment (Jer 23:11–14; Ez 22:11; Mal 3:5). And the Book of Proverbs scorns it as a senseless act by which a man destroys himself (Prv 6:23–35; cf. 7:6–27).

The NT echoes that clear condemnation. Where there is no repentance, adultery excludes those who practice it from God's kingdom (1 Cor 6:9). It is the very opposite of love of one's neighbor (Rom 13:9,10), and it stands under the judgment of God himself (Heb 13:4).

In the OT the penalty for adultery is death—for both the man and the woman (Lv 20:10; Dt 22:22). The same applies if the woman is single but engaged to another man, assuming she has not been raped (in which case only the man is to be executed—Dt 22:23–27). The refrain, "You shall purge the evil from the midst of you" (v 24) shows that adultery was considered a serious threat to society's health, not simply an attack on the family lives of the two people involved.

With such serious consequences, it was important to establish guilt beyond doubt. In cases of serious suspicion, but insufficient evidence, the wife concerned was put through an elaborate ritual test which included taking an oath and drinking bitter water. The result was not a matter of chance because she stood "before the Lord" (Nm 5:11–31).

In Roman times adultery was taken off the list of capital offenses. This fact helps to illuminate Jesus' famous confrontation with the woman caught in the act of adultery (Jn 8:1–11). Jesus did not turn a blind eye to her wrongdoing, but the gentle way he dealt with her implied that adultery is not at the very top of God's league of sin. Nor is it an offense which cannot be pardoned after repentance.

In both the OT and NT, the language of adultery is used figuratively to describe human unfaithfulness to God. The OT prophets likened God's covenant relationship with his people to marriage (Is 54:5–8; cf. Rv 21:2); so in their eyes the breaking of that relationship, especially by idolatry, was equivalent to spiritual adultery (Jer 5:7,8; 13:22–27; Ez 23:37).

Jesus used the same imagery to characterize those who either rejected his claims or showed their lack of faith in him by demanding unnecessary extra signs of his deity (Mt 12:39; 16:4; Mk 8:38). And in another vivid NT passage James describes God as a loving, jealous husband coming to deal with his adulterous people who have become "good friends" with the world and its false standards (Jas 4:4).

This is the special theme of the prophet Hosea. God used the prophet's own experience of a marriage broken by adultery to teach the seriousness of his people's unfaithfulness to him (Hos 2:2–6) and his keen longing for a full reconciliation (3:1–5). Spiritual infidelity, like physical adultery, brings God's judgment. But in both cases his overwhelming desire is for a mended relationship following sincere repentance (Jer 3:1–14; Ez 16:1–63).

DAVID H. FIELD

See DIVORCE; MARRIAGE, MARRIAGE CUSTOMS; FORNICATION.

Adummim. Pass extending from the hill country into the Jordan Valley, which formed part of Judah's northern border (Jos 15:7). It is a reference point establishing the location of Geliloth on Benjamin's southern border (Jos 18:17). The road from Jerusalem to Jericho ran through this mountain pass. The church father Jerome felt that this place was the setting for Jesus' story of the Good Samaritan (Lk 10:30–37). The modern Arabic name means "ascent of blood." The Hebrew name Adummim ("red rocks") probably stems from the natural color of the rocks rather than from the fate of many travelers through the pass at the hands of robbers.

Advent of Christ. *See* INCARNATION; JESUS CHRIST, LIFE AND TEACHING OF; SECOND COMING OF CHRIST.

Adversary. Any foe, opponent, or enemy of God and his saints. The apostle Peter's description of the devil as "your adversary" (1

Pt 5:8) has led to use of "the Adversary" as a reference to Satan in literature and popular speech.

See SATAN.

Advocate. Probable translation for Paraclete, a term used for the Holy Spirit in John's Gospel and for Jesus in 1 John 2:1.

See HOLY SPIRIT; PARACLETE.

Aeneas. Bedridden paralytic in Lydda who was miraculously healed by the apostle Peter. Many people became Christians as a result (Acts 9:33–35).

Aenon. Small town near the Jordan River. Scholars think Aenon may have been about 30 miles north of the Dead Sea. The Bible's one reference to the town merely states that John the Baptist baptized there (Jn 3:23).

Aeon. Greek word for a long period of time or age, from which comes the English word "eon."

See AGE, AGES.

Affliction. Anything causing pain or distress; suffering; calamity. From the biblical viewpoint, affliction began with the entrance of sin into the world. Both mankind and all creation were afflicted with "thorns and thistles," sin, death, and decay (cf. Gn 3:16–19; Rom 8:18–21). Because of sin, misery is a common human experience, and our short life is full of trouble (Jb 14:1–6). It is impossible for human beings to avoid natural calamity, physical injury, and interpersonal conflict (2 Chr 20:9). Yet God uses affliction to instruct and discipline his people. This aspect of affliction is graphically portrayed by the oppression during the Israelites' sojourn in Egypt (Ex 4:31), by their troubles during the period of the judges (Neh 9:26,27), and by their exile in Babylon (Is 26:16). In Israel's distress they cried out to God, who delivered them and led them into obedience (Jer 10:18; Hos 5:15–6:3).

The Bible acknowledges that it is difficult to understand the many afflictions of the righteous (Ps 34:19; 37:39; 138:7). Even the prophet and "Servant of the Lord" (Messiah) were not spared (Is 53:2–12; Jer 15:15). Jesus Christ bore the griefs and sorrows of humankind as the culmination of the affliction begun by Adam's sin (Is 53:4,5; 1 Pt 2:24). The Bible sees this affliction as the outworking of the enmity between the "seed [offspring] of the woman" and the "seed of the serpent" (Gn 3:15).

Jesus indicated that there would be many trials and sorrows for his followers (Jn 16:33).

The Jordan River, near which Aenon was situated.

Paul taught that entrance to the kingdom of God comes with many tribulations (Acts 14:22) which must not shake a Christian's faith (1 Thes 3:3). They are to be understood rather as a finishing up of the remainder of Christ's suffering for his body, the church (2 Cor 4:10,11; Col 1:24).

The biblical picture is that affliction will grow more intense as "the end" approaches (Mt 24:9–14; 2 Tm 3:13). The forces of Satan will attack in an effort to deceive and destroy the "elect" (Mt 24:24; 2 Thes 2:9–12; Rv 20:7–9). But when Jesus Christ is revealed from heaven in flaming fire, God will repay with affliction those who have afflicted believers and will bring vengeance upon those who have not obeyed the gospel of Jesus Christ (Rom 2:9; 2 Thes 1:5–10; 2:7,8).

Affliction is thus characteristic of life in a spoiled creation, but it is a means of discipline that can lead to obedience to God. Affliction is seen in the Bible as part of a cosmic conflict between Satan and Jesus Christ. Yet the afflictions experienced by Christians "will result in God's richest blessing . . . forever and ever" (2 Cor 4:16–18 LB).

See PERSECUTION; TRIBULATION.

Afternoon. Interval of the day between noon and sunset.

See CALENDARS, ANCIENT AND MODERN; DAY.

Agabus. Prophet of NT times who made two predictions referred to in the Book of Acts. His prophecy of a severe famine was fulfilled in the time of Claudius (Acts 11:27,28). He also predicted that Paul would be turned over to the Gentiles by the Jews in Jerusalem if he went there (Acts 21:10,11).

Agag. 1. Name of an Amalekite king, or perhaps a general title for their kings (like the Egyptian "pharaoh"). Balaam prophesied that Israel's king would be greater than Agag (Nm 24:7).

2. Name of another Amalekite king. God told Samuel to send King Saul to wipe out the Amalekite nation down to the last sheep. Saul conquered them but spared Agag's life and the Amalekites' best sheep and oxen. Samuel then executed Agag and told Saul that because of his disobedience, he could no longer be Israel's king (1 Sm 15).

Agagite. Term used to describe Haman, "the enemy of all the Jews," in the Persian court of King Ahasuerus (Est 3:1; 9:24). Agag, an Amalekite king, had been Saul's mortal enemy. The Amalekites probably left no descendants (1 Sm 15) so the term Agagite could simply be a derogatory expression for an enemy.

Agape. English transliteration of the NT Greek word for "love" or "love feast."

See LOVE.

Agate. Hard, semiprecious stone, a variety of chalcedony (a kind of quartz), with striped or clouded coloring.

See MINERALS, METALS, AND PRECIOUS STONES.

Age, Ages. Long, but indefinite, period of time, past or future. The ages, past and future, make up the whole of time. God is spoken of as existing and planning "before the ages" (1 Cor 2:7); He is the "King of ages" (1 Tm 1:17) and has a purpose that embraces the ages (Eph 3:11). The Bible speaks of what God will do at the close or consummation of the age(s) (Mt 13:39,49).

The NT, following on from earlier Jewish writings, speaks of the contrast between "the present age" (an "evil age," Gal 1:4) and "the age(s) to come" when in God's judgment wrongs will be righted and his people will come into their full inheritance (Mk 10:30). There is a sense, however, in which it can be said that we are both living now in "the end of the ages" (1 Cor 10:11) and that we experience "the powers of the age to come" (Heb 6:5) and its life. (The Greek word for "age," "aeon," is *aiōn* and for "eternal" is *aiōnios*.)

Two other words are sometimes connected with the word "age." One is "generation." Colossians 1:26 speaks of the mystery hidden "for ages and generations" (cf. Eph 3:21), though there is no basis in the scriptural use of these words for dividing biblical time into "dispensations" each involving some fresh development of the redemptive purpose of God. The other is the word "world." Ephesians 2:2 speaks of unredeemed humanity as "following the course [*aiōn*] of this world." Using the same word (*aiōn*), the cares of the world are spoken of, and Hebrews 1:2 and 11:3 speak of God's creation of the worlds.

The biblical expressions, "from of old" and "for ever" use the word "age," literally saying "from the age(s)" or "to the age(s)," thus referring to indefinite past or future, but only the context can show whether or not "eternal" past or future is intended.

The Bible often speaks of the age of men and women, reckoned in years or in other ways. Wisdom is seen as belonging especially to the aged (Jb 12:12), though not necessarily found there (Eccl 4:12). Age should be respected (Lv 19:32), and length of days is a blessing of God (Prv 16:31). At the same time the frailty of old age is recognized (Eccl 12:1-6), and Psalm 90:10 speaks of 70 years as the allotted human span which, if it is extended to 80, may well be "trouble and sorrow."

See ETERNITY; KINGDOM OF GOD (HEAVEN); SECOND COMING OF CHRIST; APOCALYPTIC.

Agee. Father of Shammah, one of the warriors among David's mighty men who were known as "the thirty" (2 Sm 23:11).

Agora. *See* MARKET, MARKETPLACE.

Agriculture. During Bible times agriculture took the same three main forms found in Palestine today. Emphasis on each of these has depended upon the social and technological status of the people.

Herding. Sheep raising is one of the first occupations mentioned in the Scriptures. Abel (Gn 4:2) and Jabal (Gn 4:20) were keepers of sheep or had cattle. This occupation fit the semi-nomadic life, providing both food and clothing while requiring a minimum of techniques and equipment.

The patriarchs were mainly herdsmen, pasturing their sheep and cattle on common land and generally neglecting to till the soil. Jacob and his sons entered Egypt as shepherds (Gn 47:3). Later this pastoral life is still found in the tribes of Reuben, Gad, and the half tribe of Manasseh in Transjordan (Nm 32:1) and in certain of the tribes dwelling in the western Palestinian hills (1 Sm 25:2). Herding continued to be a part of Hebrew agriculture even in post-nomadic days, partly because the animals utilized less productive lands and partly because of the people's traditions. Important among these traditions were the sacrifices performed in the temple.

Field Cropping. Most authorities agree that the Israelites learned field agriculture from the Canaanites, since contact with these people was contemporaneous with the settling of the Promised Land. Raising of grain is known to have existed before that time. Cain was a tiller of the soil (Gn 4:2), although it is uncertain what he raised. Archaeologists date the existence of grain farming around 6800 BC

Lifespans in Various Periods of Scripture

Antediluvian		Prepatriarchal		Premonarchical		Monarchical	
Adam	930	Noah	950	Sarah	127	Rehoboam	58
Seth	912	Shem	600	Abraham	175	Jehoshaphat	60
Enos	905	Arphaxad	438	Ishmael	137	Jehoram	40
Cainan	910	Salah	433	Isaac	180	Jehoiada	130
Mahalaleel	895	Eber	464	Jacob	147	Joash	47
Jared	962	Peleg	239	Joseph	110	Amaziah	54
Enoch	365	Reu	239	Levi	137	Uzziah	68
Methusaleh	969	Serug	230	Kohath	133	Jotham	41
Lamech	777	Nahor	148	Amram	137	Ahaz	36
		Terah	205	Aaron	123	Hezekiah	54
				Moses	120	Manasseh	67
				Joshua	110	Jehoiakim	36
				Eli	98		

in the Near East. Isaac sowed in Gerar (Gn 26:12), and Joseph dreamed of sheaves of grain (Gn 37:6,7). Joseph probably learned more about grain farming from the Egyptians, who raised it on the fertile soils of the Nile floodplain.

Yet it was from contact with the Canaanites that Israelites began to raise grain. The productivity of Canaan was reported by Joshua and Caleb at Kadesh-Barnea (Nm 13:26); and the Canaanites, who were later subjugated, were no doubt made to initiate their conquerors into agricultural practices. Probably such a relationship contributed to the continual Israelite lapses into idolatry (Jgs 9:27). How rapidly they made the transition from the purely nomadic life is not clear. Some tribes never did shed the nomadic way, but cultivation of the soil seems to be common by the time of the kings (2 Sm 14:30).

Of the cereals raised, wheat was one of the most important. Solomon sent great amounts of it, along with barley and oil, to Hiram (2 Chr 2:10), and it continued to be a chief item of export (Ez 27:17). Barley was second in importance. In early times it was the chief ingredient of bread (Jgs 7:13); later it became an important food for the poorer classes (Jn 6:9,13). It was also fed to cattle.

Other field crops were beans and lentils (2 Sm 17:28), which were ground into meal and sometimes used for bread (Ez 4:9). Leeks, garlic, and onions were raised for seasoning, and cumin, coriander, dill, mint, rue, and mustard for spices. Flax was important (Jos 2:6). Some cotton was grown (Is 19:9). The fiber supply was supplemented with wool. By Roman times cotton had become much more important than flax.

Fruit raising. When the Israelites became well settled, orchards and vineyards were planted and came to be symbols of prosperity. Vineyards supplied wine to drink. Olive orchards provided oil for cooking, cosmetics, and medicine. Figs and pomegranates were grown also. For all of these crops more skill and equipment became necessary.

Cultivation. Throughout biblical times much of the labor for agriculture came from the farmer himself. To plant for the first time, it was necessary to clear the land of forest (Jos 17:18), stones (Is 5:2), weeds, and thorns. Sometimes the thin soil on hillsides was terraced, and sometimes irrigation was employed. Such tasks limited the size of farms so that only the wealthy, such as Job and Boaz, had large holdings.

To till the land farmers used oxen or cows to pull very primitive plows (Jgs 14:18; Am 6:12). Occasionally an ass was used (Dt 22:10). Clods were broken with a hoe or the driver's goad. The surface was evened by drawing a simple harrow, perhaps only a thornbush, or a stoneboat over it. Seed was sown by hand, sometimes carefully in the furrow, and covered lightly with the harrow or stoneboat. Weeds were controlled by the plow, harrow, or hoe.

Implements did not change much during Bible times. The plow consisted of an upright J-shaped piece of hard wood so fixed to be drawn by oxen at one end and held by the driver at the other. Such a primitive device could break up only four or five inches of soil. After the exodus, iron became available for the tip of the plow (1 Sm 13:20), but this served mainly to cut down wear on the point.

The use of fertilizer was very limited on Palestinian farms. Of course, ceremonial law requiring that the soil lie fallow every seventh year helped to replenish water and nutrients, or at least delay their depletion. Manuring of fields was not common because dung was used for fuel. There is some mention of this practice in Scripture (Lk 13:8, where dung is placed around trees). There is mention in the Mishnah of the use of wood ashes, leaves, blood of slaughtered animals, and oil scum for fertilizer.

Harvest. Seeding was done at the beginning of the rainy season and harvesting was begun at the end. Harvesting lasted at least seven weeks. Some crops were pulled up by the roots (pulse), others were dug with a hoe (some grain), but most were cut with a sickle. Iron sickles have been found in archaeological excavations, some with cutting edges set with flakes of flint. The cut grain was tied in sheaves (Ps 126:6) and cast into heaps to be transported to the threshing floor. Barley was harvested first and wheat last.

Small quantities of grain, dill, cumin, and other small crops were beaten out with a flail (Jgs 6:11; Ru 2:17), but most grain was threshed on a floor placed on high ground so that the wind would carry off the chaff. The usual method was to scatter the loosened bundles of straw on the floor and to drive oxen over them

Olive presses at Chorazin, 3rd to 4th cent. (middle and right); a later one is on the left.

to dislodge the grains. Sometimes heavy implements were drawn over the straw (Is 28:27; 41:15). These were weighted by stones and ridden by the driver. The resulting bits of straw, or chaff, were separated from the grain by a tedious winnowing process which involved throwing the material in the air with a fork or shovel (Is 30:24; Jer 15:7). The lighter straw would be blown to the edge of the floor, and the grain would collect at the feet of the worker. The chaff was burned or used as fodder. Grain was sifted (Am 9:9), shoveled into a heap, and later stored in covered pits in the field (Jer 41:8). Sometimes storehouses or granaries were used (Dt 28:8).

Conclusion. Agricultural practices developed very slowly during biblical times. They were essentially the same in Jesus' day as they had been in David's time. Iron, introduced into Palestine after the exodus, served to improve some of the implements, but only the irrigation systems had been vastly improved by Roman times. The Romans built extensive aqueducts throughout Palestine, and agriculture reached its peak. After Roman rule was broken, agriculture suffered severe setbacks. Effects of this are seen in the primitive methods of agriculture still utilized in Arab Palestine.

ALBERT J. SMITH

See PLANTS; HARVEST; TRADES AND OCCUPATIONS (FARMER); PALESTINE; VINE, VINEYARD; FOOD AND FOOD PREPARATION; TOOLS.

Agrippa. Name of two Roman rulers of Judea from the Herodian family line.

See HEROD, HERODIAN FAMILY.

Ague. Intense fever marked by recurring chills, common in malaria. Our English word comes from the same stem as "acute." The "fever" (Dt 28:22) can "waste the eyes and cause life to pine away" (Lv 26:16, KJV "burning ague"). Both passages describe punishments the Israelites would suffer if they disobeyed God's laws. Early translators of the Septuagint used the Greek word for jaundice to translate the Hebrew word for ague, no doubt from association of both symptoms with malaria.

See MEDICINE AND MEDICAL PRACTICE.

Agur. Jakeh's son. Although not an Israelite, he wrote or collected the sayings in Proverbs 30. Agur was from Massa (Prv 30:1), an area of northern Arabia evidently settled by a son of Ishmael (Gn 25:14; 1 Chr 1:30).

See PROVERBS, BOOK OF.

Ahab. 1. Eighth king of the northern kingdom of Israel, who reigned about 874–853 BC.

His father, Omri, founded a dynasty that lasted 40 years, through the reigns of Ahab and his two sons, Ahaziah and Jehoram. Omri's dynasty had an impact beyond biblical history, being mentioned on the famous Moabite stone and in several Assyrian inscriptions. Omri was a general in the army of King Elah, son of Baasha. When Elah was assassinated, Omri was acclaimed king by his own forces in the field (1 Kgs 16:8–16). He prevailed in the resulting civil war and occupied Tirzah, the capital city (16:17–23). Soon he moved his capital to Samaria and built fortifications in the region (16:24). Omri also made an alliance with the Phoenicians, as David and Solomon had done, but was condemned for it by later generations. When Ahab succeeded his father (16:28), he pursued this alliance by marrying the Phoenician king's daughter, Jezebel (16:29–31).

Ahab's marriage to Jezebel, an immoral and fanatical pagan, strongly affected Israel (1 Kgs 21:21–26) and had consequences even in the southern kingdom of Judah. Athaliah, their daughter, married Jehoram of Judah, and the results of this marriage were disastrous (2 Kgs 8:17,18,26,27; 11:1–20). Under Jezebel's influence Ahab gave up the worship of God and took up Baal worship. Ahab's new religion was a fertility cult which featured sexual unions between priests and temple "virgins," practices explicitly contrary to the laws of God. Even in marrying Jezebel, Ahab had violated the biblical prohibition of marriage to pagans (Dt 7:1–5). As Ahab's queen, Jezebel tried to force the whole nation into Baal worship. All the prophets of God were sought out and killed except for a few who were hidden by Obadiah in caves (1 Kgs 18:4).

The biblical narrative mentions that Ahab built many cities (1 Kgs 22:39) and fought a number of wars, but for the most part it centers on the great prophetic figure, Elijah (1 Kgs 17:1; 18:1; 19:1). Early in Ahab's reign God sent Elijah to predict years of drought and famine as punishment for the king's sin (1 Kgs 17:1; 18:16–18). The drought lasted three and a half years and was such a remarkable period in Israel's history that it was remembered into NT times (Lk 4:25; Jas 5:17). It was a time of great suffering for both people and animals (1 Kgs 18:5). At the end of the three and a half years Elijah challenged Ahab to gather all the pagan prophets for a final confrontation between God and Baal. Elijah taunted the 450 prophets of Baal for not being able to attract the attention of their false god. Then he prayed to God, and fire fell from heaven on God's altar. The people shouted their belief in God and helped Elijah execute the pagan prophets (1 Kgs 18:16–40). The drought ended immediately (18:41–46).

When she heard what had happened to her

prophets, Jezebel swore revenge. Elijah fled, and on Mt Horeb, God told him to anoint Jehu to become king of Israel in place of Ahab (1 Kgs 19:1–16). This assignment was carried out by the prophet's successor, Elisha (1 Kgs 19:19–21; 2 Kgs 9:1–10). Elijah then challenged Ahab's acquisition of a vineyard owned by a man named Naboth (1 Kgs 21:1–16). When Naboth refused to sell his land to the king, Jezebel had false witnesses swear that Naboth had cursed God and the king. Naboth was stoned to death for blasphemy. Elijah denounced Ahab, saying that as a judgment God would bring a bloody end to his family (1 Kgs 21:17–24). Ahab's repentance caused God to postpone the judgment until after Ahab's death (1 Kgs 21:27–29; 2 Kgs 10:1–14).

During his reign Ahab had three major military encounters with King Ben-hadad II of Syria (Aram), largely provoked by the Syrians. In the first encounter Ben-hadad besieged Samaria, Israel's capital, and demanded heavy tribute. Ahab refused the demands and called a council of elders. As the Syrians were preparing to attack, a prophet advised Ahab to attack first (1 Kgs 20:1–14). The Syrians were routed and Ben-hadad barely escaped with his life (20:15–22). The following year Ben-hadad mounted another attack on Ahab's forces, was again defeated, and eventually surrendered to Ahab (20:23–33). Ben-hadad gave up some Israelite cities that had been overrun by his father and granted Israel trading posts in Damascus (20:34). God rebuked Ahab through a prophet for forming such an alliance with a pagan power (20:35–43).

The alliance evidently lasted three years (1 Kgs 22:1), during which Syria and Israel must have united with other Near Eastern countries to fight against the rising Assyrian power of Shalmaneser III. Ahab had allied himself with the kings of Hamath, Syria, and other smaller groups, a total of 12 states in all. Israel was evidently the dominant power of that region, with 800 chariots more than Syria could muster.

The battle of Qarqar in the summer of 853 BC, not recorded in the Bible, took place near the Orontes River in northern Syria. According to an Assyrian account, King Ahab commanded 2,000 chariots and 10,000 soldiers. The king of Aram in Shalmaneser's inscription is given as Hadad-ezer, probably meaning Ben-hadad. The outcome of the battle was not very favorable for Shalmaneser; in his own account he claims only many enemy losses, not a decisive victory. Assyrian aggression was halted, at least temporarily. Assyria drew back and did not attack the West for another five years. By that time Ahab had been killed in the last of his three engagements with the Syrians.

The importance of the battle of Qarqar for biblical scholars is that it supplies an external date for biblical events. Shalmaneser's description of the battle is given on what is known as the Monolith Inscription, now located in the British Museum. From the dating of the kings of Assyria we know when Ahab reigned and when, approximately, many OT events took place.

In Ahab's last war with Syria he had the advantage of an alliance with the king of Judah, Jehoshaphat (1 Kgs 22:2–4; 2 Chr 18:1–3). That alliance had been fortified by the marriage of Ahab's daughter Athaliah to Jehoram, son of Jehoshaphat. Ahab proposed a campaign for the recovery of Ramoth-gilead in the northeast corner of Israel. When Jehoshaphat refused to believe the optimistic predictions of Ahab's 400 prophets, a prophet of God named Micaiah was called, who foretold Ahab's death (1 Kgs 22:5–28; 2 Chr 18:4–27).

For the battle with Syria, Jehoshaphat put on his royal robes. Ahab tried to disguise himself as an ordinary soldier, but a Syrian archer hit him between the joints of his armor. Ahab died that evening, and his troops gave up the battle. His chariot and armor were washed beside the pool of Samaria, where, as Elijah had prophesied, dogs licked Ahab's blood. The fallen king was succeeded by his son Ahaziah (1 Kgs 22:29–40; 2 Chr 18:28–34).

The Bible's evaluation of Ahab is based not

The palace of Ahab in Samaria.

on his accomplishments as a warrior or politician, but on his failure to lead Israel in devotion to God. He was worse than all the previous kings of Israel (1 Kgs 16:28–30), and his marriage to Jezebel and the introduction of Baal worship "did more to provoke the Lord, the God of Israel, to anger than all the kings of Israel who were before him" (1 Kgs 16:31–33).

See ELIJAH; JEZEBEL; ISRAEL, HISTORY OF; KING, KINGSHIP; KINGS, BOOKS OF FIRST AND SECOND; CHRONOLOGY, OLD TESTAMENT.

2. Kolaiah's son, a notorious false prophet in the closing days of Judah. He was among the Jews taken to Babylon in the deportation of Jehoiachin (598–597 BC). This Ahab and his colleague Zedekiah were denounced by the prophet Jeremiah for lying in God's name and for their sexual immorality (Jer 29:21–23).

Aharah. Alternate name for Ahiram, Benjamin's third son, in 1 Chronicles 8:1.

See AHIRAM.

Aharel. Harum's son from Judah's tribe (1 Chr 4:8).

Ahasai. KJV form of Ahzai, the priest, in Nehemiah 11:13.

See AHZAI.

Ahasbai. Eliphelet's father. Eliphelet, from the city of Maacah, was a warrior among David's mighty men who were known as "the thirty" (2 Sm 23:34).

Ahasuerus. 1. Persian king better known to Western readers as Xerxes I (485–465 BC); the son and successor of Darius I (Hystaspis). In Ezra 4:6 Ahasuerus is mentioned as receiving letters of accusation from enemies of the Jews about their rebuilding the temple.

Ahasuerus played a role in biblical history in the Book of Esther. According to the Greek historian Herodotus, in the third year of his reign Xerxes (Ahasuerus) convoked an assembly of his leaders to plan an invasion of Greece. The Book of Esther begins with a banquet scene probably reflecting that period. The Greek campaign, begun in 480 BC, was unsuccessful. Afterward Xerxes turned to private matters, such as the events recorded in Esther. The Jewish heroine of that book was the second wife of Xerxes (Ahasuerus). She and her cousin Mordecai influenced the king to reverse an edict condemning all Jews to death. Ahasuerus hanged Haman, his chief minister, who had asked for the edict.

Ahasuerus, who controlled an immense area "from India to Ethiopia" (Est 1:1), was celebrated for massive building projects at Susa and Persepolis. His rule ended in 465 BC when he was assassinated in his bedchamber. He is called the conqueror of Nineveh in Tobit 14:15, but this is manifestly impossible; Nineveh was destroyed in 612 BC, over a century before Ahasuerus was born.

See PERSIA, PERSIANS; ESTHER, BOOK OF; ISRAEL, HISTORY OF.

2. Father of Darius the Mede (Dn 9:1). The identity of this father and son in secular history is uncertain.

Ahava. The name of the river (and possibly town) in Babylonia where Ezra added some Levites to the remnant of exiles. There he also declared a fast for the Jews to humble themselves before God and seek his protection before returning to Palestine (Ezr 8:15,21,31).

The gate of Xerxes in Persepolis, with man-bulls guarding the eastern doorway.

Ahaz. 1. King of Judah (735–715 BC) who was especially remembered for his apostasy. The name Ahaz (KJV Achaz, Mt 1:9) is a shortened form of Ahaziah or Jehoahaz, with an element expressing God's name (-iah, Jeho-) omitted. The three main accounts of Ahaz (2 Kgs 16; 2 Chr 28; Is 7) treat him as one of the most evil rulers of the southern kingdom of Judah. Consequently his burial was relatively dishonorable (2 Chr 28:27). He was succeeded by his son Hezekiah (2 Kgs 18:1).

There is little agreement on the chronology of this section of the OT. The chronological system that seems to have the fewest problems would place Ahaz's accession in 735 BC. If he first came to the throne as co-regent with his father, Jotham, from 735–732 BC, his entire reign covered a span of approximately 20 years, ending in 715 BC.

Ahaz reigned over Judah during a critical time in the history of the ancient Near East. The Assyrians were pushing westward, threatening the Syro-Palestinian area. Pekah, king of Israel, and Rezin, king of Syria, adopted a policy of resistance against the Assyrians and invaded Judah in order to effect a solid coalition by deposing Ahaz.

Blatantly revealing a lack of trust in God, Ahaz appealed to Tiglath-pileser III, the Assyrian king, for help. That appeal brought the wrath of the prophet Isaiah upon Ahaz. The ensuing encounter (Is 7) led to Isaiah's prediction of the birth of Immanuel as a sign of the dissolution of the countries of Israel and Syria. Those two kingdoms were ultimately destroyed by Tiglath-pileser in a campaign that lasted about two years (734–732 BC).

Ahaz's lack of trust in God seems to have stemmed from his complete rejection of the Mosaic or traditional Jewish faith rather than from the dangerous political situation. The Book of Chronicles describes him as erecting images for the Baals (deities who represented the god Baal, a Canaanite fertility deity). Ahaz is also described as engaging in human sacrifice by offering his sons in pagan worship. The Chronicler cites such practices as God's reason for the invasion by Israel and Syria (2 Chr 28:5).

Before the two kingdoms to the north were conquered by Assyria, their invasion of Judah caused great turmoil (28:8). The invaders not only carried off much spoil, but also attempted to depopulate portions of Judah by taking 200,000 people captive to Samaria. That attempt was protested by a prophet in Samaria named Obed, who condemned the act of slavery and ordered the captives returned (28:9). He was joined by several leaders of Israel (28:12) who succeeded in having the captives

returned to Jericho with provisions from the spoil that had been taken.

During that time the kingdom of Judah may have been threatened from the south as well. The Edomites, who had long been under the domination of Judah, may have taken advantage of Judah's growing internal weakness to assert their independence. The Masoretic text of the OT, preserved over the centuries by careful copying, refers to an invasion of the seaport town of Elath on the Red Sea by Aram, the Hebrew name for Syria (2 Kgs 16:6). The name Aram is quite similar to the name Edom in Hebrew, however, so many scholars think that invasion was actually by Edomites.

By virtue of the alliance he had made, Ahaz placed his country in a dangerous position of dependence on Assyria. The kingdom of Judah became essentially a vassal state under the tacit control of Tiglath-pileser. Ahaz went to Damascus, the capital of fallen Syria, to appear before Tiglath-pileser, possibly to assure his allegiance to the king to whom his nation had become tributary (2 Kgs 16:10).

While in Damascus, Ahaz saw an Assyrian altar, a model of which he sent back to Judah. Under the direction of Uriah the priest a similar altar was built in Jersualem, replacing the original bronze altar. Several other alterations were made in the temple by Ahaz, all indicating his turning away from Jewish religion.

The "dial of Ahaz" (2 Kgs 20:11; Is 38:8) later figured in a sign given to his son Hezekiah; the Hebrew word actually refers to a flight of stairs, no doubt built by Ahaz and used to tell time by the movement of a shadow across it.

See KING, KINGSHIP; KINGS, BOOKS OF FIRST AND SECOND; ISRAEL, HISTORY OF; SUN DIAL; CHRONOLOGY, OLD TESTAMENT.

2. Tarea's son and Jehoaddah's father, a descendant of Saul, otherwise unknown (1 Chr 8:35,36).

Ahaziah. 1. Ahab's son, who ruled the northern kingdom of Israel for two years as its ninth king (853–852 BC). He came to the throne when Ahab was killed while trying to recover Ramoth-gilead from Syrian control. He was a contemporary of King Jehoshaphat of Judah and of Jehoshaphat's son Jehoram. Politically, his short reign was characterized by peace with Judah, in contrast with the days of Asa and Baasha (2 Chr 20:37; cf. 1 Kgs 22:48,49). No sooner had he become king than he was compelled to launch an expedition against Mesha of Moab, who had ceased paying tribute to Israel.

Evidently Ahaziah followed not only the corrupt religion of Jeroboam I but also the overt Baal worship of his parents, Ahab and Jezebel (1 Kgs 22:51–53). The first chapter of 2

Kings is devoted to Ahaziah's terminal illness. He fell from the second story of his palace and was seriously injured. Instead of turning to the Lord for aid, he turned to the god of Jezebel, "Baalzebub, the god of Ekron." When the prophet Elijah condemned the king for his actions, Ahaziah, enraged, tried to arrest him. Two groups of soldiers were consumed by fire from God, a sign of victory over Baal since Baal was worshiped as the god of fire and lightning by his followers. Ahaziah died as predicted in Elijah's pronouncement from God (2 Kgs 1:2–18). He was succeeded by his younger brother, Jehoram, at a time when Ahaziah's brother-in-law, also named Jehoram, was king of Judah.

2. The son of Jehoram of Judah, grandson of Jehoshaphat and nephew of the Ahaziah just described. He ruled as the eighth king of Judah for only one year (841 BC) at the age of 22 (2 Kgs 8:25,26). The apostasy of the northern kingdom of Israel reached into the southern kingdom of Judah partly because this Ahaziah was a grandson of Ahab and Jezebel (his mother, Athaliah, was their daughter).

Ahaziah joined his uncle Jehoram of Israel (sometimes abbreviated Joram) in a campaign against King Hazael of Syria. In the battle Jehoram was wounded and went to Jezreel to recover. When Ahaziah went to visit his fallen kinsman at the royal residence at Jezreel (2 Chr 22:7–9), the visit proved to be a fatal mistake. Jehu, the army commander anointed by Elisha to destroy Ahab's descendants (2 Kgs 9:1–13), seized this opportunity to kill both Joram and Ahaziah together (9:14–29).

When Ahaziah's mother, Athaliah, learned of his death, she seized the throne for herself and tried to kill all of his children. One child, Joash, escaped death and eventually became king (2 Kgs 11:1–21). Ahaziah's name is sometimes given as Jehoahaz (2 Chr 21:17) or Azariah (2 Chr 22:6 KJV).

RONALD B. ALLEN

See ISRAEL, HISTORY OF; KINGS, BOOKS OF FIRST AND SECOND; CHRONOLOGY, OLD TESTAMENT; KING, KINGSHIP.

Ahban. Son of Abishur and Abihail from Judah's tribe (1 Chr 2:29).

Aher. Alternate name for Ahiram, Benjamin's third son, in 1 Chronicles 7:12.

See AHIRAM.

Ahi. 1. Abdi-el's son, a clan leader in Gad's tribe (1 Chr 5:15).

2. Shamer's brother (KJV; RSV Shemer), and therefore a member of Asher's tribe (1 Chr 7:34). The word "Ahi" in this verse, however, is probably not a name and should be translated "brother," as in most modern translations.

Ahiah. 1. KJV form of Ahijah.

See AHIJAH #1, #2, and #6.

2. Political leader who signed Ezra's covenant of faithfulness to God with Nehemiah and others after the exile (Neh 10:26, KJV Ahijah).

Ahiam. Sharar's son, and a warrior among David's mighty men who were known as "the thirty" (2 Sm 23:33). In 1 Chronicles 11:35 Ahiam's father is called Sachar.

Ahian. One of Shemida's four sons from Naphtali's tribe (1 Chr 7:19).

Ahiezer. 1. Ammishaddai's son, a leader of Dan's tribe when the Israelites were roaming in the Sinai wilderness after their escape from Egypt. As leader he presented his tribe's offering at the consecration of the tabernacle (Nm 1:12; 2:25; 7:66,71; 10:25).

2. Shemaah's son, a leader of the warriors from Benjamin's tribe who joined David at Ziklag in his struggle against King Saul. Like his men, Ahiezer was an ambidextrous archer and slinger (1 Chr 12:2,3).

Ahihud. 1. Shelomi's son, a leader of Asher's tribe. Ahihud was appointed to help Eleazar and Joshua divide the territory of Canaan among the Israelites (Nm 34:27).

2. According to some English versions (KJV, RSV), a leader in Benjamin's tribe whose father, Gera (also called Heglam), was exiled to Manahath (1 Chr 8:7). But according to the Hebrew Masoretic text, this Ahihud's father was Ehud (1 Chr 8:6), while Gera was the one who exiled Ahihud and his mother to Manahath.

Ahijah. 1. Ahitub's son who served as priest at Shiloh and had charge of the ark of the covenant at Gibeah during Saul's last campaign (1 Sm 14:3,18, KJV Ahiah). This Ahijah was evidently either the same person as Ahimelech or closely associated with him (1 Sm 21:1–9; 22:9–20).

2. One of King Solomon's secretaries (1 Kgs 4:3, KJV Ahiah).

3. Prophet of Shiloh who informed King Solomon's official, Jeroboam, of the approaching revolt of the 10 northern tribes. Before Solomon died, Ahijah acted out a prophecy before Jeroboam, giving him 10 pieces of his robe, which he had torn into 12 segments, saying that God would tear 10 tribes from Solomon and give them to Jeroboam (1 Kgs 11:29–39; 2 Chr 10:15). Later, when Jeroboam had

been unfaithful to Israel's religion, he sent his wife to ask the prophet about their son Abijah's illness (1 Kgs 14:1–5). Aware of her identity although he was now old and blind, Ahijah predicted both the child's death and the fall of Jeroboam and his family (14:6–17; 15:28–30). "The prophecy of Ahijah the Shilonite" was evidently a written source for Solomon's biography (2 Chr 9:29).

4. Father of King Baasha of the northern kingdom of Israel (1 Kgs 15:27,28,33; 21:22; 2 Kgs 9:9).

5. Jerahmeel's son from Judah's tribe (1 Chr 2:25).

6. Ehud's son (1 Chr 8:7, KJV Ahiah). The Hebrew is difficult to translate, so some English versions make Ahijah one of Ehud's sons, while others make Ahijah the one who carried Ehud's sons, Uzza and Ahihud, into exile.

7. Warrior among David's mighty men who were known as "the thirty" (1 Chr 11:36); also called Eliam the son of Ahithophel (2 Sm 23:34).

8. Levite who oversaw King David's temple treasury (1 Chr 26:20).

9. Ancestor of the prophet Ezra (2 Esd 1:2).

Ahikam. Shaphan's son, an officer of the court of King Josiah of Judah (2 Kgs 22:12). Ahikam was among the group sent to the prophetess Huldah to ask about the book of the Law (2 Kgs 22:14–20). Later, under King Jehoiakim, Ahikam was able to prevent the prophet Jeremiah from being killed (Jer 26:24). Ahikam's son Gedaliah was left as governor of Judah after Nebuchadnezzar destroyed Jerusalem and took most of its citizens to Babylon in 586 BC (2 Kgs 25:22; Jer 39:14;40:5–16;41:1–18;43:6).

Ahilud. Father of the court historian Jehoshaphat. Jehoshaphat served under both David and Solomon (2 Sm 8:16; 20:24; 1 Kgs 4:3; 1 Chr 18:15). Probably Ahilud was also the father of Baana, one of Solomon's tax officials (1 Kgs 4:12).

Ahima-az. 1. Father of Ahino-am, who was King Saul's wife (1 Sm 14:50).

2. Son of the high priest Zadok and father of Azariah (1 Chr 6:8,9,53). Ahima-az remained loyal to King David at the time of Absalom's rebellion. He and Jonathan, son of the priest Abiathar, served as couriers. News of Absalom's movements was sent from Zadok and Abiathar in Jerusalem to Ahima-az and Jonathan in En-rogel, and then communicated by them to David (2 Sm 15:27–29; 17:15–23). Ahima-az was probably well known as a fast runner. He outran the official messenger bearing news to David of Absalom's defeat (2 Sm 18:19–33).

3. One of 12 officers appointed to requisition food for Solomon's household. This Ahima-az, of Naphtali's tribe, married Basemath, one of Solomon's daughters (1 Kgs 4:15).

Ahiman. 1. One of Anak's three sons. The Ahimanites were one of the Anakim clans living in Hebron when the 12 Israelite spies scouted the land of Canaan (Nm 13:22; Jos 15:13,14; Jgs 1:10).

2. Levite gatekeeper in postexilic Jerusalem (1 Chr 9:17).

Ahimelech. 1. A priest at Nob who aided David in his flight from Saul (1 Sm 21:1–9). When he was asked for food, all that he could provide was the holy bread in the tabernacle (Jesus referred to this incident in Mt 12:1–8). Doeg the Edomite subsequently reported this action to Saul, who ordered Ahimelech put to death. Saul's guards were unwilling to execute a priest, but the informer Doeg had no such inhibitions. He killed Ahimelech and 84 other priests, plus their families and livestock (1 Sm 22:9–19). Only Abiathar, Ahimelech's son, escaped and fled to David's protection (22:20–23). Psalm 52 was written by David as an indictment of Doeg's treachery.

2. Hittite who joined David's guerrilla force during his flight from Saul (1 Sm 26:6).

3. Son of Abiathar and grandson of #1 above. This Ahimelech aided his father in the priesthood under King David (2 Sm 8:17; 1 Chr 24:3,6,31; cf. 1 Chr 18:16, where some versions have Abimelech instead).

Ahimoth. Elkanah's son, a Levite in the family of Kohath (1 Chr 6:25).

Ahinadab. Iddo's son and one of 12 officers appointed to requisition food for King Solomon's household. Ahinadab's headquarters were in Mahanaim (1 Kgs 4:14).

Ahino-am. 1. Daughter of Ahima-az and wife of King Saul (1 Sm 14:50).

2. Jezreelite woman who became David's wife after Saul took back his daughter Michal and gave her to Palti (1 Sm 25:43,44). In Hebron, Ahino-am became the mother of David's oldest son, Amnon (2 Sm 3:2; 1 Chr 3:1).

Ahio. 1. Abinadab's son. With his brother Uzzah, Ahio drove the ox cart carrying the ark of the covenant to its new home at Jerusalem (2 Sm 6:3,4; 1 Chr 13:7).

2. Elpaal's son from Benjamin's tribe (1 Chr 8:14).

3. Son of Jeiel and his wife Maacah. This

Ahio was a brother or an uncle of Kish, Saul's father (1 Chr 8:31; 9:37).

Ahira. Enan's son and the leader of Naphtali's tribe when the Israelites were roaming in the Sinai wilderness after their escape from Egypt. As leader he presented his tribe's offering at the consecration of the tabernacle (Nm 1:15; 2:29; 7:78,83; 10:27).

Ahiram. Benjamin's third son and the ancestral head of the Ahiramite clan (Nm 26:38; 1 Chr 8:1 Aharah). Two abbreviated forms of the name Ahiram in genealogies may be Ehi (Gn 46:21) and Aher (1 Chr 7:12).

Ahisamach. Father of the craftsman Oholiab, of Dan's tribe. Oholiab helped construct the tabernacle and its furnishings (Ex 31:6; 35:34; 38:23).

Ahishahar. Bilhan's son and chief of the subclan of Jediael, of Benjamin's tribe, in the time of King David (1 Chr 7:10).

Ahishar. Overseer in charge of Solomon's palace affairs (1 Kgs 4:6).

Ahithophel. King David's trusted counselor who turned traitor and joined Absalom's conspiracy. Ahithophel's counsel was highly regarded, almost as though it were an oracle of God (2 Sm 16:23). On hearing about Ahithophel's defection to Absalom, David prayed, "O Lord, I pray thee, turn the counsel of Ahithophel into foolishness" (2 Sm 15:31). Ahithophel advised Absalom to take over the royal harem (2 Sm 16:20–22). Taking possession of the harem was a public act declaring a former king to be deceased and replaced. Since David was still alive, the act was meant to bring about a final cleavage between David and Absalom. It also fulfilled Nathan's prophecy to David that because David had taken another man's wife in secret, his own wives would be taken from him in public (2 Sm 12:7–12).

Ahithophel's second stratagem was to attack David quickly with 12,000 elite troops (2 Sm 17:1–3). Absalom rejected this advice, however, and accepted a countersuggestion by Hushai, David's spy in Absalom's palace. In a speech designed to inflate Absalom's ego and gain time for David, Hushai advised a full campaign (2 Sm 17:4–14). When Ahithophel saw that his counsel was not followed, he went to his hometown and hanged himself (2 Sm 17:23).

Ahithophel is surely in David's mind in Psalm 41:9, "Even my bosom friend in whom I trusted, who ate of my bread, has lifted his heel against me." In the NT the similarity of Judas to Ahithophel is seen by Jesus' use of Psalm 41:9 to describe his own situation (Jn 13:18).

Ahitub. 1. Member of the priestly line of Aaron's youngest son, Ithamar. Ahitub was a descendant of Eli through Eli's son Phinehas and father of Ahijah and Ahimelech, who were priests during Saul's reign (1 Sm 14:3; 22:9,11,12,20).

2. Member of the priestly line of Aaron's third son, Eleazar. Ahitub was Meraioth's grandson, Amariah's son, and father of Zadok (1 Chr 6:4–7). Zadok was a chief priest during David's reign (2 Sm 8:17).

3. Possibly the same as #2 above (the scribes sometimes mistakenly copied names twice), but more likely another member of the priestly line of Eleazar, seven generations after #2 (1 Chr 6:11,12). This Ahitub's father was also named Amariah and his son or grandson Zadok (1 Chr 9:11; Neh 11:11), but his grandfather was Azariah. Ahitub is listed as an ancestor of Ezra (Ezr 7:2; 1 Esd 8:2; 2 Esd 1:1).

Ahlab. Canaanite city in Asher's territory. The Israelites failed to drive out its inhabitants in their conquest of Canaan (Jgs 1:31). It probably is identical with Mahalab in Joshua 19:29, modern Khirbet el-Mahalib near Tyre.

See MAHALAB.

Ahlai. 1. Sheshan's daughter, a member of Judah's tribe (1 Chr 2:31, 34). In verse 31 some translations refer to Ahlai as a son.

2. Zabad's father or ancestor. Zabad was one of David's mighty men who were known as "the thirty" (1 Chr 11:41).

Ahoah, Ahoh, Ahohi, Ahohite. One of Bela's nine sons, a member of Benjamin's tribe (1 Chr 8:4). Ahoah's descendants were called Ahohites, and two of them were among King David's most effective warriors: Dodo ("son of Ahohi," 2 Sm 23:9; spelled Dodai in 1 Chr 27:4) and Zalmon the Ahohite (2 Sm 23:28; called Ilai in 1 Chr 11:29). The Living Bible's use of Ahoh as a place name rather than a family name in the latter two references is probably incorrect.

Aholah. KJV form of Oholah, the symbolic name for Samaria, capital of the northern kingdom of Israel, in Ezekiel 23.

See OHOLAH, OHOLIBAH.

Aholiab. KJV form of Oholiab, a craftsman from Dan's tribe.

See OHOLIAB.

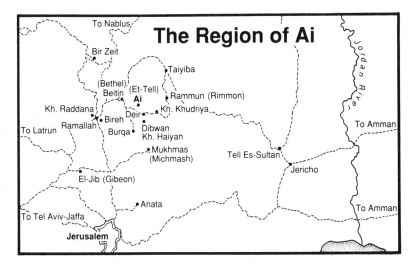

The Region of Ai

To Nablus
Bir Zeit
Taiyiba
(Bethel) (Et-Tell)
Beitin
Ai
Kh. Raddana
Rammun (Rimmon)
Deir
Kh. Khudriya
Ramallah
Bireh
To Latrun
Burqa
Dibwan
Kh. Haiyan
Mukhmas
(Michmash)
Tell Es-Sultan
Jericho
El-Jib (Gibeon)
Jordan River
To Amman
To Amman
Anata
To Tel Aviv-Jaffa
Jerusalem

Aholibah. KJV form of Oholibah, the symbolic name for Jerusalem in Ezekiel 23.

See OHOLAH, OHOLIBAH.

Aholibamah. KJV form of Oholibamah, a name associated with two members of Esau's family.

See OHOLIBAMAH #1, #2.

Ahumai. Jahath's descendant from Judah's tribe (1 Chr 4:2).

Ahuzzam, Ahuzam. Son of Ashur and Naarah, and a member of Judah's tribe (1 Chr 4:6, KJV Ahuzam).

Ahuzzath. Royal advisor to Abimelech of Gerar. Ahuzzath accompanied Abimelech to Beersheba to make a treaty with Isaac (Gn 26:26).

Ahzai. Priest of the order of Immer. Ahzai's descendant, Amashsai, was a leading priest in Jerusalem in Ezra's day (Neh 11:13, KJV Ahasai). In all probability Ahzai and Jahzerah were the same person (1 Chr 9:12).

See JAHZERAH.

Ai. Canaanite city that was settled before the time of Abraham (Gn 12:8; 13:3, KJV Hai). The name suggests a "ruin" of special significance or striking appearance. The inhabitants of Ai, as well as those of other Canaanite cities (Shechem, Bethel, Jerusalem), did not hinder Abraham in his meanderings in the hill country throughout the land. Abraham may have met with representatives of those cities and convinced their kings of his peaceful intentions. Or he may have presented such a strong front with his sizable entourage that he forestalled any Canaanite move against him.

The time of the patriarchs is generally understood to be around 2000–1750 BC, placing Abraham in the early part of the Middle Bronze Age (2100–1550 BC). The time of Joshua is usually assigned to the Late Bronze Age (1550–1200 BC), with several hundred years separating Abraham from Joshua.

The people of Israel led by Joshua entered Canaan, the Promised Land, with the intention of ridding it of its former occupants and claiming it as their inheritance. Ai, the second city to face them, withstood the first Israelite attack against it. After dealing with Achan, a disobedient soldier whose taking of booty from Jericho had caused their defeat, the Israelites attacked Ai a second time and defeated it (Jos 7:1–8:29). Joshua captured the king, executed him, and burned the city, leaving it a heap of ruins (Jos 10:1).

Ai, rebuilt and reoccupied during the monarchy (under Saul, David, and Solomon), seems to have been known under several names. It was evidently called Ayyah, one of the villages of Ephraim (1 Chr 7:28); Aiath, a village through which Assyrian armies marched toward Jerusalem (Is 10:28); and Aija, a village occupied by Benjamin's descendants during the exilic period (Neh 11:31).

Many scholars accept a ruin located about 10 miles north of Jerusalem and 2 miles southeast of Bethel, near the modern village of Deir Dibwan, as the biblical Ai. The ruin, excavated in recent years, is called et-Tell, "the Tell." Archaeologists, centering their attention on ancient Ai at et-Tell, have concluded that it was not occupied during the time of either Abraham or Joshua. Nearby Bethel, or Beitîn, has also been excavated, however, and does show evidence of occupation during the Middle Bronze Age before its total destruction. That discovery has led some archaeologists to suggest that early traditions about the destruction of Bethel became attached to Ai because Ai was not only close by but an impressive ruin. Other archaeologists and geographers have questioned the identification of et-Tell with biblical Ai. At the present time it is difficult to harmonize biblical information about Ai and the archaeological data from et-Tell.

HARVEY E. FINLEY

See CONQUEST AND ALLOTMENT OF THE LAND; JOSHUA, BOOK OF.

Aiah. 1. Zibeon's son, a Horite descended from Seir. Aiah is listed in Esau's genealogies (Gn 36:24, KJV Ajah; 1 Chr 1:35–40).

2. Father (or mother?) of Saul's concubine Rizpah (2 Sm 3:7; 21:8–11).

Aiath. Alternate name for Ai, the Canaanite city, in Isaiah 10:28.

See AI.

Aija. Alternate name for Ai, the Canaanite city, in Nehemiah 11:31.

See AI.

Aijalon. 1. City located in a valley 15 miles northwest of Jerusalem (at modern Yalo) and originally allotted to Dan's tribe (Jos 19:42, KJV Ajalon). Aijalon was designated as one of four levitical cities in Dan's area (Jos 21:24) and was later made a city of refuge by Ephraim's tribe (1 Chr 6:69). Dan's tribe had by then migrated north, having been unable to occupy its southerly allotment, including Aijalon (Jgs 1:34–36). Near Aijalon, Saul and Jonathan won a victory over the Philistines (1 Sm 14:31). Members of Benjamin's tribe occupied it at one time (1 Chr 8:13).

Camels and their drivers near the site of Aijalon. Joshua, Saul, and Jonathan won victories near Aijalon.

When the kingdom was divided after Solomon's death, Aijalon, on the northwest border of the southern kingdom, was fortified by King Rehoboam (2 Chr 11:10). It was one of 65 cities claimed to have been conquered by the Egyptian pharaoh Shishak, who invaded Palestine around 924 BC (2 Chr 12:2–12). Much later Aijalon was lost to the Philistines during the reign of Ahaz (2 Chr 28:18, KJV Ajalon).

The valley of Aijalon was part of the geographical setting of Joshua's battle to control Gibeon (Jos 10:12, KJV Ajalon). To make the Israelite victory complete, God answered Joshua's prayer to "let the sun stand still over Gibeon, and let the moon stand in its place over the valley of Aijalon" (Jos 10:12 LB).

See CITIES OF REFUGE; LEVITICAL CITIES.

2. City in the territory of Zebulun, burial place of the judge Elon (Jgs 12:12). Its site is unknown.

Aijeleth shahar. Hebrew phrase in the title of Psalm 22 (KJV), translated "according to The Hind of the Dawn" (RSV); perhaps a familiar ancient melody to which the psalm was sung.

See MUSIC AND MUSICAL INSTRUMENTS.

Ain. 1. City on the eastern border of Canaan, the Promised Land, northeast of the Sea of Galilee (Nm 34:11). The name means "well" or "spring." It may be modern Khirbet 'Ayyun.

2. Town in the territory of Simeon. Many, but not all, scholars consider the site to be En-rimmon (Jos 19:7; cf. Neh 11:29), implying a scribal error that separated "Ain" from "Rimmon."

See EN-RIMMON.

3. Place name in Joshua 21:16 resulting from another scribal mistake due to similarity of the words "Ain" and "Ashan" in Hebrew. The correct spelling is Ashan (cf. 1 Chr 6:59).

See ASHAN.

Ajah. KJV rendering of Aiah, Zibeon's son, in Genesis 36:24.

See AIAH #1.

Ajalon. KJV rendering of Aijalon in Joshua 10:12; 19:42; and 2 Chronicles 28:18.

See AIJALON #1.

Akan. Alternate name for Jaakan, Ezer's son, in Genesis 36:27.

See JAAKAN.

Akeldama. Name given to the field where Judas committed suicide after betraying Jesus; translated as "Field of Blood" (Acts 1:19).

See BLOOD, FIELD OF.

Akiba, Rabbi. Jewish leader, prominent about AD 110–35. Akiba came from a humble background and began his scholarly training at the age of 40. Having attained recognition in rabbinical study, he taught at his own school in Bene Berak, near Jaffa. During the Jewish uprising against the Romans in AD 132–35. Akiba was arrested for teaching the Jewish laws and willingly suffered a martyr's death. He had strongly supported the revolutionary leader Bar Kochba, holding him to be the long-awaited Messiah. Akiba's rabbinical activities fall into three categories.

1. *Canon of the OT.* Akiba was at Jabneh (Jamnia) when discussions were held there (AD 90?) concerning books to be included in the Jewish Scriptures and those to be left out. The discussions were less concerned with admitting new books than with reaffirming the canonical status of books that had come into question, especially Ecclesiastes and the Song of Solomon. Concerning the Song, whose literal interpretation some may have regarded as too sensual for Scripture, Akiba said, "All the writings are holy, but the Song is Holy of Holies."

2. *Oral Law.* Following a plan worked out by others, Akiba began collecting and systematizing the confusing mass of oral law. Oral law had been developed by the rabbis as a means of applying the written law to life situations not dealt with in Scripture itself. The materials were organized into six main books (orders), each further divided into tractates. This arrangement of the oral law was completed in the early part of the third century AD by Rabbi Judah Nasi, and became the basis of the Mishna and later of the Talmud, the standard body of Jewish law (which still did not contain all legal opinions).

3. *Principles of Biblical Interpretation.* Rabbi Ishmael held that the language of Scripture was to be treated as ordinary human language, following the same grammar, word meanings, etc. In contrast, Akiba insisted that Scripture was to be interpreted in a way that was not applicable to ordinary language. Ordinary language might allow different spellings of the same word with no difference in meaning, for example; but if such a thing happened in Scripture, to Akiba there had to be some reason. Other schools of interpretation accused him of twisting language to force his own interpretations on Scripture. Akiba encouraged a scholar named Aquila to make a Greek translation of the Scriptures that would embody his principles of interpretation. Aquila's translation was therefore over-literal; because it disregarded standard principles of grammar, it cannot be said to be acceptable Greek. The same influence can be seen in the Aramaic translation known as Targum Onkelos.

DAVID K. HUTTAR

See TALMUD; BIBLE, CANON OF THE; JUDAISM.

Akkad, Akkadians. Ancient Semitic city and people in Mesopotamia. The Akkadians (*akaddu*) seem to have been one of several ethnic groups living in the area at a time when the Sumerians were beginning to drain the swamps of the Tigris-Euphrates delta to lay the foundations of their own brilliant culture. The Sumerians appear to have established commercial and social contacts with other Mesopotamian peoples early in the fourth millennium BC. That Akkadians were included is clear from the Akkadian words borrowed by the Sumerians, and from the Semitic names of the later kings of Ur. A principal difference between the Sumerians and Akkadians was their languages. Sumerian has no evident linguistic links with any other tongue, ancient or modern, whereas Akkadian belongs to the East Semitic group of languages.

History and Culture. Until about 2450 BC the Semites of the Plain of Shinar displayed no particular political ambitions; but about 2360 BC, with the appearance of Sargon of Akkad, they began to come into prominence as a military and political force. Sargon founded his capital at Agade (Akkad), and from that Sumerian name his followers became known as Akkadians. The city of Akkad (spelled Accad in the Bible) was included with Babel (Babylon) and Erech (Uruk) as forming the original kingdom of Nimrod in the land of Shinar (Gn 10:10). Precise correlation of that reference with the little that is known of early Akkadian history is difficult to establish. Nimrod was a renowned ruler of antiquity who founded Babylon, one of the most celebrated cities in the ancient Near East, and named it Bab-ilu (Gate of God). It may be that the Genesis writer was referring to extremely early settlement activities, perhaps of a seminomadic nature, at the sites mentioned. If so, the form of the names preserved in the Hebrew records is doubtless a later version of the designations under which they were known originally. That would be consistent with the practices of scribes as seen in other parts of the Pentateuch and other

A cylinder seal from *c.* 2300 BC.

early historical writings, where the archaic names of sites were frequently updated by the addition of their more modern form (e.g., Jos 18:14).

About 2360 BC Sargon attacked and defeated the Sumerian king Lugalzaggesi of Uruk, occupied the land he had won, and absorbed much of Sumerian culture into his own kingdom. Sargon continued to transform his newly won territory into a Semitic kingdom, and it was not long before the Babylonian empire he founded stretched from Elam in Mesopotamia to Syria and the Mediterranean Sea.

Largely responsible for the expansion of Akkadian influence was one of Sargon's sons, Manishtusu (c. 2306–2292 BC), who launched an expedition across the Persian Gulf and conquered a number of cities unfriendly to the Akkadians. Because hostile peoples to the north and west had cut off supplies of tin, silver, and copper upon which they depended, the Akkadians were forced to open up new areas of trade in the south, which may have included even areas of southeast Persia.

Naram-Sin (c. 2291–2255 BC), the son or (more probably) the grandson of Sargon, subdued the enemies of the Akkadians in the north and west and incorporated their territory into the growing empire. The Lullubi, who lived in eastern Armenia and had long been a threat to Sargon's dynasty, were defeated in a battle which the Akkadians commemorated in a rock sculpture at Darband-i-Gawr and also on a carved stele recovered from Susa (both in Iran). In the west, Naram-Sin attacked centers that probably included Aleppo, Ebla, and other cities in northern Syria. In response to uprisings in those areas of the Persian Gulf conquered earlier, Naram-Sin marched against Magan (perhaps to be identified with Oman) and killed its ruler. Naram-Sin was the last great king of the Akkadian dynasty; before he died, he boasted that he was "king of Agade, king of the four regions of the world, and king of the universe."

Although the Akkadians placed great value on Sumerian cultural achievements, they took the important step of replacing the native tongue of the delta region with their own Semitic speech, thereby making Sumerian a classical language. Trade and commerce flourished in Mesopotamia during the Old Akkadian period (c. 2360–2200 BC), as reflected in business tablets of that time recovered from ancient Gasur. Probably the most influential feature of Sumerian culture adopted by the Akkadians was their religion. During the early fourth millennium BC the Sumerians had described the gods in terms of natural forces experienced personally. They had given names to those powers and arranged them in order of importance under the leadership of Anu the sky god and En-lil the storm deity. Thereafter myths about the gods came into being in Sumer, forming the basis of religious compositions in Akkad. So inventive and proficient were the Akkadian scribes that their religious epic poems proved superior in form and literary style to the original Sumerian compositions. One major change the Akkadians made in the Sumerian list of gods concerned Ea, the water deity and god of wisdom, whose cult was in Eridu, one of the earliest Sumerian cities: Ea was installed as head of the Babylonian gods. At a later period Marduk replaced Ea as the chief deity, but in religious literature both were described as cooperating for human benefit.

After the death of Naram-Sin his successor, Shar-kali-sharri, found it difficult to control the empire he had inherited. Thus he spent much of his time trying to crush rebellions among the Lullubi, the 36 city-states of Sumer, and the conquered peoples of Syria. In about 2230 BC he was overthrown in a palace revolt, and the Akkadian empire began to break up rapidly. Powerful cities once conquered by Sargon and Naram-Sin began to reassert themselves. The existing confusion was made worse by Elamite raiding parties from the east, some of which penetrated as far as Akkad. What marked the final days of the Akkadian empire, however, was the fact that the Semitic inhabitants of Mesopotamia were overrun by the Gutians from the Caucasus, who then began to rule Akkad and Sumer (2180 BC). A century later Sumerian culture revived under the magnificent third dynasty of Ur (2070–1960 BC), and toward the end of that period the Akkadians themselves experienced a short-lived renewal of power. While the Elamites and Subarians were sacking Sumer about 1960 BC, an Amorite chieftain occupied Akkad and brought Sargon's dynasty to an end. The site of Akkad has never been found, though its name lived on in the phrase "the land of Akkad and Sumer," a term used to describe Babylonia.

For a time the political fortunes of the Mesopotamian Semites were in the hands of military opportunists, who fought periodically with the few surviving communities to the south. Only when Babylon came into prominence under the first Babylonian dynasty, founded by Sumu-abum, did Semitic influence flourish once more. The situation was consolidated further under Hammurabi, the last outstanding king of that dynasty, who unified his empire against the dangers of Amorite attack. With that degree of political stability came prosperity and a revival of Akkadian culture.

Hammurabi's celebrated law code was only

one product of that period. He also introduced changes into the earlier Akkadian religious traditions in order to glorify the god Marduk. The result was a great epic poem about creation written on seven clay tablets, copies of which were dug up at Nineveh. Another similar poem, the Gilgamesh Epic, described the adventures of an early Sumerian king. Toward the end, the composition told of a great flood that drowned the city of Shuruppak. Both poems were more fully developed forms of earlier Sumerian traditions and have some points of contact with the Genesis accounts of creation and the flood.

From the beginning of their history the Akkadians were evidently firmly controlled by their leaders. Control was obviously necessary for groups of peoples who were seminomadic by disposition to settle in one area and establish a distinctive culture within the political and social framework of a city-state. The dramatic expansion of Sargon's empire was the result of his ability to deploy a large army and maintain it as a fighting force even in times of peace. It was thus ready at all times to put down disturbances of either a civil or military nature. Records indicate that the costs involved in supporting Sargon's standing army were met by imposing taxes on the people of Akkad, taxes collected by a centralized civil service. The bureaucracy established by Sargon set a pattern of organization that the Babylonian ruler Hammurabi adopted and expanded in his Semitic empire some centuries later. Legal texts recovered from the Akkad era describe sales of property, animals, and slaves, and include farmers' records as well as accounts of trade between cities in the empire.

Language. The Akkad texts were written in an attractive script that scholars call Old Akkadian. Old Akkadian was a northeast Semitic dialect written and spoken between about 2500 and 2000 BC. The earliest phase of Old Akkadian was pre-Sargonic; texts show that the script from that period was not nearly so well defined and regular as that from the time of Sargon. The neatness and elegance of subsequent Akkadian texts was equaled only centuries later by Assyrian scribes in the time of Ashurbanipal (669–627 BC). Old Akkadian is the first written form of any Semitic language, as far as is known, and its wedge-shaped script was an adaptation of that developed by the Sumerians. The scribes of Akkad produced a surprisingly versatile and complex language by combining phonetic writing with certain other signs (ideograms) that conveyed the idea of the meaning. Understandably, Old Akkadian contained some loanwords from the Sumerian tongue, which were normally read by the Akkadians as their Semitic equivalents.

Thus the Sumerian "idea-sign" for god, represented by a star, was pronounced *dingir*, but when read by the Akkadians it became *ilu*.

After the time of Sargon of Akkad the ideograms began to be used less often in favor of phonetic expression. That stage marked the end of Old Akkadian, ushering in the classical form of Akkadian known as Old Babylonian (c. 2000–1500 BC). At that time speech variations led to an increasing division of Akkadian into Assyrian and Babylonian dialects. Old Assyrian, which was the earliest phase of the language as spoken in the north, lasted between about 2000 and 1500 BC. It is best illustrated from tablets found at an Assyrian settlement at Kültepe in Central Anatolia. The best examples of Old Babylonian have come from the time of Hammurabi in the first Babylonian dynasty. In addition, both Assyrian and Babylonian passed through Middle and New stages of language development. From 2000 BC to just before the time of Alexander the Great (4th century BC), Akkadian in its various linguistic forms was the normal means of communication in the Near East. The cuneiform script in which Akkadian was written was syllabic and ideographic in nature rather than alphabetic, and was inscribed on the surface of soft clay tablets by means of a triangular stylus or engraved on monuments or walls. Akkadian contained several hundred basic signs, the bulk of which were syllabic, and each had at least one phonetic value. Some syllables were utilized to represent one complete word as an ideogram. For example, the combination of wedges which read *ad* also carried the value of *abu*, or "father," when it was understood as an ideogram. Many syllables often had several ideographic senses associated with them, in addition to having one or more phonetic values of their own, making for a complex linguistic structure.

Akkadian grammar had much in common with its Hebrew counterpart, and included a developed personal pronoun and five principal demonstrative pronouns as well as relative, indefinite, reflexive, and interrogative pronouns. Verbs were normally composed of three root consonants or radicals, as commonly found in Hebrew, but verbs of two and four radicals also occurred in Akkadian. The verb was conjugated in terms of four basic and three secondary stems, along with several others that occurred less often. As with the Hebrew verb paradigm, these forms expressed active and passive, causative and reflexive meanings, though in a more complex and developed manner in some respects.

Akkadian nouns could stand in a special genitive relationship to one another, known to grammarians as the construct state, and this linguistic form is found in Hebrew also. A developed system of adverbs included enclitic or appended forms which emphasized nouns, pronouns, and verbs, as well as prohibitive, temporal, and interrogative adverbs. Akkadian prepositions were also well developed in nature, being written sometimes phonetically and at other times in a less elaborate ideographic form. Thus the compound prepositions *ina muḥḥu* and *ana muḥḥu*, both meaning "on," "against," "concerning," varied only slightly in the way the wedges were used. Various particles were employed in sentence construction to express a wide variety of declarations, wishes for the future, and prohibitions, along with relative, conditional, and circumstantial clauses.

Although Akkadian became unnecessarily complex and unwieldy because of its basic syllabic form, it was the vehicle of a tremendously wide range of literary and nonliterary texts, ranging from codes of law, such as that promulgated by Hammurabi, to records of rather mundane business transactions. Akkadian texts have been unearthed by archaeologists at many sites, stretching from the Mediterranean Sea to northern and eastern Mesopotamia. As the international language of diplomacy in the second millennium BC, Akkadian made its presence felt even in Egypt, where in 1887 a collection of Akkadian diplomatic correspondence (the Amarna tablets) from various Near Eastern rulers to the Egyptian Amarna Age pharaohs was discovered. Only when the Greek language swept through the Near East did Akkadian fade into oblivion.

R.K. Harrison

See Mesopotamia; Hammurabi, Law Code of; Flood Myths.

Akkub. 1. One of Elioenai's seven sons and a distant descendant of David (1 Chr 3:24).

2. Ancestor of a family of Levite gatekeepers who returned to Jerusalem with Zerubbabel after the exile (Ezr 2:42; Neh 7:45). This family name was borne by two of his descendants (#3 and #6 below).

3. Descendant of #2 and head of a family of Levite gatekeepers who were among the first to return to Jerusalem after the Babylonian exile (1 Chr 9:17).

4. Ancestor of a group of temple assistants who returned to Jerusalem with Zerubbabel after the exile (Ezr 2:45).

5. Ezra's assistant who explained to the people passages from the Law read by Ezra (Neh 8:7).

6. Descendant of #2 above and head of a family of Levite gatekeepers who lived in Jerusalem during the time of Ezra and Nehemiah

(Neh 11:19; 12:25,26). He is perhaps the same as #5 above.

Akrabbim. A mountain pass or slope in southern Palestine between the southwestern tip of the Dead Sea and the wilderness of Zin. The pass (Nm 34:4; Jgs 1:36) of Mt Akrabbim served as part of the southern border of the land given to Judah's tribe after the conquest of Canaan (Jos 15:3, KJV Maaleh-akrabbim). During the intertestamental period Judas Maccabeus won an important victory over the Idumeans at this pass (1 Mc 5:3).

Alabaster. White or translucent stone, sometimes veined, frequently used to make vases and flasks.

See Minerals, Metals, and Precious Stones.

Alameth. KJV form of Alemeth, Becher's son, in 1 Chronicles 7:8.

See Alemeth (Person) #1.

Alammelech. KJV form of Allammelech in Joshua 19:26.

See Allammelech.

Alamoth. Hebrew term in the title of Psalm 46; perhaps a musical cue, meaning "flutes," describing the kind of musical accompaniment for the performance of the psalm.

See Music and Musical Instruments.

Alemeth (Person). 1. Becher's son from Benjamin's tribe (1 Chr 7:8, KJV Alameth).

2. Son of Jehoaddah (1 Chr 8:36) or Jarah (1 Chr 9:42) and a descendant of King Saul.

Alemeth (Place). Levitical city in the territory of Benjamin's tribe (1 Chr 6:60, NASB Allemeth); alternately called Almon in Joshua 21:18. Its site was at Khirbet 'Almit, about five miles northeast of Jerusalem.

See Levitical Cities.

Alexander. 1. The Macedonian conqueror, Alexander the Great (356–323 BC), whose life has influenced history and culture for more than two millennia, down to the present time. He was a brilliant organizer and military strategist, but his greatest achievement was the Hellenization of the empire he won. This Greek cultural influence was a unifying element among many diverse peoples, although among the Jews it produced cultural and religious conflict.

The introduction of the Greek language throughout this empire also had far-reaching effects. The OT was translated into Greek in Alexandria, Egypt, and the NT books were written in that language. The earliest Christian missionaries were bilingual, so that it was possible to bring the gospel "to the Jew first, and also to the Greek."

Alexander was the son of an illustrious father, Philip II of Macedon, whose magnificent tomb has only recently come to archaeological light. A seasoned military leader in his teens, Alexander succeeded to the throne at the age of 20 after the assassination of his father. After putting down the rebellions that broke out at his father's death, Alexander crossed the Dardanelles and conquered Asia Minor.

In 333 BC he met and defeated the vaunted Persian army of Darius III at Issus, in a battle which had a lasting historical significance. Moving down the Mediterranean coast, he captured Sidon, Tyre, and Gaza. Reaching Egypt in 332 BC, he was hailed by the oracle of Amon at Siwa as the divine pharaoh. He founded Alexandria, one of the more than 60 cities he established with this name, and then pushed on to the East. At Arbela (331 BC) he again defeated the Persians. When he reached Persia, he seized the cities of Susa, Persepolis, and Ecbatana. He forged eastward until he reached the Indus River; here, with his troops worn out and threatening mutiny, he turned back toward the West. He died in Babylon in 323 BC, a victim of fever, exhaustion, and dissipation, and master of an empire that stretched from the Danube to the Indus and south to the Egyptian Nile.

See GREECE, GREEKS; HELLENISM; HELLENISTIC JUDAISM; JUDAISM; ALEXANDRIA.

2. Brother of Rufus and son of Simon of Cyrene, the man who was passing by at the time Jesus was being led to Golgotha and whom the Roman soldiers compelled to carry the cross (Mk 15:21).

3. A member of the high priestly family, along with Caiaphas, Annas the high priest, and John (Acts 4:6). It was this group who summoned Peter and John to appear before them to account for the healing of the lame man at the Beautiful Gate of the temple (Acts 3).

4. Ephesian who was put forward by the Jews to serve as their spokesman when the silversmith Demetrius roused the Ephesians to riot (Acts 19:33). The preaching of the gospel by Paul and his companions had resulted in the conversion of many people, who left the worship of the goddess Artemis (Diana) and thus reduced the income of the silversmiths, whose revenue derived from the manufacture of images of this deity (Acts 19:23–41).

5. One who, with Hymenaeus, was mentioned as having shipwrecked his faith because of his rejection of conscience (1 Tm 1:20). Paul states that he had "delivered [them] to Satan that they may learn not to blaspheme."

6. Coppersmith (2 Tm 4:14). Paul warns Timothy to beware of this man, who had done much harm to Paul and had strongly opposed the message of the gospel. Some equate this Alexander with the apostate Alexander of 1 Timothy 1:20 (#5 above).

Alexandria.   Egyptian city established by Alexander the Great in 331 BC. Alexandria was the capital city of Egypt through the Hellenistic and Roman periods, and next to Rome was the most important city in the ancient world. It was built at the western edge of the Nile River delta on a peninsula between the mainland of Egypt and the Mediterranean Sea. Its harbor was protected by the island of Pharos, site of a huge lighthouse (the Pharos of Alexandria), one of the seven wonders of the ancient world. Pharos formed the top of a *T*, the stem of which was a long mole running out from the peninsula; on both sides of the *T* lay the ancient harbor.

Alexander built the city to provide a military base, harbor facilities, and trading center with which to control Egypt and the East. The city was laid out in a grid, with two tree-lined streets, about 200 feet wide, that intersected in the middle. It was divided into three districts: Jews in the northeast, Egyptians in the west, and Greeks to the south.

Alexandria was famous in antiquity for its architecture: the lighthouse; the Museum, greatest library and learning center of the Hellenistic age; the mausoleum of Alexander, built by Ptolemy, one of his successors; the Serapeum, a temple to Pan (in the shape of a pine cone, according to the geographer Strabo); and the commercial buildings.

Archaeological evidence of these structures of the ancient city is remarkably scarce. An earthquake damaged the lighthouse in AD 796, and it was completely destroyed some 500 years later. Only one scroll holder and a statue have been found from the Museum. One of the so-called "Cleopatra's obelisks," set up in Alexandria in honor of Roman general Mark Antony, is today in New York City's Central Park; another is on London's Victoria Embankment. The monuments actually date from the time of Thutmose III (1490–1436 BC). Pompey's Pillar, in reality a monument built by Roman emperor Diocletian in the fourth century AD, still towers 99 feet above the modern city.

Alexandria played a key role in the history of the Greco-Roman world. When Alexander the Great died in 323 BC, Egypt fell to Ptolemy, one of his four generals. Ptolemy established a dynasty that continued until Cleopatra. Because of Alexander's destruction of Tyre, Alex-

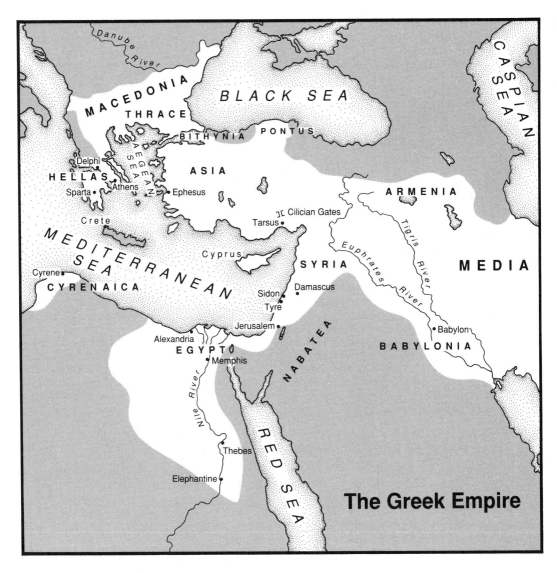

The Greek Empire

andria became the Hellenistic center of commerce with the East and with central Egypt. Julius Caesar's romance with Cleopatra led to the end of the Ptolemaic dynasty.

The Museum, not a museum in the modern sense, was actually a university and library. Founded by Ptolemy Philadelphus, it made Alexandria the intellectual center of the Greek world, with emphasis on grammatical studies, literary criticism, and textual preservation. Before its partial destruction by Egyptians and Julius Caesar's forces in 47 BC, it reportedly housed 700,000 volumes, including carefully edited texts of the Greek classics. In the late Hellenistic and Roman periods the Museum turned in the direction of the new sciences, exemplified by the building of a great lighthouse that could be seen by ingenious use of mirrors 20 miles at sea.

From its inception Alexandria had a large Jewish population. Under the patronage of the Ptolemies, Jewish scholars produced the Greek translation of the OT known as the Septuagint, so named because according to one tradition, 70 rabbis worked in 70 huts by the sea to produce it. Ethnic tension in the city grew as the Jewish populace increased and prospered. The tension erupted in AD 42 into riots by the Greeks and the expulsion of Jews from the Gentile sections into which they had spread. Jewish commercial success, particularly in the wheat trade, led to intensified anti-Semitism.

Out of the riots came two apologetic treatises by Philo Judaeus, *Against Flaccus* (Flaccus was governing in Alexandria) and *Embassy to Caligula* (Caligula was emperor in Rome). His philosophic work, eclectic in na-

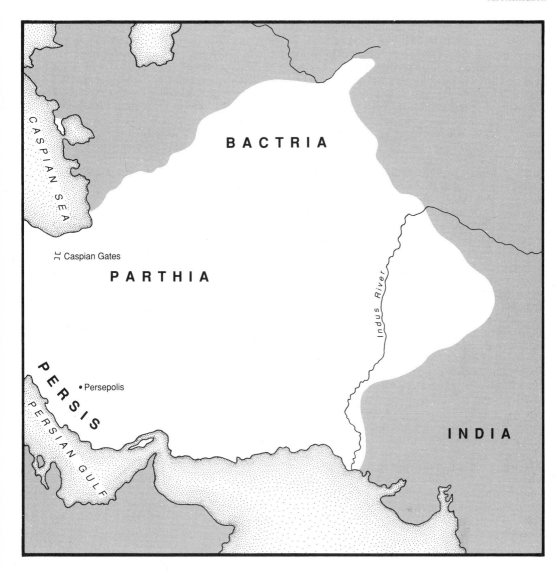

ture, attempted to reconcile Jewish monotheism with Greek philosophy.

There is little reference to Alexandria in Scripture. Stephen, who became the first Christian martyr, debated with "Jews from Alexandria" in Jerusalem concerning Jesus as the Messiah (Acts 6:9). Apollos, described as "an eloquent man, well versed in the scriptures," was a native of Alexandria (Acts 18:24). The apostle Paul made his sea journey to Rome aboard two Alexandrian ships (Acts 27:6; 28:11).

The earliest emphasis in biblical studies at Alexandria was Gnostic, under Basilides and continuing under his son Isidore. Later, an allegorizing school developed, with regular support by wealthy patrons and an organized curriculum. Clement and Origen are the names most often associated with this school. The teaching emphasized three levels of mean-

ing in the Scriptures: historical, ethical, and spiritual.

Arianism, a powerful heresy, was later formulated in Alexandria by Arius, presbyter of Alexandria. This school of thought denied the eternality of Christ, arguing that since he was begotten he therefore had a beginning. The chief opponent of Arianism, Athanasius, was also from Alexandria. It was primarily through his efforts that the heretical teaching was dissipated in the fourth century and the Symbol of Nicaea confirmed at the Council of Constantinople in AD 381.

The Muslim conquest of Alexandria occurred during the caliphate of 'Umar (AD 634–644), the invasion itself being led by the general Amr ibn al-'Ās. Beginning at Pelusium in 640, a force of 10,000 Arabs invaded Egypt and defeated a vastly superior Byzantine army at

Heliopolis. The fortress Babylon (near Old Cairo) was conquered the next year after a seven-month siege. This left Alexandria weakened, and after a siege lasting a year the city was occupied in 642 by means of a treaty negotiated by the Coptic patriarch and ratified by Constans II (Constantine III).

Iban al-'Ās's message to the caliph was filled with wonder: "I shall refrain from a description of the city. [It is sufficient to say that] it has 4,000 villas, 400 baths, 40,000 tax-paying Jews, and 400 places of entertainment." In 645 the Byzantines with 300 ships reconquered Alexandria and slaughtered the garrison of Arab defenders, numbering about 1,000. In 646 Amr captured the city again and demolished the city walls. A late tradition of the 13th century places the burning of the library at that time. The general is supposed to have said, "If these books of the pagans oppose the Qur'an they are wicked; if they agree they are unnecessary. Burn them!" Most modern scholars are skeptical of the story, viewing the tradition as a medieval Christian attempt to discredit Islam. They point out that the library was burned twice in antiquity, that very little of it survived into the 7th century, and that Islam was generally respectful of culture and learning.

ARTHUR RUPPRECHT

See ALEXANDER #1; HELLENISM; PHILO JUDAEUS; HELLENISTIC JUDAISM.

Algum. Wood imported from Lebanon (2 Chr 2:8) and possibly Ophir (9:10,11) for the construction of the temple and the palace, and for musical instruments. The term may be a scribe's error of transposition for "almug" tree.

See PLANTS (ALGUM).

Aliah. Alternate name for Alvah, Esau's descendant, in 1 Chronicles 1:51.

See ALVAH.

Alian. Alternate name for Alvan, Shobal's son, in 1 Chronicles 1:40.

See ALVAN.

Alien. *See* FOREIGNER.

Allammelech. Town in Asher's territory (Jos 19:26, KJV Alammelech).

Allegory. Strictly speaking, a device which seeks to communicate abstract ideas and concepts in pictorial terms derived from the objective world. As such, metaphors, parables, and certain types of illustrations are "allegory." "Allegory" may also refer to a literary form

employed for a part or the whole of a work, such as John Bunyan's *Pilgrim's Progress*. More often "allegory" denotes a particular method of interpretation ("allegorizing"), especially biblical interpretation, which seeks to find a deeper moral, theological, spiritual meaning behind the words and literal imagery of the text.

Allegory began among the ancient Greeks, for whom the writings of such epic poets as Hesiod and Homer provided the basis for religion and piety. Later developments in the understandings of life and the universe made these writings appear obsolete. Further, with the passage of time the significance and identity of some literal expressions of historical, geographic, cultural, and social elements in the poets was lost. In order to maintain the validity of their traditions, interpreters began to employ ingenious schemes through which abiding truths and values were sought by using the objective, literal features of the texts as symbols pointing beyond themselves.

Hellenistic Judaism, best exemplified by Philo of Alexandria (d. *c.* AD 45–50), used allegory to make the OT relevant in the Greco-Roman world. Later, a group of Christian interpreters centered around Alexandria employed allegory as their principal method of handling both the OT and NT. In one form or another allegory was the dominant interpretative method of the Middle Ages. It continues to be highly regarded by some pietistically and mystically oriented contemporary Christians, both Protestant and Roman Catholic.

Since allegorizing is a highly individualized interpretative method, its features widely differ from one practitioner to another. For all allegorists the obvious, literal, objective features and meaning of a text are either irrelevant or of only secondary importance; the significant or true meanings may well be dissociated from objective statements or the historical setting. In more advanced applications of the method the external and obvious are irrelevant and even the historicity of an account is of no consequence. Indeed, the understanding and intention of the original author may count for nothing in determining the "true," "spiritual" meaning of a biblical passage. External and obvious features of a writing are but clues pointing beyond themselves to spiritual meanings. Hence the allegorist makes free use of devices which establish arbitrary connections between ancient and contemporary events, seeks alleged meanings and derivations of word roots or the supposed relationship between similar words and sounds, and emphasizes prepositions. He assigns symbolic significance to individual parts such as persons, places, things, numbers, colors, and the like, and may claim to discover truth hidden even in the shapes of letters.

Inevitably allegorical interpretation has resulted in multiple meanings. To the thoroughgoing allegorist this commends the method and exemplifies the riches of spiritual truth. The church father Origen (c. AD 185–254) taught that every passage has three levels of meaning; Middle Age exegetes assumed a fourfold meaning (the quadriga) for each text—the literal, doctrinal, moral, and heavenly.

Typological interpretation, in contrast to allegory, takes seriously the literal content and the historical situation of the text. A writing is understood to have a single meaning, and individual parts are significant only as they contribute to it. The typological interpreter seeks to discover what the author meant in the original situation and to identify the moral and spiritual principles at work; only then does the interpreter seek, by extension or analogy, to apply the text to his own day.

Although the allegorical method has had a long history in the Christian church (and indeed is once specifically used by Paul, Gal 4:24), it has inherent difficulties. These led the Reformers Luther and Calvin to reject allegory as a valid method of interpreting Scripture. The most serious problems include allegory's separation of the "meaning" of the text from its plain statements in their original historical-grammatical-cultural setting and its inability to provide a basis for evaluating competing, contradictory interpretations of the same passage. Allegory provides no "controls" to protect the interpreter from reading his own meanings into Scripture *(eisogesis)* rather than drawing out its own message *(exegesis)*.

J. JULIUS SCOTT, JR.

See BIBLE, INTERPRETATION OF THE; HELLENISTIC JUDAISM; PHILO JUDAEUS.

Alleluia, Alleluiah. *See* HALLELUJAH.

Allemeth. NASB rendering of Alemeth in 1 Chronicles 6:60.

See ALEMETH (PLACE).

Alliance. Close association of powerful individuals or nations for a common objective. Such alliances were ratified by various means, including gifts, oaths, dowries and marriages, and covenants.

In patriarchal times Israelites entered into alliances with foreign nations without hesitation. Abraham had an alliance with three Amorites: Mamre, Eshcol, and Aner (Gn 14:13,24) and with Abimelech, king of Gerar (Gn 21:22–34). Isaac also made an alliance with Abimelech (Gn 26:26–31). Later, Moses forbade the

Israelites to make alliances with the Canaanites (Ex 23:31–33; 34:12; Dt 7:1–4), primarily for religious reasons. In the time of the judges the Israelites were reminded of that command (Jgs 2:1–3), but Joshua 9 tells how Israel was tricked into making an alliance with the Gibeonites.

During the period of the monarchy various kings formed alliances and intermarried with foreigners. David (before he was king of all Israel) made an agreement with Achish, king of Gath, under which he was expected to fight with the Philistines against the Israelite army of Saul (1 Sm 27:1; 28:2). Solomon made alliances for the purpose of trade with Hiram of Tyre (1 Kgs 5:1–18; 9:26–28) and with the king of Egypt (9:16). After the division of the kingdom, Asa formed an alliance with the king of Syria, Ben-hadad (15:18–20).

Shortly thereafter Ahab, King of Israel, joined Jehoshaphat in fighting Syria (1 Kgs 22:1–4; 2 Chr 18:1–3). About a century later King Pekah of Israel formed an alliance with Rezin, king of Syria, to fight Ahaz, king of Judah (Is 7:1–9), and Ahaz in turn made an alliance with Tiglath-pileser, king of Assyria, to fight against Pekah and Rezin (2 Kgs 16:7–9). The last king of Judah, Zedekiah, made an alliance with Egypt against the Babylonians (2 Kgs 24:20; Ez 17:1–21). In general these alliances brought foreign cults into Jerusalem (2 Kgs 16:10–18) and led the prophets to cry out against them (Hos 8:8–10; Is 30:1–3,15,16; Jer 2:18).

Following the exile alliances with foreign peoples were discouraged so that even marriage between Jews and non-Jews was condemned (Ezr 9:1–3).

During the turbulent Maccabean period Jewish national leaders negotiated alliances with Rome to ensure the security of the Jews (1 Mc 8:17; 9:70; 15:16). Political alliances continued between both good and bad Judean rulers and with Roman emperors as long as the state existed.

See COVENANT.

Allon (Person). Ziza's ancestor from Simeon's tribe (1 Chr 4:37).

Allon (Place). Landmark oak tree in Naphtali's territory, considered in some translations to be the name of a town (Jos 19:33, KJV). The RSV better reads "the oak in Za-anannim."

See ZA-ANANNIM.

Allon-bacuth, Allon-bachuth. Oak tree near Bethel under which Deborah, Rebekah's aged nurse, was buried (Gn 35:8, KJV Allon-

bachuth). The place was named "the Oak of weeping."

Allotment of the Land. Assignment of large territories of the Promised Land of Canaan to the 12 tribes of Israel following the conquest.

See CONQUEST AND ALLOTMENT OF THE LAND.

Almighty. Divine name found in 11 books of the Bible, but particularly in the Books of Job (31 references) and Revelation (9 references).

See GOD, NAMES OF.

Almodad. Son or descendant of Joktan in the family of Noah's son Shem (Gn 10:26; 1 Chr 1:20).

Almon. Alternate name for Alemeth in Joshua 21:18.

See ALEMETH (PLACE).

Almond, Almond Tree. *See* PLANTS.

Almon-diblathaim. Area in Moab where the Israelites camped during their 40 years of wandering (Nm 33:46,47). Some identify it with Beth-diblathaim (Jer 48:22).

See WILDERNESS WANDERINGS.

Alms. Charitable gifts. The practice of giving alms to the poor derives from both the OT and NT. Almsgiving has undergone many changes in both practice and importance from early biblical times to the present.

The Old Testament. The English word "alms" comes from a longer Greek word used in the Septuagint (ancient Greek translation of the OT) to translate a Hebrew word for "righteousness." The Hebrew term, in general, is unrelated to almsgiving; consequently the OT has no literal reference to almsgiving. Nevertheless, the Israelites were expected to care for the unfortunate in their midst. The Mosaic law contains many admonitions to treat the poor justly and humanely. Important among them is Deuteronomy 15:7–11, which, while recognizing the inevitable existence of poverty (v 11), commands Israel to take alleviating action. Thus, every seventh year all fields and gardens were to remain unharvested for the benefit of the poor and disadvantaged (Ex 23:10,11). Every third year one-tenth of all produce had to be given to the Levites (a Hebrew tribe that had no property), the sojourner, the fatherless, and the widow (Dt 14:28,29). Forgotten sheaves and the gleanings from grain fields at each harvest were left for the needy and the stranger (Lv 19:9; 23:22); from every vineyard and oliveyard, any fallen fruit and

the imperfect and topmost clusters were reserved for them (Lv 19:10; Dt 24:20,21). Likewise, festival pilgrims were expected to share food with those in need (Dt 16:11–14).

The OT prophets continued to champion the theme of benevolent treatment for the poor. The strongest expressions of the social justice theme are found in Isaiah (1:23; 3:15; 10:1,2; 11:4,5; 58:5–10) and Amos (2:6–8; 4:1; 5:11; 8:4). Similarly, the Psalms and "Wisdom literature" (Jb; Prv; Eccl) depict the plight of the poor, holding out hope to the afflicted and appealing to others to take up their cause or to improve their condition (Jb 20:19; 22:6; 24:2–4,9; 29:12–16; 31:13–32; 34:28; Ps 14:4; 37:14,21; Prv 14:21,31; 17:5; 19:17; 22:16; 29:7; 30:14; Eccl 5:8). The appeals were based on the conviction that all human beings are created by the one God, who had commanded Israel to deal with the unfortunate in their midst with a compassion that went beyond charity to justice.

The Intertestamental Period. During the intertestamental period the giving of alms acquired more importance. The general command to show lovingkindness (cf. Lv 19:18) became defined as specific individual acts believed to contribute to personal merit and security. Thus "almsgiving atones for sin" (Ecclus 3:30) and "delivers from death" (Tb 4:10). Along with prayer and fasting, almsgiving was elevated as one of the most important expressions of Jewish piety (Tb 12:8,9).

The New Testament. The three virtues of prayer, fasting, and almsgiving are found in a similar context in the NT. Yet Jesus criticized the way in which they were practiced by many of his contemporaries (Mt 6:2–16; cf. Acts 3:2; 9:36; 10:2,4,31; 24:17). Jesus condemned the giving of alms when done in order to be praised by others. Those who gave for this reason, he said, would receive the reward of public recognition—but that was all. In contrast, God's blessing rested on those who contributed to the poor without drawing attention to themselves.

Several NT passages testify to the early church's continued concern. The needs of the poor in the Jerusalem church were supplied from a common pooling of resources (Acts 2:45; 4:32–35). The apostle Paul recognized the problems of the poor and was active in collecting contributions for them (Rom 12:13; 15:25–27; 1 Cor 16:1–4; 2 Cor 8:1–9,15; Gal 2:10). James suggested that to demonstrate concern for widows and orphans was an example of "pure and undefiled" religion (Jas 1:27). The apostle John warned that anyone who has the world's goods but refuses to share with another in need could hardly be considered a Christian (1 Jn 3:17).

Church History. The subject of almsgiving is often mentioned by Justin Martyr, Cyprian, Ambrose, and other early church fathers who sought to inspire love for the poor and a hatred of selfish indulgence and greed. They called upon the rich to give liberally and the poor to receive thankfully. Sometimes alms were collected for the poor outside the church. Records show that early churches maintained a reserve of money, and sometimes goods, to be distributed as needed.

The medieval scholastic theologians analyzed the theology of almsgiving. Thomas Aquinas and others clarified the distinction between being merciful and giving alms. They also analyzed the essential reasons why almsgiving is obligatory for Christians.

From these foundations later casuists and moral theologians analyzed the nature and extent of obligation—that is, when is there abundance and when is there poverty, and what amount should be given as alms. The most important work in this area was Alphonsus Liguori's two-volume *Theologia Moralis* (1753–55). The papacy has issued two decrees on the methods by which alms are to be collected: *Singulari quidem* (1896) and *De eleemosynis colligendis* (1908). In recent times, however, the practice of almsgiving in the Roman Catholic Church has become less regimented and more fluid.

In Protestantism there is no developed theology of almsgiving. However, denominations, local churches or groups of churches, and especially individuals have given alms. Many charitable institutions, from famine relief to education of the deprived, exist through the almsgiving of Protestants. Normally the word "almsgiving" is not used, but equivalent terms such as "ministry of compassion" or "charity." Many American churches also take special collections or "love offerings" around Thanksgiving, Christmas, and Easter for the needy.

Almug. Wood imported from Ophir for the construction of the temple, the palaces, and for lyres and harps of the temple musicians (1 Kgs 10:11,12).

See PLANTS (ALGUM).

Aloe. Tree known for its fragrant wood; also a plant from which is pressed a juice used in embalming.

See PLANTS.

Aloth. KJV form of Bealoth, a place in one of Solomon's administrative districts, in 1 Kings 4:16.

See BEALOTH #2.

Alpha and Omega. Phrase used as a title in the NT for both God (Rv 1:8; 21:6) and Jesus Christ (Rv 22:13). The English equivalent is "the *A* and the *Z*." Similar epithets are "the beginning and the end" (Rv 21:6; 22:13) and "the first and the last" (Rv 1:17; 2:8; 22:13).

Such affirmations, which have their counterpart in the OT (see Is 41:4; 44:6; 48:12), stress the unique and faithful sovereignty of God and his Son, Jesus. They serve as comforting reminders to the Christian reader that the creation and the end of all human history are both under control of the living God (cf. Rv 1:8, "who is and who was and who is to come").

See GOD, NAMES OF.

Alphabet. Letters, characters, signs, or symbols of a language, arranged in a traditional order, and used to indicate speech sounds. The alphabet has considerable significance to readers of the Bible. "I am Alpha and Omega . . . saith the Lord" (Rv 1:8 KJV). Jesus mentioned the "jot and tittle" (Mt 5:18 KJV), referring to a letter and small projections on certain consonants of the Hebrew alphabet. The Hebrew prophets and poets often used an alphabetical "acrostic" as a poetic or mnemonic (memory) device (Pss 9; 10; 25; 34; 37; 111; 112; 119; 145; Prv 31:10–31; Lam 1–4; Na 1). From such evidence it can be concluded that knowledge of the alphabet was widespread in Bible times. Archaeology confirms that conclusion; the oldest Hebrew writing in existence is the awkward scrawling of a schoolboy. Further, the oldest decipherable Hebrew inscriptions in an alphabetic type of writing were made by miners in the Sinai peninsula before 1500 BC. Thus, the contention of some 19th-century scholars that Moses could not have written the Pentateuch because writing had not been invented in his day has been proved wrong. Even the common folk knew their Abcs.

Origin. According to Tacitus, "The first people to represent thoughts graphically were the Egyptians, with their animal pictures. . . . They also claim to have discovered the letters and taught them to the Phoenicians, who . . . introduced them to Greece and were credited with inventing what they themselves had borrowed." Though the point has been hotly debated, it does seem that the Egyptians developed an alphabetic type of writing having affinities with the Phoenician script, which is the direct source of the Greek alphabet. Greek, according to many authorities, was the first true alphabet because it was a system having symbols for both consonants and vowels. The tablet material at Ebla came from a culture that was flourishing about 2500 BC as a great

Alphabet

Syrian empire until it ultimately became lost to history. The tablets were inscribed in columns of Mesopotamian cuneiform that was about 80 percent Sumerian. The balance was in the local language, which was an ancient northwest Semitic tongue closely related to Ugaritic, biblical Hebrew, and Phoenician. It appears that Sumerian cuneiform had been adapted for communications at Ebla some time before it was used for Akkadian. The cuneiform script of the tablets is small and precise, an indication that the culture at Ebla was well developed. Though native Eblaite is similar to biblical Hebrew, it was not written according to the later principles of alphabetism.

Whether the Egyptians invented writing independently or borrowed the concept from Mesopotamia has not been established clearly, but the earliest extant Egyptian writing comes from a period when Mesopotamian influence was far-reaching. Egyptian hieroglyphs are clearly the models for many letters of alphabets which followed: Hebrew, Greek, and, ultimately, even the English letters on this page.

The principles used to create the Egyptian alphabet are important in understanding the later development of the alphabet. These principles may have been established along the following lines: When the Egyptians wished to write "cow," they drew a picture of a cow; but when they wanted to write the personal name of a particular foreign monarch, they had no symbol available. So they sounded out the name and chose words resembling the sounds.

LITERARY HIERATIC OF THE TWELFTH DYNASTY (Pr. 6, 1–5).
WITH TRANSCRIPTION

OFFICIAL HIERATIC OF THE TWENTIETH DYNASTY (Abbott 5, 1–5).
WITH TRANSCRIPTION

LITERARY DEMOTIC OF THE THIRD CENTURY B.C. (Dem. Chron. 6, 1–5).

Three types of Egyptian writing.

For example, we might express the English name "Balfour" by a picture of a ball and the numeral 4. This is known as the rebus principle. It would be quite difficult to write certain words, such as "Chattanooga," as a rebus, however. To make the system more flexible, a standardized list of words beginning with each letter of the alphabet was developed so that any word could be sounded out. For example, to express the *d* sound, the word *drt* was chosen. *Drt* meant "hand," so a hand was drawn if a *d* sound was needed. The word for pond was *sh;* so to express a *sh* sound a picture of a pond was drawn, and so on. The practice of utilizing the beginning sound of a word is known as the acrophonic principle.

Though the Egyptians were using those alphabetic principles in the earliest known inscriptions, they continued to employ picture writing along with them. They never developed a purely alphabetic system until after 310 BC, when, under the influence of the Ptolemies, they adopted and adapted the Greek alphabet to replace the ancient and beautiful hieroglyphic system.

The next step forward in the history of the alphabet is obscured by the mists of antiquity. Sometime before 1500 BC people living in the western part of the fertile crescent borrowed the acrophonic principle from the Egyptians to write their own language. From several ancient inscriptions found in various cities of Palestine and from turquoise mines of the Sinai peninsula come the first alphabetic Semitic writings. Dated between the 19th and 16th centuries BC, these inscriptions are the earliest to contain decipherable phrases written in an alphabetic, as distinct from a syllabic or hieroglyphic script. The Egyptian influence is clear. To express the *b* sound they chose the common word *baytu* ("house"). For a symbol they chose the Egyptian symbol for house. To express the velar *t* sound they chose the word *tob* ("good"), beginning with that letter. For a symbol they chose the hieroglyph of the Egyptian word for good, and so forth. The same symbols were widely adopted and became the basis for the Phoenician, Hebrew, and Aramaic alphabets.

As the alphabet concept spread throughout Syria and Palestine, it came to be expressed in three major forms: Ugaritic cuneiform (wedge-shaped) script, Aramaic script, and Canaanite script.

Ugaritic Script. Several hundred clay tablets have been dug up by archaeologists at the Mediterranean coastal city of Ugarit (modern Ras Shamra). The alphabet used at Ugarit is linked only conceptually with symbols discussed so far. To write an individual letter a certain pattern of wedge-shaped marks was made with a stylus on a wet clay tablet. The technique was borrowed from two other writing systems, Akkadian and Hittite, neither of which had an alphabet of its own. Instead they had a cumbersome syllabic system which required a separate symbol for each syllable. For example, one symbol would be needed for *ba*, another for *bi*, and still others for *be*, *bu*, *bab*, *bad*, etc., so that well over 500 signs were necessary for adequate reading or writing. That complicated way of writing continued to flourish side by side with the alphabetic systems. A linear development of hieroglyph to syllabic writing to alphabet did not occur; all three systems existed alongside each other for many centuries.

Having received their writing materials from more northern cultures, the people of Ugarit turned to the south, borrowing the idea of the alphabet and expanding it to meet their own needs. With its 30 letters their system represents the most highly developed ancient alphabet. Subtleties of sound were recorded which Canaanite and Aramaic possessed but could not express with their simpler writing systems.

Ugaritic also provides us with the oldest order of an alphabet. Removing the letters unique to Ugaritic leaves an order that is remarkably similar to the modern Hebrew alphabet. It is clear from the Abc tablets found at Ugarit that the order was standardized at least as early as the 15th or 14th century BC. As mentioned above, Hebrew poets and prophets would occasionally begin each line or stanza of their message with a letter of the alphabet, following the standard order. The KJV or NASB make this clear for Psalm 119. The order of our own English alphabet is also directly connected with the arrangement established over 3500 years ago.

The wedged-shaped alphabet of Ugarit was, however, destined for extinction. After the total destruction of the city around the beginning of the 12th century BC, the simpler Aramaic and Canaanite systems carried on in its place.

Aramaic Script. The Aramaic script, though originally similar to the first Semitic writing developed from hieroglyphs, gradually changed into the square type of lettering seen on Jewish synagogues today. The Elephantine papyri exhibit one of the earliest forms of this style, which was also the most common script of the Dead Sea Scrolls. The "jot and tittle" of the time of Christ referred to this type of script. It had especially far-reaching influence in the Orient, spawning literally hundreds of kindred alphabets including Nabatean, Arabic, Palmyrene, Syriac, Armenian, Georgian, and probably the Brahmi script of India.

The modern Hebrew alphabet, like its ancient counterpart, has 22 letters, all consonants. Vowels are marked by dots and dashes, mostly below the consonant which they follow. The system of writing consonants only is common to most Semitic languages. An important exception is Ethiopic, which developed from Old South Arabic, a language whose alphabet evolved separately, tracing its origin back to the inscriptions of the Sinai turquoise mines. Ethiopic, unlike the other major Semitic alphabets, modifies the symbol in a fixed way to indicate which vowel follows.

Arabic has 28 letters, whose shapes vary according to their position in the word.

Like Hebrew, Syriac, the language of a large number of Semitic Christians, has 22 letters, all consonants, and uses special marks above and below the letters to indicate vowels. There are three quite distinct Syriac scripts: Jacobite, Nestorian, and Estrangela. Some of the earliest NT manuscripts are preserved in Syriac.

Canaanite Script. The majority of the OT was originally recorded in the Canaanite script. This was generally used until the time of the exile (586 BC), when the Aramaic type of script began to be used. The oldest example is the Gezer Calendar, written in or before the 10 century BC. It records a little poem about the months of the agricultural year and seems to indicate that children systematically

Sumerian	Early Babylonian	Late Babylonian	Assyrian	
				Star
				Sun
				Month
				Man
				King
				Son
				Prince
				Lord
				His
				Reed
				Power
				Mouth
				Ox
				Bird
				Destiny
				Fish
				Gardener
				Habitation

were taught to write as early as the reign of King Solomon. The Siloam inscription from the time of Hezekiah (700 BC) and the Lachish ostraca describing the approach of the Babylonian army (587 BC) also reflect this ancient style, which only the Samaritan sect now uses.

Further, the Moabite Stone, dated in the reign of Mesha (c. 850 BC), uses the same style of writing. Differences between the writing on this inscription and on the Gezer Calendar are very slight.

The most significant development of the Canaanite script, however, came through the Phoenicians. Our earliest sample is the Ahiram inscription (c. 1000 BC). Because of their active trade the Phoenicians spread their form of the alphabet throughout the Mediterranean world. It found its way into Greece and formed the basis for the script in which the NT was written. Greek tradition claims that a certain Phoenician hero named Cadmus migrated to Boeotia in Greece and taught the natives there to write Greek in Phoenician letters. They even retained Semitic names for the characters. *Alpha* equals Semitic *alpu* or ox, *beta* comes from *baytu*, house, etc. The older forms of the Greek alphabet are so similar to the Phoenician forms that the borrowing can be accurately dated around 900 to 800 BC. The Greek alphabet became important in its own right and introduced a great innovation.

Greek Alphabet. The order of the early Greek alphabet came directly from the fixed Semitic order, the letters b, g, d, z, k, l, m, n, p, q, r, s, t being accepted without change. Phoenician, however, possessed four sounds not used in Greek in addition to *aleph* (a silent consonant): *he*, a soft *h* sound; *heth*, a rough *kh* sound made far back on the roof of the mouth; *yodh*, a *y* sound; and *ayin*, a deep guttural sound. Not wishing to discard the symbols for those letters, the Greeks placed the sounds *a, e, i,* and *o* in the positions occupied by those Semitic consonants. Having one more vowel, *u*, they chose Semitic *waw*, which was similar in sound to *u*, and placed it at the end of their alphabet; they called it *u-psilon* ("plain *u*"; that is, without any additional *w* sound). Since Greek at that time still retained a *w* sound, a new letter, *digamma* (which looks like a capital *F*), was chosen to represent the *w* as the sixth letter. This letter eventually came to represent our English sixth letter, *f*. Thus, the early Greek alphabet ran a, b, g, d, e, f, (z), h, (th), i, k, l, m, n, (x), o, p, (ş), q, r, s, t, u, plus three letters they developed that were combinations of other letters, such as *ph, kh,* or *ps*. The ş in parentheses equals Semitic *tsadhe*, which the Greeks later dropped and used only for the numeral 900. If all the letters in parentheses (which were part

of the original) are removed, we can see the English order very clearly foreshadowed.

The rough *h*, the eighth letter, was later (403 BC) employed to express long *e* or *eta* and a special mark developed to indicate the *h* sound. The fifth letter, *e*, which occupied the *he* (soft *h*) position of the Semitic alphabet, was then called *e-psilon* ("plain *e*"; showing that it also no longer retained its former *h* sound). At that same time, the letter *o-mega* ("great [i.e., long] *o*") was introduced into Attic, the most literary dialect.

The most brilliant contribution of the Greeks was undeniably the inclusion of the vowels with full status as letters. Even though that had been done in a limited way as far back as the Ugaritic alphabet, no system until the Greek one made the transition completely. The use of vowels removed almost all the ambiguity involved in consonantal writing and laid the foundation for some of the highest peaks in the ranges of world literature. Many scholars refuse to grant any prior system the title of "alphabet."

Greek, like the Semitic languages, was originally written from right to left. In the 6th century BC inscriptions were written back and forth, like oxen plowing a field. That style of writing is therefore called *boustrophedon* ("ox-turning"). After 500 BC the present method of left-to-right was consistently used.

In 403 BC Attic, the dialect of Athens, chose the Ionic alphabet of Miletus as its standard. The 24 letters of that alphabet are used to this day. The three accent marks (acute, grave, and circumflex) were introduced by Aristophanes of Byzantium around 200 BC.

The Greeks, like the Phoenicians, were traders and colonizers. Almost certainly through their activity the alphabet was introduced into Italy. As evidence the Marsiliana Tablet (c. 700 BC) shows the early Greek alphabet consisting of the letters borrowed from the Phoenicians plus the letters *upsilon, chi, phi,* and *psi* added at the end, written in order. The Etruscans were probably the first recipients of that Greek gift. Evidently they didn't hoard it, for it was passed on to several heirs. By far the most important of these were the people of Latium.

Latin Alphabet. The earliest Latin inscription presently known is the Praeneste *fibula* (c. 7th century BC), which has the name of the artist and owner inscribed upon it. About the same time the *cippus*, found in the Roman Forum, was carved out. For their own alphabet the Romans dropped the letter *z* from between *f* and *h* (note that they retained the *h* consonant of Phoenician and Etruscan which Greek dropped in 403 BC) and replaced the *z* with *g*, a variant of *c*, which was now in the third position. They also rejected the Etruscan *theta, xi,*

Numerical Equivalent of Letters

Hebrew Alphabet			Greek Alphabet		
Letter	*Letter Name*	*Number*	*Letter*	*Letter Name*	*Number*
א	Aleph	1	α	Alpha	1
ב	Beth	2	β	Beta	2
ג	Gimel	3	γ	Gamma	3
ד	Daleth	4	δ	Delta	4
ה	He	5	ε	Epsilon	5
ו	Waw	6	ς	Vau	6
ז	Zayin	7	ζ	Zeta	7
ח	Heth	8	η	Eta	8
ט	Teth	9	θ	Theta	9
י	Yodh	10	ι	Iota	10
כ	Kaph	20	κ	Kappa	20
ל	Lamedh	30	λ	Lambda	30
מ	Mem	40	μ	Mu	40
נ	Nun	50	ν	Nu	50
ס	Samekh	60	ξ	Xi	60
ע	Ayin	70	ο	Omicron	70
פ	Pe	80	π	Pi	80
צ	Tsadhe	90	ϙ	Koppa	90
ק	Qoph	100	ϱ	Rho	100
ר	Resh	200	σ	Sigma	200
ש	S(h)in	300	τ	Tau	300
ת	Taw	400	υ	Upsilon	400
			φ	Phi	500
			χ	Chi	600
			ψ	Psi	700
			ω	Omega	800
			ϑ	Sampi	900

and *sanpi* but retained the *chi* symbol for the *ks* sound. Thus, the Latin alphabet was ABCDEFGHIKLMNOPQRSTVX. Toward the end of the Roman republic, in the 1st century BC, they added the Greek letters *y* and *z* to the end of their alphabet, bringing the total to 23. Those letters were added because of an influx of Greek literature and terminology. The only letters not in our present English alphabet were *J*, *U*, and *W*, which were added in medieval times. The Latin alphabet used the symbol *V* for both *U* and *V*. This form of the alphabet, with slight variations according to language, serves as the primary vehicle for Western culture to this very day.

Alphabet as Numbers. Almost everyone is familiar with Roman numerals to indicate chapters, outlines, or (sometimes) clock numbers. In that system, I=1, V=5, X=10, L=50, C=100, D=500, and M=1000, etc. It is not so well known that both Greek and Hebrew alphabets were similarly used. The first 10 letters stood for the corresponding numerals, the 11th for 20, the 12th for 30, and so on. Some of the older letters of the Greek alphabet, which had dropped out before NT times, were still retained as numerals, such as *digamma, koppa, sanpi*, and *stau* (st). Thus some manuscripts of Revelation 13:18 have *chi, xi, stau* instead of 666 fully written out.

The Alphabet and the Christian Church. Christians played a very important role in spreading literacy and knowledge as well as the gospel to the uttermost parts of the earth. The register of alphabets developed after the time of Christ is largely a Christian register. The Gothic alphabet was developed by Bishop Ulfilas in the 4th century. The Armenian and Georgian alphabets are attributed to St Mesrop in the early 5th century AD. The alphabet of Slavic languages such as Russian or Bulgarian is called Cyrillic after St Cyril, its inventor.

Because of the church the Latin alphabet embraces the world, providing Abcs for such diverse cultures and languages as Icelandic, Comanche, Samoan, Mbunda, Iquito, and Sawi. The Christian missionary enterprise has reduced hundreds of languages and dialects to writing for the first time. The alphabet is the usual medium of expression; its relative simplicity places the art of reading within easy grasp of common people, who can then read the Word of God for themselves.

GLEASON L. ARCHER

See WRITING AND BOOKS; BIBLICAL LANGUAGES; INSCRIPTIONS; LATIN.

Bibliography. E. Clodd, *The Story of the Alphabet*; D. Diringer, *The Alphabet*, and *The Story of the Aleph Beth*; A.C. Moorehouse, *The Triumph of the Alphabet* and *Writing and the Alphabet*; W.M. Flinders Petrie, *The Formation of the Alphabet*; I. Taylor, *The Alphabet*, 2 vols.

Alphaeus. 1. Father of James, one of the 12 apostles (Mt 10:3; Mk 3:18; Lk 6:15; Acts 1:13), thought by some to be the same as Clopas of John 19:25.

2. Father of Levi, the tax collector (Mk 2:14) who is also known in the Gospels as Matthew (Mt 9:9).

Altar. The platform upon which offerings are made to the deity. This may include a ritual sacrifice of animals or a burning of incense before God (Ex 30:1–10). The Hebrew word for altar and the verb "to slaughter" both derive from the root *zbḥ* (Aramaic cognate *dbḥ*), terms used in connection with the ritual of sacrificing animals to God as a covering for sin. The Greek terms also point to sacrificing animals. The practice was not peculiar to Israel but was widely known in the ancient Middle East. Israel's immediate neighbors, the Canaanites, had their own altars and rituals. The altar was always a raised-up place.

Canaanite Altars. Generally altars were oblong or oval, though some were simply large field stones. The offering of sacrifice answered the universal human need to present an offering to the deity as a gift or as a covering for sin. In most cases the altar was approached by a short flight of steps or a ramp. In Israel the altar was made of earth or unhewn field stones (Ex 20:24–26). Steps were forbidden, probably to avoid any comparison with pagan altars, but also so that the "nakedness" of the offerer might not be exposed (Ex 20:26).

Israel came to a land where temples, shrines, and altars were common. In Megiddo, Canaanite temples and altars have been excavated dating to many centuries before the Israelites appeared. Generally the altars were rectangular. An exception was a large oval-shaped altar built of small field stones, about 26 feet in diameter and about 4.6 feet high. It was ascended by a flight of steps (cf. Ex 20:25,26). Bethshan, Lachish, and Hazor also preserved good examples of Canaanite shrines and altars. At Lachish there was a temple area in which three temples succeeded one another over the years 1480 to 1260 BC. The latest (from 1325 to 1260 BC) had an altar built of mud bricks 2.6 by 2.6 by 3 feet in size approached by side steps. Bones of young sheep, goats, oxen, and gazelles, mostly the right shoulders (cf. Lv 7:32), were found in the debris and in large refuse pits. There were also many smaller square-hewn limestone incense altars with four horns on their upper corners. These have been found at several places, including Megiddo, Bethshan, and Lachish. The largest is about 2.2 feet high. Archaeological evidence points to a highly developed Canaanite cult that had been in existence for many centu-

A horned altar from Megiddo.

ries before the Israelites arrived. This cult was to create difficulties for the Israelites because of a number of similarities between the two systems of worship.

Biblical Altars. Patriarchal Altars. The Bible refers to several altars built by the patriarchs. Noah offered burnt offerings (Gn 8:20). Abraham built an altar at Shechem (Gn 12:7), another at Bethel (Gn 12:8), and one on Mt Moriah (Gn 22:9). Isaac built an altar at Beersheba (Gn 26:25), and Jacob at Shechem (Gn 33:20) and Bethel (Gn 35:7). Moses built one at Rephidim (Ex 17:15) and another at Horeb (Ex 24:4). In each case the altar was erected to commemorate an event in which God had helped the offerer.

The Altars of the Tabernacle. Two altars were used in the tabernacle. One, measuring 5 by 5 by 3 cubits, was made of acacia wood overlaid with bronze and used for burnt offerings (Ex 27:1–8; 38:1–7). The other, smaller one, the golden altar, was about 1.5 feet square and 3 feet high, and was used to burn incense before the veil (Ex 30:1–10; 40:5).

Special Altars. In Exodus 20:24–26 instructions were given to Israel to make an altar of earth or of unhewn stones, upon which burnt offerings and peace offerings were to be made in every place where God caused his name to dwell. This very general prescription seems to have allowed various individuals to erect an altar from time to time. Joshua built an altar on Mt Ebal (Jos 8:30,31); the Reubenites, Gadites, and the half tribe of Manasseh built one in Transjordan (Jos 22:10–16); Gideon built one in Ophrah (Jgs 6:24); the family of David in Bethlehem (1 Sm 20:6,29); David at the threshing floor of Araunah (2 Sm 24:25); and Elijah on Mt Carmel (1 Kgs 18:30). Apart from Elijah's altar these all predated Solomon's temple.

Altars in Solomon's Temple. There were two altars in Solomon's temple. One was 20 cubits square (about 25 feet) and 10 cubits high (about 12.5 feet). It was made of bronze and used for burnt offerings. It remained the center of temple worship until the temple was destroyed, although in the days of King Ahaz it was removed from its place to the northern side of the temple at the command of the Assyrian ruler Tiglath-pileser (2 Kgs 16:14). It was later restored to its proper place by Hezekiah (2 Chr 29:18). The second, the incense altar, stood in front of the veil. It was made of cedar and overlaid with gold (1 Kgs 6:20–22).

Forbidden Altars in the Days of the Kings. The prophets refer to unlawful altars (Hos 8:11; Am 3:14). Several of these have come to light in excavations. In Beersheba a large horned altar standing 4.5 feet high was reconstructed from distinctive pieces of stone built into the city wall after its destruction. In Arad the remains of a temple included a large altar for burnt offerings built of earth and unhewn stones (cf. Ex 20:25). Other irregular shrines and high places have been found at Lachish, Dan, and even at Jerusalem.

The Temple and Altar of Ezekiel's Vision. During the exile, when the temple lay in ruins, Ezekiel had a vision of the restored temple in Jerusalem. There was an elaborate altar of burnt offering, rising in three terraces to a height of 10 cubits and resting on a base about 20 cubits square. Although the altar was visionary, it emphasized the need for atonement in

Ruins of a large altar at Dan (excavated in the summer of 1985).

Israel (Ez 43:13–17). No reference is made to an incense altar.

The Second Temple Altars. Zerubbabel built an altar of burnt offerings (Ezr 3:2) which Antiochus Epiphanes desecrated with a "desolating sacrilege," probably an image of Zeus (1 Mc 1:54). There was also an altar of incense. Antiochus Epiphanes carried off the "golden altar" (1 Mc 1:21) in 169 BC. Both were later restored by Judas Maccabeus (1 Mc 4:44–49).

Altars in Herod's Temple. Both the altar of burnt offering and the altar of incense continued in use when Herod enlarged the temple. Jesus told one offerer to leave his gift at the altar, be reconciled to his brother, and then offer his gift (Mt 5:24). Zechariah had a vision of an angel standing on the right side of the altar of incense (Lk 1:11).

The Altar in the New Testament. In Christian worship no altar was required, since in the death of Jesus Christ the final sacrifice for sin had been made. There are numerous references to both the altar of burnt offering in the temple (Mt 5:23,24; 23:18–20,35; Lk 11:51; 1 Cor 9:13; 10:18; Heb 7:13; Rv 11:1) and the altar of incense, both in the earthly temple (Lk 1:11) and in the heavenly temple (Rv 6:9; 8:5; 9:13). The Book of Acts refers to an altar to the unknown God in Athens (Acts 17:23).

See TABERNACLE, TEMPLE.

Bibliography. R. de Vaux, *Ancient Israel*, pp 406–14; P. Fairbairn, *The Typology of Scripture*, 2 vols.; G.B. Gray, *Sacrifice in the OT*; E.M. Lerner, "Altar," *Encyclopedia Judaica* 2:760–71; H.M. Wiener, *The Altars of the OT*.

Al-taschith. Hebrew phrase in the titles of Psalms 57, 58, 59, and 75 (KJV), translated "according to Do Not Destroy" (RSV); perhaps a familiar ancient melody to which the psalms were performed.

See MUSIC AND MUSICAL INSTRUMENTS.

Alush. Place where Israel encamped during the wilderness wanderings, mentioned between Dophkah and Rephidim (Nm 33:13,14) on the way to Mt Sinai. Its exact location is uncertain.

See WILDERNESS WANDERINGS.

Alvah. Esau's descendant and a chief of Edom (Gn 36:40); alternately called Aliah in 1 Chronicles 1:51.

Alvan. Shobal's son and a descendant of Esau (Gn 36:23); alternately spelled Alian in 1 Chronicles 1:40.

Amad. Town in northern Palestine near Mt Carmel, within the boundaries of Asher's territory (Jos 19:26). Its site is unknown.

Amal. Helem's son and a descendant of Asher (1 Chr 7:35).

Amalek, Amalekites. Ancient tribe of raiding nomads who lived in the Negeb desert, mentioned frequently in the OT.

Origin and Early History. Amalek was the son of Eliphaz (Esau's son) by his concubine, Timna (Gn 36:12; 1 Chr 1:36). Descendants of this tribal chief of Edom were known as Amalekites. They settled in the Negeb desert and became allies of the Edomites, Ammonites, Moabites, Ishmaelites, and Midianites. The Amalekites were notable enemies of Israel. Amalek inherited the fraternal feud that had begun with his grandfather Esau's antagonism toward Jacob. Since Jacob was one of the progenitors of Israel, the conflict between Amalek and Israel had both a theological and political basis.

The territory of the nomadic Amalekites in the Negeb ranged at times from south of Beersheba to the southeast as far as Elath and Ezion-geber. They undoubtedly raided westward into the coastal plain, eastward into the Arabah wastelands, and possibly over into Arabia. In the Negeb they blocked the path of the Israelites during the exodus (Ex 17:8–16).

Amalek and Israel in the Exodus. Israel's first encounter with the "warriors of Amalek" came at Rephidim near Sinai. Moses stood on top of a hill and held up the "rod of God" until Israel won the battle, then built an altar and named it "the Lord is my banner" (Ex 17:1,8–16). The Amalekites attacked stragglers during Israel's desert wanderings (Dt 25:17,18). After reaching the boundary of the Promised Land but rejecting Caleb and Joshua's report of it, the unbelieving and disheartened Israelites attacked the Amalekites and were defeated (Nm 14:39–45).

When Balaam was summoned by King Balak of Moab to curse Israel, he turned his curse upon Moab and in his last oracle predicted the end of Amalek's tribe (Nm 24:20). Moses, in his farewell speech, reminded the children of Israel that they had been harassed by Amalek's descendants and should blot out all remembrance of the name Amalek (Dt 25:17–19).

Period of the Judges. During the period of the judges Amalekites continued to occupy their traditional area and became associated with the Kenites (1 Sm 15:5,6), descendants of Moses' father-in-law, who settled in the Negeb south of Arad (Jgs 1:16). The Amalekites, still associated with other nomadic tribes (Moabites, Ammonites, Midianites), were rallied by Eglon, king of Moab, to defeat Israel and seize Jericho (Jgs 3:12–14). The song of Deborah cites Amalek as one of a coalition of tribes against Israel (Jgs 5:14 KJV). The name is omitted in a number of modern translations (LB), and in others translated as "into the valley" (RSV). However, Amalekite harassment is referred to in other passages of the time of Deborah and Barak (Jgs 6:3,33; 7:12). Gideon defeated the coalition (Jgs 7:12–25), but there is no evidence that the Amalekites were driven out of the Negeb.

Period of the Monarchy. Saul sent his armies out against the Amalekites (1 Sm 14:47, 48) and received a command from God to destroy them and all their possessions (15:1–3). He did attack their city (15:4–7) but did not kill their king, Agag (15:8). Saul distributed the choicest Amalekite livestock to his men (15:9), for which the Lord condemned him and sent Samuel to tell him that his kingship was ended because of his sin (15:10–31). Samuel then slaughtered Agag (15:32–35). A remnant of Amalekites must have escaped, since they appeared again as David's foes while he was still a young warrior (27:8). He rescued his two wives carried off by Amalekites and killed most of the raiding party (30:1–20). The Amalekites were Israel's sworn enemies throughout King David's reign (2 Sm 1:1). They are listed among the enemies of Israel (2 Sm 8:12; 1 Chr 18:11; Ps 83:7). Destruction of the few surviving Amalekites came several hundred years after David during the reign of Hezekiah of the southern kingdom of Judah (1 Chr 4:40–43).

WILLIAM WHITE, JR.

Amalekites, Hill Country (Mount) of the. An area near Pirathon in Ephraim, probably about six miles west of Shechem (Jgs 12:15). It is mentioned in the Hebrew Bible but not in the Greek manuscripts of the OT. Some scholars find the reference confusing; however, it is possible that based on Judges 5:14 and 12:15 an argument can be made that there was a small Amalekite district in Ephraim.

Amam. Town in the southern part of the kingdom of Judah, along the border of Edom (Jos 15:26). Its site has not been identified.

Amana. Mountain ridge, probably in the Anti-Lebanon range, mentioned along with Mt Senir and Mt Herman (Sg 4:8). It is perhaps the source of the Abana (Amana) River (2 Kgs 5:12).

See ABANA.

Amariah. Common OT name, meaning "the Lord has spoken" or "the Lord has promised."

1. Son of Meraioth in the line of Aaron's son Eleazer (1 Chr 6:7,52).

2. High priest, Azariah's son and Ahitub's father (1 Chr 6:11; Ezr 7:3).

3. Hebron's second son and Kohath's grandson from Levi's tribe (1 Chr 23:19; 24:23).

4. Chief priest during the reign of Jehoshaphat of the southern kingdom of Judah (2 Chr 19:11).

5. Levite who served faithfully under King Hezekiah of Judah (2 Chr 31:15). Amariah was one of six assistants to Kore, the "keeper of the east gate" appointed to distribute the portions of the offerings reserved for God (v 14).

6. One of Binnui's sons, who obeyed Ezra's exhortation to divorce his pagan wife after the exile (Ezr 10:42).

7. Priest who returned from Babylon with Zerubbabel (Neh 12:2,13) and who, with Nehemiah and others, signed Ezra's covenant of faithfulness to God after the exile (Neh 10:3).

8. Shephatiah's son, a descendant of Judah and ancestor of Athaiah. Amariah lived in Jerusalem after the exile (Neh 11:4).

9. Hezekiah's son and ancestor of the prophet Zephaniah (Zep 1:1).

10. Person mentioned in the Ezra genealogies of 1 Esdras 8:2 and 2 Esdras 1:2. In the first list he is Uzzi's son and Ahitub's father. In the second he is Azariah's son and Eli's father. He may be the same as Amariah #1 or #2 above, since both sources list him as Ahitub's father.

Amarna Tablets. Clay tablets, mostly letters from royal archives, the only cuneiform records ever found in Egypt. The 379 Amarna tablets were recovered from ruins located on a plain on the east bank of the Nile about 190 miles south of Cairo. The region is named after a tribe that settled there in modern times, the Beni Amran or Amarna tribe. The site of the ruins is mistakenly called Tell el-Amarna; *tell* is an Arabic word meaning "hill" or "mound," but this site lies on a plain. A village in the area bears the name "el-Till," and its name came to be annexed to the name el-Amarna.

The cuneiform script in which the tablets are written is a system that employs nail or wedge-shaped marks impressed into the writing material, usually clay, in many specific patterns. Each one of the patterns (called a "sign") represents a sound or, sometimes, a word. Cuneiform script could be used to represent a number of different languages, just as Latin script can be used to represent English, French, German, etc. The language of the Amarna tablets, with only three exceptions, is a certain dialect of Akkadian. Although its homeland was the general area of Mesopotamia, that Semitic language came to be the language of international correspondence and diplomacy in the Near East during the second millennium BC.

Reportedly the tablets were first discovered by a peasant woman collecting topsoil from among the ruins sometime during the year 1887. Word of her discovery eventually reached the ears of Westerners. The tablets unearthed by the peasants in secret (owing to strict laws against pilferage of antiquities) were transported to Luxor, where, after a series of unpleasant exchanges between Egyptian dealers and museum representatives, collections of the tablets were purchased by representatives of the Berlin Museum, British Museum, and several others. In 1889 excavation began at the site under Flinders Petrie. The ruins proved to be Akhetaten, capital of Egypt under Pharaoh Amenophis IV (Akhenaten), tenth ruler of the 18th dynasty. Between the peasants and the professional excavators, some 355 tablets and fragments of tablets were uncovered. Since the turn of the century more have come to light.

Amenophis IV (c. 1378–1360 BC), either before the death of his father, Amenophis III (c. 1413–1377 BC), or sometime afterward, commissioned the city of Akhetaten to be built on the plain now called el-Amarna. Then he moved his family and Egyptian officialdom from the traditional capital of Thebes, in southern Egypt at the bend of the Nile. To the new capital of the Egyptian empire were brought state documents including the cuneiform records, many of which had been addressed to Amenophis III. Many more cuneiform letters were received by Amenophis IV at Akhetaten. Amenophis IV changed his name to Akhenaten to show devotion to the deity he worshiped (Aten, the sun disk). About five years after his death, the capital Akhetaten was abandoned by his successors, who moved farther northward to another of the older Egyptian capitals, Memphis. Objects deemed to have no value were left behind at Akhetaten, among which were the el-Amarna tablets. Perhaps they were left because their messages had been copied onto papyrus, which was much lighter to transport and easier to store than clay tablets.

Twenty-nine of the tablets contain what appear to be copybook exercises for student scribes: lists of cuneiform signs, vocabulary lists, practice copies of sections of Mesopotamian mythological narratives. The other 350 texts are letters from the diplomatic correspondence of Amenophis III and Amenophis IV. The letters span a period of about 30 years, dating from sometime during the reign of Amenophis III to shortly after the death of Amenophis IV. They are mostly messages received from various local rulers and princes in Syria and Palestine, but there are also letters

A limestone plaque from the city of Akhetaten, depicting the pharaoh and Nefertiti.

from monarchs of more powerful nations to the far north and east.

The letters show varying relationships between the Egyptian pharaoh and the writers. Some writers were considered as more or less equals of the pharaoh, the others as inferiors. Diplomatic relationships between the correspondents were often established by treaties and confirmed by marriages. Kings who were regarded as inferiors in their diplomatic relationship with the pharaoh referred to themselves as "your servant" and to the pharaoh as "my lord," "my sun," or sometimes as "my god." Modern-day researchers call such underling rulers vassals and their domains vassal states; the pharaoh in such a relationship is referred to as a suzerain. Rulers regarded as relative equals of the pharaoh referred to themselves as "your brother" and to the pharaoh as "my brother," a relationship now described as a parity relationship.

The messages received by the pharaohs from their equals discuss such matters as exchange of gifts, negotiations for marriages, continuation of diplomatic ties, and promotion of commercial transactions. They also contain inventories of gifts sent or received,

and request presents, gold, or other goods. Such correspondence was received from rulers of the kingdoms of Babylonia, Mitanni, Assyria, Hatti (the Hittite kingdom), and Alashiya (Cyprus).

The correspondence received from vassals is often characterized by claims of loyalty to the suzerain, much complaining, and appeals for military assistance. Such letters came from the princelings of the city-states in Syria and Palestine.

Of special interest are some letters from the Palestine area containing appeals for military assistance and references to military activity. Their mention of the "Habiru" was immediately connected with the word "Hebrew." The Habiru were said to be at several locations in Palestine and to be "plundering all the lands of the king." By fastening together several pieces of information, a conclusion was initially drawn that the Amarna letters came from the general period of the Hebrew exodus from Egypt and later invasion of Palestine under Joshua. Thus, some of the letters were taken to be firsthand reports of the invasion from the point of view of the inhabitants of Palestine.

However, reconsideration of the Amarna letters, along with other available information, soon showed that conclusion to be mistaken. The Habiru were not the invading Hebrews. The word "Habiru" is a dialect spelling of the word "Apiru." This term, in both the Amarna letters and other texts, describes a class of people that may be called "outlaw" or "renegade." People of various nationalities could be labeled "Apiru." A person was not born an Apiru; rather he could join the Apiru or because of his actions become an Apiru. The Apiru ranged throughout Syria and Palestine and had no special homesite. At times groups of them hired themselves out as mercenary troops; at other times they acted as brigands.

The historical situation reflected by the Amarna letters was complex. The letters show how the balance of power was changing in the Near East in 1400–1350 BC. Although the exact sequence of events is very uncertain, and dates are difficult to establish, the following reconstruction may bring the larger picture into focus.

The Egyptians had gained control of all of Syria and Palestine between 1468 and 1450 BC. But by 1400 BC, during the reign of Amenophis III, that control had weakened considerably, so much so that northern and central Syria was controlled by the north Mesopotamian kingdom of Mitanni. Mitanni, however, was related to Egypt by treaty and marriages so that peaceful relations prevailed between Amenophis III and Tushratta, ruler of Mitanni. Between the part of southern Syria controlled by Egypt and the central part of Syria controlled by Mitanni was the kingdom of Amurru (the Amorites); to the north of Syria, in Anatolia (present-day Turkey), was the kingdom of Hatti (the Hittites), which had fallen on hard times. Hatti too was related to Egypt by treaty and marriages. About a year before the death of Amenophis III (1377 BC) a new king named Shuppiluliumash came to the throne over Hatti. Immediately he set to work to change the fortunes of the Hatti kingdom.

Sometime before Shuppiluliumash came to power, Amenophis III engaged in dealings with the vassal king of Amurru, Abdi Ashirta, in order to keep in check the Mitanni king's plans for further expansion into southern Syria. Abdi Ashirta, strengthened by Apiru, now began his own expansion and attempted to extend his control from his inland region westward to the Mediterranean coast. In so doing he began to consume territory controlled by the king of Byblos, Rib Addi. Rib Addi, also a vassal of Egypt, sent many letters to Amenophis III describing his situation. Of the Amarna letters recovered, some 67 are from Rib Addi, who continued to call for assistance from both Ameno-

phis III and Amenophis IV, each letter becoming more desperate than the last. About the same time to the south a central Palestinian chieftain, Labaya, also supported by Apiru, had begun expanding his territories in much the same way that Abdi Ashirta was expanding his. Despite all of the turmoil, the pharaohs took no definitive action.

When Shuppiluliumash came to power he conquered northern Syria and removed it from Mitannian control. Egypt, which had diplomatic ties with both Hatti and Mitanni, gave support to neither side. Moreover, Abdi Ashirta continued to expand in southern Syria, taking over even the cities that had served as provincial capitals for Egypt. But Egypt made no concerted attempt to arrest his advances. In Palestine, Amenophis IV at last had Labaya arrested. En route to Egypt, Labaya gained his release through a bribe but was assassinated before he could return to central Palestine. The Palestinian kings had no respite after the death of Labaya, since his sons continued the deeds of their father but with even more vigor.

Shuppiluliumash of Hatti continued to advance in Syria until he had removed all vestige of Mitanni power. Abdi Ashirta was finally stopped at the gates of Byblos by an Egyptian military detachment, and sometime thereafter was assassinated. Aziru, the son of Abdi Ashirta, resumed his father's program and took Byblos, which drove Rib Addi into exile. The new power balance saw Hatti in control of northern and central Syria, Egypt in control of Palestine, and the Amurru (in control of southern Syria) as a strong buffer state in between. That seemed to be the power balance Egypt wanted. For a while, matters stabilized—when Aziru was summoned to Egypt and detained for about two years. Upon his return to his own territory, however, Aziru forsook his Egyptian allegiance and made a formal pact with the king of Hatti. With Hittite power now abutting

Two tablets from Amarna.

the borderlands of Egyptian-controlled territory, confrontation became inevitable. Many events of that phase of Near Eastern history are reported or alluded to in the Amarna tablets.

JOHN E. LONG

See INSCRIPTIONS; EGYPT, EGYPTIANS.

Amasa. 1. Son of Ithra (Jether) and David's sister Abigal (2 Sm 17:25; 1 Chr 2:17, Abigail), and therefore David's nephew. Amasa was a captain who supported Absalom in his rebellion against his father David. After Absalom was killed by David's general, Joab, David pardoned Amasa and replaced Joab with him (2 Sm 19:13). Greatly offended, Joab awaited his revenge and, as soon as he had opportunity, treacherously assassinated his unsuspecting rival (2 Sm 20:4–13). David was unable to punish Joab, but instructed his son Solomon to see that Joab was executed for murdering Amasa and another of David's generals (1 Kgs 2:5,6,28–34).

2. Hadlai's son from Ephraim's tribe. Amasa supported the prophet Oded's opposition to making slaves of women and children captured from the southern kingdom of Judah in the time of King Ahaz (2 Chr 28:8–13).

Amasai. 1. Elkanah's son (1 Chr 6:25) and Mahath's father (1 Chr 6:35), listed in the genealogy of Heman the singer.

2. Leader of 30 warriors who joined David at Ziklag after deserting King Saul (1 Chr 12:18).

3. Trumpeter priest in the procession when David brought the ark of God to Jerusalem (1 Chr 15:24).

4. Father of another Mahath. This Mahath was Hezekiah's contemporary and a participant in his revival (2 Chr 29:12).

Amashsai, Amashai. Azarel's son and one of the leading priests who returned to Jerusalem after the Babylonian exile (Neh 11:13, KJV Amashai). Amashsai may possibly be identical with Maasai (1 Chr 9:12).

Amasiah. Military leader in the time of Jehoshaphat, in charge of 200,000 men. Amasiah was Zichri's son and a man of unusual piety (2 Chr 17:16).

Amaw. Region near the Euphrates River which included the city of Pethor, to which King Balak of Moab sent messengers in search of the soothsayer Balaam (Nm 22:5). The name Amaw appears in the Idrimi Inscription (1450? BC) and on the tomb of Qen-amun, who served under Amenophis II of Egypt in the latter part of the 15th century BC.

Amaziah. 1. Ninth king of Judah (796–767 BC), who at age 25 succeeded his father, King Joash, when Joash was assassinated after a 40-year reign (2 Kgs 12:19–21). Amaziah's mother was Jeho-addin. He ruled Judah for 29 years before he too was killed by assassins (14:18–20). When Amaziah began his reign, another Joash was ruling the northern kingdom of Israel (14:1,2).

Amaziah was not like his ancestor David (2 Kgs 14:3). Like his father, Amaziah did things that pleased God, but he failed to remove the pagan shrines that were corrupting the nation's religious life. He himself was respectful of the Law of Moses, at least at the beginning (14:4–6).

Amaziah was unwise in his dealings with the rival kingdom of Israel. To go to war against the Edomites, he hired 100,000 mercenaries from Israel. Warned by a prophet not to use them in battle, Amaziah discharged them. On their way out of Judah the angry soldiers raided cities and killed 3,000 people. Nevertheless, Amaziah's troops were victorious against the Edomites. At the Valley of Salt they killed 10,000 of the enemy in battle and executed another 10,000 prisoners (2 Chr 25:5–13).

Foolishly, Amaziah brought Edomite idols back with him after his conquest and was soon worshiping them. The Lord sent a prophet to announce Amaziah's doom for such spiritual rebellion (2 Chr 25:14–16). Proud of his conquest of Edom, Amaziah soon declared war on King Joash of Israel. Joash warned him in a parable that Judah would be crushed like a thistle. Amaziah refused to back down, and the two armies met at Bethshemesh in Judah. Amaziah's army was routed. Jerusalem was captured and the temple and palace looted. Amaziah was taken prisoner but was evidently left in Jerusalem. He outlived Joash of Israel by 15 years (2 Chr 25:17–26). Amaziah was murdered in Lachish, to which he had fled on learning of a plot against him in Jerusalem. His body was brought back to the capital city and buried in the royal cemetery (2 Chr 25:27,28).

See ISRAEL, HISTORY OF; CHRONOLOGY, OLD TESTAMENT; KING, KINGSHIP.

2. Father of Joshah, a member of Simeon's tribe (1 Chr 4:34).

3. Hilkiah's son, a Levite of Merari's clan (1 Chr 6:45).

4. Priest of Bethel in the days of Jeroboam II and an opponent of the prophet Amos (Am 7:10–17).

Ambassador. Messenger or envoy officially representing a higher authority.

See TRADES AND OCCUPATIONS.

Amber. Fossilized resin of certain cone-bearing plants. The resinous product of these conifers loses its volatile components and turns into a translucent yellow or orange solid. The word is used in the KJV to describe a color seen in visions of the Lord (Ez 8:2). The color is similar to that of polished brass or bronze (Ez 1:4,27).

See COLOR.

Ambush. *See* ARMS AND WARFARE.

Amen. Hebrew word meaning "so it is" or "let it be," derived from a verb meaning "to be firm or sure." Some translations of the Bible always retain the Hebrew word *amen* in the text. Others translate it by an expression such as "truly" or "I tell you the truth," or sometimes omit it altogether. Because of its use in the OT, "amen" was also used in Christian worship and religious writings, including the Greek NT. Since Jews, Christians, and Muslims all use this word in a variety of languages, it may be one of the most widely known words in the world.

"Amen" has much more significance than merely being the last word in a prayer. In fact, that practice is not evidenced in the Bible, and was not especially frequent in ancient times. In the 30 times it is used in the OT, "amen" nearly always occurs as a response to what has preceded. The significance of the response is that with it the people adopted what had just been said as if it were their own. For example, in Deuteronomy 27:15–26 (where "amen" appears 12 times) the people responded with "amen" after each statement of a curse directed toward those who disobey God. Similarly, "amen" is used as a response after statements of promise (Jer 11:5) or of praise and thanksgiving (1 Chr 16:36), and as a conclusion to the first four of the five "books" of psalms (Pss 41:13; 72:19; 89:52; 106:48). The only exceptions in the OT are two occurrences in Isaiah 65:16. There, the phrase "the God of amen" stresses that God is the one who is "firm"; that is, he is completely trustworthy and faithfully fulfills his promises.

The use of "amen" as a response to a preceding statement is continued in the NT Epistles and Book of Revelation. It appears after doxologies (Eph 3:21), benedictions (Gal 6:18), the giving of thanks (1 Cor 14:16), prophecy (Rv 1:7), and statements of praise (Rv 7:12). (The LB usually tries to give the idea without using the specific word.) From 1 Corinthians 14:16 it is clear that a response of "amen" after a statement of thanks was a means for worshipers to participate by showing agreement with what had been said. In Revelation 7:12 "amen" occurs both at the beginning and the end of a statement, but the first "amen" is a response to the praise given in 7:10. An "amen" after a statement of praise has the connotation, "That is what I say too." As a response to a benediction or a prophecy the idea is "Precisely! May God do it."

Two uses of "amen" by the early church focused special attention on Jesus Christ. In 2 Corinthians 1:20 (cf. Rv 1:7) "amen" is used almost as an equivalent to "yes." Jesus is viewed as God's means of saying "yes" to us, fulfilling his promises. Jesus is also viewed as our means of saying "yes" to God; through Jesus the "amen" response of believers is presented for the glory of God. In Revelation 3:14 "the Amen" is used as a title of Christ to emphasize his reliability and the truth of what he says (cf. Is 65:16).

The use of "amen" in the Gospels, however, is entirely different from its use in the OT, the early church, or anywhere else in Jewish literature. Excluding Matthew 6:13 (KJV) and Mark 16:20 (both passages with textual uncertainty), all of the 100 occurrences of "amen" are spoken by Jesus and always precede what is said rather than coming after as a response. In the synoptic Gospels (Mt, Mk, Lk) the form is always "Amen [Truly RSV], I say to you"; in John it is always the doubled form "Amen, amen [Truly, truly RSV], I say to you" (Jn 3:3,5, etc.). That unique use of "amen" stresses both the authority with which he taught and his majesty: Jesus' words come with absolute certainty and are binding on all.

KLYNE R. SNODGRASS

Amethyst. Purple variety of quartz used in jewelry.

See MINERALS, METALS, AND PRECIOUS STONES.

Am ha arez. Hebrew phrase translated "people of the land."

See PEOPLE OF THE LAND; JUDAISM.

Ami. Official in Solomon's court whose descendants returned to Jerusalem after the exile (Ezr 2:57). Also spelled Amon in Nehemiah 7:59.

See AMON (PERSON) #3.

Amillennialism. *See* MILLENNIUM.

Aminadab. KJV form of Amminadab in Matthew 1:4 and Luke 3:33.

See AMMINADAB #1.

Amittai. Father of the prophet Jonah from Zebulun's tribe. Amittai came from the small village of Gath-hepher northeast of Nazareth (2 Kgs 14:25; Jon 1:1)

Ammah. Hill north of Jerusalem in the area of Gibeon. A battle fought there between David's troops under Joab and Ish-bosheth's troops under Abner was the beginning of a long war between followers of Saul and followers of David (2 Sm 2:24–32; 3:1).

Ammi. Hebrew word meaning "my people." The expression "people of God" is the most common designation for the nation of Israel in the OT. It originated in God's promise to Moses before the exodus: "I will take you for my people (*ammi*), and I will be your God" (Ex 6:7). For Israel to be called "my people" emphasized the unique personal nature of their religion in contrast with the idolatry of neighboring nations. The word represented God's love for them and his faithfulness to the promises he had made to their forefathers (Dt 4:37; 7:8). In return for the privileges the name implied, God required faithfulness and obedience from Israel. Yet repeatedly the people of Israel failed, and repeatedly the prophets reminded them of their responsibility to God.

An example of such prophetic warning is found in the writings of Hosea. The prophet saw in his own marriage to an adulterous wife a picture of God's relationship to his people: God had joined himself to a people who had forsaken him for other gods. The names Hosea gave his children reflected God's attitude toward his unfaithful people. The first child was named Jezreel (Hos 1:4), a name with a double meaning. As the name of the place where King Ahab murdered Naboth (1 Kgs 21:1–16), it recalled a terrible experience in Israel's history. But the name also means "God sows," and expressed Hosea's hope that the people of Israel, despite all their failures, would soon return to God. A second child was named Lo-ruhamah ("not pitied," Hos 1:6). That name expressed God's hatred for disobedience and his inclination to turn from an unrepentant people. Hosea's third child was named Lo-ammi ("not my people," Hos 1:9). That name represented ultimate tragedy for Israel: dissolution of God's covenant relationship with them. God was saying to Israel, "You are not my people (lo-ammi) and I am not your God" (Hos 1:9). Although all seemed lost, Hosea's prophecy did not end on a note of doom. Rather, he foresaw that Israel would repent. In response, God would restore his covenant relationship with them: "And I will say to Not my people, 'You are my people'; and he shall say, 'Thou art my God' " (Hos 2:23).

Ammiel. 1. Gemalli's son, one of 12 men sent by Moses to spy out the land of Canaan. Ammiel represented Dan's tribe (Nm 13:12) and later "died by plague before the Lord" (Nm 14:37).

2. Father of Machir of Lo-debar. Mephibosheth, Jonathan's son, was hidden from David in Machir's house (2 Sm 9:4,5). Machir later helped supply David in his war with Absalom (2 Sm 17:27–29).

3. Father of David's wife, Bath-shua (or Bathsheba, 1 Chr 3:5). Ammiel is also called Eliam (2 Sm 11:3).

4. Sixth son of Obed-edom, who, along with his family, served as gatekeeper in the temple during David's reign (1 Chr 26:5,15).

Ammihud. 1. Father of a leader of Ephraim's tribe, Elishama (Nm 1:10). Ammihud was Joshua's great-grandfather (1 Chr 7:26).

2. Father of Shemuel from Simeon's tribe. Shemuel helped Moses apportion the Promised Land (Nm 34:20).

3. Father of Pedahel from Naphtali's tribe. Pedahel also helped Moses apportion the Promised Land (Nm 34:28).

4. Father of King Talmai of Geshur. Talmai gave refuge to Absalom when he fled after murdering Amnon (2 Sm 13:37).

5. Omri's son and father of Uthai from Judah's tribe (1 Chr 9:4).

Amminadab. 1. Father of Elisheba, who was Aaron's wife (Ex 6:23). Amminadab was also the father of Nahshon, Judah's tribal leader in the wilderness (Nm 1:7; 2:3; 7:12,17; 10:14; 1 Chr 2:10). Amminadab is listed in the genealogy of David (Ru 4:18–22) and, later, in the genealogy of Jesus Christ (Mt 1:4; Lk 3:33, KJV Aminadab).

See GENEALOGY OF JESUS CHRIST.

2. Alternate name for Izhar, one of Kohath's sons, in 1 Chronicles 6:22.

See IZHAR #1.

3. Levite contemporary of King David who helped bring the ark of the Lord to Jerusalem (1 Chr 15:1–4,10,11).

Amminadib. Word occurring only in the KJV rendering of Song of Songs 6:12, "or ever I was aware, my soul made me like the chariots of Amminadib" (ASV margin, NASB margin). More recent translators have not regarded the term as a proper name. Some proposals for more accurate wording are: "among the chariots of my willing people" (ASV); "in a chariot beside my prince" (RSV); "over the chariots of my noble people" (NASB); and "among my own people" (LB).

Ammishaddai. Ahiezer's father. Ahiezer was leader of Dan's tribe when the Israelites were wandering in the Sinai wilderness after their escape from Egypt (Nm 1:12; 2:25;

10:25). As leader he presented his tribe's offering at the consecration of the tabernacle (Nm 7:66,71).

Ammizabad. Benaiah's son. Both Benaiah and Ammizabad were high-ranking officers in King David's army (1 Chr 27:5,6).

Ammon, Ammonites. A Semitic people who occupied a fertile area northeast of Moab in Transjordan between the Arnon and Jabbok rivers and extending eastward to the Syrian desert. The chief city was Rabbah (Rabbath-ammon), modern Amman, capital of Jordan.

Name and Origin. The Ammonites traced their ancestry to the younger daughter of Lot (Gn 19:38). Their name in Hebrew originally meant "son of my paternal clan," preserving the remembrance of an actual clan and personal name, and suggesting a kinship between the Ammonites and Israelites. The name occurred frequently in the ancient Near East from the mid-second millennium on. One form was found in Assyrian inscriptions; other forms are seen in Ugaritic texts of the 15th century BC, in the Mari texts, in the Amarna tablets, and in the Alalakh tablets.

The Ammonites originated in the southern Transjordan region about the beginning of the second millennium BC. Though these people were of mixed ancestry, the languages they spoke were closely related to Hebrew. Ammonite was written in the Old Canaanite-Phoenician script, which could probably be read and understood by Israelites. Ammonites intermarried with Hebrews (1 Kgs 14:21,31; 2 Chr 12:13), and their personal names reflected early Arabic influences.

In language, ethnic background, and physical characteristics the Ammonites were difficult to distinguish from Amorites and were probably closely related. Both may have entered the land at about the same time, for when Joshua led the Israelites into Canaan, both the Ammonite kingdom and the Amorite kingdom of Heshbon were already well established.

History. Before the Israelite Monarchy (to the Tenth Century BC). Early archaeological studies concluded that the whole of Transjordan was unoccupied from about 1900 to 1300 BC. However, the discovery at Amman and Naur of large family tombs with numerous burial objects indicates a settled population during at least part of that period, unless those tombs belonged to seminomadic people who controlled caravan routes in the region. Excavation of a small temple at Amman uncovered large quantities of imported Mycenean and Cypriot pottery and Egyptian stone vases typical of the period from 1600 to 1300 BC, indicating sedentary occupation.

The OT states that the territory of Ammon was once occupied by a race of giants called Rephaim or Zamzummim, about whom almost nothing is known (Dt 2:20,21; Zuzim, Gn 14:5). The *Genesis Apocryphon* found among the Dead Sea Scrolls mentions them as one of the people defeated by the alliance of four kings (Gn 14:1,5). The expedition of Chedorlaomer, king of Elam (Gn 14), broke the power of those giants and probably made the occupation of the land by Esau, Ammon, and Moab much easier. King Og was "of the remnant of the Rephaim" known to the Ammonites (Dt 3:11). His bed was evidently an object of veneration because of its unusual size.

When the Israelites arrived at Kadesh, they encountered the well-organized kingdom of Edom but were refused permission to pass through Edomite territory (Nm 20:14–21). They journeyed northward to Ammonite country, which was then occupied by the Amorite king Sihon. He also refused them permission to pass through his land, but the Israelites defeated him in battle and occupied his country (Nm 21:21–24). They were instructed by God through Moses not to try to occupy Ammonite territory, as it had already been given to the descendants of Lot (Dt 2:19,37).

Continuing northward the Israelites defeated King Og of Bashan (Dt 3:1–11), then went down to the Jordan Valley, where they camped on the plains of Moab. There Balak, king of Moab, hired a soothsayer, Balaam, to pronounce a curse on the Israelites, but Balaam pronounced a blessing each time instead (Nm 22–24). For supporting the Moabites in their actions, the Ammonites were excluded from the congregation of the Lord to the tenth generation (Dt 23:3; Neh 13:1,2).

The Israelite tribes of Gad and Reuben and the half-tribe of Manasseh were attracted to the fertile Transjordan region that had belonged to the Amorites and Bashan, and decided to settle there on the Ammonite frontier (Nm 32; Dt 3:16; Jos 13:8–32). Subsequently they built an altar at the Jordan River, which the other tribes at first interpreted as an act of rebellion establishing a rival place of worship (Jos 22:10–34).

Before the Israelite conquest of Canaan, the Ammonites evidently had not attained the same level of political organization and settled life as the neighboring Moabites and Edomites. Even as late as the 7th century BC the nation was essentially nomadic. Shortly after Israel settled in Canaan, the Ammonites allied with the Moabites and Amalekites when King Eglon of Moab tried to regain former Moabite territory at the north end of the Dead Sea (Jgs 3:12,13).

By the end of the 12th century BC the Israelites, then securely established in the land of Canaan, angered God by their worship of the deities of the Syrians, Sidonians, Moabites, Ammonites, and Philistines (Jgs 10:6). The Ammonites, in their first recorded political expansion, launched an attack against Israel and were able to establish themselves in Gilead (Jgs 10:7,8). They then crossed the Jordan and attacked the tribes of Judah, Benjamin, and Ephraim (Jgs 10:9). In desperation the elders of Gilead turned for help to Jephthah, a social outcast but an able military leader (Jgs 11:1–11). He defeated the Ammonites so decisively that it was unnecessary for him to wage further campaigns against Ammonite settlements west of the Jordan (Jgs 11:12–33).

Although Jephthah's army drove the Ammonites out of Israelite territory, he evidently did not take the great Ammonite strongholds or cripple Ammonite power. Jephthah probably knew that his military resources were insufficient to pursue the Ammonites into their own land, past the massive fortresses protecting the Ammonite borders.

During the Israelite Monarchy (Tenth Century BC). Near the end of the 11th century an Ammonite king named Nahash came to power, determined to reestablish Ammonite dominion over Israelite settlements in Transjordan. He launched an aggressive military campaign around 1020 BC that took him as far north as Jabesh-gilead. The inhabitants of the town were willing to surrender to him, but delayed their surrender to appeal for help from Saul, the recently consecrated Israelite king. Saul quickly organized an army and decisively defeated the Ammonites (1 Sm 11:1–11). The victory ensured freedom from Ammonite domination in the Jordan Valley for several centuries, although later in his reign Saul was forced to fight further battles with the enemies of Israel, including Ammonites (1 Sm 14:47,48).

When David became king, he took silver and gold from the Ammonites, Philistines, and Amalekites, either as spoils or as tribute (2 Sm 8:11,12; 1 Chr 18:11). But although King Nahash of the Ammonites had been a grave threat to Israel during Saul's early reign, he became King David's friend (2 Sm 10:1,2). When Nahash died, David sent representatives to Hanun, his son and successor, to express sympathy, but the deputation was publicly insulted (2 Sm 10:3–5; 1 Chr 19:3–5). In anger David sent an army under Joab to fight the Ammonites, who imported mercenaries and invaded Gilead. Joab personally led his best troops against the Aramean (Syrian) mercenaries at Medeba and sent his brother Abishai with the rest of the Israelite army to fight the Ammonites at Rabbath-ammon (2 Sm 10:9–12; 1 Chr 19:6–13). Jo-

ab's troops put the Syrian mercenaries to flight, and the Ammonites, demoralized by news of the rout, quickly withdrew to the safety of their walled capital city (2 Sm 10:13,14; 1 Chr 19:14,15). David's troops slaughtered many of the Arameans, including their commander Shobach, and forced the Syrian king Hadadezer and his allies to make peace and become Israel's vassals (2 Sm 10:15–19; 1 Chr 19:16–19).

A year later David sent Joab at the head of a strong army to devastate the Ammonite countryside and besiege the capital city of Rabbah (2 Sm 11:1; 1 Chr 20:1). The siege lasted many months, but Joab weakened the city and David then completed its capture (2 Sm 12:26–29). In a ceremony of capitulation the Ammonite king's massive golden crown was placed on David's head (2 Sm 12:30; 1 Chr 20:2). The conquered city was plundered, and its inhabitants were enslaved. Other Ammonite cities were taken, and the nation was added to the growing number of vassal states of Israel (2 Sm 12:31; 1 Chr 20:3). David appointed a governor over the Ammonites from the Ammonite royal family. Shobi, another son of Nahash (and therefore Hanun's brother), became ruler of the Ammonites and aided David during his flight from Absalom's rebellion (2 Sm 17:27). One of David's best warriors was an Ammonite (2 Sm 23:37).

Ammonite relations with Israel remained generally peaceful during the reign of Solomon, David's successor, with the Ammonites undoubtedly sharing in the prosperity and wealth of that period. Among King Solomon's many foreign wives were Ammonite women who influenced him to build a sanctuary on a hillside near Jerusalem to their god Milcom (1 Kgs 11:1–5,33; also called Molech, 11:7). One of his Ammonite wives, Naamah, was probably a daughter of Hanun. She became the mother of Rehoboam, who succeeded Solomon as king (1 Kgs 14:21,31; 2 Chr 12:13). Thus Ammonite blood was introduced into the Israelite royal family—as Moabite blood had entered the family before David was born (Ru 4:13–22)—and the Ammonite deity was introduced into the land with royal approval.

During the Divided Israelite Kingdoms (Ninth to Sixth Centuries BC). After the death of Solomon, the kingdom split apart under Rehoboam and was further weakened by a campaign of Shishak, king of Egypt, that swept through Palestine and also through Ammonite territory. Taking advantage of the situation, the Ammonites declared their independence from Israel and Judah. Before 853 BC a king arose in Ammon named Ba'sha' who allied with Ahab of Israel and Hadadezer of Damascus to oppose a westward campaign by the

Assyrian ruler Shalmaneser III. The name Ba'sha' appears in the Monolith Inscription of Shalmaneser III in his account of the Battle of Qarqar, fought in 853 BC.

The Ammonites joined the Moabites and Meunites to make war against King Jehoshaphat of Judah (reigning 872–848 BC). In fear Jehoshaphat sought help from God in prayer (2 Chr 20:1—12). The Ammonites and their allies began fighting among themselves and destroyed each other, leaving behind great spoil for Jehoshaphat and his people—which took three days to be carried away (2 Chr 20:22–25).

With the accession of Jeroboam II to the throne of the northern kingdom of Israel (793? BC) and Uzziah (Azariah) to the throne of the southern kingdom of Judah (792? BC) both kingdoms entered an era of prosperity and stability not known since Solomon's time. King Uzziah established firm control over south Transjordan all the way from Edom to Ammon, and the Ammonites were forced to pay tribute to him (2 Chr 26:7,8). The Ammonite subjugation at the hands of Uzziah must have seemed to the prophet Amos the beginning of the fulfillment of his prophecy of judgment against them for their vicious cruelty inflicted on the Gileadites. He predicted destruction of Rabbah and exile for its rulers (Am 1:13–15).

Shortly after Uzziah's death (740 BC), the Ammonite king rebelled against Uzziah's son and successor, Jotham. Jotham successfully crushed the rebellion and forced the Ammonites to pay a tribute for three years of approximately $200,000 in silver, 10,000 sacks of wheat, and 10,000 sacks of barley (2 Chr 27:5).

Under the Assyrian king Tiglath-pileser III, all the Syro-Palestinian nations, including Judah, were forced in 732 BC to render tribute (2 Kgs 16:7,8; 2 Chr 28:16–21). The Transjordan states became Assyrian vassals, although each was permitted to retain its own native dynasty on the throne. Among the subjugated nations was Ammon, whose king Sanipu paid tribute, according to Assyrian records.

The reigns of the Assyrian kings Esarhaddon (681–669 BC) and Ashurbanipal (669–633 BC) were times of prosperity for Ammon. During the 7th century BC the Ammonites enjoyed a higher standard of living than their neighbors in Israel and Judah. The Assyrians allowed the Ammonites to retain control of the profitable caravan trade from the Syrian desert, thereby enhancing their prosperity.

When Assyrian power declined (630–612 BC), rebellion erupted throughout the Assyrian empire. Arab tribes from the desert swept through Transjordan and threatened the security of Ammon, Moab, and Edom. The Ammonites were spared destruction from the invading hordes but were unable to isolate themselves from

Arab cultural influences; several Ammonite seals from that period contain personal names. Some of the seals evidently belonged to Ammonite women officials and reflect the favorable position enjoyed by Ammonite women.

Nineveh, the Assyrian capital city, fell to the Medes and Babylonians in 612 BC. The Ammonites made good their boast to occupy part of the territory formerly held by Israel (Zep 2:8–11) by settling in cities that once had belonged to the tribe of Gad (Jer 49:1–6). By the end of the 7th century Ammon had again become completely independent and was the dominant state of south Transjordan.

After the First Deportation of Judah to Babylon (Sixth Century BC Onward). Ammonite independence was short, however, for in 599 BC, according to the Babylonian Chronicle, Babylonian king Nebuchadnezzar led his troops into Syria and began raiding southern Palestine. In 593 BC the Ammonites met in Jerusalem with King Zedekiah (Jehoiakim KJV) of Judah together with representatives from Edom, Moab, Tyre, and Sidon in a conspiracy to rebel against Babylon (Jer 27:1–3). The prophet Jeremiah warned them that God would cause their plan to fail (Jer 27:4–2). Nebuchadnezzar sent an army to crush the rebellion and attacked Jerusalem, which he destroyed after a lengthy and bitter siege (586 BC), deporting many Jews to Babylonia. Ammon was not immediately invaded, however, and many Judeans sought refuge there (Jer 40:11), including a man named Ishmael (Jer 40:13–16). Ishmael plotted with Baalis, king of Ammon, to assassinate Gedaliah, whom Nebuchadnezzar had appointed governor over Judea, now reduced to a province of Babylonia. After carrying out the assassination, Ishmael escaped to Ammon (Jer 41:1–15). Nebuchadnezzar then sent troops which sacked Rabbah and took captive many of the Ammonites. Though the city was not destroyed, the destruction of the countryside was thorough; archaeological explorations show that the area was largely depopulated before the middle of the 6th century BC, and that Ammon did not have much sedentary population again until the 3rd century BC. Arab invaders poured in and destroyed the remaining organized political structure, thus marking the end of Ammon as a semi-independent state (see prophetic warnings of destruction, Is 11:14; Jer 9:25,26; 25:21; 49:1–6; Ez 21:28; 25:2–7). Order was restored about 530 BC when the Persians took control of the former Babylonian provinces of north Arabia and Transjordan.

By the time of Nehemiah (about 445 BC) the district of Ammon extended as far west as the Jordan Valley bordering Judah. A man named Tobiah, head of a Jewish enclave in Ammon (Neh 2:10,19), led opposition to the rebuilding of the walls of Jerusalem by the returning exiles (Neh 4:3,7,8). He was the first of a long line of Tobiahs who controlled Ammon. Their home was at 'Araq el-Emir near Ammon where tombs bearing the family name have been found. Archaeological evidence shows that the city of Rabbah continued to be occupied until about 300 BC. After Alexander the Great's conquests in the area and following his death, Ammon came under the control of the Egyptian Ptolemies. Rabbah was rebuilt in the Greek style and renamed Philadelphia by Ptolemy II Philadelphus (283–246 BC). The city was captured by the Seleucid king Antiochus III about 218 BC after a long siege. In the 1st century BC the city was occupied by the Nabataeans for a short time, but they were driven out by Herod the Great about 30 BC. After the Roman conquest, the old city was rebuilt on a grand scale, removing nearly all traces of the ancient buildings in the process. The Ammonites eventually disappeared from history to be "remembered no more among the nations" (Ez 25:10).

Culture and Religion. The vitality of Ammonite culture is reflected in the architecture of their border fortresses, constructed from huge stones (megalithic style); but in other respects the Ammonites were strongly influenced by contemporary Near Eastern peoples (in matters of dress, pottery, burial customs, and the like). Their standard of literacy was probably comparatively low. In their religion they worshiped an astral deity to whom human sacrifices were offered (1 Kgs 11:5; Zep 1:5). Milcom, or Molech, their national god, was venerated at one period even in Jerusalem (2 Kgs 23:10; Jer 32:35). At the time of Jephthah's victory over them, the Ammonites were evidently worshiping the Moabite god Chemosh (Jgs 11:24).

Excavations since 1968 in the vicinity of Ammon, especially at the citadel, have produced numerous finds that help to understand Ammonite chronology, language, and religion. In 1972 a bronze bottle inscribed with 92 letters was found at Tell Siran near the University of Jordan, providing the basis for an Ammonite king list, an important anchor for chronology in the Iron Age. According to present reconstruction, kings of Ammon in the 7th century BC included Aminidab I (667? BC), Hisser-'el, Aminidab II, Aminidab III, and Ba'lay (600? BC).

Among the standing monuments on the citadel are a large temple of Hercules, an imposing Ghassanid palace, and the Ammonite defensive wall which surrounds the mountain's summit. The Roman theater opposite the citadel has been extensively restored.

F. B. HUEY, JR.

Amnon. 1. David's oldest son by his wife Ahino-am, born in Hebron (2 Sm 3:2; 1 Chr 3:1). Amnon deceived and violated Tamar, his beautiful half-sister, and was killed in revenge by Tamar's brother Absalom (2 Sm 13:1–33).

2. First son of Shimon from Judah's tribe (1 Chr 4:20).

Amok. Priest who returned to Jerusalem with Zerubbabel after the exile. Amok was the ancestor of Eber, a priest under Joiakim (Neh 12:7,20).

Amon (Person). 1. Governor of the city of Samaria during the reign of Ahab in Israel (1 Kgs 22:26; 2 Chr 18:25). Amon imprisoned the prophet Micaiah while Ahab defied Micaiah's warning against attacking Ramoth-gilead.

2. King Manasseh's son, the 15th king of Judah (642–640 BC). Amon was 22 years old when he became king. He indulged in idolatry, like

The Roman theater (with more than 6000 seats) at Amman.

his father, and after a two-year reign was assassinated in a palace coup (2 Kgs 21:19–26; 2 Chr 33:20–25). He was succeeded by his son Josiah, then eight years old, who proved to be an important reformer in Judah.

See ISRAEL, HISTORY OF; CHRONOLOGY, OLD TESTAMENT.

3. Official of Solomon, his descendants returned to Jerusalem after the exile (Neh 7:59). The spelling Ami (Ezr 2:57) is a variant of this name.

4. Egyptian god, probably a fertility deity (Jer 46:25).

Amon (Place). Part of the Hebrew name for Thebes, the capital of upper Egypt (Jer 46:25).

See THEBES.

Amorites. Semitic people found throughout the Fertile Crescent of the Near East at the beginning of the second millennium BC. Amorites are first mentioned in the Bible as descendants of Canaan in a list of ancient peoples (Gn 10:16; cf. 1 Chr 1:13–16). Some of these nomadic people seem to have migrated from the Syrian desert into Mesopotamia, others into Palestine.

Akkadian cuneiform inscriptions mention a relatively uncivilized people called *Amurrū* (translation of the Sumerian *Mar-tu*), perhaps named for a storm god. They overran the Sumerians and eventually most of Mesopotamia. The city of Mari, on the upper Euphrates River, fell to them about 2000 BC; Eshunna a short time later; Babylon by 1830 BC; and finally Assur around 1750 BC. Mari had been an Akkadian city; archaeological investigations there from 1933 to 1960 uncovered more than 20,000 clay tablets written in Akkadian but full of Amorite words and expressions. The tablets were found in a magnificent 300-room palace of the Amorite king, Zimri-lim, who ruled Mari in the 18th century BC until the city fell to King Hammurabi of Babylon. Hammurabi, also an Amorite, was known for his development of agriculture and for his famous law code.

Farther to the west, Amorites had been in Palestine and Syria as early as the third millennium BC. Egyptian texts of the early part of the 19th century BC show that additional waves of Amorite nomads were entering Canaan at that time. Many of their names are similar to the Amorite names from upper Mesopotamia. In fact, many names from the Mari tablets are identical with or similar to names in the patriarchal accounts in Genesis. People named Jacob, Abraham, Levi, and Ishmael were known at Mari, and names similar to Gad and Dan have been found there. Benja-

min was known as the name of a tribe. Nahor was found to be the name of a city near Haran. According to Genesis, Abraham lived in Haran many years before going to Canaan. Jacob spent 20 years there and married two women from Haran.

"Amorite" is considered by some to mean "westerner," but it seems unlikely that the Amorites themselves or other western Semitic peoples such as the Hebrews would refer to them as westerners. The derivation of the name remains uncertain, although the Sumerians may have thought of the Amorites as westerners. The Amorites referred to frequently in the Bible were the truly western group which settled in Canaan and adopted the Canaanite language and culture. They so predominated there that the term "Amorite" could be used to refer to the whole population of Canaan, whose wickedness in God's eyes received early biblical mention (Gn 15:16). In some passages the Amorites were simply listed as one of some 10 tribes inhabiting the land (Gn 15:21). At times the Amorites and Hittites were cited as a pair of heathen nations (Ez 16:3); possibly the whole area of Palestine and Syria was represented by Amorites in the southern part plus Hittites in the north.

In general the western Amorites remained seminomadic. In Abraham's time they occupied Hazazon-tamar in the area of Kadesh-barnea along with the Amalekites (Gn 14:7). When the cities of the plain were attacked, Abraham was dwelling at Mamre just to the north of Hebron with three Amorite brothers, Mamre, Eshcol, and Aner, who were his allies (Gn 14:13,24). Later, Abraham's grandson Jacob (Israel), on his deathbed in Egypt, mentioned to his son Joseph that he had taken land from the Amorites by force (Gn 48:22). The portion of that land given to Joseph included Jacob's well at Sychar, referred to in the NT (Jn 4:5,6).

Amorites appear prominently in the OT as major obstacles to the occupation of Canaan (the Promised Land) by the Israelites after the exodus. Calling Moses to lead Israel out of Egypt, the Lord spoke of Canaan, then occupied by Amorites and others, as a good land (Ex 3:8,17; 13:5). When the Israelites were in the wilderness, God promised to destroy those nations (Ex 23:23) and drive them out of the land (Ex 33:2). The Hebrew people were warned not to make covenants with any of them, to intermarry with them, or to tolerate their idol worship (Ex 34:11–17).

Spies sent into the land found Amalekites in the south; Hittites, Jebusites, and Amorites in the northern mountains and to the west of the Jordan River, and Canaanites by the sea and along the Jordan (Nm 13:25–29). At that time there were Amorites east of the Jordan as well (Nm 21:13).

God had instructed Israel to go up from Horeb and conquer the mountain Amorites on the west side of the Jordan all the way to the Mediterranean Sea (Dt 1:7). When they arrived at Kadesh-barnea they were at the foot of those mountains (Dt 1:19,20). But the people murmured and complained that God had brought them from Egypt only to be slaughtered by the Amorites. From the spies' reports, they pictured the Amorites as an awesome people, greater and taller than the Israelites (Dt 1:26–28). At first they refused to trust God enough to go in, so God told them to turn around and head back into the wilderness. Then they changed their minds, stubbornly attacked the Amorites against God's command, and were badly beaten (Dt 1:34–44). Finally, after 38 additional years in the wilderness, the Israelites once again faced the Amorites, but this time on the east side of the Dead Sea (Nm 21:13). The Amorite king, Sihon, refused to let them pass through his land. The Israelites were drawn up at the Arnon River, which flows into the Dead Sea about two-thirds of the way up its eastern shore.

Transjordan was controlled by two Amorite kings, Sihon and Og. Israel had to face Sihon first. His city, Heshbon, lay due east of the north end of the Dead Sea (Nm 21:21–26). Sihon himself had taken this land from the Moabites. Moses knew of Sihon's reputation and quoted a poem which boasted of Sihon's victory over Moab (Nm 21:27–30). Nevertheless, the Israelites defeated Sihon and devastated his kingdom from Dibon, four miles north of the Arnon, to Medeba, seven miles south of Heshbon. King Og, farther to the north, received the same treatment (Nm 21:31–35). King Balak of Moab heard of the Israelite victories and was terrified (Nm 22:2,3).

Moses reminded the people that by relying on God's promises they had taken all of the land of the Amorites east of the Jordan (Dt 2:24–3:10). The conquered territory was given to the tribes of Gad and Reuben and to the half-tribe of Manasseh (Nm 32:33). Then, 40 years after the exodus began Israel was standing on the east side of the Jordan, having dispossessed the two great Amorite nations there (Dt 1:1–4). But there were other Amorite kingdoms in the hills west of the Jordan, along with other nations (Dt 7:1,2). They were to be destroyed in the same way Sihon and Og had been defeated (Dt 31:3–6).

So famous was the victory of Israel east of the Jordan that Rahab and others in Jericho, west of the Jordan, knew of it and were frightened (Jos 2:8–11). The Israelites crossed the Jordan and took Jericho, but were defeated at the smaller city of Ai in the hill country west of Jericho. They immediately assumed that they would be wiped out by the Amorites in those hills (Jos 7:7).

The Israelites regained God's favor, however, and defeated Ai. Their victory made an impression on the other kingdoms west of the Jordan in the hills, valleys, and coastlands up to Lebanon, who allied to fight Joshua (Jos 9:1,2). Gibeon, an Amorite city seven miles southwest of Ai, made peace with Israel, putting more fear in the hearts of the remaining kings (Jos 10:1,2). Adoni-zedek, king of Jerusalem, was evidently the leader of the Amorite kings west of the Jordan (Jos 10:3). Jerusalem was only eight miles southeast of Gibeon. Adoni-zedek called together the kings of Hebron, Jarmuth, Lachish, and Eglon, all within 50 miles of Jerusalem, to fight against Gibeon and Joshua (Jos 10:3–5).

Joshua came to Gibeon's defense and routed the Amorites, chasing them to the northwest and southwest. The Lord fought for Israel, raining hailstones on the Amorites at Azekah, southwest of Gibeon, and causing the sun to stand still in order to provide a longer battle day (Jos 10:6–14).

In the far north, Jabin, king of Hazor, rallied the Canaanites and remaining Amorites all the way north to Mt Hermon (Jos 11:1–5). But they too were overcome (Jos 11:10–23). Toward the end of Joshua's career, he reminded the people that it was the Lord who had given them the land of the Amorites (Jos 24:1–18).

After the occupation of Canaan by Israel, Amorites still present in the land chased Dan's tribe into the mountains and continued to live near Aijalon, 17 miles west of Jerusalem. They still held the slopes toward the south end of the Dead Sea as well (Jgs 1:34–36). In the period of the judges the Amorites and their gods posed a constant threat to Israel's well-being (Jgs 6:10).

At the end of the period of the judges, relations between Israel and the Amorites improved (1 Sm 7:14). David continued to honor Joshua's treaty with the Amorite remnant of Gibeon (2 Sm 21:2–6). Solomon conscripted his labor forces from the Amorites and other peoples still surviving from Israelite conquest (1 Kgs 9:20–22).

The OT treats the deliverance of the Amorites and their land into the hands of Israel as a great event comparable with the exodus itself, a victory to be remembered and celebrated (Pss 135:9–12; 136:13–26). If the people forgot, the Lord reminded them through his prophets (Am 2:9,10). Long after Sihon and Og had been defeated, the area east of the Jordan was still remembered as the land of "Sihon king of the Amorites" (1 Kgs 4:19). When the kings of Israel and Judah began to fail God, the memory of the Amorites provided a standard of comparison of evil. King Ahab of Israel "did very abominably in going after idols, as the Amorites had done, whom the Lord cast out before the people of Israel" (1 Kgs 21:26). King Manasseh of Judah did "things more wicked than all that the Amorites did, who were before him" (2 Kgs 21:11). Thus a cycle of iniquity was completed, and Israel too was driven out of the land. Yet even after the Babylonian exile, an Amorite remnant was still capable of corrupting Jewish devotion to God through idolatry and intermarriage (Ezr 9:1,2). The Jews' continuing fascination with idolatry led God to address Jerusalem, representing the Jewish people, through the prophet Ezekiel: "Your mother was a Hittite and your father an Amorite" (Ez 16:45). In the biblical view, the Amorites stood for everything that is abominable in the sight of God.

JACK B. SCOTT

See CONQUEST AND ALLOTMENT OF THE LAND; JOSHUA, BOOK OF.

Amorites, Hill Country (Mount) of the. Central mountainous region between the plains of Philistia, Sharon, and Phoenicia on the west, and the valley of the Jordan on the east. While the KJV uses "mount," most modern translations use "hill country" (RSV) or "highlands" (JB) because the phrase does not denote a single mountain but the range running north and south through Judah and Ephraim (Dt 1:7,19,20).

Amos. Hebrew prophet of the 8th century BC. Nothing is known about the first of the "writing prophets" apart from the book that bears his name. He was a herdsman living in Tekoa, a village about 10 miles south of Jerusalem, when God spoke to him in a vision (Am 1:1,2). The kingdom was then divided, with Uzziah king of Judah in the south and Jeroboam II king of Israel in the north. In Amos' vision, the Lord was like a lion roaring out judgment on injustice and idolatry, especially among God's own people. The short biographical section of his writings shows Amos preaching only at Bethel, in Israel, about 12 miles north of Jerusalem and just over the border. Bethel had been made the royal religious sanctuary of Israel by Jeroboam I, to rival Jerusalem in Judah. Amos prophesied that Israel would be overrun and its king killed. The priest of Bethel, Amaziah, called Amos a traitor and told him to go back to Judah and do his prophesying there. Amos replied that he (Amos) was not really a prophet, but "a herdsman, and a dresser of sycamore trees" to whom the Lord

had said, "Go, prophesy to my people Israel" (7:10–15). Amos was evidently a fearless and God-fearing man who deeply felt the mistreatment of the poor by the privileged classes. He did not want to be identified with an elite group of professional prophets, who may have lost their original fervor. His writings reflect the earthy background of a shepherd (3:12). But he spoke with authority the message given him by the Lord God of Hosts: "Let justice roll down like waters, and righteousness like an everflowing stream" (5:24). The message of Amos was a call to repentance of personal and social sins and a return to the worship of the one true God and to the covenantal standards which made the Jewish people a nation.

WALTER R. HEARN

See AMOS, BOOK OF; PROPHET, PROPHETESS.

Amos, Book of. Writings of the prophet Amos, one of the 12 minor prophets of the Hebrew OT. The Book of Amos is called minor only because it is relatively short. Its message is as important as that of any of the major prophets. Indeed, Amos is one of the most powerful statements in the Bible of God's judgment against injustice, oppression, and hypocrisy. The book consists primarily of prophetic sermons preached by Amos at Bethel, royal sanctuary of the northern kingdom of Israel in the 8th century BC.

Author. The preacher of the sermons (or oracles) in the book was undoubtedly Amos, "a herdsman and a dresser of sycamore trees" from the village of Tekoa, south of Jerusalem. He received from God a vision of judgment on Israel and went north to Bethel, just across the border between Judah and Israel, to deliver his sermons. All we know about the prophet is contained in the superscription (Am 1:1,2) and a biographical section (7:10–15) of the Book of Amos, plus what can be learned about him from the style and content of the rest of the book.

Did Amos write down his prophecies himself? Although scholars have raised many questions about the authorship of Amos, there is no convincing reason to regard the book as the work of anyone else. Some have suggested that the sermons were passed on by word of mouth for a long time before they were written down in final form. The Hebrew text, however, is in much better shape than would be expected after prolonged oral transmission. The many first-person references and vigor of expression imply strongly that Amos put much of his prophecy into writing himself soon after delivering it at Bethel.

Another speculative proposal is that the visions described in the book (7:1–9; 8:1–3; 9:1–4) were compiled by Amos before he began his ministry to the northern kingdom, and the oracles (chs 1–6) were composed after that time. The two sections could have been joined into one book much later, during or after the Babylonian exile, with some sections inserted at that time. Other prophecies, however, such as Ezekiel and Jeremiah, contain both oracle and vision sections which scholars have not attempted to divide, and the internal evidence does not make such a division necessary with Amos. Both sections contain similar concerns; in both the visions (7:1–3) and the oracles (5:1–7) Amos appears in the role of intercessor on behalf of Israel.

Although it is now generally agreed that most of the text is the authentic work of Amos, some scholars think they see evidence for later insertions by another writer. For instance, some argue that short doxologies (hymns of praise, 4:13; 5:8,9; 9:5,6) have been added by someone other than Amos. The supposed additions, however, are not at all inconsistent with what a prophet of Amos's time could have included. From the beginning of Israelite prophecy, the goodness of God and his willingness to bless his repentant people were intertwined with oracles of God's judgment on the unrepentant.

Some doubt that the hope of messianic restoration (9:11,12) would have been expressed in that form until after the exile. Reference to the "City of David, which is now lying in ruins" (9:11 LB) could certainly have been made by Amos even before the Babylonian exile. With the kingdom divided, the monarchy had already fallen to a very low state, which would have grieved a sensitive man of God such as Amos.

Date, Origin, and Destination. According to the superscription, Amos prophesied during the reigns of Uzziah, king of Judah, and Jeroboam II, king of Israel (1:2), or between 792 and 740 BC. The content of his message fits what is known about the situation in Israel in that period. It is difficult to be more exact about the beginning and ending of Amos's prophetic ministry within that time span. The vision came to him "two years before the earthquake" (1:1), but another biblical reference to presumably the same earthquake places it only "in the days of Uzziah king of Judah" (Zec 14:5). Archaeological excavations at Hazor seem to have yielded evidence for an earthquake which has been dated at approximately 760 BC. Amos also contains a prophetic reference to a solar eclipse (8:9); such an eclipse has been calculated to have occurred about 763 BC. After King Uzziah was stricken with leprosy, he lived in isolation while Judah was under a co-regency (2 Chr 26:21), so mention of Uzziah as king (Am 1:2) probably sets 750 BC as the latest possible date for Amos' ministry.

The doom that came upon Israel after Amos' prophecy was conquest by the Assyrian king Tiglath-pileser III (745–727 BC). Although Amos referred to impending captivity, he never mentioned Assyria as the captor, although he did say that captivity would take Israel "beyond Damascus" (5:27). Probably Amos was not thinking specifically of the rising power of Assyria but only of the inevitable consequences of Israel's idolatry and hypocrisy. When all the evidence is taken into consideration, it seems reasonable to date the beginning of Amos's prophecies at Bethel at about 760 BC, or approximately the middle of the period during which both Uzziah and Jeroboam II were on their thrones. We do not know how long his ministry lasted; it may have been only a few months.

The campaigns of Tiglath-pileser III (bas-relief from Nineveh).

Amos had been caring for his flocks in the Judean hills south of Jerusalem when God told him, "Go, prophesy to my people Israel" (7:15). He may have been familiar with the more urban north from earlier trips there to sell wool or fruit, or the pagan worship and social wrongs there may have made a sudden impact on him after his call to prophesy. At any rate, his writings reveal not only his rural Judean background but also a firsthand knowledge of conditions in the northern kingdom of Israel. Although his prophecies were directed primarily to Israel, he also denounced the sin of Judah, predicting that its capital, Jerusalem, would be burned (2:4,5). Several passages are directed at inhabitants of Samaria, capital of Israel (4:11; 6:1), with which Amos was obviously familiar. He could have traveled on to Samaria from Bethel, or he could have learned of its splendors from the boasts of its citizens. He could have addressed them directly as they came from the capital city to worship at Bethel.

Background. The 8th century BC was a critical time in Jewish history. Both kingdoms of the divided nation had risen to heights of economic affluence that had not been experienced since the days of Solomon. Yet internal religious decay was sapping the strength of both kingdoms, and their social fabric was being destroyed. A new wealthy class was benefiting from the affluence of the time, growing ever richer while poor people became poorer than ever.

In 803 BC, the conquest of Syrian Damascus by the Assyrian king Adad-nirari III had silenced one of Israel's major enemies. With the Syrians out of the picture, the kingdom of Israel was able to expand its borders under King Joash (2 Kgs 13:25), and for a time even the thrust of Assyrian power westward was diminished. Israel and Judah entered a period of rest from constant warfare and turned their attention to internal affairs.

Joash's son, Jeroboam II, became king of Israel in 793 and reigned until 753 BC. Uzziah was on the throne of Judah from 792 to 740 BC. Under these two kings, Judah and Israel controlled a territory that made them, geographically at least, almost as great as Solomon's empire had been. Their wealth had grown both from expansion of trade and from booty from conquered territories.

Archaeology has yielded information about industrial activity within the nations, such as an impressive dyeing industry at Debir. Excavations at Samaria have produced large numbers of ivory inlays that confirm Amos's description of the wealthy in the capital city "who lie upon beds of ivory" (6:4). The city of Samaria was protected by a huge double wall of unusual thickness. A palace, probably Jeroboam's, dominated the city with a massive tower.

The splendor and prosperity of the time, however, was masking the spread of internal decay. Oppression of the poor by many in the wealthy classes not only threatened the unity of the nation but also meant that God's laws were being violated. In his denunciations of the cruel treatment of the poor (5:11–13; 8:4–10), Amos warned of the inevitable punishment for disobeying God's laws.

The nation of Israel was guilty of more than social sins against the covenant. It was also adopting pagan religious practices. Canaanite religious influence intruded into the fabric of the nation of Israel. Excavation of a palace storehouse in Samaria uncovered many ostraca (pieces of broken pottery used for writing short messages such as letters, receipts, etc.) containing Hebrew names compounded with "Baal," a chief god of the Canaanite religion.

In spite of the gradual deterioration, false optimism seems to have prevailed. A prophet contemporary with Amos described the typical response to warnings of judgment to come: "One should not preach of such things; disgrace will not overtake us" (Mi 2:6). Amos found people desiring the Day of the Lord (Am 5:18) and sought to correct their misunderstanding: the Day of the Lord prophesied in the Scriptures would be a time of judgment on all sinners.

A more immediate judgment was to come, however. Assyria began to strengthen its position in the world and to resume its expansionist policies. Under the leadership of Tiglath-pileser III (745–727 BC), Assyria regained a position of world dominance. Eventually Israel, torn by internal strife, was attacked by Shalmaneser V of Assyria. Soon afterward, in 722 BC, Samaria was occupied. No doubt when the Assyrians were sweeping into Israel, many of the people who had ignored the message of Amos then realized that a prophet of God had been among them.

Purpose and Theological Teaching. The major purpose of Amos in his prophecies was to denounce the disobedience to covenant standards that was rife in Israel at that time. Although the covenant promise given to Abraham (Gn 22:15–18) and reiterated throughout the OT is not mentioned explicitly in Amos, it is implicit in the total message of the book. Amos upheld the spiritual nature of the covenant and emphasized that its blessing was mediated through obedience.

Looking around him, Amos saw not only disobedience but hypocrisy. A basic aspect of his ethical teaching was insistence that outward adherence to religious ceremonies without a heart response to the will of God (as expressed in the Law) was wrong. The Law contained many injunctions that sought to engender love of God and fellow human beings (Ex 23:1–13). In Amos's time, those social aspects of the Law were being willfully disobeyed by the rich, who nevertheless clung to religious ritual. Amos saw what was in their hearts and condemned it. To him, religious obligations not observed in the proper spirit of responsibility to God could actually become sin (4:4). Religion could degenerate to the place where it becomes a curse, a mockery of the will of a holy God.

Amos saw the disobedience and hypocrisy of Israel as culminating in national disaster. Thus his prophecy served as a warning of impending doom to the nation. He saw that other nations besides Israel and Judah were held accountable to God because of their mistreatment of others (1:3–2:3). Their social sins were punished by God in history. Amos thus saw an aspect of the Law extending beyond Israel and Judah to other nations. They were responsible to God under what might be called a universal moral law, and they were judged for their crimes against humanity.

The prophetic concept of the Day of the Lord, regarded by the people of Amos' day as a time of vindication for their nation, was seen by Amos as a time of punishment for all sinners. Such punishment would not exclude the nation of Israel.

Yet denunciation was not the sole purpose of Amos's prophetic activity. He proclaimed a future of hope for Israel in the reestablishment of the Davidic monarchy, evidently under Messiah, in a time that would be characterized by peace (9:8–15). The relationship of the Davidic kingdom to the messianic kingdom goes back to the promise given to David (2 Sm 7:8–16). Just as those in other nations participated by extension in the demands of the Law and in judgment, so would those in other nations who belonged to God participate in the blessings of the promise (9:12).

The concepts of God drawn most sharply in the Book of Amos are God's sovereignty and God's righteousness. He is sovereign over all the nations of the world, typified by those surrounding Israel, and he brings them to judgment (1:3–2:3). He is also sovereign over nature, as recognized in his control of the universe (4:13; 5:8; 9:13,14). His righteousness demands that he cannot allow his Law to continue to be violated without retribution. But his righteousness is also the guarantee of hope for the believing remnant of Israel. It binds him to keep his promise to preserve Israel as a nation (Lv 26:44,45).

Amos held out the possibility of averting the national catastrophe looming on the horizon of world events. However, from his gloomy description of social conditions and of the hardness of people's hearts at the time, it seems likely that he did not foresee any escape.

His message was presented in bold metaphors and vivid pictures that stick in the mind. That message is still relevant, for many of the sins that characterized the people of the prophet's day are still prevalent in modern society and in the lives of individuals. Mistreatment of fellow human beings is as much a feature of the 20th century AD as it was of the 8th century BC.

Today's reader of the Book of Amos should note the prophet's insistence on the consequences of sin; his emphasis on the responsibility that always accompanies privilege; his presentation of God's faithfulness; and his message of hope, expressed in part today through the church.

If the book seems to be gloomy in its outlook, it should be remembered that the prophet faced a gloomy picture. He was watching a nation crumble because of its unfaithfulness to God. But beyond the dismal prospect that faced Israel, Amos saw a new kingdom emerging. It was a kingdom of peace in which the people of God would realize the fulfillment of God's promises.

Content. *Superscription* (1:1). The prophet introduces himself as a herdsman, perhaps implying that it is more than sheep he wants to keep from straying.

Prophetic Oracles (1:2–6:14). This section begins with a picture of the great power of God, who acts in history to judge the nations (1:2).

JUDGMENT ON SURROUNDING NATIONS (1:3–2:3). The prophet first speaks against Damascus, then moves on, pronouncing doom on various peoples in ever closer concentric circles, "homing in" on Israel. One may imagine the citizens of Israel applauding God's judgment on other nations until, with shocking effect, Amos accuses Israel of similar sins.

Damascus was the capital of Syria, northeast of Israel, and the center of Syrian influence. Syria had mistreated Israel during Hazael's reign in Damascus (842–806 BC). Hazael "whittled down" Israel in a number of campaigns (2 Kgs 10:32,33; 13:3–5,22–24). In their campaign into the territory of Gilead, the Syrians destroyed most of Israel's army as though they were dust on a threshing floor (2 Kgs 13:7). Hence Amos denounces Syria for threshing Gilead as grain is threshed with iron rods (Am 1:3). He predicts that Syria will be destroyed and its people deported to Kir, which Amos understood to be their place of origin

(9:7). (For the fulfillment of this prophecy, see 2 Kgs 16:9.)

Amos next turns to Gaza, a Philistine city in southwest Palestine. Gaza probably represents the Philistines as a whole, since three other of their five major cities are also mentioned (1:8). The fifth, Gath, had already been conquered by Hazael (2 Kgs 12:17). Amos denounces the Philistines for what must have been a border raid on Israel or Judah in which many were carried off into slavery (1:6).

The Phoenician city of Tyre is cited next. Tyre was on the Mediterranean, north of Israel and southwest of Damascus. Destruction of Tyre, like that of the Philistine cities, is predicted as punishment for making slaves of conquered Israelites.

Edom is next, south of the Dead Sea. Edom had perennially harassed the Israelites and is referred to in a negative light many times in the OT. Edom is said to have been pitiless toward Israel, "his brother," a phrase emphasizing the social nature of Edom's sin (1:11).

Ammon, just to the southeast of Israel, comes in for judgment. The particularly violent incident referred to in (1:13) evidently occurred in one of their many attempts to push northward into the Israelite territory of Gilead.

Moab is the last of the surrounding nations to be denounced, with reference to what may have been a well-known incident of desecration of the dead (2:1–3).

ORACLES AGAINST JUDAH AND ISRAEL (2:4–16). Although Judah and Israel were at peace at the time, their enmity had continued after dissolution of the united kingdom. Amos accuses Judah of rejecting "the law of the Lord" and predicts the burning of Jerusalem.

The oracle against Israel is longer than the others. Amos carefully specifies the social nature of Israel's sin, making the point that Israel is no better than the surrounding nations. Israel deserves the same punishment. Just as some of the nations were guilty of taking people into slavery, Israel is selling her own poor who cannot repay their debts (2:6). Under Mosaic law it was illegal to keep overnight a garment pledged as security for a loan, since it might be the only source of warmth the debtor had (Ex 22:26,27). Rich people in Israel were attending religious feasts in such clothing "stolen" from the poor (2:8).

Amos reminds Israel of all the good things God has done for them (2:9–11). But because Israel has chosen to continue in disobedience, the nation will not escape impending judgment (2:12–16).

DENUNCIATION AND WARNING AGAINST ISRAEL (3:1–6:14). Amos substantiates his prophetic authority with a lesson on cause and effect (3:1–8). A lion roars when it has prey, and people fear when a trumpet sounds an alarm. If calamity comes to a city, God has allowed it. God, who reveals his secrets to his prophets, has spoken Israel's doom, and Amos must proclaim it.

In a dramatic statement, Amos calls on Egypt and Assyria, great centers of oppression and cruelty, to witness Israel's crimes, as though even they will be amazed at what they see (3:9,10). Only a ragged remnant will survive the punishment to come (3:11,12). Judgment will fall on objects that symbolize Israel's religious disobedience (3:14) as well as on symbols of the wealth that led Israel away from the Lord (3:15).

Amos uses strong language to denounce luxurious and indolent living bought at the expense of the poor (4:1–3). Rich women whose love for luxuries drives their husbands to squeeze the needy still more are called "fat cows" who will someday be treated like cattle. Then Amos mocks those who worship at Bethel for going through the motions in the wrong spirit (4:4,5).

In the rest of the fourth chapter, Amos recalls incidents from Israel's history which were meant to call the people back to God: famine, drought, plagues, the destruction of some of their cities. Still they do not repent. "Prepare to meet your God, O Israel!" warns the prophet, following his warning with a hymn to the mighty power of God (4:6–13).

The fifth chapter begins in the form of a funeral dirge, as though Israel were as good as dead already (5:1,2). There is no one to help Israel, whose own armies will be decimated when the disaster strikes (5:3). Of course, God is there to help: "Seek me and live" (5:4–6). The possibility of rescue, of "life," stands in sharp contrast to the nation's "death" pictured just before. Idols, as always, are a false hope (5:5). The call to seek the Lord is again followed by a hymn to his power (5:8,9).

In spite of the hope offered to Israel, Amos has to present a gloomy picture of what he sees (5:10–13). The judicial system is corrupt; taxes and high interest charges (usury) grind down the poor. Those injustices could be corrected if the people would "hate evil and love good" (5:15), but judgment is already on the way (5:16,17).

The people are full of hypocrisy, claiming to look forward to the Day of the Lord. That day will be a day of judgment on their sins, Amos says. Instead of empty gestures of offerings and praise, God wants to let "justice roll down like waters, and righteousness like an everflowing stream" (5:18–24). Their disobedient spirit goes back to the time of the exodus from Egypt, when God's own people were attracted to pagan gods. The Lord God of Hosts will send those false gods into captivity with the people who looked to them (5:25–27).

The self-satisfaction felt by the upper classes in Israel had evidently spread to Judah, since Jerusalem as well as Samaria rates some harsh words (6:1). Amos tells those who are "lounging in luxury" to take a look at three neighboring kingdoms on which judgment has already fallen: Calneh, Hamath, and Gath. Does Israel think it will escape, since they did not? When the Day of Judgment comes, the rich, who have gone "first-class," will be the first to go (6:2–7). The destruction will leave few survivors, but they will know that punishment came from God (6:8–11). Israel is behaving stupidly to be proud of themselves when they are actually so utterly self-deceived (6:12–14).

Prophetic Visions (7:1–9:10). By describing three visions God gave him, Amos then dramatically communicates God's revelation.

ISRAEL'S DESTRUCTION (7:1–9). The first vision is in three parts. In the first, Amos pictures the threat of a locust plague in which his prayer of intercession causes God to relent and withdraw the threat (7:1–3). Then he sees an all-consuming fire, and again his prayer averts a catastrophe (7:4–6). In the third part of the vision, Amos sees the Lord standing by a wall and holding a plumb line, implying that he has a standard for his people to live up to, an element missing from the two earlier images. This time, because the people have failed to measure up, the catastrophe cannot be averted (7:7–9).

HISTORICAL INTERLUDE (7:10–17). At this point, Amos encounters Amaziah, priest of Bethel, because he has said that the vision of the plumb line means destruction of the idol altars and temples of Israel and of "the house of Jeroboam with the sword." Amaziah sends word to Jeroboam that Amos is a traitor and tells Amos to go back to Judah. Amos disclaims any relationship with professional prophets, then specifically includes Amaziah's family in another prediction of Israel's disaster.

THE RIPE FRUIT (8:1–14). In the second vision, Amos is shown a basket of ripe or "summer" fruit. The Hebrew word for summer fruit is almost the same as the word for "end," so the play on words communicates that the nation is "ripe for punishment." Their ripeness is really moral rottenness. Greedy merchants can hardly wait for religious holidays to end so they can cheat the poor some more by using false weights, selling inferior goods, and foreclosing on debtors. When the captivity comes, their festivities will turn into funerals. A fam-

ine, not just of bread and water but of the words of the Lord, is coming upon them, causing even the strongest young people to drop to the ground.

DESTRUCTION OF THE TEMPLE (9:1–10). The third vision is of the Lord destroying the shrine at Bethel when it is thronged with people engaging in their empty worship. The place where they hoped to find security is where they find destruction. Those who are not inside will be destroyed, too, no matter where they try to flee. They won't be able to hide from God in Sheol or on the heights of Carmel or in the depths of the sea (9:1–4). Another hymn to God's power follows the vision (9:5,6).

The final words of denunciation in the Book of Amos are found in 9:7–10, but they are a prelude to a message of hope. Amos shows that Israel is no better than any other nation in the eyes of God. Did he not bring Israel out of Egypt? Yes, but he also brought the Philistines from Caphtor and the Syrians from Kir. The religious significance of the exodus has been lost because of Israel's sin, so all but a faithful remnant will be lost.

The concept of the remnant was important in the prophetic preaching of the 8th century BC (cf. Is 6:12,13; Mi 5:7–9). It recalled God's promise to maintain the nation of Israel for the sake of the covenant given to the patriarchs (Lv 26:44,45). In Amos's prophecy, Israel is to be sifted by other nations like grain in a sieve; the ungodly "chaff" will be scattered across the world, but the true "grain" will be preserved.

Israel's Hope (9:11–15). The expression of hope is expanded in the last section of the book in a series of startling and beautiful metaphors.

RESTORATION OF THE CITY OF DAVID (9:11,12). The first metaphor is of the city (literally "house" or "hut") of David, a house fallen into disrepair. The monarchy, which had crumbled from internal decay and external threats, is envisioned as being restored "to its former glory." Further, an expansion of the Davidic kingdom will include all nations that belong to the Lord.

In the NT, this passage was quoted by James to support the inclusion of Gentiles in the promise (Acts 15:16–18). The wording in Acts is slightly different from that of Amos because it was based on an early Greek translation of the OT (called the Septuagint). Those called by God's name or belonging to God include not only geographical entities such as nations, but also individuals in any nation who have a close relationship to God. James saw that Amos was predicting inclusion of Gentiles in the kingdom of God, a kingdom far greater than the earthly monarchy. This prophecy has been fulfilled in part in the Christian church.

RESTORATION OF ISRAEL'S FORTUNES (9:13–15). A series of pastoral metaphors closes the Book of Amos. They depict the abundance of blessing in the coming kingdom. Israel's fortunes are to be restored, far beyond the dismal events of the century in which Amos is speaking. Theologians differ in their understanding of the application of this prophecy. If it refers to the present age of the Christian church, it pictures the blessings of the church now as "spiritual Israel." If it refers to the future, to the millennial reign of Christ, it depicts what will happen on earth at that time.

The concept of a rejuvenated earth is found elsewhere in the Bible (Rom 8:20–22). Micah uses language somewhat similar to that of Amos (Mi 4:3,4) to describe restoration of what seems to be the literal city of Jerusalem (Mi 3:12–4:2). It may be best to apply the prophetic finale of Amos to the restoration to be effected at the ultimate return of Christ. Whatever the correct application, the remnant must include the followers of Jesus Christ, and the blessings should be seen as intended for all who belong to the kingdom of God.

THOMAS E. McCOMISKEY

See AMOS; PROPHECY; PROPHET, PROPHETESS; ISRAEL, HISTORY OF.

Bibliography. R.L. Honeycutt, *Amos and His Message;* C.F. Keil, *The Twelve Minor Prophets,* vol 1, pp 233–336; G.A. Smith, *The Book of the Twelve Prophets,* vol 1; N.H. Snaith, *Amos, Hosea, and Micah;* J.D.W. Watts, *Vision and Prophecy in Amos.*

Amoz. Isaiah's father (2 Kgs 19:2; Is 1:1), not to be confused with the prophet Amos.

Amphipolis. City in ancient Greece, once the home of the Thracian Edoni tribe. Amphipolis occupied a strategic location in a fertile area on the eastern bank of the Strymon River. Its name ("around city") may refer to its being surrounded on three sides by the river. Located about 30 miles from Philippi, it eventually became an important station on the Roman Via Egnatia. On his second missionary journey Paul passed through this commercial center en route to Thessalonica (Acts 17:1).

Ampliatus, Amplias. Name of a Christian to whom the apostle Paul sent greetings at the end of his letter to the Romans (16:8, KJV Amplias). Called "my beloved in the Lord" by Paul, nothing further is known of this Christian who bore a common Roman name.

Amram. 1. Kohath's son, a member of Levi's tribe. Amram married Jochebed and had three famous children: Aaron, Moses, and Miriam (Ex 6:16–20; Nm 26:58,59). During the Israelites' wilderness journey, the responsibility of the Amramites was to care for the ark and the table, lampstand, altars, and other furnishings used in the tabernacle (Nm 3:27). Later, the Amramites were one of the groups in charge of offerings placed in the temple treasury (1 Chr 26:23).

2. Priest from Bani's family, who obeyed Ezra's exhortation to divorce his pagan wife after the exile (Ezr 10:34).

3. KJV form of Hamran, Dishon's son, in 1 Chronicles 1:41. Hamran itself is an alternate form of Hemdan (cf. Gn 36:26).

See HEMDAN.

Amramite. Descendant of Amram, Kohath's son (Nm 3:27; 1 Chr 26:23).

See AMRAM #1.

Amraphel. King of Shinar (Babylonia), who helped King Chedorlaomer of Elam quell a revolt of five vassal cities in Palestine (Gn 14:1–11). Attempts to identify Amraphel with Hammurabi of Babylon on the basis of name similarity have failed.

Amulet. Small object worn by an individual, usually around the neck, as a charm or means of protection against evil, witchcraft, disease, or other physical and spiritual threats. The word is probably derived from either a Latin or Arabic term meaning "to carry." Amulets have been made of various substances and in many forms. Pieces of metal or strips of parchment with portions of sacred writings, even herbs and animal preparations, have been used. Semiprecious gems were often inscribed with a magical formula.

Many amulets uncovered in Palestine have been Egyptian in style. They were in forms of Egyptian gods (e.g., Osiris and Isis), animals (cats and apes), fruits (lotus and pomegranates), human legs and arms, lunar discs, pierced shells, and signet rings. Amulets were often colored red because blood was vital to life or blue to ward off the evil eye.

No Hebrew or Greek word in the Bible is translated "amulet" with certainty. The practice of wearing amulets, however, is sometimes implied, generally with disapproval. The gold earrings worn by the Israelites escaping from Egypt, from which Aaron fashioned a golden calf, have been considered amulets (Ex 32:2–4). The prophet Isaiah condemned the ornaments worn by the women of his day (Is 3:16–23). Most scholars regard the phylacteries and mezuzahs used by the Jews as forms of amulets.

CARL WAYNE HENSLEY

See FASHION AND DRESS; PHYLACTERY; MAGIC; FRONTLET.

Amzi. 1. Merarite Levite and an ancestor of Ethan the musician (1 Chr 6:46).

2. Forefather of Adaiah and a priest of Malchijah's division (Neh 11:12).

Anab. Town in the hill country of Hebron inhabited by giant warriors. After Joshua eliminated the giants (Jos 11:21) Anab was allotted to Judah's tribe (Jos 15:50). Today Anab is known as Khirbet 'Anab el-Kebireh.

Anah. 1. Son of Zibeon the Hivite and father of Oholibamah. Oholibamah was one of Esau's wives (Gn 36:2,18).

2. Fourth son of Seir the Horite. Anah was a chief among the Horites who also had a daughter named Oholibamah (Gn 36:20,25,29: 1 Chr 1:38,41).

3. Son of another Zibeon, who found hot springs in the wasteland (Gn 36:24). This Zibeon was a brother to #2 above.

Anaharath. Town in the Valley of Jezreel allotted to Issachar's tribe when the land was divided by Joshua (Jos 19:19). It has been identified as modern 'en-Na'vrah, although this is not certain.

Anaiah. 1. Priest and assistant of Ezra who explained to the people passages from the Law read by Ezra (Neh 8:4).

2. Political leader who signed Ezra's covenant of faithfulness to God with Nehemiah and others after the exile (Neh 10:22). He is perhaps identical with #1 above.

Anak (Anakim). Ancestor of a race of giants in old Canaan. When Israel first reached Canaan, the Anakim were well established in Hebron. Ten of the 12 spies Moses sent into Canaan (Nm 13:17–22) were terrified by the size of the Anakim: "We are not able to go up against the people; for they are stronger than we" (Nm 13:31). Their terror led to a rebellion at Kadesh-barnea (Nm 14:39–45; Dt 1:19–46) and another 38 years of wandering. When the Israelites were finally ready to enter Canaan, God promised his help against the famed Anak giants (Dt 9:1–3).

The two spies who had not trembled before the Anakim were both involved in their defeat. Joshua defeated the Anakim living in Hebron, Debir, Anab, and all the region of Judah (Jos 11:21–23). Those who survived were left only

in the Philistine cities of Gaza, Gath, and Ashdod. The other spy, Caleb, was responsible for the defeat of the Anakim chiefs Sheshai, Ahiman, and Talmai at Hebron; Caleb's nephew Othniel was the hero of Debir (Jos 15:17). Hebron had earlier been called Kiriath-arba for Anak's father Arba, a great hero of the Anakim (Jos 14:15; 21:11).

The fact that the Anakim survived in the Philistine cities of Gaza, Gath, and Ashdod leads to the supposition that Goliath of Gath may have been a descendant of these giants (1 Sm 17:4–7).

RONALD B. ALLEN

See GIANTS.

Anamim. Unidentified group of people, possibly related to the Egyptians, mentioned in the biblical tables of earliest nations (Gn 10:13; 1 Chr 1:11).

Anammelech. Deity associated with Adrammelech, who was worshiped by the people of Sepharvaim, whom the Assyrians relocated in Samaria after 722 BC. Anammelech is evidently the Hebrew rendering of the designation for a Mesopotamian deity, Anu-melek, meaning "Anu is King." Anu was the name of the chief god of Assyria, the sky god. The worship of this deity by the Sepharvites in Samaria included child sacrifice (2 Kgs 17:31). It is not certain whether the burning of children in the Anu cult was brought from Sepharvaim or was an innovation when the Sepharvites came to Canaan.

See MESOPOTAMIA; SYRIA, SYRIANS.

Anan. One of the chiefs of the people who set his seal on Ezra's covenant to keep God's Law during the post-exilic era (Neh 10:26).

Anani. One of seven sons of Elioenai, a descendant of David (1 Chr 3:24).

Ananiah (Person). Azariah's grandfather. Azariah was one of three men who repaired the Jerusalem wall near their homes after the exile (Neh 3:23).

Ananiah (Place). Town in Benjamin's territory after the exile (Neh 11:32) which may have become the Bethany of the NT ("Bethany" is a contraction of Beth-ananiah.)

Ananias. 1. Member of the early church in Jerusalem. Along with his wife, Sapphira, he was struck dead for attempted deception with regard to some money (Acts 5:1–5).

2. Early convert to Christianity who was living in Damascus when Saul of Tarsus (Paul)

arrived there supposedly to arrest Christians. Ananias knew that Paul was a deadly enemy of Christians, but the Lord reassured him, explaining that Paul had been chosen as a special messenger of the gospel (Acts 9:13–18). The Lord sent Ananias to the newly converted Paul to restore his eyesight (Acts 9:17–19). Ananias told Paul the meaning of his unusual encounter with Christ on the road to Damascus (Acts 22:12–16) and probably introduced him to the church there as a new Christian brother rather than a persecutor. Various traditions say that Ananias later became one of the 70 disciples of Jerusalem, a bishop of Damascus, and a martyr.

3. High priest who presided over the Sanhedrin when the apostle Paul was arrested and questioned by that council in Jerusalem at the end of Paul's third missionary journey (Acts 22:12–23:10). Ananias was one of the witnesses who testified against Paul in Caesarea when he was on trial before Felix, the Roman governor (Acts 24:1). This Ananias was appointed high priest by Herod Agrippa II in AD 48 and served until AD 59. The Jewish historian Josephus wrote that he was wealthy, haughty, and unscrupulous. He was known for his collaboration with the Romans and for his severity and cruelty. Hated by nationalistic Jews, he was killed by them when war with Rome broke out in AD 66.

CARL WAYNE HENSLEY

Anath. 1. Parent of Shamgar, one of the judges of Israel (Jgs 3:31; 5:6). Since the name Anath is feminine, it is likely that Anath was Shamgar's mother.

2. Canaanite goddess of fertility.
See CANAANITE DEITIES AND RELIGION.

Anathema. Greek word meaning "cursed" or "banned," and associated with destruction.
See CURSE, CURSED.

Anathoth (Person). 1. Becher's son from Benjamin's tribe (1 Chr 7:8).

2. Political leader who signed Ezra's covenant of faithfulness to God with Nehemiah and others after the exile (Neh 10:19).

Anathoth, Anathothite (Place). Town in Benjamin's territory set aside for the Levites (Jos 21:18; 1 Chr 6:60). Anathoth may have been named by the Canaanites for their goddess Anath, or later by the Israelites for one of Benjamin's descendants (1 Chr 7:8). The town was probably located at Ras el-Karrubeh near the modern town of Anata three miles north of Jerusalem. Its residents were sometimes called Anethothites or Anetothites (2 Sm 23:27;

An aerial view of Anathoth, Jeremiah's hometown.

1 Chr 27:12, both KJV). Abiezer, one of David's military leaders, was from Anathoth (1 Chr 11:28, KJV Antothite) as was the soldier Jehu (1 Chr 12:3) and the priest Abiathar (1 Kgs 2:26). It was also the hometown of the prophet Jeremiah (Jer 1:1), though some of its inhabitants violently opposed him (Jer 11:21,23). Just before Judah fell to Babylon, Jeremiah bought a field in Anathoth as a sign that Israel would be restored to her land (Jer 32:7–9). Years later 128 men of Anathoth returned from the exile and the town was resettled (Neh 11:32)

See LEVITICAL CITIES.

Anatolia. Commonly used synonym for Asia Minor, a peninsula forming about three-fifths of modern Turkey. Anatolia is bounded on the north by the Black Sea, on the west by the Aegean Sea, on the south by the Mediterranean Sea, and on the east by a line running from the Gulf of Iskenderun northeast to the Black Sea. The total area of Asia Minor is about 200,000 square miles—equal to that of New England, New York, New Jersey, Pennsylvania, Maryland, and West Virginia.

The central part of Anatolia is a plateau 3,000 to 5,000 feet above sea level, surrounded on all sides by mountains. Although rivers flowing from the mountains into the interior provided waters for irrigation and supported a number of large cities in NT times, those waters are now swallowed up in salt lakes and swamps. With its limited resources, that area has been used primarily for grazing sheep.

Near the eastern boundary of Anatolia the

Armenian mountains fork into two ranges: the Taurus extending into southern Asia Minor, rising to about 10,000 feet, and the mountains of Pontus extending along the northern rim of the peninsula, rising to about 9,000 feet. Along the southeast edge of the plateau for about 150 miles rise groups of volcanic peaks. The Phrygian mountains on the west of the plateau thrust out spurs to the west, between which lie some of the important river valleys of the peninsula: the Caicus, Hermus (modern Gediz), Cayster, and Maeander (modern Menderes).

The mountains provided important resources (iron, copper, timber, and marble) in ancient times, though apparently much of the copper was already exhausted when the apostle Paul ministered there. Mountains descend abruptly to the sea along most of the southern shore and leave only a narrow coastal plain along most of the northern shore of Anatolia. The most important river of the peninsula, the Halys (modern Kizil Irmak) flows in a great bend to the southwest and then north through Pontus into the Black Sea, a total of 600 miles.

Though Anatolia supported important kingdoms or empires in the second millennium BC (such as the Hittites and Troy) and the first millennium BC (Lydia, Pergamum, and others), its greatest role in Scripture was played in NT times, when Rome ruled the area. The apostle Paul was born in Tarsus of Cilicia (Acts 21:39) in the southeast corner of the peninsula and traveled all across the peninsula during his three missionary journeys. The apostle Peter ministered there and addressed his first epistle to believers in several of its provinces (1 Pt 1:1). The apostle John spent his last years in Ephesus and addressed the Book of Revelation to the seven churches of the province of Asia (see Rv 1–3).

The Romans divided Anatolia into several provinces: Asia in the west, Bithynia and Pontus to the north, Galatia in the center, Cappadocia in the east, Cilicia south of Cappadocia along the Mediterranean, and Pamphylia south of Galatia and Lycia south of Asia, both along the Mediterranean coast.

HOWARD F. VOS

Anchor. Object used to keep a ship or boat stationary in the water. An anchor is attached to a ship by a cable or chain, and when thrown overboard, its weight and/or ability to dig into the sea bottom keeps the vessel from drifting. Anchors were used many centuries before the time of Christ, beginning as simple stone weights and evolving into wooden hooks weighted with lead or stone. Not long after the time of Christ, iron anchors of the familiar modern shape were used. Anchors are men-

The main entrance to the theater in Pergamum.

tioned in Luke's account of the apostle Paul's voyage to Rome (Acts 27:13,29,30,40). Hebrews 6:19 uses "anchor" in a figurative sense to indicate the immovability of God's promise of salvation to those who believe in him.

Ancient of Days. Name of God used by Daniel to describe God as judge (Dn 7:9,13,22).

See GOD, NAMES OF.

Andrew, The Apostle. One of Christ's 12 apostles. Andrew first appears in the NT as a disciple of John the Baptist (Jn 1:35,40). After hearing John say "Behold, the Lamb of God!" (Jn 1:36), referring to Jesus, Andrew and another unnamed disciple followed Jesus and stayed with him for a day (Jn 1:37–39). Andrew then told his brother, Simon Peter, that he had "found the Messiah" and brought Peter to Jesus (Jn 1:40–42). From then on Andrew faded into the background, and his brother came into prominence. Whenever the relationship of the two is mentioned, Andrew is always described as the brother of Simon Peter and never the other way around (Mt 4:18; Mk

1:16; Jn 1:40; 6:8), although Andrew is also mentioned without reference to his relationship to Peter (Mk 1:29; 3:18; 13:3; Jn 12:22). Andrew's father was John (Mt 16:17; Jn 1:42; 21:15–17), and his hometown was Bethsaida (Jn 1:44), a village on the north shore of the Sea of Galilee.

The Gospel of John mentions disciples being with Jesus (2:2; 4:2), and it is likely that Andrew was one of that early group. Evidently, however, he returned to his activity as a fisherman on the Sea of Galilee, where he shared a house with Peter and his family in Capernaum (Mt 4:18–20; Mk 1:16–20,29–33). On that occasion Andrew and Peter received a definite call to follow Jesus and become "fishers of men." From among the disciples of Jesus a group of 12 were later specially chosen as apostles. Andrew is always listed among the first four named, along with Peter and two other brothers, John and James (Mt 10:2–4; Lk 6:13–16; Acts 1:13,14).

Andrew is named in only three other contexts in the Gospels. At the feeding of the 5,000 he called attention to the boy who had five barley loaves and two fish (Jn 6:8,9). When certain Greeks came to Philip asking to see Jesus, Philip told Andrew and then the two of them told Jesus (Jn 12:20–22). Finally, Andrew is listed among those who were questioning Jesus privately on the Mt of Olives: "Tell us, when will this be, and what will be the sign when these things are all to be accomplished?" (Mk 13:3,4). The last NT mention of Andrew is in the list of apostles waiting in the upper room in Jerusalem for the promised outpouring of the Holy Spirit (Acts 1:12–14).

Various documents associated with Andrew, such as the Acts of Andrew mentioned by the early church historian Eusebius, are of doubtful value. Some traditions indicate that Andrew ministered in Scythia. According to the *Muratorian Canon*, Andrew received a revelation at night that the apostle John should write the Fourth Gospel. Tradition is rather uniform that Andrew died at Patrae in Achaia. A story developed that he was martyred on an X-shaped cross (a "decussate" or "saltire" cross), which has become known as St Andrew's Cross. Another tradition is that an arm of the dead Andrew was taken into Scotland as a relic by Regulus, and thus Andrew became known as a patron saint of Scotland. On the calendar of saints of the Roman and Greek churches, Andrew's date is set as November 30.

GEORGE W. KNIGHT III

See APOSTLE, APOSTLESHIP.

Andronicus. 1. Deputy of Seleucid king Antiochus Epiphanes. This Andronicus aroused the Jews by murdering Onias, the high priest, and was himself then executed by Antiochus (2 Mc 4:31–38).

2. Officer in charge of Gerizim after Antiochus Epiphanes sacked Jerusalem (2 Mc 5:21–23).

3. Christian greeted by the apostle Paul in his letter to the Romans (16:7), but not mentioned elsewhere. Paul called Andronicus his kinsman. The word could mean fellow countryman, fellow Jew, member of Paul's own family, or other relative. Andronicus may also have been a fellow prisoner for the cause of Christ, perhaps even in the same prison with Paul (2 Cor 6:4,5; 11:23). Paul described him as a man of "note among the apostles," and recognized him respectfully as an "older" Christian.

Anem. Town in Issachar's territory given to the priestly family of Gershom (1 Chr 6:73). It was also called Engannim (Jos 21:29) and was probably located southeast of Mt Tabor.

See LEVITICAL CITIES; ENGANNIM #2.

Anemone. Plant of the buttercup family, with cup-shaped flowers that are usually white, pink, red, or purple.

See PLANTS (LILY).

Aner (Person). Amorite ally of Abram and brother of Mamre and Eshcol (Gn 14:13). With his brothers, Aner helped Abram defeat a confederation of four kings who had plundered Sodom and Gomorrah and had captured Abram's nephew Lot (Gn 14:14–16,21–24).

Aner (Place). Levitical city in Manasseh's territory (1 Chr 6:70).

See CITIES OF REFUGE.

Anethothite, Anetothite. KJV forms of Anathothite, a resident of Anathoth, in 2 Samuel 23:27 and 1 Chronicles 27:12, respectively.

See ANATHOTH, ANATHOTHITE (PLACE).

Angel. Messenger of God or supernatural being, either good or evil, with greater than human powers.

The Concept of Angelic Beings. The only source of valid information about angels is the Bible. The cherubim (plural of "cherub," a Hebrew word) were celestial beings sent by God to guard the tree of life in the garden of Eden (Gn 3:24). They were represented symbolically on the ark of the covenant (Ex 25:18–22), in the tabernacle (Ex 26:31) and temple (2 Chr 3:7), and seen by the prophet Ezekiel in a vision of the restored Jerusalem (Ez 41:18–20). Two angels, Gabriel and the chief, or archangel, Michael, are named in the Bible (Dn 8:16; 9:21; 10:13; Lk 1:19,26; Jude 9; Rv 12:7–9).

Both Judaism and Christianity have the concept of fallen angels, of whom Satan is chief (Jb 1:6–12; Mt 25:41; 2 Pt 2:4), but neither the OT nor the NT goes into much detail about angels or demons. Scholars, poets, and artists have often gone beyond what is said about angels in the Bible. For example, the seraphim and cherubim were at times represented in the Bible as winged creatures, at least symbolically. In other passages, angels looked to observers like men clothed in white or shining garments (Lk 24:4; Acts 1:10). But even though Gabriel "flew swiftly" or "came quickly," the Bible does not describe angels as men with wings growing out of their shoulders. Some angels, however, are described in the Bible as having wings (Is 6:1–8; Ez 1:5–8,24).

Angels as Messengers. In the Bible, angels are spiritual beings who serve primarily as messengers. The English word "angel" comes directly from a Greek word for messenger. In Luke 9:52, Jesus sent "messengers" ahead of him. Usually the same word is translated "angel" and is understood to mean a spiritual messenger from God. In the OT also, one Hebrew word can refer either to a human messenger or to a spiritual being. It is not always immediately clear which is meant, especially since angels sometimes appeared in human form. In certain passages, "the angel of God" or a similar phrase may refer to God delivering his own message in a "theophany" (appearance of God himself).

Once the patriarch Abraham beheld that "three men stood in front of him" (Gn 18:2). They were clearly delivering a message from God that the elderly Abraham and Sarah would have a son. During the conversation God spoke directly (Gn 18:14). Two verses later, the men set out for Sodom, but the Lord lingered to talk to Abraham. Chapter 19 begins with "the two angels" arriving at Sodom, where they were taken to be men. Such ambiguity led a NT author to say, "Do not neglect to show hospitality to strangers, for thereby some have entertained angels unawares" (Heb 13:2).

The two major words translated "angel" appear almost 300 times from Genesis to Revelation. One or two angels, or whole hosts (armies) of angels, may appear to a specific person. The angel who announced the birth of Jesus Christ to the shepherds was joined by "a multitude of the heavenly host" praising God (Lk 2:13,14). In the garden of Gethsemane, Jesus said to one disciple, "Do you think that I cannot appeal to my Father, and he will at once send me more than twelve legions of angels?" (Mt 26:52). Such expressions as "the Lord of hosts" throughout the Bible probably refer to God as commander of an army of angels.

How the Bible Speaks of Angels. In the everyday speech of the time, humans were often compared to superhuman angels (2 Sm 14:20). Jesus said that "not even the angels" know when the end of the world will come (Mt 24:36). Peter wrote that salvation through Jesus Christ was so wonderful that it was something " . . . into which angels long to look" (1 Pt 1:12). Some passages refer to the strength or power of angels (Ps 103:20; 2 Thes 1:7; 2 Pt 2:11); others to their moral perfection (1 Sm 29:9), even though some "did not keep their own position but left their proper dwelling" (Jude 6). The reputation of angels for moral goodness was so high that Paul warned Christians of false teachers disguised as angels (Gal 1:8). Nor was Paul surprised at the success of false prophets, "for even Satan disguises himself as an angel of light" (2 Cor 11:14).

The physical appearance of angels in biblical encounters was often unusual enough to distinguish them from ordinary people. The angel who moved the stone from the entrance to Jesus' tomb had an "appearance . . . like lightning" and "raiment white as snow" (Mt 28:3). Stephen had "the face of an angel" as he prayed at his martyrdom (Acts 6:15), probably a peaceful and holy expression uncommon in such a circumstance.

Many passages about angels are descriptions of dreams or visions. "Jacob's ladder" with angels ascending and descending (Gn 28:12) is an example. In another dream an angel spoke to Jacob (Gn 31:11). An angel appeared to Cornelius in a vision (Acts 10:1–3). Major passages of this type include Isaiah 6 (the seraphim), much of the Book of Ezekiel (the cherubim), and much of Daniel and Zechariah. In the NT, over a third of the references to angels are in the Book of Revelation. In most cases there, the angelic beings are glorious or grotesque figures seen in visions and not to be confused with human persons. The language describing such visions is appropriately mystical, or at least metaphorical and difficult to interpret.

Two passages are thought by many to describe the fall of Satan and other angels. "How you are fallen from heaven, O Day Star, son of Dawn!" (Is 14:12) occurs in a denunciation of the king of Babylon. "You were in Eden" (Ez 28:13) occurs in a denunciation of the king of Tyre. If the two human tyrants were seen as personifications of evil, the statements about Satan could be regarded as metaphorical. Passages that clearly refer to the fall of angels (2 Pt 2:4; Jude 6) do not go into detail.

Some theologians think that Genesis 6:1–6 refers to fallen angels when it mentions "sons of God" who had sexual relations with women. That interpretation is based in part on Job 1:6–12, in which "the sons of God came to present themselves before the Lord, and Satan came also among them" (KJV).

Christian Angelology. Angelology, the doctrine of angels, is not a major theme in Christian theology in spite of the many references to angels in the Bible.

Spiritual Creatures. Angels are included in descriptions of all that God created (Ps 148:2; Col 1:16). There are hints that they witnessed the creation of the world (Jb 38:7). No matter how close to God angels may be, they share with humankind the status of creatures. But as wholly spiritual creatures they are free from many human limitations, such as death (Lk 20:36). They do not marry (Mt 22:30), so they could be regarded as sexless; in all biblical appearances of angels in human form they were taken to be men, never women or children. Their ability to communicate in human language and to affect human life in other ways is basic to their role in the Bible. Their power (Mt 28:2) and awesome appearance (vv3,4) sometimes tempted people to fear or worship them, but the NT does not condone the worship of angels (Col 2:18; Rv 22:8,9). Though angels are stronger and wiser than human beings, their power and knowledge are also limited by God (Ps 103:20; Mt 24:36; 1 Pt 1:11,12; 2 Pt 2:11).

Relationship to Christ. The apostle John had a vision of angels surrounding the throne of God (Rv 5:11). Paul once gave a particularly solemn command to Timothy "in the presence of God and of Christ Jesus and of the elect angels" (1 Tm 5:21). Christ became "much superior to angels as the name he has obtained is more excellent than theirs" (Heb 1:4). "When he brings the first-born into the world, he says, 'Let all God's angels worship him'" (Heb 1:6). "But to what angel has he ever said, 'Sit at my right hand, till I make thy enemies a stool for thy feet'? Are they not all ministering spirits sent forth to serve, for the sake of those who are to obtain salvation?" (Heb 1:13,14). Psalm 8 is quoted as referring to Christ, made "for a little while lower than the angels" (Heb 2:7,8).

Fallen Angels. Before Christ's final victory, Satan (literally "the adversary") must first be conquered. On earth Jesus cast out demons "by the Spirit of God" (Mt 12:28). When his disciples discovered that the demons were subject to him, Jesus said, "I saw Satan fall like lightning from heaven" (Lk 10:18). As his crucifixion drew near, Jesus said the time had come when ". . . the ruler of this world be cast out" (Jn 12:31). Many indirect references identify Satan as an angel who sinned because of pride, and Revelation 12:7–9 describes "war in heaven" in which the archangel Michael and his angels fought against Satan and his fallen angels. Although Christians are warned to be on guard against Satan who is still the "prince of the power of the air" (Eph 2:2), there is no biblical basis for excessive fear of the devil or evil spirits.

Earthly Functions. Meanwhile, "of the angels he says, 'Who makes his angels winds, and his servants flames of fire" (Heb 1:7; cf. Ps 104:4). Angels appeared to many of God's people in the Bible to announce good news (Jgs 13:3), warn of danger (Gn 19:15), guard from evil (Dn 3:28; 6:22), guide and protect (Ex 14:19), nourish (Gn 21:14–20; 1 Kgs 19:4–7), or instruct (Acts 7:38; Gal 3:19). When Christ came to earth as the Savior, angels heralded his birth (Lk 2:8–15), guided and warned his parents (Mt 2:13), strengthened him when he was tempted (Mt 4:11) and in his last distress (Lk 22:43), and participated in his resurrection (Mt 28:1–6). Jesus spoke about the guardian angels of little children (Mt 18:10). Philip was guided by an angel (Acts 8:26). Apostles were rescued from prison by an angel (Acts 5:19; 12:7–11). In a frightening situation, the apostle Paul was encouraged by an angel (Acts 27:21–25).

Role in Judgment. Christians expect angels to accompany Christ at his triumphant return (Mt 25:31; Acts 1:10,11; 1 Thes 4:16; 2 Thes 1:7). Angels will participate in the last judgment, even as they have exercised God's judgment before. It was an angel who struck Herod Agrippa dead (Acts 12:21–23). The Destroyer, whose "passing over" the Israelites as he smote the Egyptians is celebrated in the Jewish Passover (Ex 12:21–27), may have been a "death angel."

The Holy Spirit. Since NT times, many of the works previously entrusted by God to his angels have been part of the Holy Spirit's function in the lives of believers in Christ. In his guidance, illumination, protection, and empowering of Christians, the Spirit nonetheless may continue to employ angels for the sake of God and his people.

WALTER R. HEARN *and* HOWARD F. VOS

See CHERUB, CHERUBIM; SERAPH, SERAPHIM; DEMON, DEMON POSSESSION; SATAN; ANGEL OF THE LORD.

Bibliography. G.B. Caird, *Principalities and Powers;* W. Carr, *Angels and Principalities;* J. Daniélou, *The Angels and the Mission; According to the Fathers of the Church;* B. Graham, *Angels: God's Secret Agents;* A. Whyte, *The Nature of Angels.*

Angel of the Lord. Angelic being mentioned in the Bible, more properly translated the "messenger" of the Lord. In the OT the angel of the Lord, as God's personal emissary, performed special functions at particular times in the history of Israel.

The OT references portray a variety of services rendered but a basic unity of purpose: the gracious intervention of the Lord toward his people, sometimes to an individual, sometimes on a national scale. The angelic figure served Israel positively as guide and protector (Ex 14:19) and companion in the wilderness wanderings (Ex 23:20; 33:2; Nm 20:16) or negatively as assassin or destroyer (2 Sm 24:16), yet always acted to preserve the sanctity of Israel's covenant with God. Certain individuals such as Hagar (Gn 16:7; 21:17), Balaam (Nm 22:21,22), and Abraham's servant (Gn 24:7,40) were also confronted by the divinely commissioned messenger (cf. further references 1 Sm 29:9; 2 Sm 14:20; 19:27; 1 Kgs 19:7; 2 Kgs 19:35; 1 Chr 21:15; 2 Chr 32:21).

Who is the angel of the Lord? Some theologians have observed the close connection between the Lord and his messenger and have tried to explain this association as a result of Israel's taking over the idea of divine emissaries from its neighbors. Although there may be certain external linguistic and conceptual points of contact with the religions of ancient Mesopotamia and Egypt, for example, those religions spoke of celestial messengers which had acquired an independent existence. Unlike the messenger of the Lord, who is always dependent upon the existence of the Lord and subordinate to his command, the Mesopotamian and Egyptian envoys were really messenger-gods in their own right—and so fragmented the divine world in a way unacceptable to monotheistic Israel.

A second theory sees in the messenger a concept unique to Israel. As a nation, Israel developed complex and expansive traditions to narrate and proclaim the activity of God encountered in their history.

These traditions reflect the concern to preserve for Israel certain characteristics of its faith. First, while God throughout the patriarchal period may have disclosed himself by a variety of names and at a number of places (Gn 16:13; 31:13; Ex 3:6), Israel nevertheless believed that he was "one." The presence of the messenger of the Lord, in whom God's "name" resides (Ex 23:20) unites otherwise disparate accounts and assures the hearer/reader that it is one God who directs the course of history (Gn 16:7; 31:11; Ex 3:2). Further, despite its repeated witness to God's direct intervention, Israel recognized his apartness, his otherness. He was above and beyond creation

and was not to be identified with some part of it. Confrontation with the God of Israel was an awesome experience; indeed it was believed impossible to live through such an event (Ex 33:20). The figure of the messenger reflects Israel's perception of God's distinctiveness and the impossibility of realizing his complete presence. By remaining distinct from God and yet carrying out in person the activity of God himself, the messenger maintains Israel's tradition that God is both "far" and "near."

A third suggestion, coming from the time of the early church fathers, is that one can see in this figure the pre-existent "Word of God": Jesus Christ, the second person of the Trinity functioning in the OT. In certain texts, it seems impossible to distinguish between the angel of the Lord and the Lord himself (Gn 16:7–13; 21:17; 22:11–18; 24:7,40; 31:11–13; 48:16; Ex 3:2–10; Jgs 6:12–14; 13:21,22). Sometimes the angel is depicted acting for the Lord and yet is addressed as the Lord. God says "you cannot see my face; for man shall not see me and live" (Ex 33:20), and yet Hagar (Gn 16:13), Jacob (Gn 32:30), and Moses (Ex 33:11) are said to have "seen God face to face" in view of their confrontation with this angel. God promises that his very presence will be among the Israelites, and yet it is the angel who goes with them (Ex 23:23). The commander of the army of God is given reverence equal to God's (Jos 5:13–6:2). The angel seems to possess the full authority and character of God.

Some theologians think that to consider the angel of the Lord as the pre-incarnate Son of God, the Logos, is to disregard the "creaturely" character of this messenger and his clearly subordinate status to the Lord. Yet it is not inconsistent to think that the subordinate ministry of the second person of the Trinity begins as a mediatorial role between God and man in the OT.

This messenger of the Lord is an important figure, mysterious as well as intriguing, but certainly believed, reverenced, and obeyed by those confronted by him.

See ANGEL; THEOPHANY.

Anger. The word normally used in the Bible to refer to an emotion considered sinful. Psalm 37:8, for example, commands: "Refrain from anger, and forsake wrath!" Jesus paralleled anger with murder when he said that "every one who is angry with his brother shall be liable to judgment" (Mt 5:22) just as if he had actually committed the murder he felt in his angry heart. Ephesians 4:31 and Colossians 3:8 both list anger, along with bitterness, wrath, malice, and slander, as attitudes which Christians must rid themselves of once and for all. In his list of attributes for a bishop or pastor of a church, the apostle Paul said that a Christian leader should not be prone to anger, that is, easily provoked (Ti 1:7).

Anger of a good sort is also spoken of in the Bible. "Righteous indignation" refers to the extreme displeasure of a holy heart unable to tolerate sin of any kind. The anger of God contains this element: man should be good, yet he sins—and God is angry "because they forsook the covenant of the Lord, the God of their fathers, which he made with them when he brought them out of the land of Egypt, and went and served other gods and worshiped them, gods whom they had not known and whom he had not allotted to them" (Dt 29:25,26). It was in that sense also that Moses' anger burned on Mt Sinai and caused him to smash the tablets of the Law on the ground when he saw the golden calf and Israel's idolatry (Ex 32:19).

In the NT, Mark says that Jesus looked with anger at the Pharisees, who were hoping to catch him breaking their law (Mk 3:5). Jesus' anger was also shown in his cleansing of the temple (Jn 2:13–22); it should have been a place of prayer but was being used as a place of business—Jesus "drove out all who sold and bought in the temple, and he overturned the tables of the money-changers and the seats of those who sold pigeons" (Mt 21:12). His holy indignation was neither a weakness nor a sin. Such anger is an appropriate response to iniquity and injustice, especially when they are apparently unpunished.

The apostle Paul encouraged that kind of anger with a direct command: "Be angry but do not sin" (Eph 4:26a). Evidently he felt that righteous indignation could easily turn into unholy anger and sinful wrath, so he added some explanatory prohibitions: "Do not let the sun go down on your anger, and give no opportunity to the devil" (Eph 4:26b,27a). The longer a person allows permissible anger to continue, the greater the danger that it will develop sinful qualities, giving Satan a foothold for attack. James cautions, "Be quick to hear, slow to speak, slow to anger" (Jas 1:19).

The proper kind of anger on the human plane is related to the anger sometimes spoken of as "the wrath of God." In the OT, God's anger is usually directed against sin and sinners. For example, "Then the anger of the Lord was kindled against Moses" because of his excuses (Ex 4:14); and "so the anger of the Lord was kindled against Israel" because of their idolatry (Jgs 2:14). God cannot sin or even be tempted with sin of any kind (Jas 1:13); hence he cannot tolerate sin in his people. God's anger is not an unreasonable, un-warranted, or arbitrary passion but a result of the conflict between his holiness and sin.

The believer should understand that there is appropriate and inappropriate anger and attempt to insure that his anger, like God's, is proper to the situation.

WESLEY L. GERIG

Aniam. Shemida's son from Naphtali's tribe (1 Chr 7:19).

Anim. One of 44 cities of the hill country given to Judah's tribe in the allotment of the land (Jos 15:50). Anim is probably modern Khirbet Ghowein et-Tahta.

Animals. In biblical usage, nonhuman members of the animal kingdom. Animals are mentioned throughout the Bible from Genesis to Revelation. Many species have become extinct in various parts of the world, and the Holy Land is no exception; many animals of Bible times are extinct today. In 1965 a program was inaugurated by the Hai Bar Society of Israel, a private conservation agency, to save the rare and endangered animals of Bible lands, particularly those living in the desert. Land for a reserve was contributed by the government of Israel, and in 1968 the society began to acquire species of animals mentioned in the Bible from American and European zoos, from animal dealers, and from live trapping in the wild in other countries for breeding purposes. In 1971 a group of Americans concerned with conservation organized the Holy Land Conservation Fund to help the Hai Bar Society develop wildlife reserves in Israel.

At present two reserves are owned and operated. One of the reserves was opened to the public in late 1977. It is an 8,000-acre desert refuge near Yotvatah, about 12 miles north of Eilat in the Negeb desert. Some animals that had become extinct in Israel have been reintroduced there, including the addax antelope, Somali wild ass, scimitar-horned oryx, Ethiopian ostrich, and Persian onager. The Arabian oryx is being restored through breeding. The reserve also includes penned areas for domestic predators including wolves, striped hyenas, and the jungle cats.

The society's second reserve is on Mt Carmel. The land, donated by the City of Haifa, is 2,000 acres of heavy woodlands for temperate-zone animals. At present only the common gazelle and European deer inhabit it. The society hopes to introduce the Mesopotamian fallow deer, red sheep, mountain sheep, and wild goat.

The society also owns an undeveloped area in Galilee called Nahel Dishon which it hopes to develop into a nature reserve when funds permit.

At the time the Hai Bar Society's program began, small numbers of Nubian ibex, Palestinian gazelle, dorcas gazelle, and Arabian gazelle subsisted in Palestine. Through strict hunting laws, which the society encouraged, the population of a number of those animals has risen dramatically so that the Palestinian gazelle is no longer endangered. The ibex now numbers over 1,000. Recently the rare Sinai leopard was seen and photographed in the Judean desert and in the Jordan River valley by members of the society, who hope to assist in bringing it back.

Animals figured in many important biblical events, including the creation, the fall of man, the flood, the ten plagues in Egypt, the Hebrew worship system, and the life of Jesus Christ. The people of both OT and NT times lived close to the land and were well acquainted with various animals so that the scriptural writers and Jesus himself frequently used animals as object lessons.

The biblical approach to classification of animals is somewhat different from the system of classification used by biologists today. The present system of classification, which traces back to Carolus Linnaeus (an 18th-century Swedish botanist), is based on structure, both internal and external. The biblical basis of classification is habitat. Thus Genesis speaks of aquatic organisms (Gn 1:20); aerial organisms (v 21); creeping things (v 24); cattle or domesticated animals (v 24); and wild animals or "beasts of the earth" (v 24). The same system of classification is followed in Leviticus 11 and throughout Scripture.

Because of the divergence between systems of classification, the various animals of the Bible will be listed here in alphabetical order—including reptiles, fish, and even invertebrates such as insects, spiders, worms, and sponges. Birds are discussed in a separate article.

Adder. One of the 20 poisonous snakes found in Israel and surrounding countries, also referred to as cockatrice and asp. True vipers (genus *Cerastes, Echis colorata,* and *Vipera palestina*) exist there, poisonous snakes with curved fangs that spring into position when the snake strikes. The horned viper (*Cerastes hasselquistii*) may attack horses. It is 12 to 18 inches long and often lies in ambush in the sand with only its eyes and the hornlike protrusions on its head visible.

Both Jesus and John the Baptist referred to the viper several times (Mt 3:7; 12:34; 23:33). The reference in Acts 28:3 is probably to a small viper (*Vipera aspis*) that strikes rapidly and is very pugnacious. It is found in southern Europe and hisses each time it inhales and exhales. The poison of vipers attacks the respiratory system and disintegrates red blood cells.

See SERPENT, BELOW.

Ant. Social insects common in the Holy Land, though the ant is mentioned only twice in the Bible, both times in the Book of Proverbs. For many years Solomon was charged with a biological error when he referred to the ant as providing her meat in the summer and gathering her food in the harvest (Prv 6:8). Critics of the Bible were quick to point out that, so far as was then known, ants do not store up food. They assumed that Solomon had probably kicked open an ant hill and mistaken the pupal cases (pods in which immature ants grow to maturity) which he saw there for grain or had observed ants carrying bits of grain, leaves, and other matter to their nests.

At least three species of grain-storing ants are now known—two occur in Israel and the other in Mediterranean countries. The particular species referred to by Solomon (Prv 6:6–8; 30:24,25) is probably the harvester ant (*Messor semirufus*). Its granaries are flat chambers connected by galleries irregularly scattered over an area about six feet in diameter and about a foot deep in the ground. Seeds are collected from the ground or picked from plants. The head, or radicle, which is the softest part of the kernel, is bitten off to prevent germination, and the chaff and empty capsules are discarded on kitchen middens (refuse piles) outside the nest. Individual granaries may be 5 inches in diameter and a half-inch high. Some nests are known to be up to 40 feet in diameter and 6 to 7 feet deep with several entrances.

Antelope. One of several antelope-like creatures referred to in the Scriptures. One seems to be the white oryx (*Oryx leucoryx*), referred to in Deuteronomy 14:5 (KJV wild ox; RSV antelope) and Isaiah 51:20 (KJV wild bull; RSV antelope). The Isaiah reference (51:20) indicates that the animal was strong, since hunting with nets was used only for larger game. A rope was stretched tightly along the ground in a ravine near the animal's favorite haunts. A net with smaller rope was attached alongside and allowed to droop over poles which were not tightly fixed in the ground. When the animal was driven into the net, it collapsed upon him and entangled him so that waiting hunters could then make an easy kill.

The oryx was probably the antelope, commonly used for food because its long horns made it relatively easy to catch.

Another antelope mentioned in the Bible is the addax (*Addax nasomaculatus*), probably the "pygarg" of Deuteronomy 14:5 (KJV). It is a native of North Africa with grayish-white hinder parts, a white patch on the forehead, and twisted and ringed horns. The word "pygarg" comes from a Greek word meaning "white rump."

The addax is about the size of a donkey. Its body is closely covered with short hair. It has a short mane on the underside of its neck which makes the head look somewhat like that of a goat. The hooves are broad and flat, and the tail resembles that of a donkey. It is common in Africa and in Arabia, where Arabs hunt it with falcons and dogs. The addax can outrun dogs alone.

Antelopes are very graceful and run with their heads held high. Both sexes have long, permanent hollow horns. With the oryx the horns go straight back; addax horns are twisted and ringed. Antelope are alert, wary, and keen-sighted. They are usually found in herds of from two to a dozen. If injured or brought to bay, an antelope attacks with its head lowered so that the sharp horns point forward. Antelopes feed on grasses and shrubs, drinking from streams and water holes. When water is scarce, they eat melons and succulent bulbs. Both addax and oryx were ceremonially clean in Jewish law.

Ape. Primate not native to Palestine. The two references to apes in the OT (1 Kgs 10:22; 2 Chr 9:21) refer to their importation by King Solomon with other treasures on board the ships of his mercantile fleet. There is some question concerning the origin of those primates. Some believe that mention of "ivory" in the same verses suggests they came from East Africa and that they were indeed apes, that is, tailless primates. Others, believing they came from India or Ceylon, suggest that they were actually monkeys. There the baboon (genus *Papio*), a large monkey, was considered sacred to the god Thoth. Males of that genus were kept in temples, and the more docile females were often kept as house pets. Such baboons frequently had some of their teeth removed or ground down to lessen the danger of their biting. A number of mummified baboons have been found in Egypt, indicating the high regard in which they were held.

The Israelites may have been familiar with the Barbary apes of North Africa (*Macaca sylvana*) or with species of African monkeys other than *Papio hamadryas*.

Asp. Poisonous snake. Most biblical references to the asp (Dt 32:33) seem to be to the Egyptian cobra (*Naja haje*), which conceals itself in holes, walls, and rocks and has the ability to expand its neck by raising its anterior ribs so as to enlarge the front of its breast into the shape of a flat disc. Its potent poison may lead to death within 30 minutes. It attains a length of about 80 inches. The fangs are permanently erect, not movable as in the vipers (the common poisonous snakes of North America; only the coral snake in America has permanently erect fangs). Cobra poison attacks the nervous system, causing muscular paralysis. The Egyptians looked upon it as a sacred creature, regarding it as a protector since it fed on the rodents which ate their crops. The "fiery serpents" (Nm 21:6; Dt 8:15) may have been cobras; "fiery" probably refers to the burning fever caused by their venom. Isaiah 14:29 and 30:6 ("flying serpent") may refer to the hood of the cobra.

See SERPENT, BELOW.

Ass (Donkey). Beast of burden. The ass of the Holy Land (*Equus asinus*) was quite different from the European ass of today, which is usually a small, stubborn, malicious animal. In biblical times the ass was a beautiful, stately, friendly animal. Its color was usually reddish brown. Three wild races have been described, all from Africa. The race from northwest Africa is extinct; the one from northeast Africa, if not extinct, is close to extinction; the Somalian race, which survives, did not play an important part in domestication. The northeast African race, the Nubian ass, was evidently domesticated in the Nile River region in early historic times. The ass was used as a mount from the time of domestication on. It is first mentioned in the Bible among the animals that Abraham acquired in Egypt (Gn 12:16). The ass was primarily a beast of burden, driven but not bridled. From the time of the Middle Kingdom on (c. 2040 BC), it was used for riding in Egypt, but only the Jews and Nubians rode asses regularly. The ass was also used for threshing grain and for pulling the plow. In Arab countries today peasants plow with an ass and a cow or camel hitched together. In Israel the law forbade plowing with an ass and an ox hitched together (Dt 22:10). Until the time of Solomon (960 BC), horses were not used in Palestine. From that time on, the horse was ridden by warriors; the ass was used by those who were traveling peaceably.

The ass was held in high regard by the Jews and was considered an economic asset. An individual had to have an ass for minimum existence (Jb 24:3), and wealth was frequently counted by the number of asses one possessed (Gn 12:16; 24:35). The ass was considered an acceptable gift (Gn 32:13–15). It was allowed to rest on the Sabbath (Dt 5:14). Women in biblical times often used the ass as a riding animal (Jos 15:18; 1 Sm 25:23; 2 Kgs 4:24); often a special driver would help a woman guide the animal, running along at its side. If a married couple possessed only one ass, the husband usually walked alongside while the wife rode (Ex 4:20).

No real saddle was used in riding an ass; a covering was merely tied on its back and a halter affixed. That seems to have been the purpose of the disciples' putting their garments on the ass ridden by Jesus on Palm Sunday (Mt 21:7).

The people of Israel returning from Babylon had ten times as many asses as horses and camels (Ezr 2:66,67; Neh 7:68,69). Job's wealth was indicated by the fact that he had 500 she-asses before catastrophe hit him (Jb 1:3); after his recovery he had 1,000 asses (Jb 42:12). Joseph's brothers used asses to transport the grain they purchased in Egypt (Gn 42:26; 43:24). Abigail transported food on asses to David and his troops during their conflict with Saul (1 Sm 25:18). David assigned one of the 12 managers of his royal estates to look after his asses exclusively (1 Chr 27:30).

The onager or Syrian wild ass (*Equus hemionus hemihippus*) is an intermediate between the true horse and the true ass. Its ears are longer than those of a horse but shorter than those of an ass. The front hooves are narrow; there are chestnuts (callouslike spots on the inside of the knees) on the front legs only, and the tail is short-haired for a long distance from its root so that it appears to be tufted.

The Sumerians (ancient Mesopotamians) were able to domesticate the onager, which was eventually replaced by the horse. It was used to draw chariots in Ur; a number of onagers were buried with their vehicles in a royal grave that dates from about 2500 BC. Later the wild onager was a favorite hunter's prize for Babylonian and Assyrian kings.

The onager was very common in the steppe lands near Israel where it was described as a freedom-loving desert animal (Jb 24:5; 39:5–8; Ps 104:11; Is 32:14; Jer 2:24; Hos 8:9). Ishmael was described as "a wild ass of a man" (Gn 16:12), one who could not adjust to domestic life. Nebuchadnezzar lived among the wild asses when he was mentally ill (Dn 5:21). Drought seems to have been responsible for the population decline of the onager in biblical times (Jer 14:6). The modern onager (*Equus hemionus onager*) is slightly larger than the Syrian wild ass which is extinct.

See TRAVEL AND TRANSPORTATION.

Badger. Small ungulate mammal. Scholars agree that the RSV translation, "badger" (Ps 104:18; Prv 30:26) or "rock badger" (Lv 11:5; Dt 14:7), for the animal translated "coney" in KJV is incorrect. The biblical coney was undoubtedly the Syrian rock hyrax (*Hyrax syriaca*), the only species of hyrax found outside Africa. This small ungulate (having hoof-like toenails) lives among rocks from the Dead Sea valley to Mt Hermon. It is strictly a herbivorous (plant-eating) animal about the size of a hare. It resembles a guinea pig more than a rabbit, having quite inconspicuous ears and a very small tail. It has broad nails with four toes on its forelegs and three on its hind legs, the toes being connected with skin almost like a web. Pads acting as sucking discs under its feet enable it to keep its footing on slippery rocks. With its yellow and brown fur, it is sometimes called the bear rat because of its resemblance to a tailless rat. It is also equipped with black whiskers that may be 7 inches long.

Coneys, or hyraxes, live together in colonies of from 6 to 50 animals, often sunning themselves on rocks. They are difficult to catch. Guards are posted and if approaching danger is sighted, the whole group will scurry for cover, warned by the sharp whistles of the guards. Thus they are commended for taking refuge in the rocks (Ps 104:18) and are called "exceedingly wise" for making "their houses in the rocks" (Prv 30:24,26 KJV). Although they are called a "feeble folk" (Prv 30:26 KJV), when cornered they will fight back and are capable of inflicting painful bites with their incisors. They are most active during the day but also come out on warm moonlit nights.

The coney is not a ruminant (does not chew its cud), but the motion of its jaws may suggest that it chews its cud. That is probably why it was included with other cud-chewing animals in the Jewish food laws (Lv 11:5; Dt 14:7). It was forbidden to the Jews as food because it did not have cloven hooves. Some Arabs eat and even prize its meat.

Scholars also agree that the KJV translation, "badgers' skins," for a material used to make the tabernacle covering (e.g., Ex 25:5; Nm 4:6,8,10–12,14) or sandals (Ez 16:10) is correct.

Bat. Flying mammals according to modern classification. They have hair and provide milk for their young. The Bible classifies them with other aerial creatures. Bats take shelter in caves, crevices, tree cavities, buildings, and also in exposed places on trees. In colder areas they hibernate or migrate. The normal resting position for a bat is hanging head downward. Bats "swim" through the air rather than fly because they move with their legs as well as with their wings.

The bat's thumb is free and terminates in a single hook claw used for climbing and hanging. The hind feet have five toes, all pointing the same way. The large chest accommodates the powerful muscles needed for flying. Because they orient themselves by echo location, the sense of hearing is very well developed.

Most bats are insect-eaters, seizing insects in flight. Many insectivorous bats also eat some fruit. Other bats feed exclusively, usually in groups, on fruit and green vegetation.

Fruit-eating bats generally live in the tropics where fruit is constantly ripening, although some have been found in the Holy Land. These bats tend to be larger than the insectivores, having a wingspread of up to 5 feet.

A third group includes flower-eating bats which feed on pollen and nectar. These small bats with long pointed heads and long tongues are found only in tropic and semitropical regions. Three species of vampire bats, which do not occur in the Holy Land, eat blood by making a small incision and lapping it up. Carnivorous (meat-eating) bats prey on birds, lizards, and frogs. Fish-eating bats catch fish at or near the water surface.

Eight varieties of bats are known in the Holy Land. One of them, the little brown bat (genus *Myotis*) is worldwide in its distribution. It is insectivorous and probably has the widest distribution of any nonhuman terrestrial mammal. Brown bats are mostly cave-dwellers. The females form maternity colonies that may number in the tens of thousands.

Two species of mouse-tailed bats (genus *Rhinopoma*) are found in the Holy Land. Their tails are nearly as long as the head and body combined. They too are colonial, roosting in caves, rock clefts, wells, pyramids, palaces, and houses. Like the brown bat, they are insectivorous. The slit-faced or hollow-faced bats (genus *Nycteris*) are also found in the Holy Land. They are insectivorous and roost in groups of from 6 to 20.

The bats found in the Holy Land vary in size from that of a mouse to the size of a rat; the largest species measures more than 20 inches across the wings.

The bat was unclean to the Jews (Lv 11:19; Dt 14:18) and was also considered a symbol of desolation (Is 2:20,21).

Bear. Large, heavy, big-headed mammal with short, powerful limbs, a short tail, and small eyes and ears. Bears have a "plantigrade" walk: they walk on both the sole and heel as humans do. The Palestinian bear is a Syrian version of the brown bear (*Ursus arctos syriacus*). It can grow to a height of 6 feet and may weigh as much as 500 pounds.

Bears have an excellent sense of smell but less developed senses of sight and hearing. They are omnivorous (eating any kind of food); they subsist largely on vegetation, fruits, insects, and fish.

Bears are usually peaceful and inoffensive, but if they think they must defend themselves (Lam 3:10) or their young (2 Sm 17:8; Prv 17:12; Hos 13:8) they may be formidable and dangerous adversaries. David boasted of his role as a bear-killer (1 Sm 17:34–37). Since a blow from a bear's paw can be fatal, David's courage and strength as a young shepherd in running after a bear and wrenching one of his father's sheep from its jaws were noteworthy.

Some biblical passages seem to imply that bears attacked for no apparent reason (e.g., Prv 28:15; Am 5:19). At other times they were God's instruments of punishment, as in the story of Elisha and the 2 she-bears (2 Kgs 2:24). The bear and the lion, often mentioned together in the Bible (1 Sm 17:37), were the 2 largest and strongest beasts of prey in the Holy Land. Thus they symbolized both strength and terror (Am 5:19).

In biblical times bears seem to have roamed all over Palestine. Today they are found only in the Lebanon and Anti-Lebanon mountains, and even there they are rare.

Bee. One of two domesticated insects (*Apis mellifica*), the other being the silkworm. Bees gather nectar from flowers, transferring pollen from one flower to another in the process. It is believed that they convey the location of sources of nectar to other bees through a bee "dance," which may indicate both distance and direction. Bees are sensitive to four colors: blue-green, yellow-green, blue-violet, and ultra-violet (invisible to humans).

The wild bees of the Holy Land are especially noted for their ferocity in attack. Only the female "worker" bees sting people and animals, the virulence of their venom increasing in warm weather. A number of biblical passages allude to the irritable, vindictive nature of bees and to the painful stings they inflict (Dt 1:44; Ps 118:12; Is 7:18).

One reference calls attention to the fact that in semidesert regions a dead animal's carcass, stripped to the bone by jackals or vultures and dried in the sun, can provide wild bees an excellent place to start a new colony (Jgs 14:5–9).

The Egyptians considered the bee sacred. In ancient Greece candles were made from beeswax. In the Holy Land, beekeeping was probably not practiced until the Hellenistic period (c. second century BC), although Ezekiel 27:17 suggests that it may have been practiced earlier. If domestic honey was not available to the Hebrews, wild honey certainly was, and travelers would be on the lookout for caches of honey in rocky clefts and other likely places. The Philistines and the Hittites practiced beekeeping in their cities.

The Bible contains many references to bees and bee products. A bee swarm was a valuable asset, though the price of honey itself was low. Honey was sometimes eaten with the honeycomb (Sg 5:1). Honey also had uses other than food, e.g., in embalming.

The land of Israel was described as a land flowing with milk and honey. Honey was a major source of sweetening in the ancient

Near East; hence its importance (cf. Jgs 14:8,9). Actually the Hebrew word for "honey" may include not only bee honey but also the sweet syrup extracted from such fruits as figs, dates, and grapes. Thus "a land flowing with milk and honey" (Ex 3:8) does not necessarily stand for a land of bees but for a land rich in sweetness.

See FOOD AND FOOD PREPARATION; HONEY.

Behemoth. Large beast of problematic interpretation. Some early interpreters thought it referred to the elephant, others to the wild ox, the mammoth, or any large animal. Today it is generally agreed that the reference is to the hippopotamus (*Hippopotamus amphibius*), a large, thick-skinned amphibious mammal, an ungulate (having hooflike toenails) with a large head, a bulky, hairless body, and short legs.

The description in Job 40:15–24 fits closely the modern hippopotamus except for depiction of the tail. At present the hippopotamus is found only in the rivers of Africa, but there is fossil evidence that it has existed in the Holy Land, perhaps in the swamps of northern Galilee and the Jordan Valley.

The hippopotamus has highly developed sense organs, placed in such a way that it can see, hear, and smell almost without being seen; its eyes, ears, and nostrils can reach above water while the rest of the animal lies submerged. It has a large mouth, large tusks, and a short, heavy throat. The strong legs are so short that the belly almost reaches the ground when the animal is on the land. The hippopotamus lives on plants and herbs growing in rivers, but if food is scarce there it forages on land, usually at night. In spite of its heavy body it is surprisingly agile on land.

Camel. Large beast of burden. Unintelligent, ill-natured, and quarrelsome, the camel (*Camelus dromedarius*) is nevertheless a blessing to people living in the desert and on its borders because it is especially adapted to

that habitat. It has been called the ship of the desert. Having thick elastic pads of fibrous tissue on its feet, it can walk on hot desert sands. It can go without water for long periods, and can subsist on vegetation growing on the saline soils. The camel's nostrils are pinched together and can be closed at will to prevent penetration of sand during violent sandstorms.

Camels are used for transporting both goods and people. A person riding a camel can cover from 60 to 75 miles in a day. A camel can carry a load weighing 600 pounds or more. Camels were used heavily in the spice trade (Gn 37:25) and traveled regularly in camel trains between Arabia, Egypt, and Assyria. They were also ridden in time of war (Jgs 6:5). A camel can even be hitched to a plow in areas where the land is cultivated.

The hair shed by camels during the early spring is preserved and used in weaving cloth and making tents. As much as 10 pounds of hair can be sheared from one camel. A rough cloak of camel's hair, as worn by John the Baptist (Mt 3:4), is still worn by Bedouins today. A camel's hair garment was also the sign of the prophetic office (Zec 13:4).

Two varieties of camel occur within the one-humped species, the slow burden-bearing camel referred to in Genesis 37:25 and the fast dromedary of 1 Samuel 30:17.

The dromedary can stand 7 feet tall and measure as much as 9 feet from the muzzle to the tip of the tail. With its three-chambered stomach, which can hold from 15 to 30 quarts of liquid, it can go for as long as 5 days during the summer or 25 days in winter without drinking. The camel's hump is a reserve store of fat, making it possible for the animal to subsist on very little food during a desert journey.

Another species of camel, the Bactrian camel (*Camelus bactrianus*), is also resident in the Holy Land. It has two humps. It is heavier, bigger, and has longer hair than the one-humped camel, and is slower than the swift dromedary. Isaiah 21:7 may refer to the Bactrian camel; both kinds of camel are referred to in Esther 8:10 (KJV).

Camels ranked in importance with sheep, cattle, and asses in OT times. A third of the 66 biblical references to the camel lists it with other animals.

Camels are ruminants (cud-chewing mammals) but do not have cloven hooves. Thus they were included in the list of unclean beasts, forbidden to the Israelites as food (Lv 11:4; Dt 14:7). They are eaten by Arabs, however, who also drink their milk (cf. Gn 32:15).

Abraham had camels in Egypt (Gn 12:16). At first Job had 3,000 camels (Jb 1:3) and after

A camel.

his recovery 6,000 (Jb 42:12). Although wide use of camels does not seem to have begun until shortly before 1000 BC (Jgs 6:5), Sumerian texts from the old Babylonian period list camels and indicate that they had been domesticated. Camel bones and figurines have been found at various eastern archaeological sites dating from well before 1200 BC.

See TRAVEL AND TRANSPORTATION.

Caterpillar. Larval stage of insects characterized by complete metamorphosis. Such insects pass through four stages: egg, larva or caterpillar, pupa, and adult. Bees, flies, moths, and butterflies all pass through a larval or caterpillar stage.

The word "caterpillar" occurs four times in the RSV (1 Kgs 8:37; 2 Chr 6:28; Ps 78:46; Is 33:4). In the Book of Joel that same Hebrew word is translated "caterpillar" in KJV but "destroying locust" (1:4) and "destroyer" (2:25) in RSV. The locust and grasshopper to which the Hebrew word refers have an incomplete type of metamorphosis with only three stages: egg, nymph, and adult. The nymph is a miniature adult in which the wings are not fully developed, though their outline may be present. There are several nymph stages known as instars. The reference is to one of the last instars, in which the wing structures are still folded together and enclosed in a sac but are nevertheless clearly recognizable. That form of the insect is about an inch long.

See LOCUST, BELOW.

Cattle. Domestic animals of the bovine species (*Bos primigenius*). The OT often emphasized the beauty of cattle. Egypt was rich in cattle, especially in the Nile River delta area (Goshen) where the Hebrews settled under Joseph.

Some scholars believe that milk rather than meat was the foremost consideration in the domestication of cattle and that in early civilizations meat supplies came chiefly from wild game. Cattle also supplied strong hides that supplanted wood in the manufacture of shields. Their dung was a source of fuel when wood was scarce (Ez 4:15). They were used as beasts of burden and for plowing. Development of wheeled transportation was associated more closely with cattle than with any other animal.

The biblical term "cattle" often refers to all domesticated animals or livestock (Gn 1:24; 2:20; 7:23 KJV; 47:6,16,17; Ex 9:3–7; Nm 3:41,45). Occasionally the term was used to refer to all large domestic animals (Nm 31:9; 32:26), although sometimes the word as used in KJV refers only to sheep and goats (Gn 30:32,39,43; 31:8,10; Is 7:25; 43:23).

Probably several kinds of cattle were domesticated in the Holy Land. Small, short-legged, black or brown shorthorn cattle were found in the southern part of Judah; that type submitted easily to the yoke and was prominent in agricultural operations. Along the coast a larger variety was found, and the wild districts east of the Jordan River were populated with a breed of huge black cattle.

Cattle breeding was widely practiced by the patriarchs (cf. Gn 32:15; Jb 21:10). Strict laws in Mesopotamia, as well as in Israel, penalized the owner of a bull that gored a man or other cattle (Ex 21:28–36). Bulls were sometimes employed figuratively as pictures of strength or violence (Dt 33:17; Pss 22:12; 68:30; Is 10:13).

For breeding purposes one bull is normally adequate for about 30 cows, but many more were kept since bulls were preferred as draft animals.

Bulls were widely used in Israel for sacrifices. They had to be at least 8 days old (Lv 22:27). They might be used as a general sacrifice (Lv 22:23; Nm 23:1) or for special sacrifices (Jgs 6:25; 1 Sm 1:24). Particular sacrifices were offered at the consecration of priests (Ex 29:1), consecration of an altar (Nm 7), purification of the Levites (Nm 8), sin offerings (Lv 16), day of the new moon (Nm 28:11–14); Passover (Nm 28:19), feast of weeks (Nm 28:27), feast of trumpets (Nm 29:1,2), Day of Atonement (Nm 29:7,8), and the feast of tabernacles (Nm 29:12–38). The feast of tabernacles required the largest number of bulls for burnt offerings of all the annual feasts, with a total of 71 being slaughtered during the course of 8 days.

Calves were sometimes referred to as "sons of the herd" in the original Hebrew (Gn 18:8; 1 Sm 6:7; 14:32). The calf or heifer, a symbol of peacefulness (Is 11:6), was also used figuratively to refer to the Gentiles (Ps 68:30). A calf's head decorated the back of Solomon's throne (1 Kgs 10:19). Calves were sometimes fattened in stalls to keep them from running off weight in the field (Am 6:4; Mal 4:2; Lk 15:23) or were kept around the house; the witch of Endor kept a calf in her house which she killed and served to Saul and his men (1 Sm 28:24,25). Calves supplied veal (Gn 18:7), considered a delicacy by the wealthy; Amos referred to stall-fattened calves in a denunciation of luxurious and careless living (Am 6:4). Calves also supplied meat for all Saul's armies at the great slaughter of the Philistines (1 Sm 14:32). The "fatted calf" served roasted or boiled was gourmet fare, suitable for the finest banquet (Gn 18:7; Mt 22:4; Lk 15:23).

Cattle were subject to the law of firstlings (Ex 13:12). They were a mark of wealth (Gn 13:2) and were considered proper booty of war (Jos 8:2).

Aaron, the first high priest, made a golden

calf as a rival to the ark of the covenant (Ex 32; Dt 9:16,21). Even though he represented the calf as an image of the invisible God, it was especially offensive because the calf was a fertility symbol related to Egyptian and Canaanite practices. Two calves were later made by Jeroboam I of Israel (930–909 BC) for his shrines at Bethel and Dan (1 Kgs 12:28–33). Hosea's prophetic denunciations of calf worship were directed at those shrines (Hos 8:5,6; 13:2).

An ox is an adult castrated bull. A steer is a young ox. Oxen were used to do work (Nm 7:3; Dt 22:10; 25:4). They usually fed on grass (Nm 22:4; Ps 106:20), but they also ate straw (Is 11:7) and salted fodder (Is 30:24). They could be kept in a stable (Lk 13:15). Oxen could not be offered as sacrifices because they had been castrated (Lv 22:24). They could be used for food but were rarely eaten. Possession of an ox and an ass was regarded as the bare minimum for existence in the ancient Palestinian agriculture economy (Jb 24:3; cf. Ex 20:17).

In the Near East the buying of a yoke of oxen is to this day a major event. The first thing one does after the purchase is test the animals in the field to find out how much the dealer has exaggerated their worth (cf. Lk 14:19). An ox goad or stick could be a formidable weapon; Shamgar is said to have slaughtered 600 Philistines with one (Jgs 3:31). Jesus, in bringing Saul (who later became the apostle Paul) to faith, told him, "It hurts you to kick against the goads" (Acts 26:14).

Among several highly prized dairy products was the curd mentioned often in the OT, probably something like cottage cheese. Abraham offered his guests curds and milk with their fatted calf (Gn 18:8). When David and his followers came thirsty and exhausted to Mahanaim, the inhabitants brought them honey and curds (2 Sm 17:29; cf. Is 7:15). Cheese is also mentioned in the Bible (2 Sm 17:29).

For moving heavy objects, cows were favored over bulls because of their more docile nature. Thus cows were evidently used to transport the ark of the covenant to the land of Israel. When David recovered the ark after it had been lost for many years, that precaution was neglected. As a result the oxen drawing the ark stumbled, and a man named Uzzah, who put out his hand to prevent it from toppling over, was struck dead for profaning the ark (2 Sm 6:6,7). The ox was also used as a pack animal (1 Chr 12:40) although it did not have the endurance of the ass, camel, or mule.

See AGRICULTURE; FOOD AND FOOD PREPARATION; OFFERINGS AND SACRIFICES.

Chameleon. Lizard characterized by its ability to change color according to its surroundings (*chamaleon vulgaris*). To the Israel-ites the chameleon was ritually unclean (Lv 11:30). The Hebrew word for chameleon is derived from a word meaning "to pant." A lizard's lungs are very large, and in ancient times lizards were believed to live on air.

A chameleon's eyes move independently of each other, so at times one eye may be turned upward and the other downward. Chameleons live in trees and bushes, clinging to branches with their long tails.

See LIZARD, BELOW.

Coral. Calcareous (lime-containing) skeletons of relatively simple marine organisms (*Corallium rubrum*). Red coral from the Mediterranean and Red seas is widely used for jewelry and for medicinal purposes. While the animal is alive, the coral is green in color and shrublike in appearance, looking rather like an underwater plant since the coral animals are sessile (immobile). When the coral is removed from the water, it becomes hard and red in color. Red coral is fished with nets or cut off with sharp iron tools.

In ancient times coral was sometimes used as money along with precious stones, pearls, and gold. Some believe the biblical reference in Lamentations 4:7 is to pearls rather than to coral, but it is probable that the references in Job 28:18 and Ezekiel 27:16 are to the red coral.

Cricket. Insect of the order *Orthoptera* related to grasshoppers and locusts. According to Leviticus 11:22, the cricket was edible. The reference may be to one of the growth stages of the locust.

KJV translates the Hebrew word as "beetle." Beetles are insects with chewing mouth parts and two pairs of wings, the fore pair being hard and sheathlike and the hind pair being membranous and folded under the fore pair. Some beetles are carnivorous, others are chiefly herbivorous. Some are aquatic, some produce a secretion that blisters the skin, some damage fabrics, some damage crops, and some feed on other insects that are harmful to humans. In ancient Egypt the beetle, or sacred scarab, was a symbol of the sun god Ra. Scarab seals and amulets were extremely popular in Egypt.

Crocodile. Largest of all existing reptiles (*Crocodilus vulgaris*), attaining a length of well over 20 feet.

Crocodiles are characterized by large lizard-like bodies supported by short legs. The head terminates in a flattened snout armed with strong conical teeth, each of which is implanted in a distinct socket. New teeth growing from beneath continually replace those in use. The toes are webbed. The back and tail are protected by quadrangular horny shields of varying sizes arranged in regular rows and in contact with one another at the edges. The eyes are covered with movable lids which can be closed when the animal enters the water.

The crocodile spends most of its time in the water where it feeds mainly on fish but also on aquatic birds and even small animals that come down to the water's edge to drink. It is surprisingly fast and agile on dry land, even though its legs are so short that its belly and tail drag across the earth leaving a distinct path.

Until the beginning of the 20th century the crocodile was found in the marshes and small coastal rivers of western Palestine. The Egyptians considered it sacred.

A 1st-century Roman writer, Pliny, referred to a place in the Holy Land called Crocodeilopolis ("crocodile city") to the south of Mt Carmel, and visitors to the Holy Land as late as the 19th century reported seeing crocodiles in that general region.

The description of "Leviathan" in Job 41 seems to be based on the crocodile. The "dragon" of Ezekiel 29:3, used figuratively of the Egyptian pharaoh, seems to be a reference to the crocodile. In Jeremiah 51:34, Nebuchadnezzar seems to be pictured as a crocodile.

Some believe the reference in Leviticus 11:30 is to the "land monitor," a large lizard that lives in the deserts of southern Palestine, Sinai, and Egypt. It is up to 55 inches long with a long snout and sharp teeth.

Deer. Large ruminant (cud-chewing) animals. Only the males have antlers (branching horns). Deer antlers grow annually and are solid in contrast to those of the antelope and the gazelle. Fully developed antlers are devoid of any covering of skin or horn and, for all practical purposes, may be regarded as a mass of dead bone carried for a certain time by the living animal.

The end of the deer's muzzle is naked in all species. The stomach is divided into a series of compartments, some of which are used to store partly chewed food. The food is later regurgitated, rechewed, and finally swallowed into a section of the stomach where true digestion takes place.

Three species of deer were known in Palestine: the red deer (*Cervus elaphus*), the Persian fallow deer (*Dama mesopotamica*), the roe deer (*Capreolus capreolus*). All are now extinct there. The last deer were hunted in the Holy Land in 1914. The red deer referred to in the Bible as "hart" (male), "stag" (male), or "hind" (female) stood about 4 feet high at the shoulder. It was gregarious (living in herds or flocks), each group remaining in a definite territory. Red deer grazed and browsed during the morning and late afternoon (Lam 1:6). The sexes remained in separate herds. The red

deer was known for its leaping (Is 35:6) and sure-footedness in the mountains (Ps 18:33; Sg 2:8,9,17; 8:14; Hb 3:19). Its thirst was evident (Ps 42:1).

The antlers of the Persian fallow deer (1 Kgs 4:23) were large, flattened, and palmated (shaped like an open palm with fingers extended), and its coat was a yellow-brown. It traveled in small groups, feeding mainly on grass in the morning and evening.

The roe deer (Dt 14:5; 1 Kgs 4:23) was a small, graceful animal, dark reddish-brown in summer and yellowish-gray in winter. Its antlers were about a foot long and had 3 points. The roe deer preferred sparsely wooded valleys and the lower slopes of mountains, grazing in open grasslands. It usually associated in family groups made up of the doe and her offspring. They were shy, yet very curious. The roe deer barked like a dog when disturbed. They were excellent swimmers with all senses well developed.

There is some question as to whether the roe deer is actually referred to in such passages as 1 Kings 4:23; references may be to the fallow deer, although that animal does not seem to have lived in the southern part of Palestine around the Sinai desert because of its need for ample amounts of food and water. Fallow deer were found in northern Palestine.

The hart (the male red deer) was listed among the clean beasts that Jewish law permitted as food (Dt 12:15,22; 14:5), but deer were not listed among the animals appropriate for sacrifice. The hind (female red deer) normally gave birth to one calf at a time, though twins were born with some degree of regularity (Jb 39:1; Ps 29:9 KJV; Jer 14:5). The gestation period was about 40 weeks. When it was about to give birth, the hind looked for a secure hiding place, preferably in the dense undergrowth of the forest where it could find natural protection for the tiny calf. During the first few days after birth, the mother never went far from her young. The fawn was able to stand on its own legs a few hours after birth. The solicitous care of the hind for her calf during the first days of its life is hinted at in a touching way in Jeremiah 14:4,5, where only a severe drought is said to drive the hind from her calf. Job 39:1–4 describes the calving of the hinds. The hind illustrated grace and charm (Gn 49:21; Prv 5:19), and its dark, gentle eyes and graceful limbs were frequently used to describe the charm of a woman (Prv 5:18,19).

Dog. Probably the earliest domesticated animal (*Canis familiaris*), used very early in hunting. The modern dog is believed to have come from the Indian wolf (*Canis lupus pallipes*). The dogs of biblical times probably looked like a modern German shepherd, with short pointed ears, a pointed nose, and a long tail.

The dog was generally looked down upon in biblical times (Prv 26:11; 2 Pt 2:22), the biblical writers evidently having no familiarity with the warm, personal, human-dog relationships which we know today. The dog was pictured as a scavenger, haunting streets and dumps (Ex 22:31; 1 Kgs 22:38; Mt 15:26; Lk 16:21). Human corpses could become the spoil of dogs (2 Kgs 9:35,36). In general, dogs served the same function as vultures and other birds of prey. Most of the 41 references in the Scriptures to dogs show strong disfavor. Dogs were considered cowardly, filthy creatures. Isaiah 66:3 may point to a cult which sacrificed dogs.

Dogs used in hunting occur in paintings in Egyptian tombs, and there is a reference to dogs herding sheep in Job 30:1. One good quality of dogs highly esteemed by the Israelites was watchfulness (Is 56:10). In general, however, in biblical times "dog" was a term of contempt (1 Sm 17:43; 2 Sm 16:9) and was used of overly submissive persons (2 Sm 9:8; 2 Kgs 8:13) and of lascivious, evil persons (Is 56:10,11; Mt 7:6; Phil 3:2; Rv 22:15). The "price of a dog" (Dt 23:18) meant the earnings of a male cultic prostitute.

Dogs, like pigs, were voracious and omnivorous (eating any kind of food). Jesus used the metaphor of throwing household food scraps to scavenging dogs in response to a gentile woman's request that he heal her daughter (Mt 15:22–28; Mk 7:25–30). At the time of Jesus the word "dog" was a standard Jewish term of contempt for Gentiles who, like dogs, were considered unclean, although the diminutive form of the word, used by Jesus, softened this considerably. Seeing her faith, Jesus granted the woman's request, giving a non-Jew some of "the children's bread."

Dragon. Any one of a number of monstrous land and sea creatures. In biblical usage, "dragon" does not refer to the huge, fire-breathing, winged reptile of European folklore. The translators of KJV used the term to translate two Hebrew words that are usually rendered more precisely in modern translations. One word referred to desert animals; most scholars agree with RSV that "jackals" is its proper meaning (Ps 44:19; Is 13:22; Jer 9:11; Mi 1:8; Mal 1:3).

See JACKAL, BELOW.

The other Hebrew word translated "dragon" is harder to define. It was frequently used in reference to serpents (so translated in RSV: Ex 7:9,10,12; Dt 32:33; Ps 91:13). In other RSV passages it is translated "sea monster" (Gn 1:21; Jb 7:12; Ps 148:7). The exact identity of such sea monsters is not known. Several RSV

passages retain the English "dragon." In two of them (Ps 74:13; Is 27:1) the context indicates that sea monsters are meant. In three others (Is 51:9; Ez 29:3; 32:2) "dragon" seems to refer to the crocodile, a figurative reference to the Egyptian pharaoh at the time of the exodus. Jeremiah 51:34 (translated "monster" in RSV) may also refer to a voracious creature such as a crocodile.

See CROCODILE, ABOVE.

Babylonian myths described monsters and dragons in primordial conflict with the god Marduk; they represented the principle of evil. In its figurative usages in Scripture, "dragon" has a similar significance, especially in the prophetic books. In the Book of Revelation it is a symbol of Satan, the archenemy of God and his people (Rv 12:3–17; 13:2,4,11; 16:13; 20:2).

Fish. Aquatic animals frequently mentioned in the Bible without names or descriptions that enable us to identify the particular species. Since time immemorial fish have constituted one of the staple foods of humanity, and they still serve as the chief source of protein in many parts of the world. The trade in fish was highly developed in biblical times. One of the gates in Jerusalem was called the Fish Gate (Neh 3:3; Zep 1:10). The law in Leviticus 11:10–12 permitted the Jews to eat fish, but only those having both fins and scales. Such scaleless fish as catfish were forbidden even though they had fins.

Egyptian paintings depict various methods of fishing, and the Philistines fished in the Mediterranean Sea. Since the people of Israel were not a seafaring nation, it is safe to assume that most of their fish came from fresh water lakes and rivers, especially the Sea of Galilee. Some 36 species of fish have been identified in that lake, including varieties of perch, carp, barbel, "sardine," and catfish.

The method of fishing characteristic of NT times was the dragnet. After a boat had put out into the deep (Lk 5:4) a large net would be thrown out from it and then dragged toward shore by the rowers in the boat, possibly with the help of a crew in another boat. The catch was sorted out on shore (Mt 13:47,48). Fishing was usually carried out at night when the coolness of the water brought fish closer to the surface and when they could not see the approaching nets.

The Jews also fished by hook and line (Mt 17:27), a few by spear (Jb 41:7), and some by the throw net (Ez 47:10). Habakkuk refers to hook and line fishing, netting, and seining (1:15).

Fish were prepared as food in a number of ways: boiling, steaming, frying, pickling, smoking, or salting. Salt curing was probably the most common method of preserving fish that were to be transported any distance or kept for any length of time. It may have been the kind of fish that fed the 5,000 (Lk 9:10–17).

Very early in the history of the Christian church the fish became a symbol for Christ and the faith. It was scratched on the walls of Roman catacombs and may be seen today decorating walls, altars, pews, and vestments. The symbol came into use because the Greek word for "fish" (ichthus) is composed of the first letter of each word in the Greek phrase "Jesus Christ, Son of God, Savior."

The "great fish" of Jonah 2:1 was either a whale or a shark.

See WHALE, BELOW; FOOD AND FOOD PREPARATION.

Flea. Tiny, irritating insect (e.g., 1 Sm 24:14; 26:20 margin). Many species of fleas occur in Palestine, the most common being *Pulex irritans*. About a thousand species are known around the world. Fleas are wingless parasites that have sharp jaws and suck out blood from the bodies of humans and animals. The body is wedge-shaped, enabling the flea to burrow into folds of skin and hide there. The eggs, laid by the female in dust heaps in the corners of rooms, hatch into small, white larvae which pupate (a nonfeeding stage) in a cocoon. Soon adult fleas appear which immediately attach themselves to the body of a host. The female requires blood for the development of her eggs.

A flea bite is painful and causes some swelling and itching. Fleas are attracted by warmth. With favorable moisture and temperature adult fleas can live a year or longer without food, but they are voracious feeders. Fleas have a great ability to jump, and starved female fleas have been seen to jump 11 ½ inches on a smooth wooden surface.

The most dangerous fleas are those of the rat which transmit the organism responsible for bubonic plague. There were 41 recorded epidemics of bubonic plague before the Christian era.

Fly. Insects of the order *Diptera*, which have one pair of wings. Many winged insects of other orders, however, are also called flies, such as the dragonfly or butterfly.

As in almost all parts of the world, flies are abundant in Palestine. One of the most common is the common housefly (*Musca domestica*), found chiefly around dung heaps and garbage. The female lays her eggs out of which white maggots emerge that feed on refuse. After a few days the maggot develops into a cocoon out of which the adult housefly emerges. In the summer the whole cycle lasts about 12 days so that a fly can breed about 20 generations a year.

Another fly common to Palestine is the bot fly (family *Oestridae*). It causes much discomfort among livestock by irritating them and spreading diseases. Tabanid flies (family *Tabanidae*), including the horsefly (genus *Tabanus*) and related species, are also found in Palestine, but the most feared tabanid, the tsetse fly (*Glossina morsitans*), which carries sleeping sickness, does not reach as far north as Egypt or the Holy Land. Both the bot fly and horsefly are known as gadflies because of the painful wounds they inflict. Babylonian King Nebuchadnezzar is spoken of as a gadfly in view of his invasion of Egypt (Jer 46:20). Blow flies (family *Calliphoridae*) including the bright metallic-hued bluebottle (*Calliphora erythrocephala*), dog flies, midges, and numerous other flies also inhabit Palestine.

The fourth plague in Egypt just before the exodus featured "swarms of flies" (Ex 8:21–31; cf. Pss, 78:45; 105:31). Those swarms may have been made up of any or all the flies mentioned above. The maggots of Job 25:6 and Isaiah 14:11 and the worms of Exodus 16:24 and Job 7:5 and 17:14 were probably fly larvae.

Philistine inhabitants of the city of Ekron worshiped a god named Baal-zebul, meaning "Lord of the high places." The Hebrews mockingly spoke of Baal-zebub, meaning "Lord of the flies" (2 Kgs 1:2). The NT form is Beelzebul (e.g., Mt 10:25; 12:24,27).

A proverb quoted in Ecclesiastes 10:1 probably refers to the housefly, which would be attracted to an open, perfumed ointment bottle. Once inside it would drown and eventually decay, causing the ointment to spoil and stink. The fly is also referred to in Isaiah 7:18 where it symbolizes Egypt. Isaiah may have had in mind a horsefly (*Tabanus arenivagus*) which attacks both humans and animals.

See PLAGUES UPON EGYPT.

Fox. Small, doglike carnivore with a bushy tail that is about half its body length. The red fox of the Holy Land (*Vulpes vulpes palaestinae*) is similar to the North American red fox; it is smaller than a wolf and is normally a nocturnal solitary animal. The omnivorous fox eats almost any kind of food—fruits, plants, mice, beetles, and birds—but seldom touches carrion. It loves the sweet juice of grapes, but it also burrows underground tunnels that can destroy the vines (Sg 2:15). The fox is intelligent and known for its slyness (Lk 13:32). It has considerable endurance and can run at speeds up to 30 miles per hour. The Jews rebuilding Jerusalem's wall were taunted by the wisecrack that even a fox jumping on their wall would knock it over (Neh 4:3). The fox has a keen sense of sight, smell, and hearing and at times seems almost to have a sense of humor.

The Egyptian fox (*Vulpes niloticus*) is found

in the central and southern parts of the Holy Land. It is somewhat smaller than the common red fox. Its back is rust-colored and its belly light. The Syrian fox (*Vulpes flavescens*) that lives in the northern part of the Holy Land is shiny gold in color.

Some OT references such as Psalm 63:10 and Lamentations 5:18 are translated "fox" in KJV but probably refer to jackals. Jackals, not foxes, hunt in packs and tend to act as scavengers.

Frog. Amphibian (genus *Rana*), living part of its life in the water and part on land.

Frogs and toads are covered with soft, hairless skin and lack a tail in the adult stage. The hind legs are much longer and more powerfully developed than the forelegs so that the animals are able to jump large distances. It has been suggested that the frog referred to in Scripture is an edible one, *Rana ridibunda*, one of the aquatic frogs found in Egypt and in the stagnant waters of the Holy Land.

The female frog lays her eggs in the water; after about a week the eggs hatch into tadpoles. Gradually through metamorphosis the tail is lost and limbs are acquired. Frogs must maintain a moist skin since they take oxygen through the skin as well as through their lungs; thus they must always remain close to water. They feed on insects and worms.

Frogs are found throughout the Palestinian lowlands, where their croaking is heard in the spring and on summer evenings. The Israelites seem to have associated frogs primarily with sliminess and foulness. They fell into the category of creeping or swarming creatures, which in general were ritually unclean (Lv 11:29–31). Since the frog was not specifically listed, however, rabbis did not consider it one of the animals that defiled human beings through contact.

In Revelation 16:13 certain foul spirits are said to look like frogs. The ancient Egyptians made the frog a symbol of life and birth and an image of Heqet, the patron goddess of birth. She is depicted with a frog's head giving life to the newborn. Thus that deity was discredited when the power of God afflicted Egypt in the second of the 10 plagues on the Egyptians with the very animal that was her symbol (Ex 8:1–14; Pss 78:45; 105:30). The frog in question may have been the spotted frog of Egypt (*Rana punctata*), or *Rana ridibunda*.

See PLAGUES UPON EGYPT.

Gazelle. Small, dainty, graceful antelope with hollow recurved horns on both sexes. Two varieties exist in the Holy Land, the dorcas gazelle (*Gazella dorcas*), which is pale-fawn in color and up to 22 inches tall, and the Arabian gazelle (*Gazella arabica*), which is a dark smoky color and up to 25 inches tall.

Gazelles are still quite common throughout the desert and steppe areas of the Holy Land, especially in the Negeb desert. Herds usually consist of from 5 to 10 animals, but some varieties assemble in large migratory herds in the fall to relocate to lower elevations and new feeding grounds. Gazelles are herbivorous (plant-eating). They are very shy and post guards to warn the herd of approaching danger.

In biblical times the gazelle was probably the game animal most hunted by the Jews (Prv 6:5; Is 13:14). Pharaoh Tutankhamun hunted gazelles and ostriches. The gazelle is said to have graced Solomon's table (1 Kgs 4:23). Gazelles were not easy to catch because of their great speed (2 Sm 2:18; 1 Chr 12:8; Prv 6:5); they surpass even deer in swiftness. They were trapped in various ways—encircled with nets, driven into enclosures with pitfalls, or forced into narrow valleys and shot with arrows. The Bedouin hunt gazelles with falcons and dogs; the falcon annoys the gazelle, striking it on the head and injuring it so that the dogs can overtake it.

The gazelle is referred to in Song of Solomon 2:7; 4:5; and 7:3, where it is an image of feminine beauty.

Gecko. Reptile of the family *Gekkonidae*, referred to in Leviticus 11:30. In Jewish food law it was a ritually unclean lizard. There are seven species of geckos in the Holy Land (including *Hemidactylus turcicus* and *Ptyodactylus Hasselquistii*), all insectivorous (insect-eating).

Another name for the gecko is the wall lizard, so named because it can walk upside down on ceilings with the aid of the suction discs on its toes—but often plops down into the middle of the home. Since it was considered unclean, such an intrusion would have been a disgusting nuisance to Jewish households (Lv 11:31–38).

The gecko makes a low mourning sound by vibrating its tongue rapidly against the roof of its mouth. In legend the gecko was said to cause leprosy by crawling across a person's body.

See LIZARD, BELOW.

Gnat. Any very small fly, in common and biblical usage. According to the RSV the third plague in Egypt before the exodus consisted of gnats (Ex 8:16–18; Ps 105:31). The KJV translates the Hebrew word there as "lice," but the breeding pattern described in Exodus 8—insects rising from the dust—seems to fit gnats better than lice. Since "gnat" is a general term, the small flies of that plague may have included several small species such as mosquitos, harvester gnats, midges, or sand flies.

The sand fly inflicts a far more painful bite than the mosquito. Further, it does not betray itself by a buzzing noise in flight and is so small that it penetrates most mosquito netting.

Gnats were drawn to wine while it was fermenting. The Pharisees in particular would strain their wine to avoid consuming unclean insects (Mt 23:24).

See PLAGUES UPON EGYPT.

Goat. Cloven-hooved mammals (genus *Capra*) with large eyes and big, floppy ears that constantly twitch. Both males and females have backward arching horns. The Palestinian goat is a ruminant (cud-chewing animal) of lighter build than the sheep.

The goat was probably the earliest ruminant to be domesticated. Its wild ancestor seems to have been the Bezoar goat (*Capra aegagrus*). Wild goats are believed to have been domesticated very early in Palestine. The goat of Bible times was probably the Syrian or Mamber variety (*Capra hircus mambrica*). Domesticated goats may have as many as four kids in a litter, whereas wild goats bear only one or two.

The Palestinian goat was commonly black. Speckled and spotted goats were a rarity, and for that reason Jacob's request for those goats in Genesis 30:32 appeared very modest. There may also have been red goats (cf. 1 Sm 16:12; 19:13, where goat's hair was used to imitate David's hair, which was "ruddy" or auburn).

Almost every part of the goat was used by the Israelites. The whole goat was used for sacrifice. Its flesh served as meat (Lv 7:23; Dt 14:4), and it was the principal source of milk (Prv 27:27). Goats were sheared in the late spring, and the goat hair was used for weaving tent cloth and for various domestic purposes (Ex 36:14; 1 Sm 19:13,16). The "covenant tent" at Mt Sinai was made of goat's hair blankets (Ex 26:7).

Adult male goats were generally not eaten because of their strong flavor and toughness, and also because they were necessary to insure the flock's increase. Young kids, however, were usually the chief meat for a feast and were offered to visitors as a symbol of hospitality. Goat milk is richer than the milk of cows and sheep and evidently had broader uses. A good goat gives three quarts of milk a day, from which a rich butter and buttermilk can be made. The average Hebrew family could have lived almost entirely on a single goat's production.

Goatskin was tanned as leather, and the whole hide was turned into a skin bottle by sewing shut a leg and neck apertures (Gn 21:14; Jos 9:4). Goatskin had many uses, including the construction of Hebrew musical instruments. The nebal, a large harp, was made with goatskin for its sounding base. Drums had goatskin coverings.

Goats were herded with sheep in biblical times, but each group remained separate following its own bell-laden leader. Jesus was evidently referring to their common herding in his description of the last judgment (Mt 25:31–46).

Sheep are more important than goats where cattle can be kept for milk. However, where pasture and water are scarce and thorny shrubs dominate over grass, cattle are difficult to keep and goats become important. They can live under conditions that suit neither cows nor sheep, producing large quantities of milk. The goat does not supply fat as the sheep does, and since its hair is coarse its wool is rather scarce.

Goats have voracious appetites. They were responsible for much damage done to the land of Palestine, breaking down terraces, destroying forests, and bringing about soil erosion by eating off all cover.

The goat was recognized as a form of wealth, subject to the law of firstlings (Nm 18:17). It had to be eight days old before it could be offered as a sacrifice. A year-old male goat was one of the animals offered at the Passover (28:22), and two goats were offered on the Day of Atonement (Lv 16:7–10). The goat was also used for other specific sacrifices.

The goat was often used in a figurative and symbolic sense by the writers of the Bible: in Song of Solomon 4:1 and 6:5 for the bride's black hair; in Matthew 25:31–46 for the wicked; and in Ezekiel 34:17 and Daniel 8:5–8 for various human leaders.

The ibex, a type of wild goat (*Capra ibex nubiana*), still lives in small numbers on the cliffs close to the Dead Sea. That it was known

Some goats in rocky terrain.

in ancient times is evident from rock carvings. It is distinguished from the true wild goat by having a more compact rump and horns that are slender and curved back. Its slender legs and sharp cloven hooves enable it to cling to narrow rock ledges, to jump between them, and to climb steep cliffs.

Usually the ibex is found in rugged mountain country among rocky crags and meadows just below the snow line (Ps 104:18). In Job 39:1 they are referred to as "mountain goats." They frequently gather in herds of 5 to 20. They graze and browse, being active in the afternoon and sometimes feeding through the night. The large horn of the ibex was at one period made into the shofar which was blown in the second Jerusalem temple to announce the new year and the jubilee year.

Ibex flesh is excellent, superior to the drier meat of gazelles, and considered clean by the Israelites (Dt 14:5), but the ibex is difficult to hunt. It has been suggested that David and his followers lived at En-gedi in order to capture wild goats for food (1 Sm 24:2).

The satyrs of Isaiah 13:21 and 34:14 were probably wild goats. They were described as hairy creatures and may have been goat idols used in conjunction with the golden calves which Jeroboam I of the northern kingdom of Israel set up.

See Agriculture; Food and Food Preparation; Offerings and Sacrifices.

Grasshopper. Large insects of the *Orthoptera* order. They have chewing or biting mouth parts and two pairs of wings, the front pair of which is narrow and somewhat thickened and the hind pair membranous and used for flying. When not in use the flight wings are folded beneath the protective front wings like a fan against the body. By rubbing their wings together, male grasshoppers produce sounds which both males and females can detect. Grasshoppers pass through a partial metamorphosis; the egg hatches into a juvenile nymph which looks like an adult except for its smaller size and undeveloped wings. After several moults the nymph becomes a winged adult.

The terms "grasshopper" and "locust" are often used interchangeably. Actually the locust is a kind of grasshopper. Also confusing is the fact that other insects such as cicadas are sometimes called locusts. The difference between grasshoppers and locusts depends more on behavior than appearance. Grasshoppers are individual insects that lead solitary lives and do not migrate. The same insects when migrating in a swarm are called migratory grasshoppers or locusts. Elimination of their food supply by drought, flood, or fire may lead to migration. Climatic factors such as a warm dry winter also stimulate migrations.

Grasshoppers and locusts have been a staple food in the Middle East and also among the Indians of the American southwest. To the Israelites the grasshopper was considered ritually clean and could be eaten (Lv 11:22).

See Locust, below.

Hare. Animal of the genus and species *Lepus europaeus judaeus*, *Lepus capensis*, and *Lepus arabicus*. It is found in open country, often near or on cultivated lands, and in woods, usually deciduous rather than evergreen. It is an herbivorous rodent and is different from the rabbit, which is not found in Palestine. Although it is not a true ruminant according to modern classification (because it does not have a four-chambered stomach), the hare does rechew its food. It has a process of partial regurgitation of material too hard for the cells in the stomach to absorb initially; thus the hare actually chews food previously swallowed.

Near Eastern hares have very long ears and large hind feet; their feet are well furred. They are similar to American jack rabbits, which are true hares. Hares do not dig or occupy burrows the way rabbits do. Hares are mainly nocturnal and spend their inactive hours hiding in vegetation. They eat grasses and herbaceous matter as well as twigs and young bark of woody plants. Hares breed with great rapidity, the young attaining sexual maturity at six months after birth.

The hare was ceremonially unclean (Lv 11:6; Dt 14:7), evidently because although it appeared to chew its cud, it did not have cloven hoofs. Consumption of hares has also been forbidden among the Arabs, Chinese, and Lapps, but the hare was widely hunted by other people in ancient and modern times. It great speed, prolific breeding, timidity, and caution have saved it from extermination by its many enemies.

Hedgehog. Insectivore of the genus *Erinaceus*. The porcupine, often confused with it, is larger and is classified as a rodent. The hedgehog is characterized by a slow, rolling walk, but it can run rapidly. It is a good swimmer and is generally active at night. Its spines are used to cushion itself as well as for protection.

The hedgehog roots in the fallen leaves of hedges and thickets, feeding on seeds, grubs, beetles, snails, snakes, lizards, young birds, mice, and carrion. It rolls into a ball for defense, covering its vulnerable belly. There are three species of hedgehogs in the Holy Land.

The Egyptians regarded the hedgehog as a bad omen. It is used in Scripture as a symbol of an inhabited area that has become desolate (Is 14:23; Zep 2:14; rsv has "porcupine" in Is 34:11). In all three verses the Hebrew word is the same, and there is some question to what animal it refers. KJV has "bittern," a long-legged wading bird. Most scholars believe that a bird is the most appropriate translation. The debate centers on Zephaniah 2:14, where a number of animals inhabiting desolate Nineveh are listed. All but the animal in question are birds. The animal called "hedgehog" in RSV is said to "lodge in her capitals," meaning on the tops of columns. That seems to favor a bird of some sort unless we speculate that the columns were in ruins and lying on their sides. Then the animal could be a hedgehog.

Horse. Przewalski's horse (*Equus przewalskii*, an eastern race which roamed about Mongolia until modern firearms destroyed most of them after World War I) and the tarpan (a western race of southern Russia which became extinct in the Ukraine in 1851). The domesticated horse (*Equus caballus*) seems to have been derived from the tarpan. The original site of domestication is believed to have been Turkestan, a region north of Afghanistan and India now in the U.S.S.R.

The horse differs from the ass in that it has shorter ears, a longer mane with a forelock, a long hairy tail, and a soft, sensitive muzzle.

Horses were used in war not only for riding but also for pulling the heavy, springless war chariots. Two kinds of horses were needed for these different purposes, and the Hebrews distinguished between chariot horses and cavalry horses. The horse was introduced only gradually into Israel, however.

The Lord warned the early Israelites against unnecessarily amassing military strength in the form of horses and thereby following the oppressive tactics of the powerful Egyptians (Dt 17:14–16), but the demands of war caused both David and Solomon to import horses from Egypt into their kingdoms and to breed them.

Joshua was commanded to hamstring the horses of the Canaanites, that is to disable them by cutting the tendons of their legs (Jos 11:6,9). David hamstrung most of the horses captured from Zobah, though he kept enough for 100 chariots (2 Sm 8:4). Solomon greatly increased the number of horses in the Jewish kingdom and maintained large stables at various cities (1 Kgs 10:26), such as the regional defense centers of Megiddo, Hazor, and Gezar (1 Kgs 9:15–19). Ahab's horses are mentioned in 1 Kings 18:5, and records of Shalmaneser III state that Ahab furnished 2,000 chariots to a coalition against Assyria.

In early Israel, the horse was opposed as a symbol of pagan luxury and of dependence on physical power for defense (Dt 17:16; 1 Sm 8:11; Ps 20:7; Is 31:1). In addition, horses may have been used in pagan religious processions (2 Kgs 23:11). Horse trading, mentioned as early as Genesis 47:17, was carried on by Solomon between Egypt and the Syro-Hittite principalities (1 Kgs 10:28,29).

Most biblical references to horses refer to their use in war, but horses were also used for transportation. Riding seems to have been less popular than the use of chariots. Cavalry units were not introduced until the 12th century BC by the Medes. Joseph rode in Pharaoh's second horse-drawn chariot (Gn 41:43), and Absalom made a display by riding a horse-drawn chariot (2 Sm 15:1). Naaman traveled by horse and chariot (2 Kgs 5:9). Later, horses were so common in Jerusalem that the royal palace had a special horse gate (2 Chr 23:15), and a gate of the city itself was known as the horse gate (Neh 3:28; Jer 31:40). Mordecai rode a royal horse of King Xerxes as a sign of honor (Est 6:8–11).

Horses were used by the wealthy for hunting; the only biblical reference to such hunting refers to pursuit of the ostrich (Jb 39:18). Horses were forbidden as food, though they may have been eaten in Samaria during a Syrian siege (2 Kgs 7:13). There seems to have been little use of horses in agriculture or in bearing and pulling of burdens. Isaiah 28:28 may refer to the use of horses in threshing grain, though the reference is uncertain. Horses are often spoken of figuratively (Ps 32:9; Sg 1:9, stallion; Jer 5:8; 12:5), especially in the context of judgment (Hab 3:8; Zec 1:8; 6:1–8; Rv 6:2–8; 9:17; 19:11–16).

Horseshoes were unknown in biblical times, so it was regarded as a special advantage if a horse's hooves were hard (Is 5:28). Stirrups were not used, but saddle blankets were common (Jgs 5:10; Ez 27:20). The prophet Zechariah mentions different colors of horses: red, black, white, and dapple gray (Zec 6:2,3).

Since the horse was the mount of a warrior, by entering Jerusalem on an ass Jesus indicated he was coming as a prince of peace.

See ARMS AND WARFARE; TRAVEL AND TRANSPORTATION.

Hyena. Stocky carnivore (*Hyaena hyaena*); with coarse hair, an erect mane, and long hairs along the neck and back. Hyenas live in holes among rocks and banks. They are mainly nocturnal but are ordinarily neither noisy nor aggressive. Their cry, however, is a disagreeable, unearthly sound. Usually hyenas feed on carrion, crushing bones with their powerful jaws. If the carrion supply is inadequate they will kill sheep, goats, or other small animals. When threatened, hyenas growl and erect their mane, but they rarely fight. They are massively built with forelegs longer than the hind legs.

Known as scavengers in Africa, hyenas eat domestic refuse in the villages. In Palestine the striped hyena is a common predator, preferring rocky territory and even rock tombs. It may exhume human bodies.

Since hyenas were notorious for raiding the graves of the dead, all Israelites who could afford it arranged for burial in tombs protected by massive stone doors. Absalom, King David's son who was killed by Joab in the wild, was buried under a huge pile of stones to protect his corpse from molestation by hyenas (2 Sm 18:17).

The hyena is referred to in a number of other passages (Is 13:22; 34:14; Jer 50:39). The Hebrew word also appears as a proper name "Zibeon" (Gn 36:2,14,20), and as a place-name, "Zeboim" and "Zeboiim" (Gn 14:2–8; Dt 29:23; 1 Sm 13:18), perhaps indicating that hyenas were common to the area.

Jackal. Carnivore (*Canis aureus*) smaller than the true wolf and with a shorter tail. It is similar to the fox but has a broader head, shorter ears, and longer legs. The fox is solitary; the jackal tends to be gregarious. Its tail is drooping or erect, compared with the long horizontal tail of the fox. Jackals usually prowl at night, either singly, in pairs, or in packs through open savannah country. They eat small mammals, poultry, fruit, vegetables, and carrion. They spend their days in thickets and clumps of vegetation. Often they obtain scraps from kills by larger carnivores. Jackals can run at speeds of about 33 miles per hour.

The jackal can reach a height of about 20 inches, roughly the size of a German shepherd dog. Its back is pale yellow with dark, almost black, flanks. Its lips are black and its ears white on the inside.

The howl of the jackal sounds like the crying of a child or the heartrending wail of the bereaved (Mi 1:8; cf. Job 30:29). To other jackals the howl is merely an invitation calling the pack together for its nocturnal hunting.

OT references are chiefly to jackals prowling around ruined cities and wilderness areas (Neh 2:13; Ps 44:19; Is 13:22; 34:13; 35:7; Jer 9:11; 14:6; 49:33; 51:37; Lam 4:3; 5:18; Mal 1:3). Many such references are translated "dragon" in KJV, but "jackal" is more appropriate.

See DRAGON, ABOVE.

Leech. Segmented worm (class *Hirudinea*) up to 5 inches long with flat body equipped with suction pads at each end. The mouth, located at the bottom of the front suction pad, has three teeth which the leech uses to pierce the skin of its host. The leech feeds on blood, and its glands secrete an anticoagulant to prevent the blood from clotting.

The ordinary medicinal leech (*Hirudo medicinalis*) is abundant in springs and ponds from the Negeb desert to Galilee. It adheres to the bodies of human beings and animals that sub-merge themselves in water, injects its anti-coagulant, and sucks their blood.

The reference in Proverbs 30:15 is uncertain (see RSV margin) but may be to the parasitic and greedy nature of the horseleech (genus *Haemopis*) as in KJV. The small horseleech enters its host's mouth and nostrils from water while the animal is drinking. It is more attracted to horses than to humans. A leech weighing one-half ounce has been known to gorge itself with two and a half ounces of concentrated blood and then to exist for 15 months with no more to eat.

Leopard (*Panthera pardus tulliana*). Most widespread of all the large cats. In rocky areas it lives in caves, but in forested regions it lives in thick vegetation. In OT times many lived in the vicinity of Mt Hermon (Sg 4:8).

The leopard is somewhat smaller than the tiger, measuring up to 5 feet in length with a tail of about 30 inches. Its body is better proportioned than that of the tiger. The leopard takes its victim by surprise from a silent ambush, often concealing itself near villages or watering places and waiting for its prey, remaining in one spot for long spans of time.

The leopard is a wary and cunning animal, formidable and ferocious (Jer 5:6; Hos 13:7; cf. Is 11:6). It survived in the Holy Land into the present century; a few leopards still exist in remote areas near Mt Tabor and Mt Carmel.

The leopard is swift on the ground (Hb 1:8), agile in trees, and very graceful in its movements. Its color is yellowish speckled with black spots (Jer 13:23). Daniel and John saw visions in which leopards were symbols of world powers (Dn 7:6; Rv 13:2).

The leopard is dangerous not only to domestic animals but also to humans. With its natural camouflage it can hide on the forest floor, blending into the changing light and shadows.

The Israelites were terrified of the leopard because it constantly ravaged their sheep and goats. Several biblical place-names suggest that they were known for the leopards in their vicinity: Nimrah, Beth-nimrah, and Nimrim, a district northeast of the Dead Sea.

Leviathan. Sea monster mentioned several times in the Bible (Jb 3:8; 41:1; Pss 74:14; 104:26; Is 27:1). It may refer to any of the larger marine animals such as large jellyfish, whales, or sharks, or to a large reptile like the crocodile. Some biblical scholars think Leviathan may refer to animals now extinct, such as ichthyosaurs and plesiosaurs (marine reptiles similar to dinosaurs). The scriptural term might also refer to certain dinosaurs that spent part of their lives half-submerged in shallow lakes and oceans. Other scholars be-

Ashurbanipal amuses himself by hunting lions (bas-relief from Nineveh).

lieve that most of the references are to the crocodile.

See CROCODILE, ABOVE.

Lion. Large, tawny-colored carnivore (*Panthera leo*) that preys chiefly on hoofed mammals and charges by a series of leaps and bounds. Within historic times the lion ranged in Africa, Europe, and the Holy Land. In ancient times the territories of the African and Persian lions met in the Middle East.

The lion of the Holy Land was the Asiatic or Persian lion (*Panthera leo persica*). The males have heavy manes that stop at the shoulders but cover much of the belly. The Persian lion cannot climb and is mainly nocturnal, returning to its lair or a thicket by day (Jer 4:7; 25:38; Na 2:11,12).

The Persian lion is about 5 feet long with a tassled tail 30 inches or so long; its shoulders may reach a height of 35 inches. It is one of the smallest of the lion breeds.

Lion hunting was the sport of the kings of Assyria. Lions were common in biblical times in all parts of the Holy Land. Hebrew has at least 7 words for lion and young lion. The lion is referred to about 130 times in the OT—more than any other wild animal. Lions were evidently much less common in NT times. After gradually declining, they became extinct in Palestine shortly after AD 1300. The lion was present in Mesopotamia, however, until the end of the 19th century.

Lions are usually found in pairs, though sometimes in larger numbers. A small group is known as a pride. They generally prefer open country but in Palestine evidently prowled the subtropical vegetation of the Jordan River valley. Lions, which usually hunt at dusk, kill smaller animals by a blow of the paw, larger ones by a bite in the throat. A lion does not remain in the same place for more than a few days. The animal is in its prime at about 7 years of age, when it weighs from 400 to 600 pounds.

The lion does not characteristically attack humans, though like other great cats it may become a maneater (1 Kgs 13:24–28; 20:36; 2 Kgs 17:25,26; Ps 57:4; Dn 6:7–27). Ordinarily it attacks only out of great hunger or in self-defense. A very young lion that attacks humans can become dangerous if it develops a taste for human flesh. A very old lion, expelled from the pride because it can no longer keep up in the pursuit of antelope or gazelles, may choose humans as a relatively slow-moving prey.

A lion generally roars only on a full stomach, that is, after it has consumed its prey (Ps 22:13; Ez 22:25; Am 3:4). The lion is a bold (2 Sm 17:10; Prv 28:1), destructive animal (Ps 7:2; Jer 2:30; Hos 5:14; Mi 5:8), the enemy of the flock (Am 3:12); its roaring arouses fear in domestic animals (Am 3:8; 1 Pt 5:8).

Lions played an important part in the political and religious symbolism of the Near East (1 Kgs 10:19,20). In Assyria and Babylonia the lion was regarded as a royal beast (Dn 7:4). To the Jews the lion was the mightiest of beasts, having a king's regal bearing (Prv 30:29–31). Thus it symbolized leadership (Gn 49:9,10; Nm 24:9) and hence eventually became a title for Christ (Rv 5:5). It was also the ensign of Judah's tribe and was used by King Solomon in the decoration of his house and the temple.

Oriental monarchs maintained artificial lion pits as places of execution (Ez 19:1–9; Dn 6:7–16). Animals for these were captured in camouflaged nets or pits. The lion remains a favorite animal among oriental rulers; until he was deposed, the emperor of Ethiopia exhibited the "royal lions."

See HUNTING.

Lizard. Reptiles of the suborder *Lacertilia*. Their skin is covered with scales. The lizard is actually a useful creature because it captures harmful insects and worms. Like other reptiles it lays eggs with shells softer than those of a bird and with no clear division between the yolk and the white. Lizards are "cold-blooded" organisms without a temperature-maintenance mechanism; hence they become inactive in cold weather.

Lizards can survive in barren parched countryside. In the Near East they are encountered in great numbers in the Arabian desert, the Sinai peninsula, and the Judean wilderness. There may be as many as 44 different species of lizards in the Holy Land.

The Dabb lizard (genus *Uromastyx*), which attains a length of about 24 inches, is found in the Negeb desert. It is omnivorous, an unusual trait since most lizards are insectivorous. It has a hard, rough skin, green with brown spots; a short, rounded head; and a powerful tail encircled with a row of strong spines which it uses as a weapon of defense.

Lizards are listed as ceremonially unclean in Jewish law (Lv 11:29–31). The fact that lizards crawl on their bellies made them unclean, perhaps because they were in contact with the ground. Contact with a lizard's carcass defiled a law-abiding Jew (Lv 11:32–36). The RSV translates the "lizards" of Leviticus 11 as "great lizard," "gecko," "land crocodile," "lizard," "sand lizard," and "chameleon." Other translators and commentators render the original Hebrew in a wide variety of ways, including "tortoise," "ferret," "lizard," "snail," "mole," and even "water hen." The fact that most of the original Hebrew words occur only once in Scripture makes it very difficult to be certain about their appropriate translation. Proverbs 30:28 refers to "the lizard you can take in your hands" (RSV), but the KJV has "the spider taketh hold with her hands." Advocates of both translations can be found among scholars.

See GECKO, ABOVE.

Locust. An insect of the family *Acridiidae*. It is referred to by at least 12 different names in Scripture. The various Hebrew words may refer to different stages of its development from larva to adult or to the type of damage which it causes.

Locusts are characterized by swarming and mass migration. In modern times they have caused extensive and disastrous destruction to vegetation. Grasshoppers do not swarm or migrate en masse, differentiating them from the true locusts.

The OT mentions several different species of locusts. Leviticus 11:22 seems to refer to the slant-faced (bald) locust and also to the katydid or longhorned grasshopper. The reference in Deuteronomy 28:42 may be to the mole cricket. In Joel 1:4 and 2:25, and in Nahum 3:16,17, successive stages of the insect's development are described. The cutting locust (KJV palmerworm) of Joel is probably the first instar (stage of development), the swarming locusts (KJV locust) are middle stages, and the hopping locusts (KJV cankerworm) later instars but not yet fully matured insects. In the adult stage, called destroying locusts (KJV caterpillar), the color of the locust is reddish-brown, which turns to yellow with a brownish network on the wings.

Only 3 of the hundreds of varieties of locusts found in Bible lands are capable of multiplying into great swarms, and only the desert locust (*Schistocerca gregaria*) can be considered widespread in all the Bible lands. The desert locust is native to the Sudan (Africa). It is a little over 2 inches long and has a wingspread of some 5 inches. It shows two phases, a solitary phase and a gregarious phase, with a possible third phase known as transiens. There are differences in the immature and adult forms of the phases in color and physiology.

The quantity and distribution of rains are important factors in the extent of swarming. Moist soil is needed for depositing the eggs and permitting them to develop. Each female deposits from 1 to 6 egg-pods, containing 28 to 146 eggs each. The larvae emerge in 15 to 43 days.

In the gregarious phase (from the 2nd stage of metamorphosis onward), the locust is driven by a strong wandering instinct. Masses of them form a random procession of overflowing locust bodies which ignore any obstruction. They swarm over everything (Jl 2:4–9). The only regulator of their activities is temperature; they are immobilized by high or low temperatures. Taking to wing they may move 1,200 miles from their native home. They fly in compact formations large enough to blot out the light of the sun. Their movement seems to be controlled by hormones, but the direction is influenced by the wind. The swarms consume almost every plant in their path, sparing only the carob, sycamore, castor tree, and oleander bush. Locusts are still a serious problem, particularly in east Africa. Damage estimates in modern times have exceeded 30 million dollars in a single locust plague.

Harvest begins in the Holy Land in April, and in that month the locust is at the nymph stage and more voracious than at any other time. The nymph has small wings but cannot yet fly.

A locust plague was one of the most severe evils to come upon the ancient world (Dt 28:38). Joel 2:1–11 describes a locust plague in graphic terms, using it as a symbol of God's destroying judgment. Special days of prayer, fasting, and trumpet blowing were prescribed to remove locust plagues (1 Kgs 8:37,38; 2 Chr 6:28,29; Jl 2:12–17). Locusts symbolized powerful and merciless enemies that completely destroyed the earnings of human toil (Jgs 6:5; Is 33:4; Jer 46:23; 51:27; Na 3:15).

Locusts are a source of pestilence because of the putrefaction of their accumulated bodies. In some parts of Africa they have been known to cover the whole surface of the ground over areas of more than 2,000 square miles. Their excrement could be smelled 150 miles away.

Bedouins eat locusts raw, roasted, or boiled, preserving them by drying and threading. They are also crushed and ground, and the grist used in cooking or eaten with bread, sometimes mixed with honey and dates. The Greeks ground locusts in stone mortars to make flour of them.

The ancients considered the 2 large hind legs, or jumping legs, as separate limbs and had a special name for them. Hence locusts were described as having 4 legs, a reference to the 4 smaller walking legs. "Going on all fours" thus referred to creeping or walking as opposed to jumping and did not mean that the unclean insects had only 4 legs in all. Because of its 2 hind jumping legs, the locust was exempted from the prohibition against unclean insects (Lv 11:20–23). Later the Talmud, a collection of Jewish legal writings, applied the exemption only to varieties in which the wings covered the whole body.

See PLAGUES UPON EGYPT.

Mole Rat. Rodent (*Spalax ehrenbergi ehrenbergi*) from 6 to 9 inches long, which burrows in any area where the soil is suitable for digging; it is neither a mole nor a rat. It is quite common in the Holy Land, and large numbers are found in the vicinity of Jerusalem.

The mole rat has no tail and is molelike in appearance, but neither true moles nor shrews have ever been found in the Holy Land. The mole rat's teeth are strong and protruding like those of a squirrel. The neck is short and thick with a plump body shaped like a sausage. The short legs have broad paws with claws adapted for burrowing. The fur is soft, thick, and ashen gray. Its ears and almost sightless eyes no larger than poppyseeds are hidden in the fur. Folklore taught that touching a mole rat would result in blindness.

In the wet winter season the mole rat builds breeding mounds resembling those of pocket gophers. It builds less complex resting mounds in the summer, although both have rather elaborate tunnel systems. The mole rat feeds on roots, bulbs, tubers, and various other subterranean plant parts, often doing extensive damage to agriculture.

Isaiah 2:20 refers to the mole rat (RSV and KJV mole). Leviticus 11:29,30 (KJV mole) may refer to the mole rat, but some scholars believe the reference is to a lizard (RSV chameleon).

See CHAMELEON; LIZARD, ABOVE.

Moth. Insect of the genus *Tineola* that lays its eggs on wool or furs, its larvae feeding on those materials. The destructive qualities of moths are referred to in several biblical passages (Jb 13:28; Ps 39:11; Is 50:9; Hos 5:12; Mt 6:19,20; Lk 12:33; Jas 5:2). In Isaiah 51:8 "worm" refers specifically to the larva of the clothes moth. The moth symbolized disintegration, decay, and weakening. It is only the larvae that do the damage. The adult is quite harmless and feeds mainly on the nectar of flowers. It is easily crushed (Jb 4:19). There are hundreds of species of moths other than the clothes moth in the Holy Land; they are harmful to leaves, flowers, fruit, trees, and seeds. As with the clothes moth, the larvae inflict the damage.

The clothes moth reproduces in May or June. It enters human dwellings in the evening. A week after the eggs are laid the larvae appear and immediately begin their work of destruction, eating anything within reach made of animal fibers.

The moth's destructive activity is done in secret without any sound and without any dramatic appearance, such as a swarm that blots out the sun. In an age when wealth was counted more in possessions than in money, and when among those possessions wool clothing was highly valued, moths could literally cause economic disaster; hence the words of Jesus in the Sermon on the Mount (Mt 6:19,20).

Mouse. Rodent of the family *Muridae*, especially genus *Mus*. The mouse was regarded as unclean because, being short-legged, it was considered one of the creeping creatures (Lv 11:29). Mice known as commensals live in dwellings and tend to have longer tails and to be darker in color than wild mice, which are active chiefly at night. Mice are good climbers and even good swimmers. Wild mice eat many kinds of vegetation, including seeds, fleshy roots, leaves, and stems. At times they store food.

The Hebrew word for "mouse" (Lv 11:29; 1 Sm 6:4,5; Is 66:17) is probably a general term for various rats and mice. At least 23 varieties of mouselike rodents are known in the Holy Land. They cause food spoilage, damage household articles, and transport the host fleas which spread typhus, spotted fever, and bubonic plague. Plague bacteria may have caused the tumors or swellings among the Philistines (1 Sm 6:5). Isaiah 66:17 refers to a pre-exilic Canaanite cultic practice in which mice were eaten; the reference may actually be to the hamster. A number of rodents are eaten by Arabs of the Near East; the gerbil is considered a special delicacy.

The root meaning of the Hebrew word "mouse" is "destruction of corn," a reference to the damage mice do to field crops.

See VOLE, BELOW.

Mule. Hybrid offspring of a male ass and a female horse (*Equus asinus mulus*), ordinarily sterile. The offspring of a female ass and a stallion (male horse) is known as a hinny and is of little value because of its inferior size.

Because crossbreeding was forbidden in the Law (Lv 19:19, "cattle" referring to any domestic stock), Israelites procured mules from the Gentiles, perhaps from the Phoenicians, since Tyre (a Phoenician seaport in what is now southern Lebanon) imported horses and mules (Ez 27:14). Mules did not appear in Israel until David's reign (2 Sm 13:29), possibly because of the rarity of horses among the Hebrews. Mules were used chiefly by members of the royal court and by other nobles. King David rode on a mule, and Solomon rode to his anointing on King David's mule (1 Kgs 1:33). Absalom met his death riding on a mule (2 Sm 18:9). Mules were less common than horses, camels, and asses in the post-exilic community (Ezr 2:66). In antiquity Asia Minor was especially noted for breeding fine mules.

The mule is prized for riding and for carrying heavy burdens, especially in warm mountainous regions. They are sure-footed and thrive best in hot, dry climates. The mule has the frugality, endurance, and steady gait of an ass along with the size, strength, swiftness, and courage of a horse. Mules are almost never sick. They live longer than horses. They can carry a load of up to 300 pounds as far as 30 miles a day.

Mules have long enjoyed a reputation for obstinancy, but that trait is not mentioned in the Bible.

The word translated "mule" by KJV in Genesis 36:24 ("this was that Anah that found the mules in the wilderness") is not the usual word for mule in the Bible and is probably a mistranslation. Anah probably found "hot springs," not mules, in the wilderness (see RSV).

See TRAVEL AND TRANSPORTATION.

Pig. Most properly, newborn swine. "Swine" is technically the better name for the species, but it is rarely used in common speech today. The domestic pigs of the Middle East derived from the wild pig (*Sus scrofa*). The pig is the most prolific and abundant supplier of meat and fat for food. A thick layer of fat just under the skin is especially pronounced in domestic breeds. Pigs cannot be driven, so they are of value only to the settled farmer. The Hebrews were originally a nomadic people; therefore they had little use for an animal closely associated with settled life. An Egyptian prince of about 1500 BC, however, is recorded as owning a herd of 1,500 swine.

The pig is clumsily built, yet lively and able to move with agility and speed. The most conspicuous characteristic of the pig is a truncated, mobile snout terminating in a disc-shaped surface on which the nostrils are located. Most pigs have large tusks in both jaws which grow continuously in life. The tusks of the upper jaw are unique in that they curve upward instead of pointing downward as in most animals.

The excrement of a pig has an almost unbearable odor, which clings not only to the pig itself but also to swineherds, who can be identified a long way off.

Pigs were never raised in the Holy Land by Jews. The great herd into which Jesus drove the unclean spirits was encountered in the land of the Gadarenes, a non-Jewish area east of the Jordan. The Gadarene demons took refuge in a herd of pigs feeding on a bluff overlooking the Sea of Galilee (Mt 8:28–32).

Wild pigs were found in the Holy Land as in many countries today. Psalm 80:13 refers to the destructiveness of a wild boar (the male, or hog) attacking growing crops. A party of wild boars can destroy an entire vineyard or a field of crops in a single night. They devour, trample, and ravage everything within reach.

Boar hunts were common in ancient Mesopotamia. Wild boars do not attack unless molested, but they are dangerous when aroused. They travel in bands of from 6 to 50 and are most active in the evening and early morning hours. The body is covered with stiff bristles and usually some finer fur, but the body covering is often quite scanty. Wild pigs are mainly vegetarian, feeding on roots, nuts, grains, and plant stems. Wild boars were particularly abundant in the mountainous regions of Lebanon and Anti-Lebanon, in the Jordan River valley, and in wooded sections such as Mt Tabor.

Strict Jews would not even mention swine by name but would always substitute the term "the abomination." Israelites considered themselves polluted if they were even touched by a swine's bristle.

To the Hebrews the pig symbolized filth and ugliness. Pigs will eat fecal material, vermin, rodents, carrion, and the like (2 Pt 2:22). Proverbs 11:22 refers to the incongruity of a golden ring in the nose of an animal showing such characteristics. A similar metaphor occurs in Jesus' statement about casting pearls before swine (Mt 7:6). The prodigal son's degeneration was shown by his being forced in his poverty to feed pigs and eat their food (Lk 15:15,16).

Eating the flesh of pigs was forbidden to the Jews (Lv 11:7; Dt 14:8). The Canaanites in the Holy Land killed and ate pigs freely. In intertestamental times Antiochus IV (Epiphanes), a Syrian king whose territories included Israel, used the pig to "Hellenize" the Jews. He first tested their loyalty to the Jewish faith by requiring the consumption of pork, considered a delicacy by the Greeks (2 Mc 6:18). The act of desecration that drove the Jews to rebellion, however, was the sprinkling of pig blood on the temple altar in a sacrifice to Zeus (1 Mc 1:47).

Pigs were frequently used in pagan worship (Is 65:4; 66:3,17), which may account for their being forbidden to the Jews as food. Evidence in the Holy Land shows that pigs were sacrificed long before Hellenistic times. Pig bones were found in a grotto below the rock-cut place of sacrifice at Gezer. A similar underground chamber with vessels containing piglet bones at Tirzah dates to the Middle Bronze Age (about 2000 BC).

Alabaster fragments of a statuette of a pig ready to be sacrificed have been unearthed. Among the Greeks the agrarian rites of the swine god Adonis were popular. Swine were sacrificed to Aphrodite (Venus) in Greece and Asia Minor. In addition, pigs were sacrificed in connection with oaths and treaties; in the *Iliad* Agamemnon sacrificed a boar to Zeus and Helios. So it is not surprising that among the Jews the pig became a symbol of filthiness and paganism.

It is possible that eating pork was forbidden primarily because the pig may carry many worm parasites such as trichina, though that is also true of some "clean" animals. Another reason for forbidding their consumption may have been that pigs eat carrion. Some

people are allergic to pork in hot weather, another suggested reason behind the Jewish taboo. The same taboo exists among the Muslims and existed in certain social strata in Egypt.

Porcupine. True rodent, *Hystrix cristata*, which lives in forested areas, rocky hills, ravines, and valleys. The porcupine is still found in the Holy Land today. It has long quills which are raised to give the appearance of a crest. It is almost entirely nocturnal. It burrows by day into a natural cavity or crevice. The old-world porcupine rarely climbed trees, although the new-world porcupine frequently does. A porcupine may weigh as much as 60 pounds. They eat fruit, bark, roots, and other vegetation, and carrion as well. Although its flesh is edible, the porcupine was not classed among the clean animals for the Israelites. The reference in Isaiah 34:11 is probably to the porcupine, but some references in Scripture to the porcupine or hedgehog may actually be to the bittern, a long-legged wading bird.

See HEDGEHOG, ABOVE.

Scorpion. Arthropod of the same group as spiders (arachnids). A dozen species of scorpions (order *Scorpionida*) are found in the Holy Land, but 90 percent of the scorpions are yellow scorpions, usually 3 to 5 inches long. The rock scorpion, also common to the Holy Land, is as thick as a man's finger and from 5 to 7 inches in length. Scorpions are slow, nocturnal invertebrates that rest beneath stones by day and prey on insects and other arachnids by night. At the end of its long tail the scorpion carries a poisonous sting which is fatal to most prey and extremely painful to humans (Rv 9:3,5,10; cf. 1 Kgs 12:11,14). It can be very dangerous to small children (cf. Lk 11:12). Scorpions symbolized Ezekiel's evil countrymen (Ez 2:6) and the demonic forces of Satan (Lk 10:19). The scorpion is referred to as frequenting the Sinai desert (Dt 8:15).

A scorpion has from 6 to 8 eyes. It has 8 legs like a spider and 2 lobsterlike claws with which it catches and holds its prey. It feeds particularly on locusts and beetles. In many species the female scorpion eats the male after mating. Scorpions lay eggs that hatch very shortly after laying. Scorpions prefer warmer climates, and because of their desire for warmth, enter houses, especially at night, hiding in beds, blankets, footwear, and clothing.

Serpent. Various species of snake, suborder *Ophidia* (*Serpentes*). In the Bible 9 Hebrew words and 4 Greek ones refer to snakes. The most common Hebrew word is onomatopoeic, that is, an imitation of a snake hissing or of the sound it produces as it scrapes its scales along the ground (cf. Jer 46:22). Many types of snakes lay eggs (Is 59:5), although some retain the eggs in the body until ready to hatch.

Serpents are among the most widespread reptiles and are found on all continents except Antarctica; they decrease in numbers and species toward the poles but increase as one approaches the equator.

Thirty-three species of snakes are known in Palestine and neighboring countries, 20 of which are poisonous. Two dangerous characteristics of the serpent noted by biblical writers are its inconspicuous way of moving and the ease with which it hides itself.

Many serpents are able to swallow animals several times their own diameter because of their unusually flexible jaw mechanism. They lack not only legs but also movable eyelids. Snakes periodically shed their skins. The tongue is actually a hearing apparatus sensitive to airborne vibrations and probably to heat waves.

The venom of poisonous species is a clear, thin secretion, transmitted to the victim's bloodstream by means of fangs. Two types of venom are known: that of the vipers which affects respiration and disintegrates red blood cells, and that of the cobras which paralyzes the nervous system.

The "asp" referred to in the Bible is probably the cobra; the "adder" is the viper. The "cockatrice" of KJV is probably the adder.

Serpents were associated with worship in Canaanite religion and symbolized evil deities among many other peoples. Steles (upright stones bearing inscriptions) have been unearthed at several sites in the Holy Land and Syria depicting a god or worshiper with a snake winding about the legs or body. Because the Israelites were burning incense in pagan worship of Moses' bronze serpent (Nm 21:8,9) King Hezekiah destroyed it in his religious reform (2 Kgs 18:4).

Although snakes have been an object of veneration in some religions, in the Judeo-Christian tradition snakes represent evil and, more specifically, the devil. That association began in the garden of Eden (Gn 3:1–15) and is also found in the Book of Revelation (Rv 12:9; 20:2,3).

See ADDER, ABOVE; ASP, ABOVE.

Sheep. Domestic animal of the order *Ovis orientalis.* Sheep are referred to directly or by some term such as ewe, lamb, ram, or by some fact concerning them over 700 times in Scripture.

Sheep represented the chief wealth and total livelihood of pastoral peoples, providing food to eat, milk to drink, wool for the making of cloth, and hides and bones for other uses. In addition the sheep was a medium of exchange and a sacrificial animal. The number of sheep raised in ancient times was prodigious. Mesha, king of Moab, paid a tribute annually of 100,000 lambs and the wool of 100,000 rams (2 Kgs 3:4). The Israelites took 250,000 sheep from the Hagrites (1 Chr 5:21).

Sheep shearing was often a time for festival (2 Sm 13:23). The sheep was held down on its side and its legs were tied together; then it lay docilely while its wool was clipped (Is 53:7). Sheep reserved for burnt offerings were not shorn; nothing could be held back from a sacrifice to the Lord.

Wool had to be processed before it could be used for clothing. First it was washed, sometimes while still on the sheep, then carded and perhaps weighed for the market. The spinning of wool was regarded as a woman's work (Prv 31:19), but weaving the spun thread into cloth on a loom was primarily a man's occupation.

The Bible reports that Abel kept sheep (Gn 4:2). The first sheep to be domesticated was probably the argali (*Ovis ammon*), a variety of the urial (*Ovis vignei*), a mountainous species still existing in Turkestan and Mongolia. Five breeds had reached Mesopotamia by 2000 BC; all were of the urial stock.

The sheep known in Israel was the broadtailed sheep (*Ovis orientalis vignei* or *laticaudata*) of which the tail weighs from 10 to 15 pounds and has always been considered a delicacy. Thus the Lord asked for this choice part as a sacrifice (Ex 29:22–25).

Only the ram of the broadtailed sheep has horns, but in other varieties of sheep in the Holy Land the ewe also has horns. The horns, 2 to 3 inches in diameter, can be potent weapons. Ram's horns could be used as trumpets (Jos 6:4) or as oil containers (1 Sm 16:1).

Although the sheep is very similar to the goat, it is differentiated by a lower forehead, its angulated spiral horns marked with transverse wrinkles and curved slightly outward, its covering of wool, and its lack of a "goatee."

A ram.

Most sheep are white (Ps 147:16; Is 1:18; Dn 7:9; Rv 1:14).

In Scripture sheep are often mentioned as "small cattle," a term that included goats as well. Usually sheep were more numerous and more valuable than goats.

The flesh of sheep was a luxury in the biblical culture. King Solomon required a daily provision of 100 sheep for his table (1 Kgs 4:23), but the common people ate lamb or mutton only on festive occasions. A young ram was usually chosen because the ewes were more important to the future prospects of the herd. The meat was boiled in large caldrons. The milk of the sheep is extremely rich; in biblical times it was usually allowed to curdle before drinking. Possibly some Israelites kept lambs in their houses as pets (2 Sm 12:3,4).

To protect the flock at night against predatory attacks, the shepherd tried to provide a fold. In meadows near villages folds were built and watchmen hired to relieve the shepherds. The shepherds of the nativity story were "out in the field" (Lk 2:8); they had no fold but probably had set up a tent for shelter, consisting simply of goathair blankets spread across sapling supports. The scarcity of springs in the Holy Land made the watering of the flock a crucial problem for the shepherd (Gn 13:8–11).

Wild mountain sheep, varieties of *Ovis orientalis*, are known in the Mediterranean area (Dt 14:5). The Deuteronomy passage (KJV chamois) might also refer to *Ovis tragelaphus*, a sheep about 5 feet high with long, curved horns. Another possibility is the Barbary sheep which lives in small flocks in rugged mountain areas in Barbary, Egypt, and Mt Sinai. The true chamois is unknown in Palestine.

The sheep is also used figuratively in Scripture. The ram represented great strength and fittingly symbolized Medo-Persia in Daniel's vision (Dn 8:3). It is the nature of sheep to be gentle and submissive (Is 53:7; Jer 11:19), defenseless (Mi 5:8; Mt 10:16), and in constant need of guidance and care (Nm 27:17; Mt 9:36). Such qualities are regarded as desirable in the lives of believers in Christ; hence the many figurative references to sheep in the NT and to Jesus as shepherd (Mk 6:34; Jn 10:1–30; Rom 8:35–37; Heb 13:20,21; 1 Pt 2:25). The resurrected Christ told the apostle Peter to "feed my lambs" and "tend my sheep" (Jn 21:15–17).

See Food and Food Preparation; Offerings and Sacrifices; Trades and Occupations (Shepherd).

Skink. Medium-sized lizards with smooth, shiny scales. Members of the family *Scincidae* have a hard body surface with bony plates beneath the skin. Some skinks are limbless, but those with short, well-developed legs are fast-moving creatures.

The skink is the "sand lizard" that was ritually unclean to the Israelites (Lv 11:30 NIV), who were probably familiar with the common skink (*Scincus scincus*).

Snail. Invertebrate gastropods (mollusks). Land snails are very numerous in the Near East. Some freshwater forms serve as hosts for the schistosome worm, the fluke parasite causing the dread disease bilharzia (schistosomiasis). A reference to the "slime" of the snail, the substance it secretes as it moves (Ps 58:8).

Purple dyes of all shades were highly valued in the ancient world. A royal purple dye was obtained from secretions of a sea snail (*Murex trunculus* and *Murex brandaris*). Evidently that process was developed by Phoenicians, Egyptians, and Assyrians as early as 1500 BC. The purple fishermen had their own guild during the time of the Roman Empire. The snails were harvested during the fall and winter seasons; in the spring, when egg laying took place, little dye was available. The snails tended to remain concealed in the summer. They inhabited the waters off Crete and Phoenicia. Tyrian purple, produced in the Phoenician city of Tyre, the center of the purple dye industry, was obtained by a double dyeing. Large deposits of *Murex* shells from dyeing operations have been found along the Mediterranean shoreline. The Israelites had to import purple goods (Ez 27:16). Lydia was a "seller of purple" or of cloth so dyed (Acts 16:14). Purple was a sign of distinction, royalty, and wealth (cf. Ex 25:4; 28:5,6,15; "blue," Nm 15:38; 2 Chr 2:7; Est 8:15; Prv 31:22; Sg 3:10; Ez 27:7; Dn 5:7).

Exodus 30:34–35 refers to "onycha," which was an important ingredient of incense. Onycha is the horny, clawlike operculum (the plate that closes off the opening of its shell when a snail is retracted) of a Near Eastern member of the molluskan family *Strombidae*. The family is worldwide in its distribution. The operculum is sometimes used for offense or locomotion as well as for defense. When burned, the operculum gives off a sharp, strong scent, and when mixed with more fragrant but less powerful substances is even more potent. The name "onycha" is derived from a Greek word (*onyx*) for a fingernail or a claw.

See Dye, Dyer, Dyeing.

Spider. Animal of the order *Araneida*. Between 600 and 700 different species inhabit the Holy Land. Spiders are different from insects in that, like scorpions, they have 4 pairs of legs instead of 3. Spiders are equipped with poison glands, their effectiveness varying from species to species. A few can kill only insects, but others can also kill birds and mice.

Most spiders have a pair of spinnerets attached to silk glands on the underside of the abdomen; from them a web is extruded. In the Bible the spider's web is referred to as a symbol of frailty and insecurity (Jb 8:14; Is 59:5,6).

Sponge. Simple marine animals, phylum *Porifera*. The term "sponge" also refers to those animals' skeletal remains. The sponge has a porous body composed of tubules and cells.

Sponge fishing was well known in the Mediterranean area in ancient times. It was practiced particularly along the Anatolian and Syrian coasts. Sponges were harvested by divers; their work was considered "hard and woeful." The use of sponges in absorbing liquids is referred to in the Bible (Mt 27:48; Mk 15:36).

Vole. Rodent of the genus *Microtus*. One biblical reference is probably to the vole, very likely the Levant vole (*Microtus guentheri*). Some scholars, however, believe that the reference (1 Sm 6:4,5) is to a mouse or rat carrying the bacteria of bubonic plague or of a type of typhoid fever transmitted to human beings by fleas. In that interpretation the "tumors" of 1 Samuel 5:9–12 refer to bubonic plague.

Voles have short tails that distinguish them from mice. They prefer moderately moist meadow lands and swampy areas where they have clearly defined surfaced runways. Some dig short, round burrows and live among the rock crannies. The vole is strictly vegetarian and has substantial food requirements; within 24 hours most voles consume nearly their own weight in seeds, roots, barks, and leaves. The Levant vole not only ravishes agriculture but may also spread disease.

The vole is cyclic; its numbers increase and then decline.

Wasp. Social insects of the order *Vespa orientalis*. Hornets are social wasps which build large aerial apartment houses in which a thousand or more individuals may live. In the Bible the hornet seems to be a metaphor for God's use of military forces (Ex 23:28; Dt 7:20; Jos 24:12).

Weasel. Small, carnivorous mammals of the genus *Mustela*. In the Bible they are listed among the creeping things that swarm and were ceremonially unclean (Lv 11:29); it is possible that the animal referred to is not the weasel but the mole rat.

See MOLE RAT, ABOVE.

Weasels have long, slender bodies, short legs, and well-developed anal scent glands. Weasels are solitary animals and tend to be nocturnal, hunting by scent. Most are of medium or small size; one species can slip through a hole the size of a quarter. Many members of the family are clothed with fur of great brilliance and beauty, and thus are of high commercial value. Weasels were evidently plentiful in the Holy Land during biblical days.

Whale. Largest of all living creatures, including those that have become extinct. Whales are air-breathing mammals of the order *Cetacea*.

Two varieties of whales visit the shores of the Holy Land at times. The finback whale (*Balaenoptera physalus*) weighs about 200 tons and lives mainly in the Arctic region but sometimes passes through the Straights of Gibraltar to reach the eastern Mediterranean Sea. It feeds on small marine organisms which it strains through its whale bone; it does not have teeth. The finback whale's esophagus is narrow.

The sperm whale (*Physeter catodon*), about 60 feet long, has a curiously shaped head that looks like a battering ram and has teeth. The teeth in the lower jaw of the male sperm whale are about 7 inches long. It feeds on big fish, even on sharks. It has a large throat opening.

Whales are referred to in Genesis 1:21 and Job 7:12 (KJV only). A reference in Ezekiel 32:2 (KJV whale; RSV dragon of the sea) is probably to a crocodile. The "great fish" of Jonah 2:1 need not have been a whale but could have been a large shark, such as the whale shark (*Rhineodon*), which grows 70 feet long and lacks the terrible teeth of other sharks. Whatever the actual marine organism, Jonah's deliverance was miraculous. The Greek word for "whale" is sometimes used as a general term for "sea monster" or huge fish and may be used in that sense in Matthew 12:40.

Wild Ox. Large, fierce, fleet, intractable animal (*Bos primigenius*). It had a long, lean rump with a straight back and a long, narrow head. The animal described in Job 39:9–12 is clearly the wild ox. The 2 horns (Dt 33:17), its outstanding characteristic, were straight and as long as the head (Nm 23:22; 24:8; Ps 22:21). Kings often symbolized their dominion by wearing a helmet with two wild ox horns (cf. Pss 92:10; 132:17,18). The horns were often used as drinking vessels by the Israelites; some were large enough to hold four gallons.

Hunting the wild ox was a favorite sport of Assyrian kings. Tiglath-pileser I hunted it in the Lebanon mountains about 1100 BC (cf. Ps 29:6). At one time the animal referred to in Job 39:9–12 was thought to be the oryx or antelope because of the similarity between the Hebrew word in Job and the Arabian name for oryx. The translators of the KJV called the wild ox a unicorn because of representations found on Babylonian mosaics and Egyptian drawings. Those representations showed it in strict profile, showing only one horn; hence "unicorn." Jerome's Vulgate, a Latin Bible translation

(4th century AD) and Martin Luther's German version translated similarly.

Wolf. Large doglike mammal (*Canis lupus*) that travels in bands of up to 30 animals developed from a family group. They hunt singly or in relays, usually at night (Jer 5:6). Wolves have acute hearing and sight but rely chiefly on scent and usually catch their prey in a swift, open chase. The wolf has a reputation for boldness, fierceness, and voracity (Gn 49:27; Hb 1:8). It commonly kills more than it can eat or drag away and thus is known for its greediness. Its usual food is small animals (such as mice, fish, and crabs) and carrion.

From the nose to the rump the wolf measures about 3 feet; its drooping tail is about 18 inches long. It looks much like a skinny German shepherd dog. The grayish-yellow pelt is coarse and short-haired.

The wolf is a restless animal, always on the move; hunger drives it from one place to another in constant search of new hunting grounds. During spring and fall, wolves usually roam singly or in pairs, whereas in summer they may travel in family groups. In winter, several such groups may join to form a large pack. Wolves are intelligent, social creatures, faithful to their own kind. They mate for life. Individually, the wolf is a rather timid animal; it would much rather avoid human beings. But collectively wolves can be among the most dangerous animals alive.

In Egypt, Rome, and Greece the wolf was considered sacred. Wolves were well known in the Holy Land and are still found there and also in many places in Asia Minor. Shepherds continually battled with wolves that plundered their flocks (Jn 10:12).

Both the wolf's courage and its cruelty were probably in the mind of the patriarch Jacob when he predicted the fate of Benjamin's tribe (Gn 49:27).

The Bible refers to wolves in a literal sense in only three places (Is 11:6; 65:25; Jn 10:12), all other references being figurative. Usually the wolf is a symbol of enemies or the wicked (e.g., Ez 22:27; Zep 3:3; Acts 20:29).

Worm. Actually insect larvae in most biblical references, usually maggots, the larvae of flies (see *Fly,* above). For example, maggots are evidently referred to in accounts of worms feeding on spoiled manna (Ex 16:19,20), corpses (Jb 21:26; 24:20 KJV; Is 14:11), or open wounds (Jb 7:5). Mark 9:48 refers to a maggot that eats dead flesh. In Acts 12:23 a fatal abdominal worm disease of King Herod is described. In other cases (Is 51:8) the reference is to the larvae of other insects. In Deuteronomy 28:39 and Jonah 4:7 the vine weevil (*Cochylis ambiguella*) is probably referred to; it destroys vines by boring into their stems.

Comparing a man to a worm is meant to humble him (Jb 25:6; Ps 22:6; Mi 7:17 KJV). In such verses the reference may be to a segmented worm that lives in burrows consuming soil and leaf mold, namely the common earthworm (*Lumbricu terrestris*), which is a true worm in contrast to the larvae mentioned above.   JOHN W. KLOTZ

See BIRDS.

Anise. KJV translation of dill in Matthew 23:23.

See PLANTS (DILL).

Anklet, Anklet Chain. *See* FASHION AND DRESS.

Anna. Phanuel's daughter from Asher's tribe and a prophetess in Jerusalem when Jesus was a young child. Advanced in years, she worshiped with prayer and fasting day and night in the temple. When Jesus was brought by his parents and presented to the Lord in the temple, she came up, thanking God and speaking of him to all who were looking for the redemption of Jerusalem (Lk 2:36).

Annas. Jewish high priest from AD 7 to AD 15. Appointed by Quirinius, Roman governor of Syria, Annas was put out of office by Valerius Gratus, procurator of Judea. Annas was succeeded by three minor figures before the post was assumed by his son-in-law Caiaphas (Jn 18:13,24). The tenure of Caiaphas extended from AD 18 to AD 36; thus he was high priest at the time of Jesus' public ministry.

Evidently Annas's power and influence remained considerable even after his removal from that office. Like an American Supreme Court justice, the high priest held a lifetime appointment. Deposition of a high priest by the pagan Romans would have been strongly resented by the Jews. Consequently, Annas may still have been referred to as high priest among the populace, as a sort of high priest emeritus. Such a practice, evidenced in the writings of the Jewish historian Josephus, tends to clear up those references in the NT to Annas as high priest during the same chronological period as Caiaphas (Lk 3:2; Jn 18:19, 22–24; Acts 4:6).

The fact that Annas conducted a private inquiry of Jesus after he was arrested (Jn 18:13, 19–24), but before he was taken to Caiaphas, is a strong indication that Annas was still a person of considerable stature among the Jewish religious leaders. Annas questioned Jesus "about his disciples and his teaching," to which Jesus answered in a seemingly evasive and uncooperative way. OT law demanded the death penalty for those who tried to turn Israel to apostasy and idolatry (Dt 13:6–9). If Jesus was regarded by the authorities as a false prophet with such aims in view, it was legitimate that his words and his adherents be investigated. But Jewish law also required the testimony of witnesses both for and against the accused person prior to his own testimony. Only when the testimony of witnesses had been given and confirmed could the case be argued directly with the individual on trial. Thus Jesus' reply that his teaching was "spoken openly to the world" was a challenge to his questioners to bring forth proper evidence. Jesus indicated that he expected them to follow proper legal procedure.

Annas is also mentioned in the NT account of an investigation of the apostles Peter and John. Interestingly, the penalty imposed on the apostles was far less severe than the one Jesus suffered (Acts 4:6–21).

Anoint, Anointed. To pour oil or ointment onto a person or object in a ritualistic fashion.

The Practice of Anointing. As a religious act, anointing was meant to endow the anointed one with the quality of the deity involved. From ancient times the Hebrews inaugurated officers of their national community by pouring special oil on the head of the person designated for office. The same practice was used to set objects apart for special divine use. The Hebrew word for anoint first appears in Genesis 31:13, where it refers to Jacob pouring oil on the stone of Bethel (Gn 28:18,19). At a later time the ceremony was repeated (Gn 35:9–15). The ceremony was clearly religious, signifying induction into sacred use.

Scripture supplies few details of the ceremonial anointings of official things and persons. Jacob simply poured oil on a rock with an accompanying pronouncement, following some immemorial custom of the Near East. When anointing Israel's first king, the prophet-judge Samuel took Saul aside for instruction (1 Sm 9:25–27), then "took a vial of oil and poured it on his head, and kissed him and said 'Has not the Lord appointed you to be prince over his people Israel'" (1 Sm 10:1). For anointing the tabernacle and its priests, a special oil was compounded and used only for that sacred purpose. Skilled perfume makers blended the choicest spices (myrrh, cinnamon, sweet cane, cassia) in olive oil (Ex 30:22–25). The Lord specified that everything set apart for God— the tabernacle, the ark, the table and its instruments, the lampstand and utensils, the incense altar and main altar, the washbasin— was to be anointed. Aaron the high priest and

his sons the priests were also to be anointed (Ex 30:26–32). The result was a holy place with holy furnishings, holy implements of worship, and holy ministers.

Anointing, however, had more than religious or ritualistic significance. Both the Egyptians and the Syrians practiced anointing for medical and cosmetic reasons, and the Scriptures indicate that such nonreligious practice was also a part of Israelite customs (2 Sm 12:20; Ru 3:3; Mi 6:15). In fact, failure to anoint or perfume oneself indicated mourning or distress (2 Sm 14:2; Dn 10:3; Mt 6:17).

In the NT, anointing of the sick accompanied by prayer for healing by local church elders is recommended when requested by a sick person (Jas 5:14–16). Anointing with oil was also a part of the apostles' healing ministry (Mk 6:12,13).

The Anointed Leaders. The offices of prophet, priest, and king were those associated with anointing in the nation of Israel. Prophets were sometimes, but not invariably, inducted by official anointing (1 Kgs 19:16). They could be referred to as God's anointed ones (1 Chr 16:22; Ps 105:15). At the institution of the levitical priesthood, all the priests were anointed to their offices, the sons of Aaron as well as Aaron himself (Ex 40:12–15; Nm 3:3). Afterward, anointing was not repeated at the consecration of ordinary priests, but was especially reserved for the high priest (Ex 29:29; Lv 16:32).

Before they had a king of their own, the Israelites were aware of anointing as a mode of inaugurating kings (Jgs 9:8,15). Anointing became a divinely ordained rite accompanying induction of all the kings of Judah and Israel (2 Kgs 9:1–6; 11:12) from Saul onward (1 Sm 10:1; 1 Kgs 1:39). David's anointing took place in three stages (1 Sm 16:1,13; 2 Sm 2:4; 5:1–5). "The Lord's anointed" or some similar phrase became a common designation for Hebrew kings (1 Sm 12:3,5; 2 Sm 1:14,16; Ps 89:38,51; Lam 4:20).

The Anointed One. In the NT, Jesus Christ is portrayed as fulfilling the three offices of prophet, priest, and king. He is, supremely, God's Anointed One. *Messiah* is the term for "anointed one" derived directly from the Hebrew word for anointed; *Christ* is the same title derived from the Greek word for "anointee." The true anointing of Messiah (Ps 2:2; Dn 9:25,26) is spiritual; that is, it is done by the Holy Spirit (Is 61:1; Lk 4:1,18,19). That Jesus of Nazareth was indeed the Anointed One (Messiah) of OT prophecy was evidenced in his anointing by the Holy Spirit and by the miracles that followed (Jn 1:32–51; Lk 4:33–37). By extension, Christians also are said to be anointed by the Holy Spirit, enabling them to understand their faith and to live godly lives (2 Cor 1:21,22; 1 Jn 2:20,27).

ROBERT D. CULVER

See MESSIAH.

Ant. Insect used as an example of industriousness for storing up food in the summer (Prv 6:6; 30:25).

See ANIMALS.

Antelope. Swift, deerlike animal mentioned in Deuteronomy 14:5 (KJV wild ox) and Isaiah 51:20 (KJV wild bull).

See ANIMALS.

Anthothijah. Benjamite and Shashak's son (1 Chr 8:24, KJV Antothijah).

Anthropology. In a theological sense, the study of what the Bible says about man and the relation in which he stands and should stand to God.

See MAN, DOCTRINE OF.

Anthropomorphism. Representation of God in the form of a human being in speech or writing. "Anthropomorphism," derived from two Greek words, means literally "human form-ism." It can refer both to a proper, biblical representation of God and to an improper, even corrupt, manner of representing deity.

Proper Use of Anthropomorphism. Most philosophers and theologians agree that all formulated knowledge about God is "analogical." That is, declarative statements about God—such as "thou hatest all evil doers" (Ps 5:5) or "the Lord is compassionate and merciful" (Jas 5:11)—are understandable only because people know something about hate and mercy in their own experience. When we speak of these qualities, even in another human being, we are to some degree automatically projecting into that person what we know to be hate and mercy in ourselves.

In other words, all knowledge of other persons is analogical—analogous to something we have experienced—because there is no possibility of direct sensation of personality in others. To hear someone laugh gives us no direct sensation of that person's joy. But knowing how we feel when we want to laugh joyfully, we assume analogically that the same sort of feeling produces the other's laughter.

Of course, analogically perceived knowledge may be distorted by faulty self-knowledge. "But who can discern his errors? Clear thou me from hidden faults" (Ps 19:12). We all make mistakes from time to time in judging the motives (expressions of character, person, or selfhood) behind the behavior of others. We may even misjudge our own motives.

It is the "image of God" in human beings (Gn 1:26,27) that makes a degree of analogy (anthropomorphism) in our thoughts about God quite proper. But until our moral likeness to God is restored through spiritual regeneration, our analogies are likely to lead to serious error. In the extreme example, the invisible God may be represented by images (idols) to be worshiped. According to Scripture, human understanding will remain distorted until our sanctification and glorification are complete. Then we shall enjoy direct knowledge of God (the "beatific vision" spoken of by medieval mystics), for we shall see him "as he is" (1 Jn 3:2).

Meanwhile, in the broadest sense, all affirmations about God are anthropomorphic. Specifically, the Bible uses three types of figurative speech in speaking of God. The first is called *anthropoiesis*, from the Greek word for "human being" plus a word for "doing" or "making." Anthropoietic expressions picture God as doing something the way a person would do that thing. "And God said, 'Let there be light'" (Gn 1:3), yet God has no vocal cords. Similarly, God is said to have breathed into Adam's body "the breath of life" (Gn 2:7). God did confer life upon man, life of a special sort akin to God's own divine life in certain respects, but God has no lungs or other organs for breathing. The many examples of anthropoiesis in the Bible are generally distinguished from what theologians refer to as *theophany* (from Greek words meaning "God appearing"). In a theophany, the divine spirit, usually interpreted as the Logos before Christ's incarnation, assumed a temporary human form and interacted with human beings as one of them. Examples include the three men who visited Abraham in the plains of Mamre (Gn 18) and the "man from God" (Jgs 13:6) who appeared to Manoah and his wife, the parents of Samson (Jgs 13:2–25). Such theophanies are regarded by many evangelical theologians as actual appearances of the second person of the Trinity and not merely anthropomorphic figures of speech.

The figure of speech called *anthropopathy*, from the Greek for "human being" plus a word for "suffering," is used in Scripture to depict in God what would be called emotion in human beings: love, hate, joy, grief, repentance, and the like. Such statements are again analogical expressions from a human point of view. Some theologians have asserted that God is "impassible," that is, that he is incapable of suffering, and probably all would agree that God's inner, conscious essence remains undisturbed and unruffled by anything he has created. According to 19th-century theologian A.A. Hodge, when God is said in the Bible to repent, or to be grieved, or to be jealous, "it is meant only that he acts toward us as a man would when agitated by such passions. These metaphors occur primarily in the Old Testament, and in highly rhetorical passages of the poetical and prophetic books."

In the incarnation, when the Logos became Jesus of Nazareth, the divine nature joined in indissoluble union with the human nature, so affirmations about divine suffering, rejoicing, grieving, hating, are less metaphorical. That is what the incarnation is all about (Heb 2:9–18; 4:14–16).

The third variety of figurative speech about God could be called anthropomorphism proper, that is, giving God the form of a human person. The Bible contains many examples of assigning bodily parts or organs to God. As with anthropopathy, most of the examples occur in OT poetry and prophecy. God's power is referred to analogically as his hands, his knowledge as his eyes, his pleasure (an anthropopathism) as his nostrils. Hebrew statements on almost any subject can use anthropomorphism, as when "the arms of his hands" stands for military power (Gn 49:24 KJV); in that verse the "hands" are Joseph's, not God's. The Hebrew expression, "the eyes of the Lord," is used to convey sympathetic acceptance, as when Noah "found grace in the eyes of the Lord" (Gn 6:8 KJV). In other contexts the same expression conveys God's supportive attention (Dt 11:12 KJV), his moral judgment (13:18), his unslacked attention (32:10), or his omniscience and benevolence (2 Chr 16:9). Similarly, God's "ear" appears at least a dozen times in the psalms as a metaphor for his response to prayer (e.g., Pss 10:17; 17:6; 18:6). The prophet Isaiah appealed to Israel in a well-known passage containing a series of anthropomorphisms: "Behold, the Lord's hand is not shortened, that it cannot save; neither his ear heavy, that it cannot hear: but your iniquities have separated between you and your God, and your sins have hid his face from you" (Is 59:1,2 KJV).

Occasionally the metaphor of bodily parts is derived from a creature other than a human being. Thus Boaz spoke of Ruth as trusting under the "wings" of the Lord God of Israel (Ru 2:12), and the psalmist said, "He shall cover thee with his feathers, and under his wings shalt thou trust" (Ps 91:4 KJV). Simile, a figure of speech using "like" or "as" is usually a milder descriptive technique than metaphor. The difference can be seen in two translations of Exodus 19:4, where the KJV retains the metaphor ("I bare you on eagles' wings, and brought you unto myself") and LB converts it

to a simile ("I brought you to myself as though on eagle's wings"). Metaphor and simile occur together in another poetic passage: "He spreads his wings over them,/ Even as an eagle overspreads her young./ She carries them upon her wings—/ as does the Lord his people!" (Dt 32:11,12 LB).

Improper Use of Anthropomorphism. Some modern philosophers have asserted that none of our statements about God as a person or spirit with personal, spiritual attributes are even analogically correct. They claim that such statements do not in any sense conform to objective fact. To such philosophers anthropomorphic statements are of necessity invalid. Of course, when people construct images and other likenesses of God as true representations, they create a god in their own image and likeness. The apostle Paul reminded the pagan philosophers of Athens that to do so was to be not only false but also illogical (Acts 17:18–31). Likewise OT prophets sarcastically asserted that idolatry is a corrupt practice (e.g., Elijah in 1 Kgs 18:20–40). But neither Paul nor the prophets were condemning the proper use of anthropomorphic statements and concepts.

One group of early Christians who took the anthropomorphic language of the Bible literally were regarded as heretics. They have been called Anthropomorphites by church historians. The same kind of naive simplicity in biblical interpretation has in modern times often characterized the Latter Day Saints (Mormons), for example.

All anthropomorphic metaphors are analogical in character. Properly understood, however, anthropomorphisms can enrich our understanding and appreciation of biblical truth.

ROBERT D. CULVER

Antichrist. According to 1 John, anyone who denies that Jesus is the Christ, that he is the unique Son of God, or that he has come in the flesh. The biblical term, however, principally refers to a particular person in whom that denial reaches its consummate expression and who will play a key role in the final stage of history.

Antichrist in Scripture. The word "antichrist" occurs only four times, all in John's epistles (1 Jn 2:18,22; 4:3; 2 Jn 7). First John 2:18 refers also to "many antichrists." John assumed that his Christian readers knew about the antichrist and had been taught to expect his coming (1 Jn 2:18–27). The presence of many antichrists, in fact, indicated that "the last hour" or endtime had arrived. But John warned that a final antichrist who, like the others, would deny that Jesus is the Christ, would yet make an appearance.

John further described any person or message that did not "confess Jesus" as being of the spirit of the antichrist (1 Jn 4:3). In his brief Second Epistle, John referred to "many deceivers" who would not "acknowledge the coming of Jesus Christ in the flesh" (2 Jn 7). Such a person, he wrote, was "the deceiver and the antichrist."

In the Book of Revelation, John's symbol for the antichrist is probably "the beast" (Rv 13:1–18; 17:3,7–17). The beast is described, not only as an opposer of Christ, but more specifically as a satanically inspired Christ-counterfeit. Although the beast (antichrist) is clearly distinguishable from the Lamb (Christ), he receives worship from everyone except God's elect.

Another probable reference to the antichrist is "the man of lawlessness" (2 Thes 2:3). The passage is difficult to interpret, but the person described seems to be the same person later designated by John as the beast. Both the apostle Paul and John saw present events as leading up to the events of the future. Instructing the church at Thessalonica about the second coming of Christ (2 Thes 2:1–12), Paul stressed that the appearance and rebellion of the man of lawlessness must occur beforehand. That man would oppose the worship of any gods or God and even proclaim himself to be God (2 Thes 2:4). He would subsequently be destroyed by Christ at his return (2 Thes 2:8)—an indication that those events are set in the final days of history.

The concept of antichrist undoubtedly comes from the teaching of Jesus in the Gospels. A lengthy passage (Mk 13, paralleled in Mt 24, 25, and Lk 21) records the instruction Jesus gave his disciples about the tragic events and persecution which they could expect before his return as the glorious Son of Man. His coming would be preceded by the appearance of many "deceivers" and "false Christs." The term "false Christs" is used only twice (Mt 24:24; Mk 13:22). Although it has obvious similarities to John's "antichrists," the Gospel passages do not refer to "a deceiver" or "false Christ" in the singular as do John's and Paul's writings.

Antichrist in Church History. The history of the church has been marked by various attempts to identify the antichrist with some contemporary person or institution. The text that has generated the most speculation about the antichrist's identity is Revelation 13:18, which associates the number 666 (or 616, in some manuscripts) with the beast. One tradition breaks that number down into Hebrew letters of the alphabet with a total "numerical value" of 666, producing the name "Kaisar Neron." Consequently, one of the earliest and most persistent identifications of the antichrist has been with a resurrected Nero, the first major persecutor of the church. In the early 5th century, Jerome and Augustine wrote that many in their day believed that the apostle John was not dead and was waiting to identify Nero as the antichrist. Any of the early Roman rulers who systematically persecuted the church was looked upon either as having "the spirit of antichrist" (1 Jn 4:3) or as actually incarnating him. Since heresy is one obvious trait of the antichrist, another tendency was to identify him with any principal heretic, such as Arius, the 4th-century church leader who taught that Christ was a created and lesser god.

Reformation writers often identified the antichrist with the papacy. Luther was particularly fond of referring to the pope as the antichrist. In recent times, interpretation of the antichrist as a demonic, anti-Christian teaching or movement has been held by some as an alternative to the antichrist as a person. However, those who interpret the Book of Revelation literally and who hold to a premillennial view generally regard the antichrist as a person under satanic influence. During World War II, for example, advocates of that position often nominated Adolf Hitler and Benito Mussolini as likely candidates.

Historically, speculations about the antichrist's identity or nature have always proven futile. A refusal to go beyond what the Scriptures reveal would certainly prevent further cases of mistaken identity.

HOBERT K. FARRELL *and* DONALD M. LAKE

See FALSE CHRISTS; MARK OF THE BEAST; PROPHET, FALSE; BEAST; REVELATION, BOOK OF.

Bibliography. R. Anderson, *The Coming Prince;* S.J. Andrews, *Christianity and Antichristianity;* W. Bousset, *The Antichrist Legend;* A.L. Mosee, *The Parousia in the NT;* A.W. Pink, *The Antichrist;* G. Vos, *Pauline Eschatology.*

Antioch of Pisidia. City in Asia Minor between the districts of Phrygia and Pisidia to which the apostle Paul traveled to introduce the gospel. Upon arrival Paul was invited by the elders of the synagogue to deliver any message of exhortation he might have at their Sabbath meeting (Acts 13:14). Though many begged to hear more (13:42), certain Jewish leaders envied Paul's popularity and began to revile him (13:45). Paul then turned to gentile listeners (13:43, 46–48) until Jewish persecutors forced him to leave the city (13:50). The same Jews from Antioch continued harassing Paul as he traveled to Lystra (Acts 14:19). Paul passed through Antioch a second time while en route to Perga and Attalia (14:21).

The city of Antioch was founded (300? BC) by Seleucus Nicator and was named for his

An aqueduct near Antioch of Pisidia.

son, Antiochus I. As a result of the Roman conquest in 188 BC the area was declared free from the rule of the Seleucid kings, and deliberate steps toward Romanization followed. In about 36 BC, Antony made Antioch part of the domain of the Galatian king, Amyntas. Upon the death of Amyntas 11 years later the city was elevated to colony status and became Caesaria Antiochela, capital of southern Galatia.

Antioch of Syria. Principal city among 16 others of the same name built about 300 BC by the Syrian emperor Seleucus I in honor of his father Antiochus. This Antioch (modern Antakya, Turkey) occupies a fertile plain in a western bend of the Orontes River that terminates in the Mediterranean Sea. In ancient times the population numbered half a million. Because of its location on navigable waters reaching to a Mediterranean port 15 miles away, and because of its ready access through passes in the Taurus Mountains eastward to the interior, Antioch was a busy, cosmopolitan center of trade, religious ferment, and high levels of intellectual and political life. Under Roman authority Antioch received lavish attention in the form of beautiful public works, harbor improvements, and special trade advantages.

Side by side with a truly high culture were the degrading institutions of strange fertility religions, brutalizing sports spectacles, and a variety of mystery religions. Two other major influences were the large community of fully franchised Jews who flourished there and the community of government functionaries. The Jewish community supplied a number of Christian proselytes to the early church in Antioch. The government officials provided police protection, stability, and order, alternating with seemingly insatiable appetites for lavish dissipations in gambling, chariot races, brothels, exotic banquets, and the like.

Antioch of Syria.

Antioch of Syria played an important role in the Book of Acts. A certain Nicholas from Antioch became one of the first deacons in the early church (Acts 6:5). Jerusalem Christians fled to Antioch from fierce persecution (11:19). Acts 11 gives details of Barnabas and Paul's teaching in the Antioch church and of the benevolent gift of the believers there to suffering Christians in Jerusalem. The term "Christians" was first used in Antioch (11:26). Acts 13 records that the first missionaries were sent from there. The Jerusalem church council's statement on requirements for gentile believers was in part a result of the work in Antioch among Gentiles (see Acts 15 and Gal 2).

From the third century to about the eighth century, Antioch was an important center for the development of Christian theology. The approach to Scripture and to the nature of Christ taken in Antioch tended to be historical and rational, in contrast to an overly spiritualized, allegorical approach taken in Alexandria (Egypt) by such theologians as Origen and Clement.

Antiochus IV. Greek ruler (175–164 BC) from the Seleucid dynasty who forced Greek customs upon the Jews, provoking a Jewish revolt in 167 BC; also known as Epiphanes ("the manifested one").

See JUDAISM.

Antipas. 1. Early martyr in the church at Pergamum (Rv 2:13). Tradition records that he was roasted alive at the whim of a local governor.

2. Son of Herod the Great.
See HEROD, HERODIAN FAMILY.

Antipater. 1. Good-will ambassador sent out with Numenius to the Spartans and Romans by Jonathan, the high priest (1 Mc 12:16; 14:22).

2. Father of Herod the Great.
See HEROD, HERODIAN FAMILY.

Antipatris. City some 26 miles south of Caesarea rebuilt by Herod the Great in 9 BC in honor of his father, Antipater. Before its rebuilding, it was known as Aphek. Paul passed through Antipatris under Roman guard on his way from Jerusalem to Caesarea (Acts 23:31). Antipatris served as a Roman military relay station and marked the border between Judea and Samaria.

See APHEK.

Antitype. Fulfillment or resolution of a corresponding earlier type.

See TYPE, TYPOLOGY.

Antothijah. KJV spelling of Anthothijah, Shashak's descendant, in 1 Chronicles 8:24.

See ANTHOTHIJAH.

Antothite. KJV form of Anathothite, a resident of Anathoth, in 1 Chronicles 11:28 and 12:3.

See ANATHOTH, ANATHOTHITE (PLACE).

Anub. Koz's son from Judah's tribe (1 Chr 4:8).

Ape. Large, tailless primate. Apes, or perhaps other monkeys and baboons, were imported to Israel by King Solomon (1 Kgs 10:22; 2 Chr 9:21).

See ANIMALS.

Apelles. Roman Christian who received special greetings from the apostle Paul and the complimentary assessment of being one who is "approved in Christ" (Rom 16:10).

Apharsathchites, Apharsachites, Apharsites. Words used in the Book of Ezra to designate certain groups of people in Samaria who joined in writing King Artaxerxes of Babylon to stop the rebuilding of the temple in Jerusalem. Apharsathchites (Ezr 4:9 KJV) could refer to a specific ethnic group or to government leaders; a similar Old Persian word meant "messengers." Apharsachites (Ezr 5:6; 6:6 KJV) could be a shortened form of Apharsathchites or could be derived from an Old Persian word for "investigators." Apharsites (Ezr 4:9 KJV) is similar to the Hebrew word for "Persians" and has been translated that way.

Aphek. 1. Canaanite city west of the Jordan River conquered by Israel (Jos 12:18) and later included in Ephraim's territory. It was located near the source of the Yarkon River in the Plain of Sharon. (Jos 12:18 probably refers to only one person, "the king of Aphek of Sharon.") Aphek was later captured by the Philistines (1 Sm 4:1; 29:1). In Roman times Herod the Great rebuilt the city and named it Antipatris, mentioned in Acts 23:31. Its modern name is Ras el-'Ain.

See ANTIPATRIS.

2. Place in Phoenicia (modern Lebanon) that remained unconquered after Joshua's campaigns (Jos 13:4). This Aphek was probably located near the source of the River Ibrahim, east of Byblos.

3. Town given to Asher's tribe in the distribution of conquered cities (Jos 19:30). Asher's tribe failed to drive out the pagan inhabitants (Jgs 1:31; where it is spelled "Aphik"). Aphek was located on the Plain of Acco, at the pres-

ent site of Tell Kurdaneh near the source of the River Na'main.

4. City east of the Jordan River, on the main highway between Damascus and the Valley of Jezreel. The Syrian king, Ben-hadad, defeated by King Ahab of Israel, retreated into Aphek, where a falling wall demolished the rest of his army (1 Kgs 20:26,30). A century later Elisha prophesied to King Joash of Israel that he would defeat the Syrians in the same city (2 Kgs 13:17).

Aphekah. City in the hill country of Canaan given to Judah's tribe after the conquest of the Promised Land by Joshua (Jos 15:53), which is usually identified as Khirbet Kana'an near Hebron.

Aphiah. Ancestor of King Saul in Benjamin's tribe (1 Sm 9:1).

Aphik. Alternate form of Aphek in Judges 1:31.

See APHEK #3.

Aphrah. KJV for Beth-le-aphrah, possibly the name of a Philistine city, in Micah 1:10.

See BETH-LE-APHRAH.

Aphses. KJV form of Happizzez, a priest in David's time, in 1 Chronicles 24:15.

See HAPPIZZEZ.

Apocalypse. Term meaning a "revelation" or a "disclosure." The Books of Daniel and Revelation are the two apocalypses in the Bible.

See APOCALYPTIC; DANIEL, BOOK OF; REVELATION, BOOK OF.

Apocalyptic. Term derived from a Greek word meaning "revelation," and used to refer to a pattern of thought and to a form of literature, both dealing with future judgment (eschatology).

Two primary patterns of eschatological thought are found in the Bible, both centered in the conviction that God will act in the near future to save his people and to punish those who oppress them. In prophetic eschatology, the dominant form in the OT, God is expected to act within history to restore man and nature to the perfect condition which existed prior to man's fall. Apocalyptic eschatology, on the other hand, expects God to destroy the old imperfect order before restoring the world to paradise.

Origins of Apocalypticism. In Israel, apocalyptic eschatology evidently flourished under foreign domination.

From the early 6th century BC, prophetic eschatology began to decline and apocalyptic eschatology became increasingly popular. The Book of Daniel, written during the 6th century BC, is the earliest example of apocalyptic literature in existence. The prophetic Book of Malachi, written sometime during the 5th century BC, was the last Israelite prophetic book. Thereafter, the prophetic voice became silent in Israel until the rise of Christianity. With the exception of Daniel, all the surviving Jewish apocalyptic literature was written from the 3rd century BC to the early 2nd century AD. After the second Jewish revolt (led by Bar Kochba) was crushed by the Romans in AD 135, composition of apocalypses ceased and rabbinic Judaism prevailed.

Some scholars have argued that apocalyptic ideas had their origins in the Zoroastrian religion or in other religions brought into Israel after the 6th century BC by foreign invaders. In fact, however, the characteristic notions of apocalypticism were found in Israelite prophetic literature before Israel became subject to foreign empires in the 6th century BC.

Apocalyptic Patterns of Thought. *Dualism.* Antagonism between God and Satan was sharply emphasized. All men, nations, and supernatural beings (angels, demons) were seen as allies of God or of Satan. Although Satan had always been thought of as the adversary of God and man (Gn 3:1–19; Jb 1:6–12; 2:1–8), his power was restrained as long as Israel remained faithful to the covenant law of God. When Israel began to experience the long national nightmare of subjugation by foreign enemies, the reality of Satan's temporary domination of the world was brought home with great force. Though apocalyptic writers dealt with particular nations dominating Israel during one or another epoch in its history, those nations were seen as servants of Satan whose opposition to God (and God's people) would inevitably spell their downfall.

Determinism. Apocalyptic thought was dominated by the conviction that, no matter how bad circumstances might be at any given moment, God and his people would ultimately triumph over their enemies. Apocalyptic determinism was not a fatalistic conviction that everything happened by a kind of mindless necessity; rather, it clung to hope in a sovereign God who would cause his people to experience ultimate victory over all temporal and spiritual enemies. Many apocalypses contained predictions of the future historical experience of Israel (or of the Christian church), culminating in a final and decisive victory of God and his people. In Nebuchadnezzar's dream interpreted by Daniel, for example, a series of foreign empires was referred to under the symbolism of various parts of a gigantic image constructed of various materials; the image was destroyed by the kingdom of God, symbolized by a stone cut without hands from a mountain (Dn 2:31–45).

Pessimism. A major difference between apocalyptic eschatology and prophetic eschatology was that apocalypticism nearly always envisaged a cosmic catastrophe prior to the final, decisive victory of God. In some apocalypses, such as the Book of Daniel, God was expected to intervene decisively in the course of history, subdue evil, and introduce the kingdom of God. In others, such as the Revelation of John, God would first destroy the old world before creating a wholly new one (Rv 21:1; cf. 2 Pt 3:10). The general view was that things would get much worse before they got better. During the golden age of Israelite independence (10th through 7th centuries BC), the notion of future catastrophe was understandably not given much emphasis. However, after the destruction of Jerusalem in 586 BC, apocalyptists thought the Jews' problems could be reversed only by decisive and climactic intervention of God into the affairs of men and of nations.

A common apocalyptic notion based on both dualism and pessimism was the concept of two "ages." "This age," which is present and evil, was dominated by Satan and his minions, but "the age to come" would bring the blessings of the kingdom of God. A constellation of eschatological events would serve to bring the old age to a close and inaugurate the new age. When Paul spoke of the "god of this evil world" (2 Cor 4:4) he was actually referring to Satan's domination of "this age."

Imminent Expectation of the End. Another characteristic of apocalypticism was its frequent expression of intense longing for God to shorten the present evil days and quickly usher in the kingdom of God. Just as Daniel could ask, "How long shall it be till the end of these wonders?" (Dn 12:6), so John could exclaim, "Come, Lord Jesus!" (Rv 22:20). The desire for God's speedy intervention and victory made it possible to maintain hope in thoroughly adverse circumstances and encouraged God's people to conduct their lives in a manner worthy of the coming kingdom (2 Pt 3:11–13; Rv 21:5–8).

Characteristics of Apocalyptic Literature.
The Book of Daniel is the only apocalypse in the OT canon of Scripture, and the Book of Revelation the only apocalypse within the NT canon. Many noncanonical Jewish and Christian apocalypses survive, however. The Jewish apocalypses were written between the late 3rd century BC and the early 2nd century AD; the existing Christian apocalypses from the 2nd through the 4th centuries AD. Further, many apocalyptic literary patterns and structures are found outside the formal category of apocalyptic literature. The Olivet Discourse of Jesus, for example (Mk 13; Mt 24; Lk 21), has frequently been called a little apocalypse by biblical scholars. In general, most of the features enumerated below must be present for a literary work to be considered "an apocalypse."

Pseudonymity. With the exception of Daniel and Revelation, most of the surviving apocalypses are pseudonymous, that is, they were written under a false name. This characteristic is such a constant feature that apocalyptic literature has been commonly referred to as "pseudepigrapha" ("false writings"). A composite apocalypse (1 Enoch) written by several unknown authors from the 2nd century BC to probably the 1st century AD claimed to have been written by the Enoch who was an early descendant of Adam (Gn 5:21–24). Other Jewish apocalypses were attributed to such important OT characters as Adam and Eve, Moses, Isaiah, Baruch, Solomon, and Ezra. Since all were written after the close of the OT canon, their real authors probably thought that identification with some important OT personage was necessary for favorable reception. Early Christian apocalypses often bore the names of such important figures as Peter, Paul, and Thomas.

Visionary Form. The literature designated "apocalyptic" consists of compositions that either are or purport to be divine revelations received by their authors. The revelations were usually received in the form of visions. They were recounted in detail and accompanied by an interpretation. The second half of Daniel (chs 7–12) is filled with such visions, as is the whole of Revelation. Although revelatory visions also occurred frequently in OT prophetic literature (e.g., Is 6; Am 7–9; Zec 1–6), they were particularly prominent in apocalyptic literature and determined the basic literary form and structure of such writings. Sometimes (as in Daniel) the revelatory message was apprehended through a dream by the apocalyptic seer. In another form of vision (as in Revelation), the apocalyptist was caught up to the heavenly world, where he saw and heard things to be transmitted to the world of men (cf. Paul's experience, 2 Cor 12:1–4). Frequently the apocalyptist was unable to understand the meaning of the visions he received. In such instances an "interpreting angel" clarified the meaning of the vision (Dn 8:15–26; 9:20–27; 10:18–12:4; Rv 7:13–17; 17:7–18).

The visionary revelations recounted in Daniel and Revelation appear to be reports of actual experiences of the authors. Other apocalyptic authors evidently used the vision form as a literary vehicle unrelated to real experience.

Extensive Symbolism. Although biblical prophets frequently used symbolism to convey their messages, the use of symbolism in prophetic visions was relatively rare. Where it did occur it was usually uncomplicated (Is 6:6,7; Am 7:1–8:3). The complexity of symbolism in prophetic visions seemed to increase with the decline of prophecy in Israel; symbolism in the Book of Zechariah reached almost apocalyptic proportions. The symbolism of apocalyptic visions was both more complex and more bizarre than that of prophetic visions. In Daniel's vision of the four beasts (Dn 7), one beast looked like a lion, had the wings of an eagle, and stood on two legs like a man (v 4). John described four living creatures covered with eyes and each with six wings (Rv 4:6–8). Such monstrosities were common in apocalyptic visions. The bizarre nature of the symbolism underlined the importance and transcendence of the concealed realities, and their complexity made their careful interpretation more urgent and pressing. The symbolic visions of Daniel and John communicate future and supernatural realities transcending human experience and rational categories of thought.

World History Framework. The basic theme of apocalyptic literature was the history of the cosmos from creation to consummation and the central role that God and his people play in that history. The basic structure of biblical thought is salvation history; apocalypticism characteristically saw salvation history within the context of world history. Salvation history is the distinctive notion, shared by OT and NT authors alike, that God reveals himself through saving acts and revelations during the course of history, particularly the history of his chosen people.

Although Daniel's central concern was for Israel, many of his visions charted the complexities of world politics as the arena of God's sovereign activities, with Israel, of course, playing a focal role in the arena. The author of Revelation, while comforting and exhorting Christians, nevertheless dealt with the current experience of the church within the context of Roman history.

Messianism. Although messianic figures were not found in all Jewish apocalypses, Jesus in his messianic role understandably dominates Christian apocalypses, particularly the NT Book of Revelation. The expected Messiah is a marginal but important figure in the Book of Daniel (7:13,14; 9:25). The figure of a messiah is absent altogether from certain Jewish apocalypses: *Book of Jubilees, 2 Enoch, Assumption of Moses, 1 Baruch,* and *1 Enoch*

(1:36; 91–104). Some apocalyptic literature envisioned an expected priestly (levitical) messiah; others envisioned a Davidic messiah. The variegated image of the Messiah in pre-Christian Jewish apocalyptic literature indicates that no consistent concept existed in Judaism prior to the beginning of Christianity.

DAVID E. AUNE

See ESCHATOLOGY; AGE, AGES; JUDAISM; BIBLE, INTERPRETATION OF THE; SECOND COMING OF CHRIST.

Bibliography. J. Block, *On the Apocalyptic in Judaism;* F.C. Burkitt, *Jewish and Christian Apocalypses;* H.M. Hughes, *The Ethics of Jewish Apocryphal Literature;* P.S. Minear, *NT Apocalyptic;* H.H. Rowley, *The Relevance of Apocalyptic;* D.S. Russell, *The Method and Message of Jewish Apocalyptic.*

Apocrypha, Old and New Testament.

Old Testament Apocrypha. *Definition.* Collection of books dating from about the third century before Christ until roughly A.D. 100. Written well after the close of the OT during times of national unrest, the spirit of the books is characterized by the Hebrew people's response to their discordant situations and their hope for a better future. The etymology of apocrypha (meaning "hidden things") is misleading inasmuch as the writings are neither secret nor esoteric. While there is an apocrypha associated with the NT, the word customarily brings to mind the OT, not only because most of the original manuscripts were doubtless written in Hebrew or Aramaic, but also because the subject matter of the Apocrypha is decisively linked to events of the OT.

In addition to the narrow use of the term, "apocryphal" is often employed in a less restricted sense to refer to a group of writings of lesser status which circulated under false titles. Thus these writings are sometimes called Pseudepigrapha and include: Enoch, the Psalms of Solomon, the Books of Adam and Eve, the Martyrdom of Isaiah, and the Testament of the Twelve Patriarchs. Although the books of the Apocrypha were included in the Septuagint (Greek OT), it is doubtful that the early Jews ever considered these books canonical. Canonical status, when it was conferred, came by way of Greek-speaking Christians who accepted the parts of the Septuagint without making critical evaluation of books of questionable origin and content. In the Septuagint, the apocryphal books (with the exception of 2 Esdras, which was not included in the Septuagint) are generally located alongside the canonical books of the same literary genre. For example, 1 Esdras precedes Ezra–Nehemiah with the two books of the Maccabees following the Prophets. The Wisdom of Solomon and Ecclesiasticus accompany the OT Wisdom literature, with Baruch logically following Jeremiah. While the Vulgate follows a similar arrangement, English versions from Coverdale's Bible (1535) onward regularly place the books after, and separate from, those having canonical authority.

The order in which the books occur in English versions is: 1 Esdras; 2 Esdras; Tobit; Judith; Additions to the Book of Esther; Wisdom of Solomon; Ecclesiasticus (Sirach); Baruch, with the Letter of Jeremiah; Song of the Three Young Men; Susanna; Bel and the Dragon; Prayer of Manasseh; 1 Maccabees; 2 Maccabees. The overall length of these writings is roughly equal to four-fifths the volume of the NT.

Classification and Content. It is helpful to note the different types of literary genre present in the Apocrypha and consider their classifications. Books of a historical character are 1 Esdras and 1 and 2 Maccabees.

1 Esdras. Written sometime after 150 BC, 1 Esdras contains material given in biblical Ezra ("Esdras" is the Greek form), yet begins its account earlier with the observance of Passover in the 18th year of the reign of King Josiah. Its details of the final years of the kingdom of Judah closely parallel the narrative in 2 Chronicles 35 and 36. The conclusion in which Ezra reads the Law has marked similarities to Nehemiah 8, yet no mention of the prominent leader, Nehemiah, is found in the story. Historical sequencing is somewhat chaotic in the author's attempt to fill in the gaps of the Ezra–Nehemiah narrative. While much of 1 Esdras is also found in the Bible, 1 Esdras 3:1–5:6 gives the engrossing account of an intellectual contest among three young men serving as bodyguards to King Darius I. In their battle of wits each soldier writes down his answer to the king's question as to what is the strongest thing in the world. The first writes, "wine is the strongest" and defends his belief by pointing out that wine exerts a powerful, even irrepressible, influence upon all men regardless of their station in life. The second guardsman draws attention to the unlimited authority of the king, whose commands must always be obeyed by all his subjects. While his argument appears more impressive than the first, a third guardsman, who is identified as Zerubbabel, speaks in favor of the strength of women. He reasons that men are born of them and are dependent upon them for life. Moreover, a man will give all he possesses out of his passionate devotion to one captivating woman. Having said this, Zerubbabel begins a discourse upon another topic, truth. He argues that although the earth is vast, the heavens high, and the sun swift, all creation magnifies truth: "All men approve her deeds, and there

is nothing unrighteous in her judgment. To her belongs the strength and the kingship and the power and the majesty of all the ages. Blessed be the God of Truth!" (4:39,40). To this the people respond supportively, "Great is truth, and strongest of all!" (4:41). In championing the cause of truth, Zerubbabel is victorious and seeks as his prize the monarch's faithfulness to his earlier word that he would build up Jerusalem.

Among those in the early church who were influenced by 1 Esdras, Cyprian and Augustine connected the proverbial insight on the greatness of truth (4:41) with Christ who is its living embodiment (Jn 14:6).

1 Maccabees. Considered by many the most appealing apocryphal book. Martin Luther regarded 1 Maccabees as a very necessary and useful book. Samuel Taylor Coleridge declared it inspiring enough to actually be inspired. Written in Hebrew probably around 100 BC, 1 Maccabees deals primarily with the period of Jewish history from 175 to 134 BC. It tells of the Syrian ruler Antiochus Epiphanes' attempt to establish pagan worship among the Jews and how their unified revolt against him resulted in a remarkable victory for the Jewish people. In addition to that extensive military conflict, 1 Maccabees covers the period of the wars of the Hasmoneans, the rise of their dynasty, and the rule of John (identified historically as John Hyrcanus). The book concludes with a discourse in praise of that leader's notable achievements.

The main purpose of the author is to praise the heroic Maccabees and bring glory to Israel through recounting her people's mighty deeds of valor. There is a fine emphasis upon the sovereignty of God, who is acknowledged as the One who overrules the flimsy devices of men. At the same time the author stresses the importance of good military planning and the value of godly men who take the initiative in crises. It is also obvious that the writer has a profound respect for both the Law and the temple.

The account of the Maccabean victory with all its attendant details has served as the central point of reference for the Jewish celebration of Hanukkah (or Chanukah). Known as the Feast of Lights, Hanukkah commemorates the rededication of the temple consequent to the Jewish triumph over the Syrians. Tradition recalls how a very small cruse of oil burned miraculously for eight days in the sanctuary lamp. Jewish families have a special candlestick with eight receptacles, and on each day of the festal period a candle is lit in memory of that extraordinary event. It has been suggested that it was not accepted as canonical by the rabbis because of the eventual secularization of the Maccabees, which deeply offended the influential Pharisees.

2 Maccabees. Composed perhaps as early as 120 BC, 2 Maccabees is actually a shorter version of a historical document written primarily by a religious Cyrenian Jew named Jason. Its view is from the standpoint of the orthodox Pharisees, with special emphasis on such things as ritual purity, the sanctity of the temple, and the resurrection of the martyred faithful. Extensive moralization predominates, often at the cost of historical accuracy. Thus 1 Maccabees is far more reliable in its documentation of the period. The events related cover a period beginning shortly before the accession of Antiochus Epiphanes (175 BC) to the year 160 BC. The resistance of pious Jews against the paganizing influences of the Seleucid dynasty is a main concern of the narrative. Among the many issues addressed in 2 Maccabees are: faithfulness in the midst of great adversity (6:18–31); the role of angelic intercession (10:29; 13:2); the resurrection of the dead (7:11,23); the chastening love of God (6:10–12); the offering of prayers and sacrifices on behalf of the dead (12:43–46); and the uniquely creative power of God (7:28). The book pays homage to the temple at Jerusalem and delights in the intrusion of such miracles as heavenly horsemen fighting in support of the brave Maccabees. Written in Greek, the author surely hoped to inspire and instruct the people of Israel in the things of their unique faith. The cruel tortures described in chapters 6 and 7 seem to be well known to the writer of the Letter to the Hebrews (see Heb 11:35).

That which the rabbis might have termed "Haggadah" (whereby morals are communicated through tales of fiction) involves the following: Tobit, Judith, additions to the Book of Esther, and 3 additions to Daniel (Susanna, Bel and the Dragon, and Song of the Three Young Men).

Tobit. Book which dates from about 200 BC. It presents the folktale of an Israelite named Tobit who had been carried away into exile following the Assyrian conquest of Samaria. While on his way to a town of Media to collect a debt from a relative, young Tobias (Tobit's son) is assisted in his travels by the angel Raphael. This good angel helps Tobias in fending off the evil spirit Asmodaeus. Persian influences upon the tale are obvious, for the Persians subscribed to a spiritual dualism, and Asmodaeus is a name well-known to Persian demonology. In addition to the developing story, many themes and doctrinal affirmations are evident. God is identified with the ascriptions, "Holy One," "Great King," "King of Heaven," "King of the Ages" (12:12,15;

13:15; 13:7,11; 13:6,10). These titles magnifying his great power and glory are supplemented by expressions of his loving nature: he is merciful (3:2), the hearer of prayers via angelic intercession (12:12), and the restorer of his people's fortunes (14:5). His concern extends beyond the borders of Israel to other nations who will ultimately acknowledge his salvation (13:11).

The main thrust of the book is to exalt the Law with a view to stimulating obedience. In that context, performing deeds of charity is especially emphasized. Tobit 12:8,9 sees almsgiving as an example of the kind of good works which merit salvation. Fasting and prayer are also given high priority as indications of true piety. Even attending to a properly arranged burial for the dead finds its place in the life of the pious.

It is of interest to note that the 1549 edition of the Book of Common Prayer contains a prayer in the marriage service which draws from this book's account of the angel Raphael's assistance to Tobias and his wife Sarah.

Judith. Another romantic tale illustrating the way God justly provides for and vindicates his own. It takes its name from a young Jewish widow who charms a pagan general, Holofernes, and thereby finds an opportunity to rescue her city and people by beheading him. The book erroneously cites Holofernes as a general of Nebuchadnezzar and identifies the monarch as one who reigned over the Assyrians in Nineveh. While fictional and inaccurate, it is clear that the author was familiar with the geography of Palestine, despite his abundant use of cryptograms to disguise the actual places. Apparently composed shortly after the Maccabean conflict with Antiochus Epiphanes, the author attempts to encourage his people to be faithful to God and obedient to his Law.

Judith may be described as a woman of great piety: she fasts and prays with extraordinary zeal, observes all the religious feasts of Israel, and performs every act necessary for ritualistic purification. Yet she is also a woman of fierce cunning and bravery. The author seems to envision her as the female counterpart of the bold warrior, Judas Maccabeus. Hers is a long and famous life. Judith's death at the age of 105 causes great mourning throughout the land of Israel (16:21–25).

Additions to the Book of Esther. Writings partly intended to compensate for the conspicuous absence of the name of God in the Book of Esther. They extend the story line of their biblical counterpart to make the case for true religion and the uniqueness of Israel's God in the heathen world (14:3,4). The book seems disjointed because a substantial amount of material was added to the original text, which was a translation of the Book of Esther (from Hebrew to Greek) a century or so before Christ by a resident of Jerusalem called Lysimachus (11:1). The added episodes enlarge the original manuscript by 107 verses. For the sake of clarity it is advisable to read this book along with canonical Esther, especially if one is to make chronological sense out of the narrative.

Noteworthy is the book's strong reaffirmation of those tenets of Jewish theology proclaiming God's omniscience (13:12), omnipotence (13:9), and righteousness (14:6,7). God is also presented as Israel's Redeemer, whose election of the nation finds root in the covenantal promises given to Abraham (13:15–17). The Additions to Esther also looks upon prayer as a true index of godliness (13:8–14:19).

Susanna. A literary gem which has inspired writers, artists, and musicians throughout history. In Susanna, Daniel defends a virtuous woman against the slanderous accusations of two lustful elders. He vindicates her by exposing the patent inconsistencies of their stories through careful examination. Thus the heroine's honor is established and the evil of her adversaries made known.

From a moral standpoint the author shows the importance of holiness, prayer, and total trust in God. In addition, a warning is clearly implied that God will inevitably judge all whose ways fall short of his high ethical standards. Some scholars are tempted to see in the book a satirical view of the judicial system and legal processes of that historical period. Notwithstanding, Daniel's presence in the story gives hope that God will bring about needed reforms through those champions of justice he raises up.

Bel and the Dragon. Denunciation of idolatry. The brief story exposes the evil behavior of the 70 priests who minister before the image of the Babylonian god, Bel (also known as Marduk). Daniel's ridicule of the false deity enrages his adversaries, who pressure the king to cast Daniel into a den of lions. While Daniel is in the den, the prophet Habbakuk is miraculously transported from Judea by the angel of the Lord to care for all his needs. After a week of confinement Daniel is released by the king, and those who had tried to cause his death are thrown into the den, whereupon the lions immediately devour them. The book concludes with the king shouting loudly, "You are great, Lord God of Daniel, and there is no other beside You!"

Song of the Three Young Men. Addition to Daniel moored in the third chapter of that book, purporting to give an account of the events transpiring between verses 23 and 24. It is the only one of the so-called additions that attempts to supplement an actual event in the Book of Daniel.

Abednego (Azariah) prays from the midst of the fire, confessing his sins and those of his nation. He seeks God's abundant mercy (v 18), to which God responds by sending the angel of the Lord to rescue him and his godly companions from the furnace. Then follows what has been termed, The Song of the Three Holy Children. The prayer which is offered reveals those trying conditions which existed during the time of the Maccabees and Antiochus Epiphanes' persecution. Over against those tribulations the author encourages his people to seek God's face and trust in his deliverance (vv 16–18). The song strives to draw all creation to worship the one true God. A litany of sorts is apparent in the frequently recurring phrase, "Sing praise to Him and greatly exalt Him forever" (vv 35–68).

Two important entries classified as Wisdom literature: The Wisdom of Jesus the Son of Sirach (known as Ecclesiasticus) and the Wisdom of Solomon. Both entries are characteristically didactic.

Ecclesiasticus. Longest and one of the most valued apocryphal books, written about 180 BC. A man of extensive travels (34:11,12), the author is doubtless familiar with the Wisdom Literature of the OT. Having taught on a variety of topics (51:23), he sets forth in biblical Hebrew those principles which were communicated orally to his students. A half century later his writings were evidently translated by his grandson into Greek for the benefit of the Alexandrian Jews.

Like the Book of Proverbs, the material is presented in parallel couplets. Its wide scope of interest encompasses not only great theological matters but also such things as dieting, table manners (including the way to chew your food), marital relationships, and the correct treatment of children. The longest theme, in praise of famous men, occupies chapters 44 to 50. There is much of a Sadducean spirit here, for immortality is thought of largely as the remembrance and honor given by future generations to those whose lives had been lived honorably. Ecclesiasticus sees the Law as the means to live an honorable life. God's commandments are the only antidote to the sinful inclination in every man. When men pursue evil ways, God will nonetheless use their rebelliousness to suit his eternal purposes.

"Enoch pleased the Lord and was taken up from the earth" (Ecclus 44:16) finds a remarkably close parallel in Hebrews 11:5 (based on Gn 5:24).

Wisdom of Solomon. Strictly orthodox Jewish writing that employs the name of Solomon, perhaps with the hopes of gaining a wider audience. The book exalts the wisdom which God, its living embodiment, has manifested throughout history, particularly in the liberation of the Israelites. The author also attacks idolatry in a way similar to Paul's scathing indictment in Romans (1:18–23; 12:24; 13:1,5,8; 14:24,27). Some date the book around AD 40, which corresponds to the time Emperor Gaius ordered his image erected in Jerusalem's temple. While the writer firmly believes in the inherent immortality of the soul, his doctrine is not in accord with the biblical statement in Daniel 12:2 or the teaching on the resurrection as expounded in the NT.

Once again, one is tempted to see the book's influence on the writer of Hebrews (cf., e.g., Heb 12:10,11 with Wis 3:5,6).

Baruch. Work of an author believed to have lived around the beginning of the Christian era. From a literary standpoint it is modeled after OT prophetic writings. Though attributed to Jeremiah's faithful companion, at least two authors are responsible for its contents. There is a confession of Israel's sin, a treatise on the wisdom which is bound up with the Law, and a prophecy of the nation's ultimate deliverance and subsequent reestablishment in the Promised Land. The first part of the book, written in prose, speaks of the captivity in Babylon and its underlying cause, sin. Following prayers for Israel's restoration, proverbial expressions, reminiscent of biblical Wisdom Literature, abound. Thoughts of consolation are often offset by laments, although the spirited message of victory prevails.

Some early Christian writers seized upon 3:37 as a text with overtones for Wisdom's incarnation.

Letter of Jeremiah. Companion piece to Baruch. The letter was not sent by Jeremiah, nor is it, strictly speaking, a letter. Rather it is a sincere attempt by a concerned Israelite to guard his people against the folly of embracing a way of life below the standards of their ancient faith. Written perhaps as early as 300 BC, it is sermonic in character and repeatedly debunks the idolatry of the heathen by declaring, "Their idols are not gods" (vv 16,23,29,30,40,44,49,52,56,64,69).

Prayer of Manasseh. Devotional piece that first appears in literature around the third century of the Christian era. It contains a prayer of repentance and confession of sin that King Manasseh of Judah could have appropriately uttered when he was carried away to Babylon by the Assyrians (2 Chr 33:11–13). Some student of Scripture, apparently unable to find the prayer alluded to in 2 Chronicles 33:19, composed a spiritual entreaty deemed suitable for the monarch. Though very brief, the work effectively speaks of the compassion that God offers to all who are truly repentant. It sets forth the greatness of God's love as seen in his willingness to save a man whose vile 55-year reign is characterized by the evaluation, "He did much evil in the sight of the LORD" (2 Chr 33:6).

2 Esdras. Apocalyptic work that circulated in the early Christian era and the only one among many to become an accepted part of the Apocrypha. The heart of the book presents seven visions of the future, supposedly given to Ezra while in Babylon. Its slanted Jewish-Christian theology prophesies the rejection of the Jews in favor of the Christian church. The final chapters denounce sin and cite particular nations for their loathsome behavior. A poetic strain is discernible in the work despite its often bewildering and fantastic symbolism. The author's pessimism is counterbalanced by his belief in God's justice, mercy, and deliverance (16:67).

New Testament Apocrypha. Besides the 14 books of the OT Apocrypha there were unknown authors whose influential works were produced from about the 2nd century AD to perhaps as late as the 9th century. Their writings were largely modeled after the NT Gospels or Letters and sought to supplement, correct, or even replace established books of the NT. Where the four Gospels were silent, several apocryphal gospels were written to resolve questions concerning our Lord's childhood and early adulthood. Such was the motivation giving rise to the Armenian Gospel of the Infancy, the Protevangelium of James, and the Gospel of Thomas. The Gospel of Nicodemus and the Gospel of Bartholomew delve into imagined events following Jesus' crucifixion and his descent into Hades. Some gospels indulge in false and heretical ideas. Pilate's guilt is presented in a less heinous light by the Gospel according to Peter, and the Gospel of the Egyptians advances the notion (later termed docetism) that Jesus only appeared to be a human being.

Still other authors felt compelled to give more details concerning missionary activities, which Luke's account in Acts presents only in part. Such books include the Acts of John, the Acts of Paul, the Acts of Peter, the Acts of Andrew, the Acts of Philip, and the Acts of Thomas. In addition to the deeds they record, the authors moralize extensively in an attempt to motivate the reader to deeper Christian piety. In the Acts of Paul an account is given of the apostle's encounter with a ferocious lion in the amphitheater at Ephesus. This story of a talking "Christian" lion who

The amphitheater (seating 25,000) at Ephesus, the most spectacular monument of Ephesus.

befriends Paul in the arena bears a marked similarity to the old tale of Androcles attributed to Aulus Gellius around AD 160.

Certain documents imitated the form of the epistle, like 3 Corinthians and Paul's Letter to the Laodiceans (which early Syrian and Armenian churches regarded as canonical).

A number of entries bore the apocalyptic character of Daniel and Revelation, envisioning with great detail the future blessings of the saints as well as the awful judgments facing the unredeemed. Some of these apocalypses were spuriously attributed to Paul, Peter, Thomas, and the early Christian martyr, Stephen.

History and Usage of the Apocrypha. By and large, the early Greek-speaking church accepted the Septuagint in its entirety, including the Apocrypha. While some of the Greek fathers, such as Origen and Athanasius, limited the number of canonical books to those of the acknowledged Hebrew OT, they nonetheless freely quoted from the Apocrypha in their teachings. Augustine (Bishop of Hippo, 396–430) accepted Tobit, Judith, 1 and 2 Maccabees, Ecclesiasticus, and Wisdom of Solomon along with the acknowledged OT books. But the greatest biblical scholar of the Western church, Jerome (d. 420), drew a firm line between canonical and noncanonical books, using the word "apocryphal" to identify the latter. He considered the apocryphal books unsound for the formulation of doctrine, though he recognized that inspirational material could be found in them.

At the time of the Reformation, Protestants and Catholics differed sharply as to the relative worth of these books. The Catholic Church at its Council of Trent (1546) declared Tobit, Judith, the Additions to Esther and Daniel, Baruch, Ecclesiasticus, Wisdom, and 1 and 2 Maccabees to occupy an accredited place in the canon of Scripture. Some Protestants, like Lu-

therans and Anglicans, followed the position of Luther who, while denying the books biblical authority, looked upon them as "profitable and good to read." Reformed churches, on the other hand, classified the books as having no value above any other human writings. That conviction was spelled out clearly in the Westminster Confession of Faith (1643–46), which said,

> The Books commonly called Apocrypha, not being of divine inspiration, are not part of the canon of the Scripture; and therefore are of no authority in the Church of God, nor to be any otherwise approved, or made use of, than other human writings.

Nowadays the Apocrypha is not found in most editions of the Bible. However, in the early days of English Bible-printing it was simply normative to find the Apocrypha in the text.

The first English Bibles to exclude the Apocrypha were the Wycliffe Bible (1382) and some copies of the Geneva Bible of 1560 published at Geneva in 1599. Translators of the 1611 KJV translated the Apocrypha right along with the canonical books. A few years afterwards Archbishop Abbot issued a decree threatening a year's imprisonment to any Bible printer deleting the Apocrypha. In 1644, Parliament ordered only canonical books to be read aloud in church, which may have contributed to a more lenient atmosphere for printers of Scripture in the following years.

The first Bibles printed in America in English (1782) did not contain the Apocrypha. In 1826, the British and Foreign Bible Society discontinued printing Bibles with the Apocrypha altogether. Among contemporary Protestants only the Anglicans make use of the Apocrypha to any degree.

Evaluation. Notwithstanding a certain resemblance to the books of the Bible, problems in the Apocrypha of authorship, historical accuracy, and spiritual integrity abound. Termed "Outside Books" by the rabbis, it is evident that the Hebrew people never considered these books worthy of canonical status. It is also evident that our Lord Jesus Christ and his apostles accepted only that canon long recognized by their fellow Israelites. While certain parallel expressions are noticeable in the NT in conjunction with the Wisdom Literature (Eph 6:13–17 and Wis 5:17–20; Heb 11 and Ecclus 44), such correspondences do not indicate that the NT writers were dependent upon the Apocrypha for their inspiration. In no case is an apocryphal book directly cited by a NT author.

The books of the Apocrypha were not rejected by the church at a special meeting of an ecclesiastical body. Rather, the unworthiness of the books became evident as God's people simply read them alongside those highly revered books already regarded as canonical.

Nonetheless, it is also true that the Apocrypha has a valuable contribution to make, especially in its enabling us to better understand the social, political, and religious climate of Jesus' contemporaries as well as those generations following his advent. We are particularly helped through the Apocrypha's insights into the life and thought of the Jewish people during that significant period of history immediately preceding the coming of Christ. There are, moreover, writings of abiding spiritual value which have often edified the saints and inspired the arts. STUART D. SACKS

See BIBLE, CANON OF THE; APOCALYPTIC; JUDAISM; PHARISEES; WISDOM, WISDOM LITERATURE; GNOSTICISM.

Bibliography. R.H. Charles, Apocrypha and Pseudepigrapha of the OT; E.J. Goodspeed, The Story of the Apocrypha; M.R. James, The Apocryphal NT; J.M. Robinson, The Nag Hammadi Library; R.M. Wilson (ed), NT Apocrypha, 2 vols.

Apollonia. Town located on the Egnatian Way in eastern Macedonia. Paul passed through Apollonia on his second missionary journey west from Philippi to Thessalonica, a trip of about 90 miles (Acts 17:1). It is usually identified with modern Pollina.

Apollos. Native of Alexandria (Egypt), a Christian Jew who was an eloquent preacher at the time of the apostle Paul's missionary journeys. The chief biblical passage about Apollos is Acts 18:24–19:1. From Alexandria Apollos went to Ephesus in Asia Minor. Enthusiastic in spirit, learned and cultured in his ways, well-versed in the OT Scriptures, and instructed in the way of the Lord, he began to speak boldly and openly in the synagogue there. Apollos knew and preached accurately about the coming of Jesus, but knew of it only

from the message of Jesus' forerunner, John (the Baptist). Priscilla and Aquila, Paul's friends and former associates, heard Apollos speak in Ephesus and realized that he had not heard what had happened to Jesus. They took him aside privately and explained the way of God to him more accurately. Before that, he had been convinced of the value of John's baptism and John's message that Jesus was the Messiah. He was evidently uninformed, however, about such teachings as justification by faith in Christ or the work of the Holy Spirit in salvation. At such points, Priscilla and Aquila, having lived and worked with Paul, were able to help Apollos.

Soon after their instruction, Apollos left Ephesus for the Roman province of Achaia in Greece with letters from the Ephesian Christians urging the disciples in Achaia to welcome him as a Christian brother. On arrival, he vigorously and publicly refuted the Jews, using his great knowledge of the OT Scriptures to prove that Jesus was the Messiah. Paul considered Apollos's work in Corinth, capital of Achaia, so valuable that he described him as waterer of the seed which Paul had planted as the founder of the church (1 Cor 3:5–11). From 1 Corinthians it is also clear that one of the factions dividing the Corinthian church was a clique centered around Apollos, although he was not directly responsible for it (1 Cor 1:12; 3:1–4). Paul had difficulty convincing Apollos that he should return to Corinth, perhaps because Apollos did not want to encourage the continuance of that little group (1 Cor 16:12).

Apollyon. Angel of the "bottomless pit," also called Abaddon (Rv 9:11).

See ABADDON.

Apostasy. Turning against God, as evidenced by abandonment and repudiation of former beliefs. The term generally refers to a deliberate renouncing of the faith by a once sincere believer rather than a state of ignorance or mistaken knowledge. Apostasy is distinguished from heresy (denial of a part of the faith), and from transfer of allegiance from one religious body to another within the same faith. Also, it is possible to deny the faith, as Peter once did, and then at a later time reaffirm it.

Originally, "apostasy" meant literal rebellion. Thus the Jews were described as "rebels" against King Artaxerxes (1 Esd 2:23) and Jason as a "rebel against the laws" (2 Mc 5:6–8). OT descriptions of spiritual rebellion include departure from the Law, forsaking temple worship, and willful disobedience toward God himself (Jos 22:22, rebellion or unfaithful act; 2 Chr 29:19, transgression KJV, or faithlessness; Jer 2:19, backslidings KJV, or apostasy). The prophetic writings of Isaiah and Jeremiah provide many examples of Israel's defections (Is 1:2–4; Jer 2:19). Israelite kings were often guilty of apostasy (Rehoboam—1 Kgs 14:22–24; Ahab—1 Kgs 16:30–33; Ahaziah—1 Kgs 22:51–53; Jehoram—2 Chr 21:6,10; Ahaz—2 Chr 28:1–4; Manasseh—2 Chr 33:1–19; Amon—2 Chr 33:21–23).

In NT times many disciples withdrew from Christ (Jn 6:66), the most notorious example being Judas Iscariot. The Greek word from which "apostasy" is derived appears in only two passages. The apostle Paul was accused of apostasy for being "against the laws of Moses" (Acts 21:21 LB). Apostasy was given an eschatological significance in 2 Thessalonians 2:3. Christians were warned not to be carried away and deceived in the widespread apostasy to come in the end times before the Lord's return. That apostasy is linked to the rise of a "man of rebellion" who will be "Satan's tool" (2 Thes 2:3–12 LB; cf. 1 Tm 4:1–3).

Many other NT passages, using different words, convey similar warnings. In the last days, tribulation and persecution will cause many to "fall away" (Mt. 24:9,10); false prophets will arise and "lead many astray" (Mt 24:11). Other causes of apostasy include temptation (Lk 8:13) and unbelief (Heb 3:12). Paul cited Hymenaeus and Alexander as examples of those who had rejected the faith (1 Tm 1:20). The writer of Hebrews referred to those who had believed and then departed from the faith as being in a hopeless state with no possibility of further repentance (Heb 6:1–6). The consequences of willful sinning after receiving Christ are terrifying (Heb 10:26–31). The apostle Peter said that, for believers in Christ who knowingly turned away, "the last state has become worse for them than the first" (2 Pt 2:20–22). The apostle John addresses this same problem (1 Jn 2:18,19).

Ten periods of persecution intensified the problem of apostasy during the first four centuries of the church's existence. Repentance and public confession were required before offenders could be accepted again. The Roman emperor Julian (361–63) renounced the Christian faith and made such a vigorous effort to establish paganism in the empire that he became known as "the Apostate." Apostasy continues to be a danger to the Christian church, especially where the church is undergoing persecution.

JAMES D. PRICE *and* LUDER G. WHITLOCK, JR.

Apostle, Apostleship. Official designation given to certain leading individuals in the NT churches. Apostleship is the more comprehensive term denoting the functions of the one who serves in such a capacity. Questions concerning origin, function, and history of the NT apostolate are much-debated; one cannot speak of anything like consensus of opinion uniting the various church traditions. Some light is shed on our understanding of the terms by an examination of the possible linguistic and conceptual backgrounds.

Background. *Greek Usage.* The Greek word for "apostle" is not used outside the NT in the same sense as it is in the NT. It is derived from the verb "to send" and is at home in the language of the sea meaning a particular "ship" or "group of ships," a "marine expedition" or "the leader" of such. Its usage is almost always impersonal and thoroughly passive. There is no hint of personal initiative or authorization, merely the connotation of something being sent. Later papyri use the word to mean "bill" or "invoice" or even a "passport," continuing to reflect the vocabulary of maritime affairs.

Jewish Usage. Here the word is not widely used. It appears possibly twice in the writings of the historian Josephus, and not at all in Philo. Of the instances in Josephus one is important, where the word has the sense of sending "emissaries" or perhaps an "embassy."

The Septuagint (LXX) uses the word of the prophet Ahijah in 1 Kings 14:6, translating a Hebrew participle meaning "one who is sent." The Hebrew verb underlying this description had become a technical term in the OT for the sending of a messenger with a special task. Although accepting responsibility and agreeing to accomplish what is asked, the person of the messenger (whether divine or human) fades behind the importance of being so "formally" commissioned. Attention is to be focused on the initiator and his concerns. Perhaps the clearest example can be seen in the call of Isaiah (6:8): "And I heard the voice of the Lord saying, 'Whom shall I send, and who will go for us?' Then I said, 'Here am I! Send me.' " Thus when God's prophet Ahijah (1 Kgs 14:6) is described as "one who is sent," the conviction is expressed that he is a divinely commissioned representative who must convey a message to the wife of King Jeroboam. By using the word "apostle" in this passage, the translators of the Septuagint gave it a meaning beyond the classical and papyri usages, replacing the secular meaning with a theological one.

Further movement in this direction is found in the rabbinic writings. Here the verbal form in 1 Kings 14:6 (*shaliach*) has become a noun in itself, retaining the meaning "one who is sent." The rabbis used the word primarily in contexts which are neither explicitly theological nor religious but rather have to do with matters of the Law. The word is used of individuals who are temporarily authorized to carry fully in their own person the person and rights of another in the accomplishment of some act. The oft-cited passage from the Mishna provides a clear definition: "The one who is sent (*shaliach*) is the same as the one who sends." The basis for such a practice lay in the OT law of the messenger, where the reaction paid to messengers is at the same time paid to the one who sent them. For example, Abigail washes the feet of David's servants, who have come to bring her to the king as a wife, thereby accepting his proposal (1 Sm 25:40–42). Similarly the embarrassment of David's servants experienced at the hands of the Ammonites is actually an embarrassment of the king himself and, in this case, leads to war (2 Sm 10:1–8). The shift from examples such as these to the realm of legal affairs seems natural and was doubtless occasioned by the problem of individuals unable to attend personally to specific matters. Scriptural precedent and practical necessity combined in developing this later institution of the *shaliach*.

The length of this relationship extended until the successful completion of the particular task in mind. The agreement was made void upon the return of the *shaliach* to the one in whose service he was sent. And while the initiative for such a transaction is that of the one who sends, carrying out the assignment faithfully depends on the agreement and willingness of the one commissioned. In this sense one may speak of the active participation of the representative.

The exact nature of the mission given to each *shaliach* does not obtain from the designation itself. Rather it is dependent upon the specific commission of the one who sends. The term provides the form of commissioning, the content of which is fixed by the word of the initiator. So, for example, an individual may marry or divorce through a *shaliach*, purchase property, or perform certain ceremonial functions.

The rabbis applied the designation to specific OT figures as well because they performed individual acts normally reserved for God. Moses causes water to spring forth from a rock (Ex 17:5,6); Elijah brings rain (1 Kgs 17:1; 18:1) and raises the dead (1 Kgs 17:21–23); Elisha "opens the mother's womb" (2 Kgs 4:16,17) and Ezekiel receives the "key to the tombs at the reawakening of the dead" (Ez 37). Likewise, the priest is thought to act as God's *shaliach* in offering sacrifices.

Such authorized representation extended to groups of people as well. In the local syna-

gogue, one person's prayer stands as the prayer of all the congregation; certain rabbis were sent out into the diaspora representing the Sanhedrin of Jerusalem in order to regulate the calendar, announce the beginnings of a new month, and collect necessary financial aid for the scribes of that city. Some think that it is against this background that Paul carries letters of accreditation from the Jerusalem authorities to seek out Christians in Damascus (Acts 9:1,2).

To these few examples others may be added, but they are sufficient to demonstrate the most fundamental point of this institution: the term *shaliach* is not one of vocation or office. Rather it describes a relationship existing between two parties; it has to do with *function*, not *status*.

Finally it should be noted that the linguistic connection between the Greek word "apostle" and the Hebrew words "to send" and "one who is sent" do not provide the only evidence for linking the *shaliach* with the NT apostle. As early as Jerome the material closeness between the two figures was recognized, and the Syrian church actually referred to the apostles by this Semitic terminology. The above discussion therefore has led to the widely shared opinion that in the Jewish concept of the *shaliach* we have the closest parallel to the apostle.

The New Testament. *Jesus and the Apostles.* Rather than form a separatist reform within Judaism, Jesus seems to have called all Israel to repentance and to seek in faith God's help in his own person. From among the wider group of those who follow him, Jesus selects 12 men (Mt 10:1–4; Mk 3:13–19; Lk 6:12–16), who maintain with him a particularly close relationship, receiving private instruction and witnessing his miracles and controversy with the Jewish authorities. On one occasion, Jesus sends these men out to preach the message of repentance, to cast out demons, and to heal the sick, that is, to minister in ways that were characteristic of his own work (Mt 10:1–15; Mk 6:7–13,30; Lk 9:1–6). The same relationship is expressed in the saying, "He who hears you hears me, and he who rejects you rejects me, and he who rejects me rejects him who sent me" (Lk 10:16; cf. Mt 10:40). It is clear that the 12 are not merely to pass Jesus' teaching on but to represent his very person. This is exactly what the *shaliach* does, and it is in this sending that the Gospels refer to the 12 as apostles (Mt 10:2; Mk 6:30; Lk 9:10). The length of the *shaliach*'s assignment extends until his return, and consequently Matthew and Mark no longer use the term, although Luke continues to do so (11:49; 17:5; 22:14; 24:10).

From the saying in Matthew 19:28 (cf. Lk

22:29) we learn that the number of Jesus' apostles relates to the number of the tribes of Israel. The hope of Israel included the true reunification of the 12 tribes in a new world. Israel would once again be God's people in the time of salvation. Jesus' selection of these 12 men is thereby an implicit sign that in his ministry he intends to accomplish this reconstitution. It is in this sense that we understand those passages that speak of the foundational position that the 12 had for the New Israel—the church of Jesus Christ (cf. Eph 2:20; Rv 21:14; cf. also Mt 16:17–19). Among the Evangelists, Luke emphasizes this characteristic of the 12 and so relates the filling out of their number after the departure of Judas (Acts 1:15–26) but before the coming of the Spirit (Acts 2). The qualifications put forward for the election of Matthias (Acts 1:21,22) are thus not that of apostleship in general but for being one of the 12.

After the resurrection the fellowship once enjoyed between Jesus and the 12, and temporarily broken by the cross, was reinstituted and brought to completion. The Gospel appearances (Mt 28; Lk 24; Jn 20,21) not only witness to the exaltation of Jesus but include a distinct commission. The "sending" of the 12, which was limited in time and space, now becomes renewed for life. The representation, indeed the continuation of Jesus' ministry resident in the apostles, now takes the form of proclamation of God's act in Christ on behalf of all men—a claim already implicit in Jesus' own ministry.

Paul. The Pauline writings demonstrate two characteristic usages of the word "apostle." On occasion (2 Cor 8:23; Phil 2:25) it refers to persons authorized by local congregations and entrusted with the safe delivery of specific gifts for other members of the Christian community.

More important are those passages where "apostle" takes on a more technical sense through the qualifying phrase "of Jesus Christ" (1 Cor 1:1; 2 Cor 1:1; 11:13; Gal 1:1; Eph 1:1; Col 1:1; 1 Thes 2:6; cf. Rom 1:1). The "sent one" is the "sent one of Jesus Christ" (Rom 16:7; 1 Cor 9:1,5; 12:28; Gal 1:17,19; also use the word in this absolute sense). In the statements where Paul claims his own right to this title, he argues along lines assuming the same basic apostolic concept that Jesus had. He consistently links this claim to a specific event in the past in which the risen Lord had appeared to him (1 Cor 9:1; Gal 1:12,16). This appearance he ranked alongside those of the Easter witnesses (1 Cor 15:3–8). Paul understood his experience outside Damascus (cf. Acts 9:1–19a; 22:6–16; 26:12–18; Gal 1:17) as a lifelong commission to preach the now-resurrected One (1 Cor 1:17; 2:1,2) chiefly among the Gentiles (Acts 9:15; 22:15; 26:17,23; Gal 1:15,16). It was through his preaching ministry that Christ continues to work, creating the new people of God (1 Cor 9:1b,2; Gal 2:8). Here again the background of the *shaliach* is in view.

Jesus as Apostle. Hebrews (3:1) uses the word once and applies it to Jesus himself. This is in keeping with the character of the whole book (and especially with the beginning, 1:1–4), that although God has been faithfully revealed in various ways throughout history he finds his definitive representative in his son, Jesus.

Apostles and the Church Today. The grounding of the NT apostolic ministry in a personal authorization by the risen Christ raises the question to what extent we can meaningfully speak of the apostolic office in our churches today. In an important respect the position of those called apostles was unique, and yet the church continues to expand and believes that it continues to be the body of Christ with him as Lord. A final answer cannot be given here. Suffice it to say, the various ecclesiastical traditions and practices of church office and ministry are attempts to answer this question.

See ACTS OF THE APOSTLES, BOOK OF THE; APOSTOLIC AGE; JOHN THE APOSTLE, LIFE AND WRITINGS OF; PAUL, THE APOSTLE; PETER, THE APOSTLE.

Bibliography. C.K. Barrett, *The Signs of an Apostle*; F.J.A. Hort, *The Christian Ecclesia*; J.B. Lightfoot, *St. Paul's Epistle to the Galatians*; T.W. Manson, *The Church's Ministry*; K.H. Rengstorf, *Apostolate and Ministry*; B.H. Streeter, *The Primitive Church.*

Apostolic Age.

Apostolic Age. Period of growth and development in the early church associated with the leadership of the 12 apostles. The apostolic age began with the death and resurrection of Christ and ended with a persevering church at the end of the 1st century A.D. It was a dynamic age, encompassing not only the writing of the NT canon but also the development of a philosophy to guide the church in its complex relationships with both external forces (governments, other religions) and internal problems (false teachers, church discipline).

Much is still unknown about the apostolic age. Most of our knowledge comes from comments in the NT epistles and the history of the church recorded in the Book of Acts, which traces only one line of development among many during that time. For example, the ministries of most of the 12 apostles and the growth of the church in areas such as North Africa or Parthia (ancient country southeast of the Caspian Sea) are not described. From the NT materials, however, a valuable picture of the apostolic age can be obtained.

Founding of the Church. Scholars have debated whether the church was founded (1) at the confession of Peter (Mt 16:18; cf. Mt 18:17, the only other place in the Gospels where Jesus used the term "church"); (2) at the resurrection (viewed as the inaugural event of the new age); or (3) at Pentecost (the public empowering of the church by the Holy Spirit). Although arguments can be made for each view, the NT itself shows no interest in the issue. The apostles probably saw the origin of the church in a complex interplay between Jesus' ministry, the resurrection as God's vindication of that ministry, and Pentecost as a public manifestation of continuity between Jesus' ministry and the church's proclamation.

Jesus' Ministry. Jesus' choice of 12 disciples, his reference to them as the "little flock" (Lk 12:32), and his constant teaching on the "poor" and "afflicted" in the kingdom of God are reminiscent of the "remnant theology" of the OT prophets. The remnant was a group called by God out of the apostate nation of Israel, identified with the name of God, and ordained both to call the nation back to repentance and to suffer persecution in God's name. Therefore Jesus had already conceived of the separation between his band of followers and mainstream Judaism when he spoke of the church.

The term "church" (i.e., the Greek word *ecclesia*) is found over 100 times in the Septuagint, a pre-Christian Greek translation of the OT. That term, linked with the Jewish concept of the "people of God," refers to the messianic community of "the last days," an aspect of God's plan for which Jesus definitely prepared his disciples.

The Resurrection. Jesus' resurrection was the climax of his earthly ministry and the starting point of the "church age." Luke tied the two together in his theological portrayals of the ascension in his Gospel and Acts. The different narratives in his two books related different aspects of the same event. In Luke 24:51–53 the ascension is seen as the conclusion to Jesus' earthly ministry. That account thus stresses Jesus' priestly blessing of the disciples and their response in worship. In Acts 1:6–11 Luke showed that the ascension was also the beginning of the church age. There he stressed the empowering, commissioning, and preparing of the disciples for the development of the church.

Those who argue that the resurrection never really occurred have a difficult time explaining the powerful surge of faith in the disciples. For the NT writers the resurrection was the primary cause of the disciples' faith. The disciples themselves had failed. Matthew used the term "fall away" (also translated "take offense," 26:31) to describe what the disciples did after the crucifixion; normally he reserved that term for the apostate Pharisees (cf. 11:6; 13:21; 15:12; and elsewhere). The disciples could hardly have come to their later victorious proclamation on their own. In fact, they were transformed from a defeated band of stragglers into heralds of a messianic community filled with joy and enthusiasm.

The Gospels themselves indicate the relationship between Jesus' ministry, his resurrection, and the founding of the church. Mark wrote of a "messianic secret" whereby Jesus refused to allow his messianic office to be proclaimed until after the resurrection (Mk 8:30; 9:9). The disciples were told the secret but did not understand it until the resurrection (Mk 4:13; 6:52; 7:17,18; 9:10). The teaching of Jesus was both the basis of the church (Mt 28:19,20) and the content of the church's message. That message had been understandable all along but became discernible only in the light of the resurrection. Luke presented an even more complete picture, showing the continuity between Jesus' earthly ministry, which inaugurated the "messianic age of salvation," and the church's proclamation of the message of salvation. The resurrection was the connecting link between the two.

Finally, John showed that the resurrection "glory" had been visible in Jesus all along to the "eye of faith." Both salvation (Jn 20) and the church (ch 21), however, could be fully understood only through the resurrection as the key to Jesus' teaching and person. Thus all four Evangelists declared, each in his own distinctive way, that Jesus' ministry prepared for the postresurrection message of the church. The essential link was the resurrection, which pointed to the presence of the risen Christ in God's messianic community, the church.

Pentecost. The inauguration of the church age was sealed by introducing the age of the Spirit at Pentecost. John's Gospel shows that Pentecost should not be isolated from the resurrection. In what has been called the Johannine pentecost (Jn 20:22), Christ appeared to the disciples after the resurrection, "breathed" on them, and said "Receive the Holy Spirit." That was a private, personal strengthening of the disciples, whereas the Pentecost experience was a public empowering and vindication of the church, the remnant of Israel.

During the time of Jesus' appearances or shortly thereafter, the disciples moved from Galilee and made Jerusalem their permanent home, perhaps expecting the fulfillment of the prophetic promises regarding Jerusalem (Is 2:2–4; 40:1,2,9–11). During the Jewish feast of Pentecost, the church experienced the coming of the Spirit. The first Christian Pentecost had a threefold meaning: (1) It signified the outpouring of praise to God on behalf of the new messianic community (seen in the ecstatic utterances, Acts 2:4,11). (2) It began the time of universal proclamation (seen in the "nations" that understood it, Acts 2:9–11). (3) It demonstrated the power available to the church for accomplishing its task (seen in the wind and fire, Acts 2:2,3).

The Palestinian Period. *The Early Church's View of Itself.* Did the primitive church view itself as "true Israel" or simply as a part of the Jewish nation? Scholars of the 19th century argued for the second option, but many scholars have begun to see a growing "church consciousness" at the earliest stages. The early church actually saw itself as both separate from and a part of Israel itself. The church was the new Israel, hence distinct from the old, but it was also the remnant of the OT hope. As the remnant, it called the Jewish nation to the new "congregation of Jesus," to the fulfillment of its messianic hopes.

When Christians worshiped in the temple and took part in Jewish feasts, they did so in the belief that they were participating in the fulfillment of the OT promise and not merely as members of another Jewish sect. In fact, the temple and synagogue became the focus of the church's evangelistic outreach. The early church's message was one of promise–fulfillment; that is, it pointed to the OT promises of redemption and then showed how those promises were fulfilled in Christ. The earliest recorded creed (1 Cor 15:3–5) followed the promise–fulfillment pattern in stressing that the death and resurrection of Christ took place "according to the Scriptures." Every NT book except James echoes the same theme, but the early speeches in Acts especially abound with appeals to OT Scripture. The apostles sought to prove to the Jews that Jesus was indeed the Christ prophesied in the OT.

Church Leadership. Early church leadership centered around the 12 apostles, and especially Peter as the "rock" of the church (stressed in Acts 1–15). The importance of the number 12 is seen in Acts 1:21–26 when the disciples chose a replacement for Judas, and in Acts 12:2 when they did not choose a successor to James the brother of John. The two events suggest that at the outset of the church's existence the apostles felt it was crucial for the sake of its witness that they be 12 in number. When the church was fully established, however, it was no longer necessary to maintain that number. The original significance of the 12 apostles was again connected with the "remnant" motif, the 12 apostles cor-

responding to the 12 tribes of Israel. The apostleship of the chosen 12 was based on their presence with the Lord in his earthly ministry and their experience of his resurrection appearances and commission (Acts 1:21,22).

The complexity of life in the growing Jerusalem church soon proved to be too much for the 12 apostles to handle by themselves. In Acts 6:1–6, the Hellenistic Jewish faction (Jewish Christians who were from Greek territories outside Palestine) complained that the native "Hebrews" (the Palestinian believers) were favored in the distribution of the common funds given to needy widows. The apostles, realizing that they could not handle both evangelistic and domestic duties, chose deacons to handle internal matters. The term "deacon" (meaning one who "waits tables" or "serves") was uncommon both in Judaism and Hellenism; it originated in Jesus' concept of servanthood (cf. Mk 10:44).

The Scattering of the Church. Beginning with the stoning of Stephen (one of the first deacons), a wave of persecution hit the Jerusalem church, inspired by Stephen's witness before the Jewish council and by the Jewish authorities' growing realization that the Christians were not a mere splinter group within Judaism. The persecution resulted in a scattering of the church's Hellenistic Jews into outlying regions and brought about several changes.

First, the internal leadership changed from Hellenistic deacons to Jewish elders. Though it is not known precisely when the concept of "elder" originated, it was in use by the time of Paul's first missionary journey (Acts 14:23) and his visit to Jerusalem (Acts 15:2).

Second, the main leadership narrowed further from the apostles to the "pillars" (Gal 2:9), with James the brother of the Lord taking the place of the martyred James (John's brother) in the inner circle with Peter and John. James's leadership of the church's Jewish branch is evident at the Jerusalem Council (Acts 15).

Finally, an emphasis on the "charismatic" ("spiritual") gifts began to appear. The list of gifts in Ephesians 4:11 (apostles, prophets, evangelists, pastor–teachers), as well as the other lists (Rom 12; 1 Cor 12), probably go back to that early period. Many scholars have argued for a purely Spirit-led church government in the early period, but the evidence points to the presence of both institutional and charismatic elements from the beginning.

Most important, the scattering of the church became the God-ordained first step to the universal mission of the church. All the evidence suggests that in the first years the

A view of Jerusalem, looking west from the Mt of Olives toward the Old City, with St. Stephen's Gate clearly seen in the foreground.

early church interpreted the Great Commission in light of proselyte theology; that is, the church sought to reach Jews with the gospel, believing that Gentiles would come to the church by first becoming Jewish proselytes. However, the dispersion forced the church out of Jerusalem and into the Jewish communities of the diaspora. There Christians came into contact with the "God-fearers," Gentiles who followed Judaism but who had not been circumcised. There also they first faced the difficult question: Did Gentiles have to be circumcised in order to become Christians? The question plagued the church for the next few decades.

The Development of Creeds. During the earliest period the "traditions" or creeds (official doctrinal statements) of the church began to develop. At the outset the sayings of Jesus formed the core of the *didache* ("teaching") of the 12 apostles. Those sayings were not written down but were preserved through oral tradition, passed from teachers to converts in much the same way as the rabbis taught their disciples. At the same time, the apostles and teachers began to formulate creeds (e.g., 1 Cor 15:3–5), catechisms (teachings for new converts, e.g., Rom 1:3,4), confessions (liturgies for worship, e.g., Rom 10:9,10), and hymns (e.g., Phil 2:6–11), plus formulae for ethical instruction derived from Judaism through Christ's ethical teachings. Such ethical teachings quickly took on overtones of tradition as the church began to recognize the ethical limits of the new "freedom" found in Christ.

By developing traditions, the apostles and teachers sought to interpret the teaching and ministry of Jesus for later church situations.

Quite early in the church's history the traditions assumed canonical status alongside the sayings of Jesus, as can be seen in the large number of traditional sayings in the NT letters. (In fact, 1 Peter has been called a "compendium" of tradition.)

The Early Church and the Law. The religious practice of the early church also began to take form. Jewish Christians were faithful to the Law and obeyed the Sabbath commandments. In fact, as Matthew showed, the Law still had validity even though it was "fulfilled" by Christ; Jesus seemingly annulled the Law in both teaching and action, yet commanded that it be obeyed to the last detail (Mt 5:17–20). The paradox was only apparent. Before Jesus, the Law had served as a mediator between a righteous God and sinful humanity. Jesus fulfilled the Law by becoming the one true mediator between God and humanity. In so doing he called for the same basic response as the Law: repentance. Yet he also made it possible to stop hiding behind the Law from the wrath of God and to enter into true fellowship with him. Thus the Law, still valid in one respect, was transformed by the work of Christ.

So it seemed essential both to recognize the original validity of the Law and to announce its fulfillment by the Law of Christ. Yet the church ran into tremendous problems because it forgot to maintain that tension between adherence to and negation of the Law. The details are clearly spelled out in Acts, as God step-by-step led the church to the gentile mission. First, Philip was led to the Samaritans—an Israelite community that had broken from Jerusalem, established its own center of worship, and was therefore despised by Judeans. That evangelistic enterprise, at first unacceptable to the Jerusalem church, had to be confirmed by the apostles Peter and John and then by the Samaritan Pentecost (Acts 8:5–25). Evidence that the Holy Spirit worked among the Samaritans helped to wean the early church away from a purely Jewish orientation.

The next step was Peter's vision and the conversion of Cornelius. Peter's vision (Acts 10:9–16) related to the Jewish food laws as well as to laws about eating with Gentiles. Cornelius, a gentile God-fearer, was converted without being circumcised (vv 17–43). His conversion also had to be confirmed by a Pentecost experience (vv 44–48).

Finally, when Paul's gentile mission intensified the debate, Jewish Christianity split into opposing camps. Paul's opponents (the Judaizers) attacked his right to be called an apostle (Gal 1:1) as well as his motives (vv 10–12). They demanded that the new converts be circumcised before being admitted to the church. Paul saw such demands as an attack on the gospel and took the problem to Jerusalem (Acts 15). There the Jerusalem Council, after two influential speeches by Peter and James, endorsed the gentile mission, effectively ending the Palestinian period. At the same time, they requested that gentile believers respect Jewish legal sensitivities (see the "letter," Acts 15:23–29).

Early Church Discipline. Despite the pronouncement of the Jerusalem Council regarding Gentiles, the Judaizers did not suspend their opposition to Paul but rather intensified it. Jesus had given the disciples a method of dealing with unfaithful church members. If the members did not respond to personal correction, they were to be banned from the church (Mt 18:15–18; cf. Gal 6:1). Thus the Judaizers probably were banned from the church and became a cultic sect. The difference of tone between the Letter to the Galatians, where they are merely opponents, and later epistles (2 Cor 11:13–15; Phil 3:18,19), where they are called "false prophets" and servants of Satan headed for destruction, illustrates the change.

Worship. The choice of the Greek term for "church" ("called out ones") and its connection with special verbs for "gathering together" suggest that the heart of the early church was corporate worship and that worship was to characterize every aspect of the life of a believer. The practice of meeting on the first day of the week, celebrating the new creation brought about by the resurrection, probably began during the Palestinian period (cf. Acts 20:7; 1 Cor 16:2). Sunday is first called

"the Lord's day" in Revelation 1:10, though the term was probably in use before then.

At first Christians worshiped in the synagogue on *Shabbat* ("Saturday") and with other believers in homes on the following day (Acts 2:46). Acts 2:42 describes the essentials of the worship: apostolic teaching and fellowship, the breaking of bread, and prayers. In the Jewish setting, teaching was more than doctrine; it included practical application of the traditions to everyday situations. Also, teaching was not the duty merely of the leaders but of every individual. An ordinary Jew would give the synagogue sermon, and the head of each household was obligated to teach his wife, children, and servants. In the context of worship Christian teaching took on catechetical forms similar to those in 1 Peter and Hebrews. Teaching occurred in the service in connection with the sacred meal, again following Jewish precedent. "Fellowship" could refer to gifts and offerings (both giving and receiving, Acts 6:1,2; Rom 15:26), or it could refer to "table fellowship" (again the sacred meal). "Fellowship" may also have referred in a more general way to the special unity and sharing between fellow believers (note its connection with teaching in Acts 2:42). The "prayers" mentioned were probably corporate, referring to participation in the temple and synagogue prayers as well as the community prayers in the Christian service.

The "breaking of bread" was at the center of the worship. There were two aspects: table fellowship in a meal, also called the "*agape* (love) feast," and the actual eucharistic celebration (Communion, the Lord's Supper) centering on the Lord's own words (1 Cor 11:23–26). At the earliest stage, the table fellowship followed a Jewish pattern. As in the actual last supper (which was a Jewish Passover celebration), Christ's words of institution and the elements of teaching and praise were all part of the meal. The fellowship of the corporate body in sharing the meal itself was integral with the spiritual aspects of the service. The two were not separated until later, when the meal was misused in the Hellenistic branch of the church. Not understanding its significance, they tended to celebrate it like a pagan feast, replacing the sacred meaning with gluttony, and replacing the *agape* (love) with self-seeking (cf. 1 Cor 11:20–22).

Baptism early became a Christian counterpart to Jewish circumcision (cf. Col 2:11,12). The practice originated in Jesus' resurrection command, which reinstated the baptism of John the Baptist but infused it with new meaning, namely, the entrance of the believer into the kingdom of God. At the beginning, the baptismal event occurred immediately upon con-

Antioch of Syria.

version (Acts 2:38; 8:12,13; 9:18; etc.); only later did it take on a formal, institutional aspect.

Period of Expansion. *Paul's Ministry.* The apostle to the Gentiles was instrumental in bringing to a close the Palestinian period, but Paul also set the tone for the universal expansion of the church. The birthplace of the gentile mission was Antioch (Syria), a city of 300,000 with 10 percent Jews. The scattered Hellenists of Acts 8 began reaching out to the Greeks and in Antioch established a congregation that did not require circumcision for new converts; they neglected the oral tradition of the Law and other legal requirements (Acts 11:19–21; Gal 2:3–14). That group earned the name which has become the primary designation for the church, "Christians" (Acts 11:26). The Antioch church was the setting in which Paul received his call to be the apostle to the Gentiles (13:1,2).

Jewish and Hellenistic Relations. The Jewish and Hellenistic wings of the church existed in a dynamic tension but also with definite interaction, especially in the Jewish communities of the diaspora. By the 1st century AD, Hellenistic thinking had permeated Jewish thought, and the church worked creatively within both spheres. The two styles of thought mingled freely and, as their contributions were reflected in church tradition, infused each other with deeper meaning (e.g., in the concepts of meekness and love).

Further, both Hellenism and Judaism were reinterpreted on the basis of Jesus' teachings, so the valid traditions of each were maintained in the developing churches. All the NT letters exhibit the process of interpreting local situations in the light of Jesus' teachings. It seems remarkable that Paul quoted Christ so seldom until one realizes that Paul often alluded to church traditions, which themselves stemmed from the teaching and impact of Jesus. Thus the ultimate authority of Jesus' teaching provided the control for the Hellenistic (as well as Jewish) views of Christianity.

The problem of table fellowship between Jews and Gentiles did not cease with the Jerusalem Council. Scrupulous Jews felt that social interaction, especially at meals, made them unclean (cf. Acts 10:10–16; Gal 2:11–14). The Jerusalem decree (Acts 15:28,29; 21:25) was revolutionary, not only in asking the Gentiles to honor the food laws of the Jews, but even more revolutionary in thereby sanctioning table fellowship between Jewish and gentile believers. In the Pauline churches the issue was discussed in terms of the weak and the strong. The "strong" were those spiritually mature enough to free themselves of legal restrictions, such as abstaining from meat offered to idols (1 Cor 8–10) or eating only vegetables (Rom 15) without violating their consciences. Paul commanded his readers to honor the scruples of the "weak" and so to promote harmony.

The Apostolic Preaching. During the period of development, the apostles' preaching (*kerygma*) also underwent revision. Although the Jewish mission centered on proclamation of Jesus as Messiah, the gentile mission emphasized the good news that "Jesus is Lord." Pagans had no basis for understanding Jesus as the Christ, for they had no messianic expectation. In the gentile mission, "Christ" eventually became a surname rather than a title. The stress on the kingdom of God and on Jesus as king also had to be curtailed, because it caused misunderstanding and seemed to the Romans to be treason (Acts 17:7; cf. 16:21). New concepts were added, too, such as the "adoption" of a convert as a "child of God" (a metaphor well known to pagan society but not part of Jewish domestic life) and the cosmic concepts in the hymn recorded in Colossians 1:15–20.

The Jewish *kerygma* took on a stable form, but the gentile proclamation was expressed in great variety because of the many different outlooks represented in the pagan world. The speeches of Paul to the intelligentsia at Athens (Acts 17:22–31) and to the common people in Lystra (14:15–17) illustrate that variety. In both places, Paul's starting point was natural revelation (rather than the fulfillment of prophecy, as in the Jewish mission); his speech at Athens was full of quotes and allusions to Stoic and Epicurean philosophy, whereas his speech at Lystra centered on the folly of idolatry.

Nevertheless, there was a unified approach to preaching the gospel to the Gentiles. Attack on idolatry plus proclamation of the one true God became the core of the gentile mission throughout the next few centuries. An appeal to natural revelation was not stressed by the church fathers of the 2nd and 3rd centuries in their strong polemic against idolatry. It fit in well in the formative period, however, when believers took a conciliatory rather than a strongly polemical approach in gentile evangelism. Another uniting theme was Christ's resurrection and his coming return as judge (Acts 17:31; cf. 1 Thes 1:10); this theme was used to stress the saving activity of the one God in the world. Finally, the message included a demand for repentance before the triune God. Thus the gentile mission featured a unity of approach but a variety of methods that depended on each audience's background.

Missionary strategy emerged as well. Following the pattern of congregations in the diaspora that tended to settle in the urban centers, the church concentrated on populated areas, first focusing on the metropolis and then sending converts into surrounding areas. The best example of such a pattern is Ephesus, where Paul settled for two years, lecturing in the school of Tyrannus (note the further development of Paul using a Greek philosophical school to proclaim the gospel). From Ephesus the church sent out converts, such as Epaphras (Col 1:7; 4:12), to take the message into nearby regions. Paul concentrated on Corinth and Ephesus, the capitals of Achaia and Asia Minor respectively, and longed to get to Rome, the hub of the world.

Social Breadth in the Church. The appeal of Christianity in the gentile world was very broad. Writers have commonly stressed the predominance of the lower classes in the early church but have often failed to realize what Jesus and Paul meant by the "poor" and "weak." For the most part those terms referred to spiritual attitude and status rather than the economic level of a believer. Jewish monotheism held great appeal for intelligent pagans because their polytheism left a spiritual vacuum when they could no longer believe in the gods. That attraction increased with Christianity, which had all of Judaism's religious and moral advantages without its disadvantages (such as circumcision and a detailed legal code). From the outset, prominent individuals joined the church, including members of the Jewish priestly aristocracy (Acts 6:7), the wife of Herod's steward (Lk 8:3), and the proconsul of Cyprus, Sergius Paulus (Acts 13:7,12).

The freedom proclaimed by the church was especially attractive but led to many problems. Luke's stress on the disadvantaged (the lowly, women, children) in his Gospel shows that the later message of the church had its basis in Jesus' ministry. The fact that all believers have the same standing before God (Gal 3:28) must have seemed an astounding thing to slaves ("there is neither slave nor free man") and to women in cultures where women had little social status ("there is neither male nor female").

If Paul's passages on women in the church show that the assertion of freedom brought disrepute on the church among the pagans, Philippians 4:3 shows that women like Euodias and Syntyche could be considered co-workers with Paul, and Philemon 10–13 shows that Onesimus, a slave, was accepted by Paul in the same way. The social freedoms brought by Christianity were unprecedented in the pagan world.

Early Heresy. The appeal of Christianity to pagans led to the early church's greatest internal problem: false teaching or heresy. It was natural that, just as the Judaizers had tried to conform Christianity to Judaism, so pagan converts would seek to recast the traditions in Hellenistic thought-forms. A classic example was Simon Magus (Acts 8:9–13), considered by the church fathers to be the propagator of gnosticism, a philosophical school of thought that claimed special knowledge (*gnosis*) of spiritual reality. Simon's authority lay in Samaria, where he was regarded as a direct emanation from God. His attempt to buy from the apostles the authority to bestow the gifts of the Holy Spirit resulted from his claim to spiritual superiority. Simon was only one among many who plagued the church. Several NT books—1 Corinthians, the pastoral letters (1–2 Tm; Ti), John's Gospel, 1 John, Revelation, and possibly Colossians—dealt directly with the heresy of an incipient Christian gnosticism. To the later gnostics, Jesus, seen as the highest emanation from God, was a spiritual being, not a true man; salvation was acquired through esoteric knowledge centering on Jesus.

Another heresy arose in Corinth, where Paul's proclamation of liberty led to "libertinism" (1 Cor 6:12,13; 10:21–24). The Hellenistic disregard for the physical body led to asceticism (7:1,2) and even a repudiation of the physical resurrection (ch 15).

Jewish Christianity was also moving in the direction of Hellenistic philosophical thought. As Colossians and the pastoral letters show, Jewish ordinances such as food laws and the feasts were reinterpreted along ascetic lines and given a proto-gnostic stamp. "Teachers" were being exalted for their esoteric knowledge.

Changes in Leadership. Authority in the early church underwent considerable change. With the acceptance of James and then Paul as valid apostles, the central church leadership expanded beyond the original 12. Paul's apostleship was based on two factors: his vision of the risen Lord (1 Cor 9:1,2) and his divine commission to be the apostle to the Gentiles (Rom 11:13; 1 Tm 2:7). It is difficult to know how widely the apostolic office was distributed, because the term "apostle" also had a semitechnical use for appointed church emissaries (translated "messenger" in 2 Cor 8:23; Phil 2:25). Paul's enigmatic use of the plural "apostles" for his fellow workers (Rom 16:7; 1 Cor 4:9; 1 Thes 2:6) could fit either meaning, or perhaps be an even more general term used of itinerant missionaries, a meaning it came to have in the second century.

A balance between charismatic and institutional church government continued. Ephesians 4:11 shows that the offices themselves were based on spiritual gifts (cf. 1 Cor 12:28–30, which combines offices and gifts without differentiating the categories). The terms used for church offices in the pastoral letters are vague. Most scholars believe that the offices of bishop and elder were still synonymous at that late time. The three letters show, however, that at the close of the period of expansion, the institutional movement was well on its way toward the established form it took in the 2nd and 3rd centuries.

Changes in Worship. Patterns of worship in the church also underwent significant development during the period of expansion. The gentile church did not feel constrained to observe the Jewish Sabbath or feasts (Gal 4:10; Col 2:16). There is some debate concerning the development of a service devoted solely to preaching and prayer. Some scholars believe that in both Jewish and Hellenistic churches there were two basic services: the sacred meal, which included liturgy and teaching; and a missionary service, which took place in the temple or synagogue (Jewish) or a lecture hall (Hellenistic). The NT letters, however, only mention the fact that a service was held without specifying what form it took.

Two early 2nd-century works—the *Didache* (a book of instructions on morals and church order) and the letter of a Roman provincial governor, Pliny, to the Emperor Trajan—help solve the dilemma. Both allude to a separate worship service in which the preaching and teaching were paramount. Such meetings may have preceded the eucharistic celebration and prepared believers for it.

Thus, 1 Corinthians 14:23 (the presence of unbelievers in the assembly, unlikely at the sacred meal) and 14:26 (showing that the elements of the service were psalms, teaching, revelations, and speaking in tongues) may refer to a separate worship service. That service may have been followed by the *agape* meal and eucharistic celebration. As already stated, the meal and the Eucharist were celebrated concurrently in the Palestinian era, but with Hellenistic abuse the two began to diverge;

by the early 2nd century at the latest (according to the *Didache*), the Eucharist was celebrated separately following the meal. Hence the order of worship in the early church was: (1) gathering for prayer and teaching, (2) the *agape* meal, and (3) the eucharistic celebration.

Baptism was also institutionalized and at some stage, probably during the same period, became a formal ceremony. A probable reason for such formalizing was the growing complexity of the community in the later church. No description of such a service was written until the 2nd century, but the service probably centered on a confession of faith similar to Romans 10:9,10; the confession became a dialogue regarding the candidate's doctrine and conduct, as well as a time of instruction on the implications of baptism.

The First Persecution. The period of expansion closed with the first great persecution of the church—under the Roman emperor, Nero. Paul was imprisoned from AD 58 to 60—but there is considerable debate regarding his release and a second imprisonment. Acts does not mention a release and may contain a possible allusion to his subsequent execution (Acts 20:25). The pastoral letters, however, definitely presuppose Paul's release and further ministry in Asia Minor and Macedonia.

Paul's death, and probably Peter's as well, marked the end of the period of expansion. Open evangelism became difficult and Christianity went underground. Nero's decree against the Christians was not so much the cause as the result of the persecution. Popular feeling against Christians, who were seen as exclusive and individualistic, allowed Nero to use them as a scapegoat to cover up his own misdeeds.

Period of Consolidation. *Transition.* The next phase of church history was a time of great transition between the dynamic growth of the church under the apostles' leadership and the catholic church of succeeding centuries. A major feature of that era was the death of the eyewitnesses, which removed the prime apologetic strength of the early church (cf. 1 Cor 15:6). Jesus had stressed belief apart from eyewitness proof (Jn 20:29), and John's Gospel should have prepared the church for John's death (21:18–23). With the apostles' passing, the church became ever more dependent on tradition and second-generation leadership.

The Fall of Jerusalem. An important event in the final period of the apostolic age was the destruction of Jerusalem in AD 70. Shortly before that event, many Palestinian Christians had left the Holy City and fled to Pella. The church was cut off from its place of origin, a factor causing it to seek new moorings. The church was left with no center of leadership, and until mid-2nd century the church separated into regional groups such as Antioch, Rome, and Alexandria. Rome, because of its position in the empire and because it naturally attracted leaders like Peter and Paul, assumed leadership in the West, while Alexandria became the center of the eastern church.

Heresy and Growing Institutionalism. The Jewish Christians who had stayed within the church had changed from the days of the Judaizers. They no longer made salvation dependent on the Law, but they did follow Jewish customs and ways of thinking. However, the clash between the organized church and Jewish "Christians" who withdrew from the church intensified, so that by the start of the 2nd century there was only sporadic contact.

Gnosticism, however, grew in both influence and power. The reasons are primarily historical; its strength in pagan society also grew and continued to grow until its peak in the 3rd century. Some later NT works dealt with gnostic tendencies in the church. Gnosticism became especially strong in Egypt and Syria. In Syria, it flourished under the influence of Simon Magus and his pupils, who virtually changed Christianity into another Greek mystery religion. The struggles of Ignatius and other 2nd-century writers against gnosticism added to the development of the distinctive doctrines of the patristic era, such as the unity between flesh and spirit, the early emphasis on Christology (the doctrine of Christ), and the importance of the resurrection of the body.

In the Hellenistic world, the problem was not only doctrinal but also ethical. The growth of docetism (a heresy that separated the divine Christ from the human Jesus, maintaining that Christ did not truly die on the cross but left his body before death) was paralleled by a libertinism that differed little from pagan orgies (cf. Rv 2:14,20).

Two different reactions to heresy took place: one sought to answer it through the historical proclamation in the church traditions (represented in 1 Jn); the other fought gnostic thought by developing institutionalism and mystical interpretations of the church and sacraments. The pastoral letters laid the basis for the second approach, instructing the church to use excommunication procedures against false teachers (1 Tm 1:20; Ti 3:10; cf. 2 Thes 3:6,14,15). Though historical proclamation continued to be a valuable defense against heresy, the defense through institutionalism grew through the efforts of the church fathers, preparing the way for later catholicism.

Finally, the institutional approach to church discipline as a whole was growing. In the apostolic period, discipline was a corporate responsibility that centered on the daily life of each member. Principles such as confrontation, confession, repentance, and forgiveness were individualized and practiced in the fellowship of the church's life. At the end of the apostolic age, especially with the absence of apostolic leadership, such individual spiritual experiences were "institutionalized," that is, they were made the function of church officers in the context of the organization. The *Didache* shows that confession and repentance were incorporated into the church service. Also, responsibility for maintaining the purity and unity of the church was increasingly delegated to bishops rather than to individual church members.

Church Leadership. Development of the leadership continued, perhaps because of the absence of the charismatic authority of the apostles. Left without the undeniable leadership of the apostles, the church focused its attention on the remaining offices and functions. The terms "elder," "bishop," and "presbyter" (priest or pastor) often had been used interchangeably by the early church. Gradually they became distinct offices, first in the churches of Asia Minor and later in the West. For example, Clement of Rome, a church father and bishop writing around AD 97, equated bishops and presbyters (or elders). On the other hand, Ignatius, a bishop of Antioch writing in the first decade of the 2nd century, made a clear distinction between bishops, who were the highest church officials, and presbyters and deacons, who assisted the bishops. Ignatius's three-level division of church offices, known as the monarchical episcopate, gradually became the model followed by all churches. It was well established by the mid-2nd century. In that system the bishop in effect became the successor to the apostles and was alone responsible for administering the sacraments of baptism and the Eucharist (Communion).

Therefore the charismatic approach to church government gradually ceased, being replaced by the episcopacy. The lists of offices in several postapostolic writings fail to mention prophets and teachers and mention apostles primarily in a past sense. All those writers accepted the continuing validity of the prophetic or teaching functions, but for the most part they believed that the ecclesiastical officers filled those functions. At the start of the 2nd century, there were still authoritative teachers such as Clement of Rome, Ignatius, and Polycarp, but the office was disappearing. Increasingly, teaching was no longer viewed as an independent, creative act but as a recitation of the church's authoritative writings. An interest in an authoritative

NT canon (i.e., officially recognized sacred books) was developing.

Formation of the NT Canon. The process of "canonization" actually began early in the apostolic period. The sayings of Jesus were given canonical status quite early, and the creedal traditions had achieved authoritative status by the time the NT letters were written. It is difficult to know how early the Pauline letters were canonized. From the beginning they were read in the churches, with the stamp of apostolic authority (cf. Col 4:16; 1 Thes 5:27; 1 Tm 4:13). The absence of "to the Ephesians" in early manuscripts of Ephesians possibly indicates that the letter was intended for general distribution. Most scholars agree that Paul's letters replaced the sermon but not the Scripture reading in the worship service. In 2 Peter 3:15,16 the canonicity of the Pauline letters seems to be recognized. The Gospels probably attained canonical status almost immediately; the 4 were already being collected together at the end of the 1st century (according to Eusebius, a 4th-century church historian). Later attempts to collect all the canonical works developed largely in answer to heresies such as Marcionism. Marcion devised an "authoritative" canon about AD 140 in an attempt to justify his rejection of the OT. In reaction to him and others, the first true canon, the Muratorian canon, appeared about AD 180.

Worship. The worship and sacramental life of the church also became increasingly institutionalized. Both the Eucharist and baptism were seen as a celebrative part of the process of salvation and not as a memorial celebration of previously received, saving grace. At the same time, the liturgical approach to both sacraments continued to develop and was totally formalized, as was the entire worship service. The charismatic approach to worship (seen in 1 Cor 14:26) was increasingly replaced by a formal structure of readings. The free prayers of the congregation were replaced by liturgical prayers recited by the worship leader.

Conclusion. The church survived many internal struggles and seemingly irresistible external pressures in its earliest years. Its preservation and growth seem almost miraculous to Christian students of history. The church that emerged from the apostolic age became a strong and growing organized movement, scattered throughout the Roman empire.

GRANT R. OSBORNE

See ACTS OF THE APOSTLES, BOOK OF THE; APOSTLE, APOSTLESHIP; GNOSTICISM; MINISTER, MINISTRY; BIBLE, CANON OF THE.

Bibliography. J.V. Bartlett, *The Apostolic Age;* F.F. Bruce, *NT History;* H. Lietzmann, *A History of the Early Church,* 4 vols.; T.W. Manson, R.N. Moore, G.B. Laird, *A Primer of Christianity;* E.F. Scott, *The First Age of Christianity;* J. Weiss, *The History of Primitive Christianity,* 2 vols.

Apothecary. Pharmacist; KJV rendering of "perfumer" in Exodus 30:25,35; 37:29; 2 Chronicles 16:14; Nehemiah 3:8; and Ecclesiastes 10:1.

See TRADES AND OCCUPATIONS (PERFUMER).

Appa-im. Nadab's son, and the father of Ishi in Judah's tribe (1 Chr 2:30,31).

Appeal. Legal term meaning to request a higher court review of a decision by a lower one. OT Law made no provision for appeals. In the NT the apostle Paul appealed to the caesar for a hearing after his arrest in Jerusalem (Acts 25:11). Because he was a Roman citizen, Paul could have his case removed from the Jewish courts where he feared an unfair trial.

See CIVIL LAW AND JUSTICE.

Appearances of Christ. Occasions on which Jesus Christ was seen by human witnesses after his resurrection.

See RESURRECTION.

Apphia. Christian woman in Colosse, possibly the wife or sister of Philemon. The apostle Paul greeted her in his letter to Philemon (v 2). According to tradition she was martyred during Nero's persecution. On the saint's calendar of the Greek Orthodox Church, she is honored on November 22.

Appius, Forum of. Marketplace mentioned in Acts 28:15 as the place where Christians met the apostle Paul when he came to appear before the caesar. It was apparently named for Appius Claudius, builder of the Appian Way (major artery of western Italy). Around the fo-

The Appian Way.

rum was a region of swamp and marsh, notorious in the ancient world for bad water, mosquitoes, expensive taverns for travelers, nighttime noisy traffic of cargoes and passengers on mule-drawn barges along a canal cut through the area. The Appian Way passes through the Appian Forum about 40 miles south of Rome.

See FORUM.

Apple, Apple Tree. Fruit and tree not native to the Near East but used by some versions to translate certain references to fruit in the OT.

See PLANTS (APRICOT).

Apricot. *See* PLANTS (APRICOT).

Aqaba, Gulf of. Eastern branch (of two northern arms) of the Red Sea which penetrates N,NE between Saudi Arabia and the Sinai Peninsula. The gulf varies in width from 12 to 17 miles and is 100 miles long. The port city of Elath (or Eloth), located at the northern end of the gulf of Aqaba, is mentioned in the account of the Israelites' 40 years of wandering in the wilderness (Dt 2:8). From his port of Ezion-geber King Solomon sent ships down the Gulf of Aqaba to Ophir (1 Kgs 9:26–28).

Aqueduct. Conduit or artificial channel for conducting water from a distance, usually by means of gravity; also a structure carrying a conduit or canal across a valley or over a river.

In Palestine most cities were situated near an abundant water supply so that in time of siege water would be available. Ancient tunnels for the conveyance of water have been found at Gezer. The Jebusites, inhabitants of the area that later became Jerusalem, seem to have constructed some sort of aqueduct to bring rainwater into the city (2 Sm 5:8). By the time of King Hezekiah there existed a "conduit of the upper pool" (2 Kgs 18:17). In anticipation of throwing off the Assyrian yoke, Hezekiah made a 1,777-foot tunnel through the hill of Ophel to carry water from the Gihon spring to the pool of Siloam (Is 22:9–11). The famous "Siloam inscription" describes how it was done.

It is known that later 2 aqueducts, 13 and 41 miles in length, brought water into Jerusalem. They merged at the Roman reservoirs near Bethlehem. On reaching the city, the water was carried to the temple area by means of underground pipes (cf. Ez 47:1; Jl 3:18). In NT times, the Jewish historian Josephus stated, Pontius Pilate appropriated some "Corban" money from the temple treasury for work on an aqueduct. Three "pools of Solomon," which are of Roman design, were probably constructed with part of those funds.

Other cities of Bible times served by ancient aqueducts were Tyre, Samaria, Caesarea (Roman capital of the province), Jericho, and Ephesus in Asia Minor.

The Romans brought the science of aqueduct engineering to a fine art. The Appia (312 BC) was 10.3 miles long and the Ano Vetus (272 BC) was over 32 miles long. Both were underground channels that brought water into the city of Rome. Other examples of Roman engineering expertise can still be seen in the ruined arches of Aqua Claudia (Rome), begun by Emperor Caligula; the Pont du Gard of Nimes

An aqueduct, from Roman times, on the west side of Shechem.

(France); the aqueduct above the Rummel River at Constantine (Algeria); the De Los Milagros aqueduct, Mérida (Spain); and the 2,700-foot aqueduct in Segovia, also in Spain.

See SILOAM, POOL OF; SOLOMON, POOLS OF.

Aquila. Husband of Priscilla (Acts 18:2,18,26; Rom 16:3; 1 Cor 16:19; 2 Tm 4:19).

See PRISCILLA AND AQUILA.

Ar, Ar of Moab. Capital city of Moab located on the northern border (Dt 2:18,29) near the Arnon River (Nm 21:28). Ar was sometimes used figuratively to refer to all of Moab (Dt 2:9). The prophet Isaiah predicted the destruction of the Moabite cities Ar and Kir (Is 15:1).

Ara. Son of Jether, a chief among Asher's tribe (1 Chr 7:38).

Arab. City in the hill country southwest of Hebron, given to Judah's tribe after the conquest of Canaan, the Promised Land (Jos 15:52). It is thought Arab is to be identified with modern Khirbet er-Rabiyeh.

Arabah. Great valley dividing eastern and western Palestine. The Arabah extends south from the Sea of Galilee through the Jordan River valley to the Dead Sea and to the Gulf of Aqaba. Commonly known as the Rift Valley, the Arabah is about 6 miles wide and 200 miles long. The Dead Sea, located in the Aqaba, is the lowest point on the earth's inland surface, 1,275 feet below sea level.

In general the Hebrew *arabah* means a wasteland or barren district. North of the Dead Sea to the Sea of Galilee, the valley is referred to by the Arabs as the Ghor ("depression") and south of the Dead Sea as the Arabah.

In the OT the name Arabah is sometimes applied to the entire length of the valley, though at times the southern portion is alluded to (Dt 1:1; 2:8), and elsewhere the northeast portion is indicated (Dt 3:17; 4:49; Jos 11:2). It could refer to the portion east of the Jordan River (Dt 4:49) or to the part west of the river (Jos 11:16) or to the Jordan River valley (2 Sm 4:7). In the Hebrew OT, the plural of Arabah (*Arboth*) is found 17 times, and its meaning is "plains" referring to the portion of the Arabah near Jericho or Moab. The Dead Sea is sometimes referred to as the Sea of the Arabah or Sea of the Plain (2 Kgs 14:25). For the most part the section of the Arabah north of the Dead Sea was, and is today, fertile and productive.

It was from the Arabah that Joshua led the campaign to conquer Jericho. Abner fled to the northern Arabah after being defeated at Gibeon (2 Sm 2:29). The murderers of Ishbosheth crossed the area to bring his head to David at Hebron (2 Sm 4:7), and Zedekiah was fleeing to the area when he was captured by the Babylonians (2 Kgs 25:4; Jer 39:4).

The southern Arabah was the scene of Israel's wanderings before entering the Promised Land. Farther north, the Arabah was the site of the final acts of Moses (Nm 32–36), who died and was buried in the Arabah (Dt 1:1) in the plains of Moab east of the Dead Sea (Dt 34:1–6).

South of the Dead Sea there were deposits of iron and copper, and Deuteronomy 8:9 may allude to this general area when it speaks of "a land whose stones are iron, and out of whose hills you can dig copper." The land here is generally barren, though in ancient times careful use of irrigation made agriculture possible to a limited extent. Several important trade routes have passed through this area. The Arabah around the Dead Sea, prior to the destruction of Sodom and Gomorrah, was once an especially fertile area, "like the garden of the Lord" (Gn 13:10).

The rejuvenation of this area is one of the subjects of prophetic promise. Ezekiel speaks of a great river which will spring from the temple and go down into the Arabah, making the waters of the sea fresh and creating a healthy environment for fish and other living creatures (Ez 47:1–12; Jl 3:18; Zec 14:8).

PAUL L. KAUFMAN *and* R. MILTON WINTER

See PALESTINE.

Arabah, Brook of the. Dry stream bed in southern Palestine (Am 6:14).

See BROOK OF THE ARABAH.

Arabah, Sea of the. Alternate name for the Dead Sea, since that body of water lies within the area of the land of Israel called Arabah (Dt 3:17; 4:49; Jos 3:16; 12:3; 2 Kgs 14:25).

See DEAD SEA; PALESTINE.

Arabia, Arabs. Peninsula in southwestern Asia, surrounded by sea on three sides and by the Fertile Crescent on the fourth. Politically, the Arabian peninsula is bounded on the north by the modern Hashemite kingdom of Jordan and by Iraq and on the south by the Indian Ocean. The Persian Gulf forms its eastern boundary and the Red Sea its western boundary. Its area is just over a million square miles, about one-third the area of the United States.

Geography. Classical geographers such as Strabo followed the example set by the geographer Ptolemy in dividing Arabia into three divisions: *Arabia Petraea* (Rocky Arabia) in the northwest, which included Sinai, Edom, Moab, and Transjordan; *Arabia Deserta*, which included the Syrian desert; and *Arabia Felix* (Happy Arabia), which included the southern section of the Arabian peninsula.

At present Arabia is divided into several states, the largest of which is Saudi Arabia. The others are Yemen, Kuwait, Qatar, Oman, Muscat, and Aden.

In using "Arabia" as a geographical term the Bible sometimes includes both northern and southern sections. For example, 2 Chronicles 9:14 says that the kings of Arabia brought gold to Solomon as tribute. At other times the name Arabia refers only to the northwestern *Arabia Petraea*. For example, Paul said that after his conversion he went away "to the deserts of Arabia" (Gal 1:17) and referred to Mt Sinai (4:25) which is in that northwestern area. Many places named in the Bible as being in Arabia are more specifically in *Arabia Petraea*. Such sites include Buz, Dedan, Dumah, Ephah, the Hazor of Jeremiah 49:28–33, Massa, Mesha, and Midian. Hazarmaveth, Ophir, Sabtah, Sephar, Sheba, and Uzal are in the south. Havilah and Parvaim are perhaps in the northeast, and authorities debate the location of Seba. The land of Uz, mentioned in the Book of Job, is considered by many scholars to be located in the area between Edom and northern Arabia.

Climate. Arabia is thought by many to be one of the hottest countries. In some sections that conception is correct. The peninsula lies between seas on the east and west, but those bodies of water are too small to break the climatic continuity of the dry African-Asian continental masses. There are, however, some regions that enjoy temperate and semitropical climate. In the south much of the land is sufficiently elevated to avoid the intensity of tropical heat. The lowlands along the coast have a semitropical environment. Fogs and dews are common in the humid regions, but over inner Arabia the sun shines the year round, obscured only by an occasional sandstorm or an even rarer rain shower.

In al-Hijaz, the birthplace of Islam, seasons of drought sometimes extend over three years or more. In Yemen and Asir there are sufficient periodic rains to make systematic cultivation possible. There is no significant river in Arabia. Instead of a system of rivers, a network of wadis (dried stream beds) determines the routes of caravans and pilgrimages.

History. Although the queen of Sheba was probably the most famous Arabian in the Bible, many other persons and tribes were intimately connected with this land. The table of nations in Genesis 10 mentions names found preserved in many Arabic place names (vv 7,26–30). The sons of Abraham by Hagar and Keturah (25:1–4,12–18) also reflect Arabic tribes and places. Indeed, North Arab genealogists trace their ancestry back to Ishmael.

Arabia has long been desired for natural resources. Pharaohs of the first dynasty operated turquoise mines in Sinai, and the gold of Ophir and the frankincense and myrrh of South Arabia were world-renowned. The queen of Sheba brought such precious spices to Solomon (1 Kgs 10:2,10), and trade between Israel and Arabia flourished (v 15). Solomon had a seaport at Ezion-geber on the Red Sea for his opulent commerce with Ophir (9:26–28). King Jehoshaphat of Judah (872–848 BC), who also received tribute from Arabs (2 Chr 17:11), tried to revive trade with Ophir but failed (1 Kgs 22:48).

Tribes associated with Arabia played a significant role in biblical history. The Ishmaelites or Midianites who took Joseph to Egypt (Gn 37:25–36) were Arabians. So were the Amalekites who waged war with Moses in the wilderness of *Arabia Petraea* (Ex 17:8–16). Moses' father-in-law, Jethro, was a Midianite (18:1). King Uzziah of Judah fought against Arabs (2 Chr 26:7); the Meunites mentioned in the same verse were probably also from Arabia. Geshem the Arab, known also from secular inscriptions, resisted the rebuilding of the Jerusalem wall (Neh 2:19; 6:1,6).

Kedar was an important North Arab tribe condemned in Isaiah's message about Arabia (Is 21:13–17). Jeremiah also spoke against it, prophesying its destruction by Nebuchadnezzar, who did indeed subjugate it (Jer 49:28–33). Close allies of the tribe of Kedar were the Nabatean Arabs (Is 60:7), who figure prominently in later history. They captured Petra, fulfilling the prophecy of Obadiah about Edom. References to Arabia and the Arabs in the Apocrypha and NT concern mostly the Nabatean Arabs (1 Mc 11:16; Gal 1:17).

In southern Arabia four kingdoms developed: the Sabean, Minean, Qataban, and Hadramaut. Around 115 BC the Himyarite kingdom gained control of southern Arabia, keeping it until about AD 300. Three centuries later the Arabian peninsula witnessed the birth of Islam.

Culture and Religion. Some of the earliest examples of alphabetic writing come from the mines of the Sinai peninsula, dating back to at least the middle of the 2nd millennium BC. North Arabia was usually the haunt of the nomad; southern Arabia had a more sedentary agricultural civilization. Archaeologists have shown that South Arabia was considerably advanced in building and water-control technology as well as in religious sculpture.

Tombs, near the entrance to the Siq (the narrow passage leading to Petra).

Arabians were polytheists. In South Arabia the moon god was highly revered, and the sun was considered a goddess. In the northern parts Dushara, Allat, and Gad were widely worshiped. Then, with the coming of Islam, Allah became the only god recognized.

Arad (Person). Beriah's son, of Benjamin's tribe (1 Chr 8:15).

Arad (Place). Name of a Canaanite settlement or region in the Negeb desert at the time of the Israelite conquest of Canaan. The king of Arad attacked the Israelites and was defeated (Nm 21:1–3; 33:40). Consequently the Israelites renamed the place Hormah ("destruction"). Arad was later conquered by Joshua (Jos 12:14).

Until recently archaeologists thought this Arad was the modern Tell Arad. Excavations at Tell Arad, however, have shown that this site was uninhabited at the time of the Israelite conquest of Canaan. Some scholars have suggested that the Arad mentioned in Numbers and Joshua was a region and not a specific place. Others say there were two Arads, the Canaanite city located possibly at Tell Malhata about 7.5 miles southwest of Tell Arad, and the Israelite city located at modern Tell Arad. This second suggestion is supported by an inscription of Shishak, an Egyptian pharaoh (940?–915 BC), which indicates that two cities named Arad existed during the early first millennium BC.

The only possible mention of modern Tell Arad is in Judges 1:16, where Arad is used as a reference point for the land settled by the Kenites. Tell Arad had been a large important city during the Early Bronze Age, but after being destroyed around 2600 BC, it was not reoccupied until shortly before 1000 BC. From the time of King Solomon (970–930 BC) until the

Jews were taken into exile, Tell Arad served as a fortified citadel on Judah's southern border.

Several interesting discoveries were made during the excavation of Tell Arad. An Israelite sanctuary was uncovered which is very similar in plan to the tabernacle and temple, with an altar of the dimensions described in Exodus 27:1. It has been suggested that this sanctuary might have served as the worship center of the Kenite clan. Tell Arad has also provided us with a number of inscribed potsherds, called ostraca. One such ostracon contains a reference to the "house of Yahweh," a possible reference to the temple in Jerusalem.

Arah. 1. Ulla's son from Asher's tribe (1 Chr 7:39).

2. Ancestor of a group of people that returned to Jerusalem with Zerubbabel after the exile (Ezr 2:5; Neh 7:10).

Aram. 1. Shem's son and Noah's grandson (Gn 10:22,23; 1 Chr 1:17). Ancestor of the Aramaeans.

See SYRIA, SYRIANS.

2. Kemuel's son, grandson of Abraham's brother Nahor (Gn 22:21).

3. Shemer's son from Asher's tribe (1 Chr 7:34).

4. The Aram occurring in the genealogy of Jesus Christ (Mt 1:3,4 KJV) is actually a confusing Greek form of Ram, an entirely different name (Ru 4:19).

See RAM (PERSON) #1.

Aram, Aramaeans. Designation for the territory and predecessors of Syria and the Syrians.

See SYRIA, SYRIANS.

Aramaic Language. One of the three languages in which the Bible was written.

See BIBLICAL LANGUAGES.

Arameans. Alternate spelling of Aramaeans.

See SYRIA, SYRIANS.

Aram-Geshur. Small kingdom between Mt Hermon and Bashan bordering Argob.

See GESHUR, GESHURITES.

Aram-maacah (Maachah). Alternate name for Maacah in 1 Chronicles 19:6.

See MAACAH, MAACHAH (PLACE).

Aram-naharaim. Hebrew word meaning "Aram of the two rivers" and referring to the area bounded by the upper Euphrates and the Habur rivers. It is sometimes translated "Mesopotamia" (Dt 23:4) or "eastern Syria" (Jgs 3:8 LB). The major city of that area was Haran, where Terah and Abram stopped and where Terah died (Gn 11:31,32). A servant of Abraham (Abram) returned to the same region to seek a wife for Abraham's son Isaac (Gn 24:1–10). Isaac's son Jacob also returned to Haran to seek a wife (Gn 28:1–5; Paddan-aram is a synonym of Aram-naharaim). Aram-naharaim was the home of Balaam, the pagan prophet (Dt 23:4). One oppressor of Israel during the period of the judges was Cushan-rishathaim, king of Aram-naharaim (Jgs 3:8–11). Later, in King David's wars with Ammon, he had to confront mercenary charioteers hired from the Aramaean centers of Aram-naharaim, Aram-maacah, and Zobah (1 Chr 19:6; cf. Ps 60 superscription).

See SYRIA, SYRIANS.

Aram of Damascus. One of the several city-kingdoms in the land of Aram (Syria). This kingdom, whose principal city was Damascus, was subjugated by King David (1 Chr 18:3–6).

See DAMASCUS, DAMASCENE.

Aram-zobah. Syrian territory ruled in David's time by King Hadadezer, whom David defeated (2 Sm 8:3). This form of the name occurs in the superscription of Psalm 60.

See ZOBAH, ZOBA.

Aran. Dishan's son, grandson of Seir the Horite, and a descendant of Esau (Gn 36:28; 1 Chr 1:42).

Ararat. Name of a craggy, rugged range of mountains corresponding to what was, until Russian and Turkish takeover, the independent kingdom of Armenia (KJV in 2 Kgs 19:37; Is 37:38). Ararat lies just south of the Black Sea and between it and the Caspian Sea. The region overlaps extreme eastern Turkey, the southern Caucasus of Georgian Russia, and the northern tip of Iran. The mountains of Ararat are cited as the resting place of Noah's ark when the flood waters began to subside (Gn 8:4). Much speculation, several expeditions, and a Hollywood film about the legends and lore relating to Ararat in the search for remains of Noah's ark lend considerable popular interest to that remote area.

A healthy skepticism about a precise location for a singular Mt Ararat is in order, though a traditional site is pointed out between Lakes Van and Urmia in the heart of ancient Urartu (note the common consonants with Ararat), once a district of Assyria. Surrounding topography is a high plain of sparse vegetation, equally sparse habitation, and barren lava beds. Agri Dagh (Turkish for "Mt of Trouble") is one peak 17,000 feet high to which local tribesmen have given the name Kohl Nu, that is, Mt of Noah. Hence most of the searching for the ark is concentrated there.

See NOAH #1; FLOOD, THE.

Araunah. Jebusite whose threshing floor was the scene of some significant events in biblical history. (Jebus was the ancient Canaanite city which later became Jerusalem.) Araunah's threshing floor marked the place where the Lord stopped a pestilential angel after the death of 70,000 Israelites (2 Sm 24:15,16). The plague from the Lord had come upon Israel as a result of King David's prideful census. At the instruction of the prophet Gad, the repentant David purchased the floor and built an altar to the Lord (2 Sm 24:17–25). Araunah offered oxen and everything needed for the altar as a gift, but David insisted on paying him, saying, "I will not offer burnt offerings to the Lord my God which cost me nothing" (v 24). A parallel account (1 Chr 21:15–26) uses the Hebrew form Ornan for the Jebusite's foreign name. David was in too much of a hurry to go to the tabernacle to make his sacrifice, the tabernacle and altar being farther away on the hill of Gibeon (1 Chr 21:27–30). David chose the threshing floor as the site for the temple (1 Chr 22:1), and Solomon built it there on Mt Moriah (2 Chr 3:1). It was the same area to which God commanded Abraham to go for the sacrifice of Isaac (Gn 22:2). Tradition locates the present-day Muslim mosque, the Dome of the Rock, on the site of Araunah's threshing floor.

Arba. Ancestor of the giant Anakim and a great hero among them (Jos 15:13; 21:11). Arba was the founder of Kiriath-arba (city of Arba), later known as Hebron (Jos 14:15).

Arbathite. Resident of the city of Beth-arabah, and the hometown of Abi-albon (Abiel), one of David's thirty "mighty men" (2 Sm 23:31; 1 Chr 11:32).

Arbite. Title given to Paarai, warrior among David's thirty "mighty men" (2 Sm 23:35). The expression may indicate that he was a native of Arab, a village in southern Judah (Jos 15:52).

Arch. Curved structure, usually of masonry, supporting the weight over a doorway or other open space. The capstone or keystone is the most important part of an arch and the last stone put in place. It ties the two curving sides together and distributes the weight evenly through them to the foundation.

Arches were not used in the architecture of ancient Israel and appear in the Bible only through mistranslation. The Hebrew word translated "arches" throughout Ezekiel's vision of the temple (Ez 40 KJV) refers to porches rather than arches.

See ARCHITECTURE.

Archaeology. Study of the remains of ancient civilizations, frequently as the result of systematic excavations. Archaeology is a relatively young discipline, the first excavations in Mesopotamia being those of the Frenchman Paul Emile Botta at Nineveh in 1842. The earliest discoveries in the Aegean area were those of the German Heinrich Schliemann at Troy in 1870 and at Mycenae in 1876.

Egyptian antiquities were introduced to Europe by Napoleon's invasion in 1798, but most 19th-century activities in Egypt were undisguised treasure hunts and not archaeological excavations. At the end of that century the Englishman Flinders Petrie introduced order into the archaeology of Egypt. He was also the first to excavate in Palestine, in 1890 at Tell el-Hesi, 16 miles east of Gaza. Except for interludes

Arches in Chorazin.

forced by war, excavations have continued unabated in biblical lands.

In spite of a prevailing skepticism by scholars toward biblical documents in the 19th and early 20th centuries, archaeology has provided a mass of evidence that as a whole confirms the reliability of the Bible. Where such supportive evidence is still lacking, it may yet be uncovered in future digs. Present archaeological data are but a small fraction of the ancient remains potentially available for study.

Surface Surveys. Many outstanding discoveries have been entirely accidental. At Ras Shamra in Syria a peasant's plow struck a tomb that led to the ancient site of Ugarit. A Bedouin in search of a lost goat discovered the cave at Qumran which contained the Dead Sea Scrolls. In 1887 an Egyptian woman found the Amarna tablets while seeking decomposed bricks for use as fertilizer. In 1945 Egyptians hunting bird manure in caves near Nag Hammadi discovered important Coptic Gnostic manuscripts.

Such chance finds, however, are no substitute for systematic surveys. In the Middle East, excepting Egypt, numerous tells, or artificial mounds of the remains of ancient cities, dot the countryside. Because of erosion, potsherds (broken pieces of pottery) can be found on the surface, especially in gullies down the slopes. An examination of such sherds can give an idea of the periods of settlement represented in the tell. Sometimes the variation of vegetation on the surface presents clues to structures below. Leonard Woolley discovered some graves by observing patches of weeds that grew in clumps which were never more than six feet across. The deep-rooted weeds were growing over graves that had broken up the soil.

The founder of modern surface exploration was an American, Edward Robinson, professor of biblical literature at Union Theologial Seminary, New York. Together with Eli Smith, a former student and missionary in Lebanon, Robinson made a pioneer survey of sites in Palestine in 1838. Yet Robinson did not recognize the true significance of tells, because his work preceded stratified excavations.

The greatest practitioner of surface archaeology was the indefatigable Nelson Glueck, late president of Hebrew Union College in Cincinnati. Glueck began surveys in the Transjordan in 1933 and continued them year after year (except for 1940–41) until 1947. In 1952, following the Arab-Israeli hostilities of 1948, he began systematic explorations of the Negeb desert area of Israel. He located over 1,500 sites, most of them previously unrecorded. Glueck used the Bible as his guidebook and recommended that others do the same. After reading Deuteronomy 8:9 he made his famous discoveries of copper-mining operations in the Wadi Arabah. Glueck's explorations showed that there were pottery-producing settlements in the Negeb during the 20th and 19th centuries BC (Middle Bronze I), but not for a millennium before or after. His finding fits very well the period assigned on other grounds to the narratives of Abraham. He also discovered a break in sedentary occupation in the territory south of the Jabbok River between 1900 and 1300 BC. Since the biblical narrative implies opposition to the Israelites by settled communities in those areas, many scholars, therefore, put the conquest of the Promised Land in the 13th century BC, when there were such communities.

However, a number of discoveries have been made recently in Transjordan of materials from the Middle Bronze (2000–1500 BC) and Late Bronze (1500–1200 BC) periods, which may require us to qualify those conclusions somewhat. In Israel important surveys have been carried out by Saarisalo in Lower Galilee, leading to the discovery of ancient trade routes, and by Yohanan Aharoni in Upper Galilee, bringing to light the patterns of Israelite occupation. Such surveys covering broad areas can show trends that are not always reflected in the main centers, which are the usual targets of excavation.

Between 1965 and 1968 more than 500 new sites were discovered in surveys of the Negeb and Sinai regions. The Israeli surveys of 1967–68 examined the Golan Heights, Samaria, and Judah. All told, close to 2,000 sites were examined, of which 800 were previously unknown. One important result of the survey of Judah is growing recognition that the biblical site of Debir (Jgs 1:11) should be located at Tell Rabud, south of Hebron, instead of at Tell Beit Mirsim, a site excavated by W. F. Albright.

Identification of Sites. Identification of biblical sites is based on several considerations: topographical mention in the Scriptures; in some cases, retention of biblical names; and correspondence of archaeological evidence with the known history of the site. A number of sites have been continuously occupied and have retained their biblical names. Such is the case, for example, with Taanach, Jerusalem, Bethel (in the form Beitin), Gaza, Ashdod, and Ashkelon. Sometimes the ancient name has been retained not on the tell itself but at another site in the vicinity. Ancient Beth-shan, Tell el-Husn, is located 1,600 feet north of modern Beisan. Tell Beersheba is three miles from the modern town. In Byzantine times the name of biblical Beth-zur migrated to a new site at Beit Sur. The village of

Jeba lies two miles to the east of Tell el-Ful (biblical Gibeah). The fact that there were two Jerichos, OT Jericho at Tell es-Sultan and NT Jericho about a mile south, may explain the apparent contradiction between Mark 10:46 and Luke 18:35 (which describe Jesus approaching Jericho) and Matthew 20:29 (which describes him leaving Jericho) at the time he healed Bartimaeus and his companion.

There are a few situations where inscriptions from the site identify its name, as at Carchemish in Syria and Naukratis in Egypt. André Parrot at Tell Hariri found a statue with the name of the king of Mari. In Anatolia the sites of Derbe and Lystra were identified by inscriptions found on the surface. The name Lachish appeared on one of the ostraca (pottery fragments) found at Tell ed-Duweir. At el-Jib, James Pritchard found two dozen jar handles bearing the name Gibeon. Aharoni discovered a bowl at Arad with the name Arad inscribed seven times on it. Often sites can be identified only with varying degrees of probability, such as Tell en-Nasbeh as Mizpah and Tell el-Ful as Gibeah. Others cannot be identified at all.

Excavations. In Israel the chances are that excavations will be carried out at a biblical site and will be limited to a tell of such size that the areas worked can be excavated to bedrock. Since in most cases the interest centers on the earlier periods, excavators will usually avoid a tell that is covered with a great depth of modern, Muslim, and Byzantine materials. In the early days of archaeology such material was often "disemboweled" and dumped aside. Today the excavator must first deal with the top and later levels before getting to the lower and earlier strata.

Once a site for excavation has been selected, the first step is to secure permission from the country's department of antiquities. The department must be satisfied that the excavators are professionally competent, that they have the necessary resources, and that they will publish their reports with reasonable promptness. The various antiquities laws specify that the ownership of land does not mean ownership of any antiquities that are in the land—they belong to the nation.

An area to be excavated is either purchased, as at Megiddo and Dothan, or more usually rented for the requisite periods, with the understanding that the land, if used for crops, will be restored to its former condition and the owners compensated for destroyed crops. In some cases, as at Beth-shan, the land is already government property. Renting the property is often complicated by the fact that small areas of land can be owned by many families. In the case of Tell el-Ful an area of less than two acres was owned by no fewer than 66 people. They first demanded 400 Egyptian pounds. Albright finally settled for seven Egyptian pounds. Rarely, an owner will donate the land outright. Cyrus Gordon described such an occurrence in Iraq: "We were very fortunate in the case of Tepe Gawra, for it was the property of an enlightened Moslem of Mosul who donated it to the expedition for the sake of science."

The cost of financing excavations varies greatly. At one extreme was the luxury of the Chicago expedition at Megiddo with a budget of 16 million dollars. At the other extreme was the fabled austerity of Petrie's camp. He and his assistants spent only $1.20 a week for provisions, and his crew of laborers cost $140 a week (at the end of the 19th century). Margaret Murray recounted that on Petrie's expeditions one ate the sardines from tins and then the tins themselves.

Inflation has affected the cost of archaeology as it has everything else. In the mid-19th century Henry Layard paid his workers two and a half pence a day. At the end of the 19th century the first American expedition in Mesopotamia at Nippur paid ordinary workmen 12 cents a day. In 1932 Max Mallowan at Arpachiyah was paying one shilling per day; in 1949 at Nimrud he paid three shillings per day. Before the end of the expedition at Nimrud in 1963 the rate had doubled. In 1968 workers in Jordan were receiving the equivalent of $1.50 per day. In the 1968 excavations at Jerusalem, Israeli workers were receiving 10 lira per day ($2.80).

An additional expense is the payment of *baksheesh*, a reward given to workers for special finds. Some excavators give baksheesh to workers as an incentive to keep their eyes open for objects and also to keep them from pocketing small artifacts for sale to dealers. Others are sharply opposed to what Mortimer Wheeler called "bribed honesty" and counsel instead constant supervision to prevent theft. But Kathleen Kenyon, who was opposed to baksheesh, reported that in spite of the careful supervision of her excavations at Jerusalem, some inscribed weights suspiciously similar to those found in her trenches appeared in a Jerusalem shop.

Kenyon recorded her expenses for her work at Jericho from 1952 to 1958: "Seven seasons cost $84,610, or an average of $12,087 for a season of about three months of work involving a staff of about two dozen [trained people]." Her excavations at Jerusalem ran up to about $30,000 per season, subscribed by 43 universities, museums, and societies, including the British Academy.

In the past some funds often came from wealthy patrons, such as John D. Rockefeller and Sir Charles Marston. Jacob Schiff donated $60,000 to the Harvard University project at Samaria. In the 19th century, individual subscribers in Britain supported the Palestine Exploration Fund and the Egypt Exploration Fund. In recent years the United States has begun to use the so-called "counterpart" funds for excavations. These are funds for surplus American goods paid for by foreign countries but kept in those countries for developmental or cultural projects.

Along with securing the necessary funds the director must assemble a staff of trained supervisors and a work crew of laborers. Some of the workers from particular villages in Egypt and Iraq have worked so long at various excavations that they are almost a skilled craft guild. The number of workmen should be limited to the number that can be supervised adequately. In the early history of archaeology large numbers were employed without much supervision: about 300 workers at Khorsabad in 1843–44; 600 workers at Kuyunjik (Nineveh) in 1874; and an average of 200–250 workers at Babylon from 1899 to 1917. One site in Palestine in the early 20th century witnessed the use of 1,300 workers with only one supervisor present.

Workmen are usually divided into pickmen who break up the soil, hoemen who save the sherds and then scoop up the earth in baskets, and basket carriers who take the earth away. At Jerusalem in the deep trenches Kenyon used a crew of 2 pickmen, 2 to 4 hoemen, and 40 to 50 basket carriers for a given area. In modern excavations trained supervisors are generally responsible for a plot about 16 feet square. In addition, specialists on the staff work as recorders, architects, photographers, surveyors, draftsmen, and pottery restorers.

The digging season varies from a short period of 2 weeks to a lengthy season of 6 months. The rainy season in the winter curtails activity. Most expeditions take place in the summer for the convenience of participating professors and students. Exceptions include places like Jericho or Susa that are unbearably hot in the summer. Kenyon dug at Jericho from January to April.

The average workday is strenuous, beginning early in the morning after a cup of coffee, with perhaps a short break for breakfast and continuing until lunch. At Tel Anafa the present writer worked from 6 A.M. until lunch, with a short break at 8:30 for breakfast. After lunch we washed pottery until 3 P.M. At the Israeli excavations in Jerusalem we began at 7 A.M. and continued until 3 P.M., with a short mid-morning break from 10 to 10:30 A.M. The work of the supervisors and directors contin-

Some tools used in archaeological digging: hoes, pick, trowel, patish, brush, and goofa.

ues long into the night after the workmen have retired. At Hazor the workday for the staff began at 5 A.M. and did not end until 10 P.M.

Tools of the Trade. Although the spade has become the symbol of archaeology, it is actually used very little in excavations. Picks are utilized to break up the soil, and large, oversized hoes scoop up the dirt into *gufas* (baskets made from old rubber tires). For finer work a *patish*, or small pick, is used, together with a trowel and a brush. Also essential are meter sticks, levels, strings, tags, and labels for measuring and recording.

Modern technology has produced an instrument called a magnetometer, which can be used to measure variations in the magnetism of the earth. Such variations, called anomalies, are indications of buried walls and other structures. Beginning in the late 1950s, effective use of the magnetometer together with a reverse periscope and camera enabled Carlo Lerici to find and investigate hundreds of buried Etruscan tombs in Italy. Lerici was able to find a tomb with the magnetometer; then, by drilling a hole and inserting a reverse periscope with affixed camera and light, he was able to see whether a tomb was painted and thus worth excavating. At a tomb where a graffito read "Giovanni, 1947," robbers had obviously been there ahead of the archaeologists.

In the exploration of the Bar Kochba caves north of Masada in 1960–61, Yigael Yadin used a mine detector with success. The magnetometer was used to a great extent in Israel in the 1964 survey of Hebron by Philip Hammond. The rocky nature of the hill country limits the usefulness of such a device in the Holy Land, but Hammond reported some success in locating caves.

Aerial photography is another promising technique. In the recent Israeli survey of the Golan Heights, aerial photography detected a large field of thousands of dolmens (monuments) and a large Stonehenge-like circle of basalt stones. A further development of aerial photography is the use of ultraviolet and infrared film. At Sybaris the U.S. Air Force, which took pictures of the site, found that the best pictures were made by using infrared film at altitudes under 5,000 feet.

Stratigraphical Excavations. With the exception of briefly occupied sites like Khorsabad in Assyria or Qumran in Palestine, most ancient cities have left their remains behind in the stratified mounds called tells. Since there was a limited number of places that could be easily defended and that were near to water, trade routes, and fertile land, the same sites were reoccupied even after being destroyed by invading armies. Further, mud brick, the most common building material in many areas, seldom lasted more than a generation. In addition, the ancient housewife solved her housecleaning chores by covering over litter with a new dirt floor. Such processes would raise perceptibly the level of a city. The debris would be kept in a compact shape by the city wall.

The height of accumulated debris could become considerable. In Mesopotamia the tells

Excavation of Hazor under the direction of Yigael Yadin.

range from 56 feet at Kish up to 140 feet at Tell Brak. In Palestine the depth of debris at Jericho is about 60 feet; at Beth-shan and Megiddo about 70 feet. Tell es-Sa 'idiyeh in Transjordan towers 138 feet above the surrounding plain. As the tells grew higher, however, the slopes became steeper and the living area on the crown became smaller. Tepe Gawra in Mesopotamia was finally abandoned in the 15th century BC after some 20 levels had contracted the top to an area large enough only for a watchtower.

Since only limited areas can be excavated, the director needs to select strategic spots to place trenches. An exploratory trench may be dug into the flank of the mound to give an overview of the strata to be encountered. The walls of the city must be located. The gate of the city was usually placed where the approach to the mound was gradual. The main road from the gate would lead to important structures, such as a palace. An elevation may indicate the position of a citadel or temple.

The levels characterized by major rebuilding are known as strata, whereas minor alterations are known as phases. The strata are numbered in Roman numerals from the latest, or topmost, down. Since successive strata are not deposited at a uniformly level rate over a flat surface, absolute heights above sea level are useful in plotting but are not chronologically meaningful. Added complications arise from intrusions. Very often buildings have their foundation trenches cutting into earlier levels. It is highly desirable that the areas excavated should, if possible, be tested down to bedrock or to virgin soil. When the water table is reached, however, the entire trench turns quickly into a quagmire. Sometimes it is possible to dig deeper with the aid of pumps.

The general practice today is to dig in areas about 16 feet square, separated from other squares by earth partitions called balks. The faces of these balks are kept as perpendicular as possible so that the various strata can be detected and tagged. In one small area of the square the supervisor will dig a probe trench so that excavators can anticipate the levels to be encountered.

Work must proceed carefully; when a special object is found, its exact location and level are recorded. Ordinary sherds are placed in carefully labeled buckets for washing and examination later.

It is necessary to sift the soil only when small objects such as coins are expected. Bronze coins appear as tiny spots of green in the soil. On one exceptional day in the Mazar excavations in the Jerusalem temple area we found almost 100 coins by sifting the dirt. In that excavation 19,000 coins were found in the

first three years (1968–70). At Masada, Yadin had close to 50,000 cubic yards of soil sifted so that the excavation could recover hundreds of coins, scores of inscriptions on pottery, and tiny pieces of jewelry.

The Kenyon-Wheeler Methods. The older (Fisher-Reisner) methods of analysis included the careful recording of objects and of building levels. Improved methods were developed by Mortimer Wheeler from his experiences in India and were introduced into Palestine by his disciple, Kathleen Kenyon, during her work in Samaria in 1931–35 and at Jericho in 1952–58. The newer methods require the careful cutting of balks and minute analysis of different types of soils that appear in the balks.

A given stratum should include not just the floor level but the fill associated with it both above and below. A further principle is that one digs down not by predetermined levels but by layers of the same soil, no matter how uneven they may be. In contrast, the French excavated Byblos in a series of rigidly horizontal 8-inch layers without regard for the irregular contours of the site. Another insight of the Wheeler school is the rule that one must not dig along the line of a wall but at right angles to it to determine the relationship of the wall to the deposits.

Although the insights of Kenyon and Wheeler have been adopted in subsequent excavations, their methods are best fitted for small, limited operations where sizable architecture is not present. Such careful analysis demands a large staff and is time-consuming.

Sherds and Bones. The most common objects to be found in all excavations are pieces of broken pottery in enormous quantity. Petrie estimated that during his work in Egypt he had looked at about 3 million pieces. Pritchard estimated that four seasons at Gibeon produced in excess of 200,000 sherds. Of 145,000

Examples of Assyrian pottery.

Sennacherib's siege of Lachish.

sherds washed in the first season at Dothan, Joseph Free recorded 6,000 pieces.

From time to time animal bones are encountered. In view of the Hebrew prohibition against eating pork, it is interesting that pig bones have been found in an underground sanctuary dated to the 18th–16th centuries BC at Tell el-Far'ah, north (Lv 11:7,8; cf. Is 65:4; 66:3,17). Pig bones that were pierced and hence may have been used by the Canaanites in divination or as amulets were found at Megiddo and Taanach.

The most extraordinary assemblage of human and animal bones was found on the northwest slope of Lachish, from the carnage of either the Assyrian attack of 701 BC or a later Babylonian attack. From 1,500 to 2,000 bodies had been dumped into an old tomb through a hole in the roof. Over the mass of human bones was thrown a layer of animal bones, mostly of pigs. Pagan soldiers who ate pork may have purposely scattered the pig bones to desecrate the Jewish remains.

Human skeletons can sometimes provide medical information. Three of the Lachish skulls had been trephined (that is, holes had been cut into their skulls, perhaps to cure headaches). A female skeleton from a Byzantine-Roman grave at Heshbon revealed that the woman had died from a chest tumor, the calcified remains of which were about the size of an ostrich egg. The height of a population at a given time may be guessed from skeletons. Jothams-Rothschild concluded from skeletons found in the tombs of the Herodian period that the average Jew of that day was quite short, about 5 feet 3 inches tall.

In 1968 Israeli archaeologists discovered the first indisputable physical evidence of a victim of crucifixion. While clearing ground for apartments in northeastern Jerusalem at Giv 'at ha-Mivtar, builders found a number of cave tombs containing ossuaries with redeposited bones. One of the ossuaries contained the bones of an adult male and a child. It was inscribed in Aramaic with the name Yehohanan. The man's *calcanei*, or heel bones, were still pierced by an iron nail; his calf bones had been broken. Nails had also pinioned his forearms. His crucifixion may have taken place during the census revolt led by Judas of Galilee in AD 6–7 or at some time before the outbreak of the Jewish revolt in AD 66. After the latter date there would have been no opportunity for the Jews to rebury the bones so carefully in an ossuary.

Works of Art. Artistic representations are an important source of information. They give us an understanding of many items that have otherwise perished. Pictures from Egypt and reliefs from Assyria are our primary sources of information about military weapons. Art works sometimes portray historic events, the most valuable example being the relief of Sennacherib's siege of Lachish in 701 BC, now in the British Museum. It is particularly noteworthy because we have no account of that important siege in Sennacherib's annals. The famous Black Obelisk of Shalmaneser III portrays King Jehu of Israel (or his servant) prostrating himself before the Assyrian king.

Most human and animal figurines, such as the common nude figurines of Astarte, were probably made for cultic purposes. From Beth-shan came figurines and scarabs of lions, dogs, gazelles, hippopotami, asses, pigs, elephants, crocodiles—all of which may have emanated from the cult of Nergal-Mekal-Set.

The inhabitants of Gibeon incised sketches of wild birds or chickens on their cooking pots. On three potsherds from Gibeon were incised six-pointed stars, the so-called "star of David." Before the six-pointed star was found on a masonry block from Megiddo, many scholars believed that the symbol dated from the Middle Ages.

Paintings of birds, fish, and animals in red and black on pottery from about 1500 BC have been attributed to a single Canaanite painter from Tell el-Ajjul, who has been called Palestine's first artist. A unique piece of painted pottery was found at Ramat Rahel. The fragment has a drawing in black and red of a bearded man with curled hair who was probably a king. The style is similar to that of 8th- or 7th-century BC Assyrian ware, but the drawing was made by a local artist.

Ivories have been found at Samaria, appropriately in view of the references to Ahab's "ivory house" (1 Kgs 22:39). They are the remnants of "beds of ivory," ostentatious showpieces of the wealthy (Am 6:4). At Nimrud, Mallowan found thousands of ivory pieces, including master carvings which had been preserved in the mud of very deep wells.

Large statues in the round are most rare from early Palestinian levels. Two complete statues and remains of two others dated to 800 BC from the Amman citadel are about the only freestanding large statues of that early period made by native craftsmen. In the Hellenistic-Roman period statues of pagan deities and of rulers became common in the largely gentile cities such as Sebaste and Caesarea.

Many small seals bear not only important inscriptions but also fine artistic representations. The seal of Shema found in 1904 at Megiddo, dated to the time of King Jeroboam II of Israel (793–753 BC), has a magnificent engraving of a roaring lion. The seal of Jaazaniah found at Tell en-Nasbeh and dated about 600 BC is interesting because of its representation of a fighting cock. Since cocks are not mentioned in the OT, it was formerly believed that they were not known in Palestine until Hellenistic times.

In a few places small plans of buildings or of cities have been found. The actual form of the Ishtar Gate at Babylon was determined from a depiction of the gate found on a gold plaque bearing an outline plan of the citadel. The underwater expedition at Caesarea found a small coin or medallion with a representation of the harbor. In the design the entrance to the port is flanked by round towers surmounted by statues; arches border the jetty on either side of the towers.

The problem of Jewish art in the Roman period is a complex one. In the 1st century BC it seems that in Jewish areas even Herod the Great was reluctant to offend the sensibilities

The Ishtar Gate of Babylon.

of the Jews concerning representations of the human form. Thus the mosaics at Masada have either geometric or plant motifs.

Coins. Metal objects vary greatly in their preservation. Gold objects are the best preserved. Silver is usually covered with black tarnish, bronze with a greenish patina. Iron rusts very badly, at times to a reddish powder. Of objects made of metal the most valuable for a variety of reasons are coins, which are usually made of silver, copper, or bronze.

The invention of coinage is traditionally attributed to King Gyges of Lydia in the 7th century BC. It was then introduced to the Greeks about 600 BC. In the middle of the 6th century Peisistratus, a tyrant of Athens, began the practice of stamping the head of Athena on one side of a coin and an owl on the other—emblems that became widespread with the imitation of Athenian coinage in the 5th century BC.

From Palestine two coins of the 6th century BC have been published, including a coin from Thasos found at Shechem. In 1960 an Athenian coin from the time of Peisistratus was found on the surface in a suburb of Jerusalem. Three imitations of Attic coins from the 5th century BC have come from Samaria, and a fourth example from Beth Zur.

From the 4th century BC we have an interesting group of *YHD* or "Yehud" coins. They were minted during Persian rule over Judah and indicate a measure of autonomy given to the local Jewish rulers. The best-known examples are minute silver coins bearing the figure of the Athenian owl and inscriptions in Hebrew script. One particular Yehud coin, now in the British Museum, portrays a male divinity seated on a winged wheel.

The coins mentioned in the OT and NT were mainly foreign coins. Truly Jewish coins, an indication of autonomy, are rare except for coins of the Hasmoneans, to some extent those of the Herodians, and those of the two great Jewish revolts.

The "penny" brought to Jesus (Mt 22:19 KJV) was a denarius, probably of Tiberius or possibly of Augustus. That Roman silver coin, which weighed about 1/8 of an ounce, is the coin most often mentioned in the NT. It was the standard wage for a day's work for a laborer and also for a Roman soldier (Mt 20:2). The drachma was a Greek silver coin about the same weight as that of the Roman denarius. The coin mentioned in Matthew 17:24 was probably a double drachma, a half-shekel silver coin of Tyre. A half-shekel was due from every Jewish man as an annual contribution for the support of the temple. The stater found in the fish's mouth (Mt 17:27) was worth four drachmas and was probably a Tyrian shekel. The widow's mite or lepton (Mk 12:42; cf. Lk 12:59) was a diminutive bronze coin about 1/20 of an ounce.

Dating of Objects. One of the chief values of coins is the aid they may provide in dating levels of an excavation. Of course, coins, especially gold and silver issues, may be kept and used for some time, a factor that must be considered. The "heirloom" concept also applies to seals and amulets. Excavators at Beth-shan were misled in dating their levels because they did not recognize this principle. Gordon found an ancient seal at Tepe Gawra which had been treasured and kept for 1,500 years.

Apart from the discovery of written texts and the association of destruction levels with historical events, the primary means of dating levels has been the comparative typology of pottery. When a certain type of pottery can be dated, as from the known occupation dates of Masada, similar examples of such a type can usually be assigned to the same date. At Masada was found a rare example of a jar dated precisely to 19 BC by the inscribed name of the Roman consul. Paleography, or the comparative typology of handwriting, may also be used to establish relative dates.

Most OT dates are secured by synchronisms with the chronologies of Egypt and of Mesopotamia, where quite accurate lists of kings and their reigns were kept. Some of those dates can be determined by the precise fixing of astronomical observations made in antiquity.

In biblical archaeology the following chronological periods are observed:

Neolithic Age	7000–4000 BC
Chalcolithic Age	4000–3000 BC
Early Bronze Age	3000–2000 BC
Middle Bronze Age	2000–1500 BC
Late Bronze Age	1500–1200 BC
Iron Age	1200–300 BC
Hellenistic Period	300–63 BC
Roman Period	63 BC–AD 323

In recent years radiocarbon dating, first developed by W. F. Libby, has been used to date organic material. It is based on the fact that living creatures take in the radioactive isotope carbon-14 as well as carbon-12 from the atmosphere in a known ratio. Carbon-14 breaks down into nitrogen-14 at a known rate of decay. The ratio of carbon-14 remaining (after decay) to the carbon-12 (which does not decay) can be used to determine approximately how long ago the organism died (and thus stopped taking in carbon-14).

Radiocarbon dating seems to correspond quite accurately with Egyptian dates back to 2000 BC, but beyond that it seems to give dates that are too recent. One factor interfering with the results may have been a change in the earth's magnetic field. When radiocarbon dates are reported, a plus-or-minus figure called the standard deviation indicates the margin of error.

New Scientific Techniques. New scientific tools and methods are being used in other aspects of archaeology besides surveying and dating. A University of California physicist, Luis Alvarez, set up a spark chamber in the Great Pyramid of Khufu at Giza to trace the paths of cosmic rays called muons. A computer was used to record the data. By this method Alvarez hoped that he might locate any undetected passageways in the pyramids. Unfortunately he found none.

A computer is being used by Ray W. Smith of the University of Pennsylvania Museum to reconstitute the thousands of pieces of a temple of Akhnaton that had been dismantled by Akhnaton's successors. More than 35,000 sandstone blocks have been collected. As each is photographed, its characteristics are recorded on an IBM card. As the project progresses, the cards are fed into a computer to enable the archaeologists to make an accurate reconstruction.

A remarkable method called photogrammetry has made it possible to reproduce Egyptian bas-reliefs. Two stereoscopic photographs are taken of a relief. Contour lines are then plotted from the photographs. The contour plotting is then placed in a pantograver, a special device which follows every detail of the stereoscopic plotting and reconstitutes the relief on a block of plaster. The reproductions are accurate to a 50th of an inch.

The Value of Archaeology. In the period since 1843 a great deal of information has been acquired about the history, religion, and culture of the ancient world. While there is much still to be learned, the discoveries have enabled us to formulate a background of events and people against which the various scriptural narratives can be realistically set. Archaeology does not attempt to prove the "truth" of the Bible, if only because spiritual matters have to be discerned spiritually. It does show, however, that those who recorded the scriptural accounts of life in antiquity were responsible persons, writing carefully about familiar situations. The rediscovery of actual sites mentioned in the narratives puts the material in proper historical perspective, while the recovery of artifacts from the everyday life of the people gives legitimacy to their existence. By understanding the archaeological background we begin to see more clearly the life situation in the ancient world, and this enables us to appreciate better the way in which God's plan of salvation was rooted in historical processes.

EDWIN M. YAMAUCHI

See ARCHAEOLOGY AND THE BIBLE; POTTERY; INSCRIPTIONS; TELL.

Bibliography. M. Burrows, *What Mean These Stones?* A. Parrot, *Discovering Buried Worlds;* J.A. Sanders, *Near Eastern Archaeology in the Twentieth Century;* J.N. Woodall, *An Introduction to Modern Archaeology;* L. Wooley, *Digging Up the Past;* G.E. Wright, *Biblical Archaeology;* E. Yamauchi, *The Stones and the Scriptures.*

Archaeology and the Bible.

Simply defined, archaeology is the science that recovers and studies the relics of human antiquity. Biblical archaeology is concerned with the remains scattered across the Near East. Some lie buried at different levels in mounds; others survive as ruins or weathered monuments to past grandeur. Many of the artifacts bear inscriptions of sorts in a variety of ancient languages, some of which still need much study to be understood properly. Other artifacts comprise the material remains of everyday life: broken pottery bowls, charred timbers, trinkets, toys, ornaments, occasional fragments of cloth, rusted weapons, perhaps only the imprint of a woven mat. All must be interpreted carefully in the light of what is known about the period of history from which the objects have been recovered.

Modern archaeology long ago moved from the "treasure hunt" concept to become an exacting science. Potential sites are surveyed carefully, generally photographed from the air, and tested for metals and other underground anomalies by the use of complex electronic equipment. Recovered artifacts are dated according to the level where they occurred in the site and by other methods, including radiocarbon dating. The purpose is to present a chronologically accurate picture of the artifacts and also of the site itself.

The archaeologist and the Near Eastern scholar look at this testimony to ancient life in the realization that they are dealing with factual, objective data. Although there is obviously room for some speculation or difference of opinion, the objects being handled are silent but nevertheless real witnesses to people and events of the past. The relics, therefore, need to be understood in their own right as evidence, and must not be manipulated to suit the fancies of some speculative interpretation of history, culture, or religion. Near Eastern archaeology is able to help us understand Scripture by providing objective background data. If, for example, an artifact containing pictographic or other forms of writing can be dated to around 3000 BC, that alone tells us that written communications in the locality date back to at least that period. The antiquity of writing is now known to be such that all the early authors of OT material could easily have composed and written down all the narratives credited to them. Thus it is no longer necessary to suppose that Moses could not have written the Pentateuch (first five books of the Bible) on the ground that writing had not been invented in his day. In fact, archaeological discoveries have shown that Moses could, and probably did, write in Egyptian hieroglyphics, Babylonian cuneiform, and several Canaanite dialects (of which biblical Hebrew is one). Any theory of Pentateuchal composition that ignores such factual information is obviously wrong in a fundamentally important area.

Archaeology and Daily Life. The kind of housing in which the ancients lived has been revealed from excavations at many Near Eastern sites. Neolithic (Late Stone Age) dwellings were often simple "wattle-huts" of interwoven sticks, though some showed evidence of artistic interior decoration. The elegant middle-class home at Ur in the time of Abram was attractive even by modern standards. The magnificence of ancient palaces at such sites as Knossos, Persepolis, Mari, and Qantir is abundantly evident even from the ruins. Weaving is now known to be one of the oldest human crafts; the two types of knots used today in making oriental rugs originated in Mesopotamia in the remote past. Of similar antiquity was the manufacture of pottery, glazed and unglazed, some plain and some decorated.

Obscure social customs in Scripture have been illustrated by archaeological discoveries. Abram's procreation of a child by Hagar, his wife's servant, was in conformity with local customs at Nuzi and was not regarded as immoral. The adoption of Eliezer by Abram (Gn 15:2–4) is clarified by texts from Nuzi that permitted childless couples to adopt sons who, in return for certain duties to the parents, would inherit the family estate. Such children had the inheritance rights of the firstborn, but their rights could be modified if the adopting parents subsequently had their own children. Texts from Nuzi, Ugarit, and Alalakh show that heads of families could disregard the natural order and choose any one of the sons to inherit firstborn rights (cf. Gn 48:13–20,22; 49:3,4). Nuzi tablets indicate that such rights could be traded between various members of the family, which accounts for the transaction between Esau and Jacob (Gn 25:31–34).

Work of all kinds in the biblical period has been illustrated from many sources. The Beni Hasan tableau (1900 BC) shows traveling Semites bringing goods to Egypt. On one of the animals is a set of portable bellows, suggesting that the travelers may have been metalworkers. Other trades and occupations illustrated from monuments and paintings include hunting, fishing, brick making, various types of agricultural work, pottery making, and other domestic crafts. Such sources also provide valuable information about the way the ancients dressed. Men pictured on the Beni Hasan tableau were bearded and wore short skirts and sandals. Women had long, multicolored dresses fastened at the shoulder with a clasp. They wore shoes and kept their flowing hair in place by means of bands. Another Egyptian painting, dated 500 years later and showing Semites bringing gifts to the pharaoh, indicates that clothing styles had barely changed at all. These illustrations come from lands other than Palestine; the Israelites were forbidden to make representations of human beings or God.

The most common traces of everyday life are potsherds, broken pottery pieces which were discarded in great quantities in settled areas and which can still be found today. Such fragments were often used as materials on which short messages were written, as illustrated by an important group of letters dating from the time of the prophet Jeremiah. The "Lachish letters" were actually military dispatches written in 587 BC from an outpost north of Lachish to one of the officers defending Lachish itself. Centuries later in NT times potsherds were still popular as writing materials because they were more durable than Egyptian papyrus and more convenient than

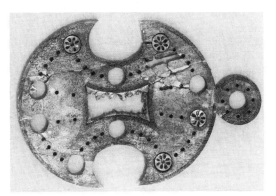

An ivory game board discovered at Megiddo.

waxed writing boards. Rectangular wooden palettes with a slot for the rush pens and rounded hollows for the little tablets of red and black ink have been found in Egypt. Remains of some of the ink actually used in writing the Dead Sea Scrolls have been recovered from the settlement at Qumran.

In antiquity various games were played by children and adults alike. From a tomb at Beni Hasan (c. 2000 BC) came a painting of pigtailed Egyptian girls keeping several balls up in the air at once. A relief in a temple at Thebes showed Rameses III playing draughts (checkers) with a concubine. Egyptian children of a later period played a game using pebbles that was perhaps the ancestor of backgammon. From Megiddo came an ivory gaming board with holes, presumably for pegs (c. 1200 BC). Children's toys recovered from Near Eastern sites include whistles, leather-covered balls, model chariots, and animals on wheels, showing that tastes have changed very little over the ages. Adult sports such as wrestling, archery, and running were depicted in Egyptian tomb paintings.

The embalming of Jacob and Joseph (Gn 50:2,3,26) represented a social custom of long standing in Egypt, and is thoroughly consistent with the background of the narrative. Jacob was buried in the Cave of Machpelah with Sarah, Abraham, and others; although the site is well known, it cannot be excavated because it is venerated by the Arabs as the sacred resting place of their ancestor Abraham.

An inscription associated with an ancient Hebrew burial site was found in the Russian Museum on the Mt of Olives in 1931. At some point it had been removed from the grave site. It reads, "Hither were brought the bones of Uzziah king of Judah—do not open." The inscription came from Christ's time, suggesting that the original tomb of the great ruler had been found during excavations in Jerusalem and that the remains had been transferred to another site. Archaeologists have shown that the kind of stone door covering the entrance to Christ's tomb was in fashion chiefly from about 100 BC to about AD 100, which is consistent with the Gospel record.

Religion. Archaeological excavations have done much to indicate the nature of biblical religion and worship. Long before Abram left Ur at the command of the one true God, pagan Mesopotamian peoples worshiped individual gods and recognized them as celestial deities or "sky gods." There is thus nothing inherently impossible or improbable about the relationship of the Hebrew patriarchs to the God whom they served and venerated. The worship of heathen deities in portable shrines has been illustrated from a relief of Rameses II, which showed the divine tent in the middle of the Egyptian encampment. In addition, 7th-century BC Phoenician writings referred to a portable shrine pulled by oxen. The Israelite wilderness tabernacle thus fits properly into that kind of background and is not of comparatively late origin, as was once supposed.

The tradition of singers participating in preexilic worship has been verified by archaeological discoveries indicating that for centuries the Palestinians had been noted for their musical abilities. Tablets from Ras Shamra (Ugarit) are full of religious poetry, some of which contains phrases similar to expressions in the Hebrew psalms. Solomon's temple was built by Phoenician (Canaanite) workmen according to a ground plan (cf. 1 Kgs 6) similar to that of the 8th-century BC chapel found at Tell Tainat in Syria. The Wailing Wall in Jerusalem is thought to contain stones going back to Nehemiah's time, but no traces of Solomon's foundations have yet been uncovered in the city. Pieces of masonry from Herod's temple, demolished in AD 70, have come to light and furnish interesting factual information about the appearance of contemporary pillars and supporting structures. Though there were supposedly many synagogues in Palestine in Christ's time, few remains of any significance have survived.

Warfare. Understanding of ancient warfare, a prominent biblical theme, has been assisted greatly by the work of archaeologists. Ancient Near Eastern peoples regarded war as conflict between the gods of the opposing nations. Military service was therefore regarded as a sacred calling, and soldiers were members of an honored profession. In his capacity as Lord of hosts, God was the commander-in-chief of the Hebrew army; he could order a city to be given up to the "ban," that is, to complete destruction (cf. Jos 6:17,24). War was waged according to well-understood rules. An enemy threatening the safety of a city would normally send its inhabitants a demand for surrender. If it was accepted, all lives were spared though property would be plundered. If the demand was rejected, the besieged city dwellers knew that if their defenses were breached, they might all be killed. Frontal assaults, spies, ambushes, and armed patrols were all used in warfare. Sometimes battles were decided by the outcome of combat between champions (1 Sam 17:38–54).

Ancient armor was pictured widely on reliefs and monuments, supplementing the artifacts that have been recovered. A magnificent golden helmet from Ur is an outstanding example of Sumerian military equipment, contrasting with the much smaller Hittite helmets depicted on a tomb wall at Karnak. Metal helmets (cf. 1 Sm 17:38) were worn initially only by leaders in the Israelite armies, but by Seleucid times all Hebrew soldiers were issued bronze helmets (1 Mc 6:35). Roman legionnaires commonly wore either leather or bronze helmets. The Hebrews used two kinds of shields: a large one protected the whole body and was designed for use by infantry; the other, smaller one was carried by archers (cf. 2 Chr 14:8). Such shields were generally of wood-and-leather construction, though occasionally made of bronze. Coats of scale armor (cf. Jer 46:4; 51:3) were used in the Near East from at least the 15th century BC, as indicated by the recovery of such scales from Boghazköy, Alalakh, and Ugarit. Swords and spears, a normal part of Hebrew weaponry, came in a variety of shapes and sizes, as illustrated on monuments and bas-reliefs. Furnaces used for manufacturing swords were found at Gerar; Bronze Age daggers have been recovered from Lachish and Megiddo. The compound Asiatic bow, made of wood, horn, and tendons attached to iron limbs, was the successor of the Semitic weapon depicted on the Beni Hasan tableau. Discovery of names inscribed on arrowheads dating between 1300 and 900 BC seems to indicate the existence of companies of archers (cf. Is 21:17). Very little is said in the NT about contemporary military equipment.

Literature. Many types of biblical literature have been paralleled in counterparts discovered in the Near East. Excavators at Ras Shamra found poetic and prose tablets that contain grammatical and literary forms occurring in the Hebrew psalms. It is now incorrect to suppose that detailed law codes such as those in the Pentateuch were not compiled until after the time of Moses, because fragmentary Sumerian codes dating from about the 19th century BC exhibit the same legislative tendencies. The code of the Babylonian ruler

Detail from the stele containing the Law Code of Hammurabi.

Hammurabi (18th century BC), based on earlier Sumerian legislation, expanded the principles of justice as the king saw them into nearly 300 sections. Hammurabi's code was an attempt to stabilize contemporary society on the basis of law and order. Its style is interesting; it commenced with a poetic prologue, followed by the prose legal section and concluded with a prose epilogue. This three-part literary pattern also appears in the Book of Job (prose-poetry-prose) and in Daniel (Hebrew-Aramaic-Hebrew), as well as in more modern writings.

The covenant structure of Exodus 20:1–17 and its fuller form in Deuteronomy have been examined in light of the literary structure of 2nd-millennium BC Hittite vassal treaties from Boghazköy. The treaties were drawn up according to a standard pattern, the elements of which occur wholly or in part in the various OT covenantal passages (Ex 20:1–17; Lv 18:1–30; Dt 1:1–31:30; Jer 31:31–37).

What appear to be 11 Mesopotamian tablet forms in Genesis can be isolated by the recurrence of the phrase "these are the generations of" in the KJV, RV, and some modern versions. The phrase and its accompanying material correspond to the colophon (notation about a publication, often found on the very last page of

modern books) of undamaged Mesopotamian tablets. Genealogical material such as occurs in Genesis was also found on clay tablets from Nuzi. The terse style of the earlier Genesis historical accounts is reminiscent of Sumerian history writing.

Hebrew wisdom literature such as Proverbs has been paralleled from Egypt by the "Instruction of Amenemope," where Proverbs 22:17–24:22 in particular is close in content to the Egyptian material. Scholars have yet to decide if one depended on the other, or if both went back to an even earlier source that has not survived.

The epistolary (letter) form was a common feature of the ancient world (2 Sm 11; 1 Kgs 21; 2 Kgs 5:10,20; Ezr 4:6,7; Neh 2:7). Many collections of Egyptian papyri, such as the Zenon documents, consisted of letters. Among the Greeks the letter form dated back to Plato. His Seventh Letter (354? BC) is interesting because it attempted to rebut contemporary misunderstandings of his teaching and personal behavior. Certain of the apostle Paul's letters (Corinthians, Galatians, Philippians, Thessalonians) also stand in that general tradition. Paul's Letter to Philemon corresponds closely to papyrus letters from Egypt of a purely personal nature.

Language. Recovery of many ancient Near Eastern languages has done much to clarify our understanding of the OT. Expressions now known to be Sumerian and Akkadian occur not only in Genesis but elsewhere in the Scriptures. Thus in Genesis 1:1 the phrase "the heavens and the earth" is a Sumerian expression (*an-ki*) meaning "universe"; the pair of antonyms (words opposite in meaning) expresses totality. Revelation 22:13 uses this literary device to express the same concept in three different ways.

Ugaritic and Eblaic, both west Semitic dialects, are closely related to Hebrew and contain striking literary similarities. Reference to archaic Ugaritic expressions has made it possible to translate properly some obscure Hebrew poetic language that is now seen to have preserved genuine ancient Canaanite phraseology.

Aramaic, another northwest Semitic language, was spoken in the 3rd millennium BC, and is represented in the OT principally by chapters in Ezra and Daniel. These were written in Imperial Aramaic, as are the Elephantine papyri of the 5th and 4th centuries BC. It is now known, on the basis of the Aramaic used, to be linguistically incorrect to assign a late date to either Ezra or Daniel.

The NT was written in *koine*, or "common," Greek, the language of the Near East and the Roman empire. Some scholars have suggested that at least some parts of Matthew and Revelation may originally have been written in Aramaic. NT common Greek differs from other Greek dialects in containing underlying Semitic expressions, which are frequently unrecognized and therefore mistranslated by the unwary.

Conclusion. From the foregoing it is evident that archaeological discoveries have done much to enlarge our knowledge of the history, religion, and culture of the ancient world. Even with the limited data at our disposal it is possible to see the men and women of Scripture as real persons, living mostly in times of stress and uncertainty but often enjoying a high degree of culture unmatched until modern times. We thus see such persons as they should be seen—not as mythical or legendary figures, but as true children of their age, grappling with life's problems and catching periodically a vision of God as all-powerful and all-holy, guiding the destinies of individuals and nations, and bringing his purposes to pass in history. Archaeology has shown that the Hebrews must never be studied separately from other ancient Near Eastern peoples, but instead must be seen as one element of a vast cultural complex that included such diverse peoples as the Sumerians and the Aegeans.

Such study must be pursued in a consistently objective fashion, arguing from relevant evidence to a proper understanding of biblical events and life. It is sometimes difficult to reconcile certain accepted interpretations of archaeological data and the evidence of Scripture. Such conflicts are few in number, however, and tend to diminish noticeably as new information is forthcoming. In principle the archaeologist has no particular interest in "proving the truth" of the Scriptures, and it is obviously impossible for a spade or a trowel to prove or disprove the spiritual revelations and assertions of Scripture. But it is fair to say that archaeology validates Hebrew history and explains many formerly obscure terms and traditions in both the OT and NT. It thus provides an authentic background for the prophecies culminating in Jesus Christ.

R.K. HARRISON

See ARCHAEOLOGY; INSCRIPTIONS; ARMS AND WARFARE; BIBLICAL LANGUAGES; LETTER WRITING, ANCIENT.

Bibliography. Y. Aharoni, *The Archaeology of the Land of Israel* and *The Land of the Bible*; W.F. Albright, *The Archaeology of Palestine* and *Archaeology and the Religion of Israel*; E.M. Blaiklock and R.K. Harrison, *The New International Dictionary of Biblical Archaeology*; J. Finegan, *The Archaeology of the NT* and *Light from the Ancient Past*; K.M. Kenyon, *Archaeology in the Holy Land*; J.A. Thompson, *The Bible and Archaeology*; G.E. Wright, *Biblical Archaeology*; E. Yamauchi, *The Archaeology of NT Cities in Western Asia Minor*.

Archangel. Chief angel; a title given to the angel Michael (Jude 9).

See ANGEL.

Archelaus. Son of Herod the Great who followed his father in governing Idumea, Samaria, and Judea (Mt 2:22).

See HEROD, HERODIAN FAMILY.

Archer, Archery. See ARMS AND WARFARE; TRADES AND OCCUPATIONS.

Archevites. KJV translation for the inhabitants of Erech (Uruk) in southern Babylonia who were transported to Samaria by Asnappar, the Assyrian King Ashurbanipal (Ezr 4:9,10). The Archevites were among the local residents who wrote to Artaxerxes of Persia, opposing the rebuilding of Jerusalem by the Jews who had returned from exile (Ezr 4:7–16).

Archippus. Contemporary of Paul whom the apostle encouraged to fulfill his ministry (Col 4:17) and referred to as a "fellow soldier" (Phlm 2).

Archite, Archi. Area between Bethel and the town Beth-horon on the Ephraim–Benjamin border (Jos 16:2, KJV Archi). Hushai, King David's friend and personal adviser, was from the Archite clan (2 Sm 15:32; 16:16; 17:5,14; 1 Chr 27:33).

Architecture. Science, art, or profession of designing and constructing buildings, bridges, etc. Architecture is the practice of combining construction and art in order to produce "beauty with purpose." The architect's synthesis of creative imagination and technical skill produces structures of interest, unity, power, and convenience. When we look at a building, monument, or tomb, we are examining its art as well as its structure.

In viewing the temples of Egypt or the columns of Corinth, we view part of the culture of past civilizations. Just as art is a window through which one can see the heritage of a people, so architecture as a form of art preserves that heritage. Thus, architecture is one important way to discover the history of past civilizations.

Special types of architecture are mentioned in Scripture, including houses, structures in particular cities, and, of course, the temples. All were influenced by the empires that dominated Israel at the time. It is therefore important to examine the architecture of empires associated with Bible history to understand the architecture of Palestine.

Sumerian Beginnings. Architecture was first developed by the Sumerians, a people of non-Semitic origin. They may have settled on the island of Bahrein in the Persian Gulf a thousand years before moving northward to the mainland. There they began to drain the marshes where the Tigris and Euphrates rivers joined together to flow into the sea. Being a highly superstitious people, the Sumerians attached great importance to the gods they believed to be at work among humankind. Consequently, religious shrines were an early and prominent part of all building activities within the settled communities of Sumer.

From the beginning of their culture the Sumerians regarded architecture as an important artistic endeavor. It found its fullest expression in the building of temples. Temple foundations were constructed of imported stone, the upper levels of mud brick. One of the earliest of such structures was excavated at Eridu. Though simpler in character than many later shrines, it set a pattern for all subsequent temples by including an offering table made of mud brick, behind which was an alcove or niche where some representation of a deity could be placed. The entire structure measured only about 12 by 15 feet. As the population of Eridu increased, the shrine was enlarged by adding extra rooms around the outside. An altar was placed along one wall, opposite the offering table, and the dull uniformity of the interior walls was relieved by adding ornamental buttresses and niches. The Eridu temple was built on a platform. A later temple at Erech (*c.* 3000 BC) was built on a hillock instead. It was of similar dimensions, but had an exterior coat of whitewash.

A more developed architectural concept can be seen in a shrine unearthed at Uqair. The platform on which it stood was only about one-third the height of the hillock at Erech, but the shrine was constructed in two stages. It is considered the prototype of the Sumerian ziggurat, or staged tower, which became Mesopotamia's most distinctive contribution to architecture, both secular and sacred. The ziggurat has often been likened to a medieval European cathedral, the highest point of which might appear to be reaching upward to God as an expression of human religious aspirations. That, however, was not the concept the Sumerians held in building their shrines. For them the ziggurat, standing on its mound or platform, represented a concentration of natural, life-giving forces. The god had already come down to his house, and it was the worshiper's duty to commune with him there.

The inside of temples soon began to be decorated. The shrine of Eanna in Erech was ornamented with thousands of small clay cones stained in several colors and placed side by side to form a variety of geometrical patterns. The Uqair shrine was decorated by a band of colored paint or wash, above which were painted patterns of a geometrical nature. The area between that band of color and the ceiling was covered with pictures of people and animals.

Distinctive as they were, the early ziggurats could never have been constructed without the important discovery by the Sumerian priest-architects of a way to absorb stresses. They invented the recessed niche structure in which walls jutted out at right angles to the basement walls toward the center of the area. That kind of construction, forming little rooms or alcoves in the bottom stories, ensured that the projecting walls could absorb the enormous stresses resulting from the weight of subsequent stories of mud brick. The recessed niches became more elaborate in later ziggurats, but the basic function of stress absorption remained unchanged. The principle was eventually copied by the Egyptians, who were thus enabled to construct the pyramids of the Old Kingdom period.

By 2000 BC a Mesopotamian temple area commonly housed the ziggurat, several storehouses, shrines, workshops, and living quarters for priests. The ziggurat usually consisted of three stages: the inner walls of sun-dried mud brick, the outer walls of baked brick set in bitumen. The upper levels were reached by flights of stairs or ramps, and sometimes a small shrine to a local deity topped off the uppermost stage.

In addition to devising decorated walls and columns, Sumerian architects discovered how to employ arches, domes, and vaults to give the impression of grandeur and space. The temple erected by Ur-Nammu at Ur was a particularly innovative building. It had very few straight lines. Rather, slightly curved lines furnished an illusion of lightness and grace to an otherwise stolid building. The same principle

The Ziggurat at Ur.

was copied many centuries later in the famous Parthenon in Athens.

Sumerian domestic architecture was quite mixed in style. Most city houses were two-story dwellings built on three sides of a square, with the opening facing away from the narrow streets. Homes of the wealthy might contain 20 rooms; some included servants' quarters. Indoor bathroom facilities were connected by means of drainpipes to an underground cesspool. Many houses had a family burial vault in the basement. There seems little doubt that the Akkadians, Hittites, Egyptians, and Greeks all benefited in various ways from the architectural innovations of Sumer.

Egyptian Architecture. The Egyptians achieved the most lasting architectural forms ever attempted by any civilization, and much of their architecture has been preserved. Such forms included temples, tombs, and pyramids. Huge stones to build those structures had to be brought from distant quarries. The Egyptians made use of slave labor and built their structures in honor of their rulers.

The outstanding examples of Egyptian architecture are the pyramids, virtually all of which were constructed in the Old Kingdom period (c. 2700–2200 BC). The Sumerian principle of the recessed niche was employed to accommodate the enormous stresses of stone masonry. Without that technique it would have been impossible to construct such a huge edifice as the Great Pyramid, the estimated weight of which is almost six million tons. The Great Pyramid is one of the most perfectly oriented buildings on earth, being just a few seconds of one degree short of true north-south orientation. Many of the huge blocks of stone were cut and fitted together so accurately that it is impossible to insert the edge of a sheet of paper between them. The pyramids were meant to serve as tombs for the remains of the persons who ordered them constructed, but the structures themselves have become monuments to human creativity.

The best known pyramids are located southwest of Cairo. Although they were built thousands of years ago, they remain almost as they were originally. Many temples were also constructed, such as the famous Sphinx at Giza and the Hypostyle Hall at Karnak, site of ancient Thebes. "Hypostyle" is from a Greek word meaning "resting on pillars"; the temple at Karnak consisted of many columns, each over 10 feet in diameter and 76 feet in height. Tombs in which kings and queens were buried are located at Saqqara and the Valley of the Kings in Luxor. Probably the most famous tomb is that of King Tutankhamen, discovered in 1922. The tomb's contents, which show how Egyptians lived at that time, can be seen in the Cairo Museum.

The major architectural style of the Egyptians was "post and lintel," with horizontal crosspieces resting on columns. As a result, buildings of any size became a forest of columns. Wall surfaces were covered with carvings, paintings, and hieroglyphics. Temples were planned on a long axis with almost perfect symmetry. The structures seem designed for imperial pageants and other ceremonies staged to impress the people with the power and authority of their rulers.

Much can be learned about Egyptian religion from a careful examination of their architecture. From early childhood an Egyptian was prepared carefully and deliberately for the time of death and subsequent judgment. That religious emphasis is seen in many of the paintings in Egyptian temples and tombs, where, for example, the deeds of the dead person's heart are weighed before Osiris on balances against the "feather of truth." If the heart was deficient in proper motivation and good works, the deceased could expect to be thrown to the crocodiles. The mortuary temples of the pharaohs depicted the ruler's activities on the inner walls of the building, which usually comprised a hall decorated with numerous pillars and surrounded by several anterooms. The mortuary temple of Queen Hatshepsut at Thebes was notable for the first occurrence in the Near East of a fluted Doric-like column, later copied and adapted by Greek architects.

Assyrian and Hittite Architecture. The Assyrians, who lived northeast of Israel, also built large buildings. These were different from Egyptian buildings because of differences in geography, building materials, and forms of religion. The Assyrians built large palaces and used sculpture such as winged, man-headed bulls. They also used Sumerian structural forms, such as the masonry arch and dome. Their structures lacked the columns and symmetry of Egyptian structures.

The Great Temple of Egypt.

The Assyrians followed the Sumerian pattern of temple construction but enlarged the ziggurats and added more stories. The great ziggurat at Borsippa was an outstanding example of seven-story temple construction. The foundation was about 272 feet square, and the building stood about 160 feet high. Each story was set back from the level beneath it in a terraced effect and painted with a different color of wash. Each story was intended to represent one of the planets. In accordance with later Sumerian practice the uppermost level had a small shrine built on its roof, where the god Nebo was thought to have taken up his residence. Many believe that the tower of Babel, which God destroyed, was a ziggurat tower (Gn 11).

Assyrian royal palaces of the 8th and 7th centuries BC were large and elegant, decorated with enormous bas-reliefs depicting the king busily occupied with a variety of activities. Assyrian art was at its height in that period, and meticulous attention to detail brought a virile character to Assyrian architecture. Large stone sculptures of protective animals were stationed at entrances to public buildings. Similar statues were a feature of Hittite architecture in Anatolia, the eastern part of Asia Minor.

Hittite buildings excavated at Boghazköy and elsewhere easily matched those of the Assyrians in extent and grandeur. Towering columns, long halls, and expansive rooms were typical of Hittite palace construction in the Bronze Age. Buildings of such size were obviously located in large cities. Boghazköy, the ancient capital, had been fortified by huge stone walls on which projecting observation and defensive towers were placed at intervals. The city gates were of interesting design. They consisted basically of two square towers set side by side and containing interior compartments which amounted to as many as six rooms. Both the outer and inner portals were made to look like elliptical doorways by having corbels jut out in inverted steps over two high monolith doorjambs. Irregular stone coursing was a construction feature of the gates. Although the huge stones varied greatly in size, they were fitted together with a precision reminiscent of the Egyptian pyramid builders. Egyptian architectural influence was likewise reflected in the sculptured reliefs from Karatepe, which portray themes also found on Assyrian reliefs.

Hittite temple design followed that which was common in Babylonia, with several buildings grouped around an open court. One difference was that the main sanctuary was approached through a series of entrances or porches extending beyond the length of adjacent buildings. The design enabled small windows to be placed at the top of the projection in order to give additional light in the sanctuary. Windows in Hittite buildings were often quite large, thereby balancing other architectural features of the construction. Most Hittite temples had colonnades, with windows in the external façades of the building often located in the panels which came between the vertical pilasters.

Greek Architecture. Architecture rose to great achievements in the Greek world. Many factors combined to produce architectural beauty that has lasted for centuries. Those factors included the climate, setting, government, and people. Perhaps the most important factor was the people, who seemed free to imagine and develop designs and structures that have continued to excite our imaginations to this day.

The chief characteristic of Grecian architecture was beauty, well illustrated by the Parthenon. That building, located in Athens, is the ideal combination of structure and setting. Following Sumerian traditions, the lines are slightly curved to make them appear straight to the eye. The corner columns tilt in slightly to keep them from appearing to tilt outward. The columns are placed so that they appear symmetrical, even though there is more space between the central ones than between those on the ends. Beauty was the goal, and the Greeks strove to attain it.

This worthy motive found its highest expression in the 5th century BC. In the time of Pericles (461–429 BC) the Parthenon and Propylea on the Acropolis were remodeled from earlier originals, and the Erechtheum was also built there. Subsequent temples in Athens included that of Hephaestus, which was a less graceful version of the Parthenon, and the shrine of Ares. Phidias, the sculptor who designed the Parthenon, was also responsible with his students for much of the 5th-century BC statuary. Although the Sumerians had been the first to execute rather stereotyped free-standing stone statues, they had done so largely with theological considerations in mind. For the Sumerian sculptors the statue had represented an individual standing before a god, ready to be judged. For the Greeks, however, the objective of good statuary was the most realistic and accurate reproduction of human anatomy possible, and like the Assyrians their sculptors studied anatomy. Eventually the Greeks became the world's most proficient sculptors.

Many Greek buildings featured appropriate combinations of structure and setting. For example, theaters were built on hills so that the structure could have tiers of seats and still have a beautiful background. Marble was used extensively. Buildings were placed so that shadows added to their beauty. All that structural beauty was seen by the apostle Paul when he visited the city of Athens, but "his spirit was provoked within him as he saw that the city was full of idols" (Acts 17:16). Many of the most beautiful buildings, such as the Parthenon, were built in honor of pagan Greek gods. In response, Paul preached his famous sermon on the Areopagus (Mars Hill), a hill that overlooked the temples of Athens.

Roman Architecture. The Romans, who took over the Grecian empire, were also great builders and therefore left their mark on the architecture of the world. The Roman emperor Augustus boasted that he found Rome a city of brick and left it a city of marble.

Several factors influenced Roman architectural styles. First was the fact that the Romans took over earlier empires and, in a sense, earlier forms of architecture. Some Egyptian influence was seen, but the Greek eye for beauty and use of marble was more important. Another factor was the Roman discovery of cement and concrete. Their cement was made from volcanic earth which, when mixed with lime, formed a mortar of great cohesion. Cement enabled the Romans to build masonry arches without supporting columns. The effect was a sense of pomp and majesty. The use of cement also allowed the Romans to build structures of more than one story, such as the Colosseum.

Another feature of Roman architecture was the use of central squares or public forums. Around the forum in the center of the city were built public buildings, temples, shops, and porticoes. The central square contained arches and monuments commemorating victorious emperors. The Roman concept of municipal planning was copied throughout the Roman empire, including Palestine.

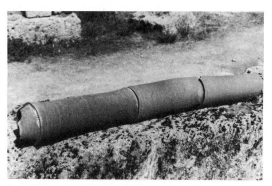

Some joints of a Roman waterpipe.

The shortage of water in a number of countries over which the Romans ruled compelled them to devise means of transporting it overland. Lead pipes could be used for only short distances, so the aqueduct was developed for longer distances. The Romans, however, were not the inventors of the aqueduct for moving water from one place to another. According to Assyrian records, Sennacherib (705–681 BC) constructed an irrigation canal across another waterway on a 90-foot bridge resting on a series of stone arches. Underground aqueducts, hewn through solid rock, were used in Palestine at least as far back as 2000 BC, but could not be considered architectural features. Like the Assyrians, Roman architects were faced with the problem of maintaining a sufficient degree of slope to enable the water to flow by gravity. Cemented channels supported by stone arches provided much of the solution to the problem, as they had for the Assyrians, though the structures were not always perfectly watertight. The architectural design of aqueduct systems remained the same throughout the Imperial period. Foundation piers were spanned by round arches. The stone channel was built on top of the archway lined with cement, and was frequently covered by a curved roof. Wherever the nature of the terrain permitted, the water was carried along in tunnels and sluices, supplementing the more spectacular elevated stone channels.

Architecture of Palestine. The architecture of Palestine resembled that of the empires already discussed, since Israel either borrowed their forms or was occupied by their forces. Today much that remains of early architecture comes from the Greek and Roman periods. Of special interest, however, is the architecture of OT and NT times: cities, fortifications, gates, houses, and the temple.

When the Israelites entered Canaan, the Promised Land, under Joshua, they soon discovered that their technology was inferior in various ways to that of the native Canaanites.

The Colosseum, construction of which was begun by Vespasian and was finished by his sons Titus and Domitian. It was officially opened in AD 80. It covered an area of about 7¼ acres, was 164 feet high, and held up to 70,000 spectators.

For example, the Canaanites knew how to construct buildings from stone. For a generation the Israelites had been tent-dwellers, living only semisedentary lives at best, without need of permanent structures of any kind, certainly not stone buildings. When the time came for them to settle down, they were handicapped by their lack of construction skills. Archaeological excavation at such sites as Shiloh, Bethel, and Debir have uncovered Israelite attempts to rebuild on earlier Canaanite foundations. Their standard of workmanship was noticeably inferior to that of the Canaanite builders, as exhibited especially in Canaanite royal cities. As Israelite towns grew up in haphazard fashion, lack of planning made for much inconvenience and ultimate overcrowding. Until the 5th century BC the buildings tended to be small and narrow, partly because the Palestinian architects had not devised any means of roofing a dwelling other than by laying beams across its width and placing a flat covering on top. The first vaulted arch in Palestine was built in the Persian period, but it was so innovative that the conservative Judeans refused to adopt it as an architectural style. Only in the Roman period did the arch and vault gain acceptance, due largely to the influence of Herod the Great.

Old Testament Architecture. *Cities.* In the OT era, cities were built on hills or mounds and surrounded with a wall for protection. Generally houses were placed in a random fashion with winding paths or alleys connecting them. People unable to afford city life lived in villages that surrounded the city. They would work the nearby fields and in time of danger flee to the city for protection.

Most essential to any city was an adequate water supply. For that reason cities were built on or near underground springs. In the archaeological museum at Megiddo in northern Israel can be seen the details of Megiddo's water supply and the way in which the water preserved the fort. Some cities used plastered cisterns and catch basins to collect rainwater to supplement the regular water supply. Underground springs were protected by stepped tunnels for access when the city was besieged.

Fortifications. During much of OT times the Israelites used the techniques of the Middle Bronze Age to defend their cities in times of war. The central feature of that defense was a wall made of stone or brick, 25 to 30 feet high. The wall was sometimes made with an artificial slope and a ditch at the bottom to fortify it against enemy battering rams.

During the Israelite monarchy, casemate walls were also built. These consisted of two parallel walls connected by a series of cross walls. The resulting rooms were then filled with dirt to give added protection against enemy battering rams (Ez 26:9). Sometimes walls 20 feet thick were built with overhangs so attackers could be subdued. The apostle Paul was let down over the wall of Damascus in a basket from a room in the wall (Acts 9:25; 2 Cor 11:33). The old city of Jerusalem even today has a wall surrounding it, although the present wall was built by the Turks long after the destruction of Jerusalem in AD 70.

Gates. For cities surrounded by walls it was important to have gates for access. Although there were many gates for the city of Jerusalem, most cities had only two. One of the gates was for camel caravans, chariots, and larger vehicles; the other, on the opposite side of the city, was used for pedestrians, donkeys, and small animals. Many gates consisted of double doors (Is 45:1 KJV; Neh 6:1) made of wood and overlaid with bronze plating (Is 45:2). The doors were secured with horizontal bars of wood, bronze (1 Kgs 4:13), or iron (Ps 107:16) which fit into openings in the gateposts (Jgs 16:3).

In times of attack the gate was the most vulnerable point of the city. That is why the location of the gate was so important to the defense of the city and why most cities had so few gates. Often the road leading up to the gate was laid out so that attackers, who carried their shields in their left hands, would have to face the wall of the city and its defenders on their right side. Sometimes the gate was part of a large tower (2 Chr 26:9). Occasionally steps were constructed on the inside of the tower, so that sentinels could reach the top to stand watch (2 Kgs 9:17). At other times the gate was so positioned that it turned 90 degrees between the portals, in order to prevent enemy archers from making a straight shot through the gate.

Ancient Palestinian city gates have been excavated at Megiddo, Lachish, and Mizpah, among other places. Such strongly defended sites were protected by elaborately designed entrances, which often ran parallel to the city walls for some distances before turning at an angle and passing through an inner gateway into the city itself. To make access even more difficult for an invader, the builders frequently included flights of steps at intervals, as well as recessed areas where defensive forces could be stationed for counterattacks.

Houses. An above-average Israelite house consisted of several rooms facing an open courtyard (2 Sm 17:18). The largest room was for the family, another was for the family's cattle, and another was used as a general storeroom. Sometimes the walls were made of stones, with the joints filled with mud. Sometimes the inside walls were plastered with mud, although more prosperous homes had cypress or cedar wood. Floors were made of clay or polished plaster stones. The flat roofs were supported by beams and made watertight with wood or brushwood. An outside stairway gave access to the roof, and some people built roof chambers which in effect made a two-story house (1 Kgs 17:19). The flat roofs of houses provided additional sleeping and recreational space for crowded households. The Mosaic Law required these roofs to be surrounded by a protective parapet to prevent people falling to their deaths (Dt 22:8). Each family built its own house, since masons worked only on royal residences and temples.

Solomon's Temple. Probably the most important piece of Israelite architecture was King Solomon's temple. Although King David had thought of building such a structure, the project was left for his son Solomon to undertake. The building was located on the site where Abraham was supposed to have offered his son Isaac (Gn 22). It took seven and a half years to build and was notable for its beauty as well as its purpose. The plan of the temple was similar to that of the tabernacle, except that the dimensions were doubled and the height was tripled. The walls were made of stone overlaid with gold (1 Kgs 6:22), with gold also covering the ceilings and floor. The partition between the Holy of Holies and the Holy Place was made of gold-covered cedar wood. The entrance to the Holy of Holies consisted of a double door made of carved olive wood overlaid with gold. The doorway stood open but was veiled. Outside the temple were two courts, an inner court for the priests and an outer court for the people.

Lack of constructional expertise in Israel compelled Solomon to hire Phoenician workmen. The result was a typically Phoenician structure, the ground plan of which closely resembled that of an 8th-century BC Canaanite chapel excavated at Tell Tainat in Syria. Columns and porticoes were doubtless a feature of the temple of Solomon, though the precise function of the free-standing pillars named Jachin and Boaz is still far from certain. Carefully dressed masonry seems to have appeared in Israel for the first time in Solomon's time; excellent specimens of hewn and squared stone have been recovered from Samaria. The Samaritan site, along with Megiddo, has also furnished interesting examples of a decorated pilaster capital, which derived its design from Canaanite artistic representations and which seems to have been of local origin.

The temple was dedicated in a week-long ceremony of thanksgiving and prayer, during which fire fell from heaven and consumed the burnt offering (2 Chr 6:13–7:1). When Babylon overthrew Jerusalem and leveled the city in 586 BC, the temple was plundered of its wealth and burned to the ground. After Israel returned from captivity, the temple was rebuilt, with the foundation being laid in 525 BC. However, that second temple was far less magnificent than Solomon's and was in great need of repair by the time of King Herod of Judea (27–4 BC).

Although OT tradition gives considerable prominence to the Solomonic temple and lauds its grandeur, the building was actually an adjunct to the royal palace, serving as a chapel. Only in the postexilic period was the temple freed from royal associations to become an independent shrine where people could observe the prescribed rituals. Both pre- and postexilic temples were quite small and narrow in their dimensions, their width being limited by the length of the wooden beams available for roofing purposes. The only way such a building could be enlarged was in the usual Near Eastern manner of attaching additional rooms to the exterior.

New Testament Architecture. The architecture of NT times consisted of Greek and Roman structures, since those rulers had most recently dominated Israel. For instance, the Greeks built more than 350 cities throughout the Mediterranean area, with over 30 of them in Palestine. The Greek cities were architectural models, containing planned streets, arches, theaters, public baths, temples, and a central marketplace called the *agora.* Jewish homes, however, continued to remain small, with flat roofs over rooms facing a courtyard.

Probably the greatest building program during NT times was that of Herod the Great (37–4 BC), during Roman domination. He built some remarkable structures including aqueducts, cisterns, dungeons, palaces, and whole cities (e.g., Caesarea). His greatest work was the rebuilding of the temple, which he did to gain favor with the Jews—although he suc-

Unique construction in Israel: opus reticulatum (diamond-shaped stone) and opus quadratum (rectangular-shaped stone)—found only in Herodian structures.

View of the eastern temple mount wall in Jerusalem showing a "straight joint" in the middle of the picture; on the left are Herodian blocks of the temple platform, and on the right are heavier, irregular stones.

ceeded only in infuriating them. Herod's temple was a remarkable structure that took 83 years to complete. It then lasted in its completed state only six years before it was destroyed in AD 70. Much of the description of Herod's temple comes from the Jewish historian Josephus. The modern nation of Israel has recently excavated part of the temple site, and with each discovery some corrections have been made in Josephus' description.

Herod's temple managed to blend the old with the new. Though it appeared to embody the latest Hellenistic architectural fashions in its colonnades, marble columns, and façades, it was still firmly rooted in the traditions of Phoenicia. The Herodian structure was an enlargement, and to some extent a rebuilding, of the 6th-century BC temple. A series of courts and porticoes surrounded the reconstructed shrine, which was given an illusion of grandeur by means of an enlarged entrance. In the middle of that porch stood an enormous doorway that gave access to the much smaller inner door of the shrine itself. Unfortunately, nothing of the building itself survived the destruction of AD 70, leaving us almost completely dependent upon Josephus' account.

EDGAR C. JAMES

See ART; CAPITAL; CITY; HOMES AND DWELLINGS; SYNAGOGUE; TABERNACLE, TEMPLE; THEATER.

Archives, House of the. Building used for storage of records, annals, and decrees; a common structure in Near Eastern nations in the second millennium BC (Ezr 5:17–6:1). In the archives at Ecbatana, a summer resort for Persian kings, King Darius (521–486 BC) found an edict of Cyrus (559–530 BC) that entitled the Jews to begin reconstruction of the Jerusalem temple following the exile (Ezr 6:2). On the basis of that edict Darius gave his support to renewed reconstruction efforts, which had

been halted for 16 years due to local opposition (cf. Hg 1:1; Zec 1:1).

Arcturus. Constellation Ursa Major (the Great Bear), referred to in Job 9:9 and 38:32 (KJV) in connection with the constellation Orion and the Pleiades.

See ASTRONOMY.

Ard, Ardite. One of the eight sons of Bela (Nm 26:40), Benjamin's firstborn son (1 Chr 8:1). Ard is called Benjamin's son in the Hebrew sense, meaning descendant (Gn 46:21). He was the founder of the Ardite family, a subclan of Benjamin's tribe. The Ard/Addar transposition in 1 Chronicles 8:3 is probably a result of scribal error.

Ardon. Caleb's third son by Azubah; a descendant of Judah (1 Chr 2:18).

Areli, Arelite. One of Gad's seven sons (Gn 46:16). After the plague of Baal-peor, Areli's descendants, the Arelites, were numbered in Moses' census in preparation for war with the Midianites (Nm 25:6–18; 26:17).

Areopagite. Member of the council or court of the Areopagus in Athens (Acts 17:34).

See DIONYSIUS.

Areopagus. Hill northwest of the Acropolis in Athens overlooking the marketplace (Acts 17:19). "Areopagus" also refers to the Athenian council or court that met there. The irregular limestone outcropping was also known as Mars Hill, Mars being the Roman equivalent of the Greek god Ares. Paul was taken to the Areopagus after he had been reasoning with Jews and God-fearing Gentiles in the Athenian synagogue and marketplace *(agora)* for several days (Acts 17:16–21). Some Epicurean and Stoic philosophers involved in those discussions brought Paul before the council, but evidently not for an official arraignment. Trials were held at the Areopagus; there, some five centuries earlier, Socrates had faced those who accused him of deprecating the Greek gods. By

Mars Hill in Athens.

Paul's day the council of the Areopagus was responsible for various political, educational, philosophical, and religious matters as well as for legal proceedings. The general tone of Paul's address does not suggest judicial proceedings. He spoke as an intelligent Christian believer who was able to meet the intellectual Athenians on their own ground (Acts 17:22–31). Some remained skeptical, but his address was convincing to a few who "joined him and believed" (Acts 17:32–34).

Aretas. Name of several kings of an Arabian people called the Nabataeans, considered to be descendants of Nebaioth, Ishmael's oldest son (Gn 25:12–16; 1 Chr 1:29). According to the Jewish historian Josephus, Ishmael's descendants inhabited an area all the way from the Euphrates to the Red Sea, calling it Nabatene. Their capital city, Sela, was called Petra in NT times.

The Aretas of 2 Maccabees 5:8, before whom Jason the priest was accused, ruled about 170 BC. The Nabataeans were evidently friendly toward the Maccabeans (1 Mc 5:24–28; 9:35). Josephus mentioned two other kings named Aretas. It was Aretas III, originally named Obodas, who extended Nabataean control and occupied Damascus during his reign (87–62 BC).

The NT contains a reference to still another Aretas. The apostle Paul had to escape from Damascus by being let down in a basket through a hole in the wall because the governor there "under King Aretas" guarded the city to seize him (2 Cor 11:32,33). That Aretas has been identified as Eneas, who took the title Aretas IV and ruled from 9 BC to AD 40. He attacked and defeated Herod Antipas over a boundary dispute and also as revenge. (Antipas had divorced Aretas' daughter in order to marry Herodias.)

Paul's mention of Aretas raises some questions about chronology, since at that particular time Damascus was under Roman jurisdiction—although it had formerly belonged to Arabian kings. If more of the history of that time were known, the facts might be that: (1) the Roman emperor had left Damascus under Aretas' rule for a while to facilitate a smooth transition; (2) Aretas was a kind of overseer of the Nabataean population in that area, though they ultimately were under Roman control; or (3) during the battle against Herod Antipas, Damascus was seized by the Nabataeans for a brief period, during which Paul visited the city.

Argob (Person). Individual supposedly killed with King Pekahiah of Israel in Pekah's revolt (2 Kgs 15:25 KJV, NIV). The early church father Jerome thought the name Argob (along with Arieh) referred to a place. Today some scholars think that Argob and Arieh may have been accidentally misplaced from a list of place names (v 29) through scribal error.

Argob (Place). Region in Bashan won by the Israelites when they defeated King Og at Edrei (Nm 21:33–35; Dt 3:4). Argob was located east of the Sea of Chinnereth (later called Sea of Galilee), beyond the regions of Geshur and Maacah (Dt 3:14). Moses assigned all of Bashan, including Argob, to half of Manasseh's tribe (Dt 3:13,14). Jair, of that tribe, subdued the villages of Argob and named them Havvoth-jair ("the villages of Jair"). First Kings 4:13 distinguishes between Argob and the villages of Jair, which are said to be in Gilead, south of Argob. Deuteronomy 3:14 may represent a textual difficulty, or perhaps the location of the villages of Jair on the border between Argob and Gilead was responsible for the apparent discrepancy. That border could have shifted during the three centuries between the conquests of Jair and the reign of Solomon. By then the name Havvoth-jair could even have referred to a different set of cities.

Aridai. One of Haman's ten sons, who was killed with his father when Haman's plot to destroy the Jews was foiled (Est 9:7–10).

Aridatha. One of Haman's ten sons, who was killed with his father when Haman's plot to destroy the Jews was foiled (Est 9:7–10).

Arieh. Person mentioned along with Argob in 2 Kings 15:25 (KJV, NIV), but possibly a scribal error which should not be read (as in RSV).

See ARGOB (PERSON).

Ariel (Person). 1. Person or thing overcome in a heroic deed by Benaiah, chief of David's bodyguard (2 Sm 23:20; 1 Chr 11:22). It is not clear that the Hebrew word *ariel* is a proper name in these passages. Benaiah may have killed two "lionlike men" of Moab (KJV) or destroyed two Moabite altar hearths.

2. One of the men sent by Ezra to ask Iddo for Levitical priests to accompany the Jewish exiles returning to Jerusalem from Babylon (Ezr 8:16).

Ariel (Place). Poetic designation for Jerusalem, used by the prophet Isaiah in a "woe" oracle warning people to turn from their wrongdoing (Is 29:1,2,7). Jerusalem, location of the altar of burnt offering, was called Ariel ("hearth of God") by synecdoche, a poetic device in which a whole thing is referred to by naming one part. In a dramatic play on words Isaiah pronounced God's judgment: Jerusalem, city of the hearth of God, would become an ariel, a pagan altar hearth, when destroyed by her enemies (v 2).

Arimathea. Hometown of the Joseph who obtained Jesus' crucified body and buried it in his own tomb (Mt 27:57; Mk 15:43; Jn 19:38). The town's location is unknown, though it may be identical to the hill town of Ramathaim-zophim, the prophet Samuel's home (1 Sm 1:1), about 20 miles northwest of Jerusalem. Luke described the place as a Jewish town, and Joseph was himself a Jewish official (Lk 23:50).

Arioch. 1. King of Ellasar, who with three other kings captured five cities and took a number of prisoners, including Abram's nephew Lot (Gn 14:1–16).

2. Nebuchadnezzar's captain of the guard (KJV) or chief executioner, who took Daniel to the Babylonian king to interpret his dream (Dn 2:14–25).

Arisai. One of Haman's ten sons, who was killed with his father when Haman's plot to destroy the Jews was foiled (Est 9:7–10).

Aristarchus. Companion of the apostle Paul; Macedonian from Thessalonica, possibly of Jewish ancestry. He is first mentioned as one of those seized by an angry mob in Ephesus (Acts 19:29). Later he accompanied Paul on the return from his third missionary journey (Acts 20:4), as well as to Rome to face Caesar (Acts 27:2). Paul described him as a fellow worker (Phlm 24) and "fellow prisoner" from whom he received great comfort (Col 4:10,11). Tradition says that Aristarchus was martyred in Rome under Nero.

Aristobulus. Nobleman to whom Paul sent greetings in Romans 16:10.

Ark, Noah's. *See* NOAH #1.

Arkite. Name of a clan descended from Ham's son Canaan (Gn 10:17; 1 Chr 1:15). The Arkites were probably residents of Arqa, a Phoenician town north of Tripolis in Syria. According to an early inscription, Arqa was captured by the Assyrian Tiglath-pileser III in 738 BC.

Ark of the Covenant. Most important piece of furniture in the wilderness tabernacle (tent-sanctuary) that God instructed Moses to build (Ex 25:10–22). The Hebrew word for ark can also mean "chest" (2 Kgs 12:9,10) or "coffin" (Gn 50:26), but it is not the same word used for Noah's ark. The ark that Moses had Bezalel make was an oblong chest made of acacia wood (Ex 31:1–5; 37:1–9). The chest measured approximately 45 by 27 by 27 inches, and was overlaid inside and out with gold. It was fitted with two pairs of rings through which poles were slid to make it portable. The ark would also serve as container for the two tablets of the Law that would be given to Moses (Ex 25:16). Since the tablets were also called the "testimony," the ark was sometimes called the "ark of the testimony." Also in the ark were placed a pot of manna, the miraculous food provided by God (Ex 16:33), and Aaron's rod that had budded (Nm 17:10; Heb 9:4).

The lid of the ark was called the "mercy

The Ark of the Covenant, with drawn curtains, pictured on the mosaic floor of the synagogue at Tiberias.

seat" or "place of mercy" (Ex 25:17). It was a slab of gold fitting over the top of the ark and having an importance of its own. Once a year the high priest was to make atonement for the people of Israel by sprinkling the mercy seat with the blood of bulls and goats (Lv 16:2–16). In fact, the English expression "mercy seat" is related to the Hebrew word for "atone." The lid was called a "seat" because the Lord was considered as enthroned between two cherubim (winged creatures) positioned opposite each other (Ps 99:1). The Lord spoke to Moses from between the cherubim (Nm 7:89).

Names. The ark was sometimes referred to simply as the ark (Ex 37:1; Nm 3:31), at other times as the "ark of [the] testimony" (Nm 4:5; Jos 4:16). The Israelites were thus reminded that the ark's holiness was not magical, but derived from the holy Law of God contained inside it. That name also confronted the Israelites with their need to follow the commands God had given in his "testimony."

Those commands were given by the God of the covenant (or promise) who had rescued Israel from slavery in Egypt, and who had promised to be the ever-present God of his people (Ex 6:6,7). Hence the ark was most widely known as the "ark of the covenant." Sometimes that name was expanded to "ark of the covenant of the Lord" (1 Chr 28:18) or, still more impressively, "ark of the covenant of the Lord of all the earth" (Jos 3:11).

At times the ark was called "the ark of God." It was a visible sign that the invisible God was dwelling in Israel's midst. It had a devastating and often deadly "holiness." The people of Beth-shemesh were severely punished after they had treated the ark without proper reverence (1 Sm 6:19). A man named Uzzah was killed by the Lord when he touched it with his hand to keep it from tumbling to the ground from a cart (2 Sm 6:6–9). The ark was dangerous to touch because it was the very symbol of God's presence. For this reason God commanded that the ark be placed in the Holy of Holies, separated from the rest of the tabernacle (and later the temple) by a heavy veil (Ex 26:31–33; Heb 9:3–5); no sinful man could look upon the glory of God above the ark and live (Lv 16:2).

History. When the Israelites journeyed from Mt Sinai to Canaan, the ark accompanied them in their trek through the desert. It was to be a constant reminder of the holy presence of their God. The ark was spoken of in the accounts of that journey almost as though it were endowed with personal features (Nm 10:33–36). Although the wrapping and carrying of the sacred objects were carefully detailed (Nm 4), God's relationship with the ark was so close that the ark seemed to be "alive."

The ark clearly played a benevolent role during the desert journey. A group of Israelites rebelled and tried to invade Canaan on their own, although "neither the Ark nor Moses" went with them (Nm 14:44). The result was defeat at the hands of their enemies (Nm 14:45). The ark played an important role in the crossing of the Jordan (Jos 3:13–17; 4:9,10), the conquest of Jericho (Jos 6:6–11), and the life of the Israelites in their new land (Jos 8:33; Jgs 20:27). There is no hint of superstitious or magical use of the ark; it was not a fetish, talisman, or charm. Yet it had solemn significance as the container of God's "testimony" and as the pledge of his presence.

A sharp contrast to the role of the ark in Joshua's day is found in later times. In the days of Eli and his sons, that is, at the end of the period of the judges, religious life in Israel was at a low ebb. The ark was still venerated but looked upon as a fetish to ensure success or victory automatically. When losing a battle with the Philistines, the Israelites rushed the sacred chest to the battlefield, thereby hoping to gain a victory (1 Sm 4:1–10). But the Lord did not tolerate such flagrant misuse of the ark. He allowed it to be captured by the uncircumcised Philistines (1 Sm 4:11) and inflicted defeat on Israel and death on the house of the high priest Eli (1 Sm 4:13–22).

At the same time, God vindicated the honor of the ark when it was offered to Dagon, the god of the Philistines. The efforts of the pagan Philistines to get rid of the ark have an almost humorous aspect (1 Sm 5,6). The biblical writer dramatically illustrated that the holy ark could neither be treated superstitiously by God's people nor mocked by his enemies.

Samuel, a great reformer and prophet, made no attempt to restore the ark to a place of prominence after it was returned to Israel. He allowed it to remain in Kiriath-jearim (1 Sm 6:21; 7:2). Samuel first had to bring Israel back to obedience to God's covenant before the ark of the covenant could be of any use.

David, described as a king after God's own heart and chosen to replace the disobedient Saul, exerted efforts to bring the ark back to a prominent place (2 Sm 6:1–17). It may have been to David's political advantage to add prestige to his newly established capital, Jerusalem, formerly the Canaanite stronghold of Jebus. But Psalm 132 describes David's concern for the honor of God and for the ark. In a moment of great religious joy and enthusiasm he addressed God directly: "Arise, O Lord, and go to thy resting place, thou and the ark of thy might" (v 8). To restless David, the ark had also been "restless" as long as Israel had not yet obtained its "rest," that is, as long as Canaan had not been completely conquered.

Some measure of peace had already come during Joshua's time (Jos 21:43–45), but much remained to be done. By conquering Jebus, David virtually completed the conquest of the Promised Land. Finally the land had rest and the Lord could then "dwell" in his temple, the suitable resting place for the ark. Nevertheless, David's desire to build a temple for the ark was not granted (2 Sm 7:1–17). He was told that his son Solomon would build a home for the ark and for the Lord. Solomon erected a magnificent temple with a place for the ark in the most holy part, behind the curtains (1 Kgs 8:1–11).

Little is known about the ark's history after that. What happened to it when Judah was exiled to Babylon is a mystery. It may have been destroyed when Nebuchadnezzar destroyed the temple and the whole city of Jerusalem in 586 BC. The new temple built after return from the exile had no ark. There is a legend in the Apocrypha that Jeremiah hid the ark in a cave on Mt Nebo until a time when God would again restore his people (2 Mc 2:4–8).

The disappearance of the ark at the exile, however, was providential. For not only had the presence of God disappeared from above the mercy seat, but God had long since rejected worship as it was offered at the temple (Lam 2:6,7; Is 1:11–14). Moreover, the very purpose and significance of the ark was ultimately to be fulfilled in the person and work of Jesus Christ.

With the coming of Jesus Christ the yearly sprinkling of the mercy seat with the blood of bulls and goats was no longer necessary. Christ, with the sprinkling of his own blood, secured an eternal redemption (Heb 9:11–14). Consequently, those who trust in him are encouraged to come with boldness before the God of grace enthroned above the mercy seat (Heb 4:14–16). Whereas before, the veil hung as a barrier between men and the ark, Christ through his death tore the veil in two and passed through it (Mt 27:51; Heb 10:20), opening the way for all worshipers to see the ark of God's covenant (Rv 11:19).

Nor was the ark necessary any longer to symbolize the presence of God with his people, because in the incarnation of Jesus Christ and the coming of the Spirit to indwell every believer the presence of God with his people was realized in a final way (Ez 36:27,28; Jn 1:14; 14:16,17). Those who live after the work of Christ already experience the reality of which the ark was only a shadow: "the dwelling of God is with men" (Rv 21:3). Jeremiah prophesied that in the future the ark would no longer be remembered because in that time all of Jerusalem "shall be called the throne of the Lord" (Jer 3:16,17). Thus, in the New Jerusalem there will be no ark or temple, for the Lord God Almighty and the Lamb are the temple (Rv 21:22).

MARTEN H. WOUDSTRA

See TABERNACLE, TEMPLE.

Armageddon. Hebrew word in Revelation 16:16 meaning "Mt Megiddo." It is generally thought that the term refers to the town of Megiddo, strategically located between the western coastal area and the broad Plain of Jezreel in northern Palestine. The area of Megiddo was important commercially and militarily, and was the scene of many important battles in Israel's history. There the Lord routed Sisera before the armies of Deborah and Barak (Jgs 4,5); Gideon was victorious over the Midianites and Amalekites (Jgs 6); King Saul and his army were defeated by the Philistines (1 Sm 31); and King Josiah was slain in battle by the Egyptian army of Pharaoh Neco (2 Kgs 23:29). Because of that long history the name seems to have become symbolic of a battlefield. Such identification was evidently the thought in the mind of the apostle John in the Book of Revelation.

Revelation 15 and 16 describe seven angels who pour out seven bowls of the wrath of God upon the earth. The sixth angel pours out his bowl upon the great river Euphrates, and its waters are dried up (Rv 16:12–16), preparing the way for the coming of the "kings of the East." Also three demonic spirits go forth to cause the kings of the whole world to gather for a battle of the great day of God the Almighty (16:13,14). Their gathering takes place at Armageddon (16:16).

Like most of Revelation the passage is difficult to interpret. A literal interpretation sees real armies gathered at an exact geographical location in the Near East. A more figurative interpretation sees John symbolically portraying a final worldwide conflict between wicked mankind and the Christ of God.

Regardless of how literally or figuratively the passage is interpreted, it clearly describes a final battle in which Christ is victorious. That battle is known as the battle of Armageddon. The term has also passed into the secular vocabulary; for example, people now speak of a "nuclear Armageddon."

See REVELATION, BOOK OF.

Armenia. KJV translation of Ararat in 2 Kings 19:37 and Isaiah 37:38, mentioned as the place where Sennacherib's two sons fled after murdering their father.

See ARARAT.

Armoni. One of Saul's two sons by his concubine Rizpah. Seven of Saul's sons, including Armoni, were handed over to the Gibeonites by David to be killed to avenge Saul's slaughter of the Gibeonites (2 Sm 21:1,8,9).

Armor, Armor Bearer. Protective gear and one who carried the armor and weapons of a warrior.

See ARMS AND WARFARE; TRADES AND OCCUPATIONS (SOLDIER).

Armory. Storehouse for weapons; an arsenal (Jer 50:25).

See ARMS AND WARFARE.

Arms and Warfare. The location of Palestine at the crossroads of three continents gave it a strategic importance in the ancient world quite out of proportion to its size. Surrounded by the great military powers (Egypt, Mesopotamia, the Hittites of Anatolia), that stretch of land was constantly the object of aggressive ambitions of other nations.

Sources of Information. The Bible is a primary witness to the role that arms and warfare played in the life of ancient Near Eastern nations. Three other sources of information have been added by archaeology: illustrated monuments, both sculptured and drawn; the ruins of fortifications with some actual weapons recovered; and written documents.

Illustrated Monuments. Reliefs and drawings illustrating military events provide a more tangible expression of the character of ancient warfare than literary description alone is capable of doing. Illustrations often depict such important aspects of warfare as weapons, fortifications, and tactics.

Much military equipment was made of perishable materials, such as wood, leather, or textiles. Even for objects fashioned from more durable material, such as metal scales used in a coat of mail, we are dependent upon monuments for knowledge of what the garment looked like and how it was worn. A battering ram consisted of many parts, most of them perishable. We understand its operation today only because we have drawings depicting the complete implement in action. Little remains of ancient fortifications beyond their foundations. Yet the upper reaches of the walls, on which were erected towers, battlements, and balconies, provided the vital features of the defense system. We can visualize their form, shape, and function because we possess graphic representations of them on monuments.

The monuments also illustrate tactical principles and methods of warfare; for example, the battle array of armies and the positioning of units on the field of battle or during the siege of a city. Although for the period of Iron Age I (1200–920 BC) reliefs and drawings related to military matters are almost completely absent, Iron Age II (920–586 BC) is unusually rich in monuments. Assyrian kings, especially, adorned their palaces with hundreds of sculptures and wall paintings, mostly concerned with warfare. Because those monuments bear the name of the person who ordered their erection, we possess documentary evidence permitting us to date with certainty new developments in arms and warfare.

Discoveries at Excavations. Archaeological excavations on the sites of ancient fortifications have uncovered their foundations and have revealed their plan and methods of construction. Such discoveries are especially important for periods for which we possess no illustrated monuments, or in which the reliefs fail to illustrate a fortified city. Excavations at Jericho have demonstrated that the city's fortifications included a moat and a massive stone tower, the earliest known defense system in the world.

Written Documents. Many written documents discovered and deciphered within the last century have advanced knowledge on a number of military subjects. Illustrated monuments and artifacts uncovered in excavations often fail to provide key pieces of information, such as the names of weapons; types of soldiers and fortifications; and the arrangement and size of field units, centers of arms production, systems of intelligence, or auxiliary services. Written records, however, have provided dates and details for important campaigns, supplementing the information in the Bible. Collections of such material include the texts of Boghazköy, capital of the Hittites in Anatolia (modern Turkey); of Ugarit, in Syria, known also as the Ras Shamra texts; of Mari on the Euphrates, where more than 20,000 documents were found dating to the end of the 18th century BC; of Tell el-Amarna, in Egypt, whose archives include letters sent to the pharaoh by kings of vassal states in Palestine, Syria, and environs during the first half of the 14th century BC; of Nuzi, in Mesopotamia, dating primarily to the 15th century BC; and of Ebla (Tell Mardikh), where the remains of a previously unknown ancient civilization are being uncovered and a library in excess of 25,000 tablets is being deciphered, illuminating the period of the Early Bronze Age (3100–2100 BC).

The Art of Warfare. War expresses the decision of one nation to impose its will upon another by force. An index to the importance of warfare in antiquity is provided by the amount of technical skill directed to perfecting devices for destruction and defense.

The invention of different weapons, fortifications, and tactics exerted a profound reciprocal influence on other inventions. Tactical innovation by one side prompted new counter-tactics by the other. The composite bow made possible increased power of penetration from long range. Its appearance was directly responsible for invention of the coat of mail for defense, which, in turn, provided the incentive for developing a suitable weapon to penetrate armor. Similarly, advances in design of city fortifications make sense in the light of standard patterns of attack on fortified structures during different periods, including perfection of the battering ram. Like a chain reaction the process continued throughout Bible times, producing advances in both offensive and defensive devices.

The three basic elements of the art of warfare are mobility, firepower, and security. The refinement of weapons, accordingly, must be studied against a background of whole systems of penetration and defense. Weapons alone seldom determined the issue of battle, particularly when both sides were evenly matched. The skill with which strategy and tactics were deployed, the spirit of the commander in directing his troops, and the precision with which the troops handled their weapons were decisive factors in many of the battles mentioned in the Bible.

The Troops. Sovereigns initiated war after consultation with their chief military advisers. Actual conduct of war was the responsibility of the troops in a king's army units. Already in the Middle Bronze period (1950–1550 BC) the powerful Egyptian and Hittite empires maintained professional armies composed of infantry supported by a chariot corps. The vassal kings in the city-states of Canaan maintained smaller armies, consisting primarily of foot soldiers, and had to depend on their suzerain (the king whom they served) for the loan of a chariot unit. The Amarna tablets record urgent requests for war chariots and more soldiers addressed to the pharaoh by vassal Canaanite kings. The army of the Israelites was essentially a militia rather than a professional army and was limited to infantry. Cavalry units did not make an appearance even in the powerful armies of the Bible lands until near the end of the 2nd millennium BC. Only in the 1st millennium BC was it common to find infantry, a chariot corps, and cavalry units together on the field of battle.

Infantry. The infantry of most ancient armies was divided into units identified with specific types of weapons. Long-range weapon troops, equipped with bows or slings, were used at the start of a conflict. Follow-up units were armed with medium-range weapons, spears and javelins. The final stage of battle was assigned to units trained in hand-to-hand combat and armed with maces, axes, and swords. A distinction was made relatively early in the Israelite army between light-armed and heavy-armed infantry. Members of a particular tribe would provide light-armed soldiers, members of another tribe the heavy-armed troops. Members of Benjamin's tribe provided a formidable unit of slingmen and archers (Jgs 20:16; 1 Chr 8:40; 12:2). Members of the tribes of Judah, Zebulun, Naphtali, and Gad, equipped with heavy armor, were experts in the use of shield, spear, and other arms for hand-to-hand fighting (1 Chr 12:8–15,24,33,34). Several illustrated monuments from the period of the judges and the first Israelite kings clearly depict such special spear units, carrying spear and shield, and wearing heavy coats of mail and helmets. Spearmen along with sword and ax bearers constituted the main power of a striking force in an assault on the wall of a fortified city or in open battle in hilly or wooded terrain.

The light infantry consisted of archers and slingmen. Evidence for the effective use of long-range archery units in battle is available from as early as the first half of the 3rd millennium BC, on a famous victory monument of the Akkadian king Naram-Sin (23rd century BC) erected at Susa. The Akkadians, successors to the ancient Sumerians, developed the composite bow, which greatly enhanced an arrow's range and power of penetration. The tactic of deploying archery units to operate from the rear and the flanks brought the art of warfare in open terrain in Mesopotamia to near perfection. Their decisive innovation, integration of archers with the chariot corps and heavy infantry, broke up the Sumerian pattern of phalanx formations based solely on chariots and heavy infantry. It permitted the Akkadians to dominate all of Mesopotamia and to penetrate distant regions as far west as the Mediterranean Sea.

Throughout the Middle Bronze and Late Bronze Ages (1570–1200 BC), both illustrated monuments and documents imply that the composite bow was the decisive weapon in all of the large armies of Bible lands. During that extended period a preoccupation with protecting the archers is evident. Since both hands were required to wield a bow, archers were particularly vulnerable to counterfire. In the Beni Hasan paintings from Egypt (20th century BC) archers fire their bows from a standing or kneeling position from the ground during an attack on a fortified city. They are unprotected by armor and are in full view of the defenders on the wall, who also have bows and who direct their fire downward. By the 18th century BC the Mari documents mention the use of siege towers, which enabled attacking archers to provide covering fire from a greater height. Such towers tended to neutralize the effectiveness of defenders on the battlements. In the Middle Bronze period, units of archers were assigned shield bearers equipped with axes or spears to screen them from enemy fire. Gradually, more effective protection was developed, both by the archer's armor and by provision of more refined shielding procedures.

In the early Assyrian reliefs of King Ashurnasirpal, and particularly of Shalmaneser, archers are equipped with heavy coats of mail that extend to their ankles. They are frequently accompanied by a special shield bearer equipped with a small round shield to protect the archer's face. Heavy armor, however, seriously impeded freedom of movement. Consequently, under Tiglath-pileser the Assyrian army abandoned that procedure. The coat of mail was shortened so that it covered only the upper portion of the body, and huge wicker shields with right-angled tops were introduced, carried by a special shield bearer assigned to protect the archer. Because the shields were slightly taller than the height of a man and were hooded, archers could direct their fire standing up and still be screened from the arrows of defenders on a wall. The monuments make clear that for all the importance of its heavy infantry, the main power of the Assyrian infantry rested with its archers, both in siege operations against fortified cities and in battle on open terrain.

Archery units were introduced early as a standard feature of the Israelite army as well. They seem to have been drawn especially from Benjamin's tribe (1 Chr 8:40). A particularly impressive fact about a unit that joined David at Ziklag was that they "could shoot arrows . . . with either the right or the left hand" (1 Chr 12:2). Asa, king of the southern kingdom of Judah, was able to rely on a contingent of archers and shield bearers from Benjamin's tribe; the biblical record specifies that they were protected by "large shields" (2 Chr 14:8).

As early as the Middle Bronze Age, units of slingmen were regularly added to the light infantry in Egypt. The famous wall-paintings from Beni Hasan depict them as a support unit, providing covering fire for archers. Although there is no documentary or pictorial evidence from the Late Bronze Age that units of slingers continued to be trained, they appear again in reliefs of a naval battle fought by the Egyptians against the invading "sea peoples" (the Philistines) at Medinet Habu (be-

ginning of the 12th century BC). Spotters in the crow's nests of Egyptian ships are shown using slings against the invaders in attacking vessels.

Slingmen constituted a separate unit within the tribal army of Israel as early as the period of the judges. At the defense of Gibeah by Benjamin's tribe, 700 left-handed men were noted for their skill and accuracy with the sling. As a result of strenuous training they could hit a target within a hair's breadth without fail (Jgs 20:16).

Slingers could be effectively deployed in an attack on a fortified city because they could direct high-angled fire up steep slopes. With skill, missiles could be projected over the walls, barraging defenders who took cover behind the battlements and walls. Slingers played an important role in the campaigns of the kings of Judah and Israel against the Moabites. When Mesha rebelled against Israel, the prophet Elisha assured Jehoshaphat, king of Judah, "You shall conquer every fortified city, and every choice city, and shall fell every good tree, and stop up all springs of water, and ruin every good piece of land with stones" (2 Kgs

Statue of a Roman soldier (in Rome).

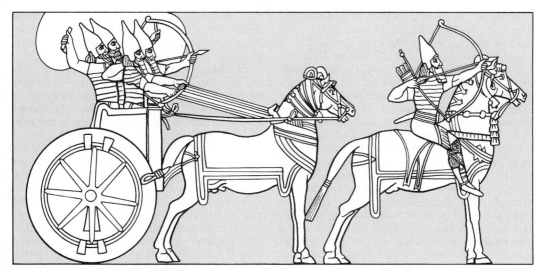

Assyrian archers in a chariot and on a horse.

3:19). That prophecy was borne out, and the cities were overthrown, "and on every good piece of land every man threw a stone, until it was covered." Finally, only the fortress of Kirhareseth, the Moabite capital, remained, but "the slingers surrounded and conquered it" (2 Kgs 3:25).

Because of their mobility in the field, units of archers and slingers continued to be used in warfare until the end of the Roman period. The Persians were dreaded for their attacks with arrows. In Greece, archery had been neglected except in Crete and in a few undeveloped parts of the Greek mainland. Cretan archers were renowned and were frequently employed as mercenaries to supplement the ranks of the ordinary citizen-soldier. Julius Caesar obtained archers and slingers from Crete and the Balearic Islands, using such units primarily in country unsuited to heavy infantry.

Chariot Corps. Chariot units were already a decisive battle force in Mesopotamia in the first half of the 3rd millennium BC, although unknown in Egypt until more than a thousand years later. The ancient Sumerians invented and developed the chariot. By coordinating its use with their infantry they attained a military superiority that permitted them to dominate Mesopotamia. Early battle chariots were either two-wheeled or four-wheeled vehicles harnessed to four draft animals, which appear on ancient monuments to be not horses but wild asses or onagers. Chariots were used principally to charge and panic an enemy, engaging the enemy at medium range with javelin throwers and at close range with spearmen. Early chariots were heavy and clumsy, lacking both speed and maneuverability.

Not until the Middle Bronze period (1950–1570 BC) were the horse and light chariot introduced, advancing the art of warfare to levels previously unattained. Documents from Mari (18th century BC) speak of horse-drawn chariots as one of the most important elements of battle in open terrain. The documents also indicate that chariots were used during a siege to seal off approaches to the besieged city and thus to forestall assistance from allies. The military power of the Hyksos—Asiatic tribes who overran Syria and Palestine and dominated Egypt in the 17th century BC—was based on light horse-drawn chariots with spoked wheels. The Egyptians succeeded in breaking the Hyksos' hold only after they had built up a chariot force of their own. Wall-paintings from the Late Bronze period often depict Canaanites offering chariots as gifts to the Egyptian royal court. The design of early Egyptian chariots was identical to that of the Canaanite chariot. The conclusion that the chariot reached Egypt from Canaan is supported by the fact that the Egyptian terms for chariot and horse are borrowed from the Canaanite language.

A battle chariot was essentially a mobile firing platform. By accelerating the movement of firepower on the battlefield, an assault could be concentrated on decisive points. A second purpose was to exploit the element of shock, creating confusion by charging into the enemy ranks. Such purposes called for a combination of speed, maneuverability, and stability for the discharge of weapons, essentially contradictory demands that taxed the technical ingenuity of military planners. Over the centuries many designs were tried before the chariot became an effective war machine that was stable, fast, and highly maneuverable. The rear axle was finally placed at the very back of the carriage body, lending stability to an otherwise flimsy vehicle. When that improvement was combined with a light body and light wheels, plus powerful but swift draft animals, the chariot achieved perfection. The complex vehicle consisted of carefully designed parts: body, wheels, axle, chariot pole, and yoke. The carriage body was equipped with fittings for weapons such as quivers, bow cases, and sheaths, and stands for axes and spears. Obviously the manufacture of battle chariots required rich resources and an advanced technology. Consequently, only the more powerful nations could develop and sustain a chariot corps. No mention is made of a chariot force in Israel's army until the time of the united monarchy under David and Solomon. Only then did the presence of a strong, central military authority with adequate resources make possible the acquisition and refinement of chariots.

In the earlier period of the judges (Iron Age I) Israel had no chariots. The fact that the Canaanites possessed an advanced form of battle chariot enabled them effectively to contain the presence of Israel in the land (Jgs 1:19). Jabin, king of Hazor, was able to exploit the northern and central tribes of Israel for 20 years because his army, consisting primarily of chariot squadrons, controlled the valley of Jezreel. His chariot corps was formidable, numbering 900 iron chariots (Jgs 4:1–3). The campaign of Deborah, a prophetess and judge of Israel, and her associate Barak against Sisera, commander of Jabin's chariots, was one of the most celebrated military encounters of that period (Jgs 4,5). The decisive battle took place near Megiddo, in the western section of the Jezreel valley. Israel's tribal army in that period was a militia, with its warriors called to arms only in a time of crisis. The Canaanite army consisted of regular soldiers supported by squadrons of battle chariots, each manned by two warriors and drawn by horses.

The strategy of the Israelite forces was to exploit topography and weather to offset the superior advantage possessed by Sisera with his chariots. The main Israelite force positioned itself on hilly ground, which afforded protection against a Canaanite chariot assault. The remainder launched a surprise attack on the chariot squadrons in the valley near the Kishon River. The timing of the attack was the decisive consideration, coinciding with heavy rains that caused the river to rise and overflow its banks, turning the valley floor into deep mud (Jgs 5:21). The Canaanite chariots became enmeshed in the mud and lost their ability to maneuver; whereupon the Isra-

elite warriors swept down and destroyed them. The biblical account underscores the serious limitation of the battle chariot to level terrain and firm ground.

Establishment of a central kingdom permitted Israel to develop a chariot corps of its own (cf. 1 Sm 8:11), although there is no evidence that King Saul possessed any chariots. During the early part of David's reign the army consisted exclusively of an infantry force. The hill territory he controlled, uncongenial to the operation of a chariot corps, provided maximum security against the effectiveness of enemy chariots. But as David's kingdom expanded he assumed control over the flatlands as well, and added chariots to his army. In a battle with the Syrians near the Euphrates River, David captured 1,000 chariots from Hadadezer, king of Zobah (2 Sm 8:3,4; 1 Chr 18:3,4). Of that number he reserved 100 for his own army and burned the rest. Mention of chariots purchased by Absalom and Adonijah also indicates that they were a familiar sight in David's army (2 Sm 15:1; 1 Kgs 1:5).

King Solomon made the chariot squadron the core unit of his army and expended enormous sums to build up its strength. He purchased horses from Cilicia (a region in Asia Minor) and chariots from Egypt (1 Kgs 10:26–29). Solomon established "chariot cities" as garrison towns to guard the approaches to his capital: he built up Hazor and Megiddo to secure the northern frontiers from invasion; Beth-horon, Gezer, and Baalath to maintain surveillance of the Philistine plains; and Tamar in the south to guard against Edomite incursion (1 Kgs 9:15–19). Each of those cities was equipped with enormous stables, with a separate stall allocated to each animal and a central courtyard for exercise and training of horses and charioteers. The exact size of Solomon's chariot corps is difficult to determine because of confusion in the numbers reported (1 Kgs 4:26—40,000 stalls for chariot horses; 2 Chr 9:25—4,000 stalls). The smaller number is consistent with the statement in 1 Kings 10:26 that Solomon had 1,400 chariots, since contemporary reliefs show each chariot being drawn by two horses, with a third held in reserve. By any reckoning, it is clear that Solomon emphasized the chariot force as the mainstay of Israel's defense.

After the division of the kingdom, most of the chariot cities—Hazor, Megiddo, Gezer, and probably Beth-horon—went to Israel in the north. Evidence that they continued to be utilized for chariotry has come from archaeology. Excavation at Megiddo uncovered an enormous stable complex, which was initially assigned to the period of Solomon. More recent excavations on the site have demonstrated that those stables belong to the period of King Ahab. The stables had room for about 450 horses, which would indicate a chariot force of 150 at that center. Since the usual strength of a squadron of chariots was 50, Ahab maintained a three-squadron formation at Megiddo. That would further suggest a chariot corps of a few hundred stationed in the other chariot cities of Israel. In an inscription, Assyrian king Shalmaneser III claimed that in the 6th year of his reign Ahab of Israel committed 2,000 chariots to the battle of the allied Aramaean kings against the Assyrians at Qarqar. That number may have included chariot units contributed by King Jehoshaphat of Judah as well (cf. 2 Kgs 3:7).

Ahab's successors were unable to recover from the defeat Israel suffered at Qarqar. The once large chariot corps of the kings of Israel and Judah in the 9th century BC became progressively smaller and poorer, until in the reign of Jehoahaz, son of Jehu, the army of the northern kingdom possessed only 50 horsemen and 10 chariots (2 Kgs 13:7). Such impoverishment of military strength encouraged the kings of Israel and Judah to rely on military alliances with the great powers to the north (Assyria) and south (Egypt), despite warnings of the prophet Isaiah (31:1,2). When Samaria, the capital of Israel, fell after a three-year siege (2 Kgs 17:5,6), the Assyrians captured only 50 chariots—barely enough to service a squadron.

Cavalry. Mounted warriors appeared on the battlefield only at the end of the 2nd millennium BC. Before that time there is evidence for the use of horses as mounts only in isolated instances when messengers were sent on distant errands.

A stone relief from the palace of Kapara in northwestern Mesopotamia (10th century BC) provides evidence for a cavalry unit at a quite primitive stage. An Aramaean mounted warrior holds the reins in one hand and a stick (spear?) in the other. Although he uses a bridle, the absence of saddle or spurs affects his stability and the control of his mount. A pointed helmet and a small, round, bossed shield slung over his shoulders provide a measure of protection in combat. Another relief from the palace of Kapara depicts a warrior on a camel. He is seated on a cushionlike saddle attached to the body of the camel by crossed straps. In a later period camels were still being used in battle by nomadic tribes in Arabia. In reliefs in the palaces of Tiglathpileser III and Ashurbanipal (8th to 7th centuries BC) depicting their campaigns against the Arabs, camels bear two men, a driver, and a warrior armed with a bow.

In David's Israelite army there appears to have been some form of cavalry, with riders

A relief of horses' heads (from Sargon's palace in Khorsabad).

mounted on mules (2 Sm 13:29; 18:9). Mules were better suited to battle in hill country than were horses. Not until Solomon did cavalry units of horsemen take their place in the defense of Israel (2 Chr 1:14,16,17).

In Iron Age II attention was directed to the problems of the mounted archer who needed both hands for discharging his weapon. In the reliefs of Ashurnasirpal cavalry archers move in teams of two. One horseman is armed with a bow; his partner at his side holds a shield and the reins of both horses. That plan of action provided a greater measure of personal protection for the warrior and greater control of his horse. A pair of horsemen frequently operated near a chariot. The pictorial detail recalls a remark of King Jehu to his military aid Bidkar, reminding him how they had ridden side by side behind Ahab on the field of battle (2 Kgs 9:25). When fording a stream or passing through a gully the archer alone remained mounted. The second horseman is shown dismounted in order to test the path ahead.

The importance of cavalry units in the Assyrian army can be gauged from a taunt offered by one of Sennacherib's generals to a truce delegation sent by Hezekiah (2 Kgs 18:23), which suggests that Judah possessed no mounted soldiers by the end of the 8th century BC. The Assyrian cavalry, however, was so large that the loss of 2,000 horses would not significantly alter the balance of power.

During the Persian period great attention was devoted to the development of the cavalry horse. The horse of Europe and Asia, an unattractive animal with a bad temper, had to be controlled with a bit. A different species, the so-called Arab or "blood" horse, was slightly built with small joints, a fine head, and a temper so gentle that it could be controlled with a nose band only. The cavalry horse of the Persians, and later of the Greeks and Romans, came from crossbreeding such Libyan horses with the Asian or European stock.

The powerful Persian military machine was based on highly trained cavalry units supported by infantry. Yet not until the military reforms ascribed to Philip II, father of Alexander the Great (356–323 BC), did cavalry become an integral part of Macedonian armies. Philip deployed his infantry in a battle array called the phalanx, a close-order arrangement of men and weapons, behind which cavalry were used to protect the vulnerable flanks and rear. In his battles against the Persians, Alexander used crack cavalry units from Thessaly and Macedonia to deliver the main thrust of his attack, exploiting charges from the flanks. His conquests made the phalanx, with its cavalry support, a primary instrument of Hellenistic strategy for the next 200 years.

In the eastern Punjab region of India the Macedonians fought a desperate battle against 200 war elephants commanded by the rajah Porus. Alexander recognized the elephant's usefulness in combat, and although he never used them in battle himself, his successors did. Indian elephants became a Seleucid (Syrian) monopoly, but Ptolemy II in Egypt and the Phoenicians in Carthage imported Indian trainers to break in African elephants as an auxiliary support to their armies. The Romans first encountered elephants (which they called "Lucanian oxen") when the Macedonian Pyrrhus invaded Italy (280–275 BC), but the Romans seldom used them in battle.

The Seleucid king Antiochus Eupator used 32 war elephants against the guerrilla army of Judas Maccabeus and his brothers in a battle near Beth-zechariah to the south of Judea (1 Mc 6:30,34–46). The Syrians "distributed the beasts among the phalanxes; with each elephant they stationed a thousand men armed with coats of mail and with brass helmets on their heads" (v 35) plus 500 picked horsemen. On each elephant was a wooden tower fastened by a special harness, with "four armed men who fought from there, and also its Indian driver" (v 37). Eleazar, Judas' younger brother, thinking the Syrian king was mounted on the largest animal, fought his way to it and killed it with his spear from underneath, dying when the elephant fell on him. The out-

numbered Jewish army, all foot soldiers, then fled from the battlefield (1 Mc 6:43–47).

Firepower: Personal Weapons. The armory of a military commander in antiquity consisted of a variety of offensive weapons designed to engage the enemy at long, medium, and short range. The bow and the sling were the principal weapons developed for long-range firepower; the javelin and the spear for medium-range; the sword, the ax, and the mace for short-range.

Bow. Early bows were fashioned from one piece of seasoned wood. No single type of bow wood, however, could provide the lightness, toughness, and elasticity required. Gradually the idea was conceived of combining several natural materials—wood, sections of animal horn, animal tendons and sinews, and glue—in the construction of a bow to meet all the demands placed on it. The resulting composite bow became a weapon of supreme importance. The composite bow gave the Akkadians a decisive edge over the Sumerians in wars for control of Mesopotamia in the 3rd millennium BC. On his victory monument erected at Susa the Akkadian king Naram-Sin (23rd century BC) provided the first representation of the composite bow.

Composite structure gave a bow lightness, strength, and elasticity. Use of a double-convex form gave increased range and power of penetration.

The bowstring was made from bindweed, natural cord, hide, or the intestines of oxen or camels. The bow was strung by hand (2 Kgs 13:16), usually bending it with the foot, which required considerable strength (cf. 2 Sm 22:35; Jer 51:3). That may explain why archers were known as "bow treaders" or as those who "tread a bow."

Improvements in bow construction were matched by comparable advances in the development of the arrow. The form of the arrowhead was a response to the enemy's defense and armor. In the Late Bronze period, for example, a battle arrowhead was generally of bronze and was thick in the middle, tapering to a spine. Its shape was dictated by the fact that the coats of mail in widespread use at the time could be penetrated only by a spined or ribbed arrowhead. The arrow shaft was usually made from reed, a material that combined strength with pliability. Well-preserved reed arrows from the period have been found in Egypt. The word for arrow in the excavated Nuzi tablets is the same word as "reed." Arrows were usually about 30 inches long and were winged with three rows of feathers. Arrow feathers were aptly designated by the Persians as "messengers of death."

Wall-paintings from the period of the Middle Kingdom in Egypt show Egyptian archers carrying their arrows in bundles, which they placed at the foot of the bow when in position. Sometime during the period of the OT patriarchs (Middle Bronze Age) the quiver (case for arrows) was introduced into Egypt from Syria and Palestine. Documents from Nuzi indicate that a quiver was capable of holding 20 to 30 arrows. Constructed of lightweight material, it was carried on the back of a bowman or over his shoulder, leaving both hands free to operate the bow.

The composite bow required technical skill in working with several types of material. The Hyksos, for example, developed bows made with laminated bone, bronze strips, horn, or ivory to increase their elasticity and penetrating power. To keep such a valuable weapon from being damaged by weather or other hazards, protective coverings were devised. Pictorial representations from the Late Bronze Age show bow cases fastened to the side of a chariot in which the bow was kept when not in use.

Sling. Complementing the bow was the sling, devised originally by shepherds to drive off animals molesting their flocks (cf. 1 Sm 17:40). It gradually assumed importance as a weapon of war, its supreme advantage being simple construction. Not only did a sling require little technical skill to produce, but the stones used as projectiles were readily available on the ground. In the hands of a trained slinger a missile could be hurled as far as 600 feet in any terrain. The sling's capacity for high-angled fire up a steep slope was particularly important in an assault on a fortified city. Its principal disadvantage was that strenuous training and experience were required to achieve accuracy in its operation (cf. Jgs 20:16).

A sling was commonly made from two leather thongs, to which were attached a pocket for holding the stone. With the thongs pulled taut the pocket became a bag. The slinger held his arms above his head, the bag in his left hand and the ends of the taut thongs in his right hand. After swinging the sling several times around his head with great force to give it momentum, he suddenly released the end of one of the thongs to discharge the missile. Lead pellets as well as smooth stones were used as projectiles. They were carried in a bag or were piled conveniently at the slinger's feet.

The importance of the sling as a long-range weapon is evident in the familiar account of David's encounter with the Philistine champion, Goliath of Gath (1 Sm 17:40–51). At that time the Philistines possessed many advanced types of weapons, but the bow was not among them. They depended on medium-range weapons like the javelin and short-range weapons like the sword (cf. 1 Sm 17:4–7,45,51). The sling gave David an advantage in range that was decisive against Goliath's superior weapons and armor (1 Sm 17:48,49).

Javelin and Spear. Two weapons employed for medium-distance warfare were similar in appearance but different in length and operation. The javelin, generally lighter and shorter than the spear, was designed for throwing. It was like a large arrow which was hurled by the hand. Sumerian charioteers of the 3rd millennium BC were armed with several javelins, carried like arrows in a quiver attached to the body of the chariot. Because of its lightness and size a javelin could be carried across a soldier's back when not in use (1 Sm 17:6). Javelin heads were designed for penetration and altered in shape and material as enemy armor became more effective. A head fashioned with sharp hooks or barbs was difficult and painful to extract from a wound. Subsequently javelin shafts were fitted with a metal point at the butt end so the weapon could be stuck in the ground when not in use. The metal tip was carefully weighted and designed to add balance and speed to the weapon's propulsion.

In the period of the judges and early Israelite kings Aegean warriors devised a means to increase the distance a javelin could be thrown. A cord with a loop on the end was added to the shaft, giving it the appearance of a weaver's leash rod. The cord was wound around the shaft with the loop retained by the hurler's fingers and would unwind swiftly as the javelin was thrown. The resultant spin provided a greater distance and a steadier course of flight. The biblical writer had such a device in mind when he compared the shaft of Goliath's javelin to a weaver's beam (1 Sm 17:7; 2 Sm 21:19). That type of javelin was unknown previously in Israel, so there was no name for it in Hebrew. A weaver's beam is the leash rod of a loom, a piece of wood to which loops or leashes of cord are tied which separate the threads of the warp to allow passage to the threads of the woof.

The dart was a lighter and smaller missile than the javelin, but little is known about it. It was evidently a sharp-pointed weapon like an arrow designed for hurling or thrusting (2 Sm 18:14).

The spear was similar in appearance to the javelin but was larger, heavier, and designed primarily as a thrusting weapon (cf. Nm 25:7,8). The oldest military monuments known indicate that the spear was already well developed. On the Egyptian hunter's slate palette and on the black granite stele from Warka

(3000? BC), the warrior's personal weapon is a long staff tipped with a leaf-shaped blade with a sharp spine. Throughout the 3rd millennium BC the spear was standard equipment for heavy-armed infantry and the most effective weapon for both chariot and infantry charges. Excavations have shown that the spear was the common weapon of the seminomadic tribes who began pouring into Palestine from the north in the Middle Bronze Age. Their spearheads were attached to the shaft by a voluted tang, a device characteristic of military weapons in Mesopotamia and Anatolia during that period. It is possible that Abraham's journey to Canaan was part of that migratory movement and that the weapons with which he equipped the members of his household included that type of spear (cf. Gn 14:14,15).

Another characteristic of spears in that early period was a metal tip attached to the butt of the shaft, enabling a spear to be stuck upright in the ground when not in use. That feature persisted into later periods and is mentioned specifically in reference to Saul's spear, which was stuck in the ground by his head while he slept (1 Sm 26:7). Occasionally the metal tip functioned as a thrusting weapon in its own right, as is evident in the account of the slaying of Asahel (2 Sm 2:23).

In the Middle Bronze period Egyptian chariots were not equipped with spears, but wall-paintings show spears as standard equipment in the chariots of opposing armies. The spear was kept in a special pipelike socket at the rear of the carriage. That Hittite innovation became characteristic of the chariot units of the Asiatic tribes. The spear was the personal weapon of the charioteer, who at times was pressed into service as an infantryman.

Throughout the Late Bronze Age illustrated monuments depict special units of spearmen carrying spears and shields. In an assault on enemy ranks they provided the main thrust of the phalanx. The spear was equally important in defense of a fortified city. Reliefs show defenders on the ramparts using spears against attacking troops climbing assault ladders.

Sword. One of the earliest objects made of iron was the sword. Already in the 3rd millennium BC Anatolian armorers had begun to fashion straight, double-edged blades for close-contact combat. The first iron blades were very short and were similar to daggers in appearance, being designed for stabbing. The blade had to be small because the process for making hard iron had not yet been discovered. A long, tough blade that would not break or bend on impact could be made only from hard iron. From Anatolia the knowledge of iron eventually spread to Syria, Palestine, and

Egypt, but not until some 1,200 years later. Eventually, after discovery of a process by which hard metals could be forged, the sword became the principal weapon in hand-to-hand fighting.

Swords were designed for either stabbing or striking. The stabbing sword developed as a long straight blade, tapered toward the point for piercing the body. Its tapered edges were sharpened so that it could also serve as a cutting instrument. The striking sword, on the other hand, had only one sharp edge, with the thickest part of the blade not along the center but along its blunt edge. Such a sword was often curved, sometimes to a degree that gave it the appearance of a sickle, but with the outer, convex edge sharpened as the cutting blade. The earliest type of "sickle sword" appeared in the second half of the 3rd millennium BC. Both the hilt, or handle, and the blade were fashioned from a single bar of metal. In the Middle Bronze Age the curved striking sword functioned essentially as an ax, with a comparatively long hilt and short blade.

That type of sword completely disappeared in the Late Bronze Age because it proved ineffective against the widespread use of the helmet and armor. In its place appeared a new design with the curved blade equal in length to the hilt and sometimes longer. It provided a cutting weapon in chariot fighting and against an enemy who possessed no armor. Widespread use of such long-bladed swords at that time explains the phrase repeatedly used in the Bible to describe Joshua's conquests of the Canaanites: "he smote them with the edge of the sword" (e.g., Jos 8:24; 10:28,30,32,35,37,39). That expression would be inappropriate for the action of a short, straight, narrow sword designed as a thrusting weapon. A fine specimen of curved sword was found at Gezer in Palestine in the tomb of a nobleman, dating to the first half of the 14th century BC. The same type of blade is also depicted on a late 13th-century BC ivory carving from Megiddo.

During those centuries advances made in the technology of forging iron were reflected in the development of the straight sword as well. The Sea Peoples, among whom were the Philistines, specialized in short-range arms. As early as the 13th century BC they began to make the straight blade more effective than the curved sickle-type sword.

The difference in the two types explains the success of Ehud's exploit in slaying Eglon, king of the Moabites (Jgs 3:15–30). Using a short-bladed, inconspicuous dagger, Ehud achieved his objective neatly and with little effort. He was able to enter the king's chamber without the guards detecting that he was armed, having concealed his straight two-edged sword of the Philistine type under his garments, fastened to his right thigh instead of the customary left (Jgs 3:16).

By the time of Saul the Philistines had used their technology to establish themselves as city-dwellers and the dominant military presence in the land. Their military superiority was based on the chariot and on an infantry equipped with personal armaments of high quality. They carefully retained the forging of hard metal under their own supervision and kept the Israelites from developing forges of their own (cf. 1 Sm 13:19,20,22). Not until that situation was altered could the balance of power pass from the Philistines to Israel.

Mace and Ax. The mace and the ax, developed as alternatives to the sword before hard metal could be forged, were designed for hand-to-hand fighting. They consisted of a comparatively short wooden handle, one end of which was fitted with a lethal head made of stone or metal. The weapons were swung like a hammer to deliver a striking blow. The critical detail was the secure fastening of the head to the handle to prevent its flying off when swung or breaking off when struck. The handle of both the mace and the ax was widened at the point of the grip, tapering toward the head, to prevent the weapon from slipping from the hand when swung. Such weapons were carried in the hand or attached to the wrist with a loop. The mace was designed to batter and smash, the ax to pierce and cut.

The mace was a very primitive weapon. The hieroglyphic sign for the verb "to fight" represents hands holding a mace and a medium-size shield. During the Chalcolithic and the first half of the Early Bronze periods (3500–2500 BC) the mace was the primary weapon for personal combat. Because the helmet had not yet made its appearance, the striking power of the mace was devastating. Ancient maceheads from that period have been found in Palestine in excavations near Beersheba and near En-gedi. Such archaeological finds demonstrate that the head, then usually of stone, was the subject of considerable experimentation. Some were shaped like a pear, others like an apple, still others like a saucer. Each type had advantages and drawbacks. With advances in defensive armor such as the helmet, the mace virtually disappeared from the battlefield. Yet long after the mace had become obsolete as a personal weapon, it continued to serve as a symbol of sovereign authority for the king or deity (cf. Ps 2:9).

Complex technical problems taxed the ingenuity of armorers in the production of the ax. The blade had to be fixed securely to the handle. The cutting ax had a short blade and a wide edge. It was an effective weapon against an enemy unprotected by armor. It was also used for tearing down the wall of a besieged city, as in the wall-painting at Saqqarah (23rd century BC). But against armor the cutting ax was ineffective. Deeper power of penetration was achieved with the piercing ax, which had a long, narrow blade ending in a short, sharp edge. Appearance of that type of ax among the Sumerians coincides with the first evidence for a high-quality metal helmet. Such a helmet could be rendered ineffective by a piercing ax swung with great force. That demanded very firm attachment of the handle to the blade. By constructing a pipelike socket into the blade itself, Sumerian armorers succeeded in producing an ax capable of penetrating the defenses of the enemy. Among the items recovered in a remarkable find of 450 copper objects at Nahal Mishmar, near En-gedi in the Judean wilderness, were a large number of socketed piercing axes forged from copper. They belong to the Chalcolithic period (3100? BC).

By the 3rd millennium BC armorers had succeeded in producing the prototype of every ax used in all subsequent periods up to the end of the Iron Age. Both tang-type and socket-type heads were developed within the first half of the 3rd millennium BC, and from that period come both the piercing ax and the cutting ax. In Sumer the ax was the personal weapon both of the spear-carrying infantry and of charioteers. So effective was the socket-type piercing ax that it spread from Mesopotamia to Anatolia, Syria, and Palestine. For some reason it did not reach Egypt, where wall-paintings show the tang-type of cutting ax as the preferred weapon of Egyptian fighters.

Security: Personal Protection. Without provision for personal protection of the individual soldier on the battlefield, the mobility and firepower of an army could be seriously compromised.

Shield. Designed to provide a barrier between the body of a soldier and the weapon of his foe, the shield was one of the oldest means of security devised. In the 3rd millennium BC the celebrated Stele of Vultures from Telloh in Mesopotamia depicts a phalanx of 6 rows of heavily armed soldiers, each of whom carries a large rectangular shield that covers the body from neck to ankles. Other shapes were also used for ancient shields. The long shield of the Sumerians served the needs of soldiers who fought without armor and who required maximum body coverage. In the Late Bronze Age, when significant advances had been made in the construction of body armor, the shield became considerably smaller. Assyrian war reliefs provide a wealth of detail for Iron Age II. They indicate the sustained attention the Assyrians devoted to the kind of shield with which to equip their spearmen. In Ashurbanipal's army, for example, in addition to a small round shield, spearmen were provided large curved shields with rounded tops which offered protection to the whole body. The large shields were constructed of plaited twigs to achieve a relatively lightweight protective device. In Tiglath-pileser's army, archers were issued huge shields over 6 feet tall, with a right-angled top.

Shields made of bronze or copper, although very heavy, provided excellent protection. A lighter type had a frame fashioned from wood or wickerwork, over which leather was stretched. Such shields were rubbed with oil to preserve them from the ravages of weather (cf. Is 21:5). Some types of shields were reinforced with a heavy boss at the center to give added protection (cf. Jb 15:26).

In the time of the judges and the early Israelite kings, persons of rank were frequently protected by a very large shield. It was carried by a special shield bearer who remained constantly at the unprotected right side of the warrior to whom he was assigned as a bodyguard (cf. Jgs 9:54; 1 Sm 14:1; 17:7; 2 Sm 18:15). The right side of an armed combatant was unprotected because he carried his weapons in his right hand and his shield in his left. The shield bearer therefore had to stand by his master's vulnerable right side to protect him (1 Sm 17:41; cf. Ps 16:8). In that period the shield was ordinarily anointed as part of the consecration of an Israelite warrior and his weapons for battle (cf. 2 Sm 1:21).

Armor. Personal armor protected the body of a combatant from injury while freeing his hands to use his weapons. The earliest type of body armor formed a substitute for the long shield. It consisted of a full-length tunic made from leather or some tough fiber. It was relatively simple to produce, was light enough to permit full mobility, and offered a measure of protection to the chest, abdomen, back, thighs, and legs. So equipped, a soldier required only a short shield to protect his arms and face.

Even armor failed to provide enough security to archers and charioteers, who had to have both hands free. The Hittites, therefore, assigned a special shield bearer to each bowman and charioteer, which meant the addition of a third man to a chariot crew (driver, warrior, shield bearer), placing a heavy strain on the light vehicle. It also meant a large number of men assigned to a defensive rather than offensive role. A more adequate means of personal security for the chariot corps and archers was clearly necessary.

In the Late Bronze period a solution was

Statue showing armor (from the museum in Corinth).

found in the coat of mail. It consisted of hundreds of small pieces of overlapping metal joined together like fish scales and sewed to the surface of a cloth or leather tunic. The method of attaching the scales to the fabric is known from armor found in Nuzi, Egypt, Palestine, and Syria. Each scale was punctured with a series of tiny holes—usually three at the top, two at the bottom, and two at one side—to permit the passage of strong thread, much as a button is sewn to a garment by hand. Written documents from Nuzi state that from 400 to 600 large scales and several hundred smaller scales went into the production of a single coat. Smaller scales and narrower rows were used where greater flexibility was needed, as at the throat and neck. The resulting garment was relatively flexible, affording freedom of movement, while the hard metal scales gave far greater personal protection than leather or fiber could provide. The coat of mail worn by the Philistine Goliath, supplemented by bronze greaves (shin armor) to protect his legs (1 Sm 17:5,6), was typical of the Aegean warrior.

The coat of mail had its drawbacks, however. Its manufacture demanded considerable technical skill and was costly. In the period of the early monarchy only King Saul and Prince Jonathan were equipped with body armor. Not even the wealthiest nations could issue scale armor to every soldier. High priorities were assigned to charioteers and archers. The weight of scale armor could hamper movement, as David discovered when he was invested with the body armor of Saul (1 Sm 17:38,39). Finally, even scale armor had points of weakness, at the joint of the sleeve to the tunic body and between the scales. This defect accounted for the mortal wound Ahab received on the field of battle at Ramoth-gilead (1 Kgs 22:34).

Helmet. Since the greatest point of vulnerability for a soldier in combat was his head, concern for some form of protective helmet can be traced as far back as the end of the 4th millennium BC. The Sumerians of the early dynastic period (3100 BC) had already developed a metal helmet. It is the most characteristic identifying feature of the Sumerian soldier in the Standard of Ur, the Stele of Vultures, and the inlaid panels of Mari. That helmet was slightly pointed and covered both the ears and the back of the neck. Modified forms were found in the excavations at Ur, covering the skulls of buried soldiers. Such metal helmets replaced earlier forms that were little more than skullcaps made of leather or tough fibers.

In subsequent periods both design and construction were modified, but because of the climate in the Near East no attempt was made to develop a helmet that covered the face. In

A gold helmet found at Ur in the tomb of Meskalamdug. The helmet was held in place by means of laces from a quilted cap that was worn underneath.

the Late Bronze Age a collar made of scales was added to the helmet, closing the gap between the original helmet and the coat of mail. Armorers continued to experiment with helmet shapes, sometimes for greater protection for the wearer, at other times for better identification. When troops were equipped with helmets especially shaped or decorated, field commanders could identify the position of each unit at any given time.

Bronze helmets were worn both by Goliath and by Saul (1 Sm 17:5,38). Although the helmet was standard equipment for the heavily-armed infantry of foreign armies for centuries, it does not seem to have been a common possession of soldiers in the Israelite army during the period of the united monarchy. Among military reforms introduced by King Uzziah in the 9th century BC was provision of helmets for the army of the southern kingdom of Judah (2 Chr 26:14).

Methods of Warfare. *Battle in Open Terrain: Standard Combat.* The earliest illustrations of warfare in open terrain are found in Mesopotamia in the Middle Bronze period (3rd millennium BC). The two most important monuments are the Standard of Ur and the Stele of Vultures, celebrating the military superiority of the Sumerians. Both are rich in content and detail, and indicate that in open battle chariots and infantry were coordinated in close harmony. Chariot units led the initial charge, confusing, scattering, and trampling the enemy by storming through their ranks. Warriors attached to the chariot corps used javelins to wound and kill. In the wake of the chariot charge the infantry followed from the flanks or center, prepared to engage the enemy with piercing axes and spears and organized as a deep phalanx. Each phalanx consisted of a column of 6 files, with 11 men in each file (probably 10 men plus an officer). The formation advanced under the protection of large rectangular shields, with spears thrust forward in horizontal position. On a right or left turn order the soldiers presented themselves for battle as a phalanx six ranks deep.

To the Sumerians' basic battle strategy the Akkadians contributed a long-range archery unit, which operated from the rear and flanks, and gave them superior firepower.

Very early material indicates that Middle Bronze Age armies were organized into units that advanced in disciplined order. A wooden model of spear-carrying Nubian archers from Egypt (2000? BC) shows a column of four 10-man files organized for a march. Written documents tend to confirm that the basic unit, the section, consisted of 10 men. In the contemporary Tale of Sinuhe the writer speaks of the size of the palace guard: "When the day had dawned, very early, they came and summoned me, ten men coming and ten men going, to usher me into the palace." Other written records provide detail on the size of armies and of units thrown into combat, indicating that standard combat entailed large-scale warfare. The Mari documents from the 18th century BC speak of militia units composed of 10,000 soldiers. They also mention smaller units containing 3,000, 2,000, 1,000, 600, and 100 men. The main assault unit evidently consisted of 300 men, representing 3 companies of 100 men each.

Cavalry units were introduced at the close of the 2nd millennium BC and the beginning of the 1st. The cavalry charge provided an additional shock force to the great armies, and the cavalry's mobility permitted concentration of firepower at decisive points. When the Assyrians coordinated their infantry, cavalry, and chariot corps into a powerful battle machine, smaller neighboring nations were more and more compelled to retreat behind their fortifications. They could not hope to engage the massive Assyrian army in standard combat in open terrain. No period is richer in illustrated monuments than Iron Age II; the Assyrian war reliefs present detailed illustrations of their conquests and the size of fortified cities. The few scenes depicting standard combat in open terrain show chariots charging from all directions and engaging the enemy at all stages of a battle. Other formations carry out mopping-up operations, finishing off pockets of enemy resistance remaining after the chariot charge.

The Assyrians were skilled in adapting to the demands of hostile terrain, such as hills, woods, and swamps. The finest monumental example of this occurs in a relief from the palace of Sennacherib (705–681 BC), commemorating his victory over an enemy who dwelt in the marshlands of southern Mesopotamia. On that occasion his infantry became an amphibious force, charging into the swamps in light boats, maneuvering among the reeds where the enemy was concealed, and burning them in their hiding places.

The Assyrian army also displayed great ingenuity and technical skill in surmounting natural obstacles such as rivers. As early as the reign of Ashurnasirpal a graphic scene depicts the crossing of a very wide river by the chariot corps, which required the transport of heavy gear, animals, and troops. The chariots were loaded on large boats propelled by oarsmen and pulled by an advance party on the opposite bank. The horses, attached to a rope held by a groom in the boat, swam behind the boats. The troops swam across the river, supported by inflated goatskins prepared in advance for the purpose. Shields and weapons were carried on their backs to prevent them from being damaged by the water. Such complicated and dangerous procedures were usually avoided. For crossing smaller streams the Assyrian engineers constructed pontoon bridges by strapping boats together and placing planking across the gunwales.

The factor of terrain was always very important. It became crucial in the battle of Samaria, an attack by Ben-hadad, king of Aram (Syria), on Ahab, king of Israel (1 Kgs 20). One of the most important roads linking Syria to Samaria passed through the valley of Succoth. Running south from Syria, it crossed the Jordan River near Admah (not far from Succoth) and then entered immediately the Wadi Fara, whose head is in the Samarian hills. The road then meandered up a hilly area until it reached the city of Samaria. Ben-hadad and a coalition of 32 allied kings marched down that road at the head of a huge army supported by chariots and cavalry, camping in the protected valley of Succoth (1 Kgs 20:12,16). Ben-hadad then dispatched envoys to the various kings on both sides of the Jordan, demanding their submission. When Ahab refused the humiliating terms imposed by the Syrians, Ben-hadad ordered his army to march on Samaria and besiege it.

Anticipating Ben-hadad's march through the narrow Wadi Fara, Ahab determined not to allow the Syrians to reach the outskirts of Samaria to set up their siege. He ordered 7,000 of his men to counterattack the advancing column while the chariot corps was still moving up the narrow valley. Syrian scouts saw Israel's forces and notified Ben-hadad, who was too drunk to perceive the danger of his position. With a comparatively small force familiar with the terrain, Ahab was able to decimate the advancing column, which scattered in panic and retreated to Succoth. Ben-hadad, recognizing the enormity of the defeat his forces had sustained, fled on horseback (1 Kgs 20:20).

The following year the Syrians chose to fight on level ground by approaching Samaria from the north rather than from the east. Ahab halted the enemy at a narrow pass near Aphek, and after seven days joined battle (1 Kgs 20:29). The Syrians tried to storm the pass but again were trapped, and 100,000 soldiers were killed. The rest fled to Aphek, but were captured along with Ben-hadad.

In standard combat on open terrain it later became conventional to place the best troops on the right side of the line. A Greek commander, Epaminondas (d. 362 BC), introduced the variant of a slanting attack by a strengthened left wing, taking the Spartan army completely by surprise. Philip of Macedon and his son Alexander continued to surprise their enemies with variations on a plan of attack based on the phalanx.

The earliest Roman battle order was probably the phalanx. In the 4th century BC the manipular system was designed for combat on open terrain to exploit the javelin and two-edged broadsword. Maniples (units of 200 men) were arranged so that the units in the rear lines covered gaps in the lines in front of them.

Subsequent experimentation led to more flexible use of the system, taking into account the topographical conditions of the terrain. Julius Caesar in particular exploited the possibilities of flank attacks and of holding troops in reserve for commitment to battle at a decisive moment. Archers and slingers were used increasingly in terrain unsuited to open-order fighting. Roman warfare, thus liberated from stereotyped theories, could rely for its success on the intense discipline of its soldiers.

Battle in Open Terrain: The Duel. During certain periods in the ancient Near East the duel presented an alternative to standard combat. The duel was a contest between two champions who represented the contending forces. The two armies would agree in advance to abide by the outcome of the fight. The duel was meant to avoid the heavy casualties of full-scale warfare. The earliest detailed written account of this unique form of warfare occurs in the Tale of Sinuhe. A chamberlain in the royal court of the 12th Dynasty, Sinuhe voluntarily went into exile and traveled to northern Palestine and Syria, where he lived among Semitic tribes. There he was challenged to a duel by a local champion whom he defeated and whose goods he then plundered.

The pattern of that early account occurs in later reports of the duel: prior negotiation, combat, and the result. From that same period come the Beni Hasan wall-paintings in Egypt, where in a series of three rows of panels the duel assumes the form of wrestling. A vase, dated in the 18th century BC, found at Tell el Far'ah in northern Palestine, depicts 2 Canaanite warriors engaged in a duel, with swords as their weapons. Those converging pieces of evidence come from the first half of the Middle Bronze Age.

Although the duel was common among other armies in subsequent periods, it was evidently unknown to Israel before the encounter between David and Goliath (1 Sm 17). The Philistine army had penetrated Judah as far as Socoh, and were arrayed on one hill. Drawn up against them on an opposite hill was the army of Saul. The valley of Elah separated the 2 camps (vv 1,2). The Israelites were challenged daily by the Philistine champion, Goli-

ath, who proposed that the battle be decided through combat between two warriors. David accepted his proposal; but when he killed Goliath, the Philistines fled, unwilling to honor the terms of the prior agreement. The Israelite army then entered the contest, pursuing the Philistines and inflicting heavy casualties (vv 50–52).

In the period immediately following the death of Saul, rivalry between Saul's and David's followers became so intense that the two armies met at Gibeon. Rather than commit his army to battle, Saul's commander-in-chief, Abner, proposed that the issue be settled by a series of duels between picked men of valor representing the two royal households (2 Sm 2:14,15). Abner's proposal and the consent by Joab, David's commander-in-chief, constituted the prior agreement. Then the contest began. Facing each other across the pool at Gibeon were the most valiant professional soldiers in the two armies. Grasping the head of one's adversary with one hand and thrusting a short sword into his side with the other was an accepted tactic in such encounters (2 Sm 2:16). That stance is depicted on a relief from the palace of Kapara in Mesopotamia from the same period (10th century BC). Because the series of duels was indecisive, there was no alternative but to commit both armies to the serious battle which ensued (2 Sm 2:17).

Assaults on Fortified Cities. Most cities in the ancient Near East were located at sites that could be defended against attack and that possessed economic advantages. In the Middle Bronze and Late Bronze periods the average size of cities in Palestine, Syria, Anatolia, and Mesopotamia was between 5 and 10 acres, although a number of principal cities covered a much larger area, sometimes extending to hundreds of acres. The population of cities can be estimated by the rule of thumb that there were approximately 240 inhabitants to an urban acre. Thus the population of most ancient Near Eastern cities ranged from 1,000 to 3,000 persons, with a few cities having up to 5,000 or 10,000. About 1 person out of 4 in the general population was enlisted to defend the city, giving a fighting force of about 300 men in the smaller cities, of perhaps 2,000 in medium-size cities. In the defense system of an ancient city primary attention was directed to the walls and subsidiary fortifications, to an inner citadel, and to the supply of water and grain. Fortifications were designed to deny the enemy two important advantages in assault: mobility and firepower. When fortifications could not take advantage of naturally defensive terrain, artificial barriers had to be erected to provide the necessary security.

An assault on a fortified city presented opposite problems for attacker and defender. The actions of one were a direct response to the actions of the other. Systems of defense were intended to thwart methods of attack, which in turn were designed to penetrate systems of defense.

There were five possible ways of conquering a fortified city: penetration from above the fortifications; direct penetration through the fortifications; penetration from below the fortifications; siege; and penetration by ruse. On many occasions a combination of two or more methods was necessary to breach the defensive network.

The biblical narrative of the conquest of Shechem by Abimelech (Jgs 9) gives an account of an assault on a fortified city in the period of the judges (Iron Age I). When the people of Shechem and their allies rebelled against Abimelech, he retaliated by attacking the city, advancing his army of mercenaries by night and launching an assault from ambush positions at dawn (Jgs 9:32–35). The men of Shechem engaged in open battle outside the city gates but were forced to retreat behind the security of the city walls. The next day Abimelech directed his assault against the city itself. Dividing his forces into 3 groups, he assumed direct command of 1, which he committed to an attack on the city gates at the decisive moment of battle (Jgs 9:43,44). The gate was breached and the main walls seized, but the city's surviving defenders fled to an inner citadel, the temple of Baal-berith.

Many reliefs depict groups of soldiers defending an inner citadel after a city's wall was breached. Archaeological excavations at Shechem confirm that its temple, like those in other Canaanite cities, was built in the form of a fortified tower, supported by stout bastions near the entrance. The tower of Shechem was thus strongly fortified and occupied only a small area, enabling its defenders to concentrate their firepower on Abimelech's troops. Since it could not be taken by storm, Abimelech ordered his soldiers to use their battle axes to cut brushwood, which was piled against the stronghold and set on fire (Jgs 9:48,49). All of the defenders within the tower died.

An assault on an inner citadel was always a hazardous undertaking for an attacking army, as shown in the sequel to the capture of Shechem's tower. Abimelech turned his attention next to the city of Thebez and followed the same plan of assault that had proved successful at Shechem. But as he was preparing to burn the door of the tower to which the defenders had fled, his skull was crushed by a piece of millstone dropped on him by a woman (Jgs 9:50–53). The incident was remembered and became proverbial for the danger of approaching too closely the walls of a fortified tower (2 Sm 11:19–21).

In the subsequent period (Iron II) the military capability of the powerful Assyrian and Egyptian armies left the smaller kingdoms in Syria and Palestine no alternative but to find a measure of security behind city fortifications. Methods of fortification were vastly improved in that period, but advances were also made in the art of warfare on fortified cities. The Assyrians became adept at exploiting all the military possibilities open to them in an assault on a fortified city. A relief from the palace of Ashurnasirpal II (885–860 BC) at Nimrud provides a comprehensive siege scene with several operations being carried on simultaneously. Archers direct steady fire against defenders on the wall. Battering rams operate against the high walls. The low outer wall is being demolished by sappers using pikes and spears to dislodge the bricks. Other troops engage in a tunneling operation beneath the walls. Storming parties mount scaling ladders set up against the ramparts. Another party attempts to burn down the doors with torches. Combining so many operations applied constant pressure on the defenders to anticipate where their defenses might be breached.

Nevertheless, the Assyrians found the fortifications in Judah and Israel so strong and the fighting spirit of the defenders so resilient that they gave particular emphasis in their war reliefs to the conquest of those cities. Samaria, capital of the northern kingdom of Israel, was captured only after a three-year siege. Every Assyrian attempt to penetrate the defenses of Jerusalem, the Judean capital, failed. Its impregnability at that time gave the inhabitants a false sense of security that proved disastrous when the city was later subjected to prolonged siege by the Babylonians.

Communications and Intelligence. From the patriarchal period (Middle Bronze Age) we have detailed written information on the use of communications systems in wartime. The documents from Mari on the Euphrates provide evidence for a well-developed communications system based on signaling. Signals were flashed by torches or firebrands at night in accordance with a prearranged code. The system was widely used in Mesopotamia and elsewhere to call for immediate help when a city was under attack.

In the Late Bronze period horsemen were sometimes employed for isolated communication functions. In one of the Amarna tablets the king of Byblos complains to the pharaoh that "the messenger of the king of Acco is more heeded than my messenger, because a horse was given to him." Such horsemen are occasionally represented in Egyptian wall-paintings of the 19th Dynasty. In a scene from the battle of Kadesh (2nd half of the 14th century BC), where Egypt was pitted against a Hittite coalition, the artist depicted a mounted messenger armed with a bow.

Intelligence services played a role in planning and executing military operations. The importance of intelligence and the use of spies or scouts is stressed in the biblical accounts of the conquest of the land of Canaan. Before entering the land, Moses sent men on an espionage mission. He instructed them to gather information on the topography of the land, to observe the relative strength of its inhabitants, to determine whether the land was fertile, to survey the cities and see if they were fortified, and to report on the character of the land—whether it was capable of sustaining a large population (Nm 13:17–20).

Tactical intelligence was very important. Joshua dispatched spies to Jericho and to Ai before beginning military operations against them (Jos 2:1; 7:2). The reports he received about the offensive spirit and strength of the Canaanites enabled him to formulate an attack plan. In the period of the judges the conquest of Bethel (Jg 1:22–26) was due directly to intelligence gathered by a reconnaissance patrol. The tribes of Joseph sent out scouts to keep the city under observation. It was strongly fortified and seemed impregnable. The scouts captured a man who emerged from the city—presumably not through the main gate, which was shut tight, but through a concealed postern or tunnel. In exchange for his own life and the safety of his family he disclosed the location of the passage leading beneath the walls. The city was penetrated through the postern and captured. In later periods good intelligence often enabled small forces to employ ambush as a regular means of warfare.

Attack and Penetration: The Breach. Direct penetration through the fortifications of an ancient city meant breaching the gate or the main walls by using hammers, axes, pikes, spears, swords, or a battering ram. Illustrated monuments and written documents indicate that early in the Middle Bronze period fortified cities were being attacked with battering rams. The earliest known illustration of a ram appears in a siege scene in the wall-paintings from Beni Hasan (20th century BC). The ram pictured is a relatively simple device, consisting of a hutlike structure with a slightly pointed roof, which could be moved near a fortress with the help of two parallel crossbars. The structure provided cover for two or three soldiers who operated by hand a very long pole with a sharp tip, presumably of metal. The point of the pole was directed against the balconies and battlements at the top of the fortress wall. By forcefully thrusting the pole against the wall to be breached, the masonry could be weakened and stones dislodged. The fact that the battering ram is depicted as the principal weapon of the attacking army indicates how effective it was in penetrating a city's defenses.

The Mari documents provide information for the period 200 years later. They mention the effectiveness of battering rams constructed largely of wood. Although very heavy, the siege weapon could be moved over long distances. One letter speaks of the use of a wagon drawn by draft animals and of a boat to transport a battering ram to the site of a besieged city.

Although the battering ram was used in warfare in Egypt, Canaan, and Anatolia in the 1st half of the 2nd millennium BC, it seems not to have played a significant role during the Late Bronze period. At that time advances made in the construction of fortifications tended to blunt the effectiveness of the battering ram, rendering temporarily obsolete a weapon that had proved devastating in an earlier period. Only with extensive improvements was the battering ram reintroduced as a major offensive weapon in assaults on fortified cities.

Moving a battering ram into position always exposed the demolition unit to heavy fire from defenders on the walls above them. Its heaviness made it cumbersome to move. Moreover, the ground adjacent to the walls was usually rough, rocky, and steep. When the chosen point of penetration was a section of the wall, an assault force had to construct an earthen ramp, occasionally strengthened on the top surface and sides with wooden planks or stones. The ramp provided a track along which the battering ram could be moved from the foot of the slope to the outer wall. Once moved into operational position, the ram had to be braked to prevent it from rolling back. The building of such a ramp was evidently necessary in Joab's campaign against the fortified city of Abel in Beth-maacah (2 Sm 20:15). The biblical account indicates that some sort of battering ram was in use in Israel under King David during the early monarchy.

The battering ram was eventually perfected by the Assyrians. Representations of the battering ram in the war reliefs of Ashurnasirpal II are the first to occur after an interval of about 1,000 years. The heavy machine was mobilized by the addition of six wheels, and a housing constructed from rectangular wicker shields was attached to the carriage. The dimensions of the ram can be calculated because the size of the shield is known and the number of shields employed is clearly visible. The body was between 13 and 20 feet in length and between 7 and 10 feet in height. The metal-tipped battering beam protruded like a tongue from a round, domed turret possibly constructed of metal.

The beam of a fully developed battering ram was suspended by a rope inside the turret so it could be swung to and fro like a pendulum. The crew operating the ram, after studying the walls through the front opening of the turret, would direct the beam to a vulnerable spot. The ax-shaped head would be forcefully lodged between the stones or bricks and levered right and left to dislodge them, causing part of the wall to collapse. An interesting detail in the Ashurnasirpal II relief is an attempt by defenders on the wall to deflect the beam by long chains. In a countermeasure two Assyrian soldiers are shown attempting to pull the chains away with heavy hooks.

Other defensive tactics included dropping lighted torches on top of the battery, generally constructed of wood and leather. This made it necessary to add another man to the demolition crew, whose assignment was to dip water from a bucket and douse the outer surface of the battery. That detail is clearly visible in murals commemorating Sennacherib's attack on Lachish. Equally visible is the action of the defenders, casting stones, torches, and even chariot wheels on the demolition units.

The earliest Assyrian reliefs show that protection of the penetration units was a major consideration. High, mobile assault towers constructed of wood operated in tandem with a battering ram. Such towers, moved into position near a breach operation and manned by archers, provided covering fire directed against the defenders on the wall. Siege towers neutralized the defenders' advantage in firepower and drew fire away from the crew engaged in breaching the walls.

Each of Ashurnasirpal's successors continued to modify the design and technique of the battering ram. His son Shalmaneser addressed himself to its cumbersomeness, a major weakness. He introduced a new type that was more mobile and less awkward. Tiglath-pileser III perfected the design, introducing an advanced type of battering ram housed within a light body on four wheels. He began the practice of assigning a pair of battering rams to operate side by side to demolish a wall. Sargon's reliefs depict a spear-pointed ram; they also indicate that he concentrated more force on the destruction of a single point in a wall, as several siege machines are shown moving in concert toward the point to be penetrated. That technique enabled the Assyrians to make

Statue of Ashurnasirpal II, one of the most powerful rulers of Assyria.

a larger breach in a shorter period of time. Under Sennacherib the ramming rod was lengthened and given a snoutlike head. By then the body was made of easily assembled and readily dismantled parts. Nevertheless, in the war reliefs of the last of the great Assyrian kings, Ashurbanipal, there is no evidence that the battering ram was used at all.

The details of the Assyrian reliefs make it possible to visualize clearly the fate of Jerusalem, as announced to the prophet Ezekiel (Ez 4:2; 21:22). The gate was the focal point of attack because it was the weakest point in the wall. Moreover, the path leading up to the gate made construction of a special ramp unnecessary. In the demolition of a gate swords were sometimes used to pry the doors loose and to tear down hinges. Wooden doors unprotected by metal were often set on fire.

The battering ram continued to be used as an engine for breaching walls in the Hellenistic-Roman period. In 63 BC the Roman commander Pompey brought up battering rams from Tyre against the defenders of Jerusalem, and with them penetrated the fortified wall that enclosed the temple (cf. Ps of Sol 2:1). The siege machine shown on Trajan's column had a beam with an iron head shaped like a ram. It was moved up to a wall in a frame protected by a wooden roof covered with clay or hides. A variation equipped for boring into a wall was used by Titus when besieging Jerusalem in AD 70.

The battering ram was not the only device used to effect a breach in a wall. Troops trained as sappers would tear down a section of the wall by using sharp-headed levers (pikes, swords, spears) or even sledgehammers (cf. Ez 26:8,9). In Ashurnasirpal's army such men were issued full-length coats of mail to cover their whole bodies. Under later Assyrian kings they were protected by both round and rectangular shields which they carried on their backs when engaged in demolition. Later, Ashurbanipal relied exclusively on such sappers for direct penetration of a fortified city. He designed for their protection a huge shield, the curved head of which could be propped against the wall, screening the sapper from missiles while he worked beneath it.

Scaling the Walls. A battle scene depicted on limestone in the tomb of Anta at Dashashe in Upper Egypt (24th century BC) provides the earliest known representation of siege activities. It shows the Egyptians raising a scaling ladder against the walls of a fortified city. A wall-painting from a 23rd-century BC tomb commemorates another Egyptian siege, and a remarkable development has taken place in the assault ladder. It rests on two solid wheels for mobility. No other example of a mobile assault ladder has been found, but it is known that such ladders were in use in other lands of the Bible. That particular ladder was evidently designed for a breaching action rather than for scaling walls. The wheels allowed the ladder to be pushed steadily closer to the wall, which soldiers battered with their axes. Reliefs indicate that during the Late Bronze period penetration of a fortified city was customarily from above by means of scaling ladders. In the reliefs of Ashurnasirpal scaling ladders figure prominently. While battering rams assaulted one section of a wall, scaling ladders were thrown up against other sections. That tactic forced the defenders to diffuse their firepower over the several points of attack or to risk entry by the Assyrians at a less-defended part of the wall.

By the time of Sargon countermeasures had been taken in the construction of fortifications. The thickness of walls was increased considerably, which permitted construction of much higher walls, more resistant to scaling. Such solid, massive walls also tended to blunt the effectiveness of a battering ram. Sargon, and especially his successor Ashurbanipal, responded by constructing longer scaling ladders, some of which could reach a height of 25 to 30 feet, judging from the number of rungs. Such ladders are a conspicuous feature in all of the war reliefs of those two kings. They were used not only to scale high, thick walls but also to cross moats. In the reliefs of Ashurbanipal archers take their place on the ladders alongside warriors equipped with swords.

Penetration Beneath the Walls. A fortified city was sometimes penetrated beneath the walls, either by undermining the foundations or by tunneling. In a siege scene in the palace of Ashurnasirpal II demolition sappers have tunneled a cavity under the walls at two points and are undermining the foundations. The action takes place in conjunction with four other conventional methods of assault, so that the presence of the sappers could go undetected.

A tunneling operation could be started beyond the range of any weapons at the disposal of the defenders. Once underground, the penetration unit was shielded from enemy fire. The tunneling could be accomplished under cover of night, so that the element of surprise could be exploited to the maximum. It was, however, a lengthy process requiring considerable technical skill. Moreover, if the operation was detected by the defenders before its completion, they could destroy the penetration unit as it emerged from the tunnel. Attempts to penetrate fortified cities by tunneling beneath the walls was a characteristic feature of warfare in Iron Age II. That is confirmed by reliefs, written documents, and archaeological excavation of sites dating to this period, where the remains of attack tunnels have been discovered.

It was not always necessary to construct a tunnel if access could be gained by means of subterranean water conduits. In 218 BC Philadelphia (Rabbath-bene-ammon), a Ptolemaic stronghold in the Transjordan, was penetrated by the Seleucid king Antiochus III in this manner. His engineers diverted the flow of the water in the city's water system, and his army entered the city through the conduit.

Siege. Particularly when a walled city was situated on a high hill, an extended siege provided an alternate method of conquering it. By encircling the city and preventing aid or supplies from reaching its defenders, the attacking army could starve the inhabitants out. That procedure minimized the element of risk for the attacking army. Its success depended upon their capacity to prevent outside assistance from reaching the city and the defenders from leaving it. An army would generally resort to siege when a city's fortifications were too powerful for direct penetration. The siege of Samaria by the Assyrians lasted for three years (2 Kgs 18:9,10).

During a siege the attacking army was itself exposed to attack from allies of the besieged city, who might approach from any direction, as well as from sorties and raids by the troops under siege. Trees in the area were cut down and used to construct fortified encampments and siege equipment. The Israelites were admonished not to destroy productive fruit trees when besieging Canaanite cities (Dt 20:19,20).

The peculiar conditions of siege produced the catapult, a major innovation of Greek artillery and a logical improvement on the bow and the sling. Designed originally as a strengthened bow mounted on a stand to fire arrows only, it was introduced around 400 BC by Demetrius I. He may have borrowed the idea from the Phoenicians at Carthage.

In the course of time the instrument was improved. The perfected weapon, called the torsion catapult, derived its power from many tightly twisted strands of elastic material, frequently supplied by women's hair, which could be tightened with a windlass and then released suddenly. Firing arrows, large stones, or fire-baskets with an effective range of 200 yards, a catapult could clear a wall of defenders while a battering ram breached it or a boarding party attacked from a mobile tower.

The catapult never replaced units of archers and slingers in the field. It could not match their mobility and rapidity of fire, nor could it be mounted on ships. Its natural function was as a siege weapon.

Although the Romans added little to siege technique, they repeatedly demonstrated strength of will. For example, the elevated Jewish fortress at Masada seemed impregnable. Yet the Romans constructed a ramp about 280 feet high, which was higher than the fortress walls, and from it they broke into Masada in AD 73.

For those in a besieged city the critical problems were food and water supplies. The horror of famine is stressed in the biblical account of the siege of Samaria by the Syrian Ben-hadad in the days of the prophet Elisha. On that occasion women were reduced to eating their children (2 Kgs 6:26–29). A besieging army would do everything in its power to aggravate such conditions. In one of the siege reliefs of Ashurnasirpal II a defender has lowered a bucket from the wall to draw water from a stream below; an Assyrian soldier is shown cutting the rope with his dagger.

Ruses, Stratagems, and Threats. Various ruses and stratagems could draw the defenders out of a city or infiltrate troops into the city. If a small force could enter a city by a cunning stratagem, it could overpower the guards and open the city gates to an attacking army. A city's fortifications were of little value once an enemy had entered the city. Moreover, penetrating a city's defenses at any one point frequently caused the entire defense system to collapse. The story of the Trojan horse is probably the most celebrated account of a stratagem circumventing the defense of a strongly fortified ancient city.

In the biblical account of the siege of Samaria by Ben-hadad, a sudden lifting of the Syrian siege led Jehoram, the king of Israel, to suspect a ruse. He refused to believe the report of four lepers that the Syrians had gone, leaving behind large food supplies (2 Kgs 7:12). That was the same kind of tactic that Joshua had employed at Ai (Jos 8:3–8).

On other occasions powerful armies sought to break down resistance by psychological warfare, as in the unsuccessful attempt by Sennacherib to capture Jerusalem in the time of Hezekiah (2 Kgs 18,19). The dialogue between the Assyrian general and Hezekiah's delegates makes clear that the Assyrian was trying to shake the confidence of the city's defenders. He called into question the reliability of the three resources upon which Hezekiah based his resistance: the help of the Lord, an alliance with Egypt, and the strength of his forces (2 Kgs 18:19–23). Hezekiah's delegation tried to get the general to speak to them in the official Aramaic language, not in the Judean dialect understood by the defenders on the walls (2 Kgs 18:26), but it was precisely the Assyrian's intention to try to demoralize the defenders (2 Kgs 18:27–35).

The discipline and adamant spirit of the Judean defenders and the depth of their trust in the Lord enabled them to resist the threats and promises offered by the Assyrian negotiator. In his annals Sennacherib was forced to concede that he had been unable to capture Jerusalem: "As to Hezekiah, he did not submit to my yoke. But I made him a prisoner in Jerusalem, his royal residence, like a bird in a cage."

Ambush and Night Fighting. The ambush was a type of ruse used to trap and destroy an enemy at a moment when he was least able to counter a sudden, unexpected blow. Its effectiveness depended almost entirely on the element of surprise. By taking advantage of good intelligence, knowledge of the terrain, and the cover of night, a small force could stage a devastating ambush against vastly superior numbers. In one of his documents the Hittite king Mursilis speaks of the trouble he encountered from a small army of irregulars who used the night ambush to disrupt his advance: "They did not dare to attack me in the daylight, and preferred to fall upon me during the night. [They said:] In the night we will attack him."

The ambush was a standard method of combat during the period of the conquest of Canaan. The fall of Ai, for example, was due directly to the tactical success of an ambush (Jos 8:1–23). Under cover of night Joshua was able to move a large force to a concealed position behind the city. He then led the remainder of the Israelite army to the edge of a valley north of the fortified city, giving the appearance of a planned assault on the city. The diversion, as calculated, drew the main force of Ai away from the city to engage Israel on the plain of Arabah. When the Israelites fell back, appearing to be badly beaten, the remaining defenders of the city were summoned to pursue Joshua's "fleeing" army. With the city left undefended, the main Israelite strike force rose from its ambush position, poured into the city, and set it on fire. Too late the men of Ai saw the smoke from their burning city and realized the stratagem. Joshua's army turned to counterattack their pursuers, who found themselves trapped between two bodies of Israelite forces. Assaulted from both front and rear, the king of Ai's army was annihilated, victim of an effectively laid ambush.

In the later period of the judges identical tactics were employed in the conquest of Gibeah by the Israelites (Jgs 20:29–48). An ambush was often accompanied by a feint, a mock assault in one direction to distract the enemy's attention from the real thrust of the attack.

Staging an ambush usually required waiting until nightfall to deploy troops. When a coalition of Amorite kings determined to destroy Gibeon, Joshua advanced the Israelite army all through the night in order to surprise the enemy at dawn (Jos 10:9). Night marches, evidently a standard procedure in that period, were mentioned at a much later time by Mesha, king of Moab (cf. 2 Kgs 3:4,5), on the famous Moabite Stone celebrating his battle against Israel: "And Chemosh said to me, 'Go, take Nebo from Israel.' So I went by night and fought against it from the break of dawn until noon." Almost identical words are used to describe King Saul's action at Jabesh-gilead, when a night march made it possible to launch a dawn attack on the Ammonites, who were unaware of the arrival of the Israelite forces (1 Sm 11:11). Capitalizing on the element of surprise, Saul's army was able to destroy the Ammonite forces of Nahash.

Ambush was frequently employed as a combat tactic even on open terrain. In the period of the divided kingdom a strike force would be posted to attack from the enemy's flank and the rear at the decisive moment in the conflict. That tactic was used by Jeroboam I of Israel in a battle with Abijah, king of Judah (2 Chr 13:13). To avoid such a simple but catastrophic snare required an efficient intelligence service.

Ambush was the key to the success of the warfare waged by Judas Maccabeus and his guerrilla army against vastly superior forces during the initial stages of the Maccabean revolt. From their refuge in the mountains of Gophna, north of Modein, Judas and his forces sallied forth against the Hellenizers living in Jerusalem under Seleucid protection. When the Syrians retaliated, Judas ambushed their troops and destroyed them (1 Mc 2:1–3:13). The Seleucid commander Seron was again ambushed at Beth-horon (1 Mc 3:13–24). Similar tactics were employed by the Maccabees in their drive to break the Syrian hold on the Jewish capital (1 Mc 3:38–4:25). Judas made equally effective use of the element of surprise in the forced march by night, as in the relief of Bostra, Dathema, and other fortresses in Gilead (1 Mc 5:3–13,24–54).

Fortifications and Defense. Most of the ancient cities of Palestine, Syria, and Anatolia were located for defensability and water supply, but the two factors were often contradictory. Tactical considerations favored locating a city on top of a hill or mountain, using the terrain as an integral component of the defense system. However, the sources of water—springs, streams, rivers—were normally found in a valley. Fortifications had to encompass at least part of the water source, because the water supply system was as important in defense of an ancient city as the walls and the inner citadel.

The earliest known fortifications in the

The top of the wall of
Jerusalem.

world, dated by some to about 7000 BC, were discovered in 1954 at Jericho. They were impressive in conception and construction. The core of the defense system was a wall, part of which, bordering the western edge of the ancient city, was still standing to a height of 21 feet. Archaeologists were able to determine that the wall encompassed the entire city, which at that time extended over an area of about 10 acres. It has been estimated that the city sustained a population of about 2,500 persons, of whom some 500 to 600 were capable of defending the city. Further excavation uncovered a large moat that had been carved out of solid rock at the base of the wall, 27 feet wide and 9 feet deep. How that feat was accomplished when the only tools assumed available were made of stone is a complete mystery. The project must have occupied a large labor force for a period extending to thousands of workdays. Although the existence of the moat suggests that the city faced the threat of a powerful assault from some neighbor, the identity and offensive capability of such a foe are unknown. A third component of Jericho's defense system was a huge stone circular tower 30 feet high, once evidently attached to the inner side of the western part of the wall. The exact purpose of the tower has not yet been determined, but Neolithic Jericho provides the earliest evidence of a fortified city supported by a wall, tower, and moat.

By the Middle Bronze period there were four components in a standard defense system: a moat, an advance (outer) wall, the main (inner) wall, and a well-fortified gate structure. The moat, advance wall, and subsidiary fortifications protecting the steep slope and lower portion of the main wall were intended to prevent breaching by a battering ram. Enormous resources of material and labor went into the construction of fortifications, reflecting the already advanced methods of assault.

City Walls. Erection of a simple wall could halt a hostile advance only temporarily, since walls could be scaled or breached. Walls therefore provided a firing platform so defenders could repel attacks. The wall system consisted of three principal components: the wall itself, constituting the barrier; an upper structure, which provided the firing platform and cover for the defenders; and a series of obstacles and traps erected in front of the wall to keep archers at a distance and to prevent operation of a battering ram. To discourage scaling, the wall had to be high; to resist breaching, it had to be thick; to withstand undermining or tunneling, it had to have deep and broadly based foundations. A wall both high and thick, whether built from stone or brick, also required the support of a series of regularly spaced buttresses.

The battlement, a crenelated parapet built along the outer top edge of the wall, provided the defenders with a measure of security, freedom for mobility, and openings through which fire could be directed. From a distance the square notches looked like a row of teeth with gaps between them. The teeth, called merlons, provided a protective barrier against hostile missiles. The gaps, called embrasures or crenels, supplied openings through which the defenders could discharge their weapons. Special towers protruded from the outer face of the wall, spaced at a distance no greater than the double range of a bow. Such towers enabled the defenders to cover the ground between them with flanking fire at enemy troops who managed to reach the walls. One way of protecting the main wall was to construct an outer or advance wall that could be breached or climbed only under heavy fire from defending units on the battlements of the main wall. Another method was to dig a wide, deep moat around the base of the main wall. A moat kept the enemy from using a battering ram unless they could bridge the moat or fill it up at certain points, under concentrated fire from the defenders. Many cities had both an outer wall and a moat. Defensive units posted outside the main wall but forced to fall back to the city were hauled to safety by their comrades with ropes let down from the top of the wall. That tactic is mentioned specifically by the Egyptian Thutmose III in the Late Bronze period in his description of the siege of Megiddo. When all else failed, defense of the wall depended on archers posted on the battlement and to spearmen who assaulted attackers reaching the top of the scaling ladders.

Casemate fortifications, introduced in the Middle Bronze period and spreading in the Late Bronze period throughout the Hittite empire, were developed from double walls built of dressed stones. The space between the walls was divided into chambers, or casemates, used for storage or dwellings. The Hittite casemate system, introduced into Palestine at least as early as the time of Saul, was widely adopted in Syria and Palestine. A fine example has been discovered at Gibeah, where Saul's citadel was located, dating to the end of the 11th century BC. The overall thickness of the double walls, including the casemates, reaches 15 feet. The same type of construction has been found in excavations of three Solomonic cities—Hazor, Gezer, and Megiddo (cf. 1 Kgs 9:15)—where the casemate walls have an overall thickness of 18 feet. At Megiddo those walls were destroyed by Pharaoh Shishak's campaign in the 5th year of Solomon's son Rehoboam. They were replaced in Ahab's time by massive solid walls with recesses and salients functioning as bastions. The radical change from the weaker casemate system to solid, massive construction was prompted by development of the improved Assyrian battering ram, which made its appearance at the beginning of the 9th century BC.

Although the divided kingdoms of Judah and Israel were not noted for technical advancements in offensive warfare, a number of their kings worked at improving fortifications and means of defense. Uzziah was especially remembered for his accomplishments in defensive warfare. Along with other measures, "in

Jerusalem he made engines, invented by skilful men, to be on the towers and the corners, to shoot arrows and great stone" (2 Chr 26:15). Those "engines" were special protective structures built to facilitate the task of the archers and to permit huge stones to be dropped on the heads of assaulting troops. A depiction of Uzziah's devices appears on the reliefs of Sennacherib commemorating the siege of Lachish. On the towers, corners, and crenelated battlements, defenders have erected structures made of wooden frames that hold their shields. The high screen formed by the shields permits the defenders to stand rather than crouch, and to use both hands freely to discharge their weapons.

Gate. It was inevitable that the gate would be the focus of action in any assault on a fortified city. City gates were therefore designed to expose an attacking army to the greatest risk while providing maximum security to the defenders. The road approaching a city on a hill would wind up the slope, climbing obliquely to the left or the right. Such roads were usually laid out to reach the gate from the right, so an attacker would have to expose the right side of his body to the defenders on the wall. Since he carried his shield in his left hand, that made him more vulnerable.

For fortification systems with an outer wall the same principle dictated placement of the gate in the advance wall to the right of the gate in the main wall. An attacker breaching the outer gate would be forced to approach the main gate with his right side exposed to the fire of the defenders on the main wall.

To prevent the heavy wooden doors of the gate from being set on fire, they were usually plated with metal. A gate wide enough for chariots required double doors, making the line at the center where the two doors met the weakest point in the barrier. Double doors were therefore fitted with huge bolts and fortified with a heavy beam running across the back of both door panels and held in place by sockets set in the doorposts.

Another component in the defense complex at a gate consisted of towers erected on either side of the gate and protruding from the outer face of the wall. Enemy soldiers trying to smash the doors with axes or set them on fire with torches were thus exposed to heavy flanking fire from defensive units on the towers. From a roof over the gate having a crenelated balcony concentrated firepower could be poured down on attackers' heads. The addition of such auxiliary structures transformed a gate into a small fortress.

Just inside the doors were rectangular columns, called pilasters, built into the walls on

The Golden Gate of the city of Jerusalem.

either side of the entrance to narrow it. Attackers forcing their way through the gates were crowded between the two pilasters and had less room for maneuvering than the defenders. Sometimes a long entrance corridor was constructed with multiple pairs of pilasters.

Inner Citadel. A major weakness of a city's walls and gate was the magnitude of the circumference. An average-size city might have a perimeter of half a mile, a larger city a perimeter of over a mile. Yet the entire wall had to be defended against breaching, scaling, or tunneling. An attacking army would use diversionary tactics to keep defenders dispersed along the entire perimeter but concentrate their primary assault at one point in the wall. Once the wall was breached, perimeter fortifications served no further defensive purpose. Therefore internal walls were often added to subdivide a city into several sections, each capable of independent defense. Also, on the highest point of land within the city a citadel would be constructed as a self-contained defensive unit.

The earliest examples of such fortifications, called migdols, are found in the Late Bronze Age. They were originally small citadels built to guard important military targets such as sources of water supply, strategic routes, cultivated farmlands, or frontiers. A migdol of that type was discovered in Israel, not far from Ashdod, in 1960. It was square in plan, with rectangular bastions, and was two stories high, just like structures depicted in Egyptian reliefs from the same period. The same design was used to fortify temples inside of cities. Such fortified temples served as places of refuge

and as a city's final defense once its walls had been breached (cf. Jgs 9:45,46,50,51).

In a later period an inner citadel could embrace a complex consisting of the fortified palace of the governor, dwellings of his chief ministers, and sometimes the temple. Such citadels resembled fortified cities, possessing a main wall, gateway, an outer wall, and occasionally a moat. Being small in area and heavily fortified, citadels could be defended in a final effort by the governor and remaining inhabitants. Presumably Zimri could have held out against Omri's army for an extended period in the citadel of Tirzah, had he not committed suicide by setting it on fire (1 Kgs 16:17,18).

Water Supply Under Siege. Unless provision was made to keep a city's inhabitants supplied with food and water during a protracted siege, no defense system could be effective. Several Judean kings made efforts to solve the food-storage problem. Rehoboam, for example, fortified a number of cities located on the western, eastern, and southern borders of his kingdom and made them centers for the storage of food, oil, and wine (2 Chr 11:5–11). In the excavation of a number of Judean cities pottery vessels have been found bearing the emblem of the Judean kings stamped on the handles together with the inscription "of the king." Such jars were apparently used for the storage of oil, wine, and flour to sustain the population during a siege. Some of the jar handles also bear the name of Hebron, Socoh, Ziph, or Mamshat. Those four cities were administrative centers for collection and distribution of stores in the various localities in Judah: Hebron for the Judean hills; Socoh for the coastal plain; Ziph for the Judean desert; and Mamshat for the southern Negeb desert.

Storage of food was easier than storage of water. Cisterns built to collect rainwater were a partial answer, but cisterns often ran dry, particularly in times of drought. Cities were sometimes built on the banks of a stream or river, using the stream as part of the city's defense system. But for a city built on a hill, the source of water might be a spring located at the foot of the slope and outside the city walls. Sometimes the mouth of the spring could be blocked and its location concealed from the enemy while still allowing access by the inhabitants. A tunnel could be cut sloping downward from the spring into a well or cistern located inside the city that could be reached by a staircase. Or a pit could be dug inside the city, and, at its bottom, a passageway cut through to the outside so the spring could be approached without detection by besieging forces. At Megiddo a vertical shaft 100 feet deep was connected by a horizontal tunnel about 220 feet long to the water supply at the western end of the city, beyond the fortifications. The work was undertaken in the time of either Solomon or Ahab.

The most celebrated measures to guarantee a supply of fresh water in a time of siege were those taken by Hezekiah at Jerusalem. That engineering achievement is recalled in all the summaries of his reign, both in the Bible and in the "Praise of Famous Men" in the apocryphal book of Sirach (2 Kgs 20:20; 2 Chr 32:30; Ecclus 48:17). The prodigious feat commemorated in those references was the sealing of the spring of Gihon and the cutting of a 1,800-foot channel through solid rock in order to bring water into a reservoir in the city. How it was accomplished was reported by Hezekiah himself in the famous Siloam inscription. Two crews, working with hammers, wedges, and pickaxes, began at opposite ends. The crew which began at the spring was able to take advantage of an older tunnel (cf. Is 22:11). They turned due south, in the direction of the city. The other crew, starting from the reservoir, began in a northeasterly direction. They then turned southeast until they reached the north-south line followed by the crew tunneling from the spring, when they turned due north to meet them. The two crews almost passed each other, being about five feet apart, but a shout from one was heard through a crevice in the rock by the other. Both parties turned sharply right, and the tunnel was completed. Hezekiah's precautionary step, taken before Sennacherib's invasion of Judah, helps to explain why the Assyrians were unable to subdue Jerusalem by the siege tactics that

Entrance to Warren's Shaft of the conduit that Hezekiah had dug in order to bring water into Jerusalem.

had earlier subdued Samaria in the time of Sargon.

Hebrew Military Organization. *Tribal Army.* In their exodus from Egypt the Israelites were organized by tribes and divisions. That systematic arrangement for their trek through the wilderness provided a precedent for military organization. After the sojourn at Mt Sinai the 12 tribes were divided into divisions or army corps, and certain grades in military rank began to appear. The "officers of the army" (Nm 31:14) had command over units of 1,000 or 100 men, which suggests that the tribal army was divided into decimal units. At a later period there is reference to units of 1,000 (the division), 100 (the company), 50 (the platoon), and 10 (the section). Except for the Levites, who were assigned as a tribe to the care of the tabernacle (Nm 2:33), men from 20 years of age who were physically able to fight were assigned to a unit in the tribal army. Certain individuals, however, were exempted from military service (cf. Dt 20:5-9; 24:5; Jgs 7:3).

Until after the conquest of Canaan the

tribal army was essentially a militia recruited in an emergency. Internal organization of the militia was the responsibility of the tribe; each clan and family sent their quota of warriors when summoned to battle by tribal leaders. Because the clan formed the basic unit, recruits were under the command of their own leaders. David's brothers, for example, served in a division composed of the fighting men from their clan under the command of a captain (1 Sm 17:18; 18:13). When the emergency passed, the militia was disbanded, and the soldiers returned to their home districts.

Because the land was divided among the tribes, no tribal or clan leader before Saul commanded the entire tribal confederation (cf. 1 Sm 11:1–11). In fact, tribal jealousies and rivalries threatened national solidarity and jeopardized united action even in a critical period. On some occasions, however, the severity of a crisis caused the armies of the various tribes to unite in common action. The multitribal armies were divided into companies of 1,000, 100, and 50, and still further into families under appointed officers. There is evidence of organization into units according to weaponry (1 Chr 12:24–38). Benjamin's tribe specialized in the bow and sling. The tribes of Gad, Judah, and Naphtali were expert with the spear and shield.

Provisioning the tribal army was the responsibility of each tribe (Jgs 20:9,10). One out of every 10 soldiers was appointed to secure food for the others, either from wealthy landowners (cf. 1 Sm 25) or from the natural resources of the land. In that early stage of military organization a soldier's pay generally consisted only of supplies and a portion of the spoils of battle (cf. 1 Sm 30:21–25).

Professional Army. Not until the time of the united monarchy did Israel have a regular army. Transition from a people's militia to a professional army took place under Saul, whose reign changed the tribal confederacy into a monarchy (1 Sm 13:2). Philistine harassment of Israel encouraged establishment of a strong standing army. The army, however, was not large; it consisted of 3,000 men organized in three formations of 1,000 each (1 Sm 13:2; 24:2). Pay for those career soldiers was sometimes in the form of a grant of land (1 Sm 8:14) as well as a share of booty. In the organization of Saul's army Abner, Jonathan, and David were given particular responsibilities. Abner was named commander of the army (1 Sm 17:55) and was probably also given direct command of one of the divisions (1 Sm 18:5,13). David's band of valorous men, "the thirty," provided the leadership core for his own military organization when he became king.

David continued the practice of maintaining a professional army. But he also developed a national militia of 12 regiments, each being called up for duty for one month of the year under professional officers (1 Chr 27:1–15). Each regiment, recruited across tribal lines, consisted of 24,000 soldiers. David's innovation provided him with a large reserve force that could be mustered for war in times of emergency. The reserves, and presumably the professional army as well, were organized into units of 1,000, 100, 50, and 10. Joab, a specialist in siege warfare (2 Sm 20:15), commanded the professional army, and Amasa was over the citizens' militia. David, however, remained commander-in-chief of the military organization.

The Israelite group in King David's professional army was an outgrowth of the small band of fighting men who had served with him during the period of conflict with Saul. That veteran group consisted of David's family and clansmen, and others who felt themselves oppressed by the central authority under Saul (1 Sm 22:1,2). It ranged in size between 400 and 600 men (1 Sm 22:2; 23:13; 27:2). The presence of mercenaries in David's army is clearly recorded. Uriah the Hittite and Ittai of Gath are conspicuous examples, along with many career soldiers of Philistine origin, such as the Cherethites and the Pelethites under Benaiah (2 Sm 8:18; 15:19–22; 23:22,23).

The Davidic dynasty maintained a permanent mercenary army until 701 BC, after which it was considered too costly. The oppressive cost of maintaining a professional army, financed by burdensome taxes and forced labor, was in fact a major factor contributing to the disruption of the monarchy after Solomon's death (cf. 1 Kgs 10:26–29; 12:4–19). After Sennacherib's invasion in 701 BC, the southern kingdom of Judah depended entirely on a citizens' militia for its defense. It is commonly held that the northern kingdom of Israel did not employ a professional army, but it is evident that King Ahab used at least some mercenary soldiers in his defense against Ben-hadad of Syria (1 Kgs 20:15–20).

Roman Military Organization. With the military intervention of Pompey in the internal affairs of Judea in 63 BC, Rome established its presence in Palestine. The census ordered by Augustus Caesar, affecting the eastern provinces as well as the rest of the Roman world (Lk 2:1,2), was a vivid reminder. Roman military presence is amply reflected in the pages of the Gospels and Acts (e.g., Mk 15:16; Lk 3:14; 7:1–8; Acts 5:37).

In the NT period, service in the legions was open to all Roman citizens. A professional volunteer army had replaced a conscripted militia. The permanent standing army was made up of legions recruited from the ranks of citizens. The legions were commanded by experienced officers of the rank of consul. Auxiliary forces were raised outside Italy, the inducement for enlistment being Roman citizenship for a soldier and his descendants after 25 years of service.

In the provinces supreme military command lay with the provincial governor or prefect. In Judea at the time of Jesus' public ministry Pontius Pilate was designated "prefect of Judea" in a Latin inscription found in Caesarea in 1961. At the official center for administration of Judea, Caesarea Maritima, one or more legions at the disposal of the governor would be garrisoned. On special occasions, particularly at the great Jewish festivals when riots and disorders could be anticipated, the provincial governor would take up residence in Jerusalem some 60 miles to the south, accompanied by a substantial contingent of troops (cf. Lk 13:1).

Augustus established a standing army large enough to defend and pacify the empire. In 15 BC there were 28 legions, each composed of some 5,000 foot soldiers plus a mounted bodyguard of 128 men. After 3 legions were destroyed in uprisings by fierce Germanic tribes in AD 9, the number remained at 25 for some time. That suggests a standing army of about 125,000 legioneers in the first century. The length of legionary service was established by Augustus first at 16 years and then at 20 years, with an additional 4 or 5 years of reserve status. Toward the end of the first century the Flavian emperors abolished the reserve corps and made the length of legionary service 25 years. Under Augustus a citizen-soldier received an annual wage of 225 denarii, plus a pension from the state treasury on his discharge.

Augustus was also responsible for establishing a permanent auxiliary army, almost the same size as the legionary army. The auxiliary forces, recruited from provincials who had not yet received Roman citizenship, included both cavalry and infantry. The cavalry was organized in squadrons, the infantry in cohorts of 1,000 under command of a military tribune (Acts 21:31–33). When the apostle Paul was in Jerusalem, the tribune was Claudius Lysias, a man of Greek birth whose purchased Roman citizenship made possible his elevation to com-

Dress of 3 Roman generals.

mander of an auxiliary cohort (Acts 22:28; 23:26). To send Paul from Jerusalem to Caesarea, Claudius could delegate a military escort of 200 soldiers commanded by 2 centurions, plus 70 mounted guards (Acts 23:23), without dangerously weakening the strength of the fortress garrison.

A cohort was made up of either 10 or 5 "centuries," units consisting of 100 men under the command of a centurion whose duties resembled those of a modern army captain. Cornelius (Acts 10:1) was a Roman centurion assigned to one of the auxiliary cohorts in Judea. There is inscriptional evidence for the presence of his unit, "the Second Italian Cohort of Roman Citizens," in Syria about AD 69. Paul was sent to Rome in the custody of another centurion, Julius, who belonged to the Augustan or imperial cohort (Acts 27:1). The term "Augustan" was a title of honor sometimes bestowed on auxiliary troops. Julius was evidently a legionary centurion assigned to the corps of officer-couriers who maintained a communication service between the emperor and his provincial armies. He had a detachment of soldiers under his command on the voyage to Rome (Acts 27:3) and on arrival handed his prisoners over to the commander of the courier corps (Acts 28:16). Probably all of the Roman centurions mentioned in the Gospels or Acts (Mt 8:5; Lk 7:2; Mk 15:39) were officers assigned to an auxiliary cohort.

Summary and Perspective. The weakening of older kingdoms provided an opening for newer nations like the tribes of Israel from the south and east and the Philistines from the west and north. They invaded and occupied areas of Palestine where formerly the mighty nations of antiquity had spent their strength in mortal combat. The occupation was accomplished through warfare, and the new peoples sustained themselves in the land through military prowess. Expansionist aims and encroachments of new regimes in Syria, Egypt, and Mesopotamia posed a constant threat of war. The debris of destroyed cities, the carnage of battle, and the wail of humiliation were too familiar a reality for the people of God ever to regard warfare lightly.

Modern readers of the Bible often have difficulty with the military emphasis of the OT, asking, "How could God be a God of love and yet lead his chosen people into bloody wars?" The fact is that the Israelites were no more belligerent than the peoples who came before them or after them. God wanted to introduce new concepts of love and justice into the world through his people, but it was necessary for them to survive in order to do that. He did not take them out of their world, a world where resources were scarce and life precari-

ous, but helped them fight for survival among far more brutal and acquisitive powers. Yet through the prophet Isaiah, God gave to his people the vision of a day when the art of warfare would be forgotten (Is 2:2–5).

The centuries that followed were characterized by a series of crises precipitated by intrigue and war. Persia, Macedonia, Parthia, and Rome successively established a military presence in the land. No display of military prowess, however, could dim the prophetic vision. No experience of an imposed peace could satisfy its terms. Indeed, Christians believe that at a time when Israel was under total military domination by Rome, God brought forth a Ruler, his Messiah, the "Prince of Peace," to establish a peace that would never end (Is 9:6,7). The promise that nations will one day beat their swords into plowshares and their spears into pruning hooks accounts for the rebirth of hope in the hearts of God's people—even when war or the threat of warfare looms imminent, or when a nation's leadership directs its attention to arms and warfare. Jesus Christ said that those to be known as God's family in the future would be "those who strive for peace" (Mt 5:9 LB). The accomplishment of Isaiah's prophecy ultimately depends not on the ingenuity or intention of human beings but on the power and achievement of the sovereign God.

WILLIAM L. LANE

See ISRAEL, HISTORY OF.

Bibliography. P. Connally, *Greece and Rome at War;* P. Craigie, *War in the OT;* R. Gonen, *Weapons and Warfare in Ancient Times;* M.C. Lind, *Yahweh Is a Warrior;* J.B. Pritchard, *The Ancient Near East in Pictures* and *Ancient Near Eastern Texts* (2nd ed); Y. Yadin, *The Art of Warfare in Biblical Lands.*

Army.   Large organized body of soldiers for waging war, especially on land.

See ARMS AND WARFARE.

Arnan.   Rephaiah's son and Obadiah's father, a descendant of David through Zerubbabel (1 Chr 3:21).

Arni.   Ancestor of Jesus according to Luke's genealogy (3:33, KJV Aram); also called Ram in Ruth 4:19 and 1 Chronicles 2:9,10.

Arnon.   River of Transjordan, the present Wadi el-Mojib, running from east to west through a canyon with walls 1,500 feet high into the Dead Sea. At the time of the Israelite conquest of Canaan the gorge served as a natural border between Moab to the south and the Ammonite kingdoms to the north (Nm 21:13–15). After the division of the land under Joshua the river Arnon became the southern boundary of Reuben's territory (Dt 3:12,16; Jos 13:16).

Arod, Arodi, Arodite. Gad's 6th son, founder of the Arodite family (Nm 26:17). He is called Arodi in the list of those who went to Egypt with Jacob (Gn 46:16).

Aroer. 1. Transjordanian city existing from Moses' time until the fall of Jerusalem (586 BC). It was among the cities that Israel conquered from Sihon the Amorite and Og the Bashanite in an area assigned to the tribes of Gad and Reuben and to half of Manasseh's tribe. Aroer was on the southern border of that territory (Jos 13:9), on the northern rim of the large Arnon canyon (Dt 2:36; 3:12; 4:48; Jos 13:9). Evidently the city was rebuilt after Israel destroyed it (cf. Jos 12:2; Nm 32:34).

Aroer was the hub city for a number of villages (Jgs 11:26) and was the city from which the census began under King David (2 Sm 24:5). The Moabites gained control of it during the later monarchy and kept it until the time of Jeremiah (Jer 48:19). King Hazael of Damascus captured Aroer, assuring Syrian control of Transjordan (2 Kgs 10:33).

Aroer has been identified with a mound beside the village 'Ara'ir, about 3 miles southeast of Dibon on the east side of the ancient north-south Transjordan highway.

2. City assigned to Gad's tribe (Jos 13:25), mentioned as a point of reference in Jephthah's victory over the Ammonites (Jgs 11:33). This Aroer has been tentatively placed in the area northwest of Amman and east of Rabbah.

3. City in the Negeb desert area of Judah. Aroer was one of the villages receiving spoil taken in David's victory over the Amalekites (1 Sm 30:28). Two of David's "mighty men" were sons of Hotham the Aroerite (1 Chr 11:44). This Aroer has been identified with Khirbet 'Ar'areh, located about 12 miles southeast of Beersheba.

4. City near Damascus (Is 17:2 KJV). The Hebrew text reads "the cities of Aroer," but the Septuagint (ancient Greek OT) has "her cities for ever" (a reading adopted by the RSV).

Aroerite. Resident of Aroer. The Aroerite Hotham, father of two of David's "mighty men," was a native of Aroer (1 Chr 11:44).

See AROER #3.

Aromatic Cane. Species of fragrant reed used by the Israelites as a perfume (Sg 4:14) and as an ingredient of the anointing oil (Ex 30:23).

See PLANTS (CANE).

Arpachshad. Shem's son and Noah's grandson, born two years after the flood. Arpachshad's descendants were probably the Chaldeans (Gn 10:22,24; 11:10–13; 1 Chr 1:17,18,24; KJV Arpaxad). Also spelled Arphaxad in Luke 3:36.

Arpad, Arphad. City in northern Syria. Arpad was overrun twice by the Assyrians: in 740 BC by Tiglath-pileser III and in 720 BC by Sargon II. The Assyrians used Arpad and Hamath as examples of the inability of any gods, including Israel's, to protect cities against Assyria's attacks (2 Kgs 18:34; 19:13; Is 10:9; 36:19; 37:13; in the latter two vv, KJV Arphad). Arpad and Hamath are also mentioned in a later prophecy against the Syrian city of Damascus (Jer 49:23). Arpad has been identified as modern Tell Erfad, north of Aleppo.

Arphaxad. KJV form of Arpachshad in Genesis 10:22,24; 11:10–13 and 1 Chronicles 1:17,18, 24. Also Luke 3:36 in RSV.

See ARPACHSHAD.

Arrow. See ARMS AND WARFARE.

Art. Knowledge of the art of the ancient Near East, and especially of Palestine, helps us understand references to art in the Bible. Further, we can explore what the biblical views of God, man, and redemption imply for a Christian attitude toward art and beauty.

Art in the Ancient Near East. Much of ancient Near Eastern culture emanated from two great civilizations: Egypt and Mesopotamia. The people of Palestine lived out their lives in the interplay of those two great powers, and a study of the cultural background of the Bible must begin with those civilizations. The focus of those ancient peoples was religious, and their material culture expressed a dominant goal: to explain the purpose of life and creation. They viewed the world as having been formed from an initial chaos, called variously the "abyss" or the "waters." The forces behind this formation were symbolized very early as the "great gods," who made use of lesser spirits in "begetting" the earth. Earthly rulers were related to the gods. In Egypt the pharaohs were seen as actual manifestations of a god; in Sumer (southern Mesopotamia) the king was a divine steward.

Egypt. Questions of life and death are prominent in all religious consciousness, but ancient Egypt seemed preoccupied with the question of life after death. Since the king was the earthly manifestation of divinity, his life certainly continued after death. An Egyptian artist's imagination was greatly influenced by the idea of immortality so he dedicated his

Egyptian mural tablet at Gebel
Silsilis.

talent to depicting its existence. By the middle of the 3rd millennium BC (Old Kingdom) most statues were cult objects made to perpetuate the memory (and thereby the existence) of the person represented. All art objects of the pyramid age, including the famous Sphinx, were grand monuments to an intense desire for eternal life. It was as if the artist wished to gather up in a monumental present form the past and future, and, by creating grand and timeless images of the present, to deny the reality of death. Anonymous artists worked in the service of the cult. Most funerary art (statues and wall reliefs made for tombs) was not even intended to be seen by the living.

The art tradition created by that faith lasted over 1000 years. An illustration from the end of the period shows the same purpose. A wall-painting from the tomb of Neb-Amon, a court official sometime during the last centuries of the 2nd millennium BC, celebrates some of the most pleasurable aspects of life, such as dancing and feasting, merriment over which the dead man and his family eternally preside. In similar scenes the owner was often shown in his official position, carrying out forever his accustomed role. No doubt such scenes formed a pleasant biographical memorial of

the deceased, but the strength of Egyptian art forms suggests a deeper certainty: belief in some eternal order.

Thus for the Egyptians, whom the Hebrews came to know quite well during their long sojourn in Egypt, art served an entirely religious function. Their art was concerned with an idea rather than with appearance; the idea of eternal existence, expressed in all their funeral monuments. Certainly Israel was exposed to one of the richest expressions of art in history. Wood carving, for example, reached a standard not equaled in Europe until the Renaissance. God employed that skill in the construction of his tabernacle after his people made their exodus from Egypt.

Mesopotamia. Very different artistic solutions to religious questions were developed by Mesopotamian peoples. For them life was too engrossing and precarious to allow so much attention to death. In contrast with Egyptians, they believed that "when the gods created man they let death be his snare, and life withheld in their own hands" (Gilgamesh Epic). To make the best of life was all they hoped for. Depending on river water to sustain life and having to endure 5 hot months of summer, they identified success entirely with the princi-

A bronze figurine (from Babylonia) with an inscription from Warad-Sin, king of Larsa (a Sumerian city) in the early 2nd millennium BC.

ple of fertility. For fertility they felt themselves dependent on distant and fearful divinities to whom there was neither recourse nor relationship.

Sumerian mythology was built on a pattern of life-giving order, and Sumerian art was almost entirely a pictorial presentation of those myths. The Bull of Heaven was the one whose fiery breath burned up the crops. Im-dugud (from c. 3000 BC), whose wings covered the heavens with dark clouds, was the image of a benevolent rainstorm ending death-threatening drought. The life-giving process was celebrated with rituals in temples dedicated to such gods. In and around Sumerian temples was found one of the earliest kinds of statue, an image worshiped and supplicated for timely rains.

Their rich mythological tradition tied Mesopotamian peoples in the closest way to natural processes. From it came an emphasis on animal and vegetable motifs that strongly influenced Palestinian art during OT times. Late in the 2nd millennium BC there was a purely secular interest in wild animals and landscapes. Somewhat later appeared the great wall reliefs on royal palaces, stone carvings forming a continuous frieze about 7 feet high around the walls, sometimes in 2 registers with a cuneiform inscription between.

A lion hunt of the Assyrian king Ashurbanipal (669–633 BC), grandson of Sennacherib, shows how religious interest had given way to secular glorification of the king. Some Egyptian influence is evident, but differences are more obvious. The violent action of the animals, the close observation of gesture, and the vitality of the design all mark this example as a high point of Assyrian art. Such carvings were often records of military history without obvious religious intent. At times they would depict "genii," winged beings hovering over protectively, but rarely an actual god. In contrast with Egyptian art the king is not oversize. In fact, his size is consistent with the melancholy Mesopotamian view of life: he seems vulnerable, his victory not certain from the beginning.

Art in Ancient Palestine. The poverty of surviving art objects from ancient Palestine is a striking fact. Much may still lie buried beneath the earth, but only a small number of artifacts have been discovered. Possibly because Palestine is situated between great empires on either side, intermittent tensions allowed no artistic tradition to develop. The Palestinian people were agricultural, often nomadic. Their conditions were unfavorable to the development of art.

Prehistoric Art. Some ancient Palestinian art does survive. Artifacts dated to the Middle Stone Age (c. 8000 BC) have been found on Mt Carmel, where cave dwellers carved and engraved bone instruments. Excavations in Jericho have uncovered interesting primitive sculpture from the Neolithic period (New Stone Age, c. 6000 BC). Ancient Jericho is the oldest urban settlement yet discovered. Amid its houses and sanctuaries many unusual statues of human beings have been recovered. The statues are two-thirds lifesize but very thin, found generally in groups consisting of a child, man, and woman. They are made of lime over reeds and touched with red paint; eyes are represented by seashells. We are not certain of the magical or ritual significance of the figures. More obviously religious is a shrine, in and around which were scattered many animal figurines and models of male sex organs, indicating that fertility cults existed at that early date.

Art from the Chalcolithic period, in which metal first appears, is seen in excavations at Teleilat el-Ghassul on the Jordan plain near the Dead Sea. The people (c. 3500 BC) lived in well-constructed houses whose mud-brick walls were covered with fresco painting in several colors. Geometrical patterns were combined with naturalistic motifs. One shows an intricate 8-point star, originally set in the midst of a complex field of which only fragments are still visible. Among the objects identifiable are stylized dragons and various masks, no doubt worn by sorcerers. Whatever its ritual significance, this fresco represents a higher level of achievement in the art of painting than was again reached in Palestine for thousands of years.

Around 3000 BC, at the beginning of the Early Bronze Age, Palestine experienced a large influx of foreign cultural influence. People from Mesopotamia streamed through to Egypt and vice versa, influencing the development of art in Palestine. A stele (stone pillar set up for commemorative purposes) from somewhat later in that period shows a warrior holding a sword, with garb that surely is Egyptian of the pyramid age.

Canaanite Art. In such a cosmopolitan setting Canaanite art developed. The ethnic term "Canaanite" refers to the peoples of Palestine before settlement of the Israelite tribes in the latter part of the 2nd millennium BC. The Canaanites, like the Hebrews, were Semitic, and were subject to a wide variety of influences. From about 2000 to 1800 BC, the inhabitants of Transjordan were mostly nomadic. Abram found Canaanite chieftains living in fortresses with their families and retainers while the poor lived in hovels. In spite of constant warring, a local art began to flourish, influenced by vigorous intercourse with nearby nations. There was no organic unity of style, but individual works of art of high quality have survived.

Noteworthy is the art of Ugarit uncovered at Ras Shamra on the Syrian coast and dating from the 14th and 15th centuries BC. Although these people are not considered Canaanite, their art demonstrates the composite style that prevailed up to the time of the Israelite conquest. A limestone stele of the period represents Baal, the thunder god, brandishing a club in his right hand while the other hand strikes with a stylized thunderbolt ending in a spearhead. Baal here personifies Canaanite faith in the providence of nature. Because they believed him able to control the unruly rainwaters (the wavy line beneath the figure probaby represents the waters in the clouds or on mountaintops) they acclaimed him as their king, on whose precarious and awesome rule their lives depended. Commonly referred to as "he who mounteth the clouds," Baal embodied the power of fertility, expressed by his association with a bull. Here he wears the horns of the cult animal on his head. Baal looms large in OT accounts, as in Elijah's contest on Mt Carmel (1 Kgs 18). Baal's essential characteristics, seen also in figurines found in Megiddo and Lachish, differ greatly from those of the God of Israel, who also "rides through the heavens" (Dt 33:26) and "treads on the heights of the earth" (Am 4:13), and whose "steadfast love endures for ever" (2 Chr 5:13).

Also from Ugarit is a fertility goddess carved on the cover of an ivory box during the 14th century BC. Egyptian influence can be seen in the shoulders portrayed full face while the head and legs appear in profile. On the other hand, the pigtails and skirt are derived from the art of Asia Minor and the pattern of dress is Mycenaen-Cretan. The radical symmetrical placement of the animals probably originated in early Mesopotamian art. In both hands the goddess holds sheaves of grain, toward which 2 he-goats are reaching.

Elsewhere in Palestine very little sculpture has been unearthed. In Beth-shan local carvers made stelae and votive plaques of limestone for the temple of the local god Mekal. Influenced by Egyptian occupation forces, the artists did their best to make their work look Egyptian, as seen in a heavy basalt panel from Beth-shan dated about the 14th century BC. A temple guardian in the form of a god and another deity, Nergal, represented by a lion, battle on one register, and a lion is assailed by a dog on another. The lion motif, also present on a stone from a temple at Hazor, is probably of Mesopotamian origin. The lion symbolized the power inherent in all gods, later becoming a royal symbol for Assyrian kings.

Clay figurines and earthenware vessels were made in the shape of human figures, often grotesque. A higher level of sculptural art is shown in the ivory carvings that decorated the palaces and furniture of Canaanite chieftains. A 13th-century BC carved frieze found in Lachish shows bulls and lions fighting, a theme no doubt derived from Mesopotamian mythology. On a carved box from Tell-el-Farah, a master and his servants are arranged in a typically Egyptian fashion, yet the costumes are Syrian, the palm trees from Mesopotamia, and the bullocks from Aegean sources.

Excavations at Megiddo have uncovered many ivories dating from the early 12th century BC. An ivory box or casket carved in high relief with lions and cherubim may give us a hint of what the biblical cherubim over the temple altar looked like. From Megiddo also comes an inlaid ivory plaque depicting what is probably the celebration of a king's triumph. On the right the king stands in his chariot, with 2 naked prisoners attached to the harness, preceded by a musician and a warrior. On the left the king is served brew (which stewards behind the throne are preparing) from a bowl while the queen presents flowers to him. Egyptian conventions are obvious, and yet Asian elements are equally important, such as the tendency to fill in space with floral motifs rather than let space itself add to the dramatic impact.

The Development of Pottery. From the beginning of the Early Bronze Age (3000 BC) the shape and design of pottery was remarkably

Various shapes of pottery lamps.

consistent in each period. Throughout the 3rd millennium BC geometric patterns of parallel lines or lattice work were common, reaching a peak in the lustrous red and black burnished ware, elegantly ribbed and fluted, which has been found at Khirbet Kerak. A marked change occurred around 1500 BC, giving rise to a style of pottery unique to Palestine. At that time pottery displayed bird, fish, and bull motifs encased in beautiful and intricate geometrical designs in red and black or sepia. Designs became increasingly complex until the Philistine period (1150–1000 BC), when much more stylized bird motifs showed a strong Mediterranean influence.

During the latter part of the Canaanite period Palestine was virtually an outpost of the Egyptian empire. Art became a barbaric reflection of Egyptian civilization, as many cities were destroyed and burned. In the time of that decline the Hebrew people, worn from their wilderness wanderings, entered Palestine.

Art in the Biblical Period. *From the Patriarchs to the Entrance into Canaan.* The household idols stolen by Rachel (Gn 31:19–35) were probably very much like those found in excavations of Mesopotamian temples. They had a long and unfortunate history in Israel (see Jgs 17:5). We know that those "teraphim" were sometimes statues the size and shape of a man (1 Sm 19:11–16).

At the time of the exodus Moses instructed the Israelites to ask for gold and silver jewelry from the Egyptians (Ex 12:35). The prohibition against idolatry (Ex 20:4,5) did not prohibit artistic activity; at the same time Moses was given the Law, he was given instructions to build and adorn the tabernacle.

The tabernacle was a notable work of art. The specific pattern for it was given by God (Ex 25:9,40). It was to include an ark of acacia wood overlaid with gold (Ex 25:10–17). Over the ark were two cherubim of beaten gold (Ex 25:18–22). The exact appearance of these creatures is not described, but they were clearly celestial beings, whose outstretched wings were thought of as protecting the sacred object below. In Mesopotamia winged lions and bulls guarded all buildings of importance (cf. Gn 3:24). The representational sculpture God requested for his holy place was clearly Mesopotamian in conception and Egyptian in execution. Is it proper to speak of artistic parallels when God revealed the design directly to Moses? The fact is that God spoke of objects similar to things already in existence in neighboring countries. It seems reasonable that for the tabernacle to be a means of genuine worship, God would design it at least to some extent according to standards his people were used to and therefore could appreciate.

God also instructed Moses to make a lampstand. It too was to be of pure beaten gold, with ornaments in the form of almond blossoms (Ex 25:31–39). Finally, curtains of blue, purple, and scarlet set off the orange-brown acacia wood of the walls, making the tabernacle a place of exquisite beauty.

For all that exacting work, including the priests' ceremonial garments, God had specific craftsmen in mind. He said he had filled Bezalel with the Spirit of God, "with ability and intelligence, with knowledge and all craftsmanship" (Ex 31:1–6). Thus the most important commission for Bezalel and his helper Oholiab was accompanied by the first biblical mention of the giving of God's Spirit for a specific project: to make beautiful objects for the service of God.

Period of the Kings. Until Saul threw off the Philistine yoke, the Israelites in the Promised Land displayed "extraordinary simplicity and lack of cultural sophistication," according to archaeologists. No doubt they continued their seminomadic ways long after settling in Palestine. There was no patrician class to sponsor and encourage the arts. Only a few clay amulets (ornaments used as charms) have been found from that period, showing women about to give birth but without the insignia of a goddess common to pagan statues.

Although neighboring peoples exhibited a rich culture, especially in Beth-shan and Megiddo, Israel continued as a primitive and pastoral state. At the time of King David's death Hebrew society was becoming more complex. Solomon's reign was one of the most prosperous periods of civilization in biblical history, a view confirmed by archaeological discoveries. But of the greatest artistic project, Solomon's temple in Jerusalem, there are no material remains.

The Bible states that the plan and pattern for the temple were given by God (1 Chr 28:11,12,19). The structure was to be of stone finished with cedarwood, overlaid with gold and garnished with precious stones (2 Chr 3:6). In the inner sanctuary were again 2 cherubim, this time made of carved olivewood overlaid

Palm tree carved into the architecture of the synagogue at Capernaum.

A spectacular furnishing of the temple was a huge bronze basin, with decorative panels of cherubim and animals, containing 12,000 gallons of water for ritual ablutions. Ten mobile lavers or basins were also made for the temple, with side panels picturing lions, oxen, and cherubim. On some of the supports were carved animals and palm leaves (1 Kgs 7:27–37). A temple laver from Cyprus gives the general idea of what these supports looked like.

None of the animal and plant figures or colors decorating the temple had any religious or magical significance. Solomon said in his dedicatory prayer: "I have built thee an exalted house, a place for thee to dwell in forever" (1 Kgs 8:13). The single purpose of the temple was to provide a place to meet with God, and all the parts served that purpose. The beautiful details added to the glory of temple occasions, playful carvings speaking simply of sheer delight experienced in worship.

In contrast with the tabernacle, foreign craftsmen were imported to build the temple (1 Kgs 5:6), to work in bronze (1 Kgs 7:13,14) and other materials (2 Chr 2:11–14). The foreign craftsmen brought the finest skills of the day, gathering the "glory of the nations" into the house of God.

Solomon's throne, built around the same time, was also a splendid work of art (1 Kgs 10:18–20). It was of ivory overlaid with gold and flanked by lions, symbols of royalty throughout the Near East. The splendor of Solomon's reign has been shown by excavation of the appropriate levels at Megiddo. A small bronze stand sheds light on the bronze supports for the temple basins and indicates that the Hebrews were themselves competent metal workers.

According to the Bible, Samaria later became a prosperous cultural center. It was the location of Ahab's ivory palace (1 Kgs 22:39) that brought on Amos' particular condemnation (Am 3:15). Archaeology richly supports the view of Samaria presented in Scripture.

with gold, 15 feet high, with a similar wingspan, together covering the whole wall (1 Kgs 6:23–28).

The walls of the temple were carved with cherubim and palm trees and covered with gold. On panels and beams were carved lions and oxen. On the olivewood doors were cherubim, palm trees, and open flowers, all overlaid with gold (1 Kgs 6:29–36). Such motifs were common in Mesopotamian and Canaanite art. More unusual were 2 pillars made of bronze for the vestibule, with 2 rows of pomegranates and lily-work at the top.

A griffin on an ivory inlay from Megiddo.

Ivory inlays dating from the 8th and 9th centuries BC and used to decorate expensive furniture have been found. Some items recovered from the area of the royal residence may actually have been part of Ahab's state furniture, as for example, an image of Harpocrates emerging from a lotus flower, a figure obviously of Egyptian inspiration. Below is a cherub amid stylized vegetable motifs. A reason for Amos' specific mention of furniture (Am 3:12; 6:4) may have been that its decoration showed Ahab's inclination to foreign superstition as well as to luxury (1 Kgs 16:29–31).

From the Exile to the New Testament. The use of art in the service of idolatry and at the expense of the poor brought down the wrath of the prophets. In their denunciations of idols Isaiah and Jeremiah both referred to techniques for making statues (Is 40:18–20; Jer 10:3–5). Kings and the rich were reprimanded for extravagantly building luxurious palaces, paneled with cedar and painted with "vermilion" (Jer 22:13–15), especially when God's house was in ruins (Hg 1:2–4). In a powerful allegorical passage (Ez 23:1–21) the southern kingdom was rebuked for "prostituting" itself (making military and political alliances with idolatrous nations); Judah was tempted by "men portrayed upon the wall," probably referring to the wall reliefs of Babylonian military splendor already noted.

Admiration also led to imitation. In a difficult passage denouncing vile things that the people of Israel were doing in secret, the prophet shows them worshiping creeping things and "loathsome beasts" portrayed on the walls (Ez 8:9–11). The word used indicates engraving rather than mere painting.

An amazing reference to art in the OT prophets is Ezekiel's vision of the restored temple (Ez 40–42). The detail is even more elaborate than for Solomon's temple but with much that is similar. The influence of Assyrian art during the exile is obvious, as in the cherubim with the face of a man and of a young lion (Ez 41:19). However, the vision is again said to come directly from God (Ez 40:1–4).

Not much can be said about art during the intertestamental period. The temple candelabra, part of the plunder from the destruction of Jerusalem in AD 70, are portrayed on the Arch of Titus in Rome. They show a strong Greek influence on Hasmonean art (2nd century BC), with animal-faced dragons and other animal and geometrical motifs. Beyond that, the principal art objects are coins, which reflect a certain crudeness. They also indicate a sudden shift from human representation to ritual symbols as rise of national feeling brought on religious prohibitions. Ossuaries (chests for the bones of the dead) were engraved with 6-point stars, rosettes, flowers, and even architectural designs, probably by a special guild of ossuary workers at Jerusalem.

Herod the Great was fully committed to the spread of Greek culture, which became the dominant influence of the intertestamental period. Although his building program was extensive, the art was imitative and commercialized, Greek art itself being in a stage of postclassical decline. What has survived tended to realism and overelaboration. The Greco-Roman sensibility that invaded Palestine brought a troupe of Greek and Roman divinities. Subsequent Christian art had an early tendency to "baptize" pagan motifs.

Conclusion. There was no defect in artistic ability on the part of Israel. Though properly speaking there was no Hebrew visual art style, one has only to think of their prose and poetry to appreciate their sensitivity to beauty. Because they were a people directed by the Word of God, their pursuits in the aesthetic realm as well as in the ethical were to be disciplined and directed by God's revelation. If that discouraged somewhat the kind of experimentation prized by modern artists, it certainly allowed no doubt as to the high calling of art. Further, having a life ordered by the Word of God, their culture tended to be oriented verbally rather than visually. The Hebrew vocabulary in the OT was able to reflect the brilliance or value of a color better than its hue.

Biblical Attitudes Toward Art. For a fuller understanding of the Bible's relation to art, we should see what is implied in some biblical passages whose relevance to art may not be immediately obvious. Most significant, of course, is the creation account. When God finished the work of making the material world, he pronounced all of it "very good" (Gn 1:31). The final thing to be done after the work of creation, just as for any artist, was to pause and enjoy it. So it is clear from the beginning that the material world—things shaped and visible—can be worthy of praise. And further, the enjoyment of such things is a spontaneous response that God himself shares. Part of what it means to be made in God's image is that we respond to loveliness.

The Bible also speaks of the tragic effects of the fall, an event transforming artistic expression. Through art fallen humanity reveals a futile and sometimes desperate attempt to appease death and to find rest, a part of the human attempt to deny mortality. In the context of such tragedy the prohibition of Exodus 20:4–6 can be understood. God forbids the making of any idols or images of any created object to worship. From the broader biblical context, from the historical setting, and from the traditional rabbinic interpretation of this

A relief of an ark on wheels, carved in the lintel of the synagogue at Capernaum and representing a portable ark of the covenant.

portion of the Law, it is clear that Exodus 20 has idolatry in view and not art in general.

During the giving of the Law, God's instructions for the tabernacle show that he did not mean to rule out representational art. God even promised to inspire the appointed craftsmen with his Spirit. Yet our brief historical survey has given ample grounds for warning. Ancient art was universally associated with idolatry and pagan practices. To check such sacrilege among a small people caught helplessly between strong cultural traditions that were thoroughly idolatrous, God gave careful instruction. At times his instruction was applied by Israel even more strictly than God intended.

Jewish application of the Law illustrates the Law's intention. In the general rabbinic view the prohibition referred to beings beheld by prophetic vision at the throne of God or to anthropomorphic visions of God. The rabbis thus forbade explicitly only the fashioning of the four figures in Ezekiel or any other angelic being. Three-dimensional human figures that might be used as objects of worship were especially forbidden, but portrait painting was never understood to be forbidden by the Law. The Law was usually observed scrupulously. During Talmudic times (after Christ) the pious avoided even looking at the pictures engraved on Roman coins, which portrayed the images of emperors who were worshiped as gods.

The OT view of God and of worship was of profound significance for attitudes toward art. Since God was as spirit perfect in goodness and holiness he must be worshiped in a spiritual way—that is, with a humble and contrite heart that expressed itself in obedience to the Law. Although the material world was never viewed as evil (cf. Ps 19), there was constant concern that sensual or corporeal beauty might detract from the way of holiness. Fear that worshipers might be distracted while at prayer has discouraged art in the synagogue generally; decoration only in honor of the Torah is permitted.

The prophets denounced those who traded the beautiful and lofty vision of a holy God for an earthly and sensual beauty. Isaiah emphasized the contrast in a striking way. The God of creation is so far above any idol (Is 40:18–21) that as he "sits above the circle of the earth," the people below "are like grasshoppers" (Is 40:22). Our idea of beauty, like our righteousness, appears as a polluted garment before the living God "who stretches out the heavens like a curtain."

The same theme is echoed in Jewish wisdom literature. "To know thee is complete righteousness," and we are not to be led astray by "the evil intent of human art," by "the fruitless toil of painters, a figure stained with varied colors, whose appearance arouses yearning in fools, so that they desire the lifeless form of a dead image" (Wisd of Sol 15:3–5). In that sense "beauty is vain" (Prv 31:30).

Paul's reaction to the classical beauty and paganism of Athens is perfectly consistent (Acts 17). When Paul rose to speak on Mars Hill, he could easily see the magnificent frieze of the Parthenon, the Temple of Wingless Victory, and the huge statue of Athena Promachos. Like the prophets before him, "his spirit was provoked within him as he saw that the city was full of idols" (Acts 17:16). Was that his only reaction to such splendor? In his address Paul quoted two Greek poets, an indication that he was by no means insensitive to beauty. Rather, he saw that art taken out of the service of God became a snare, and that God's kingdom matters more than man's achievement. The error of the Athenians was not in their view of art but in their view of God, revealed by their art.

The apostle John urged Christians to "keep yourselves from idols" (1 Jn 5:21). Rather than a denunciation of art, we see in the Bible an affirmation of an order in which all things, including art, find their relation to God.

What is the place of art in such a higher vision? First, we may remind ourselves of the care God took for the setting of worship. In the tabernacle and the temple each part was specially prepared so that the whole would display what must have been exquisite beauty. Joy and delight, dancing and singing, were everywhere a vital part of OT worship, reflecting something of the character of God.

In the Bible, beauty is seen as the working out of the order of things that God set in motion at creation. God is closely identified with such beauty or fitness, which is often called "wisdom" (Prv 8:1,22–36).

Although that kind of beauty (or wisdom) is not to be found naturally among fallen humanity (Ps 14:1–3), the NT asserts that it is offered to all through Jesus Christ. At the cross of Christ the order that art reflects is restored and the artist is retuned to the inspiration that God built into things. Creation itself is to take part in the great renewal called "salvation" (Rom 8:18–23). Heaven, where worship will become a natural life style, is seen in the NT as filled with beauty and delight. Into its eternally open doors shall be brought "the glory and the honor of the nations" (Rv 21:26). According to the Bible, every Christian whom God has gifted in the arts, and who "tunes his harp" by God's Word, has a contribution to make.

Can the experience of art help a Christian grow in grace toward the likeness of Christ? Art should be seen not as supplanting the nourishment of the Word or the life of the Spirit, but as an extension and a support. The medieval mystic Bernard of Clairvaux said that in the first stage of the vision of God "the mind focuses and sharpens its attention on simple things, on the beauty of the world around, putting down roots for its growth heavenward." The simple music David made while out alone tending sheep was taken up into his worship and is now in the Book of Psalms. Art can be part of the tuning up and sensitizing by which the Holy Spirit makes Christians more receptive to God's will and more sensitive to the tears of other human beings. Art may be part of the grand rehearsal for the heavenly chorus.

WILLIAM A. DYRNESS

See ARCHITECTURE; MUSIC AND MUSICAL INSTRUMENTS; TABERNACLE, TEMPLE; POTTERY.

Artaxerxes. Name of three kings of the Persian empire.

1. Artaxerxes I (464–424 BC), known as Macrocheir or Longimanus, son and successor of Xerxes I (485–465 BC). Xerxes I was the Ahasuerus of the Book of Esther and Ezra 4:6. A few years after the succession of Artaxerxes I the Greeks urged Egypt to revolt against Persia. Only in 454 BC was that movement crushed along with other dissension in the Persian empire. By 449 BC, when peace was made between the Greeks and Persians by the treaty of Callias, Artaxerxes had gained full control over his empire, and a period of peace resulted.

Artaxerxes I was the ruler who brought the rebuilding of Jerusalem to a temporary standstill (Ezr 4:7–23), and who commissioned Ezra to visit the city in the capacity of "secretary of state for Jewish affairs" in 458 BC (Ezr 7:8,11–26). In 445 BC Nehemiah went to Jerusalem as civil governor in the 20th year of Artaxerxes I (Neh 1:1; 2:1). By altering the text of Ezra 7:7 to read "thirty-seventh" instead of "seventh," some scholars have tried to show that Artaxerxes II was the Persian king under whom Nehemiah worked. The Elephantine papyri, however, indicate that Sanballat, governor of Samaria, was quite advanced in years in 408 BC, shortly before the death of Darius II (423–405 BC); hence Sanballat's opposition to Nehemiah must have occurred years earlier under Artaxerxes I. The dates of Ezra and Nehemiah thus fall within the lifetime of this monarch.

Artaxerxes I was notable for his kindness toward the Jews in Persia, once matters of procedure had been established clearly; his support for the work of Ezra and Nehemiah is evident from their writings.

See AHASUERUS; EZRA, BOOK OF; NEHEMIAH, BOOK OF; ESTHER, BOOK OF.

2. Artaxerxes II Mnemon (404–359 BC), grandson of Artaxerxes I and son of Darius II. His reign was a time of unrest in the Persian empire, one result of which was the loss of Egypt about 401 BC. He constructed several splendid buildings and seems to have enlarged the palace at Susa.

3. Artaxerxes III Ochus (358–338 BC), son and successor of Artaxerxes II. He brought peace to the empire by shrewd diplomacy, but

he was assassinated. Neither he nor his father is mentioned in the OT.

See PERSIA, PERSIANS.

Artemas. Christian fellow worker whom the apostle Paul considered as a replacement for Titus on the island of Crete (Ti 3:12). Later tradition describes Artemas as bishop of Lystra.

Artemis. Greek goddess of the moon, wild animals, and hunting. The cult of Artemis at Ephesus, where she is called Diana by the Romans (Acts 19:23–41), regarded her especially as a fertility goddess.

See DIANA.

Artificer. Skilled craftsman; KJV rendering of craftsman in Genesis 4:22; 1 Chronicles 29:5; 2 Chronicles 34:11; and Isaiah 3:3.

See TRADES AND OCCUPATIONS (CRAFTSMAN).

Artisan. Skilled craftsman working in the major mediums of wood, stone, metals, gems, and clay; important guild in the middle class of Hebrew society during the period of the monarchy.

See TRADES AND OCCUPATIONS (CRAFTSMAN).

Arubboth, Aruboth. Town that served as headquarters for one of King Solomon's 12 administrative districts (1 Kgs 4:10, KJV Aruboth). Arubboth was probably in Manasseh's tribal territory, about nine miles north of Samaria, at the site of modern 'Arrabeh.

Arumah. City where Gideon's son Abimelech lived after he was driven out of Shechem by its inhabitants (Jgs 9:1,22–25,31,41); perhaps alternately called Rumah in 2 Kings 23:36. It has been suggested that Arumah is modern Khirbet el-'Orma.

Arvad, Arvadite. Small fortified island about 2 miles off the coast of Syria (ancient Phoenicia) and 30 miles north of Tripolis. Arvad developed a large trading and fighting fleet, and the fame of its sailors was referred to in a description of the naval power of Tyre (Ez 27:8,11). Egyptian records recount Arvad's fall to Thutmose III about 1472 BC. Assyrian records indicate the importance of Arvad and its recurrent conquest by foreign powers from the 11th to the 7th centuries BC.

Arvad was later known as Aradus or Arados, and as such is referred to in 1 Maccabees 15:23. During the Persian and Hellenistic periods it was once again an important Mediterranean seaport, only to decline again. Today Arvad is known as Ruad.

The Canaanite tribe of Arvadites (Gn 10:18; 1 Chr 1:16) possibly had an ethnic connection with the island Arvad.

Arza. Superintendent of the palace at Tirzah belonging to King Elah of the northern kingdom of Israel. The drunken king was murdered in Arza's home by Zimri, who then declared himself king (1 Kgs 16:9,10).

Asa. 1. Third king of the southern kingdom of Judah (910–869 BC) after the split of Solomon's empire into independent kingdoms. Solomon's son Rehoboam, Asa's grandfather, had neither Solomon's wisdom nor his tact. Rehoboam failed to use diplomacy to avoid an approaching explosion of popular resentment against Solomon's oppressive policies; in fact, Rehoboam actively precipitated the explosion. Asa came to the throne just after his father, Abijam (or Abijah), had reigned only briefly (913–910 BC). Asa thus inherited a shrunken, vulnerable kingdom. Moreover, he was thrust into a suddenly unstable political arena shaken by collapse of the great world empires of Old Babylonia to the north and east in Mesopotamia, and of Egypt to the southwest. Hence until the emerging might of Assyria was firmly established (mid-9th century BC), the small Palestinian states (Israel, Judah, Syria, the Aramaeans and Phoenicians, and to some degree the peoples of Moab and Edom) were free to push and shove among themselves.

The rival states had superficial similarities, especially Judah and Israel, but were divided by deep differences and intense self-interest. Borders were in perpetual dispute—never fully settled, but seldom contested in all-out bloody conflict. Threats, expedience, bribes, payment of tribute, marriages for power-purchase, and other cunning arts in the catalog of political kingcraft were employed to shift alliances. Since all were playing the same game, a kind of fluid balance resulted.

At the beginning of King Asa's reign there was an initial decade of peace and prosperity. Then, however, he was called upon to face enemy threats and invasion. In those crises he trusted God and forced out or defeated all who attempted to conquer, divide, or destroy Judah (2 Chr 14:1–8). Further, he cleansed the land of pagan shrines and places of worship and even took away the royal prerogatives and standing of Maacah, his mother. She had erected an image of the fertility goddess Asherah (1 Kgs 15:10; 2 Chr 15:16).

Nonetheless, later in his reign Asa abruptly abandoned his trust in God. By means of a huge gift that stripped the temple treasures he entered an alliance with Ben-hadad, king of

Damascus (Syria), in order to force Baasha, ruler of the northern kingdom of Israel, to withdraw from newly conquered territory in Judah. Asa had become heedless of God's faithful protection when Israel, Judah's mortal enemy, stood triumphant and strategically poised to strike, only 5 miles from Jerusalem. Asa's power play worked. Israel had to retire from the field in the south to meet Benhadad's threat from the north. When Hanani spoke plainly to Asa about his disbelief in God, Asa was infuriated and had Hanani thrown into prison (2 Chr 16:7–10).

For the last years of his long 41-year reign, Asa was ill; "yet even in his disease he did not seek the Lord, but sought help from physicians" (2 Chr 16:12). He died and was buried in honor in the royal tombs (1 Kgs 15:24; 2 Chr 16:14).

See ISRAEL, HISTORY OF; CHRONICLES, BOOKS OF FIRST AND SECOND; CHRONOLOGY, OLD TESTAMENT; KING, KINGSHIP.

2. A Levite and Berechiah's father. Berechiah lived in one of the villages of the Netophathites after the exile (1 Chr 9:16).

Asahel. 1. Warrior among David's mighty men known as "the thirty" (2 Sm 23:24; 1 Chr 11:26). Asahel was the son of David's half sister Zeruiah and the brother of Joab and Abishai (2 Sm 2:18; 1 Chr 2:16). In the battle of Gibeon, David's general Joab engaged the forces of Abner, leader of Ish-bosheth's army. Asahel, who "was as swift of foot as a wild gazelle," pursued Abner, but in the ensuing encounter Abner killed Asahel (2 Sm 2:18–23,32).

2. One of the Levites sent out by King Jehoshaphat of Judah to teach the people the law of the Lord (2 Chr 17:8).

3. Temple aide appointed by King Hezekiah to take care of the tithed offerings given to support the Levites (2 Chr 31:13).

4. Father of Jonathan. Jonathan (not to be confused with Saul's son) opposed the appointment of a commission to take action concerning the foreign (pagan) wives of some of the Jews after the Babylonian exile (Ezr 10:15).

Asahiah. KJV form of Asaiah, Josiah's servant, in 2 Kings 22:12,14.

See ASAIAH #1.

Asaiah. 1. Royal servant sent by King Josiah of Judah to ask the prophetess Huldah about the meaning of the book of the Law found in the renovation of the temple (2 Kgs 22:12,14, KJV Asahiah; 2 Chr 34:20).

2. Clan leader of Simeon's tribe who settled in Gedor (Gerar?) during Hezekiah's reign (1 Chr 4:36).

3. Levitical leader in the time of King David. Asaiah helped bring the ark to Jerusalem (1 Chr 6:30; 15:6,11).

4. Shiloni's oldest son. Asaiah's family was among the first to resettle in Jerusalem after the exile (1 Chr 9:5). Perhaps the same as Maaseiah of Nehemiah 11:5.

See MAASEIAH #14.

Asaph. 1. Berechiah's son, an important tabernacle musician during King David's reign (1 Chr 6:31,32,39). Along with Heman the head singer and Ethan, Asaph was appointed to sound bronze cymbals during the ceremony when the ark was brought to the new tabernacle (1 Chr 15:1–19). David appointed Asaph to serve "by giving constant praise and thanks to the Lord God of Israel" (1 Chr 16:4,5 LB) and to lead Israel in a special psalm of praise (1 Chr 16:7–36). Along with his relatives he ministered daily before the ark (1 Chr 16:37; 25:6,9; 1 Esd 1:15; 5:27,59). He was also described as David's private prophet (1 Chr 25:1,2).

Asaph's name appears in the superscriptions of Psalms 50 and 73 to 83 and in the guild he established, "the sons of Asaph" (1 Chr 25:1; 2 Chr 35:15; Ezr 2:41; Neh 7:44; 11:22).

2. Joah's father. Joah was the recorder (court historian or royal scribe) in King Hezekiah's administration (2 Kgs 18:18,37; Is 36:3,22).

3. Temple guard or gatekeeper, seemingly the same person as Ebiasaph (1 Chr 26:1; cf. 9:19).

4. Keeper of the king's forest in Palestine under Artaxerxes Longimanus (Neh 2:8). Nehemiah asked this Asaph for timber to rebuild the wall, gates, and structures of Jerusalem.

Asarel, Asareel. Jehallelel's son from Judah's tribe (1 Chr 4:16, KJV Asareel).

Asarelah. KJV form of Asharelah, Asaph's son, in 1 Chronicles 25:2.

See ASHARELAH.

Ascension of Christ. Transference of the resurrected body of Jesus from this world to heaven. Of the NT writers only Luke described Jesus' ascension. Acts 1:9–11 pictures a scene in which Jesus was "taken up" and disappeared into a cloud. Luke 24:50,51 and Acts 1:12 locate that final event near Bethany, east of Jerusalem on the Mt of Olives.

Matthew concluded his history before Pentecost, but John suggested the ascension in Jesus' own comments: Jesus has departed, but he will return (21:22); he cannot be touched, for he must ascend (20:17); many will believe without having seen him (20:29). Thus, the Gospels assume that (1) after the resurrection Jesus appeared to his disciples; (2) at some point in time those appearances ceased; and (3) although physically absent, Jesus is still spiritually present in his church. Other NT writings agree. The apostle Paul wrote that God raised Christ from the dead "and made him sit at his right hand in the heavenly places" (Eph 1:20) or, as the writer of Hebrews put it, "at the right hand of the Majesty on high" (Heb 1:3).

The ascension, however, is more than merely a past event. It has further significance in the NT which can be summarized under two headings: (1) its meaning for Christ and (2) its meaning for the Christian.

For Christ, the ascension is the necessary entrance into his heavenly "glorification" in which he sits on the right hand of the Father until his enemies become his footstool (Ps 110:1—the OT text most quoted in the NT). The ascension is proof of his glorification and his superiority over such OT heroes as David (Acts 2:33–36). By his ascension he rises over all and fills all (Eph 4:10), receiving "the name which is above every name" (Phil 2:9–11). For the author of the Book of Hebrews the ascension is also proof of Christ's superiority to angels; he sits enthroned while they are constantly being sent out to serve (Heb 1:13). Angels, authorities, and powers are all subject to the ascended Christ (1 Tm 3:16; 1 Pt 3:22).

For the Christian, the ascension of Christ is meaningful in four ways. First, without it there would be no gift of the Holy Spirit, who could not come until Jesus had ascended and sent him (Jn 16:7). Without the ascension the church would have Jesus locally in one place, not spiritually present "wherever two or three are gathered" (Mt 18:20; cf. 28:20).

Second, since a truly human Jesus has ascended to heaven, human beings can also ascend there. Jesus went "to prepare a place" for his followers (Jn 14:2). The hope of those who are "in Christ" is that they will eventually ascend to be with him (2 Cor 5:1–10).

Third, the ascension proves that the sacrifice of Christ is finished and accepted by God. Jesus has passed through the heavens (Heb 4:14) and entered the presence of God (Heb 6:20), which is described as the inner sanctuary of the heavenly temple, the real temple of which the one on earth was a copy (Heb 9:24). Having brought a single, once-for-all sacrifice to God (Heb 9:12), Christ sat down (Heb 1:3; 10:12; 12:2), showing that no repetition of his sacrifice is necessary.

Fourth, the ascension means that there is a human being in heaven who sympathizes with humanity and can therefore intercede on humanity's behalf (1 Jn 2:1). Jesus has experienced everything humans experience—birth, growth, temptation, suffering, and death—and therefore he can serve effectively as an intermediary before God in heaven (Heb 2:17; 5:7–10). Christ's ascension assures the church that God understands the human situation and that Christians can therefore approach him boldly in their prayers (Heb 4:14–16).

Thus Christ's ascension is an indispensable aspect of NT teaching. It is the basis for recognition of Christ's exalted status and for the Christian's confidence and hope.

PETER H. DAVIDS

See CHRISTOLOGY; KINGDOM OF GOD (HEAVEN); JESUS CHRIST, LIFE AND TEACHING OF.

Ascent of Heres. Place mentioned in Judges 8:13.

See HERES #2.

Ascents, Song of. Superscription of Psalms 120–134.

See SONG OF ASCENTS, SONG OF DEGREES.

Asenath. Joseph's Egyptian wife who became the mother of Manasseh and Ephraim. Asenath was the daughter of the priest Potiphera (Gn 41:45,50–52; 46:20).

Aser. KJV form of Asher in Luke 2:36 and Revelation 7:6.

See ASHER, TRIBE OF.

Ash. *See* PLANTS.

Ashan. Town in the southwestern Judean foothills slightly northwest of Beersheba. Ashan first belonged to Judah's tribe (Jos 15:42), then to Simeon's (Jos 19:7), and finally to the Levites as a city of refuge (1 Chr 6:59). David roamed there with his outlaw band (called "Borashan," 1 Sm 30:30, KJV Chorashan). The city of Ain mentioned in Joshua 21:16 probably refers to Ashan (this should not be confused with Ain in the northeast of Canaan, Nm 34:11). Ashan is commonly identified with Khirbet 'Asan.

See CITIES OF REFUGE.

Asharelah. One of Asaph's four sons appointed by David to assist with prophecy and music in the sanctuary (1 Chr 25:2, KJV Asarelah); alternately called Jesharelah in verse 14.

Ashbea. Name of a family in 1 Chronicles 4:21 (KJV). The RSV is probably correct in translating the name as the family's place of residence.

See BETH-ASHBEA.

Ashbel, Ashbelite. Benjamin's son who emigrated to Egypt with his grandfather Jacob (Gn 46:21; 1 Chr 8:1). The Ashbelites, his descendants, were included in Moses' census in the wilderness (Nm 26:38). Ashbel is elsewhere called Jediael (1 Chr 7:6).

Ashchenaz. KJV form of Ashkenaz, Gomer's son, in 1 Chronicles 1:6 and Jeremiah 51:27.

See ASHKENAZ.

Ashdod, Ashdodite, Ashdothite. One of the Philistines' 5 main cities (the "pentapolis") along with Gaza, Ashkelon, Gath, and Ekron (Jos 13:3). Ashdod was located midway between Joppa and Gaza, about three miles from the coast. The ancient tell has been excavated extensively since 1962. The earliest level found was Canaanite, dating to the 17th century BC. When the Israelites arrived in the Promised Land, the city was inhabited by the giant Anakim (Jos 11:21,22). Though unconquered, it was assigned to Judah's tribe (Jos 15:46,47). Its people were referred to as Ashdodites (Jos 13:3, KJV Ashdothites; Neh 4:7). During the 12th century BC the coast of Palestine was invaded by the Sea Peoples, a group of tribes from the Aegean area. Ashdod was destroyed and reoccupied by one of these peoples, the Philistines. Excavations at Ashdod have uncovered three levels of Philistine occupation and have furnished a glimpse of the material culture of these traditional enemies of Israel.

In the days of Eli the priest, the Philistines captured the ark of the covenant and placed it first in the temple of their god Dagon in Ashdod, then in Gath and Ekron (1 Sm 5). A plague broke out wherever the ark went, so the Philistine rulers returned it with an offering of gold (1 Sm 6:1–18). Although David and Solomon controlled Ashdod, it was not until Uzziah came to the throne of the kingdom of Judah (792–740 BC) that Ashdod was actually conquered (2 Chr 26:6). However, before long Judah's military power waned, and the city became independent again. Ashdod resisted Assyrian encroachments until Sargon II attacked and destroyed it in 711 BC, a fact illumined by three fragments of a basalt stele of Sargon found at Ashdod in 1963. Those events led Isaiah to warn Judah against supporting Ashdod or counting on Egypt or Ethiopia to oppose the Assyrians (Is 20). Excavations at Ashdod show evidence of the destruction by both Uzziah and Sargon II.

Ashdod remained under Assyrian control until the Egyptian pharaoh Psamtik I (664–609 BC) took the city after a siege of 29 years (perhaps the longest in history). Later, probably at the time of the fall of Jerusalem (586 BC), Nebuchadnezzar conquered Ashdod and took its king to his court. Jeremiah and Zephaniah had prophesied about the people remaining in Ashdod (Jer 25:20; Zep 2:4). That remnant later opposed Nehemiah's rebuilding of Jerusalem, and its women married Jewish husbands (Neh 4:7; 13:23,24). Earlier, the prophet Zechariah had predicted further desolation for Ashdod (Zec 9:6).

During Maccabean times the city, then called Azotus, was attacked and plundered by both Judas and Jonathan Maccabeus because of its idolatry (1 Mc 4:12–15; 5:68; 10:77–85; 11:4). Freed by Pompey in 63 BC, Ashdod became part of the Roman province of Syria. Later Herod the Great willed the city to his sister Salome. Philip the evangelist preached the message of Christ in Azotus (Acts 8:40). The early Christian historian Eusebius regarded it as an important town in the 4th century AD, and Christian bishops were located there from the 4th through the 6th centuries. During the Middle Ages, Ashdod or Azotus began to decline, and now is only a small village called Esdud.

Ashdod was located about three miles inland and therefore had a port, separated from the city proper, called Ashdod Yam, or Ashdod-on-the-Sea. That coastal town in later years became larger than the inland city. Excavations in the area of the seaport have uncovered remains of Canaanite, Israelite, and Hellenistic occupation. One interesting find was the remains of a Hellenistic dye operation. A purple dye made from the murex shell was used to dye cloth worn by royalty and the wealthy. The site of the port continued to be occupied through the Arabic period, and today Israel has built a port near the site of ancient Ashdod Yam.

Ashdoth-Pisgah. KJV form of "slopes of Pisgah" (Dt 3:17; Jos 12:3; 13:20), referring to the slopes of Mt Pisgah.

See PISGAH, MOUNT.

Asher (Person). Jacob's son born to Leah's maid Zilpah (Gn 30:12,13). The name Asher, probably meaning "happy," was given to the child by Leah in her delight at his birth. Asher had four sons, Imnah, Ishvah, Ishvi, and Beriah, and a daughter, Serah (Gn 46:17; 1 Chr 7:30). Some have speculated that the tribe of Asher took its name from a locality mentioned in Egyptian texts of the 13th century BC. It is more likely that the tribe bore the name of its ancestor. Asher and his brothers received a special blessing and prediction from Jacob as he was dying (Gn 49:20; cf. Dt 33:24,25, where the dying Moses blessed Asher and the other tribes).

See ASHER, TRIBE OF.

Asher (Place). Place mentioned in Tobit 1:2, identified as Hazor.

See HAZOR #1.

Asher, Tribe of. Israelite tribe that inhabited the fertile coastal territory when the Promised Land was divided for settlement. Asher's allotment stretched north of Mt Carmel to a point slightly above the city of Sidon. The eastern boundary ran along the western slopes of the hills of Galilee (Jos 19:24–31,34). The tribes of Zebulun and Naphtali were Asher's eastern neighbors. Due south, the Carmel mountain range was a natural barrier between Asher and the tribe of Manasseh. The land of Asher was agriculturally rich, and is still known for its olive groves. Economically the people of Asher joined in maritime trade with the Phoenicians of the city of Tyre.

As a tribe, Asher fluctuated in size. From the few who entered Egypt with their father, Jacob, the tribe grew to 41,500 adult warriors at Mt Sinai (Nm 1:40,41). At the second census in the wilderness the tribe numbered 53,400 soldiers (Nm 26:47). At the time of King David the number varied from 26,000 to 40,000 warriors (1 Chr 7:40; 12:36). Asher was never more than fifth in size among the tribes of Israel.

The tribe joined the rest of Israel in rejecting the optimistic reports of Caleb and Joshua about the land of Canaan (Nm 13:30–14:10). As a result, that generation perished in the wilderness after 40 years of wandering (Nm 14:22–25).

At the close of the northern campaign in the Promised Land, Joshua gave the remaining seven tribes their own territory (Jos 18:2). The fifth partition went to Asher's descendants. Earlier Ahihud had been chosen by God to distribute land within the territory given to Asher's tribe (Nm 34:16,27). Certain Levites, descendants of Gershom, were allocated cities within its borders (Jos 21:6,30; 1 Chr 6:62,74).

Like all the Israelite tribes Asher was never able to possess all of its inheritance. Failure to drive out the inhabitants of Acco, Sidon, Ahlab, Achzib, Helbah, Aphik, and Rehob subjected the tribe to the degredations of pagan culture (Jgs 1:31). The "unpossessed" territory of the Sidonians and the Phoenicians stretched along the coastal region for 200 miles. Thus "the Asherites dwelt among the Canaanites, the inhabitants of the land; for they did not drive them out" (Jgs 1:32). It is possible that Asher's tribe, having become a partner in the enterprises of the successful Phoenicians, lost all desire to expel them from their cities.

After the death of the Israelite judge Ehud, Israel fell into the hands of Jabin, king of Canaan. When the judge Deborah stirred up Barak to marshal Israel's forces for battle, God gave their army a great victory and liberated them from their oppressor (Jgs 4). After the victory Deborah complained that "Asher sat still at the coast of the sea, settling down by his landings" (Jgs 5:17). Eventually, through amalgamation, the tribe succumbed to Phoenician religious and cultural influences. Foreign invasion and pagan inroads were its downfall.

Little is said in the Bible of the tribe's leadership. At the time of the exodus, when the nation was organized at Mt Sinai, Pagiel the son of Ochran became tribal chief (Nm 1:13; 2:27; 7:72; 10:26). But the Bible is silent from then on about Asher's leaders. None of the judges of Israel came from Asher, and in King David's day the tribes of Asher and Gad were omitted from the list of the nation's chief officers (1 Chr 27:16–22).

Nevertheless there are some bright spots in Asher's tribal history. The tribe answered the call of Gideon to drive out the Midianite enemy (Jgs 6:1–8,35; 7:23). They rallied with the rest of the tribes of Israel to defend Saul, their first king (1 Sm 11:7). Later, 40,000 Asherites sided with David to give him Saul's kingdom, "according to the word of the Lord" (1 Chr 12:23,36). After the fall of Samaria in 722 BC a small remnant came to Jerusalem to observe the first Passover feast in many years (2 Chr 30:5), when King Hezekiah (715–686 BC) invited all the tribes to assemble for the Passover. "The couriers went from city to city through the country of Ephraim and Manasseh, and as far as Zebulun; but they laughed them to scorn, and mocked them. Only a few men of Asher, of Manasseh, and of Zebulun humbled themselves and came to Jerusalem" (2 Chr 30:10,11).

In the NT one of Asher's descendants is mentioned, an 84-year-old widow named Anna, a prophetess. She described Jesus as "the redemption of Jerusalem" from the time of his dedication to the Lord in the temple (Lk 2:36–38, KJV Aser). CYRIL J. BARBER

See ISRAEL, HISTORY OF.

Asherah, Asheroth. Singular and plural form of the name of a Canaanite goddess associated with Baal (Jgs 3:7; 1 Kgs 18:19).

See CANAANITE DEITIES AND RELIGION.

Asherite. Member of Asher's tribe (Jgs 1:32).

See ASHER, TRIBE OF.

Ashes. Fine powder left after something has been thoroughly burned. The burning of sacrificial offerings on the tabernacle or temple

Ashkelon.

altar produced ashes which were disposed of ceremonially (Lv 1:16; 4:12; 6:10,11; cf. Heb 9:13). The ashes on pagan altars figured in several OT accounts (1 Kgs 13:1–5; 2 Kgs 23:4). Ashes thrown into the air by Moses during the contest of God with the Egyptian pharaoh spread like "fine dust over all the land of Egypt" and caused a plague of boils to break out among both people and animals (Ex 9:8–10).

Ashes are frequently mentioned in the Bible in connection with the ancient custom of putting ashes on oneself as a symbol of extreme grief, penitence, humiliation, or sense of worthlessness. The Bible refers to ashes and dust almost interchangeably in this usage. Examples of such expressions of emotion include Tamar's distress after being sexually assaulted by her half brother (2 Sm 13:19); Mordecai's agony over the Persian king's order of genocide for the Jews of his realm (Est 4:1,3); Daniel's confession and pleading for his captive people (Dn 9:3); and the king of Nineveh's repentance after hearing Jonah's preaching (Jon 3:6; cf. Lk 10:13). Ashes were spoken of as symbols of humility (Gn 18:27), worthlessness or futility (Jb 13:12; 30:19; Is 44:20), and destruction (Ez 28:18; 2 Pt 2:6).

See MOURN, MOURNING.

Ashhur. Caleb's son and Tekoa's father (1 Chr 2:24; 4:5, KJV Ashur), or perhaps the founder of a village named Tekoa (2 Sm 14:1–3; Am 1:1).

Ashima. Deity of uncertain origin, worshiped by the inhabitants of Hamath relocated in Samaria after the fall of Israel in 722 BC (2 Kgs 17:30).

Ashkelon. City dating back to ancient times, also spelled Askelon (KJV) or Eshkalon (cf. KJV Jos 13:3). In the Bible, Ashkelon was one of the Philistines' five main cities (the "pentapolis"), along with Gaza, Ashdod, Gath, and Ekron (Jos 13:3, KJV Eshkalonite). Ashkelon was located on the Mediterranean coast, 30 miles south of modern Tel Aviv, and was always an important port. Often in conflict with Egypt, it was captured by Rameses II (c. 1286 BC) and by Merneptah (c. 1220 BC).

Ashkelon is mentioned as one of the cities conquered by Judah (Jgs 1:18, KJV Askelon). After the Philistine invasion of Canaan in the 12th century BC, the city became one of the invaders' major centers. When Samson's riddle was answered through the duplicity of his Philistine wife, Samson vented his rage at Ashkelon, killing 30 men (Jgs 14:19). Ashkelon was in part responsible for pushing the tribe of Dan from its allotment, so Samson, a member of that tribe, probably had a long-standing grudge against the city. Ashkelon also figures in the story of the Philistine control of the ark (1 Sm 4–6). On hearing of the deaths of Saul and Jonathan, David lamented the loss of his king and of his friend, mentioning the city: "Tell it not in Gath, publish it not in the streets of Ashkelon, lest the daughters of the Philistines rejoice, lest the daughters of the uncircumcised exult" (2 Sm 1:20, KJV Askelon). Various OT prophets refer to Ashkelon (Jer 25:20; 47:5,7; Am 1:8; Zep 2:4–7; Zec 9:5).

In the period of Israel's decline King Pekah of Israel, King Rezin of Damascus, and the king of Ashkelon rebelled against Assyria. Tiglath-pileser III responded with three successive campaigns (734–732 BC), the first of which conquered Ashkelon. Nebuchadnezzar destroyed the city and deported many of its inhabitants to Egypt during his conquest of Palestine (604 BC). Successive invaders then took the city from each other: Scythians, Chaldeans, Persians, Greeks, and Maccabees. Ashkelon was the birthplace of Herod the Great, and ruins of his building projects are to be found there. Ashkelon is not mentioned in the NT but was a battleground in the Jewish rebellion against Rome (AD 66).

The Ashkelon of the Philistines lies just south of the Hellenistic and Roman city. It covers an area of about 15 acres. A trial excavation has shown that it was occupied from the time of the patriarchs down through that of the Israelites. The city then shifted to the north and continued to thrive through the Roman, Byzantine, and early Muslim periods, finally being destroyed in AD 1270. Most of what can be seen today at the site of Ashkelon are Greco-Roman statues, columns, and other artifacts excavated in the early 1920s by the British. Recently Early Bronze remains have been uncovered at a site some 1.2 miles northeast of the main tell. These were the first Early Bronze Age remains found at Ashkelon. Among the pottery sherds were some from pre- and protodynastic Egypt dating to the early 3rd millennium BC.

RONALD B. ALLEN

Ashkenaz. Gomer's son and Noah's great-grandson in Japheth's line (Gn 10:1–3; 1 Chr 1:6, KJV Ashchenaz). Mention of the kingdom of Ashkenaz along with Ararat and Minni (Jer 51:27, KJV Ashchenaz) suggests that he was the ancestor of the Scythians, a people who resided in the Ararat region in Jeremiah's time. An active, warlike people, the Scythians contributed to the unrest of the Assyrian empire and to its eventual collapse. The plural term "Ashkenazim," is now used for the Jews who settled in middle and eastern Europe after the dispersion, in contrast with the Sephardim, those who settled in the Iberian peninsula (Spain and Portugal).

Ashnah. Name of two towns that Judah's tribe received after the conquest of Canaan (Jos 15:33,43). No certain location for either is known, but both were in the "lowlands" separating Judah and Philistia. Although the Philistines often overran that buffer zone, they never got beyond its eastern border.

Ashpenaz. Official under Nebuchadnezzar in charge of palace personnel (Dn 1:3). Ashpenaz was reluctant to grant the captives from Judah, Daniel and his friends, a reprieve from eating the king's food, but eventually he did so (Dn 1:8–16). (Eating animal food from the table of Gentiles would have forced Daniel and his friends to violate the Law of God.) When three years later Ashpenaz presented the young men before the king, Nebuchadnezzar found them outstanding in wisdom and good judgment in spite of their vegetarian diet and abstemious lifestyle (Dn 1:18–20).

Ashriel. KJV form of Asriel, Manasseh's son, in 1 Chronicles 7:14.

See ASRIEL, ASRIELITE.

Ashtaroth. Plural form of Ashtoreth, a pagan fertility goddess associated in the OT with Baal (Jgs 2:13); also a center for the worship of that goddess.

See CANAANITE DEITIES AND RELIGION.

Ashtaroth, Ashterathite (Place). Town of Bashan, named along with Edrei as the home of King Og (Dt 1:4, KJV Astaroth; Jos 9:10; 12:4; 13:12,31). Ashtaroth is the plural form of Ashtoreth, the name of the Canaanite fertility goddess who was worshiped there. After Og was defeated by the Israelites (Dt 3:1–11), Moses gave Ashtaroth to the halftribe of Manasseh (Jos 13:12,31; Dt 3:13). Later it became a Levitical city inhabited by the Gershonites (1 Chr 6:71). Ashteroth-karnaim (Gn 14:5) is probably the same town as Ashtaroth. Its location is usually identified with Tell Ashtarah, 21 miles east of the Sea of Galilee. In 1 Chronicles 11:44 one of David's mighty men, Uzzia, is called an Ashterathite.

See LEVITICAL CITIES.

Ashteroth-karnaim. City where a coalition of four kings led by Chedorlaomer, king of Elam, defeated the tribe of Rephaim giants (Gn 14:5; cf. Dt 3:11). The area was part of the inheritance given to Abraham and his descendants by the Lord (Gn 15:18–20). It is probably identifiable with Ashtaroth.

See ASHTAROTH, ASHTERATHITE (PLACE).

Ashtoreth. Pagan mother-goddess widely worshiped throughout the ancient Near East (1 Kgs 11:5,33; 2 Kgs 23:13), also known as Astarte.

See CANAANITE DEITIES AND RELIGION.

Ashur. KJV form of Ashhur, Caleb's son, in 1 Chronicles 2:24 and 4:5.

See ASHHUR.

Ashurbanipal. Esar-haddon's son and the Assyrian ruler (669–633 BC) who reigned in the years during which kings Manasseh, Amon,

A stone stele with a figure of Ashurbanipal beginning the ceremonial work of rebuilding a god's temple.

gion, legends, and lore—comes from the cuneiform literature collected by Ashurbanipal and deposited in a large library he built in Nineveh, his capital. The remains of this library, discovered about a century ago and now in the British Museum, continue to have impact on biblical knowledge. Without doubt his library has been his most significant memorial.

Ashurbanipal was evidently the Assyrian monarch who sent alien people into Samaria (Ezr 4:10). Deportation of conquered peoples was standard Assyrian policy, which accounts for the assimilation and disappearance of the 10 tribes of Israel after its fall to Sargon II. In Ezra 4:10 the Assyrian king is called Osnappar (Asnappar, KJV), a transliteration of the Hebrew spelling. The consonantal similarity of the Hebrew word to the Assyrian name Ashurbanipal, plus the list of conquered peoples mentioned in the text, point to Ashurbanipal as the most likely identification.

By 630 BC the Assyrian empire was experiencing difficulty in maintaining its cohesiveness, and after Ashurbanipal's death it could no longer sustain itself. Innumerable Assyrian soldiers had died on faraway battlefields; mercenaries and captives pressed into the military did not serve well. Moreover, hordes of barbarians from the steppes of Asia battered Assyria from the outside. Vassal Babylon successfully revolted. Though a mere shadow of its former glory, Egypt also slipped from its Assyrian yoke. Ashurbanipal's sons were not equal to the task. Probably no one could have been. In less than 20 years a relatively weak coalition of enemies surrounded Nineveh and in 612 BC razed the city. A spark of resistance continued at nearby Haran, but within months it was snuffed out by Median troops. By the same ruthless, unrestrained cruelty with which it ruled its empire, Assyria perished.

The demise of Assyria gave a new lease on life to the tiny kingdom of Judah. Some scholars place Ashurbanipal's death in King Josiah's eighth year of reign (cf. 2 Chr 34:3–7). As Assyria lost its grip, the resulting vacuum brought back independence by default. Young King Josiah was able to begin and to consummate the most sweeping spiritual revival and political reforms in Judah's history (vv 8–33).

See ASSYRIA, ASSYRIANS; KINGS, BOOKS OF FIRST AND SECOND.

and Josiah governed the southern kingdom of Judah. The northern kingdom of Israel, whose capital was Samaria, had fallen in 722 BC to another powerful Assyrian ruler, Sargon II.

Throughout his life Ashurbanipal (also spelled Assurbanipal) had to fight continually to retain, regain, and defend his empire, which included Babylonia, Persia, Syria, and Egypt. Though his chief interests were evidently cultural, he was required to spend most of his time, and almost all the resources of his empire, maintaining the submission of conquered peoples, putting down a civil war fomented under the leadership of his brother, and coping with constant border skirmishes.

Much of what we know about the culture of ancient Mesopotamia—historical facts, reli-

Ashurite. Probably a variant spelling for Asherite, a member of Asher's tribe. The Ashurites were among those who supported Ishbosheth, Saul's son, instead of David as king over Israel after Saul's death (2 Sm 2:8,9). In Ezekiel 27:6 (KJV) the Hebrew word refers to a kind of wood rather than a group of people.

Ashurnasirpal. 1. Ashurnasirpal I (1049?–1031 BC), Assyrian king listed in the synchronistic Assyrian chronicle as the legitimate successor of Shamshi-Adad IV (1053?–1050 BC). Ashurnasirpal I ruled during a period of Assyrian weakness following the vigorous reign of Tiglath-pileser I (1115?–1077 BC).

2. Ashurnasirpal II (885–860 BC), Assyrian king, son of Tukulti-Ninurta II (890–885 BC). His grandfather, Adad-Nirari II (911–891 BC), laid the foundations of the Neo-Assyrian period (900–612 BC). Ashurnasirpal II, its first great monarch, consolidated his position by crushing rebellious Middle Euphrates tribes and then conducted campaigns against Syria (877 BC) and Philistia. In his annals he recorded the tribute received from the maritime towns of Philistia: "Gold, silver, tin, copper . . . large and small monkeys, ebony, boxwood, ivory . . . I received." Ashurnasirpal's westward expedition was the first of several Assyrian assaults on Syria, ultimately threatening Israelite forces as well. The expedition also established his reputation as a cruel and merciless opponent, a theme repeated constantly in his annals. A statue of Ashurnasirpal II recovered from Calah depicted him as a stern, egotistical despot. He fashioned the Assyrian army into a military machine that struck terror into the hearts of its opponents.

Ashurnasirpal II was an outstanding example of the way aggressive rulers in the ancient world treated their enemies. In his annals he boasted: "The heads of their warriors I cut off,

A bas relief in stone showing Ashurnasirpal II being anointed by a magical figure, perhaps a priest, dressed in the head and wings of an eagle.

and I formed them into a pillar over against their city. . . . I flayed all the chief men . . . and I covered the pillar with their skins; some I walled up within the pillar, some I impaled upon the pillar on stakes." Other atrocities included burning captives alive; mutilating prisoners by hacking off hands, noses, or ears; gouging out eyes; disemboweling pregnant women; and leaving prisoners in the desert to die of thirst.

Ashurnasirpal II made Calah (Nimrud) his capital city, employing more than 50,000 prisoners in the work of reconstruction. A. H. Layard, excavating Nimrud in 1845, uncovered the royal palace with its colossal statuary. Ashurnasirpal II was succeeded in 859 BC by his son Shalmaneser III, who reigned for 35 years.

See ASSYRIA, ASSYRIANS.

Ashvath. Japhlet's son, a great warrior and head of a clan in Asher's tribe (1 Chr 7:33).

Asia. In NT times, the Roman province immediately east of the Aegean Sea. The province was established in 133 BC out of the kingdom left to the Romans in the will of Attalus III, king of Pergamum. Greek geographers generally employed the name Asia to denote the whole eastern continent, but from the second century BC on the Romans generally referred to the kings of Pergamum as "kings of Asia." Hence the custom of using "Asia" for the peninsula alone (i.e., Asia Minor) gradually crept into popular usage.

Extent. The extent of the province of Asia differed at each stage of its history. Before Roman occupation the word was used to refer to the kingdom of the Seleucid dynasty (founded by Seleucus I; 305/4–281/0 BC). The Apocrypha referred thus to Asia (1 Mc 8:6; 11:13; 12:39; 13:32; 2 Mc 3:3), as did the early Jewish historian Josephus in his *Antiquities*. When the territory was wrested from Seleucid control by the Romans in their war against Antiochus the Great, the Romans gave it to their allies, the Attalids; Attalus III willed it to the Romans. The limits of Roman control were not firmly established until an extensive revolt had been put down. The borders then included Mysia, Lydia, Caria, and Phrygia, and (nearer the Aegean) Aeolis, Ionia, and Troas. The islands off the coast (Lesbos, Chios, Samos, Rhodes, Patmos, etc.) were also included. The mainland now forms part of modern Turkey.

In 116 BC the province was enlarged to include Greater Phrygia. Its geographic limits were then Bithynia to the north, Galatia to the east, Lycia to the south, and the Aegean Sea to the west. Even then the boundaries were not solidly fixed, for in 25 BC Augustus

Caesar augmented Rome's dominion by combining other parts of Phrygia, Lyconia, Pisidia, and possibly Pamphylia into a province called Galatia. Those geographical limits remained until AD 285, when the province was greatly reduced in size and the term Asia became restricted to the coastal areas and lower valleys of the Maeander, Cayster, Hermus, and Caicus rivers.

During Roman occupation the capital of the province was Pergamum. By the time of Augustus, however, the residence of the Roman proconsul was at Ephesus.

Natural Resources and Trade. The Roman province of Asia was the richest and best endowed of all the provinces of the peninsula. In the first century BC, Cicero wrote: "In the richness of its soil, in the variety of its products, in the extent of its pastures, and in the number of its exports, it surpasses all other lands." Its cities were centers of culture where the sciences, philosophy, and literature flourished.

In the interior the rich natural resources were developed into thriving industries. Woolen fabrics, particularly from Laodicea, were world renowned. The economy was brisk. Trade routes from the east passed down the valleys of the province to the coastal ports where costly merchandise was shipped to Greek and Roman ports to the west. Goods from western countries followed the same routes in reverse, as wealthy entrepreneurs traded with eastern importers. The Roman province of Asia became the crossroads of the empire.

With an expanding economy, banking as a profession came into prominence in Asia. Importers and exporters needed agents to arrange letters of credit, facilitate the transfer of funds, exchange one currency for another, and collect money on their behalf. Such duties were performed by bankers in all the leading cities.

Importance in the NT. In the NT, Asia generally meant the Roman province of that name. Sometimes the concept was primarily geographical, at other times primarily political. For example, at the feast of Pentecost in Jerusalem there were Jews who had come from "Asia." These included other provinces governed by Rome, such as Cappadocia, Phrygia, and Pamphylia (Acts 2:9,10). This seems to indicate that Luke, the writer of Acts, used the term to describe the province originally bequeathed to the Romans by Attalus III. Luke used the word again in Acts 6:9, providing tacit evidence of the strength of Jewish communities in Asia Minor as a whole and confirming the use of "Asia" in the restricted sense of the Roman province.

On Paul's second missionary journey, he and Timothy were prevented by the Holy Spirit from preaching in Asia (Acts 16:6–8). Evidently, from the context, Luke again had the old boundaries of the province in mind. On Paul's return from Greece he stopped briefly at Ephesus (Acts 18:19–21). On his third missionary journey he remained in Ephesus for more than two years, so that from this capital city "all the residents of Asia heard the word of the Lord, both Jews and Greeks" (Acts 19:10).

Luke further referred to Asia in Acts 19:26,27; 20:4,16,18; and 27:2. Paul also made several references to it (Rom 16:5; 1 Cor 16:19; 2 Cor 1:8; 2 Tim 1:15). The apostle Peter likewise used the term (1 Pt 1:1). In the NT the risen Christ was the last to refer to Asia. He instructed the apostle John, then living in exile on the island of Patmos, to write letters to seven specific churches on the mainland of Asia (Rv 1:1–4).

Other cities in this Roman province mentioned in the NT include Colossae and Hierapolis (Col 4:13), the lesser-known Adramyttium (Acts 27:2), and Assos (Acts 20:13,14).

CYRIL J. BARBER

Asia Minor. Peninsula synonymous with the Asia of the NT and Anatolia, identifiable with part of modern Turkey.

See ANATOLIA; ASIA.

Asiarch. Title of an official of unknown function in the Roman province of Asia. Several such officials were concerned for the safety of Paul during a silversmiths' riot in Ephesus (Acts 19:31). Nothing else is known about their qualifications, periods of tenure, or duties. Why there were a number of such officers in Ephesus at the time of the riot, or why the Asiarchs showed such concern for Paul, is not clear. Perhaps they were deputies of the "Commune of Asia," responsible to promote and protect the imperial cult (the worship practices of Rome and the emperor). The Asiarchs mentioned were evidently not adverse to a religious movement like Christianity, which embarrassed the prevailing pagan cult of Artemis. The long account in Acts 19 repeats one of Luke's themes, that Christianity was not subversive nor was Paul a political menace. Otherwise the Asiarchs would not have favored him in such a manner.

Asiel. Jehu's great-grandfather. Jehu was a prince of Simeon's tribe (1 Chr 4:35,38).

Askelon. KJV alternate form of Ashkelon, a Philistine city, in Judges 1:18; 1 Samuel 6:17; and 2 Samuel 1:20.

See ASHKELON.

Asnappar. KJV form of Osnappar, the biblical name for the Assyrian king Ashurbanipal in Ezra 4:10.

See ASHURBANIPAL.

Asp. Poisonous snake mentioned in the Bible, probably the Egyptian cobra.

See ANIMALS.

Aspatha. One of Haman's ten sons, who was killed with his father when Haman's plot to destroy the Jews was foiled (Est 9:7).

Aspen. See PLANTS.

Asphalt. Brown or black tarlike substance, a variety of bitumen, obtained in ancient times from natural oil seeps and used for mortar and caulking. Mortar, pitch, slime, and tar are other translations of the related terms in Hebrew.

See MINERALS, METALS, AND PRECIOUS STONES; BITUMEN.

Asriel, Asrielite. Manasseh's son (1 Chr 7:14, KJV Ashriel). His descendants, the Asrielites, were included in Moses' census in the wilderness (Nm 26:31) and were later given a portion of the land allotted to Manasseh's tribe (Jos 17:2).

Ass. Beast of burden used widely in the Near East.

See ANIMALS.

Assarion. Coin of small value; a farthing (Mt 10:29 KJV).

See COINS.

Assembly, Mount of. Concept of a mountain of God in the far north, an idea belonging to Babylonian and Canaanite mythology. In Isaiah 14:12–15 the king of Babylon is likened to a lesser deity who attempts to climb this mountain, to be "like the Most High," but instead is cast down "to the depths of the Pit."

Asshur (Person). Hebrew word of uncertain meaning, appearing in English translations of the Bible as Assyria, Assyrian, Assyrians, or merely "Asshur." These variants come from the Assyrian word *asshur*.

1. KJV translation of the word for Assyria in Genesis 10:11. It is improperly translated as a person, and should be understood as in the RSV, "From that land he [Nimrod] went into Assyria." In that country, east of the Tigris

River, Nimrod built four cities: Nineveh, Rehoboth-ir, Calah, and Resen.

2. Shem's son (Gn 10:22; 1 Chr 1:17). The reference may be merely a personification of the whole Assyrian people; however, since other names in the account (e.g., Arpachshad, Gn 10:24; 11:12) seem to indicate individual persons, perhaps Asshur should be taken in the same way. If so, this individual may have been the founder of the city Asshur to which he gave his name, the names of a god and nation being further derived from the city.

See ASSHUR (PLACE).

3. Patron god of the city of Asshur.

Asshur (Place). Ancient name of a city on the Tigris River whose habitation can be traced back to about 2500 BC. Asshur was not a large city (less than one-tenth the size of Babylon or Nineveh), but it formed the homeland of the later Assyrian kingdom.

Asshur had become a thriving city by the 2nd millennium BC, trading with the Assyrian colony at Kanish (in modern Turkey). It reached its peak in the Old Assyrian empire under Shamshi-adad I (1813–1781 BC), who stretched his control over most of northern Mesopotamia, including Mari. His empire fell to Hammurabi of Babylon (1792–1750 BC), and Asshur entered a dark period about which little is known. When the Assyrians once again became a major power in the Near East late in the 2nd millennium, the capital was moved away from Asshur; however, it remained the ancient holy city and the home of the Assyrian national god, Asshur.

For centuries the exact location of Asshur was unknown, but during the 19th century it was established that Qalat Shergat in Iraq was the modern location of this ancient Assyrian capital. The Germans excavated the site for a number of years prior to World War I. They uncovered a temple to Anu-adad which contained a large double ziggurat that still dominates the site today. A palace and several other buildings were also excavated. Among the literary discoveries were an Assyrian account of the Babylonian creation epic and a portion of the law code of the Assyrians.

See ASSYRIA, ASSYRIANS.

Asshurim. Descendants of Abraham and his second wife, Keturah, through Dedan (Gn 25:3). The Asshurim probably settled in Arabia.

Assir. 1. Korah's son and a descendant of Levi through Kohath (Ex 6:24; 1 Chr 6:22).

2. Ebiasaph's son and a descendant of #1 above (1 Chr 6:23,37).

3. Son of Jeconiah (Jehoiachin), king of Judah (1 Chr 3:17 KJV). It has been suggested that the Hebrew word *assir* may here be an adjective (as in RSV) describing Jeconiah and meaning "while captive" (cf. 2 Kgs 24:15). If so, his children were born while he was a captive.

Assos. Seaport of Mysia in the Roman province of Asia (Minor). The apostle Paul and Luke were reunited in Assos after Paul's journey by land from Troas (Acts 20:13,14). The Roman writer Pliny identified the town as having been founded by the kings of Pergamum and called Apollonia. Assos was located on the top and terraced sides of an inactive volcanic cone 770 feet in height. The Greek philosopher Aristotle lived there for several years. It was also the birthplace of Cleanthes, a Stoic poet quoted by Paul (Acts 17:28). Today Assos is known as Behram Kevi.

Assur. KJV transliteration of a Hebrew word (*asshur*) usually rendered Assyria (Ezr 4:2; Ps 83:8) by most English versions.

See ASSYRIA, ASSYRIANS.

Assurance. Certainty or confidence about one's beliefs or actions. The "assurance of hope" (Heb 6:11) and the "assurance of faith" (Heb 10:22; 11:1) are mentioned as qualities of wholeness that lead believers to responsible living. Paul spoke of an "assured understanding" of the gospel of Christ, which resulted in love in the community (Col 2:2), and of the "assured blessing" which was his in Christ (Rom 15:29).

A proper understanding of God's sovereignty should encourage repentant sinners and faltering believers to call upon God for salvation and to walk secure in his love. Jesus said, "All that the Father gives me will come to me; and him who comes to me I will not cast out" (Jn 6:37).

Because God has planned and purposed our salvation, we may have assurance that he will accept and forgive those who trust him (Jn 3:16). Christ's sheep hear his voice and follow him; they will never perish or be snatched out of his hand, because "my Father, who has given them to me, is greater than all" (Jn 10:29).

Such an attitude of trust in God removes the presumptive pride of the person who trusts his own good works for salvation (Mt 7:21–23; 1 Cor 10:12; Heb 3:12), or the agonizing doubt of the believer who is sensitive to his own sinfulness. Because salvation is by grace (Eph 2:8), the doubting believer may claim the finished and sufficient work of Christ and thus rest secure that "he who began a good work in you will bring it to completion at the day of Jesus Christ" (Phil 1:6).

Jesus' presence in heaven as our advocate is another significant reason to encourage assurance, because "he ever lives to make intercession on our behalf" (Rom 8:34; 1 Jn 2:2), so that "he is able for all time to save those who draw near to God through him" (Heb 7:25).

Another ground of assurance is the presence of the Holy Spirit in believers. In Romans 8:23 the Spirit is called the "first fruits"—the initial promise and pledge of a greater harvest to follow. As the Spirit produces the fruit of love, joy, peace, longsuffering, gentleness, goodness, faith, meekness, and temperance (Gal 5:22) in the lives of believers—characteristics that are not a person's attributes by nature—the Christian may know, as John says, "that we abide in him and he in us, because he has given us of his own Spirit" (1 Jn 4:13).

Assurance is provided not only to those who call upon God for salvation, but to those who have doubts in their Christian experience. First Peter 1:3–5 speaks of Christians who have "been born anew to a living hope" through Christ, who are guarded by God's power through faith for salvation. In Romans 8, Paul presents an extensive argument to assure believers. Since God "did not spare his own son but gave him up for us all, will he not also give us all things with him?" Since it is God who justifies, who is to condemn? Paul concludes that in spite of tribulation, distress, persecution, famine, nakedness, peril, or sword, "we are more than conquerers through him who loved us ... [for nothing] will be able to separate us from the love of God in Christ Jesus our Lord" (Rom 8:31–39).

See PERSEVERANCE.

Assurbanipal. Variant spelling of Ashurbanipal, the Assyrian king.

See ASHURBANIPAL.

Assyria, Assyrians. Ancient empire considered the symbol of terror and tyranny in the Near East for more than three centuries. Assyria received its name from the tiny city-state Asshur, on the western bank of the Tigris River in northern Mesopotamia (modern Iraq). The city was the seat of worship of the sun god Asshur (also spelled Ashur). The Hebrew name occurs frequently in the Bible and is translated Assyria (Gn 2:14), Assur (Ezr 4:2; Ps 83:8), or left as Asshur (Gn 10:11 KJV). The form of the name comes originally from the Akkadian language.

Originally Assyria was a small district in

northern Mesopotamia, lying in a rough triangle between the Tigris River and the Upper Zab, a tributary of the Tigris. Eventually Assyria gained control of northern Syria, securing an outlet to the Mediterranean Sea, and took possession of the fertile Mesopotamian plain, extending Assyrian domain over all of Babylonia to the Persian Gulf.

History. *Before the 8th Century BC.* By the end of the 3rd millennium BC the Sumerians were trading with Assyria and influencing its people culturally. Periodically Sumerian kings would claim political control over Assyria. Sargon of Agade (*c.* 2350 BC) brought Assyria within the sphere of his political and commercial activities, and when the Amorites overthrew the 3rd dynasty of Ur and established their own states, one of them incorporated Assyria into its territory. During the period of Hammurabi, one of the last great kings of the 1st Babylonian dynasty (*c.* 2360–1600 BC), the Assyrians supplied building materials and other goods for the Babylonian kingdom.

Trade between Asshur and the Assyrian colony of Kanish in Anatolia began at a very early time in Assyrian history. Goods were transported by caravans of up to 200 donkeys at a time. The wealth pouring in from such a trade put Assyria in a very strong position economically.

The early phase of Assyrian commercial development was followed by a long period of decline, culminating in the 15th century BC. At that time Assyria was reduced to a state of vassalage by a non-Semitic people, the Hurrians (biblical Horites) of the state of Mitanni. In the 14th century another non-Semitic people, the Hittites, overthrew the power of Mitanni. Assyria was gradually able to rise again and assume the role of a great power in the ancient Near East, largely through the policies of a shrewd prince, Asshur-uballit. His reign marked the beginning of a long process by which Assyria ultimately rose to supremacy.

Enlil-nirari (1329–1320 BC), son and successor of Asshur-uballit, attacked Babylon and defeated Kurigalzu II, the Kassite king of Babylon (1345–1324 BC). Adad-nirari I (1307–1275 BC) extended Assyria's influence by winning victories over the Kassites in Babylonia. He also added territory to the northwest.

The period of consolidation and expansion in the first Assyrian empire culminated in the capture of Babylon by Tukulti-ninurta I (1244–1208 BC), which for the first time placed Babylon under Assyrian rule. After that climax, however, Assyrian power declined.

The three centuries from about 1200 to 900 BC were marked by movements of different peoples such as the Greeks, Philistines, Aramaeans, and Hebrews. Under pressure of people migrating from Europe, the Hittite empire, which formerly had given political stability to Asia Minor and protected the trade routes, crumbled rapidly. By 1200 BC it fell to attacks by the Sea People from the Greek mainland.

During the 10th century BC Assyria began to make a slow recovery. In the reign of Adad-nirari II (911–891 BC) Assyria again launched upon a period of conspicuous economic and military expansion. For the next 60 years Assyrian kings followed a consistent policy of consolidating the work of Adad-nirari II. Ashurnasirpal II (885–860 BC) is considered the first great monarch of that new era in Assyrian history. He possessed all the qualities and defects of his successors to the extreme. He had the ambition, energy, courage, vanity, and magnificence of a ruthless, indefatigable empire builder. Ashurnasirpal's first activities were directed to the mountain area to the east, where he extended Assyria's control among the mountain people. In the west he subdued the Aramaeans with characteristic cruelty, and did likewise in Asia Minor.

Shalmaneser III (859–825 BC), son and successor of Ashurnasirpal, continued his father's work. He extended the area controlled by Assyria until everything from the Mediterranean coast to the Zagros Mountains, and from Cilicia to Babylonia, was ruled either by Assyria or by vassal princes accepting Assyrian overlordship. All the trade routes of the Near East, except those of Palestine, thus came into Assyrian hands.

Shalmaneser III is well known to historians of the biblical world for the battle of Qarqar (853 BC), considered the most fully documented event from the ancient world. He launched an invasion of Syria that was met by a coalition led by Ben-hadad of Damascus and supported by King Ahab of Israel and several other states. Since Shalmaneser was unable to rout the 60,000 troops opposing him, it was many years before the Assyrians were able to conquer Damascus and Samaria. King Jehu of Israel (841–814 BC), who later chose to pay tribute rather than fight, is represented, perhaps by an envoy, on the Black Obelisk of Shalmaneser III, excavated at Shalmaneser's capital city, Calah (now called Nimrud). Jehu is depicted as kissing the ground at the Assyrian monarch's feet and offering a tribute of silver, gold, and lead vessels.

Toward the end of his reign Shalmaneser had to put down a rebellion by some of the principal Assyrian cities. He was succeeded by his heir, Shamshi-adad V (823–811 BC). Shamshi-adad's son Adad-nirari III (810–782 BC) built a new palace at Calah and attacked King Hazael of Damascus (Syria) in 804 BC.

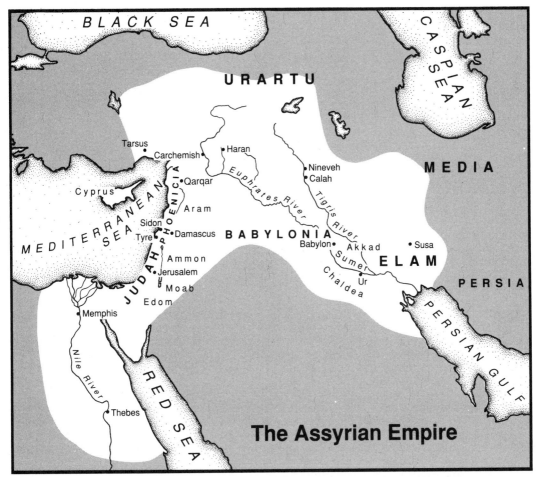

The Assyrian Empire

Assyrian pressure on the Syrians undoubtedly was a relief to Israel, which had been oppressed by Hazael (2 Kgs 13:22–25).

From the 8th Century to the Battle of Carchemish (605 BC). Beginning about 800 BC the influence of Urartu (Ararat) began to expand, especially in north Syria, at the expense of Assyria. The next half century saw a drastic decline in Assyria's fortunes. In 746 BC, during a revolt in the city of Calah, the entire royal family was murdered.

The final phase of Assyrian power was instituted by the usurper Tiglath-pileser III (745–727 BC), known also by his adopted Babylonian throne-name Pul (2 Kgs 15:19; 1 Chr 5:26). His reign began the process by which Assyria recovered and consolidated control of all its territories and established itself firmly as the dominant military and economic power in the Near East. Tiglath-pileser first secured control of the mountain passes in the north in order to eliminate the threat of invasion from that direction. Next he subjected Syria and Palestine in the west and took control of the road to Egypt and the Mediterranean Sea. Finally,

through diplomacy, he gained the throne of Babylonia also. Under the name of Pulu he governed Babylonia, creating the remarkable situation of two crowns united in one ruler bearing two different names. His political prudence was not usually found in the ruthless Assyrian monarchs.

From the year 743 BC Tiglath-pileser III waged a number of campaigns in Syria and Palestine. King Menahem of Israel (752–742 BC) paid him tribute (2 Kgs 15:19,20), as did Tyre, Byblos, and Damascus. In 738 BC he subjugated the north central state of Hamath (modern Hama). Responding to an appeal from King Ahaz of Judah (735–715 BC) to help resist the pressures of a proposed anti-Assyrian coalition, Tiglath-pileser conquered Damascus in 732 BC, and Samaria, capital of the northern kingdom of Israel, a decade later. On both occasions deportations of people to Assyria took place. The fall of Samaria in 722 BC marked the end of the kingdom of Israel.

Sargon II (722–705 BC) claimed to be the Assyrian ruler who captured Samaria, but the biblical record attributed the capture to Shalmaneser (2 Kgs 17:2–6). To the policy of deportation Sargon and his successors added that of colonization. To replace the peoples carried into captivity these Assyrian kings brought tribes from Babylonia, Elam, Syria, and Arabia, and settled them in Samaria and surrounding territory. The new arrivals intermingled with the indigenous people remaining in the land after the deportation, and became the Samaritans.

After 10 years of warfare against his enemies to the west in Syria and Asia Minor, and to the north in Urartu, Sargon concentrated his efforts on Babylonia. He chased Merodach-baladan II (721–710 BC; cf. 2 Kgs 20:12–19; Is 39:1) to Elam and made himself king of Babylon in 709 BC. He started building a new capital city for himself, Dur-Sharrukin (Khorsabad) near Nineveh, but was killed in battle before it was finished.

Sargon was succeeded by his son Sennacherib (705–681 BC), who was occupied throughout his reign in a series of bitter wars. He is especially known in biblical studies for his campaign against Judah and siege of Jerusalem during the reign of King Hezekiah (715–686 BC) and the ministry of the prophet Isaiah (2 Kgs 18:13–19:37; Is 36,37). It was during that crisis that the celebrated Siloam Tunnel was constructed to bring water into the beleaguered capital from the spring of Gihon, outside the city wall, to the Pool of Siloam (2 Kgs 20:20).

Sennacherib was murdered in 681 BC and was succeeded by Esar-haddon, who tried unsuccessfully to establish Assyrian control over Egypt. Esar-haddon was succeeded by Ashurbanipal (669–626? BC), who managed to capture No-amon (Thebes), thereby realizing the greatest victory in Assyrian history (cf. Na 3:3–10). Ashurbanipal established a great library in Nineveh, which was excavated in 1850. Many tablets made of the finest clay and ranging in size from 1 to 15 inches were found, containing a vast selection of Akkadian material. Some of the tablets contain historical records; others, astronomical reports, mathematical calculations, and private or public letters. A considerable part of the collection deals with astrology and medicine. Many of the tablets contain prayers, incantations, psalms, and religious texts in general. A copy of the Babylonian account of creation was also found. This library is now one of the principal treasures of the British Museum in London.

Very little is known about Ashurbanipal's reign after 639 BC, since his annals do not extend beyond that year. However, some information on events of his last 13 years can be gleaned from allusions in state correspondence, commercial documents, and prayers addressed to the gods. Evidently the situation in Assyria was becoming increasingly serious, and when Ashurbanipal died in 626 BC his empire declined quickly.

The Medes had entered the Assyrian annals during the reign of Esar-haddon, when they still consisted of a large number of associated but separate tribes. Later those tribes began to be welded into a single kingdom. Herodotus states that Phraortes, their king, attacked Assyria but lost his life on the battlefield and was succeeded by his son Cyaxares.

The year 626 BC marked several important events in the ancient world. Nabopolassar, a Chaldean prince, became king of Babylon (626–605 BC) toward the end of that year. An alliance between the Medes and Nabopolassar was concluded, and from that time on, the success of Nabopolassar against Assyria was almost inevitable. By the year 617 BC he had cleared Babylonia of all Assyrian garrisons. He then marched up the Euphrates to the Aramaean districts which had been part of the Assyrian empire for two and a half centuries. The plan was for Nabopolassar to attack Nineveh from the west and the Medes to attack it at the same time from the east; however, the combined forces of the Assyrians and Egyptians, now allies, compelled Nabopolassar to withdraw to Babylon.

In 614 BC the Medes carried out a massive attack on Assyria. Although Nineveh was too strong to yield to the attack, the Medes captured some of the neighboring cities, including Asshur, the ancient capital. At that point Nabopolassar arrived with the Babylonian forces. He met Cyaxares at Asshur, and they established mutual friendship and peace. Their alliance was later confirmed by the marriage of Nebuchadnezzar, Nabopolassar's son, to Amytis, daughter of Cyaxares. In 612 BC their combined forces launched a final assault against Nineveh, and after three months of siege the mighty city fell (Na 1:8).

Despite the loss of their capital, a weakened Assyrian kingdom survived for three more years. The Assyrian troops who could escape from Nineveh fled westward to Haran, where an Assyrian prince, Asshur-uballit, was made king and sought Egypt's help to restore the kingship of Assyria. Necho II (609–593 BC), known in the Bible as Neco, responded and set off with his Egyptian troops to Haran to fight against the Babylonians, who by now had annihilated Assyria. King Josiah of Judah (640–609 BC), who evidently considered himself a vassal of Assyria's heir, Neo-Babylonia, marched to oppose the Egyptian advance and was mortally wounded by an arrow on the battlefield of Megiddo (2 Kgs 23:29,30; 2 Chr 35:20–24).

When Nabopolassar and his allies attacked Haran in 610 BC, Asshur-uballit did not attempt to defend it but fled southwest to await Necho and his troops. The joint forces of the Egyptians and the Assyrians returned to mount an assault upon Haran with some initial success. But Nabopolassar's army compelled the Assyrian-Egyptian forces to abandon the siege and withdraw to Carchemish (present-day Jarablus). There, under the leadership of Nebuchadnezzar, the Babylonians made a direct attack on the powerful army. The resultant carnage on both sides was graphically depicted by the prophet Jeremiah (46:1–12). Nebuchadnezzar emerged victorious in the battle of Carchemish (605 BC). However, because of the death of his father, he did not pursue his victory but returned to Babylon to assume the throne.

There is a tradition in the Assyrian Christian church that after the collapse of the Assyrian empire under the onslaught of the Medes and Neo-Babylonians, a remnant of the Assyrian people—chiefly princes, noblemen, and warriors—took refuge in the mountains of Kurdistan. There they built a number of armed fortresses. Alexander the Great (336–323 BC), his successors, and the Roman legions made no attempt to conquer these tribes. Trajan (AD 98–117) marched at the head of the Roman armies through Armenia, touching the northern region of Kurdistan, on his way to Persia. It is asserted that the wise men, or magi, who visited the newly born king in Bethlehem, the baby Jesus, came from Edessa. According to this tradition, the magi, on returning from Bethlehem, proclaimed the amazing things they had heard and seen on their visit to the king. A Christian church was founded among the Assyrians which has survived throughout the centuries. The number of these Assyrian Christians is estimated to be between 100,000 and 200,000 at the present time.

The region that was Assyria, including all of Mesopotamia, is within present-day Iraq, an Arabic-speaking country predominantly Muslim in religion.

See ISRAEL, HISTORY OF; KINGS, BOOKS OF FIRST AND SECOND; MESOPOTAMIA.

Astaroth. KJV form of Ashtaroth, a town known for its pagan worship of the goddess Ashtoreth, in Deuteronomy 1:4.

See ASHTAROTH, ASHTERATHITE (PLACE).

Astarte. Pagan mother-goddess widely worshiped throughout the ancient Near East; also known as Ashtoreth.

See CANAANITE DEITIES AND RELIGION.

Astrology. Pseudoscience dealing with the supposed influence of the heavenly bodies on human character and destiny. Astrological conclusions are based on the apparent movement of the sun and planets through the zodiac, an arbitrary division of the celestial sphere into 12 segments identified with 12 major constellations. As the sun travels in its path, called the ecliptic, it cuts across the zodiac at various points. The movement of the sun and the planets in relation to the zodiac provides astrologers with patterns or "aspects" from which their interpretative schemes are drawn.

The 12 segments of the zodiac are called "houses." Constellations (e.g., Leo, Virgo, Sagittarius) associated with the respective houses are called "signs." One's date of birth determines the sign under which one is born. Using a rather elaborate procedure, an astrologer attempts to draw up a celestial map or "horoscope." Horoscopes are based on the supposed fact that persons born under a given sign have certain characteristics in common. Positions of the various planets with reference to the signs, or positions of the sun and moon with reference to one another, are regarded as pointing to favorable or unfavorable conditions.

Some modern astrologers maintain that the heavenly bodies influence human character and action through gravitational or electromagnetic forces emanating from those bodies. Ancient astrologers such as the Babylonians, however, worshiped the stars as deities. The influence of the stars was thus understood by them as a religious phenomenon.

History. The earliest known account of the use of astrology comes from ancient Sumer, a region in the lower Euphrates river valley. The Sumerian Gudea cylinders contain an account of a dream of King Gudea in which the goddess Nidaba came to him holding a tablet inscribed with a map of the heavens. The dream indicated that it was a propitious time for Gudea to build the Eninnu temple.

Astrology flourished in ancient Babylon under the influence of priests. It was integrally linked with the serious study of celestial phenomena. The superstitious Babylonians were intensely concerned with omens, so it is understandable that they would attempt to find omens in the observable movements of the sun, moon, planets, and stars. To the best of our knowledge the Babylonians originated the zodiac. They also drew up a monthly calendar of days that were propitious and days on which activity should be reduced to a minimum for fear of incurring the anger of one or more deities. This monthly pattern then served for the rest of the year.

Babylonian influence in astronomy and astrology spread to Greece in the 4th century BC. The Greeks' interest in science and their polytheistic religion, which allowed for the attribution of deity to heavenly bodies, undoubtedly inclined them to take up astrology and to develop it extensively.

The spread of Hellenistic culture brought the practice of astrology to Egypt, where it flourished for a long time. Herodotus, an early Greek historian, stated that the Egyptians were the first to use a person's day of birth to predict character. Herodotus also wrote that the Egyptians kept careful records of unusual phenomena, which they used as a basis for predicting consequences that might follow similar phenomena in the future. The Egyptians contributed a number of refinements to the Greek astrological system, such as division of the sky into 36 sections, each with its own deity. They also divided the day into 24 hours.

The influence of Greek astrology was felt in the Roman world as well. A Roman astrologer named Nigidius, who was strongly influenced by Greek thought, made prognostications that show considerable subtlety—and also considerable vagueness. Not much is known about other Roman astrologers, although astrological belief played an important role in Roman life. A system of lucky and unlucky days was developed. The names of the days of the week were derived from the names of planets (which bore the names of gods). The practice of naming the days of the week for the planets probably goes back to the Hellenistic period. Roman contributions to the calendar system paved the way for an even more widespread use of astrology. For example, astrological computation was made easier for ordinary people by the adoption in 46 BC of the 365-day Julian calendar.

The practice of astrology began to change with the coming of Christianity. Many Christians found astrology to be at variance with principles taught in the Bible; hence the spread of Christianity into polytheistic cultures led to a diminishing of astrological practices. Although early church fathers such as Augustine strongly opposed the practice of astrology, it flourished again during the Middle Ages. Chairs of astrology were established in certain European universities following the introduction in the 12th century of Latin translations of 10th-century Arabic texts. The Arabic texts were in turn based on earlier Hellenistic texts from about 150 BC to AD 350.

Contemporary astrology is based on concepts popular during the Renaissance (14th–16th centuries) but which then fell into disuse until the late 1800s. They were revived primarily through the Theosophical Society and the teachings of H. P. Blavatsky.

The "Age of Aquarius." Today there are an estimated 10,000 professional astrologers in the United States alone. Contemporary North American culture is filled with symbols of astrological paraphernalia: T-shirt decorations and casual greetings take for granted that each person has an astrological sign. Modern preoccupation with astrology was exemplified in the 1967 musical *Hair*, which proclaimed the dawning of a new astrological age, Aquarius, and the close of an expended age, Pisces—symbolizing the end of the Christian era.

The "dawning of the Age of Aquarius" has been chronicled by many journalists and other observers of the American scene. According to a 1970 report, for example, 350 department stores from coast to coast were supplying 30,000 customers per month with "personalized" horoscopes or "psycho-astrological portraits"; a computer produced the 15- to 20-page horoscopes from 25 million pieces of stored information. Of the nation's 1,750 daily newspapers, 1,200 were carrying astrology columns—some of them illustrated full pages. A 1976 survey by the American Institute of Public Opinion (Gallup Poll) revealed that about 32 million Americans expressed a belief in astrology, thinking that their lives were strongly influenced by the position of the stars.

Critique. Astrology posits the influence of ancient deities on the individual. It is therefore a subtle form of idolatry. Even though the zodiac names are now regarded merely as convenient labels, the planet Venus is still associated with love and Jupiter governs success.

The conclusions of astrology are often vague generalizations that might apply to individuals born under various signs. Sometimes astrological advice is harmless or even beneficial ("do not trust strangers too much"; "this is a good time to begin a new venture"), yet the value of such advice has nothing to do with its alleged astrological basis. Further, many predictions given by astrologers simply do not come true. Deuteronomy 18:22 specifies accuracy in prediction as one of the tests of a true prophet.

Astronomers have determined that over the course of centuries a shift (called "precession") has taken place in the positions of the constellations. That shift has resulted in two astrological systems, the "tropical" and the "sidereal." Although the constellations have moved out of their original "houses," astrologers generally claim that the influence remains in the original house—but original means the position existing in the time of the Egyptian astronomer-astrologer Ptolemy. Since precession has been continuing since the creation of the universe, one might question why the position of the signs in Ptolemy's time should be thought of as absolute.

Basic to the principles of astrology is the belief that one's destiny is affected by mysterious "forces" in the universe. Such a concept in effect sets up a ruling power in the world other than God. It also creates a subtle dependence on the astrological system that may lead one away from trust in God. If one's destiny is determined by a confluence of the heavenly bodies, prayer may no longer seem appropriate. Astrology can thus undercut the concept of individual responsibility to God and keep one from seeking to determine God's will.

The most serious aspect of contemporary culture's fascination with astrology is that it constitutes, for many, a substitute religion. As a pseudoreligion, it provides an apparent escape from the realities of life, both by transferring responsibility for life's decisions to the "cosmic forces" and by exploring the alleged possibility of control of one's destiny by adjusting to those forces.

Astrology in the Bible. It is often alleged that references to astrological motifs occur in the Bible. The blessings pronounced by Jacob on his 12 sons, for example, have been associated by some with the signs of the zodiac. Apocalyptic imagery of a cosmic nature is frequently regarded as having astrological significance. All such interpretations are highly speculative.

Attempts to predict the future by appeal to false deities, mediums, or objects were forbidden in the OT. The reason was that such attempts ignored God as the true source of revelation. The future was foretold by persons, like Daniel, who could interpret dreams, but the Scriptures make clear that Daniel's ability was given to him by God (Dn 2:17–23).

Specific reference to astrological prognostication is found in Isaiah 47:12–14 in an oracle dealing with the fall of Babylon. In that oracle the prophet Isaiah referred to a number of features that characterized that great empire. He spoke of enchantments practiced in Babylon. In an ironic tone he told the Babylonians to continue with their sorceries—they might bring success. He singled out the astrologers and referred specifically to the division of the heavens, evidently meaning the Babylonian division of the celestial sphere into segments (possibly the zodiac). He made reference as well to their custom of predicting the future at the time of each new moon. The point of the passage is that destruction will come to Babylon, and even its eminent astrologers will not be able to save it.

The prophet Jeremiah warned the Israelites not to be dismayed by signs in the heavens

(Jer 10:1–3). Those signs were evidently unusual celestial phenomena like eclipses, comets, and conjunctions of planets, all of which inspired dread in the hearts of most ancient people. The passage in Jeremiah indicates that it is wrong for God's people to attribute mystical influence to such phenomena or to see in them portents of the future. Prognostication on the basis of such celestial phenomena was considered "vain" (Jer 10:3 KJV).

The Book of Daniel refers to a group of soothsayers, frequently understood to be astrologers (Dn 2:27; 5:11). The meaning of the word, however, is uncertain. It is derived from an Aramaic root meaning "to cut" or "divide" and hence may be a reference to the Babylonian practice of dividing the heavens into zones. The fact that the group is mentioned along with various kinds of diviners makes it quite likely that they were astrologers. The passage in Daniel demonstrates that those who use various "mantic" arts to predict the future are ineffectual in revealing the Word of God.

The magi, who figure prominently in the account of the birth of Christ (Mt 2:1–16), may have been astrologers, although the word "magi" has broader connotations. It is possible that an unusual conjunction of planets at the time of the infancy of Christ was interpreted by them as a sign of the birth of the Jewish king. The magi could have learned about Jewish messianic belief from the Book of Daniel or from the many Jewish officials in the Persian empire. A tradition may have arisen from Numbers 24:17 that a star would be associated with the birth of the messianic king. Any unusual stellar phenomenon in the western sky might have led the magi to follow it to Palestine. The biblical account definitely does not validate astrological principles.

CLARENCE B. BASS *and* THOMAS E. McCOMISKEY

See ASTRONOMY; CALENDARS, ANCIENT AND MODERN.

Astronomy. Science dealing with the phenomena outside the earth's atmosphere but especially concerned with the observable arrangements, motions, and characteristics of the heavenly bodies. The word "astronomy" is based on two Greek words meaning "the law of the stars."

Astronomy in the Ancient World. Astronomy is by no means a modern science. Human beings have always been preoccupied with the heavens. The concern of the earliest civilizations with the universe appears to have been mainly astrological, but intellectual curiosity and the need for navigational orientation were certainly additional factors.

Mesopotamia. Evidence of astrological use of the heavens has been found as early as the

Sumerian civilization in Mesopotamia. A list of 25 stars is the only noteworthy astronomical material we have from that culture; the purpose of the list is unknown.

The Sumerians were succeeded by Semites who went on to establish the Assyrian and Babylonian empires in Mesopotamia. Under the Babylonians the science of astronomy flourished. A number of clay tablets from Babylon indicate that the Babylonian astronomers divided the heavens into zones. Arithmetical figures accompany these zonal divisions, but their purpose is unclear. Probably they were used in determining the periodic functions of celestial bodies. The zodiac may have been a basic tool for Babylonian astronomers, providing reference points for their celestial explorations. Another basic tool was the lunar calendar, for which a complex mathematical system was devised.

The outstanding feature of Babylonian astronomy was its application of mathematics to the functions of heavenly bodies. The main interest of the Babylonian astronomers seems to have been the observation and prediction of the motions of the planets. The reason for their concern is not clear. Some scholars feel that the Babylonians connected planetary movements with historical events. Thus astronomy may have been regarded as a means of predicting the course of history.

The work of the Babylonian astronomers is of great importance to modern historians. Babylonian observations of the planet Venus have provided guidelines by which certain dates, particularly in the time of Hammurabi, may be accurately ascertained.

Egypt. Early Egyptian astronomy must be described as crude, yet from it emerged a calendar concept that influenced the science of astronomy for a long time. The Egyptian calendar divided the year into 360 days with a period of 5 days added at the end of the year. That concept avoided the difficulties of the lunar calendar, which required complex adjustments because of its many variations. The benefits of the fixed calendar were recognized by the Greek astronomers who also made use of it.

Egyptian astronomy did not become a sophisticated science until after Ptolemy I (367?–283 BC) made Alexandria the capital of Egypt and one of the chief centers of learning in the known world. At Alexandria the science of astronomy flourished under the influence of Greek scholars.

The Greek mathematician Aristarchus (d. c. 250 BC) studied at Alexandria. It was he who first attempted to determine the size of the sun and moon as well as the distance between them, basing his calculations on their angular relationships with the earth. Aristarchus has been called the "Ancient Copernicus" because 18 centuries before Galileo he propounded the theory that the sun was the center of the universe. The world was not ready for a heliocentric universe, however, and his theory would be unknown to us if it had not been mentioned by the famous Greek mathematician Archimedes.

About AD 150, two centuries after the end of Egypt's Ptolemaic dynasty, an astronomer named Claudius Ptolemy worked in Alexandria, describing his observations and theories in a work later known as the *Almagest.* Although his system of the universe was taken largely from the Greek astronomer Hipparchus, it became known as the Ptolemaic system. It was the best available for 14 centuries.

Greece. Homer's epic poems, *The Iliad* and *The Odyssey* (8th century BC), refer to known constellations such as the Pleiades and Orion. The sun was understood as rising from Oceanus, the ocean-river that surrounded the earth, and setting in Oceanus.

The Pythagoreans (early 5th century BC) taught that the earth was spherical and that the sun, moon, and planets each had its own path, moving around a central fire.

Plato (427?–347 BC) set forth the concept of circular and orbital movements of the sun, the moon, and five known planets in his theory of the "whorls." He evidently knew of the theory of planet retrogradation. His concept of the celestial sphere was that of the earth at the center with the sun, moon, and planets revolving around the earth at different speeds, in literal spheres.

Aristotle (384–322 BC) argued for a fixed, spherical earth. He judged the circumference of the earth to be about 46,000 miles, nearly twice its actual circumference of 24,900 miles.

Astronomy in the Bible. *Origin of the Solar System.* The ancient Hebrews affirmed that the universe had its origin in the creative word of God (Gn 1:3). The Hebrew word translated "created" in Genesis 1:1 connotes the concept of initiating an object and implies that the universe, as we know it, came into being at that time. According to Genesis 1:14–19 the celestial bodies were made on the fourth creative day. The word used for the making of those bodies is not "create" but a word that connotes the concept of "fashioning" and emphasizes the forming of an object. The celestial bodies may have come into existence in an unformed state in the creative act of Genesis 1:1. Their final stage of formation would then have been reached on the fourth creative day.

Hebrew Cosmography. It is often said that the OT sets forth a primitive cosmography that evisioned a flat earth, resting on pillars, with the heavens forming a blue dome above. That concept is allegedly present in Job 26:9–11; 38:4–6; and Isaiah 40:22,23, for example.

In Job 26:9–11 the circle on the face of the waters may refer to the horizon that one observes on the ocean out of sight of land. The language used is probably metaphorical and need not indicate that the writer of Job had a primitive conception of the position of the earth with reference to the heavens. It is especially important to note that verse 7 speaks of the earth as being "hung on nothing," a concept quite at variance with the primitive concepts alleged to occur in the chapter.

In Job 38:4–6 God is pictured as creating the earth as one would erect a building. The picture of a builder measuring the structure (v 5) is a metaphor and is certainly not to be taken literally. The reference to foundations is also part of the metaphor. It seems unwise to assert that this highly literary depiction of creation represents the Hebrew cosmography. One must look back to Genesis 1 to see the Hebrew understanding of the nature of the universe.

In Isaiah 40:22,23 God is pictured as sitting above the horizon of the earth. The metaphor connotes a theological truth important for God's people going into exile—that is, that God is observing all that is transpiring in the sphere of history (40:27–31).

Sun and Moon. According to Genesis 1:14–19 the sun and moon, along with the stars, have the function of giving light on the earth, determining the seasons, and functioning as "signs." The word "season" may denote festal seasons as well as the annual seasons. The Hebrew calendar was a lunar-solar calendar similar to that of the Babylonians. Hebrew festal seasons were based on the phases of the moon. The function of the heavenly bodies as signs seems to relate to their delineation of the heavens, permitting human beings on earth to orient themselves, navigate, etc.

Eclipse of Sun and Moon. Although the observed occurrence of an eclipse is never mentioned in the Bible, such a phenomenon is probably behind the numerous references to the darkening of the sun and moon in certain apocalyptic passages (Jl 2:31; Am 8:9; Mt 24:29).

In Job 3:3–8 there may be an indirect reference to a mythological monster, leviathan, which was thought by many ancients to have devoured the sun or moon when an eclipse of those bodies occurred. That concept may form a background for Job's wish that the day of his birth might pass into oblivion (3:3).

Constellations. A number of constellations are cited in the OT. It is difficult to determine with certainty, however, which constellations are intended by particular Hebrew words.

The Hebrew word translated "Pleiades" (in many versions) means "cluster" or "heap." It is reasonable to suppose that the term applies to the most prominent cluster of stars in the heavens, the Pleiades. That cluster, within the constellation Taurus, is alluded to in Job 9:9; 38:31; and Amos 5:8. It is called "the Seven Stars" in Amos 5:8 (LB), although only six are generally visible to the naked eye.

A Hebrew word possibly related to the word "fool" is frequently understood to be the constellation Orion. The connection between that constellation and the word "fool" is unknown.

Other constellations seem to be intended by "the chambers of the south" and the "Mazzaroth" (Jb 9:9; 38:32). Mazzaroth may refer to division of the heavens into the signs of the zodiac, since a cognate word in the Babylonian creation epic evidently depicts such a division.

The constellation known as the Bear seems to be intended in Job 9:9 and 38:32, since the other major constellations in Job, if properly identified, occupy the eastern, western, and southern sections of the sky. The Bear (known to most Americans as the Big Dipper), occupying the northern sky, would then fill out the pattern signifying God's power in all the quarters of the sky.

Stars. The stars are often referred to in Scripture. Their vast number was used as an analogy in God's promise to Abraham (Gn 15:5). The apostle Paul referred to the varying magnitudes of the stars (1 Cor 15:41).

The writer of Jude used the concept of wandering stars to describe teachers in the early church who were propounding false doctrine (Jude 13). The metaphor is thought by some to be based on the observable movement of the stars around the polestar. It is the fixed polestar, not the stars apparently moving in paths around it, that provides the reference point for navigation. A false teacher, like the apparently moving stars, would be an unreliable guide. It seems better, however, to understand Jude's metaphor as referring to the planets. The study of astronomy by that time had advanced to the point where the regular apparent movements of the stars around the polestar and the position of constellations and star clusters were all well known. It is unlikely that all stars but the polestar were considered wandering stars. Planets, on the other hand, were regarded by ancient observers as traveling in erratic paths quite different from the fixed rotation of stars around the polestar. Some commentators think wandering stars referred to comets.

Unusual Astronomical Phenomena. Several remarkable astronomical phenomena figure prominently in the Bible, including an apparent long day (Jos 10:12–14) and the retrogression of the shadow on a sundial, which was a sign for King Hezekiah (2 Kgs 20:8–11).

Several explanations of Joshua's long day have been suggested. It is held by some that the rotation of the earth actually ceased. There is no theological difficulty involved in this event, for the Creator may perform miracles within the sphere of the universe by temporarily altering or suspending natural laws. There is a scientific difficulty in the fact that such an interruption of gravitational force probably would have caused great dislocation of everything on the earth's surface. God could have acted within the limitations of natural law to prevent such an upheaval, however.

The long day may have been the result of other changes in the natural phenomena rather than the cessation of the earth's rotation. Some have noted that the Hebrew word translated "stand still" may mean "to be quiet." When applied to the sun, the word would imply a "quieting" of the sun's activity, or a diminution of light. This would be an apt description of an eclipse of the sun. Such an occurrence would cause Israel's enemies to flee in terror. Still others see the account as a highly poetic description of Joshua's victory, not intended to be understood literally because it is a quotation from the book of Jashar. This book was probably a poetic work celebrating the exploits of Israel's heroes.

Examination of the account of the shadow's movement on Ahaz's sundial (as a sign to Hezekiah) shows that the event was purely local, since envoys came from Babylon to learn about it (2 Chr 32:31). It is possible that both the long day and retrogression of the shadow were local phenomena, perhaps caused by abnormal refraction of light. Atmospheric disturbances could have occurred at the time; the account of Joshua's battle specifically mentions hailstones (Jos 10:11).

The star of Bethlehem (Mt 2:1–11) has been identified with various astronomical phenomena such as the conjunction of Mars, Saturn, and Venus in 12 BC. In 2 BC Venus and Jupiter came into close proximity as well. That type of phenomenon does not seem to fit the description of the star, however. The star reportedly went before the magi and hovered over the site of the birth of the Christ child. Of course the writer may have been using phenomenological language, that is, describing the event as it appeared to the observers. Some think the description points to a nova or supernova, a sudden increase in a star's brightness; supernovae occur in a stellar system about once every 600 years. Although some natural event may serve to explain in whole or in part the star of Bethlehem, many Christians regard it as a miraculous supernatural phenomenon which God used to herald the event of the incarnation.

These unusual phenomena and others like them accompanied important events in the history of God's dealing with humanity. Not only do they witness to the importance of those events in God's redemptive plan, but they demonstrate God's power as well.

The attempts of some biblical scholars to explain these miracles in terms of natural phenomena is not an attempt to deny the validity of miracles. They only attempt to explain the phenomena within the sphere of observable natural order and the scope of biblical texts. Other scholars understand miracles to be the result of a supernatural alteration of physical laws, believing that the God who created the natural order continues to control that order and may perform miracles by altering the processes of nature to effect his will. In either case the power of God is central to the event, and the Bible faithfully records what took place.

THOMAS E. McCOMISKEY

See ASTROLOGY; CALENDARS, ANCIENT AND MODERN.

Asuppim. KJV transliteration of a Hebrew word meaning storehouses, a part of the temple complex, in 1 Chronicles 26:15,17.

See TABERNACLE, TEMPLE.

Asylum. Place of refuge where a fugitive from justice is immune to arrest or retribution; also, the protection afforded by such a place. An equivalent term is "sanctuary" (originally meaning "holy place"), from the ancient custom of seeking asylum at an altar or in a temple. Thus Adonijah (1 Kgs 1:50–53) and Joab (1 Kgs 2:28–31) both sought sanctuary from King Solomon at the altar of the tabernacle. In the Law of Moses asylum was provided through the establishment of cities of refuge.

See CITIES OF REFUGE.

Asyncritus. One of the Christians in Rome to whom Paul sent greetings (Rom 16:14).

Atad. Site probably in Canaan where Jacob's funeral cortege stopped on the way to Hebron. There, at the threshing floor, the household of Joseph and many Egyptians from the pharaoh's house spent seven days mourning the death of the patriarch (Gn 50:10,11). Impressed with their mourning the Canaanites called the place "Abel-mizraim."

The first word is a pun, involving the words "meadow" and "mourning," and the second is the Hebrew word for Egypt.

Atarah. Onam's mother and second wife of Jerahmeel (1 Chr 2:26).

Ataroth. 1. Town in the mountainous region east of the Jordan River. Ataroth was rebuilt by Gad's tribe (Nm 32:3,33–36). It was mentioned on the famous Moabite Stone by King Mesha, who said he brought back the "altar of David" from Ataroth. This Ataroth is probably modern Khirbet Attarus.

2. Town on the southern border of Ephraim's allotment (Jos 16:2), possibly the same as Ataroth-addar (Jos 16:5; 18:13).

3. Town in the Jordan Valley on the NE border of Ephraim's allotment (Jos 16:7).

4. Town in Judah near Bethlehem belonging to the family of Joab, Salma's son (1 Chr 2:54 KJV). The best translation of this reference, however, is Atroth-beth-joab.

See ATROTH-BETH-JOAB.

Ataroth-addar. Town on the boundary between Ephraim's territory and that of Benjamin (Jos 16:5; 18:13), about seven miles north of Jerusalem.

Ater. 1. Ancestor of a group of people who returned to Judah with Zerubbabel after the exile (Ezr 2:16; Neh 7:21).

2. Ancestor of a family of gatekeepers who also returned to Judah with Zerubbabel (Ezr 2:42; Neh 7:45).

3. Political leader who signed Ezra's covenant of faithfulness to God with Nehemiah and others after the exile (Neh 10:17).

Athach. City, probably near Ziklag in southern Judah, to which David sent part of his booty after a victory over the Amalekites (1 Sm 30:30).

Athaiah. Uzziah's son from Judah's tribe, a resident of Jerusalem after the exile (Neh 11:4).

Athaliah. 1. Wife of King Jehoram of Judah, and daughter of King Ahab of Israel and his wife Jezebel. Athaliah, Judah's only queen, ruled 841–835 BC (2 Kgs 11; 2 Chr 22,23).

Jehoram "walked in the way of the kings of Israel, as the house of Ahab had done; for the daughter of Ahab was his wife" (2 Kgs 8:16–18, Joram; 2 Chr 21:5,6). Like her mother, Jezebel, Athaliah worshiped the Canaanite god Baal and encouraged her husband to do the same. Evidently she had considerable influence over Jehoram. After his death their son Ahaziah

was made king (2 Kgs 8:25–27; 2 Chr 22:1). Like Jehoram, Ahaziah was influenced by Athaliah and "did what was evil in the sight of the Lord" (2 Kgs 8:27).

Because the kings of Israel and Judah disobeyed the Lord, Jehu was anointed by God to be the true king of Israel (2 Kgs 9:2,3). Jehu then killed Joram, king of Israel (2 Kgs 9:24), and Ahaziah, king of Judah (2 Kgs 9:27; 2 Chr 22:9). After the death of her son, Athaliah seized the throne of Judah by destroying (so she thought) all the males in the royal family (2 Kgs 11:1; 2 Chr 22:10). But Jehoshabeath, Jehoram's daughter and the wife of Jehoiada the priest, rescued Ahaziah's son Joash and hid him away (2 Kgs 11:2,3, Josheba; 2 Chr 22:11,12).

After six years Jehoiada "took courage" and resolved to reveal the young prince Joash to the people, making an agreement with some mercenary army officers who summoned to Jerusalem "the Levites ... and the heads of fathers' houses of Israel" (2 Chr 23:1–8). In a secret ceremony in the temple Joash was crowned king. Athaliah heard people rejoicing and blowing trumpets and tried to halt the proceedings by tearing her clothes and yelling "Treason!" She was immediately taken from the temple area and executed (2 Kgs 11:13–16; 2 Chr 23:12–15).

See ISRAEL, HISTORY OF; KINGS, BOOKS OF FIRST AND SECOND.

2. One of the sons of Jehoram from Benjamin's tribe (1 Chr 8:26).

3. Father of Jeshaiah, the head of the sons of Elam who returned from Babylon with Ezra (Ezr 8:7).

Atharim. Place, according to the RSV, where the Israelites sought to enter Canaan when attacked by the king of Arad (Nm 21:1). The name means "tracks" and is generally thought to be located near Tamar or Hazazon-tamar several miles south of the Dead Sea. One possible reading of the text makes it identical with Tamar. The KJV, following the Targum and Vulgate, translates it "spies."

Athbash. Hebrew cryptograph in which the first letter of the Hebrew alphabet is substituted for the last, the second for the next-to-last, etc., to produce a code. Such a code or cipher was used for the word "Chaldea" in Jeremiah 51:1 (KJV interprets the cipher as meaning "them that rise up against me"). Another athbash was used for "Babylon" in Jeremiah 25:26 and 51:41 (KJV treats that cipher as a proper name, "Sheshach"). The early Greek translation of the OT, the Septuagint, correctly deciphered these and translated them as "Chaldea" and "Babylon" respectively.

The Acropolis in Athens.

Athens. Capital of modern Greece and for centuries chief city of the province of Attica. Athens' famous landmark is the Acropolis, a steep flat rock that rises about 200 feet above the plain around it and which still holds several masterpieces of architecture. Walls dating from 1100 BC indicate an advanced community by that time.

Athens began its rise to glory in the 6th century BC, first under the leadership of Solon (d. 559 BC), who established democratic forms of government, and later under Pericles (d. 429 BC), when the magnificent buildings of the Acropolis took form. In this golden age Athens became the center of philosophy, art, architecture, and drama.

By the time Paul brought the Christian message to Athens (Acts 17:15–34) the city had only a portion of its former glory and prestige. Roman emperors continued to extend patronage by providing for new buildings and the restoration of the Agora (marketplace). Athens continued to be the home of the most prominent university in the Greek world. Both Epicurean and Stoic philosophy had worthy representatives in the city.

The Christian message was first brought to Athens by the apostle Paul on his second missionary journey about AD 50. His only reference to Athens is in 1 Thessalonians 3:1, where he indicated that he and Timothy arrived in the city together, but that shortly thereafter he sent Timothy back to Thessalonica while he remained alone in Athens.

Luke has provided a more complete account of Paul's ministry there (Acts 17:16–34). His arrival in a city marked by many statues to the gods, which surpassed anything he had seen in other cities, provoked in him strong feelings against such rampant idolatry. Reared in the strict monotheism of Judaism, Paul apparently viewed Athens as the epitome of sin, and the cultural majesty of the city could not undo this impression.

As did almost all cities of that day, Athens had its community of Jews, and Paul began to speak, according to his custom, with his own kinsmen. Before long he was also in the marketplace, speaking about Jesus to anyone who would listen, including some of the philosophers, who spoke condescendingly of him as peddling "scrap-ideas." Paul's preaching of Jesus and the resurrection sounded as though he was proclaiming a new deity, which earned him a summons before the Areopagus, a civic body responsible for the religious and moral life of Athens. As such it had to approve any new deity. The name Areopagus came from a small hill just off the Acropolis where the body formerly sat for deliberations. By Paul's time its meetings were commonly held in a portico at one end of the marketplace.

Most of Luke's account consists of Paul's message to the Areopagus, in which he referred to the many gods, even to an "unknown god." Paul declared that he was making known to them the God who was not known. He closed his address with a call to repentance and judgment. His reference to the resurrection brought division, but some individuals wanted to hear more.

Luke says only that a few followed Paul, including Dionysius, a member of the Areopagite council, and a woman named Damaris. Athens seems to be one of the few places where Paul did not succeed in establishing a church, and thus it did not figure prominently in early Christian history.

Today Athens is one of the cities that best illuminates the setting of apostolic ministry. Many of the monuments surviving today were seen by Paul. Acts 17:23 implies that he examined thoroughly the sculpture and architecture of the city.

The Acropolis was the site of palaces of the Mycenaean kings of Athens. The city was sacred to the goddess Athena, and several temples were built in her honor, including the

Erechtheum (with its porch of maidens), the small temple of Athena Nike (Victory), and the temple of Athena Parthenos (the Virgin), known as the Parthenon. A huge statue of Athena Promachos stood beside the temple, and sunlight flashing on the statue's spear was said by Pausanias to be visible to ships off Cape Sounion.

Excavations by the American School of Classical Studies since 1931 in the Athenian Agora have illuminated the city's life and its architectural pre- and early Christian history. Pottery fragments scratched with the names of political leaders were found in a ballot jar where they had been cast.

Important buildings in the Agora are the Temple of Hephaestus, the Stoa (portico) of Attalus, and the Odeum (small theater) of Agrippa. The Panathenaic Way, which led through the Agora and up to the Acropolis, was used for festival processions and ceremonial occasions. The Horologion (Tower of the Winds) in the Agora still stands. It contained sundials and a water clock.

Excavations at the Ceramicus near the Agora yielded fine grave stelae and artifacts, some of which are now at the National Archaeological Museum in Athens. At the foot of the Acropolis stands the Odeum of Herod Atticus, built in the 2nd century AD. A 535-foot stoa nearby was presented to Athens by King Eumenes II of Pergamum (197–159 BC). The theater of Dionysus, dating from the 5th century BC and later replaced in stone by Lycurgus, held more than 15,000 spectators. Add to these splendid monuments the remains of the once-massive temple of Olympian Zeus, 104 columns over 90 feet high, and it is possible to imagine what a glorious city Athens was in her prime. The temple to Zeus, begun by Pesistratus, was roofless in the time of Paul and was not completed until the reign of the emperor Hadrian, lavish benefactor of the city.

Though smaller and less influential than its rivals Corinth and Ephesus, Athens was honored as a cultural and religious center until the time of Julian the Apostate (AD 361–63), who studied philosophy there. He tried unsuccessfully to revive the city's pagan spirit.

ROBERT W. LYON

Athlai. Bebai's descendant, who obeyed Ezra's exhortation to divorce his pagan wife after the exile (Ezr 10:28).

Atonement. In Christian thought, the act by which God and man are brought together in personal relationship. The term is derived from Anglo-Saxon words meaning "making at one," hence "at-one-ment." It presupposes a separation or alienation that needs to be overcome if human beings are to know God and have fellowship with him. As a term expressing relationship, atonement is tied closely to such terms as reconciliation and forgiveness.

Biblical Data. The word "atonement" occurs many times in the OT but only once in the NT (Rom 5:11 KJV). Modern translations generally, and more correctly, render the word "reconciliation." The idea of atonement is ever present in the NT, however, and is one of the fundamental concepts of Scripture.

Foundational Concepts. God is seen as taking the initiative in man's salvation; thus atonement is the work of God, who opens the possibility for sinful human beings to receive pardoning grace. For the sinner, who cannot know God, who cannot bridge the gap between himself and God, a "new and living way" is opened up by God.

The need for atonement is bound up with man's thoroughgoing sinfulness. All of Scripture points to the radical nature of that sinfulness. The prophet Isaiah affirmed, "All we like sheep have gone astray" (Is 53:6). According to another prophet, Jeremiah, "The heart is deceitful above all things, and desperately corrupt; who can understand it?" (Jer 17:9). David the psalmist cried, "There is none that does good, no, not one" (Ps 14:3). Paul described the degeneracy of man caused by his disobedience and idolatry (Rom 1:18–32) and summed it up: "All have sinned and fall short of the glory of God" (Rom 3:23). Elsewhere Paul described men as "enemies of God" (Rom 5:10), as "hostile to God" (Rom 8:7), as "estranged and hostile in mind, doing evil deeds" (Col 1:21). Adam's race is just like Adam: "Therefore as sin came into the world through one man and death through sin, and so death spread to all men because all men sinned" (Rom 5:12).

The problem of the sinfulness of man is compounded by the holiness of God, who cannot look upon sin. Isaiah saw the holy God in the temple and drew back because of his own sinfulness (Is 6:1–5). Not only is man terribly sinful, but God is fearfully holy. Consequently man dreads God and can do nothing to change this situation. He is lost, helpless, standing under the awful judgment of God. He cannot justify himself before God and cannot merit God's concern.

The possibility of atonement, then, rests entirely with God. The nature of that atonement, as illustrated in biblical history, affirms simultaneously the nature of both God and man.

Old Testament. The Hebrew term frequently translated "atone" has the basic meaning "to wipe out," "to erase," "to cover," or perhaps more generally "to remove." In the KJV it is translated by such expressions as "to make atonement," "forgive," "appease," "pacify," "pardon," "purge," "put off," and "reconcile."

The most common OT expression of the means of atonement was the sacrifice and offering up of the blood of a victim. To appreciate the concept of sacrifice it must be understood that God provided for the sacrifice, while man performed the rite. Man is not to be viewed as attempting to do something "on his own" to obtain forgiveness. The sacrifice took place at the initiative of God and was to be seen as God's gracious provision for sin. "I have given it for you upon the altar to make atonement for your souls" (Lv 17:11). In the account of Abraham's willingness to offer up his son Isaac, God provided the sacrifice (Gn 22:9–14). In Genesis 15:17–21 God called Abraham to arrange the covenant sacrifice. Far from being something man did to satisfy God, the sacrifice was an act of God for man.

In a sacrifice the shedding of blood was the central act. Life was in the blood (Lv 17:11); in the pouring out of the blood, life was given up; that is, death occurred. Elsewhere blood may be a symbol for life, but in the sacrificial motif it symbolized death. Some scholars have argued that in the pouring forth of the blood, life was made available to the people. It was the life *of the flesh*, however, that was in the blood, and the flesh was sacrificed. In the NT it is by virtue of the resurrection that the life of Christ is made available to believers.

Not every OT mention of atonement referred directly to the shedding of blood. On the Day of Atonement one of two goats was slain, but the other was "presented alive before the Lord to make atonement" (Lv 16:10). That "scapegoat" was driven out into the wilderness bearing the sins of the people. Banishment or expulsion took the place of blood as the goat, bearing the sins of the people, suffered the fate of the sinner. The goat was a substitute for the people. Money offered for the temple was also said to make atonement (Ex 30:16). In another text Aaron and Moses prevented the spreading of a plague by carrying incense: "and he put on the incense, and made atonement for the people" (Nm 16:47). Those few special expressions do not undo the basic OT theme of atonement through provision of a substitute animal. The NT summarizes that theme by saying that "without the shedding of blood there is no forgiveness of sins" (Heb 9:22).

From atonement for sin in the OT came such terms as expiation and forgiveness. From the idea of atonement for the wrath or judgment of God came propitiation and reconciliation. Hence in modern English translations various terms attempt to express the concept of atonement provided by God.

New Testament. Throughout the NT it is made clear that the work of Christ, primarily the cross, is what provides atonement. OT language continues to find expression in the NT, especially the term "blood." Thus in the NT we have the "blood of the covenant" (Mt 26:28) and the "new covenant in my blood" (Lk 22:20) as well as the "blood of Christ" (Eph 2:13) and the "blood of his cross" (Col 1:20). Almost equivalent are the frequent references to the cross and the death of Christ. The NT is the "new covenant" of Jesus Christ, sealed by his blood. He represented the once-for-all coming of God to man and for man.

The atoning work of Christ is described as an expression of the love of Christ for humankind. The relationship was expressed clearly by the apostle John ("For God so loved the world that he gave his only Son," Jn 3:16) and by Paul ("But God shows his love for us in that while we were yet sinners Christ died for us," Rom 5:8). The atonement is the act of God's grace whereby he does for man what man could not do for himself. Man is without excuse. The judgment of God is just; yet grace is offered as coming from the very nature of God. The necessity of the work of Christ ("must suffer," Mk 8:31, etc.) is derived only from the grace and love of God.

Many terms are employed to express the atoning significance of Christ. His death is the "sacrifice to God" (Eph 5:2) and a "single sacrifice for sins" (Heb 10:12; cf. 9:26; 7:27). Paul wrote that God set Christ forth to be a "propitiation" (KJV) or "expiation" (RSV). The NIV helps to clarify the concept by using the term "atoning sacrifice," an expression that includes the ideas of both propitiation and expiation. The death of Christ is seen as the fulfillment of all that was prefigured by the OT sacrificial system.

The sacrificial nature of Christ's death is clearly expressed. He was referred to by Paul as "our paschal lamb" (1 Cor 5:7). The apostle Peter stated that believers are rescued "not with perishable things such as silver or gold, but with the precious blood of Christ, like that of a lamb without blemish or spot" (1 Pt 1:18,19). So also the references in John 1:29,36 to Jesus as the "Lamb of God" probably had in mind the idea of sacrifice.

If Christ is viewed as our sacrifice, he is also viewed as our representative. That is, he represented us in his death. One of the most difficult phrases to interpret precisely is the common biblical expression "for us" ("for me," etc.). It may mean generally "for my sake" or something more specific. Does Christ represent us? More specifically, is he a substitute for us? Some texts clearly speak of him as our representative. Thus Paul said, "We are convinced that one has died for all; therefore all have died" (2 Cor 5:14). If "substitution" were meant, the last clause would conclude that we will not, or do not, die. Hebrews speaks of Christ as our high priest before the Father, which is probably what John had in mind when he referred to Christ as our "advocate with the Father" (1 Jn 2:2).

The expression "for us" at times seems to mean much more than representation; it often carries the sense of substitution, an idea prevalent in the OT. So, "For our sake he made him to be sin who knew no sin, so that in him we might become the righteousness of God" (2 Cor 5:21). Two "ransom sayings" also portray substitution: "The Son of man came not to be ministered unto, but to minister, and to give his life a ransom for many" (Mk 10:45 KJV). He "gave himself as a ransom for all" (1 Tm 2:6). He became a "curse for us" (Gal 3:13). The unintended prophecy of Caiaphas the high priest pointed to the same reality: "It is expedient for you that one man should die for the people, and that the whole nation should not perish" (Jn 11:50).

However we describe what Christ has done by way of atonement, it remains for human beings to appropriate it by faith. The human race is not uninvolved in the atonement; the note of grace in the NT is always accompanied by a reference to faith (Eph 2:8). After the indicative of God's grace comes the imperative of personal belief.

Although many biblical expressions (some using political, military, or economic phraseology) convey the same message, no theory of atonement adequately interprets the concept. Atonement is the whole message of Scripture: God in Christ was reconciling the world to himself (2 Cor 5:19).

ROBERT W. LYON and PETER TOON

See PROPITIATION; EXPIATION; OFFERINGS AND SACRIFICES; ATONEMENT, DAY OF; REDEEMER, REDEMPTION; RANSOM; CRUCIFIXION; REPENTANCE; CONVERSION.

Bibliography. J. Denney, *The Death of Christ*; R. de Vaux, *Studies in OT Sacrifice*; P.T. Forsyth, *The Cruciality of the Cross*; R.S. Franks, *The Atonement* and *The Work of Christ*; M. Hengel, *The Atonement*; H.D. McDonald, *The Atonement of the Death of Christ*; I.H. Marshall, *The Work of Christ*; G. Smeaton, *The Doctrine of the Atonement, as taught by Apostles* and *The Doctrine of the Atonement, as taught by the Christ Himself*; R. Wallace, *The Atoning Death of Christ*.

Atonement, Day of. Yom Kippur, the most important day in the religious calendar of Israel, falling on the tenth day of Tishri (the Hebrew month corresponding to mid-September through mid-October). On that day the high priest entered the Holy of Holies of the tabernacle (or temple) to atone for the sins of all Israel. The basic idea of atonement is a "covering" of sin; the purpose is to accomplish reconciliation between man and God. In the NT the Day of Atonement was referred to as the "fast" (Acts 27:9). To the rabbis it was the "Day" or the "Great Day."

Although many additional rites were added over the centuries, the basic description of the original Day of Atonement is Leviticus 16. Complex and detailed ceremonies all focused on the central objective of complete atonement by sacrifice. First, the high priest removed his official garments, made for beauty and glory, and clothed himself in white linen as a symbol of repentance as he went about the duties of the day. Next, he offered a bull calf as a sin offering for the priests and himself. That done, he entered the Holy of Holies with a censer of live coals from the altar of incense, filling the area with incense. He sprinkled the bullock's blood on the mercy seat and on the floor before the ark of the covenant. Then he cast lots over two live goats brought by the people. He killed one of the goats as a sin offering for the nation, taking the blood inside the veil and sprinkling it as before, thus atoning even for the Holy Place. He confessed the sins of the nation over the live goat as he placed his hands on its head. Finally he sent the live goat, called the scapegoat (KJV, i.e., the escape goat), into the wilderness. Symbolically it carried away the sins of the people. Then the high priest clothed himself in his usual apparel and offered a burnt offering for himself and one for the people with the fat of the sin offering. Outside the camp the flesh of the bull calf and goat was burned.

Other OT references to the Day of Atonement include Exodus 30:10; Leviticus 23:26–32, giving the date in a list of all the annual feasts; Leviticus 25:9–16, stating that each jubilee year began on the Day of Atonement; and Numbers 29:7–11.

The Day of Atonement became so central to Judaism that it survived the destruction of the temple in AD 70 and the end of the sacrificial system. It is the highest holy day of Judaism today. Although nowhere in the books of Moses is there an explanation of "afflicting the soul" required on the Day of Atonement (Lv 23:27,29,32 KJV), the Jews have continuously interpreted it as referring to fasting (cf. Ps 35:13; Is 58:3,5,10). In biblical times celebration of the Day of Atonement showed that Israel believed the cleansing of their sins was accomplished by the rites commanded by God. The forgiveness and grace of God were granted them and were the basis for their continued fellowship with God as his covenant people. Because it was designated as a "sabbath of solemn rest" (Lv 16:31; 23:32), all work was forbidden on that day as on the weekly observance of the sabbath.

As with all the prescribed sacrifices throughout the year, the question arises as to the need for a special time for atonement. It is clear that the ritual was meant to avert God's wrath for sins already committed as well as to guarantee the continued presence of God. The sacrifice of the first goat and the sending away of the scapegoat were intended to cleanse the nation, the priesthood, and the sanctuary from sin. The intent of the whole sacrificial system reached its highest expression on that day, called by some the "Good Friday of the OT." The daily, weekly, and monthly sacrifices left something undone, so that the high priest could not enter the holiest place throughout the year. On that one day, however, he was permitted to enter with sacrificial blood as he solemnly represented the nation before the blood-stained mercy seat.

The underlying reason for the day was that other offerings for sin could not provide for unknown ("secret") sins. Because of such sins the sanctuary, the land, and the nation remained ritually unclean. The Day of Atonement was instituted by God for the complete atonement of all sin (Lv 16:33). In the person of the high priest the nation was most fully represented by the access of their mediator into the very presence of God.

In the NT the crucifixion accounts, many references in Paul's epistles, and the whole Book of Hebrews are inseparably connected to the Day of Atonement. The ritual of the day is explained as a "type" of the atonement made by Jesus Christ (Heb 9, 10). Christ, the high priest, shed his blood on Calvary and then, having atoned for the world's sins, appeared in heaven before the Father (Heb 9:11,12). Unlike the annual repetitions of the day in Israel, Christ's atonement is seen in the NT as "once for all . . . securing an eternal redemption" (Heb 9:12; see also Rom 3:25; 5:9,10; 1 Cor 5:7; 2 Cor 5:18–21; Gal 3:13,14; Col 1:14; Ti 2:14; 1 Pt 1:18,19; 1 Jn 2:2; 4:10; Rv 5:9).

CHARLES L. FEINBERG

See ATONEMENT; OFFERINGS AND SACRIFICES.

Atroth-beth-joab. Town in Judah near Bethlehem (1 Chr 2:54, KJV "Ataroth, the house of Joab"). Since the Hebrew word *ataroth* means "crowns," some scholars think that the phrase may not be a town name at all but a reference to Salma's descendants as chiefs of Joab's clan.

Atroth-shophan. City in Transjordan in Gad's allotment (Nm 32:35). The KJV mistakenly lists this compound name as two cities.

Attai. 1. Son of Sheshan's daughter and of Jarha, Sheshan's Egyptian slave. Attai was from Judah's tribe (1 Chr 2:35,36).

2. Warrior from Gad's tribe who joined David at Ziklag in his struggle against King Saul (1 Chr 12:11).

3. Son of King Rehoboam of Judah by Maachah, and Solomon's grandson (2 Chr 11:20).

Attalia. Mediterranean seaport in Asia Minor from which the apostle Paul and Barnabas sailed back to Antioch at the end of Paul's first missionary journey (Acts 14:25). The town was founded by Attalus II Philadelphus, king of the province of Pergamum (159–138 BC), which was taken by the Romans in 79 BC and became a senatorial province in AD 43. In Paul's time Attalia was part of the province of Pamphylia. Today, though its harbor is shallow, it is still an important Turkish seaport (Antalya).

Attendant. High-ranking officer in the service of the king.

See TRADES AND OCCUPATIONS (CHAMBERLAIN).

Attributes of God. Virtues, excellencies, and perfections of God.

See GOD, BEING AND ATTRIBUTES OF.

Augustus' Band. Roman military unit mentioned in Acts 27:1 (KJV). Julius, the centurion who had custody of the apostle Paul on the way to Rome, was a member of Augustus' Band. The Greek word translated "band" normally meant a Roman cohort or force of two cohorts. Some scholars, assuming that Julius was in command of that unit, have wondered why an officer normally commanding a century (100 men) should be in charge of 500 to 1000. Perhaps Julius was not in command of the whole unit, or it was not a regular cohort (tenth part of a Roman legion) but a special courier or guard detachment. Archaeological evidence has been found for the presence of a *Cohors Augusta I* in Syria in the 1st century AD.

See ARMS AND WARFARE.

Augustus Caesar. Roman emperor from 31 BC to AD 14.

See CAESARS, THE.

Aul. KJV spelling of awl in Exodus 21:6 and Deuteronomy 15:17.

See TOOLS.

Ava. KJV spelling of Avva, a Syrian district, in 2 Kings 17:24.

See AVVA.

Aven. 1. Term used by Ezekiel to describe On (Heliopolis), center of worship of the Egyptian sun god Ra (Ez 30:17). The Hebrew word *aven* ("wickedness") was a play on the name On in a prophecy against the idolatry and wickedness of Egypt.

See HELIOPOLIS.

2. Epithet for Bethel (Hos 10:8), shortened from Beth-aven, "house of wickedness" (Hos 4:15; 5:8; 10:5). The prophet Hosea was condemning the northern kingdom's idolatry, for which Bethel was one center (1 Kgs 12:28,29).

See BETH-AVEN #2.

3. Valley where Syria was to be punished because of its transgression against the Lord (Am 1:5), perhaps an oblique reference to Baalbek, the center of Syria's Baal worship in the Beqa'a Valley.

Avenger of Blood. Person who performed the duty of pursuing and ultimately executing the murderer of a near kinsman (see, e.g., Nm 35). Such a "redeemer" was expected to act in instances of deliberate murder but not of accidental manslaughter. A person guilty of manslaughter could find asylum in any one of six designated cities throughout the land (Nm 35:11) so that regular judicial processes could be set in motion. The avenger of blood can be seen in the accounts of Gideon (Jgs 8:18–21), Joab (2 Sm 3:27,30), the Gibeonites (2 Sm 21), and Amaziah (2 Kgs 14:5,6). During the monarchy the king could evidently thwart the avenger (2 Sm 14:8–11).

The custom was rooted in the ordinance of God which required a life for a life in any case of intentional homicide (Gn 9:6). Unfortunately the intent of the law—to impress upon humanity the sacredness of human life—has sometimes been greatly distorted, leading to blood feuds and the annihilation of whole families in some societies.

See CIVIL LAW AND JUSTICE.

Avim (Place). KJV spelling of Avvim, a Benjamite city, in Joshua 18:23.

See AVVIM (PLACE).

Avims, Avites (Persons). KJV forms of Avvim in Deuteronomy 2:23 and Joshua 13:3, respectively.

See AVVIM (PERSONS).

Avith. Capital city for Hadad, Edom's fourth king (Gn 36:35; 1 Chr 1:46).

Avva. District in Syria (the same as Ivvah in 2 Kgs 18:34; 19:13) conquered by Sargon of Assyria in the 8th century BC. After the deportation of the Israelites from Samaria in 722 BC,

Shalmaneser, the Assyrian king, sent inhabitants from Avva and other districts to occupy the cities of Samaria (2 Kgs 17:24, KJV Ava). These heathen Avvites continued to pay homage to their own gods in spite of learning "the fear of the Lord" from an Israelite priest (2 Kgs 17:31,32).

See IVVAH.

Avvim (Persons). Ancient people who lived in villages near Gaza before they were largely destroyed by a Philistine invasion (Dt 2:23, KJV Avim; Jos 13:3, KJV Avites).

Avvim (Place). City in Benjamin's allotment (Jos 18:23, KJV Avim), located south of Bethel.

Avvite. Designation for the inhabitants of the Syrian district of Avva who were relocated by Shalmaneser of Assyria in Samaria after its conquest in 722 BC (2 Kgs 17:31).

See AVVA.

Awl. See TOOLS.

Ax, Axhead. See TOOLS.

Ayyah. Town belonging to Ephraim's tribe (1 Chr 7:28, KJV Gaza, but different from the Philistine Gaza). Some scholars think that Aija (Neh 11:31) refers to Ayyah or to Ai, possibly a neighboring town. Many identify Aiath (Is 10:28) with Ayyah and the town with the modern Khirbet Haiyan.

Azal. KJV rendering of Azel, perhaps a place near Jerusalem, in Zechariah 14:5.

See AZEL (PLACE).

Azaliah. Meshullam's son and the father of Josiah's scribe, Shaphan (2 Kgs 22:3; 2 Chr 34:8).

Azaniah. Jeshua's father. Jeshua was a Levite who signed Ezra's covenant of faithfulness to God with Nehemiah and others after the exile (Neh 10:9).

Azarael. KJV form of Azarel in Nehemiah 12:36.

See AZAREL #6.

Azareel. KJV form of Azarel.

See AZAREL #1–5.

Azarel. 1. Warrior from Benjamin's tribe who joined David at Ziklag in his struggle against King Saul. Azarel was one of David's ambidextrous archers and slingers (1 Chr 12:6, KJV Azareel).

2. Levite selected by David to assist in the music of the sanctuary (1 Chr 25:18, KJV Azareel).

3. Chief of Dan's tribe appointed by David to be tribal leader during David's ill-fated census (1 Chr 27:22, KJV Azareel).

4. Israelite of the family of Binnui who obeyed Ezra's exhortation to divorce his pagan wife after the exile (Ezr 10:41, KJV Azareel).

5. Amashsai's father. Amashsai was a priest of Immer's family who lived in Jerusalem after the exile (Neh 11:13, KJV Azareel).

6. Priest who blew a trumpet at the dedication of the wall of Jerusalem after the exile (Neh 12:36, KJV Azarael).

Azariah. Very common Jewish name. Its numerous occurrences in the priestly genealogies has caused much confusion. The following is one of several possible arrangements.

1. Zadok's son or grandson. According to most translations, Azariah was high priest during Solomon's reign (1 Kgs 4:2). It is possible, however, that his position should be understood as that of a special counselor or keeper of the royal calendar.

2. Nathan's son, a high official in King Solomon's court. He was chief officer over the 12 regional administrators (1 Kgs 4:5).

3. Amaziah's son, king of Judah (2 Kgs 14:21; 15:1–27), more frequently known as Uzziah.

See UZZIAH #1.

4. Ethan's son, a descendant of Judah (1 Chr 2:8).

5. Jehu's son, another descendant of Judah (1 Chr 2:38).

6. Ahima-az's son and Zadok's grandson (1 Chr 6:9). If Azariah #1 was indeed a high priest, this Azariah could be identified with him.

7. Johanan's son and Amariah's father (1 Chr 6:10,11). He is identical with the Azariah of Ezra 7:3 and 2 Esdras 1:2, whose father (meaning "ancestor") was Meraioth. The parenthetical note about Solomon's temple (1 Chr 6:10b) is generally held to go with the Azariah of verse 9 (see #6 above). It is possible, however, that this Azariah served in the temple (built by Solomon) during the reign of Uzziah and is therefore identical with #17 below.

8. Hilkiah's son and Seraiah's father (1 Chr 6:13,14; Ezr 7:1; 2 Esd 1:1). Some have identified this Azariah with #10 or #11 below.

9. Zephaniah's son, an ancestor of the singer Heman. Heman sang in the worship ritual instituted by King David (1 Chr 6:36).

10. Hilkiah's son or descendant, one of the first priests to settle in Jerusalem after the exile (1 Chr 9:11; Seraiah, Neh 11:11).

11. Obed's son, a prophet in the days of King Asa of Judah. He encouraged Asa to initiate badly needed reforms in the king's fifteenth year (2 Chr 15:1–15; "Obed the prophet," v 8).

12,13. Two sons of King Jehoshaphat of Judah. Along with four of their brothers they were killed for political reasons by Jehoram, heir to the throne (2 Chr 21:1–4).

14. Alternate name for Ahaziah, king of Judah (2 Chr 22:6 KJV; cf. vv 1,2).

See AHAZIAH #2.

15. Jehoram's son, one of Judah's military commanders. This Azariah followed Jehoiada the priest in a rebellion that resulted in the execution of Queen Athaliah and the crowning of Joash as king (2 Chr 23:1).

16. Obed's son, another of the five commanders in league with Jehoiada against Athaliah (2 Chr 23:1).

17. High priest in Jerusalem during the reign of King Uzziah (2 Chr 26:16–21). He opposed Uzziah's arrogant attempt to burn incense on the altar. Perhaps the same as #7 above.

18. Johanan's son, a leader of Ephraim's tribe. Azariah and other leaders of the tribe joined the prophet Obed in protesting the capture of Judean prisoners by King Pekah of Israel and in effecting their release (2 Chr 28:12).

19. Descendant of Kohath and the father of a Levite named Joel. Joel participated in the temple cleansing instituted by King Hezekiah of Judah (2 Chr 29:12).

20. Jehallelel's son. This Azariah, a descendant of Merari, also participated in Hezekiah's cleansing of the temple (2 Chr 29:12).

21. Zadok's descendant and high priest during the reign of Hezekiah of Judah (2 Chr 31:10,13). He participated in Hezekiah's massive religious reforms.

22. Maaseiah's son, a householder in Jerusalem who participated in Nehemiah's rebuilding of the wall (Neh 3:23).

23. Leader who returned to Judah with Zerubbabel after the Babylonian exile (Neh 7:7; Seraiah, Ezr 2:2).

24. Levitical assistant of Ezra who explained to the people passages from the Law read by Ezra (Neh 8:7).

25. Priest who signed Ezra's covenant of faithfulness to God with Nehemiah and others after the exile (Neh 10:2).

26. Participant in the dedication of the rebuilt wall of Jerusalem (Neh 12:33).

27. Alternate form of Jaazaniah, the name of Hoshaiah's son, in Jeremiah 42:1 and 43:2.

See JAAZANIAH #1.

28. One of the three young Jews taken into

captivity with Daniel. In Babylon he was renamed Abednego (Dn 1:6,7,11,19; 2:17).

See SHADRACH, MESHACH, AND ABEDNEGO.

Azaz. Shema's son and Bela's father from Reuben's tribe (1 Chr 5:8).

Azazel. Hebrew term of uncertain origin and meaning, occurring in Leviticus 16:8,10,26. Since biblical or extrabiblical information is lacking, the meaning of Azazel has been interpreted in at least four ways.

1. Scapegoat (KJV). Some have thought the word refers to the scapegoat used in the ceremonies of the Day of Atonement. That interpretation is unlikely because verses 10 and 26 state that the goat was sent *to* Azazel.

2. Place to which the goat was sent. This is the view of many Jewish scholars, who attempt to support it by connecting the word *Azazel* with a high and rugged cliff from which the goat was thrown. Others regard the word as meaning "desert places."

3. Abstract "place" or state of being. Some believe Azazel comes from a Hebrew word meaning "depart" or "remove," and thus interpret it as "utter removal," "complete sending away," or "solitude." That the goat "may be sent into the wilderness to Azazel" (v 10) may be interpreted as "sent into a realm of being (or nonbeing) which is utterly removed." This possibility strengthens the idea of removal of sins: they become "nothing," since they are totally removed. Sending the goat away would then be a symbolic and ritual act through which God annihilates or removes one's past sins.

4. Personal name of a being, most likely a demon, to which the scapegoat was sent. Many modern scholars adopt this interpretation. Some support is found in the noncanonical book of Enoch, where Azazel appears as a ringleader of fallen angels who misleads mankind. Such a being would be an evil spirit to whom the sins of the people belong. Thus one goat is given to the Lord, the other to an evil being. Some have conjectured that that being was Satan himself.

Azaziah. 1. Levitical musician who played the lyre when King David brought the ark of the covenant into Jerusalem (1 Chr 15:21).

2. Hoshea's father. Hoshea was chief officer over the Ephraimites during King David's rule (1 Chr 27:20).

3. Levite appointed by King Hezekiah of Judah to help oversee the offerings stored in the temple (2 Chr 31:13).

Azbuk. Father of the Nehemiah who was ruler of half the Beth-zur district (Neh 3:16).

Azbuk's son assisted the more famous Nehemiah, the governor (Neh 10:1), in rebuilding the wall of Jerusalem.

Azekah. Town in the agricultural plain known as the Shephelah. It existed at least as early as the conquest of Canaan (the Promised Land), since Joshua drove the confederation of Amorite kings to Azekah (Jos 10:10,11). It is also mentioned in connection with the encounter of David and Goliath (1 Sm 17:1). Archaeological excavations have shown that Azekah was heavily fortified with a system of underground refuge chambers (2 Chr 11:9). Azekah, Lachish, and Jerusalem are mentioned as the only remaining walled cities of the southern kingdom of Judah at the time of Nebuchadnezzar's assault on Jerusalem (Jer 34:7). Azekah was resettled by some who returned from the Babylonian exile (Neh 11:30). Today it is known as Tell Zakariyeh.

Azel (Person). Descendant of Benjamin, Saul, and Jonathan. Azel was the son of Eleasah and the father of six sons (1 Chr 8:37,38; 9:43,44).

Azel (Place). Unknown place supposedly on the eastern outskirts of Jerusalem (Zec 14:5, KJV Azal).

Azem. KJV form of Ezem, a town in the Negeb desert area, in Joshua 15:29 and 19:3.

See EZEM.

Azgad. 1. Ancestor of a group that returned to Judah with Zerubbabel after the exile (Ezr 2:12; Neh 7:17).

2. Political leader who signed Ezra's covenant of faithfulness to God with Nehemiah and others after the exile (Neh 10:15).

Aziel. Alternative name for Jaaziel, a Levitical musician, in 1 Chronicles 15:20.

See JAAZIEL.

Aziza. Zattu's descendant who obeyed Ezra's exhortation to divorce his pagan wife (Ezr 10:27).

Azmaveth (Person). 1. Warrior among David's mighty men who were known as "the thirty." Bahurim was his hometown (2 Sm 23:31; 1 Chr 11:33).

2. Jehoaddah's son, a descendant of King Saul through Jonathan (1 Chr 8:36; cf. 9:42, Jarah's son).

3. Father of Jeziel and Pelet from Benjamin's tribe (1 Chr 12:3). Possibly the same as #1 above.

4. Adiel's son, whom King David put in charge of the palace treasuries (1 Chr 27:25).

Azmaveth (Place). Town near Anathoth. Forty-two men from the town returned from the Babylonian exile with Zerubbabel (Ezr 2:24; Beth-azmaveth, Neh 7:28; "Beth-asmoth," 1 Esd 5:18). Later, Azmaveth supplied singers to help celebrate the dedication of the rebuilt wall of Jerusalem (Neh 12:29). It has been identified as Hizmeh, a site five miles north of Jerusalem.

Azmon. City on the southern border of Judah between Kadesh-barnea and the "Brook of Egypt" (Nm 34:4,5; Jos 15:4). Its site is perhaps the modern 'Ain el-Qeseimeh.

Aznoth-Tabor. Literally the "peaks (or slopes) of Tabor," a location on the southwest border of Naphtali's tribal allotment (Jos 19:34).

Azor. Descendant of Zerubbabel and an ancestor of Jesus (Mt 1:1,13,14).

See GENEALOGY OF JESUS CHRIST.

Azotus. NT form of Ashdod in Acts 8:40.

See ASHDOD, ASHDODITE, ASHDOTHITE.

Azri-el. 1. Family chief in the half tribe of Manasseh that settled east of the Jordan River. Azri-el was taken captive along with others by the king of Assyria (1 Chr 5:23–26).

2. Jeremoth's father. Jeremoth was an official over Naphtali's tribe under King David (1 Chr 27:19).

3. Seraiah's father in the reign of King Jehoiakim. Seraiah was sent by the king to arrest Jeremiah and Baruch for prophesying against the evil ways of Israel and Judah (Jer 36:26).

Azrikam. 1. One of three sons of Neariah, a descendant of David through Zerubbabel (1 Chr 3:23).

2. One of six sons of Azel, a descendant of Saul (1 Chr 8:38; 9:44).

3. Ancestor of Shemaiah, a Levite who returned to Jerusalem after the exile (1 Chr 9:14; Neh 11:15).

4. Palace officer under King Ahaz of Judah who was killed by Zichri (2 Chr 28:7), possibly the same as #2 above.

Azubah. 1. Shilhi's daughter and mother of King Jehoshaphat of Judah (1 Kgs 22:42; 2 Chr 20:31).

2. First wife of Caleb and mother of three of his sons (1 Chr 2:18,19).

Azur. KJV form of Azzur in Jeremiah 28:1 and Ezekiel 11:1.

See AZZUR #2 AND #3.

Azzah. KJV rendering of the Philistine city of Gaza in Deuteronomy 2:23; 1 Kings 4:24; and Jeremiah 25:20.

See GAZA, GAZATHITES.

Azzan. Paltiel's father and a member of Issachar's tribe. Paltiel was appointed to help Eleazar and Joshua in apportioning the Promised Land (Nm 34:26).

Azzur. 1. Political leader who signed Ezra's covenant of faithfulness to God with Nehemiah and others after the exile (Neh 10:17).

2. Father of the false prophet Hananiah (Jer 28:1, KJV Azur).

3. Father of Jaazaniah, one of the prominent men of Jerusalem whom Ezekiel saw in a vision (Ez 11:1, KJV Azur).

Bb

Baal. Name of the most prominent Canaanite deity. As the god of fertility in the Canaanite pantheon (roster of gods), Baal's sphere of influence included agriculture, animal husbandry, and human sexuality. The word Baal occurs in the OT in combination with other terms, such as place-names (Baal-peor, Hos 9:10; Baal-hermon, Jgs 3:3), or with other adjuncts as in Baal-berith (Baal of the covenant, Jgs 8:33). Use of the name in connection with a local place-name may indicate a local cult of Baal worship.

Baal worship became prominent in the northern Kingdom of Israel during the days of King Ahab (9th century BC) when he married Jezebel of Tyre, a city in Phoenicia (1 Kgs 16:29–33; 18:19–40). It later infiltrated the Kingdom of Judah when Athaliah, daughter of Ahab and Jezebel, married King Jehoram of Judah (2 Kgs 8:17,18,24–26). Places for worship of Baal were often high places in the hills consisting of an altar and a sacred tree, stone, or pillar (2 Kgs 23:5). The predominantly urban Phoenicians built temples to Baal; while Athaliah was queen of Judah, even Jerusalem had one (2 Chr 23:12–17).

In the Ugaritic epic material Baal is pictured as descending into the netherworld, the domain of the god Mot. That descent was evidently part of a cycle intended to coincide with the cycle of seasons. In order to bring Baal up from the realm of Mot and thus insure initiation of the fertile rainy season, the Canaanites engaged in orgiastic worship that included human sacrifice as well as sexual rites (Jer 7:31; 19:4–6). Sacred prostitutes evidently participated in the autumnal religious ritual. The worship of Baal was strongly condemned in the OT (Jgs 2:12–14; 3:7,8; Jer 19).

HOWARD F. VOS

See CANAANITE DEITIES AND RELIGION.

Baal (Person). 1. Reubenite, the son of Reaiah and the father of Beerah (1 Chr 5:5).

2. Benjamite and one of the ten sons borne to Jeiel, the father of Gibeon, by Maacah his wife. His brother was Kish, the father of Saul (1 Chr 8:30; 9:36).

Baal (Place). Alternate name for Baalath-beer, a city defining a portion of the boundary of Simeon's territory, in 1 Chronicles 4:33.

See BAALATH-BEER.

Baalah. *See* BALAH.

Baalath. 1. Town of Dan which may be the same city as #2 below, although some scholars separate the two (Jos 19:44).

2. Store-city built by Solomon, probably west of Gezer in the original territory of Dan (1 Kgs 9:18; 2 Chr 8:6).

Baalath-beer. Place name meaning "mistress" or "lady of the well." Like the masculine counterpart Baal, Baalath often appears in a compound place-name. It seems to suggest that the Canaanite goddess Baalath, patron of Byblos, was associated with the particular place or well. Baalath-beer was the name of a town in Simeon's tribe, also identified as Baal (1 Chr 4:33), Ramah of the Negeb (Jos 19:8, KJV Ramah of the south), Ramoth of the Negeb (1 Sm 30:27, KJV south Ramoth), and may have marked the southern limits of Simeon's inheritance. Its site is uncertain.

Baal-berith. Pagan god worshiped in central Palestine around the city of Shechem (Jgs 9:1–4,44–46). Baal-berith ("Lord of the Covenant") was probably a local form of Baal, the leading Canaanite fertility god. During the period of the judges, the people of Israel turned

Baal, the storm god, is represented holding a club in his left hand. The lance extends upward in the form of a tree, or stylized lightning. Found at Ras Shamra in 1932.

from the Lord to worship the idols Baal and Baal-berith (Jgs 8:33).

See CANAANITE DEITIES AND RELIGION.

Baale-judah, Baale of Judah. Alternate name for Kiriath-jearim, a village on the road from Jerusalem to Tel Aviv (2 Sm 6:2, KJV Baale of Judah).

See KIRIATH-JEARIM.

Baal-gad. Site in the valley of Lebanon at the foot of Mt Hermon marking the northern border of Joshua's conquest of Canaan (Jos 11:17; 12:7; 13:5).

See HERMON, MOUNT.

Baal-hamon. Site of a vineyard owned by Solomon and rented by local farmers (Sg 8:11). The poetic context indicates that the vineyard produced superb grapes.

Baal-hanan. 1. Achbor's son, a king of Edom (Gn 36:38,39; 1 Chr 1:49,50).

2. Official appointed by King David to be in charge of the royal olive groves and orchards of sycamore figs in the lowlands bordering Philistine territory (1 Chr 27:28). He came from Geder, a town in the area.

Baal-hazor. Mountain home of King David's son Absalom. Two years after Amnon raped Absalom's sister Tamar (Amnon's half-sister), Absalom invited Amnon and his other brothers to a feast at Baal-hazor at sheepshearing time (2 Sm 13:21–30). During the festivities Absalom got his revenge: he had Amnon killed.

Baal-hazor is not to be confused with the Hazor in Benjamin's territory (Neh 11:33) or the Hazor north of the Sea of Galilee in Naphtali's territory (Jos 11:10,11; 1 Kgs 9:15; 2 Kgs 15:29). Baal-hazor was located in the territory of Ephraim at Jebel el-Asur, northeast of Bethel.

Baal-hermon. Hivite territory in Transjordan near Mt Hermon, not captured in the Israelite conquest. It was one of the regions God wanted to use to test the younger generation of Israel (Jgs 3:1–6). Baal-hermon may refer to a place on the mountain. It seems to be another name for Baal-gad (Jos 13:5).

See HERMON, MOUNT.

Baali. Hebrew title meaning "my Lord" or "my master" (Hos 2:16 KJV). The title was rejected by God because of its association with the Canaanite Baal. God chose instead to be addressed with the Hebrew word *Ishi*, "my husband," of similar meaning but untainted by pagan associations. Thus, in a prophetic play on words, God stressed his convenantal love for his people and emphatically rejected any implication that he was for Israel only what Baal was for the Canaanites.

See BAAL; GOD, NAMES OF.

Baalis. Ammonite king who arranged for the murder of Gedaliah, governor of the "remnant" left behind after Nebuchadnezzar's capture of Jerusalem and deportation of its inhabitants (Jer 40:14). Although warned by a guerrilla leader, Johanan, Gedaliah refused to take heed and was killed (Jer 41:1–3).

Baal-meon. City in northern Moab assigned to Reuben's tribe (Nm 32:38; 1 Chr 5:8). It is called Beth-baal-meon in Joshua 13:17, Beth-meon in Jeremiah 48:23, and Beon in Numbers 32:3. About 830 BC it was held by Mesha, king of Moab and was still in Moabite hands in the sixth century BC (Jer 48:23; Ez 25:9) but may have been in Israelite possession during part of the eighth century BC. Today Baal-meon is identified with Ma'in nine miles east of the Dead Sea.

Baal-peor. Moabite god worshiped on Mt Peor. It is probable that this god was Chemosh, the national deity of Moab. While camped in Shittim the Israelites were seduced by Moabite women who persuaded them to worship "Baal of Peor" (Nm 25:3). For that act of idolatry God struck Israel with a plague that killed 24,000 persons (Nm 25:9; Ps 106:28–31). Baal-peor is also spoken of as the place where Israel worshiped "the Baal of Peor" (Dt 4:3; Hos 9:10). That location may be identified with Beth-peor near Mt Nebo.

See MOAB, MOABITE.

Baal-perazim. Location near Jerusalem of a battle in which Israel's newly anointed King David defeated the Philistines (2 Sm 5:20; 1 Chr 14:11). David named the area Baal-perazim to commemorate the Lord's "breaking through" his enemies, since the phrase means the "lord of breaking through." A prophetic reference to a Mt Perazim, where the Lord came "suddenly and in anger," may recall David's battle with the Philistines (Is 28:21).

Baal-shalishah, Baal-shalisha. Home of a man who brought a sack of fresh grain and 20 barley loaves to Elisha at Gilgal. Elisha had his servant feed 100 young prophets with it and had some left over (2 Kgs 4:42, KJV Baal-shalisha). Baal-shalishah was probably located in a fertile area where early crops were raised.

Baal-tamar. Place between Gibeah and Bethel in Benjamin's territory, north of Jerusalem. There the 11 other Israelite tribes rallied their forces in a final victorious battle against the tribe of Benjamin over crimes committed in the city of Gibeah (Jgs 20:33).

Baal-zebub. Pagan god of the Philistine city of Ekron. After King Ahaziah of Israel fell from his upstairs porch (852 BC), he sent messengers to Baal-zebub to ask about his recovery (2 Kgs 1:2). He was severely rebuked for that by the prophet Elijah, who declared that his affront to Israel's God would result in the king's death.

Identification of Baal-zebub (which means "lord of the flies") is somewhat uncertain. The god may have been thought to give oracles by the flight or buzzing of a fly, or may have protected his worshipers from plagues of flies. Excavations at Philistine sites have uncovered golden images of flies. Most scholars believe that the name is a corruption of Baal-zebul ("Baal the prince"). The distortion was probably a deliberate effort to demean the god.

By NT times, the name had changed to Beelzebul (KJV Beelzebub), from the Syriac language meaning "lord of dung." It was a common practice to apply the names of the gods of enemy nations to the devils of one's own religion. Thus, the title was applied by the Jews to the devil, or Satan, the prince of demons (Mt 12:24,27). In their blasphemous criticism, the Pharisees called Jesus by this title to explain his ability to cast out demons (Mk 3:22; Lk 11:15). In Matthew 10:25 Jesus tells the disciples, "If they have called the master of the house Be-elzebul, how much more will they malign those of his household." Here Jesus seems to make his point by relying on another possible meaning of the words from rabbinic usage, "lord of *the house*," house having reference to the temple, the house of the Lord. Thus, in response to the Jewish leaders, a play on words involving contrast may have been employed. They call Jesus "Be-elzebul, lord of the dung heap" and Jesus calls himself "Be-elzebul, lord of the house." By this, Jesus claims lordship over the house of God, the truth of which is born out in his response, "If it is by the Spirit of God that I cast out demons, then the kingdom of God has come upon you" (Mt 12:28).

See CANAANITE DEITIES AND RELIGION.

Baal-zephon. Area opposite the Israelites' encampment just before they crossed the Red Sea (Ex 14:2,9; Nm 33:7). The exact location of Baal-zephon is unknown but probably was in NE Egypt. The name means "lord of the north," and a shrine to a Semitic deity was presumably located there. The god Baal-zephon is mentioned in Ugaritic, Egyptian, and Phoenician writings as a sea and storm god.

Baana. 1. Ahilud's son, one of 12 officers appointed to requisition food for King Solomon's household. He served in the district of Taanach and Megiddo (1 Kgs 4:12).

2. Hushai's son, another of King Solomon's supply officers; his district was Asher and Bealoth (1 Kgs 4:16, KJV Baanah).

3. Zadok's father. Zadok helped Nehemiah rebuild the Jerusalem wall (Neh 3:4). Possibly the same as Baanah (Neh 10:27).

Baanah. 1. Rimmon's son, a member of Benjamin's tribe. Baanah and his brother Rechab were captains under Ish-bosheth after Ish-bosheth's father, King Saul, died in battle.

Ish-bosheth, crowned king by Saul's general, Abner, was David's rival to the throne of Israel. Baanah and Rechab murdered Ish-bosheth in his sleep and cut off his head (2 Sm 4:2–7). They took the head to David, thinking he would be pleased that they had killed the son of his enemy. But David, who had wept at the death of Saul, "God's chosen king" (2 Sm 1), was angry instead. He ordered Baanah and Rechab executed. Their hands and feet were cut off and their bodies hanged (2 Sm 4:8–12).

2. Heleb's father. Heleb, from the town of Netophah near Bethlehem in Judah's territory, was one of David's 30 "mighty men" (2 Sm 23:29; 1 Chr 11:30).

3. KJV form of Baana, Hushai's son, in 1 Kgs 4:16.

See BAANA #2.

4. Leader who returned to Jerusalem with Zerubbabel after the exile (Ezr 2:2; Neh 7:7).

5. Political leader who signed Ezra's covenant of faithfulness to God with Nehemiah and others after the exile (Neh 10:27). Possibly the same as Baana (Neh 3:4).

Baara. Divorced wife of Shaharaim from Benjamin's tribe (1 Chr 8:8).

Ba-aseiah. Malchijah's son and ancestor of the temple musician Asaph (1 Chr 6:40). Ba-aseiah may be a scribal error for the common name Ma-aseiah (1 Chr 15:18).

Baasha. Third ruler of the northern kingdom of Israel from 908–886 BC and violent founder of the second of its nine dynasties. Baasha was the son of Ahijah of Issachar's tribe, an unknown whom the Lord lifted "out of the dust" to leadership in the army (1 Kgs 16:2). While the Israelite army was besieging Gibbethon (inhabited by Philistines), Baasha

assassinated King Nadab and then destroyed all other heirs of the former king, Nadab's father Jeroboam (1 Kgs 15:27–29). For much of his 24-year reign Baasha warred with Asa, king of Judah (1 Kgs 15:16,32), over control of the north-south traffic between Israel and Judah. Baasha threatened to cut off trade with Jerusalem and blockaded the northern frontier of Judah by building a fortress at Ramah, just north of Jerusalem (1 Kgs 15:17,21). Fearing the new encroachment, Asa took all the silver and gold from the temple and his palace treasures and bribed King Ben-hadad of Syria to break alliance with Baasha (1 Kgs 15:18–20). When Ben-hadad battered several of Israel's northern storage cities and captured land at the headwaters of the Jordan, Baasha lost confidence and withdrew from Judah's borders (1 Kgs 15:20,21).

The Bible's evaluation of Baasha's reign is not favorable. Baasha "did what was evil in the sight of the Lord, and walked in the way of Jeroboam and in his sin" (1 Kgs 15:34). He received God's indictment and judgment through the prophet Jehu: since Baasha had led Israel into sin and had angered God, dogs would eat the members of his family who died in the city; birds would eat those who died in the field (1 Kgs 16:1–4). Baasha died and was succeeded by his son Elah. Within two years Elah was assassinated, and all the rest of Baasha's heirs were put to death by another usurper, Zimri (1 Kgs 16:8–13).

JAMES L. MASON

See ISRAEL, HISTORY OF; KINGS, BOOKS OF FIRST AND SECOND; CHRONOLOGY, OLD TESTAMENT.

Babel. Translation of a Hebrew word in Genesis 10:10 and 11:9. Elsewhere it is translated "Babylonia" or "Babylon" (2 Kgs 17:24, etc.). The rendering *Babel* in the Genesis pas-

Merrill F. Unger's reconstruction of the Tower of Babel.

sages is intended to relate the name to the early cultural setting reflected by Genesis 11:1–9, especially to the attempt to build a "tower." The translation "Babel" is also intended to associate the tower of Babel incident with the popular understanding that Babel is derived from a root meaning "to confuse" (v 9).

Archaeological excavations have provided information about the building of towers for temples called ziggurats. The excavation of a number of such towers has made it clear they were structures consisting of several platforms, each of lesser dimensions than the one immediately below it. The top platform served as the location for a small temple dedicated to the particular deity of the builder or of the city in which it was built.

The first ziggurat at Babylon was built by Shar-kali-sharri, king of Akkad in the latter part of the 23rd century BC. Archaeologists understand that this ziggurat was destroyed and rebuilt several times across the centuries. It apparently lay in ruins from some time around 2000 BC to around 1830 BC, at which time a forebear of Hammurabi (1728–1636 BC) founded or rebuilt the city named Bab-ilu or *Babel*.

The Babylonian Creation Epic gives details concerning the construction of a "celestial city" as the proper abode of Marduk. It was with this "theological" understanding that the name Babel, "gate of god," was a significant term. Other terminology associated with the temple built for Marduk and with the ziggurat suggests the understanding that Babel for the early Babylonians was the on-earth entrance into the heavenly or celestial.

The Genesis passage reflects both the early Mesopotamian setting and the Hebrew perspective. There seems to be sarcasm in the comment: "And they had brick for stone, and bitumen for mortar" (v 3 RSV). This apparently was intended as a reflection on the poorer quality of building materials used in comparison with those available elsewhere. The narrative then recounts how God intervened and confused the builders so that they could no longer communicate with each other. The word translated "confuse" is *balal;* it means also "to babble." A preposition combined with a form of this root, *ba-bal*, meaning "in confusion" or "in babbling," became the name for the location of the tower-building project. A popular etymology replaced the original meaning of the name.

Jewish and Arab traditions associate the ziggurat or tower of Babel of Genesis with a large temple ruin dedicated originally to Nabu in the city of Borsippa, or Birs-Nimrod.

See BABYLON, BABYLONIA.

Babylon, Babylonia. Land and people of southern Mesopotamia. Politically, Babylonia refers to the ancient kingdoms that flourished in southern Mesopotamia, especially in the 7th and 6th centuries BC, whose capital city was Babylon (or *Bab-ilu*, meaning "gate of god"). The term can also be used geographically to designate a whole region (in present-day SE Iraq). The adjective "Babylonian" has an even looser meaning; it may refer to the land or its inhabitants, to the kingdom or its subjects, or to a dialect of one of the principal ancient Mesopotamian languages.

Land. The two principal features of Babylonia's geography are the Tigris and Euphrates rivers. Rising in mountainous eastern Turkey, they initially flow in opposite directions but converge near Baghdad and join farther south to flow into the Persian Gulf. Archaeologists and historians often refer to the southern area of Babylon as Sumer and the northern part as Akkad, in recognition of the two principal civilizations that flourished in those regions before Babylonia's rise.

Politically, Babylonia largely corresponded to geographic Babylonia; its centers, however, were not situated in the fertile alluvial plain between the two rivers, but rather on the banks along the main course and several side branches of the Euphrates. At times the kingdom reached eastward beyond the Tigris, into the flatlands and foothills of the Zagros Mountains, generally along the Tigris's eastern tributaries. Its political and cultural influence extended upstream along both rivers, on the Euphrates as far as Mari and beyond, on the Tigris as far as Asshur.

Sumer and Akkad: 3200–2000 BC. Babylonia emerged as a culture as the result of Sumerian influence on the diverse peoples who had migrated into the area. The Sumerian civilization began to flourish in Babylonia sometime between 3200 and 2900 BC. (Essentially all dates given in this article are approximate.) The two principal languages of the region were Akkadian, a Semitic language, and Sumerian, whose linguistic affiliation is still unknown. The Sumerian-speaking people lived predominantly between Nippur and the Persian Gulf, while the Akkadian speakers inhabited the region of Babylonia north of Nippur. At first, Sumerian manners and customs prevailed throughout Babylonia; non-Sumerian peoples evidently accommodated themselves to the Sumerian way of life. The earliest interpretable inscriptions from Babylonia, dated at 3100 BC, are in Sumerian, which was the written language throughout Mesopotamia for seven centuries. In fact, cuneiform, the wedge-shaped writing invented by the Sumerians, remained in use for almost 3,000 years.

Eventually the Akkadian way of life began to compete with the Sumerian. Political and cultural leadership was effectively wrested away from the south by Sargon I (*Sharru-kin*, meaning "true king"; 2339–2279 BC), who founded the capital Akkad (or Agade). The site of that city is not presently known, but its name has since been attached to Sargon's kingdom, to the Semitic language he spoke, and to northern Babylonia. Sargon was an empire-builder: he subjugated the cities of Sumer as well as those in the region of Akkad, then the cities in northern Mesopotamia, and finally he marched up the Euphrates to become the master of Syria.

The Akkadian empire, which lasted for nearly two centuries under Sargon and his successors (2334–2154 BC), was disrupted by the invasion of the Guti people, mountaineers from the east, who in turn were defeated by the Sumerian king Utuhegal of the city of Uruk. That event marked a period of revival of Sumerian power and culture in Babylonia, led by a dynasty of kings which established itself in the once-prominent Sumerian city of Ur. That reflowering of Sumerian influence is referred to as the "Neo-Sumerian empire of Ur," or as the "Ur III period" (2112–2006 BC). The Sumerians' fortunes soon waned, however. Many of the kings who reigned in Sumer and Akkad in the last quarter of the Ur III period had Semitic names.

First Babylonian Kingdom: 1900–1600 BC.
At the same time, Semitic-speaking people from the west—the Amurru (or Martu), nomads from Syria—were exerting migratory and military pressures on Babylonia.

Amorite Invasion. The Amurru, called by modern researchers "Amorites" after their language, were known in the pre-Sargonid period (before 2340 BC) and were looked upon as barbarians by native Babylonians who scorned their manner of life. The nomads were of mixed ancestry, partly related to the Akkadians, who differed from them principally in certain features of language and culture. During the reign of Shar-kali-sharri (2254–2230 BC), fifth king of the dynasty of Akkad, the Amorites began to appear as a menace. A century later, during the early part of the Ur III period, the first major wave of Amorites moved into Babylonia; the second wave came during the reigns of the last two kings of the Ur III dynasty. That second migration coincided with a complex political situation in Babylonia. The undermining of Sumerian political power gave rise to the kingdom of Babylon under Amorite control.

Fall of Ur. The last Neo-Sumerian king, Ibbi-Sin, was faced with military threats to his kingdom from both east and west. He also

Bronze statuette that depicts King Ur-nammu as a humble basket carrier during the building of a temple (*c.* 2100 BC). He was the founder of the Ur III dynasty.

had to deal with internal rebellion. Ishbi-Erra, vassal-governor of the city of Mari, 500 miles up the Euphrates, took advantage of the Amorite incursions to revolt against the king and establish a rival kingdom with its capital at Isin, 50 miles from Ur. At the same time, in Larsa, less than 20 miles across the Euphrates from Ur, another new dynasty was established by a ruler with an Amorite name. Meanwhile, local rulers, nominally vassals of Ibbi-Sin, as well as several newcomers, were setting up "kingdoms" for themselves in their own cities and over as much of their neighboring territories as they could control. Unable to resist those developments, the Ur III dynasty collapsed, and its capital was plundered with unusual savagery. Isin and Larsa also suffered at the fall of Ur but survived; neither kingdom, however, became the regnant power in Babylonia.

Rise of Babylon. After seven kings each had reigned at Isin and Larsa, yet a second Amorite dynasty was established, this time in the region of Akkad, at the city of Babylon. Babylon's earliest known mention was in the Ur III period; it now emerged for the first time as a capital. Three major dynasties now divided Sumer and Akkad, although numerous petty kingdoms continued to exist; some, such as Sippar, Uruk, and Kish, were ruled by Amorite chiefs.

The founder of the "first dynasty of the Kingdom of Babylon" was Sumuabum (1894–1881 BC). Little is known about him. He and his next four successors, all legitimate descendants—Sumulael (1880–1845 BC), Sabium (1844–1831 BC), Apil-Sin (1830–1813 BC), and Sin-Muballit (1812–1793 BC)—ruled peacefully and uneventfully for a century. They appear to have devoted themselves mainly to religious and defensive construction and to maintenance of an irrigation canal system, though there is some evidence of conquest and territorial acquisition. Still, the territory of the kingdom of Babylon probably extended no more than 50 miles in any direction from the capital. Hammurabi, the sixth king of that line (1792–1750 BC), enlarged the kingdom toward the dimensions of an empire. At its greatest extent it reached from the Persian Gulf up the Tigris to include some of the cities of Assyria and up the Euphrates to Mari. Babylonia's glory, however, was short-lived; under the reign of Hammurabi's son, Samsu-iluna (1749–1712 BC), the realm shriveled. It lasted for another century, but within borders narrower than those established by Sumuabum.

Minor Dynasties: 1600–900 BC. The first dynasty of Babylon was brought to an end by an attack of the Hittites who sacked Babylon about 1595 BC. With that event a Babylonian dark age—that is, a period for whose events we have no contemporaneous records—set in, lasting for over 200 years (until about 1377 BC).

First Dark Age. During this period, control of Babylon fell briefly to the dynasty of the Sealand, later called the 2nd dynasty of Babylon. Almost nothing is known of that dynasty, which had emerged from the extreme SE part of Babylonia. In about two years' time it disappeared again into obscurity, when power passed into the hands of the Kassites.

Kassites. For several centuries the Kassites had been gradually infiltrating Babylonia from the Zagros Mountains in the east. They were first mentioned in a military context by Hammurabi's successor, Samsu-iluna.

During his reign and that of his successor, Abieshuh (1711–1684 BC), the Kassites settled in the Euphrates valley in the vicinity of Terqa; there they established a dynasty of kings as early as 1740 BC. Eventually the Kassites seized Babylon, established the 3rd dynasty, and ruled for approximately four and a half centuries.

Elamites. Kassite power was challenged by the rising Aramaeans and Assyrians in the northwest, but the Kassites were ultimately brought down by the Elamites, a people from east of the confluence of the Tigris and Euphrates rivers (called the Shatt al-Arab). In turn, the Elamites withdrew or were driven out of Babylon, and princes native to the city of Isin founded the fourth dynasty of Babylon (also called the 2nd dynasty of Isin), which lasted for over a century (1156–1025 BC).

A boundary stone from the time of Nebuchadnezzar I, the most important king of the 2nd dynasty (c. 1124–1103 BC).

Second Dark Age. Over the next 50 years Babylon had seven kings divided between the 5th, 6th, and 7th dynasties. The 5th dynasty of Babylon (1024–1004 BC) was founded by a Kassite from the Sealand (and so was also called the 2nd dynasty of the Sealand). The 6th dynasty of Babylon (1003–984 BC) was the dynasty of Bazi, or Bit Bazi (*bit*, meaning "tribe"), which was founded by an Aramaean. The 7th dynasty of Babylon (983–978 BC) was Elamite and had only one ruler, who survived for six years. The history of those three dynasties and of the longer-lasting 8th dynasty of Babylon (977–732 BC) was obscured by another Mesopotamian dark age. Assyria, Egypt, and the Hittite kingdom all suffered a simultaneous decline in power between the 12th and 9th centuries, creating a power vacuum and a long period of political uncertainty and confusion. (During that time the Hebrew empire, without political hindrance, reached its height under kings David and Solomon.)

Assyrian Domination: 900–614 BC. By the end of that period of obscurity many changes had taken place, mainly in the position and role of the Aramaeans. Assyria was reasserting its power under able but ruthless kings. Four of them—Adad-nirari II (911–891 BC), Tukulti-ninurta II (890–884 BC), Ashurnasirpal II (883–859 BC), and Shalmaneser III (858–824 BC)—aggressively extended Assyrian influence north, east, and west. They also threw back the Aramaean tribes, many of which pushed their way south into Babylonia and settled between the lower Tigris and the frontier of Elam. Although the kings of the eighth dynasty of Babylon managed to remain free from Assyrian domination, the balance of power was poised delicately.

Rise of the Chaldeans. Kaldu, a country and people first mentioned in Assyrian annals in the 9th century BC, began a steady bid for power. That bid culminated 250 years later in a restoration of Babylonia's glory and empire. Originally the Kaldu, or Chaldean, tribes were situated along the Euphrates and Tigris rivers between the Persian Gulf and the southernmost cities of Babylonia, a region of swamps, lakes, and cane thickets. The Chaldeans were not Aramaeans, although they had similar economic and social structures and, at a later time, adopted the Aramaic language and writing system. For their livelihood the Chaldeans evidently relied upon fishing, hunting, small-scale agriculture, and some cattle breeding. Eventually they advanced from Kaldu and occupied lands along the two rivers. Supplied with arms and money by neighboring Elam, the aggressive Yakin tribe, one of several tribes in the area, was able to make trouble for the government in Babylon.

Fiercely independent and rural, the Chaldeans were unwilling to pay taxes or to render services to Babylonia. They recognized no loyalty beyond their clan, regularly plundering the riches of neighboring cities and waylaying their caravans. Whatever delicate balance may have been struck between the Chaldeans and the urban-dwelling Babylonians was upset when the Assyrians and Elamites intruded into Babylonian affairs.

Vassal Kingdom. The earliest incursions of Assyria into Babylonia were by Shalmaneser III. In 851 BC, the brother of Marduk-zakir-shumi, reigning king of the 8th dynasty of Babylon, made a bid for the throne with the backing of the Aramaeans. Marduk-zakir-shumi called on the Assyrians for aid. Shalmaneser defeated the rebels and entered Babylon, treating the ancient city and its inhabitants with great respect. Thereafter, advancing southward, he came to Sumer, inhabited by the Chaldeans, and pressed them back against the gulf. For whatever reasons, Shalmaneser did not annex Babylonia. Marduk-zakir-shumi remained on the throne, though he swore allegiance to the Assyrian king.

The final years of Shalmaneser III were darkened by revolts all over the Assyrian empire. His son and successor, Shamshi-adad V, spent most of his reign (823–811 BC) putting down the rebellions. He twice defeated Babylonia in battle, but the kingdom still remained independent. After his successor, Adad-nirari III (810–783 BC), the next four Assyrian administrations (782–745 BC) were ineffectual. Babylonia failed to capitalize on the situation, however, because its own government fell into anarchy.

Two strong rulers emerged from the political confusion. In Assyria Tiglath-pileser III (745–727 BC) usurped the throne. In Babylonia three years earlier a Chaldean, Nabonassar (747–734 BC), took the throne of Babylon as a successor king in the 8th dynasty. An expedition into Babylonia by Tiglath-pileser was necessary, however, to secure Nabonassar's throne against the Aramaeans.

At Nabonassar's death, an Aramaean chieftain, Nabu-mukin-zeri (731–729 BC), seized the Babylonian throne and established the 9th dynasty of Babylon. Tiglath-pileser defeated the usurper, ravaged the territory of his tribe, and had himself proclaimed king of Babylon—and thus, of Babylonia—under the name of Pulu (729–727 BC), and as the second king of the 9th dynasty. Little is known of his short-lived successor, Shalmaneser V (727–722 BC). He too was proclaimed king of Babylon as well as of Assyria. Under Shalmaneser a siege against the kingdom of Israel began, after its king, Hoshea (732–723 BC), rebelled against Assyria (2 Kgs 17:1–6).

Merodach-baladan. Sargon II (722–705 BC) succeeded Shalmaneser. His rise to power is obscure; he was probably a usurper, which is why he chose the name Sargon ("true king") like his Akkadian namesake 1,500 years earlier. Shortly before Sargon II came to the throne, Elam in the east had begun to take an active part in the affairs of Babylonia by instigating rebellions against Assyria. Whenever the Aramaean sheiks of Babylonia found themselves hard pressed by the Assyrian army, Elam would support them with men and weapons. In the same year that Sargon II came to the throne, a Chaldean ruler from the Yakin tribe, Merodach-baladan II, supported by Elam, entered Babylon and proclaimed himself king. Sargon's assault against him (720 BC) was unsuccessful; Merodach-baladan ruled Babylonia for 11 years (721–710 BC).

After the brilliant successes of his other campaigns, Sargon attacked Babylon again in 710 BC, and this time succeeded in taking it. Although he had himself proclaimed king of Babylon, he acknowledged Merodach-baladan as king of the Yakin tribe. Merodach-baladan evidently took up residence in Elam at that time. In the year that Sargon's son, Sennacherib (705–681 BC), succeeded to the Assyrian throne, Merodach-baladan, assisted by Elamite officers and troops, reappeared. He raised the whole Aramaean and Chaldean population of Babylonia against the Assyrians, took Babylon, and had himself proclaimed king again (705 BC).

During that brief period, Merodach-baladan sent an embassy to King Hezekiah of Judah (715–686 BC) "with letters and a present," ostensibly to show sympathy for Hezekiah because of the king's illness (2 Kgs 20:12). More likely, Merodach-baladan's purpose was to secure another ally against Assyrian hegemony; the account of Hezekiah's cordial reception of the Babylonian envoys shows his willingness to join the alliance. Evidently the king's vanity overruled his political sense, and he treated the Babylonians to an extensive tour of his treasury. The proud gesture was rebuked by the prophet Isaiah, who predicted Babylonia's later conquest of Judah, when the king's storehouse would be sacked and his family carried off captive (2 Kgs 20:13–19; Is 39).

At any rate, Sennacherib was able quickly to dislodge Merodach-baladan from the Babylonian throne, force him into exile, and replace him with a king of his own choice, Belibni. There is some indication that within three years Merodach-baladan was back, stirring up another rebellion (possibly with the collusion of Bel-ibni), and thus precipitating another Assyrian punitive expedition. Nevertheless, by then the fires of a Babylonian independence movement had been ignited. In 689 BC the Babylonians again revolted with the support of the king of Elam. Sennacherib's expedition was nearly defeated. To vent his fury he attacked the city of Babylon, destroyed it, and "captured" its gods.

War and Peace. Sennacherib's successor and youngest son, Esar-haddon (681–669 BC), came to the throne of Assyria after a bloody war of succession with his brothers. One of his first acts was to rebuild and enlarge the city of Babylon. Esar-haddon thus won the friendship of many of his Babylonian subjects, who enabled him to enjoy a peaceful reign in that part of his empire. Three years before his death Esar-haddon named his son Ashurbanipal as his successor (669–627 BC) and another son, Shamash-shum-ukin (668–648 BC), as viceroy in Babylonia.

At Esar-haddon's death, the transition took place smoothly. The empire was not divided by having two sons on two thrones. Ashurbanipal had precedence over his brother, bearing responsibility for the whole empire. Shamash-shum-ukin and his Babylonian subjects, on the other hand, enjoyed sovereignty; as viceroy, he was granted full authority within his realm. That arrangement lasted for 17 years until Shamash-shum-ukin, backed by the Elamites and numerous Arab tribes, rebelled against Ashurbanipal. The revolt was brutally suppressed by 648 BC, and a Chaldean noble Kandalanu was appointed Babylonian viceroy. Shortly afterward, Ashurbanipal launched a punitive expedition, devastating Babylonia and completely destroying Elam in the process. The last eight years of his reign are obscure; Assyrian records for the period cease.

Neo-Babylonian Empire: 614–539 BC.

Both Ashurbanipal and Kandalanu, his viceroy in Babylon, died in 627 BC. For a year Babylonia had no recognized ruler. Then the throne was seized by the Chaldean prince Nabopolassar (625–605 BC) who established the 10th dynasty of Babylon, which has come to be called the Chaldean or Neo-Babylonian dynasty. With the accession of the 10th dynasty the Babylonian independence movement gained its long-sought goal: freedom from Assyrian domination. Yet history depreciated the triumph; the Chaldean dynasty was Babylonia's last.

Aided by Media, the kingdom of the Iranian plateau, Nabopolassar put an end to the Assyrian empire. By 612 BC Assyria's chief cities had fallen: Asshur, then the religious center; Nineveh, the administrative center; and Nimrod, the military headquarters. The last light of Assyria was snuffed out by Nabopolassar in 609 BC. Under his son Nebuchadnezzar II (604–562 BC), Babylonia fell heir to the Assyrian empire.

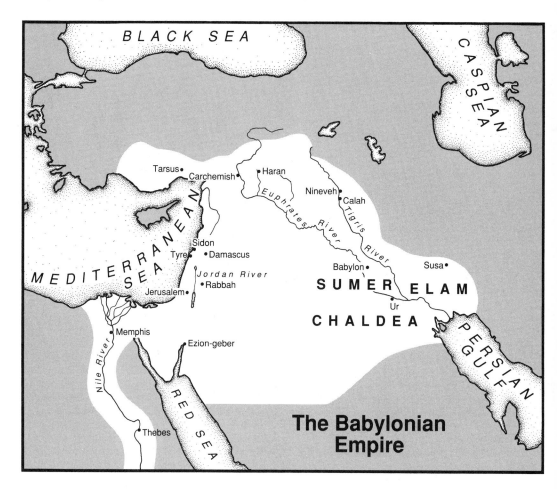

The Babylonian Empire

For a moment in history, Babylonia was master of the whole Near East. Nebuchadnezzar brought about the end of the Hebrew kingdom of Judah and the destruction of Jerusalem in 586 BC, deporting part of its population to Babylonia in the event referred to as the exile (2 Kgs 24:1–25:21).

Under Nebuchadnezzar, Babylon became the fabled city of luxury and splendor with which its name is commonly associated. Partly because of the king's haughty belief that he alone was responsible for his kingdom's glory, partly because of his tyrannical oppression of the poor, God struck Nebuchadnezzar with a fit of temporary insanity. For a period of time, according to the Book of Daniel, the great Babylonian monarch believed himself an animal, lived out-of-doors "with the beasts of the field," and "ate grass like an ox," until "his hair grew as long as eagles' feathers, and his nails were like birds' claws." When his reason finally returned, Nebuchadnezzar was a humbler king (Dn 4).

Nebuchadnezzar was succeeded by his son, son-in-law, and grandson within the space of six years. Thereafter, one of his high diplomatic officials, Nabonidus, one of history's most enigmatic personalities, took the throne (555–539 BC). During his reign, the Medes, formerly allies of the Chaldeans, came under a new ruler, Cyrus II of Persia (559 BC), who over the next 10 years conquered an empire nearly 3,000 miles in extent, from the Aegean Sea to the Pamirs (mountains in central Asia).

During Cyrus's decade of conquest, Nabonidus was strangely absent from Babylon, residing in Arabia. Although the Book of Daniel relates events occurring in the court of Babylon during Nabonidus's reign, his name is never mentioned. Instead Belshazzar, whom Nabonidus appointed regent in Babylon during his absence, is described as king (Dn 5:1). Perhaps because of his extended absence or perhaps because of his attachment to the moon god Sin and Sin's city, Harran, rather than to the Babylonian national god Marduk and Marduk's city, Babylon, Nabonidus lost the support of the Babylonians. When he finally returned to Babylon it was on the eve of Cyrus's attack on the city (Dn 5:30,31). Instead of offering resistance, however, the Babylonian army defected to Cyrus and the city gave itself up without a battle (12 October 539 BC at 3:20 AM). That surrender ended the Chaldean dynasty and the history of an independent Babylonia.

Modern Exploration. The site of Babylon was described by travelers such as Benjamin of Tudela (12th century AD) and the physician-naturalist Leonhart Rauwolff, who visited Babylon from 1573 to 1576. The modern era of exploration, however, began with a more serious scholar, Carsten Niebuhr. He visited the ruins of Babylon in 1765 and attempted to identify the hanging gardens and the "temple of Belus" (Marduk) about which he had read in the writings of Herodotus. Abbé de Beauchamp, the pope's vicar-general of Babylonia, lived in Baghdad between 1782 and 1789. During those years he made two visits to Babylon and published his observations. Claudius James Rich, a young man of scholarly interests employed by the East India Company in Baghdad, spent 10 days at Babylon in 1811, after which he wrote a description augmented by maps, drawings, and plans. In 1851 the French government sent an archaeological expedition to the Near East. From 1852 to 1854 Fulgence Fresnel directed an archaeological dig at Babylon, assisted by Jules Oppert, an Assyriologist, and Felix Thomas, an architect. Results were minimal.

Much of Nebuchadnezzar's Babylon was excavated by Robert Koldewey for the German Oriental Society in a series of campaigns beginning in 1899. Koldewey discovered that Nebuchadnezzar's Babylon was the largest city in antiquity, with an area of about 2500 acres. The older part of the city was completely enclosed by two walls made of unbaked mud bricks. The inner and higher wall, which was more than 21 feet thick, was separated from the outer wall by a military road 23 feet wide. The outer wall, though thinner, was more than 12 feet thick. Both walls were buttressed by massive fortified towers at intervals of about 65 feet. Outside the wall was a moat which reached a width of more than 200 feet in places.

During the reigns of Nabopolassar and Nebuchadnezzar another wall was built to enclose an area southeast and northeast of the older city. The remains of that 80-foot thick wall buttressed by towers at 130-foot intervals were found to be much like those described by Herodotus. The wall was actually a composite structure made up of an inner unbaked brick wall and an outer baked brick wall with a rubble filling in between. A moat 300 feet wide was fed by water from the Euphrates River and ran along the outside of this wall.

The ruins of the Ishtar Gate in Babylon.

One of the most magnificent finds was the Ishtar Gate, a double gateway 40 feet high covered with enameled brick reliefs of 575 bulls and dragons in vivid colors. (Ishtar was a goddess of love and fertility.) Through that gate ran the Procession Way, a road covered with limestone slabs three feet square. An inscription credited the road to Nebuchadnezzar. The walls along the Procession Way were overlaid with enameled bricks decorated with 120 lions representing Ishtar. The road led to the temple of Marduk and its adjacent ziggurat.

Koldewey's excavations also located the citadel, the market area, and Nebuchadnezzar's palace. Two additional seasons of work at Babylon were conducted by the German Archaeological Institute beginning in 1956.

Babylon in the Bible. The OT contains many references to Babylon. A few historical references, beginning in Genesis 10, have already been cited. The Babylon of Nebuchadnezzar's time appears frequently at the end of 2 Kings and 2 Chronicles and in the early part of Daniel. Ezra and Nehemiah record the subsequent return of the remnant of Judah from their Babylonian exile.

Among the prophetic books, Isaiah speaks of Babylon during the period of Assyrian dominance. A century later Jeremiah warns of the threat of Nebuchadnezzar, and Ezekiel and Daniel speak of Babylon from the later viewpoint of those exiled. There are as many references to Babylon in the last half of Jeremiah as in all the rest of the Bible.

Several times in the NT, reference is made to the capital city of Nebuchadnezzar to which the Jews had been deported in 586 BC (Mt 1:11,12,17); in 1 Peter 5:13 and the Book of Revelation, Babylon is used symbolically. "She who is at Babylon" was the apostle Peter's way of referring to the church in Rome, a city which had become as immoral and idolatrous as ancient Babylon. Just as that ancient cultural center had oppressed the Judean exiles, so Rome was now persecuting the Christians living there.

In Revelation 14:8; 16:19; 17:5; and 18:2,10, 21, Babylon was again used as a symbol for first-century Rome. It was pictured as "the Notorious Prostitute, who sits upon the many waters." She was gorgeously arrayed like a queen, sitting on a scarlet beast with 7 heads and 10 horns. She was "drunk with the blood of the saints," and on her forehead was written: "Babylon the great, mother of harlots and of earth's abominations" (17:1-6).

An angel helped to interpret the apocalyptic symbolism for John (Rv 17:1-18). The "many waters" symbolize nations and peoples. The "seven heads" are seven mountains, which most commentators view as representing the seven hills of Rome. Seven times Babylon is called "the great city" and is described as a dreadfully immoral center of wealth and commerce, ruling over the kings of the earth, and especially persecuting the saints of God. The wickedness personified in Babylon clearly symbolizes the historic manifestation of iniquity in 1st-century Rome.

Revelation 18 completes the picture. "Fallen, fallen is Babylon the great!" (v 2). God's final judgment upon her will be severe, repaying her "double for her deeds" (v 6). The main reason for her destruction is her immorality and persecution of the saints (19:2). The kings and merchants of the earth will mourn her demise (18:9-19), but the pronouncement is made in order that the saints might rejoice and worship God (v 20; 19:1-10).

JOHN E. LONG

The ruins of ancient Babylon, the buildings and thoroughfares that were once the pride of Nebuchadnezzar.

See POSTEXILIC PERIOD, THE; EXILE; CHALDEA, CHALDEANS; NEBUCHADNEZZAR, NEBUCHADREZZAR; DANIEL, BOOK OF.

Bibliography. E.A.T.W. Bridge, *Babylonian Life and History;* E. Chiera, *They Wrote on Clay;* B.M. Fagan, *Return to Babylon;* L.W. King, *A History of Babylon;* S. Mascoti, *Ancient Semitic Civilizations;* J. Neusner, *History of the Jews in Babylonia,* 5 vols; A. Parrot, *Babylon and the OT;* H. Ringgren, *Religions of the Ancient Near East;* H.W.F. Saggs, *Every Day Life in Babylonia and Assyria* and *The Greatness that Was Babylon.*

Babylonian Captivity. Period when many inhabitants of Judah, the southern kingdom, were exiled in Babylonia after Nebuchadnezzar's conquest of Jerusalem (6th century BC).

See BABYLON, BABYLONIA; EXILE; ISRAEL, HISTORY OF.

Baca, Valley of. Phrase in Psalm 84:6 often translated "valley of weeping." The Hebrew word *baca* obviously refers to some kind of tree in the only other context in which it occurs (2 Sm 5:23,24; 1 Chr 14:14,15), where it is translated mulberry (KJV), aspen, or balsam. It is not known whether the valley of Baca in Psalm 84 was a literal place or a symbolic expression for grief or difficulty in life. For those who seek to follow in the Lord's steps, the psalmist said, that valley becomes a pool of blessing and refreshment.

Some scholars think the valley was a specific place located near Jerusalem and the valley of Rephaim. If so, it could have been associated with weeping because (1) balsam or other trees in the valley exuded resinous gum, like tears; (2) the path was difficult to follow; or (3) it was a dreary place where waters seeped out of "weeping" rocks.

Bachrite. KJV form of Becherite, a descendant of Becher, in Numbers 26:35.

See BECHER #2.

Backsliding. To wane in religious commitment, to become less arduous in piety or less upright in morals. Grieved by the spiritual defection of his chosen people, God declared that "backsliding Israel committed adultery" (Jer 3:8 KJV). Through Hosea the Lord lamented the fact that "Israel slideth back as a backsliding heifer" (Hos 4:16 KJV). Jeremiah confessed, "Our backslidings are many, we have sinned against thee" (Jer 14:7).

The principal Hebrew word for backsliding means "turning back" or "turning away." The people of Israel repeatedly turned from God and engaged in the sin and idolatry of their pagan neighbors. In the language of the OT, backsliding Israel lusted after abominations and forsook the Lord and his commandments (Ezr 9:10; Is 1:4; Ez 11:21). They violated the sacred covenant by worshiping idols and practicing harlotry (Ps 78:10; Jer 2:11; Hos 4:10). The people forgot God's mighty works on their behalf, ignored his counsel, and rejected his instruction (Ps 78:11; 107:11; Is 30:9). Hardhearted and rebellious, they delighted themselves in all sorts of perversions (Jer 3:21). Religious leaders entrusted with the spiritual care of the nation were instrumental in leading the people astray (Is 9:16). The priests proved themselves faithless shepherds (Jer 50:6).

In the NT, backsliding is usually viewed from an individual more than from a group perspective. Jesus warned his disciples of the danger of backsliding: "No one who puts his hand to the plow and looks back is fit for the kingdom of God" (Lk 9:62). In his analogy of the vine and branches, Jesus exhorted the disciples to "abide" in him and in his words (Jn 15:4–8). Lack of continuous and vital contact with Christ would result in spiritual ineffectiveness and loss of fellowship. The parable of the prodigal son dramatically illustrated the self-willed rebellion of an erring son and the gracious forgiveness of a pardoning father (Lk 15:11–32). In a conversation on the Mt of Olives, Jesus observed that toward the end of the age evil would abound and "most men's love will grow cold" (Mt 24:12). Steadfastness and perseverance were the only reliable antidotes to backsliding.

Paul likewise warned believers of the dangers of falling away. Israel's idolatry in the wilderness and God's judgment upon their waywardness should serve as a stern warning (1 Cor 10:1–11). Paul instructed his converts in Galatia against forsaking their freedom in Christ and an enslaving religion of works. He marveled that the new believers had so quickly been deceived (Gal 3:1) and were abandoning the gospel of Christ (1:6). The new Christians who had begun so well were failing to obey the truth (5:7).

In correspondence with Timothy, Paul was grieved to learn that some believers had already turned aside after Satan (1 Tm 5:15). Love of money and philosophical speculation had precipitated their downfall (6:10,20,21). A Christian by the name of Demas turned back from serving God because he loved the world more than Christ (2 Tm 4:10).

Finally, in Revelation, the risen Christ reproached the churches for the spiritual indifference and coldness of their backsliding (Rv 2:4; 3:16).

Martin Luther once spoke of the shameful behavior of backslidden Christians: "The offenses given within the church are greater than those given among the heathen, because when Christians degenerate, they are more godless than the heathen."

From Scripture it seems clear that "born again" believers can either regress or progress in their Christian life. Paul indicated something of the inner struggle between his old carnal nature and his new spiritual nature (Rom 7:14–25). Spiritual growth results only from starving the carnal and feeding the spiritual. The apostle urged Christians to advance in faith and knowledge until they attain full maturity in Christ (Eph 4:13–16). Only then would their spiritual lives be stable. As believers purge themselves from iniquity and grow in grace, they resist the natural tendency to backslide (2 Tm 2:21). Jude expressed confidence that God is able to strengthen and sanctify believers so that backsliding becomes less and less of a threat (Jude 24).

The question arises whether Christians who backslide can lose their salvation. Those Christians known historically as Arminian in theology hold that believers can "fall from grace" and be lost. In such a case, backsliding amounts to total apostasy. Calvinists, on the other hand, insist that truly regenerated persons can never be lost. To Calvinists, backsliding means only loss of fellowship and effectiveness in the service of God, because their doctrine of perseverance teaches that God's elect will ultimately be saved (i.e., persevere in the faith).

The Bible offers practical guidance to avoid falling back into a state of sin. Christians should guard against a heart of unbelief (Heb 3:12). Their ambition should be to press on to know God more intimately (Phil 3:10–16) and to obey his commands more perfectly (Dt 8:11). God's sustaining power should be appropriated by faith (Ps 17:5). Their heart should be set upon the Lord himself rather than on the gifts he bestows (Dt 8:12–14). In short, believers should seek to "walk in the light, as he is in the light" (1 Jn 1:7).

What does God say to Christians who find themselves in a backslidden condition? First, they should face up to the consequences of their spiritual malpractice (Dt 32:29). God states that "the backslider in heart shall be filled with his own ways" (Prv 14:14 KJV). Next, they should confess all known sin and turn to the Lord in repentance (Lv 26:40; Hos 6:1,2; 1 Jn 2:2). God's promise to the penitent is "Return to me, and I will return to you" (Mal 3:7). Often it is helpful to seek the assistance of a wise spiritual counselor (Jer 3:15). Persons who are sincerely penitent will determine in their heart never again to turn to folly (Ps 85:8).

The God of the Bible is the God of all grace. Therefore, "Let us know, let us press on to know the Lord; his going forth is sure as the dawn; he will come to us as the showers, as the spring rains that water the earth" (Hos 6:3).

See ASSURANCE; PERSEVERANCE.

Badger. Small burrowing mammal with a broad back, thick short legs, and long claws on the forefeet.

See ANIMALS.

Bagpipe. Pipe instrument resembling the modern bagpipe, used in King Nebuchadnezzar's court (Dn 3:5,7,10,15).

See MUSIC AND MUSICAL INSTRUMENTS (PSANTRIN; SUMPONIA).

Bahurim, Baharum, Baharumite. Village in Benjamin's territory on the old road connecting Jericho and Jerusalem, east of the Mt of Olives. Bahurim was located at the site of the present Ras et-Temim. Palti parted from his wife Michal there at Abner's command when Michal was being returned to King David (2 Sm 3:16). At Bahurim, Shimei cursed David and threw stones at him and his servants (2 Sm 16:5; 19:16; 1 Kgs 2:8). Jonathan and Ahima-az, spying for David, were hidden from Absalom's soldiers in a well there (2 Sm 17:18). One of David's mighty men, Azmaveth, came from Bahurim (2 Sm 23:31, KJV Barhumite; cf. Baharum, 1 Chr 11:33, KJV Baharumite).

Bajith. Town in Moab (Is 15:2 KJV). Because of the uncertainty of the Hebrew text other versions of the Bible translate the word in various ways, such as "daughter" or (RSV) "temple."

Bakbakkar. Levite who returned to Jerusalem from the Babylonian exile (1 Chr 9:15). His name is missing in a parallel list (Neh 11:17), unless it is the same as Bakbukiah.

Bakbuk. Ancestor of a group of temple assistants who returned to Jerusalem with Zerubbabel after the Babylonian exile (Ezr 2:51; Neh 7:53).

Bakbukiah. 1. Shammua's son, a Levite who assisted Mattaniah at the thanksgiving services in the temple (Neh 11:17).

2. Levite who returned to Jerusalem with Zerubbabel after the exile (Neh 12:9).

3. One of the gatekeepers who had charge of collection centers at the temple gates (Neh 12:25).

It is not clear whether these references refer to one, two, or three persons.

Baker. *See* TRADES AND OCCUPATIONS.

Balaam. Beor's son, a prophet or soothsayer from northern Mesopotamia who was hired by a Moabite king, Balak, to curse the Israelites who had arrived at the Jordan Valley opposite Jericho after 40 years of wandering in the wilderness. Israel's defeat of the Amorites (Nm 21:21–25) had instilled fear in the heart of the Moabite king (Nm 22:3). Because curses and blessings were considered irrevocable (Gn 27:34–38), Balak reasoned that if he could hire a prophet to curse the Israelites in the name of their own God, the Lord, he could easily defeat them in battle and drive them away from his borders. Balak sent messengers to Pethor where Balaam lived. The town is believed to be located near Harran along the Habur River, a tributary of the Euphrates. Balak offered Balaam an impressive sum to come down and curse the Israelites.

Balaam, however, was warned by the Lord that he should not go to Moab. The king of Moab would not accept Balaam's refusal and sent his royal messengers back with offers of greater wealth and honor. Balaam revealed an inner lust for wealth and position by returning to the Lord to ask whether he should go. His words to the messengers, however, were very pious: "Though Balak were to give me his house full of silver and gold, I could not go beyond the command of the Lord my God, to do less or more" (Nm 22:18). Although Balaam would do only what the Lord allowed, he became a prime example of someone who does the right thing for the wrong reason.

Balak had sent along with his messengers "the fees for divination" (22:7), which shows that he considered Balaam a diviner of the type pagan nations commonly used. The Israelites were forbidden by the Lord to consult diviners or practice divination (Dt 18:10,11). A true prophet would not have even considered the possibility that serving Balak might be right. God's final permission to let Balaam go, with the stipulation that he say only what God told him, was the Lord's way of frustrating Balak's cause and showing God's care for his chosen people.

Although he gave his permission, God was angry that Balaam went (Nm 22:22). So the Lord placed an angel with a drawn sword in Balaam's path. His donkey could see the angel but Balaam could not. Not knowing why the donkey balked, Balaam beat her, and she was then miraculously given a voice to complain against his cruelty (22:28–30).

The purpose of this OT story is to show how spiritually blind Balaam was, no doubt because he had his mind set on the reward he would have if only the Lord would let him curse Israel. In other places in the Bible Balaam is characterized as a man "who loved gain from wrongdoing, but was rebuked for his own transgression; a dumb ass spoke with human voice and restrained the prophet's madness'' (2 Pt 2:15,16). Jude said of certain persons, they "abandon themselves for the sake of gain to Balaam's error" (Jude 11).

On the surface the story in Numbers 22 presents Balaam as a man who simply did what the Lord allowed him to do. But Deuteronomy 23:5 states that the Lord would not listen to Balaam and turned his intended curse into a blessing. When the Lord opened Balaam's eyes he saw the angel and fell flat on his face (Nm 22:31). Then he acknowledged his sin and proceeded to say only what the Lord put in his mouth.

Balaam's poems in Numbers 23 and 24 are in an archaic form of Hebrew which witnesses to their authenticity. They sometimes describe God's past blessing on his people, and at other points predict his future blessing of Israel in a unique way.

In the first poem, Balaam lamented that he could not denounce Israel but rather saw them as a unique people who would be as numerous as the dust of the earth (Nm 23:7–10). The second poem (vv 13–24) contains an introduction (v 18) followed by two stanzas. In stanza 1 Balaam extolled God as the One who brings to pass what he decrees. Balaam saw only blessing for Israel. In stanza 2 he described Israel's power, which is derived from God. The third poem (24:2–9) has a perfectly balanced poetic structure with opening and closing lines in the second person (vv 5,9b) and two antithetic stanzas between. The first stanza describes Israel at peace (vv 6,7), the second Israel at war (v 8). The fourth poem (vv 15–19) has two stanzas; in the first Balaam presented himself as a prophet of the Almighty God (Hebrew *Elyon*, Gn 14:18,22, and *Shaddai*, 17:1). In the second stanza Balaam predicted the coming of a "star from Jacob," a "ruler of Israel." He would strike the surrounding people, including Moab, and rule with dominion (Nm 24:17–19). The NT nowhere applies this prophecy to Christ, although the Essene community of the Dead Sea Scrolls did consider it messianic. It was most likely a prediction of the coming of David and his united monarchy and should be considered messianic only in a secondary sense.

The fifth, sixth, and seventh poems of Balaam are short prophecies directed against other nations: the Amalekites (Nm 24:20), Kenites (vv 21,22), and people from the coast of Kittim (vv 23,24).

Only blessings on Israel and never a single word of a curse were spoken by Balaam. The infuriated Moabite king took Balaam from one vantage point to another where they could look out over the Jordan Valley and see the Israelite encampment. When Balaam still did not curse them, Balak slapped his hands together in anger and packed the prophet off without any reward at all. But that was by no means the end of Balak's attempt to weaken Israel.

The account of Balaam is incomplete without the sequel to the story. Numbers 25 tells how the Moabite king almost succeeded in turning the Israelites against the Lord. It describes a scene at Peor where Israelite men engaged in debauchery with Moabite women. That may have meant participation in the common heathen practice of temple prostitution, for according to Numbers 31:14–16, that was Balaam's advice to Balak and the Moabites on how to weaken Israel.

Later Balaam was killed by the Israelites in their campaign against Midian (Nm 31:8; Jos 13:22). Much later, the apostle John called for repentance by those of the church in Pergamum who "hold the teaching of Balaam, who taught Balak to put a stumbling block before the sons of Israel, that they might eat food sacrificed to idols and practice immorality" (Rv 2:14).

ELMER B. SMICK

See BALAK.

Balac. KJV form of Balak, king of Moab in Moses' time, in Revelation 2:14.

See BALAK.

Baladan. King of Babylon and father of Merodach-baladan. Baladan's son sent letters and a gift to King Hezekiah of Judah after Hezekiah's recovery from a serious illness (2 Kgs 20:12; Is 39:1).

Balah. City in southern Palestine (Jos 19:3), probably identical with Baalah (Jos 15:29) and Bilhah (1 Chr 4:29).

Balak. Zippor's son, king of Moab. Balak became fearful after the Israelites defeated the Amorites, so he attempted to hire a soothsayer named Balaam to pronounce a curse against Israel (Nm 22:1–7). Balak escorted Balaam to three different mountains and offered three different sacrifices, only to have Balaam each time deliver a blessing to the Israelites (Nm 22–24). Enraged, Balak sent Balaam away. That event was later remembered as an example of God's special blessing on the Israelites and of the futility of trying to alter God's will (Jos 24:9,10; Jgs 11:25; Mi 6:5; Rv 2:14, KJV Balac).

See BALAAM.

The Egyptian Book of the Dead, depicting balances.

Balance, Balances.

Balance, Balances. Devices used to weigh an object by opposing it with a known weight. Balances or scales have been used to measure weight at least since the middle of the second millennium BC. Pictures and inscriptions in Egyptian tombs give us an idea of the appearance of the earliest scales. A pair of such balances found in Ugarit dates from about 1400 BC.

Balances usually consisted of four main parts: (1) an upright center standard, (2) a crossbar suspended from it, (3) two pans suspended from each end of the crossbar by cords, and (4) on the more elaborate models, a rod or pointer attached to the center of the crossbar at right angles to it; the rod moved in front of the standard so that when the two pans held equal weights the exact vertical position of the rod would be evident.

Scales or balances were used in the ancient world primarily to measure precious metals such as silver or gold. The "story of the eloquent peasant" dating from the Middle Kingdom of Egypt, however, mentioned the figurative measuring of a person's heart and tongue.

Balances are mentioned frequently in the OT, with much emphasis on the use of just weights in commerce (Lv 19:36; Prv 11:1; 16:11; 20:23; Ez 45:10; Hos 12:7; Am 8:5; Mi 6:10–12). The weighing of silver with a balance is described (Is 46:6), as when Jeremiah weighed the money that he paid for his nephew's field (Jer 32:8–10). In an acted-out prophecy, Ezekiel was told to cut off all his hair and beard and weigh it in balances to separate it into three equal parts (Ez 5:1,2). Job asked to be "weighed in a just balance," that God might know his integrity (Jb 31:6). Daniel said that Belshazzar had been weighed in the balances (judged) and found wanting (Dn 5:27).

One reference to scales or balances is found in the NT. "When he opened the third seal, I heard the third living creature say, 'Come!' And I saw . . . a black horse, and its rider had a balance in his hand" (Rv 6:5). The prophecy is of severe famine, when some foods can no longer be obtained, when inflation has driven up food prices, and when people check the scales carefully to be sure they are not cheated when buying even the cheapest grains, such as barley (Rv 6:6).

RALPH L. SMITH

See WEIGHTS AND MEASURES.

Bald Locust.

Bald Locust. Variety of locust considered clean and therefore edible (Lv 11:22).

See ANIMALS (LOCUST).

Baldness.

Baldness. Condition of having little or no hair on the scalp. Natural baldness due to age is referred to only indirectly in the Bible, where it is contrasted with baldness due to leprosy (Lv 13:40–42). The Israelites were forbidden to shave their heads or shape their beard in ways that resembled pagan religious practices (Dt 14:1). Such restrictions applied particularly to Israelite priests, the Levites (Lv 21:5). Shaving off the hair and offering it as a sacrifice to God was a special act prescribed for men or women taking a Nazarite vow (Nm 6:1–5,18; Acts 18:18). Baldness as an occupational hazard is referred to in connection with the siege of Tyre by Nebuchadnezzar (Ez 29:18). His soldiers wore off their hair by carrying heavy baskets of earth on their heads.

The Egyptians and other peoples shaved off their hair (and eyebrows) as a sign of respect for the dead. There are many biblical references to the non-Israelite custom of shaving the head as a sign of mourning or anguish (Jer 16:6; 48:37; Ez 27:31; Mi 1:16). Most of these passages speak of God's judgment against pagan cities or nations. Since baldness was associated primarily with leprosy, venereal disease, idolatry, or death, the prediction or threat of baldness sometimes accompanied prophetic warnings. Isaiah prophesied that "haughty Jewish women" who cared more about ornamenting themselves than about worshiping God would receive "a plague of scabs to ornament their heads" (Is 3:16,17 LB); their "well-set hair" would all fall out and they would be in shame and disgrace (Is 3:24). A difficult passage to interpret properly is 2 Kings 2:23,24. Elisha's curse and the gruesome death of some juvenile delinquents seems very severe if all they did was tease the prophet for being bald. More likely, their taunts may have been very strong accusations of idolatry or sexual immorality, or even of murdering Elijah, whose disappearance must have looked suspicious (vv 11–18). The youths who chanted "Go up, you baldhead" (v 23) may have been mocking Elisha's explanation of what happened to Elijah. In any event, disrespect for the Lord's anointed occasioned severe judgment.

WALTER R. HEARN

See FASHION AND DRESS.

Balm, Balsam. Resinous plant gum used in medicine, or the plant from which it is derived.

See MEDICINE AND MEDICAL PRACTICE; PLANTS.

Balthasar. Tradition-given name for one of the wise men who brought a gift to Jesus in Matthew 2:1,2.

See WISE MEN.

Bamah. Hebrew word meaning height, ridge, or elevation in the topography of the land (2 Sm 1:19,25; 22:34); transliterated into English once (Ez 20:29). It is a term designating hills or mountains overlooking the Arnon River (Nm 21:28). The plural form (Bamoth) alone or as the first part of a compound is used for the name of towns in Moab (Nm 21:19,20; 22:41; Jos 13:17).

Metaphorically the word connotes a place of security (Dt 32:13; Hb 3:19) as well as the high ground that a military commander wished to control in battle. Possession of an enemy's "heights" was synonymous with subjection of that enemy (Dt 33:29; Ez 36:2). The word seems to combine both literal and figurative connotations in several references to Jerusalem, a "high place" in ruin overgrown with scrub vegetation (Mi 3:12; see also Jer 26:18; Ez 36:1,2).

"High place" was also a special, or technical, term in Canaanite religion, designating a local shrine on a hill near a town or village, in contrast to the large temples located throughout the land.

See HIGH PLACE.

Bamoth, Bamoth-baal. Town in Moab allotted to Reuben's tribe by Joshua (Jos 13:17, called Bamoth-baal). It had been one of Israel's last encampments on the route into Canaan, the Promised Land (Nm 21:19,20). Bamoth-baal, a mountain or high place, was probably a shrine to the Canaanite god Baal. King Balak of Moab took the prophet Balaam there to try to get him to curse Balak's enemies, the people of Israel (Nm 22:41–23:13).

Ban. Religious practice whereby those hostile to God are devoted to destruction. It is especially associated with Israel's wartime tactics involving the total destruction of the Canaanites because of their wickedness and abominable practices (Ex 34:11–16; Dt 7:2; Jos 6:17).

See CONQUEST AND ALLOTMENT OF THE LAND; JOSHUA, BOOK OF; ARMS AND WARFARE; WAR, HOLY.

Bani. 1. Member of Gad's tribe and warrior among David's mighty men who were known as "the thirty" (2 Sm 23:36).

2. Shemer's son and ancestor of Ethan. Ethan was the Levite of Merari's line in charge of the music in the tabernacle during King David's reign (1 Chr 6:46).

3. Member of Judah's tribe and ancestor of Uthai (1 Chr 9:4). Uthai was one of the first to settle again in Jerusalem after the exile. Possibly the same as #4 below.

4. Ancestor of a family that returned to Judah with Zerubbabel after the exile (Ezr 2:10) alternately spelled Binnui in Nehemiah 7:15.

5. Ancestor of a family that returned to Judah with Ezra after the exile (Ezr 8:10; 1 Esd 8:36). The name does not occur in the KJV, but the RSV, following the Apocrypha, inserts "of the sons of Bani." Possibly the same as #4 above.

6. Ancestor of some Israelites who were found guilty of marrying foreign women (Ezr 10:29).

7. Ancestor of another group of Israelites who were found guilty of marrying foreign women (Ezr 10:34).

8. Son (descendant) of Bani (#7 above). This Bani was among those found guilty of marrying foreign women (Ezr 10:38 KJV only). Because Bani is spelled almost the same as "sons of" in Hebrew, most modern translations render verse 38 "of the sons of Binnui."

9. Rehum's father and a Levite. Rehum repaired a section of the Jerusalem wall after the exile (Neh 3:17).

10. Levitical assistant of Ezra who explained to the people passages from the Law read by Ezra (Neh 8:7). He was among those who offered praises to God on the steps of the

temple (Neh 9:4,5). He is probably the same as Binnui (Ezr 10:38).

11. Another levitical assistant who explained passages from the Law read by Ezra (Neh 9:4b).

12. Levite who signed Ezra's covenant of faithfulness to God after the exile (Neh 10:13).

13. Leader of the people representing the Bani family mentioned under #4 above who signed Ezra's covenant of faithfulness to God after the exile (Neh 10:13).

14. Uzzi's father. Uzzi was the head of the Levites in Jerusalem after the exile (Neh 11:22). Possibly the same as #9 or #10 above.

The popularity of this name and its similarity to other Jewish names (e.g., *Binnui*) has caused much confusion in the genealogical lists. The list above is one of several possible arrangements.

Banish, Banishment. Exclusion of a person from a country or group as a form of punishment.

Banishment or a similar word is used in the Bible to describe God's judgment on Adam and Eve (Gn 3:23,24) and on Cain (4:9–14), Absalom's exile from his father David (2 Sm 13:37–39; 14:13,14), and Israel's exile from the Promised Land (Dt 30:1; Is 11:12; Jer 16:15; Ez 4:13). During the exile it was included in a list of punishments for those who disobeyed God or the Persian king Artaxerxes (Ezr 7:26).

The Mosaic law specified that an Israelite should be "cut off" from the people of God for various offenses, such as failure to circumcise a male child (Gn 17:12,14), eating leavened bread during Passover (Ex 12:15), making an unholy animal sacrifice (Lv 17:1–4), eating blood (v 10), sinning deliberately (Nm 15:30, 31), or failing to undergo ceremonial cleansing after contact with a dead body (19:11–20). The term "cut off" probably meant exclusion from the social and religious life of the community (cf. Jn 9:18–23,34). After the exile, when the whole nation of Israel had been "banished," disinheritance and permanent excommunica-

tion from God's people were made official punishments (Ezr 10:7,8). The Romans, like other conquerors before them, practiced deportation in various forms. Controversy among the Jews probably because of the Christian movement led to the banishment of Jews from Rome under emperor Claudius (Acts 18:2). The author of Revelation was banished to the island of Patmos during Roman persecution (Rv 1:9). More severe forms of banishment included permanent exclusion from an area, loss of citizenship, and confiscation of all goods and property.

WALTER R. HEARN

See Exile.

Banker, Banking. *See* Money and Banking; Trades and Occupations.

Banquet. Lavish ceremonial meal, usually held in honor of some notable event or person; also a symbol of the feast to be given by Christ in the kingdom of God. Banqueting and feasting were major parts of the social and religious life of biblical times. In addition to the religious feasts prescribed by Mosaic law, banquets and feasts were celebrated on nearly any occasion of joy or solemnity: at the ratification of covenants (Gn 26:30; 31:54; Ex 24:11); at weddings (Gn 29:22; Jgs 14:10); at harvest (Jgs 9:27; Ru 3:1–3); at the shearing of sheep (1 Sm 25:11; 2 Sm 13:23–29); at the arrival of guests (Gn 19:3); at the weaning of a child (Gn 21:8); at coronations (1 Kgs 1:9,19,25); on various state occasions (Est 1:3,9; 2:18; 5:4,8); and for many other reasons.

Many customs associated with banquets in the ancient Near East are portrayed in the Bible and in extrabiblical literature; wall reliefs and carvings from some excavations also depict banquet scenes. The sequence of banquet preparation in Proverbs 9:2–5, Matthew 22:1–14, and Luke 14:15–24 is also known from the legend of King Keret in Ugaritic literature: (1) preparation of the foods, (2) sending messen-

Ashurbanipal and his queen feasting in his royal garden at Nineveh.

gers with the invitation and announcement that all is ready, and (3) the presentation of food and wine in order. The prophet Amos portrays a lavish feast and shows the main eating customs (Am 6:4–6). Meals were ordinarily taken while reclining on a couch before a table (Est 1:6; Ez 23:41; Am 6:4; Mt 9:10; Lk 7:49; 14:10,15).

Banquet imagery is prominent in both Testaments with reference to the kingdom of God. Isaiah foresaw the judgment of the nations and the deliverance of Israel followed by the Lord's reign over his people (Is 24:23); inauguration of that reign is accompanied by a huge banquet to which all peoples are invited (Is 25:6–8; cf. Lk 13:29). Meals shared following the sacrifice of animals in the OT prefigure that great feast when there will be no more death, tears, or reproach for the people of God (Is 25:7; cf. Rv 21:4). The banquet of the New Covenant likewise directs attention to the future, when the redeemed will drink fine wine (Is 25:6) with Christ in the kingdom of God (Lk 22:14–20). By participating in the Lord's Supper (Communion) all Christians anticipate that great feast.

That future, final banquet in the kingdom of God is also pictured specifically as a wedding feast; all is in readiness, the invitation is issued to many, but few are chosen (Mt 22:1–14). The church looks forward to the marriage feast of the Lamb (Rv 19:7–9).

In addition to the future joyful banquet, the Bible also has an alternate image of a banquet of judgment. In contrast to mankind being given the animals for food (Gn 6:18–21; 9:2,3; Is 25:6), the animals are pictured as feasting on the corpses of slaughtered men (Rv 19:17–20). Once animals were slaughtered as sacrifices for human sins and then eaten; in the vision of the final judgment, humans are slaughtered in a great sacrifice because of their own sins and are devoured by animals (Ez 39:17–20).

RAYMOND B. DILLARD

See FOOD AND FOOD PREPARATION.

Baptism. Term generally meaning "to dip" or "immerse," but representing a group of words employed to signify a religious rite for ritual cleansing. In Judaism there were ritual ablutions, Qumran lustrations, and proselyte baptism. In the NT it became the rite of initiation into the Christian community. The concept not only referred to the cultic rite but also was interpreted theologically as a dying and rising with Christ.

Antecedents of Christian Baptism. *Old Testament Ritual.* Ablution—ceremonial cleansing by water and/or blood—was an important part of the levitical system. The following aspects might be noted: (1) Priests (Ex 29:21; Lv 8:6) were washed and Levites (Nm 8:6–13) were sprinkled with water when initiated into their sacred offices. (2) The priests ceremonially washed their hands and feet in the bronze laver before performing the sacrifices (Ex 30:17–21). (3) The high priest on the Day of Atonement had to bathe himself and clothe himself with "holy garments," sprinkle the mercy seat with the blood of a bull offered for himself and his "house," and then sprinkle it again with the blood of a goat offered for the people; finally, he had to shed his clothes and wash himself again after performing the ritual (Lv 16:1–28). (4) Vessels, clothes, and people which had been defiled by contact with something considered unclean had to be washed in pure water (Lv 11:24–40). (5) The ashes of a red heifer were mixed with water and then sprinkled to purify one who had contact with a corpse (Nm 19:11–22). (6) Both sprinkling and bathing were elements of the ritual for leprosy (Lv 13,14). (7) After intercourse, menstruation, or birth a ritual bathing must occur (Lv 12,15). Of course, there are significant differences between the ancient rites and the sacrament in the early church. The latter practice was once-for-all rather than continual, a radical cleansing rather than a temporary measure. However, a new baptism is promised in prophetic passages (Ez 36:25; Zec 13:1).

Qumran Lustrations. Qumran was the Dead Sea community of the sect of the Essenes. It originated about 100 BC from the priestly ranks and so stressed ritual and cultic cleansing. They viewed themselves as the covenant community of the last days and so dwelt in the desert, living an ascetic life and immersing themselves daily in acts of ceremonial cleansing. At the same time they taught that internal repentance must accompany the external act (1 QS 2:3). Its sacramental nature is seen in the fact that only a full member of the community could practice it, and then only after two probationary years (1 QS 5:6). Some believe that this was the precursor of John the Baptist's baptism, but the differences are too great—they were daily acts rather than rites of admission (though for the novice the first immersion functioned somewhat in this way), private rather than public, and were of a more cultic nature. Nevertheless, they may have exerted some influence, especially in their eschatological nature (i.e., living in the time of fulfillment), the necessity of moral repentance, and the inadequacy of the temple ritual.

Proselyte Baptism. Converts from pagan religions were admitted to Judaism only after fulfilling certain obligations, which included the study of the Torah, circumcision, and a ritual bath to wash away the impurities of the gentile background. The parallels between this and the Christian practice are easily observable: the act as an initiation rite, similar terminology, similar theology (the person was considered reborn). However, there is some debate as to whether we can declare this ceremony pre-Christian. It is not mentioned in intertestamental literature, Philo, or Josephus. The earliest references are at the end of the first century. Probably it evolved concurrent with Christianity, and we may note the parallels while realizing that great differences exist, especially the necessary connection with circumcision, the Christian view of baptism as union with the Messiah, and the importance of the rite for Jews as well as Gentiles.

The Mystery Religions. There were many types of ceremonial washings in pagan religions. In Hellenistic religions, it was believed that moral sins could be washed away. Egyptians would ritually wash their dead, believing that this would renew the spark of life in the next world. The mystery religions combined eastern mystical rites with western mythology, stressing secret ritual and hidden knowledge. Among these groups baptism came to be recognized as a cultic dying and revivification. Therefore sacral baths became important elements of the Eleusinian and Mithras rites. Because of this, some have argued that Christianity borrowed the theology of this movement. However, there is no evidence that such beliefs existed before the late 2nd century, and Jewish parallels provide better background.

The New Testament Development. *The Baptism of John.* John preached a "baptism of repentance for the forgiveness of sins" (Lk 3:3). The origins of his rite are difficult to trace, for there are both parallels and differences with all three Jewish forms above. The genesis of his baptism may be found in the prophetic acted parable, which not only symbolized God's message but also intended to bring it about. John's practice had several theological ramifications: (1) It was intimately connected with radical repentance, not only of the Gentile but astoundingly (to his contemporaries) also of the Jew. (2) It was eschatological at the core, preparing for the Messiah, who would baptize "with the Holy Spirit and with fire" (Mt 3:11), and therefore looked to the final separation between God's people and the wicked at the Eschaton (i.e., "the End," cf. Mt 3:12). (3) It symbolized moral purification and so prepared the people for the coming kingdom (Mt 3:2; Lk 3:7–14). In spite of the obvious connection between John's ceremony and the early church, we cannot posit absolute dependence. In fact, it disappeared from Jesus

ministry. At first, Jesus allowed his disciples to continue the rite (Jn 3:22), but later he seemingly discontinued the practice (Jn 4:1–3), probably for the following reasons: (1) John's message was functional, while Jesus' was personal/ontological. (2) John's was forward-looking, expecting the coming kingdom, while Jesus' was backward-looking, celebrating that event. (3) John's was an interim practice, while Jesus' was sacramental. Jesus' ministry fulfilled John's, so he severed himself from the latter's modus operandi.

The Baptism of Jesus. This event has its genesis in a complex interplay of motives, divine and human, within the messianic consciousness of Jesus (see Mk 1:9–11 and parallels). For John it was Jesus' stamp of approval upon his message and ministry. Jesus was in continuity with John's kingdom proclamation. For Jesus, it was also an anointing which signified the inauguration of his messianic ministry. As seen in God's "heavenly voice" of Mark 1:11 and parallels, this has two aspects: (1) The voice alludes to Psalm 2:7, establishing Jesus' unique filial sonship. (2) It alludes to Isaiah 42:1, establishing him as the messianic "servant of Yahweh." From the standpoint of man, the event signifies Jesus' identification with his sin and suffering. It showed his solidarity with man as sinner and thereby inaugurated the time of fulfillment, wherein God's salvation would be accomplished by the Messiah.

Jesus' Resurrection Command. Here we find the true basis of the church's practice (Mt 28:19). As already stated, the disciples stopped employing it, so it is here that we see the institution reconstituted as an ordinance based on the death and resurrection of Christ. It was no longer a forward-looking phenomenon but had now become a realized activity centering on the gospel message, certified by the risen Christ who is exalted to universal lordship. It also is an essential aspect of the discipling activity, as seen in the use of the participle "baptizing" after the main verb "make disciples." Finally we might note that the act signifies the entrance of the believer "into" union with (literally "into the name of") the triune Godhead.

Baptism in the Early Church. Acts 2:38 shows that baptism was a sacral institution from the very beginning. This takes it back to the earliest days of the church. In the primitive church it was an important part of the salvation process (Acts 2:38, "repent and be baptized") and was accomplished via confession and prayer "in the name of Jesus Christ" (Acts 2:38; 8:16; 10:48; 19:5). Probably there was a question-and-answer period in which the believer confessed his faith and dedicated himself to Christ. The result was reception into and identification with the messianic community of the new covenant, signifying both forgiveness of sins (Acts 2:38; 5:31; 10:43; 13:38; 26:18) and the reception of the Holy Spirit (Lk 3:16; Acts 2:38,41; 9:17; 10:47,48; 11:16,17; 19:5–7).

The Theology of Baptism. *Pauline Theology.* Paul's basic statement is found in Galatians 3:27, "baptized into Christ." The rite of baptism is christological at the heart, signifying union with Christ. This is clarified further by Romans 6:3–8, which equates baptism with dying and rising (cf. Col 2:12,13). At the same time baptism is related to the Spirit; 1 Corinthians 12:13 connects "baptism by the one spirit" with being "given that same Spirit." Many see baptism as the outward confirmation of the inward "seal" by the Spirit (2 Cor 1:21,22; Eph 1:13; 4:30). This leads us to the eschatological dimension of baptism. In its relation to the present work of Christ and the Spirit, it externalizes the outpouring of salvation in the age of fulfillment, because it is the initiatory rite signifying the believer's entrance into the blessings of the new age (Ti 3:5).

The Covenant Relation. There is a definite link between baptism and the OT covenants. The major connection is with the Abrahamic, especially with the circumcision which characterized it. Paul in Colossians 2:11,12 combines Jewish circumcision with Christian baptism as pictures of the redemptive work of Christ. The debate today centers on the degree of continuity between them—does baptism perform the same function in the New Covenant, i.e., forensic and imputative? Whatever the theological ramifications, Paul at least cannot be made to say this. Rather, he borrows here the Judeo-Christian imagery of the "circumcision of the heart" (Dt 10:16; 30:6; Jer 4:4; Rom 2:28,29; Phil 3:3). Christians experience the fulfillment of that which circumcision merely prefigured, a spiritual, totally efficacious reality.

Baptism is also related to the Noahic covenant in 1 Peter 3:19–21. There Noah's "deliverance through the waters" is considered a picture of the effects of baptism. The debate centers on the meaning of "baptism now saves you." The answer is connected with the thrust of the ensuing clarification, "an appeal to God for a good conscience" (RSV literally "of a good conscience"). While the developed dialogue between the sacramental and baptist views is considered below, we will simply comment here that the interpretation "appeal *by* a good conscience" best fits the emphatic position of this phrase and the picture in this verse of a pledging convert. Baptism is the seal of the salvation covenant, which itself has been accomplished beforehand by the act of Christ

and the faith-decision of the individual (cf. "through the resurrection of Jesus Christ," v 21d, a major theme in Acts—5:31; 13:37,38).

The Baptismal Creeds. A great deal of recent discussion has centered on the presence of credal material in the NT and its life-situation setting within the cultic worship of the church, especially in the eucharistic and baptismal rites. The baptismal service emphasized "confession," and so many of the credal confessions in the NT (e.g., Rom 10:9,10; 1 Tm 6:12,13; possibly Phil 2:6–11; Eph 4:4–6; Col 1:13–20) may have developed in the baptismal liturgy.

GRANT R. OSBORNE

See Baptism of Fire; Baptism of the Spirit; Circumcision; Uncircumcision; Cleanness and Uncleanness, Regulations Concerning.

Bibliography. K. Aland, *Did the Early Church Baptize Infants?*; J. Baillie, *Baptism and Conversion*; K. Barth, *The Teaching of the Church Regarding Baptism*; G.W. Bromiley, *The Baptism of Infants*; J.D.G. Dunn, *Baptism in the NT*; J. Jeremias, *Infant Baptism in the First Four Centuries*; E. Schlink, *The Doctrine of Baptism*; J. Warns, *Baptism*; R.E.O. White, *The Biblical Doctrine of Initiation*.

Baptism for the Dead. Custom of uncertain meaning, referred to once in the NT (1 Cor 15:29). Many interpretations have been offered for that much-disputed verse. The important questions are the nature of the practice of baptism for the dead and whether or not the apostle Paul approved of it.

Most interpretations of the phrase "baptized for the dead" fall into one of three categories: metaphoric baptism, normal baptism, or baptism by proxy. In Mark 10:38 and Luke 12:50, baptism is used as a metaphor for suffering or martyrdom. Some scholars, interpreting "baptism for the dead" as a metaphor for martyrdom, would translate it "being baptized with a view to death." One interpreter believes that it refers to Christian leaders who had died in order to bear witness to the dead.

Many prefer to read the phrase in the normal sense of being baptized on one's own behalf. Martin Luther thought it referred to the practice of baptizing over the tombs of the dead. John Calvin believed it had to do with Christians who called for baptism because they were in danger of dying. Others think it referred to converts who were baptized because of the testimony of Christian martyrs or departed loved ones.

The most natural meaning of the words points to a practice of baptism by proxy. The phrase seems to indicate that certain people in Corinth would have themselves baptized vicariously for dead people. The Corinthians may have had a magical view of baptism. That might explain why, to them, Paul belittled his ministry as a baptizer (1 Cor 1:14–17).

Comparing the Corinthians' experience with that of Israel in the wilderness (1 Cor 10:1–13), Paul described crossing the Red Sea and gathering manna in terms clearly suggesting baptism and the Lord's Supper. Paul reminded his readers that neither of those dramatic experiences prevented the Israelites from falling into sin. Perhaps the Corinthians regarded the Christian sacraments as rites that guaranteed their salvation. If so, practitioners of baptism by proxy probably believed that the rite had some magical benefit for the departed.

There is evidence of some such rite being practiced by early heretical sects. Chrysostom, an early church father, writing about the heretical Marcionites (2nd century AD), reported that when any catechumen (candidate for church membership) among them died without baptism, the Marcionites would conceal a living person under the couch where the corpse lay and ask if it would like to be baptized. The hidden person would reply yes and then would be baptized on behalf of the dead one.

Did Paul approve of the practice of baptism for the dead? Probably not. It should be noted that in the particular arguments for the resurrection of the dead in 1 Corinthians 15:29–34, Paul separated himself from the practitioners of such baptism. After mentioning the Corinthians' practice (v 29), Paul immediately turned to his own experiences in Ephesus (vv 30–33), summarizing with an exhortation in the tone of a rebuke (v 34). In the following paragraph (vv 35–42) Paul also separated himself from his questioners. It seems clear from other passages that Paul considered the Corinthians' view of baptism inadequate (1 Cor 1:14–17; 10:1–13). Without implying approval of the practice, Paul used vicarious baptism merely as an illustrative argument: unless *some* Corinthians believed in the actual resurrection of the dead, their practice of baptizing on behalf of the dead would obviously be meaningless.

GEORGE E. CANNON

Baptism of Fire. Metaphor coined by John the Baptist. John was looking for the coming of One who would "baptize in Spirit and fire" (Mt 3:11; Lk 3:16). The context makes clear that fire in that phrase denotes judgment, a judgment that would presumably purify the penitent (cf. Is 4:4; Mal 3:2,3) as well as destroy the impenitent (Mal 4:1; Mt 3:10,12).

The prophets and apocalyptic writers frequently spoke of a period of tribulation and suffering necessary before the new age could come: "the messianic woes," "the birth pangs of the Messiah," "a river of fire." Parallels to John's phraseology are found in Isaiah 30:27,

28 and in the pseudepigraphal 2 Esdras (4 Ezr) 13:10,11. John the Baptist probably adopted that usage and reexpressed it through a metaphor drawn from his own most characteristic act (baptism).

His "baptize in fire" thus probably denoted the purifying judgment which would bring in the new age as well as bring individuals into the new age.

There is no further biblical reference specifically to baptism of fire. Mark and John abbreviate the Baptist's preaching by omitting all mention of judgment. With Pentecost and beyond, John's baptism in water is seen as fulfilled in baptism in the Spirit. But Jesus seemed to echo the Baptist's conviction that a fiery purification was necessary (Mk 9:49). And he clearly picked up the Baptist's prediction, but referred the baptism and presumably the fire to his own death (Lk 12:49,50). His death is understood as suffering the fiery baptism for others. That thought is matched by the apostle Paul in his understanding of baptism into Christ as a baptism into Christ's death (Rom 6:3). So it can be said that John's expectation of a purgative baptism in fire for the penitent is most nearly fulfilled in the believer's being united with Christ in his death and sharing in his sufferings; only in that way does one come to share fully in Christ's risen glory (Rom 6:5; 8:17–23; Phil 3:10,11).

Within the holiness movement in the late 19th century, "baptism with Holy Ghost and fire" came to be used by some groups to describe a third experience subsequent to conversion and sanctification. That "third blessing" emphasis is reflected in the names of the Fire-Baptized Holiness Church (now part of the Pentecostal Holiness Church) and the Fire-Baptized Holiness Church of God of the Americas.

JAMES D.G. DUNN

See BAPTISM; BAPTISM OF THE SPIRIT.

Baptism of the Spirit. Phrase that came into prominence in modern times in the holiness movement of the 19th century. It was used by such teachers as W.E. Boardman and Asa Mahan to describe the "second blessing" of sanctification. Toward the end of the century, partly through the influence of R.A. Torrey (1856–1928), the meaning of the phrase shifted from sanctification to empowering for service. With the turn of the century, baptism of the Spirit as evidenced by speaking in tongues became the distinctive teaching of the emerging Pentecostal movement.

For some Pentecostals baptism of the Spirit is seen as a "third blessing" distinct from and subsequent to conversion and sanctification. For others it is best regarded as a second blessing, with sanctification seen as part of conversion. But for all it is understood as a repetition of the day of Pentecost, when the disciples of Jesus received power to serve as his witnesses and spoke "in other tongues, as the Spirit gave them utterance" (Acts 1:8; 2:4).

In the 1960s increasing numbers of Christians in the older denominations claimed to experience a baptism of the Spirit and understood the experience in terms of Pentecostal theology, that is, as a second religious experience beyond conversion, evidenced by speaking in tongues. As that development broadened out in the 1970s into the charismatic movement, an increasing attempt has been made, particularly in Britain and among Roman Catholic charismatics, to understand their experience of the Spirit through their own traditional theology—as, for example, a renewal or release of baptismal grace. Whatever the precise significance attached to the phrase, "baptism of the Spirit" has come to denote a revitalization of personal religious experience of immense potential for revival.

Though popularly used, the phrase "baptism of the Spirit" never occurs as such in the Bible. Instead of the noun phrase, "baptism in the Spirit," the NT always uses the verbal phrase, "baptize [or baptized] in the Spirit." That gives it a dynamic character which the noun phrase cannot fully convey.

1. *John the Baptist.* "Baptize [or baptized] in the Spirit" occurs seven times, all in the NT. The phrase seems to have been coined by John the Baptist: "I baptize you with water; but he [the One who is to come] will baptize you in the Holy Spirit and in fire" (Mt 3:11; Lk 3:16; Mk 1:8 and Jn 1:33 omit the words "and fire").

The phrase is clearly a metaphor: it stands in contrast to and as the fulfillment of John's water baptism. First, it is a metaphor of *judgment,* as the context in Matthew and Luke makes clear. Purification or destruction in a river of fire, by a spirit of cleansing, in the fiery breath of God ("breath" and "spirit" are the same word in Hebrew), was familiar imagery in Jewish thought (Is 4:4; 30:27,28; Dn 7:10). Second, it is a metaphor of *mercy,* since the purification cleanses; after winnowing, the grain would be gathered into the barn (Mt 3:11,12). Third, it is a metaphor of *initiation,* John the Baptist's variation on "the messianic woes," the expectation that the messianic age would be introduced only through suffering and tribulation (e.g., Dn 7:19–22; 12:1; Zec 14:12–15; also the pseudepigraphal 1 Enoch 100:1–3; Sib Oracles 3:632–51).

Thus, at its earliest stage "baptism in Spirit" was John's way of speaking about the suffering through which the new age would

come to birth (the "birth pangs of the Messiah"; cf. Mk 13:8; 1 Enoch 62:4) and about the purgative experience through which the penitent would enter into the new age, refined and cleansed.

2. *Jesus.* Did Jesus speak of baptism in Spirit (and fire) during his ministry? The answer is not clear. Jesus evidently saw his ministry more as blessing than as judgment (notice where the quotation from Is 61:1,2 stops in Lk 4:18,19; and Jesus' reply to John the Baptist's puzzled question in Mt 11:3–5). In and through Jesus' ministry the blessings of the new age were already being experienced: the poor were having the gospel preached to them (Mt 11:5; 13:16,17); the kingdom was already present in power (Mt 12:28); the final rout of Satan had already begun (Mk 3:27). But looking to the end of his earthly ministry Jesus did refer to his death using the metaphors of baptism and fire (Lk 12:49,50). And he did talk about the Spirit's being given, at least to aid his disciples during the coming persecution (Mk 13:11; cf. Jn 14:15–17,26; 15:26; 16:7–15). He may have used John the Baptist's metaphor, his words in Acts 1:5 and 11:16 coming from his post-resurrection ministry (cf. Lk 24:49).

The fourth Gospel writer, John, depicts Jesus' ministry as a kind of winnowing, a separating of wheat from chaff (cf. Mt 3:12), of light from darkness, of truth from evil (see particularly Jn 3:19–21). But Mark and John, by omitting the words "and fire" from the Baptist's words, omit the judgmental or dividing effect of Jesus' ministry as a fulfillment of John the Baptist's promise.

3. *Acts.* In the two post-resurrection uses of the metaphor (Acts 1:5; 11:16) the shorter form is found: "baptize in Spirit." It is possible that the phrase "and fire" was thought of as having been fulfilled in the "tongues as of fire" on the day of Pentecost (Acts 2:3). But the fire spoken of by John the Baptist was something very different ("unquenchable," Mt 3:10–12). Luke makes no attempt to link the "tongues as of fire" and the sound "like the rush of a mighty wind" with John the Baptist's words. It is also possible that the reader is intended to understand that Jesus' death exhausted the fiery judgment of God, so that the entry of the new age ("the last days," Acts 2:17) comes only through baptism in the Spirit alone (and not in "fire").

Two group experiences are described in Acts as being baptisms "in Spirit": the disciples at Pentecost, and Cornelius and his friends at Caesarea (Acts 1:5; 2:4,17,18; 10:44; 11:15–17). Three relationships need to be explored.

(1) The relation between Spirit baptism and

water baptism. It is clear from Acts 1:5 and 11:16 that "baptized in Spirit" is being used metaphorically, for it stands in contrast to "baptized in water."

Several theological traditions within Christianity have tended to identify Christian water baptism and baptism in Spirit, maintaining that John the Baptist's prediction of baptism in Spirit (and fire) is fulfilled in baptism in the name of Jesus. Thus, in Roman Catholic tradition the Spirit typically is spoken of as given in, mediated through, or bestowed by baptism. But in Acts 2:4 and 10:44–48 baptism in Spirit cannot be identified with baptism in water (cf. 8:12–17). On the other hand, the gift of the Spirit and baptism in water are set in close association in Acts 2:38 and 19:5,6; and Acts 2:38 is probably intended as typical of what it meant in the beginning to become a Christian—the whole event involving repentance and faith, baptism in the name of Jesus, and the gift of the Spirit.

Similarly John 3:5 is best understood as describing the "birth from above" as a complex union of water (baptism) and Spirit (baptism). Some interpret *"born of water and Spirit"* as equivalent to *"baptized in water and Spirit,"* though on very questionable grounds.

(2) The relation between Spirit baptism and conversion. In the two Acts passages the metaphor retains the initiatory significance given it by John the Baptist. Acts 2:4 fulfills the promise of Acts 1:5. Since the outpouring of the Spirit was seen as *the* mark of "the last days" (Is 44:3; Ez 39:29; Jl 2:28,29), it was by being thus baptized in Spirit that the disciples *began* to experience the last days for themselves (Acts 2:17,18). Acts 11:17 speaks of Pentecost as the occasion when they came to believe in Jesus Christ as Lord. Similarly the apostle Paul sees the gift of the Spirit as the beginning of Christian experience (2 Cor 1:22; Gal 3:3), so that "having the Spirit of Christ" is the defining mark of the Christian (Rom 8:9). By being baptized in Spirit, Cornelius and his friends received the forgiveness and salvation that Peter promised them (Acts 10:43–45; 11:13–18). "Baptized in Spirit" is there synonymous with "granted repentance unto life" (11:18) and "cleansed their hearts by faith" (15:8,9).

Two passages could be taken to justify the view that baptism in Spirit is subsequent to conversion; the first is John 20:22 (cf. Acts 2:4; 8:12–17). John's purpose may have been to emphasize the theological unity of Jesus' death, resurrection, ascension, and gift of the Spirit (cf. Jn 19:30; literally, "he bowed his head and handed over the spirit/Spirit"). Even if John's account is straightforwardly historical, neither Luke nor John gives any suggestion that the first disciples' experience could be taken as typical for subsequent Christian experience (cf. Jn 20:22 with Jn 4:14; 7:37,38; Acts 2:38).

In Acts 8, the second passage, it is probable that Luke understands verse 17 as the initial reception of the Spirit. (1) In 8:12 he does not use his normal phrase for conversion (i.e., "believed into [or on] the Lord"—committed themselves to the Lord; occasionally, "believed the Lord"). He says merely that "they believed Philip," probably implying a belief that fell short of commitment. (2) In 8:16, "they had only been baptized in the name of the Lord Jesus," that and nothing more. (3) In Acts there could be no doubt as to whether the Spirit had been given or not. Luke does not know of any silent, invisible giving of or filling with the Spirit (2:4; 4:31; 8:18,19; 10:46; 19:2,6).

(3) The relation between Spirit baptism and speaking in tongues. Thus, all four occasions in Acts where the initial gift of the Spirit is actually described, his coming was evident from its effects. In three cases the effects described are inspired speech: speaking in tongues and prophesying. Similarly in 4:8,31 and 13:9–11, the filling of the Spirit evidenced itself in boldness of speech and words of effective judgment (cf. also Eph 5:18,19). According to 1 Corinthians 1:4–7, the gift of grace to the Corinthians came to expression in a wide range of spiritual gifts (gifts of grace), including "speech" and "knowledge." We may conclude that inspired speech, including speaking in tongues, was a regular manifestation of the Spirit's coming on an individual or group. But to conclude that speaking in tongues was always or ought always to be the evidence of Spirit-baptism goes beyond the intention of Luke or Paul.

4. *Paul.* The one remaining explicit use of the metaphor in the NT is 1 Corinthians 12:13. Again it is clearly *initiatory*, but also *dynamic:* it is by being baptized in one Spirit that men and women become members of the one body of Christ, the charismatic community (1 Cor 12). Baptized in Spirit is evidently just one among many metaphors used by Paul to describe conversion, becoming "in Christ" or united with Christ. Others include being drenched with or given a drink of the one Spirit (1 Cor 12:13), putting on Christ or the Spirit of Christ (Gal 3:27; cf. Jgs 6:34; 2 Chr 24:20; Lk 24:49), and being crucified with Christ (Rom 6:6). Paul, like Luke and John, speaks of an initiatory experience of the Spirit and other religious experiences, but does not describe any distinctive second (or third) experience.

"Baptized into Christ" (Rom 6:3; Gal 3:27) is probably a briefer form of the metaphor "baptized in Spirit into Christ." Many take it instead as synonymous with "baptized in the name of Christ" and hence as a reference to the baptismal ritual. That is done despite the contrast elsewhere between baptized in water and baptized in Spirit. Either way it should be noted that, for Paul, "baptized into Christ" means baptized into Christ's *death* (Rom 6:3). Thus to know Christ means not only to experience the power of his resurrection but also to share his sufferings (Phil 3:10).

JAMES D.G. DUNN

See BAPTISM; BAPTISM OF FIRE; SPIRITUAL GIFTS.

Bibliography. C.K. Barrett, *Holy Spirit in Gospel Tradition;* H. Berkhof, *Doctrine of the Holy Spirit;* J.D.G. Dunn, *Baptism in the Holy Spirit;* G.S. Hendry, *The Holy Spirit in Christian Theology;* L. Morris, *Spirit of the Living God.*

Bar (Noun). Term used in the Aramaic language to denote a close familial relationship; for example, Simon Bar-Jona means "Simon, son of John."

See BEN (NOUN).

Barabbas. Criminal who was released instead of Jesus. All four Gospel writers took note of that event (Mt 27:15–26; Mk 15:6–15; Lk 23:18–25; Jn 18:39,40), as did the apostle Peter in his temple sermon (Acts 3:14).

Barabbas was a robber (Jn 18:40) who had been imprisoned for committing murder during an insurrection (Mk 15:7; Lk 23:19). He was regarded as a "notorious prisoner" (Mt 27:16). His "insurrection" may have been an unusually violent act of robbery or an internal struggle among the Jews, but many scholars view it as a political insurrection against the Roman forces in Jerusalem. It is not unlikely that Barabbas was a member of the Zealots, a Jewish political group which sought to throw off the yoke of Rome by violence. The word translated "robber" can denote either a bandit or revolutionary.

After examining Jesus, the vacillating Roman procurator, Pilate, recognized that Jesus was innocent and wanted to free him. Yet Pilate also had an interest in pleasing the Jewish leaders in order to protect his own political position. In the face of his dilemma he offered to release a prisoner to the Jews at their Passover feast (Jn 18:39). Given the option of Jesus or Barabbas, Pilate thought that the Jewish crowd would choose to have Jesus set free. Pilate underestimated either the mood of the mob or the influence of the Jewish leaders, or both. Whatever the reason, the throng shouted for Barabbas to be released and for Jesus to be crucified (Mt 27:21,22). Consequently, Jesus was crucified and Barabbas, after being released, disappeared from biblical and secular history.

Barachel. Elihu's father, described as a Buzite (Jb 32:2,6; cf. Gn 22:21; Jer 25:23). Elihu tried to counsel Job after the failed attempts by Job's three older friends.

Barachiah, Barachias. Name attributed in the NT to Zechariah's father (Mt 23:35; KJV Barachias). Zechariah, executed in the temple by order of King Joash, was said in the OT to be the son of Jehoiada (2 Chr 24:20–22). "Son of Barachiah" could be a scribal addition, since in the parallel passage in Luke's Gospel (Lk 11:51) the name does not appear in the most reliable manuscripts. A copyist may have confused the martyred Zechariah with the postexilic prophet Zechariah, whose father was Berechiah (Zec 1:1,7).

Barak. Son of Abinoam of Kedesh in Naphtali (Jgs 4:6; 5:1) and an associate of the prophetess Deborah. Barak led an army of Israel that defeated the forces of Jabin, king of the Canaanites (Jgs 4:1–24). Barak is one of the heroes of faith listed in the NT (Heb 11:32).

See DEBORAH #2; JUDGES, BOOK OF.

Barbarian. Foreigner, especially a person from a culture regarded as primitive or uncivilized. The Greek word *barbaros,* translated "barbarian" (KJV), originated as a repeated nonsense syllable, "bar-bar," in imitation of the strange sound of a foreign language. The Greeks, viewing themselves as the only truly cultured people in the world, tended to refer to everything non-Greek as barbarian. The Romans adopted Greek culture, considered themselves equals of the Greeks, and regarded other languages, customs, and people as barbarian.

NT use of the word illustrates its several shades of meaning. The relationship to language is evident in a statement about speaking in tongues through the Holy Spirit (1 Cor 14:11). The apostle Paul said that if a Christian's spiritual language were not understood, the person speaking would be a barbarian to Paul and vice versa. Luke's account of Paul's shipwreck on Malta refers to barbarous people (Acts 28:2) and barbarians (v 4). Obviously nothing derogatory was intended, since the kindness of the natives was being described. Elsewhere (Rom 1:14) Paul used the word in the usual Greek-Roman manner, saying he was indebted both to the Greeks and to the barbarians. In a profound statement that the gospel of Jesus Christ is for everyone Paul said, "Here there cannot be Greek and Jew, circumcised and uncircumcised, barbarian, Scythian, slave, free man, but Christ is all, and in all" (Col 3:11).

See FOREIGNER.

Barhumite. KJV form for a person from the village of Bahurim in 2 Samuel 23:31.

See BAHURIM, BAHARUM, BAHARUMITE.

Bariah. Shemaiah's son, a descendant of King David (1 Chr 3:22).

Bar-Jesus. Jewish sorcerer, a "false prophet" who worked with the governor of Paphos on the island of Cyprus (Acts 13:6). When the governor, Sergius Paulus, took an interest in the message of Paul and Barnabas, Bar-Jesus tried to influence him against their teachings. Paul confronted Bar-Jesus, denounced him as a "son of the devil," and predicted that a temporary blindness would come upon him as a punishment from God. Bar-Jesus was instantly blinded (vv 7–12), and the governor apparently became a Christian.

The many superstitious people of that day were an easy prey for wonder-workers like Bar-Jesus (cf. Acts 8:9–11). The term sorcerer applied to him, however, connoted more than just a magician. It often referred to a wise man whose scientific understanding supposedly exceeded that of most others in that society.

Bar-Jesus was also called Elymas, which was his name in Greek (Acts 13:8). It was common practice for Jews with contacts in both cultures to adopt a Greek name. According to one view Elymas is based on an Aramaic word for "strong" and an Arabic word for "wise," and actually means "magician."

Bar-Jona. Aramaic form of Simon Peter's surname, meaning "son of Jonah" (Mt 16:17). Another variant of the name appears in John 1:42 and 21:15–17, where the best Greek texts have "son of John" rather than "son of Jona(s)" (KJV).

See PETER, THE APOSTLE.

Barkos. Ancestor of a group of temple servants who returned to Jerusalem with Zerubbabel after the exile (Ezr 2:53: Neh 7:55).

Barley. Important grain and dietary staple in Bible lands.

See AGRICULTURE; FOOD AND FOOD PREPARATION; PLANTS.

Barnabas. Name given by the apostles to an early convert to Christianity in Jerusalem. Formerly called Joseph, Barnabas probably earned his new name through effective preaching and teaching.

Sources for the life of Barnabas are limited to passages in the Book of Acts and from Paul's letters. The apocryphal *Epistle of Barnabas* is almost certainly a mid-second-century composition and therefore not from the hand of Barnabas. The aprocryphal *Acts of Barnabas* is from the fifth century and not useful in establishing reliable information on the person of Barnabas. Tertullian assigned to him the authorship of Hebrews, but internal evidence militates against this view.

A native of Cyprus, Barnabas was a Jew of the diaspora. His priestly family background gave him a special interest in Jerusalem. He probably came to live in the holy city. It is possible that he may even have become acquainted with Jesus in Jerusalem, but his conversion to Christianity probably resulted from the apostles' preaching soon after the resurrection of Christ.

Barnabas first appears as a property owner named Joseph (KJV Joses) in the Book of Acts who sold a field and gave the money to the Christian community (Acts 4:36,37). When persecution of Hellenistic Christians broke out in Jerusalem, Barnabas remained in the city though others of similar background fled (8:1–8; 11:19–22). His good reputation in Jerusalem may have influenced the apostles to select him as Paul's companion for missionary work.

As many of the scattered Christians gravitated to Antioch of Syria, the Jerusalem church sent Barnabas to help in the growing work (Acts 11:19–22). The writer of Acts said of Barnabas, "He was a good man, full of the Holy Spirit and of faith. And a large company was added to the Lord" (v 24). Barnabas recruited Paul, now a Christian, to help in Antioch, and the two men worked in the church for a year, teaching "a large company of . . . Christians" (v 26). When famine hit Jerusalem, Barnabas and Paul were sent with relief funds. On their return to Antioch John Mark went with them (12:25).

Barnabas was commissioned with Paul to preach beyond the boundaries of Antioch (Acts 13:2,3). The placing of Barnabas's name before Saul (Paul) may indicate the priority of Barnabas at this time. They went to Cyprus and to

The ruins of an aqueduct in Asia Minor, an area traversed by Barnabas in his missionary work with Paul.

several key centers in Asia Minor. At Lystra the citizens identified Barnabas with the mythical god Zeus and Paul with Hermes (14:8–12).

At a Jerusalem Council, Barnabas and Paul reported on their mission to the Gentiles (Acts 15). Following that council, as the two men planned another mission, a serious disagreement arose which led to their separating (vv 36–41). Barnabas wanted to take his cousin John Mark (Col 4:10), but Paul refused on the grounds that Mark had deserted them on the earlier mission (Acts 13:13). Barnabas left for Cyprus with John Mark, and Paul went to Syria and Cilicia with Silas. After that separation the focus shifted from Barnabas to Paul.

Barrenness. State of being barren or childless. A closed womb was a deep personal tragedy in OT times. God's command to men after the flood was to be fruitful and increase in number and fill the earth (Gn 9:1) and later Jeremiah offered the same advice (Jer 29:6). A barren wife in a polygamous marriage was subject to ridicule (Gn 16:4) or extreme jealously (30:1). The social pressure to bear children for her husband was so great that the barren wife sometimes offered her husband a surrogate mother (16:1,2; 30:3). If a husband died without children, it was the responsibility of his brother to have children by his wife for him (38:8).

Barrenness could be a curse (Hos 9:11,14) or a divine punishment (Gn 20:17,18). It could be removed after earnest prayers (25:21; 1 Sm 1:16,20) or by God's prophet (2 Kgs 4:16) or messenger (Gn 18:14). On one occasion a wife who had stopped having children was able to trade off some mandrakes in exchange for sleeping privileges with her husband and had three more children (30:14–21). God promised Israel no infertility if they obeyed his laws (Dt 7:14). Unique among ancient writings is the concept here that barrenness could be a result of male infertility. Finally, as bad as barrenness was, Jesus told the women of Jerusalem that barrenness and dry breasts would be better than what they were going to go through (Lk 23:29). He is teaching that physical problems are never ultimate; spiritual ones are.

DAVID E. VAN REKEN

Barsabbas, Barsabas. Biblical surname. Barsabas (KJV) means "son of Saba" in Aramaic. Barsabbas, "son of the Sabbath," is the preferred spelling in modern translations (Acts 1:23; 15:22).

See JOSEPH #12; JUDAS #6.

Bartholomew, The Apostle. Disciple of Jesus included in all four lists of the 12 apostles (Mt 10:2–4; Mk 3:16–19; Lk 6:14–16; Acts 1:13), though not otherwise mentioned in the NT. Nothing is told about him in any of the lists. Because the name means "Son of Tolmai," it has been speculated that he was known by another name in addition to his "patronymic" name. In the lists in Matthew, Mark, and Luke (the synoptic Gospels), Bartholomew is named immediately after Philip, suggesting the possibility that the Nathanael brought by Philip to Jesus (Jn 1:45–50), who seems to be linked with some of the disciples (Jn 21:2), was Bartholomew. It thus seems possible that the apostle Bartholomew is referred to in the fourth Gospel by another name; it is not certain, however, that John's references to Nathanael were intended to identify him as one of the twelve.

Eusebius (d. AD 340?), an early church historian, recorded an early tradition that Pantaenus, the first head of the catechetical school in Alexandria (AD 180?), went to India and there found Christians who knew of the Gospel of Matthew in Hebrew letters. According to Eusebius, Bartholomew had preached to them and had left the Gospel of Matthew with them. In other traditions, Bartholomew was an evangelistic partner of Philip and Thomas and suffered martyrdom in Armenia.

A number of spurious and apocryphal writings have been ascribed to Bartholomew, though certainly none of them is genuine. In the fourth century Jerome mentioned a *Gospel of Bartholomew* which is also noted by a few other writers. There are also references to the so-called *Questions of Bartholomew* (extant in Greek, Latin, and Slavonic fragments) and to a *Book of the Resurrection of Jesus Christ by Bartholomew* (extant in Coptic). Other references were made to *Acts of Bartholomew* and *Apocalypse of Bartholomew*, both otherwise unknown.

ROBERT W. LYON

See APOSTLE, APOSTLESHIP.

Bartimaeus. Timaeus's son, a blind beggar who called out to Jesus as he left Jericho on his final journey to Jerusalem (Mk 10:46–52). Seeing Bartimaeus's faith, Jesus healed his blindness. In two similar accounts (Mt 20:29–34; Lk 18:35–43) blind men who called Jesus "son of David" were instantly healed, but the accounts differ somewhat. Matthew mentions two blind men; Luke has a solitary blind man, but unidentified. Luke says the miracle took place "as they approached Jericho"; in the other accounts the incident occurred after leaving town. Various explanations for the differences have been offered: (1) Luke's words, "as they approached Jericho," may have meant "near Jericho"; (2) Mark and Luke may have mentioned only the beggar who spoke; (3) one man may have approached Jesus as he entered Jericho and then, as Jesus left, approached again, this time bringing a friend who also received healing; (4) the healing may have occurred between what was considered old Jericho (a Canaanite city) and new Jericho (a Herodian city).

Baruch. 1. Neriah's son, secretary of the prophet Jeremiah. In the fourth year of King Jehoiakim of Judah (605/4 BC). Baruch wrote down Jeremiah's prophecy of the evil which God was going to bring upon Judah unless the nation repented (Jer 36:4). God also gave Baruch a special personal message through Jeremiah about humility in service (Jer 45:1–5).

Baruch read the words of Jeremiah's prophecy to the people and to the princes (Jer 36:9–19). The message finally reached Jehoiakim, who destroyed the scroll and called for Baruch's and Jeremiah's arrest (vv 21–26). In hiding, Baruch again wrote down Jeremiah's prediction of Judah's destruction (vv 27–32).

Baruch was the brother of Seraiah, a close associate of the later King Zedekiah. Seraiah was eventually deported to Babylon with the king by Nebuchadnezzar. With Nebuchadnezzar laying siege to Jerusalem in 587 BC, a year before its final destruction, the imprisoned Jeremiah purchased a field. His act symbolized the eventual restoration of Israel to the land. Baruch was ordered by Jeremiah to keep the evidence of the purchase safe (Jer 32:12).

Two months after the destruction of Jerusalem in 586 BC, rebellious Jews murdered Gedaliah, puppet governor of Judah under the Babylonians, and sought to flee to Egypt. Jeremiah advised them to remain in Jerusalem. The rebels blamed Baruch for influencing Jeremiah to give such advice and forced both Baruch and the prophet to accompany them into Egypt (Jer 43:1–7).

Scripture does not refer to the final events in Baruch's life. The Jewish historian Josephus recorded that when Nebuchadnezzar invaded Egypt Baruch was taken to Babylon. The apocryphal Book of Baruch begins by noting that the author was in Babylon (Bar 1:1,3). Both accounts, however, are historically questionable.

2. Zabbai's son, mentioned in connection with the events surrounding the rebuilding of the Jerusalem wall (about 445 BC) under the supervision of Nehemiah (Neh 3:20).

3. Individual who signed Ezra's covenant of faithfulness to God with Nehemiah and others after the exile (Neh 10:6); perhaps the same as #2 above.

4. Col-hozeh's son, and father of Ma-aseiah (Neh 11:5); otherwise unknown.

Barzillai. 1. One of three men who offered hospitality to David and his supporters at Mahanaim during the dangerous time of Absalom's rebellion (2 Sm 17:27). After Absalom was defeated, Barzillai, a Gileadite, came to the Jordan River as David prepared to cross it in a triumphant return to Jerusalem. The 80-year-old Barzillai declined King David's invitation to be his permanent guest in Jerusalem but sent his son Chimham in his place (19:31–40; cf. 1 Kgs 2:7).

2. Adriel's father. Adriel married Saul's daughter Merab (2 Sm 21:8; cf. 1 Sm 18:19). Barzillai was thus the paternal grandfather of five of the seven men hanged in Gibeon in recompense for Saul's guilt in trying to wipe out all Gibeonites (2 Sm 21:1–9).

3. Priest who married the daughter (or descendant) of #1 above and adopted the family name. His descendants returned to Jerusalem in 538 BC with Zerubbabel after the exile. They were refused priestly status because they had lost the genealogies establishing their heritage and priestly descent (Ezr 2:61; Neh 7:63).

Basemath. 1. Daughter of Elon the Hittite. Basemath was a Canaanite woman whom Esau married against his parents' wishes (Gn 26:34, KJV Bashemath). Basemath may be the same as Elon's daughter Adah, or perhaps was her sister (36:2).

2. Ishmael's daughter, who married Esau (Gn 36:3; KJV Bashemath) and bore Reuel to him (vv 4,10). This Basemath is probably the same as Ishmael's daughter Mahalath (28:9). Since Ishmael was the son of the patriarch Abraham, this marriage would have been more acceptable to Isaac and Rebekah (vv 6–8).

See MAHALATH (PERSON) #1.

Identifications of #1 and #2 above are somewhat confused. Most scholars suspect that Esau married Elon's daughter Adah (Gn 36:2,4), who was also called Basemath (26:34). Later Esau married Ishmael's daughter Mahalath (28:9), who was likewise called Basemath (36:3,4). That two of Esau's wives should be named Basemath could be because they each had two names in their fathers' homes, because Esau chose to give both the same affectionate name (meaning "fragrant"), or for some reason not evident from the texts.

3. King Solomon's daughter who married Ahima-az, the king's administrator in Naphtali (1 Kgs 4:15, KJV Basmath).

Bashan. Region east and northeast of the Sea of Galilee. The exact boundaries of Bashan are difficult to determine, but it extended approximately 35 to 40 miles from the foot of Mt Hermon in the north to the Yarmuk

Hot baths in Jordan in Yarmuk Valley.

River in the south, and stretched some 60 to 70 miles eastward from the Sea of Galilee.

The region ("Hauran," Ez 47:16,18) is mostly a fertile tableland 1,600 to 2,300 feet in altitude. Its rich volcanic alluvium is well-watered because the low hills of southern Galilee to the west allow the rains to sweep farther inland than in most other places along the Palestinian coast. Today, as in ancient times, it is an agriculturally productive region. In NT times it was a grain-producing area of the Roman empire. Bashan was known for the quality of its cattle and sheep (Dt 32:14; Ez 39:18; Am 4:1). Reference is also made to the oaks of Bashan (Is 2:13; Ez 27:6; Zec 11:2), although the fertile farmland of Bashan would have been stripped of forests at an early time. Evidently in ancient times Bashan included Jebel Druze, a forested, volcanic mountain to the east. Two cities of Bashan, Salecah (modern Salkhad) and Kenath (modern Qanawat), were on the slopes of Jebel Druze (Nm 32:42; Dt 3:10; Jos 12:5). Botanists identify the oak of Bashan as the Valnia oak, still abundant there. The tree produces large quantities of acorns which swine and even humans can eat and which provide a good black dye.

In the patriarch Abraham's day Bashan's inhabitants were giantlike people called Rephaim (Gn 14:5). Og, the last of the Rephaim, was an enemy of the Israelites as they sought to enter Canaan after their Egyptian bondage and wilderness wandering (Dt 29:7). Og was defeated and slain by the Israelites (Nm 21:33–35). Bashan's prosperity at that time is indicated by the fact that one of its provinces, Argob, had 60 great walled cities (Dt 3:4,5). The chief cities of Bashan were Edrei, Ashtaroth, Golan, and Salecah. After Israel conquered the territory east of the Jordan River, Bashan was given to the half tribe of Manasseh (Jos 13:29,30). Golan and Ashtaroth, two cities in Bashan, were reserved for the Levites (1 Chr 6:71). Ben-geber of Ramoth-gilead administered Argob (a region in Bashan) for King Solomon (1 Kgs 4:13). In the days of Jehu (841–814 BC), King Hazael of Syria conquered the area

(2 Kgs 10:33). Tiglath-pileser III incorporated Bashan into the Assyrian empire in the 8th century BC (2 Kgs 15:29). The Nabataeans held it in the 2nd century BC, and Herod the Great (37–4 BC) ruled over it at the time of Jesus' birth. Subsequently it was the possession of Herod's son, Herod Philip (4 BC–AD 34). The tetrarchy of Philip included areas known then as Ituraea, Auranitis (Hauran), Batanaea, and Gaulanitis (Golan today).

HOWARD F. VOS

Bashan-Havvoth-Jair. KJV translation in Deuteronomy 3:14 for Havvoth-jair, 60 villages in the region of Bashan.

See HAVVOTH-JAIR, HAVOTH-JAIR.

Bashemath. 1. KJV form of Basemath, one of Esau's wives, in Genesis 26:34.

See BASEMATH #1.

2. KJV form of Basemath, another of Esau's wives in Genesis 36:3, known also as Mahalath.

See MAHALATH (PERSON) #1.

Basmath. KJV form of Basemath, King Solomon's daughter, in 1 Kings 4:15.

See BASEMATH #3.

Bat. Mouselike flying mammal with a furry body and membranous wings, and included in the two lists of unclean birds (Lv 11:19; Dt 14:18).

See ANIMALS.

Bath. Unit of liquid measure in the OT (Ez 45:10,11), equal to about 6 gallons.

See WEIGHTS AND MEASURES.

Bathe, Bathing. To cleanse, as with water; to wash oneself. In the Bible the terms "bathing" and "washing" translate, often interchangeably, a number of different words. One OT passage uses one Hebrew word for cleaning clothes, another for washing other objects, including the body (Lv 15:8–12).

Palestine's dry climate and scarcity of water discouraged bathing except where a stream or pool was available (2 Kgs 5:10; Jn 9:7). Yet people still washed babies at birth (Ez 16:4), dead bodies in preparation for burial (Acts 9:37), and sheep for their shearing (Sg 6:6). Frequent bathing of the whole body was probably reserved for the rich (Ex 2:5; Jb 29:6), but the prevalence of dust made frequent washing of the face, hands, and feet necessary (Gn 18:4; 19:2; 24:32; 43:24; Jgs 19:21; Sg 5:3).

Good grooming for the privileged demanded washing of one's body before anointing with

A wash basin (in a museum in Corinth).

A concrete Roman bathtub.

oil (Ru 3:3; 2 Sm 12:20; Ez 23:40,41). A good host provided water for a guest's feet (Gn 18:4; Jgs 19:21; Lk 7:44; Jn 13:4,5). To wash someone's feet was the task of a servant. For anyone else to do so was a sign of humility (1 Sm 25:41; Lk 7:44–47; Jn 13:3–16; 1 Tm 5:10).

Most biblical references to washing or bathing deal with ritual cleansing. Priests and Levites were required to wash their clothes and faces, and sometimes bodies, before approaching the altar and on other ceremonial occasions (Ex 29:4; 30:19–21; 40:7,12,30–32; Nm 8:21). Before a slain animal was sacrificed, its legs and intestines were washed (Lv 1:9,13; 8:21; 9:14).

Anyone who was once unclean (e.g., a leper who was healed or someone who had experienced a genital discharge) had to wash his or her clothes and bathe to be ritually pure (Lv 14:8–10; 15:5–8,10,11,21,27). Any garment that became polluted had to be ceremonially cleansed (Lv 6:27; 13:54).

A room in one of Herod's bathhouses in Jericho.

"Washing" is also used figuratively for a cleansing from sin (Ps 51:2; Is 1:16; 4:4; Jer 2:22; 4:14; 1 Cor 6:11; Heb 10:22; Rv 1:5 KJV).

Bath-Rabbim, Gate of. Gate in the city of Heshbon near which were several pools of clear water. A poetic biblical passage described a young bride's eyes as like those pools (Sg 7:4).

Bathsheba. Uriah's wife, with whom David committed adultery and whom he later married. Bathsheba, also spelled Bath-shua (1 Chr 3:5), was the daughter of Ammiel or Eliam (2 Sm 11:3) and possibly the granddaughter of Ahithophel, the king's adviser (2 Sm 15:12; 23:34). Her Hittite husband was one of David's top military heroes (2 Sm 23:39).

While Uriah was off fighting under Joab, King David saw a beautiful woman taking her evening bath. Discovering her name and that her husband was away on duty, he sent for Bathsheba and had sexual intercourse with her (2 Sm 11:1–4). When Bathsheba later informed him that she was pregnant, the king ordered Uriah back to Jerusalem, hoping that the husband's return would make Bathsheba's pregnancy appear legitimate. But Uriah considered himself still on active duty and slept with the palace guard, refusing to go home (2 Sm 11:5–13). Frustrated, David sent him back to the front and ordered Joab to put Uriah in the front lines and then pull back. In spite of the casualties suffered, David congratulated Joab on learning that Uriah was dead (2 Sm 11:14–25).

After Bathsheba's period of mourning, David installed her in the palace as his seventh wife, and she bore the child. The Lord sent the prophet Nathan to pronounce judgment on David's sin through a parable. Nathan prophesied a series of tragedies in David's household, beginning with the death of Bathsheba's infant son (2 Sm 11:26–12:14). David confessed his sin and repented, but the infant became sick and died. The prologue (or superscription) of Psalm 51 describes it as the psalm of repentance David wrote when confronted by Nathan over his adultery with Bathsheba and his murder of Uriah. David comforted Bathsheba, and eventually they had other children (2 Sm 12:15–25).

Of David's 19 sons by his 7 wives (1 Chr 3:1–9), the 4 born to Bathsheba were Shimea (also spelled Shammua, 2 Sm 5:14; 1 Chr 14:4), Shobab, Nathan, and Solomon. Nathan (Lk 3:31) and Solomon (Mt 1:6) appear in NT genealogies of Jesus Christ. At the very end of David's life the prophet Nathan told Bathsheba that David's son Adonijah (by his wife Haggith) was conspiring to usurp the throne. Bathsheba and Nathan persuaded David to make Solomon king as he had promised (1 Kgs 1:1–53). Later Bathsheba presented to her son Solomon, now king, a request from Adonijah for permission to marry Abishag, the woman who had taken care of their dying father. Solomon saw in the request a new plot and this time had Adonijah executed (1 Kgs 2:12–34).

See DAVID.

Bath-shua. 1. Canaanite wife of Judah who bore him three sons: Er, Onan, and Shelah (Gn 38:2–5, KJV Shuah; 1 Chr 2:3, Shua).

2. Alternate spelling of Bathsheba in 1 Chronicles 3:5.

See BATHSHEBA.

Battering Ram. Ancient military machine with a heavy wooden beam used to batter down gates or walls. Some battering rams had an iron ram's head at the end of the beam.

See ARMS AND WARFARE.

Battle-axe. Heavy axe with a wide blade used as a weapon of war.

See ARMS AND WARFARE.

Battlement. Defensive wall, with openings for shooting, on top of a fortress; by extension, a parapet or railing around any flat roof. Houses in the Near East were built with flat roofs, which were used for many different purposes. Rahab hid two Israelite spies on her roof (Jos 2:6). Saul slept on Samuel's roof (1 Sm 9:25). King David from his roof saw Bathsheba taking a bath (2 Sm 11:2). People celebrated on rooftops (Is 22:1,2); Peter prayed on his roof (Acts 10:9). With so much activity on rooftops it is easy to understand the need for the law, "When you build a new house, you shall make a parapet for your roof, that you may not bring the guilt of blood upon your

house, if any one fall from it" (Dt 22:8, KJV battlement).

City walls often had towers at the gates and corners from which the city could be defended from attack. Hebrew words for such fortifications are often translated "towers" (KJV) (2 Chr 26:15; Zep 1:16).

See ARCHITECTURE; ARMS AND WARFARE; HOMES AND DWELLINGS.

Bavvai, Bavai. Individual who directed the repair of a section of the Jerusalem wall under Nehemiah's supervision (Neh 3:18). Bavvai (KJV Bavai) was Henadad's son and the official of half the district of Keilah, a town 17 miles southwest of Jerusalem. Binnui (Neh 3:24), also mentioned as Henadad's son (cf. Ezr 3:9), may be a corrupted spelling of Bavvai, or the two may have been brothers.

Bay Tree. Tree 40 to 60 feet high with fragrant, evergreen leaves and native to Palestine.

See PLANTS (LAUREL).

Bazlith, Bazluth. Ancestor of a group of temple assistants returning to Jerusalem with Zerubbabel after the exile (Ezr 2:52, Bazluth; Neh 7:54).

Bdellium. Substance mentioned twice in the OT, evidently the resinous gum of an Arabian shrub (known scientifically as *Commiphora africana*). The same genus of mideastern plants includes the shrub from which myrrh is derived and possibly the one from which the biblical "balm" was obtained.

Apart from the Bible, bdellium was described by an English herbalist as an aromatic gum from a tree known in Persia and eastward. In the first century AD the Roman writer Pliny mentioned the same tree and described the gum as waxlike and looking like pearl.

The manna gathered by the Israelites is described in the Bible as having the same color as bdellium (Nm 11:7). Bdellium is also mentioned along with the gold and onyx stone found near the garden of Eden (Gn 2:12). Because it was included in that list, bdellium was once thought to be pearl or a precious stone.

See PLANTS.

Beads. *See* FASHION AND DRESS.

Bealiah. Warrior from Benjamin's tribe who joined David at Ziklag in his struggle against King Saul. Bealiah was one of David's ambidextrous archers and slingers (1 Chr 12:5).

Bealoth. 1. Town along the border of Edom in the Negeb desert area (Jos 15:24).

2. Administrative district in the time of King Solomon governed by Baana, Hushai's son (1 Kgs 4:16, KJV Aloth).

Beam. 1. Weaver's beam—round wooden roller on which the cloth or carpet was wound during the weaving process in Bible times. The spears of the giant Goliath (1 Sm 17:7; 2 Sm 21:19; 1 Chr 20:5) and an Egyptian killed by Benaiah, one of David's mighty men (1 Chr 11:23) were compared to a weaver's beam.

2. Tree trunk or log that has been squared and used for building purposes. King Solomon used "beams and planks of cedar" to build the temple (1 Kgs 6:9; 2 Chr 3:7) and his "House of the Forest of Lebanon" (1 Kgs 7:2,12). Another mention of cedar beams probably refers to their aroma (Sg 1:17). Habbakuk 2:11 states that even "the beam from the woodwork" will respond to those who do evil.

3. Crossbeam of a Hebrew balance from which the scales were hung by cords.

4. Beam (KJV) or log (RSV) referred to by Jesus (Mt 7:3–5; Lk 6:41,42). Jesus contrasted the beam in an accuser's eye with the mote (KJV) or speck (RSV) in his brother's eye.

Bean. Any of various plants of the legume family, and part of the diet of the peoples of Bible lands.

See AGRICULTURE; PLANTS; FOOD AND FOOD PREPARATION.

Bear (Animal). Large, short-tailed, shaggy animal that feeds on plants as well as small animals. The bear mentioned several times in the Bible is the Syrian brown bear still found in Syria and Turkey but no longer in Palestine.

See ANIMALS.

Bear (Astronomy). Constellation of stars (Ursa Major, also known as the Big Dipper) mentioned in Job 9:9 and 38:32.

See ASTRONOMY.

Beard. Hair growing on the lower part of a man's face, worn as a sign of maturity among all ancient Semitic peoples including the Israelites. Certain styles of beards were characteristic of specific cultures. Egyptian art objects, for example, often depict Egyptians as clean-shaven. Joseph may have shaved off his beard to avoid offending a beardless Egyptian pharaoh (Gn 41:14). Later the Greeks and Romans invading the Middle East often went cleanshaven.

Among the Israelites care of the beard took on religious significance (Lv 19:27). Levitical law prohibited priests from shaving their heads or clipping their beards (Lv 21:4–6). David's ambassadors to an Ammonite king were humiliated by having one side of their beards shaved off by the Ammonites. That indignity and others led to war (2 Sm 10:1–8). Removal of an Israelite's beard, however, was considered appropriate under certain circumstances. Suspicion of leprosy on the head or face required shaving around the suspected spot to permit better diagnosis (Lv 13:29–37). A shaven head, along with wailing and the wearing of sackcloth, was a way of proclaiming impending or prevailing doom (Is 15:1–3). Ezra dramatized Israel's spiritual disaster by pulling hair out of his head and beard (Ezr 9:3).

See FASHION AND DRESS.

Beast. Animal in both the OT and NT, having in some cases a figurative significance. The word has a variety of meanings in the OT. Some of the diversity is due to inconsistent translations of several Hebrew words which can signify "living creature" as well as "beast," but which have sometimes been translated only as "beast." In the OT, therefore, beast can refer to the following:

1. In general, any animal (e.g., Gn 1:24; Ps 36:6), but often distinguished from fish, birds, and insects (e.g., Gn 6:7; Lv 11:2; Dt 4:17; Jb 12:7; 35:11; Zep 1:3).

2. A domesticated animal (e.g., Ex 19:13; 22:10; Nm 3:13; 31:47; Jgs 20:48; Prv 12:10; Jer 21:6; Zec 8:10).

3. A wild and sometimes carnivorous animal (e.g., Gn 37:20; Ex 23:11; Dt 28:26; 1 Sm 17:44; Ez 14:15).

4. The figurative usage of the word "beast" is most apparent in the books of Daniel and Revelation. In Daniel (especially Dn 7) the beast is a symbol of a world ruler who persecutes and oppresses the people of God. In the Revelation the apostle John took over that concept with its vivid imagery to speak of the final persecution of God's people at the end of history. John's beast in its apostasy closely resembles the "antichrist" of his earlier epistles (1 Jn 2:18,22; 4:3; 2 Jn 7) and Paul's "man of lawlessness" (2 Thes 2:3). Many Bible commentators regard the three as designating the same individual.

The important NT passages describing the beast are in Revelation 13 and 17. The beast first appears coming up out of the sea, perhaps an indication of coming from a distant country. The description of the creature reminds one of the beast in the OT Book of Daniel—a wild beast, endowed with all the power of Satan, who will ravage the people of

God. The beast, as a political figure and world ruler, will fiercely persecute the church at the end of history for a short time (symbolized by the 42 months of Rv 13:5). The beast recovers from a mortal wound (13:3) as part of its conscious counterfeiting of Christ's death and resurrection.

Revelation also describes another beast, which some interpreters believe symbolizes organized religion (Rv 13:11–18). The second beast appears as innocent as a lamb and has miraculous power to deceive the world into worshiping the first beast or antichrist. Among its other extraordinary powers, the second beast has the ability to cause an image of the beast-antichrist to speak. Those who refuse to submit to worshiping the image risk exclusion from the economic system and even death.

John urged the churches to recognize the beast's satanic character, providing a cryptic number by which it might be identified. That number is 666 or, in some manuscripts, 616 (Rv 13:18). The seriousness of worshiping the beast-antichrist is brought out in Revelation 14:9–11, where the penalty for doing so is eternal punishment. Revelation 14 to 16 portrays the wrath of God, symbolized by seven bowls of unmixed wine, as poured out upon those who worship the beast-antichrist and receive its mark.

John gave another detailed description of the beast in Revelation 17. The "scarlet beast" pictured with the "great harlot" is identified (v 8) with the beast of 13:1–10 who persecutes the church. That earlier beast who was wounded and healed (13:3) resembles the scarlet beast who "was and is not." Aware of the complexity of his symbolic portrayal, John again called the church to use discerning wisdom (17:9).

John seems to have understood the beast-antichrist as a world ruler who will turn against the people he had once led who are symbolized by the great harlot. The beast will come with new allies to destroy those people and to war against the Lamb (Rv 17:9–18). Those two aspects of the final struggle are amplified in Revelation 18 and 19.

Revelation 18 pictures the destruction of the world empire that had persecuted the church. Revelation 19 pictures the destruction of the beast by Christ, whose coming in power and glory is symbolized by a rider on a white horse accompanied by the armies of heaven. Christ vanquishes the beast and the second beast ("the false prophet"), casting both into the lake of fire (v 20). The end of the beast-antichrist and the binding of Satan (in the form of a dragon) are pictured as occurring before a millennial reign of Christ (Rv 20:1–6).

HOBERT K. FARRELL

See MILLENNIUM; ANTICHRIST; ARMAGEDDON; MARK OF THE BEAST; REVELATION, BOOK OF.

Beatitudes, Mount of the. The title given to the locale where Jesus delivered the Beatitudes during his Sermon on the Mount (Mt 5:1–12). The exact site is not known. Older tradition favored the Horns of Hattin as the precise spot. Current tradition has located the area on a hill southwest of Capernaum.

Beatitudes, The. Term derived from Latin *beatitudo*, it is not used in the English Bible. Technically it means "blessedness" as described in the OT and NT. "Blessed" is translated from both Hebrew and Greek words, to refer to divine favor conveyed to man. It is used more particularly of the Sermon on the Mount, where differing literary forms are used in the two versions of Matthew (5:3–12) and Luke (6:20–23). However, the theological and

A view of the Sea of Galilee from the Mt of Beatitudes, the place usually identified as the scene of the Sermon on the Mount. Also seen are the Horns of Hattin (called Qurun Hattin), where a great battle occurred on July 4, 1187, in which Crusaders were crushed by Saladin.

ethical concept of "beatitude" has a long history in the interpretations of the church of the sense of well-being before God's presence.

The formal utterance "happy is," or "blessed is," is a common declaration in the Book of Psalms (used 26 times) and Proverbs (8 times). It is used 10 times in the other books of the OT and 13 times in the apocryphal books. These beatitudes are pronounced upon the person who is righteous, having faith and hope in God. They are signs of a life lived in proximity to Yahweh, in the experience of forgiveness, and in the love and favor of God. Such life is a totality, so such blessings are expressive of holistic enrichment, harmony, and fecundity, whether in family life, in temple worship, in public life, or in the interior of one's own being. The person so blessed is in touch with the fruitfulness of the Creater himself. Such a one lives a fulfilled life, life as God intended it to be lived before him. Only God can bless, for he alone is holy, so when the Scriptures speak of humans "blessing" God, the term has another connotation, that of acknowledgment of God's mercy, forgiveness, love, and glory.

In the NT, references to "blessing" occur seven times in the Book of Revelation, three times in the Epistle to the Romans, and once in John's Gospel. The prominence of "blessedness" in Matthew and Luke gives rise to the technical term, "beatitudes." There are interesting contrasts between Luke's "sermon on the plain" (Lk 6:20–23) and Matthew's "sermon on the mount" (Mt 5:3–12). The pronouncement of the blessings in Luke is done immediately after the selection of the 12 disciples (Lk 6:12–16). Yet the sermon is addressed to the crowd generally and speaks of the advent of God's kingdom as the reversal of the social conditions of the human race. So Luke balances four blessings with four woes—changing from the present tense to the future tense—to heighten the contrast of the impending reversal of social conditions. His purpose is eschatological consolation.

In Matthew's account, the advent of the kingdom has already commenced, indicated by the use of the present tense. It is addressed to the disciples particularly and is not a general proclamation. The sermon is set within two statements of Jesus: he has not come to destroy but to fulfil the Mosaic law (Mt 5:17); and it is necessary to have a kind of righteousness that "exceeds that of the scribes and Pharisees" (v 20). So these beatitudes are more concerned with the interior life of the disciple, to activate here and now the kind of life Jesus communicates in those who follow him. For Jesus has already inaugurated the kingdom. These eight beatitudes reflect on the traits of those who belong to that kingdom and who

therefore reflect Christ's own life. The people and situations described may seem pitiable by human standards, but because of God's presence in their lives, they are actually blessed and should be congratulated and imitated.

As a charter for sanctity, the beatitudes have had a long and controversial history in the church. First, there have been numerous attempts from Augustine onward to interpret the sequence of the beatitudes in Matthew's account in some moral progression of thought. There have been the varying interpretations of the beatific life, from the concept of deification, or becoming God-filled, as in Eastern Orthodox thought, to the vision and experience of God described by Western mystics. Especially since the 19th century, there have been several ethical interpretations of the beatitudes in the thought of Søren Kierkegaard, Leo Tolstoy, Albert Schweitzer, Johann Weiss, Hans Winchisch, Dietrich Bonhoeffer, and Jacques Dupont. Some thinkers have evaded the challenge altogether by relegating the beatitudes to another "dispensation" and not intended for the church today. One of the most reasonable positions is what T.W. Manson and others would call "an ethic of response." "In Christ" we read the ethic of the beatitudes, so we respond to his fulfilment of the Law, and "in Christ" we relate to God and his righteousness. As Christ is the content and context of the beatitudes, so as our lives are in Christ, the beatitudes express our character also.

JAMES M. HOUSTON

See JESUS CHRIST, LIFE AND TEACHING OF.

Beautiful Gate. Gate of Herod's temple in Jerusalem where a man born lame was miraculously healed through the ministry of Peter and John (Acts 3:2,10). The location of this gate is uncertain, but it was probably the gate leading from the Court of the Gentiles into the Women's Court, called the Corinthian Gate (for its Corinthian bronze) by the Jewish historian Josephus. According to him it measured 75 feet high by 60 feet wide. A burial inscription found on Mt Olivet attributes the building of the gate to an Alexandrian Jew named Nicanor.

See TABERNACLE, TEMPLE.

Beauty. Harmonious combination of qualities pleasant to see. Archaeological materials indicate that the ancient Hebrews were concerned more with usefulness than with beauty. Hebrew pottery, for example, was generally more bulky than Canaanite pottery. Yet such artifacts do not mean that the Hebrews had no aesthetic appreciation.

The OT speaks of God's creation as beautiful (Gn 2:9; Jb 26:13; Ps 19:1–6; Sg 6:10). The land of Canaan is a "pleasant land" (Jer 3:19). Jerusalem is called "beautiful" (Is 52:1; Lam 2:15), as is one of its temple gates (Acts 3:2,10). The Hebrews admired the wild grandeur of the Lebanon mountain range (Ps 104:16; Is 60:13). The Canaanite city of Tirzah ("beauty"), King Baasha's capital in the northern kingdom (1 Kgs 15:33), was so named for its attractive location.

Although the Hebrews did not exalt the human form as did the ancient Greeks, the OT does idealize physical attractiveness. A bride's beauty is described eloquently by her bridegroom in love lyrics in Song of Solomon 4:1–15; 6:4. Such praise of the bride may have been a traditional feature of Israelite weddings. Several women prominent in the OT are described as beautiful (Gn 29:17; 2 Sm 11:2; Est 2:7). But sensual beauty was secondary to industry, resourcefulness, and traditional piety in a woman (Prv 31:10–31). A number of men also were known for their physical attractiveness—for example, David (1 Sm 16:12) and Absalom (2 Sm 14:25). Cosmetics, jewelry, and other accessories were used as female beauty aids in OT times. The prophet Isaiah listed such items (Is 3:18–24), and Ezekiel mentioned cosmetic practices current in his day (Ez 16:10–13). Israelite worship was beautiful, too, with the high priest's elaborate ceremonial robes designed "for glory and beauty" (Ex 28:2,40).

The concept of beauty is applied also to God in the OT. The Lord's favor is called his "beauty" (Ps 90:17 KJV). Isaiah recorded God's promise to give his people "beauty for ashes" (Is 61:3 KJV). The psalmist expressed a desire to spend time in the temple enjoying the Lord's beauty, his "incomparable perfections" (Ps 27:4 LB). Isaiah described God as a "diadem of beauty" to the faithful Israelite remnant (Is 28:5), and the Messiah was spoken of as a beautiful king (Is 33:17). Thus in the OT the concept of beauty had a deeper meaning than simply physical attractiveness. It became a theological concept affirming God's essential glory.

The NT urges Christ's followers to live lives that will "adorn" the teaching of the Savior, making it attractive to nonbelievers (Ti 2:10). Those who preach the gospel (good news) of Christ are spoken of as beautiful (Rom 10:15). The apostles Paul and Peter warned women against being satisfied with outward beauty (1 Tm 2:9,10), reminding them that beautiful character is the true adornment of godliness (1 Pt 3:3–5). The beauty of the believer's final home in heaven is reflected in the description of the "new Jerusalem" as a bride (Rv 21:2) and in the symbolism of treasured semiprecious stones of antiquity (Rv 4:3).

Bebai. 1. Ancestor of a family that returned to Jerusalem with Zerubbabel after the exile (Ezr 2:11; 8:11; Neh 7:16). Some of the members of that family were guilty of marrying foreign women (Ezr 10:28).

2. Levitical leader of Israel who signed Ezra's covenant of faithfulness to God with Nehemiah and others after the exile (Neh 10:15). This individual was perhaps a member of the family of #1 above.

Becher. 1. Benjamin's second son, who migrated to Egypt with his grandfather Jacob (Gn 46:21; 1 Chr 7:6).

2. Ephraim's second son, from whom the family of Becherites originated (Nm 26:35, KJV Bachrites). He is also called Bered (1 Chr 7:20).

Becherite. Descendant of Becher, Ephraim's second son (Nm 26:35).

See BECHER #2.

Becorath, Bechorath. Zeror's father, a member of Benjamin's tribe and an ancestor of King Saul (1 Sm 9:1, KJV Bechorath).

Bed. *See* FURNITURE.

Bedad. Father of Hadad, one of the kings of Edom before the Israelite monarchy (Gn 36:35; 1 Chr 1:46).

Bedan. 1. One of Israel's deliverers, along with Gideon, Jephthah, and Samuel, during the time of the judges (1 Sm 12:11 KJV; RSV margin). The name Bedan may be either a shortened form of Abdon (Jgs 12:13) or a scribal error for Barak (Jgs 4:6).

2. Ulam's son, a descendant of Manasseh (1 Chr 7:17).

Bedeiah. Bani's son, who obeyed Ezra's exhortation to divorce his pagan wife after the exile (Ezr 10:35).

Bee. *See* ANIMALS.

Beeliada. Former name of Eliada, one of King David's sons, in 1 Chronicles 14:7.

See ELIADA #1.

Be-elzebul, Beelzebub. Epithet meaning "lord of the flies" or "lord of the manure pile," referring to Satan. It was used against Jesus by his enemies (Mt 10:25, KJV Beelzebub; 12:24; Lk 11:15).

See BAAL-ZEBUB.

Beer. 1. Israelite campsite on their wilderness journey, probably just north of the Arnon

River on the Moabite-Amorite border (Nm 21:16). The name means "a well." Water from the well they dug there was commemorated in a song (vv 17,18). A Moabite well that was later called Beer-elim (Is 15:8) may have been the same location.

See WILDERNESS WANDERINGS.

2. Place to which Gideon's son Jotham escaped after telling a parable against his half-brother Abimelech, who had killed all the other sons of Gideon in an attempt to become king of Israel (Jgs 9:21).

Be-era. Zophah's son, a warrior in Asher's tribe (1 Chr 7:37).

Be-erah. Chief of Reuben's tribe (1 Chr 5:6, 26) taken captive by the Assyrian king Tilgath-pilneser (a later spelling of Tiglath-pileser).

Beer-elim. One of the cities of Moab that Isaiah predicted would hear wailing at the fall of the Moabite kingdom (Is 15:8); perhaps the same as Beer (Nm 21:16).

Be-eri. 1. Judith's Hittite (Hethite) father. Judith was one of the wives of Esau (Gn 26:34).

2. Father of Hosea the prophet (Hos 1:1).

Beer-lahai-roi. Well between Kadesh and Bered where Hagar, pregnant with Ishmael, was confronted by the Angel of the Lord (Gn 16:7–14). The name given to the site means "the well of the Living One who sees me," referring to God's appearance to Sarai's servant girl. Later it became a frequent watering place for Isaac on his travels (Gn 24:62; 25:11, KJV Lahai-roi).

Be-eroth, Beeroth. One of four Hivite cities that secured Joshua's promise not to destroy them when the Israelites marched into Canaan (Jos 9:17). Be-eroth (KJV Beeroth) was later identified as a city in Benjamin's territory (Jos 18:25; 2 Sm 4:2,3). It was the home of Rechab and Baanah, assassins of King Ishbosheth (2 Sm 4:2–9, KJV Beerothite), and of Naharai, Joab's armor bearer (2 Sm 23:37; 1 Chr 11:39, KJV Berothite). The city was repopulated after the exile (Ezr 2:25; Neh 7:29). El Bireh near Ramallah and Nebi Samwil north of Jerusalem have both been suggested as possible locations for Be-eroth.

Be-eroth Bene-jaakan. Site where the Israelites camped during their wilderness journey from Egypt, near Moserah, or Moseroth (Dt 10:6); also called Bene-jaakan in Numbers 33:31,32. The Hebrew "Be-eroth Bene-jaakan" means "well of Jaakan's sons."

See WILDERNESS WANDERINGS.

The mound of Beersheba.

Be-erothite, Beerothite. Inhabitant of Be-eroth (2 Sm 4:2–9, KJV Beerothite).

See BE-EROTH, BEEROTH.

Beersheba. Scriptural designation for the southern extremity of Palestine, as Dan is for the north (Jgs 20:1), located 28 miles southwest of Hebron. It was an important Negeb site at an early time. Hagar wandered with Ishmael in this area, as did Abraham. Later Isaac (Gn 26:23) and Jacob (Gn 46:1) both had significant spiritual experiences there, and later yet it was important in the lives of numerous other Hebrews.

Beersheba of the Hebrew monarchy period was located at Tell Beersheba, two miles northeast of the modern city. Yohanan Aharoni directed a Tel Aviv University excavation there from 1969 to 1975. He discovered that the city was founded by the Hebrews in the 12th or 11th century BC and probably was the place where the sons of Samuel judged the people (1 Sm 8:2).

This city was only about two and one-half acres in size. In its ruins Aharoni found remains of a horned altar, which when reassembled stood to a height of about five feet. This is the same height as the altar found at Arad, and the two are the only Hebrew altars yet found that date to the period of the first temple. These altars were the same height as the one in the tabernacle (Ex 27:1) and probably the same as the original altar in Solomon's temple (2 Chr 6:13). A great water system was also uncovered, similar to those of Megiddo and Hazor. Aharoni concluded that Beersheba of the patriarchal period probably was located within the area of modern Beersheba.

HOWARD F. VOS

Beeshterah. City of the half-tribe of Manasseh given to the levitical family of Gershonites in the partitioning of the Promised Land (Jos 21:27). The spelling is a shortened form for Beth-Ashtaroth ("house or place of Ashtaroth"). It seems to be the same as the city of Ashtaroth found in a similar passage (1 Chr 6:71).

See ASHTAROTH, ASHTERATHITE (PLACE); LEVITICAL CITIES.

Beetle. KJV for cricket in Leviticus 11:22.

See ANIMALS (CRICKET).

Beggar. One who asks for charity, especially one who lives by begging; a mendicant.

Begging is not an OT concept. Biblical references to begging are limited to such Hebrew verbs as "to seek" or "to ask," and, as a noun, to "the poor and needy"; in the NT, Greek terms refer to being "poor" or "miserable," and to those who "ask for more." Professional beggars were unknown in Moses' time, since the Law made ample provision for taking care of the poor.

Earliest legislation assumed that the poor would always be around (Dt 15:11; cf. Mt 26:11); yet to prevent pauperism there were regulations such as the sabbath year, the year of remission to those indebted (Lv 25). In that year the produce of the land was left to the poor and destitute (Ex 23:11), and all debts were canceled (Dt 15:1). The duty of lending liberally to the poor was promulgated (vv 7–11), and hired laborers were protected (24:14, 15). The purpose was that "there will be no poor among you" (15:4). Indeed, in the early days of Israelite settlement, all Israelites enjoyed a comparable standard of living. This is evidenced by the rare allusions to exceptional wealth in the stories of Job and of David's wife Abigail.

In excavations at Tirsah near Nablus, the size and arrangements of houses of the 10th century BC are all about the same. By the 8th century BC there is a striking contrast, with houses on the same site clearly divided into the town's richer and poorer quarters. The social revolution between those two centuries was associated with the rise of the Israelite monarchy and growth of a class of officials who gained private profits from their positions. The prophets condemned the fact that wealth was ill-gotten and badly distributed in their day (e.g., Is 5:8; Hos 12:8; Am 8:4–7; Mi 2:2). The prophet Amos denounced creditors who felt no pity for the poor (Am 2:6–8; 8:6). Yet, throughout the OT, there is essentially no reference to beggars. During the intertestamental period, however, almsgiving became an important religious duty.

In the NT, begging seems to be prevalent. In the ministry of Jesus, references are made to a blind beggar (Jn 9:8,9), to blind Bartimaeus (Mk 10:46–52), and to Lazarus, a godly beggar who is contrasted with a rich man (Lk 16:19–31). The apostles Peter and John encountered a crippled beggar by the "Beautiful," or Nicanor, gate in Jerusalem (Acts 3:1–11). Jesus rebuked an ostentatious show of almsgiving (Mt 6:1–4) but stressed the importance of giv-

A woman beggar.

ing to the poor from right motives (5:42–48). By the time of Jesus, Jerusalem had become a center for beggars, probably because almsgiving in the holy city was then regarded as particularly meritorious. Begging in Jerusalem was concentrated around the holy places, although the Septuagint (the Greek version of the OT) adds to the proverb, "The blind and the lame shall not come into the house," the words "of the Lord" (2 Sm 5:8). The pool of Beth-zatha was a place of healing, and the sick, blind, lame, and paralyzed lay there to beg as well as to get into the waters for healing (Jn 5:2–9).

In the early Christian community the first organization of officers was made to provide for a fair distribution of funds to the poor (Acts 4:32–35; 6:1–6). On the first day of each week, some portion of each Christian's income was to be allotted to the needy (11:27–30; Rom 15:25–27; 1 Cor 16:1–4). Possibly the poverty of Palestine was made worse by heavy Roman taxation; tax-gatherers as well as beggars are prominent in the Gospel narratives. It has also been suggested that the rise of the Zealots was closely associated with the social factor of poverty; the revolutionary Zealots were largely comprised of society's "dregs," according to the Jewish historian Josephus. In AD 66 the Zealots burned the Jerusalem archives, no doubt intending to destroy the records of their debts kept there. Josephus reports that before the Roman destruction of Jerusalem, gangs of beggars were terrorizing the whole city.

JAMES M. HOUSTON

See ALMS; POOR, THE.

Beheading. Form of execution practiced in Bible times.

See CRIMINAL LAW AND PUNISHMENT.

Behemoth. Hebrew word in plural form usually translated "beasts" or "wild animals" (as in Dt 28:26; 32:24; Ps 50:10; Is 18:6; Hb 2:17). Most English versions refer only once to "behemoth," where the context seems to refer to a specific animal, large and powerful, believed by many biblical scholars to be the hippopotamus (Jb 40:15). In ancient times the hippopotamus was well known in Egypt and may have inhabited the Jordan Valley. Job 40:23 may, however, refer to any river "swollen like the Jordan in flood season."

See ANIMALS.

Behistun Inscription. Trilingual account of the exploits of Darius I, engraved into the side of Mt Behistun in ancient Persia.

See INSCRIPTIONS.

Beka, Bekah. Six-gram weight called "half a shekel, by the shekel of the sanctuary" (Ex 38:26, KJV Bekah).

See WEIGHTS AND MEASURES.

Bel. Title of the state god of Babylon, Marduk, mentioned disdainfully by both Isaiah (46:1) and Jeremiah (Jer 50:2; 51:44).

See BABYLON, BABYLONIA; MARDUK.

Bela (Person). 1. Beor's son, a king of Edom who ruled before Israel had a king (Gn 36:31–33). Because Balaam, the pagan prophet from north Syria, also had a father named Beor (Nm 22:5), some ancients and a number of modern critical scholars have confused the Edomite Bela with Balaam.

2. Benjamin's oldest son (Gn 46:21; KJV Belah; 1 Chr 8:1), whose descendants were called Belaites (Nm 26:38).

3. Azaz's son, a descendant of Reuben who lived in Gilead in Transjordan. So vast were his family's holdings that they pastured their cattle as far east as the Euphrates River (1 Chr 5:8). In the reign of Saul, his family successfully held their land against Hagrite opposition.

Bela (Place). Alternate name for Zoar, a city of the plain, in Genesis 14:2.

See CITIES OF THE VALLEY, CITIES OF THE PLAIN; ZOAR.

Belah, Belaite. KJV rendering of Bela, Benjamin's oldest son, in 1 Chronicles 8:1. His descendants were called Belaites (Nm 26:38).

See BELA (PERSON) #2.

Belial, Beliar. Common Hebrew noun meaning "baseness," "worthlessness," "wickedness," or "lawlessness." Belial, however, is often rendered as a proper noun. Thus such translations as "sons of Belial" appear (KJV Jgs 19:22; 1 Sm 2:12), "daughter of Belial" (1 Sm 1:16), or "children of Belial" (Dt 13:13; Jgs 20:13). Newer translations generally prefer the common noun form and give such readings as "base fellows" (Dt 13:13; Jgs 19:22; 20:13), "miscreants" (Dt 13:13 NEB), "base woman" (1 Sm 1:16), "worthless" (1 Sm 2:12; 10:27; Prv 6:12), and the like. One possible exception to this rule is found in Nahum 1:15, which some scholars think should be rendered as "Belial," a personalized designation of the Assyrian conqueror who had been a threat to the southern kingdom of Judah.

Intertestamental literature often used "Belial" as a proper noun and thus prepared the way for its NT usage. In the NT the term appears once as "Belial" (or Beliar in 2 Cor 6:15) and is identified with Satan, the personification of all that is evil. Noncanonical writings of the NT period commonly used it as a name for Satan or the antichrist.

Belief, Believe. Conviction based on testimony that something is true or that someone is reliable. As used in the Bible, to believe in God involves the element of trust, not mere acknowledgment of his existence.

See FAITH.

Believers. Those who believe; in the NT, specifically, those who believe in Jesus as Lord and follow him (Acts 5:14).

See CHRISTIANS, NAMES FOR.

Bell. Small noisemaker. Bells were intermittently attached between ornamental pomegranates around the lower hem of the high priestly robe (Ex 28:33,34; 39:25,26).

See MUSIC AND MUSICAL INSTRUMENTS (PAMONIM); PRIESTS AND LEVITES.

Belshazzar. Babylonian king who was co-regent with Nabonidus in the final days of the Babylonian empire. His name means "Bel protect the king." Daniel identifies him as the son of Nebuchadnezzar (Dn 5:2,11,13,18), though in fact he was the natural son of Nabunaid (Nabonidus). The seeming discrepancy arises from the fact that in Hebrew literature "father" may signify "ancestor" or "predecessor" and "son" may designate "descendant" or "successor in office." Some have concluded that Belshazzar's mother was a daughter of Nebuchadnezzar and that Belshazzar was therefore the grandson of the great Babylo-

The remains of the city walls of Babylon.

nian. Clearly his father, Nabunaid, was the son of a nobleman and the high priestess of the moon god at Harran. Nabunaid had usurped the throne in 555 BC.

A greater difficulty in the biblical text is the fact that Daniel presents Belshazzar as the king of Babylon when it fell to the Persians, whereas secular historical records picture Nabunaid as the last king of the Babylonian empire. Critical scholars have therefore questioned Daniel's accuracy. Inscriptions have now been found, however, which make it clear that Belshazzar's father entrusted the rule of the capital to him and was out of the city for over 10 years campaigning in Arabia. Religious concerns also took Nabunaid out of Babylon during part of his reign. When Cyrus invaded the Babylonian empire, Nabunaid marched east to meet him but fled before Cyrus's advancing armies. Later he returned to Babylon and surrendered to the Persians after the city had already fallen to Cyrus. Thus he was out of the city when the Persians overcame the royal forces there under the command of Belshazzar, the crown prince and co-regent.

While Nabunaid's armies were being routed by the Persians, Belshazzar was giving a sensual feast for the leaders of Babylonian society. Half drunk, he called for the gold and silver vessels from the Jerusalem temple to be brought in for use in a deliberate act of sacrilege. Immediately handwriting appeared on the wall, his doom was announced, and Per-

sian armies entered the city without a fight (October 12, 539 BC). They did so by diverting the waters of the Euphrates so the river would no longer serve as a moat around the city and its defenses could be easily breached.

HOWARD F. VOS

See DANIEL, BOOK OF; BABYLON, BABYLONIA.

Belteshazzar. Daniel's Babylonian name (Dn 1:7). Daniel was one of the young men taken captive to Babylon to be trained as counselors for King Nebuchadnezzar (Dn 1).

See DANIEL (PERSON) #3.

Bema. Judgment seat or tribunal of a Roman official. Although the term also means "to step" or "stride" (Acts 7:5, "a foot's

The ruins of the judgment seat of Gallio.

length"; cf. Dt 2:5), it was used in the first century primarily to denote an elevated area of platform (reached by steps) from which political orations or judicial decisions were made. Excavations in the city of Corinth have revealed a large, elaborately decorated *bema* located in the center of the marketplace.

In the NT, Jesus was questioned before the judgment seat of Pilate (Mt 27:19; Jn 19:13). Herod Agrippa I addressed the people of Tyre and Sidon from a *bema* (Acts 12:21, RSV throne). The apostle Paul was brought before the tribunal of Gallio in Corinth (Acts 18:12–17) and again before Festus' tribunal in Caesarea (Acts 25:6,10,17).

In two passages, Paul used the term to refer to God's judgment seat. In Romans 14:10 he warned those who would arrogantly judge others that all must stand before the tribunal of God. According to 2 Corinthians 5:10, the merits of each person's work will be determined before the judgment seat of Christ (cf. 1 Cor 3:13–15).

See JUDGMENT; JUDGMENT SEAT; LAST JUDGMENT.

Ben (Noun). Hebrew word often used as a prefix to describe a relationship. Literally meaning "son," it is found some 4,850 times in the OT. The Aramaic equivalent is *bar* (see Mt 16:17). *Ben* can be used in a variety of ways:

1. As a term for physical descendants and relatives (e.g., Gn 4:17), extending beyond a direct father-son relationship. It can even be used in regard to plants and animals (e.g., Jb 39:4).

2. As a term for "youths" (Prv 7:7) and "children" in a more general sense (Gn 21:10).

3. As a term showing one's relationship to a larger group, clan, or tribe (e.g., "sons of the prophets," 2 Kgs 2:15).

4. As a term indicating the relationship of a being, heavenly or earthly, to God (e.g., Gn 6:2; see RSV note, Ps 29:1).

5. As a term indicating age. Thus a male of 50 would be a "son of 50 years."

Ben (Person). Levite musician appointed by King David (1 Chr 15:18 KJV). The Masoretic text (the OT as annotated by medieval Hebrew scholars) and the KJV include the name Ben, but the Septuagint (ancient Greek translation of the OT), and RSV omit it because it is missing in verses 20 and 21. Since the Masoretic text also omits it in the later verses, the inclusion of Ben in verse 18 may be a scribal error.

Ben-abinadab. One of 12 officers appointed to requisition food for King Solomon's household. His administrative district comprised

the area around Naphath-dor, the coastal city south of Mt Carmel (1 Kgs 4:11, KJV son of Abinadab). The name means "son of Abinadab," and probably indicates that Ben-abinadab was the son of Solomon's uncle, Abinadab (1 Sm 16:8; 1 Chr 2:13).

Benaiah. Popular name meaning "the Lord has built," used primarily by Levites.

1. Son of Jehoiada the priest, from the south Judean town of Kabzeel. Benaiah was engaged in military service, and his loyalty gained for him the rank of commander in chief of the army during the reign of Solomon (1 Kgs 2:35; 4:4).

Before David became king, Benaiah distinguished himself in a number of daring military and protective feats to become one of the mighty men (2 Sm 23:20,22) during David's flight from King Saul. He attained command of "the thirty" (1 Chr 27:6), a group second only to "the three" of highest valor (2 Sm 23:23). He later had a high place in the armed forces when Joab was commander in chief and was placed over King David's elite troops, the Cherethites and Pelethites (2 Sm 8:18). He was also made third commander by David, with 24,000 men under him, and with annual responsibility for priestly service in the temple during the third month of the year (1 Chr 27:5,6).

Benaiah stayed loyal to David during the rebellion of Absalom (2 Sm 20:23; see 15:18) as well as during the attempt by Adonijah to seize David's throne (1 Kgs 1:8), and therefore had the privilege of assisting in Solomon's coronation at Gihon (1 Kgs 1:32–40). As army commander and chief bodyguard to Solomon he was responsible for executing Adonijah (1 Kgs 2:25), Joab (2:34), and Shimei (2:46) by orders of the new king.

2. Warrior from the town of Pirathon who was among David's mighty men known as "the thirty" (2 Sm 23:30; 1 Chr 11:31). Benaiah commanded the 11th division of the army in the rotation system established by David (1 Chr 27:14).

3. Prince in Simeon's tribe who participated in the conquest of Gedor during Hezekiah's reign (1 Chr 4:36).

4. Levitical musician who played the harp when King David brought the ark to Jerusalem (1 Chr 15:18,20). Afterward he was appointed to minister daily before the ark under the direction of Asaph (1 Chr 16:6).

5. Priestly musician who blew the trumpet before the ark when King David brought it to Jerusalem (1 Chr 15:24). Afterward he was appointed to play regularly before the ark (1 Chr 16:6).

6. Father of Jehoiada, King David's coun-

selor after the death of Ahithophel (1 Chr 27:34; see also 2 Sm 17:1–14,23).

7. Levite, Asaph's descendant and grandfather of Jahaziel (2 Chr 20:14). Jahaziel delivered an encouraging prophecy to King Jehoshaphat of Judah before his battle against the Moabites and Ammonites (2 Chr 20:1–29).

8. Levite appointed by King Hezekiah to help oversee the tithes and contributions brought to the temple (2 Chr 31:13).

9. Parosh's son (or descendant), who obeyed Ezra's exhortation to divorce his pagan wife after the Babylonian exile (Ezr 10:25).

10. Pahath-moab's son (or descendant), who also obeyed Ezra's exhortation to divorce his pagan wife after the exile (Ezr 10:30).

11. Bani's son (or descendant), another who divorced his pagan wife after the exile (Ezr 10:35).

12. Nebo's son (or descendant), who also divorced his pagan wife after the exile (Ezr 10:43).

13. Pelatiah's father (Ez 11:1,13). Pelatiah was a prince of the people of Israel during the time of the prophet Ezekiel.

LOUIS GOLDBERG

Ben-ammi. Son born to Lot and his younger daughter. A similar incestuous liaison between Lot and his older daughter produced a son named Moab. The two sons are identified as the ancestral heads of the Ammonite and Moabite peoples (Gn 19:38).

Although the promise made to Abraham could have been enjoyed by Lot (Gn 11:31; 12:1–4), Lot went his own way (13:2–12) and failed to trust the Lord (19:15–23,30). Lot's relationship to Abraham, however, evoked deferential treatment by the Israelites (Dt 2:8–19) toward these occasionally powerful enemies (2 Chr 20:1–12).

See AMMON, AMMONITES.

Ben-deker. One of 12 officers appointed to requisition food for King Solomon's household (1 Kgs 4:9, KJV son of Dekar). Ben-deker's administrative district comprised an area along the southern border of Dan's tribe near Beth-shemesh.

Bene-berak. One of the cities of Dan (Jos 19:45). The modern name is Ibn Ibrak, a suburb northwest of Tel Aviv.

Benediction. Pronouncement of God's favor upon an assembled congregation (Gn 27:27–29; Lk 24:50; 2 Cor 13:11,14).

See BLESS, BLESSING.

Bene-jaakan. Place where Israel camped near Edom's border (Nm 33:31,32; Dt 10:6).

See BE-EROTH BENE-JAAKAN.

Ben-geber. Literally, "Geber's son," an official in King Solomon's court who administered the sixth of 12 districts. Ben-geber's area of responsibility began at Ramoth-gilead in northern Transjordan and extended north as far as Argob in Bashan (1 Kgs 4:13). His identification with Geber, son of Uri (1 Kgs 4:19), is debatable.

Ben-hadad. Title of two or possibly three kings of Syria, meaning "son of Hadad." Hadad was the Syrian storm god probably identical with Rimmon (2 Kgs 5:18).

1. Ben-hadad I, son of Tabrimmon and grandson of Hezion. In spite of a history of Syrian hostility to Israel, Ben-hadad I entered into an alliance with King Baasha (908–886 BC) of the northern kingdom of Israel (1 Kgs 15:18–20). The pact was broken, however, when continuing hostilities between Israel and the southern kingdom of Judah erupted into a major encounter. Baasha conducted a major campaign against King Asa (910–869 BC) of Judah. In order to cut off infiltration into his kingdom and defection to the southern kingdom, Baasha fortified the city of Ramah, situated north of Jerusalem but uncomfortably close to it. His action extended Israel's territory into Judah.

In the face of that threat, Asa sent his remaining wealth to Ben-hadad I, asking him to break his pact with Baasha (1 Kgs 15:18,19). The Syrian king took advantage of the offer and sent his armies against Israel. He conquered the cities of Ijon, Dan, and Abel-beth-maacah plus the territory of Naphtali (1 Kgs 15:20), thus ensuring Syrian control of the main caravan routes through Galilee. Baasha was forced to abandon Ramah and move to Tirzah. Asa then conscripted the population of Judah to dismantle and carry off the fortifications erected by Baasha. Materials taken from Ramah were used to help build Geba in the territory of Benjamin. Asa's victory became the subject of a prophetic protest by Hanani, who berated Asa for his reliance on the king of Syria (1 Kgs 16:7).

2. Ben-hadad II. The biblical accounts in 1 Kings and 2 Chronicles do not make a clear differentiation between Ben-hadad I and II. Some scholars have therefore identified them as a single person. This view finds apparent support in the "Melqart Stele," which mentions Ben-hadad and to which a date of about 850 BC has been assigned. It seems better, however, to posit a Ben-hadad II who was the son of Ben-hadad I. If one does not distinguish be-

tween the two, Ben-hadad's activity must overlap both the reign of Ahab (874–853 BC) and that of Baasha. In each, a military encounter with Ben-hadad was recorded; one must posit an interval of up to four decades between the encounters if no distinction is made.

Ben-hadad II led a coalition of armies against Samaria during the reign of King Ahab of Israel. In the course of the siege, Ben-hadad demanded that Ahab surrender his wealth, wives, and children to him. Ahab agreed to that demand, but when Ben-hadad added the condition that he be given anything that his aides laid their hands on, Ahab refused on advice of his counselors. His refusal enraged Ben-hadad.

An anonymous prophet predicted that Ahab would defeat the armies of Ben-hadad (1 Kgs 20:13). Ahab's victory came when aides of the district governors killed the soldiers who had come out of the Syrian camp to take them captive. The Syrian forces fled. Ben-hadad was again defeated by the Israelites the next year when he attempted to engage them in battle on the plain rather than in the hill country. His reason was his belief that the "gods" of the Israelites were gods of the hills (1 Kgs 20:23). That Syrian defeat was also predicted by a prophet, who declared its cause to be Ben-hadad's misconception of the nature of Israel's God (1 Kgs 20:28).

Ben-hadad pleaded for his life, promising to restore all the cities his father had taken from Israel. Ahab agreed, but his action met with prophetic protest (1 Kgs 20:35–43). The pact established by the two kings brought about a cessation of hostilities that lasted only three years. The peace was broken by Ahab, who, at the instigation of King Jehoshaphat of Judah, sought to regain the city of Ramoth-gilead. Guidance was first sought from a group of prophets who predicted victory. Micaiah, however, a true prophet, predicted defeat (1 Kgs 22:5–28). Ahab's forces were defeated, and Ahab died in battle (vv 29–36).

Ben-hadad also figured in the life of the prophet Elisha, whom he sought to capture (2 Kgs 6:11–19). The attempt was thwarted when the Syrian army was stricken with blindness.

3. Ben-hadad III, son of King Hazael of Syria. This Ben-hadad was not related to Ben-hadad I or II but adopted the name. Because Jehoahaz (814–798 BC), king of Israel, did not follow the Lord, God allowed Israel to come under the control of Ben-hadad III. Release from the oppression of Ben-hadad III was accomplished by a "savior" (2 Kgs 13:5), probably a reference to Assyrian incursions into Syria.

THOMAS E. MCCOMISKEY

See SYRIA, SYRIANS; ISRAEL, HISTORY OF.

Ben-hail. One of five officials sent out by King Jehoshaphat of the southern kingdom of Judah to teach the people the Law of the Lord (2 Chr 17:7).

Ben-hanan. Shimon's son of Judah's tribe (1 Chr 4:20).

Benhesed. One of the 12 officers appointed to requisition food for King Solomon's household (1 Kgs 4:10, KJV son of Hesed). His administrative district comprised an area south and west of Arubboth in the western part of Manasseh's tribe.

Ben-Hur. One of 12 officers appointed to requisition food for King Solomon's household (1 Kgs 4:8, KJV son of Hur). His district was the hill country of Ephraim.

Beninu. Levite who signed Ezra's covenant of faithfulness to God with Nehemiah and others after the exile (Neh 10:13).

Benjamin (Person). 1. Youngest of Jacob's 12 sons and full brother to Joseph. Jacob named him Benjamin ("son of my right hand") after his dying mother Rachel had called him Ben-oni ("son of my sorrow," Gn 35:18). After Joseph had been sold into Egypt by his half-brothers, their father, Jacob, assumed that Joseph was lost and became very protective of Benjamin. Later, with Joseph controlling the plot, Benjamin was used in the reunion in Egypt of Jacob and his 12 sons (Gn 42–45). When prophesying concerning each of his sons, Jacob spoke of Benjamin's skill as a warrior or prophesied of the military fame of his descendants by saying, "Benjamin is a ravenous wolf, in the morning devouring the prey, and at even dividing the spoil" (Gn 49:27).

See BENJAMIN, TRIBE OF.

2. Bilhan's son and Jacob's greatgrandson (1 Chr 7:10).

3. Member of Harim's clan of the postexilic community who married a pagan wife (Ezr 10:32).

4. One who repaired a section of the wall next to his own house (Neh 3:23).

5. One of the company of Jews who participated in the dedication of the wall at Jerusalem (Neh 12:34). May possibly be the same as #4 above.

GERARD VAN GRONINGEN

Benjamin, Gate of. One of the gates in Jerusalem's old wall. The Gate of Benjamin was probably at the northeast corner, since the prophet Jeremiah passed through it on his way to Benjamin's territory northeast of Jerusalem (Jer 37:12,13). On at least one occasion King Zedekiah held court there (Jer 38:7). It was essentially opposite the west wall's Corner Gate (Zec 14:10). When the walls of Jerusalem were rebuilt at the end of the exile, a new gate known as the Sheep Gate (Neh 3:1,32) or possibly the Muster Gate (Neh 3:31) may have been at the same site. Some scholars think there were two Benjamin Gates, the other being an entrance to the temple. It seems more likely that the Benjamin Gate referred to in Jeremiah 20:2 was near the temple rather than part of the temple.

See JERUSALEM.

Benjamin, Tribe of. One of the smallest of the 12 tribes of Israel, made up of descendants of Jacob's youngest son (Nm 1:36). In the OT the tribe is often referred to as simply "Benjamin." Though small, the tribe of Benjamin played an important role in Israelite history, particularly in their conduct as great warriors (Jgs 20:13–16; 1 Chr 12:1,2).

At the Israelite conquest of Canaan, after the tribes of Judah and Ephraim had received their territory, the first lot came to Benjamin. The tribe was allotted territory between Judah and Ephraim, a strip of land between Mt Ephraim and the Judean hills. The southern boundary with Judah was clearly defined: through the valley of Hinnom immediately south of Jerusalem to a point north of the Dead Sea. Its eastern limit was the Jordan, and its northern boundary with Ephraim ran from the Jordan to Bethel, to Ataroth-addar south of Lower Beth-horon (Jos 18:11–20).

Benjamin's territory extended about 28 miles from west to east and 12 miles north to south. It was hilly country, strategically located to control key passes, but with fertile hill basins. Among its hill settlements were the important towns of Jerusalem, Jericho, Bethel, Gibeon, Gibeah, and Mizpeh (Jos 18:21–28). Not all of its towns were immediately taken from their previous possessors; Jerusalem, for example, was in the hands of the Jebusites until David's time. The environment bred a hardy race of highlanders, well described in Jacob's blessing of Benjamin as "a ravenous wolf" (Gn 49:27).

Ehud of Benjamin was one of the early judges in Canaan, a "savior" of the Israelites who killed Eglon, king of Moab (Jgs 3:15). Members of the tribe later helped Deborah and Barak defeat Sisera (Jgs 5:14). The tribe continued to produce great men: political leaders (1 Chr 27:21), captains in Saul's army (2 Sm 4:2) and David's army (2 Sm 23:29), skilled archers (1 Chr 8:40), and overseers in Solomon's labor force (1 Kgs 4:18).

Less noble traits were also shown by Benja-

min's descendants. Palti, a Benjamite, was one of the scouts making a bad report when the 12 spies returned from the land of Canaan (Nm 13:1,2,9,31–33). The tribe as a whole displayed disobedience and lack of consistent courage by failing to clear their inheritance of Canaanites (Jgs 1:21). Following the custom of the day, the whole tribe defended the lewd treatment and murder of a concubine from another tribe by a few of their members (Jgs 19,20). That act of gross immorality united the other tribes against them, and the tribe of Benjamin was almost decimated. To keep the tribe from dying out the other tribes allowed the Benjamites to take captive several hundred women who then became their wives (Jgs 21).

Three members of the tribe who lived in the early days of the monarchy receive special attention. Saul, the first Israelite king, was a rustic, impetuous, and egotistic descendant of Benjamin. Although the Lord let Israel have a king like the other nations, from the very beginning Saul gave evidence of lacking the qualifications of a shepherd of God's people. Saul hid when he was to be publicly anointed; went home after his anointing; showed jealousy against David, impatience when waiting for Samuel, and boldness in performing an unwarranted priestly duty; spared Agag and much Amalekite spoil; and continued to try to kill David (1 Sm 9–31). During King David's flight from Absalom, a member of Saul's family named Shimei is mentioned as cursing David (2 Sm 16:5) but later welcoming him back and helping him (2 Sm 19:16–23). A third member of Benjamin's tribe mentioned in the same period was Sheba, described as a hothead who led a short-lived rebellion against David after Absalom's rebellion failed (2 Sm 20:1–22).

Benjamin's tribe proved to be dependable in various ways. During the exodus from Egypt, it took its place in the organization (Nm 1:11) and the army (Nm 2:22) and made its tribal offerings (Nm 7:60). It demonstrated remarkable loyalty to the throne, initially to Saul and his family (2 Sm 2:8–31). Later David received its faithful support, as did his descendants, for Benjamin remained with Judah, loyal to Solomon's son Rehoboam when Jeroboam led a secession (1 Kgs 12:21–24).

Other men of Benjamin (often called Benjamites KJV) spoken of in the OT include Cush, of whom David sang (Ps 7 superscription); Jeremiah the prophet, who, though a Levite, lived within Benjamin's tribe (Jer 1:1; 32:8); and Mordecai, uncle and adviser to Queen Esther (Est 2:5).

In the NT the apostle Paul made no apologies for his ancestry, twice referring to himself as a Hebrew of Benjamin's tribe (Rom 11:1; Phil 3:5). In his sermon at Antioch of Pisidia,

Paul also mentioned Benjamin as the tribe of King Saul, in his brief account of Israel's history (Acts 13:21). In one other NT reference Benjamin is named with the other 11 tribes in John's apocalyptic vision (Rv 7:8).

See BENJAMIN (PERSON) #1.

Benjamite.   Member of Benjamin's tribe.

See BENJAMIN, TRIBE OF.

Beno.   Jaaziah's son in a list of Levites assigned to temple duty (1 Chr 24:26,27). It is possible that the Hebrew word is not a proper name; it has sometimes been translated "his son."

Ben-oni.   Name Rachel gave to her last son as she died in childbirth (Gn 35:18). His father Jacob changed his name from Ben-oni ("son of my sorrow") to Benjamin ("son of my right hand").

See BENJAMIN (PERSON) #1.

Ben-zoheth.   Ishi's son from Judah's tribe (1 Chr 4:20).

Beon.   Alternate name for Baal-meon, a city east of the Jordan, in Numbers 32:3.

See BAAL-MEON.

Beor.   1. Bela's father (Gn 36:32). Bela was a king of Edom.
2. Balaam's father (Nm 22:5; 2 Pt 2:15; KJV Bosor). Balaam was asked by Balak, king of Moab, to curse Israel.

Bera.   Ruler of Sodom in the days of Abraham and Lot. Bera was one of five Canaanite city-kings who unsuccessfully rebelled against King Chedorlaomer of Elam and his three allies (Gn 14:2).

Beracah, Berachah.   Warrior from Benjamin's tribe who joined David at Ziklag in his struggle against King Saul. Beracah was one of David's ambidextrous archers and slingers (1 Chr 12:3, KJV Berachah).

Beracah (Berachah), Valley of.   Place where King Jehoshaphat gathered the people of Judah to praise the Lord (2 Chr 20:26). The people were grateful for God's help in defeating the attacking armies of Moab, Ammon, and Mt Seir (2 Chr 20:1–25). It is most often identified with the area Wadi el 'Arrub, not far from Tekoa, where a ruin called Bereikut exists.

Berachiah.   KJV spelling of Berechiah, Asaph's father, in 1 Chronicles 6:39.

See BERECHIAH #2.

Beraiah.   One of Shimei's sons from Benjamin's tribe (1 Chr 8:21).

Berea.   1. Place in Palestine north of Jerusalem, where the Syrian army camped before launching an attack that killed Judas Maccabeus in 161 BC (1 Mc 9:4). Its exact location is uncertain.
2. Common spelling of Beroea (by numerous modern versions), a Macedonian city visited by Paul, in Acts 17:10,13; 20:4.

See BEROEA.

Berechiah.   1. Son of Zerubbabel and descendant of King David (1 Chr 3:20).
2. Levite, Gershon's descendant and father of Asaph (1 Chr 6:39, KJV Berachiah; 15:17). Asaph was a famous musician of Israel.
3. Asa's son and head of a family of Levites who returned to Judah after the Babylonian exile (1 Chr 9:16).
4. Levite appointed by King David as gatekeeper for the ark of the covenant (1 Chr 15:23).
5. Meshillemoth's son, a leader of Ephraim's tribe. He was one of three men in Samaria who supported the prophet Obed in sending prisoners of war back to their homes in Judah (2 Chr 28:12).
6. Meshullam's father. Meshullam assisted Nehemiah, the governor, in rebuilding the wall of Jerusalem (Neh 3:4,30; 6:18).
7. Iddo's son and father of Zechariah the prophet (Zec 1:1,7; Mt 23:35).

Bered (Person).   Alternate name for Becher, one of Ephraim's sons, in 1 Chronicles 7:20.

See BECHER #2.

Bered (Place).   Unknown site in Israel's southern Negeb desert region. God spoke to Sarai's maid Hagar at a well between Kadesh and Bered (Gn 16:14).

Beri.   Zophah's son, head of a subclan. Beri was a skilled warrior (1 Chr 7:36,40) listed with Asher's descendants (1 Chr 7:30).

Beriah.   1. Asher's son, who migrated to Egypt with his family, relatives, and grandfather Jacob (Gn 46:17). His descendants were called Beriites (Nm 26:44).
2. Ephraim's youngest son, born after several of his brothers were killed at Gath for cattle rustling (1 Chr 7:20–23).
3. Elpaal's son, head of a family in Benja-

min's tribe. This Beriah lived at Aijalon and helped repel invaders from Gath (1 Chr 8:13).

4. Shimei's son, a Levite of Gershon's clan who served in the temple at Jerusalem. Because neither Beriah nor his brother Jeush had many sons, their families were counted as a single subclan in the levitical system (1 Chr 23:10,11).

Beriite. Member of a family descended from Beriah, one of Asher's sons (Nm 26:44).

See BERIAH #1.

Berite. KJV rendering of Bichrite, a descendant of Bichri, in 2 Samuel 20:14.

See BICHRI, BICHRITE.

Bernice. Eldest daughter of Herod Agrippa I. Bernice was present during the apostle Paul's speech before her brother, King Agrippa II (Acts 25:13,23; 26:30). Bernice (also spelled Berenice) was born *c.* AD 28. At 13 she married Marcus, son of the Jewish official Alexander. After her husband's death her father betrothed her to his elder brother, Herod of Chalcis. Two sons, Bernicianus and Hyrcanus, were born to them before her second husband's death in AD 48. When the young widow's relationship with her brother, Agrippa II, deepened, there were rumors of incest. In defense, Bernice persuaded Polemo, king of Cilicia, to marry her but left him shortly afterward.

In AD 66 Bernice bravely but unsuccessfully appealed to the mad Roman procurator Gessius Florus not to ransack the temple in Jerusalem. She was at her brother's side when he warned the people against war. When war broke out that year Jewish rebels set fire to her palace as well as to her brother's. Agrippa and Bernice then swore an oath of allegiance to the Roman emperor, Vespasian.

Berodach-baladan. KJV spelling of Merodach-baladan, the king of Babylon during the reign of Judah's King Hezekiah, in 2 Kings 20:12.

See MERODACH-BALADAN.

Beroea. Ancient city of Macedonia (a region now divided among Greece, Yugoslavia, and Bulgaria), probably founded in the 5th century BC. The city was approximately 25 miles inland from the Aegean Sea on a scenic and fertile plain 600 feet high in the foothills north of the Olympian range. Conquered by Rome in 168 BC, Beroea (alternately spelled Berea in numerous English translations) was one of the most populous Macedonian cities in the time of Christ. Today the city is known as Verria.

Beroea was visited by the apostle Paul on his second missionary journey (Acts 17:10–15) and was the home of Sopater, Paul's companion (Acts 20:4). Paul and Silas left Thessalonica when violent religious and political opposition arose and went to Beroea, 50 miles southwest. There both Jews and Greeks eagerly received the gospel, but Paul had to leave the city when angry Jews arrived from Thessalonica to stir up trouble.

Berothah, Berothai. City between Damascus and Hamath mentioned by the prophet Ezekiel as lying on the northern border of the restored Israel (Ez 47:16). Berothah is probably the same as Berothai, a city captured by David (2 Sm 8:8; called Cun in 1 Chr 18:8).

Berothite. KJV form of Be-erothite, an inhabitant of Be-eroth, in 1 Chronicles 11:39.

See BE-EROTH, BEEROTH.

Berry. Fleshy fruit, usually with many seeds and having no stony seed covering.

See PLANTS (BRAMBLE; CAPER PLANT).

Beryl. Hard, lustrous mineral of various colors, mentioned in the Bible as a gemstone (Ex 28:20; Rv 21:20).

See MINERALS, METALS, AND PRECIOUS STONES.

Besai. Ancestor of a group of temple assistants that returned to Jerusalem with Zerubbabel after the Babylonian exile (Ezr 2:49; Neh 7:52).

Besodeiah. Meshullam's father. Along with Joiada, Meshullam helped rebuild a portion of the Jerusalem wall after the exile in Babylonia.

Besom. Old English word meaning "broom" (Is 14:23 KJV). The besom, or broom, of destruction is a Near Eastern metaphor signifying total destruction. It refers to the annihilation or "sweeping away" of Babylon by the Lord.

Besor, Brook of. Brook that David crossed to pursue the Amalekites southward after they had raided Ziklag, his home base. Exhausted, 200 of David's men remained at the brook while the other 400 overtook and defeated the enemy (1 Sm 30:9,10,21).

Betah. Alternate name for Tibhath, a town in the city-kingdom of Aram-zobah, subjugated by King David, in 2 Samuel 8:8.

See TIBHATH.

Beten. City allotted to Asher's tribe for an inheritance, mentioned between Hali and Achshaph (Jos 19:25). Its site is unknown.

Bethabara. Village where messengers from the Pharisees questioned John the Baptist (Jn 1:28 KJV). Modern translations have "Bethany" instead of Bethabara in accordance with older and more widely distributed Greek manuscripts. John called it Bethany "beyond the Jordan" to distinguish it from the Bethany near Jerusalem.

See BETHANY #2.

Beth-anath. Town assigned to Naphtali's tribe (Jos 19:38) from which the tribe failed to drive out the original inhabitants (Jgs 1:33).

The Israelites, who often made slaves of the remaining Canaanite people, were in many cases eventually corrupted by their pagan religious practices.

Beth-anoth. Village in the hill country assigned to Judah's tribe after the Israelite conquest of Canaan (Jos 15:59). It was probably the location of an ancient Canaanite altar, since Anath was a Canaanite fertility goddess and consort of Baal. It has been identified as modern Khirbet Beit Ainun.

Bethany. 1. Village on the eastern slope of the Mt of Olives about a mile and a half east of Jerusalem. Jesus and his disciples sometimes stayed in Bethany when in Judea, as when

The ruins of Bethany.

they attended temple observances during Passover (Mt 21:17; Mk 11:11). Jesus was eating at the home of Simon the leper in Bethany when a woman came and anointed his head with costly perfume (Mt 26:6–13; Mk 14:3–9). Bethany was also the home of Mary and Martha and their brother Lazarus, where Jesus raised Lazarus from the dead (Jn 11:1,18). The village was near Bethphage on an approach to Jerusalem (Mk 11:1; Lk 19:29) that Jesus followed in preparation for his triumphal entry into Jerusalem. In Bethany Jesus blessed his disciples after the resurrection and parted from them (Lk 24:50).

Today the town is called el-Azariyeh (the place of Lazarus) by its Arab population.

2. Village on "the other side of the Jordan" (the east side), where John the Baptist baptized (Jn 1:28). The KJV has "Bethabara," found in many manuscripts and thought correct by the 3rd-century church father Origen, who suggested that Bethabara meant "house of preparation," an appropriate location for John's ministry. The most logical site for this Bethany is the present-day Qasr el-Yehud.

Beth-arabah. One of six cities in the wilderness southeast of Jericho on the boundary between the territories of Judah and Benjamin (Jos 15:6,61; 18:22). The modern Ain Gharbeh in the Wadi el-Quelt may be the site of Beth-arabah.

Beth-aram. KJV rendering of Beth-haram, a Gadite town, in Joshua 13:27.

See BETH-HARAM, BETH-HARAN.

Beth-arbel. Town whose violent destruction at the hands of the Assyrians was compared by the prophet Hosea to Ephraim's forthcoming destruction (Hos 10:14). Betharbel is most commonly identified with present-day Irbid in Gilead, located at an important crossroads in northern Transjordan.

Beth-ashbea. Place where certain families descended from Judah were known for their production of linen (1 Chr 4:21). The KJV renders "Ashbea" as a family name rather than a place of residence. Its location is unknown.

Beth-aven. 1. Town in Benjamin's territory, located west of Michmash on the border of the wilderness, near Ai, to the east of Bethel (Jos 7:2; 18:12; 1 Sm 13:5; 14:23).

2. Term used by Hosea contemptuously to refer to Bethel, an ancient center of worship, because the "House of God" (Bethel) had become a "House of wickedness" (Beth-Aven or just Aven; Hos 4:15; 5:8; 10:5).

See AVEN #2.

Beth-azmaveth. Alternate name for Azmaveth, a town near Jerusalem, in Nehemiah 7:28.

See AZMAVETH (PLACE).

Beth-baal-meon. Alternate name for Baalmeon, a city in Reuben's territory, in Joshua 13:17.

See BAAL-MEON.

Beth-barah. Place where warriors of Ephraim's tribe under Gideon tried to block the retreat of the Midianites over the Jordan River (Jgs 7:24). Many scholars feel that originally the text read "the fords of Jordan" instead of "Beth-bara and (also) the Jordan."

Beth-biri, Beth-birei. Alternate name for Lebaoth, a city in Judah's southern territory (1 Chr 4:31, KJV Beth-birei).

See LEBAOTH.

Beth-car. Place in Benjamin's territory to which a Philistine army was pursued by the Israelites after the second battle of Ebenezer (1 Sm 7:11). Its location is unknown.

Beth-dagon. Shrine of the Philistine and Canaanite god Dagon mentioned in several sources other than the Bible. A fortress called Dagon near Jericho was mentioned by the Jewish historian Josephus, for example. Many Canaanite locations may have been known for their shrines to Dagon.

1. Town in Judah's lowlands (Jos 15:41). This Beth-dagon was mentioned both by Rameses III of Egypt and by Sennacherib of Assyria (701 BC) as having been captured by them.

2. Town on the border of Asher's territory, east of Mt Carmel (Jos 19:27).

3. Temple in Ashdod (1 Sm 5:1; called Azotus in 1 Mc 10:83,84).

Beth-diblathaim. Town in Moab (Jer 48:22), and probably identical with Almon-diblathaim.

See ALMON-DIBLATHAIM.

Beth-eden. Small Aramaean (Syrian) state north of Damascus. Assyria conquered Betheden and deported its people to Kir (2 Kgs 16:9), fulfilling the prediction in Amos 1:5 (KJV house of Eden). Beth-eden, which means "house of delight," is sometimes equated with the Eden of Ezekiel 27:23, the location of which is unknown. Its inhabitants are referred to as the "children of Eden" in 2 Kings 19:12 (KJV).

Beth-eked. Place between Jezreel and Samaria where Jehu slew Ahaziah's kinsmen at a pit or cistern (2 Kgs 10:12,14, KJV shearing house).

Bethel (God). Pagan deity mentioned in ancient texts and thought by some to have biblical reference (Jer 48:13; Am 5:5; Zec 7:2).

See Canaanite Deities and Religion.

Bethel, Bethelite (City). 1. Important OT city located about 11 miles north of Jerusalem on the north-south ridge road at the tribal borders of Benjamin and Ephraim (Jos 16:1,2; 18:13). As a trading center Bethel attracted merchandise both from the Mediterranean coast and from Transjordan via Jericho. Although the site was located in dry hill country, several springs supplied ample water for its inhabitants (the oldest artifact recovered from the site is a water jar dating about 3500 BC).

The name of Bethel, meaning "house of El (god)," may have been used as early as the 4th millennium BC by Canaanites in the area. Archaeological excavations at Chalcolithic levels (i.e., between the Stone Age and the Bronze Age) indicate that pagan worship of the Canaanite deity El took place on top of the hill at that early period. The patriarch Jacob named the place Bethel, or gave the old name new significance, after having a dream from God there (Gn 28:10–22). The site was said to be known as Bethel to the patriarch Abraham (Gn 12:8); that designation, however, could be a scribal updating of a more ancient local name, since Bethel had earlier been known as Luz (Gn 28:19). Possibly the sanctuary was known as Bethel, the nearby settlement as Luz. No doubt the name Bethel was firmly established by the beginning of the Interme-

Panorama of the city of Bethel.

diate Bronze Age (*c.* 2200 BC) and remained throughout its history. An OT passage mentioning both names records that a man from Luz founded another city of that name in Hittite territory (Jgs 1:26).

Bethel was first identified with modern Beitîn by Edward Robinson in 1838. Subsequent evacations by W.F. Albright between 1927 and 1934 and by J.L. Kelso between 1954 and 1960 have not refuted that identification. Another site two miles south of Beitîn has been suggested by David Livingston, but that area (el-Bireh) has not yet been excavated.

Bethel, one of the earliest settlements of ancient Canaan, was occupied intermittently during the Early Bronze Age (*c.* 3200–2200 BC) with continuous settlement occurring early in the Middle Bronze Age (*c.* 2200–1550 BC). The activities of the Hebrew patriarchs belong to that later period. Excavations show that Bethel was well established when Abraham and Jacob visited the area. During the Middle Bronze Age the city was surrounded by a substantial wall with several gates. In the ruins of a pagan sanctuary dating from that period, many animal bones were found along with pottery vessels used in religious rituals.

Evidence of destruction about 1550 BC suggests Egyptian conquest of Bethel in the late Hyksos period. A rebuilding phase in the 14th and 13th centuries BC was the most developed architectural period in Bethel's history. For archaeologists, Joshua's capture of Bethel (Jos 12:7,16) and Ai (Jos 8:1–29) marks the transition to the Iron Age; Israelite structures erected on the ruins of Bethel were inferior in quality and workmanship.

Although Bethel was assigned to Benjamin's tribe, Ephraim's tribe actually captured Bethel from its Canaanite fortress in their own territory (Jgs 1:22–26; 1 Chr 7:28). Under the judges, the ark of the covenant was located at Bethel, where the normal functions of Israelite worship were carried out; the ark was superintended by the high priest Phinehas, son of Eleazar (Jgs 20:18–28; 21:2,4). There is no archaeological evidence of Philistine occupation of Bethel in the time of the judges; in the days of King Saul it was bypassed when other Israelite centers were being attacked (cf. 1 Sm 12–14). Archaeological discoveries indicate that Bethel flourished in the early reign of Saul but declined when he made Gibeah his capital city.

When Israel and Judah became separate entities in the time of Jeroboam I (930–909 BC), Bethel returned to prominence as the capital of the northern kingdom of Israel, thus becoming the counterpart of Judah's capital, Jerusalem. Bethel was one of two northern cities where golden calves were worshiped (1 Kgs

12:28–33); the sanctuary area for that cultic practice has not been discovered. The city was the home of an elderly prophet (1 Kgs 13:11) who may have been connected with the prophetic colony existing there in the time of Elijah and Elisha (2 Kgs 2:2,3). During the reign of Judah's king Abijah (913–910 BC), Bethel fell under Judah's control (2 Chr 13:19) but later was returned to Israel. The prophet Amos went to Bethel to deliver scathing denunciations about contemporary social and religious life in Israel, for which the priest Amaziah had him expelled (Am 7:10–13).

There is no archaeological evidence that Bethel was destroyed during the Assyrian conquest of Israel (722 BC). In fact, one of its deported priests was returned to Bethel to instruct Mesopotamian colonists in the ways of the Lord (2 Kgs 17:28). Under Judah's king Josiah the pagan shrine was demolished (2 Kgs 23:15–20), but no damage was done to the city itself. Under either Nabonidus (555–539 BC) or Darius I (521–486 BC), however, the city was burned, so that by Ezra's time Bethel had reverted to a small village settlement (Ezr 2:28).

Prosperity returned to Bethel during the Hellenistic period, as the quality artifacts from that time indicate. Bethel was fortified by Bacchides (1 Mc 9:50) and was prosperous in the Maccabean era. Some construction took place in the northern part of the city in the early Roman period, perhaps under Emperor Vespasian, and a Roman garrison was quartered there. The city was spared the destruction that overtook Jerusalem in AD 70, although Vespasian occupied it at that time. In the Byzantine era, Bethel attained its maximum size but declined suddenly at the end of that period when the population dispersed.

Though Bethel was strongly associated with early Hebrew religion, even to the extent that God was known as the "God of Bethel" (Gn 31:13), it always had a strong pagan element in the local cultic worship. That became especially prominent under Jeroboam I and persisted in spite of prophetic warnings. The Bethelites furnished a somber forecast of Israel's destiny by rejecting Elisha's prophetic message (2 Kgs 2:23). The mocking youths in that incident have been interpreted as representing Israel in its virility rejecting the prophet's words and God's Law on which they were based. In that view, two bears symbolized Assyria and Babylon, by whom the whole kingdom was to be ravaged—fulfilling the covenant curses for disobedience (Dt 28:15–66). The Bethelites did not assist in rebuilding postexilic Jerusalem, though they once inquired there about observing certain fasts (Zec 7:2). Bethel is not mentioned in the NT.

See CANAANITE DEITIES AND RELIGION.

2. Alternate name for Bethuel, a town in Judah's territory, in 1 Samuel 30:27.

See BETHUEL, BETHUL (PLACE).

R.K. HARRISON

Beth-emek. Town on the territorial boundary between the tribes of Asher and Zebulun (Jos 19:27). It has been identified with modern Tell Mimas.

Bether. Hebrew word occurring in the phrase "upon *rugged* mountains" and regarded as a proper name in KJV (mountains of Bether, Sg 2:17). Occurrence of the phrase "mountains of spices" in an almost identical verse (8:14) suggests "spices" or a particular spice (such as cinnamon) as an appropriate translation of *bether*. Bether also occurs as the name of a city in the hill country of Judah in Joshua 15:59 (but only in the Septuagint). In 1 Chronicles 6:59 the Septuagint reads "Bether" instead of "Bethshemesh." Some scholars identify this Bether with Khir-bet el-Jehudiyeh, southwest of Bittir, which may preserve the ancient name. It is unlikely that Bether is related to the phrase "mountains of Bether."

In AD 135, Bether became the site of the last Jewish stronghold against the Romans in the Second Revolt (AD 132–35). There, Simon Bar Kochba, the designated "messiah," and the Jewish forces were massacred.

Bethesda. Name of a pool in Jerusalem to which many sick and infirm people came (Jn 5:2 KJV). Variant Greek manuscripts read Beth-zatha (RSV).

See BETH-ZATHA.

Beth-ezel. One of several small towns, probably in southwest Judah, whose destruction was lamented by the prophet Micah (1:11).

Beth-gader. Town mentioned in connection with its founder, Hareph, a Calebite (1 Chr 2:51). It is possibly the same as Geder (Jos 12:13).

Beth-gamul. City of Moab against which Jeremiah prophesied God's judgment for their ill treatment of Israel (Jer 48:23). It has been identified as Khirbet Jumeil, located eight miles east of Dibon.

Beth-gilgal. Town from which levitical singers came to Jerusalem to celebrate the rebuilding of the wall under Nehemiah (Neh 12:29).

See GILGAL #1.

Beth-haccherem, Beth-haccerem. Town in the hilly area between Jerusalem and Bethlehem. The prophet Jeremiah referred to signal fires set at Beth-haccherem (KJV Beth-haccerem) to warn of invasion from the north (Jer 6:1). Malchijah is mentioned as a political leader in Beth-haccherem in Nehemiah's time (Neh 3:14). Its exact location is uncertain, but many scholars think it was at modern Ramat Rahel.

Beth-haggan. Town to which King Ahaziah of Judah fled for his life from Jehu of Israel (2 Kgs 9:27, KJV garden house). It has been identified as modern Jenin. Beth-haggan was probably the same as En-gannim.

Beth-haram, Beth-haran. Town given to Gad's tribe at the partitioning of Canaan (Jos 13:27, KJV Beth-aram). Fortified and used to accommodate sheep herds (Nm 32:36, Beth-haran), it is probably the same as Beth-aramphtha, a city mentioned by the Jewish historian Josephus.

Beth-hoglah, Beth-hogla. City allotted to Benjamin's tribe (Jos 18:21). It was southeast of Jericho near the mouth of the Jordan River on the boundary line between the territories of Judah and Benjamin (Jos 15:6, KJV Beth-hogla; 18:19). It is identified with modern Ain Hajlah.

See HOGLAH.

Beth-horon. Canaanite place-name perhaps meaning "the house of Hauron," the god of the underworld. Beth-horon was a dual settlement 10 and 12 miles northwest of Jerusalem. Upper Beth-horon is modern Beit 'Ûr al-Fôqâ; lower Beth-horon is Beit 'Ûr al-Tahtâ, at a lower altitude and almost 2 miles farther west. Located on the boundary between the tribal territories of Ephraim and Benjamin (Jos 16:3,5), the twin settlements controlled the valley of Aijalon, one of the most important ancient routes between the Mediterranean coast and the interior hill country. The upper town controlled a strategic pass. Ephraim's "Beth-horon with its pasture lands" was assigned to the Levite family of Kohath (Jos 21:22; 1 Chr 6:68).

Many armies marched through the Aijalon Valley. Amorites pursued by Joshua's army fled past Beth-horon after being defeated at Gibeon on "the day the sun stood still" (Jos 10:1–14). A band of Philistines approached it to make war with Saul (1 Sm 13:18). The Egyptian army of Shishak passed by Beth-horon (according to his Karnak inscription). Syrian armies under Seron (1 Mc 3:13–24) and Nicanor (1 Mc 7:39–43) were defeated by Judas Maccabeus at Beth-horon. The Romans under Cestius were nearly annihilated there by the Jews, according to Jewish historian Josephus.

Beth-horon was probably destroyed and rebuilt more than once. Sheerah, Beriah's daughter and Ephraim's granddaughter, is credited with building both lower and upper Beth-horon (1 Chr 7:24). King Solomon fortified both Beth-horons after raids in the vicinity by an Egyptian pharaoh (1 Kgs 9:15–17; 2 Chr 8:5). In the intertestamental period Beth-horon was fortified by the Syrian general Bacchides after a battle with Jonathan Maccabeus (1 Mc 9:50).

Sanballat, a leader in Samaria who resisted the rebuilding of Jerusalem after the exile, was called "the Horonite," that is, a native of Beth-horon (Neh 2:10). Beth-horon is mentioned in apocryphal and pseudepigraphal writings. The apocryphal book of Jubilees (34:4) mentions a king of Beth-horon in the patriarchal period who raided Jacob's flocks regularly. Daniel was born in upper Beth-horon, according to Pseudo-Epiphanius in *The Lives of the Prophets*. In the book of Judith (4:4), the town is mentioned as being in Jewish hands when the Assyrian general Holofernes attacked Judea.

JAMES M. HOUSTON *and* R.K. HARRISON

Beth-jeshimoth, Beth-jesimoth. City assigned to Reuben's tribe (Jos 13:20), later described as a Moabite town (Ez 25:9). Prior to Israel's conquest of the Promised Land they made camp along the Jordan from Beth-jeshimoth to Abel-shittim (Nm 33:49, KJV Beth-jesimoth). The city is usually identified with Tell el-Azeimeh.

See WILDERNESS WANDERINGS.

Beth-le-aphrah. Town mentioned by the prophet Micah. Beth-le-aphrah (KJV house of Aphrah) means "house of dust," so Micah made a sarcastic pun by telling its idolatrous inhabitants to "roll yourselves in the dust" (Mi 1:10). Its location is unknown.

The Valley of Aijalon and Lower Beth-horon—the scene of Joshua's "long day."

The Church of the Nativity in Bethlehem.

Beth-lebaoth. Alternate name for Lebaoth, a city of Simeon in the southern extremity of Judah's tribe, in Joshua 19:6.

See LEBAOTH.

Bethlehem. 1. "City of David" and the birthplace of Jesus Christ, five miles south of Jerusalem. This city is sometimes called Bethlehem-judah (KJV) or Ephrath (Gn 35:19; Mi 5:2) to distinguish it from the Bethlehem of Zebulun.

As an early Canaanite settlement it was associated with the patriarchs, for Rachel died and was buried in its vicinity (Gn 35:16,19; 48:7). The earliest known historical reference to Bethlehem occurs in the Amarna texts (14th century BC) in which battle reports refer to *bit-il u-lahama* south of Jerusalem. The name may

have meant "house of (the goddess) Lahama." A branch of Caleb's family settled there, and Caleb's son Salma was known as "the father of Bethlehem" (1 Chr 2:51). Bethlehem was the home of a young Levite who served as priest to Micah (Jgs 17:8), and of Boaz, Ruth, Obed, and Jesse, the Bethlehemite, David's father (Ru 4:11,17; 1 Sm 16:1,4).

Bethlehem was the birthplace of David (1 Sm 17:12) and the home of one of David's mighty men, Elhanan (2 Sm 23:24; 1 Chr 11:26). It was the scene of a daring exploit by three of David's warriors; they broke through the cordon of Philistine marauders occupying Bethlehem to bring David water from the well (or cistern) "near the city gate" of his hometown (2 Sm 23:14–17). Much later, Bethlehem is mentioned as being adjacent to the village of Geruth Chimham, where Jews fleeing from the Babylonians stayed en route to Egypt (Jer 41:17). People from Bethlehem were among those returning from the Babylonian exile (Ezr 2:21; Neh 7:26; 1 Esd 5:17).

When Jesus was born there in NT times, Bethlehem was only a village (Mt 2:1–16; Lk 2:4–6,15; Jn 7:42). It lay near the N-S highway connecting Jerusalem with Hebron to the south. A transverse route across the Judean hill country followed the Valley of Elah to Bethlehem, one of 7 such E-W roads. The central mountain ridge of Judea sloping E and W contracts from an average width of 8 miles to only 2 miles or less between Jerusalem and Bethlehem. This feature provided a natural borderland, Jerusalem being the most southerly border town of the northern region, and Bethlehem the most important northern border town of the southern area of Judea. So although it remained small, Bethlehem was never a daughter settlement of Jerusalem.

The arid Judean wilderness extended westward right to the gates of such cities as Jerusalem, Bethlehem, Tekoa, and Hebron, enhancing their strategic locations as outposts looking out on the desert. Bethlehem is situated on one of the highest summits of the Judean tableland. Its cultivated fields still occupy patches between the many ravines. Eastward, drought and desert nomads set the limit to cultivation, the land becoming pastureland. As an ecological borderland, wheat gave place to barley, a more drought-resistant grain (Ru 2:23). We know of shepherds in the area from stories of the boyhood of David (1 Sm 17:40) and of Christ's nativity (Lk 2:8). As a border garrison, Bethlehem guaranteed the independence of Judea; hence the efforts of the Philistines to control it (2 Sm 23:14) and of Rehoboam to fortify it further (2 Chr 11:6).

Under the census decree of Caesar Augustus, Joseph had to go to Bethlehem "because he was of the house and lineage of David" (Lk 2:4). The family may still have had property there. The birth of Jesus possibly took place in a cave in the rocks outside the town. The early Christian writer Justin Martyr (c. AD 150) thought so, as did Origen some years later. Origen frequently resided in Palestine and wrote, "In Bethlehem you are shown the cave where he was born, and within the cave the manger where he was wrapped in swaddling clothes."

Jerome later described the grotto over which the Emperor Constantine had built a basilica. In excavations in 1934–35, evidence indicated a second period of building in the reign of Justinian (527–65), when Constantine's basilica was extended beyond its original proportions. Steps lead down to the grotto, the rectangular shape of which suggests that Constantine's builders reshaped the original. But there is no description of the grotto prior to the construction of Constantine's basilica.

Attempts to identify the field of the shepherds where "the glory of the Lord shone around them" (Lk 2:9) have been futile. Tradition has suggested a site at the village of Beth-sahur, half a mile E of Bethlehem, about 500 yards E of the village in an olive-yard. Another site northeast of the village has also been proposed. The shepherds would probably have pastured in the fields of those settlements only in summer after harvest, and on the surrounding hills in the early spring after the winter rains, but the date of Christ's birth is unknown.

2. Town in Zebulun (Jos 19:15), probably the home of the judge Ibzan (Jgs 12:8,10), an early ruler of Israel. It is identified today with the village of Beit Lahm, some 7 miles NW of Nazareth.

JAMES M. HOUSTON

Bethlehemite. Inhabitant of Bethlehem of Judah (1 Sm 16:1,18; 17:58; 2 Sm 21:19).

See BETHLEHEM #1.

Beth-maacah, Beth-maachah. Alternate name for Abel-beth-maacah (KJV maachah) in 2 Samuel 10:14,15.

See ABEL (PLACE).

Beth-marcaboth. City in Judah's territory given to the tribe of Simeon (Jos 19:5; 1 Chr 4:31), possibly the same as Madmannah (Jos 15:31). The name Beth-marcaboth means "house of chariots," and consequently some have seen a link to the chariot cities of Solomon (1 Kgs 9:19; 10:26). Its location is unknown unless it can be identified with Madmannah.

Beth-meon. Alternate name for Baal-meon, a town formerly belonging to Reuben's tribe, in Jeremiah 48:23.

See BAAL-MEON.

Beth-millo. House or fortress associated with the city of Shechem mentioned in connection with the crowning of Abimelech (son of Gideon) as king there (Jgs 9:6,20). Since the term "millo" probably means "mound" or "earthwork," Beth-millo is often identified with the "Tower of Shechem" mentioned later in the same chapter (vv 46–49).

Beth-nimrah. Moabite city given to and rebuilt by Gad's tribe at the partitioning of Canaan, the Promised Land (Nm 32:3, Nimrah; 32:36; Jos 13:27). Beth-nimrah has been identified with modern Tell el-Bleibil, eight miles east of the Jordan River.

Beth-palet. KJV spelling of Beth-pelet, a city of Judah, in Joshua 15:27.

See BETH-PELET.

Beth-pazzez. City given to Issachar's tribe at the partitioning of the Promised Land, apparently near Mt Tabor (Jos 19:21).

Beth-pelet. City assigned to Judah at the partitioning of the Promised Land (Jos 15:27, KJV Beth-palet). Later resettled by the people of Judah after the return from exile in Babylon (Neh 11:26, KJV Beth-phelet), Beth-pelet was possibly the hometown of David's warrior Helez the Paltite (2 Sm 23:26; 1 Chr 11:27, Pelonite).

Beth-peor. Moabite city given to Reuben's tribe in the partitioning of the Promised Land (Jos 13:20). Prior to the Israelites' entrance into the land of Canaan they made camp in a valley "opposite Beth-peor." Here the people assembled to hear Moses' final message after he had viewed the land from the top of Mt Pisgah (Dt 3:29; 4:46). It was here that Moses was buried, having been forbidden to enter the territory promised the descendants of Abraham (Dt 34:6). Baal-peor (or Baal of Peor) was the name of a local deity worshiped in this region (Nm 25:3,5).

Bethphage. Village on the Mt of Olives adjacent to Jerusalem. At Bethphage two disciples obtained the donkey colt on which Jesus rode into Jerusalem (Mt 21:1–6; Mk 11:1–6; Lk 19:29–35). Its probable site is northwest of Bethany on the summit where Kefr et Tûr stands today.

Beth-phelet. KJV spelling of Beth-pelet, a city of Judah, in Nehemiah 11:26.

See BETH-PELET.

Beth-rapha. Place or clan name listed among the descendants of Eshton in Judah's tribe (1 Chr 4:1,12).

Beth-rehob. City of district mentioned in Judges 18:28 and 2 Samuel 10:6; probably the northernmost point reached by the 12 Israelite spies when they searched out the land of Canaan. It is probably identifiable with Rehob (Nm 13:21; 2 Sm 10:8).

See REHOB (PLACE).

Bethsaida. Town NE of the Sea of Galilee. Bethsaida was the home of three of Jesus' disciples: Andrew, Peter, and Philip (Jn 1:44; 12:21). Jesus announced that calamity would come upon Bethsaida because of its unbelief in spite of the mighty works he had done there (Mt 11:21,22; Lk 10:13). A blind man was healed in Bethsaida (Mk 8:22–27), and nearby over 5,000 people were fed by the miracle of the loaves and fish (Mk 6:34–45; Lk 9:10–17).

Bethsaida is mentioned in several ancient sources, chiefly the writings of Josephus, a 1st-century AD Jewish historian. Two Bethsaidas, one on each side of the Sea of Galilee, were once postulated because the reference in Mark mentions the feeding of the 5,000 as happening across the lake from Bethsaida, whereas in Luke it seems to have taken place near Bethsaida. One solution is that the miracle occurred in the district surrounding Bethsaida, but that the quickest way to reach the city itself was to cross part of the lake. Such an interpretation questions the traditional location of the miracle (et-Tabgha on the west shore, nearer to Capernaum), but is preferable to the proposal of two Bethsaidas so close to each other.

Bethsaida was merely a fishing village until it was enlarged and beautified by Philip the Tetrarch (4 BC–AD 34), son of Herod the Great, after the death of Caesar Augustus. Philip was later buried there, according to Josephus. Bethsaida's name was changed to Julias in honor of Julia, daughter of Augustus. That city was defended by Josephus when he was its military commander during the first Jewish revolt against Rome (AD 66–70).

Josephus wrote that Bethsaida was "at the lake of Gennesareth" but "near to the Jordan River." He also said that it was in lower Gaulanitis, a district that touched the northeast quarter of the Sea of Galilee. There is, however, no ancient "tell" or ruin fitting the size or description of the city near either the lake or the river. A suggestion that the small harbor of el-'Araj is the site of Bethsaida has little archaeological support, but et-Tell, located about two miles from the lake, shows evidence of extensive Roman occupation and building activity. At present, et-Tell seems to be the most satisfactory candidate for identification of Bethsaida.

Beth-shan, Beth-shean. Strategic Palestinian town located in the sub-tropical Jordan Valley 15 miles south of the Sea of Galilee and 4 miles west of the Jordan River. Bethshan (alternately Beth-shean) stood at the eastern end of the Valley of Jezreel, guarding an important Jordan River crossing. It lay at the junction of two trade routes, one leading north toward Galilee and Damascus, the other leading from the mountains of Gilead

The ruins of Beth-shan, the rocks being from later buildings.

west through the Jezreel valley and the hills of Samaria.

When the Philistines defeated Israel under King Saul at the battle on Mt Gilboa, Beth-shan was a Philistine city. The slain bodies of Saul and his sons were hung in disgrace on the city wall, and Saul's head was displayed in the temple of Dagon, a Philistine deity (1 Sm 31:10–13; 2 Sm 21:12–14; 1 Chr 10:8–10). The city later became a part of David's kingdom.

Identification of Beth-shan with Tell-Husn is confirmed by two Egyptian texts found there that mention its name. The tell or mound is 213 feet high and about one-half mile in circumference at its base. The University of Pennsylvania Museum excavated the tell under the leadership of Clarence S. Fisher in 1921–23, Alan Rowe in 1925–28, and Gerald M. Fitzgerald in 1930, 1931, and 1933. Excavation revealed 18 levels of occupation extending from the 4th millennium BC to the early Arab period. Especially interesting was a group of temples built by Egyptian occupiers in honor of local deities, dating about 1400–1200 BC. Two later temples, erected during Philistine occupation (c. 1200–1000 BC), may be those of Ashtaroth and Dagon, where Saul's head and armor were kept. Various Egyptian inscriptions were found, including two victory stelae (inscribed stone monuments proclaiming a victory) one from the reign of Pharaoh Seti I and one from the reign of Rameses II.

At the time of Israel's conquest of Canaan, the area that included Beth-shan was allotted to Issachar's tribe, but Manasseh's tribe evidently took it over (Jos 17:11). Under King Solomon it was incorporated into the administrative district of Baanah (1 Kgs 4:12). The city is thought to have been destroyed by Shishak (Sheshonk I), pharaoh of Egypt in the 10th century BC. It was insignificant during the remainder of the OT period; occupation during the Babylonian exile and the postexilic Persian period seems to have been sporadic.

In the Hellenistic period Beth-shan re-ceived the name Scythopolis, presumably because it was settled by a colony of Scythian mercenaries serving the Egyptian king Ptolomy II. Temples to the Greek deities Dionysus and Zeus were built. Under the Hasmonean dynasty Beth-shan became an important administrative center. It prospered as a member of the league of Greco-Roman commercial cities called Decapolis (Mt 4:25; Mk 7:31) and was the only league member west of the Jordan. During the 2nd and 3rd centuries AD it was a world center for the manufacture and export of textiles.

Since 1950 several sites around the foot of the tell have been investigated, revealing occupations from the 4th millennium BC to the Byzantine period. Interesting discoveries include two synagogues (4th and 6th centuries AD), a circular Byzantine cathedral and a monastery, numerous Christian churches, Jewish graves, a Roman villa, and a Byzantine potter's workshop. Appelbaum and Negev excavated the Roman theater of Beth-shan in 1959–62 for the Israel National Parks and the Department of Antiquities. Standing about 250 yards south of the tell, the theater measures 270 feet wide and 190 feet deep and could have seated about 8,000. The structure dates to about AD 200.

Beth-shemesh. 1. Canaanite city on the northern border of Judah's territory (Jos 15:10)

Beth-shemesh.

and the southern border of Dan's (before that tribe migrated north). Beth-shemesh means "the house (or temple) of Shamash," the Canaanite sun god. As Ir-shemeth it was included in the list of cities of Dan (19:41). Beth-shemesh was one of the towns of Judah granted to the Levites (21:16; 1 Chr 6:59). Its inhabitants were called Beth-shemites (1 Sm 6:14,18 KJV). When the Philistines decided to dispose of the captured ark of the covenant because plagues were breaking out in their cities, they took it to Beth-shemesh (vv 1–20). The area was also the scene of a great victory of King Joash (Jehoash) of Israel over King Amaziah of Judah (2 Chr 25:21,23). About a century later, Beth-shemesh was captured from King Ahaz of Judah by the Philistines (28:16–20). After that the settlement fell into decline and was finally destroyed by Nebuchadnezzar in 586 BC.

Important archaeological discoveries have been made at the site of Beth-shemesh (tell er-Rumeileh, near the Arab village of Ain Shems). Beth-shemesh was excavated in 1911–12 and again in 1928–31. Six strata were uncovered by the excavators. The lowest, Stratum VI, was dated to the period shortly before 2000 BC. Little was found that belonged to this level. Stratum V, dated to Middle Bronze Age II (1750–1550 BC), had a large city wall that was traced completely around the city. It had a foundation of massive stones, with the upper part being built of clay bricks. During the Late Bronze Age, Stratum IV, the city experienced a period of prosperity. A furnace for the smelting of bronze or copper was found. The excavators also found a tablet written in Ugaritic cuneiform and an ostracon, a piece of broken pottery used as a writing tablet, upon which there was an early Canaanite inscription. The stratum was destroyed in approximately 1200 BC.

Stratum III was a period of strong Philistine influence and continued prosperity. This was the city known to Samson. It was destroyed prior to 1000 BC, probably at the same time as neighboring Shiloh, and rebuilt in the early 10th century BC. This city, called Stratum IIA, had a casemate city wall like that of Tell Beit Mirsim. The city was dominated by a large building which has been identified as the palace of the governor of a district in the Israelite government. Stratum IIA was burned by fire and rebuilt as a large, apparently unfortified village. This stratum was destroyed by the Babylonians about 600 BC.

The city moved to neighboring Ain Shems in the Roman period, but the excavators found evidence of Roman, Byzantine, and medieval occupation at Tell er-Rumeileh which they called Stratum I.

2. Canaanite city allotted to Issachar's tribe (Jos 19:22).

3. Fortified Canaanite city alloted to Naphtali's tribe (Jos 19:38). The inhabitants of this Beth-shemesh were not driven out by the Israelites (Jgs 1:33).

4. KJV reference to the Egyptian city of Heliopolis (or On) where the sun was worshiped (Jer 43:13).

See HELIOPOLIS.

Beth-shemite. Inhabitant of Beth-shemesh (1 Sm 6:14,18 KJV).

See BETH-SHEMESH #1.

Beth-shittah. Town between the Jordan River and the Valley of Jezreel to which the Midianites fled when defeated by Gideon (Jgs 7:22). Its exact location is uncertain.

Beth-tappu-ah. Town in the hill country of Judah's territory (Jos 15:53) named "place of fruit trees" because of its high ridge location and many fruitful orchards. Beth-tappu-ah is identified with modern Taffuh about four miles northwest of Hebron.

Beth-togarmah. Hebrew phrase meaning "House of Togarmah," referring to the nation descended from Gomer's son of this name, and which traded with Tyre (Ez 27:14; 38:6).

See TOGARMAH.

Bethuel (Person). Youngest son of Abraham's brother Nahor and his wife Milcah. Bethuel was thus Abraham's nephew (Gn 22:23). He was the father of Rebekah (24:15,24) and was referred to as an Aramean of Paddanaram (25:20; 28:5).

Bethuel, Bethul (Place). One of the cities allotted to Simeon's tribe within Judah's inheritance (1 Chr 4:30). Bethuel is alternately called Bethul in Joshua 19:4, and is perhaps identifiable with Chesil, a city assigned to Judah's tribe (Jos 15:30), and with Bethel in the Negeb to which David sent spoils (1 Sm 30:27).

See CHESIL.

Beth-zatha. Pool in Jerusalem. The name is generally believed to mean "house of Olives," occurring only in John 5:2. In many translations this is a variant given in the margin for Bethesda. Bethesda is an Aramaic word transliterated into Greek and is the name of a pool in Jerusalem in Jesus' day which was surrounded by five porches or colonnades that gave an arcade-like walkway around the pool. Located near the Sheepgate, it was the place where the handicapped and ill came with the

Excavations at Beth-zatha.

hope they would be miraculously healed if they could get into the pool at the proper time.

A number of other forms occur in available sources. These are *Bethsaida* ("house of fish"), *Belzetha*, and *Bezatha*, the latter two apparently variants of *Bethzaitha*. Recent studies, especially of the Copper Scroll of Qumran Cave 3, make it clear that *Bethesda* is the correct form among the several variations. Further, it is a dual form which indicates that the site of *Bethesda* was characterized by two pools. This understanding shows that the older theory that *Bethesda* meant "house of mercy" is incorrect.

The archaeological activity of the Franciscan Fathers of the Church of St. Anne near St. Stephen's Gate in the Old City has been a corrective of older views as well as the means of clarifying where the pool actually was. Their research has shown that the Pool of Bethesda is not to be identified with *Birket Israel*, a pool about 360 feet by 126 feet located between St. Anne's and the temple area to the south; or with the large cisterns under the convent of the Sisters of Zion several hundred yards west of St. Anne's on the Via Dolorosa; or with the pool adjacent to the Gihon, still farther south than *Birket Israel* on the slope of Ophel. Rather, the Pool of Bethesda is to be identified with the excavated ruin in the St. Anne Courtyard, a ruin with two pools of considerable size. Arched pillars originally bordering the two reservoirs were covered intact with 25 to 30 feet of debris. Excavated, these now stand impressively as witness to an astounding architectural achievement.

Architectural style and inscription point to Herodian times, making it one of the many magnificent building projects of Herod the Great. The debris and ruins of several centuries were dumped into the pool area filling the space around the still standing colonnades. This debris was later leveled and a Byzantine church constructed on top of it in the 5th century AD. Thus through various literary and archaeological studies, Bethesda is now correctly understood to mean "a place of two pools" located near the Sheep Market of St. Stephen's Gate.

See JERUSALEM.

Beth-zur. Hill town of Judah in the mountains north of Hebron (Jos 15:58). Beth-zur was settled by Maon, one of Caleb's descendants (1 Chr 2:45), and was one of the natural strongholds of Judah. It was fortified by King Rehoboam of the southern kingdom in the 10th century BC, even though it had begun to decline in importance (2 Chr 11:7). It served as an administrative center during the time of Nehemiah (Neh 3:16). In the Maccabean period it was known by the Greek name Bethsura. Judas Maccabeus defeated Syrian general Lysias there (1 Mc 4:29,61) and lost the town a few years later. After recapturing Beth-zur from the Syrians, Simon Maccabeus strengthened it in 140 BC, making it one of the most important fortresses on the border between Judah and Idumaea (11:65,66; 14:33).

Beth-zur, which has been identified as modern Khirbet et-Tubeiqah, 15 miles southwest of Jerusalem, was excavated in 1931 and again in 1957. A large Middle Bronze city (19th–16th centuries BC) was uncovered that was surrounded by massive walls. Scanty Late Bronze occupation agrees with the fact that Beth-zur is not mentioned in Joshua's list of conquered cities. The city once again flourished in the 12th–11th centuries BC and continued to be occupied down to the time of the exile. A large Maccabean fortress was found on the summit of the tell.

Betonim. City in the territory assigned to Gad's tribe for an inheritance (Jos 13:26). It has been identified with modern Khirbet Batneh, 16 miles northeast of Jericho.

Betrothal. First stage of marriage transaction; engagement.

See MARRIAGE, MARRIAGE CUSTOMS.

Beulah. Hebrew word used once in the KJV as a. proper name for Jerusalem, denoting a promised blessing for the people of God (Is 62:4). The word means "married" and was used symbolically by the prophet Isaiah to describe what God's special relationship would be to his restored people. The same theme recurs in NT references to the "Bride of Christ."

See BRIDE OF CHRIST.

Bezai. 1. Ancestor of a group of people that returned to Jerusalem with Zerubbabel after the Babylonian exile (Ezr 2:17; Neh 7:23).

2. Political leader who signed Ezra's covenant of faithfulness to God with Nehemiah and others after the exile (Neh 10:18).

Bezalel, Bezaleel. 1. Uri's son and the master craftsman from Judah's tribe who was specially equipped by God to be in charge of the construction and furnishing of the tabernacle (Ex 31:2; 35:30; 36:1,2; 37:1; 38:2; 1 Chr 2:20; 2 Chr 1:5, KJV Bezaleel).
2. Pahath-moab's son, who obeyed Ezra's exhortation to divorce his pagan wife after the exile (Ezr 10:30, KJV Bezaleel).

Bezek. 1. Site of a major victory for the tribes of Simeon and Judah over the Perizzites and Cannanites (Jgs 1:3–7). Adoni-bezek, which means "Lord of Bezek," was king of the city at that time. Bezek was perhaps located at Khirbet Bezqa, a few miles northwest of Jerusalem.
2. Place where Saul gathered an army to attack the Ammonites who were troubling Jabesh-gilead (1 Sm 11:8–11). This Bezek is usually located at Khirbet Ibziq, a little south of Mt Gilboa. Many scholars feel these two Bezeks were one and the same and place both at Khirbet Ibziq, 13 miles northeast of Shechem. However, this does not agree with the Book of Judges, which implies that the Bezek of 1:3 was located in the inheritance given to Judah.

Bezer (Person). Zophah's son in Asher's tribe (1 Chr 7:37).

Bezer (Place). City of refuge in Reuben's desert territory east of the Jordan River (Dt 4:43; Jos 20:8), later allotted to the Merari family of Levites (Jos 21:36; 1 Chr 6:78). It is probably a variant spelling of Bozrah in Jeremiah 48:24. According to the Moabite Stone, Bezer was among the cities rebuilt by King Mesha of Moab.

See BOZRAH #2; CITIES OF REFUGE.

Bible. Collection of 66 books that constitute the Scripture of the Christian churches. Jews accept only the first part of the Bible, the OT. Roman Catholics add apocryphal books to those adopted by other Christian bodies. The word "Bible" derives from the Greek *biblia* ("books"), which, though plural, came to be used as a singular noun and to stand for the collection which Christians regard as the Word of God. Together, according to Christian belief, these books constitute God's revelation of what all people need to know about their origins, rebellion against God, sinful nature, salvation, spiritual development, and destiny.

The idea of a collection of holy writings developed early in Hebrew-Christian thought.

Daniel in the 6th century BC spoke of a prophetic writing as "the books" (Dn 9:2). The writer of 1 Maccabees (2nd century BC) referred to the OT as "the holy books" (12:9). Jesus alluded to the OT books as "the scriptures" (Mt 21:42), and Paul spoke of them as "the holy scriptures" (Rom 1:2).

The Bible is divided into OT and NT. Of course there were no OT and NT before the coming of Christ, only one collection of sacred writings. But after the apostles and their associates produced another body of sacred literature, the church began to refer to the OT and NT. Actually "testament" is the translation of a Greek word that might better be rendered "covenant." It denotes an arrangement made by God for the spiritual guidance and benefit of human beings. The covenant is unalterable: humankind may accept it or reject it but cannot change it. "Covenant" is a common OT word; of several covenants described in the OT, the most prominent was the Law given to Moses. While Israel was chafing and failing under the Mosaic covenant, God promised them a "new covenant" (Jer 31:31).

The term "new covenant" appears several times in the NT. Jesus used it when he instituted the Lord's Supper; by it he sought to call attention to the new basis of communion with God he intended to establish by his death (Lk 22:20; 1 Cor 11:25). The apostle Paul also spoke of that new covenant (2 Cor 3:6,14), as did the writer to the Hebrews (Heb 8:8; 9:11–15). The detailed description of God's new method of dealing with people (on the basis of the finished work of Christ on the cross) is the subject of the 27 books of the NT. God's dealing with people in anticipation of the coming of Messiah (Hebrew equivalent of "Christ," meaning "anointed one") is certainly the major theme of the 39 books of the OT, though they also deal with much more than that. Latin church writers used *testamentum* to translate "covenant," and from them the use passed into English; so old and new covenants became OT and NT.

At least the first half of the OT follows a logical and easily understood arrangement. In Genesis through Esther the history of Israel from Abraham to the restoration under Persian auspices appears largely in chronological order. Then follows a group of poetic books and the Major and Minor Prophets ("Major" meaning the books that are relatively long; "Minor" meaning the books that are relatively short).

The NT also follows a generally logical arrangement. It begins with the four Gospels, which describe the birth, life, death, and resurrection of Christ and his training of disciples to carry on his work after his ascension. The

Book of Acts continues the narrative where the Gospels end and details the founding of the church and its spread through Mediterranean lands. In the latter part of the book the spotlight focuses on the apostle Paul and his church-planting activities. Next come letters Paul addressed to churches he founded or to young ministers he tried to encourage. Following the Pauline Epistles come a group commonly called the General Epistles. The last book, Revelation, is an apocalyptic work.

The OT was written almost entirely in Hebrew with a few isolated passages in Aramaic in the latter books. If one accepts the view that Moses wrote the first five books of the OT (the position the Scripture itself takes), the earliest books of the OT were written by about 1400 BC (provided one accepts the early date proposed for the exodus). If the last book written was Malachi (before 400 BC), composition took place during a thousand years of time. All the writers (some 30 in number) were Jews: prophets, judges, kings, and other leaders in Israel.

The NT was probably written entirely in Greek. If James was the first to write a NT book before the middle of the 1st century and if John was the last (composing Revelation about AD 95), the NT was written during a 50-year period in the latter half of the 1st century. All the writers (probably nine) were Jews, with the exception of Luke (writer of Luke and Acts), and they came from a variety of walks of life: fishermen, doctor, tax collector, and religious leaders.

In spite of great diversity of authorship in the OT and NT, and composition spanning over 1,500 years, there is remarkable unity in the total thrust. Christians believe that God must have been superintending the production of a divine-human book that would properly present his message to humankind.

The OT and NT are component parts of one divine revelation. The OT describes man and woman in the first paradise on the old earth; the NT concludes with a vision of the new heaven and new earth. The OT sees humankind as fallen from a sinless condition and separated from God; the NT views believers as restored to favor through the sacrifice of Christ. The OT predicts a coming Redeemer who will rescue men and women from the pit of condemnation; the NT reveals the Christ who brought salvation. In most of the OT the spotlight focuses on a sacrificial system in which the blood of animals provided a temporary handling of the sin problem; in the New, Christ appeared as the One who came to put an end to all sacrifice—to be himself the supreme sacrifice. In the OT, numerous predictions foretold a coming Messiah who would save his people; in the New, scores of passages detail how those prophecies were minutely fulfilled in the Person of Jesus Christ: the "son of Abraham" and the "son of David" (Mt 1:1). As Augustine said more than 1,500 years ago, "The New is in the Old contained; the Old is in the New explained."

See ACTS OF THE APOSTLES, BOOK OF THE; AMOS, BOOK OF; CHRONICLES, BOOKS OF FIRST AND SECOND; COLOSSIANS, LETTER TO THE; CORINTHIANS, FIRST LETTER TO THE; CORINTHIANS, SECOND LETTER TO THE; DANIEL, BOOK OF; DEUTERONOMY, BOOK OF; ECCLESIASTES, BOOK OF; EPHESIANS, LETTER TO THE; ESTHER, BOOK OF; EXODUS, BOOK OF; EZEKIEL, BOOK OF; EZRA, BOOK OF; GALATIANS, LETTER TO THE; GENESIS, BOOK OF; HABAKKUK, BOOK OF; HAGGAI, BOOK OF; HEBREWS, LETTER TO THE; HOSEA, BOOK OF; ISAIAH, BOOK OF; JAMES, LETTER OF; JEREMIAH, BOOK OF; JOB, BOOK OF; JOEL, BOOK OF; JOHN, GOSPEL OF; JOHN, LETTERS OF; JONAH, BOOK OF; JOSHUA, BOOK OF; JUDE, LETTER OF; JUDGES, BOOK OF; KINGS, BOOKS OF FIRST AND SECOND; LAMENTATIONS, BOOK OF; LEVITICUS, BOOK OF; LUKE, GOSPEL OF; MALACHI, BOOK OF; MARK, GOSPEL OF; MATTHEW, GOSPEL OF; MICAH, BOOK OF; NAHUM, BOOK OF; NEHEMIAH, BOOK OF; NUMBERS, BOOK OF; OBADIAH, BOOK OF; PETER, FIRST LETTER OF; PETER, SECOND LETTER OF; PHILEMON, LETTER TO; PHILIPPIANS, LETTER TO THE; PROVERBS, BOOK OF; PSALMS, BOOK OF; REVELATION, BOOK OF; ROMANS, LETTER TO THE; RUTH, BOOK OF; SAMUEL, BOOKS OF FIRST AND SECOND; SONG OF SOLOMON; THESSALONIANS, FIRST LETTER TO THE; THESSALONIANS, SECOND LETTER TO THE; TIMOTHY, FIRST LETTER TO; TIMOTHY, SECOND LETTER TO; TITUS, LETTER TO; ZECHARIAH, BOOK OF; ZEPHANIAH, BOOK OF.

Bible, Authority of the. View that the Bible is the Word of God and as such should be believed and obeyed. Western civilization is in a severe "authority crisis" which is not confined solely to the realm of religious faith, nor is it specially or uniquely threatening to Bible believers. Parental authority, marital authority, political authority, academic authority, and ecclesiastical authority are all being deeply questioned. Not only particular authorities—the Scripture, the pope, political rulers, and so on—but the concept of authority itself is vigorously challenged. Today's crisis of biblical authority thus reflects the uncertainties of civilizational consensus: Who has the power and the right to receive and to require submission?

Revolt Against Biblical Authority. As the sovereign Creator of all, the God of the Bible wills and has the right to be obeyed. Judge of men and nations, the self-revealed God wields unlimited authority and power. All creaturely authority and power is derived from that of God. The power God bestows is a divine trust, a stewardship. God's creatures are morally accountable for their use or misuse of it. In fallen human society God wills civil government for the promotion of justice and order. He approves an ordering of authoritative and creative relationships in the home by stipulating certain responsibilities of husbands, wives, and children. He wills a pattern of priorities for the church as well: Jesus Christ the head, prophets and apostles through whom redemptive revelation came, and so on. The inspired Scriptures, revealing God's transcendent will in objective written form, are the rule of faith and conduct through which Christ exercises his divine authority in the lives of Christians.

Revolt against particular authorities has in our time widened into a revolt against all transcendent and external authority. The widespread questioning of authority is condoned and promoted in many academic circles. Philosophers with a radically secular outlook have affirmed that God and the supernatural are mythical conceptions, that natural processes and events comprise the only ultimate reality. All existence is said to be temporal and changing, all beliefs and ideals are declared to be relative to the age and culture in which they appear. Biblical religion, therefore, like all other, is asserted to be merely a cultural phenomenon. The Bible's claim to divine authority is dismissed by such thinkers; transcendent revelation, fixed truths, and unchanging commandments are set aside as pious fiction.

In the name of humanity's supposed "coming of age," radical secularism champions human autonomy and creative individuality. Human beings are lords of their own destiny and inventors of their own ideals and values, it is said. They live in a supposedly purposeless universe that has itself presumably been engendered by a cosmic accident. Therefore human beings are declared to be wholly free to impose upon nature and history whatever moral criteria they prefer. In such a view, to insist on divinely given truths and values, on transcendent principles, would be to repress self-fulfillment and retard creative personal development. Hence the radically secular view goes beyond opposing particular external authorities whose claims are considered arbitrary or immoral; radical secularism is aggressively hostile to all external authority, viewing it as intrinsically restrictive of the autonomous human spirit.

Any reader of the Bible will recognize rejection of divine authority and definitive revelation of what is right and good as an age-old phenomenon. It is not at all peculiar to the contemporary person "come of age"; it was found already in Eden. Adam and Eve revolted against the will of God in pursuit of individual preference and supposed self-interest. But their revolt was recognized to be sin, not rationalized as philosophical "gnosis" at the frontiers of evolutionary advance.

If one takes a strictly developmental view, which considers all reality contingent and changing, where is the basis for humanity's decisively creative role in the universe? How could a purposeless cosmos cater to individual self-fulfillment? Only the biblical alternative of the Creator-Redeemer God, who fashioned human beings for moral obedience and a high spiritual destiny, truly preserves the permanent, universal dignity of the human species. The Bible does so, however, by a demanding call for personal spiritual decision. The Bible sets forth the superiority of humans to the animals, their high dignity ("little less than God"—Ps 8:5) because of the divine rational and moral image that all bear by reason of creation. In the context of universal human involvement in Adamic sin, the Bible utters a merciful divine call to redemptive renewal through the mediatorial person and work of Christ. Fallen humanity is invited to experience the Holy Spirit's renewing work, to be conformed to the image of Jesus Christ, and to anticipate a final destiny in the eternal presence of the God of justice and justification.

Contemporary rejection of biblical tenets does not rest on any logical demonstration that the case for biblical theism is false; it turns rather on a subjective preference for alternative views of "the good life."

The Bible is not the only significant reminder that human beings stand daily in responsible relationship to the sovereign God. He reveals his authority in the cosmos, in history, and in inner conscience, a disclosure of the living God that penetrates into the mind of every person (Rom 1:18–20; 2:12–15). Rebellious suppression of that "general divine revelation" does not wholly succeed in suspending a fearsome sense of final divine accountability (Rom 1:32).

Yet it is the Bible as "special revelation" that most clearly confronts our spiritually rebellious race with the reality and authority of God. In the Scriptures, the character and will of God, the meaning of human existence, the nature of the spiritual realm, and the purposes of God for humankind in all ages are stated in propositionally intelligible form that all can understand. The Bible publishes in objective form the criteria by which God judges individuals and nations, and the means of moral recovery and restoration to personal fellowship with him.

Regard for the Bible is therefore decisive for the course of Western culture and in the long run for human civilization generally. Intelligible divine revelation, the basis for belief in the sovereign authority of the Creator-

Redeemer God over all human life, rests on the reliability of what Scripture says about God and his purposes. Modern naturalism impugns the authority of the Bible and assails the claim that the Bible is the Word of God written, that is, a transcendently given revelation of the mind and will of God. Attack upon scriptural authority is the storm center both in the controversy over revealed religion and in the modern conflict over civilizational values.

The Bible's View of Itself. The intelligible nature of divine revelation—the presupposition that God's will is made known in the form of valid truths—is the central presupposition of the authority of the Bible. Much recent neo-Protestant theology demeaned the traditional evangelical emphasis as doctrinaire and static. It insisted instead that the authority of Scripture is to be comprehended internally as a witness to divine grace engendering faith and obedience, thus disowning its objective character as universally valid truth. Somewhat inconsistently, almost all neo-Protestant theologians have appealed to the record to support cognitively whatever fragments of the whole seem to coincide with their divergent views, even though they disavow the Bible as a specially revealed corpus of authoritative divine teaching. For evangelical orthodoxy, if God's revelational disclosure to chosen prophets and apostles is to be considered meaningful and true, it must be given not merely in isolated concepts capable of diverse meanings but in sentences or propositions. A proposition—that is, a subject, predicate, and connecting verb (or "copula")—constitutes the minimal logical unit of intelligible communication. The OT prophetic formula "thus saith the Lord" characteristically introduced propositionally disclosed truth. Jesus Christ employed the distinctive formula "But I say unto you" to introduce logically formed sentences which he represented as the veritable word or doctrine of God.

The Bible is authoritative because it is divinely authorized; in its own terms, "all Scripture is God-breathed" (2 Tm 3:16 NIV). According to this passage the whole OT (or any element of it) is divinely inspired. Extension of the same claim to the NT is not expressly stated, though it is more than merely implied. The NT contains indications that its content was to be viewed, and was in fact viewed, as no less authoritative than the OT. The apostle Paul's writings are catalogued with "other scriptures" (2 Pt 3:15,16). Under the heading of Scripture, 1 Timothy 5:18 cites Luke 10:7 alongside Deuteronomy 25:4 (cf. 1 Cor 9:9). The Book of Revelation, moreover, claims divine origin (1:1–3) and employs the term "proph-ecy" in the OT meaning (22:9,10,18). The apostles did not distinguish their spoken and written teaching but expressly declared their inspired proclamation to be the Word of God (1 Cor 4:1; 2 Cor 5:20; 1 Thes 2:13).

The Inerrancy Question. The doctrine of biblical authority has been subverted by attacks on its historical and scientific reliability and by allegedly tracing its teaching to fallible human sources. On the other hand, the doctrine has sometimes been unnecessarily clouded by extremely conservative apologists who have overstated what biblical authority presupposes and implies. Some conservative scholars have repudiated all historical criticism as inimical to biblical authority and distinguished "true" from "false" Christians on the basis of subscription to biblical inerrancy.

If one accepts plenary divine inspiration of Scripture—that is, God's superintendence of the whole—the doctrine of biblical authority doubtless implies inerrancy of the content. But the Christian faith can hardly hope to advance its claims through a repudiation of historical criticism. To do so would imply that to support its position it must resort to uncritical views of history. To "higher criticism," which is so often pursued on arbitrary presuppositions that promote unjustifiable conclusions, the evangelical must reply with sound criticism that proceeds on legitimate assumptions and yields defensible verdicts.

Evangelical Christianity should champion the inerrancy of Scripture as a sound theological commitment, one that is consistent with what the Bible says about itself. But it need not repudiate the Christian integrity of all who do not share that commitment, nor regard them as hopelessly apostate. J. Gresham Machen, a brilliant evangelical apologist of the 1920s and 1930s and staunch champion of scriptural inerrancy, wrote that the doctrine of plenary inspiration "is denied not only by liberal opponents of Christianity, but also by many true Christian men . . . many men in the modern church . . . who accept the central message of the Bible and yet believe that the message has come to us merely on the authority of trustworthy witnesses unaided in their literary work by a supernatural guidance of the Spirit of God. There are many who believe that the Bible is right at the central point, in its account of the redeeming work of Christ, and yet believe that it contains many errors. Such men are not really liberals, but Christians, because they have accepted as true the message upon which Christianity depends."

Yet Machen never wavered in his conviction that the whole Bible is to be considered "the seat of authority." He was convinced that the doctrine of inerrancy avoids instability in expounding authoritative doctrine and morals. He insisted that a "mediating" view of the Bible is not tenable. Modernists who claim to honor the authority of Jesus Christ rather than the authority of Scripture contradict Jesus' teaching, since Jesus held a high view of Scripture. Moreover, the full explanation of Jesus' life and work depended on his crucifixion, resurrection, and heavenly ministry, and derived from the Holy Spirit's inspiration of the apostles. It is illogical to pick and choose from the teaching of Jesus during his earthly ministry only those elements that serve one's own presuppositions. Rejection of the full trustworthiness of Scripture may finally lead one to ascribe to Jesus a life purpose different from the biblical one: that Christ died and rose bodily to be the ground of divine forgiveness of sinners.

The historic evangelical position is summed up in the words of Frank E. Gaebelein, general editor of *The Expositors' Bible Commentary:* "the divine inspiration, complete trustworthiness, and full authority of the Bible." Scripture is authoritative and fully trustworthy because it is divinely inspired. Lutheran theologian Francis Pieper directly connected the authority of the Bible with its inspiration: "The divine authority of Scripture rests solely on its nature, on its theopneusty"—that is, its character as 'God breathed.' " J.I. Packer commented that every compromise of the truthfulness of the Bible must at the same time be regarded as a compromise of its authority: "To assert biblical inerrancy and infallibility is just to confess faith in (i) the divine origin of the Bible and (ii) the truthfulness and trustworthiness of God. The value of these terms is that they conserve the principles of biblical authority; for statements that are not absolutely true and reliable could not be absolutely authoritative." Packer reinforced that argument by demonstrating that Christ, the apostles, and the early church all agreed that the OT was both absolutely trustworthy and authoritative. Being a fulfillment of the OT, the NT is no less authoritative. Christ entrusted his disciples with his own authority in their teaching so the early church accepted their teaching. As God's revelation, Scripture stands above the limitations of human assertion.

Recent Challenges. In recent debate the authority of Scripture is compromised by some mediating scholars through their willingness to grant the infiltration of culturally dependent teaching. Some of the apostle Paul's statements about women, or his views about a regathering of Israel in Palestine, are dismissed as reflective of the rabbinic teaching of the time and hence as evidence of Paul's cul-

turally limited perspective. At some points biblical teaching obviously coincides with Jewish tradition. But where Hebrew tradition was elevated into a norm considered superior to or modifying and contravening Scripture, Jesus was critical of that tradition. That the apostle Paul may at some points have taught what was also taught by tradition, historically rooted in the OT, proves nothing; at other points he was sharply critical of the rabbinical tradition.

The evangelical view has always been that what the inspired biblical writers teach they teach, not as derived from mere tradition, but as God-breathed; in their proclamation they had the mind of the Spirit to distinguish what was divinely approved and disapproved in current tradition. It is a sounder perspective therefore to speak of elements in which the Jewish tradition reflected prophetic revelation and of elements in which it departed from it. Once the principle of "culture dependency" is introduced into the content of scriptural teaching, it is difficult to establish objective criteria for distinguishing between what is supposedly authoritative and unauthoritative in apostolic doctrine. Paul's views on homosexuality could then be considered as culturally prejudiced as his views of hierarchical authority—or for that matter of the authority of Scripture.

Some recent scholars have sought to ascribe to Scripture only a "functional" authority as an inner life-transforming stimulant, setting aside its conceptual-propositional authority. For example, Karl Barth, Rudolf Bultmann, Paul Tillich, and Fritz Buri identify the supposed authoritative aspect of Scripture in radically divergent and even contradictory elements. All of them depart from the historic evangelical view (expounded, e.g., by B.B. Warfield in *The Inspiration and Authority of the Bible,* 1948) that the authority of Scripture is concentrated in its disclosure of divinely revealed truths that constitute the rule of faith and morals. The "functional" view, as reflected by David H. Kelsey in *The Uses of Scripture in Recent Theology* (1975), rejects the finality of any of the divergent views and accepts them equally (no matter how conflicting and contradictory they may be). Claims for external authority are subordinated into a supposed internal authority that dynamically alters the life of the community of faith. In spite of its profession of nondiscrimination toward divergent views, such a theory must of course explicitly exclude the traditional evangelical emphasis on the objective truth of the Bible. But once the validity of the biblical teaching in whole and part is forfeited, no persuasive reason remains why one's personal life ought to be transformed at all. One's life might be transformed in alternative and even expressly opposing patterns, or conformed sometimes in one way and sometimes in another, or transformed in correlation with ideas derived from non-Christian or anti-Christian sources as readily as in correlation with ideas derived from the Bible.

The issue of biblical authority can hardly be divorced from interest in the rational validity and historical factuality of the Scriptures. But evangelicals hold that the authority of the Bible is a divine authority; not all truths and historically accurate statements fall into that category. Scripture is authoritative because it is God's Word. The chosen prophets and apostles, some of them called by God in spite of their own indifference or even hostility—for example, the prophet Jeremiah and the apostle Paul—testify that the truth of God became theirs by divine inspiration. Judeo-Christian religion is based on historical revelation and redemption; instead of indifference to the concerns of history the Bible asserts a distinctive view of linear history alien to that of ancient religions and philosophies.

The Power of God's Word. The Bible remains the most extensively printed, widely translated, and frequently read book in the world. Its words have been treasured in the hearts of multitudes like none other. All who have received its gifts of wisdom and promises of new life and power were at first strangers to its redemptive message, and many were hostile to its teaching and spiritual demands. In every generation its power to challenge persons of all races and lands has been demonstrated. Those who cherish the Book because it sustains future hope, brings meaning and power to the present, and correlates a misused past with the forgiving grace of God, would not long experience such inner rewards if Scripture were not known to them as the authoritative, divinely revealed truth. To the evangelical Christian, Scripture is the Word of God, given in the objective form of propositional truths through divinely inspired prophets and apostles, and the Holy Spirit is the giver of faith through that Word.

CARL F.H. HENRY

See BIBLE, INSPIRATION OF THE.

Bibliography. K. Barth, *The Doctrine of the Word of God;* H. Cunliffe-Jones, *The Authority of the Biblical Revelation;* C.H. Dodd, *According to the Scriptures;* C.H. Dodd, *The Authority of the Bible;* P.T. Forsyth, *The Principle of Authority;* C.F.H. Henry, *God, Revelation, and Authority,* 6 vols.; F.J.A. Hort, *The Authority of the Bible;* M.G. Kline, *The Structure of Biblical Authority;* H.D. McDonald, *Theories of Revelation;* J. Rogers (ed), *Biblical Authority;* B.B. Warfield, *The Inspiration and Authority of the Bible.*

Bible, Canon of the. Those books in the Jewish and Christian Bible considered to be Scripture and therefore authoritative in matters of faith and doctrine. The term translates both a Greek and a Hebrew word that mean "a rule," or "measuring rod." It is a list to which other books are compared and by which they are measured. After the 4th century AD the Christian church found itself with only 66 books that constituted its Scripture; 27 of these were the NT and 39 were the OT. Just as Plato, Aristotle, and Homer form a canon of Greek literature, so the NT books became the canon of Christian literature. The criteria for selecting the books in the Jewish canon (the OT) are not known, but clearly had to do with their worth in the ongoing life and religion of the worshiping nation. The criteria of the selection of NT books revolved around their "apostolicity," according to early church writers. Like those of the OT, these books were collected and preserved by local churches in the continuing process of their worship and need for authoritative guidance for Christian living. The formation of the canon was a process, rather than an event, which took several hundred years to reach finality in all parts of the Roman empire. Local canons were the basis for comparison, and out of them eventually emerged the general canon which exists in Christendom today, although some of the Eastern churches have a NT which is slightly smaller than that accepted in the West. Judaism, as well as Christianity as a whole, believes that the Spirit of God was operative in some providential way in the production and preservation of his Word.

Old Testament Canon. The OT is a name that does not appear in Jewish literature. Jews prefer to call their 39 books of Scripture the Tanak—an acronym formed from the first letters of Torah (Law), Naviim (Prophets), and Kethubim (Writings). These are called the "Law of Moses, the Prophets and the Psalms" (the first book of the Writings in the Hebrew Bible) in Luke 24:44 (NIV). Christians called their writings the New Testament, or covenant, the latter term being a designation earlier used of the agreement God made with Abraham and the patriarchs which was repeated by Christ to his apostles (Mt 26:28). Christians in the 1st century considered their new covenant (1 Cor 11:25) from Christ to be a continuation of the one made earlier with the patriarchs (Eph 2:12), spoken of by the prophets (Jer 31:31–34), and which was therefore called a former covenant (Heb 8:7–13; 9:1,15–22) or in later centuries the OT. The terms "Old" and "New" do not appear in the apostolic fathers of the 1st and 2nd century or in the apologists of the early to mid-2nd century, but they do appear in the latter half of the 2nd century in Justin Martyr (*Dial* 11:2), Irenaeus

(*Adv Haer* 4.9.1), Clement of Alexandria (*Strom* 1:5), and in the early 3rd century in Origen (*De Prin* 4.1.1). In these authors the expression referred more to the covenant itself than to the books containing it, though the transfer was eventually made. The term "canon" was not used in the OT or NT to refer to the Jewish Scriptures. The idea of limitation inherent in the word was not appropriate to the nature of religious authority in Jewish religion during the thousand years when the OT books were being written. Only the Torah was conceived as incapable of being added to or taken from (Dt 4:2). Jewish religion existed for a millennium, from Moses to Malachi, without a closed canon, i.e., an exclusive list of authoritative books. Never in their history did the people of the OT have the entire 39 books of the OT. When their canon was closed is not known. Although some questions were being asked about religious authority by rabbis at Jamnia 20 years after the fall of Jerusalem in AD 70, we have our first list of 39 books produced by Melito of Sardis around AD 170. That list includes no books written after the time of Malachi, unless one is disposed to date Daniel to the 2nd century. The Prophets and the Writings were always considered secondary to the Law. Their composition and collection was a process rather than an event in the life of the people of Israel and functioned largely as a record of the nation's response to the Law, which was so sacred that it was kept (according to rabbinical tradition: Babylonian Talmud, Baba Bathra 14a; cf. also Cairo Damascus Document 5.2) in the ark of the covenant which stood in the Holy of Holies in the tabernacle. In Deuteronomy 31:26, however, the Levites were commanded by Moses merely to put the book of the Law *beside* the ark. Nevertheless, its very presence in the Holy of Holies establishes its uniqueness in relation to other OT books.

The 39 books of the modern OT were originally divided into only 24 according to the uniform testimony of early Hebrew tradition. The Talmud, rabbinic literature, and probably IV Esdras testify to this arrangement which included 5 books of the Law, 8 Prophets, and 11 Writings (Greek-Hagiographa). Modern Hebrew Bibles reflect this tripartite arrangement which was used in the first 3 printed editions (Soncino, 1488; Naples, 1491–93; Brescia, 1492–94). The Law contained the Pentateuch in our familiar order, Genesis to Deuteronomy. The 8 Prophets were Joshua, Judges, Samuel (1, 2), Kings (1, 2), Isaiah, Jeremiah, Ezekiel; and the Minor Prophets (12) were considered as one book and arranged in the same order as our English Bibles. The 11 books of Writings contained 3 of poetry (Ps, Prv, Jb), 5 of Rolls (Sg, Ru, Lam, Eccl, Est) which were read at the important feasts and arranged in the chronological order of their observance, and 3 of narrative or historical (Dn, Ezr-Neh, 1,2 Chr).

Apart from authentic Jewish tradition efforts were made to divide the books into 21, combining Ruth with Judges and Lamentations with Jeremiah. Josephus is the first to do

Comparison of Bible Canons

The Tanak (According to the Masoretic Text) = 24 books		
The Law (Torah) = 5 books	*The Prophets (Naviim) = 8 books*	*The Writings (Kethubim) = 11 books*
Genesis	Former Prophets = 4 books	Poetry = 3 books
Exodus	Joshua	Psalms
Leviticus	Judges	Proverbs
Numbers	1–2 Samuel	Job
Deuteronomy	1–2 Kings	Rolls = 5 books
	Latter Prophets = 4 books	Song of Songs
	Isaiah	Ruth
	Jeremiah	Lamentations
	Ezekiel	Ecclesiastes
	The Twelve	Esther
	Hosea	Others (History) = 3 books
	Joel	Daniel
	Amos	Ezra-Nehemiah
	Obadiah	1–2 Chronicles
	Jonah	
	Micah	
	Nahum	
	Habakkuk	
	Zephaniah	
	Haggai	
	Zechariah	
	Malachi	

The Septuagint (LXX) = 53 books			
Law = 5 books	*History = 18 books*	*Poetry = 9 books*	*Prophecy = 21 books*
Genesis	Joshua	Psalms	Hosea
Exodus	Judges	Odes	Amos
Leviticus	Ruth	Proverbs	Micah
Numbers	1 Kingdoms (1 Samuel)	Ecclesiastes	Joel
Deuteronomy	2 Kingdoms (2 Samuel)	Song of Songs	Obadiah
	3 Kingdoms (1 Kings)	Job	Jonah
	4 Kingdoms (2 Kings)	Wisdom (of Solomon)	Nahum
	1 Paralipomena (1 Chronicles)	Sirach (Ecclesiasticus)	Habakkuk
	2 Paralipomena (2 Chronicles)	Psalms of Solomon	Zephaniah
	(1) Esdras (Ezra)		Haggai
	(2) Esdras (Nehemiah)		Zechariah
	Esther		Malachi
	Judith		Isaiah
	Tobit		Jeremiah
	1 Maccabees		Baruch
	2 Maccabees		Lamentations
	3 Maccabees		Letter of Jeremiah
	4 Maccabees		Ezekiel
			Susanna
			Daniel
			Bel and the Dragon

The Roman Catholic Old Testament (According to the Jerusalem Bible) = 46 books			
Law = 5 books	*History = 16 books*	*Wisdom = 7 books*	*Prophecy = 18 books*
Genesis	Joshua	Job	Isaiah
Exodus	Judges	Psalms	Jeremiah
Leviticus	Ruth	Proverbs	Lamentations
Numbers	1 Samuel	Ecclesiastes	Baruch (including the
Deuteronomy	2 Samuel	Song of Songs	Letter of Jeremiah)
	1 Kings	Wisdom	Ezekiel
	2 Kings	Ecclesiasticus	Daniel (with additions)
	1 Chronicles		Hosea
	2 Chronicles		Joel
	Ezra		Amos
	Nehemiah		Obadiah
	Tobit		Jonah
	Judith		Micah
	Esther (with additions)		Nahum
	1 Maccabees		Habakkuk
	2 Maccabees		Zephaniah
			Haggai
			Zechariah
			Malachi

The Protestant Old Testament = 39 books			
Law = 5 books	*History = 12 books*	*Poetry = 5 books*	*Prophecy = 17 books*
Genesis	Joshua	Job	Major Prophets = 5 books
Exodus	Judges	Psalms	Isaiah
Leviticus	Ruth	Proverbs	Jeremiah
Numbers	1 Samuel	Ecclesiastes	Lamentations
Deuteronomy	2 Samuel	Song of Solomon	Ezekiel
	1 Kings		Daniel
	2 Kings		Minor Prophets = 12 books
	1 Chronicles		Hosea
	2 Chronicles		Joel
	Ezra		Amos
	Nehemiah		Obadiah
	Esther		Jonah
			Micah
			Nahum
			Habakkuk
			Zephaniah
			Haggai
			Zechariah
			Malachi

so, in the 1st century AD (*Cont Ap* 1.8) but is influenced by the Greek OT, the Septuagint. Origen observed in the early 3rd century that this arrangement also corresponded to the number of letters in the Hebrew alphabet (*Euseb HE* 6.25), as did Athanasius in the 4th (*Ep Fest* 39), and others including Jerome (*Prol Gal*). It was dubiously concluded that the number of books in the Hebrew Bible had been divinely ordained to agree with the number of letters of the Hebrew alphabet! Church fathers added their support to this coincidence which became providence to them. All such efforts, however, are of Greek origin and have no support in Hebrew tradition.

The oldest extant manuscripts of the OT in Hebrew are the Masoretic texts, which are no earlier than the 8th century. Only manuscripts of individual books have been found in the Dead Sea scrolls. The Masoretic scribes apparently laid down no rules about arrangement of books because there is no uniform order of the Latter Prophets or the Writings in early Hebrew manuscripts. Nor is the situation any different in ancient Greek translations of the Hebrew. Great diversity exists in the order of books in all three of our oldest manuscripts—Codex Alexandrinus, Vaticanus, and Sinaiticus. All the early Christian authors who profess to give the order and contents of the Hebrew Bible but who do not reflect the Hebrew tripartite division are clearly dependent on the Alexandrian order reflected in these Greek editions, rather than on the Hebrew Bible. Modern Protestant Bibles follow the order of the Latin Vulgate and the content of the Hebrew. Both the Vulgate and the Septuagint (Greek translation) contained the Apocrypha, which was never accepted by the Jews. The Roman Catholic Church includes the Apocrypha in its English translations because of the influence of the Vulgate on Catholic tradition. It is considered deuterocanonical.

Even though no uniformity of order was maintained, the Alexandrian order, reflected in the Greek manuscripts, generally arranged books according to their subject matter—narrative, history, poetry, and prophecy, with the apocryphal books appropriately interspersed into these categories. The Hebrew division was totally ignored.

Early Hebrew Bibles divided the text into small paragraphs and larger sections somewhat akin to our paragraphs. These were indicated by spaces left between them—three letters between the small sections and nine letters between the larger ones. The number of sections is not the same in all manuscripts. Jesus probably referred to such sections in his comment concerning the "passage about the bush" (Mk 12:26). Later, liturgical needs led to further divisions of the text for the complete reading of the Law in Babylonian synagogues in one year (54 sections) and in Palestinian synagogues in three years (154 sections). These are reflected in the lectionary cycles marked in some early Hebrew Bibles. Both systems are referred to in the Talmud (Meg 29*b*, 31*b*). The Babylonian system was better suited to the religious calendar and eventually was adopted generally, maybe as early as the 14th century. Aileen Guilding has argued that the Gospel of John may have been written and arranged according to this triennial lectionary cycle of readings (*The Fourth Gospel and Jewish Worship*, Oxford, 1960).

The division of the text into modern chapters, done in the 13th century (c. 1228) for the Latin Vulgate by Stephen Langdon, was applied to the Hebrew Bible in 1518 (Bomberg Edition), but the numbers were not given to the chapters until 1571 in the text of Arius Montanus, a Hebrew Bible with Latin interlinear translation. The verses were introduced in Bomberg's Great Bible of 1547–48 in which every fifth verse was designated by a Hebrew numeral, 1, 5, 10, and so on. Verses were inserted into the Latin Vulgate in 1555 in the small octavo edition of Stephanus.

New Testament Canon. The formation of the NT canon is no less enigmatic than that of the OT, being, like it, a process rather than an event. Authority was inherent in the commission to the apostles (Mt 28:18) but was not accepted without question by all (1 Cor 9:1–3). Not all the books written by apostles and those closely associated with them were eventually included in the canon. Paul's former letter to the Corinthians (1 Cor 5:9) and his letter to the church of Laodicea (Col 4:16) have never been identified, although some argue that the Corinthian letter is redacted into the canonical epistles, and Marcion thought Laodiceans were actually Ephesians. Polycarp, in the mid-2nd century, mentions a plurality of letters written by Paul to Philippi (Phil 3:2). Devout believers accepted any teaching by an apostle, whether oral or written, as authoritative, of course. By the late 2nd century Irenaeus considered apostolicity to be the fundamental criterion of genuineness. Nonapostolic authors were termed apostolic men.

Just when the idea of gathering together all the important and authoritative works of these early writers was conceived is not known. The Second Letter of Peter (3:16) speaks of several letters known to be by Paul. Polycarp, writing to the church in Philippi (mid-2nd century), sends at their request, all the letters of Ignatius in his possession (Phil 13:2). The death of Ignatius about 40 years earlier had not resulted in the destruction or loss of his letters by the various churches. Goodspeed's hypothesis that the Pauline Letters had "fallen into obscurity, as most old letters do," and were collected only after the publication of Acts prompted it, creates more problems than it solves. Letters were expensive to produce (on parchment or papyrus), and letters from apostles were rare blessings in a time when no NT existed and churches functioned largely through local charismatic leadership (1 Cor 14). The Colossian church was instructed to read the letter Paul wrote to Laodicea and vice versa (Col 4:16). Clearly such letters were deemed valuable and authoritative. They would not "fall into obscurity" by neglect as Goodspeed suggested. The failure of any of the Gospels or Acts to cite any of Paul's letters has no bearing on the question of when they may have been collected. Individual letters, if known, could have been cited had they been considered germane to the work being composed. Clement of Rome, for example, clearly referred to 1 Corinthians about AD 90 when he wrote: "Take up the epistle of the blessed Paul the Apostle. What did he first write to you at the beginning of his preaching? With true inspiration he charged you . . ." (1 Clem 47:1–3). Clement then refers to matters in 1 Corinthians 1.

By the late 2nd century, collections of early Christian documents would certainly have been well underway. Marcion was already making a limited collection of Paul and Luke (accepting only 10 of Paul's works). Gnostics were amassing a huge library of aprocryphal Christian documents that were found in 1945 in upper Egypt and published as *The Nag Hammadi Library* by James Robinson. Both Irenaeus and Tertullian show extensive knowledge of a wide assortment of NT books. If the Muratorian canon is to be dated in the 2nd century rather than the 4th, it provides clear evidence at this time of a canonical list (in Rome?) which contains many NT books, but also "several others which cannot be received into the Universal Church." A difference is further made between documents among the apostolic books that can be read in public service and those that cannot.

A papyrus manuscript, commonly dated to about AD 200 and containing some of Paul's letters was found in 1931 in Egypt and subsequently purchased by Chester Beatty. Although it is not an ecclesiastical list of approved books, it is evidence of a collection in the end of the 2nd and beginning of the 3rd century. The manuscript is fragmentary but contains portions of Romans, Hebrews, 1 and 2 Corinthians, Ephesians, Galatians, Philippians, Colossians, and 1 Thessalonians, in that order. Another manuscript, among the 12 that

The Canon of the New Testament in the First Few Centuries

	c. 140 Marcion	c. 130–202 Irenaeus	c. 150–70 Old Latin Version	c. 170 Muratorian Canon	c. 150–220 Tertullian	c. 200 Old Syriac Version	c. 185–254 Origen	c. 200–225 Hippolytus	c. 325–40 Eusebius of Caesarea	c. 325–350 Codex Vaticanus	c. 325–425 Codex Sinaiticus	367 Athanasius	380 Amphilocius of Iconium	c. 375–400 Peshitta	397 3rd Council of Carthage	c. 425–75 Codex Alexandrinus
Matthew	o	i	i	i	i	i	i	i	i	i	i	i	i	i	i	i
Mark	o	i	i	i	i	i	i	i	i	i	i	i	i	i	i	i
Luke	i	i	i	i	i	i	i	i	i	i	i	i	i	i	i	i
John	o	i	i	i	i	i	i	i	i	i	i	i	i	i	i	i
Acts	o	i	i	i	i	i	i	i	i	i	i	i	i	i	i	i
Romans	i	i	i	i	i	i	i	i	i	i	i	i	i	i	i	i
1 Corinthians	i	i	i	i	i	i	i	i	i	i	i	i	i	i	i	i
2 Corinthians	i	i	i	i	i	i	i	i	i	i	i	i	i	i	i	i
Galatians	i	i	i	i	i	i	i	i	i	i	i	i	i	i	i	i
Ephesians	i	i	i	i	i	i	i	i	i	i	i	i	i	i	i	i
Philippians	i	i	i	i	i	i	i	i	i	i	i	i	i	i	i	i
Colossians	i	i	i	i	i	i	i	i	i	i	i	i	i	i	i	i
1 Thessalonians	i	i	i	i	i	i	i	i	i	i	i	i	i	i	i	i
2 Thessalonians	i	i	i	i	i	i	i	i	i	i	i	i	i	i	i	i
1 Timothy	o	i	i	i	i	i	i	i	i	m	i	i	i	i	i	i
2 Timothy	o	i	i	i	i	i	i	i	i	m	i	i	i	i	i	i
Titus	o	i	i	i	i	i	i	i	i	m	i	i	i	i	i	i
Philemon	i	i	i	i	i	i	i	o	i	i	i	i	o	i	i	i
Hebrews	o	o	o	o	o	i	d	o	i	i	i	i	o	i	i	i
James	o	o	o	o	o	i	d	o	d	m	i	i	i	o	i	i
1 Peter	o	i	o	o	i	i	i	i	i	m	i	i	o	i	i	i
2 Peter	o	o	o	o	o	o	d	d	d	m	i	i	i	o	i	i
1 John	o	i	i	i	i	i	i	i	i	m	i	i	i	o	i	i
2 John	o	i	i	i	o	o	d	o	d	m	i	i	i	o	i	i
3 John	o	o	i	i	o	o	o	d	o	m	i	i	i	o	i	i
Jude	o	o	i	i	i	o	d	o	d	m	i	i	i	o	i	i
Revelation	o	i	i	i	i	o	i	i	i	m	i	i	o	i	i	i
Hermas	o	i	o	o	o	o	i	o	r	m	i	o	o	o	o	o
Barnabas	o	o	o	o	o	o	i	o	r	m	i	o	o	o	o	o
Didache	o	o	o	o	o	o	i	o	r	m	o	o	o	o	o	o
Apoc. of Peter	o	o	o	i	o	o	o	o	o	m	o	o	o	o	o	o
1 Clement	o	o	o	o	o	o	o	o	o	m	o	o	o	o	o	i
2 Clement	o	o	o	o	o	o	o	o	o	m	o	o	o	o	o	i

d = disputed (canonicity mentioned as in doubt)
i = included (canonicity definitely accepted)
m = missing (the codex omits the Pastorals and ends at Heb 9:13)
o = omitted (canonicity doubted or denied)
r = rejected (canonicity specifically denied)

were found, contains the Gospels (in the familiar order) and Acts. It dates to the first half of the 3rd century. No lists of authoritative books have yet been found in the 3rd century of which this author is aware.

Eusebius mentions several writings of Origen of Alexandria in the 3rd century containing discussions of books which he calls (for the first time among early authors, I believe) "canonical." However, Origen gives us no authoritative list of such books (Euseb, *Hist Eccl* 6.25).

The 4th century, on the other hand, contains several. Eusebius of Caesarea differentiates several categories of books. These are (1) accepted, (2) disputed, (3) rejected, and (4) heretical. The accepted books contain most of our present NT books. The disputed group contains James, Jude, 2 Peter, 2 and 3 John. The only NT book listed in the rejected group is Revelation, but with a note that many put it in group one, where Eusebius himself has already placed it. The fourth group consists primarily of pseudepigraphical books (*Eccl Hist* 3.25).

Two of our oldest and best manuscripts of the Bible in Greek come from the 4th century, Codex Vaticanus and Codex Sinaiticus. The former contains all the NT from Matthew to Hebrews, where it breaks off in chapter 9 with missing leaves. The order is: the four Gospels (in the the familiar order), Acts, General Epistles, Pauline Epistles. The latter contains the Gospels (in the familiar order), the Paulines, with Hebrews after 2 Thessalonians, followed by 1 and 2 Timothy, Titus and Philemon, then Acts followed by the General Epistles, Revelation, and the Books of Barnabas and Hermas. The last two books indicate a broader local canon than might be found in some communities. Codex Alexandrinus in the 5th century also includes 1 and 2 Clement. These manuscripts seem to represent the locality of Egypt.

The first actual list of canonical books that contains our 27 exclusively, dates to AD 367, appearing in the festal letter (#96) of Athanasius of Alexandria. The order, however, is different. The Gospels are followed by Acts and then the General Epistles. Next are the Pauline Letters with Hebrews after 2 Thessalonians, followed by 1 and 2 Timothy, Titus, Philemon, and Revelation. In AD 380 we find our 27 books in the familiar arrangement (taken from the Latin Vulgate) listed in the writings of Amphilocius of Iconium.

This means that no list containing just our 27 books in their familiar order appeared until the end of the 4th century. This seems to be the time when the process of canon formation was reaching its conclusion in the West. Lists appear in the writings of Chrysostom, Cyril, Philastrius, Gregory of Nazianzus, Epiphanius, Rufinus, and Jerome, as well as in the apostolic canons and the apostolic constitutions. Two important councils from this period, Carthage and Hippo, issued lists affirming the generally accepted books in the empire. Some of the eastern churches, Syria for example, still have a short canon of only 22 books. The old Syriac manuscripts do not have the General Epistles and Revelation. The former were not even translated into Syriac until the 6th century.

There is no "correct" order of books in the NT. The order we have is simply taken over from the Latin Vulgate, the official Bible of the Roman Catholic Church from which the earliest translations were made. The oldest

Greek manuscripts have varying arrangements of the books. The one that predominates is: Gospels, Acts, General Epistles, Pauline Epistles, Revelation. The Gospels appear in our order (Matthew, Mark, Luke, and John) in most ancient manuscripts and authors, but also in the order Matthew, John, Luke, and Mark (Codex Bezae, 5th century); Matthew, Mark, John, and Luke (Cheltenham List, 4th century); John, Matthew, Luke, and Mark (Chrysostom, 4th century).

The arrangement of the Pauline corpus varies considerably as well. In addition to our familiar arrangement, it also appears after the General Epistles, which follow Acts, in Codex Vaticanus (4th century), Codex Alexandrinus (5th century), and Codex Ephraemi (5th century). In some manuscripts Paul's Letters are placed after the Gospels (Codex Sinaiticus, 4th century) and Codex Bezae (5th century), as well as in Jerome and Augustine (late 4th century).

The arrangement of the Pauline Letters themselves vary greatly. I have observed more than 20 different arrangements in early authors and manuscripts. Further variations exist in Coptic and Latin manuscripts as well. More than 284 different sequences of biblical books have been found in Latin manuscripts alone.

The Book of Hebrews has fluctuated in relation to Paul's Letters, appearing most often after 2 Thessalonians (at the end of the letters written to churches) and sometimes after Philemon (at the end of the letters to individuals). In the two oldest collections of Pauline Letters, however, it appears among the first books. The Chester Beatty papyri, around AD 200, places it second after Romans, and Codex Vaticanus, in the 4th century, originally had it between Galatians and Ephesians. This is evident because the numbering system for paragraphs in this manuscript ends Galatians with number 58 and starts Ephesians with number 70. The sequence then follows without break through 2 Thessalonians and number 93. Hebrews next appears, but is numbered 59 rather than 94. It continues from 59 to 64 in 9:11, where the manuscript becomes defective at 9:14 and the rest is lost. Obviously an ancestor of Codex Vaticanus placed Hebrews between Galatians and Ephesians. A later scribe removed it without changing the numbering system.

These paragraph divisions in Vaticanus are the oldest known in the Greek NT. Our modern chapter divisions were introduced by Stephen Langdon for the Latin Vulgate NT as well as the OT at the beginning of the 13th century. Modern verse division is the work of Robert Stephanus, who published a Latin edition of the NT in 1551 in Geneva with the text of the chapters divided into verses.

A fresh effort is now being made by some scholars to interpret NT books in relation to their canonical status rather than in isolation, insisting that the books have come to us as a collection and must be treated as such. This approach to "canonical criticism" is being led by Brevard Childs, among others, in his most recent book *The New Testament as Canon: An Introduction* (Fortress, 1985).

JOHN R. McRAY

See BIBLE, TEXTUAL CRITICISM OF THE; BIBLE, AUTHORITY OF THE.

Bibliography. H.E. Ryle, *The Canon of the OT*; A. Souter, *The Text and Canon of the NT*, rev ed (1954); R.H. Tyle, *The Canon of the OT*; B.F. Westcott, *A General Survey of the Canon of the NT* (1855), reprint of 1889 (6th) ed by Baker (1980); S. Zeitlin, *A Historical Study of the Canonization of the Hebrew Scriptures.*

Bible, Inspiration of the.

Theological term for the influence God exerted on the writers of Scripture, enabling them to transmit his revelation of himself in writing.

For the early church, two factors were significant in their total acceptance of the OT as divinely inspired. One was the constant assertion throughout its pages that "God spoke" or "God said" this or that. Also, many OT prophecies concerning the coming Messiah had been fulfilled in Jesus, and to Christians it seemed clear that such prophecies must have been directly communicated by God himself. The second factor was Jesus' attitude toward Scripture. He declared that the OT "cannot be broken" (Jn 10:35; cf. Lk 16:17). Jesus loved the OT and lived out its essential message, demonstrating his acceptance of it as the Word of God. For the early church, his recognition of its inspiration (Mt 22:43) validated its divine origin and verified its historical accuracy.

Christ's view of the OT became the view expressed in the NT, which is saturated with quotations from the OT and allusions to it. Constant use of formulas like "the Scripture says," "it is written," "God said," or "the Holy Spirit said" shows that in the NT, Scripture is equated with the written Word of God.

But what about the inspiration of the NT itself? The first preachers of the gospel were sure that they had received divinely communicated "gospel" (Rom 1:16). The gospel message, given in oral form to the apostles "through the Holy Spirit" (Acts 1:2), was later embodied in writing by the action of that Spirit. When the NT eventually took its place alongside the OT as Scripture, it was with awareness of the specific and established meaning of the term: "Scripture" connoted "God's Word written."

The two Testaments consequently belong together and are regarded by Christians as constituting a single utterance of God. "Inscripturation" is the process by which God's self-disclosure was committed to writing so that the resulting product can be accurately designated the Word of God. God's revelation is said to be inscripturated in the biblical record. Certain NT passages specifically refer to the supernatural inspiration of Scripture, but to Christians the evidence of that reality is seen throughout the entire Bible.

The Nature of Inspiration. Before the middle of the 19th century, the church was unanimous in its view of inspiration: God gave the actual words of Scripture to its human authors so as to perpetuate unerringly his special self-disclosure. In the 2nd century, Justin Martyr called the Bible "the very language of God." In the 4th century, Gregory of Nyssa said it was "the voice of the Holy Spirit." In the 16th and 17th centuries, the Protestant reformers echoed those assertions. But in the second half of the 19th century the pervasiveness of evolutionary ideas and the rise of "higher criticism" in biblical studies led certain theologians to question the historic concept of verbal inspiration. Attempts were made to modify the concept or to replace it altogether with a new doctrine of inspiration allowing for a theory of religious development and a patchwork OT. Some theologians shifted the locale of inspiration from the objective word to subjective experience. The experience might be that of a religious genius, or of a prophet whose insights and glimpses of truth are preserved in the Bible. It might also be the experience of a person today who, gripped by a biblical word or message, avows the Bible to be an inspiring book.

Such drastically altered views do not satisfy the Bible's understanding of its own inspiration. "For it was not through any human whim that men prophesied of old; men they were, but, impelled by the Holy Spirit they spoke the words of God" (2 Pt 1:21 NEB). Thus, according to the NT, the OT prophets proclaimed a word initiated and controlled by the Holy Spirit. What they spoke was not merely their own thoughts, nor divine thoughts in their own words, but "the words of God," as they were impelled (Greek, "borne along") by the Holy Spirit. Although the passage deals specifically with spoken prophecy, the apostle Peter seems to have been using the action of the Spirit in the prophets to emphasize the divine origin of Scripture as a whole (cf. 1 Pt 1:3–25). The same Spirit of God also impelled the apostle Paul to write (cf. 2 Pt 3:15). For both the spoken and the written Word the Holy Spirit enlightened the mind and superintended the work.

According to Paul, the very language of Scripture is "God-breathed" (2 Tm 3:16). The Greek word, as Paul used it, means more than that the Scriptures are an ordinary type of writing, simply "breathed into by God." Paul also meant more than that the Bible is a book that "breathes out the Spirit." Theologian Karl Barth (1886–1968) was one who took the lesser meaning, as if to say that the Bible is the sort of religious literature than can inspire its readers with a sense of God's presence. Paul's statement means rather that Scripture is the product of God's creative breath and hence is a divine product.

In the OT, Hebrew words for "breath" are frequently translated "spirit" in English versions (e.g., Gn 1:2; 6:3; Jgs 3:10; 6:34). God's "breath" is an expression for his Spirit going forth in creative power (Gn 1:2; 2:7; Jb 33:4; Ps 104:30). That creative power is the source of those special human activities and skills required by God for the fulfillment of his purposes (Ex 35:30–35; Nm 24:2; Jgs 6:34). Throughout the OT the breath or spirit of God is specifically associated with prophecy (Nm 24:2; Is 48:16; Jl 2:28; Mi 3:8). Such observations provide a background for understanding Paul's word, "God-breathed." By "the word of the Lord the heavens were made, and all their host by the breath of his mouth" (Ps 33:6); likewise, by God's outbreathing the Scriptures were produced. By sending forth his Spirit (104:30) God performed his creative works at the beginning. God breathed into man's nostrils the breath of life "and man became a living being" (Gn 2:7). Similarly, God breathed through man the words that make up the Scriptures, which carry God's image and which alone are able to "instruct for salvation" and "train in righteousness."

Also significant throughout the OT is an association of "Spirit" and "word," the distinction between the two being comparable to that between God's "breath" and "voice." The voice is the articulate expression of a thought, whereas the breath is the force through which words are made actual.

In the NT the divine breath, the agent of God's Word, is the Holy Spirit. The relationship between the Spirit and the Scriptures is thus so close that to assert "the Holy Spirit says" is the same as saying "Scripture says" (cf. Heb 3:7). Paul asserted that what he set forth in writing to the Corinthian church was imparted "in words not taught by human wisdom but taught by the Spirit" (1 Cor 2:10,13). Paul added that through his Spirit-taught words he was "interpreting spiritual truths to those who possess the Spirit" (v 13). Theologians generally refer to the process by which the Spirit makes the Scriptures understood (by a reader) as "illumination" rather than inspiration.

Consequences of the Biblical View. Two corollaries follow from accepting the Bible's own account of its inspiration.

Inspiration Is Plenary. First the inspiration of the Scriptures can be said to be "plenary," a word meaning "full; entire; complete." That is, Scripture is God-breathed in all its parts. To say that inspiration is plenary is to reject any "illumination theory," in which inspiration is held to be only partial, or a matter of degree. The Spirit's activity is not limited to a few texts or special passages of Scripture, but belongs to the written Word as a whole. Plenary inspiration also stands in opposition to any "insight theory" that views inspiration as merely a natural activity.

Yet plenary inspiration does not require that every statement in the Bible is necessarily true. The mistaken view of Job's friends (cf. Jb 42:7–9), the falsehoods told by Peter (Mk 14:66–72), and the letters of heathen kings (Ezr 4:7–24), although quoted in the Scriptures, were not Spirit-inspired. Whether they are actually true or false must be discovered by reference to the context. The recording of such words by the writers of Scripture, however, was subject to the Spirit's inspiration; God wanted them to be part of his revelation.

Inspiration Is Verbal. A second corollary of the Bible's affirmation is that inspiration applies to the biblical *words*. God-breathed Scripture consists of God-given words. The Scriptures are "sacred writings." Inspiration functioned in the inner connection between the thought and the word, influencing them both. That understanding of inspiration historically has been referred to as "verbal." The term directs attention to the products of the divine outbreathing, the actual words. Because the Holy Spirit was concerned with the words of Scripture there is no limit to the trust and reliance a believer may place in them.

Yet to say that inspiration is verbal is not the same as declaring that the process was dictational, or mechanical. The fact that early church fathers held such views shows their high regard for the biblical Word, but hardly serves as a basis for an adequate theory of inspiration. Objectors to the historic doctrine of inspiration often associate verbal inspiration with that mechanical view, however, and consequently reject it out of hand as materialistic. To them the term "verbal" indicates that the writers of Scripture were like stenographers taking down words they scarcely understood.

When evangelical theologians today speak of verbal inspiration they are not specifying a method; they are emphasizing that the Spirit's activity was concerned with the very words of Scripture. The precise nature of inspiration cannot be given exact definition. The process should be considered God's secret—a mystery or miracle, with no explanation outside of God himself.

The term "verbal" does lend itself to ambiguity, as some conservative scholars readily admit. Most evangelical theologians agree that any statement of inspiration that regards the words of Scripture as "dictated" by the Holy Spirit to machinelike writers should be rejected. Yet they retain the word "verbal" as best able to convey that the Holy Spirit so influenced the writers of Scripture that their words are to be taken in the fullest sense as the Spirit's words (cf. e.g., 1 Kgs 22:8–16; Neh 8; Ps 119; Jer 25:1–13; Rom 1:2; 3:2,21; 16:26).

The words of Scripture, however, are at the same time fully human words. Scripture can be said to have dual authorship. It is the joint production of God and of individual human beings. Evidence of human authorship is obvious in stylistic features, historical outlook, cultural context, and so forth. From a psychological viewpoint, each biblical book is a distinctive literary creation of its author. From the theological viewpoint, its content is God's creation. Moses, the prophets, Jesus Christ, and the apostles all considered their words to be, in a literal sense, from God himself. The prophets spoke God's words (Jer 1:7; Ez 2:7); Jesus spoke the words of his Father (Jn 7:16; 12:49,50). The apostles issued commands in Christ's name (2 Thes 3:6) and claimed divine authority for them (1 Cor 14:27); their doctrines came from the Holy Spirit (2:9–13).

The doctrine of plenary, verbal inspiration thus asserts that in a unique and absolute way the Holy Spirit acted in relationship with the biblical writers so as to render them infallible revealers of God's truth; hence, the Bible may be spoken of as God's infallible Word. In Scripture, as in the person of Jesus Christ, the divine and human elements are regarded as forming one indissoluble whole, dynamically united. The language is human; the message is divine. The human writers were not passive in the process. They were God's penmen, not merely his pens. The result assures that God is the primary author of Scripture, so that the whole biblical account is rightly designated the Word of God.

Conclusion. Inspiration has been defined as that direct influence of God on the writers of the Bible by which, while they did not cease to be themselves, they were so moved, guarded, and guided by the Holy Spirit that their resulting productions constitute the written Word of God. Augustine called the Bible a letter of God Almighty addressed to his creatures. Martin Luther (1483–1546) asked "Where do we find God's word except in the Scriptures?" The Westminster Catechism (1647) affirms that since God is the author of Scripture, "it ought to be received, because it is the Word of God." Evangelical Christians continue to regard the Bible as absolutely trustworthy and wholly reliable because of its divine inspiration.

H. D. McDonald

See also BIBLE, AUTHORITY OF THE; REVELATION.

Bibliography. P. Achtemeier, *The Inspiration of the Scripture;* C.H. Dodd, *The Authority of the Bible;* N. Geisler (ed), *Inerrancy;* C.F.H. Henry, *God, Revelation, and Authority,* 6 vols.; H.D. McDonald, *Theories of Revelation;* J. Orr, *Revelation and Inspiration;* R. Preus, *The Inspiration of Scripture;* B.B. Warfield, *The Inspiration and Authority of the Bible;* E.J. Young, *Thy Word Is Truth.*

Bible, Interpretation of the.

Theological term for the process of discovering the meaning and message of the Bible. To interpret is to bring out the true meaning of something written or spoken, particularly by restating it in other words. One synonym is simply "to explain"; another is "to translate." A bilingual person who stands beside a speaker to translate the speaker's words into another language is called an interpreter. To evangelical Christians, biblical interpretation is a fundamentally important task because the Bible is considered to be God's spoken and written Word. The Creator's own revelation of himself and of his purpose for his creatures is the most significant communication human beings could possibly receive.

Most people are aware that "meaningful" communication is difficult even at the ordinary human level. Between two people who speak the same language or even live in the same household, the meaning of what is said can easily be lost or distorted. Language is quite flexible. A simple word like "early," for example, can have a whole range of meanings depending on its context: early supper means at 5:30 instead of 6:30, but early retirement means at age 60 rather than 65; Early American is a style of furniture, and Early Bronze is an archaeological period, with over 4,000 years between them. Language is continually changing. In the English of Shakespeare's day, "physics" meant "laxatives or other medicines"; what is now called "physics" would then have been known as "natural philosophy."

Such linguistic problems are faced in biblical interpretation, where they have often been formidable. By its nature the Bible stands out from all other literature, so its interpretation affords challenges beyond those of translating from one language to another and from an ancient cultural setting into a modern and rapidly changing one. The Bible is not one book but a whole library of books, written over a span of over 1500 years by many different writers with a variety of individual styles and immediate purposes. Yet its own claims and its remarkable unity demonstrate to Christians that the Bible is "God's Word in human language." The interpreter, always a finite, fallible, human creature, must try to see things from God's point of view—even though they are expressed from another human perspective.

Over the years, devoted scholars trained in the discipline called "hermeneutics" (from Greek for "interpretation") have worked out canons, or rules, for translating and interpreting Scripture. Bible students have access to their work through exegetical commentaries—"exegesis" (from Greek for "explanation") being yet another word for interpretation. The work of interpretation is never completed, partly because new data from archaeology continue to shed new light on difficult passages of Scripture, and partly because new questions are asked as human understanding changes. Errors of interpretation from reading into Scripture a meaning not really there (a process called "eisegesis") are thus discovered and corrected.

In spite of much agreement about what the Bible means, trained biblical scholars at times disagree in their interpretations of a particular passage. In the church's long history scholars have even disagreed over the basic principles of interpretation. The early church fathers in Alexandria (Egypt), influenced by Greek philosophical thought, began a whole school of biblical interpretation in which the text was largely allegorized. That is, the meaning of the text was sought not in the plain or literal meaning of the words; the words were thought to stand for spiritual ideas in the mind of God. The Alexandrians sought to understand Scripture by imagining what God would want to communicate. Imaginative interpretations piled on top of each other until they became bizarre or even fantastic, as the Alexandrian influence spread through the Western church in the Middle Ages. Another school of interpretation, not rejecting allegorizing entirely, but generally paying more attention to actual words of the Bible, grew up among the church fathers in Antioch (Syria). It had less influence than the Alexandrians on the medieval scholastic theologians, who for almost a thousand years obscured much of the literal, historical meaning of Bible passages with mystical interpretations.

The Protestant Reformation (16th century) brought the church back to an appreciation of Scripture as a direct, straightforward message from God. The Reformers laid emphasis on the study of Hebrew and Greek grammar and

of ancient Near Eastern history as the most appropriate tools for understanding the Bible. Yet they also insisted that the Bible was "perspicuous" (from Latin for "transparent"). That is, the meaning of Scripture is clear to any intelligent reader who reads it the way one would read an ordinary human document—if that person is humble enough to ask the Holy Spirit for understanding of the inspired Word of God. That is the way Christians should approach the task of biblical interpretation today.

There are two basic steps in interpretation. One must ask: (1) What did the passage mean for the person who first spoke these words or wrote them and for the people who first heard or read them? (2) What should the passage mean to a reader today? The first task is to enter into the circumstances of the person who first wrote or heard or read the passage and then try to understand the meaning in the light of the whole Bible. The second is to try to make the meaning of the passage clear in the circumstances of the present century. Interpreters in every age have struggled to be faithful in these two steps.

Sometimes Christians are so eager to proclaim what the passage means to their contemporaries that they tend to miss what it meant in its original situation. Others have spent considerable time on the OT situation but lost sight of the radical changes introduced by Jesus' life, death, and resurrection: "We have been sanctified through the offering of the body of Jesus Christ once for all ... where there is forgiveness of these [sins, lawless deeds], there is no longer any offering [that is, animal offerings] for sin" (Heb 10:10,18).

The context of the whole Bible shows the finality of Jesus' offering for sin. He brought into existence a "new people of God" (that is, both Jews and Gentiles who acknowledge Jesus as the Messiah). Many promises made to Israel in the OT are thus interpreted in the NT as applying to God's new people, the church. Because of such developments within the Bible itself, it is important to place equal weight on steps one and two. Making the proper transition from Bible times to the present takes careful study, prayer, and dependence on the Holy Spirit. Christians are responsible not to add to or subtract from the meaning God intends.

Entering into the Past. The 1500 years over which the Bible was written spanned great changes in cultural and political situations. Sometimes change came quite rapidly. The apostle Paul's situation in Athens (Acts 17:15–34), for example, was quite different from the situation he faced in Jerusalem only a few years later (21:17–23:30). Careful attention must be paid to the events of Near Eastern history.

History and Culture. Historical writings never tell everything that happened; they represent someone's selection of certain events out of all those that took place among a certain group of people over a period of time. That selection helps those who read the record see what made those people different from others around them. History can reveal the strengths and weaknesses of nations and why they have continued or why they have disappeared. But biblical history does not focus upon people alone. Its history is God-centered. The writers of the Bible saw God as revealing himself in history by choosing the Israelite people to work with in a special way. He communicated directly with individuals among them, designated as his servants, concerning the basis for his blessings and judgments upon them. Finally, God joined them on earth in the person of Jesus Christ, experiencing firsthand the full agonies of human history.

The Bible's viewpoint is that there is *one* God, *one* people of God, and *one* history. God's servants could not conceive of writing history without seeing in history the sovereign hand of God. Modern secular historians ignore or deny God's role in human history, but to interpret the Bible one must try to view history as the biblical writers did: a time, a place, an event where God disclosed himself to humanity in history.

To understand the writer's meaning, we must also understand that writer's cultural patterns. Culture includes the habits, customs, tools, material things produced, institutions, arts, music, and literary productions of any people—all the things they create and use. The culture of a particular time is a good barometer of what people consider important. The amount of money spent on amusements, liquor, and weapons shows the interests and emphases of any people. What any people do, what they actually produce, generally tells more about them than what they say.

Linguistic Structure. Language is a crucial part of the life of any people. The OT was originally written in Hebrew except for a few brief sections in Aramaic (Gn 31:47; Ezr 4:8–6:18; 7:12–26; Jer 10:11; Dn 2:4b–7:28). The NT was originally written in Greek. Each language has a particular structure, a grammar that must be mastered in order to understand what is written and to translate it accurately. All three languages are rich in vocabulary and nuances of meaning which can easily be lost in translation.

Many sentences in the Bible are long and complex. All translations break up the longer sentences of the original languages (especially the Greek) to make them read more easily in English. Paraphrases go even further in simplifying, with the results that some connections between ideas may be lost. What paraphrases show as independent sentences may in the original have been joined more closely together, revolving around one verb form. Today a student of the Bible can make use of a number of excellent translations which bring out the literal meanings of the original (such as the New American Standard Bible or the Revised Standard Version) and also a variety of carefully done paraphrases (such as the Living Bible or Phillips' New Testament in Modern English). Beyond that kind of comparison, commentaries can often help one understand why two translations differ on some passage.

Literary Context. The context of a passage means more than merely the words or paragraph immediately surrounding it. To interpret a passage correctly, one must see what comes immediately before it and what comes after, but one should also think of the whole book as the context of the passage. In a book like Daniel, the broader context includes narration of events, dreams, and visions, plus materials taken from various times in Daniel's life and that of three or four kings. Familiarity with the whole book is necessary to understand a specific part. An obscure phrase in Daniel can easily be taken out of context and given a meaning that makes sense today, but a careful look at that phrase in the light of all the rest of Daniel may show that such an "up-to-date interpretation" could not possibly be what Daniel meant. To ignore context increases the possibility of "discovering" a meaning that is not really there, that is, of practicing eisegesis. Scholars, teachers, and pastors can be as guilty of eisegesis as any ordinary reader of the Bible—if they do their work too hastily or have an axe to grind in the form of a strongly held interpretative scheme.

Distinguishing Between Literal and Figurative Language. Although the Bible uses the ordinary language of people, *its main theme is not at all ordinary.* It deals with the hostility of human beings toward God and with how those wandering away from God can come back into fellowship with him. The reality of God, the reality of sin, and the reality of redemption are themes that challenge the capacity of human language.

Meaning of the Terms "Literal" and "Figurative." Language is said to be literal when it carries its customary, socially acknowledged meaning. To say "The farmer plowed his field" is to use the verb "plow" literally. It means the farmer broke up the ground as one does to prepare a field for planting. But to say "The student plowed through a difficult

40 Notable English Versions of the Bible From The Authorized Version to the Present

Translation	Common Acronym	Year of Publication*	Translator(s)
The King James Version (The Authorized Version)	KJV (AV)	1611	54 English scholars
The Holy Bible, Containing the Old and New Testaments, in the Common Version, with Amendments of the Language		1833	Noah Webster
A Literal Translation of the Bible		1863	Robert Young
The English Revised Version	RV	1881/85	54 English scholars
The Holy Scriptures: A New Translation From the Original Languages		1871/90	John Nelson Darby
The Twentieth Century New Testament	TCNT	1898/1901	3 scholars and 32 laypeople
The American Standard Version	ASV	1901	30 American scholars
The Emphasized Bible		1872/1902	Joseph Bryant Rotherham
The New Testament in Modern Speech	Wey	1903	Richard Francis Weymouth
The Bible: A New Translation	Mof	1913/24	James Moffatt
The Complete Bible: An American Translation	AmT	1923/35	E. J. Goodspeed, J. M. P. Smith, and 3 others
The New Testament: A Translation in the Language of the People	Wms	1937	Charles B. Williams
The Revised Standard Version	RSV	1946/52	32 American scholars
The New Testament in Modern English	PNT	1947/58	J. B. Phillips
The Holy Bible: The Berkeley Version in Modern English		1945/59	Gerrit Verkuyl and 20 other scholars
The Holy Bible: A Translation From the Latin Vulgate in Light of the Hebrew and Greek Original	Knox	1944/49	Ronald A. Knox
The Holy Bible From Ancient Eastern Manuscripts		1933/57	George M. Lamsa
The Confraternity Edition of the Challoner-Rheims		1950/60	Roman Catholic scholars
The New World Translation of the Holy Scriptures	NWT	1950/60	The New World Bible Translation Committee
The New Testament: An Expanded Translation		1956/61	Kenneth S. Wuest
The Simplified New Testament		1961	Olaf M. Norlie
The Tanakh	NJPS	1962/82	14 Jewish scholars
The Amplified Bible	AB	1958/65	Frances E. Siemert and 12 others
The Jerusalem Bible	JB	1966	28 Roman Catholic scholars
The Modern Language Bible	MLB	1969	3 scholars
The Barclay New Testament		1968/69	William Barclay
The New English Bible	NEB	1961/70	C. H. Dodd and 50 others
The New American Bible	NAB	1970	50 scholars
The New American Standard Bible	NASB	1963/71	58 scholars
The Living Bible Paraphrased	LB	1962/71	Kenneth N. Taylor
The Good News Bible (Today's English Version)	GNB (TEV)	1966/76	Robert G. Bratcher and 6 others
The Holy Bible in the Language of Today: An American Translation	Beck	1976	William F. Beck
The New International Version	NIV	1973/78	115 scholars
The New Testament in Everyday English		1979	Jay E. Adams
The King James II Version	KJII	1979	Jay P. Green, Sr.
The New King James Version	NKJB	1979/82	130 scholars
The Reader's Digest Bible		1982	Bruce M. Metzger and others
The Word: New Century Version	NCV	1983/86	21 scholars
The Holy Bible: Easy-to-Read Version		1978/87	World Bible Translation Center

*When two dates are given, the first one indicates the year of publication of the New Testament or of the first portion of the project, and the second indicates the year of completion of the project.

course in physics" or "The executive plowed through a pile of paper work" is to use the word "plow" figuratively. The farmer, student, and executive all "advanced laboriously through a resistant material." Whether the word "plow" is used literally or figuratively has nothing to do with the reality of the experience. "Plowing" a field or "plowing" through paper work are both realities. Figurative language takes a common, ordinary meaning and moves it to another realm. An example from the Bible is the ordinary first-century human language of "redeeming" or "buying" a person from slavery to speak of God's "redeeming"

his people from sin. Sin is personified: it holds human beings in slavery or bondage. God redeems them from that slavery, that is, he sets people free when by faith turn their lives over to him.

Many disagreements over biblical interpretation boil down to a question of the degree of literalness intended in a passage. When John described the Holy Spirit at Jesus' baptism descending "as a dove from heaven" (Jn 1:32), did he mean simply that the Spirit "came down," like a flying dove would come down from the sky? Or did he mean that the Spirit took on the form of a literal bird that physically alighted on Jesus? Or did he mean something else entirely? Often the context provides enough clues to enable the reader to distinguish clearly; at other times the clues are missing or are themselves open to different interpretations.

Short Figures of Speech. Most of the literary devices recognized as figures of speech in ordinary literature are also found in the Bible. *Simile,* for example, is a comparison in which words such as "like" or "as" are used. A *metaphor* is a direct comparison; "He's a good sport," or (of Jesus) "Behold the Lamb of God" (Jn 1:29). Both simile and metaphor are used in a familiar passage in Isaiah (40:6–8; see also Jas 1:10,11, 1 Pt 1:24,25):

> All flesh is grass,
>   and all its beauty is like the flower of the
>   field.
> The grass withers, the flower
>   fades . . .

The metaphorical statement that "the grass withers and the flower fades" shows the power of figures of speech. "Flesh" is the Hebrew way of referring to ordinary human life. No matter how vibrant and beautiful a person may be ("like a flower"), he or she will eventually show the effects of aging and finally die. No abstract statements about aging could have the penetrating, memorable quality of that combination of metaphor and simile.

Frequently the Bible pictures God with bodily members and physical movements (anthropomorphism) or with human emotions, feelings, and responses (anthropopathism). Metaphors used about God may refer to his "ear," "mouth," "hands," or "fingers" (Ps 8:3; Is 55:11; 59:1). God is described as "angry" (Dt 1:37; 4:21) and in the Ten Commandments as "jealous" (Ex 20:5; Dt 5:9). Such metaphors do not imply that God's "anger" and "jealousy" are felt or expressed like human anger or jealousy. Human emotions are affected by human sinfulness, ignorance, and inability to maintain emotional balance.

God is free both from the physical limitations of human ears, hands, mouths, and fingers, and from the weaknesses of human emotions. Yet God can "speak," "hear," and "act." The Bible states that he loves sinners, but also that he is angry with sin and sinners. God feels it keenly when his creatures turn away from him to idolatry and to self-destruction. Anthropomorphic metaphors seem essential for human understanding of God, but one must be careful not to literalize them. God does not literally breathe in and out. When he becomes angry, he does not lose emotional control.

When Jesus spoke of "blind guides, straining out a gnat and swallowing a camel" (Mt 23:24), he was clearly using *hyperbole,* an intentional conscious exaggeration. Jesus wanted to show that the Pharisees and scribes were careful about trivial details but couldn't see important spiritual matters. Was Jesus using hyperbole when he said, "It is easier for a camel to go through the eye of a needle than for a rich man to enter the kingdom of God" (Mt 19:24)? Many wealthy Christians devoutly hope so! Was Jesus hyperbolically showing that those who have wealth usually trust in wealth rather than in God, in order to emphasize that genuine trust in God is necessary to enter into his kingdom? Or was he saying that it is literally impossible for the rich to enter the kingdom of God? The context shows that his disciples were so astonished at the literal meaning of his words that he softened them by adding, "With men this is impossible, but with God all things are possible" (vv 23,25,26).

Extended Figures of Speech. A *parable* is actually an extended simile; an *allegory* is an extended metaphor. In Luke 15:1–7 Jesus told a parable about lost sheep to Pharisees and scribes who were enraged because Jesus received sinners and ate with them (Lk 15:2). The joy in heaven over one sinner who repents, Jesus said, is like the joy of a shepherd who recovers a lost sheep. The good-shepherd figure of speech was also used in an allegory, the meaning of which Jesus had to explain (Jn 10:1–18). Unlike a parable, which in its pure form has only one main point, an allegory has several points of comparison. In the good-shepherd allegory, Jesus indicated at least four points of comparison: (1) the shepherd is Christ; (2) the door is Christ; (3) the sheep are those for whom Jesus lays down his life; (4) the flock represents the union of all believers under one shepherd.

An allegory is a story told so that certain elements can represent specific things. To allegorize illegitimately is to take a straight historical incident or narrative and make it mean something else. The tabernacle in the OT has been a favorite subject for allegorizers. For example, a sevenbranched candlestick attached to a lampstand of pure gold stood in the Holy Place (Ex 25:31–40). It provided light for the priest as he carried on his work. In the hands of a modern allegorizer, the seven burning lamps have been taken to represent the Holy Spirit and the shaft to represent Jesus Christ. The interpreter's motive was to point to Christ's work as the basis of the Spirit's manifestation in the church. Without stretching any meanings, however, one could simply say what each item of furniture was meant to do in the tabernacle and then point out how different and how effective Christ's finished work was under the new covenant. NT passages often make use of OT imagery (including the tabernacle), but rarely by allegorizing it. Any allegorizing that ignores the OT meanings does not do justice to the message of God in the OT.

Typology. NT *typology* draws attention to one point of similarity between a person, event, or thing in the OT and a person, event, or thing in the NT. Occasionally one may find two points of similarity in a single example of typology. God told King David that his unborn offspring (Solomon) would build a house or temple for God (2 Sm 7:12,13). God said of Solomon: "I will be his father, and he shall be my son" (2 Sm 7:14). By typology the writer of Hebrews later applied those words to Jesus. Hebrews 1:5 points out that God never spoke such words to any angel. Sonship is the point of emphasis in the typology. Solomon was a son called by God to occupy his father David's throne; Jesus was God's Son in a unique sense—yet both were designated "son." Typology is a kind of figurative language of comparison. A careful interpreter notes that the one point of comparison had historical reality both in the past and in the later time of application. Yet differences are also evident. God said of Solomon, "When he commits iniquity, I will chasten him" (2 Sm 7:14). In contrast, Jesus Christ "committed no sin; no guile was found on his lips" (1 Pt 2:22).

Symbols, Symbolic Actions, Apocalyptic Description. Entire books such as Daniel and Revelation, plus many OT passages, particularly in the prophets, are rich in symbolism. A *symbol* is a "visual metaphor," an object or happening that suggests a certain meaning but does not explicitly state that meaning. Daniel described a vivid dream of King Nebuchadnezzar—an image with head, arms, belly, thighs, legs, and feet all made of different metals. The symbol made sense when Daniel interpreted the meaning of each part (ch 2).

In Revelation, a beast rises out of the sea and another beast comes out of the earth (ch 13). A harlot (prostitute) stands for the capital city of a world empire (Rome, in John's day; see 17:1–18, especially v 18). The beast on which she rides stands both for rulers of a world empire and that empire itself. To use the Scriptures themselves to tell what symbols mean (as in Rv 17) is spoken of as decoding. The symbolism may seem strange, but the fact that human governments can become beastly is certainly clear in the light of 20th-century experience.

The Book of Revelation is also known as the "Apocalypse of John." *Apocalyptic* writing was a form of literature produced by Jewish and early Christian writers between about 200 BC and AD 300, depicting symbolically the power of evil, the dark chaos that evil brings, and the splendor of God's power ultimately to overcome evil.

Prophecy. The term *prophecy* has two meanings in the Bible. To prophesy means (1) to call people to a holy life—by leaving their idols and self-centeredness and returning to obedience to God and fellowship with him; (2) to predict blessing or judgment—blessing for those who obey God and calamity for those who disobey. Today many "experts" on prophecy seem to specialize in foretelling the future, neglecting the equally important prophetic role of forthtelling God's call to righteousness.

The first chapter of Isaiah begins with the prophet pleading with the people of Israel to depart from their sin and return to God. The passage also predicts judgment and promises blessing. "Prophecy" basically refers to that kind of prophetic preaching, often in quite figurative language. Nowhere in the Bible does prophecy take the form of satisfying people's natural curiosity about the future. Generally it does not give detailed predictions about the future. Just before Jesus' ascension the disciples asked him about a single detail: Would God now restore the kingdom to Israel? Jesus replied, "It is not for you to know the times or seasons which the Father has fixed by his own authority" (Acts 1:7). Predictive prophecy has revealed enough to show that God is in control of all that happens in the future. He knows clearly where history is going because he is guiding and directing. But the rest is to remain hidden; the blueprint of future history belongs only to God.

Language of Creation and Climax. What we know about the creation of the world is only what God has chosen to disclose. Not only in Genesis 1–3 but throughout the OT and NT, the fact that God created all that exists is firmly stated. Yet the passages do not answer the "how" questions typical of modern scientific thinking. To think biblically about either the creation or climax of history is to limit oneself to what the passages say. Although figurative language (as well as literal) is used to describe both the beginning and the ending of history, the narratives describe real events. With so little detail given no one should pretend to have a full picture. One should avoid trying to make an artist's conception of how it really was or how it will really be; yet one can thank God for the faithful (though partial) picture he has provided in Scripture.

Poetry. Large portions of the OT are in *poetry*, a patterned, rhythmical form of literature characterized by a focused, figurative, and generally beautiful or powerful use of language. English poetry is usually recognizable by the pattern of its sound; sometimes it even has lines that rhyme. Hebrew poetry does not depend on a pattern of sound but rather on a balanced pattern of thought. Poetry is particularly difficult to translate from one language to another, because the patterns must be conveyed along with the meanings of the words. Here is a Hebrew stanza (Is 1:3) translated into English:

The ox / knows / its owner
and the ass / / its master's crib

but Israel / does not know
my people / does not understand.

The parallelism easily seen in those four lines is the major characteristic of Hebrew poetry. Of the two pairs of lines, the second line has the same idea as the first, called synonymous parallelism. An idea is presented, then repeated in different words. In the first pair, the verb is not repeated. With three stressed units in the first line and two stressed units in the second line, the meter is said to be 3 / 2. In the second pair of lines, the two stressed units in each line form a 2 / 2 meter. The third and fourth lines are also synonymous parallelism.

To a casual reader such detail may seem irrelevant to meaning, but it is part of the writer's poetic stance. The poetic form itself conveys meaning and also alerts the reader to expect word pictures, rhythmic balance, and artistic imagery. Consequently there is an advantage in using a Bible translation that prints poetry as poetry, in a typographical format that makes it easy to recognize. That format helps the reader make the needed shift from prose to a poetic framework.

It is good to read poetry aloud, trying to feel the balance of ideas and stressed units. By doing so, a reader gets more in touch with the style of the original writer—who was carefully framing ideas in beautiful poetic language. That is part of the important first step of interpretation: finding out what a passage meant to the original writer and reader.

Conclusion. The task of interpreting the Bible is never finished. Christians must continually strive to understand its meaning correctly and to rephrase it for today's world.

Theology endeavors to state in a condensed fashion what is taught on one subject in all parts of the Bible. Many Christians naively accept the doctrines taught by their churches. Those who begin to study the Bible for themselves, carefully applying the two steps of sound interpretation, may come to a better understanding of Christianity's basic beliefs. If Bible study leads one to question some things one hears about the Bible, that is also a sign of healthy growth. No conscientious Christian should ever stop studying the Word of God; new ideas must be checked against its teachings. Weak or inaccurate statements of what God is saying today are revised on the basis of new insights into what God said to the people of biblical times.

A Christian's devotional interpretation can always be improved because personal needs keep changing. Suddenly one may see important things that were missed before, even in favorite passages that have been studied many times. The two basic steps of interpretation are important even in devotional Bible study. Suppose one faces doubts; one can turn to the account of Thomas and his experience with doubt (Jn 20:24–29). The first step is to see how Thomas overcame his doubts; the second is creatively to apply the narrative to one's own situation. Recognition that people in the Bible had the same kinds of problems can in itself be encouraging.

The two-step approach to interpretation can also keep a group Bible study from declining into mere opinion-sharing without a true biblical basis. A person with skill in that approach can help others make their own contribution to the group's understanding of any particular passage.

A. BERKELEY MICKELSEN

See APOCALYPTIC; ALLEGORY; POETRY, BIBLICAL; TYPE, TYPOLOGY; DEMYTHOLOGIZATION.

Bibliography. G.W. Anderson (ed), *Tradition and Interpretation;* C.H. Dodd, *According to the Scriptures;* F.W. Farrar, *History of Interpretation;* G.D. Fee and D. Stuart, *How to Read the Bible for All Its Worth;* I.H. Marshall (ed), *NT Interpretation;* B. Mickelsen, *Interpreting the Bible;* P. Stuhlmacher, *Historical Criticism and Theological Interpretation of Scripture.*

Bible, Textual Criticism of the.

Task of reconstructing the original text of the Bible with as great a degree of accuracy as the available materials permit. Textual criticism is sometimes designated as lower criticism to distinguish it from higher criticism, which is analysis of the date, unity, and authorship of the biblical writings.

The task of the textual critic is divided into four major stages: (1) collection and collation of the materials from existing manuscripts, translations, and quotations; (2) development of theory and methodology that will enable the critic to use the gathered information to reconstruct the most accurate text of the biblical materials; (3) reconstruction of the history of the transmission of the text in order to identify the various influences affecting the text; (4) evaluation of specific variant readings in light of textual evidence, theology, and church history.

Sources. The initial task is collection of all possible records of the biblical writings, since the originals (called autographs) no longer exist. The primary sources are manuscripts (hand-written copies). Manuscripts were usually written on animal skins, papyrus, or even metal. Secondary sources include translations into other languages, quotations used by both protagonists and antagonists of biblical religion, and evidence from early printed texts. The comparison and careful listing of the variant readings thus uncovered is known as collation.

Old Testament. Most medieval manuscripts of the OT reflect a fairly standardized form of the Hebrew text. The standardization reflects the work of medieval scribes known as Masoretes (AD 500–900); the text that resulted from their work is called the Masoretic text. Of one scholar's list of 60 important manuscripts dated from the 11th century or later, all reflect the same basic textual tradition.

The evidence or "witness" of the medieval manuscripts has been supplemented by other discoveries in recent years. The most famous discovery (or series of discoveries) was that of the Dead Sea Scrolls at Wadi Qumran in 1947. The Isaiah scroll has received the most publicity, although the scrolls contained fragments of all the books in the Hebrew Bible with the exception of Esther. The great significance of the discovery is the fact that the Dead Sea scrolls antedate the oldest Masoretic manuscripts by over a millennium. The texts found at Wadi Qumran were completed before the Roman conquest of Palestine in AD 70.

Additional evidence comes from Wadi Murabba 'at, also on the Dead Sea, from the period of the Bar Kochba revolt in AD 132–135. The biblical material found there includes fragments of the Pentateuch (the first five books of the OT) and Isaiah, and a leather scroll in Greek containing fragments of the Minor Prophets. Additional information on the transmission history of the Hebrew text is provided by a great number of biblical fragments discovered at a Cairo genizah dated AD 882. (A genizah is a room in a synagogue used to store worn or erroneous manuscripts.)

The Samaritan Pentateuch and the Septuagint are the most important translations that bear witness to the text of the Hebrew Bible. The Samaritan Pentateuch is a version of the five books of Moses written in a rounded form of Hebrew letters in contrast with the more standard square (Aramaic) form. The Samaritans accepted only the Pentateuch as canonical. A copy of the Samaritan Pentateuch came to the attention of scholars in AD 1616; it is presumably a descendant of the Hebrew text used by the Samaritans after their break with the Jews.

The Septuagint (often designated LXX, Roman numerals for 70) is the oldest Greek translation of the OT. According to tradition it was translated by a team of 70 scholars (hence LXX) in Alexandria (Egypt). The exact date of translation is not ascertainable. Evidence indicates that the Septuagint Pentateuch was completed in the 3rd century BC. Aramaic Targums (translations) and commentaries on the Hebrew Bible, the Peshitta (a Syriac translation), Old Latin, Vulgate, and Arabic translations provide additional evidence of the original Hebrew text.

Quotations and allusions from a vast amount of rabbinic commentary on the OT add to the welter of evidence collected and collated in order to reconstruct the OT text.

New Testament. Manuscript evidence for the NT is varied and voluminous. Latest statistics record knowledge of 88 papyri (manuscripts written on a very fragile paperlike material made from river reeds); 274 uncials (manuscripts written on animal skins in capital letters); 2,795 minuscules (manuscripts written on animal skins in flowing, cursive letters dated 10th century or later); and 2,209 lectionaries (manuscripts in which the biblical materials are arranged for reading according to the sequences of the liturgical calendar); a total of 5,366 sources. Most of the manuscripts are fragmentary and originally contained only a portion of the NT, such as the four Gospels. Only 59 of the manuscripts originally contained the whole NT.

The earliest NT manuscripts were written on scrolls formed by sewing pieces of leather or papyrus together. The scrolls seldom exceeded 35 feet in length—the space needed for the Gospel of Luke or the Book of Acts, for example. Early in the 2nd century the more convenient codex was introduced. A codex was formed by folding one or more sheets into a booklike shape and sewing them together. The advantages were convenience, size, and the opportunity to use both sides of the writing material.

A brief description of several manuscripts in each major category will enhance understanding of the textual critic's task.

1. Papyri. Important papyrus manuscripts include Chester Beatty Papyri P45, P46, and P47 (purchased by Sir Chester Beatty in 1930–31) and Bodmer Papyri P66 and P75 (acquired by M. Martin Bodmer in 1955–56).

P45 consists of 30 from an original 220 leaves (each leaf measures about 8 x 10 inches). Portions of each of the four Gospels and the Book of Acts have survived in this codex dated by its modern editor in the first half of the 3rd century.

P46 contains 86 leaves from an original 104. Also a 3rd-century manuscript, it originally contained the Pauline Epistles arranged as follows: Romans, Hebrews, 1 and 2 Corinthians, Ephesians, Galatians, Philippians, Colossians, and 1 and 2 Thessalonians. It is interesting to note the inclusion of the Book of Hebrews in the Pauline materials, since it is sometimes argued that Paul did not write that book.

P47 dates a bit later in the 3rd century than the first two and consists of 10 leaves from an original 32 containing the Book of Revelation.

P[66], dated by its modern editor about AD 200, is a copy of the Gospel of John. Only 104 leaves were acquired in the original purchase, and fragments of another 46 have subsequently been acquired.

P[75] is a codex containing Luke and John, of which only 102 of an original 144 leaves have survived. The editors date the codex between AD 175 and 225.

2. Uncials. Before the 9th century, Greek manuscripts were written in capital letters in a printed style. Such manuscripts are called uncials and are designated by capital letters, the major uncial manuscripts being A, ℵ (the Hebrew letter *aleph*), B, C, D, and θ (the Greek capital letter *theta*).

Codex Sinaiticus (ℵ) is a 4th-century codex written on vellum, containing all of the Greek NT plus sections of the OT. The codex was discovered in a waste receptacle in a monastery on Mt Sinai by Constantin von Tischendorf in 1844 and constitutes one of the most fascinating discoveries in the field of textual criticism. A few missing leaves were discovered at the monastery in 1978.

Codex Alexandrinus (A) is an early 5th-century vellum manuscript containing the whole Greek Bible (with some mutilation) on its 773 leaves. Only portions of Matthew, John, and 2 Corinthians are missing in the NT section. The codex was presented to King Charles I of England in 1627.

Codex Vaticanus (B) was first listed in a catalog of Vatican Library materials in 1475, although it was not fully available to the scholarly public until publication of a facsimile in 1889-90. It is an early 4th-century vellum manuscript of the whole Greek Bible. Of an original 820 leaves, 759 still exist. Missing are most of Genesis, 31 Psalms, and a large section of the NT.

Codex Ephraemi (C) is a 5th-century manuscript that was erased in the 12th century, with sermons of a 4th-century Syrian church father, Ephraem, written over the biblical materials. (Manuscripts that have one text written over another are called palimpsests.) Only 64 leaves from the OT and 145 from the NT remain. Tischendorf used chemical processes to make the original writing available to the scholarly world in 1843.

Codex Bezae (D) was presented to the library at Cambridge University (England) in 1581 by Theodore Beza. It is a 5th- or 6th-century manuscript of the four Gospels (in the order Matthew, John, Luke, and Mark) and Acts plus a fragment of 3 John. Of an original 510 leaves, 406 have survived. The outstanding characteristic of the manuscript is free addition and occasional omission. In the Book of Acts, for example, Codex Bezae presents a text about 1/10 longer than the usual text.

Codex Koridethi (θ) is a 9th-century manuscript of the Gospels with a text in the Gospel of Mark that is quite different from the tradition found in the other three Gospels.

3. Minuscules. After the 9th century, Greek manuscripts were written in a cursive style and are called minuscules. Minuscules are designated by Arabic numbers—for example, 1, 13, 33, 565, and 1839. Most of the minuscules present a rather standardized textual pattern, although occasionally they reflect a much earlier type of text. A number of manuscripts in the minuscule classification are similar enough to form a "family." Family 1 (identified by Kirsopp Lake in this century), for example, includes minuscules 1, 118, 131, and

St. Catherine's monastery at Mt Sinai.

209 (all dated from the 12th to the 14th centuries). Family 13 (identified by W.H. Ferrar in 1868) includes minuscules 13, 69, 124, 346, and several other manuscripts written from the 11th to the 15th centuries. Minuscule 33 is known as "the queen of the cursives" because of its high quality. It contains the entire NT (minus Revelation) and dates from the 9th or 10th century. Minuscule 565, beautifully written in gold ink on purple vellum, also dates from the 9th or 10th century. Minuscule 1739 is a 10th-century manuscript with significant marginal notations taken from several of the church fathers.

4. Translations. The missionary interests of the early church led to translations of the NT in a variety of languages. Those translations or versions, particularly the Syriac and Latin, provide additional information on the nature of the text at an early stage. Such evidence is complicated, however, by the transfer into a new language and by inadequate information about the textual base from which they were translated. Five different versions of the Syriac NT are available: Old Syriac, the Peshitta (the common version), the Philoxenian, the Harclean, and the Palestinian Syriac. The Old Latin version of the NT reflects a translation begun in the late 2nd century for use in North Africa. The work of Jerome near the end of the 4th century produced the famous Latin Vulgate version, represented today by more than 8,000 extant manuscripts. Other important versions include the Coptic, Gothic, Armenian, Georgian, Ethiopic, and Slavonic.

Patristic Quotations. Additional textual evidence can be drawn from quotations found in the early writers known as the church fathers. The range of such quotations, covering most of the NT, provides evidence on the history of transmission of variant readings and text types.

It is clear from the above discussion that abundant evidence is available for reconstructing the text of the NT. Much work is currently in progress using modern technology to catalog and collate every bit of that material.

History of Transmission. Reconstruction of the history of the transmission of the text is an important element in evaluating variant readings. Material from a wide variety of sources must be combined in order to arrive at even a tentative reconstruction of the text. A brief sketch of scholarly opinion for each Testament follows.

Old Testament. The early history of the text as reflected in the Dead Sea Scrolls, the Samaritan Pentateuch, the Septuagint, and the ancient Hebrew text shows a remarkable fluidity and diversity. Evidently the standardizing process did not begin at the earliest stages. For

example, the materials from the Qumran community where the Dead Sea Scrolls were found, do not reflect any frustration with varying texts within that community. Scholars have attempted to account for such diversity by theories of local texts (that various localities had differing text types) and precanonical fluidity (that until the process of canonization was complete, accurate reproduction of the manuscripts was not viewed as very important). It should be noted, however, that the basic text modern scholarship has identified as closest to the original was among the Dead Sea texts (e.g., the large Isaiah scroll).

Destruction of the temple in AD 70 provided an impetus for standardization of the consonantal text. The texts found at Wadi Murabba 'at reflect the new stage. The scholars initially reporting on the discovery were disappointed to find so few variations from the standard Masoretic text. To scholars, the very early texts from the Dead Sea discoveries had become the standard consonantal text to the exclusion of other variants. Scholars have gone so far as to identify the only slightly later Wadi Murabba 'at texts as "Proto-Masoretic."

Standardization as practiced by the Masoretes meant identifying one text as normative and copying carefully from that text. It also meant correcting existing texts by the normative text. The Hebrew text, of course, was written with consonants alone, not with consonants *and* vowels as we write English.

The next stage in the transmission of the OT text was standardization of punctuation and vowel patterns. That process, begun fairly early in the NT period, extended over 1000 years. A long series of Masoretes provided annotations known as Masora (Hebrew for "tradition"). Two different motivations are evident in their work. One was their concern for accurate reproduction of the consonantal text. For that purpose a collection of annotations (on irregular forms, abnormal patterns, the number of times a form or word was used, the enlarged letters in the middle of words that had enumerative significance, and other matters) was gathered and inserted in the margins or at the end of the text. A second concern of the Masoretes was for vocalization of the consonantal text for reading purposes. Prohibition against inserting vocalization into the text itself had required oral tradition for transmission. The origins of vocalization reflect differences from Babylon and Palestine. The Tiberian Masoretes (scholars working in Tiberias in Palestine) provided the most complete and exact system of vocalization. The earliest dated manuscript from that tradition is a codex of the Prophets from the Karaite synagogue of Cairo dated AD 896. Today the standard Hebrew text of the OT, Kittel's *Biblia Hebraica* (3rd ed and later), is constructed on the basis of the Tiberian Masoretic tradition.

Standardization of both the consonantal text and vocalization succeeded so well that the manuscripts that have survived display a remarkable agreement. Most of the variants, being minor and attributable to scribal error, do not affect interpretation.

New Testament. The history of transmission of the NT text is quite different from that of the OT. The nearness in date of extant manuscripts to the original writing, the brevity of the period of oral transmission, the shorter period of time over which the whole process took place, and the absence of early standardization have enabled the textual critic to move closer to the original text through comparison and collation.

Reconstruction has usually been associated with a so-called genealogical method. That method attempts to work back through the process of transmission in order to identify different families of manuscripts and their interrelationships. Prominent scholars in the field have been Johann Albrecht Bentley (1687–1752), Brooke Foss Westcott (1825–1901), Fenton John Anthony Hort (1828–92), Hermann von Soden (1852–1914), and Burnett Hillman Streeter (1874–1937). Streeter's work illustrates the directions of the process. Although he worked primarily from the four Gospels, his diagrams and theories pertain to the whole NT.

Streeter began his research with the intention of isolating the forms of text current in the great centers of Christendom. Using quotations of the church fathers for evidence, he identified the forms of the NT text peculiar to each center. He posited the widest divergence of text by about AD 200. The diagram represents the conclusions of his study:

Streeter's Theory of Text Types

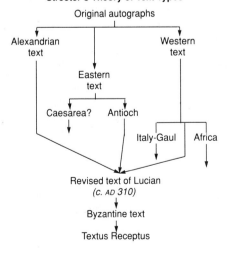

Original autographs

Alexandrian text — Western text

Eastern text

Caesarea? — Antioch

Italy-Gaul — Africa

Revised text of Lucian
(c. AD 310)

Byzantine text

Textus Receptus

Streeter's diagram delineates the primary categories of geographical distribution. The Alexandrian text (named after Alexandria in Egypt) was prepared in an area marked by scholarly traditions. The chief witnesses are Codex Vaticanus, Codex Sinaiticus, P^{66}, and P^{72}. Scholars agree that the Alexandrian is the best ancient text, on the whole, and that it reflects the original NT text from early in the 2nd century.

The Western text reflects a less standardized text which resulted from disciplined control of the manuscript tradition. Some scholars hesitate to designate it as a text type. Codex Bezae and the Old Latin manuscripts, reflecting that tradition, are characterized by additions and striking omissions. The Western text also represents an early state of the text; it was used by such 2nd- and 3rd-century writers as Marcion, Irenaeus, Tertullian, and Cyprian.

The Eastern text, represented chiefly by the Caesarean text, is found in Codex Kordethi and two different subfamilies of minuscules. That text type was brought to Caesarea by Origen (d. AD 253 or 254). It appears to be based on the Alexandrian text, but includes many Western readings. It is the least homogeneous of the three major textual families. (In fact, more recent scholarship questions even the existence of the Caesarean text.)

The Byzantine text, as the diagram indicates, is a combination of the other three. Its compilers chose to include two or more variant readings for a passage rather than make a decision about the relative value of the competing readings (the process called conflation). The result of that combination of text types is that the distinctive readings of the Byzantine text are usually secondary in quality.

Introduction of cursive writing (minuscule manuscripts) began in the early part of the ninth century. By that time the Byzantine text type had become the dominant family and nearly all manuscripts in the cursive script were copies of that inferior text type.

Introduction of printing in the 16th century soon led to the printing of a Greek NT. The first one was the Complutensian Polyglot, a collection of versions in various languages (hence polyglot) named after the Spanish town in which it was produced (Alcalá, but Complutum in Latin). It was printed in 1514–17, but was not released until 1521 or 1522. The first Greek NT to be published (i.e., released for sale) was that of Desiderius Erasmus in 1516. The textual base for Erasmus' edition was a half-dozen minuscule manuscripts. The earliest (codex 1 from the 10th century) was used least, since it was based on earlier uncial texts and Erasmus thought it to be erratic.

Robert Estienne (also known as Stephanus, 1503–59), a Paris printer, published his third edition of the Greek NT in 1550. It closely approximated the 4th and 5th editions of Erasmus. The same basic textual tradition appears in the 1633 edition of the Elzevir brothers. The preface to that edition states in Latin "the reader has the text which is now received by all, in which we give nothing changed or corrupted." From the words "text . . . received" (Latin textum . . . receptum) came the term "Textus Receptus" to designate the standard text. Subsequent editions copied the Textus Receptus faithfully. All principal Protestant translations in Europe prior to 1881 (including KJV) were based on the textual tradition of Erasmus, which was in turn based on a few relatively late manuscripts from the Byzantine "family."

Methodology. The search for an adequate methodology to handle the many variant readings found in manuscripts is inseparably intertwined with our understanding of the history of transmission. The basic issue in textual criticism is the method used to decide the relative value of those variant readings. Many factors must be evaluated in order to arrive at a valid decision.

Reading Manuscripts. Modern science has provided a number of aids for deciphering a manuscript. Scientific dating procedures help to determine the age of the writing material. Chemical techniques help clarify writing that has deteriorated. Ultraviolet light enables a scholar to see traces of ink (carbon) in a manuscript even after the surface writing has been effaced.

Each manuscript must be studied as a whole, for each has a "personality." It is important to identify the characteristic errors, characteristic carelessness or carefulness, and other peculiarities of the scribe(s) who copied the material. Then the manuscript must be compared with other manuscripts to identify the "family" tradition with which it agrees. Preservation of common errors or insertions in the text is a clue to relationships. All possible details of date, place of origin, and authorship must be ascertained.

Scribal errors fall into several distinct categories. The first large category is that of unintentional errors. Confusion of similar consonants occurred frequently. Corruptions also resulted from incorrect division of words (earliest manuscripts omitted spaces between words in order to save space). Confusion of sounds occurred, particularly when one scribe read to a group of scribes making multiple copies. In the OT, the method of vocalization (addition of vowels to the consonantal text) created some errors. Omission of a let-

ter, word, or phrase created new readings. Repetition of a letter, word, or even a whole phrase was also common. Omission (called haplography) or repetition (called dittography) could be caused by the eye of a scribe slipping from one word to a similar word or ending. (Confusion of similar endings is called homoeoteleuton.) Normally unintentional errors are fairly easy to identify because they create nonsense readings.

Intentional errors are much more difficult to identify and evaluate. Harmonizations from similar materials occurred with regularity (sometimes unintentionally—especially in the closely parallel materials of the synoptic Gospels, where the well-trained mind of a scribe could recall the wording of parallel material subconsciously). Difficult readings were subject to improvement by a thinking scribe. Objectionable expressions were sometimes eliminated or smoothed. Occasionally synonyms were employed. Conflation (resolving a discrepancy between two variant readings by including both of them) often appears. Conflation is particularly frequent in the NT family of manuscripts known as Byzantine.

Thus the more obvious errors are detected and eliminated and the peculiarities of the particular scribe are identified and eliminated. Then more subtle criteria for identifying the reading most likely to be the original must be employed. Procedures for applying such criteria are similar in both OT and NT work.

Development of Methodology. The search for an adequate methodology has engaged the attention and labor of many scholars over the years. Methodology is in a constant state of refinement in light of additional discoveries and new insights into the history of transmission. The history of the development of textual methodology is an enlightening study. Here we have room for only a brief overview of the history of NT methodology.

The first printed editions of the Bible (16th century) forced scholars to outline their principles of textual criticism. The first texts to be printed reflected the manuscripts then in greatest abundance and most readily available to the editor. Dominance of the Textus Receptus as the standard text of the Greek NT for the next 300 years overshadowed earlier and more valuable texts.

Soon after the printing of the Greek NT, the process of collecting and evaluating textual variants began. Of the many scholars who contributed to that process, only a few can be mentioned here.

John Mill (1645–1707) produced an edition of the Greek NT showing 30,000 variant readings. Johann Albrecht Bengel (1687–1752), after studying the variants that had been collected, arrived at the insight that witnesses should be "weighed" instead of being simply counted. Sheer number of manuscripts (a kind of "majority rule"), he believed, was an insufficient basis for confident decision. Johann Jakob Wettstein (1693–1754), a contemporary of Bengel, produced a two-volume Greek NT (1751–52) that contained a massive number of textual variants and provided the system of manuscript classification still in use today.

Johann Jakob Griesbach (1745–1812) carefully analyzed the processes employed in making decisions among variant readings, arriving at a set of 15 rules to be followed. Skillfully applying his canons of criticism, he produced an edition of the Greek NT that abandoned the Textus Receptus in many places. Karl Lachmann (1793–1851) was the first recognized scholar to make a complete break with the Textus Receptus, creating a complete text on the basis of recognized principles and rules.

Constantin von Tischendorf (1815–74), famous for his discovery of Codex Sinaiticus, searched avidly throughout Europe and the Near East for manuscripts of the Greek NT, published a great number of discoveries, and combined the new evidence with existing materials to produce eight major editions of the Greek NT.

The scholars most influential in the development of methodology were Brooke Foss Westcott and Fenton John Anthony Hort. Both were Cambridge professors interested in refining the processes of methodology and in rigorously applying them to the text itself. The principles they so carefully delineated became the model from which modern textual critics have operated.

On the basis of their investigations, Westcott and Hort distinguished four principal groupings or families of manuscripts. The diagram ("The Westcott and Hort Theory of Text Types") depicts their reconstruction of the relationships between the types of texts.

The Syrian family of texts was created in the 4th century by an editor interested primarily in an easy, complete text. Stumbling

blocks for the reader were reduced to a minimum, with few omissions but many additions of a harmonizing and explanatory nature. Hort described it as presenting "the New Testament in a form smooth and attractive, but appreciably impoverished in sense and force, more fitted for cursory perusal or recitation than for repeated and diligent study."

The Western Family of texts isolated by Westcott and Hort reflected an early state of transmission, being quoted by Marcion, Tatian, Justin, Irenaeus, Hippolytus, Tertullian, and Cyprian. The Western text was characterized by love of paraphrase, by freedom to change, omit, or insert materials that increased force or definiteness, by interchange of various forms, and by assimilation or harmonization.

The Alexandrian text was used by the Alexandrian fathers (Clement, Origen, Dionysius, Didymus, and Cyril). It reflected the literary taste of Alexandria in its emphasis upon correct syntax and style.

The Neutral text was best represented by the great codexes Vaticanus and Sinaiticus. Westcott and Hort felt that text was most free of mixture and corruption (hence its name) and came closest to the originals. Their high opinion of the Neutral text led them to accept its readings unless strong evidence pointed in another direction.

The work of Westcott and Hort marked a turning point in textual criticism and opened the way for modern critical editions of the Greek text and the burgeoning list of modern translations. A chief contribution of their work was identification of the Syrian text (called Byzantine by most other scholars) as a later text marked by conflations and never quoted by any church father prior to the Council of Nicaea (325).

Two other major contributors to the development of textual criticism were Hermann von Soden and Eberhard Nestle (1851–1913). Von Soden collected much manuscript evidence, worked with particular diligence on minuscules, and produced a monumental edition of the Greek NT (1902–13). He also invented a new system of nomenclature and symbolism. Von Soden's massive work has been discounted for its methodological errors and inaccuracies in collation. Eberhard Nestle initiated a compact edition of the Greek NT based upon current methodology. It was a marvel of succinctness with a wide variety of information and has now gone through 26 editions, the latest edited by Erwin Nestle and Kurt Aland.

The most recent Greek text of the NT is published by the United Bible Societies (3rd ed, Kurt Aland, Matthew Black, Carlo M. Mar-

The Westcott and Hort Theory of Text Types

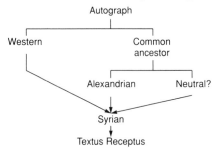

tini, Bruce M. Metzger, and Allen Wikgren). Instead of seeking to provide all available evidence, it is designed to provide a textual base for translators. Thus, only textual problems significantly affecting translations are discussed. An accompanying textual commentary outlines the method by which the editors arrived at their decisions.

Principles of Methodology. Through the work of textual critics in the last several centuries, certain basic principles have evolved. The primary principles for each of the Testaments can be briefly summarized.

A. OT. (1) The basic text for primary consideration is the Masoretic text because of the careful standardization it represents. That text is compared with the testimony of the ancient versions. The Septuagint, by reason of age and basic faithfulness to the Hebrew text, carries much weight in all decisions. The Targums (Aramaic translations) also reflect the Hebrew base, but they exhibit a tendency to expansion and paraphrase. The Peshitta (Syriac), Vulgate (Latin), Old Latin, and Coptic versions add indirect evidence, although translations are not always clear witnesses in technical details. Use of such versions does enable scholars to employ comparative philology in textual decisions and thus expose early errors for which the original reading probably has not survived.

(2) The reading that best explains the origin of other variants is preferable. Information from reconstruction of the history of transmission often provides additional insight. Knowledge of typical scribal errors enables the critic to make an educated decision on the sequence of variants.

(3) The shorter reading is preferable. The scribes frequently added material in order to solve style or syntax problems and seldom abridged or condensed material.

(4) The more difficult reading is more likely to be the original one. This principle is closely related to the third. Scribes did not intentionally create more complex readings. Unintentional errors are usually easy to identify. Thus the easier reading is normally suspect as a scribal alteration.

(5) Readings that are not harmonized or assimilated to similar passages are preferable. Copyists had a tendency to correct material on the basis of similar material elsewhere (sometimes even unconsciously).

(6) When all else fails, the textual critic must resort to conjectural emendation. To make an "educated guess" requires intimate acquaintance with the Hebrew language, familiarity with the author's style, and an understanding of culture, customs, and theology that might color the passage. Use of conjec-

ture must be limited to those passages in which the original reading has definitely not been transmitted to us.

B. NT. The basic principles in the textual criticism of the NT are similar to those in OT work. The procedures of Westcott and Hort can be reviewed briefly with some modification in light of more recent discussions.

The first step is to evaluate the strength of the evidence for competing readings. The date of the manuscripts (with attention to the date of the texts they reflect), the range of geographical distribution of the witnesses in each category, and the genealogical relationships of the major textual families must be taken into consideration.

In the second step, the probable lines of transmission are evaluated on the basis of copyists' habits. Several canons of criticism common to both Testaments come into play. (1) The more difficult reading is preferable, since copyists usually worked at a superficial level and smoothed out materials. (2) The shorter reading is preferable, unless created by an unintentional error. (3) Passages harmonized with related material are to be suspected. (4) Readings that reflect stylistic polishing of the text are probably later revisions.

A third step is to determine the author of the material by evaluating the literary style. To do so requires knowledge of the author's style and vocabulary in other writings for comparison with the work at hand, an understanding of the background against which the material was written, the immediate context of the reading, and the theology and culture of the whole setting.

Recent discussions have raised serious questions about the strength of the genealogical method, resulting in a move toward an eclectic methodology in which the textual critic attempts to use the whole range of evidence available. A textual family with a preponderance of preferable readings is not automatically given the preference in every variant. Although Hort emphasized the priority of external evidence, eclecticism tends to emphasize the internal probabilities—thus placing more weight on linguistic, stylistic, and scribal factors.

Textual criticism is obviously not a simple process. It is impossible to apply its principles and procedures mechanically. Textual criticism is an art and a skill in which a carefully prepared and alert artisan makes a calculated decision on the basis of as broad a range of factors as possible.

Conclusion. It should be remembered that textual criticism operates only when two or more readings are possible for a specific work or phrase. For most of the biblical text a single reading has been transmitted. Elimination of scribal errors and intentional changes leaves only a small percentage of the text about which any questions occur. Writing in 1940, textual scholar Sir Frederic Kenyon concluded:

> The interval then between the dates of original composition and the earliest extant evidence becomes so small as to be in fact negligible, and the last foundation for any doubt that the Scriptures have come down to us substantially as they were written has now been removed. Both the *authenticity* and the *general integrity* of the books of the New Testament may be regarded as finally established.

Similar confidence is expressed in the text of the OT.

The field of textual criticism is complex, requiring the gathering and skillful use of a wide variety of information. Because it deals with the authoritative source of revelation for all Christians, textual argumentation has often been accompanied by emotion.

Yet in spite of controversy, great progress has been made, particularly in the last century. Refinement of methodology has greatly aided our understanding of the accumulated materials. Additional aid has come from accumulations of information in related fields of study, such as church history, biblical theology, and the history of Christian thought.

Collection and organization of variant readings have enabled modern textual critics to give strong assurance that the Word of God has been transmitted in accurate and dependable form. Although variant readings have become obvious through the publication of so many manuscripts, inadequate, inferior, and secondary readings have been largely eliminated. In relatively few places is conjectural emendation necessary. In matters pertaining to the Christian's salvation, clear and unmistakable transmission provides authoritative answers. Christians are thus in debt to the textual critics who have worked, and are working, to provide a dependable biblical text.

MORRIS A. WEIGELT

See DEAD SEA SCROLLS; BIBLICAL CRITICISM, NEW TESTAMENT; BIBLICAL CRITICISM, OLD TESTAMENT; BIBLE, CANON OF THE; BIBLE; MASORA, MASORETES.

Bibliography. F.F. Bruce, *The Books and the Parchments*; J.H. Greenlee, *An Introduction to NT Textual Criticism*, and *Scribes, Scrolls, and Scripture*; F.G. Kenyon, *Handbook to the Textual Criticism of the NT*; K. Lake, *The Text of the NT* (rev ed); B.M. Metzger, *The Text of the NT* (2nd ed); A. Souter, *The Text and Canon of the NT*.

Bible, Translations of the. *See* BIBLE, INTERPRETATION OF THE

Biblical Criticism, New Testament. Analysis of the biblical text, applying historical, linguistic, and hermeneutical criteria to it in order to distinguish its true meaning. Biblical criticism answers questions of historical background (e.g., Jewish and Roman laws behind the trials of Jesus or Paul), introductory material (e.g., major themes and problems in 1 Cor), and biblical theology (e.g., the doctrine of election in Eph), as well as more specific questions of authorship, dating, and addressees.

Two Uses of Biblical Criticism. Two different approaches to biblical criticism must be delineated. One has often been destructive, dealing only with questions of authenticity or accuracy. The purpose of some scholars seems to be negation rather than open investigation of Scripture. For example, the "rationalist" critics (discussed below) were more concerned with reinterpreting Jesus' life than analyzing the meaning of biblical texts. When they were finished, very little of the Gospels as they now exist could be recognized as authentic.

The other approach to biblical criticism is primarily constructive, dealing with questions of meaning. An example is the grammatico-historical school, including J.B. Lightfoot (1828–89) and B.F. Westcott (1825–1901). Those scholars sought to discover the meaning of the text in the light of its historical context rather than to explore questions of historical truthfulness. The modern school of "canon criticism," inaugurated by OT scholar Brevard S. Childs (1923–   ), attempts to study the canonical text as it stands rather than its historical or traditional development. That method of study is akin to biblical theology rather than historical criticism.

Most scholars work between the two poles. Rudolf Bultmann (1884–1976), often identified with the extremely negative position, attempted a constructive approach through his "demythologization." Bultmann's method, destructive in conservative eyes, allows the radical critic to denote modern (existential) applications from the Scripture text. Lightfoot and Westcott also addressed questions, not only of meaning, but of authenticity as well. Most critical scholars today do the same.

Necessity of Biblical Criticism. The Bible is not a celestial book written on gold tablets and transported to earth. Though it is described as divine revelation, inspired (in Greek, "breathed out") by God (2 Tm 3:16), it was given through the Holy Spirit to the biblical writers in space and time. God did not dictate it, overpowering the writers' conscious minds. Rather the Holy Spirit guided them to answer needs of their day (Jn 14:26; 15:26), using their personalities and abilities to communicate his Word. NT letters illustrate the intention to answer specific problems in early

Christian communities. The Gospels and OT historical books also show their authors' individual traits and contemporary messages.

Thus biblical criticism is necessary to a high view of Scripture. It serves to control both the extreme liberal tendency to demote the Bible to a mere human book and the extreme conservative tendency to raise it above the possibility of academic study. Otherwise the original message may be forgotten in a search for an emotional encounter. Biblical criticism forces the reader to regard the text as more than a way to meet one's subjective needs. The inspiration of the writers if thereby honored.

Problems of Biblical Criticism. Evangelical Christians sometimes identify biblical criticism with the negative presuppositions of radical critics, who assume that a "critical" approach to the Bible automatically negates its authority as the Word of God. Such critics view the Bible as strictly a human book chronicling the faith of Israel and the church, rather than as a record of God's saving acts in history. G.E. Ladd wrote in *The New Testament and Criticism*, "To many scholars, the rigor of one's criticism is to be measured by the number of inauthentic verses he can find in the New Testament, particularly in the Gospels."

The historical books of the Bible are the crucial areas for critical study because they blend history and theology. Negative critics assume that where theological interests predominate, historical accuracy vanishes. For example, the transfiguration of Jesus is said to be a resurrection story created by the early church and read back into the life of Jesus in order to show his pre-Easter glory.

In reaction against such misuses of criticism, evangelicals have often neglected strong theological messages in the historical books. At one extreme, radical Bible commentaries can resemble a compendium of philosophical speculation. At the other, conservative commentaries can statically discuss chronology and historical meaning but pay little attention to theology.

History of Biblical Criticism. Marcion, a heretical church leader in the middle of the second century, accepted or dismissed NT literature depending on its adherence to Judaism. Martin Luther in the 16th century called the letter of James an "epistle of straw" and argued for its removal from the biblical canon. Those were isolated instances, however; the critical "movement" did not begin until the Renaissance. Theological criticism has generally followed the philosophical climate of the times. For example, German criticism has tended to be Hegelian in outlook, fol-

lowing the dialectic of G.W.F. Hegel; in recent decades critical thinking has largely been existential.

Rationalism. After the Renaissance, many scholars no longer accepted the supernatural presuppositions of the church and began to reinterpret the biblical account. For example, H.S. Reimarus (1694–1768) argued for a "rational" religion, asserting that Jesus was simply a man of his day. Jesus, he said, mistakenly followed Jewish messianic expectations and tried to make himself king; after he died, the disciples stole his body, proclaiming a resurrection and a theology of a suffering Savior.

Many rationalist critics offered a psychological explanation for NT events. H.E.G. Paulus (1761–1851) said that the miracles were legends based on natural events; for example, the feeding of the 5,000 occurred when Jesus helped a boy share his meager lunch and then everyone followed his example. Jesus used medicines and oils to heal the sick, according to such critics, and the resurrection occurred when Jesus swooned on the cross and revived in the tomb. K.A. Hase (1800–1890) and F. Schleiermacher (1768–1834) believed that Jesus was a charismatic figure who healed by the power of his personality. The NT was seen as the early church's attempt to interpret the impact of Jesus' personality on his followers.

Because of their antisupernatural bias and speculative approach to the NT records, such critics had no clear methodology for getting behind the written material to the actual events. Nonetheless, their rational approach drew attention to the human element in the writing of the biblical books. Many earlier scholars had assumed a "dictation" method in God's inspiration of Scripture, the writers simply copying what God told them. The new focus on the historical setting of the various books was a valuable advance in biblical exegesis.

Tendency Criticism. The first school of criticism developed at the University of Tübingen in Germany. F.C. Baur (1762–1860), who had been trained in Hegel's dialectic philosophy (thesis + antithesis = synthesis), applied it to his study of the development of Christianity. Baur's thesis was Peter's Jewish Christianity; his antithesis, Paul's Hellenistic Christianity. According to Baur, the two were in conflict into the 2nd century. The Books of Matthew, Mark, James, and Hebrews represented the Jewish side, viewing Christ as a prophet and making restrictions on the gospel. Paul, in his major letters (1 and 2 Cor; Gal; Rom) gave Christianity a new twist, proclaiming a divine Christ and a universal mission for the church. The synthesis began about AD 150 with the Book of Acts and concluded with 1

Peter and the Johannine writings (c. AD 200). Baur classified and dated the documents according to their "tendencies."

D.F. Strauss (1808–74) applied such a method to the life of Christ, using a literary rather than historical approach. The liberal "quest," he said, was based on a false methodology: you cannot merely align miracles with modern scientific possibility. The Gospels were "myths," a synthesis between the facts of Jesus' life (thesis) and the disciples' faith (antithesis).

The tendency school has had great influence, although Baur's theories were discarded for the most part after J.B. Lightfoot's *Apostolic Fathers* (1869–85) presented evidence that the NT's unity of thought was early and its conflict late (the opposite of Baur's conclusions). The tendency school, by pointing out the possibility of tension and conflict in the early church, allowed scholars greater freedom in pursuing the truth as they studied the Bible.

History-of-Religions Movement. Charles Darwin's *Origin of Species* (1859) made an impact on biblical scholarship through his emphasis on gradual development via natural processes. The positive influence of that concept can be seen in at least four disciplines related to biblical studies. (1) In comparative philology, scholars studied the evolution of the Greek language, especially after discovery of many papyrus manuscripts at the turn of the century provided new understanding of the Greek used in the NT. (2) In textual criticism, by tracing the mutations, or scribal errors, accumulated in copying NT manuscripts, scholars were able to discern the original form of the text. (3) In documentary research, the developmental concept enabled scholars to see how Matthew and Luke had used Mark's material in the writing of their Gospels. (4) In historical-grammatical exegesis, a scientific understanding of the development of history, language, and culture definitely enabled scholars to come closer to the true meaning of the NT text.

In the German history-of-religions movement, however, the idea that all religions grew on the same family tree, and that therefore Christianity evolved from its surrounding religious environment, approached the status of dogma. Otto Pfleiderer (1839–1908) compared Christianity to the Greek mystery religions. Richard Reitzenstein (1861–1931) believed that Christianity's source lay in the Gnostic myth of a dying and rising redeemer. Wilhelm Bousset's comprehensive work, *Kyrios Christos* (1921), pointed out parallels in Greek myth for the entire gospel portrayal of Jesus' life. The genius of Jesus the teacher lay behind the NT, Bousset believed, but it was written as the Hellenists added Greek ideas to be Jewish substructure.

The history-of-religions theory has several difficulties. (1) Data for the supposed parallels are chiefly post-Christian; therefore, the borrowing was more likely in the other direction, from Christianity to the mystery religions. (2) Use of symbols does not imply acceptance of theology. Christians could have used then-current terminology not to learn the ways of their contemporaries but to show the subordination of heathen ways to God. (3) Many so-called parallels are analogical rather than genealogical, that is, they are similar rather than directly connected. (4) Scholars now realize that many so-called Hellenistic parallels actually stemmed from 1st-century Judaism, for example, from Qumran (the Dead Sea Scrolls community) or from the OT Widsom Literature.

Consistent-Eschatology School. Johannes Weiss (1863–1914) believed that the key to the NT lay in Jewish messianic expectations. Jesus' teaching was thus "thoroughly" or "consistently" eschatological. That idea was developed by Albert Schweitzer (1875–1965), who said that Jesus was apocalyptic rather than prophetic; Jesus expected the Messianic Age to come when he sent out the 12 disciples (Mt 10). When that age did not occur, he sought to force God's kingdom to come by suffering. Jesus' cry on the cross, "Why have you forsaken me?" showed his disillusionment, according to Schweitzer. The early church overturned defeat by glorifying the resurrection, but was eventually forced to change from Jesus' apocalyptic approach (reflected in Paul's Thessalonian and Corinthian letters) to an ethical thrust (in the Ephesian, Philippian, and Colossian letters).

Schweitzer did scholarship a service by focusing attention on the Jewish background, especially upon apocalyptic concepts, but his ideas were challenged by other apocalyptic theories (such as the "realized" eschatology of Ernst von Dobschutz and C.H. Dodd, and the "inaugurated" eschatology of Joachim Jeremias and Oscar Cullmann). Also, the biblical evidence denies the kind of Christ Schweitzer portrayed. Jesus, obsessed with his mission rather than with Jewish thought-patterns, actually went against current Jewish expectations.

Modern Trends in Criticism. *Form Criticism.* In a period of two years (1919–20), three German scholars (K.L. Schmidt, Rudolf Bultmann, and Martin Dibelius) independently developed a new approach to the NT, determining chronology and authentic traditions by a literary method. According to the theory, the growing church developed needs for proclama-

Qumran monastery ruins are in the foreground, and the caves where the Dead Sea Scrolls were found are in the mountains in the background. The scrolls have many parallels with New Testament ideas (especially in the writings of John and Paul).

tion, apologetic, and teaching. As a result, the story of Jesus was divided into small units that circulated independently. As time passed, the stories took on a form dependent on the church's needs, becoming more elaborate as new situations added nuances.

Several aspects of form criticism should be noted.

1. Radical form criticism is based on an evolutionary concept. The traditional unit of the Gospels is seen as having developed from an original narrative nucleus but often does not go back to the original events in any authentic way.

2. Form criticism sees the church as the mold within which the stories as they now exist were created. To a radical form critic, the first generation was a period of oral tradition, so that stories were handled very flexibly according to the needs of the moment. Thus they were radically changed before the Gospels were written. According to that point of view the Gospels are theological treatises rather than historical documents; thus they represent the church's faith more than the literal story of Jesus.

3. In Bultmann's work, two other aspects were combined: an eschatological perspective and an existential hermeneutic. Bultmann, following Schweitzer in understanding Jesus as a thoroughgoing apocalyptist, argued that the key to the church's development was the delay in Christ's return. When Christ did not come as they believed, Christians had to change their faith to ethics. Greek ideas replaced Jewish ones, and the true history of Jesus was lost.

4. Bultmann also relied on existential interpretation, based on the philosophy of Martin Heidegger (1889–1976). In that view people are conditioned by anxiety, always living in the face of death and learning to live with that fear. Bultmann saw no clear relation between the biblical symbols of faith and faith itself, so those symbols had to be reinterpreted with reference to contemporary needs, like learning to cope with existence in the modern world. The historical nucleus about Jesus is therefore unimportant. What counts most is the early church's faith as expressed in the mythical, symbolic portrayal of Jesus.

5. The form-criticism method deals with literary units, understood as the key to chronology, which is in turn the key to authenticity. Both Bultmann and Dibelius divided the Gospels into types of literary units. Most authentic are the paradigms (Dibelius) or apo-

thegms (Bultmann), that is, concise maxims or simple sayings easy to remember and usually reflecting ideas different from those of the later church. Then come catechetical materials (teaching units, reflecting later needs), miracle stories (reflecting later theology about Jesus' impact on his disciples), and legends (without fixed form and with mythical elements—like the cloud and legendary figures at Jesus' transfiguration).

Form criticism's presuppositions and methods have many weaknesses. Bultmann especially has seemed to accept a 19th-century view with no room for the supernatural—a view many regard as abrogated in an Einsteinian age of relativity. Bultmann's approach, based on Heidegger's earlier work, ignores later developments in that philosopher's thought. Bultmann presupposes that the New Testament story-forms grew from the church's preaching needs and then in a circular argument uses the forms to prove that. Yet early preaching (*kerygma*) did not develop in a vacuum; it arose out of historical events—the life, death, and resurrection of Jesus.

Any attempt to divorce the NT from its historical roots and read "myth" into the stories is doomed to failure. It fails to allow for the creative genius of Jesus behind the church. It lays no foundation for a radical division between the historic Jesus and the kerygmatic Christ (the true life of Jesus in contrast with the picture painted in the Gospels). The early church considered the Gospel portrayals historically accurate (see Lk 1:1–5; Jn 21:25; 2 Pt 1:16).

Nevertheless, form criticism, divorced from its negative presuppositions, is an important tool for NT research. Using it, one can note different literary styles and the messages they portray. Also, recent study of early Christian creeds and hymns has enhanced our understanding of early church emphases and of the NT letters themselves. Form criticism thus can be a positive tool for tracing the growth of ideas and doctrines in the early Christian period.

Tradition Criticism. Two important offsprings of form criticism are tradition criticism and redaction criticism. Tradition criticism seeks to determine the growth of a particular Gospel story within the history of the early church. For instance, it studies the relationship and possible development of Matthew's and Luke's forms of the Beatitudes.

Standards for deciding authentic traditions have been summarized by Norman Perrin (*Rediscovering the Teaching of Jesus*) and R.H. Fuller (*A Critical Introduction to the New Testament*). Certitude is the basic criterion in tradition criticism. If any saying of Jesus can be doubted, it is considered a product of the post-Easter church.

Three major criteria have been developed by tradition critics: (1) Distinctiveness or dissimilarity. A saying is authentic only if it has no parallel in Judaism or the early church; otherwise it may be either a transfer of Jewish teaching or a later insertion by the church. (2) Cross-section method or multiple attestation. Authenticity can be accepted if a saying occurs in several or all of the primary sources behind the Gospels; otherwise it may be a later addition by the writer-evangelist. (3) Consistency or coherence. A tradition can be trusted if it is consistent with passages already authenticated on the basis of the first two standards. Authenticated sayings can thus be used as a basis for judging other passages.

Many scholars have reacted against the extreme pessimism and strictness of the criteria. It is impossible to claim that Jesus had no ties with Judaism or the early church. The former was the context within which he conducted his ministry, and the latter claimed him as its founder. The evidence shows direct continuity between the historical Jesus and the church's proclamation of him as Lord. Such critical tools betray their subjective character when they produce widely disparate pictures as different scholars study the same episode.

Removing the negative demand for certainty makes tradition criticism a more positive study tool. A study of parallel passages shows that the evangelists selected and omitted from oral traditions about Christ certain elements that highlighted important theological emphases. Also, study of creeds and hymns in apostolic letters can help clarify a writer's use of tradition.

Redaction Criticism. "Redaction" refers to the editorial reworking of Gospel stories by the evangelists in order to teach their own message. Redaction critics are open to many of the same criticisms as form critics: subjective interpretation, a misleading distinction between history and theology, and failure to allow for the foundation of the church in the Jesus of history. But the techniques of redaction criticism, when properly employed, may prove to be the finest tool yet for understanding the Bible's true message. Each Gospel writer, for instance, sought to portray a different nuance of the impact of events and teachings in Jesus' life and ministry. Thus the different theological themes in the evangelists' portrayals of the triumphal entry into Jerusalem, or of the stilling of storm, can widen and enrich a reader's understanding of Jesus' significance.

Conclusion. Although NT criticism has often been regarded with suspicion by evangelical Christians (and sometimes deservedly so), development of different techniques and schools of criticism has contributed greatly to our understanding of the NT documents and to the Christ whom they portray.

GRANT R. OSBORNE

See BIBLE, TEXTUAL CRITICISM OF THE; FORM CRITICISM; REDACTION CRITICISM; SOURCE CRITICISM; TRADITION CRITICISM; DEMYTHOLOGIZATION; BIBLICAL CRITICISM, OLD TESTAMENT.

Bibliography. R.M. Grant, *A Historical Introduction to the NT*; D. Guthrie, *NT Introduction*; H.F. Hahn, *OT in Modern Research*; P. Henry, *New Directions in NT Study*; M. Jones, *The NT in the Twentieth Century*; W. Kümmel, *The NT: The History of the Investigation of its Problems*; G. Ladd, *The NT and Criticism*; A.H. McNeile, *An Introduction to the Study of the NT*; S. Neill, *The Interpretation of the NT 1861–1961*; H.H. Rowley, *The OT and Modern Study*.

Biblical Criticism, Old Testament.

Careful analysis and scholarly study of the ancient literary sources that make up the OT. In ordinary usage, the term "criticism" is generally understood negatively, but the term is not necessarily used that way in connection with biblical studies. The task of biblical criticism is painstaking analysis of the various books in order to discover as much as possible about their origin, their historical and spiritual value, and how they were transmitted.

In general the procedures of biblical criticism are the same ones used to analyze non-biblical writings. The fact that some biblical scholars have come to negative conclusions, especially in the past, should bring into question only the critical methods they adopted, not the discipline as a whole. It is perfectly legitimate for the Scriptures to be subjected to critical scrutiny; the written record of God's revelation to humankind required conscious human participation to ensure that it would survive in written form. Human beings are a necessary part of the Scripture as it has come down to us; to that extent at least, human activities are properly open to scrutiny. Human beings have not only participated in the revelatory process but transmitted God's revelation in oral and written form.

Critical Approaches. Textual Criticism. The earliest form of biblical criticism had to do with the text, or actual wording of the Scriptures. Theologians realized that without reasonable certainty about the accuracy of what has been written, it is difficult to proclaim the Word of God with clarity and conviction. Textual critics hence worked to place at their disposal Scriptures in the original languages in a form as close as possible to what the various authors wrote. Until the Dead Sea Scrolls were discovered in 1947, it was thought that only one type of Hebrew text of the OT had been handed down over the centuries. Now it

is known that at least three different textual types circulated in Palestine and beyond in the time of Christ. Although they show no major textual differences, they do vary from each other in matters of spelling and dialect forms, and they contain some variant readings and an occasional textual insertion. For example, a manuscript scrap from the fourth Dead Sea cave includes the phrase, "he shall be a *nasîr* for ever" (i.e., a perpetual Nazirite) in 1 Samuel 1:22, although that phrase does not appear in the traditional Masoretic text found in modern Hebrew Bibles.

Textual criticism has revealed in the Hebrew certain purely human errors of copying made by ancient scribes. Although the copyists took enormous care in their work, they still committed occasional errors such as altering the order of consonants, writing a letter or word twice instead of once (dittography), failing to repeat a letter, syllable, or word (haplography), and other characteristic scribal mistakes common to every age. Before the Phoenician script was replaced by the square Aramaic characters, scribal mistakes arose from confusion in copying consonants that looked very much alike. Even some Aramaic characters resembled one another enough to lead to transcriptional mistakes. An additional problem arose because there were no spaces separating words in the Phoenician and early Aramaic scripts. Thus occasionally certain Hebrew words were incorrectly divided, as in Isaiah 2:20, where a word for "to the moles" was divided incorrectly into two words to read "to a hole of rats." In Joel 2:1,2 an incorrect division placed the words "for it is near" at the end of one verse instead of at the beginning of the next verse, where they really belong.

Occasionally a scribe faced with some unintelligible parts of the manuscript he was copying had to put down what seemed to be the best sense of the passage. In 2 Samuel 22:33 the copyist evidently reconstructed an illegible part to read "God is my refuge." By comparing the passage with the duplicate Hebrew form in Psalm 18:32, the scribe should have made it read, "God was girded with power." A mistake in copying produced "Jehoiakim" in Jeremiah 27:1 instead of "Zedekiah," which the context obviously requires. Textual criticism clears up such matters and enables the reader to see more clearly what the original writers were saying.

Early attempts to establish an authoritative text of the Hebrew Scriptures began in Jewish circles under Rabbi Akiba (d. AD 132?). The project was completed by the Masoretes, who replaced the scribes about AD 500 as guardians of the sacred Hebrew Scriptures, the form of which became known as the Maso-

One of the Dead Sea Scrolls.

retic text. Subsequently two principal Masoretic families produced two rather different texts, and still another form occurred in the rabbinic Bible of Felix Pratensis in 1516.

Scholars were once hopeful that textual criticism could restore the OT text to what had been written originally. With the discovery that several Hebrew textual types were circulated during the 1st century AD, that hope is now considered unrealistic.

Literary Criticism. Textual study was called lower criticism in contrast to a type known as higher criticism, the study of the literary materials rather than of the text itself. In its developed form, higher criticism concentrated on three areas, the first dealing with genre, or type, of literature. The aim was to discover if the original material consisted of poetry, prose, legal matter, ancient historical sources, genealogies, letters, and so on.

A second concern was to identify sources behind the finished composition. Although the OT refers occasionally to certain sources on which the writers depended, as in Kings and

Chronicles, in most instances the various books give little or no indication of their underlying sources. Literary, or higher, criticism set about to remedy that deficiency, sometimes in an elaborate but unrealistic manner. One result was that literary criticism became increasingly negative in character; in some instances it was hostile to the concepts of inspiration and revelation.

A third area of consideration had to do with questions about the authorship and date of OT books. Again much speculation took place, some of it quite radical in nature.

Historical Criticism. The third principal branch of critical activity became known as historical criticism. It endeavored to discover if the events and persons of Scripture were as historical as the narratives claim. An enormous number of archaeological discoveries have been made in the last century. Unfortunately for many literary critics, artifacts recovered from Near Eastern sites have proved the inaccuracy of many early literary critical theories. As a result, literary and historical criticism have come into increasing conflict in recent years, to the detriment of higher criticism.

Higher criticism came into being as early as the 2nd century AD, when Gnostic heretics began to attack the Christian Scriptures. Some critics were more radical than others, refusing even to recognize the OT as part of what they considered Scripture. Beginning in that period, doubts were cast on Moses' authorship of the Pentateuch (the first five books of the Bible), despite a uniform Jewish tradition attributing the Pentateuch to Moses. Part of the argument was that Moses could not possibly have written the account of his own death (Dt 34:5–12). If others had written that section of the Pentateuch how much else had they written? Even those who credited Moses with a significant role in the composition of the Torah (Pentateuch) tended to assign to Ezra a role in later compiling the finished product.

Source Criticism. Higher criticism reached a further stage of development in the 18th century as source criticism came to the forefront. When the divine names *Elohim* (God) and *YHWH* (Lord) were selected as criteria for literary analysis, a new theory emerged. It maintained that the Pentateuch had been compiled from two documentary sources, one of which used the name *Elohim* exclusively and the other the name *YHWH*. It not being known at the time that writings in the ancient Near East were never compiled by such a means, the documentary approach gained support. The search for literary sources was pursued in earnest, producing a number of conflicting opinions about the value and content of the "documents" thought to underlie the Pentateuch. The chief difficulty with those supposed sources was that they were entirely conjectural. They have never yet been confirmed by any kind of objective evidence.

The most comprehensive form of literary criticism was based on the evolutionary philosophy of G.W.F. Hegel (1770–1831). In the hands of 19th-century European scholars, the two-document theory of pentateuchal origins was expanded into a four-document one. Of the supposed Elohist (E) and YHWH (J) sources, the Elohist was regarded as the basic document of the Pentateuch. Additional sources were required, however, because parts of the Torah did not seem to belong to either J or E. The Book of Deuteronomy was a case in point. The 19th-century scholars acknowledged its basic unity, credited it with being an independent source, and gave it the symbol D. The E document, thought to be the "foundation" source, was subjected to additional scrutiny on the ground that it seemed to be the product of two writers, both of whom used the same name for God. One writer seemed closer in language and style to the compiler of the proposed J source. That, along with certain other features, required the existence of a fourth source, Priestly Code, symbolized by the letter P.

The four-document hypothesis depended for much of its success on the functioning of an imaginative editor or redactor (reviser), who took the four proposed sources and molded them into one readable account. The critics thus had a convenient but unknowable source for the existing Pentateuch; they sometimes found him a problem nonetheless, for certain details of the text continued to defy explanation according to their theories.

Up to 1850, many scholars had thought of the priestly material as being comparatively early in date, but after that time the putative "foundation" document came increasingly to be regarded as late rather than early. The criteria for that opinion were never stated very clearly and seem to have been based on feelings as much as on rationality.

From that time onward the J source came to be regarded as the basic Pentateuchal document, which had been supplemented by portions of the E source, along with Deuteronomy and priestly material. The writings of K.H. Graf (1815–69) and Julius Wellhausen (1844–1918) gave final shape to the theory, which has often been referred to by their names.

Despite protests from some scholars who thought that the priestly material should be assigned to an early period, Wellhausen maintained that the Pentateuch had been compiled from sources in the order of JEDP, thus placing priestly sources firmly at the end of the chronological sequence. Graf and Wellhausen went beyond the literary criticism of their day by assigning proposed dates to the documents which they imagined underlay the Pentateuch. Wellhausen held that the J source had originated in the 9th century BC, the E document a century later. Deuteronomy was assigned to the time of King Josiah (640–609 BC). The priestly source, regarded as the last document to take formal shape, was dated in the 5th century BC, with at least some of it seen as the work of Ezra the scribe. By about 200 BC, the theory maintained, the entire body of sources was revised thoroughly by an anonymous editor or redactor, producing the Pentateuch as it now stands.

During the whole process of developing the theory the literary critics never bothered to substantiate their speculations with any objective proof. For them, as for ancient Greek philosophical speculators, the fact that their suggestions could have any possibility of being true seemed a sufficient indication of their validity, so no further proof was needed. Wellhausen's ideas prevailed over those of his opponents, and within a short time his views were accepted as the most assured results of literary criticism. Disregarding OT tradition, Hebrew history was rewritten by enthusiastic critics to promote the contemporary idea that the priestly writings were late rather than early in origin. Although some scholars disagreed with those opinions, the theory seemed in harmony with prevailing evolutionary views in philosophy and biology. Hence the intellectual climate of the age encouraged quick acceptance of critical theories.

Much modern liberal biblical scholarship is still based on that general higher critical position with minor modifications and some shifts of emphasis. The result has been to regard the Pentateuch as one of the latest OT compositions, supposedly appearing in its final form about 200 BC.

Other Types of Criticism. In what is called *form criticism*, sources are recognized and isolated according to their specific literary form. In a sense, form criticism was a reaction against the four-source theory of pentateuchal origins. Although that theory purported to separate underlying components, it had nothing to say about the earlier history of the written material. It provided no convincing information about the way the various traditions were shaped, either by the community of Isreal or by those scribes who preserved and transmitted the traditions in written form. Literary critics constantly appealed to the functions of an editor or redactor, especially when they encountered opposition to their views

from the Hebrew text, yet said very little about the degree of control such editors exerted over their literary materials. In the end, their vagueness was a blessing, for what is now known about scribal functions in the ancient Near East is very different from what the 19th-century European writers imagined them to be.

Form criticism attempted to take the literary tradition back to a preliterary stage, in which the various spoken units (commandments, hymns, oaths, covenants, blessings, lamentations, prophetic oracles, etc.) first took the form they later exhibited in the OT.

The form-critical approach had the undoubted advantage of setting the material against a realistic Israelite life-situation; what emerged could no longer be considered unhistorical but had to be seen as actually rooted in the ongoing existence of the covenant community.

The earliest studies in form criticism, undertaken by Hermann Gunkel (1862–1932) and Sigmund Mowinckel (1884–1965) focused on the Psalms. Gunkel was concerned with each individual composition as a literary unit and how it expressed the author's thought. Mowinckel paid more attention to the life-situation from which individual psalms had emerged; for him that setting was the cultic religion of the Israelites. Gerhard von Rad (1901–71) widened Mowinckel's emphasis by recognizing the presence of a statement of God's saving acts in Hebrew history in Deuteronomy 26:1–11. That position was soon adopted by other scholars, who were able to accomplish considerable reconstruction of ancient events and institutions in Israelite life.

Gunkel also studied the Book of Genesis form-critically, but though he saw in the narratives what he described as myths, sagas, legends, romances, and folk tales, he missed completely the most obvious unit. A series of historical tablet-forms on which Genesis 1:1—37:2 is based comprises genuine ancient history written in the fashion of Mesopotamian tablets. The units of Genesis normally have a title, textual content, and a concluding colophon (notation of how a work came to be written); that three-part literary form has been amply documented from Mesopotamian sites. The tablet-units of Genesis can be discerned by recognizing each colophon, which by pointing to the contents of a tablet marks the conclusion of that particular unit.

In most English versions the phrase "these are the generations of" marks the place where a colophon occurs. Such a reading of Genesis provides a valuable corrective to much modern form criticism by showing that source materials existed in writing at an early stage.

Most liberal scholars still think that OT traditions passed through a long period of oral (that is, spoken) "folklore" before being crystalized in written form. Studies of ancient Near Eastern processes of scribal transmission have shown, however, that an oral and a written form normally existed side by side. The oral form was intended to spread the information in contemporary society; the written one was formulated as a record for posterity.

Although form criticism is useful as one means of understanding the historical situation from which the Hebrew Scriptures emerged, its limitations become evident when one realizes that it is governed by theoretical presuppositions foreign to ancient Near Eastern life and traditions. Thus form critics are unable to think of "authors" as such, being limited to collectors or editors of traditional material. Such a position cannot be supported from the OT, which repeatedly claims originality within a specific period of time for important sections of its contents.

The critical approach known as *redaction criticism* attempts to understand the main theological interests of the compilers of canonical material. Influenced by form criticism, redaction critics respect the historical continuity of the OT writings. Their principal concern is with the revision processes of the oral or literary material, in the belief that the redactor influenced the traditions he edited by giving them new emphases, sometimes relating them to central themes in Scripture.

In addition to the editorial process of interest to redaction critics, one must consider what questions an editor would try to answer for his readers. The redaction-critical approach retains one of the inherent difficulties of form criticism; it makes an artificial distinction between author and reviser, robbing the author of any real identity. Furthermore, many of the alleged revisions are purely subjective and cannot be demonstrated factually, the common weakness of the classic literary-critical approach to OT study. Finally, to presume that the community, rather than the individual, has fostered religious and cultural advances through the ages is a historic fallacy; the evidence is clearly to the contrary.

An additional kind of critical study known as *tradition criticism* seeks to examine the way in which a particular tradition (e.g., the exodus) was interpreted in various historical periods as in the Torah (Pentateuch), the Psalms, and in the Prophets. Since to some extent tradition criticism tries to unify source-critical and form-critical speculations, it appeals to some as furnishing a history of both oral and written forms of OT literature.

In a narrower sense, tradition criticism describes a particular theme, or motif, dealing with the oral phase of what allegedly became written material at a much later time. The weakness is evident, since it bases its procedures on the unproven assumption that an oral stage invariably preceded a written stage of OT material.

In spite of such weaknesses, the forms of criticism discussed above are all useful, provided they are applied to Scripture as objectively as possible.

Results of Critical Studies. The principles of analysis and development used in the literary-critical study of the Pentateuch began to be applied vigorously to almost all the other OT books. From the 3rd century AD, the Book of Daniel was regarded by some critics as a product of the Maccabean age (2nd century BC) rather than the 6th century BC, because radical criticism denied any predictive element in prophecy. That negative view of prophecy became an axiom of modern critical scholarship, and the few who challenged it were either ridiculed or ignored.

In their enthusiasm to transfer the procedures of documentary analysis from the Pentateuch to other OT writings, some critics failed to assess critically the methods they were using. Some "detected" underlying sources in the OT books simply on the basis of subjective judgment or conjecture.

One book receiving particular attention was the prophecy of Isaiah. From a study of the contents of the book, chapters 40–66 were regarded as the work of an author different from the writer of chapters 1–39. It was supposed that Isaiah 40–66 had been written in Babylonia by some "unknown prophet of the exile," also known as "second" or "deutero-" Isaiah. That division proved too simple for some scholars, who proceeded to divide up Isaiah 40–66 among several authors. As with the Pentateuch, no two scholars agreed on the details of fragmentation. By contrast with that exercise in subjectivity, the large Isaiah scroll from the Dead Sea caves at Qumran shows that the prophecy was probably written by a single author in a "bifid" (divided) form, the themes in one volume (chs 1–33) being matched by the same themes in the companion volume (chs 34–66).

In general, the tendency of literary criticism was to deny or belittle the witness of the OT to itself, and to assign the books rather arbitrarily to comparatively late dates. Historical criticism has done much to correct the subjective tendencies on which literary criticism was based.

Archaeological discoveries have confirmed the reality of many persons, places, and events of the OT scene. Such discoveries have shown, among other things, that Wellhausen was entirely wrong in assigning a late date to priestly materials in the Pentateuch. All ancient Near Eastern written priestly sources are now known to be early, the priests being educators who took care to pass on their own traditions. The antiquity of writing has been established at a period that Wellhausen would never have thought possible. Further, no evidence has come from archaeological sources to support the Graf-Wellhausen theory of Pentateuchal origins. Rather, it has become evident that no literary composition in the ancient world was compiled after the manner alleged for the Pentateuch by the documentary hypothesis.

The rediscovery of Sumerian culture has provided a fresh starting point for evaluating the materials of Genesis 1–14, which are clearly Mesopotamian in origin. Wellhausen's notion that monotheism was the end result of a lengthy process of evolutionary development in Hebrew society has been disproved by the discovery that even in the 4th millennium BC some people in Mesopotamia were monotheistic in worship.

Of the many confirmations of places and events, the most startling for many decades emerged from excavations at Tell Mardikh in Syria. That was the site of the ancient capital of Ebla, a Semitic empire that flourished as early as 2500 BC. With Mesopotamia and Egypt it formed a triad of competing military and commercial empires.

Ancient sites such as Ur, Carchemish, Gomorrah, and Jerusalem are mentioned in tablet records found at Ebla; it is even possible that Ibrum, one of the early Ebla kings, was connected in some way with Eber, an ancestor of Abraham. When the tablets from Ebla have been translated and interpreted, they will no doubt provide further background to the earliest period of Hebrew history.

As with other forms of criticism, the historical approach has its limitations, since the same archaeological data can sometimes be interpreted differently by different experts. Problems arise when archaeology is expected to "prove" the truth of the OT. What archaeology does is provide the historical and cultural background against which the OT narratives can be set and studied.

R.K. HARRISON

See BIBLE, TEXTUAL CRITICISM OF THE; DEAD SEA SCROLLS; MASORA, MASORETES; DOCUMENTARY HYPOTHESIS; DEMYTHOLOGIZATION; REDACTION CRITICISM; SOURCE CRITICISM; TRADITION CRITICISM; BIBLICAL CRITICISM, NEW TESTAMENT.

Bibliography. R.K. Harrison, *Introduction to the OT*; W.F. Lofthouse, *The Making of the OT*; P. Maas, *Textual Criticism*; D. Winton Thomas, "The Textual Criticism of the Old Testament," *The OT and Modern Study* (ed) H.H. Rowley; R.H. Tyle, *The Canon of the OT*; E. Würthwein, *The Text of the OT*.

Biblical Languages.

Hebrew, Aramaic, and Greek, the original languages in which the Bible was written.

Christians believe that God has revealed himself through a book. Hence those who read the Bible can profit from learning as much as possible about the languages in which it was written. The two major. languages of Scripture, Greek and Hebrew, represent two major language families, Indo-European and Semitic. Their contrasting linguistic traits combine to produce a thorough, progressive, propositional revelation of God. That revelation is characterized by simplicity, variety, and power.

The connection between language and thought is not a loose one; language is a product and reflection of the human soul. Language is not just a dress for thought to put on or off at pleasure, but the body of which thought is the soul. Each language that God ordained to transmit divine revelation had a personality that made it suitable for such a purpose.

No translation can replace the original languages of the Bible in primary importance for conveying and perpetuating divine revelation. Those languages should be learned not merely from the outside, with grammar and lexicon, but also from the inside, with proper appreciation for the uniqueness of each one.

Hebrew. The name "Hebrew" is not applied by the OT to its own language, although the NT does use the name that way. In the OT, "Hebrew" means the individual or people who used the language. The language itself is called "the language of Canaan" (Is 19:18), or "the language of Judah" (2 Kgs 18:26,28; Neh 13:24).

Inscription in Greek and Hebrew on the mosaic floor of the synagogue in Tiberias.

Origin and History. In the Middle Ages a common view was that Hebrew was the primitive language of humankind. Even in colonial America, Hebrew was still referred to as "the mother of all languages." Linguistic scholarship, however, has made any such theory untenable.

Hebrew is actually one of several Canaanite dialects, which included Phoenician, Ugaritic, and Moabite. Other Canaanite dialects (e.g., Ammonite) existed but have left insufficient inscriptions for scholarly analysis. Such dialects were already present in the land of Canaan before its conquest by the Israelites.

Until about 1974, the oldest witnesses to Canaanite language were found in the Ugarit and Amarna records, dating from the 14th and 15th centuries BC. A few Canaanite words and expressions appeared in earlier Egyptian records, but the origin of Canaanite has been uncertain. Between 1974 and 1976, however, nearly 17,000 tablets were dug up at Tell Mardikh (ancient Ebla) in northern Syria, written in a previously unknown Semitic language. Because they date back to 2400 BC (perhaps even earlier), many scholars think that that language may be the "Old Canaanite" which gave rise to Hebrew. By 1977, when another 1,000 tablets were unearthed, only about 100 inscriptions from Ebla had been reported on.

Languages change over a long period of time. The English used in the time of Alfred the Great (9th century AD) seems almost like a foreign language to contemporary English-speakers. Although Hebrew was no exception to that general principle, like other Semitic languages it remained remarkably stable over many centuries. Poems such as the Song of Deborah (Jgs 5) tend to preserve the language's oldest form. Changes that took place later in the long history of the language are shown in the presence of archaic words (often preserved in poetic language) and a general difference in style. For example, to a linguistic scholar the Book of Job clearly shows a more archaic style than the Book of Esther.

Various Hebrew dialects probably existed side by side even in Bible times. Variations in pronunciation, as with the word "shibboleth," seem to have developed during the period of the judges (Jgs 12:4–6). Some features of the language seem to indicate dialect differences between the northern and southern sections of the land.

Family. Hebrew belongs to the Semitic family of languages used throughout southwestern Asia. Semitic languages were spoken from the Mediterranean Sea to the mountains east of the Euphrates River Valley, and from Armenia in the north to the southern extremity of the Arabian Peninsula. Semitic languages are classified as *Southern:* Arabic and Ethiopic; *Eastern:* Akkadian; and *Northwestern:* Aramaic-Syriac and Canaanite (Hebrew, Phoenician, Ugaritic, and Moabite).

Character. Hebrew, like the other early Semitic languages, concentrates on observation more than reflection. That is, things are generally observed according to their appearance as phenomena, not analyzed as to their inward being or essence. Effects are observed but not traced through a series of causes.

Hebrew's vividness and simplicity make the language difficult to translate fully. It is amazingly concise and direct. For example, Psalm 23 contains 55 words; most translations require about twice that many to translate it. The first two lines (with slashes dividing the Hebrew words) read:

> The Lord/(is) my shepherd/
> I shall want/not

Thus eight English words are required to translate four Hebrew words. Hebrew does not use separate, distinct expressions for every nuance of thought. Someone has said, "The Semites have been the quarries whose great rough blocks the Greeks have trimmed, polished, and fitted together. The former gave religion; the latter philosophy."

Hebrew is a pictorial language in which the past is not merely described but verbally painted. Not just a landscape is presented but a moving panorama. The course of events is reenacted in the mind's sight. (Note the frequent use of "behold," a Hebraism carried over to the NT.) Such common Hebraic expressions as "he arose and went," "he opened his lips and spoke," "he lifted up his eyes and saw," and "he lifted up his voice and wept" illustrate the pictorial strength of the language.

Many profound theological expressions of the OT are tightly bound up with Hebrew language and grammar. Even the most sacred name of God himself, "the Lord" (Jehovah or Yahweh), is directly related to the Hebrew verb "to be" (or perhaps "to cause to be"). Many other names of persons and places in the OT can best be understood only with a working knowledge of Hebrew.

Grammar. Many figures of speech and rhetorical devices in the OT are more intelligible if one is familiar with the structure of Hebrew.

1. Alphabet and Script. The Hebrew alphabet consists of 22 consonants; signs for vowels were devised and added late in the language's history. The origin of the alphabet is unknown, although until the discoveries at Ebla the oldest examples of a Canaanite alphabet were preserved in the Ugaritic cuneiform alphabet of the 14th century BC.

Brief remains of a linear (noncuneiform) alphabet appear from time to time in the excavations at Ugarit (Ras Shamra, near Antioch), the oldest possibly dating from the era between Abraham and Moses. The oldest linear alphabetic remains from Canaan date from about the period of the judges (13th–11th century BC). The old style of writing was usually called the Phoenician script, predecessor of the Greek and other Western alphabets. The script used in modern Hebrew Bibles (Aramaic or square script) came into vogue after the exile (6th century BC). The older style was still used sporadically in the early Christian era on coins and for writing God's name (as in the Dead Sea scrolls). Hebrew has always been written right to left.

2. Consonants. The Canaanite alphabet of the Phoenician and Moabite languages had 22 consonants. The older Canaanite language seen in Ugaritic had fewer consonants. (Modern Arabic preserves some old Canaanite consonants found in Ugaritic but missing in Hebrew.) The older Canaanite letters were never used in either the square Aramaic script of the Hebrew Bible or the Old Hebrew or Phoenician script.

3. Vowels. Originally, in the consonantal Hebrew script, vowels were simply understood by the writer or reader. On the basis of tradition and context, a reader would supply whatever vowels were needed—much as in English abbreviations ("bldg" for "building"; "blvd" for "boulevard"). After the Christian era began, the final dispersion of the Jews and the destruction of Jerusalem led to Hebrew's becoming a "dead language," no longer widely spoken. Loss of traditional pronunciation and understanding then became more likely, so Jewish scribes felt a need for permanently establishing the vowel sounds.

The first Hebrew vowel signs were devised in about the 5th century AD and were elaborated in following centuries before being permanently "fixed." At least three different systems of vowel signs were employed at different times and places. The text used today represents the system devised by Masoretic scribes who worked in the city of Tiberias. The vowels, each of which may be long or short, are indicated by dots or dashes placed above or below the consonants. Combinations of dots and dashes represent very short vowel sounds or half-vowels.

4. Linkage. Hebrew joins together many words that in Western languages would be written separately. Some prepositions (*be-*, "in"; *le-*, "to"; *ke-*, "like") are prefixed directly to the noun or verb they introduce, as are the definite article *ha-*, "the," and the conjunction *wa-*, "and." Suffixes are used for pronouns, either in the possessive or accusative relationship. The same word may simultaneously have both a prefix and a suffix.

5. Nouns. Hebrew has no neuter gender; everything is masculine or feminine. Inanimate objects may be either masculine or feminine, depending on the formation or character of the word. Usually, abstract ideas or words indicating a group are feminine. Nouns are derived from roots and are formed in various ways, either by vowel modification or by adding prefixes or suffixes to the root. Contrary to Greek and many Western languages, compound nouns are not characteristic of Hebrew.

The Hebrew plural is formed by adding *-im* to masculine nouns (*seraphim, cherubim*), and modifying the feminine ending to *-oth*.

Three original case endings indicating nominative, genitive, and accusative have dropped away during the evolution of Hebrew. To compensate for the lack of case endings, Hebrew resorts to various indicators. Indirect objects are indicated by the preposition *le-*, "to"; direct objects by the objective sign *eth;* the genitive relationship by putting the word before the genitive in the "construct state," or shortened form.

6. Adjectives. Hebrew is deficient in adjectives. "A double heart" is indicated in the original Hebrew by "a heart and a heart" (Ps 12:2) and "two kinds of weights" is actually "a stone and a stone" (Dt 25:13); the "royal family" is "the seed of the kingdom" (2 Kgs 11:1).

Adjectives that do exist in Hebrew have no comparative or superlative forms. Relationship is indicated by the preposition "from." "Better than you" is thus "good from you." "The serpent was more subtle than any other wild creature" is literally "the serpent was subtle from every beast" (Gn 3:1). The superlative is expressed by several different constructions. The idea "very deep" is literally "deep, deep" (Eccl 7:24); the "best song" is literally "song of songs" (cf. "king of kings"); "holiest" is literally "holy, holy, holy" (Is 6:3).

7. Verbs. Hebrew verbs are formed from a root usually consisting of three letters (radicals). From such roots, verbal forms are developed by change of vowels or by adding prefixes or suffixes. The root consonants provide the semantic backbone of the language and give a stability of meaning not characteristic of Western languages. The vowels are quite flexible, giving Hebrew considerable elasticity.

Hebrew verb usage is not characterized by precise definition of tenses. Hebrew tenses, especially in poetry, are largely determined by context. The two tense formations are the perfect (completed action) and imperfect (incompleted action). The imperfect is ambiguous. It represents the indicative mood (present, past, future) but may also represent such moods as the imperative, optative, and jussive or cohortative. A distinctive usage of the perfect tense is the "prophetic perfect," where the perfect form represents a future event considered so sure that it is expressed as past (e.g., Is 5:13).

Style. Hebrew diction is characterized by a picturesque quality.

1. Vocabulary. Most Hebrew roots originally expressed some physical action or denoted some natural object. The verb "to decide" originally meant "to cut"; "to be true" meant "to be firmly fixed"; "to be right" meant "to be straight"; "to be honorable" meant "to be heavy."

Abstract terms are alien to the character of Hebrew; for example, biblical Hebrew has no specific words for "theology," "philosophy," or "religion." Intellectual or theological concepts are expressed by concrete terms. The abstract idea of sin is represented by such words as "to miss the mark" or "crooked" or "rebellion" or "trespass" ("to cross over"). Mind or intellect is expressed by "heart" or "reins" (kidneys), emotion or compassion by "bowels" (see Is 63:15 KJV). Other concrete terms in Hebrew are "horn" for strength or vigor, "bones" for self, and "seed" for descendants. A mental quality is often depicted by the part of the body thought of as its most appropriate embodiment. Strength can be represented by "arm" or "hand," anger by "nostril," displeasure by "falling face," acceptance by "shining face," thinking by "head."

Some translators have attempted to consistently represent a Hebrew word by the same English word, but that leads to serious problems. Sometimes there is considerable disagreement on the exact shade of meaning of a Hebrew word in a given passage. A single root frequently represents a variety of meanings, depending on usage and context. The word for "bless" can also mean "curse," "greet," "favor," "praise." The word for "judgment" is used also for "justice," "verdict," "penalty," "ordinance," "duty," "custom," "manner." The word for "strength" or "power" also means "army," "virtue," "worth," "courage."

Further ambiguity arises from the fact that some Hebrew consonants stand for two different original consonants which have coalesced in the evolution of the language. For this reason two roots which appear to be identical may be traced back to two different roots—for an English example, compare "bass" (a fish) with "bass" (musical term).

2. Syntax. Hebrew syntax is relatively uncomplicated. Few subordinating conjunctions (if, when, because, etc.) are used; sentences are usually coordinated by using the word "and."

English translations of biblical texts generally try to show the logical connection between successive sentences even though it is not always clear. In Genesis 1:2–3:1, all but 3 of the 56 verses begin with "and." Yet the RSV translates that pattern as "and" (1:3), "so" (1:27), "thus" (2:1), "but" (2:6), and "now" (3:1).

Its style is enlivened by use of direct discourse. The narrator does not simply state that "such and such a person said that . . ." (indirect discourse). Instead, the parties speak for themselves (direct discourse), creating a freshness that remains even after repeated reading. Hebrew is an emotional language, with feeling often overwhelming or projecting the thought.

3. Poetry. Hebrew poetry uses a variety of rhetorical devices. Some of them—such as assonance, alliteration, and acrostics—can be appreciated only in the original Hebrew. But parallelism, the most important characteristic of Hebrew poetry, is evident even in English translation. Among many forms of parallelism, four basic categories exist: *synonymous*, a repeating style where parallel lines say the same thing in different words; *antithetic*, a contrasting style where contrary thoughts are expressed; *constructive*, with a completing parallel line filling out the thought of the first; *climactic*, in which an ascending parallel line picks up something from the first line and repeats it. Hebrew literature contains a rich variety of poetic forms, including lyrics, elegies, and odes.

4. Figures of speech. Hebrew abounds in expressive figures of speech based on the Hebrew people's character and way of life. Even certain odd expressions influenced by Hebrew style, like "apple of the eye" (Dt 32:10; Ps 17:8; Prv 7:2; Zec 2:8) and "skin of my teeth" (Jb 19:20), are familiar in English literature. Some of the more striking Hebrew modes of expression are hard to transfer into English such as "to uncover the ear" meaning "to disclose, reveal." Others are more familiar, like "to stiffen the neck" for "to be stubborn, rebellious"; "to bend or incline the ear" for "to listen closely."

Legacy. English and a number of other modern languages have been enriched by Hebrew.

1. Words. English contains a small number of Hebrew loan words. Some of them have had great influence as "amen," "hallelujah," and "jubilee." Many Hebrew proper nouns are used in modern languages for persons and places, such as David, Jonathan/John, Miriam/Mary, Bethlehem (the name of several US towns and cities), Bethel, and Zion.

2. Expressions. Many common Hebrew expressions have been unconsciously accepted

into English figures of speech, as in "mouth of the cave," and "face of the earth." Some figures, such as "grapes of wrath" and "east of Eden," have been used as titles for books and movies.

Aramaic. A secondary OT language is Aramaic found in sections of the Book of Daniel (2:4*b*–7:28) and Ezra (4:8–6:18; 7:12–26). Aramaic phrases and expressions also appear in Genesis (31:47), Jeremiah (10:11), and the NT.

OT Use. Genesis 31:47 reflects usage of Hebrew and Aramaic by two individuals who were contemporaries: Jacob, the father of the Israelites, referred to a certain memorial or "witness heap" by the Hebrew term; his father-in-law, Laban, called it by its Aramaic counterpart.

Aramaic is linguistically very close to Hebrew. Aramaic texts in the Bible are written in the same script as Hebrew. The two languages are quite similar in the way they formulate their verb, noun, and pronoun constructions. In contrast to Hebrew, Aramaic uses a larger vocabulary, including many loan words and a greater variety of connectives. It also contains an elaborate system of tenses, developed through the use of participles with pronouns or with various forms of the verb "to be." Although Aramaic is less euphonious and poetical than Hebrew, it is probably superior as a vehicle of exact expression.

Aramaic has perhaps the longest continuous living history of any language known. It was used during the Bible's patriarchal period and is still spoken by a few people today. Aramaic and its cognate, Syriac, evolved into many dialects in different places and periods. Characterized by simplicity, clarity, and precision, it adapted easily to the various needs of everyday life. It could serve equally well as a language for scholars, pupils, lawyers, or merchants. Some have described it as the Semitic equivalent of English.

The origin of Aramaic is unknown, but it seems to have been closely related to Amorite and possibly to other ancient Northwest Semitic dialects barely known to scholars. Although an Aramaean kingdom as such never really existed, various Aramaean "states" developed into influential centers. A few brief Aramaean inscriptions from that era (10th to 8th centuries BC) have been found and studied.

By the 8th century BC, King Hezekiah's representatives requested the spokesman of the Assyrian king Sennacherib to "speak to your servants in Aramaic, since we understand it. Don't speak to us in Hebrew in the hearing of the people on the wall" (2 Kgs 18:26 NIV).

By the Persian period, Aramaic had become the language of international trade. During their captivity, the Jews probably adopted it for convenience—certainly in commerce—while Hebrew became confined to the learned and to religious leaders.

Gradually, especially after the exile, Aramaic influence pervaded the land of Palestine. Nehemiah complained that children from mixed marriages were unable to speak Hebrew (Neh 13:24). The Jews seem to have continued using Aramaic widely during the Persian, Greek, and Roman periods. Eventually the Hebrew Scriptures were translated into Aramaic paraphrases, called Targums. Some Targum manuscripts have been found among the Dead Sea Scrolls.

NT Use. In popular thought, Aramaic was the common language of Palestine during the time of Jesus. Yet that is by no means certain and probably oversimplifies the linguistic situation of that time. Names used in the NT reflect Aramaic (Bartholomew, Bar-jonah, Barnabas), Greek (Andrew, Philip), and Latin (Mark), as well as Hebrew. There is no question that Aramaic was widely used, as were Greek and Hebrew. Latin was probably limited to military and governmental circles. Tradition also reflects Mishnaic Hebrew, a kind of everyday Hebrew dialect used in Jesus' day; Mishnaic Hebrew documents have been discovered among the Dead Sea scrolls.

What was the "Hebrew" referred to in certain NT passages (Jn 5:2; 19:13,17,20; 20:16; Rv 9:11; 16:16)? The languages used on Jesus' cross were Hebrew, Greek, and Latin (Jn 19:19,20). Later, the apostle Paul was said to speak "Hebrew" (Acts 22:2; 26:14). The exact dialect he spoke may be debated, but as a Pharisee he was undoubtedly able to read the Hebrew of the OT. The Greek word for "Hebrew" is sometimes translated "Aramaic" and may be a general term for Semitic, or for a blend of Hebrew–Aramaic (as Yiddish is German–Hebrew). At any rate, Aramaic served as a transition from Hebrew to Greek as the language spoken by Jews in Jesus' day. In that sense Aramaic connects OT Hebrew with NT Greek.

Greek. The Greek language is beautiful, rich, and harmonious as an instrument of communication. It is a fitting tool both for vigorous thought and for religious devotion. During its classic period, Greek was the language of one of the world's greatest civilizations. In that cultural period, language, literature, and art flourished more than war. The Greek mind was preoccupied with ideals of beauty. The Greek language reflected artistry in its philosophical dialogues, its poetry, and its stately orations.

The Greek language was also characterized by strength and vigor. It was capable of variety and striking effects. Greek was a language of argument, with a vocabulary and style that could penetrate and clarify phenomena rather than simply tell stories. Classical Greek elaborately developed many forms from a few word roots. Its complex syntax allowed intricate word arrangements to express fine nuances of meaning.

Ancient History. Although the antecedents of Greek are obscure, the first traces of what could be called ancient Greek appear in Mycenaean and Minoan documents. They contain three different scripts: Minoan hieroglyphic (the earliest), linear A, and linear B (the latest). Linear B is generally considered "pre-Greek." The syllabic script of linear B is found on clay tablets discovered on the Greek mainland (1400–1200 BC).

Mycenaean civilization and script ended suddenly with the Dorian invasions (1200 BC). Writing seems to have disappeared for several centuries. Later, about the 8th century BC, Greek writing appeared in a different script. That script was based on an alphabet presum-

Tablet An 1 from Pylos—the first Linear B tablet from the Greek mainland. It describes the allocation of rowers, perhaps in anticipation of an invasion.

ably borrowed from the Phoenicians and then adapted to Greek speech sounds and direction of writing. Greek was first written from right to left like the West Semitic languages, then in a back-and-forth pattern, finally from left to right. Several dialects appeared during the archaic period (8th to 6th centuries BC): Dorian, Ionian, Achaean, and Aeolic.

During the classical period (5th to 4th centuries BC), Greek culture reached its literary and artistic zenith. Classical (or Attic) Greek was characterized by subtlety of syntax, flexibility, and an expressive use of particles (short, uninflected parts of speech, often untranslatable). As the city of Athens attained cultural and political control, the Attic dialect also gained in prestige. With the Macedonian conquests, Attic Greek, combined with influences from other dialects (especially Ionic), became the international language of the eastern Mediterranean area.

Hellenism and the Koine Dialect. The conquests of Alexander the Great encouraged the spread of Greek language and culture. Regional dialects were largely replaced by Hellenistic or koine (everyday) Greek. That language is known through thousands of inscriptions reflecting all aspects of daily life. The koine dialect added many vernacular expressions to Attic Greek, thus making it more cosmopolitan. Simplifying the grammar also better adapted it to a worldwide culture. The new language, reflecting simple, popular speech, became the common language of commerce and diplomacy. The Greek language lost much of its elegance and finely shaded nuance as a result of its evolution from classic to koine. Nevertheless it retained its distinguishing characteristics of strength, beauty, clarity, and logical rhetorical power.

It is significant that the apostle Paul wrote his letter to Christians in Rome in the Greek language rather than in Latin. The Roman empire of that time was culturally a Greek world, except for governmental transactions.

Septuagint. During the centuries immediately before Christ, the eastern Mediterranean had been undergoing not only Hellenization, but also Semitization. Both influences can be observed in the Greek translation of the OT.

Translation of the Hebrew Scriptures into Greek was an epochal event. The Septuagint (earliest Greek translation of the Hebrew OT) later had a strong influence on Christian thought. A necessary consequence of Hebrew writers using the Greek language was that a Greek spirit and Greek forms of thought influenced Jewish culture. The Jews soon appropriated from the rich Greek vocabulary expressions for ideas that were beyond the scope of Hebrew terminology. Also, old Greek expressions acquired new meanings corresponding to Jewish conceptions.

The Greek OT has been very significant in the development of Christian thought. Often the usage of a Greek word in the Septuagint provides a key to its meaning in the NT. The OT dialect of "Jewish-Greek" is at times seen in NT passages translated very literally; at other times NT translation of OT texts is very loose.

NT Greek. Although most NT authors were Jewish, they wrote in Greek, the universal language of their time. In addition, the apostle John seems to have been acquainted with some Greek philosophy. John used "Word" (Greek *logos*) in reference to Christ (Jn 1:1), and several other abstract expressions. John may have been influenced by the Egyptian center of Alexandria, where Greek philosophy and Hebrew learning had merged in a unique way.

The apostle Paul also was acquainted with Greek authors (Acts 17:28; 1 Cor 15:33; Ti 1:12). Thus Greek orators and philosophers, as well as Hebrew prophets and scholars, influenced Paul's language.

Exactly which dialect of Hebrew or Aramaic Jesus spoke is debated. However, the fact remains that the Holy Spirit inspired the Gospels as Greek texts. The records in Greek of Jesus' teaching and accomplishments prepared the way for the gospel to spread throughout a Greek-speaking culture.

The dignity and restraint of koine Greek used by Christian writers was neither so artificial and pedantic as some classical writings, nor so trivial and vulgar as spoken koine at times could be. Greek words took on richer, more spiritual meaning in the context of Scripture, influenced by the simplicity and rich vividness of Semitic style. The NT was not written in a peculiar "Holy Ghost" language (as some medieval scholars believed). Tens of thousands of papyri unearthed in Egypt in the 20th century furnish lexical and grammatical parallels to biblical language and reveal that it was part of the linguistic warp and woof of that era. Yet NT Greek was nevertheless "free," often creating its own idiom. Christian writers influenced Greek thought by introducing new expressions in order to convey their message about Jesus Christ.

Semitic Influence. Because NT Greek combines the directness of Hebrew thought with the precision of Greek expression, Greek's subtle delicacy often interprets Hebrew concepts. The Semitic influence is strongest in the Gospels, the Book of Revelation, and the Letter of James. Books like Luke and Hebrews exhibit a more typical Greek style. The NT epistles blend the wisdom of Hebrew and the dialectic philosophy of Greek. Sermons recorded in the NT combine the Hebrew prophetic message with Greek oratorical force.

In addition to direct quotes and allusions from the Septuagint, a pervasive Semitic influence on NT Greek has been noted in many areas. For example, the syntax of NT Greek contains many examples of Semitic style.

Vocabulary. The Greek NT vocabulary is abundant and sufficient to convey just the shade of meaning the author desires. For example, the NT uses two different words for "love" (for two kinds of love), two words for "another" (another of the same, or another of a different kind), and several words for various kinds of knowledge. Significantly, some words are omitted, such as *eros* (third kind of love) and other words commonly employed in the Hellenistic culture of that time.

Moreover, Greek words often took on new meanings in the context of the gospel, arising from a combination of new teachings with an exalted morality. The writers did not hesitate to use such words as "life," "death," "glory," and "wrath" in new ways to express new thoughts. Sometimes the literal meaning of a word almost disappears, as when the authors use "water," "washing," and "baptism" for Christ's spiritually purifying power. NT vocabulary also contains words found elsewhere only in the Greek OT, such as "circumcision," "idolatry," "anathema," "diaspora," and "Pentecost." Loan words from Hebrew or Aramaic include *alleluia* and *amen* (Hebrew), and *abba, mammon,* and *corban* (Aramaic).

For understanding the meaning of a NT word, then, a lexicon of classical Greek is essential but not sufficient. One must also know how the word is used in the Greek OT, in Hellenistic writings, and in the inscriptions and documents representing the language of everyday life. Papyrus documents provide many illustrations of the meaning of NT words. For example, the Greek word for "contribution" (1 Cor 16:1), at one time thought limited to the NT, is commonly used with the same meaning in the papyri. Many Greek words once defined on the basis of classical Greek have been given sharper meaning in the light of their use in the papyri.

Grammar. As in other Indo-European languages, the meaning of Greek words is affected by the addition and alteration of various prefixes and suffixes (the process known as "inflection"). Although its system of inflection was simplified compared to classical Greek, NT Greek was more inflected than many languages. Greek meaning is thus much less susceptible to ambiguity than English.

In contrast to Hebrew, Greek has a neuter gender as well as masculine and feminine. The many and precise Greek prepositions are subtle, having various meanings depending on their context. NT Greek uses only about half of the particles used in classical Greek.

The Greek verb system, much more complicated than that of Hebrew, is capable of nuances of meaning difficult to express even in English. Each Greek verb has five aspects, which grammarians call tense, mood, voice, person, and number.

1. Tense. Greek verb tense deals primarily with kind of action, rather than time of action as in English. In Greek there are three basic kinds of action: *durative,* expressed by the present, imperfect, and (sometimes) future tenses; *simple* or punctiliar, expressed by the aorist and (often) future tenses; and *completed,* expressed by the perfect tense (results of past action continue into the present) and pluperfect tense (results are confined to the past). Greek tenses are often hard to translate into English; the time of action as well as the verb stem's basic meaning (e.g., whether it takes an object) must be subtly blended with the kind of action into a single idea.

2. Mood. The mood shows how a verb's action should be understood. Is the action real? (Use the indicative mood.) Is the action demanded by someone? (Use the imperative mood.) Does the action depend on other conditions? (Use the subjunctive or optative mood.) Is the action basically descriptive of another substantive? (Use a participle.) Is the action basically substantive? (Use an infinitive.) In grammar, a substantive is a word or group of words functioning as a noun; the last two examples are not strictly moods, but they are used that way by grammarians. The moods give a Greek writer a rich choice of verbal expression.

3. Voice. A verb's voice describes whether action is directed outward (active), inward (middle), or back upon the sentence's subject (passive).

4. Person. The person of a verb tells who is doing the acting, whether I (first person), you (second person), or another (third person).

5. Number. Verb number shows whether the action is performed by one person (singular) or more than one (plural).

Style. The NT contains a variety of writing styles in its use of Greek. The Gospels especially exhibit Semitic features. Matthew uses a style less picturesque than Mark's, and in some respects close to the style of Luke, Acts, Hebrews, James, and 1 Peter. Luke's style varies from both Mark and Matthew's in its elegance. The rather simple style of John contains many Semitisms.

Among the apostle Paul's letters, differences of style have been noted. The least literary and most direct in expression are his letters to the Thessalonians. The Pastorals (1, 2 Tm; Ti) have a style nearer to the koine than much NT writing, not so Jewish, and not so much influenced by the Septuagint as his other letters.

The Letter to the Hebrews combines stylistic elegance and Jewish-Greek. James's letter, though high in cultural quality, is not as sensitive in style as Hebrews. Less elegant is 1 Peter, which is strongly influenced by the Septuagint and thus reflects Semitic style.

The Letter of Jude contains elevated, somewhat ponderous diction, and shows the influence of Jewish style. Resembling Jude in its high style, 2 Peter is even more influenced by the Septuagint.

The Book of Revelation has a generally simple style, but shows considerable Semitic influence in its use of parallelism and redundance. Linguistic scholars have identified a number of apparent grammatical mistakes in Greek in the Book of Revelation.

Conclusion. To Christians, the message conveyed by the Bible is simple and direct, yet capable of interacting with people in the most complex cultural circumstances. Although every human language has its limitations, the biblical languages have proved to be remarkably adequate vehicles for conveying God's message in all its power and richness.

LARRY LEE WALKER

See LATIN; ALPHABET; WRITING AND BOOKS.

Bibliography. G.A. Deissmann, *Bible Studies;* D. Diringer, *The Story of the Aleph Beth,* and *Writing;* G.R. Driver, *Semitic Writing, From Pictograph to Alphabet;* J.H. Moulton; W.F. Howard; N. Turner, *A Grammar of NT Greek,* 4 vols.; W.H. Simcox, *The Language of the NT,* and *The Writers of the NT.*

Biblical Theology. Branch of theological inquiry devoted to identifying distinctive themes in various sections of the Bible (e.g., the OT or the writings of the apostle Paul), tracing them from one section to another, and discovering any overall unifying theme that draws the whole Bible together.

The task of the biblical theologian is thus (1) to discern the particular emphases of individual writers (such as the social justice of Amos or human love in the Song of Solomon); (2) to compare and contrast treatments by different writers of a single theme (e.g., the different approaches to salvation in John's Gospel and Hebrews); and (3) to attempt to integrate into a single comprehensive whole all the various emphases of the biblical writers.

Biblical theology studies in detail the progressive self-revelation of God in Scripture. It focuses on the meaning of a biblical passage in the life situation at the time of its writing, rather than on its meaning or application today.

Relation to Other Disciplines. *Systematic Theology.* Biblical theology provides the foundation on which systematic theology builds. Biblical theology is descriptive: it describes the message of each biblical writer as well as the overall message of Scripture. Systematic theology then restates or reshapes the material collected by biblical theology, breaking it up into logical categories and integrating those categories into a comprehensive formulation of church teaching. For example, biblical theology notes that, according to the Gospel of John, eternal life is a present possession, which gives a believer security; on the other hand, according to Hebrews, eternal life is a future attainment, which gives a believer the responsibility of persevering.

A biblical theologian would point out that those two teachings concerning eternal life are complementary aspects of a single truth: salvation entails both security and responsibility. A systematic theologian takes such results and integrates them into a more comprehensive doctrine of salvation, discussing security and responsibility in relation to election, justification, regeneration, and sanctification. The logical structure of systematic theology is usually taken from modern thought-patterns; hence, by stating in modern terms "what the Bible means now," systematic theology becomes a bridge between "what it meant then" (the task of biblical theology) and "how it applies" (the task of homiletical theology).

Exegesis. The basis of biblical theology is "exegesis," a term derived from two Greek words meaning "to think or infer out of." As a discipline, exegesis examines biblical passages and "thinks out" their meaning on the basis of grammar (the meaning of the language and its relationship to thought) and historical considerations (the meaning of each passage in light of the culture of that day). A biblical theologian compiles such exegetical results and seeks to discover any underlying unity. Biblical theology thus stands between exegesis and systematic theology.

Historical Theology. A separate discipline studies the development of systematic theology throughout the history of the church. One might expect biblical theology, concerned only with the emphases of the biblical writers themselves, to be far removed from the debates and interpretations of later times. Historical theology, however, clarifies how different periods of church history understood various biblical teachings, and why. For example, a scholar investigating the controversy over God's sovereignty and human freedom might trace the doctrinal debate from the Augustine-Pelagius controversy of the early church through the Calvinist-Arminian debates of the post-Reformation period, to the present.

Appreciating the different turns such controversy took historically and how it affected the way related doctrines were expressed from one period to the next can help a biblical theologian gain perspective on the meaning of the biblical text. Historical theology, especially the study of the early church fathers, provides an excellent control against reading later ideas into the pages of Scripture.

Homiletical Theology. The final step of the theological process is application of biblical truth to the contemporary situation. Homiletical theology builds on the other theological disciplines, interpreting the exegetical data as organized by biblical and systematic theology and as reviewed by historical theology. Interpreters of the Bible must first understand its meaning in the biblical world before deciding how that meaning should be expressed today in preaching and in ethical decision-making.

History of Biblical Theology. *Early Centuries to the Enlightenment.* Biblical theology as a separate discipline did not develop until the 19th century. During the early centuries of the church, heresies were constantly appearing. In order to meet their threat, the church, emerging from the apostolic age, sought to systematize the apostles' teachings. As a result, systematic theology developed, producing the early creeds (Apostles', Nicene, Athanasian, Chalcedonian, and others) which are still recognized as doctrinal standards of the church.

The Middle Ages saw the appearance of philosophical theology. The authority of church dogma was so great by that time that actual biblical investigation was rarely conducted. Instead, philosophical theology like that of Thomas Aquinas (1224–74) became prominent. In the 16th century the Reformation finally set the scene for a biblical theology by undermining the authority of church tradition and establishing the principle of *sola scriptura* ("Scripture only"). Martin Luther, John Calvin, and other reformers were themselves systematic theologians, however, so it took two other movements to establish the new approach: pietism and the Enlightenment.

Pietism, a reaction to dogmatic Lutheran scholasticism, first emerged in Germany toward the end of the 17th century. It stressed the primacy of feeling and experience and considered study of the Scriptures more important than the theological formulations and speculations of Lutheran orthodoxy. As a result, the pietists turned to biblical exegesis as a more edifying discipline.

The Enlightenment, a secular intellectual movement of the 18th century which grew out of Renaissance humanism, stressed the role of reason in all learning situations and claimed to challenge all previously held assumptions. It dared to approach the Scriptures historically, trying to go behind the church's teachings to the actual events which led to the biblical record. Although its assumptions and method were increasingly hostile to supernaturalism, the Enlightenment was a strong factor in developing biblical theology.

The 18th and 19th Centuries. The foundation of biblical theology was laid by J.F. Gabler, who argued in 1787 that biblical theology was a discipline independent from systematics, centering on the description of each biblical author's theology in its historical context. From the start, that school was dominated by rationalism; it treated the Bible merely as an ancient book expressing the religious evolution of the Hebrews and Christians. The evolutionary stages were seen as the religion of the Jews, centering on the Law; the teachings of Jesus, centering on a direct relationship with God; and the dogma of the early church, centering on the development of church tradition. Those states were increasingly held to be distinct from one another.

In the 19th century that method was adopted by followers of G.W.F. Hegel (1770–1831), a philosopher who developed a dialectical theory of history. Hegelian theory stated that all historical change proceeds along the lines of compromise: a thesis (things as they are) is challenged by its antithesis (the opposing forces of social change); the interaction results in a synthesis (the integration of the two opposing forces). When applied to the OT by K.H. Graf (1815–69) and Julius Wellhausen (1844–1918), the theory resulted in a developmental hypothesis. According to those two scholars, the Pentateuch (first five books of the Bible) as it is now was not completed until the prophetic period; it was "developed" throughout the preprophetic period. A key to early stages of its development was seen in the names of God, with a Yahwist editor (using Jehovah, "Lord") and an Elohist editor (using Elohim, "God") representing two of the stages; they were later integrated with a deuteronomic segment (interest in the Law) and a priestly segment (interest in the sacrificial system of worship). The Graf-Wellhausen view of the Pentateuch is commonly referred to as the documentary hypothesis.

In the NT the same approach was applied by F.C. Baur (1762–1860) and the school of tendency criticism. Baur theorized a conflict between the tendencies of Jewish Christianity (which he identified with the followers of Peter) and those of the Hellenistic (Greek) Christianity (Paul's followers). Those two segments of the church were seen as continuing to

"war" until the middle of the 2nd century, when the NT books that represented a synthesis were thought to be written (Acts, 1 Pt, and finally Jn).

In the second half of the 19th century, a history-of-religions school applied the methods of comparative religion to the Bible and its teachings. They taught that the biblical ideas evolved out of the various religions of the surrounding cultures. In light of that, biblical theology was ruled irrelevant and was discarded in favor of a comparative approach. For example, the feasts of the OT (Lv 23; Dt 16), according to those scholars, developed from Canaanite fertility rites; the notion of a future resurrection (Dn 12:2) was not Jewish but Persian in origin. Further, it was taught that in the NT the concept of the lordship of Christ (Phil 2:9–11) developed from Hellenistic ideas superimposed on Jewish Christianity; the doctrine of the substitutionary atonement (Col 1:14,19–22) supposedly had its basis in Greek and Near Eastern mysticism.

A more conservative movement, contemporary with such theologically liberal movements but with its roots in pietism, also approached the Bible from a historical perspective. It called attention to the unity between various sections of Scripture as well as between the OT and NT. According to its scholars, the Pentateuch, rather than being written down long after Moses' death during the time of the prophets, was an authentic record of the experiences of ancient Israel; the historical books and prophetic writings accurately represented the historical and theological development of the Jewish people, building upon the pentateuchal foundation; the teachings of Paul in the NT had their roots more in Judaism than in Hellenism.

Three approaches to the unity between the Testaments were developed during that time.

J.C.K. von Hofmann (1810–77) anticipated the emphasis of later biblical theologians on salvation history, concluding that the theme unifying the Testaments was God's saving acts in history. He saw the OT as declaring even in Abraham's time that God's clear purpose was the evangelization of all humankind through his chosen people (Gn 12:3); the NT described and explained the redemptive act of Christ on the cross as the central point of history and prepared for the final act of salvation history, Christ's return.

E.W. Hengstenberg (1802–69) and others read NT Christology back into the OT—in messianic prophecies and indirectly in "types of Christ," such as Adam (Rom 5:14) and Jonah (Mt 12:40). German scholars Paul Feine (1859–1933) and Adolf Schlatter (1852–1938) took a descriptive approach to NT theology, arguing that the various writers provided different perspectives on the central theme: the impact of Jesus on the church.

J.N. Darby (1800–82) and others developed a dispensational approach, asserting that God has worked to reconcile humanity to himself through a series of dispensations, each of which is a self-contained period of history. Each dispensation exhibits a different attempt to recall human beings to God (e.g., the Abrahamic period, which centered on the Abrahamic covenant, and the Mosaic period, which centered on the Law). All are integral parts of God's economy of salvation.

The Modern Era. The reemergence of biblical theology from what had been a liberal perspective came with Karl Barth (1886–1968), who overturned the purely academic, philosophical approach which biblical scholarship had taken. In circles where the Bible had been treated as a mere chronicle of religious experience, Barth declared that Scripture is the instrument through which God continues to speak to humankind. Historical interest, he maintained, was unnecessary. World War I had dealt a death blow to the old liberal optimism; Barth's message provided a way out of the morass into which rationalism had led theology. Barth separated the message of God in the Bible from critical problems (authorship, dating, accuracy). It did not matter in Barth's theology if Israel's exodus from Egypt never occurred as recorded. What mattered was that the biblical account represents the authentic religious statement of God's people; the Bible therefore becomes the means by which God speaks to people today.

The work of Barth and his followers, which led to a "golden age" of biblical theology, was dominant for 40 years. Following Barth's lead, Otto Eissfeldt in OT studies separated rational, historical criticism (knowledge) from the systematic exposition of theological themes (faith). Walter Eichrodt in the same field stressed the theological aspect and found as a unifying core the covenant of God in the life of Israel; his was one of several theories put forward regarding the OT's central theme. G. Ernest Wright and Otto Procksch considered that theme to be God's saving revelation in history, which Procksch identified as christological in essence. Theodore C. Vriezen emphasized a promise-fulfillment theme in the OT as a theology of history in which the Lord's saving acts were portrayed in the creedal traditions of Israel. The common conviction of all the theorists, however, was that the OT should be interpreted along theological lines rather than by way of a historical criticism that discussed the historical authenticity of a passage but neglected its theological meaning.

In NT studies Oscar Cullmann (b 1902) championed the salvation-history approach. For him the Bible primarily chronicles, celebrates, and interprets God's redeeming activity in history. In the OT, God chose Israel, gave the Law, and worked through the kings and prophets—all acts of divine intervention designed to bring an estranged humanity back to himself. The NT details the fulfillment and culmination of God's salvation work in Christ. The cross is the midpoint of history; the church's proclamation of the gospel is the continuation of God's salvation work. Cullmann represented the conservative side of critical scholarship.

Rudolph Bultmann (1884–1976) became a leading radical critic. He argued for demythologizing the NT. Bultmann saw the biblical accounts as being built on an ancient belief in a three-storied universe with heaven "up there," the world "down here," and the underworld of demon forces "below." Since science had disproved that cosmology, the biblical material had to be reinterpreted by stripping off the "myth" (stories created by the ancient, superstitious approach to religious experience) and restating the timeless "existential" truth (i.e., the lessons about living and coping in a finite world). The Gospels, for example, were not actual histories of Jesus' life and ministry but instead were later products of the church, which reworked the Jewish stories of Jesus on the basis of its "kerygma" ("proclamation" in a preaching situation). More and more the historical Jesus was eclipsed as the later Hellenistic church reinterpreted the stories. According to Bultmann, the actual historical events can never be restored. Although his followers have for the most part taken a more conservative approach, Bultmann's influence still predominates in many liberal seminaries and religion departments.

Recent Movements. In the 1960s a reaction against biblical theology developed. Many critics doubted the Scripture's unity. Renewed interest in the history-of-religions approach means that the Bible is often seen as an evolving organism of sometimes conflicting theologies. Since no single theme can be cited as normative, one can only analyze the disparate theologies of the various parts. Three different schools seem to be related to that broader movement.

Redaction criticism is an attempt to get behind the forms of the gospel stories to the theologies of the individual gospel writers. Redaction critics contrast Mark's emphasis on the messianic secret with Matthew's emphasis on the kingdom of God, Luke's on salvation history, and John's on the faith-decision and the oneness between Father, Son, and Christian disciples. The attempt to separate the individual emphases has spread to all sections of the Bible and has been a major movement of the last two decades.

Canon criticism starts with the concept of the biblical canon (those books of the OT and NT, and thus recognized as being Holy Scripture) as the key principle of interpretation. According to canon critics, the true meaning of the biblical accounts does not depend on the events as they actually happened, but rather on the final form the stories of those events have assumed in the canonical books. In that view, whether those stories evolved or not is irrelevant. It is not the event but its account in the canon that is authoritative; therefore, true biblical theology must be built on those accounts. Since they describe the beliefs of ancient Israel and the early church, they are seen as the proper focus for exegesis.

Structural analysis is the most recent methodology. As its name suggests, it studies the final structure of each biblical book to determine its meaning. The analysis begins with a search for the underlying structure of a book or passage to discover its genre (its literary form: poem, chronicle, epistle, and so on). A genre significantly shapes how and what a writer writes, so that much can be learned from comparing a biblical example with other contemporary examples. Parables in extrabiblical Jewish or Greek literature can help explain why biblical parables are composed the way they are. Several works have appeared comparing the Gospel of Mark to Greek tragedy or comedy. A second task for the structural analyst is to seek the hidden agenda of the account (i.e., the meaning underlying the surface words) in order to get to its true message. Thus some see Jesus' miracles as attempts of the later church to show how his impact transcended natural barriers and the problems of human limitations.

Evangelicals have not been silent during this period. Geerhardus Vos (1862–1949) produced a biblical theology (1948) that sought to unify the two Testaments through a combination of historical and theological structures. In OT studies, E.J. Young (1907–68) has centered on the "covenant" structure; modifications have been introduced by J. Barton Payne's accent on "testament" and Walter Kaiser's on "promise." In NT studies, George Eldon Ladd has fashioned a topical approach (i.e., synoptic, Pauline, Johannine theology, and so on) built on a salvation history framework. Charles C. Ryrie has done the same in a dispensational framework.

Methodology Several different approaches to biblical theology can be undertaken, each with its strengths and weaknesses.

1. The *systematic method* traces basic theological themes through the various sections of the Bible, attempting to understand the progressive revelation of each theme. Its shortcoming is that an artificial construction and unity may be subjectively forced on the biblical data. The exodus is an example of an important biblical theme that lends itself well to systematic study. The systematic method would observe the theme's various developments beginning with the event itself in the Book of Exodus; then it would move on to its metaphorical use in the poetic and prophetic books of the OT. Metaphorically the exodus can be seen as a vivid picture of God's redemption, a type and prefiguration of Christ's work extending to the redemptive teaching of the NT. The exodus event, which in the Pentateuch detailed the liberation of Israel from bondage in Egypt, was used in the prophets as a basis for teaching deliverance from the exile and in the NT to teach deliverance from sin.

2. The *descriptive method* studies the distinctive theology of each separate book and tries to discover the unique teaching of each. The problem is that often no attempt is made to collate the data, resulting in a collage of pictures with no cohesive pattern. The exodus theme—in Exodus, Haggai, the Gospels, and Romans, for example—would be studied separately as it occurred in each individual book and only in reference to that book.

3. The *historical method* chronicles the development of religious ideas in the life of Israel or the church. Again using the exodus as an example, the historical approach would attempt to reconstruct the steps of development from Exodus to Haggai to the Gospels to the Epistles. That method can be a valuable supporting tool to the descriptive approach. When tied to the more subjective approach of historical criticism, however, results from such a method may turn out drastically different from the actual theology of the Testaments. For example, some have proposed that Paul's imagery was drawn more from Greek liberation ideas (including myths about redeemer gods) than from the Jewish exodus theme.

4. The *Christological method* makes Christ the interpretive key to both Testaments and the one princple of unity between them. That approach may cause certain hermeneutical (interpretive) difficulties, especially a tendency to read "types of Christ" into OT passages and therefore to minimize the religious experience of Israel. Examining the exodus story, for example, some theologians would read a "type of Christ" into every aspect of the exodus and thereby play it down as the central spiritual

event in Israel's history. Yet a proper christological emphasis would show how that event began a process of redemption which culminated in the cross.

5. The *confessional method* ignores critical methods, approaching the Bible as a series of faith-statements unconnected to history. Its weakness is its radical dichotomy between history and faith, an unbiblical distinction. Adherents of the confessional school would stress the theology of the exodus account but ignore its place as a historical event. Surely both aspects must be affirmed for an understanding of the Bible.

6. The *cross-section method* decides on a central unifying theme (e.g., Eichrodt on "covenant") and traces it historically through cross sections of the biblical records. The weakness of the method is a twofold danger of arbitrarily selecting the wrong theme and then forcing other themes to conform to it. Again consider the exodus theme. If "liberation" were accepted as the central theme of the Bible, one might see variations on the exodus in virtually every section of Scripture. The cross could become the early church's counterpart to Israel's tribulation. The cross-section method can be valuable, however, if a theme is placed in its proper perspective.

Most scholars recognize the necessity of combining several of the above methods to maximize their strengths and minimize their weaknesses. True biblical theology must somehow utilize the best from all the methods. Thus an approach that focuses on the message of the text helps one to avoid the radical skepticism of the liberal critics; together with canon criticism it leads to a valid examination of the Bible as it stands. Grammatical-historical exegesis alone can derive what the actual meaning of the text was and the theology behind it.

The exegetical data must then be compiled on a descriptive basis in order to discern the actual theological emphases of the Bible's various parts. Those results are further collated on the basis of historical development to discover how the various themes progressed and whether any unifying principles lie behind them. The final step, systematic compilation of the motifs into major sections and subsections, must follow the biblical pattern (descriptively) rather than an artificial reconstruction.

In the process of following those steps, a single unifying theme is sought, hopefully without forcing the subsections into an artificial conformity with the overall motif. The writings of Paul and John, for example, may provide two different perspectives on the same issue, complementary, yet still distinct. The Bible's inner unity is the result, not the cause, of the various theologies of its parts.

OT Theology. *Proposed Unifying Themes.* Many suggestions for a central unifying theme of the OT have been made. The difficulty of judging their relative worth is enormous, but four criteria should be met for any motif to be called central: the nature and character of God must be accounted for; the people of God in their relation to him must be defined; the human race as the object of God's redemptive activity must be considered; and the relationship between the Testaments must be explained.

Many of the proposed unifying themes stress one or another of the above criteria but fail to do justice to all of them. To raise one criterion to a place above the others would result in an unbalanced biblical theology. Several proposed themes will be considered here.

1. Covenant. Eichrodt defines the covenant both statically, as a legal relationship binding God and his people, and dynamically, as the manifold experiences of communion between God and humanity. Covenant therefore has both a legal and an anticipatory side, dealing with present reality and future hope. It also has both a restrictive sense, dealing with God's special relation to his covenant people, and a universal force, dealing with the cosmic God who created, sustains, and redemptively reaches out to his world. The weakness of covenant as the central theme is the absence of the idea from many parts of the OT.

2. Community. Vriezen has argued that the true relation between God and humanity is better seen as communion than as covenant. Communion is closer to the true dynamic of God's personal character and builds a better bridge to the NT. Covenant then becomes an illustration of that relationship; prophecy is the revelation of the transcendent God in immanent interaction with humankind; the poetic and wisdom writings of the OT are the expression of that communion. The chief weakness of the community theme is highlighted by the work of G. Fohrer, who posits the rule or sovereignty of God in addition to the communion between God and humanity. Any theology must take cognizance of God's sovereign majesty as well as his lovingkindness.

3. God. Gerhard Hasel argues that the OT is theocentric (focuses on God) to the same extent that the NT is Christocentric (focuses on Christ). In so doing he has sought to combine the work of many others who have put forth such themes as the holiness of God, the lordship of God, or the kingship of God as unifying themes. God is seen as absolute in himself while active in the world to restore it to fellowship with himself. Hasel views the concept of

God as dynamic rather than static. Such an approach leaves room for individual expression of peripheral themes in various sections. Although Hasel's proposal has definite advantages, his theme may actually prove to be too narrow, elevating the essential attributes of God to such an extent that relational aspects are neglected.

Redemptive History. Following von Hofmann, the theme of redemptive history has become a major school of interpretation expressed by Wright, von Rad, and others. It may be a concept broad enough to contain the other major motifs. Covenant expresses the means by which God redemptively acted within the history of Israel; communion is the goal of salvation history. The theme of redemptive history incorporates promise and privilege, judgment and responsibility, God's justice and loving kindness. Also, it broadens God's redemptive activity to include all humanity, not just the covenant people of Israel. Finally, it builds a bridge to the NT, since Cullmann, Ladd, and others find it to be the central theme motif there as well; the difference would be a theocentric core in the OT and a Christocentric thrust in the NT. Thus the theme of redemptive history seems to meet the criteria enumerated above and to include the strengths of other suggested themes.

A brief application of that theme to the other themes of the OT sections illustrates how it fits the broad trend of OT biblical theology. It has been suggested that Genesis 1 to 11 centers on the theme of blessing and cursing, uniting God's promise with human responsibility. The theme is traced throughout the rest of the Pentateuch, where God's saving acts (the Abrahamic covenant, the exodus, the Law) are wedded to a necessary human response. Salvation history is central in the scheme because both God's action and man's reaction occur within history. The historical and prophetic books focus directly on the theme as God works with and through his prophets, priests, and kings to call his people back to himself. The poetic literature is a celebration of that truth, centering on worship (Ps) or ethical responsibility (Prv), as the salvation that God has provided is worked out in history.

The major problem with the theme has to do with the meaning of the concept "history." Von Rad, for instance, uses as his key a theology of history taken from Deuteronomy; others might question why the emphasis of one section of the Bible should be imposed on all the other sections. Moreover, many scholars separate the special salvation history with its theological implications from the actual facts of Israel's history. It seems best to argue for a concept of history broad enough to cover both fact and interpretation, both history (what German scholars call *Historie*) and its theological meaning (German *Geschichte*).

Many would also argue that redemptive history is inadequate with regard to the human existential situation and to human ethics. It seems unwarranted, however, to distinguish between the vertical dimension of redemptive history and the horizontal dimension of existential experience.

In summary, the theme of redemptive history is a reasonable candidate for the overall central concept of the OT.

NT Theology. Salvation history is clearly a key concept in the NT, which centers on God's culminating act of salvation in Jesus Christ, and its implications for the age of the church. That theme is stressed more in some parts than in others. Luke, for example, has been called the theologian of salvation history for his strong emphasis on that aspect; the apostle Paul's major work on the theme is Romans (especially chs 9–11); it is also stressed in the Book of Revelation. It seems to be the one theme that binds together the diverse emphases of the whole NT, from the problem-oriented epistles to the history-oriented and theology-oriented Gospels to John's apocalyptic vision.

Thematic Diversity. Because recent scholarly trends have seemed to show the NT authors moving in their own directions, many NT theologians are reluctant to pursue a single unifying theme. The four Gospel writers, for example, covered the same basic material, but had quite different emphases. Mark focused on action, stressing Jesus as the hidden Messiah, misunderstood even by his own disciples. Matthew accented Jesus' teaching and presented his credentials as Messiah through fulfilled OT prophecy. Luke emphasized Jesus as the focal point of salvation history, carrying that over to Acts, where the church continued God's redemptive work in the world. John centered on the salvation drama of the Word becoming flesh, and on the necessity of faith-encounter and decision.

Those themes can all be woven into a larger tapestry. Since informed conservative biblical theology is a fairly recent phenomenon, students of Scripture are still discovering the individual emphases of the NT writers. Although today many feel confident that the union of those themes lies in the salvation-history concept, the matter is still debated.

History and Theology. Modern theologians sometimes argue for two different types of history: objective history, dealing with the pure facts; and interpreted history, dealing with the meaning of the events. They argue that since biblical history is interpreted history, theology must take precedence over the actual events. That view introduces a false dichotomy, however, because the OT presented revelation as occurring within the actual event; NT faith likewise included both the historical facts and the interpretation of those facts by witnesses. The witness themes of Luke and John, as well as the stress on eyewitnesses to the resurrection in 1 Corinthians 15:3–8, support the contention that the NT blended theology and history. Even those who deny Peter's authorship of 2 Peter 1:16 must accept it as the claim of the early church that they did not invent "cleverly devised myths." Proclaiming the gospel and writing history are not incompatible. For an evangelical Christian, faith must be based on historical grounds. The biblical writers' concern with theological interpretation did not necessarily hinder their accurate portrayal of the history they were interpreting.

Relation Between the Testaments. Difficult issues complicate the question of the relationship between the two Testaments. What is the exact connection between Law and grace, or between Israel and the church? Two poles have developed: dispensationalism, which teaches a dichotomy between the two, with the church age an additional historical phase not anticipated by the OT; and Reformed or covenant theology, which maintains an implicit continuity between the two, with the church age ushered in by the work of Christ and continuing the divine plan. Dispensationalism holds that the OT Law has been replaced by NT grace; covenant theology states that the Law has been fulfilled in grace.

Salvation history balances the two divergent positions. On the one hand, the two Testaments are different; promises are made in the Old that are not "kept" until the New. God's redemptive work in the OT looked forward in time to a culmination in Jesus. On the other hand, there is a flow from the OT to the NT. The church's role as the remnant of Israel is seen in Jesus' choice of 12 disciples (corresponding to Israel's 12 tribes) and his emphasis that they be sent first to Israel.

The Christocentric Core. The NT is Christ-centered, above all, and witnesses to the impact of Jesus' work and teaching. As the Gospels point out, the interpretive key to the theology of the early church was the resurrection event. Before that, even the disciples misunderstood Jesus' messiahship. The resurrection not only vindicated Jesus' own claims about his ministry but also opened the disciples' eyes to the meaning of those claims. The NT letters show the early church attempting to apply that new understanding to the practical problems of the church in the world.

Again, salvation history forms the connecting link, for the church viewed itself as carrying on God's redemptive acts in history, manifested in the believing community and proclaimed to the unbelieving.

Conclusion. Biblical theology has been described here as a scholarly discipline with its own technical jargon and developing schools of thought. To the ordinary Christian trying to study the Bible and understand God's message in it, scholarly debates among theologians may seem pedantic or irrelevant. Yet one can be grateful that some Christians faithful to the Bible have prepared themselves academically to examine it from so many different perspectives.

Bible study, usually proceeding one paragraph at a time, can give one a fragmented view unless the overall themes of individual writers, of certain types of books (the Pentateuch, Psalms, the Gospels, and so on), of the two Testaments, and of the Bible as a whole are kept in mind. By studying such themes, comparing them, and seeking to unify them, biblical theology helps serious students get the whole picture of the Bible.

GRANT R. OSBORNE

See ISRAEL, RELIGION OF; "TEACHING OF" SECTION FOR EACH BOOK OF THE BIBLE; JESUS CHRIST, LIFE AND TEACHING OF; JOHN THE APOSTLE, LIFE AND WRITINGS OF; PAUL, THE APOSTLE; PETER, THE APOSTLE.

Bibliography. B.S. Childs, *Biblical Theology in Crisis;* W. Eichrodt, *Theology of the OT*, 2 vols.; D. Guthrie, *NT Theology;* R.A. Guelich (ed), *Unity and Diversity in NT Theology;* G. Hasel, *NT Theology: Basic Issues in the Current Debate,* and *OT Theology: Basic Issues in the Current Debate;* J. Jeremias, *NT Theology;* W. Kaiser, *Toward an OT Theology;* G. Ladd, *A Theology of the NT;* R.B. Laurin, *Contemporary OT Theologians;* E. Stauffer, *NT Theology;* G. von Rad, *Theology,* 2 vols.; T.C. Vriezen, *An Outline of OT Theology.*

Bichri, Bichrite. Sheba's father in Benjamin's tribe. Sheba led a revolt against King David (2 Sm 20:1–22). Bichri's descendants were known as Bichrites (2 Sm 20:14, KJV Berites).

Bidkar. Aide of King Jehu of the northern kingdom of Israel. Bidkar fulfilled a prophecy about the fate of Ahab's family by throwing the body of Joram, Ahab's son, into Naboth's field after Jehu had killed Joram (2 Kgs 9:24–26).

Bigamy. Marrying for a second time while still legally married to another.

See MARRIAGE, MARRIAGE CUSTOMS.

Bigtha. Eunuch who served King Ahasuerus of Persia. He and six others were in charge of the royal household (Est 1:10). He is perhaps identifiable with Bigthan in Esther 2:21 and Bigthana in 6:2.

See BIGTHAN, BIGTHANA.

Bigthan, Bigthana. Eunuch who served King Ahasuerus of Persia as a palace guard. He and a fellow guard named Teresh planned an assassination attempt on the king's life. When their plot was overheard by Queen Esther's uncle Mordecai, the two conspirators were executed (Est 2:21–23; 6:2, Bigthana). In the Apocrypha, Bigthan is called Gabatha (Add Est 12:1), and he is perhaps the same person as Bigtha in Esther 1:10.

See BIGTHA.

Bigvai. 1. Ancestor of a group of people that returned to Jerusalem with Zerubbabel after the Babylonian exile (Ezr 2:2,14; Neh 7:7,19). Since his name is Persian, Bigvai may have been born or renamed during the exile.

2. Political leader who signed Ezra's covenant of faithfulness to God with Nehemiah and others after the exile (Neh 10:16); possibly a representative for the family descended from #1 above.

Bildad. One of three friends who came to comfort Job in his anguish, identified as a Shuhite (Jb 2:11). That term suggests that he was a descendant of Shuah, son of Abraham and his second wife Keturah (Gn 25:1,2). Bildad spoke to Job on three occasions. In his first speech he asserted that God upholds the just and punishes the wicked (Jb 8). Job must therefore be a hypocrite to say that he is right with God. In his second speech Bildad emphasized the immediate punishment of the wicked in this life (ch 18). Job must therefore be wicked because of his intense suffering. In his third speech Bildad proclaimed the majesty of God and called man a worm by comparison (ch 25). He implied that Job was foolish to claim to be righteous before such a holy God.

See JOB, BOOK OF.

Bileam. Alternate name for Ibleam, a levitical city in Manasseh's territory, in 1 Chronicles 6:70.

See IBLEAM.

Bilgah. 1. Head of the 15th of 24 divisions of priests whom King David assigned to official duties in the temple (1 Chr 24:14).

2. Priest who returned to Jerusalem under Zerubbabel's leadership after the exile (Neh 12:18). He is perhaps identifiable with Bilgai in Nehemiah 10:8.

See BILGAI.

Bilgai. Priest who signed Ezra's covenant of faithfulness to God with Nehemiah and others

after the exile (Neh 10:8); possibly the same person as Bilgah in Nehemiah 12:18.

See BILGAH #2.

Bilhah (Person). Servant given by Laban to his daughter Rachel when she married Jacob (Gn 29:29). Realizing her own childlessness, Rachel gave Bilhah to her husband as a concubine and accepted their two sons as her own, naming them Dan and Naphtali (30:3–8; 35:25; 46:25). Archaeological investigation has confirmed the custom of a barren wife's providing a concubine to guarantee children to her husband. Such an arrangement is mentioned in marriage contract documents dug up at Nuzi and dated from about the same time as the Genesis 29 events. Jacob's son Reuben was later guilty of incest with Bilhah (35:22).

Bilhah (Place). Town in the territory allotted to Simeon's tribe (1 Chr 4:29), probably identical with Baalah (Jos 15:29) and Balah (Jos 19:3).

Bilhan. 1. Ezer's firstborn son and a descendant of Seir (Gn 36:27; 1 Chr 1:42).

2. Jediael's son from Benjamin's tribe (1 Chr 7:10).

Bilshan. One, who with Nehemiah and Zerubbabel, led a group of Jews to Jerusalem following the exile (Ezr 2:2; Neh 7:7).

Bimhal. Japhlet's son, a great warrior and head of a clan in Asher's tribe (1 Chr 7:33,40).

Bine-a. Moza's son from Benjamin's tribe and a descendant of King Saul through Jonathan's line (1 Chr 8:37; 9:43).

Binnui. 1. Noadiah's father. Noadiah was a Levite in charge of weighing temple valuables after the exile (Ezr 8:33). Possibly the same as #4 below.

2. Pahath-moab's son or descendant. He obeyed Ezra's exhortation to divorce his pagan wife after the exile (Ezr 10:30).

3. According to the Apocrypha and KJV, one of Bani's sons (descendants) who also obeyed Ezra's exhortation to divorce his pagan wife (Ezr 10:38; 1 Esd 9:34). Because the list of Bani's descendants is proportionally very long and because verse 38 in Hebrew can easily be construed "of the sons of Binnui," most modern translations make Binnui an ancestor of a new group rather than a descendant of Bani.

4. Henadad's son who repaired part of Jerusalem's wall after the exile (Neh 3:24). He was among the Levites who signed Ezra's covenant of faithfulness to God (Neh 10:9).

Closeup of a section of the wall of Nehemiah (along the eastern edge of Mt Ophel in Jerusalem, south of the temple mount).

5. Alternate spelling for Bani in Nehemiah 7:15.

See BANI #4.

6. Levite who returned to Judah with Zerubbabel after the exile. He was one of several in charge of songs of thanksgiving (Neh 12:8).

The popularity of this name and its similarity to other Jewish names (e.g., Bani and Bavvai) has caused much confusion in the genealogical lists. The above is one of several possible arrangements.

Birds. Feathered vertebrates of the class Aves. Over 8,000 species of birds are known. Approximately 400 species are found in the Holy Land and about 40 are mentioned in Scripture.

Today scientists classify organisms on the basis of internal and external structure, but the biblical writers generally classified organisms according to habitat. Thus in the Bible bats are listed with birds as creatures of the air (Lv 11:19; Dt 14:18).

Precise identification of biblical birds is often difficult or impossible. The biblical languages were not highly specialized scientific languages. People in biblical times generally knew the difference between similar animals now categorized as separate species. For birds, however, they frequently used poetic, descriptive terms. Biblical scholars attempt to overcome the difficulties in identification by comparing the Hebrew words with similar words in related languages and by attention to the habitat, habits, and characteristics attributed to the birds in Scripture. Nevertheless, different scholars sometimes arrive at different identifications

Biblical References to Birds. The Bible refers to birds both in literal and figurative senses. The biblical writers were keen observers of nature, their awareness of birds and bird life being reflected in many passages. They asserted that God knows all the birds (Ps 50:11) and cares for them (Mt 10:29). They saw God's covenant with Noah after the flood, his promise never to destroy life again by flood, as extending even to the birds and animals (Gn 9:10).

The Mosiac law declared many birds "unclean," mostly species that were scavengers or predators, or inhabited waste places. Centuries later the early Christians came to regard unclean species as clean by God's decree, revealed in the apostle Peter's vision (Acts 10:12). Other birds, like quail, sustained the Israelites in their wanderings (Ex 16:13). The Law prescribed birds as sacrifices for a firstborn child (Lk 2:24), for a Nazirite vow (Nm 6:10), for cleansing a leper (Lv 14:22), and as a burnt offering and sin offering (12:8).

Birds are easily subject to extinction, especially through human activity. God required the Israelites to practice conservation to prevent any birds from becoming extinct in the Holy Land, both for the birds' sake and so the Israelites would have a continuous source of food. The Law allowed foraging Israelites to take eggs or the young from a bird's nest, but they were not permitted to kill both a mother bird and her young (Dt 22:6).

Biblical writers turned to nature frequently for illustrations of divine principles or human characteristics. Birds were thought by many ancient peoples to convey sacred meanings. For example, pagan artisans made idols of birds (Rom 1:23). Prophetic visions sometimes featured birds. Daniel had a vision of a composite beast having wings like a bird and representing a king (Dn 7:6).

Biblical comparisons of humans to birds sometimes carry a sense of lowness, as when King Nebuchadnezzar developed claws like a bird in his madness (Dn 4:33), or when Job remarked that birds did not know the source of wisdom (Jb 28:21). In Jesus' parable of the sower, the birds that ate the seed scattered by the wayside may represent indifference and a lack of spiritual understanding (Mt 13:4).

Scripture also contains sympathetic images of the plight of birds. A lonely man praying was likened to a lonely bird on a housetop (Ps 102:7). If someone was unjustly hunted by his enemies, he would understand a hunted bird's plight (Lam 3:52). Birds were said to be affected by curses on evildoers as they fled from Jerusalem or from the face of the earth (Jer 9:10; Zep 1:3).

In spite of such misfortune visited upon birds, Scripture affirms that, like other creatures, they are cared for and delighted in by God (Ps 50:11; Mt 6:26; 10:29). Job was instructed in God's greatness when God spoke of playing with all creatures great and small, from leviathans ("sea monsters") to birds (Jb 41:5). Both pharaoh and Nebuchadnezzar were compared to a tree that gives shelter to the birds (Ez 31:6; Dn 4:12; cf. 2:38). Human power, however, fails eventually, as when the tree representing Nebuchadnezzar was cut down, forcing the birds to flee (4:14). God's protection, by contrast, is unfailing. Jesus likened the kingdom of God to a mustard seed, growing to become a shelter for birds (Mt 13:32). God provides a habitation for birds (Ps 104:12), although Jesus, the Son of Man, had nowhere to rest his head (Mt 8:20).

Birds were considered evidence of God's handiwork (Jb 12:7). Bird lore provided examples of good sense in learning from a mistake (Prv 1:17; 6:5) and of bad judgment in failing to avoid the snares of immorality (7:23). Birds and other creatures could be tamed, unlike the wicked human tongue (Jas 3:7). A cock called Peter to repentance after he had denied knowing Jesus (Mt 26:74). Birds flying without alighting were an image of an undeserved curse (Prv 26:2). Without trust in God people might be forced by evil to flee like a bird to the mountains (Ps 11:1). Bird song was said to bring joy (Sg 2:12). The return of God's people to the Promised Land will be like birds returning (Hos 11:11). Jesus expressed his love for Jerusalem by saying that he longed to gather his people to himself as a hen gathers her brood under her wing (Mt 23:37).

Finally, birds were occasionally regarded as ominous signs. For example, pharaoh's baker learned of impending death because in a dream birds ate the food from a basket on his head (Gn 40:17). Solomon warned against cursing the king, even in private, "for a bird of the air will carry your voice" (Eccl 10:20). A vivid biblical image is that of scavenging, carrion-eating birds consuming the bodies of evildo-

ers. To the Israelites, such a desecration of humanity was an image of ultimate horror (Dt 28:26; 1 Sm 17:44; Is 46:11; Jer 7:33; 12:9; Ez 29:5; 39:4; Rv 19:17,21).

Individual Species. *Bittern.* Long-legged wading bird (*Botaurus stellaris*) similar to the heron, but with shorter legs and a smaller, more compact body. Bitterns inhabit marshes, where it is easy for them to hide with their natural camouflage. A bittern's mottled plumage of barred brown and black so duplicates the color and shape of swamp vegetation that at times the bird seems to disappear before the observer's eyes. The neck is covered with long, soft feathers, making it appear disproportionately heavy. Bitterns are wary and solitary. During mating season the bittern's larynx is modified to produce a mysterious-sounding cry. The body twists in an unusual manner in harmony with the notes. Bitterns nest alone in grassy marshes. Because they are shy they have become symbols of places of desolation and loneliness.

There is some question as to whether the bittern is actually mentioned in the Bible. The KJV has "bittern" in three places (Is 14:23; 34:11; Zep 2:14). Many biblical scholars believe the Hebrew word in those verses refers not to the bittern but to the hedgehog (Is 14:23; Zep 2:14 RSV) or porcupine (Is 34:11 RSV). The Hebrew word is similar to an Arabic word meaning "porcupine." Other scholars point out that the references suggest a bird rather than a mammal, especially Zephaniah 2:14, which speaks of the creature making its "lodge in her capitals" (i.e., above Nineveh's doorposts). Bitterns are particularly abundant in the swamps of the Tigris River (near Nineveh). The bittern's characteristics may fit the references in the three passages better than do the hedgehog's.

See ANIMALS (HEDGEHOG).

Buzzard. Hawklike soaring bird (*Buteo vulgaris* or *Buteo ferox*). It resembles the kite, though its tail is straight and not cleft. It is mentioned in the list of unclean birds (Dt 14:13). But other translations render the word as "glede" (KJV) or "kite" (NASB, NEB). The parallel list in Leviticus 11, however, substitutes "kite" (RSV, NASB, NEB), "falcon" (LB), or "vulture" (KJV) for buzzard. Thus it is difficult to determine whether the buzzard is actually mentioned in the Bible, even though it is a common resident of Palestine.

Like other great soaring birds, the buzzard is noted for its sharp eyesight, and may be the bird mentioned for that quality in Job 28:7 (variously translated "falcon," "eagle," or "vulture"). It will trail its prey for hours, and has a remarkable ability to see a carcass on which it descends to feed. Somewhat larger than the common buzzard is the long-legged buzzard, found in Palestine, western Asia, and Syria.

See KESTREL; KITE; VULTURE.

Cormorant. Large black gooselike bird (*Phalacrocorax carbo*), repeatedly depicted in art from Egypt and the Holy Land. Its length varies from 19 to 40 inches. Its feet have webs between all four toes. The feet, attached far back on the body, serve as propellers when the cormorant dives to catch its meal of fish, crustacea, or amphibia. The long bill is curved at the tip and under the bill is a sac in which the cormorant keeps the captured fish.

Cormorants live in large companies, making nests of sticks and other vegetation which they carry to trees or to rocky shelves near coasts. Up to four eggs are incubated, and the young are fed by both parents.

The cormorant frequents swamps around the Sea of Galilee, Lake Huleh (the waters of Merom), and the Mediterranean coast. Its Hebrew name originally denoted the "hurling down" of the bird at its prey. Cormorants dive into deep water and sometimes seem to zoom beneath the surface in their hunt for fish. The cormorant's greed is proverbial. It was ceremonially unclean for the Israelites (Lv 11:17; Dt 14:17).

See PELICAN.

Crane. Tall wading birds (*Grus grus*) resembling storks and herons but with shorter talons. The plumage has a silvery gloss and the tail feathers are wavy. Large flocks of cranes flying in wedge-shaped formations pass over the Holy Land during the daylight hours each fall on their way to Africa from the northern countries of Europe and again in the spring when they return north to breed. Migratory flocks may number as many as 2,000 birds. Jeremiah 8:7 refers to the crane's migratory habits.

The usual call of the crane is best described as a bellow, but during migratory flight they emit a chattering sound which may be referred to in Isaiah 38:14. Cranes have remarkably powerful voices, their calls seeming to carry for miles. Migrating flocks usually have a flock leader who does the calling.

A crane's height may reach 40 to 60 inches. Except for the ostrich the crane is the tallest bird ever to inhabit the Holy Land. A crane's wingspread may exceed 90 inches. The overall color is steel gray; the head and neck are black with a longitudinal white stripe. The crane feeds on land rather than in shallow water. It feeds primarily on grass and grain, yet may devour insects, snakes, small alligators, frogs, and worms, using its long powerful bill as a sharp hammer for killing such creatures.

The crane usually nests in solitary places,

often in shallow water or nearby. Its nest is a mass of vegetation, holding two or three eggs which are light colored with darker spots.

Cuckoo. Small drab brown bird known for its parasitic habits. The term KJV used in Leviticus 11:16 and Deuteronomy 14:15 may refer either to the common cuckoo (*Cuculus canorus*) or to the great spotted cuckoo (*Clamator glandarius*). The bird acts as a brood parasite, laying its eggs in the nest of another species after pushing out one of the eggs of the host species. The young cuckoo hatches before the young of the host species and evicts the other young. The foster parents raise it as their own.

The cuckoo, an insect eater, is considered ritually unclean in Scripture, which might imply that it is a predator or carrion-eater. For that reason some believe the Hebrew word actually refers to the sea gull or sea mew rather than the cuckoo. Gulls, terns, and petrels are all common on the seashore and lakes of the Holy Land.

Other scholars believe that the Hebrew word refers not to the cuckoo but to one of the owls, possibly the long-eared owl.

See OWL; SEA GULL.

Eagle. Large bird of prey, genus *Aquila*. Vultures were often confused, making identification of the biblical birds difficult. Eagles' heads are not bald as are the heads of vultures, but from a distance they appear similar. It is possible that the Hebrew word translated "eagle" (whch literally means "to tear with the beak") may have referred to all large birds of prey, eagles and vultures alike. A number of references to the eagle in Scripture are actually references to the griffon vulture (e.g., Hos 8:1; perhaps Mt 24:28). In certain passages, however, the true eagle may be meant.

The Holy Land has several varieties of eagle, including the imperial eagle (*Aquila heliaca*) and the less common golden eagle (*Aquila chrysaetos*). These birds are powerfully built with strong wings; their movements reveal suppleness and strength. A distinctive hooked beak, which enhances the eagle's dignified and somewhat ferocious appearance, provides it with an effective instrument for tearing and killing prey. Short, powerful legs and prehensile claws enable an eagle to apply an almost unbreakable grip on a struggling victim. The strong talons have sharp points and edges. The eagle hunts by day.

For Jeremiah and other prophets, the eagle was the epitome of swiftness. The golden eagle, which can fly three or four miles in 10 minutes, may have evoked the comparisons in 2 Samuel 1:23; Jeremiah 4:13; 49:22; Lamentations 4:19 (KJV), and Habakkuk 1:8. Moses used a similar comparison to emphasize the sudden striking power of a hostile enemy (Dt 28:49). The author of Proverbs, observing the high altitude to which the eagle soars, applied that image to the human situation (Prv 23:4,5; cf. Rv 12:14).

The eagle's strength and invincibility were mentioned often with reference to powerful nations attacking Israel. The prophet Ezekiel described Nebuchadnezzar as an eagle (Ez 17:3). Both the Babylonians and Assyrians frequently depicted the eagle in their art, especially as a deity with a man's body and an eagle's head. Nebuchadnezzar even had an experience of temporary insanity in which "his hair grew as long as eagles' feathers, and his nails were like birds' claws" (Dn 4:33).

The eagle builds its nest on inaccessible mountain peaks or at the top of the tallest trees, a fact noted by Jeremiah (Jer 49:16; cf. Jb 39:27,28; Ob 4). The brood consists of two or occasionally three eggs. Only the female sits on the nest, but the young eaglets are fed by both parents. Eagles are devoted to their offspring and train them with great care in the art of flying. Some commentators interpret Exodus 19:4 and Deuteronomy 32:11 as evidence of the eagle's practice of catching its young on its wings. There is virtually no evidence from observation, however, that any eagle can perform such a feat. In some versions the wording avoids a direct statement that eagles bear their young on their wings.

Some eagles in captivity have lived to an age of over a hundred years. This remarkable longevity caused the psalmist to speak of the eagle whose youth is renewed (Ps 103:5). Confronted by its impressive qualities, biblical authors observed the eagle with awe and wonder (Jb 39:27–30; Prv 30:18,19). Those awesome qualities also contributed to several prophetic visions, including Ezekiel's vision of a creature with an eagle's face (Ez 1:10) and the apostle John's vision of a holy beast like a flying eagle (Rv 4:7).

See VULTURE.

Fowl, Domestic. Domesticated poultry (*Gallus gallus domesticus*), probably derived from the red jungle fowl of India. They seem to have been known already in OT times (Prv 30:31). A seal of Jaazaniah (see 2 Kgs 25:23), dating from about 600 BC, bears the image of a fighting cock. A reference to fowls or poultry for Nehemiah's table, however, may be to wild game rather than domestic fowl (Neh 5:18).

Poultry symbolized fertility, and the Jews carried a cock and hen in front of bridal couples at weddings. The motherly concern of hens gathering their broods was familiar to Jesus' hearers (Mt 23:37; Lk 13:34).

Since roosters habitually crow an hour or two before dawn, the third watch of the night, from midnight to 3 A.M., was known as the cock crow. According to the Talmud (a commentary on Jewish law), keeping chickens was prohibited in Jerusalem in NT times to prevent the insects and larvae that breed in chicken droppings from contaminating sacrificial flesh. For that reason the cock that Peter heard (Mt 26:34,74; Lk 22:34,60,61) probably belonged to Romans living there or to Jews who did not follow Jewish regulations.

Goatsucker or *Night Hawk* (genus *Caprimulgus*). Migratory bird, dark in color and short-legged, similar to the American whippoorwill. The goatsucker resembles an owl with a flat head, large eyes, soft plumage, and a noiseless flight. It hunts insects at night, catches them on the wing, and during the day rests on branches. Goatsuckers were so named because they were thought by the ancients to milk goats. According to Leviticus 11:16 and Deuteronomy 14:15 they were ritually unclean. Although some scholars believe that an owl is intended, there seems to be good reason to accept the "night hawk" translation.

Goose (genus *Anser*). Long-necked, web-footed water birds with waterproof feathers. Domestic geese were known to the Greeks of Homer's day, since they are mentioned in the *Odyssey*. They were domesticated in Egypt perhaps as early as the Old Kingdom (c. 2500 BC) and certainly by the time of the New Kingdom (c. 1500–1100 BC). They were used for food and sacrifice. The breeding of geese was widespread in Canaan in biblical times; ivory carvings of the 13th or 12th century BC showing geese have been found in excavations at Megiddo in Palestine.

Many species of geese spend most of their lives on land even though they are waterfowl; some even build their nests in trees. Wild geese tend to inhabit flat lands and prairies rather than mountainous terrain.

Geese may have graced the table of King Solomon. In 1 Kings 4:23 they are referred to as "fatted fowl," a term that may also refer to ducks, swans, guineas, pigeons, or other domestic edible birds.

Hawk. Small day birds of prey found in Palestine. Most references are probably to the sparrow hawk (*Accipter nisus*). This bird is slightly larger than the kestrel, has a grayish brown back and a white belly with black and brown bars. It has short feathers, long curved talons, and broad wings, rounded at the outer ends, which enable it to soar on updrafts. The long tail, acting as a rudder, helps the bird change its course swiftly in flight. It is hence very maneuverable in the air when chasing warblers or other small birds. It does not seize its prey on the ground, as does the kestrel, but hunts and attacks small birds in flight. Hawks hunt in the daytime, unlike owls which are adapted for nighttime hunting. With their eyes located on the side of the head, hawks are very keen-sighted. They usually nest in tall trees and their nests are often occupied by the same pair year after year.

The Egyptians embalmed sparrow hawks and regarded all hawks highly. The god Horus was depicted with the head of a hawk or falcon.

The sparrow hawk was ceremonially unclean to the Israelites (Lv 11:16; Dt 14:15). It was not a permanent resident of Palestine but stopped off as it migrated from north to south. Its southward migration is mentioned in Job 39:26. A reference in Isaiah 34:11 to "hawk" ("cormorant," KJV) is uncertain.

See KESTREL; KITE.

Heron. Wading bird (genus *Ardea*) with a long thin neck and long legs. It has a characteristic comblike growth on the inner side of the third toe.

Herons are generally white, blue, green, or gray. They nest together in rookeries, and both parents bring in food for the young. Herons feed on fish, small reptiles, and insects, gulping them down in one swallow. Adults and young migrate in the late fall to warm southern climates. The white heron attains a length of more than three feet, whereas the dwarf heron is only about 22 inches long.

At least seven varieties of heron are reported in the Holy Land. The white ibis or buff-backed heron (*Buphus russatus*) was probably the most common species. The purple heron (*Ardea purpureus*) is a summer breeder found in all parts of Palestine where there is standing water.

The blue-gray heron (*Ardea cinerea*) winters in southern Europe and North Africa, migrating to northern Europe in the early spring. In Palestine it builds its winter nest near water, in swamps and along river banks, where it feeds on fish and frogs. It will stand patiently in the water for hours, and then suddenly its long pointed beak darts down with lightning speed to catch its prey. Often the blue-gray heron builds its nest in a tall tree to which it may return year after year.

According to Leviticus 11:19 and Deuteronomy 14:18, the heron was ceremonially unclean to the Israelites. Some scholars believe those references are to the cormorant, but most scholars think they refer to one of the herons.

See CORMORANT.

Hoopoe (Upupa epops). One of the Holy Land's most beautiful birds. It has vividly colored plumage, a lovely crown-shaped crest that becomes erect when the bird is alarmed, and a long, slender, curved bill. The pinkish-brown hoopoe is about 11 inches long, with black and white bands on its back, tail, and wings. Hoopoes are basically desert-dwelling birds.

The name "hoopoe" is derived from the sound of the bird's call. To emit the sound the neck feathers are puffed up and the head snapped in the air. When on the ground, the bird hammers its beak into the earth.

The hoopoe arrives in the Holy Land in February, breeds in the summer, and leaves in September. It was held in religious reverence by the Egyptians. It was listed as ritually unclean (Lv 11:19; Dt 14:18), probably because it searches for grubs and small insects in such unsanitary places as dung hills.

Ibis (Threskiornis aethiopica). Wading bird presently unknown in the Holy Land but possibly known there in biblical times. It was well known in ancient Egypt, where it was sacred to the god Thoth. Today it has practically vanished with the disappearance of swamps along the Nile.

There is some question as to whether the ibis is meant in Leviticus 11:17, where it is classified as ceremonially unclean. The same Hebrew word in Deuteronomy 14:16 and Isaiah 34:11 is translated "great owl," a translation preferred by most scholars.

See OWL, GREAT.

Kestrel or *Falcon (Falco tinnunculus).* Small hawk about a foot long with brown, black, and yellow feathers on its breast. It was abundant in the Holy Land in villages and in the countryside, nesting on rooftops and among rocks. Like most hawks the kestrel is able to hover and float in midair and then swoop down on its prey, seizing it with sharp hooklike talons. It feeds largely on mice, small reptiles, and insects.

Embalmed kestrels have been found in ancient Egyptian tombs. The Egyptians also embalmed the hunting kestrel (*Falco cherug*), which can be tamed and trained to hunt rabbits and other small game. Falconry (hunting with hawks of various species) was well known among the ancients and is still practiced today. That the Assyrians were familiar with falconry is seen in the records of Ashurbanipal. Because the kestrel is a predator it was ceremonially unclean (Lv 11:14). Some translations render the word as "kite" (Lv 11:14 KJV; Dt 14:13 RSV, KJV), an illustration of the difficulty of identifying biblical birds precisely.

See KITE.

Kite or *Glede (Milvus milvus).* Large bird of prey. The average length of the kite is about 19 inches. The upper part is generally dark but the belly is white. Kites nest high in trees and build nests of vegetation, including sticks. They rarely have more than two or three young, which they feed on snakes, grasshoppers, and so on. Sometimes kites are called snake hawks.

The kite is a migratory bird that stays in Palestine during the summer, especially in the mountains of southern Judea, in the trackless wastes west of the Dead Sea, and in the wilderness of Beersheba.

The red kite or glede is a medium-sized bird of prey. The edges of the upper part of the bill overlap with the lower one, forming a sharp scissors. The tail is forked or cleft like that of a fish. Its loud cry often includes sharp whistling notes. Other Palestinian species include the black kite (*Milvus migrans*) and the black-winged kite (*Elanus caeruleus*).

The kite is listed among the unclean birds in Mosaic Law (Lv 11:14; Dt 14:13), but the precise identification of the birds mentioned there is disputed by some scholars and translators.

See BUZZARD; KESTREL.

Lammergeier (Gypaetus barbatus). Largest of the vultures and less common than the other members of the family. It is grayish brown with white streaks and has a black tuft of stiff hairs in the facial area which gives it the name bearded vulture. Another name for it is lamb vulture.

The lammergeier has a unique way of killing its prey; since its beak is not particularly powerful it carries its victim high in the air and then drops it on rocks.

The lammergeier is especially partial to tortoises and to marrow bone. After jackals and smaller vultures have reduced a carcass to bone, the lammergeier crushes the bones to obtain the marrow, or swallows the pieces intact. Hence it is also known as the ossifrage, from a Latin word meaning "bone crusher." The lammergeier was unclean in Mosaic law (Lv 11:13; Dt 14:13; both translated "vulture" in RSV and "ossifrage" in KJV).

See VULTURE.

Ostrich (Struthio camelus). Two-toed, swift-running flightless bird that lives in deserts or in areas covered with stunted bushes.

In biblical times ostriches ranged as far north as Syria and were found over the entire wasteland of the Negeb desert, but they have since become extinct there. Its Hebrew name means "daughter of the desert." It is the largest of all living birds, attaining a height of about 10 feet and a weight of 175 pounds, though some males may weigh as much as 300 pounds. The female is considerably smaller. Powerful thighs and long legs give the ostrich great speed, reported to be as high as 40 miles per hour.

The ostrich is omnivorous. It eats grass, fruits, small mammals, birds, snakes, and lizards, as well as large pebbles which assist in the breakdown of food in its gizzard. The ostrich is hunted, but its eggs are generally more sought after than the bird itself. The empty shells are traded throughout the Mediterranean area for use as utensils, or when broken up as raw material for beads. The eggs—as many as 25 in one clutch—are laid in a shallow nest of sand, with some left uncovered. They may appear to be neglected by day, but only because they are ordinarily incubated at night. The cock does most of the incubating; the female participates only during cold days. The strong, thick egg shell protects the embryo from the heat of the desert.

Occasionally the ostrich is used for riding or even for pulling small carts. Ostrich feathers are in great demand. Ostrich plumes graced ancient royal courts as fans. An ivory-handled fan of Pharaoh Tutankhamon (King Tut) with lovely ostrich plumes, displayed during the Tutankhamon exhibition in American cities in 1977–78, is regularly on display in the National Museum at Cairo. The plumes are white in the male and brownish gray in the female. The reputation of the ostrich for stupidity comes from its behavior when hunted and cornered; it fails to take evasive action even when doing so would save it. In open country, however, it is very wary and runs at great speed to escape. In contrast to the partridge, an ostrich will run away from its eggs and chicks when pursued.

Most biblical references to ostriches emphasize their negative characteristics. They were regarded as unclean in Jewish Law (Lv 11:16; Dt 14:15). Several references associate ostriches with images of wilderness and desolation (Jb 30:29; Is 13:21; 34:13; 43:20; Jer 50:39). Their night cry, which has been compared to an ox's lowing in pain, is referred to in Micah 1:8. Biblical writers also noted the apparent indifference of the ostrich to its brood (Jb 39:13–18; Lam 4:3).

Ostriches are polygamous. Attempts at domestication have not been particularly successful, though there are ostrich farms in South Africa.

Owl (order Strigiformes). Nocturnal birds with large heads and large, forward-looking eyes. Their wing and tail feathers are soft as velvet, helping to make their flight noiseless. The owl's body is small and slender, about the size of a pigeon, but it appears bulky because of the thick covering of feathers. Owls have been considered bearers of misfortune and omens of disaster. In the Near East, owls now live in temple ruins and pyramids in Egypt, and in rock-hewn graves, ruins, and caves on both sides of the Jordan River in Israel. They seldom come near inhabited dwellings.

Owls have excellent night vision, which they

use to capture rodents or other animals. Although unusually large, the owl's eyes are almost useless in the daylight; light dazzles them.

The owl is able to swallow its prey whole because of its elastic esophagus. Indigestible hair and bones are regurgitated as pellets. The bill is short but sharply hooked.

Owls may lay up to 10 eggs. The young are cared for on the nest by both parents. Both adults and young tend to remain in the area in which they were hatched. Eight species of owls are found in Palestine, of which five are plentiful. It is difficult, however, to identify a particular species with any of the four Hebrew words translated "owl" in Scripture. A fifth word translated "owl" (KJV) is more appropriately identified with the ostrich (RSV). Owls appear in the lists of unclean birds (Lv 11:17; Dt 14:16), and although translations differ, they concur that all species of owls, being predators, are unclean.

See OSTRICH; OWL, BARN OR WHITE; OWL, LITTLE; OWL, GREAT; OWL, SCOPS.

Owl, Barn or *White (Tyto alloa)*. Large owl with a distinct heart-shaped face. It may get its Hebrew name from a snoring sound it makes when breathing in the nest. In flight it emits a frightening screech, and thus is sometimes referred to as the screech owl. Its somewhat sinister features—a large head and wide pop eyes—have led some people to consider it demonic, but they have also inspired another name, the monkey-faced owl. It is a useful bird, however, devouring rodents that raid fields and damage stored grain. Like other owls, it sleeps during the day and hunts at night with a well-developed sense of hearing and sight. Its color is light brownish yellow with a white mask around the eyes and cheeks. The whole leg is covered with feathers that protect it against the bites of struggling victims in its talons.

Some modern translations mention the barn or white owl by name (Lv 11:17 JB; 11:18 NASB; Dt 14:16 JB, NASB).

See OWL; OWL, SCOPS.

Owl, Little (Athene noctua glaux). Smallest of all nocturnal birds of prey. Chiefly insectivorous, it also feeds at times on tiny birds. It is the most common owl in the Holy Land, dwelling among ruins, tombstones, rocks, and thickets (perhaps the owl of Ps 102:6). Its voice suggests that of a dying person. On occasion it may be observed perched on a rock with its large eyes gazing off into the distance, a pose that the ancients considered a sign of wisdom. The Greeks associated the little owl with the goddess Athena. It is mentioned by name in several translations (Lv 11:17 KJV, NASB; Dt 14:16 KJV, NASB, RSV).

See OWL.

Owl, Great (Asio otus). Large owl, standing nearly two feet tall. The color is mouse gray with gray-brown spots and black stripes. As one of its names indicates, it has tufted "ears" and is sometimes called the great horned owl. It feeds on rodents, such as rats and mice. It winters in Israel among ruins and in groves.

The great owl may be the owl mentioned in the Bible among the birds of desolation that will inhabit devastated Edom (Is 34:11 NASB margin). It is also mentioned by name in some translations of the lists of ritually unclean birds (Lv 11:17 KJV, NASB; Dt 14:16 KJV, LB, NASB, RSV).

See OWL.

Owl, Scops (Otus scops). Small owl distinguished by two horn-shaped crests of hairlike feathers on its head. It perches in an inclined posture and hops and dances like a goat. During the hatching period the male's hooting sounds like a moan. The scops owl feeds on insects, rodents, and birds. During invasions of mice or locusts, these owls have appeared in large flocks and helped to destroy the pests. They have been known to attack humans who intrude on their nests. They are well-known inhabitants of Eurasia and Africa.

Some scholars suggest that the scops is the true screech owl, because of its whistling calls that resound through the night. The screech owl is mentioned only once in Scripture (Is 34:14 KJV), but that translation is the subject of scholarly debate. Following traditional Jewish mythology, some translations use the Hebrew word (*lilith*) as a proper name. In Jewish tradition Lilith was a witch-demon who, before Eve's creation, was Adam's wife. She became the mother of demons and was thought to attack children during the night; thus the name "Lilith" is translated "night hag" (RSV) or "night monster" (NASB). Most scholars favoring the mythical interpretation, however, suggest that Isaiah was using a popular legend to evoke a sense of desolation and did not himself believe in the existence of Lilith. There is little support for "screech owl" as an appropriate translation of the name.

See OWL; OWL, BARN OR WHITE.

Partridge. Most common game bird in the Holy Land. The partridge resembles a chicken in its basic anatomy but has a less chunky body and a longer tail. Two species of partridge inhabit Palestine: the sand partridge (*Ammoperdix heyi*), found near the Dead Sea, in the Jordan River Valley, and in the Sinai desert; and the chukar partridge (*Alectoris graeca*). The sand partridge is a medium-sized bird with yellow feet. The male has sandy-buff plumage, upper tail feathers penciled and barred with brown, and a chestnut and white undersurface. The female is a grayish buff.

The chukar partridge resembles the common French partridge of Europe, having a body about 16 inches long. It is covered with beautiful and radiantly colored feathers.

The biblical reference (1 Sm 26:20; probably the sand partridge because of the geographical context) alludes to the common method of catching it by chasing. It was also hunted with snares (cf. Ps 91:3) or by hunters hiding in a blind. The fast-running partridge soon becomes exhausted, which enables hunters to run it to the ground and kill it. Nevertheless, by running and jumping it can ascend very steep cliffs. The bird finds refuge among bushes into which its brownish-green feathers blend protectively. If it were not such a prolific breeder it would probably have become extinct by being hunted for food.

The biblical description of the partridge gathering a brood she did not hatch (Jer 17:11) seems to be based on the fact that the hen lays at least two clutches of eggs, one for herself and one for the cock to incubate.

Peacock. Member of the quail, partridge, and pheasant family, the peacock (*Pavo cristatus*) is actually the male peafowl. Its mate is properly known as the peahen. The male attracts attention because of a stately, luxurious appearance enhanced by magnificent feathers. The breast is a brilliant metallic blue, and each tail feather has a brilliant eye near the tip. When lowered, the unusually long tail feathers form a train behind the peacock on the ground, giving it an overall length of up to six feet. The train can also be raised to form a huge fan adorned with the multicolored eyes. During courtship the feathers are raised and vibrated to make a distinct rustling noise. The rather drab peahen lacks the long train.

Because it is not native to the Holy Land, the peacocks referred to in 1 Kings 10:22 and 2 Chronicles 9:21 are thought by some scholars to be Old World monkeys brought from east Africa, or guinea hens from the upper Nile River region. There is evidence, however, that the Phoenicians introduced peacocks to the Egyptian pharaoh, perhaps as early as the time of King Solomon. It is possible that Solomon's trade expeditions ranged as far as India where the peacock is native. The peacock was also well known to the Greeks and Romans. Alexander the Great prized its beauty and forbade his soldiers to kill the bird.

In the early Christian church the peacock became a symbol of the immortality promised in the resurrection of Christ. In addition, the eyes of its tail came to represent the all-seeing eye of God.

Pelican (Pelecanus onocrotalus). Largest of all aquatic birds, considerably larger even than the swan. It is generally about 50 inches long with a 16-inch beak, the upper part of which is hooked downward at the end, facilitating fish catching. The lower part of the bill supports a yellow pouch extending down the throat. The pouch may hold up to three gallons of food (small fish) and water. The pelican's webbed feet are peculiar in having webs between all four toes. Pelicans are expert swimmers as well as efficient fliers. The pelican's massive body, long neck, and comparatively small head give it proportions that make rising from the water difficult. To take off, a pelican must first flap awkwardly along the surface, pounding at the water with its legs.

Pelicans fly and nest in groups. Both sexes care for the naked young that hatch from the one to four eggs. Whereas most birds feed their young by placing food into their mouths, the pelican reverses the process; the young pelican sticks its head and most of its body into its mother's throat and plucks partially digested food from the mother's crop. The deep penetration of the young's beak into the mother's gullet led ancients to believe that the young were feeding on the blood of the mother's breast, thus giving rise to wide usage of the pelican as a symbol of Christ's atonement, and of charity in general.

The roseate pelican is white, at times with a faint rose tinge, and has black feathers growing from the wing joint farthest from the body. The legs, pouch, and skin around the eyes are yellow; the hook of the beak is red. This species may grow up to six feet long with a wingspread of up to eight feet. During the breeding season the coloration of the exposed areas of the roseate pelican's legs and face changes from gray to bright orange or red. At the same time the white feathers acquire a beautiful pink tint originating from an oil-gland secretion. The oil is spread throughout the plumage by the bird as it preens.

Some scholars question whether "pelican" is an appropriate translation of the Hebrew in several verses, believing rather that the word refers to one of the owls, hawks, or vultures. Most translations include the pelican in the lists of ritually unclean birds (Lv 11:18; Dt 14:17). Opinion on the other references is more sharply divided. Some scholars maintain that the desert context of the verses eliminates the possibility of a water bird like the pelican (cf. Ps 102:6, vulture, LB, RSV; Is 34:11, cormorant, KJV; hawk, LB, RSV; Zep 2:14, cormorant, KJV; vulture, LB, RSV). On the other hand, the roseate pelican frequents the rivers, lakes, and marshes of the Holy Land. After flying out to sea as far as 20 miles to swoop down on fish near the surface, the pelican often returns inland to a deserted place to digest its enormous meal. Thus the pelican may be the lonely wilderness bird of those passages.

Pigeon or *Dove.* Species of the pigeon family (*Columbidae*). In common usage the names pigeon and dove are virtually interchangeable. The common domestic pigeon familiar to city dwellers the world over, for example, is actually a descendant of the wild rock dove. Both names are used in English translations of the Bible to translate the same Hebrew word. A second Hebrew word is usually translated "turtledove." Nevertheless, it seems clear that the ancient Hebrews recognized differences between dove species.

At least six species of pigeon or dove reside in modern Palestine: the rock, ring, and stock doves (genus *Columba*), and the turtle, collared, and palm doves (genus *Streptopelia*). Of the six, the rock dove (*Columba livia*) and the turtledove (*Streptopelia turtur*) seem to be the two most often referred to in Scripture.

Pigeons vary in size from 6 to over 12 inches. The most colorful Palestinian species is the rock dove, which can be a beautiful silvery gray with grayish-green iridescent plumage on the wings (noted by David, Ps 68:13). The smaller doves (*Streptopelia*) are less colorful, mostly gray or buff with a blackish or checkered half collar on the back of the neck. Pigeons have short necks and small heads, plump bodies, and short wings controlled by strong muscles that enable them to fly considerable distances. The smaller doves have longer tails.

At present the wild rock dove is found primarily in the area around the Sea of Galilee and farther to the south in the many ravines leading down to the Dead Sea. Wild rock doves prefer to build their nests on rocks and cliff faces, a fact precisely described in Scripture (Sg 2:14; Jer 48:28). All Palestinian doves build fragile nests of scraps of vegetation. Eggs are hatched twice a year. Doves seldom lay more than two eggs. The young are cared for in the nest by both parents, who rove over the fields eating seeds and weeds. The adult's crop contains digested food in a milky condition, called pigeon's milk, which can be regurgitated and fed to the young.

During courtship there is a great deal of rivalry among the male doves. The turtledove's courtship dance is an awesome aerial display. The attention to courtship, the joint care of young, and the solicitude of the parents for each other, noted from earliest times, have made the dove one of the most popular symbols of love and peace (Sg 1:15; 2:14; 4:1; 5:2; etc.).

A major distinction between pigeons (ring doves) and turtledoves seems to have been recognized by ancient writers. Pigeons are year-round residents and easily tamable, whereas turtledoves are migratory. Turtledoves were confined in cages singly or in pairs as pets or for sacrifices. Pigeons were probably the first birds to be domesticated, perhaps as early as Noah's time (Gn 8:8–12). They were depicted on the earliest Egyptian monuments, and their edibility was mentioned in early Egyptian texts. Before long, domestic pigeons were regarded as evidence of a household's prosperity. In the more prosperous households they nested in dovecotes of molded pottery of clay fashioned in latticelike structures (hence the "windows" of Is 60:8).

In NT times there were many dovecotes in the parks around Herod the Great's palace in Jerusalem. The dove's popularity was due not only to its docility, but also to its desirability as food and as an acceptable and relatively inexpensive sacrifice. The turtledove may have been regarded more highly as a sacrifice because of its wildness and consequent lesser availability. The two biblical references to turtledoves not in a sacrificial context refer to their migratory habits and to their arrival in Israel in the spring (Sg 2:12; Jer 8:7; cf. Hos 11:11).

Most of the references to doves and pigeons in the Bible are in statements about sacrificial procedures (Gn 15:7–10; Lv 1:14; 5:7; 12:6; Nm 6:10; Lk 2:24). Other references, however, include a range of observations and symbolic usages of the dove. Its throaty moaning was often observed (Is 38:14; 59:11; Ez 7:16; Na 2:7). Its powers of flight were well known (Ps 55:6), as were its beauty (Sg 1:15; 4:1; 5:12), its gentleness and loyalty to its mate (Sg 2:14; 5:2; 6:9), its affection (Ps 74:19), and its innocence (Mt 10:16). The one negative reference to doves is in Hosea 7:11, where they are said to be senseless and foolish, perhaps in reference to their overly trusting nature.

Of NT references perhaps the most significant is the description of the Holy Spirit at Christ's baptism as a descending dove (Mt 3:16). The dove's loving nature made it natural for early Christians to connect the dove image with the concept of the Comforter. Since then the dove has remained the most popular symbol of the Holy Spirit.

See DOVE'S DUNG.

Quail (Coturnix coturnix). Short stocky birds with bills and feet similar to those of chickens; hence they are adapted to eating seeds or insects. They are the smallest of the subfamily of poultry that also includes pheasants and partridges. Quail (or "quails," another plural form) are about 10 inches long and have small rounded wings. They burst from their hiding places in the grass or bushes with a whirring sound. The belly of the quail is white. Up to 18 eggs are laid, and if the mother dies the male has been known to assume the care of the young.

Quail of the Mediterranean region winter in the Sudan and migrate northward in vast flocks in the spring. Quail cannot maintain a long sustained flight but make use of wind currents to keep them aloft.

Enormous flocks of quail twice served as food for the Israelites in the wilderness of Sinai, when the birds were driven down in the desert miraculously by winds (Ex 16:13; Nm 11:31,32; Ps 105:40). The second time they were probably flying along the Gulf of Aqaba and were blown off course by the east wind (Nm 11:31; Ps 78:26–28). Their inability to sustain long flight may account for their low flying level—two cubits, or about 40 inches. When exhausted they were easily caught by hand (Nm 11:31,32). The quail which were considered clean and the most delicate eating of all game birds, were preserved by drying in the sun (v 32). It is estimated that nine million quail must have been gathered by the hungry Israelites.

Raven (Corvus corax). Member of the crow family (*Corvidae*). The Hebrew word "raven" means "black one." The raven weighs about three pounds and varies from 22 to 26 inches in length. Its tail is broader in the middle than at either end. Eight species are found in Palestine: three ravens, two jackdaws, one crow, one rook, and one chough. The crow, about 20 inches long, is smaller than a raven, and its tail is uniform in width. The raven's most conspicuous feature is its glossy black iridescent plumage.

Ravens and crows have survived in spite of the dislike many humans have for them. Excellent fliers, they migrate by day and congregate in great flocks of up to several hundred thousand. During the nesting season they make nests of sticks in which two to seven eggs are laid. Ravens mate for life. Equipped with strong wings, a strong bill, and strong feet, ravens can live in isolated places from which they range widely for food.

Ravens are crafty, active birds. Some are capable of speaking, solving puzzles, and performing feats of memory. Bold and curious, they sometimes use their talents for theft.

The raven is the first bird mentioned by name in the Bible (Gn 8:7). A robust bird with tremendous endurance, the raven is accustomed to roam far from its home base in search of food. That it did not return to the ark was a good sign to Noah, indicating that the raven could find food and possibly a place to rest on dry mountaintops.

The raven, essentially a scavenger, was ceremonially unclean (Lv 11:15; Dt 14:14). Yet ravens fed Elijah at God's command (1 Kgs 17:4–6). Job was told that God gave the raven its food (Jb 38:41), as the psalmist and Jesus repeated (Ps 147:9; Lk 12:24). The raven's glistening black plumage inspired the bride's comparison of her beloved's hair (Sg 5:11). They prefer desolate uninhabited areas as their home territory (Is 34:11).

Sea Gull (family *Laridae*). Robust sea birds, primarily scavengers. Several species of gulls live along the seacoast of the Holy Land. They are usually gray-backed with white heads and underparts and black wing tips. The slender bill ends in a downward curve.

Sea gulls may be 8 to 30 inches long. Many species migrate, traveling long distances with their superb flying ability. Gulls can also swim easily because of their webbed feet. Their voice is like a harsh scream or squawk. In nesting season many nest together in any available place such as a cliff or tree. Both male and female incubate and care for the young.

Because gulls will eat almost anything, they are listed as ritually unclean birds (Lv 11:16; Dt 14:15, ASV has "sea mew," a common European gull). Some commentators believe that those passages refer to an owl or to the cuckoo and not to the sea gull.

See CUCKOO.

Sparrow, House. Small bird of the finch family (*Fringillidae*) or the weaver finch family (*Ploceidae*), considered to be of little worth. The Hebrew word is a general term for "bird" and refers to any small bird such as sparrow, finch, thrush, or starling. In translation, however, the word sometimes refers to the common English or house sparrow (*Passer domestica*; Ps 84:3; Prv 26:2).

Dull in color with a black throat, the male house sparrow is a noisy and energetic creature. The nest, when built in open places, has an opening on the side and is made of almost anything available. Sparrows also nest in sheltered places, in dwellings, boxes, or holes in trees. They lay four to seven eggs.

The common or house sparrow was known in ancient Greece and Egypt. There it had a reputation for invading fields in large swarms and picking the seeds from them. It is a permanent resident of the Holy Land.

The sparrow is prolific and lives in close association with humans. It was considered ritually clean. Sparrows brought low prices in countries where they were sold (Mt 10:29; Lk 12:6). Today in Near Eastern marketplaces, boys offer live sparrows for sale. Tied together in groups of four to six by strings attached to one leg, the birds fly about over the boys' heads. Evidently such a sight was common in NT times.

Stork (genus Ciconia). Long-legged white wading bird, having large, powerful wings with glossy black primary and secondary feathers. The flapping of its wings produces a loud rushing sound. Connecting membranes between the toes prevent the bird from sinking into the mud. Its red bill is sharp and long, serving to seize and lift its prey out of the water. Storks are mute, lacking a voice box.

Flocks of storks pass through the Holy Land during their September migration on the way to central and southern Africa and likewise in the spring on their return flight to their homes in northern Israel, Syria, and Europe. Storks travel in vast flocks during the day, spreading out against the sky.

The stork's faithful tending of the young is proverbial, as is its habit of returning annually to the same nesting place. Storks have the habit of adding to their nests each year, and it is possible to find nests that are 100 years old and have a height of more than three feet.

Two species of storks frequent Palestine. The white stork (*Ciconia alba*) is 40 inches tall, and its wingspread is 6 feet, enabling it to move with a slow sustained flight or to soar. In folklore the white stork is sometimes considered to be a harbinger of good fortune.

The black stork (*Ciconia nigra*), common around the Dead Sea Valley, nests in trees; hence it may be the tree-dwelling species referred to in Psalm 104:17.

The Hebrew name for stork means literally the "kindly one," or the "loyal one," a reference to the care of the bird for its young. Like the heron, the stork was ceremonially unclean because of its diet of aquatic organisms, refuse, small animals, birds, and reptiles (Lv 11:19; Dt 14:18). Jeremiah mentioned the stork's uncanny and instinctive knowledge of the time of its migration (Jer 8:7). Its impressive wings figured in one of Zechariah's visions (Zec 5:9).

Swallow (Hirundo rustica). Small, nearly black, forked-tailed bird with long, tapering wings, noted for its graceful flight. The small, weak feet are poorly adapted for walking. Swallows resemble swifts in shape and life habits but are somewhat smaller.

The swallow's large mouth enables it to catch insects while in flight. Colors vary from brown and blue to white. Swallows often nest in buildings, a feature noticed by the psalmist, who reported a swallow's home at the temple (Ps 84:3).

Swallows are basically resident in Palestine whereas the swift is a migratory bird noted for the regularity of its migratory schedule. The "swallow" of Isaiah 38:14 probably refers to a swift, as does Jeremiah 8:7, where the dependability of the bird is contrasted with the irregularity of God's people. Proverbs 26:2 may be a reference to either the swallow or the swift.

See SWIFT.

Swan. Large, graceful water birds. Two species of swan (genus *Cygnus*) are found in the Middle East as passing migrants (*Cygnus olor* and *Cygnus musicus*). Swans are known as the best musicians among the birds and were considered sacred to the god Apollo by the Greeks. Their voices sound like flutes and harps.

The references in Leviticus 11:18 and Deuteronomy 14:16 (KJV) are probably not to the swan but to the water hen or the barn owl, since there seems little reason to declare the vegetarian swan an unclean animal.

See OWL, BARN OR WHITE; WATER HEN.

Swift. Small strong flyers (genus *Apus*). Like the swallow, the swift has long bent wings and a cleft tail, enabling it to obtain great speed as it skims the ground and sweeps through the air. A swift devours a great many harmful insects, catching them in its mouth in flight. Many swifts make their nests in rooftops and in nooks and crannies of city walls. Their nests are built with strong feathers cemented together with saliva. Other swifts live in caves and clefts of rocks.

Common swifts are native to Palestine, and in the Jordan Valley they occur in large flocks. Isaiah 38:14 (NIV) seems to be a clear reference to the swift's plaintive call, since the swallow's sharp chirp is not a striking simile for a distraught king's cry. The swift has a soft delicate voice, and its cry could be easily interpreted as melodious wailing.

The migratory swifts arrive on a precise schedule in the Holy Land in late winter and immense flocks fill the cities with their cries. Thus the reference in Jeremiah 8:7 to swallows, which are largely permanent residents, is probably to swifts.

See SWALLOW.

Vulture. Subfamily (*Aegypiinae*) of the hawk family (*Accipitridae*). Each of the four species of Old World vultures is found in Palestine: the Egyptian, griffon, black, and bearded vulture (the bearded vulture is also known as the lammergeier). Those birds range in size from the 24-inch Egyptian vulture to the huge bearded vulture, largest of all flying birds in the Holy Land.

Most vultures are brown or black, having a short neck and a short, hooked bill with which they tear the dead animal flesh of which they are fond. All vultures, except the bearded, have bare or down-covered heads and necks, enabling these scavengers to penetrate deep into a carcass without spoiling the plumage. Excellent eyesight enables a vulture to locate a carcass from a lofty soaring position. Considering the decayed condition of most of its food, a vulture's poor sense of smell may be a fortunate limitation. Vultures nest in any convenient place; both parents care for the young.

The Hebrew word usually translated "eagle" in the OT may have been a general term for all large birds of prey, including vultures. Thus many of the passages about eagles may refer to either the eagle or the vulture (cf. Lv 11:13; Dt 14:12 NASB margin). Such passages include references to nesting habits (Jb 39:27, 28; Jer 49:16; Ob 4), care for fledglings (Dt 32:11), powers of flight (Ex 19:4; Dt 28:49; Jb 9:26; Lam 4:19), and extremely high soaring altitude (Prv 23:5; 30:19; Is 40:31). Despite variations among translations, the vulture clearly belongs in the list of unclean birds because of its foul diet (Lv 11:13,18; Dt 14:12,17).

Several references to the eagle in KJV have been changed to vulture in modern translations. The change seems appropriate in the references to the vulture as a sign of present or impending doom (Lam 4:19; Hos 8:1). Likewise the eye-plucking bird of Proverbs 30:17 is probably a vulture. The phrase "bald as the eagle" (Mi 1:16) clearly should read "bald as the vulture," since there are no bald eagles in Palestine and most vultures are bald. Since the vulture, like the eagle, was a symbol of sovereignty and domination in the ancient Near East, some gods were represented as vultures. Thus Ezekiel's comparison of the kings of Babylon and Egypt to eagles may be conceived alternatively as comparisons to vultures (Ez 17:3,7). Jesus' reference to the eagles congregating around corpses at the endtime (Mt 24:28) should also be revised to vultures, since eagles are usually solitary eaters, whereas vultures generally flock together around carrion.

Several KJV references to vultures are usually translated "kite" or "falcon" in modern translations (cf. various versions of Lv 11:14; Dt 14:13; Jb 28:7; Is 34:15).

See EAGLE; KESTREL; KITE; LAMMERGEIER; VULTURE, BLACK, OR OSPREY; VULTURE, EGYPTIAN; VULTURE, GRIFFON.

Vulture, Black, or Osprey (Aegypius monachus). Diurnal flesh eater a little over three feet long with a wingspread of over three yards. The feathers are black and the head and upper part of the neck are bald like those of other carrion eaters. It nests in the Jordan River Valley and seems to have been abundant in biblical times. Today it is quite rare. The black vulture is probably the osprey of Leviticus 11:13 and Deuteronomy 14:12.

See VULTURE.

Vulture, Egyptian (Neophron percnopterus). Also known as the gier eagle or as pharaoh's hen. Its plumage is basically white with a naked head and yellow neck. The Egyptian vulture breaks bones left by other vultures. Its flight is slow and easy, and its voice is a croak. Measuring about 24 inches in length, it is the smallest of all the carrion-eating birds found in the Holy Land. It may be referred to in the list of unclean birds (Lv 11:18; Dt 14:17, gier eagle, KJV; carrion vulture, NASB, RSV).

See VULTURE.

Vulture, Griffon (Gyps fulvus). One of the largest flying birds in the Holy Land. Until a generation ago the griffon vulture was one of the most common birds in Palestine. Today it is on the verge of extinction. Many have been killed by eating poisonous bait meant for foxes and jackals. In addition its reproduction is limited; the female lays only one or two eggs a year.

The griffon vulture measures about 4 feet in length and up to 10 feet between wing tips. Its beak is extremely strong, and its short toes are fitted with blunt talons. It is a light brown bird with a pale yellow head and neck that are almost bare, being covered only with a very fine down.

The griffon vulture feeds mostly on carrion, but also on locusts and small tortoises. It is able to go without food for several days with no ill effects, but when it does break its fast it gorges itself. It is found especially in the region of the Sea of Galilee. Most biblical references to the vulture are likely to be to the griffon vulture.

See EAGLE; VULTURE.

Water Hen. Small water bird of the rail family. The water hen listed among unclean birds (Lv 11:18; Dt 14:16 RSV only) may be the biblical bird most difficult to identify. Several alternatives have been suggested, including the swan (KJV), one of the owls (NASB, NEB), or the marsh hen (LB). Most scholars rule out the swan, since it is a vegetarian bird and thus should not be considered unclean. An owl remains a possibility.

The marsh hen is a rail, several species of which inhabit Palestine. One of those species is the purple gallinule (*Porphyrio porphyrio*). Rails are very thin birds varying from 6 to 20 inches in length. They live in marshes where they eat a great variety of animal and vegetable matter, thus making them a candidate for inclusion in the Mosaic lists.

JOHN W. KLOTZ

See ANIMALS.

Bibliography. A. Parmelee, *All the Birds of the Bible.*

Birds of Prey. See BIRDS (KITE; VULTURE; VULTURE, GRIFFON).

Birsha. Ruler of Gomorrah in the days of Abraham and Lot. Birsha was one of five Canaanite city-kings who unsuccessfully rebelled against King Chedorlaomer of Elam and his three allies (Gn 14:2).

Birth, New. Means of receiving "spiritual life" and entering the kingdom of God (Jn 3:3–7).

See REGENERATION.

Birthright. Right or privilege belonging to the firstborn son in a Hebrew family. The eldest son ranked highest after the father and in the father's absence had the father's authority and responsibility, as illustrated by Reuben's relationship to his younger brothers (Gn 37:19–22, 28–30). However, because he later committed incest, Reuben forfeited his birthright (49:1–4). Next in line were Simeon, Levi, and Judah (29:31–35), but Jacob, their father, passed over Simeon and Levi because of their lack of character (49:5–7). Although he praised Judah (vv 8–10), Jacob gave the birthright to his favorite son Joseph (vv 22–26; 1 Chr 5:1,2; cf. Gn 37:2–4).

Tablets recovered from Nuzi in Mesopotamia have shown that the birthright could be exchanged among members of the same family (cf. Gn 25:19–34). The holder of the birthright appears to have been in possession of the "teraphim" or household idols (31:19,32,34), which were small terra-cotta images, presumably of the particular deity worshiped locally. These tokens would reinforce the position and authority of the firstborn.

The birthright meant not only the honor of family leadership but also an inheritance of twice the amount received by every other son. In polygamous Israelite society the birthright belonged to the actual firstborn of the father and could not be transferred to the son of a favorite wife without just cause (Dt 21:15–17). However, the birthright did not belong to the firstborn son if his mother was a concubine or slave (Gn 21:9–13; Jgs 11:1,2). The rights of the firstborn son of a king included the right of succession to the throne (2 Chr 21:1–3). When King Rehoboam of Judah violated custom by making his favorite son Abijah his successor, he had to pay off his other sons to avoid trouble (11:18–23; 12:16).

In the NT, reference is made to the OT account of Esau, the son of the patriarch Isaac, who impulsively traded his birthright for a bowl of lentil stew (Heb 12:16,17; cf. Gn 25:19–34). Christians are warned not to throw away their inheritance of spiritual blessing from God the way Esau lost his birthright and his father's blessing (Gn 27).

Jesus Christ's authority over heaven and earth results from his exalted status as the firstborn Son of the heavenly Father (Rom 8:29; Col 1:17–19; Heb 1:2–6). As the second Adam, Christ is the firstborn from the dead by virtue of the resurrection (Rom 1:4; 1 Cor 15:20–28,42–50; Eph 1:22). He has received the kingdom from his Father and rules as Lord of Lords (Acts 2:36; Phil 2:9–11; Rv 5:12,13; 19:16; cf. Dn 7:13,14,26,27). Believers also share in this kingdom and inheritance and look forward to the consummation, when by virtue of union with Christ, they shall receive their inheritance in full (Rom 4:13; Gal 3:29; Eph 1:18; Heb 11:16).

WALTER R. HEARN

See INHERITANCE; HEIR; FIRSTBORN.

Birzaith, Birzavith. Malchiel's son of Asher's tribe (1 Chr 7:31). Since parallel lists fail to mention him (Gn 46:17; Nm 26:44–47), it is possible that Birzaith (KJV Birzavith) was the name of a city Malchiel founded. If so, the city may have been northwest of Bethel, near Tyre, and is now called Birzeit.

Bishlam. Resident of the vicinity of Jerusalem who opposed the rebuilding of the city after the exile. He and his associates wrote a letter complaining about the rebuilding to the Persian king Artaxerxes (Ezr 4:7).

Bishop. Official in the church whose qualifications are listed in 1 Timothy 3:2–7 and Titus 1:6–9. The Greek word from which the English title "bishop" and the adjective "episcopal" are derived is often translated in modern versions as "elder," "overseer," "shepherd," or "guardian," corresponding closely to the current term "pastor." Jesus is called "the Shepherd and Bishop of your souls" (1 Pt 2:25 KJV).

In the NT, "bishop" and "elder" refer to the

The western hill Israelite broad wall of the city of Jerusalem.

360

same office, as shown by the apostle Paul's telling Titus to appoint "elders in every town" and then referring to those same individuals as "bishops" (Ti 1:5,7). While at Miletus, Paul summoned the elders from the church at Ephesus and then addressed them as "overseers" or "guardians" (Acts 20:17,28). In his Letter to Philippi Paul greeted the "bishops and deacons" (Phil 1:1). The fact that there were numerous bishops at Philippi as well as in Ephesus, shows that the episcopal office had not yet developed into what it later became: a single bishop governing one or more churches.

Bishops obviously had positions of authority, but the duties of the office are not clearly defined in the NT. One task was to combat heresy (Ti 1:9) and to teach and expound the Scriptures (1 Tm 3:2). In addition, there is some evidence that a primary concern was with economic matters and the care of the poor, as well as with a general overseeing of the congregation. The lists of qualifications in Paul's letters to Timothy and Titus indicate that a bishop was considered a leader in the congregation and a representative to the non-Christian world (v 7).

See ELDER; PASTOR; DEACON, DEACONESS; PRESBYTER; SPIRITUAL GIFTS.

Bithi-ah. Mered's wife. Bithi-ah may have been a princess, or the phrase "daughter of Pharaoh" (KJV) may merely indicate that she was Egyptian (1 Chr 4:17,18). Her name ("daughter of Yah") seems to mean that she was a Jewish convert.

Bithron. Term in 2 Samuel 2:29 (KJV) whose meaning is uncertain. Abner, commander of Ish-bosheth's army, fled through Bithron after losing a battle to David's army. The Hebrew root has the meaning "to cut into pieces." Three explanations have been suggested: (1) It refers to a valley, perhaps the Jabbok; (2) it is the area "cut off" by a great curve in the Jabbok River; (3) it refers to the first part of the day, "all morning" (NASB) or "the whole forenoon" (RSV).

Bithynia. Roman province located in the northwest corner of Asia Minor. The apostle Paul and Silas wanted to preach the gospel in Bithynia on Paul's second missionary journey (c AD 50), but were prevented by the Holy Spirit from doing so (Acts 16:7). The apostle Peter may have ministered in Bithynia and other provinces of Asia Minor, since he addressed his first letter to believers there (1 Pt 1:1). Christianity entered Bithynia somehow, possibly through Peter.

Bithynia was occupied by a Thracian tribe that established a prosperous kingdom there in the 3rd century BC. In 75 BC, when Bithynia's last king, Nicomedes III, willed his kingdom to the Roman people, it became part of the Roman empire. For administrative purposes it was generally linked with the province of Pontus to the east.

After NT times Bithynia figured significantly in church history. Early in the 2nd century its Roman governor, Pliny the Younger, elicited from the emperor Trajan the earliest stated imperial policy on persecution of Christians. Later, the church councils of Nicaea (325) and Chalcedon (451) were held in two of Bithynia's western cities. The Council of Nicaea declared the full deity of Christ; the Council of Chalcedon made pronouncements on the nature of the person of Christ and the canonicity of the 27 NT books.

The Roman province of Bithynia was bordered on the north by the Black Sea, on the west by the Propontis (modern Sea of Marmara), on the south by the province of Asia, and on the east by Galatia and Pontus. Bithynia was mountainous, with Mt Olympus in the south rising to 7,600 feet, but had districts of great fertility near the seacoast and in its interior valleys. Beside producing fruit and grain, the province had fine marble quarries, good timber, and excellent pasturage. The principal river was the Sangarius (modern Sakarya), which flowed from south to north into the Black Sea. Transportation was largely along the river valleys.

HOWARD F. VOS

Bitter Herbs. Some kind of bitter vegetable(s), perhaps a certain variety of lettuce. The people of Israel were commanded to eat bitter herbs, roast lamb, and unleavened bread on the night when the Lord inflicted the plague of death on all the Egyptian firstborn (Ex 12:8–11).

The significance of the bitter herbs is not explained in the narrative. In the traditional interpretation, the herbs symbolize the bitterness of the Hebrews' experience of Egyptian bondage. The two other references to bitter herbs (Nm 9:11; Lam 3:15) shed no direct light upon the kind of plant or its significance. The Numbers passage specifies how the Passover commemoration was to be celebrated by persons unable to participate at the normally appointed time (9:6–12). The Lamentations passage describes the prophet Jeremiah's personal affliction. He pictures himself as suffering at the hands of the Lord who has filled him with bitterness. If the prophet's experience could be symbolized by reference to bitter herbs, it is reasonable that Israel's experience of slavery in Egypt might also have been symbolized in that way. After that night of the Hebrews' deliverance from bondage, the herbs were used annually in a commemorative observance of the Passover.

Today the Samaritans use the leaves of the wild lettuce plant as bitter herbs for their Passover observance. Jews of European origin customarily use red horseradish.

JOHN E. LONG

See PLANTS.

Bittern. KJV translation for the Hebrew word that probably designates some kind of bird (Is 14:23; Zep 2:14, RSV hedgehog; Is 34:11, RSV porcupine).

See BIRDS; ANIMALS (HEDGEHOG; PORCUPINE).

Bitterness or Jealousy, Water of. OT "trial" procedure employed when a husband suspected his wife of adultery but had no evidence to support his suspicion. The ritual, described in Numbers 5:11–31, is thought by some scholars to belong to a class of procedures known as "trials by ordeal." Such an ordeal subjected an accused person to some physical hazard for the purpose of determining that person's guilt or innocence. The effect of the hazard-producing agent on the accused individual determined the verdict. The premise was that a higher power who knew the guilt or innocence of the accused would act to influence the outcome appropriately.

In Israel as in many other ancient societies, women had few rights. An Israelite husband could resort to the trial procedure when he had no evidence of his wife's unfaithfulness, simply a "spirit of jealousy" concerning her (Nm 5:11–14). Very likely a pregnant wife would be subjected to the ritual if her husband suspected the unborn child was not his own.

The suspicious husband brought his wife to the priest with a special offering of a coarse barley meal called "a cereal offering of jealousy" (Nm 5:15; cf. "fine flour" in Lv 2:1–16; 5:11). The priest would take the woman and "set her before the Lord," mix "holy water" (probably from the tabernacle laver or basin) with dirt from the tabernacle floor, unbind the woman's hair (perhaps as a sign of shame), and place some of the barley meal offering in her hands (Nm 5:16–18). Then the priest made her swear an oath asserting that, if she had been unfaithful, drinking the "water of bitterness" would bring a curse upon her. She gave assent by saying "Amen, Amen" (vv 19–22). Somehow, after writing out the words of the curse, the priest washed them off into the water. After making a ceremonial offering of a handful of barley meal, the priest made the woman drink the water (vv 23–26).

The effect of a guilty verdict was that "the curse shall enter into her and cause bitter pain, and her body shall swell, and her thigh shall become an execration among her people" (v 27). The precise meaning of the Hebrew is not clear, but probably is intended to contrast with the effect of an innocent verdict: "she shall be free and shall conceive children" (v 28). The implication is that the sagging thigh and swelling belly refer to sterility; the term for "thigh" or "loins" is used elsewhere in the OT to denote the seat of reproductive power (e.g., Gn 46:26; Ex 1:5; Jgs 3:30, all KJV). Perhaps if only pregnant women were subjected to the ritual, the language of the curse is meant to describe a miscarriage.

There is no indication of how often the ordeal was used or how often a guilty verdict was obtained. The whole passage may seem barbarous by today's standards of justice, but at least it illustrates that the Bible has not been "cleaned up" over the centuries. Some would see this passage as an example of God's accommodation to the cultural beliefs of a still primitive people. On the other hand, under God's superintendance, however unpleasant for the woman accused, the ordeal must have "worked." A guilty woman, believing that God would expose her sin, might have become psychosomatically ill or even sterile by undergoing the ritual, whereas an innocent woman would be unaffected.

A physiological explanation for the effectiveness of certain trials by ordeal still practiced has now been found. In certain African tribes, at least until recently, a person accused of a serious crime must eat a kind of bean with the understanding that it will be fatal only to the guilty. The ordeal works because the innocent swallow the beans immediately, knowing they will not be harmed. A guilty person tends to hold the beans in the mouth, where enzymes in the saliva release a neurotoxic compound which proves fatal on absorption into the person's system.

Interestingly enough, the Israelite procedure was actually more lenient than infidelity trials among other ancient peoples. Some of the pagan trials by ordeals were brutal rituals much more likely to result in a guilty verdict than the ritual of the "water of bitterness." The Hebrew word translated "bitterness" in that expression could also be derived from a root meaning "to test"; a more appropriate translation might thus be "water of testing."

JOHN E. LONG

Bitumen. Asphalt as found in its natural state; pitch, tar. Bitumen (KJV slime) was used for mortar in the tower of Babel's construction (Gn 11:3) and to seal the reed basket in which baby Moses was concealed (Ex 2:3).

In Palestine, the Valley of Siddim was dotted with numerous bitumen pits into which a number of soldiers fell during Chedorlaomer's war against Sodom and Gomorrah (Gn 14:10).

See ASPHALT; MINERALS, METALS, AND PRECIOUS STONES.

Biziothiah, Bizjothjah. Listed in Joshua 15:28 (KJV Bizjothjah) as a city in the Negeb desert area of Judah. The Greek OT, called the Septuagint, has "and her daughters," which would mean that this was not a specific place, but rather the cluster of villages surrounding Hazar-shual and Beersheba. Such a translation is possible with a slight adjustment to the Hebrew text. It is difficult to say how the Hebrew text originally read.

Biztha. One of the seven eunuchs King Ahasuerus commanded to bring Queen Vashti to his drunken party (Est 1:10).

Black. *See* COLOR.

Blasphemy. Profane or contemptuous speech or writing about (or action toward) God. In a general sense, "blasphemy" can refer to any slander, including any word or action that insults or devalues another being. In Greek literature the term was used for insulting or deriding living or dead persons, but it was extended to cover the gods as well, including both doubting the power of or mocking the nature of a god.

In the OT, "blasphemy" always means to insult God, either by attacking him directly or mocking him indirectly. Either way the glory and honor of God are lessened, so blasphemy is the opposite of praise. An Israelite might directly insult "the Name" by cursing God (Lv 24:10–16) or deliberately disobey God's law (Nm 15:30). Either of those blasphemies was punishable by death, as was idolatry, the ultimate blasphemy (Is 66:3). It was thought that Gentiles, who had never experienced the power and majesty of the Lord, were the most likely blasphemers. Thus the king of Assyria blasphemed in equating the Lord with the gods of the nations he had already conquered (2 Kgs 19:4,6,22). For his arrogance the king was doomed by the word of the prophet Isaiah. God was also mocked when Israel was exiled (Is 52:5), when Edom derided the "desolate mountains of Israel" (Ez 35:12 KJV), and when "the enemy" scoffed that God had not protected Jerusalem (Ps 74:18 KJV; 1 Mc 2:6).

In the NT, blasphemy takes on the wider Greek meaning, for it includes slandering a human being (Mt 15:19 KJV; see also Rom 3:8; 1 Cor 10:30; Eph 4:31; Ti 3:2) as well as God. It even includes mocking angelic or demonic powers, which is just as wrong as mocking (RSV revile) any other being (Jude 8–10, 2 Pt 2:10–12). In other words, slander, derision, and mocking of any kind are totally condemned in the NT.

The most common form of blasphemy in the NT is blasphemy against God. One might insult God directly (Rv 13:6; 16:9), mock his Word (Ti 2:5), or reject his revelation and its bearer (Acts 6:11). Jesus was accused of blasphemy when he claimed a prerogative of God, the power to forgive sins (Mk 2:7). John 10:33–36 reports an attempt to stone Jesus; his accusers said to him, "you, being a man, make yourself God" (v 33). Jesus was condemned by the highest Jewish court, the Sanhedrin, on the charge of blasphemy, because he claimed to be the Son of Man (the Messiah), but in their view had given no evidence that he was such an exalted personage, thus appearing to mock the Messiah and, by extension, to mock God himself (Mk 14:64).

Naturally the early Christians viewed Jesus' trial from another perspective: the guards insulting Jesus (Lk 22:64,65) and the crowds and two dying robbers mocking him on the cross (Mk 15:29–32) were the real blasphemers. Observing how their Lord had been treated, the church was prepared to accept insult as their own lot, both personally (1 Cor 4:13; 1 Tm 1:13; Rv 2:9) and as a response to their message (Acts 13:45; 18:6). On the other hand, the church recognized that even Christians could blaspheme by giving way under persecution (26:11), by teaching false doctrine (2 Pt 2:2), or by behaving in an unbecoming fashion, which would bring others to think less of Christ (Rom 2:24; Ti 2:5).

The Bible makes clear that blasphemy is forgivable (Mt 12:32; Mk 3:28,29), but if a person will not repent, the only remedy is to turn him or her over to Satan to be taught the lesson (1 Tm 1:20).

PETER H. DAVIDS

See BLASPHEMY AGAINST THE HOLY SPIRIT.

Blasphemy Against the Holy Spirit. Sin mentioned only in Mark 3:28,29 and its parallels, Luke 12:10 and Matthew 12:31. The context in Mark portrays unbelievers reacting to Jesus' sudden popularity and startling power in two ways: (1) His family considered him insane and tried to take him home; and (2) the religious leaders, who had already proclaimed him a blasphemer (Mk 2:1–12), attributed his success to demon possession. Matthew adds that the religious leaders were Pharisees upset by a particular healing. (Luke includes the saying in a totally different context, one of confessing Christ.) Jesus, pointing out that the charge of demon possession was illogical, also stated strongly that blasphemy against the Holy Spirit can never be forgiven. Jesus was saying that to slander the Holy Spirit is worse even than insulting or blaspheming the Son of Man or God himself (a crime punishable by death in the OT; see Lv 24:16). Yet Jesus said that those sins are forgivable. Many Jews believed that death forgave all sins, so when Jesus called blasphemy against the Holy Spirit "an eternal sin," he was making it serious indeed.

The religious leaders to whom Jesus spoke had seen clear, public, and compelling evidence of the good hand of God. Jesus' healing was not a hidden God-in-flesh or God-in-his-Word, but an open demonstration of his power. By calling that power evil or demonic they were wickedly and consciously rejecting God, his power, and his saving grace. That was willful and high-handed sin by those who had seen the truth but rejected it and slandered it to others. Hebrews 6:4–6 points out that no argument or evidence will help such a person; the problem is willful rejection, not blindness. It is called "a sin that ends in death" (1 Jn 5:16 LB). The Pharisees proved their unwillingness to repent by trying to destroy Christ and later his church.

The "unforgivable sin" is not some serious moral failure nor persistence in a particular sin nor even insulting or rejecting Jesus in blindness or a fit of rebellion. It is conscious rejection of the "good power of God." It represents a perversion of the mind in which God and Satan are *willfully* confused, a free choice of evil rather than good.

How can this sin be unforgivable if God is always willing to forgive? Because it has gone beyond the possibility of recovery on the sinner's part and because God respects the freedom of persons. It is unrepentable, because the person, having refused so stubbornly to repent, finally becomes unable to repent; evidence is in, and such a one will still reject the truth while knowing it to be true.

From the definition it is clear that anyone who believes he or she has committed "the unforgivable sin" could *not* have done so; a troubled conscience and that kind of sin could never coexist. The fact that a person feels remorse proves that blasphemy against the Holy Spirit has not yet been committed. On the other hand, Jesus' teaching about it warns all who know the truth of God not to reject that truth or to abandon their faith.

PETER H. DAVIDS

See BLASPHEMY; SIN UNTO DEATH.

Blastus. Royal secretary to Herod Agrippa I (Acts 12:20). The cities of Tyre and Sidon were looked down upon by Herod, so when their delegates wanted an appointment with the king when he was in nearby Caesarea, they approached him through Blastus. Herod addressed them and was struck by a fatal illness for accepting their worship "because he did not give God the glory" (Acts 12:21–23).

Bless, Blessing. Pronouncement of the favor of God upon an assembled congregation. Worship services, especially observances of Holy Communion in Eastern Orthodox, Roman Catholic, and most Protestant churches, usually end with a blessing spoken by the senior clergyman present. This pronouncement (called "blessing" in the Roman Catholic, Eastern Orthodox, and Anglican churches and "benediction" in most Protestant churches) is based upon the widespread biblical precedent of blessing (Gn 27:27–29; Nm 6:22–27; Lk 24:50; 2 Cor 13:11,14; Phil 4:7; 2 Thes 2:16,17; Heb 13:20,21). When giving a blessing or benediction a clergyman usually raises his right hand and sometimes makes the sign of the cross.

The practice of benediction or blessing is often regarded merely as a ritual of dismissal, but it is actually a pronouncement of God's gracious favor, to be given only by his ministers on the authority of Holy Scripture to faithful believers. In this action Christians are assured that the grace of God the Father, the love of the Son, and the communion of the Holy Spirit are with them.

The term "blessing" is also applied to thanksgiving for food and drink (Mt 14:19; Mk 8:7; Lk 24:30). Eastern Orthodox, Roman Catholic, and Lutheran churches pronounce a blessing during services of Holy Communion, following the example of Christ (Mk 14:22; 1 Cor 10:16).

In some church traditions there is a blessing in the marriage service, in rogation services (blessing of the crops), and when "the faithful" take up residence in a new home.

Many Protestant churches are reluctant to bless material objects, though Presbyterian service-books, for example, contain prayers in the services for baptism and Holy Communion to set the elements of water, bread, and wine apart "from a common to a sacred use."

Benediction of the Blessed Sacrament is a service of the Roman Catholic Church (sometimes found in Anglican churches) when adoration is paid to the consecrated bread of Holy Communion and when a blessing of the congregation with that consecrated bread takes place. Such a service can occur if at an earlier Eucharist some consecrated bread has been "reserved" for this Benediction and for communions at home for the sick. This "blessing by the elements" is meaningful only because the presence of Christ is believed to be in and with the bread. As a service, its history can be traced back only to the late Middle Ages. In recent times, especially in Europe and North America, the service has lost some of its former popularity.

PETER TOON *and* R. MILTON WINTER

Bibliography. D. Daube, *Studies in Biblical Law;* J. Jeremias, *The Eucharistic Words of Jesus;* J. Pederson, *Israel: Its Life and Culture,* vols 1 and 2.

Blindness. Condition of lacking the ability to see. Physical blindness was common in the ancient Near East and is still prevalent among the poor and tribal peoples lacking the benefits of modern medicine.

Medical causes of blindness are not specified in the Bible, but poor personal hygiene and unsanitary living conditions were undoubtedly contributing factors. Newborn babies were especially susceptible. Much blindness from birth (Jn 9:1–3) was probably gonorrhea of the eyes. In the birth process germs from the mother passed to the eyes of the infant, where they found an ideal medium for growth. Within three days inflammation, pus, and swelling would be evident. In such cases, primitive treatment could not prevent some permanent or even total damage to the eye. Modern medical practice is to treat all newborn babies with antiseptic eye drops; but such treatment is not yet available to the poor, or is rejected by them in parts of the Near East today. Babies and young children also were threatened by infectious ophthalmia. Carried by flies, that disease caused heavy crusting, droopy eyelids, loss of eyelashes, and eventually clouding of the cornea, often leading to total blindness. In parts of the world one may still see a mother (because of folk superstition) permitting flies to swarm continuously on her baby's face even as she holds the infant in her lap. Blindness among adults might be due to side effects from illnesses such as malaria, long exposure to sandstorms and sun glare in the desert, accidents, punishment (as with Samson, Jgs 16:21), or old age (Gn 27:1; 1 Sm 4:15; 1 Kgs 14:4).

The OT demanded special consideration for the blind (Lv 19:14) and imposed punishment for misleading a blind person (Dt 27:18). A blind man, considered defective, was not permitted to serve as a priest (Lv 21:18).

Jesus' healing ministry brought sight to the blind in fulfillment of prophecy (Lk 4:18). His ability to restore vision was one of the proofs given to John the Baptist that Jesus was the Messiah (Mt 11:5). Jesus healed two blind men in Galilee (9:27–30), one blind man in Bethsaida (Mk 8:22–26), a man blind from birth in

Mosaic floor at Bethsaida, where Jesus healed a blind man.

Jerusalem (Jn 9), and a blind beggar named Bartimaeus and his friend at Jericho (Mk 10:46–52; cf. Mt 20:30–34; Lk 18:35–43). At times Jesus commanded immediate restoration (Mk 10:52). On other occasions he used "means" such as clay and water (Jn 9:6–11) or his own saliva (Mk 8:23). The apostle Paul was blinded at his conversion and received a miraculous cure in the presence of Ananias (Acts 9:1–9,18). Paul later afflicted a sorcerer, Elymas, with temporary blindness for opposing his ministry on the island of Cyprus (13:11).

The term "spiritual blindness" is a figurative way of defining the lost and hopeless condition of sinful mankind. Such blindness includes willful rejection of God's revelation in his creation and in Scripture, and an inability to see the truth of the gospel. Moses spoke of Israel's apostasy as "blindness" (Dt 29:4); Isaiah called it "dim eyes" (Is 6:10 NASB). Jesus charged the Pharisees with unbelief that made them "blind guides of the blind" (Mt 15:14; 23:16). Spiritual blindness is related to "hardness of heart" (Mk 8:17,18; Eph 4:17,18) and is understood as the judgment of God both upon unbelievers (Rom 1:20,21) and upon Israel (Is 29:10; Rom 11:7,8). According to Paul it is also the work of Satan, who "has blinded the minds of the unbelievers" (2 Cor 4:4). Healing from spiritual blindness is a special gift of God's grace through the "new birth" (Jn 3:3) and by seeing "the light of the gospel of the glory of Christ" (2 Cor 4:4).

JAMES C. DEYOUNG

See REGENERATION; MEDICINE AND MEDICAL PRACTICE; DISEASE.

Blood. Fluid that circulates through the body of a person or a vertebrate animal. Aside from reference to the common physical substance the term "blood" has a number of metaphorical uses in the Bible. At times it refers to a red color: "the sun shall be turned into darkness and the moon into blood" (Acts 2:20). The "blood of the grape" means wine (Dt 32:14). In the NT the expression "flesh and blood" refers to human life, to "natural" humanity: "Flesh and blood has not revealed this to you, but my Father who is in heaven" (Mt 16:17; see also 1 Cor 15:50; Gal 1:16; Eph 6:12). After betraying Jesus, Judas recognized that he had "sinned in betraying innocent blood" (Mt 27:4). In such passages "blood" has reference to life lived at the human level, natural life as opposed to spiritual or divine life.

The term "blood" is also used in the sense of shedding blood, that is, in killing or murder. Psalm 9:12 speaks of one "who avenges blood." Genesis 37:26 refers to the brothers who concealed Joseph's blood, that is, his murder. To be "burdened with the blood of another" (Prv 28:17) means to be guilty of murder. At the crucifixion Pilate said, "I am innocent of this man's blood" (Mt 27:24,25). Thus the idea of violent death is regularly connected with blood.

The logic of such expressions becomes particularly clear when one sees how closely life is associated with blood. Three passages specifically tie the two together. "Only you shall not eat flesh with its life, that is, its blood" (Gn 9:4). "For the life of the flesh is in the blood" (Lv 17:11). "The only restriction is never to eat the blood for the blood is the life . . ." (Dt 12:23 LB). Because God is the author of all life, any shedding of blood (any killing) is a serious matter. A certain sanctity associated with blood forms the basis for prohibitions against eating it. (Cf. what the apostles said in Acts 15:20.) Blood stands for the "life principle" which is from God.

Because of its association with life, blood takes on a special significance in the sacrificial motif. On the Day of Atonement (Lv 16) the blood of a bull and of a goat was sprinkled upon the altar as a "covering" of the people's sin. Life was poured out in death. Animal life was given up on behalf of the life of the people. Judgment and atonement were carried out through a transfer of the sin of the people to the animal sacrifice. Transference is de-

picted also by the scapegoat in the same ceremony (Lv 16:20–22). In the first Passover (Ex 12:1–13) the blood bore the same meaning. Animal blood posted on each door was a sign that a death had already taken place, so the angel of death passed over.

Further, because life is connected with blood, blood becomes the supreme offering to God. In the ratification of the covenant (Ex 24), Moses poured half the sacrificial blood on the altar; after reading the covenant to the people and receiving their affirmative response, he sprinkled the rest of the blood on them and said, "This is the blood of the covenant that the Lord has made with you in accordance with all these words" (24:8). Sprinkling blood on both the altar and the people bound God and the Israelites together in covenant relationship. In the cultic sacrifices of Israel, blood stood for death and depending on the context, might also stand for judgment, sacrifice, substitution, or redemption. Life with God was made possible by blood.

In the NT, apart from medical references (e.g., Mt 9:20) and references to murder (e.g., Acts 22:20), the primary reference is to the blood of Christ, an allusion to the OT motifs. The synoptic Gospels show that at the Last Supper Jesus spoke of his blood with reference to a new covenant (Mt 26:28; Mk 14:24; Lk 22:20). The language surrounding those sayings reveals the sacrificial motif; Jesus was speaking of his death and its redemptive significance. The Fourth Gospel expresses the same theology in different terms and in a different context: "Unless you eat the flesh of the Son of man and drink his blood, you have no life in you; he who eats my flesh and drinks my blood has eternal life, and I will raise him up at the last day. . . . He who eats my flesh and drinks my blood abides in me, and I in him" (Jn 6:53,54,56). The believer is said to participate by faith in the death and resurrection of the Lord (see also 1 Cor 10:16).

The apostle Paul's letters likewise associate blood with Christ's death, so much so that the word becomes—like the term "cross"—synonymous with the death of Christ in its saving significance: "making peace by the blood of his cross" (Col 1:20); and in a passage on reconciliation: "now in Christ Jesus you who once were far off have been brought near in the blood of Christ . . . thereby bringing the hostility to an end" (Eph 2:13,16). "Blood" and "cross" both stand for the death of Jesus in reconciling Jew and Gentile to God and in the creation of a new humanity. Paul evidently had in mind the sacrifice of the Day of Atonement when he said that God purposed that Christ be an atoning sacrifice by his blood (Rom 3:25). His vocabulary (from Lv 16) focused on the most important sacrifice of Jewish tradition.

Peter made reference to the blood of the covenant (Ex 24) when he described Christian exiles as having been sprinkled with the blood of Christ (1 Pt 1:2). He reminded his readers that they had been redeemed by that blood (v 19). In linking Christ to "a lamb without blemish or spot," he may have had in mind either the servant of Isaiah 53 or the Passover Lamb, both of which had redemptive significance in his readers' minds.

Finally, to the writer of Hebrews the whole OT system of sacrifices found its ultimate fulfillment in the blood of Christ, that is, in his sacrificial death (Heb 9:7–28; 13:11,12).

Thus, NT references to the blood of Christ point to the culminating and comprehensive redemption achieved by God in the death of his Son (Heb 10:20). Both justice and justification were thus achieved (Rom 3:26). The blood of Christ is therefore called the "once for all" means of redemption (Heb 9:26).

ROBERT W. LYON

See ATONEMENT; OFFERINGS AND SACRIFICES.

Bibliography. L. Morris, "The Biblical Use of the Term 'Blood,'" *Journal of Theological Studies*, vol 3 (1952) pp 216–27; A.M. Stibbs, *The Meaning of the Word "Blood" in Scripture*; V. Taylor, *Jesus and His Sacrifice*; H.C. Trumbull, *The Blood Covenant*.

Blood, Avenger of. Person who sought justice by killing a murderer. The avenger of blood was usually the nearest relative of the one who had been murdered. The Mosaic law regulated this kind of vengeance killing.

See AVENGER OF BLOOD.

Blood, Field of. Name given to the field purchased with the "blood money" Judas accepted to betray Jesus (Mt 27:8; Acts 1:19). The field was purchased by the chief priests as a burial ground for strangers (formerly, the potter's field). Judas hanged himself and burst open there. This account uses the Aramaic expression *Akeldama* (KJV *Aceldama*), translated "field of blood." The Akeldama is situated on the southern slope of the Valley of Hinnom near the Kidron Valley.

Blood, Flow of. 1. Vaginal discharge such as that during menstruation. Leviticus 15 contains social and sanitary laws which God gave to Moses concerning genital discharges. A woman with vaginal bleeding was considered ceremonially unclean during bleeding and for seven days afterward. She could not go to the tabernacle or temple for worship while unclean or mingle with crowds in the street or market. Anyone touching her or her clothes,

bed, chair, and the like was also ceremonially unclean (Lv 15:19–28). Sexual intercourse was not allowed while the woman was ceremonially unclean (v 24). Seven days after her bleeding stopped, a woman would present to the priest two turtledoves or young pigeons as offerings to atone for the time of her uncleanness (vv 29,30).

Jesus' miraculous healing of a woman who had been hemorrhaging (slowly or intermittently) for 12 years was recorded in three of the four Gospels (Mt 9:20–22; Mk 5:25–34; Lk 8:43–48). If her bleeding was vaginal, the years of ceremonial uncleanness and separation must have been particularly distressing for her. Besides being anxious and uncomfortable she would also have been unable to bear children. Further, she had "suffered much under many physicians" and "had spent all that she had, and was no better but rather grew worse" (Mk 5:26). In despair she ignored the rules about uncleanness and made her way through a crowd to touch Jesus. When she touched him the bleeding stopped immediately and permanently.

2. Bloody stools. The "bloody flux" (KJV) from which Publius' father suffered was some form of dysentery (Acts 28:8).

DAVID E. VAN REKEN

See MEDICINE AND MEDICAL PRACTICE; HEMORRHAGE.

Bloodguilt. Term used in some English Bibles to translate a Hebrew word meaning "blood" or "bloods" (Ex 22:2,3; Lv 17:4; 1 Sm 25:26,33; Hos 12:14). The translation "bloodguiltiness" occurs only in Psalm 51:14. The plural form almost invariably means the shedding of blood, but the singular can mean blood itself, bloodshed, or the guilt incurred by bloodshed (i.e., by killing). The idea that killing was punishable by death pervades the Bible; killing was generally done by literally shedding another's blood.

The first category of bloodshed resulting in bloodguilt was deliberate homicide, murder "in cold blood," as moderns say, or of "innocent blood," as the OT says (Jon 1:14). Several passages define the shedding of innocent blood and its punishment (Gn 9:6; Dt 19:11–13; 2 Kgs 24:4; Ez 33:6). The Bible prohibits any ransom for a murderer (Nm 35:31).

Another category was accidental homicide (Nm 35:9–28, Dt 19:4–10). After an accidental killing the "avenger of blood" might retaliate if he caught the offender before he reached a city of refuge. If the murderer was unknown, the town nearest the discovered corpse assumed the guilt; Deuteronomy 21:1–9 prescribes a ceremony for removing such guilt.

Blue

In ancient Israel it was possible to shed the blood of an animal and incur bloodguilt (Lv 17:3,4,10,11). An animal that was legally guilty of bloodshed was to be stoned (Ex 21:28,29).

Exceptions to bloodguilt were made in the case of self-defense (Ex 22:2), capital punishment (Lv 20:9–16), and war (1 Kgs 2:5,6).

Frequently the prophets would use the Hebrew word "bloods" or "blood" to speak of the whole nation's guilt (Is 1:15; 4:4; Ez 7:23; 9:9; Hos 1:4; 4:2, KJV; Mi 3:10; Hab 2:8,12,17; and many others).

Other crimes beside bloodshed could bring on a death sentence (Lv 20:9–16; Ez 18:10–13). Such crimes included honoring pagan deities, worshiping idols, adultery, robbery, oppressing the poor, breach of promise, and usury.

From the beginning (Gn 4:10–12), through the prophets (Is 26:21; Ez 24:6–9), and into the NT (Rv 6:10), the Bible supports the idea that God will avenge wrongs and punish those guilty of bloodshed.

ROBERT L. ALDEN

See CITIES OF REFUGE; CRIMINAL LAW AND PUNISHMENT.

Blue. See COLOR.

Boanerges. Name meaning "sons of thunder" given by Jesus to James and John, Zebedee's sons (Mk 3:17). Its derivation is uncertain. The name may have referred to the volatile personalities of the two brothers (Lk 9:54), to their possible revolutionary past as Zealots, or even to a "thundering" style of speech.

See JAMES (PERSON); JOHN THE APOSTLE, LIFE AND WRITINGS OF.

Boar. Wild or domesticated animal of the swine family (Ps 80:13).

See ANIMALS (PIG).

Boast. To speak of deeds, abilities, or characteristics in a manner showing pride or self-satisfaction. In the Bible the word also has a more positive connotation ("to glory in").

In the OT, "boasting" is often used to describe the basic attitude of the ungodly, who depend on their own resources rather than on God (Pss 52:1; 94:3,4). Enemies of Israel boasted of their victories and claimed the glory for themselves (Dt 32:27; Pss 10:3; 35:26; 73:9; Is 3:9). They boasted of their riches (Ps 49:6) and wisdom (Is 19:11). According to the Lord, the rich and wise are to "boast about this: that he understands and knows me, that I am the Lord, who exercises kindness, justice, and righteousness on the earth" (Jer 9:24). The psalmist placed primary importance upon the

object of one's boast: "Some boast of chariots, and some of horses; but we boast of the name of the Lord our God" (Ps 20:7). Job's "comforters" accused him of boasting of his innocence before God (Jb 11:3; 25:4).

Jesus depicted a proud Pharisee boasting to God in prayer (Lk 18:10–14). Most of the NT usages of the word occur in the apostle Paul's letters. The negative aspect of vaunting one's own accomplishments is contrasted with the positive counterpart of glorying in what the Lord has done (Rom 3:27,28; 2 Cor 10:17; Gal 6:14). Self-righteousness and bragging are to be avoided (Rom 1:30; 2:17,23; Eph 2:9; 2 Tm 3:2). Paul associated boasting with the attitude of those Jews who developed a feeling of self-confidence because of having kept the Law. For Paul the only legitimate boasting was to boast (rejoice) in the Lord (Rom 5:11). In Romans 5:3, the rabbinic view of glorying in one's sufferings is contrasted with Paul's view that his present sufferings pointed to God's power and toward Paul's hope for the future.

Paul's boasting was not based upon comparisons with others, in contrast to the boasting of his opponents. Because Christ worked through him (2 Cor 3:2–6) and God commended him (10:18), he could give glory to God. Paul preferred to boast of his own weakness, and of the Lord's power and strength (12:5,9).

On occasion the apostle did boast concerning a particular group of Christians (2 Cor 7:4,14; 8:24; 9:2,3), but with the implication that he was expressing confidence in *them*, not bragging about his own successes. Concerning himself, Paul boasted reluctantly and only as a means of defense against an unsupportive element in the Corinthian church. He said that those who should have commended him had instead compelled him to engage in "foolish" boasting (12:11).

JAMES D. PRICE

See PRIDE.

Boat. Small watercraft. Boats mentioned in the Bible were propelled by oars or sails and used for fishing, travel, or as lifeboats on larger vessels.

See TRAVEL AND TRANSPORTATION.

Boaz (Person). Salmon's son of Judah's tribe (Ru 4:18–22). Boaz lived in Bethlehem in the days of the judges and married Ruth, a Moabite woman. Boaz was an ancestor of Christ (Mt 1:5; Lk 3:32, KJV Booz) and a wealthy relative by marriage of Ruth's mother-in-law, Naomi. Ruth attracted the attention of Boaz when she was gleaning in one of his fields (Ru 2). His

An aqueduct at Bethlehem.

kindness to Ruth convinced Naomi that Boaz might be willing to redeem some land her husband had owned and at the same time accept the levirate marriage with Ruth that such a transaction required (chs 3,4).

See RUTH, BOOK OF; MARRIAGE, MARRIAGE CUSTOMS; GENEALOGY OF JESUS CHRIST.

Boaz (Pillar). Name (meaning "strength") given to one of the two pillars erected in front of King Solomon's temple (1 Kgs 7:21; 2 Chr 3:17).

See TABERNACLE, TEMPLE; JACHIN AND BOAZ.

Bocheru. Azel's son, a descendant of King Saul (1 Chr 8:38; 9:44).

Bochim. Place near Gilgal mentioned in Judges 2:1,5 where the angel of the Lord confronted the nation of Israel with their failure to drive out the Canaanite inhabitants of the land. For their disobedience, judgment was pronounced. The heathen peoples would become "thorns" in their sides, and their gods, "snares." The people wept, and the place was named "Bochim," meaning "weepers." Many scholars feel Bochim was merely another name for Bethel. This is supported by the Septuagint, which reads Bethel in this passage.

Bodily Resurrection of Christ. See RESURRECTION.

Body. Term used biblically in several different ways, including certain metaphorical or theological expressions. Many of the biblical references illustrate special features of Hebrew thought about human life.

OT References. The OT writers used a number of Hebrew words translated "body" in English versions, mostly with reference to physical life. The body suffers; it is plagued with illness or is injured. Sometimes it is dead, that is, a corpse or carcass. Reference is even made to the "bodies" of spiritual beings—of the cherubim in Ezekiel's vision (Ez 1:11) and of an angel (Dn 10:6). Jeremiah

spoke of the bodies of pagan gods, referring to their images in the form of idols (Jer 10:1–16). Such usages indicate that the Hebrew thought of all beings, whether heavenly or earthly, as embodied.

At times the word "body" is close to the meaning of "flesh" and frequently the same Hebrew word lies behind both terms. "Body" is man in his total physical experience. "Flesh" is generally used to refer to the sinfulness or creatureliness of man.

Human beings have bodies and a bodily existence; each person also has a spirit and a spiritual dimension in life. But in Scripture the two are not set over against each other or viewed as separate "parts" of man. The body is not seen as a hindrance to the soul (as in much Greek thought). Not until the intertestamental period did Jewish writers begin to speak of the body as evil or as something set over against the soul.

NT References. Though "body" is used in the NT in the same ways as in the OT, the concept is given new significance. The body of Jesus (i.e., his corpse) was taken down from the cross (Mk 15:43). A body could experience illness and healing (5:29) and needed to be clothed (Jas 2:16); yet the body (i.e., physical life) is "more than clothing" (Mt 6:25). Jesus said not to fear "those who kill the body but cannot kill the soul; rather fear him who can destroy both soul and body in hell" (10:28).

In the Lord's Supper Jesus said with reference to the bread, "This is my body," and then added—with the cup in his hand—"This is my blood" (Mk 14:22,24). Those terms from the OT sacrificial system were intended to underscore the sacrificial significance of Jesus' death. Under both the old and new covenants, a real, physical life was offered in death for the sake of the "covenant people."

The apostle Paul made the term "body" a fundamental reference in the understanding of Christian experience. Most of the NT references to "body" are in his letters.

The Sinful Body. In Romans 6:6 Paul spoke of the destruction of the "sinful body." The phrase did not mean that the body itself is sinful, as though sin is in some way tied to physical matter. Neither did it refer to some entity, sin, thought to dwell within human nature. Nor did it personify sin. Rather, the phrase referred to the physical life of human beings—life on earth—which is dominated by sin's influence. In Christian conversion Paul saw that familiar pattern of human experience being destroyed. To link sin with the body is only to recognize that human beings in their earthly life ("life in the body") are pervasively sinful. After describing the awful conflict in human experience, Paul cried out, "Who will deliver me from this body of death?" (Rom 7:24). Human life, "spoiled" by sin and its consequences at every point, requires Christ's redemption (7:25–8:4).

The Body of the Believer. In conversion, believers are said by Paul to experience not only the "saving of the soul" but the transformation of present life. They have "died to sin" and have been freed from sin's bondage. Paul therefore called for holiness of life "in the flesh." "Let not sin therefore reign in your mortal bodies, to make you obey their passions" (Rom 6:12). Righteousness, not sin, is to govern a Christian's physical experience. The social and personal lives of believers are to be characterized by holiness. Believers are in the world (Jn 17:11) and are to live for God in the world (i.e., in their bodily existence); they are not to be indifferent to the world.

Physical, earthly life thus takes on new significance. Paul told Christians to "present your bodies as a living sacrifice, holy and acceptable to God" (Rom 12:1). Each individual human life is to be a "living sacrifice" to God. Far from deprecating earthly existence, Paul saw that in Christ it had new potential. The reason is that the Holy Spirit is found there. "Your body is a temple of the Holy Spirit within you, which you have from God" (1 Cor 6:19). That affirmation is not to be read materialistically, as though the Spirit takes up residence in certain tissues; "body" means one's whole physical, earthly existence.

Paul also anticipated an ultimate transformation of life in the body through Christ. He spoke of the "redemption of our bodies" (Rom 8:23) and of the transformation of "our lowly bodies to be like his glorious body" (Phil 3:21). Thus the Bible, although it has a realistic view of human sin and physical deterioration, does not share the pessimism of world-views that seek escape from the world.

The Body of Christ. In his account of the Lord's Supper, Paul spoke of the bread as Christ's body "which is given for you" (1 Cor 11:24). Elsewhere in Paul's letters, similar expressions indicate that he understood Christ's death to be the means of human deliverance. In 1 Corinthians 10:16 he speaks of "participation in the body of Christ." Believers are closely identified with Christ's atoning death. They are said to have died to the Law "through the body of Christ" (Rom 7:4). Believers are reconciled in "his body of flesh by his death" (Col 1:22). Paul's repeated use of "body," "flesh," and "death" underscores his point that the vicarious ministry of Jesus in the world, culminating in physical death, is the fundamental basis of Christian faith. Peter concurred when he wrote that Christ "bore our sins in his body on the tree" (1 Pt 2:24).

Paul's most frequent use of the word "body," however, is in a metaphor of the church in its relationship to Christ. In a number of passages the church is the "body" and Christ the "head" (Col 1:18). Christ has been made "Head over all things for the church," which "is his body" (Eph 1:22,23). The body grows by "holding fast to the Head" (Col 2:19). As head of the body, Christ is its Savior (Eph 5:23). The head/body metaphor stresses the organic dependence of the church on Christ and his lordship over the church. The church finds its self-understanding in terms of its Head. The relationship is organic in that the life flows from, and is sustained by, the Head. The relationship is immediate, direct, and complete. Apart from Christ, both in his historic atoning sacrifice and in his present position at the right hand of God, the church has no existence.

An aspect of the church as the body of Christ is its essential unity within its obvious diversity. Historic distinctions are to disappear as Jew and Gentile, male and female, slave and free, become one body in Christ (Gal 3:27,28). Because there is one Spirit, there is one body (Eph 4:4). The result is a new humanity formed out of formerly alienated parties (Eph 2:11–16). The unity of the body is not a goal but a fact brought about by the baptism of believers into one body (1 Cor 12:13). The body of believers should give expression to that unity (Phil 2:2).

Paul found it necessary to add that the body's unity and corporate nature does not result in destroying or minimizing the individual. By their "incorporation" into Christ, believers belong not only to him but also to each other, "and each needs all the others" (Rom 12:5 LB). The individual "parts of the body" find their significance by virtue of their belonging to the body. In Romans 12 and in 1 Corinthians 12 Paul took note of different gifts found within the body, which he said should not be stifled but expressed. "Let us use them according to the grace given to us" (Rom 12:6). Taken together, the variety of gifts contribute to building up the body (Eph 4:12). In the process the body grows in love (v 16) and becomes the visible manifestation of divine love in every age.

The Resurrection Body. The possible separation of body and soul did not occur to the Hebrew mind. Biblically, life beyond death is not bodiless, but an existence for which a "new body" is prepared. Though Paul raised many questions in 1 Corinthians 15:35–57, it is clear that he saw continuity between the earthly body and the resurrection body. "It is sown a physical body, it is raised a spiritual body" (v 44). That expression may be derived

A body preserved in ash after the eruption of Vesuvius.

in large part from the experience of Jesus, whose dead body was not only brought to life but also transformed so that it was not bound by earth. His resurrection body was derived from the earthly. But Paul was sure that in the promised resurrection, life would return to the body without its present limitations and with new manifestations. Death, said Paul, is thereby "swallowed up in victory" (v 54).

ROBERT W. LYON

See RESURRECTION; BODY OF CHRIST; CHURCH; MAN, DOCTRINE OF.

Body of Christ.

Scriptural phrase referring to (1) the physical body of Jesus Christ, (2) his broken body and shed blood viewed symbolically and memorially in the bread and wine of the Lord's Supper, and (3) both the local and universal church viewed metaphorically.

The Physical Body of Jesus Christ. The NT declares that the Son (the second person of the Trinity) had a human body prepared for him by God the Father (Heb 10:5). The earthly body was engendered by the conceptive work of the Holy Spirit through the virgin Mary (Mt 1:20); the one thus born, humanly speaking, as a descendant of David (Rom 1:3), was also to be called the Son of God (Lk 1:35). The apostle John emphasized that the body of Christ was really human physically, not something gaseous or ethereal (1 Jn 4:2,3) as some persons in John's day were already beginning to argue. God "became flesh and dwelt among us" (Jn 1:14; cf. Is 53:1–4). Jesus' earthly body possessed ordinary human characteristics and limitations. That is, as a real human being, Jesus Christ experienced sorrow (Heb 5:7,8; Jn 11:35), weariness (Jn 4:6), thirst (19:28), and pain (vv 1–3).

When Jesus gave up his spirit, his physical body died on the cross (Jn 19:30,33). The NT proclaims that he bore the sins of the world in his body on the cross (1 Pt 2:24; 1 Jn 2:2; cf. Is 53:5,6). His death is described as a perfect sacrifice for sinners (Heb 9:12–14,26–28), a sacrifice of his body that makes believers in him holy and righteous (2 Cor 5:21; Heb 10:10).

Christ's physical body was prepared in the normal way for burial (Mt 27:59; Mk 15:46; Lk 23:53,56; 24:1; Jn 19:39,40) and placed in the rock tomb of Joseph of Arimathea (Mt 27:57–60; Jn 19:41). On the third day the body of Christ experienced a real physical resurrection, as he had predicted (Jn 2:19–22). He was seen in his physical resurrection body (Mt 28:9; Lk 24:31,36; Jn 20:10–19,26). He was heard, touched, and held onto (Mt 28:9; Lk 24:39; Jn 20:17; 1 Jn 1:1). He offered his body, scarred by his crucifixion, to be touched (Lk 24:39; Jn 20:27). The fact that he ate shows that his resurrection body was a physical one (Lk 24:42,43). In addition, Christ's body was "glorified," that is, it was not restricted as ordinary bodies are: he entered and left rooms in a remarkable way (Lk 24:31,34; Jn 20:19,26).

Christ's bodily resurrection is said in Scripture to guarantee that believers in Christ will experience resurrection of their own bodies (1 Cor 15:20–23,50–57). "But our commonwealth is in heaven, and from it we await a Savior, the Lord Jesus Christ, who will charge our lowly body to be like his glorious body, by the power which enables him even to subject all things to himself" (Phil 3:20,21; cf. vv 10,11).

The Body of Christ in the Lord's Supper. At the last supper (Mt 26:26–29; Mk 14:22–25; Lk 22:15–20; 1 Cor 11:23–26), which accompanied the Passover supper, Jesus held up a loaf of bread and said, "This is my body"; then he picked up a cup of wine and said, "This is my blood of the covenant" (Mt 26:28). Jesus meant that the bread symbolized his body, which would be broken when he was beaten at his trial and pierced at his crucifixion (Lk 23:33; Jn 19:1,2). The apostle Paul said that "Christ, our paschal lamb, has been sacrificed" (1 Cor 5:7), meaning that the Passover lamb in the OT was an object lesson pointing to "the Lamb of God, who takes away the sin of the world!" (Jn 1:29).

For Christians, the body of Christ is viewed symbolically as a broken body (Mt 8:17; 1 Pt 2:24; cf. Is 53:4,5) in the breaking of the bread at the Lord's Supper. The cup is a sign of his blood poured out, viewed as the central factor in God's covenant of grace with his people. Jesus referred to "the new covenant in my blood" (Lk 22:20). The whole ceremony of the Lord's Supper was also to be a memorial (1 Cor 11:25,26). In the ceremony believers are reminded that Christ died for sinners, that is, for the forgiveness of their sins (Mt 26:28). They are also reminded that they are participating in the body of Christ in that they are united with him (Rom 6:1–11; 1 Cor 10:16; Gal 2:20; Phil 3:10).

The Body of Christ Viewed as the People of God. The phrase "body of Christ" is also used as a metaphor for the whole church, a unity of believers connected with and depen-

371

dent on Christ. God's people are thus said to be members of Christ's "mystical body" (1 Cor 12:27), in fellowship with Christ and spiritually nourished by him (Eph 5:25b,29). A number of other metaphors are also used for the whole people of God, such as the vine (Ps 80:8), temple of God (1 Cor 3:16,17), building (1 Pt 2:5), chosen people (v 9), and family of God (Eph 3:15). Such metaphors amplify the interrelatedness, communion, and dependence of the "body of Christ" upon the living God.

The term "body of Christ" was often used by Paul to remind a local church that it was a vital part of the larger body. Paul said to the church at Rome, "For as in one body we have many members, and all the members do not have the same function, so we, though many, are one body in Christ, and individually members one of another" (Rom 12:4,5). Paul taught the Corinthian Christians that they, individually and collectively, were part of the body of Christ (1 Cor 12:27). They and Paul were all baptized by one Spirit into that one body (v 13; Eph 5:30).

In the NT the term "body of Christ" is used to mean both the universal church and each local group of believers. In both senses the church is said to be the spiritual body in which believing Jews and Gentiles are united (Eph 2:14–16; 3:6; 4:4). It is the body that Christ redeemed (Eph 5:23b), over which he presides (Col 1:18) and sovereignly rules (Eph 1:22,23) and for which he supplies strength and unity (4:15,16; Col 2:19).

Christian believers are said to be "baptized into one body—Jews or Greeks, slaves or free—and all were made to drink of one Spirit" (1 Cor 12:13). Scripture also describes this baptism as being divinely "born anew" by the Spirit of God (Jn 3:3–5), and becoming "new creations in Christ" (2 Cor 5:17) through a spiritual "washing of regeneration" of sins and renewal (Ti 3:5,6). The believers who make up the one body of Christ are said to share together in partaking of Christ the one loaf, the one who is the bread of life (Jn 6:35), set forth symbolically in the Lord's Supper (1 Cor 10:16,17).

Each member of the body of Christ has been given spiritual gifts with which to serve Christ in the body (Rom 12:6; 1 Cor 12:11). Such gifts are enumerated several times in Scripture, and range from apostleship and pastoring to encouraging and showing mercy (Rom 12:7,8; Eph 4:11). The ministry of serving is to be shared by all Christians, for example, through giving to the physical needs of others (Acts 11:29,30; 1 Cor 16:1–4; 2 Cor 8:1–5) and praying for one another (Eph 1:15–23; 3:14–19; 6:18–20). No one should look down on others or on their gifts, since God has chosen each

one to function in his or her place in the body (1 Cor 12:14–26). The gifts are given "to equip the saints for the work of ministry, for building up the body of Christ, until we all attain to the unity of the faith and of the knowledge of the Son of God, to mature manhood, to the measure of the stature of the fulness of Christ" (Eph 4:12,13). The goal is "to grow up in every way into him who is the head, into Christ" (vv 15,16).

W. HAROLD MARE

See BODY; CHURCH; LORD'S SUPPER, THE; RESURRECTION.

Bibliography. E. Best, *One Body in Christ;* A. Cole, *The Body of Christ;* P.S. Minear, *Images of the Church in the NT,* pp 173–220; E. Schweizer, *The Church as the Body of Christ.*

Bohan, Stone of. Stone marking the northeast boundary between the tribes of Judah and Benjamin. Bohan, a descendant of Reuben, is not mentioned elsewhere in the OT (Jos 15:6; 18:17).

Boil. Inflamed localized swelling on the skin. In modern medicine the term boil is restricted to a pus-filled swelling caused by infectious germs, usually staphylococci. The pus is a mixture of germs and white blood cells, which are the body's defense against germs. Although painful, boils usually heal naturally after rupturing or being lanced. A more severe boil with several openings is called a carbuncle. If the infection goes deeper and injures internal organs or tissues, it is called an abscess and can even be fatal.

In the Bible the word translated boil probably referred to a variety of skin diseases. The sixth plague that God inflicted on Egypt through Moses and Aaron was a plague of boils (Ex 9:9–11; Dt 28:27,35, KJV botch) or blisters (KJV blains). Boils or skin eruptions of a certain type were described in the Mosaic health and sanitation code as one indication of leprosy (Lv 13:1–8,18–23). Job's "loathsome sores from the sole of his foot to the crown of his head" (Jb 2:7,8,12) were probably too extensive to be boils in the modern sense; he may have had smallpox, psoriasis, tubercular leprosy, or some other disease accompanied by severe itching. King Hezekiah's boil was probably a carbuncle (2 Kgs 20:1–7; Is 38:21).

DAVID E. VAN REKEN

See MEDICINE and MEDICAL PRACTICE; DISEASE; PLAGUES UPON EGYPT.

Bond, Bondage. Anything that fastens or restrains; subjection or slavery. The basic concept in Hebrew and Greek words translated "bond" or "bondage" is "loss of freedom." The concept connotes servitude to another. The OT uses several words for bondage to describe the period of Israelite servitude in Egypt as well as the Babylonian captivity and Persian domination. Some English versions use the word "bond" to denote a state of individual servitude, such as the conditions of indenture permitted under the laws of Moses (Lv 25:39–44 KJV). The archaic "bondmaid" is used to denote a concubine or secondary wife. The concept is used metaphorically to describe the control that God exercises over the nations of the world (Ps 2:3).

In the NT the bondage metaphor has positive and negative aspects. Negatively, it indicates spiritual subjection to sin or Satan (Heb 2:14,15; 2 Pt 2:19), to the flesh (Rom 8:12–14), or to the Law (Gal 2:4; 5:1). Human beings are enslaved by forces hostile to their well-being control their actions. The term is also used to picture the subjugation of creation to physical decay (Rom 8:21), which itself is the result of human sin.

The positive aspect draws upon the broader use of bondage in the Bible to denote servanthood, especially service to God as an obligation or vow (Nm 30:2–15; "bond of the covenant," Ez 20:37 KJV). The term describes the necessity and value of suffering (Heb 10:34; 13:3 KJV). Paul especially uses it in a double sense (calling himself a "prisoner of Christ") to associate his physical bonds with his spiritual bondage to Christ (Phil 1:7–14; Eph 3:1; 2 Tm 1:8; 2:9; Phlm 9,10,13 KJV).

GRANT R. OSBORNE

See SLAVE, SLAVERY.

Bondage, House of. Expression used in the OT for Egypt, where Israel was enslaved before the exodus (Ex 13:3; Jos 24:17).

See EXODUS, BOOK OF.

Bondmaid, Bondman, Bondservant. See TRADES AND OCCUPATIONS (SERVANT).

Bone. One of the separate parts of the human or animal skeleton. After death, bones retain their form long after the soft tissues have decomposed, so bones are often associated with dead bodies or with death itself. The Israelites were concerned about proper respect for the bodies of the dead (Gn 50:25; 1 Sm 31:11–13; 2 Kgs 23:14–18; Ez 39:14–16; Am 2:1; Heb 11:22).

A valley of "old, dry bones" symbolized the people of Israel, who were without hope until the Spirit of the Lord would put life back into them (Ez 37:1–14). In a living body, however, bones are living tissue, and Ezekiel knew that broken bones could heal (30:21). Intact bones were a requirement for an unblemished lamb

for the Passover (Ex 12:46; Nm 9:11,12). Thus the NT states that when Jesus Christ, the "Lamb of God" (Jn 1:33–36), was crucified, contrary to Roman practice his legs were not broken (Ps 34:20; Jn 19:30–37).

Some references to bones in the Bible (Jb 2:5; 19:20; 30:30) carry the connotation of deep feelings, as in the phrase "I feel it in my bones." Other references are metaphorical expressions of close kinship, "flesh and bone" (Gn 2:23; 29:14; Jgs 9:2; Lk 24:39) being equivalent to the expression "one's own flesh and blood."

Book of Life. Term used to refer to a heavenly record. The phrase appears seven times in the NT: Philippians 4:3; Revelation 3:5; 13:8; 17:8; 20:12 (twice); 21:27. The Christian understanding of the phrase, however, is rooted in the OT. Passages such as Exodus 32:32; Psalm 87:6; Daniel 7:10; 12:1; and Malachi 3:16 imply or affirm a record kept by God. God is seen as keeping account of his people's faithfulness and disobedience—and possibly that of other nations as well (e.g., Ps 87:6). Psalm 69:28 uses the phrase "book of the living"; parallel poetic lines refer to physical living.

In Daniel 7:10; 12:1; and Malachi 3:16 references are linked with descriptions of final judgment and events of endtime. Names and deeds from the divine records are evidence set before a judge. Luke 10:20 and Hebrews 12:23 reflect similar thought; no concrete mention of "books" is made but a heavenly record is assumed. In Philippians 4:3 Paul uses "book of life" to encourage his fellow workers in a lively hope for the future.

"Book of life" in the Book of Revelation refers to a heavenly record with the names of persecuted Christians who remain faithful. It is used first in the letter to Sardis (3:5) where the Risen Lord, identified as "the Lamb," is custodian of the book (13:8; 21:7). If a person's name is found in the book, admittance is granted to New Jerusalem (20:15; 21:27). If one's name is not written there, the judgment is final destruction. Absolute confidence in God's care for his own is affirmed by the words "written before the foundation of the world" (13:8; 17:8).

Book of Remembrance. Divine record of the names of those who fear God, referred to once in the OT (Mal 3:16). The prophet Malachi was struggling against moral decline in his day. Arrogant individuals were seemingly "justified" in their haughtiness, and evildoers were blessed materially rather than being brought to judgment. His reference to a book of remembrance suggests that God in due time would turn things around, so that there would be a proper distinction between the righteous and the wicked.

See BOOK OF LIFE.

Book of the Covenant. Term occurring in two OT contexts. It describes, first, a document read by Moses to the people of Israel at Mt Sinai (Ex 24:7) and, second, a document discovered in the temple ("House of the Lord") by Hilkiah the priest at the time of King Josiah's program of repairing the temple (2 Kgs 23:2,21; 2 Chr 34:30). The term "covenant" refers to the covenant laws which God made with his people Israel in the time of Moses. The Hebrew term "book" means any written document, whether written on clay or stone tablets or on parchment scrolls. Ancient covenants were often in written form. The main problem in understanding the two references to "book of the covenant" is in trying to determine the concepts of those particular documents.

The book read at Mt Sinai has been taken to refer either to the Ten Commandments or to the whole section of Exodus 20 to 23 minus the narrative parts. Since the people responded, "All that the Lord has spoken we will do," it was evidently legal in its thrust, but it seems impossible to define its contents more precisely than that. The fact that Moses wrote the book (Ex 24:4) need not exclude the Ten Commandments, which are explicitly stated to have been written by God (v 12; 32:15,16). Moses could also have written them down, perhaps in a preliminary stage (19:25; 20:1).

Modern OT scholars often call Exodus 21 to 23 the "book of the covenant" without necessarily implying that that was the document read by Moses. If the phrase is taken in that sense, however, the content of the book of the covenant (Ex 20:22–23:33) may be summarized as follows:

1. Worship—Exodus 20:22–26
    Idolatry forbidden (20:23)
    Altar of sacrifice (20:24–26)
2. Civil matters—Exodus 21:1–23:12
    Slaves (21:1–11)
    Injury to person (21:12–32)
    Damage to property (21:33–22:15)
    Marriage laws (22:16,17)
    Capital religious offenses (22:18–20)
    Benevolence (22:21–27; 23:4,5,9–12)
    Responsibilities to God (22:28–31)
    Honesty (23:1–3,6–8)
3. Religious matters—Exodus 23:13–19
4. Blessings and warnings—Exodus 23:20–33

From the outline it can be seen that the laws are not rigidly categorized, nor is every problem-situation covered. Rather, a general review is given of major obligations the Israelites faced toward God and one another as they anticipated settlement in Canaan, the Promised Land. Many of the laws find close parallels in the laws of other ancient peoples.

The content of the "book of the covenant" read by King Josiah to the people of Judah is likewise uncertain. Some scholars have tried to reconstruct its contents on the basis of Josiah's reforms, concluding that those reforms were similar to principles taught in the Book of Deuteronomy. That approach has several weaknesses. First, some of the reforms are nowhere mentioned in the Law (e.g., burning the chariots of the sun—2 Kgs 23:11) and would have to represent inferences Josiah derived from the Law. It becomes unclear how much of his reform was based on explicit passages in the book of the covenant and how much on inferences. Second, the account in 2 Chronicles 34:3–7 indicates that much of the reform took place *before* discovery of the book of the covenant.

On the other hand, explicit statements in 2 Kings indicate that some of the reforms were based on the book of the covenant. Thus the book must have contained instructions on the Passover (2 Kgs 23:21). It probably dealt with mediums, wizards, and other idolatrous practices (v 24), unless that reform was an inference suggested by the wording. In addition, the book evidently contained warnings of the destruction God would bring if his words were not followed (22:16,19), even directing the judgment ("desolation and curse") against "this place." Those expressions probably indicate that Josiah's book of the covenant was larger than Exodus 21 to 23. In the older book, the Passover is mentioned only as the feast of unleavened bread (Ex 23:15). Exodus 22:18 might possibly give a basis for Josiah's action against wizards. But in Exodus 21 to 23 no statement of judgment for disobedience is sufficient to explain the wording of 2 Kings 22:16,19; the closest thing to it is Exodus 23:33.

Finally, the fact that Josiah's book of the covenant is also called the book of the law (2 Kgs 22:8) suggests that numerous references to the book of the law in the OT should also be understood as referring to the book of the covenant.

See EXODUS, BOOK OF; LAW, BIBLICAL CONCEPT OF.

Books, Production of. *See* WRITING AND BOOKS.

Booth. Small temporary hut constructed of branches and sticks when permanent buildings were unavailable. Booths provided shade during the day and protection from the dew and winds during the night (Gn 33:17; Jon 4:5). The word is also used as a figure of speech for something fragile and easily destroyed (Jb 27:18; Is 1:8).

See FEASTS AND FESTIVALS OF ISRAEL.

Booths, Feast of. One of the three great festivals of Israel, celebrating the completion of the agricultural year. The Jews built booths (temporary shelters) to commemorate their deliverance from Egypt by the hand of God (Lv 23:39–43).

See FEASTS AND FESTIVALS OF ISRAEL.

Booz. KJV NT form of Boaz in Matthew 1:5 and Luke 3:32.

See BOAZ (PERSON).

Borashan. Alternate name for Ashan, a town originally assigned to Judah's tribe, in 1 Samuel 30:30.

See ASHAN.

Born Again. Expression used by Jesus in explaining to Nicodemus how one enters the kingdom of God (Jn 3:3–7).

See REGENERATION.

Borrow, Borrowing. Receiving money or goods that one pledges to return. The Mosaic Law regulated borrowing and lending (Dt 23:19,20).

See MONEY AND BANKING.

Boscath. KJV form of Bozkath, a city in Judah, in 2 Kings 22:1.

See BOZKATH.

Bosor. KJV form of Beor, Balaam's father, in 2 Peter 2:15.

See BEOR #2.

Bottomless Pit. Phrase used in the Bible to denote the abode of the dead and of demonic forces. The Hebrew word (literally "the deep") is translated "abyss" in many versions of the Bible. In the ancient world, the concept referred to anything so deep as to be unfathomable, for example, wells or fountains. It is used in that way in the OT to describe the primeval sea (Gn 1:2) or the ocean depths (Pss 33:7; 77:16). In Near Eastern cultures the term was used to signify the inverse of the great vault of heaven; hence it came to be used metaphorically for the grave, synonymous with Sheol (Ps 71:20). In intertestamental times, it came to be used for the abode of evil spirits (Jub 5:6; 1 Enoch 10:4,11).

In the NT, the term is used in both of those metaphorical ways. The demons pleaded not to be flung into "the abyss" (Lk 8:31), which many connect with later references to a "prison" (2 Pt 2:4; Jude 6). The exact meaning of such a prison is difficult to define; recent studies of passages like the above and of 1 Peter 3:19 and 4:6 conclude that the abyss is probably not meant to be synonymous with Hades. More likely it refers to the confinement of evil spirits to their particular sphere of existence. Romans 10:7, on the other hand, uses the term for the grave, contrasting descent into it with ascension into heaven. Paul there freely adapted Deuteronomy 30:12,13, which contrasts "up to heaven" with "beyond the sea."

The major use of the term comes in the Apocalypse (the NT Book of Revelation). There the "bottomless pit" is the abode of scorpion-like locusts (Rv 9:1–11), of the prince of the underworld, named "Abaddon" or "destruction" (9:11), and of the "Beast" or antichrist (11:7; 17:8). It is also the place where Satan is confined for a thousand years (20:1,3).

Several characteristics should be noted in a study of the "bottomless pit" concept in Revelation. First, it is under the absolute control of God. The angel "was given the key of the shaft of the bottomless pit" to unlock it (9:1); the Beast "is to ascend from the bottomless pit and go to perdition" (17:8); Satan is seized, bound, thrown, and shut and locked in it (20:2,3). Second, from the beginning it is meant for eternal destruction. After it is opened, "from the shaft rose smoke like the smoke of a great furnace" (9:2). Although the bottomless pit is not the place of torment (i.e., "the lake of fire" in 20:10–15), it will be replaced by eternal punishment after the End (cf. 17:8). Finally, it is the reverse image of heaven, and from it wickedness gushes forth. This is in keeping with the metaphor and the picture throughout Revelation in which the Dragon (12:9) and the Beast attempt to duplicate the power and glory reserved for God alone. Just as heaven is the source of all that is worthwhile, the bottomless pit is the source of all that is evil.

See REVELATION, BOOK OF.

Bow, Bowman. *See* ARMS AND WARFARE; TRADES AND OCCUPATIONS (ARCHER).

Bowels, Disease of. Term used 37 times in Scripture (KJV) but only once in connection with a disease (2 Chr 21:15,18,19). The evil king, Jehoram, is punished with an incurable chronic disease of the bowels, which results in his painful death two years later. The disease caused prolapse of the intestines (v 19). Either an inflammatory bowel disease or cancer of the colon or rectum could have accounted for these symptoms.

The only fatal bowel disease recorded in the NT also occurred in a king (Acts 12:21–23). Of this final disease of Herod, Josephus the historian records that the king, aged 54, suffered with severe pains in the abdomen, which lasted until he died five days later. An acute intestinal obstruction, possibly due to roundworm infestation, could account for these symptoms. Roundworms may have been expelled during the illness, or maggots could have been seen on necrotic skin resulting in the observation by Luke that Herod was "eaten of worms and died."

See DISEASE; MEDICINE AND MEDICAL PRACTICE.

Bowl. *See* POTTERY.

Box Tree. KJV translation of a tree of uncertain identity in Isaiah 41:19 and 60:13, called "pine" in the RSV.

See PLANTS.

Bozez. One of a pair of distinctive rocks (Seneh was the other) flanking the road between Michmash and Geba. Jonathan and his armor bearer scaled one of these crags to take on a Philistine outpost (1 Sm 14:4). The two rocks are still visible in the modern Wadi Suweinet.

See SENEH.

Bozkath. Town near Lachish and Eglon in Judah's territory (Jos 15:39), home of King Josiah's mother (2 Kgs 22:1, KJV Boscath).

Bozrah. 1. Well-fortified city in northern Edom (Gn 36:33; 1 Chr 1:44) regarded as impossible to conquer because it was protected by cliffs on three sides. Located 30 miles north of Petra, at modern Buseirah, it controlled the traffic on the King's Highway. Bozrah was mentioned as one of the strongholds that would fall when God judged Edom (Is 34:6; 63:1; Jer 49:13; Am 1:12).

2. One of the cities cited by the prophet Jeremiah as collapsing with the Moabite nation (Jer 48:24); probably a variant spelling of Bezer.

See BEZER (PLACE).

3. City also called Bosorah captured by Judas Maccabeus in the course of his Gilead campaign (1 Mc 5:26,28). It is perhaps the same place as #2 above.

Bracelet. Ornamental band or chain worn on the wrist or arm in the ancient world.

See FASHION AND DRESS.

Bramble. Translation of several words designating a shrub with prickly stems and runners, often forming tangled masses of vegetation.

See PLANTS.

Branch. Literally, a shoot or sprout from a tree or bush; figuratively, a messianic or other spiritual metaphor. It is used for the three sets of arms off the main shaft of the golden lampstand in the tabernacle (e.g., Ex 25:31–36) and for the palm fronds from which booths were constructed for the ancient Jewish Feast of Tabernacles (Lv 23:40–43).

Metaphorically, the expression is found in passages where Israel is described as an olive tree (Hos 14:6), a cedar (Ez 17:23), and a vine (v 6; cf. Ps 80:8–11). "Branch," with its implication of new growth, can signify prosperity (Gn 49:22; Jb 8:16; Ps 80:8–11; Ez 36:8). Branches can be cut or broken off; hence the word may depict judgment (Jb 18:16; Is 9:14; Jer 11:16). Such passages speak of withering, being cut, or being burned; all three ideas Jesus combined into one metaphor (Jn 15:6). In a similar way, the apostle Paul wrote that "those branches, the Jews, were broken off because they didn't believe God" (Rom 11:19–21 LB).

The major use of such symbolism refers to the Davidic Messiah. Although that use of "branch" actually stems from the prophetic period, its roots go much farther back. The concept was used with reference to an influential figure, such as a king's personal servant (Gn 40:9–13), the patriarch Joseph (49:22), Job (Jb 29:19), or the Assyrian king Nebuchadnezzar (Dn 4:12). Passages such as 2 Samuel 23:4 and Psalm 132:17 speak of the Davidic line as "growing" or "sprouting forth" (the literal meaning of the Hebrew verbs there). Finally, images of agricultural prosperity were used of promised blessings of the messianic age (cf. Lv 26 with the prophetic passages below). Thus it is understandable how the term "branch" could become a technical designation for the Messiah, as illustrated in the following key passages:

1. Isaiah 4:2 is the first occurrence of "branch" as a title: "In that day the branch of the Lord shall be beautiful and glorious, and the fruit of the land shall be the pride and glory of the survivors of Israel." The majority of scholars interpret "branch" here to mean the Messiah for several reasons: (a) The whole tenor of the chapter makes it likely that it refers to the Messiah who provides the harvest

(v 2b), establishes holiness (v 3), and as the instrument of the Lord executes judgment (v 4) and creates "glory" in the land (vv 5,6). (b) Isaiah 28:5 describes the Lord in similar terms, making a messianic interpretation of Isaiah 4:2 more probable. (c) Jeremiah 23:5 and 33:15, which seem to be commentaries on Isaiah 4:2, interpret it to refer to the Messiah. Mention of a righteous remnant illustrates a concept developing along with the "branch" imagery and amplifying its meaning. The branch will become the "beauty and glory" of the remnant of Israel and will wreak destruction on apostate Israel (Is 4:4).

2. Isaiah 11:1 adds a Davidic element to Isaiah 4:2, since Jesse was David's father. The "shoot" grew out of the "stump of Jesse," that is, the "royal line of David." The Davidic line is pictured as a fallen dynasty, a tree cut down (the passage probably mentions Jesse rather than David to stress a lowly origin); the stump remains, however, and there is still life within it. That stump is insignificant in contrast to the mighty forest of Assyria, but the Lord will level that forest (Is 10:15–19,33,34) and bring forth from Jesse's stump a "fruitful" shoot who will recover the Israelite remnant (Is 11:4,11,12), destroy their adversaries (vv 13–16), and reign in wisdom through the "Spirit of the Lord" (v 2).

3. Jeremiah 23:5 and 33:15 contrast the righteous reign of the Branch to the evil leadership of King Zedekiah. In both passages a remnant is pictured under the metaphor of a flock gathered "back to their fold" under caring shepherds (Jer 23:3,4; cf. 33:12,13). The shepherds are ruled by the Branch, who is given the title "The Lord is our Righteousness" (v 6; 33:16). That phrase in Hebrew is a deliberate wordplay on the name "Zedekiah" (meaning "the Lord is my vindication"). Zedekiah was righteous in name but not in his reign. The Branch of the Lord, in contrast, will rule justly.

4. Zechariah 3:8 and 6:12 apply the Branch metaphor in a different context, the postexilic task of rebuilding the temple. Zechariah described Joshua the high priest as a symbol of the future "servant-Branch" to be sent from the Lord. The Branch is seen as performing a priestly function in restoring righteous worship to the land. The royal line would be reinstated and the glories of the priestly line would also be reconstituted in the Branch. The servant of the Branch is probably taken from Isaiah's servant songs, where similar language is used (Is 53:2). Zechariah specifically related the priestly activity to rebuilding the temple. Zerubbabel had earlier been given the task of completing the literal building (Zec 4:7–9), so the allusion must go beyond that to the "spiritual temple" to come. (Since Zerub-

babel's name means "shoot of Babylon," the connection seems deliberate). Finally, Zechariah combines the two messianic aspects of the Branch: "He will rule both as King and Priest, with perfect harmony between the two!" (Zec 6:13 LB).

"Branch" is never used as a title in the NT. Yet there are hints of that concept's influence, as in the familiar "vine and branches" metaphor (Jn 15:1–8), in the use of palm branches at Jesus' triumphal entry into Jerusalem (12:13; cf. Mk 11:8 and parallels), and possibly in the origin of the titles "Righteous One" (Acts 3:14; 7:52; cf. Jas 5:6) and "Just One" (Acts 22:14). Some have also taken an enigmatic reference to Christ, "He shall be called a Nazarene" as an allusion to the "branch" because in Isaiah 11:1 and other references *netzer* is similar to "Nazarene."

GRANT R. OSBORNE

See MESSIAH.

Brass. *See* MINERALS, METALS, AND PRECIOUS STONES.

Brazen Serpent. *See* BRONZE SERPENT.

Bread. Food made from the dough of flour or meal from grain.

Products Used in Making Bread. The Bible tells us that wheat, barley, rye, beans, lentils, millet, and manna were used in making bread.

Wheat. Wheat is mentioned frequently in Scripture (about 48 uses of four Hebrew words in the OT; 14 uses of one Greek word in the NT). The hard winter grain (*Triticum aestivuum*) remains the most popular with farmers of Palestine, who still sow in the fall and reap in the following summer.

Barley. Barley matures faster and produces more prolifically than wheat. The hail plague in Egypt destroyed the barley crop because it had ripened; at the same time wheat and rye had not matured (Ex 9:31,32). Barley is mentioned 32 times in the OT. Barley produced a crop even in time of famine (Ru 1:22; 2:17,23; 3:2,15,17) and sold cheaper than wheat (2 Kgs 7:1,16). Poorer people depended on barley. The boy who contributed his lunch to Jesus to feed 5,000 had barley bread (Jn 6:9,13). Palestinians fed barley to cattle (1 Kgs 4:28). Barley on the stalk carries a larger husk with a long wiry hair (thus the name in Hebrew means "long hair") making chaff separation more difficult. The greater likelihood of extraneous matter in the flour combined with the less-liked flavor made barley cheaper.

Rye. Rye translates a Hebrew word appearing in various versions as "vetch," "fitches," or "spelt" (Ex 9:32; Is 28:25; Ez 4:9). A hardy grass, it produces a crop even on poor soil. Rye bread gained popularity in northern Europe and to some degree in Egypt (Herodotus 2:36; Ex 9:32). Isaiah 28:24–28 summarizes the farmers' work in growing and threshing various seed crops. Jews occasionally made bread from rye (Ez 4:9), but normally used it for cattle feed.

Other Seeds. Beans, lentils, and millet were ground and mixed to make a bread, along with wheat, barley, and spelt (Ez 4:9). The prophet ate this concoction as a sign of the "defiled bread" the Jews would eat in captivity among the Gentiles.

Manna. Numbers 11:8 tells us that the people ground the manna in mills or beat it in a mortar and baked it in pans and made loaves of bread. However, in its prime state God called it bread (see Ex 16:4,8,12,15,22,29,32). It appeared as coriander seed (v 31; Nm 11:7); therefore dull white grains smaller than wheat. The Hebrews complained they had no bread, and their souls hated "this light bread" (Nm 21:5 KJV). The psalmist called it "the bread of the angels" (78:25).

Equipment Used. Bas-reliefs in Egyptian mastaba tombs illustrate most of the equipment used in ancient Near Eastern bakeries.

Sieve. A wicker strainerlike device helped separate small impurities from the grain.

Grindstones. A pair of stones were shaped so that a top stone turned against the bottom stone crushed grain into flour.

Jars. Clay jars contained olive oil, water, and liquid leaven to be mixed with the flour to make dough (Lv 2:4; 1 Kgs 17:12–16).

Bowls. Kneading bowls (Ex 8:3; 12:34; Dt 28:5,17), boards, or tables made of wood provided space for a thorough mixing of ingredients.

Pans. The poor used heated flat stones or the inside walls of their ovens as baking pans. Most people used iron griddles, plates, or pans (Lv 2:5; 6:21; 7:9; Nm 11:8; 1 Chr 9:31; 23:29; 2 Chr 35:13; Ez 4:3). These were often flat, with handles up to five feet long. The dough placed on the griddle was ready for the heat.

Ovens. Sometimes ovens had a chamber separated from the fire, but usually not. A fire of wood, dried grass (Mt 6:30; Lk 12:28), or dung (Ez 4:12,15) heated the oven (Lv 2:4; 7:9; 11:35; 26:26; Hos 7:4,6,7). While the coals and oven walls retained their heat, the plate carrying bread was inserted. Flat, hard unleavened cakes, or small leavened cakes (Mt 14:17; Mk 6:38; Lk 9:13) were done in a few minutes. Large loaves about one foot in diameter would swell to more than three inches thick, would weigh more than two pounds, and required about 45 minutes for baking (1 Sm 17:17; 2 Sm 16:1).

Eating Bread. A large proportion of the time and energy of mankind since the fall until the industrial revolution has been occupied in the production of bread. The time consumed preparing and eating bread may be illustrated by the frequent use of *lehem* (bread) in the OT: 83 times in the Pentateuch, 94 times in historical books, 118 times in poetry and prophetical books; in the NT *artos* (bread) occurs 83 times in the Gospels; 15 times in Acts through Revelation. The Hebrew verb *lāḥam* means either "to fight" or "to eat bread." Could this reflect that warfare often consisted of strife over food?

The thin, unleavened bread substituted for forks or spoons. Cupping the bread, eaters dipped into stew or cheese dishes, as Jesus and the disciples did on the eve of the crucifix-

Bakery (oven and millstones) at Pompeii.

ion (Mt 26:23; Mk 14:20). Acts 20:7,11 probably speaks of thicker loaves being broken and distributed. That bread should be known as "the staff of life" probably derives from Leviticus 26:26, and from the fact that the dried hard bread was one of the few staples that carried people through from one growing season to the next.

Figurative Uses. Genesis 49:20 says that Asher's "food shall be rich. . . ." Bread rarely has such a designation. Since Jacob speaks prophetically, he may be referring to Asher's spiritual food. Or, he may be predicting excellent wheat crops.

Judges 7:13 tells of Gideon's visit to the camp of Midian where he overheard a soldier telling his companion a dream of a barley biscuit destroying a tent. By this, God pictured Gideon and his 300 men as a loaf of barley bread.

In Matthew 16:6 (cf. Mk 8:15; Lk 12:1), the disciples understood Jesus' use of the word *leaven* to be synonymous with bread. Jesus explained his figurative use of leavened bread to mean the hypocrisy of the Pharisees.

In Matthew 7:9 (cf. Lk 11:11–13) Jesus likens bread to God's good gift, the Holy Spirit.

In "the Lord's Prayer" (Mt 6:11), some scholars have understood the Greek word for daily to mean "for the coming age," which provides the basis for the unusual interpretation: "Give us bread that will prepare us for heaven."

In John 6:32–58 Jesus repeatedly refers to himself as the Bread which men must eat to have eternal life.

Many who have studied bedouin life have concluded that eating bread together signifies reconciliation, friendship, or even confirmation of a treaty or covenant (Jos 9:14).

1 Corinthians 10:17 uses the unbroken loaf as a picture of believers in the true church, united in Christ.

Jesus quoted Deuteronomy 8:3 (Mt 4:4; Lk 4:4), which uses bread to picture "everything that proceeds out of the mouth of the Lord."

ROGER DOUGLASS CONGDON

See FOOD AND FOOD PREPARATION; MEALS, SIGNIFICANCE OF; BREAD OF THE PRESENCE; LEAVEN; UNLEAVENED BREAD.

Bread of the Presence.

Loaves of bread placed on a special table in the sanctuary or Holy Place of the tabernacle and later in the temple. Two other terms in the OT are used to describe the "bread of the Presence," which means bread that has been set before the Lord's face (Ex 25:23,30; 35:13; 39:36; 1 Kgs 7:48; 2 Chr 4:19). The term "showbread" (KJV shewbread) refers to the arrangement of the bread in rows on the table (1 Chr 9:32; 23:29;

28:16; 2 Chr 2:4; 13:11; 29:18). The term "continual bread" refers to its perpetual offering (Nm 4:7).

Although the table of showbread, the altar of incense, and the golden lampstand were not in the Holy of Holies, they were nevertheless considered to be in the presence of God. As an offering placed before the presence of God, the loaves were considered holy and could be eaten only by priests. Later in Israel, provision for offering the bread of the Presence as well as other temple services was financed by a tax of one-third shekel upon all citizens (Neh 10:32,33).

The bread of the Presence consisted of 12 very large loaves, each made of $\frac{1}{5}$ ephah of fine flour. Since an ephah was just over a bushel, two and a half bushels of finely ground wheat were required to make the 12 loaves. They were sprinkled with frankincense, arranged in two rows, the one leaning against the other, and placed on the table of showbread (Lv 24:5–9). Arranged in that way the bread became an "offering of food" to the Lord. The loaves were changed weekly on the sabbath day.

The bread of the Presence is featured in one incident recalled in the NT. The tabernacle was at Nob when David was fleeing from the presence of King Saul. David went to Ahimelech, the priest, in search of food (1 Sm 21:1–6). Ahimelech had only the showbread which he agreed to share with David's men, provided they had been sexually continent for a period of time before their eating. Jesus later referred to the incident as a parallel to his own ministry of supplying the needs of those who followed him (Mt 12:1–8; Mk 2:25,26; Lk 6:1–5). As God's anointed, David and his men were permitted to eat the holy bread. Likewise Jesus, God's anointed one, provided for the needs of others in spite of the sabbath regulations.

DAVID W. WEAD

See TABERNACLE, TEMPLE.

Breakfast.

First meal of the day, "breaking the fast."

See FAMILY LIFE AND RELATIONS; FOOD AND FOOD PREPARATION.

Breaking of Bread.

Phrase used in the NT in reference to the Lord's Supper.

See LORD'S SUPPER, THE.

Breastpiece, Breastplate.

1. Part of the ceremonial garment of the high priest (Ex 25:7).

See PRIESTS AND LEVITES.

2. Piece of armor worn to protect the chest.

The word is used figuratively in several passages. Isaiah 59:17 says that God put on righteousness as a breastplate as he prepared to take vengeance on his enemies. The apostle Paul exhorted Christians to wear a "breastplate of righteousness" in order to stand against the devil (Eph 6:14) and a "breastplate of faith and love" as they await Christ's return (1 Thes 5:8).

See Arms and Warfare.

Briar, Brier. Prickly or thorny bush, frequently mentioned in the Bible.

See Plants (Bramble; Thistle, Thorn).

Bribe, Bribery. To give a person in authority something valuable in order to influence that person's decision or action. Bribery was prohibited under OT law (Ex 23:8; Dt 16:19) and condemned by the prophets (Is 1:23; Am 5:12; Mi 3:11). Although Samuel denied that he ever took a bribe (1 Sm 12:3), his sons did not maintain the same standard (8:3).

The distinction between bribery and merely giving gifts was not always clear. "A gift in secret averts anger; and a bribe in the bosom, strong wrath" (Prv 21:14). Hence, giving something valuable is seen as a way to prevent unwanted conflict. Giving a gift is described (with neither approval nor condemnation) as a way to get ahead. "A man's gift makes room for him and brings him before great men" (18:16). The LB, on the other hand, interprets that verse to mean bribery: "A bribe does wonders. . . ."

For the most part, bribery is seen in the Bible as despicable. "A wicked man accepts a bribe from the bosom to pervert the ways of justice" (Prv 17:23; see 1 Sm 8:3). Any system that legitimizes bribery gives the rich an unfair advantage in persuading leaders and judges; the poor find it difficult to get a fair hearing. Innocent people who are poor can be condemned; guilty people who are rich can offer a sizable bribe and go free (Ps 15:5*b*; Is 5:23). In extreme cases, bribes are said to have been used to hire killers (Dt 27:25; Ez 22:12).

Brick, Brickkiln. Oblong block of shaped mud or clay that has been dried either by the sun or by burning in a kiln for use in building or paving, and the furnace in which bricks are burned and hardened. Brick was the most extensively used building material in the ancient biblical world, especially common in Babylonia. The Hebrew word for brick is taken from a verb meaning "to be white," referring to the appearance of the clay out of which brick was made.

In Babylonia, stone suitable for building was seldom at hand, so Babylonian architects used it sparingly, usually for lintels, thresholds, and door hinges. Babylonian bricks were made from the mud or clay of marshes and plains, after removing foreign substances such as pebbles. The clay was mixed with chopped straw or grass which, on decaying, released

Egyptian wall painting of brick making.

acids that gave the substance greater mold-ability. The brickmaker added water, kneaded the mixture by foot, and molded it into square bricks, each about 8 to 12 inches across and 3 to 4 inches thick. The bricks were frequently stamped with a wooden block bearing the name of the reigning king (e.g., Sargon). Some peasant houses found near Babylon today have bricks containing King Nebuchadnez-zar's stamp.

Babylonian bricks were commonly burned in brickkilns rather than sun-dried. Sun-dried bricks disintegrated easily in heavy rainfall, whereas bricks burned in a kiln were virtually indestructible. Kiln-burnt bricks were used es-pecially for facings, pavements, and important buildings. Archaeological remains of many brickkilns have been found in Babylonia.

Evidence exists of walls, temples, and store-houses constructed of brick in ancient Egypt, although almost no brickkilns have been found. Egyptian bricks were usually sun-dried rather than burned. Clay bricks were some-times made without straw, but bricks made of mud from the Nile River required straw to keep them from falling apart. Egyptian bricks were rectangular, ranging from about 4 to 20 inches long, about 6 to 9 inches wide, and about 4 to 7 inches thick. Egyptian bricks were also often stamped with an identifying seal.

The Egyptians regarded brickmaking as a lowly occupation to be imposed upon slaves. Thus during their bondage in Egypt the Israel-ites were forced to make bricks (Ex 1:11–14; 5:6–19). Their suffering was increased by deny-ing them the usual supplement of straw from the Pharaoh, since they had to take time to locate their own straw while keeping up the required production quota. The Israelites car-ried the art of brickmaking back to Palestine at the exodus, and Palestinian brickmaking to-day still follows the ancient method imported from Egypt.

See ARCHITECTURE; POTTERY.

Bride, Bridegroom. Terms used for a woman and man about to be married or just married; also used to describe the relation of Christ to his church (Eph 5:25–27).

See BRIDE OF CHRIST; CHURCH; JERUSALEM, NEW; MARRIAGE, MARRIAGE CUSTOMS.

Bridechamber. Room in which the mar-riage ceremonies were held.

See MARRIAGE, MARRIAGE CUSTOMS.

Bride of Christ. One of the NT metaphors for the church. In it Christ is pictured as a husband and the church as his bride.

Addressing the church at Corinth, the apos-tle Paul referred to himself as the one who gave the church to Christ, presenting her "as a pure bride to her one husband" (2 Cor 11:2,3). In ancient Near Eastern culture the father gave his daughter in marriage to the bride-groom, assuring him of her purity. To Paul, understanding himself as the church's spiri-tual father (1 Cor 4:15), the thought of the church as his daughter sprang readily to mind. To be Christ's pure bride requires on the church's part "pure and simple devotion." Like a concerned father, Paul was worried that the young bride (the church) might com-mit adultery by her willingness to accept "an-other Jesus," "another Spirit," or "a different gospel" (2 Cor 11:4). As between marriage part-ners, the relation between the church and Christ is governed by a covenant of mutual faithfulness. Disloyalty shatters the covenant.

The OT furnished Paul a rich background for that image of the church. God's covenant with Israel was commonly pictured as a mar-riage troth, with Israel as God's bride. Through the prophet Jeremiah, the Lord said to Israel: "I remember the devotion of your youth, your love as a bride" (Jer 2:2). He went on to lament the fact that Israel had been faithless; by going after other gods, she had actually prostituted herself and become an adulteress (3:6–9,20).

The theme of Israel's desertion of her lover (God) was explicitly treated in Ezekiel 16 and in Hosea. The terms "harlotry" and "whore-dom" were used to connote disloyalty to Je-hovah and allegiance to other gods. Thus, adultery and idolatry became synonymous. Through his own struggles with a faithless wife, the prophet Hosea experienced God's ag-ony over his bride Israel and his longing for her to return. Hosea was given a vision of a future day in which God would betroth his people to him forever "in steadfast love and faithfulness" (Hos 2:19,20). That vision may have enabled Paul to transfer the image of Israel as God's bride to the church as the bride of Christ.

In Ephesians 5:22–33 the relationship be-tween Christ and his church is compared to the relationship between a husband and wife. The image is taken from the common under-standing of the husband-wife relationship in that part of the world. The church's submis-sion to Christ is compared with the wife's sub-mission to the husband, but the stress of the passage is on the role of the husband: he is to love her "as Christ loved the church and gave himself up for her" (v 25). Christ relates to the whole church on the basis of self-sacrificial love. Just as a husband is joined to his wife, with a mutual interdependence so intimate that they become one, so Christ and his church become one body (vv 28–33). As the man's love for his wife intends her wholeness, so Christ's love of the church intends her completeness (vv 25–27).

A variation on the theme is found in John the Baptist's testimony to Jesus (Jn 3:29). John saw himself as "the Bridegroom's friend" who, according to Jewish custom, takes care of the wedding arrangements. The Messiah is identified with the bridegroom to whom the bride (his messianic community) belongs and who comes to claim that bride. John may have known of a rabbinic tradition assigning the friend's role to Moses in the "marriage" between God and Israel.

In Revelation 19 and 21 the metaphor of the church as the Messiah's bride is further developed. The vision in Revelation 19:7,8 announces the marriage of the Lamb (Christ) to the bride (church) who is clothed in the "fine linen, bright and pure" representing "the righteous deeds of the saints." In Revelation 21 the vision depicts the new Jerusalem coming down from heaven, "prepared as a bride adorned for her husband" (v 2). Then the seer is invited to behold "the Bride, the wife of the Lamb (v 9) and to see the holy city "coming down out of heaven from God" (v 10). The "new Jerusalem" is identified as the people of God, as the bride of Christ, among whom and with whom God will be present forever.

MANFRED T. BRAUCH

See CHURCH; JERUSALEM, NEW.

Brimstone.
Old name for the nonmetallic element sulfur, literally "the stone that burns." Sulfur ignites at a relatively low temperature and burns to produce acrid fumes of sulfur dioxide. Sulfur occurs naturally in volcanic regions such as the valley of the Dead Sea. "Fire and brimstone" are strongly associated in the Bible with divine retribution (Gn 19:24; Dt 29:23; Jb 18:15; Ps 11:6; Ez 38:22; and in KJV, Lk 17:29; Rv 9:17,18; 14:10; 19:20; 20:10; 21:8). The last volcanic eruptions in Palestine, which radiocarbon dating indicates took place about 4,000 years ago, probably left an impression on the inhabitants of the area that was passed on for generations.

See MINERALS, METALS, AND PRECIOUS STONES.

Broad Wall, The.
Section of the outer wall of Jerusalem which Nehemiah rebuilt in the 5th century BC. The Broad Wall was possibly located on the city's northwest side (Neh 3:8; 12:38).

See JERUSALEM.

Bronze.
Durable alloy of copper and tin widely used for ornaments, weapons, coins, and other purposes in ancient times.

See MINERALS, METALS, AND PRECIOUS STONES.

Bronze Sea.
Large tank of water in Solomon's temple yard for the priests' washing (1 Kgs 7:23–44; 2 Kgs 16:17; 25:13; 1 Chr 18:8; 2 Chr 4:2–6,15; Jer 52:17). Cast from bronze and about three inches thick (a handbreadth), it was mounted on 12 bronze oxen (three facing in each compass direction) in the courtyard at the southeast corner of the sanctuary. It was 5 cubits (about 7½ feet) high and 10 cubits (15 feet) in diameter, with a capacity of either 2,000 baths (1 Kgs 7:26) or 3,000 (2 Chr 4:5). The discrepancy possibly comes from a scribal error; the number three could have been dropped out of the Kings passage, the remaining words being understood as 2,000. The bath (originally a vessel large enough to hold a person) was a liquid measure of about six gallons, so the tank held perhaps 18,000 gallons of water.

See TABERNACLE, TEMPLE; LAVER.

Bronze Serpent.
Piece of sculpture that God commanded Moses to make when the Israelites were being bitten by "fiery serpents" (Nm 21:4–9). The serpents had been sent as a judgment because the people were grumbling against God and against Moses. When the people repented, God ordered the replica made; those who looked at it were healed.

Some connect the theological meaning of the scene with an episode in which Moses' rod became a serpent, swallowed up the serpent-rods of the Pharaoh's magicians, and then became a rod again (Ex 7:8–12; cf. 4:2–5,28–30). The serpent was a deified figure in both the Egyptian and Canaanite religions. Therefore, the triumph of God's serpent figure typified the superiority of the Lord over the pagan gods. In Numbers 21, however, such a realization must have been secondary. That event was the last of a number of "apostasies" in the wilderness (cf. 1 Cor 10:9), all of which included four elements: complaints against God, judgment, repentance, and forgiveness or deliverance. The major theological theme is not the Lord's superiority but his provision of salvation. The stress was not on a magical formula for healing but rather on the serpent as a symbol of salvation offered to all who would focus on it.

The bronze serpent appears again in 2 Kings 18:4. In the intervening centuries it had become an idolatrous object, and King Hezekiah (716–686 BC) of the southern kingdom of Judah abolished it in his reform movement. The final reference to it in pre-Christian literature is in the apocryphal book, Wisdom of Solomon, which supports the above interpretation: salvation came not through the serpent but through God's provision. "He who turned toward it was saved, not by what he saw, but by thee, the Savior of all."

Christ borrowed that thrust and said that, like Moses' serpent, he must be lifted up (Jn 3:14). The "lifting up" of the "Son of Man" is a definite reference to Christ's death and has two foci: (1) a "death as salvation" theme, seen in the Mosaic serpent imagery and the divine imperative "must" (in Jn referring to the necessity of God's ordained plan of salvation); and (2) a "death as exaltation" theme, seen in the verb itself (containing the idea of majesty) and in John's stress on the glory of Jesus' earthly ministry and of his resurrected status.

GRANT R. OSBORNE

Brood. Term used primarily for young birds, especially of the domestic fowl.

See BIRDS (FOWL, DOMESTIC; PARTRIDGE).

Brook. *See* WADI.

Brook of Egypt. Natural border between the Negeb desert area of Israel and the Sinai Peninsula, about 50 miles southwest of Gaza. The brook of Egypt, modern Wadi el-Arish (called "river of Egypt" by KJV in all places except Isaiah 27:12, where it is called "stream of Egypt") flows only during the rainy season (Nm 34:5; Jos 15:4,47; 1 Kgs 8:65; 2 Kgs 24:7; 2 Chr 7:8; Is 27:12; Ez 47:19; 48:28). A different Hebrew word, signifying an ever-flowing river, appears in Genesis 15:18, where God spelled out the boundaries of the Promised Land to the patriarch Abraham. That reference may be to the easternmost branch of the Nile (the Pelusiac), which flows into the Mediterranean Sea near modern Port Said, and to the line of ancient fortifications marking Egypt's border.

Brook of the Arabah. Unidentifiable brook presumably draining into Arabah (Am 6:14, KJV river of the wilderness). The Arabah is part of the desert rift extending from the Sea of Galilee to East Africa. A wadi (stream bed) named Arabah is south of the Salt (Dead) Sea, but in the Bible, Arabah ("desert" or "wilderness") designates portions of the Jordan Valley (Dt 4:48,49; Jos 8:14; 2 Kgs 25:4) as well as the Salt Sea (Dt 3:17). In the Wadi Arabah several springs and occasionally rainfed streams drain into the Salt Sea.

See ARABAH.

Broom. Palestinian shrub or bush which often grows quite large, providing shade (1 Kgs 19:4). KJV translates the Hebrew word as "juniper."

See PLANTS.

Brother. Man or boy in his relationship to the other children of his parents; also a close male friend or fellow member of the same race, creed, profession, organization, and the like; a kinsman.

In the OT the Hebrew word translated "brother" describes the relationship between male children who have at least one parent in common. Joseph and Benjamin were children of Jacob and Rachel (Gn 35:24), but the other sons born to Jacob are also called Joseph's brothers (42:6). The love Joseph had for Benjamin is not always found between brothers. Cain killed his brother Abel (4:8), and Esau hated his brother Jacob (27:41). A brother may be a bad influence (Dt 13:6,7), but ideally he is one who helps in times of need (Prv 17:17). The law of levirate marriage required that if a man died leaving a childless widow, the man's brother had to raise up children through her to perpetuate the family name (Dt 25:5).

David spoke affectionately of his "brother" Jonathan, although they were not related (2 Sm 1:26). A fellow Israelite could be called brother; and the relationship required certain obligations: money could not be loaned to a brother at interest, and a brother could not be enslaved (Lv 25:35–43).

In the NT the Greek word is used to describe natural brothers, such as Andrew and Peter (Jn 1:41). Four brothers of Jesus are named (Mk 6:3). (The Roman Catholic view is that they were really Jesus' cousins, but the Greek language has several words for cousin, and the word "brother" is used here; thus, it refers either to children or foster children of Mary and Joseph.) Jesus' brothers did not believe in him at first (Jn 7:5), but after the resurrection they were meeting with the Christian community (Acts 1:14). Jesus taught that his disciples had one Father (God) and were therefore brothers (Mt 23:8,9), and he graciously identified himself with the disciples as their brother (28:10).

Early in the history of the church it became customary for Christians to address one another as brother (Acts 9:17; Col 1:1); on two occasions the Christian community is called "the brotherhood" (1 Pt 2:17; 5:9, KJV brethren). Specific duties and responsibilities accompany Christian brotherhood. A Christian's love for his brother will be demonstrated in the restraint of sexual passions (1 Thes 4:6), provision of material goods when needed (Jas 2:15,16), and determination not to offend (Rom 14:13). A Christian must not go to law against a brother (1 Cor 6:5,6), but brothers must resolve their problems either personally or within the church group (Mt 18:15–17). The relationship between Christians is significant because a Christian cannot offer worship to

God if he is out of harmony with his brother (Mt 5:23,24).

E. MARGARET HOWE

See FAMILY LIFE AND RELATIONS; CHRISTIANS, NAMES FOR.

Brothers of Jesus. James, Joses (or Joseph), Simon, and Judas, identified in the NT as members of Jesus' own family (Mt 13:55; Mk 6:3). They are described as visiting Jesus with Mary, his mother (Mt 12:47–50; Mk 3:31–35; Lk 8:19–21), and hearing Jesus' statement that all who did the will of God were brother, sister, and mother to him.

They were well enough known in Nazareth that when Jesus returned to preach there, the people said, "Is not this the carpenter, the son of Mary and brother of James and Joses and Judas and Simon, and are not his sisters here with us?" (Mk 6:3). In Matthew's Gospel the order of the names of the last two brothers is reversed (Mt 13:55). When Jesus and his disciples went to Capernaum, they were accompanied by Mary and his brothers (Jn 2:12). Just before the Feast of Tabernacles the brothers visited Jesus to persuade him to go to Jerusalem for the festival. Although they were skeptical about his miracles they said he should go perform his feats in public to gain recognition: "If you do these things, show yourself to the world" (Jn 7:4). Jesus acknowledged opposition from within his family when he said, "A prophet is not without honor except in his own country and in his own house" (Mt 13:57; Mk 6:4). His brothers or other friends from home thought him to be losing touch with reality when crowds were first attracted to him (Mk 3:21).

In spite of their earlier skepticism, however, the brothers became active members of the Jerusalem church during its earliest days. They are mentioned as being frequently at prayer in an upper room with Mary, showing a sharp reversal from their earlier lack of faith (Acts 1:14). One of the resurrection appearances was made to James (1 Cor 15:7). On Paul's return to Jerusalem after his conversion, he met Peter and James, "the Lord's brother," but not the other apostles (Gal 1:19). When the apostle Peter was released from prison he went to the home of Mary the mother of John Mark, and despite the excitement of the occasion he immediately asked the group to "tell this to James and to the brethren" (Acts 12:17). A number of references in Acts show James as a strong, respected leader of the Jerusalem church (Acts 15:13–21; 21:18). In the council at Jerusalem he expressed a strong opinion on the acceptance of Gentiles into the church; he was later visited by Paul, who told him about his ministry and the many conversions among the Gentiles. Although James is mentioned more often by name, all the brothers seem to have been well respected at that time. Thus their actions were used as an example by Paul when he argued that it would be appropriate for him also to have a wife accompany him on his journeys, as Jesus' brothers did (1 Cor 9:5).

The author of the Epistle of James is generally assumed to be the Lord's brother, although he does not identify himself specifically that way (1:1). It seems clear, though, that the author wrote as a recognized leader in the church; hence to identify him as the Lord's brother seems logical. The author of the Epistle of Jude identifies himself as the brother of James. The reference would most logically be to James, the leader mentioned in Acts and probably the author of the other epistle. The author thus seems to be the Judas named as the brother of the Lord in the Gospels (Mt 13:55; Mk 6:3).

Throughout the NT the group of the 12 apostles is consistently distinguished from the brothers of the Lord. Luke named the apostles and then said: "All these with one accord devoted themselves to prayer, together with the women and Mary the mother of Jesus, and with his brothers" (Acts 1:13,14). The apostle Paul pointed to the brothers of the Lord as a group separate from the apostles (1 Cor 9:5); each mention of them in the Gospels describes them as family members and distinct from the disciples.

Whether the "brothers of Jesus" were half brothers (children of Mary by Joseph), stepbrothers (children of Joseph by a former marriage), or cousins (children of Mary's sister) is a matter of controversy. The Protestant position maintains that the brothers were actual half brothers of Jesus. The Roman Catholic position asserts that the four were cousins of Jesus. The Greek Orthodox position agrees with the Roman Catholic stance that Mary and Joseph had no other children, but assumes that the brothers and sisters were Joseph's by a former wife.

Protestants contend that not only the four brothers but at least two sisters were the children of Mary and Joseph. The plain sense of several passages is in favor of the usual meaning of the word "brother," since no instance of a wider use of that word for actual kinship appears in the NT. Consistent with that understanding of "brother," wherever brothers and sisters of Jesus are mentioned (except Jn 7 and 1 Cor 9), is their appearance in close connection with Jesus and his mother, evidently one family under Mary's care. That closeness could possibly fit their being Mary's stepchildren, but it makes less likely their being only cousins of Jesus. What is the argument for the "brothers and sister" being cousins, the children of Mary's sister? Who was that sister?

A probable reading of John 19:25 lists four women (not three) in the group at the cross: Jesus' mother, her sister (unnamed), Mary the wife of Clopas (KJV Cleopas), and Mary Magdalene. In describing the events following the crucifixion, Matthew mentions three women: Mary Magdalene, Mary the mother of James and Joseph, and the mother of the sons of Zebedee (Mt 27:56). Mark also names three women: Mary Magdalene, Mary the mother of James the younger and of Joses, and Salome (Mk 15:40). The two Marys correspond, leaving Salome as the mother of the sons of Zebedee. Some scholars feel that an identification of Salome with the unnamed sister of Mary the mother of Jesus is highly probable; the alternative would make Mary the wife of Clopas the sister of Mary, and it is unlikely that two sisters would both have been named Mary. Evidence thus points to Salome as Jesus' aunt, making the apostles John and James his cousins (rather than the four named as his brothers). The Lord's committal of his mother to John's care is understandable if the apostle was Jesus' cousin (Jn 19:26,27).

Further, the use of the expression "her firstborn son" (Lk 2:7) implies that Mary had other children after Jesus was born. Even stronger, from the Protestant point of view, is the natural implication of the words, "but knew her not until she had borne a son; and he called his name Jesus" (Mt 1:25).

The Roman Catholic interpretation of "brothers of Jesus" was originally advanced by Jerome, an early church scholar and linguist, about AD 382. It is based on the assumption that the word "brother" means "cousin." Roman Catholics argue that Galatians 1:19 means that James, "the Lord's brother" was an apostle, hence must have been James, son of Alphaeus. John 19:25 is interpreted to mean that the wife of Clopas was the sister of Mary the mother of Jesus; since Mark 15:40 mentions Mary the mother of James the younger and Joses, the assumption is that Jesus' aunt was Mary, wife of Clopas, and that James the younger was James, the son of Alphaeus. Hence Mary, wife of Clopas, must have been the wife of Alphaeus as well as the sister of Mary the mother of Jesus. Though the assumptions seem weak, Jerome's theory was the generally accepted view of theologians during the Middle Ages.

Roman Catholics have suggested that Mary took a vow of virginity, although it seems unlikely that she would have become engaged to Joseph if she had done so. In fact, taking such a vow would have been contrary to the OT view of marriage, and it is most unlikely that a young Jewish woman of the first century would have done such a thing.

The Greek church tradition is expressed in a letter of AD 336–37. The essential point of the theory is that Mary had no other children than Jesus; the brothers and sisters were Joseph's children by a former wife, and were brought up in the household of Joseph and Mary. As in the Roman Catholic Church's view, the marriage of Joseph and Mary is assumed to have been a marriage in name only. It is argued that Mary was only betrothed to Joseph, not married, and that Joseph, a just man who was himself a pattern of virginity, could never have regarded the chosen vessel of the Holy Ghost as his wife. The idea of the exaltation of virginity above marriage may have developed from misunderstood statements in the NT. The idea spread both among heretics and orthodox Christians. By the end of the 3rd century, celibate communities began to appear, and marriage among the clergy was discouraged.

Finally, it is possible that the phrase "brothers of Jesus" may have been used at times to refer simply to "believers in Christ" and hence "sons of God" (cf. Mt 23:8). In the NT passages discussed above, however, it seems most probable that the four brothers of Jesus referred to were, in fact, his half-brothers, the children of Mary and Joseph.

See JAMES (PERSON); JOSEPH #6; JUDE, THE LORD'S BROTHER; MARY #1.

Bubastis. In the Septuagint (Greek OT), the name of Pibeseth, a city on the Nile. The Greek name derives from the cat god Ubastet.

See PIBESETH.

Buckler. Small, usually round shield carried in the hand or worn on the arm in battle.

See ARMS AND WARFARE.

Build, Building. Construction, usually with wood, masonry, and similar materials. The Bible has many references to the building or rebuilding of altars, temples, houses, and whole cities. The term is sometimes used as a metaphor for God's activity among his people (1 Pt 2:4–8).

See ARCHITECTURE; INDUSTRY AND COMMERCE.

Bukki. 1. Leader of Dan's tribe who assisted Joshua in dividing up the land of Canaan (Nm 34:22).

2. Ezra's ancestor (1 Chr 6:5,51; Ezr 7:1,4,5).

Bukkiah. Heman's eldest son, who served with his father and 13 brothers as a temple musician (1 Chr 25:4,13).

Bul. Eighth month of the preexilic Canaanite calendar. In this month King Solomon's temple was completed (1 Kgs 6:38).

See CALENDARS, ANCIENT AND MODERN.

Bull, Bullock. Male, adult and young, of any bovine animal, such as oxen, cattle.

See ANIMALS (CATTLE).

Bulrush. Any of a number of reed plants that grow in marshes and beside streams and rivers.

See PLANTS (REED).

Bunah. Jerahmeel's son from Judah's tribe (1 Chr 2:25).

Bunni. 1. Levite who sang praise to God after Ezra's public reading of the Law (Neh 9:4).

2. Political leader who signed Ezra's covenant of faithfulness to God with Nehemiah and others after the exile (Neh 10:15).

3. Hashabiah's father (Neh 11:15), a Levite descended from Merari (1 Chr 9:14), possibly the same as #1 above.

Burial, Burial Customs. The Bible makes frequent reference to burial practices. A society's burial customs are a reflection of its spiritual views about death and the afterlife. The ancient Egyptians, for example, thought of life after death as a continuation of physical activities in another realm, as their elaborately furnished tombs indicate. The ancient Hebrews emphasized a more spiritual concept of union or fellowship of the departed with generations gone on before.

Graves and Tombs. Among the Hebrews, location of burial plots was generally determined on a family basis. The OT contains many references to an Israelite's desire to be buried in the family burying-place, describing his death as "going to be with his fathers" (Gn 15:15; 1 Kgs 13:22).

The cave of Machpelah at Hebron was one example of family "cohabitation" of a tomb for a succession of generations. Abraham purchased the site from Ephron the Hittite at the time of Sarah's death (Gn 23). When Abraham died, Isaac and Ishmael laid his body in the same tomb (Gn 25:9), and there Jacob in turn buried his parents, Isaac and Rebekah, as well as Jacob's wife Leah (49:31). At his death Jacob's body was carried from Egypt to be "added to his fathers," in accord with his own request (v 29; 50:13). Jacob's son Joseph made

his kinsmen promise that his remains would be preserved so they could be carried back to the homeland when God enabled his people to return from Egypt (50:25).

Individual burial sites such as that of Deborah near Bethel (Gn 35:8) and of Rachel on the road to Ephrath (vv 19,20), were an exception necessitated by sudden death at some distance from the family tomb.

Samuel is spoken of as being buried "in his house" at Ramah, evidently referring to a family graveyard plot (1 Sm 25:1). Joab was buried "in his own house in the wilderness" (1 Kgs 2:34). King Manasseh was buried in the garden of his palace (2 Kgs 21:18) and Joshua "in his own inheritance at Timnath-serah" (Jos 24:30). Kings were careful to perpetuate their memory by special burial sites, often in the City of David (that part of Jerusalem on the southeastern ridge first occupied by that great king). King Josiah designated his burial place in advance, most likely an ancestral tomb (2 Kgs 23:30).

Bodies were buried in tombs, that is, natural caves or rock-hewn sepulchers, such as that belonging to Joseph of Arimathea where the body of Jesus was laid (Mt 27:59,60), as well as in shallow graves covered with rock heaps serving both to mark them and to prevent desecration of the body by animals.

Some graves were marked by a monument erected in love (Gn 35:20) and honor (2 Kgs 23:17), but stones were sometimes heaped on a dishonorable burial place, as for Achan (Jos 7:26) and Absalom (2 Sm 18:17). Tombs often adorned or embellished, sometimes whitewashed, in part to warn against ceremonial contamination prohibited by Mosaic law. Jesus spoke of such embellishment in a rebuke of the Pharisees (Mt 23:27).

Funerals and Mourning. The interval between death and interment was very brief in Bible times, as it still is today throughout the Middle East. The account in Genesis 23 of Abraham's urgent bargaining for the field containing the cave of Machpelah is explained by that fact. Social custom (based on the biological reality of a corpse's rapid decomposition in a warm climate; see Jn 11:39) dictated rapid burial.

Immediately following a death in a home the entire neighborhood was alerted to the sad event by the wail that was suddenly raised. Wailing at the moment of death and the lamentation around the corpse during the brief period until its burial are both referred to (Ex 12:30; Mt 2:17,18; Mk 5:38; Acts 9:39).

At the first news of a death, the reaction was dramatic and demonstrative—the tearing of one's clothes (Gn 37:34; 2 Sm 1:11,12; 13:31; Jb 1:20). The Genesis reference also mentions

A corniced tomb with Nabataean inscription at Petra.

the wearing of sackcloth, a coarse material usually worn right next to the skin. A reference to walking naked and barefoot in sorrow probably refers to that crude partial garment rather than to total absence of covering (Mi 1:8); removal of shoes or sandals was another typical action of mourning (2 Sm 15:30). Headbands or other headdress was removed and hair allowed to fall loose (cf. Ez 24:17,23, where the prophet was forbidden to follow custom), but the face might be veiled or the entire head draped with a veil.

The action of putting hands on the head was a common sign of mourning (2 Sm 13:19; Jer 2:37). The first verse speaks of putting ashes on the head as well. Covering the face with hands or forearms is shown as a common pose of weeping women on Egyptian bas-reliefs and on the Ahiram sarcophagus at Byblos. The mourner might go to the extreme of rolling his head or entire body in the dust (Mi 1:10) or of lying or sitting in a heap of ashes (Est 4:3; Is 58:5; Jer 6:26; Ez 27:30). At the very least, mourners refrained from washing and from use of perfumes (2 Sm 12:20; 14:2).

Special types of food were eaten, probably prepared for the immediate family by friends or by other relatives. Such a meal was one of

387

the formalities Ezekiel was ordered to forego when his wife died (Ez 24:17). A neighborly token of wine brought in to the family was a "cup of consolation" (Jer 16:7). Food prepared in the home of the deceased would be regarded as ceremonially unclean (Nm 19:14,15; cf. Hos 9:4).

With the burial taking place so quickly, a period of shared mourning quite naturally continued afterward for a period of three days, a week, or even longer. Friends and relatives visited the immediate family of the deceased during that time, as was the situation when Jesus arrived at Bethany on the fourth day after the death of Lazarus. By then visits to the tomb for weeping at stated intervals had become a formality (Jn 11:31).

Both OT and NT mention the employment of professional mourners and the composition and singing of dirge-songs (2 Sm 1:17,18). The prophet Jeremiah described the funeral customs of his time in a metaphor of sadness over Jerusalem's fall. "Consider, and call for the mourning women to come; send for the skilful women to come; let them make haste and raise a wailing over us, that our eyes may run down with tears, and our eyelids gush with water" (Jer 9:17,18). The narrative of Matthew's Gospel describes the scene at the home where Christ healed the daughter of the synagogue ruler. "When Jesus came to the ruler's house, and saw the flute players, and the crowd making a tumult, he said, 'Depart; for the girl is not dead but sleeping'" (Mt 9:23,24; Mk 5:38,39).

A rather detailed description of a biblical burial is in the account of the death of King Asa of Judah. "And Asa slept with his fathers, dying in the forty-first year of his reign. They buried him in the tomb which he had hewn out for himself in the city of David. They laid him on a bier which had been filled with various kinds of spices prepared by the perfumer's art; and they made a very great fire in his honor" (2 Chr 16:13,14).

Treatment of the Corpse. The assurance given by God to Jacob that "Joseph's hand shall close your eyes" (Gn 46:4) probably alludes to the custom of a near relative closing the eyes of one who died with a fixed stare. Close relatives might also literally embrace and kiss the body immediately upon expiration. The body was washed and dressed in the deceased one's clothing. Pins and other ornaments found in excavated tombs are evidence that the dead were buried fully clothed. Soldiers were buried in full regalia, with shields covering or cradling the armored bodies, their swords under their heads (Ez 32:27).

Embalming was not a usual practice in Israel, Egyptian treatment for Jacob and Joseph being the exception rather than the rule.

According to Herodotus, the Egyptians commenced embalming procedures by removing the brain from the cranium through the nasal apertures piecemeal, using a long curved hook. When this had been done, the cranial cavity was rinsed out with a mixture of resins and spices. The corpse was eviscerated, and the entrails were placed in four canopic jars. The body was soaked in a solution of natron for a period of from 40 to 80 days, depending on the cost of the burial. At the time of interment, the corpse was wrapped in strips of fine linen cloth from head to foot and put in an anthropoid coffin. The canopic jars were placed in the tomb along with the body, symbolizing the reuniting of the personality and its survival after death.

Cremation of the bodies of Saul and his sons (1 Sm 31:12,13) was also an exception to normal practice. The Roman historian Tacitus wrote that in contrast with Roman custom Jewish piety required the burying rather than burning of dead bodies. Under Mosaic law such burning was reserved as a sentence of judgment (Lv 21:9; Jos 7:25).

After preparation of the body it was carried on a bier (a simple frame with carrying poles) without being placed in a coffin. The body was laid either in a prepared niche in the wall of a rock-hewn chamber or directly in a shallow grave dug in a burial plot. Neither bier nor any form of casket entered the pit with the corpse. The spices used as a perfume and temporary deterrent to decay cannot properly be considered an attempt at embalming (Mk 16:1).

As we know from the Gospel record of Jesus' burial, some cave tombs had a seal at the doorway, either a hinged wooden door or a flat stone shaped so it could be rolled into place. Such a stone seal could be reopened only with extreme effort (Mk 15:46; 16:3,4). By NT times the Jews sometimes economized on the use of a family tomb by placing the dry bones of formerly buried relatives in ossuaries. These boxlike receptacles were probably an adaptation of chests used by the Romans for holding ashes after a cremation.

OT and NT Distinctives. Under Mosaic legislation, ceremonial defilement was contracted either through physical contact with the corpse or by participation in the formalities of mourning. Especially stringent prohibitions applied to the priests of Israel. Only for a very close relative might a priest defile himself. The high priest himself could have nothing at all to do with mourning. In particular, he "shall not let the hair on his head hang loose, nor rend his clothes; he shall not go in to any dead body, nor defile himself, even for his father or for his mother" (Lv 21:10,11).

Egyptian lid of canopic jar representing a princess, made for the burial of Akhenaten.

8:10,11; 2 Kgs 1:12; 2:11; Is 6:1–6; 2 Thes 1:7; Rv 1:14; 19:12).

The burning bush was also symbolic of God's holiness. Moses was commanded not to approach, but to remove his shoes because the place where he was standing was "holy ground" (Ex 3:5). Unlike the gods of Egypt, who were pictured as living in gloomy darkness, Israel's God revealed himself as one who "dwells in unapproachable light" (1 Tm 6:16). The burning bush evidently symbolized his intent not to consume or destroy his people, but be their savior to lead them out of bondage in Egypt and into the Promised Land.

See EXODUS, BOOK OF; MOSES; THEOPHANY; GOD, NAMES OF.

Burnt Offering. Form of Israelite sacrifice in which a choice animal offered to make atonement for sin was completely consumed by fire (Lv 1).

See OFFERINGS AND SACRIFICES.

Bush. See PLANTS.

Bushel. Small vessel that could cover a light (Mt 5:15; Mk 4:21; Lk 11:33).

See WEIGHTS AND MEASURES.

Butler. Translation of a Hebrew word meaning "cupbearer" or "winetaster" in Genesis 40 and 41.

See TRADES AND OCCUPATIONS (CUPBEARER).

Buz (Person). 1. Abraham's nephew, and one of Nahor's eight sons (Gn 22:21).
2. Member of Gad's tribe (1 Chr 5:14).

Buz, Buzite (Place). Place of uncertain location mentioned along with two Arabian villages or oases, Dedan and Tema (Jer 25:23). Elihu, one of Job's protagonists, is described as being the son of Barachel the Buzite (Jb 32:2,6).

Buzi. Father of the prophet Ezekiel (Ez 1:1–3).

Buzzard. Any of a number of birds of prey declared ritually unclean (Dt 14:13).

See BIRDS.

Byblos. Greek name for a Phoenician city north of Sidon.

See GEBAL.

The Israelites were told not to duplicate certain pagan practices associated with mourning for the dead. "You are the sons of the Lord your God; you shall not cut yourselves or make any baldness on your foreheads for the dead" (Dt 14:1).

Although the customs and procedures were evidently modified little from OT to NT times, some added details are given in the NT record. For example, it is noted that the corpse was washed (Acts 9:37). The body was then anointed and wrapped in linen cloths with spices enclosed (Mk 16:1; Jn 19:40). Finally, the limbs were tightly bound and the head covered with a separate piece of cloth (Jn 11:44).

MILTON C. FISHER

See MOURNING; FUNERAL CUSTOMS.

Burning Bush. Flaming bush on Mt Horeb, where Moses experienced God's presence and received the commission to lead the people of Israel out of Egypt (Ex 3:1–15; Mk 12:26; Lk 20:37; Acts 7:30–34). The paradox of a plant burning without being consumed provided the means by which God revealed his covenant name, "I Am Who I Am." The burning bush was a theophany, a visible revelation of God's glory. Association of clouds, fire, and smoke with the manifestation of God's glory is a common biblical theme (see Ex 13:21; 19:18; 1 Kgs

C c

Cab. KJV rendering of kab, a dry measure equaling about one quart, in 2 Kings 6:25.

See WEIGHTS AND MEASURES.

Cabbon. Town in the foothills of Judah (Jos 15:40) east of Lachish, identified with Hebra and sometimes equated with Machbenah (1 Chr 2:49).

Cabul. 1. Asherite town near Mt Carmel on the border between Israel and Tyre (Jos 19:27).

2. Territory given to Hiram king of Tyre by Solomon in exchange for a gift of 120,000 talents of gold for completion of the temple. Hiram, not impressed with this northern Galilean province (1 Kgs 9:13,14), later returned it to Solomon (2 Chr 8:2).

Caesarea. City named in honor of Augustus Caesar, built by Herod the Great from 22 to 10 BC. The 8,000-acre site lies 25 miles south of modern Haifa, in the beautiful plain of Sharon on Israel's Mediterranean coast. Known as Caesarea Maritima, it became the administrative center of the country throughout the period of Roman occupation. Three Roman governors of Palestine lived there: Felix (Acts 24), Festus (Acts 25:1,4,6,13), and Pontius Pilate, who visited Jerusalem on special occasions (as in Jn 19). Archaeologists found Pilate's name carved in stone in the theater at Caesarea.

Caesarea served as the major seaport of Judea in NT times. Since the southern Palestinian coastline lacked a good harbor, Herod created one by building two huge breakwaters that could shelter ships from Mediterranean storms.

A Roman officer named Cornelius was converted to Christianity in Caesarea (Acts 10:1, 24). Later the apostle Peter visited Philip, a prominent Christian leader who lived there (Acts 21:8). Paul spent more than two years in prison in Caesarea (Acts 24:27–25:1) and embarked from there on his journey to Rome (Acts 27). In AD 70 Roman general Titus returned to Caesarea after conquering Jerusalem, as did Flavius Silva in AD 73 after defeating the fortress cities of Masada and Herodium (both in eastern Judea).

Continuous excavations since 1971 have added to the wealth of information about Caesarea. Herod built a high-level aqueduct to

An aqueduct at Caesarea.

bring fresh water from Mt Carmel to Caesarea; the water originated from springs to the northeast and traveled in an underground aqueduct to Mt Carmel. A smaller aqueduct brought brackish water from a spring north of the city for irrigation. Large sewers (mentioned by the Jewish historian Josephus) flushed by the action of the sea have been found running under the city. A 30,000-seat hippodrome (racetrack) lay on the east side of the city. It appears to have been built in the second century AD but was destroyed during the Muslim invasion of 640, along with a large archives building on the coast. Excavation of the archives building produced several inscriptions on its mosaic floors, among which were two quotations of the Greek text of Romans 13:3. Still lying beneath the ground and visible only in infrared photography is a large amphitheater northwest of the hippodrome.

Excavations in 1976 produced the first evidence of Strato's Tower, the Hellenistic site near which Herod built Caesarea, according to Josephus. A small synagogue was excavated north of a large fort built at the Herodian harbor during the Crusades. The harbor area contained many stone storerooms; although 7 have been entered, as many as 73 may still lie unexcavated. One storeroom was reused by the Roman legions as a Mithraeum (a cultic center dedicated to the Persian god Mithras), the only one ever found in Palestine. The city of Caesarea was not rebuilt after its destruction by Muslims in the 13th century.

Caesarea Philippi. City at the northern extremity of Palestine, on the southern slopes of Mt Hermon near the ancient city of Dan. Caesarea Philippi lies in a beautiful area on one of the three sources of the Jordan River, the Wadi Banias.

In the second century BC the place was called Panion because the Greek god Pan was worshiped in a cave there. It is mentioned by Polybius, a Greek historian, as the place where Syrian king Antiochus III defeated the Ptolemies of Egypt in an important battle about 200 BC. The Jewish historian Josephus (*Antiq.* 15.10.3) wrote that "Panium" was governed by Zenodorus; its cultic site was "a very fine cave in a mountain, under which there is a great cavity in the earth, and the cavern is abrupt, and prodigiously deep, and full of a still water; over it hangs a vast mountain, and under the caverns arise the springs of the river Jordan."

After the death of Zenodorus, Augustus Caesar gave the city to Herod the Great, who, according to Josephus, "adorned this place, which was already a very remarkable one" with a "most beautiful temple of the whitest stone." When Herod died in 4 BC, his son Philip was given the territory surrounding Panion, an area known as Paneas. Josephus (*War* 2.9.1) reported that "Philip built the city Caesarea, at the fountains of Jordan, and in the region of Paneas." Philip made it his capital and named it Caesarea Philippi after the Roman emperor Tiberius Caesar and himself, thus distinguishing it from the larger Caesarea Maritima on the Mediterranean coast. Josephus (*War* 3.9.7) wrote that emperors Vespasian and Titus both "marched from that Caesarea which lay by the seaside, and came to that which is named Caesarea Philippi."

It was in Caesarea Philippi that the apostle Peter confessed Jesus to be "the Christ, the Son of the living God" (Mt 16:13–16; Mk 8:27–29).

About AD 50, Agrippa II enlarged Caesarea Philippi and named it Neronias in honor of the emperor Nero. The modern name, Banias,

Caesarea Philippi.

The Caesars

Familiar Name	Full Name	Lifespan	Reign
Julius Caesar	Gaius Julius Caesar	100–44 BC	49–44 BC
Augustus	Gaius Julius Caesar Octavianus	63 BC–AD 14	27 BC–AD 14
Tiberius	Tiberius Claudius Nero Caesar	42 BC–AD 37	AD 14–37
Caligula	Gaius Julius Caesar Germanicus	AD 12–41	AD 37–41
Claudius	Tiberius Claudius Drusus Nero Caesar Augustus Germanicus	10 BC–AD 54	AD 41–54
Nero	Nero Claudius Caesar Drusus Germanicus	AD 37–68	AD 54–68
Galba	Servius Sulpicius Galba	5 BC–AD 69	AD 69–69
Otho	Marcus Salvius Otho	AD 32–69	AD 69
Vitellius	Aulus Vitellius	AD 15–69	AD 69
Vespasian	Titus Flavius Sabinus Vespasianus	AD 9–79	AD 69–79
Titus	Titus Flavius Sabinus Vespasianus	AD 40–81	AD 79–81
Domitian	Titus Flavius Domitianus Augustus	AD 51–96	AD 81–96

derives from the Arabic difficulty in pronouncing Paneas.

Caesars, The. Succession of Roman emperors. The name "Caesar," which has derivatives in the German *Kaiser*, Dutch *Keizer*, and Russian *Czar*, goes back to the family of Julius Caesar (100–44 BC), which his successors took to themselves. Luke's Gospel mentions Caesar Augustus (Lk 2:1) and Tiberius Caesar (Lk 3:1). In the Book of Acts the title "Caesar" is used to refer to Nero (Acts 25:11,12,21; 26:32; 27:24; 28:19). During NT times 12 Caesars reigned, 6 of them actually of the Caesarean lineage.

Emperors of Caesar's Lineage. *Julius Caesar.* Julius had imperial powers but never held the title of emperor. Rome had been a republic (really an aristocracy) for almost 500 years. Its citizens hated the idea of a monarch, a position Julius Caesar judiciously declined, accepting a republican office but ruling as virtual dictator. The republic was dead in practice if not in principle. Vainly hoping to revive it and fearing Caesar's imperial ambitions, a group of republicans conspired to assassinate him. Caesar was murdered on March 15 (the "Ides of March"), 44 BC, as he entered the Roman Senate. Although the conspiracy succeeded, its purpose failed. In the civil war that followed, Caesar's nephew Octavian emerged as victor and in 31 BC became the first Roman emperor.

Augustus (63 BC–AD 14). Gaius Octavianus (Octavian) was the grandson of Julia, Julius Caesar's sister. He was 18 and studying in Greece when his great-uncle was assassinated. Caesar's will, which adopted him as son and made him heir, brought him into the resulting power struggle.

Within a year and a half, a trio consisting of Antony, Lepidus, and Octavian was confirmed in power. The following year, in a battle at Philippi (in Macedonia, now Greece), Octavian defeated both Cassius and Brutus, the chief conspirators against Caesar. Antony took command of the eastern provinces (which included Greece and Egypt), Octavian led his forces back to Italy, and Lepidus assumed jurisdiction over Gaul and western North Africa. Lepidus, however, was forced into retirement, and the area he controlled fell to Octavian. Thus Octavian and Antony, who had clashed even before their alliance, became rivals again. In the battle of Actium (31 BC) Octavian defeated Antony to become sole ruler of the Roman world and its first emperor.

Octavian did not possess the military brilliance of his uncle, but he had a talent for ending strife and maintaining peace, which immediately gained him the support of the people. During his reign Roman culture enjoyed a golden age, particularly in architecture and literature. Augustus founded the Praetorian Guard, the emperor's private honor corps of 9,000 soldiers. Originally intended to secure the emperor's position, it later became so influential that it could independently depose an emperor or elect a new one without Senate confirmation.

The title "Augustus" (*Augoustos*), meaning "exalted one," was given to Octavian in 27 BC. The title reflects the practice of emperor worship that had been partly initiated in the reign of Julius Caesar, who declared himself to be "the unconquered god" and "the father of the fatherland." Augustus continued the cult, although at first he declared that he should be worshiped only in association with the goddess Roma. Later, however, Augustus' name became equated with Rome, and the emperor was regarded as the savior of the world. A temple to Augustus was built in Athens, and even Herod the Great built temples in his honor.

When Augustus became emperor he devoted himself to reorganizing his empire. Because of the chaos that had prevailed in the provinces, he took it upon himself to restructure economic and financial policies.

Though Caesar Augustus is mentioned only once in the NT, he nevertheless is known to

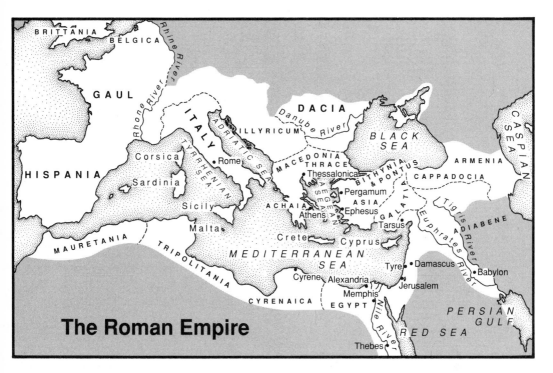

The Roman Empire

every reader of the Bible because of the census he decreed in all the provinces just before the birth of Jesus. Little information is available about that census, but Luke wrote that the first census was held when Jesus was born. The second was conducted in AD 6 and resulted in an uprising instigated by Judas of Galilee (Acts 5:37).

Augustus reigned for 44 years, from 31 BC to AD 14. During that time Herod the Great gained the emperor's trust and was allowed to rule the Jews without Roman interference. In appreciation Herod rebuilt the old city of Samaria and renamed it Sebaste to honor Augustus. Caesarea on the Mediterranean coast of Palestine was also named in his honor.

Conflicts between Herod and his sons were settled by Augustus in 12 BC. When dispute between father and sons arose again, however, Augustus ordered that it be settled in a Roman court, which ruled in 7 BC that two of them, Alexander and Aristobulus, be executed. In 4 BC, Augustus permitted the execution of Herod's son Antipater.

In Herod's last will and testament three of his sons (Archelaus, Antipas, and Philip) were appointed to rule his kingdom. Augustus' approval of those appointments was necessary. Archelaus made a personal visit to Rome immediately after the death of his father to request possible changes in his status. Likewise, Antipas journeyed to Rome to see whether Augustus might be willing to grant him royal status as well. While the two of them sought separate audiences with the emperor, a delegation representing the people of Judea appeared before Augustus with the request that the Herodian rule—which was never very popular—be terminated. At the same time riots in Judea had to be suppressed by Roman legions sent from Syria.

Augustus compromised. He converted Herod's old kingdom to a Roman province and refused kingship to all of Herod's sons. Otherwise he kept to the provisions of Herod's testament: Archelaus became ethnarch (overlord) of Judea, Samaria, and Idumea (half of the new province); Antipas became tetrarch of Galilee and Perea (one quarter of the province); Philip became tetrarch of Iturea and Trachonitis (Lk 3:1; an area east of Galilee—the final quarter of the province). Because Archelaus was unable to rule effectively, he was deposed by the emperor in AD 6 and banished to Vienne in southern France.

Augustus died in AD 14 after a brief illness, leaving the empire to his appointed successor, Tiberius.

Tiberius (42 BC–AD 37). Tiberius Claudius Nero became Octavian's stepson at the age of four, when his mother, Livia, divorced his father to marry the future emperor. Tiberius was made Augustus' co-regent in AD 13 and succeeded him the following year. When he became emperor, he changed his name to Tiberius Caesar Augustus.

Tiberius did not have an easy life. His stepfather had forced an unhappy marriage upon

Palace of the emperor Tiberius at Capri.

him. The Roman Senate often opposed him. In AD 26 Tiberius left Rome for the island of Capri, leaving the task of governing the empire in the hands of Sejanus, a Roman prefect (high-ranking official). During the next five years Sejanus secretly tried to depose the emperor and seize power for himself. His conspiracy almost succeeded, but Tiberius eventually had him executed. Despite this, Tiberius' administration was characterized by wisdom, intelligence, prudence, and duty. He continued his predecessor's policy of striving for peace and security.

In AD 26, presumably before going into semiretirement, Tiberius appointed Pontius Pilate as governor of Judea. Directly responsible to the emperor, Pilate could be immediately removed from office if word of Jewish disturbances or complaints reached Tiberius. Pilate's capitulation to the Jewish authorities during the trial of Jesus can be best understood in view of this. The Jews accused Jesus of claiming to be king, implying a rivalry with the emperor. When Pilate judged Christ innocent of the charge and sought to release him (Jn 18:33–38), the Jews insisted he could not do so and still be a friend of Caesar (Jn 19:12). If he released Jesus, they insinuated, he would risk losing the emperor's favor. Because of crimes committed at his command against the Jews, Pilate knew they might carry out their threat, resulting in his banishment. So, surrendering to their demands, he condemned Jesus to death by crucifixion.

Tiberius Caesar is mentioned only once in the NT. The Gospel of Luke states that John the Baptist began his ministry in the 15th year of Tiberius Caesar's reign, when Pontius Pilate was governor of Judea (Lk 3:1). Whether that date was calculated from Tiberius' actual accession or from the time of his co-regency is difficult to determine.

Tiberius was a strangely humble emperor. At his own request he was never officially recognized as a god (a sort of honorary title which the Senate had given to his predecessors). Interest in emperor worship had waned, and Tiberius intended to confine deity to his two predecessors. He also stopped the practice of naming months of the year after emperors; thus there is a July for Julius, an August for Augustus, but no Tiber for Tiberius. Plagued by domestic and political problems all his life, Tiberius died a tired and dejected old man. In fact, he was an excellent administrator.

Caligula (AD 12–41, reigned 37–41). At the death of Tiberius, Gaius Julius Caesar became emperor at the age of 25. He was the son of an influential general, Germanicus; Augustus had forced Tiberius to adopt Gaius and make him his heir. As a child, Gaius had accompanied Germanicus on his military duties along the Rhine River in Germany. The soldiers nicknamed him Caligula ("Little Boot") for his military attire. The name stuck.

To gain popularity with the Romans Caligula began his reign by pardoning people and recalling exiles. He squandered the money of the Roman treasury, however, and was forced to levy new taxes. His popularity was short-lived.

Six months after assuming office Caligula suffered a serious illness that left him insane. On one occasion, for example, he appointed his horse as consul (chief magistrate). He insulted many people, banished others on whim, and had others murdered without provocation. When he felt that he had been insulted by the Jews in Jamnia, a Judean town near the Mediterranean coast, he ordered a statue of himself placed in the temple at Jerusalem in revenge. The Jews were outraged, and a full-scale revolt was avoided only by the prudence of the governor of Syria, Petronius, who delayed carrying out the order. Not long afterward the emperor was assassinated by one of the many men he had insulted.

It was Caligula who appointed Herod Agrippa I (Herod in Acts 12) king over a tetrarchy northeast of Galilee—one of the first acts he performed as emperor, according to the Jewish historian Josephus. The two had become close friends before either had come to power, while Agrippa was living in Rome, where even as king he later spent much of his time. But unlike Caligula, Agrippa was a capable and popular ruler. Both king and emperor, in the tradition of many eastern monarchs, fancied themselves gods. Caligula, in fact, revived the notion in Rome of the emperor's deity and madly proclaimed himself equal to Jupiter. The Senate, however, refrained from officially recognizing that status.

Claudius (10 BC–AD 54). Tiberius Claudius Germanicus was born in Lyon (France). He was Tiberius' nephew and a grandson of Livia, the wife of Augustus. In AD 37 he was appointed consul by Caligula. After Caligula's death Claudius was proclaimed emperor by the Praetorian Guard, and the Senate approved the choice.

When Claudius became emperor, he faced the task of healing the broken relationships caused by Caligula's madness. He ended the persecution of Jews in the city of Alexandria. Josephus recorded an edict that Claudius sent to Egypt, which read, in part: "Tiberius Claudius Caesar Augustus Germanicus, high priest and tribune of the people, ordains thus. . . . I will, therefore, that the nation of the Jews be not deprived of their rights and privileges on account of the madness of Gaius; but that those rights and privileges which they formerly enjoyed, be preserved to them, and that they may continue in their own customs."

That change of policy reflected the emperor's friendship with Herod Agrippa, who had played an influential role in Claudius' succession as emperor. Claudius, in turn, added Judea and Samaria to Agrippa's kingdom, giving him the dominion that once belonged to his grandfather, Herod the Great. He also promoted him to consular rank. Further, having complete trust in Agrippa's abilities, Claudius removed Judea from Roman provincial rule.

Agrippa's rule, however, was of short duration. In order to please the Jews, he had the apostle James, Zebedee's son, killed. He also had the apostle Peter imprisoned, planning to have him executed after the Passover feast in the spring of AD 44 (Acts 12:1–3). Peter escaped. During the summer of that year Agrippa, who was wearing a glistening garment made of silver thread, gave a speech from his throne. The people acclaimed him as a god (Acts 12:22), and immediately he was struck down by an angel of the Lord. Five days later he died.

The emperor wished to stay on the right side of the Jewish people, yet five years after the death of Agrippa, Claudius issued an edict expelling all Jews from Rome. Luke related that Aquila and Priscilla were among those who had been ordered to leave the imperial city (Acts 18:2). The Roman biographer and historian Suetonius wrote that "because the Jews of Rome were indulging in constant riots at the instigation of Chrestus he [Claudius] expelled them from the city." The writer could easily have been uncertain of the spelling, because Chrestus, a common slave name, was pronounced virtually the same as Christus. It appears that Suetonius sought to convey to his readers that Chrestus was the founder of a movement (Christianity?).

Because of mismanagement by Caligula, the supply of grain for food was at an all-time low when Claudius began to reign (cf. Acts 11:28). Josephus related that during Claudius' administration famine plagued Judea, Samaria, and Galilee. To alleviate the famine in Jerusalem, Helena, mother of the king of Adiabene, bought grain from Egypt and dried figs from Cyprus. That must have taken place in AD 45–46. Various ancient historians, including Tacitus, Suetonius, and Eusebius, reported that on frequent occasions famines prevailed in Rome and elsewhere. Repeatedly, harvests were minimal and distribution of food supplies was poor.

Claudius' family life and reputation were marred by intrigue. His immoral third wife, Messalina, was eventually put to death. Causing a slight scandal, he married his niece Agrippina, who had a son by a former marriage. She wanted her son Nero to be emperor, but Britannicus, Messalina's son, stood first in line. In AD 54, when Claudius decided that Britannicus should succeed him, Agrippina poisoned her husband and made Nero emperor. The Senate officially deified Claudius, making him the third emperor to receive that honor.

Nero (AD 37–68). Nero was born Lucius Domitius Ahenobarbus. His father was a senator and consul who died when Nero was still a boy. His mother, Agrippina, Germanicus' daughter, was reputed to be one of the wealthiest and most beautiful women in Rome. When

Bust of Nero.

she married the emperor, her son received the name Nero Claudius Caesar Germanicus at his adoption by Claudius.

Nero was dominated at first by his proud mother, who wished to reign alongside her son. In those years Rome was a hotbed of political intrigue, murder plots, and assassinations. During the first five years of his reign Nero had Britannicus and Agrippina eliminated in quick succession. A few years later he banished his wife, Octavia, and had her killed.

Ironically, the church at Rome flourished at that same time. The last chapter of the apostle Paul's letter to the Romans, written from Corinth in AD 58, contains a long and impressive list of names of personal acquaintances—impressive because Paul had never been in Rome.

Nero had reigned more than five years when Paul, imprisoned at Caesarea, appealed to Caesar (Acts 25:11). Motives for the appeal may have been a prison release for Paul and an opportunity to seek legal recognition of Christianity.

Paul's appeal to Caesar, however, does not necessarily mean that he was judged by Nero. The emperor had made it known at the beginning of his reign that he would not be a judge. Instead he appointed prefects of the Praetorian Guard to judge cases for him. In the early part of AD 62 Nero changed that rule and judged a case himself. Therefore, whether Paul stood before Nero or before one of the prefects is difficult to determine. If prosecutors failed to appear, Paul's case may not have come before the judge at all. According to Philippians 1:7,12–14, Paul was still expecting a trial at the time of his writing that letter.

In AD 62 Nero's adviser Afranius Burrus died. Burrus had been a prefect of the Praetorian Guard and, together with an able senator, Seneca, had ruled the empire effectively while Nero spent his time on pleasure. After Burrus' death (Seneca was forced to commit suicide three years later), Nero began to indulge his whims unchecked. His greedy advisers, who sought self-advancement at the expense of the state, caused a severe financial crisis. Nero was also unbalanced in regarding himself the savior of the world; his doctrine of salvation was essentially the elimination of the distinction between good and evil.

In AD 64 a fire broke out at the Circus Maximus in Rome. It spread quickly, devouring everything in its path. Fanned by the wind, it raged for more than five days and devastated a large area of the city before being brought under control. At the time Nero was at Antium, his birthplace, some 33 miles to the south. He rushed to Rome to organize relief work. Because of his evil record, however, people put stock in the rumor that Nero had set the fire himself.

Nero, in turn, found a scapegoat in the Christians, whom he charged with the crime. Many were persecuted. Perhaps the apostle Peter in his first letter was referring to the sufferings of Christians during the last few years of Nero's reign (1 Pt 4:12). Nero may have been influenced by his second wife, Poppaea, to blame the Christians for the devastation of Rome. The church had increased in numbers and had become a movement. Tacitus alluded to the size of the church when he wrote that "a huge crowd was convicted not so much of arson as of hatred of the human race."

It is likely that Peter and Paul were executed during the Neronian persecution. Clement of Rome, an early church father, in his letter to the church at Corinth (written presumably in AD 95), referred to the heroes of faith "who lived nearest to our time," namely Peter and Paul, who suffered martyrdom.

In AD 66 a Jewish revolt broke out in Caesarea. Nero dispatched his general Vespasian to squelch the revolt, taking no interest himself in the affairs of state. He left Rome for a journey to Greece, leaving the responsibility of governing the empire to a Roman prefect, Helius. Because of the inescapable opposition he encountered from leading governors in France, Spain, and Africa on his return, Nero committed suicide in AD 68. He was the last emperor of the Caesarean line by blood or marriage.

Later Emperors. *Galba* (d. AD 69). The Praetorian Guard selected Servius Sulpicius Galba to become emperor at Nero's death. Galba was a popular and capable governor at various times in the provinces of France, Germany, Spain, and Africa. He was a less successful emperor and became increasingly unpopular with the army and the people for his frugality and dislike of ceremony. The German legions of the Roman army, who had only reluctantly recognized him as their commander-in-chief, withdrew their support in AD 69, proclaiming Aulus Vitellius emperor.

When Galba failed to appoint one of his chief supporters, Marcus Salvius Otho, as his successor, he in essence signed his own death warrant. Otho gained the support of the Praetorian Guard, was proclaimed emperor, had Galba killed, and was confirmed by the Senate.

Otho (AD 32–69). After being proclaimed emperor by the Praetorian Guard, Marcus Salvius Otho ruled for 95 days before committing suicide when Vitellius' army defeated him in battle.

Vitellius (reigned AD 69). While the Judean revolt raged, Vitellius entered Rome with full military regalia. He secured support only by bribing his army. The eastern armies, however, took an oath of allegiance to Titus Flavius Vespasianus, their commander. Vespasian left his son Titus in command of the armies in Judea, was proclaimed emperor by Tiberius Julius Alexander, a prefect of Egypt, and traveled to Rome. When his advance guard reached Rome, his soldiers captured and killed Vitellius.

Vespasian (reigned AD 69–79). In the fall of AD 69 Vespasian found Rome ready for a period of stability, peace, and order. The son of a tax collector, he lived frugally, reestablished Rome's finances, reorganized the armies, and reemphasized the outward forms of the old republic. According to Suetonius, no innocent party was ever punished while Vespasian was emperor. He grieved when convicted criminals were executed.

Because of Nero's financial mismanagement Vespasian had to levy new taxes and increase existing taxes in order to meet his fiscal obligations. As a result he was slandered as avaricious, although he was generous in aiding underprivileged senators and impoverished ex-consuls. Vespasian improved a number of cities in the empire that had been devastated by fire or earthquake, and he promoted the arts and sciences. In Rome he built the Temple of Peace after the destruction of Jerusalem and the defeat of the Jews, erected a forum, restored the Capitol, and began construction of the Colosseum.

During his 10-year reign Vespasian established peace throughout the empire. His son Titus ended the war in Palestine, and other Roman generals suppressed a revolt in Germany. Public confidence was largely restored with the return to earlier standards of morality. Vespasian appointed his sons Titus and Domitian to succeed him.

Titus (AD 41–81). Titus Flavius Vespasianus had served efficiently as a colonel in Germany and Britain. When the Jewish revolt broke out, he accompanied his father to Palestine. When Vespasian left for Rome five years later, Titus was appointed general of the Roman forces in Palestine. On September 26, AD 70, the temple in Jerusalem was destroyed by fire, the citadel fell into the hands of the Romans, and countless Jews were killed. Titus returned to Rome with Jewish captives and spoils from the temple to celebrate his victory with his father. The Arch of Titus was erected in Rome, depicting his conquest of Jerusalem.

Until Vespasian's death Titus was almost a coruler with his father. He served as Vespasian's secretary, drafted edicts, and addressed the Senate in session. Titus was a talented person, especially in politics and music. He had fallen in love with Queen Bernice, King Agrippa II's sister (see Acts 25,26) and allegedly had promised to marry her, but moral integrity

prevented him when rumor reached him of an incestuous relationship with her brother.

During Titus' brief reign as emperor (79–81), a series of catastrophes occurred: Mt Vesuvius in southern Italy erupted and buried the towns of Pompeii, Stabiae, and Herculaneum (August, AD 79); a fire raged for three days and nights in Rome (AD 80); and a plague spread throughout the imperial city. Suetonius wrote that during those disasters Titus cared for the people with a love resembling the deep love of a father for his children.

When Titus died unexpectedly, his death caused universal mourning; he was eulogized by senators and common people alike.

Domitian (AD 51–96). During Titus' rule his brother Domitian expressed bitterness at having to take second place, openly coveted power, and conspired to seize command of the armed forces. He secretly rejoiced over Titus' sudden death and tried to slight his older brother's reputation. As it turned out, Domitian proved to be a capable administrator: he restored the fire-gutted Capitol and built a temple to Jupiter, the Flavian Temple, a forum, a stadium, a concert hall, and an artificial lake for sea battles. He instituted the Capitoline Festival, promoted the arts and sciences, and maintained the public libraries.

After the custom of earlier emperors Domitian proclaimed himself divine and had his subjects call him "Lord God." The Senate, however, never officially deified him. Throughout his reign they resented and often opposed the power he exercised by prerogative. Domitian did not hesitate to persecute senators who made their objections known. In order to protect himself, he sought the army's support by periodically increasing their pay. He collected additional taxes and often resorted to extortion. Jewish people were especially affected by his taxation. In the last years of Domitian's reign religious persecution was revived.

The early Christian writers Irenaeus, Tertullian, and Eusebius mention the persecution of Christians during Domitian's administration. Domitian appears to have been a relentless persecutor, second only to Nero. He even put members of his own family to death; his wife, Domitia, feared for her life because of her alleged affiliation with Christianity. With friends and freedmen she plotted her husband's assassination.

After ruling the empire for 15 years, Domitian was murdered. Mourned by none, except perhaps his well-paid army, he left in the wake of his reign a bitter memory of oppression.

SIMON J. KISTEMAKER

See ROME, CITY OF.

Bibliography. E. Stauffer, *Christ and the Caesars;* Suetonius, *Lives of the Caesars;* Tacitus, *Annals.*

Caesar's Household. Term referring to imperial servants, both slave and free, in Rome and in the provinces of the Roman Empire. The apostle Paul closed his letter to the Philippian Christians with greetings from those "of Caesar's household" (4:22). The imperial household staff numbered in the hundreds, and the positions carried a certain amount of social importance.

According to the second-century *Martyrdom of Paul*, when Paul arrived at Rome he was greeted by people "from Caesar's household." He put himself in communication with the local Jewish leaders and preached and taught unhindered (Acts 28:17,31). Some men and women were convinced and believed (Acts 28:23,24), no doubt including some in Caesar's household. The message even spread to the whole Praetorian Guard (Phil 1:13).

Some scholars trace certain believers mentioned in Romans 16 to members of the imperial household.

See CAESARS, THE.

Caiaphas. High priest during the life and ministry of Jesus. As official head of the Jewish state Caiaphas presided over the council, or Sanhedrin, its highest court. Next to the Roman governor he was the most powerful man in Judea and was responsible to the Romans for the conduct of the nation. Caiaphas was, therefore, especially concerned about the popular enthusiasm and political unrest centering around the ministry of Jesus and about

its implications for the revolutionary sentiment of the time. The activities of the Zealots were increasing and were destined to break out soon into open revolt.

A huge stir among the people caused by the raising of Lazarus (Jn 11) brought matters to a head. Alarmed lest the activities of those seeking a political messiah should lead the Romans to intervene with armed force, Caiaphas advised that Jesus should be put to death (Jn 11:48–50). The Gospel writer John pointed out that in so doing, Caiaphas unwittingly prophesied concerning the atoning nature of Jesus' death (11:51,52). Caiaphas played a chief role in Jesus' arrest and trial. The leaders laid their plans in his palace (Mt 26:3–5); it was there also that part of Jesus' preliminary trial took place with Caiaphas presiding (Mt 25:57–68). That was after Jesus had first been taken before Annas, Caiaphas' father-in-law (Jn 18:13). Matthew, Mark, and Luke omit the visit to Annas, and Mark and Luke do not refer to Caiaphas by name. Upon Jesus' admission that he was "the Christ, the Son of God," Caiaphas tore his robes and charged him with blasphemy (Mt 26:63–66). After Pentecost, he, with the Jewish leaders, presided over the trial of Peter and John when the council attempted to stop the preaching of the apostles (Acts 4:5,6).

Annas, who had held the office of high priest before Caiaphas, remained influential in the affairs of the nation. That explains why Luke, in his Gospel, set the ministry of John the Baptist "in the high-priesthood of Annas and Caiaphas" (3:2), and in Acts called Annas the high priest (4:6). John's account of Jesus' visit to Annas makes plain that Annas was still popularly referred to as "high priest" (Jn 18:22).

The historian Josephus records that Caiaphas was appointed to his office about AD 18 and ruled until he was deposed about AD 36. The high priest held office at the whim of the Romans, so Caiaphas' unusually long term indicates that he was a man of considerable political skill. Caiaphas was removed from his position by the proconsul Vitellus, and nothing more is known of him.

Cain (Person). First son of Adam and Eve, who became a tiller of the soil while his brother, Abel, was a keeper of sheep. Cain's murder of Abel became proverbial of similarly violent and destructive sins (Jude 11). Each of the two brothers had brought a sacrifice to the Lord (Gn 4:3,4). According to Hebrews 11:4, Abel had acted in faith by bringing a more acceptable sacrifice than that of Cain. The latter's anger had flared against the divine rejection and, in retaliation, he killed his brother, whose offering had been accepted (Gn 4:5–8).

Steps near the house of Caiaphas in Jerusalem.

In seeking a reason for Cain's inappropriate violent reaction, biblical commentary simply says that he belonged to the evil one (1 Jn 3:12). The Lord confronted Cain with his guilt, judged him, and pronounced a curse upon him, driving him out to the land of Nod, east of Eden (Gn 4:9–16). When he complained that his punishment was greater than he could bear, that someone would find him and kill him, the Lord placed a mark on Cain and promised to take sevenfold vengeance on anyone who dared to kill him.

In the land of Nod, Cain built a city and named it after his son Enoch (Gn 4:17). Through Enoch, Cain became the progenitor of a large family that during its early generations became developers of such skills and practices as tent-dwelling herdsmen, musicians, and fashioners of metal objects and implements (Gn 4:18–22).

Cain (Place). KJV spelling of Kain, the name of a city in the southern hill country of Judah's territory, in Joshua 15:57.

See KAIN (PLACE).

Cainan. 1. A son of Arphaxad (Lk 3:36; LXX Gn 10:24; 11:12).

2. Adam's great-grandson, also called Kenan (Gn 5:9–14; 1 Chr 1:2; Lk 3:37).

Calah. One of the ancient capital cities of Assyria built by Nimrod (Gn 10:11,12). Calah is the ancient name for modern Nimrud, which is located 24 miles south of Nineveh on the east bank of the Tigris River. It was excavated by Henry Layard from 1845 to 1849 and by the British School of Archaeology in Iraq from 1949 to 1963. The site was occupied from prehistoric times down to the Hellenistic period.

Excavations at Calah revealed a large ziggurat and temples dedicated to Ninurta and Nabu. A large citadel constructed by Shalmaneser I in the 13th century BC and a palace built by Ashurnasirpal II (883–859 BC) were also uncovered there. Palaces of Shalmaneser III (858–824 BC) and Esar-haddon (680–669 BC) were partially cleared. Among other notable discoveries from the city is the black obelisk of Shalmaneser III, which is presently in the British Museum. The monument is important to biblical studies because of its record of tribute paid by King Jehu of Israel to the Assyrians.

Tiglath-pileser III (745–727 BC) and Sargon II (721–705 BC) launched their attacks on Israel and Judah from Calah. Sargon captured Samaria. Tiglath-pileser was involved with Judah when Ahaz formed a coalition with him against Israel and Syria (Is 7:1–17). Calah was eventually destroyed by the Babylonians and Medes in 612 BC.

Calamus. Variety of sweet-smelling cane (Ex 30:23; Sg 4:14; Ez 27:19).

See PLANTS.

Calcol. One of Mahol's three sons and a member of Judah's tribe (1 Kgs 4:31, KJV Chalcol; 1 Chr 2:6). He and his brothers were noted for their wisdom and musical abilities.

Caleb. 1. Son of Jephunneh the Kenizzite (Nm 32:12; Jos 14:6) and older brother of Kenaz (Jgs 1:13). Caleb was one of the 12 spies sent to scout out the land of Canaan. Although he and Joshua, another spy, recommended an immediate attack, their suggestion was rejected by the Israelite tribes because of other reports of heavily defended fortresses. Consequently entrance into Canaan, the Promised Land, was delayed for some years as a divine judgment (Nm 14:21–23,34,35).

When Israel under Joshua's leadership finally occupied Canaan, Caleb, at age 85 (Jos 14:6,7,10), was assigned Hebron, which he conquered by overcoming its Anakim inhabitants (Jos 14:13,14). Caleb offered his daughter Achsah to whoever overthrew nearby Debir (Kiriath-sepher). Othniel, Kenaz's son and Achsah's cousin, was able to claim her as his wife by conquering the town (Jos 15:16,17).

Hebron later became a Levitical city of refuge (Jos 21:13; 1 Chr 6:55–57). In some portion of Caleb's territory David spent time as an outlaw and met his future wife Abigail, then the wife of Nabal, a Calebite (1 Sm 25:3). Here also his wives were captured by Amalekite marauders who had raided southern Judah and "the Negeb of Caleb" (1 Sm 30:14).

2. Hezron's son and brother of Jerahmeel (1 Chr 2:18,42), also called Chelubai (1 Chr 2:9). Many scholars, however, believe that this Caleb is the same as #1 above because: (1) Achsah is mentioned as the daughter of both (1 Chr 2:49); (2) the prominent place of an otherwise unknown Caleb in the genealogy would be hard to account for. According to these scholars, Caleb was listed as a son of Hezron (the grandson of Judah) in order legally to establish his position and inheritance in Judah's tribe. In reality, however, Caleb was a foreigner, son of Jephunneh, a Kenizzite, who had joined himself and his clan to Judah's tribe. Some support this view by arguing that Caleb is a Horite rather than Israelite name.

3. Hur's son, according to the KJV (1 Chr 2:50). Most likely, however, the KJV joins what should be two separate phrases. The RSV correctly renders it, "These are the descendants of Caleb. The sons of Hur . . ."

Caleb-Ephratah. Possibly a Hebrew place name (1 Chr 2:24 KJV). A number of modern translations follow the Septuagint (early Greek translation of the OT) in treating Ephratah as the name of one of Caleb's wives instead of a place.

Calebite. Descendant of Caleb, Jephunneh's son (1 Sm 25:3).

See CALEB #1.

Calendars, Ancient and Modern. Systematic arrangements showing the beginning and length of each year and its division into days, weeks, and months. The modern calendar is usually taken for granted. But without a calendar it would be extremely difficult to establish a uniform chronology (that is, a system for arranging events in the time sequence in which they actually happened). Accurate prediction of the coming and going of seasons would be impossible. Relating to one another within the dimensions of time would be hampered or obstructed.

Before the calendar took on its modern format, it had to progress through a number of developmental stages.

Days and Their Divisions. The earliest attempt to mark off time was probably the simple counting of days, followed by the subdivision of each day into what eventually became 24 equal parts called hours. Since the Sumerians seem to have originated the measurement of time by minutes, hours, and days, they obviously also knew the narrower meaning of "day," which for them designated a 12-hour period.

Measurement of time in the days of King Ahaz is illustrated by reference to a sundial (2 Kgs 20:9; Is 38:8). The precise measurement of hours, however, must have been a relatively late practice. Even the use of "hour" in Daniel (4:33; 5:5 KJV) probably stood for an indefinite time period.

Early Europeans, like the ancient Egyptians, placed the beginning of the day at midnight, further dividing the period into two 12-hour segments. In the second century BC the Egyptian astronomer Ptolemy and his disciples devised an astronomically convenient method of calculating each day from high noon, when the sun reached its apex in the heavens. The Roman day began at sunrise, with the second part of the day commencing at sunset.

Astronomy and the Calendar. Ancient peoples constructed their calendars on the basis of their observation of "cycles" of the sun and moon. The solar year is the period of time in which the earth accomplishes a complete revolution in its orbit around the sun.

The life of ancient peoples was closely tied to the changes in temperature and in the relative length of days and nights characteristic of the four seasons. Seasonal changes result from the fact that while the earth is orbiting the sun, it is also rotating on its own axis, tipped at an angle to the plane of its path around the sun. In the northern hemisphere that causes the noonday sun to be highest in the sky; the longest day of the year is called the summer solstice (about June 21 on the modern calendar). At the winter solstice (December 21 or 22) the noonday sun appears lowest (farthest south) and the days are shortest. (In the southern hemisphere summer and winter are reversed by the effect of the earth's tilt.) Halfway between, at the vernal (spring) equinox about March 21, and the autumnal (fall) equinox about September 23, the sun is directly over the equator and there are as many hours of daylight as of darkness. The term "equinox" is from Latin words for "equal night." A solar year could be measured by ancient peoples as the period between two similar solstices or equinoxes.

The solar calendar marks off days by observing the period between consecutive returns of the sun to a similar position above the earth, such as its rising, setting, or highest point at midday. A "day" thus represents one complete rotation of the earth on its own axis, now divided into 24 hours. Since that rotation is not directly related to the earth's annual orbit around the sun, calendar problems arise because the true solar year does not equal a certain whole number of days but 365 days plus a fraction of a day.

The most significant calendar problems arise when the sun's motion is not the only factor taken into consideration in marking off a year. Considerable difficulties were encountered in ancient attempts to reconcile solar and lunar periods, especially when subdivisions of the year (months) were made to correspond to the more irregular phases of the moon. The fact that while the moon is orbiting the earth, the earth is orbiting the sun (and rotating at the same time) produces many complications.

The lunar calendar measured time by lunations; a lunation is the interval of time, expressed in days, between two successive new moons. Each lunar month, beginning when the thin crescent of the new moon first becomes visible at dusk, averages just over 29½ days. The moon actually orbits the earth in about 27⅓ days; because the earth is meanwhile moving around the sun, it takes the moon 2 extra days to come to the same position between the sun and earth and produce a "new moon."

A lunar year of 12 months was approximately 11 days shorter than the solar year, so additional days were inserted to make up for the difference. The practice of insertion, known as intercalation, was a device common to several lunar calendar systems. The ancient Chinese compensated by adding an intercalary month every 30 years to their calendar, which consisted of 12 months of 29 or 30 days each. The Muslim lunar calendar, still used throughout Islam, also recognized 30 years as a cycle. Beginning with the second year within each cycle, and at subsequent intervals of three years, a "leap year" (year of abnormal length) is observed. In that framework a leap year comprises 355 days as opposed to the ordinary Muslim year of 354 days. Calculation of the ancient Hebrew year suffered the same problems as other lunar calendars.

Significant Ancient Calendars. From a biblical perspective several non-Jewish calendars deserve special attention.

Egyptian. The Egyptians adopted the solar year method for marking time, a technique embraced also by the Jews before the exodus. The people of Egypt held to a 30-day month, but rather than accurately delineating the seasons by intercalation, they simply tacked on five days annually to the 12 months. Since a true annual calendar consists of 365¼ days, the Egyptians lost ¼ of a day every year. On a small scale that is insignificant; but with the loss of one whole day every 4 years, the loss over a period of 1,461 years would be one entire year. Nevertheless, the Egyptians' extensive astronomical knowledge is evidenced by their charts not only of the cycles of the sun but also of the planets, which (beginning with the most distant) they recorded as Saturn, Jupiter, Mars, the sun, Venus, Mercury, and the moon. Egyptian astronomers consecrated each day of the week to one of those seven "planets," beginning with "Saturn's day," which through Greek and Latin usage eventually became Saturday. The 7-day cycle continued without interruption despite a 2-day deficit each month. Egypt's preoccupation with the heavens is well documented. Among their gods were Re, the sun god; Nut, the sky goddess; Horus, Nut's consort; and Shu, god of the air.

Babylonian and Greek. The Babylonians invented the sundial, according to the Greek historian Herodotus. Both Babylonians and Greeks used a 12-month calendar. Because of errors in calculating months, an intercalary month was added as deemed necessary. For the Babylonians such decisions were fundamentally religious. The priests were entrusted with the sacred task of compensating for the annual loss of 6 days.

The Greeks, on the other hand, had a system of adding the appropriate days every 3rd, 5th, and 8th year within recurring 8-year cycles. Their corrections, however, still produced an inherently inaccurate calendar.

Roman. Roman ingenuity was not evident in their earliest calendar, which consisted of only 10 months. Supposedly invented by Romulus in the 8th century BC, it accounted for a scant 304 days: one month of 29 days, 4 of 30 days each, and 5 with 31 days each. The missing 2 months were included after about 700 BC. The Roman year was then composed of 12 lunar months of 29 and 30 days alternately, a principle that held until the reign of Julius Caesar in the 1st century BC.

Days of the month were not distinguished by the use of ordinals (1st, 2nd, 3rd, etc.). The Romans counted backward from three fixed points in each month called the Calends, the Nones, and the Ides. The 1st day of the month was called the Calends, from which the word "calendar" is derived. The Nones came usually on the 5th (sometimes the 7th) day; the Ides occurred on the 13th (occasionally the 15th) day. Weeks did not become a common way of designating recurrent days until after the reign of Theodosius (AD 392). Our present calendar derives many of its features from the Roman calendar, including the January new year and the names of the months.

Julian and Gregorian Calendars. Sweeping reforms in the Roman calendar were instituted by Julius Caesar in 44 BC with the help of Sosigenes, a Greek scholar who based his solar calendar on a year of 365¼ days. Although the radically transformed calendar ended much confusion, its year was about 11 minutes longer than the true solar year. Since the Julian calendar was used for more than 15 centuries, that tiny error eventually produced gross discrepancies. Bede, an 8th-century English monk and historian, and Roger Bacon, a 13th-century English Franciscan friar and scientist, were among those who reported on the problems of the Julian calendar. By AD 1580 the equinoxes were falling 10 days earlier in the year than they had in 44 BC.

By 1582 the errors of the Julian calendar were deemed too great to tolerate; in that year Pope Gregory XIII issued a decree abolishing the ancient calendar. In its place he substituted what is commonly known as the Gregorian calendar. At first few countries beyond the influence of the papacy accepted the new calendar. Some resisted the changeover for centuries. Britain, for example, refused to adopt the Gregorian calendar until 1752, Russia until 1918, and Turkey until 1928.

Gregory's edict took effect in October 1582. In that initial month the 5th day was desig-

The Hebrew Lunar Calendar

Month	Pre-exilic Name	Post-exilic Name	Babylonian Equivalent	Gregorian Equivalent	Festivals/Holy Days	Weather	Agriculture/Harvests
1	Abib (Ex 13:4; 23:15; 34:18; Dt 16:1)	Nisan (Neh 2:1; Est 3:7)	Nisanu	March/April	14th = Passover 15th (+ 7 days) = Unleavened Bread	Rainy (Latter Rain)	Flax Harvest
2	Ziv (1 Kgs 6:1,37)	Iyyar	Aiaru	April/May		Dry	Barley Harvest
3		Sivan (Est 8:9)	Simanu	May/June	6th = Pentecost (Harvest; Firstfruits; Shavuot, Weeks)	Warm and Dry	Wheat Harvest
4		Tammuz	Duzu	June/July		Warm and Dry	
5		Ab	Abu	July/August		Warm and Dry	Date Harvest
6		Elul (Neh 6:15)	Ululu	August/September		Warm and Dry	Grape Harvest Summer Fig Harvest
7	Ethanim (1 Kgs 8:2)	Tishri	Tashritu	September/October	1st = Trumpets (Rosh Hashanah) 10th = Day of Atonement (Yom Kippur) 15th (+ 7 days) = Tabernacles (Ingathering; Succoth, Booths) 22nd (+ 1 day) = Simhath Torah	Dry	Olive Harvest Grape Harvest
8	Bul (1 Kgs 6:38)	Heshvan (originally = Marheshvan)	Arahsammu	October/November		Rainy (Former Rain)	Olive Harvest Plowing
9		Kislev (Neh 1:1; Zec 7:1)	Kislimu	November/December	25th (+ 7 days) = Dedication (Hanukkah, Lights)	Cool and Rainy	Winter Fig Harvest Sowing
10		Tebeth (Est 2:16)	Tebetu	December/January		Cool and Rainy (and Snowy)	Sowing
11		Shebat (Zec 1:7)	Shabatu	January/February		Cool and Rainy	Almond Blossoms Sowing
12		Adar (Ezr 6:15; Est 3:7,13; 8:12; 9:1,15,17,19,21)	Addaru	February/March	13th = Nicanor 14th (+ 1 day) = Purim (Lots)	Cool and Rainy	Citrus Fruit Harvest Sowing

Late in Israel's history a thirteenth month (Veader) was added about every three years to align the calendar with the solar year.

nated the 15th, thereby compensating for the loss of the approximately 10 days from the Julian calendar. Simply stated, the Gregorian rule declared that a year whose number is exactly divisible by four would be a leap year, with the exception of century years (such as 1700, 1800, 1900, etc.) unless they were an exact multiple of 400 (such as 1600, 2000, etc.). In each leap year February would have 29 days instead of its normal 28. February in the Julian calendar had been shortened from 29 to 28 days by the emperor Augustus in order to add a day to his month (August)—to make it the same length as the month named for Julius Caesar (July)! The Gregorian calendar left the lengths of the months the same as in the Julian (as revised by Augustus).

The use of AD to signify the Christian year was not the contribution of Gregory (and obviously not Julius Caesar's innovation). Dionysius Exiguus, a monk living at Rome in 527 (AD by our calendar), conceived the idea of the Christian era. He reckoned back to what he believed was the 1st year of Jesus' life on earth and designated that year 1 *anno Domini*, meaning "in the year of the Lord."

The Gregorian calendar, with its irregular months consisting of 28, 29, 30, and 31 days, is at times confusing, but on the average it coincides with the astronomical solar year to within less that 27 seconds. Although societies for calendar reform exist in many countries, no proposal for reform of the Gregorian calendar has yet found worldwide acceptance.

Jewish Calendar. It is hard to imagine a people with lives more closely bound to and regulated by the calendar than the people of ancient Israel. The Jewish calendar is dated from what is supposed to have been the creation: 3,760 years and 3 months before the Christian era. Accordingly, to find the current year in the Jewish calendar, one must add 3,759 to the date in the Gregorian calendar. The system, however, will not work to the exact month, since the Jewish year (running on the civil calendar) begins in autumn rather than in midwinter.

Months. Most of the 12 months of the post-exilic Jewish calendar have names adapted from the Babylonians. The months do not correspond to but overlap the months of the Roman calendar.

The names of over half the months are mentioned in the OT: Kislev (Neh 1:1; Zec 7:1; RSV Chislev, KJV Chisleu), Tebeth (Est 2:16), Shebat (Zec 1:7, KJV Sebat), Adar (Est 3:7; 8:12), Nisan (Neh 2:1; Est 3:7), Sivan (Est 8:9), and Elul (Neh 6:15).

Since the Jewish month invariably began with the new moon, at intervals of approximately 29½ days, the Jewish year ran 354 days.

No exact information is available to explain how the Jews originally adjusted their inaccurate lunar calendar to synchronize with the actual solar year. Late in Israel's history an extra month was inserted between Adar and Nisan. That month, sometimes called Veader ("2nd Adar"), was added seven times within a 19-year cycle (at which time Adar received an extra half day).

The names for the Jewish months as now known come from the period following the return from Babylonia to Palestine. Before the Babylonian exile at least four other names were in use: Abib (Ex 13:4), Ziv (1 Kgs 6:1,37), Ethanim (1 Kgs 8:2), and Bul (1 Kgs 6:38). After the captivity they were renamed Nisan, Iyyar, Tishri, and Heshvan (originally Marheshvan), respectively. The preexilic names carried agricultural connotations. For example, Abib signified the month in which the heads of the grain became ripe; Ziv was the month for desert flowers to bloom. An agricultural orientation is apparent in what is evidently the oldest Hebrew calendar, found at Gezer (southeast of Tel Aviv) in 1908 and dating from the 10th century BC. Probably the work of a Jewish schoolboy, the calendar breaks down the year by agricultural activities such as sowing, reaping, pruning, and storage.

Primarily, however, the months were religiously significant to the Jews and enabled them to commemorate the important events of their history. Each month's beginning was considered holy. To ancient Israel the moon became a spiritual symbol of the nation itself; the sun eventually became symbolic of the Messiah (Mal 4:2). Since the moon produces no light of its own, the symbolism is especially appropriate: Israel was supposed to reflect the Messiah's light to the world.

The Jewish calendar remained unchanged during the period between the OT and NT (approximately 400 years) despite an attempt by Hellenistic rulers to introduce a modified lunar month system, presumably of Macedonian origin. According to that calendar, 5 days were added to the final month of the year, with each of the 12 months containing 30 days. Even then, it only approximated the solar year.

Reckoning of Dates. We know of no era in which the ancient Hebrews recorded dates by citing a month and day. Rather, dates were computed by reference to some significant event such as the accession year of the reigning king. In NT times the Jews continued the OT method of dating events by synchronizing them with events either in their religious calendar or within the secular sphere of the Roman world. Writers of the NT followed the same principle (Lk 1:5; Jn 12:1; Acts 18:12). Only as the calendar reforms of Julius Caesar became embedded in the culture did people change from that long-standing method to a more standardized system.

The Number Seven. Seven is a special number in Scripture. God created the world in six days and hallowed the 7th as a day of rest; "sabbath" is from a Hebrew root meaning "to rest." The 7th month in the Jewish religious calendar (Tishri) is marked by holy assemblies. The 10th day of the 7th month marks the observance of the Day of Atonement, and the 15th day, the feast of tabernacles. Leviticus 25:3,4 declares that the 7th year is also sacred to God; in it the land must remain fallow (at rest) for an entire year. When 7 "sabbatical" years had been completed, the 50th year—a year of jubilee—was commemorated by the release of servants and the return of land or homes to those who, through hardship, had been forced to sell or forfeit them.

Jewish Festivals. In addition to keeping the sabbath, Jews observe seven annual festivals.

Passover (14th of Nisan) marks the deliverance from Egypt (the exodus). The 1st day of Nisan determines the date for Passover. Passover is observed for 7 days and encompasses the feast of unleavened bread, an event recalling Israel's hasty preparation for the flight from Egypt (Ex 12:15).

Pentecost is celebrated 50 days after Passover. A time of joyful celebration for the people, Pentecost is the feast of ingathering of the first fruits of the wheat harvest (Ex 34:22; Lv 23:15–17).

Next in order is New Year's Day, the beginning of Tishri. The 1st of Tishri, according to the rabbis, was the day in which the Lord created the world. It is called Rosh Hashanah, "head of the year."

On the 10th of Tishri, Israel's most solemn day, Yom Kippur (the Day of Atonement), is observed. This holiest of days is known as "the sabbath of sabbaths," and the complex ritual for its observance is set forth in the Bible (Lv 16).

Succoth, the feast of tabernacles, occupies the 15th through the 22nd of Tishri. A largely agricultural festival, it celebrates the ingathering of the autumn harvest. The apostle John referred to it simply as "the feast" (Jn 7:37). The feast of tabernacles, sometimes called the feast of booths, is also a spiritual commemoration; it recalls God's care over his people throughout Israel's 40 years in the wilderness (Lv 23:39–43).

Of later origin is the festival of Hanukkah, the feast of dedication. It commemorates Judas Maccabeus' decisive victory over Antiochus Epiphanes and the Syrians over one and a half centuries before Christ. Since Malachi, the last of the OT prophets, had passed from the scene long before that event, tradition alone governs the manner in which the occasion is celebrated. On the 25th of Kislev and the following seven days, joyous activities mark the Jewish calendar.

Concluding the sacred festivals for the year is Purim, which falls on the 14th and 15th of Adar. The feast, which finds its origin in ancient Persia, commemorates the deliverance brought through Mordecai and Esther when they frustrated Haman's plot to destroy the Jews (Est 9).

Conclusion. As ancient sundials and modern clocks mark the passage of minutes and hours, a calendar marks the passage of days, weeks, months, years, and even centuries. A uniform, understandable way of measuring the longer units of time aids secular enterprises such as agriculture, business, and government; is essential to historians; and brings unity to the celebration of religious rites. Development of the modern (Gregorian) calendar represents an interaction between the science of astronomy and much historical and religious tradition. The religious significance of the calendar for Christians stems partly from the biblical contrast between God's timelessness and human mortality (Ps 90). The psalmist asked God to "teach us to number our days that we may get a heart of wisdom" (Ps 90:12).

STUART D. SACKS

See FEASTS AND FESTIVALS OF ISRAEL; DAY; JUBILEE YEAR; NIGHT; ASTRONOMY; ASTROLOGY; SUN; MOON.

Bibliography. J. Finegan, *Handbook of Biblical Chronology;* R.A. Parker, *The Calendars of Ancient Egypt;* J. Van Goudoever, *Biblical Calendars.*

Calf. *See* ANIMALS (CATTLE).

Calf, Golden. Calf-shaped idol fashioned at the Israelites' request from their own gold jewelry (Ex 32:1–4). Under Aaron's supervision the idol was created while Moses was receiving the Ten Commandments on Mt Sinai. Upon seeing the golden calf and the immoral carousing in which the people were engaged, Moses smashed the tablets containing the commandments. He then ground the calf to powder, scattered it on the water, and made the people drink it (Ex 32:15–20). Some of the transgressors were slaughtered (vv 25–29), while others were punished by God himself with a plague (vv 33–35).

Aaron's golden calf was probably modeled after Apis, an Egyptian bull god. Apis was connected with another Egyptian god, Osiris. Magnificent bulls worshiped in life as Apis were buried at death as Osiris-Apis, a name that became Serapis during the intertestamental period. The notoriety of Aaron's golden calf is underscored by several biblical references to it in historical summaries (Dt 9:16,21; Neh 9:18, Ps 106:19,20; Acts 7:39–41).

Jeroboam I (930–909 BC), the first king of Israel after the division of the monarchy, set up shrines at Dan in the far north and at Bethel in the south, installing a golden calf in each (1 Kgs 12:26–33; 2 Chr 11:13–15). Israel's prophets knew that such calves were not the one true God (Hos 8:5,6). Hosea called the calf at Bethel ("house of God") the calf of "Beth-aven" ("house of wickedness," Hos 10:5,6). Within two centuries after Jeroboam's time people had stooped to kissing calves (Hos 13:2), and Jeroboam's sinful act was listed as one of the main factors leading to the destruction of Samaria, Israel's capital city, and the northern kingdom's exile in 722 BC (2 Kgs 17:16).

Caligula. Roman emperor AD 37–41.

See CAESARS, THE.

Call, Calling. *See* ELECT, ELECTION.

Calneh. 1. Problematic KJV rendering in Genesis 10:10. In this context Calneh is associated with Babylon rather than with Syria. It has been suggested that the Hebrew word should be vocalized to read "all of them," yielding the translation "all of them in the land of Shinar" (RSV).

2. City identified as Kullani (Kullan Koy), about 20 miles north of Aleppo in northern Syria. This northern identification is hinted at in Isaiah 10:9, where Calno is associated with Carchemish, some 50 miles to the northeast, as well as in the context of Amos 6:2 (note the north-to-south progression—Calneh, Hamath, Gath). Canneh in Ezekiel 27:23 seems to refer to the same general location and is perhaps to be linked with Calneh. Kullani was captured

by Tiglath-pileser III, king of Assyria, about 741 BC.

Calno. Alternate name for Calneh, a city in northern Syria, in Isaiah 10:9.

See CALNEH #2.

Calvary. KJV translation of Golgotha ("the skull"), the place of Jesus' crucifixion, in Luke 23:33.

See GOLGOTHA.

Camel. Domestic animal used as a means of travel and for carrying goods in the Near East.

See ANIMALS.

Camel's Thorn. Low, thorny shrub whose root is used in making a fragrant ointment.

See PLANTS.

Camon. KJV form of Kamon, the burial place of the Israelite judge Jair, in Judges 10:5.

See KAMON.

Camphire. KJV name for henna, a shrub with pale green leaves and clusters of white, pink, or yellow blossoms which emit a delightful fragrance (Sg 1:14; 4:13).

See PLANTS (HENNA).

Cana. Galilean town that was the scene of Jesus' first miracle: changing water into wine at a wedding feast (Jn 2:1,11). Jesus was again in Cana when he told a nobleman that his son, who was seriously ill at Capernaum, would live (Jn 4:46). Cana was also the home of Jesus' disciple Nathanael (Jn 21:2).

During the first Jewish rebellion, which resulted in the destruction of Jerusalem in AD 70, Cana was made headquarters for defending

A church in Cana of Galilee.

Galilee by Josephus, a Pharisee who was captured by the Romans and later became a famous Jewish historian. After the destruction of Jerusalem and the temple, the town became the seat of the priestly family of Eliashib. John's Gospel refers to it as "Cana of Galilee," evidently to distinguish it from the Kanah located near the Phoenician city of Tyre (Jos 19:28).

The traditional site of Cana, revered as such since Byzantine and medieval times, is Kefar Kana, about four miles east of Nazareth on the main road from Nazareth to Tiberias. In the center of the village (now inhabited by Arabs) is a Franciscan church which supposedly stands on the remains of the house where Jesus performed the wedding miracle. Under the floor of the church is a mosaic pavement with a Jewish Aramaic inscription dating to the 3rd or 4th century. Nearby is the Franciscan Nathanael Chapel, traditionally said to stand on the site of Nathanael's house. But even in traditional Cana there is debate about the site of Jesus' miracle. Greek Orthodox Christians contend that their church, built close to the highway, is the true location.

Contemporary scholarship, however, has almost unanimously settled on Khirbet Kana as the site of NT Cana. That ruin is about eight miles north of Nazareth on the northern edge of the Battuf plain. The Arabs of the region call it Cana of Galilee to this day. Archaeologists exploring at the site have found pottery from the Hebrew monarchy period (c. 900–600 BC), as well as from Hellenistic, Roman, Arabic, and Crusader times.

Canaan, Canaanites. Palestinian territory (the Promised Land) west of the Jordan River, settled by the Israelites at the time of Joshua's leadership. Portions of southern Syria were also frequently considered part of Canaanite territory, the northern borders of which were never clearly defined. The pre-Israelite peoples of western Palestine, excluding northern Syria and such places as Ugarit (Ras Shamra) on the Mediterranean coast of Syria, carried the broad designation of Canaanites.

Name. Scholars once derived the word "Canaan" (KJV Chanaan; Acts 7:11; 13:19) from the Semitic root meaning "to be low." Then archaeological discoveries at Nuzi in eastern Iraq suggested that it might have come from the term *kinahhu* ("red purple") used in dyeing—since the purple murex dye was one of Canaan's most notable products. Later studies, however, show no solid linguistic grounds for that derivation. The origin of the name remains a mystery.

Land and People. In the "table of nations" (Gn 10:15–19) Noah's grandson Canaan

was progenitor of 11 groups that lived in the area of Syria and Palestine: Sidon, Heth, the Jebusites, Amorites, Girgashites, Hivites, Arkites, Sinites, Arvadites, Zemarites, and Hamathites. The first six evidently occupied territory at or south of Sidon, whereas the others lived farther north. The northerners mostly settled on the edge of the coastal plain; in the south, settlement spread eastward to the upland areas. To the north, Canaan extended to Latakia, just south of Ugarit, and inland to Hamath. To the south, Canaanite territory stretched to the Negeb desert area, with no clear boundaries. OT references specifically placed the Canaanites in western Palestine's valleys and coastal areas; the upland country was occupied by Amorites and other peoples (Nm 13:29; Jos 5:1; 7:9; Jgs 1:27–36).

One of the earliest known references to the people of Canaan is in a tablet from Mari (15th century BC) in which a military officer reported his surveillance of "thieves and Canaanites." The Canaanites were listed as a group on the Memphis stele (inscribed column) of the Egyptian pharaoh Amenophis II (c. 1440 BC). The land of Canaan was mentioned in a 15th-century inscription of Idrimi, king of Aleppo (west of Ugarit), who fled to the Canaanite seaport of Ammiya and then became ruler of Alalakh (north of Ugarit). During the Amarna Age (15th–14th centuries BC) Palestine was politically dominated by Egypt; in the Egyptian Amarna tablets the whole area was occasionally designated by foreign rulers as Canaan. To the Egyptians that territory extended from Gaza northward to the far reaches of the Lebanon mountain range and eastward to some indeterminate point, perhaps to the Orontes River. Early Egyptian texts used the name Retenu to describe Syria-Palestine and spoke of its people as "Asiatics," but by the time of Amenophis II "Canaanite" was used for the Palestinian people. In the papyrus Anastasi IIIA, the Syro-Palestinian province was known as Huru. That document fixed the southern boundary of Canaan at the Wadi el-'Arish, as in the biblical sources, which extended the border north beyond the Lebanon mountains to Lebo-Hamath in the Orontes valley, and then east to the desert (cf. Nm 34:1–12). OT Canaan also included the province of Upe, which does not seem to have been under Egyptian control, as well as the Damascus-Bashan area.

Just as "Canaan" designated the whole western Palestinian area, so "Canaanite" described its pre-Israelite inhabitants without specifying race. Of the peoples who lived in Palestine the Amorites first appeared in the 2nd millennium BC as immigrants from Mesopotamia. They settled in upland territory on both sides of the Jordan River. The Hivites (Gn 10:17–19), who lived in the Shechem area and in Lebanon, may have been Horites (Hurrians). The Hittites of Asia Minor were probably not related to the Hittites (or Hethites) native to Canaan (Gn 10:15; 15:20; 23:3).

Several OT references seem to equate Amorite territory and the land of Canaan (Gn 12:5,6; 15:18–21; 48:22), a tradition reflected in the 18th-century BC Alalakh tablets, which depicted "Amurru" as part of Syria-Palestine. Tablets from Mari from about the same period speak of an Amorite ruler of Hazor in northern Palestine. The Tell el-Amarna texts (14th–13th centuries BC) indicate that the Amurru kingdom of the Lebanon region was monopolizing coastal trade and commerce, so references to the two peoples (Amorites and Canaanites) together in Moses' time and throughout the Late Bronze Age (c. 1550–1200 BC) are not surprising.

At the end of that period the "Sea Peoples" (largely Philistines) destroyed the Hittite empire, and in the time of Rameses III (c. 1180 BC) occupied western Palestine. The Israelite conquest of Palestine broke the power of many Canaanite and Amorite city-states, while the rise of a Philistine confederacy on the southern Palestinian coast restricted further the range of specifically Canaanite territory. From the beginning of the Iron Age the cultural heirs of the Canaanites were the Phoenicians, centered in the city-states of Tyre and Sidon, who themselves liked to be known as Canaanites (cf. Mt 15:21,22; Mk 7:24–26).

Language. The various groups that inhabited western Palestine in the pre-Israelite period probably spoke related dialects of the Northwest Semitic linguistic family. The large territory covered by those peoples and the possible influence of Amorite, Hurrian, and Ugaritic languages complicate modern theories about what is properly meant by "Canaanite" as a language.

Discovery in Syria of state archives from the Canaanite kingdom of Ebla (26th–23rd centuries BC) has disclosed a cuneiform language, Eblaite, similar to biblical Hebrew and Phoenician. A millennium older than those languages, Eblaite has no affinities with Amorite, which until recently was considered the oldest West Semitic language. Although Ugaritic has been regarded as "Canaanite," because of its closeness to biblical Hebrew, the Syrian seaport of Ugarit was never really a part of the territory of Canaan. Ugaritic, Eblaite, and biblical Hebrew are the three major components of the West Semitic linguistic family, to which "Canaanite" also belonged.

History. Archaeological evidence shows that western Palestine was occupied as far back as the Old Stone Age. Mesolithic, Neolithic, and Chalcolithic deposits have also been found at several sites. It is possible that Semitic-speaking peoples inhabited places such as Jericho, Megiddo, and Byblos around 3000 BC. Discoveries at Tell Mardikh (Ebla) show that a vigorous Canaanite empire existed in Syria about 2600 BC, and there is no doubt that both Amorite and Canaanite peoples were firmly settled in Syria and Palestine by 2000 BC. The best evidence for Canaanite occupation of western Palestine has come from the Middle and Late Bronze Age (c 1950–1200 BC), when the land was dotted with Canaanite and Amorite city-states.

The Egyptians made periodic forays into Palestine during their 5th and 6th dynasties; in the 13th dynasty (2nd millennium BC) they controlled much of Syria-Palestine both politically and economically. Execration texts (inscriptions cursing enemies) from the 19th century BC list Palestine city-states and their rulers in a way that makes possible identification of certain sites. Egyptian activity in Canaan is also supported by evidence recovered from sites such as Ras Shamra, Byblos, and Megiddo.

Canaanite contacts with Mesopotamia from about 2000 BC are indicated in texts discovered at Mari and Ugarit. Evidently Amorites, Hurrians, early Assyrians, and other peoples periodically migrated to Canaan, bringing with them a diversity of political and social forms. The presence of their independent city-states plus the periodic incursions by other groups during the Middle Bronze Age impaired cultural continuity among the immigrant settlers. By the late 16th century BC most of the small Canaanite kingdoms were firmly under Egyptian control. Within two centuries the most northerly ones were subject to Hittite political influence.

Canaanite history is further complicated by the activities of the Hyksos people between about 1800 and 1500 BC. Of mixed Asiatic origin, the Hyksos owed much of their political influence to their military use of iron-fitted chariots and the compound Asiatic bow. From Canaanite locations like Hazor and Jericho they invaded Egypt and established control there from about 1776 to about 1570 BC. When they were expelled at the start of Egypt's New Kingdom (1570–1100 BC), they retreated to fortified sites in southern Canaan.

Egyptian control over western Palestine had disappeared by the time of the Israelite conquest of Canaan; Joshua met predominantly Canaanite and Amorite opposition. The Israelite occupation of Canaan was aided by the state of decay into which the small Palestinian kingdoms had fallen. Canaanite power

A relief showing Canaanite foes of Seti 1.

was further diminished when in the 19th Egyptian dynasty Rameses II campaigned in Syria against the Hittites, and Merneptah, his successor, launched a raid to punish certain Canaanite cities (including Gezer) about 1220 BC.

With the destruction of Hittite culture by the Sea Peoples and their occupation of the northern and coastal regions, the traditional city-states collapsed. From about 1100 BC Canaanite culture was restricted to Tyre, Sidon, and a few other places. The Philistines, who were apparently an important element of the Sea Peoples, introduced their own Aegean culture in the Gaza area. They warred with Israel until King Solomon's time and were eventually absorbed by the Hebrews during the monarchy. As Canaanite and Amorite centers in Syria came under Aramaean control at the beginning of the Iron Age, Canaanite culture became restricted to Phoenician territory.

Social Structure. The Canaanites and other Near Eastern peoples shared a city-state concept. For practical purposes a city and its surrounding agricultural lands and villages formed an independent social and economic unit. The unit was ruled by a king, who often owned large portions of the territory he governed. Most royal holdings were managed by overseers; arable land was worked by tenant farmers. Such a system inevitably led to bureaucracy, as excavations at Tell Mardikh have confirmed. Wealthy individuals imitated the king's pattern, so the society became an aristocracy based on land and other wealth, with freemen, "clients" or half-freemen, and slaves making up the balance of the city-state's population. The prophet Samuel's warning to those Israelites who wanted a typical Near Eastern king instead of God's appointed charismatic leaders (1 Sm 8:11–18) reflects the power such rulers wielded. Able to requisition people, lands, and money, in general they behaved like feudal monarchs.

Agriculture was essential to Canaanite city-state economy. Other trades included metalworkers, carpenters, builders, and merchants. In Canaan guilds were formed to represent priests, artisans, soldiers, and musicians. Little information is available from specifically Canaanite sources about the structure of western Palestinian society. Reconstruction must be done by using information found in tablets from Ugarit and Alalakh, neither of which was technically "Canaanite." From such sources it seems that each petty kingdom's economy was mostly monopolized by royalty, which regulated trade and controlled the population of primary workers. From 2nd-millennium BC Hurrian and Indo-Aryan sources came the concept of the *maryannu*. They were an aristocratic military group ("noble chariot warriors") mentioned by the Egyptian pharaoh Amenophis II as early as about 1440 BC in a list of Syrian captives. The *maryannu*, the equivalent of a standing army, received economic support as payment for their services to the king and city-state.

Akkadian tablets from Ugarit indicate that the king frequently gave land grants to state officials and other favored persons, which were repaid by service to the king or by a tax of money or produce. The freemen and semi-freemen of Canaan were generally natives who worked for others as farmers or artisans. Slaves were usually acquired when one city-state conquered another and took its people captive. Some domestic Canaanites were also sold into slavery for one reason or another. Such persons usually played a subordinate role in the activities of a prosperous city-state. Just how common slavery was in Canaan is difficult to estimate, but the slave population of the petty kingdoms was evidently much lower than in most Near Eastern countries.

Life in Canaan seems to have been austere in the Middle Bronze Age, judging from archaeological discoveries at burial sites. Most of the necessities of life were manufactured locally, and few objects of precious metal or expensive stones have been found. But by the time of the prophet Amos (8th century BC) the Israelites were being rebuked for indulging in the luxuries of the Phoenicians, the Egyptians, and other Near Eastern nations (Am 3:12; 6:4–6).

Literature. As with language, it is difficult to be specific about Canaanite literature. One clear fact is that our own alphabet originated in Middle Bronze Age Canaan. Before that time writing was either pictographic (words or ideas represented by pictures), cuneiform (wedge-shaped impressions in soft clay representing syllables and whole words), or hieroglyphic (Egyptian pictorial writing). Canaanites of the Late Bronze Age employed a linear alphabetic form of writing, along with the cuneiform language of Ugarit, the syllabic script used at Byblos in Phoenicia, Akkadian cuneiform, and Egyptian hieroglyphics. Alphabetical writing was passed on through the Hebrews and Phoenicians to the Greeks, who gave our present alphabet its classical form.

Until 1929 little Canaanite literature was known, but with the discoveries at Ugarit a large body of literary material came to light. Those texts are described as "North Canaanite" for linguistic purposes, in spite of some doubt that the literature is typically Canaanite.

The discoveries included portions of an epic poem about the god Baal and his consort Anath (possibly from *c.* 2000 BC), a legend about a royal personage named Aqhat (from *c.* 1800 BC), the legendary activities of King Keret (written *c.* 1500 BC), and fragmentary religious, medical, and administrative material.

The copies unearthed at Ugarit date only from about the 14th century BC but undoubtedly reproduce earlier originals. Since the Near East was a culturally unified complex in the Amarna Age, the Ugaritic sources probably reflect the general traditions of western Palestine, including Canaanite ones.

Religion. Before the Ugaritic discoveries, little was known about Canaanite religion apart from OT references to it. A few religious artifacts recovered from various Canaanite sites, and at "high places" in ancient centers like Megiddo, supplied most of the available information. The Ugaritic texts furnished a vast amount of new information about religious life at Ugarit itself. Nevertheless, Canaanite culture was sufficiently complex that Ugaritic religion should not be thought representative of all Canaanite religion. For example, although a predominant feature of Canaanite worship was sacrifice at an outdoor shrine on top of a hill, no such high place has been unearthed at Ugarit.

From what is now known of Canaanite culture, the head of the Canaanite list of gods was a shadowy personage named El, who was worshiped as the "father of man." His consorts were Athirat, known to the Israelites as Asherah, Astarte, and Baaltis. El had a son, Baal, a fertility god described in myths as the lord of rain and storm. Baal succeeded his father as head of the pantheon (list of gods) and supposedly resided in the distant northern heavens. A monument found at Ugarit represented him carrying a thunderbolt at his left side and a mace in his right hand.

According to the Baal epic of Ugarit, Baal's enemy Mot, god of drought and death, killed Baal, bringing on a seven-year famine. When Baal's violent consort Anath killed Mot, Baal revived and agriculture thrived until the cycle was repeated. Baal was worshiped in some communities as Hadad, the storm god. Hadad was associated with the god El in some texts, and in others with Dagon, the corn deity. Equally difficult to distinguish in the myths are the personages and functions of El's wife Asherah, Hadad's consort Astarte, and Baal's wife Anath.

Many small terra-cotta figurines with exaggerated secondary sexual characteristics, representing one or the other of the female deities, have been recovered from Middle and Late Bronze Age sites in western Palestine. A center devoted to the Anath cult, excavated at Byblos in Phoenicia, was evidently notorious for religious prostitution and sexual fertility rites; many naked female figurines were found there. Other Canaanite cult objects included a sacred pillar of some sort (*massebah*) and a wooden image (*asherah*), probably of the goddess herself.

In the Amarna Age Canaanite orgiastic religion was especially influential in the Near East; it infiltrated to some extent even the conservative religions of Egypt and Babylonia. Four principal festivals associated with agriculture seem to have been celebrated by the Canaanites, invariably occasions of revelry, drunkenness, and sexual excess. Canaanite religion was evidently the most sexually depraved of any in the ancient world.

Excavations in Syria and Palestine have uncovered the remains of Canaanite temples at Qatna, Ugarit, Alalakh, Lachish, Beth-shan, Jericho, Shechem, and Tell Far'ah. Megiddo and Hazor each has at least two temples. Most of the shrines were comparatively small, consisting basically of a holy place containing an image of the deity and an anteroom. At Amman a square-shaped Late Bronze Age temple had several rooms enclosing an area of worship.

Influence on Israel. Israelite morality, as defined by the covenant laws of Mt Sinai, was

A pottery jar for storage.

very different from the cultic traditions of Canaanite life. Hebrew ethical monotheism was in many ways opposite to the depraved polytheistic nature worship of Canaanite religion. It was clear that the two systems could not coexist. Hence the Law contained strict instructions that the Canaanites and their ways were to be eliminated from the Promised Land (Ex 23:24; 34:13–16; Dt 7:1–5) and that the Hebrews were to remain separate from Canaanite religion in loyalty to God's covenant. That was far from easy, if only because both peoples spoke closely related dialects and therefore used similar expressions of speech. Further, the invading Israelites under Joshua found that the Canaanites were superior to them in building stone structures and in making metal tools, implements, and weapons. The Hebrews, at a disadvantage, must have faced the prospect of requiring technical help from the Canaanites. In the time of King Solomon, Canaanites from Phoenicia were enlisted to design and construct the temple of the Lord in Jerusalem. A superficial resemblance between some aspects of Canaanite and Hebrew religion, such as peace offerings and certain divine titles, also made it difficult to maintain Israel's cultural distinctiveness.

Except for the "ban" imposed at Jericho

the Israelites were able to use Canaanite equipment captured in battle. Hence their determination to destroy all traces of the Canaanites, including their corrupt religion, was gradually weakened. By the time of King Ahab, when the worship of the Tyrian Baal was firmly entrenched in the northern kingdom of Israel, the Hebrews were in serious danger of losing their spiritual and theological distinctiveness. Their priests, who should have played a major part in maintaining the uniqueness of the covenant faith, often lapsed into Canaanite ways, emulating the immorality of their pagan neighbors and encouraging the Israelite people to do likewise (cf. 1 Sm 2:22).

As a result, Hebrew prophets proclaimed that their nation, which had almost completely succumbed to Canaanite blandishments, would have to be purified by exile before a renewed faith could become a possibility for Israel.

R. K. HARRISON

See CANAANITE DEITIES AND RELIGION; ISRAEL, HISTORY OF; PALESTINE.

Canaanite Deities and Religion. Study of the polytheistic religion of the Canaanites has contributed much to our understanding of the religion of ancient Israel. The Hebrew theological and religious structures were given by God to a people who were influenced and affected by other religions. To appreciate the Israelites' monotheistic faith fully, one must understand the polytheistic setting that challenged their life and unity as a nation.

Contact among the many religions of the ancient Near East produced not only tension but also much syncretism or borrowing of concepts and practices. When Canaanite polytheism is compared with that of Mesopotamia, striking similarities appear that probably would not have occurred had the societies been totally isolated from each other. For example, some scholars suggest that in both cultures authority resided with the sky god. That was only the *concept* of authority, however. The *implementation* of authority needed some other deity. Although the sky god of Mesopotamia was Anu, the real power was exercised by Enlil, god of wind and storm. Likewise El was the nominal head of the Canaanite gods, but the chief functions of deity were exemplified by the personification of storm, the god Hadad. He was the "Baal," or lord of gods and of humankind.

The Aramaeans and Philistines who settled in Canaan adopted the practices of the Canaanites; similarly the Amorites accepted much of the Sumerian religion as their own when they moved into Mesopotamia. Among all those peoples, however, the Hebrews took an independent course. Their God was the unique and cosmic deity who demanded exclusive allegiance. Such a concept ran against the grain of all the religions of the day.

Until the early part of the 20th century most of what was known about Canaanite religion came from the Bible. A limited amount of information was also being put together from fragmentary Phoenician sources discovered in the late 19th and early 20th centuries. The earlier extrabiblical information came from historians such as Herodotus, a 5th-century BC Greek who had heard about Canaanite mythology from secondary sources, often unreliable.

In 1928 many clay tablets were found at a site called Ras Shamra, which was the ancient Syrian city of Ugarit. They contained abundant new information about the religious life of Canaan. Most of them were in a cuneiform alphabet and written in a previously unknown Northwest Semitic language quite similar to Hebrew, Aramaic, and Arabic. The documents are often called the Ugaritic texts or the Ras Shamra tablets.

Discovery of those texts opened doors of understanding that had long been closed. The texts provided scholars with an important mythological literature that gave not only the names and functions of the gods but also much information on Canaanite society.

The Canaanite Pantheon. Canaanite deities had two striking features: an extraordinary fluidity of personality and function, and names whose meanings and sources could be easily traced. Those facts, coupled with the nature of the mythology, mark Canaanite religion as relatively primitive.

The general Canaanite word for god probably meant "the strong, powerful one." The head of the pantheon or array of gods was called El ("the mighty one"). El, a remote and shadowy figure, lived far away from Canaan "at the source of the two rivers," hence in paradise (cf. the location of the garden of Eden at the source of four rivers in Gn 2:10–14). El was called the "father of years," the "father of man," the "father of men and gods." He apparently had three wives who were also his sisters: Astarte, Athirat (Asherah, also called Elat), and Baaltis. He presided over a divine council of gods who were his children. Although he was brutal enough to slay his own son, he was called *Lutpan*, "the kindly one," and was described as an old man with white hair and a beard.

Baal, the great storm god, king of the gods, was the central figure in the pantheon and was functionally far more important than El. Baal acted as El's prime minister and eventually dethroned him. "Baal" means simply "lord" and could be applied to different gods.

Soon, however, the ancient Semitic storm god Hadad became the "Baal" par excellence. Hadad was considered to be the "lord of heaven," the "one who prevails," the "exalted, lord of the earth." He alone reigned over all else. His kingdom was "eternal to all generations." He was the giver of all fertility. When he died, all vegetation and procreation ceased. He was the god of justice, the terror of evildoers. Baal was called the "son of Dagon," the grain god and chief god of Ashdod (cf. 1 Sm 5:1–7). Baal's consort was identified both as El's daughter Anath (in Ugaritic and Egyptian texts) and El's sister Athirat (Asherah in the OT; cf. 1 Kgs 18:19).

The Canaanites explained nature by reference to their gods. Each god represented some force of nature. The moon, sun, important stars, and visible planets were each considered a god or goddess. Baal, seen as god of the thunderstorm, personified the power of all nature.

Mythological texts from Ras Shamra tell about the role Baal played in the cycle of seasons. In the story, Baal meets his archenemy Mot (death) and is killed. The god of fertility is dead, and the result is that all creation is affected adversely. Nature becomes unproductive and infertile. There is an inference that for seven years Baal remains dead, and for that period of time there is famine and drought. Baal's sister-consort, Anath, seeks to avenge his death. Having searched out Mot, she kills him in one of the most violent scenes in all mythological writings. The story reads:

> Like the heart of a cow for her calf,
>> Like the heart of a ewe for her lamb,
>> So's the heart of Anath for Baal.
> She seizes the godly Mot—
>> With sword she doth cleave him.
> With fan she doth winnow him—
>> With fire she doth burn him.
> With hand-mill she grinds him—
>> In the field she doth sow him:
> Birds eat his remnants,
>> Consuming his portions,
>> Flitting from remnant to remnant.

After Mot's demise Baal is "resurrected." He comes to life and mates with Anath, reviving the drought-stricken land.

That story became the core of the Canaanite religious system. The Canaanites' personification of the forces of nature accounted for the succession of the seasons. The dry period from April to the end of October represented the duration of Baal's death after his unsuccessful battle each spring with Mot (or with "the devourers," who at Ras Shamra performed the same general function as Mot). Revival of the rain-and-vegetation deity Baal toward the end of October signaled commencement of the autumn rains, which continued intermittently until the following April. The Canaanites believed that the land regained its fertility because of the annual mating of Baal and Anath. What better form could their own religious activities take than that of imitating the sexual behavior of their chief deities? Hence there was always a pronounced orgiastic element in Canaanite religion.

The three goddesses—Athtarat (Astarte or Ashtaroth in the OT, Dt 1:4, KJV Astaroth; Jgs 2:13), Anath (appearing in the OT in the name of the town Anathoth and as Shamgar's progenitor), and Athirat (Asherah in the OT)—presented an intricate set of relationships. Astarte was the same as Ashtar or Venus, the evening star. Anath's original character is uncertain. Athirat was primarily goddess of the sea and the wife of El. She was also called Elat, the feminine form of El. All three goddesses were concerned mainly with sex and war. Their primary function was to have sexual relations with Baal on a continual yearly cycle, yet they never lost their "virginity"; they were "the great goddesses who conceive but do not bear."

Ironically, the goddesses were considered sacred prostitutes and as such were called the "holy ones." Idols representing the goddesses were often nude and sometimes had exaggerated sexual features. In what circumstances early cultic prostitution was practiced is a matter of some debate, but there is no doubt that both male and female temple prostitutes were used in the cult of Canaanite religion.

The fertility deities were also goddesses of war. In the Baal Epic of Ugarit, Anath has a gory thirst for blood. In New Kingdom Egyptian sources Astarte appears as a nude and ferocious cavalry warrior, sporting shield and lance.

In the KJV the name Asherah was translated "grove," following the Septuagint (3rd-century BC Greek translation of the OT). She seems to have been represented by some kind of wooden cult object set up in "high places" beside incense altars and stone pillars.

The Canaanites worshiped many other deities. Resheph was lord of the underworld, the god of war and pestilence (cf. Hb 3:5, which may be an image of God driving before him the personified "pestilence"). Shulman Eshmun was the god of healing. By about 1300 BC those two were identified together as a composite deity, Rashap-Shalmon. Evidently the ancients believed that the one who caused disease was best able to heal it. Such polarities were common (e.g., Baal, the dying and reviving deity).

At Tyre, a Phoenician city on the eastern Mediterranean, the ancient god Hamon was worshiped as Melkart, king of the underworld and lord of fertile ground. In Crete, Koshar, also called Hasis (meaning "the skillful and clever one"), was the master craftsman, inventor of tools, weapons, and the arts. The sun and moon as deities played a very small part in Canaanite religion. Athtar, who as god of irrigation aspired unsuccessfully to succeed Baal, was also the morning star and appears in the Bible as Helel, "son of Dawn" (Is 14:12). He is also identified with the Moabite national god, Chemosh, in the Mesha Inscription (9th century BC). Sometimes he is called "the terrible" or "the king." He may be the god to whom human sacrifice was made, thus identified with the god Molech (Lv 18:21). The Hebrew word from which "Molech" derives, however, may simply be a noun meaning "human sacrifice."

The great Baal Epic of Ugarit is concerned with the death and resurrection of Baal and with unrelated minor myths. One episode deals with Baal and Anath. While hunting, Baal copulates with Anath, who, in the form of a wild cow, bears a wild bull for Baal. Another episode describes the victory of Anath over a series of monsters, including Yam (Sea), Tannin, and Leviathan, all mentioned in Scripture ("sea monster," Jb 7:12; "dragons," "Leviathan," Ps 74:13,14; "fleeing" or "twisting serpent," Is 27:1).

Continual struggle for survival no doubt led the Canaanites to worship things that they felt would benefit them materially. If the gods and goddesses were pleased by the worship, the result would be a plentiful harvest. Canaanite worship centered on a cultic shrine or "high place" where sacrifices were offered. Archaeological evidence indicates that animals of all sizes were offered at great temple-shrines such as Beth-shan. The city received its name from the temple located there: *beth* means "temple," and Shan was patron deity of the city.

As noted, human sacrifice became a part of religious practice in Canaan. Second Kings 3:27 mentions Mesha, king of Moab who, after defeat at the hands of a confederation of kings, offered up his son as a burnt offering to his god Chemosh.

Interaction and Conflict with OT Religion. When the Israelites appeared in Canaan, they faced a religion that was decadent and perverted. They were forbidden to adopt any such practices. The sins of the Israelites recorded in Numbers 25, idolatry and adultery, no doubt included the pagan practice of temple prostitution. God's command that the Canaanites and their religion be exterminated must be viewed in that light.

The basic idea that caused the religion of Israel to differ from that of Canaan was that the God of Israel was above nature. He was the only God the Israelites worshiped, and he was invisible. The psalmist's enemies chided, "Where is your God?" (Ps 42:3), because their gods were visible images. The Israelites viewed God as neither subject to nor a part of nature. The sun, moon, and stars were his created objects (cf. Pss 19, 29). For the faithful Hebrew, God was the Creator-Sustainer. He was almighty. No other was greater than he or even comparable to him in power and holiness: "To whom then will you compare me, that I should be like him? says the Holy One. Lift up your eyes on high and see: who created these?" (Is 40:25,26).

From the biblical perspective, the Canaanites had broken away from God's original revelation of his true nature. By the time of Abraham, progenitor of the Hebrew nation, all mankind worshiped "the gods," as did even Abraham's ancestors (Jos 24:2). Abraham received a call to a different way, to a covenant with God that meant recognition of God's authority and power as the only true God, as Creator and sovereign Lord. Obviously, then, the Israelites had no pantheon but put great stress on the singularity of God (Dt 6:4). The Hebrew language, in fact, had no word to designate a female god. The Canaanites had a general word for goddesses, but the Hebrews could refer to them only by their proper names (Asherah, etc.).

After Israel became a strong and organized nation, the influence of surrounding polytheism became a major challenge to their monotheism. God had warned them not to have other gods or to make images, but eventually the idolatrous trend triumphed; God had to allow the Israelites to be defeated by their enemies in order to chastise them for their betrayal of him. Thus came about the fall of Samaria in 722 BC and of Jerusalem in 586 BC.

Although the Hebrews were in perennial conflict with Canaanite religion, through the common denominator of language they shared some religious expressions with the Canaanites. There was nothing inherently evil in that. The basic idea of the personality of deity was a feature common to both religions. In Hebrew belief, however, all the functions of the separate Canaanite deities were performed by one personal Lord. He was indeed so much a person that the OT occasionally anthropomorphized him, that is, spoke of him as if he had human form.

Although that anthropomorphism troubled some Jews of postbiblical times, the Hebrews who wrote such lines were doing what every language does to enrich its expression, using figures of speech already available. Many anthropomorphic expressions of deity were a part of the Northwest Semitic languages be-

fore the Hebrews became a people. Some of them derive from Canaanite religion. One Ugaritic text reads: "Did I not tell thee, O Prince Baal, Nor declare, O Rider of the Clouds?" Psalm 68:4 uses a similar epithet for God ("him who rides upon the clouds").

The people of Israel handled their encounter with Canaanite religion in three ways. The first had to do with theology, the second with cultic practices, and the third with language. In the areas of theology and cultic practice the Hebrews came into collision with Canaanite religion. Israel's God presented himself as the only Creator, the absolutely unique and exclusive deity, the sovereign Ruler of the universe. That is the reason for the emphasis of the Decalogue (the Ten Commandments): "I am the Lord your God. . . . You shall have no gods before me. . . . You shall not bow down to them or serve them; for I the Lord your God am a jealous God" (Ex 20:2–5; Dt 5:6–9). The nature of Israel's God is revealed in the moral law, which is the expression of the Lord's character. In contrast to Canaanite deities, the Lord could not be bribed into behaving contrary to his moral nature (Dt 10:17).

Israel also came into conflict with Canaanite religion in cultic practice. The Israelites and the Canaanites shared certain ritual features, such as some of the terms used for sacrifices and the design of their temples. They came into conflict, however, where Canaanite practice violated the moral character of Israel's faith. Often one can understand the ritual law of ancient Israel only by realizing that those rules were a reaction to degrading Canaanite practices. "You shall not do as they do in the land of Canaan, to which I am bringing you. You shall not walk in their statutes" (Lv 18:3b).

Deuteronomy 20:17,18 gives the reason why the Israelites were told to exterminate the Canaanites: "You shall annihilate them . . . as the Lord your God commanded you, so that they may not teach you to imitate all the abominable things they have done for their gods and so cause you to sin against the Lord your God" (NEB). The most obvious of those abominable things was the worship of images. Such idolatry constituted a denial of the rightful place of the Lord as the only true God. Other reprehensible practices of Canaanite religion were sacrifice of human adults and children, temple prostitution, mutilation of the human body, and sorcery or divination. Among some of the surrounding nations there was official religious sanction for the practice of bestiality, which was punishable by death among the Hebrews (Ex 22:19). The NIV translation of Deuteronomy 23:17,18 makes the Hebrew reaction to temple prostitution very clear: "No Israelite man or woman is to become a temple prostitute. You must not bring the earnings of a female prostitute or of a male prostitute into the house of the Lord your God to pay any vow, because the Lord your God detests them both." Human sacrifice, divination, and sorcery were prohibited among the Hebrews: "Let no one be found among you who sacrifices his son or daughter in the fire, who practices divination or sorcery, interprets omens, engages in witchcraft, or casts spells, or who is a medium or spiritist or who consults the dead. Anyone who does these things is detestable to the Lord" (Dt 18:10–12 NIV).

Mutilation of their bodies was practiced regularly by the Canaanites in certain rituals for the dead. One Ugaritic text gives a typical Canaanite grief ritual:

> He pours the ashes of grief on his head,
>   The dust of wallowing on his pate.
>   For clothing he is clothed with sackcloth.
> He roams the mountain in mourning,
>   Yea, through the forest in grief.
> He cuts cheeks and chin, lacerates his
>   forearms.
> He plows the chest like a garden;
>   like a vale he lacerates the back.
> He lifts his voice and shouts:
>   Baal is dead.

That practice forms the background of Deuteronomy 14:1,2a: "You are the children of the Lord your God. Do not cut yourselves or shave the front of your heads for the dead, for you are a people holy to the Lord your God" (NIV). For Israel to practice that typical Canaanite ritual would have been a denial of the exclusive worship of the Lord.

In Exodus 34:13 the Israelites were admonished to "break down their altars, smash their sacred stones and cut down their Asherah poles" (NIV). By contrast Psalm 106:34–41 is a sad commentary on what did happen eventually in ancient Israel. The psalmist says that they failed to destroy the Canaanites, but rather fell into the Canaanite practice of idol worship and human sacrifice, thus arousing the Lord's anger so much that he abhorred them.

The Hebrews were most successful in dealing with Canaanite religion in the area of language. Every culture must find its expression of theological truth in the language that is available and commonly used. Thus many graphic Canaanite phrases, especially those that expressed the personal nature of God, were used to enhance Hebrew monotheism. Already noted, for example, was reference to the Lord as one who rides upon the clouds (Ps 68:4), a frequently used epithet for Baal. The phrase may suggest an early date for the Scripture passage but not necessarily a primitive stage of Hebrew religion. Rather, it marks a time of religious vitality and verbal fluency. Its use would have been impossible in the Maccabean period (2nd to 1st centuries BC), when the Hebrew language was rigid and when scholars opposed the use of anthropomorphisms. The poet of Psalm 68 expressed God's control over nature in an artful poetic idiom, perhaps without a thought of its originally polytheistic usage. Though Canaanite idiom was used freely, it was not used carelessly. Only theologically acceptable concepts were communicated.

Conclusion. According to the Bible, human beings originally had a true concept of deity, which they gradually distorted. The Hebrew Scriptures, however, rejected those distorted notions and progressively revealed the truth about the one God. Yet some of that truth was mingled in all religions, including idolatrous Canaanite polytheism. Some of that truth is no doubt mingled in all of today's religions.   ELMER B. SMICK

See CANAAN, CANAANITES; GODS, GODDESSES; ISRAEL, RELIGION OF; IDOLS, IDOLATRY.

Candace. Title given to ancient Ethiopian queens. Philip, an apostle and leader in the early church, met and baptized "an Ethiopian, a eunuch, a minister of the Candace, queen of the Ethiopians, in charge of all her treasure" on the road from Jerusalem to Gaza (Acts 8:27). That Candace, whose name was probably Amanitere, ruled over Nubia (modern Sudan) from AD 25 to 41.

Candle, Candlestick. KJV usage for words more correctly translated as "lamp" and "lampstand." Candles in the modern sense, typically made of wax and containing a wick, were unknown in ancient times.

See LAMP, LAMPSTAND.

Cane. See PLANTS.

Canker. KJV rendering of "gangrene" in 2 Timothy 2:17.

See GANGRENE.

Cankerworm. KJV translation of the Hebrew word meaning "locust."

See ANIMALS (LOCUST).

Canneh. Alternate name for Calneh, a city in northern Syria, in Ezekiel 27:23.

See CALNEH #2.

Canonical Criticism. See DOCUMENTARY HYPOTHESIS.

Canon of the Bible. *See* BIBLE, CANON OF THE.

Canticles. Alternate title for the biblical book Song of Solomon, derived from the Latin name of the book, *Canticum Canticorum.*

See SONG OF SOLOMON.

Capernaum. City of Galilee, mentioned only in the Gospels, which was the headquarters of much of Jesus' ministry. It lay on the northwest side of the Sea of Galilee (or Lake of Gennesaret), but its site is unknown. Its name means "village of Nahum." But it is impossible to say who this Nahum was, whether the OT writer or someone else. Matthew gives us the only location we know: "And leaving Nazareth he went and dwelt in Capernaum by the sea, in the territory of Zebulun and Naphtali" (Mt 4:13). The west shore of the lake was settled by the tribe of Naphtali. Two of the characters described as being in Capernaum help to identify its location as near the border of the Jordan and the political frontier. The story of the centurion (Mt 8:5; Lk 7:2) points to the small garrison of about 100 men found at such a frontier town. The story of Levi's call to leave the customs post controlling the taxation of the area reflects on the same border character of the town (Mt 9:9; Mk 2:14; Lk 5:27).

These are the only scant indications we have, for the supposed sites of Capernaum have not been excavated adequately to determine which it is. The two possible sites are within two miles of each other: Khan Minya (or Khirbet el-Minyeh) and Tell Hum (or Telhūm). Until the end of the last century Khirbet el-Minyeh was favored, lying at the seventh milestone on the road from Tiberias to Safed. Stones for building the road were used from this site. E. Robinson identified Khirbet el-Minyeh as Capernaum, but does not indicate why he favored the site. Josephus (*War* 3.10.8) describes in glowing terms the fertility of the countryside of Gennesaret and describes "a very copious spring" called Capernaum. This could well be the springs of the

Seven Wells in the Tabgha delta, one of which is the most abundant spring in Galilee. Its water served to drive mills and to irrigate the Tabgha plain. It also fed two cisterns which in turn supplied a Roman bath northeast of Khirbet el-Minyeh.

Older Jewish evidence has argued for Tell Hum. The Greek *Capharnaum* is rendered by the Hebrew *Kāphar nahūm* in Midrash Kohelet 1.8 and 7.26 (*c.* AD 110), proving that Capernaum still existed in the 2nd century. There is no further mention until 1160, when Benjamin of Tudela refers to "Capharnaum which is Kaphar Nachum." The Franciscans, who acquired the site, have found a considerable number of coins of that period at Tell Hum, and the ruins of the synagogue there may well date from the 3rd century AD. Preliminary excavations have failed to reveal an older synagogue lying beneath the present ruins that could be identified as the one built by the centurion in Luke 7:5. In the absence of further evidence the Israeli government has labeled Tell Hum "Kefar Nahum," leaving it an open question where Capernaum was located.

Consequently most of what we know of Capernaum is from the Gospel narrative. It was an important settlement, with a Roman garrison, adopted by Jesus as "his own city" after his rejection by Nazareth (Mt 9:1). Here he was "at home" (Mk 2:1) and performed many miracles (Mk 1:34): the healing of the centurion's servant (Mt 8:5); the healing of Peter's mother-in-law (Mk 1:31); and the exorcism of the unclean spirit (Mk 1:23; Lk 4:33). Thus highly favored by the ministry of Jesus, there was also a heavy curse imposed on the city because of its unrepentance: "And you Capernaum, will you be exalted to heaven? You shall be brought down to Hades" (Mt 11:23; Lk 10:15).

Caper Plant. Low, spreading plant whose fruit was used as an appetite stimulant.

See PLANTS.

Caphtor, Caphtorim, Caphthorim. Place name and the name of the people associated with the place.

The Caphtorim among the Hamitic peoples in the Table of Nations are listed as the "sons" of Egypt (Gn 10:13,14; 1 Chr 1:12, KJV Caphthorim). The text makes the Casluhim the parent people of the Philistines. However, prophets referred to the Philistines as "colonists from Caphtor" (Jer 47:4; see Am 9:7). This has been the basis for some to transpose the clause of Genesis 10:14 and to translate "Caphtorites, from whom the Philistines were descended" (NEB). Others understand that al-

Capernaum, as seen from the north, showing the city wall and the remains of the synagogue.

though the Philistines may have been originally a Casluhian colony, they settled in regions that became known primarily as those of the Caphtorites.

Caphtor is referred to as *Kaptara* in Akkadian, *kptr* in Ugarit, and *Keftiu* in Egyptian. These references are to be dated from as early as 2200 BC down to about 1200 BC. The Egyptian sources are especially helpful in identifying Caphtor as Crete. On the other hand there is a Jewish tradition that the Caphtorim were from Cappadocia; the Septuagint reads "Cappadocia" instead of "Caphtor." This has led some to suggest that Caphtor is to be identified with a coastal region of Asia Minor or with the island of Carpathos. Perhaps by the 13th century BC Caphtor was used in a broad sense for the Aegean area from which the Philistines came.

The Caphtorim are mentioned also as a people who invaded the region around Gaza, dispossessed the Avvim, and settled there (Dt 2:23). It appears the Caphtorim were firmly settled around Gaza before Israel crossed the Jordan at the time of the conquest. Some feel that this too is a reference to the Philistines.

Capital. In architecture, the uppermost part of a pillar, often ornately fashioned. Capitals (KJV chapter) topped the five pillars of the tabernacle during the wilderness wanderings of the people of Israel (Ex 36:38), as well as the

Ionic capital from Megiddo.

pillars called Boaz and Jachin in King Solomon's temple (1 Kgs 7:16–22; 40–42).

See Architecture.

Capital Punishment. *See* Criminal Law and Punishment.

Cappadocia. Plateau region of eastern Asia Minor intersected by mountain ranges. The name Cappadocia does not occur in the Hebrew OT. Passages that mention Caphtor or Caphtorim (Dt 2:23; Am 9:7), however, were rendered "Cappadocia" in the Septuagint (ancient Greek translation of the OT). A few scholars suggest that Cappadocia was the original home of the Philistines.

In the NT, Cappadocia was the homeland of some of the visitors to Jerusalem who were amazed at hearing their own languages spoken on the day of Pentecost (Acts 2:5–13). Cappadocia was later one of the places in Asia Minor where Christians settled, and to whom the apostle Peter addressed his first letter (1 Pt 1:1).

Cappadocia was bordered by Pontus on the north, Syria and Armenia on the east, Cilicia on the south, and Lycaonia on the west. Noted for its wheat, cattle, and horses, it also exported alabaster, mica, silver, and lead. The region was traversed by important trade routes, such as the route through the Cilician gates northward to Pontus. The area was controlled or dominated in turn by Hittites, Assyrians, Babylonians, Persians, Greeks, Seleucids, and Romans.

Reference to a letter to Ariarathes, Cappadocia's king (1 Mc 15:22), may indicate that a significant Jewish settlement was there at the beginning of the 2nd century BC. Jews from that community were apparently visiting in Jerusalem at the time of Pentecost. Christian-

Corinthian capital from Herod's palace at Masada.

ity seems to have spread northward into Cappadocia along the road from Tarsus. Cappadocia became a region of strong Christian church leaders by the 4th century AD.

Captivity, The. Period when many inhabitants of the southern kingdom of Judah were exiled in Babylonia after Nebuchadnezzar's conquest of Jerusalem (6th century BC).

See EXILE.

Caravan. Traveling group of merchants, pilgrims, or others in Bible times who joined together for mutual protection. Usually travelers used pack animals to carry their wares or personal belongings. To transport goods from one district to another donkeys were mainly used until about 1100 BC, when use of camels became more common. Ancient Palestine, situated between the Mediterranean Sea and Egypt on one side and Syria, Mesopotamia, Arabia, and lands farther east on the other, was crisscrossed by trade routes. The nation of Israel was thus intimately acquainted with caravans, many in OT times coming from Transjordan and Arabia. Arabian caravans often transported spices and incense, products that were particularly lucrative. The rulers of Sheba were engaged in that enterprise (1 Kgs 10:2). The size of a caravan depended on the amount of traffic, precariousness of the route, and availability of camels. Perhaps 40 camels might be joined by ropes attached from the saddle of one camel to the nose ring of the trailing camel. Caravans could travel in single file or with three to four camels abreast. In hot weather or on an extensive journey a camel could carry about 350 pounds; on short cool trips it could carry much more. Joseph was sold into slavery to a spice caravan going to Egypt (Gn 37:25–28). Raiding expeditions also formed caravans at times (Jgs 6:3–5; 1 Sm 30:1–20).

See TRAVEL AND TRANSPORTATION.

Carbuncle. Red or fiery colored stone such as a garnet or ruby; mentioned as one of the gems in the high priest's breastplate (Ex 28:17).

See MINERALS, METALS, AND PRECIOUS STONES.

Carcas. KJV spelling of Carkas, one of King Ahasuerus' seven counselors, in Esther 1:10.

See CARKAS.

Carchemish. Ancient city commanding an important ford on the west bank of the upper Euphrates River, about 65 miles northeast of Aleppo. Today part of the ruin is located in Turkey and part in Syria. The word is also written "Charchemish" (2 Chr 35:20 KJV). The meaning of the name is uncertain, although recent discoveries at Ebla suggest "city of Chemosh" (Moabite god).

A north-south trade route (roughly following the river) and an east-west route (connecting Nineveh with the Mediterranean Sea) both passed through Carchemish. Pottery finds indicate that the site was occupied in prehistoric times. The earliest reference to it is in the Ebla tablets (*c.* 2400 BC). Since Carchemish is about 75 miles west of Haran, Abraham probably passed through on his way to Canaan.

Early in its history Carchemish was allied first to Mari and then to Aleppo. In 1355 BC it fell to the Hittites, became a regional capital of eastern Hatti, and adopted Hittite culture and language. After several centuries of unsuccessful attempts to incorporate Carchemish into their empire, the Assyrians under Sargon II finally conquered the city in 717 BC (Is 10:9) and made it their northwestern stronghold. When Nebuchadnezzar's Neo-Babylonian kingdom succeeded the Assyrian empire, Carchemish was the last city to fall (605 BC). The Assyrians were aided in their defense by Pharaoh Neco II of Egypt (2 Chr 35:20; Jer 46:2). Thereafter, the city decreased in importance.

Excavation of ancient Carchemish began in 1911 and was continued by C. L. Woolley and T. E. Lawrence (Lawrence of Arabia) in 1912–14 and 1920. Their finds are in the Hittite museum in Ankara (Turkey). The city had features of both Hittite and Assyrian architecture. It had a casemate wall atop sloping embankments to hinder attackers. Within the city on the highest point stood a citadel surrounded by its own wall, as well as a palace with its own temple and monumental staircase.

Careah. KJV spelling of Kareah, Johanan's father, in 2 Kings 25:23.

See KAREAH.

Carkas. One of seven eunuchs or palace officers serving as personal aides to King Ahasuerus (Xerxes). Carkas and his fellows were sent to bring Queen Vashti to a feast hosted by the king (Est 1:10, KJV Carcas).

Carmel. 1. Mountainous ridge extending about 20 miles along the Mediterranean Sea and jutting southeast into the Jezreel Valley. Its greatest width at the southeast is 13 miles, its highest point 1,742 feet. Geologically the ridge is of the same Cenomanian limestone formation as the central range of Palestine. Mt Carmel forms a headland south of the Bay of Acre. The modern city of Haifa, which rises in

Crusader castle south of Haifa, which is at the foot of Mt Carmel.

tiers on Carmel's northwestern corner, has splendid harbor facilities. Nestled on Mt Carmel's slopes are also several Jewish settlements and two large Druze villages. (Druzes are members of a particular Muslim sect.) The plain of Sharon extends to the south.

Mt Carmel was renowned for its beauty and fertility (Is 33:9; 35:2); in ancient times it was forested with oak trees, olive groves, and vineyards. "Carmel" is a contraction of a Hebrew word meaning "vineyard" or "garden of God." Parts of Carmel were so covered with dense wild vegetation that, with its gorges and caves, the ridge provided refuge to robbers and outcasts (Am 9:3). Carmel is still forested, and large parts of it have been made a nature reserve. The biblical poet of love described his beloved by saying, "Your head crowns you like Carmel" (Sg 7:5), perhaps likening her hair to the thick, luxuriant foliage of Carmel.

Mt Carmel was an obstacle to north-south military and trade routes. Conquerors and traders commonly skirted its base and moved through the Jezreel Valley to the east or the Zebulun Valley to the northeast. Important passes cut through the mountain, however, such as the narrow pass through the lower slopes at its southern end linking the plains of Sharon and Esdraelon. That route was taken by Pharaoh Thutmose III early in the 15th century BC and also by British Lord Allenby when he conquered Palestine in 1918. The tribal territories of Asher, Zebulun, Issachar, and Manasseh met at Mt Carmel, but evidently possession of the heights was never fully settled.

Mt Carmel seems to have had special religious significance. It was the scene of a contest between Elijah and the prophets of Baal (1 Kgs 18); the site was fitting because Carmel was disputed territory between Israel and the Phoenicians, and thus between the Phoenician god Baal and Israel's God. Elijah was not the first to build a Hebrew altar on the mountain;

the narrative describes him as repairing a ruined "altar of the Lord" before offering his sacrifice (1 Kgs 18:30). The traditional location of that contest is Qeren ha-Carmel at 1,581 feet, overlooking the Jezreel Valley. The brook Kishon (1 Kgs 18:40) flows through that valley and around to the north of Carmel before emptying into the Bay of Acre.

The Greeks maintained an altar to Zeus on Mt Carmel during several centuries BC. Roman general Vespasian made a sacrifice on the altar of the god "Carmel" in AD 69 and obtained the blessing of its oracle on his imperial ambitions; he became emperor later that year. A monastery named for the prophet Elisha, who visited Mt Carmel (2 Kgs 2:25; 4:25), existed there as early as AD 570. The order of Carmelites, founded in 1156, built a monastery at the northwest edge of the ridge. The monastery of Our Lady of Mt Carmel, constructed in 1767, was used by Napoleon Bonaparte as a hospital for his soldiers; burned soon afterward, it was rebuilt in 1827.

The caves of Mt Carmel were used as shelters and dwellings in ancient times. While excavating caves on the lower western slopes (1929–34) archaeologists Garrod and McCown found evidence of a flint industry and human remains, perhaps from the Paleolithic and Neolithic (Stone Age) periods.

2. Town in Judah (Jos 15:55) identified with el-Kirmil (Kermel), 7 miles south of Hebron. King Saul set up a memorial to his conquest of the Amalekites there (1 Sm 15:12). Carmel was also the home of Nabal, a churlish man who refused kindness to David (1 Sm 25:2–14). After Nabal's death his beautiful wife, Abigail, married David. Carmel is mentioned as the home of Hezro, one of David's 30 heroes (2 Sm 23:35).

Carmi. 1. One of Reuben's sons; he accompanied his grandfather Jacob into Egypt (Gn 46:9; Ex 6:14; 1 Chr 5:3) and founded the family of Carmites (Nm 26:5–7).

2. Achan's father and a member of Judah's tribe (Jos 7:1,18; 1 Chr 2:7; 4:1).

Carmite. Descendant of Carmi, Reuben's son (Nm 26:6).

See CARMI #1.

Carnelian. Variety of chalcedony which may vary in color from deep red to almost white; mentioned as one of the foundation jewels in the wall of the New Jerusalem (Rv 21:20).

See MINERALS, METALS, AND PRECIOUS STONES.

Carob Tree. Evergreen leguminous tree commonly found throughout the Near East, yielding edible pealike seeds contained in a pod.

See PLANTS.

Carpenter. *See* TRADES AND OCCUPATIONS.

Carpus. Man with whom the apostle Paul left his cloak at Troas. Paul instructed Timothy to bring it when he came to see him in prison (2 Tm 4:13). Possibly Carpus was one of Paul's converts. According to tradition, Carpus became bishop of Berytus at Thrace.

Carrion Vulture. Bird of prey, also called the gier eagle in the KJV (Lv 11:18; Dt 14:17).

See BIRDS (VULTURE; VULTURE, EGYPTIAN).

Carshena. One of seven princes who were wise men of Persia and Media, and whom King Ahasuerus (Xerxes) consulted for legal advice (Est 1:14).

Casiphia. Place to which Ezra sent for Levites when he realized that his company of returnees from the exile lacked persons qualified for temple service (Ezr 8:17). Casiphia was perhaps Ctesiphon on the Tigris River near modern Baghdad.

Casluhim. Descendants of Noah through his son Ham and grandson Mizraim ("Egypt" in some versions), and ancestors of the Philistines (Gn 10:14; 1 Chr 1:11).

Cassia. Type of tree that produces a spice resembling cinnamon (Ex 30:24; Ez 27:19).

See PLANTS.

Castanet. RSV translation in 2 Samuel 6:5 for sistrum, a small hand-held percussion instrument.

See MUSIC AND MUSICAL INSTRUMENTS (MENA ʿANIM; ZELZELIM); SISTRUM.

Castor and Pollux. Twin sons of Zeus according to Greek and Roman mythology. The apostle Paul sailed from Malta to Puteoli on a ship whose sign or figurehead was the Twin Brothers (Acts 28:11).

See DIOSCURI.

Caterpillar. Wormlike larva of a butterfly, moth, and some other insects.

See ANIMALS.

Catholic Letters. Traditional name given to the epistles of James, 1 and 2 Peter, 1, 2, 3 John, and Jude. With the exception of 2 and 3 John, these epistles are all addressed to the church at large rather than to individual churches; most likely this is the reason for the designation "catholic."

See JAMES, LETTER OF; JOHN, LETTERS OF; JUDE, LETTER OF; PETER, FIRST LETTER OF; PETER, SECOND LETTER OF.

Cattle. Domesticated bovine animals such as cows and oxen, but in the Bible also sheep and goats.

See AGRICULTURE; ANIMALS.

Cauda. Small island south of Crete. The ship carrying the apostle Paul to Rome sought temporary refuge at Cauda during a storm (Acts 27:16). In the lee (calmer waters) behind the island the sailors hoisted on board a boat being towed by the ship and made efforts to strengthen the ship's hull. Even after lowering the sails they were driven past the island and eventually wrecked.

Cauda is the modern island of Gaudos (Gozzo). Ancient manuscripts are divided on the spelling of the name, some rendering it "Cauda" (RSV), others "Clauda" (KJV, NASB).

Caulker. One who works some waterproofing substance such as bitumen into the seams of a ship's planking to make them watertight.

See TRADES AND OCCUPATIONS.

Cavalry. *See* ARMS AND WARFARE.

Cedar. Tree indigenous to Palestine whose wood was used in construction (1 Kgs 6:9).

See PLANTS.

Cedron. KJV name for Kidron, the river valley between Jerusalem and the Mt of Olives, in John 18:1.

See KIDRON.

Cenchreae, Cenchrea. Seaport city that served the maritime needs of the larger city of Corinth, about 8 miles to the west. Cenchreae (KJV Cenchrea) is known as early as the 5th century BC in connection with an Athenian attack on Corinth. Before the Corinthian Canal was cut through the isthmus, traffic to Europe from Asia often passed from Cenchreae through Corinth to Lechaion.

Excavations begun in 1963 have located the harbor mole (breakwater), warehouse remains dating to the early 1st century, and a large 2nd-century stone building. A 4th-century church testifies to the influence of Christianity in the city. Portions of the ancient road leading southeast from the Cenchreaean gate in

The harbor at Cenchreae.

Corinth may still be seen among the ruins of that city's *agora* (marketplace).

The apostle Paul took an oath requiring the cutting of his hair before leaving Cenchreae during his third missionary journey (Acts 18:18). In his letter to the church in Rome, Paul commended Phoebe, a deaconess of the church in Cenchreae well known for her Christian service (Rom 16:1).

Censer. Vessel used to burn incense. On the Day of Atonement the high priest was to burn two handfuls of incense in the censer within the Holy of Holies before the Lord (Lv 16:12). The censers of the tabernacle were made of bronze (Nm 16:39); those used by the angels in the Book of Revelation were of gold (Rv 8:3,5).

See TABERNACLE, TEMPLE.

Census. Registration and enumeration of a people, usually for purposes of war or taxation. A few censuses are mentioned in the Bible.

The first census was held at Mt Sinai two years after the exodus. In order to assess Israel's military potential, all Israelite males over 20 years old were counted—603,550 in all (Nm 1:1–3,46). A special census was taken of the Levites, who were expected to serve in the tabernacle in place of military obligations. Every male Levite at least a month old was counted—22,000 in all, although of that number only 8,580 actually qualified for priestly service (Nm 3:15,39; 4:46–48).

A second census, conducted at the close of Israel's 40 years of wandering in the wilderness, is recorded in Numbers 26. It too was primarily a military census, part of the strategic calculations made at Shittim in Moab just before the Israelite invasion of the Promised Land. The number of men able to bear arms was 601,730 (Nm 26:51), again excluding the Levites. The 23,000 Levites were counted separately because they were not going to receive

an allotment of land (Nm 26:62). The rules for registration of the Israelites (given in Ex 30:11–16) included payment of ½ shekel each, about ⅕ ounce of silver. The significance of that "ransom" to the Lord, paid "that there be no plague among them when you number them," is unclear.

A third census occurred near the end of King David's reign (2 Sm 24:1–17). The two censuses under Moses had been conducted at God's command; David's census came at a time when God was angry at Israel. The record says that the Lord "incited David against them," without specifying David's own motivations for the census (cf. the later interpretation of 1 Chr 21:1). It may have been for the purpose of conscription or taxation or simply to measure the extent of the king's power by the number of his subjects. At any rate Joab, David's chief military commander, sensed that something was wrong about taking a census at that time and attempted to dissuade David. After the registration was conducted— there is some ambiguity as to whether it was ever completed (cf. 1 Chr 21:6; 27:23,24)— David realized his mistake and repented. Nevertheless, the census angered God, and as a punishment he gave David the choice of three years of famine, three months of flight before an enemy, or three days of pestilence. David chose the pestilence, in which 70,000 men died. The census identified 800,000 able-bodied men in Israel and 500,000 in Judah (2 Sm 24:9). An alternate account reported a potential militia of 1,100,000 in Israel and 470,000 in Judah (1 Chr 21:5), plus a separate count of 38,000 Levites qualified to serve in the temple (1 Chr 23:3).

Scholars have puzzled over the fact that figures for the third census (despite their variation in the two different records) approximately double the figures for the first two. Many attempts have been made to explain those variations in the strength of the military

The Two Major Censuses of Israel

Tribe	First Census Nm 1:20–42	Second Census Nm 26:5–51	Change	Percent of Change
Reuben	46,500	43,730	−2,770	−5.96
Simeon	59,300	22,200	−37,100	−62.56
Gad	45,650	40,500	−5,150	−11.28
Judah	74,600	76,500	+1,900	2.55
Issachar	54,400	64,300	+9,900	18.20
Zebulon	57,400	60,500	+3,100	5.40
Ephraim	40,500	32,500	−8,000	−19.75
Manasseh	32,200	52,700	+20,500	63.66
Benjamin	35,400	45,600	+10,200	28.81
Dan	62,700	64,400	+1,700	2.71
Asher	41,500	53,400	+11,900	28.67
Naphtali	53,400	45,400	−8,000	−14.98
Total	603,550	601,730	−1,820	−.30

The censuses include only the number of men twenty years of age and older.

and in the size of the total population they imply. So far none of the explanations is fully satisfying.

A fourth census, recorded in Ezra 2, was taken on the return of the exiles to Jerusalem. The final total included 42,360 males of Israelite descent, 7,337 slaves (male and female), and 200 singers (male and female).

In the NT a census played a role in the circumstances of Jesus' birth: "In those days a decree went out from Caesar Augustus that all the world should be enrolled. This was the first enrollment, when Quirinius was governor of Syria. And all went to be enrolled, each to his own city" (Lk 2:1–3).

Josephus, a 1st-century AD Jewish historian, records that Quirinius completed a census under the emperor's direction soon after his tenure as governor of Syria began in AD 6. Matthew 2, however, places the birth of Jesus during the reign of Herod the Great, who died in 4 BC. Several solutions have been proposed for the apparent chronological problem.

Attempts to discount the accuracy of Josephus' records have not been completely convincing. Further, Luke's care with details throughout his Gospel and the Book of Acts makes it unlikely that his report is inaccurate. Solutions based on emendations of the text, assuming some early misreading of the text (e.g., a notation of the early church father Tertullian to the effect that there was a census under Saturninus), have not received much acceptance. More popular solutions suggest that the census was ordered at the time of Jesus' birth but not actually carried out until AD 6 or 7, or that Quirinius was some type of co-regent before his elevation to the governorship in AD 6.

An alternative solution centers around the meaning of Luke's word "first" (Lk 2:2). The reference to the "first enrollment" may have been made to distinguish it from the more famous enrollment of AD 6–7. Luke was obviously aware of the later census, which he mentions in a passing reference in Acts 5:37. A series of censuses known to have been made in Egypt about the same time lend credence to the theory of a similar series in Palestine.

Thus, the most plausible solution suggests that an earlier census took place during the influential leadership of Quirinius before his full governorship.

Luke's reference to the census under Quirinius serves two purposes in his Gospel. First, it provides a date for the birth of Jesus. Second, it explains why Joseph and Mary were in Bethlehem at that time. The census under Quirinius was probably for purposes of taxation, since the Romans exempted the Jews from military service. The requirement to return to one's hometown, reflecting the patriarchal element in Hebrew religion, probably also reflects the general willingness of Caesar Augustus to let the Jews follow their own customs.

MORRIS A. WEIGELT

Centurion. Commander of 100 men in the Roman army. There were generally 6 centurions in each cohort and 10 cohorts in a legion. Each legion had 6 tribunes to whom its centurions were subordinate. In Acts 22:26, for example, a centurion appealed to his tribune for a decision concerning the apostle Paul. A centurion's authority was actually quite extensive because he was the working officer who had direct contact with the men. He went to the field with them and made spontaneous decisions according to each situation.

The office of centurion was normally the highest one within reach of the ordinary soldier. Centurions often rose from the ranks because of their experience and knowledge. After one became a centurion, further promotion could come by transfer to positions of increasing responsibility, the highest being senior centurion over the first of 10 cohorts in a legion. Thus a centurion might move about extensively throughout the Roman empire.

A centurion had many duties besides maintaining discipline among the ranks. He had to oversee executions for capital offenses (Mt 27:54; Mk 15:39,44,45; Lk 23:47). He was responsible for his troops at all times, whether they were Roman citizens or recruited mercenary soldiers. The position of centurion was prestigious and high paying; those who reached that rank usually made a career of it.

Six centurions are mentioned in the NT, at least two of whom seem to have become followers of Christ:

1. A centurion at Capernaum pleaded for the life of his dying servant because he believed that diseases would obey Jesus just as his soldiers obeyed him (Mt 8:5–13; Lk 7:2–10). In spite of his high-ranking position, he was a humble man, willing to admit his inadequacy and helplessness. He cared deeply for his servant's welfare. Jesus marveled at that example of faith and healed the sick man.

2. The centurion in charge of the squad that executed Jesus declared, "Truly this man was the Son of God!" (Mk 15:39) and "Certainly this man was innocent!" (Lk 23:47). The apocryphal *Acts of Pilate*, probably dating from the 4th century, named the believing centurion Longinus; he has been regarded as a saint in Roman Catholic tradition. A marble statue depicting his dramatic confession, sculpted by the 17th-century baroque artist Giovanni Bernini, is located in St. Peter's basilica in Rome.

3. A centurion in Caesarea named Cornelius was converted to Christ through the testimony of the apostle Peter, whose reluctance to share the gospel with Gentiles had been broken down by a vision from God (Acts 10).

4. A centurion in Acts 22:25,26 helped save the apostle Paul from a scourging when he reminded his tribune that the accused was a Roman citizen.

5. Another centurion helped save Paul from a Jewish plot to murder him (Acts 23:17–22).

6. A centurion named Julius was assigned to guard Paul on his journey from Caesarea to Rome (Acts 27:1). When their ship broke up in a storm, Julius prevented the soldiers' killing all the prisoners on board, including Paul (Acts 27:42,43).

See ARMS AND WARFARE.

Cephas. Aramaic name of Simon Peter the apostle in John 1:42; 1 Corinthians 1:12; and Galatians 1:18.

See PETER, THE APOSTLE.

Cereal Offering. One of the several types of offerings to God which reflected consecration and commitment.

See OFFERINGS AND SACRIFICES.

Certificate of Divorce. Document a man was obligated to give to his wife if he divorced her.

See DIVORCE, CERTIFICATE OF.

Chaff. Loose hulls separated from the edible grains by threshing and winnowing. In Bible times the common sight of winnowed grain remaining when the wind blew away the lighter husks gave rise to the vivid image of good people or nations surviving judgment while the wicked do not. So, for example, sinners "are like chaff which the wind drives away" (Ps 1:4).

The prophet Isaiah said of the Assyrians, "You conceive chaff, you bring forth stubble; your breath is a fire that will consume you" (Is 33:11). Likewise, in Nebuchadnezzar's dream, the nations of the world collapse and are "like the chaff of the summer threshing floors" before the victory of the coming kingdom of God (Dn 2:35).

In the NT it is said that the coming Messiah will "gather his wheat into the granary, but the chaff he will burn with unquenchable fire" (Mt 3:12).

Chalcedony. Kind of quartz, variously colored, usually grayish or milky.

See MINERALS, METALS, AND PRECIOUS STONES.

Chalcol. KJV spelling of Calcol, a man of wisdom, in 1 Kings 4:31.

See CALCOL.

Chaldea, Chaldeans. Ancient region in Mesopotamia and its inhabitants. The name comes from the Chaldean (or *Kaldu*) tribes which shared Babylonia in southeastern Mesopotamia with several other peoples, especially the Sumerians and Akkadians. After the Old Babylonian empire was absorbed by the Assyrians, the Chaldeans under Nebuchadnezzar's leadership took control and built a Neo-Babylonian empire that dominated the Middle East for nearly a century. The region called Chaldea is also associated with the patriarch Abraham, whose Mesopotamian home was "Ur of the Chaldeans" (Gn 11:28).

Land and People. Until the end of the 8th century BC Chaldea referred only to a small territory in southern Babylonia. Within 100 years, following a rapid and successful bid for power, it embraced all of Babylonia. At that time it included the territory from Baghdad on the Tigris River to the Persian Gulf and extended up the Euphrates River as far as the city of Hit. Although Chaldea is usually placed between the Tigris and Euphrates, it reached into the flatlands between the Tigris and the Zagros mountains to the east and also included some land west of the Euphrates. The Arabian desert formed its western boundary. Chaldea rarely exceeded 40 miles in width, having an area of about 8,000 square miles, approximately the size of New Jersey. On today's map Chaldea falls inside Iraq, with its southwestern tip touching the small kingdom of Kuwait.

Productivity. Chaldea was by far the most productive region of the Fertile Crescent (a geographical arc extending from the Nile delta to the mouth of the Tigris and Euphrates). Since the productivity of the land was in direct proportion to the upkeep of irrigation canals, many kings boasted of their canal building. When irrigation was neglected, as it was under Turkish rule in modern times, Babylonia became one of the most desolate places on earth.

With proper use of dikes and canals the irrigated fields produced staggering amounts of barley, wheat, and emmer (an ancient form of wheat). Figs, pomegranates, and dates grew in abundance. The Assyrian king Sennacherib praised the gardens and fruit trees of Chaldea. The higher sections of the plain were suitable for pasture mainly in the spring. Along the rivers and lagoons were large areas of marshland where cattle and sheep could graze. Fishing was another important source of food.

Trade and Transportation. Except for food products, the only raw material native to Chaldea was bitumen (asphalt), found in deposits near the city of Hit. The Chaldeans therefore depended heavily on trade to bring in building materials and other necessary items. Food and wool were traded for lumber, metals, and precious stones.

Some products came through the Persian Gulf, others via land routes from the north and east. Major roads ran from the gulf all the way to Syria, Palestine, and Egypt, and eastward to Elam and Persia. Within Babylonia itself most transportation was handled by boat. Goods were easily sent from city to city on canals and rivers. Rafts consisting of a wooden platform with inflated skins underneath plied the Tigris River. The slower-moving current of the Euphrates permitted navigation farther upstream than on the Tigris. In the Bible the majestic Euphrates was often called "the great river" (Dt 1:7; Jos 1:4; Rv 9:14) or simply "the river" (Gn 31:21 KJV). The prosperity of Chaldea hinged on the scope of its trading interests and on the effectiveness of its transportation system.

Because of the lack of both stone and lumber, the people of Babylonia were forced to use clay from the alluvium (silt) deposits to form adobe. Clay bricks were the primary building material in the land. The same clay was used to make tablets for their wedge-shaped writing called cuneiform. When baked, they lasted for centuries and have unlocked for modern archaeology many secrets of that era.

Cities. The Chaldeans had few cities at first, when they relied primarily on fishing and hunting. But in time the Chaldean population grew, and they occupied a number of famous cities whose mounds are still visible today. Most of the cities of Mesopotamia had been built by earlier cultures in its southern sectors. Near the Persian Gulf lay Eridu, Ur, Larsa, and Uruk (the Erech of Gn 10:10). Nippur was located in the center of Babylonia, and toward the north were Borsippa, Babylon, Kutha, and Kish. Some of those cities of the Sumerian and Akkadian cultures were already well known in the 3rd and 2nd millennia BC, when Chaldea was called "Sumer and Akkad." Ur and Eridu were once very close to the ancient coastline, but over the centuries alluvial deposits from the rivers have filled in the northern part of the Persian Gulf.

History. First mention of the Chaldeans is found in the Assyrian annals of Ashurnasirpal II (885–860 BC), leading some authorities to suggest that they entered Babylonia about 1000 BC. They are usually associated (though not identified) with the Semitic Aramaean tribes who were constantly pushing their way from the western deserts into Mesopotamia. They settled primarily in the southern tip of Babylonia, at the nothern end of the Persian Gulf, perhaps centuries before the Assyrian annals mentioned them.

Job 1:17 mentions three bands of Chaldeans who participated in a raid against Job's camels and servants, probably in the vicinity of Edom or northern Arabia. Their presence in those regions does not necessarily mean they lived nearby, since armies from Babylonia (Sinar) and Elam ranged as far as Palestine centuries earlier (Gn 14:1,2).

Under Assyrian Rule. Living by the marshes and lakes of the extreme south, the Chaldeans maintained a high degree of independence, even when Assyrian dominion extended over them. It was difficult for invading armies to maneuver in the Chaldean marshes. As a result, the Chaldeans resisted paying taxes or providing any form of service to the Assyrian government. When the Assyrians sought to limit their freedom, the Chaldeans turned to guerrilla warfare and political intrigue. They were quick to disregard treaties or to switch alliances as circumstances dictated. Under Assyrian rule, whereas the native residents of Babylonian cities were generally content, the Chaldeans became the leaders of a national independence movement. For 250 years the Assyrians had to enforce their dominion against persistent Chaldean attempts to assert their autonomy and influence.

Finally, in 721 BC the Chaldean leader Marduk-apla-iddina II (known as Merodach-baladan in 2 Kgs 20:12 and Is 39:1, who sent an embassy to Hezekiah, king of Judah) entered Babylon and claimed the kingship of Babylonia, a position long appointed by the Assyrian king. Crafty and resourceful, he successfully maintained his claim for 10 years before being driven back into his own southern territory by Assyria's Sargon II. On Sargon's death in 705 BC he reasserted his claim, but was defeated by the new Assyrian king, Sennacherib, who destroyed Babylon as a lesson to the Chaldeans and their allies.

Sennacherib's son and successor, Esarhaddon, pursued a policy of conciliation with the Babylonians and rebuilt their capital city, a gesture that effectively neutralized Chaldean agitation and inaugurated a period of peace that lasted over 30 years. The last unsuccessful revolt occurred under Ashurbanipal's reign and was actually instigated by his brother, whom the Assyrian king had appointed to the Babylonian throne. The Chaldeans gladly joined the rebellion, which was crushed in 648 BC.

The Neo-Babylonian Empire. Two decades later, at the time of Ashurbanipal's death, Assyrian power suddenly and dramatically slipped. Nabopolassar, a Chaldean governor, took the opportunity to drive the Assyrians out of Babylonia. He became king of Babylon in 625 BC. Allied with the Medes, the Babylonians went on to destroy the Assyrian empire, capturing the capital cities of Asshur in 614 and Nineveh in 612. They divided the conquered lands with the Medes and annexed the Assyrian regions west and south of the Tigris, creating a new Babylonian empire. (The first Babylonian empire, with which Hammurabi is associated, had flourished over a thousand years earlier.) Throughout the Middle East, Chaldea and Babylonia became synonymous.

During the long and brilliant reign of Nabopolassar's son, Nebuchadnezzar (or Nebuchadrezzar) II, the empire reached its zenith. As crown prince he won a decisive victory in 605 BC over the Egyptians at Carchemish (the battle mentioned in 2 Chr 35:20), which effectively established Babylonian supremacy in the Near East (see 2 Kgs 24:7). That same year

the southern kingdom of Judah became a vassal nation to Babylon. Nebuchadnezzar won the submission of King Jehoiachim, carried off the choicest articles from the temple for his own temple in Babylon, and took the outstanding leaders and youth of Judah captive (2 Kgs 24:1; 2 Chr 36:5–7; Dn 1:1–4). When Judah revolted several years later at the instigation of Egypt, the Chaldean army captured Jerusalem in 597 BC. Judah's new king, Jehoiachin, was deported at that time together with more of its leaders (2 Kgs 24:8–16). A second revolt in 594 BC by the Chaldean-appointed king (Zedekiah) resulted in a third invasion, the destruction of Jerusalem in 586 BC, and the exile of most of Judah's citizens (2 Kgs 24:20–25:12; 2 Chr 36:11–21). With the booty from that and other conquests Nebuchadnezzar built Babylon into one of the most dazzling cities in the ancient world. His projects included the hanging gardens (one of the seven wonders of the ancient world), the Ishtar Gate, and a 17-mile outer wall designed for defense of the city. His pride in such accomplishments eventually brought the judgment of God (Dn 4:30–33).

Nebuchadnezzar was succeeded by his son Amel-Marduk (Evil-merodach in 2 Kgs 25:27 and Jer 52:31, remembered there for his special kindness to the exiled king Jehoiachin). After two years he was killed in an armed rebellion led by his brother-in-law, Nergal-shar-usur (Nergal-sharezer of Jer 39:3), who attempted to establish his own dynasty. After a 4-year reign Nergal-shar-usur was succeeded by his son, who lasted only a few months before being ousted by a usurper, Nabonidus.

The Fall of Babylon. Nabonidus was the last of the Chaldean monarchs. His installation as king was supported by many Babylonian officials who, watching their former allies the Medes gradually become a rival power, saw in Nabonidus a ruler strong enough to meet their threat. Strong or not, his attempts to reform Babylonian religion proved extremely unpopular, and his efforts to strengthen the economy were unsuccessful. Both facts made Babylon an unpleasant residence for Nabonidus; during one extended absence from the capital city he installed his son Belshazzar as co-regent. (Belshazzar's position explains why he is described as king of Babylon in the OT Book of Daniel and why in Dn 5:7 he could make Daniel only "the third ruler in the kingdom.")

While Belshazzar was handling government affairs, the famous incident of the "writing on the wall" occurred, ominously predicting Babylon's downfall (Dn 5). The Elamites, in fact, were already attacking the empire's eastern flank. Rumors of Persian power in the north brought Nabonidus back to Babylon just in time for an invasion by the Persian king, Cyrus the Great. Cyrus took Babylon without a fight, putting an end both to Chaldean power and to the Neo-Babylonian empire.

Chaldeans as Astrologers. Long after the Chaldean empire had ceased to exist, the name "Chaldeans" lingered in Hellenistic Egypt, Greece, and Rome as a term for magicians, astrologers, and diviners. The same usage of the term appears in the Book of Daniel, where Chaldeans were linked with soothsayers, conjurers, and sorcerers (Dn 2:2,10; 4:7; 5:7).

Babylonians had long been renowned for their advanced knowledge of astronomy and for their dependence on the stars to help them predict the future. One Babylonian text from about 700 BC described the zodiacal belt and named 15 constellations. Several of the names are still used by astrologers today: the Bull, the Twins (Gemini), the Scorpion, and Capricorn. In Daniel 2:2 and 4:7 one of the terms linked with the Chaldeans is related to a Babylonian word referring to a class of priests who made use of incantations. Just how important they were for society has been shown in tablets that have been excavated which describe the priests' training. The most outstanding youths of Judah, including Daniel, were selected for a similar educational program (Dn 1:4). HERBERT M. WOLF

See BABYLON, BABYLONIA; ASSYRIA, ASSYRIANS; UR OF THE CHALDEES; DANIEL, BOOK OF; EXILE; ASTROLOGY; NEBUCHADNEZZAR, NEBUCHADREZZAR.

Chalkstone. Literally "stones of chalk," mentioned as illustrative of the destruction of the pagan altars in Judah (Is 27:9). Chalk beds cap many of the Judean hills, and since the substance easily erodes, Isaiah's prophecy is apt.

See MINERALS, METALS, AND PRECIOUS STONES; PALESTINE.

Chamberlain. High-ranking officer in the service of the king.

See TRADES AND OCCUPATIONS.

Chambers of the South. Possibly a constellation of stars, or the vast stretches of southern sky without stars (Jb 9:9).

See ASTRONOMY.

Chameleon. Any of a number of lizards having the ability to change color rapidly, declared ritually unclean (Lv 11:30).

See ANIMALS.

Chamois. Small, goatlike antelope that lives primarily in the high mountains of Eu-

rope. In Deuteronomy 14:5 "chamois" is an inaccurate translation of the Hebrew word which is better rendered "mountain sheep" (RSV).

See ANIMALS (SHEEP).

Chanaan. KJV spelling of Canaan in Acts 7:11 and 13:19.

See CANAAN, CANAANITES.

Channels of the Sea. Valleys or stream beds in the ocean floor. When the Lord delivered David from all his enemies and from King Saul, David praised God's great power, which could expose the ocean floor with a blast of his breath (2 Sm 22:16; Ps 18:15).

Chant. Recitation in song or monotonous voice (Ps 8:1; Ez 32:16).

See MUSIC AND MUSICAL INSTRUMENTS.

Chaos, Waters of. In ancient thought, the primeval seas that were divided. The world was then situated between the "waters above" and "waters below," or "the Deep."

Chapiter. KJV rendering of capital, architecturally the uppermost part of a pillar.

See CAPITAL.

Charashim. KJV rendering of Ge-harashim, a valley on the plain of Sharon's southern border, in 1 Chronicles 4:14.

See GE-HARASHIM.

Charchemish. KJV spelling of the city Carchemish in 2 Chronicles 35:20.

See CARCHEMISH.

Chariot. Ancient two-wheeled vehicle pulled by animals, usually horses, and normally thought of as an instrument of war. Chariots were also used as a means of transportation for persons of rank or wealth, and for hunting.

See ARMS AND WARFARE; TRAVEL AND TRANSPORTATION.

Charismata. Abilities the Holy Spirit gives to the church (1 Cor 12).

See SPIRITUAL GIFTS.

Charm. Small object worn around the neck to ward off evil.

See AMULET; MAGIC; SORCERY.

Charran. KJV spelling of Haran, a Mesopotamian city, in Acts 7:2,4.

See HARAN (PLACE).

Chastisement, Chasten. Correction intended to produce righteousness (Dt 21:18; 2 Tm 2:25).

See Discipline.

Chebar. Canal in Babylonia. The prophet Ezekiel, who was among the exiles from the southern kingdom of Judah, received visions from God while living in the area of the Chebar Canal (Ez 1:1,3; 3:15,23; 10:15,20,22; 43:3). Secular Babylonian texts refer to a *nar Kabaru* that is believed to be the same canal. Some scholars identify this canal with the modern Shatt en-Nil.

Chedorlaomer. King of Elam who participated with three other kings in a campaign against five cities near the southern end of the Dead Sea plain (Gn 14). Although Chedorlaomer is initially third in the list (Gn 14:1), he was evidently the leader of the four kings. Elsewhere in the chapter his name comes first or stands alone.

For 12 years the five cities of the plain had been vassals of Chedorlaomer. In the 13th year the cities rebelled, and the next year Chedorlaomer enlisted allies to enforce his lordship. The victorious kings looted the cities and took prisoners. Because the patriarch Abram's nephew Lot was among the captives, Abram mustered his servants and allies and pursued Chedorlaomer as far as Damascus. Chedorlaomer was defeated, and the captured loot and prisoners were rescued.

The first half of the name Chedorlaomer is a common Elamite word meaning "servant." The second half is probably the name of an Elamite deity. Although both elements of the name are known outside the Bible, the combination is not. It fits, however, with an early 2nd-millennium BC date for the encounter, coinciding with the biblical account.

Cheese. Milk product manufactured by curdling milk, draining the whey, pressing the curds into cakes, and drying them. The earliest biblical reference to cheese is in Job 10:10: "Didst thou not . . . curdle me like cheese?"

See Food and Food Preparation.

Chelal. Pahath-moab's son, who obeyed Ezra's exhortation to divorce his pagan wife after the exile (Ezr 10:30).

Chelluh. KJV rendering of Cheluhi, Bani's son, in Ezra 10:35.

See Cheluhi.

Chelub. 1. Shuhah's brother and the father of Mehir from Judah's tribe (1 Chr 4:11).

2. Father of Ezri. Ezri oversaw the tilling of soil in King David's fields (1 Chr 27:26).

Chelubai. Hezron's son and the brother of Jerahmeel (1 Chr 2:9); alternately called Caleb in 1 Chronicles 2:18,42.

See Caleb #2.

Cheluhi. One of Bani's sons, who was encouraged by Ezra to divorce his foreign wife after the exile (Ezr 10:35, KJV Chelluh).

Chemarim, Chemarims. Hebrew term translated "idolatrous priests" (2 Kgs 23:5; Hos 10:5; Zep 1:4). In the KJV this word appears in Zephaniah 1:4 as a proper name, spelled either Chemarim or Chemarims. The exact meaning of the word is uncertain.

Chemosh. Name of the national god of Moab (Nm 21:29); also associated with the Ammonites (Jgs 11:24).

See Canaanite Deities and Religion; Moab, Moabite.

Chenaanah. 1. Father of Zedekiah, the false prophet who incorrectly prophesied victory for kings Ahab and Jehoshaphat over the Syrians (1 Kgs 22:11,24; 2 Chr 18:10,23).

2. Bilhan's son, who was chief of the subclan of Jediael in Benjamin's tribe in the time of King David (1 Chr 7:10,11).

Chenani. Levite who participated in Ezra's public reading of the Law after the exile (Neh 9:4).

Chenaniah. 1. Levite chief who led processional singing when King David brought the ark of the covenant to the new tabernacle in Jerusalem (1 Chr 15:1–3,22,27).

2. Public administrator during David's reign. His sons also served as public officials (1 Chr 26:29).

Chephar-ammoni, Chephar-haammonai. City allotted to Benjamin's tribe for an inheritance after the initial conquest of Canaan by Joshua (Jos 18:24, KJV Chephar-haammonai). Its location is unknown.

Chephirah. Hivite city included in a treaty with Joshua that the Gibeonites secured by deception (Jos 9:17). When the Israelites conquered the land of Canaan, Chephirah became the property of Benjamin's tribe (Jos 18:26). Many inhabitants of this city came back to Judea with the repatriates after the exile (Ezr 2:25; Neh 7:29). The site is now identified as Khirbet Kefireh, located southwest of ancient Gibeon.

Cheran. Dishon's son, a member of the Horite tribe during Esau's time (Gn 36:26; 1 Chr 1:41).

Cherethite, Cherethims. Members of a tribal group that lived in southern Judah near Hebron (1 Sm 30:14), mentioned along with the Pelethites (2 Sm 8:18). The Cherethites were associated with the Philistines, according to Ezekiel 25:15–17 (KJV Cherethims; cf. Zep 2:5). They were judged with "the rest of the seacoast" for the Philistines' offense against Israel. Since the Philistines most likely originated in the islands of the Mediterranean, including Crete, the word "Cherethite" probably means Cretan. "Pelethite" is probably an alternate spelling of Philistine.

Because of the Cherethites' Philistine connections, what is known about the Philistines may shed light on them. Archaeological evidence from Cretan murals and Egyptian tomb paintings and temple reliefs shows Philistines wearing plumed headdresses. Similarities between Philistine, Cretan, and Greek pottery designs also suggest a strong link between these Mediterranean peoples.

Cherethites and Pelethites were hired by David as mercenaries, forming an elite corps of foreign soldiers faithful to him through all his troubles (2 Sm 15:18; 20:7, 23; 1 Kgs 1:38). Later kings may have continued to use them as soldiers, as suggested by mention of "Carites" (Cherethites?) in 2 Kings 11:4,19.

Cherith, The Brook. Stream where the Lord told the prophet Elijah to hide from King Ahab during a famine Elijah had predicted. There he had sufficient water to drink

The source of Cherith (near the Dead Sea).

and was fed by ravens each morning and evening (1 Kgs 17:2–6). The brook has traditionally been identified as the Wadi Qelt (in which the Greek Orthodox Monastery of Elijah is now located), west of the Jordan River near Jericho. More likely Cherith, described as "east of the Jordan River," was located in Gilead, Elijah's homeland (1 Kgs 17:3).

Cherub (Place). One of 5 Babylonian cities from which Israelites who could not trace their ancestry returned after the exile (Ezr 2:59; Neh 7:61). In the Apocrypha, Cherub is called a leader of the people (1 Esd 5:36) rather than a place from which the people came.

Cherub, Cherubim. Winged creatures mentioned occasionally in Scripture ("cherubim" is the plural form of the Hebrew "cherub"). They belong to a supernatural created order along with the seraphim and angels. Some scholars have argued that the term "cherub" had its origin in the *karibu* ("intercessor") of Akkadian mythological texts, commonly represented in Mesopotamian art as a griffin (a creature half lion and half eagle) or as a winged human. The sphinx also appears to go back to this concept. The biblical evidence, however, does not seem to support that identification.

The prophet Ezekiel described four "living creatures," each with four faces and four wings (Ez 1:5–24); those creatures corresponded to cherubim (Ez 10:2–22). The splendor of Ezekiel's vision was recaptured more modestly in his description of the king of Tyre, who in the midst of his own prosperity seemed to be playing the part of a towering or guardian cherub before being dispossessed (Ez 28:13–16). That passage has been interpreted by some as a description of Satan's "fall from grace" after he had once been in the service of God as a ranking member of a high celestial order.

Despite Ezekiel's elaborate visionary descriptions, it is difficult to be certain about the form in which cherubim appeared. Thus in Ezekiel 41:18 the cherubim that were to decorate Ezekiel's ideal temple had only two faces, a man's and a young lion's, in contrast to the four-faced creatures of the earlier visions. The four faces of Ezekiel 1:10 were those of a man, a lion, an ox, and an eagle, whereas in Ezekiel 10:14 the cherub had its own face ("the face of the cherub"), along with the faces of a man, a lion, and an eagle. If the cherub's face corresponded to that of an ox, that might account for the fact that cherubim in Near Eastern art were represented as four-footed creatures, though frequently different otherwise from biblical cherubim. In addition to their wings, the cherubim of Ezekiel's vision had stiff, unbending legs and feet with soles like those of a calf (Ez 1:7).

That complex description has led scholars to try to identify cherubim in the statues and carvings of non-Israelite peoples. The throne of Ahiram, king of Byblos, was flanked by sphinxes, which some have judged to be cherubim. The sphinx, however, seems to have been a popular decorative motif, as evidenced by an ivory box from Megiddo and ivories from Samaria, Nimrud, and elsewhere. Other decorative creatures have various combinations of human and animal bodies, with wings generally prominent. None of them adequately represents the OT descriptions of cherubim.

The four living creatures of the Book of Revelation were similar to the cherubim of Ezekiel but lacked their whirling wheels (Rv 4:6–9). Subsequent references to the creatures in Revelation (5:6–14; 6:1–8; 7:1–11; 14:3; 15:7; 19:4) add nothing to the initial description.

The cherubim of Genesis 3:24 acted as guardians or custodians. Supernatural guardians seem to have been common in Near Eastern thought. In Ezekiel 10 the cherubim were also executors of divine judgment, spreading burning coals over a city (Ez 10:2,7).

In early Israelite thought the cherubim stretched out their wings and provided God with a throne (1 Sm 4:4; 2 Sm 6:2; etc.). God spoke to Moses from such a throne on the cover of the ark of the covenant (Ex 25:22). In Ezekiel's vision (Ez 1:26; 10:1) God was seated in a four-wheeled chariot moved by the cherubim and borne aloft by their wings. In Hebrew poetry God was portrayed as employing clouds for his chariot (Ps 104:3; cf. Is 19:1) or riding on a cherub in flight (2 Sm 22:11; Ps 18:10). The idea of cherubim furnishing a seat or platform for the invisible deity found expression in Near Eastern art, where the pagan gods stood on the backs of animals.

In Israel cherubim were carved on the covenantal ark (Ex 25:18–20; 37:7–9), and representations of them were also embroidered on the curtains of the tabernacle and the veil that screened the innermost sanctuary in which the ark rested.

The Most Holy Place of Solomon's temple was adorned by two large representations of cherubim, made of olive wood and covered with gold leaf. When placed side by side with outstretched wings they spanned the entire width of the inner sanctuary. Smaller cherubim and palms were carved on the temple's wooden panels and some of the doors, and were also represented on the sides of the laver stands (1 Kgs 7:29,36). Cherubim alternating with palm trees formed part of the decor of Ezekiel's visionary temple (Ez 41:17–20).

R.K. HARRISON

See ANGEL; SERAPH, SERAPHIM.

Chesalon. City in northern Judah near the border of Dan, situated on the northern slope of Mt Jearim; usually identified with modern Kesla, about nine miles west of Jerusalem. Chesalon is mentioned only in the period of Israel's initial settlement of Palestine under Joshua (Jos 15:10).

See JEARIM, MOUNT.

Chesed. Son of Milcah and Nahor, Abraham's brother (Gn 22:22).

Chesil. City situated along the borders of Edom in the Negeb, allotted to Judah's tribe for an inheritance (Jos 15:30). In parallel lists of towns Chesil is replaced by Bethul (Jos 19:4), Bethuel (1 Chr 4:30), and perhaps Bethel—not to be confused with the Bethel north of Jerusalem (1 Sm 30:27). Bethuel or Bethul is considered by many textual critics to be the original name, with Chesil as a later textual variant.

See BETHUEL, BETHUL (PLACE).

Chestnut. KJV mistranslation for plane tree, a tree indigenous to Palestine (Gn 30:37; Ez 31:8).

See PLANTS (PLANE TREE).

Chesulloth. Town in Issachar (Jos 19:18); also called Chisloth-tabor in Joshua 19:12. It is probably to be identified with the modern Iksal, about three miles southeast of Nazareth.

Chezib. Alternate name for Achzib, a city in Judah's territory, in Genesis 38:5.

See ACHZIB #1.

Chicken. Common domestic fowl raised for its edible eggs and flesh.

See BIRDS (FOWL, DOMESTIC).

Chidon. Threshing floor where Uzzah was struck down by God as he attempted to steady the ark of the covenant (1 Chr 13:9). The parallel passage in 2 Samuel 6:6 refers to this place as "the threshing floor of Nacon." Following the death of Uzzah the place was renamed Perez-uzzah, which means either "the breach of Uzzah" or the "outbreak against Uzzah" (2 Sm 6:8; 1 Chr 13:11).

See NACON.

Chief Priest. Highest office in the hierarchy of priests and Levites. It was the chief priest who alone went into the Most Holy Place of the temple once a year to make atonement for the sins of the whole nation of Israel.

See PRIESTS AND LEVITES.

Child, Children. See FAMILY LIFE AND RELATIONS.

Childless. See BARRENNESS.

Child of God. See CHRISTIANS, NAMES FOR.

Children of Eden. KJV name for the inhabitants of Beth-eden, an Aramaic city-state conquered by Assyria, in 2 Kings 19:12.

See BETH-EDEN.

Chileab. David's second son, and the first borne to him by Abigail (2 Sm 3:3); alternately called Daniel in 1 Chronicles 3:1.

Chilion. One of the two sons of Elimelech and Naomi (Ru 1:2). He married a Moabite girl named Orpah (1:4; 4:9,10) and eventually died in Moab (1:5).

Chilmad. Mesopotamian city listed with Haran, Canneh, Eden, and Asshur as traders with Tyre (Ez 27:23). Its location is unknown.

Chimham. Son of Barzillai (according to Josephus), a very wealthy man who supplied David and his men with food while they were in Mahanaim during their flight from Absalom (2 Sm 19:32). David offered to take Barzillai back to Jerusalem with him, but Barzillai declined and suggested that David show kindness to Chimham instead (2 Sm 19:37-40). David accepted the proposal, and ordered his son and successor, Solomon, to grant Chimham a pension at the palace (1 Kgs 2:7). His name is reflected centuries later in Geruth Chimham, a place near Bethlehem where the people Johanan had rescued from Ishmael stayed, intending to go to Egypt later (Jer 41:17).

See GERUTH CHIMHAM.

Chinnereth, Chinneroth. 1. Fortified town in the territory allotted to Naphtali's tribe (Jos 19:35). It is also mentioned in an Egyptian list of towns conquered by Thutmose III in the 15th century BC. The site has been identified as Tell el-'Oreimeh on the northwest shore of the Sea of Galilee. Archaeological evidence suggests that the site was inhabited from about 2000 to about 900 BC.

2. A district in Naphtali's territory that included #1 above. It was conquered by Ben-hadad, king of Syria, in the reign of Baasha, king of the northern kingdom of Israel in the early 9th century BC (1 Kgs 15:20, Chinneroth; KJV Cinneroth).

3. Early name for the Sea of Galilee (Nm 34:11; Dt 3:17; Jos 13:27—Chinnereth; Jos 11:2; 12:3—Chinneroth). It is hard to say whether the

city (see #1 above) was named after the sea or vice versa. The name, however, means "lyres," which could be an allusion to the Sea of Galilee's shape which roughly resembles that of a lyre. In NT times the pronunciation of the name was corrupted to Gennesaret (Lk 5:1).

See GALILEE, SEA OF.

Chios. Rocky, mountainous island in the east central area of the Aegean Sea. On his third missionary journey, Paul's ship anchored opposite Chios between stops at Mitylene and Samos en route to Jerusalem (Acts 20:15). Though not particularly fertile, Chios was nevertheless noted for its wine, figs, and gum mastic. It is separated from the mainland by a five-mile strait. In Paul's day its principal city, Chios (modern Scio), was a free city in the Roman province of Asia.

Chislev, Chisleu. Third month of the Hebrew year, about mid-November to mid-December (Neh 1:1; Zec 7:1, KJV Chisleu); also spelled Kislev.

See CALENDARS, ANCIENT AND MODERN.

Chislon. Father of Elidad, leader of Benjamin's tribe during the Israelites' wilderness wanderings and one of those appointed by Moses to divide the land of Canaan among the tribes (Nm 34:21).

Chisloth-tabor. Alternate name for the city Chesulloth in Joshua 19:12.

See CHESULLOTH.

Chitlish. City assigned to Judah's tribe for an inheritance (Jos 15:40, KJV Kithlish). Its location is uncertain.

Chittim. KJV spelling of Kittim, the Hebrew name for the island of Cyprus.

See CYPRUS.

Chiun. KJV form of Kaiwan, an Assyrian astral deity, in Amos 5:26.

See KAIWAN.

Chloe. Woman whose household (possibly slaves) informed Paul in Ephesus of arguments in the Corinthian church (1 Cor 1:11). It is not known whether Chloe lived in Corinth or Ephesus, or whether she herself was a believer.

Choinix. Dry commodity measure equivalent to a little more than a quart (Rv 6:6, RSV and NIV quart).

See WEIGHTS AND MEASURES.

Choirmaster. Director of music; referred to in the superscriptions of 55 psalms.

See MUSIC AND MUSICAL INSTRUMENTS.

Choose, Chosen. *See* ELECT, ELECTION.

Chor-ashan. KJV rendering of Borashan in 1 Samuel 30:30. Borashan was an alternate name for Ashan, a town originally in Judah's territory.

See ASHAN.

Chorazin. Palestinian city on which Jesus pronounced woe (Mt 11:21–24; Lk 10:13,14). It was in Chorazin, Bethsaida, and Capernaum that "most of his miracles" had been done, but the people were generally unresponsive and had not repented (Mt 11:20).

From the biblical references Chorazin was probably in the vicinity of Capernaum and Bethsaida. The church father Jerome (*c.* AD 400) located it two miles from Capernaum, which is on the northwest shore of the Sea of Galilee. Today scholars generally agree that the ruins of Khirbet Kerazeh on the basalt hills north of Capernaum are those of Chorazin. The ruins indicate that it was a fairly im-

Ruins of the synagogue at Chorazin.

portant city. Remains of a synagogue, probably from the 4th century AD, include a carved seat with an inscription, an example of a "Moses' seat" (Mt 23:2). According to the Jewish Talmud, Chorazin was known for its wheat.

Chozeba. KJV form of Cozeba in 1 Chronicles 4:22. Cozeba was an alternate name for Achzib, a city in Judah's territory.

See ACHZIB #1.

Christ. Official title given to Jesus in the NT. It signifies his office as anointed Savior and alludes to his spiritual qualifications for the task of saving his people. The word derives from Greek *Christos*, which translates Hebrew *Messiah* (Jn 1:41). Both terms come from verbs meaning "to anoint with sacred oil"; hence as titles they mean "the anointed one." Applied to Jesus, they express the conviction that he had divine appointment for his office and function.

In the NT the title is used in combination with the given name; as "Jesus Christ" (Mt 1:1; Mk 1:1; Rom 1:4), and "Christ Jesus" (Rom 1:1; 1 Cor 1:1), or with the article "the Christ" (Rom 7:4), or with another title "Lord Christ" (Rom 16:18). It is also used alone as the one favored substitute name or title for Jesus (Jn 20:31; Rom 15:3; Heb 3:6; 5:5; 1 Pt 1:11,19).

Jesus' office and function were foreshadowed by the three groups of OT anointed officials: prophets, priests, and kings. Elisha's anointing by Elijah (1 Kgs 19:19) shows anointing of prophets was practiced, although not required by OT law. Moses was the first OT prophet (Dt 18:18) whose ministry prompted the messianic hope for the coming of the Prophet (Jn 6:14; Heb 1:1). All priests, from Aaron on, were ordained by anointing with oil in required consecration rites (Ex 28:41; 29:7–9; 30:30). The kings of Israel, beginning with Saul and David, were anointed as a sign of divine choice and approval (1 Sm 9:15–17; 10:1; 16:13). Essential to the external ceremony was pouring of perfumed olive oil upon the person's head (Ex 30:22–33). The internal reality was the gift of the Spirit to the recipient: "from that day on the Spirit of the Lord came upon David in power" (1 Sm 16:13 NIV). The anointed person was not a free agent. As prophet, priest, or king he spoke, served, or ruled in the name of the Lord and as his representative to the people of God.

The Gospels portray Jesus as modestly accepting the title and role of Messiah-Christ. His baptism should be understood as his anointing to the threefold office of prophet,

priest, and king. At his baptism by John (the new Elijah, Mt 11:14) Jesus received the outpouring of the Spirit and God's mandate to begin his ministry (Mt 3:16–4:17). John himself denied being the anointed one but tacitly identified Jesus as the Christ (Jn 1:20; Lk 3:15–17). Jesus' first disciples followed him because they knew he was the Messiah (Jn 1:41). The demons recognized him as "the Holy One [anointed] of God" (Mk 1:24; cf. Mt 8:29). The crowds followed him as the Prophet, the new Moses (Jn 6:14,32), but deserted him when they understood that his kingdom was a spiritual, not a political realm (Jn 6:66). The twelve remained loyal, saying, "We believe . . . you are the Holy One of God" (Jn 6:69 NIV). The confession of the disciples voiced by Peter and approved by Jesus as a divine revelation is: "You are the Christ, the Son of the living God" (Mt 16:16). At his trials the decisive factor in Jesus' condemnation was his claim to be the Christ (Mt 26:63,64,68; 27:11,17,22,37).

An important feature in the earliest Christian preaching was the proclamation that Jesus is the Christ (Acts 2:36; 3:18,20; 9:22; 28:23, 31). This remains the earliest (Mt 16:16) and most basic article of Christian confession (1 Cor 1:23; 1 Jn 5:1), affirming that Jesus perfectly fulfilled the role of anointed prophet, priest, and king as the servant of God for his people (Lk 7:16; 1 Cor 15:25; Heb 7:22–28; Rv 19:16).

See JESUS CHRIST, LIFE AND TEACHING OF; MESSIAH.

Christian. Name first given to the followers of Jesus Christ in Antioch (Acts 11:26).

See CHRISTIANS, NAMES FOR.

Christians, Names for. Terms used to designate Christ's early followers, as groups or as individuals. In the earliest years of the Christian era, when the church was unified, no denominational names (such as Baptist or Roman Catholic) existed. Local churches did not have names but were known by their locations (such as "the church at Ephesus"). Nor was there a single official name for the new Christian movement. Many designations were used for the followers of Christ, and these changed as the historical situation changed. Many Christians considered themselves simply Jews who followed Jesus.

What Christians Were Called by Others. As Jesus' disciples preached and won converts after the resurrection, other Jews began to see this as a new movement. They applied four names to the Christian community, not all of them complimentary.

Galileans. Since Jesus and most of the 12 disciples were from Galilee, it was natural for the term to be applied to all of his followers, especially since it implied that the movement was not as pure as Judean Judaism. Some interpreters believe that Luke 22:59 is an example of the use of "Galilean" as a title; in Acts 1:11 and 2:7 it is merely a geographical reference. One sure reference to Christians by that title appears in the work of the pagan philosopher Epictetus (AD 50?–135?), who was impressed with how Christians died for their faith. It is not clear how common the title of Galilean was, but it had obviously spread from Judea to Rome, where Epictetus lived.

Nazarenes. Jesus was known as "Jesus of Nazareth" or "Jesus the Nazarene," so it was easy to transfer that title to his followers. They were "followers of the Nazarene" or "Nazarenes." The earliest use of the term is in Acts 24:5, where Tertullus accused the apostle Paul of being "a ringleader of the sect of the Nazarenes." Certainly he did not intend the title as a compliment, but how others used it is not known. Whether the early Christians used that name for themselves is doubtful, although later Jewish-Christian and Gnostic groups did call themselves Nazarenes. One early writing was even called *The Gospel of the Nazarenes.*

Followers of the Way. Christianity was far from being simply an abstract belief; it was a whole way of life. The new way of living was obvious to those around Christians and to the Christians themselves, for they were following Jesus' life style, the way he had lived and taught. Soon the term "this Way" or "the Way" meant Christian. Thus Saul (the pre-Christian name of Paul) was sent to Damascus to arrest anyone belonging to "the Way" (Acts 9:2). Christians may also have used the term to describe themselves; Luke referred to the Christian movement as "the Way" (Acts 19:9, 23; 24:22). It is the only name Christians and non-Christians both may have used for the new movement.

Christians. When the Christian movement reached Antioch in Syria, the gospel was preached to Gentiles as well as Jews. Such evangelism marked the sect as more than a new type of Judaism; it was a new religion. The Gentiles in Antioch invented a name for the new group. Since members of the group constantly talked about Christ, they were called Christians, meaning the "household" or "partisans" of Christ. Some satire may have been intended in the name. For instance, since the "Augustinians" were an organized group who led the public praise of the emperor Nero Augustus, the citizens of Antioch may have made a comparable Latinized name out of Christ as a joke. Similar groups included Herod's partisans, the Herodians. "Christ" was an unusual and meaningless name to Gentiles, but Chrestos (meaning "good" or "kind") was a common name; some pagans called the new sect "Chrestians." Thus Suetonius wrote of the Jews being expelled from Rome in AD 49 on account of "Chrestus."

The Christians themselves apparently did not appreciate the name, but, like many other nicknames, "Christian" stuck. It appears only three times in the NT: Acts 11:26 describes its origin; Acts 26:28 records Herod Agrippa II saying satirically to Paul, "In a short time you think to make me a Christian!"; 1 Peter 4:16 instructs believers not to be ashamed if they suffer because the name has been applied to them. No further record of the name appears until the 2nd century, when Ignatius of Antioch became the first Christian to call believers Christians. The Roman governor Pliny (from the area to which 1 Peter was addressed) wrote to the emperor Trajan about people accused in his court of being Christians. From that time on, the nickname became popular among Christians. What better name could there be than one declaring that they belonged to Christ?

What Christians Called Themselves as a Group. Christians naturally had a set of names for themselves, some used to refer to individuals, others to a whole group. Three terms were used to identify Christians collectively.

Church. One way of referring to the body of Israel in the OT was simply "the congregation." Groups claiming to be the true Israel spiritually rather naturally called themselves "the congregation." The term was used by the writers of the Dead Sea Scrolls as well as by early Christians; it is the actual meaning of the word "church." Christians often referred to themselves simply as the church or the congregation (with "of God" being understood). The term could be applied either to all believers in the world or to any local group of them. It meant the total presence of God's people in a given location. That is why the NT often

Antioch, where believers were first called Christians.

uses the singular "church" even when many groups of believers are included together (Acts 9:31; 2 Cor 1:1); the term "churches" is rarely found (Acts 15:41; 16:5). Each group or the whole group was the place where God was present (Mt 16:18; 18:17); God had purchased the congregation with the blood of his Son (Acts 20:28).

Multitude. The term "the multitude" is similar to "church" as a way to describe Christians as a body. The Dead Sea Scrolls frequently refer to "the Many" or "the Multitude," meaning the gathered congregation of the true Israel. The same phrase was occasionally used to describe the early Christians (Acts 4:32 KJV; 6:5; 15:12 KJV). It also appears in the writings of Clement of Rome (AD 96?) and in the *Shepherd of Hermas* (2nd century). It was probably a shortened form of "the multitude of the righteous," "the multitude of God," or some similar title. But when Christians referred to "the multitude," they meant the whole group of Christians.

Flock. The simple designation "the flock" or "the flock of God" was sometimes used for Christians (Acts 20:28; 1 Pt 5:2,3; also in Clement of Rome's writings). The title grew out of a common Jewish metaphor for Israel found in apocryphal and pseudepigraphal writings (1 Enoch 90; Ps of Sol 17:45); Jesus also used the term (Jn 10). It became a title, so that a Christian referring to "the flock" meant the whole Christian body, whose shepherd was God.

What Christians Called Themselves as Individuals. At least nine terms were used by early Christians to describe themselves as individuals.

Disciple. Jesus was followed by a group of men and women who listened to his teaching of the Scriptures, observed his way of life, and patterned their lives after his. Those followers were called by a term common in the ancient world for a teacher's pupils: "disciples" (Mt 10:1; Lk 6:17; Jn 6:66). Jesus' command to the disciples was that wherever they went in the world they should make others into his disciples, not only baptizing them, but also teaching them to do everything he had commanded (Mt 28:19,20). It was proper for early Christians to be called disciples of Jesus of Nazareth or simply "the disciples" (Acts 6:1,2,7; 9:36; 11:26) because they were carrying on the teaching of Jesus and living the life he had exemplified. They were thus recognized as a "school" or living community that embodied the teaching of their "master" in practice. The Book of 1 John emphasizes that only those who keep Christ's commandments show real love for God (2:3-6; 3:10,11).

Slave. Five NT authors called themselves "slaves [or servants] of Jesus Christ" (Rom 1:1; Gal 1:10; Phil 1:1; Col 4:12; 2 Tm 2:24; Ti 1:1; Jas 1:1; 2 Pt 1:1; Jude 1; Rv 1:1). In many cases the term is a synonym for "Christian." Why would such a term become a name for Christians? In the OT God was viewed as a great king; the subjects of kings were their slaves, since a king could do with them as he liked. The people of Israel saw themselves in the same relationship to God: they were his slaves.

Often the title "slave of the king" meant that the person was an officer in the king's service; it was a title of honor. In Jewish literature Moses and others were called slaves of God (Nm 12:7,8; Rv 15:3). The term "slave" was thus a title both of honor and of subjugation; in the NT it is hard to know which sense is intended. Certainly subjection was often meant (1 Cor 7:22; Phil 2:7), but when applied to the apostolic writers the term probably suggested their honored position in God's household. At the same time it indicated their obedience to Christ: he commanded and they obeyed. Since obedience was characteristic of all Christians, "slaves of Christ" became a title for members of the young church.

Elect; Called. In the OT, God called the people of Israel into being as a nation. They were the "chosen people," the "elect," the "called of God." The NT presents Jesus as supremely the chosen one of God (1 Pt 2:4). His followers, who knew themselves to belong to God and indeed to be the true heirs of the election of Israel, also called themselves "the elect," "the chosen," or "the called" (Rom 1:6; 16:13 KJV; Col 3:12; 2 Tm 2:10; 1 Pt 1:2; 2 Jn 1:13; Jude 1; Rv 17:14; the same meaning may be reflected in Mt 22:14). That title pointed to the special place of Christians within God's plan as the heirs of his promises. Yet it also indicated that their position was not based on any special merit; God chose them when they could do nothing. Pride was eliminated because God had graciously given them such an honored position.

Righteous. The righteous person, who stood pious and pure before God, was prominent in the OT. Several such OT texts are quoted in the NT (Hb 2:4 in Rom 1:17; Ps 14:1 in Rom 3:10; Ps 34:16 in 1 Pt 3:12). For Christians, Jesus was the one truly righteous person (1 Pt 3:18; 1 Jn 2:1). Christians saw themselves as having been made righteous by Jesus, and, since they now lived in obedience to God, they could claim for themselves the OT title of "the righteous" (Rom 5:19; Gal 3:11; Jas 5:6; 1 Pt 4:18; Rv 22:11). The title may not have been used regularly enough to be considered a "name," but its use was not infrequent.

Saints; Holy Ones. Israel was called to be "holy" or consecrated to God (Ex 22:31; Lv

11:44); Jesus was the "Holy One of God" (Mk 1:24). The background of the title, however, is probably to be found in apocalyptic literature, where it stands for the faithful remnant of Israel, the elect people of God (Dn 7:18,21–27; 1 Enoch 38:4; cf. the language of Ps 79:2; Ps of Sol 8:40; 9:6; 10:7; note the "pious ones" of 1 Mc 2:42; 7:13). The emphasis is not on holiness as such, but rather on the fact that as a member of the elect group one must follow the laws of the kingdom, separating oneself for God.

"Saints" became the apostle Paul's favorite name for Christians (Rom 1:7; 8:27; 12:13; 15:25,26,31; 16:2,15; plus 31 other places in Paul's letters). The name is also used 14 times in the Book of Revelation. Other NT writers used it occasionally (Heb 6:10; 13:24; Jude 3). The name means that Christians are expected to be holy (Heb 12:10; Rv 22:11); they have been consecrated to God as a holy priesthood and have rejected the ways of the world (1 Pt 2:5,9; cf. 1:15,16). More than that, they are the people of the coming age, who will reign with God over the earth and over angels. The early church could hardly have found a more exalted name for itself.

Believers. One would expect the term "believers" (sometimes translated "faithful") to be a title for Christians, since the NT stresses belief in Jesus. It meant not only believing as a mental activity, but total commitment of one's whole person to Jesus. Christians were called not merely to believe something but to give themselves to someone. Although NT authors emphasized believing, they rarely used the term "believer" as a name for Christians. There are a few clear examples (Acts 4:32; 10:45; 19:18; 1 Tm 4:3,12), but in other places the term is a description, not a name (Acts 2:44; 15:5; 18:27). As a name, "believer" points to the personal commitment of Christians to Jesus.

Friends. Since Jesus called his disciples friends (Lk 12:4; Jn 15:14,15), it would have been natural for Christians to refer to themselves as "the friends (of Christ)." Such terminology was used for members of philosophical groups in the Greek world. The designation is used only once in the NT (Acts 27:3); some translations read "his friends," but the Greek has simply "the friends." Apparently "friends" seemed too cold a title, losing its place to "family" designations.

Brothers (Sisters). Good evidence exists that Jews at the time of Jesus frequently referred to themselves as brothers (Acts 2:29,37; 7:2; 22:5; 28:21; Rom 9:3). From the beginning it seemed natural for Jewish Christians to call each other "brothers" (that is, "siblings"—the term included both male and female; Acts 1:15,16; 9:30; 11:1). Members of gentile religious communities also called each other brothers, so the name found a home in the gentile churches as well (Acts 17:14; Rom 1:13; 1 Cor 1:1,10; plus dozens of other places in Paul's letters to gentile churches). In fact, along with "disciple" (in Acts) and "saint" (always plural in the writings of Paul and the Book of Revelation), it was one of the most popular names for Christians and the only one used in James and 1 John.

Each Christian was called "brother," and the Christians collectively were "the brothers." The name stressed the intimacy of the Christian community. That is, the relationship of believers to one another was as close as that of blood kin (closer, in fact—Mk 10:23–31). In 1 John and James the name underlines the claim that poorer Christians have upon those better off (Jas 2:15; 1 Jn 3:10–18; 4:20,21). It also points to equality among members of the Christian community.

Children of God. The OT refers to Israel as God's child (Ex 4:22; Is 1:2; Hos 11:1) and to the king in particular as God's son (Ps 2:7). The most important characteristic of such sonship was likeness to the Father; because the king was God's son, he would judge righteously as God did. The term was soon extended to include all righteous persons, because they acted like their Father (Hos 1:10; Wis of Sol 2:18). It was natural for Jesus to call those who behaved righteously "sons" or "children of God," stressing their moral likeness to God (Mt 5:9,45; Lk 6:35; 20:36). The church picked up that usage, referring to Christians with the term whenever their moral likeness to God needed stressing (Rom 8:14; 9:8; Eph 5:1; Phil 2:15; 1 Jn 3:1,2,10; 5:1,2).

It would be illegitimate for a person to take the name "child of God" if he or she were committed to doing evil. The title also points to Christians as God's elect, chosen to be part of his family (Jn 1:12; 11:52; Rom 8:16–21; Gal 3:26). The two ideas complement each other because anyone who is made part of a family must act like the family.

The title "sons of God" was always used in the plural to refer to Christians. The singular "Son of God" was reserved for Jesus Christ. The early Christians would speak of themselves as "children of God."

PETER H. DAVIDS

See NAMES, SIGNIFICANCE OF.

Christology. The study of the person and work of Jesus Christ. The confession that Jesus is the Christ, the Son of the living God, first ventured by Peter at Caesarea Philippi (Mt 16:16), is the heart of the Christian faith. It is this confession that makes one a Christian,

The headwaters of the Hermon River at Caesarea Philippi, the place where Peter made his significant statement about the person of Christ.

and all Christian theology is thinking, in the light of this confession, about the meaning of this confession. The first major theological decision of the church resulting from such believing thought was the affirmation of the essential deity of Jesus as the Son of God. As such he was declared to be of one essence with the Father and the Spirit (the dogma of the Trinity promulgated at Nicaea, AD 325). Since this affirmation was made with reference to the man Jesus of Nazareth, it forced upon the church, inescapably, the further question: How could one and the same person be both God and man? How could he who is infinite become finite; he who is eternal become temporal; he who is God become man?

To answer this question, the church embraced the doctrine of the incarnation. The statement of the doctrine was arrived at only after much controversy. In the course of the debate the church rejected all efforts, on the one hand, to preserve the deity of the Son at the expense of his humanity (docetism) and, on the

other, to preserve his humanity at the expense of his deity (adoptionism). In the former category were the doctrines of those who claimed that the Son only seemed to have a human body, or, like the Apollinarians, that while he had a true body and soul, the divine Logos took the place of the human spirit. In the latter category was the doctrine of those who claimed that the man Jesus, through the process of moral development, was elevated to divine sonship and so adopted into the Godhead. Some placed great stress on Jesus' endowment with the Spirit at baptism as the moment of his adoption, while others, citing Acts 13:33— "today I have begotten thee"—believed Jesus became the unique Son of God at the resurrection. The church also rejected all attempts to resolve the problem of the Savior's divinity and humanity by suggesting that he was both a divine person and a human person (Nestorianism) or, contrariwise, that the unity of his person implied a fusion of the divine and human in one nature (monophysitism).

The Chalcedonian Creed. Finally at the Ecumenical Council of Chalcedon (AD 451) the position was adopted that our Lord Jesus Christ was truly God and truly man (*vere Deo, vere homo*), "consubstantial with the Father as to his Godhead, and consubstantial also with us as to his manhood; like unto us in all things, yet without sin; as to his Godhead, begotten of the Father before all worlds; but as to his manhood, in these days, born for us men and for our salvation, of the virgin Mary, the mother of God, one and the same Christ, Son, Lord, only-begotten, known in two natures, without confusion, without conversion, without severance, and without division; the distinction of the natures being in no wise abolished by their union, but the peculiarity of each nature being maintained, and both concurring in one person and subsistence. We confess not a Son divided and sundered into two persons, but one and the same Son, and only-begotten, and God-Logos, our Lord Jesus Christ." This confession was adopted in all its essential features by the Reformers at the time of the Protestant Reformation.

Chalcedonian Christology does not remove the mystery of the incarnation but rather indicates, as it were, the boundaries of believing thought about the person of the Redeemer, boundaries that have proved significant in the history of Christian thought. As for the key terms in the creed, the following should be noted: the word "nature" (*phusis*) as used by the fathers does not have reference to the physical, material order which is the object of investigation by the "natural" sciences. "Nature" rather refers to being or reality in distinction from appearance. To say that Jesus

Christology

Christ has a divine nature is to affirm that all the qualities, properties, or attributes by which one describes the divine order of being pertain to him. In short, he is God himself, not *like* God, but just *God.* So also with the affirmation that Christ has a human nature. Christ is not God *appearing* as a man; he *is* a man. He is not *only* a man nor *only* God; he is the God who *became* a man. He did not cease to be God when he became a man; he did not exchange divinity for humanity. Rather he assumed humanity, so that he is now both divine and human. He is the God-man.

The term "person" (*hypostasis*) was used by the fathers to describe Jesus Christ as self-conscious, self-determined Subject, one who designates himself by the word "I" over against a "thou." The Mediator between God and man is *a person* who has a divine nature and a human nature. While there can be no "person" where there is no "nature," it does not follow that there is no distinction between the terms; for there can be a "nature," as defined above, where there is no "person." (An object may have the properties or "nature" of a stone: grayness, hardness, roundness, smoothness. But this object, which has the "nature" of a stone, is not a "person"; it is not self-conscious and self-determined.)

In making a distinction between the "person" and the "nature" of the incarnate Christ so as to speak of him as being a "person" with a "divine nature" and a "human nature," the fathers were teaching that while we must ascribe to Christ all the qualities which belong to the divine order of being and to the human order of being (including bodily, physical, objective being—the Word "became flesh," Jn 1:14), we cannot say that he is "two persons." He is a divine person with a human nature, not a human person as such. All human persons have a first moment; and wheresoever and whensoever we may identify that first moment for a human "I," whether at conception or at fetal quickening in the womb, whether at the moment of birth, or even as late as the first moment of self-awareness in the young child, no human "I" is aware of himself as a "subject," as an "I," before he is conceived in the womb of his mother. The man Jesus of Nazareth, however, unlike any mere man, could say, "Before Abraham was 'I' am" (Jn 8:58); and this affirmation is neither the late theological invention of Christian fancy nor the claim of a man suffering from delusions of grandeur, but rather the sober truth. This person sitting on a mountainside preaching, this person standing by the sea calling fishermen to be his disciples, is a person who always was a person, even before there were any fishermen by the sea to call or any people to preach to on the mountainside—in fact, before there was any sea or any mountain.

Christ is not the Divine Logos who inspires and uniquely endows the man, Jesus of Nazareth, with moral and religious insights. Rather, this man Jesus is the eternal Son of God, and God's eternal Son has become this man, Jesus. The Son of God did not assume a man's *person* to his own *nature,* but a man's *nature* to his own *person.* He continues the same person though he now assumes our humanity. Hence he can speak both as a Subject consciously in history and as a Subject consciously transcending history, even in one and the same sentence. "*I* have glorified thee *on the earth,* having accomplished the work which thou gavest me to do. And now Father, glorify thou me with thine own self with the glory which *I* had with thee *before the world was*" (Jn 17:4,5 KJV). Here the same person Jesus speaks as a person in the world, an "I" who has done certain things in the world, and as a person before there was any world, an "I" who shared his glory with a "thou" whom he calls "Father" before all time. All efforts at rational analysis of this mystery, which the church designates by the word "incarnation," run the risk of losing the truth by explaining it. One arrives at a position in which Christ is a divine being who appears human (docetism) or a human being who either achieves divine status for himself (adoptionism) or divine worth for us (Ritschlianism).

In order to preserve fully both our Lord's deity and his humanity, the creed employs four terms in which we are told what did *not* happen in the incarnation. The union of the two natures is declared to be "without confusion," "without conversion," "without separation," and "without division." Some have ridiculed these "four bald negatives," but they are by no means wholly without value. Should any of these basic negatives be violated, we would lose what is essential to Christian faith, the "one and the same Son, our Lord Jesus Christ, complete as to his Godhead, and complete as to his manhood."

But the creed contains not only a negative affirmation—what did *not* happen in the incarnation; it also contains a positive affirmation. The union of the two natures concurs in one Person, who is the eternal Son of the Father. The union, then, of the divine and the human in Christ is a personal one; more specifically, the union is the act of the divine Person who is the Son of God. Here we approach the very heart of the mystery of the incarnation. No one can say how the infinite God could become a finite man. Naturally, however, theologians have thought a great deal about the matter; Chalcedon does not mark the end of all inquiry.

In theological parlance it has become customary to speak of the union of the divine and the human in the Person of the incarnate Redeemer as the "hypostatic" union (*unio hypostatica*), from the Greek word for "person." It is important to note not only *that* the union is personal, but *why* it is so. The theologians speak of the union as personal because it is the act of a Person, namely the Son of God, the Word who became flesh. This means that the Person of the incarnate Redeemer is divine, the object of Christian worship. He cannot, then, be a mere human being as other men are mere human beings. To worship one who is a man and only a man would be idolatry. And because this personal union of the divine and the human is truly a *union*, the Redeemer is one Person, not two. If to worship a human person would be idolatry, to worship two persons, one human, one divine, would be an absurdity. This Person, who unites in himself as incarnate the divine and the human, is often described by theologians as a "theanthropic" person, the God-man. If one does not mean that he is a hybrid—half God, half man—then this mode of speaking is unobjectionable inasmuch as it simply says that this Person, Jesus Christ, is both divine and human, which is what the creed intends.

Christology After Chalcedon. Matters become more difficult and unanimity less in evidence, however, when the question is raised as to the personal qualities of Christ's humanity. The formulation most consistent with Chalcedon and generally held by Protestants, a formulation defended in modern times by the Swiss theologians Karl Barth and Emil Brunner and by G. C. Berkouwer of the Netherlands, speaks of the "impersonal humanity" of our Lord.

Actually the meaning of the phrase "impersonal humanity" (*impersonalitas*) is not that in the case of the incarnate Son there is no manifestation of the personal at the human level. Rather it means that this humanity, of itself, has no independent existence apart from the divine Person who assumed this humanity in the act of becoming incarnate. So far as Jesus of Nazareth is concerned, that which is human exists in and through the Word who is God himself. There is a sense in which God is present to *all* created reality (the doctrine of the divine immanence). But howsoever we may conceive of this divine presence of power (providence) and of grace (salvation), there can be no thought of *identity* between God and the creature. Even when the church, following the usage of the NT, speaks of the Christian as "indwelt by the Holy Spirit," there is no identity of *being* affirmed; there is no ontological union of the human and the divine. But in the case of the man Jesus Christ, something absolutely unique is affirmed: this man is declared to be identical with God because he, the Person, is the "Word who was made flesh and dwelt among us." "Therefore," says Barth, "he does not only live through God and with God; he is himself God. Nor is he autonomous and self-existent. His reality, existence and being are wholly and absolutely that of God himself, the God who acts in his Word. His manhood is only the predicate of his Godhead, or better and more concretely, it is only the predicate, assumed in inconceivable condescension, of the Word acting upon us, the Word who is the Lord."

In other words, Jesus our Lord is, as man, so united with God that he exists as man only and insofar as he exists as God. The doctrine of *anhypostasy* states this truth negatively. It affirms that the human nature of our Lord does not possess the mode of its being as personal in and of itself. The doctrine of *enhypostasy* states this truth positively. It affirms that the particular human nature which is our Lord's acquires its personal mode of being by union with the personal Son of God. It is not Jesus of Nazareth who becomes the Son of God (adoptionism) but the Son of God who becomes Jesus of Nazareth. The incarnation is a unique act of a divine Person, not a unique experience of the divine on the part of a human person. The Subject of the incarnation is a divine Subject who acts, not a human subject who is acted upon. But inasmuch as the divine Subject, the eternal Son, so acts as to become this man, Jesus of Nazareth, this man is—not just symbolizes, but is—the Son of God as no other man is or ever can be the Son of God.

The scriptural basis of the doctrine of the incarnation includes, of course, the entire range of data in the Gospels as well as several passages in the Pauline epistles, especially Philippians 2:6–8, which is, perhaps, the single most important christological passage in the NT. Here Paul, using the words of a primitive Christian confession, speaks of him "who, though he was in the form of God, did not count equality with God a thing to be grasped, but emptied himself, taking the form of a servant, being born in the likeness of men."

The Chalcedonian Creed does not resolve the mystery of the incarnation, and theologians have made many efforts to better understand the mystery. One of the best known is based on an inference drawn from the passage quoted above. It is known as *kenosis*, the theory that when the Son became man, he emptied himself of some aspect of his divinity. The text of Philippians does not say that he emptied himself *of* anything, but only that he emptied *himself*, a striking figure of speech denoting condescension ("made himself of no reputation" KJV). In spite of this exegetical difficulty, kenotic theory has persisted, in one form or another, especially in British theology. Another effort at understanding suggests that our Lord's humanity was the *incognito* (Kierkegaard's term) which hid his identity as a divine person from all but the eyes of faith. Thus the incarnation was a revelation that veils as well as discloses the truth.

In Reformed theology the so-called "communion of attributes" has been affirmed, whereby it is proper to speak of our Lord in any way that is true of him as God or as man or both. The statement, for example, that Jesus was born in Bethlehem in the days of Herod the king (Mt 2:1) and the sentence, "Before Abraham was, I [Jesus] am" (Jn 8:58), are both true, since he who was born of Mary during the reign of Herod is the same person as he who declares that he is before Abraham, though Herod obviously lived centuries after Abraham died. Lutherans, in contrast to the Reformed, have insisted on a "communication of attributes." According to this thesis, our Lord's human nature is informed with divine attributes by virtue of its union with the divine nature in the person of the Redeemer. The doctrine is principally applied in the Lutheran view of the Lord's Supper, the affirmation being made that although the risen Lord has ascended bodily into heaven, yet he is also present in the Eucharist, his body and blood being "in, with and under" the elements of bread and wine.

Conclusion. "Communication of attributes," "communion of attributes," "incognito," "kenosis"—these and similar theological terms all testify to the impenetrable mystery at the heart of Christology: the relation of the human and the divine in the Person of Jesus Christ. There have always been those, understandably, who have sought to illumine this mystery by viewing Jesus' uniqueness in terms of virtuosity or religious genius. Primitive attempts were made in this direction in the apocryphal gospels, which portray Jesus as something of a *Wunderkind*, the religious equivalent of the musical Mozart. (The distorted counterpart of these pious legends was the malevolent suggestion of Celsus that Jesus used Egyptian sorcery and magic.) This effort to explain Jesus as a prodigy, "one in a million," is the ruling motif of those Christologies which are grounded in German idealism; Jesus was a consummate religious genius, the high point in the religious evolution of the human race.

We are reminded of an array of data in the Gospels that show us one who transcended these human limitations in a godlike manner. These data are not arranged so as to relieve the paradox; rather at times they are so juxtaposed as to heighten it. Asleep in a ship, exhausted— how utterly human—Jesus is awakened; he rebukes the winds with a word and the sea is calm—how utterly divine (Mk 4:38). Coming from the village of Bethany, he is hungry—a very common event; but when he finds no figs on a nearby tree, he curses it and it withers to the roots (Mk 11:12–14, 21)—a very uncommon event. He inquires of his disciples, on a certain occasion, as to how much food is available—a very ordinary procedure; when he is informed, he takes the five loaves and two fish and feeds five thousand—a very extraordinary procedure (Mk 6:38–44).

Jesus confesses ignorance; he knows not the hour when the Son of Man shall come (Mk 13:32); yet at the same time he knows what is lacking in the hearts of those who profess to believe on him (Jn 2:24,25). It would be quite impossible to show why or how Jesus could be ignorant in the one instance and informed in another. The second Evangelist, who tells us that Jesus did not know the day of final judgment, reports a little later that he so perfectly knew the future he could tell a man who was a free and responsible agent exactly what he would do, exactly when he would do it, and exactly how many times. ("This day, before the cock crows twice you [Peter] shall deny me thrice" [Mk 14:30].) And all of this while the man is vehemently protesting to the contrary. How could this be? To this—and a thousand other questions—we can give no satisfying answers. To speak of a "kenosis" wherein the divine is limited by the human, or of a "communication" of attributes wherein the human is exalted into the divine, creates as many problems as it relieves.

It might be suggested at this juncture that the traditional theological impasse will be relieved as the relatively new science of psychology advances the frontiers of knowledge. A pioneering attempt to understand the ultimate reality in the person of Jesus with the help of psychology was made by William Sanday (*Personality in Christ and in Ourselves*, 1911). Applying the research of William James that located the awareness of the divine in the "subliminal consciousness," he suggested that this same faculty is the proper seat or locus of the Deity in the incarnate Son. In more recent times W. R. Matthews, in his *The Problem of Christ in the Twentieth Century* (1950), also made an approach to Christology from the perspective of psychology. Reminding us that Schleiermacher conceived his Christology in terms of Jesus' unique "God-consciousness"; that Freud and Jung had researched the nature of the unconscious; and that investigations into extrasensory perception reveal the complexities of human consciousness, he goes on to say that it is a reproach to modern theology that so little reflection appears to have been given to the bearing of this research on the doctrine of the incarnation.

The difficulty with this approach is not that psychological theory is still in an inchoate state, and what is accepted today may be discredited tomorrow. Rather, the difficulty is the inappropriateness of the method to the problem to be investigated. The "subliminal consciousness," the "unconscious," "precognition," "extrasensory perception," "genius"— these are categories by which the psychologist seeks to understand the "exceptional" man, the man with powers beyond the ordinary. But Jesus was not an exceptional man; he was the Son of God incarnate, a divine Person who assumed our humanity. And psychology has no conceptual model with which to illumine the inner life of such a Person, since such a life is necessarily unique and without analogy.

In closing it may be said that although psychology can never cut the Gordian knot of christological difficulty, theology can never endure a Christology that is psychologically absurd. And some christological speculations and pronouncements have verged on this extremity. To say, for example, that Christ had "two distinct intellects" and "two distinct wills," as some of the fathers insisted, would seem to make the incarnate Son an ontological split personality. Knowing that unity, integration, and wholeness are the prerequisites of a healthy psyche, we can hardly conceive of the divine and the human in the Person of Christ in terms of such division, severance, and disjunction as these formulas imply.

Our answer, therefore, to the question: Can we illumine the inner consciousness of Jesus? is: No, we cannot. Is, then, the doctrine of the incarnation an absurdity? To believe that God became a man—is such a belief a *sacrificium intellectus?* We answer that it is not absurd, but we confess that it is incomprehensible. To believe it is not to assassinate reason, but it is to admit the creaturely limitations of reason.

It should be noted in this respect that the doctrine that is contained in the term "incarnation" follows the structure of John 1:14: "The Word became flesh and dwelt among us." It *would* be absurd to believe that the movement could be the other way, that flesh could become the Word, that man could cross the line that separates the creature from the Creator and become God. Since Darwin, who taught us to think of evolutionary development from amoeba up to man, it might seem that it could be so. But it is not so. The christological mystery can no more be understood with the help of evolution than with the help of parapsychology. Not man's evolutionary progress upward to God, but God's condescension in coming down to man—that is what we confess when we affirm the incarnation. *God* sent forth his Son to be born of a woman (Gal 4:4), and only because of this divine act could that son of Mary be also the unique Son of God. The Word became flesh and dwelt among us, and only thus could that flesh *be* the Word. We cannot reverse the terms in these sentences. And this Word that became flesh, according to John's prologue, is the divine, creative, redeeming Word: the One who made the world into which he came, the One who grants to those receiving him the right to become children of God, the One who was with God and was himself God. And because this is who the Word is, therefore he can become a man. How he does it is God's secret; it is his mystery.

See INCARNATION; MESSIAH; JESUS CHRIST, LIFE AND TEACHINGS OF; WORD; PARABLE; KINGDOM OF GOD (HEAVEN); VIRGIN BIRTH OF JESUS; ASCENSION OF CHRIST; CHRIST; SON OF GOD; SON OF MAN.

Bibliography. E. Brunner, *The Mediator*; O. Cullmann, *A Christology of the NT*; J.A. Dorner, *History of the Development of the Doctrine of the Person of Christ*, 4 vols.; F. Hahn, *The Titles of Jesus in Christology*; W. Kramer, *Christ, Lord, Son of God*; H.P. Liddon, *The Divinity of our Lord and Saviour Jesus Christ*; H.R. Mackintosh, *The Person of Christ*; W. Pannenberg, *Jesus—God and Man*; B.L. Ramm, *An Evangelical Christology*; B.B. Warfield, *The Lord of Glory* and *The Person and Work of Christ*.

Chronicles, Books of First and Second.

Two OT books, historical records of King David and his successors in the land of Judah. The Books of Chronicles are among the most neglected books in the Bible, partly because most of the material can be found in Samuel, Kings, or elsewhere in the OT. Fourteen chapters (1 Chr 1–9; 23–27) are little more than lists of names; the rest of the material is primarily historical narrative, which some people find almost as boring as lists. Yet the content of Chronicles is not history in a professional or academic sense because the materials used are comparable to the annals compiled by ancient Near Eastern court scribes. Those sources recorded each year's most important events and were frequently more propagandistic than objectively historical. The records in Chronicles, somewhat eclectic in nature and ignoring certain facets of national history while emphasizing others, deal with only a selected portion of the history of the Israelites. A good deal of criticism that the work is historically unreliable has come from lack of understanding the book's character. Chronicles is not so much a history as a metaphysical interpretation of events in Israelite life in light of covenantal values. It was not sufficient for the Chronicler that kings rose and fell; the events were interpreted from a special religious standpoint.

Author. In the Hebrew Bible, 1 and 2 Chronicles form a single book. The Bible does not say who wrote that book or when it was written. According to the Jewish Talmud, Ezra wrote "his book and Chronicles—the order of all generations down to himself." Although many scholars defend the view that Ezra wrote Chronicles, there is still no general agreement about the date and authorship of the book.

The author is usually called "the Chronicler," a title suggesting that he was a historian. It is possible that he was a scribe, priest, or Levite. Evidently the writer had access to government and temple archives, because repeated references are made to a number of official records of kings (1 Chr 9:1; 27:24; 2 Chr 16:11; 20:34; 25:26; 27:7; 28:26; 32:32; 33:18; 35:27; 36:8) and prophets (1 Chr 29:29; 2 Chr 9:29; 12:15; 13:22; 20:34; 26:22; 32:32; 33:19).

The evidence is suggestive, but not conclusive, that the author of Chronicles also wrote the books of Ezra and Nehemiah. The last two verses of Chronicles are almost the same as the first three verses of Ezra. The language and literary style of all three books are similar. The same theological concerns for the temple and its worship and the same interest in lists and genealogies appear in all three books. In the Hebrew Bible, Ezra–Nehemiah are considered one book and stand before Chronicles. Chronicles stands at the very end of the Hebrew Bible.

Authenticity. The books of Chronicles, referred to as a single book in this article, have received considerable scholarly criticism about the nature of their content and about apparent discrepancies with material in Samuel and Kings. The differences can be classified as numerical, theological, and historical.

As an example of numerical differences, 1 Chronicles 11:11 says that one of David's "mighty men" killed 300 men with his spear at one time, but the parallel account in 2 Samuel 23:8 says he killed 800 at one time. Again, 1 Chronicles 18:3,4 says that after defeating King Hadadezer of Zobah, David took from him 1,000 chariots, 7,000 horsemen, and 20,000 foot soldiers; a parallel account in 2 Samuel 8:3,4 says that David took 1,700 horsemen and 20,000 foot soldiers. Although 2 Chronicles 22:2 says that Ahaziah was 42 years old when he began to reign, 2 Kings 8:26 says he was 22; and so on.

Many numbers in Chronicles seem exceptionally high. In 1 Chronicles 21:5 Israel had just over a million men and Judah had 470,000. In another example of a remarkably high number, the temple's vestibule is said to have been 120 cubits or approximately 180 feet in height (2 Chr 3:4). In 2 Chronicles 13:3 Judah's army had 400,000 men and Israel's army 800,000. Some 500,000 of Israel's army were slain (2 Chr 13:17). In 2 Chronicles 14:9 Zerah the Ethiopian had an army of a million men and 300 chariots.

How should such problems with numbers in Chronicles be understood? First, some of the problems in the text as it now stands may have come about from faulty copying. Also, some excessively high numbers may have been used figuratively to indicate a very large army, or perhaps as estimates. Though not all questions have been answered, scholars have found credible solutions to some of the problems. In the meantime, such matters are seen by evangelical scholars as verifying the human side of the Scriptures without necessarily detracting from their divine origin.

Chronicles also contains some different theological emphases from earlier materials. The best example can be seen by comparing 1 Chronicles 21:1 with 2 Samuel 24:1. In the Samuel account the anger of the Lord was kindled against Israel, and he incited David to harm them by taking a national census. The Chronicler's account is that "Satan stood up against Israel, and incited David to number Israel." In one account God moved David to take the census; in the other Satan was the prime mover.

The authenticity of the Chronicler has also been questioned on historical grounds. Several incidents reported in Samuel–Kings are told in a different manner in Chronicles. In 2 Samuel 8:13 David is said to have slain 18,000 Edomites at the Valley of Salt, whereas the Chronicler reports that Abishai, David's cousin, killed the Edomites (1 Chr 18:12). Again, according to 2 Samuel 21:19 Elhanan slew Goliath the Gittite, whereas the Chronicler says that Elhanan slew Lahmi, the brother of Goliath the Gittite (1 Chr 20:5; most OT scholars today believe that Chronicles preserves the true reading of the original text). A more difficult historical problem is seen by comparing 2 Chronicles 20:35–37 with 1 Kings 22:48,49. The Kings account says that the ships Jehoshaphat, king of Judah, built to bring gold from Ophir were wrecked at Ezion-geber, evidently before they ever left port. When Ahaziah, king of Israel, asked that his servants be allowed to go on the ships with Jehoshaphat's servants, Jehoshaphat refused. The Chronicler's version of what happened is different. There Jehoshaphat joined with the wicked Ahaziah in building ships at

Ezion-geber to go to Tarshish, but a prophet prophesied that the Lord would destroy the ships because of the alliance with Ahaziah. Both accounts agree that Jehoshaphat built ships at Ezion-geber and that the ships were destroyed before they left port. On the basis of the present status of the texts, however, one cannot tell whether or not Jehoshaphat joined Ahaziah. Whatever happened, the ships were lost.

In a comparison of Chronicles with Kings a serious problem arises over the war between Asa of Judah and Baasha of Israel. In 2 Chronicles 16:1 one reads that in Asa's 36th year of reign, Baasha challenged Judah by building a fortress at Ramah. But according to the chronology of 1 Kings 16 Baasha was not even alive in the 36th year of Asa's reign. First Kings 16:6–8 says that Baasha died and his son Elah succeeded him as king in the 26th year of Asa's reign.

At one time scholars were quite skeptical about the authenticity of Chronicles. Now they tend to treat Chronicles with respect and appreciation. In some instances new archaeological evidence has tended to support the historicity of the Chronicler's statement. In other instances reexamination of a discrepancy has shown it to be more apparent than real. If all the facts were known, other problems might also be cleared up to the satisfaction of impartial scholars.

Date. It is not possible to determine precisely when the Book of Chronicles was written. The book ends with a reference to the decree of Cyrus, king of Persia, permitting the Jewish captives in Babylon to return to their homeland. Since Cyrus' decree is usually dated about 538 BC, Chronicles could not have been written before that date. But if Ezra–Nehemiah are a part of the same work as Chronicles, the materials could not have been written until Nehemiah returned to Jerusalem in 444 BC.

Genealogies in Chronicles and Ezra–Nehemiah may shed some light on the dating of the books. In 1 Chronicles 3:10–24 the lineage of David and Solomon is traced through the 6th generation after the exile, which would make the date for Anani (the last person in the list) about 400 BC.

The language of Chronicles is definitely that of postexilic Hebrew. The use of the Persian word *daric* (1 Chr 29:7), plus a lack of any Greek words, places Chronicles in the Persian period (538–331 BC). The word *midrash* appears in the OT only in Chronicles (2 Chr 13:22; 24:27) but is very common in postbiblical Hebrew. Around 400 BC is probably the best estimate for the date of Chronicles based on evidence now available.

Historical Background. During the Persian period some of the Jews returned to Jerusalem from Babylon soon after Cyrus' decree. They rebuilt the temple and waited for the Messianic Age to come, but with drought, economic hardships, and moral and spiritual laxness their hopes faded. Judah was stable politically as a part of the large, dominant Persian empire. There was not the slightest possibility of restoring the Davidic kingdom.

If the kingdom of David could not be restored politically, how was a Jew of the early 4th century BC to understand history and the place of the Jews in God's plan? The Chronicler, living at that time, found the key to history in God's covenant with David. The first 10 chapters of 1 Chronicles lead up to David; chapters 11–29 detail events of David's rule. Moses is mentioned in Chronicles 31 times, David more than 250 times. David planned the temple and collected money to build it. He appointed Levites, singers, and gatekeepers. He divided the priesthood into its orders. He was responsible for the temple worship, which was tremendously important to the Chronicler and his contemporaries.

The Persian period of Israel's history is largely a silent one, both in other OT materials and in archaeological finds. Of course, all the evidence is not yet in, as archaeologists continue their investigations of the period.

Origin and Purpose. The Chronicler must have lived in Jerusalem and written for the Jewish community there. He refers to Jerusalem about 240 times and to Judah more than

The north wall of the old city. The Chronicler mentions Jerusalem by name more than 150 times.

225 times. A negative feeling toward the northern kingdom of Israel can be seen in almost total lack of references to any northern king. The Chronicler's attitude toward the north is clearly expressed in the two following verses: "So Israel has been in rebellion against the house of David to this day" (2 Chr 10:19) and "Ought you not to know that the Lord God of Israel gave the kingship over Israel for ever to David and his sons by a covenant of salt?" (2 Chr 13:5).

The Chronicler wanted the Jewish people to see that God was sovereign over all things. For example, he includes David's affirmation: "Thine, O Lord, is the greatness, and the power, and the glory, and the victory, and the majesty; for all that is in the heavens and in the earth is thine; thine is the kingdom, O Lord, and thou art exalted as head above all. Both riches and honor come from thee, and thou rulest over all. In thy hand are power and might; and in thy hand it is to make great and to give strength to all" (1 Chr 29:11–12).

Compiled in the postexilic period, Chronicles was meant to emphasize the significance of the theocracy seen in light of earlier history. The theocracy was a social configuration God planned for postexilic Judah, a religious rather than secular community. Instead of a king the Jews had a priesthood of which the Lord approved (as distinct from the corrupt priests who had been to a large extent responsible for preexilic moral and spiritual collapse of the nation).

The postexilic Judeans were to live as a holy nation, not as people with political and nationalistic ambitions. Therefore, the Chronicler demanded implicit obedience to the Mosaic covenant so that the returning Jews could find prosperity, divine blessing, and grace. The Jews were still the chosen people, purged by the experience of exile, with a new opportunity to fulfill the Sinai covenant.

The Chronicler gave great weight to divine retribution and was insistent that all action be guided by specific moral principles, to reflect God's character clearly in his people. Because the writer saw God's hand in all history, punishing the apostate and being gracious to the penitent, he saw in the chastened remnant of the exile the true spiritual heirs of the house of David. He insisted that the postexilic community adhere rigorously to the morality of Sinai, guarding against preexilic apostasy and ensuring divine blessing.

The writer wanted the Jews to know God's power. He also wanted them to believe in the Lord so that they would be "established." If they believed God's messengers, they would succeed (2 Chr 20:20). He also wanted the people to know that Jerusalem was God's chosen place of worship (2 Chr 5,6), and that the temple, priests, singers, Levites, and gatekeepers had been divinely appointed (1 Chr 28:19). The temple was meant to be a place where all their needs could be met (2 Chr 6:19–7:3).

Content and Teachings. Chronicles can be briefly outlined as follows: 1 Chronicles—genealogies (1–9); the reign of David (10–29); 2 Chronicles—the reign of Solomon (1–9); the kings of Judah (10–36); epilogue on the exile and return (36:22,23). Since the Chronicler's writings do not have a didactic format, the reader must draw out those ideas and principles that are prominent and basic.

One important idea running through Chronicles is the greatness, power, and uniqueness of God. It is expressed most beautifully and forcefully in 1 Chronicles 29:11,12, which declares that everything in heaven and earth belongs to God and he is head over all.

Other passages make a similar claim. When Sennacherib, king of Assyria, attacked Judah and Jerusalem, King Hezekiah of Judah admonished his people not to fear the king of Assyria, "for there is one greater with us than with him. With him is an arm of flesh; but with us is the Lord our God, to help us and to fight our battles."

Several times the Chronicler repeats the idea that Israel's God is unique: there is no other God like the Lord. In 1 Chronicles 16:25,26, Psalm 96:4,5 is quoted: "For great is the Lord, and greatly to be praised, and he is to be held in awe above all gods. For all the gods of the peoples are idols; but the Lord made the heavens." Both David and Solomon are quoted as saying that there is no other God but the Lord (1 Chr 17:20; 2 Chr 6:14).

Chronicles emphasizes that the Lord is "greater than all gods" (2 Chr 2:5). The classic passage which stresses the differences between God and the "god" of a nation is in 2 Chronicles 32. When Sennacherib attacked Jerusalem, he asked the people, "On what are you relying that you stand siege in Jerusalem?" (v 10). Sennacherib was saying, in effect, "Don't let Hezekiah deceive you by telling you that your God will deliver you. No god of any nation so far has been able to stand against me. Your God is like the gods of all the other nations. He will not be able to deliver you from me." The Chronicler observes that the Assyrians "spoke of the God of Jerusalem as they spoke of the gods of the peoples of the earth, which are the work of men's hands" (v 19). But God did deliver Hezekiah and the inhabitants of Jerusalem from Sennacherib (vv 21,22).

Several passages declare that God rules over the nations (1 Chr 17:21; 2 Chr 20:6). In fact, the Chronicler saw the Lord as the one who directs history. The Lord brought Israel out of Egypt and drove the Canaanites out of their land (1 Chr 17:21; 2 Chr 6:5; 20:7). Some seeming quirks of history are explained with such phrases as "it was ordained by God" (2 Chr 22:7). Over and over in telling the story of the struggles of the kings of Judah with other nations, Chronicles points out that the Lord always decided the battle (1 Chr 10:13, 14; 18:6; 2 Chr 12:2; 13:15; 20:15; 21:11–14; 24:18; 28:1,5,6,19).

To the Chronicler the Lord was a covenant-keeping God (2 Chr 6:14). He was the God of justice and righteousness (2 Chr 12:6), so human judges must judge honestly and fairly (2 Chr 19:7). The Chronicler made it clear that no individual or nation could succeed by opposing God (2 Chr 24:20); not only would people fail against God, but they were powerless without him (1 Chr 29:14; 2 Chr 20:12).

The Lord is seen not only as a unique, righteous, and powerful God, but also as a wise God as well. God "triest the heart, and hast pleasure in uprightness" (1 Chr 29:17). Solomon prayed for God to "hear thou from heaven thy dwelling place, and forgive, and render to each whose heart thou knowest, according to all his ways (for thou, thou only, knowest the hearts of the children of men)" (2 Chr 6:30; cf. 32:31).

Although God knows all about human beings and has supreme power in heaven and on earth, men and women are still free to obey or disobey the Lord. The stories in Chronicles depict people who chose to obey or disobey God. Those who obeyed succeeded; but to the extent that others, even kings, disobeyed God they failed. Three of the Chronicler's heroes were Jehoshaphat, Hezekiah, and Josiah. Each was a great reformer, and each was commended for obeying the Lord. But each one sinned near the end of his life and incurred the disfavor of God. Jehoshaphat joined an alliance with a wicked king of the north (2 Chr 20:35,37). Hezekiah sinned in receiving envoys from Babylon and "God left him to himself" (2 Chr 32:31). Josiah did not obey the word of God spoken by Pharaoh Neco and was killed (2 Chr 35:21–24).

The Chronicler believed that all human beings have sinned (2 Chr 6:36), and should repent with all their mind and heart (2 Chr 6:38). One of the greatest passages on repentance in all the Bible is in 2 Chronicles 7:14.

A prominent theme in Chronicles is the importance of the temple as the place to meet God in worship. One could say that almost everything in Chronicles is related to the temple in one way or another. For a person living in Jerusalem in the 4th century BC under the domination of the Persians, temple worship was very significant. The Chronicler expressed the importance of true community and institutional worship.

Worship was the dominant attitude of the Chronicler, whose God was worthy to be praised. A worship service is described in 2 Chronicles 29:20–30. Hezekiah commanded a burnt offering and a sin offering to be made for all Israel. The Levites were stationed in the house of the Lord with cymbals, harps, and lyres. The priest had trumpets. "And when the burnt offering began, the song to the Lord began also, and the trumpets, accompanied by the instruments of David king of Israel. The whole assembly worshiped, and the singers sang, and the trumpeters sounded; all this continued until the burnt offering was finished. When the offering was finished, the king and all who were present with him bowed themselves and worshiped. And Hezekiah the king and the princes commanded the Levites to sing praises to the Lord with the words of David and of Asaph the seer. And they sang praises with gladness, and they bowed down and worshiped" (2 Chr 29:27–30).

The Chronicler was no racial bigot or narrow legalist. Always he appealed to the people of the northern kingdom to come back to worship at the temple (1 Chr 13:2; 2 Chr 11:16; 30:1). Even Neco, a pagan king, spoke the word of God to the good King Josiah (2 Chr 35:22); Cyrus, king of Persia, obeyed the Lord's command (2 Chr 36:23). The Chronicler reported, evidently with approval, that Hezekiah allowed a multitude of people from the north to eat the Passover, even though they had not cleansed themselves. He said, "The good Lord pardon every one who sets his heart to seek God, the Lord the God of his fathers, even though not according to the sanctuary's rules of cleanness" (2 Chr 30:18,19).

RALPH L. SMITH

See KINGS, BOOKS OF FIRST AND SECOND; KING, KINGSHIP; CHRONOLOGY, OLD TESTAMENT; ISRAEL, HISTORY OF.

Bibliography. P.R. Ackroyd, *I and II Chronicles, Ezra, Nehemiah*; I.W. Slotki, *Chronicles*; A.C. Welch, *The Work of the Chronicler*.

Chronology, New Testament. Branch of biblical studies that attempts to discover the sequence of NT events and the amount of time that elapsed between them. Chronology is essential to historians, whose task it is to determine the causes and effects of past events. Generally, for a historian's purpose, assigning absolute dates is less important than knowing the sequence of events that may have influenced each other. Very few NT happenings, in fact, can be given exact dates.

A remarkable testimony to the influence of Christianity is the fact that the entire Western world now divides history into BC (before Christ) and AD (*anno Domini*, "in the year of the Lord"). Before that method of dating became widespread in the Middle Ages, events were dated by their relation to other important events such as the founding of Rome or the beginning of a king's reign. When a monk named Dionysius Exiguus (6th century) invented our present method of dating, with the birth of Christ dividing history, he made a mistake in his computations. The odd result is the historical anomaly that Jesus himself was born no later than 4 years "before Christ."

Chronology of Jesus' Life. *Birth.* According to Matthew 2:1 Jesus was born "in the days of Herod the king." A 1st-century AD historian, Josephus, recorded that Herod died in the spring of the year we identify as 4 BC. Hence Jesus was born sometime before that, but how much before is uncertain. Luke 2:1,2 records that Jesus' birth occurred when "Caesar Augustus," the Roman emperor, decreed that a census, or enrollment, should be taken throughout the nation. "This was the first enrollment, when Quirinius was governor of Syria" (v 2). Those statements raise two questions: When was such a census taken, and when was Quirinius governor of Syria? Neither question has received a completely satisfying answer.

Census documents discovered in Egypt, together with earlier references, suggest that such enrollments were held every 14 years. That would put a census roughly in 8 or 9 BC. In view of the time needed to carry out the census (which required a person to travel to his birthplace), the birth of Jesus may have been somewhat later than the actual year of the decree (perhaps 7 BC).

Josephus recorded that Quirinius became governor of Syria in AD 6, rather late as a date for Jesus' birth. But some scholars have argued from ancient inscriptions that Quirinius also served in Syria as a special legate of the emperor Augustus before 6 BC. That could be the period referred to in Luke 2:2. Why did Luke choose to cite Quirinius instead of the regular governor of Syria at that time? Perhaps by so doing he could provide a more exact date for the birth of Jesus, since Quirinius was in authority for a shorter time than the regular governor of Syria.

A reasonable conclusion is that Jesus was born about 7 BC. That fits with Matthew 2:16, which seems to say that Jesus was born at least two years before Herod's death in 4 BC. No clear evidence exists concerning the day and month of his birth. Celebration of December 25 as Christmas originated in the 4th century, probably as a Christian alternative to the pagan winter solstice festival (Saturnalia).

The Beginning of Public Ministry. Luke 3:23 says that Jesus, "when he began his ministry, was about thirty years of age"; since the age given is only approximate, he may have been two or three years older or younger (cf. the pseudegraphic Testament of Levi 2:2; 12:5). If exactly 30 is added to the suggested date of birth, one gets AD 24. That date cannot be right, because Jesus' ministry began after John the Baptist appeared; Luke 3:1–3 dates John's public appearance precisely in "the fifteenth year of the reign of Tiberias Caesar" while Pilate was procurator (governor) over Judea. Pilate governed from AD 26 to 36, and the fifteenth year of Tiberias was most likely AD 27. Therefore Jesus did not begin his public ministry before AD 27. If only a short time elapsed between the beginning of John's ministry and the beginning of Jesus' ministry, then Jesus probably began in AD 27 or 28 when he was approximately 33 years old.

Death. All four Gospel records seem to imply that Jesus ate the last supper with his disciples on Thursday evening, was crucified on Friday, and rose from the dead early Sunday morning (Mt 28:1; Mk 16:1; Lk 24:1). The claim that Jesus rose on the third day (1 Cor 15:4) comes from the Jewish custom of counting a part of the day as a whole day. According to Matthew (26:19), Mark (14:12), and Luke (22:15), the last supper was the Passover meal, a yearly celebration of Israel's escape from Egypt (Ex 12–15). But according to John 13:1 and 19:14, the Passover meal had not yet been eaten on Friday; hence the last supper in John was not the Passover meal.

No completely satisfying solution to the apparent discrepancy has been put forward. Some scholars suggest plausibly that the use of two different calendars was responsible. According to that theory Jesus was following a calendar that placed the Passover meal on Thursday night. Temple officials, on the other hand, followed an alternate calendar that placed the killing of sacrificial victims on the next day. John may have used the second system to emphasize the fact that Christ was offered as the Passover sacrifice (cf. Jn 19:36; 1 Cor 5:7).

To find out how long Jesus' public ministry lasted and thus the year in which he died, one can turn to time references in John's Gospel. John referred to at least three Passovers (2:13; 6:4; 13:1) and possibly four (5:1). Since the Passover was a yearly feast, the ministry of Jesus would have lasted at least two and possibly three years. In Matthew, Mark, and Luke the Friday of Jesus' death occurred on the 15th of the Jewish month Nisan (which overlaps March and April). According to John, Jesus died on 14 Nisan. The question is: In which years from 26 to 36 (when Pilate was procurator in Judea) did 14 or 15 Nisan fall on a Friday? The answer is AD 27, 29, 30, and 33. Of those, the year 27 is too early and 33 is probably too late. Thus Jesus was probably crucified in 29 or 30, his public ministry lasted two or three years, and he was 35 or 36 years old when he died.

Events from 30 to 50 AD. Acts is the only NT book that records how much time elapsed between Jesus' death and his ascension: "To them he presented himself alive after his passion by many proofs, appearing to them during forty days and speaking of the kingdom of God" (Acts 1:3). The next key event after the ascension of Jesus into heaven was Pentecost (Acts 2:1). Pentecost, the Greek word for "fiftieth," referred to a celebration of the feast of weeks (cf. Ex 34:22; Dt 16:9–12) 50 days after the Passover. Since Jesus was crucified during the Passover season, the Pentecost of Acts 2:1, during which the disciples were filled with the Holy Spirit, took place in AD 30, some 50 days after the crucifixion and about 10 days after the ascension.

After that, events of the early chapters of Acts are hard to date because no precise statements are made about the amount of time between various events. Therefore the usual method for dating events of the apostolic age is first to find at least one event that can be dated with relative certainty from sources outside the NT; one then dates events before and after that event by figuring out how much time elapsed between them. Sometimes Acts records how much time passed between two events; usually it does not, so dating can be only approximate.

One pivotal starting point is the great famine prophesied by Agabus, which befell Palestine during the reign of Roman emperor Claudius (Acts 11:28,29). Josephus, who was alive at the time, gives enough information to locate the famine sometime between the years 46 and 48. We also know from the Mishna, a collection of Jewish laws, that the autumn of 47 to the autumn of 48 was a sabbatical year, when the Jews let the land rest and harvested nothing (cf. Lv 25:2–7). That could have aggravated and prolonged a famine, but one cannot be sure how early the famine started; some scholars propose 46 and some 47.

At first it seems peculiar that Luke, the author of Acts, should have recorded that famine (Acts 11:28) before recording the death of Herod Agrippa (Acts 12:20–23). From facts reported by Josephus the death of Herod (a grandson of Herod the Great) can be dated in AD 44, probably in the spring. That means that Herod must have died several years before the famine Luke recorded earlier. Some scholars

think that Luke simply got his chronological facts wrong. Others see Acts 12:1–24 as a kind of flashback to bring the history of the church in Jerusalem up to date. Such a practice was common among ancient historians, who often followed one source up to a suitable stopping point before moving on to another source. To charge Luke with inaccurate dating, it is argued, is to misunderstand the techniques of historical writing he was using.

Since Herod died in AD 44 (Acts 12:23), the apostle James, whom Herod put to death with the sword (Acts 12:2), must have died soon before 44, perhaps during the Passover season of 43 (Acts 12:3). The apostle Peter's imprisonment and his miraculous escape (Acts 12:3–17) also belong to that period.

When the Christians of Antioch decided to send relief to the Christians in Jerusalem in the midst of the great famine (Acts 11:29), Barnabus and Paul were appointed to transport the money to Jerusalem. That was Paul's second visit to Jerusalem after his conversion. The first visit is recorded in Acts 9:26–30. The third comes in Acts 15 when Paul and Barnabas were sent to discuss with the apostles and elders whether gentile converts to Christianity had to be circumcised. How one dates the first and third visits to Jerusalem, as well as Paul's conversion, depends on how those Jerusalem visits are related to those reported in Paul's letter to the Galatians.

The basic problem, which still divides NT scholars, is this: In Galatians 1:15–2:10 Paul recounted that his conversion was followed by two visits to Jerusalem, one three years after his conversion (Gal 1:18) and one 14 years after that (2:1–10). All scholars agree that the first visit three years after his conversion is the same as the first visit recorded in Acts 9:26–30. Answers differ, however, to the question of whether Galatians 2:1–10 refers to the second (famine) visit to Jerusalem in Acts 11:30 (in which case the third visit of Acts 15 is the one omitted from Galatians) or whether Galatians 2:1–10 refers to the visit in Acts 15 (in which case the famine visit was the one omitted from Galatians).

Two Possible Reconstructions

Reconstruction 1			Reconstruction 2		
Acts		*Galatians*	*Acts*		*Galatians*
9:26–30	=	1:18	9:26–30	=	1:18
11:30	=	2:1–10	11:30	=	omitted
15:1–29	=	omitted	15:1–29	=	2:1–10

Those who favor the first reconstruction offer six arguments: (1) The reason Paul gave such a rigorous account of his comings and goings in Galatians 1:15–24 was to show that he "did not get his gospel from men, nor was he taught it" (1:12). In other words his visits to the Jerusalem apostles were not for the purpose of receiving his gospel. If that is so, for Paul to omit the second Jerusalem visit would jeopardize his integrity and his authority with the Galatians. The first reconstruction avoids that difficulty; omission of a third Jerusalem visit from Galatians 2:1–10 could mean that it had not yet happened when Galatians was written. (2) Galatians 2:1–10 pictures a private meeting between Paul and Barnabas on one hand and the "pillar" apostles on the other. But the meeting in Acts 15 was public and before the whole church. Hence Galatians 2:1–10 more likely refers to a private meeting during the visit of Acts 11:30, which Galatians does not record. (3) Paul's eagerness to give to the poor mentioned in Galatians 2:10 connects naturally with the second Jerusalem visit when he was in fact delivering relief to the poor (Acts 11:30). (4) If Galatians 2 recorded the same trip as Acts 15, one would expect some mention of the decision reached by the Jerusalem council, especially since that decision related directly to the problem of circumcision which Paul was handling in his letter to the Galatians. (5) Further, it seems unlikely that the Jerusalem council preceded the event of Galatians 2:11–21, when Peter was rebuked by Paul for withdrawing from fellowship with gentile believers; that incident could hardly have happened so soon after the issue of gentile status in the church had been settled in Jerusalem. (6) According to Galatians 1:6 the letter was written "quickly" after Paul had established the Galatian churches. That makes sense if Galatians was written soon after the first missionary journey, hence just before the Jerusalem council of Acts 15; that would make Galatians Paul's first letter.

Scholars who favor the second reconstruction offer four arguments: (1) The main purpose of Paul's visit in Galatians 2:1–10 appears to be the same as that in Acts 15:1–29; both dealt with the issue of whether circumcision should be required of gentile converts (Gal 2:3–5; Acts 15:1,5). That similarity is obvious, but there is no explicit similarity between Galatians 2 and Acts 11:30. (2) On the basis of form and content Galatians is similar to Romans and to 1 and 2 Corinthians; it would thus seem to come from the same period—considerably later than the Jerusalem council. If so, it is likely that Paul would have included a reference to the Jerusalem council (namely Gal 2:1–10) in his recollections, since its outcome supported his own stance on circumcision set forth in the letter. (3) Acts 11:30

pictures Barnabas as the leader of the Barnabas/Paul team, since his name is given first place (as in Acts 12:25; 13:1,2,7; cf. 11:25,26). But in the description Paul gives of the visit in Galatians 2 he sees himself as the leader of the team. Since Acts does picture Paul as the leader from the time of the first missionary journey (Acts 13:9,13,43,46,50), including the third Jerusalem visit (15:2), it is more likely that Galatians 2 records the trip of Acts 15. (4) Finally, in Galatians 2:7,8 Paul was recognized as an apostle to the Gentiles with a standing equal to that of Peter. But if Galatians 2 recorded the events of Acts 11:30 and the first missionary journey had not yet occurred, the "pillar" apostles could hardly have recognized Paul's authority as apostle to the Gentiles. It is more likely that Galatians 2 followed the first missionary journey, just as Acts 15 followed the first missionary journey in Acts, and that both refer to the same event.

The significance of those arguments for chronology is that according to the first view Paul's conversion came 17 years before the famine visit of Acts 11:30 (cf. Gal 1:18; 2:1). According to the second view Paul's conversion took place 17 years before the Jerusalem council in Acts 15. The difference amounts to only one year, however.

It is helpful to consider one more date that can be fixed with high probability; namely, Paul's arrival in Corinth on his second missionary journey (Acts 18:1). On the second missionary journey (Acts 15:40–18:22) Paul and Silas set out on land through Syria, Cilicia, Phrygia, and Galatia, visiting churches founded on the first missionary journey. They came to Troas, then passed over to Philippi and continued down the coast through Thessalonica and Beroea. Paul went on to Athens before arriving at Corinth. From Acts 18:12 we know that Gallio was a proconsul in Corinth while Paul was there. An inscription discovered at nearby Delphi indicates that in all likelihood Gallio's term of office was from mid-51 to mid-52. The incident recorded in Acts 18:12–17 probably occurred at the beginning of Gallio's term, since the Jews hoped to get a ruling against Paul from their new proconsul. Not long after that, Paul left Corinth, probably in the summer or autumn of 52. According to Acts 18:11 Paul had spent 18 months in Corinth, which means that he probably arrived in the early months of 50 or the end of 49. That arrival date is confirmed by Acts 18:2, which says that Aquila and Priscilla had only recently been exiled from Rome when Paul came to Corinth. A 5th-century historian, Orosius, dated the edict of Claudius expelling the Jews from Rome in AD 49. Therefore Paul and Aquila and Priscilla probably arrived close together late in 49 or early in 50.

Early in his 18-month stay Paul wrote his first and second letters to the Thessalonians.

The two fixed dates, then, are 46 or 47 for the famine visit (Acts 11:30) and late 49 or early 50 for Paul's arrival in Corinth (Acts 18:1). Taking into account the time gaps mentioned in Galatians 1:18 and 2:1, as well as the supposition that the first missionary journey lasted about a year, the two reconstructions are presented in the following table. Keep in mind that they are approximations and that they reflect the ancient custom of counting a part of a year as a whole year.

Two Possible Chronologies

1		2
31 or 32	Paul's conversion (Acts 9:3–19)	32 or 33
33 or 34	First Jerusalem visit (Acts 9:26–30)	34 or 35
46 or 47	Famine visit (Acts 11:30)	46 or 47
47–48	First missionary journey (Acts 13:4–14:28)	47–48
48	Jerusalem council (Acts 15:1–29)	48
late 49 or early 50	Paul's arrival in Corinth on second missionary journey (Acts 18:1)	late 49 or early 50
autumn 51	Paul's departure from Corinth (Acts 18:18)	autumn 51

Events from AD 50 to 70. Acts 24:27 describes an event that helps us date events in the rest of the book, namely Porcius Festus' replacement of Felix as the procurator of Judea. A careful analysis of the evidence given by Eusebius, a 4th-century historian, leads to the probable conclusion that Felix was replaced in the summer of 59.

Working backward from that date, Paul's arrest in Jerusalem (Acts 21:33) must have occurred in 57, some two years before the coming of Festus. More precisely, Paul's arrest probably occurred in the late spring or summer of 57; Paul's goal (Acts 20:16) was to arrive in Jerusalem by Pentecost of that year, and Pentecost occurred at the end of May. He was not long in the city before he was arrested.

The Passover festival, 50 days before Pentecost, was celebrated by Paul with the church in Philippi (Acts 20:6). That would have been April 7–14, AD 57. Only after the feast did he continue his hurried journey to Caesarea and Jerusalem (Acts 20:6–21:16). Before his Passover visit to Philippi, Paul had spent three months in Greece (Acts 20:3). Allowing some time for him to travel through Macedonia and visit the Thessalonians and Beroeans, those three months were probably the winter months of 56–57 (Acts 20:3; cf. 1 Cor 16:6). No

doubt they were spent in the main church of Greece, Corinth, and were used in part for the writing of the letter to the Romans.

Between Paul's departure from Corinth on the second missionary journey (Acts 18:18) in the autumn of 51 and his arrival in Corinth on the third missionary journey (Acts 20:2) in the late winter of 56 are five years of activities that cannot be given exact dates. Paul said that he worked during three of those years in Ephesus (Acts 20:31; cf. Acts 19:1–20:1). With enough time allowed for the travels before and after, that stay at Ephesus probably lasted from 52 or 53 to the summer of 55 or 56 (cf. 1 Cor 16:8). During his long stay in Ephesus Paul wrote his first letter to the Corinthians. Then, on his way to Corinth in 56, he wrote 2 Corinthians from Macedonia.

Festus arrived as governor in the summer of 59, after Paul had been in prison in Caesarea for two years. Within a matter of days Paul was tried before Festus (Acts 25:1–12). Not wanting to be remanded to the Jewish authorities, Paul appealed to Caesar (Acts 25:12), which meant that he would go to Rome. The account in Acts gives no hint of a delay, so the voyage most likely began in the summer or fall of 59 (Acts 27:2).

Luke reported that when Paul the prisoner got to Fair Havens on the island of Crete, the weather had become dangerous for sea travel "because the fast had already gone by" (Acts 27:8,9). One ancient writer said that sailing became dangerous between mid-September and mid-November, and after that, impossible until spring. The fast referred to was no doubt the one in preparation for the Day of Atonement, which in the year 59 fell on October 5. It is not surprising that 14 days after leaving Fair Havens, the ship in which Paul was traveling was wrecked on the coast of Malta, south of Sicily (Acts 27:27–44). Three months later Paul set sail for Rome again in a ship that had spent the winter at Malta (Acts 28:11). Soon he was welcomed into Rome by Christians who came out to meet him (Acts 28:15). Thus Paul arrived in Rome in the early part of AD 60. The Book of Acts closes with the remark that "For two whole years Paul stayed there in his own rented house" (Acts 28:30 NIV). The NT does not report the outcome of his trial. During that period, according to the traditional view, he wrote Ephesians, Philippians, Colossians, and Philemon.

Eusebius wrote, "Tradition has it that after defending himself the Apostle was again sent on the ministry of preaching, and coming a second time to the same city suffered martyrdom under Nero." Nero, who was the Roman emperor from 54 to 68, put to death a multitude of Christians in Rome soon after a disastrous fire in July of 64, according to the Roman historian Tacitus. A number of early Christian writings (e.g., Clement) seem to indicate that Peter and Paul were both killed in Rome during that savage persecution. If so, and if Eusebius was right, then Paul may have spent the two years from 62 to 64 freely ministering back in the eastern provinces. Many conservative scholars date Paul's first letter to Timothy and his letter to Titus from that period. Written from Rome shortly before Paul's martyrdom in 64, 2 Timothy was probably his last letter (2 Tm 2:9; 4:6).

In Jerusalem, within three years after Paul had been carried off to Rome, James the brother of Jesus was stoned to death by the Jewish authorities. According to Josephus that occurred in 62. Not long afterward, according to Eusebius, the church in Jerusalem received a prophecy warning them to leave that doomed city and settle in Pella, one of the cities of the Decapolis ("ten cities") east of the Jordan. Thus when war broke out between the Jews and the Romans in 66, the Christians for the most part escaped its fury. That war ended in 70 with the destruction of Jerusalem and the temple (cf. Mk 13:2; Lk 21:24).

Conclusion. The results of NT chronological inquiry can be summarized in the following table of key events giving the approximate dates when they happened.

Summary of NT Chronology

Birth of Jesus (Mt 2:1)	7 BC
Beginning of Jesus' public ministry (Lk 3:23)	AD 27
Death of Jesus (Mk 15:37)	30
Pentecost (Acts 2:1–41)	30
Paul's conversion (Acts 9:1–19)	32
Paul's first Jerusalem visit (Acts 9:26–30)	34
Death of James the apostle (Acts 12:2)	43
Paul's second (famine) visit to Jerusalem (Acts 11:30)	47
Paul's first missionary journey (Acts 13:4–14:28)	47–48
Paul's third Jerusalem visit (Jerusalem council) (Acts 15:1–29)	48
Paul's arrival in Corinth on second missionary journey (Acts 18:1)	early 50
Paul's departure from Corinth (Acts 18:18)	autumn 51
Paul's stay in Ephesus on third missionary journey (Acts 19:1–20:1)	52–55
Paul's winter in Corinth (Acts 20:3; 1 Cor 16:6)	56/57
Paul's celebration of Passover at Philippi (Acts 20:6)	57
Paul's arrival in Jerusalem and imprisonment (Acts 21:17–23:31)	mid-57
Paul's journey to Rome after two years in prison in Caesarea (Acts 24:27; 25:10,12; 27:1,2)	59
Paul's arrival in Rome (Acts 28:14)	early 60
Paul's two years in Rome (Acts 28:30)	60–62
Paul's final ministry in the east?	62–64
Martyrdom of James, Jesus' brother	62
Peter and Paul's martyrdom under Nero	64
Destruction of Jerusalem	70

JOHN PIPER

See "DATE" UNDER EACH NT BOOK; GENEALOGY OF JESUS CHRIST; JESUS CHRIST, LIFE AND TEACHING OF; APOSTOLIC AGE; ACTS OF THE APOSTLES, BOOK OF THE; PAUL, THE APOSTLE; FIRST JEWISH REVOLT.

Bibliography. J. Finegan, *Handbook of Biblical Chronology*; J.J. Gunther, *Paul, Messenger and Exile: A Study in the Chronology of His Life and Letters*; R. Jewett, *A Chronology of Paul's Life*; G. Ogg, *The Chronology of the Life of Paul* and *The Chronology of the Public Ministry of Jesus*.

Chronology, Old Testament. Branch of biblical studies that attempts to assign dates and sequences to OT events.

Both biblical and nonbiblical materials are utilized by students of OT chronology. Biblical data include: (1) genealogies showing personal and tribal affiliations among various peoples; (2) specific numbers given by biblical authors to indicate a person's longevity, a king's reign, or duration of a specific event; (3) synchronizing statements which date an event in a specific year of a king's reign or relate it to a natural phenomenon assumed to be common knowledge at the time of writing (Am 1:1; Zec 14:5).

From the abundance of such chronological passages in the OT, one might conclude that establishment of OT dates and sequences would be a simple procedure. Each of the three kinds of biblical material, however, exhibits special problems that must be solved first.

Nonbiblical materials that shed light on OT chronology are quite numerous, and more are discovered year by year. They include: (1) official records of important affairs such as military campaigns from countries like Egypt or Babylonia; (2) official inscriptions that are dedicatory or commemorate a great victory; (3) annals listing major accomplishments of a ruler year by year; (4) ostraca (inscribed pieces of pottery) containing letters, tax transactions or other economic records, military dispatches between field leaders and command headquarters, or other information. Ostraca may be dated archaeologically and are often used to supplement the biblical record.

The chronologist tries to examine the pertinent biblical and nonbiblical information, note areas of correlation among all the data, and finally establish a working system into which the most facts can be fitted. New evidence uncovered at any time may necessitate shifts in the present working system. Although the basic structure of biblical chronology seems reasonably firm, many details will no doubt be subject to change as new evidence is discovered.

As a general rule, the earlier the period the less certain one can be of one's dating. In the 2nd millennium BC, for example, many dates can be assigned within a range of about 100 years. By the time of David and Solomon (c. 1000 BC), the margin of error over which scholars debate is a decade or less. The range narrows as one comes toward the present, so that, with the exception of one or two problem eras, dates accurate to within one or two years are possible by roughly the middle of the 9th century BC. Such limitations must be kept in mind in any examination of the major periods of OT history.

Prepatriarchal Period. *Biblical Evidence.* In the first 11 chapters of Genesis are found accounts of the creation (Gn 1, 2), the fall (Gn 3), Cain and Abel (Gn 4), the flood (Gn 6–9), and the tower of Babel (Gn 11). Those events are set within a certain chronological framework.

According to Genesis 5 a period of 10 generations elapsed between the creation and the flood. Although the individuals listed enjoyed an average life span of a hefty 847 years plus, the total time elapsing between Adam and the flood was only 1,656 years.

According to Genesis 11 another 10 generations elapsed from the time of the flood until the time of Abraham (at least in the Septuagint, the 3rd-century BC Greek translation of the OT; the Hebrew Masoretic text has nine). In that period the average age attained by individuals in the list is only 346 years (using a figure of 460 for Arpachshad's son Kainan, who is included in v 13 of the Septuagint; cf.

Lk 3:36); the total elapsed time from the flood to Abraham is only 520 years. Taken literally, that would mean that all of Abraham's ancestors as far back as Noah's son Shem were still alive at Abraham's birth, and that a total of only 2,176 years elapsed from the time of creation to Abraham.

Interpretation of the Biblical Data. A literalistic or slavishly mathematical interpretation of the figures, as now appears in the margin of many KJV Bibles, requires a number of assumptions: that no names are omitted from the genealogies, that all the numbers given are consecutive, and especially that numbers used in an ancient biblical source carry the same meaning as that associated with them in the modern Western mind. Each assumption needs serious examination in the light of other established facts.

A cursory reading of other biblical genealogies, for example, reveals that not all the names of a given family were always included. Even in more recent NT times Matthew recorded a total of 28 generations (two sets of 14 each) between David and Jesus, and comparison with OT genealogies reveals that Matthew omitted several names. Luke listed a total of 42 generations for the same interval. Omissions are also obvious when one compares the genealogical lists given in 1 Chronicles 1–8 with those recorded earlier in Genesis, Exodus, Numbers, Joshua, 1 and 2 Samuel, and 1 and 2 Kings.

Further, ancient peoples thought of numbers in a schematic or stylized way. Use of numbers among the ancient Near Eastern nations differed sharply from current Western practice.

Examples of that practice are known from both biblical and nonbiblical sources. For example, a list of eight Sumerian kings who ruled in the city of Shurruppak before the "great flood" of the Jemdet Nar era (c. 3000 BC) assigns each man an average reign of more than 30,000 years. Berossus, a Babylonian priest of Marduk living in the 3rd century BC, added two names to the eight found in that earlier list of kings and assigned an average of 43,200 years to each king. Such extraordinarily high numbers provide a perspective for considering the numbers of Genesis.

In light of the present evidence, therefore, although one can assume that the numbers assigned to the ages of the patriarchs preceding Abraham in Genesis "had real meaning for those responsible for their preservation," according to OT scholar R. K. Harrison, they should not be employed in a purely literal sense to compute the length of the various generations mentioned in the text. Further, the numbers given in the Septuagint and the Sa-

Significant Old Testament Dates
(According to Various Authorities)

Biblical Event	Rabbi Jose c. 150	Ussher 1650	Anstey 1913	Unger 1954	Anderson 1957	Schultz 1960	Mauro 1961	Thiele 1965	Kitchen 1966	Pfeiffer 1973	Bright 1981	Merrill 1987
The creation of Adam	3759	4004	4124				4046					
The flood	2103	2348	2469				2390					
The birth of Abraham	1811	1996	2117	2161	1750	2166	2038		(?) c. 1950	c. 2000	(?) c. 1950	2166
Jacob's entrance into Egypt		1702	1827	1871	(?) c. 1550	1877	1748		c. 1700	1720		1876
The exodus	1311	1491	1612	1441	1290	1447	1533		c. 1280	1290	(?) c. 1280	1446
The crossing of Jordan	1271	1450	1572	1401	1250	1406	1493		c. 1240	1250	1250	1406
The anointing of Saul		1095	1102	1020	1020	1026	1023		c. 1050	1020	1020	1051
The division of the kingdom	795	974	982	925	922	931	903	931	c. 937	925	922	931
The fall of Samaria		721	718	721	722/21	722	640	722		722	722/21	722
The fall of Jerusalem	421	588	585	587	587	586	507	586	587/86	587	587	586
Cyrus' decree to return			538	539	538	538	457		538	538	538	
Second Temple	351	515	520		515	515			515	515	515	
Ezra's return		467	515	c. 458	428 (398)	457			457	c. 428	458	
Nehemiah's return			502	444	445	444			445	445	445	
Malachi			488	c. 400	500 (450)	460 (444)			c. 525	c. 450	432–425	

Sources: Rabbi Jose, Seder Olam Rabbah, Niddah, 46b; (c. 150) James Ussher, *Annales Veteris Testamenti* (London, 1650); Martin Anstey, *The Romance of Bible Chronology*, 2 vols. (London: Marshall, 1913); Merrill F. Unger, *Archaeology and the Old Testament* (Grand Rapids: Zondervan, 1954); Bernhard W. Anderson, *Understanding the Old Testament* (Englewood Cliffs, N.J.: Prentice-Hall, 1957); Samuel J. Schultz, *The Old Testament Speaks* (New York: Harper & Row, 1960); Philip Mauro, *The Wonders of Bible Chronology* (Swengel, Pa.: Bible Truth Depot, 1961); Edwin R. Thiele, *The Mysterious Numbers of the Hebrew Kings* (Grand Rapids: Eerdmans, 1965); K. A. Kitchen, *Ancient Orient and Old Testament* (Chicago: Inter-Varsity, 1966); Charles F. Pfeiffer, *Old Testament History* (Grand Rapids: Baker, 1973); John Bright, *A History of Israel*, 3rd ed. (Philadelphia: Westminster, 1981); Eugene H. Merrill, *Kingdom of Priests* (Grand Rapids: Baker, 1987).

maritan Pentateuch, another early version of the Pentateuch, diverge in many details from those of the Hebrew Masoretic text. That means, among other things, that the Genesis numbers caused problems for even the earliest scholars of Scripture.

Nonbiblical Evidence. Archaeology provides no evidence that may be used to date either the creation or any other account preserved in Genesis 1–11. The flood is an example that illustrates some of the difficulties. Many claims have been made by persons from a wide variety of backgrounds (scientists, explorers, theologians, and others) to the effect that archaeology has proven the Genesis flood narrative to be true. Yet no city so far excavated in Palestine and Syria (including some of the oldest towns in the world) shows archaeological evidence of the flood.

Although several cities in Mesopotamia do exhibit evidence of a flood, three factors make it difficult to link that evidence with Genesis 6–9. Each of the flood levels so far discovered dates from a different period. Further, since nearby sites show no evidence of flooding, all of the Mesopotamian flood evidence points to relatively small local floods. Finally, the evidence indicates no great cultural discontinuities of the sort that would result from destruction of an entire population. Thus it seems that the ancient Mesopotamian floods discovered through archaeological research are of the same kind as the floods that still occur in the Euphrates river valley.

Clearly, certain questions one might ask of the Genesis narratives simply cannot be answered. Many who regard the Bible as the Word of God have concluded that the date of events found in Genesis 1–11 must be less important than the theological truths of salvation, faith, and obedience that these accounts present.

From Abraham to Moses. *The Patriarchal Age.* The date of Abraham is still a lively topic among biblical scholars who agree that Abraham, Isaac, and Jacob were indeed historical persons. Opinions range from an early-date view estimating that the patriarchal age extended from 2086 to 1871 BC, to a late-date view placing Abraham at around 1400 BC. Since each position claims to fit the biblical data, a closer look at the two points of view is in order.

Many OT passages seem to support the view that puts Abraham at a comparatively early date. First Kings 6:1 computes 480 years back from the founding of the temple in the 4th year of Solomon's reign (961 BC, according to the early-date view) to the exodus from Egypt, which would then be dated 1441 BC. Counting 430 years as the period of Israelite

sojourn in Egypt (see Gn 15:13; Ex 12:40) takes the date back to 1871 BC. To that date are added the 215 years demanded by the total of (1) Abraham's age upon entering Canaan (75 years according to Gn 12:4); (2) 25 additional years before the birth of Isaac (Gn 21:5); (3) 60 more years to the birth of Jacob (Gn 25:26); (4) the appearance of Jacob before the pharaoh at age 130 (Gn 47:9). Those 215 years added to the previous total give a date of 2086 BC for the entrance of Abraham into Canaan and a date of 2161 BC for his birth.

Such a calculation does not use all of the chronological evidence presented in the OT; consequently the date for Abraham is open to challenge. For example, the 480 years between the exodus and Solomon's 4th year represent a period of time into which the wilderness wanderings, the career of Joshua and his immediate successors, the period of the judges, Samuel, Saul, and David must be placed. Although the OT does not specifically say how long were the careers of Joshua, Samuel, or Saul, even a modest reckoning pushes the total years required by all the biblical data together to approximately 600.

In addition, the length of time to be assigned to the Egyptian sojourn is problematic. The Samaritan Pentateuch and the Septuagint both view the number 430 (in Ex 12:40) as applicable not only to the years in Egypt but to the years of Abraham, Isaac, and Jacob in Canaan as well. Evidently Paul followed the Septuagint tradition when he dated the giving of the law 430 years later than the time of God's promise to Abraham (see Gal 3:15–18). That means the Septuagint figure cannot be dismissed lightly.

The late dating of Abraham (c. 1400 BC) is based on two propositions. (1) The picture of patriarchal society portrayed in Genesis most closely parallels that reflected in the cuneiform tablets recovered from Nuzi, a town in northeastern Mesopotamia about 175 miles north of Baghdad. (2) Because those tablets must be dated in the 15th and 14th centuries BC, the parallel patriarchal age must have fallen within the same general time period.

Those who hold the late-date view are aware that their date for Abraham cannot be equated with the set of numbers on which the early-date view depends. They point to other data, also from the OT. Joseph, who was already a highly placed Egyptian official when Jacob moved to Egypt, lived to be 110 years old (Gn 50:26). Moses was a great-grandson of Levi, Joseph's older brother. Since Joseph lived to see his own great-grandchildren born (who would probably be younger than Moses since their great-grandfather was younger than his), the late-date view concludes that Joseph could have been alive when Moses was born. The four-generation genealogy of Moses (Levi-Kohath-Amram-Moses, in Ex 6:16–20; Nm 3:17–19; 26:58,59; 1 Chr 6:1–3) was evidently thought to be complete according to Genesis 15:16, which predicted that Abraham's descendants would be freed from Egyptian bondage "in the fourth generation."

However, a date of around 1400 BC for Abraham cannot be aligned with certain other biblical data, including the long Egyptian sojourn demanded by Genesis 15:13 and Exodus 12:40 and a 40-year (or "one-generation") wilderness existence. Some normally moderate scholars are forced to reduce the wilderness time to two years in order to maintain their late date for Abraham.

In short, the late-date theory is consistent with part of the biblical evidence (the genealogies of Moses), but the early-date theory conforms to another part (the actual year figures listed in scattered verses from Gn and Ex). The late-date theory holds that the genealogies represent more reliable information in Semitic societies generally, whereas the early-date theory computes years given in the biblical account literally throughout its scheme.

Because of problems attached to both positions, a large group of scholars take a middle ground in dating the patriarchal age. Archaeologically, they say, Abraham and his life and times fit perfectly within the early 2nd millennium, but imperfectly within any later period. By placing Abraham roughly between 1800 and 1600 BC, they provide enough latitude for a merging of all the available evidence, biblical and nonbiblical, into a workable chronological scheme. Archaeology provides four major bits of evidence for an early 2nd-millennium patriarchal era.

(1) Though the Nuzi tablets furnish a clear parallel to patriarchal social life, other tablets from other towns and an earlier era reflect many of the same customs common to Nuzi and Genesis. Since the Nuzians were Hurrians who came to northeastern Mesopotamia from elsewhere (perhaps Armenia), their social customs originated no doubt much earlier than the time of their tablets now in our possession. Accordingly, the 15th-century BC date of the Nuzi tablets does not preclude an earlier date for Abraham.

(2) The names of several of Abraham's ancestors listed in Genesis 11 can now be identified with towns in the northern area of Mesopotamia around Haran, the city from which Abraham migrated to Canaan (Gn 11:31–12:3). Significantly, Haran flourished in the 19th and 18th centuries BC.

(3) Shortly after 2000 BC Semitic nomads from the desert invaded the civilized communities of the Fertile Crescent. Those invaders, called Amorites in the OT, established themselves in several cities in northern Syria and Mesopotamia. One of the Amorite cities was Babylon, ruled by Hammurabi sometime around the beginning of the 18th century BC. Although the Amraphel of Genesis 14:9 is not linguistically identifiable with the Babylonian king Hammurabi, as earlier scholars believed, the picture of the times following the Amorite invasion still accords well with the Genesis narratives generally.

(4) Mari, another Amorite town, is now well known because of more than 20,000 tablets recovered from its royal palace and archives. Geographically, Mari is located in the general area of Haran. Chronologically, the tablets recovered come from the 18th century BC. One 18th-century king of Mari, Zimri Lim, carried on extensive correspondence with Hammurabi of Babylon. The tablets from Mari also furnish valuable information about tribal and ethnic groups and their movements in the general region. Of basic importance for dating the Genesis materials are certain documents from Mari which include personal names very similar to Abraham (Abi-ram), Jacob, Laban, and several other West Semitic names.

Archaeological evidence neither proves nor disproves the actual existence of Abraham, Isaac, or Jacob. That is admitted on all sides. What archaeology has done is to provide a framework of probabilities within which the biblical patriarchal narratives appear more and more to be at home.

Date of the Exodus. The problem of dating the patriarchal age is closely related to the problem of assigning a date to the exodus of the Israelites from Egypt. Since the evidence does not permit a precise date for Abraham, a precise date for the entry of Joseph or Jacob into Egypt is likewise unobtainable. Further, the biblical evidence does not yield an exact figure for the length of the Israelite sojourn in Egypt.

For years biblical scholars viewed 1 Kings 6:1 as a foundation upon which to build an unshakable date for the exodus. Because Solomon's 4th year could be unquestionably fixed to within at least a 10-year span (967–958 BC), the exodus too could be dated with the same precision simply by adding 480 years. But other biblical data raised serious questions about that simple procedure. When the Bible deals with all the events between the time of the exodus and the founding of Solomon's temple, that is, from Numbers to 1 Kings 5:18, the precise numbers given total not 480 but closer to 600 years.

Because the evidence is insufficient to allow a precise date for the exodus, scholarly opinion remains divided between two possibilities. A 15th-century exodus is supported by several pieces of evidence. The chronology in 1 Kings 6:1 appears to be independently corroborated by a passage in Judges 11:26. It claims that Israel had occupied the area around Heshbon for 300 years preceding his own day. If Jephthah is dated at roughly 1100 BC, one is obviously led back to an exodus in the middle of the 15th century. Also, three successive generations of pharaohs who ruled in the 16th and 15th centuries produced no male offspring, making it more likely that Moses would have become the foster son of a royal princess during that time; all of the 19th-dynasty kings (1306–1200 BC) had legitimate male heirs.

In addition, a 15th-century date makes possible a connection between the Habiru invasion of Canaan (1400–1350 BC) described in the Amarna letters found at Tell el-Amarna, Egypt, and the invasion of Canaan by the Hebrews described in the OT Book of Joshua. Related to that is a reference to "Israel" in the Merneptah stele, a stone pillar inscribed with the deeds of the Egyptian king, Merneptah, of about 1220 BC; it implies that the people referred to, met by Merneptah in the course of a Canaanite military campaign, had been in existence for some time. Finally, an excavator of Jericho, John Garstang, placed the destruction of that city at around 1400 BC.

Other evidence, however, strongly implies not a 15th- but a 13th-century date for the exodus. Many scholars assign a date between 1290 and 1275 BC on the basis of that evidence. First, the 480 years of 1 Kings 6:1 discussed above may be interpreted as schematically representing 12 generations, as indicated by 1 Chronicles 6:3–8. Thus if 12 generations averaged 25 years instead of 40 years, reduction of 480 schematized years to 300 actual years would point to an exodus date of around 1266 BC. Second, archaeological evidence exists that dates destruction at the assumed sites of several cities conquered by Joshua (Lachish, Debir, Bethel, and Hazor) to the late 13th century. Third, there is no biblical mention of Egyptian military campaigns (such as Merneptah's 1220 BC incursion); Israelites living in Canaan before the time of the militarily active pharaohs Seti I (1319–1301 BC) and Ramses II (1301–1234 BC) would certainly have been affected by such activity. Fourth, Exodus 1:11 mentions the city of Ramses, the capital built by Ramses II, according to his own inscriptions.

A fifth line of argument comes from archaeological conclusions that Transjordan and the Negeb desert were not occupied by sedentary people between 1900 and 1300 BC, whereas the Bible states clearly that the Israelites encountered stiff opposition from groups in that same region. Thus, it is argued, the Israelites must have entered that region after 1300 BC. Sixth, connecting the Habiru with the Israelites of the conquest lacks weight because many texts besides the Amarna tablets attest to the existence of Habiru groups virtually all over the ancient Near East. "Habiru" seems to be a much broader term, possibly meaning "trespasser," and is probably unrelated etymologically or semantically to "Hebrew." Seventh, and finally, Garstang's work at Jericho has now been revised by archaeologist Kathleen Kenyon, who showed that the fallen walls that Garstang had dated about 1400 BC in reality were destroyed in 1800 BC or earlier.

So far it has been impossible to decide with precision between the two centuries proposed for the exodus. The majority opinion among OT scholars generally, including a growing number of moderate or conservative scholars, is in favor of the 13th-century option. On the other hand, many other conservative scholars continue to favor the 15th-century date. Dogmatism is unwarranted since problems remain unresolved with either option.

In accordance with the majority opinion, however, a date of about 1290 BC for the exodus will be used in dealing with subsequent problems.

Conquest and Consolidation. The chronological task for the period of conquest and consolidation is to fit all the events narrated by the OT, chiefly in Joshua and Judges, between the exodus (*c.* 1290 BC) and the times of David (*c.* 1000 BC) and Solomon (d. 930 BC). In other words, one must fit roughly 550 years of biblical events between Moses and David into a 290-year span.

Although assigning an early date for the exodus (*c.* 1447 BC) would make the task somewhat easier, the mere addition of about 157 years does not by itself solve all the problems. Neither date allows enough time for all the OT events from Joshua to David to take place singly and consecutively. Accordingly, advocates of both dates assume that some of the judges ruled simultaneously rather than consecutively. The difference is one of degree only.

The Book of Joshua furnishes most of the OT evidence regarding the conquest of Canaan by the Israelites. Unfortunately, the Book of Joshua has no chronological notes that specify the amount of time elapsing during Joshua's career. Further, there are no biblical references to major contemporary events in other parts of the ancient world, the dates of which could be used to fix the chronology. Rather, in what is obviously a telescoped account, the Book of Joshua records the fall of Jericho and Ai, followed closely by a southern and then a northern campaign. After those victories, covering much of the total territory of Canaan, various parcels of land were distributed to the tribal groups of Israel; the tribes were expected to complete the task of destroying whatever Canaanite inhabitants remained in their particular region. One seeks in vain, however, for any statements indicating how long those events took.

In the Book of Judges a slightly different circumstance prevails. There the OT furnishes a rather complete list of figures to indicate the duration of periods of foreign oppression, judgeships, and ensuing peace. The total number of years described for that period is 410, but that total does not include any time for the many "minor" judges. It seems obvious, therefore, that most if not all of the judges were simply local chieftains whose activity was simultaneous with that of other judges, at least for part of their reign. Unfortunately the Book of Judges provides no crossreference system to indicate which judges were contemporaries of which others. Perhaps the best one can do is to assume general guidelines for the chronology of that period between Moses and David.

Two significant facts should be kept in mind. First, archaeological information seems to demand a conquest date beginning about 1250 BC rather than 200 years earlier. Assuming concurrent careers for the judges allows one to compress the literal OT figures into the general scheme demanded by other evidence.

Second, the ancient scribes evidently related the chronology of the period to a 40-year or generation-based schema, a practice that lasted until the time of the divided kingdom, when a regular dynastic chronology was introduced. In the face of so many careers being assigned exactly 40 years, the fact remains that the literal totals of such numbers cannot be harmonized with either the biblical or the archaeological evidence for the period. Accordingly, most scholars doubt that the number 40 was ever intended to be an exact mathematical calculation. That view permits enough leeway for cautious fitting of biblical and other evidence into a general timetable.

The Monarchy. Types of Evidence. For the period of the Israelite monarchy chronological evidence is abundant.

The OT itself strives to provide all the information necessary for the chronology of the period, including (1) a complete list of all the kings in Israel and in Judah both before and after the division of the kingdom; (2) the age of each king (except Saul) at his accession; (3) synchronisms of the northern kingdom of Israel and the southern kingdom of Judah showing in what year of his contemporary in the other kingdom each king came to the throne; and (4) precise calculations of the length of each king's reign.

In addition, some important events are dated by reference to another event; others are coordinated with concurrent events in secular history.

Outside the OT an abundance of material provides evidence for a chronology of the period. By far the most important single source is a collection of Assyrian *limmu* lists. In Assyria a record of each king's reign was kept on a particular kind of an annal. Each year of reign was named after an individual of high rank in the court; the first year was named after the king himself, the second after the next highest-ranking official (though that name appears to have been selected by lot originally), and so on, down until the death of the king. The word *limmu* was used to introduce the name of the official after whom the current year was to be named, hence the designation "*limmu* lists."

Assyrian *limmu* lists are tied precisely to the solar year, making the documents highly reliable. Further, in addition to many events in Assyrian history, notable natural phenomena were dated on the basis of the *limmu* in which they occurred. For example, a solar eclipse dated by the Assyrian scribes in the *limmu* year of Bur-Sagale has been computed astronomically as June 15, 763 BC. Beginning with the year 763, then, and working both backward and forward, a complete list of Assyrian *limmu* officials has been obtained for the period between 891 and 648 BC.

With the accuracy of the Assyrian *limmu* lists corroborated by a number of sources, they can be used with confidence in reconstructing the chronology of the corresponding period of biblical history. That is especially true where a biblical writer related an Israelite or a Judahite event to a particular year in the reign of an Assyrian king whose *limmu* list indicates the precise years of his reign.

There are also records from Chaldean (Babylonian) king lists and from later Greek historians. Ptolemy, in the 2nd century AD, for example, gave dates for Babylonian kings from 747 BC and continued with dates for Persian, Greek, and Roman rulers down to AD 161. Finally, useful information is found in inscriptions from monuments, stelae, and other artifacts from Assyria and elsewhere.

Problem Areas. Despite a wealth of evidence both in and outside the Bible, however, the problems of OT chronology of the monarchical period are not easily solved. Taken at face value, the biblical totals appear to be hopelessly out of harmony with the Assyrian dates. Further, the totals given respectively for the northern kingdom of Israel and the southern kingdom of Judah do not match precisely either. Hence one must consider four variable factors which, in general, provide enough flexibility to fit all the data into a single system.

1. Israel and Judah did not always use the same method for reckoning the accession year of a king. Confusion has arisen also because each kingdom changed its system. In the accession-year system, year one of a king's reign began with the first new year's day following his inauguration. In the nonaccession-year system, the remainder of the calendar year in which a king was crowned counted as year one of his rule—but also counted as the last year of his predecessor. Judah followed an accession-year reckoning from 931 to about 850 BC, switched to a nonaccession-year reckoning until 796, and then returned to an accession-year pattern from 796 to the exile. Israel, on the other hand, reckoned by the nonaccession-year pattern from 931 to 792 BC and then switched to the accession-year system until conquered in 722. Obviously the totals computed by scribes of the two countries would not match a total reached strictly sequentially.

2. Another problem is related to the first one. When scribes from Judah computed the regnal years of a king in Israel, they used their own system rather than Israel's, and vice versa. Unrecognized, that factor can lead to confusion in attempting to correlate the years assigned to kings of the two countries.

3. A final problem is that of co-regencies (having two rulers in one country simultaneously) and the way in which they were figured into the numerical totals of the kings. Biblical authors sometimes counted a particular king's total from the beginning of his co-regency; at other times they reckoned his years only from the time he began to rule independently.

Monarchical Chronology. The *limmu* list of the Assyrian king Shalmaneser III provides a basis for the first comparison of dates among Assyria, Israel, and Judah. In the *limmu* of Daian-Assur, Shalmaneser's sixth year on the throne, Ahab of Israel was listed as one of the kings who fought against the Assyrians in the battle of Qarqar. Thus the date for that battle may be placed confidently in 853 BC.

Assyrian records also indicate that Shalmaneser III came into contact with an Israelite king 12 years later, in 841 BC. That king was Jehu. Thus two fixed points are available for correlating the biblical information. Following the death of Ahab, which is not dated exactly by reference to the Assyrian records, two of his sons came to power. The first, Ahaziah, reigned two years (1 Kgs 22:51); the second, Joram (also called Jehoram), reigned a total of 12 years (2 Kgs 3:1). Recognizing a nonaccession-year reckoning by the Israelites in that era, the apparent total of 14 years may be reduced to an actual total of 12. Thus it seems evident that Ahab not only fought Shalmaneser III in 853 BC, but also died in that year. Ahab was then followed by his two sons for a total of 12 years before the accession of Jehu in time to account for his contact with Shalmaneser III in 841 BC. Further, because Jehu murdered both the king of Israel (Jehoram) and the king of Judah (Ahaziah) at the same time (2 Kgs 9:24–27), a fixed synchronism is provided between the two kingdoms for the year 841 BC.

The first nine kings of Israel ruled an apparent total of 98 years or an actual total (taking into account Israel's nonaccession-year policy) of 90 years. Zimri, who ruled only seven days (1 Kgs 16:15–18), counts as one of the nine but does not insert an extra year in either the actual or apparent totals. The accession of Jeroboam I thus occurred in 930 BC (adding 90 years to 841 BC), and Rehoboam of Judah began to rule in that same year as well. Allowing Solomon the 40-year reign indicated in 1 Kings 11:42 points to the year 970 BC for his accession. The death of David would also be pinpointed in that period, although allowance must be made for the possibility of a short co-regency of David and Solomon before David's death. The reign of Saul then falls approximately in the late 11th century BC.

In Judah the period between the death of Solomon in 930 BC and the murder of Ahaziah by Jehu in 841 BC was occupied by the kingships of six men whose time on the throne totals 95 biblical years. Computation of that era in Judah is not as simple as for the Israelite kings for several reasons. Problems include a change from accession- to nonaccession-year reckoning sometime around 850 BC, at least two co-regencies (Jehoshaphat with Asa and then Jehoram with Jehoshaphat), and the calendar differences between the two kingdoms. It is clear that the 95 apparent years must be reduced, on the basis of the differences in computation and calendar, to 90 actual years in order to bring the Judahite figures into line with the established Assyrian and Israelite synchronisms.

After the year 841 the next biblical event to be certified by nonbiblical materials is the fall of Samaria in 722 BC. That date is furnished by the annals of Sargon II of Assyria (722–705 BC), successor to Shalmaneser V (727–722 BC). Although that date comes just 120 years after the fixed point of 841 BC in Israelite history, the chronological materials for that period are quite difficult to interpret accurately. In the past, scholars resorted to assumptions of extensive co-regencies, to presumed confusion on the part of certain scribes over methods to be followed in computations, or to other theories in attempting to understand the period. In spite of the many difficulties, however, all the biblical and Assyrian dates for the period of the divided monarchy have been harmonized—with the exception of four figures related to the closing years of the Israelite kingdom, all connected in some way with the problematic reign of Hoshea.

The basic agreement among scholars regarding the chronology of the period of monarchy in Israel and Judah is illustrated in the table titled "The Monarchy to 722." The names heading the columns of years are those of OT scholars W. F. Albright, E. R. Thiele, and R. K. Harrison, who proposed the computations under their names.

Judah After the Fall of Israel. Following the fall of Samaria in 722 BC OT chronology is concerned only with the southern kingdom of Judah until its destruction some 135 years later. Two events in the biblical record important for establishing a chronology for that period are the siege of Jerusalem by Sennacherib of Assyria in the late 8th century and the eventual fall of Jerusalem to the Babylonians in the early 6th century.

Sennacherib's Invasion of Judah. The Assyrian invasion (704–681 BC) is recorded in 2 Kings 18:13–16, where verse 13 dates the event to the 14th year of King Hezekiah. Sennacherib's own inscriptions include a lengthier version of the affair. From them the date of 701 BC is established, placing the accession of Hezekiah in 715 BC. That much is simple, but problems still arise. For example, 2 Kings 19:9 reports that Sennacherib was in contact with an Ethiopian king, Tirhakah (c. 690–664 BC), during the course of his campaign, which included a siege of Jerusalem. Obviously, contact with a ruler who came to power in 690 BC at the earliest could not refer to events in 701 BC. It is possible, however, that Sennacherib actually made two invasions of Judah, the first in 701 and the second sometime later. The date of that supposed second invasion is not assured, although 2 Kings 19:35–37 may imply that Sennacherib was murdered only shortly after his withdrawal from Jerusalem. Since Sennacherib was succeeded by his son Esarhaddon in the year 681, the presumed second invasion of Judah would have occurred somewhere in the last half of the same decade.

A number of scholars oppose the assumption of a second invasion of Jerusalem by Sennacherib. They suggest the possibility that Tir-

The Monarchy to 722 BC

Israel	Judah	Albright	Thiele	Harrison
Jeroboam I		922–901	930–909	931/30–910/09
	Rehoboam	922–915	930–913	931/30–913
	Abijah	915–913	913–910	913–911/10
	Asa	913–873	910–869	911/10–870/69
Nadab		901–900	909–908	910/09–909/08
Baasha		900–877	908–886	909/08–886/85
Elah		877–876	886–885	886/85–885/84
Zimri		876	885	885/84
Tibni			885–880	885/84–880
Omri		876–869	885–874	885/84–874/73
	Jehoshaphat	873–849	872–848	873/72–848
Ahab		869–850	874–853	874/73–853
Ahaziah		850–849	853–852	853–852
Jehoram [Joram]		849–842	852–841	852–841
	Jehoram [Joram]	849–842	853–841	853–841
Jehu		842–815	841–814	841–814/13
	Ahaziah	842	841	841
	Athaliah	842–837	841–835	841–835
	Jehoash [Joash]	837–800	835–796	835–796
Jehoahaz		815–801	814–798	814/13–798
Jehoash [Joash]		801–786	798–782	798–782/81
	Amaziah	800–783	796–767	796–767
Jeroboam II		786–746	793–753	793–753
	Uzzah [Azariah]	783–742	792–740	792/91–740/39
	Jotham	750–735	750–732	750–732/31
Zechariah		746–745	753	753–752
Shallum		745	752	752
Menahem		745–738	752–742	752–742/41
Pekahiah		738–737	742–740	742/41–740/39
Pekah		737–732	752–732	752–740/39
	Ahaz	735–715	735–715	735–716/15
Hoshea		732–724	732–723	732/31–723/22

hakah, though king only from 690 BC, may have led troops against Sennacherib as early as 701, before acceding to the throne. The reference to Tirhakah in 2 Kings 19:9 would then be understood as use of his eventual title in an effort to identify him to a later generation of readers.

However the question of the number of invasions is decided, it is certain that Sennacherib invaded Judah in 701 BC, the 14th regnal year of Hezekiah. Such a synchronism establishes Hezekiah's accession year as 715 BC, but that date raises another problem. The fall of Samaria, now established at 722, is dated by 2 Kings 18:10 in the sixth year of Hezekiah's reign. The most likely solution is that Hezekiah began a co-regency with his father, Ahaz, six years before Samaria fell. The possibility for confusion arises from the fact that one verse (2 Kgs 18:13; repeated in Is 36:1) synchronizes Sennacherib's 701 invasion with the 14th year of Hezekiah's independent reign; another verse (2 Kgs 18:10) correlates the fall of Samaria with the beginning of Hezekiah's co-regency. Thus from about 728 to 715 BC Hezekiah was co-regent with Ahaz. From 715 to 697 he reigned alone. From 696 to 686 his son Manasseh was co-ruler with him.

According to the chronological information given by a number of verses in 2 Kings, a total of 128 years and six months elapsed between the time of Hezekiah's accession in 715 and the capture of King Jehoiachin in 597, a date to be discussed below. Thus another problem is to explain the more than 10-year excess apparently demanded by the biblical totals. The best solution appears to lie in the assumption that Manasseh first came to power in 697 as co-regent with his father, Hezekiah. Manasseh died in 642, following what 2 Kings 21:1 states was a 55-year reign. Hezekiah, who came to the throne in 715, is said to have reigned 29 years (2 Kgs 18:2), which would mean that he was king until 686, roughly 11 years after the time when Manasseh must have come to the throne in order to have completed a 55-year reign by 642.

Fall of Jerusalem. Contemporary Babylonian records are available to shed valuable light on the last few years of Judah's existence. For the years 626–623, 618–595, and 556 BC the Babylonian Chronicle, a formal record of Babylonian affairs of state, has been recovered. From information contained in that chronicle and other cuneiform documents of the period, three dates in Judah's history may be fixed firmly. The first is the death of Josiah in 609; the second is the battle of Carchemish in 605; the third is the end of the reign of Jehoiachin, which is dated by the Babylonian Chronicle to the second month of Adar

in the 7th year of Nebuchadnezzar, or March 16, 597.

After Jehoiachin's capture, Zedekiah became puppet king of Judah for 11 years (2 Kgs 24:18). On the 10th day of the 10th month during Zedekiah's 9th regnal year (2 Kgs 25:1), the final siege of Jerusalem was begun by the Babylonian army. That day was January 15, 588. On the 9th day of the 4th month during the 11th regnal year of Zedekiah, after a siege of almost 18 months, the wall of Jerusalem was broken through (2 Kgs 25:3,4). The temple was burned on day 7 of the following (5th) month.

The chronology of the kings of Judah after the fall of Samaria is shown (see "Chronology of Judah After the Fall of Samaria [Israel]"), again listing the estimates of Albright, Thiele, and Harrison.

Beyond 586 BC. Following the tragedy of 586 BC several further developments are given chronological notice in the OT. Jeremiah 52:30 records a third deportation of Jews to Babylonia in the 23rd year of King Nebuchadnezzar (582 or 581 BC). Both 2 Kings 25:27 and Jeremiah 52:31 give evidence of the release of King Jehoiachin from prison; the Babylonian Chronicle dates that event at 27 Adar, or March 21, 561 BC.

In 539 BC the Babylonians themselves were destined to learn the meaning of defeat. In that year a Persian ruler, Cyrus the Great, launched a successful campaign against Babylon and its king, Nabonidus. Inheriting control over the exiled Jews and many other groups of people conquered earlier by Babylonia, Cyrus moved quickly to initiate a policy of tolerance toward his new subjects. In the first year of his rule Cyrus issued an edict making it possible for Jews to return to their former land (Ezr 1:1). On the first day of the following year, 1 Tishri (Ezr 3:6), an altar was set up in Jerusalem. In Nisan of the following year (March/April 537) work was begun on the temple itself (Ezr 3:8).

After a period of frustrating work stoppages of varying lengths, the preaching of Haggai and Zechariah spurred on the Jews to com-

Chronology of Judah After the Fall of Samaria (Israel)

Ruler	Albright	Thiele	Harrison
Hezekiah	715–687	715–686	716/15–687/86
Manasseh	687–642	696–642	697/96–643/42
Amon	642–640	642–640	643/42–641/40
Josiah	640–609	640–608	641/40–609
Jehoahaz	609	609	609
Jehoiakim	609–598	609–598	609–598
Jehoiachin	598	598–597	598–597
Zedekiah	598–587	597–586	597–586

plete the temple. Work resumed in 520 (Ezr 4:24; Hg 1:1,15) and was finally completed on 3 Adar, or March 12, 515 (Ezr 6:15).

The final stages of OT chronology pertain to the careers of Ezra and Nehemiah. The traditional view of their era places Ezra in the seventh year of Artaxerxes I (458 BC) and Nehemiah in the 20th (445 BC). Recently many scholars have reversed the traditional order of the two, dating Nehemiah about 445, with Ezra's arrival in Jerusalem placed at 428. The basis for that reversal is a supposed textual error in Ezra 7:7, where not the seventh year (458) but the 37th year (428) of Artaxerxes should be understood.

Other scholars have chosen not only to reverse the traditional order of Ezra and Nehemiah but also to move the arrival of Ezra in Jerusalem down to 398 BC. They assume that the Artaxerxes mentioned in Ezra was Artaxerxes II (404–359) rather than Artaxerxes I (464–424). The year 398 is the seventh year of Artaxerxes II (Ezr 7:7).

Actually, none of the three positions solves all the problems of the period. All of Jewish tradition is uniform in placing Ezra first. The supposed error in Ezra 7:7 commands absolutely no textual support in the ancient versions. Further, it is unlikely that the careers of Ezra and Nehemiah should be completely separated, as required by the third view. Accordingly, a traditional sequence (Ezra–Nehemiah) and corresponding traditional dates appear to be at least as probable as any other alternative.

Conclusion. Clearly, OT chronology is beset with difficulties. A dogmatic stance seems unwarranted for periods as far separated as the age of Abraham and the career of Ezra.

Chronology is a science. It deals with evidence, theories, assumptions, and the balance of probabilities. Often it boils down to a matter of choosing among theories that are equally unable to solve all the problems raised by other points of view. OT chronology is an accredited branch of biblical studies primarily because it is essential for understanding the proper historical background of the biblical texts. In general, the chronology of the OT is understood well enough to vindicate the basic accuracy and sequential order of Scripture.

On the other hand, the biblical teachings about God and humankind, about sin and salvation, grace and redemption, are affected very little by one's ability to understand numbers, sequences, synchronisms, and schemas. For Christians, the most important chronological statement in the Bible is no doubt that of the apostle Paul: "When the time had fully come, God sent forth his Son" (Gal 4:4).

See "DATE" UNDER EACH OT BOOK; PATRIARCHS, PERIOD OF THE; EXODUS, THE; WILDERNESS WANDERINGS; EXILE; CONQUEST AND ALLOTMENT OF THE LAND; POSTEXILIC PERIOD, THE; ISRAEL, HISTORY OF.

Bibliography. E.F. Campbell, Jr., "The Ancient Near East: Chronological Bibliography and Charts," *The Bible and the Ancient Near East,* ed. G.E. Wright; J. Finegan, *Handbook of Biblical Chronology;* D.N. Freedman, "The Chronology of Israel and the Ancient Near East," *The Bible and the Ancient Near East,* ed. G.E. Wright; E.R. Thiele, *The Mysterious Numbers of the Hebrew Kings.*

Chrysolite. Magnesium iron silicate, usually olive green; mentioned in Ezekiel's vision of the four wheels (1:16) and as one of the gems in the foundation wall of the New Jerusalem (Rv 21:20).

See MINERALS, METALS, AND PRECIOUS STONES.

Chrysoprase, Chrysoprasus. Light green variety of chalcedony; mentioned as one of the gems in the foundation wall of the New Jerusalem (Rv 21:20, KJV chrysoprasus).

See MINERALS, METALS, AND PRECIOUS STONES.

Chub. KJV spelling of Cub, a place in Ezekiel 30:5 identified as Libya (RSV margin).

See LIBYA, LIBYANS.

Chun. KJV spelling of Cun, a city from which David took much bronze, in 1 Chronicles 18:8.

See CUN.

Church. A group or assembly of persons called together for a particular purpose. The term appears only twice in the Gospels (Mt 16:18; 18:17) but frequently in the Book of Acts, most of the letters of Paul, as well as most of the remaining NT writings, especially the Revelation of John.

The use of this word in the NT is somewhat dependent upon the OT and the Greek world. In the former, the word designated the *congregation* of the Israelites, especially when they are gathered for religious purposes and specifically for the purpose of hearing the Law (Dt 4:10; 9:10; 18:16; 31:30; Jgs 20:2; Acts 7:38). In the Greek world the word "church" designated an *assembly* of people, a meeting, such as a regularly summoned political body, or simply a *gathering* of people. The word is used in such a secular way in Acts 19:32,39,41.

The specifically Christian usages of this concept vary considerably in the NT. (1) In analogy to the OT, it sometimes refers to a church meeting, as when Paul says to the Christians in Corinth: ". . .when you assemble as a [in] church" (1 Cor 11:18). This means that Christians are the people of God especially when they are gathered for worship. (2) In texts such as Matthew 18:17; Acts 5:11; 1 Corinthians

4:17; and Philippians 4:15, "church" refers to the entire group of Christians living in one place. Often the local character of a Christian congregation is emphasized, as in the phrases, "the church in Jerusalem" (Acts 8:1), "in Corinth" (1 Cor 1:2), "in Thessalonica" (1 Thes 1:1). (3) In other texts, house assemblies of Christians are called churches, such as those who met in the house of Priscilla and Aquila (Rom 16:3; 1 Cor 16:19). (4) Throughout the NT, "the church" designates the universal church, to which all believers belong (see Acts 9:31; 1 Cor 6:4; Eph 1:22; Col 1:18). Jesus' first word about the founding of the Christian movement in Matthew 16:18 has this larger meaning: "I will build my church, and the powers of death shall not prevail against it."

The church, both as a universal reality and in its local, concrete expression, is more specifically designated in Paul's writings as "the church of God" (e.g., 1 Cor 1:2; 10:32) or "the church of Christ" (Rom 16:16). In this way a common, secular Greek term receives its distinctive Christian meaning, and sets the Christian assembly/gathering/community apart from all other secular or religious groups.

It is clear from the NT as a whole that the Christian community understood itself as the community of the end time, as the community called into being by God's end-time act of revelation and divine presence in Jesus of Nazareth. So Paul tells the Christians in Corinth that they are those "upon whom the end of the ages has come" (1 Cor 10:11). That is, God had visited his creation, had called out of both Judaism and the gentile world a new people, empowered by his Spirit to be present in the world, sharing the good news (gospel) of his radical, unconditional love for his creation (Eph 2:11–22). The Gospels tell us that Jesus chose 12 disciples who became the foundation of this new people. The correspondence to the 12 tribes of Israel is clear, and shows that the church was understood both as grounded in Judaism and as the fulfillment of God's intention in calling Israel to become "a light to the nations, that my salvation may reach to the end of the earth" (Is 49:6; Rom 11:1–5). It is this recognition that allows Paul to call this new gentile-Jewish community, this new creation, "the Israel of God" (Gal 6:15,16). In this new community the traditional barriers of race, social standing, and sex—barriers that divided people from one another and categorized them into inferior and superior classes— are seen to be shattered: "There is neither Jew nor Greek, slave nor free, male nor female; for you are all one in Christ Jesus" (Gal 3:28 NIV).

This broad understanding of the church is furthered and amplified throughout the NT through a variety of concepts and images, each revealing a particular facet within the early church's understanding of itself, its nature and mission.

Community of the Spirit. The two-volume work of Luke the Evangelist, Luke–Acts, presents the church as that community of people in which and through which the Spirit of God is working. Insofar as the church is that, it is an extension of a reality already begun in Jesus of Nazareth. In the Gospel, John the Baptizer announces the coming of one who would baptize with the Holy Spirit (Lk 3:16). In Acts, this promise is seen fulfilled in the outpouring of the Spirit (1:5; 2). As Jesus is empowered for his mission by the Spirit (Lk 3:21,22), so the early Christian community is empowered for its witness in the world (Acts 1:8). As Jesus, the Man of the Spirit, is confronted at the outset of his ministry with great obstacles (the temptation, Lk 4:1–13, 28–30), so the church, as the community of the Spirit, faces the temptation to yield to pressures that would compromise its mission (Acts 2:12,13; 4:1–22; 5:27–42). As Jesus, empowered by the Spirit, proclaims the good news and touches the lives of people with reconciliation, release, and restoration (Lk 4:18,19), so the church is empowered by the Spirit to become a community of caring and sharing (Acts 2:43–47; 4:31–37). As Jesus, the Man of the Spirit, reaches out to the weak, poor, and rejects of the Palestinian society (this is a special emphasis throughout Luke's Gospel), so the community of the Spirit is concerned with concrete human need (Acts 4:34, 35; 6:1–6). These parallels could be multiplied; they illustrate Luke's understanding of the oneness of Jesus' ministry with that of the church. The latter is the extension of the former, yet is impossible without that foundation provided in Jesus' own ministry.

Body of Christ. Paul alone among NT writers in speaking of the church as "the body of Christ" (1 Cor 12:27; Rom 12:5; Eph 1:22,23; 4:12; see also 1 Cor 10:16,17; 12:12,13), or as "the body" of which Christ is the "head" (Eph 4:15; Col 1:18). The origin of this way of speaking about the church is not clear. Among a number of suggestions, two are particularly revealing about Paul's thought: (1) The Damascus Road experience. According to the account in Acts (9:3–7; 22:6–11; 26:12–18), Jesus identifies himself with his persecuted disciples. By persecuting these early Christians, Paul was actually fighting against Christ himself. It is possible that later reflection on this experience led Paul to the conviction that the living Christ was so identified with his community that it could be spoken of as "his body," that is, the concrete expression of his real presence. (2) The Hebrew concept of corporate solidarity. Paul was a Hebrew of the Hebrews (Phil 3:5), and his thinking was thoroughly Jewish. In that context the individual is largely thought of as intimately tied into the nation as a whole; the individual does not have real existence apart from the whole people. At the same time, the entire people can be seen as represented by one individual. Thus, "Israel" is both the name of one individual and the name of a whole people. The "servant" of Isaiah 42–53 can be both an individual (Is 42; 53) and the nation of Israel (Isa 49:1–6). This idea of corporate solidarity (or personality) is the background for the intimate connection Paul makes between "the first Adam" and sinful humanity as well as between "the last Adam" (Christ) and renewed humanity (1 Cor 15:45–49; see also Rom 5:12–21).

The reality of the intimate relation between Christ and his church is thus expressed by Paul as the organic unity and integration of the physical body (Rom 12:4–8; 1 Cor 12:12–27). For Paul, the Lord's Supper is a specific manifestation of this reality: "The bread which we break, is it not participation in the body of Christ? Because there is one bread, we who are many are one body, for we all partake of the one bread" (1 Cor 10:16b–17). Since this is the case, Paul goes on to argue, all the functions of the body have their legitimate and rightful place. Division within the body (i.e., the church) reveals that there is something unhealthy within. It is this image of the church as the "body of Christ" which lies behind Paul's repeated call for and insistence upon unity within the Christian community.

The equation of Christ and the church in this image of "body" leads to a very particular understanding of the nature of Christian existence. Paul speaks of the life of faith as life "in Christ." To be "in Christ" is to be a "new creation" (2 Cor 5:17). But for Paul, this is not just an individual experience, a kind of mystical union between the believer and Christ. For in a real sense, to be "in Christ" is at the same time to be in the church. To be "baptized into Christ" (Gal 3:27) is to become one with a community where the traditional barriers of human society are overcome—"for you are all one in Christ Jesus" (Gal 3:28). Again, to be "in Christ" is to be "baptized into one body" (1 Cor 12:12,13), for "you are the body of Christ and individually members of it" (1 Cor 12:27). There is then for Paul no such thing as a Christian in isolation, nurturing an individual relationship with Christ. To be a Christian is to be incorporated in a community of persons that is growing toward expressing, in its "body life," the reality of Christ, fleshing out this reality in its common life and work.

Temple of God. In his attempt to overcome the divisions within the church at Cor-

inth, Paul pictures the church not only as the body of Christ, but also as God's temple, as the dwelling place of God's Spirit (1 Cor 3:16,17). Contrary to much interpretation, this passage is not concerned so much with individual Christians as "temples" of God but with the Christian community, in its common life and work, as God's temple. For Paul the church at Corinth, and the Christian community everywhere, is God's option, God's alternative to the brokenness and fragmentation of human society. Therefore, to be involved in destroying that temple—by disunity, lack of concern and love, etc.—is to invalidate the potential of the church as God's option and to bring upon oneself the judgment of God (1 Cor 3:17). The community of believers is "God's building" (1 Cor 3:9), and Christians are responsible to be involved in its construction with "materials" that endure (1 Cor 3:10–13). Indeed, Christians themselves are seen as the building blocks which form the structure of "a holy temple in the Lord" (Eph 2:20–22).

The roots of the idea that a community of people can be the dwelling place of God's presence go back into the pages of the OT, and are mediated to Paul through Jesus' own understanding and that of the earliest Christian community. In the faith of ancient Israel the tabernacle/temple was considered the visible sign of God's presence among his people (Ex 25:8; 29:42–46; Lv 26:11,12; Ez 37:27). That is why there was such despair among the exiles in Babylon. The temple had been destroyed; how could the people still come into the presence of God? Yet, side by side with this exclusive location of the presence of God in the temple, there is the frequent recognition that God's presence with his people could not be localized (Is 66:1,2). The Law would no longer be engraved on stone, signifying God's presence upon the ark of the covenant in the inner sanctuary of the temple; rather, God says, "I will write it upon their hearts; and I will be their God, and they shall be my people" (Jer 31:33). Jesus pushes this concept further. In his discussion with the Samaritan woman he rejects the idea that proper worship of God is tied to a particular sanctuary and affirms that God is present wherever people respond to him in authenticity and integrity (Jn 4:20–24). Jesus also envisioned the final dissolution of the temple in Jerusalem (Mt 24:1,2; Mk 13:2; Lk 21:5,6). Stephen, in his defense before the Sanhedrin (the Jewish council), takes a similar critical attitude toward the temple (Acts 7:48, "The Most High does not dwell in houses made with hands"), and cites Isaiah 66:1,2 for support. John interprets Jesus' word about the destruction and subsequent raising of the temple (Jn 2:19) as referring to Jesus' own body and his resurrection. Since the church came into being as a result of the resurrection, the identification of Jesus' resurrection body as "temple" and its correspondence to the new community established through that event lie close at hand.

Whether Paul was directly dependent upon these ideas is difficult to determine. What is clear is that he is part of a tradition that increasingly understood God to be present among his creatures in and through a living community of people, consecrated for a particular purpose, like the temple of old.

Minor Images of the Church. There are several images and metaphors for the church that are not as prominent as those discussed above. Nonetheless, they convey perspectives which add to the total NT understanding. Two may be briefly discussed here.

Bride of Christ. Several times the church is pictured as the bride and Christ as the groom/husband (2 Cor 11:2,3; Eph 5:22–31; Rv 19:7,8; 21:2–14). This picture of intimacy is based on the common OT image of Israel as God's bride (Jer 2:2; Hos 2,3). The common element in these concepts is the call to faithfulness and love.

People of God. It is a common strand of Israel's faith that it became the people of God because he chose it to be his own possession (Ex 6:6,7; 19:5; Dt 7:6; 14:2; 26:18). The idea of the covenant is linked to this (Lv 26:9–12). In the preaching of the prophets, where the judgment of God is often seen as leading to complete destruction, there is also the vision of the reestablishment and re-creation of the people of God (Jer 32:37,38; Hos 2:1,23; Ez 11:20; 36:28). In the development of Judaism after the exile, the idea emerges that it is only the Israel of the future, the final messianic community, which will be "people of God" in the full sense of that term.

It is evident from a number of passages in the NT that the church knew itself to be this future people of God. The clearest passage is 1 Peter 2:9: "You are a chosen race, a royal priesthood, a holy nation, God's own people." The expressions "royal priesthood" and "holy nation" are taken from Exodus 19:6, which so powerfully expresses both the participation in God's reign and the priestly service of the people of God in the world. Just as the original people of God were called to proclaim God's mighty acts of deliverance (Is 43:20,21, Greek OT), so the new people of God are called to "declare the wonderful deeds of him who called you out of darkness into his marvelous light" (1 Pt 2:9). Hosea 2:1,23 is cited as support for the contention that the Christian community is the new people of God (Rom 9:25,26; 1 Pt 2:10).   MANFRED T. BRAUCH

See BODY OF CHRIST; BRIDE OF CHRIST.

Bibliography. G.C. Berkouwer, *The Church*; A. Cole, *The Body of Christ*; R.N. Flew, *Jesus and His Church*; E.G. Jay, *The Church*; K.E. Kirk, ed, *The Apostolic Ministry*; P.S. Minear, *Images of the Church in the NT*; E. Schweizer, *The Church as the Body of Christ*; H.B. Swete, ed, *Essays on the Early History of the Church and Ministry*.

Church Officers. *See* BISHOP; DEACON, DEACONESS; ELDER; PASTOR; PRESBYTER; SPIRITUAL GIFTS.

Chushan-rishathaim. KJV spelling of Cushan-rishathaim, a Mesopotamian king and oppressor of Israel, in Judges 3:8,10.

See CUSHAN-RISHATHAIM.

Chuza. Steward of Herod Antipas, either a manager of Herod's property or a political appointee; a man of influence and prestige. He was married to Joanna, who was healed by Jesus and subsequently accompanied Jesus and his disciples on their travels (Lk 8:3).

Cilicia. Province of the Roman empire, located in southeastern Asia Minor. Its capital was Tarsus, Paul's hometown (Acts 21:39; 22:3), hence permitting Paul Roman citizenship (Acts 16:37) even though a Jew.

Jewish presence in the area probably dated to the time when Antiochus the Great settled 2,000 Jewish families in the Asia Minor regions of Lydia and Phrygia in the 2nd century BC (Josephus, *Antiq.* 12.3.4).

In antiquity Cilicia (called Kue in OT times) formed a bridge between the country

Mountains in Cilicia.

now known as Turkey and Syria, its neighbor to the southeast. Geographically the country was divided between Cilicia Tracheia, the mountainous region in the western half, and Cilicia Pedias, the lovely plains to the east. Entrance into Turkey (ancient Asia Minor) was possible through the Cilician Gates, a narrow pass in the Taurus mountains. Cilicia Pedias was early attached to the province of Syria (c. 38 BC) and was known in the NT times as Syria and Cilicia (Gal 1:21). The western part, Cilicia Tracheia, was given by Mark Antony to Cleopatra in 36 BC, but by the time of Paul it was ruled by the Hellenist king, Antiochus IV of Commagene (AD 38–72). In AD 72 the two areas were unified into one Roman province, called Cilicia, by the Roman emperor Vespasian.

Jews from Cilicia participated in the persecution of Stephen (Acts 6:9). After his conversion to Christianity Paul eventually returned to Tarsus, later accompanying Barnabas to Antioch (Acts 11:25,26). Syria and Cilicia thus became the first major center of non-Jewish Christianity, and from this region Christianity spread to the rest of the gentile population of the Roman empire.

See KUE.

Cinnamon. Spice made from the dried inner bark of several oriental trees.

See FOOD AND FOOD PREPARATION; PLANTS.

Cinneroth. KJV spelling of the place-name Chinneroth in 1 Kings 15:20.

See CHINNERETH, CHINNEROTH #2.

Circumcision. Surgical removal of the foreskin of the male reproductive organ. In Bible times circumcision was the seal of God's covenant with Abraham (Gn 17:1–14). While circumcision originated as an ancient tribal or religious rite, since the early part of this century it has been practiced in Western nations for hygienic purposes. Many physicians believe that circumcision helps prevent genital cancers in both men and their wives, so that this minor operation is performed a few days after birth on nearly all newborn males in North America. Outside of Judaism the procedure no longer carries religious significance.

In the Ancient World. The rite of circumcision is far older than the Hebrew people. Cave paintings give evidence that it was practiced in prehistoric times. Egyptian temple drawings show that the operation was common in 4000 BC and probably earlier. Peoples practicing circumcision lived on almost every continent. The rite was observed among Central and South American Indians, Polynesians, the

peoples of New Guinea, many Australian and African tribes, Egyptians, and pre-Islamic Arabs. The rite is not mentioned in the Koran, but because Mohammed was circumcised tradition dictates that male Muslims follow the ancient custom. Arab ancestry is traced to Abraham through Ishmael (Gn 17:20), so a common age for Muslim circumcisions is 13, because Ishmael was circumcised at that age (Gn 17:25).

Among the West Semitic peoples the Ammonites, Edomites, Midianites, Moabites, and Phoenicians all practiced circumcision (Jer 9:25); the Philistines, however, did not (Jgs 14:3; 15:18; 1 Sm 14:6; 17:26,36; 18:25,27; 31:4; 2 Sm 1:20; 3:14; 1 Chr 10:4).

Young men were usually circumcised at puberty, evidently in preparation for marriage and entrance into full tribal responsibilities. The Hebrews were the only ancient practitioners of circumcision to observe the rite in infancy, thus freeing it from association with fertility rituals.

In the Old Testament. In the Bible the practice of circumcision began in Genesis 17 as a sign of the covenant between God and Abraham. God promised Abraham a land and, through a son yet to be conceived, numerous descendants, from whom kings would come. Blessing would come upon Abraham and through him to all nations (Gn 12:1–3). After the covenant was formally inaugurated (Gn 15), God sealed it, ordering Abraham to be circumcised along with all the males in his household (Gn 17:9–13).

Circumcision was to be an expression of faith that God's promises would be realized. Because Abraham's faith had lapsed (Gn 16) even after he had seen the awesome display of God's majesty (Gn 15:9–17), a permanent reminder of God's covenant promises was placed on his body and the bodies of his male descendants (Gn 17:11). This sign was so closely related to God's covenant promise that the rite itself could be termed the "covenant" (Gn 17:10; Acts 7:8).

Circumcision was to be performed on the eighth day after birth (Gn 17:12; Lv 12:1–3; see Gn 21:4; Lk 1:59; 2:21; Acts 7:8; Phil 3:5), customarily by the boy's father (Gn 17:23; 21:4; Acts 7:8), at which time a name would be given (Lk 1:59; 2:21). Flint knives were used in the early days (Ex 4:25; Jos 5:2,3). Later the rite was carried out by a trained practitioner called a *mohel.* Medical research has determined that prothrombin, a substance in the blood that aids in clotting, is present in greater quantity on the eighth day than at any other time in life.

Theological Meaning. Circumcision had to do with the fulfillment of God's promise concerning Abraham's descendants (Gn 17:9–12). Because it was applied to the reproductive organ, the sign involved the propagation of the race. Its application to the eight-day-old infant demonstrates the gracious character of God's promise to Abraham's descendants and indicates that God's people are in need of cleansing grace from birth (Lv 12:1–3). The promises of the covenant were reaffirmed to each generation before the recipients were able to respond in either faith or unbelief; nothing in the hearts of the chosen people could either bring about or thwart the ultimate fulfillment of the promises given to Abraham and his posterity.

Circumcision also had to do with the fulfillment of God's promise concerning the land (Gn 17:8). The land was God's holy possession, and the Israelites had to be holy to possess it. When Joseph and his descendants were in Egypt, they continued to circumcise their sons. But following the great sin at Mt Sinai after the exodus the unbelieving Israelites failed to place the covenant sign upon their children as they wandered in the wilderness. Because the new generation had not been circumcised, the people were unprepared to enter the Promised Land. Therefore God ordered Joshua to circumcise the men of Israel. The people's obedient response was an act of faith, since the armies of the enemy were camped nearby as the Israelite warriors lay incapacitated by the surgery (Jos 5:2–9).

From the beginning, participation in the covenant promises was open to persons outside Abraham's household (Gn 17:17). Exodus 12:43–49 gives non-Israelites the opportunity to participate in the Passover if they are willing to fulfill the same stipulation placed upon the Jews—that of circumcision.

The provision for admission to God's people by reception of the covenant sign was abused by Jacob's sons when circumcision was made a precondition for intermarriage with the Shechemites: while the Shechemites were disabled by their wounds, Simeon and Levi killed them, plundering the city and raping the women to exact retribution for the rape of their sister Dinah (Gn 34).

The sign of the covenant was not to be treated lightly. The penalty of excommunication rested upon the uncircumcised (Gn 17:14). The strange incident recorded in Exodus 4:24–26 seems to have been God's reminder to Moses of the stipulations of the covenant made with Abraham. Moses had proved an unfaithful servant of the Lord by neglecting to circumcise his son, but was rescued from judgment when his wife Zipporah took a flint rock and circumcised the boy, throwing the bloody foreskin at her husband's feet.

Spiritual Significance. The hygienic act of circumcision symbolized the need for cleansing if the holy God was to enter into relationship with an unholy people.

At first it was God's intention to let the ritual teach its own lesson. In Genesis 17:9–27 the observance merely serves as the covenant seal; Abraham is given little explanation of the significance of the rite itself. Later Moses used the expression "uncircumcised lips" to describe his unskilled speech (Ex 6:12,30). When Israel entered the Promised Land, the yield of its fruit trees was to be considered "uncircumcised" for the first three years; after that it would be holy to the Lord (Lv 19:23,24).

By the time of the exodus it became evident that circumcision had to do with ethical as well as physical considerations. In Deuteronomy 10:16 Moses exhorted the people to circumcise the foreskins of their hearts, and in Deuteronomy 30:6 this command assumes the form of a promise: "The Lord your God will circumcise your heart and the heart of your offspring, so that you will love the Lord your God with all your heart and with all your soul."

Sin in the lives of the chosen people made their circumcision meaningless before God. Thus Moses told the Israelites to humble their uncircumcised hearts (Lv 26:41). The prophets further develop this teaching. Jeremiah urged the citizens of Judah to remove the foreskins of their hearts to avoid God's wrath because of their evil ways (Jer 4:4), warning that the "uncircumcised ears" of Israel were not sensitive to the word of the Lord (Jer 6:10, RSV margin). Judgment will come upon Egypt, Edom, Ammon, Moab, and Judah, declares God, for "I am going to punish all who are circumcised only in flesh . . . for all these nations, and the whole House of Israel too, are uncircumcised at heart" (Jer 9:25,26 JB). Through Ezekiel the Lord complains that the temple has been profaned by the admission of aliens uncircumcised in heart and flesh (Ez 44:7,9). Isaiah looks forward to the day when there will be a new Jerusalem into which the uncircumcised and unclean would no longer come.

In the Intertestamental Period. During the Babylonian exile (586–530 BC) circumcision became a distinctive symbol of Judaism. After Judea was conquered by Alexander the Great (332 BC), a strong Hellenistic influence was introduced. A gymnasium was built in Jerusalem near the temple. Greek athletes ridiculed the Jews because they were circumcised, so that some of the Jews underwent a painful operation called epispasm to make themselves appear uncircumcised (1 Mc 1:15; see 1 Cor 7:18). Antiochus Epiphanes (175–164 BC) attempted to stamp out the Jewish religion, forbidding circumcision on penalty of death (1 Mc 1:48,60,61; 2 Mc 6:10). A revolt led by Mattathias resulted in the forcible circumcision of those boys whose parents had submitted to Antiochus' decree (1 Mc 2:46). Thus, in the two centuries before Christ's birth circumcision became an important mark of Jewish fidelity. Strict rules were laid down for its proper observance (see Jn 7:22,23), and care was taken to make sure epispasm could not later be performed.

In a move to suppress Judaism the Roman emperor Hadrian (AD 117–138) decreed that the rite was a capital crime. The edict was one of the causes of the Jewish revolt led by Bar-Kochba (AD 132–135).

In the New Testament. John the Baptist was circumcised, as were Jesus and Paul (Lk 1:59; 2:21; Phil 3:5). Jesus recognized the cleansing significance of circumcision (Jn 7:22,23), contrasting the rite with his healing ministry that made a man completely well and therefore ceremonially "clean." Just before he was stoned, Stephen referred to the covenant of circumcision, charging that his Jewish accusers, like their ancestors, were stiff-necked and uncircumcised in heart and ears, always resisting the Holy Spirit (Acts 7:8,51).

For a time the first Christians continued to participate in the Jewish rites and customs, even attending the services of the temple (Acts 3:1; 5:21,42). As Gentiles came to Christ, controversy arose between those who said that participation in the covenant community required circumcision and those who believed the rite was unnecessary. It was argued that since the covenant promise of the Messiah was given to the Jews, Gentiles must first be circumcised and become Jews before they could receive salvation in Christ.

In the time of Christ many Jews misunderstood the significance of circumcision, believing that the physical act was necessary for and a guarantee of salvation. Thus for Jews the observance became not only a symbol of religious privilege, but a source of racial pride (Phil 3:4–6). These Jews associated the ceremony with the Mosaic Law rather than the promise to Abraham (Jn 7:22; Acts 15:1). Because Greeks and Romans did not practice circumcision, Jews had come to be called "the circumcision" (Acts 10:45; 11:2; Rom 15:8; Gal 2:7,9; Eph 2:11; Ti 1:10), and following OT practice (Ez 28:10; 31:18,19; 32:19–32) Gentiles were termed "the uncircumcision" (Gal 2:7; Eph 2:11).

While visiting Caesarea, Jewish believers were amazed to realize that uncircumcised Gentiles received the purifying gift of the Holy Spirit (Acts 10:44–48). Moses had promised that God would circumcise the hearts of his people to love the Lord with heart and soul (Dt 30:6), and Ezekiel had prophesied that the Lord would sprinkle clean water upon his people, giving them a new heart and putting his Spirit within them (Ez 36:25–27). As these Jewish believers saw the prophecy that God would pour out his Spirit upon all flesh (Jl 2:28; Acts 2:17) being fulfilled, they realized that the inward reality symbolized by circumcision could be accomplished without the physical sign. Thus the gentile believers were immediately baptized.

Not all the Jewish believers were immediately willing to accept Gentiles into the church. When Peter returned to Jerusalem after his visit to Caesarea, "the circumcision party" criticized him; but after telling how the Spirit had fallen upon the Gentiles, Peter asked, "If then God gave the same gift to them as he gave to us when we believed in the Lord Jesus Christ, who was I that I could withstand God?" At this the Jewish believers were silenced and glorified God that repentance unto life had been granted to Gentiles (Acts 11:1–3, 15–18).

Certain "Judaizers" of the Pharisaic party taught the Christians in Antioch that circumcision was necessary for salvation (Acts 15:1,5). After debating these persons, Paul and Barnabas went to Jerusalem to consult with the other apostles and elders (Acts 15:2). Peter argued that God had given the Spirit to Gentiles and "cleansed their hearts by faith," affirming that "we believe that we shall be saved through the grace of the Lord Jesus, just as they will" (Acts 15:8,9,11). Therefore James and the other Jerusalem leaders agreed that circumcision should not be imposed on the Gentiles (Acts 15:13–21).

It was decided that Peter, James, and John would be entrusted with the gospel to "the circumcised," while Paul and Barnabas would preach to "the uncircumcised" (Gal 2:7–9). Because of his evangelistic policy to be "all things to all men" with respect to spiritually indifferent matters of custom (1 Cor 9:19–23), Paul circumcised Timothy, who was reckoned by Jews as one of their race because his mother was Jewish (Acts 16:2). But Paul resisted attempts to have Titus circumcised, since he was a Gentile (Gal 2:3). Paul apparently allowed Jewish believers to circumcise their sons (Acts 21:21).

Yet Paul charged that those who argued that the Galatian Christians must be circumcised and keep the law did not keep it themselves, but wanted to boast in the Galatians' flesh and avoid persecution for the cross of Christ (Gal 6:12,13)—persecution Paul was willing to bear (Gal 5:11). Granting for the sake of argument the Pharisaic assumption that salvation could be merited by keeping the law, Paul declared that those who received circumcision "must always obey every other Jewish law or perish" (Gal 5:2,3 LB). Christ would be "of no advantage" to those who "would be justified by the law"; this attempt at works-righteousness would evidence that the Galatians were "severed from Christ," having "fallen from grace" (Gal 5:2–4). These Christians were being tempted to turn to "a different gospel" (Gal 1:6,7).

Because of the serious threat the Judaizers posed to the gospel of free grace, Paul wished that those who unsettled the Galatians would "mutilate themselves" (Gal 5:12). He termed the Judaizers "dogs" and "evil workers" (KJV "concision"), asserting that Christians are "the true circumcision," because they worship God in spirit and glory in Christ Jesus, putting no confidence in human works to merit salvation (Phil 3:2,3).

Paul taught that circumcision was indeed of value to Jews, for it was the sign that to them had been committed the "oracles of God," that is, God's word concerning the promise of salvation (Rom 3:1–3). He reminded the prideful Ephesians that as Gentiles they had once been "strangers to the covenants of promise," not bearing the covenant sign in their flesh (Eph 2:11,12; see Col 2:13). Likewise Jews had no cause for pride, for disobedience could cause outward circumcision to be counted as uncircumcision (Rom 2:25).

Paul and the other apostles followed Moses and the OT prophets in teaching that true circumcision was a matter of the heart. The teaching of the NT goes further to affirm that a faithful believer, though physically uncircumcised, is regarded by God as circumcised, "for he is not a real Jew who is one outwardly, nor is true circumcision something external and physical" (Rom 2:26–29). Both Jews and Gentiles are saved by grace (Acts 15:11) and circumcised and uncircumcised alike are justified on the ground of their faith, apart from works of the law (Rom 3:28–30).

Abraham served as an example of a person whose faith "was reckoned to him as righteousness" (Rom 4:3; see Gn 15:6). Paul argued that both Gentiles and Jews are justified by faith, because Abraham was accounted righteous before he was circumcised. Abraham did not receive circumcision to obtain righteousness, but as a "sign or seal of the righteousness which he had by faith while he was still uncircumcised." Thus, Abraham is the father of all who believe without being circumcised, as well as those who are circumcised but also follow the example of Abraham's faith (Rom 4:9–12; see Gal 3:6–9).

No Christian need either be circumcised or seek to remove the marks of his circumcision for spiritual reasons, for "neither circumcision counts for anything nor uncircumcision"; what matters is "keeping the commandments of God" in the heart (1 Cor 7:18, 19), or "faith working through love" (Gal 5:6), and most of all that believers are "a new creation" (Gal 6:15). For this reason there can be no racial distinctions among Christians (Col 3:11), for all who are Christ's are Abraham's offspring (Gal 3:28,29).

The circumcision of the new covenant believer is accomplished "in the circumcision of Christ"—a circumcision "made without hands" as that person is "buried with him in baptism" and "raised with him through faith" (Col 2:11,12). In Paul's thought circumcision and baptism symbolize the same inner reality, so that circumcision may be called the OT counterpart of Christian baptism.

The "circumcision of Christ" fulfills God's promise in the OT to perform an inward work by circumcising the hearts of his people (Dt 30:6), making a new covenant in which sin would be forgiven and his law written upon their hearts (Jer 31:31–34), and placing his spirit within them (Ez 36:25–27). To be "in Christ" (Col 2:11) is to have a circumcised heart (Col 2:12; Rom 2:29). The presence of the Spirit in the lives of believers is the sign that God has performed in Christ this inward work promised to believers (Acts 11:15–17).

Only one Christian church retains the observance of ritual circumcision, the Abyssinian Orthodox Church of Ethiopia, which administers the rite between the third and the eighth day, prior to baptism.

In some churches which observe the liturgical year, January 1 is celebrated as the Feast of the Circumcision, to commemorate Christ's obedience to the law in our behalf, as evidenced by his circumcision (Lk 2:21). The festival originated in the 6th century in Spain and Gaul (France), not being established at Rome until the 11th century.

See BAPTISM; CLEANNESS AND UNCLEANNESS, REGULATIONS CONCERNING; UNCIRCUMCISION.

Cis. KJV form of Kish, King Saul's father, in Acts 13:21.

See KISH #1.

Cistern. Place to store water; a man-made catch basin or reservoir. Stone cisterns plastered with lime came into common use in Palestine in the 13th century BC.

Leaky or abandoned cisterns were often used as burial, torture, or prison chambers. For example, the dungeon into which the prophet Jeremiah was lowered was an aban-

A cistern found at Lachish.

doned muddy cistern (Jer 38:6). Ishmael threw the bodies of 70 murdered men into a large cistern originally constructed by King Asa for a wartime water supply (Jer 41:4–7,9).

Cisterns were vitally important in the arid Near East. King Uzziah of Judah is described as hewing out many cisterns in areas where springs or wells were lacking (2 Chr 26:10). An Assyrian general taunting King Hezekiah and his people promised that, if they would submit, every one would "drink the water of his own cistern" (Is 36:16; cf. 2 Kgs 18:31). Much earlier, Moses had assured the Israelites that cisterns already hewn out would be among God's blessings in the Promised Land (Dt 6:11).

The word "cistern" is also used figuratively in the Bible. Through the prophet Jeremiah, God rebuked Israel for rejecting him, the "fountain of living waters." Instead, they had "hewed out cisterns for themselves, broken cisterns, that can hold no water" (Jer 2:13). Ecclesiastes 12:6 refers to a broken wheel at a cistern as a figurative description of old age.

Citadel. A city's stronghold, tower, or fortification of last resort where people sought safety during an attack. The citadel of Penuel was destroyed by Gideon after he captured two Midianite kings (Jgs 8:17). The citadel of El-berith at Shechem was burned to the ground by Abimelech and his men (Jgs 9:46–49). Abimelech was killed shortly thereafter when a woman in the citadel at Thebez dropped a millstone on his head and crushed his skull (Jgs 9:50–54). David conquered Jerusalem by capturing its citadel (2 Sm 5:7–9; 1 Chr 11:5–8).

During the Maccabees' struggle for independence in the 2nd century BC, the citadel in Je-

rusalem often aided the party in power (1 Mc 1:29–33; 11:41,42; 13:49–51). The Fortress of Antonia, the Jerusalem citadel in the day of Jesus, fell to the Romans in AD 70.

Cities of Refuge. Six cities, three in Canaan and three in Transjordan (area east of the Jordan River), designated as places of safety for persons suspected of manslaughter. The 6 cities were among the 48 assigned to the Levites (Nm 35:6). The 3 Transjordian cities were "Bezer in the wilderness on the tableland for the Reubenites, and Ramoth in Gilead for the Gadites, and Golan in Bashan for the Manassites" (Dt 4:43; Jos 20:8). The 3 cities west of the Jordan were "Kedesh in Galilee in the hill country of Naphatali, and Shechem in the hill country of Ephraim, and Kiriath-arba (that is, Hebron) in the hill country of Judah" (Jos 20:7). They were distributed so that east of the Jordan, Golan was located in the north, Ramoth in the center, and Bezer in the south. West of the Jordan, Kedesh, Shechem, and Hebron were located north, center, and south respectively. That made it possible for an accused manslayer to reach a city of refuge quickly.

In ancient Israel the nearest relative of a murder victim was required to take the life of the murderer (Nm 35:19–21). It was his duty to the widow, other family members, and to society. Murderers were not allowed to live, and there was no way to ransom them (Nm 35:31).

Accidental death, however, was another matter. Manslaughter without malice or premeditation had a special provision in the Law of Moses. A man who accidentally killed someone could flee to the nearest city of refuge, where the local authorities would grant him asylum (Dt 19:4–6). When the case came to court, if the man was found guilty of premeditated murder, he was handed over for execution (Dt 19:11,12). If the death was deemed accidental, the person was acquitted. Nevertheless he had to pay a penalty. The manslayer had to stay in the city of refuge as long as the current high priest was in office (Nm 35:22–28). That would be a considerable hardship in some cases. It meant either separation from one's family or the expense and risk of moving from one's ancestral land and trying to make a livelihood in a new city.

See ASYLUM; CIVIL LAW AND JUSTICE.

Cities of the Valley, Cities of the Plain. Group of five cities in the plain or basin of the Jordan River. Since the region in which these cities were located was particularly fruitful, it attracted Abraham's nephew Lot when the growing size of the flocks and herds forced a

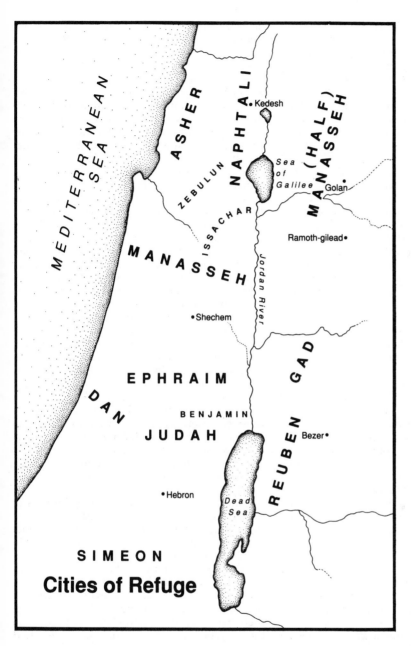

ASHER

NAPHTALI

Kedesh

ZEBULUN

ISSACHAR

MANASSEH (HALF)

Sea
of
Galilee

Golan

Ramoth-gilead

MEDITERRANEAN SEA

MANASSEH

Jordan River

Shechem

EPHRAIM

GAD

DAN

BENJAMIN

JUDAH

REUBEN

Bezer

Hebron

Dead
Sea

SIMEON

Cities of Refuge

division of these two patriarchal communities (Gn 13:10–12). The cities are enumerated as Sodom, Gomorrah, Admah, Zeboiim, and Bela or Zoar. Evidently each was a city-state with its own king.

These cities entered the biblical narrative in four connections. (1) They provided a region where Lot could settle; he ultimately decided to make his home in Sodom.

(2) The five kings of the cities of the plain fought with a superior force led by four kings of lands far to the east. In the struggle they were defeated and their cities ransacked. The plunder was great, as was the number of captives—especially women and children (Gn 14). Since Lot was among those carried off, Abraham felt an obligation to launch a rescue operation. In this he was immensely successful, recovering not only Lot but also the other captives and the booty.

(3) The wicked cities of the plain later came in for God's judgment. Their evil was so great that Abraham's intercession on their behalf was to no avail (Gn 18:22–33). Their depravity is illustrated by the account of the homosexual mob at Lot's door in Sodom (Gn 19). Soon

thereafter Lot and his family were ordered to flee before the cities were wiped out. Lot's wife was turned into a pillar of salt for her disobedience in turning back. Brimstone and fire obliterated the cities, changing the composition of the whole area.

(4) References to the destruction of these cities appear in numerous passages in both the OT and NT to serve as a warning of divine punishment for sin (Is 3:9; Jer 50:40; Ez 16:46–56; Mt 10:15; Rom 9:29).

The question of the location of the cities of the plain has been an intriguing one in biblical study. Today scholars generally conclude that these cities stood at the south end of the Dead Sea. Scripture itself connects them with the valley of Siddim. Either they stood in the valley or the valley lay adjacent to the plain where they were located. Between the days of Abraham and Moses the water level of the Dead Sea evidently had risen enough to cover at least part of the Valley of Siddim; Genesis 14:3 declares that the valley of Siddim was "the Salt Sea" (in Moses' time). The southern part of the Dead Sea is now only 12–15 feet deep, whereas the northern part reaches a depth of 1,300 feet. Josephus, a 1st-century historian, declared that ruins of the five cities were still to be seen at the south end of the Dead Sea. No trace of these ruins has been discovered in modern times.

Though much of the region south of the Dead Sea is now burned out and sterile, the area to its southeast is still fertile. Three streams pour down from the mountains of Moab into this area and furnish water for irrigation. W. F. Albright, a 20th-century archaeologist, noted that five streams flow into the south end of the Dead Sea. A town could have stood on each of them.

HOWARD F. VOS

Citizenship. In NT usage (1) designation of belonging to the city or city-state where one was born and reared, and (2) status of sharing in the privileges and responsibilities of the Roman empire. Thus the apostle Paul claimed to be a citizen of both Tarsus (Acts 21:39) and Rome (Acts 22:28).

The right of Roman citizenship most commonly was acquired by birth, as was true of Paul (Acts 22:28). The status of a child whose parents were married was determined by the status of the father at the time of conception. The status of a child born out of wedlock was determined by that of the mother at the child's birth. Slaves automatically became citizens when freed by their masters. Although known as "freedmen," they were often denied the rights of regular freeborn citizens. Greedy magistrates frequently sold the right

of citizenship for a high price. The tribune Claudius Lysias received his citizenship in that manner (Acts 22:28). Citizen rights could also be granted by treaty or imperial declaration. Following the Social War (about 90–85 BC), citizenship was granted to all the inhabitants of Italy. Julius Caesar extended the right to colonies in Gaul (France) and provinces in Asia Minor. According to the census of the emperor Augustus (Lk 2:1), there were approximately 4,233,000 Roman citizens at the time of Christ's birth. By the time of Paul's ministry the number had reached 6,000,000.

Roman citizens were often required to give proof of their citizenship. That was usually accomplished by reference to the census archives, where the name of every citizen was recorded. In addition, freeborn citizens possessed a small wooden birth certificate containing information about their status at birth. Military documents and taxation tables also carried the names of registered citizens. Further, every Roman citizen had three names, whereas noncitizens generally had only one.

The rights of Roman citizenship were extensive, including the right to vote; to hold office; to serve in the military; to purchase, possess, sell, and bequeath property; to enter into a legal contract; to have a fair trial; and to appeal to Caesar. Thus Paul, upon mention of his Roman citizenship, received an apology from magistrates at Philippi for having been imprisoned without a trial (Acts 16:39). He also avoided a scourging in Jerusalem (Acts 22:24–29) and was able to request a trial before Caesar (Acts 25:10–12; cf. 26:32).

Since the privileges and responsibilities of citizenship originated in Rome, that city came to be a symbol of power, success, and national purpose for people throughout the empire. In that light, Paul reminded the Christians at Philippi, a Roman colony, of their identity as citizens of heaven and their responsibility to live accordingly (Phil 3:20). Paul evidently wanted the Philippian Christians to recognize that their new relationship to God conveyed upon them certain rights and duties, as did their Roman citizenship.

City. Settled group of people living in permanent dwellings and bound together by political, economic, and (in biblical times) kinship ties. The Bible does not generally distinguish between city, town, and village. The emphasis upon walls (Lv 25:29–31) and fortifications (Jos 19:35), with repeated references to towers, gates, and sieges, indicates that cities provided the primary security for the surrounding towns and villages.

Origin and Antiquity. *Practical Prerequisites.* The existence of settled communities depended upon a controlled food supply. In contrast to the city dweller, the nomad lived in a portable tent, appropriate for a never-ceasing search for food. Nomadic peoples (e.g., today's Bedouin of the Middle East) do not build cities. The contrast between settled city life and the nomadic experience is illustrated by a NT reference to seminomadic Abraham: "For he looked forward to the city which has foundations, whose builder and maker is God" (Heb 11:10).

Since food production was a key factor in the establishment of cities, fertility of the land had a direct bearing on the size of early settlements. The semiarid marginal land of much of Palestine could support only modest cities as compared with the well-watered river valleys of Mesopotamia and Egypt.

As city dwellers became more adept in farming adjacent land, the harvests increased, leading to increased population and social stratification. When the entire population was no longer needed for food production, some individuals became specialists in a growing number of occupations: pottery making, metal working, stone masonry, and carpentry. Their products in addition to farm surpluses made the ancient city the center of trade and commerce.

The First Biblical City. The first biblical reference to a city is in Genesis 4:17. The Hebrew verb indicates that Cain "was building" the city. Probably he did not complete it, nor did he permanently reside there; he had earlier been condemned to a vagabond's existence (Gn 4:12).

The Genesis account, affirming that city life came early in human existence, is internally consistent. The first human offspring, Cain

and Abel, were involved in food production (Gn 4:2). Cain was an agriculturist and Abel tended domesticated flocks. Genesis 4 shows both the prerequisite of food production and the resulting specialization. With Jabal, tent making was associated (Gn 4:20); with Jubal, music (Gn 4:21); and with Tubal-cain, metal working (Gn 4:22).

Archaeological Evidence. The testimony of archaeology generally agrees with an early date for the origin of cities. The oldest city thus far discovered in Canaan was Jericho. Using carbon-14 analysis of wood materials from the site, Kathleen Kenyon assigned a date prior to 7000 BC. Although less than 10 acres, it was a well-developed city with an impressive wall 6 feet thick and a round stone tower almost 30 feet high equipped with an inside staircase from top to bottom. Even though pottery and writing had not yet been developed, Jericho had substantial public buildings and assorted material artifacts. Perhaps the abundant fresh-water springs and the climate attracted the early settlers.

Jericho seems to be 3,000 years older than other Canaanite cities. A date comparable to that of Jericho has been given to Jarmo in northern Mesopotamia and to a number of other sites in the Near East. Most of the great Sumerian cities such as Ur, Kish, Lagash, and Uruk were founded later, in the 4th or early 3rd millennium BC.

Location and Name. *Topographical Prerequisites.* There were four primary considerations in the selection of a site for a city.

1. A city with its permanent homes, private possessions, and public buildings represented substantial investment of the time and effort of its citizens. Thus the city stood as a tempt-

Important Biblical Cities

Old Testament		New Testament	
Ai	Golan	Alexandria	Jericho
Ashdod	Gomorrah	Antioch of Pisidia	Jerusalem
Ashkelon	Haran	Antioch of Syria	Joppa
Babylon	Hebron	Athens	Laodicea
Beersheba	Jericho	Berea	Lystra
Bethel	Jerusalem	Bethany	Nazareth
Bethlehem	Jezreel	Bethlehem	Paphos
Bethshemesh	Kadesh Barnea	Bethsaida	Perga
Bezer	Kedesh	Cana	Pergamum
Damascus	Lachish	Caesarea	Philadelphia
Dan	Megiddo	Caesarea Philippi	Philippi
Debir	Mizpah	Capernaum	Rome
Ekron	Nineveh	Colosse	Salamis
Gath	Ramoth-gilead	Corinth	Sardis
Gaza	Samaria	Damascus	Smyrna
Gerar	Shechem	Derbe	Tarsus
Gezer	Shiloh	Ephesus	Thessalonica
Gibeah	Sodom	Gadara	Thyatira
Gibeon	Tyre	Gerasa	Tiberias
Gilgal	Ur	Iconium	Troas

ing prize for plunder by a marauding desert tribe. The topographical situation of the ancient city had to contribute to its defense. A city built on a natural hill tended to be less vulnerable than one in the valley. Substantial advantage was given to the defenders if an enemy was forced to attack up an incline.

The topography of Jerusalem illustrates the factor of security in the selection of a site. Although surrounded by higher mountains (Ps 125:2), Jerusalem originally was established on a limestone ridge protected on the east by the deep Kidron Valley and on the west by the equally formidable Tyropean Valley. The two valleys met, thus affording Jerusalem protection from the south. To complete the security, walls were constructed around the city, with special emphasis on the northern side where Jerusalem was otherwise exposed (cf. 2 Sm 5:6).

2. A water source conveniently located was an absolute necessity for a city's existence. The city spring or well became the center of social intercourse, particularly for the women, who were traditionally the water carriers. Biblical examples of socializing at the village well are numerous (Gn 29:1–12; 1 Kgs 1:38,39). Gihon was the spring that supplied Jerusalem with water (Jn 4:5–26).

In general, water sources were located in valleys, so the nearest spring to a city was frequently outside the walls. If an attacking enemy seized the water source, a city could be forced to surrender when the water supply stored within the walls ran dry. Such a situation is vividly described in the apocryphal book of Judith (Jth 7). In Jerusalem, King Hezekiah constructed a water tunnel to neutralize the impending attack of the Assyrian king Sennacherib (2 Chr 32:30; 2 Kgs 20;20). His amazing engineering feat, more than 1,700 feet long and over 2,500 years old, can still be seen by visitors to Jerusalem.

3. Every city needed adequate food for its inhabitants. Ancient agriculturalists lived in a village or city and walked each day to their fields. The existence of a city, therefore, depended upon nearby cultivable fields adequate to meet the needs of the population. The maximum size of the city depended to a considerable extent upon the fertility of the surrounding land.

4. As urban populations became more diversified in economic interests, cities became more interdependent. Contact with other communities was needed to acquire raw materials not locally available. In addition, surplus production required outside markets. To facilitate importation of raw materials and exportation of finished products, proximity to local and international roads was desirable if not impera-

tive. The important cities of the Bible were located along primary arteries of commerce.

The relative importance of these four factors has changed over the centuries. With the appearance of strong nation-states such as Rome, cities could depend upon standing armies and thus give up their inconvenient hilltop sites. Development of plastered cisterns and aqueducts made possible the founding of cities some distance from water sources; for example, Caesarea, built by Herod the Great, was 12 miles from Mt Carmel's springs. Trade routes shifted with changing international conditions, causing the demise of some cities and the development of others.

Origin of City Names. The name given to a city was not accidental. Generally it contained the name of a god, clan, or topographical feature. Most of the city names that include *Beth* (Hebrew word for "house") refer to the worship of some god (e.g., Bethel). The name Jerusalem recalls its early inhabitants, who were called Jebusites. Joppa, meaning "beautiful," was so named because of its spectacular location along the Mediterranean Sea.

Historical Development. *Neolithic Age (7000–4000 BC).* According to some archaeological research the first cities appeared in the "New Stone Age." Major sites like Tell es-Sultan (OT Jericho) and Jarmo (in Iraq) reveal that inside the walled cities people lived in small, rectangular houses positioned randomly.

Chalcolithic Age (4000–3200 BC). During this period settlements were for the first time dispersed throughout Palestine. Villages were small and unwalled. Surviving from this period are the underground dugout houses of Abu Matar near Beersheba and the intricate frescoes of Teleilat Ghassul on the Jordan plain across from Jericho. Material artifacts (of copper, ivory, basalt) from remote Chalcolithic sites give evidence of communication and trade.

Early Bronze Age (3200–2100 BC). This period witnessed the development and multiplication of substantial cities in the ancient Middle East. Although urban development tended to concentrate in the well-watered areas of Mesopotamia and Egypt, Palestine had flourishing strategic communities such as Lachish, Megiddo, Beth-shan, and Shechem. Canaanite settlements were small, as evidenced by comparing Lachish's 18 acres with the more than 150 acres of Abraham's home city of Ur in Mesopotamia. Canaanite cities played a role in biblical history far out of proportion to their size. The cities of that period were generally protected by heavy walls up to 30 feet thick. Many cities contained impressive public buildings, including temples and "high places" (outdoor shrines).

Middle Bronze Age (2100–1570 BC). The beginning of this age was marked by destruction. Throughout the Middle East the great cities of the Early Bronze Age lay destroyed and unoccupied. The most substantial evidence for the period 2100–1900 BC comes from tombs rather than from cities.

What occasioned the widespread destruction is still debated. Two historical factors may have been significant. (1) Migration of the Amorites ("westerners") into the area took place at this time. Although the Amorites were not innovators, their sudden influx in considerable numbers effected change and disruption. Abraham's appearance in Canaan at this time, in obedience to divine command, fits into this restless period. (2) Excessive exploitation of human and natural resources in building the cities and great structures of the Early Bronze Age may have contributed to the collapse. Consider the time and energy invested in the Great Pyramid of Cheops, built around 2500 BC. The ancients had their ecological problems too.

The major part of the Middle Bronze Age witnessed the rebuilding of cities. Written records in Egypt and Mesopotamia mention several biblical towns as existing during that time. During a significant part of the age (1700–1570) a Semitic people called the Hyksos dominated Syria, Canaan, and Egypt. Several cities were enlarged. Hazor, located about 10 miles north of the Sea of Galilee, became a city covering over 175 acres, making it the largest Palestinian city built during the biblical era. In addition, the Hyksos greatly strengthened the defenses of cities.

Late Bronze Age (1570–1230 BC). The Egyptians succeeded in expelling the Hyksos from Egypt by 1570 BC, and Hyksos influence in other areas soon vanished. The Amarna letters show that Canaanite cities such as Jerusalem, Shechem, Gezer, and Megiddo were independent of each other, although all somewhat answerable to Egypt. That there were many Palestinian cities and towns during the Late Bronze Age is evidenced by the records of the Egyptian ruler Thutmose III. His records list 119 Canaanite settlements as rebelling against Egypt in about 1450 BC.

Archaeological surveys of the mountainous areas of Palestine show that those areas were sparsely occupied by the Canaanites. Many of the settlements in the hills were first established by the Hebrews after the exodus from Egypt. Some scholars conjecture that living in the mountains was made feasible by two developments. (1) Development of mortar cement made possible the lining of cisterns. Without such a lining the porous limestone of the area could not store water over the long dry season.

With the capacity to store water, cities were not so dependent upon water sources located in the valleys. (2) The spread of the iron industry developed by the Hittites meant better tools. Equipped with such tools the Hebrews were able to clear forests and till the rocky soil of mountainous areas. Many new settlements came into existence during the latter part of the Late Bronze Age.

Iron Age (1230–330 BC). In this age the majority of the settlements in the hilly areas of Palestine were Israelite. The 12 tribes gave up their independence and the united monarchy was born. Jerusalem, which had resisted Israelite attacks, was conquered by David and made the political and religious capital of the new nation. During Solomon's reign the city was enlarged to accommodate the temple. Other cities grew in size, strength, and status in order to implement the economic, military, and administrative demands of the prosperous kingdom.

With the division of the kingdom during the reign of Rehoboam, northern cities challenged Jerusalem for political and religious leadership. First Shechem, then Tirzah, and finally a totally new city, Samaria, took turns as the political capital of Israel. The northernmost city of Dan and ancient Bethel took on new roles as they became religious centers of the northern kingdom. Later during the Iron Age both Israel and Judah fell, and many of the cities were made desolate as thousands of captives were deported first by the Assyrians and later by the Babylonians.

Hellenistic Period (330–63 BC). Under Greek occupation cities showed evidence of better planning: wide streets, orderly arrangement of houses and shops, amphitheaters, gymnasiums, and stadiums. Many new cities were founded. Seleucus I (305–281 BC) alone took credit for establishing 37 cities, many of which he named after his father, Antiochus, or himself. The best known of these cities was Syrian Antioch, which played a vital role in the expansion of the church into the gentile world.

The Roman Period (63 BC–AD 300). With the Romans came peace and the building of roads, factors that stimulated trade and in turn resulted in increased size and population of cities, especially those established along the highways. Alexandria, Antioch, Ephesus, and Corinth became congested, each with a population of about 500,000. Rome likely supported a population of well over 1,000,000.

In this period Herod the Great attempted to transform his Judean kingdom into a Roman showcase. Jerusalem was embellished with a magnificent new temple, a strong citadel named after Mark Antony, a vast palace complex, an amphitheater, and a hippodrome. Her-

The Lechaion Road going
north out of Corinth to the
Corinthian Gulf.

od constructed Palestine's largest port, naming it Caesarea in honor of Augustus. Samaria was enlarged and graced with impressive public buildings. What Herod did in Judea was rather typical of a period that brought forth grandiose buildings to adorn important cities.

Identification. Although the biblical period terminated almost 2,000 years ago, many of its cities still remain. Most of them, however, are no longer living cities. Instead they lie buried underneath huge mounds of earth called "tells" (Arabic for "mounds"). Actually a tell consists of several cities built one upon another. At Tell el-Hosn (ancient Beth-shan) and at Tell el-Mutesellim (ancient Megiddo) there are approximately 20 levels of occupation. Because of topographical advantages associated with its site, a city that was destroyed by famine, earthquake, pestilence, or war would later be rebuilt using the older foundations. The heavy city walls tended to keep artifacts within the tell in spite of destruction due to war or erosion from heavy rain. Thus through several successive rebuildings over centuries of time, the tell grew higher and higher, preserving in part the history of an ancient settlement.

The problem of identifying a biblical city with a present tell or *khirbet* (ruin) presents a serious challenge to archaeologists. According to the Israeli archaeologist Yohanan Aharoni, out of 475 Palestinian place-names in the OT about 262 have been identified with some degree of certainty. Specialists in this field rest their identifications on three lines of evidence.

Literary Evidence. Among ancient writings the most important primary source for identification of biblical cities is the Bible itself. Not only does the Bible make reference to many cities, it often gives significant clues about their locations. Three main types of geographical texts can be observed in the Bible. (1) There are historical texts in which cities are mentioned as a part of the narrative. The itinerary of the Israelites during the 40 years in the wilderness is an example (Nm 33). (2) Territorial and administrative lists that established boundaries and facilitated government rule are also important. Boundary lists (Jos 15:1–12) are more decisive than rosters of towns (1 Kgs 4:7–19), since the former are arranged in geographical sequence. (3) Records of military movements and conquests are useful. The account of Sennacherib's march on Jerusalem helps in locating certain towns of Ephraim and Benjamin (Is 10:28–32).

Although the biblical references are the most important, they do not constitute the sole written evidence. Additional geographical data come from both Egyptian and Mesopotamian records. The earliest Egyptian references to biblical cities are 12th dynasty (2000–1776 BC) execration texts (curses on enemies). These consisted of city names written on pottery vessels. The deliberate smashing of the vessels was tantamount to placing the cited cities under a curse. Egyptian sources also include tomb and temple annals that detail military campaigns of several pharaohs. The 18th and 19th dynasty rulers (especially Thutmose III, Amenhotep II, and Ramses II) undertook numerous expeditions against Syria and Palestine. Many of the settlements mentioned are biblical cities.

The best-known Egyptian documents containing references to Canaanite cities are known as the Amarna tablets. These are about 400 letters written in cuneiform script by minor Canaanite kings to their Egyptian overlords. They not only reveal general conditions at the time (14th century BC) but also supply clues useful in locating specific cities.

Mesopotamian documents about Canaan are not so numerous as those from Egypt. Perhaps the greater distance from Canaan is the primary reason. However, the Mari tablets plus military annals of Shalmaneser III, Tiglath-pileser III, Sargon II, Sennacherib, Esarhaddon, and Ashurbanipal all contribute to our knowledge of Palestinian geography. The famous bas-relief of Sennacherib's conquest of Lachish confirmed the identification of Tell ed-Duweir with that important biblical city.

Few written records have been uncovered in Palestine. Among the most important are the Lachish ostraca (inscribed potsherds). Written at the time of Nebuchadnezzar's final invasion of Judah, these letters made reference to other cities in the vicinity.

In addition to these early sources there are later writings (e.g., from the Talmud, Eusebius, Jerome, and medieval Christian pilgrimages). These, however, do not enjoy the same credibility among scholars as do the earlier records. All in all, epigraphic evidence to support the identification of biblical sites is considerable.

Archaeological Evidence. Only rarely does the archaeologist uncover an artifact that conclusively identifies a site. Rather, archaeology supports other evidence. Archaeology can show the time of occupation. It is essential to know the ages associated with the various strata of a tell in order to correlate with the written sources. If the written documents, including the Scriptures, indicate that a certain city was in existence at a particular time, a projected site must show occupation at that time. In addition, excavation can reveal size, special structures (temples, citadel, water tunnel), nature of the population, and general orientation. Any or all of these factors might contribute to identification.

Present Place Names. According to Aharoni, in about 40 percent of the sites that have been identified with a high degree of certainty, identification is based on preservation of the name. The city or village name generally has been carried from generation to generation with little alteration. Evidence of the continuity of place-names is seen in the results of the pioneering work of Edward Robinson and Eli Smith undertaken in 1837 and 1852. With the use of only the Scriptures and current Arabic names, scores of biblical sites were identified. The majority of these identifications have been confirmed by subsequent archaeological

research. It is evident, however, that in some locations the name has been transferred to a nearby site.

It is clear that Bible students can use a Bible atlas with confidence. The identification of biblical sites rests on increasing evidence which is already substantial.

GORDON G. CEPERLEY

See ARCHAEOLOGY; ARCHAEOLOGY AND THE BIBLE.

City of David. 1. Southeastern hill (Ophel) in the present-day city of Jerusalem, the site occupied by King David as his royal city; also called Zion (e.g., 1 Kgs 8:1). David captured the Jebusite fortress of Jerusalem and transferred his capital to it from Hebron (2 Sm 5:1–10).

See JERUSALEM.

2. Alternate name for Bethlehem, David's hometown, in the NT (Lk 2:11).

See BETHLEHEM.

City of Destruction. KJV translation in Isaiah 19:18 (RSV, City of the Sun), generally understood as a reference to the Egyptian city Heliopolis.

See HELIOPOLIS.

City of Moab. Phrase in Numbers 22:36 referring to Ar of Moab, the place where Balak went out to meet Balaam.

See AR, AR OF MOAB.

City of Palm Trees. Phrase referring to Jericho, so named for its many palms (Dt 34:3).

See JERICHO.

City of Salt. City located near the Dead Sea, assigned to Judah's tribe for an inheritance (Jos 15:62). Its exact location is uncertain.

City of the Sun. Phrase in Isaiah 19:18, generally taken as a reference to the Egyptian city Heliopolis.

See HELIOPOLIS.

Civil Law and Justice. Civil law deals with private disputes between individuals occasioned by debt, divorce, inheritance, or other relationships. In contrast, criminal law deals with crimes, that is, actions the state prohibits and takes steps to punish, such as murder, treason, or theft. In civil cases the guilty party is asked to compensate the victim in an appropriate way.

This distinction between civil and criminal law is quite foreign to biblical thinking.

Nearly all offenses were matters for private prosecution. If someone was murdered, his relatives were responsible for killing the murderer or chasing him to the nearest city of refuge, where a trial would be held. All offenses in Israel had a religious dimension: theft or adultery was not merely an offense against one's neighbor but was a sin against God. This meant that in theory every Israelite would be shocked by such behavior and would want it punished. If such acts continued, God himself might step in to punish the individual, his family, or even the whole nation. This religious dimension gave an aura of criminality to every offense, even though in most cases prosecution was left in the hands of individuals. Some religious offenses, such as sabbath breaking (Nm 15:32–36) or idolatry (Dt 13), were regarded as so heinous that the whole nation was responsible for prosecuting and punishing the offenders. They thus correspond most closely to the modern understanding of a crime, though few modern states would prosecute those particular sins.

Ownership of Property. Basic to the OT view of property was the conviction that God had given Israel the land in fulfillment of his promise to Abraham and the other patriarchs (Gn 15:18; 28:13; Ex 3:17). Furthermore, each tribe had been allocated its territory by lot, symbolizing the fact that God chose where each tribe was to live and how much land each was to hold. Within each tribe every family was assigned a plot of ground to own and work in perpetuity. That family land could not be sold or given to any person outside the family, but had to be passed on from father to son.

The inalienability of family land is illustrated in various laws. Deuteronomy 19:14 says, "You shall not remove your neighbor's landmark, which the men of old have set" (see also Prv 22:28; 23:10). People who fell into debt could sell their land, but the sale was valid only until the next jubilee year occurred, a maximum period of 50 years. Then the land went back to the original owner without payment. In effect, the owner could only rent his land out for a maximum of 50 years (Lv 25:8–31). Naboth refused to sell his land to King Ahab, claiming it as "the inheritance of my fathers" (1 Kgs 21:3).

The eighth commandment, "You shall not steal," expresses the same idea that personal property is a gift from God and therefore should not be taken by someone else (Ex 20:15). When theft occurred and the thief was caught, restitution had to be made to the person robbed. The amount repaid depended on the thief's actions and attitudes. The thief who later repented and confessed voluntarily simply had to restore the stolen goods plus 20 per-

cent and offer a sacrifice (Lv 6:1–7). Someone who had been entrusted with a neighbor's property and then decided to keep it had to make double restitution. If anyone stole an animal and killed it or sold it, four- or fivefold restitution had to be made (Ex 22:1–9). Some of these penalties seem severe, but in Israel property offenses were treated more leniently than in other ancient societies. The laws of Hammurabi, for example, provide for up to thirtyfold restitution or even death for stealing state or religious property.

In general, the Hebrew law of restitution is stated in Leviticus 24:19,20. The penalties laid down were actually for the protection of the offender, since the punishment was not allowed to exceed the crime. The humanitarian nature of Hebrew civil law is seen in a prohibition against charging an impoverished fellow Israelite interest on a loan (Lv 25:36,37). Under Hammurabi's code, by contrast, interest rates could be as much as 20 percent. Israel was more concerned about offenses against religion or the family, and punished them more severely than did many ancient societies.

Inheritance. Fixed rules governed the distribution of the family estate when the head of the household died. As far as we know, no wills were made. If a man wished to give his favorite child something extra, he had to make the gift before he died. On his death, family property was normally divided between his surviving sons. Daughters usually did not share in the inheritance because they would have taken the land out of the family when they married, conflicting with the principle of the inalienability of family land. However, the same law did provide specifically for the inheritance rights of daughters where no son had been born into the family (Nm 27:8–11). The so-called "levirate law" (Dt 25:5–10), which provided for the needs of a widow who had not borne a son, had similar considerations in view.

When family land was divided among a man's surviving sons, the eldest son received a double portion (Dt 21:17). That may have reflected his responsibility to look after a widowed mother. The double portion of the eldest son is also mentioned in Assyrian law.

Biblical law does not explicitly mention what widows inherited from their husbands. Babylonian law distinguished between childless widows and those who had borne children, and there are hints in the Bible that Israel did the same. A childless widow returned to her father's home, and her husband's property reverted to his nearest relatives (see Lv 22:13). Widowed mothers received a portion of property equal to a son's share, unless husbands had previously presented them with property. Naomi, the widowed mother of two deceased sons, sold to relatives a piece of land that had belonged to her husband, Elimelech (Ru 4:3).

If a man died childless, his land passed to his brother or, failing that, to his father's brother or the next nearest relative (Nm 27:8–11).

Marriage and Property. The property rights of most women in ancient times were tied up with their marriages, and these financial arrangements did much to stabilize unions and prevent capricious divorce. As in the case of the laws governing inheritance, the Bible does not give many details about these payments; but whenever they are mentioned, they appear to be more or less the same as those of Mesopotamia and Israel's other neighbors.

When a man wished to marry a girl, he or his parents had to seek the consent of her parents. Then he had to make them a betrothal gift or engagement present. This is referred to as the "marriage present" or "dowry" in Exodus 22:16,17. Comparison with Deuteronomy 22:29 suggests that 50 shekels was a typical payment. (In the 2nd millennium BC a laborer could expect to earn about 10 shekels a year.) Those who did not have such funds available could enter their father-in-law's service, as Jacob did. He worked seven years for Leah and another seven for Rachel (Gn 29:20–30).

Another important gift was made at the time of the wedding: the bride was given a dowry by her father. This was generally an even larger present than the betrothal gift. Among the generous dowries mentioned in the Bible are servant girls (Gn 29:24,29), land (Jos 15:17–19), and the city of Gezer (1 Kgs 9:16). Usually dowries were smaller gifts of land, money, jewelry, or furnishings. The dowry always belonged by law to the woman, but her husband could use the property as long as the marriage lasted. When her husband died, a widow could claim the dowry because it did not form part of the husband's estate. A dowry would be shared by any sons at a mother's death. If a woman was divorced, she could take the dowry back with her to her father's house, a tradition common to most ancient Near Eastern peoples.

Under Babylonian law a third payment associated with marriage was the optional "settlement." That was a gift from the husband to his wife, designed to maintain her in her widowhood in case he should die before her. If no settlement was made, the widow was entitled to a share in her husband's estate. Presumably the Hebrews made similar provision for widows, though exactly what these were is uncertain.

The size of these various wedding gifts had profound consequences. Though polygamy and divorce were permitted in OT times, both were rare in practice. Only rich patriarchs and kings could afford the betrothal gift for more than one wife. An exception was Elkanah, father of Samuel, who took a second wife (1 Sm 1:2) because his first was barren. There are no stories of divorce in the OT (save for religious reasons) though the law evidently permitted it. One reason may be that the dowry was too valuable to dispense with for most husbands.

Choice of Marriage Partner. Genesis suggests that marriages between cousins were regarded with special favor in Israel.

Israelites were forbidden to marry foreigners because of the danger of accepting their foreign gods. Except for prohibitions against incestuous relationships, Israelites could intermarry as they pleased. Consanguineous unions were encouraged in Egypt, but Leviticus 18 and 20 give lists of close relatives with whom marriage was regarded as incestuous and therefore prohibited. Deuteronomy 25:5–10 recommends one exception to this: if a man died leaving a childless widow, his brother was encouraged to marry the woman "so that his name will not be forgotten."

Divorce. The only law governing divorce in the OT is Deuteronomy 24:1–4, which is concerned with remarriage after divorce rather than divorce itself. It states that if a woman was divorced by her husband, married again, and then was divorced a second time (or widowed), she could not return to her first husband.

Deuteronomy 24:1 suggests infidelity may be a reason for divorce, but not necessarily. A husband could probably divorce his wife for any cause he liked, but the mandatory loss of the dowry meant that divorce would be the last resort in very desperate marriages. Babylonian law required heavy extra payments besides the refund of the dowry when the wife's behavior had been blameless. Biblical law also mentions the "bill of divorce" (Dt 24:1) that the husband had to give his wife. This was a letter stating that he had divorced her and she was free to marry another man. Without such a document a woman could have been charged with adultery, which was a capital offense in ancient times. It is interesting to note that whereas Hammurabi's law code allowed women equal rights of divorce, this privilege was not even mentioned in Hebrew law (see Dt 24:1–4).

Sexual Offenses. OT law exacts the death penalty for adultery and incest (Lv 20:10–21). Other ancient peoples also rejected such practices and often exacted the death penalty as well. The Hebrews, unlike the Hittites and some Canaanites, also rejected the practice of homosexuality (Lv 20:13).

The OT definition of adultery was somewhat narrower than ours. Sexual relations between a married woman and a man who was not her husband were considered adulterous, while relations between a married man and an unmarried girl were not. This imbalanced definition of adultery is a corollary of permitting polygamy. It does not mean that the OT approved of extramarital sex by husbands; in fact, husbands could be heavily penalized, but they could not be accused of adultery with its punishment of death.

The death penalty was only imposed when a couple was caught in the act—"If a man is found lying with the wife of another man, both of them shall die" (Dt 22:22). If the circumstances suggested that the woman was an unwilling victim, only the man was put to death (Dt 22:25–27). As in other ancient Near Eastern countries, intercourse with an engaged girl by someone who was not her fiancé also counted as adultery (Dt 22:23,24). It seems likely that in Israel, as among its neighbors, the death penalty was not mandatory for adultery; but if a man wished to pardon his wife, he had to let her lover off too. Proverbs 6:35 warned a would-be adulterer not to count on buying off an angry husband, implying that the death penalty was not always demanded.

Two laws dealt with the suspicious husband who believed his wife or fiancée had been unfaithful but could not prove it. Numbers 5:11–31 describes the ritual that a wife could be asked to undergo in such circumstances. She was brought to the priest, who made her curse herself if she had been guilty and drink water into which the curses had been sprinkled. If she was guilty, the water would make her body swell and her thigh rot; if she was innocent, it would have no effect. Deuteronomy 22:13–21 deals with an accusation of unfaithfulness by a husband against his bride. The girl's parents were required to "bring out the tokens of her virginity" to prove she had not committed adultery while under their care. What these tokens were is uncertain: possibly the girl's underwear or bedclothes stained with blood from first intercourse.

Intercourse with an unbetrothed girl was heavily penalized, but it never demanded the death penalty. The proper thing to do was for the pair to marry and the man to give his father-in-law the normal betrothal gift (Ex 22:16). Deuteronomy 22:28,29 fixes this at 50 shekels and removes the man's right of divorce. The girl's father, however, could refuse to let them marry and still insist that the betrothal gift be given (Ex 22:17).

The Prophets and the Law.

The prophets preached a sensational message: God's age-old covenant with Israel had been broken. The covenant, instead of guaranteeing Israel's security, would now be the cause of its ruin. Drought, crop failure, poverty, and exile to foreign lands would be the people's lot. When Amos and Hosea appeared in the middle of the 8th century BC, this prophetic message seemed wildly improbable. The two kingdoms of Israel and Judah were enjoying a peace and prosperity they had not known since King Solomon's reign (10th century BC). Within 50 years the truth of the prophets' preaching had been demonstrated; the northern kingdom was destroyed, and the southern kingdom had submitted to Assyria.

In proclaiming God's word the prophets had to explain why his judgment was falling on the people. Their explanation was simple: God's promises of protection depended on the people observing the Law, but the Law was being so flagrantly disobeyed that God would inevitably punish such a wicked nation. The prophet Isaiah condemned the way the rich were oppressing the poor and confiscating their family property: "Woe to those who join house to house, who add field to field, until there is no more room, and you are made to dwell alone in the midst of the land" (Is 5:8). Jeremiah compared his countrymen to "well-fed lusty stallions, each neighing for his neighbor's wife" (Jer 5:8). Hosea declared that most of the commandments were being broken: "There is swearing, lying, killing, stealing, and committing adultery; they break all bounds and murder follows murder" (Hos 4:2).

Yet despite these lax moral attitudes people were still attending divine worship. At the official festivals the temple was thronged with worshipers, and many people were faithful in offering their tithes and private sacrifices. But the great discrepancy between religious enthusiasm and immoral lives was an insult to God. The Law commanded, "Love the Lord your God with all your heart" (Dt 6:5) and "your neighbor as yourself" (Lv 19:18). The people apparently deceived themselves that they were loving God by being such good worshipers while ignoring the needs of their neighbors.

The prophets clearly saw the hypocrisy of such behavior and attacked it fiercely: "Bring no more vain offerings; incense is an abomination to me. New moon and sabbath and the calling of assemblies—I cannot endure iniquity and solemn assembly. Your new moons and your appointed feasts my soul hates; they have become a burden to me, I am weary of bearing them. When you spread forth your hands, I will hide my eyes from you; even though you make many prayers, I will not listen; your hands are full of blood" (Is 1:13–15). Micah similarly attacked the emptiness of religious rituals without good works: what God requires is "to do justice, and to love kindness, and to walk humbly with your God" (Mi 6:8).

Jesus and the Law. Like the prophets before him, Jesus accepted the Law as God's rules for his people. "Think not that I have come to abolish the law and the prophets; I have come not to abolish them but to fulfil them" (Mt 5:17). He goes on to explain in the Sermon on the Mount that God is not concerned merely with outward acts but with thoughts and feelings. It is as much a sin to be angry as to murder, to lust as to commit adultery (Mt 5:21–30). The righteousness of Jesus' followers must exceed "that of the scribes and Pharisees" (Mt 5:20).

Jesus' preaching is summarized in Mark 1:15: "The kingdom of God is at hand; repent, and believe in the gospel." With the coming of Jesus, God's kingdom had come, and Jesus was indeed the long-expected king. In this call he invites men to acknowledge his kingship by repenting (forsaking their sins) and accepting God's forgiveness (believing in the gospel). In this respect, then, Jesus is very much like the prophets; he does not question the Law's demands, but urges men to live in full obedience to it.

However, in the realm of civil law there are changes of emphasis in Jesus' teaching over against the OT. In earlier times land could not be transferred from family to family, because God had given it. Jesus called men to forsake their occupations and sell their property to follow him (Mk 1:17–20; 10:21). Money can easily become a form of idolatry. Men love and serve it instead of God (Mt 6:24). The follower of Jesus must trust in God, not in his wealth (Mt 6:25–34). He must lay up treasure in heaven, not on earth (Mt 6:19,20). Not all Jesus' disciples gave everything away. Peter owned a house (Mk 1:29), rich women supported Jesus (Lk 8:3), and Zacchaeus gave away half his goods to the poor (Lk 19:8). We should not regard these followers as mistaken in retaining some of their property, but they show what Jesus meant when he attacked wealth. How men use it is all-important. When used for the service of the kingdom, money has its place. When it is served instead of God, money is the chief obstacle to entry into the kingdom.

The other change in emphasis over against the old civil law concerns marriage. The OT permitted polygamy, divorce, and remarriage, and did not regard infidelity by a husband as adultery against his wife, though in practice all these things were rare in OT times. When challenged by the Jews, Jesus said that these customs were only tolerated by God because of the sinfulness of Israel. Originally God had made one wife for a man; therefore there should be no divorce (Mk 10:2–9). Further, he stated if a man does divorce his wife and marry again, "he commits adultery against her" (Mk 10:11). This is stricter than the OT and apparently implies that any second marriage is forbidden. Thus, Jesus abolished polygamy and remarriage after divorce, and made man and woman equal as regards adultery. An unfaithful husband is just as adulterous as an unfaithful wife. This revolutionary teaching struck the disciples as severe (see Mt 19:10), but it illustrates what Jesus meant when he said their righteousness must be greater than that of the Jewish leaders (Mt 5:20).

There is a slight difference in Matthew's account of Jesus' teaching, which has led some scholars to argue that Jesus was not quite as strict as the above summary suggests. According to Matthew 19:9 a wife's unchastity" (probably some sexual misconduct) allows an aggrieved husband to divorce her and marry again. If this remark concluded the passage, this interpretation would be the simplest. However, from the context it is more likely that Jesus allowed innocent spouses to separate from their wives but not to remarry. This explains why the disciples were so shocked (v 10) and why Jesus went on to speak about some who "refuse to marry for the sake of the kingdom of heaven" (v 12). This was also the way the church interpreted the passage for the first five centuries. They allowed Christians to separate but not to remarry (cf. 1 Cor 7:11).

GORDON J. WENHAM

See CRIMINAL LAW AND PUNISHMENT; DIVORCE; DIVORCE, CERTIFICATE OF; LEVITICUS, BOOK OF; HAMMURABI, LAW CODE OF; MARRIAGE, MARRIAGE CUSTOMS; COURTS AND TRIALS; LAW, BIBLICAL CONCEPT OF; TEN COMMANDMENTS, THE; DIETARY LAWS.

Bibliography. H.J. Boecker, *Law and the Administration of Justice in the OT and Ancient East;* D. Daube, *Studies in Biblical Law;* B.N. Kaye and G.J. Wenham, eds, *Law, Morality and the Bible;* J.A. Motyer, *Law and Life;* J. Pedersen, *Israel: Its Life and Culture,* 4 vols.; A. Phillips, *Ancient Israel's Criminal Law;* R.E.O. White, *Biblical Ethics.*

Clauda. Ancient name of a small island south of Crete, in Acts 27:16.

See CAUDA.

Claudia. Christian woman known to the apostle Paul and to Timothy (2 Tm 4:21).

Claudius. Roman emperor from AD 41 to 54, mentioned twice in the NT (Acts 11:28; 18:2).

See CAESARS, THE.

Claudius, Edict of. Marble slab inscription from Nazareth prohibiting grave robbing, dated to Claudius' reign (AD 41–54).

See INSCRIPTIONS.

Claudius Lysias. Commander of the Roman garrison in Jerusalem who wrote a letter to the Roman procurator Felix concerning the apostle Paul (Acts 23:26). His title in Greek (*chiliarch*) identifies him as a commander of 1,000 troops. Although Claudius Lysias is unknown outside the NT, some information about him is supplied by the Book of Acts. His surname Lysias is Greek. The Roman name Claudius was evidently taken at the time he purchased his Roman citizenship (Acts 22:28).

Stationed in the Antonia fortress overlooking the northern sector of the temple area in Jerusalem, he rescued Paul from a Jewish mob that was about to kill him there. He allowed Paul to speak to the Jews from one of the two staircases that led from the "court of the Gentiles" in the temple up to the Antonia (Acts 21:40) and prevented Paul from being scourged when he learned of Paul's Roman citizenship (Acts 22:22–29). Claudius Lysias sent Paul secretly to Caesarea under heavy guard when Paul's nephew informed the tribune of a Jewish plot to murder the apostle in Jerusalem (Acts 23:16–25).

How Luke, the writer of Acts, obtained a copy of the official letter about Paul written by Claudius to Felix the governor is not known, but the document provides an important vindication of Paul's character and conduct in the face of his opponents' accusations.

Clay. *See* MINERALS, METALS, AND PRECIOUS STONES; POTTERY.

Clay Tablet. *See* WRITING AND BOOKS.

Cleanness and Uncleanness, Regulations Concerning. Aspect of Hebrew religion having physical, ceremonial, moral, and spiritual significance. Though these senses of clean and unclean can be distinguished with reference to their contexts, they also merge into and illustrate each other; the physical and ceremonial contexts point to a moral state of the worshiper and to a spiritual relationship between God and his people.

The OT vision of a people's relationship with God is along moral and personal lines, God's personal nature being expressed in his giving of the Law to Moses. The personal and uniquely consistent character of Israel's Lord made him morally a completely different being from the many gods of pagan cultures. Unlike the Lord, the baals of the Canaanites were capricious and vicious; nobody expected them to be ethically consistent. Israel's Lord, on the other hand, could be trusted to keep his word (a verbal communication through his chosen prophets). Nobody, not even the high priest or the king, was above the Law, which expressed not only God's character but also his sovereign will for the individual and the nation. His moral consistency carried over into his miraculous interventions into history to protect his people, to judge them and their enemies, and to redeem humanity itself.

Cleanness as defined in the Book of Leviticus, therefore, was always conditioned by the presence of the personal God who gave the Law. As the people sought to approach the Lord, they necessarily did so on his terms and therefore within the framework of the cultic ceremonies he had prescribed. Details of the Levitical ceremonies were designed to illustrate the moral implications of the sinner's approach to God and God's provision for his people to become morally clean in his sight.

The meaning of the Levitical system was stated clearly in the psalmist's words: "Who shall ascend the hill of the Lord? And who shall stand in his holy place? He who has clean hands and a pure heart, who does not lift up his soul to what is false, and does not swear deceitfully" (Ps 24:3,4). One's state of cleanness depends not only on external actions, but also on an internal relationship with God. As a result, the sinner's inability to satisfy the moral demands of a holy God leads to his or her complete dependence on God and on God's provision for satisfying his own demands. That provision was detailed in the Law.

Early History. *Gentile Religious Background.* The gentile conscience was no doubt a strong influence on the development of ethnic notions of clean and unclean. The subjective sense of sin's uncleanness is universally encountered in one form or another in the literature of every great religion, whatever explanation is given for it. Many religions have rites of purification based on water and washings. The Hebrews' ritual avoidance of certain objects, some because of their holiness and others because of their unholiness, finds an analogy in the taboos of many primitive religions, including some of those with which the early Hebrews came into contact.

The similarities between Hebrew and other ancient religions are easily established by superficial comparison. It would be surprising if there were none. Those differences that give biblical religion its distinctive character, however, must be accounted for.

Biblical Religion Before the Mosaic Era. The few references to notions of clean and unclean in Genesis bear certain similarities to other religions but also point to the development of those notions in Hebrew thought after the exodus. For example, God referred to the distinction between clean and unclean animals in his instructions for Noah's ark (Gn 7:2–9). Birds were included in the clean things offered to God by Noah as an act of worship after the flood (Gn 8:20). Such references imply a concept of clean and unclean things even before the flood.

Rachel excused herself from standing up and showing due respect to her father because, she said, "the way of women is upon me" (Gn 31:35). If she was referring to her menstrual period, the household idols in her camel saddle were ritually unclean because she was sitting on them (cf. Lv 15:19). In another instance God told Jacob to go to Bethel and build an altar there. Jacob's response was to "destroy the idols" and to demand that all those in his household "purify" themselves and change their clothing (Gn 35:1–3). Clearly, some kind of ritual purity was thought appropriate for such an act of worship.

Levitical Prescriptions. *Ceremonial and Moral Law.* The relationship between the external ceremonial details of the Mosaic Law and the internally directed moral requirements of such parts of it as the Ten Commandments is one of the fundamental issues of OT theology. It is possible to demonstrate that throughout the OT, uncleanness and sin are virtually synonymous. In many passages sin is described as uncleanness (e.g., Lv 16:16,30; the ordeal of the bitter water in Nm 5:11–28; Zec 13:1).

The relationship between ceremonial and moral cleanness can be illustrated from passages mentioning clean hands on the one hand (2 Sm 22:21; Jb 17:9; 22:30) and a clean heart on the other (Pss 24:4; 51:10; 73:13; Prv 20:9). The prophet Isaiah felt convicted of "unclean lips" when he was in God's presence; a purifying coal, perhaps representing forgiveness and atonement, cleansed him (Is 6:5–7). In many passages cleanness represents innocence before God (Jb 11:4; 33:9; Ps 51:7–10; Prv 20:9), and uncleanness is said to come from sin (Ps 51:2; Is 1:16; 64:6).

Causes of Uncleanness. From the Mosaic Law a number of causes of uncleanness can be derived.

1. Some foods were not to be eaten. Various laws concerning animals make a "distinction between the unclean and the clean and between the living creature that may be eaten and the living creature that may not be eaten" (Lv 11:46,47). Permitted food was what was acceptable to God (see also Dt 14:3–21; Acts 15:28,29).

2. Diseases, especially leprosy, produced an unclean state (Lv 13,14). The story of Naaman refers to leprous defilement (2 Kgs 5:1–14). The Gospels refer often to lepers (e.g., Mt 8:1–4; 10:8; 11:5; Lk 4:27). Many swellings, sores, and rashes were included under that heading, including Hansen's disease (modern leprosy). The defilement of disease included all things touched by a diseased person (Lv 14:33–57).

3. Bodily discharges were unclean, and contact with them defiled a person for various periods of time. Emission of semen produced uncleanness until the evening, whether in intercourse (Lv 15:16–18) or inadvertently during the night (Dt 23:10). An unnatural dis-

A ritual bath for Jewish purification in preparation for worship in the temple.

charge, since it usually indicated disease, made a person unclean for seven days after it had ceased (Lv 15:1–15). Menstruation also produced uncleanness lasting seven days after it ceased (Lv 15:19–24; 2 Sm 11:4). Sexual intercourse during that time made both partners unclean (Lv 15:19–24; 20:18). Contact with the spittle of an unclean person produced uncleanness for a day (Lv 15:8).

4. Dead bodies, or even parts of them such as bone, caused uncleanness (Nm 19:16). Persons who touched a dead body were unclean for a month, and only after that period could they celebrate their own Passover if they had missed it (Nm 9:6–11). The high priest could not even bury his own parents because of his special ritual responsibilities (Lv 21:10,11; cf. Nm 6:7; Hg 2:13; Mt 23:27).

5. Idolatry was the greatest source of spiritual defilement. The entire nation of Israel was defiled because of it (Ps 106:38; Is 30:22; Ez 36:25), as were the Gentiles (Jer 43:12). Consequently, contact with Gentiles was thought to produce defilement. The gospel's universal appeal confronted that conviction (e.g., Jn 4:9; Acts 10:28; cf. Gal 2:11–14). Closely related to the defilement of idolatry was the defilement caused by unclean spirits (Zec 13:2; cf. Mt 10:1; Mk 1:23–27).

Laws About Objects. Certain laws illustrate the principle that uncleanness was transmitted much like a contagion. Dead bodies contaminated what they touched, as did dead insects and certain crawling things (Lv 11:29–38). It is interesting that dry grain, running spring water, and water in a cistern were expressly excluded from that law of contamination; perhaps otherwise starvation would have resulted, dead insects and mice being found in grain and water every day in an agricultural community. Unclean pottery had to be broken, but wooden vessels merely required washing (Lv 15:12). Even uncovered pots in a house where a person had died became unclean (Nm 19:15); everyone who entered the house was unclean.

Because of their idolatrous associations the possessions of pagans were unclean; therefore booty taken in war had to be cleansed by fire or washing (Nm 31:21–24). Clothing of wool, linen, or leather could contract unclean "leprosy" from diseased persons and had to be tested. If the leprous spots (greenish or reddish patches) spread after a test period, the garments had to be burned (Lv 13:47–59; 14:33–53).

Laws About Places. The land and people of Israel were holy; they could be defiled by the uncleanness of economic oppression or idolatry (Jos 22:17–19; Ez 22:24). Jerusalem was a holy city, but it could be defiled by the sins of its people (Jer 13:27; Lam 1:8) or by the blood of its slaughtered inhabitants (Lam 4:15).

The temple could be defiled by unclean persons. It was necessary for Hezekiah to cleanse the temple after Ahaz's idolatrous worship (2 Chr 29:15–19); Nehemiah had to cleanse the rooms in which Tobiah had been (Neh 13:9). One of the functions of the Day of Atonement was removal of impurities transferred to the temple by the sins of the Israelites during the past year (Lv 16:16–19,31–33).

An unclean place received the pieces of a leprous house after its demolition (Lv 14:45). The Valley of Hinnom became Jerusalem's garbage dump in later years, giving rise to the visions of "Gehenna" as a place of eternal punishment in NT eschatology. Since the Israelite camp was a holy place, care was taken to bury human excrement outside its boundaries (Dt 23:12–14). The value of that simple expedient in preventing disease during military excursions can hardly be exaggerated, since plagues were a great scourge of ancient armies.

Laws About Food. Certain kinds of animals were unclean and thus could not be eaten (Lv 11; Dt 14:3–21). Animals that died of old age, disease, or injury, or had been wounded by predators were unclean. Animals that did not both chew the cud and have a cloven hoof were unclean, a definition that included pigs, camels, badgers, and rabbits among others. Among fish Israelites could eat only those that had both fins and scales. Birds of prey and scavengers were unclean. All winged insects were unclean except hopping insects (locusts, grasshoppers, and crickets). A large classification of "crawling things" was prohibited, including worms, lizards, snakes, weasels, and mice. In addition to all those was the ancient prohibition against eating blood (Gn 9:4; Lv 17:14,15; Dt 12:16–23; Acts 15:28,29).

Purification Rites. *Purification by Lapse of Time.* Secondary contamination could often be canceled simply by waiting until the evening (Lv 11:24) or for 7, 14, 40, or 80 days. Dead bodies contaminated what they touched for 7 days (Nm 19:11), as did menstruation (Lv 15:19). When a child was born, the mother's unclean state lasted 7 days for a boy and 14 days for a girl. For 33 days afterward for a male child, and 66 days for a female, the mother could not touch any sacred thing.

Purification by Water. Contact with unclean things such as bodily discharges often required washing of hands and clothing, usually accompanied by a time lapse of a day (Lv 15:5–11).

Purification by Ceremonial Substances. Ceremonial substances used in purification rites included the ashes of a red heifer mixed with water (Nm 19:1–10), and (in cases of leprosy) cedarwood, scarlet cloth, hyssop, and blood (Lv 14:2–9). When the altar was used in a purification ceremony, only blood was suitable, since the altar was the place of sacrifice for sin (Lv 16:18,19; Ez 43:20).

Purification by Sacrifice. Sacrifice was the ultimate source of both ritual and moral purification. All bodily discharges except sexual ones were purified by offerings of doves and pigeons (Lv 15:14,15,29,30). Childbirth required a lamb and a bird (Lv 12:6). Poor people could offer birds in place of an animal (Lv 12:8; 14:21–32; Lk 2:24).

In sacrifice, blood was symbolic of a life given and therefore a death experienced; the uncleanness of disease or sin was thought of as being transferred to the victim, thus removing the uncleanness (Lv 14:7). Sacrificial death therefore always had a substitutionary element. Only blood sacrifice could provide the moral cleansing necessary for sin itself; such sacrifice was therefore the basis of all cleansing, including that of disease.

Purification by Fire. Some contamination could be removed only by fire, such as contamination of metal pots (Nm 31:22,23). Incest was punishable not only by death but also by burning the bodies (Lv 20:14). Idolatry had to be put away by total destruction of the objects and by burning (Ex 32:20). Cities consecrated to pagan deities were to be burned.

New Testament Development. The NT did not reject the OT concept of clean and unclean, but rather reinterpreted it in a new context. It stresses in particular the moral sense of the concept as well as the identification of uncleanness with sin.

The Teachings of Jesus. The Gospels were written in the context of OT law and its Pharisaic and Sadducean accretions. Jesus obeyed the Law, but was often at odds with the practical casuistry (moral system) that had grown up around it.

Jesus taught that true defilement came from the sinner's heart and not from outside contamination (Mk 7:14–23; Lk 11:41). A central element in his teaching was his attack on the ceremonial externalism of the Pharisees. Thus it has been said that Jesus "internalized" the Law. It would be more correct to say that he forced attention to the Law's demands on people's inner lives.

The intrinsic wickedness of demons is underscored by the use of the term "unclean spirit" throughout the Gospels. In fact, the word "unclean" itself always appears in the Gospels in the context of spirit, a detail that illustrates the NT shift of emphasis from ritual uncleanness to sin and its guilt.

Acts and the Epistles. An important episode in the life of the early church came in Acts 10, when God taught the apostle Peter that Gentiles were not unclean in themselves and that Peter was obliged to receive them. The result was Cornelius' conversion.

Jesus' assertion that uncleanness originates in the heart bore fruit in the apostle Paul's doctrine of Christian freedom. Paul, a Pharisee who could say of himself that he had never broken an external law, came to see that nothing is unclean in itself (Rom 14:14); rather, "everything is indeed clean" (Rom 14:20). Although everything is lawful, not everything is expedient (1 Cor 6:12), because everything that "does not proceed from faith is sin" (Rom 14:23). The statement that everything is lawful was a repudiation of ceremonialism.

Throughout the epistles cleanness is the result of obedience of the heart flowing from regeneration; it is based on the cleansing power of the atonement (see Rom 6:19; 1 Thes 2:3,4, where uncleanness is strictly moral). Repentance and confession procure the cleansing power of Christ's blood (1 Jn 1:7–9).

The Atonement. The atonement was the final cleansing agent for sin and its moral results (Heb 9:14,22; 1 Jn 1:7), doing in reality what the blood of bulls and goats only typified. Thus those who are "washed . . . in the blood of the Lamb" (Rv 7:14) are seen as wearing clean white robes (Rv 15:6; 19:8–14).

The cleansing power of Christ's blood in the unrepeatable historical event of the cross is not mystical. His blood, symbolizing the life given and the death died by the Son at the behest of the Father, satisfies the attributes of personal justice of the triune God. Because the personal character of a righteous Father was vindicated, the personal forgiveness of sinners is morally possible. God can be in history only what he is eternally: he is both just and the justifier of believers in Christ (Rom 3:24–26).

Regeneration and Faith. Even OT believers recognized that an internal change had to accompany the sacrifices in order to bring about true cleanness. Thus David invited God to "create in me a clean heart" (Ps 51:10), noting that ceremonial sacrifice is no substitute for real repentance (Ps 51:16,17). Jesus showed his disciples the connection between cleansing and regeneration: "You are already made clean by the word which I have spoken to you" (Jn 15:3). The apostle Paul described regeneration as a "washing" (Ti 3:5) effected by the Holy Spirit applying the cleansing Word (Eph 5:26). The apostle Peter likewise used the language of cleansing to describe the Word's regenerating action in connection with faith (1 Pt 1:22).

See Baptism; Circumcision; Uncircumcision; Offerings and Sacrifices; Law, Biblical Concept of; Dietary Laws.

Cleanthes. Leader of the Athenian Stoic school of philosophy from 269 to 232 BC. Cleanthes' poem, "Hymn to Zeus," was adapted in part by another Stoic poet, Aratus, in his own creation, "Phaenomena." Centuries later the apostle Paul quoted the fifth line of "Phaenomena" as he spoke to a crowd on the Areopagus in Athens: "For we are indeed his offspring" (Acts 17:28).

Clement. Fellow laborer with Paul at Philippi who worked side by side with him in the furtherance of the gospel there (Phil 4:3). Paul includes him in the group of those whose names are written in the book of life. Even though some early church fathers identified this Clement with the third bishop of Rome, there is no evidence to substantiate their claims.

Cleopas. Follower of Jesus who conversed with him on the way to Emmaus (Lk 24:18). Some identify Cleopas with Mary's husband, mentioned in John 19:25 (RSV Clopas; KJV Cleophas). However, there is little evidence to support this conclusion.

See CLOPAS.

Cleophas. KJV form of Clopas, Mary's husband, in John 19:25.

See CLOPAS.

Cloak. Translation of several words referring to outer garments.

See FASHION AND DRESS.

Clopas. Husband of Mary, one of the women who was present at Jesus' crucifixion (Jn 19:25, KJV Cleophas). From the Greek it cannot be determined if Mary the wife of Clopas was also the sister of Jesus' mother or a different person. One tradition identifies Clopas as the brother of Joseph. Another links him with Cleopas of Luke 24:18, even though "Clopas" is of Hebrew origin and "Cleopas" is Greek. A third possibility is to equate him with Alphaeus. This is feasible only if James, son of Alphaeus (Mt 10:3; Lk 6:15; Acts 1:13) is the same as James, son of Mary (Mt 27:56; Mk 15:40), and Mary is the same person mentioned in John 19:25. These suggestions are theoretical; it is possible that Clopas, Cleopas, and Alphaeus are all separate individuals.

Closed Womb. *See* BARRENNESS.

Cloth, Cloth Manufacturing. Since antiquity cloth has been made from such natural fibers as flax, wool, cotton, silk, and hair. Linen (spun from flax), wool, and sackcloth (woven from goat's or camel's hair) are the fabrics most frequently mentioned in Scripture. The Bible also refers to silk and cotton.

The most primitive form of clothing was made of hides, or leather, which could be sewed to make garments or blankets. As far back as the Stone Age wool shed by sheep was made into a thick, feltlike fabric. Balls of red and blue wool 4,000 years old have been found in Egypt, as well as linen cloth made before the first Egyptian kings ruled (3100 BC). Silk was first manufactured in China around 3000 BC. Thus the use of animal and plant materials in cloth making developed in areas as far apart as China, India, Egypt, and the Near East. With the spread of trade the basics of cloth-manufacturing techniques were also transmitted.

Fibers for Weaving. Linen. Flax was cultivated extensively in the Near East. In Palestine it flourished around the Sea of Galilee. The stalks were gathered into bundles and steeped in water, causing the fibers to separate from the nonfibrous stem. The bundles were then opened and spread out to dry in the sun. Rahab hid Hebrew spies on the roof of her house amid stalks of flax laid out to dry (Jos 2:6). After drying, the stalks were split and combed to separate the fibers for spinning and weaving into linen. Biblical references to flax include Exodus 9:31; Judges 15:14; and Proverbs 31:13.

The quality of linen varied considerably. The ordinary linen used for everyday clothing was inferior to that used for temple decorations or for the more elaborate garments of the priests (Ex 26:1; 39:27). The type of fabric from which the priestly coats, girdles, and caps (Ex 28:40) were made is not stated, though the mention of linen breeches may imply that most if not all of the priestly garments were made of linen. An artistically woven band of gold, blue, purple, and scarlet thread decorated the bottom part of the linen outer garment, or ephod (Ex 28:8). The gold threads would be made of finely drawn wire, but the nature of the silver and bronze mentioned in Exodus 25:3 is uncertain.

The finest linen, worn by kings and nobles, served as a mark of honor or as a special gift. Joseph was given a garment of fine linen when he was made ruler of Egypt (Gn 41:42). When the Hebrews left Egypt at the time of the exodus, they took with them a high-quality linen and donated it to the tabernacle (Ex 25:4; 35:6). The Phoenicians imported embroidered Egyptian linen for use as sails on their merchant ships (Ez 27:7). Other Bible references to linen include Leviticus 6:10; Ezekiel 9:2; Daniel 10:5; and Revelation 15:6.

About 2000 BC in Ur, statues of gods were

draped in linen, a fabric considered too valuable for ordinary clothing. Temple workshops were evidently set up as small factories for weaving linen. Linen became an important commodity in the economy of Babylonia and certain other regions. By the 3rd century BC small factories for linen weaving had developed in Egypt, and a flourishing export business was in progress. Other centers of export were Byblos, Tyre, and Berytus (Beirut). Despite the quantity of linen manufactured in Palestine, a craftsman who was trained to work in fine linen came from Tyre to work for Solomon on temple hangings (2 Chr 2:14).

Wool. Wool was another extremely important fiber in the Near Eastern economy. Tablets from Ur dating back to 2000 BC indicate that thousands of sheep were kept in the city, and that several thousand may have been shorn in a single day. Large storehouses were built to accommodate such quantities of wool. During that period slaves and free women were employed as weavers, earning wages of dates, oil, fish, and possibly beer. In the area around Lachish 6,400 weavers were employed in a particular five-month period.

Wool could come in any shade from creamy yellow to tan or black. Sometimes to obtain pure white wool a sheep was kept wrapped to prevent its fleece from being soiled. Preparation of wool was a home craft in antiquity (Prv 31:13; cf. Ex 35:25). Wool had to be washed thoroughly, dried, and then beaten to detach the fibers and remove the dirt before being carded and spun. Women spun their own yarn and wove garments for their families. Wool was the fabric of seminomadic, sheep-raising people; by contrast, the growing of flax required a more settled life style. That difference contributed in part to wool's remaining the material of everyday usage, while linen became the "haute couture" of priests and the upper classes.

Goat's Hair. A thick cloth that was extremely warm as well as waterproof was woven from goat's hair (Ex 35:23,26). Clothing worn by the poor was often manufactured from goat's or camel's hair. That coarse-haired fabric (sackcloth) on occasions was worn next to the skin as a form of penitence (Neh 9:1; Dn 9:3; Mt 11:21), as a mourning vestment (Gn 37:34; 2 Sm 3:31), or even as a prophetic protest against luxurious living (Rv 11:3). Sackcloth also made warm blankets. The cloak that the apostle Paul asked Timothy to bring to keep him warm against the prison's penetrating cold may have been made of that material (2 Tm 4:13).

Cotton, Silk, and Gold Thread. The people of Judea would certainly have been aware of cotton during their Persian exile (beginning in 538 BC). Cotton is mentioned once in a description of elaborate hangings in the Persian king's palace (Est 1:6). It is doubtful, however, that cotton was cultivated in ancient Palestine or even found there until after the exile.

The finest-quality silk was imported from China to Antioch, but other types of wild silk were known and used in the Near East in Roman times. Although silk was sometimes associated with extravagance and decadent luxury (Rv 18:12), the veil of the temple may have been made of that expensive material.

Earlier in Israel's history part of the tabernacle fabric was woven with gold thread, evidently made from thin sheets of beaten gold cut into fine wire strips (Ex 39:3). A wider type of gold wire with a flat surface was used to adorn expensive Palestinian and Syrian garments. An ancient hank of fine gold thread was uncovered during excavations at Dura on the Euphrates River.

Spinning. The fact that vegetable fibers tend to twist when wet may have given ancient peoples the idea of spinning such fibers into thread. The most primitive technique was probably simply to roll fibers between the fingers or hands. A spindle rotated against the thigh or by the fingers was the earliest spinning implement. In Bible times a spindle was a slender rounded stick, tapered and notched at one end and weighted at the other end with a "whorl" of clay, stone, glass, or metal to serve as a kind of flywheel. The thread spun at the tapered end was wound on the spindle. Another thin stick, called a distaff, held the fibers to be fed onto the twirling spindle.

The earliest collection of spindle whorls used for fine thread was found at Nagada in Egypt and dates from the end of the 4th millennium BC. Many early spindle whorls of clay and stone were recovered from the Sumerian sites of Ur and Lagash.

Threads could be doubled by respinning. According to Jewish tradition a 24- and 72-ply yarn was spun for the last curtain of the temple. Two different kinds of fiber were never spun together, either because of undesirable properties of such threads or from a general religious concern for "purity" in all aspects of life (Dt 22:9–11).

Looms and Weaving. Weaving is the interlacing of "warp" threads stretched on a loom by threads of "weft" or "woof" passed from side to side over and under the warp. A primitive warp could be stretched around pegs or rods tied to a tree or roof beam and sometimes connected to the weaver's waist. As weaving technique developed, three types of loom emerged: the horizontal ground loom, the vertical two-beamed loom, and the warp-weighted loom. In a horizontal ground loom the warp was stretched between two wooden beams fastened to the ground by four pegs. Traveling nomads could pull out the pegs and roll up the unfinished weaving on the beams. Early in the development of such looms the odd and even threads were separated by a "heddle," which made the weaving of the weft much faster than the original darning method of simple basketry. Delilah wove Samson's hair on a horizontal ground loom (Jgs 16:13, 14). Many biblical passages refer to fabrics probably made on such looms (see 1 Sm 2:19; 2 Kgs 23:7; Prv 31:21–24; Acts 9:39).

The vertical two-beamed loom had its warp stretched on a rectangular wooden frame. In addition to the two uprights and two warp beams, another beam was often used to maintain the tension of the warp, especially on longer lengths. The vertical loom was probably invented in Syria or Palestine. The OT contains a number of references to a "weaver's beam" (1 Sm 17:7; 2 Sm 21:19; 1 Chr 11:23; 20:5).

The warp-weighted loom, also on a vertical frame, was worked from the top down. The lower edge was weighted with loom weights, often shaped lumps of clay. Many such weights dating from 3000 to 2500 BC have been found at Near Eastern sites. The warp-weighted loom was the only type used in Greece and is depicted on Greek vases from the 6th century BC. A disadvantage of such a loom was that the weaver had to stand to operate it.

The degree of sophistication in weaving techniques in biblical times is seen in the specifications for fabrics for the tabernacle and its court. Hangings for the court were to be 50 yards long and probably a standard two yards wide (Ex 27:9–18). The tabernacle veil (Ex 26:31) and screen for the entrance (Ex 26:36) were to be "blue and purple and scarlet stuff," probably highlighted or embroidered with linen.

Garments such as the tunic that Jesus wore were woven in one piece with the selvage (edge of the weaving) coming at the neck and hem, the areas of greatest wear. A tunic woven on a narrow loom would be constructed of three pieces.

Linen thread was strong and could be spun very fine and woven to an extremely sheer degree. Woven linen did not necessarily have equal numbers of warf threads and weft threads passing over each other together. Often three or less weft threads were interwoven with four in the warp, the warp tending to bend more than the weft. A striped warp could easily be set up on a loom, but other designs in weave or color were unusual.

Cotton had a very short fiber which was therefore difficult to spin. The tendency of cotton fiber to readjust itself when wet had to be counteracted in the weaving, which was frequently done on a horizontal loom.

Wool with its long, scaly fiber could be set up on a widely spaced warp that had to be kept taut to prevent bagging. Bands of color were often used to form a design in wool.

Silk fibers were long and slippery. Although easier to weave than short fibers, silk tended to slither out of place when taken off the loom. A special crossover technique was developed for weaving sheer fabrics to overcome that problem.

Cloth Dyes and Dyeing. Like the fibers, the dyes used in antiquity were also of animal or plant origin. A red dye was obtained from the body of an insect. Purple came mainly from two kinds of mollusks found in many parts of the eastern Mediterranean seaboard. The purest shade of purple could be obtained from mollusks found on the shore at Tyre, so a large industry developed there (Ez 27:1–3,16). Purple, the most expensive dye, remained the distinguishing color of kings and nobles. The first Christian convert in Europe, Lydia, was a businesswoman who sold the costly purple cloth (Acts 16:14). Yellow was obtained from the petals and flower heads of the safflower. Saffron (orange-yellow) came from the stigmas of the crocus that grew extensively in Syria and Egypt. Green was usually concocted from a mixture of other dyes. In Hellenistic times woad, a plant of the mustard family, was cultivated in Mesopotamia for its blue dye. Indigo was grown in Egypt and Syria. Dyeing in antiquity was often carried out in large vats, pictures of which have been found in paintings and on pottery. The ruins of structures including vats have been excavated at some Palestinian sites.

HAZEL W. PERKIN

See DYE, DYER, DYEING; FASHION AND DRESS; INDUSTRY AND COMMERCE.

Clothing. *See* CLOTH, CLOTH MANUFACTURING; FASHION AND DRESS.

Cloud, Pillar of. Supernatural phenomenon of God's presence which guided the Israelites through the wilderness.

See PILLAR OF FIRE AND CLOUD; SHEKINAH; WILDERNESS WANDERINGS.

Cnidus. Port city situated off the southwest corner of Asia Minor, mentioned as a harbor passed by the apostle Paul en route to Italy (Acts 27:7). During the 2nd century BC it had a Jewish colony (1 Mc 15:23). The island on which Cnidus was built is now joined to the mainland by a sandbar.

Coal. Translation of several Hebrew or Greek words in the Bible referring primarily to charcoal (mineral coal is not found in Palestine). The glowing embers from a wood fire were used for heating (Is 47:14; Jn 18:18), cooking (Is 44:19; Jn 21:9), and by blacksmiths (Is 54:16). Coals from the altar were used in religious ritual (Lv 16:12).

Figuratively the term is used in descriptions of God's infinite brightness and glory (2 Sm 22:9,13), of his revelation (Ps 18:8), of divine judgment (Ps 140:10), and of creatures associated with God's throne (Ez 1:13; 10:2). In other metaphorical passages glowing coals stand for a life (2 Sm 14:7), the breath of a huge beast ("leviathan," Jb 41:21), and the risk of being "burned" by sexual sin (Prv 6:28).

Coat. Translation of several words referring to various garments.

See Fashion and Dress.

Coat of Mail. Piece of armor covering the body from the neck to the girdle, probably made of leather with small interlaced metal plates sewn onto it.

See Arms and Warfare.

Cock. Adult male of the domestic fowl.

See Birds (Fowl, Domestic).

Cockatrice. KJV rendering of serpent, adder, and viper in Isaiah 14:29; 11:8; and 59:5, respectively.

See Animals (Serpent).

Cockle. KJV term for "foul weeds" in Job 31:40.

See Plants (Thistle, Thorn).

Codex. Earliest form of the book, consisting of sheets of papyrus or vellum folded and bound together and enclosed between two wooden leaves or tablets.

See Writing and Books.

Coffin. *See* Burial, Burial Customs.

Coins. Pieces of metal used and accepted as a medium of exchange. A coin has a specific weight and bears some type of authentication to make it easily recognizable. The word "coin" originally referred to a wedge-shaped die or stamp used to "strike" the metal blank. The first coins may have been minted in the late 8th century BC (the words "mint" and "money" are both derived from the Latin *Moneta*, a designation of the goddess Juno, in whose temple in Rome money was once

coined). According to Herodotus, a 5th-century BC Greek historian, the earliest coins were made of electrum (an alloy of gold and silver) and minted by King Croesus of Lydia (560–546 BC), who traditionally was also responsible for the introduction of gold coins. The resistance of gold and silver, and to a lesser extent of bronze, to corrosion and the fact that coins often bear a mintage date as part of their inscription have given coins a special importance to archaeologists of the Near East.

General acceptance of coinage as a medium of exchange did not stamp out fraud. Coins were sometimes minted from inferior metal and coated with silver. For that reason many ancient coins show a sharp gash, which proved that the coin was silver throughout. Such clipping of coins was common from antiquity until well into the 18th century, when coins began to be minted with milled edges.

Earliest Coins in Palestine. Not until the time of Darius the Great (Darius I of Persia, 521–486 BC) did an official government-sponsored coinage become current in Palestine. Those earliest coins were oval-shaped gold darics, along with some silver coins. On both varieties the obverse (front side) was the same: the Persian king robed and crowned, facing right, and kneeling with his left knee up and his right knee down. In his left hand he held a bow and in his right a long arrow or lance. The gold coin, exactly the same size as the silver, was worth about 15 times as much. The reverse (back side) of all Persian imperial coins carried no markings.

"Dram" is another term for the Persian gold daric. It is mentioned in Ezra 2:68,69 (KJV), where Zerubbabel's caravan offered gold darics amounting to $30,000 toward rebuilding the temple, which had been destroyed by Nebuchadnezzar. This passage is the first mention of an actual coin in the Bible. It is interesting to note how quickly after that time values are recorded in the monetary units of drams rather than in the earlier weights of talents and shekels. Nehemiah reported the collection of 41,000 drams (KJV) of gold in addition to thousands of "minas" of silver (Neh 7:70–72). The mina was not a coin but a Babylonian unit of weight equivalent to 70 Mesopotamian drachmas.

· Almost at the same time that the Persian coins became current in Palestine, the widely popular silver tetradrachmas (four-drachma pieces) of Athens began to find their way to the mercantile centers of the Phoenician, Israelite, and Philistine coasts. Archaeologists have unearthed them in hoards throughout the eastern Mediterranean region. They continued to be used through the Persian period, which lasted until the Persian empire was conquered by Alexander the Great in 334–330 BC. Tetradrachmas scarcely varied in weight or design throughout the period of their usage. The obverse carried the head of the goddess Athena, facing right and wearing a garlanded helmet; the reverse had an owl facing the viewer, with its body tilting to the right. In the right border were Greek letters meaning "Of the Athenians." In the upper left was a sprig of olive, Athena's gift to the city of Athens. The coin was thick and heavy in appearance, but being of high-quality silver it was in great demand for international commerce. Presumably Greek merchants found they could obtain the most desirable Asiatic imports in exchange for that particular form of currency.

So admired was the tetradrachma in Palestine that imitations of it were designed for use in the province of Judea, inscribed with letters resembling "YHD" for Judah. One type, probably minted by some city on the Philistine border, had the bearded head of a man or a god, facing right and wearing some sort of oriental headpiece. The reverse had the Athenian owl and olive sprig, but done in a rather crude style. The fact that few such coins have ever been discovered may mean that they had only limited circulation. The silver didrachma or half-drachma, in general use in the Greek empire from the 4th century BC, continued through Roman times. After Alexander's conquests, of course, Greek coins were used throughout the Macedonian empire from present-day Yugoslavia to Pakistan. They were almost certainly employed for business purposes in Judea, for example.

The shekels of the Phoenician trade centers of Tyre and Sidon, which had contributed substantially to the money supply in the Persian period, continued to be accepted in Judea even after the Alexandrian conquest. Typical of Sidon was a silver shekel portraying the battlements and walls of Sidon's harbor, with a ship lying at anchor and two prancing lions in the foreground. A two-shekel coin showed the Persian king with two attendants mounted on a chariot and driving toward the left. The reverse showed a war galley riding on the waves.

A typical Tyrian shekel showed the god Baal robed and wearing a tiara. He was riding a hippocamp (winged horse with the tail of a fish) on the sea, with a fish or dolphin beneath. The reverse showed an Egyptian-type owl facing right, plus a shepherd's crook and flail, both royal insignia in Egypt. During the Greek period and later during the Seleucid period of Syrian rule, Tyre began to issue a larger Greek type of tetradrachma (or shekel). The obverse showed the head of Baal-Heracles (Hercules) with a garland of victory;

on the reverse a large eagle strode leftward and an inscription said "Of Tyre, the holy city of refuge." Such coins often carried dates representing an era. The later ones date from 126 BC, when autonomy was granted to the city by the Seleucid government. When the monastic center of Qumran near the Dead Sea was completely abandoned because of a severe earthquake in 31 BC, a large jar containing four-drachma and two-drachma pieces from Tyre was hidden under the floor of a storeroom and unearthed only in the 20th century. Archaeological discoveries of hoards dating from Jesus' time suggest that Tyrian shekels circulated widely in Palestine many years after their mintage.

The stater (or tetradrachma) found by the disciple Peter in a fish's mouth and used to pay the temple tax for himself and Jesus may have been a Tyrian coin (Mt 17:27, RSV shekel). Many of the 30 pieces of silver paid to Judas Iscariot for betraying Jesus were probably of the same type. Some of the Tyrian tetradrachmas Judas received could have come from the reign of Philippus Philadelphus, who ruled from 92 to 83 BC in the declining days of the Seleucid empire. The obverse showed the king's curly-headed portrait; the reverse depicted a seated Zeus holding in his hand a statuette of Nike (goddess of victory). The coin carried a large inscription, "Of king Philip Epiphanes Philadelphus"; Epiphanes meant "illustrious" or "manifestation" (of a god) and Philadelphus, "brother-lover." Philip, who was constantly at war, so abundantly minted and widely circulated his coinage that his tetradrachmas are found more commonly than coins of other Seleucid kings.

Before the Seleucid tetradrachmas with their Apollolike heads appeared in Palestine, Egyptian coinage had also circulated there. The Ptolemies controlled the Holy Land from the breakup of Alexander's empire until defeat of Ptolemy V by Antiochus III of Syria in 200 BC. The Seleucid kings were at first tolerant toward Jewish religious practices, as the Egyptians had been, but then began an intense persecution. In December of 175 BC the Jewish patriot leader Judas Maccabeus had the Jerusalem temple cleansed of pagan pollution and rededicated to the worship of the Lord, an event celebrated thereafter by the annual feast of Hanukkah.

The talent, which represented a certain weight of gold or silver, was a common medium of exchange before the development of coinage. During the Maccabean period John Hyrcanus saved the city of Jerusalem from destruction in 133 BC by paying a ransom from a 900-year-old hoard stored in David's sepulcher. Three thousand talents of silver were sent to the Seleucid king Antiochus VII Sidetes in return for his promise to withdraw his troops. Treasure plundered from the temple by the Romans in AD 66 is recorded as amounting to 17 talents. In gold talents that sum would represent the equivalent of the purchase price of 17 large houses in a modern Western city.

Coinage from the Maccabees to Herod Agrippa I. Even though a native Jewish dynasty assumed the government of the Holy Land, it was many years before any indigenous Jewish coinage was minted. Presumably the inhabitants continued to use the coinage of Tyre and Egypt and of the Seleucid empire for their commercial transactions. It was formerly supposed that silver shekels bearing images of the chalice and pomegranate cluster dated from the reign of Simon Maccabeus (142–134 BC); more recent archaeological discoveries prove that those coins date from the First Jewish Revolt (AD 66–70).

When the time came to issue the first Jewish coins, the die makers faced several problems. No mint was available, and no local people were skilled in design or die sinking. Coins current in the Near East at that time, which showed a high degree of design and craftsmanship, each bore the portrait head of a ruler or a god. For the Jews to make such coins would have meant contravening the second commandment, "You shall not make for yourself a graven image" (Ex 20:4). Not until well into Roman times was a coin struck in Palestine bearing a portrait head of a Roman emperor.

The earliest coinage of the Hasmonean dynasty (the regnal name of the Maccabees) was the small bronze lepton (plural, lepta) of John Hyrcanus I (134–104 BC), son of Simon Maccabeus. The obverse showed two cornucopias with a pomegranate between them. That image symbolized the fertility that God had granted to the land. The reverse contained an inscription within a wreath, "John the high priest and the community of the Jews." Small bronze lepta from the reign of Alexander Jannaeus, son of Hyrcanus I, have been found in great numbers. They were evidently much in demand for transactions at the temple, where money changers converted the gentile currency of visiting worshipers into the more acceptable Jewish money. Undoubtedly Hasmonean lepta were the coins Jesus scattered over the pavement of the court of the Gentiles when he over-turned the tables of the money changers (Mt 21:12; Jn 2:15). The lepton or "mite" of bronze or copper, worth 1/400 of a shekel, was mentioned by Jesus on another occasion. He praised a widow's gift of two mites to the temple treasury with the comment that the rich "contributed out of their abundance; but she out of her poverty has put in everything she had, her whole living" (Mk 12:44).

In 63 BC Hyrcanus II, grandson of the founder of the Hasmonean dynasty, was in a dispute over the Jewish throne with his younger brother, Aristobulus II. To arbitrate the dispute, appeal was made to the marauding armies of Pompey, a Roman general. The result of bringing Pompey into the quarrel was that the Holy Land came under Rome's control. Although John Hyrcanus II still held the title of ruler of the nation, the government was actually falling increasingly into the hands of Antipater, whose son Herod I ("the Great") retained the favor of the Roman overlords. Herod I came to power under the patronage of Mark Antony and secured the allegiance of the pro-Hasmonean Jews by marrying Mariamne, granddaughter of Hyrcanus II, in 38 BC. After Antony's defeat at the battle of Actium in 31 BC, Herod managed to make his peace with the victor, Octavian (Caesar Augustus). Herod was confirmed as vassal king over the whole of Palestine.

Herod was empowered to strike his own bronze coins. Although he had a free hand to introduce innovations, Herod's lepta followed tradition quite faithfully. The lepta carried an anchor with letters meaning "Of King Herod." The reverse bore the double cornucopias with a pomegranate (or poppy) between them. Herod also minted a large bronze coin with what appears to be a Macedonian helmet on the obverse and a slender tripod on the reverse along with an inscription of Herod's name. Other designs he employed included wheat, eagles, and wreaths. He issued no silver coinage, relying instead on the available supplies of silver coins from Tyre, Syria, Asia Minor, Greece, and Rome.

After Herod's death in 4 BC, his son Herod Archelaus assumed control. Lepta from that period bore a hanging cluster of grapes with a Greek inscription, and on the reverse a two-plumed Macedonian helmet. Such a grape cluster, which had already appeared in a cruder form on coins of John Hyrcanus II, was the type used on the first coins of the modern state of Israel (1948). Grapes were an allusion to Israel as the Lord's vine (Is 5).

When Herod Antipas began his rule in AD 4, he had no authority in Judea or Samaria. That portion of the former Jewish kingdom was placed under the control of Roman governors, or procurators, appointed directly by the emperor himself. The first of the procurators, Coponius, was under the authority of Quirinius (Cyrenius, KJV), governor of Syria (cf. Lk 2:2). A new series of bronze lepta was begun, featuring symbols of agricultural wealth such as palm branches, date palms, wreaths, and

Coins

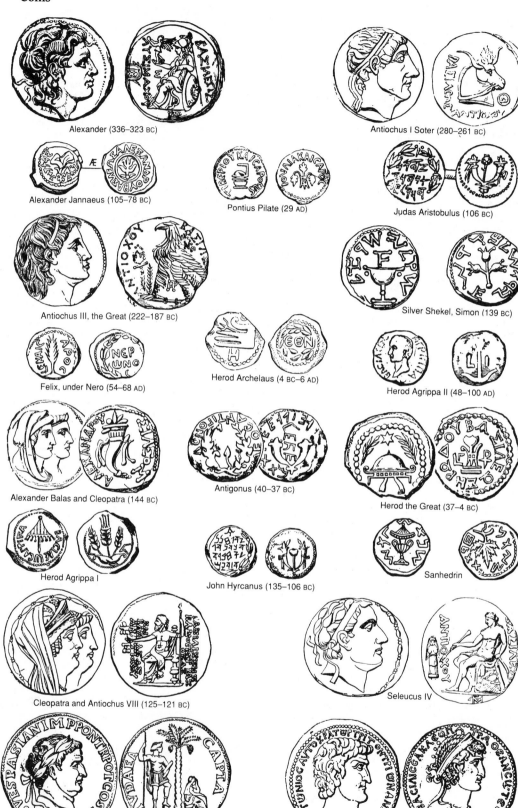

Alexander (336–323 BC)

Antiochus I Soter (280–261 BC)

Alexander Jannaeus (105–78 BC)

Pontius Pilate (29 AD)

Judas Aristobulus (106 BC)

Antiochus III, the Great (222–187 BC)

Silver Shekel, Simon (139 BC)

Felix, under Nero (54–68 AD)

Herod Archelaus (4 BC–6 AD)

Herod Agrippa II (48–100 AD)

Alexander Balas and Cleopatra (144 BC)

Antigonus (40–37 BC)

Herod the Great (37–4 BC)

Herod Agrippa I

John Hyrcanus (135–106 BC)

Sanhedrin

Cleopatra and Antiochus VIII (125–121 BC)

Seleucus IV

Vespasian (71 AD)

Antony and Cleopatra (30 BC)

Tarsus

Chios

Brutus at Philippi

Nero at Thyatira

Colossae

Attalus II Philadelphus

Samothracia

Colossae

Miletus

Ephesus

Paphos in Cyprus

Thessalonica

Attalia

Alexandria Troas

Smyrna

Ephesus

Melita (Malta)

Thyatira

Samos

Ephesus

Coins

Macedonia under Roman Rule

Syracuse

Sardis

Philetairus of Pergamus

Nero

Laodicea in Asia

Philippi

City of Antioch

Laodicea

Cenchrea, Port of Corinth

Ephesus

Sardis

Ephesus

Perga in Pamphylia

Iconium

Chios

cornucopias. Similar designs remained popular through succeeding years.

Most familiar of the Roman procurators of Judea was Pontius Pilate (AD 26–36). His bronze coinage showed some bold innovations; his designs included representations of instruments used in the Roman religion such as the augur's wand, resembling a shepherd's crook in shape, and a ladle used in connection with broth prepared at sacrifices. The reverse bore a wreath enclosing the regnal date indicating AD 30–31. The two lepta put into the temple treasury (Lk 21:2) could have been lepta issued by Pilate or his predecessor. More likely, however, they were the Hasmonean lepta of Hyrcanus or Jannaeus, which were free of any taint of pagan Roman influence.

Herod Agrippa I (AD 37–44), grandson of Herod the Great, continued the family tradition of ingratiating himself with the Roman overlords. During his reign several notable coins were struck. Many of Herod Agrippa's lepta have been found, showing a conical tasseled umbrella (perhaps symbolizing his royal protection of the people of Palestine) plus a Greek inscription indicating his reign. The reverse showed a bound cluster of three wheat ears and bore the regnal year as the legend. For the administrative capital of Caesarea, however, Herod Agrippa struck a larger bronze coin seldom found by archaeologists. It bore his own head in portraiture and the inscription "The great king Agrippa, the friend of Caesar." The reverse showed a standing figure holding a rudder and a horn of plenty, with the inscription "Caesarea at the Augustan Harbor."

Another large bronze coin, an inch in diameter, carried the emperor's head with an inscription reading "Tiberius Caesar Augustus." The reverse showed a temple porch with the regnal year in the gable, plus the same inscription as on the coin's obverse. Two figures faced each other in the temple entrance, probably the temple of Augustus in Caesarea. The figures may have been those of Tiberius and Herod themselves. The regnal year favors the interpretation that the emperor portrayed on the coin was actually Claudius (AD 41–54), although even after his accession to the throne his official name was Tiberius Claudius Drusus. With the death of Herod Agrippa I (Acts 12:20–23) the last pretense of a real Jewish kingdom vanished.

Roman Coins in New Testament Times. The Roman "as" came into circulation about 348 BC as a bronze coin bearing the figure of an animal. The coin was named after the Roman one-pound weight, equivalent to 12 ounces in our modern system. At first the coin actually weighed that much, making it especially cumbersome for merchants traveling abroad. De-

veloping into the typical round shape, the coin gradually shrank in size until by 241 BC the as weighed two ounces. Within 50 years it was half an ounce. At the time of Christ's birth the Roman as minted for use in the Asiatic provinces bore the head of the emperor Augustus, with a laurel wreath on the reverse. A smaller bronze quadrans or quarter as was also minted by the Romans.

Another bronze coin found in Greek and Roman currency was the assarion, first minted in the 1st century BC but still in use in the Christian period. One type was stamped with a winged sphinx, with an amphora on the reverse. It is still debated whether the coin described as a "farthing" in the KJV was in fact a Greek assarion or a Roman as or quadrans. The coin is mentioned four times in the NT, most familiarly in the question, "Are not two sparrows sold for a farthing?" (Mt 5:26; 10:29; Mk 12:42; Lk 12:6, RSV penny). There is no doubt that the KJV translators decided to make the coin seem more familiar to their readers by using the name of the smallest copper coin in circulation in England at that time.

The word translated "penny" in the KJV is the Greek form of "denarius," the normal daily wage for a laborer in NT times. In the parable of the laborers in the vineyard, for example, the master agreed to pay each man "a penny" for his day's work (Mt 20:2 KJV; RSV a denarius). "Two pence" was the amount paid to the innkeeper by the good Samaritan (Lk 10:35 KJV). Because of the influence of the Roman denarius on British currency, the English penny has always been represented by the initial letter of its Roman equivalent, *d*.

When the denarius or "penny" is recognized as a normal day's wage, the astonishment of Jesus' disciples when they were expected to find food for 5,000 people is better understood. They exclaimed that "two hundred pennyworth" of food would not feed such a crowd (Jn 6:7 KJV); that sum represented more than six months' work.

Argyrion is a general Greek term for silver found in the NT (Lk 9:3; Acts 8:20). In a broad sense it meant "money." The reference would probably be to either of the popular silver coins then in use, the tetradrachma or the Roman denarius.

As might be expected, the silver and gold coinage current in Palestine during the time of Christ and for the remainder of the 1st century AD came primarily from Rome. The larger silver coins, however, which are referred to as tetradrachmas or staters in the NT, came from Egypt, Phoenicia, or Antioch. The silver coin most frequently mentioned in the NT was the Roman denarius or the Greek drachma. Since few drachmas have been found in excavations dating from the 1st century, it is possible that the term was used in popular speech to refer to the denarius (plural, denarii), which was approximately the same size as the average Greek drachma. Actually, few Greek cities were permitted by their Roman overlords to continue minting drachmas.

It is conceivable, though unlikely, that some denarii of Julius Caesar were still current in the Near East during Jesus' boyhood. Only toward the end of his rule did Julius Caesar's portrait appear on coins that bore his name. The earliest issues showed the head of Venus, mythical ancestor of Julius Caesar's line, or an elephant or some other martial symbol connected with Caesar's conquest of Gaul. One interesting denarius showed Caesar wearing a priestly veil as pontifex maximus, the high priest of the Roman hierarchy. The inscription read "Dict(ator) Perpetuus Caesar" ("Caesar, perpetual dictator"), a status granted to him in 45 BC by the Roman senate. The reverse had Venus standing with a bronze staff in her left hand and a statuette of Victoria (Roman name for Nike) in her right. The legend spelled the name of the mint master.

Caesar Augustus issued a decree for all the Roman world to be enrolled (Lk 2:1,2) in an empire-wide census just about the time that Jesus was born (6 or 5 BC). During his long reign (27 BC–AD 14) Augustus authorized a large variety of denarii. They generally carried his likeness on their obverse with the inscription "Augustus, son of the divine one" (that is, son of Julius Caesar, who had been voted divine honors by the Roman senate). One type of reverse showed Augustus' grandson Gaius galloping to the right, with three legionary standards in the background. That coin first appeared about 8 BC, shortly before Jesus was born. A second reverse a few years later (2 BC–AD 3) showed Gaius and Lucius, another grandson, dressed in togas, facing each other with shields and spears in between. Above them were sacrificial implements. The legend read "Gaius and Lucius Caesar, the sons of Augustus, consuls elect, leaders of the youth." Tragically for the hopes of Augustus, both of those grandsons, who he had hoped would follow him on the throne, died before he did—Lucius from illness in AD 2 and Gaius a year later from a wound received during military service in Armenia.

In Matthew 22:19 Jesus asked those trying to trick him with a question to show him a coin used to pay the government tax. They handed him a denarius bearing the portrait and inscription of "Caesar" (Mt 22:21). That coin could have been a denarius of Augustus, who had died some 16 years before, or of Tiberius (AD 14–37), who was then on the throne.

The silver denarius of Tiberius read "Tiberius Caesar Augustus, son of the divine Augustus." The reverse showed the high priestess of the vestal order, flaming torch in hand, seated on her throne facing right. The title "pontif(ex) maxim(us)" referred to Tiberius rather than to the priestess. A companion coin was the golden aureus bearing a similar portrait of Tiberius and reading the same as the denarius. The reverse showed a four-horse chariot with words referring to Tiberius' seven triumphal entries into Rome and to his 17th term as a tribune of the Roman people. That pinpoints the date of the coin at AD 15 or 16.

Tiberius, who died perhaps seven years after the crucifixion of Christ, was succeeded by his grandnephew Gaius Caesar, also known as Caligula. Early in his reign Caligula removed Pontius Pilate from office and placed control of Judea in the hands of Herod Agrippa. Believing himself to be divine, Caligula gloried in sadistic excesses and acted without restraint of morality or law. The denarius of the period showed his portrait with an inscription. The reverse commemorated Augustus, who was seen accompanied by stars and exalted to divine status in heaven.

After the assassination of Caligula in AD 41, Claudius was chosen as successor by the Praetorian Guard. During his reign a severe famine afflicted the Near East, necessitating the collection of a relief fund by Paul among the new Christian churches in Macedonia and Greece. The denarius of Claudius gave the emperor's title and on the obverse showed a winged figure of Peace with a healing wand of entwined serpents and a snake to the right, with the words "For the peace of Augustus." His reign did not remain peaceful very long. Claudius was murdered in AD 54, and his stepson Nero succeeded to the throne.

According to early church tradition the martyrdoms of the apostles Peter and Paul took place during Nero's reign, at a time when Christians were being made scapegoats for a disastrous fire that raged through the city of Rome in AD 64. Peter and Paul would have been familiar with the coins of Nero's reign. The denarius usually had an inscription naming Nero as emperor and giving him the title "Father of his country." The reverse showed a seated goddess facing left. Her name, Salus, could be translated as "salvation," "health," or "well-being." On the gold aureus the obverse gave the information that it belonged to the reign of the emperor Nero. The reverse showed a soldier facing left with a spear, with an inscription that referred to Nero's 10th term as a tribune of the Roman people, which would place the coin in the year AD 63.

Besides the denarii in circulation in the

time of Christ, larger silver coins also existed. Since the Romans themselves minted no silver coins above the size of a denarius, payment in large silver coins had to be made in Greek or Near Eastern issues, with legends in Greek rather than in Latin.

Palestinian Coinage After Herod Agrippa I.

After Herod Agrippa's death a succession of obscure Roman procurators were appointed by Claudius to administer Judea. We have no evidence that they minted coins during their terms of office. During the six-year administration of Antonius Felix, however, a fairly plentiful quantity of bronze lepta was issued, first under Claudius until AD 54, then under Nero. In AD 59 Felix was replaced by Festus (Acts 24:27), a freedman from the household of Claudius. The bronze lepta from his period showed the name of the emperor and on the reverse a wreath containing the name of the empress. Lepta from Nero's time featured two tall shields crossed with two javelins, plus an inscription. The reverse showed a fruiting date palm, with another name used by Nero. No procurator ever ventured to put his own name on any of the bronze lepta of the period, inscribing instead the name and title of the reigning emperor or his empress.

The lepta of Festus, less plentiful than those of Felix, carried a vertical palm branch with the regnal date and the simple inscription "Of Nero Caesar." The reverse bore the single name of Nero with a wreath. No other issues are known from that period.

Herod Agrippa II (see Acts 25, 26) also minted bronzes, always of a non-Jewish type. Under emperors Nero, Vespasian, and Domitian he struck coins, largely at Caesarea Philippi, featuring the reigning emperor's portrait and titles on the obverse, and such reverse images as Nike, Tyche (another Greek goddess), a war galley, or a palm tree. The legend often included the regnal year, and always the emperor's name.

Coins of the Jewish Revolts.

Coinage was minted during both the first (AD 66–70) and second (AD 132–35) Jewish revolts. During the four years of the First Revolt a great surge of patriotic fervor and hope arose as the rebels looked for the coming of the Messiah to crush the power of Rome. At that time the revolutionaries set up a mint in Jerusalem and issued many coins, not only lepta but larger bronze coins plus silver shekels and half shekels. The designs were Jewish, the inscriptions in Hebrew only. One lepton carried an amphora or chalice, with dates indicated as "Year 2" or "Year 3"; since AD 66 was considered the beginning of a new messianic age, the hopeful freedom fighters measured time from that date. The reverse of the lepton showed a vine leaf, symbolic of Israel as the Lord's vineyard, with a legend reading "The freedom of Zion."

One larger bronze coin had two bundles or baskets of fruit and branches on the obverse with the date "Year four and a half." The reverse showed a palm tree with two baskets of fruit below it and the legend "Of the redemption of Zion." The silver shekel displayed a chalice without handles but adorned with a border of pearls. The inscription, "The shekel of Israel," proclaimed the establishment of the new state; over the chalice appeared the date "Year 2." The reverse had a sprig of three pomegranates (or possibly the head of Aaron's rod that budded) with the inscription "Jerusalem the holy." The legends were in an ancient epigraphic style of alphabet, probably intended to conform to the times of David and Solomon, although the spelling was generally that of the intertestamental period (4th to 1st centuries BC).

The silver half shekels carried the same chalice and abbreviated date, plus a legend reading "The half shekel." The reverse was identical to that of the shekel. All the devices used on the First Revolt series have been adopted for the coinage of modern Israel, a testimony to the artistic quality of those designs. One modern Israeli coin, the half lira of 1961, carries on its reverse a careful replica of the chalice side of the half-shekel coin just described, complete with the old epigraphic Hebrew script.

After the fall of Jerusalem in AD 70 one might expect that no more official coins were minted in Palestine. For the most part that was true, at least for Jewish state mintage, although certain cities continued to issue bronze coins even after the destruction of the Jewish state. After the revolt had been crushed and Jerusalem destroyed, the Roman government issued victory commemoratives. Best known is the large bronze sestertius series, which bore a portrait of Vespasian on the obverse with his title and a numeral serving to date the coin. The reverse displayed a tall date palm, a familiar symbol from earlier Jewish coinage, with either a Roman commander standing at the left or a mournful, bearded Jew. Sitting to the right, bent over with grief, was a mourning Jewish woman. The inscription read "Captive Judea." The word "captive" did not appear on the silver denarius of the same series.

Coinage of the Second Jewish Revolt was bronze and silver, and many of the designs of palm trees, palm wreaths, vine leaves, and grape clusters familiar on earlier Jewish coins were used. One unusual design depicted a four-column portico surmounted by a star with the ark of the covenant in the background. Because the temple treasury had been seized, metal was in short supply during the Second Jewish Revolt. As a result, many coins of earlier times were simply overstruck with the words "Deliverance of Jerusalem." The coins of the Second Revolt were the last Jewish issue minted in Palestine until establishment of the modern state of Israel in 1948.

HAZEL W. PERKIN

See MONEY AND BANKING; MONEY CHANGER; MINERALS, METALS, AND PRECIOUS STONES.

Bibliography. F.A. Banks, *Coins of Bible Days*; K.A. Jacob, *Coins and Christianity*; F.W. Madden, *History of Jewish Coinage and of Money in the Old and New Testaments*; H. Mattingly, *Roman Coins*; C.H.V. Sutherland, *Coinage in Roman Imperial Policy 31 BC–AD 68*; R.S. Yeoman, *Moneys of the Bible*.

Col-hozeh. The father of Shallum, who was ruler of the district of Mizpah (Neh 3:15). Col-hozeh, the son of Hazaiah in Nehemiah 11:5, may be another person.

Color. The OT and NT have no exact word for "color," although the word appears several times in our English Bibles. The words translated "color" have quite different meanings in the original languages.

The word most frequently translated "color" in the KJV literally means "eye" and suggests "appearance" (Lv 13:55; Nm 11:7; Prv 23:31; Ez 1:4,7,16,22,27; 8:2; 10:9; Dn 10:6). Only Leviticus 13:55 retains the translation "color" in the RSV. Other words translated as "color" in the RSV refer to facial appearance (Dn 5:6,9,10; 7:28), fabrics of variegated colors (Prv 7:16; Ez 17:3; 27:24), stones (1 Chr 29:2), and breastplates (Rv 9:17). Joseph's "coat of many colors" (Gn 37:3 KJV) and Tamar's "garment of divers colors" (2 Sm 13:18,19 KJV) were either long-sleeved robes or richly ornamented tunics that served as a mark of preferred status.

In the NT, a word that means "pretense" is used archaically in Acts 27:30 and was interpreted as "color" by the KJV translators. They also added the word "color" to Revelation 17:4, evidently to clarify the meaning.

Though many colors are mentioned in the Bible, colors are not particularly singled out for emphasis. Natural colors are seldom mentioned in descriptions. Colors that appear frequently and that are most carefully differentiated are manufactured colors, especially dyes.

Colors Mentioned in the Bible. Because the Hebrews perceived color differently than we do in Western culture, it is sometimes difficult to translate precisely the various Hebrew words denoting colors. Thus there is often a wide variation in translations of such words in English Bibles. To provide a base for comparison this article will follow the RSV except as noted.

Colors mentioned most often in the OT and NT are the following:

Black is the translation of five words in the OT and one in the NT, expressing varying degrees of darkness. The words describe the color of lambs (Gn 30:32,33,35,40), hair (Lv 13:31,37; Sg 5:11; Mt 5:36), skin (Jb 30:30), horses (Zec 6:2,6; Rv 6:5), the sky (1 Kgs 18:45, Jer 4:28; Is 50:3), the day (Jb 3:5; Mi 3:6), the darkened sun (Rv 6:12), and an invading army (Jl 2:2). Job's "blackness" (Jb 30:28) has been understood as disease or sadness.

Blue probably refers to a blue-purple dye obtained from Mediterranean mollusks. A popular color, it was considered less desirable in antiquity than "royal" purple. Both dyes were produced in Tyre, which at one time had a monopoly on the manufacture of blue and purple dye (2 Chr 2:7,14; Ez 27:24). Ships of Tyre had awnings of blue and purple (Ez 27:7). Blue was used in the tabernacle fabrics (Ex 26:1; Nm 4:6,7,9), the priests' garments (Ex 28:5,6), in Solomon's temple (2 Chr 2:7,14), and in the Persian court (Est 1:6; 8:15). Blue is not mentioned in the NT.

Crimson is the English translation of three different Hebrew words. This red color of varying shades was derived from certain insects. The word describes certain fabrics in Solomon's temple (2 Chr 2:7,14; 3:14) and was used figuratively to describe sin (Is 1:18). The word translated "crimsoned" to describe garments from Bozrah (Is 63:1) probably means "vivid colors" rather than a specific hue.

Gray, a color found only in the OT, is used exclusively to describe old age—as in gray hair or gray-headed (Gn 42:38; 44:29,31; Dt 32:25; 1 Sm 12:2; 1 Kgs 2:6,9; Jb 15:10; Ps 71:18; Prv 20:29; Is 46:4; Hos 7:9). A different word used to describe dappled gray horses (Zec 6:3) probably means "spotted" or "speckled."

Green translates seven words in the OT and two in the NT. Most of the words refer to vegetation and are descriptive of the fresh or moist condition of plants rather than their color. The following are described as "green": plants (Gn 1:30), trees (1 Kgs 14:23), branches (Jb 15:32), pastures (Ps 23:2; Jl 2:22), herbs (Ps 37:2), olive trees (Ps 52:8; Jer 11:16), thorns (Ps 58:9), leaves (Jer 17:8), grass (Mk 6:39; Rv 8:7), and wood (Lk 23:31). In addition to various plants, a dove's wing (Ps 68:13), a couch (Sg 1:16), and a righteous person (Ps 92:14) are also described as "green." Idolatrous worship practices took place under "every green tree" (Dt 12:2; 2 Kgs 16:4; Is 57:5; Jer 2:20; Ez 6:13), although the word actually describes the luxurious growth of the leaves rather than their color.

Another word, "greenish," is derived from

one of the OT words for "green" and refers to disease (Lv 13:49) and fungus that forms on the walls of houses (Lv 14:37).

Purple was the most highly valued dye in the ancient world. Encompassing shades varying from actual purple to red, it was obtained from mollusks of the Gastropoda class. The first people to use the dye were perhaps the ancient Phoenicians, whose name may come from a Greek word meaning "blood-red." At any rate, the Phoenicians monopolized the purple industry for many years. Some of the fabrics used in the tabernacle (Ex 25:4; 26:1), in the garments of the priests (Ex 28:5–8,15,33), in Solomon's temple (2 Chr 2:7), in the upholstery of Solomon's chariot (Sg 3:10), and in decorations of the Persian court (Est 1:6) were purple. Purple was customarily worn by wealthy people and royalty (Jgs 8:26; Prv 31:22; Dn 5:7). Mordecai was rewarded with a garment of purple (Est 8:15). Daniel was given a similar garment (Dn 5:29). It was worn by Assyrian soldiers (Ez 23:6). Jeremiah described idols that were robed in blue and purple garments (Jer 10:9). Ships of Tyre had awnings of blue and purple (Ez 27:7), and purple dye was an item of trade between Tyre and the people of Aram (Ez 27:16). It is used once to describe the color of hair (Sg 7:5).

References to purple in the NT are fewer than in the OT but affirm the continued economic importance of the dye. Purple clothing denoted wealth (Lk 16:19). Jesus was robed in purple by Roman soldiers (Mk 15:17,20; Jn 19:2,5; cf. Mt 27:28, "scarlet"). The purple and scarlet garment of the harlot Babylon symbolized royal rank (Rv 17:4). Lydia of Thyatira was a seller of purple fabrics (Acts 16:14).

Red frequently refers to the natural color of certain objects mentioned in the Bible: skin (Gn 25:25), pottage (Gn 25:30), the eye (Gn 49:12, though the word used here may mean "sparkling" or "dark"), a sacrificial heifer (Nm 19:2), water (2 Kgs 3:22), the face of a weeping person (Jb 16:16), wine (Prv 23:31), the eyes of one drinking wine (Prv 23:29), clothing (Is 63:2), a shield (Na 2:3), and horses (Zec 1:8; 6:2). It is used figuratively to describe sin (Is 1:18). A leprous disease (Lv 13:49), a spot on the skin (Lv 13:19,24,42,43), and fungus on the wall of a house (Lv 14:37) were discolored with a reddish hue.

The Red Sea is mentioned frequently in the OT (Ex 10:19; 15:4), but the Hebrew words thus translated actually mean "Sea of Reeds." However, in the NT the Greek word is actually the word "red" (Acts 7:36; Heb 11:29).

In the NT, red is used to describe the color of the sky (Mt 16:2,3), a horse (Rv 6:4), and a dragon (Rv 12:3).

Scarlet, a brilliant red hue derived from cer-tain insects, was used for fabrics and yarns and was highly valued in the ancient world (Rv 18:12). It is difficult to distinguish between "scarlet" and "crimson" in the Bible.

A scarlet thread was bound to the hand of Zerah at birth (Gn 38:28,30). The word describes certain fabrics in the tabernacle (Ex 25:4; 26:1,31,36; 27:16), the priests' garments (Ex 28:5,6,8,15,33), rope (Jos 2:18,21), clothing (2 Sm 1:24; Prv 31:21; Jer 4:30), lips (Sg 4:3), and soldiers' uniforms (Na 2:3). Some kind of scarlet material was used during the ratification of the covenant at Sinai (Heb 9:19), for the cleansing of a leper (Lv 14:4,6) and of a house (Lv 14:49,51,52), for covering the articles on the table of the bread of the Presence (Nm 4:8), and for the ritual of the red heifer (Nm 19:6). Matthew described Jesus' robe at his trial as scarlet (Mt 27:28). The woman of Revelation 17:3,4 was dressed in purple and scarlet and seated upon a scarlet beast. The luxury associated with Rome is suggested by the description of clothing of purple and scarlet (Rv 18:16). Scarlet, like crimson and red, is also used figuratively of sins (Is 1:18).

Sorrel was the color of a horse in Zechariah's vision (Zec 1:8). Some believe that the Hebrew word translated "sorrel" was a bright red color; others visualize a pale yellow or speckled.

Vermilion, a red pigment obtained from red ocher (an iron oxide), is mentioned only twice in the Bible. It describes the houses of the wealthy (Jer 22:14) and Chaldean garments (Ez 23:14). Vermilion was also used for painting idols and pottery.

Violet translates a Hebrew word found in Jeremiah 10:9 (RSV). Elsewhere the word is translated "blue."

White translates a number of words found in the Bible. It is generally the color of natural objects such as goats (Gn 30:35), hair (Lv 13:10; Mt 5:36; Rv 1:14), diseased skin (Ex 4:6; Lv 13:4,17), manna (Ex 16:31), snow (2 Kgs 5:27), milk and teeth (Gn 49:12), horses (Zec 1:8; 6:3; Rv 6:2; 19:11), a donkey (Jgs 5:10 KJV, RSV tawny), wool (Ez 27:18), special stones (Rv 2:17), light (Mt 17:2), clouds (Rv 14:14), and fields ready for harvest (Jn 4:35). It is used to describe the color of curtains (Est 1:6), clothing (Est 8:15; Eccl 9:8; Dn 7:9; Mk 16:5; Rv 3:5,18; 4:4), the garments of angels (Jn 20:12; Acts 1:10), and a throne (Rv 20:11). It is used figuratively to describe cleansing from sin (Ps 51:7; Is 1:18; Dn 12:10) and the appearance of princes (Lam 4:7).

Yellow is mentioned rarely in the OT and not at all in the NT. It refers to the color of hair when a leprous disease is present (Lv 13:30,32,36) and to the greenish-yellow color of a dove's wings (Ps 68:13, KJV, RSV green).

Symbolic Uses of Colors. It is difficult to determine what the different colors symbolized in the ancient world. Some interpreters find no significance at all in the colors found in the Bible, whereas others do. According to Philo, a Greek-speaking Jewish writer who lived at the time of Christ, white represented the earth; purple, the sea; blue, the air; and scarlet, fire—reminiscent of the four basic elements of earthly matter in Aristotle's philosophy. Ancient rabbis thought they could identify nations with the colors of Zechariah's horses (e.g., red stood for Babylon because that empire had shed much blood). The Scofield Reference Bible (1909) interprets the colors in the tabernacle symbolically: gold represented deity; silver, redemption; bronze, judgment; blue, heaven; purple, royalty; and scarlet, sacrifice.

It is probably unwise to insist that each color in the tabernacle hangings symbolized something. Only a few colors are given explicit significance in the Bible; further, no rule says that a color given symbolic meaning in one usage will always retain that meaning. The following colors frequently have symbolic meaning in the Bible: red, war and bloodshed (2 Kgs 3:22); black, gloom or mourning (Is 50:3); white, purity or righteousness (Is 1:18); green, prosperity and health (Ps 92:14); purple, royalty or honor (Mk 15:17). Those colors have maintained similar symbolic associations to the present day.   F. B. HUEY, JR.

See CLOTH, CLOTH MANUFACTURING; DYE, DYER, DYEING.

Colossae. Ancient city in Asia Minor, located in the southwestern part of present-day Turkey, and remembered primarily for the apostle Paul's letter to the church there (Col 1:2). Colossae was near the Lycus River, a tributary of the Meander. The city flourished during the 6th century BC. According to Herodotus, an ancient Greek historian, when the Persian king Xerxes came to Colossae, it was a city of great size. Another Greek historian, Xenophon, related that Cyrus the Great, founder of the Persian empire, had passed Colossae still earlier on his way to Greece.

Colossae was situated in the region known as Phrygia and was a trading center at a crossroads on the main highway from Ephesus to the east. In Roman times relocation of the road leading north to Pergamum brought about both the growth of Laodicea, a city 10 miles away, and Colossae's gradual decline. Colossae and Laodicea shared in the wool trade. Thus the name Colossae was derived from a Latin name *collossinus,* meaning "purple wool."

In the apostle Paul's time Colossae was a small city with a mixed population of Phrygians, Greeks, and Jews. During his extended stay in Ephesus, Paul may have taught Jews and Greeks who lived in Colossae (Acts 19:10). Epaphras, a Colossian, visited Paul in Rome and informed him about the condition of the church at Colossae (Col 1:7; 4:12), then was later imprisoned with Paul (Phlm 23). Others from the Colossian church included Philemon, Apphia, Archippus, and Onesimus, a slave who became a Christian (Phlm 16). Subsequent history is silent on the church at Colossae. The city was weakened under Islamic rule and was eventually destroyed in the 12th century.

In 1835 archaeologists discovered the acropolis, theater, and other structures together with inscriptions from ancient Colossae at a site near Chonas. Recent archaeological investigations have been conducted near Tell Hüyük.

Colossians, Letter to the. NT book, one of four "prison letters" attributed to the apostle Paul. As with Philippians, Philemon, and Ephesians, Paul said he was in prison when he wrote Colossians (Col 4:3,10; cf. Eph 3:1; 4:1; 6:20; Phil 1:12–14; Phlm 9,10). He sent three of the letters to churches in Asia Minor and linked them with his colleague, Tychicus (Col 4:7–9; Eph 6:21,22). That seems to indicate

Colossae, the city in which tradition says Paul wrote Colossians.

that he wrote them at approximately the same time and that Tychicus delivered them.

Author. Though tradition that Paul wrote Colossians stands on solid ground, many scholars today debate its authorship. Reasons for their doubts fall into two main categories—theology and style.

First, some scholars question Paul's authorship on theological grounds. Development of certain major theological themes in Colossians differs from the way they are set forth in the undisputed letters of Paul. In Colossians the doctrine of Christ is developed on the basis of a hymn about Christ in 1:15–20. There he is seen as the "firstborn of all creation"; all things owe both their origin and continuing existence to him. In him resides all the fullness of deity. His death is interpreted not as a victory over sin, law, and death, but as a triumph over the cosmic authorities and powers.

To some scholars that suggests that the Christology in Colossians is much more "exalted" than in any of the undisputed letters. Yet Paul characteristically regarded Christ as highly exalted. He declared Christ to be creator of all things (1 Cor 8:6) and set forth his lordship over the whole cosmic order by citing another hymn (Phil 2:6–11). Further, the kind of statements made about Christ in Colossians was demanded by the situation that had arisen in the city of Colossae. The heresy that had broken into the congregation required such statements.

Colossians also appears to teach doctrines about "the last things" and baptism that are somewhat different from the doctrines in the undisputed letters. In Corinthians, Paul based his teaching about the last things on the Jewish doctrine of the "two ages." Judaism taught that in "this age" the world is under the tyranny of the evil powers, but that in "the age to come" God would set it free. In contrast, Paul's teaching was unique in holding that the age to come had already come in the advent of Christ—though not in its fullness. Paul saw the time between the first and second advents of Christ as a period of conflict. Christ "must reign until he has put all his enemies under his feet" (1 Cor 15:25). Christ by his mission is liberating the present age from the evil powers, but the conflict will not end until his second coming. Therefore Christians live in hope of his future appearing. That future element of hope is not stressed in Colossians (though see 3:1–4); rather, the emphasis is on a hope already present in heaven (1:5).

The doctrine of baptism in Colossians has been influenced by the stress on the realized aspect of hope. In his letter to the Romans, Paul taught that baptized Christians live by faith in the resurrected Lord and are filled with hope for their future resurrection (Rom 6:1–11, especially vv 5,8). In Colossians he declared that baptized believers have not only died with Christ, but have already been raised with him (2:12,13; 3:1). The hope for the future is not for resurrection, but for the manifestation of the life that is already "hid with Christ in God" (3:2,3). Further, in Romans Paul stated that in baptism Christians have died to sin, so they no longer need serve it. Colossians, on the other hand, states that in Christ, Christians died to what can literally be translated as the "rudiments of the universe" (2:20). Many interpret that phrase to mean the basic religious teaching of the world. In Colossians, however, a strong case can be made that the phrase means "the elemental spirits of the universe" (as RSV translates it). In either case the emphasis, if not the meaning, differs from Romans.

Such theological matters have led many to believe that Paul could not have written the letter to the Colossians. Rather, they see the letter as the product of a disciple of Paul who wrote at a later time. It should be noted, however, that the differences are of perspective or emphasis. They are not differences that result in contradiction.

The second reason for questioning Paul's authorship of Colossians is literary, pertaining to vocabulary and style. The brief letter uses 34 words that occur nowhere else in the NT. Also, common Pauline terms are absent from passages where they might be logically expected. Further, the style of the letter, though similar to Ephesians, is notably different from other undisputed letters of Paul. In those letters the thoughts are usually developed in an argumentative style similar to the discussions of the Jewish scribes. Colossians is marked by stylistic features that one finds in hymns, liturgies, and early Jewish and Christian catechisms.

But some obvious differences in theological perspective and literary style do not force one to conclude that someone other than Paul wrote Colossians. Scholarly opinion is divided. Perhaps the following discussion about the use of tradition in Colossians provides a solution to the problem.

Understandably, Paul's originality has sometimes been exaggerated in the past. His conversion was dramatic; he needed to declare defiantly his independence from the Jerusalem apostles. Hence many have come to regard him as a sort of "solitary colossus" whose extraordinary intellectual power made him the innovator of great theological ideas. Paul was certainly a man of unusual intelligence, but to say that his theology was completely independent of his predecessors is untrue.

Paul's great respect for the traditions of

the early church is shown by his frequent references to those traditions in his letters. He often used the semitechnical terms "to deliver" and "to receive" when citing an authoritative tradition. Sometimes the traditions had to do with doctrine (e.g., 1 Cor 11:23–25; 15:3–7). At other times the traditions had to do with behavior (1 Cor 11:2,17; 1 Thes 4:1–8; 2 Thes 2:5; 3:6). Many passages in his letters appear to be quotations from or allusions to hymns sung about Christ (Phil 2:6–11; Col 1:15–20), to confessional sayings (Rom 1:3,4; 3:24,25; 4:25), to words from the Lord (1 Cor 7:10,11; 9:14; 1 Thes 4:15), or to other kinds of traditional materials.

In no other letter attributed to Paul are traditional materials more common than in Colossians. Although it is difficult to isolate the traditions with precision, the following passages are based on materials the early church probably used in worship and teaching:

1. Colossians 1:12–20 and 2:14,15 are hymns and confessional units celebrating the creating and redeeming activity of Christ.

2. Colossians 3:5–14 is a highly structured catalog of vices and virtues, perhaps based on early Christian baptismal materials.

3. Colossians 3:18–4:1, the so-called "household code," consists of a series of admonitions to the members of a household. The same kind of series is also found in Ephesians, 1 Peter, the pastoral epistles, and many early Christian writings outside the NT.

Add to all this the fact that the structure of Colossians reflects an established letter-writing form, and nearly one-third of the letter can be seen to be based on traditional materials, which clearly influenced the style, vocabulary, and theological perspectives of the letter. Further, the problems concerning authorship cluster in precisely those sections.

The impressive amount of traditional mate-

rial shows that Paul regarded it as extremely important for his readers. He demonstrated that by his admonition, "As therefore you received Christ Jesus the Lord, so live in him, rooted and built up in him and established in the faith, just as you were taught, abounding in thanksgiving" (2:6,7). Note his use of "received" and "taught." Paul's readers were to base their ethical conduct on the authoritative teaching about Christ. For that reason the apostle warned the Colossians not to be deceived by the "philosophy" and "empty deceit" of their opponents, which was "according to human tradition, according to the elemental spirits of the world, and not according to Christ" (2:8).

Date, Origin, and Destination. The date of Colossians depends on where Paul was imprisoned when he wrote. Traditionally scholars have held that all four "prison letters" came from Rome. If so, Paul would have written them between AD 60 and 62.

The Book of Acts indicates three places where Paul was imprisoned: Philippi, Caesarea, and Rome. Paul, writing 2 Corinthians before either of the last two imprisonments, suggested that he had already been in prison many times (2 Cor 11:23). Ephesus is a likely place for one of those imprisonments (cf. Acts 19, 20; 1 Cor 15:32; 2 Cor 1:8–10). Consequently an increasing number of scholars name that city as the probable place where Paul wrote the prison letters. If that is correct, Paul wrote Colossians sometime between AD 52 and 55.

The Ephesian theory is especially appropriate for Philippians, but the Roman hypothesis seems better for Philemon, Colossians, and Ephesians, thus leading to AD 60–62 as the date of Colossians.

Background Material. To identify the teaching that endangered the church at Colossae is a difficult task. The problem is not insufficient

Villa on Palatine Hill in Rome.

data, but the opposite. Historical research has uncovered a wealth of information about the religious beliefs and practices that proliferated in the 1st-century Roman world. Asia Minor was a particularly fertile region for religions. Many people even belonged to more than one religious sect, and it was common to select ideas and practices of several religions. Christians were not exempt from those tendencies.

Colossian Heresy. Paul gave no formal definition of the Christian heresy in Colossae. Rather, he dealt with a number of issues without precisely identifying them. If one is given only the answers to a number of questions, however, it may be possible to re-create the questions from them. The reader of Colossians must attempt to define the tenets of the false teaching on the basis of Paul's response to them.

Some scholars have concluded that the heresy rose out of the flesh-spirit dualism that became characteristic of later Greek and oriental Gnosticism. The later Gnostics taught that the material order of things is evil, so only what is free from matter is good. Other scholars, noting Paul's injunctions against certain food laws, festivals, sabbaths, and external circumcision, have concluded that the false teaching rose out of Jewish beliefs. Since the tendency to blend a variety of ideas was so prevalent, both theories are probably true.

Paul regarded the heretical teaching as a "philosophy" based on human tradition (2:8). His prayer for the Colossians (1:9–11) and certain other remarks (1:26–28; 2:2,3) suggest that he was countering the notion that for certain people "philosophy" led to some special, perhaps magical, understanding. That philosophy was based on "the rudiments of the universe."

That phrase, "the rudiments of the universe," is open to two main lines of interpretation. (1) The basic meaning of rudiments is "objects that stand in a row or series," such as the letters of the alphabet. It can readily be extended to mean rudimentary principles or basic teaching. Such is the meaning in Hebrews 5:12, where the term refers to the "first principles" of God's Word. (2) The Greeks applied the phrase to the four physical substances they thought made up the world: earth, water, fire, and air.

A 1st-century BC Greek text, referring to the followers of the philosopher Pythagorus, uses several of the same words that Paul applied to the Colossian heresy. A messenger of the highest gods carries the soul through all the elements of the world, from the lowest of earth and water to the highest. If the soul is pure, it remains in the highest element. If not, it is returned to the lower ones. The required purity is achieved by self-denial and certain cultic observances. The upper air contains the sun, moon, and stars, regarded as gods who control human destinies. In addition, the atmosphere around the earth is filled with spirit powers who are to be reverenced. In that way the elements of the world become associated with the gods and spirit powers who hold all people captive and determine their fate. With the help of magical knowledge and cultic ceremonies human beings could not only escape from the destiny imposed by the spirit powers but even manipulate them for their own advantage.

To summarize, the phrase "rudiments of the universe" can refer either to basic religious teaching or to the spirit powers of the universe. The statements in Colossians make the latter meaning probable. Through his cross Christ has triumphed over the rulers and authorities and has publicly exposed them (2:15). They do not rule the world order; he does (1:16–20). The divine "fullness" dwells in Christ, not in a remote deity (1:19; 2:9). The spirit powers are under the authority of Christ (2:10) and owe their existence to him (1:16). The "worshiping of angels" (a practice probably including homage paid to heavenly powers) is so wrong that it may have disastrous consequences (2:18).

Main Features of the Heresy. A major dogma of the Colossian philosophy seems to have asserted that God was remote and inaccessible. Two factors point in that direction. First, the fascination with the angels and spirit powers just discussed seems to indicate that the remote God was accessible only through a long chain of intermediaries. Christ seems to have been regarded as one of them, perhaps enthroned above them. Second, the philosophy evidently held to a dualism that separated the high God from creation. To approach him seekers first had to be delivered from the evil influence of the material order.

How could human beings short-circuit or manipulate the angelic star powers who hindered them from reaching the high God? How could they be delivered from the enslaving power of matter? The philosophy evidently offered magical wisdom and insight as the answer. Through worshiping angels and observing special days and cultic practices (2:16–18), seekers could placate or please the intermediaries and get through to the divine "fullness." By voluntary self-abasement, self-denial, and the achievement of visions (2:18,21–23) they could escape the pull of the material order. The practice of self-denial through abstinence from food and possibly from sexual relations ("touch not" in 2:22) seems to have been limited to special seasons for attaining the "vision" of God. Otherwise the philosophy seems to have permitted freedom to engage in libertine practices (3:5–11).

Purpose and Teaching. A warning in Colossians 2:8 points to the main purpose of the Colossian letter. The readers are admonished against following anyone who "makes a prey of you by philosophy and empty deceit, according to human tradition, according to the elemental spirits of the universe, and not according to Christ." A false teaching was settling in and threatening the health of the congregation, so Paul wrote Colossians to counter it.

Paul approached the heresy by contrasting its teachings with the correct teaching his readers had received in the traditions previously delivered to them, probably by Epaphras (1:7; 4:12,13). God through Christ had qualified them to be uniquely his own people, his church (1:12–14). The proponents of the false teaching threatened to disqualify the Colossians from that favored position by persuading them not to hold fast to Christ, the Head of the church (2:18,19). Consequently the traditions Paul cited mainly teach about Christ or about the church. The former are primarily related to the impressive hymn about Christ (1:15–20; referred to again in 2:9,10—the latter mainly associated with baptism).

Christ. In 1:15–20 Christ is celebrated as the preexistent creator of all and as the divine redeemer of all. The "all" has cosmic dimensions. It includes the earth and the heavens, the visible and the invisible, the church and the universal powers. All things, including the heavenly powers, own their existence, sustenance, and destiny to Christ. He is not to be regarded as one of the heavenly mediaries. He is the preeminent one in whom all the fullness of God dwells (1:19; 2:9) and in whom human beings find fulfillment (2:10).

Paul gave special attention to the significance of Christ's death. In the hymn of Colossians 1 he explained the reconciling work of Christ by the phrase "making peace through the blood of his cross" (1:20). He contrasted the past and present experiences of the readers. Formerly they were alienated from God both in attitude and behavior. Now they are reconciled "in his body of flesh by his death" (1:21,22). As a consequence of that reconciliation, God transforms human character.

The death of Christ not only brings about restored relationships between individuals and God, but it also liberates them from the hostile intentions of the "principalities and powers." Those powers seem to be demonic agents who bring accusations against human beings—accusations grounded on a "certificate of indebtedness" based on ordinances (laws). Paul proclaimed to the Colossians that God had removed the ground of those accusations, nailing it to the cross (2:14), and that in the cross he had publicly exposed and triumphed over the accusers (2:15). Christ's death was not a tragedy but a life-changing, liberating triumph over sin and evil powers.

The Church. The church is the "body" of Christ (1:18,24), over which Christ is the Head and source of life (2:19). It is a community that the Father has qualified to participate in the heavenly inheritance with the saints; he has delivered it from the powers of the evil age and made it participate in the power of the age to come, "the kingdom of his beloved Son" (1:12,13). The church, therefore, should not live in fear of the "rulers" and "authorities," but should participate in Christ's triumph over those hostile powers.

Baptism. How does the church participate in this victory achieved by Christ's death? To answer that question Paul referred to circumcision and baptism. He linked both of those sacramental terms to Christ's death and the Christian's participation in its consequences (2:11–15). The baptismal theme is implicit in the admonitions that follow: "If with Christ you died" (2:20–23); "If then you have been raised with Christ" (3:1–4); "Put to death therefore what is earthly in you" (3:5); "You have put off the old nature with its practices and have put on the new nature" (3:9,10); "put on then, as God's chosen ones, holy and beloved" (3:12). Christians have been baptized into Christ; by virtue of that fact they participate in the liberating triumph of his death and the energizing power of his life.

Content. In writing to the Colossians, Paul followed a standard letter form of salutation, thanksgiving, prayer, main body, and concluding remarks. The salutation (1:1,2) carries greetings to the church from himself and Timothy. Then follows a statement of thanksgiving for the good condition of the community (1:3–8) and a prayer that the Colossians may be filled with a knowledge of God's will, which will result in worthy conduct (1:9–11).

The first part of the body of the letter summons the Colossians to praise and then quotes and applies the great hymn about Christ (1:12–23). Specifically, the first part begins with a confessional thanksgiving to the Father for calling them to be his own unique people (1:12–14). A hymn follows, celebrating Christ as the sovereign Creator and Redeemer of all that exists (1:15–20). The Colossians are participants in the results of Christ's reconciling ministry (1:21–23).

The second part of the body of the letter describes Paul's apostolic ministry (1:24–2:5). His was the task of making known the mystery of God concerning Christ to the Gentiles in general (1:24–29) and to the churches of Colossae and Laodicea in particular (2:1–5).

The third part of the body of the letter introduces Paul's primary concern for the Colossian congregation: they are to follow the received tradition about Christ (that is, the teachings about Christ they had first accepted), and not to fall prey to the current false teaching (2:6–23). They are to walk in the light of the received tradition (2:6,7), and they are warned against the false philosophy (2:8). The hymn of 1:15–20 is again referred to, here stressing Christ's divine lordship (2:9,10) and proclaiming his victory over the principalities and powers (2:11–15). Because of such a Christ, the Colossians are exhorted not to submit to the regulations and tenets of the false teaching (2:16–23).

The fourth part of the body of the letter summons the church to a life befitting Christians (3:1–4:6). Those who have been raised with Christ are to seek the things that are above (3:1–4). That means they are to put off the traits and attitudes listed in a catalog of vices (3:5–11) and to put on the traits and attitudes listed in a catalog of virtues (3:12–14). In worship they are to conduct themselves in a unified and orderly way (3:15–4:1). The so-called "household code" concerning marriage, children, and slavery (3:18–4:1) appears in a context dealing with worship (3:15–17; 4:2–6). The most pressing admonitions in the code are addressed to wives and slaves, groups that especially would crave the equality promised in the gospel (Gal 3:28; note Col 3:11). So Paul probably used the code to call for order in the public worship service.

Paul concluded his letter by first stating that Tychicus and the recently converted slave, Onesimus, would inform the church about his circumstances (4:7–9), and then adding a series of greetings (4:10–18).

GEORGE E. CANNON

See COLOSSAE; PAUL, THE APOSTLE; APOSTOLIC AGE; ACTS OF THE APOSTLES, BOOK OF THE.

Bibliography. F.F. Bruce, *The Epistles to the Colossians, to Philemon and to the Ephesians*; G. Demarest, *Colossians*; R.C. Lucas, *Fullness and Freedom*; R.P. Martin, *Colossians and Philemon*; H.D. McDonald, *Commentary on Colossians and Philemon*; H.C.G. Moule, *Colossians and Philemon Studies*; E. Schweizer, *The Letter to the Colossians*.

Comforter. KJV translation of the Greek word *parakletos* in John 14:16,26; 15:26; and 16:7.

See PARACLETE.

Command, Commandment. See COMMANDMENT, THE NEW; LAW, BIBLICAL CONCEPT OF; TEN COMMANDMENTS, THE.

Commandment, The New. Christ's commandment for Christians to love each other. The phrase "new commandment" occurs four times in the NT, all in the writings of John (Jn 13:34; 1 Jn 2:7,8; 2 Jn 5). Initially it was a command given by Jesus to his disciples on the night of his arrest: "A new commandment I give to you, that you love one another; even as I have loved you, that you also love one another" (Jn 13:34). The same command occurs elsewhere (Jn 15:12,17; Rom 13:8; 1 Pt 1:22; 1 Jn 3:11,23; 4:7,11,12), but is not called "new" in those passages.

Love as a Commandment. Jesus had already commanded his disciples to love their enemies (Mt 5:43–45) and to love their neighbors as themselves (Lk 10:25–37). The "new commandment" demanded that Christians love each other. In no sense did it overrule the other two love commands. Jesus' command to love those within the church was intended to produce a compelling testimony to those outside the church. It would offer them demonstrable proof (1) that his followers were Christlike in their love toward one another; (2) that the basis for vital human community could be found "in Christ"; and (3) that, by extension, what Jesus said about himself and his work was really true (Jn 13:35; 17:21–23).

Jesus chose the word used to describe the OT Law, giving similar authority to his new commandment. In fact, the Law included commands to love (Lv 19:18,34; Dt 10:19). The apostle Paul thought of love as the "law of Christ" (Gal 6:2), and James called the love command "the royal law" (Jas 2:8) and "the perfect law of liberty" (Jas 1:25; 2:12).

The word "commandment" had another meaning as well. Many Jews in Jesus' day wrongly supposed that the commandments were given in order that men, by obeying them, could show themselves worthy of God's blessing (Rom 9:32; Gal 3:2). Jesus made it clear, however, that love was a natural result of God's blessing, not a necessary condition for it. For Jesus the commandment expressed how one who is already living in the joy of God's blessing should act. Disciples were commanded to love in the same sense that branches were "commanded" to bear fruit: the branch by abiding in the vine; the Christian by abiding in Christ (Jn 15:4).

What Made It New? The character of the new commandment comes from the "new covenant" (Jer 31:31–34; Lk 22:20; 1 Cor 11:25) which Jesus inaugurated at the Last Supper. Under the new covenant, God "writes" his law on the hearts of believers (Heb 10:16). That is, he actively works in them in the person of the Holy Spirit (Ez 36:27; 2 Cor 3:3), and gives them a new willingness to obey him (Rom 8:4;

Gal 5:16). The new commandment of love is the all-embracing, single requirement of the new covenant (Rom 13:8,10; Gal 5:14). Obedience therefore is a gift, because "love is from God; and every one who loves is born of God" (1 Jn 4:7 NASB). It is the fruit of faith (1 Jn 3:23) and part of the gospel itself (1 Jn 3:11).

The close relationship between the new covenant and the new commandment may explain partly why the command to love was called "new." Christ's incarnation inaugurated a new age. "The darkness is passing away," John wrote, "and the true light is already shining" (1 Jn 2:8). Anticipating his ascension into heaven (Jn 13:33–35), Jesus left one inclusive commandment to preserve his disciples in the new age until its consummation at the judgment day (Jn 5:28,29; 1 Jn 4:17). Obedience to the new commandment was supposed to identify them as Jesus' disciples during his absence (Jn 13:35; 17:21–23). The love command was thus new in the sense that it had a special function in the new age.

What made the age new was that Jesus Christ's coming had revealed God the Father with an unprecedented and incomparable clarity (Jn 1:18; 10:30; 17:6–8). No prophet had ever been able to say, "He who has seen me has seen the Father" (Jn 14:9). Therefore Jesus' demand that the disciples love each other "as I have loved you" (Jn 13:34) was, by every human standard, new and astonishing. No human had ever loved perfectly like Jesus ("to the uttermost," Jn 13:1, NASB margin). To follow his example of love, then, was a new commandment. The greatness of Jesus' love moved him to "lay down his life for his friends" (Jn 15:13). Accordingly John drew the conclusion that "we ought to lay down our lives for our brothers" (1 Jn 3:16 NIV). It follows that love means never shutting one's heart against another Christian in need (1 Jn 3:17), but rather rejoicing to sacrifice one's temporal good for another's blessing.

In the new commandment Christians are called not just to copy but to share in the love of God. Jesus prayed to his Father, "I made known to them thy name, and I will make it known, that the love with which thou hast loved me may be in them, and I in them" (Jn 17:26). The prayer followed naturally from two things Jesus said: "Love one another as I have loved you" (Jn 15:12); "As the Father has loved me, so have I loved you" (Jn 15:9). Thus to love as Jesus loved is to love *with* the very love of the Father for the Son (Jn 17:26). As John put it, "If we love one another, God abides in us and his love is perfected in us" (1 Jn 4:12; cf. 2:5). Therefore the love commandment is new because it summons us not only to mirror, but also to experience, God the Father's love for

his Son—a love that had never been so clearly revealed before the incarnation.

Why, then, does 1 John 2:7,8 stress that the new commandment is *not* new but old? The phrase "from the beginning" (also found in 1 Jn 2:24; 3:11; 2 Jn 6) no doubt refers to the beginning of the readers' Christian experience, that is, when they first heard the word of the gospel. Thus John meant that he was not teaching anything beyond the original message. His command was the same old "new commandment" that they heard when they first believed. He probably stressed its "oldness" because of false prophets in the churches (1 Jn 4:1) who were leading people into heresy by new and different teaching (2 Jn 9). The best protection against that deception was to obey what Jesus taught "of old," including the new commandment (2 Jn 6,7).

See TEN COMMANDMENTS, THE; LAW, BIBLICAL CONCEPT OF; NEIGHBOR.

Commerce.   See INDUSTRY AND COMMERCE.

Communication.   Archaeological excavations have uncovered thousands of ancient business and family letters written on clay tablets. As early as 2000 BC the Assyrians maintained an informal postal service with eastern Anatolia (Asia Minor), using the caravans that frequently went between them. Later, Assyrian roads used by the army were also traveled by royal messengers of an efficient government mail service. A network of postal officials stationed in key population centers supervised the couriers and the mail. Clay tablets listing the place-names along a given route and the distances between them served as travel guides. Many royal letters of Assyria and other parts of the Middle East now help to reconstruct ancient history.

After the Persians ascended to power, they expanded the Assyrians' postal service. The Persian "royal road" was built for government messengers, but it was open to all. It extended more than 1,600 miles from Sardis in Asia Minor to Susa, the Persian capital located near the head of the Persian Gulf (Est 3:13; 8:10). Royalty and officials traveling that highway found rest houses and inns about 15 miles apart, forts at strategic points, and ferries for river crossings. Ordinary travelers, averaging 18 miles a day, would spend three months traveling the full length of the road. The Persian dispatch service, however, relaying messages on fresh mounts between regular stages, probably traversed the same distance in two or three weeks. Describing a Persian messenger, the Greek historian Herodotus in the 5th century BC reported that neither snow nor rain

The Appian Way—a road that Paul traveled as a prisoner on his way to Rome.

nor heat nor gloom of night prevented the swiftest possible completion of their appointed rounds.

At the same time as the Persians, the Chou dynasty in China had built up an efficient postal system. By the 3rd century BC, the Han dynasty of China and the Ptolemies of Egypt were operating the closest thing to a modern postal system that the ancient world was to know. A system of communication necessary to rule the large Roman empire was devised in the reign of Caesar Augustus (27 BC–AD 14). The idea for the system came after the Romans annexed Egypt in 30 BC. The Roman system did not stress speed or regularity, and although the mail moved speedily over short distances, it could take weeks over long distances or over water. Usually the mail system of the emperors did not benefit the ordinary public; rather, it was an added tax burden. Wealthy families had their own slaves deliver mail, businesses employed letter carriers, and the poor asked traveling friends to carry messages.

A letter written by Christian leaders in Jerusalem to the churches of Asia Minor was delivered by the apostle Paul and Barnabas (Acts 15:22–29). Later, Paul requested Timothy (1 Thes 3:2), Tychicus (Col 4:7,8), and Epaphroditus (Phil 2:25; 4:18) to serve as messengers.

One means of local communication was the Roman *album* (Latin for "white"), a white-painted public bulletin board displayed in the center of a city on which messages were painted in black.

Fire, light, and smoke signals were probably the earliest methods of communicating over any distance. The Babylonians were the first to employ a primitive heliograph system (reflected sunlight) for signaling over short distances. A classic use of fire beacons was related by Aeschylus, a Greek dramatist, who described the news of the fall of Troy being relayed to Clytemnestra of Mycenae (c. 1084 BC) by a dozen or more fires lighted on mountaintops. Similarly, the Lachish letters mention use of fire signals to coordinate Israel's defense against the Babylonians in 587 BC. One letter concludes, "Let my lord know that we are watching for the fire signals of Lachish according to the signs my lord has given, because we do not see Azekah" (see Jer 6:1; 34:7). Later, fire signals were communicated from lighthouses such as the famous one at Alexandria (Egypt).

Projected sounds have been used as a means of communication for thousands of years. Around 550 BC, Cyrus of Persia built a network of towers from which a soldier shouted a message to a soldier in a nearby tower. According to legend, Alexander the Great had a giant megaphone that could carry a voice several miles. The historian Severus said that the Romans had brass speaking tubes to aid in defense along the northern wall in England. The Hebrews used the shofar, a ram's horn trumpet, to announce the new moon, the beginning of the sabbath, and the approach of danger (Jos 6:4; Jgs 7:16; Hos 8:1). Also, drum tatoos were used in communication. Even today Ashanti drummers in Ghana can render high and low tones that correspond to the tonal values of their language.

Thus in the ancient world the chief ways of communicating were writing in various forms, fire signals, and magnified sounds.

AUSTIN H. POTTS

See TRAVEL AND TRANSPORTATION.

Communion, Holy. *See* LORD'S SUPPER, THE.

Compassion. Quality of showing kindness or favor, of being gracious, or of having pity or mercy. In the Bible, God is described as being like a compassionate father to those who revere him (Ps 103:13). Jesus Christ exemplified God's compassion in his preaching and healing (Mt 9:36; 14:4), in his concern for the lostness of humanity (Lk 19:41), and finally in his sacrifice on the cross (Rom 5:8). The church is to demonstrate compassion as one facet of the love Jesus commanded (Mt 5:4–7; Jn 13:34; Jas 2:8–18; 1 Jn 3:18). In scriptural usage compassion is always both a feeling and the appropriate action based on that feeling.

In the OT, compassion describes one aspect of God's covenantal relationship with his people. One of the Hebrew words translated compassion is derived from a root word meaning "womb," thus comparing God's love with maternal love. God's compassion, however, went beyond simply feeling the emotion; it was always demonstrated by definite acts that testified to his covenant with Israel. In spite of Israel's rebellions God still had compassion on his people (2 Kgs 13:23; 2 Chr 36:15; Ps 78:38), as well as on all his creation (Ps 145:9). When Israel was chastised, the nation often feared that God had permanently withdrawn his favor (Ps 77:9; Is 27:11; 63:15; Jer 13:14; 21:7; Hos 13:14). Yet God's compassion would revive, and he would restore his people (Dt 30:3; Ps 135:14; Is 14:1; 49:13; 54:7,8; Jer 12:15; 30:18; Mi 7:19; Zec 12:10), especially when they returned to him and cried out for deliverance (1 Kgs 8:50; Ps 79:8).

In the NT, Jesus Christ, the Son of God, exactly reflected the Father's compassion in his dealings with a fallen humanity. Jesus healed diseases and infirmities, cast out spirits, and empowered others and sent them out to do likewise. He fed hungry people and, in response to a mother's grief, raised her only son from the dead. Following Jesus' example, Christians are to show compassion in dealing with others. Jesus set forth the example in the parables of the good Samaritan, who had compassion on a wounded traveler (Lk 10:33), and the prodigal son, whose father had compassion on him when he returned home (Lk 15:20).

The apostle Paul listed a number of qualities that the Colossian church "as God's chosen ones" was to incorporate; the first was compassion (Col 3:12). It was to be an integral part of the concept of Christian community. The Greek word means literally "to be moved in one's bowels." The term thus pointed to the very core of one's inner feelings, much as the term "heart" does today. One's intense inner feelings should always lead to outward compassionate acts of mercy and kindness.

Conaniah. 1. Levite and chief officer who supervised tithes, contributions, and the dedicated things given to the temple during the reign of Hezekiah (2 Chr 31:12,13, KJV Cononiah).

2. One of the chief Levites during the time of King Josiah (2 Chr 35:9); perhaps identifiable with Jeconiah in 1 Esdras 1:9.

Concision. KJV translation in the text of Philippians 3:2, meaning "mutilation of the flesh."

Concubinage. Practice of a man cohabiting with a woman who is regarded only as his sexual partner or as a secondary wife in his household, of lower station than his primary wife. Concubinage was practiced in many ancient cultures, especially in Mesopotamia, where the king maintained a harem and where a private citizen might have one or two concubines in addition to his primary wife. Both types of concubinage are referred to in the Bible. A concubine was often a slave or part of the booty of war (Jgs 5:30).

A man might have a concubine simply as an economical form of marriage, since no dowry or bride-price was required. A concubine could add to a man's prestige by giving him two wives and thus an increased capacity for children. Such offspring were normally delivered onto the knees of the legal wife, thus establishing their legitimacy as family members. The concubine was also another servant to add to his work force.

In the patriarchal period, concubinage was customary (Gn 22:24; 35:22; 36:12), especially when the primary wife was childless (Gn 16:1–3; 25:5,6; 1 Chr 1:32). A concubine could exercise certain rights and secure recognition and inheritance for her offspring (note Gn 49:1–28, where sons of Bilhah and Zilpah were included along with the sons of Leah and Rachel; cf. Gn 35:22–26). The custom was not suppressed by the Mosaic law, which must have included concubines in its treatment of multiple wives (Dt 17:17; 21:15–17).

Concubinage continued through the period of the judges. Gideon had a concubine (Jgs 8:31), as did an unnamed man of Levi's tribe (Jgs 19). Abuse of that man's concubine by men from Benjamin's tribe caused a bloody civil war (Jgs 20, 21).

During the period of Israel's monarchy the luxury of concubines could be afforded only by kings such as Saul (2 Sm 3:7), David (5:13; 15:16), Solomon (1 Kgs 11:3), and Rehoboam (2 Chr 11:21). Royal harems existed in many other cultures of that time, including Egypt, Persia (Est 2:14), and Babylon (Dn 5:2,3,23).

Concubines were thus a legitimate part of many ancient cultures, even when a society acknowledged the superiority of monogamous marriage. Concubinage was fostered by a desire for prestige and a large family, but could at times degenerate into a license for sexual freedom (cf. Eccl 2:8). Concubinage was part of the contemporary Greek and Roman cultures, but it was not in keeping with the teachings of Jesus (Mt 19:1–9).

See FAMILY LIFE AND RELATIONS; CIVIL LAW AND JUSTICE; MARRIAGE, MARRIAGE CUSTOMS.

Conduit. Water tunnel or channel. In the OT the Hebrew word can mean rivulets in the ground made by rain (Jb 38:25 channel; Ez 31:4 stream) or a simple trench such as Elijah dug around the altar in his encounter with the prophets of Baal, a Canaanite fertility god (1 Kgs 18:31–38).

A water tunnel was constructed during King Hezekiah's reign to bring water from the Gihon spring, located outside the walls of Jerusalem, to inside the city proper (2 Kgs 18:17; 20:20; Neh 2:14 pool; Is 7:3; 22:9,11 pool; 36:2). The mouth of the spring was sealed and its water diverted into the city through the conduit to keep Israel's enemies from using the spring during a siege of the city. That tunnel expanded a tunnel begun by earlier inhabitants of the city, the Jebusites. David and his men may have entered Jerusalem through that first tunnel to overthrow the Jebusites (2 Sm 5:8).

See ARCHITECTURE; SILOAM, POOL OF.

Coney. Small, rabbitlike animal declared unclean in Leviticus 11:5 and Deuteronomy 14:7 (KJV; RSV rock badger).

See ANIMALS (BADGER).

Confectioner. KJV rendering of perfumer in Exodus 30:35 and 1 Samuel 8:13.

See TRADES AND OCCUPATIONS (PERFUMER).

Confession. Admission, especially of guilt or sin; also, a statement of religious belief. "To confess" can mean to agree, to promise, or to admit something.

In the Bible. Two types of confession occur in the Bible. First, individuals confess that

they have sinned and are therefore guilty before God, often confessing a particular sin (Lv 5:5; 1 Jn 1:9). In such confession one agrees or acknowledges that he or she has broken God's Law (Ps 119:126), that its penalty is justly deserved (Rom 6:23), and that in some specific way God's standard of holiness has not been met (Lv 19:2; Mt 5:48).

In OT times the high priest would confess the sins of the whole nation (Lv 16:21); the nation of Israel was expected to confess when it had rebelled against the Law of God (Lv 26:40; 2 Chr 7:14). Pious Jews were quick to confess; Daniel, Ezra, and Nehemiah confessed their nation's sins, agreeing with God that his punishment of the people (including themselves) was just, yet praying for God's mercy and deliverance (Dn 9:20; Ezr 10:1; Neh 1:6).

Second, individuals confess that God is God and that he rules the world (1 Chr 29:10–13), that he is faithful in showing his love and kindness (Ps 118:2–4), and that he has helped his people (Ps 105:1–6). Such confession or agreement, expressed publicly in worship or song (Ps 100:4), is spoken of in the OT as "blessing the Lord."

The two types of confession are often combined in the Bible, producing many psalms of thanksgiving. In general those psalms contain some or all of the following ideas: (1) I sinned; (2) I became ill and nearly died; (3) I prayed to God, who delivered me; and (4) now I offer this song of confession, which I promised him (Pss 22; 30; 32; 34; 40; 51; 116). The same Hebrew word means both "praise" and "confession of sin"; the two meanings were part of a single concept. The psalmist began by admitting sin and God's justice and ended by confessing God's forgiveness and delivering power.

Both those meanings also occur in the NT. Christians confess (that is, they declare as a matter of conviction and allegiance) that Jesus is the Christ and that they belong to him. "Whosoever therefore shall confess me before men, him will I confess also before my Father which is in heaven" (Mt 10:32 KJV). Not to confess Christ is the same as denying him (Mt 10:33; Lk 12:8; cf. 2 Tm 2:11–13; Rv 3:5). The Christian life therefore begins with a confession of faith, a public delaration before witnesses (Rom 10:9,10; 1 Tm 6:12). An additional dimension of the Christian's confession is provided in 1 John 4:2: one must confess that "Jesus Christ has come in the flesh," that is, acknowledge Jesus' divinity and preexistence as the Son of God (that he "has come"; see also 1 Jn 4:15) as well as Jesus' humanity and incarnation (that he has come "in the flesh"). The Greek word "confession" literally means "saying the same thing." The Christian's "good confession" is modeled after the pattern of Christ's confession (1 Tm 6:12,13).

In only a few passages does the NT discuss confession of sin. Those being baptized by John the Baptist publicly admitted their sins and repented (Mk 1:4,5). All Christians, in fact, must agree with God that they are sinners; otherwise "we deceive ourselves, and the truth is not in us" (1 Jn 1:8). James presented a fuller picture: when a Christian is ill, the elders are to visit and give the person opportunity to confess any sins. As in the psalms, forgiveness and healing (the moral and the physical) are tied to confession. Recalling that principle, James urged Christians to confess their sins to one another (Jas 5:13–16).

In the Church. Both types of confession continued to be practiced in the church. During the first 300 years of the church, confessing Christ publicly, especially in a court of law, was very important. Those who did so were honored with the title "martyr" (from a Greek word meaning "witness" or "confessor"), whether or not they were actually put to death for their faith. During that same period, in addition to congregational confessions of sin (which continue in virtually all churches), any Christian who sinned seriously was required to make a public confession in church.

After Constantine legalized Christianity and accorded it privileged status, confessing Christ in court became obsolete. Personal confession of serious sin continued, although Leo I (pope, AD 440–61) made it private rather than congregational. The Celtic monks in Ireland in the 6th century initiated the practice of confessing all sins to a spiritual director. That practice was brought to the European continent by British scholars in the early 9th century. It became widespread, and at the Fourth Lateran Council (AD 1215) annual confession to a priest became mandatory on penalty of excommunication.

Formal, secret confession continued as an important practice in the Roman Catholic Church. By the late Middle Ages it was a central part of an elaborately refined sacrament of penance. The sacrament consisted of contrition (remorse and repentance), confession (admission of the sin to a priest), and satisfaction (restitution or punishment, at the priest's instruction). Penance culminated in absolution, a formal declaration that the sinner was forgiven, which could be pronounced, according to Roman Catholic doctrine, only by a priest.

The Roman Catholic Church distinguishes between venial sins (minor transgressions that may be excused or overlooked) and mortal sins (serious transgressions that deprive the

soul of saving grace). In Roman Catholic belief a Christian who commits a mortal sin and dies without formally confessing it hazards damnation. The Reformation largely rejected that belief, holding that one who embraces Christ as Savior is delared by God to be forgiven and acquitted once and for all.

Having rediscovered the concept of justification by faith, Martin Luther called the Roman Catholic practice of penance "a means of oppression and extortion." At first he retained a modified form of penance but later dropped it as a sacrament. After 1520 Luther held that confession of sins was still "obligatory" and that "secret confession" to another Christian, although not required by Scripture, was "useful and even necessary."

John Calvin also commended private confession for any believer who is "troubled and afflicted with a sense of sins, so that without outside help he is unable to free himself from them." Calvin suggested that the pastor be turned to as a source of comfort, but approved of confessing to any other church member.

The Prayer Book of the Church of England provides for the private confession of sins by the sick to the clergyman who visits to give Holy Communion. This provision, made in the 16th century, was used by Anglo-Catholics of the 19th century to revive and defend the practice of auricular confession prior to the receiving of Holy Communion by all communicants. This practice still continues in parts of the Anglican Communion much the same as it does in the Roman Church.

From time to time various Protestant groups have taught the value of confessing sins to one another or to the whole church. Sometimes this is based on scriptural suggestions and sometimes on psychological theories. However, in general, confession of sins is made by Protestants only to God in the privacy of personal prayer. In church a general confession is often used, but this is couched in general terms and thus allows for the private confession of sins to God.

PETER H. DAVIDS

See FORGIVENESS; REPENTANCE; CONVERSION.

Congregation. Assembly of people, particularly for religious purposes. The Bible describes Israel as the congregation of the Lord because it was a covenant nation. The whole nation was considered to be the people of God (Ex 3:6–8,15,16; 4:22; 12:6; Is 1:2–4).

As a chosen nation, Israel had a unique position (Is 42:1; 45:4; 65:9,22). It was to display God's greatness in the midst of other nations during the OT period (Dt 4:6–14). Because of its function the whole nation was called "the assembly of the congregation of the people of Israel" (Nm 14:5; see also Lv 4:13; Nm 16:3).

The church of the NT owes much to the spiritual heritage transmitted by the OT congregation of God's people. This relationship of the church to the OT people of God is highlighted in several places (Heb 2:10–13; 1 Pt 2:9,10; see also Gal 6:16; Rom 9:1–8).

See CHURCH.

Congregation, Mount of the. KJV translation for "mount of assembly," the name of a mountain that figured in Babylonian and Canaanite mythology, in Isaiah 14:13.

See ASSEMBLY, MOUNT OF.

Coniah. Alternate name for Jehoiachin, king of Judah, in Jeremiah 22:24,28 and 37:1.

See JEHOIACHIN.

Cononiah. KJV spelling of Conaniah the Levite, in 2 Chronicles 31:12,13.

See CONANIAH #1.

Conquest and Allotment of the Land. Terms referring to Israel's winning of the Promised Land and the distinctive way in which it was divided among the Israelite tribes.

Conquest. The conquest of Canaan by the Israelites is one of the remarkable events of OT history: a loosely organized nomadic people successfully invaded a long-established culture secure in its protected urban centers. That achievement, according to the Scriptures, was a necessary consequence of a promise God had made to Abraham, Isaac, and Jacob that their descendants would possess the land (Gn 17:8; 26:4; 28:13; Ex 3:15–17). Dispossession of the pagan inhabitants was a divine judgment on false religion and its associated immorality (Dt 7:1–5).

Scholars who attempt to reconstruct the history of the conquest face certain problems. Critical scholarship has run into conflict with statements in the Bible at three key points: chronology, rate of occupation, and the issue of Israel's military annihilation of portions of the population of the Canaanite city-states.

Date. Reference works and scholarly treatments of OT history often suggest a date for the exodus from Egypt in the 13th century BC (1280 BC or later). Several biblical references to that event would seem to call for an earlier date. According to 1 Kings 6:1, construction of Solomon's temple was begun in the fourth year of his reign, 480 years after the exodus. Since Solomon's fourth year was about 960 BC, that would place the exodus at 1440 BC. In

Judges 11:26–28 when Jephthah, 8th of the named judges, argued with the king of Ammon about Israelite possession of land east of the Jordan River, he indicated that Israel had occupied this territory 300 years. Saul's accession to kingship about 1020 BC was still some decades off, so the later date proposed for the exodus does not allow sufficient time for the period of the judges. Further, the apostle Paul referred to a period of about 450 years from the exodus to Samuel's day (Acts 13:19).

Archaeological evidence is inconclusive. Conflicting arguments have been drawn from the same data, depending on whether the interpreters are adherents of the early or late date for the exodus. The controversy extends to excavations done at sites overrun in Joshua's campaigns. A notable example is Bethel, where a level showing that the town was burned (dated *c.* 1200 BC by archaeologists) is assumed to be evidence of Joshua's capture of the town. The Bible, however, makes no mention of his burning that city.

Joshua's Campaigns. A picture of a concentrated period of Israelite conquest of Canaan is given in the Book of Joshua. Yet many scholars insist that an earlier gradual penetration occurred (by Hebrews who supposedly did not accompany Jacob into Egypt), plus an extended mopping-up procedure that continued down to the time of the monarchy. Although the biblical record allows for later acquisitions in some areas (Megiddo and Bethshan, e.g.), there is no valid reason for rejecting the description of the major conquest given in Joshua 1–12.

The conquest began on the east side of the Jordan River under Moses. After Moses' death Joshua led Israel across the river, capturing first the fortified cities of Jericho and Ai. Those strategic victories provided access to the hill country and drove a wedge into the middle of Canaan. Two major campaigns followed—a southern and then a northern—which won for Israel in six years' time the key cities of Canaan, defeating 31 kings and concluding the initial and principal stage of the conquest.

Numbers 32 records the earlier assignment of territory east of the Jordan (Gilead and Bashan, acquired by the defeat of two kings, Sihon of the Amorites and Og of Bashan) to the tribes of Reuben, Gad, and half the tribe of Manasseh. Though their land had already been acquired, the men of those tribes were obligated to cross the Jordan with the rest to participate in the military conquest of Canaan itself.

Joshua 2–8 records the unusual events of the destruction of Jericho and Ai in the initial thrust westward. Those victories tended to de-

A tomb at Jericho (c. 1600 BC).

the service of their gods, and so to sin against the Lord your God" (Dt 20:18). Bloodthirsty caprice was not the cause of what would today be considered racial genocide. It was the righteous command of the Lord of life, the Judge of all people.

In Abraham's time the wickedness of the Amorites was not yet "complete" (Gn 15:16), but by Joshua's time it was. Archaeology has documented the sexual perversions, child sacrifices, idolatry, and cruelty of the Canaanites. The Land of Promise was intended to be swept clean of such abominations so that Israel could live an unhampered life, ordered by the covenant law of their God.

Allotment. The Promised Land was divided among the Israelite tribes by "casting lots," a method analogous to drawing straws or tossing a coin. The same method was used at other times in Bible history as a means of determining the divine will.

The specific territory in Canaan to be occupied by each of the 12 tribes of Israel was not left to their own initiative. They were not to possess whatever land they could wrest for themselves by military conquest. Rather, they were ordered to fight unitedly and then divide the total area by casting lots. Besides avoiding arguments or intertribal fighting, the procedure had theological significance. The outcome was placed solely in God's hands (see Prv 16:33). The Lord thereby reminded his people that the land was his to apportion as he saw fit. In Numbers 26:52–56 the Lord's order for such a lottery was given (see also Nm 34). In Joshua 13–19 the allotment was planned and carried out, ending with the statement that this was done "at Shiloh before the Lord, at the door of the tent of meeting" (Jos 19:51).

Assignment of the southern part of Transjordan to two and a half tribes had already been made by Moses (Nm 32). West of the Jordan the remaining nine and a half tribes received portions by lot after their faithful leader, Caleb, got his choice of the region around Hebron. The order in which the tribes were named somewhat follows their relative locations. The territory of the major southern tribe, Judah, included Caleb's lands and extended north to the yet unconquered Jerusalem. Next came the large central portions of the tribes of Ephraim and (half-) Manasseh, the patriarch Joseph's sons. Benjamin's area lay between Judah and Ephraim. Then Simeon's territory was named, lying in southern Judah. The remaining tribes listed in Joshua 19, with one exception, received territorial inheritance north of Manasseh. They were Zebulun, Issachar, Asher, Naphtali, and Dan. Dan's tribe drew an allotment west of Judah, but because the Philistines held the coastline,

moralize the remaining cities of the land. Chapters 9 and 10 describe the southern campaign, including the Gibeonites' procurement of a treaty by deception. In the subsequent fighting an alliance of five Amorite kings was crushed, the kings were killed, and the city-states of the area were destroyed, except for Jerusalem (later captured by David). Joshua 10, with its account of the remarkable rout of the enemy forces (vv 9–12) and miraculous prolonging of daylight, is the central passage about the southern campaign.

In his northern campaign Joshua confronted a more formidable alliance. Yet even the powerful king of Hazor, largest of the Canaanite cities, supported by his local vassals, was no match for Israel's armies. Joshua 11 describes that phase, then sums up the entire conquest in verses 16–23 and on through chapter 12.

Treatment of the Canaanites. Many have expressed objection to the apparent cruelty of the Israelites in wiping out the Canaanite people, sometimes calling it "barbarism." It should be noted, however, that total annihilation was not practiced everywhere, but only in Jericho and Ai and the later punishment of the Amalekites under Saul (1 Sm 15). As in the earlier conquest of the Midianites (Nm 31:17, 18), not all the population was killed. In Deuteronomy 20:10–18 and 21:10–14, a distinction is drawn between the treatment of Canaanites (actually a heterogeneous group; see Dt 20:17) and other captive peoples. With the Canaanites, the command to "save alive nothing that breathes" (Dt 20:16) was given "that they may not teach you to do according to all their abominable practices which they have done in

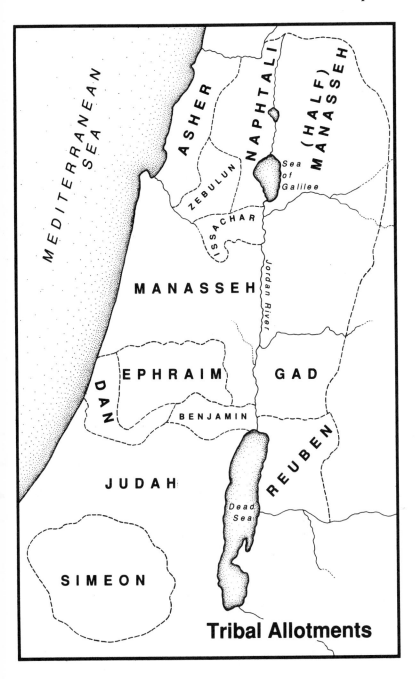

Tribal Allotments

Dan's tribe migrated north and renamed the captured city of Laish for their tribal ancestor, Dan (see Jgs 18). From then on, "from Dan to Beersheba" meant all of Israel.

Such a method of assigning real estate seems strange to present-day economics, yet with respect to the customs of that time, it made theological sense. Kings and emperors in the ancient Near East were considered sovereign representatives of their gods. They held the ownership right to all lands and gave portions to whomever they pleased. From the time of the exodus, Israel was a theocracy. God was king. No human authority was sovereign or possessed sovereign property rights. God was the Israelites' sole benefactor, as Moses reminded them shortly before their entrance into Canaan: "For the Lord your God is bringing you into a good land, a land of brooks of water, of fountains and springs, flowing forth in valleys and hills" (Dt 8:7). Because God owned the land, he would apportion it and bless it.

The allotment of the land led to fulfillment of a prediction made several hundred years earlier by Jacob about his sons Simeon and Levi: "I will divide them in Jacob and scatter them in Israel" (Gn 49:7). Simeon later disappeared through assimilation into neighboring Judah. The Levites, on the other hand, were scattered throughout Israel for special service to the Lord. "Therefore Levi has no portion or inheritance with his brothers; the Lord is his inheritance, as the Lord your God said to him" (Dt 10:9).

The theme of Israel's inheritance of Canaan recurs throughout the rest of the Bible with rich spiritual overtones. Psalm 37:9, 29 refers to the land as the portion of the godly. By their sins the people eventually lost out and became exiles from their heritage, as some of the prophets predicted (Mi 2:3–5). But the prophet to the exiles, Ezekiel, envisioned an idealized alignment of tribal territories (see Ez 48), and at the end of the Scriptures the Book of Revelation returns to the theme of the 12 tribes (Rv 7:4–8). In that vision the surety of the inheritance of God's people is seen: God himself in the Spirit will live in all believers and provide them with all things (Rv 7:9–17). Those words echo the provisions of the Land of Promise (Dt 8:7–10; 11:11,12; Is 25:8; 49:10).

MILTON C. FISHER

See ISRAEL, HISTORY OF; JOSHUA, BOOK OF; CHRONOLOGY, OLD TESTAMENT.

Conscience.   Self-awareness that judges whether or not an act one has carried out or plans to carry out is in harmony with one's moral standards.

Both the English word "conscience" and the Greek word translated as "conscience" in the NT literally mean "to know together." In the OT, Adam and Eve hid themselves from God in shame because their consciences passed moral judgment on their disobedience (Gn 3:8–10). All human beings normally have the power of moral judgment: "The spirit of man is the lamp of the Lord, searching all his innermost parts" (Prv 20:27). Conscience, then, is a gift of God to provide light in matters of good and evil.

In the New Testament.   The word "conscience" is found 31 times in the NT, especially in the writings of the apostle Paul. Conscience, in Paul's writings, is regarded as passing judgment not only on conduct that has already taken place, but also on what ought to be done in the future. The behavior of people who are without God's Law shows that the Law's requirement is "written on their hearts" (Rom 2:14,15). Paul's statement that every person should "be subject to the higher authorities" to avoid God's judgment and "for the sake of conscience" presupposes that conscience can establish obedience as a moral requirement (Rom 13:5).

To approve, or pronounce "not guilty," is a function of conscience just as important as self-condemnation. Paul said, "I am not aware [using the same root word from which 'conscience' is derived] of anything against myself" (1 Cor 4:4). Yet conscience is neither a final court of appeal nor an all-sufficient guide: Paul went on to say, "I am not thereby acquitted. It is the Lord who judges me." In another passage Paul called on his conscience to verify his truthfulness, linking the verdict of conscience with the Holy Spirit (Rom 9:1; cf. 2 Cor 1:12) without developing the nature of that relationship.

Justifying his ministry to the Corinthians, Paul asked them to judge his conduct in the light of their own consciences (2 Cor 4:2). Insisting that God knew the motivation behind his conduct (that is, the "fear of the Lord"), he hoped that the Corinthians' conscience would also recognize it (2 Cor 5:11). When Paul wrote to Timothy, he linked a good conscience with sincere faith (1 Tim 1:5); when people depart from the faith, their consciences can become "seared" or rendered insensitive by their persistence in evil (1 Tm 4:2).

Answering a question about meats offered to idols, Paul spoke of the conscience as exercising judgment on prospective as well as on past behavior (1 Cor 8–10). Some had a conscience that was "weak" due to ignorance (1 Cor 8:7); they failed to understand that "everything is indeed clean" (Rom 14:20). Yet even a "weak conscience" should not be violated (1 Cor 8:10–13). Paul insisted that those who had a "strong conscience," who understood that "the earth is the Lord's, and everything in it" (1 Cor 10:26), should not encourage others to violate their consciences (1 Cor 8:9–13).

As a Guide.   In the apostle Paul's thought, conscience is not an infallible guide but a guide that requires instruction by the revealed will of God. Because he viewed humanity as fallen, Paul differed sharply from certain philosophical evaluations of conscience as an adequate barometer of the moral life. Conscience judges between right and wrong, but its judgment is made according to the standard furnished. For the Christian, conscience must operate within a framework of revelation, having its validity conditioned by scriptural instruction. Though human beings are made in the rational, moral, and spiritual image of God, hence with an interior moral sense, that sense is marred by a sinful nature. That is why Paul urged Christians not to be "conformed to this world" but to be "transformed" by the renewing of their minds, in order to "prove what is the will of God, what is good and acceptable and perfect" (Rom 12:2).

When Jesus said, "If you then, who are evil, know how to give good gifts to your children" (Mt 7:11), the implication was that everyone has some knowledge of good, however elementary or distorted. To crowds of people he said, "And why do you not judge for yourselves what is right?" (Lk 12:57); in the Greek, Jesus' words suggest that he expected an affirmative answer such as "That's right. We should." Paul's assertion of the universality of conscience, even in the pagan world, has already been mentioned (Rom 2:15).

Since knowledge of what is good has been distorted by sin, can conscience be a valid moral guide? Many ethicists hold that all moral intuitions are developed entirely through social training; others take a less extreme view. Certainly children's consciences are influenced by reinforcement of approved conduct and by discipline of misbehavior within the framework of family life. From a Christian point of view, although one's conscience is an inner witness to spiritual and moral truth, it cannot be regarded invariably as the voice of God. Jesus said, "If your eyes are good, your whole body will be full of light. But if your eyes are bad, your whole body will be full of darkness. If then the light within you is darkness, how great is that darkness!" (Mt 6:22,23 NIV; cf. Lk 11:34–36). No one has such a grasp on moral truth that his or her sinful nature may not overwhelm the conscience and render it unreliable.

The existence of conscience argues strongly for God's existence and reveals something about his nature; namely, that God always does what is right and that he punishes the transgression of his laws. Even unbelievers, simply from recognition of their moral nature, sense that they are ultimately responsible to God (Rom 1:19,20,32). The 18th-century philosopher Immanual Kant, for example, posited belief in God, freedom, and immortality on the basis of conscience. The Christian knows that behind conscience is a God who is personal, ethical, self-revealing, and the Creator, Sustainer, and moral Governor of the universe.

In essentially every culture certain kinds of conduct are approved or disapproved. Such evidence suggests that conscience cannot be explained merely on the basis of social convention or the preferences of individuals. Within the Christian community, where considerable diversity also exists, the standard of morality is not provided primarily by a narrow social structure but by a broad allegiance to biblical truth. Maturity comes as Christians recognize

themselves as part of a larger body, under the lordship of Christ, in which individuals "consider how to stir up one another to love and good works, not neglecting to meet together . . . but encouraging one another" (Heb 10:24,25). Fellowship is maintained and a good conscience preserved by "walking in the light" (1 Jn 1:7). A bad conscience is cleansed by confession of sin and the acceptance of God's forgiveness (1 Jn 1:9).   PAUL L. KAUFMAN

See MAN, DOCTRINE OF.

Bibliography. M.S. Enslin, *The Ethics of Paul;* C.A. Pierce, *Conscience in the NT;* A.M. Rehwinkel, *The Voice of Conscience;* N.D. Stacey, *The Pauline View of Man;* G.B. Stevens, *The Pauline Theology.*

Consecration. Separation of persons, utensils, buildings, or places from everyday secular uses for exclusive dedication to holy or sacred use. In the Bible consecration was effected through an appropriate rite or vow. Hebrew expressions imply "separation" (Ex 13:2; Lv 8:10–12; Dt 15:19), "dedication" (Lv 21:12; Nm 6:9), or "ordination" (literally, "filling the hand," Ex 28:41; 1 Kgs 13:33). NT references are fewer, but they frequently connote the idea of holiness (Jn 10:36; 1 Cor 7:14; 1 Tm 4:5).

In church usage, especially among hierarchical denominations, the term describes solemn rites that establish a bishop or other official in his office. It is also used to describe dedication of shrines, reliquaries, cathedrals, elements of the Mass, and lesser objects or buildings set aside for ecclesiastical functions.

Protestant teaching stresses the priesthood of every believer. Thus all Christians are "saints" (from the same root word as "consecration"), that is, devoted to God for life. In Roman Catholic doctrine the church consecrates (canonizes) great Christians as saints after they have died.

Consecration is significant in relation both to God and to the world. The apostle Paul spells out the term's Godward meaning in Romans 12:1,2. Its importance in relation to people and things is a basic theme of the apostle Peter's first letter. In everyday life each Christian is meant to live out a "holy" and "royal" priesthood for God's glory (1 Pt 2:9).

Christians consider the consecration of one's own personality by the work of the Holy Spirit to be an important mark of spiritual maturity.

Constellation. Certain number of stars in the sky, arbitrarily chosen as a group and named for an object, animal, or person which the outline of the group is said to resemble. A number of constellations are mentioned in the Bible.

See ASTRONOMY.

Consumption. Medical term historically referring to pulmonary tuberculosis. The word "consumption" appears twice in the Bible (Lv 26:16; Dt 28:22). However, it does not specifically mean tuberculosis but rather any chronic wasting disease process, perhaps including cancer, diarrhea, malnutrition, malaria, kidney failure, and other disorders.

In the biblical references consumption is listed as one of many medical symptoms threatening those who do not follow the commandments of the Lord.

See MEDICINE AND MEDICAL PRACTICE; DISEASES.

Conversion. Total change in one's direction in life or moral orientation. For Christians this means a change from an orientation that does not take God into account to one in which the person is submitted to Christ. Conversion is the process of which repentance is the entrance and faith the new direction; the same Hebrew and Greek words may be translated either "repentance" or "conversion."

In the OT conversion is basically a turning or returning from one's former course of life toward the Lord, the God of Israel. Israel often had to return to their God (Dt 4:30), either as individuals (Ps 51) or as a nation (Jer 4:1); foreign nations needed to turn to God for the first time (Ps 22:27). The characteristic feature is that one turns from wickedness (Ez 18:21,27; 33:9,11; Jer 26:3; 36:3), from a life of disloyalty to God to a life of obedience to God (Jer 34:15; Is 10:20,21; 44:2; Hos 14:4). Conversion means a change in inward orientation which finds expression in a changed life style.

In the NT John the Baptist begins the call to conversion (Mt 3:2; Mk 1:4; Lk 3:3), giving a prophetic call for people to change their minds (which is the root meaning of the Greek term) in the light of the nearness of God's kingdom. This change of life must include a change in actions to prove its reality (Mt 3:8; Lk 3:8). Jesus preached the same message (Mt 4:17; Mk 1:15), adding that since the kingdom had arrived in his person, obedience to him was part of the good news of conversion. Yet it was also bad news, for one would be damned if he failed to make this radical change (Mt 11:20; Lk 13:3,5). Conversion is radical but also simple, for it requires the simplicity of a child who commits his whole self, not the calculating self-protectiveness of the adult (Mt 18:3).

Outside the Gospels conversion is not a frequently used term except in Acts, where it forms the call to commitment climaxing evangelistic sermons (2:38; 3:19; 8:22), describes the commitment of new Christians to the Lord (9:35; 11:21), and pictures the change of life as a turning from darkness to light (26:18,20). Later writers look back upon conversion (2 Cor 3:16), worry about Christians converting to paganism or Judaism (Gal 4:19), and call for the reconversion of Christians who have left the faith and are in danger of judgment (Jas 5:19,20; Rv 2:5,16,22; 3:19).

As in the OT and in the preaching of John and Jesus, conversion has three factors. First, it is a turning *from* something, which includes specific sins, false gods, or simply a life lived for oneself (1 Thes 1:9; Rv 9:20,21; 16:11). Second, conversion is a product of the will of God and his gracious working in the world (Acts 11:18; Rom 2:4; 2 Cor 7:10; 2 Tm 2:25; 2 Pt 3:9). Third, conversion is a turning *to* someone, a commitment of one's whole life to God in Jesus Christ (Acts 14:15; 1 Thes 1:9; 1 Pt 2:25). It is thus a total reorientation, whether spectacular or undramatic, sudden or gradual, emotional or calm, in which a person transfers his or her total allegiance to God.

See REPENTANCE; JUSTIFICATION; SANCTIFICATION; GRACE; FAITH.

Bibliography. J. Bailke, *Baptism and Conversion*; W.E. Conn, ed, *Conversion*; E. Rontley, *The Gift of Conversion*; J. Schniewind, "The Biblical Doctrine of Conversion," *Scottish Journal of Theology* 5 (1952) pp 267–81.

Convocation, Holy. Solemn assemblies celebrated in Israel at appointed feasts in order that the people and the temple might be sanctified; the days were specially devoted to rest and sacrifice to God. Holy convocations were times set aside to make the nation holy enough to worship the Lord (Lv 19:2).

Holy convocations were included in the most important feasts and the Day of Atonement (Lv 23:27). The assemblies occurred on the first and seventh days of the feast of unleavened bread, or Passover (Ex 12:16; Lv 23:7,8). Work was forbidden, except cooking. Each sabbath was considered a holy convocation (Lv 23:2–4). The feasts of Pentecost, trumpets, and booths (tabernacles, KJV) each included days of holy convocation (Lv 23:21, 24,35–37).

It is thought by some that the holy convocation in Israel's fall harvest festival (the feast of booths) replaced the Canaanite celebration of the new year. The final assembly of that festival may have proclaimed the triumph of Israel's God over the forces of evil and famine. Lavish meals and festive garments accented the occasion.

In the feast of unleavened bread, atonement, sin, whole burnt, meal, and drink offerings combined to cleanse the Israelites before God (Nm 28:18–25). Abstaining from work allowed time for fasting and prayer. The feast of trumpets was a time "to blow the trumpets"

(Nm 29:1), a time for letting God speak without interruption.

The Hebrew words for "holy convocation" also referred to the time of the reading of the Law (Neh 8:8). Eventually the words became the technical name for the sacred Scriptures, since through the Scriptures the people were convoked or "called out" to become holy.

The holy convocation was prophetically viewed as a promise of the coming triumph of the kingdom of God (Is 4:5). The time of rest and communion with God pointed to a day of joy when God would come in power to triumph finally over his enemies and to sanctify his people.

See FEASTS AND FESTIVALS OF ISRAEL; ATONEMENT, DAY OF; SABBATH.

Cook, Cooking. *See* FOOD AND FOOD PREPARATION; TRADES AND OCCUPATIONS.

Coos. KJV spelling of Cos, an Aegean island and city, in Acts 21:1.

See COS.

Copper. Reddish-brown, malleable metal found in the ground (Dt 8:9) and fashioned into ornaments, tools, and coins.

See MINERALS, METALS, AND PRECIOUS STONES.

Coppersmith. *See* INDUSTRY AND COMMERCE; TRADES AND OCCUPATIONS.

Cor. Large dry measure.

See WEIGHTS AND MEASURES.

Coral. Calcareous skeletal deposits of marine organisms of a low order. The red coral of the Mediterranean was used for jewelry.

See ANIMALS; MINERALS, METALS, AND PRECIOUS STONES.

Corban. Greek transliteration of a Hebrew term (*korban*) that occurs only in Mark 7:11, where Mark provides an editorial explanation: corban is "given," that is, "dedicated or given to God." Hence, corban is an offering.

Jewish law allowed individuals to earmark their service or property as "dedicated to God," thus removing it from profane use and giving it the character of an offering intended for God. To do this was a serious decision (see Mishna, *Nedarim*) and was rarely reversed (*Ned* 5), for violation of a corban vow risked the severe consequences of divine judgment. In Mark 7 Jesus chastises the scribes because, theoretically, a son could exclude his parents from gaining any benefit from his estate by declaring his property "corban to them." This

in effect nullifies the fourth commandment (see Ex 20:12), setting rabbinic traditions against the Law of Moses. Worse still, if the son repented of his vow—arguing that it had been given in haste—a rabbinic tribunal would no doubt forbid a reversal of corban (Mk 7:12; cf Nm 30:1,2).

See OFFERINGS AND SACRIFICES.

Core. KJV spelling of Korah, Izhar's son, in Jude 11.

See KORAH #3.

Coriander. Annual herb native to Palestine. The fragrant seeds of this plant are mentioned twice in the description of manna (Ex 16:31; Nm 11:7).

See FOOD AND FOOD PREPARATION; PLANTS.

Corinth. Prominent city of Greece, formerly the capital of the ancient province of Achaia, in which the apostle Paul preached. The site of ancient Corinth lies to the west of the isthmus separating the Peloponnesian peninsula from mainland Greece. The ancient ruins, largely of Roman origin, are situated about 4/5 mile from present-day Corinth. The area was inhabited from Neolithic times. Corinth is dominated by an outcrop of rock known as Acrocorinth (Upper Corinth). The grandeur of the Greek period is evident in the remains of the temple of Apollo, whose massive columns dominate the site. Entrance to the ancient city is by means of a very broad avenue which lies in a straight line from the city gate. That avenue ends in the marketplace, with roads

Acrocorinth.

leading from there to the Acrocorinth. In the apostolic period the city was a bustling commercial and industrial center boasting a population of almost 700,000.

History and Archaeology. By the mid-8th century BC, Corinth, strategically located along east-west trade routes, was a flourishing city-state. From 350–250 BC it was the most prominent city in Greece. Then the Roman military machine began a relentless march to forge a vast empire. In 146 BC Corinth was completely destroyed and lay in ruins for a century. In 46 BC Julius Caesar moved a mixed group of Italians and dispossessed Greeks onto the site, and once more a magnificent city arose, this time as a Roman colony. As in most Roman cities, marble temples dominated the landscape. The city was supplied with water from an underground well. It became a cosmopolitan city attracting tradespeople from all over the world, though its reputation grew simultaneously as a center of luxury, indulgence, and vice. A large colony of displaced Jews (part of the diaspora) developed in the city, the group which undoubtedly attracted the apostle Paul.

In 1896 the American School of Classical Studies at Athens secured permission to begin excavation of the ancient site. The finds are of special interest for study of the NT Corinthian epistles. An important archaeological find was a doorway lintel bearing a portion of an inscription designating the building as the "Synagogue of the Hebrews." It may have marked the synagogue in which the apostle preached (Acts 18:4). Another discovery was the *bema*, or judgment place (Acts 18:12–17), located in the center of the *agora*, or marketplace. There Paul appeared before Gallio, proconsul of Achaia. The dates of Gallio are well established by other inscriptions. He must not have arrived in Corinth before July, AD 51. Paul appeared before him after having ministered in the city for almost 18 months. That would date Paul's arrival in Corinth at the beginning of AD 50.

Isthmian Games. Corinth was also prominent because of the Isthmian Games, which occurred in the first and third years of the Olympiad (the four-year period between Olympic games). They were supposedly originated by the mythical King Sisyphus and date from 523 BC. Competition centered on three kinds of events: equestrian, gymnastics, and music. By the NT period the games were influenced by Roman civilization, so chariot racing and other spectacles were probably added to the Hellenistic competitions. In an allusion to athletic contests Paul mentioned both running and boxing (1 Cor 9:24–26). The prize for winning the games was a wreath made of myrtle, olive, or pine branches, plus additional benefits: a stipend from the state; remission of taxes; and special benefits for the champion's children. Winners were national heroes.

Religion. The distinctive cult of Corinth was veneration of Aphrodite, goddess of love, beauty, and fertility, who is identified with the Roman Venus. The summit of Acrocorinth was dominated by a temple dedicated to her worship, served by over 1,000 sacred prostitutes or slave-priestesses. Associated with such religious practices was a general moral degradation. Corinthian morals were notoriously corrupt, even when compared with pagan Rome.

Corinth is significant in the history of the church because of the ministry of the apostle Paul in response to his Macedonian vision (Acts 16:9,10). He established churches in Philippi, Thessalonica, Beroea, and possibly Athens on his way to Corinth. Acts 18 describes Paul's work at Corinth, first with the Jews, among whom he met with violent opposition (Acts 18:6). At Corinth, Paul engaged in the longest ministry up to that time in either of his first missionary journeys. The Corinthian church, born in such a crucible of paganism, had to go through serious birth pangs. Paul's letters to the group of believers there reflect a large catalog of troubles for Christians in the 1st century, a list not unlike the problems of Christians today. RICHARD I. MCNEELY

See CORINTHIANS, FIRST LETTER TO THE; CORINTHIANS, SECOND LETTER TO THE.

Corinthians, First Letter to the.

Author. There is no doubt about who wrote 1 Corinthians, for all scholars agree that the apostle Paul wrote it on his third missionary journey while he was living in Ephesus. By this time Paul was a mature, middle-aged (perhaps 55 years old) missionary, fully seasoned from planting churches around a quarter of the Mediterranean world.

Date and Origin. Paul worked in Corinth from about AD 50 to 52. After a brief stay in Jerusalem, he returned to his missionary work, this time at Ephesus (Acts 19), where he ministered for three years (AD 53–55/56). During this period he wrote at least three letters to Corinth and made a visit as well. His first letter, often called "the previous letter," is referred to in 1 Corinthians 5:9–11. We know from this reference that the letter was misunderstood, but we know little of its content, for it has been lost.

Some time in AD 55, after hearing reports from Chloe's household (1 Cor 1:11), who were probably members of Chloe's house church, he dictated a second letter to Corinth, our 1 Corinthians 1–4. Before this was dispatched, Paul received a letter from Corinth. The messenger probably supplied the news to which Paul responds in 1 Corinthians 5–6, but 1 Corinthians 7–15 is a direct response to questions in the letter (see 7:1), with chapter 16 the closing. The completed 1 Corinthians was probably sent off in the hands of Stephanus, Fortunatus, and Achaicus (16:17).

Paul would later write a third letter to Corinth, called "the letter of tears" (2 Cor 2:3,4) and then finally 2 Corinthians.

Background. Corinth was a seaport city, destroyed by the Romans in 146 BC and rebuilt in 46 BC by Julius Caesar. After 27 BC it was the Roman capital of Achaia, where the proconsul had his residence (Acts 18:12). The city itself was really three cities: the port of Cenchrea, about eight miles to the east, where ships from the Aegean would unload; the port of Lechaeum, about a mile to the west on the Gulf of Corinth, where the ships would be reloaded, their goods having been transported in wagons over the isthmus and the ships on rollers; and the city itself on the high ground in between.

The acropolis of the city on top of the steep, high Acrocorinth, contained the temple of Aphrodite, where 1,000 female slaves were dedicated to the service of this goddess of love. Down in the city was the synagogue (Acts 18:4); for while the city as a Roman colony was largely populated by Italians, it had attracted other peoples from the Mediterranean, among whom were the Jews.

Purpose and Theological Teaching. The main concern of Paul in 1 Corinthians is the unity of the church. There was a self-centeredness in Corinth which resulted in building cliques within the church, in flaunting knowledge and liberty in the face of others scandalized by it, and in selfish displays in the services.

Two other major concerns also surface in the book. First, along with other pagan practices the lax sexual ethics of Corinth had influenced the church; Paul needed to erect some barriers. Second, there was a problem in accepting the resurrection of the body; Paul realizes that this issue has implications for the core of the faith and vigorously affirms the resurrection.

Both of these latter two areas, as well as aspects of the unity issue (particularly their concern with knowledge), have been identified by some scholars as gnostic motifs, leading to the conclusion that Paul was opposing a gnostic party in Corinth. Careful examination reveals, however, that while some of the elements floating in the Corinthian milieu would later contribute to the development of Gnosticism, it would be anachronistic to call them gnostic. Gnosticism itself was a 2nd-century movement, developing out of a combination of Christianity with Hellenistic and Eastern pagan elements. While recognizing protognostic ideas in the Corinthian situation, it is important to keep interpretation within the 1st-century context.

Thus the focus of Paul's concern is the church, its unity and purity. Paul is fighting to keep this church from disintegrating into a number of competing and bickering factions divided over moral and doctrinal issues. Furthermore, he wants to keep the focus of the church on Jesus, the exalted Lord.

Content. *Greeting, 1:1–9.* Paul begins with a standard greeting, followed by his usual thanksgiving prayer. Two features stand out. First, the greeting associates Sosthenes with Paul. While we cannot be sure who Sosthenes was, he was surely well known to the Corinthians; probably he was the Sosthenes whom Acts 18:17 identifies as the ruler of the synagogue, following the conversion of Crispus.

Second, Paul stresses the Corinthians' abilities in speech, knowledge, and spiritual gifts. They had all of these, and these were genuine, but it was precisely these good things that they were abusing. Paul's solution is not to suppress these gifts (indeed, he thanks God for them), but to place them in a new context.

The Report from Chloe's People, 1:10–4:21. The Corinthians had made Paul, Cephas (Peter), Apollos, and even Christ into party leaders. We are not sure what each of these groups stood for, but one might guess that the Pauline group stressed Paul's slogans of liberty, the Petrine group the need to hold to Jewish practices, and the Apollos group the value of philosophical understanding and oratory. Whatever they stood for, Paul is appalled that it breaks the unity given in Christ. His first response is to argue that his behavior was not calculated to build a following but to point to Christ. That is, he did not insist on personally baptizing converts; who performed these acts did not matter, since they were all baptized into Christ.

Paul immediately moves to the underlying issue, that of various persons wanting to show themselves better or wiser than others who did not have the insights of their party in the church. Their seeking for wisdom contradicts Paul's preaching of the gospel.

First, the message of a crucified and resurrected Jesus ("the word of the cross," 1:18) made no sense within the wisdom and values of either Jews or Greeks. It demanded a whole new way of looking on life, God's way.

Second, God had not chosen them on the basis of their status in society; quite the contrary, he had made their only status the equal status they received from him (1:26–31).

Third, their faith had not been based on Paul's oratory, but on the gifts of the Spirit that Paul had manifested ("demonstration of the Spirit and of power," 2:4), which had convinced them that God was acting in Paul. Thus it was not argument that led them to God, but God's Spirit. Therefore it is the Spirit, not human reasoning, that will continue to reveal God to them. Unless they become fools with respect to the world's ways of reasoning, they will never be able to rethink life from the perspective of the Spirit, who gives true wisdom and makes them one in Christ.

Fourth, they are not acting on this spiritual level when they claim Paul and others as party leaders; this activity demonstrates the evil impulse in human beings ("the flesh" or "fallen human nature") at work since it elevates mere servants rather than the God who works equally in each of them.

Fifth, these servants are working together to build one "temple" for God based on the one foundation in Jesus Christ, that is, the church. God alone will judge how each Christian contributes to the work of building the church. But woe to the person who divides the church, for "if anyone destroys God's temple, God will destroy him" (3:17). Note that here the temple imagery is used collectively; the church is the temple. In chapter 6 it will be used individually; each Christian is the temple.

Finally, he points to their overrealized eschatology, for with their spiritual gifts (which were genuine) and vaunted wisdom (which was worldly) they claimed they were reigning with Christ (4:8–13). Paul, with ironic sarcasm, points out how different this claim is from the life style of the apostles. The apostles lived like Jesus—a life of suffering, expecting exaltation later. The Corinthians were trying to have their exaltation now without crucifixion, that is, self-denial, first.

Paul closes this section with an admonition. He softens his words toward some who would be responsive, urging them to copy him, for teaching in the NT includes demonstration of a proper life style along with speech. The teacher was the message (4:14–16). Timothy will also faithfully live the truth before them. Then he threatens the "arrogant" (4:18), pointing out that he will not challenge their words but their spiritual power if he comes. However many doctrinal arguments they might win, they had better repent before they wither in the face of the Spirit, "for the kingdom of God does not consist in talk but in power" (v 20).

The Report from the Corinthian Messengers, 5:1–6:20. Paul now turns to three issues raised by oral reports from the messengers bearing the Corinthians' letter to him.

The first issue is that of church discipline (5:1–13). Paul cites a case of flagrant immorality, probably marriage to or cohabitation with a young stepmother after the death of a man's father. It is not as much the nature of the sin (sexual immorality) that disturbs Paul, for in 5:11 he will cite a number of other sins for which he would prescribe the same remedy. Rather, this immorality is so clear (even pagans considered it immoral), that it is not a case of ignorance of Christian principles; further, the church has taken no action but rather boasted in its tolerance, perhaps on the basis of a misunderstanding of Paul's teaching on freedom from the Law.

Paul presents three principles in this section: (1) the primary goal of church discipline is the repentance and restoration of the offender; (2) the secondary goal of church discipline is the protection of the church (5:6–8); and (3) the church is not to seek to judge or control the actions of evil persons in the world—they are God's responsibility—but it is to discipline those within the church (5:9–13). Paul will use these principles also in the following chapters (cf. 7:12–16).

The second issue is that of lawsuits between Christians (6:1–11). The Corinthian society was as prone to litigation as our own, and Christians did not see anything wrong in suing each other. Paul is horrified. If Christians are to judge the world, they certainly should not bring the world in to judge issues within the church. Rather than put their cases before "those who are least esteemed by the church" (6:4, i.e., pagan judges), they should decide the cases within the church (a scene reflected in Jas 2:2–4).

Paul has an even better way than bypassing the pagan courts, and that is to simply suffer the wrong (6:7). Applying the teaching of Jesus quite literally (Mt 5:38–42), Paul argues that it would be best to allow themselves to be defrauded. Instead, the Corinthians are willing to step on their brothers in Christ to get what they feel are their rights.

This raises the issue as to whether greed is not still in their hearts (6:9–11). While Paul accepts people who formerly did all sorts of evil (for Jesus has cleansed them), he makes it very clear that anyone presently practicing greed or immorality is not part of the kingdom, whatever their doctrinal commitments may be. Thus the fact of the lawsuits should lead to deep self-examination.

The final issue in this section is that of casual sexual intercourse (6:12–20). In a world where virginity was important if a woman wished to be married and where slaves in the temple of Aphrodite were available as prostitutes, prostitution was the major form of casual sex. The libertine party used two slogans, "All things are lawful for me," a saying that may well have been derived from Paul's teaching, and "Food is meant for the stomach and the stomach for food"—that is, since the body works this way, it must be the Creator's purpose. Paul qualifies rather than contradicts their slogans. Freedom is subordinate to other goals (6:12,20). The body is not made to be used as we wish, but is to be dedicated to the Lord, as the doctrine of the resurrection demonstrates (6:13,14).

Furthermore, sexual intercourse is an act of the whole person, unlike eating (Paul cites Gn 2:24; cf. Jesus in Mt 19:5). Therefore this act takes a member (i.e., the person) from the body of Christ and makes him a unity with a prostitute (6:15–17). Thus immorality is unlike other sins that are external to the self, for it changes the self and thus defiles the body, the place where the Holy Spirit dwells. It disregards the fact that Christ has redeemed the body, and that the whole of the Christian belongs to God, not to the Christian.

The Answer to the Letter from Corinth, 7:1–16:4. Now Paul turns to the Corinthians' own issues, building on the answers he has already given to questions they did not ask.

The first issue is that of marriage (7:1–24). The slogan of the ascetic party in Corinth (perhaps a reaction against the libertines of ch 6) was "It is good for a man not to have sexual intercourse" (not "not to marry," NIV). The Corinthians applied this slogan to both married and unmarried, arguing that married Christians should abstain from sexual relations. Again Paul accepts this statement, for he does not believe every person needs sexual intercourse, but immediately destroys the argument through qualifications. First, it is unrealistic, for total abstinence would lead to immorality (7:2,7–9). Second, when people get married they no longer own their own bodies; their bodies belong to each other for their mutual benefit (7:3,4). Sexual refusal denies a spouse what rightly belongs to him or her. Third, abstinence is allowed for limited periods by mutual agreement as a type of fast to help focus on Christ (7:5).

While Paul will handle the unmarried more fully in 7:25–40, in a side remark he indicates that he is himself content unmarried. But since some do not have this gift, full sexual expression in marriage is far better than fighting passion (7:7–9).

Returning to the married, divorce for Christians is unthinkable. A clear word of Christ

proves this (Mt 5:31–32; Mk 10:11,12; Lk 16:18 and parallels), so there are no exceptions (Paul either does not know of the exception clause in Mt 19:9, or he understands it as referring to something like premarital unchastity discovered before the wedding, not to adultery after the wedding). Although in some cases a Christian couple must live separately, it is always with a view to reconciliation. The teaching of Jesus does not allow him to think of the marriage as ending (7:10,11).

But what if the spouse is not a Christian? Paul applies his principles to a situation for which Jesus did not leave a clear word. First, since Jesus told Christians not to divorce, even in this situation the Christian may not initiate a divorce (7:12,13). Second, since Christians are not to control or judge non-Christians (6:12,13), the Christian does not need to continue the relationship if the non-Christian insists on a divorce (7:15). Third, far from defiling the Christian (as the relationship in 6:15 does), the Christian will make the relationship holy, with positive results for the children and the possible salvation of the spouse (7:14,16). While this is no call to remain in situations of physical or sexual abuse, it is a call to remain faithful to a mixed marriage situation.

Paul does not believe that one normally needs to change one's life situation to serve Christ (7:17–24). Therefore normally each person should remain in that state of life in which he or she was when called to Christ. Paul's examples show that he is thinking in terms of marriage or singleness, Jew (circumcision) or Gentile, slave or free, not in terms of situations that might be immoral in themselves. In the case of slaves, they can accept freedom if it becomes available, but it does not make an essential difference in their real state before God or their ability to serve Christ (7:21–23).

The second issue is that of the unmarried (7:25–40). Paul argues that single people and widows may marry—it is not wrong. Yet he advises them to remain single. Since all in this age is passing away, it would be good to stay single so as to avoid the extra suffering to which marriage exposes one (7:25–31). What is more, marriage always divides one's attention between the Lord and the legitimate needs of the spouse. One must not abandon the spouse or ignore his or her needs in order to serve the Lord, but one can remain single so that the Lord can be the sole focus of life and devotion (7:32–35). Finally, if one is in a situation in which marriage is expected, the person must make his own decision as to whether he should marry the woman for her sake (and perhaps that of the wider family) or whether he can and should simply care for her as a single

The Pirene Fountain in the agora of Corinth, the main source of water for Corinth.

person (7:36–38). Paul closes this section by repeating his general principles (7:39–40).

The third issue Paul deals with is that of food which has been offered to idols (8:1–11:1). Most meat that was available in the marketplace came either from animals slaughtered as sacrifices in the temples or from groups of animals from which one was offered as a dedicatory sacrifice. To scrupulous Jews all of this meat would be suspect. Furthermore, pagans invited Christians to feasts in their homes and to private feasts held in the precincts of pagan temples, where trade guilds also held feasts. Paul discusses these issues and uses them to teach wider principles of Christian conduct.

First, love, not knowledge, is the key to correct behavior (8:1–13). Some Corinthians felt superior because they were convinced that idols had no reality (there is only one God) and therefore any food offered to them was still fit to eat. Paul again accepts their slogans, but counters with " 'Knowledge' puffs up, but love builds up" (8:1). God is not concerned with what we know or eat, but he is concerned with whether or not we love our fellow Christians. The concern is not that a fellow Christian might become enraged because one indulged, but that he or she might have a vulnerable conscience and indulge himself, even though he believed it wrong and thus in his own eyes apostasizes from the

faith (i.e., rebels against Christ). Such leading astray is not love. It would be better never to eat meat than to lead a fellow Christian into sin.

Second, he points out that one should subordinate one's own interests to those of others, especially those of Christ and his gospel (9:1–23). Both the example of the apostles, who expected the church to support them and their families (cf. Lk 10:5–7), and Scripture prove that Paul had the right to demand support from the Corinthians. This had not been his practice, for he had normally made tents to support his ministry, though he did accept gifts from other churches. Paul did this to prevent people from thinking he was peddling religion for profit (9:12) and for the personal satisfaction of doing more than he had to do (9:16,17). This was part of Paul's larger policy of subordinating his own personal preferences and interests to those of Christ and his gospel (9:19–23).

Third, the bravado of the "strong" who demonstrate their liberty with disregard of fellow Christians is spiritually dangerous (9:24–10:22). It is not who begins, but who completes the Christian life that counts; therefore it is a life of discipline, not relaxed license (9:24–27). Israel in the wilderness presents an example of failure in this regard. They had "baptism" and "the Lord's Supper" (10:2–4) just like the church, yet most of them did not make it to the Promised Land. The reason God destroyed them was simple: They turned to sin. Likewise the Christian has to be careful not to be so proud about faith and freedom that he becomes careless about sin and falls from the faith (10:12). On the other hand, Christians need not be fearful, for the temptation is not more powerful than they are; God has provided a way of escape, if they will take it (10:13).

One application of this is to the issue at hand, idols (10:14–22). In the Lord's Supper there is a sharing of the blood and body of Christ, just as real as Israel's sacrifices on the altar. Food offered to idols is also a sharing, not with the supposed god, but with the real demon which is behind the idol. To try to share at both tables is to provoke God's jealousy just as Israel did (10:22). This means that the Christian must not participate in dinners given in pagan temples, even if they are the official dinners of his trade guild.

A summary of the discussion draws the three chapters together (10:23–11:1). Since the food is not changed by being offered to idols, and since all food really belongs to God, one may eat anything sold in the market—do not ask any questions (10:25,26). Likewise the Christian may eat anything served at a dinner in the home of an unbeliever. However, if someone points out that the food was offered to idols, the Christian should pass it by, not because it would hurt him, but because it is an issue with the person who raised the question, and the Christian is concerned about the good of his neighbor (10:27–30). In other words, follow Paul's example as he patterns himself in turn after Christ, who served others rather than himself. Act so that God's reputation and character shine through even in what one eats (10:31); try to offend no one but to benefit each person in moving him toward salvation (10:32).

The fourth issue Paul deals with is that of order in church meetings (11:2–14:40). The Corinthian house churches had lively meetings, but rather than showing unity in Christ they demonstrated selfishness. Paul had no desire to change what they did; he did want to change how they did it.

The first problem in the meetings was the behavior of married women (11:1–16). The sign of marriage in that day was the wearing of a veil or distinctive hair style, as a ring is today. Women praying and delivering prophecies in church was no issue for Paul, but the women felt that this foretaste of resurrection life (cf. ch 15) temporarily loosed them from their husbands (cf. Mk 12:25), and therefore was reason to toss off their veils. Paul argues that husband and wife are intimately joined, just as humans are to God (11:3). Therefore as humans should not shame, but glorify God, so the wife should act toward her husband. And because the unveiling would look like a sexual come-on, it was improper to do this in a church attended by the holy angels (11:10). There were also cultural reasons for such decorum (11:13–16). On the other hand, the veil was a sign of authority to actively minister (11:10); Paul approves of ministry by women, but puts marriage first.

The second problem in the meetings was that of making class distinctions (11:17–34). Until the weekly Lord's Supper began to be turned into the sacrifice of the Mass in the 3rd century, it was a full shared meal. Middle- and upper-class Christians could come earlier to the church gatherings and also provide better food and drink for themselves. Following the customs of pagan clubs, they had no scruples against starting early and feasting as befit their class, so long as at least simple food was provided for the slaves and peasants who could not come as early (11:21). This shamed the poorer Christians and made them feel class distinctions keenly (11:22). This, argues Paul, is not the Lord's Supper but a blasphemy (11:20).

Paul repeats the words of institution to point out that they all are participating in Christ's body and blood (cf. 10:16,17), not their own meal. To do it in an unworthy manner, with divisions and class distinctions among them, is to profane his meal by failing to demonstrate the unity of his body the church ("without recognizing the body," 11:29 NIV) and thus invite his judgment, which they were already experiencing. Instead, they should examine their own motives and truly gather as one to eat this common meal.

The third problem in their meetings was the use of spiritual gifts (12:1–14:40). It is possible that some people in these house churches, under the influence of gnostic ideas in which the spiritual is good and the material evil, and feeling inspired by a spirit, cried out, "Jesus [meaning the human Jesus as opposed to the spiritual Christ] be cursed." It is not the Spirit of God saying this, argues Paul, for the Spirit in us cries the basic Christian confession, "Jesus is Lord."

Others in these churches were exalting their own particular gift, especially the gift of tongues, shouting down others or refusing to give them a turn. There is only one Spirit and he gives all the gifts, Paul argues (12:4–6). The Spirit manifests himself sovereignly in each Christian, not simply for the Christian's own benefit, but for the good of all (12:7). Since it is the Spirit, not a given manifestation, which the Christian has, the gifts manifested could change from meeting to meeting and different manifestations could be requested.

That same Spirit has made all Christians into one organic unity in Christ (12:12,13). Thus not only does the one Spirit give all the gifts—all are equally inspired—but all the gifts are equally needed for the proper functioning of the body of Christ (12:14–26). No one can say that his lack of a given gift makes him less a part of the body; indeed, the less noticeable gifts may well be the more important. Thus within the body of Christ there are not only different manifestations of the Spirit through individuals in a given meeting, but different ministries or functions of individuals in the body (12:27–31).

Therefore it is not the demonstration of a particular gift that shows one's spirituality, but how one demonstrates it; that is, whether one manifests it with love (13:1–13). Any gift exercised for selfish purposes may be a genuine gift of the Spirit, but it is worthless to the individual (13:1–3). This is because love is the opposite of selfishness (13:4–7). In fact the gifts of the Spirit are only for the period between Jesus' first coming and his second coming, when the kingdom of God will be perfectly revealed and the King will be present in person, and thus the intermediary gifts of the

Spirit will be no longer necessary (13:10,12). It is not giftedness, but faith and hope which will have a reward then, and love, which is the greatest, because it will continue as Christians live in perfect love with each other and with Jesus (13:13).

Applying this to Corinth, Paul argues that while one should desire all the gifts, love dictates that prophecy should be the gift of choice in the church meetings (14:1–25). The Corinthians had evidently been stressing tongues. Tongues without interpretation is of little value to anyone except to the speaker himself. Therefore it does not build anyone up; its confusion seems madness to outsiders. Outside the church meetings there is a role for tongues, both as a sign of judgment (14:21) and for private devotion (14:18), but inside only with interpretation. Prophecy, however, builds up and convicts, and thus is to be sought in the meetings.

In the church meetings, then, both gifts and order are to prevail (14:26–40). All types of gifts are allowed expression with a goal to mutual edification, not selfish demonstration (14:26). Tongues speakers must have an interpreter; both they and prophets must speak in turn, with time being taken to evaluate the utterances after every few speakers (14:27–33). Furthermore, the women, who were perhaps chatting in the service, perhaps due to habits learned in Jewish synagogues, where they were segregated and did not participate, are to cease their chattering, pay attention, and learn, asking questions at home if they do not understand (14:34–36).

In his concluding summary, Paul states that the truly spiritual will recognize that this is the Lord's command. Paul has not forbidden speaking in tongues in church, but simply stressed the value and importance of prophecy, and that all should be done in an orderly manner (14:37–40).

The fifth issue Paul deals with is that of the resurrection of the dead (15:1–58). Some of the problems mentioned earlier concerning either loose morals (ch 5,6) or ascetic denial or sexuality (ch 7) or feeling one was resurrected already (ch 11) point to the fact that some Corinthians did not believe in the resurrection of the body, though they apparently believed in the resurrection of Jesus and the immortality of the human soul.

Paul reaffirms that the resurrection of Jesus is an essential part of the gospel message (15:1–19). The unified voice of the church was that Jesus not only died, but rose again and appeared to numerous witnesses (15:3–11). If they were consistent in their antiresurrection argument, Christ could not have been raised. Yet if this were the case, the whole gospel message is false and all their hopes for salvation in vain (15:12–19).

Since Christ has been raised, Christians will also be raised because of their solidarity with him (15:20–28). As they had experienced the results of being in Adam, so now they will experience the results of being in Christ. But resurrection does not happen at once. There are progressive stages: (a) Christ was first; (b) Christians will be raised at his coming; (c) Christ must reign until he extends kingdom rule over the whole world, destroying all demonic powers (including death itself); and (d) then he will turn over the perfected kingdom to the Father (15:23–28).

Resurrection hope also explains Christian practices such as baptizing people on behalf of others who had died (probably people who had turned to Christ but had died before they could be baptized, 15:29), and willingness to risk death for Christ (15:30–32).

Paul admits that there are intellectual problems involved, but these are solved when one realizes that resurrection includes both continuity and discontinuity (15:35–50). Just as seed and plant are the same and yet different, and just as many types of bodies exist, so it is with the resurrection. What was perishable, dishonorable, weak, and physical (i.e., in Adam) will be raised imperishable, glorious, powerful, and spiritual (i.e., in Christ). Indeed, it is only as Christians thus become like Christ, the heavenly man, that they can become part of God's kingdom.

With excitement Paul shares his real hope, that of transformation (15:51–58). At the coming of Christ the dead will be raised transformed. But the living will also need transformation, and this will happen in a split second, making all of them impervious to death. Then they will truly know the victory already present in Jesus' resurrection (15:54–57). A concluding summary draws the practical conclusion that this teaching should give them assurance of a reward for anything done for Christ now (15:58).

The sixth issue Paul deals with is that of the collection for the needy Jerusalem church (16:1–4). Because of famine in Judea in the 40s, the church there had become impoverished. Partly because of the need and partly to further the unity of the church, Paul took up a collection in some of his churches for the Judean church. He answers the Corinthians' practical queries by stating that the collection should be made weekly according to ability, not all at once when Paul arrives (16:2). When he comes, he will send off the money with their own messengers. Paul remains vague about whether or not he will accompany them, allaying suspicions that somehow he plans to profit from it (cf. 2 Cor 8–9).

Final Remarks and Closing, 16:5–24. Having come to the end, Paul discusses his travel plans, including his intention for a lengthy visit whenever he leaves Ephesus (cf. 2 Cor 1). Timothy was either coming with the letter or else would arrive shortly after another mission; they are to respect him and help him return. Paul points out that he urged Apollos to visit Corinth, in case some suspect he is against him. A closing formal exhortation to firm faith and love leads into his final customary greetings. He praises the Corinthian messengers who had brought him their letter (16:15–18) and sends greetings from Aquila and Prisca (Priscilla), his co-missionaries who had helped him found the church in Corinth (Acts 18:2,3,18). Referring to the customary greeting in the church, he tells them to greet each other with a kiss on each cheek (16:20). Paul then takes the pen from the scribe, as was normal, and writes the closing exhortation, a curse on those who do not love Jesus, the common Aramaic expression used in the church "Come, O Lord" (*Marana tha,* perhaps used to close services), and an assurance of his own love for them (16:21–24).

PETER H. DAVIDS

See CORINTHIANS, SECOND LETTER TO THE; ACTS OF THE APOSTLES, BOOK OF THE; PAUL, THE APOSTLE; CORINTH.

Bibliography. C.K. Barrett, *The First Epistle to the Corinthians*; T.C. Edwards, *A Commentary on the First Epistle to the Corinthians*; C. Hodge, *An Exposition of the First Epistle to the Corinthians*; A. Robertson and A. Plummer, *First Epistle of St. Paul to the Corinthians* (ICC); G.B. Wilson, *I Corinthians*.

Corinthians, Second Letter to the.

Author. The apostle Paul is the acknowledged author of 2 Corinthians. While some scholars argue that 2 Corinthians 2:14–7:4 and 10–13 are separate letters, only in the case of 6:14–7:1 is Paul's authorship disputed. This section is admittedly a strange digression, but stranger still would be the thought that an editor could have inserted it in such an unusual place. Also the repetition of thought in 7:2 from 6:13 indicates that Paul is aware that he has digressed from his topic and is repeating a phrase to bring his readers back to the subject, a not unusual practice for him.

Date and Origin. After writing both the "previous letter" (1 Cor 5:9) and 1 Corinthians from Ephesus in AD 55, Paul continued to work there. Sometime during the next year a crisis arose in Corinth. Paul made a quick trip across the Aegean Sea, but he could not resolve the crisis, and due to the personal opposition of a leader in the church (likely an interloper bearing letters of recommendation from Jerusalem) had to withdraw (2 Cor 2:1,5). Returning to Ephesus from this "painful visit," Paul dispatched Titus with a blistering "letter of tears" (2 Cor 2:4; 7:8,12, his third letter to that church), which led to the excommunication of the leader and the repentance of the church. This letter has been lost. Meanwhile a situation erupted in Ephesus during which death (probably execution) seemed so certain that Paul despaired of life (2 Cor 1:8,9; Rom 16:4; Acts 19:23–41 may be the origin of the problem, if Paul were later arrested, although 1 Cor 15:32 indicates that he may have had earlier problems in Ephesus). Paul was not killed, but his escape seemed miraculous.

Leaving Ephesus in early AD 56, Paul traveled north to Troas seeking Titus and news of Corinth. Unable to endure without news, he abandoned a promising mission in Troas and sailed to Philippi. There he met Titus, who explained the change of heart in Corinth. Second Corinthians 1–9 responds to this situation, with 8,9 preparing the Corinthians for an upcoming visit. Later Paul received further news from Corinth that renewed opposition to him was present. In response he penned the self-

The temple of Apollo at Corinth.

defense found in 2 Corinthians 10–13. Paul followed up the letter with a visit later in the year (Acts 20:2). We do not know the response to 2 Corinthians or the outcome of his final visit, but later the troubled history of the Corinthian church continued, with another Christian leader needing to write a letter at the end of the century (1 Clement).

Background. The Corinthian house churches always had great diversity. While those who liked Apollos undoubtedly despised Paul's crude style, others who preferred Peter likely appealed beyond Paul to the more genuine "original" apostles in Jerusalem with their Jewish customs (1 Cor 1). Traveling teachers with letters of commendation from these apostles (who would have disliked what these teachers did with the letters) easily drew a following when they came to Corinth and undermined Paul's authority and even his character. Furthermore, because of this outside influence the collection for the poor in Jerusalem which Paul had initiated (1 Cor 16:1–4) was left in abeyance, both because it was connected to Paul and because the teachers themselves were taking money from the church. Paul writes to reaffirm his love in the context of the recent reconciliation between him and Corinth and (later) to set this situation of interlopers to rights.

Purpose and Theological Teaching. In the first section of the letter Paul has two main purposes. The first is to cement his restored relationship with Corinth, explaining situations, forgiving those who opposed him, and reflecting on the nature of ministry. For Paul, ministry meant both intense suffering and comfort. Physical and emotional suffering came from the situations and people he worked with, but his knowledge of future reward and his experience of the power of God working in him brought profound joy and comfort. Due to his own recent brush with death, Paul also reflects on what happens at death. His expectation is to receive a resurrection body and be in the presence of Jesus at death, so it is a goal more than a terror for him as he keeps these unseen realities in view.

The second purpose of this section is to get the collection for Jerusalem on track again. In this context he gives major teaching on giving and Christian economics: Christians are to follow Christ in giving freely; economic equality is the principle governing who gives to whom.

The second section of the letter is an impassioned self-defense, refuting the interlopers' claims to superiority. Neither oratory nor pedigree counts in Christian ministry, but the call of God.

In both sections one observes Paul's deep desire for the unity of the church, both unity within the local community and unity with leaders appointed by God, such as Paul.

Content. *Greeting, 1:1–7.* A standard greeting (1:1,2) comes before Paul's usual thanksgiving (1:3–7). The topic of the thanksgiving, comfort in the midst of suffering, is the topic of chapters 1–7. Paul knows what it is to suffer, but it is in suffering that he has experienced God's comfort, which he passes on to the Corinthians.

Paul's Explanation, 1:8–2:13. Paul informs them of the danger he had suffered in Ephesus, one so great that he did not believe he would survive. His eventual survival seemed like a virtual resurrection, reinforcing his conviction that God, not human strength, is the only Christian refuge (1:8–11). In that and all situations Paul's one boast is that of a clear conscience before God (1:12–14).

Paul had told them of plans for a double visit (cf. 1 Cor 16:5,6), but except for his brief "painful visit" he had not fulfilled his plan (2 Cor 1:15–2:4). He defends himself from charges of either not planning in the Spirit or hypocritical vacillation. He was indeed as good as his word (cf. Jas 5:12), for his life reflected God's fulfilled promise in Jesus, but he had changed plans so as not to repeat the "painful visit" of the previous year. It was love, not fickleness, that motivated the delayed visit.

The Corinthians had responded to Paul's "letter of tears" by excommunicating the person who had opposed Paul (not the same person as 1 Cor 5); the person is now repentant, and Paul calls for his restoration to the community, freely and graciously forgiving the man who had hurt him. Excommunication is for the unrepentant; its purpose is over the moment the person repents (2:5–11).

Paul begins to recount his journey from Ephesus to Philippi, when he sought news of the response to the "letter of tears" (2:12,13). After telling how he left an opportunity to minister in Troas to go to find Titus in Philippi, he breaks the narrative with a long digression.

Nature of Apostolic Ministry, 2:14–7:4. The apostolic ministry in which Paul takes part is like the ministry of Jesus, one of suffering and glory.

Even in suffering there is triumph in Christ, for Christians share Christ's triumph. Yet just like the perfumes of a Roman triumph were joy to the victors but meant death for prisoners on their way to execution, so Jesus' triumph is life to the believer and death to the unbeliever (2:14–17).

This triumph may have sounded like a boast, but Paul is not engaging in self-exaltation. Indeed, he has no need of the letters of commendation which the interlopers in

Corinth carried from Jerusalem, for the Corinthians are themselves the proof of his ministry (3:1–3). His boast is not in himself but in the new covenant in the Spirit, which unlike the old covenant is not fading (here Paul follows one Jewish interpretation of Ex 34:29–35, that Moses put the veil over his face so the people would not see the glory fade), nor does it veil the presence of God, but is permanent and reveals God directly in the Spirit. There is no deceit or hiddenness, for the message is not about Paul, but about Jesus who is light itself (3:4–4:6).

Paul the messenger, however, is simply the cheap, breakable pot that contains the priceless treasure, revealing by way of contrast that the only power in the gospel is God's power. This contrast of weakness and power is seen in the sufferings of the apostle, a type of living death modeled on the sufferings of Jesus, out of which the life of Jesus flows to others (4:7–15).

Therefore, despite intense suffering Paul has courage, for he looks beyond this life to the rewards of the coming life. His whole motivation is one of faith, not sight, for he lives already for unseen realities (4:16–18). When he dies, Paul expects to receive an eternal resurrection body. His hope is not of becoming a disembodied soul ("naked"), but of passing immediately into glorified bodily life, already guaranteed by the presence of the Spirit. This hope was likely the fruit of his near brush with death in Ephesus, when he must have meditated and prayed about what would come at death (5:1–5). Because this future includes Christ's judgment, Paul makes every effort now to live in the light of that judgment, which he already sees by faith (5:6–10).

Far from trying to commend or exalt himself, Paul is simply presenting what he is (which they of all people should recognize), a person filled with the love of Christ and convinced that all should live not for themselves but for Christ (5:11–15). No one should be valued from merely a human point of view, not Paul nor even Christ (for Paul before his conversion had a human opinion of Christ which his conversion had radically changed); everyone should be valued from the point of view of the new creation. Paul's job is simply to announce the reconciliation of the new creation, which God has already effected on his side and which only awaits a person's ratification on the human side (5:16–20).

Paul, then, is a co-worker with God, announcing salvation, using every means consistent with God's character to proclaim the message, and suffering everything imaginable to demonstrate the extent of God's love (6:1–10). Therefore Paul has nothing against the Corin-

thians. If there is any blockage in their relationship with him, it must be on their side (6:11–13).

Excursus on Purity, 6:14–7:1. Perhaps suspecting that the real block in the relationship is their love of the world, or that the Corinthians might not be totally over the problems mentioned in 1 Corinthians, Paul breaks off his argument and argues for separation from unbelievers. There are two groups, light and darkness, Christ and the devil, believers and unbelievers. Therefore, as Exodus 25:8; Leviticus 26:11,12; Isaiah 52:11; Ezekiel 37:27; and Hosea 1:10 show (phrases from these passages flow into each other in a style of chain quotation familiar to Jews), Christians should not be closely bound to unbelievers in marriage or in business, for it will affect their moral purity.

Return to the Nature of the Apostolic Ministry, 7:2–4. Picking up from 6:13, Paul points out that the Corinthians have nothing substantival against him. He is not criticizing but simply appealing to them in love; even now he is prepared to die for them.

Explanation Concluded, 7:5–16. Having concluded his digression, Paul now returns to his journey, which he left in 2:13. When he met Titus, he received good news about Corinth. He was relieved that his "letter of tears" had been effective, not in simply making them sorry but in bringing them to true repentance that yielded zeal and moral purity and joy. Furthermore, their behavior toward Titus had been so impressive that Titus' enthusiastic report of his own impressions had further cheered Paul.

Collection for Jerusalem, 8:1–9:15. In the context of restored relationships Paul turns to the sensitive topic of the collection for the church in Jerusalem, which had been impoverished through famines in Judea in the 40s. This collection was both an act of charity (cf. Acts 11:27–30; Gal 2:10) and a symbolic act of unity and fellowship between the gentile and Jewish branches of the church.

The impoverished and suffering church in Macedonia (Philippi) had given eagerly. Therefore Titus was coming back to help the Corinthians complete what they had begun the previous year (and probably dropped during their controversy with Paul, 8:1–7). The principles of the collection are (1) the Corinthians should follow the example of Jesus, who became poor for them; (2) they should give freely what they can without regretting that they cannot give more, for God values the eagerness to give expressed in action, not the net amount of the gift; and (3) there should be an economic equality among sections of the church, no one section being enriched at the expense of another (cf. Ex 16:18). This economic equality extends to the relationship between two churches a continent apart (8:8–15).

Titus and two absolutely trustworthy men appointed by the churches for this work will come to supervise the final gathering—Paul will have nothing to do with the money personally—for it is important that not only God but the world be able to see the honesty and integrity of the way the church handles money (8:16–24).

Paul points out that he does not need to argue the reasons for this collection; they were aware of them when they began to gather money the year before. This letter is not an argument for the collection but an encouragement to finish the work, so that when Paul arrives with representatives of other churches carrying their contributions, the Corinthians would not be embarrassed by their relatively wealthy church's not being ready or able to give generously, despite Paul's boasts about their previous eagerness. In saying this, Paul shows himself diplomatic and insightful in motivating human behavior; he makes the best assumptions possible about the present situation (9:1–5). However, no person from Achaia is listed among his companions on his last trip to Jerusalem (Acts 20:4).

Paul would not want the Corinthians giving out of guilt, although he, like Jesus (Mt 6:19,20), points out that the only real value of money is in giving; rather, he wants them so convinced of God's generosity and ability to provide that they give freely and joyfully. God wants to enrich them so that they can give more. The giving will result in thanksgiving to God by the recipients, who will also pray for those who gave the gift, binding the church together. A closing reminder of the extent of God's own giving finishes the section (9:6–15).

Paul's Self-Defense, 10:1–13:14. There is an abrupt change in tone between 9:15 and 10:1. Now, instead of the tone of conciliation found in 1:1–7:16, there is argument and defense, even threat. Paul's apostleship has been attacked, and he will defend it with vigor.

Paul is indeed a humble person who prefers not to use his authority. Yet when forced, he has something more than authority; he has spiritual power, capable of destroying opposing arguments and bending all to obedience to Jesus. He will use that power in Corinth if he must, though up to that time he had been gentle and had shown this side of his ministry only in letters (10:1–11).

His opponents talk of their qualifications and compare themselves favorably with other ministers. Paul will not enter into this game of comparisons. God has set the sphere of his la-

bors, which was the area in which he founded churches. He was the one who pioneered the church in Corinth, so it is his sphere of ministry, not the interlopers'. They boast in having reaped the benefits of his ministry; he can point to an original ministry given by God; for it is God's commendation in the end which counts (10:13–18).

Yet the Corinthian rebellion is serious enough to force him into self-defense, ridiculous as such an exercise is. He is shocked by how readily they turn away to every novel doctrine that comes along. This tendency strikes fear in Paul's heart (11:1–6).

Paul had been criticized for refusing financial support from Corinth (even though he accepted gifts from other churches; cf. 1 Cor 9). He will continue to refuse such support, for he wants to undermine the claims of the interlopers. If they are really serving God alone, let them work on the same basis as he! But since they are false at heart, serving Satan and not God, they seek money from the church. Paul is astonished that in the Corinthians' vaunted wisdom they do not see through this hypocrisy; yet he hopes that even if he must play the fool in making a self-defense, they will at least accept him; they feel so wise that they can condescend to tolerate "fools" like Paul. The irony is that his very tender care and concern for the church, his gentleness, is being used against him as a supposed "weakness." Paul, the opponents argued, knows he is false, so therefore does not dare take money from you as we do (11:7–21).

The interlopers claimed to come with authority from Jerusalem. They had letters from the apostles; it is unlikely, however, that the apostles would have approved of their activities. Still, they were Jews with respectable authority behind them. Paul feels compelled to state his own credentials. If they are Jews, he is just as pure a Jew. If they have served Christ, can their work and sufferings match his? The list of sufferings both gives historical information not found in Acts and points to tireless labor, including days of fasting ("gone without food") and nights spent in prayer ("gone without sleep") (11:21–29).

But this boasting is repulsive to Paul, so he shifts to one particular suffering, his escape from Damascus, when he had to hide and slip out of the city in a basket. The story at once shows his effectiveness as an evangelist (in that he was a target of persecution) and shames him, for he could not defend himself and had to slip away under cover of darkness, his oriental pride deeply wounded. Yet that weakness is indeed his glory (11:30–33).

His opponents boasted in revelations from God. Paul knows that this boasting is senseless; but if he must, he will tell them of a revelation superior to theirs, a time when he actually saw the inside of heaven (he is not sure whether it was a vision or an actual bodily experience). This happened about AD 42, while Paul was in Tarsus before Barnabas came for him (Acts 9:30; 11:25). Paul dislikes telling about this, for God's power is more easily seen in his weakness. In fact, Paul's opponents are an affliction of Satan which God allows to keep Paul humble and to demonstrate his power in Paul's weakness. (The image of a "thorn in my flesh" is one of enemies, Nm 33:55; Jos 23:13; Paul also describes what he means more clearly in 12:10.) If vulnerability shows God's power, Paul willingly accepts the weakness (12:1–10).

Paul feels shamed that he had to boast. The opponents boasted in coming from Jerusalem "superapostles." Paul points out that he is their equal, although both are nothing. God had set his mark upon Paul's work. With biting irony he asks forgiveness for not having taken money from the Corinthians (12:11–13).

Yet Paul will come a third time, and he will keep to the same policy of not taking any support from them but giving himself freely to them, just as Jesus had done on earth. Not only he, but all his envoys, kept to the same policy. No one could accuse him of deceit or inconsistency (12:14–18).

However, he feared coming to them, for he knew that the community had not just rebelled against him, but was also in internal disorder. This disunity and immorality would humble and pain Paul; he would have to deal with the sin, and he would deal with it firmly, using the power of God (12:19–13:4; cf. 1 Cor 5; 1 Tm 1:20).

Therefore the Corinthians had better examine themselves. Are they really following Jesus or not? If so, they should see that Paul is also following Jesus. Yet Paul's concern is not his own position—he is content to be rejected ("weak")—but their following the truth. He hopes for their repentance, not to protect himself, but so that he need not be severe when he comes (13:5–10).

Probably taking the pen from the scribe at this point, Paul closes with a final appeal to repent and come to unity as a church. Brief greetings from the church in Macedonia and a formal blessing closes his correspondence with the Corinthians (13:11–14).

PETER H. DAVIDS

See CORINTHIANS, FIRST LETTER TO THE; PAUL, THE APOSTLE; CORINTH.

Bibliography. C.K. Barrett, *The Second Epistle to the Corinthians*; C. Hodge, *An Exposition of the Second Epistle to the Corinthians*; J.E. McFudgen, *I–II Corinthians*; A.P. Stanley, *The Epistles of St. Paul to the Corinthians*.

Ruins of the old city of Corinth, with Acrocorinth in the background.

Cormorant. Large, black, webfooted water fowl, considered ceremonially unclean for the Israelites (Lv 11:17; Dt 14:17).

See BIRDS.

Corn. Word used in the KJV to denote grain, especially wheat. Maize, the plant known in America as corn, was unknown in the Middle East in biblical times.

See PLANTS (BARLEY; WHEAT).

Cornelius. Roman centurion and the first gentile Christian mentioned in the Book of Acts.

The story of Cornelius' conversion through the preaching of the apostle Peter is recorded in Acts 10:1–11:18. Before his conversion Cornelius was well known to the Jews as a person who feared God, prayed continually, and gave alms.

At first the church was composed only of Jews, who were reluctant to preach the gospel to Gentiles because law-abiding Jews never had fellowship with "pagans." Peter, a law-abiding Jew, had scruples about entering a Gentile's house and eating "unclean" food. Through a vision, however, God led Peter to Cornelius' house to preach the gospel to him and his family and close friends. Before Peter had finished speaking, and before baptism or the laying on of hands could be administered, God dramatically demonstrated his acceptance of Gentiles into the fellowship of the church by giving them the gift of the Holy Spirit. Peter remained several days in Cornelius' house, no doubt rejoicing in the centurion's conversion and instructing him in his newfound faith.

Cornelius' conversion represented a significant step in the separation of the early church from Judaism. Cornelius did not have to submit to any of the Jewish practices, such as circumcision or eating only ritually "clean" animals. For the first time a gentile believer was accepted into the church on equal terms with Jewish Christians.

See ACTS OF THE APOSTLES, BOOK OF THE.

Corner Gate. Gate presumably located in the northwest corner of the Jerusalem wall. After King Jehoash of Israel captured King Amaziah of Judah, he tore down a section of the Jerusalem wall from the Corner Gate to the Ephraim Gate (2 Kgs 14:13; 2 Chr 25:23); later King Uzziah of Judah built towers at this gate (2 Chr 26:9). Jeremiah (31:38) foretells a time when the Jerusalem wall will be rebuilt from the tower of Hananel to the Corner Gate; Zechariah (14:10) also envisions a period of security and prosperity epitomized by the presence of the Jerusalem wall, including the Corner Gate.

See JERUSALEM.

Corners of the Earth. Figurative term denoting the borders and extremities of the earth (Jb 37:3; Is 11:12; Ez 7:2; Rv 7:1; 20:8).

Cornerstone. Term used in the NT to describe the exalted position of Jesus.

Jesus used this term to speak of himself in the parable of the wicked tenants (Mt 21:42; Mk 12:10; Lk 20:17). The setting for this parable was his final ministry in Jerusalem after he had cleansed the temple. The Jewish leaders had questioned him about his actions, and part of his reply was this parable, which symbolically addressed the situation between Jesus and the leaders. The Jewish leaders were represented in the parable as the tenants who were caring for the vineyard, which symbolized God's people. Those tenants wickedly refused to honor the owner, who represented God, ultimately putting his son to death. The parable speaks of the coming death of Jesus in symbolic terms, and Jesus concluded it by referring the Jewish leaders back to their own Scriptures, Psalm 118:22,23 (cf. Is 28:16), which he understood as speaking of his rejection and exaltation. That is, the

Jewish leaders rejected Jesus, but God will exalt him as the cornerstone.

Second, the term is used in Acts 4:11, which describes Peter's defense before the Jewish rulers in Jerusalem. Peter explained to them the healing of the lame beggar by the temple gate, stressing that the healing took place by the name of Jesus Christ, the Nazarene whom they crucified but whom God raised from the dead (v 10). He then quotes Psalm 118:22 to confirm the events as being according to Scripture. It seems clear that Peter intended the rejection of the stone to refer to Jesus' death and the placing of the stone as the cornerstone to refer to Jesus' resurrection and exaltation. Thus, cornerstone designates Jesus in his exalted position with the Father.

The term is also used in 1 Peter 2:6,7. In verse 4 Peter combines the idea of the rejection of the stone in Psalm 118:22 with the idea of the chosen and precious stone in Isaiah 28:16, adding the idea of living from his own experience of Jesus' resurrection. Peter is encouraging his readers to come to Jesus, that they may be built up as a spiritual house to God (v 5). This rich imagery is used to bring out the exalted nature of Jesus. In verse 6 Peter quotes Isaiah 28:16, which speaks of the chosen and precious cornerstone, and relates this to believers. In verses 7,8 he quotes Psalm 118:22, referring to the rejection of the stone, and Isaiah 8:14, which speaks of a stone of stumbling, and relates these to unbelievers. Peter's purpose is to set before his readers the exalted position of Jesus and to encourage them to remember him to whom they were called.

It is evident that the OT concept of cornerstone is applied to Jesus to emphasize his exalted position with the Father and so to encourage the believer. In Ephesians 2:20 brief reference is also made to Christ Jesus as the cornerstone upon which the church is built.

Cornet. *See* MUSIC AND MUSICAL INSTRUMENTS (HATZOTZROT).

Correction. *See* DISCIPLINE.

Corruption, Mount of. Southern end of the Mt of Olives, called "corruption" because King Solomon built idols there for his foreign wives (1 Kgs 11:7; 2 Kgs 23:13). The term is possibly an ironic play on the Hebrew word for "anointing." The site may have originally been called the "Mt of Anointing" because oil from the many olive groves on its slopes was used in consecration ceremonies.

See OLIVES, MOUNT OF, OLIVET.

Cos. Island of the Sporades group in the Aegean, containing a city of the same name, located off the coast of Caria in Asia Minor. Cos was the apostle Paul's first stop beyond Ephesus on his voyage to Jerusalem at the end of his third missionary tour (Acts 21:1, KJV Coos). In the Apocrypha, Cos and other areas are mentioned as recipients of a decree by the Roman consul Lucius forbidding war against the Jewish population (1 Mc 15:23).

Cos (modern Kos) was a major shipping center, famous for its wheat, ointments, wines, and silk. It eventually became one of the financial centers of the eastern Mediterranean.

Hippocrates, the "father of medicine," was born and practiced there in the fifth and fourth centuries BC. Under King Herod's rule Cos received perpetual revenues, and a statue was built there to honor his son Herod Antipas.

Cosam. Ancestor of Jesus, Addi's father and Elmadam's son, listed only in Luke's genealogy (3:28).

See GENEALOGY OF JESUS CHRIST.

Cosmetics. *See* FASHION AND DRESS.

Cotton. Soft, white, fibrous hairs surrounding the seeds in the boll of various plants of the mallow family (genus *Gossypium*), woven into thread and cloth (Is 19:9).

See CLOTH, CLOTH MANUFACTURING; PLANTS.

Couch. Article of furniture for reclining in sleep or rest.

See FURNITURE.

Counsel, Counselor. Advice; adviser, especially on legal matters (such as a lawyer). In Bible times a counselor in a king's court was like a U.S. cabinet member today. A counselor might at times have been in line to succeed the king. Ahithophel, counselor to David and Absalom, gave advice as sound as the "oracle of God" (2 Sm 16:23). The elders of Israel counseled King Rehoboam (1 Kgs 12:6), as did the friends with whom Rehoboam had grown up (1 Kgs 12:8), although his friends gave poor advice. The Bible mentions official counselors in Egypt (Is 19:11) and Babylon (Dn 3:2,3).

A wise person seeks counsel when making plans: "Without counsel plans go wrong, but with many advisers they succeed" (Prv 15:22). One's counselors may be one's parents (Prv 1:8), older people (Ez 7:26), prophets (2 Chr 25:16), wise men (Jer 18:18), or friends (Prv 27:9 KJV). Some counselors are evil, giving deceitful advice (Prv 12:5).

According to the Bible, God also counsels.

He frustrates the counsel of "the nations who oppose him" (Ps 33:10 LB), but his own counsel endures for many generations (Ps 33:11). No one may counsel the Lord (Is 40:13). His Messiah is called "Wonderful Counselor" (Is 9:6).

In the NT the Spirit counsels or comforts believers (Jn 14:16,17). Christ sends the Holy Spirit to his people (Jn 16:7), and the Spirit, also called the Spirit of truth, bears witness to Christ (Jn 15:26). The ascended Jesus Christ is seen as a counselor in God's heavenly court (1 Jn 2:1, advocate).

See HOLY SPIRIT.

Court. Area enclosed by buildings or walls and without a roof. The temple had courts for priests, women, and Gentiles. Courts were common in private homes as well.

See ARCHITECTURE; HOMES AND DWELLINGS; TABERNACLE, TEMPLE.

Courts and Trials. Legal disputes were as much a part of life in Bible times as they are today. The ways that courts operated and trials were conducted, however, were quite different. Unless those customs are understood, modern readers of the Bible, thinking of contemporary legal procedures, may misunderstand the judicial accounts contained in the Bible.

Although the Bible never explains exactly how courts functioned in ancient times, a reasonably reliable picture can be pieced together from the bits of information it contains. Archaeology has provided additional information about the legal practices of Israel's neighbors. Among the records of ancient Mesopotamia and Egypt are descriptions of court cases that illuminate OT legal practice. Jesus and the apostle Paul were both tried under Roman law, which is much better documented.

Mesopotamian Legal Procedures. Many collections of laws and records of legal cases exist from ancient Mesopotamia (the area between the Tigris and Euphrates Rivers, approximating modern Iraq and eastern Syria). Those records reveal how the legal system operated there between about 2500 and 500 BC. Of particular interest is the period of Hammurabi (1792–1750 BC), a king of Babylon whose laws were renowned in ancient times. At some point before the time of Hammurabi, the patriarch Abraham and his family migrated from Mesopotamia to Canaan, undoubtedly bringing with them legal ideas and customs from their past.

In ancient Babylon the king was supreme lawgiver and judge. The gods were supposed to have endowed him with special intelligence to make good laws. Difficult cases could be referred to the king from lower courts. Those courts often sat in temples, or sometimes in an open public space such as at a city gate. The judges included priests, professional lawyers, and (in lower courts) the town's leading citizens or elders. Except for the king, who presumably had advisers, cases were always tried before a group of judges rather than by a single judge.

In general, a legal action was brought by an aggrieved party, not by a state prosecutor. If one citizen had a grievance against another, both parties would appear in court to make their accusations and defenses. To substantiate a charge, more than one witness was required. In theft cases an accused person had to be caught in the act or in possession of the stolen goods. Where evidence was inconclusive, accused persons could be cleared by taking a solemn oath inviting the gods to bring them harm if they were lying. Refusal to take such an oath was seen as an admission of guilt. Where the court had considerable grounds for suspicion that a charge was true but no clear proof, the accused might be taken to a river and forced to jump in. Whether the defendant sank or floated would determine guilt or innocence.

Normally when all the evidence had been heard, the judges pronounced their verdict and that verdict was written down. One copy of the judgment was given to the plaintiff and another kept in court. Anyone convicted of bringing a false charge was liable to suffer the punishment that would have fallen on the accused had the charge been true; that same principle was part of the Mosaic Law (Dt 19:18,19). Enforcement of a Mesopotamian court's decision was the responsibility of the successful litigant, perhaps at times with the help of court officials.

Egypt's Legal Procedures. Ancient Egypt was also famous for its legal codes; in contrast to Mesopotamia, however, few of its laws have been preserved. The meager evidence suggests that the legal system was like that of Mesopotamia. The king was supreme lawgiver and judge. Lower courts were run by his deputies or district officials sitting as a team, not individually. As in Babylon the legal system was essentially one of civil law; that is, prosecution and enforcement of the court's decision was the responsibility of the individual, not the state.

Old Testament Legal Procedures. *Exodus to Deuteronomy.* The books of Exodus, Leviticus, Numbers, and Deuteronomy contain most of the law in the OT, plus much other information about courts and legal procedures. Those books reveal how trials were conducted before Israel had kings. Certain changes in the legal system occurring after establishment of the monarchy (*c.* 1000 BC) are described in other OT books.

The OT depicts God as supreme lawgiver and judge, with Moses and later the kings as God's deputies. But Moses did not create the law or decide the most difficult cases, which were referred directly to God for decision (see Lv 24:10–23; Nm 15:32–36; 27:1–11). When disputes arose between Israel's leaders, God intervened, judging the guilty party directly (Nm 16, 17). Thus law is seen in the OT as a divine revelation, not a human creation, as it was regarded in ancient Babylon.

Usually it was not necessary to seek God's direct guidance; precedent was sufficient. Elders were appointed in Israel to serve as judges of all but the most serious cases, relieving Moses of the burden of judging all the people himself (Ex 18:13–27). Deuteronomy 16:18 specifies that "judges" be appointed in every town; in other passages those responsible for punishing criminals are called "the elders" (Dt 19:12). The local judges were obviously nonprofessionals selected from the most respected members of each tribe or village. Difficult cases were referred to a central court of justice to be decided by the priests and, in the period of the judges, by the civil and military leader (Dt 17:8–12). Deborah and Samuel were both examples of such "judges of Israel." Samuel even conducted a circuit court in a number of different centers (Jgs 4:4,5; 1 Sm 7:15–17).

In Israel, as in other ancient societies, private prosecution was the norm. An individual with a grievance had to bring the case before the court. Only in situations of idolatry or other serious religious crimes were public prosecutions instituted (Dt 13; 17:2–7). Even in murder cases prosecution was left in the hands of the victim's relatives. One relative called the "avenger of blood" had to pursue the alleged murderer to the nearest city of refuge, where a trial was held (Nm 35:10–34; Dt 19:1–13).

Trials were held in a public place, such as the open space near a city gate (Dt 21:19). During the trial the judges were seated, but the parties to the dispute and the witnesses stood. At least two witnesses were required to convict (Dt 19:15). They had to be eyewitnesses who had caught the accused red-handed. Where such clear-cut evidence was lacking, for example in disputes over ownership, the litigants could take an oath to demonstrate their honesty (Ex 22:8–13). If a husband suspected his wife of infidelity but had no proof, he could require her to undergo an ordeal of drinking "bitter water" to demonstrate her innocence (Nm 5:6–31).

When all the evidence had been presented, the judges gave their verdict. Those who had brought the accusation had the duty of enforcing the court's sentence. Thus a witness of idolatry had to throw the first stone at the guilty person's execution (Dt 17:7). Certain administrative officials may have had the job of writing down the court's decision and seeing that it was enforced (Dt 16:18). At times it may have been difficult for people to uphold their legal rights if their opponent came from a strong and wealthy family.

Other OT Books. When Israel became a kingdom, certain changes were made in its judicial system. Most obviously, the king became the supreme judge who dealt with the most difficult cases. Solomon demonstrated his great wisdom in adjudicating between two women who both claimed to be the mother of a particular baby (1 Kgs 3:16–28). Kings, who had all the power necessary to enforce their decisions, were expected to use it to help the weak members of society such as orphans and widows: "For he delivers the needy when he calls, the poor and him who has no helper" (Ps 72:12).

In practice, however, Israel's kings did not always live up to that ideal. Absalom sowed the seeds of a revolution by telling those who came to the royal court that his father, King David, did not administer justice well (2 Sm 15:1–6). One notable trial in the OT illustrates how royal judicial powers could be completely misused by unscrupulous rulers. Naboth was put to death on a trumped-up charge of blasphemy so that King Ahab could extend his palace grounds by taking over Naboth's vineyard. Though the charge was false, the trial followed correct legal procedures. Two scoundrels were found to give evidence that they had heard Naboth curse God and the king (1 Kgs 21:10); one witness would have been insufficient to secure conviction. Naboth was tried by the elders of the city in a public place. After being convicted he was taken outside the city and executed (21:11–13). In other trials the prophet Jeremiah was charged with subversive activities more than once (Jer 26; 37:11–21; 38).

The prophets sometimes pictured God as taking Israel to court to answer for the nation's misdeeds. God would list Israel's sins and invite the people to explain their behavior. Sometimes heaven and earth, or the mountains, were called to be witnesses confirming the truth of God's accusations. Finally judgment was pronounced (e.g., Is 1:2–26; 43; Jer 2:4–37; Mi 6).

A theme running through the Book of Job is Job's request for a trial. Job thought that if he were given a fair hearing, his innocence would be demonstrated and God would stop causing him so much suffering (cf. Jb 13; 23). Eventually God heeded Job's request and a long cross-examination began, finally reducing Job to silence (42:1–6).

New Testament Legal Procedures. Numerous trials occur in the NT. Jesus was tried by the Sanhedrin (the supreme Jewish religious court) and also by the Roman governor. The Book of Acts mentions various court actions designed to stop the spread of Christianity. Luke, the author of Acts, presents a vivid and accurate description of how courts operated in provinces of the Roman empire. Acts reaches a climax with Paul traveling to Rome to have his case heard by the Roman emperor Nero. Legal procedures in Roman courts were governed by complicated rules broadly resembling modern judicial technicalities. Serious crime was handled by public prosecutors, and trials were usually conducted by one judge. There were lawyers for the prosecution and lawyers for the defense.

In Judea and other provinces of the empire the local legal system was not suppressed. Traditional Jewish courts were allowed to try minor and religious offenses (Acts 4; 6:12–7:60) but were not permitted to handle serious cases where the death penalty was appropriate. For that reason, when the Sanhedrin found Jesus guilty of blasphemy for claiming to be the Son of God and the Messiah, they had to transfer the case to Pontius Pilate, the Roman procurator (governor) of Judea. The Jews considered blasphemy worthy of death but, as they admitted to Pilate, "it is not lawful for us to put any man to death" (Jn 18:31). The rule throughout the Roman empire was that only governors could pronounce the death sentence. Execution of the apostle James by Jewish authorities, mentioned by the Jewish historian Josephus, took place during an interregnum between two governors. The stoning of Stephen was probably an irregularity deliberately overlooked by Pilate (Acts 7).

The Trials of Jesus. Jesus was first tried by the Sanhedrin, presided over by the high priest. By later standards of Jewish legal practice that trial was somewhat irregular. For example, it seems to have been held both at night and on the eve of a festival. Criminal trials were not supposed to take place at such times. It is uncertain that those rules existed in Jesus' day, but even if they did, little can be made of that technicality since the Jewish court had no power to carry out its sentence.

After conviction by the Sanhedrin, Jesus was taken to Pilate, whose Jerusalem residence, the old royal palace called the Praetorium, was on the western side of the city near the modern Jaffa gate. The Romans were unlikely to sentence anyone to death in a religious matter, so the Jewish authorities presented their charges against Jesus in political language: he violated the law by "forbidding us to give tribute to Caesar, and saying that he himself is Christ a king" (Lk 23:2). Perhaps sensing something false about those charges, that they were actually religious rather than political, Pilate sent Jesus to Herod, the ruler of Galilee, who was in Jerusalem at the time. Pilate, who did not have to send Galileans to Herod for trial, probably saw a means of avoiding an uncomfortable decision. Herod, however, pronounced Jesus innocent and returned him to Pilate.

Pilate offered to give Jesus a disciplinary beating traditionally given to troublemakers as a warning to behave themselves in the future (Lk 23:16). But that did not satisfy Jesus' accusers, who pressed the charge of insurrection, threatening to report Pilate to the emperor if he did not convict Jesus. Pilate, who had not been a very successful governor, feared official complaints about his administration, so the threat worked. He sentenced Jesus to be crucified on the charge of being king of the Jews. The heavy scourging that preceded the crucifixion was never a punishment by itself but was a frequent accompaniment to other punishments. Another feature of Roman legal practice illustrated in the Gospels was the division of Jesus' clothes among the soldiers; executioners were allowed to keep such personal effects as a fringe benefit.

The Trials of the Apostle Paul. Paul's trials recorded in the Book of Acts also reflect the division between Jewish and Roman authority in legal matters. When arrested, Paul had a preliminary hearing before the Sanhedrin (Acts 23). He was then transferred to the governor for a formal trial in Caesarea, the governor's usual headquarters. There he was tried before Felix, who adjourned the case for two years until a new governor could be appointed. Luke reported that Felix (another unpopular governor) did that to please the Jews, but it was quite common for governors to leave cases to be dealt with by their successors.

When the new governor, Festus, arrived, he suggested that Paul be tried in Jerusalem. Paul, disliking the prospect of being tried there, exercised his right as a Roman citizen to be tried in Rome before the emperor (Acts 25:10–12). The rest of the Book of Acts tells how Paul eventually reached Rome and had to wait another two years before his case was heard. No details of Paul's trial in Rome are known, but Nero, who was emperor when Paul arrived, tried very few cases himself. He appointed judges to handle appeal cases such as Paul's, so it is unlikely that Paul was actually tried by Nero.

The right of appeal to the emperor was not the only legal right possessed by Roman citizens. They were also protected from being beaten without a trial, a right asserted by Paul in Philippi and Jerusalem (Acts 16:37; 22:24–29).   GORDON J. WENHAM

See CRIMINAL LAW AND PUNISHMENT; CIVIL LAW AND JUSTICE; AVENGER OF BLOOD; SANHEDRIN; CITIES OF REFUGE.

Covenant. Arrangement between two parties involving mutual obligations; especially the arrangement that established the relationship between God and his people, expressed in grace first with Israel and then with the church. Through that covenant God has conveyed to humanity the meaning of human life and salvation. Covenant is one of the central themes of the Bible, where some covenants are between human beings, others between God and human beings.

The covenant theme in the OT, implicit in the garden of Eden, is developed from Noah to Abraham and reaches its first climax in the covenant formed between God and Israel at Mt Sinai. After King David's time, the history of the covenant becomes a less prominent theme.

At a low point in covenant history the Bible introduces the prophet Jeremiah's prophecy of

The bema in Corinth.

a "new covenant" in Israel's future. Christians believe that Jeremiah's prophecy eventually found fulfillment in the person and work of Jesus Christ. It is not accidental that the two volumes of the Christian Bible have been called the Old Covenant and New Covenant (the word commonly translated "testament" means "covenant").

Meaning of Covenant. The essence of covenant is to be found in a particular kind of relationship between persons. Mutual obligations characterize that kind of relationship. Thus a covenant relationship is not merely a mutual acquaintance but a commitment to responsibility and action. A key word in Scripture to describe that commitment is "faithfulness," acted out in a context of abiding friendship.

In the OT the word "covenant" was used in an ordinary human sense as well as in a theological sense. An understanding of human covenants provides a starting point for understanding the covenant between God and human beings.

Human Covenants. A variety of human relationships, from profoundly personal to distantly political, may be described as covenantal. The deep brotherly love that David and Jonathan shared led to a formal covenant between them (1 Sm 18:3). Their covenant of friendship was more than a token of esteem; it bound them to demonstrate mutual loyalty and lovingkindness in certain tangible ways. Jonathan's covenant faithfulness was typified on an occasion when David was out of favor with the king; Jonathan braved his father's wrath to speak favorably for his friend. Subsequently he warned David secretly to flee into hiding (1 Sm 19, 20).

To appreciate the many OT laws on marriage and divorce, one must understand that marriage itself was a covenant relationship (Mal 2:14). The solemn promises exchanged by a man and woman became their covenant obligations. Faithfulness to those promises brought marital blessing (cf. Ps 128; Prv 18:22); violation brought a curse.

An individual could, at least figuratively, make a covenant or vow with himself or herself (something like a New Year's resolution). Job, arguing his integrity before God, referred to a covenant he had made with his eyes to keep him from looking at a woman licentiously (Jb 31:1).

Covenants could also have a national or international character. The elders of Israel made a national covenant with King David in Hebron (2 Sm 5:3). Probably it contained explicit promises both from the elders on behalf of the people to submit themselves to the king's authority and from David to rule the nation justly and according to the Law of God

(Dt 17:15–20). That covenant relationship described mutual obligations between a senior partner (the king) and junior partners (the Israelites). In international relationships OT covenants were similar to modern treaties or alliances. King Solomon entered into such a covenant with Hiram, king of Tyre; that covenant, like many modern international treaties, was a trade agreement between the two nations (1 Kgs 5:12).

Covenant is thus an interpersonal framework of trust, responsibilities, and benefits, with broad application to almost every human relationship from personal friendship to international trade agreements. In Scripture covenant is also the most comprehensive concept covering an individual's relationship to God.

Divine–Human Covenants. The same basic characteristics of a strictly human covenant are present in a divine covenant: (1) a relationship between two parties (God and a human being or nation), and (2) mutual obligations between the covenant partners. To the OT believer, religion meant covenant. OT religion was faithfulness to the covenant relationship between God and his chosen people; religious responsibilities for both the faith and practice of Israel were covenant responsibilities.

The concept of a divine–human covenant in the OT was not static. Although the fundamental character of covenant remains the same throughout the Bible, the specific nature and form of the covenant changed and developed in the course of ancient Israel's history. A brief survey of covenant history will further clarify its dimensions.

Beginnings of the Covenant Tradition. *Adam.* Adam and Eve were placed in the garden. God was their Creator; they were his creatures. The meaning of their lives was to be found in relationship with each other and with God, the giver of the garden. The fall, however, brought a disruption of the divine relationship, and they were expelled from the garden.

The fall substantially influenced the nature of subsequent religious covenants. The separation of humankind from God clarifies the nature of the human predicament. Created for a relationship with the Creator, sinning humans are excluded from that relationship and cannot, on their own accord, reestablish it. From that circumstance emerges a distinctive feature of divine–human covenants; namely, that God alone can initiate the relationship of covenant.

Noah. The first explicit mention of covenant in Scripture refers to the initiative taken by God to bind himself again to human beings in a covenant, despite human faithlessness. When God warned Noah to build an ark in order to escape the impending flood, he also promised to establish a covenant with him (Gn 6:18). The corruption and violence of the human race had provoked God's anger, but his grace was shown in his dealings with Noah. The promised covenant provided that God would maintain a relationship with one family, even though other divine–human relationships were being formally severed. Significantly, God's covenant promise to Noah came in a context of demand: God ordered Noah to build an ark (Gn 6:14). Noah's receipt of the covenant blessing depended on his obedience to a divine command.

The covenant was elaborated only after the flood, when Noah had made an offering to God (Gn 8:20–22). The covenant with Noah was in fact a universal covenant with humankind and all living creatures (Gn 9:8–10). God promised never to send such a flood again as judgment on the world. The sign of that covenant was the rainbow.

The covenant with Noah affords some perspective for understanding the "covenant God." Although human beings may deserve destruction because of their wickedness, God withholds that destruction. The covenant of Noah did not establish an intimate relationship between God and each living being; nevertheless, it left open the possibility of a more intimate covenant. Human beings, in spite of their evil, are allowed for a time to live in God's world; during those years they may seek a deeper relationship with that world's Creator.

In the Jewish tradition the "Laws of Noah" were understood from the time of the ancient rabbis to be laws binding on all peoples. To the reverence for human life demanded in Genesis 9:5,6 the rabbis added such matters as prohibitions against idolatry, blasphemy, and theft. They affirmed those prohibitions to be universally binding, reflecting the theme of justice that was central to the covenant with Noah. The flood which preceded the covenant was an act of divine justice; God judged a sinful world. Yet God's grace balanced his justice; God made a covenant with Noah for all humankind. The demand for justice, particularly with respect to life, was expressed clearly at the heart of the covenant: "For your lifeblood I will surely require a reckoning" (Gn 9:5). Justice is essentially the negative aspect of the moral law regulating the lives of human beings with each other and with God. Justice is corrective rather than creative. On the other side of the covenant "coin" from justice is righteousness. That quality was first articulated in God's covenant with Abraham.

Abraham. The first explicit reference to God's covenant with Abraham is in Genesis 15. When the Lord called the 75-year-old Abram (as he was first called) to leave his home city of Haran and set out on a journey, a relationship already existed between God and Abram. In that relationship, which enabled God to command Abram's obedience, God made certain promises to him: "I will make of you a great nation, and I will bless you, and make your name great, so that you will be a blessing" (Gn 12:2).

Formal establishment of the covenant with Abram is described in Genesis 15 as a profound religious experience. The initiative lay entirely with God, who approached Abram in a vision and spoke with him. Abram raised a fundamental objection: how could he experience the blessing of God if it was to come to him through a son he did not have? His wife Sarai was past the childbearing age, and he himself was "as good as dead" (Rom 4:19). God assured the old man that he would have a son through whom his descendants would eventually be as numerous as the stars of heaven. Abram's belief at that point introduced the theme of righteousness central to the covenant concept: Abram "believed the Lord, and he reckoned it to him as righteousness" (Gen 15:6). At the end of that day Abram knew that his own future and the future of his descendants were firmly in the hands of the covenant God. "On that day the Lord made a covenant with Abram, saying,'To your descendants I give this land' "(Gn 15:18).

The covenant is more fully expressed in Genesis 17, which probably records a renewal of God's covenant with Abram. The initiative once again lay with God (Gn 17:1). God addressed the 99-year-old Abram in words that made clear that the covenant was not a relationship between equal partners. God was the Almighty; Abram was a human being to whom an extraordinary privilege had been granted.

Yet the details of the covenant in Genesis 17 show that both partners assumed responsibilities. God committed himself voluntarily to Abram and his descendants, in turn requiring certain commitments from Abram. The blessing Abram would receive as a covenant partner became clear from the new name God gave him. "No longer will you be called Abram; your name will be Abraham, for I have made you a father of many nations" (Gn 17:5). God would give to Abraham, through his descendants, the land of Canaan as an everlasting gift and would be the personal God of Abraham and his family in perpetuity (Gn 17:7,8).

God's giving required a response of obedience from Abraham: "Walk before me, and be blameless" (Gn 17:1). Those simple words indicate the essence of covenant relationship: to relate to God is to live in his presence; since God is holy, one who "walks before him" is expected to live a life of integrity and blamelessness.

The covenant also had a more formal aspect. Abraham and the male members of his household were to undergo the rite of circumcision as a symbol of covenant commitment. Abraham was an old man when he was circumcised (Gn 17:24), though male children born into the covenant family were to be circumcised when they were eight days old (Gn 17:12). Circumcision was not in itself a ritual peculiar to the Hebrews; it was practiced in most societies in the ancient Near East (the Philistines were one exception). The distinctiveness lay in what the act symbolized: among other things, a continuing and faithful relationship with the living God.

God's covenant with Abraham was characterized by both present and future realities. The covenant established a continuing relationship between Abraham and his Creator. Yet its thrust pointed to future blessings: in the children yet to be born, the "chosen people," and in the land that eventually his descendants would call their own.

Another dimension of the covenant lay still further in the future: "In you all the families of the earth shall be blessed" (Gn 12:3). Early in the OT the idea of election (God's unconditional preference; cf. 2 Thes 2:13) is present. God chose to enter a covenant relationship with a particular man and his particular descendants. Yet God always elects a person to serve: Adam, to cultivate the garden; Noah, to build an ark; Abraham, to leave his home for another land and to live blamelessly before God (cf. Eph 2:8–10). Further, the "particularity" of Abraham's election contained within it a universality: through his descendants the blessing of God would be offered to all.

Thus the future aspects of Abraham's covenant reflect two stages. From Abraham's perspective, in the relatively near future his descendants would possess a land given them by God. But in the more distant future was the prospect of a universal blessing, the culmination of God's work in the world. The initial fulfillment of that distant future is perceived in the NT, but the more immediate fulfillment of God's promise was the Sinai covenant at the time of Moses.

The Sinai Covenant. The covenant established between God and Israel at Mt Sinai is the focal point of the covenant tradition in the OT. It was anticipated in the covenant of Abraham and lay behind the covenant of David and the proclamation of the prophets. It was central to OT religion, laying down the foundations of Judaism which continue into the modern world. The Sinai covenant was the formal institution of a relationship between God and his chosen people, Israel. Although matters of chronology in Hebrew history cannot be fixed with certainty, it is probable that the Sinai covenant was established during the first half of the 13th century BC.

In order to appreciate the impact of the Sinai covenant one must understand its historical context. It was preceded by the exodus of the Hebrew people from Egypt under the leadership of Moses. The exodus was an extraordinary act of liberation in which God intervened in the normal course of history to free his people from slavery in Egypt. The exodus is interpreted in the OT as a divine act comparable to creation, the act through which God "created" the nation of Israel. Examination of the two versions of the fourth commandment (Ex 20:11; Dt 5:12–15) shows that the exodus from Egypt directly parallels the creation of the world as a basis for sabbath observance. Although Israel was created in the exodus, the nation had neither constitution nor land. The covenant provided the nascent state of Israel with a constitution making it a theocratic state (a state ruled by God).

The basic account of the Sinai covenant is contained in Exodus 19 and 20. The initiative came from God, who gave instructions through Moses to prepare for the covenant; God spoke the words that contained the covenant offer. There was no doubt that the God of Israel was the senior partner in the relationship made formal at Sinai. The God who had revealed himself through his acts in the exodus then revealed himself in words. Those two aspects—the God who acts and speaks—are central to OT theology. And although the covenant contained law, it was preceded by the exodus, an act of divine grace.

God's offer of covenant carried with it a divine promise: "You shall be to me a kingdom of priests and a holy nation" (Ex 19:6). The promise was one of extraordinary privilege; an entire nation was called upon to represent all other nations before the God of the universe. But the priestly office, though it carried privilege, was also a demanding office. A priest had to be pure and had to know the God whose presence he was required to enter. Thus Israel, the priestly nation, received a law that would provide direction in living, in loving God, and in serving all people. The law given with the covenant expressed the requirements for God's covenant people.

The Covenant Law. The covenant law had two principal parts. First, the Ten Commandments expressed God's requirements of Israel in a concise form (Ex 20:2–17). The commandments specified the covenant people's relationship both to God and to other human beings. Although the tendency in the 20th century is to view the Ten Commandments as a system of ethics or morality, they had a different role in ancient Israel. The covenant law was the foundation or constitution of a new nation, a special "nation of priests." The head of the nation-state was God. Hence, in ancient Israel the status of the Ten Commandments was approximately that of the code of criminal law in a modern nation-state. To break one of those laws was to commit a crime against God, the head of the state. Yet the laws had a positive purpose. They set down a way of life that would result in a full and rich communion with God and community with others.

The second part of the covenant law was a detailed law code covering the activities of everyday life. Examples of such laws are found in Exodus 21–23. These laws were compiled and recorded in the "Book of the Covenant" (Ex 24:7). Although many laws were contained in this book, it was impossible to codify every aspect of human behavior. The diversity of the examples given indicates that for the covenant member no area of human life was beyond the influence of the covenant. Persons who entered a relationship with God entered into a relationship that impinged on every possible aspect of their lives.

Covenant Renewal. The covenant at Sinai was made with a particular group of people under the leadership of Moses but was binding on future generations. Consequently the covenant was renewed from time to time. Covenant renewals are recorded in the time of Joshua (Jos 8:30–34; 24:1–28) and, much later, during the reign of King Josiah (2 Kgs 23:1–3).

The most important passage in the Bible for understanding covenant renewal and the nature of covenant is the Book of Deuteronomy. The entire book describes a particular covenant-renewal ceremony that occurred at a critical juncture in Israel's early history. The Sinai covenant was renewed just before Moses' death, before the transition of leadership to Joshua, and before a major military campaign to possess the Promised Land.

The covenant since the time of Abraham had contained a promise of land. Immediately before they entered that land (c. 1250 BC), the covenant vows were renewed with a new generation of Israelites, most of whom had not stood at the foot of Mt Sinai some 40 years earlier. Although covenant renewal is the central theme of Deuteronomy, the writer focused primarily on Moses' sermon rather than on a detailed account of the renewal ceremony.

Many aspects of the ceremony were simply a repetition of what happened at the original ratification of the covenant. The Ten Com-mandments were repeated (Dt 5:6–21), and the laws of the Book of the Covenant were expounded in greater detail (Dt 12–26). Two points emerging in Deuteronomy are particularly significant for an understanding of covenant: a clear statement of covenant love and a detailed statement of the blessings and curses that accompanied the making and renewing of the covenant.

1. Love underlies all covenants. That principle had been implicit in the fact that the Sinai covenant was preceded by the exodus, a remarkable demonstration of God's grace to and love for his people. It is clarified in Deuteronomy: the covenant was established with the chosen people in the first place because God loved them (Dt 7:8). Consequently it is not surprising to discover that central to all the commands placed upon Israel was the command to love: "Love the Lord your God with all your heart and with all your soul and with all your strength" (Dt 6:5 NIV). Jesus later called that commandment "the great and first commandment" (Mt 22:38), essential for any member of the covenant community. To enter into covenant with God was to have a relationship with one who loves and to return that love. His love came first.

2. The renewal ceremony also clarified that covenant carried with it divine blessings and curses (Dt 27, 28). If Israel loved God and kept the covenant law, the nation would experience God's blessings (Dt 28:1–14). But if Israel did not obey the covenant law and thereby failed to demonstrate its love for God, the curses of the covenant would ensue (Dt 28:15–68). Ultimately the curse could culminate in an end to the covenant, loss of the land, and a return to the slavery that characterized Israel's life before the exodus (Dt 28:68). The tension between divine grace and the contingency of human obedience, at the heart of Deuteronomy's covenant renewal, was eventually resolved during the dark days in which the prophet Jeremiah lived (Jer 31, 33).

Form of the Covenant. Modern biblical scholarship has established that the Sinai covenant and its renewals were formally patterned after a particular type of human covenant, namely the suzerainty treaty of the ancient world (an agreement between a great power and a lesser power). Archaeological discoveries in the 20th century have brought to light a number of such international political documents, the most interesting coming from the ancient Hittite empire and dating from approximately the 14th century BC. Study of those treaty documents has revealed a fairly consistent pattern. Comparison with biblical passages describing the Sinai covenant shows a remarkable parallel. The structural parallel

Parallels Between Hittite Suzerainty Treaties and the Book of Deuteronomy

Structure of Hittite Suzerainty Treaties (14th Century BC)	Structure of Deuteronomy, a Hebrew "Covenant Document"
1. Preamble. "These are the words of the Great King. . ."	*1. Preamble* (1:1–6). "These are the words which Moses spoke. . ."
2. Historical Prologue. The events leading up to the treaty.	*2. Historical Prologue* (1:7–4:49). Events leading up to the making and renewing of the covenant.
3. General Stipulations. The loyalty due to the suzerain.	*3. General Stipulations* (5–11). The loyalty due to God.
4. Specific Stipulations. Detailed law relating to the vassal's obedience to the suzerain.	*4. Specific Stipulations* (12–26). The detailed Hebrew casuistic law.
5. Divine Witnesses. Called to witness the making of the treaty ("heaven and earth").	*5. Divine Witness* (32). The witness of "heaven and earth" (30:19; 32:1).
6. Curses and Blessings. Contingent upon disobedience or obedience.	*6. Curses and Blessings* (27,28). Contingent upon disobedience or obedience.

between the suzerainty treaties and the Book of Deuteronomy is outlined in the table, "Parallels Between Hittite Suzerainty Treaties and the Book of Deuteronomy," which omits many minor details of similarity.

In Deuteronomy the Hebrews seem to have adapted the form of international suzerainty treaties to express their own covenant relationship with God. Why did they choose that particular form? Perhaps the Hebrews had been bound to their Egyptian masters by that kind of treaty, so they wanted to dramatize their liberation by making a new treaty, this time with their God at Sinai. Also, the Sinai covenant formed the constitution of a new but small Near Eastern nation. Whereas other small nations commonly depended for their existence on the generosity of a suzerain power (e.g., Egypt), Israel was to be a free nation, owing allegiance only to God. Israel's "treaty" with God meant that it could acknowledge no other master. Its freedom and strength lay in its wholehearted commitment to God alone.

The Covenant with David.
The covenant tradition underwent modification during the time of King David (c. 1000 BC). The Sinai covenant had been established between God and Israel, with Moses acting as mediator. In David's time an additional element was added; God entered a covenant with David as king. That royal covenant was intimated to David through the prophet Nathan (2 Sm 7:8–16), indicating once again the divine initiative. It was to be an everlasting covenant with David's royal lineage (2 Sm 23:5).

Christians generally interpret the covenant with David as a messianic covenant. For several centuries the dynasty established by David ruled a united Israel, then ruled the remaining southern kingdom of Judah. But in 586 BC Judah was conquered by the Babylonians. At that point a descendant of David was

no longer ruling an independent kingdom of God's chosen people. The everlasting nature of the covenant with David was brought out, however, not in the pages of ancient history but in the expectation of a Messiah who would be born of David's descendants. Matthew and Luke both pointed to Jesus' Davidic descent (Mt 1:1; Lk 3:31). The NT thus extends the covenant acts of God into the new age in the person of Jesus.

The New Covenant in the Old Testament.
Although David's covenant with God was eternal, in a sense the covenant established with Israel on Mt Sinai was temporal. The Sinai covenant included conditional clauses, stated in the blessings and curses of Deuteronomy. Israel's disobedience of the covenant law would at worst bring exile from the Promised Land, a central covenant theme from Abraham to Moses and beyond.

The Hebrew prophets often perceived the danger of an end to the covenant as a result of Israel's sins. Some of the prophets, especially Hosea and Jeremiah, also perceived a deeper truth; namely, that the covenant was rooted in divine love and that therefore even the curse of God could not be final.

Hosea dramatically expressed that truth through the "living parable" of his marriage (Hos 1–3). He married Gomer at God's command, but later, as a result of her unfaithfulness, the marital covenant was dissolved by divorce. Although Gomer's adulterous acts compelled Hosea to divorce her, he did not cease to love her. God later commanded Hosea to go back to Gomer (Hos 3:1); despite her unfaithfulness the prophet was to take her again into the covenant relationship of marriage. That acted-out parable depicted God's actions with Israel. Israel's sin would inevitably culminate in a divorce from God, but Hosea perceived a new marriage. In the new covenant between God and Israel, Israel would be graciously accepted back into a relationship with God (Hos 2:14–18).

The new covenant is given powerful expression in the writings of the prophet Jeremiah, who lived through the end of the 7th and beginning of the 6th centuries BC. In his lifetime Jeremiah saw the kingdom of Judah defeated in war. The nation lost its independence and became a vassal of the Babylonian empire. In an external sense, that defeat in 586 BC marked the end of the Sinai covenant. Israel could no longer call the Promised Land its own. Yet Jeremiah perceived a truth beyond the contemporary political realities. God's work in the world, like his love for the world, was not over.

Thus Jeremiah spoke of a new covenant that God would bring into effect: "The days are coming, says the Lord, when I will make a new covenant with the house of Israel and the house of Judah" (Jer 31:31). The new covenant would be marked by an act of God within human hearts, a radical spiritual transformation (Jer 31:33). At the last supper Jesus declared to his disciples that "this cup which is poured out for you is the new covenant in my blood" (Lk 22:20). To the writer of Hebrews the new covenant was central to a full understanding of the ministry of Jesus Christ (Heb 8:8–12).

Conclusion. Covenant is a concept central to the message and the history of the OT. The covenant theme continues into the NT as a way of interpreting the Christian gospel. Meaning in human life is to be found in a covenant relationship with the living God. Yet sinful human beings cannot work their way into such a relationship; God alone can initiate it. According to the NT, God's act in giving his son Jesus to die opened up the covenant relationship to all human beings. The forgiveness made available by Jesus' "blood of the new covenant" makes it possible for any individual to enter into a covenant relationship with God. Entry into such a relationship, today as in Abraham's time, hinges upon faith (Gal 3:6–14).

PETER C. CRAIGIE

See COVENANT, THE NEW; LAW, BIBLICAL CONCEPT OF; OATH; VOW; ALLIANCE.

Bibliography. G.W. Buchanan, *The Consequences of the Covenant;* D.R. Hillers, *Covenant: The History of a Biblical Idea;* J. Jocz, *The Covenant: A Theology of Human Destiny;* M.G. Kline, *Treaty of the Great King;* D.J. McCarthy, *Treaty and Covenant;* T.M. McComiskey, *The Covenants of Promise;* G.E. Mendenhall, *Law and Covenant in Israel and the Ancient Near East.*

Covenant, Book of the.

Phrase used by Moses in reference to the Ten Commandments and the laws and stipulations recorded in Exodus 20:22–23:33.

See BOOK OF THE COVENANT.

Covenant, The New.

Sovereign administration of grace instituted by God through Jesus Christ for the redemption of fallen humanity, replacing and fulfilling the old covenant, which was expressed primarily through the Mosaic law. The expression "new covenant" is found principally in the NT; the word "testament," in fact, is better translated "covenant."

Old Covenant. Although the concept of a new covenant is found in several places in the OT (Ez 34:23–31; 37:24–28; Jl 2:12–32), the actual phrase occurs only once (Jer 31:31). That passage contrasts the new covenant which the prophet Jeremiah saw God making with Israel "after those days" (Jer 31:32–34) with the covenant God had made with his people in the days of Moses. The contrast is seen first of all in the internal nature of the new covenant. Whereas the old covenant was written on tables of stone (Ex 31:18; 34:27–32; Dt 4:13; 5:22; 9:11; 10:3,4) and in a book (Ex 24:7; cf. the phrase "old written code," Rom 7:6), the new covenant is to be "written on the human heart." One result is a clearer revelation of what God demands; another is the enablement of believers to fulfill those demands (see Rom 8:2–4). The interior nature of the new covenant is spoken of in several other passages (Ez 11:19–21; 36:26,27) and made explicit in the prophet Joel of a time when God "will pour out [his] spirit on all flesh" (Jl 2:28–32).

A second contrast is in the way God's people know him under the two covenants. There is no doubt that Israel under the old covenant "knew" God; God had revealed himself, though at times the nation tended to forget this (Jgs 2:10; Hos 4:1,6). What the prophets envisioned in the new covenant is a unique personal knowledge of God by each individual member of the covenant community.

Finally, the two covenants differ in regard to God's dealing with human sin. Jeremiah promised that God would forgive the iniquity of his people and blot out their sin. Israel already knew that God delighted in mercy and forgiveness (Ex 34:6,7), but Jeremiah was saying that God would "remember their sin no more" (Jer 31:34). Under the old covenant there was a "reminder of sin year after year" (Heb 10:3); under the new covenant no remembrance of sin remains, "for by a single offering he has perfected for all time those who are sanctified" (Heb 10:14).

Intertestamental Period. During the intertestamental period the nation of Israel looked forward to the establishment of the new covenant. The pseudepigraphal Book of Jubilees spoke of a time when God would circumcise the people's hearts and give them "a holy spirit"; then they would fulfill his commandments and never again turn away from him

(Jub 1:21–25). The people of Israel looked forward to a time when God's Spirit would be active in the nation once again through prophecy (1 Mc 4:46; 14:41) and in a unique way act in individual lives (Test Judah 24:2,3; Test Levi 18:11).

Expectation of the new covenant was most clearly seen and emphasized by a Jewish sect known as the Essenes, who had a monastic community at Qumran and related sectarian communities. The Essenes, however, believed that their community itself was the new covenant that had been promised by Jeremiah. In the Dead Sea Scrolls found at Qumran the community is described as "the men who have entered into the new covenant in the Land of Damascus," or as "members of the new covenant in the Land of Damascus." The community is referred to as "the community of the everlasting covenant." The Hebrew term for covenant occurs over 110 times in the literature of Qumran. Evidently initiation into the sect was regarded as a way of entering into the new covenant. In the Qumran concept the new covenant, like the old, centered around the Law of Moses; it was thought that through the founder of the sect, the "Teacher of Righteousness," God had given to the community the true interpretation of the Law.

New Covenant. The expression "new covenant" is found at least six times in the NT (1 Cor 11:25; 2 Cor 3:6; Heb 8:8,13; 9:15; 12:24; and probably Lk 22:20). In certain Greek manuscripts the phrase is also found in Matthew 26:28 and Mark 14:24, where "new" seems to have been added by various scribes to "blood of the covenant," in order to make these accounts conform to parallel accounts of the Lord's Supper in 1 Corinthians or possibly in Luke.

Even though the term "new" is not found in the accounts in Matthew and Mark in the best Greek manuscripts, and was therefore probably not part of the original text, it is clear from all four accounts that Jesus saw the Lord's Supper as instituting a different and therefore "new" covenant. The covenant was being sealed by his sacrificial death, that is, by his blood, just as the Mosaic covenant was sealed by the "blood of the covenant" (Ex 24:6–8). The cup of the Lord's Supper symbolizes the blood of Christ's sacrifice, sealing the new covenant God has at last made with his people. The new covenant, ratified by Christ's death, is what the church therefore commemorates each time it celebrates the Lord's Supper.

In his institution of the Lord's Supper, Jesus did not elucidate what the "newness" of the covenant entailed. Elsewhere he mentioned a "baptism with the Holy Spirit" (Acts 1:5; 11:16; cf. Mt 3:11; Mk 1:8; Lk 3:16; and Jn 1:33, where this promise is found on the lips of John the Baptist; cf. also 1 Cor 12:13). Yet both OT prophecies refer to the same new covenant that God would establish in the future, as shown in 2 Corinthians 3:6. There the apostle Paul stated that God "has made us competent to be ministers of a new covenant" (Jer 31:31), not "in a written code but in the Spirit" (Jl 2:28–32), for "the written code kills, but the Spirit gives life."

Superiority of the New Covenant. In 2 Corinthians 3, Paul was showing that in contrast to the old (Mosaic) covenant (v 14), which was a "dispensation of death, carved in letters on stone" (v 7), the new covenant instituted by Jesus is one of far greater splendor (vv 8,9), written on the human heart by the Spirit of the living God himself (v 3).

The new covenant concept is treated most exhaustively and systematically in the Book of Hebrews. In Hebrews 8:8–12 the quotation of Jeremiah 31:31–34 is the longest OT quotation found in the NT. In Hebrews 12:24 a different Greek word for "new" is used, but the meaning remains the same. The theme of the new covenant dominates the Book of Hebrews, which was written to encourage faltering Christians by demonstrating the superiority of the Christian faith over their old Jewish beliefs and practices. In Hebrews the new covenant is seen as better than the old "obsolete" covenant in a number of ways.

1. The new covenant has a better priesthood than the old covenant, since there is no longer any need for a continual change of priests due to death (Heb 7:23). One continual priest now lives forever to make intercession before God on behalf of his people (7:24,25).

2. The new covenant priest is better than those of the old covenant, since Jesus does not have to offer sacrifices continually for his own sins and then for the sins of his people. He has instead made one complete and perfect offering (7:27; 9:25–28; 10:12).

3. The new covenant has a better sacrifice than the old covenant; what the blood of bulls and goats could not do, since the atonement they brought could at best be only partial (10:2,3), the blood of Christ has done once for all (9:11–14; 10:1–10).

4. The new covenant is built on "better promises" than the old (8:6).

5. Whereas the old covenant was imperfect (8:7) and thus became obsolete (8:13), the new covenant is perfect and eternal (13:20).

6. Whereas the old covenant provided a believer with no direct access to God (9:6–8), the new covenant provides a direct access to God that can purify and perfect the believer's conscience (cf. 9:14 with 9:9).

7. The new covenant possesses a better "surety" or guarantee, an oath sworn by God himself (7:20–22).

8. The new covenant assures the presence of the Holy Spirit in the life of each believer. The new covenant community has been touched by the promised Spirit (6:4) who, according to Paul, is both the seal and guarantee of their inheritance (see 2 Cor 1:22; 5:5; Eph 1:13,14).

Similarities of the Covenants. Having examined some features that make the new covenant "new," one should be careful not to think of it as contrary or antithetical to the old covenant. The new covenant is not a refutation of the old, but a fulfillment and "interiorization." The continuity and essential unity between the two are as obvious as the differences between them.

Both covenants were instituted by the sovereign initiative of God on the basis of grace (cf. Ex 19:4,5; Jer 31:31). Both were addressed to the same people, the seed of Abraham—though the new covenant also includes the gentile world that was at one time "alienated from the commonwealth of Israel, and strangers to the covenants of promise, having no hope and without God in the world" (Eph 2:12). By faith Gentiles can become the children of Abraham (Rom 4:16; Gal 3:7) and thus become participants in the new covenant. Both covenants required the seal of a sacrifice (cf. Ex 24:4–8; 1 Cor 11:25), and both have the same object: that "I will be their God" (cf. Ex 6:7; Lv 26:12; Jer 31:33).

Further, the new covenant results in a new commandment, just as the old covenant was coupled with a code of commandments. Within both covenants, *being* and *doing* go hand in hand; being God's children by his election and doing his commandments cannot be separated. Under the old covenant the children of Israel promised to do "all that the Lord has spoken" (Ex 19:8). Under the new covenant those who have the Law written on their hearts keep the "new commandment" of a better covenant (Jn 13:34; 1 Jn 2:7,8; 2 Jn 5). Yet that new commandment is also a fulfillment, since "he who loves his neighbor has fulfilled the law" (Rom 13:8; cf. Mt 22:40; Rom 13:10; Gal 5:14).

Conclusion. The new covenant and its accompanying new commandment are both fulfillments of what was implicit in the old. The new covenant is "written on the heart" of each member of the new covenant community by the Holy Spirit. The power of God's Spirit within, enabling the believer to carry out the new commandment (Rom 8:2–4; Gal 5:16–25), is a distinctive feature of the new covenant.

ROBERT H. STEIN

See COVENANT.

Covenant of Salt. Biblical phrase for a two-way agreement, the inviolability of which was symbolized by salt. A Middle Eastern saying, "There is bread and salt between us," meant that a relationship had been confirmed by sharing a meal. Salt symbolized the life and enduring nature of the alliance. In the OT salt appears in the relationship between God and Israel (Lv 2:13). As a purifying agent and preservative in the cereal offering, salt symbolized the indissoluble nature of the covenant between God and Israel.

An everlasting "covenant of salt" (Nm 18:19) was made between God and Aaron, who represented the whole priesthood of Israel. Since the Levites received no inheritance in the Promised Land, God himself was to be their special portion forever. God's covenant with King David and his sons was also called a covenant of salt (2 Chr 13:5).

See COVENANT; COVENANT, THE NEW.

Covering of the Head. Problem discussed by the apostle Paul in 1 Corinthians 11:2–16. In Paul's day Jewish women always wore veils in public and Greek women generally went veiled—a practice that showed deference to authority and dignified the wearer.

Disagreement arose in the church at Corinth when women prayed publicly with uncovered heads. Since women had traditionally covered their heads out of respect for men (or "husbands"), it seemed shameful for a woman to pray or prophesy unveiled; it was viewed "as if her head were shaven" (v 5), a sign of dishonor.

Paul responded to that confusion with a brief theological excursus about creation (v 8). An enigmatic reference to "angels" (v 10) precedes his statement on the interdependence of men and women (vv 11,12). Some interpret the word translated "veil" (v 10) as a symbol of new authority, since in the synagogues women were permitted no part in Jewish worship services. In contrast, a Christian woman could participate in Christian worship provided she wore a veil.

Paul spoke of "nature" as teaching men and women on the subject. Some scholars think he meant that since a woman's long hair was "her pride" (v 15), she should cover her head. Some think that the phrase referred to hair style. Others believe Paul was saying that a veil was not needed since "her hair is given to her for a covering" (v 15).

Paul encouraged freedom but also insisted on order in the churches. He upheld certain customs to avoid offense (see 1 Cor 9:19–23). Yet he challenged other customs for the sake of the gospel's integrity (see Gal 6:12).

In most church traditions covering the head is considered necessary only in societies where it is proper for women to be veiled. Some groups, however, believe that all women should still wear hats or something on their heads in church services. In a few groups women regularly wear small "coverings" in their hair so they will always be able to pray with their heads "covered."

See CORINTHIANS, FIRST LETTER TO THE.

Covetousness. The desire to have something for oneself, a craving or passionate desire. Three Hebrew words are translated "covet" in the OT. In one recital of the Ten Commandments (Dt 5:21) the text reads, "You shall not covet your neighbor's wife." The same Hebrew word occurs in Proverbs 21:26: "All day long the wicked covets." Another word implies dishonest gain (Hab 2:9). In the Exodus listing of the Ten Commandments a third word is used for craving a neighbor's wife (Ex 20:17). The same word is used of Achan's coveting of the spoils of Ai (Jos 7:21; cf. Mi 2:2). To covet is to desire inordinately, to place the object of desire before love and devotion to God.

That idea is conveyed in the NT by a Greek word literally meaning "inordinate desire to have more." The apostle Paul listed that kind of covetousness among earthly attitudes of which Christians are to rid themselves. "Put to death therefore what is earthly in you: fornication, impurity, passion, evil desire, and covetousness, which is idolatry" (Col 3:5; cf. Eph 5:3; 1 Cor 6:10).

Covetousness is pictured as a grave sin that leads to a variety of other sins. The love of money is "the root of all evils" (1 Tim 6:9, 10; cf. Prv 15:27). It was the sin of Ananias and Sapphira (Acts 5:2,3; cf. 1 Sm 15:9,19; Mt 26:14,15; 2 Pt 2:15; Jude 11). Jesus warned: "Take heed, and beware of all covetousness; for a man's life does not consist in the abundance of his possessions" (Lk 12:15). Another Greek word translated "covet" in KJV is better translated "earnestly desire" in a positive sense (1 Cor 14:39).

The translators of the OT who produced the Septuagint used still another Greek word for the three Hebrew words rendered "covet" in English versions. In the NT the verb form of that word is used in both a positive and negative sense. It means "to desire or long for," whether food (Lk 15:16), the divine mysteries (Mt 13:17; 1 Pt 1:12), some good thing (Phil 1:23; Heb 6:11), or some evil thing (Mt 5:28; 1 Thes 4:5; 1 Jn 2:17). The noun form of the same word generally reflects an attitude of disobedience to the law of God in which desire has

given place to an evil impulse that results in sin (Jn 8:44; Rom 1:24; 6:12; 7:7,8; 13:14; Gal 5:16,26).

See TEN COMMANDMENTS, THE.

Cow. *See* ANIMALS (CATTLE).

Coz. KJV spelling of Koz in 1 Chronicles 4:8.

See KOZ #1.

Cozbi. Midianite woman with whom a Hebrew named Zimri entered into an illicit relationship. Phinehas, the grandson of Aaron, stopped a plague on Israel by executing Zimri and Cozbi (Nm 25:15–18).

Cozeba. Alternate name for Achzib, a city in Judah's territory, in 1 Chronicles 4:22.

See ACHZIB #1.

Craftsman. *See* TRADES AND OCCUPATIONS.

Craftsmen, Valley of. Place named for a community of craftsmen who lived in a valley on the southern border of the Plain of Sharon (1 Chr 4:14; Neh 11:35).

See GE-HARASHIM.

Crane. Translation of a Hebrew word in Isaiah 38:14 and Jeremiah 8:7, the meaning of which is uncertain.

See BIRDS.

Crawling Things. Translation of various Hebrew words primarily referring to reptiles.

See ANIMALS (ADDER; ASP; GECKO; LIZARD; SERPENT; SKINK).

Creation, Doctrine of. One of the two central themes in Scripture comprising the backbone of its theological teaching, the other theme being redemption. Creation is not the same as redemption; nor can redemption so overshadow creation as to cut short its theological validity. Both doctrines belong together but in a unique relationship. The God of Israel is also the God who created the heavens and the earth out of nothing. Redemption occurs within the creation, which serves as its presupposition and backdrop. The end of redemption is the creation of the new heavens and the new earth.

Human beings unaided by divine revelation cannot arrive at the biblical doctrine of creation by theological, philosophical, or scientific speculation. According to the Bible, human knowledge of creation must come by God's revelation (cf. Heb 11:3). That creation is known only by faith means that it is known only by revelation.

Understanding Creation. To start a discussion of the doctrine of creation with a comparison of the Genesis record and modern science is to begin at the wrong place. One should first ask what the creation account would have meant to a Hebrew person in Bible times; then one should ask what use the prophets of Israel made of the doctrine of creation. The following are some points to be noted:

1. Creation was a conquering of chaos. Most creation accounts from the ancient world began with a primeval chaos. The God who could conquer chaos was understood as the true and living God. Genesis 1 is a magnificent account of how the God of Israel brought the chaos of Genesis 1:2 into an ordered cosmos.

One aspect of this motif that often puzzles modern Christians is the biblical reference to Behemoth (Jb 40:15) and Leviathan (Jb 41:1). Both the hippopotamus and the crocodile were fierce, terrible, powerful, and awe-inspiring creatures in biblical times. A hippopotamus can weigh up to 4½ tons and in short spurts can outrun a man. The crocodile is armor-plated, has jaws that snap in two rather than crush, and can measure up to 20 feet long. The Lord has made such creatures. The Lord controls such creatures. No other gods can. Therefore, the Creator and Lord of the hippopotamus and the crocodile is the true God.

2. Creation is the result of grace. It was not asked for by man but was a free act of God. It is good (1:4,10,12,18,21,25,31). On the basis of that fact Christians assert that life is a gift of grace and is good. The Christian affirmation stands against all the nihilisms and pessimisms found in religious and philosophical history.

3. Creation is opposed to all dualisms (two ultimate realities). Good and evil do struggle with each other, but the biblical record is clear that good eventually wins. Matter and spirit may be opposed to each other but God, who is a Spirit, has the final word (Rom 8:1–11; 1 Cor 15:42–58; Rv 20). God and the devil may seem to compete on equal terms, but that is not so. God conquers both death and the devil in the Bible's final chapters.

4. Creation is under the shadow of sin (Rom 8:18–25). Scripture teaches that creation today is not seen in its original pristine purity but rather is seen as a world with a large measure of ambiguity.

5. Creation is dependent upon God. The relationship of God to his creation is set out in Ephesians 4:6. God is above all; that is, he is transcendent. God is through all; that is, he works in all things. God is in all; that is, he is divinely present or immanent in the entire creation (Pss 90;104; cf. Jn 1:3; 1 Cor 8:6; Col 1:16,17).

6. Creation is by the word of God (Gn 1; Heb 11:3). Students of literature have said that the creation of the world by the "word of God" is one of the most sublime of all human thoughts. Among other things it means creation by a Person. The vast expanse of the universe and the enormous number of stars and galaxies can numb a thoughtful person into a sense of meaninglessness. But when one knows that it was all created by the word of God, one knows that a Person is behind the frigid mask of the stellar spaces (Pss 8;19; Rom 1:20).

7. Creation as depicted in the Bible stands up to critical examination. Scholars have studied parallel accounts of other peoples of biblical times, and none of them has the majesty and theological purity of the Genesis account. American archaeologist W. F. Albright said that, given the same limitation of space, it would be difficult to imagine a modern scientist improving on Genesis 1.

Creation and Theology. The doctrine of creation is built on the sum of all the biblical teachings on creation. Examination of that material leads to a number of further conclusions.

1. The doctrine of creation gives us our fundamental understanding of humanity. Men and women are in the image of God (Gn 1:26,27). That means at least that a human being is more than an animal, even though both are from the dust of the earth and have much in common. Many surmises have been made about the positive meaning of the expression "image of God." If there is a common denominator, it is that human beings find their meaning, their destiny, and their worth in their special relationship to God.

2. Parallel to the statement of humanity's relationship to God is the affirmation that humanity is to be lord of God's creation. Again human beings are separated from the animal world, and their responsibility before God is specified (Gn 1:28; 2:15; Ps 8).

3. Both male and female are in the image of God. That means that the divine image is borne equally by both sexes. It also means that sexuality in human beings has many more dimensions than sexuality among animals. The sexual life of human beings is therefore vastly richer than that of animals and subject to deeper corruption (Mk 10:2–9; 1 Cor 7:1–5; Eph 5:25–31; cf. Heb 13:4).

4. The doctrine of prayer as "asking and receiving" is grounded in the providence of God, which in turn is grounded in creation. There is meaning in petitionary prayer only if there is a sovereign Creator who can answer

the petitions of his own creatures (Mt 6:5–13; Col 4:2; 1 Pt 5:6,7; Rv 8:3).

5. The history of humankind and of Israel begins with Genesis 1. Creation begins history; it is not merely the premise of history. The God of creation is the God of Abraham, of Moses, of the prophets, and of Jesus Christ.

6. Creation is a witness to the existence and nature of God (Ps 19; Rom 1:18,19). In theology the expression used is "general revelation." "General" means that it is a revelation witnessed by all people.

7. Creation is a total creation. The Genesis account mentions certain bodies in the skies, certain creatures in the seas, certain plant and animal life on the earth. The number of species runs into the millions. Genesis does not attempt to list them but merely suggests such a list. God has made all that there is (cf. Jn 1:1,2). Therefore there is never a threat to the believer in the Lord from any part of the universe. There is only one Lord, not many gods and lords, to whom all are called in obedience. The personal meaning is found in Romans 8:38,39, where the apostle Paul searches the entire universe and can find nothing in it, anywhere or at any time, that can separate a believer from the love of God in Christ.

8. The chief theological use of the doctrine of creation in the OT is to label idolatry for the sin that it is. Idolatry is the primeval lie and it leads to immorality, making a lie of one's life.

9. One of the remarkable doctrines of the NT is the "cosmic Christ." Christ is set out as the Creator (Jn 1:1,2; Heb 1:3; Col 1:16). The purpose of linking Christ with creation is to show that he is more than a 1st-century Jew, more than an inhabitant of Palestine.

Creation and Science. Does science prove creation? Some scientists have thought that the innumerable conditions necessary for life, which do as a matter of fact exist on the earth, is such a proof. That argument has been called "cosmic theology."

Another so-called proof of creation from science is the "big bang" theory of the origin of the universe. Although that view has forged ahead of its competitors, it is a theory of "first states" and not of the absolute origin of all things. The Christian doctrine of creation from nothing (Latin, *ex nihilo*) means more than that: it means that the absolute origin, sustaining, and meaning of all things is in the living Lord of Israel and of the church.

Another argument comes from the second law of thermodynamics and the concept of entropy. Heat systems cool off. The universe is not infinitely old or it would now be cool (entropy refers to the leveling off of energy or temperature to a state in which no energy is available). Since there are still stars and suns, the universe must have been created a finite time ago. Another argument is that it was necessary to create a universe that would run down. In so running down, it supplies heat to the earth so that the drama of God and man could unfold.

The Issues Around Evolution. When Charles Darwin proposed biological evolution in the middle of the 19th century, many evangelical Christians took exception to it. They objected even more strenuously when books were written about human evolution. Two famous debates resulted from that controversy. In England the issue was debated in 1860 before the British Association at Oxford. That debate pitted Bishop Samuel Wilberforce (against the theory) against T. H. Huxley (for the theory). Although there was no formal decision, sentiment was with Huxley. The second debate was the famous Scopes trial in Dayton, Tennessee, in 1925. William Jennings Bryan defended the law which said that John T. Scopes should be found guilty of teaching evolution in the classroom. Clarence Darrow defended Scopes. Again, the sentiment was with the proponent of evolution, Darrow (although Bryan gave a sturdier defense of his beliefs than is generally acknowledged).

Both orthodox Roman Catholics and evangelical Protestants have taken various views of the controversy, of which only a few can be mentioned.

1. Some argue that evolution is contrary to the teachings of Scripture and is—in the name of science—actually the supreme defiance of Scripture's authority. Thus, no quarter must ever be given in the battle against evolution.

2. Others find a satisfactory resolution in "theistic evolution." They try to show due regard for both science and Scripture.

3. Many see the parallels between the order of fossil-bearing strata in the so-called "geological column" and the six days of creation as too close to be accidental. For them there is essential harmony between "Genesis and geology."

4. Many regard evolution as a theory like all other theories, which will be made or broken in the laboratory or in field work. They see the doctrine of creation as neither for nor against evolution. It is on a different level of explanation: "Science tells how; Scripture tells why."

5. Jesuit paleontologist Teilhard de Chardin attempted to save Christianity from evolution by "christifying" the whole evolutionary process.

6. British author C. S. Lewis, among others, seems on target in distinguishing evolution from what might be called "evolutionism."

Lewis says that the validity of evolution as a narrow scientific thesis is for scientists to decide. But the notion of a total, all-encompassing evolutionary myth, as a human pseudo-doctrine of creation, is clearly not scientific.

Creation, Science, and Morality. The growth of world population and the spread of industrialization have produced the problem of local and worldwide pollution. The ecological crisis has been said by some scholars to be the fault of Christian faith, which inspired man—as the "lord of creation"—to exploit creation. But that is hardly the meaning of Genesis 1:26, which is an injunction to responsibility. A number of OT texts show clearly that the concern of Scripture is for human responsibility in God's world; hence Scripture parallels modern ecological concerns.

Science stretches theological understanding by continually revising our knowledge of the universe, but the biblical doctrine of creation does not retreat as science advances. For the Christian, the world studied by scientists and pondered by philosophers remains God's created world.   BERNARD L. RAMM

See CREATION MYTHS; GOD, BEING AND ATTRIBUTES OF.

Bibliography. K. Barth, *Church Dogmatics III;* J.M. Houston, *I Believe in the Creator;* S. Jaki, *Cosmos and Creator* and *The Road of Science and the Ways to God.*

Creation, New. *See* NEW CREATION, NEW CREATURE.

Creation Myths. Religious stories explaining the origin and order of the universe. Parts of some Mesopotamian creation myths bear a close resemblance to the biblical accounts of creation and earliest times.

Stories explaining creation were known throughout the ancient Near East. Many were based on stories originating in Sumer, one of the earliest Mesopotamian civilizations. Although now commonly regarded as fanciful and even entertaining explanations for why things were as they were, the myths seem to have fulfilled an important political function. Their recital at religious festivals was believed to have magic power to revitalize nature and society. The creation stories assured worshipers that the original state of order created by the gods would continue to overcome the forces of chaos that threatened illness, ruin, sterility, and death.

Sumerian Creation Myths. The Sumerians flourished in southern Mesopotamia between 4000 and 3000 BC. Although they were non-Semitic, their cosmology influenced the Semites (various peoples inhabiting Palestine, Phoenicia, Assyria, and Arabia), who eventually adopted the Sumerian chief deities. About 5,000 tablets and fragments inscribed with an assortment of Sumerian literary works have been discovered. Although most of those tablets were inscribed in the early post-Sumerian period (*c.* 1750 BC), the compositions belong to at least the latter half of the 3rd millennium (2500–2001) BC. As yet, no Sumerian account dealing directly with the origin of the universe has been uncovered. What is known about their notions of creation has been gleaned in part from brief passages scattered throughout their literature, especially from the introductions to poems, where Sumerian scribes were accustomed to writing several lines dealing with creation. In addition, nine myths have survived about the gods who organized the universe, created human beings, and established civilization.

The Sumerian religion, like that of all ancient Near Eastern peoples except the Israelites, was a naturalistic polytheism: they worshiped as gods the natural forces governing fertility (rain, wind, clouds, sun, moon, rivers, seas, and so on). Consequently, people understood the origin of the universe (cosmogony) as accompanying the origin of the gods (theogony).

Heaven and Earth. In a tablet cataloging the Sumerian gods the sea goddess Nammu is described as "the mother, who gave birth to heaven and earth." In another text she is described as "the mother, the ancestress, who gave birth to all the gods." Evidently the Sumerians looked upon the primeval sea as the first cause and prime mover of all things, believing that "the heaven and earth" were somehow engendered in that sea. Moreover, in their view the major components of the universe were heaven and earth; their term for universe was a compound word meaning "heaven-earth" (exactly as in the opening verse of the Book of Genesis, where "heavens and earth" designate the entire organized universe). Before Enlil, the air god, separated them, heaven–earth was conceived of as a mountain whose base was the earth and whose peak was heaven.

Enlil, called "the king of heaven and earth" or "the king of all the lands," was the most important of the Sumerian gods. His creative work in organizing the earth is celebrated in "The Creation of the Pickax," which describes his fashioning and dedicating that valuable agricultural instrument. In part it reads:

> Enlil, who brings up the seed of
> the land from the earth,
> Took care to move away heaven
> from earth,
> Took care to move away earth
> from heaven.

... He brought the pickax into
  existence, the "day" came
  forth,
He introduced labor, decreed the
  fate,
Upon the pickax and basket he
  directs the "power."

Thus Enlil separated heaven from earth, brought seed to fruition, and fashioned the pickax for agriculture.

Sun and Moon. The Sumerians believed that their city Nippur was inhabited by the gods even before the moon and sun existed. One Sumerian myth describes the creation of moon and sun. The "old woman" of Nippur, Nunbarshegunu, preens her daughter Ninlil and teaches her how to win the air god Enlil's affection. Ninlil succeeds, but Enlil's advances terrify her. She refuses him, and Enlil then rapes her. Scandalized by that misdeed, the gods banish Enlil to the netherworld (the place of the dead). Ninlil, now pregnant by him with the moon god Nanna, follows him into exile.

Regretting that their child, the moon, will thus become a denizen of the gloomy netherworld rather than the sky, Enlil impregnates Ninlil with three other children. Those offspring take up residence as netherworld deities as a substitute for their brother Nanna, the moon god. Freed, Nanna ascends to heaven, where he and his mate Ningal become parents of Utu, the sun god.

Civilization. The water god Enki was also god of the abyss and wisdom. Although Enlil drew up "blueprints" for the universe, Enki did most of the work carrying them out. His efforts went beyond fashioning the natural world to initiating the most important aspects of culture and civilization. In "Enki and the World Order," the water god makes his way to the banks of the Tigris and Euphrates, the two rivers that water the sandy Mesopotamian valley, and fills them with life-giving rains and winds. Then, preparing the earth for cultivation, he "turns the hilly ground into fields, ... directs the plow and ... yoke, ... opens the holy furrows, and grows the grain in the cultivated field." Then the god lays the foundations of houses, stables, and sheepfolds, and builds them. He fixes the "borders" and sets up boundary stones. Finally he invents weaving, called "that which is woman's task." Having organized the earth, Enki entrusts each place and element to a special deity.

Sumerian Eden. Another myth, "Enki and Ninhursag: A Paradise Myth," bears a remote resemblance to the biblical story of the garden of Eden. The myth seems to take place before the creation of animals or humans in Dilmun, a land in the east where the gods reside—

"pure," "clean," "most bright," and probably without sickness or death. Having filled that land with fruitful fields, Enki successively impregnates three goddesses: Ninhursag, "the mother of the land"; Nimmu, his daughter by that union; and Ninkurra, his granddaughter by Nimmu.

Ninhursag seems to use Enki's semen to make eight new plants. Evidently they are "forbidden fruit," because when Enki eats them, Ninhursag curses him and leaves the garden, adding, "Until he is dead I shall not look upon him with the eye of life." Under the curse, the garden languishes and the gods mourn. Enlil, the king of the gods, seems unable to cope with the situation. Enki lies dying. The fox, evidently already present in Dilmun, saves the day by luring Ninhursag back to Dilmun, where she heals Enki and revives the garden.

Humankind. Regarded as the mother of all gods, Ninhursag may have personified Earth. In "The Creation of Man," she plays an important role along with Enki.

Having come into existence before there was meat or bread for them to eat, the gods face a dilemma:

They knew not the eating of
  bread,
Knew not the dressing of garments,
Ate plants with their mouth
  like sheep,
Drank water from the ditch.

To relieve that situation Enlil and Enki fashion a cattle god and a grain goddess. Cattle and grain suddenly abound, but the gods are unable to utilize them. Something is still needed to tend the animals and make grain into bread. The gods complain to Enki and command him to create servants to take care of their needs.

Coming to their aid, Enki takes "clay that is over the abyss" and with Ninhursag oversees its fashioning into human beings who are pressed into the gods' service, especially to make them bread. At a feast afterward Enki and Ninhursag get drunk and ineptly make several abnormal human types, including the barren woman and the eunuch. But whole or flawed, man and woman are the clay of the abyss and are related by nature to chaos. Moreover, their individual fates are decreed by the gods. That partly explains why the Mesopotamian kings ruled as gods and reigned with absolute authority. Only a god's rule could maintain order in the state and check the human tendency toward chaos.

Akkadian Creation Myths. The Babylonian and Assyrian cultures, both Semitic, shared the Akkadian language, which distin-

A cuneiform tablet of the Babylonian account of creation.

guished them from the non-Semitic and linguistically different Sumerians. By far the most familiar creation myth of the ancient Near East is the Babylonian creation epic known as *Enuma Elish* (from its opening words). It deals explicitly with the creation of the universe and contains some striking parallels to the biblical account. A later Assyrian version of the myth appropriately substituted the national god Asshur for Babylon's god Marduk.

In *Enuma Elish* the human race is made from the blood of Kingu, leader of a rebel horde against the creator god Marduk. Consequently, in the Babylonian myth, man and woman are again related to chaos. In another myth preserved in an Old Babylonian fragment, humankind is made from the blood of a slain god:

> ... Let [man] appear!
> He who shall serve all the gods,
> Let him be formed out of clay,
>   be animated with blood!
> Enki opened his mouth,
> saying to the great gods:
> ... Let them slay one god,
> ... With his flesh and his blood
>   let Ninhursag mingle clay. . . .

The later Assyrian version describes how the goddess Mamu accomplished creation of humans with a block of clay:

Fourteen pieces she pinched off,
  seven pieces she put on the right,
Seven pieces she put on the left;
  between them she cast a brick,
. . . The seven and seven wombs:
  seven gave origin to males,
Seven gave origin to females;
  . . . She perfected them in pairs;
  . . . Mamu formed them into the forms
  of actual people.

According to another Akkadian myth, the gods created man as a perverse being, presenting him with twisted speech, lies, and untruth.

Egyptian Creation Myths. The customary Egyptian myth of creation (found, e.g., in the dedication ritual of a royal pyramid or in the *Book of the Dead*) relates that before the creation there was a watery void, accompanied by darkness, formlessness, and invisibility. That watery chaos bore the name Nun, "the great god who came into being by himself, . . . the father of the gods." The void subsides, leaving a primordial mound of earth with the creator god Atum ("totality") upon it. Atum brings into being the rest of the universe and assigns places and functions to its parts. How he accomplished that feat differs in the myth's various versions. In one, Atum produces children by masturbation. (He has no mate.) The resulting male and female deities carry on the work of generation and creation. In another version he brings the other gods into existence by dismembering his own body to make them.

In the Bremmer-Rhind papyrus, containing material dating back to around 2300 BC, the god Ra copulates with himself and spits the new generation of gods from his mouth.

In a detail similar to the Mesopotamian myths, the air god Shu separates heaven-earth by lifting the sky goddess Nut from the earth god Geb and placing himself between the two.

The most significant Egyptian creation myth is the so-called "Memphite Theology" (*c.* 2700 BC), which sought to move the Egyptian capital to Memphis by claiming it to be the site of the original creation mound. Rather than describing the creation in purely physical terms, that myth conceives of the universe as coming into existence through the mind ("heart") and commanding speech ("tongue") of the creator god. According to that myth, then, an intelligent will controlled the universe.

Levantine Creation Myths. Ebla, only recently excavated at Tell Mardikh, was the ancient capital of an empire that dominated the Levant (eastern Mediterranean region from Greece to Egypt) not later than 2250 BC. Ebla was located about 43 miles south of Aleppo in northwest Syria. Initial study of its myths indicates that the ancient West Semitic people at Ebla borrowed the Sumerian myths.

Among the Canaanite gods worshiped at Ugarit on the northwest coast of Syria in the 14th century BC, El was regarded as titular head. He was evidently thought of as the creator god. The hero god of the Canaanites was Aliyan Baal ("victorious lord"), also known as Hadad, the storm god and fertility god who usurped the kingship of the gods. To the Amorites, who brought their gods with them when they moved into Canaan, Hadad was the son of the grain god Dagan or Dagon; temples to Baal and to Dagon, but not to El, have been found at the site of Ugarit (Ras Shamra). Though Baal, unlike El, is never called "creator" in the Ras Shamra tablets, he was believed responsible for the life-giving storms and rain that the Canaanites worshiped.

In the initial fragment of one myth, "Baal Versus Yam," El has granted Yam (the chaotic primeval sea) dominion over the gods and ordered that a palace be built for him. Anxious to protect his position, Yam demands that the gods surrender to him Baal, who represents the forces of life and order. But Baal refuses to submit and destroys Yam in deadly combat:

Baal drags him forth, he scatters
  him!
He annihilates Judge River!
. . . Baal shall reign!

The opening lines of another fragment call for a banquet in Baal's honor:

Serve Baal the Victor,
Exalt the Prince, Lord of the
  Earth!
Arise, let preparation be made
  for him, that I may dine him.

Baal then assumes the titles once ascribed to Yam. The banquet in Baal's honor turns into a massacre. Baal's sister and mate, Anat, slaughters all of Baal's enemies, wading waist-deep in their blood and gore. Baal then invites Anat as the goddess of love and fertility to restore fertility and well-being to the battle-scarred earth:

The Message of Baal the Victor,
The speech of the most valiant
  of heroes:
"Meet me in the turbulent earth,
Diffuse love across the land,
Purr out peace in the midst of
  earth,
That I may increase love amidst
  the fields."

Baal demonstrates his own creative power by making lightning. Finally, a palace is built for him in heaven so that he can pour out rain and fertility from its window.

Hebrew poetry occasionally compares the victory of God (Hebrew *Yahweh*) over his political and spiritual enemies to a victory over Rahab-Leviathan, evidently a repressive monster similar to Yam (Ps 74:13,14). The prophet Isaiah portrayed the Lord's final victory over his enemy using a similar metaphor: "In that day the Lord with his hard and great and strong sword will punish Leviathan the fleeing serpent, Leviathan the twisting serpent, and he will slay the dragon that is in the sea" (Is 27:1). In calling for a second exodus, this time from the oppressive Babylon, the prophet cried:

> Awake, awake, put on strength,
> O arm of the Lord;
> awake, as in days of old,
> the generations of long ago.
> Was it not thou that didst cut Rahab in
> pieces,
> that didst pierce the dragon?
> (Is 51:9,10).

Those and other biblical allusions (Jb 3:8; 26:12,13; Ps 89:9,10) suggest that the Canaanites, whom Israel dispossessed, had a creation myth similar to other myths found throughout the ancient Near East. According to that myth, the god who represented life and order and who served as king of the pantheon (roster of gods) achieved his exalted position by vanquishing the hostile cosmic forces which inhibit and destroy life. Defeating them, he released and organized the forces essential for life.

Creation Myths and Genesis. Mythological allusions occurring in some of the poetic passages in the OT give the poetic imagery color and vividness. They indicate that the Israelites were acquainted with the creation myths of Mesopotamia and Canaan. To infer, however, that the Hebrews accepted those myths is unwarranted. The biblical poets borrowed their imagery, not their theology. The Bible's own creation accounts seem to have been written consciously to exclude mythological elements.

The Genesis account of creation differs from pagan myths in at least two ways. First, the accounts differ in their purpose. The pagan myths served principally to preserve life and society by magical recitation. Although the biblical account has implications for life and society, it serves primarily to teach a covenant people about God and is devoid of any occult claims or power.

Second, the accounts differ in their quality. The Genesis creation narrative presents a straightforward theology with a minimum of adornment. Told as a story, it rings true even in an age of scientific discovery, when people are accustomed to mechanistic explorations of natural phenomena. An intelligent, well-informed person can accept Genesis as an authoritative statement of nature's meaning and purpose, and on it base a life of devotion to the divine Creator. In contrast, the creation myths present a debased theology and an even more debased morality. The most ancient myths, which may appeal to modern practitioners of "occult sciences" for various reasons, are simply unbelievable as religious truth. The gods of the ancient myths have been buried in the rubble of long-dead civilizations or transmuted into the gods of modern polytheistic religions; the God of the Bible lives on.

The literary form of Genesis is not theology; that is, it does not make analytical statements about God. Yet it presents a view of God distinctively different from the gods of the pagan myths. God is present "in the beginning." He is one; he creates with singleness of purpose, unchallenged. In contrast, the pagan myths portray the beginning as impersonal and chaotic. Chaos evolves into a cosmos, out of which the gods emerge by chance. The subsequent development of heaven and earth is viewed as a cosmic power struggle between rival gods. Again, the Creator in Genesis is different from and "bigger" than the heavens and earth he creates. The pagan gods are material and made up of the same cosmic stuff as the world; the world is bigger than they are.

Biblical and pagan anthropologies are also significantly different. In Genesis man and woman are creatures distinct from the Creator, although bearing his "image." They are created for the purpose of ruling the earth as God's agents and are accordingly assigned clear responsibilities. In pagan mythology human beings come from the same stuff as the gods, though humans are more closely related to chaos than to the gods who fashioned them. The pagan gods made humans as slaves to take care of the gods' material needs, so the gods treat them with either contempt or indifference. The Near Eastern world view was not only pessimistic but fatalistic. Human beings, far from being responsible or significant, were assigned at birth an inexorable destiny that they could not overrule.

The best that most Near Eastern inhabitants could hope for was a relatively prosperous and regular life before their fated end, and for that they thought they had to manipulate their deities through recital and reenactment of the ancient myths. Genesis, on the other hand, as part of the larger OT teaching, sought to bring the human community into a living, personal covenant relationship with God.

BRUCE K. WALTKE

See CREATION, DOCTRINE OF.

Creature, New. *See* NEW CREATION, NEW CREATURE.

Credit, Creditor. Acknowledgment of payment on a debt incurred through goods or services sold on trust, and the one who operates the business of selling on credit. The Mosaic Law regulated credit and creditors (Dt 23:19,20).

See MONEY AND BANKING; TRADES AND OCCUPATIONS (BANKER).

Creeping Things. Reference to insects, reptiles, and some other animals that crawl on the belly or creep on four or more feet.

See ANIMALS.

Crescens. Co-worker of the apostle Paul. Crescens went on to Galatia when Paul was imprisoned in Rome (2 Tm 4:10).

Crete. Fourth largest island in the Mediterranean, lying approximately 60 miles SE of Greece and 110 miles SW of Turkey. In size it is 160 miles long from east to west, with a width of approximately 36 miles, an area of 3,200 square miles. Through the island stretches a mountain range dominated in the center by the sacred Mt Ida (altitude 9000 feet). These mountains slope down sharply to the southern coast, with the result that most of the inhabitants live on the more gradual northern slopes.

Civilization in Crete reached its climax with the Minoan era (3000–1100 BC). The spectacular remnants of this high civilization may be seen best at Knossos, thanks to the labors of British archaeologist Arthur Evans. About 1950–1900 BC beautiful pottery was produced and exported. Metallurgy was highly developed, and hieroglyphic writing was introduced. This civilization was suddenly and dramatically destroyed in a mysterious manner about 1700 BC, perhaps by volcanic eruption or earthquake. Following this, the towns and palaces were rebuilt, and the island enjoyed its greatest prosperity. The partially restored palace of Knossos amazes today's visitor with superb frescoes, stairways, and pillars. All this ended in total destruction about 1450 BC. Some think it was caused by the volcanic explosion at the nearby island of Santorini.

Crete is important in the history of the Christian church. When Paul went to Rome as a prisoner, the ship sought refuge from a storm at Fair Havens (Acts 27:8). The ship tried in vain to reach the more commodious harbor at Phoenix (Acts 27:12), but was blown off course and sought refuge at an island off the southwest coast of Crete, called Cauda (Acts 27:16). Paul may have visited Crete after imprisonment in Rome, for in his letter to Titus, he said, "I left you in Crete" (Ti 1:5). On the basis of this and other evidence many scholars conclude that Paul was released and had an extended ministry before his second imprisonment and execution (2 Tm 4:6). Paul had little good to say about the people of Crete, quoting one of their own poets as characterizing them as "liars, evil beasts, lazy gluttons" (Ti 1:12). But the gospel must have made quite a difference there, for today the name of Titus is honored in many villages, churches, and monasteries.

A Cretan vase and a Mycenean vase.

547

Because of its location and its relative fertility, Crete over the years has been a prize of war and of commerce. The island was conquered by Rome in 67 BC and became a separate province. The inhabitants prospered under the Romans and later under the Greek Christians (Byzantines). The Saracens (Moslems) occupied the island for over a century (AD 823–960). After centuries of Christian leadership it was conquered by the Turkish sultan, and civilization languished (1669–1898). In the 20th century Crete has been a part of Greece, except for a period of German occupancy during World War II.

Cricket. RSV name for a four-footed winged insect, considered edible by the Israelites (Lv 11:22).

See ANIMALS.

Criminal Law and Punishment.
The science or philosophy of law is called jurisprudence. Although modern jurisprudence bears little resemblance to biblical concepts of law, the Scriptures have played a definite role in its development. Today criminal law is clearly distinguished from civil law; in Bible times the distinction was much less clear. Today offenses against civil law (torts) are distinguished from minor crimes (misdemeanors) as well as from serious crimes (felonies). In the Bible, "crimes" included all punishable offenses, even religious offenses such as idolatry (worshiping a false god) or blasphemy (speaking or behaving with contempt toward God).

Near Eastern Context. In ancient societies as in modern ones, laws were considered necessary to regulate individual behavior for the good of the community, state, or nation. Today laws are thought of as made by people for their own protection. In contrast, all ancient Near Eastern law codes were considered to have come directly from some divine source. Hebrew law, though distinct, followed the general pattern of Near Eastern law codes, as is known from those that have survived—such as the code of Hammurabi and Assyrian and Hittite laws.

Conclusions about the "origin" of ancient laws should be made cautiously. Although evidence indicates that Hammurabi based his legislation partially on earlier Sumerian codes, he declared that his code had been received from Shamash, god of justice. That declaration must have been intended to convey primarily that his code had the express sanction of Shamash, since at least some people would recognize it as a compilation based largely on earlier laws. Similarly, the clear biblical statements about Moses receiving the Law on Mt

Sinai (Ex 19–24) do not rule out the possibility that parts of the Decalogue (the Ten Commandments) may have existed in earlier codes. Possibly the Mosaic legislation included some social rules adapted from the period of Israel's sojourn in Egypt.

The Code of Hammurabi dates from the first Babylonian (Sumerian) kingdom (c. 1780 BC) and is named for its royal compiler. It is a collection of separate Semitic and Sumerian laws, precedents, and judgments put into a composite form so that the same laws would be applicable throughout the kingdom. The laws reflect a people who enjoyed a high degree of civilization and stable government. They were a settled, responsible group whose laws were valid not merely for a single city, as was usual at the time, but for a wide area. The amount of detail suggests that the laws were based on vast experience and a variety of court hearings and decisions. The purpose of the code was establishment of social justice, continuation of political order, and maintenance of a stable economy.

Although the surviving Assyrian laws, probably dating from the 15th century BC, did not apply to a whole empire, they show a number of similarities to the earlier Code of Hammurabi. The Assyrian laws, however, were suited to a society with a lower level of civilization and development. Private retribution was widespread, savagery was common, and the death penalty was imposed for many crimes.

The Hittite laws, probably dating from the 14th century BC, reflect a considerably higher level of civilization than the biblical laws but a less advanced ethical content. Maintenance of social order was the primary purpose of the Hittite code; and since agriculture was the basis of the economy, many laws dealt with agricultural questions. In general the punishments meted out by the Hittites were far less severe than those of the Sumerians or Assyrians. Fines were imposed frequently, but death, forced labor, imprisonment, and even facial mutilation were sometimes ordered.

The Code of Hammurabi and Hebrew Law. Although the law code of Hammurabi and the biblical laws have many general similarities, close inspection shows many more differences in detail. Hebrew law had an independent and original character. The civil development of the Mesopotamians differed greatly from the primitive social and cultural level of the Hebrews, who did not even define a detailed court procedure.

In general, offenders received a more drastic punishment for the same offense under Hammurabi's law code than under biblical law. Capital offenses, however, were numerous in biblical law. Perhaps because the Hebrews were to maintain a monotheistic religion in a polytheistic environment, many crimes of a religious nature were capital offenses. The worship of strange gods, idolatry, sorcery, blasphemy, and the breaking of the sabbath were all punishable by death, as were crimes related to sexual morality.

Some laws were in complete contrast in the two law codes, as for example those concerning the treatment of runaway slaves. Under Hammurabi's code, aiding a runaway slave was a capital offense: "If a man aid a male or a female slave of the palace, or a male or female slave of a common man, to escape from the city, he shall be put to death." In a similar biblical law the Hebrews were told to accept a runaway slave into their homes so that he or she might remain there with impunity (Dt 23:15,16). On the other hand, the Code of Hammurabi stated that "if a man strikes his father, they shall cut off his hand," but the Book of Exodus states, "Whoever strikes his father or his mother shall be put to death" (Ex 21:15). In general, though, the Hebrew law exhibited a greater sense of humanity and a tendency toward leniency. Few modern readers realize that the "law of retribution," paying "eye for eye, tooth for tooth," and so on (Ex 21:24), was really a limitation on retribution. That is, *no more* than one eye or one tooth should be exacted. The tendency in ancient societies (and perhaps in modern ones as well) was for retribution to escalate (cf. Gn 4:24,25). Hebrew law also showed concern to protect the poor. In ancient times there was a striking lack of protection for widows, a matter that was gradually altered.

The purpose of biblical law was more encompassing than that of other Near Eastern law codes. Going beyond the maintenance of morality and justice, biblical law sought to develop a strong ethical sense and a faith in the one God, plus a sense of human understanding, love, and thought for one's neighbor.

Assyrian Laws and Hebrew Law. Direct influence of the Assyrian laws on the Hebrew code was negligible, although several parallels can be seen. One Assyrian law states: "If a woman in a quarrel injure the testicle of a man, one of her fingers they shall cut off. And if a physician bind it up and the other testicle which is beside it be infected thereby, or take harm; or if in a quarrel she injure the other testicle, they shall destroy both of her eyes." A comparable law in Deuteronomy gave an equally drastic but different punishment. It says that: "When men fight with one another, and the wife of the one draws near to rescue her husband from the hand of him who is beating him and puts out her hand and seizes him by the private parts, then you shall cut off her

hand, your eye shall have no pity" (Dt 25:11,12). The great emphasis on family continuity in Near Eastern cultures demanded special protection for the human reproductive process.

A close resemblance is also seen in the punishment for a man who struck a pregnant woman and caused her to have a miscarriage. In Assyrian law, if convicted, he paid a fine in lead, received 50 blows, and had to work for the king for a month. Restitution often had to be made for a lost life. (The Code of Hammurabi contained similar provisions: "If a man strike the daughter of a man and bring about a miscarriage, he shall pay ten shekels of silver for her miscarriage. If that woman die, they shall put his daughter to death.") The Book of Exodus recommended that the fine be suggested by the husband and decreed by the judges. If any harm to the wife followed, however, the law read, "You shall give life for life" (Ex 21:22,23). Witchcraft, homosexuality, and adultery were penalized harshly in both Assyrian and biblical law codes.

Hittite Laws and Hebrew Law. Among the surviving Hittite laws the only one with a strong resemblance to biblical law concerns rape: "If a man seize a woman in the mountain, [it is] the man's wrong, he shall die. But if he seize [her] in the house, [it is] the woman's fault, the woman shall die. If the man find them and then kill them, [there is] no punishing him." The Book of Deuteronomy stated, "If there is a betrothed virgin, and a man meets her in the city and lies with her, then you shall bring them both out to the gate of that city, and you shall stone them to death with stones, the young woman because she did not cry for help though she was in the city, and the man because he violated his neighbor's wife.... But if in the open country a man meets a young woman who is betrothed, and the man seizes her and lies with her, then only the man who lay with her shall die. But to the young woman you shall do nothing; in the young woman there is no offense punishable by death ... because he came upon her in the open country, and though the betrothed young woman cried for help there was no one to rescue her" (Dt 22:23–27).

The Hittite law code must have had at least an indirect effect on the biblical laws because of the close association of the two peoples. The Hittites, referred to in the Book of Genesis, had evidently settled in Palestine long before the time of the patriarchs and had intermarried with the local people. People of Hittite stock, such as Uriah (2 Sm 11:3) and a woman in Solomon's harem (1 Kgs 11:1), are mentioned from time to time in the OT.

Egyptian Influences. The extent to which Egyptian social practices may have been reflected in Hebrew legal enactments is difficult to determine, since no ancient Egyptian law codes have yet been discovered. The basis of codified Hebrew law was the covenant enacted at Mt Sinai, which became the norm throughout Hebrew history. Perhaps some of those laws had already been in operation during the time the Hebrews settled in Egypt and even prior to that.

Hebrew Criminal Law. *Laws Governing Offenses Against God.* Since Hebrew law was designed for a group of people for whom religion was of paramount importance and whose faith was endangered by the influence of the beliefs of their pagan neighbors, it is not surprising that so much of Hebrew law dealt with crimes committed against God. Prohibition against worshiping idols is stated and repeated in the Torah, or Pentateuch (first five books of the Bible): "You shall not make for yourself a graven image, or any likeness of anything that is in heaven above, or that is in the earth beneath, or that is in the water under the earth; you shall not bow down to them or serve them" (Ex 20:4; Dt 5:8,9). Sacrifice of infants, practiced in some pagan religions, was specifically prohibited in Israel. The penalty for that crime, as for the other forms of murder, was stoning to death (Lv 20:2).

In the Book of Leviticus, death by stoning was recorded as the appropriate punishment for blaspheming the name of God (Lv 24:11–16). False prophecy was also a criminal offense; that accusation could apply to a person making a prediction in the name of a god other than the Lord, or implying falsely that one's prophecy resulted from a communication with God. Jeremiah, whose prophecy of Nebuchadnezzar's victory over the southern kingdom of Judah was for a time considered to be false, was almost lynched by a mob (Jer 26:8,9).

The idea of keeping the 7th day holy stemmed from the celebration of God's work in creating the universe in 6 days and resting on the 7th. Keeping the sabbath required cessation of manual work for the entire family, including farm animals (Ex 16:23; 20:8–11). People were also required to meet together on the sabbath for worship, which at a later period in Hebrew history included the reading of Scripture, prayer, and preaching. Anyone breaking the sabbath could be sentenced to death, as happened to a man caught gathering firewood on the sabbath (Nm 15:32–36).

Any type of premeditated crime was considered an offense against God, the giver of all law; hence was punishable by death (Nm 15:30,31). Hebrew law also insisted on donation of the firstfruits of harvest to the Lord without delay. That requirement was some-times carried over to include a first child, whose life was dedicated to service in the temple (Ex 22:29,30; Dt 15:19).

Personal Injury. Murder, an offense against "God's image," was one of many crimes punishable by death in OT times. The Book of Exodus stated unequivocally that "whoever strikes a man so that he dies shall be put to death" (Ex 21:12). A murderer who killed by using a weapon such as a stone or a piece of wood or iron could be killed in revenge by a relative of the deceased. If the original death happened accidentally, the community would sometimes help to conceal the killer and encourage him to hide in a nearby city of refuge, where he would be safe as long as he remained within its gates. He had to stay in that sanctuary until the death of the high priest then in office, after which he was free to return to his own city (Nm 35:10–28). The sixth commandment enjoined, "You shall not kill" (Ex 20:13). The Hebrew word used referred specifically to murder, not to all forms of killing. Killing an enemy in battle and the execution of a murderer were considered necessary and were not prohibited. More than one witness was required for any conviction, particularly in a murder case (Nm 35:30; Dt 17:6; 19:15).

In the Code of Hammurabi a man responsible for an accidental injury to another was required to pay for the services of the physician. If the victim died, a fine was payable according to the victim's rank. In a sense the Hebrews went further by requiring payment for any loss of time suffered by the injured person (Ex 21:18,19).

Kidnapping was punishable by death in the OT. Exodus states that "whoever steals a man, whether he sells him or is found in possession of him, shall be put to death" (21:16). Joseph's being sold into slavery by his brothers illustrates that motive for kidnapping—rather than the extortion of ransom, which is the common purpose today.

Laws Concerning Property. The Book of Exodus was quite specific about anyone responsible for damage to the property or crops of another. If a field caught fire and the fire spread, damaging crops in other fields, the person who started the fire, or perhaps the owner of the first field to catch fire, was responsible for the damage (Ex 22:6). Hammurabi's code cited a similar instance of a man who neglected to keep a dike in repair and was therefore responsible for flood damage to his neighbor's crops.

Injuries to animals, especially oxen, or injuries to people or property caused by such animals formed an important area of Hebrew law. If an ox that had been previously good-tempered killed a man, the owner would be blameless, although the ox would be put to death—a severe financial penalty for the owner. If an ox with a history of goring killed a man because its owner failed to restrain it adequately, both ox and owner would be put to death. The owner's life could be ransomed by payment of an agreed sum. If the person an ox gored was a servant, the ox was stoned and the owner paid a fine (Ex 21:28–32). The Code of Hammurabi also recommended no punishment for a first offense by an animal, but if the owner knew that the ox was dangerous and had taken no steps to prevent harm, a fine in silver was payable—a very large fine for an upper-class victim, slightly less if the victim was a slave. However bad the circumstances and however vicious the ox, the Code of Hammurabi stopped at a fine for the offense, never imposing a death penalty on either the animal or the owner.

Negligence causing injury to an animal was also punished in Hebrew law. If an ox or an ass fell into a pit carelessly left uncovered, the owner of the animal was reimbursed for its loss (Ex 21:33–36).

In ancient cultures women were generally considered chattel (personal property), much like animals or slaves. A daughter was considered to be her father's property until her marriage, then the property of her husband. Therefore, any offense against a married woman was regarded as an offense against the property of the husband. According to the Code of Hammurabi, a child could be sold into slavery as a servant or bondsman, usually in payment of the father's debt (cf. Ex 21:2–7; Neh 5:5–8; Is 50:1). Parental authority was so highly regarded in biblical law that a stubborn and rebellious son could be brought before the elders on the grounds of being disobedient and a glutton or a drunkard. He might then be convicted and stoned to death on the spot by the men of the city (Dt 21:18–21). Even that, however, was a protection of the child's rights; some Near Eastern legislation allowed a parent to order the death of his offspring without reference to the elders or to anyone else. With daughters in particular being held in such low esteem, it is perhaps remarkable that a daughter could inherit property if there were no sons (Nm 27:8).

Adultery, prohibited in the Decalogue, was another crime against a man's property, specifically his wife. The Book of Deuteronomy goes into considerable detail about cases of adultery, the punishment for both persons being death (Dt 22:22). If a man seduced a young woman who was not betrothed, he was required to pay her father the bride price (50 silver shekels); he could not divorce her but had to keep her as his wife for the rest of his life (Ex 22:16; Dt 22:28,29).

In a situation where a wife was accused of adultery but without evidence, a trial by ordeal was conducted. The husband would bring his wife to a priest and present a small offering (a tenth of a measure of barley meal, with neither oil nor frankincense on it), indicating the low esteem in which he now held his wife. The woman then stood before the Lord holding an earthen jar of "holy water." Dust from the floor of the tabernacle was mixed with the water, and the cereal offering was placed in her hands. Her hair was loosened by the priest to show not only her grief but also to give an impression of abandonment. She was then required to take an oath. After that, the priest pronounced a curse upon her to the effect that her womb would be fertilized easily, but that she would have many miscarriages. She had to give her consent to that pronouncement. The priest then wrote the curses in a book and symbolically washed them off into the "bitter water." The woman was required to drink the water while the priest waved the cereal offering from her hands before the Lord and burned some of it on the altar. The priest told her that if she was guilty, the water would make her thigh rot and her abdomen swell. If that happened, she would become an outcast; but if she were proved innocent, she would be free. Whatever the result, no blame for false accusation fell upon the husband (Nm 5:12–31).

The punishment of "burning" for loss of chastity may have referred to branding on the forehead or possibly to the burning to death of the guilty individual. That punishment was probably reserved for an unchaste daughter of a priest or for a man having intercourse with a mother and her daughter (Lv 20:14; 21:9).

If a slave was struck by his master in such a manner as to cause instant death, the slave's death had to be avenged. If the slave lingered, possibly for days, he did not need to be avenged, his loss being a sufficient punishment for the owner (Ex 21:20,21). It is unlikely that the Hebrews had much experience with that law, which had no parallels in Hammurabi's code. If an owner injured his slave by causing the loss of an eye or a tooth, Hebrew law required that the slave be set free (Ex 21:26, 27). The Code of Hammurabi gave an example of a man injuring another man's slave; the owner had to be paid half the slave's value.

Little emphasis was placed on burglary or larceny in the Hebrew law code. A burglar was presumed to be repentant and ready to make restitution. After return of the stolen property and payment of a small additional fine, a thief could again "approach the Lord" (Lv 6:2–7). By contrast, the Code of Hammurabi prescribed the death penalty for burglary.

In Hebrew law theft of an animal required restitution to be made in the ratio of at least two to one; if a bull or a cow had been stolen or sold, the thief had to restore the property five-fold. The Code of Hammurabi contained a similar statute: "If a man steal ox or sheep, ass or pig, or goat—if it be from a god or a palace, he shall restore thirtyfold; if it be from a freeman, he shall render tenfold. If the thief have nothing wherewith to pay, he shall be put to death." In Hebrew law goods stolen from a home were simply to be restored without additional penalty. If the thief no longer had the goods and was unable to pay the equivalent value, he might be sold into slavery until restitution was made (Ex 22:1–4).

General Laws. The Hebrew code as contained in Exodus and Deuteronomy included many general prohibitions. Some concerned business dealings such as the removal of boundary markers (Dt 19:14). The use of false weights and measures was condemned (Lv 19:35; Dt 25:15; Prv 11:1; 20:23; Mi 6:11). Bribery was strictly forbidden: "You shall take no bribe, for a bribe blinds the officials, and subverts the cause of those who are in the right" (Ex 23:8); yet no punishment was specified for those who broke that law. In the Code of Hammurabi, if a judge changed his decision and was unable to give a satisfactory explanation, particularly if bribery was suspected, the judge had to pay 12 times the amount of the penalty and lost his seat on the bench. In the Hebrew code, perjury was also dealt with, although again no punishment was specified. The Code of Hammurabi stated that for perjury in cases where the punishment was death, persons giving false testimony were to be sentenced to death themselves (cf. Ex 23:1).

A number of Hebrew laws reflected concern for the poor. For example, poor people were not to be subjected to usury if they were in debt, or left cold at night if their coats were taken as a pledge. Widows, orphans, and strangers were also to be treated with mercy and understanding (Ex 22:21–24,26,27; 23:9; Dt 23:19; 24:17).

Some Hebrew laws concerned family behavior, such as those already mentioned concerning cursing, disobeying, or disparaging parents (Ex 21:17; Lv 20:9; Dt 27:16; cf. Prv 20:20; 30:17). Family responsibilities were strong; an entire family frequently suffered punishment for the crime of one of its individual members (Jos 7:20–26; 2 Sm 3:29; 21:1–9; 2 Kgs 5:27; Lam 5:7). Over a period of time, as individual responsibility came to be recognized, parents were no longer put to death for the crimes of their children, or vice versa (cf. Jer 31:29,30).

Sorcery and witchcraft were forbidden. The Book of Exodus stated explicitly, "You shall not permit a sorceress to live" (Ex 22:18; Dt 18:10,11). Sexual perversions, such as intercourse with animals, were forbidden under penalty of death. Regulations prohibiting marriage with close relatives were given in detail (Lv 20:17–21).

In Hebrew law no parallel existed for some interesting items in the Code of Hammurabi concerning surgery. That code mentioned veterinary surgery and even operations on the human eye. A Babylonian surgeon had to be wary, for, "If a physician makes a deep incision upon a man with his bronze lancet and causes the man's death or operates on the eye-socket of a man with his bronze lancet and destroys the man's eye, then they shall cut off his hand." Surgery was virtually unknown among the ancient Israelites except for the ritual practice of circumcision.

Punishments. As noted, Near Eastern punishments for murder and personal injury were retaliatory and often of the same nature as the offense. Other methods of punishment tended to vary with individual countries or traditions. Many kinds of punishment were inflicted on people defeated in a full-scale war or a small insurrection.

Physical Punishment. Many forms of punishment stopped short of killing but could nevertheless be quite severe.

1. In the OT beating with rods or switches was the traditional form of discipline for children, fools, and slaves (Ex 21:20; Prv 13:24; 26:3). Scourging (also called flogging) was more severe than beating. The whip employed could be made of several strips of leather fastened at one end or of two interwoven leather strips. A whip nicknamed "scorpion" (because of the barbs in its end) was one of the cruelest instruments of punishment mentioned in the OT (1 Kgs 12:11,14). The severity of punishment could be increased by inserting pieces of metal or bone into the leather.

Before a scourging the victim would be examined for physical fitness. If death resulted from the blows, no blame was attached to the person administering the punishment. The victim was stripped to the waist and tied to a pillar, his hands bound with leather thongs. The severity of a scourging depended on the crime, although the Mosaic Law set an upper limit of 40 lashes (Dt 25:1–3). To guard against a miscount, that number was later lowered by one (2 Cor 11:24). Lashes might be administered both on the chest and the back. Under some law codes scourging could be used as a private punishment; in that case, if the victim died, another life was forfeit.

In offenses against the law synagogue authorities administered scourgings (Mt 10:17). A husband might be scourged by the elders of the city for defamation of his wife's character (Dt 22:18). Scourging was also used as a means of interrogating a prisoner; hence a Roman captain's comment that the apostle Paul should be "examined by scourging" (Acts 22:24).

The Romans usually reserved scourging for non-Roman citizens such as slaves or aliens, as well as for those condemned to death. Normally criminals were scourged after they had been condemned to death; it is therefore unusual to find the scourging of Jesus taking place before his condemnation. Pilate may have hoped to soften the people's hearts by Jesus' suffering so that they would not demand the death penalty (Lk 23:16,22; Jn 19:1).

Citizens of the Roman empire could never be beaten or scourged before sentencing (Acts 22:25). Hence the magistrates were afraid when they heard that Paul, a Roman citizen, had been beaten under those circumstances (Acts 16:37–39).

2. The gouging of the eyes of prisoners and captives was a common practice in the Near East. The Philistines blinded Samson before imprisoning him (Jgs 16:21). The Babylonians did the same to King Zedekiah in 587 BC before taking him into captivity (2 Kgs 25:7). The Ammonite king Nahash was prepared to accept peace overtures from the men of the city of Jabesh on condition that all their right eyes be gouged out. Nahash's purpose was to disgrace them and prevent them from further active participation in warfare (1 Sm 11:1–4).

3. Several forms of mutilation served as punishments in the Near East. The Israelites considered their own bodies sacred and made in God's image, but that did not prevent them from mutilating their enemies by cutting off their thumbs and large toes.

The Code of Hammurabi and the Assyrian law code prescribed mutilation of the eye, nose, ear, breast, tongue, lip, hand, and finger as punishments for specific crimes. In Assyria punishment was often inflicted by the victim of the crime under supervision of court officials. The Code of Hammurabi also contained safeguards so that criminals were not punished in excess of the law's sentence.

4. Stocks are mentioned as a form of punishment in the later OT period. The prophets Hanani (2 Chr 16:10) and Jeremiah (Jer 20:2,3) suffered the indignity of being placed in stocks. Both ankles, and sometimes the wrists and head as well, were placed in holes in two large pieces of wood. In Roman times, stocks were converted to a form of torture, with a prisoner's legs stretched to holes increasingly far apart. In the NT, Paul and Silas had their feet placed in stocks by a Philippian jailer (Acts 16:24). The same Greek word, meaning "con-

finement," can refer to fetters chaining a prisoner or to an iron collar like that worn by runaway Roman slaves.

Capital Punishment. Capital punishment was common in many Near Eastern countries. Several methods were used.

1. Those who offended a king were beheaded with a sword (2 Sm 16:9; 2 Kgs 6:31,32), as were idolaters and murderers (according to the Mishna, the Jewish commentary on the Law). The sword was probably used for private executions as well. Inhabitants of entire cities were sometimes "put to the sword" for their denial of the faith (Ex 32:27; Dt 13:15).

2. Certain sexual offenses were punished with death by burning (Lv 20:14; 21:9). Tamar, Judah's daughter-in-law, was accused of adultery and ordered to be burned to death outside the city (Gn 38:24). The Lord instructed that anyone whose feet touched the holy ground of Mt Sinai was to be shot with arrows or stoned (Ex 19:13).

3. Hanging was not a form of execution in biblical times but a means of exhibiting a corpse as a warning to local inhabitants (Gn 40:19; Jos 8:29; 10:26; 2 Sm 4:12). Corpses were exhibited only for one day and were buried before nightfall. The hanging corpse was considered a defilement of the land which God had given (Dt 21:22,23). The hands were tied together and the body hanged from the arm of a wooden gallows, according to the Mishna.

4. Some writers think that the word translated "hanging" or "hanging on a tree" actually meant impalement (Nm 25:4; Dt 21:22,23; Jos 8:9; 2 Sm 21:6,9; Est 9:14). A spiked wooden stake was set in the ground and the victim's body was forced onto the spike, the tip of which probably protruded from the chest or mouth. Commonly practiced by the Assyrians, that form of execution was reserved for those guilty of the worst crimes and for prisoners of war or deserters. The Persian king Darius is reputed to have impaled 3,000 men when his army entered Babylon. Impalement was the penalty Darius set for changing his edict concerning the rebuilding of the temple (Ezr 6:11,12).

5. Crucifixion was a punishment employed by the Syrian king Antiochus IV Epiphanes in 167–166 BC; according to Josephus, a first-century Jewish historian, Jews who refused to give up their traditional faith were so executed. During the Maccabean period (167–40 BC) Alexander Jannaeus crucified 800 rebellious Pharisees in an attempt to reestablish his authority. Crucifixion was a widespread form of execution: it was used in most places in the Roman empire, including India, North Africa, and Germany. Between 4 BC and AD 70, on some occasions the number of people crucified at one time reached into the thousands.

Three types of crosses seem to have been used: a cross with the crossbar below the head of the upright bar (Latin cross); a T-shaped cross (St. Anthony's cross); and an X-shaped cross (St. Andrew's cross). Matthew records that an inscription, "This is Jesus the King of the Jews," was placed over Jesus' head (Mt 27:37). That indicates that for Jesus' crucifixion a Latin cross was used, as artists have traditionally depicted it. In crucifixions the victim was most likely affixed to the cross while it was still lying flat on the ground. Then the cross was raised into position and dropped into a hole. The hands were either nailed or bound to the cross; it is uncertain whether the feet were nailed with one or two nails. The weight of the body was supported by a piece of wood at the feet and possibly by another which was like a spike between the legs.

6. Stoning was the most common Hebrew death penalty. The first stones were thrown by the prosecution witnesses, who were then joined by spectators. Stoning was the punishment for certain religious offenses (Lv 24:16; Nm 15:32–36; Dt 13:1–10; 17:2–5), adultery (Dt 22:23,24), child sacrifice (Lv 20:2), divination of spirits (Lv 20:27), and rebellion (Dt 21:18–21). Before his conversion the apostle Paul witnessed and consented to the stoning of Stephen (Acts 7:58,59). Paul himself later survived a stoning at Lystra (Acts 14:19). In Roman times a person would occasionally be stoned as he stood on a gallows.

Conclusion. Hebrew law was part of the Torah ("instruction") given by God to make his covenant people holy. At that time the Israelites were a seminomadic band of former slaves. Although there are similarities with the Code of Hammurabi and other laws of settled Near Eastern cultures, there are also many differences. Hebrew law often had a broader view, even in its less sophisticated cultural setting, as though its purpose was more to teach godly behavior than to stabilize society. The simplicity and directness of the Ten Commandments in particular continue to influence jurisprudence, even in modern secular society.

The Bible's primary message is God's love for his covenant people, yet it never overlooks the harsh realities of life in a fallen world. Human beings sin and they commit crimes; they suffer estrangement from God because of their sin and are punished for their crimes. Christians are constantly reminded of the realism of God's love by the cross as the symbol of Christian faith. They see the crucifixion of Jesus Christ as the fulfillment of OT prophecy that "the Lord has laid on him the iniquity of us all" (Is 53:5,6). The NT conviction is that "Christ died for our sins in accordance with the scriptures" (1 Cor 15:3); for those estranged from God, Jesus Christ has made peace "by the blood of his cross" (Col 1:20).

HAZEL W. PERKIN

See CIVIL LAW AND JUSTICE; LAW, BIBLICAL CONCEPT OF; HAMMURABI, LAW CODE OF; COURTS AND TRIALS.

Bibliography. A.J. Boecker, *Law and the Administration of Justice in the OT and Ancient East;* H.B. Clark, *Biblical Law;* D. Daube, *Studies in Biblical Law;* B.S. Jackson, *Theft in Early Jewish Law;* J. Pedersen, *Israel: Its Life and Culture,* 4 vols; A. Phillips, *Ancient Israel's Criminal Law;* J.M.P. Smith, *The Origin and History of Hebrew Law.*

Crimson. *See* COLOR.

Crispus. Synagogue leader at Corinth (Greece) who was converted "with all his household" during the apostle Paul's 18-month missionary visit to the city (Acts 18:8,11). Paul referred to Crispus as one of the few persons he personally baptized in Corinth (1 Cor 1:14).

Crocodile. Large aquatic, flesh-eating reptile with a lizardlike body, long pointed head, long powerful tail, and short legs. Although specifically mentioned once (Lv 11:30), it is often identified with the Leviathan of Job 41.

See ANIMALS.

Crookedback. KJV reading for hunchback in Leviticus 21:20.

See DEFORMITY.

Cross. *See* CRUCIFIXION.

Crown. Headpiece symbolizing honor or high office. The OT refers to three kinds of crowns in addition to using the word metaphorically.

One type of crown was worn by the high priest and Hebrew kings. The high priest's "holy crown" was a gold plate engraved with the words "Holy to the Lord" fastened to the front of a turban (Ex 29:6; 39:30). It symbolized his consecration as the people's representative before God. The Hebrew kings wore a crown light enough to be worn into battle (2 Sm 1:10), perhaps a narrow band of silk studded with jewels. Like the high priest's, the king's crown also indicated a divinely appointed office (2 Kgs 11:12; Ps 89:39; 132:18). A second type of crown was a massive gold and jeweled symbol of office worn by pagan kings and idols (2 Sm 12:30; Est 1:11). The prophet Zechariah placed such a crown on Joshua the high priest to indicate the union of royal and priestly functions (Zec 6:11,14). A third type of crown was a wreath of flowers used at a banquet to symbolize joy and celebration (Sg 3:11; Is 28:1; Wisd of Sol 2:8).

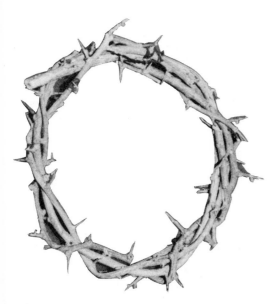

A crown of thorns.

The word "crown" is used metaphorically to indicate rule or royalty (Nah 3:17 KJV), glory or honor (Jb 19:9; Ps 8:5; Ez 16:12), joy (Ez 23:42), or pride (Jb 31:36; Is 28:3).

In the NT the most common word for crown means a laurel wreath worn at banquets or given as a civic or military honor. The apostle Paul alluded to its use as an athletic prize when he urged Christians to be disciplined in striving for a "crown" that would not wither (1 Cor 9:25 KJV; 2 Tm 2:5). Paul regarded his converts as his "joy and crown" (Phil 4:1; 1 Thes 2:19).

A victor's wreath symbolizes the glory of Christ (Heb 2:7,9) and the eternal life of Christians who have persevered (Jas 1:12; 1 Pt 5:4; Rv 2:10; 3:11). In the Book of Revelation the victories of the locusts (9:7), the woman (12:1), and Christ (6:2; 14:14) are symbolized by laurel crowns. A different Greek word, meaning a royal crown, is used for the diadems on the heads of the dragon (12:3), the beast from the sea (13:1), and Christ (19:12).

Jesus' crown of thorns was a circlet formed from a prickly shrub, an ironic parody of a victor's wreath (Mk 15:17,18). Its combination with the robe, scepter (Mt 27:27–29), and satirical inscription on the cross that Jesus was "the King of the Jews" (Mk 15:26), were all meant to mock him as a defeated messianic aspirant.

Crucifixion. Form of execution employed in the death of Jesus Christ. Two concepts related to crucifixion occur in Scripture: the "cross," a pagan mode of capital punishment, and the "tree," which was a Jewish form. Jesus' crucifixion was the means by which he procured atonement for humanity. The term "cross" was also used figuratively by Jesus to portray the sacrifice required in discipleship and by the apostle Paul to symbolize the death of self in the process of sanctification.

Background. *The Pagan Mode.* Literally, the word "cross" in Greek referred to a pointed stake used for various purposes, including a means of agonizing execution. As an instrument of death it could be an upright stake, used to impale a victim, or a vertical stake with a crossbeam either across the top (T) or across the middle (+), used to hang or crucify a criminal, with the added disgrace of public display. Evidently crucifixion was practiced first by the Medes and Persians and later by Alexander the Great (356–323 BC), the Carthaginians, and the Romans. Both Greeks and Romans restricted its use to slaves, considering it too barbaric for citizens. In the imperial era the Romans extended the use to aliens, but even so it was used mainly for crimes against the state.

Crucifixion was universally recognized as the most horrible type of death. In the East, in fact, it was used only as a further sign of disgrace for prisoners already executed, usually by decapitation. In the West the condemned criminal was scourged (beaten), usually at the place of execution, and forced to carry the crossbeam to the spot where a stake had already been erected. A tablet stating the crime was often placed around the offender's neck and was fastened to the cross after the execution. The prisoner was commonly tied or sometimes nailed to the crossbeam (with the nails through the wrists, since the bones in the hand could not take the weight). The beam was then raised and fixed to the upright pole. If the executioners wished a particularly slow, agonizing death, they might drive blocks or pins into the stake for a seat or a step to support the feet. Death came about through loss of blood circulation followed by coronary collapse. That could take days, so often the victim's legs would be broken below the knees with a club, causing massive shock and eliminating any further possibility of easing the pressure on the bound or spiked wrists. Usually a body was left on the cross to rot, but in some instances was given to relatives or friends for burial.

The Jewish Mode. The Eastern form of crucifixion is seen in the OT. King Saul's body was decapitated and affixed to a wall by the Philistines (1 Sm 31:9,10). The Persian king Darius made impaling the penalty for altering his decree (Ezr 6:11). According to Deuteronomy 21:22,23 the Eastern form was employed by the Jews with the added proviso that the body must be removed from "the tree" before nightfall, because the victim was "accursed by God" (cf. Gal 3:13) and must not remain to "defile the land." The Western form was not employed by the Jews. The only exception was a mass crucifixion of 800 rebels by the Jewish ruler Alexander Jannaeus in 76 BC, reported by the Jewish historian Josephus as being universally condemned by the Jews. Some believe that Jewish courts did practice the Western method of crucifixion after the second century BC.

Christ's Crucifixion. *The Predictions.* The Gospels record three predictions by Christ of his own crucifixion (Mk 8:31; 9:31; 10:33,34 and parallel passages). In addition, John recorded three sayings about the Son of man being "lifted up" (Jn 3:14; 8:28; 12:32,33), which parallel the synoptic predictions. Several themes are interwoven into those passages. (1) Christ's passion (a term used for his suffering on the cross) was part of God's redemptive purpose (Mk 8:31, "must"). (2) Both Jew and Roman were guilty of "delivering" and of "killing" Jesus. (3) His death would be followed by vindication via the resurrection. (4) His death itself, in a paradoxical way, was "glory" (seen in the symbolism John attached to "lifted up"). Other sayings that hint at Jesus' fate are his comment about the murder of the prophets (Mt 23:29–39; Lk 13:33); his parables about the death of the prophets and the "son" (the great feast, Mt 22:1–14; the wicked husbandman, Mk 12:1–10); and his teachings about the coming similar suffering of his disciples (Mt 10:24–28; Mk 8:34,35; Jn 15:18–25).

The Historical Event. The crucifixion of Jesus combined Roman and Jewish elements. Although the Gospel writers stressed Jewish guilt for their own polemical purposes, they were careful to distinguish between the leaders and the common people. It was the leaders who initiated Jesus' arrest (Mk 14:43) and his trial by the Sanhedrin (Mk 14:53–64). Though Pilate seemed to vacillate and in the end surrendered weakly to the crowds by "washing his hands" of any guilt (Mt 27:24), Rome was clearly implicated in the crucifixion. Since the Sanhedrin did not have the power to inflict capital punishment, Pilate's decision was necessary before crucifixion could occur. Further, Romans actually carried out the execution.

At Jesus' crucifixion Roman custom was observed in his scourging, his mock enthronement and stripping, the bearing of his own crossbeam, his being nailed to the cross, and the breaking of the two thieves' legs. The elevated site fits the custom of displaying certain criminals publicly. So does the height of Jesus' cross, probably seven to nine feet, as indicated by the hyssop reed. The presence of a tablet bearing the inscription "the King of the Jews" on the cross suggests that the crossbeam was fixed somewhere below the top of the stake. Jewish elements are seen in the wine mixed with myrrh (Mk 15:23), the vinegar on the hyssop reed (Mk 15:36), and the removal of the body before sunset and the beginning of the sabbath (Jn 19:31).

Although the fact of Jesus' crucifixion is seldom challenged historically, the varying details in the four Gospels are sometimes regarded as later additions due to the influence of prophetic "fulfillment," to Christian-Jewish polemics, or to cultic considerations. However, one cannot conclude from the differences in the Gospel accounts that the details are not historical. Narrative selectivity on the part of the Gospel writers is in no sense evidence of fabrication.

The Emphasis in Each Gospel. The elements found in the individual passion narratives were selected by each writer to present a particular view of the crucifixion scene. It has been realized for some time that the Gospel writers were not only historians but also theologians, selecting scenes and portraying them to show the significance of the events for the Christian faith. Their selection is poignantly evident in the crucifixion narratives.

Mark and Matthew both show the horror of the Messiah being put to death by human beings. The first half of Mark's scene contrasts the taunts of the crowd with the true significance of Jesus' death. The twofold "save yourself" (Mk 15:29–31) repeats Jesus' words about rebuilding the temple in three days, prophetically pointing to the resurrection. The second half of Mark's description stresses the horror of the scene, progressing from a darkness motif (Mk 15:33) to the cry of abandonment (v 34) to further taunts (vv 35,36).

The Gospel of Matthew extends Mark's im-

The Church of the Holy Sepulchre, which stands over the traditional site of the crucifixion, burial, and resurrection of Jesus Christ. Construction of the church began in 335, ordered by Queen Helena, the mother of Emperor Constantine.

agery in certain important directions, adding that Jesus refused the stupefying drink (a drugged wine to alleviate pain) "when he tasted it" (Mt 27:34) and adding "yielded up his spirit" to the death scene (27:50). Matthew thus emphasizes that Jesus voluntarily faced his death fully conscious and in complete control of himself. Matthew's irony and allusion also bring out the disparity between Jesus' suffering and his vindication. Elements of vindication include the ripping of the temple veil (27:51) and the centurion's testimony (27:54). In the remarkable supernatural scene of Matthew 27:52,53, Jesus' death is followed immediately by an earthquake that opened tombs and revived "many bodies of the saints" who had died. For Matthew those events and others inaugurated the last days, the new age of salvation, when the power of death is broken and life is made available for all.

The account in Luke's Gospel is also quite remarkable. It has two major thrusts. First, Jesus is portrayed as the perfect example of the righteous martyr who forgives his enemies and by his attitude converts some of his opponents. The taunts of the rulers and soldiers are reversed when the crowd returns home "beating their breasts" (Lk 23:48) and the centurion cries, "Certainly this man was innocent!" (23:47). Second, in Luke the entire setting has an atmosphere of reverence and worship. Omitted are the wine and myrrh, the cry of abandonment, and the Elijah taunt. Other episodes are noted instead, in particular the prayers of Jesus. In Luke alone are related: (1) Jesus' prayer that God forgive his executioners, placing it in contrast with the soldiers' mockery; (2) the promise in answer to the prayer of the "believing" criminal; and (3) the commitment of Jesus' spirit to the Father. Luke's awesome stillness compared to Matthew and Mark makes the crucifixion a kind of worshipful commemoration.

In the Gospel of John also one finds a change of theological focus. It goes further than Luke in removing shocking details such as the darkness and the taunts. Calm pervades throughout. Stress is laid on Jesus' sovereign control of his situation, as the crucifixion virtually becomes a coronation procession. John alone states that the inscription on the cross was written in Hebrew, Latin, and Greek; the charge thus becomes a worldwide proclamation of Christ's enthronement. The inscription, "Jesus of Nazareth, King of the Jews," continues Pilate's dialogue on kingship beyond Jesus' trial. John thus adds to Matthew's emphasis: Jesus has not only become king but has been sovereign all along. The king is pictured as performing the priestly function and himself becoming the sacrifice. John alone mentions the hyssop (which had been used to sprinkle the blood of the lamb at the Passover, Ex 12:22), and Jesus' cry, "It is finished" (Jn 19:29,30). Further, the piercing of Jesus' side (19:31–37), which shows the reality of his death, may also be seen symbolically, along with the "rivers of living water" (7:37,38), as typifying the outpouring of salvation in the new age.

Thus, each Gospel pictures the meaning of Jesus' death from a different vantage point. To combine their pictures gives new understanding of the significance of the cross. Rather than contradiction, one sees separate parts of a compelling whole.

The Theology of the Cross. The cross plays a dual role in Christian theology. Some theologians emphasize the significance of the historical crucifixion of Jesus Christ and what it accomplished for the believer. Others focus on the symbolism of the cross in each believer's life.

Literal Interpretation. The death and resurrection of Jesus of Nazareth are the central events of Christian theology. The cross has meaning because of the significance of the person who was put to death on it and because of what his death accomplished.

1. Creedal basis. Most commentators assert that the apostle Paul originated the "theology of the cross," since in the NT it is found mainly in his epistles. It can be demonstrated, however, that Paul followed the emphasis of the primitive creeds. Probably the earliest creed is found in 1 Corinthians 15:3–5, which employs two rabbinic code words for tradition— "delivered" and "received." That creed was evidently given to Paul on his first visit to Jerusalem (Gal 1:18,19). Its first affirmation, that "Christ died for sins in accordance with the Scriptures" (1 Cor 15:3) combined two major themes: fulfillment of OT prophecy and substitutionary atonement. That proto-creed also emphasized that Christ's death led to exaltation (1 Cor 15:4), the primary motif in all the early creeds. Other creedal statements containing that motif are Romans 4:25; 6:1–8; 8:32; Colossians 2:11,12; 1 Peter 1:21; 3:18–22.

2. The power of the gospel. "The word of the cross" was central in the salvation proclamation of the early church. Above all, the event of the cross was God's principal saving act in history; hence the cross, though a past event, has present significance. Christ crucified and risen is the core of the church's message (Gal 3:1). The central passage is 1 Corinthians 1:17–2:5. There the "word of the cross" (1:18) is contrasted with "eloquent wisdom" (1:17). Sounding like foolishness, it is offensive to both Greek philosophy and Jewish legalism (cf. Gal 6:12–15), but that very "weakness" in human

eyes opens the door for the "power of God" (1:18), "the mighty power . . . in the simple message of the cross of Christ" (1:17 LB). The cross in the church's *kerygma* (proclamation) illustrates the pattern of God's action: he forges out of the debilitated things of life both power and wisdom (1:26–30). Because philosophical speculation replaces God's message with human wisdom and thus empties the cross of its significance, Paul rejected "lofty words" and preached only the "crucified Christ." The "Holy Spirit's power" thus became evident in Paul's "weakness" (2:1–5). The central core of the gospel is God's demonstration of victory emerging from seeming defeat, of power arising out of infirmity.

3. Salvation. The cross as the basis of atonement is the principal emphasis in the epistles (see Eph 2:16; Col 1:20; 2:14), whereas in the Book of Acts the resurrection seems more central (see 2:33–36; 3:19–26; 13:37–39). The reason for the different emphasis is found in the different purposes of those writings: the cross tends to be used in didactic (instructional) sections, the resurrection in apologetic (persuasive) or kerygmatic sections, when the basis for salvation is being presented. In actuality they were a single event in salvation history. Jesus "was put to death for our trespasses and raised for our justification" (Rom 4:25).

Paul expressed the significance of the cross in the words "redemption," "propitiation," and "justification." The first two concepts have the "for us" theme traceable to the suffering servant (Is 53:10–12), whose death was for "the sin of many." The idea of redemption in both Testaments is the payment of a price to "ransom" those held captive. That price, the NT explains, was paid on the cross, and humanity was thereby freed from sin (Mk 10:45; Ti 2:14; 1 Pt 1:18). The connection between Jesus' death and the substitutionary preposition "instead of" is also seen in Galatians 3:13, which adds to the curse of Deuteronomy 21:23 the interpretation "for us" (cf. Rom 5:10,11,18; 1 Cor 11:24; Eph 1:7; 2:13). Similarly, Paul's concept of justification centers on the cross. It is "Christ crucified" who declares humanity righteous and makes freedom from sin possible (Rom 6:6; Gal 2:19–21). Human guilt was transferred to the cross and expiated there, opening up God's forensic (legal) forgiveness of all who avail themselves of its power (1 Pt 1:18–21; 2:24; 3:18). Finally, the result is "reconciliation"—both vertically, between humans and God (Col 1:20), and horizontally, between previously opposed human forces (e.g., in Eph 2:13–16, between Jew and Gentile).

Figurative Interpretation. Beyond the theological meaning of the literal cross on which Jesus Christ was put to death in Judea nearly two thousand years ago is the symbolic significance of the cross for his followers today.

1. Bearing the cross. Jesus made "bearing the cross" a condition of discipleship in five passages. There are two major variants: one, found in the material common to Matthew and Luke (Mt 10:38; Lk 14:27), is phrased negatively ("cannot be my disciple"); the other, which is found in all three synoptic Gospels (Mt 16:24; Mk 8:34; Luke 9:23), is phrased positively ("If any man would come after me"). Two major motifs are found in the sayings. The major motif comes from the imagery of a condemned man carrying his cross to an execution site; a necessary part of discipleship is a daily (Lk 9:23) willingness to sacrifice all and to suffer for the sake of Christ. The central point is not death but disgrace; the disciple must be ready to become an outcast from society. A secondary motif may stem from Ezekiel 9:4–6, where the righteous are given a "mark upon their foreheads" to separate them from the guilty. That mark was a tau, the last letter of the Hebrew alphabet, which in ancient manuscripts was written as an X or + . Some have asserted that "bearing the cross" was a sign of confession, an indication of being "sealed" for Jesus in the last days. Whatever the validity of that interpretation, the major theme is clearly self-denial and surrender to the possibility of suffering.

2. The crucified life. Paul extended Christ's metaphor to the death of self. Again, he may have taken the idea from the early catechism, as seen in the baptismal creed of Romans 6:1–8, which identifies baptism as being "buried therefore with him." Paul interpreted the Christian's identification with Christ's death to mean that "our old self was crucified with him so that the sinful body might be destroyed, and we might no longer be enslaved to sin" (Rom 6:6). As further developed in 2 Corinthians 5:14–17, the believer participates in the death and resurrection of Christ, so that the "old has passed away, behold the new has come" (5:17). The same view is found also in Galatians, which contrasts the mystical death of self to the legalistic system of the Judaizers. The believer is "crucified with Christ," with the result that "it is no longer I who live" (Gal 2:20); "the flesh with its passions and desires" is "crucified" (Gal 5:24); and "far be it from me to glory except in the cross of our Lord Jesus Christ, by which the world has been crucified to me, and I to the world" (Gal 6:14). Believers must experience the cross before they can find the resurrection life.

GRANT R. OSBORNE

See ATONEMENT; CRIMINAL LAW AND PUNISHMENT; REDEEMER, REDEMPTION; ELI, ELI, LAMA SABACHTHANI; SEVEN LAST WORDS, THE; GOLGOTHA.

Bibliography. J.A. Fitzmyer, *To Advance the Gospel*, pp 125–46; M. Hengel, *Crucifixion;* E.C. Hoskyns and N. Davey, *Crucifixion–Resurrection;* L. Morris, *The Cross in the NT;* H.W. Robinson, *The Cross in the OT;* V. Taylor, *Jesus and His Sacrifice.*

Cruse. Small earthern vessel or flask, about four to six inches tall, used for holding liquids (1 Kgs 17:12–16). In the KJV two other Hebrew words are translated "cruse." However, a bottle or jar is probably in view in 1 Kings 14:3, and an open dish or bowl in 2 Kings 2:20.

See POTTERY.

Crystal. Variety of quartz, usually clear or nearly so. Two Hebrew words and two Greek words are translated "crystal."

See MINERALS, METALS, AND PRECIOUS STONES.

Cub. Name of a place, identified as Libya (RSV margin), in Ezekiel 30:5.

See LIBYA, LIBYANS.

Cubit. Linear measure, about 18 inches, the length of a man's forearm from the elbow to the tip of his middle finger.

See WEIGHTS AND MEASURES.

Cuckoo. KJV translation of a Hebrew word better rendered "sea gull" in Leviticus 11:16 and Deuteronomy 14:15 (RSV).

See BIRDS.

Cucumber. Garden vegetable of the gourd family, mentioned as one of the foods desired by the wandering Israelites (Nm 11:5).

See FOOD AND FOOD PREPARATION; PLANTS.

Cummin. Herb of the carrot family cultivated for its aromatic seeds, which are used for seasoning food (Is 28:25,27; Mt 23:23).

See FOOD AND FOOD PREPARATION; PLANTS.

Cun. Syrian city belonging to Hadadezer, king of Zobah. David raided Cun, taking away large quantities of bronze (1 Chr 18:8, KJV Chun). In a parallel account Berothai may be the same place (2 Sm 8:8).

See BEROTHAH, BEROTHAI.

Cuneiform. *See* WRITING AND BOOKS.

Cup. The word may refer either to the vessel itself or to its contents and may be intended literally or figuratively.

1. A small drinking vessel, made of various materials (leather, metal, or pottery), sizes, and designs.

2. A figure of speech to represent one's por-

A design from the inside of a Greek cup.

tion of or participation in something. It is associated with consolation (Jer 16:7), demons (1 Cor 10:21), divination (Gn 44:2,5), drunkenness (Prv 23:31), immorality (Rv 17:4; 18:6), inheritance (Ps 16:5), judgment (Ps 11:6; 75:8; Is 51:17,22; Jer 25:15; 49:12; Ez 23:33; Zec 12:2; Rv 14:10; 16:19; 18:6), the Lord (1 Cor 10:21), prosperity or blessing (Ps 23:5), salvation (Ps 116:13), suffering (Mt 20:22; 26:39; Mk 10:39; 14:36; Lk 22:42; Jn 18:11), and thanksgiving (1 Cor 10:16).

See CUP OF BLESSING.

Cupbearer. Official whose primary duty was to taste the wine served to the king as a precaution against poisoning.

See TRADES AND OCCUPATIONS.

Cup of Blessing. Theological phrase used in two contexts: (1) in Jewish usage, a cup of wine drunk at the end of a meal and having special Passover significance; (2) in Christian usage, the Communion goblet.

In the Passover feast the cup of blessing is the third of four cups required in the ceremony of the paschal meal. It derives its name from the prayer offered over the cup: "Blessed art thou, O Lord our God, who givest us the fruit of the vine."

The apostle Paul used the term in reference to the wine of the Lord's Supper (1 Cor 10:16). His words are taken by many interpreters as evidence that the early church saw the Lord's Supper as a transformation and fulfillment of the Passover celebration. To participate in drinking the cup of blessing is to commit oneself to Christ, "our paschal lamb" (1 Cor 5:7), whose death it commemorates, and to enter into "communion" or fellowship with him. The phrase "cup of the Lord" (1 Cor 10:21; 11:27) or simply "the cup" (1 Cor 11:25) is also used. Paul added that true communion with

Christ, signified by the cup of blessing, should exclude communion with spiritual forces opposed to Christ, signified by the "cup of demons" (1 Cor 10:21).

See LORD'S SUPPER, THE.

Curse, Cursed. Invocation of evil or injury against one's enemies. As practiced in Bible times, cursing was the opposite of blessing and should not be confused with profanity in the modern sense.

Pagan Beliefs. Curses and blessings were linked to the ancient pagan belief that spirits or "the gods" could be invoked to act on behalf of a person who repeated certain incantations or performed certain deeds (such as sacrifices). It was thought that a spoken curse possessed an occult power to work calamity on one's enemies. In some pagan cultures curses were written on clay jars that were then smashed, symbolically initiating or effecting the intended curse.

Tombs were protected against would-be desecrators by means of curses. Royal inscriptions were protected by maledictions aimed at anyone who might alter, destroy, or defy the written decree (Ezr 6:11,12).

Curses in Old Testament Times. Among the Hebrews a curse, valid only within a covenant framework overseen by God, was spoken for the sake of justice. In the OT the curse was an integral part of a covenant relationship—between God and the community, between God and an individual, or among members of the community. To break the terms of a covenant was to merit the covenant curse or curses. A curse invoked under other conditions was powerless. "Like a sparrow in its flitting, like a swallow in its flying, a curse that is causeless does not alight" (Prv 26:2). A curse could be retracted by pronouncing a blessing (Ex 12:32; Jgs 17:1,2; 2 Sm 21:1–3).

The Mosaic law forbade the cursing of parents (Ex 21:17; cf. Prv 20:20; Mt 15:4), the ruler (Ex 22:28), and the deaf (Lv 19:14). A man who suspected his wife of unfaithfulness could require that she submit to a test administered by the priest that would result in a curse upon her if she was guilty (Nm 5:11–31). Individuals might pronounce a curse upon themselves to show the truthfulness of their assertions or promises (Nm 5:19–22; Jb 31:7–10,16–22; Ps 137:5,6). In the NT the apostle Peter followed the OT practice when he used a curse to deny that he knew Jesus (Mk 14:71); certain men who wished to kill the apostle Paul proved their sincerity by such a solemn curse (Acts 23:12,14,21). Cursing God was punishable by death (Lv 24:10–16; cf. Ex 22:28; Is 8:21,22).

Curses in Bible history include God's curse on the serpent, Adam, and Eve (Gn 3:14–19); on Cain (Gn 4:11, 12); on those who might curse the patriarch Abraham and his descendants (Gn 12:3); and on those who put their trust in human strength instead of in the Lord (Jer 17:5). When the people of Israel passed through Moab on their way to the Promised Land, Moab's king Balak hired Balaam to curse the Israelites; he and Balaam learned, however, that they could not curse those whom God had blessed (Nm 22–24). Joshua cursed anyone who might try to rebuild Jericho (Jos 6:26; fulfilled in 1 Kgs 16:34). King Saul made a curse that almost cost his son Jonathan's life (1 Sm 14:24,43–45). Many other curses are mentioned in the OT (see, e.g., Gn 9:25; 49:5–7; Jos 9:22,23; Jgs 9:7–21,57; 2 Sm 16:5–13; 1 Kgs 21:17–24; 2 Kgs 2:24; Mal 2:2; 4:6). The pronouncement of "woe" is also the language of curse (Is 5:8–23; cf. Mt 23:13–33, where "alas" and "woe" can be used synonymously and may be either an exclamation of sorrow or of impending doom and calamity).

Psalm 109 contains a lengthy imprecation against the psalmist's enemies, evidently because they had spoken some words against him falsely (see also Pss 58:6–11; 69:19–28; 143:12; but contrast Prv 24:17,18). The prophet Jeremiah was not averse to calling on God to punish his tormentors (Jer 11:20; 12:3; 15:15; 17:18; 18:21,22; 20:11,12) or asking God not to forgive them (18:23). Such imprecations against one's enemies are difficult for Christians today to understand. OT examples of cursing contrast sharply with the NT commands to "bless those who curse you" (Lk 6:28; cf. Rom 12:14). Jesus' injunction to "love your enemies" (Mt 5:44) may be intended to point beyond the cursing practiced in the OT to a fuller understanding of God's command to love one's neighbor as one's self.

Covenant Curses. Protection of a contract or treaty by invoking a curse on the violator was common in OT times. Sometimes a covenant was sealed by cutting up an animal and having the covenanting individuals walk between the severed pieces; the slain animal symbolized the curse to befall the violator. God agreed to submit to such a curse on himself if he broke the covenant he made with the patriarch Abraham (Gn 15:7–18). Later God accused the leaders and people of Israel of breaking their covenant with him and warned them of the consequences to follow (Jer 34:18,19). An essential part of the covenant God made with Israel at Mt Sinai was the promise of blessings for keeping the covenant and curses for breaking it (Dt 11:26–28; 27:15–26; 28:15–68; 30:19; cf. Lv 26:3–39). Israel suffered those curses in the time of the prophets Jeremiah and Ezekiel;

the covenant breakers, including the king, were threatened with a curse (Jer 11:3; Ez 17:11–21).

The Ban on "Devoted Things." A special kind of curse was the ban or anathema. Strictly speaking, it was a vow to devote persons, animals, or objects under such a curse to God. In some cases the priests could use objects that had fallen under the ban (Nm 18:14; Ez 44:29), but that provision did not apply to living beings; all persons or animals under the ban were sacrificed or destroyed (Lv 27:28,29). The ban was commonly used in Israel's wars against its pagan neighbors. Sometimes everything was declared anathema (Jos 6:17–19), but normally only persons and heathen images were destroyed (Dt 2:34; 3:6; 7:2,25,26—not even the melted gold of images was to be kept). To violate the ban by preserving any part of the cursed things was to come under the ban oneself. Because Achan did not respect the ban placed upon Jericho, the terms of that curse came upon all Israel until Achan confessed and was executed (Jos 7).

After the exile the Jews did not practice the anathema (or ban) by putting people to death; people who violated a curse were excommunicated and put out of the congregation of Israel (Ezr 10:8). That meant that the person was no longer part of God's people and was considered "dead."

Curses in New Testament Times. Jewish synagogues practiced excommunication or anathema in the NT period (Lk 6:22; Jn 9:22; 12:42; 16:2). Later, Christians excommunicated persons by declaring them outside of the redeemed community (Mt 18:17) or "delivered to Satan" (1 Cor 5:5; 1 Tm 1:20). Both practices stemmed from the OT ban. Unlike that curse, however, the excommunication could be removed as soon as the person repented.

Since the anathema branded a person as "rejected" or "cursed by God," Saul of Tarsus, before his conversion, tried to compel Christians to renounce Christ by calling him accursed (cf. Acts 26:11). Later, as an apostle, Paul (Saul) warned that no one speaking by the Spirit of God could call Jesus accursed (1 Cor 12:3). Paul pronounced anathema (destined for judgment and perdition) upon anyone who preached another gospel than the one he and the other apostles preached (Gal 1:8,9). Paul said he wished he could be accursed, cut off from salvation and the people of God, if that could lead to the salvation of his fellow Israelites (Rom 9:3). His desire reflected the love of Christ, who accepted the "curse of the Law" upon himself in submitting to suffering and death on the cross in order to redeem human beings from that curse (Gal 3:8–14; cf. Dt 21:22,23). The NT promises that a time will come when "there shall no longer be any curse" (Rv 22:3 NASB).

F. B. HUEY, JR. & PETER H. DAVIDS

See WAR, HOLY.

Curtains. *See* FURNITURE; HOMES AND DWELLINGS; TABERNACLE, TEMPLE.

Cush (Person). 1. Eldest of Ham's four sons (Gn 10:6; 1 Chr 1:8). Because the other three (Egypt, Put, and Canaan) are place-names, it is likely that Cush also is a place. It is usually identified with Ethiopia.

See CUSH (PLACE); ETHIOPIA.

2. Benjamite and presumably David's enemy, mentioned in the title of Psalm 7.

Cush (Place). Egyptian, Akkadian, and Hebrew term broadly referring to the countries of the Upper Nile south of Egypt. In a narrower sense Cush consisted of the territory between the 2nd and 4th cataracts of the Nile, roughly the present northern Sudan (equivalent to ancient Nubia). The OT generally uses the term in that sense. The Greeks called it Ethiopia, which eventually gave its name to modern Ethiopia (farther to the south and east).

The meaning of Cush in the Book of Genesis, however, is problematic. In the garden of Eden narrative (Gn 2:13) Cush seems to be located in Mesopotamia, the region of the Tigris and Euphrates rivers (Gn 2:14). Perhaps the term there should be equated with Kassite (Cossaean), the usual designation of the Babylonian rulers who held sway in Mesopotamia for about half a millennium down to the 12th century BC. The Cush of Genesis 10:6–8, then, could be divided into two locales, Nubia (Gn 10:6,7) and Mesopotamia (Gn 10:8), since the latter reference is tied in with a Cushite individual, Nimrod, whose activities took place entirely in Mesopotamia (Gn 10:9–12). Alternatively, the Cush of Genesis 2:13 and 10:8 could be Kish, the Mesopotamian city that was traditionally the seat of the first Sumerian dynasty after the flood.

Less uncertainty exists over use of the term "Cushite." With one possible exception (Nm 12:1) Cushite always refers to people from Nubia, the African Cush.

The first messenger whom Joab, King David's commander in chief, sent to announce Absalom's defeat to David was a Cushite (2 Sm 18:21–32). That messenger's foreign origin is reflected in the fact that he was unaware of a shortcut as well as in his insensitivity to the feelings of King David when he gave him the message. The KJV transliterates the Hebrew word as a proper name (Cushi), but that rendering is unlikely.

Moses had a wife who was known as a Cushite (Nm 12:1). In that context it is possible to understand Cushite in several ways: as a person from Nubia—which would make her a second wife, different from Zipporah; as a person from Cushan—making her possibly a Midianite, perhaps identical with Zipporah; or as a reference to her darker skin and foreign origin—possibly but not necessarily a reference to Zipporah.

Most English versions translate the other occurrences of Cush and Cushite as Ethiopia and Ethiopians.

See CUSHAN; CUSHI #1; ETHIOPIA.

Cushan. Name of a tribe or place mentioned only once in the Bible (Hab 3:7). Some have identified Cushan with the people and land referred to in the OT as Cush, or Ethiopia in most English versions. The parallel position of "Cushan" to "the land of Midian" in Habbakuk 3:7, however, as well as the location of the other places mentioned in the passage (Teman, Mt Paran) seems to place Cushan in the vicinity of Edom and Midian, south and southeast of the Dead Sea.

See CUSH (PLACE).

Cushan-rishathaim. King of Mesopotamia whom Israel served for eight years. The Lord raised up Othniel, Kenaz's son, to deliver Israel out of his hand; later, Cushan-rishathaim was defeated by Othniel in war (Jgs 3:8,10, KJV Chushan-rishathaim). His exact identity is uncertain.

Cushi. 1. Joab's messenger sent to David to announce Absalom's defeat (2 Sm 18:21–32 KJV). However, the Hebrew word transliterated "Cushi" should more likely be translated "Cushite"

See CUSH (PLACE).

2. Jehudi's great-grandfather. Jehudi was a prince in the court of King Jehoiakim of Judah in the time of Jeremiah the prophet (Jer 36:14).

3. Father of the prophet Zephaniah (Zep 1:1).

Cushite. Person from the African region of Nubia (2 Sm 18:22).

See CUSH (PLACE).

Custodian. Servant whose responsibility was to accompany, protect, and sometimes discipline his master's son until the boy reached maturity.

See TRADES AND OCCUPATIONS.

Customs in Bible Times. *See* AGRICULTURE; BURIAL, BURIAL CUSTOMS; CIVIL LAW AND JUSTICE; CLEANNESS AND UNCLEANNESS, REGULATIONS CONCERNING; CRIMINAL LAW AND PUNISHMENT; COURTS AND TRIALS; DIETARY LAWS; EDUCATION; FAMILY LIFE AND RELATIONS; FASHION AND DRESS; FEASTS AND FESTIVALS OF ISRAEL; FOOD AND FOOD PREPARATION; FURNITURE; HOMES AND DWELLINGS; INDUSTRY AND COMMERCE; INHERITANCE; MARRIAGE, MARRIAGE CUSTOMS; MEDICINE AND MEDICAL PRACTICE; MONEY AND BANKING; MUSIC AND MUSICAL INSTRUMENTS; OFFERINGS AND SACRIFICES; SLAVE, SLAVERY; TOOLS; TRADES AND OCCUPATIONS; TRAVEL AND TRANSPORTATION; WAGES.

Cuth, Cuthah. Town in southern Babylonia (2 Kgs 17:24), from which some people were taken and relocated in Samaria after the Assyrian conquest (722 BC). The name appears also in Assyrian and Babylonian sources. In 1881–82 Hormuzd Rassam identified Cuthah as an ancient city whose towering ruins are located at modern Tell Ibrahim, about 20 miles northeast of Babylon. Cuthah was the location of a temple dedicated to Nergal, its patron deity (2 Kgs 17:30).

The Cuthans seem to have been a predominant segment of the population of postexilic Samaria, since Jews in later centuries applied that name to Samaritans in general. The religious syncretism of which the Cuthans were a part produced hostilities between Judah and Samaria following the Jews' return from their exile. That animosity between Jews and Samaritans continued across the centuries to Jesus' day (Jn 4:7–9).

Cylinder Seal. *See* SEAL.

Cymbal. Percussion instrument consisting of two round, thin, slightly concave, metal plates which are struck together. Cymbals were used in the worship of God (2 Sm 6:5; Ezr 3:10; Ps 150:5).

See MUSIC AND MUSICAL INSTRUMENTS (ZELZELIM).

Cypress. Evergreen tree with dark foliage and distinctive symmetrical form. Cypress is mentioned as one of the materials in Solomon's temple (1 Kgs 5:8).

See PLANTS.

Cyprus. Island country located in the northeastern Mediterranean Sea, 50 miles south of Turkey (Asia Minor), 70 miles west of Syria, and 245 miles north of Egypt. This island, about 110 miles long and 50 miles wide, supports the Kyrenia and Troodas Massif mountain ranges separated by the fertile Mesaoria plain. A narrow strip of land 40 miles long and 5 miles wide extends from the northeastern

A mirror from Cyprus.

Alashiya, as attested in the ancient documents of Ebla (24th century BC), Mari (18th century BC), Ugarit, and Tell el-Amarna (14th century BC). Elishah, an OT name for this island, is perhaps identifiable with the extrabiblical Alashiya (cf. Ez 27:7). Alashiya (Cyprus) established a network of trade with Syria, Palestine, and Egypt and became known for its exports, especially copper, oil, wood, and pottery. Pieces of Alashiyan pottery have been found at over 50 sites in Egypt, 25 sites in Palestine, and 17 sites in Syria. The ancient texts of Ebla, Mari, and Amarna record the business transactions involving Alashiya's treasured copper. Toward the end of the Bronze Age (c. 1270–1190 BC) the Mycenaean and Achaean Greeks began to migrate to Cyprus. During this period the Greek colonies of Salamis and Paphos were founded.

In the ninth and eighth centuries BC the Phoenicians settled their people and asserted their dominance on Cyprus. King Hiram II of Tyre (741–738 BC) included Cyprus in his royal domain, according to the inscriptions found at Mt Sinoas. Kition, near modern Larnaka, was a Phoenician settlement whose inhabitants were called Kittim. The Hebrews named the whole island Kittim (Nm 24:24, KJV Chittim) and eventually referred to any maritime country by this name (Dn 11:30; Jer 2:10; 1 Mc 1:1). Isaiah announced that from the ports of Kittim (Cyprus), the reports of Tyre's destruction would be confirmed to its homeward-traveling sailors (Is 23:1,12).

Assyria, rising as the superior power in the Middle East during the eighth and seventh centuries BC, made Cyprus one of its tributaries. The stela of King Sargon II (721–705 BC) records the tributes received by seven kings of Cyprus. The prism of Esar-haddon (c. 670 BC) registers ten Cypriot kings with their cities. During the Assyrian occupation Cyprus was called Iadnan. After the dissolution of the Assyrian empire Cyprus was governed by Amasis, king of Egypt (569–527 BC), and later by King Cambyses II of Persia (529–522 BC).

After Alexander the Great's decisive defeat of the Persian army at Issus in 333 BC, Cyprus sent 120 ships to help support his siege against Tyre. The Ptolemies of Egypt (a subdivision of the Greek empire) gained possession of the island after Alexander's death in 323 and retained control of Cyprus from 294–58 BC. This period brought relative peace and prosperity to the island. Cyprus, meaning copper in Greek, was the name assigned to it.

Cyprus was annexed to Rome in 58 BC, and Cicero was appointed its governor in 52. In 22 BC Rome made Cyprus into a senatorial province; Sergius Paulus was selected as its proconsul in AD 46. Later, Hadrian suppressed a vio-

part of the island. Cyprus is rimmed with a number of natural harbors. In antiquity these harbors provided a strategic meeting place of sea routes from Asia Minor, Syria, Palestine, and Egypt. The Cypriot copper mines, though now largely depleted, have long been a source of revenue for its inhabitants.

During the Bronze period (later 4th–2nd millenniums BC) Cyprus experienced an increased growth in population and economic importance among the Mediterranean communities. The island at that time was named

lent Jewish revolt in 117, after which he banished all Jews from the island.

In the NT, Cyprus is first mentioned as the birthplace of Barnabas (Acts 4:36). Later, Jewish believers sought refuge at Cyprus from the persecutions that arose in Jerusalem on account of Stephen (Acts 11:19,20). On Paul's first missionary journey he and Barnabas set sail from Seleucia, crossing to Cyprus before going on to Asia Minor (*c.* AD 47). Landing at the eastern seaport of Salamis, they gradually made their way westward across the island until they reached the western harbor town of Paphos. Here they met Bar-Jesus, the false prophet, and converted the Roman proconsul Sergius Paulus. From Paphos, Paul and Barnabas sailed to Asia Minor, docking at Perga in Pamphylia (Acts 13:4–13). Paul bypassed Cyprus on his second missionary journey; however, Barnabas with John Mark revisited the island (Acts 15:39). On Paul's final trip to Jerusalem, Cyprus was used as a navigational landmark in crossing from Patara to Tyre (Acts 21:3). On the journey to Rome, Paul's ship sailed under the lee of Cyprus to avoid rough winds (Acts 27:4).

Cyrene, Cyrenians. City on the coast of North Africa which was the capital of Cyrenaica. It was founded in the 7th century BC by Greeks who engaged primarily in agricultural pursuits. Herodotus comments in his fifth-century BC *Histories* that "the land of Cyrene, the highest of that part of Libya which is inhabited by Nomads, has the remarkable peculiarity of three separate harvest-seasons . . . making for the fortunate people of Cyrene, a continuous autumn of eight months on end" (4.199). It was conquered by Alexander the Great in 331 BC and later became a part of the Roman empire. During the period of the NT the city contained a large Jewish population which had come from Alexandria. One such person, named Simon, was visiting Jerusalem during the Passover feast the year Jesus Christ was crucified and was forced to carry his cross (Mt 27:32). Fifty days later Peter preached to Jews from Cyrene on Pentecost day in Jerusalem (Acts 2:10). Stephen was attacked by Jews associated with a synagogue that included people of Cyrene (Acts 6:9), some of whom were later converted and became preachers (Acts 11:20). They appear to have traveled as far north as Antioch, where a prominent Christian teacher was Lucius of Cyrene (Acts 13:1).

Cyrenius. KJV rendering of Quirinius, the governor of Syria when Christ was born, in Luke 2:2.

See QUIRINIUS.

Cyrus the Great. Persian king (559–530 BC) who founded the Achaemenid dynasty and the Persian empire. Cyrus (II) was the son of Cambyses I (600–559 BC), who ruled the unified territories of Parshumash-anshan and Parsa. Cyrus' mother was Mandane, daughter of the Median king Astyages (585?–550 BC). The ancestor of the dynasty was Achaemenes. Cyrus succeeded his father and established himself in Pasargadae about 559 BC. Ambitious and daring, he aligned his kingdom with neighboring peoples and tribes into a solid block of Persian power, then revolted against Astyages of Media. When it became evident that Cyrus would win in the struggle to control Media, the troops of Astyages mutinied and deserted to Cyrus. When Cyrus conquered the Median kingdom, however, he came into conflict with Babylon, since the two kingdoms claimed much of the same territory.

Cyrus consolidated his power before fighting with Babylon. First, he conquered Asia

The Cyrus cylinder.

Minor. Wealthy King Croesus of Lydia and the Lydians submitted to him. Then he overran the northern mountainous region between the Caspian Sea and the northwest corner of India.

By 539 BC Cyrus was ready to move against Babylon. The Babylonian governor of Elam defected to Cyrus and joined his army. With a minimum of opposition the armies of Cyrus entered the Babylonian capital in 539 BC. Nabonidus was taken prisoner but was treated with respect and mercy. Sixteen days later Cyrus himself entered the city, to the acclaim of many of its inhabitants.

Isaiah's prophecy spoke of Cyrus as the Lord's anointed (Is 45:1). Israel regarded him as called and empowered by their God to free them. Under Cyrus the Jews were allowed to rebuild Jerusalem and its temple (Is 44:28). Documents preserved in the OT state that in his first year in Babylon, Cyrus issued a decree permitting the reconstruction of the house of God at Jerusalem (2 Chr 36:22,23; Ezr 1:1–3; 6:2–5). He also returned sacred vessels taken from the temple by Nebuchadnezzar. Biblical descriptions of the decree say nothing about rebuilding the city, but that would be in harmony with the king's policy.

During excavations (1879–82) at Babylon, archaeologist Hormuzd Rassam discovered a clay barrel inscription on which Cyrus told of taking the city and of his resulting policies. Isaiah and Chronicles reflect the content of the Cyrus Cylinder, which says that captured peoples were allowed to return home and build sanctuaries to their own gods.

Nothing is known about the death of Cyrus. Accounts that have been preserved make it clear that he was killed in battle, but the statements are conflicting. Probably the Greek historian Herodotus is right in indicating that Cyrus died in a terrible disaster which destroyed the Persian army fighting the Massagetae. The tomb of Cyrus can still be seen at Pasargadae in Iran.

See PERSIA, PERSIANS.

Dd

Dabareh. KJV spelling of the town Daberath in Joshua 21:28.

See DABERATH.

Dabbesheth, Dabbasheth. Designation for a camel's hump (Is 30:6). The name also refers to a town ("camel's hump hill") situated on the western border of the land allotted to Zebulun's tribe for an inheritance (Jos 19:11, KJV Dabbasheth). Its exact location is unknown.

Daberath. Town in Issachar's territory given to the Levite family of Gershon (Jos 21:28, KJV Dabareh; 1 Chr 6:72). It was located west of Mt Tabor on the Issachar-Zebulun border, and has been identified with the modern Debuyiyeh.

See LEVITICAL CITIES.

Dagger. Short sword.

See ARMS AND WARFARE.

Dagon. Deity worshiped throughout the Mesopotamian world. In the OT, Dagon is the principal god of the Philistines (Jgs 16:23; 1 Sm 5:2–7; 1 Chr 10:10). Shrines to Dagon were found in Israel's territories (Beth-dagon, Jos 15:41; 19:27).

See PHILISTIA, PHILISTINES; CANAANITE DEITIES AND RELIGION.

Dalaiah. KJV spelling of Delaiah, Elioenai's son, in 1 Chronicles 3:24.

See DELAIAH #1.

Dalmanutha. Area on the west side of the Sea of Galilee near the southern end of the plain of Gennesaret. Its exact location is uncertain. Jesus and his disciples stayed there briefly after the incident of the feeding of the four thousand (Mk 8:10). The Pharisees came to him seeking a sign from heaven in order to test him. After his answer that "no sign shall be given to this generation" (Mk 8:12), he departed from there.

The word "Dalmanutha" is present in the best manuscripts, although other sources record Magadan or Magdala. The parallel passage in Matthew 15:39 cites Magadan. Because of this, the exact name and location have been difficult to pinpoint. Probably the various names are meant to designate the same site or at least two places in the same area.

See MAGADAN; MAGDALA.

Dalmatia. Mountainous region on the eastern shore of the Adriatic Sea, across from Italy. The Dalmatians were an Illyrian (Greek) tribe, or group of tribes banded together, coming from the area around the town of Delmion (or Delminium). Their piracy gave the Romans considerable difficulty until Octavian thoroughly subjugated them in 33 BC.

At the time of Paul, Dalmatia was the name of the Roman province; its southern boundary was Macedonia, and its northern boundary is not clearly known. There is one reference to the province in the NT: Titus is mentioned as going there in 2 Timothy 4:10. We are not told why he went. It may be that Paul had organized some churches there, or Titus may have been opening up a new mission field.

Dalphon. Haman's son killed by the Jews in the aftermath of the plot against Mordecai (Est 9:7).

Damaris. Woman mentioned (Acts 17:34) as one of the first converts in the city of Athens, following Paul's preaching there. Since Luke singles her out by name, she may have been a person of importance (see Acts 13:50; 17:12).

Damascus, Damascenes. Syrian oasis city protected on three sides by mountains, and situated on trade routes about 160 miles northeast of Jerusalem. The name Damascus can also refer to the surrounding area and to the southern Syrian state. Though close to the desert, the district is rich in almonds, apricots, cotton, flax, grains, hemp, olives, pistachios, pomegranates, tobacco, vineyards, and walnuts. These crops grow well because the land is watered by two rivers, the Nahr Barada, "the Cool" (biblical Abana), which runs from the northwest mountains through a deep ravine to the city, and the Nahr el-A waj, "the Crooked" (biblical Pharpar), which flows west to east. Together the two rivers irrigate 400 square miles of land. Their beauty and importance in biblical times is conveyed by the haughty words of Naaman, a resident of the area, who almost refused to wash his leprosy away in the Jordan, as Elisha had prescribed, because it was such a poor river in comparison with the Abana and Pharpar (2 Kgs 5).

Of the several trade routes which converged in the area, one led to Tyre and down the Mediterranean coastline, another to Megiddo and eventually to Memphis and Egypt, and a third to the Gulf of Aqaba.

Though Damascus is thought to be one of the oldest cities in civilization, a precise date for its founding is unknown. According to the Jewish historian Josephus it was Uz, son of Aram, grandson of Shem and great-grandson of Noah, who was the founder. Scripture does record that the name "Aram" was applied to the Syrian area (Nm 23:7), and especially to the northern Syrian-Mesopotamian district. This lends some credibility to Josephus, since it is quite likely that Aram's son would have moved south along natural travel routes.

The name "Damascus" is first used in geographical lists compiled about the 16th century BC by Thutmose III, and it is mentioned several times in the Amarna tablets (c. 15th and 14th centuries BC). Damascus was a kingdom of some importance, and the tablets indicate that the ruler was frequently seeking to throw off the yoke of Egyptian domination. Nevertheless Damascus remained generally under the control of Egypt until about the 12th century BC. Abraham may have passed through Damascus while traveling the caravan routes, and it is possible that he acquired Eliezer as his chief steward there. Eliezer became heir apparent to Abraham until the birth of his son Ishmael (Gn 15:2). It is possible that Eliezer was the servant sent to Nahor to find a bride for Isaac.

The first biblical mention of Damascus (Gn 14:15) refers to the city in connection with Abraham's successful attack upon the confederation of kings who kidnapped Lot and his family. The Bible does not refer to the city again until the time of David (c. 1000 BC).

Israel occupied a strategic position along the trade routes between Mesopotamia and Egypt, and although in the time of Joshua and the judges Israel was in conflict with its immediate neighbors, the Amorites, Moabites, Philistines, Ammonites, and Midianites, there was relatively little opposition from Syria.

By the time of Saul, Zobah, an Aramaean kingdom to the north of Damascus, was menacing the Israelites. Damascus was possibly in alliance with Zobah at this time, and the Israelites fought a defensive action (1 Sm 14:47). David subsequently defeated Hadadezer of Zobah and gained control over southern Syria and Damascus, where he garrisoned his troops. David's forces under Joab continued to be successful, and tribute was sent from Damascus to Israel. One of Hadadezer's officers, Rezon, deserted and formed a guerrilla band in the Damascus area. Subsequently in Solomon's reign he eroded even the Israelites' economic control of the region and set himself up as king in Damascus around 940 BC (1 Kgs 11:23–25).

In the reign of Ben-hadad I, about 883–843 BC, soldiers from Damascus besieged Samaria and sent reasonable terms to Ahab, which were accepted swiftly. Ben-hadad replied with new terms that included the unconditional surrender and plundering of the city. Ahab rejected this move and turned a seemingly sure Damascene victory into a resounding defeat. A second Syrian campaign was equally unsuccessful, and Ben-hadad and Damascus were at the mercy of the Israelites. In setting terms Ahab was concerned mainly with trading profits and not with the total destruction of Syria. When Assyria reappeared menacingly in the north, Ahab and Ben-hadad formed a coalition, but were defeated by Shalmaneser III. Alliances were soon reshuffled, and Ben-hadad faced a Hebrew coalition of Ahab and Jehoshaphat of Judah. Ben-hadad assumed correctly that if Ahab were killed, the coalition would collapse. Despite a disguise, Ahab was killed at the battle of Ramoth-gilead, around 851 BC (1 Kgs 22:34–36).

Damascus was at the height of its power when Ben-hadad was campaigning successfully against the Assyrians. At this time, when Jehoram, Ahab's son, was king of Israel, Naaman the leper, a Syrian captain, was healed by the prophet Elisha when he accepted humbly the prescribed cure.

The strategy of overcoming the kingdom by killing the king had been successful for Ben-hadad in his fight with Ahab, and he continued to follow the same policy. Shortly afterward, in a further effort to subdue Samaria, he sent assassination squads to murder either Jehoram or the prophet Elisha. The Lord preserved the lives of the pursued, and the Syrians attacked without success. Several years later, Elisha, who had gained the respect of the Syrians, entered Damascus boldly and announced that Ben-hadad's illness was not fatal but that his death was imminent. Ben-hadad was thereafter murdered by Hazael, who then succeeded him. Although Damascus was soundly defeated by Assyria about 838 BC, Hazael rebounded quickly, and by 830 BC other predictions of Elisha were fulfilled. Damascene troops then controlled large areas of Palestinian territory, and the temple treasure was used to bribe the Syrians and save Jerusalem (2 Kgs 12:17,18).

Planning to continue the subjection of Israel, Ben-hadad II, probably the son of Hazael (2 Kgs 13:3), found himself having to contend instead with resumed attacks from Assyria. In 803 BC Damascus became a tributary of Assyria, but the northern forces were unable to hold the area. After a further campaign in which Assyria again proved dominant, a weakened Damascus was unable to quash an Israelite rebellion in 795 BC. By the time of Jeroboam II the Damascenes were forced to pay tribute to Samaria (2 Kgs 14:28).

About 738 BC the Syrians, led by their new leader Rezin, joined forces with Pekah, king of Israel, to subjugate Judah. Much land was captured, although their siege of Jerusalem was unsuccessful (2 Kgs 16:5,6; 2 Chr 28:5). At this time of seeming success for Damascus the city's doom was predicted by Isaiah (8:4; 17:1), Amos (1:3–5), and Jeremiah (49:23–27). Rejecting God, Ahaz of Judah turned for protection to an alliance with the Assyrians, whom he bribed with the temple treasure. The Assyrian king Tiglath-pileser III ("Pul") agreed and marched against the Syro-Israelite confederation. After defeating Israel he attacked Damascus, plundered the city, deported the population, and replaced them with foreigners from other captured lands. Damascus was no longer an independent city-state.

Due to its key location Damascus remained important, and the Assyrians used the city as a provincial capital. Their records mention it in 727, 720, and 694 BC, and in the days of Ashurbanipal (669–627 BC). Assyrian world dominance succumbed to that of Neo-Babylon, which was later replaced by that of Medo-Persia. During the period of Persian control Damascus was a noted administrative center. Under the regime of Alexander the Great the importance of Damascus was diminished by the rise in commercial significance of Antioch.

During intertestamental times Damascus passed from one ruler to another. Following the death of Alexander, the city was controlled by the Ptolemies of Egypt and the Seleucids of Babylon. Somewhat before 100 BC Syria was divided, with Damascus becoming the capital of Coele-Syria. Its non-Syrian kings were constantly in trouble at home with the economy and abroad with the Parthians, Hasmoneans, and the Nabataeans, who under Aretas controlled Damascus from 84 to 72 BC. Subsequently authority passed to the Hasmoneans, descendants of the Maccabees, and then to the Idumeans (the Herods). The area was subjected to Roman dominance after the defeat of Syria by the Romans in 65 BC.

Shortly after the death of Christ the Nabataeans regained control of the area, ruling Damascus from Petra through an ethnarch. It was under the control of an Arab appointee, probably Aretas IV, when Saul of Tarsus sought Jewish authority to purge Damascus of its Christians (2 Cor 11:32). Luke's report in Acts 9, corroborated by Paul's own confession (Acts 22:5–21; 26:11–23), relates Saul's vision, blinding, and subsequent conversion "on the road to Damascus." This may have been close to the place where Syrian soldiers were blinded when planning to assassinate Elisha (2 Kgs 6:18–23). After Saul's sight was restored in a house on the street called "Straight," he preached Christianity. Apparently the uproar in the Jewish quarter concerning his preaching was so great that the ethnarch was willing to condone Saul's murder by orthodox Jews. Acts 9:23–25 describes his escape to Jerusalem. Damascus is not mentioned thereafter in biblical history.   HAZEL W. PERKIN

See SYRIA, SYRIANS.

Damnation.   *See* HELL; JUDGMENT.

Dan (Person).   Fifth son of the Jewish patriarch Jacob. Dan's mother was Bilhah, maid of Jacob's wife Rachel (Gn 30:1–6). Dan's descendants settled in Israel overlooking the Huleh plain, in territory actually assigned to Naphtali, Dan's full brother (Gn 30:7,8; 35:25; Jos 19:32–48). The two brothers are mentioned together in a number of references (e.g., Ex 1:4).

Dan's name was given him not by Bilhah but by Rachel, who considered the child her own. Rachel had long been childless—a shame to women in ancient cultures—and she was jealous of Jacob's other wife, Leah, who had already borne him four sons. Rachel viewed the birth of Bilhah's son as averting her shame and as God's vindication of her status as wife. The name Dan ("he judged") meant that God had judged her and had vindicated her through the child's birth (Gn 30:6).

An area of the wall of Damascus where Paul was let down and made his escape (Acts 9:25).

Evidently Dan had only one son to continue his line, Hushim (Gn 46:23; Shuham, Nm 26:42,43). In Jacob's patriarchal blessing Dan was promised the role of "judge" among his people but was also spoken of as one who would be stealthy and dangerous, like a serpent (Gn 49:16,17). How that blessing worked out in the life of his descendants is unknown. The small amount of information given about Dan himself parallels the insignificance of his tribe in later times.

See DAN (PLACE); DAN, TRIBE OF.

Dan (Place). 1. Phoenician city, originally named Leshem (Jos 19:47) or Laish (Jgs 18:7), which was conquered by Dan's tribe when it migrated northward. The city lay a day's journey from Sidon in the valley near Beth-rehob (Jgs 18:28) at the southern base of Mt Hermon. It was the most northerly point of the ancient Israelite kingdom, and was used as a topographical marker in the phrase "from Dan to Beersheba" (cf. Jgs 20:1; 1 Sm 3:20).

The site of Dan guarded a major trading route running between Damascus and Tyre, and was therefore an important commercial center. The Nahr el-Leddan, one of the principal sources of the Jordan, rose in the area, and this made the Huleh valley below Dan lush and fertile, even in the heat of summer. Consequently the territory around the city produced grain and vegetable crops in abundance, as well as supplying the needs of flocks and herds adequately.

It is possible to identify the site of ancient Dan quite confidently with Tell el-Qâdi ("mound of the judges"), a large quadrangular area occupying about 50 acres. Excavations at the site commenced in 1966 and indicated that the locality had been settled during the Early Bronze Age, perhaps even by 3500 BC. The

site was attractive because of the numerous springs and its location on the trading route. A strong fortified city was uncovered at Middle Bronze Age levels, and this is undoubtedly the one mentioned in the annals of Thutmose III (c. 1490–1436 BC) as Ra-wi-sa. The Middle Bronze Age city was also mentioned in the 19th-century BC Egyptian execration texts, as well as in cuneiform records recovered from Mari in Mesopotamia. To the Canaanites, Dan was known as Leshem (Jos 19:47) or Laish (Jgs 18:7), and the Iron Age levels have produced a large number of Canaanite pottery artifacts as well as some Philistine containers from the middle of the 12th century BC. At that time the city was fortified by means of a solid earthen rampart. Of archaeological interest was the presence of a Mycenaean tomb containing the remains of 45 skeletons of adults and children. Locally made containers and stone implements competed with various types of imported Mycenaean pottery vessels. This ceramic evidence indicates that the tomb was

One of the sources of the Jordan River, near Tel Dan.

used for about 60 years from the middle of the 14th century BC.

In the Early Iron Age Dan was a prosperous city, as indicated in Judges 18:7, but by the middle of the 11th century BC it had been destroyed, evidently as a result of occupation by the Danites. When Jeroboam I became king of the separate northern kingdom of Israel, Dan was one of two shrines where the golden calves were worshiped. The high place at Tell el-Qâdi (Tell Dan), a square masonry platform some 61 by 20 feet, has been excavated, but by 1977 no trace of the golden image had been found.

The cultic worship of Baal at Dan survived even Jehu's drastic purge (2 Kgs 10:28–31), but during Ben-hadad's reign the city fell under Syrian control (cf. 2 Kgs 10:32). When the Syrians were attempting to ward off Assyrian attacks on their eastern border during the time of Jeroboam II (793–753 BC), Dan was reconquered by the northern kingdom. It did not remain in Israelite hands for long, however, for its inhabitants were deported to Assyria (2 Kgs 17:6) by Tiglath-pileser III (745–727 BC). Nevertheless, the site continued to be inhabited (cf. Jer 4:15; 8:16), and its high place or acropolis at the northern extremity of the mound was used for worship. This particular area was enlarged periodically in both Greek and Roman times, and it is from the latter period that a statue of Aphrodite came. In NT times Dan was eclipsed by Caesarea, which was only four Roman miles distant. Josephus (*War* 4.1) recorded that Titus crushed a revolt at Dan in AD 67.

See DAN (PERSON); DAN, TRIBE OF.

2. KJV rendering of an obscure Hebrew word in Ezekiel 27:19, alternately translated "wine," a commodity from Uzal, in the RSV.

See UZAL (PLACE).

Dan, Tribe of. Israelite tribe named for the patriarch Jacob's fifth son. The tribe of Dan, descended from Dan's only known son, Hushim (cf. Shuham in Nm 26:42,43), had little distinction in its early years. Some Danites are mentioned in the wilderness narratives: Oholiab, a craftsman of the tabernacle (Ex 31:6; 35:34; 38:23); another whose mother married an Egyptian and who blasphemed God (Lv 24:11); and Ahiezer, chief prince of Dan during the exodus (Nm 1:12).

Dan was the second largest tribe at the first census taken in the wilderness (62,700 warriors, Nm 1:38,39). They were instructed to encamp on the north side of the Israelite's camp along with Asher and Naphtali (Nm 2:25–31), and were to bring up the rear in the line of march (Nm 2:31; 10:25). At the second census 40 years later, just before entering the Prom-

ised Land, they had grown only to 64,400 (Nm 26:42,43), still second in size. The tribe does not stand out in the conquest narratives (Dt 2:16–3:29; Jos; Jgs 1). Dan is listed among the tribes who reminded Israel of the covenant curses at Mt Ebal (Dt 27:13; cf. Jos 8:30–33). The tribe is called a "lion's whelp" in Moses' blessing (Dt 33:22). Some believe that the reference to "Bashan" in that blessing prefigured the Danites' migration to the northern territory where they eventually settled.

One of the most significant references to Dan's tribe is the account of its northward migration (Jos 19:40–48; Jgs 18). The Danites had been allotted a portion of Canaan between Judah and Ephraim bordering the Mediterranean seacoast (Jos 19:40–46; cf. Jgs 5:17), but were unable to occupy their territory except for the valley at Zorah and Eshtaol (Jgs 13:25; 18:2), the rest being retained by the Amorites and later by the Philistines. As a result a group of Danites, discouraged with their situation, marched north and captured Laish, located about 25 miles north of the Sea of Galilee and just below Israel's northernmost border. Laish was renamed Dan at that time (Jgs 18:27–29). Their association with that northern territory eventually gave rise to the expression "from Dan to Beersheba" (Jgs 20:1; 1 Sm 3:20) as designating Israel's northern and southern borders.

Southern Dan continued for some time, as illustrated in the exploits of Samson of the tribe of Dan (Jgs 13–16). Evidently the southern Danites gradually merged into the tribe of Judah, and no historical reference is made in the rest of the OT. The Danites were mentioned in King David's time as mustering a considerable army loyal to David (1 Chr 12:35; 27:22).

The Danites were among the tribes who did not drive the Canaanites from their territory (Jos 13:4,5; cf. Jgs 1:34,35). Joshua had to prod them into the task at the Shiloh assembly (Jos 18:1–4; 19:40–48). Eventually the Danites gave up the effort and sought other lands in the north, where conquest was easier. Their disobedience was further manifested in their open sin of setting up a "graven image" and establishing a rival priesthood, even though their priest was a Levite (Jgs 18:30,31). The result of that idolatry was that, at the division of the Israelite kingdom at the end of King Solomon's reign, King Jeroboam of the northern kingdom of Israel chose the city of Dan as one of the idol shrines in which to set up the "golden calves" (1 Kgs 12:28,29). The Danites' apostasy, and that of the other northern tribes, continued throughout their history (2 Kgs 10:29), and because of it they were eventually carried captive to Assyria (2 Kgs 17:1–23).

The tribe name is mentioned in the prophet Ezekiel's idealized description of the restored land and Jerusalem (Ez 48:1,2,32). In the NT, the apostle John omitted the tribe from a list of Israel's tribes (Rv 7:4–8).

See ISRAEL, HISTORY OF; DAN (PERSON); DAN (PLACE).

Dance. Form of artistic expression incorporated into Israel's worship, used especially during times of celebration.

See MUSIC AND MUSICAL INSTRUMENTS.

Daniel (Person). 1. David's second son, the first by his wife Abigail (1 Chr 3:1). Also called Chileab (2 Sm 3:3).

See CHILEAB.

2. Priest, descendant of Ithamar. He signed Ezra's covenant of faithfulness to God with Nehemiah and others after the exile (Ezr 8:2; Neh 10:6).

3. Jewish statesman and seer in the Babylonian court whose career is recounted in the Book of Daniel. Daniel's early life is cloaked in silence. Nothing is known of his parents or family, though he was probably descended from Jewish nobility (Dn 1:3). If born during the time of King Josiah's reforms (c. 621 BC), Daniel would have been about 16 when he and his three friends—Hananiah, Mishael, and Azariah—were deported from Jerusalem to Babylon by King Nebuchadnezzar. They may have been hostages to assure the cooperation of the royal family in Judah.

Daniel, renamed Belteshazzar (meaning "may [god] protect his life"), was trained for court service. He quickly established a reputation for intelligence and for absolute fidelity to his God. After three years of instruction he began a court career which lasted nearly 70 years (Dn 1:21). Daniel had hardly finished his training when he was called on to interpret one of Nebuchadnezzar's dreams, in which a great image collapsed and disintegrated when struck by a stone. God revealed its meaning to Daniel, who explained it to the king. In gratitude Nebuchadnezzar offered him the post of governor of Babylonia, but Daniel requested that the honor be conferred on his three companions in captivity.

Near the end of Nebuchadnezzar's life Daniel was able to interpret a second dream (Dn 4). That dream intimated the king's impending insanity. Daniel urged the king to repent (4:27), but he did not, and subsequently for a period of time he became deranged.

After the death of Nebuchadnezzar in 562 BC, Daniel dropped from public view and evidently occupied an inferior position in the royal court. Although he received visions (Dn

Balances, reminiscent of part of the interpretation of the handwriting on the wall—"weighed in the balances and found wanting" (Dn 5:27).

7,8) in the first and third years of the Babylonian regent Belshazzar's reign (555 and 552 BC), it was not until 539 BC that Daniel made another public appearance. During a banquet hosted by Belshazzar, the king profaned the sacred vessels pillaged from the Jerusalem temple. A disembodied hand suddenly appeared and wrote on the palace wall the mysterious words, "Mene, Mene, Tekel, Parsin." Summoned to explain the message, Daniel interpreted it as a forecast of the imminent end of the Babylonian kingdom. That same night Belshazzar was killed by the Persians, who attacked and successfully overran the capital city (5:30).

Under Darius the Mede, Daniel became one of three "presidents" of the realm (6:2). Daniel's rank, along with his capable and distinguished management, infuriated his political enemies. They persuaded Darius to pass a decree forbidding petition to any god or man but the king, under penalty of being cast into a lions' den. Daniel's religious integrity forced him to violate the law. Thrown to the lions, he remained miraculously unscathed. Vindicated, he was restored to office (6:17–28).

The latter part of the Book of Daniel describes several visions he received of future events. The visions dealt with four beasts (7:1–28), future kingdoms (8:1–27), the coming of the Messiah (9:1–27), and Syria and Egypt (11,12). The prophet Ezekiel alluded to Daniel's great wisdom (Ez 28:3) and ranked him in righteousness with Noah and Job (Ez 14:14,20).

DONALD K. CAMPBELL & R. K. HARRISON

See DANIEL, BOOK OF; EXILE; PROPHET, PROPHETESS.

Daniel, Book of.

Daniel, Book of. Fourth book of the Major Prophets in the OT, characterized by vivid symbolism and reflecting heroic historical events during the Babylonian exile of the Jewish people. Because Daniel is not an easy book to understand, its interpretation requires careful study and reflection. Daniel himself wrote, when reflecting on the meaning of one of his visions, "But I was appalled by the vision and did not understand it" (Dn 8:27).

In the old Jewish division of the OT Daniel is part of the third section, called the Writings, along with such books as Psalms, Proverbs, and Job. It was not included in the second section of the OT, called the Prophets. Although portions of his book may be interpreted from a prophetic perspective, Daniel is never explicitly identified as a prophet. The book's two major divisions are narratives about Daniel's life (1–6), and Daniel's visions (7–12).

Author. In terms of having a known author, the Book of Daniel is anonymous, as are many books coming from the ancient world. The existing text bears only a title, "Daniel," identifying the key subject matter of the book: the man himself.

The first six chapters of the book contain information about Daniel written in the third person; beginning in Daniel 7:2, however, the book purports to contain words written by Daniel in the first person. Although the traditional view within Judaism, later adopted by Christianity, was that Daniel wrote the entire book named for him, there is little confirming evidence. Jesus' words about things "spoken of by the prophet Daniel" (Mt 24:15) do not clarify who wrote the whole book, since the words in question appear in the second half of the Book of Daniel, explicitly identified as his words. Thus the problem of who wrote the first part remains.

Whether or not Daniel wrote the entire book, he is definitely the key character. The only source of information about him is the book itself. Daniel was a Hebrew from Judah, probably of royal lineage, born late in the seventh century BC. As a young boy he was taken from his homeland to Babylon (in what is now southern Iraq) around 605 BC. There, after three years of formal education in language and literature (Dn 1:4,5), he became an official in the royal household. The first six chapters tell of particular incidents in Daniel's life but do not provide a comprehensive biography of his life and times.

Daniel's name means "God is my judge." As a foreign resident in Babylon, he was given another name, Belteshazzar, which may have meant "(let god) protect his life" in the Babylonian language.

Date. Uncertainty about the authorship of the Book of Daniel naturally contributes to uncertainty about the date of its writing. If Daniel was the author of the whole book, a date in the second half of the sixth century BC is likely. If he was not the author, a later date is possible. The conservative interpretation has usually been that the book was written in the sixth century BC. The most widely held alternative maintains that the book was written about 165 BC.

Evidence exists to support both the early and late dates of Daniel. Those who argue for a late date and non-Danielic authorship normally use two lines of argument, one historical and the other linguistic.

Historical Argument. According to the historical argument, the writer was thoroughly familiar with the history of Near Eastern imperial power from the sixth to the second centuries, but had an incomplete, erroneous view of the historical details in the second half of the sixth century, Daniel's era. Such an imbalance in knowledge implies a late date of writing.

The first part of the historical argument must be conceded by those holding a more conservative view. The Book of Daniel does present a remarkable knowledge of Near Eastern history. The critical question is whether that knowledge was normal human knowledge, gained after the events, or special knowledge revealed to Daniel beforehand. That question is answered in different ways by different people, depending on their view of prophecy and other factors.

The second part of the historical argument is technically more complex. Was the writer's knowledge of history in the late sixth century BC really erroneous? The most significant problem is that of the identity of Darius the Mede (Dn 5:30,31). The Book of Daniel says that Darius the Mede conquered Babylon and was succeeded at a later date by Cyrus. External historical sources contain no reference to a Darius at that time, but show clearly that it was Cyrus who conquered Babylon. Advocates of a late date consider that strong evidence. Those who advocate an early date have no simple solution to the problem. One proposed solution is that Darius and Cyrus are two names for the same person. A basis for that hypothesis is that Daniel 6:28 can be translated: "Daniel prospered in the reign of Darius, even [that is] the reign of Cyrus the Persian." An analogy appears in the use of the names Pul and Tiglath-pileser in 1 Chronicles 5:26. In summary, the dating of Daniel on the basis of the writer's historical knowledge is difficult, whether one suggests an early or late date.

Linguistic Argument. The linguistic arguments for the date of Daniel are also complex, especially for a person not familiar with the original languages of the book (Hebrew and Aramaic). Advocates of a late date use three related arguments: (1) the Aramaic language of the book is typical of late Aramaic (second century BC and later); (2) the presence of Persian loan words is a further indication of the late date of the book's Aramaic; and (3) the presence of Greek loan words in the Aramaic shows that the language must be dated after the time of Alexander the Great's conquest of the Orient (c. 330 BC). For many advocates of a late date for the book's composition, the last argument is most compelling. It would be impossible, they affirm, to find Greek loan words in Aramaic two centuries before Alexander's time.

Although the arguments are at first convincing, on closer examination they are less persuasive to those who hold the conservative view. Each of the three parts of the argument has been answered.

(1) Aramaic was in common use in the Near East from about the ninth century BC, being recognized as an official language in Assyria from the eighth century BC. Ninety percent of the Aramaic words in Daniel were used in that older language, in both the Old and Imperial Aramaic dialects. The remaining 10 percent, known only in later texts in the light of present evidence, might indicate a late date, but they could equally be early uses of the words in question.

(2) The evidence of Persian loan words in Aramaic can function like a boomerang. It is true that later Aramaic has many Persian loan words (about 19 appear in Daniel), but one can give an alternative explanation for Persian loan words in Daniel at an early date. The story of Daniel is set, in part, in the context of life in a Persian-controlled court. The Persians used Aramaic in their administrative control of the empire, and their own language inevitably penetrated Aramaic. If one assumes an early date for the Book of Daniel, then it was being written in precisely the period when Persian would be having its greatest influence on Aramaic.

(3) The evidence of Greek words in Daniel's Aramaic (a total of three) is not altogether compelling. Greek (or "Ionian") traders traveled in various parts of the Near East from the eighth century BC onward. Greek mercenaries fought for Near Eastern states in and after the seventh century BC. In Daniel's lifetime King Nebuchadnezzar is known to have employed Greek artisans in the city of Babylon. Thus it is unnecessary to limit the possibilities of Greek penetration of the Aramaic language to the period after Alexander. The conqueror was by no means the first Greek to set foot in the Orient.

Conclusion. The historical and linguistic arguments for the date of Daniel are inconclusive for either an early or late date of writing. To a large extent, dating the book depends on other matters, such as authorship, intention, and the extent to which one takes a "prophetic" interpretation of portions of the book. To postulate that Daniel was the author is consistent with the evidence currently available. Further, evidence provided by some of the Daniel material from the Dead Sea Scrolls at Qumran does not support a late date for the book. All Daniel manuscripts and fragments are second century BC copies, thus requiring an earlier date for the original. One manuscript, related paleographically to the large Isaiah Scroll, must have come originally from the same period—estimated to be several centuries before the Qumran copy of Isaiah. Other manuscripts from Qumran show that no OT canonical material was composed later than the Persian period. Thus no evidence exists for a second-century BC date for Daniel.

Language. One of the most curious features of the Book of Daniel is not immediately evident to a reader of the English Bible. The book is bilingual. Daniel 1:1–2:4a and Daniel 8–12 are written in Hebrew, the language of the other OT books. The middle section (Dn 2:4b–7:28), however, is written in Aramaic, a different but related language. Various explanations have been offered. Some have suggested that an original Aramaic book was expanded by a Hebrew writer, with additions to the original book at the beginning and the end. Others suggest that a portion of the original Hebrew book was lost, so the missing section was replaced from a surviving Aramaic translation. More complex and ingenious suggestions have also been made, but none has been commonly accepted.

Another suggestion is possible. The Book of Daniel (whatever date one prefers) may simply reflect the bilingual character of its cultural setting. (As a modern example, consider the many written materials in Canada that appear in both English and French.) Finally, one can regard the bilingual character as another of the mysterious aspects of the book which make its interpretation difficult.

Background. The background of the Book of Daniel can be examined from two perspectives. It may be viewed from the perspective of the Babylonian exile, of which Daniel was a part (early sixth century BC), or in the light of future historical events (second century BC), toward which the visions in the book's second half seem to point.

The Babylonian Exile. Although Daniel himself was exiled about 605 BC, the major phase of the Babylonian exile began in 586 BC, following the defeat of the kingdom of Judah and the destruction of Jerusalem. The account extends through the reigns of Nebuchadnezzar (properly Nebuchadrezzar) and Belshazzar, culminating in the early years of the Persian king Cyrus, who took over the city of Babylon in 539 BC. For the Jews the exile was a time of hardship, but also a time of renewed theological understanding. Both aspects are reflected in the Book of Daniel.

The Seleucid Period in Palestine. Daniel's visions in the latter half of the book appear to refer to the Seleucid period in Palestine, specifically the time when the Jews were ruled by Antiochus Epiphanes, a member of the Seleucid dynasty (175–163 BC). Whether the visions were prophetic anticipations of future events or reflections of contemporary culture, the Seleucid period is important to a full understanding of the book.

Under Antiochus, Palestinian Jews experienced a time of considerable hardship. The ancient faith was severely undermined, the high priesthood in Jerusalem was sold to the highest bidder, and the temple was desecrated in several ways. Pressure was exerted on the Jews to adapt their lives and faith to Hellenistic (Greek-influenced) culture. Although some capitulated, others refused and steadfastly held firm to the old faith. A rebellion against the oppressive measures of Antiochus began in 168 BC. By 164 the rebels had largely succeeded in getting rid of the objectionable practices. But the Seleucid period was generally a bad time for faithful Jews, when all the forces of history seemed to work against the true faith. Part of the Book of Daniel's greatness lies in its theological understanding of history, which enabled men and women to continue living in faith through a time of terrible crisis.

Purpose and Theological Teaching. The scriptural section called the Writings served a variety of purposes. The psalms, for example, were used primarily in Israel's worship. The proverbs may have been part of Israel's school curriculum. The Book of Job addressed a specific human and theological problem.

The purpose of the Book of Daniel is not so easy to determine, since it is essentially a story, a partial biography of Daniel. It is not strictly a prophetic book, nor is it history in the modern sense. Much of it is concerned with dreams and their interpretations.

Nevertheless, the word "history" provides a clue to its purpose. Daniel seeks to provide theological understanding of history. The first six chapters tell about Daniel and his companions, not merely to satisfy historical curiosity but to teach the reader. OT theology insisted that the God of Israel participated in human life and history. To read biblical history, therefore, is to discover God's participation in human affairs, and to learn how God and human beings relate to each other. In the opening chapters of Daniel one reads of events in the life of a man of remarkable faith, the kind of history from which one may learn how to live.

The last six chapters focus on Daniel's dreams. Although neither the dreams nor the interpretations are easy to understand, it is possible to see the theme of history emerging again. The emphasis in chapters 7–12 is not on history as a record of past events, but on the meaning of history and the world's future. In the biblical perspective the movements of human societies in the present and future matter as much as past history. Though Daniel's visions are dominated by nations and superpowers, they have a more basic theme: God's power over human beings and nations. History often appears to be a conglomeration of chaos and human conflict. Yet God ultimately controls history and moves it toward a goal. In spite of ambiguous details at the end of the book, Daniel provides hope for people living in a time of crisis. Even if what is said about the "time of the end" cannot be understood now (Dn 12:9), the end of history is full of hope for those with faith in God (12:13). The purpose of the Book of Daniel thus has to do with the meaning of history, both what can be learned from the past and what can be hoped for in the present and future.

The book also contains specific theological statements on such matters as human faith, divine salvation, and the nature of revelation. One theological matter in Daniel deserves particular attention: the doctrine of resurrection.

The NT's clear doctrine of resurrection followed by judgment is not a central theme in the OT. For the most part the Hebrews' faith was fixed on the realities of earthly life. Hope for life beyond the grave is hinted at in many texts but remains implicit. Only in the later writings of the OT, especially those of Ezekiel and Daniel, does a more explicit doctrine of resurrection develop.

The focal point of that doctrine in the Book of Daniel is 12:2: "And many of those who sleep in the dust of the earth shall awake, some to everlasting life, and some to shame and everlasting contempt." The doctrine of personal resurrection provides a basis for individual hope within an understanding of present and future history. Nations move against nations in apparent turmoil. God is believed to be in ultimate control, but what becomes of all the people who die while history is still in motion? The dead shall rise again, says Daniel, and in resurrection bodies shall be judged according to their deeds. Some will be rewarded with everlasting life, but others will be condemned to shame.

The kind of life beyond death depicted in Daniel's words is not merely immortality of the soul, a concept common among the Greeks. The Jews understood a full person to comprise both body and soul, both outer and inner life. The continuity of a disembodied soul, acceptable to the Greeks, would for the Jews have to mean physical life beyond the grave, a concept full of mystery.

To the readers of the Book of Daniel the doctrine of resurrection provided hope in an otherwise bleak and hopeless world. It was a reminder that the actions of earthly life are important: they form the basis of future judgment. The world has a larger horizon of life beyond the body's death. Ultimately there will be justice, even though justice is rarely seen in the present existence. Evildoers may live without ever being punished. Yet beyond the death of the body lies a final judgment characterized by God's justice.

So the Book of Daniel is about history and hope. Life must be lived now; for that, the book offers in the first six chapters the insight of Daniel's experience. Life is lived in the context of war and international chaos; for that, chapters 7–12 depict God's sovereignty and his purposes in history. Individual life moves toward death; for that, the writer speaks of resurrection and judgment.

Content: Stories About Daniel (1–6). *Daniel and His Companions (1:1–21).* Daniel and his companions, Hananiah, Mishael, and Azariah, were exiled to Babylon some 19 years before the main exile following the destruction of Jerusalem. The four healthy young men, selected from among many Jewish exiles, were at the command of King Nebuchadnezzar assigned to a special three-year training program to make them court aides.

As soon as the four Jewish youths entered Babylon's high society, they faced a dietary problem. The king provided them with the best food and wine from the royal kitchens, but a Jew's diet was restricted by the laws of God (see Dt 14). The four asked for a diet of vegetables and water, not to be fussy or ungrateful, but to remain faithful to their God. The story tells how the dietary situation

worked out and sees them through their education and Daniel's appointment as a royal counselor.

The first episode thus focuses on a key issue faced by all Jewish exiles. How could one live in a foreign land, with foreign food and customs, yet remain faithful to God and his laws? Daniel provided a model. He was courageous enough not to compromise, but wise enough to seek a solution acceptable to all. His faithfulness was rewarded by God. By the end of the episode Daniel is seen as a person with special wisdom and gifts from God. The rest of his life was marked by the exercise of those gifts.

Nebuchadnezzar's Dream (2:1–49). The king had a dream and, although he could not remember its substance, it weighed heavily on his mind. When his corps of professional interpreters could do nothing for him, he ordered that they be executed. The king's order included Daniel and his companions, whose training qualified them as interpreters. Daniel obtained a stay of execution by offering to interpret the dream. After prayer, Daniel received from God both the substance of the dream and its interpretation, which he relayed to the king. The grateful Nebuchadnezzar promoted Daniel and his companions to important positions in Babylon.

Although the writer recorded both the king's dream and Daniel's interpretation, the problem for a modern reader is how to interpret the interpretation. The king saw in his dream a statue, with head of gold, chest and arms of silver, belly and thighs of brass, legs of iron, and feet of part iron and part clay. The interpretation identified Nebuchadnezzar as the head of gold. His kingdom would be followed by three other kingdoms, each represented by the statue's parts and substances. At that point modern interpretations begin to diverge.

A common interpretation of the four sequential kingdoms is as follows: Chaldean empire (gold), Medo-Persian empire (silver), Greece (brass), Rome (iron and clay). Others suggest an alternative interpretation: Chaldean empire (gold), Media (silver), Persia (brass), Greece (iron and clay). To focus too much attention on identifying the four kingdoms can result in failure to see the chapter's key feature. From the midst of those human kingdoms, "the God of heaven will set up a kingdom which shall never be destroyed, nor shall its sovereignty be left to another people" (2:44). The Babylonian king's dream anticipated the coming of a greater kingdom, that of Jesus Christ.

The Furnace (3:1–30). The story continues, focusing on Daniel's three friends and using their Babylonian names, Shadrach, Meshach, and Abednego. King Nebuchadnezzar constructed a massive golden statue, 90 feet high. At its dedication ceremony everyone was required to bow down and worship as a band began to play. The three young Hebrews, who refused to worship, were summoned before the king. Their continued firm refusal led to a sentence of execution, and they were thrown into a fiercely burning furnace. Remarkably, they did not burn, and a fourth being appeared with them in the furnace. As they emerged unharmed from the ordeal, the king acknowledged God's power of salvation and rewarded them.

The story illustrates a second dilemma of the Jews in exile. Faithfulness to God's first commandment, "You shall have no other gods before me" (Dt 5:7), could lead to death. The three young men were faithful—not out of confidence that God would rescue them, but whether or not he chose to spare their lives (3:17,18). As it happened, God delivered them; they were tossed into the furnace bound, but they came out free men. The message was profound: certainly the Jews should believe in a God able to deliver from the flames of persecution, but they should believe and hold fast even if no deliverance could be seen beyond the trial.

Nebuchadnezzar's Second Dream and Madness (4:1–37). On two occasions Nebuchadnezzar had confessed faith in the living God: when Daniel had interpreted his dream of the statue (2:47), and on the release of Daniel's three companions from the furnace (3:28). Nonetheless, the king's faith was shallow. The story in chapter 4 recounts a lapse of faith that brought terrible consequences. After eight years, when those consequences had run their course, the king again acknowledged God (4:37).

The entire story is presented in the form of a proclamation, written by Nebuchadnezzar and widely circulated after the events in the story had transpired. The king dreamed of a tall tree growing in a field to ever greater heights. A divine messenger ordered the tree cut down, with only a stump and roots left in the ground. The stump and roots then took the form of a man, but the man's mind was replaced with that of an animal. For seven years that semihuman creature behaved like a beast.

Daniel showed the king how the dream applied to the king himself. Nebuchadnezzar was the great tree that would be cut down; he would behave like a beast in the field for seven years. One year after the king had been told that interpretation, the judgment came. For seven years he behaved like an animal until his sanity returned.

The moral of the king's story is that his madness was no accident but rather divine judgment. His arrogant belief that he had the power of God led to heavy retribution (4:30). The king was afflicted with a rare and peculiar form of mental illness today called "boanthropy." The true meaning of the story lies at a deeper level: to think that one is God, having absolute power and control of one's own life, is madness. That kind of madness can be cured and overcome only with the realization that absolute power and authority belong to God alone.

Belshazzar's Feast (5:1–31). The scene shifts to the reign of a later king in Babylon. Belshazzar, son of Nabonidus, was probably co-regent with Nabonidus (555?–539 BC), with special authority in the region of Babylon. The theme of his story is similar to that of chapter 4. Belshazzar, in the course of an enormous feast, called for the sacred vessels captured from the temple in Jerusalem. With the sacred vessels the Babylonians toasted the local gods, a sacrilegious act that invited divine judgment. It came in the form of words written on the wall by a finger, which Daniel interpreted for the king as words of judgment (5:26–28). Although he praised Daniel for the interpretation, the king missed both the true meaning of the words and the lesson taught to Nebuchadnezzar, his predecessor (5:18–22). Belshazzar was killed that very night when Darius the Mede entered the city and captured it. The theme continues remorselessly: human pride and arrogance do not pass unnoticed by the God of history, who controls and directs human events toward the fulfillment of his purpose.

The Den of Lions (6:1–28). The theme of chapter 6 is similar to that of chapter 3, but with Daniel as the story's central figure. He is portrayed as one unwilling to compromise, fully obedient to Darius as long as that was possible, but unwilling to disobey the law of God. Hence Daniel knowingly disobeyed a royal decree that prohibited prayer to any other than the king himself. Although he was aware of the consequences, Daniel remained faithful to God. The immediate outcome, when his enemies reported him, was an order of execution; Daniel was thrown to the lions. He was delivered from the hungry cats, and the king, relieved of a terrible predicament, had the plotters punished.

A double message emerges from the story. On the one hand, God's servant must be faithful in prayer and worship, regardless of the outcome; God delivers, and in that case did deliver Daniel from disaster. On the other hand, the effect of Daniel's faithfulness was that the king, who had ordered his subjects to worship him, learned about true worship (6:25–27). The effects of faithfulness, like ripples from a pebble tossed in a pool, spread far beyond the one who is faithful.

Content: Daniel's Visions (7–12). With the beginning of chapter 7 the chronological sequence of the Book of Daniel changes; Daniel's first vision goes back to the first year of Belshazzar (7:1), but subsequent visions take place as late as the reign of Cyrus, the Persian king (10:1). Chapters 7–12 emphasize the meaning of history and God's sovereignty in history, expressed in the mysterious symbolism of dreams. The whole section can be divided as follows: (1) vision of four beasts (7:1–28); (2) vision of the ram and the goat (8:1–27); (3) Daniel's prayer (9:1–27); (4) vision of the end times (10:1–12:13).

The first vision again takes up the theme of four kingdoms, already seen in Nebuchadnezzar's dream (ch 2). In the second vision the focus is narrowed down to two kingdoms, Persia and Greece. Much of the final vision of the end times deals with events occurring during the reign of Antiochus Epiphanes in the second century BC. All the visions play on the same theme. Although human kingdoms may exert their might in a chaotic world, the sovereign God acts through history's apparent chaos toward an ultimate goal of salvation.

The primary interpretation of the visions can be perceived in past historical events, but a further messianic dimension can be seen in the light of the NT. That dimension is most evident in chapter 7. In the context of the four kingdoms a divine court of judgment is established, presided over by the "Ancient of Days—the Almighty God" (7:9). Then Daniel sees the arrival of "one like a son of man" (7:13). Though the phrase "Son of man" was later perceived to be a messianic title, it did not technically have that meaning in the Book of Daniel. Daniel 7:13 is a principal source for the title "Son of man," which Jesus commonly used to designate himself. His most significant use of that term was at his trial, where he directly associated his title with Daniel 7 (Mt 26:63,64).

Earthly kingdoms dominate Daniel's visions but Jesus established the kingdom of God. That kingdom, however, has only partially come, and will reach its fullness in Christ's second advent. The message of Daniel speaks within that tension of a kingdom already come and yet still to come in its fullness. The modern world reveals not the universal kingdom of God but the clamorous kingdoms of humanity. They are powerful and often appear to hold the world's future firmly in their hands. Daniel's message is that they do not: God is sovereign, and his kingdom will finally come in its full power.

To say more than that with respect to Daniel's visions is a delicate business. Trying to identify the nations of Daniel's dreams with modern nations misses the intention of the book. If Daniel, even with the help of angelic interpreters, found it difficult to understand his own visions, caution is appropriate for the modern reader. Yet Daniel ended his mysterious book with a note of hope: "But go your way till the end; and you shall rest, and shall stand in your allotted place at the end of the days" (12:13).   PETER C. CRAIGIE

See DANIEL (PERSON) #3; EXILE; PROPHECY; ISRAEL, HISTORY OF; PROPHET, PROPHETESS.

Bibliography J.G. Baldwin, *Daniel*; D. Ford, *Daniel*; C.F. Keil, *Biblical Commentary on the Book of Daniel*; J.A. Montgomery, *A Critical and Exegetical Commentary on the Book of Daniel*; R.S. Wallace, *The Lord Is King*; D.J. Wiseman, et al, *Notes on Some Problems in the Book of Daniel*; E.J. Young, *The Book of Daniel* and *Daniel's Vision of the Son of Man*.

Danite. Member of Dan's tribe (Jos 19:47; 1 Chr 12:35).

See DAN, TRIBE OF.

Dan-jaan. Geographical landmark denoting the northern limit of David's kingdom (2 Sm 24:6 KJV). Joab's census-taking stopped here. Some feel that this is a copyist's error, because no town with a similar name is known to have existed in that area. Others believe that it means "Dan in the wood," referring simply to Dan (RSV). Still others think it refers to a town within Dan, perhaps Jaan, of which all traces have vanished.

Dannah. Town located in the hill country of Judah between Socoh and Kiriath-sepher (Debir) (Jos 15:49).

Darda, Dara. Mahol's son (1 Kgs 4:31), a Judahite of the family of Zerah (1 Chr 2:6). With Ethan the Ezrahite and Heman and Calcol, also sons of Mahol, Darda is mentioned as the proverbial type of wisdom, though he is surpassed by Solomon (1 Kgs 4:31,32). First Chronicles 2:6 gives the name as Dara, probably the error of a copyist, and includes a fifth man, Zimri. That there are two different fathers (Mahol and Zerah) mentioned in the two passages may be explained by making Mahol the natural father and Zerah the Ezrahite an earlier ancestor.

Daric. Persian gold coin.

See COINS.

Darius. Name of three emperors in the Persian dynasty of the legendary King Achaemenes. A Darius appears in the biblical books of Ezra, Nehemiah, Haggai, and Zechariah as a Persian king, and in the Book of Daniel as a Mede "who became king over the realm of the Chaldeans" (Dn 9:1).

Darius I (521–486 BC). Also known as Darius Hystaspes and Darius the Great, Darius I seized the throne of the Persian empire after the death of Cambyses II. Although he was an Achaemenid, he was from a different branch of the royal family than Cyrus and Cambyses, and his authority was not accepted in all the provinces. After Darius quelled several revolts, however, his power was firmly established, and he turned his attention to expanding the empire. His military campaigns extended Persian borders to the Danube River in the west and to the Indus River in the east, making him ruler of the largest empire the world had known. Greco-Persian conflict, which continued until Alexander the Great conquered the empire in 330 BC, began when Darius launched two invasions of Greece after conquering Thrace and Macedonia. The first expedition was destroyed by a storm in the Aegean Sea; the second was defeated by the Athenians in the famous battle of Marathon in 490 BC.

An able administrator, Darius did much to promote trade and commerce. He instituted a uniform system of weights and measures. During his reign a canal from the Nile River to the Red Sea was completed, and a sea route from the Indus River to Egypt was explored.

During Darius' reign, Persian architecture developed a style that continued until the end of the Achaemenid dynasty. Darius built at Babylon, Ecbatana, and Susa, his capital. A great royal road was constructed from Susa to the Lydian capital of Sardis. His greatest architectural accomplishment was the founding of Persepolis, a new royal city to replace the emperor's residence at Pasargadae. Darius also allowed temples to be built in Egypt and in Jerusalem, continuing Cyrus' policy of respecting the religious customs of his subjects.

Darius I is the Darius, king of Persia, mentioned in the books of Ezra, Haggai, and Zechariah. Ezra 5–6 record that Zerubbabel and Jeshua, with the help of Haggai and Zechariah, finished rebuilding the temple during Darius' reign while Tattenai was governor of the province "Beyond the River" (Syria-Palestine). Zerubbabel and Jeshua had returned to Jerusalem under Cyrus II about 538 BC (Ezr 2:2). They completed the temple in the sixth year of Darius (Ezr 6:15). That must have been the sixth year of Darius I (516 BC), since the sixth year of Darius II (417 BC) would certainly be too late. That identification was confirmed by discovery of a Babylonian document, dated June 5, 502 BC, which refers to Tattenai as "the governor of Beyond the River."

In chapter 4 of Ezra three Persian rulers are mentioned: Darius (vv 5,24); Ahasuerus (probably Xerxes I, v 6); and Artaxerxes (probably Artaxerxes I, vv 7–23). The chapter is a brief record of resistance to Jewish efforts to rebuild the city of Jerusalem and the temple. Verse 24 states that work on the temple "ceased until the second year of Darius"; yet the temple was completed in the sixth year of Darius I. Obviously work on the temple could not have stopped in the second year of Artaxerxes' son, Darius II (421 BC), if it had already been finished in 515 BC. Therefore Ezra 4:24 should be understood not as a chronological continuation of the first 23 verses but as an

The palace stairway of Darius.

introduction to the next two chapters, which discuss the building of the temple.

Darius II (423–404 BC). Also known as Ochus (his real name) and Darius Nothus ("Darius the bastard"), Darius II was the son of Artaxerxes I by a Babylonian concubine. Before he became emperor, Ochus was a satrap (governor) of Hyrcania, a region on the southeast coast of the Caspian Sea. In 423 BC his half brother, Sogdianus (or Secydianus), killed Xerxes II. Ochus then seized the throne from Sogdianus, whom he executed, and adopted the name Darius II. His reign was plagued with revolution and corruption. His own full brother, Arsites, revolted soon after Darius seized the throne, and Darius had him executed.

After an alliance with Sparta was formed against Athens, Persia joined the Peloponnesian War. Several successful military campaigns succeeded in recovering the Greek coastal cities of Asia Minor and breaking Athenian power in the Aegean area. Darius II died in Babylon in 404 BC, the year the Peloponnesian War ended.

The Darius mentioned only once in the Book of Nehemiah probably refers to Darius II. The passage states that Jewish priests were recorded "until the reign of Darius the Persian" (Neh 12:22b); descendants of Levi were recorded "until the days of Johanan son of Eliashib" (Neh 12:23). An Aramaic document found in Elephantine (Egypt) refers to Johanan the high priest in Jerusalem. The document was written in 407 BC, thus placing Johanan in the reign of Darius II.

Darius III (336–330 BC). This Darius, also known as Darius Codomannus, was the grandson of Ostanes, who was the brother of Artaxerxes II. Darius was governor of Armenia when the eunuch Bagoas, who had poisoned Artaxerxes III and placed Arses on the throne, then poisoned Arses and placed Darius on the throne. Bagoas later attempted to poison Darius when the king broke from the eunuch's control; Darius, however, forced Bagoas to drink his own poison. Yet Darius did not enjoy control of the empire for very long. In 334 BC Alexander the Great crossed the Hellespont and defeated the Persians at Granicus. After his defeat in a crucial battle at Issus (333 BC), Darius III attempted to form an alliance with the Greeks, who were rapidly subduing Phoenicia, Palestine, and Egypt. Having refused all offers of an alliance, in 331 BC Alexander again met the Persians in battle at Gaugamela, just west of Nineveh. Darius, soundly defeated, fled to Ecbatana. Alexander took Babylon and Susa and burned Persepolis, then pursued Darius to Ecbatana and into Hyrcania. In July of 330 BC Darius III was killed by Bessus, the rebellious governor of Bactria. His death brought an end to the Achaemenid dynasty, which had ruled Persia and most of the Middle East for more than two centuries.

The Jewish historian Josephus, in the first century AD, wrote that an old man named Jaddua was high priest when Alexander the Great invaded the Persian empire. If Josephus' account is accurate, that Jaddua could be the Jaddua of Nehemiah 12:22; if so, and if "Darius the Persian" was meant to be read as a contemporary of Jaddua rather than Johanan in that verse, then Nehemiah's Darius may have been Darius III instead of Darius II.

Darius the Mede. Unknown in historical documents of the period of the Babylonian and Persian empires, this biblical Darius has been identified with several known figures. The most important efforts have identified Darius the Mede as another name for Cyrus II ("Cyrus the Persian," Dn 6:28); for Cambyses II, Cyrus' son; or for Gubaru, who was governor of Babylon and the province Beyond the River during the reigns of Cyrus II and Cambyses II.

According to the Book of Daniel, "Darius the Mede received the kingdom" when Belshazzar, king of Babylon, was slain (Dn 5:30, 31). Darius was about 62 years old (Dn 5:31) and was "the son of Ahasuerus, by birth a Mede" (Dn 9:1). Daniel never suggested that Darius was king of Media or of the whole Persian empire, only of the Chaldean (Babylonian) kingdom. The Babylonian empire included Mesopotamia (Babylonia and Assyria) and Syro-Palestine (Syria, Phoenicia, and Palestine). In the Persian empire that huge area became known as the province of Babylon (Mesopotamia) and Beyond the River (Syro-Palestine). Daniel also recorded that Darius appointed governors in the kingdom. By the third year of Cyrus the Persian (536 BC), the first year of Darius the Mede had already passed (Dn 10:1–11:1).

According to Nabonidus' Chronicle and the Persian Verse Account of Nabonidus, two cuneiform documents from Nabonidus' reign, Nabonidus was in Tema until Cyrus' invasion of Babylonia. While away he "entrusted the kingship" to his son Belshazzar. On October 12, 539 BC Babylon fell to Ugbaru, general of Cyrus' army. Cyrus entered Babylon on October 29, 539 BC and appointed a person named Gubaru governor of Babylon. Gubaru then appointed other governors under him. General Ugbaru died on November 6, 539 BC.

Clearly there is no place for Darius the Mede between the reigns of Nabonidus/Belshazzar and Cyrus II. Thus Darius the Mede must be either Cyrus, or a subordinate of Cyrus, or Cambyses, crown prince under Cyrus. But Cyrus II is mentioned as a separate person (Dn 6:28; 10:1–11:1), and it seems unlikely that the author would name the same figure both "Cyrus the Persian" and "Darius the Mede." Cambyses II could not have been 62 years old; and since he was not made king of Babylon until he became king of the empire in 529 BC, Cambyses' first year could not precede Cyrus' third year (536 BC). Further, neither Cyrus nor Cambyses had an Ahasuerus anywhere in his ancestry. Although they may have had Median mothers, both Cyrus and Cambyses traced their ancestry paternally to Achaemenes, founder of the dynasty of Persian emperors. They considered themselves Persians, not Medes.

Darius the Mede was thus probably a subordinate of Cyrus who was made ruler of "the realm of the Chaldeans" after Belshazzar and who could have been considered a king by his subjects. Accordingly, the reign of Darius (Dn 6:28) should be understood as simultaneous with that of Cyrus, not as a preceding reign. Thus, Gubaru was made governor of Babylon immediately following the reign of Belshazzar, and he appointed governors as did Darius the Mede. There is no record of Gubaru's age, nationality, or ancestry. He may well have been a 62-year-old Mede whose father was named Ahasuerus. The Ahasuerus of the Book of Esther and of Ezra 4:6 must be identified with a later king, probably Xerxes I.

Many Babylonian texts record that Gubaru was governor of Babylon and the province Beyond the River for about 14 years (539–525 BC). The documents attribute much power to him. His name is a final warning to officials who might disobey the laws. In documents that mention Cyrus II or Cambyses II, crimes in Babylon are stated to be sins against Gubaru, not against Cyrus or Cambyses. The province of Babylon and Beyond the River was the richest and most populous in the Persian empire, encompassing many nations and languages. For a powerful governor of such a region to be called "king" by his subjects seems only natural.

The case for Gubaru is admittedly circumstantial, but it remains the best solution to the problem. Until further evidence comes to light, it is safe to assume that Darius the Mede, "king over the realm of the Chaldeans" was actually Gubaru, the known governor of that realm.

JOHN R. McRAY

See PERSIA, PERSIANS; MEDES, MEDIA, MEDIAN.

Darkness. Absence of light or brightness. Although the Bible seldom refers to literal dark-

ness, a number of words translated "darkness" are used in a figurative or metaphorical sense.

When God created the world, there was no light until he commanded that light appear. He then made a distinction between light and its opposite, darkness, which he called night (Gn 1:2,4,5,18). Literal darkness is also mentioned in the account of the plagues God inflicted on Egypt; the ninth plague was an intense darkness that could be "felt" (Ex 10:21–23). That darkness lasted three days and was selective; wherever Egyptians were, it was dark, but where the Israelites were, there was light. The Israelites left Egypt accompanied by a cloud that separated them from their enemy, evidently giving light to the Israelites but making darkness for the Egyptians (Ex 14:20). The Bible notes that thieves or adulterers are likely to do their evil deeds in the dark or at night (Jb 24:16,17).

In the NT "darkness" is used twice in its literal sense. At the crucifixion of Jesus, for a three-hour period from noon to three o'clock, there was no light (Mt 27:45; Mk 15:33; Lk 23:44). The other reference is to Christ's second coming, when "the sun will be darkened, and the moon will not give its light" (Mt 24:29).

Several biblical passages speak of a darkness surrounding God, evidently moving from a literal sense of absence of light to a more profound meaning. God spoke to Moses on Mt Sinai in a dense, black cloud (Ex 20:21; Dt 4:11) or from the darkness (Dt 5:23). Darkness is pictured as a shelter or cloak around God (2 Sm 22:12; Pss 18:11; 97:2). God sets a boundary for light and darkness (Jb 26:10), brings darkness (Pss 104:20; 105:28), and creates light and darkness (Is 45:7). God dwells in thick darkness (1 Kgs 8:12; 2 Chr 6:1), and thick darkness is under his feet (2 Sm 22:10; Ps 18:9).

Most figurative references to darkness appear in poetic material, such as Job, Psalms, and Isaiah. Generally, such darkness depicts ignorance about God's will. Knowledge of God is "light"; hence lack of such knowledge is "darkness" (Jb 12:24,25; Mt 4:16; Jn 1:5; 8:12; 12:35,46; 1 Jn 1:5; 2:8,9,11).

Job spoke of darkness as equivalent to nothingness in referring to the day of his birth (Jb 3:4–6). In other references darkness stands for death, a land of shadows and gloom, the dwelling place of the dead far from the light of day (Jb 10:21,22; 15:23; 17:12,13; 18:18; Eccl 6:4; 11:8).

Darkness frequently stands for distress and anxiety, or for the confusion and destruction experienced by the wicked (Gn 15:12; Jb 5:14; 12:25; 15:22,30; 19:8; 22:11; Pss 35:6; 107:10,14; Eccl 5:17; Is 5:30). Moral depravity is sometimes described as darkness (Prv 2:13; 4:19; Is 5:20; 60:2). In the NT darkness is generally a metaphor of moral depravity and spiritual ignorance (Mt 4:16; 6:23; Lk 1:79; 11:35; 22:53; Rom 2:19; Col 1:13).

A major theme of OT prophets was the Day of the Lord, often associated with darkness (Ez 32:8; Jl 2:2,31; Am 5:18,20; Zep 1:15); the NT also links darkness with judgment in connection with Christ's second coming (Mt 8:12; 22:13; 25:30; 2 Pt 2:17; Jude 6,13). Those who come to know God are said to come out of darkness (Is 9:2; 29:18; 42:7); darkness cannot be a hiding place from God (Jb 34:22; Ps 139:11,12; Is 29:15).

The apostle John's emphasis on the conflict between darkness and light depicts the continuing struggle between the evil one (Satan) and Jesus. The light has come and the darkness has not overcome it (Jn 1:5). The world is a realm of darkness into which Jesus has brought light (Jn 3:19; 8:12; 12:46). God himself is light (1 Jn 1:5). True light comes only through Jesus (Jn 1:9). Anyone, therefore, who does not know God remains in darkness, in spiritual ignorance.

The conflict of light against darkness was carried further by the people at Qumran, the Dead Sea Scrolls community. They developed a dualism of two spirits: a spirit of truth and a spirit of perversity. According to their *Manual of Discipline*, both spirits were given in equal measure, and both were created by God. Anyone who practiced righteousness was controlled by the "Prince of Light," but one who acted perversely was dominated by the "Angel of Darkness."

See Light; Plagues upon Egypt.

Darkon. Ancestor of a group of people that returned to Judah with Zerubbabel after the exile (Ezr 2:56; Neh 7:58).

Dart. Sharp, pointed weapon used as an arrow or light spear for thrusting.

See Arms and Warfare.

Date, Date Palm. Fruit and tree mentioned only once in the Bible (Sg 7:7).

See Plants (Palm).

Dathan. Reubenite, son of Eliab and brother of Abiram; one of the leaders of Israel who, with Korah, rebelled against Moses during the wilderness wanderings (Nm 16:1–27; 26:9; Ps 106:17).

Daughter. *See* Family Life and Relations.

Daughter-in-law. *See* Family Life and Relations.

David. Israel's most important king. David's kingdom represented the epitome of Israel's power and influence during the nation's OT history.

The two books in the OT devoted to David's reign are 2 Samuel and 1 Chronicles. His earlier years are recorded in 1 Samuel, beginning at chapter 16. Almost half of the biblical psalms are ascribed to David. His importance extends into the NT, where he is identified as an ancestor of Jesus Christ and as a forerunner of the messianic king.

Early Years. Family. David was the youngest son in Jesse's family, part of Judah's tribe. The family lived in Bethlehem, about six miles south of Jerusalem. His great-grandmother was Ruth, from the land of Moab (Ru 4:18–22). Genealogies in both the OT and NT trace David's lineage back to Judah, son of the patriarch Jacob (1 Chr 2:3–15; Mt 1:3–6; Lk 3:31–33).

Training and Talents. Little is known about David's early life. As a boy he took care of his father's sheep, risking his life to kill attacking bears and lions. Later David publicly acknowledged God's help and strength in protecting the flocks under his care (1 Sm 17:34–37).

David was an accomplished musician. He had developed his ability as a harpist so well that, when a musician was needed at the royal court of King Saul, someone immediately recommended David.

In Jesse's family David was regarded as unimportant. When the nationally known prophet Samuel visited Jesse's home, all the older sons were on hand to meet him; David had been tending the sheep. Samuel had been instructed by God to anoint a king from Jesse's family, not knowing beforehand which son to anoint. Sensing divine restraint as seven brothers passed before him, he made further inquiry. When he learned that Jesse had one other son, David was immediately summoned. David was anointed by Samuel and endowed with the Spirit of the Lord (1 Sm 16:1–13). Whatever Jesse and his family understood by that anointing, it seems to have made no immediate change in David's pattern of living. He continued to tend the sheep.

Preparation for Kingship. During his youth David was willing to serve others even though he had been anointed king. It was his willingness to take supplies to three of his older brothers in the army that gave him his opportunity for national fame.

As a young man David was also sensitive toward God. While greeting his brothers on the battlefield he was disturbed by the Philistine Goliath's defiance of God's armies. Although rebuked by his brothers, David accepted the challenge to take on Goliath. He had a reasonable confidence that God, who had helped him encounter a lion and a bear, would aid him against a champion warrior. So, with faith in God and using his ability to sling stones, David killed Goliath (1 Sm 17:12–58).

National Fame. Killing Goliath made David a hero to the nation of Israel. It also brought him into close relationship with the royal family of Saul. But success and national acclaim brought on the jealousy of Saul and ultimately resulted in David's expulsion from the land of Israel.

In the Royal Court. After promising David his oldest daughter, Merab, in marriage, Saul went back on that promise and offered David another daughter, Michal. The dowry of trophies from dead Philistines demanded by Saul was designed to bring about David's death at Philistine hands. But again David was victorious. Women sang praises of his exploits, intensifying Saul's jealousy and further endangering David's life (1 Sm 18:6–30).

In the meantime David and Saul's son Jonathan developed an intimate friendship. When they made a covenant, Jonathan gave David his choicest military equipment (sword, bow, and belt). Although Saul tried to turn Jonathan against David, the friendship deepened. Because Saul was trying to kill him, David had to flee from the court and live as a fugitive.

After Jonathan had warned David of Saul's continuing designs on his life, David went to Ramah to see the prophet Samuel. Together they went to Naioth, near Ramah. After sending several groups of men after David, Saul finally went with them himself. All his attempts to seize David were thwarted by the Spirit of God, who caused Saul and his men to prophesy all night in religious fervor (1 Sm 19).

Conferring again with Jonathan, David realized that Saul's jealousy had developed into hatred. Jonathan, aware that David would be the future king of Israel, requested assurance that his descendants would receive protection under David's rule (1 Sm 20).

Life as a Fugitive. Fleeing from Saul, David stopped at Nob. By deceiving Ahimelech, who was officiating as priest there, David obtained food supplies and Goliath's sword (kept as a trophy). An Edomite named Doeg, chief of Saul's herdsmen, saw what happened at Nob. David continued his flight, taking refuge temporarily in Gath with King Achish (1 Sm 21), then finding shelter in the cave of Adullam, located 10 miles southwest of Bethlehem. There his relatives and about 400 fighting men joined him. He went to Mizpeh in Moab, appealing to the Moabite king for protection, especially for his parents. When the prophet

Gad warned him not to stay there, David moved back to Judah to the Hereth woods (1 Sm 22:1–5).

David's freedom of movement enraged Saul, who charged his own people with conspiracy. When Doeg reported what he had witnessed at Nob, Saul executed Ahimelech and 84 other priests, then massacred all of Nob's inhabitants. One priest named Abiathar escaped to report Saul's atrocities to David, who assured him protection (1 Sm 22:6–23).

The Philistines were always ready to take advantage of any weakness in Israel. David's reprisal after a Philistine raid on Keilah, 12 miles southwest of Bethlehem, gave Saul an opportunity to attack David, who escaped to the Wilderness of Ziph, a desert area near Hebron. David and Jonathan met for the last time in that wilderness. Pursued by Saul's army, David fled still farther south. He was almost encircled in uninhabited country near Maon when Saul had to march his army off to respond to a Philistine attack (1 Sm 23).

At his next place of refuge, En-gedi, on the western shore of the Dead Sea, David was attacked by Saul with 3,000 soldiers. David had an opportunity to kill Saul but refused to harm the "Lord's anointed" king of Israel. Learning of David's loyalty, Saul confessed his sin in seeking David's life (1 Sm 24).

During the years they roamed the wilderness in the Maon–Ziph–En-gedi area, David's band provided protection for Nabal, a rich man living in Maon with large flocks of sheep at Carmel. In exchange for that protection David proposed that Nabal share some of his wealth. Nabal's scorn angered David, but Nabal's wife Abigail appealed to David not to take revenge. When Abigail told Nabal of his narrow escape, he was evidently so shocked that he had a heart seizure. He died 10 days later, and Abigail later became David's wife (1 Sm 25).

Once more Saul came with an army of 3,000 men into the Ziph desert. Entering Saul's camp during the night, David once again passed up an opportunity to harm the king. Realizing the folly of seeking David's life, Saul finally abandoned pursuit (1 Sm 26).

Refuge in Philistia. David continued to feel unsafe in Saul's kingdom. Returning to Gath in Philistine country, he was welcomed by King Achish. His followers were allotted the city of Ziklag, where they lived for about 16 months, attracting new recruits from Judah and the rest of Israel (1 Sm 27; 1 Chr 12:19–22).

The Philistine army marching up to the Megiddo valley to fight Saul's army was uneasy with David's guerrillas in their rear column, so the commanders put pressure on Achish to dismiss David. When he returned to

Ziklag, David found that the city had just been raided by the Amalekites. He pursued the enemy, rescued his people and goods, and divided the spoils with those who had remained behind to guard the supplies (1 Sm 29,30). Meanwhile the Philistines routed the Israelites at Mt Gilboa, killing Jonathan and two of Saul's other sons in a fierce battle. Saul, badly wounded, killed himself with his own sword (1 Sm 31).

David as King. David ruled over Israel for about 40 years, although the accounts of his reign do not contain enough information for an exact chronology. He began his rule at Hebron, and reigned over Judah's territory for seven or eight years. With the death of Saul's successor, Ish-bosheth, David was recognized as king by all the tribes and made Jerusalem his capital. During the next decade or so he unified Israel through military and economic expansion. Then came approximately 10 years of disruption in the royal family. The last years of David's reign seem to have been devoted to plans for the Jerusalem temple, which was built in the reign of his son Solomon.

The Years in Hebron. David was subjected to an unusually rugged period of training for his kingship. Serving under Saul he gained experience in military exploits against the Philistines. Then during his fugitive wanderings in the desert area of southern Judah he ingratiated himself with the landholders and sheep raisers by giving them protection. Being recognized as an outlaw of Israel even enabled him to negotiate diplomatic relations with Moab and Philistia.

David was in Philistine country when news came to him that both Saul and Jonathan had been slain. In a beautiful elegy he paid tribute to his friend Jonathan as well as to King Saul (2 Sm 1).

Sure of God's guidance, David returned to his home, where the leaders of Judah anointed him king at Hebron. He sent a message of commendation to the men of Jabesh for providing a respectable burial for King Saul, probably also bidding for their support.

Hebron, David's first capital.

Confusion probably swept through Israel when Saul was killed, because the Philistines occupied much of the land. Various leaders gathered whatever fighting men they could find, as old tribal loyalties reasserted themselves. David had most of Judah's tribe firmly behind him.

A kind of civil war broke out between the followers of David and those of Saul, with David gaining the allegiance of more and more people. Saul's general, Abner, eventually negotiated peace with David, who requested the restoration of Michal as his wife, indicating that he held no animosity toward Saul's dynasty. With the consent of Saul's son Ish-bosheth, whom Abner had enthroned as king, Abner went to Hebron and pledged Israel's support for David. But Abner was killed by Joab, one of David's captains, in a family vendetta, and soon afterward Ish-bosheth was assassinated. David publicly mourned Abner's death and had Ish-bosheth's two murderers executed. Thus when Saul's dynasty ended, David was seen by the people not so much as a challenger as a logical successor. Hence he was recognized as king by all Israel (2 Sm 2–4).

Consolidation in Jerusalem. When the Israelites turned to David as king, the Philistines became alarmed and attacked (2 Sm 5; 1 Chr 14:8–17). David was strong enough to defeat them and thus unify the people of Israel.

In search of a more central location for his capital, David turned toward the city of Jerusalem, a Jebusite stronghold. Joab responded to his challenge to conquer the city and was rewarded by being made general of David's army. Jerusalem became known as the "city of David" (1 Chr 11:4–9).

In the same way that he had organized his earliest followers into an effective guerrilla band (1 Chr 11:1–12:22), at Hebron David began organizing the whole nation (1 Chr 12:23–40). Once established in Jerusalem, he quickly gained recognition from the Phoenicians, contracting for their artisans to build him a magnificent palace in the new capital (1 Chr 14:1,2). He also made sure that Jerusalem would become Israel's religious center (2 Sm 6; 1 Chr 13–16). His abortive attempt to move the ark of the covenant by oxcart (cf. Nm 4) reminded the powerful king that he still had to do things God's way to be successful.

With Jerusalem well established as the nation's capital, David intended to build God a temple. He shared his plan with the prophet Nathan, whose immediate response was positive. That night, however, God sent a message via Nathan that David should not build the temple. David's throne would be established eternally, the prophet said, and, unlike Saul,

David

Warren's shaft (which goes down to Hezekiah's Tunnel and the Gihon Spring); David's captain took the city of Jerusalem through this tunnel and shaft.

King David would have a son to succeed him and perpetuate the kingdom; that son would build the temple (2 Sm 7; 1 Chr 17).

Prosperity and Supremacy. Little is recorded about the expansion of David's rule from the tribal area of Judah to a vast empire stretching from the Nile River of Egypt to regions of the Tigris-Euphrates valley. Nothing in secular history negates the biblical perspective that David had the most powerful kingdom in the heart of that "Fertile Crescent" about 1000 BC.

It is likely that skirmishes with the Philistines to the west were frequent until they finally became subservient to David and paid him tribute. In Saul's day the Philistines had enjoyed a monopoly on the use of iron (1 Sm 13:19–21). The fact that David freely used iron near the end of his reign (1 Chr 22:3) hints at profound economic changes in Israel.

David's kingdom expanded southward as he built military garrisons in Edomite territory. Beyond Edom he controlled the Moabites and Amalekites, who paid him tribute in silver and gold. To the northeast, Israelite domination was extended over the Ammonites and

the Aramaeans, whose capital was Damascus. David's treatment of both friends and enemies seemed to contribute to the strength of his kingdom (2 Sm 8,10).

Although he was a brilliant military stratigest who used all the means and resources available to bring Israel success, David was humble enough to glorify God (2 Sm 22; see Ps 18). He continued to show kindness toward Mephibosheth, a son of Jonathan (2 Sm 9).

Sin in the Royal Family. A lengthy section of the Book of 2 Samuel (chs 11–20) gives a remarkably frank account of sin, crime, and rebellion in David's family. The king's own imperfections are clearly portrayed; the king of Israel himself could not escape God's judgment when he did wrong.

Although polygamy was then a Near Eastern status symbol, it was forbidden for a king of Israel (Dt 17:17). David practiced polygamy, however; some of his marriages undoubtedly had political implications (such as his marriages to Saul's daughter Michal and to princess Maacah of Geshur). Flagrant sins of incest, murder, and rebellion in his family brought David much suffering and almost cost him the throne.

David's sin of adultery with Bathsheba, committed at the height of his military success and territorial expansion, led him further into evil: he planned a strategy to have Bathsheba's husband Uriah killed on the front line of battle.

David seems to have excluded God from consideration in that segment of his personal life. Yet when the prophet Nathan confronted the king with his sins, David acknowledged his guilt. He confessed his sin and pleaded with God for forgiveness (as in Pss 32 and 51). God forgave him, but for nearly 10 years David endured the consequences of his lack of self-restraint and his failure to exercise discipline in his family. Although unsurpassed in military and diplomatic strategy, David lacked strength of character in his domestic affairs. Evil fermented in his own house; the father's self-indulgence was soon reflected in Amnon's crime of incest, followed by Absalom's murder of his brother.

Having incurred his father's disfavor, Absalom took refuge in Geshur with his mother's people for three years. Joab, David's general, was eventually able to reconcile David with his alienated son. Absalom, however, having taken advantage of his position in the royal family to gain a following, went to Hebron, staged a surprise rebellion, and proclaimed himself king throughout Israel. His strong following posed such a threat that David fled from Jerusalem. David, still a master strategist, gained time through a ruse to organize his forces and put down his son's rebellion. Absalom was killed while trying to flee; his death plunged David into grief.

On his return to Jerusalem, David had to work at undoing the damage caused by Absalom's revolt. His own tribe of Judah, for example, had supported Absalom. Another rebellion, fomented by Sheba of Benjamin's tribe, had to be suppressed by Joab before the nation could settle down.

David's Last Years. Although David was not permitted to build the temple in Jerusalem, he made extensive preparations for that project during the last years of his reign. He stockpiled materials and organized the kingdom for efficient use of domestic and foreign labor. He also outlined details for religious worship in the new structure (1 Chr 21–29).

The military and civic organization developed by David was probably patterned after Egyptian practice. The army, rigidly controlled by officers of proven loyalty to the king, included mercenaries. The king also appointed trusted supervisors over farms, livestock, and orchards in various parts of his empire (1 Chr 27:25–31).

David took, or at least began, a census of Israel (2 Sm 24; 1 Chr 21). The incompleteness of the accounts leaves unanswered such questions as the reason for God's punishment. The king overruled Joab's objection and insisted that the census be taken. Since David later seemed keenly aware that he had sinned in taking the census, it may be that he was motivated by pride to ascertain his exact military strength (approximately one and a half million men). God may also have been judging the people for their support of the rebellions of Absalom and Sheba.

Through the prophet Gad, David was given a choice of punishments for his sin. He chose a three-day pestilence. As David and the elders repented, they saw an angel on the threshing floor of the Jebusite Ornan (Araunah). David offered sacrifice there and prayed for his people. Later he purchased the threshing floor, located just outside the city of Jerusalem, concluding that it should be the site for the temple to be built by his son Solomon (1 Chr 21:28–22:1).

David's Influence. Psalms. The OT Book of Psalms became one of the most popular books in ancient Israel, and has remained so among countless millions of people throughout the centuries. These words of praise prepared by David were intended for use in the temple worship (2 Chr 29:30). The 73 psalms ascribed to David generally grew out of his own relationship to God and to other persons.

Some Psalms from David's Experiences

Psalm	Historical Reference
59	(1 Sm 19:11)
56	(1 Sm 21:10)
34	(1 Sm 21:13)
142	(1 Sm 22:1)
52	(1 Sm 22:9)
54	(1 Sm 23:19)
57	(1 Sm 24:1)
7	(1 Sm 24:11,12)
18	(2 Sm 7:1;22)
32	(2 Sm 12:13,14)
51	(2 Sm 12:13,14)
3	(2 Sm 15:16)
63	(2 Sm 16:2)

David probably compiled Book I of the Book of Psalms (1–41) and Book IV (90–106), since most of those psalms were written by David himself. Other psalms of his (Ps 51–71) are in Book II (42–72), which was probably compiled by Solomon. As those psalms were used for worship in later generations, various people added others until the time of Ezra.

David's psalms provided much of the poetry that was set to music for Israel's worship. His organization of the priests and Levites and his provision of instruments for worship (2 Chr 7:6; 8:14) set the pattern for generations to come in the religious life of Israel.

Prophets. David, recognized as the greatest Israelite king, is often mentioned as a standard of comparison in the writings of the OT prophets. Isaiah (as in Is 7:2,13) and Jeremiah often referred to their contemporary kings as belonging to the "house" or "throne" of David. Contrasting some of David's descendants who did not honor God, both Isaiah and Jeremiah predicted a messianic ruler who would establish justice and righteousness on the throne of David forever (Is 9:7; Jer 33:15). When Isaiah described the coming ruler, he identified him as being from the lineage of Jesse, David's father (Is 11:1–10). Predicting a period of universal peace, Isaiah saw the capital in "Zion," identified with the city of David (Is 2:1–4).

Ezekiel promised the restoration of David as king in an eschatalogical and messianic sense (Ez 37:24,25), and of "my servant David" as Israel's shepherd (Ez 34:23). Hosea likewise identified the future ruler as King David (Hos 3:5). Amos assured the people that God would restore the "tabernacle" of David (Am 9:11) so that they could again dwell in safety. Zechariah referred five times to the "house of David" (in Zec 12,13), encouraging the hope of a restoration of David's glorious dynasty. The concept of the eternal throne promised to David during his reign was delineated in the message of the prophets even while they were announcing judgments to come on the rulers and people of their time.

New Testament. David is frequently mentioned by the Gospel writers, who established Jesus' identity as the "son of David." The covenant God made with David was that an eternal king would come from David's family (Mt 1:1; 9:27; 12:23; Mk 10:48; 12:35; Lk 18:38,39; 20:41). According to Mark 11:10 and John 7:42, Jews of Jesus' day expected the Messiah (Christ) to be a descendant of David. While stating that Jesus came from the lineage of David, the Gospels also clearly teach that Jesus was the Son of God (Mt 22:41–45; Mk 12:35–37; Lk 20:41–44).

In the Book of Acts, David is recognized as the recipient of God's promises that were fulfilled in Jesus Christ. David is also seen as a prophet whom the Holy Spirit inspired to write the psalms (1:16; 2:22–36; 4:25; 13:26–39).

In the Book of Revelation, Jesus is designated as having the "key of David" (3:7), and as being "the Lion of the tribe of Judah, the Root of David" (5:5). Jesus is quoted as asserting that "I am the root and the offspring of David, the bright morning star" (22:16).

Theological Significance. David, one of the most gifted and versatile individuals in the OT, is second only to Moses in Israel's history. He was keenly conscious that God had enabled him to establish a kingdom (Ps 18; cf. 2 Sm 22); it was in that context that he was given the messianic promise of an eternal kingdom.

From David's own suffering, persecution, and nearness to death came prophetic psalms that portrayed the suffering and death of the Messiah (e.g., Pss 2; 22; 110; 118). Even the hope of the resurrection is expressed in Psalm 16, as the apostle Peter noted on the day of Pentecost (Acts 2:25–28).

Awareness of a vital personal relationship with God is expressed more consistently by David than by any of the faithful men and women who preceded him. He knew that it was not legalistic observance of rules or rituals that made him acceptable to God. Offering and sacrifice could not atone for sin if one had no accompanying contrition and humility. Many of David's prayers are as appropriate for Christians as they were for God-fearing people in the OT.

David's writings show that "knowing God" was as real in OT times as it was for the apos-

tle Paul, even though the full revelation of God in Jesus Christ was still in the future.

SAMUEL J. SCHULTZ

See ISRAEL, HISTORY OF; MESSIAH; CHRISTOLOGY; KING, KINGSHIP; KINGDOM OF GOD (HEAVEN); CHRONOLOGY, OLD TESTAMENT.

Bibliography. W.G. Blaikie, *David, King of Israel;* R.E. Clements, *Abraham and David;* G. de S. Barrow, *David: Shepherd, Poet, Warrior, King;* D.M. Gunn, *The Story of King David;* W.O.E. Oesterley and T.H. Robinson, *A History of Israel,* vol I, pp 200–238; D.F. Payne, *David: King in Israel;* A.W. Pink, *The Life of David.*

David, City of. 1. In the OT, the city of Jerusalem. "City of David" referred originally to the old Jebusite stronghold captured by King David (2 Sm 5:6–9). David, Solomon, and many of their descendants who ruled over Judah were buried in the city of David (1 Kgs 2:10; 11:43). Solomon considered it a holy place because of the presence of the ark of the Lord. He therefore moved his pagan wife, Pharaoh's daughter, away from the city of David and built a house for her in another place (2 Chr 8:11).

After Solomon's time the term "city of David" was also used in a larger sense to describe the entire city of Jerusalem, including the newly built temple area. The old section of Jerusalem below the temple site was still specifically designated as the "city of David," however (Neh 3:15). David's tomb was close to

Excavations at the City of David.

the pool of Siloam and to the staircase that descended from the city of David (Neh 3:15,16).

King Hezekiah was concerned about that area when he prepared to defend Jerusalem against the Assyrian king Sennacherib in 702 BC. Having plugged up the water sources outside the city, Hezekiah repaired the city wall and the great tower "Millo in the city of David" (2 Chr 32:5). After the angel of the Lord had destroyed the Assyrian army besieging Jerusalem (2 Chr 32:21), Hezekiah wisely provided a new water source for the city of David. A spring in the cliff beneath the east wall of the city had flowed into the Kidron Valley. To remove that water supply from future enemies and to make it available for his own defenses, Hezekiah "closed the upper outlet of the waters of Gihon and directed them down to the west side of the city of David" (2 Chr 32:30). That required a remarkable engineering feat. Two crews, working from opposite sides, penetrated the rocky Ophel ridge. When they met, they had completed a wandering tunnel one-third of a mile in length through solid rock. The tunnel carried water from the spring, underneath the city of David, and into the pool of Siloam, which was within the city wall.

See JERUSALEM; ZION.

2. In the NT, the town of Bethlehem. Bethlehem was David's birthplace and home until he went to Saul's palace as a musician (1 Sm 16:16–23). When David became Judah's king, he chose Hebron to be his capital, as the Lord had instructed him (2 Sm 2:1–11). Bethlehem was the birthplace of Jesus, who was a descendant of David (Mi 5:2–4; Lk 2:11).

See BETHLEHEM #1.

David, Root of. Phrase applied to Jesus Christ in the Book of Revelation (Rv 5:5; 22:16). Though "root" usually means "source," the metaphor depicts Jesus as David's royal descendant, as indicated by the parallel word "offspring" in Revelation 22:16. That is, Jesus came from King David's family as a branch grows from a rooted tree (cf. Is 11:1).

See JESSE, ROOT OF.

David, Tower of. 1. Fortress built by David, with a thousand shields hung on it, commemorated in Song of Songs 4:4 but otherwise unknown.

2. David's Tower in Jerusalem, near the Jaffa gate, built in medieval times.

See JERUSALEM.

Day. Most literally, a period of time delimited by the earth's rotation around its axis, such as the period between two consecutive sunrises; also, the portion of that period in which the sun is visible, the other portion being called "night." The word "day" occurs over 2,000 times in the OT, over 350 times in the NT. The Hebrew word for day is used in a variety of ways, not merely in the literal sense. The Hebrew day began in the evening and continued until the following evening, a reckoning presumably based on the Torah (cf. Gn 1:14,19). That kind of literal solar (24-hour) day is known as a civil day. Among other ancient Near Eastern nations the civil day began at different times. Greek custom agreed with that of the Hebrews; the Babylonians started their day at sunrise; the Egyptian and Roman day stretched from one midnight to the next.

Biblical Days and Weeks. Commonly recognized units of the visible (12-hour) day were morning, noonday, and evening (Ps 55:17). Those divisions were sometimes defined by terms for dawn (Jb 3:9), the heat of the day (1 Sm 11:11), noon (Gn 43:16), the cool of the day (Gn 3:8), and evening (Ru 2:17). The Hebrew phrase "between the two evenings" (Ex 16:12) probably referred to dusk, the dark part of twilight. Division of days into consecutive hours did not take place until the time of Christ. The closest OT approximation to such a unit was division of the day into quarters (Neh 9:3), perhaps a counterpart of the preexilic division of the night into watches.

The ancient Hebrews did not name the days of the week other than the sabbath. Rather, they referred to them numerically, a practice carried over into NT times (Lk 24:1). Because of the traditional Hebrew emphasis on the sabbath it was important for the Jews to know the exact time when the sabbath began. The Pharisees therefore decided that the appearance of three stars following sunset would determine the sabbath day's beginning.

Days of Creation. Many people believe that the days mentioned in the Genesis creation narrative were 24-hour periods. The phrase "there was evening, there was morning" is used to support that idea. That expression, however, is actually a Sumerian literary figure that pairs opposites together to describe totality. Thus "evening-morning" means a complete phase of time within the total creative cycle; it emphasizes the completeness or comprehensiveness of the process, not the specific period of time in which that process was accomplished. The totality of creation, phase by phase, may have been thus depicted without any necessary reference to a defined time period.

Since the Sumerian civil day included only the visible (12-hour) period, a legal day of other nations was actually a "double day" (24 hours). If the early Genesis material reflects Sumerian culture, the use of "evening-morning" would preclude current concepts of a day and point instead to a phase or general time period.

Old Testament. In the OT, "day" frequently has a figurative meaning—for example, the "day of the Lord" (Jl 1:15; Am 5:18), the "day of trouble" (Ps 20:1), and the "day of God's wrath" (Jb 20:28). The plural form is sometimes used to describe a king's reign (1 Kgs 10:21) or the extent of an individual's life (Gn 5:4; 1 Kgs 3:14; Ps 90:12). God is described in the Book of Daniel as the "Ancient of Days" (Dn 7:9,13).

In addition to the sabbath (Gn 2:3; Ex 20:8–11), which was reserved for rest and worship, "day" was applied to the Passover celebration each spring (Ex 12:14; Lv 23:5) and the Day of Atonement (Lv 16:29–31) each autumn. As with the sabbath, no work was performed on those occasions; prescribed religious rituals were observed.

New Testament. In the NT the use of "day" followed Semitic usage to some extent, although the four military night watches were of Greek and Roman origin. The 12-hour day of NT times was a legacy of Babylonian astronomy (cf. Jn 11:9).

In addition to the literal usage of "day," NT authors sometimes employed it figuratively, as in such expressions as the "day of salvation" (2 Cor 6:2) and the "day of Jesus Christ" (Phil 1:6). Or they described specified periods of time, as in the "days of his Temple duties" (Lk 1:23 LB). Special feasts mentioned include the Passover (Jn 12:1), the days of unleavened bread (Acts 12:3), and the day of Pentecost (Acts 2:1).

As in the OT, the period of human life is described as days (Jn 9:4). Christians are called "sons of light and sons of the day" (1 Thes 5:5). Longer periods or eras are referred to as days (2 Cor 6:2; Eph 5:16; 6:13; Heb 5:7). The ominous note struck by the Hebrew prophets about a day of judgment is matched by NT stress on a day of final divine judgment when the Son of man (Jesus) will reveal himself as Lord (Lk 17:30; Jn 6:39–44; 1 Cor 5:5; 1 Thes 5:2; 2 Pt 2:9; 3:7,12; 1 Jn 4:17; Rv 16:14). The "day of eternity" marks that point at which time will become eternity (2 Pt 3:18). The new Jerusalem, dwelling place of God's people, is described as a place of perpetual day (Rv 21:25).

R. K. HARRISON

See CALENDARS, ANCIENT AND MODERN; DAY OF THE LORD; ESCHATOLOGY.

Day of Atonement. *See* ATONEMENT, DAY OF.

Day of Christ. Phrase used by the apostle Paul in reference to the second advent of Christ (Phil 1:10; 2:16).

See DAY OF THE LORD.

Day of the Lord. Expression used by OT prophets (as early as the eighth-century BC prophet Amos) to signify a time in which God actively intervenes in history, primarily for judgment. Thus "the day of the Lord" is also called "the day of the Lord's anger" (Zep 2:2 KJV).

Sometimes "the day of the Lord" is used in the OT to speak of a past judgment (Lam 2:22). More often an impending future judgment is in view (Jl 2:1–11). Ultimately, though, the term refers to climactic future judgment of the world (Jl 3:14–21; Mal 4:5). Often prophecy of a near-future event and an end-time prophecy are merged, the immediate judgment being a preview of the final day of the Lord. The prophecy of Isaiah against Babylon is an example (Is 13:5–10). Jesus combined events described there with other prophecies to explain his second coming (Mk 13:24–37). Another example is Joel's prophecy of the day of the Lord (Jl 1:15–2:11). Though the prophet initially spoke of God's judgment on Israel by a locust plague, that judgment prompted further pronouncements about a final day of the Lord far beyond Joel's time (Jl 2:31; 3:14–17). That day of the Lord extended even beyond the outpouring of the Holy Spirit at Pentecost predicted by Joel's prophecy (Jl 2:28–32; Acts 2:16–21; Rv 6:12,13). The NT uses the term exclusively to mean the end time.

The final day of the Lord is characterized in the Bible as a day of gloom, darkness, and judgment. Associated with God's judgment is language depicting changes in nature, especially a darkening of the sun, moon, and stars (Is 13:10; Jl 2:31; 3:15; Mt 24:29; Rv 6:12). Nations will be judged for their rebellion against God's anointed people and king (Jl 3:19; cf. Ps 2). Israel is counseled not to be eager for that day, because it will also include judgment on the chosen nation (Am 5:18–20). But the prophets promise that a believing "remnant" will be saved by looking to the Messiah they once rejected (Jl 2:32; Zec 12:10).

Following the judgment, the future day of the Lord will be a time of prosperity, restoration, and blessing for Israel (Jl 3:18–21).

The more explicit NT expressions—"the day of our Lord Jesus Christ" (1 Cor 1:8), "the day of the Lord Jesus" (1 Cor 5:5; 2 Cor 1:14), and "the day of Christ" (Phil 1:10; 2:16)—are more personal and more positive. They point to final events related to Christian believers, who will not experience the wrath of God (1 Thes 5:9).

When the day of the Lord comes, the earth will be renewed and purified through a judgment of fire (2 Pt 3:10–13). In the Book of Revelation the final purging seems to come after the millennium—that is, the 1,000-year reign of Christ (Rv 21:1).

Evangelical scholars differ about the beginning point of the day of the Lord in relation to other prophesied future events. Various views suggest it will start: (1) at the beginning of a seven-year period preceding Christ's coming to earth, when a "man of lawlessness" is to be revealed and make a covenant with Israel (2 Thes 2:3; cf. Dn 9:27); (2) following an "abomination of desolation," in which the "man of lawlessness" will pose as God (Mt 24:15 KJV; 2 Thes 2:4) at the middle of the seven-year period; or (3) later in the seven years at the outpouring of God's wrath (Rv 16:1).

Concerning the future day of the Lord as it is prophesied in the Scriptures, one should note: (1) biblical passages mentioning the impressive celestial signs of that day (Is 13:10; Jl 2:31; 3:15; Mt 24:29; Rv 6:12); (2) the sequence of the judgments that focus on seals, trumpets, and bowls in the Book of Revelation; (3) the relationship of the wrath of Revelation 6:16 to the series of "seal" judgments; and (4) the revelation of the "man of lawlessness" in 2 Thessalonians 2:3.

See Eschatology; Last Judgment; Last Days.

Day's Journey. Way of estimating distances in Bible times. A day's journey approximated 20 miles, but depended on such things as mode of travel, the terrain, and the weather. Scripture refers both to a day's journey (Nm 11:31; 1 Kgs 19:4; Lk 2:44) and to a sabbath day's journey (Acts 1:12). A sabbath day's journey was probably about 3,500 feet.

See Sabbath Day's Journey.

Day Star, Dayspring. KJV translations in Job 38:12 (dawn, RSV), Luke 1:78 (day, RSV), and 2 Peter 1:19 (morning star, RSV) referring to Venus, the star that heralds the dawn, or to first light of dawn itself.

In Isaiah 14:12 Day Star is a designation for the haughty king of Babylon (Lucifer, KJV) who, having aspired so high at the cost of Israel, will surely be brought down in shame and disappointment by God.

See Morning Star.

"D" Document. Designation used by some biblical critics for the Book of Deuteronomy. According to a number of proponents of the documentary hypothesis (a critical theory that attributes the five books of Moses to several authors and redactors), the Book of Deuteronomy was written in the time of Judah's king Josiah (reigned 640–609 BC) and not by Moses, as traditionally believed by Jews and Christians. According to the critical view, the "book of the law of the Lord" found in Josiah's time about 621 BC (2 Kgs 22:8; 2 Chr 34:14,15) was written by a group (possibly under the direction of the high priest Hilkiah) who then buried the document in the basement of the temple and later claimed to "discover" it there.

The "D" document was supposedly written to defend the prophetic positions that true religion was love for God (Dt 6:5), that moral righteousness was as important as offering sacrifices to God, and that worship should be centralized in Jerusalem.

See Documentary Hypothesis.

Deacon, Deaconess. Terms designating an officer in a local church, derived from a Greek word meaning "servant" or "minister." The term "diaconate" is used for the office itself or for the collective body of deacons and deaconesses. As with many other biblical words used today in a technical sense, the words "deacon" and "deaconess" began as popular, nontechnical terms. Both in secular first-century Greek culture and in the NT, they described a variety of services.

Origins of the Concept. *Greek Usage.* References have been found in extrabiblical writings where the Greek word "deacon" meant "waiter," "servant," "steward," or "messenger." In at least two instances it indicated a baker and a cook. In religious usage the word described various attendants in pagan temples. Ancient documents show "deacons" presiding at the dedication of a statue to the Greek god Hermes. Serapis and Isis, Egyptian deities, were served by a college of "deacons" presided over by a priest.

General NT Usage. The same word was used by biblical writers in a general sense to describe various ministries or services. Not until later in the development of the apostolic church was the term applied to a distinct body of church officers. Among its general usages "deacon" refers to a waiter at meals (Jn 2:5,9); a king's attendant (Mt 22:13); a servant of Satan (2 Cor 11:15); a servant of God (2 Cor 6:4); a servant of Christ (2 Cor 11:23); a servant of the church (Col 1:24,25); and a political ruler (Rom 13:4).

The NT presents servanthood in the sense of ministry or service as a mark of the whole church—that is, as normative for all disciples (Mt 20:26–28; Lk 22:26,27). Jesus' teaching on the final judgment equates ministry with feeding the hungry, welcoming strangers, clothing the naked, and visiting the sick and imprisoned (Mt 25:31–46). The entire NT emphasizes compassionate care for individuals' physical and spiritual needs as well as the giving of one's self to meeting those needs. Such service is ultimately a ministry to Christ himself (Mt 25:45).

Ministry in church life is based on spiritual gifts distributed to "members of the body" (1 Cor 12:12). The apostles Paul and Peter in their treatment of spiritual gifts made reference to "service" as a form of the Holy Spirit's ministry (Rom 12:7; 1 Pt 4:11).

Origin of the Office. There is little question that before the end of the first century the general term for service or ministry became a kind of title for a position or office in the church. That development evidently went through several stages.

Some biblical scholars emphasize a relationship between the *hazzan* of the Jewish synagogue and the Christian office of deacon. The *hazzan* opened and closed the synagogue doors, kept it clean, and handed out the books for reading. It was to such a person that Jesus handed the scroll of Isaiah after finishing his reading (Lk 4:20).

Other NT scholars give considerable attention to the choosing of the seven (Acts 6:1–6); they see that action as a historical forerunner of a more developed structure (Phil 1:1; 1 Tm 3:8–13; the two specific references to an "office" of deacon). Luke devoted considerable attention in Acts to the selection of a new set of church leaders. Overworked with a variety of responsibilities, the 12 apostles proposed a division of labor to ensure care for the Hellenist (Greek-speaking) widows in the church's daily distribution of food and alms. "Seven men of good repute, full of the Spirit and of wisdom" (Acts 6:3) subsequently became prominent in the Jerusalem congregation, doing works of charity and caring for physical needs.

Some scholars caution that the diaconate should not be exclusively linked with charitable works, since the Greek word used in Acts 6:2 is related to the word translated "ministry of the word" in verse 4. Those chosen to oversee the care for physical needs were people of spiritual stature. Stephen, for instance, "full of grace and power, did great wonders and signs" (Acts 6:8). Philip, appointed as one of the seven in Acts 6, "preached good news about the kingdom of God and the name of Jesus Christ" (Acts 8:12). Philip also baptized (Acts 8:38) and is referred to as an evangelist (Acts 21:8).

Deacons in the Early Church. *Preliminary Stage.* Those who cite Acts 6 as a preliminary stage of the office of deacon refer to the spread of the practice from the church in Jerusalem to the gentile congregations sprouting elsewhere. Many churches probably took the appointing of "the Jerusalem seven" as a pattern to follow, some even adopting the number seven. In a letter of the third-century pope Cornelius, for example, the church of Rome was said to have maintained seven for the number of deacons.

By the time the church of Philippi received its instructions from the apostle Paul (c. AD 62), and Timothy had Paul's first letter in hand, "deacon" had become a technical term referring to a specific office in the churches. In Philippians 1:1 Paul addressed the church in general and then added "with bishops and deacons." Some interpreters consider that to be a clear establishment of two distinct groups within the larger church body, though no further description is given. Possibly the deacons of that congregation were responsible for collecting and then dispatching the offerings referred to (Phil 4:14–18).

In 1 Timothy 3:8–13 instructions are given about qualifications for the office of deacon. Although that is the most detailed treatment of the subject in the NT, it is actually quite

The west wall of Samaria, the city where Philip the deacon evangelized.

sketchy. Most of the qualifications, dealing with personal character and behavior, are similar to those for a bishop. For instance, a deacon is to be truthful, monogamous, "not addicted to much wine," and a responsible parent. Verse 11, requiring that "the women likewise must be serious, no slanderers, but temperate, faithful in all things," may refer not to deacons' wives but to deaconesses, as several translations note (NIV, NEB). In any event, it is clear that women participated in the work of the diaconate.

In contrast to the office of bishop (1 Tm 3:2), deacons are not described as providing teaching or hospitality. In fact, no mention is made of any functional qualifications to clarify deacons' or deaconesses' roles in the early church. The character qualifications listed are appropriate for those with monetary and administrative responsibilities (as Acts 6:1–6 suggests). Timothy is told that good deacons will not go unrewarded; not only will their faith increase, but also their good standing among those whom they serve (1 Tm 3:13).

The NT writings indicate that to be chosen as a deacon or deaconess is a high compliment and affirmation. Named as "deacons" were Timothy (1 Thes 3:2; 1 Tm 4:6), Tychicus (Col 4:7), Epaphras (Col 1:7), Paul (1 Cor 3:5)—and even Christ (Rom 15:8, "servant"). Biblical "deaconing" is not characterized by power and prominence but by service to others. In imitation of Jesus' life, the deacon or deaconess followed the servant pattern. The Christian diaconate thus contrasted sharply with the prevailing Greek thought of service, which was considered unworthy of the dignity of free men. (The Greek philosopher Plato wrote, "How can man be happy when he has to serve someone?")

The office of deacon differed from the office of elder, which was adapted from a definite Jewish pattern in the OT (see Nm 11:16,17; Dt 29:10). The diaconate, on the other hand, developed from the strong, personal, historical example of Jesus, the servant who compassionately met concrete human needs.

Later Developments. As the office of deacon became more firmly established, its duties could be defined as those of pastoral care. The poor and the sick received their service, not only physically but also with instruction and consolation. The homes of church members became familiar territory to a deacon or deaconess. A pattern of visitation was established to discover and then meet the needs of the church body at large. Although that included the administration of funds, it went far beyond it. Those who served as deacons and deaconesses undoubtedly became symbols of loving care for the church in general.

Where the office of deacon fits into the larger pattern of church order within the NT is difficult to determine because of the obvious variety present during the formative years. Some church historians conclude that as ecclesiastical structure developed, elders provided congregational leadership. Deacons assisted them, especially in social services and pastoral care. The late first and early second centuries witnessed a distinctive threefold ministry of deacons, elders (presbyters), and bishops. Bishops or "overseers" began to exercise authority over areas or groups of churches.

Deaconess. Where did women fit into the ministry of the early church? Paul's inclusion of references to women in ministry is striking when compared with the role of women in general in the first century. He commended Phoebe for her service in the church at Cenchreae, using the word "deacon" to describe her (Rom 16:1). He praised her as a "helper" (Rom 16:2), a word that denotes leadership qualities (cf. Rom 12:8; 1 Tm 3:4,5). Some scholars have used that reference as an example of early development of the office of deaconess. Others have interpreted it in a nontechnical sense, meaning that Phoebe functioned in a generally serving role and thus was worthy of recognition at Rome. Whether "deacon" was used technically or descriptively, ministry for both women and men in the NT was patterned after the example of Jesus, who "came not to be served but to serve" (Mk 10:45). Because of the large number of female converts (Acts 5:14; 17:4), women functioned in such areas of ministry as visitation, instruction in discipleship, and assistance in baptism. Deaconesses are mentioned in third-century documents as administering baptism to female converts.

Considering the rigid separation of the sexes in the Near East at that time, female participation in church ministry stands out in bold relief. A governor of Bithynia, Pliny the Younger (d. 113?), in his *Correspondence with Trajan* verified women officeholders in the church. Pliny also mentioned two deaconesses who were martyred for the cause of Christ.

MANFRED T. BRAUCH

See BISHOP; ELDER; PASTOR; PRESBYTER; SPIRITUAL GIFTS.

Bibliography. J.M. Barnet, *The Diaconate;* F.J.A. Hort, *The Christian Ecclesia;* E.M. Howe, *Women and Church Leadership;* J.B. Lightfoot, "The Christian Ministry" in *Philippians;* C. Robinson, *The Ministry of Women;* E. Schweizer, *Church Order in the NT.*

Dead, Abode of the. Term covering a number of descriptive biblical images of the whereabouts of those who have died. Those images include Sheol and "the pit" in the OT, plus Hades, Gehenna, Paradise, and "Abraham's bosom" in the NT. As their understanding of God advanced, the Hebrews' idea of what happens at death changed from rather hazy beginnings to a developed concept found in the NT.

Old Testament. The OT contains meager information about the dead. At death, according to some OT passages, one descends to Sheol (often translated as "grave," "hell," "pit," or simply "the dead"), which at times means merely that one is laid in a grave (Nm 16:30,33), but more often indicates an underworld. The abode of the dead is pictured as a place beneath the earth to which one "goes down" (Gn 42:38; Prv 15:24; Ez 26:20) and as a place of gloomy darkness (Jb 10:21,22), silence (Pss 94:17; 115:17), and forgetfulness (Ps 88:12). God is not remembered there and his praises are never sung (Pss 6:5; 30:9; 115:17). Even God himself, it was believed, does not remember those who are there (Ps 88:5,11; Is 38:18). The dead were seen as permanently cut off from contact with the Lord and from participating in his activity in history. Even though the border between life and death was considered fluid (as shown by a resurrection in 2 Kgs 4:32–37 and by Samuel's ghost in 1 Sm 28:7–25), communication with the dead was forbidden to the Jews (Dt 18:11). Worshiping the dead was a common practice in the nations surrounding Israel.

Although one's fate in the underworld could not properly be called life, it was a kind of existence, perhaps even in the company of one's countrymen and ancestors (Gn 25:8; Ez 32:17–30). The realm of the dead was not beyond the reach of God's power (Ps 139:8; Am 9:2; Jn 2:2). Although Sheol was pictured as a hungry monster wolfing down the living (Prv 27:20; 30:16), God's power could save one from its grasp (Pss 49:15; 86:13). By the end of the OT period there was even hope that one would finally be delivered from Sheol, although only Daniel expressed that hope clearly (Jb 14:13–22; 19:25–27; Pss 49:15; 73:23–28; Dn 12:1,2). So although the ancient Hebrews never looked forward to death in the same way that the apostle Paul could in the NT (2 Cor 5:1–8; Phil 1:21–23), nevertheless they did come to understand that death was not a hopeless state.

Intertestamental Writings. Between the exile and the beginning of the NT period (586 BC–AD 30, overlapping with the end of the OT), contact with the religions of Persia and Greece stimulated the Jews to clarify their ideas about life after death. When the OT was translated into Greek, the Greek name for the underworld, "Hades," was used to translate the Hebrew "Sheol." In the NT, Hades was carried over to become the common name for the abode of the dead.

Along with new names came new ideas. Many different notions circulated about the place of the dead. A common one appears in the pseudepigraphal 1 Enoch 22, where the dead are said to be kept in hollow places in a great mountain waiting for the final judgment. One relatively pleasant section was described as for the righteous and one full of torments for the wicked. Other writers continued the OT concept of Hades or Sheol as a place of separation from God and from happiness (Ecclus 14:12,16; 17:27,28).

During that period the Jews also began to use a new term, "Gehenna" (Hebrew "Hinnom"), the name of a valley south of Jerusalem. The valley was noted in the OT period for the abomination of child sacrifices (2 Kgs 16:3; 21:6; 23:10) and in the NT period for its smoldering garbage. Gehenna became a designation for the final place of the wicked dead, a place of fiery torment (1 Enoch 90:20–27; 2 Esd 7:70). Over against that place of punishment stood Paradise (a Persian name for a pleasure garden), a place where the righteous would enjoy blessedness.

All those concepts—Hades, Gehenna, Paradise—were molded by NT writers into forms most appropriate to the revelation of Christ.

New Testament. Although the NT uses a variety of terms for the abode of the dead, it contains surprisingly few references to it—about 35 verses in all. Those passages are concentrated in the Gospels and the Book of Revelation. The apostle Paul said a lot about heaven, but only Jesus and John said much about hell.

The word "Hades" is attributed to Jesus only once, in the parable of the rich man and Lazarus (Lk 16:23). In that parable Hades is a place of torment where the wicked go at death. The torment is described as a "flame" that afflicts a person physically despite bodily death. All comfort is refused to those in agony.

Although the wicked go to Hades as soon as they die, their ultimate destination is Gehenna, a place of fire and worms, both indicating corruption (Mt 5:22,29,30; 18:9; Mk 9:48, quoting from Is 66:24; Jas 3:6). Jesus also referred to Gehenna as "the outer darkness" where there will be "weeping and wailing and gnashing of teeth" (Mt 8:12; 22:13; 25:30). Evidently, after the final judgment the wicked are sent there at the command of Christ (Jn 5:22,27; Acts 10:42; 17:31; 2 Tm 4:1). That place of torment picks up the negative side of the OT concept of Sheol as a place of separation from God.

As a preacher of repentance, Jesus stressed the danger of Gehenna. He had much less to say about the place of the righteous when they die. Ultimately, though, the righteous would enter into "the kingdom" instead of Gehenna after the last judgment (Mt 25:34). Jesus twice indicated that the righteous enter a blessed state immediately at death. Luke 16:22 refers to the dead Lazarus as being in "Abraham's bosom," a place of comfort and peace. Luke 23:43 calls the same place Paradise in a promise that the dying thief would join Jesus there at death. Paul later added that Paradise is in fact in heaven (2 Cor 12:2,3), a fact that John also confirmed (Rv 2:7).

Paul and other writers of the NT epistles had little to say about the abode of the wicked dead. Paul spoke only in passing of "the abyss," his term for the pit of Sheol (Rom 10:7). His reference to Christ's descent to the "lower parts of the earth" (Eph 4:9) is probably only his way of saying that Christ, having died, went to the place of the dead. ("The lowest earth" was a term used by Jewish rabbis for Sheol/Hades/Gehenna.) Peter spoke of Christ's going in "spirit" after his death to some "prison" where he "preached to the spirits" (1 Pt 3:18–20). Interpretations of that passage differ. Some think that Christ entered Hades and preached to the fallen angels of Noah's day ("sons of God," Gn 6:1–4), not that he preached to imprisoned human spirits. In 2 Peter 2:4 the prison for spirits (translated "hell" in RSV) is called "Tartarus," another Greek name for the underworld.

Paul had much to say about the abode of the righteous dead. In his earliest letters he never mentioned their location, only that they would be resurrected (1 Cor 15; 1 Thes 4:13–17). After facing almost certain death himself (2 Cor 1:8–11), he began to discuss where the dead "went." To die means to be with Christ, Paul said, and thus is better than life (Phil 1:23). To be "absent from the body" is to be "at home with the Lord" (2 Cor 5:8). Paul probably meant that the righteous dead went directly to Paradise to be with Jesus (cf. 2 Cor 12:2–4, where Paul called Paradise "the third heaven"). Death has absolutely no power to separate Christians from Christ (Rom 8:38,39). Instead, it brings them into the presence of God.

The Book of Revelation contains much about the abode of the dead, especially the wicked dead. It uses two names for that place: "the abyss," the home or prison of all evil spirits, and "Hades," the name for the place of the human dead. From the abyss (or bottomless pit) come the demonic forms that torment humanity (Rv 9:1–11) and the satanic "beast," who kills the two witnesses and carries the "great prostitute" on its back (11:7; 17). There Satan himself will be imprisoned (20:2,3). Jesus described it as a place prepared for the devil and his angels (cf. Mt 25:41). The good news for Christians is that the abyss or Hades is not an autonomous realm. The Book of Reve-

lation begins with Jesus' announcement that he has the keys to Hades (1:18), and in the end he will force it to give up its dead (20:13). Until then, the key to the abyss is not in the hand of Satan, but hangs on a heavenly key ring to be distributed only to the messengers of God (9:1; 20:1). In the end, Hades, Death, and the wicked will be cast into the lake of fire (Gehenna), where they will suffer eternal torment (19:20; 20:10,14,15; 21:8).

John, the writer of the Revelation, agreed with Paul that the righteous will not share the fate of the wicked at death. Instead of going to Hades, they go to heaven. The martyrs appear under the altar, calling to God to avenge them (Rv 6:9–11). In another image innumerable Christians appear before the throne of God praising him (Rv 7:9–17). Those believers, shepherded by Christ himself, suffer no hunger, thirst, discomfort, or sorrow.

Conclusion. In summary, the abode of the dead began in the OT as an undifferentiated, hazy idea of a place of separation from life and God. Later writers came to see that instead of one place for all (Sheol), there must be two. According to Christian teaching, the wicked enter the underworld, Hades, a place of torment, where they suffer until the time of judgment; ultimately they will be cast into Gehenna, the lake of fire. Christ, however, rather than the devil, is in control of Hades as he is of the rest of creation. The righteous do not go to Hades, but go directly to Paradise ("Abraham's bosom" or heaven). There they are with Christ; faith has become sight, suffering has become blessedness, and prayer has become praise. Christians believe that death, although fearful as the "last enemy," has no torment for them. It has no power to separate them from their Lord. Rather, it brings them face to face with the One they love.

PETER H. DAVIDS

See GEHENNA; HADES; HEAVEN; HELL; INTERMEDIATE STATE; PARADISE; SHEOL.

Dead Sea. A large salt-water lake into which the River Jordan empties. Since the Greek era Western civilization has referred to this mysterious body of water as the "Dead Sea." However, the frequent OT term for this sea is the "Salt Sea" (Gn 14:3; Nm 34:3,12; Dt 3:17; Jos 3:16; 12:3; 15:2,5; 18:19), the name deriving from that most important and valuable commodity traded in antiquity. It is also designated the Sea of the Arabah (KJV "Plain"; Dt 3:17; 4:49; Jos 3:16; 12:3; 2 Kgs 14:25) and the Eastern Sea (Ez 47:18; Jl 2:20; Zec 14:8). Apocryphal, classical, and Talmudic authors make reference to the Sea of Sodom, Sea of Asphalt, and Sea of Lot. The NT makes no reference at all to the sea.

Dead Sea

Location and Description. The sea lies in the great trough of the Jordan Valley, known also as the Rift Valley. This valley forms part of the longest and deepest crack in the earth's crust, extending from the Taurus mountains in southern Turkey, through Syria, Lebanon, Palestine, the Gulf of Aqaba, the Red Sea, and East Africa to Mozambique (there called the Great African Rift Valley). The chasm measures between 2 to 15 miles wide, and in its deepest spot, along the shoreline of the Dead Sea, it plummets to about 1,300 feet below sea level, marking this as the lowest area on the earth not covered by water. The sea itself is oblong in shape, measuring approximately 53 miles from the mouth of the Jordan River in the north to the Sebkha region in the south, and some 10 miles in width, enclosed on both sides by steep, rocky cliffs. It is divided into two basins by the 8½-mile Lisan peninsula, which juts out from the eastern shore. The northern basin is larger, and at its deepest point (in the northeast sector), a water depth of about 1,300 feet has been measured by W. F. Lynch. The southern basin is flatter, and its water depth ranges between 3 and 30 feet.

The forces of nature seem to have conspired against the Dead Sea. Fed by the Jordan River, four or five perennial streams, and numerous wadis (an average daily inflow totaling some seven million tons has been computed by J. Neumann), the sea possesses no outlet for this water except evaporation. This condition, coupled with aridity (with an average annual precipitation of two to five inches) and enormous heat (with the mercury sometimes soaring as high as 125° F in the summer), quite often creates an extremely high rate of evaporation and a dense haze virtually impenetrable to human eyesight. Most of the streams that feed the Dead Sea are unusually saline, flowing through nitrous soil and sulphurous springs. At the same time, springs under the waters of the sea pump chemicals (especially bromine, magnesium, and calcium) into the sea. And along its shores are extensive sulphur deposits and petroleum springs. In the southeast corner there is a 300-foot-thick rock-salt ridge, which is only the tip of an estimated 4,500-foot salt plug stretching some five miles. Finally, the bed of the sea contains salt crystals. All these factors combine to produce a total salinity of approximately 26 percent, the average ocean salinity being only 3.5 percent. This makes the Dead Sea the earth's most saline water body, completely devoid of marine life, with an ever-increasing solidity.

Mineral Extraction. In ancient times the Dead Sea was valued for its salt and bitumen (a commodity prized for waterproofing properties, consisting of petroleum hardened by evaporation and oxidation). During the NT era the Dead Sea bitumen trade was apparently controlled by the Nabataeans, who also exported the product to Egypt for use in embalming. It has been suggested that Cleopatra's desire to govern the Dead Sea region was stimulated by her desire to regulate the bitumen trade.

The 20th century has witnessed the importance of yet another mineral in the Dead Sea: potash (an essential element in the production of chemical fertilizer). In 1932 the Palestine Potash Ltd. began extracting potash from the northern shore of the sea. In 1937 a second factory, constructed along the southern shore, began production. But the obstacles of intense heat and aridity, limited fresh water supply, and transportation inaccessibility hindered large-scale production. Then in the 1948 War of Independence, both plants were seized by Jordanian forces, and all potash operations ceased. However, in 1952, the State of Israel decided to resume potash extraction, founding the Dead Sea Works and undertaking to construct a highway from Beersheba to the Dead Sea. This undertaking has signalled both the revitalization of potash production at the sea and the foundation of numerous new towns in the Negeb, Israel's last frontier. In this context it may be stated that the Dead Sea is coming to life for the first time in its modern history.

Historical Role. The ominous desolation and barrenness of the Dead Sea apparent to the gaze of the modern onlooker is also reflected in the pages of history. The events of Genesis 19, the destruction of Sodom and Gomorrah, transpired in this vicinity. Mt Sedom, the salt plug located at the southeast corner of the sea, obviously reflects the name Sodom. The archaeologist Nelson Glueck affirms that the region surrounding Sedom was occupied by as many as 70 towns dating back to about 3000 BC. The exact nature of the destruction rained upon Sodom and Gomorrah is variously interpreted either as a volcanic eruption or as the spontaneous explosion of subsurface pockets of bitumenous soil. Karstic salt pillars, known as "Lot's wife," are a frequent phenomenon in this locality.

The howling wilderness which surrounds the sea provided a suitable refuge for the fugitive David (1 Sm 23:29–24:1ff), the contemplative company of Qumran Essenes, and the disenfranchised Jewish insurgents of the second Jewish rebellion. On the other hand, Ezekiel envisioned (47:1–12; cf. Zec 14:8) a time when even the brinish waters of the Dead Sea would be re-created afresh and the stark, lifeless character of the sea would issue forth in life.

BARRY J. BEITZEL

See PALESTINE.

594

Rolled scrolls, part of the Dead Sea Scrolls.

Dead Sea Scrolls. Collection of biblical and extrabiblical manuscripts from Qumran, an ancient Jewish religious community near the Dead Sea. The discovery of the scrolls in caves near the Dead Sea in 1947 is considered by many scholars to be the most important manuscript discovery of modern times.

Before the Qumran find, few manuscripts had been discovered in the Holy Land. The early church father Origen (third century AD) mentioned using Hebrew and Greek manuscripts that had been stored in jars in caves near Jericho. In the ninth century a patriarch of the eastern church, Timothy I, wrote a letter to Sergius, metropolitan (archbishop) of Elam, in which he too referred to a large number of Hebrew manuscripts found in a cave near Jericho. For over 1,000 years after that, however, no other significant manuscript discoveries were forthcoming from caves in that region of the Dead Sea.

Discovery of the Dead Sea Scrolls. The history of the Dead Sea manuscripts, both of their hiding and of their finding, reads like a mystery-adventure story.

Discovery by Scholars: February 1948. The modern drama of the Dead Sea Scrolls began with a telephone call on Wednesday afternoon, February 18, 1948, in the troubled city of Jerusalem. Butrus Sowmy, librarian and monk of St. Mark's Monastery in the Armenian quarter of the Old City of Jerusalem, was calling John C. Trever, acting director of the American Schools of Oriental Research (ASOR). Sowmy had been preparing a catalog of the monastery's collection of rare books. Among them he found some scrolls in ancient Hebrew which, he said, had been in the monastery for about 40 years. Could

the ASOR supply him with some information for the catalog?

The following day Sowmy and his brother brought a suitcase containing five scrolls (or parts of scrolls) wrapped in an Arabic newspaper. Pulling back the end of one of the scrolls, Trever discovered that it was written in a clear square Hebrew script. He copied several lines from that scroll, carefully examined three others, but was unable to unroll the fifth because it was too brittle. After the Syrians left, Trever told the story of the scrolls to William H. Brownlee, an ASOR fellow. Trever further noted in the lines he had copied from the first scroll the double occurrence of an unusual negative construction in Hebrew. Translating the passage with the use of a dictionary, he discovered it was from Isaiah 65:1:

> I revealed myself to those who did not ask for
> me;
> I was found by those who did not seek me.
> To a nation that did not call on my name,
> I said, "Here am I, here am I" (NIV).

The Hebrew script of the scrolls was more archaic than anything he had ever seen.

Trever then visited St. Mark's Monastery. There he was introduced to the Syrian archbishop Athanasius Samuel, who gave him permission to photograph the scrolls. Trever and Brownlee compared the style of handwriting on the scrolls with a photograph of the Nash Papyrus, a scroll inscribed with the Ten Commandments and Deuteronomy 6:4 and dated by scholars in the first or second century BC. The two ASOR scholars concluded that the script on the newly found manuscripts belonged to the same period. When ASOR director Millar Burrows returned to Jerusalem from Baghdad a few days later, he has shown the scrolls, and the three men continued their investigation. Only then did the Syrians reveal that the scrolls had been purchased the year before, in 1947, and had not been in the monastery for 40 years as first reported.

Discovery by Bedouin: Winter 1946–47. How did the Syrians come to possess the scrolls? Before that question could be answered, many fragmentary accounts had to be pieced together. Sometime during the winter of 1946–47 three Bedouin were tending their sheep and goats near a spring in the vicinity of Wadi Qumran. One of the herdsmen, throwing a rock through a small opening in the cliffs, heard the sound of the rock evidently shattering an earthenware jar inside. Another Bedouin later lowered himself into the cave and found 10 tall jars lining the walls. Three manuscripts (one of them in four pieces) stored in two of the jars were removed from the cave and offered to an antiquities dealer in Bethlehem.

The War Scroll of the Sons of Light and the Sons of Darkness, produced by the Qumran community.

Several months later the Bedouin secured five more scrolls from the cave and sold them to another dealer in Bethlehem. During Holy Week of 1947, St. Mark's Syrian Orthodox Monastery in Jerusalem was informed of the scrolls, and Metropolitan Athanasius Samuel offered to buy them. The sale was not completed, however, until July 1947, when the scrolls were bought by the monastery. They included the complete Book of Isaiah, a commentary on Habakkuk, the Genesis Apocryphon (originally thought to be the apocryphal book of Lamech, but actually an Aramaic paraphrase of Genesis), and two scrolls making up a manual of discipline of an ancient religious community.

Discovery by Other Scholars: November 1947. In November and December of the same year an Armenian antiquities dealer in Jerusalem informed E. L. Sukenik, professor of archaeology at the Hebrew University in Jerusalem, of the first three scrolls found in the cave by the Bedouin. Sukenik then secured the three scrolls and two jars from the antiquities dealer in Bethlehem. They included an incomplete scroll of Isaiah, the Hymns of Thanksgiving (containing 12 columns of original psalms), and the War Scroll. (That scroll, also known as "The War of the Children of Light and the Chil-

dren of Darkness," describes a war, actual or spiritual, of the tribes of Levi, Judah, and Benjamin against the Moabites and Edomites.)

Publication: April 1948. On April 11, 1948, the first news release appeared in newspapers around the world, followed by another news release on April 26 by Sukenik about the manuscripts he had already acquired at the Hebrew University. In 1949 Athanasius Samuel brought the five scrolls from St. Mark's Monastery to the United States, where they were exhibited in various places. Finally, on July 1, 1954, they were purchased in New York for $250,000 by Sukenik's son for the nation of Israel and sent to the Hebrew University in Jerusalem. Today they are on display in the Shrine of the Book Museum in Jerusalem.

Further Discoveries. *Wadi Qumran.* Because of the importance of the initial discovery of the Dead Sea Scrolls, both archaeologists and Bedouin continued their search for more manuscripts. Early in 1949 Lankester Harding, director of antiquities for the kingdom of Jordan, and Roland de Vaux, of the Dominican École Biblique in Jerusalem, excavated the cave (designated Cave I or 1Q) where the initial discovery was made. Several hundred caves were explored the same year. So far 11 caves in the Wadi Qumran have yielded treasures. Almost 600 manuscripts have been recovered, about 200 of which are biblical material. The fragments number between 50,000 and 60,000 pieces. About 85 percent of the fragments are leather; the other 15 percent are papyrus. The fact that most of the manuscripts are leather has contributed to the problem of their preservation.

Probably the cave next in importance to Cave I is Cave IV (4Q), which has yielded about 40,000 fragments of 400 different manuscripts, 100 of which are biblical. Every book of the OT except Esther is represented in those manuscripts.

In addition to the biblical manuscripts the discoveries have included apocryphal works such as Hebrew and Aramaic fragments of Tobit, Ecclesiasticus, and the Letter of Jeremiah. Fragments were also found of pseudepigraphal books such as 1 Enoch, the Book of Jubilees, and the Testament of Levi.

Many sectarian scrolls peculiar to the religious community that lived at Qumran were also found. They furnish historical background on the nature of pre-Christian Judaism and help fill in the gaps of intertestamental history. Manuscripts of the Zadokite Fragments, or the Damascus Document, a writing which had first come to light in Cairo, have now been found at Qumran. The Manual of Discipline was one of the scrolls found in Cave I; fragmentary manuscripts of it have also been discovered in other caves. The document

gives the group's membership requirements, plus regulations governing life in the Qumran community. The Thanksgiving Hymns include some 30 hymns, probably composed by one individual. There were also many commentaries on different books of the OT. The Habakkuk Commentary is a copy of the first two chapters of Habakkuk in Hebrew, accompanied by a verse-by-verse commentary. The commentary gives many details about an apocalyptic figure called the "Teacher of Righteousness," who is persecuted by a wicked priest.

A unique discovery was made in Cave III (3Q) in 1952. It was a scroll of copper, measuring about 8 feet long and a foot wide. Because it was so brittle, it was not opened until 1966, and then only by cutting it into strips. It contained an inventory of some 60 locations where treasures of gold, silver, and incense were hidden. Archaeologists have been unable to find any of this. Those treasures, perhaps from the Jerusalem temple, may have been stored in the cave by Zealots (a revolutionary Jewish political party) during their struggle with the Romans in AD 66–70.

During the Six-Day War in June 1967, Sukenik's son, Yigael Yadin of the Hebrew University, acquired a Qumran document called the Temple Scroll. That tightly rolled scroll measures 28 feet and is the longest scroll found so far in the Qumran area. A major portion of it is devoted to statutes of the kings and matters of defense. It also describes sacrifices, feasts, and rules of cleanliness. Almost half of the scroll gives detailed instructions for building a future temple, supposedly revealed by God to the scroll's author.

Wadi Murabba'at. In 1951 Bedouin discovered more manuscripts in caves in the Wadi Murabba'at, which extends southeast from Bethlehem toward the Dead Sea, about 11 miles south of Qumran. Four caves were excavated there in 1952 under Harding and de Vaux. They yielded biblical documents and important materials, such as letters and coins, from the time of the Second Jewish Revolt under Bar Kochba in AD 132–35. Among the biblical manuscripts was a magnificent Hebrew scroll of the Minor Prophets, dating from the second century AD.

Khirbet Mird. Another watercourse, lying between the Wadi Qumran and the Wadi Murabba'at, is the Wadi en-Nar, a continuation of the Kidron Valley extending southeast toward the Dead Sea. There about nine miles southeast of Jerusalem lie the ruins of a Christian monastery of the Byzantine period called Khirbet Mird. In 1952 the same Bedouin discovered further manuscripts having a later date than the documents found in the other valleys. The

Cave 4 at Qumran (just to the left of the center of the picture).

Khirbet Mird fragments were written in Arabic, Syriac, and Greek, and date from the fifth to the eighth centuries AD. They include Greek fragments of Mark, John, and Acts, and Syriac fragments of Matthew, Luke, Acts, and Colossians. All of the biblical fragments found there were of Christian origin, whereas those found at Qumran and Murabba'at were of Jewish origin.

Date of the Scrolls. Early conclusions about the antiquity of the first scrolls were not accepted by everyone. Some scholars were convinced that the scrolls were of medieval origin. A series of questions relate to the dating problem. When were the nonbiblical texts at Qumran composed? When were the biblical and nonbiblical manuscripts copied? When were the manuscripts deposited in the caves? Most scholars believe the manuscripts were placed in the caves by members of the Qumran community when Roman legions were besieging Jewish strongholds. That was shortly before the destruction of Jerusalem in AD 70.

Internal Evidence. Careful study of the contents of a document sometimes reveals its authorship plus the date when it was written. An example of internal evidence for dating the nonbiblical works is found in the Habakkuk Commentary. It reveals the people and events in the days of the author of the commentary, not in the days of the prophet Habakkuk. The commentator described the enemies of God's people as "the Kittim." Originally that word denoted Cyprus, but later came to mean more generally the Greek islands and the coasts of the eastern Mediterranean Sea. In Daniel 11:30 the term is used prophetically, and most scholars seem to identify the Kittim with the Romans. Thus the Habakkuk Commentary was probably written about the time of the Roman capture of Palestine under Pompey in 63 BC.

External Evidence. An important item to consider is when a manuscript was copied. Although the vast majority of manuscripts are undated, it is often possible to use paleolography, the study of ancient handwriting, to determine the date a manuscript was written. That was the method initially employed by Trever when he compared the script of the Isaiah Scroll with the Nash Papyrus. His conclusions were confirmed by William F. Albright, then the foremost American archaeologist. During the time of the Babylonian captivity, the square script became the normal style of writing in Hebrew (as well as in Aramaic, a cousin of Hebrew). The evidence of paleography clearly dates the majority of the Qumran scrolls in the period between 200 BC and AD 200.

Archaeology provides another kind of external evidence. The pottery discovered at Qumran dates from the late Hellenistic and early Roman periods (200 BC–AD 100). Earthenware articles and ornaments point to the same period. Several hundred coins were found in jars dating from the Greco-Roman period. A crack in one of the buildings is attributed to an earthquake that, according to Josephus, a first-century AD Jewish historian, occurred in 31 BC. The excavations at Khirbet Qumran indicate that the general period of occupation there was from about 135 BC to AD 68 (the year the Zealot revolt was crushed by Rome).

Finally, radiocarbon analysis has contributed to the solution of dating the finds. (Radiocarbon analysis is a method of dating material from the amount of radioactive carbon remaining in it; the process is also known as carbon-14 dating.) Applied to the linen cloth in which the scrolls were wrapped, the analysis gave a date of AD 33 plus or minus 200 years. A later test bracketed the date between 250 BC and AD 50. Although there may be questions concerning the relation of the linen wrappings to the date of the scrolls themselves, the carbon-14 test agrees with the conclusions of both paleography and archaeology. The general period in which the Dead Sea Scrolls can be safely dated is from about 150 BC to AD 68.

The Qumran Community. On the north side of the Wadi Qumran, about one mile south of Cave I, lie the ruins of a Jewish monastery known as Khirbet Qumran. The ruins had been noted by travelers for years.

Excavations at Khirbet Qumran. Preliminary investigations of Khirbet Qumran were made in 1949 by Harding and de Vaux. Systematic excavations were carried out, beginning in 1951, under the auspices of the Jordanian Archaeological Museum and the École Biblique. They uncovered the main building in the complex, concluding that it was the center of a well-organized community. An estimated 200 to 400 people lived at Qumran at one time, most of them in tents outside the buildings or in nearby caves. A large cemetery, with smaller secondary graveyards, was located to the east toward the Dead Sea. De Vaux concluded that Khirbet Qumran was the headquarters of a Jewish sect called the Essenes.

Investigations at the site have shown that it had been occupied at various times in antiquity. The earliest level of occupation dates back to the eighth and seventh centuries BC. Some have suggested that the buildings and cisterns may have been built during the reign of King Uzziah (cf. 2 Chr 26:10). Evidence of occupation of the site in the Greco-Roman period is abundant. A major settlement began shortly before 100 BC, probably in the time of Hyrcanus I (the first ruling priest of the Hasmonean dynasty, 134–104 BC), and ended with an earthquake in 31 BC. The site was probably reoccupied about the time of the death of Herod the Great (4 BC). That occupation ended when the area was captured by the Romans in AD 68. A Roman garrison remained there until about AD 90. Finally, Jewish rebels used the site in the second revolt against the Romans (under Bar Kochba in AD 132–35).

The largest building was the main assembly hall, with adjoining rooms. Pottery was found in abundance, not only for kitchen use, but also probably for housing the scrolls, which were copied in the writing room, or scriptorium. Although no manuscripts were found in the ruins of Khirbet Qumran, the pottery was similar to that in which the scrolls were found in Cave I, thus establishing a link between the ruins and the manuscripts. Low plaster tables or benches, together with ink wells dating from Roman times, were found in the scriptorium.

An interesting feature of the area was an elaborate water system, with many round and rectangular cisterns supplied with water from the mountains to the west. The cisterns were probably used for ritual purification and baptismal ceremonies of the Qumran sect. Hundreds of coins from the Greco-Roman period have also helped in dating the various layers of occupation. An oasis and spring known as 'Ain Feshka, about two miles to the south, appears to have been an agricultural outpost of Khirbet Qumran.

Identity of the Qumran Sect. The Qumran community was a sectarian group of Judaism. It originated in the second century BC, probably as a result of the imposition of Greek culture on the Jews by rulers of the Seleucid dynasty. The community repudiated the temple at Jerusalem and withdrew into the desert. "Damascus" was probably the designation of their community at Qumran. As the "community of God," the members believed they were obedient to God's will and were keeping his covenant.

The sect has been identified with various groups, including the Hasidim, Pharisees, Sadducees, Zealots, Ebionites, and others. The best identification seems to be with the Essenes, a sect mentioned by such first-century writers as Josephus, Philo, and Pliny the Elder. They described the Essenes as an ascetic group then living along the western shores of the Dead Sea. In addition to the geographical and chronological arguments in favor of that identification, a more important argument is based on similarities in beliefs and practices between the Qumran community and the Essenes. Both had a probationary period of about two years for entrance into the group, ranked the members in their community, held

their property and wealth in common, ate communal meals, practiced immersion and ritual cleansings, and were subject to the discipline and examination of overseers.

The Qumran sect was composed of both priests and laity. The council of the community consisted of 15 men: 3 priests and 12 laymen. A superintendent or examiner was over the whole group. There are some discrepancies and alleged differences between the Qumran sect and the Essenes. Unlike the Essenes the Qumran members were allowed to marry, and women were permitted entrance into the sect. Although the Essenes were pacifists, the people of Qumran were not.

Beliefs of the Qumran Sect. Like both orthodox Jews and Christians, the Qumran sect held the Scriptures in high esteem. Considering themselves God's covenant people, they separated themselves from the mainstream of Jewish life to study the Law of God and prepare the way of the Lord. As Jews they believed in the God of the OT: the Lord of creation, sovereign over all things, predestining human beings to either salvation or condemnation. Angels played an important role in their theology as spiritual creatures who would fight beside the "elect" in a final war against evil and darkness. The sect strongly emphasized knowledge and, within their basic framework of monotheism, viewed the world as evil and good, but God as the author of both.

Qumran teachings pictured humans as frail creatures of dust who were utterly sinful and who could be saved only by God's grace. Cleansing came only as one obeyed God's ordinances and the community's teachings as given by the Teacher of Righteousness. The anonymous Teacher of Righteousness described in the Habakkuk Commentary and other scrolls was not the founder of the sect, but had been raised up by God to teach the community the

The Manual of Discipline of the Qumran sect.

way of life. He had been given special insight into God's purposes, which would be accomplished in the end times. He was a priest who had received understanding from God to interpret the words of the prophets, but he was not the Messiah. The Teacher was opposed and persecuted by a "Wicked Priest." Attempts to identify the Teacher of Righteousness and the Wicked Priest with specific historical figures, as some scholars have tried to do, are purely conjectural.

The Qumran sect had a strong messianic hope. They believed that they were living in the last days before the coming of the Messiah (or Messiahs) and the final battle with wickedness. The Damascus Document used the expression "the anointed ones [messiahs] of Aaron and Israel." Many scholars see in the expression a reference to two messiahs: a superior priestly messiah (descended from Aaron) and a lesser kingly messiah (descended from Israel). Some scholars even see three messianic figures: one descended from David, a messianic king; one from Aaron, a messianic priest; and one from Moses, a messianic prophet (cf. Dt 18:18). The Teacher of Righteousness may even have had the role of the anticipated prophet. Members of the community believed in the resurrection of the dead and the immortality of the righteous. The wicked, they taught, would be punished and annihilated by fire. The righteous would enjoy God's blessings, which they regarded as essentially "this-worldly" and material.

A writing table and bench from the Qumran scriptorium.

Significance of the Dead Sea Scrolls. *Importance for OT Studies.* Before the Qumran discoveries the oldest existing Hebrew manuscripts of the OT dated from about AD 900. The oldest complete manuscript was the Firkowitsch Codex from AD 1010. The greatest importance of the Dead Sea Scrolls, therefore, lies in the discovery of biblical manuscripts dating back to only about 300 years after the close of the OT canon. That makes them 1,000 years earlier than the oldest manuscripts previously known to biblical scholars. The most frequently represented OT books are Genesis, Exodus, Deuteronomy, Psalms, and Isaiah. The oldest text is a fragment of Exodus dating from about 250 BC. The Isaiah Scroll from Cave I dates from about 100 BC.

The Dead Sea Scrolls show that the OT text has been handed down along three main lines of transmission. The first is the Masoretic text, which was preserved in the oldest Hebrew manuscripts known before the Qumran discoveries. The Masoretes, whose scholarly school flourished between AD 500 and 1000 at the city of Tiberias, standardized the traditional consonantal text by adding vowels and marginal notes (the ancient Hebrew alphabet had no vowels). Some scholars dated the origin of the consonantal Masoretic text to the editorial activities of Rabbi Akiba and his colleagues in the second century AD. The discoveries at Qumran, however, proved them wrong, by showing that the Masoretic text went back several more centuries into antiquity and had been accurately copied and transmitted. Although there are some differences in spelling and grammar between the Dead Sea Scrolls and the Masoretic text, the differences have not warranted any major changes in the substance of the OT. Yet they have helped biblical scholars gain a clearer understanding of the text.

A second line of transmission of the OT text has been the Greek translation of the Hebrew OT known as the Septuagint. The majority of OT quotations in the NT are from the Septuagint. That translation was made about 250 BC and ranks second in importance to the Masoretic text for reconstructing an authentic OT text. Some scholars used to attribute differences between the Septuagint and the Masoretic text to imprecision, subjectivity, or laxity on the part of the Septuagint's translators. Now it seems that many of those differences resulted from the fact that the translators were following a slightly different Hebrew text. Some Hebrew texts from Qumran correspond to the Septuagint and have proved helpful in solving textual problems. Septuagint manuscripts have also been found among the Dead Sea Scrolls.

A third line of OT transmission has been in the Samaritan preservation of the Hebrew text of the Pentateuch dating from the second century BC. The copies of the Samaritan Pentateuch were written in the same script used in some of the Qumran documents. Some of the Hebrew biblical texts found at Qumran have closer affinities with the Samaritan version than with the one handed down by the Masoretic scholars. All of the manuscripts have shed new light on grammatical forms, spelling, and punctuation.

Whatever differences may have existed between the community at Qumran and the mainstream of Jews from which they separated, it is certain that both used common biblical texts. The discovery of the Dead Sea Scrolls is thus a witness to the antiquity and accurate transmission of the biblical text.

Importance for NT Studies. Continuing investigations around the Qumran area have become increasingly important for NT studies. Because Qumran was a Jewish, not a Christian community, scholars were not expecting to find NT documents there. The 1955 discovery of Cave VII (7Q), therefore, caused some surprise.

The contents of Cave VII, not made known until 1962, were unique in that they yielded only Greek fragments, whereas most of the fragments of the Dead Sea Scrolls were written in Hebrew. Of the 19 papyrus fragments found in Cave VII, only two—one from the Book of Exodus and the other from an apocryphal book known as the Letter of Jeremiah—had been deciphered and identified by 1962. The remaining 17 unidentified fragments were assumed to belong to the OT. In 1972, however, José O'Callahan, a Spanish Jesuit scholar and papyrologist from the Pontifical Biblical Institute in Rome, suggested that certain fragments found among the scrolls should be identified with various NT writings. Using the science of paleography he deciphered nine NT fragments, including four from Mark's Gospel and one each from Acts, Romans, 1 Timothy, James, and 2 Peter. The dates assigned to those fragments are in the range AD 50–100. O'Callahan's report has shaken the scholarly world. If true, it means that the fragments are the oldest NT documents so far discovered. (The earliest, before that announcement, was the John Rylands fragment of the Gospel of John, dating from about AD 130.)

One problem is how to account for the scrolls' presence in Cave VII if the Qumran community disbanded about AD 68. One possible explanation is that they were placed there by someone fleeing from the Romans during the Second Jewish Revolt (AD 132–35). There is no evidence that the NT fragments are necessarily connected with the Qumran community or its scrolls found in other caves.

Many suggestions and widely differing opinions have been offered on the relationship of the earlier Qumran discoveries to Christianity. Most scholars agree that some NT references give evidence of a background similar to that furnished by the documents from Qumran.

Because of John the Baptist's ascetic life in the wilderness (Lk 1:80; 3:2), his use of OT Scripture (Lk 3:4–6; cf. Is 40:3–5), and his rite of baptism by water, some have suggested that he was a member of the Qumran community. In spite of such comparisons, no evidence proves that John had any contact with Qumran. One clear difference is that John's baptism was a single rite, whereas the Qumran sect practiced repeated washings and baptisms.

Comparisons have been made of the Teacher of Righteousness with Jesus Christ, but more differences than similarities exist. Qumran was an ascetic, separationist, and legalistic group. Christ's teaching, on the other hand, struck at the religious formalism and hypocrisy of the religious leaders. Far from being separatist, Jesus sent his disciples into all the world to preach the gospel (Mk 16:15). No evidence from Qumran suggests that the sect regarded their Teacher of Righteousness as divine, as having redeemed humanity from their sins by his death, or as having been the Messiah who was also a priest "after the order of Melchizedek" (Heb 7:17). There is no indication of crucifixion, burial, resurrection, or ascension. Parallels can be made between the teachings of Christ and the Qumran teachings, but there are serious gaps and differences between the two.

Many parts of the NT have received new light from the Qumran discoveries. Some scholars have thought that John's Gospel owed some of its alleged dualistic language (e.g., its "light versus darkness" imagery) to Hellenistic influences; consequently they have dated the book in the second or third century AD. Now it can be shown that the same kind of language appears in 1st-century anti-Hellenistic Jewish writings. Thus John's ideas and writings can now be confidently placed in a 1st-century Palestinian Jewish background.

Some similarities also surface between the writings of the apostle Paul and the Qumran texts. They include baptism, Communion (the Lord's Supper), the concept of the "new covenant," and elements of interpretation of biblical ideas of sin, the flesh and the spirit, the sabbath, and so on. In the life of the early church, similarities to Qumran may be seen in the communal society's life, order, and discipline.

The Dead Sea Scrolls provide a new background against which one can study the NT and the beginnings of Christianity with greater understanding. They also furnish valuable material for the study of a sectarian Judaism at Qumran. Many similarities between the two may be accounted for largely by their common environment and by the fact that both drew from a common source, the OT. Yet the differences outweigh the similarities, leaving a definite chasm between Qumran and the Christian faith.   PAUL S. HAIK

See ESSENES; BIBLE, TEXTUAL CRITICISM OF THE; BIBLICAL CRITICISM, OLD TESTAMENT.

Bibliography. M. Burrows, *The Dead Sea Scrolls;* and *More Light on the Dead Sea Scrolls;* F.M. Cross, *The Ancient Library of Qumran and Modern Biblical Studies;* J. Daniélou, *The Dead Sea Scrolls and Primitive Christianity;* R. de Vaux, *Archaeology and the Dead Sea Scrolls;* J.T. Malik, *Ten Years of Discovery in the Wilderness of Judea;* H. Ringgren, *The Faith of Qumran;* G. Vermes, *The Dead Sea Scrolls in English.*

Deaf, Deafness.   Inability to hear; term used in Scripture to describe both a literal, physical inability and a figurative, spiritual defect. The spiritually deaf were those who either refused to hear the divine message or were rendered incapable because of their lack of spirituality (Ps 38:13). The prophet Isaiah forcefully addressed both types of deaf persons (the figurative in Is 42:18; 43:8; the literal in Is 29:18; 35:5). In the OT, although the condition was considered the result of God's judgment (Ex 4:11; Mi 7:16), it was wrong to curse a deaf person (Lv 19:14). In the NT the deaf were among those Jesus healed (Mt 11:5; Mk 7:32–37; Lk 7:22). An epileptic boy whom Jesus healed was afflicted with a "deaf and dumb spirit" (Mk 9:25). Such healings authenticated Jesus' role as Messiah.

See MEDICINE AND MEDICAL PRACTICE.

Death.   Cessation of life (physical death) or separation from God (spiritual death).

Old Testament View.   In the OT death was accepted as the natural end of life. The goal of an Israelite was to live a long and full life, produce many descendants, and die in peace with the children and grandchildren gathered about. The OT contains many protests against an early death (e.g., Hezekiah's, 2 Kgs 20:1–11). An early death might appear to be the result of God's judgment; hence Job saw in the possibility of an untimely death a need to vindicate his character (Jb 19:25,26). Only in Ecclesiastes 3:19,20 is outright pessi-

A restored jar from Qumran, used for storing scrolls.

mism expressed in the face of death—and that book probably shows considerable non-Hebraic influence.

Death, although a natural ending to life, was never viewed as pleasant. Death cut one off from human community as well as from the presence and service of God. God may offer comfort in the face of death (Ps 73:23–28), but he is rarely portrayed as present with the dead, and that only in later biblical literature (Ps 139:8). For that reason, suicide is rare in the OT (1 Sm 31:4,5; 2 Sm 17:23). Death was never viewed as the threshold to a better life.

The relationship of sin to death is seen in the death penalty in the Law of Moses. A serious offender was put to death. The punitive phrase "He shall be cut off" implied that although the nation went on living, the criminal was separated from it by death. The Israelites were warned that to disobey God's commandments could bring premature death as a consequence of breaking fellowship with God (Dt 30:15–20; Jer 21:8; Ez 18:21–32).

In the intertestamental period, as Jewish ideas of afterlife and resurrection developed more explicitly, so did Jewish thinking about death. Death itself, not just a premature death, came to be seen as an evil result of sin (2 Esd 3:7; Ecclus 25:24; 2 Bar 54:19). Sometimes all death is depicted as the result of the "first sin" (Adam and Eve's disobedience). In other references everyone dies as a result of his or her own sin. The first clear indication in Scripture of a resurrection of the dead and a final judgment or punishment occurs in the Book of Daniel (Dn 12:2), one of the last OT books to be written. That teaching is echoed throughout the intertestamental period (2 Esd 7:31–44). During that time it was believed that the soul survived death either in some immortal form (Wis of Sol 3:4; 4:1; 4 Mc 16:13; 17:12) or awaiting the resurrection (1 Enoch 102). Some of those extrabiblical writings incorporated Greek ideas that the body was a burden to be gotten rid of, a notion foreign to Hebrew thought.

The concept of resurrection and a life redeemed from death, however, set the stage for the NT revelation focusing on Christ's resurrection and his conquest of death.

New Testament View. In the NT death is seen more as a theological problem than as a personal event. Death goes beyond the simple ending of physical life, which the authors accept almost without difficulty. Death is seen as affecting every part of a person's life. God alone is immortal, the source of all life in the world (Rom 4:17; 1 Tm 6:16). Only as human beings are properly related to God's life can they live. But it has been unnatural for people

to be in personal communion with the divine source of life since sin was introduced into the world (Rom 5:12,17,18; 1 Cor 15:22). When Adam separated himself from God, that separation brought death. Each human being has followed in Adam's footsteps (Rom 3:23; 5:12), bringing death for everyone as the absolutely necessary result (Rom 6:23; Heb 9:27). Death, then, is not merely something that happens to people at the end of their lives; it is also the living out of their lives apart from fellowship with God.

The extent of death's domination is vast. It affects every aspect of culture. All of human life is lived under the shadow of the fear of death (Rom 8:15; Heb 2:15). Death reigns over all that is "of the flesh" (Rom 8:6). Anyone not living in relationship to Christ lives in a state of death (Jn 3:16–18; 1 Jn 5:12). The devil, who rules the world, is the lord of death (Heb 2:14). Death is sometimes personified as a demonic power at large in the world, but finally brought to bay by Christ himself, the only one who could master it (1 Cor 15:26,27; Rv 6:8; 20:13,14).

Christ died, was buried, and rose again on the third day (Rom 4:25; 1 Cor 15:3,4; 1 Thes 4:14). Through that historic event the power of death was broken. The NT in various ways expresses Christ's subjection to death in payment for sin. He "became obedient unto death" (Phil 2:8); he died as a sacrifice for the sins of all (1 Cor 5:7; 2 Cor 5:15); he descended into Hades, the place of the dead (1 Pt 3:18,19). The major point of all such passages is that he did not remain dead but defeated the devil, took the power (keys) of death, and ascended in victory (Heb 2:14,15; Rev 1:17,18). Jesus Christ worked not for his own benefit, but for those who commit themselves to him (Mk 10:45; Rom 5:6–8; 1 Thes 5:9,10). By accepting a death he did not deserve, Christ has broken the power of death for his followers.

The Christian is thus delivered from "this body of death" (Rom 7:24) by the power of Christ. Salvation comes through being "baptized into his death" (Rom 6:3,4), and "dying with Christ" to the world and the law (Rom 7:6; Gal 6:14; Col 2:20). That is, the death of Christ is counted by God as the believer's death. The rebellious world's sin (Rom 6:6) and self-idolatry (living for oneself; 2 Cor 5:14,15) become things of the past. The death of Jesus for his people is the means by which his life is given to them (2 Cor 4:10). The result is that believers are separated from the world just as they were once separated from God. From the world's point of view they are dead; Christ is their only life (Col 3:3).

The apostle John expressed it somewhat differently. Jesus came into the world to give life to the dead (Jn 5:24). That life-giving will not happen at the resurrection; it is already happening. All who commit themselves to Jesus pass immediately from death to life. Or, to put it another way, those who keep (obey) his words will never see death (Jn 8:51,52). The point is that all who are outside Christ are already dead, and those trusting in Christ are already enjoying life. The radical difference between the Christian and the non-Christian is a difference between life and death.

Naturally, the NT writers knew that Christians die; their problem was to find words to explain the difference from non-Christian death. Believers who die physically are said to be "dead in Christ" (1 Thes 4:16). Or they are not dead at all, but merely "asleep" (1 Cor 15:6,18,20,51; 1 Thes 4:13–15; cf. Jesus' words, Jn 11:11–14). Although their bodies are dead, deceased believers are not separated from Christ; that is, they are not really dead. All the powers of death and hell cannot separate believers from Christ (Rom 8:38,39). For them, death is not a loss but a gain; it brings them closer to Christ (2 Cor 5:1–10; Phil 1:20,21). What is more, believers will share in Christ's victory over physical death as well. Because he is the "first fruits" of those rising from the dead (1 Cor 15:20; Col 1:18), those "in Christ" will rise "on the last day" to be with him, whole and complete.

On the other hand, for those who do not belong to Christ there is a final, total separation from God. At the last judgment all whose names "were not written in the book of life" are consigned to a lake of fire, in the company of death itself and Hades. That final separation from God is the "second death" (Rv 20:14). Christians, however, have been saved from death (Jas 5:20; 1 Jn 3:14). The second death has no power over those who are faithful to Christ (Rev 2:11; 20:6). Instead they will live with God, in whose presence there can be no death, for he is life itself (Rv 21:4).

PETER H. DAVIDS

See DEAD, ABODE OF THE; INTERMEDIATE STATE; WRATH OF GOD.

Bibliography. O. Cullmann, *Immortality of the Soul or Resurrection of the Dead?*; O. Kaiser and E. Lohse, *Death and Life*; L. Morris, *The Wages of Sin*; K. Rahner, *On the Theology of Death.*

Death, The Second. Term used in the NT only in the Book of Revelation, to describe God's eternal judgment on sin. Originally a rabbinic expression, the second death will be experienced by those whose names are not written in the "book of life" (20:15). The second death is equated with the "lake of fire" (20:14), or the lake that burns with "fire and brimstone" (21:8 KJV), and is described as the lot of "the cowardly, the faithless, the polluted, . . . murderers, fornicators, sorcerers, idolaters, and all liars" (Rv 21:8). Those who are victorious in this life have nothing to fear from the second death (Rv 2:11).

See DEATH; ESCHATOLOGY; FALL OF MAN; LAST JUDGMENT.

A Roman sarcophagus from Jerusalem.

Death of Christ. *See* ATONEMENT; CRUCIFIXION; JESUS CHRIST, LIFE AND TEACHING OF.

Debir (Person). One of the kings of Eglon who became an ally of Adoni-zedek, the king of Jerusalem. Debir was executed by Joshua (Jos 10:22–27).

Debir (Place). 1. Canaanite city originally held by the Anakim before being conquered by the Israelites (Jos 11:21; 15:15). There are two accounts of the conquest of Debir (Jos 10:38,39; 15:13–17). One of these lists Joshua as the conqueror, and the other lists Othniel as the conqueror (by request of Caleb). It is possible that the Othniel account is simply a further elaboration of the Joshua account, or it is possible that Debir was retaken by the Canaanites and the Othniel-Caleb account tells of the subsequent recapture by the Israelites. The latter explanation, however, does not seem to accord well with the apparent finality of the Joshua account. Thus, it would seem that the former explanation is more probable.

Debir, with its pasture lands, was finally given to the priestly descendants of the Aaronites (Jos 21:15; 1 Chr 6:58). This might seem fitting since prior to its capture by the Israelites, Debir was known for its pagan temple. Debir was also known as Kiriath-sannah (KJV Kirjath-sannah), meaning "city of the scribes" (Jos 15:49), and Kiriath-sepher (KJV Kirjath-sepher), meaning "city of the books" (Jos 15:15). Its exact location is disputed among scholars, but most likely it was located near Khirbet Rabûd in the southern Judean hill country.

2. Gadite town east of the Jordan River near the Sea of Galilee (Jos 13:26). It is possibly the same site as Lo-debar (2 Sm 9:4,5; 17:27; Am 6:13), where Mephibosheth once lived before David summoned him.

3. Town on the northern border of Judah some 10 miles northeast of Jerusalem (Jos 15:7). The name may be the same as Tugret el-Debr, 8 miles northeast of Jerusalem.

Deborah. Name of two OT women. The word in Hebrew means "honeybee" (Ps 118:12; Is 7:18).

1. Rebekah's nurse (Gn 35:8). Deborah died as she was traveling to Bethel with her master Jacob's household. She was buried in a spot remembered as *Allon-bacuth* ("the oak of weeping"), indicating that she had been well loved. She was probably Rebekah's longtime companion (see Gn 24:59–61).

2. Prophetess and judge (Jgs 4,5). Deborah's position as a prophetess, indicating that her message was from God, is not unique in the Bible, but it was unusual. Other prophetesses included Miriam (Ex 15:20), Huldah (2 Kgs 22:14), and Anna (Lk 2:36). Deborah was unique in that only she is said to have "judged Israel" *before* the major event that marks her narrative (Jgs 4:4). Her husband, Lappidoth, is otherwise unknown.

Deborah, heralded as a "mother in Israel" (Jgs 5:7), remained in one location and the people came to her for guidance. Evidently over 200 years later, when the Book of Judges was compiled, a giant palm tree still marked the spot. Though residing within the boundary of Benjamin (Jgs 4:5; cf. Jos 16:2; 18:13), Deborah was probably from the tribe of Ephraim, the most prominent tribe of northern Israel. Some scholars, however, place her in the tribe of Issachar (Jgs 5:14,15). At that early time the tribes were loosely organized and did not always occupy the territory they had been allotted.

Under Deborah's inspired leadership the poorly equipped Israelites defeated the Canaanites in the plain of Esdraelon (Jgs 4:15); flooding of the Kishon River evidently interfered with the enemy's impressive chariotry (Jgs 5:21,22). The Canaanites retreated to the north, perhaps to Taanach near Megiddo (Jgs 5:19), and never reappeared as an enemy within Israel. The Song of Deborah (Jgs 5) is a poetic version of the prose narrative in Judges 4.

See JUDGES, BOOK OF; BARAK.

Debt. Something owed to another person such as goods, property, or money. In the Bible, righteous conduct is something one "owes" to God; hence, in theology, sin is described figuratively as being "in debt."

In Hebrew culture debt was usually connected with usury (the business of lending money on interest). The Hebrew verbs describing usury picture a painful situation. One word for usury means "to bite," a vivid image for the way high interest "ate up" any kind of business transaction so that borrowers never received the full value of the money. People could be ruined financially by heartless exaction of interest (2 Kgs 4:1–7). Another verb is usually translated as "increase" or "profit" (Lv 25:37), since lenders profited from others' labor. Ancient Near Eastern interest rates on produce and goods might be as much as 30 percent of the loan per year, on money as much as 20 percent. Clay tablets from Nuzi, a town in northeastern Mesopotamia, indicate interest rates of even 50 percent.

The Law of Moses. The Mosaic covenant given to Israel immediately after the exodus sought to eliminate extortionist practices from Hebrew life. Thus God's revelation had many rules and restrictions relating to debt and credit in Israel.

Protection for the Poor. Portions of the legislative sections of the Pentateuch (the first five books of the Bible) regulated the practice of lending in a way that protected the poor and secured each person's right to earn a living and support a family. Many popular Hebrew proverbs dealt with that theme. The positive thrust of the biblical laws was to ensure help for the financially needy, without interest. No personal profit was to be made at the expense of the poor (Ex 22:25; Dt 23:19,20); God was their special advocate. Thus by lending without interest, the Israelites could demonstrate their reverence for God (Lv 25:35–37).

That point was reemphasized 40 years later when Moses renewed the covenant with Israel just before their entrance into the Promised Land. God was the landlord, and his tenants were to respect his Word. God promised the Israelites that if they would lend so as to alleviate human misery, they would be unusually blessed by the Lord (Dt 15:6; 23:19,20; 28:12). Interest could be charged to a foreigner not living under the Mosaic Law, however, a situation parallel to commercial treaties prevalent in the ancient Near East.

In ancient Israel, financial ruin was frequently brought about by poor harvests. Often they were taken as an indication that the relationship between God and his people was not right (Lv 26:14,20). The wealthy were expected to help, not to add more burdens to those who suffered from poor harvests.

Violation of the Law. The law was so often violated that eventually exorbitant interest became a social plague, making the situation of debtors hopeless. Many of the fighting men who rallied around David early in his military career were "outlaws" unable to repay their loans and interest (1 Sm 22:2). The prophet Ezekiel called people to task for their failure to observe God's commands about usury (Ez 18:5–18; 22:12). When Nehemiah returned from the exile to rebuild the walls of Jerusalem, he brought charges against the government officials whose interest rates had enslaved the people (Neh 5:6–13).

The Wisdom Literature, which included Job, Proverbs, and Ecclesiastes, added that those who acquired riches by usury would not profit in the long run because God would give their profits to others who looked after the welfare of the poor (e.g., Prv 28:8). The prophet Amos gave a similar warning to corrupt merchants in Israel: "Because you trample upon the poor and take from him exactions of wheat, . . . you have planted pleasant vineyards, but you shall not drink their wine" (Am 5:11). In spite of such warnings the law was often ignored, and burdensome interest charges were laid on borrowers who were already poor.

Pledges and Surety. When it was necessary to borrow, the law provided alternatives to the unfair practice of usury. When taking out a loan, a borrower would surrender some movable property as collateral to ensure repayment. That "pledge" represented a tangible sign of the debtor's intention to repay the loan. Certain restrictions applied to such pledges. For example, a creditor could not take a widow's clothes (Dt 24:17). Tools (such as millstones) or animals (such as oxen) necessary for daily life were forbidden as pledges (Dt 24:6). Clothing absolutely essential to the borrower (to keep warm, e.g.) could be temporarily offered as a pledge, but the temporary token had to be returned before nightfall (Ex 22:26,27; Dt 24:10–13).

In drastic circumstances, where there was no collateral, a debtor could pledge a son, daughter, or slave. The value of the child's or slave's labor could then be credited against both interest and principal. An account in the Bible of a widow's two sons about to go into slavery shows how cruel the custom could be (2 Kgs 4:1–7). Pledging labor or their children's labor was the only way slaves could pay off a debt when they had to borrow.

A borrower could also have a wealthy friend assume responsibility as a cosigner on a loan and thus become the pledge or surety. The Book of Proverbs cautioned against standing surety for others, however, especially for strangers (Prv 6:1–3; 11:15; 17:18; 22:26; 27:13).

Sabbatical and Jubilee Years. Two legal provisions to curb the enslavement of people by longstanding debts were the sabbatical year and the jubilee year. The sabbatical year, or "year of release," took place every seventh year. At that time debts were cancelled and slates wiped clean (Dt 15:1–12; cf. Ex 21:2; 23:10,11; Lv 25:2–7). The law clearly forbade lenders to withhold loans to those in desperate need during a sixth year. Jewish tradition held strict injunctions against a lender trying to collect on a loan that should have been forgiven in the sabbatical year. The idea of acquitting certain debts in the seventh year after they are contracted is still seen in certain legal practices. For example, in some states a savings account inactive for seven years is considered to be abandoned and the money becomes the property of the state.

Every 50 years Israel had its year of jubilee. In that year land reverted to its original owner if it had not already been redeemed by some relative. That provision prevented the buildup of landed estates by the wealthy few while the many poor suffered in slavery (Lv 25:13–17). Although the Mosaic law could not guarantee economic utopia, it sought to curb the greediness in human nature. It also aimed at providing everyone with an equal opportunity and a fresh start every 50 years.

Debt in the New Testament. The NT shows how various cultures handled the matter of loans and debts. There were Jewish people who adhered strictly to the Mosaic law and refused to charge their fellow Jews high interest. Hellenistic and Roman legal practices, however, penetrated parts of Jewish society.

Jesus' Parables. Jesus alluded to non-Jewish economic practices in his parable of a servant who jailed a fellow slave for not repaying a loan (Mt 18:23–35). The parable illustrates the ordinary Hellenistic and Roman custom of jailing or restraining such a person as surety. That practice forced a debtor to sell his property, to ask family and friends to cover the loss, or to sell himself into slavery. The parable of the talents (Mt 25:14–28) and the parable of the pounds (Lk 19:12–24), speaking allegorically about the kingdom of God, mention earning interest on money invested with bankers.

Economic and Theological Instruction. The apostle Paul instructed Christians to "owe nothing to anyone" (Rom 13:8 NASB), which means at the very least that Christians should make good promptly on loans. On the other hand, a Christian's economic activity should be characterized by kindness toward those in need, generosity, and willingness to help (Mt 5:42; Lk 6:35).

The NT also presents a number of lessons in doctrine based on a figurative use of "debts" and "debtors." Jesus once referred to sinners (Lk 13:2) with a word literally meaning "debtors" (RSV offenders, Lk 13:4). In the Lord's Prayer "debts" is paralleled with "sins" (Mt 6:12; Lk 11:4).

Sin is seen as an enslavement (Jn 8:34), and all men and women as debtors to God. Redemption can be made only by God, who "gave his only Son" to set people free (Jn 3:16–18). The writer to the Hebrews showed that Jesus was made the "surety of a better covenant" (Heb 7:22).

The apostle Paul felt indebted to all people because of his own salvation, a debt he could pay by preaching the gospel (Rom 1:14,15). The NT teaches that all who receive the gospel are likewise in debt, and therefore should devote themselves to serving others as a way of serving God (cf. Rom 15:26,27).

LOUIS GOLDBERG

See MONEY AND BANKING.

Decalogue. Greek term meaning "ten words," referring to the Ten Commandments.

See TEN COMMANDMENTS, THE.

The theater at Sythopolis (Beth-shan), a city of the Decapolis.

Decapolis. Group of city-states where Greeks settled following Alexander the Great's conquest of the area in the fourth century BC. They were located to the southeast of the Sea of Galilee, with the exception of Scythopolis, which was west of the Jordan River. About AD 77 Pliny gave what is the earliest known list of the cities: Canatha, Damascus, Dion, Gadara, Gerasa, Hippos, Pella, Philadelphia, Rephana, and Scythopolis.

With the rise of Jewish nationalism in the second century BC, the Jewish king Alexander Jannaeus seized control of a few of these cities; they remained in the hands of Israel until they were recaptured by Pompey in 63 BC. During the lifetime of Jesus the cities of the Decapolis, which had become moderately prosperous trade centers, were consolidated into a Roman alliance against a possible Jewish uprising.

The Decapolis is mentioned three times in the NT. The first is in Matthew 4:25, where great crowds (mostly Greeks and Canaanites) followed Jesus during his early ministry. In Mark 5:20 the demoniac who was healed by Jesus went and proclaimed Jesus throughout the Decapolis region. Finally, in Mark 7:31 Jesus passed through the Decapolis region on his way from Tyre and Sidon to the Sea of Galilee.

Decision, Valley of. Place mentioned in Joel 3:14, where the Lord will judge the heathen nations gathered against Judah. It is the same as the Valley of Jehoshaphat (see Jl 3:2).

See JEHOSHAPHAT, VALLEY OF.

Decrees of God. *See* FOREORDINATION.

Dedan (Person). 1. Grandson of Cush in the list of Noah's descendants. His father was Raamah, and his brother's name was Sheba (Gn 10:7; 1 Chr 1:9).

2. Grandson of Abraham through Keturah (Gn 25:3). His father was Jokshan, his brother was Sheba, and his sons were Asshurim, Letushim, and Leummim.

Dedan (Place). Region located in the Arabian peninsula. The Dedanites were listed among those who rejoiced at the downfall of Israel during the time of the Babylonian captivity. Jeremiah and Ezekiel foretold Dedan's approaching destruction "by the sword" (Ez 25:13; 38:13; Jer 25:23; 49:8). Apparently the Dedanites were merchants who traveled by caravan and dealt in "precious clothes for chariots" (Is 21:13; Ez 27:20 KJV). Some scholars interpret the "precious clothes" as simply being saddlecloths and various garments associated with riding. Dedan is believed to have been located at or near an oasis called El-'ula in the central portion of the Arabian peninsula. This oasis was part of the ancient trade routes, and undoubtedly played a role in the Dedanites' mercantile way of life.

Dedication, Feast of. Designation by the apostle John for the feast of lights, or Hanukkah (Jn 10:22). The feast lasts eight days and begins on the 25th day of Kislev (November to December).

See FEASTS AND FESTIVALS OF ISRAEL.

Deer. Hoofed, cud-chewing mammal, considered clean by the Law.

See ANIMALS.

Defile. To make ethically or ritually unclean.

See CLEANNESS AND UNCLEANNESS, REGULATIONS CONCERNING.

Deformity. Any obvious physical abnormality. In the OT sacrificial system both the animal to be sacrificed (Lv 1:3; 4:3) and the priest who performed the sacrifice (Lv 21) had to be perfect physical specimens, without defect or blemish. By being perfect, they are both OT types of Christ.

Of the 11 defects that would exclude a man from becoming a priest (Lv 21:17–20), 7 are in the musculoskeletal system, 2 are in the eye, 1 is of the skin, and 1 is in the reproductive system.

The deformity of the "flat nose" (KJV) or "disfigurement" (NIV) in Leviticus 21:18 does not refer to a normal variant, but to a severely diseased nose. There are a large number of genetic syndromes and inherited diseases that feature very deformed noses. Likewise, the acquired infectious diseases of syphilis, tuberculosis, and leprosy can cause destruction of the bone and cartilage support of the nose. With the support gone, the skin of the nose sinks inward. This is referred to today as a "saddle-shaped" deformity of the nose. The individual with a serious nasal deformity would not have the sense of smell that may have been necessary for a priest to perform his duties properly. The Babylonian Talmud numbers at least 11 ingredients in the incense used in the sanctuary. In Babylon, Assyria, and Egypt prisoners of war and some criminals were sometimes mutilated by having their noses cut off (cf. Ez 23:25).

Both the OT and the NT describe an instance where a man has a defect of a "withered" (KJV) or "shriveled" (NIV) arm or hand. Such a defect occurs when the nerves supplying an extremity are damaged and the muscles atrophy. An injury from a sword striking an arm can cause this (Zech 11:17). From the NT we learn that Jesus had the power to instantly heal a man with a chronically paralyzed hand (Mt 12:10; Mk 3:1; Lk 6:6). Note that only the physician, Luke, bothers to record that the defective hand was the *right* hand. While handedness is not important to the layman, it is very important to a medical person.

See MEDICINE AND MEDICAL PRACTICE; DISEASE.

Degrees, Song of. Superscription of Psalms 120–134 (KJV).

See SONG OF ASCENTS, SONG OF DEGREES.

Dehavites. Group of people among those colonized in Samaria by the Assyrian king Ashurbanipal (Ezr 4:9 KJV). The Dehavites, whom some scholars associate with the Daoi (a Persian tribe originating near the Caspian Sea), wrote to Artaxerxes to protest the rebuilding of Jerusalem by the returning Jewish exiles. Some interpreters suggest that the word translated "Dehavites" could mean "that is," so that the phrase would read "the Susaites, that is, the Elamites" (RSV).

Dekar. KJV spelling of Deker, one of King Solomon's officials, in 1 Kings 4:9.

See BEN-DEKER.

Delaiah. 1. Son of Elioenai who traced his line of descent through Zerubbabel to David (1 Chr 3:24, KJV Dalaiah).

2. Priest in the time of David (1 Chr 24:18).

3. Head of a postexilic family that returned with Zerubbabel to Judea. The group was unable to prove true Israelite descent (Ezr 2:60; Neh 7:62).

4. Father of a 5th-century BC man named Shemaiah. Shemaiah opposed Nehemiah (Neh 6:10).

5. Counselor in the reign of Jehoiakim (609–598 BC) who urged the king not to destroy Jeremiah's scroll which Baruch had just read (Jer 36:12,25).

Delilah. Samson's mistress, who betrayed him to his Philistine enemies (Jgs 16). Because Philistia held southern Israel in vassalage at the time (c. 1070 BC), Samson was chosen by God to begin the delivery of Israel. His success prompted the five Philistine rulers to offer Delilah a bribe if she would help capture him by discovering the secret of his enormous strength.

Delilah was from the valley of Sorek, in the southeast corner of Dan's territory, only a few miles from Samson's home in Zorah. Whether she was a Philistine or an Israelite is unclear, although the large reward she accepted (5,500 pieces of silver) implies that her motivations were other than Philistine loyalty. Her unhindered contact with men probably indicates that she was a prostitute.

On her fourth attempt Delilah finally tricked Samson into revealing his secret. His strength was from God, and his long hair, which signified that he was under a Nazirite vow (see Nm 6:1–8) and thus "set apart" by God for special service (Jgs 13:5), was never to be cut. Delilah lulled him to sleep, shaved his head, and delivered him (still unsuspecting) into the hands of his enemies.

Probably no painting more brutally depicts the theme of betrayal than that of the 17th-century Dutch artist Rembrandt. Delilah is hurrying out of her room, scissors and her lover's streaming hair in hand, while Samson's captors gouge out his eyes. The Bible makes no further mention of Delilah after the betrayal.

See SAMSON.

Deliverance, Deliverer. Rescue or redemption and the agent of such a rescue. Scripture teaches that God's ultimate goal in history is to rescue people from the curse of sin, death, Satan, and hell. The OT depicts God as delivering his chosen people from Egyptian slavery, from Babylonian captivity, and from oppression at the hands of various Palestinian tribes. To Christians those deliverances foreshadow the coming of Jesus Christ as supreme deliverer.

The noun "deliverer" occurs a number of times in the OT. Three times the word refers to a human being. Othniel delivered Israel from subjugation to Cushan-rishathaim, king of Mesopotamia (Jgs 3:8–10). Ehud delivered Israel from Eglon, king of Moab (Jgs 3:15,30). Judges 18:27–29 states that "there was no deliverer" to protect Laish from conquest by Dan's tribe. Other uses of "deliverer" refer to God himself as personal deliverer of his people (2 Sm 22:2; Pss 18:2; 40:17; 70:5; 144:2). The basic OT concept of deliverer is expressed in a Hebrew word for "next of kin." A close relative was responsible to aid an individual in distress and to redeem him or her from slavery. God sent deliverance when his people were in danger, or God himself acted as deliverer, uniquely and forcefully in the exodus from Egypt (Ex 3:7,8).

In the NT, Jesus quoted a messianic passage (Is 61:1,2) as describing his own mission "to proclaim release to the captives" (Lk 4:18, KJV deliverance). The KJV also has "deliverance" instead of "release" in Hebrews 11:35, where certain "heroes of the faith" are said to have accepted torture because of their faith, "refusing to accept release." In Acts 7:35 Moses is called a "deliverer" of Israel. In Romans 11:26 the apostle Paul used the term in place of "Redeemer" to paraphrase Isaiah 59:20 ("The Deliverer will come from Zion"), referring to Jesus Christ.

See MESSIAH; REDEEMER, REDEMPTION.

Deluge, The. *See* FLOOD, THE.

Demas. One of Paul's associates who was with him during one of his imprisonments. Little is known about Demas beyond the brief information given in the NT. Initially he supported Paul's ministry and was mentioned in the salutations of Paul's letters to the Colossians (4:14) and to Philemon (v 24). However, in 2 Timothy 4:10 Paul writes that Demas deserted him because of his love for the present world.

Demetrius. Name ("son of Demeter") of five persons in biblical times: three Syrian kings and two NT figures.

1. Successor to Antiochus V Eupator. Demetrius I was king (160–151 BC) when the Jewish uprising led by Judas Maccabeus was under way. He attempted several unsuccessful campaigns against the Jews (1 Mc 7:1–10; 2 Mc 14:1–15; 15:25–28). Toward the end of his reign Demetrius was challenged by Alexander Balas and was killed in battle (1 Mc 10:46–50).

2. Son of Demetrius I. After his father's defeat and death, Demetrius II sought refuge in Crete, then challenged Alexander Balas by invading Syria with an army of foreign mercenaries. Demetrius eventually concluded a treaty with the Jews and gained the Syrian throne in 145 BC (1 Mc 11:32–37). The Jews also helped Demetrius against another rival, Trypho, until he broke his word to them (1 Mc 11:54,55). In the subsequent contest between Demetrius and Trypho, the Jews, under Jonathan's brother Simon Maccabeus, achieved independence (1 Mc 13:35–42). Demetrius was captured by Arsaces VI (Mithridates I), king of

Ephesus, one of Turkey's most important cities of antiquity. Marble streets, known as the arcadian way, lead to the Celsus Library (2nd century AD), with its elaborate facade.

Parthia, around 138 BC (1 Mc 14:1–3). He returned to the Syrian throne 10 years later and reigned briefly until his assassination (125 BC).

3. Grandson of Demetrius II. Demetrius III ruled Syria (95–88 BC) in the turbulent years of the Seleucid era. One ruling party in Israel, the Pharisees, unsuccessfully enlisted his aid in their contest with the priest-king Alexander Jannaeus.

4. Pagan silversmith in the city of Ephesus. He provoked a riot against Christian evangelists whose preaching had detrimental effects on his trade (Acts 19:23–41). The city of Ephesus was a center of the worship of Diana (Latin counterpart of Greek Artemis), the goddess of hunting. A huge temple, one of the seven wonders of the ancient world, had been erected there for her worship. Among the commercial enterprises connected with the cult of Diana was the making of religious images out of various materials, including silver.

Demetrius, speaking for the silversmiths, said that both his business and the worship of Diana were threatened by the preaching of the apostle Paul and his companions. Gathering the other silversmiths together, he denounced Paul. The meeting caused a general uproar, and a mob dragged three of Paul's companions to the amphitheater. Finally the town clerk, who was responsible to the Roman authorities for maintaining civic order, was able to quiet the mob, persuading them to take any grievances they might have to the courts.

5. Christian believer whom the apostle John commended in his third NT letter (v 12). Demetrius may have been the bearer of that letter.

See JOHN, LETTERS OF.

Demon, Demon Possession. Demons are fallen angels, divinely created supernatural beings who, under the leadership of Lucifer (Satan), rebelled against God. Demonism is the activity of demons, while demonology is the study of demons and their activity, for the purpose of knowing the tactics of the enemy (2 Cor 2:11) in order to properly exercise authority over them (Lk 10:19).

Who Demons Are. The English word "demon" is derived from the Greek *daimōn*, which essentially means "a divinity, a deity" (i.e., a false deity, a demon; cf. 1 Cor 10:20). Any deity other than the one true God is a spirit opposed to him; therefore such a spirit is an evil spirit or demon. The word "demon" does not appear in the KJV, which mistranslates *daimōn* as "*devil*." There is only one devil (Greek *diabolos*), who is known by a variety of names, titles, and epithets in the Bible. He is the prince or ruler of all the other demons, who are subject to him.

Often in the Bible the word "spirit" is used for demon, along with a descriptive or identifying phrase; for example, "evil spirit" (Acts 19:12,13), "unclean spirit" (Mt 10:1; Mk 1:23,26; Acts 5:16), "spirit of infirmity" (Lk 13:11), "dumb and deaf spirit" (Mk 9:25). Spirits may be identified by their specific role or function, such as a spirit of murder, suicide, lust, depression, fear, lying, etc., associating them with various sins or attitudes contrary to God, the kinds of things that the Bible lists under the "works of the flesh" (Gal 5:19–21).

Demons may have personal names which sometimes are strange or foreign in sound. An instance is known of a demon whose name is derived from that of the ancient Egyptian scorpion goddess (Selket, Pselchis), who appears as a protective deity on the shrine of Tutankhamen.

In the Hebrew OT there is no word for "demon." The term "evil spirit" occurs (Jgs 9:23; 1 Sm 16:14–23; 18:10; 19:9). There is reference to "a lying spirit" (1 Kgs 22:22,23; 2 Chr 18:20–22). Others are "familiar spirit" (1 Chr 10:13; 2 Chr 33:6 KJV), "spirit of confusion" (Is 19:14), "spirit of deep sleep" (Is 29:10), and "spirit of harlotry" (Hos 4:12; 5:4).

A specific powerful demon referred to by title in the OT is "the prince of the kingdom of Persia," who hindered the archangel Gabriel from coming to bring information to Daniel, so that the archangel Michael came to Gabriel's assistance (Dn 10:13).

The number of demons is unknown; it appears that it is a vast number, perhaps incalculable. From Revelation 12:4 it is inferred that one-third of the angels were led astray by Satan. This means that the hosts of heaven outnumber Satan's minions by two to one. Ephesians 6:12 suggests an order or rank of demons: "principalities," "powers," "world rulers of this present darkness," "spiritual hosts of wickedness in the heavenly places."

Demons are created beings, personal, immortal, and incapable of reconciliation with God. They have great power as compared with humans, but little power as compared with God. God has given us authority over them, so that in the name of Jesus they must obey God's people, even as they must obey the Lord himself.

What Demons Do. Angels were created to worship and praise God, to serve him, and to act as his messengers. The Bible states that they are "ministering spirits sent forth to serve, for the sake of those who are to obtain salvation" (Heb 1:14). The fallen angels have a similar function, but a different master. Their allegiance is to the devil, whom they serve out of fear and delusion. They desire to work with human beings, but their purpose is to carry out the schemes of Satan and to oppose God. They tempt, deceive, and delude people so as to bring them to eternal damnation. In opposing God they attack, oppress, hinder, and accuse the people of God.

Since Satan is not omnipresent, he uses his demonic hosts to execute his will; for example, in the parable of the sower (Mt 13:3–9; Mk 4:1–20; Lk 8:4–15) they snatch away the Word before it can take root (Mk 4:15). By persecution Satan causes some to fall away before they have made a genuine commitment (Mk 4:17). By "the cares of the world, and the delight in riches, and the desire for other things," he chokes the Word, so that little or no fruit is produced (Mk 4:19).

How Demons Operate. Basically, demons operate according to the pattern set by Satan in his threefold approach with Eve: (1) they deny the truth of the Word of God and challenge its statements; (2) they deny the reality of death (typically they substitute something like reincarnation); and (3) they appeal to human vanity and pride by telling men and women that they can become like God or be gods (Gn 3:1–5). These also are the basic methods and teachings underlying most cults and false religions.

Demons work by lying, deceit, and oppression, and when the opportunity arises they enter the body of a person (Lk 8:30; 22:3), in order to control the individual's thoughts and actions. Sometimes a distinction is made between demonic oppression and demonic possession; this supposedly differentiates an attack from without and control from within. Although a non-Christian may be said to be "possessed" by a demon, the Christian cannot be so possessed, for he belongs to Christ and his human spirit has been sealed by the Holy Spirit (Eph 1:13). Demonic spirits somehow know and acknowledge this seal.

The term "possession" is misleading and is not the best translation for the Greek word *daimonidzomai*, which literally means "to be demonized" and can often best be translated as "to have a demon."

Demons can also enter the bodies of animals, as in the case of the swine in Mark 5:13. Demons are associated with books of magic (Acts 19:19), idols (1 Cor 10:19–21), fetishes, and amulets. Demons often cause illness or physical disability; Luke 13:11 tells of a woman who had a "spirit of infirmity" for 38 years but was delivered and healed by Jesus. Since evil spirits often attack the mind and the emotions, many symptoms of mental illness may be attributed to their activity. The boy whom Jesus delivered just after the transfiguration exhibited symptoms of epilepsy. Paranoia may be the work of a spirit of fear. Some individuals suffering from schizophrenia (split or multiple personality) may in reality be demonized by a number of spirits. It is possible for a person to have many demons. Jesus cast seven of them out of Mary Magdalene (Lk 8:2). The spirit in the Gerasene demoniac gave his name as Legion, "for we are many" (Mk 5:9; Lk 8:30); in the time of Augustus a Roman legion consisted of 6000 foot soldiers, usually accompanied by an equal number of auxiliary troops.

A "familiar spirit" is a demon who masquerades as the spirit of a person who is dead. (There is no such thing as a "ghost." The spirits of the dead are confined to their places [Lk 16:26] and are not able to come or go. In the case of Samuel [1 Sm 28:8–25], God sent him to convey a message to Saul. The medium of Endor did not call him up, nor could she have done so.)

Demonization occurs in various ways. Some people are demonized by a hereditary curse, which may continue to the third or fourth generation (Ex 20:5). The curse against illegitimacy was particularly strong, for the bastard could not enter the congregation of Israel until the tenth generation (Dt 23:2). Curses may also be placed upon someone by spells, incantations, or similar practices such as voodoo or other forms of witchcraft. Galatians 3:13 speaks of redemption from the curse of the law through Christ's having become a curse for us. Usually believers are immune from curses made against them, unless they have given grounds to the devil (Eph 4:27). Such grounds may be provided through drugs, illicit sex, the occult, or any other avenue forbidden in the Bible. Involvement with tarot cards, horoscopes, or any other form of fortune-telling may give demons opportunity to enter. Such contacts may seem innocuous, but Satan utilizes the smallest foothold to gain advantage over people.

Manifestation. Often demons prefer to hide rather than to make their presence known, for then they can exercise control without hindrance. When they do manifest, often when challenged, all sorts of strange and frightening things may occur. They possess supernatural powers (cf. Rv 16:14) which they exhibit outright or through their victims. The Gerasene demoniac had superhuman physical strength, so that he could not be bound with fetters or chains (Mk 5:4,5); he lived in tombs and went about night and day screaming and injuring himself with stones.

The spirit in the demonized boy in Mark 9 rendered him dumb and deaf, threw him on the ground, and caused him to roll about and to foam at the mouth (vv 18,20). The demon caused him to grind his teeth and become rigid; he had tried to kill the boy by throwing him into the fire and into the water on various occasions (vv 18,22). Before leaving at the command of Jesus, the demon cried out (cf. Mk 1:26), convulsed the boy terribly, and left him lying like a corpse. Jesus took him by the hand and raised him up (v 27). Similar manifestations take place today.

Exorcism. Casting out demons, or exorcism, was a regular and frequent part of the ministry of Jesus, and he taught and commanded his followers to do the same. This command has never been abrogated, and the ministry of deliverance should be even more important today, when the forces of evil are so rampant. The following principles are derived from the practice of Jesus, the Scriptures, and personal observation and involvement.

(1) Jesus spoke to demons and commanded them to come out (Mk 1:25; 9:25). He cast them out "with a word" (Mt 8:16). Jesus gave his followers authority to use his name in casting them out and used this as a sign of the believer (Mk 16:17). His name is not a magical formula, and its use depends on the relationship between the Lord and the person using his name, as the sons of Sceva found out to their dismay (Acts 19:11–18).

(2) Jesus cast out demons by "the Spirit of God" (Mt 12:28). "God anointed Jesus of Nazareth with the Holy Spirit and with power"; Jesus healed all who were oppressed by the devil, "for God was with him" (Acts 10:38).

(3) The Lord gave clear teaching about "the binding of the strong man" in deliverance (Mt 12:29; Mk 3:27) and about binding and loosing (Mt 18:18).

(4) Prayer is an important weapon in spiritual warfare. When the disciples asked (Mk 9:28) why they could not cast out a demon, Jesus replied that this kind comes out only with prayer. Other ancient manuscripts add "with fasting." Fasting is often coupled with prayer in waiting upon God.

(5) Revelation 12:11 testifies to the power of "the blood of the Lamb" in overcoming Satan. Demons do not like to hear of the blood of

Jesus and often become agitated at the mention of it.

(6) The same verse speaks of the effectiveness of the testimony of the saints in defeating the devil. He does not like to be reminded of his failures and shrinks from hearing praise to the Lord.

(7) God has equipped the believer with armor for defense in spiritual battle (Eph 6:10–17).

(8) The Lord answered Satan with correctly applied texts from the Bible. We have been given the sword of the Spirit, the Word of God (Eph 6:17; Heb 4:12), as a means of defense and for attack against the enemy.

(9) Followers of Jesus must use the spiritual gifts in spiritual warfare (1 Cor 12–14). These are divine enablements for combating powers far superior to our human capabilities.

(10) We must come against the hosts of hell from our position "in the heavenly places" (Eph 2:6), not from our limited earthly station.

(11) We must recognize that the ultimate victory has already been won by Jesus, who came to destroy the works of the devil (1 Jn 3:8) and to destroy him who has the power of death (Heb 2:14–16). When Jesus cried out on the cross, "It is finished," he meant that the redemptive work was done; and when he arose from the dead, he demonstrated his power over death. We win only as we enter into his victory.

The Final Destiny of Demons. It is written concerning the angels who sinned that God "cast them into hell and committed them to pits of nether gloom to be kept until the judgment" (2 Pt 2:4). The Lord spoke of "the eternal fire prepared for the devil and his angels," into which the cursed among humans are also to go (Mt 25:41). Eventually Satan and his host will be thrown into the lake of fire (Rv 20:10), which is also the place of eternal torment for all whose names are not written in the book of life (Rv 20:12–15).

Carl E. DeVries

See SATAN; ANGEL.

Bibliography. E. Langton, *Essentials of Demonology* and *Good and Evil Spirits;* S.V. McCausland, *By the Finger of God;* H. Schlier, *Principalities and Powers in the NT;* M. Unger, *Biblical Demonology* and *Demons in the World Today.*

Demythologization. Hermeneutical program proposed and followed by the German NT theologian Rudolf Bultmann. Speaking to a pastors' conference in 1941, Bultmann challenged the theological world to take up the task of freeing the NT message from the mythological worldview of the first century. Similar challenges had been issued by others before; but Bultmann's call, especially in its developed form, was unique in several crucial respects.

Prior proposals for "demythologizing" regarded myth as the product of a discredited, prescientific way of thinking, which simply required elimination. Applied to the NT, this "demythologizing" was essentially a surgical, rather than a hermeneutical, procedure: everything unacceptable to rational, Enlightenment man was cut away in hopes of salvaging a residue of religious or ethical principles. It was understood that the gospel itself, based as it was on such fantastic notions as incarnation, atonement, and resurrection, could not be salvaged.

Bultmann incorporated aspects of this earlier outlook on myth and the NT into his own program. He too regarded myth as the product of outmoded, prescientific ways of thinking and agreed that it was precisely in its formulation of the gospel that the NT betrayed its dependence on myth most clearly. But here Bultmann parted company, for he was also committed to other philosophical and theological positions not even articulated until the late 19th and 20th centuries. Influenced by the history of religions school early in his career, Bultmann rejected liberalism's reduction of Christianity to a set of tame and timeless ethical principles. Moreover, his own form critical studies led him to conclude that the only thing we really have in the NT is the preaching of the early church. Thus, if being a Christian (in any historical sense of the word) was important, the gospel could not be thrown out, no matter how myth-encrusted. For the next decade Bultmann struggled with a problem that occupied many other young scholars of the post–World War I period: how could a myth-imbued message about God's grace still speak to modern, scientific man?

Bultmann's answer to that question was shaped decisively by an even more basic, life-long commitment. This commitment gradually led him to redefine not only the question, but also the key terms, "myth" and "gospel." Bultmann inherited from his professors at the University of Marburg a peculiar amalgam of 19th-century Lutheranism and Marburg Neo-Kantianism. The brand of Neo-Kantianism that was the rage at Marburg during Bultmann's student days there posited mathematical physics and logic as the pattern for explaining all valid forms of "knowing." Knowing, they argued, was not (logically, as Kant maintained, or otherwise) dependent on sensory data, but was solely the activity of reason as it "objectifies," that is, forms objects, in accordance with universal laws. As a knower, man objectifies or creates the world but loses his individuality, since with all men he is part of a transpersonal, infinitely rational system determined by the universal laws of reason—a system that does not admit freedom and uniqueness. Individuality was not completely disinherited, however; the Neo-Kantians also posited a qualitatively distinct realm of "feeling," "immediate experience," or religion on the fringes of the realm of "objectifying knowledge." As the subject of religious experience, man, though passive, is an individual—utterly unique, free, and unbound by the claims of reason.

The Neo-Kantians abandoned this epistemological theory after World War I, but Bultmann, following the lead of his teacher Wilhelm Herrmann, clung to it as essential for understanding the doctrine of justification by faith over against works. For Bultmann all knowing (scientific, theological, etc.), inasmuch as it is essentially "objectifying in accordance with the principle of law," falls under the category of "works." It is an activity whereby man alone forms, manipulates, and systematizes the world, God, and even himself with reference to laws. Categorically opposed to knowing is religious experience, which man receives "by grace" and to which he can only respond in faith and loving obedience.

From the point of view of this peculiar epistemology the problem with NT mythology is not so much its prescientific picture of the world as its objectifying representation of the gospel. If the NT is taken at face value, the gospel is about a direct relationship between a God spatially above and man spatially below, made possible by the theoretically verifiable life, death, and bodily resurrection of a miracle-working Jew in Palestine two thousand years ago. This fantastic story is certainly nonsense to modern man, Bultmann argued, but much more importantly, it cannot be the gospel. The NT story reduces God's act in Christ to a series of past events subject to man's objectifying knowledge. Man cannot at the same time be a creator, researcher, verifier, and the recipient of grace. Even if fully verified, the NT version of the gospel could only call men to confidence in human works, not to faith in the transcendent God.

Thus for Bultmann the original problem was broken down into two: it was necessary not only to make the gospel intelligible to modern man, but also to recapture and safeguard its character as a message of grace. To solve the latter, all forms of objectifying thinking, not only myth, had to be avoided. Restating the gospel in terms compatible with a scientific picture of the world might, therefore, solve the first problem but never the second; the scientific picture, even though correct, was as much the product of man's objectifying thinking as any other understanding of the world, including the mythological. Bultmann found himself in a hermeneutical dilemma—the gospel must be restated in a form absolutely independent of any understanding of the world, yet it must speak to men whose thinking is always determined by some such understanding. It was clear that a new conceptuality for understanding and communicating the gospel was needed, a conceptuality free of objectification.

The answer to Bultmann's dilemma came to him by way of the philosopher Martin Heidegger, a faculty colleague from 1923 to 1927. Heidegger was attempting to elucidate the meaning of "being" in a way that, among other things, avoided objectifying thinking. He believed he could do this by first analyzing "human being," not in order to formulate some new psychological or anthropological theory, but to disclose that mode of existence in the world which humans experience prior to any objectifying analysis or thought. Heidegger wanted to spell out our "self-understanding." Taking certain cues from Heidegger's existential analysis, Bultmann argued the gospel must also concern man's self-understanding. When the preacher preaches about God's decisive act in Christ, the hearer is challenged to make a decision between an old self-understanding based on his own ability to attain security and manipulate the world ("works") and a new self-understanding based on the revelation that there is no security except that which is received by faith in the transcendent God. The second choice made repeatedly at each point of decision leads to the "new life" of freedom.

But how could anyone be sure that Bultmann's existential gospel had anything to do with the gospel found in the NT? Bultmann appealed at this point to the work of Hans Jonas, one of Heidegger's students. Jonas applied some of Heidegger's insights to the gnostic myths of antiquity and concluded that the central purpose of those myths was not to describe the universe as it really is, but to express a gnostic self-understanding. Bultmann, in effect, generalized Jonas' findings by incorporating them into his final, comprehensive definition of myth: myth is the prescientific, objectified repository of an authentic self-understanding that can be unlocked by an existential hermeneutic. By definition, then, the gospel mythology in the NT was intended to be interpreted existentially. In fact, Bultmann claimed, within the NT itself we already find sporadic attempts at existential, deobjectifying interpretations—for example, when Paul eschews a futuristic eschatology in favor of a personal, "in Christ" understanding of the last things.

Thus, unlike earlier proposals for "demythologizing," Bultmann's program was truly a hermeneutical one. It did not aim at the immediate elimination of myth, but at the interpretation of myth prior to its elimination. Bultmann was supremely confident that the residual meaning salvaged by this hermeneutical step was the gospel—faithful to the real intent of the NT, free of myth, and intelligible to modern man.

Few have shared Bultmann's confidence, however. Insofar as greater intelligibility for modern man was one of his goals, his program must be judged a failure. Only the theological and philosophical intelligentsia has been able to understand his demythologized gospel—and this with great difficulty and debate. So if the ability to elicit widespread response and to change lives are accepted as criteria of intelligibility, the "objectified" gospel of the NT continues to bridge the hermeneutical gap far more effectively than Bultmann's version. To be sure, Bultmann's existential gospel is remarkably free of "myth," but only trivially so, since Bultmann has repeatedly reshaped the problem by redefining all the principal terms. The demythologization program is, therefore, not so much a solution to the original hermeneutical problem as it is a testament to Bultmann's consistency as a thinker. Yet even Bultmann's consistency has been questioned; some of his more radical critics have pointed out that his system logically has no place for a crucified Jewish rabbi. Bultmann's insistence on the preaching of the cross of Jesus as the only catalyst for a new self-understanding is seen by them as a last-minute capitulation to the mythology of the NT. For the evangelical this is a happy inconsistency, but one which, unfortunately, does not mitigate the crucial problem posed by Bultmann's hermeneutical program. His program (despite his appeal to Jonas) does not translate the gospel; it transforms it, and thus betrays the trust of a responsible hermeneutic. At too many crucial points Bultmann was more committed to ultimately unworkable philosophical positions than to a careful restatement of the NT message. This is not to deny the enduring value of some of Bultmann's interpretive insights (e.g., into Pauline anthropology); it is simply to recognize that his program, viewed from the perspective of his uncritical philosophical commitments, comes across as a contrived solution to a series of false problems.

STEPHEN TAYLOR

See DOCUMENTARY HYPOTHESIS; FORM CRITICISM; REDACTION CRITICISM; SOURCE CRITICISM; TRADITION CRITICISM; BIBLE, INTERPRETATION OF THE.

Bibliography. R. Bultmann, "New Testament and Mythology" and "Bultmann Replies to His Critics," in *Kerygma and Myth,* ed H.W. Bartsch, and "Religion and Culture," in *The Beginnings of Dialectic Theology,* ed J.M. Robinson; R.A.

Johnson, *The Origins of Demythologizing*; R.C. Roberts, *Rudolf Bultmann's Theology: A Critical Interpretation*; A.C. Thiselton, *The Two Horizons*.

Denarius. Roman silver coin, equivalent to one day's wage.

See COINS.

Deputy. 1. Official of superior rank whose authority is normally granted by a king (1 Kgs 22:47; Jer 51:28).

See GOVERNOR.

2. KJV translation for "proconsul," an officer appointed over provinces by the Roman senate, in Acts 13:7–12; 18:12; and 19:38.

See PROCONSUL.

Derbe. A city of Asia Minor located in the district of Lycaonia (Ac 14:6) in the province of Galatia. Derbe was the last city on Paul's first missionary journey (14:20), the first city on his second journey (16:1), and likely one city he revisited on his third journey (18:23). Gaius, one of Paul's missionary companions on his third journey, was from Derbe (20:4).

Desert. Empty waste place, often arid, sandy, and incapable of sustaining vegetable life, as for example the Negeb of southern Palestine. A desert frequently includes local areas where marginal life is possible. The most common Hebrew term for desert means "wilderness," and is perhaps related to a verb meaning "to drive," as a shepherd drives sheep to pasturage. The Greek word commonly used in the NT and in the Septuagint (ancient Greek translation of the OT) implies an unenclosed, uncultivated area where wild beasts roam (Dt 32:10; Jb 24:5). The wilderness is also sometimes a place of pasturage (Ex 3:1; Ps 65:12; Jer 23:10; Jl 2:22).

The churches of Derbe, Lystra, and Iconium were located in this general area. The Taurus mountain range dominates this section of modern Turkey.

The Bible often refers to wilderness regions (e.g., Gn 16:7; 21:20; 1 Sm 17:28; Mt 3:1; Mk 1:13; Lk 15:4). "Wilderness" is usually a place with no settled population (Nm 14:33; Dt 32:10; Jb 38:26; Prv 21:19; Jer 9:2) but is the dwelling place of wildlife: the vulture (Ps 102:6, KJV pelican), wild asses (Jb 24:5), jackals (Mal 1:3), and ostriches (Lam 4:3). The term is also used figuratively (Hos 2:3; Jer 2:31).

Another Hebrew term for desert, from a root meaning "to be arid," refers to an infertile, desolate, bare steppe (Jb 24:5; Is 33:9; Jer 51:43). The plural form of that word describes topographical features of the desert plains of Moab (Nm 22:1; 26:3,63; Dt 34:1) and of Jericho (Jos 4:13; 5:10; 2 Kgs 25:5). With the definite article, that word (the Arabah) is the plain of the Jordan Valley and of the environs of the Dead Sea. The geography of that region contains sharp contrasts; the Jordan Valley, dense with jungle-like forest sheltering wild beasts (including lions in biblical times), gives way to the steppe lands of the Dead Sea area which have always been desert. The RSV identifies "the Arabah" in certain references to desert lands (2 Sm 2:29; Ez 47:8).

Two other Hebrew terms, meaning "waste" and "ruin," refer to districts or settlements once inhabited but later devastated (Is 1:7; 5:9; 6:11; Jer 42:18; Ez 35:7). They are also used more generally for any desolate or waste place (Lv 26:31,33; Jb 3:14; Pss 9:6; 109:10; Is 5:17; 44:26; 51:3; 52:9; Jer 7:34; Ez 5:14). One of them is also used once for the wilderness of the exodus (Is 48:21). Another word meaning waste (Ps 78:40; Is 43:19,20) when prefixed with the definite article, is a proper name for Jeshimon, a tract of land west of the Dead Sea (Nm 21:20; 1 Sm 23:24; 26:1).

In the NT the noun for "wilderness" and the adjective "desert" (Mt 3:1; 24:26; Lk 5:16; Jn 6:31; Acts 8:26) come from the same Greek root.

The whole of biblical history has been interpreted as having a desert or wilderness motif. It can be seen in the realm of disobedient human experience outside the garden of Eden; in the wandering of Israel in the exodus; in the struggle between pure faith in the desert and soft, idolatrous city life. The desert is viewed as a realm of demons and death (Dt 32:17; Is 34:13,14); its demonic wildness resembles the primeval chaos of the creation (Gn 1:2; Jb 26:7). Several moving passages of Scripture deal with renewal of life in a desert valley (Ez 37), or with transformation of arid land into a productive garden (Is 41:18–20).

The desert is also a place where God is close to his people (Dt 32:10–12), both watching over them and testing their obedience (Jer 2:2; Hos 2:14,15). Finally, the desert is a place of refuge, cleansing, and consecration. The desert fathers of the early church and the hermits of the Middle Ages emulated the prophet Elijah and John the Baptist (1 Kgs 19:4–8; Mt 3:1–6). In the Gospels the desert theme of the exodus recurs in the 40 days and nights in which Jesus was tempted in the wilderness (Mk 1:13; cf. Ps 91).

See PALESTINE; NEGEB; WILDERNESS.

Desire. To long for, want, or covet; also the object so desired. The word "desire" occurs many times in the KJV. As a noun it translates 12 Hebrew words and 3 Greek words. As a verb it represents about 12 each of Hebrew and Greek verbs. Some of the original words simply mean "ask" or "seek," and are translated that way in modern versions.

Desire is a basic part of life, neither good nor bad in itself. The important moral issue is how one responds to his or her desires. It is possible to let them control one's conduct, or to control one's desires and use them to serve their God-appointed purposes.

Christians have differed on the appropriate reaction to desire. Ascetics have claimed, for example, that the desire for food and the enjoyment of eating is sinful. But Jesus' example in the Gospels shows that he enjoyed good meals—so much so that his critics called him a glutton (Lk 7:34). His first miracle in John's Gospel was performed at a wedding in Cana of Galilee, where the feasting probably went on for several days (Jn 2:1–11).

Many think that sexual desire is bad, but it is of itself no more evil than the desire for food. God created people with both desires, and they both must be kept under control, in obedience to God's Law.

How does one distinguish between good desire and bad desire? Ultimately there is one basic issue: Is a person's desire self-centered or a desire for God's will? The Bible teaches that the essence of sin is a determination to have one's own way. Although King Saul never committed the dual crimes of adultery and murder that King David did, David was honored and Saul was reproached. The reason given by the Bible is that David was "a man after [God's] heart," who wanted to do God's will (Acts 13:22). But Saul was stubborn and self-willed, and he was rejected for that reason (1 Sm 15:23).

Evil desire, therefore, is not necessarily a desire for something that one might label as wicked. It is essentially the desire to have one's own way. As such it is idolatry, putting self in place of God. Without desire, nothing is accomplished in life. But one's actions must always be in accord with God's will as it is revealed in his Word. The Bible even promises that if one takes "delight in the Lord," then God will "give you the desires of your heart" (Ps 37:4; cf. Ps 145:16,19; Prv 10:24; Mt 6:33). When God is one's greatest desire, all other desires become properly oriented and can thus mirror God's own desires for his people's well-being.

Destiny. 1. Pagan god (Meni) mentioned in connection with another pagan god (Gad); presumably a deity of good luck or fortune (Is 65:11).

See MESOPOTAMIA.

2. Foreordination of the Hebrews as God's elect people (Ex 19:5,6). In the NT eternal destiny depends upon one's relationship with Christ (Acts 17:30,31; 1 Jn 5:1–5).

See ELECT, ELECTION; FOREORDINATION.

Destroyer, The. 1. Divine agent sent to carry out a sentence of destruction. The destroyer killed Egypt's firstborn, culminating the plagues and releasing the Hebrews from slavery (Ex 12:23; cf. Heb 11:28). The apostle Paul used the term for God's judgment on the rebellious Israelites in the wilderness (1 Cor 10:10; cf. Nm 16:44–50).

2. In plural form, "destroyers" implies destruction carried out by a group of agents, whether angelic or human (Jb 33:22 KJV; Jer 22:7).

3. In a broader sense, any agent of destruction (Jb 15:21; Jer 4:7).

4. Samson was called a destroyer by his Philistine captors (Jgs 16:24 KJV).

Destruction, City of. Phrase in Isaiah 19:18 (KJV), generally taken as a reference to Heliopolis.

See HELIOPOLIS.

Deuel. Eliasaph's father. Eliasaph led the tribe of Gad during the Israelites' wilderness wanderings (Nm 1:14; 7:42,47; 10:20). In Numbers 2:14 the name is spelled Reuel in most manuscripts (KJV, RSV) and Deuel is some others, due to a confusing similarity between the Hebrew letters "d" and "r."

Deutero-Isaiah. Alleged second author of the Book of Isaiah. Since the 18th century certain Bible critics have questioned the unity of the Book of Isaiah. Late in the 19th century a theory emerged that ascribed chapters 40–66 to an unknown prophet—a deutero ("second") Isaiah presumably living among the exiles in Babylon. Some scholars have even posited the existence of a third author (Trito-Isaiah), limiting the extent of Deutero-Isaiah to chapters 40–54.

The theory was first prompted not by problems of stylistic unity but by the issue of whether OT prophets could really foretell future events, especially with Isaiah's amazing accuracy. Rationalist critics doubted that Isaiah could have possibly foretold the fall of Jerusalem, the later restoration of Palestine, and especially the name of the Persian king (Cyrus, see Is. 45:1) who would permit the Jews to return to their homeland from exile—events that did not occur and a person who was not even born until well over 100 years after the prophet had died.

Most conservative biblical scholars, however, affirm with ancient Jewish tradition the unity of the book, its single authorship, and the supernatural origin of its prophetic passages.

See ISAIAH, BOOK OF.

Deuteronomist. Name assigned by adherents of the Documentary Hypothesis of OT origins to the supposed author or compiler of an ancient document roughly corresponding to the Book of Deuteronomy. Julius Wellhausen (1844–1918), a chief exponent of the hypothesis, taught that King Josiah's religious reforms in Judah (621 BC) formed a necessary backdrop for the Deuteronomic material. Josiah's book of the law (2 Kgs 22:3–23:25) would thus be a basic part of Deuteronomy.

See DOCUMENTARY HYPOTHESIS; FORM CRITICISM.

Deuteronomy, Book of. Fifth book of the OT, and last of the Pentateuch (the five books of the Law). In it Moses restated to the people of Israel various laws and precepts of the covenant which God had revealed to them at Mt Sinai. Thus the book has become known in Greek and Latin tradition as Deuteronomy ("second law"). That name has led some to misinterpret the significance of its contents as secondary. The book makes an important contribution to God's unfolding revelation of his purpose for the nation of Israel. Moses' reminders of the wilderness wanderings and the Ten Commandments, plus his instructions for life in the Promised Land, are a vital part of the OT covenant literature.

Date and Authorship. Two basic views (with variations) on the date and authorship of Deuteronomy are advocated by modern biblical scholars. Those who consider Moses the author date the book in the 14th or 13th century BC. Others believe that it was composed by an unknown author in the 7th century BC, when Josiah was king in the southern kingdom of Judah.

The Case for a 7th-Century Date. As early as 1805 W. M. L. de Wette advocated that Deu-

teronomy was used by Josiah in his 7th-century reforms, and that it was written shortly before that. Biblical critic Julius Wellhausen adopted that view, which has been advocated by many scholars ever since S. R. Driver publicized it in his *Introduction to the Literature of the Old Testament* (1891). According to that view the book was written late but ascribed to Moses.

Many modern scholars, such as Gerhard von Rad and G. E. Wright, regard Moses as the founder of Israel's faith. They argue that whatever in Deuteronomy is from Moses was transmitted orally until about the 7th century BC. Denying that Moses actually wrote Deuteronomy, they attribute its present form to numerous writers and editors over an extended period of centuries.

The Case for Mosaic Authorship. In recent decades studies of Hittite suzerainty treaties from the 2nd millennium BC have yielded interesting comparisons between those treaty forms and the Books of Exodus and Deuteronomy. In 1954 G. Mendenhall suggested that the form of the covenant at Mt Sinai was the same literary form used by Hittites in treaties with Syrian vassal states during the 14th and 13th centuries BC. In 1960 M. G. Kline applied that idea to the Book of Deuteronomy, seeing it as a renewal of the Sinaitic covenant and outlining its structure as a literary unit reflecting the pattern of Hittite covenant forms.

The Book of Deuteronomy does contain certain parallels to Hittite vassal treaties. As a renewal treaty it appeals to the covenant of God with Israel at Mt Sinai, recorded in the Book of Exodus.

(1) The "preamble" in ancient Hittite treaties usually identified the suzerain or ruler. In Deuteronomy 1:1–5 (Ex 20:1) Moses as the speaker represents God the King of Israel. As his death approaches, Moses makes an appeal for the renewal of the covenant.

(2) In the "historical prologue" the suzerain usually cited the benefits he had bestowed on his vassal. In Deuteronomy 1:6–4:49 (Ex 20:2) Moses declares what God has done for Israel since his revelation at Mt Sinai. Moses reminds the people of Israel of God's faithfulness even when they had been unfaithful.

(3) The "stipulations" were usually stated by the suzerain in the treaty's third division. In Deuteronomy 5:1–26:19 Moses outlines the stipulations for Israel in their covenant relationship to God. The basic requirement in Deuteronomy 5:1–11:32 (Ex 20:3–17) is exclusive, wholehearted love for God. In the following chapters, Deuteronomy 12:1–26:19 (Ex 21–23; 25–31), the basic principle of exclusive love for God is applied to specific areas of cultic-cere-monial consecration (Dt 12:1–16:17), judicial

justice in government (16:18–21:23), the sanctity of God's order (22:1–25:19), and public acknowledgment of God as their Redeemer and King (26:1–19).

(4) "Covenant ratification" usually contained a provision for treaty renewal and a formula for curses and blessings. In Deuteronomy 27 provision is made for Joshua to conclude the renewal of the covenant after the Israelites occupy the land. In addition, the divine threat and promise are expressed in blessings and curses as Israel swears its oath of allegiance on the plains of Moab.

(5) "Sucession arrangements" were usually the concluding part of suzerainty-vassal treaties. In chapters 31–34 Joshua is designated as Moses' successor. The written text is deposited in the sanctuary with the song of witness and a testamentary blessing by Moses. The Book of Deuteronomy thus constitutes the documentary witness of God's covenant as it concludes with the death of Moses.

The fact that the literary structure of Deuteronomy parallels the legal forms characteristic of ancient Hittite treaties supports the traditional viewpoint that Moses is the author of Deuteronomy. When Moses is recognized as the mediator between God and Israel in the Sinaitic covenant, it is significant that the Book of Deuteronomy represents Moses' renewal of the covenant in the literary form current in the culture of his day.

Historical Setting. Moses led the Israelites from Egypt through the wilderness to the plains of Moab east of the Dead Sea. Exodus 1–19 gives an account of the enslavement of the Israelites in Egypt, the birth and preparation of Moses, his contest with the pharaoh, the miraculous deliverance out of Egypt, and the journey to Mt Sinai (also known as Mt Horeb).

In that desert area God's great revelation came to Israel through Moses (Ex 20–40; Lv 1–27; Nm 1–9). At Mt Sinai, God identified himself as the one who had delivered the Israelites. There he established an agreement by which they would be exclusively devoted to him as his holy nation. There the tabernacle was built and the priesthood established. Instructions were given for making sacrifices and offerings, and for observing feasts and seasons, so that Israel's pattern of living would show that they were God's holy people. The tribes were also organized for encampment around the tabernacle and for the march to Canaan, the Promised Land.

Numbers 10–21 is an account of 38 years the Israelites spent in the wilderness. In 11 days they marched from Mt Horeb to Kadesh-barnea, about 40 miles south of Beersheba. From there 12 spies were sent into Canaan. Their report produced a crisis in the form of a revolt against God. Subsequently Israel wandered in the wilderness for 38 years, during which those who had been at least 20 years old when they left Egypt died. The new generation moved to the plains of Moab, located east of the Dead Sea and north of the Arnon River. Numbers 20–36 tells of the conquest and occupation of the land east of the Jordan River.

The Book of Deuteronomy presents Moses' address to the new generation of Israelites. In Exodus and Numbers God frequently speaks to Moses; in Deuteronomy, Moses is speaking at God's command to the Israelites (Dt 1:1–4; 5:1; 29:1). In contrast to the preceding books, Deuteronomy has a style of exhortation in which Moses admonishes the new generation

The Dead Sea, with the mountains of Edom in the background. It was in this region that Israel camped while Moses addressed them with the contents of what is now the Book of Deuteronomy.

about their responsibility in view of the preceding generation's failures. Whatever repetition occurs in Deuteronomy is carefully selected, with the specific purpose of warning the new generation so that they will not fail to conquer and occupy Canaan. Deuteronomy is not primarily retrospective; its outlook is optimistic about the future, offering hope for fulfilling the promises God made to the Israelites in Egypt.

Importance of Deuteronomy. Deuteronomy (with Genesis, Psalms, and Isaiah) is among the most frequently quoted books in the early Christian centuries. More than 80 OT quotations in the NT are references to Deuteronomy.

Jesus focused attention on Deuteronomy when he summarized the essence of the entire OT Law and Prophets in two great commandments of love for God and neighbor (Mt 22:37; see Dt 6:5; 10:19). Jesus also quoted Deuteronomy (6:13,16; 8:3) in his temptation experience (Mt 4:4–10).

Deuteronomy unfolds the essence of what God revealed to Moses at Mt Sinai. In Deuteronomy, Moses shares with the Israelites the core of God's revelation without repeating details of sacrifices, observances, or rituals. He expounds the character of Israel's faith and nationhood. Most important is their relationship with God, Moses says, repeatedly emphasizing his concern that they faithfully maintain that relationship. An exclusive devotion to God expressed in everyday life is the key to a lifetime of blessing.

The primary need of love toward God and neighbor eventually became a basic requirement for the followers of Jesus Christ (Lk 10:25–28). The Book of Deuteronomy is thus crucially important to the Christian concern to maintain a vital relationship with God.

Deuteronomy and the Law. To designate the Book of Deuteronomy as a "second law" or a repetition of the law is misleading. Moses' emphasis is not legalistic. Details of worship and ritual are not repeated or delineated to any great extent. Although the Ten Commandments are repeated, emphasis is placed on the first commandment, explicitly requiring exclusive devotion to God. Moses is primarily concerned with Israel's relationship with God and their determination to maintain it in their own and their children's lives.

The NT reveals that a legalistic interpretation of the Mosaic revelation was held by the Jews of the 1st century AD. Such legalism developed in Judaism especially during the intertestamental era. The Judaistic legalism of NT times has in modern times been ascribed wrongly to Moses. Moses did warn of the necessity of keeping all of God's Law (Dt 28:1,58),

but in Deuteronomy his message as a whole makes it clear that he was not exclusively concerned about legalistic observance. Rather, the central theme of Deuteronomy is the unique relationship that had been established by a unique God with a unique people, the Israelites.

Content of Deuteronomy. *Brief Historical Review (1:1–4:43).* Moses is identified as the speaker, addressing the Israelites on the plains of Moab during the last year of his life. The Israelites were on the verge of entering the Promised Land of Canaan.

Moses began with a reference to Mt Sinai, scene of the greatest revelation in OT times. He focused attention on God's explicit command for them to move up to Canaan and occupy the land promised to Abraham, Isaac, and Jacob. Their rebellion brought divine judgment, so the conquest of Canaan had been delayed 38 years while an entire disobedient generation died in the wilderness.

Instructed by God not to molest the Edomites or Moabites, Moses had led the Israelites to the Moab plains north of the Arnon River. The Israelites defeated Sihon, the Amorite king of Heshbon, and Og, king of Bashan. The tribes of Reuben and Gad and half the tribe of Manasseh appropriated the territory east of the Jordan River as their land (Nm 32). On the basis of that conquest, Moses encouraged Joshua to believe that God would aid him and the Israelites in the conquest of the land of Canaan west of the Jordan River.

The Israelites should learn from the mistakes of the generation that died in the wilderness (Dt 4:1–49). They should consider the fact that the Word of God had been spoken to them. The revelation that had come to them through Moses was unique, and the most important thing was for them to revere the God who had revealed himself. The uniqueness of Israel's God among the nations that worship idols should never be forgotten.

Moses reminded the Israelites that they had entered into a contractual agreement with their unique God. That covenant was mentioned 26 more times by Moses. No nation had ever experienced anything like it. If Israel obeyed, they would enjoy God's blessing and favor.

Hortatory and Legal Application (4:44–26:19). The circumstances in which Moses addressed the Israelites are reported in a short transitional passage (4:44–49). From the slopes of Mt Pisgah (or Nebo), with Israel encamped in the valley opposite Beth-peor, where they could partially view the land already conquered, Moses made his appeal to the people before they crossed the Jordan River.

Moses' exposition of the "great commandment" is centered in the agreement made between God and Israel. He repeated the Ten Commandments as the essence of God's revelation at Sinai. As Moses explained what God expected of Israel, he elaborated the first commandment: "I am the Lord your God, who brought you out of the land of Egypt, out of the house of bondage" (5:6). Their relationship with God was of basic importance, since God's wrath will be against those who worship other gods (5:9).

Love is the key word in the relationship between God and Israel. Moses boldly asserted, "The Lord our God is one Lord; and you shall love the Lord your God with all your heart, and with all your soul, and with all your might" (6:4,5). All other commandments are significant because they bear on that relationship (as spelled out in chs 5–11).

Exclusive love and devotion to God are essential. In a relationship of wholehearted love, no idols can be recognized or tolerated. Yet Moses wanted Israel to convey its consciousness of God to future generations by many external things: signs on their hands, frontlets or "phylacteries" on their foreheads, Scripture verses on their doorposts, and so on. By precept and example they should convey to their children that they love God (6:1–25).

The Israelites should never forget that God had chosen them to be his people (7:1–26). They were to execute God's judgment on the Canaanites, who had been spared judgment since Abraham's time (Gn 15:16). Although the Israelites themselves did not merit God's love, in love and mercy he had redeemed them out of Egypt.

Moses appealed to the people to remember what God had done for them (8:1–20). To God's sustaining provisions they should respond with thankfulness, recognizing that the power to achieve anything they had done had been God's gift.

The Israelites had repeatedly failed in their faith and commitment to God (9:1–10:11). Through Moses' intercession they had been spared. It was for no merit of their own that they would enter Canaan; that was God's gracious provision for them.

Moses' appeal for a wholehearted commitment is summarized in Deuteronomy 10:12–11:32. It is necessary to display reverence, respect, love, and obedience to God (see also 6:5,13,24).

The God whom the Israelites must love sincerely and without reservation is Lord of the cosmos. He is the righteous judge who rules supreme over all nature and history. God loved their forefathers, the patriarchs. He redeemed the Israelites from Egyptian enslavement and gave them his covenant. He manifested himself in helping the orphans, widows, and strangers. He multiplied Israel to be as numerous as the stars of the heavens.

Moses gave two basic instructions to apply in daily life to maintain their relationship with God as a reality: "circumcise therefore the foreskin of your heart" (10:16); "love the sojourner" (10:19). He did not refer to physical circumcision, a sign of the covenant between God and Abraham (Gn 17). Circumcision, which was not observed during the years of wilderness wanderings, was reinstituted under Joshua after the Israelites crossed the Jordan River (Jos 5:2–9). Moses referred to "spiritual circumcision" (see Lv 26:40,41; Jer 4:4; 9:25; Rom 2:29). All things that might restrict, interfere with, or negate total devotion to God were to be cut away (circumcised) so that the Israelites would continue to love God "with all [their] heart."

"Love the sojourner" ranks second in importance to wholehearted love for God. Love for the stranger or neighbor is basic to all other human obligations (see Lv 19:9–18). Social obligations issue out of a person's relationship with God. Being recipients of God's love, the Israelites were to love others. They were to remember God's love for them when they were slaves and strangers in Egypt. God loves the stranger, the widow, and the orphan; therefore, if anyone loves God, he or she is under obligation to love other people. God is concerned about justice and righteousness; a person who professes to love God must be concerned about just treatment for other people.

The Israelites were to be known for their concern for people whose social position exposed them to exploitation and oppression. The profound humanitarian spirit of the Mosaic Law stands in unique contrast to the Babylonian Code of Hammurabi and the Assyrian and Hittite law codes of that day. In those codes human relationships reflected no vital consciousness of a love relationship with deity.

In the 1st century AD Jesus Christ came into conflict with Jewish religious leaders who had lost the essence of God's law in a maze of legalism. For Jesus, the greatest commandment was to love God; the second was to love one's neighbor. Those two commandments (which constitute the essence of the entire OT revelation) would, if kept perfectly, provide the basis for eternal life (Mt 22:37–39; Mk 12:29–31; Lk 10:27,28). Christians believe that the climax of God's revelation of love came in Jesus Christ. For them, responding to God's love means to accept Jesus Christ in wholehearted devotion, and to love one's neighbor as Jesus exemplified in his life.

In Deuteronomy 12:1–26:19 Moses gave instruction in practical living for a God-related people when they resided in the land God had promised to them. Having once survived on manna supplied directly by God, in Canaan they would enjoy the fruit and produce of the land. They would also encounter a culture permeated by Canaanite religion.

In worshiping God in their new setting they were cautioned to maintain due sanctity (12:1–14:21). They were not to worship at pagan shrines. They should bring their offerings to divinely appointed places for fellowship and rejoicing together "before the Lord." Idolatry was not to be tolerated in any form. Any prophet who deviated from the Law of Moses in advising the worship of other gods should be stoned. Exclusive devotion to God was to be daily practice.

Canaan's abundant blessings should be shared with neighbors (14:22–15:23). Tithes should be brought to the central sanctuary where Levites assisted the priests in religious ministration. Joy in sharing life's blessings and opportunities was to characterize Israel's pattern of living.

Moses prescribed three annual pilgrimages (16:1–17). The people should remember their deliverance out of Egypt by observing the feast of Passover and unleavened bread. Seven weeks later, when the grain harvest was completed, they should spend time rejoicing before the Lord in a one-day festival called the feast of weeks. When the vintage as well as the grain harvest was completed, they were to observe the feast of ingathering (or booths), a time of thanksgiving and sharing with others. Every seven years the Law was read at the feast of ingathering.

In human relations justice was to prevail among the Israelites (16:18–21:23). The book of the Law kept at the main sanctuary was their divine authority, providing God's instructions for them. The king was to have a copy of this law and govern his life in accordance with it. Prophets and priests played an important role as religious leaders in the life of Israel. Judicial authority was vested in the priests. In contrast to the brutality of other nations, humanitarian principles were to prevail in Israel's warfare. Fathers were responsible for their own family households.

In domestic and social relationships the law of love was to prevail (22:1–26:19). Many regulations governed family life. In matters of sustenance, wages, and business dealings the Israelites were admonished to be compassionate and just. Promises and warnings raised their consciousness about using the resources of land and animals entrusted to them so that their stewardship would please God.

In Deuteronomy 26:1–19 Moses instructed the Israelites in two liturgical confessions and a reaffirmation of the covenant. By acknowledging that God was the giver of all they had, and by confessing before God that they shared his gifts with others, they confirmed their covenant with God.

Alternatives: Blessings and Curses (27:1–30:20). Moses set before the Israelites the alternatives of blessings or curses. Under Joshua they were to renew the covenant publicly. At Mt Ebal a stone was to be erected for inscribing the Law and an altar constructed for offering sacrifice. The curses were to be read from Mt Ebal and the blessings from Mt Gerizim. Conditional self-curses were read regarding offenses against God and other human beings (27:15–26). Thus they acknowledged their accountability to God. Though their sins might be hidden from people, it was God to whom they were primarily and ultimately accountable. Blessings as a way of life and curses as a way of death were clearly set before the Israelites (28:1–68). Setting them in the perspective of history, Moses appealed to the new generation to take advantage of their present opportunity (29:1–29). Warning that should they fail to love God they would ultimately be subjected to dispersion, Moses admonished them to choose the way of life and good rather than the way of death and evil (30:1–20).

Transition: Moses to Joshua (31:1–34:12). When the life and ministry of Moses were nearing completion, and transfer of leadership was near (31:1–34:12), Joshua had already been designated by God as Israel's new leader. Moses assured the Israelites that God would be the same with Joshua in charge. The revelation given through Moses had been put in writing and now was committed to the priests, the custodians of the Law. Joshua, who had already distinguished himself in responsible leadership, was publicly confirmed at the door of the tabernacle (31:1–29).

The "Song of Moses" is the covenant's document of witness (32:1–47). In it Moses spoke with prophetic understanding as he recounted Israel's past experience. Reiterating the consequences of their attitude toward God, he assured the people of restoration if in the future they again failed. He encouraged them to fix their hearts on what God had revealed to them and to impress it on their children. Keeping the covenant by maintaining a wholehearted love for God would be important for all future generations as well as for those then listening to Moses.

After final brief instructions (32:48–52) Moses pronounced his blessings on the Israelites, whom he had led for 40 years (33:1–29). In his final blessing, also called the "Testament of Moses," the greatness of God and his special relationship with Israel are delineated. Israel is unique among all the nations of the world.

The Book of Deuteronomy appropriately ends with an account of the death of Moses, the greatest prophet in OT times (34:1–12).

SAMUEL J. SCHULTZ

See MOSES; ISRAEL, HISTORY OF; SHEMA, THE; DOCUMENTARY HYPOTHESIS.

Bibliography. P.C. Craigie, *The Book of Deuteronomy;* A. Harper, *The Book of Deuteronomy;* A.H. McNeile, *Deuteronomy, Its Place in Revelation;* A.C. Welch, *Deuteronomy: The Framework to the Code.*

Devil, The. *See* SATAN.

Devoted Things. Persons, animals, or objects that God forbade the children of Israel to possess (Lv 27:28,29; Nm 18:14).

See CURSE, CURSED.

Dew. Moisture condensed from warm air during a cool night, usually found as small droplets on surfaces the next morning. Dew was an important source of moisture for the people of the ancient Near East, replacing some of the moisture lost during the hot days in that region. It was important to the growth of plants and a successful harvest (Hg 1:10). In the Bible dew and rain are spoken of together as of great value (1 Kgs 17:1). During the exodus, dew was a source of sustenance (Ex 16:13–21; Nm 11:9). Figuratively "dew" was sometimes used as a symbol of blessing; for example, Isaac blessed Jacob by asking that "the dew of heaven" be given to him (Gn 27:28; cf. Dt 33:13 KJV; Mi 5:7). Dew was also a symbol of refreshment, renewal, or prosperity (Jb 29:19; Hos 14:5). A king's favor was said to be "like dew upon the grass" (Prv 19:12). Dew could represent stealth, coming silently by night (2 Sm 17:12); it also depicted circumstances that could change rapidly, since it evaporated so quickly in the morning (Hos 6:4). A passage in one of David's messianic psalms declares of the Lord that his strength will be renewed like the morning dew (Ps 110:3).

Diadem. *See* CROWN.

Diamond. Precious gem, usually colorless, consisting of crystalized carbon. In the Bible "diamond" seems to indicate hardness, rather than the actual identification, of the stone.

See MINERALS, METALS, AND PRECIOUS STONES.

Diana. Roman name for the mythological Greek goddess Artemis, daughter of Jupiter and Latona and the twin sister of Apollo. She renounced all idea of marriage, supposedly because she was appalled at the birth pains her

Diana of the Ephesians.

mother had suffered in bearing her, and remained the unattainable virgin goddess. Although goddess of the moon, Diana was more often portrayed as the huntress with two dogs beside her.

The temple of Diana at Ephesus was one of the seven wonders of the ancient world. The impressive building was supported on 100 large columns. The local legend was that there her statue fell from the sky (Acts 19:35). This may have been a reference to a meteorite. Pliny described a large stone over the doorway, which, according to tradition, had been put in place by Diana. Ceremonies and services of worship in her honor were conducted by eunuch priests.

Among the statues that have been excavated some show Diana as a multibreasted female; others show a shrine with the goddess attended by lions. Models of the temple were sold as souvenirs by the silversmiths, who were reluctant to see any slackening of this lucrative trade when Paul began his preaching in Ephesus (Acts 19:23–20:1). The discontent and agitation of the silversmiths led to the riot of the crowd, culminating in the roar "Great is Diana of the Ephesians" (Acts 19:28,34 KJV). Inscriptions in the British Museum refer to the goddess as "Artemis the Great." If the silversmiths are to be believed, she was worshiped throughout the known world. The form of worship is not known for certain, but the worship of the goddess Diana may have been associated with a fertility cult.

Diaspora of the Jews. Dispersion of Jewish people from Israel to foreign lands. *Diaspora*, a Greek noun meaning a "sowing" or "scattering," is regularly used in the Septuagint to mean "exile" (Jer 25:34; cf. Is 11:12; Ez 20:23; Zep 3:10). The word occurs twice in the NT (Jas 1:1; 1 Pt 1:1), referring to Christian Jews residing outside Palestine as a result of the several dispersions in Israel's history. Diaspora sometimes refers to the exiled people, sometimes to the place of exile.

Causes of Jewish Dispersions. Israel's dispersions were at times a result of its political or economic successes and at other times a result of its religious failures.

Voluntary Dispersion. Military, political, and commercial gains necessitated a certain amount of outward movement. Israel's ambition led to expansion. David expanded his kingdom northward to Damascus (Syria) and eastward to the Euphrates River. In order to occupy and supervise that new territory he "put garrisons in Aram of Damascus; and the Syrians became servants to David and brought tribute" (2 Sm 8:6). Solomon extended Israel's borders even farther. He "ruled over all the kingdoms from the Euphrates to the land of the Philistines and to the border of Egypt; they brought tribute and served Solomon all the days of his life" (1 Kgs 4:21). Military occupation provided bases for a series of colonial expansions and commercial ventures. After a military presence in a tributary nation was no longer necessary, political supervision generally continued.

Commerce provided a number of occasions for dispersion of the Israelites. Shipbuilders at Ezion-geber, a port at the tip of the Red Sea, produced the ships of King Solomon's merchant marine centered there. The ships sailed on three-year voyages to trading centers along the African coast and perhaps as far as India and Ceylon (1 Kgs 9:26–28). The Cilicians, Egyptians, Hittites, and Syrians bought from Solomon's traders and sold horses to them (1 Kgs 10:28,29). A hundred years later the Syrian

king Ben-hadad II bargained for his life by promising commercial rights in Damascus to King Ahab of the northern kingdom of Israel (874–853 BC). To make the most of that opportunity in a city over 100 miles from Israel's capital, a sizable colony had to be established in Damascus (1 Kgs 20:34).

Jewish merchants sometimes moved to a foreign city for a year to trade (Jas 4:13). Initially having planned to return to Israel, they might be kept in "voluntary exile" by commercial success. Distance might make the trader nostalgic, but success held him in the trade city. Periodic pilgrimages often replaced permanent return.

Forced Dispersion. Dispersion also came to the Israelites as a divine judgment, always prophesied long before the dispersion took place. When Moses forewarned Israel of exile, he delivered the Lord's promise of blessing for obedience: "I will give peace in the land, and you shall lie down, and none shall make you afraid" (Lv 26:6). But disobedience would bring destruction and dispersion. God warned, "If you will not hearken to me, and will not do all these commandments, . . . and if your soul abhors my ordinances, so that you will not do all my commandments, but break my covenant, I will do this to you" (Lv 26:14–16). Crops would fail, "sudden terror" would strike, disease would waste, wild beasts would ravage, and even enemies would be amazed at Israel's desolation. Ultimately God would disperse his people among the gentile nations (Lv 26:16–33). Forty years later, when Canaan was about to be conquered, Moses solemnly repeated the warning against religious unfaithfulness. If Israel forsook God, they would be scattered until they repented (Dt 4:27,30,31; 28:64–68; 30:1–5).

When the forcible dispersion of exile finally came, God's prophets pointed not to enemy superiority as the cause, but to God's sentence on Israel's sinfulness. Greed, oppression, dishonesty, pride, idolatry, and a catalog of other crimes against God, and especially against the poor, had called forth divine judgment (Is 3:16; 5:8; Jer 5:28; Ez 8; Am 2:7; 4:1; 8:4–6; Mi 2:2; 3:2; 6:11).

Major Diasporas. From the end of the 8th century BC onward, Jewish history was marked by several major dispersions.

Diaspora of the Northern Kingdom. After Solomon's death his kingdom broke in two. The northern kingdom of Israel sunk deeper into idolatry and immorality (2 Kgs 17:14–18). Jeroboam, the first king of the divided Israel, established a pattern of apostasy ("falling away" from faith). Epitaphs for succeeding kings regularly recorded that the deceased ruler "did not turn from the sins of Jeroboam" (2 Kgs 10:31;

13:11; 14:24; 15:9,18,24,28). Assyria conquered the northern kingdom in 722 BC and took over 27,000 Israelites into exile, as had been predicted (2 Kgs 17:23). They were settled in cities along the tributaries of the Euphrates River and in Media. Assyrians from cities around Babylon in turn colonized Israel (2 Kgs 17:6,24).

Diaspora of the Southern Kingdom. The southern kingdom of Judah suffered exile to the east in Babylonia and to the south in Egypt. The Babylonian king Nebuchadnezzar captured Judeans in several expeditions from 605 BC to the fall of Jerusalem in 586 BC. The first deportation to Babylon took Jerusalem's treasures from the temple and palace, and "all the princes, and all the mighty men of valor, ten thousand captives, and all the craftsmen and the smiths; none remained, except the poorest people of the land" (2 Kgs 24:12–14; cf. 2 Chr 36:10; Jer 52:29,30).

A year later a second expedition focused on the rebellious Jewish vassal king Zedekiah and his sons (2 Kgs 25:1,6,7; Jer 52:4–11). In the 19th year of Nebuchadnezzar's reign, Babylonia struck Judah a third time, destroyed the temple and the king's palace, and broke down the city's walls. All but the very poorest people were carried away captive (2 Kgs 25:8–21; Jer 52:12–16).

Shishak, king of Egypt, deported exiles from Judah as early as the 10th century BC. Judah lost people and also temple gold at that time (1 Kgs 14:25,26; 2 Chr 12:9). About 400 years later Johanan, a Judean, thought he could escape from Nebuchadnezzar by fleeing to Egypt. Johanan forced Jeremiah and a group of other Jews to go with him; they settled at Migdol, Tahpanhes, and Memphis. Nevertheless the Babylonians pursued them, took control of Egypt, and executed many of the Jews there (Jer 43:5–44:30). Records of property ownership and artifacts of an altar suggest that the few surviving exiles established permanent colonies in Egypt (Is 19:18,19).

Other Dispersions. The Egyptian king Ptolemy I (323–285 BC) captured many Jews and carried them off to Egypt about 300 BC. Those exiles populated Alexandria, a city thereafter noted as a center of both Greek and Jewish scholarship. Elsewhere large colonies of Jews were exported from Babylonia to Phrygia and Lydia by Antiochus III (the Great) of Syria (223–187 BC). The Romans transplanted a sizable group of Jews to Rome. The Roman general Pompey took many there as slaves in the 1st century BC.

How widely the Jews were scattered is suggested in the NT Book of Acts, where Luke listed Jerusalem's visitors: "Parthians and Medes and Elamites and residents of Mesopotamia, Judea and Cappadocia, Pontus and Asia, Phrygia and Pamphylia, Egypt and the parts of Libya belonging to Cyrene, and visitors from Rome . . . , Cretans and Arabians" (Acts 2:9–11). Those Jews of "the diaspora" were in Jerusalem to celebrate the feast of Pentecost.

Other Jewish communities were located in the Macedonian cities visited by the apostle Paul on his missionary journeys: Thessalonica, Beroea, and Corinth (Acts 17:1,10; 18:2–4). Around the middle of the 1st century AD the Roman emperor Claudius "commanded all Jews to leave Rome" (Acts 18:2). Scholarly estimates of the Jewish population in Palestine at the time of Jesus' birth range from about 4 to 6 million. The dispersion population numbered several times that of Palestine; communities with more than 1 million each flourished in Asia Minor, Mesopotamia, and Alexandria. Today, with a national homeland, far more Jews still live outside Israel than inside.

Conditions Among Diaspora Jews. Jews of "the diaspora" over the centuries have known suffering and rejection, but also prosperity and blessing.

Social Status. Although Jews often suffered discrimination in foreign lands (Dn 6:5–17; Heb 11:37,38), positions of influence and favor came to certain scattered individuals. For instance, a young Jewish woman named Esther was chosen to be queen by the Persian king Ahasuerus, also known as Xerxes I (485–465 BC), because of her beauty and wisdom. "The king loved Esther more than all the women, . . . so that he set the royal crown on her head and made her queen" (Est 2:17). She precipitated the downfall of Haman, an anti-Semitic Persian prime minister. To replace Haman she requested the elevation of her uncle Mordecai, another pious Jewish exile (Est 7:3–6; 8:2).

Later the Persian king Artaxerxes I (464–424 BC) awarded Nehemiah, a Jew, the position of cupbearer, a powerful and highly esteemed office in the Persian court (Neh 2:1–8). Daniel, another Jewish exile, rose to political power in Babylonia (Dn 1:19,20; 2:48).

Historically, dispersed Jews have made a cultural name for themselves as scientists, philosophers, musicians, and statesmen. But they have also been the persecuted victims of racial and religious hatred under kings, popes, czars, and dictators.

Jewish Unity. In spite of their scattering Jews of various diasporas retained a basic unity with Palestinian Jews through several practices. (1) The great national feasts—Passover, harvest, and tabernacles (Ex 23:12–17; Dt 16:1–17)—continued to be observed abroad. (2) The temple tax used for the temple's upkeep (Ex 30:11–16) was collected in foreign Jewish communities, even after the temple

Center medallion in the mosaic floor of the synagogue in Tiberias, showing pagan influence in Jewish religion by depicting what is probably Sol Invictus or Helios.

had been destroyed. (3) All Jews everywhere recognized the authority of the Sanhedrin (the Jewish religious council) over them.

Positive Aspects. In exile the Jews tended to abandon the idol worship that had in part alienated them from God. Their exile led them to establish synagogues as institutions for prayer and education. Alexandrian Jews translated the OT Scriptures into Greek, at that time the international language. The result, called the Septuagint, was the version often cited by NT writers.

From the Christian point of view, the network of dispersed Jewish communities had a special significance. They provided strategic bases for the spread of Christianity, which quickly broke out of those communities and into the surrounding gentile world. Thus God used the dispersions to bring the gospel to the Gentiles (Rom 1:11–15; 1 Cor 10:11,12; cf. Ps 67; 3:28,29; 4:34–37).

Finally, the arts, sciences, and humanities have been greatly enriched by the Jews scattered throughout Western culture. Few other peoples have endured so much ferocious ethnic bigotry as the Jews, yet rewarded that rejection with cultural gifts and graces of such excellence. Although the church of Jesus Christ has become a "new Israel" and the "chosen race" (1 Pt 2:9), the testimony of history and of Scripture indicates that God still has a unique interest in the Jews.

JAMES L. MASON

See ISRAEL, HISTORY OF; POSTEXILIC PERIOD, THE; JUDAISM; JEW; EXILE.

Diblah, Diblath. ASV and KJV forms of Riblah, the name of the place from which King Nebuchadnezzar directed operations against Jerusalem in 588–86 BC (Ez 6:14; cf. Jer 52:9–27).

See RIBLAH.

Diblaim. Father of Gomer, Hosea's wife (Hos 1:3). The name Diblaim is thought by some to be an allusion to Gomer's harlotry, since the name means "raisin cakes" and raisin cakes were used in ancient fertility-cult rites.

Dibon. 1. City in Moab, east of the Dead Sea and north of the Arnon River. It was located on the King's Highway in Amorite territory and was a camping station for the Israelites during the exodus (Nm 33:45). Israel asked permission of Sihon, the Amorite king, to pass through his territory, but he refused. Israel then fought and defeated Sihon, thus gaining control of Dibon. Following the Hebrew conquest of Palestine and its division among the 12 tribes, Dibon was given to Gad (Nm 32:3, 34), being also referred to as Dibon-gad (Nm 33:45,46). One biblical reference assigns it to Reuben (Jos 13:17).

During the period of the judges, Moab under King Eglon oppressed Israel and apparently retook Dibon. It was probably recovered under the leadership of Ehud (Jgs 3:12–30). Subsequently Dibon was ruled by Israel under King David (2 Sm 8:2).

In the preexilic period Dibon was again under Moabite influence (Is 15:2; Jer 48:18,22). Isaiah condemned Dibon (Dimon) as chief among the wicked cities of Moab (Is 15:9). Dimon is probably a play on words (from the root "blood") predicting Dibon's bloody and disastrous fate.

In 1868 excavations uncovered the famous Moabite Stone at Dibon, erected by Mesha, king of Moab, who built "Qarhah" as his capital. This may have been a new capital city replacing Dibon, or a renaming of Dibon by Mesha. Most likely Qarhah referred to the fact that Dibon was built on two elevations. The higher one was Qarhah, the defensive citadel of the city, surrounded by a wall and possessing a water reservoir, several cisterns, the royal palace, and a shrine ("high place," Is 15:2) to Chemosh, the principal god of Moab.

Excavations conducted in 1950–56 at Dibon (modern Dhiban) uncovered remains of the city from a period about 3000 BC. Evidence indicated that it contained only a nomadic population in the period 2100–1300 BC and that it was settled again about 1300 BC. The earliest excavations found five city walls, the oldest dating to about 3000 BC. The heaviest wall was from 7½ to almost 11 feet thick, built with large, well-squared blocks, and is considered to have been built in Mesha's time.

2. Town in the Negeb of Judah inhabited by Babylonian exiles who returned to Palestine during Nehemiah's time (Neh 11:25).

Dibon-gad. Alternate name for Dibon, a Moabite city, in Numbers 33:45,46.

See DIBON #1.

Dibri. Father of Shelomith from Dan's tribe. Shelomith married an Egyptian man, and her son by this marriage was stoned in the wilderness for blaspheming the name of God (Lv 24:10,11).

Dichotomy. *See* MAN, DOCTRINE OF.

Didrachma. Greek silver coin worth 2 drachmas and equivalent to the Jewish half-shekel. Every Jew was required to pay this amount as the annual temple tax (Mt 17:24, KJV tribute).

See COINS.

Didymus. Greek word for "twin" and another name for the apostle Thomas in John 11:16; 20:24; and 21:2.

See THOMAS, THE APOSTLE.

Dietary Laws. Regulations of food preparation and consumption provided by God for his people in OT times. The dietary laws formed part of broader regulations on "cleanliness"

which were designed to maintain Israel's status as a holy people.

The Meaning of Holiness. Biblical laws concerning diet and cleanliness were based on the idea of holiness. The underlying meaning of the Hebrew word for "holiness" is difficult to ascertain but most probably was "to cut," or "to be separate," or "to set apart." The Lord told Israel, "You shall be holy to me, for I the Lord am holy, and have separated you from the peoples, that you should be mine" (Lv 20:26). God is the supreme example of holiness; he is the one uniquely separate in his character and being (Is 6:3). But God wanted his covenant people to be holy, too. One of the ways that God made the Israelites different from the other peoples of the world was by giving them dietary laws: "I am the Lord your God; consecrate yourselves and be holy, because I am holy" (Lv 11:44 NIV). Keeping the dietary laws did not automatically make the people "holy" (i.e., separated to God); rather, it was one of the ways OT believers could show their gratitude to God for his deliverance and hence could demonstrate their faith in him.

Before Moses. From the creation, God approved all varieties of fruit and vegetables as legitimate, clean food (Gn 1:29). After the fall of humanity God distinguished between clean and unclean animals. At the time of Noah, God directed that additional specimens of clean animals be taken aboard the ark (Gn 7:2; 8:20). After the flood, God prohibited the eating of blood because blood represented life (Gn 9:4). To commemorate the patriarch Jacob's wrestling with the angel of the Lord, Jacob's descendants refrained from eating a certain hip muscle (Gn 32:32), though that was not a command from God.

The Mosaic Law. The primary revelation of the Lord's dietary standards for Israel was given through Moses. Dietary laws are found among the ceremonial regulations received at Mt Sinai (Lv 11). Moses repeated many of those laws 39 years later, shortly before the people entered the Promised Land (Dt 14:3–21). The dietary laws concerned only animal products, except for the prohibition of wine to certain people (Lv 10:9; Nm 6:3,4; cf. Jgs 13:14; Jer 35:6).

Five categories of living things were regulated for food. To be edible an animal had to have cloven (divided) hooves and had to chew its cud. That requirement ruled out camels, horses, rabbits, and pigs (Lv 11:2–8). Sea life had to have fins and scales (11:9–12). Birds were edible if they were not predatory (11:13–19); Moses went on to list 20 species specifically prohibited because they were birds of prey or scavengers. Winged insects were forbidden (11:22–23) except for certain types of locusts and grasshoppers (food commonly eaten by desert nomads). Finally, "the animals that move about on the ground," including reptiles and rodents (11:29–31 NIV), were ruled out.

Further prohibitions were made about food that otherwise would have been considered clean. For example, nothing found "already dead" (Dt 14:21 NIV) or that had been "torn by beasts" (Lv 17:15) was to be eaten. Food could become defiled by contact with some other thing that was unclean, like a dead mouse that happened to fall into a food container (Lv 11:32–34). A young goat was not to be boiled in its mother's milk (Ex 23:19; 34:26; Dt 14:21). When clean animals were slaughtered, their blood was to be drained out (Lv 17:14). All pieces of fat (Lv 3:16; 7:23), especially a sheep's fat tail (Ex 29:22; Lv 3:9), were restricted for use only in sacrifices to the Lord. Through Moses the Lord reiterated the prohibition against eating blood (Lv 17:10; 19:26; Dt 12:16; 15:23).

Several reasons, stated in or inferred from Scripture, account for the dietary laws and apply to the Bible's cleanliness regulations in general. Some seem to be natural reasons; others may be symbolic or relational.

Hygiene. Some dietary laws, such as those against eating vermin or decomposing flesh, circumvented obvious health hazards and were given for the people's protection. But hygiene alone cannot account for all the regulations; in fact, some foods that might have been acceptable from a hygienic viewpoint, such as rabbit or clams, were excluded.

Aversion. Worms and snakes are generally considered loathsome, whatever their actual food value. Such animals were not *kosher* (proper).

Relationship to Pagan Practice. Boiling a young goat in its mother's milk has now been documented as a pagan rite among Moses' contemporaries, the Canaanites. God's people were not to imitate the practices of the peoples around them (Dt 18:9).

Symbolism. Certain food products were ruled out because of something they symbolized. God said not to eat blood: "Be sure that you do not eat the blood; for the blood is the life, and you shall not eat the life with the flesh" (Dt 12:23). Blood had a ritual function. It was used to make atonement on God's altar and therefore was not to be eaten (Lv 17:11,12). The NT writers recognized the sacrificial blood of the OT as a "type" or foreshadowing of the blood of Jesus Christ shed on the cross as a sacrifice for sin (Heb 10:1,4,12; 1 Pt 1:18,19). A symbolic regard for maternal life may explain why one who came upon a bird's nest was allowed to take the eggs or the

young but had to leave the mother bird unharmed (Dt 22:6,7); the need to preserve a fragile desert ecosystem may also have been a factor.

Expression of Holiness. The basic idea of holiness is separation. God selected certain means, sometimes seemingly arbitrary, by which his people could demonstrate their devotion to him. Some of the choice parts of a sacrifice, such as the fat tail, were thus reserved for the Lord and were offered in visible dedication on the altar.

The dietary regulations were rigorous, but their simplicity provided God's people with a practical basis for maintaining good eating habits while they sojourned in a harsh environment or a strange land.

After Moses. The dietary laws given at Mt Sinai continued to be recognized throughout Israel's history. Before the birth of Samson, the child's mother was warned, "Now see to it that you drink no wine or other fermented drink and that you do not eat anything unclean" (Jgs 13:4,7 NIV). During the Philistine wars of the next century (c. 1041 BC) King Saul's soldiers sinned by disregarding requirements about the proper draining of blood from animals (1 Sm 14:32–34).

Later, when the Israelites were exiled in heathen lands, they were faced with situations in which the selection of food and its preparation could render it unclean (Ez 4:12–14). Daniel's refusal to be defiled by pagan delicacies at Nebuchadnezzar's Babylonian court (605 BC) illustrated his loyalty to God (Dn 1:8).

From the prophet Isaiah's day (740 BC) onward, the most abhorrent food to the Israelites was the meat of swine (Is 65:4; 66:3,17). In the Maccabean period the "abomination of desolation," which the Jewish hero Judas Maccabeus and his followers resisted to the death, included sacrifices of pigs on the temple altar in Jerusalem by the pagan ruler Antiochus Epiphanes (1 Mc 1:54,62,63; 2 Mc 6:5; 7:1).

Relevance Today. In principle the dietary laws that were based on hygienic reasons continue to be relevant for Christians today. A person's body deserves care: "Your body is a temple of the Holy Spirit within you, which you have from God" (1 Cor 6:19). But according to the NT the dietary laws that were based on ceremony and "typology" are no longer binding. "Therefore do not let anyone judge you by what you eat or drink, or with regard to a religious festival, a New Moon celebration or a Sabbath day" (Col 2:16,17 NIV). Jesus stressed moral cleanliness; the thoughts that come out of a person, not the food that goes in, are defiling (Mt 15:17,18; Mk 7:15). To Pharisees who criticized him for not ritually washing before eating, Jesus said, "Give that which is within as charity, and then all things are clean for you" (Lk 11:41 NASB).

Contemporary Orthodox Judaism continues to observe the kosher laws of the OT, though many of its practices are based on later traditions. For example, rules about two sets of dishes, one for meat and the other for dairy products, were developed to prevent any possible contact between meat from a young goat and its mother's milk.

At first the early church, with its Jewish background, found it difficult to break away from Hebrew dietary traditions. The apostle Peter was given a vision, repeated three times, about no longer calling either non-Jewish food or the non-Jews who ate it "unclean" (Acts 10:9–16; 11:1–10). Later, a council at Jerusalem officially decided not to retain Moses' ceremonialism in the church, except that gentile Christians should abstain "from food polluted by idols, from sexual immorality, from the meat of strangled animals and from blood" (Acts 15:20,29 NIV) in order not to offend Jewish Christians. That was an application of the NT teaching of consideration for those with sensitive consciences. "Do not destroy the work of God for the sake of food. All food is clean, but it is wrong for a man to eat anything that causes someone else to stumble.... But the man who has doubts is condemned if he eats, because his eating is not from faith; and everything that does not come from faith is sin" (Rom 14:20–23).

Jewish dietary laws also have relevance to Christians because of certain OT promises. God promised, first to Abraham and, by reiteration or allusion, throughout the OT, that the Gentiles would be included in his covenant. By preserving the health of the Hebrew people, God was ensuring their continuation as a nation. According to the NT the salvation of both Jews and Gentiles was achieved by Christ, a Jew. The nation through which Christ came was protected in order that God's promise could be fulfilled. Thus the dietary laws need not be seen as burdensome restrictions of the Law; they were part of God's way of working out his redemptive plan.

See LEVITICUS, BOOK OF; CLEANNESS AND UNCLEANNESS, REGULATIONS CONCERNING; CIVIL LAW AND JUSTICE.

Diklah. Son of Joktan in the list of nations descended from Noah's sons (Gn 10:27; 1 Chr 1:21); perhaps the name refers to an Arabian tribe or territory, living in or near a palm-bearing area, as the name suggests.

Dilean. Obscure Judean village near Lachish. It is mentioned only once in the OT (Jos 15:38), and its site is unknown today.

Dill. Herb from an annual plant known in Bible times. Dill has been widely used as a seasoning, especially for pickles, and for certain medicinal purposes. The KJV translation of "anise" instead of "dill" is considered incorrect by most scholars.

See PLANTS.

Dimnah. Alternate name for Rimmon, a Levitical city in Zebulun's territory, in Joshua 21:35.

See RIMMON (PLACE) #2.

Dimon. RSV translation of a Moabite city in Isaiah 15:9, alternately named Dibon in the large Dead Sea Isaiah Scroll. The site of Dimon is identified with Khirbet Dimneh, nearly 3 miles northwest of Rabbah.

See DIBON #1.

Dimonah. Town mentioned in Joshua 15:22 as being located in the Judean Negeb close to Edomite territory. It was one of 29 towns in the general area of Beersheba, and some scholars have identified it with the Dibon mentioned in Nehemiah 11:25. Its actual site is unknown.

Dinah. Daughter born to Jacob and Leah (Gn 30:21), whose name means "judgment." Living with her family in Shechem, a Canaanite city (Gn 33:18), Dinah went out to visit some neighboring pagan women (Gn 34:1). Shechem, the Hivite prince of the area, saw her and, while Dinah's brothers were away in the fields tending their herds, he raped her. Shechem then requested Dinah from Jacob as a wife.

Jacob's sons, enraged at the dishonor done to their sister, plotted revenge. They agreed to the marriage on the terms that all the Hivite males be circumcised. Hamor, Shechem's father, consented. While the Canaanite men

A vat, a storage jar, and a platter unearthed in a residential district of Shechem, the city where the incident over Dinah occurred.

were still incapacitated from their surgery, Dinah's brothers Levi and Simeon led a massacre in the city and killed every male. Dinah was retrieved and the city plundered. The brothers excused their action as a just retribution for one of the Canaanites having treated their sister as a harlot (Gn 34:27,31). For their use of "weapons of violence" (Gn 49:5) Simeon and Levi were later cursed by Jacob.

Dinaite. Postexilic group involved in a protest to Artaxerxes about the rebuilding of the Jerusalem temple (Ezr 4:9 KJV). The name is evidently an Aramaic title, "judge" (RSV); such judges are mentioned in 5th century BC Aramaic administrative papyri.

Dinhabah. Capital city of Edom before the time of Israel's monarchy, whose king Bela is mentioned in the Bible (Gn 36:22; 1 Chr 1:43). Its site is unknown.

Dion. One of the cities of the Decapolis, built after the death of Alexander the Great by some of his soldiers. The city (not mentioned in the Bible) was culturally Greek, attracting many Greek immigrants; it was also a mercantile center of exchange. Dion was one of only two Decapolis cities having a Macedonian name (the other being Pella). It was located in Palestine east of the Jordan, possibly near the Yarmuk River and the town of Gadara.

See DECAPOLIS.

Dionysius. Prominent citizen of Athens; a member of the Areopagus, the Athenian supreme court, and one of Paul's few converts during his brief ministry at Athens (Acts 17:34).

Dioscuri. Twin sons of Zeus known as Castor and Pollux. In Greek mythology they were the patron deities of navigation and represented in the constellation Gemini. The Dioscuri (the "Twin Brothers") were the figurehead of the Alexandrian ship on which Paul sailed to Rome (Acts 28:11).

Diotrephes. A church member whom John reprimanded for his contentious behavior (3 Jn 9). He spoke against John "with evil words" (v 10); had resisted John's authority by refusing to receive an earlier letter; and refused to show Christian hospitality, urging others to do likewise. He may have been an official in the church who abused his position since he liked "to put himself first" (v 9).

Diphath. Alternate spelling of Riphath, Gomer's son, in 1 Chronicles 1:6.

See RIPHATH.

Discerning of Spirits. *See* SPIRITUAL GIFTS.

Disciple. Someone who follows another person or another way of life and who submits himself to the discipline (teaching) of that leader or way. In the Bible the term "disciple" is found almost exclusively in the Gospels and the Book of Acts, the only exceptions being Isaiah 8:16 and less directly Isaiah 50:4 and 54:13, where the same Hebrew word is translated "learned" and "taught," respectively. Yet clearly wherever there is a teacher and those taught, the idea of discipleship is present.

In the Gospels the immediate followers of Jesus, called by his authority from a wide variety of circumstances, not only the 12 but all those who were sympathetic to his teaching and committed to him, are called "disciples." The calling of these disciples took place at a time when other teachers had their disciples, most notably the Pharisees (Mk 2:8; Lk 5:33) and John the Baptist (Mt 9:14). It is evident from the practice of John the Baptist that different leaders called for different disciplines from their followers. John's way was considerably more ascetic in character than that of Jesus (Mt 9:14); but it too involved not only teaching regarding conduct and manner of life but also a distinctive pattern of praying (Lk 11:1).

The disciples of Jesus were in a unique if rather anomalous position. Not only did they benefit from the immediate teaching of Jesus, his looks and tones of voice (Mk 10:21) as well as his words; they were also witnesses of the unfolding drama of redemption which had Christ as its center. They followed a teacher who embodied the substance of that teaching. The first disciples could be taught by Christ only little by little, not only because of the need to remove their misconceptions (Mt 16:21), but also because the full significance of what Jesus said and did could not be most fully appreciated until after the events of his death and resurrection (Mt 28:9). It is not surprising that the period of "discipling" covered the time before and after Christ's death and resurrection, and also after Pentecost, when the Holy Spirit taught the disciples about matters which they could not "bear" while Jesus remained on earth (Jn 16:12).

Groups of Jesus' first disciples, both the 12 and the 70 (Mt 26:20; Lk 10:1), received his teaching, taught others in turn (Lk 10:1–11), and were given power to heal (Mt 10:1). They were also to proclaim the message of salvation through Christ. Yet the 12 were given special prominence and, with the exception of Judas Iscariot (whose place was taken by Matthias, Acts 1:26), they became the foundation teachers of the newly emerging Christian church. Their authority in the church, given by Christ (Mt 16:19; 28:16–20), was to be characterized by a unique style of self-giving service (Lk 22:24–30). To this group of disciples, who came to be known as the apostles (though this term is occasionally given to a wider application), Saul of Tarsus was added. At his conversion on the road to Damascus he saw the risen Lord and was immediately commissioned by Christ (Gal 1:12,16) as the apostle to the Gentiles (Acts 9:15).

At the time of his ascension Christ commissioned the first disciples to "make disciples of all nations" (Mt 28:19); hence, the term "disciple" is also used in the Book of Acts to describe believers, those who confess Christ (6:1,2,7; 9:36; 11:26). Though they have not been directly called by Christ himself, such disciples are called by Christ's Spirit through the message delivered by the first disciples; disciples called later are not in any sense inferior to the first disciples, even though they are less privileged.

The discipline of the Christian disciple is whatever is involved in being a follower of Christ (Mt 16:24,25). In the case of the first disciples this involved literally going where Christ went, sharing in his privations and joys (Lk 22:28) and, beyond this, conforming minds and wills to his teaching (Phil 2:5). Such service was not a matter of following a set of abstract moral principles enunciated by a leader; much less was it a discipleship based on gaining the favor or goodwill of the master by righteous obedience. It was a discipleship of loving obedience based on gratitude for Christ's work as the Messiah, service that was made possible by the strength and motivation that come from union with Christ in his death and resurrection secured by faith and by the indwelling of the Holy Spirit.

NT Christian discipleship is firmly rooted in the OT, in the idea of the forming and calling of Israel out of the nations to be God's peculiar treasure (Ex 19:5) and to bear testimony to his name among the nations (Dt 4:6–8). The call was buried in Jewish exclusivism until the advent of the desire of all nations (Hg 2:7) and the commissioning of the worldwide preaching of the gospel (Mt 28:19). The NT is also emphatic that, viewed from the perspective of the history of redemption, the Israelite disciple under the OT was immature and preparatory (Gal 3:19–4:7).

Although the word "disciple" occurs infrequently outside the Gospels and Acts, it would be a mistake to think that the idea of discipleship is either absent or less dominant in the remainder of the NT. Rather it is filled out and enriched, the emphasis falling not on following Jesus but on being united to him, though the idea of following Jesus is by no means absent (1 Pt 2:21–23). As Christ called both for self-denial (Mk 8:34) and for following his example (Jn 12:26), so Paul wrote of the need for those who are in Christ to mortify their old nature and to yield themselves to God in consecrated obedience (Rom 8:13). As Christ spoke of the need for his disciples to be separate from the world, to be light and salt (Mt 5:13,14), so Paul spoke of Christians as lights in a dark world (Eph 5:8), as awake and sober (1 Thes 5:6). As Christ taught his disciples to pray (Lk 11:2), so Paul and the other disciples insisted on the need for prayer (1 Thes 5:17). As Christ laid down the pattern of righteous obedience through the true understanding of the Law of God (Mt 5), so Paul frames the rule of Christian obedience in terms of the Law (Rom 13:9). Yet while the Gospels refer to "disciples," the apostles refer to those who are "saints" (1 Cor 1:2), "the called" (Eph 4:4), "in Christ" (2 Cor 5:17), "pilgrims" (1 Pt 2:11 KJV), and "servants" (1 Pt 2:16). This variety of expression is evidence of the richness of the idea of discipleship in the full NT conception.

The discipline of the Christian disciple involves other people in human society, especially those who are in Christ, and more immediately those who make up the fellowship of the local church. Such churches are to consider themselves as under the discipline of apostolic authority, the Word of God, and individuals are open to rebuke and even to excommunication if the discipline is flouted to the point of impenitence. Yet such a regime is to be exercised in a spirit of mutual submission to the rule of Christ (Eph 5:21), with caution and restraint (Gal 6:1), by ministry and the use of reason and not by undue force (2 Cor 4:2), and with the aim and desire of recovering those disciplined (1 Cor 5:5). At the same time the NT is equally emphatic on the place in the church of individual differences in gifts, personality, and temperament, and of liberty in behavior regarding those matters that are "indifferent," neither commanded nor forbidden by God.

In the history of the Christian church the ideals and even the practice of Christian discipleship have tended to veer between extremes. For some being a Christian disciple has amounted to nothing other than a carefully cultivated and controlled worldliness. Others have identified discipleship with the adoption of an ascetic discipline. This has been a feature of medieval Catholicism and of certain Anabaptist communities, and has been a recurrent tendency in Protestant pietism and fundamentalism. More recently discipleship has come to be thought of by some in wholly secular terms, as involving emancipation from "religion" in any of its forms. Such extremes indicate that the balance between a Christian disciple being in the world (Jn 17:15; 1 Cor 5:10) but not of the world (Jn 17:16) is difficult to achieve and to sustain.

PAUL HELM

Bibliography. E. Schweizer, *Lordship and Discipleship.*

Discipline. Learning that molds character and enforces correct behavior; from a Latin word meaning "instruction" or "training." To discipline a person or a group means to put them in a state of good order so that they function in the way intended. Discipline, in spite of a popular misconception, is not inherently stern or harsh. Bible translators chose "disciple" as an appropriate term for one who learns by following.

Biblical Teaching. Although used only once in the KJV (Jb 36:10), the word "discipline," in various noun and verb forms, occurs frequently in modern versions of the Bible. The Hebrew and Greek words commonly rendered "discipline" are sometimes translated as "reproof," "warning," "restraint," "correction," or (especially in KJV) "chastisement." More positive synonyms include "upbringing," "training," "instruction," and "education."

OT usage of "discipline" is noticeably more negative than in the NT, principally because of the legal aspect of God's approach to Israel under the old (Mosaic) covenant. The "new covenant" approach to the church leads to a more positive language of discipline in the NT. Yet both covenants had the same goal: righteousness. Considered in that light, even the OT emphasis on punishment proceeds from a positive motive toward a constructive goal. Where the OT emphasized retaliation, it was to teach offenders the nature of their offense by showing them an effect like the one they had caused. Vindication of a wronged person's rights also vindicated God's righteousness. Vindication was an important way of upholding God's justice. Retribution was also important. Covenant-breaking brought on the covenant curse (Dt 27:26) in the form of punitive discipline. Retribution reestablished the authority of God's law and taught respect for his standards of righteousness.

Complementary to punitive discipline, positive discipline can be thought of as reinforcive discipline. God always disciplines; he does so punitively when necessary, but reinforcingly when possible.

Discipline is frequently spoken of as being exercised by God over Israel (Lv 26:23; Dt 4:36; 8:5; Jer 31:18), over the nations (Ps 94:10), or over individuals (Jb 5:17; Ps 94:10,12; Heb 12:5–11; Rv 3:19). In Israel parental responsibility to discipline children was taken seriously (Dt 21:18). Fathers were solemnly charged to discipline their sons (Prv 13:24; 19:18; 22:15; 23:13; 29:17; cf. Eph 6:4; Heb 12:7–10). In the church, disciplining was a pastoral responsibility (2 Tm 2:25).

It is understandable that people fear discipline from God (Ps 6:1), but it is his wrath that should be feared. His wrath is directed only against those who have proved themselves by their actions to be God's enemies (Dt 11:2,3). God's discipline is different from his wrath and should not be despised (Prv 3:11) or taken for granted (Heb 12:5). Only a fool or wicked person hates it (Ps 50:17; Prv 5:12; Jer 31:18). God disciplines his people as a loving father disciplines a beloved son (Dt 8:5; Prv 3:11,12; Heb 12:5–7). In fact, according to Scripture, a wise person loves discipline (Prv 12:1; 13:24; 2 Tm 1:7; Heb 12:5,9).

The fruit of discipline is knowledge (Prv 12:1) and parents' delight (Prv 29:17). One who is disciplined can be spoken of as "blessed" (Jb 5:17; Ps 94:12). Where the purpose of discipline is left unspecified, the discipline is nevertheless understood as good and righteous (Dt 4:36; Jb 36:10; Prv 13:24; Rv 3:19). Specifically, discipline is called "the way of life" (Prv 6:23). It saves one from destruction (Prv 19:18) and allows one to escape both folly (Prv 22:15) and God's condemnation of the world (1 Cor 11:32). It eventually leads to sharing God's holiness (Heb 12:7), and yields "the peaceful fruit of righteousness" (Heb 12:11).

In contrast, the consequences of a lack of discipline are stipulated to be abandonment by God (Lv 26:23,24), death (Prv 5:23), and destruction (Prv 19:18).

The Book of Proverbs speaks of discipline as necessary to avoid sexual immorality (5:12–23; 6:23,24). Loose or wicked women probably symbolize many kinds of deceptive and enticing situations. To be able to act maturely and responsibly in such situations requires that young people respond to wise and loving parental discipline so that they learn to live disciplined lives. They then do by "bent of nature" what is right because their nature has been shaped to what is right. Evil can then be shunned even when it is encountered unexpectedly.

Both Proverbs and the Book of Hebrews urge their readers to respond to discipline rather than to react against it. In Hebrews two harmful reactions are stipulated and the helpful response is identified. On the one hand, no individual should "regard lightly" (Heb 12:5) or "despise" (Prv 3:11) "the discipline of the Lord." Discipline should be regarded neither as worthless nor as being of little value. On the other hand, one should not "lose courage when you are punished by him" (Heb 12:5) or "be weary of his reproof" (Prv 3:11). That is, preoccupation with the negative aspect of the disciplinary procedure must not obscure its goal or demoralize persons being disciplined. Rather, they are to be aware that "it is for discipline that you have to endure" (Heb 12:7). There is a purpose for what happens, which should be sought and realized: "it yields the peaceful fruit of righteousness to those who have been trained by it" (Heb 12:11). The exhortation is not to reject discipline or be dejected by it, but to accept it and be instructed by it.

Self-discipline. Jesus' ethics of righteousness both fulfill and surpass the stringent code of the old covenant (Mt 5:17–48). Yet Christians are not therefore inherently more legalistic than were the Pharisees. Set free from "the law of sin and death," Christians have "the law of the Spirit of life in Jesus Christ" (Rom 8:1–8) to provide a built-in dynamic to fulfill the will of God. Beyond slavish obedience to the letter of the law, believers are enabled by the indwelling Spirit of God to exercise self-discipline. Spiritual transformation is accompanied by renewal of the mind (Rom 12:2), which brings fresh understanding of oneself, one's motivations, and one's attitudes.

Over the centuries the church has realized the value of certain "spiritual disciplines" encouraged in the NT. In the Roman Catholic tradition they formed the basis for the way of life of "the religious" (priests, nuns, monks, etc.). Prayer (cf. Lk 6:12; Acts 6:4; Rom 12:12; 1 Pt 4:7), fasting (Mt 6:16–18), study of Scripture (Acts 17:11; 2 Tm 2:15; 3:16,17), and charity or almsgiving (Mt 6:1–4; Acts 11:29,30; 2 Cor 9; 1 Tm 6:17–19) have always been included among the spiritual disciplines. Protestants have been less inclined to establish religious orders or communities based on the spiritual disciplines, more often trusting the Holy Spirit to produce self-discipline in individual lives and seeking fellowship and exhortation in the context of the church. Among evangelicals there seems to be a new appreciation of the need for spiritual discipline. A well-ordered, wholesome, liberated life that releases the Christian for service is almost always a self-disciplined life.

Such ideals and the lifestyle they engender run counter to much of the prevalent permissiveness in Western culture. Young people are surrounded by superficial commitments, short-term relationships, instant gratification, the quest for freedom without responsibility, and obsession with self-centered indulgence. Christian parents need to help their children develop the self-discipline to stand against such pressures. Adult self-discipline often has its roots in a biblical pattern of discipline and an appreciation for the desirability of such discipline inculcated in childhood.

Parental Discipline. The family constitutes the basic unit of the human community. Within that cell of intimate relationships parents are entrusted with the responsibility of guiding and correcting their children (Dt 6:7; Prv 22:6). The biblical view is essentially pessimistic about the perfectibility of human nature. Hence parents are urged not to leave children at the mercy of their own natural tendencies. Undisciplined children are potential victims of the powerful conditioning exerted by a predominantly pagan culture. To exercise their responsibilities properly, parents must model values, practices, and attitudes to their children, besides teaching them through instruction and correction.

The parents' educational task is best accomplished through positive means such as advice, exhortation, counseling, family devotions, and Christian training in church and Sunday school. But it also may require negative measures such as prohibitions and disciplinary action. When verbal admonitions are not heeded by small children, corporal punishment becomes an effective form of persuasion (Prv 13:24). Physical discipline, however, should be administered on the basis of clearly stated and understood principles. Christian parents must avoid punishing out of anger or personal animosity, and must never cause injury to a child. Physical discipline should be viewed as a last resort intended to obtain maximum educational results with minimum outrage to children (Eph 6:4).

Human fallenness (Gn 3) means that self-centeredness infects even children (cf. Ps 51:5). Somehow children must learn respect for themselves and for others. Left on their own and then battered by a fallen society, they can become rebellious social misfits leaving a trail of heartache in their own lives and in the lives of other people. Love for one's children does not preclude the use of negative disciplinary measures. As distasteful as they may seem to both parents and children, genuine love may require them. A family environment regulated by consistent and loving firmness will enhance the chances for children to mature as responsible and considerate individuals.

Church Discipline. The church is basically a large family of which each believer is a member. The nature of the church—as a community intended to reflect in the faith, worship, and lives of its members the true character of God—distinguishes it from all other groups.

At the same time, the church is called to be

an open community of concern, reaching out in compassion to desperately needy human beings. Christian lifestyles clearly differ from pagan lifestyles. That difference often creates a barrier isolating the "lost" from the very people who could extend to them God's deliverance from loneliness, addictions, disorientation, broken relationships, and so on. The church has a responsibility not to place unscriptural obstacles in the way of its outreach to unbelievers; yet the tension between openness and purity is difficult to resolve. Without a careful balance, a church can easily become unduly restrictive or overly permissive. In either extreme its witness is impaired.

The solution to the dilemma lies in formulating church discipline that is authentically biblical. The Scriptures provide the church with ample guidance for the formulation of standards of conduct (e.g., Ex 20:1–17; 1 Cor 5:11; 6:9–11; Eph 4:25–32; 5:1–21; Col 3:5–11). As those standards are spelled out, however, it is necessary to differentiate between biblical absolutes and cultural norms. For instance, though drunkenness is expressly forbidden in the NT, there is no scriptural prohibition on the drinking of wine. Some churches allow drinking but decry drunkenness, others recommend abstinence to their members, and still others make abstinence from alcoholic beverages a condition of membership. The NT, recognizing that conflict sometimes occurs between Christian liberty and Christian responsibility, gives guidelines for resolving such conflicts (1 Cor 8).

For the sake of scriptural consistency and in order to be credible, church discipline should oppose sins of attitude with the same severity as for "gross sins." The NT condemns immorality, murder, and drunkenness—but along with them envy, jealousy, anger, selfishness, complaining, and criticism. Each of those vices is an impediment to entering the kingdom of God (Gal 5:19–21). Unbelievers are often made to feel unwelcome in the church because of secondary matters such as smoking or drinking. Yet gossiping, complaining, and selfishness among church members are seldom exposed and properly disciplined. A more consistent position would promote the purity of the church and would also enhance its ministry as a supportive, accepting center of Christian love.

In addition to affirming the necessity for discipline within the church, the NT delineates a procedure for carrying out disciplinary action (Mt 18:15–18; 1 Cor 5:3–13; Gal 6:1). Offenders are first to be approached and admonished privately. If they refuse to repent or mend their ways, the case is to be presented before the leadership of the church and then,

Oenochoes (wine pitchers or jugs) from Corinth, the location of the church that needed much discipline by Paul.

if necessary, before the whole congregation. Should offenders persist in their error, they are to be ostracized, not out of vindictiveness but with the hope of bringing them to repentance and restoration (2 Thes 3:14,15).

The Bible's emphasis on the necessity for self-discipline, parental discipline, and church discipline seems underscored by the moral decline evident in many areas of modern society. God's love, as depicted in the Bible and exemplified in Jesus Christ, is intended to teach all people how to live. Those who spurn God's "positive reinforcement" encounter the negative aspects of his discipline. Christians who discipline themselves, their children, and each other in a loving way honor Christ and model his way of life, thus helping others to understand God's purposes.

GILBERT BILEZIKIAN

Disease. Term used in Scripture synonymously with sickness, infirmity, illness, plague, and pestilence. However, plague and pestilence are generally used when there are large numbers of victims, as in epidemics. "Pestilence" literally means "destruction" and usually describes an epidemic with a high mortality rate. "Affliction" and "torment" are other terms that may include disease, but are broader and are not used synonymously with disease.

Biblical Concept of Disease. During the time the Bible was written people did not have a detailed concept of anatomy or of how the specific organs of the body functioned. Disease was thought of as abnormal, something that limits one's ability to function with strength and vitality. The Hebrew word translated "sickness" as a noun means "to be weak" in its cognate verb form. The ill man by the pool of Bethesda is described as being "impotent" (Jn 5:7 KJV), being unable to get around by himself.

Additional insight into the concept of disease can be obtained by looking at what the Bible says about health. To be healthy means to be whole, and to be healed means to be restored to wholeness (Mt 12:13). Central to this idea of health is the concept that a person exists as a unity, one single person, but has several parts. Each part or member has a specific function, and all must work together in concert with the other parts. When Paul describes how a group of believers should function, he utilizes this concept of the healthy human body (1 Cor 12). Paul perceptively points out that the smaller, hidden parts of the body are more vital to life and health than some of the larger, more obvious members (1 Cor 12:22–25).

But the biblical concept of health does not stop with properly functioning physical parts. The key to health for a person is right relationships with oneself, with others, and with God. Jesus taught that one's relationship with God was more important than having eyesight (Mt 5:29). He also taught his disciples not to fear those who can kill the body but to fear the one who can send people to hell (Lk 12:4,5). The Bible clearly places greater value on a person's spiritual condition than on physical or mental condition in evaluating the person's overall wholeness or health.

Origin of Disease. The etiology of disease has four sources: (1) God, (2) Satan, (3) sins of ancestors, and (4) breaking of physical, mental/emotional, or moral laws of nature.

God. All early peoples attributed events and phenomena to the supernatural, either to various gods or to evil spirits. The Hebrews were different by being strong monotheists, attributing all phenomena to the one true God who had revealed himself to them (Is 45:21). God was responsible for everything, including disease and evil (Is 45:7). This same God could also give material blessings, health, and heal all diseases (Ps 103:3). To the Hebrews, God could give health or sickness, and in either case he had his purpose or reason.

One purpose of disease was punishment for wrongdoing (2 Sm 24:1,12–16; 1 Cor 10:8). In the Hebrew mind, even when the immediate cause of the disease and death was obvious— as many poisonous snakes biting people in the camp—the response was not to kill all the snakes but to pray to God for forgiveness (Nm 21:4–9). Leprosy, which literally means "a smiting," was a devastating disease sent by God to punish individuals who sinned (Nm 12; 2 Kgs 5:27).

God also sent disease to demonstrate his power or to protect his people. The ten plagues in Egypt illustrate the former; the elimination of Sennacherib's army the latter (2 Kgs 19:34–36).

Satan. Satan and other evil spirits could also be responsible for disease. In the biblical scheme of things Satan's ability to bring disease is in the permissive will of God. The restriction on Satan's capacity for harm is clearly spelled out in the case of Job (Jb 1:12). The message of the NT is also clear, that despite cases of demon possession and of people acting under Satan's influence, Satan's time is finite and his ultimate total defeat and destruction are certain.

Sin of Ancestors. Sickness could also come about because of the sins of one's ancestors (Ex 20:5; Lv 26:29; 1 Kgs 17:18; Jb 21:19; Lam 5:7). The most striking example of this is the death of David's son as a result of his sin with Bathsheba (2 Sm 12:15). This concept of the origin of disease continued into NT times and was familiar to the disciples of Jesus (Jn 9:2).

Breaking of Natural Laws. This idea is pivotal, for it sets the Hebrews apart from the other peoples of their day. With the understanding that disease can follow the violation of fixed physical, mental/emotional, and moral laws comes the idea of personal accountability in obeying these laws and avoiding disease. A person is responsible for his and the community's health and is not merely a passive victim of supernatural forces.

Based on this concept the books of Moses set up elaborate codes of behavior to maintain personal health and the health of the community. The Mosaic law covers the areas of diet, personal hygiene, sabbath observance, sanitary regulations in the camp, cleanliness, and sexual relations. In following these natural laws established by God the Hebrews could expect freedom from disease (Ex 15:26) and long life (Prv 3:1,2). These health laws of Moses make a lot of sense from a public health point of view even today, and are far more rational than the approach of any other ancient people.

Another major consequence of understanding that disease can follow the breaking of the laws of nature is the shift away from the priest and toward physicians in looking for cures. As long as diseases were of supernatural origin, there was no basis for attempting to learn about disease processes in the search for cures. The Hebrews were familiar with physicians in Egypt (Gn 50:2), where they seem to have functioned as embalmers. Physicians were practicing in Israel throughout its history, but only gradually developed the capacity to be of much help (2 Chr 16:12; Jer 8:22; Mk 5:26; Col 4:14). While validating the use of physicians for sick people (Mt 9:12) and of drugs for medicinal purposes (Prv 31:6; 1 Tm 5:23), the Scriptures emphasize the role of the Christian community and its elders in ministering to the sick (Jas 5:14).

Jesus Christ and Disease. Christ's approach to people with disease is distinctly different than that of the OT. He was nonjudgmental, interacting with them as people of worth, not as social outcasts. He was full of genuine compassion for them as suffering people, touching them, comforting them, healing them, and speaking normally and naturally with them.

Jesus evidently thought of disease as a hindrance that prevented people from being the whole persons they were created to be. When confronted by a woman with a severe back deformity of 18 years duration, he healed her, saying she had been "bound by Satan" (Lk 13:16). His healing of incurable diseases was one of the proofs he offered that he was the Messiah (Lk 7:19–23). His ministry was directed toward releasing men and women to live life more abundantly (Jn 10:10). He did not fully subscribe to the punitive concept of disease (Jn 9:3). When a leper mentioned the possibility that it might not be God's will for him to be well, Jesus healed him instantly (Mk 1:40; Lk 5:12,13).

Jesus was always concerned with the person's total health or wholeness, rather than merely the symptoms of disease. He frequently dealt with spiritual issues first, even though the sick person was brought to him for a physical problem. His conversation with the Samaritan woman at the well focused on the basic conflicts in her disturbed personality (Jn 4:5–30). And the Sermon on the Mount, which basically deals with right attitudes and motives for human behavior, would greatly reduce personal and social suffering if it were followed. To Jesus, health is more than the mere absence of physical and mental disease; it is whole persons being all that they were meant to be.

DAVID E. VAN REKEN

See MEDICINE AND MEDICAL PRACTICE; PESTILENCE; PLAGUE.

Dish. A vessel, usually made of baked clay or metal, used in everyday life and in religious ceremony. Dishes were to serve or preserve food (Jgs 5:25; Mt 26:23; Mk 14:20). They had to be wiped and left to dry (2 Kgs 21:13), but later the Pharisees added a ritual cleansing as well (Mt 23:25–26; Lk 11:39). Dishes were used in connection with the meal offering (Nm 7:13) and with the table of showbread for worship in the OT tabernacle and temple (Ex 25:29; 37:16; Nm 4:7).

Dishan. Chieftain in the land of Seir, a mountainous area southwest of the Dead Sea. Dishan's father was Seir the Horite (Gn 36:21; 1 Chr 1:38). The Horites were driven out of their territory by the Edomites (Dt 2:12). Later OT references often use Seir and Edom synonymously.

Dishon. 1. Seir's fifth son and a Horite leader in Edom (Gn 36:21; 1 Chr 1:38), whose people were eventually displaced by the Edomites.

2. Grandson of Seir and son of Anah, a Horite leader. This Dishon was also the brother of Oholibamah, Esau's wife (Gn 36:25; 1 Chr 1:41).

Dispersion of the Jews. *See* DIASPORA OF THE JEWS.

Dives. Traditional name of the rich man in Christ's parable about the beggar Lazarus (Lk 16:19–31). It came from the Latin term *dives*, translating a Greek word for "rich," "wealthy." Though the rich man was not named in the parable, this name was already well accepted in the church by the 3rd century.

See LAZARUS #1.

Divination. *See* MAGIC.

Divine Presence. *See* GOD, BEING AND ATTRIBUTES OF; PRESENCE OF GOD, THE.

Diviners' Oak. Place apparently near Shechem (Jgs 9:37); mistakenly called "the plain of Meonenim" in the KJV. The Diviners' Oak may have been associated with those who practiced divination, hence the name.

Division of the Land. Assignment of portions of the Promised Land to the 12 tribes of Israel following the conquest.

See CONQUEST AND ALLOTMENT OF THE LAND.

Divorce. Biblical provisions regulating divorce are closely bound up with the various definitions given to marriage within the successive phases of God's progressive revelation in history.

In the Genesis creation account, marriage is defined as the "one flesh" union established by God in the context of a sinless environment (Gn 2:24). Given such conditions, the dissolution of the marriage relationship was inconceivable. During his ministry Jesus affirmed this aspect of God's original design for marriage. He described the implications of the "one flesh" relationship as the abrogation of the separatedness of the spouses and the creation of an inviolable union (Mt 19:6).

Old Testament Regulations. The disruptions brought about by the fall had grievous consequences for the male/female relationship. Having allowed sin to sever their primary dependency on God, man and woman became respectively subject to the elements from which they had been originally made.

Man became subject to the dust of the ground whence he had come (Gn 2:7; 3:19), and woman became subject to the man from whom she had been formed (Gn 2:22; 3:16). Prior to the fall man and woman had enjoyed a relationship of equality as cosharers in the divine image (Gn 1:27) and as partners in the divine mandate to exercise dominion over creation (Gn 1:28). After the fall man became ruler over woman, and woman became subject to man (Gn 3:16).

As a result of these new conditions man assumed rights of disposition over woman that he did not possess prior to the fall. The "one flesh" relation was violated when the right of rulership opened the way for the male ruler to multiply the number of his female subjects. This disparity between male and female resulted in the practice of polygamy (Gn 4:19; 16:3; 29:30) and of serial monogamy, which required the termination of each successive marriage by an act of divorce (Dt 24:1–4). Thus, the emergence of the practice of divorce appeared as the inevitable consequence of the principle of male rulership. Neither rulership nor divorce was part of God's original design for the marriage relationship. The Mosaic regulation on divorce was a concession made by God to the fallen condition of mankind (Mt 19:8). Characteristically, the option of divorce was a right available only to the male rulers. As subjects of their male rulers, wives became the victims of divorce. Men could divorce their wives; women could not divorce their husbands.

As unfair as it may seem, the Deuteronomic provisions for divorce were actually intended to offer a modicum of protection for its female victims. A husband had to justify a divorce action against his wife by citing something indecent about her. He was to give his divorced wife a bill of divorce that accounted for her marriage to him (Dt 24:1). Moreover, a divorced husband was forbidden to remarry his ex-wife after her subsequent marriage, since his original divorce was viewed as a defilement of her (Dt 24:4).

Although the Mosaic dispositions on divorce were granted as a divine concession to the "hardness of heart," the OT emphatically states that God hates divorce (Mal 2:16). The right of divorce was grudgingly granted as an accommodation to the principle of male rulership that had resulted from the fall. But God's original design, reflected in the "one flesh" marital relation, remained the standard for the union of man and woman in marriage.

Jesus' Teaching on Divorce. Inasmuch as Christ's ministry of redemption signaled a return to God's original purposes in creation, the old covenant regulations on divorce were abrogated in the Christian community. In order to justify the inviolability of the marriage bond among his followers, Jesus directed them to the creational model. Referring negatively to the intervening Mosaic allowance for divorce, Jesus upheld God's original creation order by stating that "from the beginning it was not so" (Mt 19:8). Christ repudiated the fall and affirmed the creation design.

In Matthew 5:31,32 Jesus explicitly abrogated the Mosaic legislation that allowed men to divorce their wives. He viewed the practice as a violation of the integrity of women. Adulterous men who divorce their wives reduce them to the status of whores, using them as commodities to be passed around through the expedient of easy divorce. By divorcing their wives, men treat them as adulteresses. By marrying a woman discarded from a previous marriage, a man perpetuates the demeaning process and becomes guilty of adultery.

Jesus deliberately withdrew from men the ruler's right of discarding a wife at will and reinstated the creational pattern of the lifelong "one flesh" union. His disciples understood his intent accurately. But the principle of male privilege was so deeply ingrained in their mentality that they declared the freedom available in celibacy preferable to a commitment to lifelong monogamous marriage (Mt 19:10).

Not only did Jesus reaffirm the validity of the "one flesh" union for the community of redemption, but the NT reinforced the inviolability of the marriage bond by defining it as an earthly copy of the relationship between Christ and the church (Eph 5:25).

Despite such strong sanctions for the permanency of the marriage bond, the NT permits divorce as an exception intended to protect the innocent spouse in the case of immorality and desertion. Jesus made exceptions that established the right of a spouse wronged by an unfaithful mate to press for divorce (Mt 5:32; 19:9). Obviously the wronged spouse has the option of maintaining the marriage bond despite the breach of commitment by the unfaithful mate. But in view of the exception allowed by Scripture, the obligation to maintain or reinstate the disrupted marriage may not be imposed upon the innocent spouse.

The other exception that justifies divorce according to the NT is desertion. Although the provisions of 1 Corinthians 7:15 refer primarily to desertion by an unbelieving spouse, it should be noted that a believer guilty of desertion is to be treated as an unbeliever (1 Tm 5:8). Behavior equivalent to the abandonment of the marriage relationship constitutes a breach of conjugal commitment and becomes subject to the provision stated in 1 Corinthians 7:15.

In either case, adultery or desertion, the aggrieved party has the right to seek divorce from the offending spouse and, having obtained it, becomes again a single person. Should repentance and reconciliation fail to restore the violated union, the aggrieved spouse is not bound to the marriage. According to Scripture, a person who is not bound is free to remarry, but only "in the Lord," meaning to another Christian (1 Cor 7:39). The injunction for a single person who does not have the gift of celibacy to marry (1 Cor 7:9) applies to a person formerly married but who has become single by a scripturally legitimate divorce. In keeping with Christ's teaching in Mark 10:11,12 and Luke 16:18, the remarriage of believers may not be approved when the divorce has been used as a means of changing mates, since such intent makes the divorce adulterous.

Many factors usually combine to destroy a marriage; therefore it behooves the church to deal with each case of divorce and remarriage on an individual basis, taking into account God's inexhaustible capacity to forgive sin and to restore broken lives. Obviously, the scriptural restrictions on divorce do not apply to believers whose broken marriages predate their conversion, since God's forgiveness wipes clean the sins of their pre-Christian past and makes them new creatures in Christ.

Divorce is a devasting experience that commonly leaves its victims broken and scarred. The church has a special opportunity to minister in love and compassion to divorced persons by reaching out to surround them, support them, and integrate them into the redemptive fellowship of the new community, and thus provide favorable conditions for their healing and restoration.   GILBERT BILEZIKIAN

See CIVIL LAW AND JUSTICE; MARRIAGE, MARRIAGE CUSTOMS; SEX, SEXUALITY; ADULTERY.

Bibliography. D. Atkinson, *To Have and to Hold;* L. Boettner, *Divorce;* R.H. Charles, *The Teaching of the NT on Divorce;* S.A. Ellisen, *Divorce and Remarriage in the Church;* K.E. Kirk, *Marriage and Divorce;* J. Murray, *Divorce.*

Divorce, Certificate of.

A document declaring the separation of a husband and wife mandated by Mosaic law (Dt 24:1–4; see Mt 5:31; 19:7; Mk 10:4). The certificate of divorce protected the woman's rights, providing evidence of her freedom and ensuring that her husband could not claim her dowry. An example of the wording of such a certificate is Hosea 2:2: "She is not my wife, and I am not her husband." The OT prophets used this statement figuratively to portray God's desire to separate himself from his rebellious people (Is 50:1; Jer 3:8).

See CIVIL LAW AND JUSTICE; DIVORCE; MARRIAGE, MARRIAGE CUSTOMS.

Di-zahab.

Name, listed along with Paran, Tophel, Laban, and Hazeroth, meant to designate the locale of Moses' final address to Israel (Dt 1:1). Its precise location is unknown, though it was east of the Arabah.

Doctor of the Law.

KJV for Teacher of the Law in Luke 2:46; 5:17; and Acts 5:34.

See PHARISEES; TRADES AND OCCUPATIONS (TEACHER); GAMALIEL #2.

Documentary Hypothesis.

A critical attempt to explain the present composition of the Pentateuch, the first five books of the Bible. The Pentateuch is analyzed as a composite of four documents (JEDP), each of which had its own background and development before it was edited into the five books. The hypothesis arose from a serious concern with the duplications, stylistic differences, seeming contradictions, various names for Deity, and different perspectives in the books of the Pentateuch. Apart from several post-Mosaic passages, Jewish and Christian scholars had generally assumed the essential Mosaic origin of the Pentateuch.

Though it was not the intent of Jean Astruc to father a critical approach, his work on Genesis (1753) made a distinction between pre-Mosaic and Mosaic sources (A and B). Eichhorn (1780), Geddes (1800), Vater (1802–05), de Wette (1806–07), Ewald (1823), Vatke (1835), and Hupfeld (1857) each contributed significant critical analyses, which led to a consensus under the influential writings of Graf, Kuenen, and Wellhausen. Graf's thesis proposed a postexilic date for the Levitical legislation. The order and dates of the documents were established: J (Yahwist, early monarchy, c. 850 BC); E (Elohist, shortly before Israel's exile, c. 750 BC); D (Deuteronomist, 621 BC); and P (Priestly, time of Ezra, 450 BC). The documentary sources were seen as having been edited in stages by redactors from 650 to 400 BC. All the material of the Pentateuch and Joshua could now be divided according to source documents, hence the name "Documentary Hypothesis."

Graf's thesis was later supported by Kuenen and Wellhausen. Wellhausen further developed the Documentary Hypothesis by intertwining the analysis of the documents with a reconstruction of Israel's history along evolutionary lines. J and E represent the beginning of Israel's awareness of God, their world, and their distinct place, when Israel was composed of many clans with different traditions and local temples. Through the impetus of the prophets, ethical monotheism gradually developed; but it was not until Josiah's reform (621

BC) that a synthesis of the cultic traditions and the prophets took place. Out of this synthesis arose a concern with centralization of the cult and cohesiveness of the people (Deuteronomist). Israel's history was written largely from the perspective of the Deuteronomist and hence gives the impression of unity. The cultus developed especially after the exile, and to this process we owe the Priestly additions and codes. Thus, the Documentary Hypothesis had been transformed into a model for historical reconstruction.

Development of the Hypothesis. The dogmatic attitude of those who embraced the Documentary Hypothesis facilitated the enthronement of documentary and historical investigation along the lines proposed by Wellhausen. There was little internal criticism; instead, Wellhausen's views were hailed as a Copernican revolution and accepted as dogma. The doctrinaire spirit and the antagonism to conservative approaches were sure to arouse a reaction from those who held to the essential Mosaic authorship (W. H. Green, O. T. Allis, E. J. Young, G. C. Aalders) or to the unity of the Pentateuch (Umberto Cassuto).

The gulf between conservative and critical scholarship widened as research focused on further fragmentation of the critical sources (O. Eissfeldt, R. H. Pfeiffer) and called into question more tenets of Israel's history and faith (A. Alt, M. Noth, G. von Rad). Other scholars questioned the existence or the dating of certain documents (A. C. Welch, G. von Rad, Y. Kaufmann).

In 1951 H. H. Rowley (*The Old Testament and Modern Study*) observed that the history of each document had proved to be as complex as the history of all four documents together. This was due to the highly speculative studies on the development of the oral traditions, the life situation (geographical, cultic, wisdom, prophetic, etc.), and the redactional stages.

Current Debate. Criticism arose along three major lines. First, the "documentary" aspect was criticized from a religio-historical perspective. Hermann Gunkel argued that it was not enough to analyze the sources behind the biblical writings, as each literary piece must be understood in its original life setting (*Sitz im Leben*). The different accounts reflect different settings, the study of which provided Gunkel and his form-critical school insight into the development of Israel's faith. A related development is the traditio-critical approach, which has shown great interest in the development of the oral traditions behind the written materials (I. Engnell). Dependent on the insights of form criticism, redaction criticism arose.

Second, archaeological evidence has necessi-tated a historical reevaluation. The Albright, or American, school of archaeology has done much to establish the essential correctness of biblical history. Rather than assuming that all of Israel's history was open to question and subject to the analytic knife of source criticism, W. F. Albright, J. Bright, and G. E. Wright, among others, wrote significant volumes on Israel's history and faith, aiding in establishing a more comprehensive framework.

Third, comparative literary evidence (from Ugarit, Mari, Nuzi, and Ebla) has thrown light on the literary development of the Bible. Discoveries at Ugarit have called for significant alterations in the use of literary evidence. Materials that on linguistic and stylistic grounds had been assumed to be late occur in early documents. Names, customs, and phrases which caused problems more than 100 years ago have been explained from the ancient Near Eastern background.

More recently, B. Childs has introduced the approach of canonical criticism, according to which the Mosaic authorship of the Pentateuch as a theological affirmation stands side by side with an openness to critical investigation of the origins. Childs' approach begins with an openness to further investigation without leaving the student of the Pentateuch with the bits and pieces resulting from critical analysis. "Because the present shape of the Pentateuch offers a particular interpretation of how the tradition is to be understood, the critical task at hand is both to describe the actual characteristics of the canonical shape and to determine the theological significance of that shape" (Childs, p. 128).

Evaluation. The assumption of criticism has been that the critical method establishes historical facts and that the facts thus established illuminate biblical faith. Evangelicals welcome refinement of literary methods and historical reconstruction, but reject the historic factuality as the model for developing their faith. The last 100 years have resulted in a splintering of methods, conclusions, and theologies. The canonical approach offers an openness to continued exploration and research; it suggests creative ways of approaching the theological contribution of each biblical book and encourages a deeper understanding of the hermeneutical relationship between the ancient books and the modern reader.

Evangelicals have made significant contributions in the study of the ancient Near East (K. A. Kitchen, D. J. Wiseman), the covenant form (M. G. Kline), and the question of post-Mosaic material (Aalders). Their criticism, however, has had little if any impact on the direction of critical thinking (for a summary, see R. K. Harrison, *Introduction to the Old Testament*, pp. 516–

41). Positively, the defense for the unity and the essentially Mosaic origin of the Pentateuch has established a firm foundation for evangelical OT scholarship. Negatively, in response to the dogmatism of critical scholars, the evangelical position may have been overstated. Regrettably, the cautious approach of Aalders has not stirred much interest. Now that evangelicalism has come to a period of relaxation and growth, it is most urgent to intensify the study of the Pentateuch with openness to the text and to its canonical shape.

Though the Documentary Hypothesis has undergone significant shifts in the last 100 years, Wellhausen's approach has vindicated itself in critical circles. The subsequent development of form criticism and redaction criticism is considered complementary and corrective, rather than destructive, of the hypothesis. The grand gulf between evangelical and critical scholars is likely to remain and deepen. As confidence in the archaeological consensus and skepticism of the literary materials erodes the relatively conservative results of the Albright school, evangelicals will be challenged to respond to the issues rather than react in fear of the slippery slopes of criticism.

WILLEM A. VANGEMEREN

See REDACTION CRITICISM; SOURCE CRITICISM; TRADITION CRITICISM; FORM CRITICISM; DEUTERONOMIST.

Bibliography. B.S. Childs, *Introduction to the OT as Scripture;* R.E. Clements, *One Hundred Years of OT Interpretation;* K.A. Kitchen, *The Ancient Orient and the OT;* M.G. Kline, *Treaty of the Great King: The Covenant Structure of Deuteronomy;* G. Maier, *The End of the Historical-Critical Method.*

Dodai. Ahohi's descendant and a commander of one of Israel's 12 contingents of soldiers (24,000 men each) during David's reign (1 Chr 27:4). Dodai is perhaps alternately called Dodo, Eleazar's father, in 2 Samuel 23:9 and 1 Chronicles 11:12.

See DODO #2.

Dodanim. Descendants of Noah's son Japheth (Gn 10:4). The name is emended to Rodanim in 1 Chronicles 1:7 (RSV).

See RODANIM.

Dodavahu, Dodavah. Inhabitant of Mareshah and father of Eliezer the prophet. Eliezer spoke against King Jehoshaphat of Judah because of his alliance with King Ahaziah of Israel (2 Chr 20:37, KJV Dodavah).

Dodo. 1. Grandfather of Tola, a minor judge who judged Israel from his native city Shamir (Jgs 10:1).

2. Father of Eleazar, one of David's mighty men known as "the 30" (2 Sm 23:9; 1 Chr

11:12). Dodo is perhaps identifiable with Dodai the Ahohite in 1 Chronicles 27:4.

See DODAI.

3. Father of Elhanan, one of David's mighty men known as "the 30" (2 Sm 23:24; 1 Chr 11:26). Dodo lived at Bethlehem.

Doe. Female deer (Prv 5:19).

See ANIMALS (DEER).

Doeg. Official of Saul who was commanded to slay the innocent priests at Nob (1 Sm 21,22). An Edomite, he was either a proselyte or a prominent Edomite chieftain captured by Saul (1 Sm 14:47). He was subsequently given supervision over Saul's flocks (1 Sm 21:7; cf. 1 Chr 27:30, where David had a foreign head over his herd). The reason for his presence at the sanctuary at Nob (1 Sm 21:7) is not clear, though he had some religious purpose in being there, maybe being detained while in a purification process (e.g., a Nazirite vow, Nm 6:13). Possibly he secretly hid there as a spy for Saul. Whatever the case, it is evident that he saw an opportunity to gain favor with Saul when he observed David hospitably treated by the priests, who even supplied him with a weapon—the sword of Goliath (1 Sm 21:9). Shortly thereafter he had occasion to report this to Saul (22:9,10; Ps 52 title), hoping thereby to demonstrate his loyalty. His brutal slaying of the priests and the inhabitants of the city of Nob (1 Sam 22:18,19) show his ruthless character and intimate further that he was not an Israelite.

Dog. *See* ANIMALS.

Doleful Creature. Designation for animal of uncertain identity in Isaiah 13:21 (KJV), better rendered "howling creature." The context implies such beasts are unclean; hence suggested creatures include the horned owl, hyena, jackal, and leopard.

See ANIMALS; BIRDS.

Domitian. Roman emperor (AD 81–96) who persecuted both Jews and Christians. Tradition says that under Domitian the apostle John was banished to Patmos, where he wrote the Book of Revelation (Rv 1:9).

See CAESARS, THE.

Donkey. Domesticated ass.

See ANIMALS (ASS).

Doorkeeper. *See* TRADES AND OCCUPATIONS (GATEKEEPER).

Dophkah. Name of an area near the Wilderness of Sin where the Israelites camped on their way to Mt Sinai (Nm 33:12,13). Its site is perhaps identical with Serabit el-Khadem, an Egyptian turquoise mining center.

See WILDERNESS WANDERINGS.

Dor. Fortified Palestinian city (modern el-Burj) situated along the Mediterranean coast, south of Mt Carmel and eight miles north of Caesarea. It is mentioned occasionally in connection with events in the period of the judges and the united monarchy (Jos 17:11; Jgs 1:27; 1 Chr 7:29). Dor is probably the same city as Naphath-dor (Jos 12:23; 1 Kgs 4:11) and Naphoth-dor (Jos 11:2). During the days of the conquest the king of Dor joined Jabin's confederacy against Joshua (Jos 11:2), but was defeated (12:23). The city was assigned to Manasseh's tribe, but the tribe failed to dispossess its inhabitants (Jgs 1:27).

Dorcas. Christian woman in Joppa of Judea, noted for her acts of charity (Acts 9:36–41). Dorcas is called a disciple in verse 36, which is the only instance where the feminine form of the word is used in the Greek NT. Her ethnic origins are not known, since Dorcas, her Greek name, was in common use among both Jews and Greeks. The Aramaic equivalent, Tabitha, meant "gazelle."

When Dorcas died, the apostle Peter was nearby at Lydda. In response to news of his healing ministry there, two men were sent to bring Peter to Joppa. When he arrived, the body had been prepared for burial and placed in an upper room. Peter sent the mourners from the room, knelt to pray, and raised Dorcas back to life. Her restoration was the first of such miracles performed by an apostle.

Dothan. Ancient city located about 60 miles north of Jerusalem, 13 miles north of the city of Samaria, and about 5 miles southeast of Megiddo. The two cities of Engannim (modern Jenin) and Ibleam guarded a narrow pass on the road leading to Dothan and on to the coastal plain.

The mound of Tell Dotha, site of Dothan, rises 200 feet above the surrounding plain to a height of 1,200 feet above sea level. The top of the mound comprises some 10 acres. From there one can today look out upon fertile land boasting good crops. Flocks pasture here as they did in biblical times, drawn to the area in part by the adequate water supplied by its springs.

Dothan was the place where Joseph's brothers sold him to a caravan of Ishmaelites (Gn 37). A millennium later the city was surrounded by Syrian forces in an attempt to capture Elisha, who lived there and who was thought to be betraying the Syrian plans to the Israelite king (2 Kgs 6:8–14). Dothan was mentioned also in the lists of places conquered by Thutmose III and, in the intertestamental period, in connection with the military campaigns of Holofernes (Jud 39,46,73).

Dothan was excavated from 1953 to 1964 by Dr. and Mrs. J. P. Free. The site was occupied from the Early Bronze Age (3000–2000 BC), and was fortified by a large city wall. Its base was 11 feet thick with a vertical exterior face and sloping interior face. The wall was 9 feet wide at its existing 16 feet height, and may have

Aerial view of Jaffa, showing the old town. In the center is the Church of St. Peter the Apostle, where tradition says Peter brought back Dorcas from the dead.

The mound of Dothan.

measured 25 feet high in its original state. Next to the large city gate was found a gray-cream bowl of the same type as that found in first Egyptian dynasty tombs (c. 3000 BC).

The city was heavily fortified in Abraham's day. Free discovered a ten-room fortress constructed inside the city wall. This Middle Bronze Age (1950–1550 BC) building had walls four feet thick. In the Late Bronze Age (1550–1200 BC) this citadel was destroyed in the Israelite occupation of Canaan. A tomb from this period was used continuously with four separate burial levels until about 1100 BC. Pieces of jugs, jars, bowls, and other fragments representing Cypriote and Mycenaean ware were recovered from the various levels, along with daggers, spear points, lamps, and over 160 skeletons.

Dating from Iron Age I (1200–1000 BC), corresponding to the last of the judges and beginning of the monarchy, two walls were discovered which marked the two sides of a street the archaeologist named "Wall Street."

Excavations of the Iron II period (1000–600 BC), that of the Hebrew monarchy, gave indications that Dothan was an administrative center under Solomon. A street from this period was also unearthed, measuring 4 feet wide and excavated a distance of 111 feet. Houses had been built on either side of the street. From the ruins came more imported pottery, toys, and a large 14-handled bowl. Other houses excavated from this period contained the usual domestic remains.

Dothan was destroyed by fire at the end of the ninth century BC, perhaps by Ben-hadad or Hazael of Syria. The city was rebuilt, but it was destroyed again by Tiglath-pileser III (2 Kgs 15:29). A fourth city, built about 700 BC, lasted for over a century.

Very little evidence was found from the Persian period (500–300 BC). The few metal bowls and pottery samples discovered may reflect a declining occupation during this time of the exile and after. In the Hellenistic age (300–50 BC), however, a settlement was established, at least on the top of the mound. Hellenistic lamps, glazed ware, Rhodian jar handles, and a coin bearing the name "Antiochus the King" all give evidence of a Greek settlement at Dothan. During the Roman period the site was also occupied, as attested by a stamp found with the letters SC, "Senatus Consultus," noting the approval of the Roman Senate.

Dove. Small pigeon.

See BIRDS (PIGEON).

Dove's Dung. Source of food eaten when Samaria was besieged by Ben-hadad, king of Syria (2 Kgs 6:25). Taken literally as pigeon excrement, the reference indicates how desperate conditions were in the famished city.

Some scholars suggest that dove's dung refers to the small, edible bulb of the star-of-Bethlehem plant, also known as bird's milk or bird's dung. The bulb could be boiled or roasted to make flour for bread. The "kab" in verse 25 is a unit of measure approximating 1.3 quarts.

Dowry. Gift of property or goods from the bride's family to the bride or groom prior to marriage.

See MARRIAGE, MARRIAGE CUSTOMS.

Drachma. Greek coin made of silver, roughly equivalent to the Roman denarius.

See COINS.

Dragon. Term indicating a number of monstrous land or sea creatures.

See ANIMALS.

Dragon Well. *See* JACKAL'S WELL.

Dram. KJV for daric, a Persian gold coin, in 1 Chronicles 29:7; Ezra 2:69; 8:27; and Nehemiah 7:70–72.

See COINS.

Dreams. Dreams have always fascinated people; the events experienced in dreams are too vivid and real to be ignored.

Scientific Explanation. Many superstitiously believe that dreams are a strange forewarning of serious trouble. On the other hand, psychological research has given many new insights into the nature and causes of dreams. Brain scanning equipment which records unusual mental activity during sleep has enabled scientists to determine the occasions and frequency of dreaming.

To the child a dream is what you look at when you are sleeping. But dreams consist also of ideas and emotions. The sensations of happiness, fear, sorrow, or excitement are so lifelike that the dreamer believes the dream is actually happening.

The details of a dream usually follow a relatively meaningful sequence. The dream may seem to last a long time, but its actual duration is very brief. Dreams often bring together people or events totally unrelated in one's past. Childhood acquaintances may appear vividly in random grouping with friends from adult life. Whereas it is a relief to wake up from a nightmare, there is often disappointment when a pleasant dream is abruptly interrupted.

Dreams are the combined product of memory and sensation. They project information recorded and stored in the mind since earliest childhood, open the window of the mind, and give a glimpse of a person's unconscious self. A dream may be triggered by anything—perhaps a noise, odor, or touch—that physically disturbs the sleeper. Indigestion or an emotional state can produce dreams. Worry and fear often give rise to nightmares.

Ancient Understanding. From the earliest times people viewed dreams as a mystery, provoking speculation about another actual sphere of existence in which the person lived and acted while the body slept. Dreams, especially those of emperors and kings, were held to be messages from the gods.

Ancient recorded dreams focused on three main areas: religion, politics, and personal destiny. Religious dreams called for piety and devotion to the gods. Political dreams supposedly forecast the outcome of battles and the future destiny of nations. Personal dreams guided family decisions and presaged serious crises.

Sometimes the god took the initiative and forewarned the person about something unexpected. Sometimes the ruler or general would go to a pagan temple or holy place and sleep there, hoping to bring on a dream that would help him cope with some serious problem. In some dreams the message was clear; more often it had to be discovered by individuals who specialized in dream interpretation. Records were kept concerning specific dreams and the subsequent events.

Old Testament Use. Dreams played an important part in the lives of God's people. Of the 116 references to dreams listed in *Young's Concordance*, 52 come in Genesis during the early patriarchal period and 29 in the Book of Daniel. In reality, however, only 14 specific dreams are recorded in the OT. Most of them are in Genesis and reflect God's direct revelation to the patriarchs. Even Daniel tells about only two of Nebuchadnezzar's dreams—the

large manlike image and the gigantic tree chopped down—and his own dream about the four beasts and the Ancient of Days.

The OT understanding of dreams had several significant features. Like the rest of the ancient world, people of God believed that God communicated in dreams. Yet there is in the OT accounts a reserve lacking in the perverse and obscene scenes often described in pagan dream records. Another distinction is that God is the initiator; he gives the revelatory dreams when, where, and to whom he pleases—a truth painfully learned by Saul (1 Sm 28:6,15). More significantly, the secular approach to interpretation was specifically rejected. Understanding of dream symbols came not by research in dream books or by natural human ability. When Joseph interpreted the dreams of his two Egyptian fellow prisoners and later of the pharaoh himself, he insisted on giving full credit to God (Gn 40:8; 41:7,25,28,39).

Similarly Daniel informed Nebuchadnezzar that the "God in heaven that revealeth secrets" would make known the king's dream and its meaning, in which task professional dream interpreters had failed (Dn 2:27,28).

Unlike their neighbors, the OT saints knew that a dream was a mere "vision of the night" (Jb 33:15), and figuratively represented unreality (Jb 20:8; Pss 73:20; 126:1; Is 29:7,8).

God used dreams in OT days to protect his servants (Gn 20:1–18); to reveal himself to people in a special way (Gn 28:12); to provide guidance in specific circumstances (Gn 31:10–13); and to forewarn about personal future events (Gn 37:7–19). Dreams were also used to predict the history of nations (Gn 40,41) and to foretell the four great successive world empires that would be replaced by God's eternal kingdom (Dn 4:19–27).

During the approximately 1,000 years between Joseph and Daniel, only two dreams are recorded. One assured Gideon that God would defeat the Midianites (Jgs 7:13–15); the other concerns how Solomon became so wise after his humility and unselfish request for "an understanding heart" (1 Kgs 3:9) thoroughly pleased God.

In the final OT dreams God gave Nebuchadnezzar an overview of future world history (Dn 2:31–45) and a prediction of the king's temporary insanity (Dn 4:19–27). Daniel's dream of the 4 beasts was similar to the king's first dream, but added details concerning future international relations (Dn 7:13,14).

Dreams were seen as one means by which God would speak to prophets (Nm 12:6). But how could the people of God distinguish true prophet from imposter? God gave two tests: ability to predict the immediate future (Dt 18:22) and consistency of message with previously revealed truth (Dt 13:1–4). False prophets were put to death (Dt 13:5). False prophecy was a serious problem in the days of Jeremiah (23:25–32) and Zechariah (10:2). Despite repeated warning by Jeremiah (23:32; 27:9,10; 29:8,9), the people preferred to listen to the false prophets with their empty messages of hope.

Dreams also were a part of Israel's prophetic hope (Jl 2:28).

New Testament Use. The few specific dreams in the NT all come from Matthew, five of these in the first two chapters. They emphasize the divine care and protection of the baby Jesus. First there was God's provision that Jesus would grow up in a home with a father and mother and thus avoid the cruelty and shame of being unjustly called an illegitimate child (Mt 1:19–23). The wise men were instructed in a dream not to tell Herod where Jesus was living (Mt 2:12). Jesus was further protected from jealous King Herod by the dream that told Joseph to flee to Egypt with Mary and the child (Mt 2:13). On Herod's death, Joseph was divinely advised in a dream to return home from Egypt (Mt 2:20). Finally, God warned Joseph to avoid Judea, where Herod's evil son Archelaus reigned, and to settle in Galilee instead.

The only other specific dream mentioned in the NT prompted Pilate's wife to warn her husband, "Don't have anything to do with this innocent man" (Mt 27:19).

KERMIT A. ECKLEBARGER

See PROPHECY; VISION.

Dress. *See* FASHION AND DRESS.

Drink Offering. *See* OFFERINGS AND SACRIFICES.

Dromedary. Swift-footed camel of the Arabian species.

See ANIMALS (CAMEL).

Dropsy. Old medical term for excessive accumulation of watery fluid in any tissue or space of the body. Dropsy, mentioned in Luke 14:2, is a symptom of several serious disorders such as heart, kidney, or liver disease; Jesus healed a man "who had dropsy" but whose underlying illness is not described. The word "dropsy" has generally been replaced with more specific medical terms: excessive abdominal fluid is now referred to as ascites, cutaneous or subcutaneous dropsy as edema, and pleural dropsy as hydrothorax. Dropsy is not mentioned directly in the OT. A reference to swollen feet (Dt 8:4) could refer to pedal edema or simply to the formation of blisters.

See MEDICINE AND MEDICAL PRACTICE.

Drusilla. Third and youngest daughter of Herod Agrippa, king of Judea. A Jewess, Drusilla was born about AD 38 and had two sisters, Bernice and Mariamne. She became engaged to Epiphanes, prince of Commogene, but the engagement was broken as a result of his refusal to convert to Judaism.

Drusilla's brother, Agrippa II, then arranged for her to marry Azizus, king of Emesa, who agreed to be circumcised. Soon after her marriage Felix, a gentile governor of Judea, fell in love with the 16-year-old Drusilla. Around AD 54 he persuaded her to break the Jewish law and leave her husband to marry him.

Drusilla and Felix heard the apostle Paul's proclamation of the gospel while Paul was held in custody at Caesarea (Acts 24:24). Their son, Agrippa, perished when the Italian volcano Vesuvius erupted in AD 79.

Dulcimer. KJV mistranslation for bagpipe in Daniel 3:5,10,15.

See MUSIC AND MUSICAL INSTRUMENTS (PSANTRIN).

Dumah (Person). Ishmael's son who founded an Arab tribe (Gn 25:14; 1 Chr 1:30). Perhaps his descendants lived in the el-Jôf area, but this is difficult to establish.

Dumah (Place). 1. Region of the 12 tribes of Ishmael (Gn 25:14; 1 Chr 1:30) where there were a number of oases; identified with el-Jôf, modern Dumat el-Jendel. This place was located about three-fourths of the way from Damascus to Medina.

2. Town in the highlands allotted to Judah's tribe for an inheritance (Jos 15:52). Its site is probably identifiable with ed-Domeh, 10 miles southwest of Hebron.

3. Hebrew term referring to the land of silence or death; that is, the place of graves (Pss 94:17; 115:17).

4. Perhaps a designation for Edom or Idumaea in Isaiah 21:11.

Dumbness. The inability to speak. Dumbness (now generally called muteness or aphasia) can be a momentary phenomenon or a permanent handicap. It may result from mental retardation, brain lesion, or deafness.

The Bible records several examples of dumbness. Zechariah was "struck dumb" by the angel Gabriel for not believing he would become the father of John the Baptist (Lk 1:18–22). That condition persisted at least nine months until the baby was born and named (Lk 1:62–64).

Inability to speak is usually associated with neurological diseases or severe structural deformities. When Jesus healed people who were thus afflicted, or "hearing-impaired" (Mt 9:32, 33; 12:22,23; 15:30,31; Mk 7:32–37; 9:17–27; Lk 11:14), observers were understandably astonished.

Other scattered biblical passages refer to muteness in people (Prv 31:8; Is 35:6) and in animals (Is 56:10; 2 Pt 2:16). The fact that false gods and idols cannot speak (Hb 2:18–20; 1 Cor 12:2) was frequently pointed out by the prophets, who contrasted them with the living God of Israel.

See MEDICINE AND MEDICAL PRACTICE.

Dung Gate. One of the 11 gates in the Jerusalem wall in Nehemiah's time (Neh 2:13; 3:14). It was located near the southwest corner of the city and led to the Valley of Hinnom, where rubbish and refuse were dumped. This particular gate had been reconstructed by Malchijah, son of Rechab (Neh 3:14), and was situated between the Fountain Gate and the Valley Gate. When the restored walls of Jerusalem were completed, the ceremony of dedication took place near this gate. Josephus knew it as the Essene Gate.

See JERUSALEM.

Dura, Plain of. Location in "the province of Babylon" where Nebuchadnezzar set up the great image of gold which all his subjects were ordered to worship (Dn 3:1). Its exact location is uncertain. It may be situated to the southeast of Babylon, or perhaps even located within the great outer wall of the city itself. The image was doubtless in a prominent place, probably in an open area used for public gatherings. Since *dur* means "rampart," the phrase should probably be read as "the plain of the rampart" within Babylon.

Dwarf. See DEFORMITY.

Dye, Dyer, Dyeing. Method of coloring textiles practiced in the Near East with natural materials even before the time of the patriarch Abraham. The Bible mentions four colors of dyes: purple, blue (actually a shade of violet), crimson, and scarlet. The purple and blue dyes were extracted from small murex shellfish found along the Phoenician coast. The dye, a glandular secretion of the mollusk, changed color on exposure to air from whitish-yellow to red, violet, or purple, depending on how it was treated. Because that dye was costly to produce, only the rich could afford purple clothing; purple, therefore, became a symbol of royalty and luxury. The dye was commonly known as "Tyrian purple" because the Phoenician cities of Tyre and Sidon were the major suppliers (Ez 27:16).

Crimson and scarlet were among several shades of bright red obtained from the kermes insect, a grub that feeds on a species of oak growing in southern Europe and Asia Minor. Some Syrian dyers still use the kermes in spite of the availability of artificial European dyes. The "tanned rams' skins" mentioned in Exodus 25:5 are still made in Syria. The tanned skin is rubbed with dye made by boiling the kermes in water. When dry, the skin is oiled, polished, and used for Bedouin slippers and other beautiful leather articles.

The "purple goods," sold by Lydia of Thyatira (Acts 16:14) was actually a dull red, now sometimes called "Turkey red." It was produced from the root of the madder plant, both for export to Europe and for local use in dyeing cotton and wool for rugs and clothing. Cultivation of madder was a major industry in Cyprus and Syria. A father customarily planted a new madder field for each son born, which would eventually be that son's inheritance. Thyatira had a dyers' guild.

Although not mentioned in the Bible, an "indigo blue" dye produced from pomegranate rind may have been familiar to the Israelites. Egyptian tombs have been discovered that contain cloths dyed with that blue and with yellows and browns of uncertain origin. The Jews, who learned the dyeing trade from the Phoenicians, evidently produced only reds and purples. The Jewish dyeing trade flourished in Asia Minor at least through the 12th century AD.

Yellow was obtained from the petals and flower heads of the *Carthamus tinctorius*, while saffron was derived from the stigmas of the crocus, which grew in large quantities in Syria and Egypt. Green was usually concocted from a mixture of other dyes.

Excavations at Tell Beit Mirsim (Debir) have uncovered the remains of domestic dyeing vats, basins, and drains dating from the Iron Age. The size of the vats indicates that yarn rather than woven cloth was dyed. Storage jars containing agents for stabilizing the colors of the dyes were also found. The ancient processes of dyeing are not clearly understood, but excavations indicate that dyeing was a flourishing industry throughout Bible times.

See CLOTH, CLOTH MANUFACTURING; INDUSTRY AND COMMERCE.

Dysentery. Diarrhea caused by parasitic bacteria, protozoa (amoeba), or worms in contaminated food or drink. Dysentery is accompanied by intestinal spasms and ulceration, with the appearance of blood and pus in the excrement. On the island of Malta the apostle Paul miraculously cured a person of dysentery (Greek *dysenteria,* Acts 28:8). As the verse indicates, high fever accompanies acute dysentery, epidemics of which still plague Malta. A disease described in the OT was probably amoebic dysentery, in which intestinal tissue can be sloughed off "day by day" (2 Chr 21:14–19). A sporadic form of dysentery occurs when the body is able to tolerate the disruptive organism for the most part. Chronic dysentery can be protracted over many years.

See MEDICINE AND MEDICAL PRACTICE.

Ee

Eagle. Large, carnivorous bird of the falcon family noted for its strength, keen eyesight, and graceful flight.

See BIRDS.

Earring. *See* FASHION AND DRESS.

Earth. Term used for our inhabited planet; the world, as distinguished from heaven and hell; land; soil; and in several other ways. Biblical usage is as broad as modern usage.

One Hebrew word translated "earth" is also used generically for "man," or Adam (Gn 2:7,19). That word refers to reddish soil from which Adam's body was made. Another Hebrew word translated "earth" or "land" can refer to a country (Gn 21:21). A word translated "dust" can mean simply earth or dry ground (Gn 3:19). In the NT one Greek word translated "earth" can refer to a land or country (Mt 27:45). The Greek word from which "ecumenical" is derived refers to the whole inhabited earth (Lk 21:26) or the Roman Empire of those days (Lk 2:1).

In the beginning "God called the dry land Earth, and the waters that were gathered together he called Seas. . . . And God said, 'Let the earth put forth vegetation' " (Gn 1:10,11). In some passages "the earth" is used in essentially the modern sense for the whole planet (Jb 1:7), hanging in empty space (Jb 26:7). References to the earth's four corners (Is 11:12; Ez 7:2) allude to the points of a compass, not to the earth's shape. The circle of the earth probably refers to the circumference of the horizon (Is 40:22; cf. Jb 38:13). The earth is sometimes pictured as supported on pillars (Jb 9:6; Ps 75:3) or foundations (Ps 104:5; Prv 8:29; Is 24:18; Jer 31:37). Since many of the biblical usages are found in figurative passages of poetry or prophecy, they reveal little about the Hebrews' cosmological understanding.

"Earth" sometimes refers to the soil or ground that a farmer works (cf. 2 Kgs 5:17). According to the Bible the original condition of the earth (Gn 2:6) was affected by the curse of human sinfulness (Gn 3:17–19); modern ecologists seem to agree that the earth suffers because of human greed and arrogance. After Abel's blood was spilled on the ground, Cain's difficulty in making the soil produce for him was a constant reminder that he had murdered his brother (Gn 4:8–12).

The Israelites, who lived as tenants on God's land (2 Sm 20:19), were instructed to let the land be at rest every seventh year (Ex 23:10–12; Lv 25:4,5), allowing the soil to replenish nutrients used up by crops. After seven such "sabbath years," in the 50th "jubilee year" the land reverted back to original family holdings (Lv 25:10–17). That provision not only reminded the people of God's ultimate ownership but kept potential "land barons" from amassing huge estates.

The Mosaic law instructed the Israelites that the land's condition would be a spiritual barometer of their relationship with God. Drought or lack of productivity was a sign that the relationship had been broken (Lv 26; Dt 28). Israel was warned that their wickedness could become so great that the Lord would evict them from his land (cf. Lv 26:37; Dt 28:64). Even if that happened, however, God would eventually restore his people so they could again be "wedded" to the land (Is 62:4).

In the NT the earth, or world, is said to lie in the power of the evil one (1 Jn 5:19), a reminder that many of the earth's inhabitants are living outside of fellowship with God (cf. Eph 2:1,2). Jesus emphasized the fundamental difference between "earthly" and "heavenly" things (Jn 3:1–12), a theme repeated by James (Jas 3:13–17) and Paul (Col 3:1–5). Earthly wisdom is natural and cannot comprehend the things of God (1 Cor 1:20,21). A Christian's earthly body, although a "temple of the Holy Spirit within you" (1 Cor 6:19), is hardly to be compared with the future immortal body (1 Cor 15:40–44; 2 Cor 5:1–4).

Many passages point to a "coming age," when the earth will be set free from its "bondage to decay," a deliverance for which the whole creation is said to be "groaning" in anticipation (Rom 8:19–23). The Bible pictures a period of prodigious renewal of the earth's fertility (Ez 47; Jl 3:18,19; Am 9:13–15; Zec 14:6–9). One day, however, "the heavens will pass away with a loud noise, and the elements will be dissolved with fire, and the earth and the works that are upon it will be burned up" (2 Pt 3:10). Yet in the apostle John's apocalyptic vision, when "the first earth had passed away, and the sea was no more," he looked up and saw "a new heaven and a new earth" (Rv 21:1).

LOUIS GOLDBERG

Earth, New. *See* NEW HEAVENS AND NEW EARTH.

Earthenware. *See* POTTERY.

Earthquake. Frequent geologic disturbance in Palestine due mostly to the volcanic nature of the regions around the Dead Sea and the Sea of Galilee. The primary centers of earthquakes in Palestine are upper Galilee, the Samaritan country near Shechem, and the western edge of the Judean mountains near Lydda.

The Hebrew word for earthquake indicates a great noise or a tremendous roaring, suggesting that the Israelites were impressed with the rumbling connected with earthquakes.

Instances of earthquakes are (1) at Mt Sinai in connection with God's giving the Law to Moses (Ex 19:18); (2) during the wilderness wandering of the Israelites, when Korah and his followers rebelled against Moses and were destroyed as punishment for their rebellion (Nm 16:31–33); (3) among the Philistines on the occasion when Jonathan and his armor bearer fought a garrison of Philistines (1 Sm 14:15); (4) after Elijah killed the prophets of Baal and fled Jezebel's wrath, when he sat under a juniper tree feeling sorry for himself (1 Kgs 19:11); (5) in the reign of King Uzziah (Am 1:1); (6) at the death of Jesus on Calvary (Mt 27:51–54); (7) at the resurrection of Jesus (Mt 28:2); and (8) at Philippi while Paul and Silas were in jail (Acts 16:26). Earthquakes are also mentioned as one of the phenomena in connection with the "Day of the Lord" (Zec 14:4,5) and the consummation of this age (Rv 6:12–24; 11:19; 16:18).

The Jewish historian Josephus described a quake that occurred during the battle of Actium in which many animals and more than 30,000 people were killed. Eusebius recorded the destruction of Caesarea and Emmaus by an earthquake during the reign of Hadrian. In spite of much ancient and modern earthquake activity in Palestine, Jerusalem has remained relatively undamaged.

East, People of the; Children of the. Phrases used in reference to those nations that were east of Israel.

See PEOPLE OF THE EAST.

Eastern Sea. Alternate name for the Salt Sea, or Dead Sea, derived from the sea's location on the eastern boundary of the land of Israel (Ez 47:18; Jl 2:20; Zec 14:8).

See DEAD SEA.

East Gate. Gate in the walled city of Jerusalem (Neh 3:29). "East gate" also refers to the gate of the temple mentioned in Ezekiel 10:19; 11:1; and 43:1.

See JERUSALEM.

East Sea. KJV name for the Eastern Sea, an alternate name for the Dead Sea, in Ezekiel 47:18.

See DEAD SEA.

East Wind. Wind coming mostly in May, September, and October. This scorching wind, also called a sirocco, destroyed vegetation (Gn 41:6; Ez 17:10; Jn 4:8), withered flowers (Ps 103:16), and dried up fountains and springs (Hos 13:15). With an east wind the Lord drove back the waters of the Red Sea for the Israelites to cross (Ex 14:21). The east wind also depicts God's judgment (Is 27:8; Jer 4:11; 18:17). An east, northeast wind drove the apostle Paul's ship off course (Acts 27:14, KJV Euroclydon). That wind, which is frequent in the western Mediterranean, is called a "levanter."

See PALESTINE.

Ebal. 1. Shobal's son and descendant of Seir the Horite (Gn 36:23; 1 Chr 1:40).

2. Joktan's son and descendant of Shem (1 Chr 1:22). He is called Obal in Genesis 10:28.

Ebal, Mount. Mountain just over 3000 feet high in the central hill country of Israel. Mt Gerizim is usually mentioned with it (Dt 11:29; 27:13; Jos 8:33). There is no certain known meaning to the word. It is quite unlikely that it was connected in any way with a son of Shobal, whose name is spelled the same as the mountain (Gn 36:23; 1 Chr 1:40; cf. 1 Chr

1:22, where Ebal is a variant of the spelling Obal of Gn 10:28).

Years before the entrance into the Promised Land, God, through Moses, designated the twin mountains Ebal and Gerizim as the place for the recitation of the curses and blessings of Deuteronomy 27, 28. According to Deuteronomy 27:12 six tribes of Israel were to stand on Gerizim and shout the blessings. These were Simeon, Levi, Judah, Issachar, Joseph, and Benjamin. Joseph here would mean the tribes of Ephraim and Manasseh in whose territory these two mountains belonged. The other six tribes, Reuben, Gad, Asher, Zebulun, Dan, and Naphtali, were to recite the curses from Mt Ebal. It is interesting that Ebal is north of the east-west valley that separates the two mountains and it is the more northerly tribes that stand on it.

The fulfillment of the divine directive is recorded in Joshua 8:33. Joshua also obeyed in another matter—that of building on Mt Ebal an altar of unhewn stones (Jos 8:30) as Moses had commanded (Dt 27:4).

Ebed.   1. Gaal's father (Jgs 9:26–35). Gaal led the men of Shechem in an unsuccessful revolt against Abimelech, judge of Israel.

2. Adin's descendant and son of Jonathan. Ebed was the head of a family that returned to Judah with Ezra after the exile (Ezr 8:6).

Ebed-melech.   Ethiopian eunuch in King Zedekiah's court. He secured the king's permission to rescue the prophet Jeremiah out of a cistern where he had been thrown to die (Jer 38:6–13). For this righteous act Ebed-melech was promised God's safety at the fall of Jerusalem (Jer 39:16).

Ebenezer.   1. Site where the Israelite army encamped before a battle with the Philistines (1 Sm 4:1–11). It is thought to have been near Aphek, where the Philistines were encamped. The Israelite army was badly defeated in the battle, and 4,000 of its men were slain on the field. The elders of Israel tried to change their fortunes by bringing the ark of the covenant into their camp; but Israel was again defeated with a loss of 30,000 foot soldiers, and the ark of God was captured (1 Sm 4:3–11; 5:1).

2. Site near Mizpah, where God gave Israel a great victory over the Philistines. To commemorate the victory Samuel set up a stone between Mizpah and Jeshanan "and called its name Ebenezer; for he said 'Hitherto the Lord has helped us' " (1 Sm 7:12). The location of this site is unknown.

Eber.   1. Abraham's ancestor (Gn 10:21–25; 11:14–17; 1 Chr 1:18–25; Lk 3:35, KJV Heber)

from whom the word "Hebrew" may be derived. Eber lived 464 years and was the ancestor of the "sons of Eber," a phrase possibly equal to the "Hebrews," as "sons of Heth" equals the "Hittites" (Gn 23:10 NASB). However, the term "Hebrew" may be an indication of social class rather than of descent from Eber. Eber had a son in whose time the earth was divided, a division possibly into nomadic and sedentary groups.

2. Gadite leader registered during the reigns of Jotham, king of Judah (950–932 BC), and Jeroboam II, king of Israel (993–953 BC; 1 Chr 5:13, KJV Heber).

3. Benjamite and Elpaal's descendant (1 Chr 8:12).

4. Benjamite and Shashak's descendant (1 Chr 8:22, KJV Heber).

5. Head of Amok's priestly family during the days of the high priest Joiakim (Neh 12:20).

Ebez.   City in the plain of Esdraelon, allotted to Issachar's tribe for an inheritance (Jos 19:20, KJV Abez). Its site is unknown.

Ebiasaph.   Kohathite Levite, Elkanah's son and the father of Assir (1 Chr 6:23,37; 9:19); alternately called Abiasaph in Exodus 6:24.

Ebla.   Ancient Syrian city-state identified with the contemporary site of Tell Mardikh.

According to one text discovered there, Ebla was a huge city, with a population of 260,000. That a quarter of a million people could crowd into a city the size of Old Jerusalem is explained by the fact that many of the farmers and workers lived in the surrounding area in tents or possibly in beehive houses made of clay brick. Such beehive villages are found even today in the vicinity of Tell Mardikh. Only the palace, the treasury, the storerooms, and

A part of the king's palace at Ebla. The podium for the royal throne is at the lower left.

the essential facilities and personnel for operation of the city-state, would as a rule be located within the city walls. Even so, the population density in the city would be extremely high.

Ebla was a commercial center, manufacturing items of textiles, wood, ceramics, gold, silver, and other metals. A large number of the clay tablets unearthed are economic documents, recording transactions with many other cities, stretching from Asia Minor to Egypt and from Cyprus to Iran (Persia). Thousands of cities are named in these documents, according to archaeologist Giovanni Pettinato. Included are many familiar biblical names, such as Hazor, Megiddo, Dor, Joppa, Gaza, and Uru-salim (Jerusalem, or possibly "city of Salem"). In one text Ur is described as "in the territory of Haran" (cf. Gn 11:31). Most amazing is Pettinato's reference to the "cities of the plain" (Gn 13:10), reportedly in the same order in which they occur in the Bible: Sodom, Gomorrah, and Zoar. Zoar is described as "in the territory of Bela" (cf. Gn 14:2). According to the biblical account, Sodom and Gomorrah were destroyed in the days of Abraham (Gn 19:24–29); hence the details recorded in Genesis 14 and 19 could not have been reconstructed at a later date unless there was a living tradition recording the events. This claim has been denied by a later epigrapher at Ebla.

The date of the Eblean documents is a very important question; the answer is a bit complex, but nevertheless quite certain. For one thing, the pottery from Tell Mardikh IIB-1 is contemporary with the pottery from Amuq I (a well-known site in the plain of Antioch on the Orontes in Turkey, not far from Tell Mardikh), and Amuq-I pottery is contemporary with the dynasty of Akkad (c. 2360–2180 BC). Furthermore, the royal palace was found burned to the ground, and Naram-Sin (c. 2269–2234 BC) boasts of his conquest of Arman and Ebla, "cities uncaptured since the creation of man." The archaeologists conclude that Naram-Sin burned Ebla about 2250 BC. Still another line of evidence is found in a text from Tell Mardikh, dated in the reign of Ebrum, where Sargon of Akkad is mentioned. Sargon and Ebrum were therefore contemporaries, and Sargon is dated about 2350–2295 BC. Igrish-Khalam was the first king of Ebla, so the archaeologists conclude that he built the royal palace about 2400 BC, possibly a few years earlier. It should be mentioned that other scholars lower the dates for the Akkadian dynasty by about 110 years. In any system, the period covered from the beginning of the reign of Sargon to the end of the reign of Naram-Sin is about 120 years, an average of 30 years per reign. On the basis of known datable dynastic successions (from father to son), this

seems a bit high—the first son was usually born when the father was 20 years old or thereabouts—but it is not unreasonable. If we work from this figure, it would put the beginning of the known kings of Ebla around the year 2430 BC.

Kings of Ebla	Dynasty of Akkad
Igrish-Khalam	
Ar-Ennum	
Ebrum	Sargon
Ibbi-Sipish	Rimush
Dubukhu-Ada	Manishtusu
Irkab-Damu	Naram-Sin

The name Ebrum is remarkably similar to Eber, the ancestor of Abraham. According to Genesis 11, the genealogy consists of Eber, Peleg, Reu, Serug, Nahor, Terah, and Abram (Abraham). The suggestion has been made that since Ebrum was such a mighty king, he may well be the Eber of Genesis 11. According to the figures in Genesis 11, the birth of Abram occurred 191 years after the birth of Peleg, at which time Eber was 34 years old. Since Ebrum was contemporary with Sargon, this could suggest a date of about 2180 BC for Abraham's birth—which is remarkably close to the date given in older biblical chronologies. This, however, is not proof that Ebrum and Eber are the same person; it merely demonstrates that the identification lies within the realm of chronological possibility.

Many other personal names appear in the tablets from Tell Mardikh. Included in those mentioned by Pettinato are many biblical equivalents—e.g., Abram (ab-ra-mu), Israel (ish-ra-ilu), Saul (sha-u-lu), and David (da-u-du). To some, this fact raises questions, while others find it to be a confirmation of the biblical record. For example, it might be asked how the name "Israel" could be found four or more centuries before God gave the name to Jacob. The Bible does not suggest that the name was new. Names in those days were often composed of the name of a deity plus a verbal form (e.g., Isaiah = "Yah is salvation"). It is entirely conceivable that parents named their children ish-ra-ilu, "El (God) has prevailed (or shall prevail)" before the days of Jacob. What was new in the biblical experience was the personal encounter with God and the blessing that it brought on Jacob.

A number of the names from Ebla seem to appear in two forms, one compounded with -ilu (El), the other with -ya (Yah). Thus the names mi-ka-ya (Micaiah, Micah) and mi-ka-il (Michael) are reported by Pettinato, along with other theophoric (God-bearing) names. The appearance of the ending -ya, if it has been properly interpreted as a divine name (Yah, the Lord), raises an important question. According to Exodus 6:3, God told Moses that he appeared to Abraham, to Isaac, and to Jacob as El Shaddai, "but by my name Yahweh I did not make myself known to them." This seems to say that the name Yahweh was not known prior to the revelation to Moses at Sinai. On the other hand, the name Yahweh is found many times in Genesis, not only in narrative portions (where a later author or editor might have inserted a name, such as was done with certain place names), but also in oaths taken in the name of Yahweh and in quotations that imply that the name of Yahweh was actually in use. This problem has long been recognized, and biblical scholars have divided into two groups: those who held that the name was *not* known prior to the time of Moses, and those who held that the name *was* known, but that it took on a new meaning in the light of the Sinai-exodus event. If the interpretation of the Eblean materials proves to be correct—namely that *-ya* is a divine-name element in personal names—then we shall have to conclude that the name Yah(weh) was known in patriarchal times, but its true significance, that Yahweh is the ever-living and life-giving God, only began to be fully revealed in his deliverance of his people from Egyptian bondage.

The whole problem becomes moot, however, since scholars (some of whom seem to be apprehensive of displeasing the Syrian government) are now inclined to reject many of Pettinato's earlier claims. Even Pettinato seems to have retracted some of them.

The Eblean texts contain many other names of gods and goddesses, most of them already known to us. According to Joshua 24:2, Abraham's ancestors "worshiped other gods." Yah may have been one of those gods whom they worshiped in ignorance. The revelation that he was not just another god among many was given to Abram when the Lord called him out of Mesopotamia and sent him to Canaan to become the father of the people of faith in Yahweh.

The Eblean materials have certainly opened a new door to a rich storehouse of knowledge. It will be many years—well into the 21st century—before all the implications of this discovery are fully realized. But certain facts are already clear, and among these is this very important truth: the patriarchal stories in Genesis 11–35 can no longer be ascribed to 8th- or 7th-century authors. To assume that such an author could have included hundreds of names of places and persons, items of trade, and the many details that are found in these chapters, and then to suggest that it is mere coincidence

A cylinder seal from Ebla.

that has brought to light the same names, places, trade relationships, and countless other details through modern archaeological discoveries, is simply unreasonable. Ebla has delivered the coup de grace to such theories.

The discoveries at Tell Mardikh, astounding as they are, do not "prove" the Bible, for it does not need the proof of archaeology or of any other human skill. The Bible is God's Word. Any attempt to "prove" it only exhibits our doubts (Jn 5:41–47). The discoveries at Ebla will help us to see, as other archaeological discoveries have done, what kind of men and women God was dealing with, what kind of world they were living in, and how much he must have loved them to want to deliver them from the ways of the world to walk in his way. We still have much to learn, and Ebla will supply some of the background for that learning process.

WILLIAM SANFORD LaSOR

See INSCRIPTIONS; ARCHAEOLOGY.

Bibliography. P. Matthiae, *Ebla: An Empire Rediscovered;* G. Pettinato, *The Archives of Ebla: An Empire Inscribed in Clay.*

Ebony. Dark black wood, highly prized in antiquity for use in home furnishings.

See PLANTS.

Ebron. Town belonging to Asher's tribe (Jos 19:28, KJV Hebron). Its location has not been identified. Ebron may be a copyist's error for Abdon (Modern Abdeh), a levitical city located some 15 miles south of Tyre and inland from Achzib on the Mediterranean coast.

Ebronah. KJV form of Abronah, an Israelite stopping place in the wilderness, in Numbers 33:34,35.

See ABRONAH.

Ecbatana. Greek name for the capital of the ancient Median empire, later one of the capital cities of the Persian and Parthian empires. It is often spelled Achmetha (Ezr 6:2 KJV), approximating its Aramaic name. The Old Persian name, Hangmatana, may have meant "place of assembly." Modern Hamadan covers most of the ruins of the ancient city.

The city is at 6,300 feet on the eastern slopes of Mt Orontes (Alvand), a granite peak reaching to a height of 12,000 feet above sea level, part of an impassable range broken only by the pass leading to Ecbatana. Major trade routes converged on this pass and gave Ecbatana its strategic importance.

The altitude of the city also accounted for its popularity as the summer residence of Persian and Parthian kings. In the winter, blizzards pile snow several feet deep and temperatures plummet below zero, but the summer climate is cool and comfortable; mountains shade the afternoon sun while melting snows bring ample water. Greek general Xenophon reported that the Persian king Cyrus annually spent three months of spring in Susa, seven months of winter in Babylon, "and in the height of summer two months in Ecbatana."

Greek historian Herodotus recorded that the city was established by Deioces, founder of the Median dynasty early in the 7th century BC. In 550 BC Cyrus captured the city from a Median king, Astyages. It was from Ecbatana that Cyrus issued his 538 BC degree that all Jews throughout his kingdom might return to Jerusalem to rebuild the temple of the Lord (Ezr 1:2–4). Later an Aramaic memorandum regarding this decree was found in the records at Ecbatana after a fruitless search of the archives in Babylon (Ezr 6:1–12). After Darius I (522–486 BC) quelled a revolt in securing the throne, he had the famous Behistun inscription carved in the side of Mt Orontes high above the city. The city was taken and pillaged by Alexander the Great in 330 BC.

Although Ezra 6:2 is the only explicit biblical reference to the city, Ecbatana could have been one of the Median cities receiving exiles from the northern kingdom (722 BC), if the city were in existence before fortification by Deioces (2 Kgs 17:6). The apocryphal book of Tobit places Jewish exiles in Ecbatana in the 7th century (Tob 3:7; 7:1; 14:14), though that is of questionable historical worth. The apocryphal book of Judith records a battle between a Median king Arphaxad and an Assyrian king Nebuchadnezzar in which the Assyrians capture Ecbatana (Jth 1:1,2,14), but the account is dubious because the identity of those kings is unknown. Antiochus Epiphanes may have died there in 164 BC (2 Mc 9:1–3, 19–28).

Ecbatana is the only one of the three Per-sian capitals that has yet to be excavated. Ancient Greek authors gave elaborate descriptions of the city and its wealth. Polybius, for example, reported that it "greatly exceeded all the other cities in wealth and the magnificence of its buildings." Incidental archaeological discoveries of two foundation inscriptions in silver and gold from the time of Darius I and column bases from Artaxerxes II suggest the great promise of excavations there. Excavations have been forestalled, however, because extensive demolition of modern Hamadan would be necessary for access to much of the ancient city below.

The tomb of Esther and Mordecai is alleged to be at Ecbatana, but it is probably the tomb of the wife of a Sassanid (Persian) king of the 5th century AD.

See PERSIA, PERSIANS.

Ecclesiastes, Book of. OT book of wisdom literature. Ecclesiastes is philosophical in character, posing deep questions about the meaning and nature of human existence.

"Ecclesiastes" is the Greek title for the book and has come into English from the Septuagint (Greek translation of the OT). In keeping with an early Jewish practice of adopting the first few words of a book as the title, the Hebrew title of Ecclesiastes is "The Words of Qoheleth, the Son of David, King in Jerusalem." It is also known simply as "Qoheleth."

The term "Qoheleth" is the author's title for himself throughout the book (1:1, 2, 12; 7:27; 12:8–10). It is the Hebrew participial form of a verb meaning "to assemble," and thus it seems to designate one who speaks in an assembly. The word has often been translated "the preacher" in English. Because of the philosophical nature of the book, however, the title possibly indicates the author's function or station as a leader in the community of wise men.

Author. The authorship of Ecclesiastes presents complex questions, on which biblical scholars disagree. Early Jewish tradition was divided over the issue, ascribing the book to King Hezekiah and his school as well as to King Solomon.

Internal evidence is often appealed to for support of Solomon as the author of Ecclesiastes. The first verse ascribes the authorship of the book to "the son of David." Other passages (e.g., 1:16–17; 2:6–7). also seem to refer to Solomon, who succeeded David as king of the united kingdom of Israel. Those who reject Solomonic authorship interpret such references as literary devices, written by a later unknown author in order to use Solomon's devotion to wisdom as a context for his own ideas about life's purpose and meaning.

A number of passages in the book have been appealed to in support of non-Solomonic authorship. Some scholars allege that if the book had been written by Solomon, he would not have used the past tense about his reign "over Israel in Jerusalem" (1:12). Proponents of Solomonic authorship point out, however, that the Hebrew verb "was" can also mean "became," thus stating that Solomon had become king in Jerusalem.

It is also alleged that 1:16 supports a date of writing by an author who lived much later than Solomon. They say that Solomon could not have said that he was wiser than "all who were over Jerusalem before me," for that would point to a long succession of kings before him. But the author may have meant prominent wise men rather than kings (see 1 Kings 4:31).

One of the chief difficulties with Solomonic authorship is the fact that OT history does not record a period of spiritual revival in Solomon's life as a context for the Book of Ecclesiastes. That is not a conclusive argument, however, for the thoughts recorded in the book are intensely personal in nature. The historical books of the OT deal primarily with historical developments, mentioning personal aspects of human life only where they bear upon God's purposes as reflected in the national history. It would in fact be surprising if the extremely personal struggles recorded in Ecclesiastes were cited by the historical writers.

The question of authorship is a difficult one, but there seems to be no conclusive evidence against Solomon as the author of Ecclesiastes.

Date. The majority of scholars who hold to the Solomonic authorship of Ecclesiastes date the book in Solomon's final years as king (c. 940 BC). The book would then have been written in the golden era of Israelite wisdom, by one of the foremost proponents of wisdom teaching.

Those who deny Solomonic authorship disagree among themselves as to when the book was written, but most date it in the postexilic period. A Maccabean date (c. 165 BC) is somewhat difficult to maintain, because fragments of the book, dated in the 2nd century BC, have been found at the Dead Sea site of Qumran. Also, the apocryphal book of Ecclesiasticus, probably written in the early 2nd century BC, was heavily influenced by Ecclesiastes. Such factors would allow little time for the writing and circulation of the book in the Maccabean period.

A number of conservative scholars, such as F. Delitzsch and E. J. Young, have assigned a 5th-century date to the book. Many others consider it a 3rd-century document.

Internal Evidence. Attempts have been made to determine the date of the Book of Ecclesiastes from alleged historical allusions. But the somewhat gloomy observations found in such passages as 1:2–11 and 3:1–15 need be nothing more than the author's conclusions about the emptiness of life. They do not necessarily indicate that the book was written in a time of national decline or social decay within Israel, a time that would not fit with the reign of Solomon.

It is also alleged that the book contains allusions to Greek philosophical concepts. That would indicate that it was written sometime after the Hellenization of the Syro-Palestinian world effected by the conquests of Alexander the Great (356–323 BC).

One of those philosophical concepts is the "golden mean" propounded by Aristotle. The golden mean calls for avoiding extremes in the pursuit of satisfaction in life, and it is reflected in Ecclesiastes 7:14–18. The same concept is found in Egyptian Wisdom Literature (*Instruction of Amen-em-opet* 9.14), as well as in Aramaic wisdom literature. In one of the finest examples of Aramaic wisdom, *The Words of Ahiqar*, the golden mean is expressed in the words "Be not (too) sweet, lest they [swallow thee]: be not (too) bitter [*lest they spit thee out*]." But the golden mean concept need not indicate one particular period of thought; it may simply represent a basic kind of wisdom shared by people of all times and ethnic backgrounds.

Linguistic Considerations. The most critical issue in dating Ecclesiastes is the nature of the book's language. The Hebrew of Ecclesiastes is unique, differing stylistically and linguistically from such 5th-century OT books as Ezra, Nehemiah, and Zechariah.

Some scholars maintain that the language of Ecclesiastes was heavily influenced by Aramaic, and thus the book was written at a time when the Aramaic language was influential in the Hebrew-speaking world. Others have argued that the peculiarities of the Hebrew should be understood as affinities with Canaanite-Phoenician dialects.

It is often asserted that the Hebrew of the book is similar to later Mishnaic Hebrew, particularly in its use of the relative pronoun. Yet the language of Ecclesiastes is dissimilar to the Mishna in other ways.

The linguistic evidence could point to a late date for the book, but it is also possible that Solomon wrote in a literary style that was heavily influenced by Phoenician literature. Such a style may have become a standard for the literary genre into which Ecclesiastes falls. During the reign of Solomon, contacts between Palestine and Phoenicia were quite common.

Purpose and Theological Teaching. The Book of Ecclesiastes demonstrates the meaninglessness of a world view that does not press beyond the limits of human experience to include God. It seeks to show that meaningful satisfaction may be attained in a universe that seems to be nothing more than a succession of wearying cycles—a universe in which people are locked with no apparent means of escape. According to Qoheleth, freedom can be achieved by fearing God and believing that God will ultimately judge everything fairly. Thus, life has a goal and purpose that it will reach, although in the course of history and the processes of the physical world it may not look that way.

The book's chief theological tenet is that God is not disinterested in the course of human events with its gross injustices. He will judge every deed. Life therefore has a purpose, and human deeds have meaning, for they will be judged by the ultimate standard—the mind of the Creator himself.

Qoheleth is often accused of having a pessimistic view of life. One cannot read such passages as 1:12–14,18 and 2:1–9,18–23 without feeling his helplessness as he viewed what seemed an empty existence. But Qoheleth's pessimism had to do with life apart from God. To him such a life had no meaning.

A positive good emerges from the book, however, which is often overlooked. Qoheleth speaks in terms of absolutes as he spins his argument. There is an absolute good for people as they live in a seemingly meaningless world. That good is the enjoyment of God's gifts to his people. Thus Qoheleth is not an utter pessimist. When he lifts the horizons of his world view to include the hand of God at work in the world, he becomes an optimist. But when he looks at life without God he is pessimistic, for such a view offers only despair.

Qoheleth's "theology of contentment" is clear in such passages as 2:24,25, 3:10–13, and 3:22. The first passage seems to express a hedonistic view of life, making eating and drinking the main purpose. The expression "eat and drink" is a Semitic idiom that seems to express the everyday routines of life (cf. Jer 22:15; Lk 17:27,28). Qoheleth's use of the phrase, then, simply means that one should enjoy God's providence. Life is meant to be enjoyed, not endured.

In 3:10–13 Qoheleth sets forth the great enigma of humankind: God has put the knowledge of eternity in the human mind. That is, he has made the mind able to go beyond the limits of physical existence. Yet even that ability to conceptualize the eternal does not explain all of God's purposes. So it is good for a person simply to accept human limitation and enjoy whatever knowledge God gives.

Ecclesiastes 3:22 is part of a difficult section of the book, for 3:16–22 seems to present an agnostic view of life. There Qoheleth observes the inequities of life and concludes that God allows such things for the purpose of "sifting" people to show them that they are no more than beasts. The same principle appears in 8:11, where Qoheleth observes that when evil goes unpunished, the wicked are encouraged to continue to do evil. In 3:18 he asserts that injustice is present in the world to distinguish the good from the wicked. The Hebrew in that assertion should be translated "in and of themselves." That is, viewed alone, apart from God, humankind is no better than animals. If one adopts a world view that omits God, there can be no way of knowing what lies beyond the grave (3:21). The inequities that Qoheleth observes will be corrected only in the day of judgment. Thus it is best for a person to be content with God's providence and not to be anxious about tomorrow (3:22).

The key to understanding the Book of Ecclesiastes is the recurring phrase "under the sun." That phrase defines Qoheleth's perspective. He is not judging all human experience as vain. Rather, he is observing life "under the sun," or apart from God, as vain. The apostle Paul rendered the same verdict on the created world in Romans 8:20–23, but went on to say that God uses all things in his world to work out good results for his people (Rom 8:28). Qoheleth's viewpoint is similarly hopeful.

Qoheleth has often been interpreted as expressing an Epicurean view of life, that eating and drinking are humanity's highest good. In 2:1–8, however, he tests pleasure and finds it futile. He concludes that pleasure is not an absolute good. The passages that speak of eating and drinking refer only to the enjoyment of those good and necessary things that come from God's hand.

Content. *The Vanity of the Cycle of History and Nature (1:1–11).* Qoheleth begins his recital of the vanity of life by observing its emptiness and the apparent lack of purpose in the processes of nature. Human toil is fruitless (1:3), and the endless cycle of life and history is meaningless (1:4–11).

The Vanity of Qoheleth's Own Experience (1:12–2:26). In this dramatic section Qoheleth looks back to observe the futility of aspects of his life that some might have regarded as possessing great value. He recalls his search for wisdom, but pronounces human philosophy futile (1:12–18). His search for pleasure (2:1–11) also ended in futility. In the light of this conclusion, Qoheleth hardly sets forth the attainment of pleasure as life's highest good. The search for valid philosophical verities is wearisome and futile in its outcome (2:12–17). Human toil is also vain (2:18–23), because one can never be sure who will inherit the reward of one's toil (2:21). Qoheleth concludes that the greatest good is to accept God's providence joyfully (2:24–26), an optimistic note in his message.

The Plight of Humanity Apart from God (3:1–22). Qoheleth's familiar statement that everything in life has its time (3:1–9) has often been interpreted as crassly fatalistic. But those verses more probably set forth the unalterability of life's circumstances. Humankind is locked into a continuum from which there is no escape, yet people are able to think in terms that go beyond the physical (3:11). That is the enigma of humankind. Viewed apart from God, people really are no better than animals (3:19,20).

Conclusions Resulting from Qoheleth's Observations (4:1–16). The author begins with a gloomy outlook on life (4:1–3) but goes on to draw conclusions of permanent value. He points out, for example, that life's difficulties are better faced with a partner than alone (4:9–12).

The Vanity of Living Only for Oneself (5:1–6:12). Qoheleth gives a powerful denunciation of a self-seeking life by focusing on God (5:1,2,4–6). His condemnation of the misuse of riches and his concern for the poor (5:8–6:9) are themes later emphasizes in the NT.

Wisdom for Living (7:1–8:17). This fine example of OT Wisdom Literature uses a proverbial pattern (7:1–13) and personal references (7:23–29) to give insight into how one may find true satisfaction. The whole passage upholds the virtue of godly wisdom. Qoheleth's theology of contentment underlies his observation that God is the source of adversity as well as prosperity (7:14). He affirms that one should accept both as coming from God. Applying wisdom to governmental authority (8:2–9), Qoheleth counsels the reader to obey the authorities. The apostle Paul gave the same advice in Romans 13. Qoheleth strikes an optimistic note (8:13), exalting the fear of God. The author is not totally pessimistic, for he shows that fearing God leads to genuine satisfaction.

Observations on Life's Seeming Injustices (9:1–18). "Under the sun," apart from God, there are no apparent differences among human beings (9:1–6,11,12). Great deeds often go unnoticed and unthanked (9:13–16). A person should nonetheless be content, for life does offer certain benefits (9:7–10).

Wisdom and Folly (10:1–20). Wisdom in the OT basically means knowing God, and folly is rejection of God. Qoheleth shows how wisdom can lead to honor and satisfaction, and folly can lead to ruin.

Qoheleth's Conclusion—Fear God (11:1–12:14). The Book of Ecclesiastes began with a pronouncement of vanity on all creation, and it ends with Qoheleth looking beyond his gloomy vistas to see God. Chapter 11 begins with a statement of human inability to understand the ways of God. Though people are meant to enjoy life, they must remember that the future will bring God's judgment (11:9,10). After a beautiful description of old age (12:1–8) and encouraging the reader to fear God in youth, Qoheleth states his conclusion. A person's whole duty is to fear God (12:13,14). The pleasures of youth will burst like a bubble and, without God, one will finally have nothing. Satisfaction can come only as one fears God. Life without God is the ultimate vanity.

THOMAS E. McCOMISKEY

See WISDOM, WISDOM LITERATURE; SOLOMON (PERSON).

Bibliography. G.A. Barton, *A Critical and Exegetical Commentary on the Book of Ecclesiastes*; F. Delitzsch, *Commentary on the Song of Songs and Ecclesiastes*; R. Gordis, *Koheleth—The Man and His World* and *The Wisdom of Ecclesiastes*; A.H. McNeile, *An Introduction to Ecclesiastes*; A.L. Williams, *Ecclesiastes*.

Eclipse. Total or partial obscuration of the sun as a result of the passing of the moon between the sun and the earth; thus the possible explanation for certain unusual astronomical events in the Bible.

See ASTRONOMY.

Ed. Name of an altar built in God's honor by the Reubenites, Gadites, and the half tribe of Manasseh (Jos 22:10,34) when these tribes took possession of Gilead. The tribes west of the Jordan opposed the erection of the altar (v 11). The Hebrew Masoretic text and the Greek Septuagint do not contain the word, but the KJV and RV insert it on the authority of a few manuscripts.

Edar. KJV spelling of Eder in Genesis 35:21.

See EDER (PLACE) # 1.

Eden. 1. Place where Adam and Eve lived until their sin against God (Gn 2:8,15; 3:23,24).

See GARDEN OF EDEN.

2. Alternate form of Beth-eden in Ezekiel 27:23.

See BETH-EDEN.

Eder (Person). 1. Member of Benjamin's tribe and the son of Beriah, a leader in the town of Aijalon (1 Chr 8:15, KJV Ader).

2. Levite of Merari's clan and the son of Mushi (1 Chr 23:23; 24:30).

Eder (Place).   1. First camping place of Jacob between Ephrath (Bethlehem) and Hebron following Rachel's death. The tower of Eder, meaning "the tower of the flock," was perhaps a watchtower constructed for shepherds to guard their flocks (Gn 35:21, KJV Edar). It was located a short distance from Bethlehem. Its exact location is unknown.

2. One of the 29 cities located near the border of Edom in the southern extremity of the land allotted to Judah's tribe for an inheritance. It is listed between Kabzeel and Jagur in Joshua 15:21. Its site is unknown.

Edom, Edomites.   Land and its inhabitants found on the high plateau to the south and southeast of the Dead Sea. The biblical term Edom, meaning "red," denotes either the name of the land or the name of Esau, in remembrance of the red pottage for which he exchanged his birthright (Gn 25:30; 36:1,8,19). The country of Edom was also known as Seir (Gn 32:3; 36:30; Nm 24:18).

Geography.   The northern boundary of Edom was the Wadi Zered, the "Brook of the Willows" (Is 15:7). In ancient geological times the area was thrust up to a considerable height, and dark red sandstone cliffs were exposed along the western side where the land falls steeply into the Arabah, the southern extension of the deep depression in which the Dead Sea and the Jordan Valley lie. The Edom plateau rises to over 5000 feet, reaching over 5600 feet in places. The area divides into two unequal parts. The region of Punon forms something of a valley between the smaller northern part and the longer southern part. The northern section is not quite so high,

though in a limited area near Rashadiyeh it reaches 5300 feet. The southern section is longer and generally higher, being over 5000 feet throughout the central ridge and touching 5687 feet at one point. To the east the escarpment does not fall below 4000 feet except in the north. The desert lies beyond and limits expansion eastward. To the west the land falls away rather steeply into the Arabah. The extent of Edom to the west varied from time to time. It was comparatively easy to gain access to the Negeb of southern Judah in this area, and Edomite encroachments were made from time to time. The southern frontier was marked by an extensive limestone scarp at the southern edge of the plateau. This ran eastward from Ain Gharandal in the Arabah. Beyond this barrier to the south lay rocky uninhabitable desert, through which merchants must have journeyed to the port at Eziongeber for trade.

The land of Edom was, on the whole, inhospitable though there were areas where farming could be undertaken, particularly in the northeast. Here too herds of animals could be grazed. Edom's wealth, however, came largely from the caravan trade which came up from the south and brought goods from India and South Arabia to the Mediterranean coast and Egypt. The important King's Highway (Nm 21:22) passed through Edom on its way north.

History.   Biblically, the name Edom does not appear in the genealogy in Genesis 10. It first appears in the story of Esau in Genesis 25:30. Esau was called Edom from the red color of the pottage for which he sold his birthright to his brother Jacob. In Genesis 36 there is reference to an Edomite kingdom at a time

The Wadi Tubgha and the mountains of Edom, looking north from the Snake Monument at Petra.

well before the appearance of an Israelite kingdom, though it is possible that the "chiefs" of Edom were tribal chieftains or nondynastic leaders like the Israelite judges.

The earliest nonbiblical references come from Egypt and seem to confirm this. Amarna Letter No. 288 (early 14th century BC) refers to the "lands of Seir," the crossing of the Shashu tribes of Edom into Egypt is mentioned by Seti II (1214–1208 BC) and Rameses III (1198–1166 BC). There are no Egyptian references to towns or rulers, only to tribal Bedouin from Seir-Edom. There is some evidence that Rameses II was in Transjordan about 1280–1270 BC, but there is no clear evidence that there was a centralized government before the 13th century BC. Rather, the land was occupied by mainly seminomadic people. From then on, permanent settlements began to appear, a fact that has relevance for the date of the exodus. The Song of Moses in Exodus 15 refers to the "chiefs of Edom." By the time of the exodus there appears to have been a kingdom of Edom (Nm 20:14,18,20–23; 33:37; 34:3). The Israelites skirted round Edom on their journey to the Promised Land (Jgs 5:4; 11:17,18).

At the time of the rise of the Israelite monarchy Saul fought successfully against Edom (1 Sm 14:47). Doeg the Edomite was the chief of Saul's herdsmen (1 Sm 21:7; 22:9,18,22). At the beginning of the 10th century BC David defeated Edom in the Valley of Salt and slew many Edomites (2 Sm 8:13; 1 Chr 18:12). Thereafter David placed garrisons in Edom and the Edomites became his subjects (2 Sm 8:14). It is not clear whether David saw in these people a military threat or whether he was interested in the supply of copper from their land and the potential wealth that would flow from the caravan traffic passing through Edom. David's successes resulted in the flight of a certain Hadad, who was "of the royal house of Edom" to Egypt (1 Kgs 11:14–17), where he married a member of the Egyptian royal family (1 Kgs 11:18–20). On David's death Hadad returned to Edom, where he became king. It would seem that a monarchical form of government had developed by David's time. Solomon continued to exert influence in Edom. He had access to the port of Ezion-geber (1 Kgs 9:26). It is not clear how strong the government was in Edom.

The biblical records provide no information about Edom from the end of Solomon's reign until the days of Jehoshaphat of Judah (872–848 BC). Jehoshaphat was able to occupy the port of Ezion-geber, although his ships were wrecked there, possibly by the Edomites (1 Kgs 22:48; 2 Chr 20:36,37). Israel combined with Judah and Edom in an unsuccessful campaign against King Mesha of Moab (2 Kgs 3:4–27). Edom was able to throw off Judah's au-

thority under King Jehoram (853–841 BC) and set up a king of its own (2 Kgs 8:20–22). It remained independent until the days of King Amaziah of Judah (796–767 BC), who conquered Edom as far south as Sela, defeating a large army of the Edomites in the Valley of Salt (2 Kgs 14:7; 2 Chr 25:11–13). This gave Judah control of the copper mines in the Punon area. King Uzziah of Judah (792–740 BC) was able to push his control south to Elath (Ezion-geber; 2 Kgs 14:22; 2 Chr 26:1,2). Before the end of the 8th century BC, in the days of Ahaz (735–715 BC), Edom defeated Judah and recovered Elath (2 Kgs 16:6). Thereafter Judah lost control over Edom.

During the 8th century BC the Assyrians began to move into Transjordan. About 800 Adad-nirari III (810–782) claimed to have conquered several of these western states and to have imposed tribute. Then Tiglath-pileser III (745–727) received tribute from Qaus-Malaku of Edom. Sargon II (722–705) spoke of an unnamed ruler of Edom who was involved in the rebellion of Ashdod in 713. Sennacherib (705–681) spoke of a certain Aiarammu, who brought gifts from Edom. Esar-haddon (681–669) referred to Qaus-Gabri king of Edom, who came to Nineveh with 22 vassals to swear allegiance. Under Ashurbanipal (669–627) Edom appears on Assyrian records. Thereafter Assyria itself was defeated by the Babylonians. Under the Babylonians Edom seems to have remained a subservient vassal, although in 594 it joined other small nations in discussing rebellion (Jer 27). When Nebuchadnezzar attacked these, however, Moab and Edom were not involved. In the overthrow of Jerusalem in 586 Edom remained neutral and even allowed some refugees from Judah to shelter there for a time (Jer 40:11). The prophet Obadiah castigated Edom for not assisting Judah at the time of the Babylonian invasion (Ob 11). Instead, they raided Judah, handed over captives to Babylon, and possessed lands in the Negeb area to the south (Ez 35).

A long history of enmity existed between Judah and Edom, and several prophets spoke unfavorably about Edom (Is 11:14; 34:5–17; Ez 32:29; Jl 3:19; Am 1:11,12; Mal 1:2–4). In the 6th century BC Edom entered a period of decline. Several cities were abandoned. At the same time Edomite colonies west of the Arabah in the southern hill country of Judah emerged, and by Roman times there was a province of Idumaea, which was the descendant of the Persian province of Edom, with its administrative center at Lachish. In the old Edomite homeland Arab groups began to move in. Finally, ancient Edom became the home of the Nabataeans.

The urn tomb, located in the southern part of the city of Petra.

Archaeology. Limited archaeological research has been carried out in Edom. Tawilan, Tell el-Kheleifeh, Umm el Biyara, Petra, and some small border fortresses have been excavated, and an extensive surface survey has been undertaken. The Edomites proper emerged at the end of the Late Bronze Age, about 1300 BC, and from the Early Iron Age onward evidence of settled towns has been found. Some aspects of Edomite culture have become clear. A few pieces of writing, notably a seal from Tell el-Kheleifeh, have shown that the Edomites used a script not unlike the Hebrew and Moabite scripts. A number of ostraca have produced personal names and names of deities, such as Qaus, which appears as an element in personal names. Artifacts such as pottery, tools, and ornaments are becoming available in increasing quantities, and architectural features are becoming known. At present, however, archaeological information is comparatively sparse.

Edrei. 1. City of residence for Og, king of Bashan (Dt 1:4; 3:10; Jos 12:4; 13:12). It was located on the southern branch of the Yarmuk River, which was the southern border of Bashan. At this strategic point Og could look over the neighboring region for invaders from the south or from the east, where the land turned into a desert. At Edrai, Moses was able to defeat Og before destroying the city (Nm 21:33–35; Dt 3:1–6). The territory was allotted to the Machirites, the eastern clan of the tribe of Manasseh (Jos 13:31). The modern site for Edrei seems to be Derba, a town of 5,000 in Syria. Many important remains from antiquity survive in this town, including shops, cisterns, streets, and underground caves.

2. Fortified city allotted to Naphtali (Jos 19:37). It was near Kadesh, and may possibly be identified with the modern Tell Khureibeh.

JOHN A. THOMPSON

Education. The original purpose of Jewish education was to teach children to know and understand their special relationship with God, to teach them to serve him, and to educate them in "holiness." Later Jewish education included character development and the history of God's people (particularly through rehearsing his acts of deliverance). Because of that education, the Jews knew the Mosaic law and their own history, and during periods of subjection to foreign powers they were able to maintain their national pride. In modern times they have reestablished themselves as a nation (1948).

Education in the Home. The priority given to education stemmed from the value of children in the Jewish family. Children were a great joy and reward (Ps 127:3–5). Education in the home began soon after a child could talk, and certainly by the age of three. Parents taught prayers and songs which children learned by repetition, just as children today learn nursery rhymes.

At home, children became aware of certain religious items and symbols. They were encouraged to ask about the meaning of the annual Passover ritual (Ex 12:26), which served throughout Hebrew history as a fundamental means of instruction about the nature and significance of God's power in human life. Children undoubtedly had questions about objects they encountered, whether sacred vessels, ornaments, or clothing used in the tabernacle or temple worship, or more mundane things of everyday life.

Parental responsibility for education was clearly defined. A father was expected to give his son instruction in religion and in the history of the Hebrew people. He was also specifically required to teach his son a trade, often his own, since a boy without a trade was thought to have been trained for life as a thief. A father's other responsibilities included finding his son a wife and teaching him to swim.

Rabbis held that women could not study the Law because they were "of light mind." Influential women in the Bible include Deborah (Jgs

4:4,5), Jael (Jgs 4:18–24), the wise woman of Tekoa (2 Sm 14:2–20), the wise woman of Abel (2 Sm 20:16–22), Lois, Eunice, and Priscilla (Acts 18:2; Rom 16:3; 1 Cor 16:19; 2 Tm 1:5).

The Jewish mother played a considerable role in a child's education, particularly in the earliest years. A mother was expected to assist in teaching her sons, but her major responsibility was to train her daughters. Since daughters were less highly esteemed than sons, a girl's education took place entirely in the home. The mother was responsible for educating her daughters to be successful homemakers: obedient, capable, and virtuous wives. Girls learned the skills of cooking, spinning, weaving, dyeing, caring for children, and managing slaves. They learned how to grind grain and at times helped with the harvest. Occasionally they were expected to help guard the vineyard or, if they had no brothers, to help care for the flocks.

Girls probably learned music and dancing and were expected to have good manners and high moral standards. They were taught to read, and some learned to write and reckon weights and measures. In exceptional circumstances a girl might receive an advanced education privately at home from a tutor.

Even when education was entirely home-centered, it is probable that most wealthy and especially royal children were instructed by a tutor, following a tradition established by other Near Eastern peoples.

Religious Education. At an early age children accompanied their parents to religious services. At the great festivals they were introduced to important episodes in Jewish history. The Jews, an agricultural people, believed that agricultural knowledge had been revealed by God and that tending the ground was a basic human responsibility. Like some other Near Eastern nations, they believed that the land belonged to God. They were merely tenants. If a crop failed, it was because God withheld rain, but he would do that only if the people were sinful.

The celebrations of the Passover, Pentecost, and the feast of tabernacles were associated with the harvest. Throughout the biblical period those festivals remained closely identified with the growing season. Such occasions became educational opportunities for children. They learned that the Passover commemorated the deliverance of their ancestors from slavery in Egypt. At Pentecost the Jewish people remembered God giving the Law to Moses on Mt Sinai. The feast of tabernacles, with its green booths made from tree branches, commemorated God's faithfulness to the Jews on their seemingly endless journey to the Promised Land.

An example of a ceremony used as a teaching tool is the Passover ritual, which of the three great festivals was the least directly connected in origin with the harvest. That feast, which was immediately followed by a seven-day period known as the feast of unleavened bread (Lv 23:6), was associated with the beginning of the barley harvest in April. (The exodus from Egypt had taken place at that time of year.)

In the Passover ceremony the priest would take one of the first sheaves of the barley harvest and wave it before the Lord (Lv 23:9–11). Before that, the men would choose a barley field at random and bind some of the best sheaves, leaving them standing. The following evening three men would go out to that field with sickles and baskets to reap those specifically prepared sheaves. As onlookers, including the children, gathered to observe the ceremony, the reapers would ask the crowd certain traditional questions. Year by year the children saw that ritual and heard the answers. The barley was cut and taken to the temple court, where it was threshed and winnowed. Some of it was mixed with oil and incense, and used as an offering. The remainder went to the priests.

Formal Education. Jewish education during the biblical period consisted of acquiring an intimate knowledge of the Law, studying the history of the Jewish people, and becoming proficient in reading, writing, and a certain amount of arithmetic. To that, incidental information such as the medicinal value of certain herbs (see 1 Kgs 4:33) might sometimes be added.

Teachers. As one of their functions priests had from the time of Moses instructed the people in the knowledge of God. As officers of the synagogue the Levites also performed a teaching role (cf. Dt 33:10; 2 Chr 35:3). Before the exile the prophets assumed the role of instructors, teaching the historical heritage of the people and acting as critics of injustice and improper social behavior. Their responsibility was to interpret the Law for contemporary society. By the 4th century BC the prophets' role as instructors had passed to the scribes and to others designated as teachers.

In the centuries before Christ, scribes not only transcribed and preserved the traditions in written form but were students and interpreters of the Law. The scribes were known as doctors of the Law (Lk 5:17 KJV), lawyers (Mt 22:35), and rabbis (Mt 23:8). All higher education was in their hands, and they developed a complex system of instruction known as "the tradition of the elders" (Mt 15:2–6). Although the scribes needed leisure for their scholarly pursuits, they did not despise workers. Most of them, in fact, when necessary practiced a trade as a means of support.

Although the scribes were influential in the time of Christ (Mt 23:1,2), they undoubtedly found, like the prophets before them, that their words were not always heeded. The scribes, who exercised an important influence over contemporary life and morals, were notable for their fierce opposition to Jesus (Mk 2:6) and to the early church (Acts 4:5; 6:12).

By the NT era the entire community was expected to establish and maintain elementary schools. The community was also responsible for financing the education of poor or orphaned children. Out of high regard for earlier priests, prophets, and scribes, and because of the eminent position given to education, teachers were highly esteemed by the Jewish people. Because God had given them the Law, it was of greatest importance. One who worked as God's servant expounding the Law was therefore the most important person in the community. To be a teacher was life's highest privilege, the most significant task a man could perform.

Teachers were expected to demonstrate exceptional character along with their academic qualifications. They were expected to keep children from having contact with anything harmful. They were not to show bitterness or give preference to one child over another. Rather than threatening, they were to explain right and wrong and the harmfulness of sin. Teachers were expected to keep promises to children lest the students grow accustomed to broken words and lies. Teachers were to be even tempered, never impatient or lacking in understanding, always prepared to repeat explanations. It was said that children should be treated like young heifers, with their burdens increased daily. Yet any teacher who was too severe was dismissed.

A teacher was warned not to jeopardize the dignity of his position by familiarity with students, such as joking, eating, or drinking in their presence.

Subject Matter. Early education consisted of learning the Law through listening and oral repetition, along with the study of the written text. The content of the Law covered three main areas: ceremonial, civil, and criminal. Students needed to master these, preparing themselves to take responsibility for observing the Law as adults.

The Scriptures contained such a variety of writings that pupils learned about religion, history, law, morals, and manners, plus reading, writing, and arithmetic. They studied from great literature; along with the Law they used the books of Psalms, Proverbs, and Ecclesiastes extensively as texts. The Dead Sea Scrolls have shown that some classical Hebrew was still being spoken in NT times. Students who commonly spoke Aramaic or Greek were faced with a difficult situation when learning the Hebrew of the OT. The problem was especially complex because the Hebrew was written without any vowel sounds. Those had to be memorized in association with the consonants of the text.

Since the ancient Hebrews were generally regarded as the most proficient musicians and singers in the Near East, it is probable that basic instruction in singing and playing instruments, such as the pipe and harp, was received at home. Even in later times it is unlikely that music formed part of the regular academic education of Jewish boys, although persons who served as temple musicians and singers must have received some formal instruction. Although no Hebrew hymns have survived in musical form, temple singers would almost certainly have been familiar with the kind of music theory known among the Canaanites. (A musical text recovered from Ugarit [Ras Shamra] consisted of a ballad or a hymn inscribed on clay with curious musical symbols that long defied identification. Dating to perhaps 1800 BC, that Canaanite text has been described as the "oldest sheet music in the world.")

During the exile especially, great emphasis was placed on recording and preserving ancient customs and ceremonies in order to maintain the distinctiveness of Hebrew culture. The captives recognized the importance of keeping alive their national heritage and the Law during the years they were living in an alien culture.

The synagogue developed during the exile as a place for the study of religion and for prayer, becoming the center of instruction in the Jewish faith. Previously the temple at Jerusalem had been the only place for sacrifice. Because that ritual could not be performed in Babylon, it was natural for the synagogue to increase in importance in worship as well as in education.

The exile brought about fundamental changes in Jewish life in areas other than the purely religious. Education received considerable stimulation from the Jewish exiles' contact with the more sophisticated culture of the Babylonians. The Babylonian law code was a precise and well-established feature of life. Schools and libraries in Babylonia had been in existence for many centuries. Mesopotamian knowledge of medicine, astronomy, mathematics, architecture, and engineering was far superior to that of the Jews. In that intellectual environment the literature of the Jews took on new meaning; it was from that period that the books of Ezekiel and Daniel emerged.

In the postexilic period, teaching was based extensively on Proverbs and the apocryphal books of Ecclesiasticus and the Wisdom of Solomon. From those works the Jews received practical training for a successful life. The scribes taught that wisdom came from God and that those who obeyed the commandments would bring joy and honor to others.

Under Persian rule in the 6th century BC the Jews had been encouraged to return to Jerusalem and rebuild the temple. After 332 BC, when Alexander the Great defeated the Persian king Darius, strong efforts were made to Hellenize the conquered peoples. The Greek language was introduced along with Greek religion, political procedures, and educational methods. The drive for Hellenization continued under the rule of the Ptolemies (a Macedonian family line that ruled Egypt) and the Seleucids (a Syrian dynasty). Coincident with the establishment of foreign rule came the dominance of the Jewish priesthood in Judean political matters. Greek influence was seen in the enriched aesthetic appreciation typical of certain Jewish rulers.

Although Greek philosophy and sports remained outside the realm of Jewish education, there was a noticeable decline in Jewish religious and moral standards in the Hellenistic period. Some Jews were eager to obtain advancement from the foreign masters by adopting the Greek culture. Others fought desperately to preserve their Jewish heritage. During Roman times the foreign influence was again ignored by faithful Jews whenever possible.

Teaching Methods. Teaching methods, developed from memorizing the Law, stressed the importance of retentiveness and recollection. Children were taught to memorize as soon as they could talk, and were trained to repeat the exact words so that no nuance of meaning would be altered. The alphabet was taught and memorized by being repeatedly written and drilled. Students copied and recopied passages from the written Law in precise, neat handwriting. Any piece of writing containing a mistake was considered dangerous, since it might imprint the wrong word or spelling on the learner's mind. Reading aloud was recommended as an aid to memorization.

To aid learning, each boy was also given a personal text beginning with the first letter of his name and ending with the last. As soon as he demonstrated his ability to read, he received a scroll which contained the first words of Deuteronomy 6:4: "Hear, O Israel: The Lord our God is one Lord." That was recited every morning and evening in postexilic times, along with the Hallel (or psalm of praise), the

story of creation, and the main part of the Law contained in Leviticus.

Teachings also came in the form of proverbs or parables, a device later used by Jesus (Mk 4:1,2). An open sharing of knowledge occurred in "question and answer" periods (for example, the visit of the 12-year-old Jesus to the temple in Jerusalem, Lk 2:46,47).

Very little information is available on education in the early Christian era. We know that Jesus could read and expound the Scriptures and was knowledgeable enough to discuss theology with the learned men in the temple. He probably learned at home and received the elementary education common to most Jewish boys at that period.

Discipline. Discipline, almost always an important element in education, was important to the ancient Hebrews. A system of reward and punishment was used in which corporal chastisement was normal. Punishment was considered to be an outward symbol of God's love and concern for the instruction of his people (Ps 94:8–13), although the Jews as a people did not always learn from those corrections (Jer 5:3; Am 4:6–13). A child was thought to need "breaking" like a horse: "A horse that is untamed turns out to be stubborn, and a son unrestrained turns out to be wilful" (Ecclus 30:8).

Adult Education. When Ezra the scribe returned from Babylon with a copy of the Law, he taught it to the Levites and to the people. That material, together with the Book of Proverbs and literature from both the preexilic and exilic periods, became basic in Jewish education. In the postexilic period, priests traveled to the towns, addressing people in the synagogue on the sabbath and in the square on market days, when a large crowd would be gathered. Some individuals may have extended their learning through discussion with the elders (cf. Ez 8:1).

For those who continued their education, the next phase was probably instruction by scribes. The scribes, leaders of a Jewish sect called Pharisees, had developed Ezra's principles into strict rules on tithing, ritual purity, and synagogue worship. As a young man, Saul of Tarsus came to Jerusalem to study with Gamaliel, an honored rabbi (Acts 22:3). At that time the curriculum was an advanced study of theological law, both written and oral, along with the rites and ceremonies of Jewish culture.

School Buildings. By NT times some schools operated in special buildings and others in the teachers' own houses, but most were attached to the synagogue. When a separate building was designed, it was considered inadvisable to construct it in a crowded area. In a large town the community was expected to provide two schools, especially if a river divided the town. A school did not operate in the heat of the day (between 10 AM and 3 PM), and would meet only four hours a day in July and August. Class size was expected to be 25, with a teacher and an assistant for 40 students and two teachers for 50. At school the boys sat on the ground at the teacher's feet and learned from the Scriptures. Thus the school became known as the "House of the Book."

Education in Surrounding Cultures. The theological emphasis of Hebrew education contrasted sharply with the aims of education in Greece and Rome. Those societies, however, were also concerned to develop a particular type of character.

In Sparta the purpose of educational training was to develop young men to be fighters who would subject themselves to the welfare of the state. Character development was achieved by eliminating luxuries and by systematically disciplining mind and body through physical activity. Survival techniques encouraged resourcefulness and initiative. Girls received the same education, since it was considered important to develop women who could give birth to strong warriors.

In Athens education was deemed essential to life. Because transmission of culture would enable boys to become perfect citizens, they were taught letters, music, morals and manners, mathematics, and gymnastics (development of a healthy body). Education was ideally a noble pursuit, a training of the mind, the birthright of every citizen; but in practice it was restricted to a small section of the aristocracy. Earning a living was despised by the educated as a way of life suitable only for slaves. Women received no education. The teacher in elementary schools was a lowly individual.

Roman education prepared a boy mentally and physically for farm, battlefield, or wherever his services were required by the state. Education was a family responsibility, the boy learning first from his mother, then from his father. Basic reading, writing, arithmetic, language structure, and debating skills were taught, sometimes by private tutors. When schools were developed, they seem to have been noisy, storefront activities operated by poorly paid teachers. Girls were taught housekeeping skills at home.

Egyptian boys attended the "House of the Books" for their studies and learned reading and elementary arithmetic. Writing in hieroglyphs on papyrus was the most difficult task. Like students in other cultures, boys were subject to corporal punishment. Egyptian teachers considered that "a boy's ears are in his

Egyptian uniconsonantal sign list.

back," following up that conviction with frequent use of a cane.

Literacy Among the Jews. The extent of literacy among Jews over the centuries is difficult to determine, but indications can be found from specific examples. The Book of Joshua describes three men chosen from each tribe who had to prepare a written report about the land of Canaan (Jos 18:4,8,9). Later, Gideon captured a youth who was able to make a written list of the important men of the city (Jgs 8:14). Writing was probably a common skill since the Israelites were exhorted to use it frequently (Dt 6:9; 27:2–8). Simple mathematical terms could be written and understood by boys, and there are indications of familiarity with the geometrical relationship of a circle's radius and circumference (the concept of pi; 2 Chr 4:2). The development of cursive script implies widespread use of writing from at least the 8th century BC. It is noteworthy that a synagogue service could be performed by any 10 men in the congregation, which presupposes that there were more than 10 men in any synagogue who were literate enough to fulfill that duty.

When fears of Hellenism were strong and the existence of Judaism was threatened in the 1st century BC, it was decreed that every Jewish boy should attend elementary school. Since such a system probably already existed, that decree merely made attendance compulsory for all males up to 16 or 17 years of age. No doubt the reason was that thorough knowledge and careful observance of the Law were vital to the survival of the Jewish heritage.

Joshua ben-Gamala (high priest, AD 63–65) is considered the founder of universal education. His instructions for setting up schools in towns and villages were precise, requiring attendance of boys from the age of six or seven years. The community was responsible for setting up a school and maintaining a teacher in any town where there were 10 Jewish families. Fathers were required to see that their sons attended school. When a family lived in an isolated area, a teacher often lived with the family. Teachers were probably paid either by the family or from a community tax, although scribes were not paid directly for the instruction they gave. It is difficult to know how far the goal of universal elementary education was attained.   HAZEL W. PERKIN

Bibliography. J.A. Grassi, *The Teacher in the Primitive Church and the Teacher Today;* G. Hodgson, *Primitive Christian Education;* H.I. Marrou, *History of Education in Antiquity;* N. Morris, *The Jewish School;* F.H. Swift, *Education in Ancient Israel.*

Eduth. Hebrew word usually translated "testimony," "witness," or "commandment." It is used with reference to the tabernacle (Nm 17:7,8; 18:2; 2 Chr 24:6), the ark (Ex 25:16), the Ten Commandments (Ex 31:18), and the Law of God in general (Ps 19:8).

The transliterated form appears only in the title of Psalm 60 in the Hebrew phrase *Shushan Eduth.* The phrase means "Lily of Testimony."

See MUSIC AND MUSICAL INSTRUMENTS.

Eglah. One of King David's wives and mother of Ithream (2 Sm 3:5; 1 Chr 3:3). Born while David was still in Hebron, Ithream was the 6th son.

Eglaim. Town mentioned in Isaiah 15:8. It cannot be located with certainty, but it was probably in southern Moab. A village called Aigaleim was mentioned by Eusebius and another called Agalla by Josephus (*Antiq.* 14.1.4) However, their identification with Eglaim is uncertain.

Eglath-shelishiyah. Place in Moab mentioned in Isaiah 15:5 and Jeremiah 48:34 in pronouncements of judgment. The name means literally "the third Eglath." It was probably near Zoar at the southern end of the Dead Sea, but its exact location is uncertain.

Eglon (Person). Moabite king who captured Jericho and held it for 18 years, exacting a tribute from Israel. Ehud, an Israelite judge pretending to bring tribute, killed Eglon (Jgs 3:12–30).

See MOAB, MOABITE.

Eglon (Place). Town situated 7 miles southwest of Lachish, assigned to Judah's tribe for an inheritance (Jos 15:39). It is generally identified with the modern Tell el-Hesi.

Egypt, Brook of. *See* BROOK OF EGYPT.

Egypt, Egyptians. Egypt figured significantly as a stage on which the biblical narrative was enacted. Here Abraham lived in time of famine. Joseph, his great-grandson, was sold into slavery in Egypt and rose to a position equivalent to that of prime minister. Through Joseph's intercession, Jacob and the rest of the Hebrew patriarchal family living in Palestine came to reside in the eastern delta region of Goshen, again as a result of famine. Initially treated favorably, they were later reduced to bondage; crying to God, ultimately they were released through the 10 plagues. Thereafter for 40 years they wandered in the Egyptian Sinai, where they received the Law, specifications for building the tabernacle, and instructions for the priestly and sacrificial systems.

After the destruction of Jerusalem in 586, a group of Jews forced Jeremiah to go with them to Egypt (Jer 43:6,7), where they became numerous during the intertestamental period and gradually forgot their Hebrew. At Alexandria, Jews translated the OT into Greek (the Septuagint) between about 250 and 150 BC. This became the Bible of the early church, especially of those outside Palestine.

When the NT opened, Egypt served as a refuge for Joseph, Mary, and Jesus as they fled to escape the assassination attempts of Herod the Great (Mt 2:13–23). At several other points, Hebrew and Egyptian history intersected—for example, when Shishak I invaded Palestine in the days of Rehoboam (1 Kgs 14:25–28).

Geography. Egypt is the gift of the Nile, without which it could not exist. From time immemorial the Nile has deposited a thin layer of rich silt each year as it overflowed its banks. This ribbon of loam along its course contrasts vividly with the sterile sands which stretch from the river valley often as far as one can see. Then, having deposited this soil, the Nile provides water for its irrigation. This is necessary in a land that receives only 6 to 8 inches of rainfall per year along the Mediterranean, 2 inches or less per year at Cairo, and less than that farther south.

The Nile valley is a tube, shut in on either side by cliffs and corked up at the southern end by cataracts, six places where the river has failed to cut a clear channel and where rocks are piled in irregular masses in the stream bed. From cliff to cliff the Nile valley ranges from about 10 to 31 miles in width between Cairo and Aswan. But the cultivated area along this stretch is only about 6 to 10 miles wide, and narrows to 1 or 2 miles in width around Aswan. This cultivated tract is only about 5,000 square miles.

But Egypt is more than the valley. It is also the delta, a pie-shaped area north of Cairo also deposited by the Nile over the millennia. The delta measures some 125 miles north and south, and 115 miles east and west. Its more heavily populated southern region provided ancient Egyptians with some 5,000 square miles of farmland—making the total of valley and delta about 10,000 square miles, roughly equal to the state of Maryland.

West of the Nile extends a chain of oases, the largest of which is the Fayum, about 70 miles southwest of Cairo. In the center of the Fayum is Lake Qarun, which today covers 90 square miles and is about 17 feet deep. It is surrounded by about a half million acres of good farmland.

Ancient Egypt extended some 125 miles from the Mediterranean to Cairo (Lower Egypt) and another 600 miles from Cairo to Aswan (Upper Egypt). At the height of its power, Egypt also controlled the valley from the 1st cataract at Aswan south to the 4th cataract (Nubia). Thus its domain extended a total of some 1,100 miles south from the Mediterranean.

Egypt's most important resource was the rich loam along the Nile. On it in antiquity farmers raised grains, such as barley, emmer, and wheat. Onions, leeks, beans, and lentils were common vegetables. Dates, figs, and grapes were the most widely grown fruits. Oil came from castor-oil plants and sesame rather than from the olive, as in other Mediterranean lands. Flax provided linen for clothing. Domesticated animals included oxen, cattle, sheep, goats, pigs, donkeys, and horses.

Another important resource was an abundant supply of stone. Granite mountains rise between the Nile and the Red Sea, and deposits of alabaster and other fine stone are found in the same region. South of Aswan stand the granite mountains of Nubia. The quarries of Syene at Aswan are famous for their extremely hard and durable red granite. Gold was reasonably plentiful in the Nubian mountains, and gold-bearing quartz veins were found in the mountains east of the Nile. Egyptians controlled the copper and turquoise mines of the Sinai during much of their important historical periods. In early antiquity some timber was available in Nubia for building the barges that carried the huge loads of stone for construction of pyramids, temples, and other magnificent structures.

The Nile itself was an all-weather highway. One could float northward with the current and sail southward against the weak current (3 miles per hour) by means of the prevailing northerly winds. In fact, the Nile was the road of ancient Egypt. Land routes normally conducted traffic only to the river's edge. In addition to the massive north-south commerce, ferry boats regularly moved from shore to shore.

Along the river grew papyrus reeds, from which writing material could be made. And along the Nile, clay was deposited from which could be made pottery and sun-dried bricks for the houses of the poor.

The ancient Egyptians lived in comparative isolation and peace in their valley home. The cataracts on the south, the deserts on east and west, and the harborless coast of the Mediterranean protected them from invasion and left them free to develop a homogeneous culture. Outside influences could sift in chiefly at the two northern corners of the delta. There were Semitic incursions from the east and Libyans, possibly of European origin, from the west. Defenses were erected to protect against both. The security of their valley home and the regular provision of the sun and the Nile gave the Egyptians a sense of confidence and well-being that was not the lot of other peoples of the ancient Near East.

History. It is wrong to think of the contemporary rulers of Egypt as descendants of the pharaohs or the present inhabitants of the land as Egyptians in any but a geographic sense. Egypt as an area of distinctive civilization ended with the Arab conquest in the 7th century and was greatly diluted during the several preceding centuries by Greco-Roman influences.

Origins. Though the origins of the ancient Egyptians are imperfectly understood, physically they show affinities to Hamites, Semites, and Mediterraneans. Hamites with negroid characteristics moved north from Nubia. Asiatics migrated across the isthmus of Suez into the delta, and the small, brown, finely boned Mediterranean people dominated the Nile valley from early times. However diverse their origins may have been, Egyptians of the ancient period were conscious of themselves as a nation, a distinctive people. Men stood about 5 feet 6 inches in height and women about 5 feet. They were slight but strong-boned, with round heads and oval faces. The men had little face or body hair, and throughout antiquity they were commonly smooth-shaven while Semites were bearded.

Archaeologists list a series of successive predynastic cultures—Fayumic, Merimdian, Tasian, Badarian, Amratian, Gerzean, and Semainean—who mastered basic techniques and learned how to build a civilization with minimal resources. Of course, they developed an irrigation system for the maintenance of an effective agricultural program. At a very early time they discovered how to turn flax into linen and thus to produce clothing. Boats were made from papyrus reeds and trees that grew along some of the stream beds in the south. Sun-baked bricks provided building material, and clay was available for pottery. The latter was made by hand; the pottery wheel did not appear until dynastic times.

Writing appeared in Egypt about the end of the predynastic period. Their hieroglyphs, or sacred signs, were called "the words of God" and were believed to be of divine origin. By 2700 BC they had learned how to make "paper" by crisscrossing strips cut from the pith of the papyrus plant and forming them into sheets. About the same time they developed techniques for cutting stone from the quarry. Commonly they cut a groove along a line where a block was to be split off. There they drove in wedges of dry wood and wetted them to swell the wood and split the block off. Sometimes they lit a fire along the groove to heat the stone and then poured water over it to split it away from the main rock.

Unification of Egypt. In the period just before about 3100 BC Egypt consisted of the two separate kingdoms of Lower Egypt and Upper Egypt. Then about 3100 apparently the king of Upper Egypt conquered Lower Egypt and unified the two lands under his sole rule. But the division was never quite forgotten, and Egypt was referred to as the "Two Lands" throughout its history. The pharaohs wore a double crown, a combination of the low red crown of Lower Egypt and the white crown of Upper Egypt. The king's palace was called the "double palace," and even the royal granary was double. The Hebrews recognized this duality, for throughout the OT they called Egypt *Mitzrayim*—a word with a dual ending.

The pharaoh who was credited in the ancient sources with the unification of Egypt was sometimes called Narmer and sometimes Menes; presumably these were merely different names for the same person. Narmer-Menes began the 1st dynasty of united Egypt. Though the ancient Egyptians did not reckon in dynasties, modern historians follow the practice of Manetho, an Egyptian priest of the mid-third

Stone pillars with papyrus and lotus representing Upper and Lower Egypt respectively.

century BC, who compiled a list of kings down to the Persian period and divided it into 30 dynasties; later others added a 31st dynasty. The ancients did not use such terms as "Old Kingdom" and "Middle Kingdom" either, but modern scholars find them a convenient way of organizing Egyptian history.

Early Dynastic Period (3100–2700). Kings of the first two dynasties ruled at This, or Thinis, some 300 miles south of Cairo, but they built Memphis as another administrative center. They consolidated their hold over the land and developed the theory that the king was divine. Contacts with the outside world were considerable, and there are many indications in Egypt of influences from Mesopotamia at this time.

Old Kingdom (2700–2200; Dynasties 3–6). The Old Kingdom is especially remembered for its building operations. The great monuments known as the pyramids were erected at that time. The capital was located at Memphis (biblical Noph), southwest of modern Cairo. Contacts with Phoenicia were numerous, and some believe Egyptians were so heavily involved there and elsewhere that it is proper to speak of the "Old Empire." Artistic standards were being developed, and literary and medical beginnings were significant. Egypt was an absolute monarchy. The divine king was served by an army of officials; the whole population might be regimented during his lifetime to prepare his tomb.

The first king of the 3rd dynasty was Djoser, who built the step pyramid at Saqqara. The earliest great stone structure in the world, it consists of six layers or steps rising to a height of 204 feet. The architect was Imhotep, his vizier or prime minister, who later was deified and credited with the beginnings of architecture, literature, and medicine, and identified by the Greeks with the god of medicine, Asklepios.

The 4th dynasty pharaohs were the great pyramid builders. They were responsible for erecting the three great pyramids at Giza between about 2600 and 2500 BC. The greatest of these, attributed to Khufu, covers 13 acres, originally rose to a height of 481 feet, and contains about 2,300,000 blocks of limestone averaging 2½ tons each. The second pyramid stands 447½ feet high and is accompanied by the sphinx, a couchant lion with the face of the king. The third pyramid is 204 feet high. These pyramids are not isolated examples. Several more small pyramids were built at

Giza, and there were 9 pyramid fields in all scattered along the western bank of the Nile south of Memphis. During the 5th and 6th dynasties appeared the pyramid texts, carved and painted inscriptions, magical spells, and hymns which were supposed to aid the deceased in the afterlife.

The artistic standards of Egypt were established during the Old Kingdom. The king and the gods were portrayed in a stylized form. Art tended to be conceptual rather than perceptual; that is, instead of reproducing what he saw, the artist painted what he knew to be there. For example, a school of fish became individual fish painted whole instead of being pictured naturally with one fish obscuring part of the fish next to it. In a similar manner the saddlebags on a donkey were shown with the one facing the viewer reproduced in a natural way; the other one, known to be behind the donkey's back, was flipped up in the air above the donkey's back.

The importance of an individual determined his size in a pictorial representation. In a battle scene the pharaoh would be the largest figure, his commanding officers next in size, the common soldiers smaller yet, and enemy troops smallest of all.

Egyptian art was intended to tell a story; much of it was more like a motion picture than a snapshot. A wine-making scene might

Two of Egypt's great pyramids, with the sphinx in the foreground.

include picking the grapes, treading out the juice (normally done by stomping with bare feet), and storing the juice in jars.

Evidently Egyptian medical knowledge was also developing during the Old Kingdom. Though the sources for knowledge of Egyptian medicine are the great papyri of the Middle Kingdom, there is some indication that medical knowledge claims far greater antiquity. Numerous archaic expressions appear in the texts. Perhaps Egyptians knew something of the circulation of the blood; they talked about feeling the "voice of the heart." Egyptian medical practice combined a hodge-podge of home remedies, charms and incantations, and scientific expertise. The Edwin Smith Surgical Papyrus is a remarkable study dealing especially with the treatment of broken bones.

During the 6th dynasty the Old Kingdom began to break up as a result of poor rulers, aggressive nobles, fiscal difficulties, Nubian incursions in the south, and Asiatic attacks in the northeast.

First Intermediate Period (2200–2050; Dynasties 7–11). During the Old Kingdom there was political stability and prosperity. The Nile flood came predictably and not devastatingly. There was enough for all to eat. If one behaved himself and worked hard and studied diligently in school, he could count on the proper promotions and general success in life. Familiar social, political, economic, and religious institutions remained constant and could be counted on to assume their regular place in the rhythm of life.

Now the old aristocracy had fallen. The central government had broken down; nobles ruled many districts and took the title of kings. It was no longer true that if one did certain things he could count on success. The collapse of the whole philosophy of life of the Old Kingdom brought a spiritual upset and spawned attempts at reevaluation of life. Some of the literature of the time advocated the hedonistic approach of drowning one's problems in pleasure; some recommended a stoical approach—to steel oneself against the hardships of life; and some anticipated the coming of a messiah who would right the wrongs of society and become the ideal shepherd of all.

Middle Kingdom (2050–1780; 12th Dynasty). Late in the 11th dynasty princes of Thebes (440 miles south of Memphis) struggled to restore order and royal control and were partially successful. The Middle Kingdom was the period of the 12th dynasty, native Thebans who made their capital at Lisht in the Fayum. The six rulers of this dynasty took the names of Amenemhet and Sesostris. Each of them ruled some 30 years, and most of them took

their sons on the throne as co-regents before death. Thus the danger of a usurper was eliminated. Since these kings did not dare to deprive the nobles of their largely independent power, a feudal condition existed during much of the period.

Unable to function as absolute kings, these pharaohs had to rule by persuasion and the development of good will. Their rendering of *ma'at* (social justice) was constantly emphasized; and if a person could not obtain *ma'at* at the hands of the nobles, he was promised it at the hands of the king. Their propaganda program also portrayed the pharaoh as concerned with responsible leadership instead of merely exercising authority. The pharaoh was the shepherd of his people. The art of the time represented the king with a worn look on his face—a result of constantly bearing the burdens of his people.

Middle Kingdom pharaohs were wise enough not to exhaust the treasury on great pyramids; instead, they undertook public works such as a massive effort to increase cultivable acreage in the Fayum, construction of a defensive wall across the isthmus of Suez, and systematic working of the Sinai copper mines. Trade was extensive with Crete, Lebanon, Syria, and the legendary land of Punt. Scholars debate whether Middle Kingdom pharaohs dominated Palestine and Syria by means of military action or as part of their economic imperialism. There is no debate, however, about their conquest of Nubia south to the 2nd cataract.

The Middle Kingdom was a time when Amon began to emerge as the great god of Egypt. He was grafted onto the sun god Re as Amon-Re and came to supersede the gods who had formerly stood for Thebes. As god of the nation, he was to become the great imperial god under the empire and thus to assume a universal quality. Religious texts, which had graced the walls of the pyramids during the Old Kingdom, now were inscribed on coffins instead, and their use was available to nobles as well as kings.

A literary flowering occurred during the Middle Kingdom. Scientific literature is represented by such outstanding works as the Rhind Mathematical Papyrus and the Smith Surgical and Ebers Medical Papyruses. The "Instructions of Merikare" portrays something of the Wisdom Literature of the period, and the "Tale of Sinuhe" introduces the genre of entertainment literature.

If one holds to the early date of the exodus (*c.* 1446) and adds 430 years for the period of Israelite sojourn in Egypt (Ex 12:40), he will conclude that the Israelites entered Egypt about 1876. This would be early in the reign of

Sesostris III (or Senwosret or Sen-Usert; 1878–1840). Sesostris was a vigorous king who extended Egyptian control south to the 2nd cataract and campaigned up into Syria. He was also able to reverse the feudalistic conditions of the earlier period; he took away the power of the nobles and appointed royal officials in their stead. Possibly this achievement was somehow related to famine in Joseph's day and Joseph's use of that famine to fasten royal control on all the populace of the land (Gn 47:13–26).

Second Intermediate Period (1780–1570; Dynasties 13–17). With the passing of the strong 12th dynasty, Egypt relapsed once more into a period of disintegration. The Hyksos ("rulers of foreign lands"), Semites from Syria and Palestine, gradually infiltrated into the delta region and took control there about 1730, maintaining their capital at Tanis, or Avaris, in the eastern delta. Meanwhile Theban princes ruled weakly in the south and were commonly vassals to the Hyksos.

Apparently as a result of Egyptian hatred of the Hyksos and stringent efforts to obliterate their memory, the Hyksos are a very shadowy people. Little remains on which to base a reconstruction of their history. Presumably they were responsible for introducing new kinds of bronze swords and daggers, the powerful compound bow, and above all the horse and chariot. The Egyptians adopted these with good success and used them to overthrow Hyksos power and then to build an empire in Palestine and Syria. The struggle of Theban princes to gain release from Hyksos control was prolonged and apparently fierce at times. The effort began late in the 16th century BC and was completed by Ahmose I (1570–1546).

The Empire Period (1570–1090; Dynasties 18–20). Ahmose launched the 18th dynasty, and may be viewed as initiating the Empire, or New Kingdom, period as well. After defeating the Hyksos in Egypt, he carried on successful campaigns against Nubia and Sharuhen in southern Palestine. Subsequently he was forced to subdue nobles who had managed to gain independence from the central government during the Hyksos era. Amenhotep I (1546–1525) was also forced to fight the Nubians in the south and Libyans in the northwest.

Dying without a son to succeed him, Amenhotep was followed on the throne by his sister Ahmose, who married a Thutmose (Thutmose I, 1525–1508), probably a relative. Thutmose had to resubjugate rebellious Nubians during the first year of his reign and in subsequent campaigns considerably expanded Egypt's Nubian holdings. Between those two Nubian attacks he mounted an offensive in Syria; thus he could claim an empire that stretched from the Euphrates to the third cataract of the Nile. Moses may have been born early in his reign. Thutmose began the practice of carving out royal tombs in the Valley of the Kings west of Thebes.

Evidently the only surviving child of the union of Thutmose and Ahmose was a daughter, Hatshepsut, who was married to Thutmose II (1508–1504), a son of Thutmose I by a secondary princess. Thutmose II had to quell rebellious Nubians, but little else is known of his reign. Since his marriage to Hatshepsut produced two daughters but no sons, he decided to marry his daughter Marytre to a son by a minor wife (Thutmose III, 1504–1450).

Hatshepsut continued to rule during the minority of Thutmose III and refused to step aside when he came of age. She dominated Egypt from 1504 to 1482. During her reign Egypt enjoyed economic prosperity. Her building activities were considerable; not the least of her achievements was the erection of two great obelisks at the Temple of Karnak at Luxor. The one remaining shaft stands 97½ feet high and weighs about 700,000 pounds. She also conducted trade expeditions to the Land of Punt. Hatshepsut is sometimes identified as the pharaoh's daughter who rescued Moses from the Nile (Ex 2:5).

Finally, in 1482, Hatshepsut met an untimely end, probably at the hands of Thutmose III as he burst his bonds and assumed rule over the realm. Within 75 days he had assembled an army and was leading it north into Palestine-Syria to subjugate rebellious princes there. A great initial victory at Megiddo and a sack of the city after a 7-month siege cowed northern Palestinians but did not break their will to resist. Thutmose found himself campaigning in Palestine or Nubia almost annually for the next 2 decades.

What started out as an Egyptian impulse to punish the Hyksos turned into a spirit of imperialism, which enjoyed a sense of power in victory. As the frontiers expanded, there was almost always a peril to attend to somewhere during subsequent generations; some of them were real and some remote. Thus the sense of security which Egyptians had enjoyed during earlier centuries when they were shut up in their valley home gave way to a feeling of insecurity. And as the god Amon-Re smiled on Egyptian military efforts, he was rewarded with quantities of booty and handsome gifts. In time the temples gained so much wealth and power that they came to exercise great clout in political and economic circles. Especially great was the power of the priesthood of Amon at the temple of Karnak.

Thutmose III was one of the greatest of

Egypt's ancient pharaohs. A conqueror and empire builder, he is often called the Napoleon of ancient Egypt. There was hardly a city of any size in the kingdom where he did not engage in building activities. With him began an effort to glorify the pharaoh as sportsman, athlete, and warrior that was to last for several generations; he had the powers of a god in conducting the affairs of men. If one accepts the early date of the exodus, Thutmose III is often considered to have been the pharaoh of the great oppression of the Hebrews.

Thutmose was succeeded by his son Amenhotep II (1452–1425 BC), who then may have been the pharaoh of the exodus. Serving briefly as co-regent with his father, he enjoyed an easy transition to sole rule over the empire. Though forced to conduct 2 campaigns into Syria and Palestine to subdue rebellious towns, he seems generally to have enjoyed a peaceful reign. Like his father he sought to be known for his prowess as a sportsman and his ruthlessness as a warrior.

After the little-known reign of Thutmose IV (1425–1412), Amenhotep III (1412–1375) ascended the throne of Egypt. Frequently called "the magnificent," he reveled in the wealth that poured in from the empire. Once, in the brief space of only 14 days, he had excavated for his wife a lake 6,400 feet long and 1,200 feet wide. Here on the west bank of the Nile at Thebes a royal barge could float about while musicians aboard provided entertainment for the king and queen. Amenhotep built several temples, including a mortuary temple at Thebes, to which were attached the famous colossi of Memnon, seated statues of the king about 70 feet high. Though obsequious priests dutifully represented him as a great conqueror on temple walls, he seems to have engaged in stifling only one uprising in Nubia and probably never set foot in Palestine or Syria.

Just as Amenhotep III made no effort to maintain the empire, neither did his son Amenhotep IV (1387–1366). Because of ill health Amenhotep III made his son co-regent in 1387, but the son paid little attention to the affairs of state. Of a mystical bent, he devoted himself to the establishment of the cult of the sun god Aton at a new capital named Amarna. Aton worship was almost monotheistic (the king being worshiped along with the god) and thus constituted a virtual religious revolution, but it had few adherents outside the court. Religious changes, political changes connected with the move of the capital, and artistic changes were 3 of the main elements of the so-called "Amarna Revolution." The loose naturalism in art, almost bordering on caricature, was not new, however, since it had been accepted as early as

Amenhotep III, 18th-dynasty ruler of the New Empire.

the reign of Thutmose IV. Amenhotep IV took the name Akhnaton ("spirit of Aton").

Akhnaton paid no attention to numerous appeals (the Amarna letters) from loyal princes of Palestine and Syria for help to repel invaders, and the empire disintegrated. Acceptance of the early date of the exodus would place the Hebrew conquest and the subsequent settling in process during the reigns of Amenhotep III and IV, precisely when Egyptian power over Palestine disappeared. However, the Habiru, which some of these appeals name as attackers, should not be identified as Hebrews. Much of what is said about them could not have been true of Hebrews.

When Amenhotep IV died, Tutankhamon (1366–1357) succeeded to the throne. A young boy of 8 or 9, he was associated with Eye, a favorite of Akhnaton, as co-regent. When Tutankhamon died 9 years later, Eye continued to rule until 1353. Because of the discovery of his magnificently furnished, unrifled tomb in

Akhenaton, his wife Neferti, and his daughter presenting offerings to the sun-god, Aton.

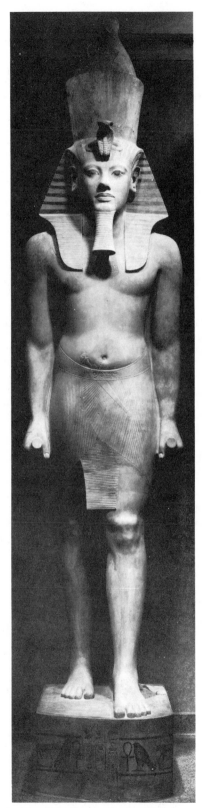

Colossal statue of Tutankhamun (from c. 1360 BC).

1922, Tutankhamon has received attention out of proportion to his significance in antiquity. The thousands of objects from his tomb illustrate the wealth, grandeur, and artistic achievements of ancient Egypt and help to demonstrate what it meant for Moses to turn his back on the riches of Egypt (Heb 11:26).

When Eye died, Harmhab, commander-in-chief of the army, succeeded to the throne (1353–1319). He reorganized the state and reestablished a strong government. Dying childless, Harmhab designated as his successor Rameses I, commander of the army and vizier, or prime minister. Rameses (1319–1318) and Seti I (1318–1299) made valiant attempts to restore the Asiatic empire lost by Akhnaton. In connection with their efforts the capital was moved to Tanis in the delta, from which military campaigns could be more effectively launched.

Rameses II (1299–1232) continued the effort to restore Egyptian control in Palestine. In the 5th year of his reign he met the Hittites in battle at Kadesh on the Orontes in Syria and narrowly missed destruction of his forces. Subsequently he fought battles all the way from

669

southern Palestine to northern Syria. If the Hebrews were then in the land, as an early date of the exodus requires, they probably never made contact with the Egyptians because they were shepherds and vinedressers in the hills of Palestine, and Rameses moved along the coastal road. Finally, in his 21st regnal year, Rameses made a peace treaty with the Hittites and kept it to the end of his days. He built massively all over Egypt, notably at his capital of Tanis, at Thebes, at Abu Simbel (south of Aswan), and at Memphis. Many believe he was the pharaoh of the exodus.

Rameses' 13th son, Merneptah (1232–1222), was the only Egyptian king who claimed to have defeated the Hebrews in battle. But some scholars argue that he never invaded Asia and that this statement is to be interpreted as a customary claim of victory over the king's opponents in surrounding lands, whether or not he ever met them in battle. Merneptah did turn back a Libyan invasion in his 5th regnal year, however.

Rameses III (1198–1164) also fought off Libyan invasions of the delta in his 5th and 11th regnal years, and in his 8th year repulsed an invasion of Sea Peoples, among whom were Philistines. He was the last ruler of the empire period to maintain outposts in Palestine and Syria. In his later years the Egyptian economy deteriorated, and inflation and breakdown of the government's ability to meet the public payroll brought great suffering. Hunger marches resulted.

During the reigns of Rameses IV–XI (1167–1085) there was a steady decline of the state. Graft and inflation increased. During the reign of Rameses IX (1138–1119) unpaid mercenary troops seem to have roamed as marauders in the delta, and tomb robbery reached epidemic proportions. Finally Herihor, viceroy of Nubia and commander of military forces in the south, seized control of upper Egypt and made himself high priest of Amon in Thebes. The empire had come to an end.

The Postempire Period. In the postempire period, Egypt came under the rule of Libyan kings (945–712) and Ethiopian kings (712–670). After a brief period of Assyrian domination (670–663) a native dynasty asserted itself (663–525). Then the Persians conquered and held the land until Alexander the Great marched through in 331. Thereafter the Ptolemies ruled Egypt until the death of Cleopatra in 30 BC. At that point the Romans took over. They controlled the land when Mary and Joseph fled there after the birth of Jesus. During the Greco-Roman period Hellenistic culture dominated Egypt.

During the early postempire period, when Egyptian culture was still dominant, several kings figured in biblical history. During the 5th year of Rehoboam, king of Judah (probably 926 BC), Shishak I of Egypt invaded Judah and wrought great havoc there (1 Kgs 14:25, 26). He even marched into the territory of Israel, as archaeological discoveries show. About 700 BC, in the days of King Hezekiah and the prophet Isaiah, Tirhakah of Egypt led an army into Palestine to help the Jews against invading Assyrians (2 Kgs 19:9). Near the end of the seventh century BC, Pharaoh Neco led an army through Judah to come to the aid of weakened Assyria. When King Josiah tried to stop him, the Hebrew monarch lost his life (2 Kgs 23:28–30). During the last days of the kingdom of Judah, while Nebuchadnezzar was besieging Jerusalem (588–86), Pharaoh Hophra invaded Palestine in a vain effort to aid the Hebrews and defeat the Babylonians. Jeremiah predicted the Egyptians' destruction (Jer 44:30).

Social Life. *Social Classes.* In theory and in practice the king owned all the land of Egypt. He was divine, and the gods had assigned to him the deeds to all the land. Of course, he made gifts—to the gods for the support of the temples, to his most loyal supporters, and to maintain his own worship cult after his death. Thus large parts of the kingdom slipped from his hands, but much remained as the possession of the crown. Although by the beginning of the Middle Kingdom nobles held great tracts of land, the king managed to sweep aside their power and repossess a considerable amount of acreage. During the Empire the king made large grants to the temples, especially the temple of Amon at Thebes. This generosity enhanced the power of the priesthood at the expense of the crown.

As increasing amounts of land passed out of the control of the crown, and as social and economic life became more complex, a complicated class structure developed. The major division in Egyptian society was between the educated elite and the uneducated masses, but such an observation is too simplistic. At the top were the royal family and the great nobles. Below them was a group of lesser nobles and officials. Lower yet was a class of craftsmen who served both of the upper classes. Then, at least during the Empire, there were farmers who owned small plots which they worked themselves. At the bottom of the social structure were free serfs and slaves. Slavery became common only under the Empire, when slaves were obtained as prisoners of war, primarily in Palestine and Syria to the north and Nubia to the south. Some slaves found their way into domestic service at the palaces and on the large estates, but most of them worked on the land and some served in the mines. Slavery was never as necessary and important in Egypt as in other Near Eastern countries. Also during the Empire a class of professional soldiers appeared on the scene; probably these should be rated just below the lesser nobles and officials.

Family Life. Egyptians apparently married in early adolescence. Children were weaned at 3. Boys were circumcised between the ages of 6 and 12. Although education was designed for boys of the upper classes, girls—especially of royal families—frequently received some formal education. Egyptian women evidently enjoyed much greater freedom and prestige than women of other Near Eastern countries. They went about rather freely; they accompanied their husbands in the conduct of business and even at social events. The family might even accompany the husband and father on an outing when he went fishing or hunting, though they did not take part in the action. Egyptians normally were not monogamous, the size of the harem being dictated by economic considerations. But the status of the chief wife was protected, and her first son was her husband's heir. Professions open to women included the priesthood, midwifery, mourning, dancing, and perhaps scribal activity (there was a feminine word for scribe).

Furniture was meager in an Egyptian house. Beds, chairs, stools, footstools, and stands for water jugs seem to have been the main items. Dining tables do not appear to have been used; there were stands on which trays of food might be placed. The poor simply sat on the floor, slept on mats on the floor, and spread out their meals on the floor.

Houses were normally built of mud brick. Those of the wealthy were set amid gardens and frequently had decorative pools. Rooms might be color-washed on the inside and even decorated with frescoes. Roofs were flat and provided a second bedroom in the hottest months. Houses sometimes had a second story. Though remains of 2 or 3 villages of workmen on government projects have been found, virtually nothing is known of the layout or size of the important cities of ancient Egypt.

Dress. Women wore long linen garments extending from the armpits to the ankles and held up by straps over the shoulder. During the Empire period the skirt was made fuller and pleated. Men wore loincloths fastened with a belt and extending to the knee. The upper classes often wore it pleated in front. During the Middle Kingdom and the latter part of the Empire the loincloth was extended to mid-calf, and men sometimes also wore a short-sleeved tunic. As a result of Asian influence, Egyptians of the upper classes frequently wore colored clothing during the Em-

pire, instead of the prevailing white of other periods.

Men were clean-shaven, but the king and a few top officials wore false beards for ceremonial purposes. Both men and women wore wigs, and both men and women used eye paint for medicinal and decorative purposes. Women wore lipstick and rouge, and applied henna to their nails, the palms of their hands, and the soles of their feet. Men and women of the upper classes wore a variety of jewelry. People of all classes applied oils and fats to their skin to protect them in the hot, dry climate. The use of perfume was also universal.

Entertainment. There were no organized games in ancient Egypt. Sportsmen went out alone or with their families. They might hunt in the desert with bows and arrows and dogs, go fishing, try to knock down birds with a boomerang in a marsh, or go driving in a chariot. Boys and young men among the peasants especially enjoyed wrestling. Soldiers participated in war dances, which were a sort of physical drill. A game on the order of checkers was the chief indoor game of men and women alike.

Law and Punishment. The king was viewed as the source of all law, and apparently there was no written code to which all could appeal. Courts followed precedent set in past cases, and periodically the king modified the legal system by new edicts. Procedure in the courts involved administering an oath to tell the truth, speeches by accuser and accused, judgment of the court, and note-taking by a court recorder. In some cases torture was used to extract a confession.

Treason, murder, and perjury were among the capital crimes. The latter was so serious because the court oath was taken "by the life of Pharaoh"; thus, swearing falsely meant injury to the king. Other serious crimes were punishable by mutilation (cutting off nose or ears) or hard labor in the mines and quarries (a living death). A person convicted of theft might be sentenced to repay double or triple what he had taken. Beating was the usual punishment for minor offenses. At least during the Empire, Egypt had a kind of police force with a contingent in each town.

Cultural Affairs. *Language and Writing.* Ancient Egyptian was related to both Semitic and Hamitic languages. By about 3100 BC both hieroglyphics (pictorial characters used in inscriptions and more formal writing) and hieratic (a more running hand) were in use. Hieroglyphs may stand for a letter, a syllable, a sound, a word, or an idea. François Champollion cracked the decipherment of the hieroglyphs in 1822, primarily with the help of the Rosetta Stone. About 700 BC a more rapid script called demotic came into being, and con-

The Rosetta Stone, the trilingual inscription (Egyptian hieroglyphic, Egyptian demotic, and Greek) that contained the key to the decipherment of hieroglyphics; it contained a decree in honor of Ptolemy V, Epiphanes, voted by the priests of Egypt assembled at Memphis. It was discovered in 1799 at Rashid in the Egyptian delta.

tinued to be written until early Christian times. Thereafter Coptic, the ancient Egyptian language, came to be written down in a Greek script with a few extra letters.

Education. Egyptian education, available almost exclusively to upperclass boys, was designed to provide trained personnel for the priesthood, government offices, or the professions. Very few had a chance to obtain any education at all. Boys began their training at a very early age, commonly about 4. Classes started early in the morning and normally ended about noon, in order to avoid the heat of the day. Reading, writing, and arithmetic were the standard fare. Good handwriting and the ability to compose letters were essential for all leaders in society. Eloquence was also valued. Learning by imitation was achieved through copying handwriting samples and

model letters. Pieces of stone and potsherds provided inexpensive writing tablets, with papyrus being reserved for final drafts of important compositions. Knowledge of arithmetic was especially important for workers in government offices where taxes were collected in kind.

The highest form of education was priestly training, and a prince might enroll in a school for priests. But often he was educated by tutors in classes held at the palace. Such classes normally were designed for children of the harem; princesses and nonroyal children might also attend them.

After lower school a boy might attend a "House of Life," a kind of academy or senior college. There outstanding persons might lecture on a variety of subjects (including medicine). Presumably resembling Plato's academy in Athens, such "Houses" did not have a prescribed curriculum or regular examinations. They were equipped with libraries.

Religion. All of Egyptian life was bound up with religious considerations. As the "gift of the Nile," Egypt worshiped the great river as Hapi. The sun, which gave life to all things, was deified under such names as Amon-Re and Aton. The king was the offspring of the gods and was in some sense god incarnate. Thus it is obvious that the 10 plagues in Moses' day were an attack on the gods of the Egyptians. Turning the Nile into blood, bringing intense darkness on the land, and smiting the firstborn of the divine pharaoh involved a discrediting of Egyptian gods, as did the other plagues in various ways.

The greatest concern of all individuals was immortality and the blessing of the gods upon them in the next life. Egyptians were not morbid in that they were preoccupied with death; they sought to project or continue as many of the pleasant aspects of this life as possible into the next life.

Ancient Egyptians, unlike modern Western peoples, had no concept of an inanimate world. All natural phenomena were personalized, and acted as friendly or unfriendly beings whenever they affected human activity. The gods were looked on as patrons of various activities or functions. Thus Bes, a bandy-legged dwarf, was the patron of music and conception, and the goddess Taurt (a combination of hippopotamus, lioness, and crocodile) was associated with childbirth. Charms of both were made in abundance, and these two seem to have been more widely regarded among the masses than the chief gods of Egypt.

Most important of all the gods was Re or Ra, the sun god. The pharaoh was his physical son and earthly embodiment. When he died, he rejoined his divine father in the sky. Re generated the god Shu, personification of air, and the goddess Tefnut, personification of moisture. These gave birth to two children, Geb the earth god and Nut the sky goddess. Mankind came into being variously according to the legends; one has Re generating them with his tears, another has Khnum forming them on his potter's wheel. During the Empire the god of Thebes, Amon, was identified with Re, and the sun god henceforth became known as Amon-Re. The great triad of Thebes was Amon, his consort Mut, and their son Khonsu (the moon god).

Rivaling Amon-Re in importance was Osiris, apparently originally a king of the delta city of Busiris. Murdered by his brother, Osiris was brought back to life by his son Horus through various magical devices; thereafter he ruled in the west as king of the blessed dead.

Eventually the experience of Osiris became that of every human being. Through magical formulas of the sort used by Horus, the individual could come to Osiris and even in some sense become Osiris. In addition to the knowledge and pronouncement of such formulas, the individual had to appear at a judgment for the weighing of his heart in the balance of righteousness. If declared innocent of wrongdoing, he was allowed to enter the kingdom of Osiris and enjoy a blessed hereafter.

Some of these formulas connected with transit into the next life began to appear on the walls of pyramid tombs in the Old Kingdom ("Pyramid Texts"); during the Middle Kingdom they were recorded on coffins ("Coffin Texts"); during the Empire they were compiled as the "Book of the Dead." Portions continued to be inscribed on the walls of tombs from the Empire period to about AD 300.

Countless other Egyptian gods could be mentioned. A few of the more important include Anubis, jackal-headed patron of embalming and guardian of the tomb; Hathor, a sky goddess, patroness of love and the necropolis; Imhotep, patron of learning (especially of medicine); Ptah, patron of arts and crafts and creator of man; Sekhmet, woman with a head of a lioness representing the destructive powers of the sun; Thoth, a man with a head of an ibis, inventor of hieroglyphic writing, god of scribes, and lord of wisdom and magic.

Science. The ancient Egyptians excelled in applied mathematics, astronomy, and medicine. The annual flood of the Nile required an early development of the ability to resurvey the land rapidly after waters receded. Engineering skills were necessary to produce the irrigation system on which all Egyptian life depended. Moreover, their massive building projects necessitated a knowledge of mathematics. Egyptians could add and subtract but had cumbersome procedures for multiplication and division. They could calculate the area of a square, a triangle, a rectangle, and a

The Egyptian god Amon.

A frieze from the Temple of Denderah Tentyris in Egypt.

circle and could do simple exercises in geometry. It is thought that experience rather than mathematical reasoning ability was responsible for most of their mathematical successes. They understood that the calendar must have 365¼ days in it, and they divided the year into 12 months and the months into three 10-day weeks. They invented an adequate water clock by 2000 BC.

With their elaborate practice of embalming, one would expect their knowledge of anatomy to be superior. They distinguished between injuries and diseases and performed some amazing surgery. Treatment was a curious combination of scientific and superstitious efforts, however. Egyptian scientists, with a practical rather than theoretical motivation, amassed a vast collection of facts about astronomy, chemistry, geography, medicine, surgery, mathematics, and natural history.

Architecture. As the ancient Egyptians built their great temples, they were most concerned with stability and enduring qualities. They were to last forever. Thus they were made of stone (commonly limestone or sandstone) and roofed with great stone slabs supported on massive columns. The capitals generally were lotus, papyrus, or palm leaf in design. Great statues of a king were placed inside these temples; as mere architectural decoration, these sculptures appear stiff and formal. Light entered the temple through windows in the side of the raised central hall; the side aisles were lower. Though the roofs of these temples were flat, Egyptians knew how to construct a round arch at least by 2700 BC. Greatest of the remaining temples is the temple of Karnak at Luxor. The hypostyle hall there, built by Rameses II, has a forest of 134 sandstone columns, the central avenue of which has 12 columns which soar to a height of 70 feet, the tallest columns in the ancient world.

Pharaohs of the Old Kingdom built great pyramids as burial places along the west bank of the Nile south of Memphis. Pharaohs of the Middle Kingdom constructed smaller pyramids in the Fayum area. During the Empire they carved tombs out of the cliffs west of Thebes. Pharaohs as divine beings covered the walls of their tombs at Thebes with religious scenes. The nobles had their tombs decorated with scenes of everyday life—a life which they wished to perpetuate beyond the grave.

Houses were constructed of sun-dried brick and have generally disappeared; a few remain at Amarna and in a couple of abandoned workers' camps.

Music. All that is known of Egyptian music must be gleaned from musical instruments found in tombs or representations of musical instruments painted on tomb walls. Three instruments used in religious exercises were the sistrum, tambourine, and castanets. The sistrum was a metal loop fastened to a handle. Holes were cut in the sides of the loop so that three metal rods could be loosely fastened in it. When the sistrum was shaken, the rods would rattle. This is the instrument referred to in 2 Samuel 6:5. Miriam used the Egyptian timbrel or tambourine in the celebration after crossing the Red Sea (Ex 15:20).

Stringed instruments in ancient Egypt included the harp, lyre, lute, and a kind of guitar. Wind instruments included the single and double flute and the trumpet, the latter apparently used only for military purposes. At first, instruments were used singly to accompany a singer or dancer. Orchestras existed during the Empire period, when Israel escaped from Egyptian bondage.

Commerce and Crafts. Long before Egypt became a united nation trade was extensive, both along the Nile and with foreign countries. Timber and other forest products, especially from Lebanon, were chief among the imports during the 4th millennium BC. Copper and turquoise came from Sinai, lapis lazuli from Western Asia, gold from Nubia, gold and silver from Asia Minor, and perfumes from Asia or Africa. Trade contacts with India and Mesopotamia were also established. During the Old Kingdom, Crete was added to the list. During the Middle Kingdom, trade was widespread, including Mediterranean lands and Black Sea, Red Sea, and Indian Ocean regions. With the advent of the Empire, trade was even more fully developed. Much of the commerce was carried on as a government monopoly and with government protection. Trade continued to be extensive during the Ptolemaic and Roman periods.

It was not always necessary for Egypt to send commodities in exchange for goods from abroad. It simply sent expeditions to the Sinai, overpowered the Nubians and Palestinians, and exacted tribute. And it extracted quantities of gold from the region between the Nile and the Red Sea; this added to the gold of Nubia, could purchase many foreign commodities.

Egyptian craftsmen produced endless quantities of quality goods that could have been sent abroad. Jewelry production was unsurpassed; metallurgy and carpentry reached levels of excellence at an early date. Manufacture of linen cloth, pottery, and stone vessels provided abundant supplies for the home market and some to spare for export. Beer and wine production was also extensive.

HOWARD F. VOS

See EXODUS, THE; PLAGUES UPON EGYPT; PHARAOH.

Bibliography. J.H. Breasted, *A History of Egypt from the Earliest Times to the Persian Conquest;* J. Černý, *Ancient Egyptian Religion;* H. Frankfort, *Ancient Egyptian Religion;* K.A. Kitchen, *The Joseph Narrative and its Egyptian Background;* S. Moscati, *The Face of the Ancient Orient;* T.E. Pect, *Egypt and the OT;* S. Sauneron, *The Priests of Ancient Egypt.*

Egyptian, The. Unidentified antagonist of Rome who led a revolt into the wilderness with a host of barbarous assassins (Sicarii). After an uproar at the Jerusalem temple, the tribune Claudius Lysias challenged the apostle Paul, asking if he was the Egyptian insurrectionist (Acts 21:38). According to Josephus, the Egyptian led a Jewish rebellion that was suppressed by the procurator Felix. Accounts vary as to the number of assassins involved, but all point to a revolt led by an Egyptian who apparently escaped.

Ehi. Benjamin's son (Gn 46:21); perhaps a scribal error for Ahiram.

See AHIRAM.

Ehud. 1. Judge of Israel from Benjamin's tribe who delivered Israel from Eglon, king of the Moabites (Jgs 3:12–30). He was notable because he was left-handed (Hebrew "hindered in the right hand"). Before taking Israelite tribute to Eglon, he made an iron dagger, with which he assassinated the unsuspecting Eglon during a private audience. He then rallied the Israelites west of the Jordan to encircle the Moabite troops before they could return south to Moab. When the 18-year rule of Eglon over the Israelites ended, an 80-year period of peace began. Some scholars have supposed that Judges 3:18,19 is an insertion into the main deliverance narrative, but this is difficult to prove.

2. Bilhan's son, a member of Benjamin's tribe (1 Chr 7:10; 8:6).

Eker. Jerahmeelite and the son of Ram from Judah's tribe (1 Chr 2:27).

Ekron, Ekronites. Most northerly city among the major Philistine settlements. During the Hebrew conquest of Palestine, Ekron was not taken by Joshua (Jos 13:3). When the land was divided among the 12 tribes, Ekron was given first to Judah and then to Dan (Jos 15:11,45,46; 19:43). It was eventually taken by Judah (Jgs 1:18), but subsequently fell back to the Philistines.

Ekron played a prominent role in the story of the capture of the ark of the covenant. After the ark brought disaster to Ashdod and Gath, it was taken to Ekron (1 Sm 5:1–10). The Ekronites did not want the ark, so they consulted with the "lords of the Philistines" and proposed that the ark be sent back to Israel (1 Sm 5:11).

After David killed Goliath, the Israelites pursued the Philistines to the gates of Ekron, which at that time apparently was the nearest walled city in which fugitives could take refuge (1 Sm 17:52).

Ekron was apparently the center of the worship of the god Baal-zebub. When Ahaziah injured himself and lay ill, he preferred to consult with Baal-zebub rather than with God. Elijah was sent by God to denounce Ahaziah and tell him that he would die (2 Kgs 1:2–18). Baal worship may have been increasing in Israel at this time. Ekron is included in the denunciations of several prophets: Jeremiah (25:20), Amos (1:8), Zephaniah (2:4), and Zechariah (9:5–7).

Assyrian records inform us that Ekron revolted against Sennacherib in 701 BC. The rebels deposed Padi, the ruler of Ekron who was loyal to Assyria, and handed him over to Hezekiah in Jerusalem for imprisonment. Sennacherib moved against Ekron, and Ekron called for aid from the king of Mutsri (either Egypt or a district of northwestern Arabia). Sennacherib lifted his siege of Ekron long enough to defeat the army of Mutsri, and then returned to take Ekron. He executed the rebels, made captives of their followers, forced Hezekiah to release Padi, and restored Padi as ruler of the city. Padi also received some territory taken from Judah. Padi's successor, Ikausu, was not so fortunate. He, along with Manasseh of Judah, was forced to pay heavy tribute to both Esar-haddon and Ashurbanipal.

In 147 BC the king of Syria, Alexander Balas, gave Ekron to Jonathan Maccabeus as a reward for his loyalty (1 Mc 10:89). In the 4th century AD it still had a large Jewish population.

Archaeologists disagree concerning the exact location of Ekron. Three places are suggested: ʿAqir, Qatra, and Khirbet el-Muqannav̇.

See PHILISTIA, PHILISTINES.

El. Ancient Semitic name for deity, perhaps meaning "power" (cf. Gn 17:1); used by the Hebrews generally in a poetic sense to denote the true God of Israel. The same word was used for the senior Canaanite god and the god in Ugaritic mythology. The "Il" or "El" of ancient Canaanite mythology (before 3500 BC in the region of Syria) was not as active as the god Baal, who struggled with Death and triumphed over Chaos. But Il was the father god of the Canaanite pantheon. OT critics have suggested that the Hebrews adopted the clan gods of the Canaanites, including Il. Yet both Phoenician and Ugaritic literature use Il in the feminine form for the names of goddesses. The Hebrew avoids such usage. El is combined with other adjectives to describe the numerous attributes of God; for example, God Most High (Gn 14:18–24), the seeing God (Gn 16:13), the jealous God (Ex 20:5), the forgiving God (Neh 9:17), and the gracious God (Neh 9:31).

See CANAANITE DEITIES AND RELIGION; GOD, NAMES OF.

Ela. Father of Shimei, one of the 12 officers appointed to requisition food for King Solomon's household (1 Kgs 4:18, KJV Elah).

Eladah. KJV form of Ele-adah, Ephraim's descendant, in 1 Chronicles 7:20.

See ELE-ADAH.

Elah. 1. Esau's descendant and a chief of Edom (Gn 36:41; 1 Chr 1:52).

2. KJV rendering of Ela, Shimei's father, in 1 Kings 4:18.

See ELA.

3. Baasha's son and 4th king of Israel. Elah reigned for only two years (886–885 BC). While in a drunken stupor he was murdered by one of his generals (1 Kgs 16: 8–14).

See ISRAEL, HISTORY OF.

4. Father of Hoshea, the last king of the northern kingdom of Israel (2 Kgs 15:30; 17:1; 18:1,9).

See ISRAEL, HISTORY OF.

5. Caleb's 2nd son and father of Kenaz (1 Chr 4:15).

6. Uzzi's son, descendant of Benjamin (1 Chr 9:8). Elah was among the first to resettle in Jerusalem after the Babylonian exile. He is not mentioned in the parallel list of Nehemiah 11.

Elah, Valley of. Southernmost valley in the Shephelah, starting at Hebron and descending in a northerly direction before turning west. At the Wadi al-Sant it comes together with other valleys, and at this juncture there is a wide, level valley about one-half mile wide. It was here that the great struggle between David and Goliath took place, with the Philistine army camped on the southern hills and Saul's army on the north or northeast (1 Sm 17:2,19; 21:9).

Elam (Person). 1. Firstborn son of Shem and a grandson of Noah (Gn 10:22; 1 Chr 1:17).

2. Benjamite and the son of Shashak (1 Chr 8:24).

3. Korahite Levite and the 5th son of Kore from the house of Asaph (1 Chr 26:3).

4. Forefather of 1,254 descendants who returned with Zerubbabel to Judah following the exile (Ezr 2:7; Neh 7:12). Later 71 members of Elam's house accompanied Ezra back to Palestine during the reign of King Artaxerxes I of Persia (464–424 BC; Ezr 8:7). In postexilic Judah, Shecaniah, Elam's descendant, urged Ezra to command the sons of Israel to divorce their foreign wives (Ezr 10:2); a number from Elam's house eventually did so (Ezr 10:26).

5. Another forefather of 1,254 descendants who returned with Zerubbabel to Judah (Ezr 2:31; Neh 7:34).

6. One of the chiefs of Israel who set his seal on Ezra's covenant (Neh 10:14).

7. One of the priestly musicians who performed at the dedication of the Jerusalem wall (Neh 12:42).

Elam (Place). Occupying an area roughly the size of Denmark, Elam was located in southwest Asia, east of Babylonia and north of the Persian Gulf, on a plain known to the Iranians since the Middle Ages as Khuzistan. The region today corresponds to southwest Iran. Mountainous areas to the north and east, known as the Anshan range, formed a peripheral part of Elam. The land's fertility was linked to several waterways, the most significant of which—the Karkheh—forms Elam's western boundary. It was probably this river of which Daniel speaks when he says, "and I heard a man's voice calling from across the river" (Dn 8:16 LB).

History. A people with a culture and history spanning more than 2000 years, the Elamites seem to have lived in constant strife with the Sumerians, Babylonians, Assyrians, and finally the Persians, by whom they were absorbed. As a race, the Elamites were a mixture of dark-skinned aboriginals of questionable origin and Semites who had spilled over into the land from Mesopotamia. In Genesis 10:22 Elam appears as a descendant of Shem, attesting to the presence of Semites in the region. Some scholars have suggested that Elam's link to Shem has more geographical than genealogical significance; the Elamites were often ruled and to some degree colonized by Semites. The Semitic influence on Elamite culture in the time of Sargon I (24th century BC) is well attested by archaeological evidence.

Elamites established a substantial dynasty at Susa several hundred years before God called Abraham out of Ur, a city 100 miles to the west of Elam. With the ascendency of Sargon of Akkad (a region northwest of Elam) open hostility resulted in the absorption of Elam and its adjacent northerly area, Warahshi, into his empire. A subsequent Elamite revolt was crushed by Sargon's grandson, Naram-Sin (2291–2255 BC), who managed to repress Elamite power until his death. After nearly a century of submission to the Akkadians, Elam asserted its strength once again during the reign of Sharkalisharri, Naram-Sin's heir. Around 2000 BC a militant, autonomous Elam invaded and conquered several cities in Babylonia, reducing Ur and its Sumerian overlords to subservience. It is probably at this time that the Elamite Chedorlaomer (in Elamite Kuter-Lagamar, meaning "the [goddess] Lagamar is protectress") undertook his Transjordan tribute-collecting expedition (Gn 14:1–7). Although the Babylonian Hammurabi expelled the Elamites approximately ten years later (c. 1760 BC), both Elamite and Babylonian forces were eclipsed by the mighty Kassites, a people of Asiatic stock, who swooped down invincibly from the northerly Zagros mountains. The pendulum of power, which had swung back and forth between Elam and its Mesopotamian adversaries for centuries, now came to a full stop as the Kassites launched what would ultimately be a 400-year dynasty.

Elam does not become historically significant again until around 1300 BC, when a resurgence of power under the Elamite Pahirishshan enabled the country to exert political influence in the Near East. For the following 200 years the Elamite dynasty was unrivaled in power, controlling the Tigris Valley, including most of the area of the Persian Gulf as well as the Zagros mountain range. During this period the famous codified law of Hammurabi (inscribed upon an upright pillar called a stela) was taken as a trophy to the chief Elamite city of Susa.

From about 1000 BC until the campaigns of Sargon the Assyrian (c. 721–705 BC) Elamite history is obscure. Their complete subjugation to Assyria in the time of Sennacherib (705–681 BC) marked the end of their historical significance. When Ashurbanipal's Assyrian empire collapsed, Elam was annexed by the Indo-European Persians. With the subsequent rule of Cyrus II (539–530 BC) Elam vanished from the scene.

Religion. Like virtually all of their neighbors, the Elamites were polytheistic. Archaeological finds reveal innumerable deities, both male and female. Chief among their goddesses was Pinikir, who was somewhat on the order of the Mesopotamian Ishtar (Ashtaroth in biblical references). The male consort of this mistress of heaven was called Humban. In Elamite religion it was possible for one deity to gain prominence over others during the course of time. Inshushinak, once known simply as "father of the weak" was eventually addressed as "the Lord of Susa." It was commonplace for gods to have two or three mothers, also the objects of adoration.

An elaborate priesthood apparently exercised most of their functions in sacred groves and temples. Snake worship and the deification of the sun and the moon were also essential to Elamite religion.

Law. Certain idiosyncrasies mark Elamite law as unique. Civil proceedings were handled exclusively by secular judges; priests could serve only as witnesses in court. Such dissociation seems strange in view of the fact that the trials were held within the sacred temples. Witnesses were of extreme importance in Elamite law. The majority of texts show that between 5 and 20 witnesses appeared during an average trial. Criminal law called for the severe mutilation of certain offenders. Whoever committed perjury had his hand and tongue cut off. In spite of polygamy, Elamite women were highly favored by the law, enjoying both elevated social and administrative positions.

Biblical Significance. Western civilization would know virtually nothing of Elam were it not for the biblical witness. Elam is mentioned in conjunction with Shem's progeny (Gn 10:22), and in the Book of Acts it is reported that among the Israelites present in Jerusalem for the feast of Pentecost were some from the old area of Elam (2:9). Isaiah prophesied that the Jews carried away in the Babylonian exile would return from such places as Elam (Is 11:11); however, these were most likely Aramaic-speaking Jews who had decided not to return to their homeland following the repatriation edict of Cyrus of Persia (Ezr 1:1–4). The name Chedorlaomer, king of Elam (Gn 14:1), is demonstrably an authentic Elamite name, thereby lending additional support to the accuracy of the historical narrative in Genesis. Daniel's vision at Shushan in the province of Elam (Dn 8:2) reveals precise knowledge of the geography of the area and its waterways. In such accounts the Bible shows itself to be a valuable adjunct to extrabiblical literature.

In the 8th century BC Isaiah summoned Elam to participate in the shattering of Babylon as an act of Yahweh's judgment (Is 21:2); there is little information, however, about Elam's role in the overthrow of Babylon in 540 BC. Elam, with other rebellious nations, would eventually experience the cup of God's wrath (Jer 25:15–26). Even its world-renowned archers would prove to be no match for the Lord of Hosts (Is 22:6–12; Jer 49:35; Ez 32:24). Ezekiel's dirge over Elam dramatically illustrates the horror of a godless grave (Ez 32:24,25). Jeremiah warns the Elamites that they cannot escape the judgment of God, made certain by the presence of his throne among them (Jer 49:38). Yet Elam's destruction, though politically complete in Persia's conquest, would not be altogether irremediable (Jer 49:39). Though its dislocation would rival those of its contemporaries, Jeremiah spoke of a time when God would extend mercy to descendants of the Elamites. Such an expectancy, following the phrase, "in the latter days," may point to the messianic age. The prophet may well have envisioned that momentous day of Pentecost, when many from Elam would be among those in Jerusalem upon whom the Spirit of the Lord fell. STUART D. SACKS

Elasah. 1. Priest of Pashur's clan who obeyed Ezra's exhortation to divorce his pagan wife after the exile (Ezr 10:22).

2. Shaphan's son and King Zedekiah's envoy to King Nebuchadnezzar of Babylon. On his trip to Babylon, Elasah also carried a letter of encouragement from the prophet Jeremiah to the Jewish exiles there (Jer 29:3).

Elath. Edomite city (also spelled Eloth), at the head of the Gulf of Aqaba (Dt 2:8; 1 Kgs 9:26), on the eastern border of the wilderness of Paran (Gn 14:6, where it is alternately called El-paran). It probably owed its name (which means "grove of trees") to the many palm trees in the area and may have been located in

Elath, seaport on the Gulf of Aqaba.

a grove of sacred trees. Elath was strategically located along a primary trade route running from southern Arabia and Egypt to Phoenicia, making it a valuable city to possess.

Elath was taken by Chedorlaomer from the Horites (Gn 14:5,6). Later the chief of Edom lived there (Gn 36:41), and it was regarded as the southern limit of the territory of Edom (Dt 2:8). David no doubt captured it when he conquered Edom (2 Sm 8:14). During the reign of Joram, Jehoshaphat's son, revolt restored it to the Edomites (2 Kgs 8:20–22). A few years later it was recaptured and rebuilt by Judah's King Uzziah (2 Kgs 14:22). It remained under Judah's rule until the time of Ahaz, when it was taken by Rezin of Syria and occupied by Syrians (2 Kgs 16:6). From about 753 BC onward it remained an Edomite city until it was abandoned sometime between the 6th and 4th centuries BC. Then the Nabataeans, who controlled the area, built a city a little farther east of the original site and renamed it Aila.

See EL-PARAN.

El-berith. Local god worshiped at Shechem (Jgs 9:46). He is usually identified with the god Baal-berith (Jgs 8:33; 9:4).

El-bethel. Name Jacob gave to the place at Luz (Bethel) where he built an altar after he returned from Haran with his family (Gn 35:7).

See BETHEL, BETHELITE (CITY).

Eldaah. Midian's 5th son and a descendant of Abraham and his wife Keturah (Gn 25:4; 1 Chr 1:33).

Eldad. One of the 70 elders of Israel who were commissioned to assist Moses in governing the people (Nm 11:26,27). Though Eldad and another elder, Medad, were not among the 68 elders who had gathered around the tabernacle at Moses' command, they too received the Spirit and prophesied. When Joshua, out of concern for Moses' authority, asked Moses to stop them, Moses showed great humility and sensitivity to God's will by answering, "I wish that all the Lord's people were prophets" (Nm 11:29 NIV).

Elder. Person who, by virtue of position in the family, clan, or tribe; or by reason of personality, prowess, stature, or influence; or through a process of appointment and ordination, exercised leadership and judicial functions in both religious and secular spheres in the ancient world, both among biblical and nonbiblical peoples. The roots of the development of the presbytery (group of elders) in the NT and postapostolic church originate in Judaism and the OT, though the figure of the elder or groups of elders can also be found in the world surrounding ancient Israel and in the Greco-Roman world of the NT period.

In the Old Testament. The elder, or the institution of elders, is closely linked with the tribal system. Tribes were composed of clans, and clans of large, extended family units. By virtue of age and function in a patriarchal society, the father of a family ruled. This fact of age, as well as the wisdom and maturity invested in older persons, is undoubtedly the origin of the authority that these elders exercised. A clan was ruled by the heads of the families constituting it, forming a council of elders. In time of war, each clan furnished a contingent; these were led by a chief, probably chosen from the ranks of the elders.

In Israel's premonarchy period local administration and judicial action was largely in the hands of those elders. In the exodus narrative it was the elders of Israel (heads of families) who were instructed by Moses concerning the first Passover meal (Ex 12:21,22). It was these elders who, in Exodus 18:12, met with Jethro, Moses' father-in-law, and from whose ranks were chosen worthy representatives to assist Moses in the interpretation of the Law of God and the administration of justice (Ex 18:13–23). Similarly, according to Numbers 11:16,17, Moses was instructed by God to select 70 men from among the elders of Israel to assist him in leadership of the people. In this latter account the elders were marked by a special endowment of God's Spirit. In the former the elders—chosen as co-administrators with Moses—were those known to be trustworthy, who "hate a bribe."

A central function of elders was the administration of justice. They were the "judges," who sat "in the gate," the traditional courtroom of ancient villages and towns. Here disputes and trials were settled by the elders, and community affairs were discussed and decisions made (Gn 23:10,18; Jb 29:7; Prv 24:7;

31:23). The preservation and application of the Law was clearly in the hands of "elders at the gate of the town" (Dt 21:19; 22:15) or "elders of the town" (Dt 19:12; 21:3,6; 25:7–10). Ruth 4:1–12 provides an excellent description of such a process.

During the period of the monarchy, local administration and judicial authority continued to be invested in councils of elders. At end of Saul's reign David sent messages and gifts to the elders of the towns of Judah (1 Sm 30:26), obviously recognizing that his efficient rule would depend on their goodwill and allegiance. In the time of Jehu (2 Kgs 10:5) we hear of elders in Samaria, side by side with a governor and master of the palace. To facilitate her plot against Naboth, Jezebel wrote instructions to the elders and nobles of Yizreel (1 Kgs 21:8–11). Again, Josiah convened the elders of Judah and Jerusalem to hear the reading of the Law and to enter with him into a new covenant of obedience (2 Kgs 23:1). It is clear that the elders of Israel were now responsible for the application of the Law within their jurisdictions. Beside administrative and judicial functions, elders also assumed cultic roles (Ex 24:1,9; Lv 4:15) and were participants in the royal covenant with David (2 Kgs 19:2).

The institution of the elders survived the collapse of the royal institutions. Elders were present during the exile (Ez 8:1; 14:1; 20:1–3) as well as after the return (e.g., Ezr 10:16).

In Judaism of the New Testament Period. While use of the title "elder" to designate officers of various Greek cult associations and village magistrates may have influenced the development of community structure in the gentile churches, the Christian office (or function) of elder stems in the main from a very similar institution within Judaism. In the first three Gospels and in Acts there are numerous references to elders as functionaries within the communal and religious life of Judaism. Generally they are mentioned together with one or more other groups of functionaries: "elders and chief priests and scribes" (Mt 16:21); "chief priests and elders of the people" (Mt 21:23; 26:3,47,57); "scribes and elders" (Mt 26:57); "chief priests and elders" (27:1,3,12, 20,41); "rulers and elders and scribes" (Acts 4:5); "rulers of the people and elders" (Acts 4:8). From these NT passages we cannot determine what exactly their functions were, or how they differed from rulers or scribes. However, the duties of Jewish elders are clearly described in the tractate *Sanhedrin* in the Mishna, as well as in the community rule books of the Qumran ascetics, discovered among the Dead Sea Scrolls.

Each Jewish community had its council of elders, who had general administrative oversight and represented the community in relations with Roman authorities. Their primary duty was judicial. They were custodians of the Law and its traditional interpretations (see Mt 15:2) and were charged with both its enforcement and the punishment of offenders. The most important of these councils of elders was the Sanhedrin in Jerusalem, a group of 71 men who acted as the final court for the entire nation.

In the Christian Community. Since the primitive church eventually regarded itself as the new Israel (Mt 21:43; Gal 6:16) it is easy to see why it should gradually adopt the institution of elders. Though it is difficult to make out the order that prevailed in the first Christian communities, because it apparently varied according to place and time in both form and extent, the presence and functioning of elders was part of the reality of early church life.

In Luke's account of the origin and spread of Christianity the elders are already present in the church at Jerusalem. In Acts 11:30 we find Christians at Antioch sending famine relief "to the elders [of the Judean churches] by Barnabas and Saul." On their first missionary journey Paul and Barnabas appoint elders in every church (14:23). Later, Paul and Barnabas are sent from Antioch to Jerusalem "to the apostles and elders" about the question of circumcision of gentile Christians (15:2), and are "welcomed by the church, and the apostles, and the elders" (15:4) who gathered to hear the case and resolve the issue (15:6–23).

Who these elders were, and how they were chosen, we are not told. It seems possible to argue, on the basis of Jewish precedent, that age and prominence gave them the privilege of rendering special service within the community. Veneration for age was a deeply rooted sentiment among Jews, and the name "presbyter" (elder) was derived from Jewish usage. It is also possible that, like the appointment of "the seven" for special service by the laying on of hands (Acts 6:1–6), the first elders in the Jerusalem church were appointed by the apostles. Apparently they functioned in the Christian community in ways comparable to elders in the Jewish communities and the Sanhedrin (Acts 11:30; 15:2,4,6,22,23; 16:4; 21:18).

Paul apparently continued the practice among the gentile churches, though elders are not mentioned in the earliest Pauline writings. They are mentioned only in the pastoral epistles (1 Tm 5:17, 19; Ti 1:5). On his last journey to Jerusalem, Paul summons the elders of the church at Ephesus to Melitus (Acts 20:17) to bid them farewell, and to instruct them to be faithful in their task of overseeing and caring for the Christian flock, the church of God (20:28).

Although elders are not explicitly mentioned in Paul's early letters, they may be among the leaders who presided over the congregations in pastoral functions (Rom 12:8; 1 Thes 5:12,13). It is probably wrong, as many interpreters have done, to draw a sharp line of distinction between the so-called "charismatic" leadership in the Pauline churches (e.g., 1 Cor 12) and a more hierarchial structure in Jewish Christian congregations. Philippians 1:1 certainly reveals a definite stratification of leadership ("overseers and deacons") within a young Pauline congregation. And 1 Timothy 5:17, reflecting what is often considered a later phase in the development of church government, attributes the more "charismatic" functions of preaching and teaching to the ruling elders. Further, that Christian elders exercised pastoral functions may be inferred from 1 Peter 5:1–5 and James 5:14.

There is only one passage where we find a possible identification of an apostle and elders: "I exhort the elders among you, as a fellow elder and a witness of the sufferings of Christ" (1 Pt 5:1a). This text may indicate that elders were appointed and functioned as extensions of apostolic servanthood. Paul's practice of appointing elders in the churches before his departure may support such a suggestion. The fact that in the tradition of the later church the "elder" of 2 and 3 John was identified as the apostle John points in a similar direction. Though such an identification is implicit, apostles and elders were never confused.

The matter of distinction between elders and other officers in the church is not so easy. Though in Paul's listing of gifts and functions (1 Cor 12:28; Eph 4:11) a distinction is made between prophets, evangelists, pastors, teachers, etc., it is clear that in practice two or more of these functions were often invested in the same individual. For example, 1 Timothy 5:17 speaks of elders as involved in preaching and teaching; James 5:14 sees them involved in a healing ministry; 1 Peter 5:2 exhorts them to tend the flock. Thus, the prophets and teachers who led the church at Antioch (according to Acts 13:1–3) may well have been the elders of this community.

The diaconate, too, whose roots are to be seen in the selection of "the seven" for service to those in need (Acts 6:1–3), was not restricted to purely external service. Two of these men, whom Luke introduces to us as deacons, appear at the same time as evangelists who were particularly effective as preachers of the Word, performers of miracles, expounders of the Scriptures (Stephen, Acts 6:8–10; Philip, Acts 8:4–13,26–40).

Whereas in the later church bishops and elders were clearly distinguished, the NT reflects an early period when these offices were virtually synonymous. In Paul's farewell speech at Melitus (Acts 20), addressed specifically to the Ephesian church elders (20:17), he tells them that the Holy Spirit has made them "overseers to care for the church of God" (20:28). Whether "overseer" is used here in the later technical sense of bishop or the more general sense of guardian is not clear. However, in Titus 1:5–7, the elders of verse 5 are clearly the same persons as the bishops of verse 7. Again, the bishops of Philippians 1:1 are likely to be understood as the elders appointed by Paul upon leaving this mission station.

It is clear that church government in the NT period was still relatively fluid, but the seeds for the later structures were surely planted. The institution of the elders, on the basis of Jewish precedent, was central. The episcopate (overseers/bishops) probably emerged out of the presbytery (elders), one elder being appointed as overseer by the entire council of elders. MANFRED T. BRAUCH

See BISHOP; PASTOR; DEACON, DEACONESS; PRESBYTER; SPIRITUAL GIFTS.

Bibliography. G. Berghoef and L. DeKoster, *The Elder's Handbook*; T.M. Lindsay, *The Church and Ministry in the Early Centuries*; I.M. Ross, *What Is an Elder*; B.H. Streeter, *The Primitive Church.*

Elead. Ephraim's descendant who was killed in a raid against the Philistine city of Gath (1 Chr 7:21).

Ele-adah. Ephraim's descendant (1 Chr 7:20, KJV Eladah).

Elealeh. Town in the Transjordan northeast of Heshbon conquered by Reuben and Gad (Nm 32:3,37). It was taken back by the Moabites and is associated with Heshbon in the prophetic denunciations of Moab (Is 15:4; 16:9; Jer 48:34).

Eusebius refers to it in the 4th century AD as a large village. It is identified with the modern el-'Al, a village 2,986 feet above sea level in a region rich in vineyards. The remains of walls from the prepatriarchal period have been uncovered by archaeologists.

Eleasah. 1. Helez's son and member of Judah's tribe (1 Chr 2:39,40).

2. Raphah's son and descendant of King Saul (1 Chr 8:37; 9:43).

Eleazar. 1. Third of Aaron's four sons (Ex 6:23). Eleazar ("God has helped") was consecrated as a priest with his brothers and Aaron in Sinai (Ex 28:1; Lv 8:2,13). When his brothers Nadab and Abihu were slain by God as they offered "unholy fire" to the Lord (Lv 10:1–7),

Eleazar and Ithamar took leading positions as Aaron's sons (Nm 3:1–4).

Eleazar is described as "chief of the leaders of the Levites" (Nm 3:32). Under his supervision were the sanctuary and its vessels (Nm 4:16; 16:37,39; 19:3,4). Eleazar was installed as high priest by Moses when Aaron died on Mt Hor (Nm 20:25–28; Dt 10:6). He was then considered Moses' assistant (Nm 26:1,3,63; 27:2,21). Joshua was commissioned by Moses in the presence of Eleazar (Nm 27:18–23). In the conquest of Canaan, Joshua and Eleazar served together as leaders. It was Eleazar's function as Joshua's counselor to inquire of the Lord (Nm 27:18–22). He also had his share in the census-taking at Shittim. He took part in the partitioning of Canaan, the east bank (Nm 34:17), and the west bank (Jos 14:1; 17:4; 19:51; 21:1).

When Eleazar died he was highly regarded and memorialized in the land of Ephraim (Jos 24:33); his son Phinehas followed him as high priest.

In the oversight of the priests 16 divisions were assigned to Eleazar's descendants and 8 to Ithamar's (1 Chr 24). The ancestry of the prominent priests Zadok and Ezra is traced to Eleazar (1 Chr 6:3–15,50–53; 24:3; Ezr 7:1–5). In King Solomon's time the priests of Zadok replaced Abiathar, a descendant of Ithamar (1 Kgs 2:26,27,35). The descendants of Eleazar would be the only ones permitted to minister in Ezekiel's ideal temple (Ez 44:15).

See AARON.

2. Abinadad's son charged with caring for the ark by the people of Kirjath-jearim, when it was brought from Beth-shemesh and placed in the "house of Abinadad on the hill" (1 Sm 7:1).

3. Dodo's son, one of the three mighty men whose exploits against the Philistines gained him great fame (2 Sm 23:9; 1 Chr 11:12).

4. Merarite Levite, son of Mahli. Eleazar died without sons, so his daughters were married to their first cousins (1 Chr 23:21,22; 24:28).

5. Priest descended from Phinehas. This Eleazar helped inventory the temple treasure on returning from the exile with Ezra (Ezr 8:33).

6. Parosh's son, listed with others who divorced their foreign wives in the reform under Ezra (Ezr 10:25).

7. Priest in attendance at the dedication of the rebuilt walls of Jerusalem following the exile (Neh 12:42).

8. Person in the lineage of Joseph, husband of Mary (Mt 1:15).

See GENEALOGY OF JESUS CHRIST.

Elect, Election. In modern English, terms referring to the selection of a leader or representative by a group of people. An element of choice is involved, since usually there are several candidates out of whom one must be chosen.

When the verb "elect" is used theologically in the Bible, it usually has God as its subject. In the OT it is used for God's choice of Israel to be his people (cf. Acts 13:17). Israel became God's people, not because they decided to belong to him, but because he took the initiative and chose them. Nor did God's choice rest on any particular virtues that his people exemplified, but rather on his promise to their forefather Abraham (Dt 7:7,8). God also chose their leaders, such as Saul and David (1 Sm 10:24; 2 Sm 6:21), apart from any popular vote by the people. The word thus indicates God's prerogative in deciding what shall happen, independently of human choice.

The same thoughts are found in the NT. God's people are described as his "elect" or "chosen ones," a term used by Jesus when speaking of the future time when the Son of· man will come and gather together God's people (Mk 13:20,27). He will vindicate them for their sufferings and for their patience in waiting for his coming (Lk 18:7). In 1 Peter 2:9 God's people are called an "elect nation." This phrase was originally used of the people of Israel (Is 43:20), and it brings out the fact that the people of God in the OT and the Christian church in the NT stand in continuity with each other; the promises addressed to Israel now find fulfillment in the church.

In Romans 9–11 Paul discusses the problem of why the people of Israel as a nation have rejected the gospel, while the Gentiles have accepted it. He states that in the present time there is a "remnant" of Israel as a result of God's gracious choice of them. This group is called "the elect." They are the chosen people who have obtained what was meant for Israel as a whole, while the greater mass of the people have failed to obtain it because they were "hardened" as a result of their sin (Rom 11:5,7).

Nevertheless, God's choice of Israel to be his people has not been cancelled. Most Jewish people have aligned themselves against the gospel, so that the Gentiles may come in and receive God's blessings in their place; but they still remain beloved by God, and God will not go back on his original calling of them (Rom 11:28). Consequently Paul is confident that in due time there will be a general return to God by the people of Israel.

The word translated "elect" is generally found in the plural and refers either to the members of God's people as a whole or to those in a particular local church (Rom 8:33; Col 3:12; 1 Thes 1:4; 2 Tm 2:10; Ti 1:1; 1 Pt 1:1;

2 Pt 1:10; Rv 17:14; Rom 16:13 and 2 Jn 13 have the singular form). The use of the plural may partly be explained by the fact that most of the NT letters are addressed to groups of people rather than to individuals. More probably, however, the point is that God's election is concerned with the creation of a people rather than the calling of isolated individuals.

The use of the word "election" emphasizes that membership of God's people is due to God's initiative, prior to all human response, made before time began (Eph 1:4; cf. Jn 15:16,19). It is God who has called men and women to be his people, and those who respond are elect. God's call does not depend on any virtues or merits of humankind. Indeed, he chooses the foolish things by worldly standards to shame the wise, the weak to confound the strong, and the low and insignificant to bring to nothing those who think that they are something (1 Cor 1:27,28). The effect of election is to leave no grounds whatever for human boasting in achievement and position. Whatever the elect are, they owe entirely to God, and they cannot boast or compare themselves with other people.

God's elect are a privileged people. Since they now have God to uphold them, no one can bring any accusation against them that might lead to God's condemnation (Rom 8:33). They constitute a royal priesthood; they are God's servants with the right of access to him (1 Pt 2:9). It is for their sake that the apostles endured hardship and suffering, so that they might enjoy future salvation and eternal glory (2 Tm 2:10).

The elect are distinguished by their faith in God (Ti 1:1), and they are called to show the character that befits God's people (Col 3:12). They must make their calling and election sure; that is, they must show that they belong to God by the quality of their lives (2 Pt 1:10). They must continue being faithful to the One who called them (Rv 17:14).

The relationship between God's call and human response is explained in Matthew 22:14: "For many are called, but few are chosen." Although God calls many through the gospel, only some of those respond to the call and become his elect people. The text sheds no light on the mystery of why only some become God's people. Certainly, when a person does respond to God's call, it is because the gospel comes to him or her "in power and in the Holy Spirit and with full conviction" (1 Thes 1:4,5). When men and women refuse the gospel, it is because they have become hardened as a result of sin and their trust in their own works. Scripture does not go beyond that point in explanation, and neither should Christians.

"Election" can also be used of God's choice

of people to serve him. Jesus chose the 12 disciples out of the larger company of those who followed him (Lk 6:13; Acts 1:2). The same thought reappears in John's Gospel; Jesus commented that although he chose the 12, one of them turned out to be a devil (Jn 6:70; 13:18). When a replacement was needed for Judas, the church prayed to Jesus and asked him to show them which of the two available candidates he would choose to fill the gap in the 12 (Acts 1:24). Peter attributes his evangelism among the Gentiles to God's "election"of him for that purpose (Acts 15:7). Similarly, Paul was an elected instrument for God's mission to the Gentiles (Acts 9:15). The initiative in Christian mission rests with God, who elects people to serve him in particular ways.

Jesus is called "God's Chosen" (Lk 9:35; cf. the taunt in Lk 23:35). The heavenly voice at Jesus' transfiguration spoke in language that echoed Isaiah 42:1 and identified Jesus as God's Servant, chosen to do his work of bringing light to the nations. In the same way, Jesus is a "chosen cornerstone" (1 Pt 2:4,6; cf. Is 28:16).

In the teaching of Augustine and Calvin, the doctrine of election is of fundamental importance. They taught that God had chosen before the creation of the world to save a number of specific individuals from sin and judgment and to give them eternal life. Those whom he chose did nothing to deserve it; their merits are no better than the rest of humankind who will be judged for their sins. But in his mercy God decided to save some; therefore, he chose them and sent Jesus to be their Savior. The Holy Spirit regenerates and brings to faith through an "effectual calling" those whom God has elected. God's Spirit effectively persuades each of them to submit to the gospel, so they are guaranteed recipients of eternal life.

This choice by God selectively to save some may seem unjust. But in fact, God is not obliged to show mercy to anybody; he is free to show mercy as he pleases. People cannot protest that because they were not the elect, they never had a chance of being saved. They never deserved that chance anyway. But anybody who hears the gospel and responds to it with faith can know that he is one of the elect. Whoever rejects the gospel has only his own sinfulness to blame.

Many Christians reject that explanation of God's election. They maintain that although it appears to be logically consistent with Scripture, it makes God the prisoner of his own plan. His predestination of certain individuals to salvation commits him personally to a detailed, predetermined, unilateral course of action that reduces human action to a charade

and renders it insignificant. God ceases to be a person dealing with persons.

The Augustinian and Calvinist view of election, according to its critics, also makes God out to be arbitrary in his choice of the elect. In effect, chance becomes the arbiter of human destiny rather than a holy and loving God. Those difficulties arise because, they say, the teaching of Scripture has been pressed into an artificial logical system that distorts it.

Some Christians avoid the difficulties by saying that God elects "those whom he foreknew" (Rom 8:29), that is, those whom he knew beforehand would respond to the gospel in faith. Augustine briefly held that view but eventually rejected it. Many believe that the "solution" produces even greater logical problems and undermines the sovereignty of God.

Karl Barth has proposed an alternative solution. Instead of teaching that God has chosen to save some of mankind and has passed by the others or chosen to reject them, Barth has noted how Jesus is spoken of in Scripture as "the elect One." Jesus is the object both of God's rejection and of his election. In him the human race was rejected and endured judgment for its sins, Barth argued, but in him also the race is chosen and appointed to salvation. It is thus in Jesus Christ that we are chosen by God (Eph 1:4). Barth's interpretation could conceivably lead to universalism (that is, the view that all humanity will be saved), but Barth explicitly rejected that as a necessary conclusion. He insisted that a person may reject his or her calling and election. Nevertheless, difficulties remain. It has been argued that Barth's view places too much weight on one text and also that it confuses God's election of Jesus for service with his election to salvation of the whole human race.

The teaching of Scripture should not be overly systematized. In the words of the Westminster Confession, election is a "high mystery . . . to be handled with special prudence and care, that men attending the will of God revealed in his word, and yielding obedience thereunto, may, from the certainty of their effectual vocation, be assured of their eternal salvation" (3:8).   I. HOWARD MARSHALL

See FOREKNOWLEDGE; FOREORDINATION.

Bibliography. G.C. Berkouwer, *Divine Election*; F. Davidson, *Pauline Predestination*; P.K. Jewett, *Election and Predestination*; J. Jocz, *A Theology of Election: Israel and the Church*; H.H. Rowley, *The Biblical Doctrine of Election*; B.B. Warfield, "Predestination" in *Biblical Doctrines*.

Elect Lady. Greeting found in 2 John 1:1. The phrase has been interpreted two ways.

Some interpreters regard 2 John as addressed to a particular woman. Ancient Greek manuscripts show that the word *kuria* (translated as "lady" or "mistress") was used by letter writers as a personal term for family members or close friends of either sex. Thus, the phrase could be translated, "to my dear friend, Eklete." Some scholars associate the elect lady with Martha of Bethany (whose name in Aramaic also means "mistress").

Other interpreters regard the phrase as signifying a local congregation. John possibly portrayed this Christian community as a mother, the members as her children, and other congregations as sisters (v 13; cf. 1 Pt 5:13). The phrase could thus be translated, "the lady elect."

See JOHN, LETTERS OF.

El-Elohe-Israel. Name of an altar built by the patriarch Jacob on land he purchased from the "sons of Hamor," near Shechem (Gn 33:20). Jacob used the Canaanite deity's name, El, as a designation for Israel's God.

Some scholars, thinking this a strange name for an altar, have suggested that the combination of names reflects later scribal emendations of the scriptural texts. They argue that the Septuagint corrects the difficulty by saying that Jacob had called "upon" the God of Israel. Others speculate that Jacob built a pillar, not an altar (cf. Gn 35:14,20).

See GOD, NAMES OF.

El-elyon. Hebrew for "God Most High" (Gn 14:18).

See GOD, NAMES OF.

Elemental Spirits, Elements. Alternative translation of a Greek word used in the NT, "elemental spirits" being spiritual forces at work in the world, and "elements" being either the basic constituents of the physical world or of human life or the basic principles of a system of thought. In three passages the meaning is clear (Heb 5:12; 2 Pt 3:10,12). The other four passages, however, have caused considerable debate. The difficult phrase "the elements of the world" appears in three of the four passages (Gal 4:3; Col 2:8,20). The meaning of "elements" in the fourth passage (Gal 4:9) is probably the same as in the other three because of its similar context.

Range of Meanings. The basic meaning of the Greek word is "basic or fundamental component." The word, however, occurs frequently in ancient Greek literature and takes on a variety of connotations in the different contexts in which it appears. Most frequently it was used literally to refer to the physical elements of the world: earth, air, water, and fire. This is probably the meaning of the term in 2 Peter 3:10,12, which state that the world's

elements, the physical matter, will be destroyed by fire.

In antiquity the word also commonly referred to the letters in a word, notes in music, the "elementary" rules of politics, or the foundations or basic principles in science, art, or teaching (particularly logical propositions basic to the proof of other propositions). The last is clearly the meaning of the word in the Epistle to the Hebrews (5:12), which describes people's need to have someone teach them the basic principles or elementary truths of God's Word.

In the 3rd century AD another meaning of "elements"—elemental spiritual beings—became current. The development of this meaning has led to the current debate over its suitability in Paul's context.

Elementary Spirits. A difficulty with Paul's use of "elements" is that any of three possible meanings makes sense. One can understand "elements" to mean spiritual beings and view Paul's reference as similar to his mention of the principalities and powers (e.g., in Eph 6:12). Paraphrasing Galatians 4:3 according to this view (adopted by RSV), Paul would have been saying that before conversion a person is enslaved to spiritual forces who rule this world. In 4:9, he asks how the Galatians could wish to be enslaved to these forces again. The references to "beings that by nature are no gods" (Gal 4:8) and to angels through whom the law was mediated (Gal 3:19) are both used to substantiate the meaning "elemental spirits."

Similarly, Colossians 2:8 would be warning Christians against being led away captive through the philosophical speculations and empty deceit that are perpetrated by human traditions and the elemental spirits. Only two verses later Paul declares that Christ is the head of every principality and power (Col 2:10). Many commentators now believe that Paul intended "principalities and powers" to refer to demons who temporarily ruled various spheres of life in the world. Paul announces that Christ has conquered them and displayed them publicly as captives in his triumphal procession (Col 2:15). Thus Colossians 2:20 might mean that Christians have "died" to those elemental spirits as elsewhere Paul wrote of "dying" to sin (Rom 6:2).

However, despite the fact that Paul spoke of the principalities and powers as spiritual forces, and despite the ease with which this meaning fits Paul's use of "elements of the world," many scholars regard this interpretation as the least likely of the three possibilities. The earliest certain evidence for the use of "elements" to mean spirits is from the 3rd century AD, which is far too late to reflect common usage in Paul's day. In addition, nowhere else did Paul speak of Christians being in bondage to angels or having died to demonic powers.

Elementary Principles. Some scholars understand "the elements of the world" to refer to elementary religious teaching (as in Heb 5:12). Paul may have been appealing to the "ABC's of religion"—perhaps the elementary character of the Law (cf. Gal 3:24; 4:1–4) or pagan religious teaching (Gal 4:8). The "weak and beggarly elements" may be explained by the fact that the Galatians were legalistically observing special days, months, seasons, and years as if their righteousness before God depended on it.

Similarly, in Colossians the elements of the world seem to be parallel to human traditions (Col 2:8). The problem again is the same as in Galatians, legalism (Col 2:16,20–23). In both contexts the bondage warned against is bondage to elementary religious thinking that comes merely from humans and would be equivalent to contrasting a kindergarten level of thought with the advanced teaching that comes in Christ. Some scholars believe that this interpretation has more in its favor than the meaning "elemental spirits," but others argue that it is not precise enough.

Elementary Existence. By far the most frequent use of "elements" in ancient literature is literal, referring to the physical elements of the world, which were usually considered to be earth, air, water, and fire. The third interpretation, which many scholars prefer, draws on this understanding of "elements of the world." The meaning of the phrase "of the world" determines how the passages in question are to be interpreted. In the NT writings "world" was not merely physical. Frequently "world" was viewed in an ethical sense, standing for human life apart from God or even lived in opposition to God and Christ. The world often represented unregenerate humanity with its culture, customs, worldview, and ethics—the part of creation that had not yet been redeemed and was helpless to save itself. Thus, the elements of the world, in this view, are the "basics" of a merely human existence. According to this interpretation, Paul warned the Colossian Christians against being led away captive by philosophical speculation and empty deceit that were in accord with human traditions and with the basics of a merely human existence and not in accord with what they had in Christ (Col 2:8). They had died from the basics of a merely human life (Col 2:20), and being no longer bound to that level of existence, they possessed a life that came from Christ (Col 3:1–4).

This interpretation still leaves the precise meaning of Galatians 4:1–3 uncertain. Was Paul addressing both Jews and Gentiles or only Jews (the "we" in Gal 4:3)? No doubt Paul viewed both Jews and Gentiles as being in bondage to a merely human existence. Even though the Jews possessed God's Law, it was ineffectual for salvation. Christ's coming broke that bondage and brought the Holy Spirit, who would give Christians a completely new quality of human life. Therefore Paul warned against becoming enslaved again to such weak and poverty-stricken basics of a merely human existence (Gal 4:9).

In this view, then, the elements of the world are the "basics" of existence before and outside of Christ. Paul nowhere recorded specifically what he included in those basics. The contexts of both Galatians and Colossians, however, seem to imply that the basics at least included the Law and "the flesh" (that is, life lived ethically apart from God). Such a view of "elements" accords well with the wider context of these passages and with other passages (especially Rom 6–8; Gal 3:2,3,23–25; 4:1–10).

KLYNE R. SNODGRASS

Eleph. KJV translation for the town Haeleph in Joshua 18:28.

See HAELEPH.

Eleven, The. Designation for the 12 disciples after the resurrection of Jesus (Mk 16:14; Lk 24:9,33), and at Pentecost (Acts 2:14), Judas Iscariot having committed suicide.

See APOSTLE, APOSTLESHIP.

Elhanan. 1. Hebrew soldier who distinguished himself by killing a Philistine giant. In one passage he is named as the son of Jaare-oregim of Bethlehem, and is said to have killed Goliath the Gittite (2 Sm 21:19). In another passage he is named as the son of Jair, and is said to have killed Lahmi, the brother of Goliath (1 Chr 20:5).

2. Dodo's son and warrior among King David's mighty men (2 Sm 23:24; 1 Chr 11:26).

Eli. Priest in the sanctuary of the Lord at Shiloh in the period of the judges (1 Sm 1:3,9). Shiloh, about 10 miles north of Jerusalem, was the central shrine of the Israelite tribal confederation. Eli had two sons who were priests, Hophni and Phinehas (which are Egyptian names; 1 Sm 1:3). No lineage is recorded for Eli, but there are two possible suggestions: he is a descendant of Ithamar, Aaron's younger son (1 Sm 22:20; 1 Kgs 2:27; 1 Chr 24:3); or he comes from the house of Eleazar (Ex 6:23,25; 2 Esd 1:2,3). In 1 Samuel 1, Eli blessed the childless Hannah, Elkanah's wife, after learning of her prayer for a son (v 17). Subsequently Sam-

A tomb at Shiloh.

uel was born, and when weaned was brought by his mother to Eli for service and training in the sanctuary, according to her promise to the Lord (vv 27,28).

Hophni and Phinehas were corrupting the Israelites despite Eli's protests, and for this sin God promised judgment upon Eli's family (1 Sm 2;27,36). The sons of Eli were to die on the same day (1 Sm 2:34), and the fulfillment came in a battle with the Philistines at Aphek (1 Sm 4:11,17). Eli too died when he heard of the defeat and the loss of the ark of the covenant to the Philistines. At his death he was 98 years old, and besides being priest he also had judged Israel for 40 years (1 Sm 4:15,18). Eli's daughter-in-law, Phinehas' wife, died in childbirth, brokenhearted over the loss of her husband and the ark. She named her son Ichabod because she felt that there was no more hope (1 Sm 4:19–22).

Eli was not characterized by a firm personality. He was no doubt sincere and devout, but he was also weak and indulgent.

Eli, eli, lama sabachthani.

One of Jesus' cries from the cross, properly translated "My God, my God, why have you forsaken me?" That form of the "cry of dereliction" (Mt 27:46) is slightly different from its other recorded form, "Eloi, eloi, lama sabachthani?" (Mk 15:34). Both versions are adaptations of Psalm 22:1 into Aramaic, the common language of first-century Palestine. The only difference in the two accounts is that Mark's version is completely Aramaic whereas Matthew retains the Hebrew word for God (which was not uncommon for Aramaic-speaking Jews). The fact that some of Jesus' hearers thought he was calling Elijah indicates that Matthew's version is probably the original. Elias (Elijah) could have been confused with "Eli" more easily than with "Eloi" (Mt 27:47; Mk 15:35).

The textual variants that exist suggest the difficulties copyists and interpreters have had

with Jesus' words. After meditating on the passage, Martin Luther exclaimed, "God forsaken of God! Who can understand it?" Luther's statement of the major theological problem, that Jesus was forsaken by God, is not the only possible understanding of the text. Debate has focused on two questions: whether in fact abandonment by God was expressed by Jesus' use of the psalmist's words, and why the onlookers spoke of Elijah.

Meaning of the Cry. At one extreme, many have been struck by the starkness of Jesus' words. Some have even seen in them a realization on the cross that he had failed and that all hope was lost for the coming of God's kingdom. From that perspective Jesus' words were a cry of despair over a lost cause. Such a view hardly fits the rest of the NT presentation of Jesus, however.

At the opposite extreme, some interpret the words as neither stark nor negative in any sense. They view the cry as an affirmation of Jesus' faith in committing himself to God (Lk 23:46). To such interpreters the fact that Jesus began his question with "My God, my God" and used a biblical quotation indicates religious reverence and continued faith. In Jewish practice sometimes the first line of a psalm or song would be quoted to refer to the whole work. Hence Jesus might have been quoting Psalm 22:1 as a way of referring to the whole psalm. Psalm 22 is clearly the lament of a righteous sufferer. Psalms of lament always expressed a prayer of confidence in God and praise to God as well as a prayer for help from God. Thus, from a certain point of view the cry from the cross can be seen as a confident prayer.

Many biblical scholars find the second extreme view as unconvincing as the first. The Gospel writers did not clarify the meaning of the cry. Yet if the words were an expression of confidence or praise, some indication would be expected in the text. As they stand, the words are hardly an expression of religious reverence. The words themselves and the fact they were expressed in a loud cry do not suggest a prayer of confidence or praise.

Another approach views the words as expressing Jesus' feeling of isolation in a moment of extreme anguish but rejects the notion that he was actually forsaken by God.

The interpretation that has become "traditional" is that Jesus was actually forsaken by God. In that view the context of the garden of Gethsemane (Mt 26:36–46; Mk 14:32–42; Lk 22:39–46) indicates the kind of conflict expressed in Jesus' cry on the cross. Jesus' identification with sinners was so real that taking on their sin broke the closeness of his communion with the Father. Thus Jesus' abandonment by God is seen as an important aspect of the atonement. Although stressing that Jesus was actually forsaken, the traditional view goes on to stress that the unity of the Trinity remained unbroken.

The explanation of such a paradox is not easy. Some view it as a divine mystery and make no attempt to explain it at all. Others attempt to make some kind of distinction between what happened on the cross and the reality of God's being. For example, in the early centuries of the church the view was expressed that only Jesus' humanity was affected by the separation, so that his deity remained intact with God. Others argue that Jesus was separated from the Father "functionally" in the work of salvation but not "really" with respect to his existence.

The refusal of the Gospel writers to explain Jesus' cry should make scholars hesitate to give precise or dogmatic explanations. At the least, one can confidently state (1) that the cry reflects the reality of Jesus' humanity in the face of death, (2) that the particular kind of death ("even death on a cross," Phil 2:8) was especially scandalous, and (3) that Christ's identification with sinners was a horribly painful experience. Thus, although the cry is somehow related to the atonement, the biblical texts do not discuss whether Jesus was absolutely abandoned. Further, they do not explain how God could recoil from sin at the same time that "in Christ God was reconciling the world to himself" (2 Cor 5:19). In doing justice to the depth of emotion expressed in the cry, one should be cautious not to force the text to say something the author did not intend.

Elijah and the Cry. Various possibilities of connections between the cry and Elijah have been offered. If the cry refers to the whole of Psalm 22, mention of Elijah by the bystanders would show that they understood Jesus' words as expressing confidence in salvation. A salvation mediated by Elijah would have seemed natural to the Jews, who often saw Elijah as a deliverer of the righteous oppressed. Others claim that the bystanders were willfully and maliciously distorting Jesus' words in order to mock him. Still others view the mention of Elijah as an honest misunderstanding because of the similarity of the words. The view that one adopts will depend to some extent on how Jesus' cry is understood.

KLYNE R. SNODGRASS

See SEVEN LAST WORDS, THE; CRUCIFIXION.

Eliab. 1. Heron's son and leader of Zebulun's tribe when the Israelites were roaming in the Sinai wilderness after their escape from Egypt (Nm 1:9, 2:7; 10:16). As leader he pre-

sented his tribe's offering at the consecration of the tabernacle (Nm 7:24,29).

2. Member of Reuben's tribe and son of Pallu. Eliab was the father of Nemuel, Dathan, and Abiram. Dathan and Abiram rebelled against Moses and Aaron in the wilderness (Nm 16:1,12; 26:8,9; Dt 11:6).

3. Jesse's eldest son and brother of King David. An impressive person physically, he was rejected by God for the kingship in favor of David (1 Sm 16:6; 1 Chr 2:13). Eliab served King Saul when Goliath defied Saul's army (1 Sm 17:13,28). He was appointed leader of Judah's tribe during David's reign (1 Chr 27:18, Elihu). His granddaughter Mahalath married King Rehoboam of Judah (2 Chr 11:18).

4. Variant name for Elihu in 1 Chronicles 6:27.

See ELIHU # 1.

5. Warrior from Gad's tribe who joined David at Ziklag in his struggle against King Saul (1 Chr 12:9). Eliab was an expert with the shield and spear (1 Chr 16:5).

6. Levite musician assigned to play the harp in the procession when King David brought the ark to Jerusalem (1 Chr 15:18). He was assigned permanently to service in the tabernacle (1 Chr 16:5).

Eliada. 1. One of King David's sons, born in Jerusalem (2 Sm 5:16; 1 Chr 3:8). He is also called Beeliada in 1 Chronicles 14:7.

2. Father of Rezon, the king of Damascus and an adversary of Solomon (1 Kgs 11:23, KJV Eliadah).

3. General under King Jehoshaphat. Eliada and the 200,000 warriors he commanded were from Benjamin's tribe (2 Chr 17:17).

Eliadah. KJV spelling of Eliada, Rezon's father, in 1 Kings 11:23.

See ELIADA # 2.

Eliah. KJV form of the name Elijah in 1 Chronicles 8:27 and Ezra 10:26.

See ELIJAH # 2,4.

Eliahba. Warrior among David's mighty men who were known as "the 30" (2 Sm 23:32; 1 Chr 11:33).

Eliakim. 1. Hilkiah's son and a royal officer in the household and court of King Hezekiah (2 Kgs 18:18,26,37). His position had increased in importance since Solomon's reign (1 Kgs 4:2–6) until he was second only to the king. As such Eliakim had absolute authority as the king's representative.

When Sennacherib of Assyria moved against Jerusalem in 701 BC, Eliakim was one of the diplomatic emissaries who conferred with the Assyrian officers on behalf of Hezekiah (2 Kgs 18:18,37). He was also sent by Hezekiah in sackcloth to Isaiah to ask for prayer on Jerusalem's behalf (2 Kgs 19:1–5).

2. King Josiah's second son. When Eliakim was made king of Judah by Pharaoh Neco, his name was changed to Jehoiakim (2 Kgs 23:34; 2 Chr 36:4).

See JEHOIAKIM.

3. One of the priests who assisted at the dedication of the Jerusalem wall after it was rebuilt by Zerubbabel (Neh 12:41).

4. Abiud's son in Matthew's genealogy of Jesus (1:13).

See GENEALOGY OF JESUS CHRIST.

5. Melea's son in Luke's genealogy of Jesus (3:30).

See GENEALOGY OF JESUS CHRIST.

Eliam. 1. Alternate name for Ammiel, Bathsheba's father, in 2 Samuel 11:3.

See AMMIEL # 3.

2. Alternate name for Ahijah the Pelonite in 2 Samuel 23:34.

See AHIJAH # 7.

Elias. KJV rendering of the prophet Elijah's name in the NT.

See ELIJAH # 1.

Eliasaph. 1. Leader of Gad's tribe appointed by Moses. He was the son of Deuel (Reuel) (Nm 1:14; 2:14; 7:42,47; 10:20).

2. Gershonite Levite and the son of Lael. His responsibility in the tribe was to take charge of the tabernacle coverings, the curtains of the court, and the main altar (Nm 3:24).

Eliashib. 1. Elioenai's son and a descendant of Zerubbabel in the royal lineage of David (1 Chr 3:24).

2. Aaron's descendant chosen by David to head the 11th of the 24 courses of priests taking turns in the sanctuary services (1 Chr 24:12).

3. High priest in the second succession from Jeshua (Neh 12:10). Eliashib assigned a chamber of the temple to Tobiah the Ammonite, a relative by marriage. When Nehemiah returned from exile, he had Tobiah removed from his temple lodge (Ezr 10:6; Neh 3:1,20; 13:4,7,28).

4. Levite and temple singer. He pledged to put away his foreign wife at Ezra's command (Ezr 10:24).

5, 6. Two men, a son of Zattu and a son of Bani, similarly persuaded by Ezra to put away their foreign wives (Ezr 10:27,36).

Eliathah. Son of Heman appointed to assist in the temple service during David's reign (1 Chr 25:4,27).

Elidad. Benjamite, of the sons of Chislon, appointed to work under Eleazar and Joshua in allotting Canaanite territory west of the Jordan to the 10 tribes (Nm 34:21).

Eliehoenai. 1. Korahite Levite who, with his 6 brothers and his father, Meshelemiah, served as a temple doorkeeper during David's reign (1 Chr 26:3, KJV Elioenai).

2. Zerahiah's son, who came to Jerusalem with Ezra, bringing his family and others from Babylon (Ezr 8:4, KJV Elihoenai).

Eliel. 1. Warrior and head of a family of the half tribe of Manasseh that lived east of the Jordan River (1 Chr 5:24).

2. Tola's son, a Kohathite who was one of the Levitical singers in the time of David (1 Chr 6:34); possibly the same as Elihu son of Tohu (1 Sm 1:1) and Eliab (1 Chr 6:27).

See ELIHU # 1.

3. Shimei's son and a chief of Benjamin's tribe (1 Chr 8:20).

4. Shaahak's son and a chief of Benjamin's tribe (1 Chr 8:22).

5. Warrior among David's mighty men (1 Chr 11:46), called a Mahavite.

6. Another warrior among David's mighty men (1 Chr 11:47).

7. Warrior from the Gadites who joined David at Ziklag in his struggle against King Saul. Eliel was one of those "experts with shield and spear." Whether the Eliel of 1 Chronicles 12:11 should be equated with either of the two Eliels of 1 Chronicles 11:46,47 is impossible to say.

8. Levite and chief of the family of Hebron, who was involved in bringing the ark to Jerusalem in David's time (1 Chr 15:9).

9. Priest who assisted in bringing the ark to Jerusalem (1 Chr 15:11); possibly the same as # 8 above.

10. Levite who assisted Conaniah in the administration of the tithes, contributions, and dedicated things given to the temple during Hezekiah's reign (2 Chr 31:13).

Elienai. Benjamite and the son of Shimei (1 Chr 8:20). His name may be a contraction of Elioenai (see 1 Chr 26:3 KJV).

Eliezer. 1. Native of Damascus and Abraham's servant, who according to custom was the adopted heir before Ishmael and Isaac were born (Gn 15:2).

2. Moses and Zipporah's second son (Ex 18:4; 1 Chr 23:15,17).

3. Benjamite and Becher's son (1 Chr 7:8).

4. One of the seven priests who blew a trumpet before the ark of the covenant when David moved it to Jerusalem (1 Chr 15:24).

5. Zichri's son and a chief officer in Reuben's tribe (1 Chr 27:16).

6. Son of Dodavahu of Mareshah, who prophesied against King Jehoshaphat of Judah because of his alliance with Ahaziah, king of Israel (2 Chr 20:37).

7. One of the leaders sent by Ezra to Iddo at Casiphia to request Levites for the house of God (Ezr 8:16).

8, 9, 10. Three men of Israel—a priest, Levite, and Israelite—who were encouraged by Ezra to divorce their foreign wives during the postexilic era (Ezr 10:18,23,31).

11. Ancestor of Christ (Lk 3:29).

See GENEALOGY OF JESUS CHRIST.

Elihoenai. KJV spelling of Eliehoenai, Zerahiah's son, in Ezra 8:4.

See ELIEHOENAI # 2.

Elihoreph. Prominent official in the time of Solomon (1 Kgs 4:3) who, with his brother Ahijah, was a royal secretary. Attempts to regard Elihoreph as the title of an official and not a personal name find no support in the Hebrew text.

Elihu. 1. Ephraimite, Tohu's son and an ancestor of Samuel the prophet (1 Sm 1:1); perhaps also called Eliab and Eliel in 1 Chronicles 6:27,34, respectively.

2. One of the soldiers of Manasseh's tribe who joined up with David's army at Ziklag (1 Chr 12:20).

3. Korahite Levite and a gatekeeper of the tabernacle during David's reign (1 Chr 26:7).

4. Alternate name for Eliab, David's eldest brother, in 1 Chronicles 27:18.

See ELIAB # 3.

5. One of Job's friends, a Buzite, the son of Barachel (Jb 32:2). He spoke about suffering as a form of discipline after three of Job's friends failed to answer Job's arguments (chs 32–37).

Elijah. 1. Ninth-century BC prophet of Israel. Elijah's name means "my God is the Lord"—appropriate for a stalwart opponent of Baal worship. The Scriptures give no information regarding his family background except that he was a Tishbite who probably came from the land of Gilead on the east bank of the Jordan River. He lived primarily during the reigns of kings Ahab (874–853 BC) and Ahaziah (853–852 BC) of Israel. The biblical account of Elijah runs from 1 Kings 17 to 2 Kings 2.

Elijah was called by God at a critical period in Israel's life. Economically and politically the northern kingdom was in its strongest position since its separation from the southern kingdom. Omri (885–874 BC) had initiated a policy of trade and friendly relations with the Phoenicians. To show his good faith, Omri gave his son Ahab in marriage to Jezebel, the daughter of Ethbaal, king of Tyre. She brought Baal worship with her to Israel, a false religion whose rapid spread soon threatened the kingdom's very existence. Elijah was sent to turn the nation and its leaders back to the Lord through his prophetic message and miracles.

Warning of drought. Elijah began his recorded ministry by telling Ahab that the nation would suffer a drought until the prophet himself announced its end (1 Kgs 17:1). He thus repeated Moses' warning (Lv 26:14–39; Dt 28:15–68) of the consequences of turning away from God.

Elijah then hid himself in a ravine on the east bank of the Jordan River by the brook Cherith (possibly the valley of the Yarmuk River in north Gilead). There he had sufficient water for his needs, and ravens brought him food twice daily. When the brook dried up, Elijah was directed to move to the Phoenician village of Zarephath near Sidon. A widow took care of him from her scanty supplies, and her obedience to Elijah was rewarded by a miraculous supply of meal and oil that was not depleted until the drought ended.

While Elijah was staying with the widow, her son became ill and died. By the power of prayer, the child was restored to life and good health.

In the drought's third year the Lord told Elijah to inform Ahab that God would soon provide rain for Israel. On his return, Elijah first encountered Ahab's officer, Obadiah, who was searching for water for the king's livestock. Elijah sent Obadiah to arrange a meeting with Ahab. At first Obadiah refused. For three years Ahab had searched Israel and the neighboring kingdoms in vain for the prophet, no doubt in order to force him to end the drought. Obadiah was certain that while he went to bring Ahab, Israel's most wanted "outlaw" would elude them again, thus enraging the king. When Elijah promised him that he would stay until he returned, the officer arranged for Ahab to meet the prophet.

In the subsequent meeting Elijah rejected the king's allegation that he was the "troubler of Israel" (1 Kgs 18:17). He was only obeying God, he insisted, in pointing out Ahab's idolatry. Ahab had even permitted Jezebel to subsidize a school of Baal and Asherah prophets. Elijah then requested a public gathering on Mt Carmel as a contest between the prophets

Elijah and Elisha:
A Comparison of the Lives and Ministries

	Elijah	Elisha
OT references	1 Kgs 17–19; 21; 2 Kgs 1–2; 2 Chr 21:12–15; Mal 4:5	1 Kgs 19; 2 Kgs 2–9; 13:21
NT references	Mt 11:14; 16:14; 17:3–4,10–12; 27:47–49; Mk 6:15; 8:28; 9:4–5, 10–13; 15:35–36; Lk 1:17; 4:25–26; 9:8,30–33; Jn 1:21,25; Rom 11:2–4; Jas 5:17–18	Lk 4:27
Meaning of the name	"My God is the Lord"	"God is salvation"
OT parallel	Moses	Joshua
NT parallel	John the Baptist	
Call		Through Elijah (1 Kgs 19:16,19–21)
Theme of Ministry	Yahweh vs. Baal	Yahweh's sovereignty
Nation to which his ministry was directed	Israel (the northern 10 tribes)	Israel (the northern 10 tribes)
Rulers during ministry	Ahab and Ahaziah	Ahab, Ahaziah, Jehoram, Jehu, Jehoahaz, and Jehoash
Object of the wrath of rulers	King Ahab and Queen Jezebel (1 Kgs 18:10; 19:1–2)	King Joram (2 Kgs 6:31)
Association with chariots of fire	a chariot of fire and horses of fire separated Elijah from Elisha at Elijah's translation to heaven in a whirlwind (2 Kgs 2:11)	his servant saw hills full of horses and chariots of fire all around Elisha (2 Kgs 6:17)
Tone of prophecies	generally negative	generally positive
Prophecies	3-year drought (1 Kgs 17:1) God's judgment on Ahab for murdering Naboth (1 Kgs 21:17–24) Ahaziah's death (2 Kgs 1:4,16)	victory of Judah, Israel, and Edom over Moab (2 Kgs 3) Syrian army's plans (2 Kgs 6:8–23) much food; a prince's dying without eating any (2 Kgs 7:1–2,17–20) a 7-year famine (2 Kgs 8:1–3) the death of Ben-Hadad, Syria's king, Israel's enemy (2 Kgs 8:7–15) Jehoash's defeat of the Syrians (2 Kgs 13:14–20)
Similar miracles	multiplication of flour and oil (1 Kgs 17:16) feeding of Elijah by ravens (1 Kgs 17:2–6) resuscitation of son of widow of Zarephath (1 Kgs 17:17–24) parting of the Jordan (2 Kgs 2:8) two companies of 50 soldiers each are consumed by fire from heaven (2 Kgs 1:10,12,13)	multiplication of oil (2 Kgs 4:1–7) feeding of 100 people (2 Kgs 4:42–44) resuscitation of the Shunammite's son (2 Kgs 4:8–37) parting of the Jordan (2 Kgs 2:14) 43 youths cursed by Elisha are consumed by 2 bears (2 Kgs 2:23–25)
Other miracles	fire on Mt Carmel (1 Kgs 18) wind, earthquake, and fire at Mt Horeb (1 Kgs 19)	healing of waters (2 Kgs 2:19–22) purifying of food (2 Kgs 4:38–41) healing of Naaman (2 Kgs 5) leprosy on Gehazi (2 Kgs 5) the floating ax head (2 Kgs 6:5–7) Syrian soldiers' loss and recovery of sight (2 Kgs 6:18–20)
Final miracle associated with him	translation to heaven in a whirlwind (2 Kgs 2:11)	resuscitation of a dead man when his bones touch Elisha's (2 Kgs 13:21)
Appointment of successor(s)	the appointing of Elisha to succeed him (1 Kgs 18:10; 19:1–2)	sends a young prophet to anoint Jehu to succeed Joram (2 Kgs 9:1–13)

of Baal and the prophets of the Lord to determine who was the true God.

Confrontation on Carmel. One of the highlights of Elijah's ministry was the contest on Mt Carmel. Ahab assembled all Israel along with 850 prophets of Baal and Asherah. The famous challenge was issued: "How long will you go limping with two different opinions? . . . If the Lord is God, follow him; but if Baal, then follow him" (1 Kgs 18:21). Sacrificial animals were to be placed on two altars, one for Baal and one for the Lord, and the prophets representing each were to ask for fire from their God.

All day long the pagan prophets called in vain on Baal. They danced a whirling, frenzied dance, cutting themselves with knives until their blood gushed. But there was no answer. Finally Elijah's turn came. He repaired the demolished altar of the Lord and prepared the sacrifice. For dramatic effect, he built a trench around the altar and poured water over the sacrifice until the trench overflowed. Then he said a brief prayer, and immediately fire fell from heaven and "consumed the burnt offering, and the wood, and the stones, and the dust, and licked up the water that was in the trench" (1 Kgs 18:38).

When the people saw it, they fell on their faces in repentance, chanting, "The Lord, he is God; the Lord, he is God" (1 Kgs 18:39). At Elijah's command the people seized the prophets of Baal and killed them by the brook Kishon. Then Elijah, at the top of Carmel, began to pray fervently for rain. Dramatically, the sky became black with clouds and rain began to pour, ending the long drought. Ahab rode back in his chariot to Jezreel, 20 miles to the east. God's Spirit enabled Elijah to outrun Ahab, and he arrived in Jezreel first.

Jezebel, furious over the massacre of the Baal prophets, sent a message to Elijah: "So may the gods do to me, and more also, if I do not make your life as the life of one of them by this time tomorrow" (1 Kgs 19:2). When Elijah received her message, he panicked and fled to Beersheba. His greatest defeat followed his greatest triumph.

Experience at Horeb. Elijah left his servant in Beersheba, going another day's journey into the desert alone. There he lay down under a broom tree and, in despair and exhaustion, asked God to take his life. Instead an angel appeared, nourishing him twice with bread and water. After he had slept, Elijah continued on his way.

After 40 days Elijah arrived at Mt Horeb, where he found shelter in a cave. There the Lord spoke to him, asking what he was doing there. The prophet explained that he was the only prophet of God left in Israel, and now even his life was threatened. In response, the mighty forces of nature—a great wind, an earthquake, and fire—were displayed before Elijah to show him that the omnipotent God could intercede on his behalf with a powerful hand. Finally God encouraged Elijah in a "still small voice." The Lord had further tasks for him to accomplish. God also told Elijah that he was not the only faithful person in Israel, but 7,000 others remained true to the Lord.

Since Elijah had faithfully delivered God's message to Ahab, the Lord commissioned him to deliver another message, one of judgment on Israel's continuing failure to listen to God. The instruments of retribution were to be Hazael, who would become king in Syria (c. 893–796 BC), and Jehu, who would become king of Israel (841–814 BC). Elijah was instructed to anoint both of them. He was also told to anoint his successor, Elisha, to be his understudy until it was time for Elisha's full ministry to begin.

Naboth. After his return to Israel one of Elijah's boldest confrontations with King Ahab was over Naboth's vineyard. Although Ahab wanted Naboth's property, he was sensitive to the law regarding ownership of land. Further, Ahab never completely abandoned the faith of his fathers (1 Kgs 21:27–29). Jezebel, however, had no regard for the Mosaic law and conspired to have Naboth put to death on a false charge.

When Ahab then took possession of the vineyard, Elijah branded him as a murderer and a robber. He predicted divine judgment—the fall of Ahab's dynasty and Jezebel's horrible death (1 Kgs 21:17–24). Ahab repented, however, and the judgment was postponed.

Ahaziah's folly. The Lord's judgment on Ahab was finally executed when the king was killed in a battle with Syria in 853 BC. The dogs licked up Ahab's blood, as the prophet had predicted (1 Kgs 21:19). Shortly after Ahaziah had succeeded his father as king, he suffered a crippling fall. While lying ill, he sent messengers to ask Baal-zebub, the god of Ekron, whether he would recover. The Lord sent Elijah to intercept them and give them a message for the king: a rebuke for ignoring the God of Israel and a warning of the king's impending death.

Ahaziah angrily sent a captain with 50 soldiers to arrest Elijah. They were consumed by fire from heaven at Elijah's words. A second captain and another 50 soldiers were sent but met the same fate. The third captain who came begged the prophet to spare his and his soldiers' lives. Elijah went with this captain and delivered God's message to the king personally. The king would not recover but would die, because he had inquired from pagan gods rather than from the true God.

Warning to Jehoram. Elijah had been called primarily to minister to Israel, but he also delivered God's word of warning to Jehoram, king of Judah, rebuking him for following Israel in its idolatry and for not walking in the godly ways of his father and grandfather (2 Chr 21:12–15).

Elijah's Translation. When the end of Elijah's ministry drew near, Elisha refused to leave him. After a journey which took them to schools of the prophets at Bethel and Jericho, the two crossed the Jordan River miraculously; Elijah struck the waters with his mantle and they parted. Elisha requested a double portion (the firstborn's share, cf. Dt 21:17) of his master's spirit, for he desired to be Elijah's full successor. Elisha knew his request was granted because he saw Elijah pass into the heavens in a whirlwind bearing a chariot and horses of fire. The young prophets who had accompanied Elisha searched in vain for Elijah in the mountains and valleys around the Jordan, but God had taken his faithful prophet home. Elijah thus joined Enoch as the only other man in the Bible who did not experience death.

Elijah's Message and Miracles. As the Baal worship of Tyre made inroads into Israel through Jezebel, Elijah was sent to check its spread by emphasizing again that Israel's God was the only God of the whole earth. He began a vital work that was continued by Jehu, who slaughtered many of the Baal worshipers among Israel's leaders (2 Kgs 10:18–28). Elijah's specific mission was to destroy heathen worship in order to spare Israel, thus preparing the way for the prophets who were to follow in his spirit.

Miracles were prominent in Elijah's ministry, given as a sign to confirm him as God's spokesman and to turn Israel's kings back to God. Some scholars have rejected these miracles or tried to explain them away. The OT, however, clearly testifies to their validity, and the NT affirms them.

Elijah and the New Testament. Malachi named Elijah as the forerunner of the "great and terrible day of the Lord" who will "turn the hearts of fathers to their children and the hearts of children to their fathers" (Mal 4:5,6). Jewish writers have often taken up the same theme in their literature: Elijah will "restore the tribes of Jacob" (Ecclus 48:10); he is mentioned in the Qumran Manual of Discipline of the Dead Sea Scrolls; he is the central sign of the resurrection of the dead according to the Mishna, the collection of Jewish oral law; and he is the subject of songs sung at the close of the sabbath.

In the NT, Malachi's prophecy was interpreted in the angelic annunciation to Zechariah as pointing to John the Baptist, who was to do the work of another Elijah (Lk 1:17; KJV Elias) and was confirmed by Jesus himself (Mt 11:14; 17:10–13).

Jesus also alluded to Elijah's sojourn in the land of Sidon (Lk 4:25,26), and the apostle Paul referred to the prophet's experience at Mt Horeb (Rom 11:2). The apostle James used Elijah to illustrate what it means to be a righteous man and a man of prayer (Jas 5:17).

Elijah appeared again on the mount of transfiguration with Moses as they discussed Jesus' approaching death (Mt 17:1–13; Lk 9:28–36). Some Bible scholars believe that Elijah will return as one of the two witnesses of the end times (Rv 11:3–12), in fulfillment of Malachi's prophecy that he is to come before the dreadful judgment day of God.

See ISRAEL, HISTORY OF; PROPHECY; PROPHET, PROPHETESS.

2. Chief of Benjamin's tribe (1 Chr 8:27, KJV Eliah).

3. Priest who married a gentile wife (Ezr 10:21).

4. Layman who also married a foreign wife (Ezr 10:26, KJV Eliah).

RICHARD L. SCHULTZ

Bibliography. W. Milligan, *Elijah: His Life and Times;* H.H. Rowley, *Men of God;* R. Wallace, *Elijah and Elisha.*

Elika. Harodite, listed as one of David's mighty men (2 Sm 23:25). His name is not included in a similar list in 1 Chronicles 11:27.

Elim. Early encampment of the Israelites after their passage through the Red Sea (Ex 15:27; 16:1). Elim was situated between Marah and the desert of Sin. It had 12 springs of water and 70 palm trees (Nm 33:9,10).

Most scholars identify Elim with the Wadi Gharandel, 63 miles from Suez. At this wadi the vegetation consists of palm trees, tamarisks, and acacias. But if Mt Sinai is to be located somewhere in Arabia, Elim would be much closer to the Gulf of Aqaba.

See WILDERNESS WANDERINGS.

Elimelech. Man from Bethlehem who took his wife, Naomi, and his sons, Mahlon and Chilion, to sojourn in Moab because of famine in Judah (Ru 1:2,3). While in Moab, he died; then his sons also died; and Naomi decided to return to Judah. One daughter-in-law, Orpah, preferred to remain in Moab; the other, Ruth, chose to accompany Naomi. Boaz, a kinsman of Elimelech, bought Elimelech's land and married Ruth (4:9,10). From this union came a great-grandson, David, and the royal line in which the Messiah would eventually be born.

See RUTH, BOOK OF.

Elioenai. 1. Postexilic descendant of Solomon and the father of Hodaviah (1 Chr 3:23,24).

2. Simeonite chieftan (1 Chr 4:36).

3. Head of a Benjamite family (1 Chr 7:8).

4. KJV spelling of the Levite Eliehoenai in 1 Chronicles 26:3.

See ELIEHOENAI # 1.

5. Man of the priestly family of Pashhur who divorced his foreign wife in Ezra's day (Ezr 10:22).

6. Zattu's son, who was encouraged by Ezra to divorce his foreign wife during the postexilic era (Ezr 10:27).

7. Postexilic priest who assisted in the dedication of the rebuilt Jerusalem wall (Neh 12:41).

Eliphal. Ur's son and one of David's mighty men (1 Chr 11:35); alternately called Eliphelet, son of Ahasbai, in 2 Samuel 23:34.

See ELIPHELET # 2.

Eliphalet. KJV spelling of Eliphelet, David's son, in 2 Samuel 5:16 and 1 Chronicles 14:7.

See ELIPHELET # 1.

Eliphaz. 1. Oldest son of Esau and his wife Adah (Gn 36:4–16; 1 Chr 1:35,36). He was the ancestor of a number of Edomite clans.

2. One of Job's friends, called the Temanite (see Jer. 49:7). Teman was traditionally associated with wisdom; hence Eliphaz's speech depicts the orthodox view of sin and punishment. His three addresses (Jb 4,15,22) failed to grapple with the essence of Job's problem because he assumed previous major sin in Job's life.

See JOB, BOOK OF.

Eliphelehu, Elipheleh. Levitical musician who played the lyre when the ark was brought to Jerusalem in David's time (1 Chr 15:18,21; KJV Elipheleh).

Eliphelet. 1. One of David's nine sons born in Jerusalem (2 Sm 5:16; 1 Chr 3:8; 14:7; KJV Eliphelet).

2. Ahasbai's son and one of David's mighty men (2 Sm 23:34); perhaps the same as Eliphal, Ur's son, in 1 Chronicles 11:35.

See ELIPHAL.

3. Another of David's sons born at Jerusalem but perhaps earlier than # 1 above (1 Chr 3:6; 14:5, KJV Elpalet, RSV Elpelet).

4. Eshek's son and a descendant of Saul and Jonathan (1 Chr 8:39).

5. One of Adonikam's three sons who returned with Ezra from Babylon (Ezr 8:13).

6. Hushum's son whom Ezra persuaded to divorce his foreign wife during the postexilic era (Ezr 10:33).

Elisabeth. KJV spelling of Elizabeth, John the Baptist's mother.

See ELIZABETH.

Elisha, Eliseus. Prophet in Israel during the 9th century BC.

Background and Call. Elisha is first mentioned in 1 Kings 19:16, where he is described as the son of Shaphat, who lived at Abelmeholah. That place has been tentatively identified with the modern Tel Abu Sifri, west of the river Jordan, though many scholars place it to the river's east. The prophet Elijah had been ordered by God to anoint Elisha as his successor, but the narrative does not make it clear whether Elisha was already one of Elijah's disciples. When the two met, Elisha was busy plowing a field, and he does not seem to have greeted Elijah with the respect that a disciple would normally show to his teacher.

Elisha's use of 12 yokes of oxen in his agricultural work has been taken as a sign that he was wealthy, for normally two yoked oxen would be handled by one person. When Elijah passed by and placed his cloak on Elisha's shoulders, the latter man knew it was a sign that he should inherit the great prophet's mission. The nation needed a prophet, for it was increasingly indulging in Canaanite idolatry with the encouragement of King Ahab and his Phoenician wife Jezebel.

After Elijah commissioned him symbolically and strode away, Elisha hurried after the prophet to request a brief interval of time to announce his new vocation to his parents before leaving home. The prophet's reply, "Go back again; for what have I done to you?" (1 Kgs 19:20), helped Elisha to make up his mind immediately. Delay in implementing his vocation would almost certainly have been fatal for Elisha (cf. 2 Kgs 8:21,22; Lk 9:61,62).

To mark the change in his way of life, Elisha made a great feast for his neighbors, roasting two oxen, another hint that he came from a wealthy family. From that time he was no longer a farmer; by associating with Elijah he began to prepare for his own ministry. There is no record of Elisha being anointed to the prophetic office, but the transfer of prophetic authority by means of the cloak would leave no doubt in anyone's mind that Elisha was the next official prophet in Israel.

"Sons of the Prophets." That there could have been some question of Elisha's authority is implied by the existence of groups of people known as "sons of the prophets." The phrase meant that those persons were heirs of the prophetic teachings and traditions, though apparently none of them was a major prophet. The prophet Amos even denied any connection with such groups, which seem to have died out in the 8th century BC (Am 7:14). In the time of Elisha the "sons of the prophets" were located in Gilgal, Bethel, and Jericho, and seem to have exercised a primarily local ministry. They may have gone out under the instructions of Elijah and Elisha to teach people God's Law and to pronounce divine revelations, as in the days of Saul (cf. 1 Sm 10:5,10).

Just before Elijah was taken to heaven he and Elisha visited such prophetic groups, and Elijah tried in vain to persuade Elisha to stay behind at Gilgal and at Bethel (2 Kgs 2:1–4). The prophetic group at Bethel may have been warned by God that Elijah would be taken from them, for they questioned Elisha about the matter and ascertained that he also was aware of the situation.

Successor to Elijah. After miraculously parting the waters of Jordan, Elijah asked his successor what he might do for him (2 Kgs

2:8). Elisha requested a "double share" of his spirit as they parted, the share of an inheritance normally given to a firstborn son (Dt 21:17). His request was granted when Elisha saw his master taken up to heaven in a fiery chariot, and it took immediate effect when Elisha parted the Jordan's waters and crossed over (2 Kgs 2:14).

His prophetic authority now recognized, Elisha began his ministry to Israel at approximately the end of King Ahab's reign (c. 853 BC). His work lasted for half a century, and, in contrast with the harried, austere, and sometimes dramatic ministry of Elijah, the activities of Elisha were mostly quieter and took place among the ordinary people of Israel. But he also addressed the royal court, though not in conflicts with Canaanite priests such as Elijah had experienced.

Miracles. The miraculous element was prominent in Elisha's ministry. When the people of Jericho reported that the local spring water was brackish, Elisha purified it with salt (2 Kgs 2:19–22), and to this day it is the only significant fresh-water spring in the area (Tell es-Sultan).

As the prophet left for Bethel, he encountered a group of youths who mocked his baldness (2 Kgs 2:23,24). He cursed them in the name of the Lord, and two bears came from the woods and mauled the offenders. What at first sight seems to be an immoral act on God's part was actually full of foreboding for the nation. The youths at Bethel were a generation of Israelites who had so absorbed the immoral, pagan culture of their city that they rejected both the person and the message of God's prophets. They were not merely irreligious but also unbelievably discourteous, according to ancient Near Eastern standards, in ridiculing a bald man instead of respecting his seniority.

The curses Elisha pronounced "in the name of the Lord" were not his own reactions to the treatment he had received, but instead were covenant curses (Dt 28:15–68) that would come upon all who rejected the Sinaitic laws and went back on their promises to God (see Ex 24:3–8). The two bears were also symbolic of Assyria and Babylonia, which would tear apart the nation at different times. One small incident was thus a somber forecast of what the future held for a wicked and disobedient people.

In one of his contacts with royalty Elisha gave a message (although unwillingly) from God to King Jehoram of Israel (852–841 BC). The king had allied with King Jehoshaphat of Judah (872–848 BC) and the Edomite ruler against Mesha, king of Moab. The allied forces were deep in Edomite territory when they ran out of water, and in despair they turned to Elisha, the local prophet. He refused to say anything at first, but finally predicted ample supplies of water and victory for the coalition. Both occurred on the following day (2 Kgs 3:1–27).

Miracles of Charity. The kind of work for which Elisha was justly renowned was usually performed for people who could not help themselves. Such a person was a poor widow who had almost pledged her two children to a creditor. Her only asset was a jar of oil. Elisha instructed her to borrow empty jars from her neighbors and fill them with the oil from her own jar. In a miraculous manner every jar was filled. Elisha then told her to sell the oil, pay her debts, and use the balance of the money for living expenses (2 Kgs 4:1–7).

A similar act of charity was performed for a Shunammite woman, who had persuaded her husband to provide a room where the prophet could stay when in the area. In return for her kindness Elisha predicted that the woman, previously childless, would have her own son. About a year later it happened (2 Kgs 4:8–17). The boy later contracted a severe ailment, perhaps meningitis, and died suddenly. His mother laid the body on Elisha's bed while she hurried to Mt Carmel to seek the prophet. Elisha was apparently unaware of the situation until the distraught mother informed him of the boy's death. As an emergency measure Elisha dispatched his servant Gehazi to put the prophet's staff on the child's face. That did not revive the child, but when Elisha arrived

An oil storage jar (in the museum in Jaffa). The result of the miraculous multiplication of oil in the jars was that "the vessels were full" (2 Kgs 17:6).

and lay down on the body, the boy was healed and returned to his parents (2 Kgs 4:18–37).

Another beneficial incident was the correction of a potentially disastrous situation. When some poisonous gourds were accidentally cooked and served, Elisha rendered the mixture harmless by adding meal to the contents of the cooking pot (2 Kgs 4:38–41). A miracle similar to Christ's multiplying the bread loaves (see Mt 14:16–21; 15:32–38) occurred when someone brought the prophet several loaves of bread and fresh ears of corn. Elisha instructed his servant to set the food out for 100 people, presumably the inhabitants of the area, and when that was done the people ate and had food left (2 Kgs 4:42–44).

The healing of Naaman, a Syrian commander, came through the influence of a Hebrew maid in the man's household, who persuaded Naaman's wife that Elisha could heal her husband. The Assyrian king sent his general to the Israelite ruler with instructions for Naaman to be healed. The afflicted man was sent to Elisha, who ordered him to wash in the Jordan River. Reluctant at first, Naaman finally obeyed and was cured of his affliction. In gratitude the Syrian leader acknowledged the power of Israel's God (2 Kgs 5:1–19).

Elisha's periodic association with the "sons of the prophets" proved helpful to them on one occasion when they were expanding their buildings. Needing additional wood, they went to the Jordan River to cut down trees, and in the process one of the workers lost a borrowed ax head in the water. Elisha remedied the situation by throwing in a stick, whereupon the ax head came up to the surface and was retrieved (2 Kgs 6:1–7).

Encounters with Royalty. When Syria attacked Israel, Elisha revealed the movements of the Syrians to the Israelite king. Syrians tried to capture the prophet at Dothan, but God blinded them and Elisha led them to the Israelite capital of Samaria. Their sight returned, and Elisha advised the Israelite king to spare the captives, feed them well, and send them home. Because their evil was rewarded with good, the Syrians did not attack Israel for a while (2 Kgs 6:8–23).

When the Syrian king Ben-hadad besieged Samaria years later, famine conditions there became so severe that the king threatened to execute Elisha. In response, the prophet promised an abundance of food the following day. The Syrians fled from their camp for some unspecified reason, and the prophecy was fulfilled (2 Kgs 6:24–7:20). In an unusual encounter with the ailing king of Syria, Elisha was visited by Hazael, servant of Ben-hadad, who had been sent to ask about the prospects for his master's improvement. Elisha sent back a reassuring re-

ply, but at the same time said that Hazael would shortly succeed Ben-hadad (2 Kgs 8:7–13). On another occasion Elisha sent a prophet to Ramoth-gilead to anoint Jehu, son of Jehoshaphat, as king of Israel to replace Joram, whom Jehu proceeded to kill in battle (2 Kgs 9:1–28).

Elisha's final contact with Israelite rulers came at the time of his own death, when Joash the king visited him to lament the prophet's illness. On that occasion, by the symbolic handling of arrows, the dying prophet promised Joash that he would defeat the Syrians in battle but would not exterminate them (2 Kgs 13:14–19).

The prophet also intervened a second time on behalf of the Shunammite woman whose son he had healed, instructing her to move her household into Philistine territory during a seven-year famine in Israel. When she came back, her house and property had apparently been occupied by others, so she appealed to the king for help in recovering it. Elisha's servant Gehazi told the ruler about her, and on interviewing her himself the king ordered all her property to be returned (2 Kgs 8:1–6).

Continuing Influence. Elisha's final miracle occurred after his death, when a corpse that was tossed hurriedly into the prophet's tomb came abruptly to life (2 Kgs 13:21; Ecclus 48:14). Jesus mentioned Elisha once in connection with the healing of Naaman, declaring that God's mercy was not restricted to the Israelites (Lk 4:27, KJV Eliseus).

R. K. HARRISON

See ELIJAH; ISRAEL, HISTORY OF; PROPHECY; PROPHET, PROPHETESS.

Elishah. Javan's son (Gn 10:4; 1 Chr 1:7). The Hebrew term for Greece is Javan, hence Elishah could designate the western Aegean islands or coastlands (cf. Gn 10:5) that supplied dye stuffs to the inhabitants of Tyre (Ez 27:7). The Jewish historian Josephus identified Elishah with the Aeolians; other suggestions are Carthage in North Africa, Hellas, Italy, and Elis. A Mediterranean site seems probable from the context of Ezekiel 27:6,7, perhaps an area of Cyprus which exported copper. This location may be the Alashia of cuneiform and hieroglyphic texts.

Elishama. 1. Ammihud's son and leader of the Ephraimites at the beginning of the journey in the wilderness (Nm 1:10; 2:18; 7:48,53). His was the seventh tribe in line during the wilderness march (Nm 10:22). Elishama was the father of Nun and grandfather of Joshua (1 Chr 7:26).

2. One of David's nine sons born in Jerusalem to a legitimate wife (2 Sm 5:16; 1 Chr 3:8; 14:7).

3. Ishmael's ancestor. Ishmael killed Gedaliah, the governor of Israel appointed by Nebuchadnezzar (2 Kgs 25:25; Jer 41:1).

4. Man of Judah, descended through Jerahmeel and Sheshan (1 Chr 2:41).

5. Another of David's sons (1 Chr 3:6); alternately called Elishua in 2 Samuel 5:15 and 1 Chronicles 14:5.

See ELISHUA.

6. Priest sent by Jehoshaphat to instruct the Judeans in the Law of God (2 Chr 17:8).

7. Prince and scribe in Jeremiah's time (Jer 36:12). He heard Baruch read the words of God, and later the scroll of the Lord remained in Elishama's chamber until the king requested it to be read (Jer 36:20,21).

Elishaphat. Military commander in Judah who supported Jehoida the priest in overthrowing Queen Athaliah and making the young Joash king (2 Chr 23:1).

Elisheba. Wife of Aaron (Ex 6:23), who bore him Nadab, Abihu, Eleazar, and Ithamar. Her father was Amminadab and her brother was Nahshon, the leader of Judah (Nm 1:7; 2:3), the tribe to which Elisheba also belonged.

After Aaron died (Nm 20:28), Moses invested Eleazar, Elisheba's third son, with the office of chief priest.

Elishua. One of the 13 children fathered by David during his reign in Jerusalem (2 Sm 5:15; 1 Chr 14:5). In the parallel passage of 1 Chronicles 3:6 the name Elishama appears in Elishua's place.

Eliud. Achim's son, Eleazar's father, and an ancestor of Jesus Christ according to Matthew's genealogy (1:14,15).

See GENEALOGY OF JESUS CHRIST.

Elizabeth. Woman of priestly descent (Lk 1:5) and a relative of Mary, mother of Jesus (Lk 1:36). The name Elizabeth (KJV Elisabeth), which derives from the same Hebrew word as Elisheba, wife of Aaron (Ex 6:23), means "my God is an oath." Only Luke's Gospel, which characteristically focuses greater attention upon the role of women, mentions Elizabeth and her husband, Zechariah.

Luke emphasized Elizabeth and Zechariah's godly character and blameless conduct (Lk 1:6) before stating that the elderly couple had not been favored with children. Although in Jewish culture childlessness was regarded as a reproach (Gn 30:22,23; Lk 1:25), the devout pair continued to steadfastly worship and serve God. Unexpectedly, an angel of the Lord appeared to Zechariah with the announce-

ment that Elizabeth would conceive and bear a son, who would be the forerunner of the promised Messiah (Lk 1:13–17). When Elizabeth conceived, she withdrew from public life for five months, during which time her kinswoman Mary visited her.

See JOHN THE BAPTIST.

Elizaphan. 1. Kohathite Levite and Uzziel's son (Nm 3:29,30), who assisted in removing the bodies of Nadab and Abihu from the camp (Lv 10:4). Elizaphan's descendants were responsible for caring for the ark, the table, the lampstand, and vessels of the sanctuary (cf. 1 Chr 15:8; 2 Chr 29:13). His name is alternately spelled Elzaphan (Ex 6:22; Lv 10:4).

2. Parnach's son and a leader from Zebulun's tribe, who helped Eleazar and Joshua divide the Canaanite territory west of the Jordan among the 10 tribes (Nm 34:25).

Elizur. Shedeur's son and leader of Reuben's tribe at the start of Israel's wilderness journey (Nm 1:5; 2:10; 7:30,35; 10:18).

Elkanah. 1. Levite of Korah's family (Ex 6:24) and the head of Izhar's house (v 25). He was Assir's son, and fathered Ebiasaph (1 Chr 6:23).

2. Father of the prophet Samuel (1 Sm 1:19). He was the son of Jeroham of Ephraim, from Ramathaim-zophim (v 1). Elkanah had two wives, Hannah and Peninnah, the former being barren (v 2). Hannah begged God repeatedly for a son whom she would give to the Lord's service. Samuel was subsequently born, and after weaning was brought to the aged priest Eli for training. Elkanah had other sons and daughters by Hannah (2:21), and became the forefather of Heman, a singer in David's time.

3, 4. Name of two Kohathite Levites descended from Korah's line and ancestors of Heman the singer (1 Chr 6:26,27,34,35).

5. Levite who dwelt in the village of the Netophathites and later lived in Jerusalem in the postexilic era (1 Chr 9:16).

6. Benjamite warrior who joined David's mighty men at Ziklag (1 Chr 12:6).

7. Gatekeeper for the ark of the covenant during David's reign (1 Chr 15:23). He is perhaps the same as # 6 above.

8. One who held an authoritative post in King Ahaz's court. Elkanah was slain by Zichri, an Ephramite, for having forsaken the Lord (2 Chr 28:7).

Elkosh. Home or birthplace of the prophet Nahum (Na 1:1). Different places have been suggested:

(1) Al-Qush, about 50 miles north of modern Mosul. This was a medieval tradition, but evidence from the Book of Nahum does not support it.

(2) Hilkeesei, a village in Galilee, perhaps corresponding to modern el-Kauzeh.

(3) Capernaum near the Sea of Galilee, where Jesus frequently taught.

(4) Beit Jebrin in southern Judea.

Ellasar. Place in Babylonia; a few scholars have suggested that Arioch was its king. He joined a coalition which included Chedorlaomer, king of Elam, and together they raided the Jordan Valley during the time of Abraham (Gn 14:1,9). Some Near Eastern scholars identified Arioch with a king of Larsa known as Eri-Aku, a name subsequently read as Warad-Sin. This was conjectural at best, and has now been abandoned. To the present it has not been possible to identify either Ellasar or Arioch with any confidence.

Elm. KJV mistranslation for terebinth, a large Palestinian tree, in Hosea 4:13.

See PLANTS (TEREBINTH).

Elmadam, Elmodam. Ancestor of Jesus Christ according to Luke's genealogy (3:28, KJV Elmodam).

See GENEALOGY OF JESUS CHRIST.

Elnaam. Father of two mighty warriors in David's army, Jeribai and Joshaviah (1 Chr 11:46).

Elnathan. 1. Grandfather of King Jehoiachin. His daughter, Jehoiachin's mother, was Nehushta (2 Kgs 24:8).

2, 3, 4. Three Jewish leaders whom Ezra sent to Iddo at Casiphia to obtain Levites and temple servants for the caravan of Jews returning to Palestine from Babylonia (Ezr 8:16).

5. Achbor's son, who was ordered by King Jehoiakim to bring back Uriah from Egypt to be executed for prophesying against the king (Jer 26:22,23). Elnathan was present with other princes when Baruch read the Lord's words of warning written at Jeremiah's dictation on a scroll (36:12); he tried unsuccessfully to prevent Jehoiakim from burning the scroll (v 25).

Eloah. Hebrew name for God which stresses that he alone is deserving of worship.

See GOD, NAMES OF.

Elohim. General name for God in the OT. The etymology of Elohim is uncertain, but it is generally agreed that it is based on a root that means "might" or "power." The word is plu-

ral in form, but when applied to the true God it is used in a singular sense and most frequently with verbal elements. The most common explanation for the plural form of Elohim as applied to God is that it is "plural of majesty," that is, all the majesty of deity is encompassed by him.

Elohim also occurs as a designation of deity in other languages, such as Assyrian and Ugaritic; it is used of other nations' gods, thus demonstrating its more general sense. It seems to be used in a general sense in the OT, particularly the Pentateuch (the five books of Moses), denoting God's transcendence and capacity as Creator of the universe. It is thus somewhat different from the designation Yahweh, which usually connotes God in his personal relationships to people.

Elohim is used as a designation of Israel's rulers and judges (Ps 82:1,6), perhaps denoting their function as God's earthly representatives (Ex 21:6). That meaning of the word was used by Christ (Jn 10:34–36) in a defense against his detractors.

The word is also used of angelic beings (Ps 8:5 KJV; cf. Heb 2:7), and in the expression "sons of God" (Jb 1:6).

See GOD, NAMES OF.

Elon (Person). 1. Hittite who was the father of Basemath (perhaps also called Adah, Gn 36:2), one of Esau's wives (Gn 26:34).

2. Second of Zebulun's three sons (Gn 46:14) and the founder of the Elonite family (Nm 26:26).

3. Judge from Zebulun who judged Israel 10 years. He was buried in Aijalon (Jgs 12:11,12).

Elon (Place). Village near Timnah, the home of Samson's first wife. Elon was included in the inheritance allotted to Dan's tribe in Joshua's distribution of the Promised Land (Jos 19:43; cf. 14:1,2). It is generally identified with Khirbet Wadi 'Alinm near 'Ain Shems.

Elonbeth-hanan. Administrative district in Dan during the reign of Solomon (1 Kgs 4:9). It is perhaps identifiable with the Danite town of Elon.

Elonite. Descendant of Elon, Zebulun's son (Nm 26:26).

See ELON (PERSON) # 2.

Eloth. Alternate spelling of the Edomite town Elath, in 1 Kings 9:26; 2 Chronicles 8:17; and 26:2.

See ELATH.

Elpaal. Benjamite and one of Shaharaim's sons (1 Chr 8:11,12,18).

Elpalet. KJV spelling of Elpelet, an alternate name for David's son, Eliphelet in 1 Chronicles 14:5.

See ELIPHELET # 3.

El-paran. Place located on the edge of the wilderness of Paran, probably at the southern tip of the mountains of Seir in the Sinai peninsula, present-day Arabia. It was the farthest point south to which King Chedorlaomer and his allies pushed their punitive raid against the rebellious kings of Sodom and Gomorrah (Gn 14:5,6). Presumably El-paran was later called Elath, which was near or at Eziongeber on the northern tip of the Gulf of Agaba.

See ELATH.

Elpelet. Alternate name for David's son Eliphelet in 1 Chronicles 14:5.

See ELIPHELET # 3.

El Shaddai. Hebrew for "God Almighty" (Ps 68:14).

See GOD, NAMES OF.

Elteke, Eltekeh. City allotted to Dan's tribe for an inheritance (Jos 19:44, where it is spelled Eltekeh); it was later assigned to the Kohathite Levites (Jos 21:23). An important battle was fought near Elteke between King Sennacherib of Assyria and the Egyptians. The Egyptians were subsequently routed, and the city was captured by the Assyrians. From here Sennacherib went on to invade Judah (2 Kgs 18:13). Eltekeh was located north of Ekron and west of Timnah, but its exact site is uncertain.

Eltekon. Town located in the hill country of Judah. It was assigned by Joshua to Judah's tribe (Jos 15:59), and may be the modern Khirbet ed-Deir, west of Bethlehem.

Eltolad. Town assigned to Simeon's tribe in the southern portion of Judah's inheritance (Jos 15:30; 19:4). It is alternately called Tolad in 1 Chronicles 4:29. Its site is unknown.

Elul. Hebrew month corresponding to mid-August to mid-September (Neh 6:15).

See CALENDARS, ANCIENT AND MODERN.

Eluzai. One of the men of Benjamin who came to join David in Ziklag (1 Chr 12:5). Eluzai was an ambidextrous slinger and bowman.

Elymas. Another name for Bar-Jesus, a Jewish magician and false prophet, in Acts 13:8.

See BAR-JESUS.

Elyon. Hebrew name for God meaning "Most High."

See GOD, NAMES OF.

Elzabad. 1. Military leader from Gad's tribe who joined David at Ziklag (1 Chr 12:12).

2. Korahite Levite from Obed-edom's family, and a gatekeeper of the sanctuary (1 Chr 26:7).

Elzaphan. Alternate spelling of Elizaphan, a Levite chief, in Exodus 6:22 and Leviticus 10:4.

See ELIZAPHAN # 1.

Embalm. *See* BURIAL, BURIAL CUSTOMS.

Embroidery, Embroiderer. *See* FASHION AND DRESS; TRADES AND OCCUPATIONS.

Emekkeziz. City allotted to Benjamin's tribe for an inheritance; it was mentioned between Beth-hoglah and Beth-arabah (Jos 18:21, KJV valley of Keziz). Its location is uncertain.

Emerald. Rich green variety of beryl, regarded as a precious stone.

See MINERALS, METALS, AND PRECIOUS STONES.

Emerod. 1. KJV rendering of ulcer in Deuteronomy 28:67.

See SORE.

2. KJV rendering of tumor in 1 Samuel 5:6–12 and 6:4–17.

See TUMOR.

Emim. Name given to the original inhabitants of Moab (Gn 14:5) by the Moabites who ousted them from their land. They were a tall people, known also as Rephaim (Dt 2:10,11), and were compared with the Zuzim, Avim, and Horim for size. This phenomenon is evidently an indication of genetic isolation.

See GIANTS.

Emmanuel. Alternate spelling of Immanuel in Matthew 1:23.

See IMMANUEL.

Emmaus. Town in Judea which appears only once in Scripture (Lk 24:13). It was the destination of two disciples to whom Jesus appeared after the crucifixion. Following the resurrection, Cleopas and a friend were going to Emmaus when they encountered another traveler. They walked the road and talked together, but the disciples did not recognize that the stranger was Jesus. Jesus asked them the nature of their conversation, and was told of the crucifixion, the empty tomb, and their dis-

A garden of old olive trees in Emmaus.

couragement that things had not worked out as they hoped. Jesus then rebuked them (v 25), and "beginning with Moses and all the prophets, he interpreted to them in all the scriptures the things concerning himself" (v 27). When they reached their destination, Jesus accepted an invitation to spend the night. As they ate the evening meal, he blessed the bread, broke it, and gave it to them to eat. At that moment they recognized him. After Jesus vanished from their sight, they returned to Jerusalem to report the event to the apostles.

Though Emmaus, which means "warm wells," was near Jerusalem, its exact location has never been determined. Several locations have been suggested:

(1) Colonia (Qaloniyeh), about four miles west of Jerusalem on the main road to Joppa.

(2) El-Qubeibeh, about seven miles northwest of Jerusalem on a Roman road passing by Nebi Samwil. Its identification with Emmaus dates back to AD 1099, when the Crusaders found a Roman fort there named Castellum Emmaus.

(3) Abu Ghosh, about nine miles west of Jerusalem. Identified with the OT Kiriath-jearim, it is also known as Kiryat el-'Enab, where a Crusader church was built over a Roman fort. This site appears to be too far from Jerusalem to be the biblical Emmaus.

(4) Amwas, also known as Nicapolis, about 20 miles west of Jerusalem on the Jaffa road.

This is the Emmaus of 1 Maccabees 3:40,57. This site has the earliest claim to being Emmaus and also has two "warm wells." Eusebius and Jerome accepted it as the site. The primary objection to its being the NT Emmaus is its distance from Jerusalem, which exceeds the distance given by Luke.

(5) El Khamsa, southwest of Jerusalem.

(6) Artas, south of Bethlehem.

No conclusive evidence has been offered to substantiate the claim for any of these sites as being Emmaus; hence, its location remains unknown.

Emmor. KJV rendering of Hamor, Shechem's father, in Acts 7:16.

See HAMOR.

Emperor. Official designation of the Roman sovereign beginning in 27 BC with the reign of Caesar Augustus; a derivation of imperator, an honorary title of supreme command conferred by the Roman Senate upon one of its victorious generals. Nero is the only Roman ruler addressed as emperor in Scripture (Acts 25:21,25).

See CAESARS, THE; EMPEROR WORSHIP.

Emperor Worship. Exaltation of human rulers as divine, especially the Roman emperors, a practice that included dedicating temples and offering sacrifices to them.

Emperor worship had its origins in the Near Eastern practice of considering the king divine. The Egyptian pharaoh was considered a descendant of the sun god Ra, and Mesopotamian legends speak of kingship "descending from heaven." Alexander the Great and other Greek heroes were worshiped after their deaths. The idea of a ruler's divinity was encouraged by the central place of the king in pagan cults. Israel was directly affected by such worship during the Babylonian exile (see Dn 3).

Such a background set the pattern for the Seleucid king Antiochus IV Epiphanes, who believed himself to be an incarnation of the Greek god Zeus. He desecrated the temple in Jerusalem by setting up an altar to Zeus in it (167 BC). That event, which the Jews never forgot, triggered the Maccabean war for the liberation of Palestine.

Roman generals and emperors likewise picked up the trappings of godhood as soon as they penetrated Asia Minor, especially after Augustus Caesar came to full power (27 BC). Augustus saw his reign as the inauguration of a new age of peace for Rome and the world. Although the Romans acclaimed him as "savior," he claimed for himself only the high priesthood. In the eastern provinces coins were minted with a double temple for Rome and Augustus. In Antioch coins depicted Augustus as the incarnate Zeus or "worship-worthy Son of God," and altars were erected in his honor. Augustus encouraged the cult as a unifying element in his diverse empire and as a type of patriotism. After his death temples were built in his honor and the symbols of divinity were transferred to succeeding emperors. For decades all new temples were for the imperial cult. (In Mk 12 and parallel passages about paying taxes, the coin was probably inscribed "Tiberius Caesar . . . Son of the Divine Augustus.")

Gaius Caesar, nicknamed Caligula (AD 37–41), was the first emperor to be worshiped in Rome during his own lifetime. On hearing of a dispute between Jews and Gentiles over worshiping him in Jamnia, he ordered a statue of himself placed in the temple in Jerusalem. His plan, which would surely have caused a general revolt, was averted only by the intercession of Herod Agrippa I. Under the succeeding emperors, Claudius (AD 41–54) and Nero (AD 54–68), the cult reached ridiculous extremes. Later emperors varied in how seriously they took the imperial cult, but it remained a test of loyalty to the empire, similar to loyalty oaths or pledging allegiance to the flag. For the sake of the empire's unity other religions had to accommodate emperor worship one way or another.

Emperor worship naturally caused problems for Christians, since the titles given to the emperor ("Lord," "Prince of Peace," "Son of God," "Savior") were the same as those used for Christ. The confession "Jesus is Lord" (Rom 10:9) was bound to conflict with the claim "Caesar is Lord." Christians who would not sacrifice to the emperor were charged with treason. The conflict between emperor worship and Christianity remained a focal point for the persecution of the church until the time of Constantine (AD 306–337).

Enaim, Enam. Obscure Hebrew term used only in Genesis 38:14,21, translated "open place" in the KJV. It was probably the name of a place located in the hill country of Judah, southeast of Jerusalem, between Timnah and Adullam. It may have been a variant form of Enam (Jos 15:34), a location in the Judean Shephelah. Its location is unknown.

Enan. Ahira's father. Ahira was appointed by Moses as the commander of the tribe of Naphtali during the first census of Israel in the desert of Sinai (Nm 1:15; 2:29; 7:78;83; 10:27). The name is apparently preserved in the name Hazar-enan (-enon), a town somewhere between Damascus and Hauran (Nm 34:9; Ez 47:17; 48:1).

Enchantment. Act of casting charms or incantations to influence others or to obtain knowledge. Balaam could place no enchantment upon Israel, but could only bless them (Nm 23:23). Enchanters were present among the wise men of Nebuchadnezzar's court; however, Daniel and his three friends were found to be ten times wiser than they (Dn 1:20). The enchanters were unable to recall King Nebuchadnezzar's forgotten dream (2:2–27) or to interpret his second one (4:7); later, under Belshazzar, they could not read or interpret the handwriting on the palace wall (5:7–15). According to the prophet Isaiah, even the great powers of Babylon's enchantments would not save it from eventual destruction (Is 47:9,12). In a more figurative sense the psalmist writes: wickedness "does not hear the voice . . . of the cunning enchanter" (Ps 58:5).

See MAGIC; SORCERY.

End of the World. *See* DAY OF THE LORD; ESCHATOLOGY; LAST JUDGMENT.

Endor. Ancient Canaanite city, four miles south of Mt Tabor, assigned to the tribe of Manasseh though never fully taken by them (Jos 17:11). The city witnessed the defeat of Jabin and Sisera by Barak (Ps 83:9,10). Endor is not actually mentioned in Judges; despite this omission, it is not necessary to alter "Endor" (Ps 83:10) to "En-harrod" (cf. Jgs 7:1). Endor is best known as the dwelling place of the famous witch who was called upon by King Saul (1 Sm 28:7). On that occasion Saul disguised himself because his journey to Endor took him near the Philistine army encamped at Shunen.

Today there is a kibbutz located at or near the ancient city of Endor which bears that name.

En-eglaim. Place mentioned in Ezekiel 47:10 where, in a description of the millennial age, it is said that "fishermen will stand beside the sea; from En-gedi to En-eglaim it will be a place for the spreading of nets; its fish will be of very many kinds, like the fish of the Great Sea." This condition will be in sharp contrast to the present lack of marine life in the Dead Sea. The location is on the shore of the Dead Sea, probably south of Khirbet Qumran, perhaps 'Ain Feshkha.

Engagement. Act of binding oneself to another by a pledge to marry.

See MARRIAGE, MARRIAGE CUSTOMS.

Engannim. 1. Village in the lowland of Judah near Beth-shemesh (Jos 15:34). Some identify it with the modern Beit Jemal, but this is doubtful.

2. Town on the boundary of Issachar (Jos 19:21). It was a levitical city of the Gershonites (21:29) and the Anem of 1 Chronicles 6:73, which may be a copyist's mistake. It seems to be the Ginaea of Josephus (*Antiq.* 20.6.1). Its site is the modern Jenin, a village on the southern edge of the plain of Esdraelon, 5 miles northeast of Dothan and about 68 miles north of Jerusalem.

See LEVITICAL CITIES.

En-gedi. A vital oasis on the west side of the Dead Sea about 35 miles southeast of Jerusalem. Allotted to Judah's tribe for an inheritance (Jos 15:62), En-gedi contained a hot-water spring coming from the side of a limestone cliff, producing semitropical vegetation. The area became known for its palms, vineyards, and balsam (Sg 1:14; Josephus, *Antiq.* 20.1.2). The ancient site was southeast of the oasis at Tell ej-Jarn near modern 'Ain Jidi.

En-gedi was called Hazazon-tamar in 2 Chronicles 20:2, and figured in several OT events. There Chedorlaomer conquered the Amorites (Gn 14:7); David sought refuge from Saul (1 Sm 23:29); and in Ezekiel's vision of Israel's restoration, fisherman would catch fish from the Dead Sea from En-gedi to En-eglaim (Ez 47:10).

Engines of War. Mechanical devices used in war, such as battering rams.

See ARMS AND WARFARE.

Engraver, Engraving. *See* TRADES AND OCCUPATIONS (STONECUTTER).

Enhaddah. City allotted to Issachar's tribe for an inheritance, mentioned between Engan-

A wadi at En-gedi in Judea near the Dead Sea.

nim and Beth-pazzez (Jos 19:21). Its location is uncertain.

En-hakkore. Spring of water that burst forth when Samson cried to the Lord after he had slaughtered the Philistines (Jgs 15:19). Though many have attempted to locate this spring, using Lehi, the battle site, as a geographical key, it still has not been found.

En-hazor. Fortified city of the OT (Jos 19:37). Of several Hazors in the OT, En-hazor was probably located in Galilee. Its exact location, however, is uncertain.

Enmishpat. Early name for Kadesh, mentioned in the account of Chedorlaomer's battles (Gn 14:7).

See KADESH, KADESH-BARNEA.

Enoch (Person). 1. Cain's son and grandson of Adam (Gn 4:17,18).

2. Jared's son among the descendants of Seth; Methuselah's father (Gn 5:18–24; 1 Chr 1:3, KJV Henoch). He lived in such close relationship to God that he was transferred to heaven without having died.

Enoch (Place). City which Cain named for his first son, Enoch (Gn 4:17). Its location is unknown.

Enosh, Enos. Seth's son and the grandson of Adam (Gn 4:26; 1 Chr 1:1). He became the father of Kenan at 90 years of age, after which he fathered other sons and daughters, dying at the age of 905 (Gn 5:6–11). He is mentioned as Jesus' ancestor in Luke's genealogy (Lk 3:38, Enos).

See GENEALOGY OF JESUS CHRIST.

En-rimmon. Town assigned first to Judah and then to Simeon (Jos 15:32; 19:7, KJV Remmon; 1 Chr 4:32). These verses refer to two places, Ain and Rimmon, but this was probably a scribal error for the one town, En-rimmon (see Jos 19:7). It was resettled after the exile (Neh 11:29), and is perhaps the Rimmon south of Jerusalem mentioned in Zechariah 14:10. En-rimmon is thought to be the modern Khirbet Umm er-Rumamin, 9 miles north of Beersheba.

En-rogel. Spring which was an important landmark identifying the boundary line between the tribes of Judah and Benjamin (Jos 15:7; 18:16). Jonathan and Ahimaaz hid at En-rogel when they were spying on Absalom's troops for King David (2 Sm 17:17), and from there a maidservant delivered their messages

to the king. Here also Adonijah sacrificed sheep, oxen, and goats when he anticipated David's death and wished to set himself up as king (1 Kgs 1:9).

Of the two suggested locations for En-rogel, the older identifies it with a spring in a cave near Siloam, on the west side of the Kidron Valley, known as the Virgin's Fount. There is strong evidence, however, that this is actually the Gihon spring (1 Kgs 1:33), which is mentioned as distinct from En-rogel. A more likely suggestion is another spring south of Jerusalem known as the Well of Job.

Enrollment. Registration of people according to tribe, family, and position.

See CENSUS.

En-shemesh. Place mentioned only in Joshua 15:7 and 18:17 as a boundary marker between Judah's northern border and Benjamin's southern border. The usual identification is with 'Ain el-Hod, about 3 miles east of Jerusalem on the road to Jericho. On the basis of a tradition that the apostles drank there, it is sometimes referred to as the Spring of the Apostles.

En-tappuah. Canaanite town located on the border between Ephraim's and Manasseh's territory (Jos 17:7). It is usually identified with the modern Sheikh Abu Zarad, about 8 miles south of Shechem.

See TAPPUAH (PLACE) # 2.

Enuma Elish. Title of the Babylonian creation epic found during excavations at Nineveh (1848–76). The words *enuma elish* mean "when on high" and are the first two words of the epic, introducing the reader to a time when the heavens "on high" had not been named and the earth did not yet exist. The cuneiform tablets containing the epic were found in the library ruins of the Assyrian king Ashurbanipal. The epic was probably composed in the time of the Babylonian king Hammurabi (1792?–1750? BC). One of the chief purposes of the epic is to show the sovereignty of the Babylonian god Marduk.

See ASHURBANIPAL; CREATION, DOCTRINE OF; CREATION MYTHS.

Epaenetus. Believer greeted by Paul in Romans 16:5 as "my beloved" and "the first convert in Asia for Christ." It is not known if Epaenetus was a personal convert of Paul. Mention of his name has been used to promote the hypothesis that the letter was written for the Ephesians, but contrary evidence has refuted this.

A theater at Hierapolis.

Epaphras. Co-worker with the apostle Paul. Epaphras, a native of Colossae, was responsible for the city's evangelization, as well as that of Laodicea and Hierapolis. Through him Paul learned of the progress of the Colossian church and thus wrote his letter to the Colossians. Paul's high regard for Epaphras was evidenced by his use of such terms as "beloved fellow servant," "faithful minister of Christ" (Col 1:7), and "servant of Christ" (4:12), a title of esteem Paul bestowed only on one other person (Timothy in Phil 1:1). Epaphras was in prison with Paul at the time the letter to Philemon was written (Phlm 23).

See COLOSSIANS, LETTER TO THE.

Epaphroditus. Leader in the Philippian church. Epaphroditus was sent to the apostle Paul during Paul's first Roman imprisonment to deliver gifts (Phil 4:18) and to assist the apostle in his work (Phil 2:25). While in Rome, Epaphroditus became seriously ill and nearly died. After a period of convalescence he returned to Philippi with Paul's letter instructing the church to "receive him in the Lord with all joy" (2:29). Epaphroditus' devoted service endeared him to the Philippian believers and to Paul, who termed him "brother, fellow worker, fellow soldier" (2:25).

See PHILIPPIANS, LETTER TO THE.

Ephah. Measure of grain, about half a bushel.

See WEIGHTS AND MEASURES.

Ephah (Person). 1. Son of Midian, an offspring of Abraham through his concubine Keturah (Gn 25:4; 1 Chr 1:33). Isaiah mentions him as a gold trader (60:6). Some manuscripts mention two sons of Midian with the same name, Ephah, but that is an error of misspelling.

2. Caleb's concubine, who bore him three sons (1 Chr 2:46).

3. Jahdai's son from Judah's tribe (1 Chr 2:47).

Ephai. Netophathite (resident of the town Netophah, near Bethlehem), whose sons fought against the Babylonian army (Jer 40:8). They, with others, approached Gedaliah, the governor of Judah appointed by Babylon, and requested his protection. They died, along with Gedaliah, in an uprising led by Ishmael, the son of Nethaniah (Jer 41:3).

Epher. 1. Son of Midian and grandson of Abraham through his concubine Keturah, whose tribe was sent to the east. Some were supportive of Abraham's descendants and others became enemies (Gn 25:4; 1 Chr. 1:33).

2. Son of Ezrah from Judah's tribe (1 Chr 4:17).

3. Head of a household and a great warrior in the half tribe of Manasseh. He lived between Bashan and Mt Hermon (1 Chr 5:24).

Ephes-dammim. Location between Socoh and Azekah in Judah (1 Sm 17:1) where the Philistines encamped. It was called Pas-dammim in 1 Chronicles 11:13. The reference to blood (dammim) in the name probably has to do with the number of battles fought there, or it may refer to the red earth of the area. Traditionally identified with the ruins of Damun, about 4 miles northeast of Socoh, the exact location of the site is unknown. A recent suggestion identifies it with Beit Fased, southeast of Socoh.

Ephesians, Letter to the. Letter to the Christians in the great city of Ephesus and vicinity written with a magnificence that both instructs and inspires the reader. It provides a sweeping view of the role of the church as history moves toward the ultimate recognition of the universal headship of Christ.

Author. The writer of the letter identifies himself as the apostle Paul (1:1; 3:1). He also describes his own ministry in terms that reflect what we know of Paul (3:7,13; 4:1; 6:19,20). There are some characteristics of the letter, however, that have caused many scholars to question its clear claim to Pauline authorship. Some of these characteristics would be a problem only if the letter were intended exclusively for people in Ephesus, but such was probably not the case. Otherwise it would be hard to understand why, after establishing the church there over a three-year period, Paul would write as though author and recipients had only a secondhand knowledge of each other. It would also be strange that the warm personal words of greeting to various individuals which are found in other Pauline letters are missing here. There is instead only a general greeting to "the brothers" (6:23).

For these reasons, and assuming that this letter was written to the Ephesians, some scholars have felt compelled to reject the Pau-

line authorship of the work. Further reasons were advanced to support the theory that someone other than Paul had written the work, drawing on the ideas and vocabulary of Paul's other letters. For example, it was noted that the author spoke of the apostles and prophets as the foundation of the church, referring to them in the third rather than the first person, as though the writer were not one of them (2:20). Also he called this group "holy" (3:5), a term which was thought would be used only by a later Christian who held the early apostles in special awe. Yet Paul himself wrote in the third person of the "saints" (Col 1:26), although he certainly counted himself as one of them. The biblical writers used the words "saints" and "holy" (which are linguistically related to each other) in a way different from our usage, to refer to those especially set apart for God.

It was also thought that the great apostle Paul would not write so deprecatingly of himself as to say he was "less than the least of all God's people" (3:8 NIV). This, however, is precisely the way Paul did humbly view himself, conscious of his sinfulness and former opposition to the gospel.

There are several other arguments that have been employed to disprove Pauline authorship. Some of these call for careful study; others are more subjective and unpersuasive. A survey of the vocabulary of Ephesians reveals many words that do not otherwise occur in the Pauline letters. Also some words found both in the other letters and in Ephesians are used in the latter with somewhat different meanings.

But statistical studies have shown that each of Paul's letters typically contains unique words, and many scholars therefore do not consider these arguments substantial. Where similar words are used in a different sense, one must decide whether or not it is likely that an author will vary and enrich his own concepts, with consequent expansion of meaning, and whether or not differing contexts call for differing aspects of word meaning.

An example of a term which is allegedly used with a unique meaning in Ephesians is "mystery" or "secret plan." In Ephesians it refers to God's plan to have Jews and Gentiles brought together in one body, the church. Colossians, which has many ideas similar to those in Ephesians, refers to Christ, rather than the church, as the "secret" (1:27; 2:2). However, Romans 16:25,26 does apply it to the inclusion of Gentiles in the church. Actually the word has a slightly different application each time it is used throughout the NT.

Detailed studies also include a comparison of literary style and of concepts in Ephesians with those in the other letters attributed to Paul. Although there are some unique concepts, the basic theological themes of Ephesians, such as the grace of God, are typically Pauline. Discussion of the authorship of Ephesians thus takes into account many factors.

Since resolution of the various problems mentioned is possible, it is reasonable to accept the clear testimony of leading figures in the early history of the church that Paul is the author. This has always been the position of those who consider the Bible to be without error. There is no doubt that the letter itself contains the name of Paul twice, along with other indirect evidence that he is the author. Unless one can justify the use of Paul's name by a later anonymous Christian, the issue becomes one of truth or error in the biblical text.

Date, Origin, and Destination. Ephesians 4:1 and 6:20 indicate that the letter was written while Paul was a prisoner. Since he was imprisoned several times, it is necessary to narrow the options. The first major imprisonment may have been at Ephesus itself, but this is obviously not in consideration. The second was at Caesarea for two years (Acts 24:27; cf. 23:23,24,33; 24:2). It is possible that Paul wrote some letters at that time, but most scholars think that Ephesians (along with Colossians, Philemon, and probably Philippians) was written during Paul's imprisonment at Rome (Acts 28:16,30). This probably took place sometime between AD 59 and 63 and lasted for two years.

This period of time, following about 25 years of spiritual growth and 12 years or so of missionary experience, gave Paul a splendid opportunity for reflection and writing. Written at approximately the same time as Colossians, Ephesians displays both striking similarities and significant differences in comparison with that letter. By studying these, some knowledge can be gained about the composition of Ephesians.

There are many words and phrases which appear in almost identical form in the two letters. This is often more obvious in the Greek text than in modern translations. One example is found in Ephesians 1:4 and Colossians 1:22, where at the end of each verse Paul states that God will not charge the believer with any fault. There are also longer passages that are parallel to one another. These include teachings on adopting a new way of life (e.g., Eph 4:22–24; Col 3:8–10), singing praise (Eph 5:19, 20; Col 3:16,17), and living together in harmony (Eph 5:22–6:9; Col 3:18–4:1).

These similarities are not absolute, however. In the passages just cited on human relationships, Ephesians has a detailed section on husbands and wives that is lacking in Colossians. Also, in Ephesians some unique sections

are interspersed that are thought to have a liturgical character (1:3; 3:20,21; 4:5,6; 5:14). Others sound as though they were intended for public exhortation, some think at a baptism or for renewal of dedication (4:17–5:2; 5:3–21).

Further, some verses in Ephesians seem to be conflations of verses from various parts of Colossians. For example, Ephesians 1:7 seems to combine thoughts found in Colossians 1:14 and 20. The ideas of Colossians 1:3, 4, and 9 seem to be brought together in Ephesians 1:15–16. A similar instance is Ephesians 2:1–5, which combines two widely separated verses, Colossians 2:13 and 3:6.

Theories abound to account for such similarities and differences. A few have proposed that Ephesians was written first; most grant priority to Colossians. Some think that a preliminary version of one was used in the other, and was then expanded into its present form. According to one popular theory, which assumes that Paul is not the author, Ephesians was written by a later Christian who prepared it as an introduction to a collection of Paul's genuine writings, drawing material from Colossians and other Pauline letters.

The most satisfying reconstruction is that Paul wrote Colossians to meet the specific needs of the church at Colosse, planning to ask his friend Tychicus to take the letter there (Col 4:7). Meanwhile, Paul was reflecting on several of the themes touched on in Colossians. He thought also about the ultimate goals of his missionary endeavors. God had revealed to Paul his comprehensive plan for the church and the universal headship of Christ. Paul wrote Ephesians by drawing on some of the phrases and sentences that were fresh in his mind from Colossians.

This reconstruction also explains why some of the terms are used in a somewhat diffferent way than they are in Colossians. Paul's purposes were different. Colossians is polemical, dealing with the problem of false teachers and teaching. Ephesians is reflective, dealing with the general subject of the church. There are other topics that are distinct in Ephesians but barely touched on in Colossians.

It is then clear why, in the example cited earlier, the term "mystery" is applied differently. In Colossians, where the issue revolves largely around the person of Christ, the "mystery" is applied to the Lord himself. In Ephesians, with its emphasis on the church, the term is applied to the unity of Jews and Gentiles in the church. Neither usage exhausts the comprehensive meaning of the term.

If this is an accurate understanding of the relationship between the two letters, and if Paul is the author of both, why does Ephesians give the impression that Paul did not have a recollection of, and regard for, individuals in Ephesus? First, the very nature of the letter—a comprehensive treatment of expansive themes—does not lend itself to this as much as do his other letters. Second, it is not certain that the letter was intended specifically for the Ephesians. Since the time when the KJV was prepared, a great deal has become known about the early manuscripts of the NT. It is now known that the words "at Ephesus" did not appear in two of the earliest manuscripts (Vaticanus; Sinaiticus), nor did it appear in an early papyrus (P47), or in early copies of some citations of early Christian writers.

Since the words do appear in later manuscripts, the letter must have had some connection with Ephesus. The fact that this letter, like Colossians, was to be delivered by Tychicus (Eph 6:21; Col 4:7) suggests that it may have been intended for several churches along the way, the most notable being at Ephesus. Ephesians 6:23 implies some limitation of readership, while verse 24 is more general. The words "at Ephesus" could then be accounted for if it were a circular letter with an original copy sent there, or with one copy left there, which was later identified with those words. This would account both for the lack of personal references and for the inclusion of the words "at Ephesus" in many later manuscripts and versions. It has also been theorized that the letter went to Laodicea, among other places, and is the letter that was to be forwarded from there to Colossae (Col 4:16).

Background. Ephesus was the most important city in Asia Minor, located on the Cayster River, with a harbor on the Aegean Sea. With this location it became a center for commercial travel, and major trade routes led

One of the marble streets of Ephesus.

to it from several directions. A great pagan temple dedicated to the goddess Artemis (Diana) was located in Ephesus. Paul made the city a center of evangelistic and church-building ministry (Acts 19), spending three years there (20:31). It was very natural, therefore, for a letter intended for a wide readership in that part of Asia Minor to have Ephesus as its main destination.

Purpose and Theological Teaching. It may be said that the purpose of Ephesians is "doxological"; that is, it should cause the readers to glorify God, both in grateful praise and in manner of life. This is seen in the opening section, which is like a hymn in style: "Praise God, the Father of our Lord Jesus Christ" (1:3; cf. the Doxology often sung in church). Paul says three times in the first chapter that the result of God's blessings should be praise (vv 6,12,14).

While the letter contains much doctrinal and moral instruction (with the latter solidly based on the former), its purpose is not only teaching or exhortation, important as these are. It is rather to lift its readers up to a new vantage point that will help them to identify with the risen, ascended Christ and to share his perspective on the church and its role in the world.

In this connection a significant term occurs in 1:3 and elsewhere. It is perhaps best translated "heavenly realms." It is different in form from the usual word for "heaven" and seems to have a special significance in Ephesians as the realm of Jesus' victorious reign in the present age. This is seen in 1:20, read in the context of verses 19–23. Whatever beings there may be, Christ is above them all. The believer, although obviously on earth physically, "sits with Christ" in the heavenly realms (2:6) and is "blessed" (1:3), while drawing on the unlimited resources of heaven for his daily life. It is also in this realm that the spiritual conflict takes place (6:12).

Paul thus makes it clear that Christians are not to have a limited or merely earthly viewpoint. Those who do will mistakenly think that our enemies are people (6:12) and our resources human (2 Cor 10:3–4). With this orientation to the heavenly world of the Lord's present exaltation, the reader is prepared to understand that the church does not function merely to carry out routine activities here, but that it displays the wisdom of God to beings who exist in the heavenly realms (3:10). Even the function of church leaders is discussed in terms of the gifts of the Christ who has ascended to the heavens (4:8–10).

There is a strong sense of ultimate purpose in Ephesians. The first chapter contains a number of different expressions of purpose. The great goal of history is expressed in 1:10. The sense of purpose is never lost. The church is even seen, in chapter 3, as the expression of God's ancient secret plan. There is also a movement throughout the letter, from (1) reconciliation of individuals to God to (2) their reconciliation to each other to (3) their life together in the church. There is no arguing of points along the way, such as one finds in most of the letters, but rather a connected series of affirmations, each leading the reader on to the next.

Paul discusses a number of topics from this heavenly perspective and the sense of purpose this provides. These topics will be discussed below in such a way as to show their interconnection, rather than necessarily in the order of their importance or prominence in Ephesians.

The Church. Paul employs a number of figures of speech to describe the church, including a household, a temple, and a body (1:22–23; 2:19–22). Actually it may be insufficient to call the word "body" a figure of speech, because it seems to be more than that. There is a sense in which Christ and the church have an actual organic relationship, in which he functions as the head and believers as parts of his body.

The church is the result of the reconciling work of Christ, whose death has made peace between mutually hostile Jews and Gentiles (2:11–18). The ensuing unity was long planned by God (3:2–6), and is furthered by a proper attitude and mutual ministry (ch 4).

An especially remarkable feature of Ephesians is the parallel drawn between the relationship between a husband and wife and that between Christ and the church (5:22–33). In this comparison the prior reality is not marriage, with the relationship of Christ and the church only providing an illustration. Rather, the essential reality is Christ and the church.

The Headship of Christ. Not only is Christ the head of the church, but he is head over all things to the church's benefit (1:22). The meaning of 1:10 is that the presently disparate parts and beings of the universe will be brought into order under the headship of Christ. This universal headship is anticipated in the ascension and present exaltation of Christ. The expression of universal domination—"God has put all things under his feet" (1:22, from Ps 8:6)—fortifies this expectation.

The "Mystery" or "Secret Plan." The Greek word "mystery" has a special meaning in early Jewish and Christian literature. It refers to the private eternal decisions of God concerning his saving work and his ultimate purposes in history, which are revealed stage by stage. The term is used in connection with the kingdom in the Gospels (Mt 13:11), with the preaching of the gospel in 1 Corinthians 1:18–2:16,

with the destiny of Israel in Romans 11:25, and elsewhere with differing applications. Finally, Revelation 10:6–7 declares that there will be no more delay, but that God's "mystery," initially announced by the prophets, will reach its completion.

The aspect of God's plan that Paul presents in Ephesians 3:3–6 is not only the inclusion of Gentiles among God's people but their complete integration with Jews in the church. The extent of this was not revealed prior to the time of Paul's ministry.

The Trinity. Each member of the Trinity is mentioned several times in chapter 1. God is described as the "glorious" Father in 1:17. The first member of the Trinity is both the God and Father of our Lord Jesus Christ (1:3), but at the same time Father and Son are equally the source of grace and peace (1:2). The essential fatherhood of God is the basis for the existence of family relationships among humans, especially, of course, of the family of believers (3:14). In the passage just cited, Paul prays to the Father, in accordance with the pattern of the Lord's prayer (Mt 6:9; Lk 11:2).

The believer's relationship to God as Father is possible only through Jesus Christ (1:5), who is described as "his beloved Son" (7:6; cf. Col 1:13). This expression recalls the words spoken from heaven at the baptism and the transfiguration of Christ, "This is my beloved Son" (Mt 3:17; 17:5). The believer becomes the recipient of the same love given the Son by the Father. Many of the topics in chapter 1 are said to be accomplished, or are imparted to the believer "in Christ" (vv 3,10,12; cf. vv 7,14). The phrase "in Christ" is common throughout Paul's writings. The entire second chapter expands on the fact that redemption is through the death and resurrection of Christ.

Chapter 1 also contains a section that centers on the work of the Holy Spirit. The Spirit marks a believer as belonging to Christ, just as someone in the 1st century would use an impressed wax seal to identify a scroll or other item (v 13). The Spirit is also a guarantee (v 14, i.e., a deposit or down payment) of God's ownership of the believer. Paul further describes the believer's relationship to the Holy Spirit by indicating that a bad attitude toward others, expressed for example in intemperate language, brings sorrow to the Spirit (4:30). This fact is indirect evidence that the Holy Spirit is capable of what we would call feelings, thus not an impersonal being.

Perhaps the most noteworthy mention of the Spirit in Ephesians is in 5:18. Here Paul teaches that rather than losing control of one's behavior by imbibing too much liquor, the believer should submit to the filling—that is, the control—of the Holy Spirit. Colossians has a similar statement: "Let the Word of Christ dwell in you richly" (Col 3:16) instead of "be filled with the Spirit." Assuming that the same basic truth is taught in both passages, one may conclude that the Spirit-filled Christian is the one who obeys the Lord Jesus.

Content. *The Divine Purpose: The Glory and Headship of Christ (1:1–14).* This whole section constitutes a "doxology." Paul reminds readers, by expressing his own prayer of praise, of all the blessings God has given believers. These include being chosen to live in God's presence without guilt (v 4), being given the destiny of full sonship (v 5), and being forgiven because Christ died for them.

But Paul is not only giving a recitation of what God has done. He interweaves a number of words and phrases indicating *why* God has acted, that is, what God's *purposes* are. Various translations use different English words to represent Greek expressions of purpose, such as "chose," "predestined," "plan," "will," "secret reason," "good pleasure," "purpose" (vv 4–10). Perhaps the most comprehensive statement is in verses 11–12.

It is clear from this that the ultimate purpose of God's saving work is not merely the happiness of believers but the glory of God through the Lord Jesus Christ. The Spirit is given to guarantee not only the believer's security, but God's investment, so to speak, in the believer.

Prayer That Christians May Realize God's Purpose and Power (1:15–23). Paul's prayer issues from his opening section, constituting a request that believers may appropriate all that is contained in that statement. It is here that the fact of Jesus' death, resurrection, and ascension is cited as the basis for the believer's present vantage point and power.

Steps Toward the Fulfillment of God's Purpose (2:1–3:13). The first step was the death of Christ in order to save individuals from sin and death (2:1–10). Since this was at God's initiative, not man's, and since man was spiritually "dead" and helpless, salvation can only be by grace.

The second step was the reconciliation of people not only to God but to each other (2:11–18). Paul thus moves from the individual to the corporate aspect of salvation. This was particularly significant for Gentiles, who previously did not have even a formal relationship with God. One of the key words in this section is "peace" (vv 14,15,17).

Step three goes beyond reconciliation to the actual uniting of Jews and Gentiles in one "household" (2:19–22). God has not only brought people individually to himself, and to each other as individuals, but has formed a new corporate entity, a new society that is described both in political and family terms. Ultimately believers together form a corporate body in whom God is exalted, a living temple.

This third step is amplified in a fourth step, the revelation of God's eternal purpose in the formation of this one body, the church (3:1–13). Using the biblical concept of the "mystery," Paul shows how the church displays the wisdom of God to all who may be looking on throughout the universe. This immediately gives the believer a new awareness of the reason for his salvation and participation in the church. Self-centeredness and boredom with the routine of church activity give way to a sense of meaning and purpose.

These steps are now summarized in a second prayer (3:14–21). An exalted series of petitions culminate in another "doxology." This expresses Paul's awe over the infinite power of God to accomplish all that he has described in the epistle thus far, and his desire that this will indeed result in great glory to God both in the church and in Christ.

Practical Ways to Fulfill God's Purpose in the Church (4:1–6:20). Doctrine and life are never separated in Paul's thinking, but in Ephesians the connection is even more vital than usual. The believer's life is to be lived in a manner worthy of the great purposes of God. The believer's "calling" is not merely to be saved or eternally happy, but to participate with the entire body, the church, in bringing glory to God. This contributes to the realization of the prayer in 3:20–21.

The first way to fulfill God's purpose is to maintain the unity he established in the church. This is accomplished by recognizing the strong basis for unity ("one Lord, one faith," etc., vv 5–6). Then believers must acknowledge diversity in that unity, remembering that God has given each one special abilities (vv 7–8). These abilities are to be used to bring the church both individually and corporately to maturity. This diversity in unity constitutes the second way in which God's purpose is fulfilled. Christian maturity enables the individual members of the church to relate to each other in love (v 26).

The third way to accomplish the purposes of God is by renewal of personal life (4:17–5:21). Paul emphasizes the kind of life-style that is expected of a Christian by contrasting the behavior patterns which had characterized the believers before their conversion. But the new life of the believer is not simply structured as a reaction against the old. Rather, the Lord has given both his teachings and the example of his own sacrificial love (4:20–21,32; 5:1–2). The believer should cast off his old way of life, his old self or character. (The actual term is "old man" in Paul's wording, not, as is often thought, "old nature.") He should at the same time put on the "new man," which, in Paul's words in verse 24, is "created according to God" (NIV, "created to be like God"). The section closes with the important exhortation to be filled with the Spirit (5:18).

The expression of the new character in interpersonal relations is the fourth way in which believers can forward the purposes of God in the church. Unity is either achieved or broken in accordance with the presence or absence of the proper submission described in 5:22–6:9. The basic principle of submission is first expressed by verse 21 as a result of the Spirit's full control.

Marriage then provides the first example of mutual submission. The wife submits to the husband, and this in turn is an expression of her submission, along with that of the whole church, to the Lord. The husband loves his wife as Christ loved the church. While the husband's love is not described as submission, in effect love does cost the lover his freedom. Jesus thus expressed his love for the church by his death (5:25). Further, husband and wife are bound together in a unity, just as God intended at the time of creation (Gn 2:24, quoted here in 5:31). This unity portrays that spiritual unity that exists between Christ and the church.

It should be noted that this list of examples is similar to a pattern used elsewhere in the NT (e.g., Col 3:18–4:1; 1 Pt 3:1–7). Thus, following the example of marriage, Paul turns to the relationship that should exist between parent and child. The child obeys the father; the father refrains from excessive reactions (6:1–4). The last example is that of slaves and masters.

The final way in which believers forward God's great purposes is to carry on the spiritual conflict by depending on spiritual resources (6:10–20). Drawing on imagery both from the OT and from contemporary Roman warfare, Paul shows that the heavenly perspective is essential for victory. This includes dependence on God as expressed in prayer (6:18–20). He acknowledges his own need in this respect.

The conclusion to the letter (6:21–24) is a word of encouragement and an explanation of Paul's decision to send the letter in the good hands of Tychicus. One of the concluding words is "grace," a word which underlies the entire divine process described in Ephesians.

WALTER L. LIEFELD

See PAUL, THE APOSTLE; COLOSSIANS, LETTER TO THE; EPHESUS.

Bibliography. F.F. Bruce, *The Epistles to the Colossians, to Philemon, and to the Ephesians*; D. Guthrie, *Epistles from Prison*; C. Hodge, *A Commentary on the Epistle to the Ephesians*; C. Leslie Mitton, *Ephesians*; E.F. Scott, *The Epistles to the Colossians, to Philemon, and to the Ephesians*; J.R.W. Stott, *God's New Society*.

Ephesus. Most important city of the Roman province of Asia, located on the western shore of Asia Minor (modern Turkey). Ephesus was built on a natural harbor whose waves, according to the Roman writer Pliny the Elder, "used to wash up to the temple of Diana." Ephesus was described by Strabo, an early Greek geographer, as the largest commercial center west of the Taurus mountains. It was also well known as the "guardian" of the temple of Artemis or, as the Romans called her, Diana (Acts 19:35).

Christianity's threat to that pagan temple and to the commerce it produced for the makers of idols almost cost the apostle Paul his life (Acts 19:24,30,31). Priscilla and Aquila were associated with the early preaching in Ephesus (Acts 18:18,19), as were Timothy (1 Tm 1:3) and Erastus (Acts 19:22). According to Irenaeus, an early Christian writer, the apostle John, after his exile on the island of Patmos (Rv 1:9), returned to live in Ephesus until the time of the emperor Trajan (AD 98–117). The commendable practices of the Christian community described in the letter to the Ephesians had been largely abandoned by the time John wrote the Book of Revelation (Rv 2:4).

Ephesus was founded by Ionian Greeks at a location where the Cayster River emptied into a gulf of the Aegean Sea. It had been a city for about a thousand years when Paul arrived there on his third missionary journey. The worship of Artemis in Ephesus was as ancient as the city itself. The temple, built in the middle of the 6th century BC, was the largest edifice in the Hellenistic world and the first of monumental size ever to be constructed entirely of marble. Two excavated images of Artemis, magnificently sculpted in marble, date to the period of emperors Domitian and Hadrian (the lifetime of the apostle John). The temple of Diana, "mother of the gods," was considered one of the seven wonders of the ancient world. Although persistent effort by British archaeologist J. T. Wood resulted in the temple's discovery in 1869, its great altar was not found until recently. Excavation has shown the altar to be larger than the later altar of Zeus at Pergamum. The original temple was partially destroyed in 356 BC but was later rebuilt on its original plan.

Excavations have also uncovered the theater mentioned in Acts 19:29. Situated next to the main shopping area (*agora*), it is known to have seated 24,000 people in three tiers. The theater was 495 feet in diameter with two doors opening to the most impressive street in Ephesus. That street, leading to the harbor, was about 35 feet wide and was flanked by tall columns. It passed through a magnificent monumental gateway on its western end.

View down from the seats of the Grand Theater (seating about 25,000), the most spectacular monument of Ephesus. This is where the riot occurred and the crowd shouted, "Great is Diana of the Ephesians."

In the other direction the road continued around the theater and marketplace, making its way southeast between Mt Koressos and Mt Pion. It became narrower and was bordered by lovely fountains, civic buildings, houses, shops, a library, baths, and a small theater which probably doubled as a council chamber for city officials.

Ephesus was a wealthy city. The multi-storied residences of its upper-middle-class society rested on the north terraces of Mt Koressos. Some homes had mosaic floors and marble walls. Two were found with heated bathrooms. Many had running water. The moral status of the city can be partially ascertained from a centrally located house of prostitution and gambling tables; fertility motifs are evident in the exaggerated sexual features of the Diana statues.

The impact of Christianity was felt in Ephesus for centuries. The 3rd ecumenical council was held there in AD 431 (in the Church of Mary northwest of the theater), a council that established Mary's place as the "Mother of God" in Western Catholic theology. By that time Diana, whose temple had been burned by the Goths in AD 262, was no longer influential among the Ephesians. The truth of Paul's message that "gods made with hands are not gods" (Acts 19:26) had to some extent been realized.

See EPHESIANS, LETTER TO THE.

Ephlal. Jerahmeel's descendant, who could trace his ancestry through Perez to Judah (1 Chr 2:37).

Ephod. Upper garment worn during religious services associated with the tabernacle or temple. "Ephod" generally referred to the ornamented vest that the high priest wore over a blue robe (Ex 28:31). Included with the ephod were the Urim and Thummim, the sacred lots. Sometimes "ephod" meant the complete dress of the high priest (1 Sm 2:28; 23:6,9; 30:7) or similar garments worn by lesser priests.

Made of dyed material and fine linen, the garment was embroidered in blue, purple, scarlet, and gold. At the upper end were attached two shoulder straps, each having an onyx stone inscribed with the names of Israel's 12 tribes. The breastplate, also containing the tribal names, was bound to the ephod by an elaborate series of cords and chains (Ex 28; 39).

Jewish writers suggest various appearances for the ephod: (1) apronlike, covering the body from the chest to the heels; (2) enveloping the body only from the waist down, the upper body covered by the breastplate; or (3) sleeved and jacketlike, with the middle of the breast uncovered so the breastplate could be inserted easily.

Prior to the Babylonian exile the ephod served as a means of revelation from God, especially concerning military operations. Abiathar the priest brought the ephod into David's camp on one occasion for consulting the Lord (1 Sm 23:6–9; 30:7). It is uncertain whether the priest donned or held the ephod while seeking counsel from the Lord by means of the Urim and Thummim.

During the period of the judges the ephod was often misused, as by Gideon (Jgs 8:27), Micah (Jgs 17:5), and Jonathan, grandson of Moses (Jgs 18:30; cf. vv 14,17,20). Either the garment itself or an image that represented God, on which the garment was placed, was worshiped as the people sought revelation in a manner condemned by God. Household idols (teraphim) were also associated with this ungodly practice (Jgs 17:5; Hos 3:4).

Besides the high priest, other priests wore

an ephod for certain religious services (1 Sm 22:18), and even Samuel (1 Sm 2:18) and David (2 Sm 6:14) wore one. By the postexilic period, and perhaps as early as Solomon, the ephod was no longer consulted (Ezr 2:63; Neh 7:65). There was no need for ephod or Urim revelation once there was the more complete revelation of the prophetic ministry promised by Moses (Dt 18:15–22). However, the high priest continued to wear this vestment until the destruction of Jerusalem in AD 70.

See PRIESTS AND LEVITES.

Ephod (Person). Father of Hanniel, the prince of the children of Joseph (Nm 34:23). Hanniel was responsible for distributing Canaanite territory among the Israelite tribes.

Ephphatha. Transliteration in the imperative voice of the Aramaic expression "be opened," used by Jesus in the healing of a deaf mute (Mk 7:34). No attempt at establishing a magical word formula was intended; the author apparently desired simply to preserve the actual wording. A connection with Isaiah 35:5 may have been implied.

Ephraim (Person). Joseph's younger son, born of Joseph and Asenath before the 7 years of famine in Egypt (Gn 41:52). He was the ancestor of an Israelite tribe, and his name came to designate the northern kingdom of Israel (Is 7:5,8; Jer 31:18,20; Hos 5:3,5). Ephraim's boyhood overlapped the last 17 years of his grandfather, the patriarch Jacob, who migrated to Egypt during the years of plenty. Thus Ephraim could learn of God's promises and blessings directly from Jacob. After Jacob exacted an oath to bury him in Canaan from his grandsons Ephraim and Manasseh, he adopted them. That adoption gave the two brothers the position and legal rights equal to Jacob's eldest sons, Reuben and Simeon (Gn 48:5).

See EPHRAIM, TRIBE OF.

Ephraim (Place). 1. Area allotted to Ephraim's tribe for an inheritance (Jos 16:5–8; 17:7–11). Ephraim and Manasseh originally were recognized as "the people of Joseph" (Jos 16:4). Together they occupied the central highlands area between Jerusalem and the plain of Esdraelon. Ephraim's territory lay to the south of Manasseh. The area was relatively high, and the expression "the hill country of Ephraim" (1 Sm 1:1) was an apt description. In places the hard rocks form steep and difficult slopes, and the valleys leading to the west are steep. Roads followed the spurs between the valleys rather than the valleys themselves. Movement between Ephraim and the coastal plain along the edge of the rocky Sarida valley was not easy, but it was possible. Another road followed by the Philistine invaders (1 Sm 4) led up from Aphek. Because of their relative inaccessibility the Ephraimites became a leading tribe in Israel very early. The expression in Joshua 16:9, "the towns which were set apart for the Ephraimites within the inheritance of the Manassites," suggests that there had once been a disputed boundary; however, Ephraim was evidently able to strengthen itself and to emerge as a dominant force in Israel. Indeed the name Ephraim is sometimes used as the equivalent of Israel (Hos 4:17; 5:3,11–14; 6:4,10, etc.)

The extent of the tribal area of Ephraim is given in Joshua 16:5–8 and 17:1–11. It would appear from the abundant detail given in these passages that the main topographical features of Ephraim's boundaries would be easy to determine. Yet the precise identification of a number of the places mentioned is uncertain. The eastern boundary began at Michmethah, tentatively identified with Khirbet en-Nabi. It continued south through Taanath-shiloh, Janoah, Ataroth, and Naarah to a point near Jericho. The southern boundary seems to have passed westward toward Bethel, Beth-horon, and Gezer to the Mediterranean Sea. The western boundary is not defined and probably encroached on Canaanite areas in early times. The northern boundary separating Ephraim from Manasseh went from Michmethah, which was "before Shechem," toward Tappuah and then ran along the Wadi Qana to the Mediterranean Sea north of Joppa. But it must be stressed that the precise definition of the boundaries is by no means clear. Immediately to the south of Ephraim lay the tribal area of Benjamin.

The rainfall in the hill country of Ephraim is greater than in Judea, which lay further south, and the soil is reddish in color, rich and fertile. Because of this Ephraim was very productive. Today the country is dotted with orchards, and olive trees are abundant. The description in Deuteronomy 33:14–17 of an area which yielded "the choicest fruits of the sun, and the rich yield of the months, with the finest produce of the ancient mountains, and the abundance of the everlasting hills, with the best gifts of the earth" gives an excellent picture of the general nature of the region.

See EPHRAIM, TRIBE OF.

2. Town near Baal-hazor to which Absalom invited his half brother Ammon in order to have him put to death (2 Sm 13:23–29) for incest with Absalom's sister Tamar. The town lay to the north of Jerusalem and was possibly identical with Ephron (2 Chr 13:19).

3. Town near the wilderness to which Jesus

retired after raising Lazarus from the tomb (Jn 11:54). It is generally identified with eṭ-Ṭaiyibeh, 13 miles northeast of Jerusalem and 4 miles northeast of Bethel.

Ephraim, Forest of.

Rocky, wooded stretch of country east of the Jordan in the area of Mahanaim. It was here that David's army defeated Absalom (2 Sm 18:6, KJV wood of Ephraim). The connection of this location with the territory of Ephraim is difficult. The most probable explanation is that Ephraim once extended farther to the east, but was lost by the tribe after its defeat by Jephthah and the Gileadites near Zaphon (Jgs 12:1–6). The name may have been used while the Ephraimites held the land, or perhaps been given at a later date as a reminder of Ephraim's defeat. Some speculate that Ephraimites once established a colony in the area (Jos 17:14–18).

Ephraim, Gate of.

Gate in the Jerusalem wall positioned about 600 feet east of the Corner Gate (2 Kgs 14:13; 2 Chr 25:23). It was rebuilt in Nehemiah's day (Neh 12:39) and was situated close to the Water Gate and courts of the temple.

See JERUSALEM.

Ephraim, Mount.

KJV expression referring to the hill country in central Palestine where Ephraim's tribe was located (Jos 20:1; Jgs 19:1,16,18; 1 Sm 1:1, etc.). The area was one of the most productive in Palestine.

See EPHRAIM (PLACE) # 1.

Ephraim, Tribe of.

Tribe descended from the patriarch Joseph's second son. Both Ephraim and his brother Manasseh were regarded as sons also by their grandfather Jacob and became his heirs.

Many Bible commentators think that in naming his son Ephraim (Gn 41:52), Joseph was making a play on words based on a Hebrew root meaning "to be fruitful." In support of this theory they note that the hill country later assigned to Ephraim's tribe was one of the most fertile areas in Palestine, and at present is still planted with vines and fruit trees such as olive, pomegranate, and carob. Prior to Israelite settlement, the area was wooded (Jos 17:18). During the monarchy wild animals still roamed there (2 Kgs 2:24).

It is difficult to determine the exact limits of Ephraim's territory, since it is often mentioned with Manasseh's tribe. Ephraim was allotted land in the heart of Canaan, the Promised Land, between the Jordan River and the Mediterranean Sea. One half of Manasseh's allotment formed Ephraim's northern boundary (Jos 16:5–9).

Ephraim became a great tribe, and its members often held prominent positions. The first census taken in the wilderness lists the total of Ephraimite soldiers as 40,500 (Nm 1:33). After the wilderness wanderings the number of warriors dropped to 32,500 (Nm 26:37). In Israel's encampment around the tabernacle, Ephraim was the leader of the western camp, supported by the tribes of Manasseh and Benjamin (Nm 2:18–24).

Joshua the son of Nun, one of the 12 spies, was descended from Ephraim (Nm 13:8, Hoshea). Under Joshua's leadership Ephraim and the other tribes conquered Canaan and received their promised inheritance (Jos 16).

In the days of the judges the Ephraimites felt slighted when they were not called upon to assist others in their battles. They quarreled with Gideon because of his belated invitation to help against the Midianites (Jgs 8:1–6) as well as with Jephthah of Gilead, who defeated the Ammonites (Jgs 12:1–6). The judge Abdon came from Ephraim's tribe (Jgs 12:13). The idolatrous Micah (Jgs 17:1) as well as the prophet Samuel lived in Ephraim (1 Sm 1:1). The military and political importance of the Ephraimites is reflected in the Song of Deborah (Jgs 5:14), an ancient biblical poem.

Judah was Ephraim's main rival, and even under David that animosity was evident (2 Sm 18; 19:41–20:22). Discontent in the north with Solomon's rule (1 Kgs 11:26–40), combined with a foolish decision by Rehoboam, Solomon's son, brought about the division of the kingdom. The 10 northern tribes (Israel) were then ruled by Jeroboam I.

After the northern tribes seceded, the capitals of the northern kingdom—Shechem, Tirzah, and Samaria—were situated in Ephraim. The establishment of Samaria by King Omri of Israel gave the Ephraimites more direct access to the great north-south trunk road (Via Maris) through the western plain. This contact with trade routes gave the northern kingdom greater world consciousness and brought greater temptation to depart from God and his commands.

The prophets proclaimed that Ephraim and the other northern tribes would one day be reunited with the southern kingdom of Judah in the messianic kingdom (Hos 1:11). The division introduced by Jeroboam I would be healed when a king descended from David would rule over Judah, Ephraim, and all the tribes of Israel (Ez 37).

AUSTIN H. POTTS

See ISRAEL, HISTORY OF; EPHRAIM (PERSON); EPHRAIM (PLACE) # 1.

Ephrain. KJV form of Ephron, a town near Bethel, in 2 Chronicles 13:19.

See EPHRON (PLACE) # 2.

Ephrath, Ephrathah, Ephratah (Person). Mother of Hur and Caleb's second wife (1 Chr 2:19; alternately spelled Ephrathah, KJV Ephratah, in v 50).

Ephrath, Ephrathah, Ephratah (Place). 1. Town in the Judean hill country later named Bethlehem. It was on the road to Ephrath (also spelled Ephrathah, KJV Ephratah) that Rachel died while giving birth to Benjamin (Gn 35:16,19). This town was the home of Naomi's family, who identified themselves as Ephrathites (Ru 1:2). Ephrath was the dwelling place of Ruth and Boaz (Ru 4:11), the childhood home of David (1 Sm 17:12), and the announced birthplace of the Messiah (Mi 5:2).

See BETHLEHEM # 1.

2. District in which the city of Kiriathjearim was situated and where the ark of the covenant was kept (Ps 132:6).

Ephrathite. Inhabitant of the town of Ephrath (Bethlehem) in Judah (1 Sm 17:12).

See EPHRATH, EPHRATHAH, EPHRATAH (PLACE) # 1.

Ephron (Person). Hittite from whom Abraham purchased the cave of Macpelah with its adjoining field for 400 shekels of silver (Gn 23:8–17). Sarah was buried there, as was Abraham (Gn 25:9) and Jacob (Gn 50:13).

Ephron (Place). 1. Mountainous district on the northern edge of Judah (Jos 15:9).

2. City near Bethel, captured by Abijah (2 Chr 13:19, KJV Ephrain); perhaps the Ophrah of Joshua 18:23.

Epicureans. Those who followed the teachings of the Greek philosopher Epicurus (342–270 BC). Paul encountered some of them while in Athens (Acts 17:18).

Epicurus spent his childhood on the island of Samos near the western coast of what is today Turkey. In his late teens he moved to Athens for military service. After his tour of duty, he devoted his time to the study and teaching of philosophy. This work took him from Athens, but he returned in 307 BC to found a school. He attracted a considerable following, and his disciples spread his message throughout the civilized world. The fact that Paul met Epicureans over 3 centuries after the death of Epicurus shows both the attractiveness of his teachings and the commitment of his disciples. In the 1st century BC these teachings found expression in the writing of the Roman poet Lucretius. His *On the Nature of Things* is a helpful guide to understanding Epicurus, especially since only fragments of Epicurus' writings remain.

The Epicureans were empiricists; they relied upon sense experience for knowledge. This put them in opposition to those who chose to make statements about the world on the basis of reason alone, distrusting or rejecting the data of the senses. Epicureans were concerned with natural evidence and with practicalities, thus showing a somewhat scientific character. They were unenthusiastic about mathematics because of what they took to be its abstract quality, having little to do with the important matters of living. Ethics, the study of right behavior, was their focus.

The Epicurean judged the value of an action or thing in terms of the pleasure or pain it brought, a position called hedonism. It was egoistic hedonism because the person sought his own pleasure rather than the pleasure of others. This description can bring to mind the image of an irresponsible glutton or lover of wild parties; but the image, encouraged by the modern sense of the word "epicurean" is misleading. Epicurus rejected just such behavior. He realized that momentary pleasure can lead to enduring pain and that some pain can be beneficial. He viewed pleasure more as a quality of life than a series of thrills. What he sought is better called happiness. Basing his counsel on experience, he urged moderation, calm, friendship, a simple life. He avoided feasting, sexual passion, and strife. In fact, he avoided pain more than he sought pleasure. The pleasure of tranquility, of peace, could be found in the absence of pain, and this was his aim. To ensure tranquility, a man must tend to his stomach; but he must also attend to his mind, directing it toward wisdom.

Epicurus saw belief in gods as a serious threat to tranquility. Gods were generally viewed as emotional, meddling, and powerful beings who terrified ordinary mortals— sources of insecurity, not peace and happiness. Epicurus taught that the gods were not, in fact, like this but were tranquil hedonists who stayed away from men. They avoided the strife involved in contact with people on earth. In short, they were nothing to fear.

Epicurus taught that we, and everything in our world, are made up of atoms of different qualities. For example, the atoms of the human soul are smooth and round. Although atomic theories often lead to the conviction that all human actions are determined by the laws that rule the motion of atoms, Epicurus' theory did not. He allowed for human freedom by claiming that some atoms spontaneously leave their straight paths, thus setting off an unpredictable chain of collisions. Man's behavior is then free and not machinelike.

In spite of his freedom, man is still a collection of atoms, and when the atoms separate, the man ceases to exist; he is not immortal. Epicurus saw this as reason no longer to fear death. For after death, all experience ceases. There will be no pain, and so there is no cause for anxiety.

Epicurean themes can be found in the Bible—for example, moderation (Phil 4:5) and the peace that comes from the exercise of wisdom (Prv 3:13–18). But the differences are clear. The Bible reveals a God who is intimately involved in the world; the immortality of man's soul; and the truth that genuine happiness depends upon communion with and service to God. (Rom 8:6; Phil 4:6–7).

See PHILOSOPHY.

Epilepsy. Disease of the central nervous system characterized by unconsciousness and convulsions. Seizures can be either "petit mal" (twitching of the face or hands, brief but sharp abdominal pain, and possible momentary unconsciousness) or "grand mal" (convulsions, foaming at the mouth, and unconsciousness lasting from 5 to 20 minutes). Although the causes of epilepsy are still not known, drugs are available to prevent or control the seizures.

In biblical times epilepsy, known as the "falling sickness," could not be treated effectively. Jesus healed a boy evidently suffering from that affliction (Mt 17:14–18; Mk 9:17–27; Lk 9:37–42). The KJV description of the boy as a "lunatic" (from Latin *luna*, "moon") is an incorrect usage. The Greek word in Matthew (literally "moonstruck") reflected anicent belief in a connection between certain diseases and the lunar phases. According to the biblical account, the youth was healed when Jesus called forth a demon or "unclean spirit" from him.

See MEDICINE AND MEDICAL PRACTICE.

Epistle. *See* LETTER WRITING, ANCIENT.

Er. 1. Eldest son of Judah and Bath-shua, a Canaanite woman (Gn 38:3). The Lord killed him before he and his wife Tamar could have any children (Gn 38:7; 46:12; 1 Chr 2:3).

2. Grandson of Judah and father of Lecah (1 Chr 4:21); a nephew of # 1 above.

3. Joshua's son and an ancestor of Joseph, the husband of Mary (Lk 3:28).

See GENEALOGY OF JESUS CHRIST.

Eran. Grandson of Ephraim and the oldest son of Shuthelah (Nm 26:36), from whom

Erastus inscription (Rom 16:23).

came the Eranite family. In 1 Chronicles 7:20, Eran was replaced by Ele-adah, which may be a copyist's error.

Erastus. Name mentioned three times in the NT. Whether only one individual is being referred to cannot be ascertained, although in each case Erastus is an associate of Paul. The mentions include: (1) a helper of Paul sent with Timothy into Macedonia (Acts 19:22); (2) the city treasurer of Corinth (a steward of financial affairs, possibly a slave or freedman of some wealth and an important man in the Corinthian community), who sends greetings with Paul to the church in Rome (Rom 16:23); (3) a friend of Paul's who "remained at Corinth" (2 Tm 4:20).

Erech. Important Sumerian city, located at what is now called Warka near the Euphrates river, 40 miles northwest of Ur and 160 miles south of Baghdad. Genesis 10:10 refers to Erech as the second of four cities founded by Nimrod. Partial excavations have uncovered the city walls, 6 miles in circumference, canals, and the remains of elegant buildings with fluted walls decorated with colored cones and inscriptions. Two ziggurats are among the oldest ever discovered, and several temples date back to the late 4th or early 3rd millennium BC. The use of clay cylinder seals began in Erech, and from the same period have come hundreds of pictographic inscriptions.

Ancient inscriptions indicate that Erech and its surroundings were regarded as extremely beautiful and fertile. Its religious pantheon centered around the aggressive goddess of love, Inanna, who was supposed to have brought to Erech the "divine laws" to which it owed its greatness. She helped Erech to subjugate its enemies and married King Dumuzi to ensure the fertility and prosperity of Sumar. Dumuzi, in turn, was identified with Tammuz, the fertility god widely worshiped in Mesopotamia and Palestine.

Among Erech's rulers in the 3rd millennium was Gilgamesh, hero of the great Akkadian epic. From the time of Hammurabi, Erech became part of Babylonia, and continued to flourish until after 300 BC. Ezra 4:9 refers to "Archevites," or men of Arku, the Assyrian name from which the Hebrew "Erech" is derived. Strabo, Ptolemy, and Pliny mention its renown as a center of learning, chiefly astronomical. They refer also to the practice of banking the waters of the Euphrates, forcing them to flow into the Tigris.

Eri. Gad's 5th son (Gn 46:16) and founder of the Erite family (Nm 26:16).

Eruption. *See* SORE.

Esaias. KJV form of Isaiah, the prophet, in the NT.

See ISAIAH (PERSON).

Esar-haddon. King of Assyria (681–669 BC). Though probably not the eldest son of Sennacherib, he was the eldest surviving son following several internecine murders. Sennacherib was assassinated by his sons Adrammelech and Sharezer, and civil war ensued between their supporters and those who accepted the youthful newly proclaimed king, Esar-haddon. As the threat from the brothers was eliminated by death or exile, Esar-haddon solidified his position. He ruled from Nineveh and proclaimed his twin sons, Ashurbanipal and Samas-sum-ukin, crown princes of Assyria and Babylonia. His attempt thus to ensure a smooth changeover of rule at his own death was frustrated.

Esar-haddon's immediate task was to settle the rebellious border areas, which he did by launching military campaigns. He installed governors he could rely on, and increased substantially the level of tribute required. Some kings were replaced and others subsequently restored. Of the latter, Manasseh (2 Chr 33:11), taken in chains to Babylon, later continued to reign in Jerusalem, although this incident may not have taken place until the reign of Ashurbanipal. Of the strong cities, Sidon was finally subdued, but Esar-haddon was forced to come to terms with Baslu, king of Tyre. In 675 BC, Esar-haddon invaded Egypt and destroyed the royal city of Memphis together with many other towns and cities. Prince Taharqa, who had fled to Nubia on the initial invasion, continued to rule over Egypt, and subsequently led a rebellion against Esar-haddon. During his second Egyptian campaign Esar-haddon succumbed to a fatal sickness.

Esar-haddon was a strong, cruel, and fearless ruler who was proud of his achievements.

A stele of Esar-haddon that shows a seed plow and other implements.

He maintained dominion over a vast area, claiming control not only of Babylonia and Syria but also of Egypt and Ethiopia, the lands bordering on Assyria, and some of the islands of the eastern Mediterranean. He built a palace at Kar-esarhaddon near Nineveh and restored the fabled temple of Ashur originally constructed by Shalmaneser I about 1250 BC. He commemorated the deeds of his reign on numerous stelae and prisms. Esar-haddon is mentioned in 2 Kings 19:37; Isaiah 37:38; and Ezra 4:2 (v. 10 is possibly also a reference).

See ASSYRIA, ASSYRIANS.

Esau. Isaac's son, and the older twin brother of Jacob (Gn 25:24–26), who was given this name because of the hair on his body at birth. The reddish color of the baby together with the color appearing in the episode of the lentil soup (Gn 25:30) led to the use of the term Edom, or "red." The Edomites claimed to be descended from Esau, and naming their land Seir may have been an attempt to retain an association with the word *sair*, meaning "hairy."

A proficient hunter, Esau brought tasty wild meat to his father, who enjoyed its stronger flavor much more than that of the mild meat provided from the family flocks by Jacob. When hungry one day following an unsuccessful hunting expedition, Esau was persuaded to surrender his right of primogeniture in return for food (Gn 25:29–34). Archaeological information from Nuzi shows that giving up the birthright to another member of the family was not unknown. Esau's marriage to two local women who were not descendants of Abraham made life extremely difficult for his parents (Gn 26:35). This may have been the reason why his mother, Rebekah, decided to tutor Jacob in the means of obtaining the patriarchal blessing rightly belonging to his elder brother Esau (Gn 27).

Esau's anger on discovering the perfidious deception of his brother prompted Jacob to leave for Haran, though 20 years later, through the generous forgiveness of Esau, the brothers were reunited (Gn 33:4–16).

At birth Jacob had come into the world grasping the heel of Esau, an omen that was interpreted to show that the Edomite descendants of Esau would be subject to the offspring of Jacob. The subservient relationship between the Edomites and the Israelites in the time of David (2 Sm 8:11–14; 1 Chr 18:13) continued until the time of Jehoram (2 Kgs 8:20–22; 2 Chr 21:8–10). Following a rebellion in 845 BC the Edomites gained their independence for a while but were reconquered by Amaziah (796–767 BC). Regaining their freedom in 735 BC, they subsequently remained independent of Judah.

See EDOM, EDOMITES.

Eschatology. Branch of systematic theology concerned with the study of the last things, whether in relation to the individual or the world.

Topics of Eschatology. *Death.* The Bible teaches that all humans will die (Heb 9:27). The only exceptions will be those who are still alive when Christ returns (1 Thes 4:17). Physical death, or the "first death," is the separation of the soul from the body. Because of the presence of sin in the world, death has come upon everyone (Rom 5:12).

The Intermediate State. This refers to the condition of the person between the time of death and the resurrection. The traditional orthodox view is that believers experience a state of conscious bliss in the presence of the Lord, while unbelievers are tormented by separation from the presence of God. This, however, is a relatively incomplete state when compared with the final destiny of each. Some groups, such as Seventh-day Adventists, have held a belief in a type of "soul sleep," or unconsciousness, between death and resurrection. Still others, notably Roman Catholics, believe in a place of purging in preparation for the future life.

The Second Coming. Scripture teaches that at the end of time Christ will return in a personal, bodily form (Acts 1:11). No one knows exactly when this will occur, and it will consequently catch some by surprise, coming as a thief in the night (Lk 12:39,40). Although the time is not known, the fact that it will occur is very definite. Many of Jesus' parables (esp. in Mt 24,25) refer to this fact and to the appropriateness of alert, faithful, and intensive activity.

The Resurrection. All who have died will come to life. This will be a bodily resurrection, a resumption of bodily existence of each person. For believers this will take place in connection with the second coming of Christ, and will involve the transformation of the body of this present flesh into a new, perfected body (1 Cor 15:35–56). The Bible also indicates a resurrection of unbelievers, unto eternal death (Jn 5:28,29).

The Judgment. There will be a time of judgment, in which the Lord will determine the spiritual condition of all who have lived, based on their relationship to him. On these grounds some will be sent off to everlasting reward and others to eternal punishment. Some theologians distinguish between the time when believers and unbelievers will be judged. Some see as many as seven different judgments occurring.

The Final States. The Bible teaches the existence of heaven, a place of eternal joy, where Christians are in the presence of God, and of hell, a state of anguished separation of unbelievers from the presence of God. These are fixed states, determined by the decisions made within this life.

The Millennium. Many Christians believe there will be an earthly reign of God, called the millennium, immediately preceding the final judgment. This belief is based on Revelation 20:4–7. Those who hold that Christ will return personally to inaugurate this period are called premillennialists. Others, who teach that the kingdom will be established through the progressive successful preaching of the gospel, are termed postmillennialists. Still others, called amillennialists, do not believe that there will be any earthly reign of Christ at all, interpreting the 1,000 years of Revelation 20 symbolically.

The Great Tribulation. The Bible speaks of a time of great anguish or tribulation, which will come upon the earth, exceeding anything that has ever occurred before. Some, identifying this with the 70th week of Daniel 9:24–27, believe it will be of seven years duration. Some believe the church will be present to experience this, the Lord not returning until the end of the period. These are termed posttribulationists. Others, known as pretribulationists, believe that the Lord's second coming will be in two stages, or phases—that, in addition to his public second coming, Christ will come for his church, to remove them from the world, or "rapture" them, before the great tribulation. Still others, known as midtribulationists, believe that the church will be present for the first half of the seven years but will be removed before the severe part of the tribulation begins.

Recent History. In recent years there has been an increased interest in eschatology. Some have defined it in such a way that it is almost all-inclusive, rather than merely a part of theology. Since the Christ-event was the introduction of the new age, much of the NT must be considered eschatology.

Some have carried this so far as to suggest that the supposedly future events were already accomplished. Thus, the second coming of Christ took place at Pentecost. There is no future event to look forward to. This view is termed "realized eschatology."

The theology of hope has extended this eschatological conception into all areas of theology, even into the doctrine of God. Thus, whereas the transcendence of God had been thought of as the God who has his being above or beyond us, these people think of him as lying before us. He is the God who is to be. His transcendence is thought of in relation to time, not to space.

Conservatives have retained a more traditional conception of eschatology. There has been great interest in the predictive prophetic passages of Scripture, as indicated by the popularity of books like *The Late Great Planet Earth* (1973). Many have seen a correlation between current events in the Middle East and passages such as Daniel 9, Matthew 24,25, 1 Thessalonians, and Revelation.

Cautions. Sometimes eschatology has been a divisive force within Christian circles, as believers quarreled over minor points. In some cases denominations in which there was agreement on the major doctrines of eschatology have split over a minor point, such as the tribulational views. Another danger to be avoided is date setting. While we are to be alert to the "signs of the times," we must remember that God has not revealed the exact time of our Lord's return to any human being, or even to the angels (Mt 24:36). Some have believed that they could determine the exact time of the Lord's return. When their calculations proved incorrect, these believers had their faith jeopardized as a result.

Practical Values. Properly understood and applied, eschatology has a powerful positive significance for Christians. It is to be a source of comfort (1 Thes 4:18), of encouragement (1 Cor 15:58), of challenge to watchfulness and faithful service, and the assurance of reward (Mt 25:14–30). Because the time is limited, Christians are to use faithfully the opportunities that are theirs. Because of the certainty of our Lord's return, we are to be filled with hope and courage. MILLARD J. ERICKSON

See DEATH; SECOND COMING OF CHRIST; TRIBULATION; MILLENNIUM; HEAVEN; HELL; RESURRECTION; INTERMEDIATE STATE; JUDGMENT; ETERNAL LIFE; LAST JUDGMENT; DAY OF THE LORD; LAST DAYS; WRATH OF GOD; APOCALYPTIC; SEVENTY WEEKS, DANIEL'S.

Bibliography. G.R. Beasley-Murray, *Jesus and the Future;* J.A. Beet, *The Last Things;* O. Cullmann, *Christ and Time;* T.F. Glasson, *The Second Advent;* A.A. Holkema, *The Bible and the Future;* G.E. Ladd, *The Presence of the Future;* A.T. Lincoln, *Now and Not Yet;* J.D. Pentecost, *Things to Come;* H. Ridderbos, *The Coming of the Kingdom;* G. Vos, *The Pauline Eschatology;* L.J. Wood, *The Bible and Future Events.*

Esdraelon, Plain of. Greek name, in the Apocrypha, for a portion of the valley of Jezreel, which separates the hills of Galilee and the hills of Samaria.

See JEZREEL, VALLEY OF.

Esek. Name Isaac gave to a well dug by his servants in the valley of Gerar (Gn 26:20). When the herdsmen of Gerar claimed it belonged to them, Isaac relinquished Esek and another well, called Sitnah, to induce the men of Gerar to allow him to live peacefully in the land.

Eshan. Town in the hill country of the territory allotted to Judah's tribe for an inheritance (Jos 15:52, KJV Eshean). Its exact location is unknown.

Esh-baal. King Saul's fourth son, who became Israel's king after his father's death. Esh-baal literally means "man of Baal," or "Baal exists" (1 Chr 8:33; 9:39). During the period of the judges and the early monarchy many Hebrew names were compounded with "baal," a word that can mean "master" or "possessor." Later generations were reluctant to speak the name "baal," so "bosheth" (shame) was substituted (cf. Hos 2:16,17). Thus Esh-baal was altered to Ish-bosheth (2 Sm 2:8), which means "man of shame." Perhaps later copyists changed the name in the Book of Samuel because it was read aloud in synagogue services, whereas Chronicles was not.

After the death of Saul and his older sons, Abner, commander of Saul's army, installed Ish-bosheth as Israel's king (2 Sm 2:8,9). Judah's tribe, however, followed King David, who struggled with Ish-bosheth for leadership of all the tribes. The conflict lasted a long time, but the house of David gradually overwhelmed the house of Saul (2 Sm 3:1). Abner deserted Ish-bosheth and was murdered by Joab, one of David's men (2 Sm 3:27), thus removing an important leader of Israel and causing the people to despair (2 Sm 4:1). Soon afterward Ish-bosheth was murdered by two of his captains (2 Sm 4:7). Although David disapproved of the deaths of Abner and Ish-bosheth, the last obstacles to his kingship over all the tribes were now removed.

See DAVID; ISRAEL, HISTORY OF; SAUL # 2.

Eshban. Dishon's second son and grandson of Seir the Horite (Gn 36:26; 1 Chr 1:41).

Eshcol (Person). Amorite who, with his brothers Mamre and Aner, helped the patriarch Abraham defeat the forces of Chedorlaomer and rescue Lot and his family (Gn 14:13,24).

Eshcol (Place). Valley near Hebron from which the spies sent by Moses brought back pomegranates, figs, and a large cluster of grapes (Nm 14:23,24; 32:9; Dt 1:24). This site may be identifiable with 'Ain Eshkali, just north of Hebron.

Eshean. KJV spelling of the town Eshan in Joshua 15:52.

See ESHAN.

Eshek. Descendant of Jonathan, Saul's son. Eshek's grandsons were "mighty men of valor" in the tribe of Benjamin (1 Chr 8:38–40).

Eshkalonite. Inhabitant of the Philistine city Ashkelon (Jos 13:3 KJV).

See ASHKELON.

Eshtaol. Lowland town on the border between Judah and Dan (Jos 15:33; 19:41), always mentioned along with nearby Zorah. In this area the young Samson began to be moved by the Spirit of the Lord (Jgs 13:25), and here he was later buried (Jgs 16:31). Dan's tribe sent out five brave men from Zorah and Eshtaol to seek additional land for tribal expansion. When they reported the vulnerability of the city of Laish, 600 men from Zorah and Eshtaol attacked it, opening the area for occupation by the Danites (Jgs 18).

Eshtemoa (Person). 1. Ishbah's son from Judah's tribe (1 Chr 4:17).
2. Ma-acathite from Judah's tribe (1 Chr 4:19).

Eshtemoa, Eshtemoh (Place). City south of Jerusalem allotted to Judah when Palestine was divided among the 12 tribes (Jos 15:50, Eshtemoh). Eshtemoa was assigned to the Levites (Jos 21:14; 1 Chr 6:57). After an Amalekite victory David sent booty to his allies in Eshtemoa (1 Sm 30:26–31). The site may be modern al-Samu'a, 8 miles south of Hebron.

See LEVITICAL CITIES.

Eshton. Mehir's son and the grandson of Chelub from Judah's tribe (1 Chr 4:11,12).

Esli. Naum's father and ancestor of Jesus, according to Luke's genealogy (3:25).

See GENEALOGY OF JESUS CHRIST.

"E" Source. Designation used by proponents of the Documentary Hypothesis (a critical theory that attributes the five books of Moses to several authors and redactors) for those portions of the Pentateuch supposedly written or edited by someone who preferred the name Elohim, one of the Hebrew names for God used in the OT.

See DOCUMENTARY HYPOTHESIS.

Espousal. *See* MARRIAGE, MARRIAGE CUSTOMS.

Esrom. KJV rendering of Hezron, Perez's son, in Matthew 1:3 and Luke 3:33.

See HEZRON (PERSON) # 2.

Essenes. Jewish sect or community in Palestine in the last century BC and the 1st century AD.
The Name. The sect is called *Esseni, Osseni, Ossaei, Essaeans,* and other variations; sometimes two different forms are found in the same author. No satisfactory explanation of the name has been given, but a number of scholars tend to prefer "healers" (Heb. *'iśśiyīm,* Aram. *'ăsīyâ*), which hardly seems likely since the term describes the Therapeutae ("Healers"), a sect that was only distantly related to the Essenes, if at all.
Sources of Information. The principal sources of information about the Essenes are (1) Philo of Alexandria, a Jew who lived in Egypt from about 30 BC to some time after AD 40, in his works, *Let Every Good Man Be Free* and *Apology for the Jews;* (2) Flavius Josephus, a Jew of Palestine and later of Rome, who lived from AD 37 to about AD 100, in his works *War of the Jews* and *Jewish Antiquities*—our most extensive sources; (3) Pliny the Elder, a Roman who died in AD 79 and who may have been in Palestine with Titus during the Jewish War, in his *Natural History;* and (4) Hippolytus of Rome, in his work *A Refutation of All Heresies,* written about AD 230 and largely dependent on Josephus. Other writers sometimes mentioned are: Hegesippus, who was at Rome sometime in the 2nd century, known only through quotations by Eusebius; Epiphanius (310–403; bishop of Constantia, Cyprus); and Porphyry (347–420; bishop of Gaza). Nothing significant is added by these last three, and indeed little of reliable value is added by Hippolytus, so we are principally dependent

on Philo, Josephus, and Pliny. Josephus tells us that he determined to know the three Jewish "sects" intimately, so he joined the Essenes when he was 16. But since he was a Pharisee by the time he was 19, and since it took at least three years for the initiatory rites of the Essenes, we must conclude that he did not have time or opportunity to learn much about the inner life of the Essenes.

Origin and History. The first mention of the Essenes, as well as that of the Pharisees and the Sadducees, is in the time of Jonathan (160–143 BC), successor of Judas Maccabeus (see Josephus, *Antiq.* 13.5.9). Josephus calls these groups "sects" (Greek *haireseis*), a term that sometimes connotes heretical movements, but this is a later meaning of the word. Luke uses the very same term for Pharisees (Acts 15:5; 26:5), Sadducees, (Acts 5:17), and Christians (Acts 24:5,14; 28:22).

The Maccabean revolt began in 167 BC. The background of the uprising had been a struggle between the Seleucid Greeks and the Ptolemaic Greeks, with Palestine as the object of the struggle. The Seleucids won in 198 BC, but there were pro-Syrian and pro-Egyptian parties in Judea. Moreover, Hellenism, which was strongly promoted by the Seleucids, had taken a deep hold on many Jews. In order to participate in the athletic games, some Jews even resorted to operations to obliterate the sign of circumcision (1 Mc 1:15). The Seleucid king Antiochus IV Epiphanes sold the Jewish high priesthood to the highest bidder, Menelaus, in 168; and when this was rejected by the Jews, violent persecution broke out. Somewhere along the line a group of pious Jews came into existence, and they joined the Maccabees in the revolt. We know them as the Hasidim (or Hasideans, Assideans, "pious ones"; cf. 1 Mc 2:42).

Because of numerous similarities in doctrine it is generally accepted that the Pharisees are either the direct descendants of the Hasidim or one of two or more groups of descendants. It is further generally accepted that the Essenes are a group that split either from the Pharisees or from the Hasidim. Qumran (the community of the Dead Sea Scrolls) is looked upon either as a branch of the Essenes or as another closely related group of separatists whose origin was at approximately the same point in time.

Josephus speaks of only three Jewish sects: Pharisees, Sadducees, and Essenes (*Antiq.* 18.1.2). Therefore it is often concluded that these were the only Jewish sects at that time. This is a false conclusion. We know of at least seven Jewish sects, and perhaps as many as 12. There is probably some overlap, and it is not always clear whether a particular group

Ruins at Qumran, with a mill in the foreground.

should be described as a religious party (e.g., the Zealots). But we can argue against Josephus' number of sects by other data he supplies. According to Josephus, there were 6,000 Pharisees (*Antiq.* 17.2.4), 4,000 Essenes (*Antiq.* 18.1.5; cf. Philo, *Every Good Man* 75), and the Sadducees were fewer in number than the Pharisees (cf. *War* 2.8.14). This would account for, at most, 16,000 persons, and the population of Judea was well beyond that figure. Moreover, Josephus himself speaks of a "fourth philosophy" (*Antiq.* 18.1.6), which some scholars identify with the Zealots, although Josephus never does so. We can only conclude that in Josephus' view there were three principal or significant sects or groups of Jews.

The Essenes left the cities of Palestine and lived in the towns and villages. Pliny locates them west of the Dead Sea and says, "Below them was En-gedi" (*Natural History* 5.15.73), a statement which could mean either that En-gedi was at a lower elevation or that it was to the south. Scholars are not unanimous in the interpretation of this statement.

Admission to the Sect. Admission to the Essenes was a long, complicated process, consisting of one year as a postulant and two additional years of limited participation in the community. The novice took solemn oaths, which included his relationship to God and to his fellow members. He swore to hate the wicked and to love truth, to conceal nothing from the community and to reveal nothing to outsiders, and to transmit doctrines exactly as he received them. Until he took these oaths he could not touch the common food.

Community Life. When a new member joined the Essenes, he turned over all property to the community. The individual members were without goods, property, or homes. They lived frugally, having only what was necessary for life. They despised riches, had no slaves, and did not engage in commerce. They worked in fields or at crafts that contributed to peace, and would not make instruments of war. They dwelt in brotherhoods, ate together, held property in common, had a common purse and a common store of clothing. They always wore white clothing.

Evidence is somewhat confusing about their views on marriage. They either banned it entirely or disdained it, counting continence as one of their virtues. There were Essenes who did marry, but these looked upon the marriage relationship as existing only for the purpose of raising children so that the race might continue.

There is also mixed evidence concerning children. According to Philo, they had no children, no adolescents, not even young men. Josephus, on the other hand, tells us that they adopted children, and the Essenes who married raised children of their own.

The Essenes were divided into 4 lots or ranks, and would do nothing unless ordered by superiors, except for works of mercy. They obeyed their elders. When 10 sat, one would not speak if the 9 were opposed. They refrained from spitting in assembly or spitting to the right. Justice was dispensed at an assembly of 100 members or more. For serious offenses the penalty was expulsion from the community, and the expelled member usually starved to death because of the tremendous oaths he had taken.

A Typical Day. Josephus describes a typical day in the life of the Essenes. They rose before dawn and recited prayers to the rising sun (which probably is not to be interpreted as sun worship). Then each man worked at his craft until the 5th hour (11 AM). At that time the community assembled, put on linen loincloths, bathed in cold water, and then went to the building that was restricted to members, to a dining hall that was further restricted to those who were pure. Each Essene received bread and one bowlful of food. The priest said a prayer before anyone was permitted to touch the food, and another prayer after the meal. Then the members laid aside their sacred garments and resumed their work until evening. The evening meal was in the same manner as the noon meal. They ate quietly and spoke only in turn, eating and drinking only what they needed to satisfy them.

Religious Beliefs. It is somewhat risky to attempt to reconstruct Essene theology from Josephus and Philo, for both of these writers thought in philosophical rather than theological forms.

The Essenes were not concerned with logic or natural philosophy, but rather devoted themselves to ethics. Josephus likens them to the Greek Pythagoreans (*Antiq.* 15.10.4), but he does not explain this further. The Essenes were concerned with purity and holy minds. They rejected oaths (apparently excepting the tremendous oath they took upon entering the sect), and considered their word sufficient. They observed the 7th day, going to synagogues and sitting according to age. One would read and another explain, making use of symbols and the triple use of definitions (which may be a reference to the rabbinic method of exegesis). They would do no work on the sabbath. There is confusion concerning the matter of sacrifices; either they did not offer sacrifices (Philo, *Every Good Man*), or they sacrificed among themselves and did not send sacrifices to the temple (Josephus, *Antiq.* 18.1.5). They sent offerings to the temple, according to this same passage in Josephus. The name of the lawgiver (Moses? or God himself?) was an object of great veneration.

The Essenes studied holy books and were skilled at predicting the future. Josephus tells of one Essene, Menahem, who foretold that Herod would be king (*Antiq.* 15.10.5). They also studied the works of the ancients (which appears to mean works other than the Scriptures), and became proficient in the knowledge of healing, of roots, and of stones. The Essenes believed that their souls were immortal; but, as Josephus seems to have understood this doctrine, the body was "corruptible and its constituent matter impermanent" (*War* 2.8.11), which may imply a denial of the resurrection.

The material available to us is hardly satisfactory for reconstructing Essene theology. It is clear, however, that they were Jews, devoted to the Law, but with certain emphases or aberrations that set them apart from both the Pharisees and the Sadducees. They were ascetic, although some of them married, and they were pacifists, although Josephus tells of an Essene named John who was a general in the army (*War* 2.20.4). Above all, they were exclusivistic, withdrawing from other Jews and living a communal or communistic type of life.

The Essenes and the Qumran Community. There are many similarities between the Essenes and the people of the Dead Sea Scrolls. Both were Jewish sects. Both were communal groups that had withdrawn from the common stream of Judaism. Both were located west of the Dead Sea. Both had long and rigid processes for admission of new members. Both had an oath of admission. Both hated the wicked and loved the members of the community. Both required handing over all property to the sect. Both kept their secrets to their own group. The daily life—prayers, ritual bathing, common meals, the study and interpreta-

The Manual of Discipline from Qumran.

tion of the Bible, and concern with purity—is markedly similar. Scrupulous observance of the sabbath, the division into ranks or lots, and the authority of elders and superiors are features of each group. Both had injunctions against spitting in assembly. Both had a minimum group of 10. Both had laws of expulsion for serious offenses.

The differences are also noteworthy, and not as often pointed out. Obviously the Qumran community could not have constituted all of the Essenes, but were at most a small fraction (perhaps 200) of the 4,000 Essenes. Moreover, they were at best only one of the towns and villages of the Essenes. If Qumranians worked at crafts, we know nothing of it either from their texts or from the archaeology of Qumran. Similarly, we know nothing of their attitude toward war or the implements of war. But we do know from the War Scroll (1QM) that they had an elaborate concept of the final war, with an army, weapons, maneuvers, and the like, and they do not sound like pacifists (cf. 1QS 9:16,22,23; 10:18; 1QSa 1:19–21). It appears that the Qumranians did engage in commerce (CD 13:14,15). We have no information about any common store of clothing at Qumran. From the Dead Sea literature we know that there were provisions for marriage, for young children, adolescents, and young men. Of course, the Qumranians may have been the marrying Essenes to whom Josephus refers. Admission to the Qumran group was a two-year process; to the Essenes it was three years.

We know nothing of Qumran prayers to the sun or of daily bathing, although some of the "cisterns" were probably immersion pools. Unlike the Essenes, the Qumranians did use oaths, and there are extended sections on oaths in their literature (CD 9:8–12; 15:1–10; 16:6–18). The Qumran attitude toward sacrifices is not entirely clear, but there is provision for sending sacrifices to the temple. We know of no aversion to oil among the Qumranians such as is described for the Essenes.

There is no evidence that the Qumranians used triple definitions in their biblical interpretation. There is a minimum use of symbols in their writings. There is no evidence that they studied the knowledge of healing, roots, or stones. If they were experts at predicting the future, we have no record of it.

The seating arrangement at Qumran was by rank and not by age, as among the Essenes. Rank was altered by an annual examination at Qumran. There is no indication that justice at Qumran was handled by 100 men; rather, it seems to have been administered by a council of 15 (1QS 8:1) or 10 (CD 9:4,5).

In view of the similarities we must conclude that there was some kind of relationship between the Essenes and the Qumran community. In view of the differences we are forced to the conclusion that they were not exactly the same. There are several possible explanations: (1) The Essenes and the Qumranians may have started out as the same split-off from the Hasidim, and then later split again. In fact, the Dead Sea Scrolls, particularly the Damascus Document (CD), hint at some kind of split in the earlier period of the group. (2) The Essenes of Josephus and Philo are about a century later than the literature of the Qumranians, and may have altered somewhat during that period of time. (3) The Essenes were located in a number of towns and villages, and may have developed significant local variations, so that Josephus may have drawn his description from one location, Philo and Pliny from others, while the Qumran group represents yet another local variant form. There is little to guide a preference for any one of these explanations.

The Essenes and Christianity. From time to time there have been attempts to show that Jesus and the early Christians were Essenes. A full treatment of the discussion can be found in J.B. Lightfoot, *St. Paul's Epistles to the Colossians and to Philemon* (London: Macmillan, 1875), pp. 82–95, 114–179. There is nothing to be gained in reopening this discussion, unless, of course, we substitute the Qumran materials for what Philo, Josephus, and Pliny have told us about the Essenes, a methodology that would be highly objectionable.

It is possible to take certain sayings of Jesus in the Gospels, certain passages in Acts, and certain statements in Paul's epistles, and construct a fantasy Christianity that is ascetic, communal, and legalistic. Point by point we could demonstrate parallels with Essene beliefs and practices. But such techniques are a denial of true scholarship. Taken as a whole, the teachings of Jesus exalt marriage and the family, and place the rights and proper use of property in the conscience of the owner, while legalism is strongly rejected. The same can certainly be said for the early church as portrayed in Acts and for the teaching of Paul in his epistles. By no proper use of the materials can Christianity be equated with Essenism, or, for that matter, with Qumranism.

This is not to deny, however, that there are elements of Essenism that can be compared with elements of Christianity. We should not object to the theory that some Essenes may have heard the gospel and become Christians. Nor is there any sufficient reason to reject the notion that certain Essene ideas could have been influential in the early church. A careful study of the NT will show that there were many currents and crosscurrents in the early church. The differences between Peter and Paul provide only one example out of many. If the ultimate redemptive purpose of God is to remove the divisions that man has erected, to make one those who are divided (cf. Eph 2:14), then we may properly conclude that the church on earth must be the mixing bowl where all kinds of ingredients are brought together, to be sifted, blended, and purified by God's Spirit (cf. Eph 4:13).

The Essenes were a part of God's people who were following a way which they believed to be the right way. Some of their beliefs were good, such as the sanctity of their word, their concern for works of healing and deeds of mercy, and their self-denial and devotion to honest work. Some of their beliefs were not good, such as their exclusivism, their low view of the place of women, and their legalistic attitude toward God's Law. But is it not so with all man-made systems? Only the Scriptures of the OT and NT are the Word of God, the infallible rule of faith and life; and only as we let the Spirit apply God's Word to our faith and life can we develop into representative members of the community of God.

WILLIAM SANFORD LASOR

See DEAD SEA SCROLLS; JUDAISM; PHARISEES.

Bibliography. C.D. Ginsburg, *The Essenes;* D. Howlett, *The Essenes and Christianity;* K. Kohler, "Essenes," *Jewish Encyclopedia;* W.S. LaSor, *The Dead Sea Scrolls and the NT,* pp 131–41; R. Marcus, "Pharisees, Essenes, and Gnostics," *Journal of Biblical Literature* 73 (1953): 157–61.

Esther (Person).   One of two names borne by the Jewish queen of Persia. Hadassah (Hebrew "Myrtle") apparently was her Jewish name (Est 2:7) and Esther (Persian "Star") her name as queen of Persia. Some scholars speculate a connection with the Babylonian goddess Ishtar, since exiled Jews were occasionally given pagan names (see Dn 1:7).

Esther was an orphan from the tribe of Benjamin who lived with the Jewish exiles in Persia. She was reared by her cousin Mordecai, a minor government official and covert leader of the Jewish community (see Est 3:5,6) in Susa, capital of the Persian kingdom. Esther became queen after King Ahasuerus (Xerxes) became displeased with Queen Vashti when she refused to obey his command to attend a festival (Est 1:11,12).

After Esther's coronation she discreetly won Xerxes' confidence by informing him of an assassination plot (Est 2:21–23). The favor she won in the king's eyes enabled her to deliver her family and her people from a massacre by Haman, a high official to the king.

The feast of Purim was instituted to celebrate God's deliverance of his people through Esther and Mordecai. This festival is still observed annually by Jews.

See ESTHER, BOOK OF.

Esther, Book of.   OT book telling the story of a Jewish woman's protection of her people after her marriage to a gentile king.

Author.   The Book of Esther is an anonymous composition. The reference in 9:20 that Mordecai "recorded these things" implies that part, if not all, of the book was written by him. The absence of God's name in the Book of Esther may be due to the fact that the author intended the book to become part of the official Persian court record. The use of God's name might have prevented that from happening.

The author of the book had considerable knowledge of Persian court life and customs. Thus, Mordecai might be identified with a *Morduka*, mentioned as a Persian court official in the reign of Darius I (521–486 BC) and Xerxes (485–465 BC).

Date, Origin, and Purpose.   Immediate impressions favor a date for the Book of Esther shortly after 465 BC, if Ahasuerus is identified with Xerxes, who died that year. Many contemporary scholars, however, favor a later date. The apocryphal book of Ecclesiasticus, written about 180 BC, refers to that period. Jewish heroes are mentioned there, but Esther and Mordecai are not included. Some also suggest the period of the Maccabees as the time of the book's writing. Others have identified it with a cultic story from ancient Babylon, associating Esther with the goddess Ishtar and Mordecai with the god Marduk. The earliest postbiblical reference to the feast of Purim is 2 Maccabees 15:36, probably written around 75 BC.

The Book of Esther claims to record events in Persia sometime during the 5th century BC, surrounding the selection of Esther as queen. If a later date is preferred, the book can be viewed as written to encourage Jews during a time of persecution. One definite purpose of the Book of Esther is to explain the origin of the Jewish feast of Purim (9:16–28). The term "purim" is probably related to the Assyrian word *puru*, meaning a small stone used for casting lots.

Teaching and Canonicity. The major theological problem with the Book of Esther is the absence of any mention of God and the lack of even an intimation of divine providence. As a result, some scholars in both Jewish and Christian circles question its canonicity. But closer observation reveals an obvious providential dimension in the book. The reference to "fasting" in 4:16, for example, implies prayer as well as abstinence from food. Esther's being in the right place at the right time is no accident. The fall of Haman is also not accidental. On the negative side, the extreme measures taken in hanging Haman's sons reflect a collective view of guilt that is probably not acceptable today (9:13,14). Implicit too is the theme of God's protection of his covenant people even in times of persecution. That fact has made the Book of Esther a favorite of Jews throughout history.

Its practical implications, however, have not kept some from questioning the book's genuineness as a part of the Bible. The Book of Esther appears in the third part of the Jewish canon, as part of the five scrolls known as the Megilloth; its companions there are Ruth, Song of Songs, Ecclesiastes, and Lamentations. The Septuagint (Greek version of the OT) contains 107 extra verses in the Book of Esther. These additions form part of the Apocrypha in English versions of the Bible. Even as late as the Reformation era Esther's canonicity was being debated, and some contemporary evangelicals have raised doubts about its value. Its canonicity is favored by (1) its history of acceptance in both Judaism and the Christian church, and (2) its illustrative value for teaching God's providential care of the Jewish people (see Rom 9–11; Rv 7,14).

Content. The Book of Esther portrays the reign of King Ahasuerus, whose empire stretched from India to Ethiopia (1:1–9). The center of his empire was in Susa (Shushan), in Persia. Because Queen Vashti disgraced the king by refusing his order to appear in court, she was removed, and a search began for a new queen (1:10–22). A young Jewish woman named Hadassah, without parents and living with her kinsman Mordecai, was selected to replace Queen Vashti (2:1–18). Early in her reign Esther and Mordecai helped to save the king's life (2:19–23). A man named Haman, who was promoted to an influential position in the palace court, plotted to kill the Jews because he hated Mordecai (3:1–15). Mordecai intervened through Queen Esther, and the queen called on the Jews in Susa to fast for deliverance (4:1–17). Esther's intervention with the king led to a sleepless night for Ahasuerus (5:1–6:1). He re-

viewed the records of "memorable deeds," and discovered that Mordecai's earlier help had gone unrewarded. When Haman arrived to initiate his plot against the Jews, the king ordered him to honor Mordecai (6:1–14). When Haman's plot was then discovered, the schemer was hanged (7:1–10). The king honored Mordecai and sent out an edict protecting the Jews from harm (8:1–17). The Jews, by the king's permission, slew the soldiers who would earlier have killed them in Haman's plot (9:1–16). To celebrate their national deliverance the Jews planned a great celebration (9:17–10:3). That celebration became the festival of Purim, a time of feasting and distribution of gifts to all, especially to the poor.

Historical Background. A number of historical problems have been noted: (1) Xerxes' known wife was named Amestris, according to the historian Herodotus; but it is possible and likely that the king had more than one wife. (2) The implication that Mordecai went into exile in 597 BC would have made him about 120 years old during the reign of Xerxes; but the text of 2:5,6 might mean that Mordecai's great-grandfather was the original exile rather than Mordecai. (3) Various details seem fanciful to some modern readers: a banquet lasting 180 days; Esther's 12-month beauty treatment; a gallows 83 feet tall; the Jews killing 75,000 of Xerxes' subjects. But what appears mythological sometimes turns out to be truly historical (see 1:4; 2:7,12; 7:9; 9:16).

Several elements in the Book of Esther point to a genuinely historical setting for the book. Ahasuerus is usually identified with Xerxes. Xerxes' father was Darius, from whom have come some notable inscriptions and relief sculptures, one of them showing Darius seated on his throne with Xerxes standing behind him. Xerxes is believed to have been a weak-willed man in domestic affairs, easily influenced by flattering and scheming courtiers. On the field of battle, however, he was a vigorous leader who ferociously pursued his objectives. His energetic suppression of a revolt in Egypt was a prelude to mustering a navy to attack Athens. Only the skill and daring of the Greek forces at the naval battle of Salamis (480 BC) saved Greece from complete Persian occupation. Xerxes eventually lost the war and retired to his elegant palaces at Persepolis and Susa. He rejected the traditional gods of Egypt and Babylon and became a devotee of Ahuramazda, the Persian spirit of good.

DONALD M. LAKE

See ESTHER (PERSON); PERSIA, PERSIANS.

Bibliography. S.B. Berg, *The Book of Esther;* C.F. Keil, *The Books of Ezra, Nehemiah, and Esther;* L.B. Paton, *A Critical and Exegetical Commentary on the Book of Esther;* A. Raleigh, *The Book of Esther;* A.W. Streane, *The Book of Esther.*

Scene south of Bethlehem and presumably near Etam.

Etam. 1. Rocky area in western Judah where Samson hid from his pursuers (Jgs 15:8,11).

2. Unknown site located in Simeonite territory (1 Chr 4:32).

3. Town in the Judean uplands near Bethlehem fortified by Rehoboam of Judah after the division of the kingdom (2 Chr 11:6). It is identified with Khirbet el-Khokh, just southwest of Bethlehem. The spring at Etam supplied Jerusalem with additional water in the Greek and Roman periods.

Eternal Life. Mode of existence referred to in Scripture characterized by either timelessness or endlessness, and especially by a qualitative difference from mortal life. The perspective of the biblical writers flowed from an understanding of a living God who existed prior to the world's creation, and will continue to exist when the end of time arrives. God's gift to those who are obedient and responsible to him is designated as eternal life or some such synonym. John's Gospel provides the most definitive material on such eternal life.

The phrase "eternal life" occurs only once in the Greek version of the OT (Dn 12:2, with the basic meaning of "the life of the age," designating the life of the age beyond the resurrection from the dead). The primary meaning of "life" in the OT, however, is the quality of well-being in earthly existence.

In the intertestamental period, the rabbinic distinction between "this age" and "the age which is to come" emphasized that the concept of life in the new age consisted of a qualitative, rather than simply a quantitative, distinction from the present age.

The Greek word translated "eternal" is derived from the word for "age" or "eon." The setting of the NT within the context of Judaism, with its concept of a living God and the consequent promise of "the age which is to come," gives depth and color to the meaning of the adjective "eternal." Jesus Christ's coming as God's definitive revelation brings the possibility of the qualities of life in the future messianic age into present reality.

The rich young ruler came to Jesus and asked for directions on how to inherit eternal life (Mk 10:17). He was obviously thinking of resurrection in the age to come. Jesus answered in the same terms (Mk 10:30).

In his response to the rich young ruler Jesus equated the reception of eternal life with entrance into the kingdom of God (Mk 10:23–25). The kingdom of God is not simply a future event but is already inaugurated in Jesus' life, ministry, and teachings. The kingdom is a gift of life available while the follower still lives within the present age. Many of Jesus' parables emphasize this point (e.g., those in Mt 13). The Beatitudes in the Sermon on the Mount (Mt 5:3–12) reinforce the concept of a present blessedness that includes salvation, forgiveness, and righteousness. Thus eternal life is a present blessing available to those who submit to God's reign and are enjoying the blessings of this new era of salvation before the final consummation at the present age's end.

The apostle Paul's summary of eternal life is found in 2 Corinthians 5:17: "Therefore, if any one is in Christ, he is a new creation; the old has passed away, behold, the new has come." God's redemptive activity in Christ at Calvary provided full reconciliation with God. The new life is life "in the Spirit" or "in Christ." The quality of life anticipated in OT prophecy has now become a reality. The "new creation" is the climax and goal of God's redemptive activities through the ages.

The presence of the new life—the eternal life—is vividly described in 2 Corinthians 3:18: "And we all, with unveiled face, beholding the glory of the Lord, are being changed into his likeness from one degree of glory to another; for this comes from the Lord who is the Spirit." The transforming presence of God through Christ is a "treasure in earthen vessels, to show that the transcendent power belongs to God and not to us" (2 Cor 4:7).

It is surprising that Paul never clearly referred to "eternal life" in the way John did, but he was describing the same experience in different metaphors. Paul's usages of "eternal life" (Rom 2:7; 6:22; Gal 6:8; 1 Tm 1:16; Ti 1:2; 3:7) have primary reference to the consummation of all things at the end of history as we know it. The numerous passages in which Paul speaks of walking "in newness of life" (e.g., Rom 6:4), however, clearly indicate that he understood that eternal life must not be limited to the hereafter.

The definitive discussions of eternal life come from John's Gospel. John's purpose delineates the crucial significance of the concept: "But these are written that you may believe that Jesus is the Christ, the Son of God, and that believing you may have life" (Jn 20:31). The earliest Johannine reference to eternal life is found in John 3:15.

John clearly shared in the Jewish expectation of the age to come with its anticipated blessings (e.g., Jn 3:36; 4:14; 5:29,39; 6:27; 12:25). Eternal life is defined by the special gifts of the messianic age when it arrives at consummation. Lazarus' resurrection (Jn 11) was a living parable demonstrating the future life available to those who trust in Christ. Martha, before her brother's actual resurrection, asserted her belief that Lazarus would be raised on the last day (Jn 11:24). Jesus responded that he himself is the resurrection and the life, and that those who believe in him will never die, even if they die physically (Jn 11:25,26).

The central emphasis of John's Gospel, however, does not lie in the anticipated future, but in the present experience of that future life. The life of the age to come is already available in Christ to the believer. The metaphors with which Jesus defined his own mission emphasize the present new life: living water that is "a spring of water welling up to eternal life" (Jn 4:14); living bread that satisfies the world's spiritual hunger (Jn 6:35–40); the light of the world who leads his followers into the light of life (Jn 8:12); the good shepherd who brings abundant life (Jn 10:10); the life giver who raises the dead (Jn 11:25); the way, the truth, and the life (Jn 14:6); and the genuine vine who sustains those who abide in him (Jn 15:5).

Jesus was very careful to note that the accomplishment of his mission did not rest in his own nature and ability, but in the Father who sent him. Jesus' submission to the Father highlights again the fact that life is a gift of God. Those who are obedient to the Father through Christ are recipients of the life that God alone gives—eternal life. Thus the promise of resurrection for all believers, made explicit in Lazarus' resurrection and guaranteed in Christ's resurrection as the "first fruit" (in Pauline terminology), is the natural consequence of God's gift (Jn 5:26–29).

Jesus added further content to the concept of eternal life by connecting it with knowing the true God (Jn 17:3). In Greek thought knowledge referred to the result of either contemplation or mystical ecstasy. In the OT, however, knowledge meant experience, relationship, fellowship, and concern (cf. Jer 31:34). This connotation of knowledge as intimate relationship is underlined by the usage of the verb form to designate sexual relations between male and female (cf. Gn 4:1). Jesus stated, "I am the good shepherd; I know my own and my own know me, as the Father knows me

and I know the Father" (Jn 10:14,15). The intimate and mutual relationship of Father and Son is the model for the relationship of the Son and his disciples. This knowledge does not come by education or manipulation of the mind, but by revelation through the Son (Jn 1:18; cf. 14:7).

Closely related to the concept of knowledge of God as the definition of eternal life is Jesus's reference to truth: "And you will know the truth, and the truth will make you free" (Jn 8:32). Again the primary content of "truth" in the OT is faithfulness, reliability, and stability. Truth is frequently used to describe God's essential character. God's continuing covenant love for Israel was now definitively revealed in Christ. Knowledge of that utterly trustworthy God brings freedom and eternal life. Thus Jesus is the "true light" (Jn 1:9) who spoke of the "true God" (Jn 17:3). From that base doing the truth (Jn 3:21) is the proper response to the faithful God.

A brief survey of the primary elements in the concept of eternal life clearly shows that it is not simply an endless or everlasting life. Although there are no final boundaries to eternal life, the Bible's primary emphasis is on the quality of life, especially its redemptive elements. Eternal life is the importation of the qualities of the age to come into the present through the revelation of a faithful God in Christ, and brings knowledge of God's relationship with him.   MORRIS A. WEIGELT

See LIFE; MAN, OLD AND NEW; NEW CREATION, NEW CREATURE; REGENERATION; SALVATION.

Bibliography. J. Baillie, *And the Life Everlasting;* L. Berkhof, *Systematic Theology;* L. S. Chafer, *Systematic Theology,* IV, 24–26, 389, 400–401; VII, 142, 227; P.T. Forsyth, *This Life and the Next;* A.H. Strong, *Systematic Theology.*

Eternity. Duration of time that cannot be measured.

The OT does not have a clearly worked out concept of time; it simply records sequences of events without struggling to understand the philosophical implications of that record. God has revealed himself within the historical realm, implying his control of history and leading to the understanding that there is a goal and purpose in the historical process. Out of this complex of ideas arose the necessity to express the endless duration of time commonly designated as eternity.

The OT does not have a single word corresponding to our English word "eternity." The concept grows out of such expressions as "from generation to generation" and "from age to age." The understanding of God as the Creator and controller of history very early led to the understanding of his endless life span. Thus God himself is designated by the adjective "eternal" (cf. Gn 21:33; Is 26:4; 40:28). The Hebrews simply understood that God is the God of the past and the God who will always be, in stark contrast to humans whose days on earth are specifically limited. Before the world was created God obviously was being the Creator. His purposes and promises for the future frequently include the word "forever."

The NT picked up these concepts from Judaism and the OT. In Greek the same root word is used to describe the ages of time and God's agelessness. For example, the word "eternal" used in Romans 16:26 comes from the Greek root transliterated into English as "eon." The God who rules the ages or eons is himself the ageless one who brings continuity and stability into the human life so severely bounded by this age. The clear understanding that time will come to an end, provided by NT revelation, added to the OT's vivid understanding of creation, serves to underline and clarify the concept of an eternal God. God's preexistence and postexistence is yet another way of expressing his eternal being.

The NT regularly spoke of the temporal sequences of God's revelation in Christ in much the same way as the OT spoke of God's self-revelation to Israel. The NT usage of prepositions with "eon" is particularly instructive: for example (translated literally) "out of the age" (Jn 9:32), "from the age" (Lk 1:70; Acts 3:21), "into the age" (Jude 13), "into the ages" (Jn 4:14). The first two phrases reflect an indefinite time preceding the present moment, and the last two point to a future indefinable time (often translated as "forever").

The biblical concept of eternity stands in contrast to other cultures of the time, which often thought in cyclical terms. The Greek world particularly thought of time in the analogy of a circle—an ever-recurring sequence of events—and redemption was to find an exit from that vicious cycle, thus being freed from time in order to experience timelessness. The biblical concept pictures time as a line with beginning and end guaranteed by the eternal God. Thus for the Greeks salvation could not occur within a designated sequence; it only occurs in the experience of the individual and moves on to the historical consummation directed by the eternal God.

The contrast between the Greek and biblical ways of viewing time raises the question of the exact nature of eternity. Is it to be understood as merely unlimited time or, in direct contrast to present time, as timelessness? The biblical view seems to be that eternity is not timelessness and does not stand in contrast to present time as its opposite, since present time and eternity share basic qualities.

The NT (following Judaism) uses "eon" or "age" to divide time into "this present eon" and "the eon that is about to be" or "the coming eon." The contrast is not simply between time and timelessness, for the "eon that is about to be" is future and shares a specific and identifiable character. The biblical picture of the start of the "coming age" is dramatically painted with broad sequential brush strokes. The new age is not simply a restoration to the primitive and naïve innocence of the earliest stage, but a consummation according to the purposes of "him who is and who was and who is to come" (Rv 1:4). Thus it is designated as the new creation.

The NT clearly teaches that the "age that is to be" has now begun in the life and ministry of Christ, although there is a definite overlap in the two ages. The frequency of such terms as "the first fruits," "the earnest of the Spirit," and "the last days," reflects this understanding (e.g., Heb 6:5: "and have tasted . . . the powers of the age to come"). The believer enjoys the blessings of the future age imported into the present through Christ's redemptive work.

The concept of eternity, then, does not stand in opposition and contrast to time as timelessness. Eternity is the unlimited and incalculable space of time bounded at its beginning by the introduction of the kingdom of God in Christ and stretching out into the unlimited future. Both time ("the present evil age," Gal 1:4) and eternity are governed by God as the Lord of all time, the one who gives content and meaning to both. For the believer the midpoint of time (even though the second coming of Christ and the consummation of the present eon have not yet occurred) is found in the first Easter. It is not the consummation that brings eternity; eternity is the accomplishment of God's sovereign and eternal purpose in Christ for the whole universe.

MORRIS A. WEIGELT

See AGE, AGES; GOD, BEING AND ATTRIBUTES OF.

Etham. First encampment of the Hebrews after leaving Succoth (Ex 13:20), perhaps located on the border of the wilderness of Shur (Ex 15:22; Nm 33:6–8). The suggestion that it was an Egyptian fortress is improbable.

See WILDERNESS WANDERINGS.

Ethan. 1. Wise man comparable to Solomon (1 Kgs 4:31) and probably the author of Psalm 89. It is uncertain if he was a contemporary of Solomon.

2. Descendant of Judah and son of Zerah (1 Chr 2:6), perhaps the same man as # 1 above. However, they are given different fathers in the two passages.

3. Son of Zimmah, a descendant of Gershon, Levi's oldest son (1 Chr 6:42).

4. Descendant of Levi through his son Merari, and the son of Kishi (1 Chr 6:44) or Kushaiah (1 Chr 15:17). He was one of three outstanding musicians, along with Heman and Asaph, appointed by David (1 Chr 15:16–19). It was probably this Ethan whose name is ascribed to Psalm 39 (as "Jeduthun," which he is called in 1 Chr 16:41; 25:1) as "chief musician"; it is likely that he composed the music for the psalm.

Ethanim. Early name for the seventh month in the Jewish calendar (1 Kgs 8:2).

See CALENDARS, ANCIENT AND MODERN.

Ethbaal. King of Sidon whose daughter Jezebel entered into a political marriage with Ahab of Israel (1 Kgs 16:31). Ethbaal was credited with building Botrys in Phoenicia and founding the colony of Auza in Libya. He also established commercial relations with Damascus.

Ether. 1. City situated in the Shephelah of the territory allotted to Judah for an inheritance, listed between Libnah and Ashan (Jos 15:42). Its site is perhaps that of Khirbet el-'Ater.

2. City located in the land given to Simeon within the borders of Judah's inheritance, mentioned between Rimmon and Ashan (Jos 19:7). Its location is probably identifiable with Khirbet 'Attir, northeast of Beersheba.

Ethiopia. In the OT, Ethiopia was generally referred to as Cush (Gn 10:6; 1 Chr 1:8; Is 11:11 KJV), which is a transliteration of the only Hebrew word used to describe the land lying to the south of Egypt. The Greek version, however, spoke of this territory as Ethiopia, and

kept the name Cush for the lists of peoples in Genesis 10:6–8 and 1 Chronicles 1:8–10. English translations have generally followed the Greek, except in cases where Cushi appears as a personal name (2 Sm 18:21–23,31,32).

Location. The Hebrew name Kush is actually an old Egyptian loanword that came into use in the early Middle Kingdom period. At that time it was used of a small area between the Second and Third Cataracts of the Nile. Later on, in the New Kingdom period (*c.* 1570–1160 BC) it was applied to a larger area which extended some distance to the south. This broader designation corresponds geographically to the modern lands of Nubia and the northern Sudan. It is misleading to think that the Ethiopia of Scripture is the same territory as the Ethiopia of modern times, which in an earlier period was called Abyssinia. The name Ethiopia was of Greek origin, and according to some interpreters meant "burnt-faced" (cf. Acts 8:27). This tradition has been perpetuated by the Arabic name Beled es Sudan, or "land of the blacks," from which the designation Sudan comes.

The use of Cush by the OT writers seems to have paralleled the Egyptian geographical terminology in thinking of an arid land stretching south of Aswan, the Syene of Ezekiel 29:10. The borders of Ethiopia were never clearly defined, even by the Egyptians, so the territory may be regarded as extending to some indeterminate point in the Sudan beyond Meroë.

Ethiopia consisted predominantly of desert lying east of the Nile, and the topography of the region made travel hazardous. Even the river itself presented obstacles to navigation in the form of cataracts. Outcroppings of hard stone forced the Nile down narrow channels

The ruins of a crusader castle built by the sea at the city of Sidon, on the coast of Lebanon, where Ethbaal was king.

and produced rough water that swamped boats easily. Such forbidding natural obstacles protected Egypt against invasion from the south, but also gave an inhospitable character to Ethiopia. Nowadays the Nubian desert is crossed by a railway running from Wadi Halfa to Abu Hamed and on to Khartoum. Wadi Halfa is situated just below the Second Cataract of the Nile, and was one of the places to be affected when the High Dam at Aswan, the Sadd el Aali, was constructed. Almost all the land suitable for farming in Egyptian Nubia and part of northern Sudan was inundated, and the Nubians were compelled to move below Aswan to Kom Ombo.

Since the area covered by Nubia is predominantly desert, it is hardly surprising that the rainfall is minimal, except for the upstream areas. The territory around Meroë, which was the capital during the Meroitic period, experiences seasonal rains: and an area bordered on the west and north by the Nile and the Atbara, the so-called "island of Meroë," was apparently quite fertile in antiquity and may have been heavily forested.

History. The First Intermediate period (c. 2200–2000 BC) saw some attempt by the Egyptians to exert influence over Kush as a means of protecting the southern approach to Egypt. In the Middle Kingdom period (c. 2000–1780 BC) they gained control over the territory, the extent of which in the time of Sesostris I (c. 1971–1930 BC) comprised an area stretching from Aswan to the Second Cataract. The 12th dynasty rulers established their frontier farther south, at Semna, where fortifications were erected as part of a defensive chain reaching into northern Nubia. The 12th dynasty pharaoh Sesostris III was perhaps the best-known Egyptian ruler in Nubia, and after his reign the connections between the two countries became less marked until the end of the Second Intermediate period. Under Thutmose I in the New Kingdom period (c. 1570–1150 BC), Egyptian influence extended into lower Nubia and probably as far as Meroë. Amenhotep III built a magnificent temple at Soleb, while the splendid structure at Abu Simbel was carved out of the Nubian sandstone cliffs in the days of Ramses II. During this period Ethiopia was governed by a series of viceroys who were known by the title "king's son of Kush." These people controlled territory which stretched from Nekhen (Hierakonpolis) to Napata in the Sudan. One such governor whose activities were illustrated pictorially in his tomb at Gurnet Murai was a man named Huy. Egyptian officials stationed in Ethiopia during the New Kingdom period were frequently buried there instead of in Egypt. Their graves consisted of deep rectangular shafts with burial chambers excavated at one or both ends. Multiple burials occurring over a period of time have been encountered by excavators.

Towards the close of the New Kingdom period Egyptian power declined, and about 1100 BC Kush became independent, establishing its capital at Napata near the Fourth Cataract. The Ethiopians launched an expedition into Palestine during the time of Asa of Judah, but were defeated (2 Chr 14:9–15). In the 25th dynasty a Kushite family came to power in Egypt under Kashta and Pi-ankh, and for the next 60 years Ethiopian rulers controlled the Nile valley. One member of this dynasty, Taharqa, the Tirhakah of the OT, apparently allied with Hezekiah in an effort to stop the advance of Sennacherib's forces (2 Kgs 19:9; Is 37:9). Kushite power waned when Esarhaddon and Ashurbanipal made Egypt and Ethiopia tributaries to Assyria, and the end came with the destruction of Thebes by Ashurbanipal in 663 BC (cf. Is 20:2–6; Nah 3:8–10).

The Kushites continued to control the Sudan, however, and when the Egyptians suffered defeat at Carchemish (605 BC), they considered regaining control over Egypt. This expectation ended permanently when the conquests of Cambyses (525 BC) brought both Egypt and Ethiopia into the Persian empire.

Biblical References. In Esther 1:1 and 8:9 Ethiopia is described as the most distant southwesterly province in the Persian empire. Its "rivers" were presumably the Nile and the Atbara (cf. Is 18:1; Zep 3:10). The products of Kush were referred to in Job 28:19 and Isaiah 45:14, which according to Egyptian lists included semiprecious stones, animal and agricultural products. Some prophets expected exiled Jews in Ethiopia to return (Ps 87:4; Is 11:11), while others foresaw divine judgment coming upon the land (Is 20:3; Ez 30:4; Zep 2:12). But since Kush was under God's sovereignty, it could hope for divine blessing as well as punishment; hence the expectation in Psalm 68:31; Isaiah 45:14; and Zephaniah 3:10 that its peoples would be converted to the Hebrew faith. The Ethiopia of Acts 8:27 was the kingdom of Candace ("queen"), who ruled from Meroë, where the capital of Kush had been moved about 300 BC.

Archaeology. A good deal of excavation has taken place at Meroë. Large slag heaps indicate the extent of the iron-processing industry in antiquity, while Egyptian culture is reflected in the ruins of pyramids, cemeteries, temples, and other structures. As the result of an international movement to preserve the monuments of Nubia, the famous rock-cut temples of Abu Simbel were preserved from destruction when the Aswan High Dam was built. There were also significant deposits of gold in Nubia, and it was this source that enriched the Egyptian kings of the Amarna Age. Gold was still being mined in Kush during the Roman period. When Meroë became capital of Kush, its location provided better trading opportunities with other nations than had been the case previously, and the Meroitic territory was mentioned by several classical writers. The people were slow to accept Roman rule, but were eventually subdued by Petronius in 23 BC. Excavations show that the Kushites used hieroglyphs and also an alphabetic script, but far less study has been made of Kushite than other Near Eastern languages.

R. K. HARRISON

See CUSH (PLACE).

Eth-kazin. One of the towns marking the eastern boundary of Zebulun's tribe (Jos 19:13, KJV Ittah-kazin). Its exact location is unknown, but the context indicates that it was probably in the vicinity of Gath-hepher and Rimmon.

Ethnan. Member of Helah's family from Judah's tribe (1 Chr 4:7).

Ethni. Alternate name for Je-atherai, Zerah's son, in 1 Chronicles 6:41.

See JE-ATHERAI, JEATERAI.

Eubulus. Roman believer who sent greetings to Timothy during Paul's second Roman imprisonment (2 Tm 4:21). His Greek name indicates his probable gentile origin.

Eucharist. *See* LORD'S SUPPER, THE.

Eunice. Timothy's mother, daughter of Lois (2 Tm 1:5), and the wife of a pagan Greek; a "Jewish woman who was a believer" (Acts 16:1). She apparently taught her son the OT Scriptures "from childhood" (2 Tm 3:15) and was converted to Christianity during Paul's first trip to her home in Lystra, previous to his visit mentioned in Acts 16:1.

Eunuch. Officer or chamberlain in the court or household of a ruler, often assigned to the women's quarters. Many of these men were emasculated, though not always (cf. Gn 39:1,7 NEB). Eunuchs were public officials in Israel (1 Sm 8:15 NEB; 1 Chr 28:1 NEB), Persia (Est 2:3), Ethiopia (Jer 38:7; Acts 8:27), and Babylon (Dn 1:3). Eunuchs were not included in public worship in Israel (Dt 23:1), but the prophet Isaiah referred to their restoration in the messianic kingdom (Is 56:3–5; see Acts 8).

The Ethiopian eunuch of Acts 8:27–39 was probably minister of the treasury, and has been credited with founding Christianity in Ethiopia.

Jesus mentioned three classes of eunuchs (Mt 19:12), including those "who have made themselves eunuchs for the sake of the kingdom." This is generally understood in a metaphorical sense of voluntarily foregoing marriage in order to serve the kingdom (e.g., John the Baptist, Jesus, and the apostle Paul).

See TRADES AND OCCUPATIONS (CHAMBERLAIN).

Euodia, Euodias. Prominent woman in the Philippian church whom Paul asked to resolve her differences with Syntyche (Phil 4:2, KJV Euodias). The nature of their disagreement is not known, but it was of enough severity to reach Paul in Rome. Both women had labored with him in the work of the gospel (4:3).

Euphrates River. Largest river in western Asia, formed by the union of two rivers in Asia Minor, the Kara-Su and the Murat-Suyu. Its source is in central Armenia. The river flows generally in a southeasterly direction for some 1,800 miles until it reaches the Persian Gulf. At Korna, about 100 miles from the Gulf, it joins with the Tigris River. The Euphrates is shallow until it combines with the Tigris and can be navigated for about 1,200 miles by small boats only. After the union of the Tigris and Euphrates, ocean liners can proceed as far as Basra. Melting snows at the source cause the river to rise about from the middle of March until about June. Control and storage of water in flood canals during the overflow of the river made possible abundant harvests that sustained large populations in antiquity.

Some have suggested that there were two branches of the Euphrates that began near Sippar. One, the Arachtu, flowed through Babylon, but after about 1000 BC became the main portion of the Euphrates. The older course ran south from Sippar to Kish, capital of the first dynasty of Mesopotamia before 3000 BC. From Kish it flowed on to Nippur, city of the sun god Enlil, the main religious center of Sumer which is dated earlier than 3000 BC. After Nippur the river passed through Shuruppak (modern Fara). According to mythology Ziusudra, the Sumerian counterpart of Noah, built his ark there. The river then flowed south to ancient Erech, famous as the city of Ishtar. The *Enuma Elish* epic describes this center as home of the mythical hero Gilgamesh. The river then continued to Ur, birthplace and early home of the patriarch Abraham.

The Euphrates was one of four branches issuing from the river that watered the garden of Eden (Gn 2:14). In the promises made to Abraham, the northern boundary of the land of Israel was to be the upper division of the river (Gn 15:18; Dt 1:7; 11:24). These boundaries were approximately reached during the period of kings David and Solomon (2 Sm 8:3; 10:16; 1 Kgs 4:24). The Euphrates is called "the River" (Nm 22:5; Dt 11:24; Jos 24:3,14) or "the great river" (Jos 1:4). People living east of the Euphrates referred to Israel and its surrounding territories to the west as "beyond the river" (Ezr 4:10; Neh 2:7,9). It was to this river that Jeremiah sent Seraiah with a book of prophecies relating to the destruction of Babylon. After reading them Seraiah was to throw the book into the Euphrates as a symbol of the way Babylon would sink to rise no more (Jer 51:63).

Two NT references to the Euphrates figure in the message of the Book of Revelation (9:14; 16:12).

See BABYLON, BABYLONIA; MESOPOTAMIA.

Euroclydon. KJV transliteration of the Greek word for the northeasterly wind mentioned in Paul's journey to Rome in Acts 27:14.

See NORTHEASTER.

Eutychus. Common slave name, mentioned only in Acts 20:9. It was Eutychus' misfortune to become sleepy while sitting on a windowsill listening to the apostle Paul preach at Troas. He sank into a deep sleep and fell from the ledge, which was in the third loft. Though he was "taken up dead," the apostle declared him alive, giving great comfort to the people (Acts 20:7–12).

Evangelist. NT term referring to one who proclaims the gospel of Jesus Christ. There are only three occurrences of the word in the NT. The apostle Paul exhorted the Ephesian church to walk worthy of their calling (Eph 4:1–12). The exhortation stressed the gifts given to each within the unity of the Spirit. Paul explained that the ascended Christ has given "some as apostles, and some as prophets, and some as evangelists, and some as pastors and teachers" (4:11 NASB). Paul was saying that Christ calls persons to these ministries and gives them to the church. The evangelist is one of Christ's gifts to the church. The meaning of the term indicates that the task of such a person is to function as a spokesperson for the church in proclaiming the gospel to the world. An evangelist is similar to an apostle in function, except that being an apostle involved a personal relationship to Jesus during his earthly ministry (Acts 1:21,22). The evangelist stands in contrast to the pastor and teacher. The former makes the initial proclamation, and the latter provides continuing follow-up ministry that develops maturity in the believer. The reference to Philip the evangelist (Acts 21:8) supports the idea of evangelism as a gifted ministry to which Christ calls some in the church.

More than one gift or ministry may be performed by the same person. Paul charged Timothy with his responsibilities as a pastor and teacher, and also exhorted him to "do the work of an evangelist" (2 Tm 4:5). Therefore, evangelist can refer to a person called to that distinct ministry, and also to a function that may be performed by others.

See SPIRITUAL GIFTS.

Eve. First woman, "the mother of all living" (Gn 3:20). The Book of Genesis recounts that after God had finished his creation, he saw that it was not good for Adam to be alone. He decided to create "a helper fit for him" (Gn 2:18). The woman is called *ezer* (in Hebrew literally "help"), a word that appears elsewhere in the OT in reference to God as Israel's help (Dt 33:7,26,29; Pss 33:20; 70:5; 115:9,10,11; 146:5). Causing Adam to fall into a deep sleep, God took one of his ribs and used it to fashion Eve (Gn 2:18–25).

Eve was given two names by Adam. The first was "woman," a generic designation with theological connotations that denote her relationship to man (Gn 2:23). The second, Eve ("life"), was given after the fall and refers to her role in the procreation of the human race (3:20).

Adam and Eve are pictured as living in Eden, serving God and fulfilling each other's needs. Then evil entered. Eve was tempted by the serpent to disobey God's command, which forbade their eating the fruit of the "tree of the knowledge of good and evil" (Gn 2:17; 3:3). Tricked by the serpent's subtle persuasion, Eve transgressed God's will by eating the fruit. Adam did the same when she brought some to him, although he was not deceived as she had been. Both then recognized their nakedness and made garments of fig leaves.

When God came to commune with them, they hid from him. When he demanded an account, Adam blamed Eve and Eve blamed the serpent. God told Eve that as a result of their sin, childbirth would be a painful experience and her husband would rule over her (Gn 3:16). Eve later became the mother of Cain, Abel, Seth, and other children (Gn 4:1,2,25; 5:4).

Eve is mentioned twice in the NT. In his letter to Timothy the apostle Paul referred to her when discussing whether or not women could teach (1 Tm 2:13). He said that woman could not teach or have authority over man because of man's priority in creation and Eve's responsibility for the original transgression (see 2 Cor 11:3).

Several early church fathers, including Justin and Irenaeus, compared Eve with Mary the mother of Jesus. They pictured Mary as the "new Eve," contrasting the disobedience and sin of the first Eve with the obedience and faith of the second. They regarded Eve as restored to wholeness in Mary. Since Protestants are strongly opposed to the Roman Catholic veneration of Mary, and see newness and wholeness as totally centered in Christ (Gal 3:28), they have not developed that particular typology.

See ADAM (PERSON); GARDEN OF EDEN.

Evening. *See* DAY.

Evening Sacrifice. *See* OFFERINGS AND SACRIFICES.

Everlasting Life. *See* ETERNAL LIFE.

Everyday Life in Bible Times. *See* AGRICULTURE; BURIAL, BURIAL CUSTOMS; CIVIL LAW AND JUSTICE; CLEANNESS AND UNCLEANNESS, REGULATIONS CONCERNING; CRIMINAL LAW AND PUNISHMENT; COURTS AND TRIALS; DIETARY LAWS; EDUCATION; FAMILY LIFE AND RELATIONS; FASHION AND DRESS; FEASTS AND FESTIVALS OF ISRAEL; FOOD AND FOOD PREPARATION; FURNITURE; HOMES AND DWELLINGS; INDUSTRY AND COMMERCE; INHERITANCE; MARRIAGE, MARRIAGE CUSTOMS; MEDICINE AND MEDICAL PRACTICE; MONEY AND BANKING; MUSIC AND MUSICAL INSTRUMENTS; OFFERINGS AND SACRIFICES; SLAVE, SLAVERY; TOOLS; TRADES AND OCCUPATIONS; TRAVEL AND TRANSPORTATION; WAGES.

Evi. One of five Midianite kings killed in a battle against Israel under the leadership of Moses (Nm 31:8). Apparently God directed Moses to go to battle against Midian because the Midianites had led the Israelites into pagan religious practices. In Joshua 13:21 Evi is called a prince of Sihon, the Midianite king.

Evil. *See* SIN.

Evil-merodach. Son and successor of Nebuchadnezzar as king of Babylon, who reigned for two years (561–560 BC). During his reign he released Jehoiachin, former king of Judah, from imprisonment (2 Kgs 25:27–30; Jer 52:31–34). Aside from this fact, little is known about his reign. He was killed by his brother-in-law Neriglissar, who succeeded him to the throne.

See BABYLON, BABYLONIA.

Evil One. NT designation for Satan.

See SATAN.

Evil Spirit. Another name for demon.

See DEMON, DEMON POSSESSION.

Ewe. Female sheep.

See ANIMALS (SHEEP).

Execution. *See* CRIMINAL LAW AND PUNISHMENT.

Exhortation. Translation of a Greek word literally meaning "a calling of someone alongside to help." Its primary meaning in the NT is the urging of someone to do something, more specifically some ethical course of action. In some contexts the same Greek word may also include the idea of comforting and consoling. The given context will determine which meaning to use.

A passage that most clearly illustrates "exhortation" in the sense of inciting or spurring people on to action is Luke 3:7–18. John the Baptist exhorts (v 18) his Jewish hearers to bring forth fruits in keeping with repentance (v 8), to stop resting on descent from Abraham as protection from punishment for sin (v 8), and to share clothing and food (v 11). He exhorted tax gatherers to collect no more money than they had a right to take (v 13), and soldiers not to take money from anyone by force, not to accuse anyone falsely, and to be content with their wages (v 14).

The ability to exhort is said to be a spiritual gift that God has given to some in the church for the benefit of the whole (Rom 12:8). In addition, exhortation is one of the results of a proper use of the gift of prophecy as seen in 1 Corinthians 14:3,31. It was also one of the responsibilities that Paul commanded of Timothy: "Give attention to the public reading of Scripture, to exhortation and teaching (1 Tm 4:13 NASB). The writer to the Hebrews also refers to an exhortation addressed to the readers lest they regard lightly the discipline of the Lord or faint when they are reproved (Heb 12:5).

In 2 Corinthians 1:3–7 the Greek word is used in the sense of consolation or encouragement. The context is one in which serious suffering for Christians is evident. Paul writes that God encourages us in our times of testing so that we may be able to do the same for those experiencing similar trials. Acts 15:31 refers to the encouragement and consolation which came to the church at Antioch when the decree of the Jerusalem council was read in their hearing. They had been fearful that the Judaizers might have their way and that Christians would be required to become circumcised in order to be saved. Another clear illustration of this word meaning "comfort" is in 1

Thessalonians 4:18, where Paul instructs the believers that those who die in Christ will not miss out on the blessings of the day of Christ; he then exhorts them to "comfort one another with these words."

See SPIRITUAL GIFTS.

Exile. Mass deportation of large population groups practiced in ancient times usually for political purposes, frequently to destroy the power of an enemy nation and to prevent rebellion. Sometimes the exile of a conquered people was carried out to colonize an area, to create a cultural fusion. Captivity removed people from familiar associations and patriotic memories and put the defeated under the eye of the central government. Deportation was generally resorted to as an extreme measure when other means, such as the imposing of tribute, failed.

"Exile" and "captivity" have the same meaning in the OT and are used interchangeably. The principal allusions are to the Assyrian captivity of 722 BC, in which Israel was transported to Mesopotamia by the Assyrians, and the Babylonian exile of 605–582 BC, in which a similar fate overtook the inhabitants of Judah. There are references in preexilic writings to other captivities of peoples (Am 1:6,9), as well as predictions that Egypt (Is 20:4; Jer 46:19), Ethiopia (Is 20:4), Moab (Jer 48:7), Rabbah (Jer 49:2,3), and Nineveh (Na 3:10) would themselves be exiled. An apocalyptic reference to the final captivity of Jerusalem occurs in Zechariah 14:2.

Assyrian Exile. As early as 842 BC King Jehu of Israel paid tribute to Shalmaneser, king of Assyria. But it was not until 734 BC, in the reign of Tiglath-pileser III (745–727 BC), that the first deportation recorded in the OT

occurred. Tiglath-pileser had received tribute from King Menahem of Israel (2 Kgs 15:19), but later had marched against King Pekah of Israel and King Rezin of Syria (734–732 BC) because together they had made war against his vassal, King Ahaz of Judah. Tiglath-pileser punished Israel by carrying some of its inhabitants, especially from Naphtali's tribal territory, into exile (2 Kgs 16:7–9). During this campaign Gilead, a region just east of the Jordan River, was devastated, and the Israelite leaders in the Transjordan were deported (1 Chr 5:6,26). A fragmentary cuneiform inscription from Tiglath-pileser lists several thousand male captives whom he exiled from eight cities around the Sea of Galilee. The Israelites avoided a worse fate by assassinating their hostile king, Pekah, before Tiglath-pileser came. A new king, Hoshea, was elected, who immediately submitted to the Assyrians. That timely action helped to preserve part of the kingdom of Israel.

Nevertheless, insurrection in Israel came soon after Tiglath-pileser was succeeded by his son Shalmaneser V (727–722 BC). Hoshea refused to pay the annual tribute to Assyria and by that act tested the new monarch's power early in his reign. In 724 Shalmaneser marched on Israel (2 Kgs 17:3–6). Hoshea was taken captive, and the Assyrian armies moved up to surround the capital, placing Samaria under siege. Since Israel's king was already imprisoned, it was expected that Samaria would fall quickly, but it stubbornly resisted from 724 to 722. Finally Samaria fell; the days of Israel as a sovereign nation were over, and many more captives were taken into exile. The Bible attributes Samaria's capture to Shalmaneser V, but in his inscriptions Shalmaneser's successor Sargon II (722–705) boasted of his conquest of the city and the removal of

A relief of Assyrian court officials.

27,290 captives. Evidently Shalmaneser began the siege, but his successor, Sargon, finally took Samaria and carried out the exile.

The exiles were transplanted to sparsely populated areas in the provinces of Halah, Gozan, and Media (2 Kgs 17:6), where apparently they were permitted to live fairly normal lives. The Assyrian records state that there were 27,290 captives, which was probably only a fraction of the Israelite population.

Assyrian documents dating from the end of the 8th to the 7th centuries BC are of particular significance, since they record what may be Israelite names. There are traces of Israelite captives and possibly exiles from Judah in the lists of personal names on an 8th-century BC Aramaic ostracon (potsherd) found at Calah on the Tigris River, then capital of Assyria. Included are common names in Israel such as Elisha, Haggai, Hananel, and Menahen. Various other Assyrian documents contain Hebrew names, but it is difficult to determine that they belong to descendants of the Israelite captives.

Babylonian Exile. *History.* Around 705 BC King Hezekiah of Judah tried to restore the religious unity of Israel and Judah by inviting the people of Samaria to worship in Jerusalem. His attempt, however, was nullified by the invasion of Judah by King Sennacherib of Assyria. Later King Josiah of Judah took advantage of the decline of Assyrian power to extend his rule and religious reformation into regions formerly belonging to the kingdom of Israel (621 BC). Further evidence of expansion of the kingdom under Josiah is seen in his attempt to prevent Egypt's advance under Pharaoh Neco at Megiddo, but he was killed in battle in 609 BC (2 Kgs 23:29,30).

The overthrow of the Assyrian empire brought only temporary relief to the kingdom of Judah. The newly established Neo-Babylonian dynasty (626 BC) joined forces with Media to destroy Nineveh (612), and after the battle of Carchemish in 605 Nebuchadnezzar of Babylon became the new world leader. As he marched south through the newly conquered lands, he demanded that the large cities submit and that the finest young men be relocated in Babylon as prospective government personnel. From Jerusalem, Daniel and his three friends, Hananiah, Mishael, and Azariah, were sent (Dn 1:1–7). While subjugating Judah in this way, Nebuchadnezzar was interrupted by the death of his father, Nabopolassar. In August of 605 Nebuchadnezzar quickly returned to Babylon to secure the crown. The carrying away of captives at that time was the first of four times during Nebuchadnezzar's reign when prisoners were taken from Jerusalem to Babylonia.

The second Babylonian invasion of Judah occurred in 597 BC. By withholding tribute from Babylonia, King Jehoiakim invited calamity. Since Nebuchadnezzar was involved elsewhere, he urged the surrounding nations to make a number of raids against Jerusalem. Jehoiakim may have been killed in one of the attacks, leaving the throne of Judah to Jehoiachin, his 18-year-old son. Jehoiachin's reign ended after 3 months. Nebuchadnezzar came to punish Judah for renouncing allegiance to Babylonia, and Jehoiachin and his mother were taken captive along with 7,000 soldiers and thousands of craftsmen, smiths, chief officials, princes, together with temple and palace treasures (2 Kgs 24:10–16). Babylonian sources confirm that this invasion took place in March of 597 BC. The Lachish letters and the excavations of such fortress towns as Beth-shemesh and Lachish give graphic illustration of Judah's defeat at that time. Further evidence of this phase of the exile was found by German archaeologists who discovered cuneiform tablets naming "Yaukin (Jehoiachin) king of Judah" with those who received rations of grain in captivity. Though Jerusalem maintained some form of government for another 11 years, the siege of 597 had a devastating effect.

Nebuchadnezzar left Zedekiah, Jehoiachin's uncle, on the throne. Though warned by the prophet Jeremiah, Zedekiah was easily swayed by popular opinion. This weakness proved his undoing and made inevitable Jerusalem's utter desolation and a third deportation. For a few years, Zedekiah remained in submission to Babylonia, and in the 4th year of his reign journeyed to Babylonia, evidently to renew his pledge of loyalty (Jer 51:59). Later he negotiated alliances with neighboring nations, especially Egypt (Jer 37:6–10). Eventually Judah was invaded, and the temple, the palace, and private homes were destroyed. The temple treasuries were confiscated and more people were deported. The siege of the city lasted from January, 587, to July, 586, when the Babylonians breached the city wall. Archaeological excavations show clear evidence of destruction in Judah at sites such as Lachish, Beth-shemesh, and Beth-zur. On the other hand, the evidence thus far shows that the land of Benjamin was not attacked. Judah was added to the province of Samaria, and ceased to exist as a national state.

Tyre and other lands of western Asia resisted Babylonia's supremacy. Tyre preferred an alliance with Egypt to submission to Babylonia. Nebuchadnezzar besieged Tyre for 13 years (585–573). Finally Tyre was overrun, but the Babylonians found only an empty shell; the people and wealth had been evacuated to an island off the coast and probably to Egypt. Pharaoh Hophra was defeated, deposed, and replaced by Amasis, an Egyptian general. For a few years there was peace; then in 568 Amasis revolted against Nebuchadnezzar, who returned and occupied part of the land of Egypt.

A fourth deportation from Judah occurred in 582 (Jer 52:30). After vengeance had been taken for the revolt under Zedekiah, Nebuchadnezzar appointed Gedaliah as governor over the sadly reduced territory of Judah. Gedaliah opposed the pro-Egyptian policy; he set up his administration at Mizpah, and he had the prophet Jeremiah in his entourage. The irreconcilable resistance party considered Gedaliah a traitor to the national cause. Ishmael, a disappointed member of the royal family, ruthlessly assassinated Gedaliah and his supporters. Since the assassins could not remain in Judah and face Nebuchadnezzar's revenge, they fled to Egypt, compelling Jeremiah and the people of Mizpah to accompany them. The prophet warned that they could not escape the Babylonians, because Nebuchadnezzar would soon attack Egypt, including the frontier city (Tahpanhes) settled by the fleeing Jews.

The total number of captives taken in all the deportations from Judah probably did not exceed a total of 70,000 men, women, and children.

Effects of Exile. Of the many crises Judah experienced, none presented greater danger than the Babylonian exile. It was an event that challenged the faith of the most orthodox Jew. The Lord who worked so mightily for Judah before had now apparently gone down in defeat, or so it seemed. Battles among nations in ancient times were thought of as reflecting a parallel warfare among the gods. When Jerusalem was destroyed and the temple vessels seized, many concluded that Marduk, Babylonia's god, had proved himself stronger than Judah's God. Yet Jeremiah prepared Judah for the crises of exile with words of hope (Jer 29:10,14). God would use the Babylonians to chasten his people, and in turn would punish the Babylonians. Those who were weak in faith were destined to be absorbed among the Gentiles; however, the remnant that believed in God's power and purposes, even in captivity, would someday return and rebuild the temple and Jerusalem.

The internal religious causes of the exile were lack of faith in God and his covenant, disregard of the admonitions of the prophets, turning to idolatry, and trust for the nation's sustenance not in the provision of God but rather in their own industry and wisdom. Despite the danger of falling into idolatry in Babylonia, the great effect of the exile lay in the anchoring of the Jews in the Law and in their trust in God. The contrast between monotheism and polytheism was sharpened. The renewed dedication to monotheism later helped the Jews withstand the bewitching fascination of Greek culture and the repeated onslaught of Seleucid power. The exile brought desires for revenge and stirrings of repentance (Jer 51; Lam). The sabbath and festivals continued to be observed, and regular commemorative fasts were initiated (Zec 7:1–3; 8:18,19).

Life in Exile. The lot of the captives was one of servitude, at least at the beginning; they were forced to supply labor for many of Nebuchadnezzar's building projects. Sometimes the work was made harsh by false prophets who provoked the Babylonians to cruel acts of repression (Jer 29:21–23). After the first shock of expatriation was past, however, the exiles' life became more a liberal internment than a concentration camp. The experience of Daniel and his colleagues portrays the generally favorable treatment accorded the captives. Education, position, and responsibility were given to many.

While in captivity the Jews could no longer observe the sacrifices that had been made at the central sanctuary in Jerusalem. As a result, there was a renewed emphasis on reading and observing the Law, an emphasis that led to the development of the synogogue as a place of worship. The institution of the prophets and priests, however, continued to function; that is evident in Jeremiah's address to the captives, naming first the elders, then the prophets, priests, and people (Jer 29:1).

The captives were permitted, within limits, to come and go as they pleased and to marry and establish families. There was liberty for correspondence with the homeland; Jeremiah wrote letters to the exiles and he mentioned correspondence by the captives (Jer 29:1,25). Not only did the Jews engage in skilled slave labor for the Babylonians, but clay tablets give evidence of activity in business—buying, selling, and renting. Many were so successful financially that they were able to send money to Jerusalem; and when the Jews were allowed by the Persian king Cyrus to return home, large numbers refused because they were unwilling to leave the possessions they had acquired. Another favor granted the Jews was permission to settle as a large community on fertile, irrigated land (Ez 1:1,3; 3:15,23).

Calendar. While in Babylonia the Jews adopted a Babylonian calendar that is still the basis for the Jewish year. The Babylonians had a lunar calendar with 12 months, each numbering 30 days. Early in history they learned that it was necessary to add an extra

Maurice Bardin's concept of ancient Babylon. The painting shows a procession moving along Marduk's Way and entering the precincts of Nebuchadnezzar's palace through the Ishtar Gate. The hanging gardens are in the upper right.

(intercalary) month every six years to make the lunar and solar years coincide. Both Babylonians and Hebrews reckoned their days from sunset to sunset (Gn 1:5). The use of the Babylonian calendar is especially found in postexilic writings (the month of Nisan in Neh 2:1; Est 3:7; and the month of Adar in Ezr 6:15). Before the exile, years were reckoned according to the year of the Jewish monarch (2 Kgs 22:3). In postexilic times the years were designated according to the year of the gentile monarch, whether Neo-Babylonian or Persian (Jer 25:1; Ezr 1:1; 6:15).

Language. When Sennacherib besieged Jerusalem in the days of Hezekiah, Aramaic was the language used in international diplomacy. The leader of the Assyrian forces challenged the defenders of Jerusalem in the Hebrew language, much to the dismay of Hezekiah's officials who knew the official Aramaic. Sennacherib's rabshakeh (cupbearer), however, wished to undermine the morale of the defenders by issuing the ultimatum in language all the people could understand, so he spoke in the Hebrew vernacular (2 Kgs 18:26).

While in exile the Jews learned Aramaic as a means of communication with their non-Jewish neighbors. When they returned to Palestine they brought the Aramaic language with them. By the time Ezra read the Law to the people of Jerusalem, it was necessary to give an interpretation of the Hebrew Scriptures, probably in the Aramaic tongue (Neh 8:8). Aramaic letters to and from kings Artaxerxes and Darius may have been copies of the original texts kept in the Persian archives (Ezr 4:11–22; 5:7–17; 6:6–12; 7:11–26). In addition the Israelites from the northern kingdom, who were already in Mesopotamia, undoubtedly were fluent in both Hebrew and Aramaic. Hebrew continued to be used as a living language; the postexilic books of Haggai, Zechariah, and Malachi were written in Hebrew, as was the later literature from a community at Qumran, the source of the Dead Sea Scrolls. Most of the people, however, spoke only Aramaic in Syria and Palestine during NT times and until the Arab conquest of the 7th century AD.

Conditions in Judah After the Exile. Unlike the Assyrians, who repopulated the northern kingdom after its fall in 722 BC (2 Kgs 17:24), the Babylonians did not resettle areas from which captives had been taken. Only the poorest Jewish people remained in the land, truly sheep without a shepherd, pressed between the Edomites and Arabians edging in from the south, Ammonites and other tribes from the east, and the Samaritans from the north. The Jews who remained in the land, in common with their Samaritan neighbors, accepted the Mosaic law and worshiped Israel's God. Sacrifices were still offered on the temple hill, but amid the prevailing gloom and poverty superstitions and crude religious beliefs flourished anew. Judging by the problems Ezra and Nehemiah faced in a later day, the Jews and Samaritans got along well together, and intermarriage became quite common (Ezr 10:18–44, Neh 13:23–28).

Ezekiel spoke often of the spiritual conditions in Judah during the exile. He was taken in the spirit to Jerusalem, where he was shown an idol, the "image of jealousy," in the inner temple court (Ez 8:1–6). Then he was taken to the temple wall and ordered to dig until he came into an inner secret room. The walls of the room were adorned with serpents and wild beasts similar to the Procession Way in Babylon, which was adorned with lions, bulls, and dragons. Seventy elders were seen burning incense to the idols (Ez 8:11–13). At the temple's north gate Ezekiel saw women weeping for Tammuz, the Babylonian god of vegetation whose death was mourned annually (Ez 8:14,15). The worst offense of all was the sight of 25 people worshiping the sun (Ez

8:16). Finally, Ezekiel saw God's departure symbolized by the departure of the divine glory (Ez 11:23).

Release from Exile. While the Jews were held captive, Babylonia was conquered by the Persians under Cyrus in 539 BC. The edict of Cyrus, issued in 538, released the Jews to return home to rebuild the temple in Jerusalem (Ezr 1:1–4). Cyrus showed greater kindness than most rulers to conquered and subject peoples. Some say that he favored the Jews because he saw some similarity between Judaism and Persian religion. Probably permission was freely given to the Jews so that eventually a strengthened Judean province would serve as a buffer between Persia and Egypt. In addition an economic factor was the hope that the restored province would soon contribute taxes to Persia's treasury.

Exile and Judaism's Future. The exile was the watershed between Israel as a political unit and the religion known as Judaism. National life came to an end; the Jews were gradually scattered throughout the ancient world and became identified with a religion and a tradition rather than a nation. The remnant that lingered in Palestine was governed by Babylonia, Persia, Greece, and Rome successively, and never achieved independence except for a short time under the Maccabees during the 2nd and 1st centuries BC. Thus the exile proved the people; their religious and racial consciousness was intensified to prevent assimilation into their heathen environment. Hence a more spiritual remnant emerged, detached from local limitations and physical structures. During the exile an "Israelite" came to be called a "Jew," and the idealization of Zion began among the people.

The prophets spoke of the Babylonian exile as divine retribution and judgment for Judah's rejection of their message and for persistence in sin and idolatry. If this judgment were accepted, it would eventually lead to restoration and a revelation of divine love for Israel (Is 54:9,10; Jer 31:3–6). Out of the experience would come a new covenant (Jer 31:31–34). The exile brought a more profound comprehension of the Law and the prophets. There came also a deeper understanding of God's universality and sovereignty. The exile is one of the primary historical incidents upon which the hope for the Messiah's coming was established.

AUSTIN H. POTTS

See CHRONOLOGY, OLD TESTAMENT; POSTEXILIC PERIOD, THE; DIASPORA OF THE JEWS; ISRAEL, HISTORY OF; JUDAISM; JEW.

Exodus, Book of.

Second book of the Bible, containing the story of God's liberation of the people of Israel from slavery in Egypt. Few books of the OT are as important historically and theologically as the Book of Exodus.

Historically, the exodus event was the birth of Israel as a nation. At Mt Sinai a group of tribes who were descendants of Abraham became a nation ruled by God. The Book of Exodus explains how the Israelites were able to resettle the land God had promised to Abraham and gives the basis for this religious, political, and social life.

Theologically the Book of Exodus is so frequently referred to in the OT and NT that theologians speak of an "exodus motif." In Psalm 37, for example, David received assurance in remembering that his God was the same one who rescued Israel from Egypt. The prophet Jeremiah compared the future regathering of Israel to their exodus from Egypt as an even more miraculous event (Jer 16:14,15). The return of Jesus and his parents from Egypt is associated with the exodus in Matthew 2:13–15. The deliverance of the Jewish people from Egypt was interpreted as a prototype for God's freeing of all his people, both Israel and the church. Thus the message of the Book of Exodus is foundational to understanding God's plan of salvation throughout the Bible.

The English title "Exodus" comes from the Septuagint, a pre-Christian translation of the OT into Greek. The word means "a way out" or "departure," and refers to Israel's rescue from Egypt. The Hebrew title is *Shemoth* ("these are the names"), from the book's opening words, referring to the names of the sons of Jacob who joined Joseph in Egypt.

Author. According to tradition, Exodus and the entire Pentateuch (first five books of the Bible) were written by Moses. Exodus was probably written at Mt Sinai or shortly after the events there, according to this view. There is much to support that claim:

(1) The book states that Moses wrote God's words in at least one book (Ex 17:14; 24:4,7; 34:27,28). According to Deuteronomy 31:9,24, Moses incorporated God's Law in a book that was deposited beside the ark of the covenant as a witness for God.

(2) Many OT writers referred to portions of Exodus as the "law of Moses" (1 Kgs 2:3; 2 Chr 34:14; Neh 8:1; 13:1). The NT, including the testimony of Jesus, calls Moses the author (Mk 7:10, 12:26; Jn 1:45; 7:19).

Various other theories about the origin of Exodus have been proposed. Some scholars credit Moses with writing nearly the entire book. One writer claims that Moses was an unknown desert sheikh who never even met the Israelites. Some critics think they detect in the book several documents from various periods in Israel's history that were finally put together by an editor, centuries after Moses' death. Others have isolated various literary forms, such as the "Song of Moses" (Ex 15), and traced their development. Another interpretation says that the exodus story was passed on by word of mouth for many generations before being written.

Although such theories are held by biblical scholars, they deny what the text of the book repeatedly affirms: that Moses wrote Exodus. The Book of Exodus contains evidence of being written by an eyewitness. Only such a person would recall, for example, that there were 12 fountains and 70 palm trees at Elim (Ex 15:27). The author shows a thorough knowledge of Egyptian court life, customs, and language. Some of the materials used to construct the tabernacle, such as acacia wood for its furniture (Ex 25:10) and rams' skins for the outer covering (Ex 25:5), are found in Egypt and the Sinai peninsula, but not in Palestine. The book thus seems to have had a desert setting.

Moses was not only commissioned by God to write the Book of Exodus, but he was also well qualified. He was "instructed in all the wisdom of the Egyptians, and he was mighty in his words and deeds" (Acts 7:22). In addition, the 40 years spent in the wilderness of Midian and Sinai gave him a thorough knowledge of the geography and wildlife of the regions through which the Israelites traveled. The events of the exodus—deliverance from the Egyptians and God's giving of the Law—were so central to the history of Israel that Moses took special care to preserve the record so it could be passed on to following generations.

Date. If one accepts the traditional view that Moses wrote Exodus, then the book is to be dated in the time of Moses. Two dates are generally suggested for the exodus from Egypt.

The "Late Date" View. This view says that the pharaoh who oppressed the Israelites was Seti I (Sethos, *c.* 1304–1290 BC) and the pharaoh of the exodus was Rameses II (Ramses, *c.* 1290–1224 BC). The exodus would thus have occurred in 1290, and the conquest of Canaan would have begun in 1250. The two principal arguments for this view are: (1) According to Exodus 1:11, the Israelites were forced to build the store city of Rameses; therefore Rameses II must have been ruling at the time. But the city of Rameses could have existed earlier under a different name and then been renamed after Rameses II when he rebuilt it. Or there could have been an earlier monarch named Rameses who commissioned its construction. (2) There is archaeological evidence of movements of people and widespread destruction in Canaan around 1250 BC. If this destruction

was caused by the Hebrew conquest under Joshua, it would place the exodus around 1290. But it could just as easily have been the result of social turbulence and anarchy in the period of the Israelite judges, or of the military activities of neighboring peoples.

The "Early Date" View. This says that the pharaoh of the oppression was Thutmose III (*c.* 1504–1450 BC) and the pharaoh of the exodus was Amenhotep II (*c.* 1450–1424 BC). Thus the exodus would have occurred about 1440, and the conquest would have begun around 1400. Chief arguments supporting that view are: (1) If the 4th year of King Solomon was 966 BC, then the 480 years of 1 Kings 6:1 would place the exodus at 1446. (2) If the time of Jephthah was 1100 BC, then the 300 years of Judges 11:26 would date the conquest at 1400. (3) The late date would not leave enough time for the period of the judges, which most chronologies indicate lasted between 300 and 400 years. On the basis of such biblical references to the date of the exodus, the early date appears preferable.

Background. Some events in Egypt during the period covered by the Book of Exodus shed additional light on the biblical record. Exodus 12:40 records that the Israelites lived in Egypt for 430 years. That would place the settling of Jacob and his family in Goshen (Gn 47:4,11) at about 1870 BC, during the powerful 12th dynasty of Egypt's Middle Kingdom. Around the turn of the century two weaker dynasties followed. Semite invaders from Asia began to infiltrate northern (or Lower) Egypt. Those outsiders, known as the Hyksos, were able to displace the native dynasty with their own king around 1730. That was the "new king" who "did not know Joseph" (Ex 1:8). Being foreigners themselves, they were naturally concerned about the Israelites, who were "too many and too mighty" for them (1:9). In event of war the Israelites might "join our enemies [the Egyptians] and fight against us" (1:10). Enslavement was thus the easiest solution to the problem of the Israelites. The Hyksos kings could use the new source of labor to enlarge Rameses, at that time the capital of Lower Egypt.

Not until about 1580 BC were the Egyptians, led by Ahmose, able to drive out the Hyksos and reestablish an Egyptian line of kings. Because the Israelites were still multiplying despite their hard labor, the pharaohs of the 18th dynasty continued their bondage and decreed that all male children must be killed. When Moses was born (*c.* 1560 BC), that edict was still in effect. Thutmose I (1539–1514), the great empire builder and third of that dynasty, was pharaoh.

Thutmose I's only surviving legal heir was

The temple of Queen Hatshepsut at Deir el-Bahri.

a daughter, Hatshepsut. Her husband assumed the name Thutmose II (1514–1504). When he died, another of the pharaoh's descendants was named successor—Thutmose III (1504–1450), who was 10 years old at the time. Hatshepsut took the kingdom from the young ruler and controlled it for 22 years (1503–1482). Such a strong-willed woman could have the nerve to disobey her father's command by saving the life of a Hebrew baby and raising him in the palace at Thebes.

Hatshepsut, who continued to rule despite Thutmose III's coronation, possibly intended for Moses to have the throne, or at least a high position in the realm. Thutmose III, once he had full power after Hatshepsut's death, would have been eager to do away with Moses. Moses' hurried flight into the wilderness after slaying the overseer fits well with such historical possibilities. Thutmose III's death in 1450 BC opened the way for Moses to return and confront Pharaoh Amenhotep II with God's command, "Let my people go."

An interesting inscription has been found on a granite column between the paws of the great Sphinx of Gizeh. The god Horus is said to have promised the throne of Egypt to Thutmose IV (1424–1417), Amenhotep II's successor. Thus Thutmose IV was possibly not the rightful heir to the throne. If so, then the biblical account that the pharaoh's eldest son died in the tenth and final plague is verified (Ex 12:29).

Purpose and Theological Teaching. The purpose of the Book of Exodus is to show how God's promise to Abraham (Gn 15:12–16) was fulfilled when the Lord rescued the Israelite descendants of Abraham from Egyptian bondage. It also explains the origin of the Passover festival, the beginning of the nation by God's establishment of a covenant with Israel, and the giving of the Law on Mt Sinai.

The Book of Exodus tells the moving story of a mighty God, Creator of the universe, beyond all limitations of time and space, who intervenes in history on behalf of a helpless group of slaves. God defeats the ruler of the greatest empire on earth, and leads his oppressed people from that land to freedom. Exodus is the story of a single family that providentially grows into a multitude. Through God's covenant a nation is formed, and through his Law the nation is given stability and set apart from all its neighbors. The Book of Exodus tells of an unusual man, whose 80 years of preparation are equally divided between the palace of a king and the pasture of a nomadic priest. Moses is a reluctant leader, but he defies the pharaoh, speaks with God face to face, and writes nearly one-fourth of the Hebrew Scriptures.

The God of Exodus is above all faithful. He makes promises and keeps them. Genesis 15:13–16 records an amazing prophecy: "Then the Lord said to Abram, 'Know of a surety that your descendants will be sojourners in a land that is not theirs, and will be slaves there, and they will be oppressed for four hundred years; but I will bring judgment on the nation which they serve, and afterward they shall come out with great possessions. . . . And they shall come back here in the fourth generation.' " In response to this promise, Joseph, "at the end of his life, made mention of the exodus of the Israelites and gave directions concerning his burial" (Heb 11:22).

That promise provides a background for the drama of redemption on which the Book of Exodus focuses. Redemption can be defined as "deliverance from the power of an alien dominion, and enjoyment of the resulting freedom." It speaks of a deliverer and what he does to achieve deliverance. The Book of Exodus is full of the vocabulary of redemption. It tells of the God who "remembers" his promise to the Hebrew patriarchs (2:24; 6:5). God "comes down to deliver" the Israelites (3:8), or "save" them (14:30; 15:2), in order to "bring them" out of the land of Egypt (3:10–12).

(1) The Lord is the author of redemption. In Exodus 6:1–8, as God answered Moses' prayer to deliver his people, he used the pronoun "I" 18 times to emphasize that he was the one initiating the action. The Hebrew descendants of Abraham had known God primarily by the Hebrew name "El," a common title in the ancient Near East for the supreme deity. But in Exodus Israel learned that God is "Jehovah" or "Yahweh." That is his personal name, a reminder that he is the God of the covenant who personally cares for his people's welfare. In Exodus 3:14, God told Moses, "I am who I am" or "I will be who I will be." Some scholars think that statement shows that the name "Yahweh" comes from the Hebrew verb "to be." In any case, the concept of "name" in the Hebrew culture is synonymous with "character." To know the name of God is to know something of his character. Israel knew God as the one who is eternally self-existent, yet present with them wherever they would go, acting on their behalf (Ex 3:12; 33:14–16).

(2) The reason for redemption was God's promise to the forefathers of the Israelites. When God heard the groaning of the people of Israel, he "remembered his covenant with Abraham, with Isaac, and with Jacob" (Ex 2:24; cf. 6:5). In response to their need he selected an agent of redemption, the unwilling Moses. Moses exhausted every possible excuse, but God would not take "no" for an answer. Moses is a vivid example of how God prepares, empowers, and sustains his chosen servants, and uses them to accomplish his purpose.

(3) The motive of redemption was God's grace and love (Ex 15:13; 20:6; 34:6,7). The purpose of redemption was that Israel and the Egyptians might know God (Ex 6:7; 7:5; 8:10; 14:18). The Lord worked so that all who were involved—Moses, the Israelites, Pharaoh, and the Egyptians—would be sure that he alone is God. The Hebrew understanding of knowledge is not primarily intellectual but experience oriented. The desired response to God's action is not mere mental assent, but also faith and obedience.

(4) Redemption is achieved in Exodus by miracles (4:21), natural processes controlled supernaturally by God. They are variously described as "signs and wonders" (7:3), "great acts of judgment" (6:6; 7:4), and "the finger of God" (8:19). Such miracles were not frivolous "fireworks," but purposeful works of God. Some of the miracles prove that Moses was sent by God. The miraculous plagues proved that God is supreme, for each of them was a direct challenge to one of the gods of Egypt: Osiris the river god, Yeqt the frog god, Ra the sun god, Athor the cattle god. The miracles in the wilderness proved that God fulfills all the needs of his people.

(5) The pharaoh was the villain in redemption, a picture of rebellious humanity confronted by God's command (Ex 4:21–23). Ten times the pharaoh hardened his heart, and 10 times it was God who hardened it, in effecting the king's decision to defy him.

(6) The Passover marked the purchase of redemption (Ex 12:23–27; 15:16). It was a clear example of salvation by substitution. When the death angel saw the blood on the doorposts and lintels, he passed by. The word used for redemption (Ex 6:6; 15:13) means to "act as a kinsman redeemer," as God prescribed in Leviticus 25:25–37 (cf. Ru 3:12,13).

(7) The recipients of God's redemption in Exodus were the Israelites. God took them as his own special people (6:7), and they were no longer free to do as they pleased. Even before the exodus he had claimed them, telling Pharaoh, "Israel is my first-born son, and I say to you, 'Let my son go that he may serve me'" (4:22,23).

(8) The demand of redemption was obedience. On the basis of his deliverance of the Israelites from bondage, God set forth the Ten Commandments (20:1–17) and the rest of the Law for them to obey. The people, though quick to pledge their obedience (Ex 19:8; 24:3), were even quicker to disobey (32:8). Because the Lord is holy and wants his people holy and wholehearted in devotion (34:14), he must punish iniquity. But, being compassionate, he also forgives. Throughout the centuries of Israel's history God pleaded with his people through the prophets to remember the exodus and repent (see Mi 6:3,4). The faithful responded in gratitude with Moses' "song of redemption" (Ex 15; cf. Rv 15:3,4).

Content. The Book of Exodus can be divided into four sections, each describing one aspect of God's dealings with the Israelites during the 15th century BC.

The God Who Descends: Revelation (Ex 1–6). The Book of Exodus begins with the 70 descendants of Jacob who joined Joseph in Egypt for the duration of a famine that was afflicting their land (cf. Gn 46–50). After more than a century of prosperity for the Israelites in the land of Goshen, a new dynasty is established in Egypt whose leaders are not friendly toward Israel. In order to stem the rapid growth of the Hebrew people, the Egyptians force them to do hard labor, building storage cities for the pharaoh.

A further command requires all Israelite male children to be killed at birth. The superintendents of the midwives do not comply, however, and God rewards them, not to show his approval of their lie but because they fear and obey God rather than the pharaoh. A new command calls for all male Israelite babies to be drowned in the Nile River. One special child, who escapes when Pharaoh's daughter has his basket fished out of the Nile, is Moses. Ironically, Moses' mother is paid by the princess to raise her own child, who grows up in the palace as the princess's adopted son.

As an adult, Moses chooses to identify with his Hebrew kin, a tribute to the early instruction given him by his godly parents (see Heb 11:24–26). He sets out to liberate Israel from the Egyptians, one man at a time. But he has to flee to Midian, at the eastern edge of the Sinai peninsula or in Arabia beyond the northern top of the Gulf of Aqaba. Moses marries into the household of Jethro, also named Reuel. Reuel ("friend of God") is probably the man's personal name, and Jethro ("excellence") his title. Because he is called a "priest of Midian" (Ex 2:16), some scholars have maintained a "Kenite hypothesis," suggesting that Moses adopted the religion of his father-in-law and taught it to the Israelites. The Bible states that Moses received his religion by a direct revelation from God. Jethro seems to believe only after he sees that God has rescued Israel from the Egyptians (Ex 18:10,11).

While their future deliverer is in Midian, the Israelites continue to be oppressed and cry out to God in their misery (2:23–25). God responds by descending to his people. He "comes down to deliver" (3:8), to intervene on Israel's behalf. He appears to Moses in a burning bush and identifies himself as the same God who promised the patriarchs a land "flowing with milk and honey" (3:17). Moses will lead the Israelites there, assisted by his brother Aaron.

Assured that God's presence and miraculous signs will accompany him, Moses takes his wife Zipporah and his two sons and departs for Egypt. On the way, the Lord meets him and seeks to put him to death (4:24). That is probably the Hebrew way of saying that God strikes him with a mortal illness. Moses, who is going to deliver God's people, has neglected the sign of the covenant in failing to circumcise one of his sons (Gn 17:14). Moses

recovers after the rite is performed and continues on to Egypt, meeting Aaron at Mt Sinai. Their reception by the Israelites is more cordial than that of Pharaoh, who refuses to honor the God who sent Moses. Instead of releasing the Israelites to offer sacrifices to their God in the wilderness, he increases their burdens. The people complain to Moses, and Moses complains to God. God appears again to Moses (Ex 6), reassuring him that Israel will be delivered by divine power. God's plan is not a failure—he is just beginning to put it into action.

The God Who Delivers: Redemption (Ex 7–19). Chapters 7–12 record 10 plagues with which God afflicts the Egyptians. Even before the first of them the pharaoh has hardened his heart to defy God (7:13). There are three cycles of three plagues each:

	1st cycle	*2nd cycle*	*3rd cycle*
Announced in the morning	blood	flies	hail
Announced before Pharaoh	frogs	cattle	locusts
Unannounced	gnats	boils	darkness

The first three plagues affect both the Egyptians and the Israelites; the Israelites are protected from the final six. The Egyptian magicians are able to duplicate the first two plagues, but when the third strikes, they admit, "This is the finger of God" (8:19). After the plague of flies covers the land, the pharaoh offers Moses the first of four compromises, but Moses refuses all of them (8:25–29; 10:8–11,24–29). The first plagues are merely unpleasant, but the final ones are destructive and inflict much suffering. Since all of the plagues are common to that area, they themselves are not miraculous. The miracle is how the phenomena are multiplied, the exact prediction of their beginning and end, and their limitation to just the land of Egypt.

The nine plagues only serve to further harden the pharaoh's heart, so God prepares one final stroke. The death of every firstborn male, among both animals and humans, will be the fatal blow. God warns the Israelites to get ready to leave. To avert the death angel, they must put blood from an unblemished yearling male sheep or goat on their doorways. While they are eating the Passover meal, the death angel begins moving through the land of Egypt. In anguish the pharaoh drives the Israelites from the land; the slaves are free at last. The Passover must be celebrated annually as an eternal reminder of God's deliverance. Just as he has promised, the Lord goes before the children of Israel (about 2 million in number, Nm 1:46), in a pillar of cloud by day and of fire by night.

Once again the pharaoh's heart is hardened and he gives pursuit. God parts the waters of the sea with a great wind. The literal meaning of the name given that body of water is "sea of reeds." It could refer to any shoreline where the water is sufficiently shallow for such plants to grow (see 1 Kgs 9:26, where the same term refers to the Gulf of Aqaba near Eloth). Whatever the location, there God hands the Egyptians their final defeat; the deliverance is complete.

Moses and the Israelites respond with renewed faith in the Lord and with a song of victory and praise (Ex 14:31–15:21). Soon, however, thanksgiving turns into grumbling because of bitter water (15:22–26), lack of meat and bread (16:1–15), and lack of water (17:1–7). In each situation God provides for their need. He also gives them victory over the Amalekites (17:8–16). As the Israelites approach Mt Sinai, Moses' family rejoins him, accompanied by Jethro. Jethro now confesses his faith in the God of the Israelites and shares in a fellowship meal with the leaders. He also assists Moses in reorganizing the judicial system before returning to Midian (Ex 18).

The Israelites arrive at Mt Sinai, also called Horeb (3:1), and prepare to meet the Lord who has rescued them in fulfillment of his promise to Moses (3:12). The Lord establishes his covenant with Israel, taking them as his own possession, a "kingdom of priests and a holy nation." They quickly respond, "All that the Lord has spoken we will do" (19:5–8).

The God Who Demands: Instruction (Ex 20–24). The God who redeems a people, who literally "buys them back from slavery," has a right to make certain demands of them. The commandments God gives to Israel at Sinai are not burdensome requirements, but protective guidelines for demonstrating their gratitude and obedience (Ex 20:2,3).

The Law (or Torah, "instruction") revealed at Sinai consists of three parts: (1) The Ten Commandments (Ex 20), addressing a person's relationship to God and other people. Based on God's nature, and therefore permanent, the Ten Commandments are unique in the history of the nations. (2) The judgments (Ex 21–23), social regulations for governing the people as a theocracy, similar in many ways to the law codes of Israel's neighbors. (3) Ordinances (Ex 24–31) regulating religious ceremonies. All of the laws are given to Moses during the weeks he spends with God on the mountain.

The Ten Commandments form the basis of all other laws in Israel (20:1–17). The first five deal with honoring the Lord, the second five with respecting one's neighbor. The last commandment deals with one's thoughts and intentions, rather than with specific actions. It thus forms a safeguard against all sins not included in the first nine. The people are terrified as nature responds to the Lord's presence, and they ask Moses to intercede on their behalf (20:18–20).

The judgments recorded in chapters 21–24 deal with master-slave relationships (21:1–11), offenses punishable by death (21:12–17), compensation for injury to persons or damage to property (21:18–22:15), various interpersonal relationships (22:16–23:9), and sabbaths, feasts, and the offering of firstfruits (23:10–19). Many of the judgments would not take effect until Israel settled in the Promised Land. Accordingly, that section of the Law closes with a solemn warning against being rebellious and adopting pagan ways. It also contains a bright promise that God will drive out Israel's enemies, protect his people from sickness, and grant them prosperity, "if you . . . do all that I say" (23:22).

Exodus 24 records a reaffirmation of the covenant between God and Israel, as Moses seals it with the blood of a sacrifice. In response, God appears to the leaders of the people, giving them a glimpse of his splendor. Then Moses ascends the mountain one more time to receive the stone tablets containing the commandments, as well as further instructions regarding the meeting tent (tabernacle), the priesthood, and worship.

The God Who Dwells: Fellowship (Ex 25–40). The Lord told Moses that after he redeemed the Israelites, "I will take you for my people, and I will be your God" (6:7). Moses has seen that wonderful promise fulfilled, yet one further step remains to be taken. "Let them make me a sanctuary, that I may dwell in their midst" (25:8). God's dwelling among his people is possible because God has descended to deliver the people and because they have pledged to meet his demands. God calls for a contribution from all whose hearts are willing to give, and he shows Moses a detailed pattern of the tabernacle and its furniture. Aaron and his sons are set apart to serve in the tent. Stipulations for the various offerings, including the Day of Atonement, are given. God tells Moses that he has chosen Bezalel and Oholiab to build the tabernacle and to craft its furnishings, having filled them with his Spirit.

In the meantime the Israelites, who so recently promised total obedience, grow impatient as Moses lingers for 40 days on the mountain. They demand that Aaron make an idol for them. Under pressure, Aaron complies and forms a molten calf, a representation of a pagan deity. "These are your gods, O Israel, who brought you up out of the land of Egypt," he tells them (32:4).

The Lord informs Moses of the people's idolatry, revelry, and immorality, and says that he is angry enough to destroy all of them and start again with Moses' offspring. Moses pleads for Israel until the Lord relents, then descends from the mountain to punish the people. He pleads again for forgiveness for Israel, and God in mercy pardons their terrible sin (34:8–10).

Once more God offers to make a covenant with the people (34:10). Moses spends another 40 days with the Lord, writing the commandments on tablets to replace those smashed when he saw the golden calf. When he returns to the people, his face shines from being in God's presence, and he must keep it veiled.

Now that Israel has been restored to God's favor, the construction of the tabernacle can begin. The contributions are so generous that Moses must restrain the people from bringing any more. Finally, all is ready. Moses examines the tabernacle, and it is erected on the first day of the first month, nearly a year after the first Passover. The priests are consecrated, the lamps are lit, and the first burnt sacrifice is offered. A cloud descends, filling the tabernacle with the glory of the Lord. God dwells among his people, the goal of redemption has been attained, and the drama of the Book of Exodus has come to an end.

KENNETH L. BARKER & RICHARD L. SCHULTZ

See EXODUS, THE; FEASTS AND FESTIVALS OF ISRAEL; ISRAEL, HISTORY OF; PLAGUES UPON EGYPT; TABERNACLE, TEMPLE; TEN COMMANDMENTS, THE; MOSES; EGYPT, EGYPTIANS; DOCUMENTARY HYPOTHESIS; CHRONOLOGY, OLD TESTAMENT.

Bibliography. H. Alford, *The Book of Genesis and Part of the Book of Exodus*; S.R. Driver, *The Book of Exodus*; J.G. Murphy, *A Critical and Exegetical Commentary on the Book of Exodus*.

Exodus, The.

Departure of Israel from Egypt led by Moses. The exodus was one of the most significant events in the history of the Hebrews. It was a unique demonstration of God's power on behalf of his people, who were working under conditions of forced labor for the Egyptians. So dramatic were the circumstances in which the exodus occurred that they were mentioned frequently in subsequent OT periods. When the Hebrews were oppressed, they looked back to that great historical event and trusted God for their future liberation.

The historicity of the exodus from Egypt is beyond question, being one of the pivotal historical and religious points of the Jewish tradition. It is quite another matter, however, to assign a firm date to the event, partly because certain scriptural references can be interpreted in various ways, and partly because little archaeological evidence from Egypt exists that bears on the question. Since the Egyptians regularly ignored defects in their records and defaced inscriptions belonging to unpopular fellow countrymen, it is improbable that anything approaching an Egyptian literary record of the exodus will ever be obtained. Much of the information regarding the date of the exodus is therefore inferential in character, and that presents biblical historians with one of the most complex problems of chronology.

Date of the Exodus. *The Problem of Dating.* Determining the date of the exodus has long been a problem for biblical scholars. At the beginning of the 20th century many scholars, both liberal and conservative, placed the date toward the end of the 13th century BC. Not all of them agreed that the exodus was a single event, however, some believing that the Hebrews entered Palestine twice at widely separated times. Such a view, which occasionally resulted in Joshua being placed before Moses chronologically, could only be maintained by disregarding completely the biblical tradition.

According to Exodus 12:40 the length of time that Jacob's descendants resided in the land of Egypt was 430 years. God had already predicted that interval of time to Abram (Gn 15:13). The Genesis prophecy, however, did not indicate when that occupation would begin.

The Septuagint (the first Greek translation of the OT), in its version of Exodus 12:40, reduced the period of occupation in Egypt to 215 years. That may mean that two traditions of exodus history existed. A stay of four centuries may have been reckoned from the period when an Asiatic people known as the Hyksos invaded Egypt (1720? BC) and governed it for about a century and a half. The period of 215 years preserved in the Septuagint may be the interval of time between the expulsion of the Hyksos and the exodus itself.

More specific information from Israel's early monarch, however, has a bearing on the time when the Hebrews escaped from Egypt. Solomon, says 1 Kings 6:1, constructed the temple in Jerusalem 480 years after the Israelites were led out of Egypt by Moses. Taking that figure at face value, and allowing a date of 961 BC for the reference to Solomon, the exodus would have occurred about 1441 BC. On the basis of such biblical data some scholars argue for a 15th-century BC date for the exodus, connecting it with the reign of Pharaoh

Amenhotep II, who many think was the pharaoh of the Exodus, stands in his chariot and shoots arrows at a copper target.

Amenhotep II (c. 1450–1425 BC) as the time of Israel's oppression. Other scholars feel equally persuaded that the exodus occurred in the 13th century BC.

Early Date Theory. The early date received support from archaeologist John Garstang's excavations at OT Jericho (Tell es-Sultan). Garstang identified several levels of debris there, indicating that the city had been rebuilt a number of times. He concluded that the one built about 1500 BC was the Jericho overthrown by Joshua's forces (Jos 6). Garstang's statement that Jericho had fallen before 1400 appeared to support the time frame of 1 Kings 6:1, and was received enthusiastically by supporters of the 15th-century BC date.

Garstang also stated that diplomatic connections between Jericho and Egypt had been severed under Pharaoh Amenhotep III (1412–1377 BC), thus making Amenhotep II the pharaoh of the exodus and Thutmose III the ruler during the oppression period. A mural from the tomb of Rekhmire, vizier (minister of state) under Thutmose III, showed a brick-making scene, complete with Egyptian overseers, bearing the inscription "The rod is in my hand; be not idle," all of which seems to suggest the Hebrews in captivity. Further evidence for the early date theory came from the discovery of the Tell el-Amarna letters, a body of correspondence addressed to Pharaoh Amenhotep IV and his father, Amenhotep III, between 1400 and 1360 BC. Proponents of the early date theory assume that references in the letters to invading "Habiru" allude to the conquering Hebrews under Joshua, since the term "Habiru" is thought by some to be equivalent to "Hebrew." The letters, which contain pleas from native Canaanite rulers to Egypt for help against the marauding Habiru, are taken as a Canaanite account of Joshua's invasion and are offered in support of a 15th-century BC exodus date. The most direct evidence for the early date, however, remains the literal interpretation of 1 Kings 6:1.

Late Date Theory. Arguments for a 13th-century BC date take Exodus 1:11 as referring to the time when the Egyptian cities of Pithom and Rameses (or Raamses) were being enlarged or rebuilt with the help of Hebrew slaves. Pharaoh Rameses II (c. 1290–1224 BC) moved the Egyptian capital from Thebes to Avaris, the old Hyksos capital, which was known to the Hebrews as Rameses. Late-date theorists argue that, since the Exodus account used the name by which the city was known for about two centuries only (c. 1300–1100 BC), the Hebrew tradition of the exodus must also date from that period. In such an event Rameses II would have been the pharaoh of the oppression, and his son Merneptah (1224?–1214 BC) the pharaoh of the exodus.

Archaeological surveys by Nelson Glueck in Transjordan indicated that during the time of Isaac and Jacob, the population of Edom and Moab declined until about the middle of the 13th century BC. Thus, it was argued, the difficulties experienced by the invading Hebrews in Transjordan (Nm 20,21) could not have occurred until the 13th century BC, when Edom was a strong nation. In support of a late date for the exodus appeal is also made to the Merneptah stela, a stone slab inscribed about 1220 BC recording a list of conquered peoples. Among the names listed, Israel's is the only one to be written in such a manner as to imply a people rather than a territory, suggesting that although the Hebrews were in Canaan (the Promised Land) at the time, they were not in complete occupational control of the territory.

Difficulties with Early and Late Dates. Both 15th- and 13th-century BC dates, however, meet with difficulties. The 480 years mentioned in 1 Kings 6:1 are open to a symbolic interpretation if the number is regarded as the product of 12 (tribes) and 40 (wilderness years). If the 480-year figure is symbolic in nature, it is of no help in determining the date of the exodus.

A 15th-century BC date presents problems for the chronology of Abram. Archaeological evidence relating to the overthrow of Sodom and Gomorrah seems to date Abram's arrival in Canaan around 1900 BC. The Genesis narratives place Jacob's migration to Egypt about 215 years later. On the basis of the 430 years of Exodus 12:40 it would seem that Abram came to Canaan about 2086 BC, some 645 years before the exodus. That would date his birth (cf. 12:4) about 2161 BC. If the Sodom and Gomorrah evidence is correct, Abram's arrival in Canaan would harmonize with a 13th-century BC date.

Garstang's discoveries at Jericho have been modified seriously by the subsequent work of another archaeologist, Kathleen Kenyon. She found no trace of Late Bronze Age walls, which indicates that the city Garstang thought to have been conquered by Joshua was considerably earlier than his time. Unfortunately, the mound has been so ravaged by erosion and human pillaging that it reveals almost nothing about the Jericho of Joshua's day, and thus does not help to simplify matters.

Archaeological evidence from Canaanite sites such as Bethel, Debir, Lachish, and Hazor indicates destruction at 13th-century BC levels, a fact generally regarded as relating to the Hebrew occupation under Joshua. Scholars who maintain an early date for the exodus think of Bethel falling to Joseph's tribe (Jgs 1:22), while Debir's collapse would be described first in terms of its inhabitants (Jos 10:38), and second of the city proper under Othniel (Jgs 1:11). Evidence from Philistine sites tends to favor a late rather than an early date for the exodus. Against that, however, must be set the fact that the major Philistine occupation of the southern Palestinian coastlands only occurred around 1175 BC, in the time of Rameses III.

The relationship between the "Habiru" of the Amarna letters, the "Apiru" in 13th-century BC Egypt, and the biblical Hebrews has been examined minutely by scholars. Widely differing opinions have been offered. Some believe that the three are variations of the name of one people. To others, however, it seems far from clear that there was any significant relationship between the names. Such disagreement also tends to intensify the problem.

Some scholars have criticized Glueck's statements about the sparse Transjordanian population in the 15th century BC, arguing on the basis of excavations at Amman, Heshbon, and elsewhere that there were more people in the locality than Glueck imagined. Such a position would tend to support a 15th-century BC date for the exodus.

Other scholars have argued that the reference in Exodus 1:11 is to the original construction of the Hyksos capital of Avaris about 1720 BC, not to its reconstruction as Rameses under Rameses II. A stela recovered from Rameses and dated about 1320 BC recorded that the city had been founded 400 years earlier, thus authenticating its establishment. Such a view assumes that the Hebrews entered Egypt in the Middle Kingdom period (2000–1780 BC), perhaps about 1870 BC, and that their oppression commenced under Hyksos rule. This view has to contend with the unlikely prospect of the Hebrews being treated preferentially by Egyptians, who heartily disliked the "hated Asiatics," but being enslaved by the Hyksos, who were fellow Semites.

As is evident from such a range of opinion, the date of the exodus is one of the most complex problems of Hebrew history. Understandably enough, the exodus has been correlated with the pattern of Egyptian history, but the lack of conclusive data from Egypt precludes a ready solution to the difficulties. Only if new information is forthcoming from an unforeseen area is there any prospect of resolving the problem satisfactorily.

Route of the Exodus. The biblical data concerning the route of the exodus placed the beginning of the flight at Rameses (Ex 12:37). This place was identified with Tanis (Sân el Hagar) by early investigators; but more recent work suggests Qantir, about 17 miles southwest of Tanis, as the preferred site. It now seems certain that the monuments at Tanis apparently erected by Rameses have been misunderstood. None of those monuments seems to have originated at Tanis but were brought there by later kings who reused them. Thus the primary evidence for identifying Tanis with Rameses has proved to be misleading. Excavations at Qantir, on the other hand, have revealed indications of palaces, temples, and houses, all of which were local in origin.

Beni Hasan tomb painting that shows Semites entering Egypt during the 19th century BC.

Such evidence suggests that Qantir, not Tanis, was the Rameses from which the exodus commenced. In addition, Rameses, unlike Tanis, was located beside a body of water (the "Waters of Re" mentioned in Egyptian sources), which again conforms to the biblical account.

From Rameses the Israelites moved to Succoth (Nm 33:5), generally identified with Tell el-Maskhuta, a fortification in the eastern area of the Wadi Tumeilat, west of the Bitter Lakes. From Succoth they journeyed to Etham (Ex 13:20), which was probably a fortress on the frontier of the wilderness of Shur. The Hebrews were then instructed to return northwestward in order that the stage might be set for the events of the exodus proper. Accordingly they encamped between Migdol and the "sea," close to two sites called Pi-hahiroth and Baal-zephon. Pi-hahiroth may have been a lake, the "Hi-waters," mentioned in Egyptian documents. Baal-zephon has been identified with the later Tahpanhes (Tell Defenneh) near Qantara. Both identifications lack certainty, but these places were probably located in the northeast part of the Nile River delta area near Lake Menzaleh. The "sea" was a lake of papyrus reeds, described in Exodus 15:22 as the "reed sea," the English equivalent of an Egyptian phrase meaning "papyrus marshes." In most English translations from the time of the KJV onward the Hebrew for "reed sea" was rendered as "Red Sea."

Sources from the 13th century BC mention the existence of a large papyrus marsh in the area of Rameses which could be the one referred to in Scripture. Other suggestions equate the reed sea with the southeast exten-

The Nile delta—with the Mediterranean Sea to the left, the Suez Canal and the Red Sea at the top right.

sion of lake Menzaleh, or with some body of water just to the south, perhaps Lake Ballah, all of which are reasonably close to each other. The topography can never be determined with complete accuracy, since the construction of the Suez Canal drained a series of lakes and swamps, of which the reed sea was probably one.

At the camp at Migdol the Hebrews were overtaken by the pursuing Egyptians and appeared to be trapped hopelessly. Then the Lord worked one of the great miracles of history. He prevented the Egyptians from encountering the Hebrews that night by means of a pillar of cloud (Ex 14:19,20). Moses raised his rod over the reed sea, and a strong east wind blew on the water all night. By morning a strip of the "sea" bottom had been exposed and dried out, enabling the Israelites to flee across it. When the Egyptians pursued their former slaves, Moses again raised his rod, the wind ceased, and the waters returned to normal levels, trapping the Egyptian chariots and soldiers and causing heavy losses. A victory song (Ex 15:1–21), typical of ancient Near Eastern customs in warfare, was the liberated captives' immediate response to God.

The parting of the waters is a phenomenon that has been observed periodically in various parts of the world. It always occurs in the same manner and involves a strong wind displacing a body of water. Shallow lakes, rivers, or marshes are parted readily under such conditions. The scriptural reference to the east wind indicates that God miraculously employed that natural phenomenon to rescue his people.

Having escaped successfully from the Egyptians, the Hebrews journeyed to the wilderness of Shur, three traveling days away from the bitter waters of Marah (Ex 15:22–25). In Numbers 33:8 the wilderness of Shur is identified with Etham, which the Israelites had already left. Thus it appears that they had moved north from Migdol, after which they moved south again to the wilderness in the area of Etham. The Israelites were not able to go into the Sinai peninsula along the normal routes, which were guarded by Egyptian fortresses. In addition, they had been instructed not to travel along the northward road going to the "way of the land of the Philistines" (Ex 13:17) into Canaan. Consequently, the best means of satisfying both conditions was to move southeastward to Sinai as unobtrusively as possible, taking care to avoid the access routes to Serabit el-Khadem in the central peninsula region, where the Egyptians mined turquoise and copper.

The narratives of Numbers 33:9–15 show that the Israelite camps were located in an area south of the reed sea, proving that the refugees had not taken the northerly, or "Philistine," route, as earlier liberal scholars had suggested before the discovery of Rameses and its identification with Tanis.

The Exodus Theme in Scripture. *Old Testament.* The motif of deliverance from captivity in Egypt became etched indelibly upon the Hebrew mind, particularly since it was reinforced each year by the celebration of the Passover meal, at the institution of which all the Egyptian firstborn had died (Ex 12:12–14,29). At each celebration thereafter the Hebrews were made aware that they had once been captives, but by the provision and power of God they were now free people, favored with his choice as an elect nation and a holy priesthood (Dt 26:19).

In later periods psalms were written recounting Israel's history in the light of the great liberating event of the exodus (Pss 105;106;114;136). Those compositions resound with triumph and thanksgiving. Hebrew accounts of the bondage in Egypt depict the rigorous life, the oppression, and the hard labor. It is now known that there were a number of foreign groups in Egypt at the time, and that the corporal punishment suffered by the Hebrews was a normal feature of everyday Egyptian life. In short, there was no discrimination against the Hebrews as a group; instead, they enjoyed the dubious distinction of being treated like ordinary Egyptian workers. Ever after, when they were oppressed, the Hebrews could look back to the great miracle of the exodus and believe that what God had done once he could do again. That was of great consolation to the faithful exiles weeping by the waters of Babylon (Ps 137:1) as they looked forward to another exodus when God would lead them in triumph from a destroyed Babylon (Ps 137:8) back to Palestine.

New Testament. God's mighty work at the time of the exodus was recalled on a few occasions by NT writers, even though Christ had been sacrificed as "our Passover lamb" (1 Cor 5:7 NIV) by that time. In his speech before the Jerusalem council Stephen gave a traditional recital of OT history, mentioning the event of the Red Sea (Acts 7:36) as part of a demonstration of God's power to change human affairs. The apostle Paul used the experience of the exodus to remind his hearers that many who were delivered from oppression at that time never reached the Promised Land (1 Cor 10:1,2,5). Instead of committing themselves wholly to God in trust and obedience, the Israelites fell victim to temptations of various kinds in the wilderness. Though all of them were called to be part of a holy nation, few were actually chosen. Thus Paul stressed that

since it is possible for Christians to become castaways (1 Cor 9:27), they should cling to Christ the Rock and take their spiritual responsibilities seriously. In Hebrews 11:27–29 another historical recital lists the heroes of faith, mentioning especially Moses and his role at the exodus. R. K. HARRISON

See EXODUS, BOOK OF; CHRONOLOGY, OLD TESTAMENT.

Exorcism, Exorcist. Art of expelling demons and evil spirits, and the practitioner of this art.

See DEMON, DEMON POSSESSION; TRADES AND OCCUPATIONS.

Expiation. Atonement, purification, or removal of sin or its guilt. The term occurs in some English translations for KJV "reconciliation" (Heb 2:17) or "propitiation" (Rom 3:25; 1 Jn 2:2; 4:10). "Expiation" also appears in some English translations of some OT passages (Nm 35:33; Dt 32:43; 1 Sm 3:14; Is 27:9). The word does not appear in the more recent Bible translations.

The Hebrew family of words translated by "expiation" speaks fundamentally of a solution for sin, and the most common association is with the idea of atonement. Expiation has to do with the blot of sin, and hence the term is related to such words as "forgive," "purge," "cleanse," or "atone."

All NT references to expiation have to do with the sacrifice of Christ for human sin. In the Bible both expiation and propitiation are part of God's atoning work. Christ's sacrifice both propitiates (turns away) the wrath of God and expiates (covers) human sin. God's redemptive work is both personal, or relational, and objective. When a biblical context concentrates on God's wrath, propitiation is involved; when human sin is the focus, then redemption provides expiation.

The best solution to the problem of relating expiation and propitiation is not to choose between them—both terms are proper biblical concepts—but to read the prominent idea or ideas in context. In Romans 3:25, for example, both wrath and sin are part of the context (see Rom 1:18; 2:5,8; 3:5). Thus the broader term "atonement," which can include both ideas, is preferable (cf. NIV).

The biblical writers sought to do justice to every aspect of God's redemptive work, and so a number of related expressions were used to describe it. That expiation means "removal of sin" underscores a fundamental dimension of redemption: "as far as the east is from the west, so far does he remove our transgressions from us" (Ps 103:12).

See OFFERINGS AND SACRIFICES; PROPITIATION; ATONEMENT; WRATH OF GOD.

Bibliography. C. Brown, ed., *New International Dictionary of New Testament Theology*, vol. 3, pp. 151–60. L. Morris, *The Apostolic Preaching of the Cross*; R.V.G. Tasker, *The Biblical Doctrine of the Wrath of God.*

Eye Paint. See FASHION AND DRESS.

Ezar. KJV spelling of Ezer, Seir's son, in 1 Chronicles 1:38.

See EZER # 1.

Ezbai. Father of Naarai, one of David's elite force known as "the 30" (1 Chr 11:37). In 2 Samuel 23:35 he is called Paarai the Arbite. This has led some interpreters to suggest that "the son of Ezbai" in the 1 Chronicles passage is a corruption of "the Arbite" and that the correct reading of his name should be Naarai the Arbite.

Ezbon. 1. Gad's son (Gn 46:16), called Ozni in Numbers 26:16; perhaps an eponym of a Gadite family.

2. Benjamin's grandson (1 Chr 7:7). It has been proposed that 1 Chronicles 7:6–11 is a genealogy of Zebulun assigned to Benjamin by error, and that Ezbon suggests Ibzan (Jgs 12:8–10), a minor judge of Bethlehem.

Ezekias. KJV spelling of Hezekiah, Judah's king, in Matthew 1:9,10.

See HEZEKIAH # 1.

Ezekiel (Person). Priest and prophet during Israel's Babylonian exile. Ezekiel was a descendant of the influential priestly family of Zadok (Ez 1:3). He was probably reared in Jerusalem and was familiar with the temple ritual, though whether he served as a priest there is not known. All that is known of his personal life is obtained from the OT Book of Ezekiel.

Ezekiel was married (24:16–18) and lived at Telabib in Babylonia (3:15), in his own house (3:24; 8:1). Most of the Judean captives had settled by the Chebar canal (1:3), which went from Babylon by Nippur to Erech. The elders of Israel there sought out Ezekiel for counsel (8:1; 14:1; 20:1). In the fifth year of the exile, when Ezekiel was between 25 and 30 years old, he received God's call to the prophetic office (1:1–3:11). His wife died suddenly during the exile, but he was forbidden to mourn for her in public (24:16–18). Her sudden death was meant to convey a striking and solemn warning of what would occur in the captives' homeland (24:15–27).

The time of Ezekiel's ministry was unusual in many ways. It was a period of great pro-

phetic activity. With the prophets Jeremiah and Daniel, Ezekiel spoke to the nation's needs at the time of the Babylonian captivity. It was an era of upheaval and uprooting for the southern kingdom of Judah, and a time of persistent apostasy, idolatry, and general disobedience to the Mosaic law. It was also a period of international conflict and shifting power balances throughout the Middle East.

Ezekiel's ministry seems to have extended from 592 BC to at least the 27th year of the exile (29:17), and falls into two main periods. During the first period (592–587 BC) his messages were repeated warnings, in prose discourse and symbolic acts, intended to lead the exiles to repentance and faith in God. During the second period (586–570 BC) after Nebuchadnezzar's destruction of Jerusalem and the temple, the prophet comforted the exiles and encouraged them to look to the future in hope (chs 33–48). There were 13 years in which no prophetic utterances were delivered, namely 585 BC (32:1,17; 33:21) to 572 BC (40:1). The prophet learned of the fall of Jerusalem while in Babylon (33:21,22).

The burden of Ezekiel's message was that Judah was ripe for judgment. His preparation for speaking God's message is given in the picture of his eating the written prophecies (2:8–3:3). At first the messages were not accepted, but later his prophecies were vindicated as they began to come true and as the nation was purged of its idolatry. Ezekiel has been called "the father of Judaism" because of his supposed influence on Israel's later worship. His greatest contribution to postexilic Jewish worship consisted in establishing the basis of the synagogue. He stressed the teaching of personal immortality, resurrection, and the ritual law, a unique feature among the prophets.

Ezekiel carried out his messages with vivid and dramatic acts of symbolism (e.g., 4:1–8; 5:1–17). His style has been characterized as heavy and repetitious, but it was designed with the themes of apostasy and subsequent judgment in view. The place and circumstances of his death are unknown, Ezekiel is not mentioned elsewhere in the OT.

CHARLES L. FEINBERG

See EZEKIEL, BOOK OF; EXILE; PROPHET, PROPHETESS.

Ezekiel, Book of. Prophetic book of the OT, originating in the time of the Babylonian exile.

Author. Ezekiel was the son of Buzi (1:3), a member of a priestly family. It is unclear whether he actually served in the temple as a priest, but such was his training. His writings show that he knew the regulations for sacrifices, the rituals, and the people's expectations of a priest. In exile Ezekiel the priest spoke God's word about the future of the temple to his fellow exiles. Settled at Telabib, on the canal of Chebar, the thousands of deportees eked out a meager existence. They hoped for a speedy return to Judah and a change for the better in the international situation. Their hope was flamed by the spirited preaching of false prophets, likened to foxes among the ruins (13:4). They piously said, "The Lord declares . . . ," but they were actually self-commissioned (13:6). They deceived the people with a message of peace at a time when God's judgment was about to be poured out on his people (13:10). They had led the people to distrust prophecy to such an extent that a proverb circulated among the people that "the days grow long, and every vision comes to nought" (12:22). Much time had passed since visions of God's judgment had been given to the people, and nothing could be interpreted as a fulfillment of those visions. Ezekiel was called to serve his community by symbolic acts, visions, and verbal messages in order to convince the people that God's judgment was imminent (12:23).

Background. The ministry of the prophet Ezekiel can be understood best against the backdrop of his time. If, as the church father Origen believed, the vague reference "in the thirtieth year" (1:1) marks the prophet's age at the time of his first vision, Ezekiel was born during the rule of King Josiah of Judah (c. 640–609 BC). Josiah was the grandson of King Manasseh, whose sacrilegious acts had brought God's judgment on the kingdom of Judah (2 Kgs 21:10–15).

Though Judah's political situation was perilous, Josiah led the nation in a radical reformation that began with the finding of the "book of the law" (2 Kgs 22) in the year that Ezekiel was born (c. 621 BC). Idolatry was done away with and the people turned back to God, but God's judgment on Judah was unchangeable (2 Kgs 23:26,27). Josiah erred in trying to make Judah a kingdom with which other states had to reckon. He was threatened when the Egyptian pharaoh Neco passed through Judah, to aid the weakened Assyrian kingdom. Josiah marched to meet the Egyptian forces, but his troops were unable to stand against the Egyptians, and he died in battle (2 Kgs 23:29). Egypt took control of Judah, and Pharaoh Neco placed Jehoiakim in power over Jerusalem. Egyptian control did not last long, however, for in 605 BC Egypt and Assyria were defeated by Babylonia's king Nebuchadnezzar at Carchemish. The Babylonians then pushed south to Jerusalem, and the first deportation of Judean leaders, among them the prophet Daniel, took place.

Although Scripture contains no record of the death of Ezekiel or of the location of his grave, tradition suggests that he died in Babylon during the reign of Nebuchadnezzar and that he was buried at this spot—Kefil, near Babylon, between the Chebar and the Euphrates.

Jehoiakim was permitted to continue ruling over Judah as a vassal king of Nebuchadnezzar. His dealings with Egypt brought him the emperor's wrath. Before the Babylonians could address the Judean situation, Jehoiakim died and his son Jehoiachin was crowned. When the Babylonian forces arrived at the gates of Jerusalem, Jehoiachin and thousands of the aristocracy were taken to Babylon (2 Kgs 24:10–17). Among those deportees was Ezekiel, then about 25 years old.

Although the book says otherwise, many scholars think that Ezekiel lived and taught in Judah for the duration of the siege and the fall of Jerusalem (586 BC). They conclude this from Ezekiel's familiarity with idolatry in the temple and his vivid descriptions of Jerusalem's last days (Ez 8:11). Others believe that Ezekiel ministered both to the exiled community and to the Judeans living in Judah. Neither interpretation does full justice to the claims of the book itself. Ezekiel was exiled in 597 BC. He was called to bring God's word to the deportees at Telabib; he was granted a vision of the horrible practices in the temple court; and he was familiar with Jerusalem and Judah from having lived there and from reports on affairs in Jerusalem coming to the exiles through messengers. Jeremiah, Ezekiel's contemporary, was prophesying in Jerusalem, but there is no evidence that Jeremiah and Ezekiel knew of each other's ministry. If Ezekiel had brought God's word to Jerusalem during the siege, some reference to Jeremiah might appear in his writings. If Jeremiah was supported by Ezekiel's ministry in Jerusalem, he probably would have included a positive word for his colleague in his book. The Book of Ezekiel plainly says that Ezekiel lived and preached in exile (see 1:1,3; 11:24,25).

Content. The prophecy of Ezekiel is easily outlined by subject matter and chronology.

The chronology of the period permits a division before and after 586 BC (the fall of Jerusalem). Chapters 1–24 cover the pre–586 ministry of Ezekiel, whereas chapters 33–48 represent his post–586 ministry. Chapters 25–32 (oracles against the foreign nations) function as a transition between the book's two major divisions.

The book's outline according to subject matter divides into four parts: Ezekiel's call (1:1–3:21); prophecies of judgment against Israel (3:22–24:27); oracles against the nations (25:1–32:32); and proclamation of hope (33:1–48:35).

Ezekiel's Call (1:1–3:21). The prophet's call in one sense was similar to that of Isaiah and Jeremiah. Isaiah received his mission in a vision of God's glory in the temple (Isa 6:1–13). Jeremiah was called unexpectedly in his youth, and received signs which solemnly set forth the nature of his mission (1:11–15). The call of Ezekiel combined those two elements. Revelation of God's glory to the prophet at the same time revealed the nature of the prophet's mission. Ezekiel's call contained a uniquely full description of God's glory. Isaiah briefly stated that he saw the Lord enthroned in the temple, and concentrated on the seraphim representing and magnifying God's glory. Ezekiel elaborated on the revelation of the Lord's glory as well as on the ministering angels who went before the Lord as part of his royal entourage. The vision of God's glory, though difficult, is the key to the Book of Ezekiel.

Ezekiel, as a priest, was concerned about the future of the temple. That sacred place had been ordained by God as his home among his people. The glory, presence, and holiness of God were symbolized in the temple (see 1 Kgs 8:10,11). In exile Ezekiel could not serve his people as a priest, for they were far from Jerusalem, the city God had chosen. Against all expectations the Lord revealed himself to Ezekiel in the land of Babylon. In calling Ezekiel to a prophetic ministry, God assured his servant that he had not forsaken his people, even though they had been banished from the Promised Land.

Ezekiel's vision of God's glory has been interpreted in various ways. In the pseudepigraphical writings of the intertestamental period, pious Jews made mystical speculations on the "chariot chapter" (Ez 1). Some modern readers interpret the vision of God's glory as an appearance of an unidentified flying object, an idea that in no way appreciates God's glory.

The prophet's vision began with a storm. As a large cloud approached from the north, Ezekiel saw a brightness surrounding the cloud, four creatures, and four wheels. The combination of creatures and wheels suggests that the Lord appeared in a chariot. God's chariot is a familiar OT representation of his coming in judgment (see Is 66:15,16). The wheels within wheels and the position of the four living creatures may signify God's total control over the whole earth, as he could move his "chariot of judgment" in any direction. It is also possible that the living creatures with their four faces, and the wheels full of eyes, may be separate symbols showing that God sees all that happens, that he knows the plight of the exiles. In the vision the prophet's attention was drawn to a throne above the heads of the creatures. On the throne was "the appearance of the likeness of the glory of the Lord" (1:28). In his vision of God's coming in judgment, Ezekiel received his call to the prophetic ministry: "Son of man, I send you to the people of Israel, to a nation of rebels who have rebelled against me" (2:3). During a dark hour of Israel's history, Ezekiel had to prophesy, rebuke his fellow exiles (3:11), and be responsible as a watchman over the house of Israel (3:17; cf. 33:1–9). Symbolic of his mission was a scroll filled with lamentations and woe (2:9,10), which when eaten became sweet as honey (3:1–3). Difficult as the mission was, God's presence and the certain fulfillment of the prophecies sweetened Ezekiel's task. Such encouragement was intended to take away any fear of the rebellious Israelites (2:6,7). Instead of being elated with his mission, however, Ezekiel became despondent.

A week later the word of the Lord came to Ezekiel to remind him of his important role as a watchman (3:16,17). Ezekiel became responsible for Israel as a nation, not just for individuals. His witness to Israel had the express aim of national repentance (3:18,19).

Ezekiel was confined to his house by God (3:25). The house ministry was to be carried on only with those Israelites who sought God's Word and will, for the Lord had abandoned those who continued in their apostasy. The prophetic word would not help the apostates (3:26). The principle of Ezekiel's ministry is found in 3:27: "He that will hear, let him hear; and he that will refuse to hear, let him refuse; for they are a rebellious house" (cf. 3:11; also see Mt 11:15; 13:43).

Prophecies of Judgment Against Israel (3:22–24:27). Symbolism figures prominently in Ezekiel's writing. His priestly background and preparation probably suited him to receive and communicate God's word in symbolic acts and speech. Chapters four and five contain four symbolic acts. (1) Jerusalem's siege is portrayed on a brick (4:1–3); (2) Israel's iniquity is represented by Ezekiel's lying on his sides (4:4–8); (3) Jerusalem's grief and horror in the last days of the siege are represented by Ezekiel's food and drink (4:9–17); (4) Jerusalem's fate is represented by the prophet's hair being cut off (5:1–4).

Ezekiel's instructions were further illuminated by God's explanation of Israel's apostasy (5:6,7) and his judgment on Israel (5:8–12). The judgment will last until the Israelites admit that in covenant faithfulness their Lord has inflicted righteous judgment on them (5:13).

God would direct his judgment first against the people and the city of Jerusalem. Next in line were the mountains of Israel (ch 6) and the land (ch 7). God's wrath included the cities and cultic sites in the hill country of Judah, leaving no protection for the people (6:3–6). Abominations that were practiced throughout the land caused God's judgment to fall on the land as well as on the people (7:2,3,10,11,23). But because God is righteous, he judged the people according to their ways of life, desiring that they would once more acknowledge him as their God (7:27).

The prophet then (chs 8–11) focused on the abominations practiced in Jerusalem, particularly idolatry in the temple courts, which caused the judgment announced in chapters 1–7. An idol had been erected in the inner court (8:3,5). By the wall of the court, elders of the city were paying homage to the idols that surrounded the court (8:11,12). Closer to the temple, women were weeping for Tammuz (8:14), and men were worshiping the sun (8:16). In preparation for the ultimate judgment on the land, the prophet placed a mark on the foreheads of the few faithful Israelites so that they would survive (9:4–6). Then (ch 10) the glory of God, which had filled the temple from the time of Solomon, gradually left, until it "went up from the midst of the city, and stood upon the mountain which is on the east side of the city" (11:23). The people, now without divine protection, were being handed over to the Babylonians (11:9).

The message of doom for Jerusalem contains four elements of hope: restoration of the people (11:17); restoration of the land (11:17); purification of the people (11:18); renewed fellowship between God and his people (11:19,20). The prophet develops those four themes in chapters 33–48.

The visions of chapters 10 and 11 made clear that when God removed his presence from Jerusalem, the exile was approaching. Those who were already in Babylon were unwilling to believe that such an extensive devastation of Jerusalem would happen or that the people would all be exiled and the land become desolate.

Ezekiel acted out the certainty of God's word of judgment by packing his bags and showing the baggage to his fellow exiles. First, he placed the bags in the courtyard outside his modest home. Next, he went out by making a hole through the wall. Finally, the prophet walked about the settlement with his bags in full view. Skeptical observers did not understand Ezekiel, and probably thought he was crazy. The believers who saw him understood His strange actions dramatized how the king's aides would do all they could to help King Zedekiah escape just before the fall of Jerusalem. Second Kings 25 tells how the king and his soldiers left Jerusalem for the wilderness to be overtaken by the Babylonians at Jericho and brought before Nebuchadnezzar at Riblah. As a captive, Zedekiah witnessed the murder of his sons; then his eyes were pierced, and he was sent into exile with the other Judeans (cf. Ez 12:13). The prophet's explanation concluded with a word of comfort. Because of his covenant with Abraham, God promised not to destroy the people completely. A remnant who overcame the sword, famine, and pestilence, would live to tell the story of God's judgment (12:15,16).

Ezekiel further illustrated the nation's plight by eating as though full of fear, suggesting the great trauma that all of Judah's inhabitants would soon undergo.

Both symbolic acts, packing his belongings and eating, emphasized the truthfulness of God's Word. The people needed to face the nature of their God: He is magnificent; and when he speaks, his words are powerful and come to pass. Thus, the devastation of the land and the people's exile were a fulfillment of God's Word through the prophets. The judgment was meant to produce a recognition of the Lord, repentance, and return to God. Some in Judah doubted the efficacy of God's prophecies, saying, "The days grow long, and every vision comes to nought?" (12:22). Others thought God's Word would come true in the distant future (12:27). The prevailing attitude of distrust in God's Word had been stimulated by the popular preaching of false prophets (ch 13). Never commissioned by the Lord, they deceived God's people by lying and misdirecting them with messages of peace (13:8,10). Wickedness, lying, and deceit were encouraged among the people by such false prophets (13:22). The magnitude of their sin and their great responsibility for Judah's fall would be matched by the Lord's heavy judgment. God will save his people from such evil and will prepare a righteous nation with whom to maintain his covenant (13:23).

The certainty of the judgment has been connected with the truthfulness of God's Word. Ezekiel's difficult task of affirming the doom of Jerusalem to stubborn hearers was intensified by the people's idolatry. Their whole way of life denied the existence of God. They practiced idolatry in their worship, and they had "taken their idols into their hearts" (14:3). Before the covenant with God could be restored, they had to be purified from their idolatry. Even so, repentance would not guarantee immunity from judgment. Sword, famine, wild beasts, and plagues would ravage the population (14:21). After the execution of his judgment God would take back those survivors who had turned to him for mercy. God would surely accomplish all that he intended for his people's good (14:23).

In chapters 15–17 Ezekiel uses three parables to set forth the apostasy, present uselessness, and judgment of Israel. Jerusalem and Judah are compared to a piece of charred wood, an adulterous woman, and a vine.

Chapter 15 reviews Jerusalem's case. Jerusalem is compared to a piece of wood, both ends of which have been charred with fire, so that the wood is of no value. As the whole piece of wood is burned instead of being saved, so Jerusalem would undergo complete devastation (15:7,8).

Chapter 16 presents God's case against Jerusalem from a different perspective, stressing his care for Jerusalem in the past. The beginnings of her history are compared to the birth of a female child, left abandoned by her mother (16:3–5). God adopted the child, washed and clothed her (16:6,7). He made a covenant with her (16:8), making her his own possession. He generously gave her all the fine things of life (16:9–13). In the height of her development Jerusalem's fame spread to the nations (16:14). Her self-reliance made her a spiritual prostitute as she took up the religious practices and way of life of the nations (16:15–34). The cities of Sodom (Gn 19) and Samaria (2 Kgs 17:6), known for their immorality, are called Jerusalem's sisters (v 46). They had been judged by God, but the corruption of those cities was little compared to the lewdness of Jerusalem (16:48–51). Thus, Jerusalem also would surely fall and become desolate. Yet Ezekiel anticipates the judgment's final outcome: Jerusalem will be restored to covenantal blessing (16:62,63) after her repentance.

The third parable (ch 17) brings in the dimension of God's sovereignty over political developments. Assyria was no longer a power to be reckoned with. Babylonia and Egypt both exercised dominion, although the balance of power was veering in favor of Babylon. Their extension of power is likened to an eagle. Nebuchadnezzar, "a great eagle with great wings and long pinions, rich in plumage of many colors," took control over the affairs of Judah by removing Jehoiachin, "the top of the cedar," from office and by exiling

him with young leaders of the Judean state, "the topmost of its young twigs" (17:3,4). Ezekiel was among them. Nebuchadnezzar let the Judeans control their own affairs under Zedekiah, but expected them to be subject to Babylon and not to any other power. But Judah (likened to a vine) tried to ally itself with Pharaoh Hophra of Egypt, "another great eagle with great wings and much plumage" (17:7), against Nebuchadnezzar. Zedekiah's folly in turning to Egypt would cause Nebuchadnezzar to pull up the vine by its roots and make it wither (17:9,10). In explaining the parable, God told the exiles that Judah's fall was a result of its unfaithfulness to king Nebuchadnezzar, to whom Judah owed allegiance by covenant (17:13–18). Judah's unfaithfulness thus extended to all of its relationships: religious, cultural, and political. After the exile, God promised, he would restore his people to their land under a Messiah, "a tender one" (17:22). The messianic rule is signified by the young twig, which when planted in the land will become a magnificent cedar, giving shade and protection to the birds. Chapter 17 is an inspiring affirmation of the sovereignty of God in human affairs ("I the Lord bring low the high tree, and make high the low tree," 17:24).

Chapters 18–22 contain Ezekiel's oracles to Judah, its leaders, and the exiles. First he enunciates God's standard of righteousness: "The soul that sins shall die" (18:4). The people are charging God with injustice, for they believe themselves to be under God's judgment for the sins of their ancestors (18:25,29). Although the Ten Commandments do say that God may punish "the iniquity of the fathers . . . to the third and the fourth generation" (Ex 20:5), the prophet vindicates God's justice, telling the people that they are not being punished merely for their ancestors' sin. Each person must be directly accountable to God; the sinner will die in wickedness, and the righteous will live by righteousness. A life of faithfulness to God's moral and civil law will be rewarded (18:5–9). Even if one's father was a sinner, the father's sin is not transferable (vv 14–18). God is ready to forgive any sinner who repents (18:27). The prophet's vindication of God's justice becomes a call to repentance. The sinners in Judah and in exile were thus warned of the consequences of their evil, and exhorted to return to their God and his standard of right and wrong (18:31,32).

Chapter 19 contains two parables in the form of a lamentation. The first portrays a lioness and her two cubs. The lioness is Hamutal, the wife of King Josiah (2 Kgs 23:31), who bore two sons: Jehoahaz and Zedekiah. Jehoahaz is referred to in verses 3 and 4 as a cub

An artist's reconstruction of Babylon, showing the sacred quarter and the Euphrates River in the foreground.

rael's past and future. In view of the people's doubts of the coming judgment on Jerusalem, he stresses the necessity of judgment and the need for repentance. Still, the future restoration of a remnant is touched upon here and there as the counterpart of his message of judgment. After announcing the fall of Jerusalem, the prophet shifts from a message of judgment to one of hope.

The prophet returns to the proclamation of judgment in four oracles (20:45–21:32). He speaks against the Negeb desert area (20:45–49), Jerusalem and the land of Israel (21:2–17,20–27), and against the Ammonites (21:8,28–32). God permitted the sword of Nebuchadnezzar to be his instrument of judgment upon the Judeans (21:19). He would see to the judgment on the Ammonites. The Judeans would recover their previous glory, but the memory of the Ammonites would perish (21:27,32). The oracle against the Ammonites anticipates a larger treatise on Israel's other neighbors: Moab, Edom, Philistia, Tyre, Sidon, and Egypt (Ez 25–29).

Chapters 22–24 contain a renewed series of indictments against Jerusalem. Jerusalem's religious and civil leadership (the prophets, priests, and princes) are corrupt, and the people have followed their example (22:25–30). The parable of the two sisters, Oholah and Oholibah, is a variation of the parable of adulterous Jerusalem (ch 23; cf. 16). It differs in that the comparison drawn between Jerusalem, soon to be exiled, and Samaria, already in exile, is more explicit in the parable of Oholah and Oholibah. In chapter 16 Jerusalem was charged with greater sins than Sodom and Samaria, but was promised restoration. Only the adulterous nature of the two sisters and God's judgment on them is emphasized in chapter 23, with no word of restoration. This parable is a fitting introduction to that of the boiling pot (ch 24), in which Jerusalem is compared to a rusty pot boiling with water. The Jerusalemites, likened to pieces of meat in the boiling pot, will die in the city. The parable was pronounced on the day of Nebuchadnezzar's siege of Jerusalem. Thus, the exiles were divinely forewarned of God's intent to destroy the temple (24:21) and were prepared for messengers bringing the bad news of Jerusalem's fall.

Those oracles and parables conclude the first division of the book. Ezekiel has stated God's case against the rebellious house of Judah in many ways. His metaphors have likened Judah to a burnt piece of wood, to an uprooted vine, to a baby who grew up to be an adulteress, and to Oholibah, the adulterous woman. He has countered arguments against the fulfillment of God's Word and against the

who grew up and was taken to Egypt (by Pharaoh Neco in 508 BC; see 2 Kgs 23:31–34). Zedekiah succeeded to the throne 10 years later. In the lamentation the prophet imaginatively represents Zedekiah as a young cub who is ultimately taken to Babylon as a rebellious ruler (19:7–9). The second parable changes the imagery to a vine, representing Israel (v 10). In its early days God blessed Israel with strong rulers, but now the vine was wilting as Zedekiah irresponsibly led Judah to its last days. Ezekiel's lamentation stresses the lack of a good candidate for the throne and the lack of life in the vine (19:13,14).

In chapter 20 the prophet concludes God's argument against his people. He reviews the history of Israel's past, starting with God's self-revelation in Egypt (vv 5,6). He took to himself a stubborn nation, tied to idolatry (20:8) and prone to apostasy (20:13,21). Israel wanted to be one of the great nations (v 32) instead of a sanctified people (v 12). As a result of its spiritual hardness, Israel is dispersed to live among the nations (20:35). Yet God had a solemn covenant with Israel, made by oath to the patriarchs Abraham, Isaac, and Jacob. On the basis of that covenant God will reach out with compassion to those who repent of their sinful ways (20:37–40,43,44). In Israel's judgment and restoration the nations will see the holiness of God, which does not tolerate unfaithfulness in Israel (v 41).

Ezekiel's prophecies alternate between God's judgment on Israel's sin and his restoration of Israel, spanning the bridge between Is-justice of God. He has reassured the exiles that God will not leave the righteous and that the future of Israel begins with a righteous remnant. The pendulum of Ezekiel's writing has swung from judgment to restoration, while the clock was bringing Judah closer to the hour of its fall.

Oracles Against the Nations (25:1–32:32). Ammon, Moab, and Edom were Israel's neighbors to the east. Because they were ethnically related to Israel, they were not attacked by the Israelites on their march to the Promised Land. Ammon and Moab were descendants of Lot, Abraham's nephew, and the Edomites descended from Esau, the brother of Jacob. Although God forbade war with them, relations between Israel and its eastern neighbors were always tense. Israel had been overrun by the Ammonites, but whenever Israel was strong, the other three nations suffered domination. But Israel was never successful in controlling the Edomites' competitive trade relations. Those neighboring nations joined the Babylonian attack against Jerusalem, and rejoiced when Jerusalem fell and the temple was devastated (Ez 25:3,6,8,12). They were ready to take over and loot Judah's cities, and to instigate trouble in the hour of Jerusalem's distress. Therefore, says Ezekiel, God's judgment will also extend to Ammon, to Moab, and to Edom (vv 4,9,13,14).

The Philistines had been Israel's enemy to the southwest. During the period of the judges and the united monarchy, the Philistines had controlled much of Israel's territory. King David successfully limited the Philistine threat by confining them to their own territory. But in Ezekiel's day they were still considered Israel's "everlasting" enemy (25:15), possibly intensified by Philistine support of the Babylonian invasion of Judah.

The city of Tyre had received reports of the overthrow of Jerusalem and was ready to exploit the opportunity for its own advantage (26:2). Tyre's trade position was unrivaled; its ships crossed the seas to exchange goods with many distant lands (Ez 27). But Tyre would soon be broken by the Babylonians, its wealth dried up with the destruction of the fleet and the murder of its sailors (27:26).

The prince of Tyre is singled out in chapter 28, but verse 12 refers to the "king" of Tyre. Interpreters disagree whether they are one person or two. Those who distinguish between the two understand the prince of Tyre to be the ruler of that city, but they consider the "king" of Tyre to represent Satan (28:13–15). The garden of Eden with all its splendor is an appropriate setting for the original glory of an angelic Satan before his fall. But there is no reason within the context to distinguish between the prince and the king of Tyre. Each is said to have exalted himself, and both took authority over men as if they were gods and enjoyed all the splendor and royalty that belong to God. And both prince and king fall from their high position. The passage is a magnificent example of Ezekiel's literary ability. He draws a glorious picture of the garden of Eden, reworking the same theme as he depicts the glory and fall of the king of Tyre. Ezekiel presents him as a cherub, in accordance with the local belief that the king was divine. He wore the finest clothing, with nine kinds of precious stones (28:13). Though God had elevated him to the royal throne (28:13,14), the king's heart turned to materialism and to religious and judicial corruption (vv 16–18). In a sense the king (prince) represents the people of Tyre. They were all guilty of corruption, injustice, and violence. If God judged his covenant people for their perversion of justice and for their sins, his judgment would surely come also on the city of Tyre (vv 18,19). When the Babylonians marched on Tyre, they laboriously built a jetty from the mainland to the city. At the same time Tyrian ships loaded with goods and treasures sailed out across the Mediterranean, so that when Nebuchadnezzar's troops finally breached the walls, little loot could be taken (29:18).

The city of Sidon also cheered at Jerusalem's destruction. Sidon was a port city in Phoenecia, to the north of Tyre. By pestilence and war, the inhabitants of Sidon would learn the justice of Israel's God.

Six nations (Ammon, Moab, Edom, Philistia, Tyre, and Sidon) scorned Israel at the fall of Jerusalem. Because God had invested his holiness in the temple of Jerusalem and in his people, the temple's destruction and the people's exile signified to the nations that Israel's God was impotent. They did not realize that the reason for Israel's fate was God's intolerance of his people's sin. God's holiness required the punishment of sin, and it also required vindication for his name (28:22,23). God was still concerned for his people, that Israel might know he had removed the scorn of their neighbors (28:24). In the restoration of Israel the Lord would further manifest his holiness before the nations. Israel would receive back the land, vineyards, and houses, and would enjoy the bounty of the Lord in peace (vv 25,26).

Egypt had convinced the people of Israel and Judah that with its help the Assyrians and the Babylonians could not stand their ground in Canaan. In 722 BC the Assyrian troops took the northern capital of Samaria, and in 586 the Babylonians conquered Jerusalem, while Egypt remained passive. The Egyptians had

A limestone relief of the head of an 18th-dynasty princess from Tell el-Amarna.

of chapters 1–24. (1) He was called to be a watchman over Israel (33:1–9; cf. 1–3:21). (2) Israel had sinned against the Lord and had to receive a righteous judgment (33:10). (3) Jerusalem was to be taken by the Babylonians (33:21). (4) Israel's repentance is necessary for restoration (33:11,14–16).

Thus far his ministry had not met with success. The exiles who had heard his messages were full of appreciation for Ezekiel's rhetorical and literary abilities (33:32). They readily accepted Ezekiel as a watchman who warned the people of the impending catastrophe at Jerusalem, and they may have admitted that their sin was the reason for God's judgment on Israel and Jerusalem. But they were slow in applying the prophetic word to their own lives. God was ready to forgive their sins if they repented, acknowledged him, and demonstrated their renewed spirit by practicing the Law of God (33:32). Now that the news of Jerusalem had been reported to the exiles (33:21), the necessity for the people to act responsibly was even more urgent. The Lord had demonstrated that Ezekiel was a true prophet (33:33).

The success of Ezekiel's ministry was not measured in numbers. He faithfully declared the Word of God in word, sign, and parable. The exiles had followed the false hopes proclaimed by false "shepherds" (Ez 13,34), who had fattened themselves at the expense of the flock (34:2,3). They did not take care of those in need (34:4), and they allowed the flock to be scattered (34:5,6). God promised his people that he would be the faithful shepherd, to bring the sheep together, feed them, and care for them (34:11–15; cf. Ps 23). God would also distinguish between the sheep and the goats, to find out whose hearts were right with him, so that the true sheep could be restored to God's flock (34:20–22). God's promise included the restoration of the land and the restoration of the divinely appointed Davidic dynasty (34:24). The renewed fellowship between the Lord and Israel under the messianic ruler would be sealed with a new covenant, the "covenant of peace." That covenant assured the people of God's blessing on their labor, bringing them abundant harvests (34:26,27). The people would not be forced to fight against nature in their pursuits (34:25,28). They would not have to struggle against other peoples who might try to share in their blessings by force (34:27–29). The prophetic vision telescoped the events of the restoration of Israel after the exile, the coming of Jesus the Messiah (cf. Jn 10), and the full restoration of the sin-cursed world.

It is possible to forget in reading the following chapters that the prophet has set the prop-

desired control over Canaan for economical reasons, but not at the expense of their own welfare. Egypt, too, would lose its leadership under God's judgment (29:9,10,12,14–16). Reduced to dependence on foreign powers, Egypt would no longer be a stumbling block for Israel. First, Babylonia was permitted to break Egypt's power (30:1–32:21); and later the Persians, Greeks, and Romans would incorporate Egypt as a province. The fall of Egypt coincided with the fall of several great and small kingdoms: Assyria (32:22,23), Elam (32:24,25), Meshech-Tubal (32:26–28), Edom (32:29), and Sidon (32:30).

Proclamation of Hope (33:1–48:35). After the visions of God's judgment on the surrounding nations, Ezekiel returns to the future hope of Israel. In the first major section of his book he dealt with the reasons for Judah's exile and the destruction of the temple, alluding often to the future of Israel. But the prophet's organization of his material included, between prophecies of Israel's judgment and restoration, the oracles of God's judgment on Israel's neighbors who had encouraged and rejoiced in its fall. Throughout its history Israel had allowed foreign nations to influence its religion, culture, and form of government. The reduction of their powers meant Israel, restored to the Promised Land, would be more free for faithfulness to God. Before taking up the theme of the restoration, Ezekiel reviews the emphases

er stage for interpretation. Chapter 34 is the key to the messages of restoration. The emphases include the outworking of the frequently repeated verse "They shall be my people, and I will be their God" (11:20; cf. 34:30; 36:28). The most significant aspects of the restoration theme include (1) God's gracious restoration of his people to covenant blessing (36:20–36; 37:23,26; 39:25); (2) God's restoration of the nation of Israel to the land (36:1–15,24; 37:14–23; 39:27); (3) God's new covenant, giving his Spirit to his people (36:25–27; 37:14; 39:29), and his blessing on his people (36:8–12,29–30,33–35,37,38; 39:9,10,26), assuring them of victory over their enemies (35:1–15; 36:36; 37:28; 38–39:24); (4) God's appointment of a Davidic king, the Messiah, over his people (37:24,25); and (5) God's temple restored among his people (37:26,27).

(1) The People of God. The rejection of the exiles did not last forever. Based on the Abrahamic covenant, the Lord promised to bless the faithful remnant and to make of them a new people. The imagery of a valley of dry bones is particularly fitting. The dry bones represent God's people without hope (37:11). Ezekiel proclaims to them the good news that God will renew and restore them (37:11,12). The Lord's purpose for his people is that all the nations may honor his holy name through his people (39:7,25,27).

(2) The Land. The promise also extends to the land, originally given to Abraham and his descendants. The Abrahamic covenant included a messianic element, for through the family of Abraham living in the Promised Land all nations would receive God's blessing (Gn 12:3). In a vision Ezekiel saw the boundaries and described the division of the land (Ez 47,48). The royal city of Jerusalem is the central symbol of God's presence among his people; its name will be "The Lord is there" (48:8–35).

(3) The New Covenant. The Abrahamic covenant is renewed, a gracious covenant that expresses the restored relationship. "Covenant of peace" fittingly describes its nature and benefits. The restless people of God are promised rest from their searching, their enemies, and their toil. The change in relationship is further emphasized by God's sending of his Spirit, who will add a new dimension to the life-style of his people. Obedience to God will be no longer constrained, for God's Spirit helps his people to do his will. A new heart, controlled by the Spirit of God, is given to the Lord's people (36:26,27). The presence of the Spirit also signifies a new life for the people (37:14; see Jn 3:8,16; Acts 2:38; Rom 8:2,4,15).

(4) The Messiah. The OT hope of a messianic king is crystalized in Ezekiel's message.

His rule will be everlasting (37:25), over all God's people who have new hearts (37:15–25).

(5) The Temple. As a priest, Ezekiel remained keenly interested in the temple, priesthood, sacrificial regulations, and festivals. A large section of the prophecy's last division describes the temple's revived worship (40–46:24). His vision of the glory of God, so important in the messages of God's judgment on Jerusalem (chs 1,10,11), now assures the remnant that God did not forsake his people (43:2–5). He will dwell among them, for the temple is a symbol of God's presence (37:27). Some interpreters believe that the temple, with its ritual as described in Ezekiel 40–46, will be restored in the messianic era before the last judgment. Others believe the promises about the temple provide a positive symbolic answer to Ezekiel's greatest concern: whether God will return to be with his people (48:35; see Jn 2:21; Rv 21:22).

There are various interpretations of chapters 34–48. As a watchman to Israel, Ezekiel had a message for the exiled Jewish community. Thus the prophecy's fulfillment must have begun with the decree of Cyrus I (538 BC), permitting the Jews to return to their land (Ezr 1:1–3). Two rival schools of interpretation exist on how the prophecy is fulfilled beyond Israel's restoration to the land. Those who interpret Israel as simply the nation view the modern return of Jewish people to the land of Israel as a continuation of God's prophetic promise. They believe that God's plan for Israel is being fulfilled along with, and in addition to, his plan for the Christian church. The fulfillment of those prophecies will be inaugurated by the coming of the messianic king, who will give earthly peace to the Jewish people. The temple worship (Ez 40–48) will be restored in some way during the period of the messianic kingdom. The church will enjoy a small share in all the events centered on the Jews. The promises of Ezekiel's vision are thus limited to the nation of Israel and must be fulfilled before the coming of a new heaven and earth.

Other interpreters believe that Ezekiel wrote for the benefit of spiritual descendants of Abraham who believe, as Abraham did, in God's promises (Gn 15:6; cf. Rom 4:11,13; Gal 3:6–9,29). All who have faith like Abraham, whether Jews or Gentiles, are regarded as Abraham's offspring (Gal 3:28,29). Ezekiel's message thus would include all of God's gracious work among Christian Gentiles, who have become the recipients of God's promises and benefits. It is possible, on the basis of 1 Peter 1:10,11, to interpret Ezekiel's language as a prophetic expression of how God's grace would come to all those who become reconciled to God through faith in the gospel.   WILLEM A. VANGEMEREN

See EZEKIEL (PERSON); EXILE; PROPHECY.

Bibliography. G.A. Cooke, *A Critical and Exegetical Commentary on the Book of Ezekiel;* W. Eichrodt, *Ezekiel;* H.L. Ellison, *Ezekiel, the Man and His Message;* P. Fairbairn, *An Exposition of Ezekiel;* C.F. Keil, *Biblical Commentary on the Prophecies of Ezekiel,* 2 vols.; J. Skinner, *The Book of Ezekiel.*

Ezel.   Hebrew word designating a stone where Jonathan and David met prior to David's departure from the court of Saul (1 Sm 20:19, RSV stone heap).

Ezem.   City alloted to Judah's tribe (Jos 15:29, KJV Azem), then later to Simeon's tribe, for an inheritance (Jos 19:3, KJV Azem; 1 Chr 4:29). Joshua 15 locates the city in the extreme southern part of Canaan (v 21). Its exact location is in question, but Umm el-'Azem near Beersheba has been suggested.

Ezer.   1. Chieftain of a Horite tribe (Gn 36:21; 1 Chr 1:38, KJV Ezar).

2. Descendant and probably the son of Ephraim. He was killed while making a raid on the cattle of the Philistines (1 Chr 7:21).

3. Man of Judah, descended from Hur (1 Chr 4:4).

4. Gadite who joined David at Ziklag (1 Chr 12:9).

5. Jeshua's son, who ruled Mizpah and repaired the Jerusalem wall (Neh 3:19).

6. Priest who took part in the ceremony at the dedication of the Jerusalem wall (Neh 12:42).

Ezion-geber, Ezion-gaber.   Important port near some significant ruins at the head of the Gulf of Aqaba. Ezion-geber (KJV Ezion-gaber) was one of the stations where the Israelites encamped while on their way to the plains of Moab (Nm 33:35,36; Dt 2:8). The city is not mentioned again until Solomon's time. From this port Solomon and Hiram, king of Tyre, carried on a profitable commercial venture. Solomon had copper (mined in the Arabah at Timna, 15 miles north of Ezion-geber), olive oil, and possibly products bought from Egypt, linen and chariots (1 Kgs 10:28,29). The "ships of Tarshish" with the ships of Hiram made a round trip of three years from Ezion-geber to many ports along the coasts of Africa, and Arabia, and possibly even as far as India (1 Kgs 10:22). In exchange the fleet brought back gold from Ophir, along with precious stones, almug wood (1 Kgs 10:11,12), silver, ivory, apes, and peacocks (1 Kgs 10:22). Solomon's alliance with the Phoenicians of Tyre gave him a port on the Mediterranean (which he himself did not have). The alliance also gave Hiram and

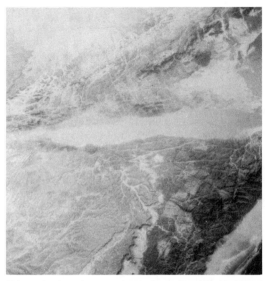

Ezion-geber is at the top center, and a portion of the Red Sea is near the bottom of this photograph.

the Phoenicians an outlet at Ezion-geber for trading in the Indian Ocean.

With the division of the kingdom after Solomon, the port was under Judah's control. It was burned and destroyed by Shishak of Egypt in his invasion of Judah in Rehoboam's 5th year (925 BC). A second city was built on the ruins, but there is no mention of a navy. Jehoshaphat was able to restore the fleet to sail once again, but some storm or other disaster wrecked the ships (1 Kgs 22:48). In subsequent Judean history, Judah was able to use the port when it was strong, but in times of weakness other nations did (e.g., Edom, 2 Kgs 8:20–22; 16:6).

In 1934 Ezion-geber was first identified with Tell el-Kheleifeh, where Early Iron Age pottery had been found. Beginning in 1936 Nelson Glueck excavated the site, finding four settlement levels, each of which had been burned. Glueck assigned the first settlement to the Solomonic period, since he thought that the area was a copper and iron refinery for the Arabah ores. What may have been a seal of king Jotham was also recovered, perhaps indicating a restoration of port facilities in his day. Pieces of 5th-century BC Greek black ware indicated trade with the Aegean in Persian times. In 1962 Beno Rothenberg suggested that Glueck's "smeltery" was a storehouse for grain and caravan supplies. Perhaps the port of Ezion-geber should be identified with the island of Jazirat Farun.

See EXODUS, THE; WILDERNESS WANDERINGS.

Eznite.   KJV designation for the preeminent leader of David's mighty men in 2 Samuel

23:8. Most consider Adino the Eznite a later scribal alteration of the Hebrew text and prefer the reading "Jashobe-am, a Hachmonite" in the parallel passage of 1 Chronicles 11:11 (RSV omits "Adino the Eznite" in the 2 Sm passage, replacing it with "Josheb-basshebeth a Tah-chemonite").

Ezra (Person). 1. Religious reformer following Israel's return from exile. Ezra's genealogy (Ezr 7:1–5; cf. 1 Chr 6:3–15) places him in the high priestly Aaron-Zadok family line, which accounts for the importance of his scribal and priestly activities. He is called "priest" (Ezr 10:10,16; Neh 8:2), "scribe" (Ezr 7:6; Neh 12:36), and "priest and scribe" (Ezr 7:11,12; Neh 8:9; 12:26). The OT scribe was not a mere copyist, as in Christ's time, but a profound student of God's laws and commandments (Ezr 7:11,12; Jer 8:8). In the commission of the Persian king Artaxerxes to Ezra, the king described him as "scribe" (Ezr 7:6–11). It was Ezra who began the traditional view of the scribe as a religious leader, a "bookman"; the view lasted until 200 BC. Scribes were qualified to teach and preach the Scriptures as well as interpret them, but by the 1st century AD the scribe's function was more specialized.

As "Secretary of State for Jewish Affairs" in the Persian empire, Ezra visited Jerusalem about 458 BC, and on his return reported his findings. Little was done, however, until Nehemiah went to Jerusalem in 445. Once the city walls had been rebuilt, Ezra instituted a religious reformation in which the ancient Torah (the Law) was made the norm for Jewish life. He also demanded that Jews who had married foreigners must divorce them to maintain the Jewish purity the Torah required. Ezra set an example of piety and dedication through prayer and fasting, and this placed his reforming zeal in proper spiritual perspective. He set the pattern for life in the postexilic Jewish commonwealth, making God's Word and worship central features. The date and place of his death are unknown.

LOUIS GOLDBERG & R. K. HARRISON

See EZRA, BOOK OF; POSTEXILIC PERIOD, THE.

2. KJV rendering of Ezrah in 1 Chronicles 4:17. See EZRAH.

Ezra, Book of. One of the historical books of the OT, associated with 2 Chronicles and Nehemiah.

Name. In the Talmud tractate *Baba Bathra* 15a, the rabbis and scribes regarded Ezra and Nehemiah as one book. Josephus (*Apion* 1.8) also considered the two books to be one when the number of OT books was given as 22. Some church fathers, such as Melito of Sardis and Jerome, thought of them as one book. The Septuagint (Greek translation of the OT) also grouped the two books as one, referring to them as 2 Ezra to distinguish them from an apocryphal book known as 1 Ezra. The Latin Vulgate, however, calls Ezra "1 Ezra" and Nehemiah "2 Ezra."

Historical Background. The Jewish people came under the rule of the Persian empire when Cyrus conquered Babylon in 539 BC. From then until Ezra's time the Persian kings were: Cyrus (539–530 BC), who allowed the Jewish people and other captives to return to their homeland (Ezr 1); Cambyses (529–522 BC); Gaumata, a usurper of the throne (522 BC); Darius I (521–486 BC; Ezr 5:6); Xerxes I (OT Ahazuerus, 485–465 BC; Ezr 4:6); Artaxerxes I (464–424 BC; Ezr 4:7–23; 7:1–10:44). Both Ezra's and Nehemiah's work fall within the period between Cyrus and Artaxerxes I. Some scholars, however, place Ezra during the reign of Artaxerxes II (404–359 BC).

The Sources. By tradition, the Jewish leader Ezra researched and put together the material that forms his book. Chapters 7–10 are written in the first person singular, and Ezra may have used the autobiographical passages as the core of this book, adding information from other sources. That the book contains portions written in Aramaic has been used as justification for assigning a date later than Ezra's time. But the Aramaic of Ezra bears a remarkable similarity to 5th century BC Aramaic papyri from the Jewish community at Elephantine, in Egypt.

The book is largely a compilation, using autobiography, official documents, edicts, and other material. The present Book of Ezra contains four identifiable strata of source material.

Memoirs of Ezra. Certain sections appear in the first person singular (7:27–9:15), located between third person narratives (7:1–26; 10). The memoirs were probably part of Ezra's own official reports.

Aramaic Documents. Aramaic was the diplomatic language in the Persian empire, and a number of documents appear in the Book of Ezra. A letter of complaint was written to Artaxerxes I about the rebuilding of the city walls, for example, and Ezra also included the official reply (4:8–23). There is also a letter of Darius I and the king's reply (5:1–6:18). An official authorization by the Persian court of Artaxerxes permitted Ezra to return, and included a description of material entrusted into his keeping (7:12–26). All of those sections were official correspondence, so the record naturally is written in Aramaic.

Hebrew Lists. Ezra included Hebrew documents listing people's names for a number of purposes. One such document indicated the

Persian government's permission for Jewish immigrants to return to the land of Israel (Ezr 1:2–4). It was a Jewish version of Cyrus' general edict expressing concern for all his subjects. The edict in Aramaic is repeated by Ezra in 6:3–5, and that version is probably taken from an original memorandum of a royal decision. Ezra included lists of the immigrants who returned to begin the second commonwealth of Israel (ch 2, repeated in Neh 7). The book also contains a list of immigrants who returned with Ezra by permission of Artaxerxes I (8:1–14). Lists of those who had married pagan wives are provided as well (10:18–43).

Narrative. The rest of the book comprises narrative by Ezra himself. For the period of the first return prior to his own time, he probably drew upon existing sources, either oral or documentary. Material in the book that was contemporary with the scribe would be his personal account about his own work.

Date. Traditionally the Artaxerxes in Ezra 7:1 has been identified with Artaxerxes I Longimanus. Ezra's arrival in Jerusalem would thus have been in 458 BC ("the 7th year of the king," 7:8). Therefore Ezra's work at Jerusalem started before Nehemiah, who came in 445 BC.

But the traditional dates are questioned from a number of sources. One alternative is to place Nehemiah during the reign of Artaxerxes I (464–424 BC) and Ezra at a later date, in the reign of Artaxerxes II Mnemon (404–359 BC). Such a suggestion creates a difficulty with Nehemiah 8:2, because there Ezra is named as Nehemiah's contemporary and fellow worker.

In addition, the Elephantine papyri (407–400 BC) mention the high priest Johanan in Jerusalem, and Sanballat as governor of Samaria. Johanan is considered a grandson of Eliashib, but Nehemiah was a contemporary of Eliashib (Neh 3:1,20). The biblical material that speaks of Nehemiah going to Jerusalem in the 20th year of Artaxerxes (Neh 1:1, 445 BC) and again during the 32nd year (Neh 13:6, 433 BC) refers to Eliashib's contemporary high priesthood with Ezra. The traditional position thus furnishes a better date for the Book of Ezra. If the scribe were placed during the reign of Artaxerxes II (c. 397 BC), his ministry would be too late for the high priesthood of Johanan.

More recently scholars suggest that Ezra's return and work should be dated in Artaxerxes' 37th year (c. 428 BC). The assertion is that Ezra 7:8 contains a copyist's error and should read "thirty-seventh year of the king" rather than "seventh year," thus allowing for a return by Ezra later than Nehemiah but still within the reign of Artaxerxes I. A number of possibilities are advanced to counter this proposal.

(1) If "seventh year" is an error in Ezra 7:7,8, and "thirty-seventh" should replace it, then there seems to be a difficulty because the reforms of Nehemiah were carried on in the "thirty-second" year of Artaxerxes (Neh 13:6). It is difficult to accept the idea that measures against intermarriage with foreigners would have to be repeated only five years after Nehemiah had dealt with the problem. It is much easier to hold to the traditional dates, maintaining that Nehemiah had to address the same problem after Ezra's reform.

(2) Another argument in favor of the 37th year of Artaxerxes is a supposed difficulty in reconciling Ezra's description of Jerusalem as fairly well organized (8:33–35) with Nehemiah's description of the city as "broken down and . . . destroyed by fire" and desolate (Neh 1:3; 2:17). Therefore some suppose that Ezra came after Nehemiah, when the city was better organized and more fully populated. But the scriptural record does not describe the situation that way. When Nehemiah arrived in Jerusalem, his complaint was not that the city was uninhabited, but that the city walls had not been rebuilt and that some areas of the city still showed the effects of war. Nowhere does Ezra say that the city was totally repopulated in his day. But it was not secure, and that was what Nehemiah desired. As long as Jerusalem was not militarily protected, neighboring peoples didn't care. Only when the Jewish people began to rebuild the walls did the surrounding states make problems for Nehemiah. The point is that Ezra returned to Jerusalem in 458 BC to do a specific job in making the Law the civic standard for the Jewish community. Nehemiah's journey to Jerusalem in 445 BC was prompted by deep concern for the people's welfare, as they were at the mercy of their neighbors in the defenseless city. The urgency of the situation impressed itself upon him so much on his arrival that he bent every effort to secure the city and create the means by which the population could protect themselves.

(3) Still another charge against the traditional position is that if Ezra's reforms (chs 9,10) preceded Nehemiah (ch 8), then Ezra had failed in his ministry. If Ezra's reforms were considered contemporary with Nehemiah, the two accounts could be more easily put together. But the Scripture specifically indicates that Ezra dealt only with the problem of intermarriage with pagans (9:10) about 458 BC. Nehemiah, though also confronting intermarriage, dealt with additional problems: unfair interest (ch 5), temple quarters given to Tobiah the Ammonite (ch 13), neglect in presenting tithes, and the desecration of the sabbath. It would seem that there are two alto-

gether different accounts in view in the books of Ezra and Nehemiah. It is quite possible that the evil of foreign intermarriages could have arisen again and therefore required the attention of Nehemiah a second time.

Languages. The language of Ezra for the most part is Hebrew; the exceptions are 4:7; 6:18; and 7:12–26, which are written in Aramaic. The Hebrew portion appears to resemble the language of Daniel, Haggai, and 2 Chronicles much more than later Hebrew, such as that of Ecclesiasticus. As indicated, the Aramaic portions resemble the Elephantine papyri, dated at about 407–400 BC. In addition, Persian personal and family names and Persian words and expressions occur in the book, such as *Bigvai, Mithredath,* and *Elam.* All of these evidences serve to place the book in about the 5th century BC.

Text and Versions. The Hebrew Masoretic text of Ezra seems well preserved. The Septuagint version is a bit shorter than the Masoretic text. Only parts of Ezra 4 and 5 have been found among the Dead Sea Scrolls.

Some Critical Problems. There seems to have been an unsuccessful attempt to build the walls and foundation of Jerusalem (Ez 4:6–23). The passage is actually a history of opposition to rebuilding the ruined temple (4:1). It narrates the frustrations experienced by the Judean community from the time of return to their homeland during Cyrus' rule up to the time of King Darius. The prophet Haggai (520 BC) aroused the people with his message and persuaded them to lay the foundations of the new temple. When the building was only partly complete, another lengthy interval ensued during the reign of Ahasuerus, or Xerxes, and the early part of Artaxerxes' regime. During this period complaints were made to the Persian authorities that the returned Judeans were rebuilding the city wall of Jerusalem, and as a result the work was halted for some time. In Ezra 4 the writer recorded the opposition launched against the reconstruction of the temple. Accordingly he shows that in the days of Cyrus (4:1–5) and Darius I (4:24; 5:1–17) the project met with opposition. This continued through the reign of Xerxes I (4:6) and was finally dealt with under Artaxerxes I (4:7–23), when Nehemiah appeared on the scene. Construction stopped in Jerusalem until the second year of Darius. Ezra resumes the theme of the book in chapter 5.

Note the type of building activities set forth in Ezekiel 5:6–23, when "walls" and "foundations of the city" are mentioned but not the temple (vv 12,21). Note in contrast that when telling the story of the problem of the erection of the temple, Ezra pointed out the problems, frustrations, and hindrances the Jewish people had with its construction. It was not until a diligent search had been made in the archives by the Persian authorities that the original edict granting permission to build the temple was found (5:7–6:5). Internal evidence suggests that a long historical insertion existed, having to do largely with the matter of the walls of the city (vv 5–23). It readily can be seen that Ezra was dealing with the evil intentions of Judah's enemies and that the opposition of Rehum and Shimshai did not appear in the 520s because they lived in the 460s, early in the reign of Artaxerxes I. We should recognize that Ezra's approach is topical rather than chronological where, in the middle of describing the earlier opposition to building the temple, he complained that the same kind of opposition was being repeated in his day concerning the attempt to rebuild the city walls and repair the fortifications of Jerusalem.

Still another problem has to do with the differences in the versions of Cyrus' edict, the Hebrew one in Ezra 1 and the Aramaic version in Ezra 6. However, the edict in the latter was found in Ecbatana in Persia, while that in Ezra 1 was given in Babylon to the Jewish people in Hebrew. The Aramaic copy was on file for preservation in the archives, whereas the Hebrew form was given to the Jewish people themselves. It is interesting to note that Cyrus dealt with a number of refugee peoples and that he gave permission to each of them to return to their own lands and rebuild their temples. The set form of such edicts would provide for acknowledging various gods. When dealing with the God of the Jews, Cyrus inserted the name of Yahweh, who is related to Israel; on the other hand, when he spoke to the Babylonians, he addressed himself to Marduk.

Purpose. The Book of Ezra is a straightforward account of one of the most important events in Jewish history. From a priestly point of view, it is an account of the restoration of Jewish people to their homeland following the Babylonian dispersion. The record tells of two distinct returns, one under the leadership of Zerubbabel (ch 1–6; 538 BC) and, 80 years later, the second return led by Ezra (chs 7–10; 458 BC). The book emphasizes Ezra's leadership and the reestablishment of the people on their land, both of which were to have important future consequences.

Little is known about the political activity of Ezra in the Persian court. He appears to have been a man of considerable influence, however, and could well be described as an official who held a position corresponding to that of "Secretary of State for Jewish Affairs." To what extent that function applied to the Persian empire as a whole is uncertain, since Ezra's recorded activities took place only in the area known to the Persians as the province "Beyond the River," that is, the territory lying to the west of the Euphrates. The importance of Ezra's position in the Persian empire is indicated by the fact that King Artaxerxes gave him full authority to do whatever he thought necessary for the welfare of his people and the empire (7:21–26). Ezra's genealogy is given in 7:1–5, and he is consistently spoken of as a scribe learned in the Mosaic law. As a descendant of Zadok the priest he would have the authority to instruct others in the Torah.   Louis Goldberg

See Postexilic Period, The; Ezra (Person) # 1.

Bibliography. L.W. Batten, *A Critical and Exegetical Commentary on the Books of Ezra and Nehemiah;* C.F. Keil, *The Books of Ezra, Nehemiah, and Esther;* H.G.M. Williamson, *Ezra, Nehemiah.*

Ezrah. Father of four sons from Judah's tribe (1 Chr 4:17, kjv Ezra).

Ezrahite. Word occurring only three times in the OT. Twice it is used as a title for Ethan (Ps 89 title; 1 Kgs 4:31) and once as a name given to Heman (Ps 88 title). It is no longer thought to be a family name, but instead signifies a member of a pre-Israelite family.

Ezri. Son of Chelub and one of the men who supervised the tilling of David's lands (1 Chr 27:26).

Ff

Fair Havens. Small harbor, identifiable with modern Limenes Kali, positioned along Crete's southern coast about five miles east of Cape Matala near the city of Lasea. Here Paul's ship sought shelter from contrary winds on his voyage to Rome (Acts 27:8).

Faith. State wholly and steadfastly in God. Faith lies at the very heart of Christianity, and its importance for today's Christian is clear from the fact that Protestantism was born through the rediscovery of the great words "The just shall live by faith" (Rom 1:17 KJV).

Definition. Faith in the OT and NT carries several meanings. It may mean simple trust in God or in the Word of God, and at other times faith almost becomes equivalent to active obedience. It may also find expression in the affirmation of a creedal statement. Thus it also comes to mean the entire body of received Christian teaching or truth. So in Colossians 2:7, the term suggests something to be accepted as a whole and embodied in personal life. In 2 Timothy 4:7 Paul witnesses to having "kept the faith."

The OT. In the OT, faith first involved God as the Creator, Sustainer of life, and the Controller of history. Psalms such as 19 and 24 are evidence of the trust in God as the Creator, whose sovereign power continues to operate in the creation.

The OT also strongly emphasizes faith as confidence in God's covenant or in the covenant God has made with Abraham and his descendants. The call of Abraham and the promise that his descendants would be used in the history of redemption became the basis of the narratives of the OT, being seen as the working out of that covenant. Once the nation Israel is brought into being, God sustains and protects it. The land which was promised to Abraham and his descendants remains theirs. The exodus from Egypt is a prominent indica-

tion that God is at work restoring his people to the Promised Land. The obedience of the people of God as the proper expression of faith is seen clearly in the OT. Without seeing God, his people believe and obey him. Abraham leaves his native land to go into unknown territory. The people of Israel leave Egypt following the leadership of God to a land they cannot see. The promise of God gives them courage to possess the land that has been promised to them. After the exodus the covenant of Abraham was confirmed with the people of Israel by the sprinkling of blood (Ex 24:6,7). There was to be strict obedience to God's commands as an expression of faith. This response of human faith to Jehovah's faithfulness was national and collective: There also were, however, commands to and instances of personal faith.

Not only the narrative and legal portions of the OT, but also the poetic and prophetic writings emphasize faith. The Psalms abound in expressions of personal confidence in Jehovah even in dark times. Habbakuk points out that "the righteous shall live by his faith" (2:4). From such instances it is clear that as Jehovah's education of Israel proceeded, the matter of faith in God's faithfulness became more and more a matter of individual and personal response, and it is in the prophets that several ingredients such as trust, obedience, fear, and certainty blend into the understanding of such personal faith.

The NT. As over against the OT, where the accent is on the faithfulness of God, in the NT the emphasis is placed on the active, responding faith of the hearer to the promised, final revelation in the Messiah, Jesus Christ. Both verb and noun regularly describe the adequate response of man to Jesus' word and deed and to the gospel of the primitive church.

The Synoptic Gospels. The most striking feature of the synoptic Gospels is the use of

The restored portion of the synagogue at Capernaum, the city where Jesus saw the faith of the men who lowered the paralytic through the roof of a house (Mk 2:5).

faith without identifying its object. "If you have faith as a grain of mustard seed" (Mt 17:20). "Your faith has saved you" (Lk 7:50). "When Jesus saw their faith" (Mk 2:5). Jesus is portrayed as one who by his work and word opens the door to faith and makes faith possible. The question is not whether the faith is in Jesus or in the Father; the implication is undoubtedly both, but as with every true bearer of the Word of God the eye of faith is turned to the One who sends.

On more than one occasion Jesus denies the request for a miracle to substantiate his words (Mt 12:38,39; 16:1–4). Faith is response to the Word alone without any supporting props. No sign is to be given but the sign of Jonah. In the story of the rich man and Lazarus (Lk 16:19–31) Jesus denies the request for the spectacular and insists that the hearer must respond to the word given to him (cf. Jn 20:29). The Word demands self-surrender and commitment. Hence, the very nature of the Word and of faith becomes an obstacle to the proud and the powerful.

Faith is the medium by which the power of God is made visible. It moves mountains, heals the sick, and is the means of entrance into the kingdom. It may be mingled with doubt, as with the father who sought healing for his son ("I believe; help my unbelief!" [Mk 9:24]), or as with John the Baptist in prison, who, even with his doubts, was confirmed by Jesus as the greatest of the offspring of woman (Mt 11:2–15). Peter's (and the other disciples') perception was very faulty, but Jesus affirms Peter's confession as the foundation stone of the church. The synoptic Gospels portray the early faith of the disciples in all its limitations and weaknesses, yet it is still faith in that it is their positive response to Jesus' word and work.

The Fourth Gospel. Faith is an especially significant concept in the Gospel of John, though the word (in the Greek) occurs only as a verb. Quite often the reference has to do with the acceptance that something is true, that is, simple credence, or belief: "Believe me that I am in the Father and the Father in me" (Jn 14:11); "If you had believed Moses, you would believe me" (Jn 5:46). This is consistent with the importance of "truth" in the fourth Gospel. (Cf. also Jn 8:24; 11:27,42; 16:27,30; 17:8.)

Even more significant is the special expression "to believe into" in the sense of putting one's trust into another. The particular form of the expression is without parallel before the fourth Gospel and may well express the strong sense of personal trust in the eternal Word made flesh. In John 3:16 whoever puts trust in him has eternal life. Those who put their trust in him are given power to become sons of God—to be born of God (Jn 1:12). They will never thirst (6:35); they will live, even though they die (11:25).

In other places John speaks of trust or faith in an absolute sense, that is, without referring to the one in whom trust is placed. In John 11:15 Jesus arrives after the death of Lazarus and is glad "in order that you might believe." The outcome is going to be faith. Similarly in the prologue (Jn 1:7), John the Baptist bears witness in order that through him all might believe. As Jesus satisfies the doubt of Thomas concerning the resurrection, he says, "Have you believed because you have seen me? Blessed are those who have not seen and yet believe" (20:29). In these and other passages the fundamental outcome of Jesus' witness to himself is trust.

Faith and knowledge are closely related. In John 6:69 Peter says, "We have believed, and have come to know that you are the Holy One of God." In his priestly prayer Jesus says that eternal life is to "know thee, the only true God, and Jesus Christ whom thou hast sent" (Jn 17:3). Also, God is seen through the eyes of faith. No one has ever seen God, but the Only Begotten has revealed him (1:18). He who has seen Jesus has seen the Father (14:9).

To believe is also expressed in the verb "receive." Those who receive Christ are given power to become the sons of God (Jn 1:12). Trust is that form of knowing or seeing by which the glory of God (1:14; 17:4) is made present.

Paul. In his letters Paul writes about faith from a number of angles. He sets faith over against "works of the Law" as the only and true basis for righteousness (Rom 1–4; Gal 1–4) and appeals to Abraham to prove his point: "Abraham believed God and it was reckoned to him for righteousness" (Gn 15:6; Rom 4:5; Gal 3:6). This is entirely apart from the Law (Rom 3:21); righteousness is the gift of God

through faith in Christ, specifically in his atoning work. Behind Paul's conviction lies his awareness of the radical and pervasive sinfulness of humans which renders each one helpless. Humanity is dead in sin, but is made alive by faith in the word and work of Jesus mediated through the gospel.

Faith, then, is faith in Jesus Christ. The number of metaphors Paul employs to describe the consequences of faith is staggering. It is by faith that believers are justified (Rom 5:1), reconciled (2 Cor 5:18), redeemed (Eph 1:7), made alive (Eph 2:5), adopted into the family of God (Rom 8:15,16), re-created (2 Cor 5:17), transported into a new kingdom (Col 1:13), and set free (Gal 5:1). Faith is, for Paul, the *sine qua non* of every aspect of salvation, from the grace that convicts to the receiving of the full inheritance at the coming of the Lord.

In Paul's letters faith is bound up with love so that the great exponent of justification by faith becomes also the articulate exponent of distinctive Christian love. To say that faith is indispensable to salvation is only part of the truth, for faith expresses itself through love: "For in Christ Jesus neither circumcision nor uncircumcision is of any avail, but faith working through love" (Gal 5:6); "If I have all faith, so as to remove mountains, but have not love, I am nothing" (1 Cor 13:2). Love is both the genesis and the ultimate expression of faith. Hence, even for Paul there can be no *total* separation between faith and works. This love of which Paul speaks is the essential fruit of the Spirit through whom the life of faith is lived. Only by virtue of the indwelling Spirit does faith find expression in love.

Rest of the NT. James speaks of faith as being completed by works (Jas 2:22). He is opposing that concept of faith which thinks primarily of creedal assent, of believing that something is true without acting upon it. James assumes, like Paul, the primacy of faith but is warning against those who would draw wrong conclusions. Faith apart from works is not faith; it is barren (v 20). The practical dimension of faith is the burden of much of this epistle.

The writer of Hebrews recognizes that faith has always been characteristic of the people of God and their specially called leaders. Faith makes substantial what is otherwise nebulous and uncertain; it makes evidential what is not visible. By faith the people of God have a more certain ground for their lives and their action than the world is able to discern (Heb 11:1). The great cloud of witnesses (12:1) bear testimony by their faith to the faithfulness of God.

Faith is opened up by the Word of God, finds expression through the Holy Spirit who is given, and bears witness to the lordship of Jesus Christ.

Faith and Reason. Any serious discussion of faith must give some attention to the relation of faith to reason. Historically, three major views have emerged regarding this relationship.

The Thomistic View. Reason precedes faith in the sense that the truth of at least some of the objects of belief can be rationally demonstrated. Thus, the existence of God can be proved to any rational human being willing to honestly examine the evidence. Some forms of this position undertake to prove the whole of the teachings of Christianity, so that faith is virtually a function of reason. In other forms, faith takes over where reason leaves off, accepting on the basis of authority what cannot be established by reason.

The Augustinian View. Faith precedes reason, but makes reason possible. From the perspective of faith, understanding can emerge. Thus, while faith does not result from reason, it is in harmony with it. Neither faith nor reason can dispense with each other.

The Tertullian View. Faith and reason do not support one another. Hence one believes virtually in spite of reason. This position, often referred to as fideism (faithism), may either take the form that faith and reason are quite independent of one another, or that they are opposed. In the latter case, there is a disjunction between the two, leading to conflict or tension.

There arise here three questions: (1) the internal relation of God as Creator to the God who reveals himself to his creatures; (2) the structure of humankind as the crownpiece of God's creation; and (3) the meaning of religious statements in general and of Christian thought in particular.

As Creator, God built a pattern of structures into the world. In placing man within that world, he addressed himself to man's mind. This involved a capability upon the part of man to receive, not only impressions, but information. The fall of man made the issue especially crucial, for any plan for recovery would need to appeal to his thinking processes. This would suggest the necessity for points of clear contact between the human mind and what man would need in order to believe in, and respond to, the call of grace.

As the culmination of God's creation, man was placed in a world which flashed all sorts of signals, and these would include data concerning the nature of the world. With the fall, the need became urgent for some harmony between knowledge gained by his usual reasoning powers, and that addressed to him by God in saving love and grace. In such a situation man could scarcely act purposively, to say nothing of acting morally and spiritually, if there were no possibility of relating the intimations of grace to the signals from his world. After all, one can scarcely act on the basis of two vital abilities (i.e., reason and faith) if these have no connection with one another.

The question of the meaning of religious statements has, of course, historical dimension. While truth does not change, human understanding of truth does. Certainly no one would maintain seriously that we are asked to accept in faith what is absurd. What is true must have value to the thinking mind, and where religious faith touches the mind, it must appeal to the best modes and ways of thought.

It is well known that much thinking of our time is undergirded by the idea that everything is in process, that there is nothing which can be regarded as final and fixed. The relation of faith to reason is particularly crucial here, for Scripture clearly indicates that there are realities in the Judeo-Christian tradition which are enduring. This suggests that in relating faith to reason, one must at times go outside the usual ways of viewing the world, man, God, and man's relation to him.

Scripture gives valuable assistance here. Paul states that "the man without the Spirit" (NIV) (the "natural man") cannot accept God's thoughts which the Holy Spirit teaches (1 Cor 2:14). It is also asserted that faith is closely related to understanding. Note, for instance, the words of Hebrews 11:3: "By faith we understand that the world was created by the Word of God, so that what is seen was made out of things which do not appear."

From the foregoing, it seems clear that Scripture takes for granted that reason and faith are not two separate and unrelated abilities; rather, they are both inescapably bound up in the structure of the total person. In the final analysis, neither can safely stand alone. Reason without faith may deteriorate into a mere gathering of facts—facts that are never really put together. Faith without reason, on the other hand, can trail off into vagueness and lack of meaning.

ROBERT W. LYON

Bibliography. D.M. Baillie, *Faith in God;* G.C. Berkouwer, *Faith and Justification;* D.M. Emmet, *Philosophy and Faith;* R.M. Hals, *Grace and Faith in the OT;* P.S. Minear, *The Obedience of Faith.*

Faithfulness. Maintaining faith or allegiance; showing a strong sense of duty or conscientiousness. In biblical Hebrew, "faith" and "faithfulness" are grammatically related. Although both concepts are important in the OT, there is no English word exactly equivalent to the Hebrew terms. The most relevant Hebrew verbal root (related to our word "amen") carries such meanings as "strengthen," "support," or "hold up." In a physical sense it is used of pillars that provide support for doors (2 Kgs 18:16). Moses used the word when he disclaimed any role as supporter of the Israelites (Nm 11:12). God, however, is an eternally firm support for his people (Dt 7:9; Is 49:7).

With that notion of firm support as the bedrock for faith, words such as "firmness," "constancy," or "trustworthiness" best convey the related concept of faithfulness. Trustworthiness, or steadfastness of character, is ascribed to the object of one's trust. To be unfaithful is to be unworthy of confidence or belief. In the OT a synonym for "faithfulness" is "truth." Since God is consistently true he is the logical object of human trust (Ps 71:22; Is 61:8). When used of God in the OT, the word "faithfulness" frequently refers to his unwavering commitment to his promises.

Human Faithfulness. Faith and faithfulness are logically and linguistically one in the OT and NT. That is, the major words for faith in both Testaments also connote the concept of "faithfulness." This indicates that faith is more than momentary assent to the truth of God. It is commitment to that truth, and it manifests itself in continued obedience. Abraham's life in this regard is instructive. He assented to, relied upon, and acted in conformity to the revealed Word of God. He received God's revelation as true (i.e., demonstrating faith), and his subsequent actions proved his faithfulness. He left home and country, settled in a strange land, and offered up his son Isaac as God commanded. His willingness to sacrifice his only son is an unparalleled expression of faithfulness in the OT. It is no surprise, therefore, that Abraham is commended for his steadfastness and is set forth in the NT as one whose behavior should be imitated by Christians (Gal 3:6–9; Heb 11:8–10). Faithfulness, then, must not be viewed as an isolated act. Rather it is an attitude that should characterize the entire life of those who say they have faith in God. Although by definition all unbelievers are characterized by unfaithfulness, God's children are called to manifest faithfulness as a fruit of the Holy Spirit (Gal 5:22; cf. Eph 2:8).

God's Faithfulness. In spite of Israel's faithlessness (Dt 32:20; cf. Rom 3:3), God showed himself to be absolutely reliable. His faithfulness is great (Lam 3:23). He is loyal to his covenant and will always manifest his steadfast love to his people (Ps 136).

The pinnacle of faithfulness in the Bible is seen in the work of Jesus Christ, who showed himself faithful to his Father (Heb 3:2) and in

his witness (Rv 1:5). God calls men and women to be faithful by following Christ, relying on him for all things (Hab 2:4; cf Rom 1:17).

STUART D. SACKS

Falcon. Bird of prey noted for keen eyesight, and declared unclean in the OT (Lv 11:14).

See BIRDS (KESTREL).

Fall of Man. Transition from a state of moral innocence and favor with God to a state of condemnation and death, which occurred in the history of mankind with Adam's eating of the forbidden fruit.

Biblical Evidence. The narrative of creation in Genesis 1 and 2 affirms the distinctiveness of both man's nature and task. Man was created in the image of God for the purpose of communion and fellowship with God. As God's vicegerent, he was given dominion on the earth to cultivate and use its resources for the glory of God. Man was created righteous with a disposition and with every encouragement to do good.

In addition to the cultural mandate, man also received a specific command. He was authorized to use the vegetation of the garden of Eden for food, but he was expressly forbidden to eat of the tree of the knowledge of good and evil. The purpose of this command was to introduce into the human consciousness the radical antithesis between good and evil and to confirm man in service of the Creator. As a faithful and loyal servant, man was to enjoy all the blessings bestowed by his father in heaven and at last be led into the fulness of eternal life with God.

Man was made a living creature as were the animals, but the core of his life was to be union and communion with God. Fellowship with God was to become Adam's conscious possession, in contrast to the animals which know neither the possibility of sin nor conscious communion with God.

In full awareness of the evil of the alternative, man was to serve God willingly and lovingly. His life before God was therefore to be religious rather than instinctive.

The purpose of God in giving the command not to eat was to establish man in the ways of righteousness and faith, but Satan used the command as an occasion to tempt man to rebel against God. Although there was no evil for man in being tempted, it was evil for Satan to tempt man to sin. This means that there was evil in the universe prior to the fall of man. It was the apparent purpose of Satan to subject man to himself, and through man to extend his kingdom of darkness over the earth. The fall of man and the subsequent program of redemption must be understood in the context of the cosmic conflict between God and Satan, in which the ultimate triumph of God is assured.

Satan approached Adam by way of Eve, using as his instrument the serpent and urging them to eat of the tree of the knowledge of good and evil.

The difference between good and evil was not concealed from man prior to the fall, though man's experiential knowledge was only of the good. Adam was to receive instruction concerning the nature of this distinction and the consequences of eating or not eating only from God. As he had received life in the beginning from his Creator, so he was to live in obedience to every word that proceeded from the mouth of God. Such obedience was believing trust in God. Adam was a righteous man whose destiny was to live by faith.

The point of the temptation was to urge independence from God. Satan called into question the truth of God and challenged his authority. He led man to think that he could determine for himself the difference between good and evil and that he could control the consequences to his own advantage. It was the temptation for man to be a god to himself.

Adam fell when he yielded to the temptation of Satan and, together with his wife, ate of the forbidden fruit. As it is impossible to establish the date of the creation, so it is impossible to establish the date of the fall or the length of time between the creation and the fall. The length of this period is not theologically significant, but the historicity of it is. The sin of man is not eternal, nor is the fall given with the creation or existence of man. The fall took place in calendar history at a point subsequent to the creation as an act of rebellion by the creature against the Creator.

The act of rebellion was an act of disobedience, disloyalty, faithlessness, and unbelief. As the command not to eat summarized and brought to a focus all that was involved in righteousness before God, so the transgression epitomized radical apostasy from God. Satan attacked Adam precisely at the concentration point of man's covenant loyalty. Undivided obedience to God gave way to whole-souled rebellion and complete revolt: the authority of God was repudiated; the goodness of God was doubted; the wisdom of God was disputed; and the truth of God was contradicted. A whole new complex of affections and emotions took possession of the heart and mind of man.

The cause of the fall is not located in God, for he is not the author of evil. Nor is the cause to be found in Satan, since the tempta-

tion was the occasion for the fall, not the cause of it. There is no rationale for man's voluntary acquiescence to the temptation and the overt act flowing from this acquiescence.

Effects of the Fall. The immediate effects of the fall are visible in the loss of boldness and joy in the presence of God and the emergence of fear and shame. They are visible also in the alienation of Adam and Eve from God and in the revolution in the relation that God sustains to man. This is exemplified in the curse in relation to man, but more pointedly in the expulsion of Adam and Eve from the garden. The garden was the dwelling place of righteousness, the sphere of union and communion between man and God. Expulsion was inevitable once the communion was severed by unrighteousness.

As God had warned, the consequence of sin was death. Righteousness is the way of blessedness and life in communion with God; sin is punished by the suffering of hell in separation from God's beneficent presence. Since death intervenes at every point where there is life, it works itself out also in the dissolution of the body in the grave.

The consequences of the fall are not limited to Adam and Eve but extend to all those descended from the first pair by natural generation, because there is a unique relation of solidarity existing by divine institution between Adam and the rest of the race. Some theologians accent the generic connection between Adam and his descendants, while others focus on the covenant relationship of Adam as the head and representative of his posterity. The consequences of Adam's transgression for the human race are the imputation of his sin to all his descendants, their consequent liability to death, and their inheritance of a depraved nature.

The results of the fall are also manifest in the cosmos as the curse works itself out in the resistance offered to the accomplishment of the original cultural mandate. Only with the pain and danger attendant upon childbirth is the world populated, and only with arduous, toilsome labor is the food, clothing, and shelter necessary to sustain life provided.

However, the fact that death does not descend *immediately* upon man after the fall as *final* judgment is indicative of God's saving purpose for man. Adam does not hear the curse pronounced until he has heard the promise of a savior (Gn 3:15). An indirect consequence of the fall, and one which by no means justifies or explains it, is the magnificent display of grace in the redemption wrought by Christ.

After Genesis 3, the Bible only infrequently refers to the fall of man, but this historical event is the indispensible presupposition of all that follows. The thrust of the Bible is toward the future—the widening effects of sin and the unfolding of God's remedy.

Contemporary Understanding. Within contemporary theology of all confessional varieties there is widespread denial of the historicity of the biblical account of the fall. It may be granted that the Genesis account is told as history continuous with subsequent history and that within the worldview of the writers of the Bible, the account is alluded to as history. But it is argued that moderns can receive the story of the fall only as myth. This view has its source in the development of an evolutionary view of human origins coupled with a negatively critical evaluation of the literary history of the Genesis account.

Although the historicity of Adam may be abandoned, there is usually an attempt to appreciate the "truth" conveyed by the myth. For example, it is said that every person is Adam, and that everyone living is a sinner as far back as he or she can remember.

Others see in the myth not a fall, but an ascent to conscious and independent responsibility. Sin is thought of as necessary to religious maturity in the same way that exposure to competition from opponents strengthens the prowess of an athlete.

Because of the way the Bible parallels Adam and Christ (Rom 5:12–19; 1 Cor 15:22), a mythological understanding of Adam leads to a mythological understanding of Christ. As Adam becomes a symbol for the universality of sin and death, so Christ becomes simply a symbol for the inherent righteousness and redemption of all men.

The modern isolation of the message from the history of Genesis 1–3 violates the integrity of the account without offering a valid explanation for the universality of sin and death. Christian doctrine holds that sin entered the world within the horizon of man's daily life and is overcome by Christ within the arena of human history by his death and resurrection.

NORMAN SHEPHERD

See SIN; MAN, DOCTRINE OF; DEATH; ADAM (PERSON).

Fallow Deer. KJV translation of roebuck, a ruminant and member of the deer family, in Deuteronomy 14:5.

See ANIMALS (DEER; GAZELLE).

False Christs. Those who falsely claim to be the Christ or Messiah. False christs are mentioned only in the eschatological discourse of Jesus recorded by Matthew (24:24) and Mark (13:22).

In that discourse Jesus instructed his disciples about the future. He prophesied the destruction of the temple in Jerusalem and warned about deception and persecution that would confront the disciples. With a foreshortened perspective characteristic of biblical prophecy, Jesus blended together the destruction of Jerusalem and his return as the Son of man.

He especially warned his disciples that during the terrible days surrounding the destruction of the temple they were not to be deceived by false christs and false prophets (Mk 13:21–23). In this particular form of deception some would claim that the Christ was in a particular location (v 21). Those deceivers would perform signs and wonders to try to deceive the elect. But Jesus prepared his disciples by instructing them that there will be cosmic signs preceding his return as the Son of man (vv 24–25) and that his coming will be with great power and glory visible to all.

From history we know Jesus' instruction enabled Christians to flee the destruction of Jerusalem and the temple in AD 70, and to withstand the deception of false christs. The church still awaits Jesus' return as the glorious Son of man.

HOBERT K. FARRELL

See ANTICHRIST.

False Prophets. *See* PROPHET, FALSE.

Family Life and Relations. In Bible times, the family comprised members of a household, including not only parents and children, along with other relatives and concubines, but also servants, travelers, aliens, and anyone else who happened to be within the house and

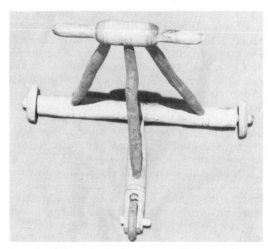

An ancient baby walker (in the museum in Tel Aviv).

was therefore under the protection of the head of the family. The family of Jacob, for example, comprised three generations (Gn 46:8–26). Biblically, the term "family" is interchangeable with "house," and "founding a house" can refer to setting up a separate dwelling as well as establishing a family. In the broader sense "house" may refer to an entire nation ("house of Israel"). The heads of families returning from Babylon in the postexilic period controlled sometimes several hundred family members (Ezr 8:1–14). The family was a smaller part of a clan and tribe. In nomadic times the responsibilities and allegiances centered on the larger family group.

Those who belonged to the clan knew that they had to work for common interests and accept responsibility for the whole group. All members of the family were to be protected and assisted in time of need.

As the life of the Israelites became more settled, families in the wider sense of the term lived in villages surrounded by fields of wheat, barley, and flax, with areas of grazing land for sheep and goats. Each group of villages consisted of an intermarried, interdependent family group, such as that of the Danites of Zorah and Eshtaol (Jgs 18:11). The hard life of those days demanded a sharing of work and the loyal cooperation of the entire family for survival.

As crafts and trades developed, along with a more sedentary lifestyle, sons learned their fathers' skills and continued the family trade. Consequently the whole village might follow a particular craft (1 Chr 4:14; Neh 11:35). By specializing in such trades, however, the villagers became less self-sufficient, depending more on farmers for food and on other specialized villages for the production of cloth (1 Chr 4:21) or pottery (v 23).

With the growth of cities, related groups lived together in specific areas. Many members of the tribes of Benjamin and Judah were listed in the census of Jerusalem by Nehemiah (Neh 11:4–8), and by the writer of Chronicles (1 Chr 9:4–9). One consequence of life in the cities was the fragmentation of the family group. As the bonds of the wider family were loosened, the unit consisted increasingly of a husband and wife with their children, living in one house. The size of houses that have been excavated precludes the idea of any larger family unit as the norm in OT societies.

During the kingdom period, although King David's unmarried daughter Tamar lived with him at the palace, his sons Amnon and Absalom set up their own separate houses (2 Sm 13:7,8,20). At that time there were few slaves in Hebrew society, but they also were considered members of the family. As bonds of the wider

family loosened, and the master of the household lost a degree of authority, the society became one in which the king was sovereign and all the people were his subjects.

The early kings of Israel promoted such a change in order to establish a central ruling authority for the entire country. The king's subjects fell broadly into the categories of employers and employees, corresponding to the rich and poor of society. By the 8th century BC, members of the wider family no longer worked for the communal good under the authority of the clan's head; rather, individuals worked primarily for the good of their own immediate family. Hence one's labor and devotion were focused more narrowly, and the greatest beneficiary was the king, the personal symbol of the nation.

Emphasis on the smaller family unit increased, and old duties that had been willingly accepted by the wider groups in former times came to be neglected. People did not always help relatives in times of need, and they frequently had to be reminded of their obligations, particularly toward widows and orphans (Is 1:17; Jer 7:6). Family feuds also declined, because members no longer felt responsible to take vengeance as a way to uphold the honor of the clan (2 Sm 3:27; 16:8; 2 Kgs 9:26). Nevertheless, Nehemiah expected Israelites to fight for their family honor (Neh 4:14). In NT times, the family was such a unit that it could be sold for a debt incurred by one of its members (Mt 18:25).

The Hebrew religion's emphasis on family participation in certain celebrations strengthened the small unit. The Passover, for example, was always celebrated as a family thanksgiving meal (Ex 12:3,4,46). The prophet Samuel's parents made a traditional annual pilgrimage to the shrine at Shiloh (1 Sm 2:19). In modern times, a young Jewish boy's arrival at the threshhold of manhood is celebrated with the Bar Mitzvah ceremony. Being so honored in the midst of a religious family preserves the ancient Hebrew tradition of family participation in religious ceremonies.

In his preaching Jesus used the family as a symbol for the relationship of God to his people (Mt 19:14; 23:9; Lk 8:21). From the cross he handed over responsibility for the care of his mother to his disciple John (Jn 19:27).

In NT times, the communion meals in the Jerusalem church took place by households (Acts 2:46). Early Christian meetings were held in the homes of believers because of opposition by the authorities. The Book of Acts contains examples of entire families being converted to Christianity (Acts 10:24,44–48; 16:15, 31,32). Timothy learned the gospel from his grandmother and mother (2 Tm 1:5).

Status of Family Members. From nomadic times a father's authority held the family group together in their encampment, and he became the symbol of their security. In ancient patriarchal societies, the father was an absolute master who had the power of life and death over family members, ruling with unchallenged authority. Although he had extensive responsibilities for those under his care, his power was awesome and his status unquestioned.

A man's possessions included his wife, servants, slaves, and animals (Ex 20:17; Dt 5:21). In fact, the phrase "to marry a wife" comes from a Hebrew root meaning "to become the master of a wife." A husband was as much the master of his wife as he was of his home or his fields. Consequently the wife addressed him in a subservient manner, as a slave would address a master (Gn 18:12 KJV; Jgs 19:26). This low status for a woman extended to a daughter's position in the ancient household. Females were always under the authority of a male relative: first the father, then a husband, and if a woman became a widow she was subject to her husband's nearest male relative, who became her "redeemer." The bride-price (Gn 29:18,27; Ex 22:16,17; 1 Sm 18:25; 2 Sm 3:14) paid by her husband was not exactly a purchase of the woman from her father, but the exchange of money did stigmatize her. The amount of a bride-price depended on the father's status (Gn 34:12). The usual price was probably 20 to 30 shekels of silver. The price for a virgin who had been raped was 50 shekels, a figure set presumably as a punishment of the man who had violated her (Dt 22:29). The bride received gifts of jewelry, ornaments, and clothing from her future husband, and she occasionally enjoyed some sort of financial or material return from the bride-price for her own use (Jos 15:19; Jgs 1:15). When her father or husband died the money frequently reverted to her.

An engaged woman was considered her fiance's property just as much as if she were already married to him (Dt 22:23–27). The woman left her own family at marriage, to live with and become part of her new husband's family. Normally any succeeding marriages would be with members of that family.

In Mesopotamia, according to the law of Hammurabi, a bridegroom gave presents to his bride's parents. If the engagement was broken off, the bride's family had to restore double the amount of the gifts received. Under Assyrian law both the bride and her parents received presents, though most if not all of those gifts seem to have reverted to the bride for her personal use. There was nothing resembling a dowry, but a Babylonian woman received gifts from her father upon marriage, which could be used by her husband, although they did not belong to him. Their ownership remained with her if she became a widow.

Despite the low legal status of the mother of the family, her life was not as bad as one might suppose. She was the legal wife, not an unpaid servant, and she frequently took a strong role as advisor to her husband in family affairs. Her most important function, aside from childbearing, was organization of the household, of which she was generally the respected manager. Even though the wife might have been acquired through capture in war (Dt 21:10–14), she could not be sold as a slave or daughter could (Ex 21:7; Neh 5:5).

Nevertheless her position was precarious, in that she could be disowned or divorced by her husband as the result of a simple renunciation: "She is no longer my wife and I am no longer her husband." Perhaps he had found fault with her culinary skills, or possibly he was casting his eyes on another woman. In any event, a husband knew that if his wife did not obey even a signal or a glance he was within his rights to obtain a divorce (cf. Ecclus 25:26). The wife, however, obtained a certain degree of protection in the letter of repudiation, by which her freedom was formally restored. Under Jewish tradition a wife could not divorce her husband.

In ancient Mesopotamia, the law of Hammurabi permitted a man to divorce his wife by pronouncing a stated formula, but despite that he was still responsible for paying her compensation. The wife also had the right to secure a divorce if she could obtain a judgment about her husband's guilt. Under Assyrian law no compensation was payable to a discarded wife, and she had no right of divorce at all.

In matters of domestic protocol, the Hebrew wife was not introduced to her husband's guests, a tradition that subsequently led to considerable embarrassment for Abraham's wife Sarah and for Rebekah (Gn 20:16). A woman normally remained veiled in public (24:65; 38:14; Is 47:2), which accounts for Ruth's mother-in-law Naomi failing to recognize her when she returned home (Ru 3:15,16).

During the period of the monarchy the queen mother took precedence over the queen consort (1 Kgs 2:19), a custom probably showing more respect for age than for women.

The imagery in Proverbs 19:13 and 27:15 draws a vigorous comparison between a contentious woman and water dripping from a leaky roof. The OT leaves little doubt about the type of behavior expected from a woman. She was expected to be charming, soft-spoken, discreet, and calm (Prv 9:13; 11:16,22; 21:9). She was also to be responsible, well-organized, intelligent, thoughtful, reverent, and a good manager of both the household and the family purse (31:10–31). A woman should also be pious and beautiful, and, in NT tradition, submissive to her husband, as befitted a woman adorned with the priceless jewel of a gentle and quiet spirit (Ti 2:4,5; 1 Pt 3:2–6).

The actions of a few women whose roles in life do not seem to fit the pattern of the meek, passive female pictured above, are recorded in the Bible and the Apocrypha. The books of Judith and Esther recount heroic tales of how national fortunes were saved by women. Deborah and Jael were renowned heroines (Jgs 4,5), and the kingdom of Judah was ruled by a vicious woman, Athaliah, for several years (2 Kgs 11). The women who stepped to the forefront of public life were exceptional and few in number. Judith was a rich widow, an unusual thing in Israel.

The Rights of Children. The nature of patriarchal society made for unfortunate distinctions between male and female children. The position of a daughter, who could be sold into slavery or sold to be the concubine of a man and then possibly sold again (Ex 21:7–11), was certainly inferior to that of a son. In the patriarchal period, however, both a son and a daughter could be put to death for disobeying the head of the family. One's children could also be sacrificed in worship rituals (see Gn 22; Jgs 11). It is probable that infant sacrifice was practiced by nations neighboring Israel, including Canaan and Ammon.

The rights of children were improved considerably with the promulgation of the code of Mosaic law. A father was no longer permitted to put his child to death without referring the case to the elders (Dt 21:18–21). Both sons and daughters could be brought before such authorities and accused of being disobedient, gluttonous, or drunkards. If convicted, they were stoned to death. A father's absolute authority even extended to his married son and family if they were living under his roof. The law also prohibited children from being held responsible for the crimes of their parents (24:16). In King David's time a person convicted by the community had the right of appeal to the king (2 Sm 14:4–11).

In Hebrew families both parents were held in high respect. Honor had to be given to both mother and father (Ex 20:12), and the law condemned offenses against either parent (21:17; Lv 20:9; Dt 21:18; 27:16). Respect due to the mother is a recurrent theme in the Wisdom literature (Prv 19:26; 20:20; cf. Ecclus 3:1–16).

Marital Security. The security of a wife's position improved considerably when she produced her first child, particularly if it was a

An ancient cradle (in the museum in Tel Aviv).

son. A woman's primary duty to her husband and his family was procreation (Gn 1:28; 9:1), and until she gave birth to a son she feared displacement by a second wife or a concubine. Polygamous marriages were by no means rare, especially in wealthy families. They resulted in two ill-defined family groups, controlled by the mothers but under the overall authority of fathers; there were inevitable jealousies and frictions.

The legal status of a woman was consistently poor in Bible times. With no evidence at all, a husband could accuse his wife of adultery, and she was compelled to face a trial by ordeal. She had to abase herself, taking an oath, eating dust and a cereal offering, and drinking bitter water. A priest meanwhile made pronouncements regarding the dire results that would come to her if she were guilty: she would become an outcast with no hope of survival. But if she maintained her serenity, and her thigh did not rot nor her abdomen swell, she was considered to have "proved" her innocence. In such an event she would go free, and her husband bore no blame whatsoever for his false accusation (Nm 5:12–31).

If a woman took a vow, it was only legal as long as her father or husband approved it. If she became a widow, the vow still remained in force and could be used against her (Nm 30:4–15).

A woman in Israel was always under the protection of a male, be it her father, grandfather, great-grandfather, brother, husband, or some other member of her husband's family. She had few legal rights and, in contrast to Babylonian traditions, could not inherit at her husband's death. It is small wonder that widows were classed with orphans and aliens as the pitied poor. A childless widow could on occasion return to her father's family (Gn 38:11; Lv 22:13; Ru 1:8), thus becoming subject again to the authority of her father. A Hebrew widow could also remain with her late husband's family. She would then come under the protection of her "redeemer," a male relative of her husband's family who assumed responsibility for her. If a husband died leaving a woman childless, it was the responsibility of the husband's brother to marry her. The first son born of such a union was then regarded as the heir of the first husband.

It was normal for a brother to accept the obligation for such a marriage (levirate). It could be refused on various grounds, but such refusal was considered dishonorable, for it was a man's duty to perpetuate his brother's name and to safeguard the family fortune.

A redeemer's responsibilities were considerable. In addition to the marriage, he was perhaps involved in avenging the family reputation, and he had to ensure that family property increased and remained within family control.

If an Israelite fell into debt and was forced to sell himself into slavery, he would normally be "redeemed" by one of his relatives (Lv 25:47–49). If in his penury an Israelite had to sell his land or his house, the redeemer had the right of first refusal over all other prospective purchasers. It was as much his duty as his right to prevent family property from passing into the hands of strangers (Lv 25:25). The prophet Jeremiah bought his cousin Hanamel's field under similar circumstances (Jer 32:6–15).

The most familiar OT story of a childless widow and her "redeemer" and their levirate marriage is recorded in the Book of Ruth. One of Naomi's two sons married Ruth. When Ruth was widowed, her impoverished mother-in-law Naomi left her home in Moab and returned to Bethlehem to sell some of the family property. Although a close relative was prepared to buy the land and keep it in the family, he was not ready to marry Ruth as well (Ru 3:12; 4:4). He knew that a son of that union would be deemed a son of the deceased, bearing the dead husband's name, and thus ultimately inheriting the land (vv 4–6). The next relative in order of kinship was Boaz, who became Ruth's "redeemer." He was prepared to accept the double obligation of purchasing the land and marrying Ruth (vv 9,10).

Names. In the ancient Near East, the naming of an object or person implied power and authority over what was named (Gn 2:19, 20). Thus a person not knowing another's name could do neither harm nor good to that person (Ex 33:12,17). In the ancient world a name described the person or his work in some way. When the individual or his situation changed, so did the name, as with Abram (Abraham) and Jacob (Israel). Pharaoh, as master of the patriarch Joseph, changed Joseph's name when his status al-

tered, calling him Zaphenath-paneah (Gn 41:45). When Eliakim was made king of Judah, the pharaoh changed the Jewish king's name to Jehoiakim (2 Kgs 23:34). In captivity, Daniel, Hananiah, Mishael, and Azariah were forced to change their names to Belteshazzar, Shadrach, Meshach, and Abednego by order of the eunuch (Dn 1:6,7).

In the NT, John the Baptist was named by an angel who represented God, and similarly Jesus was given his name by an angel. The naming of those children symbolized God's authority over John the Baptist and his special relationship as Father to Jesus. In biblical times an infant received his or her name at birth from its mother (Gn 4:1,25; 35:18; 1 Sm 1:20) or father (Gn 4:26; 5:29).

Position of Children. Children were generally well loved, but their childhood was short and they were often regarded as laborers for the house or fields. According to the law of primogeniture, the eldest son received a double portion of the estate as his birthright (Dt 21:17). Thus he was assured of the position of family head. Even during his father's lifetime, the eldest son took precedence over his brothers and sisters (Gn 43:33). Where twins were born, the first to emerge from the womb was considered the elder, with all the attendant privileges (Gn 25:24–26; 38:27–30).

For a serious offense the eldest son could lose the right of primogeniture (Gn 35:22; 49:3,4; 1 Chr 5:1), or it could be surrendered voluntarily as Esau did by selling his birthright to his brother Jacob (Gn 25:29–34). There was a law protecting the eldest son from his father's favoritism for a younger brother (Dt 21:15–17). Nevertheless King David gave his kingdom to Solomon, his youngest son (1 Kgs 2:15).

In a family with no sons, a daughter could inherit property (Nm 27:8). Frequently parents consulted neither sons nor daughters when marriage partners were arranged for them. Marriage was often an alliance or contract between two families, and thus the wishes and concerns of individuals were considered unimportant. Love matches were few, although occasionally a son would marry in defiance of his parents, as Esau did (Gn 26:34,35). Although it was rare for young people to express their feelings and preferences about marriage in an open fashion, Saul's daughter, Michal, made known her love for David (1 Sm 18:20). It is not certain what the normal age for marriage was in biblical times.

There is no record of legal adoption among the Hebrews, but it was practiced from ancient times in Mesopotamia. It was especially useful as a means of ensuring a childless couple that their land would be tilled and that they would be cared for in their old age. All examples of adoption mentioned in the OT took place outside the land of Israel (Ex 2:10; 1 Kgs 11:20; Est 2:7,15), and are not examples of true adoption as a lifetime member of a family.

Daily Life of the Hebrew Family. In the everyday affairs of a Hebrew household, it was the father's responsibility to maintain the family fortune and to be the provider. He might work in the fields, most probably with crops of flax, barley, or wheat. Or he would work at a trade, possibly as a weaver, builder, potter, dyer, fuller, or a worker in copper or bronze. If he lived near the shore, he might be a fisherman.

The father was also responsible for the religious well-being of the family. It was his duty to take over his sons' education from the mother at an early age, teaching them the tenets of Hebrew religion (Ex 10:2; 12:26; Dt 4:9; 6:7). He also explained all the facets of the Law and the interwoven history of the nation.

The father was the disciplinarian of the family, with the rod being used to drive home the lessons taught (Prv 13:24; 22:15; 29:15,17). Though children were loved and valued, they were not pampered (Ecclus 30:9–12). In postexilic times education also took place within the precincts of the synagogue, and shortly before the time of Christ a general elementary education was introduced. It was also imperative that a father teach his sons a trade, normally his own, for a man without a trade either starved or became a thief. Another important paternal responsibility was to provide wives for male offspring in the household.

The mother was responsible for her sons' and daughters' early education (Prv 1:8; 6:20), teaching them religious songs and prayers as soon as they could talk. A father took over the education of his sons, but the mother continued with the daughters, training them to spin, weave, cook, clean, trim the lamps, and generally to become competent in all the household duties (31:13–31).

With little furniture, keeping a house clean meant sweeping the floors to keep them free from dust and dirt. Cooking was at once simple and difficult. It was simple in that much of the food was cooked in the form of a soup or stew, or else made into a cake and cooked on a griddle. It was difficult in that the corn had to be ground by hand and bread was baked daily.

A mother was expected to take wool, card it, spin it, and often weave and make clothes for her family. In addition, she would help her husband in the fields at harvest time. Because many families had one or more olive trees, a few grape vines, and fig trees, the mother would also assist in picking the fruit. She would sometimes work at the press when the olives or grapes were being processed. Frequently the treading of grapes in the family vat would be done together by husband and wife. Drawing water from the well was considered a menial task and was generally the wife's responsibility, although sometimes it was assigned to the children (Gn 24:15,16).

As in all societies, there was a time when children laughed and played together (Zec 8:5; Mt 11:16), although childhood and adolescence were not recognized as specific stages of development. Children were considered as sucklings if under three, but were regarded as boys or girls when they were able to take care of themselves. A small child sat on his mother's lap and was played with (Is 66:12). There is no evidence of organized sports for children. Toys including whistles, rattles, dolls, and miniature cooking utensils have been excavated at Palestinian sites.

As soon as a boy was old enough, he took his place in the family and accepted his appointed task. Among other things, children were expected to gather fuel (Jer 7:18). Young boys and girls tended the flocks. The sheep had to be protected from marauding wild beasts, guarded against their own folly when they wandered near crevices, steered toward good pasture and water, and carried home when sick or injured (Gn 29:6; Ex 2:16). The care of cattle was also the responsibility of children (1 Sm 16:11). Of necessity, boys were trained in the various arts of war.

Children sometimes joined their fathers in the fields, and their presence was always welcome. From earliest times, boys in particular would watch their fathers until they too picked up a tool or implement to try their skill; girls watched and learned from their mothers. Young children frequently listened to the talk of the elders at the city gates or in the villages. A visit to a sanctuary at festival time was a family affair, furnishing an ideal learning experience. As a child, Jesus accompanied his parents Mary and Joseph to the temple in Jerusalem (Lk 2:42–47).

Young girls were surprisingly free to go about their appointed tasks. They were not secluded or veiled, and could visit unhindered with friends and neighbors (Gn 34:1). They were also able to converse with men without embarrassment (24:15–25; 29:11,12; 1 Sm 9:11–13).

Mealtimes were strictly family times. It is doubtful whether a meal comparable to a breakfast was eaten, and a farmer would probably have a light lunch in the fields. The main meal of the day was prepared by the mother, and would be eaten in the early evening. Although the variety of food available was limited, its preparation was time-consuming.

Feast times were periods of great religious significance, and also the days when family members participated in the symbolic rituals of their faith. Among the Israelites several kinds of food were fundamental to their religious ritual. Family unity and the national religion were molded together by special meals in the home.

Light played an important part in the daily habits of the people in antiquity. Although oil lamps were readily available in later periods, it was customary to rise with the sun and go to bed relatively soon after dark. The wife would probably be up before sunrise and might continue her labor after dark.

By NT times, for those who followed the Greek and Roman style, life became more elegant. Despite that, the status of many family members did not change substantially. Wealthier families had more slaves, and the children were more likely to have formal education, sometimes spending less effort on family chores. Even in Roman times, however, the father still had a legal right to accept or reject his child.

The status of the woman had definitely improved by the NT period. A Roman matron was highly respected, and exerted a strong influence over her husband. She was not sequestered in a particular section of the house, as a Greek woman was, but managed and supervised tasks in any part of her home. She helped her husband in business, had her own place in theaters, games, and religious festivals, and sometimes managed her own property. Palestinian women began to enjoy a new status and dignity as the result of Jesus' attitude toward women and its influence on the early Christian church.

HAZEL W. PERKIN

See MARRIAGE, MARRIAGE CUSTOMS; EDUCATION; FOOD AND FOOD PREPARATION; MEALS, SIGNIFICANCE OF; SEX, SEXUALITY; WIDOW.

Bibliography. A.C. Bouquet, *Everyday Life in NT Times* and *Everyday Life in OT Times*; R. de Vaux, *Ancient Israel*, pp 19–55; A. Edersheim, *Sketches of Jewish Social Life in the Days of Christ*; E.A. Judge, *The Social Pattern of Christian Groups in the First Century*; A. Van Duersen, *Illustrated Dictionary of Bible Manners and Customs*.

Famine. Prolonged and extreme lack of food. Famine along with other disasters (such as war and disease) have always been part of the human experience. Sometimes there was enough rainfall, properly timed, but occasionally rainfall was too early or late or insufficient (Lv 26:19; Am 4:7,8). The Hebrews and other people in the Near East viewed famine as a judgment of God. God as Creator and Sus-

tainer had power over the natural world. He could use his created order as he chose; it was no accident when there was famine. Whether a famine occurred through lack of rainfall, hailstorms, or any other event, God was the agent.

The most prevalent cause of famine in the ancient world was lack of rain. Such famines occurred in the time of Abraham (Gn 12:10) and Isaac (26:1). Joseph was greatly concerned about overcoming the famines in Egypt (41–47). The Nile River usually provided the Egyptians with enough water for their crops; a failure to receive adequate water supplies from upland regions meant famine for Egypt.

Besides lack of rainfall, famine could result from other causes, such as hail and thunderstorms (Ex 9:28,31; 1 Sm 12:17). Sieges on crops by locusts and other pests sometimes caused famine (Ex 10:15; Am 4:9). Invasion by foreign armies also brought on famine (Dt 28:53; 2 Kgs 6:25; 25:3; Lam 4:9,10). Disease often accompanied famine (1 Kgs 8:37; Jer 14:12; 21:9).

Famine brought changes to the lives of Naomi and Ruth (Ru 1:1). God raised Joseph to a position of power in famine conditions. Famine also affected the lives of King David (2 Sm 21:1), Elijah (1 Kgs 17), Elisha (2 Kgs 4:38; 6:25), and Zedekiah (2 Kgs 25:2,3).

Famine was used by God to warn (1 Kgs 17:1), correct (2 Sm 21:1), and punish God's people or the heathen (Jer 14:12,15). The famines predicted by Jesus and the writer of the Book of Revelation were signs of judgment (Mk 13:8; Rv 18:8).

The famine of Acts 11:28 was of great severity.

Farmer, Farming. See AGRICULTURE; TRADES AND OCCUPATIONS.

Farthing. 1. KJV translation for penny, a copper coin equivalent to 1/16 of the silver denarius (Mt 10:29; Lk 12:6).

2. KJV translation for another word translated "penny" (RSV), a coin equivalent to 1/4 of #1 above, or 1/64 of the denarius (Mt 5:26; Mk 12:42).

See COINS; MONEY AND BANKING.

Fashion and Dress. Clothing, especially as related to Bible times. Clothing mentioned in the Bible is usually referred to in such general terms as "inner garment," "outer garment," or "tunic." Few descriptions give specific details of costumes or clothing, and it is therefore necessary to rely on paintings, pottery, decorations, statues, and bas-reliefs to show

Statue that illustrates a typical dress in ancient Rome.

As the seminomadic Israelite tribes became more sedentary in nature, flax was cultivated. It was woven into linen, which became a commonly used fabric. Flax was manufactured in several qualities, ranging from very coarse to extremely fine. Goat's hair and camel's hair were also used for making coarse, heavy fabrics. At the beginning of the Middle Bronze Age (c. 2000 BC), fine silks began to be imported from China, and wild silk was produced in some areas of the Near East. Cotton was known in Egypt, but it does not appear to have been produced anywhere in Palestine in the biblical period.

Attitudes Toward Clothing. Articles of clothing were frequently regarded as objects of wealth. Clothing was sometimes taken after a battle, as during the Israelite conquest of Canaan. Thirty linen garments formed the prize when Samson tested the Philistines with a riddle (Jgs 14:12,13). Elisha's servant Gehazi exhibited greed in his request for two festal garments (2 Kgs 5:22,26). Excessive quantities of clothing were frowned upon as an unnecessary extravagance. Similarly, anxious concern for items of clothing was considered a materialistic approach to life (Mt 6:25; 10:10). The Jews pictured God as the supplier of food and clothing for his people (Dt 10:18). A significant contrast in social standing was reflected in the clothes described in the story of the rich man and Lazarus (Lk 16:19–31). In contrast to the poor beggar, the rich man was clothed in purple and fine linen. That cloth was so expensive that it was considered inferior only to the purest silk imported from China, which was as valuable as gold. Fine linen was imported either from Egypt (see Ez 27:7) or India.

The general care of fabrics was of great importance in the Near East, especially where fine quality materials were involved. For Jews, laundering or changing clothes often had religious connotations, as seen in the instructions that Jacob gave to his household on the changing of clothes as part of a purification rite (Gn 35:2,3). Washing clothes was also part of a complex levitical ritual for diagnosing leprosy (Lv 13:47–59), purifying healed lepers (14:8,9), and cleansing those in contact with any cultic uncleanliness (15:2–27).

Garments were also changed in times of grief. Thus David changed his attire after the death of his child (2 Sm 12:20). As one indication of mourning or anger, it was common for garments to be torn (2 Sm 1:11; 2 Kgs 5:7). Sackcloth (woven goat's hair) was also worn during mourning (Gn 37:34) or as an act of repentance (Jer 4:8).

Clothing also served as a token of joy and festivity. Ruth was instructed to put on her best clothes when she presented herself to

the clothing styles of the period. It should be remembered that many Egyptian and Babylonian artifacts depict the people of Israel as captives and supplicants, and as such their clothing would be different from that normally worn by the various ranks of their society.

Many ancient Near Eastern peoples (including the Israelites) kept flocks of sheep before the discovery of spinning and weaving and used the leather of their hides for clothing. Later, wool plucked from the sheep and from branches on which the fleece had accumulated as the animals brushed past was made into a feltlike fabric. Wool remained one of the most important fabrics for clothing throughout the biblical period.

Another Roman statue depicting a woman's dress.

Boaz (Ru 3:3). Garments and jewelry were used as gifts by Abraham's servant when he went to encourage Rebekah to return with him as Isaac's bride (Gn 24:22,47,53). Weddings were occasions for special garments: "The princess is decked in her chamber with gold-woven robes" (Ps 45:13).

In later periods Jewish attitudes toward clothing were expressed in talmudic regulations. An example is the law concerning rescue of garments from a house that had caught fire on the sabbath. According to rabbinic traditions, the salvaging of articles of clothing under such conditions would have been thought of as work and prohibited on the sabbath. On the contrary, a person was permitted to salvage 18 specified articles, but only on condi-

tion that they be worn and not carried from the fire.

Male Clothing. Early in biblical times the loincloth formed an important item of male clothing that was worn by all levels of society. Prior to 2000 BC, a type of loincloth was also the customary piece of clothing for all Egyptians, from the lowliest laborer to the pharaoh. At a later period, however, it appeared only as part of military dress (Ez 23:15). The inner garment (a tunic or shirt) was made of wool or linen. It had openings for the neck and arms, and appears to have had long sleeves, although some styles had half-sleeves. It was worn next to the skin, and fell either to the knees or, more often, to the ankles, frequently being belted at the waist. The Greek *chitōn* ("coat") and the Roman tunic would have been undergarments of a similar character. A man who was wearing nothing except this undergarment was considered "naked." The young man who followed after Jesus at Gethsemane at his arrest was probably attired in this manner (Mk 14:51,52).

Generally speaking, the outer garment, formed out of a square-shaped piece of cloth, was referred to as a cloak or mantle. It had openings for the arms, and was draped over one or both shoulders.

A Hebrew man was considered improperly dressed without his cloak, and one was forbidden to demand another's mantle as a loan or pledge. At night when the other items of clothing were removed, the cloak, which was often made of animal skin or wool, was used as a blanket (Ex 22:26,27; Dt 24:13). Cloaks made of goat's hair or camel's hair, such as John the Baptist wore (Mt 3:4; Mk 1:6), would have been particularly warm at night. Those tough outer garments were probably the clothes described as longlasting by the Israelites, following the exodus (Dt 29:5). The mantle was removed while working.

The coat of many colors which Jacob gave to Joseph was probably a striped shirt or tunic made of leather or wool felt. The entire garment may have been bound with a woolen border (Gn 37:3). The garment Hannah made each year for the young Samuel was probably a coat or mantle (1 Sm 2:19).

Cloaks were usually made with a hem, and in Matthew 9:20 it was this that the woman touched when she came to Jesus for healing. The robe that Roman soldiers placed derisively upon Jesus to symbolize his kingship was probably a purple military cloak such as Roman officers commonly wore (Mt 27:28,31; Mk 15:17; Jn 19:2).

In Greek and Roman times, the outer garment often had tassels at the four corners. The best-known item of Roman men's apparel was the toga. It was a heavy, voluminous garment that fell in luxurious folds. The toga symbolized the strength and wealth of Rome and was intended strictly for Roman citizens. It was worn over a white tunic that came to the knees. A robe similar to the Greek *himation* was the type of outer garment placed on the prodigal son (Lk 15:22) when his father celebrated the son's return with his best food, clothing, and jewelry. The cloak that Paul wore (2 Tm 4:13) may well have been a circular style of cape that was popular in the 1st century AD.

Girdles, used as belts for undergarments, consisted of fabric folded to about 5 inches in width. These were sometimes made of leather (Mt 3:4) or linen (Prv 31:24), but wool, a tougher and longer-lasting material, was more common. Coins, knives, or food could be carried in the girdle as in a pocket. On dusty journeys or when manual work was being performed, the undergarment was often tucked around the girdle. The messianic descendant of Jesse is depicted as wearing a girdle of righteousness and faithfulness (Is 11:5). The writer of the Book of Revelation envisaged "one like a son of man, clothed with a long robe and with a golden girdle" (Rv 1:13).

Garments were of different qualities and signified rank or office (Is 3:6). The scribes and prophets wore special mantles symbolic of their professions. Elijah wore a prophet's mantle (1 Kgs 19:13,19; 2 Kgs 2:8,13,14). In NT times scribes wore special robes (Mk 12:38; Lk 20:46).

Israel's kings wore a linen ephod and robe (1 Chr 15:27). David wore a garment of linen when the ark of the covenant was transferred to Jerusalem (2 Sm 6:14). Foreign princes were often notable for their luxurious embroidered garments (Ez 26:16). Outer garments with tassels at the corners were a favorite item of royal attire. Turbanlike conical headwear was also a mark of kingship (21:26). On special occasions royalty wore perfumed garments (Ps 45:8). Royal robes were frequently voluminous, dyed scarlet and purple and embellished with tassels and beaten gold or silver thread. The seriousness of an occasion was indicated when a king discarded his royal robes and put on sackcloth. This occurred when the ruler of Nineveh proclaimed a time of mourning after hearing the preaching of Jonah (Jon 3:6). King Herod appeared on his throne "arrayed in royal robes" and awed the populace into believing he was divine, as was Roman custom of that time (Acts 12:21).

Christ and his disciples probably wore tunics, sandals, and carried moneybags and staffs (Mt 10:9,10; Mk 6:8; Lk 9:3; 10:4). When Roman soldiers divided Jesus' clothing after the crucifixion (Jn 19:24), they cast lots for the inner garment, one woven without any seams and probably made of wool. This was the most valuable of Jesus' items of clothing.

The Hebrew Priest's Clothing. The garments of the priests, particularly the high priest, were elaborate full-length linen tunics with long sleeves and decorated with embroidery. The belt or sash worn by the priest was also exquisitely crafted of fine linen. Exodus 28:4–8 specifies in detail the garments to be made for the high priest.

Breeches or drawers as an undergarment are mentioned only in connection with priestly clothing. These linen breeches were designed to cover the area from the loins to the thigh (Ex 28:42). Breeches were worn during two ceremonies: during the removal of the ashes of the burnt offering from the altar (Lv 6:10) and on the Day of Atonement (16:4). In the Book of Ezekiel the priests are again exhorted to wear the correct linen garments for their sacred duties, including the breeches (Ez 44:17,18).

On top of the tunic or undershirt, the high priest wore a robe of blue linen with blue, purple, and scarlet pomegranates, which were either woven into the fabric or embroidered on it. Between the pomegranates were gold bells which gave a soft tinkling sound as the high priest moved about (Ex 28:31–35). Over the robe from the shoulder to the waist was the ephod (similar to a vest) made of fine linen interwoven with gold, blue, purple, and scarlet cloth. A heavily jeweled breastplate made of similar material was prescribed for wearing on top of the ephod (vv 15–28). The attire of Aaron's sons was much less elaborate than that of the high priest and was of fine white linen. The special headdress worn by the high priest was made of fabric, often linen, and was a type of turban. Other priests wore a less elaborate cap (29:9; 34:28).

Women's Clothing. The woman's undergarment was similar to the man's but slightly longer, reaching the ankle. It also had a higher neckline. It was made in such a way that it could be worn draped across one shoulder.

Hebrew women also wore a robe that could have special significance when worn by the virgin daughters of a king (2 Sm 13:18). The robe depicted on one of the Megiddo ivories is elaborately decorated with a fringe. Roman women wore a long tunic that reached to the ankles, while their outer garment was a rectangular woolen cloth or *stola*, which could be pulled over the head when in public.

As a sign of mourning a widow probably wore a garment of sackcloth (Gn 38:14,19; 2 Sm 14:2). This coarse, uncomfortable fabric was most probably made of goat's hair and

Typical attire of two Greek women.

could be worn over the tunic or next to the skin. In Deuteronomy 24:17 the Israelites were forbidden to take a widow's robe as a pledge, since, like a man's cloak, this article of clothing was used as a blanket at night.

The girdle was also part of a woman's clothing as mentioned in the detailed description of wealthy women's attire in Isaiah 3:18–24. The woman's girdle was often quite elaborate and could be more valuable than the dress.

Head Coverings. Carvings on monuments frequently depicted Israelites with simple headbands or caps of conical shape made from strips of cloth. At a wedding, the bridegroom also wore special headgear for the ceremony (Sg 3:11).

The type of head covering most frequently used by both men and women was a piece of fabric, sometimes referred to as a veil, which would be placed on the head and fall below the shoulders, covering the upper part of the body (Gn 24:65; 38:14). The woman's veil was often held in place by a circlet, frequently made from the coins that formed part of her dowry. The man's headwear would probably have been very similar to the prayer shawl worn by many Jews today. It was probably held in place by a piece of twisted fabric or cord.

Footwear. In Bible times footwear consisted of shoes and sandals, which were an essential part of a person's wardrobe (2 Chr 28:15; Acts 12:8). Occasionally sandals had wooden soles, but usually they were leather. Sometimes they had an enclosed upper front and open back. The upper part was typically made of open strips of leather, and sometimes the sandal merely consisted of a sole with thongs laced around the leg or ankle. A woman's sandals were considered an attractive and fashionable part of her wardrobe (Jth 10:4; 16:9).

On a long journey through the country, one's sandals might be carried and saved for the arrival in the next town, so that they would not be worn out. (Being barefoot in a town or city was a sign of abject poverty.) Since sandals were so open in design one can easily understand the necessity for the ritual foot washing of a guest.

Decorated shoes or boots are seen in the Tell Beni-Hasan (Egypt) paintings. Most people would have been unable to afford such elaborate shoes in Bible times. A closed type of shoe was worn occasionally in parts of the ancient Near East. The sandals worn by a bride or bridegroom would have been made from fine quality leather, possibly cowhide. In a prophetic passage concerning the fate of Jerusalem, Ezekiel used the imagery of a bride wearing shoes made from expensive badgers' skin (Ez 16:10).

Shoes were not worn in the temple or on any holy ground (Ex 3:5; Jos 5:15) and were

Two sides of a palette from Egypt, the obverse showing a recess in which to grind cosmetics.

also taken off when a person was in a house. It was customary to remove the sandals at a time of mourning. The shoes which the Israelites wore in their wilderness wanderings did not wear out (Dt 29:5).

Cosmetics. Eye paint originally served the medical purpose of preventing flies from spreading infection by settling on the eyes, especially of sleeping persons. Substances such as kohl, malachite, and stibium had astringent and antiseptic properties and so were useful medications. These minerals were ground and made into a paste by mixing them with gum arabic or water. The paint was compounded in a small bowl and applied either with a spatula or with the finger. Many such bowls dating to 800 BC have been found at various Palestinian sites. Much earlier ones have been recovered from Egypt, where women used green malachite as an eye paint. In the Roman period antimony came into popular use.

When eye makeup became fashionable as a cosmetic procedure, the eyes were outlined in black, using balena or lead sulphide to make them look large, a practice that was followed particularly in Egypt, Palestine, and Mesopotamia. Eyebrows were also darkened by the application of a black paste. Jezebel decorated her eyes with cosmetics just before her dramatic death in about 841 BC (2 Kgs 9:30). In biblical Jewish society, painted eyes were associated with women lacking in virtue (Jer 4:30; Ez 23:40). Henna was used as a paint and was applied to parts of the body, including the hands and feet, as well as the fingernails and toenails.

Although not mentioned specifically in the Bible, rouge for coloring cheeks was used by both men and women in Egypt and Babylonia. It has become apparent from excavations that red ochre, yellow ochre, and lead carbonate were used to make red, yellow, and white face powders. In the makeup of the Sumerians yellow predominated, while the Babylonians favored red. The single reference in the Bible to a cosmetic use of powder is found in Song of Solomon 3:6. The powders used for cosmetic purposes were most probably carried in boxes or pouches. Among general toilet articles, the earliest known powder puff was recovered from an Egyptian site, while lipstick was also a familiar commodity. In Greek and Roman times, painted lips were particularly popular.

Oils, often perfumed, were used as a protection for the skin against the sun. Anointing with oil was considered so important that when the troops of the Israelite king Ahaz were repatriated in about 730 BC, they were clothed, fed, and anointed (2 Chr 28:15). Anointing a guest's feet was a normal act of hospitality. The process may also have had hygienic significance. Many persons found it far more convenient to apply perfumes than to wash the body, particularly when water was in short supply.

An alabaster jar of ointment (Lk 7:37) was an extremely expensive gift since it would have to be imported. At the archaeological dig of Lachish an excellent ivory ointment flask from about the 13th century BC was unearthed. A Babylonian inscription described a fragrant ointment made from the root of gingergrass, which was imported from Arabia. In NT times costly ointments most probably came from India. Excavators at Mari discovered the remains of a flourishing perfume factory in 18th-century BC palace buildings. Perfumes and ointments were mentioned frequently in the Bible and were used as gifts and applied for personal adornment (Est 2:12; Sg 1:12).

Hair and Beards. In Palestine and throughout the Near East, men wore their hair short. Women's hairstyles were long. In NT times a woman who cut her hair might be mistaken for a pagan priestess, and thus be disgraced (see 1 Cor 11:15).

Women's hair in Greek and Roman society was often twisted into a knot at the nape of the neck, while the forehead was surrounded by a mass of stiff curls. Braided hair became popular among women and was copied to a limited extent by men also. Bands of gold thread or beads were used to keep the long, elaborate hairstyles in position.

The apostle Peter warned Christian women against preoccupation with elaborate styles of hair (1 Pt 3:3). When a woman married, it was customary to change her hairstyle slightly, in favor of a more mature appearance. Curling tongs and hair oils were used by some married women.

Dark hair was more popular in Bible times, although gray hair represented maturity and was respected. Some persons preferred to make use of popular black and red hair dyes. According to tradition, Herod the Great dyed his graying hair with henna.

Hair was anointed at times of festivity and also as a mark of hospitality (Ps 23:5; Lk 7:46). Reference is made to the anointing with oil of the high priest Aaron's beard (Ps 133:2) as part of his priestly consecration (Ex 30:22–30). Christ commanded his disciples to anoint their heads when they were fasting (Mt 6:17), which was contrary to the Pharisees' custom.

Beard and hair trimming was performed in a specialized manner in Jewish culture. An Israelite man was instructed not to cut the hair on his temples or trim the corners of his beard (Lv 19:27). This was done to maintain a contrast in every way between the Israelites and the members of idolatrous cults in Canaan and elsewhere (Dt 12:29,30). Beards distinguished Hebrews from Egyptians, who were clean shaven, although they sometimes wore false beards on ceremonial occasions. Shaving or cutting off the beard of enemy captives was considered the gravest humiliation that the victor could impose. A shaved head, however, was also a recognized symbol of purification at the termination of a vow (Lv 14:8,9; Acts 18:18). Shaving a beard was the usual sign of mourning (Is 15:2). It could also symbolize the approach of doom (Is 7:20; Jer 41:5; 48:37). A beard which was well cared for was a source of great pride to its owner.

When Roman males shaved, they most likely used hot water and oil to first soften the beard. As early as the 1st century AD, the Romans had discovered the process for making tempered steel. Their sharp but somewhat expensive razors were a great advance upon the awkward flints or knives used in earlier periods. About the beginning of the

A tribute bearer, with hair in spiral curls (which was a convention of archaic Greek art).

Christian era, the moustache put in an appearance in Palestine.

Baldness was unpopular in OT times, possibly because of its association with the practice of shaving all hair. There seem to have been periods when priests, young boys, and soldiers had shaved heads.

Dishevelled hair was a sign of mourning, while tearing the hair was the action of a distraught person (Ezr 9:3). Mutilating a beard brought dishonor upon the bearer (2 Sm 10:4–6).

Jewelry. Items of jewelry were worn by both men and women in the Near East. Gold was used in considerable quantities, and silver was also very popular. Semiprecious stones were frequently incorporated into necklaces and other pieces of jewelry. Royal headdresses from the graves at Ur near the Persian Gulf give an indication of the skill of jewelers around 2700 BC. Hairbands and pins were a necessary part of hair adornment and have been recovered from numerous Near Eastern archaeological sites. Rings, often with delicately carved stones, were extremely popular, and nose rings were also in use by the Middle Bronze Age (see Gn 24:47). Fine gold chains were frequently worn. A signet ring or a heavy gold chain was a decorative symbol of office (41:42). Bracelets and amulets were worn either around the wrist or on the upper arm. Decorative pins, similar in design and intent to the modern safety pin, were often used to hold clothing together.

An excellent description of women's clothing and jewelry is found in Isaiah 3:18–23, where the prophet warns: "In that day the Lord will take away the finery of the anklets, the headbands, and the crescents; the pendants, the bracelets, and the scarfs; the headdresses, the armlets, the sashes, the perfume boxes, and the amulets; the signet rings and

A mirror and jewelry box found in Judea.

nose ring; the festal robes, the mantles, the cloaks and the handbags; the garments of gauze, the linen garments, the turbans, and the veils."

Conclusion. In general, clothing styles changed very little in the Near East during the biblical period. Climate and occupation dictated the most suitable styles. Natural fabrics have remained popular even to modern times, as they are best suited to the heat in Near Eastern lands.

HAZEL W. PERKIN

See CLOTH, CLOTH MANUFACTURING.

Fast, Fasting. Eating sparingly or abstaining from food altogether, either from necessity or desire. In medical terms, fasting is the detoxification of the body through the restriction of food.

Spiritual fasting entails setting aside activities as well as reducing the intake of food and replacing these activities with the exercise of prayer and preoccupation with spiritual concerns. The NT word which is translated "fasting" literally means one who has not eaten, one who is empty.

Three types of fast are generally recognized: *normal*, in which there is no intake of food for a prescribed period of time, though there may be an intake of liquids; *partial*, in which the diet is limited, though some food is allowed; and *absolute*, in which there is a total abstinence from food and liquids in all forms.

In the OT the fast was regarded as an act of self-renunciation designed to mollify God's wrath and move him to act in gracious disposition. In times of emergency, the people fasted to persuade God to spare them from impending calamity (Jgs 20:26; 1 Sm 7:6; 1 Kgs 21:9; 2 Chr 20:3; Jer 36:6,9). Individuals fasted in the hope that God would liberate them from trouble (2 Sm 12:16–20; 1 Kgs 21:27; Pss 35:13; 69:10). Fasting was regarded as concomitant to prayer to assure that God would answer the prayers (Ezr 8:21; Neh 1:4; Jer 14:12). Throughout the OT, fasting is associated with a mournful attitude of importuning God to aid the supplicant.

Regular fasts were usually for one day, morning to evening, with food permitted at night (Jgs 20:26; 1 Sm 14:24; 2 Sm 1:12), although there are reports of longer fasts, such as Mordecai's call for a 3-day fast (night and day specified) (Est 4:16) and the 7-day fast at Saul's death (1 Sm 31:13; 2 Sm 3:35). Among special fasts were Moses' 40 days on Mt Sinai (Ex 34:28) and Daniel's 3-week fast prior to receiving visions (Dn 9:3; 10:3,12).

In general, in the OT, fasting was abused. Instead of a sincere act of self-renunciation and submission to God, fasting became externalized as an empty ritual in which a pretense of piety was presented as a public image. Hence, the prophets cry out against the callousness of such hypocrisy. Jeremiah records Yahweh as saying, "Though they fast, I will not hear their cry" (14:12; see Is 58:1–10.).

The setting for the NT understanding of fasting lies in the development of the rabbinic tradition that grew out of the period between the Testaments, during which fasting became the distinguishing mark of the pious Jew, even though it was largely still ritualistic. Vows were confirmed by fasting (Tob 7:12), remorse and penitence were accompanied by fasting (4 Esd 10:4), and prayer was supported by fasting (1 Mc 3:47). Special fast days were observed, some voluntarily imposed (2 Mc 13:12; 4 Esd 5:13).

This developed into a rabbinic tradition in which fasting was viewed as meritorious and therefore became the primary act of demonstrating piety. It was, however, a false piety consisting mostly in the externals of fastidious observance of fast days, both public and private. With the exception of ascetic groups such as the disciples of John the Baptist, the prevailing mood of fasting when Jesus appeared on the scene was one of mournful sadness, an obligatory necessity, a self-imposed requirement to produce the discipline of self-denial.

Jesus' understanding of fasting is significant in that it represents a shift in the role of fasting. His initial attitude undoubtedly reflected the fact that he grew up participating in the regular fasts and therefore shared the prevailing teachings of his day. Yet, his mature teaching about fasting breaks with the rabbinic tradition.

Two accounts relating to Jesus and fasting are important: his fast as a part of his temptation in the wilderness (Mt 4:2; Lk 4:2), and his teaching about fasting in the Sermon on the Mount (Mt 6:16–18).

His temptation was born out of the context of struggle. Immediately after his baptism, he was cast out into the wilderness by the Spirit to face as the Second Adam the temptation of Satan. In the midst of his temptation, he fasted and prayed, quoting from Deuteronomy 8:3 and Psalm 91:11,12. His fasting is associated with dependence upon God.

Jesus' words about fasting in the Sermon on the Mount constitute a radically different approach to voluntary fasting. In condemning the type of fasting which seeks favor with men by an ostentatious display of outward piety, Jesus taught instead a robust faith that sought genuineness of relation to God through a pure heart. Jesus does not condemn fasting as such,

nor does he forbid it. He does, however, give it a new meaning. Fasting is service to God.

This new understanding of fasting is set within the context of the dawning of the time of salvation. The bridegroom is here. It is a time of joy, not of sorrow. Consequently, the prevailing mood of fasting as mournful stress and pretended piety is inconsistent with the mood of the new age that has begun.

Jesus' teachings may be summarized: Fasting is transcended by the beginning of the eschatological times. The rule of the Messiah has broken the power of the evil age. Fasting would appear to be no longer consistent with the spirit of thanksgiving and joy that marks the framework of the new age, since the Christian life is not to be dominated by tragedy but by joy and happiness. Yet, the kingdom is not fully realized. There is a place for fasting, properly understood. Fasting must be done within the context of the joyful thanksgiving of the new life in Christ.

The context of fasting is prayer. It should conform to the same conditions as prayer: unostentatious quietness before God, arising out of gratitude, expressing thanksgiving, grounded in faith, as a means of spiritual growth.

CLARENCE B. BASS

See PRAYER.

Bibliography. I. Abrahams, *Studies in Pharisaeism and the Gospels*, vol 1, pp 121–28; D. E. Briggs, *Biblical Teaching on Fasting*; H. von Campenhausen, *Tradition and Life in the Church*.

Father, God as. *See* GOD, NAMES OF.

Father, Human. *See* FAMILY LIFE AND RELATIONS.

Father-in-law. *See* FAMILY LIFE AND RELATIONS.

Fathom. Unit of measure equivalent to about 6 feet (Acts 27:28).

See WEIGHTS AND MEASURES.

Fawn. Designation for a young animal, usually a deer.

See ANIMALS (DEER).

Fear. Emotional foreboding or dread of impending distress or misfortune. Often spoken of as the source of religion. Yet fear alone can never account for true religion, since men are impelled to draw near unto God, the object of their worship. One does not desire to come close to the being he fears.

The biblical conception of fear embraces a much wider dimension than our common English word, which simply denotes some sort of dread or terror. While this meaning forms an essential part of the scriptural picture, it is by no means the primary significance, especially when the fear of God—an awe-inspiring reverence—is referred to.

There is, of course, a legitimate place for the fear of God in the lower, anxious sense. We are told, "It is a fearful (terrible) thing to fall into the hands of the living God" (Heb 10:31). Jesus taught that we should fear him (God) who has power to punish sin and consign men to utter destruction (Lk 12:4,5). Fear has a constructive role to play in enabling men to realize both the degeneracy of their souls and their need of divine forgiveness. The first occurrence of such fear may be found in Genesis 3 where Adam and Eve recoiled from the presence of the Holy God whose commandment they had blatantly spurned. Their fear was entirely reasonable for they had been sternly warned that disobedience would incur a grave judgment. Fear is quite naturally the logical consequence of sin (Gn 3:10; 4:13,14; Prv 28:1). The Bible presents an array of people who are plagued with deep-reaching anxiety (e.g., Cain, Saul, Ahaz, and Pilate). Anxious fear seizes the wicked (Jb 15:24), surprises the hypocrite (Is 33:14), and consumes evildoers (Ps 73:19), whose faithless lives are characterized by fear (Rv 21:8). Pharaoh's mighty host was virtually paralyzed by fear as God moved against them (Ex 15:16), and Job's associate Bildad spoke of men driven to their knees by the judgments of God (Jb 18:11).

Fear has a tendency to either immobilize men or seriously affect their activity. This is especially true of the spiritually uncommitted. Saul's fear of the people caused him to transgress the commandment of God (1 Sm 15:24). The parents whose blind son was miraculously healed by Jesus were afraid to support Christ because they feared the Jews (Jn 9:22). In the parable of the talents Jesus told of a man whose fear prevented him from doing his reasonable duty (Mt 25:25).

Jesus Christ, by his atoning death, resurrection, and heavenly intercession for believers, is the unique liberator from fear. The apostle Paul encouraged the Romans by informing them that in their conversion to Christ, they received the Holy Spirit, not as a spirit of fear and bondage, but as the spirit of adoption, whereby they could address God as "Abba" (Rom 8:15; the Aramaic word commonly used by Jewish children to address their fathers). This is the word by which our Lord Jesus addressed his heavenly Father and which Christians, by virtue of their adoption into the family of God, may also use in speaking to God (Gal 4:6). Recipients of God's love have received a dynamic force for casting out their anxieties (1 Jn 4:18). A sense of God's intimate love inspired Paul to say, "If God is for us, who is against us?" (Rom 8:31).

Unwarranted fear may harm the efforts of the people of God. Jeremiah was warned by God not to fear the faces of his opponents (Jer 1:8) lest God allow calamity to befall him (v 17). Similar calls to courage were given to Jeremiah's contemporary, Ezekiel, and to a great many others (Jos 1:7,9; Ez 2:6). We realize that even godly people are tempted to fear and may be temporarily overwhelmed (Ps 55:5). So God repeatedly counsels his people not to succumb to that temptation (Is 8:12; Jn 14:1,27). He tells them to heap their anxieties upon the God of their redemption, whose care for his sheep is infinitely great (1 Pt 5:7). Faith, then, is the indispensable antecedent of fearlessness as seen in the words of Isaiah: "Thou dost keep him in perfect peace, whose mind is stayed on thee, because he trusts in thee" (Is 26:3). The psalmist repeatedly stresses the role of faith in conquering fear (37:1; 46:2; 112:7).

Genuine faith is expressed in, and animated by, a reverential awe, and this is the basic meaning of the biblical idea of the fear of God. Unless there is personal awareness of the awesome and majestic sovereignty of God, it is impossible to have a meaningful faith existing in one's heart (Pss 5:7; 89:7). When God was called "the fear of Isaac" (Gn 31:42) it showed the patriarch's understanding of the immutable greatness of Yahweh. Isaac's father, Abraham, anxiously observed the absence of this holy fear in the people who dwell in Gerar (20:11). Even Jesus carried out his ministry in the fear of God (Is 11:2,3; Heb 5:7). Though Christians are to be liberated from the fear of men (Heb 13:6), death (2:15), and life in general (2 Tm 1:6,7), they must never lose their sense of the awesomeness of God. Such awareness not only leads to true wisdom (Ps 111:1) but also provides direction for the child of God throughout life (Phil 2:12; Eph 5:21).

Godly fear is characterized by total allegiance to the one true God. The Samaritans, in attempting to serve Yahweh and their idols simultaneously, were rejected by God (2 Kgs 17:33,41). Those who love God learn of wholesome fear by searching the Scriptures (Prv 2:3–5), the Word of God, which the ancient Israelites were commanded to cleave to and obey as evidence of their reverence for God (Dt 6:2). In Acts 10:2 Cornelius and his family were called "God-fearers" because of their high regard for the God of Israel and because they stood in awe of his person. True reverence for God must invariably express itself in good works and holy living (2 Cor 7:1). To truly revere the Lord entails avoiding sin (Ex 20:20) and translating the directives of the Word of

God into everyday experience (Eccl 12:13). This holy fear is actually a source of joy (Ps 2:11) and a veritable fountain of life (Prv 14:27). The fear of the Lord is more valuable than the greatest material riches (15:16) because the Lord takes pleasure in those who hold him in such high regard (Ps 147:11).

STUART D. SACKS

Feast of Lights.

Alternate name for Hanukkah, one of Israel's festivals celebrating the rededication of the temple in 164 BC.

See FEASTS AND FESTIVALS OF ISRAEL.

Feasts and Festivals of Israel.

Occasions of public or private rejoicing to commemorate some significant event or personage. The element of celebration has a special meaning in the cycle of religious occasions and the rites and ceremonies associated with these particular days. While the idea of a feast commonly implies a banquet with plenteous food and drink, this element is not indispensable. Sometimes there is only a token amount, as in the celebration of Holy Communion.

In contemporary usage "festival" usually refers to activities extending over a period of time, while "feast" indicates one part of the celebration, often a meal. However, in religious usage, both ancient and modern, the two words are used interchangeably. The ancient Hebrews employed the words *mo'ed* ("seasons") and *hag* for their great public celebrations, while feasts of a more private nature were commonly described by the term *mish-*

teh. The majority of English translations of Scripture do not differentiate between these words.

Feasts and Their Functions. A festival places great emphasis on community participation and on the continuity of social or religious tradition, especially where the celebrations are elements of a regular civil or religious calendar. Without community backing, even in a family celebration, no festival can be successful. When there is communal participation, a festival can reinforce the individual and community memory of specific occasions, and can perpetuate that store of recollection over years and generations. Such shared memory has a cohesive effect upon a cooperating community, large or small, and serves to establish the traditions by which the group lives. If the festival commemorates a particular event or celebrates some lofty ideal, that theme becomes more firmly embedded in the minds of the participants by being associated repeatedly with the rites and ceremonies performed. The feasts of the ancient Hebrews had this positive function. The great festivals of their religious calendar commemorated specific occasions when God had reached out in power to intervene for his people or had provided for them in their distress. By celebrating these feasts on a regular basis, the Hebrews were keeping at the forefront of their minds the power and greatness of their covenant God in directing their destiny. Their repeated rehearsal of God's help and love for them reminded them that he was still able to sustain them. Especially in times of hardship, it

Annual Feasts and Festivals of Israel*

Feasts and Festivals	Day(s) and Post-(Pre-)exilic Month	Gregorian Month	Major References
Passover	14th of Nisan (Abib)	March/April	Ex 12:11–30; Lv 23:5; Nm 9:1–5; 28:16; Dt 16:1–8
Unleavened Bread	15th (+7 days) of Nisan (Abib)	March/April	Ex 34:18–21; Lv 23:6–8; Nm 28:17–25; Dt 16:1–8,16–17
Pentecost (Shavuot, First fruits, Harvest, Weeks)	6th—Sivan	May/June	Ex 34:22; Lv 23:15–21; Nm 28:26–31; Dt 16:9–12,16–17
Trumpets (Rosh Hashanah)	1st of Tishri (Ethanim)	September/October	Lv 23:23–25; Nm 29:1–6
Day of Atonement (Yom Kippur)	10th of Tishri (Ethanim)	September/October	Lv 16:29–34; 23:26–32; Nm 29:7–11
Tabernacles (Succoth, Booths, Ingathering)	15th (+7 days) of Tishri (Ethanim)	September/October	Ex 34:22; Lv 23:33–43; Nm 29:12–38; Dt 16:13–17
Simhath Torah	22nd (+1 day) of Tishri (Ethanim)	September/October	
Dedication (Lights, Hanukkah)	25th (+7 days) of Kislev	November/December	1 Mc 4:41–49; 2 Mc 10:6–8; Jn 10:22
Nicanor	13th of Adar	February/March	1 Mc 7:49
Purim (Lots)	14th (+1 day) of Adar	February/March	Est 9:21,27–28

*Beginning with Nisan (Abib), the first month in the calendar of Israel.

pointed to the reality of God's presence and activity among them. Faith sustained by this means furnished an invaluable spiritual dimension to the life of the nation and provided a sense of continuity under divine provision and guidance. Only when corrupt or pagan elements were introduced into festive occasions did this important ingredient of national life begin to lose its vitality.

OT Festivals. 1. General festival occasions were surprisingly numerous in Israel, considering the rather austere mode of life reflected in much of the OT. No doubt such celebrations offset or compensate for the hardships and insecurities of existence in the ancient Near East, and the Israelites made the most of every opportunity. A wedding was one of the most obvious occasions for celebration, and it is not surprising that a feast was prepared for the marriage of Rachel and Jacob (Gn 29:22) in which the whole neighborhood participated. Just how long this particular feast lasted is unknown, but some marriage festivals continued for a week, as in the case of the marriage between Samson and the woman of Timnah (Jgs 14:17). A festival, still observed in some parts of the Near East, was held when a child was weaned. On such an occasion the child, then from two to three years old, was introduced to semisolid food and was not thereafter nursed again. It was during such a feast that an emotional scene occurred when Sarah saw the son of Hagar playing with Isaac (Gn 21:8–10). The canons of Near Eastern hospitality required the host to prepare a feast when guests arrived (19:3) or left (26:30). Wine that makes glad man's heart (Ps 104:15) was consumed freely on such occasions.

Birthdays were often observed in a festive spirit, especially where a royal person was concerned (Gn 40:20). Solomon's dream was commemorated with a feast provided for his servants (1 Kgs 3:15), and when the temple was dedicated the occasion was celebrated for a full week (8:65 RSV, NEB). Kings and queens held feasts periodically to mark certain occasions or to express goodwill (cf. Est 1:3; 2:18; 5:4,14; 7:2,7; Dn 5:1). Herdsmen traditionally made a feast for the shearing of the first sheep, and this occasion was consecrated when the wool was sent to the levitical priests (Dt 18:4).

2. Preexilic Feasts. In addition to the general festivals, which were frequently of a secular nature, communal feasts were prescribed for the Israelites that had a specifically spiritual significance. They were meant to emphasize the activity of God on behalf of his people and to remind them that continued divine blessing depended upon their obedience to his will. The catalog of festivals in Leviticus 23:2 began with an injunction to observe the sabbath. The seventh day, in which God ceased from creating (Gn 2:3), was holy, though it is difficult to determine the extent to which it was kept until the time of Moses (Ex 20:8–11). From that time on, sabbath observance stressed refraining from all work so as to commemorate properly God's own rest from creative activity (31:17) and his deliverance of his people from bondage in Egypt (Dt 5:12–15). Sabbath celebration was the sign of a special relationship between God and the Israelites. During this 24-hour period even trivial tasks like making a fire (Ex 35:3) or gathering wood (Nm 15:32,33) were prohibited on pain of death. Journeys of any distance also came under the sabbath ban (Ex 16:29). Special offerings were part of the observance (Nm 28:9,10), and the bread of the presence was replaced in the tabernacle (Lv 24:5–8). Despite the restrictions on activity, the sabbath was meant to symbolize a time of happiness and security in the presence of God (cf. Is 58:13,14), since its observance would bring blessing to the individual and to the whole land.

The new moon was a monthly celebration based on the lunar calendar. It was especially appropriate for an agricultural people, since all could tell when the moon was new. Special offerings were prescribed for this festival, consisting of a burnt sacrifice, a cereal offering, and a drink offering (Nm 28:11–15). In addition, a male goat was sacrificed to God as a sin offering, and trumpet blasts were sounded over the sacrificial offerings as a memorial before God (Nm 10:10). The sacrifices prescribed for the new moon festival were significantly greater than those required in Numbers 28:9, 10 for the weekly sabbath. This lunar feast was popular throughout Israelite history; during the monarchy the Levites were required to assist the Aaronic priests at the new moon festival, as well as on the sabbath (1 Chr 23:29–31). The preexilic prophets may well have taken advantage of the large gatherings to give guidance to the people or proclaim prophetic oracles (cf. 2 Kgs 4:23), though to what extent this was done is uncertain. Not everyone found the period of rest and celebration valuable, however, and Amos (Am 8:5) complained about those avaricious Israelites who felt that such observances interfered with the business of making a living. The feast could not be observed when the Judeans were in exile in Babylonia (cf. Hos 2:11), but under Ezra and Nehemiah its observance was restored (Neh 10:33). In Isaiah 66:22,23 it was related to Israel's final destiny and was an accepted part of the ordinances for Ezekiel's ideal temple (Ez 45:17). The purpose of the festival was to enhance the unity of national life by reminding the Israelites that God's covenant with their ancestors was permanent and still binding upon the nation. It also stressed the loving nature and providence of a God who could begin such a relationship and carry out his promises with complete faithfulness (cf. Ps 104:19; Ecclus 43:6–8). By implication it was also a constant reminder to the Israelites that they, too, had responsibilities under the covenant which they would neglect at their peril.

The feast of trumpets was celebrated on the 1st day of the 7th new moon. This month, subsequently named Tishri, was especially holy, and for this reason was governed by certain regulations different from those of ordinary new moon festivals. The trumpets were blown on the 1st day (Lv 23:24) as the animal and cereal sacrifices were offered. From Numbers 29:2–6 it appears that the offerings required for this particular feast exceeded those prescribed for normal sabbath sacrifice, but were somewhat less than those required for the regular new moon festival (cf. Nm 28:11). This feast was to be observed as a day of solemn rest and as a holy convocation, and the trumpets were sounded as a triumphant memorial to God's great provision for his people through the Sinai covenant.

The 7th month was particularly sacred, partly because of its place in the hallowed cycle of sevens, but also because the day of atonement (or Yom Kippur) and the feast of tabernacles, or booths, occurred during this period. The latter feast followed the day of atonement by some 5 days (Ex 23:33), and its joyful character served to offset somewhat the solemnity of the annual penitential occasion when the nation confessed its collective sins and saw them banished symbolically into the wilderness as the scapegoat was driven from the congregation.

Another feast closely connected with the institution of the sabbath was the sabbatical year. At the end of each cycle of 6 years the following 12 months were observed as a "sabbath of rest for the land." During this interval the ground was to lie fallow (Ex 23:11) without any form of cultivation, and whatever sprouted and grew from it naturally was assigned to the poor and needy (Lv 25:6). This provision for the land itself constituted one of the most important ecological principles of Scripture. Like God's people, the land was holy, and just as they needed to have regular intervals of rest from daily work in order to regain their energy and spiritual vitality through worship, so the ground needed to rest and recuperate from the strain of constant cultivation. The festival reminded the Israelites that the land on which they lived had been given to them by God in fulfillment of his covenantal undertaking to provide richly for

their physical needs (cf. Dt 8:7–10). To keep the Israelites from experiencing any shortages or other hardships during the year of sabbath, God promised that in the year immediately preceding the sabbatical period the land would bear fruit to suffice for the next 3 years (Lv 25:21). This assurance was based upon the experience of the wilderness wanderings, when on the 6th day of the week sufficient manna appeared to last through the sabbath (Ex 16:5).

In this festival period God's absolute claim over the land was reaffirmed (cf. Lv 25:23), and the faith of the nation in God's ability to provide for future needs was reinforced. The provisions that freed for a year from agricultural bondage were paralleled in the 7th year of rest by those requiring liberation of slaves and debtors. These underprivileged members of society were to be released from their obligations of servitude. As a result, men and women who had become slaves for one reason or another found personal liberty (Ex 21:2–6), and under proclamation of the Lord's release the provisions applying to debt were rescinded (Dt. 15:1–6). The sabbatical year seems to have been a regular part of preexilic Israelite life, although some abuses were noted in Jeremiah 34:8–22. There the prophet took advantage of the opportunity presented to instruct the people in the nature and purpose of the sabbatical year ordinance. He also warned the wayward Judeans that because they had disobeyed the commands of God in denying proper liberty to their slaves, they would have their own freedom taken away in a far more serious manner by being carried captive to Babylonia after seeing their land destroyed. The lesson was not lost upon those who returned from exile, for under the administration of Nehemiah the Jews bound themselves by a covenant to observe the principle of the sabbatical year (Neh 10:31). This undertaking evidently took its impetus from the reading of the Law of Moses at the feast of booths, which coincidentally occurred at the beginning of the sabbatical year (Neh 8:13–18).

Still another feast based on the principle of the sabbath was the year of jubilee or pentecostal year (Lv 25:8–55; 27:17–24). As the sabbatical year was related to the concept of the 7th day, so the pentecostal ("50th") year marked the completion of a cycle of 7 sabbatical years. The commencement of a jubilee year was proclaimed on the day of atonement throughout the land by means of trumpet blasts (Lv 25:9). The activities which took place during the pentecostal year were similar to those prescribed for the sabbatical year. A special feature was that land that had been sold during the preceding 49 years was returned to its original owners, a procedure which sometimes involved financial adjustments. To prevent abuse of the process through opportunism or speculation, the Hebrews were instructed to deal fairly and honestly with one another in the fear of God, who was the real owner of the land (Lv 25:14–17). As in the sabbatical year, God promised to make provision so that no one would suffer hardship. It was during the year of jubilee those who were slaves in Hebrew households were given their liberty, so that everyone in the land would commence a new cycle of sabbatical years on the same footing, as free persons under God.

Three annual feasts which followed the seasons of the year rather than phases of the moon furnished important occasions for commemorating God's power and provision in national life. These festivals were designated by the term *hag*, indicating a festival usually observed by some sort of pilgrimage. These three festivals were prescribed in Exodus 23:14–17 and Deuteronomy 16:16, and consisted of the feast of Passover and unleavened bread, the feast of weeks (Pentecost), and the festival of booths (tabernacles). On these occasions all the males of Israel were commanded to make pilgrimage to the sanctuary and celebrate

The mosaic floor of the synagogue in Tiberias depicts a menora, as well as other objects used at the feast of Tabernacles (including shofar, incense shovel, lulav [palm branch stem], and etrog [a citrus fruit]).

these "feasts of the Lord" (Ex 12:14). The Passover and the feast of unleavened bread were originally separate ordinances, but since the latter always followed immediately upon the Passover rite, they naturally blended into a single festival.

The Passover was of supreme theological significance for the Israelites, since it marked one of the most momentous acts of divine intervention in their history, the beginning of their deliverance from bondage in Egypt when, in the final plague, God destroyed the firstborn of the Egyptians but spared those Israelites whose homes had blood smeared on the doorposts (Ex 12:11–30). God commanded that the day was to be observed as a memorial feast (12:14), and the next Passover celebration occurred in the Sinai desert (Nm 9:1–5). In the Hebrew calendar the Passover festival came in the first month, called Abib in Deuteronomy 16:1, but known after the exile as Nisan (cf. Neh 2:1). The Passover rite took place the 14th evening (Lv 23:5), and this was followed by a seven-day period during which nothing leavened was to be eaten. The principle for removing all leaven from bread was similar to that underlying the draining of blood from animal flesh. Both leaven and blood had quickening power and were to be kept separate as an offering to God. The 1st and 7th days of this period were marked by a holy assembly, during which the only work permitted was the preparation of food (Ex 12:16). This period when unleavened bread was eaten was described as a feast because it opened the 7-day period of grain harvest (Dt 16:9). During this feast special burnt sacrifices were offered, along with a sheaf of newly harvested barley. By NT times the festivals of Passover and unleavened bread were well-attended celebrations and were known as the "days of unleavened bread" (Lk 22:1; Acts 12:3). The theme of Israel's deliverance from the power of Egypt by divine intervention assured the Israelites that God was always ready to act on behalf of a faithful and obedient covenant people. It also reminded them that they had once been slaves (Dt 16:12). In Israelite life the early Passover and unleavened bread observances were comparatively simple in character, but during the monarchy more elaborate passover rituals came into use (cf. 2 Kgs 23:21–23; 2 Chr 35:1–19).

The 2nd great festival, Pentecost, or weeks, lasted for 1 day only and was observed on the 50th day after the newly harvested corn sheaf had been waved before the Lord at the feast of unleavened bread (Dt 16:9–12). The festival marked the end of the grain harvest and the beginning of the period when first fruits could be offered (cf. Ex 23:16; 34:22; Nm 28:26). The feast day was marked by the presentation of 2 wheaten flour loaves along with sacrifices of 7 lambs, a ram, and a bullock (Lv 23:15–20). Freewill gifts to God were presented to reflect gratitude for his blessings, and the entire occasion was one of communal rejoicing (Dt 16:10,11). Since Pentecost was essentially a harvest festival (Ex 23:16), the Israelites were called on to recognize that they depended entirely upon God for their material prosperity. In Deuteronomy 26, specific instructions were given for the ritual of presenting first fruits. It comprised a great confession of faith set within the framework of Israel's history and recounted God's deliverance of the nation from Egyptian oppression and his provision of a land which could amply supply the needs of his people.

A festival known variously as the feast of booths, tabernacles (Lv 23:34; Dt 16:13), or ingatherings (Ex 34:22) was the 3rd great occasion that all Hebrew males were required to observe annually. It began on the 15th day of the 7th month (Tishri), shortly after the observance of the day of atonement, which fell on the 10th day. The feast of booths lasted for 1 week and involved pilgrimage (*ḥag*). It was associated initially with the end of the year (Ex 34:22), when the agricultural work had been completed. The 1st day was marked by a symbolic cessation from all activity, after which burnt offerings were presented to the Lord. The 8th day was also one on which the congregation of Israel abstained from manual work and again offered burnt sacrifices. Leviticus 23:39–43 furnished details for the rituals which gave the festival its special name of booths or tabernacles. The fruit of "goodly trees" was to be gathered on the 1st day of the feast, along with palm fronds, willow branches, and boughs from trees in full leaf. From these, rough shelters or booths were to be constructed in which the people lived for the week of the feast. Every 7th year the observances were marked by a public recital of the covenant provisions to which the Israelites under Moses had committed themselves, a procedure designed to keep fresh in their minds the obligations as well as the blessings of the covenant relationship. A particularly significant observance of the feast of tabernacles took place in the time of Ezra, when the Judean community returned from Babylon— celebration of a kind unknown for centuries was held (Neh 8:13–18). From the context it appears that observance of the feast had lapsed during the monarchy. The feast at Shiloh where Hannah was mistaken for a drunken woman and the feast referred to in Judges 21:19 were evidently the feasts of booths. In a prophetic vision in which he saw all nations coming to Jerusalem to observe the festival of booths, Zechariah warned that those who did not continue this tradition could expect hardship and shortages of food (Zec 14:16–19).

Postexilic Feasts. There are a few minor festivals which took their rise in the period of the return, some of which had their origin in specific historical occasions. The feast of Purim, or lots, was a joyful occasion occurring on the 14th day of the 12th month (Adar). It celebrated the way in which Esther and Mordecai were used by God to deliver his people in the Persian empire from extermination by Haman (Est 9:21,24–28). The feast was observed on the 14th day of Adar by those living in villages, and on the 15th by the inhabitants of walled towns and cities. The explanation of the name of the festival is given in Esther 9:24–26, and its observance reminded the Hebrews of God's ability to save them during a time of anti-Semitic activity in Persia. This hope of deliverance memorialized in this festival has consoled the Jews on other occasions when they have suffered persecution. Traditionally the scroll of Esther was read aloud in the synagogue on the evening before the feast, and there was a great outcry, especially among the children present, whenever the names of the hated Haman and his sons were mentioned.

Another joyous festival which lasted for 8 days was the feast of the dedication of the temple (1 Mc 4:52–59; 2 Mc 10:6–8), familiar to modern readers as Hanukkah, or the festival of lights. The specific dedication which prompted the feast occurred in 164 BC, when Judas Maccabeus reconsecrated the temple after it had been defiled by Antiochus IV Ephiphanes. The celebrations commenced on the 25th day of the 9th month (Kislev), and were marked at night by blazing lights and lanterns. The stories of brave opposition by the Maccabees to the crushing forces of paganism were recounted, and the feast was one of praise to God for his marvellous deliverance of the Jews during the Maccabean period.

A 3rd minor feast was that of the reading of the Law (cf. Neh 8:9; 1 Esd 9:50), held on the 1st day of the 7th month. This soon became attached to the end of the feast of booths. The feast of Nicanor (1 Mc 7:49) on the 13th of Adar similarly became part of the feast of Purim. Both expressed gratitude for divine guidance and deliverance.

NT Festivals. In Christ's time the sabbath was observed rigorously and was the occasion for synagogue worship (cf. Lk 4:16; Acts 13:14; 18:4). Pharisaic law prohibited all work, and Jesus came into conflict with the authorities periodically for breaches of the sabbath regulations (cf. Mt 12:1–4; Mk 3:1–5; Lk 13:10–17). In the primitive church, worship occurred on "the first day of the week" (i.e., Sunday) to commemorate Christ's resurrection. The early Christians initially participated in Jewish ceremonies (cf. Acts 20:16; 1 Cor 16:8), and it was on the feast of Pentecost after Christ's resurrection and ascension that the Spirit was poured out (Acts 2:1–4), fulfilling Joel 2:28–32 and commencing the history of the Christian church as such.

The Passover and feast of unleavened bread were of great significance in the life of Christ (cf. Jn 4:45; 5:1; 6:4; 12:1–26), for the occasion was a very popular one in NT times (cf. Jn 12:20). On the Passover, Pilate had instituted the custom of clemency to a prisoner nominated by the populace (Mt 27:15; Mk 15:6). Jesus participated actively in the Passover rituals (cf. Lk 2:42; Jn 2:13; 6:4). The last supper with his disciples occurred just prior to the Passover (Jn 13:1), when Judas Iscariot betrayed Jesus to the Pharisees (Lk 22:4–6). The breaking of bread and the drinking of wine at that Passover celebration (Mk 14:22–25) were related directly to Christ's forthcoming death on the cross in a sacramental manner. Christ's disciples were instructed to observe this rite as a memorial of his suffering and death for human sin (1 Cor 11:24–26) and as a proclamation of the power of the cross until the Lord returns in glory. Some scholars have suggested that Christ was actually hanging on the cross when the Passover lamb was being slaughtered, and if that chronology is correct it would represent Jesus graphically as the "Lamb of God, who takes away the sin of the world" (Jn 1:29). Jesus was also present once when the feast of tabernacles was celebrated (Jn 7:2). In his day water was carried in procession from the pool of Siloam as an offering to God, and the ceremony most probably prompted Christ's discourse on living water and eternal life (Jn 7:37–39). On one occasion at least Jesus was in Jerusalem when the festival of lights occurred (Jn 10:22) and narrowly missed death by stoning.

Jesus was entertained occasionally at private feasts (cf. Lk 5:29), and once remedied an emergency situation when the wine ran out at a wedding ceremony (Jn 2:8–10). He was critical of the Pharisees for securing the chief seats at feasts (Mt 23:6; Mk 12:39; Lk 20:46) and taught that festivals ought to benefit the poor (Lk 14:13).

Symbolism of Feasts. Many aspects of the ancient Hebrew feasts were interpreted symbolically in the early church. Paul regarded the earliest Hebrew Christians as the first fruits of the Israel of God (Rom 11:16). In Romans 8:23, the Holy Spirit as possessed by Christians was regarded as only a token of what was to come, and as such was the first fruit of the Spirit. Christians themselves were described in James 1:18 as the first fruits of God's creatures who were brought forth by the word of truth. The resurrection of Jesus was considered by Paul to be the first fruits of those who slept (1 Cor 15:20,23). In an allusion to OT festivals, Paul spoke of the sabbaths, new moons, and feasts as merely comprising a shadow of good things to come (Col 2:16,17). The Passover was used figuratively to emphasize that Christ our passover lamb had been sacrificed for us. Believers were urged to keep the feast with the unleavened bread of sincerity and truth, and not with the old leaven of malice and evil (1 Cor 5:7,8). The OT prophets looked for a divinely appointed banquet at the end of the age (cf. Is 34:5; Ez 39:17,20; Zep 1:7–9) in which God's judgments would be poured out on unbelievers. The Qumran brotherhood also expected a great banquet at the appearing of the Messiah, but without the threat of judgment. In Revelation 19:17,18, carrion birds will be summoned to a great feast on the flesh of God's enemies, in stark contrast to the destiny of the elect (cf. Mk 14:25).

R.K. HARRISON

See ISRAEL, RELIGION OF; PRIESTS AND LEVITES; OFFERINGS AND SACRIFICES; ISRAEL, HISTORY OF; JUDAISM; TABERNACLE, TEMPLE.

Bibliography. R. de Vaux, *Ancient Israel*, pp 424–517; W. Eichrodt, *Theology of the OT*, vol 1, pp 119–33; A.J. Heschel, *The Sabbath*; H.J. Kraus, *Worship in Israel*; H. Schauss, *Guide to Jewish Holy Days* and *The Jewish Festivals*.

Felix, Antonius.

Roman procurator (governor) of Judea (AD 52–60) succeeding Cumanus, appointed by Claudius and succeeded by Festus Porcius. Felix's brother, Pallas, a prominent, more influential Roman, interceded on his behalf after he was recalled from his procuratorship by Nero. During his oppressive rule, Felix utilized the aid of robbers to have Jonathan, the high priest, murdered. His tyranny has been cited as the cause for the Jewish War that broke out 6 years after he was recalled. Felix had 3 wives: one unknown, another the granddaughter of Mark Antony and Cleopatra, and another the Jewess sister of Agrippa II, whose name was Drusilla. At the age of 16, Drusilla left her husband, King Azizus of Emesa, to marry Felix. She later bore him a son, Agrippa.

Felix was serving as governor when the apostle Paul was brought before him in Caesarea to answer charges against him after the riot in Jerusalem (Acts 23:24–24:27). After a 5-day delay, Tertullus, spokesman for the Jews, and others arrived to state their charges. Felix put off a decision until he could hear from Lysias, the tribune. In the meantime, Paul was placed in limited custody. Felix hoped to obtain bribe money for his release. As a result, Paul was detained for 2 years, during which time he and Felix often conversed. The apostle's message of "justice, self-control, and future judgment" alarmed Felix greatly (24:25). Record of his life after being recalled by Nero is not available.

Fellowship. The essence of the Christian life—fellowship with God and fellowship with other believers in Christ.

In the beginning, Adam was placed in the garden to enjoy friendship and communion with God. When the creature chose to assert his own autonomy rather than live under the Creator's gracious care, fellowship was broken. Hence Adam and Eve hid themselves from the Lord's presence (Gn 3:8). Yet God immediately sought them out (v 9) and revealed his plan for the ultimate restoration of sinners through the work of the Redeemer (v 15).

The OT tells how God began to draw a special people into fellowship with himself. Enoch is described as a man who walked with God (Gn 5:22,24). Noah, likewise, walked in communion with the Lord (6:9). And Abraham, the father of Israel, is called "the friend of God" (Jas 2:23). No OT saint had deeper fellowship with God than did Moses during his 40-day encounter with the Lord on Mt Sinai (Ex 24). Later in Israel's history David wrote psalms that reflect a heart vitally in tune with the living God (Pss 16,34,40,63).

As a result of Christ's finished work on the cross, God now makes his permanent abode in the believer's heart (Jn 14:23). Hence the fellowship which now prevails under the new covenant is nothing less than the vital, spiritual union of the believer with Christ (Jn 14:20,21). Fellowship with God is the goal of the Christian life (1 Jn 1:3), and this relationship will be perfected forever when we see our Savior "face to face" (1 Cor 13:12), when God dwells with his people in the heavenly kingdom (Rv 21:3).

The gospel restores fellowship not only with God, but among believers as well. Jesus' last supper with his disciples illustrates the relationship between the vertical and horizontal dimensions of fellowship (Mk 14:22–25). In the upper room Jesus shared with his disciples a sacred love feast. The hearts of the Lord and his followers were knit together by a deep sense of love and commitment. Later the disciples discovered that their own hearts were strongly united out of their common loyalty to Jesus. Following the cross and the outpouring of the Spirit the church was born, that new society of people in fellowship with God and with one another.

The depth of comraderie among the first Christians is portrayed in the early chapters of Acts. Daily the believers met together in house groups for teaching, fellowship, the Lord's Supper, and prayer (Acts 2:42,46). So profound was their sense of togetherness that the Christians pooled their possessions and distributed them to brethren in need (vv 44,45; 4:32–35). Perhaps the dominant characteristic of this early Christian fellowship was "love of the brethren" (1 Thes 4:9; 1 Pt 1:22). Constrained by love, Paul organized among the gentile churches a collection for poor believers in Jerusalem. In Romans 15:26, which speaks of the gifts of the churches in Macedonia and Achaia, the word translated "contribution" is the common Greek word for "fellowship." Similarly, the fellowship which the Philippian church shared with Paul assumed the form of gifts to support the apostle's ministry (Phil 1:5; 4:14,15).

Scripture uses several images to describe the spirit of togetherness which characterized the early church. The first is "the household of God" (Eph 2:19; 1 Tm 3:15), or "the household of faith" (Gal 6:10). In God's household, love and hospitality are to be the rule (Heb 13:1,2). Further, the church is depicted as the family of God on earth (Eph 3:15). God is the Father and believers are his faithful sons and daughters. The life of God's family is to be governed by love, tenderness, compassion, and humility (Phil 2:1–4). Finally, the Christian fellowship is represented as the "one new man" or the "one body" (Eph 2:15,16). In spite of great natural diversity, the Holy Spirit binds believers together into a single organism (4:4–6). In this fellowship of love, no believer is insignificant. Each member has been endowed with gifts for the spiritual edification of the entire body.

Scripture lays down the basis of fellowship in 1 John 1:7: "If we walk in the light, as he is in the light, we have fellowship with one another." Jesus Christ, then, is the source and fount of all spiritual communion. Only when rightly related to the Lord do we experience true fellowship with another Christian. Just as light and darkness are incompatible, so a believer can have no real fellowship with an unbeliever. Neither can the Christian be in fellowship with one who walks contrary to the teaching of Christ (2 Jn 9–11), or a professing brother who is immoral, idolatrous, a drunkard, or a thief (1 Cor 5:11).

Scripture lays down several guidelines for enhancing the communion of believers in the body. (1) Love one another with the same compassion that Christ displayed to his own (Jn 13:34,35; 15:12). The law of the fellowship should be the rule of love (Heb 13:1). (2) Cultivate that spirit of humility that seeks the other person's honor (Phil 2:3–5). (3) Lighten fellow believers' load by bearing one another's burdens (Gal 6:2). (4) Share material blessings with brothers and sisters in need (2 Cor 9:13). (5) Tenderly correct a sinner while helping to find solutions to the problems (Gal 6:1). (6) Succor a fellow believer in times of suffering (1 Cor 12:26). And (7) Pray for one another in the Spirit without ceasing (Eph 6:18).

The Christian will want to seriously regard the saying of an anonymous saint, "You cannot draw nigh to God if you are at a distance from your brother." BRUCE A. DEMAREST

Bibliography. M. Burrows, *More Light on the Dead Sea Scrolls*; J.Y. Campbell, *Three NT Studies*; A.L. George, *Communion with God in the NT*; R. Schnackenburg, *The Moral Teaching of the NT*.

Ferret.   KJV translation for gecko, a kind of reptile, in Leviticus 11:30.

See ANIMALS (GECKO; LIZARD).

Fertility Cults. *See* CANAANITE DEITIES AND RELIGION.

Festival. *See* FEASTS AND FESTIVALS OF ISRAEL.

Festus, Porcius. Roman procurator (governor) of Judea, who succeeded Felix Antonius and who was succeeded by Albinus. The precise date of Porcius Festus' accession to power is debatable but has been narrowed to sometime between AD 55 and 60. The only sources mentioning Festus are the Book of Acts and the writings of Josephus, a Jewish historian who lived in Rome in the 1st century AD (*Antiq.* 20.8.9–11; 9.1).

Josephus wrote that Festus ruled wisely and justly in contrast to Felix and Albinus. Sicarii bandits (named after the small swords they carried) who had terrorized the Palestinian countryside were eliminated under Festus' rule. In spite of this, he could not reverse the damage incurred by his predecessor, Felix, who had aggravated the conflict between pagans and Jews.

The NT recounts that as new procurator, Festus traveled from Caesarea (where Paul was in custody) to Jerusalem (Acts 25:1). The Jewish leaders confronted him there and brought charges against Paul. Upon returning to Caesarea, Festus heard Paul's defense (v 4). He granted the apostle's appeal to be heard by Caesar (the right of any Roman accused of a capital offense) in an effort to avoid further religious disputes in his jurisdiction (vv 11,12). When King Agrippa arrived a few days later, Festus was in a quandary, unable to understand the Jews' charges against Paul (vv 25–27). After Paul's address before the king, Festus loudly declared him to be mad (26:24),

though still agreeing that Paul had done "nothing to deserve death or imprisonment" (v 31).

Field of Blood. *See* BLOOD, FIELD OF.

Fiery Serpent. Brazen symbol made by Moses on God's instruction to save the Israelites.

Deadly snakes sent by God to punish the Israelites for their rebellious grumblings, many of whom died from the poisonous bites (Nm 21:4–9). Recognizing their sin they cried out to God for deliverance and he instructed Moses to make a fiery (bronze) serpent and set it on a pole; healing was granted to those who gazed at the uplifted figure.

Jesus Christ referred to the bronze serpent incident as a witness to the saving power of his crucifixion. A person who looks in faith to the uplifted Christ will receive forgiveness for sin and have eternal life (Jn 3:14,15). The apostle Paul also drew upon the OT event as a warning to those who might arrogantly test God (1 Cor 10:9).

Fig, Fig Tree. *See* PLANTS.

Filigree. Wirelike setting (usually gold) for a precious stone or ornament (Ex 28:11–25; 39:13–18).

See FASHION AND DRESS.

Finance. *See* INDUSTRY AND COMMERCE; MONEY AND BANKING.

Finger (Measure). Linear measure equivalent to the width of a finger (Jer 52:21).

See WEIGHTS AND MEASURES.

Fir Tree. Translation of several Hebrew words in the OT that possibly designate a conifer type of tree. Positive identification is not possible.

See PLANTS.

Fire, Lake of. *See* LAKE OF FIRE.

Fire, Pillar of. Supernatural phenomenon of God's presence which guided the Israelites in the wilderness.

See WILDERNESS WANDERINGS; PILLAR OF FIRE AND CLOUD.

Firkin. Measure of about 10 gallons. In John 2:6, firkin is the KJV translation for the name of a Greek liquid measure. The RSV converts the amount to gallons.

See WEIGHTS AND MEASURES.

Firstborn. Term used in the Bible to describe a family's oldest son (Gn 22:21). Israel was called God's firstborn because of that nation's miraculous beginning and special deliverance out of Egypt (17:5,15,16; Ex 4:22). As God's firstborn, Israel had unique privileges over all other nations. Gentiles were "blessed" only in relation to their kindness to Israel (12:3; Ex 19:6; Dt 4:5–8). The prophet Isaiah foresaw a day when Israel would have a double portion of inheritance (Is 61:7). Thus, firstborn implies priority or preeminence, as well as an inheritance.

The expression "firstborn of the poor," (Is 14:30) means one who is supremely poor, the poorest of the poor. Another figurative expression, "firstborn of death" (Jb 18:13), implied that Job's disease was fatal.

Because God delivered Israel's firstborn from death in Egypt, he expected each firstborn to be sanctified to him (Ex 11:4–7; 13:12). The first male child was a representative of the entire offspring (Gn 49:3; Ex 22:29; Nm 3:13). The firstborn of all animals used in sacrifice was to be sanctified to the Lord (Ex 13:2,15).

Firstborn and Redemption. The firstborn of every tribe except Levi's was to be redeemed by a sum not to exceed 5 shekels (Nm 18:15,16). Redemption implied a previous bondage and was to remind Israel of their redemption from bondage in Egypt (Ex 13:2–8).

The firstborn of ritually clean animals was devoted to the Lord. It was brought to the tabernacle (or later, the temple) within a year from the 8th day after birth. This animal was then sacrificed and its blood sprinkled on the altar. The meat of the sacrificed animal was for the priests (Ex 13:13; 22:30; cf. Nm 18:17). The firstborn of unclean animals could be redeemed with an addition of $\frac{1}{5}$ of the value as determined by the priest. If not redeemed these animals were sold, exchanged, or destroyed by the priests (Lv 27:27). The colt of an ass was to be redeemed with a lamb (Ex 13:13). If not redeemed, it was to be killed. Meat from unclean animals was not eaten.

Firstborn and Birthright. The firstborn acted as priest of the family in the father's absence or death. Esau and Reuben are both examples (Gn 27:19,32; 1 Chr 5:1,2). This position of the firstborn ceased when the priesthood was committed to Levi's tribe (Nm 3:12,13). All the firstborn of succeeding generations had to be redeemed. The redemption money became part of the Levites' yearly income (8:17; 18:16).

A double portion of the family inheritance was the right of the firstborn. This protected the firstborn when there was a polygamous marriage. The son of a favorite wife could not take the place of the first son born of the household (Dt 21:17).

The title "firstborn" is applied to Christ (Lk 2:7; Rom 8:29; Col 1:15,18; Heb 1:6; Rv 1:5). It stresses Christ's right or preeminence or his position as first to rise from the dead. As firstborn, Christ is heir of all things (Heb 1:2) and the head of the church (Eph 1:20–23; Col 1:18,24; Heb 2:10–12).

R.K. HARRISON

See PRIMOGENITURE; HEIR; INHERITANCE; BIRTHRIGHT.

First Day of the Week. Sunday.

See LORD'S DAY, THE.

First Fruits.
Firstborn child or animal or first parts of any crop which, in Hebrew thought, were considered as holy and belonging to the Lord. The first fruits, as a foretaste of more to come, were offered to God in thanksgiving for his goodness in providing them.

First-fruit offerings could include produce either in its natural state or prepared or processed in some way—such as dough, bread, wine, olive oil, wool. The firstborn son and the firstborn of the animals that one owned were to be treated as belonging to God. The firstborn children and the firstborn of the unclean animals were "redeemed" (paid for) with money by the offerer, and the firstborn of the cows, sheep, and goats were offered in sacrifice to God (Nm 18:14–17).

First fruits of any kind were reserved for those whom God designated, namely, the priests. At least 3 times "the first of the first fruits" is mentioned in the OT. This may be a reference to the first ripened of the first fruits, or it may refer to the choicest of them. These offerings were especially designated for the priests and could be eaten by any of them who was ritually clean (Nm 18:12,13). For other references to the first fruits, see Exodus 23:15–19; 34:22,26; Leviticus 2:14; 23:10–17; Numbers 15:20,21; 28:26–31; and Deuteronomy 26:1–11.

The first fruits were presented to God by bringing the offering to the priest at the tabernacle and, in later times, at the temple (Dt 26:2). The priest took the offering and on the first day of the week with arms outstretched waved it before the Lord. On the same day, the person presenting the first fruits offered a male lamb as a burnt offering to the Lord, a meal offering of fine flour mixed with olive oil, and a drink offering of wine. Fifty days later another meal offering was to be made. Each family was to give two loaves of bread to the Lord as a special gift. These were also given with appropriate animal, meal, and drink offerings (Lv 23:9–22).

In the NT the apostle Paul referred to Jesus Christ's resurrection as the first fruits of the resurrection of believers which will occur at Jesus' return (1 Cor 15:20,23). The Holy Spirit, who indwells all believers (Rom 8:9), is also said to be the first fruits of the full redemption that is yet to come (v 23). "First fruits" is sometimes used of the first believers in a geographical area (16:5; 1 Cor 16:15 KJV). They were a kind of promise of a spiritual harvest to follow in that particular locality.

Christian believers are said to be first fruits, referring to their being a unique and sacred possession of God out of all he has created (Jas 1:18). Similarly, in the Book of Revelation the 144,000 are said to have been redeemed from humanity as first fruits belonging to God and to the Lamb, Jesus Christ (14:4).

WESLEY L. GERIG

See OFFERINGS AND SACRIFICES; FEASTS AND FESTIVALS OF ISRAEL.

First Jewish Revolt. Uprising in AD 66–70, occurred as the result of a series of ineffective Roman governors in Judea. The last Jewish king, Agrippa I (the Herod of Acts 12), died in AD 44, and the next 20 years were filled with persecution and humiliation for the Jews in Palestine. The unrest needed only a spark to flame into open revolt; the spark was provided by Florus, the Roman governor appointed in AD 64. His demand for money from the temple treasury, and the slaughter and pillage by Roman soldiers, provoked the Jews into an uprising in the year 66.

Rebellion quickly spread throughout Palestine, accompanied by a general struggle between Jews and pagans in several eastern Mediterranean cities. The revolt in Palestine was led by the Zealots, a Jewish group that had long wanted the Romans to leave Palestine. After an initial Jewish victory at the pass of Beth-horon, the emperor Nero dispatched his most able general, Vespasian, to direct the operation of punishing the rebels. By the autumn of AD 67 all of Galilee and other northern lands were back in Roman hands. In 67 and 68 further operations in Samaria and Judea left only four strongholds in Jewish control. At this point the Roman campaign slackened. Nero committed suicide in AD 68, and after three short-lived emperors, General Vespasian gained control of the empire in AD 69. His son Titus took command of the forces in Palestine, and laid siege to Jerusalem in AD 70.

The Jews in the capital might have been better prepared had they taken advantage of the turmoil in Rome to consolidate their own position and resolve disputes among warring

Arch of Titus in the forum in Rome. It commemorates Titus' conquest of Jerusalem in AD 70.

Jewish factions. As it was, the arrival of Titus with 80,000 soldiers forced them to unify for a last defense of the city.

The siege of the city lasted for some 5 months. Jerusalem held out heroically against the advancing Romans, forcing a step-by-step conquest of the city. A tragic moment in Jewish history came early in August, AD 70, when for the first time in centuries, the morning and evening sacrifices were not offered at the temple. About August 29, under circumstances still not clear, the sanctuary was put to the torch and the temple destroyed, thereby fulfilling Jesus' prophecy (Mt 24:1,2; Mk 13:1,2; Lk 19:43,44; 21:5–7). For another month some resistance continued, but by the end of September the conflict was over in the desolated city. In all, perhaps 1,000,000 Jews were killed and 900,000 taken captive during the course of the revolt.

WILLIAM TRAVIS

See JERUSALEM; JUDAISM; ISRAEL, HISTORY OF.

Fish. *See* ANIMALS.

Fisherman, Fishing. *See* INDUSTRY AND COMMERCE; TRADES AND OCCUPATIONS.

Fish Gate. Gate probably located in the north wall of the city of Jerusalem. The Fish Gate was built in David's time and later formed part of Manasseh's fortifications (2 Chr 33:14). After the Babylonian exile it was restored under Nehemiah (Neh 3:3; 12:39) and is mentioned along with the Mishneh or Second Quarter (Zep 1:10).

The gate was probably so named either because fish were brought into the city from the north, or because it was located near the city's fish market.

See JERUSALEM.

Fitch. KJV translation of two Hebrew words. "Fitch" is actually an older form of the word "vetch," the name of many species of leguminous plants. The "fitch" of Isaiah 28:25,27 (RSV dill) is the nutmeg flower, the seeds of which are used as a condiment. The "fitch" of Ezekiel 4:9 (RSV spelt) is probably emmer, an inferior kind of wheat.

See PLANTS (NUTMEG FLOWER; SPELT).

Flag. KJV rendering of an uncertain marshland plant in Job 8:11.

See PLANTS (PAPYRUS; REED; RUSH).

Flax. Cultivated plant providing one of the oldest of textile fibers. The term may also refer to the fiber itself, thread spun from it, or the woven linen cloth.

See PLANTS; CLOTH, CLOTH MANUFACTURING.

Flea. Small, wingless insect with strong legs for jumping. The flea is mentioned only in 1 Samuel 24:14 and 26:20 (KJV), where David refers to himself as a flea.

See ANIMALS.

Flesh.
In the OT. Term commonly used to designate the material stuff of the body, whether of men (Gn 40:19) or of animals (Lv 6:27). However, "flesh" is used in the OT with a variety of meanings. Sometimes it is used as equivalent for the whole body (Prv 14:30; Hebrew has no separate word for "body"), and the meaning is extended to designate the whole person ("my flesh also shall rest in hope," Ps 16:9 KJV). This idea leads to the union of two different persons, man and wife as "one flesh" (Gn 2:24), and a man can say of his relatives "I am your bone and your flesh" (Jgs 9:2). The idea of flesh as the whole person leads to the expression "all flesh," denoting the totality of mankind, sometimes including also the animal world.

Perhaps the most distinctive use of "flesh" in the OT is found in those passages where it designates human weakness and frailty over against God. "My spirit shall not abide in man for ever, he is flesh" (Gn 6:3). In Psalm 78:39, God attributes sin to the fact that men are but flesh. In 2 Chronicles 32:8 the arm of flesh of the king of Assyria (i.e., his weakness) is contrasted with the all-powerful God. The one who puts trust in God need not fear what "flesh" can do (Ps 56:4), but the one who puts trust in human flesh instead of in God is under a curse (Jer 17:5). In Isaiah 31:3 flesh is contrasted with spirit as weakness is with strength.

However, nowhere in the OT is flesh viewed as sinful. Flesh is conceived as being created by God of the dust of the earth (Gn 2:7), and, as God's creation, it is good.

In the NT. Paul makes the most distinctive use of "flesh" in the NT, one being unique to him. The more common uses include:

Flesh as the Stuff of the Body. "Flesh" is frequently used to describe the tissues that constitute the body and is thus contrasted with its other parts. There are different kinds of flesh—"of men," "of animals," "of birds," "of fish" (1 Cor 15:39). Pain and suffering may be experienced in the flesh (2 Cor 12:7). Circumcision is done in the flesh (Rom 2:28). While "flesh" in such references is not sinful, it is corruptible and cannot inherit the kingdom of God (1 Cor 15:50). Jesus' body was also a body of flesh (Col 1:22).

Flesh as the Body Itself. By a natural transition, the part is used for the whole, and in many places "flesh" is synonymous with the body as a whole rather than designating the fleshy part of the body. Paul may thus speak either of being absent in the body (1 Cor 5:3) or in the flesh (Col 2:5). Paul can say that the life of Jesus may be manifested in our body or in our mortal flesh (2 Cor 4:10,11). "He who joins himself to a prostitute becomes one body with her. For, as it is written, 'The two shall become one flesh' " (1 Cor 6:16).

Flesh as Person with Reference to Origin. Following an OT usage, "flesh" is used to refer not merely to the stuff of the body or to the body itself, but concretely to the person as constituted by flesh. In this usage the word may refer to the person's human relationship, the physical origin and the natural ties that bind that one to other humans. Paul speaks of his kinsmen "according to the flesh," his fellow Jews (Rom 9:3 KJV), and even uses "my flesh" (11:14 KJV) as a synonym for these kinsmen. The "children of the flesh" (9:8) are those born by natural generation in contrast to those born as a result of divine intervention. Christ was descended from David according to the flesh (1:3). The phrase does not designate merely the source of his bodily life, but of his entire human existence including both his body and his human spirit.

Flesh as Human Existence. Another use of "flesh" simply designates human existence. As long as a person lives in the body, that one is "in the flesh." Thus Paul can speak of the life which he lives "in the flesh" as lived by faith in the Son of God (Gal 2:20). Referring to Jesus' earthly ministry, Paul says that he abolished "in the flesh" the enmity between Jew and Gentile (Eph 2:15). Peter has the same meaning when he speaks of Jesus having been put to death "in the flesh" (1 Pt 3:18). So also John: "Jesus Christ is come in the flesh" (1 Jn 4:2). This usage is reflected most notably in the Johannine saying, "The Word became flesh and dwelt among us" (Jn 1:14).

Flesh as Human Existence in Terms of Outward Appearance and Conditions. "Flesh" also extends beyond man in his bodily life to include other factors crucial to human existence. Thus, "confidence in the flesh" (Phil 3:3–6) does not mean confidence in the body, but confidence in the whole complex of the outward realm of human existence. It includes Paul's Jewish ancestry, his strict religious training, his zeal, and his prominence in Jewish religious circles. The phrase to "glory after the flesh" (2 Cor 11:18 KJV) is rendered "boasting of worldly things" by RSV. A good showing "in the flesh" is practically synonymous with worldly prominence (Gal 6:11–14). The Judaizers insisted upon circumcision to promote a sense of prideful attainment in the religious life so that they might have a ground of glorying. But these external distinctions and grounds for glorying no longer appealed to Paul, because the world had been crucified to him and he to the world.

"Flesh" is also used of outward relationships, as when describing the social ties existing between slave and master (Eph 6:5; Col 3:22; Phlm 16). "In the flesh" also describes the realm of marital relationships, which entails certain troublesome problems (1 Cor 7:28).

This usage illuminates an otherwise difficult saying, "Henceforth know we no man after the flesh; yea though we have known Christ after the flesh, yet now henceforth know we him no more" (2 Cor 5:16 KJV). The RSV correctly renders the phrase, "from a human point of view." The verse does not mean that Paul had heard and seen Jesus in Jerusalem at some previous time and had gained some acquaintance with Christ "after the flesh." "After the flesh" modifies the verb "to know," not the noun "Christ." Before his conversion, Paul knew all people "after the flesh"; that is, he judged them by worldly, human standards. To know Christ "after the flesh" means to look at him through merely human eyes. As a Jew, Paul had felt that Jesus was a false, deluded messianic pretender. According to the Jewish understanding, the Messiah was to reign over the earth as Davidic king, save his people Israel, and punish the hated Gentiles. Now Paul has surrendered this false human view and knows Christ as he really is—the incarnate Son of God, the Savior of all who believe. Now as a Christian, Paul no longer judges others according to the flesh. He no longer thinks of the Gentiles as dogs in the usual Jewish way. He sees both Jews and Greeks as beloved of God, as people for whom Christ died.

Flesh as Fallen Human Nature. The expression, "flesh and blood" designates fallen humanity seen over against God. After his conversion, Paul says that he did not confer with flesh and blood (Gal 1:16) but rather went away for three years into Arabia. He means that he did not seek the meaning of his Damascus Road vision from anyone else but drew apart for a considerable time to confer with God.

When Paul says that "flesh and blood cannot inherit the kingdom of God" (1 Cor 15:50), he means, not that humanness cannot inherit the kingdom of God, but that human fallenness cannot; as the next clause shows, "neither doth corruption inherit incorruption" (KJV). The weak, fallen, corruptible body cannot inherit the kingdom of God; there must be a change; the "corruptible must put on incorruption, and this mortal must put on immortality" (1 Cor 15:52 KJV). This is not the salvation of the soul or spirit, but the exchange of one kind of body for another that is suited to the final glorious kingdom of God.

When Peter confessed the messiahship of Jesus, Jesus replied, "flesh and blood has not revealed this to you, but my Father who is in heaven" (Mt 16:17). The meaning of this verse is obvious. This knowledge of Jesus' messiahship was not a human deduction; it could be achieved only by divine revelation.

Flesh as Fallen Sinfulness. There remains a group of ethical references that are distinctly Pauline. The most important feature of this usage is that man is seen not only as fallen and weak before God, but as fallen and sinful. Flesh is contrasted with Spirit—the Holy Spirit, not man's spirit, and without the aid of the Spirit one cannot please God. The most vivid passage is the first part of Romans 8, where Paul sharply contrasts those who are "in the flesh" with those who are "in the Spirit." To be "in the Spirit" in this sense does not mean to be in a state of ecstasy, but to be living one's life in that spiritual realm which is controlled by the Spirit of God. Those who are "in the flesh," that is, unregenerate, cannot please God: "Because the carnal mind is enmity against God: for it is not subject to the law of God, neither indeed can be. So then they that are in the flesh cannot please God" (vv 7,8 KJV). The translation "carnal mind" is unfortunate, for "carnal" in our idiom means to be surrendered to bodily appetites, especially to the sexual. The Greek is "the mind of the flesh." Then Paul says, "But you are not in the flesh, you are in the Spirit, if in fact the Spirit of God dwells in you" (v 9). There are two contrasting and mutually exclusive realms: "in the flesh" and "in the Spirit." To be "in the Spirit" means to be indwelt by God's Holy Spirit, that is, to be a regenerate person.

Those who are unregenerate cannot fulfill the Law of God and thereby please him. The highest demand of the Law was to "love the Lord thy God with all thy heart, and with all thy soul, and with all thy mind," and then "to love thy neighbor as thyself" (Mt 22:37–39 KJV). Paul claims that he had blamelessly kept the formal demands of the Law as a Jew (Phil 3:6) and was therefore blameless so far as legal righteousness was concerned. But the one thing formal commandments could not do was to give him a new heart so that he would love God. Indeed, the flesh boasted in the conformity to the legal demands of the Law and was uplifted in pride. Romans 8:8 means that the unregenerate heart cannot please God by loving and serving him as God requires. Thus the Law was unable to make mankind truly righteous, because the flesh is weak (Rom 8:2). To live after the flesh is death; to live after the Spirit is life (v 6). Elsewhere Paul says, "For I know that in me [i.e., in my flesh] dwelleth no good thing" (v 18 KJV). Flesh here cannot be the physical flesh, for the body of flesh is the temple of the Spirit (1 Cor 6:19) and a member of Christ (v 15) and is to be the means of glorifying God (v 20). Paul means that in his unregenerate nature, there dwells none of the goodness that God demands.

While Paul makes a sharp and absolute contrast between being "in the flesh" (unregenerate) and "in the Spirit" (regenerate); when one becomes regenerate and comes to be "in the Spirit," that person is no longer in the flesh, the flesh is still in him. In fact, there remains in the believer a struggle between the flesh and the Spirit. Writing to people who are "in the Spirit," Paul says, "For the flesh lusteth [strives] against the Spirit, and the Spirit against the flesh; and these are contrary the one to the other; so that ye cannot do the things that ye would" (Gal 5:17 KJV). Because the Christian life is the battleground of these two opposing principles, it is impossible to be the perfect person that one would wish to be.

The same situation is reflected in 1 Corin-

thians 2:14–3:3 where Paul describes three classes of people: the "natural" (2:14), the "carnal" that is, fleshly man (3:1,3), and the "spiritual man" (3:1). The "natural man" is unregenerate. Those who are "in the flesh" (Rom 8:9), have devoted the whole of their life to the human level and hence are unable to know the things of God. "Spiritual man" refers to those whose life is ruled by the Spirit of God so that the fruits of the Spirit (Gal 5:22,23) are evident in their life. Between these two there is a third class—those who are "fleshly," yet who are babes *in Christ.* Therefore they must be "in the Spirit," yet they do not walk "according to the Spirit." Because they are "babes in Christ," the Spirit of God dwells in them, yet the Holy Spirit is not allowed to have full control over them, and they are still walking "like men" (3:3), manifesting the works of the flesh in jealousy and strife. Those who are "in the Spirit" and no longer "in the flesh" have yet to learn the lesson of walking after the Spirit and not after the flesh.

Works of the Flesh vs. Fruit of the Spirit. In Galatians 5:19–23 Paul contrasts the life in the flesh and the life in the Spirit. "Now the works of the flesh are manifest, which are these: adultery, fornication, uncleanness, lasciviousness, idolatry, witchcraft, hatred, variance, emulations, wrath, strife, seditions, heresies, envyings, murders, drunkenness, revellings, and such like" (vv 19–21 KJV). The important thing to note about this list is that while some of these are sins of bodily and sexual appetite, others are religious sins—idolatry, witchcraft—and several are sins "of the spirit," that is, of the disposition—hatred, variance, emulations, wrath, strife. The words "seditions" and "heresies" refer not to theological heresies but to a factious, divisive spirit. This proves conclusively that for Paul the "flesh" is not synonymous with the body but includes the whole person, with all the inner attitudes and disposition.

On the other hand, the fruit of the Spirit is love, joy, peace, longsuffering, gentleness, goodness, faithfulness, meekness, and self-control (vv 22,23). These are mostly characteristics of the inner self; "against such there is no law" (v 23); that is, when one is characterized by such traits as these, there is no need for an external law to indicate what is right and wrong.

Victory over the Flesh. While a struggle remains in the Christian between the Spirit and the flesh, Paul knows of a way of victory for the Spirit. The flesh of the body comes within the sphere of sanctification (1 Thes 5:23), but the flesh as the unregenerate human nature can only be put to death.

This is called the tension between the indicative and the imperative. Because certain things have happened in Christ (indicative), certain inevitable results should accrue (imperative). In Paul's view, the flesh has already been put to death in the death of Christ. Those who belong to Christ have already crucified the flesh with its passions and desires (Gal 5:24). Paul elsewhere says, "I have been crucified with Christ" (2:20) and "our old self was crucified with him" (Rom 6:6). Such references make it clear that "flesh" and the "self" are in some ways to be identified. This identity is further supported in the teaching about crucifixion, for Paul means the same thing by the crucifixion of the flesh that he means when he says, "How shall we that are dead to sin, live any longer therein? We were baptized into his death. We are buried with him by baptism into death" (vv 1–3). It is I myself who have died with Christ.

The same idea is expressed in a different idiom in Colossians 3:9. "Lie not one to another, seeing that ye have put off the old man [the old nature of the flesh] with his deeds, and have put on the new man" [the regenerate nature]. The "old man" denotes the sinful, unconverted being. This is another way of saying that the old self has been crucified with Christ (Rom 6:6). Paul views this as something that has already happened when one comes to faith in Christ.

This crucifixion and death of the flesh does not, however, work automatically. It is an event that must be appropriated by faith. This involves two aspects. First, believers are to recognize that the flesh has been crucified with Christ. "Reckon ye also yourselves to be dead indeed unto sin, but alive unto God through Jesus Christ our Lord" (Rom 6:11 KJV). One cannot consider the self dead with Christ unto sin unless that person has actually died and been crucified with Christ; but because this has already happened at the moment of saving faith, it can be put into daily practice. Those who have died with Christ are to "put to death the deeds of the body" (8:13 KJV). "Body" is here used as a vehicle for the works of the "flesh"—the sensual life of the unregenerate nature. Those who have been brought from death into life are to yield their members to God as instruments of righteousness (6:13). One who has died with Christ is to "mortify" (KJV), that is, put to death what is earthly—fornication, uncleanness, covetousness (Col 3:5). Having already put off the old nature and put on the new, the believer is to put on compassion, kindness, lowliness, and the like (v 12).

Victory over the flesh is sometimes described as walking in the Spirit. "Walk by the Spirit, and do not gratify the desires of the flesh" (Gal 5:16; cf. Rom 8:4). Walking in the Spirit means to live each moment under the control of the Holy Spirit.

GEORGE E. LADD

See BODY; MAN, DOCTRINE OF; SIN.

Bibliography. W. Barclay, *Flesh and Spirit;* E.D. Burton, *Spirit, Soul, and Flesh;* W.P. Dickson, *Paul's Use of the Terms Flesh and Spirit;* R. Jewett, *Paul's Anthropological Terms;* W.G. Kümmel, *Man in the NT;* W.D. Stacey, *The Pauline View of Man.*

Flint. Dark, fine-grained, hard silica (rock) used for blades of tools. Flint when struck against other hard surfaces produces sparks and so was used for lighting fires.

See MINERALS, METALS, AND PRECIOUS STONES.

Flogging. Beating a person with a whip or other instrument, sometimes used as a legislated punishment.

See CRIMINAL LAW AND PUNISHMENT.

Flood, The. Rising and overflowing of water to cover the land, specifically the flood of Noah.

Biblical Account. The narrative of the Noahic flood, found in Genesis 6–9, constitutes one of the longest connected stories in the Pentateuch (first five books of the OT). The flood is referred to frequently elsewhere in the Bible, in each case being mentioned as a historical event (Gn 10:1,32; 11:10; Mt 24:38,39; Lk 17:27; 2 Pt 2:5). According to the biblical account, God brought about the flood because of human society's increasing deterioration, which finally reached a point where "the wickedness of man was great in the earth" (6:5). God determined to destroy the race and to begin again with a new people who would obey him (cf. Gn 1:26–28). Of all the people on earth, only Noah, his sons, and their wives remained faithful to the Lord. They became God's means of repopulating the earth following its watery destruction. After a period of 120 years' preparation, during which Noah built a great ship and preached of God's coming judgment, the flood came in the form of heavy rain and the rise of subterranean waters (Gn 6:3, 7:11; cf. Heb 11:7; 1 Pt 3:20; 2 Pt 2:5). Only the selected pairs of land animals brought aboard the vessel were saved from the onslaught. For more than a year the waters prevailed, until finally the waters receded and the earth was dry and habitable again (Gn 7:6,10–12,24; 8:3–6,10,12–14). When Noah and his family left the ark, they offered sacrifices to God in thanksgiving. God then promised that he would never again destroy the earth by a flood.

The Chronology of the Flood

The 600th–601st year of Noah's Life	Day from the Flood's Beginning	Event	Genesis Reference
10th day of 2nd month	−7	Animals and 8 people enter ark.	7:4,7–10
17th day of 2nd month	0	Rains begin to fall.	7:11
27th day of 3rd month	40	Underground springs erupt and rains cease.	7:12,17
17th day of 7th month	150	Water covers the mountains.	7:19,24; 8:3
		The ark lands on the mountains of Ararat.	8:4
1st day of 10th month	224	Other mountain peaks appear.	8:5
11th day of 11th month	264	Noah sends out a raven and a dove.	8:6–8
18th day of 11th month	271	The dove is sent out again.	8:10
25th day of 11th month	278	The dove is sent a third time.	8:12
1st day of 1st month	319	The water has dried up.	8:13
27th day of 2nd month	375	The ground is dry; animals and 8 people leave ark.	8:14–19

Nonbiblical Traditions. No theme is more widely circulated in the world's epic and mythic literature than that of a great flood which long ago destroyed either the entire world or some vast portion of it. Such stories are found among the Chinese, Indians, Greeks, Mayas, islanders of the South Pacific, and elsewhere. Many stories have aspects similar to the Genesis accounts, but none is so strikingly similar as that of the ancient Babylonians. Their story was based on that of their historical and cultural predecessors, the Sumerians of Lower Mesopotamia. The Babylonian version, known as the Gilgamesh Epic, dates in its present form to the period of Hammurabi (c. 1750 BC). It professes, however, to narrate the life and career of Gilgamesh, a celebrated king of Uruk in the 3rd millennium BC. The epic tells how a pious man named Utnapishtim was saved from a devastating flood which the gods sent upon Shuruppak by building an ark. After seven days afloat, the storm ended and the ship landed on Mt Nisir. After sacrificing to Ealil, Utnapishtim became immortal.

Though few deny a connection between the Genesis account and flood stories like the Gilgamesh Epic, how they are to be related is a debated matter. The possibilities are: (1) the Genesis account is adapted from the extrabiblical ones; (2) the extrabiblical stories are adapted from the Genesis account; (3) all find a common source. The nonmythical, transcendent, and monotheistic character of the biblical narrative seems to rule out the first option. The earlier dating of the extrabiblical stories in their written versions excludes the second, unless earlier copies have been lost. The best solution, to those who understand the Genesis record as inspired narrative history, is to see all the major early accounts as reflections of the same vast deluge recounted in written form.

Extent of the Flood. Scholars who view the flood account as history are divided as to its geographical extent. An objective reading of the story would seem to indicate that the whole earth was flooded, even to the height of the highest mountains (Gn 7:17–20; 8:4,21). Some have argued that waters high enough to cover "all the high mountains under the whole heaven" (7:19) would extend over the entire earth. Some advocates of a local flood respond that the narrative uses the language of appearance (that is, to Noah it *appeared* that all the earth was flooded). Thus a universal flood was unnecessary, for God wished to destroy only the human race, which at that time may have lived in Mesopotamia. Others point out translation difficulties in the use of the word "earth." In Genesis 1:1, it is part of an ancient idiomatic expression denoting totality ("heaven and earth" means "cosmos"). Sometimes "earth" describes a person's country (Gn 47:13), the soil itself (23:15), and so on. Thus one should not assume that the use of the word in the Genesis flood story implies the complete inundation of the world.

Some advocates of a universal flood use the presence of marine fossils on the tops of the world's highest mountains in support of their arguments. But all the mountains originally emerged from the seas (Gn 1:9), so they would be expected to preserve traces of their marine ancestry on their summits. One's view on the matter must be determined in the final analysis on theological considerations as well as interpretative factors.

Scientific Evidence for the Flood. With the beginning of modern archaeology in Mesopotamia, it became popular to associate evidence of flood destruction in sites such as Kish, Ur, and Shuruppak with the biblical flood. Those places, however, were destroyed by different floods at different times. Their floods were also much too limited in scope to suit any interpretation of the Genesis account. More recently a "catastrophism" movement has developed within conservative circles, interpreting the world's great geologic upheavals as chaotic remnants of the destruction caused by Noah's flood. That view suggests, among other things, that such geological formations may have taken shape in a short time (during the flood) and in a relatively recent era (the time of Noah). Though that theory satisfies many, its opponents point out that some means of dating show the formations to be much earlier than the time of Noah.

Geologists exploring the Mt Ararat region have discovered on the mountain what is called "pillow lava," volcanic rock formed under water. Such lava structures have been located up to the mountain's ice cap at 13,500 feet, so water evidently reached that height at one period. That phenomenon has been taken by some as a confirmation of worldwide scope for the Genesis flood, but it does not prove that the lava was formed on Mt Ararat in the time of Noah. All it really indicates is that the structures originated under water, just as all land masses did.

The presence of "conglomerates" on Mt Ararat is cited as yet another proof of a universal deluge. Such rocks, varying in size from pebbles to boulders, resulted from a process of fusion in which eruptions of lava interacted with a violent disturbance of water. But again, the presence of such material at the 13,000-foot level merely indicates that Mt Ararat was born in precisely the same manner as modern islands and that the highest levels involved an eruption of volcanic rock in the ocean. Nor can such geological structures be used to imply that Mt Ararat was in the process of growth even while the flood occurred. The Genesis account says nothing about the mountain erupting during Noah's deluge. In any event, the material deposit would have been silt, not lava.

Interest in the nature of the Genesis flood has been stimulated periodically since 1856, for some 200 persons have claimed to have seen Noah's ark on Mt Ararat in 23 separate sightings. At least one report was a hoax, but many of them agree on the general nature of the object that has been sighted. Despite such apparent evidence, all concerned must admit that no conclusive proof exists that Noah's ark is located on Mt Ararat. From a crevasse near the top of the mountain, Fernand Navarra in 1955 recovered a five-foot piece of wood, which was hand-tooled and originated at some distance from the mountain. Carbon-14 dating techniques, however, produced widely differing dates for the artifact. It has so far been impossible to locate what many have thought to be remains of the ark, despite the use of sophisticated photographic techniques.

The nature of the Genesis flood will continue to be a matter of debate among interested parties, but it seems unlikely that the issue will be resolved unless some new archaeological or scientific evidence of a compelling nature is forthcoming. That there was a flood of enormous proportions is hardly to be doubted in the light of the Genesis account and other ancient traditions. However, the precise nature and extent of the biblical deluge must remain a matter of interpretation and speculation until incontrovertible evidence settles the issue.   EUGENE H. MERRILL

See NOAH #1; FLOOD MYTHS.

Bibliography. F.A. Filby, *The Flood Reconsidered*; H.M. Morris and J.C. Whitcomb, Jr., *The Genesis Flood*; A.M. Rehwinkel, *The Flood*; D.A. Young, *Creation and the Flood*.

Flood Myths. Traditional stories which seek to explain a catastrophic, possibly universal flood. Such myths are found among nearly all nations and tribes, though most commonly on the Asian mainland and the islands immediately south of it as well as on the North American continent.

Although these traditions have been modified through the ages and have occasionally taken on fantastic elements, they share three common features: (1) destruction of human beings and other living things by water; (2) some sort of ark or boat provided as a means of safety for one person or a few; (3) one or more human beings preserved to repopulate the earth; and sometimes (4) wickedness of man as a cause of the flood. The universality of these flood myths may lend support to the view that the flood was worldwide, at least as far as the inhabited world was concerned.

Examples of Flood Accounts. A few random examples will demonstrate the nature of these myths. A Mexican flood tradition has Concox (also known as Tezpi) embarking in a boat with his wife and children, some animals and some grain to escape a great flood. As the waters receded, Concox first sent out a vulture, which did not return because it feeds on carrion. Then he sent out other birds; finally a hummingbird returned with a branch covered with leaves, indicating it was now safe to disembark.

In Greenland there is a tradition that after 100 generations had lived on the earth a flood came and destroyed the whole human race, with the exception of one man who managed to save himself. Subsequently, when he struck the earth with his rod, a woman was created for him; this pair became the progenitors of a new human race.

A Hawaiian myth describes how, a long time after the first man, mankind became very wicked. One among them was righteous, Nu-u.

He built a great canoe with a house on it and stocked it with food and took plants, animals, and his family aboard. Then came a flood which destroyed all humankind except those on the canoe. Subsequently the great god put a rainbow in the sky as a token of forgiveness.

In India the Hindus revere Manu the righteous as the progenitor of the race. A great fish warned him that the earth was about to be covered by water. He was instructed to build a ship, stock it with all kinds of seeds, and take aboard seven holy beings (a total of eight—equivalent to the number on Noah's ark). Then the flood came, and a great fish towed the ship to a summit of the Himalayas, where Manu was permitted to create a new human race.

Chinese tradition identifies Fahhe as the flood hero. He escaped the universal deluge with his wife, 3 sons, and 3 daughters. From these the whole earth was repeopled.

The Roman flood tradition appears in Ovid's *Metamorphoses* (1st century AD) which tells of the creation of man, his innocence and happiness in Paradise, his fall, and finally the flood as punishment for human rebelliousness. Jupiter, enraged, caused a great flood to engulf all humanity; the rains from above were joined in their destructiveness by the release of subterranean waters, as in the biblical account. Only the righteous Deucalion and his wife Pyrrha escaped in a boat to Mt Parnassus. After the flood they were instructed to throw stones over their backs; these became men and women who then repeopled the earth.

The Babylonian Flood Account. By far the most interesting flood myth is that of the Babylonians because of its alleged or actual similarity to the biblical flood account. Some have argued that the Babylonian story helped to confirm the biblical narrative because of similarities in the accounts and because it came from the same geographical area as that intimated in the biblical story. Others have used the Babylonian account to cast doubt on the biblical account, claiming that the biblical narrative is only a myth like the other myths of the world and merely a sanitized or monotheistic version of the Babylonian account.

Discovery. The world first became aware of the Babylonian flood story on December 3, 1872, when George Smith of the British Museum reported it in a paper read before the Society of Biblical Archaeology in London. What Smith described was part of a flood account found among the tens of thousands of clay tablets comprising the library of King Ashurbanipal of Assyria (669–633 BC). Hormuzd Rassam, conducting a British excavation at Nineveh, had found this library in 1853 and had sent it to the British Museum.

Smith's report led to demands for reopening the Nineveh excavations in order to find the missing portion of the account. The following May, Smith arrived at Nineveh and found the flood fragment after only about a week of excavation! This flood story turned out to be the 11th tablet of a 12-tablet piece, the Gilgamesh Epic. It is an account of Gilgamesh's obsession with the fact that all must die and of his search for immortality. In the 11th tablet Gilgamesh (king of Uruk, biblical Erech) interviewed Utnapishtim, the "Babylonian Noah," and learned from him the story of the flood and his securing of immortality.

Smith later reported on fragments of an earlier Akkadian story of the flood, written in Mesopotamia about 1600 BC. This is now known as the Atra-hasis Epic, which has been properly understood only since 1967. Meanwhile, an earlier Sumerian version of the Babylonian flood story (dating perhaps *c.* 1700 BC) was found at Nippur and published in 1914. Without going into all the archaeological detail, it should be said that fragments of the myth have been found in Mesopotamia, in the Hittite archives in Asia Minor, and even among the Ras Shamra texts in Syria. The effect of all these discoveries has been to provide clearer understanding of the narrative as a whole and to make possible an accurate reading of doubtful passages. The story in all these texts is similar, and the flood hero is known variously as Ziusudra in Sumerian and Atra-hasis or Utnapishtim in Akkadian.

The Flood Narrative. As the account goes, the god Enlil could not sleep because the increasing number of people on earth made too much noise. So he decided to reduce their numbers by plague. But the god of plague was appeased, and the people began to increase again and to make more noise. Next Enlil decided to reduce the earth's population by drought and famine. This effort was frustrated by Enki or Ea, the god who controlled subterranean waters. Finally Enlil decided to destroy mankind by flood.

Enki, partial to Utnapishtim (or Atra-hasis) was forced to take an oath to cooperate with Enlil. Enki found a way around the commitment, however, by communicating with the flood hero, first in some sort of enigmatic dream and more specifically by speaking to the wall of a reed hut, so Utnapishtim, inside the house, could get the message and prepare to escape destruction. The instruction was to pull down the house and build a boat, to make it watertight by coating it with pitch, and then to load it with his family and possessions and with animals and birds. The Gilgamesh Epic specifies construction of a very large ship, while the Atra-hasis Epic indicates that

The Gilgamesh **Epic**.

the boat was fairly small and that the occupants had only 7 days to build it and get ready for the flood.

The flood lasted for 7 days and 7 nights, after which the boat landed on Mt Nisir and the hero sent out 3 birds (a dove, a swallow, and a raven) to reconnoiter the situation. Upon disembarking, Utnapishtim made an offering to the gods, after which he was granted immortality.

Comparison of Mesopotamian Accounts with Genesis. Comparing the Genesis and Mesopotamian flood stories, one is impressed with the number of similarities. Both accounts indicate that the flood was divinely planned and that the disaster was revealed to the flood hero. Both accounts assert that the hero was divinely instructed to build a boat which was pitched within and without, that a limited number of persons embarked in these ships with a considerable number of other living creatures to be saved alive, and that those not on board were destroyed. Both accounts also specify the physical causes of the flood, its duration, the landing place of the boat, and the sending out of birds. And in both accounts the heroes offer a sacrifice after the flood is over, receive a divine blessing, and are given some assurance that a similar catastrophe will never again overtake mankind.

The degree of similarity between the Genesis and Mesopotamian flood narratives has often been so emphasized that the extent of differences between them has been obscured. Actually the differences are far greater than the similarities. Most significant among these differences is the gross polytheism of the Babylonian and Assyrian stories, while the Genesis narrative is characterized by an exalted monotheism.

The reason for the flood is different in the two accounts. Genesis clearly indicates that God judged man with the deluge because of his sin. At the beginning of the Gilgamesh Epic the caprice of the gods seems to be responsible for the curse. The Atra-hasis Epic states that Enlil sent the flood to destroy man because he was so noisy Enlil could not sleep.

In addition, there are several lesser differences between the biblical and non-biblical accounts.

1. A period of grace. Genesis 6:3 notes that

man was granted a reprieve of judgment for 120 years, during which time he had ample opportunity to repent. The Mesopotamian deities jealously guarded their secret, giving man no opportunity for repentance.

2. Nature of the boat. Figuring the biblical cubit as 18 inches, Noah's ark was 450 feet long, 75 feet wide, and 45 feet high, with a displacement of about 43,300 tons. Supposing that the Babylonian cubit mentioned in the Gilgamesh Epic was the usual 20-inch measure, Utnapishtim's ship was cubical, measuring 200 feet on a side, with a displacement of 228,500 tons. Moreover, the latter vessel had 7 stories; Noah's had 3.

3. Occupants of the boat. Utnapishtim took aboard his family and relatives, craftsmen, boatmen, gold and silver, and "beasts of the field," while Noah took only his wife, sons and their wives, and a specific number of living creatures according to God's instructions (Gn 6:19–21; 7:2,3).

4. Length of the flood (or rain). The Sumerian narrative says it rained for 6 days and nights; the Babylonian, 7 days and nights. The Hebrew account declares it rained 40 days and nights (Gn 7:11).

5. Landing of the boat. Utnapishtim's ship landed on Mt Nisir, usually identified with a mountain east of the Tigris River and 400 miles north of the Persian Gulf, whereas Noah's ark landed in the Ararat Mountains, considerably farther north, either in eastern Turkey or adjacent territory in Russia.

6. The birds. According to the cuneiform account, a dove was sent forth first, then a swallow, and finally a raven. Noah sent a raven first and a dove on 3 separate occasions.

7. Blessing on the hero. Utnapishtim was granted immortality after the flood was over; Noah was not.

Though we have noted the differences, the similarities are considerable and scholars long have puzzled over the relationship between the accounts. There seem to be only 3 possibilities: (1) the Babylonian borrowed from the Hebrew; (2) the Hebrew borrowed from the Babylonian; (3) both descended from a common original. The first seems highly unlikely because the Mesopotamian accounts antedate the Pentateuch, though the Hebrew account could have existed orally long before it was written. While many in the past have suggested that the Hebrews borrowed the flood and many other accounts from Babylonian sources and merely purified them of polytheistic elements, even liberal scholarship now finds this view increasingly unacceptable.

The position that Hebrew and Babylonian accounts descended from a common original is very appealing. After all, Genesis gives Meso-potamia as the original home of the Hebrews and the place where civilization first began and where it made a fresh start after the flood. What would be more likely than that many accounts of an early tragedy of such magnitude would be preserved by peoples who lived in Mesopotamia or who had migrated from there. In accepting such a conclusion, we do not rule out divine inspiration. Biblical writers did not always write without access to source materials, but God ruled and directed the choice of such materials, guaranteeing accuracy of the finished product.

HOWARD F. VOS

See FLOOD, THE; NOAH #1; INSCRIPTIONS.

Flour. Fine, powdery substance produced by grinding the inner kernels of wheat. Called "the finest of the wheat" (Dt 32:14), flour was used in baking and also for cereal offerings (Lv 2).

See FOOD AND FOOD PREPARATION.

Flower. *See* PLANTS.

Flute. Translation of several words designating various kinds of wind instruments played by blowing across or through a hole.

See MUSIC AND MUSICAL INSTRUMENTS (HALIL).

Fly. Two-winged insect. In Scripture, several species are in view, including the common housefly (Eccl 10:1) and the horsefly (Is 7:18).

See ANIMALS.

Followers of the Way. Designation for Christians in the Book of Acts (9:2; 19:9,23; 24:22). In its early years, Christianity was called "the Way."

See WAY, THE; CHRISTIANS, NAMES FOR.

Food and Food Preparation. Substances required by the body to sustain life and the methods of making them edible. Food consumed in Bible times included bread, milk products, fruit, meat, and fish. Food was also offered sacrificially or given as gifts. The availability of food was a perpetual concern because of the recurrent scarcity: droughts were frequent (2 Kgs 4:38; Jer 14:1,4–6; Hg 1:11), hail storms wrought devastation among crops (2:17), farming was frequently interrupted by warfare with neighboring nations (2 Kgs 6:25), and intermittent plagues of locusts ravaged large areas.

Food was more plentiful in Palestine (described as a "land flowing with milk and honey") than in many other parts of the Near East. Shallow cultivation of the soil, however, made crops highly reliant on regular rainfall. Egyptian crops were far less susceptible to weather variations, because the Nile provided a dependable source of water.

Food shortages were considered warnings or punishment from God (Lam 4:9,11; Am 4:6–9) to teach the Hebrews that life is more than food and that faith must continue despite scarcity, famine, or even death (Dt 8:3; Hb 3:17,18).

Adam and Eve were given their choice of all the vegetation (except the fruit of the tree of the knowledge of good and evil) in the garden of Eden (Gn 1:29; 2:16,17), but there is no indication that meat was eaten at that period.

In patriarchal times of the OT, food was often scarce. Esau, a hunter, sold his birthright for a bowl of lentil soup (Gn 25:33,34), which indicates a shortage of meat in the household at that time. Joseph, a Jewish official in the Egyptian empire, was informed in a dream of an impending famine. He was able, therefore, to convince the pharaoh of the need to build storehouses and make adequate preparation. As a result, the available food in one area was used to supplement the disappearing stocks among other nations. Jacob probably cultivated grain, and thus needed to go to Egypt when his crops failed (Gn 42:2).

The staple of nomadic Hebrews was milk, curds, and cheese. As the people became more stationary, they grew grains and vegetables, and planted orchards and vineyards. Grain would sometimes be grown for a season, and then after the harvest, the tribes would move their flocks to other pastures and find other arable land. Religious sacrifices and festivals were not only times of solemnity but of rejoicing and great feasting. Victories were also celebrated with banquets and feasting on the food obtained from the camp of the vanquished enemy.

Dairy Products. Milk and its by-products formed a vital part of the Hebrew diet (see Jgs 4:19). Goat's milk was most frequently used, although milk from camels, cows, and sheep was also available (Gn 32:15; Dt 32:14; Prv 27:27).

Since fresh milk could not be preserved in Palestine's hot climate, it was processed into buttermilk, curds, and cheese. Milk was poured into goatskins, where it soured and thickened because of the unsterile condition of the previously used skins and the movement as it was transported. That movement of the pouch (often made from a cow's stomach, containing the enzyme rennin used in cheese-making) produced curds. Curds are first mentioned in the Bible as part of the meal that Abraham provided for his extraordinary guests (Gn 18:8).

The Hebrew word for curds (*chena*) is also translated "butter" (Jb 10:10). This butter would be similar in consistency to yogurt from which the water has been squeezed out. When pressed and rolled into small balls, it kept indefinitely, despite the climate. Thus, compressed curds were particularly valuable for journeys in arid regions where food was scarce.

Grain Crops. The most frequently mentioned food in the Bible is bread. The term refers in a general sense to all foods but also to food prepared from grain. In biblical times bread was prepared from several grains. Wheat, barley, and spelt were grown in Egypt (Ex 9:31,32).

Wheat was the most expensive grain. Fine wheat flour was a luxury only the rich could afford (Gn 18:6; Ez 16:13,19). In later periods wheat became a valuable export crop that was shipped from Tyre to other ports in the Mediterranean.

Because barley could grow in less productive soil and was more tolerant of drought conditions, it became a popular grain crop in the ancient Near East. Barley could also be harvested several weeks earlier than wheat. Barley bread (Jgs 7:13; 2 Kgs 4:42) and barley cakes (Ez 4:12) were eaten by the average laborer. Jesus miraculously multiplied a young boy's five barley loaves and two fishes and fed five thousand (Jn 6:9,13).

Millet, a cereal with a small grain head growing on a stalk less than two feet high, and spelt, a type of wheat, were also used in times of need as a border around the edges of fields.

An Egyptian physician named Sinuhe, living in the mid-20th century BC, recorded that bread was baked daily in Palestine and Syria, and it is probable that it was served with every meal. This bread was probably a wafer or flat cake made from barley or emmer (an early form of wheat), since these were the two grain crops that Sinuhe mentioned seeing.

The most primitive way of processing grain was to rub the ears between the hands to separate the kernels, as Jesus and his disciples did (Lk 6:1). To perform this act on the sabbath (the day of rest) was considered the equivalent of reaping and was therefore forbidden.

Parching (roasting the grain lightly in a pan) was another simple method of preparation (Jos 5:11; 1 Sm 17:17). It formed a quick and easy meal for laborers or kings (Ru 2:14; 1 Sm 25:18; 2 Sm 17:28). Parched corn was ideal for taking on journeys.

Bread-making was a strenuous task. Mortars, pestles, and simple mills with upper and lower stones were used for grinding flour in ancient Egypt around 2900 BC. These primitive mills were normally placed on the ground, and one was compelled to kneel in order to do the back-breaking work. The resulting meal

A millstone for grinding grain.

was coarse and filled with small pieces of husk.

When the flour had been prepared, water was added and it was kneaded together in a special trough. The dough could then be made immediately into cakes, pancakes, or unleavened bread (Gn 19:3). These flat cakes or wafers were often baked on previously heated stones, on the inner walls of small conical ovens, or in larger communal ovens. Leaven was added to make a lighter dough. The leaven was normally a piece of dough left over from an earlier mixing, and allowed to ferment before being used.

The flour meal was also mixed with a porridge made of lentil beans in order to stretch the food supply.

God provided a different kind of bread for the Israelites in the wilderness (Ex 16:14,15,22). This manna was made into cakes (Nm 11:7,8) which fed the Israelites for the following 40 years, providing valuable food for the people (Jos 5:12).

Animal Products. The introduction of meat as part of the diet seems to coincide with the time when Noah and his family left the ark (Gn 9:3). After this time, however, the animals normally eaten for food were so valuable that only the wealthy could afford to slaughter them. So in biblical times the peasant had a simple, somewhat monotonous diet, while the rich feasted on meat, delicacies, and imported commodities. As a result, meat was a luxury item which the poor would rarely enjoy except on such occasions as the Passover celebration or sacrifices in which the worshiper ate part of the offering (Ex 12:8). Although it was clearly uneconomic to slaughter an animal that produced such staples as milk, curds, and cheese, the rules of hospitality in the Near East dictated that an animal should be killed to entertain an honored guest or an unexpected traveler (2 Sm 12:2–4).

Domestic sheep, goats, and oxen provided the main source of meat, although venison was popular with the upper classes. When the blind Isaac was deceived by his son Jacob, the father was offered the luxury of both kid's meat and wild game (Gn 27:3,9,19). The ox kept in a stall or the fatted calf were reserved for occasions of great festivity (Mt 22:4).

The use of meat for sacrifice was given definitive form in the provisions of Leviticus and Deuteronomy. The Law forbade anyone to slaughter an animal and its offspring on the same day (Lv 22:28). Another prohibition, perhaps directed at pagan Canaanite sacrificial rituals, would not allow a kid to be stewed or poached in its mother's milk (Dt 14:21). Mosaic law was emphatic in prohibiting the consumption of blood in any form. Animal blood was considered the source of the animal's life

Ovens on Cyprus.

and was offered by priests as a sacrifice to God to atone for human sin (Lv 17:11). In the Mosaic law, pigs, camels, badgers, and rabbits were considered unclean and were therefore forbidden for food, principally on hygienic grounds (11:4–8).

Many food regulations were not strictly followed by the nobility (Am 6:4). This deviation from the Law inspired the distinctive ritual holiness of the covenant people of Israel (Lv 11:44,45).

In the ancient world, meat was usually boiled or stewed. Roasting an ox or a kid would usually occur only as part of a special feast or sacrificial ritual. Animals might also be roasted for members of the royal palace or for a king's special guests.

Despite the fact that hunting was enjoyed by all who were able to participate, wild game provided only a minor part of the diet. Among the game found in Palestine and mentioned in the Bible are gazelle, roebuck, wild goat, and deer (Dt 14:5; 1 Kgs 4:23). It is probable that pheasants were available, and there were certainly turtledoves, pigeons, quails, and partridges, although the precise quantities of food that these birds provided is not certain (Gn 15:9; Ex 16:13). Goose was the most popular dish in Egypt, and marsh ducks were also highly esteemed as game. After the Persian period, chickens were eaten (2 Esd 1:30), and eggs and omelettes were popular in Rome in early Christian times. The eggs mentioned in Deuteronomy are probably wild birds' eggs (Dt 22:6,7; Is 10:14).

Thirty varieties of fish were available in the Jordan, and an extensive fishing industry existed on the shores of the Sea of Galilee at the time of Christ. Supplies of fish were readily available from the Mediterranean coast during the Roman period, but at an earlier time inhabitants depended to a large extent upon whichever nation had control of the coastline. In the postexilic period the people of Tyre supplied the city of Jerusalem with fish, which was sold near the Fish Gate (Neh 3:3). In the regulations concerning the types of fish suitable for food, only those that had fins and scales were acceptable (Lv 11:9–12).

In NT times many of the distinctions concerning food were eliminated. In the Gospel of Mark, Jesus, challenging the Pharisees' hypocrisy, upset the Jewish food laws by saying that evil thoughts, not certain foods, make a person unclean (Mk 7:19). As Christianity spread into gentile areas, there was, however, a continuing concern about eating meat that had been offered to idols. The question came to a head in Corinth. The apostle Paul maintained that though the meat was acceptable, one should take care not to cause spiritual damage to another Christian with a more sensitive conscience.

Insects and Their By-Products. Wild honey was found in Palestine, but there is no evidence of beekeeping. Egyptians, however, did practice beekeeping at that time.

The honeycomb is mentioned specifically in 1 Samuel 14:27 and Song of Solomon 5:1; liquid honey is referred to in 1 Kings 14:3. Honey was to be found in crevices of rocks and on trees (Dt 32:13). It was the primary sweetener in cooking. Although it could not be used in a sacrifice to the Lord (Lv 2:11), honey was prized as a delicacy. In the 15th century BC, when Thutmos III was campaigning in Syria and Palestine, he brought back vast quantities of honey as tribute from his newly conquered lands.

Locusts were probably first eaten in desperation after they had devastated crops. They are one of the few insects mentioned as a permissible source of food (Lv 11:22). Locusts were fried in flour or honey, or were preserved by being dried. Locusts and wild honey formed John the Baptist's basic diet in the wilderness (Mt 3:4; Mk 1:6). Although locusts contain little protein, they are rich in fat and have some mineral content.

Vegetables and Seasoning. The Hebrew people wandering in the Sinai wilderness bemoaned the loss of the flavorful vegetables they had become accustomed to during their Egyptian captivity. In particular, they expressed a longing for cucumbers, melons (possibly watermelons), leeks, onions, and garlic (Nm 11:5). Many of these vegetables were later grown in Palestine, the Gaza area in particular producing excellent onions. When cucumbers were first cultivated they were regarded as luxury items and had to be protected by guards who lived in shacks overlooking the gardens (Is 1:8). Beans, lentils, and parched grain were among the items brought to David and his soldiers at Mahanaim (2 Sm 17:28).

Lentils were known in Egypt from at least the 13th century BC and were used extensively both then and in later times by the Israelites. Lentil soup is mentioned in Genesis 25:34.

In times of hunger the husks of the carob tree, normally fed to cattle, could be used for food. Those would have been most acceptable to the prodigal son (Lk 15:16). There were many other kinds of green herbs which could provide a meal for the poor in time of need (Prv 15:17). In cases of extreme hunger, some kinds of mallow and juniper roots could also be used as food. In Elisha's time a group of prophets at Gilgal prepared a stew of wild vegetables, to which they mistakenly added poisonous wild gourds. Elisha somehow rectified the situation by adding meal to the pot (2

Kgs 4:38–41). While there is no actual record of the kinds of bitter herbs used as part of the Passover offering (Ex 12:8; Nm 9:11), mint and cummin were most probably included. Dill, cummin, rue, and mint were common garden herbs (Mt 23:23; Lk 11:42).

Seasonings were welcome additives to the rather bland character of typical Israelite fare. Salt came mainly from the Dead Sea area, and was essential as a seasoning and preserving agent. Salt was so important in the diet that it became part of the vocabulary of moral obligation. The sharing of salt with a person at a meal sealed a covenant or pact (Nm 18:19). In the levitical sacrificial ritual, salt was part of meat and cereal offerings, since it signified the sealing of God's covenant with Israel (Lv 2:13; Ez 43:24).

The mustard tree, which was probably grown for its oil content, grew from a minute seed to the height of 15 feet (Mt 13:31,32). Anise, coriander, and cinnamon were also available (Ex 16:31; Nm 11:7). Perhaps the most popular and widely used spice, apart from salt, was garlic. Vinegar was also probably used as a flavoring agent and a preservative. From the number of seeds and plants found in Egyptian tombs from the 18th dynasty, it is obvious that the use of seasoning was widespread in antiquity.

Fruits, Nuts, and Wine. Olive trees grew abundantly in Palestine and were an excellent source of food and oil. Even in poor soil, one tree could sufficiently supply a family for a whole year. Some green olives were pickled in brine and eaten with bread, but the olive was most important as a source of oil. Workers are

recorded as receiving rations of 20,000 measures of wheat and 20 measures of pure oil. Olive oil was used in baking bread and cakes, and in frying foods. The best quality olive oil was used in the temple sacrifices.

Oil was extracted from olives by a simple process: for the finest quality oil, olives were picked before fully ripe and then crushed by hand with a stone mortar and pestle. Usually, however, pickers beat the olives from trees with long poles and collected them in baskets. The oil was then trodden out, probably in the same vat used for grapes (Mi 6:15), which were harvested approximately four weeks later.

An oil mill was developed subsequently, and the heavy upper grinding stone was turned by two people. As the oil dripped through, it was collected in another stone vat and was allowed to settle and purify. When refined, the oil was stored in skins or jars.

Fig trees grew in all areas of Palestine. They required little attention and provided two or three crops per year. The most abundant of these was the second, which ripened in late summer. The first figs of the season were considered a great delicacy (Is 28:4; Mi 7:1). The prophet Hosea suggested that the Israelites were like the first fruits of the fig tree (Hos 9:10). Another prophet, Jeremiah, spoke of those who had gone into exile as being like

A mortar and a pestle for grinding grain in small quantities.

An olive press for making olive oil.

the first figs, while those who were left behind were the bad figs, fit only for destruction (Jer 24:1–10).

Figs were usually eaten fresh from the trees, but some were pressed into cakes to use when traveling (1 Sm 25:18; 30:12; 1 Chr 12:40). Figs were also valuable for medicinal purposes, since effective poultices could be made from them (2 Kgs 20:7; Is 38:21). Sycamore trees produced small, figlike fruit eaten primarily by the poor. A short time before harvest, the fruit was slightly incised, making it swell and ripen more quickly. The prophet Amos notched sycamore fruit before his call (Am 7:14).

Fruit from the date palm could also have been pressed into flat cakes for travelers, as figs were. The Bible, however, makes no specific reference to its fruit as food (see Jgs 4:5; Ps 92:12; Jl 1:12; Jn 12:13).

Another popular Near Eastern fruit was the red pomegranate. It was eaten whole, or the seeds were pressed to provide refreshing drink. The pomegranate is mentioned in temple ritual as one of the fruits brought back from Canaan to Moses by his spies (Ex 28:33), and as an exotic drink (Sg 8:2).

The "apple" mentioned in Scripture (Prv 25:11; Sg 2:5) was most likely a type of apricot or quince, not an apple as we know it today.

Nuts were used for additional flavor in cooking. Almonds and pistachio nuts were among the gifts sent by Jacob to ransom his sons (Gn 43:11).

Grapes were popular and plentiful from the Early Bronze Age. In addition to being eaten fresh from the vine, grapes were dried as raisins (Nm 6:3; 1 Sm 25:18) or pressed, their juice drunk either as new wine or fermented into an alcoholic drink. One of the duties of the cupbearer in ancient royal courts was to provide grape juice or wine for the king, his family, and guests (Gn 40:9–13).

The juice of grapes also provided vinegar when wine deteriorated. Vinegar was used as a flavoring agent in cooking and as a preservative. When diluted with water, it supplied a refreshing drink for workers in the fields. A type of jelly was made in the Near East by boiling grapes until they assumed the consistency of molasses. This syrup could also be used as a sweetening agent in cooking.

Wine was the universal drink in antiquity. It could be diluted with water or mixed with spices or honey to make a mulled wine (Sg 8:2; Is 5:22). The Hebrew word for "banquet" or "feast" means literally "drinking," which reveals much of the character of such occasions. While a certain amount of merriment was considered proper at a festival or banquet (Gn 43:34; Jgs 9:13; Lk 5:34), Scripture contains stern warnings against excessive drinking and drunkenness (1 Sm 1:14; Prv 20:1; Is 5:11).

Wine making was similar in many respects to the production of olive oil. Clusters of grapes were cut from the vine with a sickle, collected in baskets, and taken to the winepress, where they were trodden by men and women. The juice ran into a lower vat, where, under the hot sun, fermentation began almost immediately. The wine was left to settle so that any twigs or skins would form a sediment; after that the wine could be strained off. In about six weeks the wine was ready to drink or store in earthenware jars or wineskins.

HAZEL W. PERKIN

See ANIMALS; MEALS, SIGNIFICANCE OF; FAMILY LIFE AND RELATIONS; BREAD; LEAVEN; PLANTS; UNLEAVENED BREAD.

Footstool. Low stool used to support one's feet. Part of King Solomon's great revenue of gold was used to fashion a footstool for his ivory throne (2 Chr 9:18). Both the ark of the covenant and the temple are referred to as God's footstool because they were places where God rested (his glory resided there) and reigned (1 Chr 28:2; Pss 99:5; 132:7; Lam 2:1; cf. Is 60:13). Though Solomon's throne and footstool were spectacular, the heavenly throne and earthly footstool of God dwarf them (Is 66:1).

The enemies of the Messiah were to become his footstool, that is, they would be fully subjected to him by the power of God (Ps 110:1). Many of the NT references to a footstool (lit., "something under the foot") parallel the OT expectation of the final conquest of Messiah's enemies (Mt 22:44; Mk 12:36; Lk 20:43; Acts 2:35; Heb 1:13; 10:13).

Another OT concept repeated in the NT is that of the earth being God's footstool (Mt 5:35; Acts 7:49).

See FURNITURE.

Fords of the Jordan. Shallow places where people and animals could wade through the Jordan River. Many OT personalities crossed over the Jordan at its two main fords: Jacob (Gn 32:10), Gideon (Jgs 8:4), David (2 Sm 10:17; 17:22), Absalom (17:24), Abner and his men (2:29). Joshua led his followers across the Jordan on dry land during a flood, truly a God-given miracle (Jos 3:15,16). Jesus crossed the Jordan on several occasions on his trips between Galilee and Jerusalem.

The two main fords of the Jordan were at Jericho (Jos 2:7; Jgs 3:28; 2 Sm 19:15) and at Bethabara, where John baptized (Jn 1:28 KJV). In certain places and at certain times the Jordan was not fordable: after the melting of the snows in the Lebanese mountains, and near the Dead Sea, where the Jordan is about 100 feet wide and from 5 to 10 feet deep (Jos 3:15).

See JORDAN RIVER.

Foreigner. Noncitizen or alien, temporary guest, sojourner, or stranger. The Greek word for "proselyte" ("foreigner") means a stranger in sympathy with Judaism (Mt 23:15; Acts 2:10; 6:5); it can also mean a convert to Christianity.

The Hebrew word meaning foreigner is rendered correctly on all occasions in the RSV, but the KJV uses it in its truest sense on only two occasions (Dt 15:3; Ob 11). In most cases KJV translates the word as "alien" (Dt 14:21; Jb 19:15; Ps 69:8; Lam 5:2) or "stranger" (Gn 15:13; Ex 2:22; Lv 25:35). Another Hebrew word means "dweller" (Lev 25:35; 1 Chr 29:15; Ps 39:12), or "settler." For the most part, however, it is rendered "foreigner."

A temporary guest or sojourner was usually someone who wanted to take up temporary residence or had moved from one tribe or people to another, and then attempted to obtain certain privileges or rights belonging to the natives. A whole tribe might be sojourners in Israel. This was the case with the Gibeonites (Jos 9) and the Be-erothites (2 Sm 4:3; cf. 2 Chr 2:17). The Israelites themselves were sojourners in the land of Egypt (Gn 15:13; 23:4; 26:3; 47:4; Ex 2:22; 23:9) and in other lands (Ru 1:1).

Foreigners or sojourners had certain rights but also certain limitations while in Israel. They could offer sacrifices (Lv 17:8; 22:18) but could not enter the sanctuary unless circumcised (Ez 44:9). They were allowed to participate in the three great Jewish festivals (Dt 16:11,14) but could not eat the Passover meal unless circumcised (Ex 12:43,48). Foreigners were not obliged to follow the Israelite religion, but shared in some of its benefits (Dt 14:29). They were not to work on the sabbath and the Day of Atonement (Ex 20:10; 23:12; Lv 16:29; Dt 5:14) and could be stoned for reviling or blaspheming God's name (Lv 24:16; Nm 15:30). Foreigners were forbidden to eat blood (Lv 17:10,12) but could eat animals that had died a natural death (Dt 14:21). Israel's code of sexual morality also applied to the foreigner (Lv 18:26). There were prohibitions against Israelite intermarriage with foreigners, but it was nevertheless a common occurrence (Gn 34:14; Ex 34:12,16; Dt 7:3,4; Jos 23:12).

Civil rights were provided for foreigners by the Law of Moses (Ex 12:49; Lv 24:22), and they came under the same legal processes and penalties (Lv 20:2; 24:16,22; Dt 1:16). They were to be treated politely (Ex 22:21; 23:9), loved as those under the love of God (Lv 19:34; Dt 10:18,19), and treated generously if poor and receive the fruits of the harvest (Lv 19:10; 23:22; Dt 24:19–22). They could receive asylum in times of trouble (Nm 35:15; Jos 20:9). Foreign servants were to receive treatment equal to Hebrew servants (Dt 24:14). A foreigner could not take part in tribal deliberations or become a king (17:15). The prophet Ezekiel looked forward to the messianic age when the foreigner would share all the blessings of the land with God's own people (Ez 47:22,23).

One Hebrew word specifically describes one who goes out of the way to visit a foreign country (Ez 7:21; Ps 54:3; Hos 7:9; 8:7 KJV).

In the NT, "foreigner" refers variously to Samaritans (Lk 17:18) and Canaanites (Heb 11:9,34). The work of Christ allowed all foreigners to become members of God's household (Eph 2:11–19). Christians should consider themselves foreigners in this world (Heb 11:13; 1 Pt 2:11).

See BARBARIAN; NEIGHBOR.

Foreknowledge. Knowledge of things or events before they exist or happen.

In the NT the Greek equivalent of "foreknowledge" appears only seven times. It refers to the Christian's advance warning about false teachers (2 Pt 3:17); the Jews' previous knowledge of Paul's early life (Acts 26:4,5); God's previous knowledge of the death of Christ (Acts 2:23; 1 Pt 1:18–20); and knowledge of his people (Rom 11:2) and of the church (8:28–30; 1 Pt 1:1,2).

The concept of foreknowledge does, however, appear throughout the Bible in other ways. First, the all-inclusiveness of the knowledge of God is clearly taught. God's understanding is unlimited (Ps 147:5). He knows every heart and thought (1 Chr 28:9). Psalm 139 provides an extended poetic description of God's knowledge of all human thoughts, words, and actions. This knowledge extends to the flight of a sparrow and the number of hairs on the head (Mt 10:29,30). From such limitless knowledge, it may be inferred that God also knows the future events of human history.

In addition, Scripture directly teaches that God is aware of events before they happen. This sets him apart from heathen idols who lack the ability to foresee the future (Is 44:6–8; 45:21; 48:14). It is God's foreknowledge that provides the basis for the predictions of the prophets. God announced to Adam and Eve that the seed of the woman would certainly defeat the serpent and his seed (Gn 3:15). Promises of future blessing were given to Abraham (12:3). God said to Moses, "I know that the king of Egypt will not let you go" (Ex 3:19). The coming glory of the Messiah was declared by the OT prophets. (See, e.g., Is 9:1–7; Jer

23:5,6; Ez 34:20–31; Hos 3:4,5.) In Daniel 7 (see also Dn 2:31–45) God reveals the rise and fall of future world empires and the establishment of the kingdom of God. In many places the NT sees Christ's ministry and the establishment of the Christian church as fulfillment of predictions made beforehand by the OT prophets (Mt 1:22; 4:14; 8:17; Jn 12:38–41; Acts 2:17–21; 3:22–25; Gal 3:8; Heb 5:6; 1 Pt 1:10–12; etc.).

For many of the early Greek philosophers, fate rigidly controlled all future events, including not only the events of human history but the fortunes of the gods as well. Occasionally a future event might be known by the gods and revealed to men, and such foreseen events could in no way be altered. This view is, of course, far different from the biblical view of the personal Creator who knows the future and guides history according to his own purpose.

Nevertheless the question of the relationship between God's foreknowledge and human responsibility and freedom has occupied the attention of theologians and philosophers over the centuries. It is sometimes argued that if God knows infallibly what will happen in the future then it must happen. Therefore it makes no difference at all what choice a person makes since it could not have been otherwise.

The theologians of the early church emphatically denied that foreknowledge implies any predetermination of events. Justin Martyr, for example, said, "What we say about future events being foretold, we do not say it as though they come about by fatal necessity."

Other theologians, fearing that foreknowledge destroys human freedom and responsibility, insist that God does not know future events either certainly or completely. Modern process theology, for example, conceives of God as growing and developing along with nature and man. This God, it is argued, can at most know only those events which have already taken place. Hence the future remains open and uncertain for God as well as for man. An older theologian, Adam Clarke, suggested that although God can know all future events, he chooses not to know some events beforehand.

Augustine denied foreknowledge for a different reason. He argued that God lives in eternity where all things are present. For God, then, there is no past or future. Hence he would not know things before they happened, since he would see all events from the vantage point of an eternal "now." Augustine, of course, did not deny God's knowledge of all things, even of things which are still in the future as far as we are concerned.

Because of the clear biblical teaching regarding God's foreknowledge, evangelical theologians have generally held that God has complete knowledge of all future events. There is a further distinction, however. The followers of Augustine and Calvin insist that God knows all events precisely because he sovereignly determines what is to happen in human history right down to the tiniest detail. Here foreknowledge is closely tied to, if not identified with, foreordination. At the same time, most Calvinistic theologians assert that human beings are nonetheless responsible for their choices—not victims of a blind fate. It is also generally held that God is not the author of sin. Rather, sin is the result of the rebellion of angels and men against a holy and righteous God.

Evangelicals in the Arminian tradition, on the other hand, distinguish foreknowledge from foreordination of events. While the plan of salvation of the world and human history in broad outline are predetermined by God, it is argued that individual response to God is not so predetermined. Hence God can foreknow an event without directly decreeing that event to take place.

While evangelical Christians differ in their descriptions of the relationship between the eternal all-knowing God and the events of human history, it should be kept in mind that Scripture teaches both God's foreknowledge of all things and the responsibility of humans for their choices.

WILLIAM S. SAILER

See ELECT, ELECTION; FOREORDINATION.

Foreordination. Activity of God by which he establishes events and outcomes before they occur. In common usage, "foreordination" and the term "predestination" are synonymous. "Predestination" or "election," however, specifically refers to the destiny of persons.

Foreordination underlies the whole plan of God: his decision to create the universe, to care for it (providence), and to determine its destiny "according to the counsel of his will" (Eph 1:11). The Westminster Shorter Catechism states the teaching in this way: God has decreed "his eternal purpose according to the counsel of his will, whereby, for his own glory, he hath foreordained whatsoever comes to pass." Foreordination, then, is at the foundation of all Christian teaching, for it concerns the history and destiny of the whole world, the universe, and all that it contains.

The apostle Paul spoke of God's plan for the fulfillment of all creation: "For the creation waits with eager longing for the revealing of the sons of God; for the creation was subjected to futility, not of its own will but by the will of him who subjected it in hope; because the creation itself will be set free from its bondage to decay and obtain the glorious liberty of the children of God" (Rom 8:19–21). Scripture gives only a glimpse of the redemption of the whole creation. It speaks of new heavens and a new earth in which righteousness dwells (2 Pt 3:13). Those things that mar human existence and demonstrate human fallenness and sinfulness (i.e., depravity) will all pass away. God will make "all things new" (Rv 21:1–5). So the destiny of everything rests with God himself.

Foreordination creates problems for theology and commonsense thinking, particularly in relation to human freedom and responsibility and that aspect of foreordination concerned with salvation. How can people be held responsible for their actions and decisions if they have been predetermined? To remove that difficulty some have denied God's foreordination as it relates to human freedom. In creating free beings, they argue, God must have limited his determination of things that "must" come to pass. Otherwise free and responsible human activity has no meaning.

Calvinism rejects such an argument, insisting that free activity is possible even though it is foreordained and foreknown. The problem remains, however, for humanly speaking there seems to be no possibility for a last minute change of mind.

On the other hand, denial of the doctrine of foreordination implies that God does not control his creation. If that were true, the existence and happenings in the universe, including human activity, would be determined either by something above or beyond God, or by occurrences whose ultimate causes are unknown. God's providence and care revealed in the Bible and human experience make such a view untenable. Christian thought generally states that God foreordains and controls his creation and that humans are able to act freely and responsibly within that larger control. The apparent contradiction or paradox remains unresolved because there is a limit to human understanding.

Foreordination was referred to by many early church fathers and was a major emphasis in the theology of Augustine of Hippo (354–430). Augustine greatly influenced the reformers, particularly John Calvin. Reformed theologians begin the study of the doctrine of foreordination with the eternal decree of God, as indicated by creeds such as the Westminster Confession of Faith. The decree of God is one, but for purposes of discussion and explanation it is usually referred to as "the decrees of God." Martin Luther believed in foreordination but did not stress it as much as Calvin. Luther's theology is generally silent on foreor-

dination, primarily discussing predestination or election. Contemporary Lutheran thought stresses conditional, rather than absolute election, that is, election or predestination based on foreseen faith.

Foreordination in Scripture. There are many references to foreordination (including predestination, or election) and the related idea of foreknowledge in the Bible. Foreordination can be thought of as logically prior to foreknowledge, but there is no actual priority since both activities are eternal in God.

Speaking of judgment to come upon Babylon, God said: "This is the purpose that is purposed concerning the whole earth; and this is the hand that is stretched out over all the nations. For the Lord of hosts has purposed, and who will annul it? His hand is stretched out, and who will turn it back?" (Is 14:26,27). God also declared that he has determined the end from the beginning. "My counsel shall stand, and I will accomplish all my purpose" (46:10). Paul stated that the purpose of God is carried out "according to the counsel of his will" (Eph 1:11; cf. Ps. 119:89–91; Dn 4:35).

With respect to human affairs it is said that one's life span is determined (Jb 14:5), that God's concern extends to his creatures (Ps 104:14–30; Mt 10:29), and even the hairs on our heads are numbered (Mt 10:30). Furthermore, God's plan extends to peoples and nations, for "he made from one every nation of men to live on all the face of the earth, having determined alloted periods and the boundaries of their habitation" (Acts 17:26).

God knows and even uses people's evil acts for his own ends. For example, although Joseph's brothers sinned by selling him into slavery, Joseph later said, "As for you, you meant evil against me; but God meant it for good, to bring it about that many people should be kept alive, as they are today" (Gn 50:20). Judas Iscariot betrayed Jesus, but God used that sinful intent. Jesus said, "For the Son of man goes as it has been determined; but woe to that man by whom he is betrayed!" (Lk 22:22). On the day of Pentecost the apostle Peter said "this Jesus, delivered up according to the definite plan and foreknowledge of God, you crucified and killed by the hands of lawless men" (Acts 2:23; cf. 4:27,28). Paul refers to God's determining authority over pharaoh's acts (Rom 9:17). Revelation 17:17 says, "God has put it into their hearts to carry out his purpose." God, then, foreordains the events of nature and history, and even evil acts are subject to his control and are made to fulfill his purposes.

Election of sinners to salvation through Christ is also included in God's foreordination (Rom 8:28–39; cf. Acts 13:48; Phil 2:12,13; 1 Pt

2:9). God's choosing or electing is not arbitrary, "since all have sinned and fall short of the glory of God" (Rom 3:23). God's plan of salvation is grounded in his eternal love and good pleasure (Eph 1:3–14; Rom 5:6–11). The Christian is the recipient of God's grace in that the believer knows God and is known (i.e., loved) by God (Gal 4:9). Both election and believers' faith are part of the salvation process.

Foreordination and Providence. The doctrine of foreordination is implied in the doctrine of providence or God's care. Providence is the working out of God's plan for the world. God's care and control of the whole creation point to his plan of redemption for man and woman made in his image. God sovereignly controls the events that take place in the world, but God is not responsible for sin. He created human beings who may say no to God as well as yes. That does not mean that God's plan can be thwarted; it goes on in spite of opposition. God's ultimate plan is being realized through all the events of human history, evil and good. Yet, his sovereignty is not imposed arbitrarily. God is not a tyrant, but holy, loving, and righteous. His plan is effected according to his nature, which is expressed in care and concern for the whole creation and in steadfast love for undeserving sinners.

Natural law refers to the rules God has laid down (foreordained) to control the universe. What about destructive forces of nature, such as earthquakes, tornadoes, and hurricanes? Why are such apparent evils necessary in a world made and controlled by a loving God? It is no answer to suggest that God is unable to act or control nature fully. If life's total meaning resided in the temporal, physical world, there might be reason for complaint. But considering the whole plan of God and his ultimate redemptive purpose, the answer takes on a different dimension. God's ultimate purpose transcends the present life and centers in the fulness of the redemptive kingdom yet to be revealed (Rv 11:15; 21:1–4). The doctrine of foreordination is a great mystery, but it should be a source of joy and comfort to believers whose loving Lord has brought them to a knowledge of his great plan.

WARREN C. YOUNG

See ELECT, ELECTION; FOREKNOWLEDGE.

Forerunner. Scout sent in advance of troops, or a herald who precedes a high official to announce his coming. The term is used to describe the man who ran ahead of Joseph when he was viceregent of Egypt (Gn 41:43), and to refer to the first grapes of the season in the land of Canaan (Nm 13:20). In the Apocrypha, hornets were said to be sent as forerunners of the Israelite army, who were to bring judgment on the people of Canaan (Wis of Sol 12:8).

Although John the Baptist is commonly viewed as the forerunner of Jesus Christ, the term is not used with reference to him. The word occurs only once in the NT, where Christ himself is described as a "forerunner on our behalf" (Heb 6:20). Under the old covenant, the people never accompanied the high priest into the most sacred place of the temple. The Book of Hebrews, in discussing the new covenant, describes Jesus as a high priest who has entered heaven—the holy place—ahead of those who believe in him (cf. 2:17–3:2; 5:1–9).

Forest. *See* PLANTS.

Forgiveness. Ceasing to feel resentment for wrongs and offenses; pardon, involving restoration of broken relationships. Primarily, forgiveness is an act of God, releasing sinners from judgment and freeing them from the divine penalty of their sin. Since only God is holy, only God can forgive sin (Mk 2:7; Lk 5:21). Forgiveness is also a human act toward one's neighbor, given new incentive and emphasis in the NT because of God's forgiveness in the death of Christ. Hence forgiveness is a uniquely Christian doctrine.

In other religions, forgiveness does not have the same force. In animism, there is no awareness of a personal relationship with God. In Hinduism, all have to pay the inexorable consequences of *karma* in the wheel of reincarnations. Buddhism likewise knows nothing of a forgiving God. The idea is present in Islam, but there is no personal God and Father. Even in Judaism, forgiveness remains a limited experience, though forgiveness as developed in the NT adds dimension to the teaching of the OT.

Expressions of Forgiveness in the OT. The idea of forgiveness is expressed in various metaphors. The command is *nasa*, to "send away," as the scapegoat was sent away into the wilderness to bear the sins of the Israelites. It is also rendered "to be merciful" (Lv 4:20; 1 Kgs 8:30,34; Pss 86:5; 103:3). The Hebrew word *kapar* is commonly used of atonement, meaning "to cover up," as the sacrifice was offered to cover the deficiency of the worshiper (Ex 29:36; Dt 21:8; Jer 18:23; Ez 43:20; 45:20). Cognates of *salah* always refer to God's act of forgiveness (Nm 30:5,8,12; Pss 86:5; 130:4; Dn 9:9). God lets go of the transgression; he removes it. Another expression is *maha*, to "wipe away" (Ps 51:1,7; Is 43:25; 44:22).

The OT teaches that God is a forgiving God (Ex 34:6,7; Neh 9:17; Dn 9:9), yet he is just and punishes sin. Many incidents are also given where God refuses to forgive when the proper conditions are not met, or when certain serious offences are committed (Dt 29:20; 2 Kgs 24:4; Jer 5:7). Forgiveness is rooted in the character of God, but his forgiveness is never indiscriminate, for man must also be penitent. God will "by no means clear the guilty." The OT uses vivid imagery to indicate the magnitude of God's forgiveness. Sin is cast "into the depths of the sea" (Mi 7:19), removed "as far as the east is from the west" (Ps 103:12), hid behind God's back (Is 38:17), "remembered no more" (Jer 31:34). The stain and soil of sin is bleached white (Is 1:18). Sin, which burdens like a weight, is forever lifted and remitted.

The dynamic of forgiveness in the OT is thus releasing one from the past. The past acts and deeds of sin are not denied, but there is no longer any bondage. Forgiveness brings freedom.

Forgiveness in the NT. In the NT, the concept of the unmerited forgiveness of God is extended, intensified by the death of Christ, offered on our behalf. The human creature is an insolvent debtor (Mt 18:23–35) who has no hope of repayment. Sinners all, we cannot keep the Law or save ourselves (Mk 10:26,27). This highlights the NT teaching that it is in the person of Christ himself that there is forgiveness. He alone has the power to forgive sins (Mk 2:5,7,10). It is his death that is redemptive (Mt 26:28; Mk 10:45) and his blood that is the basis of a new covenant (1 Cor 11:25). It is through him that one can enter into the living experience of forgiveness (Heb 9:15,22). So forgiveness is inseparable from the proclamation of Jesus Christ (Acts 13:38; Eph 1:7; Col 1:14; 1 Jn 2:12).

There are other distinctively NT concepts of forgiveness. The Greek word *charizomai*, meaning "to forgive sins," is distinctively developed by Paul in terms of God's gracious pardon (2 Cor 2:7; 12:13; Eph 4:32; Col 2:13; 3:13). Sin is considered as a debt, and *aphesis* denotes the discharge of a debt ("putting it away," Lk 6:37). Forgiveness is also treated as remission, *paresis*, ("passing over"). God has not executed the full retribution called for by sin (Acts 14:16; 17:30); instead, he has shown mercy.

Yet the NT speaks of two limitations to forgiveness. One is the unpardonable sin (Mt 12:31,32; Mk 3:28–30; Lk 12:10). In this regard Christ speaks of those, who like the Pharisees, are so warped in their moral judgments that they cannot distinguish between acts of Satan and the good deeds of Christ. There is also "the sin against the Holy Ghost" (1 Jn 5:16) that is "sin unto death." This sin is not specifically defined, but its essence seems to be consistent rejection of the grace of God.

The ethics of forgiveness in the NT insists not only on penitence as a condition for forgiveness (2 Cor 7:10), but also on the need to forgive others (Mt 6:14,15). If in the midst of receiving forgiveness one does not forgive others, it is a clear sign that repentance is not complete. "As the Lord has forgiven you, so you also must forgive" (Col 3:13). Several times in his parables, the Lord insists that the readiness to forgive others is a sign of true repentance (Mt 18:23–35; Lk 6:37). So Christ taught that to forgive is a duty, and no limits can be set on it. It must be granted without reserve, even to seventy times seven (Mt 18:21,22). Forgiveness is part of the mutual relationship of believers: since all are dependent upon God's forgiveness, all are required to forgive one another.

The Christian Experience of Forgiveness. The Christian understanding of forgiveness has broad implications.

1. It reflects the character of God as one who pardons and enters into a meaningful relationship with his creature, producing a change in human relationship with him. This has been done in the costly anguish of the cross of Christ.

2. It expresses the efficacy of divine atonement in the reconciliation of man with God. Those who truly realize their condition as sinners know that God can remove sin and redeem sinners. This must be experienced, not just comprehended intellectually. In Christ's death, sin is condemned and absolutely judged, and yet Christ bears the penalty on our behalf by his sacrifice.

3. For the apostle Paul the bare concept of forgiveness did not convey deeply enough the full consequences. Instead, he speaks of *being justified*. To be "treated as righteous" is a rich consequence of forgiveness (Rom 4:5), a gift of God's grace (3:24), a present experience (1 Cor 4:4) for those who have a faith relationship with Christ (Rom 3:26). Thus justification is the positive relationship that forgiveness provides.

4. Forgiveness implies that God has reconciled man to himself (Eph 2:14–17). The outcome is peace with God (Phil 4:7; Col 3:15), a reconciliation accomplished by the cross (Col 1:20). This is the implication of all the references to being justified, reconciled, and trusting in Romans 5. It also includes the idea of divine sonship (Mt 5:9,44; Jn 1:12).

5. Forgiveness includes the theme of fellowship with God the Father (1 Thes 1:3), Son (1 Cor 1:9), and Holy Spirit (2 Cor 13:14). It is expressed in the Pauline phrase "in Christ" or "in the Lord" (used some 164 times), indicating a profound relationship of communion and union with God. Forgiveness as reconcilia-

tion and restoration to fellowship with God comprehends, in effect, the whole nature of the Christian life. Sanctification is its fruit, and glorification is its objective. In forgiveness, God ultimately remains God, and the erring sinner is brought home to the Father who has eternally loved him.

JAMES M. HOUSTON

See CONFESSION; REPENTANCE.

Bibliography. W. Eichrodt, *Theology of the OT*, vol 2, pp 380–95; E.M.B. Green, *The Meaning of Salvation*; J. Jeremias, *The Prayers of Jesus*; P. Lehmann, *Forgiveness*; H.R. Mackintosh, *The Christian Experience of Forgiveness*; I.H. Marshall, *Kept by the Power of God: A Study of Perseverance and Falling Away*; E.B. Redlich, *The Forgiveness of Sins*; V. Taylor, *Forgiveness and Reconciliation*; W. Telfer, *The Forgiveness of Sins*.

Form Criticism.

Study of biblical tradition which may be presumed to have existed originally in oral form.

Definition and History. The concern of form criticism is to get behind the sources which literary criticism may identify to the preliterary stage of the tradition. It seeks to describe what took place as the tradition was transmitted orally from person to person and from community to community. Its special concern is the modification of the tradition by the life and thought of the believing community. In the case of the OT, form criticism presupposes that the dynamic life of Israel exerted a creative influence on the tradition when it circulated orally, and seeks to recover the earlier forms of the individual units within a larger cycle of tradition. In the NT, form criticism has concerned itself primarily with an investigation of the synoptic Gospels. It has focused upon the individual units of tradition in the Gospels in an effort to distinguish those strata which reflect the concerns of the church from the elements which might be thought to go back to Jesus himself or to some contemporary source in Judaism or Hellenism.

Form criticism was developed as a critical tool in 1901 by Hermann Gunkel. In a commentary on Genesis he broke new ground by attempting to recover the earliest form of the tradition which was given its final literary expression in Genesis. Gunkel accepted the current literary-critical analyses, but was convinced it was possible to recover an earlier stage of the tradition than source criticism had envisioned. He postulated that before there were written documents or structured collections of tradition there was a preliterary oral stage in which the individual stories circulated as independent accounts. The stories must therefore be isolated from the context in which they now stand in Genesis and studied as individual units against the background of similar accounts in the ancient Near East.

Gunkel was persuaded that these originally oral stories had been developed and modified over an extended period of time in response to social and cultural changes in the life of Israel.

Gunkel classified the stories in Genesis in terms of their purposes: "ethnological legends" were accounts told to explain the relations of the tribes to each other; "etymological legends" were popular accounts explaining the origin and meaning of the names of races, mountains, wells, sanctuaries, and cities; "ceremonial legends" were devised to explain the sacred customs of Israel; while "geological legends" were told to explain the character of a particular region or locale.

Gunkel attempted to detect how an earlier account had been altered by additions which show more concern for the thought than for the form of the story. He argued that these additions could be recognized by the fact that they disrupted an otherwise harmonious story and by the fact that they were relatively general in character. His analysis tended to eliminate speeches and short narrative notes from the accounts as they stand in Genesis. In his analysis of the individual units Gunkel sought to find reasons for the transformation of an original account and so to describe the inner history of the units of the tradition.

Gunkel was convinced that this method of identifying and classifying smaller units of narrative, didactic, and liturgical tradition behind the literary text was applicable to the study of the synoptic Gospels as well. This insight was developed by one of his pupils, Martin Dibelius, in a study of the primitive Christian tradition concerning John the Baptist (1911). In this early work Dibelius expressed two methodological conclusions concerning the synoptic Gospels and the tradition embedded in them which became programmatic for form criticism: (1) The Gospel writers are not authors but collectors and preservers of tradition, who have edited their material by adding such items as time and place references, connecting links, and summary reports. (2) Both sayings and narrative material existed in fixed oral forms before they received literary expression by the writers of the Gospels. The second of these insights Dibelius developed in a small brochure, "The Form Criticism of the Gospels" (1919), in which he distinguished five "forms" that he could recognize behind the units of tradition now found in the synoptic Gospels. Three months later his own student, K.L. Schmidt, applied Dibelius' insights to the framework of the synoptic Gospels and sought to demonstrate that the order of the paragraphs even in Mark, the oldest connected narrative source for the ministry of Jesus, was casual and arbitrary.

Traditional birthplace of John the Baptist, who was the subject of Martin Dibelius' study.

In 1921 Rudolf Bultmann published his own independent research into the history of the synoptic tradition. He examined systematically the entire material of each of the synoptic Gospels and sought not only to classify the units by form but to distinguish between the tradition which owes its present form to the early Palestinian church from that which received its form from the later Hellenistic community.

Methodology of Form Criticism. There are three stages in the form criticism of the synoptic Gospels. In the first, the stories and sayings in the Gospels are separated from the framework in which they now appear. K.L. Schmidt had compared a Gospel, with its several units of tradition, to a string of pearls, where each pearl is held in place by the string to which it has been attached artificially. This initial stage of form-critical investigation simply cuts the string so that each of the pearls (the individual units of tradition) may be examined independently.

In the second stage, internal criticism is ap-plied to these units of tradition in order to recover the original form of each. It is presup-posed that the units which have been isolated by removing the framework are not yet in their earliest form. A first step toward the re-covery of the original form of the tradition is the classification of the material according to its type. Much of the tradition of Jesus' say-ings, for example, may be classified as pro-nouncement stories containing important ut-terances. Some of these occur in the context of a controversy (e.g., Mk 2:23–28, where the pro-nouncement occurs in vv 27,28), while others may be assigned to catechetical instruction (e.g., 12:28–34, where the pronouncement is preserved in vv 32,33). The words of the Lord sometimes assume the form of a proverb (2:17a), a prophetic statement (9:1), a mission pronouncement (2:17b; 10:45), or a parable (4:30–32). Narrative material about Jesus can be similarly classified (e.g., 1:40–45 is a mira-cle story).

Once the material has been classified, stylis-tic considerations established through the study of oral communal "literature" are applied to each unit to determine its original form. It is assumed (1) that each of the several forms possesses a certain stereotyped character; (2) that each unit is complete in itself, stylistically marked off, expressing a single thought or event; (3) that by analysis of the forms it is possible to detect modifications of the tradition; and (4) that since these considerations apply to the popular literature of the day, whether Jewish or Hellenistic, they must apply to the Gospels as well. Working with these assumptions Bultmann, for example, judged that Mark 2:19 preserved a brief parable told by Jesus, but that verse 20 was an allegorical addition appended to the parable after Jesus' death to interpret the parable and apply it to the worshiping community.

In the third stage, external criticism is applied to the units of tradition to recover the setting in the life of the early church which accounts for their preservation. At this stage the form critic must seek to reconstruct the actual course of early Christian history in order further to classify the material embedded in the Gospels. It is assumed that the gospel tradition served the church in its concern to advance its cause through evangelism, to defend itself through apologetics, and to mature its life through worship and discipline. These several types of concern are reflected in the tradition and account for the modification of the original core of the tradition in some instances, while in others they explain how the tradition actually originated within the developing life of the church, according to Dibelius, Bultmann, and others.

Evaluation of Form Criticism. There are positive features in the form-critical method. (1) The emphasis upon the period of oral transmission prior to the writing of the Gospels balanced earlier approaches which had stressed literary sources almost exclusively. (2) The interest in the role of the community of faith as the guardian and transmitter of the biblical tradition is sound. (3) The Gospels are "occasional writings," in the sense that they were composed for a particular occasion. The emphasis placed by the form critics on the life situation of the believing community is, therefore, proper. (4) Finally, the isolation of particular units of tradition, especially the different groups of pronouncement stories, and the insistence upon the centrality of the passion narrative in the tradition about Jesus, has been helpful for the interpretation of the Gospels.

Negatively, criticism must be directed to each of the three stages of form criticism. There is an element of truth in the estimate of the character of the synoptic Gospels expressed in the first stage. There are fewer precise links to the aspects of the tradition than one might suppose. Nevertheless, this does not imply that there was an indifference to historical sequence or factual truth in the early church. Schmidt's method was to play one Gospel off against another. His method presupposed a rigid literary criticism of the synoptic Gospels and failed to take into account the element of oral tradition which may clarify some of the differences he observed. Form criticism also fails to appreciate the distinct historical, theological, and communal concerns of each of the Evangelists. Moreover, the gospel could not be proclaimed apart from some framework. Since the evangelical message involved a life story, there was a demand for a sequence, at least to some extent. The actual framework discovered by Schmidt conforms to the outline of Peter's preaching in Acts 10:36-41.

A basic weakness in the second stage is that the classification of the material frequently reflects not form, but content. The objectivity claimed by the discipline, consequently, is not evident. Moreover, the appeal to stylistic considerations may be seriously challenged, because the assumptions upon which they are based are not as established as is generally claimed. That they can be applied in a rigid way to materials which have been transmitted orally can be questioned. Such a presupposition precludes diversity which may originate in the authority of the individual responsible for the tradition. In the synoptic Gospels, content is more important than form; it is inappropriate to bring a critical judgment upon the tradition from narrow considerations of form.

One other objection is substantial. The determination of the "laws of style" was based upon a study of material which circulated in an oral state for an extended period of time. It is inappropriate to apply such criteria to traditional units which were written down within a generation or two from the time of their origination.

It is in the third stage of form criticism, the application of external criticism to the units of the tradition to recover their life setting in the experience of the community, that the radical character of the presuppositions of the form critics becomes evident. Dibelius and Bultmann felt that the demands of preaching and worship accounted for most of the modification of the tradition. Bultmann assigned to the (later) Hellenistic community everything that suggests worship, such as interest in the person of Jesus, the birth narratives, most of the accounts of Jesus' miracles, the resurrection narratives in their present state, the mission pronouncements of Jesus (Mt 11:27; Mk 10:45; Lk 19:10), and the words of institution of the

Lord's Supper. To the Palestinian community Bultmann assigned almost all the rest of the narrative portions and of the teaching, including the distinctly eschatological features of the Gospels and those sayings which indicate that Jesus was conscious of being the Messiah.

The basis of this negative evaluation was Wilhelm Bousset's reconstruction of early Christian history. Bousset distinguished sharply between Palestinian and Hellenistic Christianity and maintained that the title "Lord" was applied to Jesus first by the Hellenistic Greek-speaking Christians in the course of worship. The early Palestinian Aramaic-speaking Christians referred to Jesus only as the Son of man. This overly sharp distinction between the Palestinian and Hellenistic churches was adopted by Bultmann and others in the determination of the social setting in the life of the church in which the tradition first assumed its distinctive shape.

It is now widely recognized that this reconstruction of the course of early Christian history and development is not accurate. The distinction between Hellenistic and Palestinian Christianity is overdrawn. Palestine was not an island isolated from all Hellenistic influences; Jerusalem itself had Hellenistic synagogues. Moreover, it was primarily Christians from Jerusalem and other Palestinian communities who carried the gospel into Hellenistic regions. Consequently, the disparity between Palestinian and Hellenistic Christianity postulated by Bousset is difficult to maintain.

Moreover, this stage of form criticism tends to separate the gospel tradition from Jesus and those who were the eyewitnesses to what had been said and done unjustifiably. The presence of the apostolic witnesses within the early church exercised a stable influence upon the formation and transmission of the tradition which must be appreciated when seeking to recover the earliest form of the tradition about Jesus' words and deeds.

WILLIAM L. LANE

See DOCUMENTARY HYPOTHESIS; REDACTION CRITICISM; SOURCE CRITICISM; TRADITION CRITICISM; DEMYTHOLOGIZATION; BIBLICAL CRITICISM, NEW TESTAMENT; BIBLICAL CRITICISM, OLD TESTAMENT.

Bibliography. R. Bultmann, *History of the Synoptic Tradition;* M. Dibelius, *From Tradition to Gospel;* W.G. Doty, "The Discipline and Literature of NT Form Criticism," *Anglican Theological Review* 51 (1969), 257–319; K. Koch, *The Growth of the Biblical Tradition;* E.V. McKnight, *What Is Form Criticism?* E.B. Redlich, *Form Criticism: Its Value and Limitations;* V. Taylor, *The Formation of the Gospel Tradition* (4th ed.), 1957; G.M. Tucker, *Form Criticism of the OT.*

Former Rain. Important rainfall which begins the agricultural year in Palestine, usually in October (Dt 11:14; Jer 5:24; Jas 5:7).

See PALESTINE.

Fornication. Unchastity, sexual immorality. The word "fornication" is used in the Scriptures to mean several different things.

Its general meaning refers to every kind of illegal sexual intercourse, that is, any intercourse except that between a husband and wife. For example, in 1 Corinthians 5:1 (KJV) the word is used twice to refer to a sin which was being tolerated by the church: a man apparently was living with his stepmother as though with a wife. In a list of terrible sins in Romans 1:29, the apostle Paul included fornication, apparently intending the term to mean all acts of sexual immorality (KJV). In 1 Corinthians the context suggests that Paul used the word in reference to all sorts of illicit sexual activity (vv 13, 18 KJV). In 1 Corinthians 7:2 (KJV) Paul used the plural Greek word for "fornications" to imply the various ways in which the sin may manifest itself. He thus gave a reason why people in Corinth, should marry and live together properly. One of the sins included in the word's general sense is adultery.

"Fornication" also has a more limited sense of immoral sexual activity between unmarried people. Such a meaning is implied in those biblical lists where both fornication and adultery come together. Jesus' list of the defiling sins that proceed out of a person's heart includes "fornication" and "adultery" (Mt 15:19; Mk 7:21). Paul's list of those sinners who will not inherit the kingdom of God also contains both fornicators and adulterers (1 Cor 6:9 KJV).

"Fornication" in Matthew 5:32 and 19:9 (KJV, "unchastity" RSV) is usually taken by biblical students today to refer specifically to adultery. The conclusion has to do with interpretation rather than translation. Conservative scholars disagree whether Jesus' exceptive phrase relative to divorce has to do with fornication in a general or limited sense. He might have meant adultery alone, or he might have been including it generally with other sexual sins. He also could have used the term in a more limited sense of unlawful premarital sex.

A figurative use of the word "fornication" appears in both the OT and NT. Originating in descriptions of Israel and the church as the Lord's wife or the bride, apostasy from God and idolatry are called fornication (see, e.g., Jer 2). Ezekiel 16 uses marriage and unfaithfulness to marriage vows as a symbol of God's relation with sinful Jerusalem, which had become an "unfaithful wife" to him. The first three chapters of Hosea use the relationship of the prophet Hosea and his unfaithful wife Gomer as an illustration. The nation Israel was guilty of fornication against its "husband," the Lord, by going after other gods. In the Book of Revelation the same figurative use of "fornication" and "impure passion" appear (Rv 14:8; 17:2,4; 18:3; 19:2).

Fornication is a category of sin that the Christian must continuously shun and persistently avoid (1 Cor 6:18; 1 Thes 4:3). The apostle Paul even counseled against carelessly talking about it and other sins (Eph 5:3,4).

WESLEY L. GERIG

See ADULTERY.

Fort, Fortification. Walls, citadels, and sometimes moats protecting most cities in the ancient world. Fortifications followed the natural contour of the area encircling a city. Early city defenses consisted of simple banks of earth tossed against the walls and outer structures to make it difficult for hostile forces to approach and enter the city. Wherever possible, the site chosen for the location of a city would be a naturally favorable topographical situation, such as a steep elevation in an isolated place or a hill that afforded natural protection. Some sites were so strategic because of ample water supply, good navigation, or a central location at crossroads of traveled highways, however, that they were chosen even if they had no natural defenses. The difficulty and cost of fortifications were then obviously much more serious.

In general, whatever materials were available were used for construction of fortifications, including old debris, rubble, and beaten earth. Those materials were faced with hard-packed clay or lime plaster to prevent an enemy from knowing the quality of the underlying filling. Commonly a ditch or moat was dug or cut out of solid rock in front of the walls. This hindered an enemy's advance, and made any attempt to tunnel under the walls and into the city more difficult.

The eastern wall of Jerusalem, with Bedouin tents pitched next to it.

Towers were built for added strength and protection at potentially weak spots, such as corners, gateways, or openings for water supplies. Towers had inner access stairways, and chambers for use by soldiers who manned the structures and for watchmen who announced the approach of danger. Gateways were provided with massive piers and bronze or iron bars and bolts. Gates were hung on pivots driven into the pavement below and into the lintel above and had to be strongly fortified and carefully protected. Often they consisted of a series of entrances, one inside the other, with guard rooms between them.

Excavations of ancient forts reveal the development of fortifications from primitive beginnings to NT times. Earliest strongholds were constructed with crude brick and rough stone work. Masonry was irregular, and large stones of various sizes and shapes and field boulders were roughly trimmed and crudely placed into the wall structures. Stone facings and wall joints were packed with pebbles or limestone chippings. During later times carefully prepared mortar was used to cover the walls to give greater strength and support to the fortifications. Not until late in the Hebrew period were stones with ornamentation and skilled drafting used.

Scripture uses the imagery of a fortress or high tower to picture the confidence that believers can have in God's strength and protection. The prophets realized that the strength and defense of the nation lay not in fortifications of brick and stone, but in God, and they urged the people to put their trust in him as a secure refuge (2 Sm 22:2,3,33; Prv 10:29; Is 25:4; Jer 16:19; Hos 8:14; Jl 3:16; Na 1:7).

God is also able to make his chosen servants "a fortified city" (Jer 1:18; 15:20). In the messianic age cities will no longer need bars or gates (Ez 38:11) but will be protected by God's salvation (Is 26:1; 60:18).

RALPH E. POWELL

See WATCHTOWER; CITY; ARMS AND WARFARE.

Fortunatus. Member of the church at Corinth. Fortunatus is a Roman proper name written in Greek and found only once in the NT (1 Cor 16:17). Paul rejoices that he, along with Stephanas and Achaicus, had come to be with him in Ephesus. The Textus Receptus (a 16th-century compilation of Greek NT manuscripts) has a subscript naming these three men as the carriers of Paul's letter to the Corinthians.

Forum. Open area in Roman cities used for commerce, political affairs, and judicial matters. The forum was usually on level ground, rectangular in shape, and surrounded by temples, law courts, colonnades, and other public buildings.

The forum of Appius was a traveler's stop on the Appian Way, 43 miles south of Rome, where Paul was met by Christians from Rome on his way to the capital under guard (Acts 28:15).

The most important of the forums were those located in the city of Rome. These were built at different times in its history, and existing forums were changed through continued building. The Rome to which Paul went for his trial had several forums, including those of Julius Caesar (begun by him but actually completed by Augustus Caesar) and Augustus Caesar. Most important was the Roman Forum, center of the world in Paul's day. It lay between the two central hills of the seven hills on which the city was built. It contained many columns, statues, works of art, and buildings important in the political and religious life of the empire.

If Paul was brought directly into the city by the centurion who had charge of him, he would have passed on his way to the forum the triumphal arch of Augustus, the temple of Castor and Pollux, and the temples dedicated to Julius and Augustus for emperor worship. Arriving at the Roman Forum proper, he would have noticed on the northwest the famous ideal center of the city (and thus of the empire), and on the southwest the gilded milestone, giving distances to places as far away as London to the west and Jerusalem to the east. In the background was the temple to Jupiter, chief god in the Roman pantheon. On the south side was a large public building, the Basilica Julia, completed in AD 12, the probable site of the pronouncement of Paul's death sentence. On the north side was the Basilica Aemilia, a building from which marble columns were taken and used in the building of a church over the traditional site of Paul's tomb. That church was completed in AD 398 and stood for 1400 years.

A short distance to the northwest of the Roman Forum was the Mamertine prison, the place where, according to tradition, both Paul and Peter were confined before their executions under the emperor Nero in the AD 60s.

See APPIUS, FORUM OF.

Foundation Gate. Structure mentioned in 2 Chronicles 23:5, in the narrative about Queen Athaliah's execution. The parallel passage in 2 Kings 11:6 reads "gate of Sur," while the Septuagint has "gate of the ways," indicating some difficulties within the Hebrew text.

See JERUSALEM.

Fowl. KJV common translation for bird. In modern usage and the RSV, the term is reserved for domestic birds or wild fowl which are eaten.

See BIRDS.

Fowler. One who traps or shoots wild birds.

See HUNTING; TRADES AND OCCUPATIONS.

Fox. Small, wild, carnivorous, doglike mammal, several species of which existed in Palestine in the biblical period.

See ANIMALS.

Frankincense. Fragrant gum resin that can be ground into powder and burned to produce a balsam-like odor. It was often associated with myrrh (Sg 3:6; 4:6; Mt 2:11). Frankincense is obtained from balsam trees of the genus *Boswellia*, specifically the species *B. carterii*, *B. papyrifera*, and *B. thurifera*. These trees, which are related to turpentine trees, have star-shaped flowers that are pure white or green, tipped with rose. To obtain the resin a deep incision is cut into the trunk, yielding an amber-colored gum. Since these trees were native only to Saba (Sheba) in southern Arabia (Is 60:6; Jer 6:20) and Somaliland, the resin was a very costly item transported into Palestine by caravan. The so-called frankincense tree growing in Palestine (Ecclus 50:8) was probably *Commiphora opobalsamum* whose resin was used to produce perfume.

Frankincense was used alone or with other materials for incense. It was one of the ingredients of the holy incense used for worship in the tabernacle (Ex 30:34). It was placed on the bread of presence (Lv 24:7) and mixed with oil on the cereal offerings (2:1,2, 14–16; 6:15), but excluded from the sin offering (5:11). A supply of frankincense was maintained in the Jerusalem temple (Neh 13:5,9). It was later used in cosmetics and perfume (Sg 3:6). Both the costly value and its use for worship made the presentation of frankincense to the infant Jesus an appropriate gift (Mt 2:11).

F. DUANE LINDSEY

See PLANTS.

Freedom. *See* LIBERTY.

Freedmen. Members of a Jewish synagogue in Jerusalem (Acts 6:9), descended from Jews who had been captured and taken to Rome by the general Pompey (106–48 BC), then later released. Pompey found that the Jews adhered so strictly to their religious and national customs that they were worthless as slaves.

Not all the freedmen returned to Jerusalem; some stayed in Rome. In the time of the Roman writer Pliny, a freedman was described as a "mean commoner." The freedmen derived their name from a Latin term for one manumitted, or the son of such a former slave.

See LIBERTINES.

Freewill Offering. Voluntary peace offering (Lv 7:16; Dt 12:6).

See OFFERINGS AND SACRIFICES.

Fringe. KJV translation for "tassel," four of which were worn on the upper garments of Jewish men according to the Lord's commandment (Dt 22:12). Those tassels were to be reminders of God's laws.

See FASHION AND DRESS.

Frog. Aquatic, tailless, smooth-skinned amphibian, mentioned in connection with the second plague in Egypt (Ex 8; Pss 78:45; 105:30; Rv 16:13).

See ANIMALS.

Frontlet. Translation of a Hebrew word referring to anything bound on the forehead (Ex 13:16; Dt 6:8; 11:18). The phylacteries of Jesus' day (Mt 23:5) were worn daily at morning prayer by every male Israelite over the age of 13. They consisted of four Scripture passages (Ex 13:1–10; 13:11–16; Dt 6:4–9; 11:13–21) written on parchment and placed in small leather boxes tied to the forehead and the left arm. Whether the phylacteries were the parchments or the leather boxes is debated. There is no evidence that the Israelites in Moses' day made such phylacteries. It is probable that the commands were to be understood figuratively, portraying the memorial value of the feast of unleavened bread, and the importance of the Law in the people's lives. For the Pharisees the outward observance had replaced the obligation to apply the power of God's Word to the heart (Mt 23:5).

See PHYLACTERY; AMULET.

Frost. Frozen water vapor or dew (Pss 78:47; 148:8; Jer 36:30; Zec 14:6).

See PALESTINE.

Fruit. *See* FOOD AND FOOD PREPARATION; PLANTS.

Fruit of the Spirit. Expression taken from Galatians 5:22,23. As listed there, this fruit is the manifest evidence one may expect from a life in which the Spirit of God is living and reigning. Jesus also implied that the character of a life can be determined. In the context of

Matthew 7, the test for false prophets is, among other things, the kind of life they live. Consequently, even though Jesus did prohibit censorious criticism of others by his followers (Mt 7:1), he encouraged fruit inspection. The secret to exhibiting spiritual fruit in abundance is described in John 12:24. Using as an illustration a grain of wheat sown in the ground, Jesus encourages death to self and to the desires of the old nature and resurrection to the new life of "much fruit."

The fruit of the Spirit, as listed in Galatians 5, is love, joy, peace, patience, kindness, goodness, faithfulness, gentleness, and self-control. Love is that outgoing, self-giving kind of action, not necessarily emotion, that characterized God himself when he loved the world so much that he *gave* his only Son (Jn 3:16). Goodness is the translation of a Greek word that includes the idea of generosity. The word "faith" refers usually to trust or confidence in someone or something. However, the word can also refer to that which causes trust and faith, namely faithfulness and reliability. Both meanings are in the use of the word here as another evidence of the Spirit-controlled life. Another fruit, translated "temperance" by the KJV, is the Greek word for self-control, that ability to hold oneself in, to keep oneself in check. It is significant that the Spirit is said to be the one responsible for this fruit. Since these qualities are the fruit of the Spirit, it is self-evident that legalism and obedience to law cannot originate or produce them.

This fruit appears in a context within Galatians where Paul is emphasizing Christian freedom from obedience to the Law as a meritorious means of being justified before God. He warns the Galatian Christians, who were in danger of returning to the Law, that physical circumcision is an outward sign of a return to legalistic means of justification and that to attempt to obtain it this way is impossible (Gal 5:3). However, lest the Galatians overemphasize their freedom in Christ, Paul cautions that this liberty does not mean license to sin, an opportunity for gratifying the desires of the flesh, but rather an opportunity to continue as loving bondservants belonging to one another (v 13). Life in the Spirit will mean that one will not fulfill the lusts or desires of the flesh (v 16). Then Paul identifies both the works of the flesh and the fruit of the Spirit. A person who is abstaining from the works of the flesh and is demonstrating the fruit of the Spirit in his life will be loving, joyful, peaceful, patient, kind, good, dependable, gentle, and self-controlled. These are not said to be gifts of the Spirit, however, but graces that will adorn the life that is under the Holy Spirit's control.

There has been some confusion about the

relation of this fruit to the gifts (Greek, *charismata*) of the Spirit listed in 1 Corinthians 12:4–11; 12:28–31a; Romans 12:3–8; and Ephesians 4:11–14. First Corinthians 12:31b explicitly relates the gifts of the Spirit to the fruit. The first fruit of the Spirit mentioned in Galatians 5:22 is love, the very item which Paul mentions as "a more excellent way" (1 Co 12:31b) rather than as a gift to be listed with the others.

It is significant that the works of the flesh, are many, while the fruit of the Spirit is singularly one. Hence some have interpreted Galatians 5:22 to mean that the fruit of the Spirit is singular, namely, love, and that what follows (vv 22,23) are varying facets of love. Correlating this Galatians reference with 1 Corinthians 12:31b demonstrates that the fruit of the Spirit is love with all of its many aspects and also the more excellent *way* in which the various gifts are to be used. To underscore that love is not itself a gift, Paul goes on to describe the fruit of the Spirit, in 1 Corinthians 13, the great love chapter of the Bible. Comparing these two passages it is interesting to note how many of the facets of love appear in both places. Paul is saying in essence that the gifts of the Spirit are only effective, worthwhile, and capable of edifying, when they are exercised in a proper *way*, that is, with the qualities given in Galatians 5:22 and 23 and 1 Corinthians 13.

It becomes apparent then that the fruit of the Spirit and not the gifts or any particular gift is the evidence of a Spirit-controlled life. The Corinthians were blessed with many of the gifts (1 Cor 1:5,7; chs 12,14), but they were still immature (1 Cor 3:1–4). The proof of a Spirit-led, sanctified life is not the gifts of the Spirit but the fruit of the Spirit, chief of which is love.

WESLEY L. GERIG

Fuller. One who cleans, shrinks, and thickens, or dyes cloth or newly shorn wool.

See TRADES AND OCCUPATIONS.

Fuller's Field. Place in Jerusalem which was linked to a spring or pool by a causeway (2 Kgs 18:17; Is 7:3; 36:2). It has been generally identified with an area near En-rogel ("spring of the fuller"). The spring was south of Jerusalem in the Kidron Valley. It was originally the tribal boundary between Judah and Benjamin (Jos 15:7; 18:16). When Absalom rebelled and King David fled from Jerusalem, two of David's men stayed at En-rogel to gather information about the rebellion (2 Sm 17:17).

En-rogel has been identified with the modern Bir Ayyub, or "Job's Well," on the left bank of the Wadi en-Nar. The well sinks deep into the rock, reaches an underground stream, and gushes forth following rainfalls.

See JERUSALEM.

Fullness of Time. Expression meaning "when the time was ripe," occurring in English translations of Galatians 4:4 and Ephesians 1:10. In Galatians the reference is to the time when "God sent forth his Son." The apostle Paul used the image of a child coming of age to say that Jesus came at a point in human history when the time was ripe and released humanity from bondage to the Law.

Traditionally theologians have seen indications of the ripeness of the time of Jesus' birth in the historical circumstances of his day. Rome's conquests had produced "Roman peace," so that travel was both safe and easy. That political unity was built on the earlier victories of Alexander the Great, whose expansion from Greece to Egypt to India left in its wake the Greek language and culture, which later made the spread of the gospel easier. Greek-speaking Jews lived in every city of the Roman Empire. Their religion was protected by Roman law, and that law protected Christianity for its first half century. Many Gentiles who were interested in the monotheism and morality of Judaism went to the Jewish synagogues. Thus the synagogue was a natural starting point for the church's early outreach to Gentiles.

In Palestine the Jews were longing for a Messiah (deliverer) since they were politically subject to the Herods and the Romans. Messianic rebellion simmered constantly, and repeatedly broke out in open battle. Socially, peasants were oppressed by large landholders, who used every opportunity and legal loophole to expand their properties. Many of those oppressors were from the chief priestly families, whose greed was well known to all. Throughout Palestine messianic speculation was at a high point. The Pharisees talked about what would happen when the Messiah came, and the scribes at Qumran (Dead Sea Scrolls community) wrote books about it. The time was ripe for Jesus' coming, as he himself indicated (Mt 13:11,16,17; Mk 1:15).

In Ephesians 1:10 Paul used a slightly different Greek expression, which covers the whole of the time between Jesus' first coming and his future return to complete God's plan in history. Jesus revealed this plan (or mystery, as Paul called it—Rom 16:25,26; Eph 1:9; 3:4,5; Col 1:26), which works out in the church as people repent and are joined to him. In the ultimate sense, the full "ripeness" will come when God's plan or purpose ("dispensation"

KJV) is completed and Christ becomes Head over all things. Paul knew that this completion was in progress, but he awaited its total realization in what he hoped would be the near future.

PETER H. DAVIDS

Funeral Customs. Practices and rites that encompass the dying and death of human beings. Funerary rites have been practiced by all social groups from their very beginnings.

Most anthropologists believe that funeral customs fulfill certain important social functions for the living. However, the general meaning these customs provide for any given culture is a matter of longstanding dispute. On the one hand, some behavioral scientists believe that funeral rites alleviate the sudden anxiety which death brings for the grieving. On the other hand, some believe that the purpose of death customs is not to dispel anxiety but rather to foster the feelings of religious awe or group solidarity. In varying degrees both these factors probably underlie most funeral rites. Funerary customs remind the participants that death must be taken seriously, while at the same time providing a comforting interpretation of death.

Belief patterns have profoundly influenced funeral customs. A conception of immortality is one of the more commonly held beliefs. The discovery of artifacts such as tools, ornaments, and even food in the oldest known human graves may be evidence of the pervasive conviction that human beings continue to exist in some form after death. Proper funeral rites were believed to assist the dead in reaching their final habitat, which usually included a journey fraught with various perils, such as crossing mythical rivers or wide chasms. The rites also assured the living that the spirits of the dead would not harm them.

Disposing of the Corpse. A common form of disposing of a corpse has been burial in the earth (inhumation). This practice may have emerged because of the belief that the abode of the dead was located under the ground. Often the grave was considered the entrance to the underworld, although some groups considered the habitation of the dead to be in the sky. Above-ground disposal has also been practiced by many. Some communities place the corpse on a rack to be devoured by birds or other animals. A few groups have been known to eat the corpse, believing that the good qualities of the deceased could be ingested. Many Asian societies have traditionally practiced cremation, or the burning of the corpse. In the past it was not uncommon for the wife and slaves of a deceased man to throw themselves on the burning pyre. Cremation is becoming

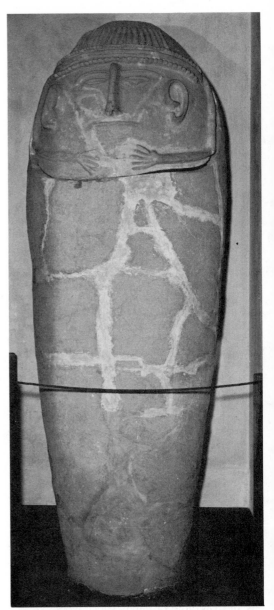

Philistine coffin with lid.

popular in the West and may become more widely practiced because of the increasing scarcity of land for grave sites.

Nearly every society observes special mourning customs during the disposal of the body. These include the wearing of special clothing, emotional outbursts, seclusion, and food taboos. Most societies mark the experience by a ceremony which may include purification rites and the sharing of special meals by the friends and relatives of the dead. In almost every cultural group status symbols infiltrate the funeral customs and rituals. For instance, if the deceased were of a high social standing, then the funeral ceremonies would be more elaborate.

Funeral Customs and the Bible. While the Bible does not provide a detailed picture of proper burial procedures, it does allude to the common practices of the Hebrew people, and contains some scattered prohibitions relating to death. Placing the corpse in the ground or in a cave was the principal method for disposing of their dead. One of the worst indignities was to be left unburied or become "food for beasts of prey" (Dt 28:26; 1 Kgs 11:15). If possible the deceased were to be buried on the day of death (Dt 21:23). While embalming was not practiced, the corpse was dressed in special burial clothes and sprinkled with various perfumes (Mk 15:46; Jn 11:44).

Intense weeping surrounded funerary rites during biblical times. This mourning did not simply result from spontaneous grief, but was part of the funeral ritual (Mt 11:17). In ancient Israel, groups of paid mourners emerged who could wail on ritual cue. Much of the funeral service centered around these professional mourners who sang psalms and delivered elaborate eulogies for the dead (2 Chr 35:25; Jer 9:17–22). The emphasis upon mourning resulted from the Hebrew appreciation of human life and health, which was considered one of God's greatest gifts (Ps 91:16), and also from a view of human nature which affirmed embodied existence (Ps 16:9–11). This latter belief may have contributed to the OT's lack of a full-fledged doctrine of immortality, even though it implies that the dead partake in the "shadowy existence" of Sheol and will some day be resurrected (Jb 14:13; Ez 37).

The early Christian church affirmed the Jewish belief in embodied existence, but highlighted a belief in existence after death. Unlike the Greek dualists who asserted the immortality of only the soul, the NT writers, following the OT, emphasized a belief in eternal life which entailed not only the soul, but also the body. This view became the fulcrum for the belief in the bodily resurrection, which undergirded Christian funeral customs. Nearly every practice symbolized a belief in the resurrection and eternal life. Thus, the emphasis upon lamentation gave way to joyful singing of psalms. The body was washed, anointed with perfumes and spices, wrapped in linen, and surrounded by candles, all of which represented eternal life. Friends and relatives usually held a vigil at the home of the deceased, and scriptural passages dealing with the resurrection and eternal life were read. Whenever possible the Lord's Supper was observed, symbolizing the sacrifice of Christ. At the church or the gravesite, a funeral oration was delivered both to eulogize

the dead and to comfort the living. Many of these practices are still observed by Christians today. In opposition to the common cultural practice of not touching a corpse, Christians often kissed the dead as a sign of both love for the person and reverence for the body. The body was usually buried. Because pagans often desecrated Christian tombs and burned bodies, however, Christians began to affirm that any form of disposal was acceptable—no method could impede the resurrection. Consequently, Christian customs surrounding disposal of the corpse tended to reflect local practices.

DOUGLAS J. MILLER

See BURIAL, BURIAL CUSTOMS; MOURNING.

Bibliography. R. de Vaux, *Ancient Israel*, pp 56–61; A. Edersheim, *Sketches of Jewish Social Life*, pp 161–81; A. Van Deursen, *Illustrated Dictionary of Bible Manners and Customs*.

Furlong. Linear measure of about 202 yards.

See WEIGHTS AND MEASURES.

Furnace. Brick or stone structure varying in size and shape, depending on whether it was to be used domestically or commercially. A typical furnace consisted of a firebox, a flue, a chamber for the material to be heated, and an opening to give the refiner access from the outside. Common uses of the furnace were to smelt ore, melt ore for casting, heat ore for forging, fire ceramic materials, fire bricks, and make lime.

Various types of furnaces are mentioned in Scripture. The potter's kiln was used to make lime and to fire and glaze pottery (Gn 19:28; Ex 9:8,10; 19:18). It was commonly made of limestone, was dome-shaped, had a chimney for smoke to escape, and a hole at the bottom for fuel. Such a furnace emitted a thick, dark column of smoke.

Larger furnaces used for smelting ore were seldom employed by the Hebrews, except possibly in the time of King Solomon. The Hebrews, however, knew of this type of furnace, probably from its extensive use in Lebanon. Most OT references to such furnaces are figurative (Dt 4:20; 1 Kgs 8:51; Prv 17:3; 27:21; Is 48:10; Jer 11:4; Ez 22:18,20,22). This kind of large, ore-smelting furnace is central in the story of Shadrach, Meshach, and Abednego, the three Jewish men whom King Nebuchadnezzar threw into the fiery furnace for refusing to bow down and worship his golden idol (Dn 3).

A small, household oven for baking bread (Gn 15:17; Neh 3:11; 12:38; Is 31:9) was a necessary item in biblical times; baking as a commercial trade was a later development.

The most common use of "furnace" in the Bible is to describe figuratively God's discipline or punishment, and his refining of character (Dt 4:20; 1 Kgs 8:51; Is 48:10; Jer 6:27–30; Ez 22:17–22). The NT preserves the Hebrew distinction between the furnace (Mt 13:42,50; Rv 1:15; 9:2) and the oven (Mt 6:30; Lk 12:28). Furnace is used as a symbol for hell (Mt 13:42,50; Rv 9:21). The refining image is used to refer to the trials of life which prepare a person for life after death (Jas 1:12; 1 Pt 1:7). In John's vision, the one who is like the Son of man has "feet like unto fine brass, as if they burned in a furnace" (Rv 1:15 KJV). This reference to refined brass, an extremely hard metal, is symbolic of Christ's power to conquer his enemies.

WAYNE C. HENSLEY

See HOMES AND DWELLINGS; INDUSTRY AND COMMERCE.

Furnaces, Tower of the. KJV rendering of Tower of the Ovens in Nehemiah 3:11 and 12:38.

See OVENS, TOWER OF THE.

Furniture. Items of material culture used in homes, palaces, and temples. Because of the close geographical proximity to other nations, Israel had extensive contact with neighboring cultures. Historical surveys document parallels between the furniture of Israel and that of other tribes and countries.

Sources: Archaeology and the Bible. Archaeological investigations provide the most specific cultural information. Sometimes items of furniture are discovered in graves and tombs; notable examples have come from Egypt and Mesopotamia. Particularly in Egypt, murals or stone bas-reliefs adorning tomb walls provide information. Similar data are often obtained from scenes painted on Greek pottery. Items of cultic furniture occur in excavated temples. Terra-cotta models of furniture items have been discovered in various lands. There are numerous references to household tables, beds, couches, chairs, stools, and such, as well as more uncommon items used in shrines and temples. As a result, knowledge of Egyptian, Greek, and Roman furniture is quite extensive.

The Bible refers to beds, stools, reclining couches, tables, curtains, ivory (inlay), and lamps in the domestic scene. The furniture of the tabernacle is described in some detail in the Book of Exodus. The Israelite kings' palaces included thrones, footstools, tables, curtains, and more.

Egypt. Egypt had many cultural contacts with the people of Palestine over the centuries, reaching Israel to the north by caravan and shipping routes. Thus it is possible that Egyptian furniture styles influenced the furniture craft in Palestine.

Archaeologists have found an Egyptian bed from the 1st dynasty (c. 3000 BC). Soft linen strings, closely plaited and lashed to the low wooden frame, form a mattress—a common style for Egyptian beds in all periods. A more elaborate bedroom set, including a chair and canopy overlaid with gold, came from a tomb at Giza of the 4th dynasty (c. 2600 BC) Queen Hetepheres. The original bed with its silver headrest and detachable footboard of inlaid faience can be seen in the Egyptian Museum today. Some of the finest examples of beds come from the tomb of Pharaoh Tutankhamen who lived late in the New Kingdom period (c. 1552–1306 BC). The beds of this period had frames that curved up at the head and were furnished with a high footboard. The legs of these beds were generally elaborately carved—a characteristic of furniture in wealthy Egyptian households.

There are many examples of chairs and thrones of royalty and nobility, although little is known about chairs in other economic levels. Perhaps the earliest example of an Egyptian chair is a representation from Hierakonpolis of two seated figures which dates to about 3000 BC. Another early picture shows the 1st dynasty (c. 3100 BC) King Narmer seated on a throne watching a dance. His throne was merely a stone block hollowed out for a seat with no back or arms. Chairs came into use for the nobility after the time of Zoser, a ruler of the 3rd dynasty during the pyramid age (c 1600 BC), These were constructed of wood with a cushion resting on a plaited leather seat. Later, arms and backs were added, and the carved legs resembled those of animals.

Ornate footstools were often used by royalty. The symbolic representation of crushing one's foes beneath one's feet was common in Near Eastern art and literature (cf. Ps 110:1). Less elaborate stools standing about a foot high with square legs and plaited leather seats were used by other citizens.

In ancient Egypt, tables were evidently not used. Where food is shown in reliefs and paintings the "table" is merely a tray and stand. In the Old Kingdom period (c. 2900–2200 BC) wooden stands holding water jars and wine jars were placed at household entrances or in gardens with other stands for food beside them. Bas-reliefs and paintings also depict ornate boxes for storing cloths and household objects.

With the advent of the Middle Kingdom (c. 2100–1700 BC), furniture usage seems to have increased so that less affluent people had beds, chairs, stools, and tables.

The 18th dynasty period (*c.* 1552–1306 BC) evidenced a degree of luxury in many homes. Patterns established during that period continued during the centuries that followed.

Mesopotamia. Contact between Palestine and lands to the east was longstanding. The first Hebrew tribes came from Mesopotamia (later the nations of Assyria and Babylonia). Assyria had a profound political effect on the Jewish people during the Babylonian exile (see 2 Kgs 25) and postexilic times. Such contacts may well have introduced new ideas about furniture into Palestine.

Beds, stools, chairs, and boxes were the main items of furniture in ancient Mesopotamia as evidenced by bas-reliefs. Their construction resembled Egyptian furniture but was heavier and lacked the curves which distinguish Egyptian patterns. Ornamentation was applied in thin strips of bronze, bone, or ivory. Metal studs and rings were characteristic decorations.

Since most soil conditions in Mesopotamia do not preserve wooden objects, the furniture of lower economic classes has disappeared, leaving a somewhat distorted impression since only the wealthy could afford to have bas-reliefs made depicting their way of life.

Wooden beds were evidently in common use, at least among the upper classes. The mention of beds in extant medical texts probably means they were available for patients. Some bas-reliefs depict the gods using tables for meals. Other reliefs show well-to-do citizens dining from tables. Chairs with legs, a back, and even arms were common in Assyrian palaces. Artisans' footstools appear as early as the 3rd millennium BC. In some excavated palaces, mud brick benches have been found. There were also wooden storage boxes and chests of various sizes.

Babylonian (southern Mesopotamian) furnishings are quite similar to Assyrian. Poor, and even middle-class, Babylonians may have slept on mats, rugs, or mattresses. Wealthier citizens, nobles, and rulers slept on high beds with one end built up to form a bolster.

As in Assyria, bas-reliefs show patients on sickbeds and tents of soldiers (probably officers) furnished with beds.

The Babylonians sat on stools made of palm wood or on a kind of armchair with a deeply curved back of plaited reeds. Chests and boxes completed the household furniture.

It has been conjectured that Mesopotamian styles influenced features of later furniture in both Asia and Europe. Those features include heavily turned furniture legs, fringes on furniture covers, couches for reclining while eating or conversing, small tables to hold food, and low chairs on which servants or musicians sat to entertain and attend reclining superiors. The recognized conventions about who might recline and who might sit persisted through classical times, the Middle Ages, and still exist in some forms today.

Palestine in OT Times. OT passages supply most of the information about furniture in ancient Palestine, although there are also significant archaeological data. There are many references to beds in the OT, using at least three Hebrew nouns. Jacob is pictured as sitting up in bed (Gn 48:2) and as dying on his bed (49:33). Moses threatened that frogs would invade the bedroom and bed of the Egyptian pharaoh (Ex 8:3). Michal, Saul's daughter, placed an effigy in David's bed (1 Sm 19:11–17) when Saul sent messengers to capture him there (vv 15,16). King David condemned the practice of killing a defenseless person sleeping in bed (2 Sm 4:7,11). The prophet Elijah laid a dead boy on his bed and revived him (1 Kgs 17:19).

King Ahab sulked on his bed (1 Kgs 21:4), and King Ahaziah lay on his sick bed (2 Kgs 1:4,6,16). The prophet Amos criticized the rich who lay on beds of ivory and stretched out on their couches (Am 6:4). The prophet Ezekiel spoke symbolically of disobedient Jerusalem as a prostitute sitting on a stately couch with the Lord's incense and oil on a table nearby (Ez 23:41). Isaiah promised that the righteous would rest in their beds (Is 57:2) and also spoke of the unrighteous setting their beds among false worshipers (vv 7,8). The psalmist flooded his bed with tears (Ps 6:6), and Proverbs refers to a sluggard on his bed (26:14).

"Table" in the OT refers both to the temple table for the bread of the Presence and to the table used in the palace or home for meals or banquets. King Adoni-bezek had his captives scrambling for scraps under his table (Jgs 1:7). David absented himself from Saul's table (1 Sm 20:29). Saul's son Jonathan showed his anger by leaving his father's table (v 34). Jonathan's disabled son Mephibosheth was allowed to sit at David's table (2 Sm 9:7,10–13; 19:28). Solomon's table is described several times (1 Kgs 2:7; 4:27). The Queen of Sheba was particularly impressed by the food and table service in Solomon's palace (10:5). The prophets frequently refer to tables (Is 21:5; 28:8; 65:11; Ez 40:39–43).

The few references to chairs describe people reclining at meals and indicate couches rather than actual chairs (Am 6:4). There are numerous mentions of thrones, including those of (1) the pharaoh (Gn 41:40; Ex 11:5), (2) David (2 Sm 3:10; 7:13), (3) Solomon (1 Kgs 10:18), (4) the kings of Israel and Judah (1 Kgs 22:10), and (5) God (1 Kgs 22:19; Pss 9:4,7; 11:4;

93:2). The OT writers sometimes indicate thrones decorated with ivory (1 Kgs 10:18).

The exact character of furniture in Palestine is difficult to determine. Bas-reliefs and wall paintings are more common among Israel's neighbors. Excavations in Jericho, however, have unearthed some valuable archaeological clues. Tombs of the Middle Bronze Age produced reasonably well-preserved tables, stools, and boxes, making possible a study of ancient joinery methods. A variety of small trinket boxes show evidence of bone inlay and incised decoration. Some large slabs of timber may have been beds. Although primarily Canaanite styles, the furniture reflects the household furniture used in Israel in the centuries to follow.

Greece. Historians are more informed about Greek furniture because of the abundance of decorated vases, bas-reliefs, bronze and terra-cotta statuettes, and literary descriptions. That archaeological evidence indicates that Greek furniture was influenced by preceding civilizations. The picture is generally one of comparative simplicity, far removed from the cluttered and crowded rooms of later civilizations.

The Greeks made several types of seats: (1) the throne, often with a back, legs of various shapes, and armrests, (2) the lighter curved-back chair with arm supports, (3) the four-legged stool, (4) the folding stool with crossed legs traceable to Egyptian models, (5) and the bench. Representations which regularly appear on monuments dating from the 8th to the 2nd century BC link Greek chairs to Egyptian and Assyrian prototypes.

Greeks used couches for sleeping and for reclining at meals. Footstools were used to rest the feet or as a step up to higher couches. Like chair legs, couch legs varied in style. Some were carved in the shape of animal legs, some were turned, some were rectangular. From about the 6th century BC, the legs projected above the frame. Such projections later became headboards and bootboards. In Hellenistic times these headrests and footrests were carved and carried bronze medallions in high relief depicting children, satyrs, and animals. Turned legs replaced the rectangular ones. Couches were normally in wood, although bronze and marble couches are known.

Tables were used during meals to hold dishes and food and were removed after the meal. They were made of wood, bronze, and marble and normally had four legs, but three-legged tables were occasionally used.

Chests, large and small, served to store clothes, jewelry, and other articles. They were normally of wood, although some were bronze.

A carbonized bed found at Herculaneum and typical of those in use in Herculaneum and Pompeii in the 1st century AD.

Rome. Roman furniture continued many Greek patterns. The eruption of the volcano Vesuvius in AD 79 preserved actual pieces of Roman furniture in its lava flow.

Chairs with backs were heavier than their Greek counterparts and widely used. There were several types of stools: the folding stool, mostly wooden though sometimes metal; and a newly developed decorative stool often of bronze which was supported by four curved legs ornamented with scrolls.

A variety of couches were in use. Some followed Greek models, but others were a Roman invention. Excellent examples of bronze bed frames have been preserved. Presumably, interlaced strips of leather or cords were stretched crisscross on the frame. Gold, silver, tortoiseshell, bone, and ivory decoration were used along with veneer work in rare timber. Later, couches in Italy and in other lands had high backs and sides. The Romans seem to have used tables more widely than Greeks. They appear often as permanent supports for vases and other possessions. Tables were normally rectangular with four legs, but table-makers also constructed some with three legs, or even resting on a single support. Round table tops and legs of animals became popular from the 4th century BC on. Plain, undecorated wooden tables and benches were used in kitchens and workshops. Outdoor tables were usually of marble with carved animal legs or decorative figures of animals and monsters.

There were various chests and boxes in daily use. Shelves and cupboards became much more popular than in Greek times.

Palestine in NT Times. The nature of furniture in the NT is probably best understood in relation to contemporaneous Roman models. The NT refers to beds in several passages. People brought a paralytic lying on his bed to Jesus (Mt 9:2,6; Lk 5:18). When the apostles went into Solomon's portico, people brought the sick to them on beds (Acts 5:15). A Syrophoenician woman's sick child lay on a bed (Mk 7:30). Jesus spoke of setting a lamp on a stand and not placing it under a bed (Mk 4:21;

Lk 8:16), and described what would happen to people in bed when the day of the Lord came (Lk 17:34). In another parable Jesus spoke of a needy person begging for bread at midnight from a friend who was already in bed with his family (Lk 11:7). Beds of the poor and sick were probably only pallets or mattresses (Mk 6:55; Jn 5:8). When people reclined at meals, they would have been lying on a couch (Jn 13:23).

There are numerous NT references to tables. Jesus mentioned crumbs falling from a rich man's table (Mt 15:27; Mk 7:28; Lk 16:21).

Jesus overthrew the money-changers' tables in the temple (Mt 21:12; Mk 11:15). Jesus sat with his disciples at a table for the Passover meal (Lk 22:21) and promised his disciples that they would sit at his table in God's kingdom (v 30). The apostles were relieved of serving tables in order to preach (Acts 6:2).

The household lamp is referred to a number of times (Mt 25:1; Mk 4:21). Terra-cotta domestic lamps have been found in abundance in excavations.

JOHN A. THOMPSON

See HOMES AND DWELLINGS.

Gg

Gaal. Ebed's son, who persuaded the men of Shechem to revolt against Abimelech, the judge of Israel. The revolt, however, was quickly crushed and Shechem was destroyed (Jgs 9:26–41).

Gaash. 1. Mountain about 20 miles southwest of Shechem. Joshua was buried at Timnath-serah (Timnath-heres) in the hill country of Ephraim, near Mt Gaash (Jos 24:30; Jgs 2:9).

2. Stream in the vicinity of the mountain, mentioned as the home of Hiddai, one of King David's mighty soldiers (2 Sm 23:30; 1 Chr 11:32).

Gaba. KJV spelling of the Benjamite city, Geba, in Joshua 18:24; Ezra 2:26; and Nehemiah 7:30.

See GEBA.

Gabbai. Head of a family that returned to Jerusalem with Zerubbabel after the Babylonian exile (Neh 11:8).

Gabbatha. Transliteration of an uncertain Aramaic expression, which is rendered in Greek as "paved with stones," and refers to the raised area before the palace in Jerusalem where formal sentencing by the governor occurred. Pilate seated himself on the elevated judgment seat here in order to preside over the trial of Jesus (Jn 19:13). The site today is identified by many as the basement of the Convent of Our Lady of Zion, adjacent to Herod's Tower of Antonia. A paved court measuring approximately 25,000 square feet has been excavated here.

Gabriel. One of the two angels mentioned by name in the Bible (the other is Michael). Gabriel appeared in human form to Daniel to reveal to him the meaning of a vision, to show what would transpire on the day of judgment, and to give Daniel wisdom and understanding (Dn 8:16; 9:21,22). In the NT Gabriel appeared to Zechariah the priest as he served in the temple, to announce the birth of Zechariah's son, John the Baptist (Lk 1:11–20). Six months later Gabriel appeared to Mary to announce that she would become the mother of Jesus, the long-awaited Messiah (vv 26–33). Gabriel is commonly called an archangel, but is not referred to as such in the Bible.

There is an abundance of material about Gabriel in the noncanonical writings of the Jews. In the books of Enoch he is pictured as one of the four chief angels, along with Michael, Raphael, and Uriel (1 Enoch 40:3,6). He is one of the holy angels (20:7) who looks down from heaven and is a principal intercessor (9:1; 40:6; 2 Enoch 21:3). He is to destroy the wicked (1 Enoch 9:9,10) and cast them into the furnace (54:6) and is set over all powers (40:9). Michael sits at God's right hand and Gabriel sits on the left (2 Enoch 24:1). Michael, as guardian angel of Israel (cf. Dn 12:1) and a high priest of heaven, is more occupied with affairs in heaven, but Gabriel is God's messenger who goes from heaven to execute God's will on earth.

CARL WAYNE HENSLEY

See ANGEL.

Gad (Person). 1. One of the 12 sons of Jacob (Gn 35:26; 1 Chr 2:2). He was the first of the two sons born to Jacob by Zilpah, Leah's maid. Delighted with giving Jacob another son, Leah named the boy Gad, meaning "good fortune" (30:11). Later he moved his family with Jacob to Egypt (Ex 1:4). When Jacob blessed his sons, he predicted that Gad would constantly be troubled by foreign invaders but would successfully withstand them and put them to flight (Gn 49:19). Gad became the father of 7 sons (46:16) and the founder of the Gadites (Nm 2:14), one of the 12 tribes of Israel (Dt 3:12,16).

See GAD, TRIBE OF.

2. Prophet and seer of David. He counseled David to leave Mizpah of Moab and return to the land of Judah (1 Sm 22:5). Gad communicated David's punishment for numbering the fighting men of Israel (2 Sm 24:11–14,18,19; 1 Chr 21:9–19), assisted David and Nathan in setting up the order of worship in the sanctuary (2 Chr 29:25) and later wrote an account of David's life (1 Chr 29:29).

3. Canaanite god of fortune whom the Israelites worshiped (Is 65:11).

WAYNE C. HENSLEY

See CANAANITE DEITIES AND RELIGION.

Gad, Tribe of.

Descendants of Jacob's 7th son Gad (Gn 30:11; Nm 1:24,25), and 8th largest of the 12 tribes that came out of Egypt with Moses (according to the number of warriors in Nm 1:1–3,24–25). They were cattlemen and had a reputation for being fierce in battle (32:1; Dt 33:20).

During the wilderness period, they were led by Eliasaph's son Deuel (Nm 1:14; 2:14, Reuel; 7:42; 10:20). When Israel encamped, Gad was located south of the tabernacle behind the tribes of Reuben and Simeon (2:14,15). They are mentioned at the tribal offering to the tabernacle, and after the plague, which God brought upon Israel (7:42–47; 26:15,18). Machi's son Geuel represented the tribe as one of the 12 spies sent by Moses into Canaan (13:15).

At the close of the wilderness period, Gad, Reuben, and half of Manasseh's tribe requested permission to settle east of the Jordan, for it had good pasture land (Nm 32:1,2). This was permitted on the condition that they would help in the conquest of Canaan (32:20–22; Jos 1:12–18).

During the conquest under Joshua, Gad is mentioned only at the battle of Jericho (Jos 4:12). After the cessation of conflict Gad, Reuben, and half of Manasseh settled their land east of the Jordan (cf. Nm 34:13,14; Jos 12:6; 13:8).

Gad's inheritance was between Manesseh's tribe to the north and Reuben's to the south. The Arabian desert formed its eastern border and the Jordan River its western. There seem to have been no fixed borders between the three tribes, and the whole area was often referred to as Gilead and Bashan (2 Kgs 10:33). Its land ran north to the Sea of Chinnereth (Galilee), but among the mountains it seems to go east only as far as the Jabbok River. To the south the cities of Aroer and Heshbon mark their southern limits (Dt 3:12,13; Jos 12:1–6; 13:24–28).

The history of Gad from its settlement to the captivity was closely tied with the two neighboring Hebrew tribes. Shortly after returning to their lands, the three tribes almost started a civil war by erecting a large altar (Jos 22:10–34). During the time of the judges, Gilead (including Gad) was threatened, if not occupied, by the Ammonites until they were defeated by Jephthah (Jgs 11). Some Gadites joined David at Ziklag during his exile (1 Chr 12:14,37). In the 14th year of David's reign the three tribes were formally brought together under an overseer named Jerijah (and his brothers, 26:30–32).

During the time of the divided kingdom, the tribes east of the Jordan were constantly under attack. During Jehu's reign (841–814 BC), Hazael annexed all the lands east of the Jordan, and they were later carried off into captivity by Tilgath-pileser, king of Assyria (2 Kgs 15:29; 1 Chr 5:26,27). Subsequently the Ammonites occupied Gad's land (Jer 49:1).

In the postexilic period Gad is mentioned only once—in Ezekiel's vision of the restoration of Israel (Ez 48:1,27,28,34).

In the NT Gad is mentioned only in the Book of Revelation, in the list of the seals (Rv 7:5).

See ISRAEL, HISTORY OF; GAD (PERSON) #1.

Gad, Valley of.

Translation of a Hebrew phrase in 2 Samuel 24:5, meaning literally "the river or streambed of Gad." It is rendered "in the midst of the river of Gad" (KJV), "in the middle of the valley, toward Gad" (RSV), and "the valley of Gad" (ASV). The valley of Gad was the beginning point for David's census, and the "river" or "valley" is undoubtedly the Arnon.

Gadara, Gadarenes.

City of the Decapolis and its inhabitants, mentioned only once in the better manuscripts of the NT (Mt 8:22). Jesus had crossed to the eastern side of the Sea of Galilee and healed the demoniac, Legion, whom he encountered in "the country of the Gadarenes" (Mt 8:28, KJV Gergesenes). Mark's account in 5:1 and Luke's in 8:26,37 read "Gerasenes" (KJV Gadarenes). The variant readings may be due to the fact that Gerasa was the wider geographical area of which Gadara was a chief city. Geographers conclude that the most likely location for the leap of the swine into the sea would have been a strip of steep coastline near Gergesa, a smaller, less important town of the area. This would fit another suggestion that Matthew was a native of the region and so he pinpointed the precise place, while Mark and Luke intended to point out the general lo-

Gadara, the location where, according to the vast majority of Greek manuscripts (Mk 5:1; Lk 8:26,37), Jesus sent demons from a man into a herd of swine.

cation for their Greek and Roman readers, since Gergesa was small and relatively unknown, while Gadara was a Greek city of some importance.

The name "Gadara" indicates that the city was of Semitic origin. It was located 5 to 6 miles southeast of the Sea of Galilee, and its territory included the hot springs of el Hamme, north of the Yarmuk River. The first reference to it in history was when it was captured by Antiochus III (218 BC). It was taken by the Jews under Alexander Jannaeus (103 BC), and the inhabitants were enslaved and forced to receive the Law of Moses as proselytes of justice. The city was demolished by the Jews, but when the area was reconquered by Pompey, it was rebuilt (63 BC). It became a free city under Pompey and joined the federation of Greek cities in the Transjordan known as the Decapolis. Augustus Caesar added Gadara to the territory of Herod the Great (30 BC), and at Herod's death it was annexed to Syria (4 BC). During the Jewish rebellion (AD 66–70), Vespasian took the city, and it continued to flourish for many years. It was the seat of a Christian bishopic from AD 325 until the Moslem conquest.

Gadara is identified with the modern Um Qeis on the east edge of the Jordan Valley. Although it has not been excavated, visible signs indicate that it had a circumference of two miles and that it had characteristic Greek features, including two theaters, a basilica, a temple, public baths, a colonnaded street, and an aqueduct.

WAYNE C. HENSLEY

See DECAPOLIS; GERASA, GERASENE, GERGESA, GERGESENE.

Gaddi. Man from Manasseh's tribe sent by Moses to search out the land of Canaan (Nm 13:11).

Gaddiel. Sodi's son from Zebulun's tribe, sent by Moses to search out the land of Canaan (Nm 13:10).

Gadfly. Any of a number of large flies, including the horsefly and botfly, which sting livestock. King Nebuchadnezzar is called a gadfly in the only biblical reference to this insect (Jer 46:20).

See ANIMALS (FLY).

Gadi. Father of Menahem. Menahem revolted and killed Shallum, king of Israel, placing himself on the throne as king in his stead (2 Kgs 15:14,17).

Gadite. Member of Gad's tribe (Dt 3:12,16).

See GAD (PERSON) #1; GAD, TRIBE OF.

Gaham. Son of Nahor, Abraham's brother, and his concubine Reumah (Gn 22:24).

Gahar. Ancestor of a group of temple assistants that returned to Jerusalem with Zerubbabel after the exile (Ezr 2:47; Neh 7:49).

Gaius. 1. Native of Macedonia and traveling companion of Paul during the apostle's third missionary journey. He and Aristarchus were both seized at Ephesus during the riot caused by Demetrius, the silversmith (Acts 19:29).

2. Native of Derbe in Lycaonia, who traveled with Paul from Ephesus to Macedonia (Acts 20:4). Some have identified him with #1 above.

3. Prominent believer in Rome and host to Paul and the whole church there (Rom 16:23).

4. One of two Corinthians whom Paul personally baptized (1 Cor 1:14). Since Romans was written in Corinth, this Gaius has been equated with #3 above.

5. Man to whom John addressed his third letter (3 Jn 1).

Galal. 1. Levite and Mica's son, who returned from exile in Babylon (1 Chr 9:15).

2. Levite and forefather of Obadiah (Abda). Obadiah returned from exile in Babylon (1 Chr 9:16; Neh 11:17).

Galatia. Ancient kingdom resulting from migrations of Gallic people from the west and settlement on the central plain of Asia Minor. An earlier migratory movement resulted in the sack of Rome by the Gauls (or Celts) in 390 BC, but in a later attempt to overrun Greece the Gallic invaders were repulsed. That unsuccessful invasion into Greece led the Gauls to turn their attention to Asia Minor. They penetrated the larger part of the area but were defeated by Attalus I in 230 BC. As a result they became restricted to that part of Asia later known as Galatia. By that time, the Gauls consisted of three tribes, the Trocmi, Tolistobogii, and Tectosages, which settled into the towns of Tavium, Pessinus, and Ancyra, respectively. In 189 BC these Galatians were subdued by Romans but were allowed to govern themselves.

After the death of Amyntas in 25 BC Galatia became a Roman province. Within its boundaries were the ethnic areas of Galatia proper, Lycaonia, Isauria, and part of Phrygia and Pisidia. The new province, therefore, included the towns of Derbe, Lystra, Iconium, and Pisidian Antioch, all of which the apostle Paul visited on his first missionary journey. The term "Galatia" was used in two different ways, one to describe the area occupied by the Gauls in the north, and the other to describe the whole Roman province, including the southern towns. That ambiguity has given rise to a problem over the destination of Paul's letter to the Galatians.

The original inhabitants of north Galatia were Phrygians, many of whom still remained in the 1st century AD, together with some Greeks and a fairly large community of Jews. Although the area was cosmopolitan, the Celtic element predominated. These people were known for their sturdy independence, but also for their drunkenness and revelings. They were of an inquisitive disposition and were easily impressed with new ideas, particularly of a religious kind. They were nevertheless easily turned aside and had a reputation for fickleness. In religious matters there is evidence that they were highly superstitious and were especially attracted to the wild rites of the goddess Cybele. It is not difficult to imagine the impact the Christian gospel may have made on a people of such temperament. Paul's letter to the Galatians reflects several of the traits of the Gallic peoples.

In towns of the southern region, Greek influence was more pronounced, especially among the more educated members of the communities. But the Phrygian element was still strong among the humbler inhabitants. They too were predominately devotees of Cybele, although there the cult had become modified by Greek influences. In Pisidian Antioch, for instance, the goddess was known as the Genius of Antioch, while in Iconium she was known as Athena Polias.

Geographically the northern towns, situated on a well-watered plateau and served by a major road from the Aegean shores to the west, became prosperous centers of commerce. But access from north to south was difficult and communication poor because of the mountainous terrain leading up to the plateau. The southern towns were situated on the route between Syria and Asia. Their strategic location explains why churches were established in those towns on Paul's first missionary journey (cf. Acts 13, 14).

Galatia, linked with Phrygia, is mentioned in Acts 16:6 and 18:23, but it is not clear whether Paul ever visited or established churches in the northern area.

The only other references to Galatia in the NT are probably to the southern towns (1 Cor 16:1; 2 Tm 4:10; 1 Pt 1:1).

DONALD GUTHRIE

See GALATIANS, LETTER TO THE.

Galatians, Letter to the.

Galatians, Letter to the. This letter has an important place in the NT. It reveals much of Paul's character and sheds light on his teaching. It has appropriately been called the charter of Christian liberty.

Author. The letter gives some brief but telling glimpses of the writer's experience before he became a Christian. He mentions his former life in Judaism (1:13). The fact that he had been a thoroughly devout Jew has an important bearing on what he writes in this letter. He remembers his passionate devotion to his former faith, in whose cause he had violently persecuted the church of God. He reminds the Galatians about this, for the Jewish traditions had meant a great deal to him. There is no doubt that he had once regarded his violent opposition to the church as a religious act of the highest order. Indeed, his strong devotion to Judaism sets in clear relief the remarkable transformation which occurred when he became a Christian. A revelation from God, he is convinced, gave him special authority to write the way he does.

He mentions two features of his conversion experience which have had a profound effect on him. One is the purpose of God for his life which he recognizes as reaching back even before he was born (1:15). He does not go into detail, but he never tires of talking about the grace of God. His present position is none of his own doing. He has turned his back on the idea of earning merit through his own efforts. The second aspect of his conversion which deeply impresses him is the recognition that his call to preach can be traced to that occasion. When he preached to the Galatians he did so with divine authority because he was conscious of having received a divine commission. The apostles and elders of the church did not decide it would be a good thing for him to preach the gospel. It was God who planned it. Moreover, Paul is equally convinced that the gospel he preaches is not of his own making. He has received it through a revelation of Jesus Christ (v 12). It is in no sense a human gospel.

Why does Paul place so much emphasis on his own position? He goes to some lengths to demonstrate that he has received his apostleship from God (1:1). He is conscious not only of a call to preach but also of a call to exercise apostolic authority on an equal footing with the Jerusalem apostles. He certainly seems to be on the defensive, but this is prompted by the special situation that had arisen among the Galatians and that caused this letter to be written.

Paul gives one biographical detail in this letter which is not mentioned in his other letters. He states that after his conversion he went away into Arabia (1:17). The apostle does not tell us what he did there, but probably he was quietly reorientating his thoughts. According to the Book of Acts, when he returned to Damascus he powerfully proved that Jesus was the Messiah (Acts 9:22). He also refers to traveling in Syria and Cilicia (Gal 1:21), which must have been prior to his first missionary journey.

Date and Destination. It is impossible to determine the date of this letter before discussing its destination.

The Destination. Paul addresses his letter to the Galatians; but there has been much debate over where they lived, because the term "Galatia" was used in two different senses. It was used of the province which stretched from the borders of Pamphylia in the southern part of Asia Minor to the borders of Pontus toward the northern sea coast. The term was also used of a part of the province in the north where a group of people from Gaul had settled and given their name to the whole area. Hence "Galatia" could mean either the geographical area in the north or the whole province. It is not easy to decide what the term meant when used by Paul. The debate is between the view that the term was used geographically, in which case some churches in the north are in mind (North Galatian Theory), or politically, in which case Paul may be referring to the churches in southern Galatia founded on his first missionary journey (South Galatian Theory). It may at first sight seem a quite unimportant issue, but since the decision affects the date of the letter and to some extent its occasion and purpose, a brief glance at the lines of evidence on both sides must be made.

Until the beginning of the 20th century no one seems to have questioned that Paul was writing to the inhabitants of the geographical district in the northern part of the province. This view agrees with the oldest use of the term, since the province did not come into existence until 25 BC, whereas there were Galatians in the north some time before this. It is reasonable to suppose that the southerners would not have taken too kindly to being addressed as "Galatians." It may be argued that most people in those days would have thought of the northern peoples when hearing the name.

Luke's habit when writing Acts was to use geographical rather than political descriptions of places. He refers, for instance, to Lystra and Derbe as cities of Lycaonia, not as cities of Galatia. It is reasonable, therefore, that when he refers to Phrygia and Galatia in Acts 16:6 and 18:23, he means that Paul went through the northern area. There were three main towns in that district, Ancyra, Tavium, and Pessinus, and it would therefore follow that Paul must have established churches there. Nevertheless the evidence is not quite as straightforward as it seems, for Luke sometimes uses political terms when referring to Paul's movements, as when he says that the Spirit would not allow Paul and Silas to go into Asia or Bithynia (Acts 16:6,7). Since this is in the same context as the reference to Galatia, some caution is needed before reaching conclusions.

The map shows that if Asia and Bithynia were closed to the missionaries, it would have been quite natural for them to go to the north of Galatia, although this would be something of a detour. It would be more convincing if we had other evidence of churches having been established in that area.

Another point often made is the reputation of the Gallic people for being fickle and the possibility that this would explain why they had so quickly turned aside from the gospel Paul had preached to them (cf. 1:6). This is an interesting point, but it cannot be shown that this would not equally apply to the people of the southern area.

This traditional North Galatian view has been challenged. It is pointed out that although Luke prefers geographical descriptions, Paul prefers political ones for grouping his churches. In this letter he mentions the churches of Christ in Judea (1:22). Elsewhere he mentions the "churches of Asia" (1 Cor 16:19). Several times Paul refers to the believers in Macedonia (e.g., 2 Cor 8:1; 9:2; 1 Thes 4:10) and in Achaia (1 Cor 16:15; 2 Cor 1:1), while both are mentioned together in Romans 15:26; 2 Corinthians 9:2 and 1 Thessalonians 1:7. This seems to be Paul's normal habit, in which case a letter addressed to the Galatians would be circulated to all the existing churches in the province of Galatia.

South Galatian supporters do not agree that the southern people would not have resented the name "Galatians," maintaining that there would have been no other name available with which to describe them. One fairly positive piece of evidence is found in Paul's statement that it was because of a bodily ailment that he first preached to the Galatians (Gal 4:13). But a glance at the map, particularly a relief map, would show that the route to the northern area was over mountainous terrain, and it is difficult to think that a sick man would have attempted it. Under the southern theory the journey would have been much shorter and less arduous.

Another argument in support of the South Galatian Theory assumes that Acts 20:4, which mentions the names of those who accompanied Paul to Jerusalem, is referring to delegates appointed by the churches in support of the collection to aid the poor churches of Judea. If this assumption is right it is noticeable that no representative is included from the northern area, although both Gaius and Timothy were from the south. This would be more weighty if Acts had actually mentioned the collection.

One last point is that Barnabas is mentioned three times (2:1,9,13) suggesting that he is known to the readers. Yet according to Acts he accompanied Paul only on the first missionary journey.

It is difficult to reach a conclusion, but it seems that the arguments for the South Galatian Theory have a slight edge on those for the older theory.

Date. Under the North Galatian Theory, it is claimed that the letter was written after the events mentioned in Acts 18:23, that is, during the course of the third missionary journey, possibly while Paul was at Ephesus or soon after.

If on the other hand, the letter was addressed to the south Galatian churches founded on the first missionary journey, any date after that journey is possible, including during the third journey as mentioned above. But a further possibility opens up since a much earlier date might more readily fit into the background of the letter. In fact it is possible that this letter is among the earliest that Paul wrote.

The main problem is that in Galatians 1 and 2 Paul mentions two visits to Jerusalem (1:18; 2:1), whereas Acts mentions (or implies) three visits (Acts 9:26; 11:29,30; 15:2). It has traditionally been supposed that the second visit (2:1) can be identified with the events of Acts 15. This would mean that Paul is giving his own account of the decisions of the so-called council of Jerusalem. There is much to be said for this view. There are similarities between the two passages. In both, Barnabas is mentioned. In both, questions are asked about the circumcision of the Gentiles, and in both, Paul and Barnabas give a report about the matter to the Jerusalem leaders. The main difficulty is that Paul's wording in Galatians 2:1 suggests that this event took place on his *second* visit to Jerusalem, whereas Acts 15 relates his *third* visit. It is traditionally explained that on the second visit Paul and Barnabas had no contact with the apostles but simply handed over the collection from the Antioch church to the Jerusalem elders (cf. Acts 11:30). Another difficulty with this view is that Galatians 2 speaks only of conversations with the three leading apostles at Jerusalem and does not mention the whole church (as Acts 15 clearly does). Paul does not refer to the decision reached by the church, but only to his agreement with those he calls the "pillar" apostles. It could of course be that before the general meeting of Acts 15, Paul and Barnabas had a behind-the-scene meeting with the leaders and preferred to mention the decision reached with them rather than quote an ecclesiastical edict. This may also explain another difficulty—the lack of any mention of the prohibitions which the Jerusalem church imposed on the Gentiles (15:20). Paul simply mentions the need to remember the poor (Gal 2:10). Yet another difficulty with the traditional view is the fact that Paul mentions his dispute with Peter over the question of Gentile-Jewish fellowship (vv 11–14) *after* his account of the agreement reached with the Jerusalem apostles. This places Peter in a compromising position. It is difficult to explain his inconsistency. He may have agreed that Gentiles should not be circumcised, but then vacillated over the question of fellowship.

An alternative view suggests that when Paul and Barnabas went to Jerusalem with the collection they also had private talks with the leading apostles. Acts 11:29,30 is set in a period of political activity against the apostles (Acts 12 records the martyrdom of James and the arrest of Peter), and this may explain the private nature of the meeting. This interpretation would explain why Paul makes no mention of the church's decision because the meeting happened before the Jerusalem council. It would also make it easier to explain Peter's action at Antioch, if this was before the church as a whole had discussed and resolved the matter. According to this view Paul's Letter to the Galatians may be the earliest of his letters.

There are, however, some difficulties with this view. Acts 11:30 mentions no apostles as meeting Paul and Barnabas. Nor is there any reference to Titus, whom Paul says they took with them (Gal 2:1). Further, Paul's references to preaching among the Gentiles (v 2) would seem to require a date after the first missionary journey, unless he was thinking of his work in Antioch, a Jewish-Gentile church.

It is difficult to decide between these two views. Chronological considerations (based on Paul's mention of 14 years in 2:1) slightly favor a later date. The same may be said for doctrinal considerations, since Galatians is so closely akin to the thought of Romans, which must be dated at the end of the third missionary journey.

Purpose and Theological Teaching. Difficulties had arisen in the Galatian churches because a group of people had been insisting that Gentiles must be circumcised. These people must have been Judaizers, that is, Christian Jews who could see no hope for Gentiles unless they accepted circumcision as an initiatory rite. Linked with this was a criticism of Paul's apostolic status. The opponents were claiming the support of the Jerusalem apostles, whom they regarded as superior to Paul. This would explain why Paul sees the issue so clearly as a challenge to the gospel which he preached. His letter strongly expresses his understanding of the seriousness of the situation.

Interpretations will vary slightly according to which date one assigns to the letter. If it was written before the Jerusalem council (Acts 15), the circumcision issue had not yet been thrashed out and the Galatian situation would be the first major crisis over it. But if the Jerusalem council had already happened, the south Galatian churches would already have received those decisions (16:4), and apparently had allowed themselves to be affected by Judaizers who took a harder line than the Jerusalem apostles had. If the northern churches are indicated, there is no direct evidence to show that they had received the decrees.

We may conclude that the apostle's aim in this letter is twofold—to maintain the validity of his apostleship and the character of the gospel which he preached. In the first part of the letter he is concerned to show his relationship with the Jerusalem "pillar" apostles in order to demonstrate his equality with them, while at the same time claiming his independence of them. His apostleship was from God, not from men. Moreover, he asserts that there is only one gospel, which suggests that his opponents were charging him with preaching a different gospel. But he claims to have received his gospel from God, not from men.

In the course of his letter Paul gives expression to some important theological truths. The main body of the letter issues a strong warning against legalism that is applicable, not only to the situation Paul confronted in the Galatian churches, but wherever dependence on legal observances is considered essential for salvation. If a Gentile could not become a Christian without being circumcised, it would not only make an external rite a condition for Christian salvation, but would imply a commitment to keep the whole Jewish Law. Paul is arguing against justification by works of the Law and in doing so shows the superiority of justification by faith. The whole letter extols the doctrine of grace.

Nevertheless in contesting the doctrine of works the apostle lends no support to spiritual license. He sees clearly that the alternative to legalism is not the absence of all restraint. Although Christ has secured freedom for the believer, that freedom must not be used to indulge the flesh (5:13). Indeed, Paul's exposition of the Christian life in this letter is of a high moral order. He sets the standard himself by declaring that he has been crucified with Christ (2:20). Not only is this letter a charter for Christian liberty, but also a chart for Christian living.

Contents. *Introduction* (1:1–5). The opening to this letter is more abrupt than in Paul's other letters. He omits the usual thanksgiving and expands the usual greeting. In the first words he strongly affirms the divine origin of his apostleship.

The Opponents (1:6–10). Paul is astonished that the Galatians have allowed themselves to be influenced so quickly by those who were perverting the gospel. He expresses an anathema against any who preach another gospel.

A Defense of His Apostleship (1:11–2:14). There are several stages in Paul's argument about his own position. He states that his teaching has come from God, not from men, showing his awareness that God has not only called him to be an apostle, but has also sanctioned his gospel. It is important for him to make clear that he is not dependent on others for his position, although he proceeds to show that there is no difference between him and the leading apostles (1:11–12). He next contrasts his former zeal in Judaism with his calling to preach the gospel, again emphasizing the divine nature of his call (vv 13–17).

He then proceeds to mention that he has on two occasions had meetings with the Jerusalem apostles. As a result he has been offered the right hand of fellowship, a way of showing that there is no disagreement between them. It was agreed that Paul should be entrusted with the gospel for the uncircumcised, and that Peter should go to the circumcised. There was no questioning of Paul's apostleship. They all agreed on the Christian responsibility to remember the poor (1:18–2:10).

In order to give a tangible example of his apostolic position, Paul mentions the occasion of his public rebuke of Peter. Peter had acted inconsistently for fear of certain men who had come from James in Jerusalem, and who were representatives of the circumcision party. Paul's challenge to Peter sets the scene for the introduction of the doctrinal part of the letter (2:11–14).

A Defense of the Gospel (2:15–4:31). Paul at once introduces the issue of justification by works of the Law and contrasts it with justification by faith. He sees the whole situation as a choice between Christ and the Law (2:15–21).

His aim is to show the superiority of Christianity over Judaism in the matter of salvation. He notes first that the Galatians had become Christians through the Spirit and wonders what is possessing them to want to return to the works of the Law, which Paul then equates with the "flesh" (3:1–5).

Abraham is brought into the discussion presumably because the opponents were maintaining that only Abraham's seed would receive the inheritance, and circumcision was regarded as an indispensable sign of a son of the covenant. But Paul points out that even Abraham was justified by faith, not by the law (3:6–9).

Indeed, the Law could only bring a curse on those who disobeyed. This leads Paul to show how Christ had become a curse for us. Hence he claims that in Christ we may still inherit the blessing promised to Abraham (3:10–14).

Paul anticipates that some may say it is invalid to appeal to the promise to Abraham to counteract justification by works of the Law. He shows that the promise preceded the Law by four centuries and cannot be invalidated by it (3:15–18).

This leads the apostle to reflect on the function of the Law. He points out that it served to prepare the way for Christ by showing mankind's need and by revealing its own inability to give life. Paul calls the Law our custodian, thinking in terms of the person whose function it was to guard and guide a son until he reached the age of independence (3:19–29).

The contrast between those under a guardian and fully independent sons causes Paul to reflect on the superior position of sons. The Spirit of God has enabled believers to call God "Abba" (Father), something the Law could not do (4:1–7).

The apostle has made his point, but he supports it with a personal appeal. He reminds his readers of their state of bondage before they became Christians and deplores that they have returned to such a state in wanting to observe ritual feast days after the Jewish manner. He also reminds them of the former affectionate relationship they had with him when they first became Christians. He is deeply affected by their present attitude (4:8–20).

Paul appeals to a scriptural allegory in support of his argument. He sees Isaac and Ishmael, both sons of Abraham, as representing the distinction between sonship and slavery, which he has already mentioned (4:21–31).

Practical Advice (5:1–6:10). Paul proceeds to draw out the practical consequences of his doctrinal arguments. He sets out the way in which those who are liberated in Christ should live. They should not commit themselves to Judaism by submitting to circumcision (5:1–6). Paul again attacks those who were leading the Galatians astray (5:7–12). The new principle which must replace legalism is love. Love is possible only by living in the Spirit. This will lead not only to a rejection of the works of the flesh, but to the development of the fruit of the Spirit (5:13–26). The spiritual man will have a concern for the burdened and will seek to help others, particularly fellow Christians (6:1–10).

Conclusion (6:11–18). Paul now takes the pen and writes his final word with his own hand. He sees fit to contrast his own aim in glorying in the cross of Christ with his opponents' aim to glory in the flesh.

There are no greetings at the end of this letter, only a request that no one should bother him further.

DONALD GUTHRIE

See PAUL, THE APOSTLE; JUDAIZERS; GALATIA; LAW, BIBLICAL CONCEPT OF.

Bibliography. H.D. Betz, *Galatians*; F.F. Bruce, *Commentary on Galatians*; E.D. Burton, *A Critical and Exegetical Commentary on the Epistle to the Galatians*; R.G. Gromacki, *Stand Fast in Liberty*; D. Guthrie, *Galatians*; J.B. Lightfoot, *St. Paul's Epistle to the Galatians*.

Galbanum. One of the ingredients used to make a special perfume for the tabernacle (Ex 30:34). Galbanum comes from a waxy, brownish gum excreted from the lower part of a plant that is a member of the carrot or parsley family and native to Syria and Persia. It is a tall herb which bears small, greenish-white flowers and fruit at the stem tip in bunches or clusters. Its leaves are compound and divided into many fine parts like the leaves of parsley or carrot. An incision made in the stem a few inches above soil level yields a milky sap that hardens. Galbanum is presently used as an antispasmodic and in the manufacture of varnish.

Galbanum is mentioned in the apocryphal book of Ecclesiasticus as having a pleasant odor (24:15). Although galbanum is not an agreeable perfume when used alone, it was evidently mixed with other substances to yield a fragrant ointment.

See PLANTS.

The Horns of Hittin, the traditional site of the Sermon on the Mount. The twin peaks were on the road from Tiberias (on the Sea of Galilee) to Cana and Nazareth.

Galeed. Name meaning literally "a heap of witness." Jacob gave this name to a pile of stones erected as a witness to the pact of friendship made between himself and his father-in-law, Laban, who named the cairn Jegar-sahadutha (Gn 31:47,48). Its location is unknown. The name Galeed is not to be confused with the name Gilead, designation of the territory east of the Jordan.

Galilee, Galileans. Area in northern Palestine which, in Israel's earlier history, had boundaries which were not clearly defined but which became more precisely defined in the period of Roman rule. The English name "Galilee" comes from two Hebrew words meaning "circuit" or "district."

Historical Background. In OT times Galilee was not significant in Israelite life, but in NT times it was a prominent Jewish population center. Galilee is first mentioned in the Bible as the location of Kedesh, a city of refuge in the hill country of Naphtali (Jos 20:7; cf. 21:32; 1 Chr 6:76).

Galilee originally designated the area occupied by the tribes of Naphtali, Zebulun (Is 9:1), and possibly Asher (if Cabul in Jos 19:27 is the same city as in 1 Kgs 9:11–13). None of those tribes was able to completely expel the original Canaanite inhabitants (Jgs 1:30–33; 4:2), and as a result Galilee tended to be racially intermixed. The cities that King Solomon gave to Hiram, gentile king of Tyre, were within Galilee (1 Kgs 9:11), and the gentile intermixture in that area may have influenced Solomon's choice of those cities for a gift. This racially mixed condition is also the probable basis for the designation in Isaiah 9:1, "Galilee of the nations" (cf. 1 Mc 5:15; Mt 4:15).

During the monarchy, Galilee was a buffer zone between Israel and Syria, and it bore the brunt of Syrian invasions against Israel. This fact is cited by the prophet Isaiah (Is 9:1), but he saw it as the prelude to a brighter day when the messianic king would reign. Galilee was conquered by Syrian King Ben-hadad (1 Kgs 15:20) and was probably recovered by Israel's King Ahab. Galilee was later subjugated by the Aramaeans under Hazael (2 Kgs 10:32; 12:18; 13:22) and regained by Jeroboam II (2 Kgs 14:23–25). As a result of Assyrian conquests in the area of Damascus and Galilee in 732 BC by Tiglath-pileser III (15:29), more Gentiles were imported into the area while many of the Jewish inhabitants were deported. This naturally led to greater gentile influence and domination in Galilee. Under the successive influence of Babylonia, Persia, Greece, and Syria, Galilee was constantly experiencing infiltration and migration. From the time of the Assyrian conquest of Israel to about the end of the 2nd century BC, Galilee's population was dominated by Gentiles, with only a few Jews.

The Jews remaining in Galilee were brought to Judea by Simon Maccabeus in 164 BC (1 Mc 5:21–23). Galilee was conquered by Aristobulus I (104–103 BC), who forced the inhabitants to be circumcised and to submit to Jewish laws, a work that probably already had been initiated by John Hyrcanus (134–104 BC).

Herod the Great (ruler under Rome, 37–4 BC) affixed Galilee to his kingdom, and more Jews were attracted there. Josephus recorded that Galilee had 240 cities and villages and 100,000 men available to fight against the Romans. After the death of Herod the Great, Galilee was included in the tetrarchy of Herod Antipas (4 BC–AD 39). With the banishment of Herod Antipas in AD 39, Galilee was added to the territory of Herod Agrippa I who ruled it until he died in AD 44. Rome directly administered Galilee until it was put under the rule of

Herod Agrippa II. By siding with the Romans during the Jewish revolts, he was able to retain his position until AD 100. In spite of the Galileans' attempt to gain independence, the revolutionary faction was brought under subjection by Vespasian in AD 67. After Herod Agrippa II's death, Galilee became part of the Roman province of Syria.

Following the fall of Jerusalem in AD 70, the Sanhedrin and many other Jews of southern Palestine flocked to Galilee. As a result, such cities as Tiberias and Sepphoris became Jewish, and the dispersed Jews came to think of Galilee as their center. Tiberias became a center for Jewish learning, and it was there that such major contributions as the Tiberian system of vowel pointing the Hebrew consonantal text were made, as well as the formulation of the Mishnah and the Palestinian Talmud.

From about AD 451 until the Muslim rule over Galilee began in the 7th century, Galilee was governed by the Christian patriarchate of Jerusalem, set up by the Council of Chalcedon in AD 451. Muslim rule from the 7th century on was continuous except for the intervals caused by the 12th century Crusades and World War I. All of Galilee has been included in the modern state of Israel since its establishment in 1948.

Boundaries. Galilee was bounded on the east by the upper Jordan River and the Sea of Galilee and on the south by the plain of Esdraelon, which served as a natural boundary between Galilee and Samaria. At times the plain was included in Galilee as it was during the intertestamental period (1 Mc 10:30; 12:47,49). While the northern boundary was uncertain and variable during Galilee's history, in NT times it reached to Lake Huleh. The western boundary followed along the Mediterranean Sea to Mt Carmel.

From the time of the divided kingdom until the Assyrian conquest of Galilee (734 BC), it was the northernmost part of the kingdom of Israel. The area was divided into upper Galilee and lower Galilee by the Plain of Ramah which ran between Capernaum and Ptolemais (cf. Jth 1:8; 1 Mc 12:49; and Josephus *Wars*, 3.3.1). In the Mishna (compilation of early rabbinical interpretation of the Law) Galilee is divided into 3 parts corresponding to the natural divisions of plain, hill country, and mountain. Under Roman rule, Galilee was about 25 to 30 miles from east to west and about 35 to 40 miles from north to south.

Geography. The attractive Galilean landscape is made up of volcanic limestone hills and alluvial fertile plains. Its climate is cooler than any other part of Palestine, and its beauty and fertility contrast sharply with the sunbaked, barren hills of southern Palestine.

The physical features range from the high mountains in the north to the plain of Esdraelon in the south. Mt Tabor is prominent on the east while Mt Carmel stands out on the west. Much of upper Galilee is 3000 feet above sea level, and in NT times it was largely forested and less densely inhabited than lower Galilee. Lower Galilee starts at 1500 to 2000 feet above sea level and descends sharply to the Sea of Galilee more than 600 feet below sea level.

Besides the average annual rainfall of 25 inches, Galilee is watered by the streams that flow from springs in the hills and are the main sources of the beautiful Kishon River at Janin, and the headwaters of the Jordan River, the largest river in Palestine. The ground is also moistened by heavy dews resulting from climatic conditions created by the Lebanon mountain range to the north.

Cities. Among the more notable cities in Galilee's early history were Kedesh-Naphtali, a city of refuge (Jos 20:7; 21:32; 1 Chr 6:76), and Hazor, about 10 miles north of the Sea of Galilee (Jos 11:10; 1 Kgs 9:15). During the time of Christ, Chorazin (Mt 11:21) and Capernaum (4:13; 11:23) were prominent cities located in the northeast near the Sea of Galilee. Capernaum seems to have been a center for Jesus' ministry in the area (Mt 4:13; Mk 2:1; 9:33; etc.). Nazareth is especially significant as the city of Christ's childhood (Mt 2:22,23; Lk 2:39; 4:16; etc.). Nain (Lk 7:11–17), located on the north edge of the mountain now called Little Hermon, and Cana of Galilee (Jn 2:1–11) also figured prominently in Christ's ministry. Sepphoris and Tiberias were important cities during Roman administration.

Roads and Travel. Many roads traversed Galilee, and those in NT times were superior due to Roman construction and maintenance.

Seats along the wall of the synagogue at Chorazin, one of the cities that Jesus upbraided (Mt 11:20–21).

Among the best known trade routes was the Via Maris (the Way of the Sea) which ran through Galilee on its way from Damascus to Egypt. Another main road ran from Tiberias near the Sea of Galilee to Acco (Ptolemais), a port on the Phoenician coast. Major caravan routes also connected Galilee with the markets of the East. The area was tied together by a network of spurs and connecting roads that branched from the main highways.

Inhabitants. The occupants of Galilee were basically Jewish in religious and patriotic orientation, but they were composed of various ethnic elements. The influence of this mixture was sufficient to cause recognizable differences in speech from that of southern Palestine (cf. Mt 26:69,73). The Galileans absorbed more Greek and Roman influences than did the Judean Jews. The racial mixture, differences in speech, and location caused Judean Jews to view Galilee and its inhabitants with contempt (Jn 1:46; 7:41,52).

Lower Galilee was densely settled with villages, and in NT times the population was probably about three million. The fertility of the soil and resultant fruitfulness of the country produced a prosperous Jewish populace, particularly in the centuries immediately after the time of Christ.

Government. Galilee was under the Roman rule of emperors Augustus and Tiberius during the time of Christ. Roman fortifications throughout Galilee were a constant reminder of the presence and influence of the Roman Empire. During Christ's ministry Rome installed the tetrarch, Herod Antipas (Mt 14:1; Lk 23:5-7) to rule the territory. He was appointed to office when 17 years old. Sepphoris was his first capital, and about AD 22 he built Tiberias on the shore of the Sea of Galilee as his new capital, in honor of the emperor.

Products. Abundant crops enabled Galilee to provide produce for the neighboring Phoenician cities of Tyre and Sidon around the middle of the 1st century AD. Main crops included grapes, pomegranates, olives, and grains. Fishing in the Sea of Galilee was a prominent business in NT times (Mk 1:14-20).

Jesus and Galilee. Jesus was raised in Galilee (Lk 4:16), and 11 of his 12 disciples were from there (Judas was the only Judean).

The culture, commerce, farming, and fishing business of the area formed the background for much of Jesus' ministry, as his parables show (Mt 20:1-8; 21:33; Mk 4:3; Lk 13:6-9). The first three Gospels are largely occupied with Christ's ministry in Galilee with much of it being spent around the Sea of Galilee. Most of his parables (19 of 32) were spoken here and the vast majority of his miracles (25

of 33) were performed in Galilee. Jesus received his greatest response in this region. The Sermon on the Mount was spoken in Galilee, and one of its mountains was the scene of the Lord's transfiguration. Many of the women who followed Christ and ministered to him also came from here (Mt 27:55). Two of Christ's most significant postresurrection appearances took place in Galilee (Mt 28:16-20; Jn 21:1-23), and one of Christ's own titles, Jesus of Nazareth (Jn 1:45), identified him as a Galilean.

HENRY W. HOLLOMAN

See PALESTINE; GALILEE, SEA OF.

Galilee, Sea of. Perhaps the most familiar body of water in the Near East to the readers of the Gospels. It has had many names in its history. In the OT the Sea of Galilee was known as the Sea of Chinnereth (Nm 34:11), named for the town (Jos 19:35), or as Chinneroth (12:3). Later the name was changed to Lake of Gennesaret because the city of Gennesaret was located on the site of Chinnereth or Tell Ureime (Lk 5:1; 1 Mc 11:67). The most familiar name (the Sea of Galilee) was due to its connection with the province of Galilee to the west (Mt 4:18). It derived the name Sea of Tiberias (Jn 6:1,23; 21:1) from the town of Tiberias on its southwestern shore. About AD 26 Herod Antipas, son of Herod the Great, built the town near the warm springs of Hamath by the sea and named it for the emperor. In the Gospels "the sea" usually identifies the Sea of Galilee. Its modern Hebrew name is Yam Kinneret.

Location. The sea lies in the lower section of the Jordan Valley about 60 miles north of Jerusalem, located in a range of mountains. The mountains of Upper Galilee are northwest of the lake and rise to a height of 4000 feet above sea level, while the mountains on the east and west ascend about 2000 feet. On the west, south, and east is the Decapolis.

At the northwest corner of the lake the mountain wall flattens into the rich plain of Gennesaret, and on the east at 2000 feet above sea level it gives way to the fertile El Batila in the northeast, where the Jordan enters the sea. At the time of the NT the Sea of Galilee was surrounded by the towns of Capernaum, Bethsaida, Chorazin, Magdala, Tiberias, and others.

The sea is an integral part of the Jordan River which feeds it with water from the snow-capped Mt Hermon (towering over 9000 ft. above sea level) and the Lebanons. In its 65-mile course from the Sea of Galilee to the Dead Sea, the Jordan River drops 590 feet, an average of 9 feet per mile.

A view of the Sea of Galilee from its western shore.

Description. The lake is approximately 13 miles long and 6 miles wide (7½ at its broadest point opposite Magdala). It lies almost 700 feet below the Mediterranean Sea, and its greatest depth is 200 feet. Its shape resembles a harp, and some scholars think the name "Chinnereth" comes from a Hebrew word meaning "harp." The climate is semitropical. Because of this climate, combined with the sulphur springs at Tiberias, it became a resort to which sick people traveled for centuries. The lake abounds in fish, so fishing became an important industry (Mt 4:18–22; Mk 1:16–20; Lk 5:10,11). Sudden and violent storms (Mt 8:23–27; Mk 4:35–41; Lk 8:22–25), caused by the collision of the warm and cold air, occur regularly.

Importance. Most of the events of Christ's life took place in Galilee, especially around Gennesaret, the most densely populated area of Palestine. He is said to have lived at Capernaum (Mt 4:13), and he did many miracles there (11:23). Because the area on the west of the lake was a health resort, Jesus found many infirm people there and healed them (Mk 1:32–34; 6:53–56). Other important occurrences in relation to the sea were the Sermon on the Mount, traditionally near Capernaum (Mt 8:1,5); the drowning of the Gadarene swine in Gadara; the curse on Chorazin (11:21); the calming of the sea (Mt 8:23–27; Mk 5:35–41; Lk 8:22–24); and Jesus walking on the water (Mt 15:22,23; Mk 6:45–51; Jn 6:15–21).

See PALESTINE; GALILEE, GALILEANS.

Gall. 1. Yellowish-brown, bitter secretion of the liver (Jb 16:13) or the organ containing the gall (20:25).

2. Very bitter, poisonous herb which cannot be identified with certainty, although the hemlock, colocynth, and poppy have been suggested. The Hebrew word occurs periodically in the OT and refers to (1) "gall" in Deuteronomy 29:18 (KJV); (2) the "poison" of a venomous snake in Job 20:16; (3) "gall" or "poison" given to a person for food in Psalm 69:21; (4) divine punishment upon Israel as "water of gall" (Jer 8:14; 9:15; 23:15 KJV, or poison RSV). (5) Israel's bitter experience of divine judgment (Lam 3:5,19); (6) divine judgment upon Israel sprouting up like "hemlock" in the furrows of the field (Hos 10:4 KJV, or poisonous weeds RSV); and (7) Israel's perversion of justice by turning "judgment into gall" (Am 6:12 KJV).

3. "Substance of an unpleasant taste" in the NT. Matthew 27:34 mentions the gall mixed with wine which was offered to Christ on the cross. Mark 15:23 speaks of "myrrh" which may be a more specific identification of the liquid mixed with the wine. In Acts 8:23 Peter described the spiritual state of Simon the magician as being "in the gall of bitterness."

See PLANTS (GOURD, WILD).

Gallim. Village near Gibeah of Saul and Anathoth in Benjamin, north of Jerusalem and close to Bahurim (1 Sm 25:44; Is 10:30); probably present-day Khirbet Kakul.

Gallio. M. Annaeus Seneca's son, and brother of the philosopher Seneca, who lived from 3 BC–AD 65. Born in Cordoba, Spain, Gallio came to Rome during Tiberius' reign. His given name was Marcus Annaeus Novatus, but he assumed the name Gallio after his adoption by the rhetorician Lucius Junius Gallio. The wealthy Lucius trained him for his career in administration and government.

Gallio served as Roman proconsul of Achaia sometime between AD 51 and 53. During the apostle Paul's first visit to Corinth the Jews brought the apostle before the proconsul, accusing him of having persuaded people to practice religion in an unlawful manner (Acts 18:12–17). Gallio abruptly dismissed the charge since it dealt with Jewish and not Roman law. His action reflected the characteristic behavior of Roman governors toward religious disputes.

Forced to leave Achaia because of illness, Gallio returned to Rome as consul suffectus under Nero. His involvement in a conspiracy against Nero resulted in temporary pardon but eventual obligatory suicide.

Gallio Inscription. Dated Greek inscription found in Delphi, Greece mentioning Gallio as proconsul, and establishing the time of Paul's initial visit to Corinth (cf. Acts 18:12–17).

See CHRONOLOGY, NEW TESTAMENT; INSCRIPTIONS.

Gallows. Upright frame with a crossbeam and a rope for hanging criminals. In the Book of Esther, a gibbet is mentioned, upon which men were impaled and left to hang in scorn.

See CRIMINAL LAW AND PUNISHMENT.

Gamad. Home of mercenaries who served in the army of Tyre, according to Ezekiel's prophecy (Ez 27:11, KJV Gammadims). Gamad may have been located in Syria and is identified as *Kumidi* in the Tell el-Amarna Letters.

Gamaliel. 1. Pedahzur's son and captain or prince of Manasseh's tribe (Nm 10:23). Gamaliel was chosen by Moses to help take the census in the wilderness near Mt Sinai (1:10) and to organize the tribe for the journey to the Promised Land (2:20). He participated in the special 12-day ceremonial offering by the princes at the dedication of the altar following completion of the tabernacle (7:54,59).

2. Jewish scholar. This man lived in the 1st century AD and died 18 years before the destruction of Jerusalem in AD 70 by Titus, the Roman general.

Gamaliel is mentioned in Acts 22:3 as the rabbi with whom the apostle Paul studied as a youth in Jerusalem.

When Peter and the other apostles were brought before the enraged and threatening council in Jerusalem, Gamaliel, who was highly respected by the council, offered cautionary advice that probably saved the apostles' lives in that situation (Acts 5:27–40).

During that period in Israel a number of rabbinical schools evolved. Two of the most influential were the rival Pharisaic schools of Hillel and Shammai. Both of those teachers had vast influence on Jewish thinking. Hillel's school emphasized tradition even above the Law. Shammai's school preserved the teaching of the Law over the authority of tradition. Hillel's school was the most influential, and its decisions have been held by a great number of later rabbis.

Traditionally Gamaliel is considered to be the grandson of Hillel, and was thoroughly schooled in the philosophy and theology of his grandfather's teaching. Gamaliel was a member of the Sanhedrin, the high council of Jews in Jerusalem, and served as president of the Sanhedrin during the reigns of the Roman emperors Tiberius, Caligula, and Claudius. Unlike other Jewish teachers, he had no antipathy toward Greek learning.

The learning of Gamaliel was so eminent and his influence so great that he is one of only seven Jewish scholars who have been honored by the title "Rabban." He was called the "Beauty of the Law." The Talmud even says that "since Rabban Gamaliel died, the glory of the Law has ceased."

Gammadims. KJV form of "men of Gamad" in Ezekiel 27:11.

See GAMAD.

Gamul. Priest assigned to temple duty in David's time (1 Chr 24:17).

Gangrene. Death of tissue due to the loss of the vital blood supply to that part of the body. Often the most distal tip of an extremity, such as fingertips or toes, will turn black and surgeons will amputate the dead part to prevent extension and harm to more of the limb or to life itself.

The term "gangrene" or "consumption" occurs only once in Scripture (2 Tm 2:17, KJV canker). Paul warns Timothy that godless talk will encourage more godlessness, just like gangrene tends to spread to surrounding tissues.

Although not identified by name, Asa's disease of the feet (2 Chr 16:12) could have been gangrene. Miriam's leprosy was likened to the flesh of a macerated, gangrenous, stillborn's body (Nm 12:12).

See MEDICINE AND MEDICAL PRACTICE.

Garden House. KJV translation of Beth-haggan in 2 Kings 9:27.

See BETH-HAGGAN.

Garden of Eden. Location east of Eden (Gn 2:8) in the Tigris-Euphrates area of Mesopotamia, referred to 14 times in the OT. The data in Genesis 2:8–10 show that it was in the Shinar Plain area, and that four "heads" were formed from the one river flowing through Eden to water the garden. The heads were the Tigris and Euphrates (both of which are familiar modern rivers), and two rivers which have disappeared—the Pishon and Gihon. The latter were most probably irrigation canals, since in cuneiform there is no separate word for "river" and "irrigation canal." Thus the Eden area was irrigated after the Sumerian manner, making for a highly fertile garden. If Pishon and Gihon were in fact irrigation canals, the narrative places Adamic man firmly in a historic high culture, and takes him out of the realm of myth and legend. If the above identification is correct, Cush referred to the land of the ancient Kassites, while Havilah may have indicated Arabia.

The notions that the rivers were the four encircling the earth and that Eden is to be identified with the Sumerian Dilmun are based on inadequate geographical information.

Eden was the testing ground of man's fidelity to God's commands, and through disobedience, the garden was lost. It will be regained in the form of the new paradise (Rv 22:14).

See ADAM (PERSON); FALL OF MAN; EVE; TREE OF KNOWLEDGE OF GOOD AND EVIL; TREE OF LIFE.

Gareb (Person). Warrior among David's mighty soldiers (2 Sm 23:38; 1 Chr 11:40).

Gareb (Place). Hill near Jerusalem mentioned in Jeremiah 31:39 as a future boundary of the city, perhaps on the south or west side.

Garlic. Bulbous herb cultivated for use in cooking (Nm 11:5).

See FOOD AND FOOD PREPARATION; PLANTS (ONION).

Garmite. Designation for Keilah in 1 Chronicles 4:19. The word seems to denote strength and means "bony" (the same Hebrew word is used in Jb 40:18 and Prv 25:15). Some feel that the word refers to a place, although no such place is known.

Gashmu. KJV spelling of Geshem the Arab in Nehemiah 6:6.

See GESHEM.

Gaspar. Traditional name for one of the wise men who brought a gift to Jesus in Matthew 2:1,2.

See WISE MEN.

Gatam. Esau's grandson, the fourth son of Eliphaz and an Edomite chief (Gn 36:11,16; 1 Chr 1:36).

Gate. See ARCHITECTURE; CITY.

Gate Between the Two Walls. Entrance in the southeast part of the city of Jerusalem, possibly the same as the Fountain Gate (2 Kgs 25:4; Jer 39:4).

See JERUSALEM.

Gatekeeper. *See* TRADES AND OCCUPATIONS.

Gath. Walled city (2 Chr 26:6) and one of the five chief cities of the Philistines, which also included Gaza, Ashdod, Ashkelon, and Ekron (Jos 13:3; 1 Sm 6:17), all situated on or near the southern coast of Palestine. Although frequently involved in conflict with the Israelites, the city was apparently not subdued until David's time (1 Chr 18:1). It was a Canaanite city, the home of the giant Goliath (1 Sm 17:4) and other men of great height (2 Sm 21:18–22). A remnant of the Anakim was left even after the extensive campaigns of Joshua (Jos 10:36–39; 11:21,22).

When the Philistines captured the ark of God, they carried it from Ebenezer to Ashdod, from there to Gath, and then to Ekron (1 Sm 5:8). After many of the Philistines died or were stricken with tumors the ark was returned to Israel, first to Beth-shemesh and then to Kiriath-jearim (6:14; 7:1). When David fled from Saul he came to Gath and feigned madness before Achish, the king of the city (21:10–15). During the rebellion of Absalom, 600 Gittites served among David's mercenaries (2 Sm

Gath, the city of the Philistines that is mentioned most frequently (33 times) in the OT.

15:18). According to 2 Chronicles 11:8, Rehoboam fortified the city of Gath, and 2 Kings 12:17 relates that it was taken by Hazael, king of Syria, in the 9th century, but it was apparently again in Philistine control when Uzziah broke down its walls (2 Chr 26:6). The city disappeared after being besieged and conquered by Sargon II in the 8th century BC (cf. Am 6:2). Today its location is uncertain. The scriptural data suggests a site in the Shephelah, probably a few miles northeast of Ashkelon and about 10 miles east of Ashdod. Tell es-Safi has been suggested as the site of ancient Gath. Due to the widespread culture of grapes in ancient Israel there were a number of cities by the name of Gath ("winepress") in Palestine (e.g., Gath-rimmon, Jos 19:45; 21:24,25; Gath-hepher, 2 Kgs 14:25), several mentioned in the Amarna Tablets without any additional identifying name.

See PHILISTIA, PHILISTINES.

Gath-hepher. Town in Galilee, in Zebulun's territory, which was the birthplace of Jonah (Jos 19:13, KJV Gittah-hepher; 2 Kgs 14:25). Modern el-Meshad occupies the site of Gath-hepher and boasts a Muslim tomb in honor of Jonah.

Gath-rimmon. 1. City located in the land allotted to Dan's tribe for an inheritance (Jos 19:45). It was assigned as one of the four levitical cities for the Kohathites in Dan (Jos 21:24). Lost to the Canaanites, Gath-rimmon was later regained by Ephraim and included as one of its cities for the sons of Levi (1 Chr 6:69). Its site is identifiable with the modern Tell ej-Jerisheh.

See LEVITICAL CITIES.

2. One of two cities given to the Levites in Manasseh west of the Jordan River (Jos 21:25), suggesting a possible transcription mistake better read as Bileam (cf. 1 Chr 6:70).

Gaulanitis. Small province east of the Sea of Galilee, situated between Mt Hermon and the Yarmuk River, and extending perhaps to the Jordan River. It took its name from the ancient town of Golan. Archaeologists have discovered extensive ruins 17 miles east of the Sea of Galilee, which they consider to be the remains of Golan. Moses named Golan as a city of refuge for Manasseh's half tribe east of the Jordan (Dt 4:41,43), and Joshua assigned it to the Gershonite Levites (Jos 20:8; 21:27; 1 Chr 6:71). According to Josephus, Alexander Jannaeus suffered a heavy defeat in this place and later destroyed the town (*Antiq.* 8.2.3). Josephus also identified a Judas, who led a tax revolt, as being from Gaulanitis (18.1.1), where-

as Luke called him a Galilean (Acts 5:37). Later, Josephus called him a Galilean as well (20.5.2; *Wars* 2.8.1). It is quite possible that this Judas lived in these places at different times.

After Herod's death in 4 BC, Philip inherited Gaulanitis, making his capital Bethsaida Julias which he had rebuilt and named after Augustus Caesar's daughter. Jesus traveled in this area (Mk 6:45; 8:22), and it remained under firm Roman control until AD 66 when the Jewish war broke out. Jewish revolutionaries subsequently hid in its heights and the Romans fought several campaigns here.

See GOLAN; HEROD, HERODIAN FAMILY.

Gaza, Gazathites. City near the Palestinian coast, about 50 miles W, SW of Jerusalem. It has been occupied almost continuously since ancient times; modern Gaza (Arab. Ghazzeh) has played an important part in the conflict between Arabs and Israelis. Gazite and Gazathite are biblical names for the residents of the town. Azzah is a variant transliteration of the Hebrew name (KJV).

Set about midpoint of the length of the plain of Philistia, Gaza was in a rich agricultural area, where wheat and similar grains flourished. Situated some three miles from the Mediterranean, Gaza's position as the greatest trading center of ancient Palestine did not come from the sea but from the highways, which brought caravans from all parts of the Fertile Crescent. This accessibility was also a handicap, for the roadways along the coast were the easiest route for the armies of Egypt, Assyria, Babylonia, Persia, Greece, and Rome. Often Gaza was the victim of their passage.

In the records of secular history, Gaza first shows up in the annals of Thutmose III in the temple of Karnak. Thutmose wisely scheduled his Asiatic campaigns just after the Egyptian harvest and in time to seize the harvest of Palestine.

In Amarna Letter No. 289, Abdu-Heba of Jerusalem acknowledged that Gaza was loyal to the king of Egypt, but complained that Addaya, the Egyptian ruler of Palestine whose residence was at Gaza, had taken the garrison the pharaoh had sent for Jerusalem. From the late 13th century BC there is a satirical letter which was composed as an exercise for training scribes. In this letter, written from one scribe to belittle another, various itineraries are traced, including one from the frontier of Egypt to Gaza.

Pharaoh Neco (610–595 BC) captured and chastised Gaza and Ashkelon in the reign of Josiah of Judah (cf. Jer 47:1,5).

Tiglath-pileser III (745–727 BC) refers to Hanno of Gaza, who fled to Egypt just prior to the capture of Gaza by the Assyrians. On the Oriental Institute Prism and the Taylor Prism, Sennacherib (705–681 BC) tells of his invasion of Palestine and of how he shut up Hezekiah "like a bird in a cage." He captured 46 of Hezekiah's fortified cities and gave them to three minor kings, including Sillibel of Gaza, who is also mentioned by Esar-haddon (681–669 BC) and Ashurbanipal (669–633 BC). Reference to "the king of Gaza" also appears in the records of Nebuchadnezzar II of Babylon (604–562 BC).

In 332 BC Gaza was captured and punished by Alexander the Great. He was angered because it had held out against him for two months, so he killed all of the men and sold the women and children into slavery. During the Maccabean period it was taken by Alexander Jannaeus, who slaughtered its inhabitants.

In the Bible, Gaza is first mentioned in Genesis 10:10, where it is said that the territory of the Canaanites extended from Sidon to Gaza. In a summary of the conquests of Joshua, one of the dimensions of the conquered area is "from Kadesh-barnea to Gaza" (Jos 10:41). Joshua destroyed all the Anakim in the land, but some remained in Gaza and other Philistine cities (Jos 11:22). Another ancient people, the Avvim, "who lived in villages as far as Gaza," were annihilated and replaced by the Caphtorim from Caphtor (Crete) (Dt 2:23). Gaza, along with its towns and villages, was listed among the tribal inheritance of Judah (Jos 15:47). At the time of Joshua's advanced age, Gaza and the other four cities of the Philistine Pentapolis are said to be among the territories not yet taken (Jos 13:3); in Judges 1:18,19, however, it is reported that Judah took it.

During the time of the judges, Midianite raiders swept through Israel, looting and destroying, even as far as Gaza (Jgs 6:4).

In this period, the main biblical interest in Gaza centers in the life and exploits of Samson. Philistine women were Samson's weakness. He went to Gaza and found a prostitute with whom he had relations (Jgs 16:1). The people of Gaza learned that he was there and determined to kill him in the morning, but Samson arose at midnight and went to the gate of the city, took the doors, posts, and the bar of the gate and carried them to the top of a hill facing Hebron.

His involvement with another Philistine woman, Delilah, resulted in his capture by the Philistines, who gouged out his eyes and took him to Gaza (Jgs 16:21), where he was bound and forced to grind at a mill in the prison. On a festival day in the temple of Dagon, the reveling worshipers called for Samson to be brought so they could make sport of him. His strength was returning and God answered his prayer for vengeance. Samson dislodged the two pillars which were the support for the stone slab roof of the pagan temple; so Samson died, along with a great number of Gazites.

In the days of Eli, the high priest, the Philistines captured the ark of the covenant in battle and took it as a prize of war to the temple of Dagon in Ashdod (1 Sm 5:1,2). After the Lord sent afflictions upon this false deity and the Philistine cities, the rulers of the five cities determined to send the ark away, placing with it guilt offerings of gold to appease the Lord (6:17).

Gaza is named as the southern boundary of Israel during the time of Solomon, who ruled over "all the region west of the Euphrates from Tiphsah to Gaza" (1 Kgs 4:24).

Hezekiah defeated the Philistines as far as Gaza (2 Kgs 18:8). When he rebelled against Assyria, Sennacherib came and took 46 of Hezekiah's cities and gave them to the king of Gaza and two other kings.

Jeremiah 47 records a prophecy against the Philistines, which the Lord gave to the prophet "before Pharaoh smote Gaza" (v 1; cf. v 5; see Neco, above). Amos gives specific prophecies of judgment against Gaza (1:6,7). Zephaniah also states that Gaza would be deserted (2:4). Zechariah 9 gives an oracle of judgment, in which it is said that Gaza will be afraid and "writhe in anguish" and that its king shall perish (v 5).

In the NT there is only one reference to Gaza (Acts 8:26). Philip, who was preaching in Samaria, was told by an angel to go south to "the road that goes from Jerusalem to Gaza." Here he met the treasurer of Cush, who was reading Isaiah 53 as he rode in his chariot. Philip preached the gospel to this man and baptized him. CARL E. DEVRIES

See PHILISTIA, PHILISTINES.

Gazelle. Medium-sized Asian or African antelope.

See ANIMALS.

Gazer. KJV alternate spelling of the town, Gezer, in 2 Samuel 5:25 and 1 Chronicles 14:16.

See GEZER.

Gazez. 1. Caleb's son by his concubine Ephah and the brother of Haran (1 Chr 2:46).

2. Son of Haran and the nephew of #1 above (1 Chr 2:46).

Gazite. Resident of Gaza (Jos 13:3).

See GAZA, GAZATHITES.

Gazzam. Ancestor of a group of temple assistants that returned to Jerusalem with Zerubbabel after the exile (Ezr 2:48; Neh 7:51).

Geba. Modern Jeba', and a levitical city in the territory of Benjamin (Jos 18:24, KJV Gaba; 21:17), about seven miles N, NE of Jerusalem and south of the pass of Michmash (1 Sm 14:5; Is 10:29). It is easily confused with Gibeah, the home town of Saul, which is also in Benjamin, to the southwest of Geba. Both names mean "hill." The phrase "from Geba to Beersheba" indicated the north and south extremities of Judah's tribe (2 Kgs 23:8).

In the time of Saul the Philistines had a garrison at Geba (1 Sm 10:5; 13:3). Jonathan defeated this outpost and stirred up the Philistines, who swarmed into Israel with an army vastly outnumbering the forces of Saul. Saul and his men were at Geba (13:16) and later approached Gibeah (14:2). The Philistines had set up a garrison at Michmash, just opposite Geba. Jonathan proposed to his armor-bearer that they go over to this outpost and suggested that if the Philistines called to them to come over that would be a sign that the Lord had given their enemy into their hand. The Philistines did just that, so the two Israelites approached and killed some 20 of the Philistines, putting the garrison and the entire army to rout.

During the reign of David another horde of Philistine invaders was struck down by him "from Geba to Gezer" (2 Sm 5:25). Asa, king of Judah, built up Geba and Mizpah of stones taken from Ramah, which Baasha, king of Israel, had been building (1 Kgs 15:22; 2 Chr 16:6).

Isaiah prophetically traces the advance of the Assyrian army toward Jerusalem: "At Michmash he stores his baggage; they have crossed over the pass, at Geba they lodge for the night" (Is 10:28,29). Zechariah prophesied that the land would become a plain "from Geba to Rimmon south of Jerusalem" (14:10).

Men from Geba are mentioned among the Jews who returned from the Babylonian exile (Ezr 2:26, KJV Gaba; Neh 11:31). At the dedication of the rebuilt Jerusalem wall, singers from the area of Geba participated (Neh 12:29).

CARL E. DEVRIES

Gebal. 1. One of the earliest villages in Phoenicia and Syria (along with Ras Shamra and Tell Judeideh); also called Byblos ("books") by the Greeks. It was situated on the Mediterranean about 20 miles north of modern Beirut and was an important commercial center and outlet for the hardwoods of Lebanon in the period when it was an Egyptian colony and

Gebal, the place with "all the ships of the sea with their mariners" (Ez 27:9).

when the diplomatic and commercial interests of Egypt reached all over Syria. It was a city-kingdom according to the el-Amarna Letters (c. 1400–1350 BC), and seal impressions found there from a very early period suggest that it was on a major exchange route through Palestine and Syria. Its inhabitants were called Gebalites (Jos 13:5, KJV Giblites). While it was a great commercial center, a more important achievement of the Gebalites was the development of a syllabic script modeled on the Egyptian. Passed on from Phoenicia to Greece, it became the ancestor of our own alphabet. Excavations begun by Dunand in 1919 revealed a succession of remains from Neolithic (5000 BC) to Crusader times. Prior to 4000 BC a people who lived in one-room rectangular houses settled in Byblos and buried their dead beneath the plastered floors of their houses. Heavy tribute was collected from the kings of Tyre, Edom, Moab, Gaza, Ashkelon, Ekron, Byblos (Gebal), Arvad, Samsimuruna, Beth-ammon, and Ashdod by the Assyrians. It was then successively under the control of Babylonia, Persia, Greece, and Rome.

2. Territory southeast of the Dead Sea, associated with Ammon and Amalek as hostile to Israel (Ps 83:7).

PAUL L. KAUFMAN

Gebalite. Inhabitant of Gebal (Jos 13:5).

See GEBAL #1.

Geber. 1. Alternate name for Ben-geber, one of Solomon's commissariat officers, in 1 Kings 4:13.

See BEN-GEBER.

2. Uri's son, who was responsible for providing food for Solomon's household. His territory was probably south of Ramoth-gilead (1 Kgs 4:19). Perhaps #1 and #2 were related.

Gebim. Small town just north of Jerusalem. Isaiah 10:31 prophesied that its inhabitants would flee when the Assyrian army came to invade. Its exact location is unknown.

Gecko. Small lizard, incorrectly identified with the ferret by the KJV in Leviticus 11:30.

See ANIMALS.

Gedaliah. 1. Ahikam's son, and grandson of Shaphan (King Josiah's royal scribe). In 586 BC Nebuchadnezzar, the Babylonian king, appointed Gedaliah as governor over the Jews remaining in Israel to work the fields, vineyards, and orchards (2 Kgs 25:12,22).

Gedaliah established his headquarters at Mizpah, where he was joined by the prophet Jeremiah and the Jewish commanders and their guerrilla forces who had escaped capture during the fall of Jerusalem (Jer 40:6–8). Gedaliah assured them that if they would settle down and live in peaceful subjection to Babylon all would be well (2 Kgs 25:23,24; Jer 40:9,10). On the basis of that assurance many of the Jews who were dispersed in the Transjordan and other countries returned to Israel to work the land into great productivity (Jer 40:11,12).

Though warned about a plot against him by Ishmael, Gedaliah entertained the schemer at a meal and was killed (2 Kgs 25:25; Jer 40:11,12; 41:1–3). Along with some pilgrims visiting the temple, Ishmael fled with hostages to Ammon, escaping the vengeance of Johanan (Jer 41:10,15,16).

See ISRAEL, HISTORY OF.

2. Jeduthunite temple musician in the time of King David (1 Chr 25:3,9).

3. Jeshua's son and one called to divorce his foreign wife during Ezra's reforms (Ezr 10:18).

4. Pashhur's son and one of the Jerusalem officials who urged King Zedekiah to put the prophet Jeremiah to death for his pro-Babylonian prophetic pronouncements (Jer 38:1).

5. Amariah's son, grandson of King Hezekiah, and grandfather of the prophet Zephaniah (Zep 1:1).

Gedeon. KJV spelling of Gideon, Joash's son and judge of Israel, in Hebrews 11:32.

See GIDEON.

Geder. One of the 31 royal cities in Canaan, whose kings were defeated by Joshua (Jos 12:13). Its location is uncertain. Geder is perhaps identifiable with Gedor in the mountains of Judah (15:58) or with Beth-gader (1 Chr 2:51).

Gederah, Gederathites. Town and its inhabitants situated in the Shephelah (hill country) of the territory allotted to Judah's tribe for an inheritance (Jos 15:36). It was a place where potters lived (1 Chr 4:23). A man from Gedarah, Jozabad the Gederathite, is mentioned in 1 Chronicles 12:4. The town is perhaps the modern Jedireh, and not the Gadara (Um Qeis) of the Gospels.

Gederoth. Town (modern Qatra) in the Shephelah assigned to Judah's tribe for an inheritance (Jos 15:41) and later captured by the Philistines from King Ahaz (2 Chr 28:18).

Gederothaim. Village in the Judean Shephelah (Jos 15:36) of unknown location. The Hebrew list contains 14 cities without Gederothaim (vv 33–36), while the Greek version reads, "Gederah and her sheepfolds" (v 36). Gederothaim probably reflects a later scribal error where the copyist accidently made the term "sheepfold" into a 15th city.

Gedor (Person). Joel's son, who was an ancestor of King Saul. Gedor's family lived in Gibeon (1 Chr 8:31; 9:37).

Gedor (Place). 1. City in the Shephelah allotted to Judah's tribe (Jos 15:58) named with Halhul, Beth-zur, Maarath, Bethanoth, and El-tekon. It has been identified with Khirbet Gedur north of Hebron near Bethlehem.

2. Place founded by Penuel, one of the families of Judah (1 Chr 4:4).

3. Settlement established by Jered of Judah (1 Chr 4:18).

4. City settled by the Simeonites (1 Chr 4:39).

5. Town in the territory of Benjamin and the home of Joelah and Zebadiah, the sons of Jeroham (1 Chr 12:7); perhaps the same as #1 above.

Ge-harashim. Name for a richly wooded valley near Lod and Ono, settled by Joab from Judah's tribe, whose posterity called the valley Ge-harashim, meaning "valley of craftsmen," after their own trade (1 Chr 4:14, KJV valley of Charashim). In the 5th century BC the area was resettled by people from Benjamin's tribe (Neh 11:35, valley of craftsmen).

Gehazi. Servant of Elisha (2 Kgs 5:25) who instructed the prophet how best to recompense the generous Shunammite woman for her kindness to him (4:25–31). Gehazi took Elisha's staff to use in reviving the woman's dead son, but he was unsuccessful, and the prophet himself had to revive the child (4:32–37). His greed in securing from Naaman presents declined by Elisha resulted in his contracting Naaman's leprosy (5:20–23). In 2 Kings 8:1–6 Gehazi again encountered the Shunammite woman as she was petitioning the king of Israel.

Gehenna. English transliteration of the Greek form of an Aramaic word which in turn is derived from the Hebrew phrase "the Valley of [the son(s) of] Hinnom." The name properly designates a deep valley delimiting the territories of the tribes of Benjamin and Judah (Jos 15:8; 18:16). It is commonly identified with the Wādi er-Rabābi which runs from beneath the western wall of the Old City, forming a deep ravine south of Jerusalem.

The place became notorious because of the idolatrous practices which were carried out there in the days of Judah's kings Ahaz and Manasseh, especially involving the heinous crime of infant sacrifice associated with the Molech ceremonies (2 Kgs 16:3; 21:6; 2 Chr 28:3; 33:6; Jer 19:56; 32:35). The spiritual reformation of King Josiah brought an end to these sinister proceedings (2 Kgs 23:10). The prophet Jeremiah referred to the valley in picturing God's judgment upon his people (Jer 2:23; 7:30–32; 19:5,6).

The Valley of Hinnom, with Jerusalem in the background.

Subsequently, the valley appears to have been used for the burning of the city's refuse and the dead bodies of criminals. Interestingly, a well-established tradition locates the scene of Judas' suicide and the consequent purchase of the Potter's Field on the south side of this valley.

The ravine's reputation for extreme wickedness gave rise, especially during the intertestamental period, to use of its name as a term for the place of final punishment for the wicked (Enoch 18:11–16; 27:1–3; 54:1 ff.; 56:3,4; 90:26; 2 Esd 7:36; cf. Is 30:33; 66:24; Dn 7:10). Jesus himself utilizes the term to designate the final abode of the unrepentant wicked (Mt 5:22; 10:28; 18:9). Since Gehenna is a fiery abyss (Mk 9:43), it is also the Lake of Fire (Mt 13:42,50) to which all the godless will ultimately be consigned (23:15,33), together with Satan and his hosts (Mt 25:41; Rv 19:20; 20:10,14,15).

Gehenna must be carefully differentiated from other terms relative to the afterlife or final state. Whereas the OT "Sheol" (cf. NT "Hades"), uniformly designates the temporary abode of the lost between death and resurrection when referring to the place of the departed spirit of man, "Gehenna" specifies the final place where the wicked will suffer everlasting punishment (cf. Ps 49:15,16 with Mt 10:28). "Tartarus" occurs only in 2 Peter 2:4 and identifies the particular abode of the angels who fell in the primeval satanic revolt.

Significantly, the hideous nature of Gehenna is laid hold of by James (Jas 3:6) to depict the grave sinfulness of the unbridled tongue.

See DEATH; HELL; HADES; DEAD, ABODE OF THE; SHEOL.

Geliloth. Place mentioned in the boundary line of Benjamin (Jos 18:17), usually identified with Gilgal.

See GILGAL #4.

Gemalli. Father of Ammiel, one of the 12 spies sent by Moses to explore the land of Canaan (Nm 13:12).

Gemara. Summary of the important points of rabbinic discussion on the Mishna (the oral tradition). The Gemara and Mishna together form the Talmud (which many Jews consider authoritative for their faith). In Aramaic *Gemara* means "acquired learning." That meaning reflects the teaching method of the rabbis, who passed on the Gemara by committing it to memory rather than writing it down. The word's Hebrew root means "to complete." Since the Gemara takes the form of a running commentary on the Mishna, it serves to supplement and hence complete it.

Two basic schools contributed to the development of Gemara material. One arose in Palestine in the third or fourth century AD (mainly in Tiberias). The other came from the Babylonian cities of Pumbedetha, Sura, and Nehardea (3rd century to the end of the 5th century AD).

The Gemara, developed from rabbinic discussions and debates, represents the distilled wisdom of the rabbis on the Mishna. Where there was an apparent conflict between the Mishna and the Law or among different rabbis, later rabbis would attempt to resolve it. An obscure quotation from an earlier rabbi they would attempt to clarify and apply to their own situation.

The Gemara, then, contains many different strands of tradition and perspective. Some predate the NT, some parallel it, and others are much later. It stands as an important source for understanding the thought world of the Jews.

Pages of the Talmud are arranged with the Mishna in the middle and the Gemara in blocks of print on the side. The Gemara does not necessarily quote the same sources twice when dealing with similar passages from the Mishna on the same problem, nor does it always contain commentary on the Mishna. The Gemara also includes folklore, astronomy, astrology, medicine, homiletic parables, and examples from great rabbis' lives.

See TALMUD.

Gemariah. 1. Hilkiah's son and emissary to Nebuchadnezzar from King Zedekiah. He carried Jeremiah's letter to the exiles in Babylon (Jer 29:3).

2. Son of Shaphan the scribe. In the temple chamber of Gemariah, Baruch read Jeremiah's scroll (Jer 36:10–12,25).

Genealogy. Record or study of descent involving a tracing backward or forward of the ancestry of a nation, tribe, family, or individual. The Hebrews were not the only people in the ancient world to take an interest in maintaining genealogical records. The Sumerian king list of the 3rd millennium BC contains records of the early rulers of Mesopotamia. In Babylonian records the word "son" was frequently used in the sense of "descendant of." King Tirhakah of Egypt (c. 685 BC) referred to his "father," Sesostris III, who lived some 1200 years before him. Greeks and Romans also kept genealogical records. However, the biblical genealogies, especially those in Genesis and 1 Chronicles 1–9 are unique in the litera-

The Sumerian King List, the earliest record of Sumerian rulers before and after the flood.

ture of the ancient Near East. Only at the beginning of the Islamic age are such broad genealogical records found. Even today among tribal Semites, such as Arab nomads, there is an intense interest in genealogy, and it is not unusual for an Arab to be able to recite accurately the names of his ancestors for 10 or 15 generations back, covering a period of several hundred years.

Terms Used. The word "genealogy" occurs only once as a noun in the OT (Neh 7:5), where it refers to a register of those who returned to Jerusalem with Zerubbabel at the end of the exile. The verbal form of the same word is found a total of 20 times in 1,2 Chronicles, Ezra, and Nehemiah. The terms "generations" and "book of the generations," used in Genesis and elsewhere in the OT, convey the same idea. The equivalent NT terms are found in 1 Timothy 1:4 and Titus 3:9 ("genealogies") and Matthew 1:1, which refers to the "book of the genealogy" of Jesus Christ.

Purpose of Genealogical Records. The keeping of genealogical records in ancient Israel was an important activity and served a number of useful purposes. God's promise of a land to Abraham and his descendants made such records necessary to establish and preserve the allotment of the land; a genealogical record served as evidence of a legitimate title to the ancestral property. Genealogies were essential for the preservation of the exclusively hereditary priesthood that had been established by the Mosaic law. In the time of Josephus every priest was supposed to be able to prove his descent.

One of the most important reasons for keeping genealogical records was to establish and maintain the right of royal succession in Judah through the family of David. The belief that the Messiah would come from the Davidic house made such records even more important.

Other purposes served by these family records included the imposition of military duty according to families (Nm 1:2,3). Position in camp and on march from Egypt was determined by tribes and families (2:2,17; 10:1–28). Also God's blessings were passed from one member of the family to his descendants (Gn 27). The stress placed on purity of the congregation (Dt 7:1–4; 23:1–8) required complete family records, particularly in the postexilic period. With the insistence of Ezra and Nehemiah upon racial purity and the purging of foreign elements from among the people (Ezr 2:59–63; 10:9–44; Neh 13:23–28), written evidence of purity of descent became essential; and interest in the compilation of genealogies became intense after the exile.

Lineage was ordinarily traced through the male members of the family, with females being mentioned only rarely (e.g., Gn 11:29, Sarah and Milcah; 22:23, Rebekah; and Nm 26:33–27:11, where the property inheritance of the daughters of Zelophehad was involved).

Principal Genealogical Lists in the Bible. The principal sources of genealogical material in the OT are found in Genesis, Numbers, 2 Samuel, 1 Kings, 1, 2 Chronicles (which contain the greatest amount of genealogical material in the Bible), Ezra, and Nehemiah. The genealogies of Jesus Christ in Matthew 1 and Luke 3 are the only NT records. Together they contain a genealogical record from Adam to Christ.

Grouped together by historical periods, the following are the principal genealogical lists found in the Bible:

Before the Flood. Three lists are from this period. The first, found in Genesis 4:17–22, traces the descendants of Cain through seven generations and explains the hereditary origin of certain occupations and crafts. The second Genesis 4:25,26, begins the account of the descendants of Seth, the posterity of Adam whose faithfulness to God is contrasted with the ungodly posterity of Cain. The third list Genesis 5:1–32 (cf. 1 Chr 1:1–4), traces the descendants of Adam through Seth down to Noah and his sons at the time of the flood.

From Noah to Abraham. Genesis 10:1–3 (cf. 1 Chr 1:4–23), frequently called the "table of nations," contains a list of the nations descended from the sons of Noah (Shem, Ham, and Japheth). Genesis 11:10–27 (cf. 1 Chr 1:24–27) traces the descendants of Shem to the time of Abraham, and Genesis 11:27–30 (see also Gn 22:20–24) lists the descendants of Nahor, Abraham's brother.

From Abraham to the Descent into Egypt. The descendants of Abraham by Hagar, Sarah and Keturah are found in Genesis 16:15; 21:1–3; and 25:1–4 (introducing the Arabs as descendants of Abraham). Genesis 19:37,38 links the Moabites and Ammonites to Abraham through his nephew Lot. A very important genealogical list during this period is that of the descendants of Jacob, giving the account of the parentage, birth, and naming of the founders of the 12 tribes of Israel (Gn 29:31–30:24; 35:16–26). Esau is acknowledged as the ancestor of the Edomites; his Edomite descendants are traced through his three wives (Gn 26:34; 36:1–43; 1 Chr 1:35–54). The list of Jacob's family at the time he entered Egypt, numbering 70, is found in Genesis 46:1–27 (cf. Ex 6:14–16; Nm 26:1–51; 1 Chr 2–8). A partial list of the heads of the fathers' houses of Reuben, Simeon, and Levi is found in Exodus 6:14–25; the chief purpose of this genealogy is to establish Aaron and Moses as members of Levi's tribe.

From the Exodus to the Conquest of Canaan. While the tribes were still in the desert after leaving Egypt, a census was taken to determine the total number of Israelites (Num 1:4–54; 2:2–33). During this same period a genealogy of the family of Aaron was compiled, and a separate census was taken of the Levites (3:1–39). A list of the 12 spies who searched out the land and the tribes they represented is given in Numbers 13:4–16, the most important names on this list being Caleb and Joshua. Near the end of the wilderness wanderings another census of the people was ordered; the total number was approximately the same as that of the first census almost 40 years earlier (26:4–51,57–62). As the tribes neared the Promised Land, a list was prepared of the tribal representatives who would take part in the division of the land (34:16–29).

Period of the Judges. The period of the judges contains very little helpful genealogical information. This history is given in the ac counts of the various judges rather than through a genealogical format. One exception is the account of the ancestors of David found in Ruth 4:18–22 (cf. 1 Chr 2:9–15).

The Monarchical Period. During the entire period of the monarchy, over 400 years, the only genealogical records of any consequence are those that pertain to David. His descendants are traced through 20 rulers who sat upon the throne of Judah until the nation fell to the Babylonians in 586 BC (1,2 Kgs; cf. 1 Chr 11:1–2 Chr 36:21). A list of David's children is found in 2 Samuel 3:2–5 and 5:14–16 (cf. 1 Chr 3:1–9; 14:4–7). His mighty men, an elite group of soldiers, are named in 2 Samuel 23:8–39 (cf. 1 Chr 11:10–47). His recruits at Ziklag are recorded in 1 Chronicles 12:1–22. Those who were his musicians and doorkeepers when the ark was brought to Jerusalem are named in 1 Chronicles 15:1–24 (cf. 1 Chr 16:5, 6,37–43). David's political and religious organization of the kingdom that included the Levites, priests, singers, porters and other household officers, and military officers is found in 1 Chronicles 23–27. In spite of the literary activity associated with the reign of Solomon, the only genealogical record preserved from this period is that of Solomon's princes and 12 officers (1 Kgs 4:1–19). The genealogy of one prophet is traced back four generations (Zep 1:1).

The Postexilic Period. During the postexilic period the keeping of genealogical records probably received its greatest impetus through the activity of Ezra and Nehemiah, primarily because of their insistence upon racial purity and the purging of foreign elements from the community. A list of the exiles who returned with Zerubbabel is found in Ezra 2:1–70 (cf. Neh 7:6–73, where the same list is found). A list of those who returned with Ezra is in 8:1–20. Ezra's own genealogy is also recorded (7:1–5). There is a list of the Jews who married foreign women that included priests, Levites, singers, porters, and other Israelites (Ezr 10:18–44). Nehemiah 8:4–7 names the Levites and others who assisted Ezra when he read the Law publicly. Nehemiah also contains a list of those who participated in the ceremony of sealing the covenant (Neh 10:1–27) and a list of those who lived in Jerusalem and other cities (3–36). His interest in the priesthood is reflected in the list of priests and Levites who returned with Zerubbabel (12:1–9), of the high priests from Jeshua to Jaddua (vv 10–11), of the heads of the priestly families (vv 12–21), of the Levites and porters who served under the high priest (vv 22–26), and of the princes and priests who were present at the dedication of the rebuilt wall of Jerusalem (vv 31–42).

The final genealogical record that must be mentioned is the genealogy from Adam to Saul (1 Chr 1–9), the longest section of genealogical material in the Bible. It is properly included with the genealogies compiled during the postexilic period, as the unknown Chronicler (some think he was Ezra) prepared this list around 400 BC from extant records and documents available to him. His purpose seems to have been to conserve the purity of blood in the restored nation and to insist that the nation's well-being depended on its faithfulness to God's law.

The NT Period. The only genealogies of consequence in the NT are those concerning Jesus Christ in Matthew 1:1–17 and Luke 3:23–38.

F.B. HUEY, JR.

See GENEALOGY OF JESUS CHRIST.

Genealogy of Jesus Christ. Account of Jesus' human descent. The NT records Jesus' genealogy twice in great detail: in Matthew 1:1–17 and in Luke 3:23–38.

Matthew's Genealogy (1:1–17). Matthew 1:1 presents Jesus Christ as "the son of David, the son of Abraham." By those two names Matthew highlights Jesus' earthly relationship to the Abrahamic (Gn 17:1–8) and Davidic (2 Sm 7:12–16) covenants of promise. Then beginning with the patriarch Abraham, Matthew traces Jesus' human ancestry through King David to Joseph, "the husband of Mary, of whom Jesus was born, who is called Christ" (Mt 1:16). Matthew summarizes his account: "So all the generations from Abraham to David were fourteen generations, and from David to the deportation to Babylon fourteen generations, and from the deportation of Babylon to the Christ fourteen generations" (v 17).

An examination of Matthew's handling of this genealogical material discloses several interesting peculiarities:

(1) The arrangement of the names into three groups of 14 seems to be an artificial device. Furthermore, there are 41 and not 42 names in the genealogy, as verse 17 implies.

(2) The list of names in the first group (vv 2–6) totals 14; the list in the second group (vv 6–11), if reckoned "from David to the deportation to Babylon," totals 15. The third group (vv 12–16) totals 14 counting Jeconiah. If Jeconiah is restricted to the third group David has to be counted twice, as the name concluding the first group and beginning the second group.

(3) To have 14 names in the second group, Matthew omits three kings, Ahaziah, Joash, and Amaziah, between Joram and Uzziah (v 8) and one, Jehoiakim, betweeen Josiah and Jechoniah (v 11).

(4) In the first group Matthew mentions three women: Tamar, Rahab, and Ruth; and

The Genealogy of Jesus Christ

Matthew 1:1–17 (that of Joseph?)	Luke 3:23–38 (that of Mary?)	Matthew	Luke
		Asa	Menna
		Jehoshaphat	Melea
	God	Joram	Eliakim
	Adam	Uzziah	Jonam
	Seth	Jotham	Joseph
	Enos	Ahaz	Judah
	Cainan	Hezekiah	Simeon
	Mahalaleel	Manasseh	Levi
	Jared	Amos	Matthat
	Enoch	Josiah	Jorim
	Methuselah	Jechoniah	Eliezer
	Lamech	Shealtiel	Joshua
	Noah	Zerubbabel	Er
	Shem	Abiud	Elmadam
	Arphaxad	Eliakim	Cosam
	Cainan	Azor	Addi
	Shelah	Zadok	Melchi
	Eber	Achim	Neri
	Peleg	Eliud	Shealtiel
	Reu	Eleazer	Zerubbabel
	Serug	Matthan	Rhesa
	Nahor	Jacob	Joanan
	Terah	Joseph	Joda
Abraham	Abraham	(Jesus)*	Josech
Isaac	Isaac		Semein
Jacob	Jacob		Mattathias
Judah	Judah		Maath
Perez	Perez		Naggai
Hezron	Hezron		Esli
Ram	Arni		Nahum
Amminadab	Admin		Amos
Nahshon	Amminadab		Mattathias
Salmon	Nahshon		Joseph
Boaz	Sala		Jannai
Obed	Boaz		Melchi
Jesse	Obed		Levi
David	Jesse		Matthat
Solomon	David		Heli
Rehoboam	Nathan		Joseph
Abijah	Mattatha		(Jesus)*

*Both Gospels are careful to not connect Joseph to Jesus in a physical father-son relationship.

in the second group alludes to Bathsheba, an uncommon practice in genealogies and all the more strange when it is noted that these four represent what could be regarded as moral blemishes in the history of the Davidic dynasty—Tamar, a victim of incest, Rahab, a prostitute, Ruth, a Moabitess, and Bathsheba, an adulteress.

(5) In the first group Matthew mentions Judah's brothers and Zerah, Perez's brother. In the second group he refers to Jeconiah's brothers.

(6) In verse 6 David is called "the king."

From these data, it is obvious that Matthew does not intend to present a strict genealogy; the arrangement is contrived, and extraneous material is included, probably for some other purpose than merely to present Jesus' forebears. Matthew's arrangement of the names into groups of 14, probably guided (here as throughout the Gospel) by an interest in portraying Jesus to Jews as the promised king of Israel and rightful heir to the Davidic throne, gives a definite historical movement to the genealogy by dividing it into three periods of time. These respectively highlight the origin, rise to power, and decay of the Davidic house, the last point represented by the lowly birth of the promised heir to a carpenter of Nazareth.

The 14 names in each group may be an effort to call attention to the thrice-royal character of Mary's son by focusing on the numerical value 14 of the Hebrew letters in David's name (d=4, v=6, d=4). This number also happens to be twice the sacred number seven, so that the whole list is composed of three sets of two sevens each. It may be, however, that the contrived groupings were merely intended to aid in memorization.

With respect to the second peculiarity—the "missing name" in the third group—one must conclude either that David or Jechoniah are to be counted twice, being the pivotal names separating the three groups, or that a name was mistakenly dropped out in a later copy of Matthew's Gospel.

The third peculiarity presents no difficulty at all. Numerous genealogies in Scripture omit some names. Ancient Near Eastern writers often used the phrase "the son of," or the word "begat" quite flexibly, relating grandsons or great-grandsons, for instance, to earlier forebears without indicating every intervening ancestor. The modern mind should not require a precision in ancient records that ancient writers themselves did not insist on.

The women listed in the genealogy—the fourth peculiarity—may have been intended to disarm Jewish criticism about Jesus' birth (1:18–25) by showing that irregular unions were not disqualifications for the Messiah's legal ancestry.

The reason for including several brothers in the genealogy at three points—the fifth peculiarity—is not readily discernible. The mention of "Judah and his brothers" (v 2) may simply be following an established practice of speaking of the 12 patriarchs together.

Finally, David's description as "the king" (v 6) underscores the Davidic or royal character of the list.

The sources employed in compiling the first group in the genealogy, drew upon records preserved in Chronicles 1:27–2:15 and in Ruth 4:18–22. The second group followed the records found in 1 and 2 Kings, and 2 Chronicles. The third group relied mainly on public or private records from the intertestamental period; the nine names from Abiud to Jacob are not mentioned elsewhere in Scripture.

On the basis of this genealogy, if there had been a Davidic throne in Joseph's day, the lowly carpenter would have been the legal heir to it, and Jesus stood after him as the next in line to inherit the royal seat.

It has been argued against this understanding of Matthew's genealogy that the presence of Jechoniah in the list (v 11) jeopardizes, if not completely negates, the legal claim to the Davidic throne of every one descending directly from him, inasmuch as the Lord declared of him: "Write this man down as childless, . . . for none of his offspring shall succeed in sitting on the throne of David, and ruling again in Judah" (Jer 22:30). Therefore, it is said, it could not have been Matthew's intention to represent the men from Shealtiel to Joseph as legal heirs to the throne.

This is a point which admittedly could dispose of the view that the list presents David's descendants if it were not for the fact that Shealtiel, who in Matthew's record is represented as the son of Jechoniah, appears also in Luke's genealogy as the son of Neri (Lk 3:27). Neri's name is unique to Luke's Gospel so it is impossible to check its use elsewhere to discover the actual parentage of Shealtiel. But it is not surprising in the light of Jeremiah 22:30 to find him listed in both accounts with different parents. Neri most likely was Shealtiel's real father, and while it is impossible to determine Neri's precise relationship to Jechoniah, it may be that those responsible for determining and keeping the record of the legal heirs to the Davidic throne looked to the collateral line of Neri and selected Shealtiel as the man to be legally adopted into the line and the one through whom the line would continue. Shealtiel may well have died without a male descendant which made it necessary to look to Zerubbabel, the son of Pedaiah, Shealtiel's brother by adoption, as the legal heir to the Davidic throne. By this pair of adoptions the curse upon Jechoniah was fulfilled while an actual grandson of Jechoniah continued the line, inasmuch as the grandson was legally the son of Shealtiel, who in turn was the actual son of Neri. Jechoniah's presence in the genealogy is a strength, rather than a weakness, for the interpretation that Matthew's Gospel intended to present the legal heirs of the Davidic throne, since only a writer conscious of the problems surrounding Jechoniah's lineage, but also aware of an explanation, would present such an ancestry to a Jewish audience he was seeking to convince that Jesus was indeed the royal Messiah.

Luke's Genealogy (3:23–38). Luke's genealogy also has peculiarities.

(1) Some expositors have thought it significant that Luke's genealogy appears not at the beginning of the Gospel, but at the beginning of Jesus' ministry.

(2) Luke's account, in contrast to Matthew's, begins with Jesus and traces his lineage back through OT history. This seems irregular, for most genealogies follow the order of succession.

(3) Luke's account, furthermore, does not end with Abraham, but goes all the way back to "Adam, the son of God" (3:38).

Some have seen the first peculiarity as a result of Luke's desire to bring a period of sacred history to its close, and to signal the beginning of another with the person and especially the ministry of Jesus. The genealogy, located as it is, sets off the work of Christ from the accounts of his birth and preparation.

Many have suggested that the regressive order in the genealogy is probably Luke's instrument to focus attention on Jesus. The fact that Luke traced Jesus' ancestry back to Adam, "the son of God," was probably due to the fact that he wrote for Romans and Greeks. By tracing Jesus' ancestry back to Adam, he shows Jesus to be related to the whole human race. In Luke's genealogy Jesus and Adam are both "sons of God;" Jesus, of course, is the son of God by nature, Adam, the son of God by having been created in God's image.

As to his sources, it is rather certain that Luke used the Septuagint version (ancient Greek version of the OT) of Genesis 11:12, which inserts the name Cainan between Shelah and Arphaxad (Lk 3:36), and the records of 1 Chronicles 1–3 for the history down to David. For the period from David to Jesus most expositors agree that Luke relied upon information probably received directly from Mary or from persons close to her. It was a common practice among the Jewish people for genealogical records to be maintained both publicly and privately. There was special concern in families of Davidic descent to preserve their ancestral records because of OT prophecies that Messiah would be born in the house of David.

Luke no doubt intended to accomplish more by his list than merely a presentation of a number of Jesus' ancestors. Since Luke did not highlight David in his list, it may be assumed that he was not zealous to present a list of legal heirs to the Davidic throne, not that the issue is of no concern to him (cf. 1:27,32,69; 2:4,11). Rather a concern throughout Luke's Gospel is this emphasis—that of portraying the Christ as the savior of Romans and Greeks, indeed, of the world. Therefore, though Luke traced Jesus' ancestry through Joseph's ancestral line to David, he continued beyond David to Adam. Jesus is a member of the race to which all people belong.

The Relationship Between the Two Records. Even a cursory examination of the two genealogies of Jesus will show several differences. For example, Matthew's genealogy comprises 41 generations, while Luke lists 76. Luke includes the period between Adam and Abraham, Matthew does not. While the two lists are practically identical from Abraham to David, they diverge for the period from David to Jesus, Matthew tracing Jesus' lineage from David through Solomon in 27 generations, whereas Luke traces Jesus' lineage from David through Nathan, another son, in 42 generations. Furthermore, at only one point do the lines converge during this period: at the names of Shealtiel and Zerubbabel, who are doubtless the same men in both lists. Finally, Matthew represents Joseph as the son of Jacob (1:16), whereas in Luke's account he is the son of Heli (3:23).

How are these differences to be explained? The differences between these lists stem from the purposes for which they were compiled and the meanings they were intended to convey.

A widely held explanation is that Matthew gives Jesus' ancestry through Joseph and that Luke gives his ancestry through Mary. On this interpretation Jacob was Joseph's real father, and Heli, probably Mary's father, became Joseph's foster father, that is, Joseph was Heli's "son," or heir, by his marriage to Mary, assuming that Heli had no sons (cf. Nm 27:1–11; 36:1–12). This view is certainly a possibility and should not be rejected out of hand. If Mary was a direct descendant of David, it could be literally said of any son of hers, "he is the seed of David."

On the other hand, many scholars prefer to regard Luke's genealogy as that of Joseph rather than Mary, since it is to Joseph's ancestry that Luke calls the reader's attention (1:27; 2:4). Furthermore, nowhere in Scripture is Mary said to be of Davidic descent. If the fact that Joseph was not the actual father of Jesus nullifies any value which Joseph's lineage might otherwise possess for a real son, why does Luke point to Joseph's lineage twice, and to Mary's not at all?

A major difficulty for the view that regards both genealogies as Joseph's is related to Joseph's two fathers. One solution is that Matthew gives the legal descendants of David, but Luke gives the actual descendants of David in the line to which Joseph belonged. This would mean that Heli was Joseph's real father and that Jacob was his legal foster father. How this could be is readily explainable. Assuming that Jacob's father, Matthan (Mt 1:15), and Heli's father, Matthat (Lk 3:24), are the same person, then Jacob [the elder] may have died without a male descendant so that his nephew, the son of his brother Heli, would have become his heir.

If Matthan and Matthat are not the same person, one might postulate that Jacob, the legal heir to the throne, died without a descendant and that Joseph, son of Heli, became the legal heir immediately upon the death of Heli and was counted as Jacob's son in a list of legal heirs to the throne. Possibly Heli, a relative, married Jacob's widow making Joseph, the son of that union, Heli's son and Jacob's son by levirate marriage. In other words, there are a number of possible explanations of this divergence.

One other major objection to the view that regards both genealogies as Joseph's is that, because of the virgin birth of Jesus, one may in no sense speak of Jesus as being literally the seed of David, a proposition that Scripture seems to insist upon. This objection has been adequately countered: (1) because of the realistic manner in which the Jews looked upon adoptive fatherhood; and (2) because the relationship in which Jesus stood to Joseph was much closer than a case of ordinary adoption, there being no earthly father to dispute Joseph's paternal relation to Jesus. Jesus could and would have been regarded as Joseph's son and heir with complete propriety, satisfying every scriptural demand that he be the "seed of David." The question, therefore, whether Mary as well as Joseph was descendant of David does not need to be answered one way or the other by one who desires to defend Jesus' Davidic descent.

It is beyond human reach to discover for certain the full solution to the divergencies between the two genealogies of Jesus, or the actual relationship of Jesus to them. Enough has been said to demonstrate that they are reconcilable, and the purposes of each, suggested here, indicate that either of the ways outlined above does full justice to the Davidic descent of Jesus, as rightful heir to his ancestor's covenanted throne, and also to his virgin birth by Mary.

ROBERT L. REYMOND

See GENEALOGY; VIRGIN BIRTH OF JESUS; INCARNATION; JESUS CHRIST, LIFE AND TEACHING OF.

Genesis, Book of.
First book of the Bible.

Name. The name "Genesis" comes into English as a transliteration of the Greek name meaning "origin" or "beginning." This name was given to the book in the Greek translation of the Hebrew Scriptures, known as the Septuagint. Genesis reflects both the content of the book and the Hebrew name for it, which is taken from its first word *bereshith*, "in the beginning."

Authorship. The authorship of Genesis is closely related to the authorship of the entire Pentateuch (lit. "five-volumed," the first five books of the Bible, which in Hebrew are called the Torah). It is clear that the Bible regards the human author of these books as Moses. On several occasions the Lord commanded Moses to write down various things; "in a book" (Ex 17:14); "write these words" (34:27). The Pentateuch reports that "Moses wrote all the words of the Lord" (24:4); he wrote the itinerary of the exodus wanderings (Nm 33:2); "Moses wrote this law" (Dt 31:9). (Here it is not certain that all five books are meant, but it must refer to at least the greater part of Deuteronomy.) In Exodus 24:7 it is said that Moses read the book of the covenant, which he must have just completed.

The rest of the OT bears witness to the writing of the Pentateuch by Moses. David referred to "the law of Moses" (1 Kgs 2:3). In the time of Josiah there was found in the temple the "book of the law of the Lord given through Moses" (2 Chr 34:14). Day by day Ezra read from "the book of the law of God" (Neh 8:18); cf. "the book of the law of Moses," 8:1).

In the NT, Jesus refers to "the book of Moses" (Mk 12:26; Lk 20:37) and otherwise mentions the commands or statements of Moses

Three stages in the development of the alphabet—the top row being Proto-Sinaitic (before 1446 BC), the middle row being transitional (c. 1200 BC), and the bottom row being later Phoenician (9th cent. BC).

(Mt 8:4; 19:8; Mk 7:10; cf. Lk 16:31; 24:44). The Jews also quoted from the Torah as coming from Moses, and Jesus did not contradict them.

Of Genesis in particular, it may be said that Moses had the opportunity and ability to write the book. He could have written it during his years in Egypt or while exiled with the Kenites. As the recognized leader of the Israelites he would have had access to, or perhaps even custody of, any records which Jacob brought from Canaan. He was "instructed in all the wisdom of the Egyptians" (Acts 7:22); and probably could have written in several languages and in several scripts (hieroglyphic, cuneiform, old Hebrew). Although Moses was admirably fitted for the task of writing, one must remember that he was not putting together a human composition, but was writing under the inspiration of God (2 Pt 1:21). We may with confidence conclude that Moses was the human author of Genesis.

The liberal view of the authorship of Genesis is that the book is an editorial composite, a view first put forward by a French physician, Jean Astruc, who suggested that the different names for God indicated different documents or sources for the writing of the book. This position is still held today, even by some who profess to be conservative, for the divine names are in actuality reflections of the various attributes of God.

The German higher critics expanded the view of the use of documents in the writing of Genesis and developed it into the Graf-Wellhausen-Kuenen or Documentary Hypothesis, which may also be called the JEDP theory of the authorship of the book. This view holds that there were four basic documents: (1) J, which uses the name YHWH for God, dates about the 9th century BC and comes from Judah; (2) E uses the name Elohim, dates from the 8th century, and comes from the northern kingdom; (3) D is Deuteronomy and is supposed to come from the time of Josiah, about 621 BC; (4) P is the priestly element, which deals with matters of the priesthood and ritual, dating to the 5th century BC or later. Some may date portions of Genesis as late as the Hellenistic period. According to this theory, the various documents were blended together by editors, so that there was a JE, JED, and so on.

The science of archaeology broke down many of the extreme postulations of these critics, and the work of W.F. Albright and his followers did much to restore confidence in the historicity of Genesis. Within the last several decades the patriarchal narratives and the account of Joseph have again come under strong attack, but these views are extreme, and much of the evidence adduced by Albright and earlier scholars like R.D. Wilson, W.H. Green, and others still has validity.

Date. The date of the book is also a matter of debate. Even among those who accept the Mosaic authorship the date for Moses varies. Based on the biblical data, Moses must be placed in the 15th century BC (cf. Jgs 11:26; 1 Kgs 6:1), but many scholars incline toward a 13th century date.

As outlined above, the liberal view of the date of Genesis would be from the 9th to the 5th centuries BC, with the final editing coming around the 5th century or perhaps even later.

Purpose. Genesis sketches the origin of many things: the universe, the earth, plants, animals, and mankind. It gives the beginnings of human institutions, professions, and crafts. It describes the origin of sin and death, and illustrates the insidious working of Satan in human life. Above all, Genesis relates the beginning of the history of redemption with the announcement of a Redeemer who was to come (Gn 3:15). It names the early progenitors in the lineage of the Messiah and the beginning of the Hebrew people through whom the Bible and the Savior came. Genesis also gives a selective history of people and events as viewed from the purposes of God.

Structure. The book is divided into 11 parts of uneven length, each set off by the expression "these are the generations [descendants, history] of" (2:4; 5:1; 6:9; 10:1; 11:10; 11:27; 25:12; 25:19; 36:1; 37:2). Only three times does the formula coincide with the first verse of a chapter; usually called a heading or superscription, the expression serves as a kind of link between what precedes and what follows.

Content. *The Creation (1:1–2:25).* These two chapters have been a scientific-theological battleground for many years, as researchers and students have tried to probe the origins of the universe and of life. Much of the evidence is not subject to scientific scrutiny, for science by definition requires that the evidence must be reproducible by experiment.

The statement of Genesis 1:1 remains the grandest, most precise, and most accurate statement of origins: "In the beginning God created the heavens and the earth." He did this *ex nihilo* ("out of nothing") by his word (Heb 11:3); he spoke the word of command and it was done (Gn 1:3,6,9,11,14,20; Ps 33:6,9).

The date of the beginning is unknown; time meant little to the ancients, and it appears that the duration of time also means little to God (cf. 2 Pt 3:8), who is more concerned about timing (Gal 4:4, "when the time had fully come"; Rom 5:6, "at the right time"). Uniformitarian cosmogonists (students of the origins of the universe who believe that natural events have always followed a uniform pattern, cf. 2 Pt 3:3–7) have speculated that the beginning of the universe was billions of years ago, but creationists posit a world thousands of years old.

To accommodate geological ages and the existence of extinct animals, some interpreters have proposed a gap between Genesis 1:1 and 1:2, with Genesis 1:2–2:3 representing a second or new creation. The notion that the days represent geological ages has little to commend it and much to controvert it. The days are called evening and morning, and the term "day" in the OT points to the days as 24-hour periods. Theistic evolution in its various forms is another attempt to bridge the gap, or to straddle the fence, between evolution and creationism; generally it is rejected by both sides.

There is a correlation between the first three days and the second three days. Day one saw the creation of light; day four, the light-bearers. Day two was the time of the creation of the firmament (better, "expanse"), which divided the waters; day five, birds and swarming water creatures. On day three, God made the dry land and plants; on day six he created the land animals and man. He made man in the image of God (1:26), "a little less than God" (Ps 8:5), and gave him dominion over the earth. He made everything "according to their kinds," so that each kind is distinct and unique. The perfection of his work is affirmed in that "God saw that it was good" (1:4,10,12, 18,21; "very good," 1:31).

The seventh day was a time of cessation from the activity of creating and served as a type for mankind's day of rest (2:1–3).

Critical scholarship eyes 2:4–25 as a doublet in conflict with Genesis 1:1–2:3. To conservative scholars the second chapter is the same account from a different perspective. Chapter 1 gives the creation from the standpoint of sequence; chapter 2 shows it in view of the centrality of mankind in God's creative work.

Chapter 2 gives details of the creation of man of "dust from the ground" (v 7) and woman from a rib of the man (vv 21,22). She was created to be "a helper fit for him" (vv 18,20). They were created as mature adults, with the gift of speech and with great intelligence. Adam had imagination and vocabulary sufficient for naming all of the animal species (v 19).

The location of the Garden of Eden is given (vv 10–14). Two of the four rivers, the Tigris and the Euphrates, can be identified with certainty. So man lived in this beautiful garden in the bliss of innocence.

The History of Mankind from Eden to Babel (*3:1–11:26*). THE FALL. The loss of Eden and the break in fellowship with God is the saddest chapter in human history. The serpent, the devil, approached Eve with the same philosophy he always uses: doubt of God's word (3:1), denial of death (v 4), and the suggestion of equality with God (v 5). He gained access to her will by a three-fold attack (v 6; cf. 1 Jn 2:16): (1) "good for food," "the lust of the flesh"; (2) "a delight to the eyes," "the lust of the eyes"; and (3) "to be desired to make one wise," "the pride of life." Eve was deceived, but when she offered the fruit to Adam he took it willingly, knowing what he was doing (Gen 3:6; cf. 1 Tm 2:14), but later he had the audacity to blame God for giving him the wife that gave him the fruit (Gen 3:12). Fellowship with God was broken (v 8), yet God came seeking Adam and found him.

With sin came judgment, and the Lord pronounced righteous judgment on the serpent, the woman, and the man. The earth was also "subjected to frustration" and now groans as it awaits renewal (Rom 8:21,22). God gave hope to man and a promise of a Redeemer (Gen 3:15), who was to bruise the serpent's head. Adam and Eve were forced out of the garden, and it was made inaccessible to them.

The impatience of humankind is shown in Eve's expectation that her son Cain was the promised Deliverer. Instead, he developed a wrong-hearted attitude toward God and became so jealous of his younger brother that he murdered him. Apprehended by God and confronted with his crime, Cain showed only self-pity and went east from Eden where he built a city (4:1–16). Chapter 4 closes with another contrast: the brazen poetic effrontery of Lamech, who called for vengeance while others began to call upon the name of the Lord.

THE GENERATIONS OF ADAM. This genealogical table brings mankind to the time of Noah and the flood. The longevity of the antediluvian patriarchs seems very striking to us, but one must remember that the earth had not yet been subjected to pollution and the effects of sin on the human race were still nominal. The refrain "and he died" reminds us of man's mortality; for Enoch there was something better—he "walked with God; and he was not, for God took him" (5:24).

THE FLOOD. With population explosion came an eruption of sin (6:1–5). As men multiplied, so did their corruption. The universal condemnation of verse 5 shows a world ripe for judgment. Noah, however, "found favor in the eyes of the Lord," for he was a righteous and blameless man who walked with God (vv 8,9).

The Lord then moved to annihilate the human race, but he determined to save Noah and his family. Intending to cover the earth with a flood, God instructed Noah in building the ark. Noah was directed to take animals aboard the ark, two by two, male and female, for the preservation of each species. When all was in readiness, the flood came; "the fountains of the great deep burst forth, and the windows of the heavens were opened" (7:11). It rained for 40 days and 40 nights. The highest mountains were covered, and life outside the ark perished. "But God remembered Noah" and sent a wind to evaporate the waters (8:1). Eventually the ark came to rest on the mountains of Ararat (v 4). Noah made a sacrifice to the Lord, and the Lord determined that he would never again bring such destruction upon the earth.

The flood is another of God's acts which has been much debated. Many have argued for a local flood, which affected only part of Mesopotamia. Archaeologists have pointed to various flood strata in the excavation of Mesopotamian city-mounds as evidence for the account of the flood and have cited the various flood stories from that area as the source of the Genesis record. The epic of Gilgamesh gives an interesting tale of this hero, who went on a mission to visit Utnapishtim, the cuneiform Noah, in quest of eternal life. The flood story told by Utnapishtim has many parallels to Genesis, but there are greater contrasts, which demonstrate that the Bible preserves the true account.

Both the Genesis account and the references to it in the NT (cf. 2 Pt 3:6) favor the view that the deluge was not a minor episode in the Tigris-Euphrates area but was an unprecedented worldwide catastrophe. Christian geologists affirm that the flood had far-reaching effects on the earth itself. Flood stories are almost universally known, lending support to the conclusion that the flood covered the whole earth.

Following the flood, God blessed Noah and his sons, Ham, Shem, and Japheth. God made a covenant with Noah, promising that he would never again send a worldwide flood. As a sign of this he established the rainbow.

Noah was the first tiller of the soil, and he planted a vineyard (9:20). Noah became drunk from wine he made and lay uncovered in his tent. Ham saw him and reported this to his brothers, who discreetly covered him. Ham and his son, Canaan, were cursed; Shem and Japheth were blessed.

THE TABLE OF NATIONS. "These are the generations of the sons of Noah (10:1). This chapter lists the descendants of Noah's three sons, in the order of Japheth (vv 2–5), Ham (vv 6–20), and Shem (vv 21–31). Many of the names of their descendants are preserved in tribes and nations of the world.

THE TOWER OF BABEL. The building of the tower of Babel ("Gate of God") illustrates man's perversity and his tendency to want independence from God. The desire of man to displace God follows the fateful example of Lucifer and is a basic tenet of many cults. God thwarted the designs of the builders of Babel by confusing their languages, so that the project came to a halt (11:1–9). The site of this tower is not known with certainty. Some associate it with Birs Nimrud, not far from the ruins of the city of Babylon.

Genesis 11:10–25 picks up the line of Shem and carries it down to Terah, the father of Abram.

The History of Abraham (11:27–25:10) and Isaac (21:1–28:5). Abram came from Ur of the Chaldees, an urbane and prosperous city. Large-scale excavations at the site of Ur were conducted by C.L. Woolley. The city had an imposing ziggurat (temple-tower), with many temples, storehouses, and residences.

Abram and Sarai, his half-sister and wife, went with his father to Haran in Syria, which like Ur was a center of the worship of the moon god, Sin (or Annar).

ABRAM'S CALL. The call of God came to Abram directing him to leave his relatives and move to a land which the Lord would show him (12:1; cf. Acts 7:2,3). Abram obeyed and at age 75 he, Sarai, and his nephew Lot left Haran and went to Shechem where the Lord appeared to him and promised that land to his descendants.

Famine drove Abram down to Egypt (12:10–20). Because of Sarai's beauty, he feared that someone might kill him to get her, so he passed her off as his sister. She was taken into the pharaoh's harem. When the Lord plagued pharaoh because of this, Abram's lie was discovered and Sarai was returned to him.

Critics have assailed the record of 12:16 because camels are included among Abram's possessions, and there is no word for "camel" in

ancient Egyptian and very little evidence for them from Egyptian archaeology. There is, however, sufficient evidence to account for his ownership of such animals, and if they were rare they were of that much greater value.

ABRAM AND LOT. Abram and Lot returned to Canaan, where strife broke out between Abram's herdsmen and those of Lot. Abram suggested that they should separate and he gave Lot his choice of territory. Lot chose the well-watered Jordan valley and the cities of the plain, Sodom and Gomorrah (ch 13).

THE INVASION OF THE FOUR KINGS FROM THE EAST. The four kings who invaded along the King's Highway in Transjordan cannot be identified with certainty. Those kings were successful in their attack against the five cities of the plain, and they moved off with much booty and many captives, including Lot. Abram took 318 retainers, born in his household, and set off after them. By surprise attack Abram recovered both Lot and the loot. On his return he was met by Melchizedek, king of Jerusalem, to whom Abram paid tithes (ch 14).

THE COVENANT. The Lord promised Abram a son as heir, and in an impressive nighttime ceremony God made covenant with Abram and promised him the land from the River of Egypt (wadi el Arish) to the Euphrates (ch 15). Because of her own barrenness, Sarai gave her Egyptian maid, Hagar, to Abram. Hagar gave birth to Ishmael, the progenitor of the Arab peoples. When trouble arose between the women, Sarai sent Hagar away, as was her right according to Near Eastern custom as illustrated by the Nuzi tablets. God showed mercy to Hagar and promised that she would have a great posterity (ch 16).

God repeated his promise to Abram concerning his descendants and changed the names of Abram ("exalted father") and Sarai to Abraham ("father of many") and Sarah ("princess"). A covenant sign of circumcision was given to Abraham (ch 17). This operation had already been practiced among the Egyptians for several centuries.

THE DESTRUCTION OF THE CITIES OF THE PLAIN. The Lord and two angels appeared to Abraham and announced the birth of the promised heir within a year as well as the impending destruction of Sodom and Gomorrah, concerning which Abraham bargained with God (18:22–33). Lot and his immediate family were rescued from Sodom and the cities were destroyed by God with brimstone and fire (19:24–25). Lot's two daughters, wishing to preserve their family line, got their father drunk and had sexual relations with him. Moab and Ammon, enemies of Israel in later times, were the result.

In Genesis 20:1–18, Abraham again represented Sarah as his sister and got into trouble with Abimelech, king of Gerar.

Isaac. When Isaac was born (21:1–3) trouble again broke out between Sarah and Hagar, who was driven out a second time, and once more was befriended by the Lord.

A disagreement arose between Abraham and Abimelech concerning a well, but they made a covenant of peace at Beersheba (21:25–34).

God tested Abraham's faith by asking him to sacrifice Isaac on Mt Moriah, which probably is the same site David later bought from Araunah the Jebusite (2 Sm 24:16–25), the place where the temple was to stand. As Abraham was about to use the knife, God called to him and showed him a ram caught in a thicket. Isaac was freed and the animal was sacrificed in his stead.

Sarah died at Hebron, and Abraham purchased the cave of Machpelah as a burial place from Ephron the Hittite (ch 23), in a transaction typical of Near Eastern business dealings. To find a wife for Isaac, Abraham sent his servant Eliezer back to the area of Haran, and the Lord directed Eliezer to Rebekah (ch 24).

Chapter 25 records the marriage of Abraham to Keturah, who bore him a number of children. Abraham died at the age of 175 years and was buried in the cave of Machpelah by his two sons, Isaac and Ishmael (vv 7–10).

The History of Jacob and Esau (25:19–37:1). Rebekah bore twin sons, Esau and Jacob. When the boys were grown, Esau sold his birthright to Jacob for a meal of red pottage (25:27–34).

When famine came to the land, Isaac went to Gerar as his father had done (ch 20) and repeated his father's lie by calling his wife his sister (26:1–11). Trouble arose with the Philistines over wells, but Isaac was a peaceable man and preferred digging new wells rather than fighting over old ones (vv 17–33).

In Isaac's old age, when his sight had failed, Rebekah connived with Jacob to trick Isaac into giving to Jacob the blessing of the firstborn, which was rightfully Esau's. This oral blessing had legal validity and was irrevocable, according to the Nuzi tablets. Fearing for Jacob's life at the hands of Esau, Rebekah arranged to send Jacob to Haran to find a wife from among her own people. At Bethel God appeared to Jacob in a dream of a ladder (stairway?) leading up to heaven and renewed with him the promise made to Abraham and Isaac (28:10–22).

Jacob reached Haran, found his uncle Laban, and was employed by him (ch 29). His wages for seven years labor were to be Laban's younger daughter, Rachel, as his wife,

but Laban substituted Leah, so that Jacob had to work another seven years for Rachel. The Lord prospered Jacob, but difficulties continually came about with Laban. The Lord directed Jacob back to Canaan (31:3), so he left secretly with his wives, children, and property. Laban pursued them because his household gods were missing (possession of these "gods" made the holder heir to the owner's estate according to Nuzi custom). Rachel had taken them but successfully concealed them from her father, and Laban went back to Haran.

Fearing a meeting with Esau as they passed through Edom, Jacob sent gifts to his brother and divided his own party into two camps for security. On this return journey, Jacob had an unexpected wrestling bout with the angel of the Lord, and he was left with a limp and a new name, Israel (ch 32).

The meeting with Esau was friendly, and Jacob went on to Shechem (ch 33), where his sons killed the male Shechemites because of the rape of their sister Dinah (ch 34). God told Jacob to go to Bethel and build an altar to the Lord. All idols of foreign gods were put away (35:1–4). At Bethel God reaffirmed his promise of a posterity and the land (vv 9–15).

Rachel died on the way to Bethlehem, while giving birth to Benjamin, Jacob's 12th and last son. Isaac died at Hebron at age 180 and was buried in the cave of Machpelah by Esau and Jacob.

Genesis 36 records "the generations of Esau" (v 1). Here Esau is also named Edom ("Red"; cf. 25:30).

The History of Joseph (37:2–50:26). Joseph was Jacob's favorite son and thus incurred the jealousy of his brothers. This was heightened by Joseph's dreams of lordship over them, and their resentment climaxed when Jacob gave Joseph a beautiful coat. The brothers determined to kill Joseph, but compromised by selling him to a caravan of merchants, who took him to Egypt and sold him as a slave to Potiphar, an Egyptian captain of the guard (37:36; 39:1).

Chapter 38 relates a historic case of levirate marriage. Judah failed to give his widowed daughter-in-law to his third son. She deceived him into fathering twin sons and forced him to acknowledge his faults. The elder son, Perez, is named in Luke's genealogy of Christ (38:33).

The Lord blessed Joseph, who soon was put in charge of Potiphar's household (ch 39). The young man attracted the attention of Potiphar's wife who, after many attempts to seduce him, at last accused him of attempted rape. Sentenced on this charge, Joseph met with favor in prison and had opportunity to interpret dreams for two of the pharaoh's servants (ch 40). When the king had dreams that his magicians and wise men could not interpret, Joseph was remembered and was summoned from jail. Joseph told pharaoh that the dreams meant seven years of plenty, followed by seven years of famine. Joseph was then exalted to the office of vizier, or prime minister, second only to the king and put in charge of the administration of the land (41:37–44).

When the famine came to Palestine, Jacob sent his sons to Egypt to purchase grain. Joseph recognized his brothers but did not reveal his identity to them. Joseph put them to the test by accusing them of being spies (42:9), by keeping one of the brothers (Simeon) hostage (v 19), and by demanding that if they came to Egypt again they must bring their youngest brother with them (v 20; 43:3). The famine became so severe in Canaan (43:1) that Jacob at last allowed Benjamin to go with his brothers to Egypt. The brothers were again set up by Joseph, who had his silver cup put into Benjamin's grain sack and then had him apprehended as a thief (ch 44).

At this point Joseph revealed himself to his brothers (45:4–15) and there was much rejoicing. Joseph pointed out that it was God who had sent him to Egypt (vv 7,8), in order to preserve the lives of all the family.

Jacob was then sent for (46:1), and Joseph met him in the land of Goshen (vv 28,29). The Israelites were assigned land in the region of Goshen where they prospered (47:27).

In Jacob's final illness, Joseph brought his two sons, Manasseh and Ephraim, to his father for his blessing. Jacob gave the primary blessing to the second-born Ephraim (48:13,14,17–20).

Jacob blessed each of his own sons and then died at the age of at least 130 years. Joseph arranged for Jacob's body to be prepared for burial according to Egyptian custom (50:2,3). After the burial of their father in the cave of Machpelah at Hebron, Joseph's brothers worried about vengeance, but Joseph declared "you meant evil against me, but God meant it for good, to bring it about that many people should be kept alive" (v 20).

Joseph died at age 110 with the prophetic request that when the Israelites went up from Egypt they would take his bones with them (50:25; cf. Ex 13:19; Jos 24:32).

CARL E. DeVRIES

See PATRIARCHS, PERIOD OF THE; DOCUMENTARY HYPOTHESIS; ADAM (PERSON); EVE; NOAH #1; ABRAHAM; ISAAC; JACOB #1; JOSEPH #1; FALL OF MAN; NATIONS; ISRAEL, HISTORY OF; COVENANT; FLOOD, THE; CREATION, DOCTRINE OF; CIRCUMCISION.

Bibliography. G.Ch. Aalders, *Genesis*, 2 vols; W. Brueggemann, *Genesis*; R.S. Candlish, *Studies in Genesis*; M. Dodds, *The Book of Genesis*; W.H. Green, *The Unity of the Book of Genesis*; J. Skinner, *A Critical and Exegetical Commentary on Genesis*.

Gennesaret. Area on the northwest shore of the Sea of Galilee between Capernaum and Magdala, where many of Jesus' healing miracles took place (Mt 14:34; Mk 6:53).

The Plain of Gennesaret, as the district was called, curves along a distance of about four miles with an average width from sea to mountains of approximately one mile. The topography is generally level, with the land rising slowly as it nears the bordering mountains. The unusually fertile soil is laced with flowing streams and rivers and noted for its productivity. Temperatures ranging from hot to mild allow for a long growing season and abundant crops. The fruits of Gennesaret were so exceptional that the rabbis did not allow them in Jerusalem during feast observances, fearing many would attend only to enjoy their succulence. Rabbis termed this area the Garden of God. During Jesus' lifetime, the area was considered the garden spot of Palestine. Trees such as the walnut, palm, olive, and fig, which require a wide diversity of growing conditions, all flourished here. Rich harvests of grapes, walnuts, rice, wheat, vegetables, and melons, as well as wild trees and flowers, were common. Later, centuries of neglect caused the plain to be largely overgrown with thorn bushes, although in more recent years, certain areas have been cleared and productivity restored.

In Luke 5:1, the Sea of Galilee is referred to as the Lake of Gennesaret, the alternate name undoubtedly derived its origin from the bordering plain.

Gennesaret (more accurately termed Ginnesar) was also the later name of the town Chinneroth (Jos 11:2), an ancient city which had long since fallen into ruin by Jesus' day.

Gennesaret, Lake of. Alternate name for the Sea of Galilee in Luke 5:1.

See GALILEE, SEA OF.

Gentiles. See NATIONS.

Gentiles, Court of the. Large outer portion of King Herod's temple complex. The court was of irregular oblong shape, somewhat broader at the north than the south. In that court, which was open to Gentiles as well as Jews, sacrificial animals were sold and money was exchanged. A warning was posted on a partition wall instructing Gentiles not to stray into the temple's inner courts. Jesus' "cleansing of the temple" probably occurred in the Court of the Gentiles (Mt 21:12,13; Mk 11:15–18; Jn 2:14–16).

See TABERNACLE, TEMPLE.

Genubath. Son of Hadad, the Edomite prince who, as a young lad, was taken to Egypt to escape Joab's slaughter. There Hadad married a sister of Queen Tahpenes. She bore Genubath, who was raised by the queen as a son of pharaoh (1 Kgs 11:20).

Gera. 1. One of Benjamin's sons (Gn 46:21). The name, however, does not appear in a similar list in Numbers 26:38–41.

2. Father of the judge Ehud (Jgs 3:15).

3. Shimei's father. Shimei cursed and threw stones at David during Absalom's rebellion; later he sought David's pardon (2 Sm 16:5; 19:16–18; 1 Kgs 2:8).

4. Bela's son from Benjamin's tribe (1 Chr 8:3,5); alternately called Heglam in verse 7.

Gerah. Measure of weight defined as 1/20 of a shekel, the latter being the basic weight among Semitic peoples.

See WEIGHTS AND MEASURES.

Gerar. City located in the western Negeb. It was used as a geographical landmark defining the western boundary of the Canaanite territory from Sidon to Gaza (Gn 10:19). Abraham resided temporarily in this city, at which time he deceived Abimelech the king by giving him the impression that Sarah was his sister (20:1,2). Later, Isaac settled in this city and also disguised his marriage to Rebekah for fear of reprisals from the men of the city. Isaac eventually left the town, moving to the nearby valley of Gerar on account of his conflicts with the Philistines. Here the herdsmen of Gerar quarreled with Isaac's servants over a newly dug well, and Abimelech king of the Philistines made a covenant with Isaac (26:1–26). It is doubtful that King Abimelech of Gerar (Gn 20:2) was the same person as Abimelech, king of the Philistines (Gn 26:8). Abimelech was probably a surname or an official title.

During the patriarchal period, Gerar appeared as a dominant Canaanite city in the Negeb; however, in Joshua's recounting of the conquest, this town was not named among the Philistine cities yet to be conquered (Jos 13:2,3) or in the list of cities already defeated (15:21,22). Later, in the period of the kings, Gerar was mentioned as the southernmost city to which the Ethiopian army fled before it was completely destroyed by King Asa of Judah (910–869 BC) and his army (2 Chr 14:13,14). Perhaps the fertile valley of Gedor (1 Chr 4:39; cf. Gn 26:17), formerly inhabited by the sons of Ham (cf. Gn 10:9), was identical with the valley of Gerar. Gedor was possibly a later scribal error where the copyist confused the Hebrew letter *r* for a *d*.

Cliff (upper left) where pigs that were possessed by demons may have run off.

The site of Gerar is identifiable with Tell Abu Hureireh along the northwestern bank of the Wadi esh-Sheri'ah, 15 miles northwest of Beersheba and 12 miles southeast of Gaza.

Gerasa, Gerasene, Gergesa, Gergesene. City and district in the Decapolis. Gerasa was a well-known Roman city situated in the hills of the Transjordan about 35 miles southeast of the Sea of Galilee and 19 miles east of the Jordan River. Although the city is not named in the NT, Mark 5:1 and Luke 8:26,37 mention the "country of the Gerasenes" (RSV) as the place where Jesus healed the demoniac and the swine drowned in the Sea of Galilee. The parallel account in Matthew 8:28 reads the "country of the Gadarenes" (RSV).

The reading of "Gerasenes" in Mark and Luke is preferred by the better manuscripts of the NT over the later scribal alterations of "Gadarenes" and "Gergesenes." Gadara was an important city of the Decapolis whose political jurisdiction extended to the eastern shores of the Sea of Galilee. It was added perhaps by later copyists to harmonize Mark and Luke's account with Matthew's Gospel. Gergesa was a city along the eastern coastline of the Sea of Galilee and the name was probably inserted in the texts of Mark and Luke to make better geographical sense of Jesus' miracle. Nonetheless, the district of the Gerasenes has the best textual support and should be understood as the intended site of Mark and Luke for Jesus' exorcism and miracle. To the non-Palestinian Roman and Greek readers of Mark and Luke's Gospels, the small regional district of Gadara would be unknown; however, the affluent Roman city of Gerasa would be widely known and suitable as a geographical designation for Jesus' miracle at the Sea of Galilee.

Gerasa was established as a Greek city by Alexander the Great around 333 BC. In 85 BC, the Jewish monarch Alexander Jannaeus conquered the city. Gerasa remained in Jewish

Mt Gerizim, as seen from the vicinity of Shechem.

hands until Pompey brought it under Roman control in 63 BC, at which time it was incorporated into the province of Syria and later included in the Decapolis. The site of Gerasa is identical with the modern Jerash.

H. DOUGLAS BUCKWALTER

See DECAPOLIS.

Gerizim, Mount. Mountain (modern Jebel et-Tor) from which the blessings were to be pronounced just as the cursings were to come from Mt Ebal (Dt 11:29). The two mountains designated by God were opposite each other, and the setting was a memorable one with six tribes positioned on Mt Gerizim and six on Mt Ebal, the Levites standing in the valley between with the ark of the covenant reciting "with a loud voice" the blessings and the cursings (27:11–28:68; Jos 8:33–35). The mountain is near Shechem, about 10 miles southeast of the city of Samaria, and it is referred to by the woman of Samaria in John 4:20–23 as the mountain where "our fathers worshiped." Abraham, indeed, had built an altar in this area (Gn 12:6,7; 33:18–20), and it had been the revered site for Samaritan worship for centuries. Jesus answers the woman's implied question as to which is the correct place to worship, Gerizim or Jerusalem, by pointing out that where one worships is not the important thing, but the attitude of heart with which one worships.

It was in this area that the bones of Joseph were buried (Jos 24:32) and that Joshua called upon the people to renew their allegiance to the God of their fathers (vv 25–27). Josephus records in his *Antiquities* Sanballat's promise to Manasseh to preserve for him the honor of the priesthood and also to build a temple on Mt Gerizim like that at Jerusalem (11.8.2,4). It was apparently destroyed later by the Maccabean forces under Hyrcanus (13.9.1). The Samaritans still worship at Nablus, which lies at the foot of Mt Gerizim, but are a diminishing community precariously held together. The so-called Samaritan Pentateuch, while ancient, is not in the opinion of most scholars, as old as it is claimed to be.

PAUL L. KAUFMAN

Gershom. 1. Moses' son by Zipporah, born in Midian during Moses' exile from Egypt (Ex 2:22; 18:3; 1 Chr 23:15,16).

2. Jonathan's father. He and his sons were priests to Dan's tribe. They made a graven image for the Danites to worship (Jgs 18:30).

3. Alternate spelling of Gershon, Levi's oldest son (1 Chr 6:1,16,17,20,43; 23:6,7).

See GERSHON, GERSHONITE.

4. Ancestor of Shebuel, the chief officer over the temple treasury during David's reign (1 Chr 26:24).

5. Phinehas' son who returned with Ezra after the exile (Ezr 8:2).

Gershon, Gershonites. Levi's oldest son (also spelled Gershom) who went into Egypt with Israel (Gn 46:11; Nm 3:17; 1 Chr 6:1) and was ancestor of a division of Levites (Gershonites) who came out of Egypt with Moses (Ex 6:16,17; Nm 3:18,21).

In the list of the allotment of levitical cities, the Gershonites were listed as one of the largest levitical groups in Israel (Jos 21:1–7). Some passages indicate that they were at times dominant among the functioning levitical groups (Gn 46:11; Ex 6:16; Nm 3:17; 26:57; 1 Chr 6:1,16; 23:6).

During the wilderness wandering the Gershonites were encamped behind the tabernacle to the west (Nm 3:23). Early in the second year after the exodus from Egypt the Gershonite males numbered about 7500 (v 22). Only those between the ages of 30 and 50 could serve in the tabernacle, which at the time of that early census totaled 2630 men (4:39,40). They were responsible for the care and transportation of the external furnishings of the tabernacle (3:25–27; 4:24,27,28) and were given two wagons and four oxen for the purpose, being supervised by Aaron and his sons (4:27).

After the initial settlement of Canaan, the Gershonites were allotted 13 cities among the tribes of Issachar, Asher, Naphtali, and Manasseh in the northern part of Palestine (Jos 21:6).

During the time of King David they were listed among the Levites appointed to service in the temple (1 Chr 23:6–11). The Gershonite families of Ladan and Jehieli were in charge of the treasury of the house of God (26:20–22). At David's request music in the temple was partly directed by Asaph and his family, who were Gershonites (25:1,2).

In the reign of King Hezekiah the Gershonites are mentioned among the Levites who cleansed the temple (2 Chr 29:1–6,12).

In the postexilic period the descendants of Asaph celebrated the laying of the temple foundation (Ezr 3:10) and the dedication of the city walls (Neh 12:46) with music.

See LEVI, TRIBE OF; PRIESTS AND LEVITES.

Geruth Chimham. Plot of land (meaning "the lodging place of Chimham") near Bethlehem. Geruth Chimham possibly was given to Chimham for the service his father, Barzillai the Gileadite, had rendered to King David (2 Sm 19:31–40; 1 Kgs 2:7). After the fall of Jerusalem (586 BC) Geruth Chimham was the camp of Johanan son of Kareah and his band as they prepared to flee to Egypt (Jer 41:17).

See CHIMHAM.

Geshan, Gesham. Jahdai's son and a descendant of Judah through Caleb's line (1 Chr 2:47, KJV Gesham).

Geshem. Arab opponent of Nehemiah who derided those seeking to rebuild the walls of Jerusalem (Neh 2:19; 6:1,2,6, KJV Gashmu). He was likely an inhabitant of the North Arabian desert and has been identified with Gashm, son of Shahr in a Dedanite Arabian inscription. Like Sanballat and Tobiah, his economic interests were threatened by the rebuilding of Jerusalem.

Geshur, Geshurites. 1. District and its inhabitants east of the Jordan River, in the tribal allotment of the half tribe of Manasseh (Jos 13:11). Most Bible geographers place it near Bashan, on the E, NE shore of the Sea of Galilee. In their conquest of the land, the Israelites defeated Og, king of Bashan, and Jair of Manasseh took Bashan as far as the border of the Geshurites and Maachites (Dt 3:14). Though the land of the Geshurites was given to the Transjordanian tribes (Jos 13:11), Israel did not drive them out (v 13). Later, Geshur and Aram took 60 towns from the Israelites in Transjordan (1 Chr 2:23).

David married Maacah, daughter of Talmai, king of Geshur, and she bore Absalom (2 Sm 3:3; 1 Chr 3:2).

After the vengeful murder of Amnon, Absalom fled to Geshur for refuge with his grandfather, Talmai (2 Sm 13:37) and stayed there three years.

See SYRIA, SYRIANS.

2. Name of an area and its people south of Philistia. Among the lands not yet taken at the time of Joshua's advanced old age are listed "all the regions of the Philistines and Geshurites: from the Shihor River on the east of Egypt to the territory of Ekron on the north" (Jos 13:2 NIV). When David lived at Ziklag, in the territory of Achish, king of Gath, David made raids upon the Geshurites and others, "as far as Shur, to the land of Egypt" (1 Sm 27:8).

CARL E. DE VRIES

Gether. Aram's son and the grandson of Shem (Gn 10:23). In 1 Chronicles 1:17 he is listed as one of the sons of Shem.

Gethsemane. Place to which Jesus and his disciples walked after their last supper together in the upper room. In Gethsemane Jesus underwent a great inner struggle as he realized the hour of his betrayal was at hand (Mt 26:36–56; Mk 14:32–50; Lk 22:39–53).

The name "Gethsemane," used only in the Gospels of Matthew (26:36) and Mark (14:32), means "oil press," suggesting the presence of an olive grove. The use of the Greek word "place" indicates that Gethsemane was an enclosed piece of ground. It may be that the grove was privately owned and that Jesus and his disciples had special permission to enter.

Though the Gospels of Luke and John do not mention the word "Gethsemane," they both record Jesus' agony before his betrayal. Luke says the location was on the "Mount of Olives" (22:39). John describes the area as "across the Kidron valley" (18:1); John's is the only Gospel to call the spot a garden. From those accounts it is also evident that Jesus and his disciples gathered in Gethsemane often for fellowship and prayer (Lk 22:39; Jn 18:2).

The Gospel narratives indicate that the garden was large enough for the group to separate into different parts of it.

Though the Franciscan, Russian, Armenian, and Greek Orthodox churches have all claimed otherwise, the precise location of Gethsemane remains a matter of conjecture.

JAMES D. PRICE

Geuel. Machi's son from Gad's tribe, and one of the 12 spies appointed by Moses to search out the Promised Land of Canaan (Nm 13:15).

The Garden of Gethsemane.

Gezer. Modern Tell Jezer (also known as Tell Abu Shusha), and an important ancient city in a strategic position in the north Shephelah, about 18 miles W, NW of Jerusalem. It was identified by C. Clermont-Ganneau in 1873, and excavations there were conducted by R.A.S. Macalister (1902–09), A. Rowe (1934–35), and G.E. Wright, W.G. Dever, et al. (1964–73). An early non-Semitic people who lived here apparently cremated their dead. The city of the 3rd millenium BC was protected by a brick wall, which was replaced by a 13-foot thick stone wall. The Canaanite city reached its zenith during the 20th–14th centuries BC. The so-called outer wall was 14 feet thick and enclosed an area of 27 acres. There was a Canaanite high place (c. 1600 BC) with 10 pillars or standing stones (up to 10 feet high) and a stone altar or basin. A 216-foot tunnel with steps led down to a spring in a cave, so that there was safe and ready access to water in time of siege, as at Gibeon and other Palestinian sites. Objects found indicate cultural and commercial contacts with Egypt. The Gezer Calendar, a stone tablet with a Hebrew inscription that gives the months of the year in terms of agricultural activities, was dated to the 10th century BC.

Gezer (KJV Gazer) first appears in Egyptian sources in the list of cities taken by Thutmose III (c. 1469 BC). The 14th-century Amarna tablets include letters from kings of Gezer, Milkilu and his successor, Yapahu, and show that Gezer controlled an area that included Ajalon and Zorah.

Horam, the king of Gezer, was defeated by the Israelites under Joshua (Jos 10:33). Gezer was a levitical city in the tribal territory of Ephraim (16:3; 21:21) but Ephraim was unable

A stone serpent for Baal worship, found in a cave at Gezer and dated 1800–1200 BC. Both the Jebusites and the Canaanites used the snake in their idol worship.

to drive out the Canaanites (Jgs 1:29). Merneptah (c. 1225–1215 BC) of Egyptian dynasty 19 lists Gezer, along with Ashkelon and Yanoam, on the Israel Stela, which gives an account of his conquests.

During the reign of David, the Philistines invaded the plain of Rephaim, but the Lord instructed David in a successful ambush and David struck down the Philistines "from Geba to Gezer" (2 Sm 5:25).

After Solomon's marriage to the daughter of the king of Egypt, the pharaoh, whose identity is uncertain, captured and burned Gezer and gave it as a dowry to his daughter (1 Kgs 9:16). Solomon rebuilt Gezer, along with a number of other cities which served as store-cities or chariot-cities (cf. vv 15–17). He fortified Gezer and made a strong gate with four sets of piers, like those at Hazor and Megiddo.

In the 5th year of Rehoboam, Solomon's son, Shishak (Sheshonk), king of Egypt, invaded Israel (1 Kgs 14:25). Gezer is included in the list of captured cities inscribed on the wall of the temple of Karnak.

The capture of Gezer by the Assyrian king, Tiglath-pileser III (745–727 BC), was shown in reliefs on the walls of his palace at Nimrud (biblical Calah). The Assyrians brought to Gezer conquered people from other areas, as they did at Samaria (2 Kgs 17:24). Cuneiform tablets of contracts testify to their presence.

CARL E. DeVRIES

See LEVITICAL CITIES.

Gezrite. KJV spelling of Girzite in 1 Samuel 27:8. The Girzites were raided by David's men while he was at Ziklag.

See GIRZITES.

Ghost, Holy. *See* HOLY SPIRIT.

Giah. Unidentified place along the descent from Gibeon to the Arabah to which Joab and Abishai pursued Abner (2 Sm 2:24).

Giants. English translation of four different Hebrew words. One of these words occurs in Job 16:14, where the Hebrew word means "mighty man, warrior" in the RSV, and "giant" in the KJV. Another Hebrew word is translated "giants" in the KJV and "Nephilim" (a transliteration of the Hebrew) in the RSV (Gn 6:4; Nm 13:33). The original meaning of this Hebrew term is unknown, but it seems to be used of a group or race of people. Since none of the terms translated "giants" has that actual meaning, we cannot be sure that the Nephilim were of unusual physical stature.

In several passages the KJV translates "giants" where the RSV translates "Rephaim" (e.g., Dt 2:11,20; 3:11; Jos 12:4). That word, usu-

ally in plural form, refers to several tribes of people who inhabited Palestine and who may have been unusually large in physical size. They included the Anakim of Judah's coastal area and hill country around Hebron (Dt 2:11), the Emim of Moab (v 10), the Zamzummim of Ammon (v 20), and the inhabitants of Bashan (3:11). The word also appears in Joshua (12:4; 13:12; 15:8; 17:15; 18:16). Some interpreters have suggested that these people were the original inhabitants of Palestine who were distinct tribes of tall people and who were eventually conquered and absorbed by the Canaanites, Philistines, Hebrews, and other invading peoples. Other interpreters contend that they were not distinct racial tribes but were individuals of great stature, perhaps the result of disease, who were found among the various races and tribes of Palestine. Neither contention can be established with certainty. Another Hebrew term is translated "giant" in both the KJV and RSV (2 Sm 21:16,22; 1 Chr 20:8).

Perhaps the most famous giant in biblical literature is Goliath of Gath, the Philistine soldier who challenged King Saul's army at the Valley of Elah and caused them to be dismayed and afraid (1 Sm 17). He is said to have been 6 cubits and a span tall, which has been variously interpreted as being between 7½ and 9½ feet. David's defeat of Goliath brought the youth prominence in Israel (18:5–7). Goliath is not referred to in the text as a "giant," but his height marks him as one of "gigantic" size. King Og of Bashan was another unusually tall person (Dt 3:11).

See NEPHILIM.

Giants, Valley of the. KJV translation for "Valley of Rephaim" in Joshua 15:8 and 18:16.

See REPHAIM, VALLEY OF.

Gibbar. Forefather of a family that returned to Jerusalem with Zerubbabel (Ezr 2:20). The parallel list in Nehemiah 7:25 reads "sons of Gibeon," suggesting that "Gibbar" may be a textual corruption. Some support for this view lies in the fact that Ezra 2:21 begins listing descendants by home city rather than by family.

Gibbethon. City in the western part of central Palestine. It was located in the territory of Dan (Jos 19:44) and allotted to the Levite clan of Kohath (21:23). Baasha killed King Nadab at Gibbethon when Israel was taking the city from the Philistines (1 Kgs 15:27). About 26 years later, Omri was proclaimed king at Gibbethon (16:17).

See LEVITICAL CITIES.

An aerial view of Gibeah.

Gibea. Caleb's grandson from Judah's tribe (1 Chr 2:49; see also Jos 15:57).

Gibeah. 1. Gibeath-haaraloth (Jos 5:3 RSV, KJV hill of the foreskins); a place located between the Jordan River and Jericho, in the vicinity of Gilgal, where Joshua conducted the circumcision of the Hebrew males born in the wilderness during the 40 years of wandering.

2. Town in the hill country of Judah (Jos 15:57). Its exact location is uncertain. Gibeah is listed as being among other towns located in the section of Judah southeast of Hebron and probably was in the fertile plateau containing Maon, Ziph, and Carmel.

3. Town in the province of Benjamin, also called "Gibeah of Saul" (1 Sm 11:4, 15:34; Is 10:29), and its inhabitants are called Gibeathites (1 Chr 12:3). It is first mentioned in the description of the territory assigned to Benjamin (Jos 18:28, KJV Gibeath) and comes to prominence in the biblical narrative as a result of the atrocity recounted in Judges 19–21 of the Levite and his concubine.

Gibeah was also noted as the home of Saul (1 Sm 10:26). After his anointing as king of Israel, Saul returned to Gibeah, and it probably remained his home and his capital (10:26; 22:6; 23:19).

Another tragic event is recorded in 2 Samuel 21. A famine had afflicted Israel for three years, and the text assigns the reason for it to Saul, "because he put the Gibeonites to death" (v 1). So, David asked the Gibeonites what he could do to recompense them, and they asked for seven sons of Saul to be hanged at Gibeah; David gave them two sons and five grandsons of Saul, and the Gibeonites hanged them there (1 Sm 21:8,9).

The site of ancient Gibeah has been generally identified as the modern Tell el-Ful. The OT references place Gibeah north of Jerusalem, between Jerusalem and Ramah, and situated near the primary south-to-north road through the hill country (Jgs 19:11–19). Tell el-Ful is about 3½ miles north of Jerusalem and is situated on one of the highest areas in that mountain range. Excavations reveal that an early Israelite village was there about the 12th century BC and was destroyed by fire. Probably during the 11th century a stone fortress was built, and its corner tower is still evident. It probably was the citadel of Saul and his royal residence. A second fortress was built about 1000 BC, but fell into disuse when David established the Israelite capital at Jerusalem. It then served as an outpost for the capital city. The tower was alternately destroyed and rebuilt through the centuries until its final destruction in the war between Antiochus III and Ptolemy V. Josephus wrote that a village existed at the site of Gibeah during the Roman period, but it finally ceased to exist with the Roman destruction of Jerusalem (AD 70).

4. Town in the hills of Ephraim which was given to Phinehas, son of Eleazar. It was the burial site of Eleazar (Jos 24:33). An addition to the Septuagint indicates that Phinehas was also buried here. Its exact location is unknown, and several sites have been suggested: Nibi Saleh, about 6½ miles northwest of Jifna; Jibia, 4 miles northwest of Jifna; et-Tell, northeast of Jifna and south of Sinjil; and Awertah near Shechem.

5. Gibeath-elohim (1 Sm 10:5 RSV, KJV hill of God). At this site Samuel, following Saul's anointing as king, predicted that Saul would meet a company of prophets and would prophesy with them. This was to be a sign of God's selection of Saul as Israel's king. Some have suggested that this is the same place as Gibeah of Benjamin, the home of Saul, but the context suggests that Saul reached this place before he arrived at his home.

6. Hill near Kiriath-jearim, where the ark of the covenant was housed by Abinadab, after its return from the Philistines and until it was moved by David to the house of Obededom (2 Sm 6:1–4).

WAYNE C. HENSLEY

Gibeath. KJV spelling of the town Gibeah in Joshua 18:28.

See GIBEAH #3.

Gibeath-elohim. Place where Samuel foretold an event that would confirm Saul as Israel's king (1 Sm 10:5).

See GIBEAH #5.

Gibeath-haaraloth. Place situated between Jericho and the Jordan, near Gilgal (Jos 5:3).

See GIBEAH #1.

Gibeathite. Inhabitant of the Benjamite town of Gibeah (1 Chr 12:3).

See GIBEAH #3.

Gibeon, Gibeonites. Place and its inhabitants figuring prominently in the OT from the days of Joshua to the days of Nehemiah, though both were in existence outside these time limits. The site may be identified with confidence as el-Jib some 5½ miles north of Jerusalem. This identification was proposed as early as 1838 by Edward Robinson. Since the excavation of this site in the years 1956, 1957, 1959, 1960, and 1962, and the discovery of 31 jar handles bearing the names of Gibeon the identification is placed beyond doubt. Certain geographical and chronological considerations also support this. The location of Gibeon, north of Jerusalem and accessible to that city in the days of David, Solomon, and Jeremiah, as well as its location southwest of Ai combine geographically to support this identification. Further, the periods of occupation at el-Jib revealed by excavation are parallel to historical data supplied by the OT.

Biblical Data. The first mention of Gibeon and its inhabitants comes in Joshua 9 and 10 in the days of Joshua, perhaps about 1200 BC. Hearing of the success of the people of Israel at Jericho and Ai the people of Gibeon, Chephirah, Be-eroth, and Kiriath-jearim plotted to obtain a covenant of peace from them. By pretending that they had come from afar and displaying worn-out clothing and footwear as well as dried bread, they were able to deceive Joshua into making a treaty with them. When their deception was discovered they were sentenced to become "hewers of wood and drawers of water" (Jos 9:21,23,27). Neighboring groups of people from Jerusalem, Hebron, Jarmuth, Lachish, and Eglon, led by Adoni-zedek king of Jerusalem, launched an attack on Gibeon because of its defection to Joshua. The Gibeonites appealed to Joshua, and the Israelites made a forced march from Gilgal to assist them. The enemies of Gibeon were driven down the road to Beth-horon. Their rout was completed with the assistance of hailstones. In that day the sun stood still over Gibeon (Jos 10:9–13). Only Gibeon made peace with the incoming Israelites (11:19). In due course the town became part of Benjamin's territory (18:25; 21:17).

In the days before David was king, Saul's general encountered some of David's men at Gibeon and engaged in an unusual contest at the "pool of Gibeon." Twelve men from each side fought and were all thrust through by the swords of their opponents (2 Sm 2:12–17). This encounter was followed by a further skirmish where David's men were successful (2:18–32). Later, David's nephew Amasa, captain of the rebel army of Absalom, was attacked by Joab at the "great stone which is in Gibeon" (20:8) and left to die in the highway

in his blood. In David's time also seven sons of Saul were executed "at Gibeon on the mountain of the Lord" (21:1–9) in retribution for Saul's violation of the ancient covenant between Gibeon and Israel when he slew men of Gibeon (21:1–6).

There was an important high place still operating at Gibeon in David's time. The tabernacle of the Lord rested there and an altar of burnt offering as well (1 Chr 16:39; 21:29). It was at Gibeon according to 1 Kings 3:3–9 that Solomon dreamed after offering a sacrifice and asked for an understanding mind to govern Israel well (cf. 2 Chr 1:2–13). A second time God appeared to Solomon at Gibeon to assure him that his prayer had been heard and to urge him to walk in God's ways (1 Kgs 9:2–9). Gibeon was among the cities taken by Pharaoh Shishak in the second half of the 10th century BC. Presumably Gibeon remained an important center during the days of the kings. There was a prophet in Gibeon in the days of Jeremiah, although he prophesied falsely (Jer 28:1–4). In the months following the fall of Jerusalem in 586 BC when the traitor Ishmael slew Gedaliah, the Babylonian governor, and his garrison and took loyal Jews captive, Johanan led a force to capture him and to rescue his captives. They came upon Ishmael at the great pool in Gibeon. The captives were rescued but Ishmael escaped (41:11–16).

Some of the Gibeonites went into exile in Babylon and a small group returned (Neh 7:25) and assisted Nehemiah in repairing the Jerusalem wall (3:7,8). Later still Josephus relates that Cestius pitched his camp at Gibeon on his march to Jerusalem in AD 66 (*War* 2.515–516). Biblical references cover a period from about 1200 BC to about 445 BC, in archaeological terms from the beginning of the Iron I period, through the Iron II period, and into the Persian or Iron III period. We would expect, therefore, to find evidence for at least these periods in an excavation. In fact the whole period of occupation reaches from Early Bronze I, about 3100 BC, into the early Roman period.

Archaeological Data. Gibeon was occupied extensively in the Early Bronze Age I (3150–2850 BC) well before the biblical story begins. There was some occupation during the Middle Bronze Age (2200–1550 BC) and the Late Bronze Age (1550–1200 BC), but the remains from these periods are limited. With the coming of the Iron I period (1200–1100 BC) Gibeon began to flourish, and it remained a thriving city throughout the Iron II period (1000–586 BC). There is scant evidence of occupation from the end of the 6th century until the beginning of the 1st century BC when it began to flourish once again.

Apart from some preliminary work, the ma-

The pool of Gibeon.

jor excavation of Gibeon was undertaken by J.B. Pritchard in five seasons during the summers of 1956 to 1962. Several features of these excavations are significant.

The Great Pool. This is referred to several times in the Bible and can now be identified. It was 37 feet in diameter and 82 feet deep, cylindrical in shape with perpendicular sides cut into bed-rock. There was a spiral stairway of 79 steps which gave access to fresh water 80 feet below street level. The pool lay inside the city walls.

The Stepped Tunnel. There was a second plan for obtaining water in time of siege. An underground sloping tunnel which descended by a series of 93 steps led to an underground reservoir fed by a spring originating in the rock mass below the city. This spring had been traced and a feeder tunnel enabled its water to flow more readily to the reservoir. Any overflow found its way via a conduit to the village below. This was a remarkable engineering achievement. The stepped tunnel reached down to a depth of 80 feet and was 167 feet long. In its walls were niches to hold oil lamps. Probably it was here that the "drawers of water" (Jos 9:27) obtained their supplies.

Inscriptions and Royal Stamp Seals. Sixty-one jar handles have been found on which inscriptions were cut in the archaic Hebrew script. On 31 of these is the word for Gibeon in whole or in part. Another 80 jar handles carry the letters *lmlk*, "belonging to the king." Several well-known OT names such as Azariah, Amariah, Hananiah, and Neriah and a number of place-names such as Hebron, Socoh, and Ziph appear on these inscriptions.

Industrial Area. A remarkable industrial area came to light in the excavations, located both north and south of the pool. Here there were numerous winepresses, fermenting basins, and 63 underground cellars for cooling large wine jars. The whole area covered over 1100 square yards with cellars sunk into the limestone, some of these being over seven feet deep and equipped with stone covers. It is estimated that up to 25,000 gallons of wine could be stored in the jars. Some of the cellars were used as tombs in Roman times, but in Byzantine and modern times their use as wine cellars continued. In detail the cellars were bottle-shaped and averaged 7.2 feet in depth and 6.6 feet across at the bottom. The opening to the cellars averaged 2.2 feet in diameter at the top. The jars in which the wine was stored had a capacity of 9.75 gallons. It is clear that the manufacture of wine was an important element in the economy of Gibeon in OT times.

Fortifications. Gibeon was a walled city. Two impressive stone walls which encircled the city at different periods have been exposed. No traces of walls were found that could be dated to the Early, Middle, or Late Bronze periods although the remains of house walls, pottery, and tombs demonstrate that the city was occupied then. The excavator concluded that the construction of the earlier wall dates to the 12th century BC and the later wall was built in the 10th century BC and continued in use to the end of the 7th century BC. The average thickness of the wall was about 13 feet. The circumference of the fortification was 3125 feet.

The Necropolis. The burial place of Gibeon was situated to the west of the city halfway down the rock scarp. Many of the graves contained skeletal remains, pottery, scarabs, and other artifacts. The size of the tombs varied considerably, but most consisted of a vertical cylindrical shaft about 3.7 feet in diameter, the depths varying from 3.3 feet to 13 feet. The tombs were sealed by either one large stone or several smaller ones at the foot of the vertical shaft where the burial chamber opened to one side.

JOHN A. THOMPSON

See GIBBAR; CONQUEST AND ALLOTMENT OF THE LAND.

Giblite. KJV rendering of Gebalite, an inhabitant of Gebal, in Joshua 13:5.

See GEBAL #1.

Giddalti. Heman's son and a temple singer appointed by David to serve under the direction of his father (1 Chr 25:4). The 22nd of the 24 divisions of service fell to Giddalti (v 29).

Giddel. 1. Ancestor of a group of temple assistants that returned to Jerusalem with Zerubbabel after the exile (Ezr 2:47; Neh 7:49).

2. Another ancestor of a group of people that returned with Zerubbabel after the Babylonian exile (Ezr 2:56; Neh 7:58).

Gideon. Judge of Israel, son of Joash, of the clan of Abiezer and the tribe of Manasseh. Of the 12 judges of Israel more verses are devoted to Gideon than any other, Samson running a close second. The narrative in which he is the central character antedates the Christian era by roughly 11 centuries.

Following seven years of cruel oppression by the Midianites, Israel cried out to the Lord for relief (Jgs 6:6). An unknown prophet informs the Israelites that their miserable conditions stem from their forgetting to give exclusive devotion to the one true God. God sends his angel to Gideon. A touch of humor earmarks the angel's greeting, for the "mighty warrior" (v 12) is threshing wheat secretly for fear of the Midianites. Yet God addresses Gideon in realization of what his mighty power is able to accomplish in him (vv 14,16,34). Conscious of his own weakness and the formidable task before him, Gideon is an ideal vehicle for God's tremendous work of deliverance (cf. 1 Cor 1:27; 2 Cor 12:10).

Gideon's first task is to tear down his father's altar to Baal and the adjacent one to Asherah, Baal's female consort (cf. Is 42:8). Conscious of the people's resistance to such an act, Gideon and his servants destroy these images of debased Canaanite religion at night. The following day the men of Ophrah confront Gideon and seek his life in retaliation for the act. Surprisingly Joash pleads the cause of his son, inviting Baal, if he indeed is deity, to contend for himself. Out of this confrontation the name Jerubbaal ("let Baal contend") is ascribed to Gideon (Jgs 6:32).

Yet Gideon is a man of inconstant faith, and his desire for further assurance is not rebuked as God graciously and patiently accedes to his requests concerning the dew and the fleece (Jgs 6:36–40). Subsequently Gideon is informed that mere numbers will not assure victory (cf. Pss 118:8,9; 147:10; Eccl 9:11a). Moreover, there must be no doubt whatever as to the true source of Israel's liberation (Jgs 7:2). From 32,000, Gideon's troops are trimmed down to only 300 by an unusual method of reduction (vv 3–7). A secret reconnaisance mission to the outskirts of the opposition's camp enables Gideon to receive further strengthening as he and his servant Purah overhear a Midianite soldier reveal his dream indicating Israel's imminent victory (vv 13,14). In response to this additional encouragement he worships the Lord (v 15; cf. 6:24).

Divided into three companies, Gideon's army stations itself at night outside the Midianite stronghold. At Gideon's signal each man blows a trumpet (made from an animal's horn) and smashes an empty jar, shouting, "a sword for the Lord and for Gideon!" (Jgs 7:20). The effect of the clamor is overwhelming. Thinking themselves outnumbered, the confused and disheartened Midianites flee eastward across the Jordan. In hot pursuit, Gideon's men are joined by Israelites from Naphtali, Asher, and Manasseh, who follow the enemy into the Transjordan area. The men of Ephraim, whose efforts are now called upon for the first time, capture and kill two of the Midianite leaders. Angry with Gideon for failing to enlist their services earlier, the Ephraimites are nonetheless appeased by Gideon's tactful response to their queries (8:1–3).

Perhaps out of chronological sequence, we learn of the uncooperative Israelites of Succoth (in the region of Gad) and their nearby eastern neighbors of Penuel (cf. Gn 32:22–32) who refuse aid to their Jewish brethren for fear of possible retaliation by the Midianites, whose kings Zeba and Zalmunna are still at large. True to the rough justice of that time, Gideon vows terrible reprisals upon these fellow countrymen (Jgs 8:7–9; cf. vv 15–17).

Following the devastating victory at Karkor, a remote wadi east of the Dead Sea, the Midianite host is finally and totally dispersed. It is at that point that Gideon's noble unselfishness shines in response to the people's desire to make him king (Jgs 8:22,23). He does, however, receive an immense personal fortune from the spoils of war (vv 24–26).

The unfortunate conclusion of Gideon's story relates to his making an ephod from the gold won in battle. Perhaps a garment patterned after the high priest's or a free-standing image, the object ensnares the people, and they worship it at Ophrah (Jgs 8:27). In 2 Samuel 11:21 Gideon's alternate name, Jerubbaal, becomes Jerubbesheth, "Baal" being replaced with the Hebrew word for "shame" (bosheth).

No longer a man of modest means, an affluent Gideon enjoys peace for the remainder of his lifetime. Seventy sons are born with lineages through his Abiezrite clan. Yet Abimilech, whose treachery is described in chapter 9, is the son of a concubine of Shechem, a Canaanite city.

Following Gideon's death there is a large-scale reversion to idolatry, chiefly the worship of Baal-berith (Lord of the covenant). The Israelites not only forget the Lord their God but also forget to show honor to the memory of their former general (8:35).

A humble man who spoke firmly for the rightness of theocracy and not a hereditary monarchy (8:23), Gideon has been singled out in the Letter to the Hebrews as a hero of the faith whose trust in God—not the arm of flesh—brought glory to the Lord (Heb 11:32, KJV Gedeon). As far back as the time of Isaiah, "the Day of Midian" had become proverbial for deliverance accomplished by the hand of God apart from human strength (Is 9:4).

STUART D. SACKS

See JUDGES, BOOK OF.

Gideoni. Abidan's father and leader of Benjamin's tribe when the Israelites were roaming in the Sinai wilderness after their escape from Egypt (Nm 1:11; 2:22; 10:24). As leader, Gideoni presented his tribe's offering at the consecration of the tabernacle (Nm 7:60–65).

Gidom. Place to which the Benjamite army was driven during a civil war between Benjamin and the rest of Israel (Jgs 20:45). Its location is unknown.

Gier Eagle. KJV translation for carrion vulture in Leviticus 11:18 and Deuteronomy 14:17.

See BIRDS (VULTURE, EGYPTIAN).

Gifts, Spiritual. *See* SPIRITUAL GIFTS.

Gihon, Spring of. Site in Jerusalem where Solomon was anointed as king (1 Kgs 1:33,38, 45). There are two sources of running water in Jerusalem: (1) the 'Ain Umm el Daraj' (also known as the Spring of the Mother of Steps, Gihon in the OT, and to Christians as the Virgin's Fountain), which lies at the eastern ridge, and (2) Bir 'Ayub, or the well of Job. The importance of the spring of Gihon for the defense of Jerusalem in time of siege is emphasized by Hezekiah's measures to deny his enemies access to the water supply and provide access for those who defended the city (2 Kgs 20:20; 2 Chr 32:30; cf. 2 Kgs 25:4; 2 Chr 32:3,4; Is 7:3). Hezekiah's tunnel brought the waters from the spring of Gihon in the Kidron valley

Excavations on Mt Ophel near the Spring of Gihon.

(eastern) into the central valley where the present-day Pool of Siloam is located. The spring was unable to supply all of Jerusalem's needs after the exile, and in the Roman period aqueducts were built to bring in additional water.

See SILOAM, POOL OF.

Gilalai. Musician present at the dedication of the Jerusalem wall, rebuilt during Ezra's time (Neh 12:36).

Gilboa, Mount. Mountain on the east side of the plain of Esdraelon between Galilee on the north and Samaria on the south (modern Jebel Fuqu'ah). Many battles were fought in the area, including Deborah's defeat of Sisera. At that time the flooding of the Kishon, which rose in Gilboa, greatly helped in the victory (Jgs 5:21). This region was the probable location of Gideon's camp when he attacked the Midianites (Jgs 6:33). Gilboa is only mentioned by name in connection with Saul's defense of the area against the Philistines. Here his sons were killed, and he himself committed suicide (1 Sm 31:1,8; 2 Sm 1:6,21; 21:12; 1 Chr 10:1,8). Had the Israelites stayed in the uplands instead of moving into the Philistine plain and posing a threat to the trading route between Egypt and Damascus, Saul and his family would not have been killed.

Mt Gilboa towers over the valley of Jezreel. It is a weathered limestone ridge reaching to a height of 17,000 feet above sea level.

See SAUL #2.

Gilead, Balm of. Substance of uncertain identification and one of several resins used in the Near East for medicinal purposes. It did not grow in Gilead, however, but may have received its name from being exported to Egypt and Phoenicia from Gilead (Gn 37:25; Ez 27:17). The substance supposedly had astringent, antiseptic, and other therapeutic qualities.

See MEDICINE AND MEDICAL PRACTICES; PLANTS.

Gilead, Gileadite (Person). 1. Machir's son from Manasseh's tribe (Nm 26:29,30; 27:1; 36:1) and head of the clan of his descendants (26:29; 36:1) during the time of Moses (26:29).

2. Father of Jephthah during the period of the judges (Jgs 11:1,2). Jephthah was the head of the Gileadites and judge over Israel.

3. Michael's son from Gad's tribe, who lived in Bashan during the initial settlement of Palestine (1 Chr 5:14).

Gilead, Gileadite (Place). 1. Region east of the Jordan River. Generally used to designate

The Yarmuk River, the northern boundary of Gilead.

the territory occupied by all the Transjordanian Israelite tribes (Jgs 20:1; 2 Kgs 10:33; Jer 50:19; Zec 10:10). Specifically, Gilead is the area of the Transjordan lying between the Yarmuk and Arnon rivers and divided by the Jabbok River.

The so-called Dome of Gilead is an extension of the central hill country of Judah, rising to heights of more than 3000 feet above the Jordan Valley. The valleys and hills were well watered by numerous rivers and tributaries, making flatter portions of the countryside well-suited for agriculture, especially olive trees, grape vines, and grains (cf. Jer 8:22; 46:11; Hos 2:8). The densely forested and rugged hills were sometimes compared to those of Lebanon (Jer 22:6; Zec 10:10) and made the land a refuge for those in flight, since the terrain prohibited ready pursuit by enemies (cf. Gn 31:21; 1 Sm 13:7).

Originally the region of Gilead was allotted to the tribes of Reuben, Gad, and Manasseh (Nm 21). The period of the judges saw Israelite security there assailed by the Midianites and Amelekites, only to be checked by the military exploits of Gideon (Jgs 6,7). Half a century later Jephthah was recalled from his banishment to rescue Gilead from oppressive Ammonite rule (Jgs 10,11). During the united monarchy Saul delivered Jabesh-gilead from Ammonite dominance (1 Sm 11:1–11; 31:8–13; 2 Sm 2:1–7); Abner installed Ish-bosheth as a rival to David in Gilead (2 Sm 2:8,9); David conquered the Ammonites controlling Gilead as he extended the borders of Israel (2 Sm 8:12; 10:1–19). He fled there for refuge in the face of Absalom's rebellion (chs 15–17) and was finally restored to the throne when Absalom was slain in the forest of Ephraim (chs 18,19). Gilead remained a battleground during the divided monarchy, as first the Israelites warred with the Syrians (Aramaeans; 1 Kgs 20:23–43; 22:1–4,29–40; 2 Kgs 13:22; Am 1:3) and then with the Assyrians, who wrested the territory from Pekah in 733 BC and deported the Israelite population, thus severing Gilead's tie to the northern kingdom (2 Kgs 15:27–31).

See DECAPOLIS; PEREA.

2. "City of evildoers, tracked with blood" (Hos 6:8). This may be an abbreviated name for Jabesh-gilead or Ramoth-gilead (cf. Jgs 10:17,18).

ANDREW E. HILL

Gilgal. 1. Town near Jericho. Gilgal was assigned to Benjamin's tribe when Palestine was divided among the tribes of Israel. For many years it was a center of religious, political, and military importance, especially during the periods of the conquest of Canaan and the early monarchy under Saul.

Gilgal was the first place where Israel encamped in Palestine after the miraculous crossing of the Jordan River (Jos 4:19). No doubt the tabernacle was set up here, since Israel occupied Gilgal for some time and used it as center of the commonwealth. Several significant religious events occurred at Gilgal: the circumcision of all Hebrew males born in the wilderness during the 40 years of wandering (Jos 5:2–9), the celebration of the Passover (v 10), the cessation of the manna (v 12), and a divine manifestation to Joshua by the "commander of the army of the Lord" (vv 13–15).

Militarily, Gilgal was Israel's first foothold in Canaan and the base of operations for the conquest. From here Joshua led Israel to the conquest of Jericho (Jos 6) and Ai (8:3), formed a treaty with the Gibeonites (9:3–15), attacked the five Amorite kings (10:6–43), and launched his northern campaign (ch 11). At Gilgal Judah, Manasseh, and Ephraim were assigned their portions of Palestine (chs 15–17).

After the relocation of the tabernacle at Shiloh, Gilgal retained its importance to Israel. It was one of the towns visited regularly by Samuel in his annual circuit as judge (1 Sm 7:16) and was one of the primary places for offering sacrifices (10:8; 13:9,10; 15:21). At Gilgal Saul, a Benjamite, was crowned king (11:14,15), and later rejected (13:4–15; 15:17–31). Here the men of Judah met David returning to Palestine after Absalom's rebellion (2 Sm 19:15). That Gilgal was still a religious center of some importance as late as the 8th century BC is indicated in the denunciation by Hosea and Amos of the sanctuary and sacrificial cult located there (Hos 4:15; 9:15; 12:11; Am 4:4; 5:5).

The exact location of Gilgal is disputed among archaeologists. Some locate it at Khirbet en-Nitleh about two miles east of modern Jericho. Others prefer Khirbet Mefjir, a mound about one mile from ancient Jericho (Tell es-Sultan). Joshua 4:19 places it on the eastern border of Jericho, and Josephus gives the distance from the Jordan fording place to Gilgal as 50 stadia (c. 5.8 miles), with Gilgal being about 10 stadia from Jericho (Antiq. 5.6.4). These distances fit best with Khirbet Mefjir.

2. Place perhaps near Jericho (Dt 11:30); however, the language of the passage implies that it is located in the neighborhood of Mt Ebal and Mt Gerizim.

3. KJV rendering of "Goiim in Galilee" in Joshua 12:23. Although its location is uncertain, the context places it in northern Palestine in the area of Galilee.

See GOIIM #2.

4. Place describing the northern border of Judah (Jos 15:7). It was near Adummim and was perhaps identifiable with Geliloth in Joshua 18:17.

5. Place mentioned in connection with Elijah and Elisha (2 Kgs 2:1; 4:38). It was apparently a town farther from the Jordan River than #1 above. In the story of Elijah's translation into heaven, he and Elisha were going from Gilgal to Bethel to Jericho. Since the account places Bethel between Gilgal and Jericho, it could not have been the first Gilgal. It may refer to the modern Jiljiliah, a town on top of a hill in central Palestine, about seven miles north of Bethel.

WAYNE C. HENSLEY

Gilgamesh Epic. Twelve-tablet Babylonian story of Gilgamesh's quest for immortality. The 11th tablet records a version of the flood.

See FLOOD MYTHS.

Giloh, Gilo, Gilonite. Village, and the inhabitants, in the mountains of southern Judah (Jos 15:51). David's counselor Ahitophel was a Gilonite (2 Sm 15:12; 23:34, RSV Gilo). It has been identified with modern Khirbet Jala just northeast of Hebron.

Gimzo. Town of Judah captured by the Philistines during King Ahaz's reign (2 Chr 28:18). It is modern Jimzu, located southeast of Ludd (Lydda).

Ginath. Tibni's father. Tibni unsuccessfully attempted to gain the throne of Israel. Omri became king instead (1 Kgs 16:21,22).

Ginnethoi, Ginnetho. Priest who set his seal on Ezra's covenant during the postexilic period (Neh 10:6, alternately spelled Ginnethon; 12:4, KJV Ginnetho).

Ginnethon. 1. Alternate spelling of Ginnethoi, a postexilic priest, in Nehemiah 10:6.

See GINNETHOI, GINNETHO.

2. Priest and head of Meshullam's household during the postexilic days of Joiakim the high priest (Neh 12:16).

Girdle. Various articles of clothing worn about the waist.

See FASHION AND DRESS.

Girgashites. Canaanite tribe (Gn 10:16; 1 Chr 1:14) whose land was promised to the Jews (Gn 15:21; Dt 7:1; Jos 3:10) and was ultimately acquired (Jos 24:11; Neh 9:8). The tribe's location is unknown, though they may have lived in Karkisha, a city mentioned in Hittite texts, or in Kirkishati, an area east of the Tigris. The name Gresh appeared in 13th century BC Ugaritic texts, and might indicate a tribe. In Matthew 8:28; Mark 5:1; and Luke 8:26, a name variously translated as "Gergesenes" (KJV), "Gerasenes," and "Gadarenes" may preserve the tradition of Girgashite occupation in Palestine.

Girzites. People living in southwest Canaan who were raided by David when at Ziklag (1 Sm 27:8, KJV Gezrites). The Hebrew text has girzi, while the marginal variant transposes two consonants to read gizri, "Gezrites." The Greek version follows the Hebrew marginal variant. The confusion of the names is obviously early. If "Gerzites" is the original, they could have been a Canaanite tribe living in the Mt Gerizim area. If "Gezrites" originally, the people could have migrated from Gezer. They are otherwise unmentioned in the OT.

Gishpa, Gispa. Overseer of the temple servants in Nehemiah's time (Neh 11:21, KJV Gispa); perhaps alternately called Hasupha in Ezra 2:43 and Nehemiah 7:46.

See HASUPHA.

Gittah-hepher. KJV form of the town, Gath-hepher, in Joshua 19:13.

See GATH-HEPHER.

Gittaim. Town in Benjamin to which the inhabitants of Be-eroth fled, where they remained under civil protection (2 Sm 4:3). Nehemiah 11:33 lists Gittaim as one of the places where the returned exiles later settled. The two references may indicate two different places. If so, the second Gittaim may be located northwest of Jerusalem. Some scholars, however, believe that there is only one Gittaim, the one near Be-eroth. No site has been established as yet.

Gittite. Inhabitant of Gath, the Philistine city (2 Sm 6:10,11; 1 Chr 13:13).

See GATH.

Gittith. Obscure Hebrew term in the superscriptions of Psalms 8, 81, and 84; perhaps a musical instrument or a musical cue, signaling a mood, to which the psalms were to be performed.

See MUSIC AND MUSICAL INSTRUMENTS.

Gizonite. Designation for Hashem, one of David's mighty men (1 Chr 11:34). Gizon may describe an ancient Canaanite settlement. Some scholars have emended the text to read "Gunite" (cf. 1 Chr 5:15; 7:13) or "from Gimzo" (cf. 2 Chr 28:18).

Glass. KJV mistranslation for "mirror" in Isaiah 3:23; 1 Corinthians 13:12; and James 1:23. Since mirrors of Bible times were polished metal sheets, "glass" is incorrect.

See MIRROR.

Glean, Gleaning. Practice of allowing the poor to follow reapers in a field to pick up missed spears of grain (cf. Lv 19:9,10; 23:22; Dt 24:21; Ru 2:2–23). Vineyards, as well as fields of grain, were to be available for gleaning (Lv 19:10; Dt 24:20,21). Olive trees, however, were not to be gone over a second time (cf. Jgs 8:2; Is 17:6; 24:13; Jer 6:9; 49:9 [figuratively]; Mi 7:1). The word "gleaned" is also used to describe the killing of men who fled from a battle (Jgs 20:45 KJV).

Glede. KJV translation for "buzzard" in Deuteronomy 14:13.

See BIRDS (KITE).

Glorification. Doctrine of an aspect of salvation built upon the broader biblical concept of the glory of God. The Hebrew word for "glory" originally meant "weighty, heavy, or important." From there it moved to the idea of an influential, rich, or prominent person. In ancient cultures the wealthy and the powerful were marked by the finery of their dress and jewels. Hence a person's glory meant the ostentatious signs of wealth and power. Glory also suggested beauty, since fine clothes and jewels were items of beauty. The concept was then extended to God.

Glory of God. In the OT the glory of God means something obvious about God. The Book of Exodus is rich with references to God's glory. There was the fiery pillar and the glory that entered into the Holy of Holies in the tabernacle (cf. 40:34–38).

In the making of the tabernacle (Ex 25–27), the concepts of glory and beauty are joined. There is evidence that the goodness of the Lord that Moses saw (33:19) could also be translated as beauty. Hence God's glory is his beauty.

The NT continues the theme of the OT, that God is a God of glory (cf. the vision of God in his glory in Rv 4). The main NT evidence, however, centers on the glory of Christ. John's Gospel is uniquely the Gospel of glory. In the incarnation, the Son of God showed the glory that was his as the only begotten of the Father (Jn 1:14). The raising of Lazarus was a manifestation of the glory of God by Christ (11:40). Jesus' prayer in John 17 is filled with comments on the glory of Christ, including the affirmation that the disciples of the Lord would share in that glory.

The transfiguration of Christ was a breaking out into the open of his glory (Mt 17:1–8). The apostle Paul called Jesus the Lord of glory (1 Cor 2:8) and wrote that the glory of God radiated from his face (2 Cor 3:18).

Glorification of the Believer. In 2 Corinthians 3:18 sanctification is described as a changing from glory to glory. Glorification is implied as the last event in the change from glory to glory. In the process of salvation Paul lists glorification as the last and final event (Rom 8:28–30). The verb used (v 30) is in the past tense, which some have taken to mean the certainty and finality of glorification. Glorification is the completion, the consummation, the perfection, the full realization of salvation.

Glorification is a perfect, incontestable

standing before God in the day of judgment (Rom 5:6–11). Christ died for believers while they were ungodly, helpless, sinners, and enemies of God. By faith believers have now been justified. Paul, anticipating the day of the wrath of God, said that if believers are now saved by the death of Christ, in that day they shall be totally vindicated by the life (or intercession) of Christ (v 9). In Romans 8:38,39 Paul says that nothing shall separate believers from the love of Christ, now or in the age to come. In glorification believers shall be in a state of complete exoneration from any possible charge.

Glorification is the perfection of sanctification, and that pertains to one's inner character, self, person. No one passage treats this theme extensively, but Ephesians 5:27 may be taken for all. In that passage Paul wrote of presenting the church to Christ, but what he says of the church is true of each Christian. Jesus will present the church to himself in "splendor, without spot or wrinkle or any such thing, that she [the church] might be holy and without blemish." Or in the language of 2 Timothy 2:10, "Therefore I endure everything for the sake of the elect, that they also may obtain salvation in Christ Jesus with its eternal glory."

Another aspect of glorification is that Christians shall reign with Christ. Paul sets out the reign of Christ in general terms (1 Cor 15:20–28). In one passage of admonition he says that those who endure shall reign with Christ (2 Tm 2:12). Another view of reigning with Christ as an experience of glorification is found in Ephesians, where it describes the state of the Christian in the age to come. Especially relevant is Ephesians 2:7, where believers are seen seated and viewing the immeasurable riches of God in Christ for the redeemed.

The strongest passages of reigning with Christ as part of the Christian's vindication and share in glorification are the martyr chapters in the Book of Revelation (1,11,15,19,21). Paul wrote that believers are heirs of God and joint heirs with Christ, and those who suffer with him shall be glorified with him (Rom 8:17).

Just as the inner person undergoes glorification so does the believer's body. Paul calls the resurrection of the body the redemption of the body (Rom 8:23). In Philippians 3:21 Paul speaks of the transformation of bodies of humiliation (i.e., humiliated by sin and mortality) into bodies of glory identical to that of Christ. The power that shall do this is the power of God by which he subjects all things to his reign.

The most extensive treatment on the glorification of the body is found in 1 Corinthians 15

with some additional material in 2 Corinthians 5. Paul's theme in 1 Corinthians 15 is that as Christians have borne the image of the mortal clay of Adam, they shall bear the image of the immortal Son of God. Paul contrasts the two bodies. The present body is perishable, the resurrection body will be imperishable. This body is one of dishonor, the resurrection body will be one of glory. This body is one of weakness, the resurrection body is one of power. This body is of the current physical order, the resurrection body will be of the future, spiritual, eternal order.

The final event of glorification is God's re-creation of all things: "Behold, I make things new" (Rv 21:5). This means that the old age of sin, defeat, and corruption will be effaced, and the new order of eternal glory shall replace it. Hence there will be a new heaven, a new earth, and a new Jerusalem. Without making all things new the entire plan of salvation would be incomplete.

Salvation involves justification, regeneration, and sanctification in this life. In the life to come it means the glorification of the inner person and the resurrection of the body in glory. But such a glorified person must live in a glorified environment. Hence Scripture must logically end the course of salvation with a glorious new heaven, new earth, and new Jerusalem.

BERNARD L. RAMM

See GLORY; HEAVEN; NEW CREATION, NEW CREATURE; RESURRECTION.

Glory. The singular splendor of God and its consequences for mankind.

The Glory of God. The glory of God can be described in two senses: (1) as a general category or attribute, and (2) as a specific category referring to particular historical manifestations of his presence.

As an Attribute. God's glory refers primarily to his majestic beauty and splendor and the recognition of it by mankind; however, it is also an ethical concept and embraces his holiness, for to sin is to fall short of the glory of God (Rom 3:23). The Scriptures record praise to his glorious name (Neh 9:5), describe him as the glorious Father (Eph 1:17) and the King of glory (Ps 24); he is exalted above the heavens and his glory is over all the earth (Pss 57:5,11; 108:5; 113:4). He is the God of glory that appeared to the patriarchs (Acts 7:2). He is jealous to maintain his glory and unwilling that it be given to another (Is 42:8); he acts to bring glory to himself (Ps 79:9; Is 48:11).

The glory of God is proclaimed by the creation (Pss 19:1; 97:6; Rom 1:20). It is revealed by his mighty acts of salvation and deliverance (1 Chr 16:24; Pss 72:18,19; 96:3; 145:10–12; Jn 11:4,40). His glory is the theme of the praise of men (1 Chr 16:24–29; Pss 29:1,2,9; 66:1,2; 96:7,8; 115:1; Is 42:12; Rom 4:20; Phil 2:9–11).

As His Presence. References to the glory of the Lord are often to particular historical manifestations of his presence; images of light and fire are prominently associated with these occurrences. The foremost example is what is known in rabbinical literature as the *Shekhinah* glory, a phrase meaning the "dwelling glory" and referring primarily to the presence of God in the pillar of cloud and fire in the OT.

The first explicit reference to the glory cloud is found in Exodus 13:21,22; however, earlier examples of God's visible presence should probably be included as well. The presence of the Spirit of God hovering over the waters (Gn 1:2) is likely the same glory cloud that hovered over Israel in the empty wastes of the wilderness at the exodus (Dt 32:10,11). The smoking fire and flaming torch seen by Abraham (Gn 15:17) should also be understood as the glory presence of God. The flame of the burning bush (Ex 3:2) anticipates the later presence of the glory of God on Sinai (Ex 24:16–18).

At the time of the exodus the glory of God appeared in the pillar of cloud and fire to lead the people through the sea and wilderness (Ex 13:21,22; Neh 9:11,12,19). At Sinai with Israel encamped around the mountain, the glory of God comes in the cloud and fire to speak with Moses in the sight of the people (Ex 19:9,16–18; 24:15–18; Dt 5:5,22–24). When Moses is given a glimpse of that glory unconcealed by the cloud and fire, his own face becomes radiant and must be veiled because of the people's fear (Ex 33:18–23; 34:29–35; 2 Cor 3:7–18).

The picture of Israel encamped around the glory of God on Sinai portrays the Immanuel concept of God in our midst, God in the midst of his people. When the tabernacle is completed and the people set out on their march, the glory cloud of God's presence dwells above them throughout their journey (Ex 40:34–38; Nm 10:11,12). When they encamp, the tribes encircle the tabernacle (Nm 1:50–2:2), and the cloud reminds them of his presence in their midst. The cloud is present to quell their rebellions (Lv 10:1–3; Nm 12:5; 14:10,21,22; 16:19,42), to give them manna from heaven (Ex 16:10), and water from a rock (Nm 20:6).

When the ark is lost in battle against the Philistines, a child is named Ichabod, "for the glory has departed from Israel" (1 Sm 4:21,22). The cloud makes no appearances before Israel until the ark is recovered; then the glory cloud fills the new temple that Solomon built and fire devours the offerings (2 Chr 5:13–6:1; 7:1–3). The psalmists celebrate Jerusalem and the

Moses' Peak at Sinai, where the glory of God came in cloud and fire.

temple as the place where his glory dwells (Pss 26:8; 63:2; 85:9); God was in their midst.

Israel, however, did not obey the God in their midst. They denied his glorious presence (Is 3:8) and exchanged the glory of the Lord for idols made by human hands (Ps 106:20; Jer 2:10,11; cf. Rom 1:23). Because of their disobedience judgment came against Jerusalem; the penalties of covenant violation were enforced. God would no longer be the God of a disobedient people (Hos 1:9). God's presence in the glory cloud leaves the temple (Ez 10:4,18,19; 11:12), and Israel goes into exile (12:1–15).

Yet out of this judgment God determined to bring a remnant to rebuild the city and the temple. In his visions Ezekiel sees the glory of the Lord return to dwell in the temple again (Ez 43:2–9), a time when the glory would return to a purified people and dwell among them forever. When the exile is over and the second temple is under construction, Haggai and Zechariah urge the people on with the promise of the return of the glory of God to "fill the house" as it had done in the first temple and to "be glory in their midst" (Hg 2:3–9; Zec 2:5,10,11).

The *Shekhinah*, however, never returned to the second temple—not, that is, until Jesus "became flesh and *dwelt* among us," and we "beheld his *glory, glory* as of the only Son" (Jn

1:14). Isaiah had foreseen that the Messiah, "the Branch," would be glorious (Is 4:2–6; 11:10). John came preaching to prepare the way for the coming of the glory of the Lord (Is 40:2–5; Mt 3:3; Mk 1:3). After the messenger prepared the way, the Lord would suddenly come to his temple (Mal 3:1). Ezekiel had seen the glory of God in the form of a man (Ez 1:28). When Jesus comes to the second temple, he does it as "the radiance of God's glory and the exact representation of his being" (Heb 1:3 NIV). God is again in the midst of his people; Immanuel is present. Christ is the very image of God; to see the light of his face is to know the glory of God (2 Cor 4:4–6). The disciples who witnessed the transfiguration (Mt 17:1–8) saw his glory (2 Pt 1:16,17). To see Jesus was to see a "light to the Gentiles and the glory of Israel" (Lk 2:30–32).

That glory which was Christ's before the foundation of the world (Jn 17:5; Phil 2:4–7) and in his incarnation is enhanced yet more in his resurrection and ascension. Because he humbled himself and was obedient to the point of death, God has highly exalted him (Phil 2:8,9). The Christ who glorified the Father on earth (Jn 7:16; 8:50–54; 12:28; 13:31,32; 17:4) prays that he himself be glorified by the Father (17:1–10). He suffers the death of the cross and enters into his glory (Lk 24:26). He is vindicated and taken up in glory (1 Tm 3:16; 1 Pt 1:21). His resurrection is to a new and glorious body (1 Cor 15:39–43; Phil 3:21). Like the glory cloud of the OT he ascends in the clouds to receive dominion, glory, and a kingdom (Dn 7:14); he is crowned with glory and honor (Heb 2:6–10). He is worthy (Rv 5:12).

The glorified Christ also appears to his servants. Stephen sees the glory of God (Acts 7:55), and Saul is blinded by its splendor (9:3).

That same Christ is to return in glory. He will sit on his throne in judgment (Mt 25:31); evil will be punished (16:27; 24:30; Mk 13:26; Lk 21:27; 2 Thes 2:9,10). Those who have professed him before men need not fear his glorious appearing (Mk 8:38).

At the consummation "the whole earth will be filled with his glory" (Ps 72:19; Is 6:3; Hb 2:14). No longer will a glory cloud rest above a temple to mark the holy place, for there will be a new heaven and a new earth (Rv 21:1). The whole city will have the radiance of the glory of God (vv 10,11), and the glory and honor of the nations shall be brought to its light (vv 22–26).

Glory and the People of God. The people of God experience the glory of the presence of God. The glory cloud of the OT was *their* glory (Ps 106:20; Jer 2:11). Christ came as the embodiment of the glory of God; God was in the midst of his people. When Christ ascended he

sent his Spirit (Jn 16:7–14). God is still in the midst of his people. But he did not come in a pillar of fire over one place, but in tongues of flame at Pentecost as the Spirit filled those in whom he would dwell. The Spirit of glory rests on those who suffer for the name of Christ (1 Pt 4:14); that Spirit is the guarantee of the glorious inheritance of the saints (Rom 8:16,17).

God has given to his people the hope of glory (Rom 5:2; Phil 3:21; Col 1:27; Jude 24,25). Those whom he has chosen he will also glorify (Rom 8:30; 9:23); they will share in the glory of Christ (Col 3:4; 2 Thes 2:14; 2 Tm 2:10). The sufferings of this age do not compare with the glory that will be revealed (Rom 8:18; 2 Cor 4:17). The whole of creation longs to see the glorious freedom of the children of God (Rom 8:21). This hope of glory is so certain that Peter can speak of participating in it even now (1 Pt 5:1) while looking forward to that eternal glory (v 10).

As partakers in the glory of Christ, the church is called to glorify God. Because of the hope that is in them they purify themselves (1 Jn 3:3).

They are called to do all to the glory of God (Rom 15:6; 1 Cor 10:31), to glorify him in their bodies (1 Cor 6:20), and to live such lives that those who see their good works will give glory to God (Mt 5:16,48). They readily endure suffering and persecution to bring glory to him (Rom 5:1–3, 2 Cor 12:9). Their lives are lived "to the praise of his glory" (Eph 1:12,14), depending on his glorious might (Col 1:11). They share in the ministry of the glorious gospel (2 Cor 3:7–18). They are a glorious church (Eph 5:27).

Glory and Mankind. The Bible does speak of the glory of mankind and of the individual in two different ways, one positive and the other negative.

The word in the OT usually translated as "glory" can also be translated as "wealth, honor, status" as the context may demand (Gn 31:1; 45:13; Nm 24:11; 1 Sm 2:8). Men and women strive for wealth and honor as their glory in the world. This status is given them by God (1 Kgs 3:13; 1 Chr 29:12; Pss 21:5; 84:11; Prv 3:16; 8:18), but he can also take it away (2 Chr 26:18; Jb 19:9).

On the whole, however, the attitude of the Bible toward the glory achieved by mankind is negative. It is transitory, and "you can't take it with you" (Ps 49:16,17). All flesh is like grass that withers (Is 40:6), a vapor that vanishes (Jas 4:13–16). Pride in appearance and boasting come from evil motives; faith in the glorious Lord discounts human glory (Jas 2:1–4); pride should not be in appearance but in a pure heart (2 Cor 5:12). All the glory of Solomon could not compare with that of a flower (Mt 6:29). The glory of nations can be toppled in a moment (Is 10:16; 16:14; 17:4; 21:16; Jer 48:18; Ez 31:18; Hos 4:7); the glory of all the kingdoms of earth could not tempt Christ to forsake the law of God (Mt 4:8,9). Rather than seek self-glorification (Lk 14:10,11; Jn 12:43; Rom 2:7,8), all people should give praise to God (1 Cor 1:29–31; Eph 2:9). Pretensions to the glory of God bring only death (Acts 12:23).

RAYMOND B. DILLARD

See GOD, BEING AND ATTRIBUTES OF; PILLAR OF FIRE AND CLOUD; SHEKINAH; THEOPHANY; BOAST; WEALTH.

Bibliography. I. Abrahams, *The Glory of God;* F.D. Coggan, *The Glory of God;* A.M. Ramsey, *The Glory of God and the Transfiguration of Christ.*

Glossolalia. Transliteration of a Greek expression meaning, "speaking in tongues."

See TONGUES, SPEAKING IN.

Gnat. Small flying insect. The word as found in Matthew 23:24 is a general word for a small fly.

See ANIMALS.

Gnosticism. Religious thought distinguished by claims to obscure and mystical knowledge, and emphasizing knowledge rather than faith. Until the mid-20th century Gnosticism was regarded as a Christian heresy which developed through the interweaving of Christian experience and thought with Greek philosophy. More recently, many scholars define the Gnostics more broadly as devotees of a religious view which borrowed ideas from many religious traditions. The meanings of these borrowed terms and practices were shaped into mythological expressions of experiential salvation.

Gnosticism as a Heresy. Prior to the 20th century most of the information available concerning the Gnostics came from early Christian writers (heresiologs) who penned treatises against heretics, and in the process described some of their beliefs and practices. These heresiologs, such as Irenaeus, Tertullian, and Hippolytus, viewed the Gnostics as distorters of Christianity. The Gnostics developed many misinterpretations of the Bible, especially of the creation account and the Gospel of John. Indeed, the Gnostic writers Heracleon and Ptolemaeus are the first known commentators on the fourth Gospel. The anger of the Christian apologists is well summarized by Irenaeus when he likens the Gnostic interpreter to one who tears apart a beautiful picture of a king and then restructures it into a picture of a fox.

Apparently a number of Gnostics continued as members of local churches and some served in high offices. Indeed, there is speculation that Valentinus may have been considered as a possible candidate for bishop at Rome. Moreover, Marcion, the fabled Christian heretic, reinterpreted Paul in such a way that the OT God became the god of evil and Christ became the messenger of the good god of grace. Many Gnostic heretical tendencies have been associated with Marcion, who developed his own censored canon of the NT and thereby forced the Christians to counter by clarifying their own canon. The early Christian historian, Eusebius (d. AD 339), who excerpted some of the early lost works of heresiologs like Hegesippus, also provides insight into the hostility of Christians against various Gnostics like Marcion, Basilides, Tatian, Satornil, Dositheus, and the so-called father of all heresy, Simon the sorcerer.

The wide variety of sects mentioned by heresiologs like the Samaritans, Essenes, and perhaps the Encratites, Nazarenes, Ebionites, and Osseans may suggest the question, Who are the Gnostics? Nevertheless, the view of the heresiologs was so well accepted up to the close of the 19th century that, despite some broadening and generalizing by scholars of the meaning, Adolph von Harnack could still define Gnosticism as the "acute secularizing or hellenizing of Christianity."

During the first third of the 20th century, however, scholars began the task of translating Mandean materials which appeared to be related to Gnosticism. Even though these documents are late—some as late as the 19th century—a number of speculations were made at that time concerning the pre-Christian nature of Mandean literature, primarily by scholars associated with Bultmann.

From this turmoil of "Mandean fever," Hans Jonas, a student of Bultmann, arose to challenge the heresiolog's view of Gnosticism. For Jonas, Gnosticism had emerged because of the mixing of Oriental religions (not merely Christianity) with Greek culture. While Greek culture was superior to the cultures of the Orient, the Hellenistic world experienced a failure of nerve. Because of the religious and philosophic upheaval in the Greek culture, at least three religious traditions made an impact on the Hellenistic world: (1) Jewish monotheism, (2) Babylonian astrology with its view of fate, and (3) Iranian dualism with its basis for understanding evil. The ability of the Greek mind to fuse these ideas into mythological expressions which sought to answer the deep problems of mankind provided for Jonas the context of Gnosticism. While this broader understanding is still debated, Jonas has provided a foundation for distinguishing the two basic types of Gnostic systems as well as for categorizing the library of documents recently discovered in Nag Hammadi, Egypt.

The Gnostic Types. (1) The Iranian type of Gnostic myths that arose in Mesopotamia is an adaptation of Zoroastrianism. The myths are constructed with a horizontal dualism in which the opposing powers of good (light) and evil (darkness) are regarded as fairly equal in strength. In the first stage of the myth, a segment of the light is captured by the jealous darkness when the light transcends itself and reaches into the realm occupied by the darkness. The capture of the light had been viewed by some scholars as the Iranian cosmic "fall." Since the Gnostics themselves are usually identified with the captured light particles, a major task of their myths is to describe the process by which the light particles (encapsulated within the bodies of Gnostics) are released. The body, or flesh in the Greek sense, is merely a worthless covering or tomb, while the spirit—the spark in man linked to the divine—is the part that seeks release and return to the heavenly bliss. In the Iranian system the light forces regroup and make a partially successful counterattack on the forces of darkness. Then, primarily through the work of an alien messenger of strength who has gained a foothold in the world, the good forces are able to challenge the work of the evil captors and supply advice (gnosis) to their devotees. This gnosis leads to salvation or release.

(2) The Syrian type of Gnostic myth that arose primarily in Syria, Palestine, and Egypt, is more complex and involves a vertical dualism. In these systems there is only one ultimate being or group of divinities (not two as in the horizontal systems). Their dualism is usually explained as the result of a flaw, or error, in the good. The error in good, for example, is frequently attributed to the least aeon or member in the good pantheon. The guilty deity is usually designated as Sophia (the Greek term for "wisdom"—which indicates the Gnostic's low opinion of the Greek philosopher's quest for wisdom). This Gnostic myth details how, instead of being satisfied with her station in life, Wisdom lusts for the Ultimate Depth. Since this ultimate god cannot tolerate distortion and weakness in the godhead, he must exclude Wisdom's lust from the heavenly realm. This lust is exiled to a lower heaven, is personalized as the Lower Wisdom (sometimes called the demiurge), and becomes the creator of the world. As lesser deities, the creator and the subordinate gods (often called fates) are unable to perceive the upper heavenly realm and falsely consider themselves to be ultimate. The upper godhead deviously maneuvers the Lower Wisdom to create human beings and give life to them through the pro-

cess of passing on the breath of life. Unknowingly, in the act of creation the Lower Wisdom not only gives life to human beings, but also passes on the divine light particles. Thus, with the help of a savior—an alien messenger of knowledge sent by the upper godhead and often designated as Jesus—humanity is enabled to perceive even more than the creator and to conquer the spiritual stupor that has come upon him when his spirit was encased by the creator in an earthly body.

As a result of the split within the deity in this system, the biblical garden of Eden story becomes radically reinterpreted. The creator provides a tree of life which is a misnomer and actually offers humanity bondage instead. The lower god also forbids access to the tree of knowledge (gnosis), which appears in his creation without his authorization, being provided by the upper godhead for the purpose of awakening Gnostics to the state from which they have come.

Because only those people who have light particles are capable of being saved, the process of salvation in most Gnostic myths is very deterministic. Moreover, salvation really occurs at the end of the Gnostic's life when he seeks to escape from the created world. Concurrent with the escape, the Gnostic strips off the created elements of the body from his spirit and climbs through the fates to the heavenly realm.

With respect to both systems of Gnosticism, recent discoveries have clarified our understanding of the myths. New primary sources for the Iranian type of Gnosticism became available during the first half of this century and include the publication of a Manichean Psalter (1938) and a Manichean book of Homilies (1934). New primary sources for the Syrian type of Gnosticism were made available through the publication of the Berlin manuscript in 1955, but more significantly, our knowledge has recently increased through the discovered codices usually designated as the Nag Hammadi library.

A New Library. In 1947, the area of Jabal al-Tariff (near Chenoboskion and Nag Hammadi in Egypt) gave up a magnificent collection of 12—not 13 as first reported—Coptic codices containing 52 tractates or documents, 6 of which are duplicates. One volume was smuggled out of Egypt and was finally purchased in 1952 by the Jung Institute in Zurich (Gnosticism is important to the study of the psychology of religious experience). After publication the owners agreed to return the pirated manuscript to Egypt, and, together with the remainder of the Nag Hammadi documents, it is now housed in the small but very significant Coptic Museum in Cairo. The documents in the Nag Hammadi library can be divided into several categories.

(1) *Gnostic Texts with Christian Orientation.* In this category, those which have received considerable attention are: *The Gospel of Thomas* which is a series of sayings and was thought at first by some scholars to be a sayings-source for the canonical Gospels of Matthew and Luke; *The Gospel of Truth* which some scholars have thought came from the pen of the well-known heretic Valentinus; *The Gospel of Philip* which contains a unique series of logia related to Gnostic sacraments; and the *Apocryphon of John* which has close affinities to the theories of the Ophites and Sethians as described by the heresiologs and provides a full-scale primary source for the Syrian Gnostic reinterpretation of the garden of Eden story, as outlined above. Some of the other documents in this category which show indisputable signs of Christian influence on Gnosticism are: *The Treatise on the Resurrection,* the several apocalypses of *Peter* and *James, The Book of Thomas the Contender,* and *Melchizedek.*

(2) *Gnostic Texts with Less Than Clear Christian Orientation.* Some scholars have considered that these texts suggest a pre-Christian Gnosticism, but such a conclusion does not seem to be fully substantiated. *Eugnostos* is the document usually cited in this matter and is frequently viewed as an undeveloped stage of the more Christianized form of the text known for some time as *The Sophia of Jesus Christ.* Even the so-called pre-Christian *Eugnostos,* however, seems to bear unmistakable signs of being related to the Alexandrian school of Christian writings and has been found to contain some allusions to the NT. *The Paraphrase of Shem* is another document frequently assigned to this category. Its references to baptism and the redeemer, however, may be the result of a reinterpretation of Christian views and may reflect the conflict between the church and the Gnostics rather than arising from a totally non-Christian context. Other documents in the library usually assigned to this category and subject to similar doubtful interpretations by those who seek to sustain the theory of the presence of a pre-Christian Gnosticism are: *The Apocalypse of Adam, The Three Steles of Seth,* and *The Thunder.*

(3) *Non-Gnostic, Christian Documents.* There are also in the library several non-Gnostic, Christian documents which include: *The Acts of Peter and the Twelve, The Sentences of Sextus,* and *The Teachings of Silvanus.*

(4) *Miscellaneous Documents.* In addition, there are several documents which are neither Christian nor technically Gnostic but which

were probably read with great interest by the Gnostic scribes. Of particular note are the hermetic treatises that are Egyptian in orientation but contain a less radical dualism than is evident in typical Gnostic literature. Hermetic literature has long been known by scholars through the publication of a hermetic library known as the *Corpus Hermeticum* (Eng. trans. *Thrice Greatest Hermes*). The first tractate, "Poimandres," is probably of the greatest interest to biblical students because of its rather positive view of creation and its interesting parallels with some of the theological ideas such as "light" and "life" in the fourth Gospel.

Understanding the Gnostic Purpose. Perhaps one of the greatest problems for the uninitiated readers of Gnosticim is understanding the purpose of the Gnostic myths. The myths often seem so strange that the readers are tempted to scratch their heads and wonder how anyone with any intelligence could believe such wild stories. One must realize, however, that the myth writers were seeking to communicate elements of the unexplained relationships between the human and the divine.

The bondage of evil in the world and its relationship to a good god has stretched the minds of the greatest theologians and philosophers of history. The Gnostics devised their answer to the problem of evil by shifting the blame from this world back to either God himself or to divisions within the divine realm. By compartmentalizing good and evil, it was possible to decide one's destiny by the alignments one made.

But the role of evil was seen as so strong in this world that the Gnostics, like the Greek philosophers before them, concluded the world was a hopeless context for the victory of the good. Accordingly, they abandoned the world to the evil god and developed a theology which focused on salvation as the process of escape from the world. Their theory also provided a salvation while on earth: Since the Gnostics contained divine light particles, they were in fact immortal, and their spirits, though existing in an evil context, would not ultimately be contaminated. The body and all its lusts and lower animal desires would be shed from the spirit as it rose through the realms of the lower godhead to be reunited with the divine spiritual realm after death. Some Gnostics, indeed, carried the idea of noncontamination to ridiculous lengths and devised systems whereby sexual relations with various persons represented divine-human encounters—the more the better! Others tended to affirm more ascetic tendencies whereby they sought to conform the miserable body to the life-style of the incorruptible spirit.

One of the realities the Gnostic interpreters encountered was the fact that not everyone accepted their theories. Accordingly, they devised mythical methods to distinguish between various types of people. Using ideas suggested by Paul in 1 Corinthians 2 and Romans 8, the Gnostics developed a highly sophisticated categorization of people. The pneumatic or spiritual (i.e., Gnostic) persons were divine in origin, being from light particles. The sarkic or fleshly persons were formed totally from the substances made by the creator and could never inherit the divine realm. The Christians whom they saw as struggling to be obedient to the biblical message, however, were a kind of mixture. They needed desperately to work out their salvation, and if they were obedient as psychic people they might gain some form of acceptance. This elitism of the Gnostics and their distortion of the Christian message clarifies the hostility of the Christians against the Gnostics.

The myths were the methodological formulations the Gnostics used to express their theological constructs. To understand them the reader needs the key of gnosis, or knowledge. Interpretation of the myths was in fact an early type of demythologizing, not unlike the process Bultmann employed in interpreting the Bible. The Gnostic writers were among some of the brightest minds of their day. Their creativity is to be admired. Their theology, however, is to be rejected as a distortion of the biblical message.

GERALD L. BORCHERT

Bibliography. R.M. Grant, *Gnosticism* and *Gnosticism and Early Christianity*; H. Jonas, *The Gnostic Religion*; E. Pagels, *The Gnostic Gospels*; J.M. Robinson (ed.), *The Nag Hammadi Library*; R.M. Wilson, *The Gnostic Problem*; E. Yamauchi, *Pre-Christian Gnosticism*.

Goad. Pointed rod, sometimes tipped with metal, used for driving or guiding cattle, especially oxen in plowing.

See TOOLS.

Goah. Location mentioned in connection with the hill of Gareb to which the restored city of Jerusalem will extend. Goah is situated south of Gareb (Jer 31:39, KJV Goath).

Goat. See ANIMALS.

Goath. KJV spelling of Goah in Jeremiah 31:39.

See GOAH.

Gob. Location where David and his men twice encountered the Philistines in battle (2 Sm 21:18,19). In the parallel description of 1 Chronicles 20:4, Gezer is mentioned as the place of war instead of Gob.

God, Being and Attributes of. Inherent characteristics of God revealed in Scripture and displayed in God's actions in biblical history. They are characteristics equally of the Father, the Son, and the Holy Spirit. God's attributes are revealed in progressively richer and fuller ways within the history of redemption.

According to the Bible, the entire creation shows God's glory, deity (Godhead KJV), and eternal power (Ps 19:1–6; Rom 1:20). God's providence also reveals certain of his attributes (Mt 5:45; Lk 6:35; Acts 14:16,17; 17:22–31). The fullest revelation of God's attributes is seen in his work of redemption through Jesus Christ.

How does Scripture express the characteristics of God? First, in the divine names by which God revealed himself (Gn 1:1; 2:4; 17:1; Ex 3:6,14,15; 6:2–5). Some of God's attributes are revealed implicitly in the biblical accounts of creation, fall, flood, Babel, and the exodus, and more fully in the various covenants God made with his people. To Israel he identified himself as the God of Abraham, Isaac, and Jacob (Ex 3:15). To the pharaoh he identified himself as the "God of Israel" or the "God of the Hebrews" (5:1,3).

By the time the people of Israel had reached Mt Sinai the revelation of God's attributes in the biblical narrative had become more explicit: "The Lord, the Lord, a God merciful and gracious, slow to anger, and abounding in steadfast love and faithfulness, keeping steadfast love for thousands, forgiving iniquity and transgression and sin, but who will by no means clear the guilty, visiting the iniquity of the fathers upon the children and the children's children, to the third and the fourth generation" (Ex 34:6,7). This summary is repeated elsewhere with slight variations (Nm 14:18; Neh 9:17; Ps 103:8; Jer 32:18; Jon 4:2).

Historically, theologians have often discussed the attributes of God in abstract, speculative, scholastic ways. That never happens in the Bible. God's disclosure of his attributes led Moses to fall on his knees in worship to confess Israel's sin and pray for pardon (Ex 34:8,9). In other summary passages the response was similar. A sinful appeal to God's attributes was made by Jonah in his angry prayer (Jon 4:1–4). To Christian believers, Scripture presents God's attributes as a standard for living: his people are to be holy, loving, and the like, because God is (Lv 19:2; 1 Jn 4:8,11).

Essence and Attributes. Under the influence of Greek philosophy, scholastic theologians of the Middle Ages usually separated

God's attributes from his "essence." God's essence was viewed in an abstract way; they spoke of "pure Being" or "absolute essence." His essence was generally considered unknown, or known only as "pure Being," whereas his attributes could be known by humankind.

Some theologians have thought that the essence of God could be defined by one attribute—independence, infinity, or absolute will. From a liberal perspective, Albrecht Ritschl (1822–89) thought of love as the chief attribute of God, a view prominent in contemporary theology. Rudolf Otto (1869–1937) described God as "the Holy"; some contemporary theologians also regard holiness as God's chief attribute. Others think of the essence of God as being more complex so that each attribute is part of God's total essence.

All such views are speculative. The attributes should be viewed as inherent characteristics of God, and no separation should be made between essence and attributes. The attributes are the biblical description of God's essence; they state who God really is and what he is like. God revealed himself in relation to his creatures, but in that revelation he gave an authentic description of himself.

Classification of Attributes. The historic Christian confessions refer to various characteristics of God without calling them attributes or classifying them. The Westminster Shorter Catechism (1647) shows a tendency toward classification, describing God as "a Spirit, infinite, eternal, and unchangeable in his being, wisdom, power, holiness, justice, goodness and truth." The first four attributes qualify the others.

Several ways of classifying the attributes have been suggested. Generally such schemes divide the divine attributes into pairs: negative and positive, natural and moral, absolute and relative, immanent and emanent, intransitive and transitive, quiescent and operative, antithetical and synthetical, or incommunicable and communicable. Roman Catholics prefer the distinction of negative and positive, or natural and moral. Lutherans generally favor the distinction between quiescent and operative attributes. Reformed and evangelical scholars usually distinguish incommunicable and communicable attributes. Karl Barth (1886–1968) grouped the attributes under freedom and love and then proposed pairs of attributes that reflect freedom-love or love-freedom. In spite of the diversity of labels given the groups of attributes, surprising agreement exists in the attributes listed under each group.

This article will make a distinction between incommunicable and communicable at-

The Attributes of God

Incommunicable	Communicable
Eternity	Intellectual
Immensity	Knowledge
Immutability	Veracity
Independence	Wisdom
Spirituality	Moral
Unity	Holiness
	Love
	Volitional
	Omnipotence
	Sovereignty

tributes without considering the classification itself as significant. No classification of God's attributes is fully satisfactory. The *incommunicable* attributes emphasize the absolute distinctness of God, his transcendent greatness and exalted nature. Such attributes have little or no analogy in God's creatures. The *communicable* attributes find some reflection or analogy in human beings created in God's image. They indicate the immanence of God in relation to creatures. Yet all the attributes are God's attributes; the distinction between God and man, between Creator and creature, is always basic.

Incommunicable Attributes. Acknowledging some diversity of theological opinion, the following attributes will be considered incommunicable: unity, spirituality, independence, immutability, eternity, and immensity. In addition, the incomprehensibility of God must be mentioned.

God's *incomprehensibility* is sometimes included in lists of his attributes. It seems preferable to regard it as a description of human inability to understand God fully. Incomprehensibility is therefore not an attribute, although it is a given in every discussion of God. Through his revelation God is truly known by faith, yet no creature will ever comprehend God the Creator. Likewise, no one will ever fully understand any one of God's attributes. Acknowledgment of God's incomprehensibility should contribute to a spirit of humility in every consideration of God and his attributes (Pss 139:6; 145:3; Is 40:28; 55:8,9; Mt 11:25–27; Rom 11:33–36; 1 Cor 2:6–16; 13:8–13).

God's *unity* is an expression of monotheism—the fact that the God of Scripture is the only, living, true God (Dt 6:4; Mk 12:29; Jn 17:3). All other gods are idols and figments of human imagination. This attribute is reflected in the first commandment: "You shall have no other gods before me" (Ex 20:3; Mt 4:10).

God's *spirituality* indicates that God is not physical and is invisible. Positively it means that God is personal, living, self-conscious, and self-determining. The invisible God cannot be seen by human eyes (Ex 33:20), so the second commandment forbids every visible representation of God (20:4). Because God is Spirit, he must be worshiped in spirit and in truth (Jn 4:24).

God's *independence* or self-existence indicates that he is not dependent upon anything outside himself. He is self-sufficient in his existence, in his decrees, and in all his works. God has "life in himself" (Jn 5:26) and he "gives to all men life and breath and everything" (Acts 17:25). To Israel he revealed himself as " 'I Am' " (Ex 3:14), and he made Israel a covenant people for his own possession. God continues to work out his will in the world, and even though he uses various means, his independence remains intact. Thus he enters into fellowship with his covenant people, and he publishes the gospel through human agents.

God's *immutability* or constancy expresses his changelessness and his faithfulness to himself, to his decrees, promises, and works. He remains forever the same true God who undergoes no change from within or from anything outside himself. And so in James 1:17 (RSV) we read: "Every good endowment and every perfect gift is from above, coming down from the Father of lights with whom there is no variation or shadow due to change." God's oath to Abraham expressed his immutability so that his covenant people could be sure of the "unchangeable character of his purpose" (Heb 6:17). Samuel told King Saul that the Lord would not "change his mind; for he is not a man" (1 Sm 15:29 NIV; cf. Nm 23:19). "For I the Lord do not change" (Mal 3:6). That was God's explanation for not destroying sinful Judah; he shows mercy and keeps his covenant. Because "Jesus Christ is the same yesterday and today and forever," Christians are warned not to be "led by diverse and strange teachings" (Heb 13:8,9).

God's immutability or constancy does not imply that he is static or immobile. He is a dynamic, living God who is constantly working (Jn 5:17). Sometimes God is described as being sorry, repenting, or changing his mind (Gn 6:6,7; 1 Sm 15:11; Jon 3:10). In their contexts, such figurative expressions show the constancy of God who, in holiness and righteousness, always abhors sin and reacts against it. In his grace and mercy he forgives the penitent, and he carries out his promises without fail (Jer 18:7–10; Ps 110:4; Is 46:10; Eph 1:11). Thus the constancy of God is significant in all human relationships with him, including petitions offered in prayer.

God's *eternity* indicates his transcendence over time. He is timeless and everlasting. He has no beginning or end; he does not undergo growth, development, or maturation. He ex-

isted before the creation of the world; he dwells now in eternity; he will continue as the eternal God even when history ends. Scripture speaks of God as "eternal" (Dt 33:27), "the King" (1 Tm 1:17 NIV), "the beginning and the end" (Rv 22:13). He "inhabits eternity" (Is 57:15) and his "years have no end" (Ps 102:27; cf. 2 Pt 3:8). Although God is above time and is timeless, time is his creation and history is the arena of his work. "When the time had fully come God sent forth his Son" (Gal 4:4); Jesus Christ died on a Friday and rose on the third day. In response to the eternal God, Christians confess that their "times are in thy hands" (Ps 31:15), the powerful hands of the Lord of history.

God's *immensity* and *omnipresence* express his transcendence over space. God fills heaven and earth (Jer 23:23,24). Heaven is his throne and the earth his footstool, so he is not restricted to temple buildings (Is 66:1; Acts 17:24). Yet God is immanent in the world and is actively at work in it to establish his kingdom. No one can hide from the omnipresent God (Ps 139:6–12). Jesus promised "I am with you always, to the close of the age" (Mt 28:20). Since Pentecost (Acts 2) the Holy Spirit is said actually to dwell within the bodies of believers (1 Cor 6:19).

Communicable Attributes. Many attributes of God can be classified under this heading, although it is sometimes difficult to say which biblical references to God should be regarded as attributes. A rich diversity of terminology is found in Scripture, with many synonyms. For convenience the communicable attributes are often classified as intellectual, moral, and volitional.

Intellectual Attributes. God's *knowledge* indicates that in a unique way God knows himself and all things possible and actual. *Omniscience* means that "he knows everything" (1 Jn 3:20). "Even before a word is on my tongue, lo, O Lord, thou knowest it altogether" (Ps 139:4), the secret thoughts of a person's heart. God's righteous judgment is rooted in the fact that he "knows the thoughts of man" (Ps 94:11). Acknowledging that God's omniscience is incomprehensible, the psalmist finds it a source of comfort (139:1–5). All the "treasures of wisdom and knowledge" are hidden in Christ (Col 2:3); therefore the Christian is told to bring every thought captive to obey Christ (2 Cor 10:5). Christian sanctification includes renewal in knowledge to become more like Christ (Col 3:10).

God's *wisdom* indicates that he uses his knowledge in the best possible manner to achieve his goals. God's works are varied, but they are all done in wisdom (Ps 104:24). "The Lord by wisdom founded the earth" (Prv 3:19);

his providence also displays his wisdom (Gn 50:20). Redemption through Jesus Christ reveals God's wisdom (1 Cor 1:24) and awakens awe and praise (Rom 11:33–36). Human beings should seek wisdom (Prv 3:21)—wisdom rooted in the fear of God (Jb 28:28; Ps 111:10; Prv 9:10). Christians are said to be "wise in Christ" (1 Cor 4:10), and Christ charges them to act wisely (Mt 10:16), thus emulating the wisdom of God.

God's *veracity* expresses his truthfulness and faithfulness. He is the truth and he is faithful to himself, to his Word, and to his promises (2 Tm 2:13). "God is light and in him is no darkness at all" (1 Jn 1:5); therefore his followers are to walk in the light (vv 6,7). Jesus is "the way, and the truth, and the life" (Jn 14:6); hence Christians are to walk in the truth and show faithfulness in their lives.

Moral Attributes. The most comprehensive description of God's moral character is his *goodness*. God deals bountifully and kindly with all his creatures. He is "good to all" (Ps 145:9). Jesus insisted that "No one is good but God alone" (Mk 10:18; Lk 18:19). The redeemed praise God for his goodness (1 Chr 16:34; 2 Chr 5:13; Pss 106:1; 107:1; 118:1; 136:1; Jer 33:11) and are called upon to emulate this divine characteristic (Mt 5:45; Lk 6:27–36).

God's *love* is the heartbeat of the gospel. Perfect love flows between the Persons of the Trinity (Jn 3:35; 17:24). At Sinai God revealed himself as "abounding in steadfast love and faithfulness" (Ex 34:6,7), and all his covenantal relations with Abraham's descendants showed his steadfast love. The chief manifestation of God's love was the sending of his Son, Jesus Christ (Jn 3:16). The apostle John, who declared that "God is love," pointed to the cross to indicate what that love really meant: "he loved us and sent his Son to be the expiation for our sins" (1 Jn 4:8,10).

Since the rise of liberalism, many theologians have cheapened God's love for sinners by suppressing God's holiness and righteousness. The catastrophe of sin is minimized, and the cross as an atoning sacrifice and satisfaction of God's justice is denied. But God's holy and righteous love should not be romanticized or cheapened. Love is neither God's chief attribute nor a full description of his nature. Yet Jesus Christ and the cross do express the marvelous love of God—a sovereign, righteous, holy, immutable love (Rom 8:29,30,35–39).

God's love shown to undeserving sinners is called *grace* (Eph 1:6–8; 2:7–9; Ti 3:4). *Mercy* is God's love (sometimes his goodness) shown to those in misery and distress. God is *longsuffering* or patient in his love; he gives time for repentance.

God's *holiness* depicts the moral purity and excellence of God. The description of Jesus' holiness is applicable to each of the Persons of the Trinity: "holy, blameless, unstained, separated from sinners, exalted above the heavens" (Acts 3:14, Heb 7:26). The root idea of holiness is to be separate or set apart. Because of his inherent holiness, God is distinct from everything impure or unholy. God alone is holy; his name is holy, and he bears the name the "Holy One" (Pss 78:41; 89:18; 99:3,9; 111:9; Is 12:6; Jer 51:5; Rv 15:4). Angels praise God's holiness (Is 6:3; Rv 4:8); that revelation led the prophet Isaiah to recognize his own unholiness (Is 6:5). Objects, places, and people are called holy when set apart for the worship of God. Because God is holy his people are called to holiness (Lv 11:44,45; 19:2; 1 Pt 1:14,15). God's discipline of his people is aimed at making them "share his holiness" (Heb 12:10). The holiness of God is so prominent in Scripture that some have (mistakenly) regarded it as God's chief attribute.

Volitional Attributes. God's *sovereignty* indicates the divine authority with which he rules the entire creation and in his sovereign good pleasure does whatever he wills. God is king over the entire creation, and he rules the destiny of human beings and nations. He restores his kingdom through Jesus Christ; the risen Lord revealed that "all authority in heaven and on earth" was given him (Mt 28:18). Election to salvation in Christ is "according to the purpose of him who accomplishes all things according to the counsel of his will" (Eph 1:11). God's sovereign will, though free, is not arbitrary; it is righteous and holy. He created the world and gave his Law as the rule for his people's lives; he covenants, blesses, and judges. God is the "King of kings and Lord of lords" (1 Tm 6:15); he calls all his subjects to obedient love (Dt 6:4,5; Mt 22:37–40; 1 Jn 5:3).

God's *sovereign power* means that he is without bounds or limit in ability; he is *omnipotent* or almighty (Rv 4:8). By his powerful word he created all things, and upholds "the universe by his word of power" (Heb 1:3). There is nothing too hard for the Lord God Almighty (Gn 18:14; Jer 32:27; Mt 19:26); he keeps his gracious covenant and fulfills all his promises (Lk 1:37; Heb 6:18; 2 Tm 2:13). The gospel is "the power of God for salvation" (Rom 1:16) for Christ is "the power of God" to save (1 Cor 1:24). Hence believers must come to know "the immeasurable greatness of his power in us who believe, according to the working of his great might which he accomplished in Christ when he raised him from the dead and made him sit at his right hand in the heavenly places" (Eph 1:19,20).

God's Glory. All the attributes of God are summarized in Scripture's references to the glory of God. The majesty, splendor, beauty, and brilliance of God who dwells in unapproachable light are expressed by this indefinable term. "The God of glory appeared to our father Abraham" (Acts 7:2); God showed his glory to Moses (Ex 33:18,19; 34:6,7). The God of the Lord Jesus Christ is "the Father of glory" (Eph 1:17). The heavens declare the glory of God (Ps 19:1); "the majesty and glory" of God fill heaven and earth (8:1). When finally every tongue shall confess Jesus as Lord, it will be "to the glory of God the Father" (Phil 2:11). Human beings were created for God's glory and Christian believers are instructed to do everything for the glory of God (1 Cor 10:31), thus reflecting in themselves his inherent glory.　　　　　　　　FRED H. KLOOSTER

See GOD, NAMES OF; MONOTHEISM; REVELATION; GLORY.

Bibliography. S. Charnock, *The Existence and Attributes of God*; L.R. Farnell, *The Attributes of God*; D.L. Hocking, *The Nature of God in Plain Language*; J.M. Houston, *I Believe in the Creator*; R.G. Jones, *Our God*; J.I. Packer, *Knowing God*; H. Schultz, *OT Theology*, vol 2, pp 142–79; P. Toon, *God Here and Now*; A.W. Tozer, *The Knowledge of the Holy*.

God, Names of. Cumulative self-disclosure of God to his people. When the Scripture employs the phrase "name of God," God in his fullness is meant. When men and women call on the name of God, God himself is worshiped (Gn 21:33); when they forget the name of God, they depart from God himself (Jer 23:27); when they take the name of God in vain, God himself is personally profaned and affronted (Ex 20:7).

The Biblical Idea of Name. In the Scriptures the name and person of God are inseparably related. This is in keeping with the biblical conception of what a name signifies.

In the Hebrew language, the term for "name" most probably meant "sign" or "distinctive mark." In the Greek language, "name" (*onoma*) is derived from a verb which means "to know"; a name then indicates that by which a person or object is to be known. But the idea of name is not to be taken in the sense of a label or an arbitrary means of identifying or specifying a person, place, or object. "Name" in biblical usage correctly describes the person, place, or object and indicates the essential character of that to which the name is given. Adam names the animals according to their nature (Gn 2:19,20); "Noah" means "one who brings relief and comfort" (5:29); "Jesus" means "savior" (Mt 1:21). When a person was given a new position or a radical change took place in his life a new name was given to indicate that new aspect, for example, Abraham ("father of many," Gn 17:5); and Israel ("one who strives with God" or "God strives,"

32:28). The name of a person or people expressed what the person or people thought the proper description or statement of character was. But with regard to the names of God there are considerable differences, and these are most clearly seen when biblical scholars and theologians confront the question of whether the names of God are ascriptions given by God concerning himself or they are ascriptions given to God by people who observed his acts and reflected on his character as discerned through a study of divine deeds.

Some scholars consider the names of God as human ascriptions. They choose to speak about God as unknowable; they speak of the names and attributes of God as limiting concepts and as hindrances to a fuller understanding of the God who is only known by acts and events. The suggestion is that people should study the acts of God in the present as well as past rather than pay too much attention to the names and attributes ascribed to God by people of ancient times. This view implies that God is still revealing himself as he did in biblical times.

Evangelical scholars, however, insist that the Bible clearly states that God employs names to reveal himself. No one name God employs states all that can be said by God about himself; in fact, all the names taken together do not reveal all that God is. God is infinite; he cannot be fully known. But he has revealed much concerning himself, so much that if one studies the names of God one is struck by the greatness, holiness, majesty, glory, indescribable goodness, and justice of God. And, it should be added, evangelical biblical scholars and theologians are quick to assert that a study of the acts of God increases one's understanding of the self-revealing names and attributes. These same evangelical scholars, while disagreeing with Emil Brunner on some aspects of his view concerning divine revelation, readily agree with him when he writes that if one point is clear from the outset it is that God is not an object which man can manipulate by means of verbal activity or reasoning: "God is mystery in the depths of 'inaccessible light...' God's name is wonderful" (Jgs 13:18). Why ask about it? The answer is that by his name(s) God has chosen to reveal himself. But, the better we know God, the more we know and feel that his Mystery is unfathomable" (*Christian Doctrine of God*, p. 117).

At this point, it should be stated that there is a difference of opinion among biblical scholars and theologians on how to classify the names, ascriptions, descriptions, and attributes of God. For example, J. Calvin and C. Hodge do not discuss the names of God except as they aid in the understanding of his attributes. Others, such as A. Kuyper, have separate discussions of God's attributes and names. H. Bavinck and L. Berkhof deal with the nature of God under three headings: (1) proper names, (2) essential names, and (3) personal names. If one consults these works and goes on to those of scholars like A. Jukes, H. Stevenson, L.S. Chafer, and a group of works designated biblical theology, one would conclude that the names (in the broadest sense) fall into six categories:

(1) Proper names: El, Yahweh, Adonai, Theos, Kurios (God).
(2) Personal names: Father, Abba, Son, Jesus, Holy Spirit.
(3) Titles: Creator, Messiah/Christ, Paraclete/Comforter.
(4) Essential names: Light, Love, Spirit.`
(5) Descriptive names: Rock, Ba'al, Master, Rabboni, Shepherd.
(6) Attributes: names of virtues or characteristics of the triune God-head.

The OT Names of God. *El and Related Names.* The name *El* is found over 200 times in the Hebrew Bible. It is best translated as "God." The term *El* has a number of possible meanings. The root is thought by some to be *Ul*, which means "to be first" or "to be strong." Others suggest the root is *Alah*, which means "to precede," and suggests "leader" or "commander." It can also mean "to be afraid," thus God as *Alah*, as the strong one, is to be feared. Still others suggest the preposition *el* ("to, toward") as the root; the idea then is of "one giving self to others" or of "one to whom others go for help." Some scholars suggest that the word *Alim*, meaning "to bind," should be considered as a root also; that is "the strong one binds and holds firm control." Common to these four suggested root meanings is the idea of strength, power, and of supreme excellence and greatness.

Recent discoveries of tablets inscribed with poems about Canaanite deities indicate this meaning. It is the case in the "Epic of Baal" found at Ras Shamra and thought to have been written in patriarchal times. This epic sets forth Baal as the chief hero, but El [or Il] is referred to numerous times. He is the father of the gods Baal, Amoth, Mot, and the male counterpart of the female goddess Asherah from whom came 70 sons. El is also referred to as the creator of creatures and the father of mankind. He is thus the highest of all Canaanite deities; the king, ruler, the strong one over all things and people. This Canaanite god is very likely referred to in the OT. Isaiah says that a throne will be set above the stars of El (Is 14:13), and Hosea accuses Judah of unfaith-

Ruins at Ugarit, where the "Epic of Baal" was found.

fulness to God because he still is roaming with El. From these passages it can be understood that the God of the Scriptures called El, is not to be identified with the Canaanite god El. The Canaanite god was conceived of as mortal, the Hebrew El as the eternal Living One. The point is that both the Hebrews and the Canaanites used the word *El* to refer to their deity as the strong and powerful one and the first and preeminent one.

El in the OT is used particularly in the earlier books, where it describes God's exercising dynamic power as distinguished from authority. *El* speaks of God as the great doer and producer. He is the One who exercises such power that whatever is made, done, kept, or destroyed is his doing (cf. Ex 15). *El* is also used to express the idea that God is not to be identified as part of creation but as the One who is above, behind, and beyond creation (Ps 19:1). In relation to man, the crown of creation, God as El is totally other (Ez 28:2; Hos 11:9).

Elohim is also commonly used as the name of God, occurring over 2500 times in the OT. There are differences of opinion concerning the exact origin and meaning of this plural name. Some have suggested that *Elohim* is the plural form of *El*, but it seems more likely that it is a plural of *Eloah*, which appears in the poetical writings. Some critical writers have suggested that this plural form is borrowed from pagan polytheistic sources; but no such plural form is found among pagans as the name of a deity. Others have suggested that the plural form is used to indicate the triune nature of God, and support for this has been seen in the use of a singular verb with this plural noun. The biblical doctrine of the Trinity, as it is developed throughout the Scriptures, does not appear to be based on the use of this plural form of God's name, even though the two positions are not contradictory.

The plural form, *Elohim*, is best understood as expressing intensity. God makes himself known by this name as the Lord of intense and extensive glory and richness as he exercises his preeminence and power in the created cosmos. Hence, when the Scripture speaks of creation, it states, "In the beginning Elohim created the heavens and the earth" (Gn 1:1). This name is repeated 35 times in Genesis 1 and 2 in connection with God's power revealed in creation. In the Book of Deuteronomy the name *Elohim* is used repeatedly to stress the majestic power of God which was shown in Israel's release from bondage in Egypt, her preservation in the wilderness, and her preparation for entrance into the Promised Land. In this context, God (*Elohim*) is also recognized as the lawgiver who will powerfully execute judgment on covenant-breakers. The psalmists also used this name repeatedly as they acknowledged and praised God the majestic ruler who had demonstrated his omnipotence in many dimensions of life (see Ps 68, in which *Elohim* appears 26 times.)

Evangelical scholars such as A. Juke and G. Campbell Morgan have interpreted *Elohim* as an expression of God's covenant relationship with his people. They point to the use of *Elohim* when God spoke to Abraham and said he would be Elohim to the patriarch and his seed, that is, God would be in a covenant relationship to them (Gn 17:1–8). Included in this relationship is the idea that God is ever ready to use his power on behalf of those who are in covenant with him. Thus *Elohim* also expresses the concept of God's faithfulness in regard to the covenant and the promises and blessings involved in it.

The name *Eloah* occurs mainly in the poetical writings, no less than 41 times in Job. Isaiah used it to express the incomparable character of God (Is 44:8). In like manner David asked, "Who is Eloah, but the Lord?" (2 Sm 22:32). Moses was the first to use the name *Eloah* in his song (Dt 32:15–17) referring to Israel's God in the context of the "no-gods," which had been chosen in place of the rock of salvation and the incomparable One. This name was probably used to stress the fact that God is the only true and living One, the One to be adored and worshiped; he is to be reverenced with a holy fear.

Another closely related name is *Elah*, found in Ezra and Daniel. Some think *Elah* is a Chaldee form of *Eloah*. Its root is said to be *Alah*, which means "to fear" or "to be perplexed." God as Elah is the God to be feared and worshiped accordingly. In view of this meaning it can be understood why, in the time of Israel's exile and immediately after their return this name was commonly used.

Three other names of God include the term *El: El Elyon* (or *'Eljon*) is the name used to designate the God of Melchizedek (Gn 14:18–

22) as God Most High. In Psalms 57:2 and 78:56 the Hebrew reads *Elohim Elyon*. It is believed that the term *Elyon* is derived from the verb *Alah*, meaning "go up, be elevated, to be exalted." There are a number of instances where the term *Elyon* is used alone, but the context indicates that it is then used as a synonym for God (e.g., Nm 24:16; Ps 83:18; Is 14:14). The term *Haelyon*, translated the Most High, also occurs (e.g., Gn 40:17). The term *elyon* is used quite frequently as an adjective; it is then translated as "high, highest, upper, uppermost." The basic ascription given to God when this name is employed is to One who is above all things as the maker, possessor, and ruler. He is incomparable in every way; he is subject to no one and no thing; he is the Exalted One. Some evangelical biblical scholars have noted that this term is used particularly of God's ruling in the millennial kingdom, a conclusion based on the fact that Yahweh is called *Elyon* in passages construed to refer to Israel's final and full restoration (Dn 4:25; Ps 83:18). It would seem, however, that *El Elyon* is a name that is applicable to God in all ages and in all circumstances. In all dimensions of life, in worship, military activities, political and economic involvement, God is to be acknowledged as the incomparable, the exalted, the maker, possessor, and ruler of all people, all things, and all events.

El Shaddai is used in the longer form seven times in the Scriptures (Gn 17:1; 28:3; 35:11; 43:14; 48:3; Ex 6:3; Ez 10:5). In the shorter form (*Shaddai*), it appears more frequently: in Job 30 times, in Psalms 19:1 and 68:14, once in Isaiah (13:6), Ezekiel (1:24), Joel (1:15), and Ruth (1:21). In these passages the combined ideas of God as the all-powerful, all-sufficient, transcendent, sovereign ruler and disposer are present. This meaning is generally accepted, but there are differences as to the exact meaning of the term *Shaddai*. Some have begun with *shad* as the first concept to be considered; its meaning is "breast, pap, or teat," and it is considered a "precious metaphor" of God who nourishes, supplies, and satisfies. The root of *shad* (*shadah*) in Semitic usage, is to moisten; this meaning is not the preferred one in the context in which El Shaddai appears; nor is *shed* (demon), which some scholars have sought to use because it appears in Deuteronomy 32:17 and Psalm 106:37 speaking of Israel's idolatry. In addition to the fact that *shed* is spelled differently, the connection between the concept of demon and God as all-powerful is difficult to establish. More acceptable is the suggestion that Shaddai is a composite term of *sha* ("the one who") and *dai* ("is sufficient"). The later Greek versions have adopted this meaning. The most preferred explanation is that Shaddai is derived from the verb *shadad* ("to overpower, to deal violently, or to devastate"). A clear connection between *shadad* and *Shaddai* is said to be found in Isaiah 13:6 and Joel 1:15. God as *El Shaddai* is presented as the all-powerful One, totally self-sufficient, absolute ruler, and the One who can and does make final disposition. The Septuagint has adopted this meaning; it translates *El Shaddai* as *Pantokrator*, the "All Ruler or Sovereign One."

G. Vos points out that *El* and *Elohim* emphasize God's relation to nature, and *El Shaddai* points to God's overpowering nature in the service of his grace and compelling her to further her designs. L. Berkhof (*Systematic Theology*) points out that whereas God as *El Shaddai* is indeed presented as the all-powerful One who overpowers nature, the name, where it occurs in the Bible, does not present God as an object of fear or terror, but rather as a source of blessing and comfort.

El Olam is used to refer to God as the everlasting or eternal one, a clear instance where the name of God and an attribute of God are combined. The term *olam* has a wide range of uses. It is usually defined in lexicons as meaning "long duration, antiquity, and indefinite futurity." It is used to speak of God's existence, God's covenant and promises, and of the Messiah's reign. The psalmist said, "Thou art from *olam* (everlasting) to *olam* (everlasting)" (90:2), and the prophet Isaiah spoke of God as the everlasting Creator (40:28), as everlasting strength (26:4), and Jeremiah spoke of God as everlasting King (10:10). Berkhof points out that God's everlastingness or eternity speaks of his infinity in relation to time. *Olam*, as ascribed to God, should not be thought of as duration prolonged indefinitely backward and forward. Rather, the word speaks to God's transcending all temporal limits; in addition, *olam* refers to the quality of God which differs essentially from time. The Scriptures speak of *El Olam* in contexts where the believer's assurance of well-being, security, and hope are presented as prized possessions.

El Gibbor is a name that speaks of God's power and might. *Gibbor* alone is used in reference to mighty and heroic men. The two terms together always refer to God, and in some instances *Haggadol* ("the greatest"), is added (Dt 10:17; Jer 32:18) to emphasize the greatness and awesome majesty of God. *El Gibbor* is also used to describe the Messiah in Isaiah 9:6 (cf. also Pss 45:4; 89:20).

El Roi is used once to describe God as the seeing One. Hagar described the Lord this way when she was found in the wilderness (Gn 16:13). Psalm 139:1,2 expresses this concept of God as the all seeing One from whose eye nothing is hidden (cf. also Ps 33:18).

Yahweh (Joseph). *Yahweh* is a distinctly proper name of God. It is never used to refer to any pagan gods; neither is it used in regard to men. It appears 6823 times in the OT, occurring first in Genesis 2:4, where it is joined with *Elohim*. Yahweh is used 164 times in Genesis, and it appears 1800 times in Exodus through Joshua. It never appears in a declined form in the Hebrew language, and it never occurs in the plural form or with suffixes. It is abbreviated as *Yah* and *Yahu* (cf. Ex 15:2; Ps 68:4; Is 12:2, etc.).

The exact meaning of the name "Yahweh" is difficult to determine. Some have sought the root in the verb *hayah* ("to be") or in an ancient form of that same verb *hawah*. There is no agreement as to whether or not the *qal* or *hiphil* form of the verb should be considered as the root. Those who opt for the *hiphil* form read Yahweh to mean, "cause to be"; thus Exodus 3:14 would read, "I will cause to be what has come to be." Others look to the *qal* form and then translate the name as "I Am" or "I Shall Be." Still others are inclined to disassociate the name from the verb *hayah* and regard it as an original and independent term, expressing the uniqueness of Israel's gracious God.

Translators of the OT have not agreed upon the correct translation of the name "Yahweh." Since it is translated into the Greek as *kurios*, which means "Lord," many have rendered Yahweh as "Lord." But "Adonai," which is best rendered "Lord," appears with Yahweh in various instances. Many modern translators have chosen to use Yahweh. The name "Jehovah," as used in the ARV (1901) is judged unacceptable. This name arose due to the Jewish practice of not pronouncing Yahweh because of Leviticus 24:16, "He that names the name of Yahweh shall surely be put to death." This warning against a vain or blasphemous use of the name was taken in an absolute sense, especially after Israel's deportation (cf. Am 6:10). Hence, when reading the OT the Jews substituted either Elohim or Adonai for Yahweh. From this, the practice of adding the vowels of Adonai to YHWH (JeHoWaH) became established.

An interesting question is whether Yahweh was used initially in a specifically geographical area. Some scholars have concluded that Moses first learned of the god called Yahweh while in the desert of Midian. Later it became the name used of the god worshiped in southern Canaan, that is, the area of Judah and Simeon. These scholars posit that Elohim was the name used in northern Canaan. They also suggest that each area developed its own religious traditions and wrote its "records of religious beliefs," each employing the divine name in use in its respective area. Later, when the nation of Israel was united, the two documents were joined, and the names "Yahweh" and "Elohim" were both used to refer to their common god. This view of the origin and use of the names of God finds no basis in the text of the OT. Both names are used in unique combinations and are also shown to have been known and used long before the time of the exodus. Abraham, for example, spoke of lifting his hand to Yahweh, El Elyon (Gn 14:19–22), and Abraham and Isaac built altars to Yahweh and called on his name (13:4; 26:25).

The interpretation of Exodus 6:2,3 has caused much debate. "And God said to Moses, 'I am Yahweh; I appeared to Abraham, to Isaac, and to Jacob, as El Shaddai, but by my name Yahweh I did not make myself known to them.'" This passage has been understood to mean that the name Yahweh was not known or used prior to the time of Moses. But that is not what the passage states; rather it speaks of the patriarchs not knowing God *as* Yahweh. They knew him as El Shaddai in actual revelatory historical deeds. They had not come to know God according to his unique character, that is, as Yahweh. In other words, God had always been Yahweh; he is saying to Moses that the descendants of the patriarchs would come to know the full rich meaning of the name by the way God dealt with them.

This name "Yahweh" reveals God's nature in the highest and fullest sense possible. It includes, or presupposes, the meaning of the other names. Yahweh particularly stresses the absolute faithfulness of God. God had promised the patriarchs that he would be their God, that he would be with them, would deliver and bless them, keep them, and give them a land as a place of service and inheritance. Moses is told by God that Israel is about to behold and experience the unchangeableness of God as he steadfastly and wondrously remembers his word and executes it to the fullest degree. God would prove to be a faithful, redeeming, upholding, restoring God. In working out this redemption, God would demonstrate that he is all that his name implies: merciful, gracious, patient, full of loving-kindness, truthful, faithful, forgiving, just, and righteous (Ex 34:5,6). Truly, Jacob had received an insight into the meaning of the name when he exclaimed, "I wait for thy salvation, O Yahweh" (Gn 49:18).

Yahweh, then, is the name par excellence of Israel's God. As Yahweh he is a faithful covenant God who, having given his Word of love and life, keeps that Word by bestowing love and life abundantly on his own.

In view of the richness of the name Yahweh, it can be understood why there were stringent rules regarding its proper use (Lv 24:11,16). It also explains why thankful, rejoicing, worshiping Israelites used the abbreviated form of Yahweh in song when they sang Hallelujah: "Praise Yah" (Pss 104:35; 106:1; 149:1; 150:1).

Yahweh is used in a number of phrases which are considered names of or ascriptions of God. The most common of these compound names is *Yahweh Sabaoth* ("hosts"). The word "hosts" is used very frequently in the Pentateuch to refer to the armies of Israel (cf. e.g., Nm 10:14–28). This is because the word is derived from the verb *saba* which means "to wage" war. It also means "to serve" in some contexts; for example, Numbers 8:24 clearly has reference to the service performed in the tabernacle. The noun *sabaoth* first occurs in Genesis 2:1, where it refers to the many components of the earth and heaven. Some would limit the reference in these contexts to the stars. Still others would suggest that the *sabaoth* refers to the angels, appealing to Psalm 33:6 for confirmation.

The compound name, Yahweh Sabaoth first appears in 1 Samuel 1:3. In view of the frequent use of *sabaoth* in 1 and 2 Samuel to refer to armies (1 Sm 12:9; 14:50; 17:55; 2 Sm 2:8; 8:16; 10:16, etc.), it is thought that the compound name refers to Yahweh as the God of armies, that is, God has his armies to serve him. These are considered to be armies of angels who are ministering servants to God. It has been correctly pointed out that the compound name, Yahweh Sabaoth, is used most frequently by the prophets (Jeremiah 88 times, Zechariah 55 times, Malachi 25 times, Haggai 14 times) at times when God's people had either suffered defeat at the hands of enemy armies or were threatened by defeat. So the compound name was used to remind them that their covenant God had great hosts to fight and work for him on behalf of his people. Thus, though Israel's armies failed, their covenant God was sufficient for every possible circumstance. And it was to this Yahweh Sabaoth that Israel's commanders were to give allegiance (Jos 5:14,15), and in whose name Israel was blessed (2 Sm 6:18).

Other compound names which occur infrequently are:

Yahweh-Nissi (*nissi*, "my banner") is the name that Moses called on when he built an altar celebrating Israel's God-given victory over the Amalekites (Ex 17:15). Isaiah uses the term *nissi* when speaking of the coming Messiah who is to be the conqueror (Is 11:10; 59:19).

Yahweh-Rapha (*rapha*, "healer") appears in

Exodus 15:26, when Israel is assured that God, their healer, will prevent the diseases of Egypt from affecting Israel. Although the name is only used once, God was often called upon and praised as the healing One (e.g., Ps 103:3; Is 30:26; Jer 6:14, etc.).

Yahweh-Rohi (*rohi*, "my shepherd") appears in Psalm 23:1. The concept of Yahweh as shepherd is explicated in Ezekiel 34. "I myself will be the Shepherd of my sheep" (v 15). Jesus demonstrated this concept's full meaning when as a shepherd he gave his life for his sheep.

Yahweh-Jireh (*jireh*, "to see ahead or to provide") appears in Genesis 22:14. Abraham gave this name to the place where God provided a substitute for his son Isaac, whom Abraham was to offer as a sacrifice to God.

Yahweh-Shalom (*shalom*, "peace") is the name Gideon gave to the altar he built when the angel of the Lord came to give him orders to fight the Midianites (Jgs 6:24). In Ephesians 2:14, Christ is called the peace for sinners, a peace which passes all understanding and guards believers' hearts and thoughts (Phil 4:7).

Yahweh appears with a few forms of the term *zadaq*, "righteousness." Yahweh is spoken of as our righteousness in Jeremiah 23:6; the thought evidently is that David's Righteous Branch (the Messiah) will impute God's righteousness to those who are incorporated in the new covenant. This concept is expressed in the Pentateuch a number of times when it is said that God has provided a way for living righteously; that is, God provides a way of sanctification (cf. Lv 20:8; 22:9; etc.).

Adonai. This name for God appears some 360 times in the OT, though it is not uniformly used. It is first found in Genesis 15:2,8, when Abram requests more definite information concerning a son and the Promised Land. It appears only 14 times after that in the Pentateuch. It appears repeatedly in the Psalms (over 50 times), and certain of the prophets use it frequently (Is 47; Jer 29; Ez, over 150; and Am 27 times).

The word *adan*, meaning "master, ruler, owner, lord" is thought to be the root of the noun *adon* which is frequently used of men. For example, in Genesis and 1 and 2 Samuel the term is used often for men who own slaves or are in positions of authority.

In reference to its use as a name for God, some have argued that it was used frequently in early times but that it was later replaced by Yahweh. This hardly seems likely in view of its frequent use during the monarchy by kings, servants, and prophets. It is a name by which people addressed God, and when so used, it was in combination with Elohim. Adonai is

correctly described as the name of personal communication between the believer and God. In such communication the worshiper acknowledged God's intense majesty and greatness and also the sense of belonging to this God. Adonai, coming from human lips, expressed honor for God and humble submission on the part of the believing person. Adonai, thus, is the name that expresses faith, assurance, security, ready service, and thanksgiving (Pss 16:2; 57:9,10, etc.).

Old Testament Combinations. In the OT the names of God appear in various combinations. For example Elohim-Yahweh, Elohim-Yahweh-Adonai, and Elohim-Adonai are very common. These combinations were an effort to express the fullness of God's being and character as these had been revealed. Names of God in combination with "Israel" occur also as, for example, Yahweh-God-Israel (Jgs 5:3; Is 17:6), God is also invoked in relation to Israel without the mention of one of his names, for example, Qedosh Yisrael (Holy One of Israel, Is 43:14, etc.) and Abir Yisrael (Mighty One of Israel Gn 49:24; Ps 132:2; Is 49:26, etc.). By means of these phrases the covenantal relationship between God and his people was expressed and God's unchanging character was positively acknowledged.

Old Testament Personal Names. The personal names of God are Father, Son, and Holy Spirit and variations of these.

H. Lockyer has correctly stated that there is no revelation of God as Father in the OT comparable to that of Jesus in his prayer, "Our Father."

The term *Abh* ("father") appears more frequently in Genesis than in any other book, and in the Pentateuch more than in any other division of the OT. But it is not used there of God, but of one who has generated children (i.e., the male parent), the progenitor—head, chief, and ruler of the family group or clan. It is used often in the sense of the responsible one through whom God has spoken, with whom God has dealt, and through whom he has given a rich heritage to the children and descendants of the patriarchs.

In the poetical books, God is referred to as Father, but is not directly named as such. Job is asked "Has the rain a father?" (Job 38:28). The reference is to God as the maker, source, and controller of rain. In Psalm 68:5 God in his holy dwelling place is the "Father of the fatherless"; the parallel phrase, "protector of widows," indicates the sense. Psalm 89:26 says that David will cry to God, "Thou art my Father," and the parallels use the terms "God" and "Rock of my Salvation." The idea here is of God as creator and savior who raised up, delivered, and protected David. In Psalm 103:13,

"Father" is used analogously, "As a father pities his children."

Isaiah uses the term "Father" in relation to God four times. Three times it refers to the One who has made, saved, formed, kept, and directed Israel (Is 63:16; 64:8). Isaiah says the promised child is to be named Everlasting Father (9:6). Used in this sense, the term establishes the Son's equality with the Father in stature, function, ability, and responsibility.

Jeremiah also refers to God as father in 3:4,19, meaning the origin, keeper, and friend of his people Israel. Malachi in 1:6 and 2:10 speaks of God as the parent who deserves honor from his children and as the origin and ruler of all people.

The term "son" is one of the most used terms in the OT; it commonly occurs in the sense of offspring and descendant. It also appears in the sense of follower or successor. There are a few indirect references to the second person of the Trinity.

The messianic Psalm 2 has such a reference, "You are my son" (v 7). It is stated in the context of the king speaking to one who rules and is to rule with and under the sovereign. The immediate reference may be to the theocratic king; however, the reference is revealed in the NT to be the second person of the Trinity (Acts 13:33). Thus the term "son" is applied to the promised Messiah who is set forth as the divine sovereign ruler and judge of the nations. The Son is perceived to be equal with Father in deity and function. Not all biblical scholars accept this interpretation, but support is found in such NT passages as Hebrews 1:8 which quotes Psalm 45:6. As stated above, Isaiah speaks of the son to be given (9:6), the One born of the virgin (7:14) who is Immanuel, Almighty God, Everlasting Father, Prince of Peace.

The name Holy Spirit occurs only a few times in the OT. The Spirit is referred to frequently by terms and phrases such as the Spirit of God (Gn 1:2), the Spirit of the Lord God (Is 61:1), the Spirit of the Lord (Ez 37:1), the Spirit (Nm 11:17; 27:18), my Spirit (Gn 6:3), and thy Spirit (Ps 51:11). Though the character of the Spirit is not developed as clearly in the OT as in the NT, it can be safely stated that the relationship posited between God and the Spirit is such that there is no doubt that the OT teaches the deity of the Spirit. The character and function of the Spirit is referred especially in relation to the work of creation (Gn 1:2; Ps 33:6, etc.) and the equipping of servants for the service of God, for example, craftsmanship (Ex 35:31), leadership (Nm 11:17; 27:18), prophecy (1 Sm 10:6; 2 Sm 23:2; 2 Chr 15:1; Ez 11:5; etc.).

Old Testament Titles of God. Titles are employed in the OT in reference to offices and functions. It is not suggested that God has an office as such, but the terms are used to indicate the concept of functions with authority, full right, and responsibility. In this sense, God possesses office in fullness and totality.

God is entitled the Creator of men (Eccl 12:1), of the entire earth (Is 40:28), and of Israel his people (43:15). God is spoken of as Redeemer in a personal manner (Jb 19:25; Ps 19:14) and also as *the* universal Redeemer (Is 59:20). Other titles are employed which refer to God's functions, such as maker, (Is 54:5), king (Ps 29:10; Is 43:15), judge (Gn 18:25; cf. Ancient of Days, Dn 7:9,13,22), keeper (Ps 121:5).

Messiah is the title that is given to the one who is to come as the True Prophet, the Only High Priest, and the Eternal King. The term *Messiah* comes from the Hebrew word *Meshiah* ("to be anointed"). When a person was anointed to be a prophet, priest, or king, it meant that he was designated for the position, assigned the duties of the position, authorized to function, and qualified or enabled to fulfill the requirements of the respective office. The anointing oil symbolized the Holy Spirit particularly in respect to qualifying a person for the tasks assigned. The Holy Spirit is not referred to by any specific title in the OT.

Old Testament Essential Names. The group of names included under this heading are more common in the NT, but when used there, they reflect an OT source.

God is light. The psalmist sang, "The Lord is my light" (Ps 27:1); he undoubtedly had in mind the pillar of fire that gave light and direction to the Israelites in the wilderness. The cloud that stood before the tabernacle and filled the temple is described as a radiant light of glory. Hence, to speak of God as light is to speak of him as the source and dispenser of glory.

God is also spoken of as the one who loves his people (Dt 7:8,13), but he is not said to *be* love in the NT sense. Nor does the OT speak of God as spirit, although it does teach that he is spirit.

Old Testament Descriptive Names of God. The OT writers employed a wide variety of symbolic names to describe some specific aspect of God and of his relationship with his people. Only a few of the more common and striking ones will be listed.

Baal is used to express the concept of God as owner and possessor. The term must be understood as carrying both the idea of a position of sovereignty combined with a personal relationship; this explains why the term is often translated as "husband."

The verbal root of *Baal* means "to marry, take possession of, to rule over."

Baal is used very frequently, either alone or in compounds (e.g., Baal Peor), of the pagan gods of Canaanites and Philistines. It is used of the God of Israel by Isaiah: "Your Maker is your husband" (54:5). In Hosea 2 God is spoken of as husband also, but the Hebrew word used there is *'ish*.

Qanne' is said to be God's name in Exodus 34:14. The word originally meant "to possess," and the idea of becoming protective over that which was possessed seems to have given the meaning of "to be red or to be jealous." God's name is Jealous because he presses his claim on those with whom he has covenanted; he will not tolerate their covenanting with other gods.

Zur ("Rock") is used by Hannah in her song of exultation to describe God (1 Sm 2:2). It conveys the idea of God as a support and defense. God had upheld and protected scorned and despised Hannah. Isaiah accuses God's people of not remembering the "Rock of your refuge" (17:10). The psalmist sang to God to be his rock (31:2) and then sang, "Thou art my Rock and my fortress" (31:3, cf. also Ps 71:3). The most striking reference to God as Rock is in Moses' song: "The Rock, his work is perfect; for all his ways are justice. A God of faithfulness . . . just and right is He" (Dt 32:4). Moses expresses complete confidence in God's unfailing and permanent demonstration of his virtues as he performs his Word and work.

Ro'eh, from the verb *ra'ah* ("to feed, shepherd") is used by the psalmist to sing of God's care and concern for his people (23:1). Psalm 80:1 appeals to the Shepherd who leads Israel to bestir himself and to restore Israel to her place and blessing. Jacob used the name when blessing Joseph, speaking of God as the Shepherd and Rock who had kept and protected Joseph and who would continue to do so (Gn 49:24). Ezekiel presents an expanded description of the Shepherd's character and work (Ez 34). Jesus undoubtedly drew from these OT passages when he said, "I am the good shepherd" (Jn 10:11). It should be noted that in taking the OT name of shepherd Jesus was identifying himself with Yahweh of the OT.

Divine names which are descriptive of the promised Messiah are very common in the OT, for example, Root, Branch, Star, Scepter, and the like.

The NT Names of God. *Proper Names of God.* Theos is the NT equivalent of the OT names El and Elohim; Elyon appears in the NT as *Hupsistos Theos*, the Highest God (Lk 1:32,76; Mk 5:7, etc.). *Pantokrator* (El Shaddai) appears with *Theos* (2 Cor 6:18; Rv 16:7, etc.). This name was used not only to express God's transcendency, power, sovereignty, and lordship; but also, the fact that God is a personal God in close relationship with his people. This fact is established by the very frequent use of personal pronouns used with *Theos*. L. Berkhof says this is so because in Christ God is the God of each of his children. *Theos* appears over 1000 times in the NT. *Kurios*, "Lord," is used to express the OT names Yahweh and Adonai in the Septuagint and the NT follows it. *Kurios* means "power," so the meaning is not the same as "Yahweh"; yet the NT does give *Kurios* the full weight of meaning that the OT gave to Yahweh, especially when applied to Jesus Christ (cf. Acts 2:36; Phil 2:9–11; etc.).

Despotes is used five times of God or of Jesus in the NT (Lk 2:29; Acts 4:24; 2 Pt 2:11; Jude 4; Rv 6:10). It expresses the idea of authority; the idea of brutality conveyed by the modern concept "despot" is absent from the NT usage even when applied to men, where its central thought is ownership (2 Tm 2:21).

Personal Names of God. In the baptismal formula, which is part of the Great Commission, the three personal names of God appear, Father, Son, and Holy Spirit. These names carry the OT meaning, but since the relationship of the three persons is explicated, the NT meaning of the names is enriched.

Abba is used as a personal name of God in the NT. It is an Aramaic word which is translated as "Father" (Mk 14:36; Rom 8:15; Gal 4:6). The name expresses a very intimate and inseparable relationship between Christ and the Father and between believers (children) and God (Father).

"Jesus" is the personal name of the Son, the second person of the triune Godhead. It means "savior" (Mt 1:21). The root of this name "to save" gave rise to names such as Joshua, Hoshea, and Hosea. The basic meaning of the OT root is "to bring into a safe, wide, open place." Joshua, bringing Israel into Canaan, did in person what his name meant. The NT explanation ("save from sin") is not contrary to the OT meaning. To be saved from sin is to be restored to fellowship with God and to enter into the paradise of the heavenly kingdom.

Titles of God. As in the OT, the title "Creator" is applied to God (Rom 1:25; 1 Pt 4:19). It expresses specifically the idea of God as originator, sole possessor, and absolute ruler of the cosmos.

"Christ" is the title applied to the Son, Jesus. It is the Greek translation of the Hebrew "Messiah."

"Paraclete" is the title given to the Holy Spirit by John (14:16,26; 15:26; 16:7). The Greek word *parakletos* means "intercessor, advocate, consoler, comforter." When Jesus spoke to his disciples concerning his departure he emphasized that he would send his Spirit, through whom he would be present. In addition, the Spirit would minister to them in their specific needs, particularly in times of stress, persecution, and threats of death. The Spirit would render whatever service was deemed necessary for Christ's disciples.

The Essential Names of God. Jesus often used a wide variety of terms to express who and what he was. According to John's Gospel he repeatedly said, "I Am," and then used such terms as "light," "manna/living bread," "water." These self-appropriated names can be fully understood only if they are studied in their OT contexts (cf. above).

Jesus spoke of God as spirit (Jn 4:24). The essential nature of the triune God must be understood as spiritual, that is, noncorporeal. Spirit carries with it the idea of transcendence of space, time, or any other limitation.

John specifically stated that God is love (1 Jn 4:8). Love expresses in the fullest manner how God gave himself in his Son Jesus Christ.

Descriptive Names. "Shepherd," "door," "vine," and similar names are terms Jesus Christ used to describe himself when he spoke of what he came to do on behalf of those the Father had given him.

Rabbi is used to describe Jesus Christ. It means "my great one." *Rabboni* is an intensified form of the word. Applied to Christ it suggests a recognition of his divine status and character. The term *rabbi* was used to refer to the teachers who had mastered the Law of God and were able to communicate its truth to the unlearned. "The Highest," *Hupsistos*, is used to refer to God as the transcendent, exalted One. It carries much the same meaning as El Elyon in the OT.

GERARD VAN GRONINGEN

See GOD, BEING AND ATTRIBUTES OF; MONOTHEISM; NAMES, THE SIGNIFICANCE OF; CHRISTOLOGY; MESSIAH; HOLY SPIRIT; JESUS CHRIST, LIFE AND TEACHING OF.

Bibliography. W. Eichrodt, *Theology of the OT*, vol 1, pp 178–205; L. Koehler, *OT Theology*, pp 21–58; G. Oehler, *Theology of the OT*; D. Patrick, *The Rendering of God in the OT*; H.H. Rowley, *The Faith of Israel*; H. Schultz, *OT Theology*, vol 2, pp 116–41.

God-fearer. One who fears God. This can be a term of reverence, an emotional reaction of terror, or a dread of God's vengeance.

Phrases describing the God-fearer in the OT are frequently coupled with such terms as "stood in awe" and "held in awe" (1 Chr 16:25; Ps 22:23). Reverence for the Lord is used less frequently, but is used with this meaning when Obadiah hid the prophets in a cave to save them from being assassinated by Jezebel (1 Kgs 18:3,4,12). A man could expect to receive

justice from a God-fearing ruler (2 Sm 23:3; 2 Chr 19:7), and long life was a reward for those who feared the Lord (Prv 10:27; 14:27; 19:23). A God-fearing family would rely on the Lord for practical help in time of trouble (2 Kgs 4:1; Prv 14:26). The fear of the Lord was effective in driving away sin and was itself the beginning of wisdom (Sir 10:24; 40:14–20).

In the NT fear of God is frequently used in conjunction with admonitions to love and serve the Lord (Col 3:22; 1 Pt 2:17), and in the Magnificat, Mary's statement "His mercy is on those who fear him" is used in the sense of revere and obey (Lk 1:50). In Acts, the term "God-fearer" is given a specific interpretation, being used with reference to Gentiles who attended the synagogue. Paul mentions them separately when introducing his address: "Men of Israel, and you that fear God" (Acts 13:16). Cornelius was an honest, generous, and God-fearing Roman centurion who, although not a Jew, was recognized as leading a life acceptable to the Lord (Acts 10:2,35).

The fear of God was also used in both the OT and the NT to denote dread or terror of the mighty power and judgment of the Lord (Gn 3:10; Dt 9:19; Jb 6:4; 9:28,29; Ps 76:8; Mt 17:7; 28:10; Lk 5:10; 12:5; Acts 5:5,11; 1 Tm 5:20).

HAZEL W. PERKIN

See PROSELYTE; FEAR.

Gods, Goddesses. Pagan male and female deities. Although the Bible teaches that there is only one God (Is 45:18,21,22; Mk 12:32), heathen people in ancient times quickly developed a belief in large numbers of so-called gods (Jer 10:11) and goddesses. Eventually each nation created and worshiped its own deities, usually more than one in number. Many of these "foreign gods" (1 Sm 7:3) are named in the Bible, and in most cases we are told to what nation each belonged. The list from Mesopotamia, a center of idol worship, is the longest: Adrammelech and Anammelech (2 Kgs 17:31), Bel (also known as Marduk; Is 46:1; Jer 50:2; 51:44), Kaiwan (Am 5:26), Nebo or Nabu (Is 46:1), Nergal (2 Kgs 17:30), Nisroch (19:37; Is 37:38), Rephan (Acts 7:43), Sakkuth (Am 5:26), Succoth-benoth (2 Kgs 17:30), Tammuz (Ez 8:14), and Tartak (2 Kgs 17:31). The Syrians were devoted to Ashima (v 30) and Rimmon (5:18), who was also worshiped under the compound name Hadad-rimmon (Zec 12:11). Israel's eastern neighbors, Ammon and Moab, worshiped Milcom or Molech (1 Kgs 11:5,7,33; 2 Kgs 23:13) and Chemosh, respectively, although the Moabites also worshiped a local manifestation of Baal (Nm 25:3,5). Philistine gods were Dagon and Baal-zebub (2 Kgs 1:2,3,6,16), who is the equivalent of the NT Beel-

A four-headed god from Babylon.

zebul (Mt 12:24; Lk 11:15). One Canaanite god, Baal, and two Canaanite goddesses, Asherah and Ashtoreth, are mentioned frequently in the OT; Ashtoreth was the same as the Mesopotamian Ishtar, also known as the "Queen of Heaven" (Jer 7:18; 44:17–19,25). The gods of Egypt are represented by only two names in the Bible: Amon (46:25) and Apis (v 15). Nibhaz (2 Kgs 17:31) was probably an Elamite god.

At least three Greco-Roman deities are mentioned in the NT: the Greek goddess Artemis (Acts 19:24,27,28,34,35), known as Diana by the Romans, and the Greek gods Zeus and Hermes (Acts 14:12,13), known as Jupiter and Mercury, respectively, by the Romans.

The Bible clearly teaches that the gods of the nations have no objective reality (Jer 2:11), even though their worshipers sincerely believe that they actually exist (v 28). But the Lord proclaims that "they are no gods," (v 11; 16:20), "gods that are not gods" (5:7 NIV), they "are nothing" (Is 41:24), "beings that by nature are no gods" (Gal 4:8). The NT further

declares of idols that "an idol has no real existence" (1 Cor 8:4) and that "gods made with hands are not gods" (Acts 19:26). It is not surprising, then, that when the Israelites began to encounter other nations in significant ways—that is, as early as the time of the exodus—they were told repeatedly that the Lord is greater than all other gods (Ex 15:11; 18:11; Dt 10:17; Jos 22:22; 1 Chr 16:25; 2 Chr 2:5; Pss 86:8; 95:3; 96:4,5; 97:7,9; 135:5; 136:2; Dn 2:47; Zep 2:11).

Such so-called gods were not worthy of Israel's attention or veneration. Since there is only one God, other gods could not claim and did not deserve Israel's worship (Ex 20:3; Dt 5:7). The Hebrew language did not even have a word for "goddess" and therefore had to use its word for "god" to express that concept (see 1 Kgs 11:5,33). The Israelites were to make no images (Ex 20:4,23; Lv 19:4; Dt 5:8) or mention (Ex 23:13; Jos 23:7) of the gods and goddesses of their heathen neighbors.

Yet despite all God's warnings, idolatry was Israel's besetting sin from the earliest times. During the patriarchal period God's people were attracted to the "household idols" (Gn 31:32) of their relatives, and they continued to worship other gods throughout most of their history (Ex 32:1,4,8,23,31; 34:15; Hos 11:2). Idolatry eventually led to the destruction of the northern kingdom (2 Kgs 17:7–18) in 722 BC and of the southern kingdom (2 Kgs 22:17; cf. Dt 29:25–28) in 586 BC. During their time of exile in Babylonia the Jewish people saw idolatry at its worst and turned away from it, but their ancestors could have avoided untold agony if they had simply followed the example of Joshua: "As for me and my house, we will serve the Lord" (Jos 24:15).

Refusing to worship the one true God in the

Red-figure ware (dated in the 5th cent. BC) from Athens, picturing Leto, Apollo, and Artemis.

proper way leads inevitably to other evil activities (Rom 1:21–32). An example applicable to modern times is given to us by Paul, who warns that we are not to "worship the good things of life, for that is idolatry" (Col 3:5 LB).

RONALD F. YOUNGBLOOD

See CANAANITE DEITIES AND RELIGION; IDOLS, IDOLATRY; HIGH PLACE.

Gog. 1. Reubenite, Shemiah's son (1 Chr 5:4).

2. Individual described as the prince of Meshech who ruled over the land of Magog (Ez 38:2–21; 39:1–16). Magog was evidently a territory located far from Palestine whose inhabitants would attack Jerusalem in a final attempt to overthrow God's people. The Lord, through Ezekiel, promised Gog a catastrophic defeat.

Attempts to identify Gog with some historical ruler have not been convincing. Gyges of Lydia, who drove out Cimmerian invaders, has been suggested, but equally probable are Gaga, mentioned in the Amarna tablets, and Gagi, king of the city-state of Sabi. Some have maintained a mythological interpretation, in which Gog is a symbol of evil actively opposing good. Certainly Gog, connected in Scripture with godless nations such as Gomer, Put, Persia, Sheba, and Tarshish, is depicted as leading an alliance of world powers in opposition to God. Gog also appears in Revelation (20:7–9), where Satan mobilizes Gog and Magog (i.e., the nations of the world) against God's saints in a final battle. A literal view contemplates an attack on Jerusalem by hostile forces (cf. Zec 14) while a symbolic interpretation envisions a climactic conflict between good and evil.

R.K. HARRISON

Goiim. 1. People or region mentioned in Genesis 14:1,9 as ruled by a king named Tidal. The word is variously translated "nations" (KJV) and "Goiim" (RSV). Tidal, together with three other kings—Amraphel of Shinar, Arioch of Ellasa, and Chedorlaomer of Elam—attacked several cities in the Valley of Siddim near the Dead Sea (v 3). They defeated the five kings of the valley region, looted their towns, and captured Lot, Abraham's nephew, who lived in Sodom (v 12). When Abraham heard of this, he gathered his soldiers, pursued the victorious kings, defeated them, and rescued Lot (vv 13–16).

2. People mentioned in connection with Joshua's victory over an unknown king of Goiim (Jos 12:23, KJV king of the nations of Gilgal). The location of these people is uncertain, since the verse reads "Gilgal" in the Hebrew text and "Galilee" in the Septuagint.

Golan. City and a district in the territory given to Manasseh in Bashan. It was the northernmost city of refuge east of the Jordan River (Dt 4:43; Jos 20:8), given to the Levite family of Gershon (Jos 21:27; 1 Chr 6:71). Of uncertain identification, it was known to Josephus as a fertile area, and to Eusebius as a village. The best current suggestion places it at Sehem el-Jolan, east of the river el-'Allan.

See CITIES OF REFUGE; LEVITICAL CITIES.

Gold. Soft yellow metallic element.

See COINS; MINERALS, METALS, AND PRECIOUS STONES; MONEY AND BANKING.

Golden Calf. *See* CALF, GOLDEN.

Goldsmith. *See* INDUSTRY AND COMMERCE; TRADES AND OCCUPATIONS.

Golgotha. Place where Jesus and two thieves were crucified, in the vicinity of Jerusalem. The term appears in the NT only in the accounts of the crucifixion. Three of the Gospels use the Hebrew-Aramaic term, "Golgatha" (Mt 27:33; Mk 15:22; Jn 19:17), while one uses the Greek equivalent, "Calvary" (Lk 23:33, meaning "skull or cranium").

The reason why this place was called "the skull" is unknown, although several explanations have been offered. (1) An early tradition, apparently originating with Jerome (AD 346–420), asserted that it was a common place of execution and that the skulls of many who had been executed were strewn around the site. No 1st-century evidence has been found to substantiate this viewpoint. (2) Some suggest that it was a place of execution and that "skull" was used figuratively, simply as a symbol of death. (3) Origen (AD 185–253) mentioned an early, pre-Christian tradition that the skull of Adam was buried in that place and hence its name. This is probably the oldest explanation of the name, and is referred to by several writers after Origen. (4) Others have said that the name resulted from the fact that the place of the crucifixion was a hill which had the natural shape of a skull. No early evidence from any sources has been found to substantiate this view, and the NT accounts do not refer to the place as a hill.

The location of the site is disputed. The biblical references give us only general indications. It was outside the city proper (Jn 19:20; Heb 13:12). It may have been on an elevated site since it could be seen from a distance (Mk 15:40). It was perhaps near a road since "passersby" are mentioned (Mt 27:39; Mk 15:29). John's account places it near a garden which contained the tomb in which Jesus was buried

Gordon's Calvary/Golgotha.

(Jn 19:41). The use of the definite article, "*the* place of the skull," would indicate that it was a well-known place.

There seems to have been little interest in the site of Golgotha until the early part of the 4th century. Eusebius, who lived in Jerusalem for several years, said that Constantine the emperor instructed Bishop Marcarius to find the site of the crucifixion and burial. Later accounts said that the bishop was guided to the site by a vision of the Queen Mother Helena. The site which he settled on contained a Hadrianic temple of Aphrodite, which Constantine destroyed; and there tradition says he found fragments of the cross of Christ. On that site he built two churches, and this is the site of the modern Church of the Holy Sepulcher. Although destroyed and rebuilt several times, this has remained a fixed site since the time of Constantine.

In 1842 Otto Thenius contended that Golgotha was a rocky hill about 250 yards northeast of the Damascus Gate. He based his contention on the assertions that it had been a Jewish place of stoning, lay outside the city wall, and was shaped like a skull. Later General Charles Gordon also advocated this spot, and it has come to be known as "Gordon's Calvary."

WAYNE C. HENSLEY

See CRUCIFIXION; JERUSALEM.

Goliath. Eleventh-century BC Philistine warrior from Gath, who challenged Israel to battle (1 Sm 17). He was subsequently felled and decapitated by the youthful David. Goliath was over 9 feet tall (v 4), wore armor weighing about 125 pounds, and carried a spear of 15 pounds weight. His sword, kept at Nob, was later given to David (21:9; 22:10). He may have descended from the Anakim (see Jos 11:22), but his height could have resulted from an anterior pituitary tumor. In 2 Samuel 21:19 his death is attributed to Elhanan, who in 1

Chronicles 20:5 is credited with killing Goliath's brother.

Gomer. 1. Son of Japheth, who was a son of Noah (Gn 10:2; cf. 1 Chr 1:5). He had three sons: Ashkenaz, Riphath, and Togarma (Gn 10:3; 1 Chr 1:6). He is the progenitor of the ancient Cimlerians, who according to Ezekiel's prophecy would join with Gog, the leader of the Magogites, in an effort to stamp out Israel (Ez 38:6).

2. Diblaim's daughter, a prostitute and wife of Hosea by divine command. Having borne Hosea children, she lapsed into immortality but was redeemed. Her behavior served as an illustration of Israel's infidelity to God (Hos 1–3).

See HOSEA (PERSON).

Gomorrah. One of the "cities of the valley" destroyed by God because of its wickedness (Gn 19).

See CITIES OF THE VALLEY, CITIES OF THE PLAIN; SODOM AND GOMORRAH.

Goose. *See* BIRDS.

Gopher Wood. Material Noah used to build the ark (Gn 6:14).

See PLANTS (CYPRESS).

Goshen. 1. Geographical region in Egypt occupied by the Israelites during their sojourn in Egypt from the time of Joseph to the exodus. Genesis 46,47 gives us several pieces of information concerning Goshen. (a) It was a definite part of Egypt. (b) It was the place where Joseph met his father after their years of separation, when Jacob moved his family to Egypt. (c) It was an area good for grazing flocks. Goshen has been associated with Egyptian bull cults and as being important for animal husbandry. At one period the princes of Thebes sent their cattle to the Delta for pasture, even though it was controlled by the Hyksos. Sacred cattle were probably pastured there by Egyptians also. (d) It is called "the best of the land" in two different verses (Gn 47:6,11) and is identified as the "land of Rameses." (e) It probably had a military outpost on its eastern border and may not have been heavily inhabited by Egyptians.

The name "Goshen" is not of Egyptian origin, but is Semitic and attests to the occupation of the region by Semites before the New Kingdom of Egypt. The Septuagint reads "Gesem of Arabia" instead of "land of Goshen" in Genesis 45:10 and 46:34. Ptolemy the geographer said that "Arabia" was an Egyptian name for the eastern border of the Nile Delta, and

Delta, and this would account for the terminology of the Septuagint.

Goshen was a region of about 900 square miles, consisting of two districts. The western half ran from Zoan to Bubastis, a distance of about 35 miles from north to south. This district was an irrigated plain containing some of the most fertile land in Egypt. It is about 15 miles wide at the Mediterranean Sea and narrows to about 10 miles between Zagazig and Tell el-Kebir on the south. The eastern sector contains a large desert area between the Nile plain and the Suez. As it stretches to the south from Daphnai to the Wadi Tumilat, it increases in width to about 40 miles from east to west. South of this section more desert area stretches to the Suez on the south and from the Bitter Lakes on the east to Heliopolis on the west. The physical arrangement of Goshen is important in determining the route of the exodus. Given the above description, the Wadi Tumilat would have been the most logical route to the Red Sea for people who were driving flocks and herds. The route would have led from the south side of the field of Zoan near Bubastis, east to the edge of the wilderness and the head of the Bitter Lakes.

2. Area in the territory conquered and occupied by the Israelites under Joshua (Jos 10:41, country of Goshen; Jos 11:16, land of Goshen). It was probably in the hill country of Judah between Hebron and the Negeb.

3. Town in the territory of Judah (Jos 15:51). It may have been the central city of the district discussed in #1 above, but this is uncertain.

Gospel. Word derived from the Anglo-Saxon *godspell* denoting "glad tidings" or "good news."

The OT. *The Gospel Declared.* Glad tidings may concern the birth of a son (Jer 20:15); deliverance from personal affliction (Ps 40:9); the choice of a king (1 Kgs 1:42); victory in battle (1 Sm 31:9; 2 Sm 1:20; 4:10; 18:19–31; 2 Kgs 7:9; 1 Chr 10:9; Ps 68:11); or Israel's salvation from foreign powers (1 Chr 16:23; Ps 96:2), particularly Assyria (Na 1:15) and Babylon (Is 40:9; 41:27; 52:7; 61:1)—a theme eventually taken up by the Gentiles themselves (Is 60:6). Naturally such news is proclaimed *widely* (e.g., 1 Sm 31:9; Pss 40:9; 96:2,3; Is 40:9; 52:7), spread *rapidly* (2 Sm 18:19–31; 2 Kgs 7:9; note also the "great host" of evangelists in Ps 68:11), and declared and received *joyfully* (2 Sm 1:20; Ps 96:2,11,12; Is 52:7–9; 61:1–3; Jer 20:15).

God the Savior. Where the message is gospel for the Israelites (cf. 1 Sm 31:9) and is based on fact (cf. 1 Kgs 1:42–43), the news is in every case but one (Jer 20:15) expressly related

to God. Gospel owes its existence and bears its witness to action which he has taken, action moreover that is *saving* in character. In 2 Samuel 18, the good news is not merely that David has been delivered from his enemies, but that the Lord has accomplished this (vv 19,28,31). A direct act of God causes the Syrians to flee (2 Kgs 7:1–9). The "glad news" of Psalm 40:9 concerns the Lord's "saving help" (v 10; cf. 1 Chr 16:23 and Ps 96:2). The kings whose flight the maidens celebrate (Ps 68:11) have been scattered by the Almighty (v 14). The gospel of Nahum 1:15 is that the Lord has broken the Assyrian yoke (v 13). God's saving work is the main theme of Isaiah 40–66. The good news is that the mighty God is returning to Zion (40:9,10), having conquered Babylon by the hand of Cyrus (41:25,27). The "peace" and "salvation" announced in 52:7 are won by his sovereign power ("Your God reigns"). Having witnessed his saving deeds, the nations praise the Lord (60:6, cf. vv 4,9,16). There are "good tidings for the afflicted" (61:1) because "the year of the Lord's favor" has arrived (v 2).

The Basis of Salvation. Of all the passages cited, those of Isaiah provide the most important background for gospel in the NT. According to Isaiah's gospel, it is God alone who saves, and there is no explanation for his saving action except in his own nature. Israel's deliverance is undeserved; she is no more worthy of the divine love now than when she went into captivity. In whatever measure she has paid the just due for her past sins (Is 40:2), she remains a sinful people (42:25; 46:12,13; 48:1). It is only by God's *grace* that she is saved (55:1–7). By God's design, Israel's salvation depends not upon her own righteousness but upon his (41:10; 45:24; 46:13; 51:5,6). There being no righteousness to reward, the Lord acts to *create* righteousness in Israel (45:8; 61:3,10, 11). Yet as these references indicate, salvation is not accomplished at the expense of justice. The penalty for Israel's sins is to be paid in full. God's mercy is not hereby called into question. On the contrary, it is precisely here that his mercy is most poignantly expressed; for the penalty is exacted not from his people but from the Servant appointed to stand in their place (53:4–12). Through the Servant's work, many shall be justified (v 11); those who could present no case for their own righteousness (43:25–28) shall be acquitted.

The Effects of Salvation. The joy which attends the proclamation and reception of gospel finds its ultimate expression in the praise of God. In reporting victory to David, Ahimaaz exclaims, "Blessed be the Lord your God, who has delivered" (2 Sm 18:28). The gospel of Psalm 40 is declared amidst public worship (vv 9,10). It is during a festal procession celebrating God's enthronement that the glad tidings of Psalm 68:11–14 are recollected. At the heart of the evangel in Isaiah 40:9 is the exclamation "Behold your God!" The herald of 52:7 declares, "Your God reigns"; it is not primarily the appearance of the herald or the release of the captives that causes the watchmen to "sing for joy," but rather "the return of the Lord to Zion" (v 8). The identity of the evangelist in 61:1 is not disclosed; what is certain is that the Lord has anointed him (v 1), that he proclaims the year of the Lord's favor (v 2), and that God will be glorified through his preaching (v 3). According to 60:6, the nations "shall proclaim the praise of the Lord." Psalm 96 calls upon the whole earth to tell of God's salvation (vv 1,2) and thereby to "bless his name" and "declare his glory" (vv 2,3).

The Promise of Salvation. With the return of the exiles from Babylon, the salvation announced in Isaiah's gospel is only partly realized. Israel's suffering is by no means over: the foreign nations, far from becoming her fellow worshipers (as envisaged in Is 60 and Ps 96), would remain her oppressors. Nor was Israel altogether liberated from her sin: her unrighteousness was to persist (cf. Mal), and the Servant appointed to bear her iniquities (Is 53) had not yet appeared. As Isaiah makes clear, the full realization of this salvation awaits the dawn of a new age—an age which is itself created by God's saving activity. At the close of the OT, the inauguration of this new age is still awaited. We are thus prepared for gospel as set forth in the NT.

The NT: Stage One. The gospel as declared before the death of Jesus must be examined.

Gospel and the OT. In only two places (Gal 3:8; Heb 4:2,6) does the NT speak of the proclamation of gospel prior to the Christian era. This is quite remarkable, given (1) the unmistakable presence of gospel in the OT, (2) the extent of gospel terminology in the NT (the noun appears 76 times, and the verb 54), and (3) the fact that the NT presents Christ as the fulfillment of the OT and draws heavily on the OT to interpret his person and work. Not only is it remarkable, it is very significant. It indicates that the NT usage depends not only upon the *character* of the message (truth about salvation), but also upon *historical events*. Almost without exception, the NT restricts its application of gospel-terminology to proclamations made during the time of fulfillment—the age in which the salvation promised in the OT is *actually accomplished*. The NT is preoccupied, not with promises of salvation, but with news of salvation. According to Mark 1:1–4, the gospel "begins" not in the OT but with John the Baptist, in whose work OT prophecy

is fulfilled. In Romans 1:1–5 the gospel is represented as a blessing promised in the OT but not actually given until Jesus comes (see also Acts 13:32,33). Galatians 3:8 is not so exceptional as might first appear, for the word used here to denote an advance proclamation of the gospel to Abraham is not *euangelizomai* but *proeuangelizomai*.

Good News of Christ's Coming. The promised birth of John the Baptist is good news (Lk 1:19), not only for his parents (1:7,24,25) but for all the people: John is sent to prepare them for Messiah's coming (vv 14–17,67–79). John's own preaching is gospel (3:18) for the same reason. Messiah is coming to execute judgment, a process that involves both condemnation and salvation (vv 3–17). John's message is gospel for sinners in that they are warned of impending doom and urged to repent before the axe falls (vv 7–9); it is gospel for the repentant in that they are promised forgiveness (v 3) and membership in Messiah's community (v 17). The birth of the Savior himself is announced as "good news of a great joy" (Lk 2:10,11).

Gospel According to Jesus: The Coming of the Kingdom of God. Jesus is authorized by God and anointed by the Spirit to evangelize (Mk 1:14; Lk 4:18). At the heart of his preaching stands the announcement, "The time is fulfilled, and the kingdom of God is at hand; repent, and believe in the gospel" (Mk 1:15). (For further references to this gospel, see Mt 4:23; 9:35; 24:14; 26:13; Mk 8:35; 10:29; 13:10; 14:9; Lk 4:43; 8:1; 16:16.) The message is good news for several reasons: (1) The kingdom is coming. The God whom Jesus worships is eternally sovereign over all that he has made. Yet paradoxically his rule is incomplete: his will is not done on earth as it is in heaven; wrong, not right, prevails. But these conditions are not final, according to Jesus. With the *coming* of the kingdom, God's rule will be completed; wrong will be judged, righteousness established, and his people blessed. (2) The kingdom is *now* being inaugurated. "The time is fulfilled," declares Jesus (Mk 1:15a). The time appointed for the fulfillment of the OT promises has arrived. (3) The consummation of the kingdom is therefore no longer a distant prospect; the full realization of God's rule is "at hand" (v 15b). (4) God is establishing his rule for a saving purpose. This is implied in Jesus' call to repentance (v 15c). It is especially clear in the passages to which we now turn.

Gospel According to Jesus: The Salvation of the Poor. Invited to read the Scripture in the synagogue at Nazareth, Jesus turns to Isaiah 61: "The Spirit of the Lord is upon me, because he has anointed me to preach good news to the poor. He has sent me to proclaim release to the captives and recovering of sight to the blind, to set at liberty those who are oppressed, to proclaim the acceptable year of the Lord" (Lk 4:18,19). Having read the prophecy, Jesus announces its fulfillment in his own ministry (v 21). Included among those whom Jesus has come to free are the *physically* infirm such as the blind (v 18) and the leprous (v 27). (cf. the references to healing miracles in 4:23,33–41; the close connection between evangelizing and healing in Mt 4:23; 9:35; 11:5; Lk 7:21,22; 9:6; and the description in Mt 12:22–29; Lk 13:11–16, of the physically afflicted as captives of Satan now liberated by Jesus.) Also included are the *materially* poor—people like the widow helped by Elijah during the famine (Lk 4:25,26). It is the literally poor and hungry whom Jesus pronounces "blessed" in Luke 6:20,21 (cf. the woes upon the rich and well-fed in vv 24,25, and the commands to give to the needy in vv 30–38). Yet it is primarily *spiritual* poverty which is in view. Still applying Isaiah 61, Jesus speaks in Matthew 5:3 of the "poor in spirit." These are people broken and grieved by misery and poverty, oppression and injustice, suffering and death, national apostasy and personal sin—people who in their extremity turn to God and longingly wait for him to bring forth justice, bestow his mercy, and establish his kingdom. It is to just such people that Jesus brings good news (Mt 5:3–10). God has sent him to usher in the kingdom, to rescue the lost, to liberate the enslaved, to cure the afflicted, to bind up hearts that are broken, and to forgive the guilty (Mk 2:5,10,17; 10:45; Lk 4:18–21; 7:48–49; 15:1–32; 19:10).

Gospel According to Jesus: The Grace of God. The coming of the kingdom is not the effect or the reward of human effort, but God's answer to the human predicament—the gift of his favor (Lk 12:32). Correspondingly, the explanation for the salvation of the poor lies nowhere but in God's own character. As the prodigal himself recognizes, he hardly deserves to be his father's servant, much less his son. Nothing he has done, not even his repentance, accounts for the father's love (15:11–32). In the parable of Matthew 20:1–16, it is owing entirely to the goodness of the employer that the last workers to be hired receive a full day's wages. The first debtor in the story of Matthew 18:23–35 has earned nothing but the right to be sold into slavery; instead the king cancels his enormous debt. The publican who has nothing to offer God but a confession of sin and a plea for mercy, goes home justified (Lk 18:13,14). The same holds true for the more virtuous among the poor, such as the persons described in Matthew 5:7–10. Their virtue is real, not imagined. Yet in keeping God's commands, they do not put him in their debt; they are simply doing their duty (Lk 17:7–10). Fur-

thermore, even the most merciful need divine mercy (Mt 5:7). For even those most zealous to obey God's Law are unable to fulfill all its requirements (cf. 11:28–30). The first servant in Matthew 18:23–35 owes far more money than someone in such a situation could possibly pay—which serves to magnify the generosity of the king. Grace depends for its exercise upon the inability of its objects (Lk 14:12–14).

Gospel According to Jesus: The Call to Salvation. The Israelites are without exception a sinful people, all of them needing the salvation which Jesus brings (Mt 1:21; Lk 1:77). In demonstration of God's grace, Jesus proclaims his gospel to the entire nation (Mt 4:23; 9:35; 15:24; Lk 4:43; 9:6; 20:1). From the most respectable to the least, all are summoned to submit to God's rule, all are invited to come and partake freely of the banquet he has spread (Lk 14:16–24). But the gift of salvation must be received if it is to be experienced (Mk 10:15). And while it is indeed a gift which costs nothing, it is also a priceless treasure for which a wise person will freely sacrifice everything else (Mt 13:44–46; a sacrifice exceeded only by the cost of rejecting the gospel: Mt 11:20–24; Mk 8:34–39; Lk 14:24,33). "Repent and believe in the gospel," commands Jesus (Mk 1:15). The self-righteous and the self-sufficient must be jolted out of their false sense of security and humbly recognize their need of God (Lk 6:24–26). Only then will Jesus' message to the poor be seen as gospel. An announcement of liberation (4:18–19) is good news only to people who are enslaved and know they are. The command applies also to the destitute and the afflicted. Those among them who bemoan their lot without repenting of their sin, must learn that it is being personally related to God as subject to sovereign and as child to father which makes one "blessed" (Mt 5:3–10). But something further is needed for the response to be complete: a person cannot believe Jesus' gospel without a commitment to the person (11:28; 18:6; cf. Jn 3:16). Even those who are already "poor in spirit" in the sense defined earlier, are not really "blessed" until they acknowledge the truth of Jesus' claims (Mt 11:6) and commit themselves to a life of obedience on his terms (7:21–27). This prepares us for the next point.

Approaches to Stage Two. Throughout Jesus' earthly ministry, the theme of his gospel remains the dawning kingdom of God (Mt 4:23; 24:14; Lk 4:43; 16:16), a message that is furthermore preached almost exclusively to Jews (Mt 10:5,6; 15:24). Yet Jesus also provides glimpses into what the gospel is to become once his work on earth is accomplished. (1) In Mark 8:35 and 10:29 Jesus speaks of individuals who make great sacrifices "for my sake and for the gospel." While distinguished from each other, the person of Jesus and the gospel are here associated in the closest possible way. The time is approaching when the Proclaimer of the gospel will become the Proclaimed. (2) In Mark 13:10 and Matthew 24:14 (and the textually doubtful Mk 16:15) Jesus foretells the preaching of the gospel of the kingdom to the gentile nations. (3) In Mark 14, having interpreted a woman's action (v 3) as an anointing of his body beforehand for burial (v 8), Jesus declares, "And truly, I say to you, wherever the gospel is preached in the whole world, what she has done will be told in memory of her" (v 9; cf. Mt 26:13). This statement strongly implies that both the person of Jesus and the event of his death will figure prominently in the message that is to be proclaimed; otherwise it is strange that the gospel and this particular act should be so solemnly bound together. Thus here already there is an indication how crucial Jesus' death is both for the provision of the salvation announced in his gospel (cf. Mk 14:22–24) and for the launching of the evangelistic mission to the Gentiles (Mt 20:28 is vital for explaining the shift from Mt 15:24 to 28:18–20).

The NT Stage Two. It remains to consider gospel as declared after the resurrection of Jesus. Our main sources are the Book of Acts and the letters of Paul. Of the 43 instances of *euangelizomai* ("evangelize") beyond the Gospels, 15 occur in Acts and 21 in Paul; of the 64 instances of *euangelion* ("gospel"), 2 occur in Acts and no less than 60 in Paul.

The Gospel of God. God is the author of the gospel and the one who authorizes and enables men to proclaim it (Acts 15:7; 16:10; Rom 1:1–5; 15:15,16; 16:25–27; 2 Cor 11:7; Gal 1:11–16; 2:7–9; Eph 3:6–8; 6:13–15; 1 Thes 2:2,4,8,9). Not only so, God himself is an evangelist, personally declaring his own gospel through human agents, and by this means calling people to salvation (Acts 10:36; 2 Cor 4:4–6; Gal 1:6; 2 Thes 2:13,14; Rv 10:7). Paul's gospel is both a witness to and an expression of God's *grace* (Acts 20:24; Col 1:5,6) and *power* (Rom 1:16; 16:25; 1 Cor 1:17–25) and *glory* (2 Cor 4:4–6; 1 Tm 1:11). Thus to accept the gospel is to turn to God (Acts 14:15; 1 Thes 1:5–9). Conversely, to disobey the gospel is to be deprived of the knowledge of God (2 Thes 1:8). What especially distresses Paul about the Galatians' abandonment of the true gospel for a false one, is that in the process they are turning away from God (Gal 1:6). The "eternal gospel" of Revelations 14:6,7 summons the nations to recognize and revere the one true God before judgment falls (cf. 1 Pt 4:17).

The Gospel of Christ. Having risen from the dead, Jesus Christ again evangelizes (Eph 2:16,17), doing so now through his appointed representatives (Rom 15:16–18; 1 Cor 1:17; 9:12–18; Gal 4:13,14; Eph 4:11; 2 Tm 1:9–11). More than that, Christ has become the *central theme* of the gospel; the Proclaimer is now the Proclaimed. This is repeatedly affirmed in Acts (5:42; 8:4,5,35; 11:20; 17:18) and in Paul (Rom 1:1–4; 10:8–17; 15:19,20; 2 Cor 4:4–6; 11:4; Gal 1:16; Eph 3:8; Phil 1:15–18; 2 Tm 2:8). Mark describes his whole book as "good news about Jesus Christ" (1:1; the thought of Christ as evangelist may also be included, cf. vv 14–15). The NT always speaks of the *gospel*—never the Gospels—of Christ. A second gospel is as inconceivable and as unnecessary as a second Christ. This is the one gospel which God authorizes (e.g., Rom 1:1–17) and proclaims (e.g., 2 Thes 2:13,14; according to one interpretation of 1 Thes 3:2, Timothy is called "God's fellow worker in the gospel of Christ"). Galatians 2:7–9 speaks not of two gospels but of two mission fields. Paul (the apostle to the uncircumcised) and Peter (the apostle to the circumcised) are both entrusted with "the gospel of Christ" (Gal 1:7; cf. 1 Cor 15:1–11), the message which God has ordained for the salvation of Jews and Gentiles alike (Rom 1:16). The "different gospel" which Paul denounces in Galatians 1:6–9 and 2 Corinthians 11:4 is not another gospel about Jesus, but a message about "another Jesus"—not the real one, but one who exists only in the minds and the messages of those who proclaim him. On the other hand, to preach the true Christ is to preach the true gospel, however questionable one's motives (Phil 1:15–18,27); and to respond rightly to the gospel is to turn to Christ (Acts 11:20,21; Rom 10:8–17; Gal 2:14–16).

The Gospel as a Witness to Saving Events. The gospel bears witness to every aspect of Christ's saving work, from his birth (Rom 1:3; 2 Tm 2:8) and public ministry (Mk 1:1; Acts 10:36–38) to his second coming (Col 1:5,23, cf. 3:1–4; 1 Thes 1:5–10) and the last judgment (Rom 2:16). But it is the *death* and the *resurrection* of Christ that are most crucial for the accomplishment of salvation, and that are therefore most prominent in the gospel's witness. These are the events with which Mark's proclamation climaxes (chs 15,16), and for which everything else prepares (8:31; 9:31; 10:33,34; 12:6–8); special stress is placed upon Jesus' death as the means of salvation from sin (10:45; 14:3–9,22–24). In Paul's gospel too the death and resurrection of Jesus are central (Rom 4:25; 1 Cor 15:1–4), with the cross occupying the very center (1 Cor 1:17–2:5). Had Christ not risen from the dead, Paul argues, the preaching of the cross would be a waste of time (1 Cor 15:14,17; cf. Rom 6:3–11); but now that Christ has risen, his death deserves special emphasis as the place where God provides atonement for sins (Rom 3:21–26; 5:6–11; 2 Cor 5:14–21; Eph 1:7). The gospel according to Acts proclaims Jesus' death (8:35; 20:24,28; cf. 10:36–43), and preeminently his resurrection, the event by which he conquered death and was exalted as Lord and coming Judge (10:36–43; 13:32,33; 17:18,31). According to 1 Peter the bearers of the gospel (1:12) concentrated, as had the OT prophets, on "the sufferings of Christ and the subsequent glory" (1:11; cf. 1:18,19; 2:21–24; 3:18–22).

The Gospel as a Power for Salvation. The gospel is much more than a report of past events and an exposition of doctrine. Paul declares in 1 Corinthians 1:17,18 and again in Romans 1:16 that the gospel is "the power of God"—not merely a witness to his power but an *expression* of his power. Thus it cannot be fettered (2 Tm 2:8–9). "Our gospel came to you not only in word, but also in power," Paul writes in 1 Thessalonians 1:15. His point is not that the gospel was accompanied by mighty works (though this happened; cf. Rom 15:18, 19), but that the gospel itself is a mighty work. God makes it so through his Holy Spirit (Rom 15:18,19; 1 Cor 2:1–5; 1 Thes 1:6). Furthermore, God's singular purpose in thus exercising his power is to change men's lives, to liberate them from sin and death, and to reconcile them to himself—in short, to *save* them. The gospel has power to effect the salvation it announces and to impart the life it promises (e.g., Rom 1:16; 10:8–17; 1 Cor 1:17,18; 15:1,2; Eph 1:13; 2 Thes 2:13,14; 2 Tm 1:8–11; 1 Pt 1:23–25). If men are to experience salvation, they must hear and believe the gospel. It is precisely in and through this message that the saving power manifested in the person and work of Christ (especially in his death and resurrection) is conveyed to men and made effective in their lives. Similarly it is in association with the gospel, or as a direct result of the reception of the gospel, that the Holy Spirit is imparted to believers (Acts 10:36–44; 15:7,8; 2 Cor 11:4; Gal 3:1,2). In short, the gospel is the decisive place of encounter between man the sinner and God the Savior.

The Gospel of Grace. According to Peter's testimony at the Jerusalem Council (Acts 15:7–11), an essential part of the gospel—for Gentiles and Jews alike—is salvation "through the grace of the Lord Jesus" (v 11; cf. 1 Pt 1:10–12). Toward the close of his missionary career, Paul states that his basic concern has been "to testify to the gospel of the grace of God" (Acts 20:24; cf. Col 1:5,6). This statement can be understood only in relation to Paul's concept of the *righteousness of God*, particularly as set forth in Romans. Paul is here not merely expounding a divine attribute. Rather he is dramatizing a divine activity—the manifestation of God's righteousness now, "in the present time" (Rom 3:21,26), in the New Age inaugurated by the coming of Jesus. The manifestation is twofold. Viewing the two aspects together, and doing so in the light of the gospel declared by Isaiah and by Jesus, respectively (both of whom strongly influenced Paul), will help us to understand why Paul speaks of "the gospel of the grace of God." (1) The gospel is a *witness* to God's grace. In offering his Son as a sacrifice for sins (Rom 3:25a), God demonstrates his righteousness (vv 25b,26). That is, in the death of Jesus sins formerly "passed over" (v 25c) become the object of God's wrath (cf. 1:18) and judgment. Yet in the very place where God deals justly and decisively with sins, he shows his grace to sinners. For the judgment against sin is focused not upon the sinners themselves but upon the One appointed to act on their behalf and to stand in their place (4:25; 5:6,11; cf. 2 Cor 5:21; Gal 3:13). On this basis sinners are freely pardoned (Rom 3:24). "The grace of the Lord Jesus" (Acts 15:11) toward the sinful is also in evidence, for he willingly bears their iniquities and suffers the consequences of their wrongdoing (Gal 2:20; cf. 2 Cor 8:9; Phil 2:6–8). (2) The gospel is a *channel* of God's grace. "The righteousness of God is revealed" in the gospel, says Paul (Rom 1:17). By this he means, not that the gospel talks about the righteousness of God (though it does), but that God's righteousness is actively at work in the gospel. This activity in turn explains how the gospel becomes "the power of God for salvation" (v 16). And just how does God demonstrate his righteousness at this stage? In short, by *bestowing* it as a free gift on sinful human beings. It remains the righteousness of God, but by God's grace it is a righteousness in which humans may share. Furthermore, partaking of God's righteousness depends on being personally united with Jesus Christ. In Paul's view the saved person is one who has been acquitted, justified, "declared righteous," by God the judge. The basis for the verdict is not that I *in myself* am righteous (God justifies the ungodly, 4:5). Nor does God treat me *as though* I were righteous. According to Paul I am declared righteous because I really *am* righteous—not in myself but *in Christ* (1 Cor 1:30; 2 Cor 5:21; Phil 3:9). This union is established through the revelation—and the free offer—of God's righteousness in the gospel (Rom 1:16,17).

Responding to the Gospel. The gospel calls for a threefold response. (1) Believing. The gospel, says Paul, is "the power of God for salvation to every one who has faith" (Rom 1:16). For Paul, faith is the abandonment of all reliance upon "works of law" for justification (3:28) and utter dependence instead upon the grace of God as demonstrated in the work of Christ, especially his death (v 25). Accordingly the "different gospel" of Galatians 1:6 and 2 Corinthians 11:4 is spurious, for it preaches salvation by personal merit rather than (or together with) the work of Christ (cf. Gal 2:16). Ultimately faith rests upon God (Rom 4:24; 1 Thes 1:8,9) and upon Christ (Rom 3:22,26; Gal 2:16,20). Yet it is imperative that one believe the gospel also (Acts 8:12; 11:20,21; 15:7; Rom 1:16; 10:8–17; 1 Cor 1:17–24; Phil 1:27; Heb 4:2), for it is just by this means that God's salvation is made known and mediated. Moreover, believing the gospel entails repentance (Acts 14:15; 20:21,24; 1 Thes 1:5–10) and obedience (Rom 1:5; 15:16–18; Heb 4:6). Those who refuse to obey the gospel are imperiling their lives (2 Thes 1:5–10; 1 Pt 4:17; cf. Rv 14:6,7). (2) Growing. The gospel is more than a message to be received; it is also a place in which to stand (1 Cor 15:1,2). It is sustainer of life as well as giver of life. One grows as a Christian not by turning from the gospel to other things (to turn away from the gospel is to abandon God and Christ, Gal 1:6), but by going ever more deeply into the gospel. In Romans 1:15 Paul expresses his eagerness to proclaim the gospel to the Christians in Rome. In the ensuing chapters, anticipating his visit, he offers his profoundest exposition of the gospel—one whose truth has never been fathomed and whose power has never been exhausted. (3) Hoping. "The hope of the gospel" (Col 1:23) includes not only the return of Christ and the glory of heaven (Col 1:5; 3:1–4; 2 Thes 2:14–16), but the final judgment as well. For those who embrace the gospel the last judgment holds no terrors, because the Judge is the very one who rescues them from the wrath to come (1 Thes 1:10). Those who are united to him need not dread condemnation now or at the end (Rom 8:1); instead the last judgment will mark their final vindication (1 Cor 4:5; Gal 5:5). Accordingly this theme is not just a corollary but an integral part of the good news (Rom 2:16). Those who have died since believing the gospel (1 Pt 4:6) may seem to have suffered a fate common to all men, or even the condemnation reserved for the lawless; in fact, their response to the gospel assures them of approval by the coming Lord (vv 5,6; 5:4) and of a share in the imperishable inheritance of heaven (1:4).

J. KNOX CHAMBLIN

Bibliography. K. Barth, *God, Grace, and Gospel*; C.F. Burney, *The Gospel in the OT*; J. Denney, *Jesus and the Gospel*; C.H. Dodd, *The Apostolic Preaching and its Development* and *Gospel and Law*; J.A. Fitzmyer, *To Advance the Gospel*, pp 149–61; R.H. Mounce, *The Essential Nature of NT Preaching*; E.F. Scott, *The Gospel and Its Tributaries.*

Gospels, Apocryphal. Writings preserving stories about Christ and some varied teachings; being mostly fanciful in nature, they never became canonical. There are three broad classes:

1. A type similar to the synoptic Gospels, represented by the Gospel of Peter and the Gospel of the Egyptians, as well as papyrus fragments including Oxyrhynchus 840 and papyrus Egerton 2. Other papyrus collections of sayings show affinities with the canonical Gospels.

2. Gospels that disseminated Gnosticism, a 2nd-century AD heresy stressing philosophical knowledge (*gnosis*) of the cosmos and man. They are often in the form of dialogues between Jesus and his disciples, for example, the Coptic Gospel of Thomas, the Apocryphon of John, the Wisdom of Jesus Christ, and the Dialogue of the Redeemer. Into this category also come those "gospels" attributed to the Twelve as a group, such as the Memoirs of the Apostles.

3. Infancy gospels, purporting to supply otherwise unknown information of a legendary nature about Christ's earliest years. Passion "gospels" also come into this category. These narratives were written to satisfy curiosity about Christ's birth and childhood or to embellish the canonical accounts of his crucifixion and resurrection.

See GNOSTICISM; APOCRYPHA, OLD AND NEW TESTAMENTS.

Gouging. Common practice among the Philistines. Amorites, Babylonians, and other nations surrounding Israel (Jgs 16:21; 2 Kgs 25:7) of forcibly removing the eyes. The practice was not only intended to disable but to bring extreme disgrace upon the person (1 Sm 11:2). Although the Israelites seem to have known about it from their sojourn in Egypt (Nm 16:14), there is no evidence that it was a common practice in Israel.

See CRIMINAL LAW AND PUNISHMENT.

Gourd. Trailing or climbing plant.

See PLANTS (CASTOR OIL PLANT; GOURD, WILD).

Governor. Biblical term translated from at least 10 different Hebrew root words and 5 Greek roots. English versions do not render these words consistently: they use a variety of titles, such as "overseer," "officer," "leader," "judge," and "deputy," to translate the same Hebrew word. The situation is similar in the Septuagint (Greek OT).

A governor was someone of superior rank who exercised authority over persons, territory, or both. Sometimes rank and power were his by virtue of the office; other times accession to office was based on noble lineage, wealth, public attainment, and the like. A governor normally received authority from a king; hence he was a deputy in the territory he governed. Such was the case with Joseph (Gn 42:6), Gedaliah (Jer 40:5), Daniel (Dn 2:48), and Zerubbabel (Hg 1:1). One Hebrew term for "governor," however, could mean "absolute ruler" (Jos 12:2) as well as a person who acted under authority.

The term most frequently used in the OT is evidently from an Akkadian expression meaning "lord of a district." Such governors normally relied on military power to maintain their rule (2 Kgs 18:24; Jer 51:23,28; Neh 2:7). The satrap of the Persian and Greek periods was most probably a civil governor. The leader of a city-state was often known as "governor" in the preexilic period (1 Kgs 22:26; 2 Chr 34:8). The writer of Psalm 22:28 used that title to describe God as the ruler of his people. A temple official who imprisoned the prophet Jeremiah in the stocks (Jer 20:1) was described in the KJV as a "governor" (RSV "officer"). One who governed an army probably commanded one or more military units. What appears to be a special title is rendered "governor" by the RSV in Ezra 2:63 and Nehemiah 7:65.

Translation problems from the Greek are also numerous. Different levels and functions in leadership were obviously intended by the various words used. This is most clearly indicated by the use of such terms as *ethnarch* (1 Mc 14:47; 2 Cor 11:32 NASB), one who governed as a deputy of a king, and by another word referring to Roman provincial officials. Such governors were mentioned in NT writings (cf. Mt 10:18; Lk 2:2; 3:1; Acts 23:24; 1 Pt 2:14) and were responsible for maintaining law and order in their assigned territory. In NT times Judea was under the control of the governor of Syria. Archaic uses of "governor" occasionally appear in the KJV. The "governor" of KJV James 3:4 is the ship's pilot.

Pool built north of Hebron by Pontius Pilate, mentioned in Scripture as governor of Judea (Lk 3:1).

Gozan. City and district near the Euphrates River. The Harbor River (modern Khabur) flowed through it. The Assyrians conquered it sometime before Sennacherib's invasion of Judah (701 BC). This fact is mentioned by Sennacherib, king of Assyria, in a blasphemous letter sent to Hezekiah, king of Judah (2 Kgs 19:12; Is 37:12). Later, it became one of the places in Assyria where conquered Israelites were deported. Gozan has been excavated, and excellent pottery has been found.

Grace. One of the distinctive features of the religion of the Bible. No other system of religious thought, past or present, contains an emphasis on divine grace comparable to that of the Bible.

As a general definition, the doctrine of grace pertains to God's activity rather than to his nature. Although God is gracious, this trait of his nature is revealed only in relation to his created works and to his redemptive enterprise. In other words, grace is to be understood in terms of a dynamic expression of the divine personality rather than as a static attribute of God's nature. Grace is the dimension of divine activity that enables God to confront human indifference and rebellion with an inexhaustible capacity to forgive and to bless. God is gracious in action.

The doctrine of divine grace underlies the thought of both OT and NT. However, the OT merely anticipates and prepares for the full expression of grace that becomes manifest in the NT.

Early in the narrative of the OT, God reveals himself as "a God merciful and gracious, slow to anger, and abounding in steadfast love and faithfulness" (Ex 34:6). As a result, it becomes possible for undeserving humans to approach him with the prayer, "If now I have found favor (or grace) in thy sight, O Lord, . . . " (v 9). Through divine initiative, human alienation from God is turned by him into a state of unmerited acceptance that opens the way for reconciliation and redemptive usefulness.

Divine grace was already operative in the garden of Eden when God responded to the debacle of the fall with the promise of redemption (Gn 3:15b) and solicitous watchcare (v 21) rather than with abandonment or retributive annihilation. The call to Abraham was an extension of grace, not only to him as an individual, but through him as a means of universal outreach. As an inseparable part of God's promise of individual blessing to Abraham and of a national blessing to his descendants, the indication was given that the individual and the national blessings would be instrumental in bringing about a universal blessing to "all the families of the earth" (12:2,3). Consequently, both the election of Abraham and the promise of universal blessing find expression in a God-given covenant, the object of which is to extend God's grace to the whole human race. In a solemn confirmation of the promise to Abraham, God affirmed, "My covenant is with you, and you shall be the father of a multitude of nations. . . . And I will establish my covenant between me and you and your descendants after you throughout their generations for an everlasting covenant" (17:4,7). This promise was to be understood as finding fulfillment on the basis of grace, not of race, so that it would become applicable to all Abraham's offspring—not only to Jewish believers, his racial descendants, but also to his spiritual descendants, believers from all nations who profess a faith like Abraham's (Rom 4:16). Thus, from the perspective of divine grace, the election of Abraham and of national Israel was not an end in itself. It was God's plan for extending his redemptive designs to all believers, from all nations. In extending his grace to Abraham, God was establishing the beginnings of the church, the community of grace.

The divine particularism evidenced in the election of Abraham and in his becoming the recipient of God's grace provides a model for the selection of all the individuals used by God in the history of redemption. Beyond the benefits of grace accorded to individuals such as Abraham, David, the prophets, and later the apostles by virtue of their call, loomed the potential of their contributions to the fulfillment of the covenant of God on behalf of the community of those who share the faith of Abraham, the church. In the gracious dealings of God with Israel, with its patriarchs and its leaders, God was laying the basis for his outreach of grace to the church universal. God's gracious interventions in the old covenant were intended to manifest the ultimacy of the church in his redemptive purposes. In the exercise of their ministries, the prophets of the old covenant knew that they were serving not themselves but the church (1 Pt 1:10–12).

As a transitional, mediatory expression of divine grace, the institutions of the old covenant possessed only a temporary validity that has been superseded by the ultimate manifestations of God's grace in the new covenant (Heb 8:6,7). Consequently, the old covenant was to become obsolete and replaced by a new covenant that would display the full manifestation of God's grace (v 13). The proverbial tension between law and grace becomes intelligible in this perspective. Like the election of racial Israel, the Law, as one of the most visible institutions of the old covenant, was a temporary measure of divine grace accorded to anticipate and prepare the covenant of justification through grace by faith in Jesus Christ (Gal 3:23–29; Heb 10:1).

The concept of grace defined as God's active involvement on behalf of his creatures in their states of need receives a sharper focus in the NT. Divine grace becomes embodied in the person of Jesus Christ who demonstrates visibly the dynamic nature of God's grace and fulfills in his ministry of redemption the old covenant promises relative to God's gracious dealings with humanity (Jn 1:14,17).

God's grace manifested in Jesus Christ makes it possible for God to forgive sinners and to gather them in the church, the new covenant community. During his ministry, Jesus repeatedly pronounced the words of forgiveness on a great number of sinners and ministered God's benevolent succor to a variety of desperate human needs. Through teachings such as the father's forgiveness of the prodigal son and the search for the lost sheep, Jesus made it clear that he had come to seek and save those who were lost. But ultimately, it was his redemptive death on the cross that opened wide the gate of salvation for repentant sinners to find access to God's forgiving and restorative grace. This simple truth is formulated in the doctrine of justification by faith through grace (Rom 3:23; Ti 3:7). According to this teaching, God's gracious provision of the substitutionary death of Christ enables him to pronounce a verdict of "just" or "not guilty" on repentant sinners and to include them in his eternal purposes. As a result, they enter into the realm of God's gracious activity, which enables them to implement the process of individual sanctification in cooperation with the Holy Spirit.

God's grace manifested in Jesus Christ makes it also possible for God to bestow on believers undeserved benefits that enrich their lives and unite them together in the church, the body of Christ. Their acceptance on th basis of grace endows them with a new status as children of God, members of the household of God, so that they relate to him as to their heavenly father (Gal 4:4–6). Consequently, they become members of a community where race, class, and sex distinctions are irrelevant since they all became equal inheritors of God's age-long promise to Abraham of universal blessing (3:28,29). In order to enrich their individual lives and to assure the usefulness of their participation in the life of the new community, the Holy Spirit graciously energizes believers with a variety of gifts for the performance of ministries designed to benefit the church (Rom 12:6–8). Foremost among those ministries is that of apostle, itself closely linked to God's gracious provision (1:5, 15:15,

16) since it combines with the ministry of the prophets of old to provide the foundational structure of the church (Eph 2:20). Because the riches of divine grace are freely lavished upon believers in their community life upon earth (1:7,8), the church translated into eternity will demonstrate, by its very existence, the immeasurable riches of God's grace in Jesus Christ (2:6).

Finally, God's grace manifested in Jesus Christ makes it possible for God to cause believers to reflect his grace in their character and relationships. The irreducible condition for receiving God's grace is humility (Jas 4:6; 1 Pt 5:5). Such humility in relation to God enables believers to practice humility in regard to other people. From a position of grace, they can set aside selfishness and conceit in order to treat others with deference (Phil 2:3,4) in an attitude of mutual servanthood (Eph 5:21), and in a spirit of mutual forgiveness (Mt 18:23–35) so that even their communication can exhibit divine grace (Col 4:6). Since the grace of Jesus Christ constitutes the existential context of the lives and relationships of believers, they are exhorted not to pervert the grace of God into ungodly practice (Jude 4) but instead to grow in the grace of the Lord (2 Pt 3:18).

The essential meaning of grace in the Bible refers to God's disposition to exercise goodwill toward his creatures. This favorable disposition of God finds it supreme expression in Jesus Christ. By its very definition, this grace is rendered fully accessible to all humans with no other precondition than a repentant desire to receive it (Ti 2:11,12). As a result, the human condition of alienation from God and from his purposes becomes replaced with access to the otherwise inapproachable majesty of God represented by a throne, so that his grace may become available to meet human need (Heb 4:16). The tragic alternative to receiving God's grace is to remain in hopeless alienation or to pursue sterile attempts to merit God's favor through human efforts doomed to futility (Rom 1:21). God's unconditional acceptance of sinners may be conditioned only by their rejection of his acceptance.

Because Christ represents the fulfillment, the embodiment, and the dispenser of divine grace, the early Christians freely referred to God's grace as "the grace of our Lord Jesus Christ." This grace was conceived as being so basic and so pervasive to their individual lives and to the existence of their communities of faith that they naturally coupled the traditional greeting of *shalom* ("peace") with a reference to the grace of Jesus Christ. This is the reason for the ubiquitous repetition of numerous variations on the basic greeting formula found in almost every book of the NT, "The grace of our Lord Jesus Christ be with you all" (2 Thes 3:18).

GILBERT BILEZIKIAN

See GOD, BEING AND ATTRIBUTES OF; LOVE; MERCY.

Bibliography. P. Fransen, *Divine Grace and Man*; R.M. Hals, *Grace and Faith in the OT*; E. Jauncey, *The Doctrine of Grace*; J. Moffatt, *Grace in the NT*; C.R. Smith, *The Biblical Doctrine of Grace*; N.P. Williams, *The Grace of God*.

Grain. See AGRICULTURE; PLANTS (BARLEY; MILLET; SPELT; WHEAT).

Granary. See AGRICULTURE.

Grape. Smooth-skinned, juicy berry which grows in clusters on woody vines. Grapes are eaten fresh or dried, and are fermented for wine.

See AGRICULTURE; PLANTS (VINE); VINE, VINEYARD; WINE.

Grass. See PLANTS.

Grasshopper. Plant-eating insect equipped with long hind legs for leaping.

See ANIMALS.

Grate, Grating. Network of bronze surrounding the lower half of the altar of burnt offering in the tabernacle (Ex 27:4).

See ALTAR; TABERNACLE, TEMPLE.

Gratitude. Natural expression of thanks in response to blessings, protection, or love. In the Judeo-Christian tradition, gratitude is not a tool used to manipulate the will of God. It is never coerced or fabricated in one's mind; rather, gratitude is a joyful commitment of one's personality to God.

In the OT, gratitude to God was the only condition in which life could be enjoyed. For Jews, every aspect of creation provided evidence of God's lordship over all life. The Hebrew people thanked him for the magnificence of the universe (Pss 19:1–4; 33:6–9; 104:1–24). When they received good news they thanked God for his goodness and great deeds (1 Chr 16:8–12). When they received bad news, they also gave thanks, trusting that he was a just God (Jb 1:21).

These same sentiments are found in later Jewish writings such as the Talmud (6 Ber, 35*a*, 54*a*). The people of Israel thanked God for his faithfulness to covenant promises: (1) for deliverance from enemies (Pss 18:17; 30:1; 44:1–8) and from death (Ps 30:8–12; Is 38:18–20; (2) for forgiveness of sin (Pss 32:5; 99:8; 103:3; Is 12:1); (3) for answers to prayer (Pss 28:6; 66:19); (4) for compassion toward the afflicted and oppressed (34:2; 72:12); (5) for executing justice (Dt 32:4; Ps 99:4); (6) and for continuing guidance (Ps 32:8; Is 30:20,21).

Gratitude was such a vital part of Israel's religion that it pervaded most ceremonies and customs. Thank offerings acknowledged blessings from God (Lv 7:12,13; 22:29; Ps 50:14). Shouts of joy (Ps 42:4), songs of praise (145:7; 149:1), and music and dance (150:3–5) all added to the spirit of thanksgiving in worship. Feasts and festivals were celebrated in remembrance of God's steadfast love throughout their history (Dt 16:9–15; 2 Chr 30:21,22). King David appointed levitical priests to offer God thanks (1 Chr 16:4). This custom was carried on by the kings Solomon (2 Chr 5:12,13) and Hezekiah (31:2), and by those who returned from the exile (Neh 11:17; 12:24,27).

In the NT, the object of thanksgiving is the love of God expressed in the redemptive·work of Christ. The apostle Paul thanked God for that gift of grace (1 Cor 1:4; 2 Cor 9:15) and the ability to preach the gospel (2 Cor 2:14; 1 Tm 1:12). Paul thankfully participated in the spiritual gifts (1 Cor 14:18). Gratitude for love and faith among believers pervades his letters (Rom 6:17; Eph 1:15,16; Phil 1:3–5; Col 1:3,4; 1 Thes 1:2,3).

Because the expression of gratitude is tied so closely to the response of faith, Paul encouraged believers to give thanks in all things (Rom 14:6; 1 Thes 5:18). He commanded Christians to pray with thanksgiving (Phil 4:6; Col 4:2) in the name of Christ, who has made all thanksgiving possible (Eph 5:20). In his teaching on how to celebrate the Lord's Supper, Paul specified that Christians should give thanks, just as the Lord "had given thanks" (1 Cor 11:24).

Grave. *See* BURIAL, BURIAL CUSTOMS.

Grave Clothes. *See* BURIAL, BURIAL CUSTOMS.

Graven Image. Image or representation of a deity made of wood, stone, or metal.

See IDOLS, IDOLATRY.

Great Lizard. One of the reptiles which the Jewish Law listed as ceremonially unclean (Lv 11:29).

See ANIMALS (LIZARD).

Great Owl. Name of one of the great horned or eagle owls (Dt 14:16).

See BIRDS (OWL; OWL, GREAT).

Great Sea, The. Alternate name for the Mediterranean Sea. It was given this name by the ancient Near Eastern peoples because of its great size in comparison to the other seas they knew (Nm 34:6; Jos 1:4).

See MEDITERRANEAN SEA.

Greaves. Protective piece of armor worn over the shank of the leg (1 Sm 17:6).

See ARMS AND WARFARE.

Greece, Greeks. Location and inhabitants of a country in southeastern Europe. The biblical references to Greece and Greeks are often ambiguous. In the OT some references have been understood to mean Greece or Greeks. Javan, the fourth son of Japheth in the table of the nations (Gn 10) seems to fit a Greek identification (vv 2,4; 1 Chr 1:5,7; Is 66:19; Ez 27:13). The name Greece occurs clearly in Daniel 8:21; 10:20; 11:2; and Zechariah 9:13, and Greeks are mentioned in Joel 3:6. In the NT the term "Greek" appears to have the special sense of Hellenist, that is, Jews living in Hellenistic cities (Acts 6:1; 9:29; 11:20). The term in John 12:20; Acts 14:1; 16:1,3 seems to refer to Greeks specifically. But often in the NT the term "Greek" was used for non-Jews because the Jews recognized only Jews and non-Jews. Hence the term was virtually synonymous with Gentiles (Rom 1:16; 10:12; 1 Cor 1:22,24; Gal 2:3; 3:28). Sometimes the term "Greek" refers to the language (Jn 19:20; Acts 21:37; Rv 9:11). The use of the term "Greek" for the Syrophoenician woman (Mk 7:26) may be a cultural term. In Acts, references are made to Greeks in the synagogues as observers. These may have been Greeks as such, although certainty is not possible (Acts 14:1; 17:4; 18:4).

Geography. The ancient Greek homeland comprised the southern end of the Balkan peninsula. But at times Greek speakers were to be found in the islands of the Aegean Sea, Western Asia Minor, South Italy, and Sicily. Small Greek republics were also established quite early throughout the Black Sea area and Asia Minor, to the east and as far west as Marseilles and Spain. After the days of Alexander there were Greek states as far to the east as India. But always, the core of Greek culture was in the Balkan peninsula and in the Aegean islands.

Greece and the Greeks in History. *Origins.* Precisely who the Greeks were originally remains an enigma. Their language belongs to the Indo-European family. One of the ancient scripts, the Linear B, which has been found both on the mainland and in Crete dating to the 15th century BC in association with the Mycenaean civilization is a primitive Greek.

Bronze Age people came to the Aegean perhaps by way of Asia Minor prior to 2000 BC when mass migrations, probably of Indo-European origin, began. They imposed their culture on the original population of the area, the Aegeans, and occupied the islands as well as the mainland. Immigrants arrived in four waves: (1) the Achaeans who came overland from the north and the east about 2000–1900 BC and settled in the central area (Arcadia) and in Thessaly, Boeotia, and the northeastern Aegean area; (2) the Dorians who settled in east Peloponnesus and the isthmus, Crete and the islands of the south Aegean and the southwest corner of Asia Minor about 1500–1200 BC; (3) the Ionians who settled in Attica, Euboea, the islands of the middle Aegean and parts of the mainland of western Asia Minor; and (4) the Aetolians who occupied west central Greece, the northern Peloponnesus, Aetolia, and the offshore islands. Unfortunately the accounts of these migrations are largely preserved in legend, and exact dates and locations are far from certain.

The Minoans. The first significant civilization among these Greek-speaking peoples was the Minoan on the island of Crete, named after Minos the legendary king of Crete. It was a remarkable culture with fine buildings, pottery, painting, art work, and technical skills. Writing was in use. Two scripts have been discovered, Linear A showing affinities with Akkadian and Linear B, a primitive Greek. This civilization collapsed about 1400 BC for unknown reasons.

The Mycenaeans. The Mycenaean civilization benefitted greatly from the contact of the mainland Achaeans with the people of Crete. The first mainland settlers produced the so-called Helladic civilization, which was not particularly distinguished although its pottery was quite distinctive. The Middle Helladic civilization (c. 2000–1550 BC) from the mainland combined with the Cretan influences from 1500 BC onward to produce the Mycenaean civilization, named after the great fortress of Mycenae on the Peloponnesus. This civilization was distinguished by great palaces, strong fortresses, great wealth, and a powerful army. Writing was known and the Linear B script has been found both on the mainland and in Crete. It has been conjectured that the destruction of the Minoan civilization about 1400 BC was partly due to the Mycenaean invaders, although internal strife and natural causes such as earthquakes played a part. Certainly Greek invaders sacked and destroyed Cnossus in Crete, the center of the Minoan civilization and scattered the survivors over the

The rocky ruins of Troy, a major Mycenaean city in northwest Asia Minor and the site of the Trojan War.

eastern Mediterranean. Some of these reached the coastlands of Palestine. The Mycenaean civilization has left a good archaeological record. Archaeologists have been able to subdivide the period into a number of distinct subdivisions. About 1200 BC a Greek expedition to the mainland of western Asia conquered and destroyed the prosperous city of Ilium (Troy) which lay on the northwest coast of Asia Minor near the entrance to the Dardanelles. This event gave rise to the story of Helen of Troy, vividly recounted by the poet Homer. The Trojan war was a major military exploit which weakened the Mycenaeans and led in part to their collapse before the Dorian invaders, although part of the reason for the collapse was climatic. The rain belt of southern Europe receded to the north at that time, and important centers like Mycenae were depopulated as people fled to more hospitable lands. The Dorians entered a land that was already depopulated. Greece and the Aegean area entered a dark age that lasted for about four centuries.

The City-States. From about 800 BC onward Greece settled down, reorganized itself, built cities, cultivated the land, absorbed the survivors of earlier cultures on the mainland and in the islands, and developed Greek as a common language although it was spoken in a variety of dialects. Small city-states developed as scattered villages united for protection. The villages of Attica merged into a city-state around ancient Athens. Similar developments occurred around Thebes and Sparta. The process began with "kings" though monarchy soon gave place to oligarchy in which an aristocracy governed the people. But the aristocracy was often incompetent, especially in crises and people rallied round individuals—often a noble turned democrat—and overthrew the aristocracy. These individuals were the "tyrants" (leaders or dictators). They were not necessarily cruel men, but the opportunity for the development of corruption and despotic rule was a natural consequence. Athens resisted "tyranny" in 630 BC, and by 594 BC Solon, a rich representative of a new industrial class, was empowered to institute constitutional reforms on a broadly democratic basis. There were further crises with the tyrants but in 507 BC Cleisthenes introduced a genuinely democratic constitution. The assembly of citizens held sovereign power. By 500 BC the age of the tyrants had passed.

Other states also broke free. Sparta was slow to follow. It was dominated by a Dorian group that oppressed the subject population and built up a military society that was to destroy Athens in a great war which lasted from 431 to 400 BC.

City-states were independent of one another so that there is strictly no history of Greece in these years but rather a history of Greek states. Even so there were some unifying elements such as pan-Hellenic games, important sanctuaries to which all Greeks might come, the oracle at Delphi, and an underlying sense of a common origin, heritage, and destiny.

Colonization. From about 770 BC onward sea trade developed greatly and colonization began. Colonies developed in the form of city-states in Spain, southern France, southern Italy and Sicily, the Black Sea, and the African coast. There was no penetration inland, but powerful states developed at Massilia in southern France, Tarrentum in southern Italy, Syracuse in Sicily, and many other places. Rome was strongly influenced by the Greek civilization that flourished around the coasts of Italy.

The Crisis of the Fifth Century BC: The Persian Wars. In the 7th century BC Greek settlements on the western coast of Asia Minor known as Ionia, fell under the control of the inland empire of Lydia based on Sardis. But by 546 BC Lydia was overcome by Persia which was expanding to the west and looking toward the Aegean. In 499 BC the Ionian cities revolted against Persia and Athens, which had helped them, and was marked down for invasion by the Persians. Darius I attacked from the sea in 450 BC but was driven back by the Athenians at Marathon in 486 BC. Within 10 years the Persian Xerxes sent forces by land and sea. The army was held up for a short time at Thermopylae by the Spartans who were supporting Athens. But the Persians pressed on into Attica and sacked Ath-

ens, whose citizens drew back to the island of Salamis. In the Straits of Salamis the Greek fleet struck a severe blow to the Persian fleet and Xerxes had to withdraw. He left an army in Boeotia that was defeated by a united Greek force at Plataea in 479 BC. The final debacle for the Persians came when the Greeks crossed into Asia Minor, defeated the remnants of the Persian army, and burned their warships, also in 479 BC. It was the end of the Persian threat, and Greece was free to continue her own system of government.

The Delian Confederacy. The confederate Greeks determined to liberate the Greeks of Asia Minor and assembled a fleet under the Spartan Pausanias. He proved arrogant and inclined to come to terms with the Persians, and Aristeides the Athenian replaced him and the Spartans withdrew. Athens came to an agreement with the Greek allies to form a confederacy which would meet annually in the Temple of Apollo at Delos and contribute money and ships each year till the Persians were driven out of Asia Minor. This was achieved within 10 years. When the center was moved from Delos to Athens about 455 BC tensions arose because Athens became despotic and used the annual payments to the league for her own ends. The tension reached a climax in the days of Pericles, the Athenian leader. Finally came a clash with Sparta in 431 BC which ended Athenian greatness. The disastrous 27-year war with Sparta left the way open for the emergence of Philip II of Macedon who united Greece into a Macedonian empire.

The Climax of Greek Culture. The end of the Persian wars saw Athens enter upon a remarkable period of greatness. Athens was rebuilt and its port at Piraeus was fortified. When the Athenian citizens embarked on a course of unbridled democracy, chaos seemed to threaten, but Pericles, a brilliant leader, restored the equilibrium of the state and Athens soon regained her glory. Vast buildings were erected on the Acropolis, notably the Parthenon (dedicated to Athena, the goddess of Athens). Athens became wealthy, partly from the contributions to the Delian League. Athenian sea power grew. There was an abundance of slaves, artisans, craftsmen, foreign traders, artists, poets, philosophers, teachers, actors, athletes, scientists, physicians, historians, religious teachers, and experts in military and naval affairs. The great writers of the 5th and early 4th century BC included the dramatists like Aeschylus, Sophocles, and Euripedes, historians like Thucydides and Herodotus, and philosophers like Socrates, Plato, and Aristotle. There was a flowering of art and architecture. It was a golden age of spectacular achievement in art, thought, literature, and architecture.

The Age of Hellenism. The great glory of Athens withered before the 4th century BC was over. Philip of Macedon, with ambitions of empire, drove west, and by 338 BC Athens and Thebes were overwhelmed and Greece became united into a Macedonian empire. Philip was assassinated in 366 BC, but Alexander his son, educated in Athenian tradition, took up his father's work and before his own death in 323 BC had finally conquered Persia and reached to the Punjab in India. In the end he exerted his control from the Caucusus to the Libyan desert and the borders of Ethiopia as well. On the death of Alexander, his vast territories were divided among four generals. After some adjustments three divisions emerged—Egypt under Ptolemy; Asia Minor, Syria, and the East under Seleucus; and Macedonia under Antigonus.

Finally the whole of the Greek area came under the control of the Romans, who moved into Greek areas in 198 BC and over the years established a number of Roman provinces such as Achaia (Acts 18:12). It was into the world of Hellenism, now under Rome, that the Christians moved with the message of the gospel in the 1st century AD.

The Greeks in Palestine. Excavations have shown that there was contact between Palestine and the Aegean areas over many centuries. From the Middle Bronze period (patriarchal age) Middle Minoan II pottery has been found at a number of sites. The Philistines who formed part of the Sea Peoples in the 13th century BC settled in areas of coastal Palestine and developed their own culture there, leaving a great deal of their distinctive pottery. During the period around 1370–1200 BC various peoples from the Aegean and western Asia Minor found their way to Palestine. Mycenaean pottery has been found in a number of sites. From a later period still, numerous examples of Attic black-figure ware from the 6th century BC, and Attic red-figure ware from the period around 530–300 BC have been found in excavations. Silver coins struck in imitation of Attic drachmas come from the same period. With the rise of Hellenism and the occupation of Palestine by the Ptolemaic and Seleucid rulers, Greek influence increased greatly. The presence of Greek pottery like Rhodian jars, and the influence of Greek architectural features in buildings emphasize how significant the Greek influence in Palestine was, as well as throughout the Levant region and the hinterland. With the coming of the Romans these influences continued. Greek was the language of commerce. Indeed the NT was written in the Greek of ordinary people, and a wide variety of Greek inscriptions has come to light from Roman times.

JOHN A. THOMPSON

See ALEXANDER #1; ALEXANDRIA; HELLENISM; HELLENISTIC JUDAISM; JUDAISM.

Bibliography. M.I. Finley, *The Ancient Greeks*; G. Glotz, *The Greek City and Its Institutions*; W.K.C. Guthrie, *A History of Greek Philosophy*, 3 vols; M. Hengel, *Judaism and Hellenism*, 2 vols; P. Jonquet, *Macedonian Imperialism and the Hellenization of the East*; G. Murray, *The Five Stages of Greek Religion*; D.S. Robertson, *A Handbook of Greek and Roman Architecture*; M. Rostovtzeff, A History of the Ancient World, vol 1, *The Orient and Greece*; *Out of the Past of Greece and Rome*; W.W. Tarn, *Hellenistic Civilization*.

Greek Language. See BIBLICAL LANGUAGES.

Greyhound. KJV mistranslation in Proverbs 30:31 (RSV strutting cock).

See BIRDS (FOWL, DOMESTIC).

Grief. Emotional suffering brought on by bereavement, mishap, or disaster. To grieve is either to cause or feel sorrow or distress. The concept is found in the Scriptures under a variety of circumstances. Isaac and Rebekah experienced grief when their son Esau married a Hittite woman (Gn 26:35 KJV). God mourned the misery of Israel brought upon them by disobedience (Jgs 10:16 KJV). Hannah was so sad because she had no son that she appeared to be drunk while praying (1 Sm 1:16 KJV). Similarly, Samuel, distraught at King Saul's disobedience, prayed all night. Job was exceedingly sorrowful over his personal loss (Jb 2:13; cf. 6:2; 16:6), and the psalmist poetically demonstrated distress and sorrow (cf. Pss 6:7; 31:9,10; 69:26 KJV; 73:21 KJV; 95:10 KJV; 112:10 KJV). The Book of Lamentations is devoted to the expression of grief, and the prophets in general speak of judgment because Israel had grieved a holy God.

Jesus experienced sorrow and distress (Mk 3:5; Jn 11:33), including the death of a friend (Jn 11:35). The Jews are said to have been grieved as the apostles taught about Christ (Acts 4:2 KJV). The apostle Paul instructed believers not to grieve one another (Rom 14:15 KJV) and did not want to cause any sorrow himself (2 Cor 2:1–5 KJV). Most of all, the believer is not to grieve the Holy Spirit (Eph 4:30). A believer may, of course, suffer grief and suffering in an alien world (1 Pt 2:19 KJV). In Bible times grief was given particular expression at a time of death by means of shrieks, wails, and laments (cf. Jer 9:17,18; Am 5:16; Mk 5:38).

See MOURNING.

Grove. Mistaken KJV translation of a Hebrew word that was the name of a Canaanite goddess, Asherah. Often sacred trees were designated as symbols of that fertility goddess; sometimes wooden poles were erected. God commanded the Israelites to destroy those symbols (called *Asherim, Asheroth*) by cutting them down (Ex 34:13) and burning them (Dt 12:3). Because the poles were wooden, archaeologists have been unable to find any clear remains. In an early sanctuary at Ai, however, a large piece of carbonized wood was discovered lying between incense burners. It may have been a tree trunk from which the branches had been trimmed. Some researchers suggest it was an Asherah.

God strictly forbade the Israelites to worship Asherah or to erect sacred symbols in her honor. From time to time Israel disobeyed God and engaged in false worship. One account of the downfall of the northern kingdom attributes its failure to the existence of groves and the worship of the pagan goddess and her male counterpart, Baal (2 Kgs 17:7–18). Jezebel, a priestess of the Tyrian Baal, promoted the spread of such idolatry. The "grove" of Genesis 21:33 (KJV) was actually a tamarisk tree.

See HIGH PLACE; CANAANITE DEITIES AND RELIGIONS; GODS, GODDESSES; IDOLS, IDOLATRY.

Guard, Court of the. Perhaps an emergency detention area in 7th-century BC Jerusalem when the city was under Babylonian attack. Although the prophet Jeremiah was placed under arrest there, he was still able to maintain his normal activities, indicating that the area was probably a small courtyard (Jer 32:2–12; 33:1; 37:21; 38:6–28; 39:14,15; KJV court of the prison).

Guard, Gate of the. Gate located in the north or northwest part of Jerusalem, although unrelated to the Court of the Guard (Neh 3:25), which was connected to the palace (12:39, KJV Prison Gate). Perhaps it was the same as the Muster Gate.

See JERUSALEM.

Guardian Angel. *See* ANGEL.

Gudgodah. Alternate name for Hor-haggidgad, one of the stopping-places in the wilderness wanderings of the Israelites (Dt 10:7).

See HOR-HAGGIDGAD, HOR-HAGIDGAD.

Guilt Offering. *See* OFFERINGS AND SACRIFICES.

Gull. Any of a number of birds from the family *Laridae*. The RSV "sea gull" (KJV cuckoo) in Leviticus 11:16 and Deuteronomy 14:15 is uncertain.

See BIRDS (SEA GULL).

Gum. General name for the sap of shrubs of the *Astragalus* species (Gn 43:11, KJV spices), used in trade. *Astragalus* shrubs grew widely in the Near East. Gum tragacanth, from the *Astragalus Tragacantha*, is still used commercially.

See PLANTS (ALOE; BALM; MYRRH).

Guni. 1. Naphtali's son and the grandson of Jacob (Gn 6:24; 1 Chr 7:13). His descendants were the Gunites (Nm 26:48).

2. Abdiel's father from Gad's tribe (1 Chr 5:15).

Gunite. Descendant of Guni, Naphtali's son (Nm 26:48).

See GUNI #1.

Gur, Ascent of. Elevated place near Ibleam where Ahaziah, king of Judah, was smitten by the soldiers of Jehu of the northern kingdom. From Gur Ahaziah fled to Megiddo where he died (2 Kgs 9:27). Though its location is uncertain, some identify it with the Akkadian Gurra, about one-half mile south of Jenin.

Gurbaal. Town in the Negeb occupied by Arabs, possibly in the neighborhood of Edom, which Uzziah of Judah conquered (2 Chr 26:7). Its location is uncertain.

Hh

Haahashtari. Naarah's son from Judah's tribe (1 Chr 4:6).

Habaiah. Head of a priestly family who returned to Palestine with Zerubbabel after the exile. He was unable to prove his priestly genealogy and so was not allowed to do priestly service (Ezr 2:61; Neh 7:63, Hobaiah).

Habakkuk (Person). Author of the eighth book of the Minor Prophets. The meaning of Habakkuk's name is uncertain. It was probably derived from a Hebrew word meaning "to embrace."

Nothing is known about Habakkuk apart from what can be inferred from his book. Several legends purporting to give accounts of his life are generally regarded as untrustworthy. The apocryphal book Bel and the Dragon describes a miraculous transporting of Habakkuk to Daniel while Daniel was in the den of lions. A Jewish legend makes Habbakkuk the son of the Shunamite woman mentioned in 2 Kings 4:8–37. That legend apparently is based on the fact that it is said she would "embrace" a son. Chronological difficulties make both accounts unlikely.

Habakkuk lived in the period before the rise of the Chaldeans (Hb 1:6), that is, during the reign of the Judean king Jehoiakim. The dates 605–589 BC delineate the probable period of his prophetic activity.

The Book of Habakkuk reveals a man of great sensitivity. His deep concern about injustice and his prayer (Hb 3) show that Habakkuk was characterized by profound religious conviction and social awareness.

THOMAS E. MCCOMISKEY

See HABAKKUK, BOOK OF; PROPHET, PROPHETESS.

Habakkuk, Book of. Eighth book of the Minor Prophets in the OT.

The Habakkuk Commentary from the Dead Sea Scrolls.

Author. Little is known about the prophet Habakkuk apart from information that may be gained from the Book of Habakkuk itself. In 1:1 and 3:1 he is called a prophet, a spokesman for God to his fellow Israelites.

The prayer of chapter 3 contains several musical designations (3:1,3,9,13,19). Such technical notations suggest that the author had some responsibility for the temple music. If that is so, he may have been a member of one of the levitical families. The apocryphal book, Bel and the Dragon, contains a reference to Habakkuk as "the son of Jesus of the tribe of Levi," possibly reflecting such a tradition.

The book portrays Habakkuk as a man of deep moral sensitivity who rebelled at the injustice that characterized the society of his day.

Date. Although it is difficult to date the prophecy of Habakkuk precisely, several clues to its date appear in the text. In 1:5,6 the prophet refers to the Chaldeans whom God is "rousing." The Chaldeans were originally a group of loosely organized tribes who occupied a large portion of the Assyrian Empire. They were a constant source of trouble to their Assyrian lords. Eventually, the Chaldeans successfully rebelled against the Assyrian power, placing Nabopolassar on the throne (625–605 BC). The Chaldeans then ruled all of Babylonia, establishing the Babylonian empire and inaugurating a period of extensive expansion. Because the Chaldeans came to power about 625 BC, many scholars think that the prophecy of Habakkuk was written shortly before that time. The book would have been written, then, within the reign of Josiah (640–609 BC). Habakkuk 1:6 does not necessarily refer to the initial rise of the Chaldeans. Their reputation was already established as warlike and cruel, for the prophet described them as "bitter and hasty"; they "seize habitations not their own," and "their horsemen come from afar" (1:6–8). Their reputation for military prowess seems to fit best with a time after the battle of Carchemish (605 BC), when Nebuchadnezzar II defeated the Egyptians and established the Babylonians as an important world power. It is also possible that their reputation was gained from the Babylonian conquest of Nineveh in 612 BC.

The term "rousing" need not imply that the Chaldeans were being raised up on the scene of world history as a new nation. The term may also signify the concept of "stirring up," indicating that God was preparing the already powerful Babylonians to be a tool of his wrath against the kingdom of Judah.

The social conditions in Habakkuk's day seem to fit best with a time after the death of Judah's king Josiah in 609 BC. Josiah's reign was characterized by far-reaching religious reforms, initiated by the discovery of the Book of the Law during renovations in the temple (2 Kgs 22:8). Habakkuk describes his society as filled with "destruction and violence" (1:3). An unfair judicial system led to oppression of the righteous (v 4). Such conditions contradict the national reforms initiated by Josiah. It thus seems best to date Habakkuk's ministry between 608 and 605 BC, early in the reign of Jehoiakim (609–598 BC).

Background. The historical period inaugurated by King Josiah's death was one of the most bitter in the history of the kingdom of Judah. In 612 BC the Babylonians destroyed the Assyrian city of Nineveh, and in two years they eliminated the last vestiges of formal Assyrian rule in Mesopotamia. The Egyptians, who had been allies of the Assyrians, sought to solidify their hold on the western portion of the former Assyrian Empire. They marched to Carchemish, an important city on the Euphrates River, where they were opposed by Josiah, who died in that battle.

The Egyptians placed Jehoiakim on the throne in place of Jehoahaz, the rightful successor of Josiah. Jehoiakim was an Egyptian vassal, and the land of Judah was forced to pay heavy tribute, its independence gone forever.

The faith of many people might understandably have begun to falter in that time. The religious reforms under Josiah had resulted not in national blessing, but in the loss of their freedom. The tenor of society had changed from one of relative stability to one of oppression and violence (see Jer 22:17).

In 604 BC the Babylonians advanced into the Syro-Palestinian area, encountering only weak resistance. At that time Jehoiakim transferred his allegiance to Nebuchadnezzar, who continued his advance to the south. When Pharaoh Neco's army challenged the invaders, both sides suffered heavy losses and Nebuchadnezzar retreated to Babylon. The vacillating Jehoiakim then transferred his loyalty to Egypt. In 598 BC the Babylonians advanced again to Syro-Palestine, beginning a campaign that led to the fall of Jerusalem in 586 BC.

Purpose and Theological Teaching. The main purpose of Habakkuk's prophecy is to explain what a godly person's attitude should be toward the presence of evil in the world. It also addresses the nature of God's justice in punishing moral evil.

The teaching of the book is set forth in an interesting pattern of crucial questions by the prophet about God's activity in history. His questions may reflect deep doubts and concerns, or they may be a literary device for reflecting the questions that people in his society were asking. In the psalm at the end of the book, the prophet shows that he has reached an understanding of God's purposes, and he rests in utter submission to God. One of the prophet's chief problems was the seeming inactivity of God, as evil continued unpunished. God's answer was that he does punish evil in his own time and with his chosen instruments. The world is not an arena in which evil continually triumphs. History testifies to the fall of tyrants and wicked nations. The godly person thus interprets history in terms of faith, trusting God and affirming God's righteous rule in the world.

The Book of Habakkuk does not explain why God has allowed evil in the world. It does affirm that a righteous person will see God's activity in history through the eyes of faith. Chapter 3 eloquently expresses that theme as Habakkuk looks at history and recounts all God's gracious activity on behalf of his people.

One of the most important theological concepts in the book is that of God's sovereign activity in history. Habakkuk affirms God's control of all history and demonstrates that even the godless nations are subject to his control. Their rise and fall is determined not by the fortuitous course of events but by God.

Content. *The First Complaint and Its Response (1:1–11).* The prophecy of Habakkuk begins with a series of questions reflecting the prophet's deep feelings over the wrongs rampant in his society. He begins by asking how long he shall have to cry to God who does not seem to hear. Many have asked that question as they see evil present in a world governed by the sovereign God.

The answer that the prophet received was unusual. The Lord was surely doing something about the evil in his society; he was raising up the Chaldeans as an instrument of his wrath to punish the people of Judah.

The description of the Chaldeans in 1:6–11 is filled with bold metaphors that depict them as an awesome force pillaging as they advance in their conquests. One might well wonder, as the prophet did, why God would use such a tool to accomplish his purposes.

The prophet's first complaint reflects a number of perplexing problems. Why does God not do something about evil? Why does he allow it to continue? God does not always seem to respond when people want him to.

Furthermore, when God did answer he said he would punish the evil in Judah by using the Babylonians. The prophet's prayer was answered, but in a way he did not expect. God would use a hated and wicked nation to punish the wrongs of his own people. Habakkuk must have been perplexed at this, but he could take comfort in one fact: God was still in control of history (1:6). God governed the rise and fall of nations, using even wicked ones to accomplish his will.

The Second Complaint and Its Response (1:12–2:5). The answer to the first complaint was not enough for Habakkuk. He acknowledged that God had "ordained them as a judgment" and "established them for chastisement" (1:12). But he goes on to say that God is "of purer eyes than to behold evil," and he wonders why God looks on "faithless men" and is "silent when the wicked swallows up" those who are more righteous (v 13). He implies that God observes the wicked Chaldeans, but does not punish them for their wrongs. Habakkuk still cannot understand how God can use a wicked nation to punish his own people.

But Habakkuk did learn something from God's first response. He began his second complaint with the affirmation, "Art thou not from everlasting, O Lord my God. . . . We shall not die" (1:12). The prophet probably had in mind the previous verse (v 11), that declared that the god of the Chaldeans was their own military might. In contrast, Judah's God is eternal and not transitory like the fleeting strength of armies and nations.

Habakkuk's problem was still not resolved for he next described the rapacious nature of the Chaldeans, wondering how God could use them to punish Judah. The Chaldeans were like fishermen, catching people in their nets and then worshiping their nets (1:15,16). Habakkuk asked God if the Chaldeans would continue emptying their nets and slaying the nations (v 17).

Having posed his questions, the prophet waited to see what God's response would be (2:1). The Lord replied that his answer should be written in large clear letters for it was certain (v 2); but it would not be fulfilled immediately (v 3).

What follows is one of the greatest verses about faith in the whole OT (2:4). The words "the righteous shall live by his faith" became the touchstone of the Protestant Reformation. The apostle Paul appealed to Habakkuk 2:4 in his exposition of the doctrine of justification by faith (Rom 1:17; Gal 3:11). This passage was also important in the NT Book of Hebrews (10:38,39).

The word "faith" in the OT basically means "firmness" or "strength." The root of the word is used to describe the supporting posts of a door (2 Kgs 18:16) and firm support for a peg (Is 22:23). When used of God, the word has the sense of faithfulness, or unwavering commitment to his promises. Referring specifically to human faith, it means unwavering trust in the God who promised. Faith in the OT is not an abstract concept, but commitment to God. It is not characterized by works, but by an attitude of wholehearted trust in God.

God affirms in 2:4 that a truly righteous person will live by unwavering trust in God, trust that remains firm in spite of trials. Jesus taught the same thing in the parable of the sower (Mt 13:21), and it is also expressed in James 1:12.

God's answer to Habakkuk's complaint was that he does punish evil, but in his time and his way. A truly righteous person will not lose faith because evil is not immediately eliminated or the wicked quickly punished. Faith trusts in the sovereignty of God's righteous rule in this world.

A Taunt-Song Celebrating the Fall of the Chaldeans (2:6–20). After hinting at the fall of the Chaldeans, the prophet composes a taunt-song in which he depicts the gloomy future of that nation. When the Babylonian Empire fell to a oalition of Medes and Persians, the prophetic elements in Habakkuk's poem became historical reality.

The prophet affirms that Babylon's "debtors" will arise against her (2:7). This expression implies that some nations would suddenly arise to bring about Babylon's downfall.

The reason for the destruction of Babylon is cited in 2:8: "Because you have plundered many nations, all the remnant of the peoples shall plunder you." The OT principle of retributive justice teaches that God's moral law extends not only to believers but to unbelievers as well.

The great building efforts of the Babylonian king Nebuchadnezzar seem to be implied in verses 9–11. The prophet says that even the stones and beams of his cities will cry out, as though protesting the fact that the city was built with blood (vv 12–14).

Habakkuk condemns the Chaldeans, not only for their inhuman cruelty, but for the shameful way in which they treated their captive peoples. The prophet pictures this degrading treatment in a vivid metaphor, saying it is like making others drunk in order to gaze on their shame (2:15).

Habakkuk concludes his taunt-song with a denunciation of Chaldean idolatry, pointing out the folly of those who make gods from wood and stone (2:18,19). The Chaldeans, like other pagan peoples, attributed their success to their idols. The prophet implies that because such trust is groundless—their idols are powerless to help them—Babylon will fall.

Habakkuk goes on to make a striking contrast between the Lord and the idols created by people (2:20). "The Lord is in his holy temple" in heaven, and all the earth must keep silence before him. God is real and he is sovereign. The prophet's word is that the earth should wait in hushed silence for the judgment that will surely come.

The Prayer of Habakkuk (3:1–19). The prophecy of Habakkuk closes with a prayer, reminiscent of some of the OT psalms. It contains a superscription (3:1) and several musical notations. Some have argued that this chapter is not originally Habakkuk's, because it does not fit the narrative flow of the book. They regard the chapter as originating in the postexilic period.

The psalm could have been written by the prophet and added to his prophetic oracles, either by himself or by a secretary. The musical notations do not necessarily point to a later period, because many psalms have such musical directions, and their preexilic date has been substantiated by linguistic and historical studies.

The prayer is similar to the message of Habakkuk. In it he affirms that God will judge his enemies (3:16), and he praises God's sovereignty (v 3). Both themes are prominent in the prophetic oracles of chapters 1 and 2.

The prayer is filled with assurances of God's power and justice. It forms a fitting conclusion to the body of the book, in which the prophet questioned divine providence. It demonstrates that the prophet had come to a place of unshakeable faith as he observed God's activity in history.

THOMAS E. McCOMISKEY

See HABAKKUK (PERSON); ISRAEL, HISTORY OF; PROPHECY; PROPHET, PROPHETESS.

Bibliography. D.E. Gowan, *The Triumph of Faith in Habakkuk;* C.F. Keil, *Biblical Commentary on the OT: The Twelve Minor Prophets,* vol 2; D.M. Lloyd-Jones, *From Fear to Faith: Studies in the Book of Habakkuk;* E. Marbury, *Obadiah and Habakkuk;* G.A. Smith, *The Book of the Twelve Prophets,* vol 2; C. von Orelli, *The Twelve Minor Prophets.*

Habazziniah, Habaziniah. Jaazaniah's grandfather. Jaazaniah was a leader of the Rechabites, warriors tested by Jeremiah with regard to their forefather's command not to drink wine (Jer 35:3, KJV Habaziniah). They remained loyal to the command, and Jeremiah used their loyalty in an appeal to Judah to be faithful to God.

Habergeon. KJV translation for coat of mail, part of a soldier's defensive armor (2 Chr 26:14; Neh 4:16; Jb 41:26).

See ARMS AND WARFARE.

Habiru. Term, more accurately rendered Hapiru, referring to certain groups of people appearing in texts from virtually the whole ancient Near East from the 19th century BC to the 12th century BC. Despite more than a half-century of discovery and research, no agreement has been reached on the spelling, etymology, and meaning of the name; whether the term represents a people, a social class, an occupational group, or something similar; and whether or not they were related to the Hebrews.

The Name. With the discovery of the Ugaritic language and the identification of these same people in Egyptian texts, it has become virtually certain that the word is West Semitic in origin and is to be correctly spelled 'Apiru. The traditional forms *Habiru/Hapiru* come from the attempt of Akkadian scribes to render a foreign name. The alternate form with *b* or *p* arises from the fact that the second syllable can be read with either sound in the cuneiform orthography of the period. In cuneiform texts they are also frequently referred to by the ideogram SA.GAZ. Unfortunately the meaning of the name is quite unclear. The only meaning attested in West Semitic in this period for the root '*pr* is "dust." The word would then signify "dusty," people covered with dust from the sands of the desert, or from long journeys, but this etymology seems forced.

Brief Survey of the Evidence. Hapiru have appeared in virtually every major textual find from the 2nd millennium BC in a wide diversity of roles. Frequently they function as armed units in service to local princes or cities (e.g., Mari, Alalah), stationed in garrisons for protection (e.g., in Hittite texts from Asia Minor), or provided with rations and clothing from the state (e.g., in Babylonia and Nuzi). On the other hand, they are frequently pictured as hostile to the established order and engaged in looting and pillaging (e.g., at Mari and in the Amarna tablets). Elsewhere they appear as wealthy persons detained for ransom (Cappadocia); kings make treaties with them (Alalah and the Hittite capital); while other texts refer to the "gods of the Hapiru" (Hittite) or "Aleppo of the Hapiru" (Ugarit). At Nuzi several texts are concerned with Hapiru men and women who enter voluntarily into slavery to wealthy persons.

The largest body of evidence comes from the Amarna texts, about 1400–1350 BC. Here the Hapiru are a powerful force hostile to the pharaoh and his loyal princes. Local princes are allied with them, and the complaint is often made that the pharaoh's land has been taken over by them. Yet the Egyptian commissioner at Damascus has Hapiru troops in his army. It is clear that here they are mercenary soldiers.

They were present in large numbers in Palestine throughout the Egyptian Empire, about 1500–1200 BC. Several pharaohs report bringing large numbers of Hapiru prisoners from campaigns there, and Egyptian texts of the 19th dynasty (c. 1300–1200) mention Hapiru, probably prisoners of war, as employed in Egypt working vineyards and quarrying stone.

The Identification of the Hapiru. The above evidence is so diverse in date and origin and in the role that the Hapiru play that it is exceedingly difficult to construct a coherent picture from it. The most common view regards them as an underprivileged class in society, soldiers of fortune, refugees or outlaws, stateless or uprooted persons who work for food or who rebel against constituted authority. Serious objections to this view include the fact that none of these definitions fits all, or even most, of the texts, and it is very unlikely that a group would be known by exactly the same designation for almost a millennium among widely separated people who spoke different languages. The facts are best explained by the view that Hapiru is an ethnic term or

had an ethnic connotation, referring to r lated Semitic nomadic or seminomadic trib groups living in the border areas and also i side Syria, Mesopotamia, and Palestine, wh were in the process of settling down, eith peacefully in cooperation with the ruling po ers or in opposition to them.

The Hapiru and the Hebrews. The que tion of their connection to the Hebrews ca only be answered tentatively. The view th "Hapiru" is the same word as "Hebrew" now made difficult, although not impossib by the recognition that the true form of t word is '*Apiru*. That the two are historica identical is made impossible by the wid spread temporal and geographical distrib tion of the Hapiru. Further, there is extrabiblical text dealing with the Hapiru th bears any relation to the Hebrews. But th does not mean there is no connection at all.

The term "Hebrew" is not used in the O after the time of Saul, about 1000 BC, and regularly used only by foreigners to identi the Israelites, or by the Israelites when spea ing to foreigners. Thus, the word disappears Israel at about the same time as the ter "Hapiru" disappears from nonbiblical tex Further, numerous close analogies exist b tween the Hapiru and the Hebrews. Both a seminomadic tribal societies in the process settling down, mainly by armed conflict. The move in the same areas: for example, both a pear as state slaves in Egypt, both appear armed conflict with the city-states of Pale tine; and the Hapiru appear frequently northwest Mesopotamia, the region the Bib gives as the homeland of the patriarchs. A this can be explained by the hypothesis th the Hebrews were part of the broad moveme represented by the Hapiru/ 'Apiru, groups semisedentary West Semitic tribes in the pr cess of settling down by various means in var ous places.

FREDERIC W. BUS

Habor. Modern Habur (Chaboras) Rive The Habor River runs from the mountains north-central Assyria, in Gozan, into the E phrates River at a junction about 250 mil south and west of Nineveh. Numerous tributa ies feed the Habor farther to the north. The O names the river as the site to which King Sha maneser carried the captive Israelites (2 Kg 17:6; 18:11; 1 Chr 5:26).

Hacaliah, Hachaliah. Nehemiah's fath (Neh 1:1; 10:1; KJV Hachaliah).

Hachilah. Unidentified site in Hebron which David fled when Saul attempted to ki him (1 Sm 23:19; 26:13).

Hachmoni. Name of Jehiel's family. Jehiel was David's servant (1 Chr 27:32), apparently a companion or tutor of David's sons.

Hachmonite. Designation for Jashobeam (also named Josheb-basshebeth in 2 Sm 23:8), one of David's personal guards (1 Chr 11:11). He is alternately called a Tahchemonite (KJV Tachmonite) in 2 Samuel 23:8, but this is probably a textual error.

Hadad. 1. Eighth of the 12 sons of Ishmael, and thus a grandson of Abraham (Gn 25:15; 1 Chr 1:30). The KJV reads "Hadar" in Genesis 25:15 and "Hadad" in 1 Chronicles 1:30, whereas RSV and ASV read "Hadad" in both passages.

2. Edomite ruler, son of Bedad, who reigned before the Hebrew captivity in Egypt, and who won an important victory over the Midianites in the plain of Moab (Gn 36:35,36; 1 Chr 1:46,47).

3. Another king of Edom, one of the few whose wife, Mehetabel, was mentioned by name. His capital city was Pau (Gn 36:39; 1 Chr 1:50,51).

4. Prince of the royal house of Edom who fled to Egypt after David and Joab conquered Edom and occupied the land. He grew up in Egypt and gained favor with the pharaoh who gave him his sister-in-law as a wife. Later, when David was dead, he desired to return to Edom and lead a revolt against Solomon (1 Kgs 11:14–25). Some scholars have identified him with #3 above.

Hadadezer. King of Zobah in Syria during David's reign in Israel. He apparently ruled a region from Ammon in the south to the Euphrates in the east. In 2 Samuel 8:3–12 (see also 1 Chr 18:3–10; KJV Hadarezer) Hadadezer "went to restore his power at the river Euphrates"; David engaged him in battle and defeated him. When the Syrians came to his aid, David defeated them and occupied Damascus. In 2 Samuel 10:1–3 David sent servants to comfort Hanun when his father, Nahash king of Ammon, died. The servants were mistreated and humiliated (v 4). So David sent Joab against Ammon, after Ammon allied with Syria as protection against Israel (v 6). Joab defeated the combined armies (vv 15–19; see also 1 Chr 19:16,19). After Joab's victory Hadadezer sent more troops from "beyond the river." The armies met at Helem, David was victorious, and Hadadezer sued for peace, becoming tributary to Israel.

See ISRAEL, HISTORY OF; SYRIA, SYRIANS.

Hadadrimmon. Combination of two storm deities, Hadad (mentioned in the Ugaritic texts) and Rimmon (Babylonian storm god). Hadadrimmon was formerly thought to be a place. The Ras Shamra material equated Hadad with the vegetation god Baal, who was worshiped to ensure agricultural productivity. Canaanite fertility rituals included periodic mourning for the deceased Baal by the goddess Anat, his consort. It is to that rite that Zechariah 12:11 alludes. The messianic reference in the previous verse likens the grief in Jerusalem to the lamentation for Hadadrimmon at the rites near Megiddo.

See CANAANITE DEITIES AND RELIGION.

Hadar. 1. KJV spelling of Hadad, Ishmael's son, in Genesis 25:15.

See HADAD #1.

2. Alternate spelling of Hadad, king of Edom, in Genesis 36:39.

See HADAD #3.

A view of the Dead Sea and the mountains east of it near Lisan and the area where Hadad defeated the Midianites.

Hadarezer. KJV alternate spelling of Hadadezer, king of Zobah.

See HADADEZER.

Hadashah. Town in the lowlands of Judah, near Gath, in the vicinity of Zenan and Migdal-gad (Jos 15:37). Its site is unknown.

Hadassah. Original name of Esther (2:7).

See ESTHER (PERSON).

Hadattah. Name of a city (KJV) incorrectly derived from the name of the town Hazorhadattah in Joshua 15:25.

See HAZOR-HADATTAH.

Hades. Abode of all the dead (in Greek and some Jewish literature) or the abode of the wicked dead (in Christian literature).

In Greek mythology Hades was originally the god of the underworld (also named Pluto), a brother of Zeus. He was the abductor of Persephone and thus the cause of winter. His realm, which was called by his name (and also called Tartarus), was the dark land where the dead existed. Odysseus entered that realm and fed the ghosts with blood to get directions back home (Homer, *Odyssey* 4,834). Originally the Greeks thought of Hades as simply the grave, a shadowy, ghostlike existence that happened to all who died, good and evil alike. Gradually they and the Romans came to see it as a place of reward and punishment, an elaborately organized and guarded realm where the good were rewarded in the Elysian Fields and the evil were punished (so described by the Roman poet Virgil, 70–19 BC).

Hades became important to the Jews as the stereotyped term used by the translators of the Septuagint to translate the Hebrew name "Sheol" into Greek. This was a very suitable translation for the Hebrew term, for both words can signify the physical grave or death (Gn 37:35; Prv 5:5; 7:27), and both originally referred to a dark underworld (Jb 10:21,22) where existence was at best shadowy (J 38:17; Is 14:9). Sheol is described as under the ocean (Jb 26:5, Jon 2:2,3) and as having bars and gates (Jb 17:16). All people go there whether they are good or evil (Ps 89:48). In the earlier literature there is no hope of release from Sheol/Hades. C.S. Lewis describes this concept well in *The Silver Chair:* "Many sink down, and few return to the sunlit lands." Of course all these descriptions are in poetic literature: how literally the Hebrews (or the Greeks for that matter) took their descriptions of Hades/Sheol is hard to say. They may have simply used the older picture-language of Greek poetry to describe that for which prose words were inadequate.

Jew and Greek alike came in contact with Persia, the Jews at the time the postexilic writers were composing their books (e.g. Malachi, Daniel, and some psalms) and the Greeks somewhat later (they fought the Persians 520–479 BC and conquered them 334–330 BC). Whether because of Persian influence or these groups or not, during this period the idea of reward and punishment after death developed, and Sheol/Hades changed from a shadow-land to a differentiated place of reward and punishment for both Greeks (and Romans) and Jews. Josephus records that the Pharisees believed in reward and punishment at death (*Antiq.* 18.1.3) and a similar idea appears in 1 Enoch 22. In these and many other cases in Jewish literature, Hades stands for the one place of the dead, which has two or more compartments. In other Jewish literature Hades is the place of torment for the wicked, while the righteous enter Paradise (Pss Sol 14; Wis of Sol 2:1; 3:1). Thus by the beginning of the NT period Hades has three meanings: (1) death, (2) the place of all the dead, and (3) the place of the wicked dead only. Context determines which meaning an author intends in a given passage.

All these meanings appear in the NT. In Matthew 11:23 and Luke 10:15 Jesus speaks of Capernaum's descending to Hades. Most likely he simply means that the city will "die" or be destroyed. Hades means "death," in this context as "heaven" means "exaltation." Revelation 6:8 also exemplifies this: Death comes on a horse and Hades (a symbol of death) comes close behind. This personification of Hades probably comes from the OT, where Hades/Sheol is viewed as a monster that devours people (Prv 1:12; 27:20; 30:16; Is 5:14; 28:15,18; Hb 2:5).

Matthew 16:18 is a more difficult use of Hades. The church will be built upon a rock and the gates of Hades will not prevail against it. Here the place of the dead (complete with gates and bars) is a symbol for death: Christians may in fact be killed, but death (the gates of Hades) will no more hold them than it held Christ. He who burst out of Hades will bring his people out as well. This is also the meaning of Acts 2:27 (quoting Ps 16:10): Christ did not stay dead; his life did not remain in Hades; unlike David he rose from the dead. It is uncertain in either of these cases whether Hades is simply a symbol for death or whether it means that Christ and the Christian actually went to a place of the dead called Hades; probably the former is intended. Whatever the case, since Christ did rise, he has conquered death and Hades. He appears in Revelation

1:18 as the one holding the keys (the control) to both.

Two NT passages refer to Hades as the place where the dead exist: Revelation 20:13,14 and Luke 16:23. In Revelation 20 Hades is emptied of all who are in it (either all dead or the wicked dead, depending on one's eschatology)—the resurrection is complete. When the wicked are judged and cast into the lake of fire (Gehenna) Hades is also thrown in. Luke 16:23, however, clearly refers to Hades as the place of the wicked dead. There the rich man is tormented in a flame, while the poor man Lazarus goes to heaven (Abraham's bosom).

Hades, then, means three things in the NT as it did in Jewish literature. (1) Death and its power is the most frequent meaning, especially in metaphorical uses. (2) It also means the place of the dead in general, when a writer wants to lump all the dead together. (3) It means, finally, the place where the wicked dead are tormented before the final judgment. This is its narrowest meaning. The Bible does not dwell on this torment—Dante's picture in *The Inferno* draws on later speculation and Graeco-Roman conceptions of the Hades more than on the Bible. Yet it also knows that the Christian cannot go to the same place as the wicked, for the progress of revelation has revealed that death is conquered and cannot separate us from Christ. Thus death for the Christian means not the gloom of Hades (Sheol), but the light of seeing Christ face to face.

PETER H. DAVIDS

See HELL; SHEOL; DEAD, ABODE OF THE; GEHENNA.

Hadid. City in Benjamin (Neh 11:33) mentioned with Lod and Ono (Ezr 2:33; Neh 7:37) as the home of 720 Benjamites returning from the Babylonian captivity (Neh 11:34). In 1 Maccabees 12:38 and 13:13 the place is identified with Adida, which was fortified by Simon Maccabeus and later by Vespasian. A more likely suggestion identifies it with the modern site of el-Had<u>i</u>theth, about three to four miles northeast of Lydda.

Hadlai. Amasa's father from Ephraim's tribe (2 Chr 28:12). Amasa opposed the taking of prisoners from Judah's tribe after a battle.

Hadoram. 1. Joktan's fifth son; Hadoram and his brothers were the sixth generation from Noah (Gn 10:27; 1 Chr 1:21).

2. Alternate spelling of Joram in 1 Chronicles 18:10.

See JORAM #1.

3. Alternate spelling of Adoniram in 2 Chronicles 10:18.

See ADONIRAM.

Hadrach. Settlement in northwest Lebanon mentioned only in association with Tyre, Sidon, Hamath, and Damascus (Zec 9:1). The last two cities were listed in Assyrian records with Hatarivia, with which Hadrach is now identified.

Haeleph. City given to Benjamin's tribe for an inheritance after the initial conquest of Palestine (Jos 18:28, KJV Eleph). Its location is unknown.

Hagab. Ancestor of a family of temple servants returning with Zerubbabel to Palestine following the exile (Ezr 2:46).

Hagaba, Hagabah. Forefather of a family of temple servants that returned to Jerusalem with Zerubbabel after the Babylonian exile (Neh 7:48; also spelled Hagabah in Ezr 2:45).

Hagar. Egyptian handmaid of Sarai, the wife of Abram. At Sarai's insistence Abram took Hagar as his concubine and she became the mother of his son Ishmael (Gn 16:1–16; 21:9–21).

When God commanded Abram to leave Mesopotamia, he promised to make a great nation of him and to give the new land to his seed (Gn 12:2,7). After 10 years in Canaan and still childless, Sarai suggested to Abram that he take Hagar as his concubine and have children by her. It was the custom in northeast Mesopotamia when a wife failed to produce an heir for her husband, she could give him a slave for that purpose. Any son born of the union of husband and concubine was considered the child of the wife (cf. Gn 30:1–6).

During her pregnancy, Hagar became disrespectful to Sarai. Sarai dealt so harshly with Hagar that she fled to the desert. An angel of God appeared to her at a well in the desert and told her to return to Abram's house, promising that she would have a son, Ishmael ("God heard"), who would be a wild and quarrelsome man. Hagar then named the place Beer-lahai-roi, "the well of one who sees and lives."

Ishmael was born when Abram was 86 years old, and 14 years later God gave Abraham and Sarah the promised son, Isaac. At the time of Isaac's weaning (at approximately three years of age), a feast was held. At the weaning feast Ishmael mocked Isaac (Gn 21:9), and Sarah in anger asked Abraham to send Hagar and Ishmael away. Abraham hesitated until God spoke to him and told him to do so (v 12).

Hagar and Ishmael left to wander in the wilderness of Beersheba. When their water was exhausted, God miraculously rescued Ha-

An animal skin used for carrying water, such as the waterskin that Abraham gave to Hagar when he sent her and Ishmael away (Gn 21:14).

gar and Ishmael from death and assured Hagar that Ishmael would be the father of a great nation (21:17–19). Ishmael lived in the wilderness of Paran, became a hunter, married an Egyptian, and became the father of the Ishmaelites.

In an allegory developed by Paul (Gal 4:22–31), Hagar represents the old covenant of Sinai. As Ishmael was Abraham's son by human arrangement, the Judaizing Christians who would bind all Christians to the Law of Moses are the bondslave Hagar's spiritual children. Sarah, the freewoman, represents the new covenant of Christ. As Isaac was Abraham's son by faith in the divine promise, Christians who are free of the fleshly ordinances of the Law are spiritual children of Sarah. The contrast is between salvation by works, which is bondage to the Law, and salvation by grace and faith, which is freedom.

See SARAH #1; ABRAHAM.

Hagarene, Hagarite. KJV alternate forms of Hagrite, the name of a member of an Arabian tribe descended from Hagar living east of Palestine.

See HAGRITE.

Hagerite. KJV rendering of Hagrite, a descendant of Hagar, in 1 Chronicles 27:31.

See HAGRITE.

Haggadah. Method of Jewish interpretation that is homiletical in character. Haggadah is usually defined negatively, that is, as that part of rabbinic teaching that is *not* Halakah. Haggadah and Halakah complement each other: the latter is interpretation which gives the rule, statute, or religious law Jews are to follow, while Haggadah aims at edification, inspiration, inner piety, and religious devotion, covering the entire field of religion and ethics. Halakah states the fact; Haggadah stirs one to action. Halakah means literally "walking," thus showing the devout Jew how to walk in "the way of the Lord." Haggadah means literally "narrative," or "storytelling," which includes proverbs, parables, and sermons. Within these artistic forms of instruction are contained moral and ethical principles intended to show one how to live correctly. Among the two types of interpretation, Haggadah is the more "popular," having a wider appeal. Its way of storytelling is designed to touch the human heart "so that one should recognize Him who created the world, and so cling to His ways" (*Sifrei-Deuteronomy* 49). As one Jewish scholar has said, its purpose is "to bring Heaven down to earth and to elevate man to Heaven." Because Haggadah is not Halakah, but rather interpretation, it also contains other material, such as metaphysical speculations, historical and legendary tales of Israel's past, visions of its furture, and remarks on scientific subjects such as astronomy and medicine.

See TALMUD; HALAKAH.

Haggai (Person). Prophet whose book is the 10th in a series of 12 brief prophetic books concluding the OT. Haggai's name probably came from a word for "festival." We have no information concerning his family or social background. He is referred to merely as Haggai the prophet (Hg 1:1; Ezr 5:1; 6:14). His place in the postexilic community seems to have been a conspicuous one, and according to Jewish tradition he was known as a prophet in Babylon during the exile. The major concern of his prophetic ministry was to encourage the people to rebuild the temple, which had been destroyed during the earlier years of the exile.

See HAGGAI, BOOK OF; PROPHET, PROPHETESS.

Haggai, Book of. Tenth in the 12 short prophetic books at the end of the OT.

Author. Haggai was among the Jewish colonists at Jerusalem in the year 520 BC when his prophetic words were recorded (Ezr 5:1,2; 6:14). The four messages which the Lord gave to Haggai were to be directed to specific individuals. The first was to Zerubbabel the governor and Joshua the high priest (Hg 1:1). The second was to Zerubbabel, Joshua, and the remnant of the people (2:2). The third was a word to the priests (v 11). The final message was limited to Zerubbabel (v 21).

Purpose. The key phrase of Haggai's prophecies is "Consider your ways" or "Consider" (1:5,7; 2:15,18). The purpose of God's messages to the Judean leadership and people, therefore, was to awaken them to spiritual responsibilities. Two different classes of Judeans had to be turned from their indifference. The true believers needed to be reminded that God was yet merciful. The conditions which they thought were the result of unforgivable sins committed by their fathers could be remedied. The hypocrites among the Judeans had only sought the promised blessings. They had only exchanged one form of idolatry for another. When the blessings did not materialize they were disappointed.

The unifying message was: Today gives no key to what God will do tomorrow. God's fulfillment of his promises cannot be judged by appearances. Haggai's message was twofold: reproof and encouragement. The colonists needed to be chastised for their indifference and consoled in the midst of their troubles.

Teaching. Haggai is a practical book, dealing with the believer's service to God. Procrastination and indifference have been debilitating sins among God's people throughout all ages. Concern and a sense of urgency are always pleasing to God (Rom 13:11–14).

The presence of God is the primary motivation for boldness and the means of banishing discouragement (Mt 28:19,20; Eph 3:8–21; Heb 13:5,6).

Separation from contaminating influences and sin is demanded of all believers (2 Cor 6:14–7:1). Without this quality of life the believer cannot expect to be found fit for God's service (2 Tm 2:19–26).

The disobedient child of God can expect removal of blessing and chastisement from God (2 Cor 9:8–11; Heb 12:3–13; Jas 4:1–3).

The message concerning God's judgment of sin and the establishment of the messianic kingdom is a message of hope to the NT believer as well as the Jews of Haggai's day (Rom 15:4–13; 2 Pt 3:10–18).

The key phrase of Haggai ("consider your ways") has echoes in 1 Corinthians 11:28 and 2 Corinthians 13:5, as do his writings about the effects of sin and the blessings of God (Jude 1–25).

The God of Haggai is given the title "Lord of hosts" 14 times in the book. This title is characteristic of the postexilic prophets (Hg; Zec; Mal) where it is found more than 80 times. It teaches that God is all-powerful and is Master of all spirit beings in heaven and all created beings on the earth.

Haggai also testifies to the God-breathed quality of the Word of God and its divine authority. Over and over the prophet announces ways that God has spoken to him and is the author of these messages (at least 25 times in the space of 28 verses).

Content. *First Message.* The first message Haggai was to deliver to the Judeans was given to him "on the first day of the month" (1:1). Upon the first day of each month the Jews were to bring special offerings to the sanctuary (Nm 28:11–15). God chose this special time to reveal the sin of the people with regard to the unfinished sanctuary.

The leaders of the Judeans were singled out for the first message from the Lord (Hg 1:1). Zerubbabel was the civil leader or governor and Joshua was the spiritual leader or high priest. Together, they were responsible for the activity (or inactivity) of God's people.

The Word of the Lord revealed the procrastination of the people (1:2). God's temple had not been completed because his people had determined for themselves that "the time is not come." The energies and finances of God's people had been channeled selfishly into their own homes (v 4).

"Now" (1:5) focused the attention of the Jews upon the present requirement of God in the light of their sinful indifference. They were to give attention to their own condition spiritually and materially: "Consider how you have fared" (v 5). This key phrase of Haggai's prophecies is literally, "Set your heart to your ways" or "Lay your ways to your heart." Self-examination would reveal that their procrastination had robbed them of more than just 16 years.

Verse 6 reveals the poverty in which the Jews were living as a result of God's chastisement for their sin. The blessings of God had been withdrawn in accord with his covenant (see Dt 28:15–31).

Following another exhortation to "consider" their ways (1:7), the Lord revealed the remedy for the Jews' cursed condition: "build the house" (v 8). The disobedience with regard to the completion of the temple was the reason for their poverty (vv 9–11).

The response of the leaders and the people was encouraging. The resumption of the construction of the temple was a definite manifestation of belief in the Word of God (1:12). Immediate obedience also testified to the acceptance of the ministry of Haggai, who was "the Lord's messenger" delivering "the Lord's message" (v 13).

Second Message. Approximately one month later Haggai was summoned again by the Lord (2:1). The second message continued the note of encouragement with which the first message closed. Perhaps the builders had begun to feel the pressures of their service. Perhaps the old doubts and discouragements had plagued their faith again. The adversaries had reappeared to hinder them (Ezr 5:3–6:12). Haggai's second message was similar to Ezra's claim that "the eye of their God was upon the elders of the Jews" (5:5). The Lord not only sees his servants' needs, but also sends relief and encouragement.

The day of this second message was the last day of the feast of tabernacles (Lv 23:33–43). Perhaps this reminder of God's glorious presence with their ancestors in the wilderness made their present situation all the more discouraging. Therefore, the Lord spoke to all the people rather than just their leaders (Hg 2:2). Was there any survivor of the preexilic days who had personally beheld the glory of God as it resided in the Solomonic temple (cf. 1 Kgs 8:1–11; Ez 9:1–11:23)? Was the present temple "as nothing" in comparison (Hg 2:3)? The Babylonian Talmud listed five things that were absent in the new temple that had been present in the Solomonic temple: (1) the ark of the covenant, (2) the sacred fire, (3) the Shekinah glory, (4) the Holy Spirit, and (5) the Urim and Thummim.

Again, "now" calls attention to God's remedy. Three times the command "take courage" is proclaimed (Hg 2:4). Each time the command is given, one of the recipients of God's message is addressed (cf. v 2). The concluding command was "work." The reason for the strength and the activity was God's presence. The Holy Spirit might seem to be absent from the temple, but he would remain among the people "according to the word" of God (v 5).

To encourage the workers further, God revealed the future glory of his house (2:6–9). That glory would come to pass after a time of judgment (vv 6,7a), when "the treasures of all nations shall come in" (v 7b). The exact meaning of this verse has been variously interpreted. The views center around two different translations: "the desire of all nations shall come" (KJV) and "they will come with the wealth of all nations" (NASB).

The arguments for the messianic interpretation based on the first translation may be summarized as follows: (1) The vast majority of both Christian and Jewish interpreters took this phrase as a reference to the Messiah. (2) The abstract noun "desire" may have the concrete concept of the one who is desirable. (3)

Though the verb in the Hebrew is plural, it is grammatically possible for the agreement of subject and predicate to be based upon the second noun ("nations") in a genitive relationship. (4) The time element is suitable since God has just judged the nations and the hour of Christ's coming would be at hand. (5) An alternate translation is available which meets the grammatical difficulties but retains the Messianic import: "they (the nations) have come to the desire of all the nations."

In spite of the weight of the arguments for this first view, it seems better to accept the second translation and corresponding view. The arguments are as follows: (1) The vast majority of early Christian and Jewish interpreters base their view on the Latin Vulgate translation (c. AD 400) while the second translation is in agreement with an older version, the Greek Septuagint (c. 300 BC). (2) The singular "desire" may be taken as a collective noun referring to "features," "wealth." (3) The principle of Hebrew grammar which allows the noun "nations" to be the one with which the verb agrees is a rare occurrence in poetic books for such constructions as this. It is unlikely that such phraseology would be used without Haggai declaring the exact meaning in the immediate context. (4) The immediate context does solve the difficulty by the plain declaration that the silver and the gold belong to the Lord (2:8). (5) The kingdom context of these verses accords well with such parallel passages as Isaiah 60:5,11 and Revelation 21:24.

The conclusion to this message of encouragement is that the future glory of the temple (cf. Hg 2:3, "first glory") will be greater than in the days of the Solomonic temple (v 9), because the Shekinah glory will return (v 7c; Ez 43:1–5) and the building will have great beauty (cf. Hg 2:8; Is 60:13,17). God will also grant peace (Hg 2:9) in his kingdom at the time of this future glorious temple (see Is 9:6,7; 66:12; Zec 6:13).

Third message. About two months later Haggai received a third message from God (2:10). This time exhortation would be the theme, and the message was directed to the priests alone (v 11). Haggai used questions concerning the Law of Moses, to instruct the priests in the polluting character of sin. Something clean or holy cannot transfer its sanctity to something else (v 12). On the contrary, that which is unholy can transfer its character to something clean, defiling it (v 13; cf. Lv 22:4–6; Nm 19:11).

The application of this principle to the Judeans was clear: the offerings they brought during their years of disobedience were unacceptable to God because of Judah's uncleanness (Hg 2:14).

By reviving the memory of past disobedience and chastisement, God was exhorting the Jews to constantly "consider" (2:15,18) the consequences of disobedience. Such consideration should prevent future spiritual indifference. The conclusion of the message was a reminder of the blessing of God upon the obedient (v 19).

Fourth Message. On the same day Haggai received another message from God (2:20). This message was to be directed toward Zerubbabel (v 21) who was to be encouraged by the permanency of his inherited Davidic office (cf. 1:1; 1 Chr 3:1,5,10,17–19; 2 Sm 7:4–17). The gentile nations would be judged and the kingdoms of the world overthrown (Hg 2:6,7,21,22). This would be but the preparation for God's rule (cf. Rv 11:15–18).

The promise to Zerubbabel in Haggai 2:23 was God's means of confirming that his promises to David were still operative even after the 70-year Babylonian captivity and the 16-year stagnation among the Judeans who had returned to Jerusalem. Zerubbabel was appointed "as a signet" by God. A signet was a personal cylinder or ring seal with which men demonstrated their authority and the authenticity of their signature. Kings used them for identifying their decrees (Est 3:10; 8:8–10) and for confirming the authority of their deputies (Gn 41:42). God's appointment of Zerubbabel "as a signet," therefore, meant that Zerubbabel would be God's seal of authority on the continuation of the Davidic line from which the Messiah should come and reign (cf. Mt 1:12; Lk 3:27).

See HAGGAI (PERSON); ISRAEL, HISTORY OF; POST-EXILIC PERIOD, THE; PROPHECY; PROPHET, PROPHETESS.

Bibliography. J.G. Baldwin, *Haggai, Zechariah, and Malachi*; N.E. Barnes, *Haggai and Zechariah*; C.F. Keil, *Biblical Commentary on the OT: The Twelve Minor Prophets*, vol 2; E.B. Pusey, *The Minor Prophets*, vol 2; G.A. Smith, *The Book of the Twelve Prophets*, vol 2; C. von Orelli, *The Twelve Minor Prophets*; H. Wolf, *Haggai, and Malachi*.

Haggedolim. Father of Zabdiel, overseer of 128 mighty men of valor who lived in Jerusalem in Nehemiah's day (Neh 11:14).

Haggeri. KJV rendering of Hagri, Mibhar's father, in 1 Chronicles 11:38.

See HAGRI.

Haggi. Gad's son and founder of the family of Haggites (Gn 46:16; Nm 26:15).

Haggiah. Merarite Levite, Shimea's son and the father of Asaiah (1 Chr 6:30).

Haggite. Descendant of Haggi (Nm 26:15).

See HAGGI.

Ruins at Hebron, the city in which Haggith gave birth to Adonijah.

Haggith. One of David's wives and the mother of Adonijah (2 Sm 3:4; 1 Kgs 1:5,11; 2:13; 1 Chr 3:2). She gave birth to Adonijah in Hebron while David maintained his capital there. In 2 Samuel she and her son are fourth in the list of David's wives and sons.

Hagri. Mibhar's father according to 1 Chronicles 11:38 (KJV Haggeri). The parallel list in 2 Samuel 23:36, however, has "Bani, the Gadite" instead of "Mibhar, son of Hagri." Due to some textual difficulties in the 1 Chronicles passage, the 2 Samuel reading is preferred.

Hagrite. Arabian tribe descended from Hagar, Abraham's concubine. Being nomads, the Hagrites roamed the desert east of Gilead. Relations between Israel and the Hagrites were usually hostile. During Saul's reign Reuben's tribe fought them and were defeated (1 Chr 5:10, KJV Hagarites). Later, however, with the help of Gad and the half-tribe of Manasseh, Reuben was able to take their land and hold it until the exile (1 Chr 5:19,20, KJV Hagarites). In the light of that hostility it is easy to understand Asaph's prayer against them in Psalm 83:6 (KJV Hagarenes). David, on the other hand, made a Hagrite, Jaziz, the steward of all his flocks (1 Chr 27:31, KJV Hagerite).

Hahiroth. Alternate form of Pi-hahiroth in Numbers 33:8.

See PI-HAHIROTH.

Hai. KJV form for the Canaanite city Ai in Genesis 12:8 and 13:3.

See AI.

Hair. See FASHION AND DRESS.

Hakkatan. Member of Azgad's family, the father of Jonathan, and one of the exiles who returned to Jerusalem with Ezra (Ezr 8:12).

Hakkoz. Name borne by a priestly family during the monarchy (1 Chr 24:10). In Ezra's time, the family pedigree could not be documented properly; consequently the privilege of priestly service was withdrawn (Ezr 2:61; Neh 3:4,21; 7:63; KJV Koz).

Hakupha. Forefather of a family of temple assistants that returned to Jerusalem with Zerubbabel after the exile (Ezr 2:51; Neh 7:53).

Halah. Place in Assyria where the inhabitants of Samaria were taken after its fall in 722 BC (2 Kgs 17:6; 18:11; cf. 1 Chr 5:26).

Halak, Mount. Mountain listed as marking the southern boundary of Joshua's conquests (Jos 11:17; 12:7). It is located in the western Arabah, and is probably identical with Jebel Halaq on the northwest side of the Wadi Marra.

Halakah. Overall term for Jewish law. Halakah, which means literally "walking," gives the authoritative Jewish way of life as contained in the Mishna. It shows the Jew how he is to walk and what he must do (see Ex 18:20).

First of all, Halakah rests upon the biblical laws and commandments found in the written Law (the Pentateuch, the first five books of the Bible) and the oral Law (according to Jewish tradition the unwritten law supposedly given to Moses on Mt Sinai and passed down through generations, finally to be recorded in the Talmud). In the Pentateuch, then, Halakah is given as law; for example we are told not to work on the sabbath. But what, in this context, does "work" mean? The written Law gives us no help, but in the Talmud we have Halakah, which is interpretation of the written Law, and in the Talmud we learn what "work" means.

Second, Halakah rests upon all the rabbinic legislation and decisions handed down through the ages by great Jewish scholars. All these things, then, taken together provide the basis for making religious-legal decisions in the orthodox Jewish community. All these things, the written and oral Law plus the history of Jewish legal scholarship, provide us with Halakah.

Halakah is intended to be all-encompassing, to handle every situation in life. One's eating habits, sex life, business ethics, social activities, entertainment; these and much more, are dealt with by Halakah. For this reason it has been called "the Jewish way," that way in which we can hope to find the mind and character of the Jewish people exactly and adequately expressed. Halakah is the Jewish legal and practical guide to living.

See TALMUD; HAGGADAH.

Halhul. City assigned to Judah's tribe for an inheritance after the initial conquest of Palestine. It was located between Beth-zur and Beth-anoth, four miles north of Hebron (Jos 15:58).

Hali. Town mentioned among those which formed the border of Asher's tribe (Jos 19:25). Hali may have been located west of Mt Carmel, but this is uncertain.

Hallel. Hebrew term describing a song of praise to God. It was later used in the Talmud and in rabbinical writings to refer to several groups of psalms of praise to God. Psalms 113–118 were known as the Egyptian Hallel, and 1st-century AD Jewish tradition assigned them to Moses. During the temple period this Hallel was recited on 18 days in the year, but only once at night, on the Passover. For that occasion it was recited in parts. Psalms 113,114 preceded the meal, prior to drinking the second cup, and Psalms 115–118 were recited after the last cup was filled. This is probably the song that is meant in the reference to the last supper of Jesus and his disciples, "when they had sung a hymn" (Mt 26:30; Mk 14:26). This Hallel was also used for the feasts of unleavened bread, Pentecost, tabernacles, and dedication.

The Great Hallel consisted of Psalm 136, but sometimes included Psalms 120–136. Psalms 146–148 were also considered as a single Hallel. These were used in the daily morning service of the synagogue.

See TALMUD; HALLELUJAH.

Hallelujah. Important Christian term figuring extensively in the church's worship and liturgy from early times. Hallelujah is a transliteration into Greek, and thence into English, of two Hebrew words which mean "Praise ye the Lord." This combination of the two Hebrew words forms the characteristic call to praise. Jews living in the dispersion in pre-Christian times were already using the transliteration in their synagogue worship. "Hallelujah," according to ancient Hebrew tradition, is to be written as one word, except in Psalm 135:3. It occurs nowhere in the OT but in the Psalter, where it occurs 23 times, and for the first time in Psalm 104:35. In Psalms 111–113 each one begins with "Hallelujah"; in 115–117 each ends with the word; and 146–150 each begins and ends with it.

In the Septuagint version of Psalms 113–118 all the individual psalms are headed "Allelujah." Through the Vulgate, this form of the word "Hallelujah" has come into use in the church. Like another famous Hebrew liturgical term "Amen," "Hallelujah" has passed from the OT to the NT, and thence to the Christian church. But in the AV and RV the phrase is rendered, "Praise ye the Lord."

In Hebrew liturgical usage the Hallel, or Hymn of Praise, Psalms 113–118, is sung at the three great religious festivals of Passover, Pentecost, and tabernacles. At the domestic celebration of Passover, Psalms 113 and 114 are sung before the meal, and Psalms 115–118 are sung after it. Matthew 26:30 and Mark 14:26 refer to the singing of 115–118 as the "hymn" sung by the Lord and his disciples after their celebration of the Passover and before they left the upper room.

"Hallelujah" does not appear anywhere in the NT except in Revelation 19:1,3,4,6. There it is a chant of the saints in heaven, and was taken over into the liturgy and hymnody of the church at an early date. It became the characteristic expression of joy, and was, therefore, sung especially at Eastertide, as is witnessed by Augustine. The choice by the Christian church of Psalms 113, 114, and 118 from the Hebrew Hallel as the psalms to be sung on Easter Day marks the liturgical connection of Easter with Passover, which it succeeded.

J.G.S.S. THOMSON

See HALLEL.

Hallohesh, Halohesh. Shallum's father (Neh 3:12, KJV Halohesh) and one who set his seal on Ezra's covenant (10:24).

Ham (Person). Second son of Noah (Gn 5:32; 6:10; 7:13; 9:18,22; 10:1,6,20). Ham had four sons whose names were Cush, Mizraim (Hebrew for Egypt), Put, and Canaan (Gn 10:6; 1 Chr 1:8). Ham, then, is seen as the ancestor of the Egyptians (though a mixed race apparently occurs later), as well as of peoples in Africa, Arabia, and Canaan.

After the flood Noah began cultivating vineyards, and on one occasion exposed himself while drunk (Gn 9:20–24). Ham saw his father lying naked and related the incident to Shem and Japheth, who covered Noah up discreetly. When Noah awoke and learned what his youngest son (seen by some as Ham) had done, he cursed Ham's son Canaan, saying his brothers (Cush, Mizraim, and Put) and Shem and Japheth would rule over him. But if Ham is the one referred to in 9:24 as offending Noah, why should the curse fall on his son Canaan? The most likely answer is that Ham is not being referred to in verse 24. The expression is "his youngest son" (the "younger" of the AV is hardly possible in Hebrew), whereas Ham is repeatedly seen as the second of the brothers, not the youngest (Gn 5:32; 6:10; 7:13; 9:18;

10:1), the explicit order of the sons indicating age. Instead "his youngest son" refers to Canaan, and to some base deed not being recorded, on whom the curse falls. "Son" used for "grandson" is common in Semitic material, and it seems to have been used here in this way since Canaan is the "youngest" of the (grand)sons. The curse, then, as the text clearly says, is on Canaan rather than Ham. Canaan (and his posterity) is to be subjugated by Japheth and Shem with the Canaanites, finally disappearing by NT times.

See NATIONS; NOAH #1.

Ham (Place). Place where Chedorlaomer and his cohorts defeated the Zuzim (Gn 14:5). The name is probably preserved by Tell Ham, near the modern village on the Wadi er-Rejeilah. Bronze and Iron age settlements have been unearthed there.

Haman. Son of Hammedatha the Agagite, a high official under King Ahasuerus (Xerxes) in Persia during the time of Esther. Haman became angry with Mordecai, the uncle of Esther the queen, because Mordecai would not bow down to him as all others did. In anger he planned to exterminate all the Jews in Persia (Est 3:8). While he was plotting Mordecai's hanging, Esther was gaining the favor of Ahasuerus and telling him of Mordecai's valuable services. Haman's plot to kill all Jews was revealed, and he and his ten sons went to the gallows made for Mordecai. In the Hebrew Bible the sons' names are written in a perpendicular manner, supposedly to show their relative positions on the gallows. The carnival atmosphere of the feast of Purim sometimes resulted in Haman being hanged in effigy, or his name being written on the soles of shoes to express contempt.

See ESTHER, BOOK OF.

Hamath. 1. City and district located about 125 miles north of Damascus (Syria), on the Orontes River. The early residents apparently were of the Hamitic race from the descendants of Canaan (Gn 10:18), but later inhabitants were Semitic. It was to be the northern boundary of the nation of Israel (Nm 34:8; Jos 13:5), described as the "entrance of Hamath" (Hebrew, Lebo Hamath), but actually it was such only in the early monarchy and under Jeroboam II (793–753 BC). The location is uncertain, but was between the Lebanon and Anti-Lebanon ranges. Some scholars have thought of it as an actual place-name, Lebo-hamath, and have identified it with modern Lebweh on the Orontes. Others have located it elsewhere in Syria.

Hamath was established during the Neolithic period and destroyed about 1750 BC, perhaps by the Hyksos. It was later rebuilt and conquered by Thutmose III (1502–1448 BC), and while Egypt controlled Syria, Hamath prospered. Several Hittite inscriptions have been discovered which disclose that Hamath had become the capital of a small Hittite kingdom prior to 900 BC.

When David fought Hadadezer, king of Zobah, and defeated him, Toi, king of Hamath, sent his son to congratulate David (2 Sm 8:10). Since Solomon built stone-cities in the region of Hamath (2 Chr 8:4), it has been suggested that Hamath had become a tributary kingdom to Israel. During the reign of Ahab of Israel, the Assyrian royal inscriptions state that Irhulini, king of Hamath, allied with Damascus, Israel, and the 12 kings of the coast to resist the advances of Shalmaneser III (860–825 BC). The league halted Shalmaneser, although he continued to harass Syria, and about 846 BC he conquered the Syrian league, when Hamath became subject to Assyria. In 730 BC Eni-Ilu, then king of Hamath, paid tribute to Tiglath-pileser III. About 720 BC Sargon II colonized Hamath with 4300 Assyrians and moved many people from different areas of his kingdom, including Hamath, to Samaria (2 Kgs 17:24). Israelites also were apparently colonized in Hamath (Is 11:11). Other OT references to the Assyrian conquest of Hamath include 2 Kings 18:34; 19:13; Isaiah 10:9; 36:19; 37:13; and Amos 6:2. Later the city seems to have been subject to Damascus (Jer 49:23). Some of the prophets predicted that Israel would eventually extend its boundaries once again to Hamath (Ez 47:16,17; 48:1; Zec 9:2).

During the Maccabean period Jonathan Maccabeus and his army met the army of Demetrius at Hamath (1 Mc 12:25). According to Josephus, Antiochus Epiphanes changed its name to Epiphania (Antiq. 1.4.2), the name by which it was known to the Greeks and Romans.

The modern city of Hama is built at the location of ancient Hamath.

2. Hamath-zobah is mentioned in 2 Chronicles 8:3 as a town conquered by Solomon. Some have suggested that is was the same city as the Hamath above while others suggest that it was a different town in the district of Zobah. Its identification remains uncertain.

See HAMATH-ZOBAH.

Hamath, Entrance of. Place of uncertain identification, marking the northern border of the Canaanite territory promised to Israel by God (Nm 34:8), but only attained by the time of the monarchy (1 Kgs 8:65 1 Chr 13:5, KJV Hemath; 2 Chr 7:8).

After the death of Solomon the kingdom was divided and the northern boundary shrank. It was not until the reign of Jereboam II, son of Joash (793–753 BC), king of the northern kingdom (called Israel), that the northern boundaries extended again to the entrance of Hamath (2 Kgs 14:23–25).

Both Amos and Ezekiel refer to the entrance of Hamath in their prophecies concerning Israel (Am 6:14; KJV Hemath; Ez 47:15–20; 48:1). Some authorities regard the place as the ancient town, Lebo-hamath, identified with modern Lebweh.

Hamathite. Resident of Hamath (Gn 10:18; 1 Chr 1:16).

See HAMATH #1.

Hamath-zobah. City captured by King Solomon of Israel (2 Chr 8:3,4). Its identity is uncertain. It occurs only once in the Bible, and is not mentioned in any of the cuneiform inscriptions from that period. Some scholars have suggested that there were two Hamaths, and Zobah was added to distinguish it from the better known city (cf. Ez 47:17). The city is mentioned with Hamath and Tadmor, and was perhaps located in northeastern Syria.

Hammath (Person). Ancestor of the house of Rechab (1 Chr 2:55, KJV Hemath), about whom nothing else is known.

Hammath (Place). Fortified outpost identified with the modern Hamman Tabariyeh (Jos 19:35). This place is located among hot springs on the western shore of Galilee and is probably identifiable with Hammon (1 Chr 6:76) Hammoth-dor (Jos 21:32), and perhaps the Emmaus of Josephus (Antiq. 18.2.3).

Hammedatha. Father of Haman, a chief advisor to the Persian king Ahasuerus and a sworn enemy of the Jews according to the Book of Esther (3:1,10; 8:5; 9:10,24).

Hammelech. Hebrew word meaning "the king," taken to be a personal name by the KJV but more correctly translated as "the king" by other versions (Jer 36:26; 38:6).

Hammer. *See* TOOLS.

Hammolecheth, Hammoleketh. Machir daughter and Gilead's sister (1 Chr 7:18, KJV Hammoleketh).

Hammon. 1. One of the cities of Asher mentioned in Joshua 19:28. Its exact location is unknown, but it was somewhere south of Tyre on the west border of Asher.

2. Alternate name for Hammath in 1 Chronicles 6:76.

See HAMMATH (PLACE).

Hammoth-dor. Alternate name for the levitical town Hammath in Joshua 21:32.

See HAMMATH (PLACE).

Hammuel. Member of Mishma's family from Simeon's tribe (1 Chr 4:26, KJV Hamuel).

Hammurabi, Law Code of. Law code devised by Hammurabi, the last great king of the first Babylonian dynasty (*c.* 1790–1750 BC), to safeguard the rights and define the responsibilities of Babylonian citizens. The laws were inscribed on stelae, which were usually erected in marketplaces or near temples for all to see. The most complete example discovered so far dates from the latter part of his reign. The black diorite stela was found at Susa in 1901 by French archaeologists. It stood eight feet high, and showed a bas-relief of Hammurabi receiving the symbols of kingship and law from the god Shamash. Beneath this was a poetic introduction, followed by the 282 articles of the code, and an epilogue in an equally poetic style extolling the virtues of Hammurabi, his concern for his people, and the way in which he had followed the wishes of the great god Marduk and Shamash, god of justice. The gods are called upon to curse any who defy the stela.

It had been carried to Susa as a battle trophy by the Elamites in 1160 BC, and it is now in Paris in the Louvre. The code is a collection of laws based on Sumerian and early Semitic laws. Similarities between the code of Hammurabi and those of the Assyrians, Hittites, and Hebrews are numerous.

Hammurabi began his code by setting out punishments for the most obvious crimes such as kidnapping, theft, or receiving stolen property, breaking and entering, looting, perjury, false accusation, and harboring a fugitive. All these could be punished by death, especially where robbery involved the theft of temple or state property, and where perjury was committed by a witness giving testimony in a case involving a capital offense.

All valid transactions took place before witnesses, and it was essential that their testimony was trustworthy in disputed cases. Summary justice was meted out to the man found guilty of breaking and entering: "If a man made a breach in a house, they shall put him to death in front of that breach and wall him in" (Sect 21), and to the looter at a fire: "If a fire broke out in a man's house, and a man, who went to extinguish (it) cast his eye

The Law Code of Hammurabi—black diorite stele, about 7 feet high, inscribed with about 250 laws and a scene at the top showing the sun-god Shamash committing the law to Hammurabi. It was found at Susa in three pieces by Jacques de Morgan (1901–2), having been set up first at Babylon.

on the goods of the owner of the house and has appropriated the goods of the owner of the house, that man shall be thrown into that fire" (Sect 25).

The protection of feudal rights and responsibilities are outlined in the next section. The officer was responsible for soldiers under his command in the same way that the soldier was required to fulfill his duty to the state. The law also protected his property while he was in the army. A tenant was under obligation to use his rented property carefully and advantageously. If a tenant rented land that became flooded before the harvest, the law protected him from having to pay rent for that year. He also had to be thoughtful toward his neighbors' crops and ensure that he didn't inundate their fields by his own overzestful irrigation (Sects 30–56).

The detail in which contracts and commercial laws are discussed indicates the extent and variety of such transactions. If money was borrowed from a merchant who foreclosed and the borrower was unable to repay the loan, he had to make payment in kind, for example, in dates from his own crop. The permissible interest rate was approximately 20 percent. The borrower was also protected by law from the practice of the lender using a small weight of grain or money and insisting on the return with interest at a large weight. Anyone caught doing this forfeited whatever he had lent. Female wine sellers were also cautioned against selling with short weight (Sect 108). High interest rates were prescribed for obtaining wine on credit, and it is unlikely that many took advantage of this early form of credit.

To ensure an equal division in the breaking-up of a partnership, the transaction was performed in the presence "of God," presumably in the temple. A trader borrowing money at interest was expected to make a profit. If he did, he repaid the principal and the interest. If he did not, it was presumed that he was a poor trader, and he was penalized by having to repay the merchant double the amount that he had borrowed. If the money was loaned as a favor, however, and the trader then suffered a loss, the principal only was repayable without interest. A trader who was set upon by bandits on the road was not required to make payment. Sealed receipts were used as a safeguard of fair trading practices. In disputes between a merchant and a trader over a loan, if the merchant proved his case the trader had to return three times the amount of the money originally borrowed. Where the merchant disputed with a trader who then proved his case, the merchant paid the trader six times the amount of the principal involved (Sects 98–107).

A creditor could not come and take a debtor's money or grain without his permission. If he did so, he had to return what he had taken and forfeit the loan. In several instances a person could be held as a pledge. If he died of natural causes during that period, no claim could be made, but if he died as a result of maltreatment, compensation was payable according to rank. If the pledge was a slave (the lowest level of Mesopotamian society), the amount payable was one-third of a mina of silver and the loan was forgiven. If the pledge was a man's son, the creditor's son was put to death as a recompense. Where a wife, son, or daughter was bound over for service to pay a debt, the maximum period of servitude was three years (Sects 113–17).

A man was responsible for the security of anything left with him for safekeeping. If the property was lost through robbery because the building was not secure, restitution had to be made to the owner of the property. Anyone claiming falsely that his property was lost had to pay the city council double the amount of his claim.

Extensive laws relate to sex and marriage (Sects 127–62). Like most transactions, marriage was not valid without a contract. Adultery was frequently punished by death, but a man might plead to have his wife's life spared. The victim of rape was not punished. According to Mosaic law such a person was equally guilty if the act took place within the city, as she was expected to scream for help. If it occurred outside the city walls, however, she was not held responsible, on the theory that her screams could not have been heard. Hammurabi's code shows concern for the woman who was deserted or whose husband was taken captive. She was permitted to live with another man if she had insufficient means to be self-supporting.

A woman's dowry was returned when she was divorced, or if there had been no dowry, a payment of one mina of silver was made to her, or one-third of a mina of silver if her husband was a peasant. If a woman neglected her household duties to set herself up in business, her husband might divorce her without payment or he might remarry without divorcing her, thus forcing her to live on in the house as a servant.

A slave who had borne her master's child could not be sold. If a man married a woman who was sick, and he then decided to marry another, the sick wife might continue to live in the house and her husband had to support her for the rest of her life. A woman who killed her husband for her lover was impaled on stakes (Sect 153). Incest was punishable by death or banishment. Breach of promise cases usually resulted in the repayment of double the value of the dowry. When a wife died, her dowry became part of her inheritance for her children, but if she died childless and her father returned her marriage price, her husband might not lay claim to her dowry, which had to be returned to her father (Sects 162–63). The rights of a younger unmarried son were protected, as were those of the children of a master and his slave. A son was protected against being disinherited by his father unless he had committed some serious offense. A widow was protected against the over-zealous financial demands of her children. If a free woman married a slave, their children were free. If the slave died, his widow retained her dowry and half the goods acquired since the marriage, the slave-owner being entitled to the remainder. Women temple personnel were also protected by law.

Under Hebrew law it was a father's duty to teach his son the means of earning a livelihood. Hammurabi's code prescribed that an adopted son had to be similarly trained, and if in any way he was not reared as a natural child within the family, he might return to his own home.

If a man subsequently had a family of his own and the foster child was sent away, he had the right to take with him one-third of the man's goods, although none of his land or his house, since these were the inheritance of the natural children. If a child died in a nurse's care and she took another assignment without informing the new employers of the previous death, her breast was cut off.

The most famous section of Hammurabi's law code concerns assault: "If a (man) has destroyed the eye of a member of the aristocracy, they shall destroy his eye." Similarly if he broke a man's bone or knocked out a tooth, he would suffer the same fate (Sects 196,197). If the injured person was a commoner, however, a fine of one mina of silver was charged for destroying an eye or breaking a bone. When the injured man was a slave, payment of half his value had to be made. Punishments for simple assault depended upon the rank of the two protagonists. Where a man swore that the blow was not deliberate, he might simply pay the physician's bill. Other penalties were set out for instances where the blow was fatal or caused a woman to miscarry (Sects 209–14).

Surgeons' fees were also specified. For saving a life or for eye surgery the fee was ten shekels of silver when the patient was an aristocrat, but only five for a commoner, and two for a slave. If an aristocratic patient died under the surgeon's bronze knife, or lost an eye, the surgeon could have his hand cut off (Sect 218). If a slave died during surgery, the surgeon had to replace the slave with another. For setting a broken bone or healing a sprained tendon the physician charged five, three, or two shekels, depending on the patient's status (Sects 221–23).

The final section of laws concerns the protection of people from the poor workmanship of house and boat builders, rules and regulations for those who rent animals or hire people, theft of agricultural implements, rates for hiring and paying wages, and rules for the purchase and sale of slaves (Sects 228–82).

A man who fraudulently let out his mas-

Limestone relief with part of Hammurabi's law code and a figure representing Hammurabi; the monument was dedicated to a goddess.

ter's oxen for hire rather than using them on his own fields would be required to pay the normal rental of grain for the field. If he was unable to do so, he was to be dragged through that field by the oxen.

Because of similarities in culture, it is hardly surprising that there should be areas of correspondence between Hammurabi's code and the Mosaic law. Thus both bodies of legislation prescribed the death penalty for adultery (Hammurabi Sect 129; Lv 20:10; Dt 22:22), and for the kidnapping and selling of an individual (Hammurabi Sect 14; Ex 21:16). The *lex talionis*, or principle of retaliation, in Exodus 21:23–25 and Deuteronomy 19:21 is reflected widely in Hammurabi's laws, including Sections 197, 210, and 230. The differences, however, are equally significant. Whereas Hammurabi's legislation allowed women equal rights of divorce (Sect 142), these were denied under the Mosaic law by simply not being included (cf. Dt 24:1–4). Hammurabi's code was basically pragmatic in nature, and although promulgated under the authority of Shamash, god of justice, the legislation took little notice of ethical and spiritual principles. By comparison with the Mosaic enactments, Hammurabi's laws placed a lower value upon human life.

HAZEL W. PERKIN

See LAW, BIBLICAL CONCEPT OF; CRIMINAL LAW AND PUNISHMENT; CIVIL LAW AND JUSTICE.

Hamonah. Site in the Transjordan where the marauding armies of Gog will be destroyed by the Israelites (Ez 39:16).

Hamon-gog. Valley in the Transjordan where the dead of the armies of Gog will be buried (Ez 39:11,15).

Hamor. Hivite or Horite prince of the country about Shechem (Gn 34:2), from whom Jacob bought land when returning with his family from Paddan-aram. At this time Hamor's son, Shechem, committed fornication with Dinah, the daughter of Jacob. At his son's request Hamor asked Jacob for a marriage alliance between Shechem and Dinah, offering a dowry. Simeon and Levi in pretended friendship persuaded the males of the city to be circumcised, but then attacked and killed them before they were healed in revenge for their sister's humiliation (vv 1–31).

"Hamor" is the word which Jacob uses to denote Issachar in blessing his sons (Gn 49:14), and is the usual word for *ass* in OT (e.g., Gn 42:26; Ex 20:17; Jgs 15:15; Is 1:3; Zec 9:9).

In the NT, Emmor is the KJV form for Hamor in Acts 7:16.

Hamran. Alternate name for Hemdan, Dishon's oldest son, in 1 Chronicles 1:41.

See HEMDAN.

Hamuel. KJV spelling of Hammuel, the Simeonite, in 1 Chronicles 4:26.

See HAMMUEL.

Hamul, Hamulite. Perez's younger son (Gn 46:12; 1 Chr 2:5) and founder of the Hamulite family (Nm 26:21).

Hamutal. Daughter of Jeremiah of Libnah, one of King Josiah's wives, and the mother of two kings: Jehoahaz and Zedekiah (2 Kgs 23:31; 24:18; Jer 52:1).

Hanamel, Hanameel. Shallum's son, from whom Jeremiah bought a field in Anathoth (Jer 32:7–12, KJV Hanameel). This purchase signified that God would restore the nation and that possession of the land would again be possible.

Hanan. 1. Shashak's son and one of the chief men of Benjamin (1 Chr 8:23).

2. Azel's son from Benjamin's tribe (1 Chr 8:38; 9:44).

3. Warrior among David's mighty men who were known as "the thirty" (1 Chr 11:43).

4. Ancestor of a group of temple assistants that returned to Jerusalem with Zerubbabel after the exile (Ezr 2:46; Neh 7:49).

5. Levitical assistant who explained to the people passages from the Law read by Ezra (Neh 8:7).

6. Levite who signed Ezra's covenant of faithfulness to God with Nehemiah and others after the exile (Neh 10:10).

7.,8. Two political leaders who signed Ezra's covenant of faithfulness to God with Nehemiah and others after the exile (Neh 10:22,26).

9. One of the Levites whom Nehemiah appointed as treasurer over the storehouses (Neh 13:13).

10. Igdaliah's son and head of a prophetic guild occupying the room in the temple where Jeremiah offered the Rechabites wine to drink (Jer 35:4).

Hananel, Tower of. Tower on the north wall of Jerusalem, located near the Sheep Gate (Neh 3:1; 12:39; KJV Hananeel). Later in Israel's history John Hyrcanus erected a Maccabean fortress on this spot which Pompey destroyed in 63 BC. Still later, Herod the Great built the Tower of Antonia here to oversee the temple area. Two prophecies refer to the Tower of Hananel as a boundary point in the rebuilding of Jerusalem (Jer 31:38; Zec 14:10).

Hanani. 1. Seer who rebuked King Asa for giving treasure to Ben-hadad of Syria to persuade him to attack Israel. Hanani was imprisoned for his preaching (2 Chr 16:1–10). Hanani was the father of the prophet Jehu who inveighed against Baasha, king of Israel (1 Kgs 16:1,7), and Jehoshaphat, king of Judah (2 Chr 19:2).

2. Heman's son, David's seer, and a musician in the temple (1 Chr 25:4,25).

3. Priest who obeyed Ezra's exhortation to divorce his pagan wife after the exile (Ezr 10:20).

4. Brother of Nehemiah who induced him to act on behalf of the Jews when he reported the state of Jerusalem and Judah (Neh 1:2). Hanani was later given responsibility for the city of Jerusalem (7:2).

5. Priest and musician who participated in the dedication of the rebuilt walls of Jerusalem (Neh 12:36).

Hananiah. 1. Zerubbabel's son and a descendant of David (1 Chr 3:19,21).

2. Benjamite and the son of Shashak (1 Chr 8:24).

3. Heman's son and the leader of the 16th of 24 divisions of musicians trained for service in the house of the Lord (1 Chr 25:4,23).

4. One of the commanders of King Uzziah's army (2 Chr 26:11).

5. Bebai's son, who returned with the exiles from Babylon and was later encouraged by Ezra to divorce his foreign wife (Ezr 10:28).

6. Perfumer who helped Nehemiah rebuild the Jerusalem wall (Neh 3:8).

7. Shelemiah's son, who with Hanun repaired a section of the Jerusalem wall during the days of Nehemiah (Neh 3:30). He is perhaps identical with #6 above.

8. Commander of the citadel of Jerusalem who was assigned by Nehemiah to rule the city jointly with Hanani, Nehemiah's brother. Hananiah, described as a faithful and God-fearing man, was appointed the task of seeing that the city walls and gates were regularly guarded (Neh 7:2,3).

9. One of the leaders of the people who set his seal on the covenant of Ezra (Neh 10:23).

10. Head of the priestly family of Jeremiah during the days of Joiakim, the high priest, in postexilic Jerusalem (Neh 12:12).

11. One of the priests who blew a trumpet at the dedication of the Jerusalem wall during the days of Nehemiah (Neh 12:41).

12. Gibeonite and the son of Azzur. Hananiah prophesied during the fourth year of King Zedekiah of Judah's reign (597–586 BC). He openly declared in the temple that in two years the Lord would break the yoke of Nebuchadnezzar, king of Babylon (605–562 BC), from the neck of Judah and return its exiles and sacred possessions to Palestine. Told by the Lord that Hananiah's prophecy was false, Jeremiah reproached Hananiah for lying and foretold his imminent death. Hananiah died two months later (Jer 28).

13. Father of Zedekiah, an official of King Jehoiakim of Judah (609–598 BC; Jer 36:12).

14. Grandfather of Irijah, the captain of the guards, who arrested Jeremiah at Jerusalem's Gate of Benjamin for apparently deserting to the Babylonians (Jer 37:13).

15. One of the three Jewish friends of Daniel exiled in Babylon. He was assigned the Babylonian name Shadrach (Dn 1:6–19; 2:17).

See SHADRACH, MESHACH, AND ABEDNEGO.

Hand. Unit of measure among the Hebrews. The fingers, up to four (Jer 52:21), made a handbreadth; three handbreadths made a handstretch (Ex 28:16). Figuratively, hand meant power (Dt 2:15; Ps 31:15; Mk 14:42). Indeed, in Joshua 8:20 "hand" is translated "strength" (see Ps 76:5). Conversely, limp hands symbolized irresoluteness and weakness (Is 35:3). Clasping the hands signified friendship (2 Kgs 10:15). To seat someone on one's right hand denoted favor (Pss 16:11; 77:10). Clean hands symbolized innocence (Ps 18:20), while striking hands sealed a bargain (Prv 6:1 KJV). Lifting the hand symbolized violence (1 Kgs 11:26). The hands were used in supplicatory prayer (Ex 17:11; Lv 9:22; Is 1:15; 1 Tm 2:8) and in making vows (Gn 14:22 KJV; 24:2).

Other idiomatic uses of the hands expressed jeopardizing one's life (Jgs 12:3), gladness (2 Kgs 11:12), generosity (Dt 15:11), grief (2 Sm 13:19), humility (Prv 30:32), and undertaking a duty (Lk 9:62). Manual labor is an expression of man's dignity and duty (Eph 4:28; 1 Thes 4:11), the marks of which Paul was not ashamed to display (Acts 20:34; 1 Cor 4:12). Ritual hand-washing was obligatory for the priests before fulfilling their office (Ex 30:19–21; 40:30–32). The scribes and Pharisees so misapplied this that Jesus ignored ceremonial hand-washing (Mt 15:1–20; Lk 11:38). Pilate's hand-washing (Mt 27:24) disclaimed responsibility for, or professed innocence concerning, a wrong which, however, could not be done without his consent.

When Israel went out of Egypt "with a high hand" (Ex 14:8 KJV), the reference is to the hand or help of the Lord. The hand of the Lord represented God's resistless power (Dt 2:15), judgment (Acts 13:11; Heb 10:31), divine inspiration (Ez 8:1; 37:1), providential care (Ezr 7:6; Jn 10:28,29), and blessing (Mt 19:13–15); although the latter refers to an act of prayer.

The laying on of hands had a profound significance and occurs frequently in the Bible. Before making a blood sacrifice the person making the offering, not the priest, laid hands on the victim. The act signified the transference of guilt to, or self-identification with, the victim (Lv 1:4). Laying on of hands signified appointment to an office: as when Moses commissioned Joshua (Nm 27:12–23), the apostles made seven disciples their associates or deputies in the ministry (Acts 6:5,6), and Paul and Barnabas were appointed missionaries and representatives of the church in Antioch (13:3). By laying on of hands a person was made an associate with the holder of an office and was admitted to the status of that office (1 Tm 4:14; 2 Tm 1:6). The act was accompanied by prayer and was, in itself, a form of prayer. As Augustine remarks: "What else is the laying on of hands but a prayer over one?"

The laying on of hands accompanied healing in the ministry of the Lord (Mk 6:5; Lk 4:40; 13:11–13) and of the disciples (Mk 16:18; Acts 9:12,17; 28:8). This expressed the self-identification and sympathy of the healer with and for the sufferer, as well as reinforcing of the patient's faith, and God's imparting health to him in answer to prayer.

J.G.S.S. THOMSON

See LAYING ON OF HANDS; RIGHT, RIGHT HAND.

Handbreadth. Linear measure equivalent to one-sixth of a cubit or just under three inches in length.

See WEIGHTS AND MEASURES.

Handmaid, Handmaiden. *See* TRADES AND OCCUPATIONS.

Handpike. Wooden staff with pointed metal tip (Ez 39:9).

See ARMS AND WARFARE.

Hands, Laying on of. *See* LAYING ON OF HANDS.

Hands, Washing of. Jewish religious ritual.

See HAND.

Handstaff. KJV rendering of handpike in Ezekiel 39:9.

See ARMS AND WARFARE.

Hanes. City in Egypt included with Zoan (or Tanis) in Isaiah 30:4 as a center of Egyptian government to which ambassadors would be sent. This indicates that it was one of the dynastic centers. It has been identified with Heracleopolis Magna, south of Memphis, the capital of northern Egypt in Roman times, and also with Heracleopolis Parva in the eastern delta region.

Hanging. *See* CRIMINAL LAW AND PUNISHMENT; IMPALEMENT.

Haniel. KJV spelling of Hanniel, Ulla's son, in 1 Chronicles 7:39.

See HANNIEL #2.

Hannah. Wife of Elkanah from Ephraim's tribe and the mother of the prophet Samuel. The childless Hannah prayed annually at Shiloh for a son, whom she vowed to dedicate to the Lord.

The Lord answered her prayer, and she called her son Samuel. When he was weaned (probably about age three), she dedicated him at Shiloh to the service of the Lord in the sanctuary. Henceforth, Samuel lived with Eli the priest and was visited by his parents on their annual pilgrimages. Hannah had three more sons and two daughters (1 Sm 1:1–2:21).

Her prophetic psalm (1 Sm 2:1–10) anticipates the Magnificat (Lk 1:46–55).

Hannathon. Northern border town of Zebulun (Jos 19:14), mentioned in the Amarna tablets (c. 1370 BC) and in the annals of Tiglath-pileser III (745–727 BC). Not yet precisely located, it has been identified with Kefr 'Anau near Rimmon, or with Tell el-Bedeiwiyeh, north of Nazareth.

Hanniel. 1. Ephod's son and leader of Manasseh's tribe who represented his tribe in apportioning land to Israel under Moses (Nm 34:23).

2. Ulla's son and warrior in the tribe of Asher (1 Chr 7:39, KJV Haniel).

Hanoch. 1. Midian's third son, and grandson of Abraham by Keturah (Gn 25:4; 1 Chr 1:33; KJV Henoch).

2. Reuben's first son (Gn 46:9; Ex 6:14; 1 Chr 5:3) and ancestor of the Hanochites (Nm 26:5).

Hanochite. Descendant of Hanoch, Reuben's firstborn son (Nm 26:5).

See HANOCH #2.

Hanukkah. *See* FEASTS AND FESTIVALS OF ISRAEL; JUDAISM.

Hanun. 1. Nahash's son and successor to the Ammonite throne. When King Nahash died, King David of Israel sent messengers to console Hanun, and to express his continued friendship. But Hanun insulted David by humiliating his messengers and accusing them of spying. This action led to war and the defeat of Ammon (2 Sm 10:1–14; 11:1; 12:26–31; 1 Chr 19:1–20:3).

2. One who helped repair Jerusalem's Valley Gate during the time of Nehemiah (Neh 3:13).

3. Zalaph's son who repaired a section of the Jerusalem wall during the time of Nehemiah (Neh 3:30); perhaps the same as #2 above.

Hapharaim, Haphraim. Town included in the territory allotted to Issachar's tribe for an inheritance (Jos 19:19, KJV Haphraim). Its location is uncertain, though some have identified it with et-Taiyibeh, about 10 miles northwest of Beth-shan.

Happizzez. Head of a division of priests whom David assigned to official duties in the temple (1 Chr 24:15, KJV Aphses).

Hara. Place where Tiglath-pileser exiled Reuben, Gad, and the half-tribe of Manasseh (1 Chr 5:26). A possible miscopying of 2 Kings 17:6 and 18:11 may have substituted Hara for "cities of Media." The Greek version reads "Mountains of Media," indicating an area east of the Tigris Valley. A district rather than a single site seems to be indicated.

Haradah. Twentieth wilderness encampment of the children of Israel, and the ninth from Sinai; listed between Mt Shepher and

Makheloth. Its location is unknown (Nm 33:24,25).

Haran (Person). 1. Terah's son, youngest brother of Abraham, and the father of Lot (Gn 11:26–31).

2. Caleb's son by his concubine Ephah, a member of Judah's tribe and the father of Gazez (1 Chr 2:46).

3. Shimei's son, a member of the Gershonite division of Levi's tribe (1 Chr 23:9).

Haran (Place). City of northern Mesopotamia, first mentioned in Genesis 11:31 as the destination of Terah, Abraham's father, in migrating from Ur of the Chaldees, and his home until his death. At age 75, Abraham was commanded by God to move to a land which God had for him (Gn 12:1–4). There were relatives who remained in Haran, however, to whom Jacob, Abraham's grandson, fled in fear of Esau (27:42,43; cf. 29:1–14). Jacob stayed in Haran many years while serving his uncle Laban and acquiring Leah and Rachel as wives, as well as many cattle, servants, camels, and donkeys (30:43).

This "city of Nahor" (Gen 11:27–29; 24:10; 27:43) was established in the 3rd millennium BC, and its location on a branch of the Euphrates soon made it an important commercial center. Perhaps the ancient trade route which linked Damascus, Nineveh, and Carchemish passed by Haran. Ezekiel mentions trade between Haran and Tyre (Ez 27:23). Haran was an Aramaean city and was famous for its worship of the lunar Sin-and-Nikkal cult. This system was an offspring of the cult found in Sumerian Ur. Sin and his wife Nikkal were not only revered here, but throughout Canaan and even in Egypt. The cult persisted past NT times, its temple being finally destroyed by Mongols in the 13th century. It is little wonder that God commanded Abraham to leave this seat of idolatry. Modern Harran preserves the ancient cuneiform spelling of the name. Acts 7:2,4 (KJV) has Charran.

Hararite. Term applied to several names which appear in the accounts of King David's "mighty men." Shammah, one of David's mightiest men, and Jonathan's father (a different Jonathan than Saul's son and David's friend) is called a Hararite (2 Sm 23:11,33; 1 Chr 11:34 has Shagee), as is Agee, Shammah's father (2 Sm 23:11). Sharar, Ahiam's father, is also so named (v 33; 1 Chr 11:35 has Sachar). The meaning of the term is uncertain.

Harbona. One of King Ahasuerus' seven personal attendants. They were ordered by Ahasuerus to parade Queen Vashti before a drunken banquet to satisfy his vanity (Est 1:10). Harbona later suggested that Haman be hanged on the gallows he had built for Mordecai (7:9).

Hare. Small, swift, long-eared mammal similar to the rabbit; condemned as unclean (Lv 11:6; Dt 14:7).

See ANIMALS.

Hareph. Caleb's son from Judah's tribe and founder (or perhaps father) of Beth-gader (1 Chr 2:51).

Hareth. KJV spelling of Hereth in 1 Samuel 22:5.

See HERETH.

Harhaiah. Father of Uzziel, a goldsmith who worked to rebuild the wall of Jerusalem in Nehemiah's time (Neh 3:8).

Haran.

Harhas. Shallum's grandfather. Shallum's wife was Huldah the prophetess who delivered an oracle on the discovery of Josiah's Book of the Law (2 Kgs 22:14; spelled Hasrah in 2 Chr 34:22).

Har-heres. Mountain in Aijalon of Dan's territory (Jgs 1:35).

See HERES #1.

Harhur. Ancestor of a group of temple assistants that returned to Jerusalem with Zerubbabel after the exile (Ezr 2:51; Neh 7:53).

Harim. 1. Priest whom King David appointed to official duties in the temple (1 Chr 24:8).

2. Ancestor of a Jewish family which returned from the Babylonian exile with Zerubbabel (Ezr 2:32; Neh 10:5). Members of this family were guilty of marrying foreign women (Ezr 10:31), but they divorced their wives and a representative of the clan signed Ezra's covenant (Neh 10:27).

3. Ancestor of a family of priests who returned from the exile with Zerubbabel (Ezr 2:39; Neh 7:42). Some identify him with #1 above. Members of this family were guilty of marrying foreign women.

4. Ancestor of Malchijah. Malchijah repaired a section of the Jerusalem wall during Nehemiah's time (Neh 3:11). This Harim could be the same as #2 above.

5. Priest who returned from the exile with Zerubbabel (Neh 12:3, here incorrectly spelled Rehum). His son (or grandson), Adna, is listed as a leading priest during the high priesthood of Joiakim (12:25). Later, under Ezra, a representative of the family signed the covenant of faithfulness to God (10:5).

Hariph. Ancestor of a family that returned to Jerusalem with Zerubbabel after the exile (Neh 7:24). The name Jorah appears in the parallel list of Ezra 2:18. A representative of this family signed Ezra's covenant of faithfulness to God with Nehemiah and others (Neh 10:19).

Harlot. Woman guilty of illicit sexual relationships, figuratively, one who worships an idol. The term "harlot" translates four different words found in the Bible. One type of harlot was the man or woman, married or unmarried, who committed immoral acts (Gn 34:31; Jgs 19:2; Prv 23:27). A different harlot was the temple prostitute of heathen religions in which fornication was part of the worship (Gn 38:21,22; Dt 23:17; Hos 4:14). Such prostitution was forbidden by the Law of Moses (Lv 19:29; 21:9). The "strange woman" was another har-

lot (1 Kgs 11:1; Prv 5:20; 6:24; 7:5; 23:27). There are different opinions why that name was given to harlots. One explanation is that it referred to a man leaving his own wife for another, who ought to be a stranger to him (Prv 5:17,18,20). It may also have referred to a foreign woman (Nm 25:1; Jos 23:13). "Harlot" also refers to any woman, married or single, who practices unlawful sexual indulgence, whether for lust or gain (Mt 21:31,32; Lk 15:30; 1 Cor 6:15,16; Heb 11:31; Jas 2:25).

Harlotry appeared early in Israel's life and continued throughout biblical history. Most biblical passages strongly condemn the practice of harlotry in any form. The priestly law of Leviticus 21:9 provided that a priest's daughter who practiced harlotry was to be burned to death. A priest could not marry a harlot (Lv 19:29) and the wages of harlotry could not be used to pay vows in the temple (Dt 23:18). These prohibitions served to keep the worship of the Lord free from the practice of cult harlotry.

The sons of Jacob killed Hamor and his son Shechem, justifying their act by saying: "Should he treat our sister as a harlot?" (Gn 34:31). Amaziah's wife was to become a harlot (Am 7:17) as punishment for his treatment of the prophet Amos.

In the 1st century harlots and tax collectors were equally detested by the Jews (Mt 21:32). According to Paul, the body of a Christian belongs to Christ, and should not be joined to a prostitute's (1 Cor 6:15,16). Proverbs is replete with warnings to those who would go in to harlots.

A number of biblical passages do, however, seem to accept the harlot as a member of the community. Tamar temporarily served as a temple harlot to remind her father-in-law of his promise to her (Gn 38:14,15), and Rahab the harlot had a special place in Hebrew history because she had befriended the Hebrew spies (Jos 2:4–16; Heb 11:31).

The words "harlot" and "harlotry" were used figuratively for idolatry, especially in the prophetic books (Is 1:21; Jer 2:20; Rv 17:1,5, 15,16; 19:2). This figurative use was based on the marriage-like relationship of the Lord and the nation of Israel (Jer 3:20). When the people gave their allegiance to idols rather than God he charged that they "went a whoring after" other gods (KJV) or "played the harlot after" other gods (Jgs 8:33). The same idea is found in the NT (Rv 17). These condemnations are directed toward that inner harlotry which is a rejection of the Redeemer.

WILLIAM B. TOLAR

Harmon. Place mentioned by the prophet Amos to which the inhabitants of Bashan would be exiled (Am 4:3, KJV palace). Harmon occurs only once in the Bible, and there is no known place with such a name. There are problems with the text and numerous emendations have been proposed. Some Hebrew manuscripts render it as a common noun, meaning "palace" (KJV), rather than a proper name. The Septuagint renders it "the mountain of Rimmon," perhaps referring to a hill east of Rimmon (see Jgs 20:45,47; cf. Jos 15:32; 19:13).

Harnepher. Zophah's son from Asher's tribe (1 Chr 7:36).

Harod. 1. Spring beside which Gideon and his army camped before their encounter with the Midianites (Jgs 7:1). Perhaps this is the same spring by which Saul and his army pitched their tents prior to their battle with the Philistines (1 Sm 29:1). The spring of Harod is at 'Ain Jalud by the northern side of Mt Gilboa, about two miles E, SE of Zerin.

2. Home of Shammah and Elika, two of David's valiant warriors (2 Sm 23:25). In the parallel passage (1 Chr 11:27), Elika's name is omitted and Shammah (Shammoth) is listed as a Harorite instead of a Harodite. Harorite reflects a later scribal error where the copyist mistook the Hebrew letter "d" for an "r."

Harodite. Designation for Shammah and Elika, two of David's mighty men (2 Sm 23:25).

See HAROD #2.

Haroeh. Alternate name of Reaiah, Shobal's son, in 1 Chronicles 2:52.

See REAIAH #1.

Harorite. Alternate description of one of David's mighty men (1 Chr 11:27).

See HAROD #2.

Harosheth-ha-goiim. Town in Canaan which was the home of Sisera. This Canaanite general led his forces from Harosheth against Deborah and Barak (Jgs 4:2,3,16, KJV Harosheth of the Gentiles). After his soldiers were defeated they fled back to Harosheth (v 16). The exact location is unknown, but it has been identified with both Tell 'Amr and Tell el-Harbaj, though not convincingly. Some authorities have identified Harosheth with a place described in the Tell el-Amarna tablets as Muhrashti, but this too is uncertain.

Harp. Stringed instrument.

See MUSIC AND MUSICAL INSTRUMENTS (NEBEL).

Harrow. Agricultural term for implement or procedure, though no implement corresponding to the modern harrow is known from Palestine or Egypt. Job 39:10 speaks of an ox performing the harrowing, while Isaiah 28:24 notes that previously plowed ground was levelled in the process. Like the foregoing references, Hosea 10:11 speaks of harrowing in connection with plowing. Most probably harrowing consisted of branches being pulled behind an animal or plow to smooth the land and cover seed.

See AGRICULTURE; TOOLS.

Harsha. Ancestor of a group of temple assistants that returned to Jerusalem with Zerubbabel after the exile (Ezr 2:52; Neh 7:54).

Hart. Adult male red deer.

See ANIMALS (DEER).

Harum. Aharhel's father from Judah's tribe (1 Chr 4:8).

Harumaph. Jedaiah's father. Jedaiah helped repair the wall of Jerusalem during the time of Nehemiah (Neh 3:10).

Haruphite. Name applied to Shephatiah, one of David's ambidextrous warriors from Benjamin's tribe who joined him at Ziklag (1 Chr 12:5). Whether the name refers to a family or a place is uncertain.

Haruz. Maternal grandfather of Amon, king of Judah (2 Kgs 21:19).

Harvest. The gathering in of a crop, especially for food. There was no single harvest time in ancient Israel. Olives were harvested in September–November, flax in March–April, barley in April–May, and wheat in May–June. Fruits such as figs and grapes were harvested at the end of the summer, in August or September. The Israelites' calendar revolved very much round the harvest periods (cf. Jgs 15:1; Ru 1:22).

In the OT, harvest was one of the three major feasts which the Israelites were required by the Lord to keep annually (Ex 23:16). In doing so they would remember that the rich land into which they had been brought from Egypt (Dt 8:7–10) was the gift of God. In offering the firstfruits of the harvest (Lv 23:10,11) the Israelites showed gratitude and acknowledged their dependence on the Lord. Moreover, as the harvest was a gift, they were not to be selfish in enjoying it, but leave some for the underprivileged (19:9).

NT references to harvest are largely figura-

A grain bin, for storage of a harvested crop.

tive. In one parable (Mt 13:24–43) harvest represents the final judgment and the reapers are angels, gathering in the righteous and excluding the wicked from the kingdom. In another, the harvest refers to those who have not yet heard the gospel, and the "laborers" are those who bring it to them (9:37,38).

See AGRICULTURE; FEASTS AND FESTIVALS OF ISRAEL; VINE, VINEYARD.

Hasadiah. One of Zerubbabel's sons (1 Chr 3:20).

Hasenuah. KJV rendering of Hassenuah in 1 Chronicles 9:7

See HASSENUAH.

Hashabiah. 1. Ancestor of Ethon, a Levite and descendant of Merari. Ethon was a musician in the temple during the reign of David (1 Chr 6:45).

2. Ancestor of a group of Levites who helped rebuild the temple after the Babylonian exile (1 Chr 9:14; Neh 11:15).

3. Jeduthun's son, a Levite and musician in the temple during the time of David (1 Chr 25:3,19).

4. Head of a group of Hebronites who was given the position of overseer of Israel west of the Jordan. He was in charge of both political and religious activities (1 Chr 26:30).

5. Kemuel's son, a Levite and head of a household during the reign of David (1 Chr 27:17).

6. Chief of the Levites who participated in the Passover kept by King Josiah in the kingdom of Judah (640–609 BC; 2 Chr 35:9).

7. Merarite Levite who returned to Jerusalem from Babylon with Ezra (Ezr 8:19).

8. Priest who returned to Jerusalem from Babylon with Ezra (Ezr 8:24).

9. Parosh's son, who obeyed Ezra's exhortation to divorce his pagan wife after the exile (Ezr 10:25, KJV Malchijah); possibly the same as Asibias (1 Esd 9:26).

10. Ruler over half the district of Keilah (a city of Judah in the Shephlah district of Libnah-Mareshah) who participated in rebuilding the city wall in his district after the exile (Neh 3:17).

11. Levite who signed Ezra's covenant of faithfulness to God (Neh 10:11).

12. Ancestor of Uzzi, an overseer of Levites in Jerusalem after the exile (Neh 11:22).

13. Priest and head of a household in Palestine after the exile during the time of the high priest Joiakim (Neh 12:21).

14. Chief of the Levites and a temple musician after the exile during the time of Joiakim the high priest (Neh 12:24); perhaps the same person as #10 above.

Hashabnah. One of the leaders who signed Ezra's covenant of faithfulness to God with Nehemiah and others after the exile (Neh 10:25).

Hashabneiah, Hashabniah. 1. Hattush's father. Hattush assisted in rebuilding the walls of Jerusalem during Nehemiah's day (Neh 3:10, KJV Hashabniah).

2. Levite who joined with others in an invocation at the covenant-signing ceremony (Neh 9:5; KJV Hashabniah).

Hashbaddana, Hashbadana. Man, possibly of Levite origin, who stood on Ezra's left when Ezra read the Law to the people (Neh 8:4, KJV Hashbadana).

Hashem. Warrior among David's mighty men (1 Chr 11:34); alternately called Jashen in 2 Samuel 23:32.

See JASHEN.

Hashmonah. One of the places where the Israelites stopped during the 40 years they wandered in the wilderness (Nm 33:29,30). Its location is unknown.

See WILDERNESS WANDERINGS.

Hashub. KJV alternate spelling of Hasshub.

See HASSHUB.

Hashubah. One of Zerubbabel's sons (1 Chr 3:20).

Hashum. 1. Ancestor of a family that returned from Babylon with Zerubbabel after the exile (Ezr 2:19; 10:33; Neh 7:22).
2. Israelite who stood to Ezra's left at the reading of the Law (Neh 8:4).
3. Leader who signed Ezra's covenant of faithfulness to God with Nehemiah and others after the exile (Neh 10:18).

Hashupha. KJV alternate spelling of Hashupha in Nehemiah 7:46.

See HASUPHA.

Hasidim. Transliteration of a Hebrew word meaning "the pious." The influence of Greek customs and ways threatened the preservation of Jewish patterns of life in the 3rd and 4th centuries BC. Jews were required to employ the Greek language in their daily lives and with the language came the influence of Greek culture. This process was quite apparent in Palestine during the 2nd century BC, and the Jewish people responded in two antagonistic ways: one party was friendly to the Greeks; the other party set as their goal strict adherence to the principles of Judaism. The latter group, known as "the pious" or Hasideans, cherished the ideals of responsible covenant observance (Dt 7:9), and in the Maccabean period became militants in their efforts to worship God according to the Mosaic law. They were probably one of several religious groups in Judea. The Apocrypha identifies them by the alternate name of Asideans. When Antiochus Epiphanes ruled (176–164 BC), he attempted to abolish Jewish worship and institute purely Greek rites; the Hasidim and the majority of the people rose up to preserve the old faith. In 1 Maccabees 2:42 they are described as "mighty warriors of Israel, every one who offered himself willingly for the law" (cf. 1 Mc 1:63; 2:34; 2 Mc 6:18–20). Although they had accepted the leadership of Judas Maccabeus (2 Mc 14:6), the Hasideans later questioned the Maccabean claims to the high priesthood, and their break with Judas contributed significantly to their decline. Both the Pharisees and the Essenes may have had early roots in the Hasidim movement.

R.K. HARRISON

See ESSENES; JUDAISM; PHARISEES.

Hasmonean. Family name of the Jews who instigated the Jewish revolt against the Greeks in 167 BC.

See JUDAISM.

Hasrah. Variant spelling of Harhas, Shallum's grandfather, in 2 Chronicles 34:22.

See HARHAS.

Hassenaah. Alternate name for Senaah in Nehemiah 3:3.

See SENAAH.

Hassenuah. Ancestor of a Benjamite family that returned to Judah with Zerubbabel after the exile (1 Chr 9:7; KJV Hasenuah; Neh 11:9; KJV Senuah); perhaps alternately called Senaah (Ezr 2:35; Neh 7:38), and Hassenaah (Neh 3:3).

See SENAAH.

Hasshub. 1. Merari clan leader of Levi's tribe. Hasshub was the father of Shemaiah, a settler in Jerusalem after the return from captivity (1 Chr 9:14; Neh 11:15; KJV Hashub).
2. Pahath-moab's son, who repaired a section of the Jerusalem wall and the Tower of the Ovens during the time of Nehemiah (Neh 3:11, KJV Hashub).
3. Another Hasshub who repaired the Jerusalem wall opposite his house (Neh 3:23, KJV Hashub).
4. Leader who signed Ezra's covenant of faithfulness to God with Nehemiah and others after the exile (Neh 10:23, KJV Hashub).

Hassophereth. Ancestor of a family of temple assistants that returned to Jerusalem with Zerubbabel after the exile (Ezr 2:55, KJV Sophereth). He is perhaps identifiable with Sophereth in Nehemiah 7:57.

Hasupha. Ancestor of a group of temple assistants that returned to Jerusalem with Zerubbabel after the exile (Ezr 2:43; Neh 7:46; KJV Hashupha). He is perhaps the same person as Gishpa in Nehemiah 11:21.

See GISHPA, GISPA.

Hat. *See* FASHION AND DRESS.

Hathach, Hatach. Eunuch appointed by the Persian king, Ahasuerus, to wait on Esther. Hathach brought Esther messages from Mordecai. In this way, Esther learned of Haman's plot against the Jews (Est 4:5–10, KJV Hatach).

Hathath. Othniel's son and the grandson of Kenaz (1 Chr 4:13).

Hatipha. Ancestor of a family of temple servants that returned to Jerusalem with Zerubbabel after the captivity (Ezr 2:54; Neh 7:56).

Hatita. Ancestor of a family of gatekeepers that returned to Jerusalem with Zerubbabel after the exile (Ezr 2:42; Neh 7:45).

Hattil. Forefather of a family of temple servants that returned to Jerusalem with Zerubbabel after the exile (Ezr 2:57; Neh 7:59).

Hattush. 1. Shemaiah's son and a descendant of David (1 Chr 3:22). Huttush returned from the Babylonian exile with Ezra (Ezr 8:2).

2. Son of Hashabneiah, who helped Nehemiah rebuild the walls of Jerusalem (Neh 3:10).

3. Priest who returned from Babylon with Zerubbabel (Neh 12:2). One of his descendants signed Ezra's covenant of faithfulness to God (Neh 10:4). His name is omitted from Nehemiah 12:14 through scribal error.

Hauran. Region in northeastern Transjordan mentioned in Ezekiel's description of the borders of the land (Ez 47:16,18). In biblical times it corresponded to the modern Jebel ed-Druze of the Leja. This area is mentioned as early as the reign of Shalmaneser III of Assyria in his description of a military campaign in 841 BC. His army marched to Mt Khauranu after a siege of Damascus and before crossing Galilee to Mt Carmel.

In 733–732 BC Tiglath-pileser III of Assyria conquered Damascus and its surrounding region and organized it into provinces, one of which was Khaurina, or Hauran. The same province is mentioned in the Annals of Ashurbanipal during his campaign against the Arabians (639–637 BC).

The Greek version of the OT calls Hauran by the name Auranitis. It was evidently under the control of the Ptolmies, the Macedonian rulers of Egypt, in the 3rd century BC as indicated by a reference to Aurana in the Zenon Papyri. A great deal is said about the area by Josephus, who records that Hauran (Auranitis) and the adjacent area, Trachonitis, were part of the territory assigned to Herod the Great and later given to his son Philip.

Havilah (Person). 1. Descendant of Cush (Gn 10:7; 1 Chr 1:9).

2. Descendant of Shem through Joktan (Gn 10:29; 1 Chr 1:23).

Havilah (Place). Land in the neighborhood of Eden, now unknown but said to be watered by the River Pishon and containing supplies of gold, bdellium, and onyx stone (Gn 2:11,12). The location of Havilah has been a matter of much dispute. It cannot have any connection with the Havilah of 1 Samuel 15:7, where Saul fought against certain Amalekites, because the locale of the Eden narratives is Mesopotamian and not Palestinian. On the same basis any attempt to locate Havilah in southern Arabia, Somaliland, or India would be mistaken. The "river" Pishon may have been an irrigation canal, since Akkadian does not have a separate word for these two different bodies of water and the Mesopotamian custom was to name large irrigation canals as if they were rivers. This would help to account for the survival of the name "Pishon" long after the canal had disappeared. The Pishon was one of four branches which the river formed once it left Eden, hence Havilah must have been to the north since the narrative assumes an upstream perspective. Probably Havilah was in the general area of the Shinar plain and was watered by a major irrigation canal. Both Havilah and the canal have long disappeared.

Havvoth-jair, Havoth-jair. Series of settlements on the edge of Bashan across the Jordan captured by Jair, according to Numbers 32:41. Because of their location they fell into the allotment of the half-tribe of Manasseh. The number of these villages is given in Joshua 13:29,30 as 60, and they are probably included in the list of cities and towns of 1 Chronicles 2:22,23, although only 23 cities are specified as belonging to Jair. The KJV rendering as Bashan-havoth-jair (Dt 3:14) makes the location as specific as the Hebrew. In Judges 10:4, a judge named Jair had 30 sons who controlled 30 cities named Havvoth-jair; but he is obviously different from the Jair of Numbers 32:41. If his sons controlled only 30 settlements, he himself probably governed the remaining 30. In 1 Chronicles 2:21–24, which reflects a relationship between Judah and Manasseh, Jair was said to have 23 cities in Gilead when Geshur and Aram captured 60 towns from the tent-settlements of Jair and Kenath and its dependencies. While the variant numbers presents difficulties, the narrative itself may be the chronicler's way of indicating Judah's sense of sovereignty over Gilead.

Hawk. *See* BIRDS.

Hay. Dried grass used as animal fodder. *See* PLANTS (GRASS).

Hazael. King of Syria (843?–796? BC) who came to power by assassinating his ruler Ben-hadad (2 Kgs 8:7–15) and establishing a new dynasty. An inscription of Shalmaneser speaks of Hazael as a "son of a nobody," and mentions that he had "seized the throne." The Hebrew prophet Elijah was told to anoint Hazael as the next king of Syria (1 Kgs 19:15).

Upon becoming king, Hazael continued the policy of Ben-hadad in resisting the Assyrian military influence in Palestine. Although most of Palestine came under Assyrian control in 841 BC, Hazael was able to retain independence by withstanding the siege of Damascus. Failing in a final attempt to subdue Damascus in 837 BC, the Assyrians withdrew. This allowed Hazael the freedom to begin a series of attacks against Israel which resulted in Syrian domination of most of Palestine.

Toward the end of Jehu's reign in Israel, Hazael occupied Israelite territory in the hills of Galilee and east of the Jordan (2 Kgs 10:32). After Jehu's death, the Syrian king continually harassed Israel, captured much of Philistia, and spared Jerusalem only because Joash, king of Judah, sued for peace and was willing to pay heavy tribute (12:17,18). The Syrian oppression continued during the reign of Hazael's son until Adad-nirari III, king of Assyria, marched into Syria causing Damascus to submit and pay heavy tribute. This took the pressure off Israel and provided opportunity for her to regain territory taken by Hazael (13:24,25).

Archaeologists found the remains of a bed at Arslan Tash (Hadathah) which may have been included in the tribute taken from Damascus. Part of the inscription on a piece of ivory inlay from the bed reads "to our Lord Hazael." Evidently there was a high level of culture in Damascus under Hazael. According to Josephus, Hazael was long remembered for his part in building temples in Damascus.

GEORGE BLANKENBAKER *and* R.K. HARRISON

See SYRIA, SYRIANS.

Hazaiah. Maaseiah's descendant from Judah's tribe, who was one of the leaders in Jerusalem after the exile (Neh 11:5).

Hazar-addar. Town, which with Azmon, defined the southern border of Judah (Nm 34:4), usually identified with Khirbet el-Qudeirat near Kadesh-barnea. The parallel passage in Joshua 15:3,4 lists four places—Hezron, Addar, Karka, and Azmon—instead of two. Some have suggested that Hazar-addar and Addar are the same place; others, that it was renamed Hezron to distinguish it from Addar.

Hazar-enan, Hazar-enon. Place describing the northeast corner of Israel's border (Nm 34:9,10); alternately spelled Hazar-enon in Ezekiel 47:17,18 and 48:1. It is identified with modern Hadr at the base of Mt Hermon.

Hazar-gaddah. City in the southern extremity of the land assigned to Judah's tribe for an inheritance (Jos 15:27). Its site is unknown.

Hazar-hatticon. KJV spelling of the place Hazer-hatticon in Ezekiel 47:16.

See HAZER-HATTICON.

Hazar-maveth. Descendant of Shem through Joktan (Gn 10:26; 1 Chr 1:20) whose progeny lived in southern Arabia (Gn 10:30) in the Wadi Hadhramaut. Excavations there revealed a flourishing economy in the 5th century BC, based on frankincense trade. This trade, revived in the 2nd century BC, made the area prosperous and influential.

Hazar-shual. Simeonite city located in the southern section of Judah (Jos 15:28; 19:3; 1 Chr 4:28). It is also listed among those cities occupied by the Jews who returned from captivity (Neh 11:27).

Hazar-susah, Hazar-susim. City assigned to Simeon within the territory allotted to Judah for an inheritance (Jos 19:5); alternately called Hazar-susim (1 Chr 4:31). Solomon probably used it as a transfer point for horses brought from Egypt for sale to the Hittites and Syrians, as suggested by its name, meaning "horse station." Hazar-susah has been identified with Sbalat Abu Susein, east of the Wadi Far'ah.

Hazazon-tamar. City identifiable with En-gedi in 2 Chronicles 20:2. During the time of Abraham it was inhabited by Amorites who were subdued by Chedorlaomer as he and other eastern kings swept through the area (Gn 14:7, KJV Hazezon-tamar). It has been suggested that it may be the Tamar which Solomon fortified (1 Kgs 9:18), placed by Ezekiel southeast of Israel (Ez 47:18,19; 48:28). Wadi Hasasa has apparently been named after the ancient site.

Hazel. KJV mistranslation for almond in Genesis 30:37.

See PLANTS (ALMOND).

Hazelelponi. KJV spelling of Hazzelelponi, Etam's daughter, in 1 Chronicles 4:3.

See HAZZELELPONI.

Hazer-hatticon. Boundary marker along Israel's northern perimeter (Ez 47:16, KJV Hazar-hatticon). In conjunction with the use of Hazar-enon in this context and in comparison with Numbers 34:9,10, it appears that Hazer-hatticon may represent a scribal error for Hazar-enan.

Hazerim. KJV transliteration of the corresponding Hebrew word in Deuteronomy 2:23. Instead of the proper name for a city, it may be a generic term for "villages," a rendering favored by the ASV and RSV; NEB has "hamlets."

The mound of Hazor.

Hazeroth. Camp of the Israelites during their wanderings in the desert. It was the third camp from Mt Sinai (Nm 11:35; 12:16; 33:17,18; Dt 1:1). Here Miriam and Aaron spoke against Moses for marrying a Cushite woman and questioned whether God spoke only through Moses (Nm 12:1,2). The site is probably modern 'Ain Khadra, about 30 miles northeast of Jebel Musa.

See WILDERNESS WANDERINGS.

Hazezontamar. KJV spelling of the city Hazazon-tamar in Genesis 14:7.

See HAZAZON-TAMAR.

Haziel. Levite and son of Shimei during David's time (1 Chr 23:9).

Hazo. Nahor's fifth son (Gn 22:22); probably used as the name for a Nahorite clan. It has been identified with the name "Hazu" which designated a mountainous region in northern Arabia mentioned in an inscription telling of Esar-haddon's Arabian campaign.

Hazor. 1. City in northern Palestine in the territory of Naphtali, called "head of all those kingdoms (of Canaan)" in Joshua 11:10 and Asher in Tobit 1:2. Located 5 miles southwest of Lake Huleh and 10 miles north of the Sea of Galilee, it is known as Tell el-Qedah (or Tell Waggas) today. At its peak it numbered 40,000 inhabitants and was by far the largest Canaanite city in area and population. It was a great commercial center on the trade routes between Egypt and Babylon.

Hazor was identified by J.L. Porter in 1875, but the first excavations were made by John Garstang in 1928. More extensive excavations were made in 1955–58 and again in 1968 under the direction of Yigael Yadin. Excavators uncovered remains of 22 cities, from its beginnings around 2700 BC to its final destruction around 150 BC, and have been able to reconstruct its history based on their findings.

Hazor is first mentioned in the 19th-century Egyptian Execration Texts. It is given promi-

nence in the archives of Mari (18th century), being the only Palestinian city to be mentioned in these documents. It is frequently mentioned in Egyptian documents from the time of Thutmosis III to Ramses II, including the Tell el-Amarna correspondence.

The OT mentions Hazor a number of times—first, concerning the conquests of Joshua in which Hazor was completely destroyed (Jos 11:1–15; 12:19). At that time Hazor was a Canaanite royal city whose king Jabin headed a northern Canaanite federation against the invading Israelites. Hazor figures in the revolt led by Deborah and Barak against another Jabin (a dynastic name?) that resulted in a rout of Jabin's forces under Sisera (Jgs 4,5). Hazor was fortified by Solomon (1 Kgs 9:15); the remains of Solomon's Hazor are clearly preserved. King Ahab (874–853 BC) also added to the fortifications; the elaborate water system Ahab constructed when he rebuilt the whole upper city and fortified it to withstand long siege has been found. The city was destroyed by Tiglath-pileser III about 732 BC, thus bringing to an end its use as a fortified Israelite city (2 Kgs 15:29). Fortresses of the Assyrian, Persian, and Hellenistic periods respectively have been found in various strata of the city. Hazor is not mentioned again in the OT, but 1 Maccabees 11:67 says Jonathan encamped on the plain of Hazor while he fought against Demetrius (147 BC). The last mention of Hazor in ancient sources was by Josephus.

The site of Hazor is composed of two distinct elements: (1) the tell proper, an area of about 25 acres, rising about 130 feet above the surrounding plain; and (2) a large rectangular enclosure north of the tell about 175 acres in area, on the west side of which was a beaten earth wall about 350 feet wide. Temples, tombs, palaces, and numerous artifacts, found at different levels, have enabled archaeologists to reconstruct the history of Hazor through successive centuries. One temple was very similar in plan to Solomon's with an antechamber, holy place, and holy of holies. Archaeologists believe the city suffered severe destruction by earthquake during the time of Jeroboam II (Am 1:1).

Hazor has been of particular interest for the light it sheds on the conquest of Palestine described in Joshua. Excavations clearly show that the great city was destroyed by fire in the last half of the 13th century BC, and was never rebuilt. Archaeological finds support the biblical picture of a violent conquest under Joshua. The meager Israelite occupation in the 12th and 11th century BC was replaced by a well-fortified city during the Solomonic era.

The excavations at Hazor have been particularly illuminating for the picture they give of Canaanite temples and religious practices. One sanctuary was found with a basalt statue of a god seated on a throne, holding a goblet in his right hand. Beside a nearby pillar was a basalt lion, still keeping watch. Beside the deity were bowls and dishes apparently used for sacrificial purposes. Sacrificial high places have been found with altars and incense stands. In the antechamber of a temple whose pattern has been compared to Solomon's was found a deep trench in which a standing lion of basalt almost six and one half feet long had been buried.

2. Town in southern Judah (Jos 15:23). It is perhaps el-Jebariyeh, on the Wadi Umm Ethnan near Bir Hafir, about 9 miles southeast of el-'Auja.

3. Another town in southern Judah, called Hazor-hadattah (Jos 15:25). The KJV translates as separate cities, "Hazor, Hadattah."

See HAZOR-HADATTAH.

4. Alternate name for Kerioth-hezron (Jos 15:25), probably situated in southern Judah. The KJV translates as separate cities, "Kerioth, and Hezron."

See KERIOTH #1.

5. Town north of Jerusalem occupied by Benjamites after their return from exile (Neh 11:33). The name has been preserved in Khirbet Hazzur, west of Beit Hanina.

6. Place somewhere in the Arabian desert east of Palestine, called a kingdom of his oracle of judgment against Kedar and Hazor (Jer 49:28–33).

F.B. HUEY, JR.

Hazor-hadattah. One of the cities located in the southern extremity of Judah, near the border of Edom (Jos 15:25). The KJV translates the term as two different cities, "Hazor and Hadattah." The Aramaic adjective "Hadattah" indicates this as a settlement from Hazor, but this is unsure. Its location is uncertain.

Hazzelelponi. Etam's daughter from Judah's tribe (1 Chr 4:3, KJV Hazelelponi).

Head. Term with many figurative uses in Scripture. Frequently it designates prominence or authority. The OT commonly uses parts of the body to refer to the whole person (e.g., Dt 6:5). Thus, the number of soldiers in an army or the inhabitants of a nation could be determined by a "head count" (Nm 1:2).

To raise one's head was considered an act of pride (Ps 140:9) or honor (Gn 40:20; Pss 3:3; 27:6). Bowing the head signified humility (Is 58:5) or sadness (Lam 2:10). The Hebrew word is used metaphorically of mountain peaks (Gn 8:5), the tops of buildings (Gn 11:4) or trees (2 Sm 5:24), and river sources (Gn 2:10). The term was commonly used to designate positions of political, military, or familial authority. In this sense the "head" exercised control over all those subjected to him (Jgs 10:18; 1 Sm 15:17; Ps 18:43; Is 7:8,9; Jer 31:7; Hos 1:11). David was called the "defender of the head" (KJV) when he served as the bodyguard of Achish (1 Sm 28:2; cf. Jgs 9:53; Ps 68:21).

Greek philosophers used the image of the body to represent the universe. The head of this body—called Zeus or Reason—was considered responsible for the creation and sustenance of the remaining members (celestial beings, humans, animals, plants, and inanimate objects). The universe or "body" owed its existence to the "head."

Between 460 BC (the date usually ascribed to the first writings of Hippocrates) and AD 200 (the death of Galen, who developed Hippocrates' findings), Greek medical science came to understand the head as the seat of intelligence. The body was able to operate efficiently only because the brain was capable of interpreting data received from the body (eyes, ears, skin, and so on), and because it was able to send out appropriate impulses to the various members of the body, based upon the data received. The ability of the brain to interpret and direct made the existence of the body completely dependent upon it.

In the NT, the term refers to the actual human head (Mt 5:36; 6:17; 14:8; 26:7; Mk 6:27; 14:3; Lk 7:46; Jn 13:9; 20:7); to apocalyptic beings (Rv 1:14; 4:4; 12:1) and animals (Rv 9:7,17,19; 12:3); and appears in such expressions as "to heap coals of fire upon the head," meaning to return good for evil (Mt 5:44; Rom 12:20); to "shear" or "anoint the head," expressing a vow (Acts 21:24); or "to lay down the head," meaning to sleep (Mt 8:20; Lk 9:58).

The apostle Paul drew from the OT metaphorical understanding of the term to express the authority of God over Christ, Christ over man, and man over woman (1 Cor 11:3–16; cf. Eph 5:23). In the light of these relationships, Paul encouraged women at Corinth to wear veils in worship. The veil gave a woman the authority to worship as an equal with men before God. The term is used again with the meaning "authority" to express the lordship of Christ over the universe (Eph 1:21,22; Col 2:10).

Paul used the image of the head and body to express the relationship between Christ and his church (Eph 4:15; 5:23b; cf. 1 Cor 12:12–27). In addition to the OT sense, the contributions of medical science in Paul's day may provide insight into this image—for Christ is not only the dominant ruler over the church, but he is also the dynamic force that provides its direction and unity. The ability of the church to exist and the focal point of its activity are rooted in the work of its "head," Jesus Christ.

Bibliography. J. Bannerman, *The Church of Christ;* K. Barth, *Church Dogmatics,* vol 3, pp 309–16; H. Ridderbos, *Paul: An Outline of His Theology;* H.W. Wolf, *Anthropology of the OT,* pp 40–58.

Headband. *See* FASHION AND DRESS.

Head Covering. Something used to cover one's head either for protection or for religious reasons.

Men wore either a cap, turban, or head-scarf to protect against the sun. The cap was similar to a modern skullcap and was sometimes worn by the poor. The turban (Is 3:23) was made of thick linen wound around the head with the ends tucked inside the folds. The priest's turban had a plate strapped to it bearing the inscription "Holy to the Lord" (Ex 28:36). The head-scarf was made from a square yard of cloth, folded in half to form a triangle. The sides fell over the shoulders and the V-point down the back, and it was held in place by a headband made of cord. About the 2nd century BC male Jews began to wear phylacteries on their foreheads, small leather boxes containing special scripture passages, at morning prayers and at festivals, but not on the sabbath.

Women were often veiled in public, although this custom changed over the centuries. Thus Rebekah was unveiled when she first saw Isaac (Gn 24:65). In NT times, women usually wore veils (1 Cor 11:6). Women also wore a cloth similar to the head-scarf, but the fabric was different in quality and color from that worn by men. It was often pinned over a stiff hat and set with ornaments. If a woman was married, these and other important coins covered the front of the hat and constituted her dowry (cf. Lk 15:8–10). Women also adorned their heads with an elaborate "plaiting" of their hair, prompting Peter to warn Christian women about too much concern with external beauty (1 Pt 3:3,4).

See FASHION AND DRESS.

Heal, Healing. To make sound or whole. The OT provides the proper background for a Christian understanding of the concept of healing. In the OT the basic point is made that God is the healer of his people. In Exodus 15:22–26, after God has delivered his people from Egypt, led them through the sea, and sweetened the water at Marah, he speaks of

Three Egyptian ceremonial headdresses and five styles of Greek headdresses.

A headcovering from Ur.

withered hand (3:1–6), the multitudes by the sea (vv 7–12), the Gerasene demoniac (5:1–20), the woman with a hemorrhage, and Jairus' daughter (vv 21–43). Jesus then commissioned the 12 to proclaim repentance, to cast out demons, and to heal the sick (6:7–13); and he himself continued with healings at Gennesaret (vv 53–56), casting out the unclean spirit from the daughter of the Syrophoenician woman (7:24–30), healing the deaf and dumb man (vv 31–37), the blind man of Bethsaida (8:22–26), the boy possessed with a dumb spirit (9:14–29), and blind Bartimaeus (10:46–52).

Certainly healing is an important aspect of Jesus' ministry. Those healings expressed not only his compassion for the suffering but also constituted a revelation of his person. This is brought out by the climactic statement of Jesus in healing the paralytic, "that you may know that the Son of man has authority on earth to forgive sins" (2:10). It also seems that Mark intended his readers to understand that the healing of the deaf and dumb man (7:31–37) and the blind man of Bethsaida (8:22–26) symbolize the awakening of spiritual understanding in the disciples of who Jesus is. It is also significant that Mark has placed the healing of Bartimaeus (10:46–52) immediately after Jesus' third announcement of his own coming death (vv 32–34) and the disciples' third failure to understand that his being the Messiah entailed the necessity of suffering (vv 35–45).

Matthew also portrays Jesus as teaching, preaching, and healing (4:23–25), and parallels the accounts in Mark, except the healing of the demoniac in the synagogue (Mk 1:23–28) and the blind man of Bethsaida (8:22–26). However, according to his special purpose and structure, Matthew has placed many of Jesus' healings together in a "mighty works" section (chs 8,9) following and complementing the "great words" ("sermon") section (chs 5–7). Matthew views Jesus' healings as directly fulfilling the OT, as he states in 8:17. The unique way in which the healings of 8:16 are spoken of as fulfilling Isaiah 53:4 seems to indicate that Jesus' power over sickness derives in some way from his death for sin which was to be accomplished at the end of his ministry.

It is also interesting that Matthew, in relating Jesus' healing of the multitudes by the sea (12:15–22), cites Isaiah 42:1–4. This OT passage speaks of God's servant anointed with the Spirit to proclaim justice to the nations. As used by Matthew, the quotation explains why Jesus commanded those healed not to make him known. Jesus did not want too much publicity about himself to thwart God's plan for him as the Suffering Servant who was to bring forth justice or salvation to the nations. This

himself as their "healer." This refers primarily to physical sustenance, but it points to the more encompassing concept of God sustaining his people in an eternal relationship with himself. In a similar manner Deuteronomy 32:39 speaks of God as the One who heals. The context in Deuteronomy implies that this healing power derives from the fact that God is God. This concept of God as the healer is echoed throughout the OT by the psalmists (Pss 6:2; 41:4; 103:3) and prophets (Is 19:22; Jer 17:14; Hos 7:1; Zec 11:16).

The NT significantly emphasizes Jesus as the healer. Mark portrays him as a teacher and healer in his opening account of Jesus' ministry in Capernaum with the healing of the demoniac, Peter's mother-in-law, the sick brought to him in the evening, and the leper (1:21–45). Indeed, healing sickness and casting out demons characterize Jesus' ministry as Mark presents in rapid succession his healing of the paralytic (2:1–12), the man with the

action demonstrates that Jesus' healings are revelations of his person.

Again another quotation from Isaiah (6:9, 10) in Matthew 13:14 brings out the fact that healing is understood primarily in the spiritual sense of hearing Jesus' proclamation of the kingdom of God.

Further indication of Matthew's special interest in Jesus' healing in his inclusion of the healing of the blind and lame (21:14–16) in his account of Jesus' cleansing the temple (21:12–17).

Luke, like Matthew and Mark, portrays Jesus preaching and healing. After the account of the birth of John and Jesus and the ministry of John the Baptist, Luke presents Jesus preaching in Nazareth (4:16–30). Here in the synagogue of his hometown Jesus himself affirms, using a quotation from Isaiah 61:1,2, that the Spirit has anointed him to proclaim good news and to announce release for the captives and a recovery of sight for the blind (v 18). The healing aspect of Jesus' ministry occupies an important place in the rest of the Book of Luke. Indeed, Luke has all the healing incidents noted by Mark, except for those in Mark 6:45–8:26, which have no parallels in Luke. However, Luke's opening scene in Nazareth seems to underscore that Jesus' healing is to be understood, not as merely expressing Jesus' compassion for the needy, but primarily as a sign of the arrival of the kingdom of God as promised in the Scriptures.

This emphasis may be seen in the distinctively Lukan account of the commissioning of the 70 (10:1–12), where Jesus instructs them to heal the sick in any city they enter and announce to the people there that the kingdom of God has come near to them (vv 8–10).

The first three Gospels take up the OT understanding of God as the healer of his people and see this as fulfilled in Jesus. This fulfillment signifies the presence of God's reign in the ministry of Jesus and points to him as the One through whom God is at work in the midst of his people.

John's Gospel has only four healing incidents: the official's son (4:46–54), the man ill for 38 years (5:1–18), the man born blind (9:1–41), and the climactic raising of Lazarus in (ch 11). The special purpose and structure of this Gospel indicate that these incidents are carefully related to the accompanying discourses and are clearly intended as signs revealing the person of Jesus. This heightened emphasis on healings as revelatory signs in this Gospel confirms the similar intention in the first three Gospels.

The Acts of the Apostles tells of the continuation of Jesus' ministry through the Spirit at work in his disciples, though now they are em-powered by the Spirit. The primary focus in Acts is on proclamation as 1:8 indicates. However, the healing of the lame beggar in Jerusalem indicates that the disciples were able to exercise the power of healing in the name of Jesus (3:12–16; 4:8–16). The healing is clearly intended to point to and glorify the person of Jesus and lead to faith in him (3:12–16,17–26). The balanced twofold ministry of the disciples may be seen in the prayer of 4:29,30. "Lord, look upon their threats, and grant to thy servants to speak thy word with all boldness, while thou stretchest out thy hand to heal, and signs and wonders are performed through the name of thy holy servant Jesus."

The ministry of Philip in Samaria was devoted to proclaiming Christ (Acts 8:5) and healing the sick and those with unclean spirits (v 7). Peter heals Aeneas and raises Tabitha (9:34,40), and in each case the effects are that many believe in the Lord (vv 35,42). Paul is also described as preaching the gospel (14:7), healing (vv 8–11; 28:8), casting out spirits (16:18), and raising a dead man (20:10).

The letters of the NT say little about healing. First Corinthians speaks of the gifts of healing (12:9,28). The implication is that such gifts are intended to be part of the ministry of the church, but the context indicates that not all are given such gifts (v 30) and that it is God who sovereignly distributes gifts for the good of the body.

James indicates that a believer who is ill should request the church to pray for his healing (Jas 5:14–16; cf. Heb 12:13). The clear implication is that God is willing and able to minister to his people for healing today.

HOBERT K. FARRELL

Bibliography. E. Frost, *Christian Healing*; A.J. Gordon, *The Ministry of Healing*; M.T. Kelsey, *Healing and Christianity in Ancient Thought and Modern Times*; K. Seybold and U.B. Mueller, *Sickness and Healing*; R.A. Torrey, *Divine Healing*.

Healing, Gift of. *See* SPIRITUAL GIFTS.

Heart. Vital bodily organ; however, all modern assumptions concerning circulation of the blood, the intellectual and directive functions of brain and nervous system, must be set aside when considering Scripture's remarkably consistent physiological language. "Heart" (Hebrew *léb*; Greek *kardia*) occurs approximately 1000 times, often disguised in translation, and the range of meaning is immense.

Physical Heart. That the beating heart indicates life seems implied in 1 Samuel 25:37,38 despite the delay in Nabal's death; perhaps "heart" means "midriff" (cf. 2 Sm 18:14; 2 Kgs 9:24). Physical food and wine affect the heart (Jgs 19:5; Ps 104:15; Acts 14:17), and the heart an "faint," and "tremble." The heart's position yields an obvious metaphor for "the center" (Dt 4:11; Mt 12:40).

Psychological Heart. The heart attends intellectually (e.g., Jer 12:11); it also perceives (Jn 12:40), understands (1 Kgs 3:9), debates (Mk 2:6), reflects (Lk 2:19), remembers (Lk 2:51), thinks (Dt 8:17), imagines (Lk 1:51), is wise (Eccl 1:17 KJV) or mad (Eccl 9:3), has technical skill (Ex 28:3 KJV), and much more.

Emotionally, the heart experiences intoxicated merriment (1 Sm 25:36), gladness (Is 30:29), joy (Jn 16:22), sorrow (Neh 2:2), anguish (Rom 9:2), bitterness (Prv 14:10), anxiety (1 Sm 1:13), despair (Eccl 2:20), love (2 Sm 14:1), trust (Ps 112:7), affection (2 Cor 7:3), lust (Mt 5:28), callousness (Mk 3:5), hatred (Lv 19:17), fear (Gn 42:28), jealousy (Jas 3:14), desire (Rom 10:1), discouragement (Nm 32:9), sympathy (Ex 23:9), anger (Dt 19:6 KJV), irresolution (2 Chr 13:7 KJV), and much besides.

Volitionally, the heart can purpose (1 Cor 4:5), incline to (1 Sm 14:7), prompt (2 Kgs 12:4; cf. Prv 4:23), be steadfast (Acts 11:23), willing (Ex 35:22), or willful (Ez 13:2 KJV), contrive evil (Acts 5:4), or follow its "treasure" (Mt 6:21).

Morally, the heart can be gentle, lowly (Mt 11:29), holy (1 Thes 3:13), faithful (Neh 9:8), upright (Ps 97:11), pure, singleminded (Jas 4:8), clean (Acts 15:9), loving toward God (Mk 12:30) and others (1 Pt 1:22), or hardened (Ez 11:19). Scripture's emphasis falls upon the heart's evil (Gn 6:5 and throughout), as self-deceiving (Jas 1:26), deceitful (Jer 17:9), avaricious (Mt 6:19–21), lustful (Mt 5:28), arrogant (Is 9:9), impious (Acts 7:51), perverse (Ps 101:4), and impenitent (Rom 2:5). Nothing defiles a man but his own heart (Mk 7:18,19).

Yet, as conscience the heart can smite (1 Sm 24:5; cf. Acts 2:37). Moreover, out of the heart can come good (Lk 6:45, 8:15). Even when frustrated by circumstances or by fear, the heart's good intention remains good, its evil intent, bad (1 Kgs 8:18; Mt 5:28).

Being so complex, man's heart is sadly divided, and Scripture often extols a perfect, whole, true (i.e., united) heart (Gn 20:5; Acts 8:37 mg; Ps 86:11). For "heart" signifies the total inner self, a person's hidden core of being (1 Pt 3:4), with which one communes, which one "pours out" in prayer, words, and deeds (Gn 17:17; Ps 62:8; Mt 15:18,19). It is the genuine self, distinguished from appearance, public position, and physical presence (1 Sm 16:7; 2 Cor 5:12; 1 Thes 2:17). And this "heart-self" has its own nature, character, disposition, "of man" or "of beast" (Dn 7:4 KJV; 4:16; cf. Mt 12:33–37).

Religious Heart. The heart is especially important in biblical religion. The mystery of the hidden self is fully known to God and to Christ (Jer 17:10; Lk 9:47; Rom 8:27; and throughout), and the heart is the seat of our knowledge of God (2 Cor 4:6). The state of heart governs the vision of God (Mt 5:8); from the heart one speaks to God (Ps 27:8); the heart is the locus of divine indwelling (2 Cor 1:22; Gal 4:6; Eph 3:17).

On the other hand, moral evil in the heart is seen in biblical perspective as sin against God. Senseless hearts are darkened, often secretly idolatrous, far from God, "not right" before God (Dt 29:18,19; Mt 15:8; Acts 8:21; Rom 1:21). Yet the Lord will not despise a broken, contrite heart (Ps 51:17); if when one's heart is turned toward God, he promises to make it sensitive to divine things, renewed and purified (Dt 4:29; 2 Kgs 23:25; Ps 51:10; Jl 2:13; Ez 36:25–27). God's law shall then be written on the heart, as the inward guide and incentive (Jer 31:33; Heb 8:10; cf. 2 Cor 3:2,3).

In Christian terms, such transformation involves believing the gospel from the "honest and good heart" that provides fruitful soil for the Word of God (Lk 8:15; Rom 10:9). The true heart draws near to God, loves him with all its intellect, feeling, and will (Lk 10:27; Heb 10:22). Then God becomes to the heart strength, reward, renewal, grace, peace, and joy (Ps 73:26; Is 57:15; Acts 2:46; Phil 4:7; Heb 13:9). So the ancient ideal becomes possible again, that of being "a man after God's own heart" (1 Sm 13:14; Acts 13:22).

The high value which Scripture places upon such heart-religion does not discourage corporate worship and prayer, nor the uniting of individual hearts in spiritual fellowship (Jer 32:39; Ez 11:19; Acts 4:32). But it is directed against the external legalism, which judges according to visible outward acts rather than inward dispositions (Mt 5:21–48); against the heartless "hardness" of prevailing regulations concerning the sabbath, marriage, religious obligations (Mk 3:5; Mt 19:8; 23:4); against hypocrisy and self-display that belie the true state of heart (Is 29:13; Jer 3:10; Mt 6:1–18).

One fundamental assumption of Scripture is that the human heart is constantly open to influences from above and from below. God would "lay hold of [human] hearts" (Ez 14:5), "incline hearts" to his truth and ways (Ps 119:36), "put into . . . hearts to carry out his purposes," both for judgment and for salvation (Rv 17:17). The alternative to divine "possession" is the demonic influence that can drag the heart down to utmost evil (Jn 13:2; Acts 5:3). The same heart that can be "deceitful above all things, and desperately wicked" (Jer 17:9) can also become the shrine of divine love and the Spirit (Rom 5:5).

In that openness to infinite good or evil, the

scriptural dimensions of the human heart are revealed.   R. E. O. WHITE

Bibliography. R. Bultmann, *Theology of the NT,* vol 1, pp 220–27; R. Jewett, *Paul's Anthropological Terms;* A.R. Johnson, *The Vitality of the Individual in the Thought of Ancient Israel;* H.W. Wolf, *Anthropology of the OT,* pp 40–58.

Hearth.   See HOMES AND DWELLINGS.

Heath.   Type of evergreen shrub; KJV mistranslation for shrub and for wild ass in Jeremiah 17:6 and 48:6, respectively.

See PLANTS (JUNIPER).

Heaven.   Realm (or realms) designated by a Hebrew term used to represent the sky and air, and also heaven. The form of the word in Hebrew is dual (implying two of something). Although this dual form may only represent an ancient device for expressing the plural, it is supposed by some to imply the existence of a lower and an upper heaven—a physical and a spiritual heaven.

The OT.   The OT writers viewed the physical heavens as a "firmament" appearing as a great arch supported on foundations and pillars (2 Sm 22:8) and spread out above the earth, with rain descending through its doors (Ps 78:23). The keynote of the OT revelation about the physical heavens is set forth in Psalms 8 and 19:1–6. Elsewhere the OT speaks of the atmospheric heavens as the region of the clouds (Ps 147:8), winds (Zec 2:6), rain (Dt 11:11), thunder (1 Sm 2:10), dew (Dt 33:13, mg), frost (Jb 38:29), and the abode of birds (Gn 1:26,30). It is also the locale of such destructive forces as hail (Jos 10:11) and fire and brimstone (Gn 19:24). In the NT this notion of the vaulted expanse of the sky as the region in which the elements, clouds, and tempests gather (Mt 16:2; Lk 4:25) and birds fly (Lk 9:58) is continued.

In addition to the atmospheric regions, the Hebrew idea of the physical heavens includes stellar space, which ultimately embraces the universe. The heavenly bodies of the stellar heavens were viewed by the Hebrews as inexpressibly glorious manifestations of God's handiwork without having any power or vitality of their own. These include the sun, moon, planets, and stars, which were but lights in the firmament of the heavens (Gn 1:14; 15:5). As such, they were regarded as unworthy of worship because God had, by his own will and grace, made humans superior to them. In fact, the Hebrews were expressly forbidden to worship the stellar bodies (Ex 20:4), the gods and goddesses who represent them (Jer 44:17–25), or to participate in astrological speculation (Is 47:13). Hence, this unique theological ordinance differentiated the Hebrews, who viewed

the heavenly bodies as made and moved by the will of God, from the superstitious heathen, who worshiped them.

From the theological viewpoint, the most important use of the term "heaven" is its reference to the spiritual domain, the abode of God himself. Numerous passages of Scripture speak of God as "the high and lofty One who inhabits eternity" (Is 57:15), who has a parallel dwelling on earth and in heaven (1 Kgs 8:12), and of whom Solomon said, "Behold, heaven and the highest heaven cannot contain thee" (v 27). It is that abode to which the Lord Jesus Christ said he was about to return (Jn 14:2; cf. Pss 61:4; 65:4). There is where the true tabernacle stands, of which the earthly tabernacle was merely a shadow (cf. Heb 8:1–5). That abode of God was in view when the apostle Paul wrote of "the third heaven" (2 Cor 12:2). As such, it is often seen as a synonym for God himself (cf. Mt 23:22; Lk 15:18).

The term "heaven of heavens" (Dt 10:14; see also KJV 1 Kgs 8:27; Pss 68:33; 148:4) is the literal English rendition of the Hebrew idiom for the superlative "the highest heaven." Some have thought this the counterpart to Paul's expression, "the third heaven" (2 Cor 12:2), which parallels the classical Greek conception of three heavens. This notion was subsequently adopted by the Roman Catholic medieval church and in the Latin form of *Coelum Aqueum, Coelum Sidereum,* and *Coelum Empyreum.* The basic concept followed the Greek view, and coincides with the OT view of the physical and spiritual heavens as indicated earlier. Those who follow this approach tend to regard this third heaven as the place reached by the souls of the blessed as they pass through the two lower regions of the atmosphere and outer space containing the celestial bodies, and enter into the uttermost reaches of the universe.

The NT.   The Lord Jesus indicated that heaven is the dwelling place of God, or the place from which his presence is made manifest (cf. Mt 6:9; Rv 11:1–3); the Scriptures tell how Christ came from heaven to declare the glory of God (Jn 1:14,18); Jesus, during his earthly ministry, repeatedly claimed that he had come from heaven (Jn 3:13; 6:33–51); and on at least three occasions utterances from heaven confirmed these claims (Mt 3:16,17; 17:5; Jn 12:28). In the upper room, Jesus said that he was about to return to his Father's house and that it was a genuine place (Jn 14:1–6). In his high priestly prayer (ch 17), he tells of his eternal preexistent glory with the Father in heaven. After his ascension in Acts 1:6–11, two angels reminded the disciples that Jesus would return again from heaven. This was later confirmed by the apostle Paul (1 Cor

5:1–11; Eph 4:7–16; 1 Tm 3:16) and reiterated in the summary of the teachings of the NT known as the Apostles' Creed. In all, the relationship of Jesus Christ to the heavenly abode of God is inextricably interwoven in the NT and is inseparable from the gospel message itself. Indeed, it is from the "right hand of God" that Christ ever lives to make intercession for those who have come to him by faith (Heb 7:25; cf. Mk 14:62).

Paul presents one of the fullest statements in Scripture of the relationship of the believer to heaven. He asserts that in heaven the believer will be made conformable to the glorious body of Jesus Christ (Phil 3:20,21). In so doing Paul confirms John's teaching (1 Jn 3:2,3) and adds that the believer's true citizenship is in heaven. The term "citizenship" (KJV) or "commonwealth" (RSV) implies a colony of individuals who live in a foreign country while observing the laws of their homeland instead of the land in which they reside (cf. Acts 22:28). The implication for believers is quite clear: They are to live according to the moral and ethical principles of God as revealed from heaven regardless of the standards proclaimed by the world. They have been raised together with Christ and have been instructed to "seek the things that are above, where Christ is, seated at the right hand of God" (Col 3:1). From there Christ has blessed his followers "with every spiritual blessing in the heavenly places" (Eph 1:3). The expression "in the heavenly places" is peculiar to Ephesians (see 1:3,20; 2:6; 3:10; 6:12), suggesting that the blessings of the spiritual world are not relegated to some remote future time or place, but can be perceived by faith here and now. That is why believers are said to have been made partakers already in the heavenly calling (Heb 3:1; 6:4).

In addition to the absence of tears, sorrow, pain, and death, there will be no night or need of light in heaven, because the Son of God will be there (Rv 21:4,27; 22:3,5), and in the resurrected state there will be no marrying or giving in marriage (Lk 20:27–38). At least two OT saints, Enoch (Gn 5:22–24; Heb 11:5) and Elijah (2 Kgs 2:1), were translated directly into the presence of God—into heaven. In addition to Paul's statement about the third heaven, John was called into heaven (Rv 4:1), a heaven that is intended to be populated (cf. 1 Thes 4:16,17; Rv 19:1). All believers will ultimately dwell in heaven in their resurrection bodies, which they will receive when the Lord comes for them from heaven (1 Thes 4:16,17; Rv 19:1–4). The Lord will also give treasures and rewards at that time (Mt 5:12; 1 Cor 9:25; 2 Cor 5:1; 2 Tm 4:8; Jas 1:12; 1 Pt 1:4; 5:4; Rv 2:10; 4:10). Meanwhile, the souls of the redeemed abide with Christ in heaven (2 Cor 5:8,9).

See ABRAHAM'S BOSOM; NEW HEAVENS AND NEW EARTH; PARADISE.

Bibliography. J.S. Bonnell, *Heaven and Hell;* P.J. Krieft, *Heaven: The Heart's Deepest Longing;* R. Lewis, *A New Vision of Another Heaven;* A.T. Lincoln, *Paradise Now and Not Yet;* D.L. Moody, *Heaven;* K. Schilder, *Heaven: What is it?;* W.M. Smith, *The Biblical Doctrine of Heaven.*

Heavenlies, The. Term unique to Paul's letter to the Ephesians, also translated "heavenly places" or "realms," and referring to the super-earthly upper regions of the air. Since the term "in the heavenlies" carried with it associations from pagan cultic vocabulary, it was perhaps used by the apostle in an apologetic manner.

The heavenly places indicates the sphere where the risen Christ has been seated at the right hand of God in a position of authority, power, and dominion, reigning as conqueror and ruler high above the heavenly world (Eph 1:20,21). Other usage points to the idea of the realized hope of those who are in Christ, in that believers have already been blessed with "every spiritual blessing in the heavenlies" (v 3) and are raised with Christ, made to sit with him in the heavenlies (2:6). The church will make known the wisdom of God to the principalities and powers in the heavenlies (3:10). She will thus participate in the victory over the spiritual hosts of wickedness, also present in the heavenly places (6:12).

See HEAVEN; PRINCIPALITIES AND POWERS.

Heavens, New. See NEW HEAVENS AND NEW EARTH.

Heave Offering. Portions of the sacrifices and offerings set aside for the Lord and for the priests.

See OFFERINGS AND SACRIFICES.

Heber. 1. Descendant of Jacob through Asher and Beriah (Gn 46:17) and father of the family of Heberites (Nm 26:45; 1 Chr 7:31,32).

2. Husband of Jael, the woman who deceptively killed Sisera, known as Heber the Kenite (Jgs 4:11–21; 5:24).

3. Judahite, Mered's son and the father of Soco (1 Chr 4:18).

4. Elpaal's son from Judah's tribe (1 Chr 8:17).

5. KJV spelling for Eber in 1 Chronicles 5:13; 8:22; and Luke 3:35.

See EBER #s 1,2,4.

Heberites. Descendants of Heber in the family of Jacob (Nm 26:45).

See HEBER #1.

Hebrew Language. *See* BIBLICAL LAN-
GUAGES.

Hebrews, Letter to the. One of the most
profound and enigmatic books in the NT. The
identity of its author, the time of its writing,
and the people and place to which it was sent
are all shrouded in mystery. Yet in spite of the
uncertainty, Hebrews remains one of the most
timely and relevant books in the Bible. Some
300 years ago John Owen, the English Puritan,
appropriately remarked: "No doubt the Epistle next in importance to Romans is this to the
Hebrews." The letter is both doctrinal and
practical, theological and pastoral. In short, it
builds a compelling case for the finality of
Christianity.

Yet in addition to the excellence of its doctrine and apologetic, Hebrews reflects the impassioned concern of a pastor's heart. Those
who have experienced God's ultimate work of
grace in Christ are urged to hold fast to God's
final word of revelation in his Son.

Unlike most other NT epistles, Hebrews
does not begin like a letter. There is no intro-
ductory salutation, the writer is not identified,
and no mention is made of those to whom the
document is addressed. The author characterizes the work as a "word of exhortation"
(13:22) which suggests a sermon or oral homily
(cf. Acts 13:15). The phrase "time would fail
me to tell" (Heb 11:32) suggests a spoken
rather than a written discourse. Yet although
the general character of Hebrews is sermonic,
its conclusion is that of a conventional letter
(13:22–25).

Some have detected a gradual transition in
the document from an 'essay' to a more specifically 'epistolary' form (cf. 2:1; 4:1; 13:22–25).
The evidence thus suggests that the author
may have cast the original homiletic "word of
exhortation" into letter form when the need to
communicate in writing with his Christian
friends became urgent.

Author. Who wrote Hebrews is not directly stated in the letter. Since the late 2nd
century, various authorities have linked the
document with the apostle Paul. Clement of
Alexandria (d. 220) theorized that Paul wrote
the letter in Hebrew for Jews and that Luke
translated it into Greek. However, this suggestion has not been widely received by modern scholars. Clement's pupil Origen (d. 254)
stated more generally that the thoughts of the
letter are Pauline, but that the style is unlike
that of the known writings of the apostle.
Other early authorities such as Jerome (d. 419)
and Augustine (d. 430), persuaded that canonicity demanded apostolic authorship, likewise
affirmed that Paul was the author.

Yet a number of factors argue against the
Pauline authorship of Hebrews. The anonym-
ity of the letter is contrary to the consistent
pattern of Paul's introduction in the opening
salutation of his letters. Moreover, Hebrew 2:3
indicates the writer was discipled by eyewitnesses of the Lord. Yet Paul insists that his
knowledge of Christ was gained from an encounter with the risen Christ (cf. Gal 1:12). F.F.
Bruce evaluates the authorship of Hebrews as
follows: "We may say with certainty that the
thought of the epistle is not Paul's, the language is not Paul's, and the technique of OT
quotations is not Paul's."

Early Christian tradition suggests that Barnabas may have written Hebrews. According
to Tertullian (d. 220), many early authorities
believed that Barnabas was responsible for
the letter. Acts 4:36 speaks of him as a "son of
exhortation" (cf. Heb 13:22). Furthermore, as a
Levite, Barnabas would have been familiar
with the Jewish sacrificial ritual so prominent
in the letter.

Luther was the first to suggest that Hebrews may have been penned by Apollos, "an
excellent man of learning, who had been a disciple of the apostles and learned much from
them, and who was very well versed in Scripture." As a native of Alexandria (Acts 18:24),
Apollos would have been familiar with the typological interpretation evident in Hebrews.
Clearly Apollos was the sort of man who was
qualified to write Hebrews.

Other names have been suggested as possible authors. Calvin surmised that either Luke
or Clement of Rome was responsible for the
letter. It is noted that the Greek of Hebrews
resembles the language and style of the third
Gospel and Acts. Others theorize that Hebrews
may have been written by Silas, a Jewish
Christian from Jerusalem who would have
been thoroughly familiar with the levitical ritual. Silas is described as one of the "chief men"
among the brethren" (Acts 15:22). He was a co-
worker with Paul in the gentile mission, and
apparently was known in Rome as well as in
Jerusalem (1 Pt 5:13).

In conclusion, it is probable that the author
of Hebrews was a second-generation Jewish-
Christian, a master of classical Greek whose
Bible was the Septuagint, conversant with
first-century Alexandrian philosophy, and a
creative apologist for the Christian faith. As to
the identity of that author we can affirm no
more than Origen in the 3rd century: "But as
to who actually wrote the Letter, God alone
knows."

Historical Background. The very early
title of the letter, "To Hebrews," suggests that
the book concerns Jewish Christians living in
the dispersion. The letter itself offers a few
hints of the historical circumstances surround-

ng its composition. Not long after becoming Christians, the readers of the letter were exposed to severe persecution (10:32–36). During their trial the new believers endured imprisonment, confiscation of personal property, and public ridicule and contempt. Yet the persecution had not been fatal; they had not yet been called upon to lay down their lives in martyrdom (12:4). Amidst the excitement of their new-found faith in Christ they had demonstrated practical concern and love by ministering to fellow believers in need (6:10) and comforting others who had been harassed for their faith (10:34).

But since those earlier trials the readers had made little progress in Christian maturity (5:11–13). Moreover, in the face of a new wave of persecution, and despondency caused by an apparent delay in the Lord's coming, the believers began to waver and abandon hope. Indeed, they threatened to renounce Jesus Christ and to revert back to the security of the Jewish religion which enjoyed the protection of Roman law.

Thus we read that because of the "diverse and strange teachings" of certain Judaizers who sought to draw them back to their former religion (13:9), the wavering believers have neglected to assemble together (10:25) and have lost confidence in their spiritual leaders (13:17). Faced with the possibility that these Jewish Christians might abandon their faith altogether, the writer sternly warns them of the tragic consequences of renouncing the Son (13:12–19; 6:4–6; 10:26–31) and urges them to renew their commitment to Christ, God's foremost and final revelation.

Date. Lacking firm information as to the author and recipients of the letter, no certainty exists as to the date of the writing. We have noted that the author of Hebrews, and probably his readers as well, had been discipled by those who were personally acquainted with Jesus (2:3). Further evidence in the letter suggests that Paul probably was not alive. Timothy, Paul's younger associate, was still living (13:23).

The absence of any mention in Hebrews of the destruction of the Jerusalem temple is significant for dating the letter. In terms of his argument that the old covenant had passed away and the legal priesthood had been superseded, the writer would scarcely have omitted mention of the temple's destruction had he written the letter later than AD 70. Hebrews 9:6–10 and 10:1–4, 11–14 plainly suggest that the Jewish sacrifices were still being offered. Hence it may be supposed with some degree of certainty that the letter was written prior to AD 70.

Some scholars point to Hebrews 3:7–19 (quoting Ps 95:8–11) and suggest that the argument of Israel's 40 years wandering in the wilderness would be more forceful if the 40th year from the Lord's death was approaching. Such a scheme of reckoning would date Hebrews about AD 66. In conclusion, the various strands of evidence suggest that Hebrews was written between AD 60 and 70, possibly near the middle of the decade.

Origin and Destination. The place from which Hebrews was written is also uncertain. Some old manuscripts of the letter bear the subscriptions, "written from Rome," or "written from Italy." Such notations are educated deductions drawn from the statement: "Those who come from Italy send you greetings" (13:24). Most probably this indicates that the writer is extending greetings to a church in Italy on behalf of Italian Christians associated with him in another land, possibly Asia. Nevertheless, we cannot locate the point of origin with any certainty.

It has been suggested that the letter was written to a group of Jewish converts to Christianity. Yet the precise community to which it was sent is a matter of debate. Opinions vary

Latin inscription in Rome, where some believe that the Book of Hebrews was written or was its destination.

943

from Judea to Spain. Tradition has it that Hebrews was directed to Jewish Christians living in Palestine. But against a Palestinian destination it may be argued: (1) no allusion is made to the temple in Jerusalem; (2) the readers had had no personal contact with Jesus (2:3), an unlikely event for mid-1st century residents of Palestine; (3) the statement in 12:4 that his readers "had not yet resisted to the point of shedding blood" could hardly be said of Palestinean Christians of the period; (4) the generosity of the believers (10:34; 13:16) was inconsistent with the poverty of the Jerusalem church; and (5) the general tone of the letter is Hellenistic rather than rabbinical.

Other proposals for the destination of Hebrews include (1) Caesarea, on the supposition of Lukan authorship; (2) Syrian Antioch or Cyprus, assuming Barnabas wrote the letter; (3) Ephesus, in the light of the conversion of many Jews during Paul's ministry in that city; (4) Colossae, noting certain similarities between the Colossian heresy and the false beliefs of the "Hebrews"; and (5) Alexandria, because of the apparent influence of the philosopher Philo Judaeus in the letter.

The thesis that Hebrews was directed to a group of Jewish Christians in Rome has found favor with a number of scholars. Arguments in support of a Roman destination include: (1) the letter was first known in Rome no later than AD 96; (2) Romans 11:13,18 suggests that the church at Rome consisted of a Jewish-Christian minority; (3) references to persecution and suffering endured by the readers (10:32,33; 12:4) is consistent with known repressive measures exacted by the Roman authorities; (4) the possibility that saints who "come from Italy" convey greetings to their brethren in Rome; and (5) the Jewish community in Rome preserved certain features of nonconformist or sectarian Judaism that would explain several notable similarities between the theology and praxis of the Qumran community and that expressed in Hebrews.

It is likely that the letter was addressed to a small subgroup within a local church. The exhortation in 5:12, "by this time you ought to be teachers," hardly would have been relevant to an entire congregation. Hebrews 13:7,24 lends further support to the theory that the letter was sent to a small group, perhaps to a "house church" within a larger assembly.

Tentatively, one might conclude that the addressees were converts from Judaism who dwelt in the dispersion. Hence they were familiar with OT Judaism and were acquainted with the religious philosophy of the Greek world. Possibly the readers comprised a house fellowship which tended to disassociate itself from the parent group (10:25). The existence of such house churches in Rome is confirmed by Romans 16:5,14,15.

Purpose. In response to the threat that his Jewish-Christian friends might renounce Christianity and revert back to Judaism, the writer by a "word of exhortation" (13:22) communicated to them the finality of the Christian revelation. He sought also to inform his despondent, vascillating readers that Christ, the object of God's final revelation, is vastly superior to the greatest of Judaism's heroes. The author, in addition, affirmed the heavenly and eternal character of the salvation wrought by Christ. Whereas the legal sacrificial system was powerless to effect the remission of sin, Christ the eternal high priest "is able to save for all time those who draw near to God through him" (7:25).

In short, the writer commended to his readers the need for patient endurance amidst the persecution and sufferings to which the heirs of eternal salvation are inevitably exposed. Just as Jesus, the forerunner of our faith, suffered and patiently endured in anticipation of eternal reward, so ought harassed, oppressed believers "lift up the hands which hang down, and the feeble knees" (12:12 KJV) in anticipation of their reception in that eternal "kingdom which cannot be shaken" (v 28).

The author's final purpose for writing was to proclaim the fearful judgment that awaits those who repudiate Jesus Christ. Since "our God is a consuming fire" (12:29), "how shall we escape if we neglect so great salvation" (2:3).

Contents and Theology. Next to Romans, Hebrews is the most doctrinal book in the NT. The writer develops a series of weighty arguments to demonstrate the superiority of the gospel of Christ to the religion of Judaism. Since Jesus is final both as to his person and his work, Christianity is the ultimate and normative faith. The book's particularism runs counter to the spirit of the modern world.

The Superiority of the Son to Former Revelation (1:1–4). The writer acknowledges that God revealed himself to the prophets of old in many ways—through dreams, visions, audible speech, and mighty acts. But "in these last days" (the advent of the endtimes, cf. 9:26) God spoke finally and definitively through his own Son (v 2). Central to the argument is the fact that in one way or another the prophets received an eternal word from God. Yet given the intimate relation of the Son to the Father, God's latest revelation has come forth from the very depths of his own being.

Identification of the Son as the pinnacle of divine revelation leads to a concise but profound statement of Christ's person and his cosmic work. The Son "reflects the glory of God" n that the sum of the divine attributes brilliantly shine through his person. Moreover, he bears the very image and stamp of God's nature (v 3), as the wax bears the impress of the seal. Jesus as God's final word of revelation is truly the divine and eternal Son of God. Christ's excellence is further displayed in the fact that he is the mighty agent through whom the universe was created (v 2) and by whom the cosmic order is sustained (v 3). In the moral realm he has wrought the purification of sins and now sits enthroned on God's right hand (cf. 8:1). God's pleasure toward the Son is seen in that he has appointed Christ heir and head of all (1:2). His name is surpassed by none save God the Father (v 4).

The Superiority of the Son to Angels (1:5–:18). Angels enjoyed an exalted status in biblical and postbiblical Judaism. Traditionally the Jews believed that angels praised God upon his throne, mediated God's revelation to men, attended to God's will, and gave succor to the people of God. Angels were far superior to men in power and knowledge. According to the Jewish Apocrypha angels ruled the stars and were responsible for the rise and fall of civilizations. In Qumran thought angelic beings would engage in a final cosmic struggle with Belial and the forces of evil at the end of the age.

Against this background the writer of Hebrews argues that the Son is vastly superior to the angels. To prove his point the author assembles a string of well-known OT texts and applies them directly to the Son. God never said of any angel, "You are my Son, today I have begotten you" (Ps 2:7). Yet just such a claim was made on behalf of the Son (Heb :5). When the Son incarnated himself in the world he received the obedient worship of angels (v 6). His is the sovereignty and the eternality and the majesty at God's right hand (vv 8,11,12). By contrast, angels are "ministering spirits" (v 14) that rank below the Son in dignity and might.

In Hebrews 2:1–4 the writer parenthetically warns his wavering congregation of the danger of drifting away from the truth of God. If disobedience to the Law mediated by angels resulted in stern punishment, how much more severe would be God's judgment on those who trampled under foot the revelation delivered by the Son. If God's saving grace in Christ is neglected, retribution will surely follow (v 3).

The mention of angels turns the writer's mind to Jesus' humiliation and exaltation 2:5–18). Psalm 8, a song about the smallness and yet the significance of man, is applied to the experience of Jesus. In assuming human flesh and blood, Jesus was made "for a little while lower than the angels" (4:7). But subsequent to the completion of his earthly work he was elevated above the angels and crowned with the glory and honor of heaven (v 9). The theological implications of Christ's descent and ascent are carefully spelled out: Christ descended to earth (1) to bring many children to glory (v 10); (2) to destroy the devil (v 14); (3) to deliver his people from the bondage of death (v 15); and (4) to make expiation on the cross for the sins of the people (v 17). He ascended to heaven (1) to intercede on our behalf as a faithful high priest (v 17); and (2) to succor those who are sorely tempted (v 18). The perfect summary of Christ's person and work is given in Hebrews 2:9: "But we see Jesus, who for a little while was made lower than the angels, crowned with glory and honor because of the suffering of death, so that by the grace of God he might taste death for every one."

The Superiority of the Son to Moses and Joshua (3:1–4:13). Jewish-Christians contemplating reversion to Judaism surely believed that Moses was one of the greatest figures in Israel's history. So esteemed was the one who led Israel out of Egypt through the wilderness, the one to whom God delivered his holy Law, that there was no one in Israel's history quite like Moses. Yet the author of Hebrews argues that Moses, though faithful to his calling, was but a servant in the house of God. Jesus by contrast was no a mere servant, but a Son; he was not a mere dweller in the house, but the very builder of the structure. Jesus, therefore, far transcends the revered figure of Moses.

Practical implications are drawn from Jesus' superiority to Moses. From Psalm 95:7–11 the writer rehearses the tragic experience of Israel under Moses during the desert wanderings (Heb 3:7–19). Throughout the 40-year wilderness experience the people hardened their hearts and rebelled against God. In turn God "was provoked" (v 10) by their stubbornness and swore that those who sinned would never enter the rest he was going to provide (v 11,18). The writer thus argues that if disobedience to God under Moses had serious consequences, forsaking Christ will be much more perilous. Hence the wavering Christians are urged to watch lest due to an evil, unbelieving heart they should fall away from the living God (v 12). Nothing short of steadfast persistence will lead to the attainment of the heavenly goal (v 14).

Joshua, likewise, was regarded as a great leader of Israel. Yet because of disobedience the people under Joshua's leadership failed to enter the rest that God had planned. That rest spoken of corresponds to the sabbath rest of God (4:3,4), and is a concept closely related to salvation. It is a spiritual reality that is achieved by turning from our own empty works and trusting in the finished work of Christ (v 10). The author reminds the readers that "there remains a sabbath rest for the people of God" (v 9) that only Christ can provide. Christians not only benefit from this sabbath rest in the present age, but anticipate its full realization in the age to come. One of the chief means of ensuring entry into the sabbath rest of salvation is the Word of God (v 12). The living and powerful Word penetrates the innermost depths of the soul, reveals our impoverished condition, and strengthens the trusting heart.

The Superiority of the Priesthood of the Son (4:14–7:28). More than 40 percent of Hebrews is devoted to the priesthood of Jesus Christ. The writer goes to great lengths to demonstrate that the revered Aaronic priestly system has been superceded by the high priest "after the order of Melchizedek" (5:6; 6:20; 7:11). This central theme had been anticipated earlier when Christ was referred to as "a merciful and faithful high priest in the service of God" who has made atonement for sins (2:17).

Hebrews makes the claim that Jesus' priesthood is the ultimate ground of the believers' confidence (4:14–16). On three counts Jesus surpasses the old legal priestly order. First, he is an *exalted* high priest (v 14). The Jewish high priest climbed the mount to enter the temple sanctuary. But Jesus, our great high priest, has ascended to heaven itself and entered the sanctuary on high. He ministers in no earthly tabernacle, but in the very presence of God. Second, Jesus is an *empathetic* high priest (v 15a). Fully God and fully man, Jesus suffers along with his people in their trials and afflictions. From heaven's perspective he knows fully what his people are called upon to endure. He "feels" our hurts, and he does so perfectly. Finally, Jesus is a *sinless* high priest (v 15b). Day in and day out (7:27), year in and year out, the levitical priests were required to bring sacrifices for their own sins. Yet Jesus had no sin that needed cleansing, for he was "holy, blameless, unstained, separated from sinners" (v 26). In view of Jesus' priestly perfections, sorely tempted Christians are urged to "draw to the throne of grace" to "receive mercy and find grace to help in time of need" (4:16).

For those not convinced that Jesus was, indeed, a legitimate priest, two prerequisites for priesthood are detailed. First, if the high priest is to represent humanity before God he must be taken from among men (5:1,2). And second, he must be called by God to high priestly office as was Aaron (v 4). Christ has fully satisfied these qualifications. From Psalms 2:7 and 110:4 it is shown that Jesus did not take this office upon himself, but was appointed by God (5:5,6). Moreover, from the obedience which he had to learn (v 8) and from the agony of the Gethsemane experience (v 7) it is clear that Jesus was in every way a man. Nevertheless, Hebrews makes it perfectly clear that Jesus was not a priest after the order of Aaron but a "high priest after the order of Melchizedek" (v 10).

After introducing the theme of Christ as a Melchizedekian high priest the writer recalls that his readers were not ready for such advanced teaching. Although not new converts (5:12), his friends had remained spiritually immature and sluggish. Hence the writer issues the challenge to press on to Christian maturity, to be ready for the solid food of advanced teaching.

In his digression the writer warns not only against spiritual immaturity but also against "apostasy." The question now arises whether the author's apostasy teaching in Hebrews 6:4–8 and 10:26–31 contradicts the NT doctrine of the perseverance of the saints. Undoubtedly it does not. Some authorities hold that those addressed were not true Christians, hence the issue is not one of apostasy. It is possible, like Judas Iscariot or Simon Magus (Acts 8:9–24), to possess considerable knowledge of the gospel and fall short of personal commitment. But the writer makes it quite clear that in the case of his addressees he is persuaded otherwise (Heb 6:9). The most reasonable view is that in these two hortatory passages the writer advances a hypothetical argument warning his friends of the utter seriousness of reverting back to Judaism. That is, if a falling away were to occur, renewal would be impossible unless Christ were to die a second time. The writer sums up the point of these difficult passages with the words, "it is a fearful thing to fall into the hands of the living God" (10:31). Nevertheless, followers of Christ may confidently lay hold of God's promises, confirmed by solemn oath, to see them through their trials (6:13–18). The believer must practice "hope" (v 11), "faith," and "endurance" (v 12). God may be trusted to hold the believer fast.

Hebrews 7 contains an intricate argument for the superiority of Christ, a priest like Melchizedek, over the old legal order. Melchizedek, the ancient priest-king of Salem (Gn 14:18–20), is regarded as a primordial type of Christ. He is "king of righteousness" and "king of peace" (Heb 7:2). The solemn priest from Salem has figuratively what Christ possesses actually: neither mother nor father, neither beginning nor end of life (v 3). Melchizedek is shown to be superior to Abraham on three counts: (1) Melchizedek blessed the patriarch (vv 1,7); (2) he accepted tithes from

Abraham (vv 2,4,6); and (3) Melchizedek lives on since the OT nowhere mentions his death (v 8). It follows that since Levi was in the loins of Abraham as seed (v 10), Melchizedek is superior to the levitical priests. And inasmuch as Christ is a priest after "the likeness of Melchizedek" (v 15), it follows that the Son of God is more excellent than the old legal priesthood.

The result is that the old levitical priesthood has been superseded by the priesthood of Christ. The demise of the old order was inevitable, for its repetitive animal sacrifices could never effect spiritual perfection (7:11). It was a system characterized by "weakness and uselessness" (v 18). By contrast, Christ's priesthood is indestructible, eternal, uninterrupted, efficacious, final, and perfect (vv 16,21,24,25, 27). Forgiveness and reconciliation is possible only through Christ, our great high priest.

The Superiority of the Priestly Work of the Son (8:1–10:39). Since Christ's priestly office far excels the old order, it follows that his priestly ministration is superior to all that has gone before. The theme of Christ as high priest in a better sanctuary is introduced (8:1–5). The writer utilizes Plato's distinction between the ideal form in heaven and the imperfect copy on earth to argue that the levitical sanctuary and sacrifices are mere shadows of the heavenly realities: (1) Christ ministers in "the true tent" which is the "heavenly sanctuary" (vv 2,5); (2) he discharges his high priestly service in the very presence of the Father, which results in a far more effective ministry (vv 1,6); and (3) his oblation on the cross was the ultimate sacrifice (v 3). How unreasonable it is that his Christian readers should go back to the old Jewish priestly system.

Christ is the minister of a new and better covenant (8:6–13). The old covenant established by God with the fathers was not to be despised, nevertheless, it had become ineffectual and obsolete (v 13). Indeed, the prophet Jeremiah (31:31–34) foresaw the new covenant that God would inaugurate with his people. This new covenant sealed by Christ involves (1) the immediate work of the Holy Spirit on the mind and heart (v 10); (2) a personal and intimate knowledge of God (v 11); and (3) the full absolution of sins (v 12). This new and better covenant has been established on the work of Christ, the great high priest.

Chapter 9 gives a detailed comparison of the efficacy of priestly service under old and new covenants. The levitical priests ministered in a material sanctuary on earth (vv 1–5). Features of the tabernacle and its furnishings are described to highlight their obsolescence. More important, however, is the character of the sacrificial ritual conducted in the earthly sanctu-

ary. The Jewish priests in their daily service were not permitted to enter the Holy of Holies, which contained the ark of the covenant and the mercy seat—the place of propitiation of sins (v 6). The high priest alone could enter the Holy of Holies, and then but once a year on the Day of Atonement, and only after sacrificing for his own sins (v 7). The inaccessibility of the Holy of Holies signified that access to the presence of God had not been opened. The presence of the curtain symbolized that the people had no way to the throne of God, the priests had no way, and the high priest had a limited way and only once a year. Moreover, the sacrifices brought by the Jewish priests could not purify the conscience, but merely dealt with external ritual cleansing (vv 9,10). A truly effectual sacrifice must await "the time of reformation" (v 10).

Christ's priestly ministration is shown to be far more efficacious. First, the Christian's high priest has brought a better sacrifice (9:11–14), and here we arrive at the heart of the message of Hebrews. Employing the imagery of the tabernacle the author demonstrates that Christ our high priest has accomplished what the Jewish priests failed to do. He entered the heavenly Holy of Holies, not repeatedly, but *once* for all, thereby effecting a completed redemption (v 12). Christ brought to the altar, not the blood of bulls and goats, but his own life's blood. The Lord did not merely lay down a material body, but he presented himself to God through the eternal Spirit (v 14). Christ's better sacrifice thus goes beyond cleansing of the flesh to the purification of the defiled conscience.

Second, Christ through his death has instituted a better covenant (9:15–23). The teaching of Hebrews 8:6–13 is developed further. The old covenant was sealed with the blood of calves and goats (v 19). But the new covenant was ratified with the blood of Christ, God's own Son. The new covenant thus could accomplish what the old covenant merely foreshadowed—forgiveness and cleansing of sins (v 22).

Third, Christ ministers in a better tabernacle (9:24–28). Our Lord entered, not into a merely earthly sanctuary, but into the holy place of heaven there to represent us (v 24). Access to the throne is not limited to one day per year, for he is continually in the presence of the Father. Nor is it necessary that repeated sacrifices be made. Christ's single sacrifice on the cross has conquered sin once and for all (v 26). In sum, as regards the sanctuary, the covenant, and the sacrifices, the Christian's high priest is vastly superior to the old Jewish order.

In order to drive home these crucial points the writer expands on the theme of the absolute finality of Christ's high priestly work in chapter 10. The earlier argument concerning the futile character of the levitical sacrifices (9:6–14) is repeated for emphasis (10:1–4). The Mosaic ceremonial legislation called for repetitive sacrifices, which could never perfect the worshiper (v 1). Instead of purifying one's life, they served only as a yearly reminder of sin (v 3) until Christ should come.

The writer discovers in Psalm 40:6–8 a prediction that the eternal Christ would become man for the purpose of offering himself as the ultimate sacrifice for sin (Heb 10:5–10). Once again the sanctifying power of Christ's single self-oblation is emphasized (v 10). The vivid contrast is again drawn between the ineffective ministrations of the Jewish priests who stand during the daily ritual (v 11), and the effectual single sacrifice of Christ who is now seated at the right hand of God (v 12). Since Jesus "has perfected for all time those who are sanctified" (v 14), nothing can be added to what the seated Sovereign has accomplished (v 18).

In view of the manifest superiority of Christ's priestly office and work, the struggling Christians are exhorted to appropriate the means of grace at their disposal (10:19–39). In the midst of trials and persecution they should remember that Christ has effectively opened the way to God (vv 19,20). They are summoned to come to God in faith with hearts cleansed by Christ's sacrifice (v 22). Those tempted to revert to legal religion should hold fast and support one another in love (vv 23,24). The means of grace afforded by corporate worship should not be neglected (v 25). In short, the wavering Jewish-Christians are summoned to renewed endurance and fidelity to their Lord (vv 26–31). What God has promised to his people he will surely make good.

The Superiority of the Life of Faith (11:1–12:29). The discussion of faith and endurance as the solution to despondency (10:36,38) prompts a fuller consideration of the faith theme. Faith is a prominent concept in the Book of Hebrews, as attested by the fact that the word occurs some 35 times in the letter. The Pauline idea of faith as the means of legal justification is adapted to the particular circumstances of the threatened Jewish-Christians. The concept of faith is broader in this book than the strictly 'saving' faith discussed by Paul, in that it leads to spiritual salvation (11:39,40). But uniquely faith is the power by which heaven's unseen realities are laid hold of to satisfy the soul. Faith enables the Christian disciple to view the world and interpret the flow of history from the divine perspective. Faith is the means of victory over the world of sin and woe. Through faith the be-

liever approaches the throne of grace (4:16) with the confidence and assurance that God will enable him to overcome.

The victory faith affords is amply illustrated from the history of God's OT people. Abel, Enoch, and Noah in the primal history, Abraham the father of faith, Moses the leader of the young nation, and many valiant prophets and martyrs serve as living memorials to faith's overcoming power. And yet God has something better in store for his sanctified people, the church (11:40); that is the reality of the living Christ.

Yet the greatest model of steadfast endurance in suffering is Jesus, "the pioneer and perfector of our faith" (12:2). When surrounded with trials the Christian needs to recall Christ, who in anticipation of the heavenly crown endured the cross and its shame. The Christian's trials are trivial compared with what Jesus Christ was called upon to suffer (v 3). Moreover, for the people of God suffering and persecution prove to be disguised blessings. The rod of discipline confirms our status as children of the living God (vv 5–10). But beyond this, the sovereign God is able to transform the Christian's suffering into inestimable blessing (v 11). Hence the wavering saints should strive for spiritual wholeness and maturity, taking care lest they be overtaken by bitterness and resentment (v 15).

Final Exhortations and Benediction (13:1–25). The writer in his closing words challenges his Christian friends to be faithful to the tasks that lie right at hand. They are to show continued love to the brethren, to extend hospitality to strangers, to uphold the sanctity of marriage, to be content with what they now possess, and to be obedient to their spiritual leaders (13:1,2,4,5,7).

The readers are warned against the trickery of the Judaizers who would lead them astray from Jesus Christ, the One who remains "the same yesterday and today and forever" (13:8). Spiritual determination is strengthened by recalling the example of Christ, who "suffered outside the gate" for their salvation (v 12). As the people of God they are challenged to follow Christ out of the camp bearing abuse for him (v 13). Patient endurance is possible when the Christian realizes that he has no enduring city here (v 14). His goal is the heavenly Jerusalem, the eternal city of God.

The anonymous letter to the unknown "Hebrews" closes with a glorious benediction. The Christian's God is described as the great "God of peace" (13:20), and Jesus is "the great shepherd of the sheep," who established a new and eternal covenant and then rose triumphant from the dead. And the promise is made to the trusting soul that the triune God would "equip you with everything good that you may do his will, working in you that which is pleasing in his sight" (v 21).

The letter to the Hebrews is rich in doctrinal teaching. It discloses more about the historical Jesus than any other NT letter. It alone explains the atoning work of Christ under the rubric of the Melchizedekian priest. The letter's discussion of repentance, justification, sanctification, and perseverance makes it a mine of soteriological teaching. Its explication of old and new covenants, impending judgment, and the world to come make a significant contribution to Christian theology. And the letter's teaching on faith, endurance, and the practical Christian combine to make Hebrews one of the most glorious documents God has given to the church.

BRUCE A. DEMAREST

Bibliography. R. Brown, *Christ Above All: The Message of Hebrews;* F.F. Bruce, *Commentary on the Epistle to the Hebrews;* F. Delitzsch, *The Epistle to the Hebrews,* 2 vols.; W.A. Henrichsen, *After the Sacrifice;* R. Jewett, *Letter to Pilgrims: A Commentary on the Book of Hebrews;* S.J. Kistemaker, *NT Commentary: Exposition of the Epistle to the Hebrews;* N.R. Lightfoot, *Jesus Christ Today: A Commentary on the Book of Hebrews;* W.S. Plumer, *Commentary on the Epistle of Paul, the Apostle to the Hebrews.*

Grains being sold at a Bedouin market in Hebron.

Hebron (Person). 1. Third of Kohath's four sons, Hebron was a descendant of Levi (Ex 6:18; Nm 3:19; 1 Chr 6:2,18; 23:12). Hebron's sons were Jeriah, Amariah, Jahaziel, and Jekameam (1 Chr 23:19). Hebron's descendants were called the Hebronites. They are mentioned in a census taken in the wilderness near Sinai (Nm 3:27) and again in a census taken in the plains of Moab (26:58). The Hebronites are mentioned in connection with the transfer of the ark to Jerusalem in David's time (1 Chr 15:9; 26:23,30,31).

2. Mareshah's son and Korah's father (1 Chr 2:42,43).

Hebron (Place). 1. City of antiquity still standing today. It was built on the southern end of the highlands which run north to south through the length of Palestine. In patriarchal times it was known as Kirjath-arba (or Kiriath-arba; see Gn 23:2), and stood on the hill known as El Arbain. The modern city straddles both ridges of the mountain range.

Hebron is situated 25 miles S, SW of Jerusalem and less than 2 miles from Mamre, where Abraham spent much of his life. It is 3000 feet above sea level and marks the southern end of the Judean highlands. From this elevation the land slopes down rapidly to the east, but gradually to the west and south. The soil is relatively fertile, and a variety of fruits (apples, plums, figs, pomegranates, apricots), nuts, and vegetables are grown easily. To the

south is the Negeb, where the grazing land is excellent. A large number of springs and wells dot the landscape and assure residents of an abundance of water.

Between 1964–66 a team of American archaeologists excavated portions of ancient Hebron. They found evidence of occupation dating back to about 3000 BC. Because of Hebron's location, the fertility of the soil, and the plentiful supply of water, it seems to have enjoyed almost continuous occupation. The city must have been destroyed, however, perhaps by the Hyksos, for it was "built" (or rebuilt) seven years before Zoan (also known as Tanis), approximately 1730 BC (Nm 13:22).

In OT times Hebron included Mamre, the place where Abraham built an altar to the Lord after parting from Lot (Gn 13:18). It was here too that he learned of the capture of his nephew Lot (14:12–16); and, years later, entertained three angels and was told of the judgment soon to fall on Sodom and Gomorrah (ch 18).

It is most unlikely that the "oaks of Mamre" (probably terebinth trees) known by the patriarch are still standing. Two ancient oak trees in the vicinity of Hebron, nevertheless, have been associated with Abraham: the one stands near the traditional site of Mamre, and the other on the western edge of the Wadi Tuffa in the grounds of the Russian Orthodox church. The site where the trees probably once stood is now enclosed. Walls bearing evidence of the Herodian era may be seen to the south and west of this enclosure, and the "well of Abraham" in the southwest corner still is used by shepherds to water their flocks. The basilica located on this piece of land was erected by Constantine. Arab remains have been unearthed, and artifacts from the time of Abraham have been discovered.

Sarah died in Hebron, and Abraham purchased the cave of Machpelah from Ephron the Hittite (Gn 23:8,9,17; 25:9; 49:29–32; 50:12, 13) in which to bury her. This cave is now within the walls of the modern city, and the famous mosque of Harân el-Khalîl was built over it.

At the time of the exodus of the Israelites from Egypt, spies were sent into the land. They began in the south and traversed the central highlands of Palestine from Kadesh-barnea through Hebron to Rehob (Nm 13:17–21). On their return they brought back evidence of the productivity of the land (Nm 13:23,24).

From Numbers 13:33 we know that giants ("sons of Anak") lived in Hebron. The sight of these men filled 10 of the spies with fear. Only Caleb and Joshua proved equal to the occasion. On account of their faith they were promised a possession in the land, and Caleb was given Hebron (Jos 14:9,13). The unfaithful spies died in a plague in the presence of the Lord (Nm 14:36,37).

During the period of the judges Hebron is mentioned in connection with Samson. When trapped inside the city of Gaza, he carried off the gates and left them at Hebron (Jgs 16:3).

Following the death of Saul, the first king of Israel, David was crowned king of the tribes of Judah and Benjamin in Hebron (2 Sm 2:1). He made this city his capital, for it was more centrally located than Benjamin, and its position at the southern end of the mountain range removed it as far as possible from the 10 northern tribes that followed Ish-bosheth, the son of Saul. It was far enough from the Philistines to the west and the Amalekites to the south to avoid notice, and it was also easily defensible. Hebron also lay at the junction of several important trade routes, and this insured its prominence. Later, however, when David was made king over all Israel, he moved his capital to Jerusalem—an act which must have displeased the people of Hebron.

When Absalom wished to obtain support for his claim to the throne, he initiated his revolt from Hebron (2 Sm 15:7–12).

Following the death of Solomon, David's son, the kingdom was divided. Rehoboam, fearing an attack by the Egyptians on his southern border, fortified Hebron (2 Chr 12:1–12). From this time onward the city disappears from the OT record.

In the intertestamental period Hebron is again mentioned. Judas Maccabeus defeated the Edomites who had invaded the Negeb from Edom and had established themselves as far north as Hebron. Shortly before the birth of Christ, Herod erected a "haran" ("enclosure") around the ancient burial site of the patriarchs and their wives.

Hebron is not mentioned in the NT. However, because it preserves the cave of Machpelah, the last resting place of Abraham and Sarah, Isaac and Rebekah, Jacob and Leah, it became in the centuries that followed one of the most sacred places for Christian and Moslem pilgrims.

2. KJV translation of the town of Ebron, in Joshua 19:28.

See EBRON.

CYRIL J. BARBER

Hebronite. Descendant of Hebron from Levi's tribe (Nm 3:27; 26:58; 1 Chr 16:23,30,31).

See HEBRON (PERSON) #1.

Hedgehog. Small, insect-eating mammal with a coat of short spines and similar to the porcupine (Is 14:23; Zep 2:14).

See ANIMALS.

Hegai, Hege. Chamberlain of Ahasuerus and keeper of his harem when Esther was chosen as queen (Est 2:3, KJV Hege).

Heglam. Alternate name for Gera, Bela's son, in 1 Chronicles 8:7.

See GERA #4.

Heifer. Young cow.

See ANIMALS (CATTLE).

Heir. One who inherits something or who is entitled to a future inheritance; the one who receives the property of a deceased person, particularly on the basis of law and usually by means of a will. In both the OT and NT, the Hebrew and the Greek words encompass these ideas.

In Genesis 15, after God had reiterated his special promise to Abraham (vv 5,13–16), Abraham wondered how the fulfillment of the promise might occur. At the time, only his steward, Eliezer of Damascus, was "the son of his house," that is, the one of his large household who would inherit. There was no natural-born son of Abraham within the family (see 15:3,4). Without a son in patriarchal times, a man's chief steward could be his heir as a substitute. Later, after the birth of Ishmael (Abraham's son by Hagar, Sarah's maidservant) and of Isaac (his son by Sarah his wife), trouble erupted between the women, and Sarah demanded that Abraham send Hagar and her son away, because Sarah did not want Ishmael to be an heir with her own son, Isaac (Gn 21:10).

A maidservant, at Joab's instigation, told David a story about herself and her two sons. She said that one son killed the other, and that her family now wanted to kill the remaining son for the murder. If this happened, she claimed, the heir of her deceased husband would be destroyed and he would be left with "neither name nor remnant upon the face of the earth" (2 Sm 14:7). Another biblical illustration of this normal use of the word "heir" is seen in a parable told by Jesus. The workers in the vineyard who saw the son of their master coming, said among themselves, "This is the heir; come, let us kill him and have his inheritance" (Mt 21:33–43; Mk 12:7; Lk 20:14).

In a number of references in the NT, the word "heir" is used to refer to the believer in Christ, who has an inheritance coming because of being a child of God the Father and consequently a joint heir with Christ (Rom 8:16,17). The inheritance of salvation is variously referred to in different sections of the NT. In Hebrews 6:17, Christians are called "heirs of the promise" made to Abraham when God said, "Surely I will bless you and multiply you" (vv 13,14). In Hebrews 11:7, Noah is described as "an heir of the righteousness which comes by faith." In James 2:5, the poor in the world who are rich in faith are said to be "heirs of the kingdom which he has promised to those who love him." Paul writes that those who are justified by God's grace are made heirs according to the hope of eternal life (Ti 3:7).

In Hebrews 1:2, the word "heir" is used with a singular reference to God's Son, who is said to have been appointed "heir of all things" by his Father. Here is an instance where someone has been designated to receive an inheritance but will actually enter into full possession much later.

In biblical times the right of primogeniture prevailed, that is, the right of the eldest son in the family to be the primary heir in the household. In OT times, the firstborn son possessed the birthright, which included inheriting a double portion of his father's possessions and headship of the family (Dt 21:15–17). The other sons shared the remainder equally. If there were no sons to inherit, the daughters became the heirs (Nm 27:8; 36:1–12), although there was a stipulation that the daughters could not marry outside their tribe. This was to preserve the tribal territory intact. If there were no daughters, then the dead man's brothers inherited; if no brothers, then his uncles; and if no uncles, then the nearest relative (Nm 27:9–11). Because the matter of tribal possession was so important, it is easy to understand why there was such a concern for genealogical records among the Hebrew people.

WESLEY L. GERIG

See INHERITANCE; FIRSTBORN.

Helah. One of Ashhurs' wives who bore him Zereth, Izhar, and Ethnan from Judah's tribe (1 Chr 4:5,7).

Helam. Place east of the Jordan where David defeated the armies of Hadadezer, king of Syria (2 Sm 10:16,17). Its location is uncertain.

Helbah. One of the Canaanite strongholds that was not conquered by the Asherites after taking possession of the land under Joshua (Jgs 1:31). Its location is unknown.

Helbon. District north of Damascus, which produced choice wine (Ez 27:18); perhaps identifiable with modern Halbun, where the vine is still cultivated.

Heldai. 1. Baanah's son, described as a Netophathite in the line of Othniel. He appears first as one of David's mighty men (2 Sm 23:29; Heleb; 1 Chr 11:30, Heled). In 1 Chronicles 27:15, he is commander of an army division of 24,000 which served during the 12th month of the year.

2. One of the exiles returning from Babylon from whom the prophet Zechariah took gold and silver to make a crown for Joshua, the high priest (Zec 6:10, KJV Helem in v 14).

Heleb. Alternative name for Heldai, Baanah's son, in 2 Samuel 23:29.

See HELDAI #1.

Helech. Term mentioned in Ezekiel's prophecy against the city of Tyre (Ez 27:11, KJV thine army), perhaps referring to mercenaries from Cilicia southeast of Asia Minor. Assyrian texts indicate that Cilicia was once called Hilakku, but little is known about the people. They are first mentioned by Shalmaneser III, king of Assyria (854–824 BC) in his conquest of Asia Minor. Their history under the Assyrians was quite violent. Sargon, Sennacherib, and Esarhaddon had to put down revolts from the Hilakku. Later, they gave tribute to Ashurbanipal.

Heled. Alternate name for Heldai, Baanah's son, in 1 Chronicles 11:30.

See HELDAI #1.

Helek, Helekite. Gilead's son from Manasseh's tribe (Jos 17:2) and founder of the Helekite family (Nm 26:30).

Helem. 1. Member of Asher's tribe (1 Chr 7:35), called Hotham in verse 32.

2. KJV rendering for Heldai in Zechariah 6:14.

See HELDAI #2.

Heleph. Village on Naphtali's southern border (Jos 19:33), northeast of Mt Tabor. Its site may be modern Khirbet 'Arbathah.

Helez. 1. One of David's valiant warriors, called a Paltite in 2 Samuel 23:26 and a Pelonite in 1 Chronicles 11:27. The former is probably correct and refers to a person from Bethpelet. Most scholars feel that he is the same man as the officer in charge of the seventh course during David's reign (1 Chr 27:10).

2. Jerahmeel's descendant from Judah's tribe (1 Chr 2:39).

Heli. Ancestor of Joseph in Luke's genealogy of Christ (3:23).

See GENEALOGY OF JESUS CHRIST.

Heliopolis. Ancient Egyptian city famed as a center for worship of the sun god Re. Heliopolis ("city of the sun") was located in the Nile River delta region of Lower Egypt, a few miles northeast of modern Cairo. Heliopolis became important from about 2400 BC, with the emergence of Atum-Re as the cult deity. Many pharaohs embellished the city's temples and put up various public monuments, especially in the New Kingdom period (1570–1150 BC).

Since the temples contained the royal archives, the priests became the official historians of Egypt. Herodotus, a Greek historian of the 5th century BC, said the priests at Heliopolis were famous for their knowledge of Egyptian history. There were also training schools for priests and a medical school in the city.

Other Egyptian sun worship centers existed at various times, but Heliopolis maintained its popularity for some 2000 years. Though the city was of little importance politically, it was of primary religious influence. Among Egyptian religious buildings, the temple of Re at Heliopolis was second in size only to the temple of Amon at Thebes.

In the OT Heliopolis is called On. When Joseph was a member of the Egyptian official class he married Asenath, the daughter of Potiphera the priest of On (Gn 41:45,50; 46:20). The prophet Ezekiel warned of coming destruction in Egypt by Babylonian king Nebuchadnezzar,

citing Heliopolis (On) as one of the cities to be destroyed (Ez 30:17). In Amos 1:5, the RSV has an alternative rendering, "On," for "valley of Aven," and the same reading in Ezekiel 30:17 for the KJV "Aven." The prophet Jeremiah also predicted the destruction of the obelisks (sacred pillars) of Heliopolis (43:13, KJV Bethshemesh). Isaiah 19:18 (KJV City of Destruction) may be a reference to Heliopolis, but this is not certain.

The city fell into decay in the 4th and 3rd centuries BC, partly because of Egypt's declining fortunes and partly because of the library founded at Alexandria early in the 3rd century BC. Alexandria replaced Heliopolis as the leading intellectual center in Egypt.

Little remains today from the ancient city of the sun, but an obelisk erected by Sesostris I (1971–1928 BC) can still be seen at the site of Heliopolis. Several obelisks from Heliopolis, erected by Thutmose III (1490–1436 BC), have been moved to various parts of the world in modern times.

WILLIAM TRAVIS

Helkai. Head of Meraioth's priestly house in the time of Joiakim the high priest (Neh 12:15).

Helkath. First of 22 cities mentioned in the territory allotted to Asher's tribe for an inheritance (Jos 19:25). Helkath was one of four cities in Asher given to the levitical Gershonite families (Jos 21:31). It is alternately spelled Hukok in 1 Chronicles 6:75. Its ancient site is perhaps located at the modern Tell el-Harbaj.

Helkath-hazzurim. Area near the pool of Gibeon, where 12 champions from Joab's army and 12 from Abner's battled. All 24 died in the fight, each fighter killing his opponent (2 Sm 2:16). Some feel that the name may mean "field of the crafty," that is, "field of ambush," or "field of the adversaries."

Hell. Place of future punishment for the lost, unrepentant, wicked dead.

Definition and Description. Hell is the final destiny of unbelievers and is variously described by the figures of a furnace of fire, eternal fire, eternal punishment (Mt 13:42,50; 25:41,46); outer darkness, the place of weeping and torment (8:12); eternal sin (Mk 3:29); the wrath of God (Rom 2:5); everlasting separation from the Lord, never to see the glory of his power (2 Thes 1:9); the bottomless pit (Rv 9:1,11); continuous torment (14:10,11); the lake of fire, the second death (21:8); a place for the devil and his demons (Mt 25:41). The foregoing designations clearly show that the state of those in hell is one of eternal duration.

Other expressions that indicate that the final state of the wicked is eternal are: "burn with unquenchable fire" (Mt 3:12); "to the unquenchable fire . . . where their worm does not die, and the fire is not quenched" (Mk 9:43,48); there is sin which "will not be forgiven, either in this age or in the age to come" (Mt 12:32). When Scripture is understood properly, there is no hint anywhere of the termination of the terrible state of unbelievers in hell. Their doom is unending; there is a solemn finality about their miserable condition. (It is significant that the most descriptive and conclusive utterances about hell come from the lips of our Lord.)

A summary of all Scripture that speaks of hell indicates that there is the loss and absence of all good, and the misery and torment of an evil conscience. The most terrifying aspect is the complete and deserved separation from God and from all that is pure, holy, and beautiful. In addition there is the awareness of being under the wrath of God and of enduring the curse of a righteous sentence because of one's sins that were consciously and voluntarily committed.

Although the biblical descriptions of hell are stated in very physical and literal terms, the essential character of hell should not be conceived in or limited to designation such as the worm that devours, the stripes that are inflicted, the burning or being consumed by fire. This affirmation does not detract from the horror or the gravity of the situation in hell, because nothing could possibly be worse than separation from God and the torment of an evil conscience. Hell is hell for those who are there essentially because they are completely alienated from God, and wherever there is alienation from God there is always estrangement from one's fellows. This is the worst possible punishment to which anyone could be subject: to be totally and irrevocably cut off from God and to be at enmity with all those who are around oneself. Another painful consequence of such a condition is to be at odds with oneself—torn apart from within by an accusing sense of guilt and shame. This condition is one of total conflict: with God, one's neighbors, and oneself. This is hell! If the descriptions of hell are figurative or symbolic, the conditions they represent are more intense and real than the figures of speech in which they are expressed.

Punishment for sin is a persistent teaching of the Bible. The doctrine of judgment is as extensive as the canon itself. Typical of such passages are Genesis 2:17; 3:17–19; 4:13; Leviticus 26:27–33; Psalm 149:7; Isaiah 3:11; Ezekiel 14:10; Amos 1:2–20; 2:1–11; Zechariah 14:19; Matthew 25:41,46; Luke 16:23,24; Romans 2:5–12; Galatians 6:7,8; Hebrews 10:29–31; and Revelation 20:11–15.

Biblical Terms. The Hebrew word "Sheol" in the OT is predominantly used for "the grave, the pit, the place of the departed dead" (Gn 37:35; Jb 7:9; 14:13; 17:13–16; Pss 6:5; 16:10; 55:15; Prv 9:18; Eccl 9:10; Is 14:11; 38:10–12,18). There does not seem to be a very clear distinction in the OT between the final destiny of the good and the evil. They all alike go to the grave, to the world below, a world of gloom, weariness, darkness, decay, and forgetfulness, where one is remote from God (Jb 10:20–22; Ps 88:3–6), yet accessible to him (Jb 26:6; Ps 139:8; Am 9:2). It is a place characterized by silence (Pss 94:17; 115:17) and rest (Jb 3:17). Other texts, however, seem to suggest some aspect of consciousness, hope, and communication in Sheol (Jb 14:13–15; 19:25–27; Pss 16:10; 49:15; Is 14:9,10; Ez 32:21). A few texts seem to suggest the threat of divine judgment after death (Pss 9:17; 55:15). On the whole, Sheol was regarded with dismay and foreboding (Dt 32:22; Ps 39:13; Is 38:18).

It was not until the time of the postcanonical Jewish literature, the writings which were developed between the close of the OT and the beginning of NT times, that clear distinctions were made between the final destinies of the righteous and the unrighteous. The idea of separate divisions within Sheol for the good and the evil was developed. It is unmistakable that there was in Jewish thought, as reflected throughout the OT, a belief in a future and continued existence beyond death, however shadowy and indefinite the concept.

The Greek word "Hades" in the NT is used very similarly to "Sheol" in the OT. It was, in fact, used by the translators of the Septuagint, the Greek version of the OT, for Sheol. It designated in general the place or state of the dead, the grave, or death itself. In some versions the word is not translated at all, but is transliterated simply as "Hades." The NT is not always very explicit about the meaning of Hades, other than what has just been described. Use of the word often does not reveal much about the specific condition of the dead. There are some passages, however, which indicate a distinct advance over the use of Sheol in the OT. Some NT passages definitely describe Hades as a place of evil and punishment of the wicked, and may appropriately be translated "hell" (Lk 16:23).

Some Bible scholars held on the basis of the Luke passage (16:19–31) that Hades consists of two compartments where the dead are kept, "the bosom of Abraham," or Paradise, where Lazarus resided, and the place of torment where the rich man suffered. This teaching seems derived more from a pagan Greek origin than from the Gospel of Luke. The contrast here seems to be a distinction between "the bosom of Abraham" and an altogether different place, antithetical and exclusive of the place where Lazarus was. It does not naturally seem to be speaking about two separated divisions both included in Hades, but about two altogether different locales and conditions separated by an impassable and fixed gulf. The intent of the passage is not to give topographical information about the realm of the dead, but to give a warning to those who are not prepared for life after death.

The Greek word "Gehenna" is used in a number of NT texts to designate the fiery place for punishment of sinners and is often translated "hell" or "the fires of hell" (Mt 5:22,29,30; 10:28; 18:9; 23:15,33; Mk 9:43,45,47; Jas 3:6). It is usually used in connection with the final judgment and often has the suggestion that the punishment spoken of is eternal. Gehenna is derived by transliteration from the Hebrew of the OT, "valley of Hinnom" or the "valley of the son of Hinnom," a ravine on the south side of Jerusalem. This valley was the center of idolatrous worship in which children were burned by fire as an offering to the heathen god Molech (2 Chr 28:3; 33:6). In the time of Josiah it became a place of abomination, polluted by dead men's bones and the filth of Jerusalem (2 Kgs 23:10–14) and by garbage and rubbish dumped there. A fire burned continuously in this valley. It thus became a symbol of the unending fires of hell where the lost are consumed in torment. It was a symbol of judgment to be imposed on the idolatrous and disobedient (Jer 7:31–34; 32:35).

Another Greek word used to designate hell or "the lower regions" is Tartarus (2 Pt 2:4), a classical word for the place of eternal punishment. The apostle Peter uses it for the fallen angels who were thrown into hell, "committed . . . to pits of nether gloom to be kept until the judgment."

As noted above, there are, in addition to these terms, the very explicit and vivid phrases that clearly teach the doctrine of hell, as developed at the beginning of this article. The biblical doctrine is determined much more by these decisive phrases than by the somewhat indecisive but frequently used terms "Sheol" and "Hades."

Justice of Eternal Punishment. It is difficult for us as sinners to understand the righteous judgment of a holy God who, on one hand, hates all evil, yet, on the other hand, loves the evildoers enough to sacrifice his only Son for their salvation from sin. Divine wrath is the necessary reaction of a holy God who hates all that is contrary to his righteous nature. When the only remedy for human sin is rejected and all appeals of a loving, seeking God for the reconciliation of rebellious sinners are refused, there is no other course of action which God himself can pursue but to leave the sinner to his self-chosen destiny. Punishment for sin is then the inevitable and inescapable response of holiness to that which is morally opposite, and it must continue as long as the sinful condition requiring it continues. There is no indication anywhere in Scripture that lost sinners in hell are capable of repentance and faith. If in this life they did not turn away from sin and receive Christ as Savior with all the favorable circumstances and opportunities afforded them on earth, it is unreasonable to think they will do so in the life to come when none of the encouragements to believe and to forsake sin are present. Punishment cannot come to an end until guilt and sin come to an end. When the sinner ultimately resists and rejects the work of the Holy Spirit whereby he is convicted of sin, there remains no more possibility of repentance or salvation. He has committed an eternal sin (Mk 3:29; Rv 22:11), which deserves eternal punishment. (Incidentally, the same word "eternal" is applied to the duration of the punishment in hell as is used for the duration of the bliss in heaven, Mt 25:46.)

The impossibility of faith and repentance in hell is seen also from the tragic reality of the depraved will, conditioned and determined by its repeated rebellion against God. Sin reproduces itself in the will, and character tends to become irrevocably fixed. God responds to endless sinning with the necessary counterpart of endless punishment.

If the question be raised, How can a loving God send men to an everlasting Hell? it must be replied that God does not choose this destiny for men; they freely choose it for themselves. God simply concurs in their self-chosen

The Gehenna Valley outside of Jerusalem, the location of the garbage dump with its fire that was never quenched (Mk 9:43,44,45,46,48).

way and reveals the full consequences of their evil choice. It must always be remembered that God is not only loving; he is also holy and righteous, and there must be some adequate reckoning with justice in the universe where a revolt against God has brought evil consequences of enormous proportions.

While the duration of punishment in hell is eternal for all who have chosen that destiny for themselves, there are degrees of punishment proportional to the degrees of guilt of each individual. Only God is able to determine what those degrees are, and he will assign the consequences with perfect justice according to the responsibility of each one. Evidence of such gradations in future punishment is found in Scripture (Mt 11:20–24; Lk 12:47,48; Rv 20:12,13; cf. Ez 16:48–61). An obvious comparison is made in these texts between the differing intensities of punishment that are involved in the contrasting privileges, knowledge, and opportunities.

From all that has been said it should be obvious that a variety of nonbiblical views must be ruled out, however attractively they may be presented by their advocates and however popular they may be from time to time. Among these views are the erroneous, but sometimes persuasive, doctrines of universalism, annihilationism, and second probation. It must always be remembered that the Bible is our rule of faith for the doctrine of hell, however difficult the doctrine may seem for natural reason or for human sentiment. Scripture leaves no doubt about the terrible nature and the eternal duration of hell. Rejection or neglect of this doctrine will have dire effects upon the true health and mission of the church.

RALPH E. POWELL

See DEATH; DEAD, ABODE OF THE; SHEOL; HADES; INTERMEDIATE STATE; GEHENNA; ABRAHAM'S BOSOM; WRATH OF GOD.

Bibliography. J.A. Beet, *The Last Things;* J.S. Bonnell, *Heaven and Hell;* H. Buis, *The Doctrine of Eternal Punishment;* W. Eichrodt, *Theology of the OT,* vol 2, pp 210–28.

Hellenism.

That unique blend of Greek cultural, philosophical and ethical ideals which after Alexander the Great had a profound effect on the development of culture throughout the Mediterranean world. While the antecedents of the movement occur long before, the Hellenistic Age is seen by most to have begun in 323 BC, with the death of Alexander, and to have continued until either 30 BC, when Rome conquered Egypt, or (more likely) AD 300+. Rome itself was culturally conquered by Hellenism.

Historical Development. The Antecedents. The Hellenistic spirit can be traced as far back

as the Archaic period (750–500 BC), which was a time of growing population and prosperity. The *polis* or city-state became the center of political and social life. As a result, the era became increasingly characterized by a strong individualism and realistic approach to life. This cultural factor must be seen in the light of the major development of that period, the growing specialization of war. The Greeks developed a new approach, that of the *hoplite* or infantrymen. Previously, warfare had been under the province of the aristocracy and was fought by individual champions. The Greeks introduced the idea of the finely molded unit and taught peasants how to fight. This made the art of warfare a Greek specialty, and their mercenaries were known throughout the ancient world.

Some city-states, such as Sparta, specialized in military matters while others, like Athens, moved in the direction of political reform, evolving a democratic form of government from the "tyrannies" of earlier times. The result was that Sparta ambitiously extended her influence, conquering and colonizing neighboring lands, while Athens seemed to be characterized by internal squabbles and atrophy. However, in the 5th century BC Athens had settled her problems and became a major force in the wars against the Persians. These were also the times of Greek alliances; the Peloponnesian league of the 6th century was followed by the Delian league of the 5th.

The Classical Period. These political developments provided the basis for the evolution of a vigorous, dynamic new spirit that was to characterize art, drama, and philosophy. Sculpture and painting were revitalized, and the stylized figures of the past were replaced by the realistic forms associated with the classical period. The Greek tragedy developed vigorously. Schools of philosophy flourished, notably Pythagoras', whose mathematical approach set the stage for the marriage of science and ideas so crucial to Greek philosophy; and Parmenides', who wedded physics to metaphysics. After a period of war between Athens and Sparta, Pericles transformed both architecture (by building the Parthenon in Athens) and government (by adding a new dimension to Athenian democracy, allowing even foreigners to participate). During this time, the Greeks developed the idea that was to transform their way of life: that human intellect or reason was the highest good and the path to happiness. From this nucleus arose the sciences, the arts, and the Hellenistic philosophies.

The Great Peloponnesian War (431–404 BC) accelerated the cultural changes. The political and economic tensions produced first the Sophists, who exalted rationalism and rhetoric, then Socrates and Thucydides, both of whom stressed a rigorous cross-examination of all truth-claims. The war ended with the defeat of Athens by Sparta, but during the next few decades Sparta began to decline from lack of good leadership, while Athens restored its democracy and built a Second Athenian League. Yet even this was only temporary, and the common Greek tendency to individualism and dissension soon led to its failure as well.

It remained for Philip of Macedonia to pick up the pieces. Through a series of wars he succeeded in finally uniting the Greek city-states. His untimely assassination left his son, Alexander, the task of spreading his kingdom throughout the then-known world.

Philosophy during this period became the handmaiden of politics. Plato was primarily a statesman-philosopher who never ceased in his search for a "philosopher-king" who could unite Greece. The death in 399 BC of his mentor, Socrates, turned Plato from active politics and he established his Academy, primarily a school of political philosophy which sought to use truth to reform the state. His most famous pupil, Aristotle, became the tutor of young Alexander and thereby achieved his master's dream. Platonic idealism and Aristotelian realism were to become the two poles of Greek thought for generations to come.

The Hellenistic Age. Alexander the Great was more than a military conqueror. He made Hellenistic culture the norm throughout his realm. He taught conquered people the Greek language and customs, and he built new Greek cities like Alexandria in Egypt (34 in all), which became bastions of Hellenism. His major accomplishment was not so much territorial as cultural; after him Hellenism controlled the Western world for centuries. It was Alexander who spearheaded the triumph of the Attic *koine* (common) dialect over the other Greek dialects, and this became the primary force in the Hellenization of the East. The *koine* dialect was to be the basis for the acceptance of Hellenism by subject peoples. The first period after his death would be characterized by the dissolution of Alexander's empire and an emerging balance of power between the forces of Ptolemy, who controlled Egypt and Palestine; Seleucus, who ruled Babylon and Asia Minor; and Antipater (followed by Antigonus), who reigned over Macedonia and the Hellespont.

In the East the next century was typified by intermittent skirmishes between the Ptolemies and Seleucids, with the result that Palestine became a buffer state between the two. An important difference is that the Ptolemies had a unified kingdom and so were not interested in change; under their rule Palestine

was autonomous both culturally and religiously. However, the Seleucids controlled many different groups and so tried to unite them by forcing Hellenization on them. This finally led to the successful revolt of the Jews under the Maccabees and the disintegration of both empires. In the West, Rome became progressively involved in Greek affairs and by 149 BC controlled the Greek lands politically, while they themselves were overtaken by Greek ideals culturally.

During this period there was a growing middle class, which was brought about partly because Alexander's conquests led to a vast dispersion of Greeks into the conquered lands. The redistribution of wealth this engendered was based upon a Greek education and an acceptance of Hellenistic ideals. The term "civilized" came to be identified with the Greek way of life. Education was controlled by the idea of sound rhetoric, so that style triumphed over truth. Greek drama turned to comedy, which stressed realism in human emotions, and Hellenistic art grew even more naturalistic than in the classical period.

Philosophy also developed, with at least three schools arising to dominate Greek thought for the next few centuries. Interestingly, all three centered on practical ethics rather than the classical quest for truth and knowledge. The Cynics, founded by Diogenes, stressed a total self-sufficiency which left the individual in a social vacuum but taught him how to deal with human misery. The two most influential schools were the Epicureans and the Stoics. Epicurus sought freedom from anxiety or fear and taught that peace of the soul could only be derived from a disciplined, moderate experience of pleasures. The result was a retreat from society into one's own selfhood. Stoicism, founded by Zeno and named after the *stoa* (porch) in Athens where he taught, was similar to cynicism in its emphasis on self-sufficiency, but it combined this with a stress on the brotherhood of man. Every person was to strive after virtue and live above the vicissitudes of life. This last philosophy had become the center of Hellenism by the time of Christ.

Hellenism and Judaism. Judaism was virtually the only culture that resisted the encroachment of Hellenism. Therefore the power of this movement can be seen in the degree to which it permeated Judaism.

The pull of Hellenism was always felt primarily by the upper class nobility, and it was strongest in Jewish communities of the dispersion. However, under the Seleucids the temple priesthood was pro-Hellenist, so this added a religious dimension to the economic pressure upon the wealthy. From the beginning Palestine was split into two factions, the urban nobility, who tried to make Jerusalem another *polis* or Hellenistic city-state by adding such things as gymnasia and Greek drama; and the agricultural, poor peasants who saw in Hellenism a threat to the very existence of the Mosaic system.

Jews had to learn *koine* Greek to make business transactions and participate in legal matters. Archaeology shows that almost all inscriptions in Palestine from the 3rd century BC were in Greek, and the translation of the Torah into Greek in the Septuagint shows the permeation of the language in the Jewish communities outside of Palestine (diasporate communities). The gymnasium was the school in Hellenistic cities, and Greek education was the key to citizenship. Alexandria (Egypt) in this regard became the intellectual center of the Greek world, and its influence on the strong Jewish community in that city was considerable. Well-to-do Jews in lands of the dispersion and in Jerusalem itself were expected to procure a gymnasium education. Many followed the Greek practice of participating naked in sports, as can be seen from the literature of the intertestamental period, which is strongly antagonistic a century later (due to Jewish aversion to such public display). Jewish synagogue schools, as a result of competition with the gymnasia, adopted Greek ways. In fact, the development of the scribal tradition is partly due to this interaction; the movement was away from the oligarchical system of the temple era and toward a democratic instruction of the whole people.

Jewish literature and philosophy became permeated by Hellenistic patterns. This is seen in 1 and 2 Maccabees, which reflect Greek historiography, and Hellenistic influence can be seen in virtually every Jewish work of this period. The major exponent, of course, was Philo of Alexandria, whose allegorical interpretation of the OT was designed to make Jewish teachings palatable to the Hellenistic world and vice versa. This attitude was quite common. The symbolism of Jewish apocalyptic was influenced by a combination of Hellenistic and oriental (primarily Persian) themes, and even the hyper-conservative Essene movement used thought-forms which had been molded via Judaism's penetration by Hellenistic and Persian ideas. The stress on "eternal knowledge" and "revealed mystery" and the dualistic combination of salvation history and anthropology are evidence of this. Of course, the influence was not all one way. The development of Greek philosophy was strongly influenced by Semitic forms, especially Phoenician; and the strong Jewish piety was very attractive to the Greek mind.

It is accurate to say that even the Judaism of Palestine in the 1st century BC was a Hellenistic Judaism. The universality of the *koine* Greek, the infiltration of Greek learning and thought-patterns, the presence of Jewish literature in Greek, and the permeation of Hellenistic rhetorical devices, even into the very literature of the opposition movement, shows the power of Hellenism in Palestine.

Hellenism and Christianity. Some scholars have attempted to stratify early Christianity into periods typified by Palestinian, Hellenistic-Jewish, and Hellenistic outlooks. However, as the evidence above has shown, this is by no means an easy task, since even Judea was penetrated by Greek thought-patterns. To be sure, the reactionary stance against Hellenism in Judaism is paralleled by the Hellenist-Hebrew conflict of Acts 6 and by the opposition of the Judaizers to Paul and the gentile mission. However, from the very earliest stages the influence of Hellenism on the church can be traced. Moreover, it becomes virtually impossible to know whether a phrase is drawn from Palestinian or from Hellenistic sources, due to the mutual penetration of both into diasporate communities as well as Palestine itself, and to the bilingual nature of the church from the beginning.

This does not mean that there were no differences at all. The Hellenistic background of Stephen allowed him to see the logical implications of Christ for the land and the temple (cf. Acts 6,7) while the more conservative Jerusalem church did not. Also, a study of the speeches in Acts shows that the kerygma (preaching) developed differently for Jewish and gentile audiences. The first centered on OT fulfillment and the second on the active penetration of history by the one true God, who unlike dead idols involved himself in the affairs of man.

The very fact that the NT was written in *koine* Greek makes the influence very direct. Strongly Jewish-oriented works, such as Hebrews or James, are written in polished Greek, and even the Gospels, which record the life of Jesus in a Jewish setting, reflect Hellenistic historiography (e.g., an interest in the theological meaning of the historical events). Most obviously Hellenistic, of course, are ideas found in the epistles stemming from the gentile mission. Early hymns like Colossians 1:15–20 use terminology from the Hellenistic environs to describe the incomparable superiority of Jesus over pagan ideals. The stress on the universal mission, while based on the teachings of Jesus, developed during the gentile mission; the primitive church interpreted it in keeping with Jewish proselyte theology, which was that the Gentiles became Christians after becoming Jews.

Further Developments. Two Hellenistic schools of thought evolved during the time of the early church, coming to full fruition only later. One was Gnosticism, which seemed to develop simultaneously from Babylonian mythology, Persian dualism, Egyptian mysticism, and Jewish Christian theology. In fact, Gnosticism has been called one of the earliest syncretistic movements. In the past it has been common to regard the movement as a Christian development, since the sources for most information about it were early church fathers writing against these "heresies." However, it is now more common to recognize the movement as a broader Hellenistic conception which arose out of the general intellectual and metaphysical milieu of the late 1st century AD. The stress on knowledge (*gnosis*) as the saving way of escape in the dualistic battle between good and evil, defined in terms of the spiritual versus the material, and the central place of the "savior" as the means of leading the soul into the higher realms of salvation are both Hellenistic in their essence. While many have seen these ideas in the NT, it seems more likely that the movement was just in its beginning stages and was not fully developed until the 2nd century. However, this "incipient" or "proto" Gnosticism is definitely opposed in later writings like Colossians, the pastoral Epistles, or 1 John.

The second aspect of Hellenistic thought is the mystery religions, which appeared early in the Hellenistic period, as in the Greek cults of Eleusis or Dionysus. These eastern cults became popular in the West only after the spread of Christianity. These popular movements, for example, the Isis (Egyptian) and Mithraic (Persian) cults, were primarily oriental and exotic, appealing to the Greek sense of myth and ritual. They primarily taught that every person had a divine essence trapped inside the flesh which could be released only through solemn initiatory rites and communion with the deity around which the particular cult revolved. While the details of the rites differed, the meaning and significance was much the same. Salvation was found by participation in the mystery rites of the cults, which for the most part resembled ancient fertility rites centering on the renewal of vegetation in the spring. The popularity of these groups shows the highly syncretistic nature of Hellenism, which adapted itself to new ideas and worked them into the Greek way of life.

GRANT R. OSBORNE

See HELLENISTIC JUDAISM; STOICS, STOICISM; EPICUREANS; JUDAISM; GREECE, GREEKS; GNOSTICISM.

Hellenistic Judaism.
Branch of Judaism which maintained the Jewish way of worship but accepted Greek cultural and linguistic peculiarities. It originated from four factors: (1) the forced dispersion of the Jews into Greek-speaking lands under the Assyrians (2 Kgs 17,18) and Babylonians (2 Kgs 24,25). Other forced deportations took place under Ptolemy I (to Egypt, 300 BC) and Pompey (to Rome, 63 BC); (2) unsettled conditions in Palestine, especially in the latter stages of the Hasmonean period, which led many Jews to prefer an uncertain future in foreign lands to the assured deprivations at home, with wars, persecutions, and hard taxation; (3) economic opportunities abroad, which led Jews to take advantage of agricultural and commercial opportunities in nearly every country of the known ancient world; and (4) the growing proselyte movement, which reached its peak at the time of Christ (Mt 23:15).

Estimations of population density in the Roman Empire vary, but most scholars favor 10 million. This means that one of every 20 people in the empire was Jewish! The areas of greatest density were Rome, Egypt, and Parthia, but the economic strength was negligible. While some rose to positions of power (e.g., Daniel or Nehemiah), the majority were farmers or belonged to the lower middle class. While they were not paupers, they were neither wealthy nor influential.

Hellenistic Judaism in Palestine. The historical origins of Hellenism and its impact on main-line Judaism are not only chronicled in the dispersion movements of the people but are also to be found in the strong influence of Hellenism in Palestine itself. After the Greek takeover of Palestine (332 BC) the power turned from the priests to the scribes, and the religious emphasis thereby shifted from cultus to Torah. This introduced the dialogue method of interpretation into Jewish life, and inevitably Greek logic entered the picture. Originally, the subtle encroachment of Hellenistic ideals took the form of cultural borrowing, that is, the Jews copied their more sophisticated cultural (but not religious!) practices. Problems began when cities and especially the upper classes (called "Hellenes") began to emulate Greek practices in political as well as cultural areas. The gymnasiums became popular, a thing abhorrent to the orthodox Jew who hated nakedness and display. Theater and drama were also considered depraved.

These caused bitter debates among Palestinian Jews, many of whom refused to separate the cultural from the religious. The situation came to a head when the Ptolemies, who wished to purge strong nationalistic ties, elected pro-Hellenists to the high priestly office. Onias III, Jason, and Menalaeus (175–163 BC) built gymnasiums, encouraged Greek dress, and forced "reform" upon Palestine. This led first to rebellion, then to the "abomination," the desecration of the temple, by Antiochus Epiphanes, and finally to the successful revolt by Matthias and his sons that eventually freed Palestine from Greek rule. For a time the strong surge of puritanism controlled the land, but even here the Hellenistic thought patterns were so ingrained that they could not be eradicated (for the most part, the people did not even realize this, for they were imbedded in external practices).

However, later in the period of the Maccabees and Hasmoneans the strong influence of Hellenism was again felt. When that period came to an end and the Herodian dynasty was inaugurated, the forces of change intensified. To solidify the break with the Hasmonean past, Herod brought in diasporate Jews from Egypt and elsewhere to take over the high priesthood, a situation that continued into the time of Christ. For all these reasons Hellenistic Judaism had a strong influence within the borders of Palestine itself.

Relations Between the Diaspora and Palestinian Judaism. Historically, the unity between the Hellenistic Jews of the diaspora and those in the homeland varied, depending on the political situation and the orthodoxy of the Jews in the particular area. There are records of communities which combined the worship of Yahweh with the Greek pantheon, but for the most part these were isolated and had no influence on Hellenistic Judaism. Diasporate Jews followed the Torah publicly as well as privately.

As noted, Hellenistic Jews accepted the Greek culture but at the same time regarded themselves as aliens and believed that Palestine was their true homeland. They identified strongly with the traumas of their fellow Jews, and their literature contains a strong expectation of deliverance for their homeland from the foreign oppressors. The Promised Land and temple worship were the centers of their religious longing, and they did not consider themselves significantly different from the Palestinian Jews. Five factors especially contributed to the unity:

1. The presence of the temple in Jerusalem bound them to Palestine. They believed that God was present in the Holy of Holies, and so God could only be worshiped there. While there was the Temple of Onias at Heliopolis in Egypt, it was only built for the military force there and had no influence even among the Jews of Egypt. Diasporate worship centered in the synagogue; but sacrifices, the core of Jewish cultic life, could only be offered in the temple. Of course, the legal regulations were softened for Jews of the Diaspora, who could

hardly make it to Jerusalem for each festival. Nevertheless, many often tried to send a sacrifice when they could not take it themselves.

2. The temple tax united the Jews. While Jews outside Israel did not have to support the land of Palestine, the half-shekel temple tax, which went for the public sacrifices, was an obligation upon all Jews. From written records of the large amounts gathered in various communities, it was faithfully met. In fact, when the amount greatly exceeded the needs, the excess was applied to the maintenance of Jerusalem, which was thought to be part of the temple area. The feeling of unity engendered by this is seen in the temple prayers, which included the "exile Jews" in other lands.

3. The pilgrimages to the three major feasts (Passover, Pentecost, Tabernacles) tied Hellenistic Jews to Israel. Exodus 23:17, 34:23, and Deuteronomy 16:16 commanded every Jewish male to "appear before the Lord" at these three feasts. Of course, it was impractical, even within the confines of Palestine, and so the requirement was not rigidly enforced; but Jews from every land streamed to the feasts each year, as may be seen in the famous Pentecost passage (Acts 2:9–11). Often young Jews would remain in Jerusalem for a time to study the Torah under a famous rabbi, as did Saul of Tarsus (later the apostle Paul) under Gamaliel.

4. Many diasporate families actually settled down in Jerusalem. Acts 2:5 says, "Now there were dwelling in Jerusalem Jews, devout men from every nation under heaven." Acts 6:9 speaks of synagogues "of the Freedmen ... and of the Cyrenians, and of the Alexandrians. . . ." In fact, while it was impractical for all Hellenistic Jews to return to their homeland, it was the desire of every devout diasporate Jew to do so.

5. Another unifying influence was the envoys or traveling rabbis who acted as emissaries from the homeland to the Hellenistic Jews of the diaspora. These were often the most famous scholars of the period, such as Gamaliel or Akiba. These men, called sages, traveled in pairs and functioned in every way like local rabbis—preaching, teaching, settling legal disputes, or collecting contributions. Their influence was enormous, and they more than any other force solidifed the authority of the Sanhedrin in Jerusalem over the Jewish communities in other lands.

Religious Practices. Jews of the dispersion were generally quite orthodox. It was Hellenistic Jews who instigated the trial against Stephen (Acts 6:9–15) and who started the riot against Paul for allegedly bringing Greeks into the temple (Acts 21:27–36). While their cul-

The synagogue at Herodium.

tural practices followed Hellenistic customs, their religious life was Jewish to the core. The center, of course, was the synagogue. The great synagogue at Alexandria was reputedly so large that flags had to be waved to tell the congregation when to say the Amen. A typical service is described in Acts 13:15, with prayers, readings from the Law and the prophets, respectively, then an address. The service was designed for the public rather than for specialists like the priests (unlike temple worship), and laymen were asked to deliver the readings or the address (as was the case with Jesus and Paul). The most important difference within Hellenistic Judaism was the use of Greek in the worship service rather than Hebrew or the Aramaic Targums. As a result, it had an important social role in the community. In fact the head of the synagogue functioned with the elders as the "ruler" of the community (there being no distinction between religious and civic matters), especially in lands which allowed the Jewish community to govern its own internal affairs (common Roman practice). His assistant, the "attendant" of Luke 4:20, not only managed the practical affairs of the synagogue but also functioned as town "manager."

The synagogue, because of its unique function, came to be used for many purposes within Hellenistic Judaism. Civic business was conducted there, and in most communities it also functioned as the school. In addition, the public tribunals met in the synagogues. There are scriptural examples of public floggings given there (Mt 10:17; Acts 22:19), and Acts 9:1,2 tells of Paul procuring letters to the diasporate synagogues so that the tribunals there would allow Paul to extradite Christians to Jerusalem.

Education naturally centered around the study of the Torah, which was not just the prerogative of priests and rabbis but was a community responsibility. Here there was little difference between the diaspora and Judea except for the refusal to teach or use Greek in the schools of the homeland. The child began studying the written Scriptures at the age of five or six and then added the oral law at the age of ten. At 12 or 13 he finished school and after bar mitzvah entered the adult world. Adults would continue studying Torah, but mainly would confine themselves to the oral law.

Another area peculiar to the diasporate communities was the training of proselytes and God-fearers; the difference between the two groups was often that the latter had not undergone circumcision and so could not be considered a legal part of the covenant people. A perusal of the Book of Acts shows that the God-fearers provided the nucleus of the converts in most of the cities Paul evangelized. Gentiles were particularly susceptible to Judaism and Christianity due to the deterioration of faith in the pagan religions. The religious conviction and moral strength of both had great appeal. So the Hellenistic synagogues became missionary centers.

Finally, we might mention here the development of the guilds. As was common in the ancient world, the various guilds (e.g., the tentmakers or weavers) became mini-communities. We know that in the synagogue of Alexandria, each guild sat in a different section, and this may well have been the universal practice.

Differences with Palestinian Jews. As already intimated, the distinctions should not be overstated, for Hellenistic Judaism was far more Jewish than Hellenistic, and Hellenistic influence can certainly be demonstrated in Palestine itself. The major differences are seen in the daily life, business practices, and the mind-set of diasporate Judaism. Naturally, after the first generation there was a tendency to accept the external way of life of the nation within which they lived, so long as it did not interfere with their religious convictions. For example, some Jews would favor the games or plays, the artistic tastes and ways of expression observed in the lives of their neighbors. In Alexandria, some even sought a Greek education, a necessary prelude to citizenship. However, the majority of Hellenistic Jews probably refused to succumb even this far and remained in their isolated communities. The aristocracy naturally was more inclined to Hellenization. The average diasporate Jew had contact with Greek-speaking neighbors only on the commercial plane. At the same time, however, Hellenistic Judaism was forced out of its cocoon by a widespread anti-Jewish movement about the time of Christ. Jews in Palestine remained aloof from an active propagandizing of pagans; for example, there was very little polemic against idolatry in Judaea. They connected the disappearance of idolatry with the appearance of the kingdom of God and refused to get involved in an active way against pagan ways. In the diaspora conditions were different; Jews were forced to defend their ways and then to develop an active polemic.

This propaganda was couched in terms of Greek philosophy and led to a vigorous output of Hellenistic Jewish literature. The Septuagint was probably produced, not only to provide a Bible for Greek-speaking Judaism, but also to show that Judaism and Greek thought were not mutually exclusive. The writings of Philo went even further, attempting to couch Jewish theology in Hellenistic thought-forms. Scholars list four types of literature: (1) Historical works (e.g., Josephus) that sought to show the meaning of Jewish history in contrast to pagan; (2) theological and philosophical writings that presented Jewish beliefs in Greek forms (e.g., Wisdom of Solomon); (3) Jewish poetry that employed Greek stylistic traits; (4) apologetic works that answered pagan charges and then went on to ridicule pagan ways. However, it is important to modify this by noting that it was the intelligentsia rather than *hoi polloi* (the people) who produced these works. The common Jews remained isolated from much of this, even in diasporate communities.

GRANT R. OSBORNE

See HELLENISM; JUDAISM; PHILO JUDAEUS; ALEXANDRIA.

Bibliography. W. Foerster, *Palestinian Judaism in NT Times;* M. Hadas, *Hellinistic Culture: Fusion and Diffusion;* M. Hengel, *Jews, Greeks, and Barbarians;* M. Hengel, *Judaism and Hellenism,* 2 vols; M. Stone, *Scriptures, Sects, and Visions;* V. Tcherikover, *Hellenistic Civilization and the Jews.*

Hellenists. Name used in Acts 6:1; 9:29; and possibly 11:20 for a distinct branch of the early church that was characterized by Greek modes of thinking. Their actual identification is disputed, and the following possibilities have been propounded: (1) Greek-speaking Jews rather than Aramaic-speaking Jews (but "Hebrews" as in 6:1 was seldom used in a linguistic sense); (2) proselytes or "Greeks" as opposed to true Jews (the list of deacons in 6:5 makes this doubtful, for it is unlikely that they were all proselytes); (3) diasporate Jews living in Palestine (fits 6:1–6 but not the other passages); (4) pro-Hellenist sect within Judaism (this does not fit the whole tenor of the passages); (5) Gentiles who joined the church at an early date (this does not really fit the context of all three passages); (6) a general not specific term and simply referring to one who either speaks Greek or follows Greek customs (or both). This is the best answer, as a study of the contexts will illustrate.

In 6:1 the group was probably made up of Hellenistic Jews then living in Palestine. This is seen in the deacons chosen in 6:5 (Luke used Greek names for all of them, probably not because they were Greek but to symbolize the desire of the apostles to unify the separate groups; most Jews in the ancient world had three names—a Jewish, a Greek, and a Roman name—and used one or the other depending on the occasion) but especially in the synagogues mentioned in 6:9. Hellenistic Jews differed sufficiently in their background and worship habits (especially in the use of Greek in the service) that there would be separate synagogues for them (there were seven such in Jerusalem alone). This created a potentially divisive situation for the early church, and the schism here was the result. The "Hebrews" would naturally tend to allocate the common pool to those they knew, and so the very separation between the groups would add to the problem.

In 9:29 the "Hellenists" are members of the same group. Paul, a diasporate Jew himself, would naturally go to his old compatriots on his first visit to Jerusalem after his conversion. In 11:20 the manuscript evidence is equally divided between "Hellenists" and "Greeks."

As "Hellenist" is used in 11:20, it designates the Greek-speaking populace of Antioch, therefore Gentiles in general. This is different from the usages in 6:1 and 9:29.

GRANT R. OSBORNE

See HELLENISTIC JUDAISM; JUDAISM; ACTS OF THE APOSTLES, BOOK OF THE.

Helmet. *See* ARMS AND WARFARE.

Helon. Father of Eliab, prince of Zebulun's tribe at the taking of the first census (Nm 1:9; 2:7; 7:24,29; 10:16).

Helps, Gift of. *See* SPIRITUAL GIFTS.

Hemam. KJV spelling of Heman, Lotan's son, in Genesis 36:22.

See HEMAN #1.

Heman. 1. Lotan's son, the brother of Hori and a descendant of Seir the Horite (Gn 36:22, KJV Hemam); alternately spelled Homam in 1 Chronicles 1:39, reflecting a later scribal error.

2. Mahol's son, descendant of Zerah from Judah's tribe and one of the sages whose wisdom was surpassed by King Solomon's (1 Kgs 4:31; 1 Chr 2:6). He is perhaps the Ezrahite and author of Psalm 88.

3. Kohathite Levite, Joel's son and one appointed, along with Asaph and Ethan (also

called Jeduthun), by David to lead the musicians in the sanctuary (1 Chr 6:33; 15:17; 16:41). During the transport of the ark from Obed-edom's house to Jerusalem, he was responsible for sounding the bronze cymbals (1 Chr 15:19; 2 Chr 5:12). Heman fathered 14 sons and 3 daughters, all of whom served as musicians in the Lord's house (1 Chr 25:1–6); later, his descendants participated in the cleansing of the temple during King Hezekiah's reign (715–686 BC; 2 Chr 29:14) and assisted with the Passover celebration initiated by King Josiah (640–609 BC; 2 Chr 35:15).

Hemath. KJV form of Hammath, the Rechabite, in 1 Chronicles 2:55.

See HAMMATH (PERSON).

Hemath, Entering of. *See* HAMATH, ENTRANCE OF.

Hemdan. Dishon's son and a descendant of Seir the Horite (Gn 36:26). He is also called Hamran in 1 Chronicles 1:41 (KJV Amram).

Hemlock. KJV mistranslation for poisonous weeds and for wormwood in Hosea 10:4 and Amos 6:12, respectively.

See PLANTS (WORMWOOD).

Hemorrhage. Issue of blood, coming from any cut or nosebleed (Prv 30:33). However, in Scripture it almost always refers to vaginal bleeding. Laws concerning normal and abnormal menstruation are given in Leviticus 15:19–30. A woman with normal menstruation was considered unclean for seven days, along with anything that came into contact with her (vv 19–24). A woman who bled longer than seven days was unclean as long as she was bleeding seven additional days (vv 25–28).

All the Gospels except John give an account of the miraculous healing by Jesus of the woman who had a hemorrhage for 12 years (Mt 9:20–22; Mk 5:25–34; Lk 8:43–48). By touching Jesus' garment, the woman was actually violating the OT laws concerning menstruation and making Jesus' garment unclean (Lv 15). Jesus knew that she was made whole through her courageous act of faith in him, but he wanted her to testify before the crowd as to what had happened.

See MEDICINE AND MEDICAL PRACTICE.

Hen. *See* BIRDS (FOWL, DOMESTIC).

Hen (Person). KJV alternate name for Josiah, Zephaniah's son, in Zechariah 6:14.

See JOSIAH #2.

Hena. One of the six cities that Rabshakeh boasted fell before the armies of Sennacherib, in spite of their gods (2 Kgs 18:34). Rabshakeh hoped the example of these cities would strike fear in King Hezekiah's heart and make him doubt the Lord's deliverance as the same hordes surrounded Jerusalem. The kings of the five other cities are mentioned along with Hena again in 2 Kings 19:13 and Isaiah 37:13.

Henadad. Head of a Levite family that participated in the rebuilding of the temple (Ezr 3:9). Members of this family also helped to build the Jerusalem wall (Neh 3:18,24), and signed Ezra's covenant of faithfulness to God together with Nehemiah (10:9).

Henna. Fragrant, flowering shrub mentioned in Song of Solomon 1:14 and 4:13.

See FASHION AND DRESS; PLANTS.

Henoch. 1. KJV form of Enoch, Jared's son, in 1 Chronicles 1:3.

See ENOCH (PERSON) #2.

2. KJV form of Hanoch, Midian's son, in 1 Chronicles 1:33.

See HANOCH #1.

Hepher (Person). 1. Manassite and founder of the Hepherite family (Nm 26:32).

2. Ashhur's son from Judah's tribe (1 Chr 4:6).

3. One of David's valiant warriors (1 Chr 11:36).

Hepher (Place). Canaanite city located southwest of Jerusalem. It was captured by Joshua (Jos 12:17) and later used as an administrative district under Solomon (1 Kgs 4:10).

Hepherite. Descendant of Hepher from Manasseh's tribe (Nm 26:32).

See HEPHER (PERSON) #1.

Hephzibah. 1. Mother of Manasseh, king of Judah (2 Kgs 21:1).

2. Symbolic name (KJV) for the restored city of Jerusalem, meaning "my delight is in her" (Is 62:4).

Herb. *See* PLANTS (GRASS).

Herdsman. *See* TRADES AND OCCUPATIONS.

Heres. 1. Region from which the Amorites were not expelled by the Israelites, known as Mt Heres (Jgs 1:34,35, RSV Har-heres). In Joshua 19:41,42 Mt Heres is synonymous with the town of Ir-shemesh (Beth-shemesh).

2. Ascent of Heres (Jgs 8:13 RSV; KJV before

the sun was up). Though the text and the exact nature of the terrain is unclear, it was the place on the Jordan River from which Gideon returned after his victory over Zebah and Zalmunna.

Heresh. Levite who returned to Jerusalem following the exile (1 Chr 9:15).

Hereth. Section of forested land in the territory of Judah where David and his men hid for a time as they fled from King Saul (1 Sm 22:5, KJV Hareth).

Hermas. Christian to whom Paul sent greetings in his letter to the Romans (16:14).

Hermeneutics. Practice of interpreting Scripture.

See BIBLE, INTERPRETATION OF THE.

Hermes. 1. Greek god and the son of Zeus by Maia. He was identified with Mercury in the Roman pantheon of deities. In Greek mythology, Hermes was the messenger of the gods and the escort of the dead to Hades. He was the god of fertility, the patron of music, the guardian of travelers, and the god of eloquent speech.

While ministering at Lystra, Paul was acclaimed by its people to be Hermes because of his miraculous work and role as chief speaker. The Lystrans thought Paul was a god visiting them in bodily form (Acts 14:11,12, KJV Mercurius).

2. Christian to whom Paul sent greetings in his letter to Rome (16:14).

Hermogenes. Prominent Asian believer who "turned away" from Paul (2 Tm 1:15). His actions may have been the result of doctrinal disagreement, but more likely involved his unwillingness to come to Paul's defense during the apostle's second Roman imprisonment for fear of suffering the same fate himself.

Hermon, Mount. Mountain often mentioned as the northern extremity of the territory conquered by Joshua and Moses in Transjordan; it is also the northern boundary of the inheritance of the half-tribe of Manasseh as well as of Israel in general (Dt 3:8; 4:48; Jos 11:17; 12:1,5; 13:11; Jgs 3:3; 1 Chr 5:23). Hermon is said to tower over the Valley of Lebanon (Jos 11:17; 13:5) and over the land of Mizpah in the valley of Mizpah to whence Joshua pursued the kings of Canaan after his victory over them at the waters of Merom (Jos 11:3,8). Biblical poetry praises Hermon for its height and for causing the dew on Zion (Ps 133:3),

The southern slope of Mt Hermon.

and it was famed for its wildlife (Sg 4:8). It also appears in tandem with Mt Tabor (Ps 89:12) and with the Jordan (Ps 42:6; KJV Hermonite); the plural in the latter passage expresses majesty and not a multiplicity of peaks.

Though Hermon does not appear in epigraphic sources from the biblical period, it has other names in the Bible that do play a role in the extrabiblical records. According to Deuteronomy 3:9, "the Sidonians call Hermon Sirion, while the Amorites call it Senir" (KJV, Shenir). Scholars have suggested that Sirion is mentioned in the Execration Texts from Egypt (19th century BC), but this is uncertain. Sirion and Lebanon appear in Ugaritic poetry as the sources for choice woods. Similar parallelisms between Lebanon and Sirion or Senir occur in the Bible (Ps 29:6 Ez 27:5). Shalmaneser III called it "Saniru, a mountain facing the Lebanon" (841 BC). Deuteronomy 4:48 (mg) gives Sion as another name for Hermon; the Greek version supports this reading but the Syriac has Sirion.

It would appear that Senir/Sirion is the name for the Ante-Lebanon range while Hermon is the name of the highest peak, today called Jebel esh-Sheikh, "the Mountain of the Elder," because of its snowy white mane. This identification is related to that of Baal-hermon (Jgs 3:3; 1 Chr 5:23) and Baal-gad (Jos 11:17; 12:7; 13:5). These places are also border points for Manasseh and are either identical or else represent two cult centers on the lower slopes of the mountain.

The mountain itself is about 13 miles long and rises to a height of 9166 feet.

ANSON F. RAINEY

Hermonite. KJV mistranslation for Hermon (Mount) in Psalm 42:6. Mt Hermon, a sacred site since antiquity, lies on the northernmost boundary of Joshua's conquest (Jos 12:5; 13:11).

See HERMON, MOUNT.

The Herodian Genealogy

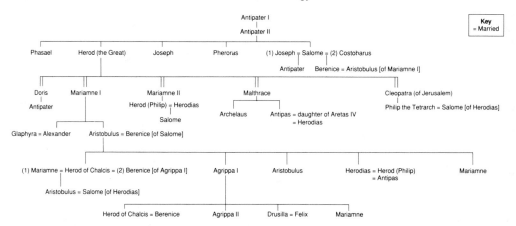

Herod, Herodian Family. Political rulers during the lifetime of Christ. Christ was born when Herod the Great was ruling. Herod's son, Herod Antipas, was the ruler of Galilee and Perea, the territories in which Jesus and John the Baptist carried out most of their ministries. It was this ruler who beheaded John the Baptist and tried Christ just before his death. Herod Agrippa I is persecutor of the church in Acts 12, and Herod Agrippa II heard Paul's testimony (Acts 26) just before he went to Rome to be tried by the caesar. Without a knowledge of the Herodian family one can hardly have a proper understanding of the times of Christ.

The Herodian Dynasty (67–47 BC). The Herodian dynasty became prominent during the confusion that resulted in the decay of the Hasmonean dynasty, the transference of Syria and Palestine to Roman rule, and the civil wars that marked the decay of the nation.

The first member of this dynasty was Antipater, who was appointed governor of Idumaea. He came into prominence after the death of Alexandra, the Maccabean queen. Her eldest son, Hyrcanus II, assumed power in 67 BC. He was set aside by his younger brother, Aristobulus, after only three months. Antipater, with the help of the Roman general Pompey, restored Hyrcanus II to power, rallying the people to support him as their ruler. However, Antipater secretly considered him an unsuitable leader to rule Judea. Consequently, while continuing his loyalty to Hyrcanus he was definitely the power behind the throne, appointing his son Phasael as governor of Jerusalem and his second son Herod as governor of Galilee (Josephus, *Antiq.* 14.9.1–2 §§156–58; and *War* 1.10.4 §§201–3).

Herod the Great (47–4 BC). As Governor of Galilee (47–37 BC). Herod the Great became governor of Galilee at 25 years of age. Although he gained the respect of both the Romans and the Galilean Jews for quickly capturing and executing the bandit leader Ezekias, some in Hyrcanus' court thought that he was becoming too powerful and arranged to have him brought to trial. He was acquitted and released and thereafter fled to Sextus Caesar at Damascus. Sextus Caesar, governor of Syria, appointed Herod governor of Coele-Syria, and thus he became involved with Roman affairs in Syria. He remained in this position under a series of rulers and was successful in collecting taxes and suppressing various revolts. Thus, in 41 BC when Antony came to power under Octavius Caesar, after asking the advice of Hyrcanus II, he appointed Herod and Phasael as tetrarchs of Judea (*Antiq.* 14.13.1 §§324–26; *War* 1.12.5 §§243–44).

The new tetrarchs of Judea enjoyed their office for only a brief period. The next year (40 BC) the Parthians appeared in Syria. Pacorus, a Parthian prince, joined with Antigonus (son of Aristobulus and nephew of Hyrcanus) in the effort to place the latter on the throne held by Hyrcanus. This began a complicated series of incidents which resulted in Jerusalem's being besieged by the invaders (*War* 1.13.2 §§327–29; cf. also 12.3 §240; *Antiq.* 14.13.3 §335). A civil war was inevitable with daily skirmishes occurring between the two forces. The Parthians gained the upper hand and captured Phasael and Hyrcanus. To prevent Hyrcanus from being restored to the priesthood he was mutilated which disqualified him. Phasael died either by suicide, poisoning, or in battle. (*Antiq.* 14.13.10 §§365–69; *War* 1.13.10–11 §§271–73). Herod, with his family and troops, fled to Masada, and finally moved to Petra, the capital of the Nabatean kingdom (*Antiq.* 14.13.7–9 §§352–64; *War* 1.13.6–7 §§261–64). Malchus, the Arabian king from whom Herod had expected help, ordered him to leave. Herod departed to Egypt and then to Rome, where he was welcomed by Antony and Octavius. After hearing Herod's story, they, with the senate's confirmation, designated him king of Judea (*Antiq.* 14.14.6 §§381–85; *War* 1.14.4 §§282–85; cf. also Strabo 16.2.46; Appian, *Civil Wars* 5.75; Tacitus, *Hist.* 5.9). From Italy he sailed back to Ptolemais in late 40 BC or early 39 BC, marched through Galilee, captured Joppa, and finally moved to Masada, where his relatives were under attack (*Antiq.* 14.15.1 §§394–98; *War* 1.15.3–4 §§290–94). With the help of the Roman armies, Herod then proceeded to encamp on the west side of Jerusalem. He proclaimed that he was rightful king and promised to forget all past offenses against himself. Antigonus made counter-proclamations, announcing that Herod was a commoner and an Idumean, that is, a half-Jew, and thus not a legitimate heir to the throne.

In 38 BC after putting down guerrilla bands in Galilee, Herod went to Samosata where Antony was besieging Antiochus, king of Commagene, who had sided with the Parthians. Herod hoped that his timely assistance to Antony, who had been unsuccessful with the siege, would move the general to help him in return. Antony was pleased with Herod's unsolicited loyalty, and after the defeat of Samosata he ordered his legate Sossius to use the Roman army to support Herod against the Parthians. Thus in the summer of 37 BC Jerusalem fell, and Antigonus was captured by Sossius (*Antiq.* 14.16.2 §§470–80; *War* 1.18.2 §§349–52; Tacitus, *Hist.* 5.9; Dio Cassius 49.22). During the course of this siege Herod took time to journey to Samaria to marry Mariamne, to whom he had been betrothed for about five years. This was a contemptuous move against Antigonus, Mariamne's uncle. Since she was a Hasmonean it strengthened Herod's claim to the throne.

It is recorded that Antigonus fell beneath the axe (*War* 1.18.3 §357; Plutarch, *Antony* 36; cf. also Dio Cassius 49.22). This ended the Hasmonean rule of 129 years.

As King (37–4 BC). The reign of Herod is divided by most scholars into three periods: (1) consolidation from 37 to 25 BC; (2) prosperity from 25 to 12 BC; and (3) the period of domestic troubles from 14 to 4 BC.

The period of consolidation extended from his accession as king in 37 BC to the death of the sons of Babas, the last male representatives of the Hasmonean family. During this period he had to contend with many powerful adversaries—the people and the Pharisees, the ruling class, the Hasmonean family, and Cleopatra.

The first adversaries, the people and the Pharisees, objected to his being an Idumean, a half-Jew, and a friend of the Romans. Those who opposed him were punished, and those who took his side were rewarded with favors and honors (*Antiq.* 15.1.1 §§2–3; *War* 1.18.4 §358).

The second adversaries were those of the aristocracy who sided with Antigonus. Herod had executed 45 of the wealthiest and had confiscated their properties thus replenishing his own coffers.

The third group of adversaries were the Hasmonean family. Herod's chief problem was his mother-in-law, Alexandra. She was upset that he had not appointed another Hasmonean to the high priesthood to replace Hyrcanus, specifically her son Aristobulus. She wrote to Cleopatra asking her to influence Antony to force Herod to remove the appointed high priest, Ananel, and replace him with Aristobulus. Finally, Herod gave way to the pressure, even though it was unlawful to set aside a high priest once he had been appointed. This brought about a temporary truce between Herod and Alexandra. Herod, however, never really trusted either her or Aristobulus. Much hostility developed between the three. In the end, after a celebration of the feast of tabernacles, Herod had Aristobulus drowned, making it look like an accident. Alexandra never believed the official report of accidental drowning, and she reported to Cleopatra that Herod had murdered her son. Antony summoned Herod to give an account for his actions, but through eloquence and bribery Herod persuaded Antony to free him of any charges. Herod put Alexandra in chains and placed her under guard to keep her from causing him more trouble (*Antiq.* 15.3.3–9 §§50–87; *War* 1.22.2–5 §§437–44).

Herod's fourth adversary was Cleopatra. First, she had cooperated with Alexandra in the matter of Aristobulus. Next, she asked Antony to increase her territory, which he did by including the district of Jericho, the most fertile area of Herod's kingdom (*Antiq.* 15.4.1–2 §§88–96; *War* 1.18.4–5 §§360–63). When civil war broke out between Antony and Octavius, Herod wanted to help Antony. But Cleopatra persuaded Antony to set Herod in battle against the Arabian king Malchus who had failed to pay tribute to her. When she saw Herod winning she ordered her troops to help Malchus, hoping to weaken both parties to the breaking point so that she could absorb them both. After a catastrophic earthquake in his domain in 31 BC Herod defeated the Arabs and returned home (*Antiq.* 15.5.1–5 §§108–60; *War* 1.19.3–6 §§369–85).

Soon after, on September 2, 31 BC, Octavius

defeated Antony in the Battle of Actium, resulting in the suicide of Antony and Cleopatra.

Immediately Herod felt it was necessary to ingratiate himself with Octavius and persuade him that he, Herod, was the rightful ruler of Judea. He first eliminated Hyrcanus II, his only possible rival, by making false charges against him and then executing him (*Antiq.* 15.6–14 §§161–82; *War* 1.20.1 §386). He then set out for Rhodes and skillfully persuaded Octavius that Herod's loyalty would be beneficial. Shortly after, Octavius returned Jericho to Herod's territory and also gave him Gadara, Hippos, Samaria, Gaza, Anthedon, Joppa, and Straton's Tower (later Caesarea). Octavius also made Herod king (*Antiq.* 15.6.5–7.3 §§183–217; *War* 1.20.1–3 §§387–97). During this time Herod continued to have domestic problems. Convinced that Mariamne had been unfaithful to him while he was in Rhodes, he had her executed at the end of 29 BC (*Antiq.* 15.7.1–5 §§202–36). He became very ill as a result of this, and when recovery seemed doubtful, Alexandra took the opportunity to win the loyalty of those in charge of the two fortified places in Jerusalem. When Herod recovered and learned of this, he had Alexandra executed in 28 BC. Herod's sister Salome, wanting to get rid of her husband Costobarus, revealed to Herod that Costobarus had concealed and protected the influential sons of Babas who were loyal to Antigonus and who spoke ill of Herod. Herod executed Costobarus and the sons of Babas (25 BC). This act eliminated the possibility of any of Hyrcanus' line becoming king (*Antiq.* 15.7.6–10 §§237–66).

The second period of Herod's reign was one of prosperity (25–14 BC). It was a period of splendor and enjoyment interrupted by an occasional disturbance.

According to Josephus the most noble of all Herod's achievements was the building of the temple in Jerusalem, begun in 20/19 BC (*Antiq.* 15.8.1 §380). Rabbinic literature claims: "He who has not seen the Temple of Herod has never seen a beautiful building" (Babylonian Talmud: Baba Bathra 4a). Prior to this he had built theaters, amphitheaters, and race courses for both men and horses (*Antiq.* 15.8.1 §§267–76). In 24 BC Herod built himself a royal palace and built or rebuilt many fortresses and gentile temples, including Strato's Tower, later renamed Caesarea (*Antiq.* 15.8.5–9 §§292–341).

During this time he became very interested in culture and gathered around him men accomplished in Greek literature and art. Greek rhetoricians were appointed to the highest offices of the state. One of these was Nicolas of Damascus, Herod's instructor and advisor in philosophy, rhetoric, and history.

In late 24 BC he married Mariamne, daugh-

Part of the palace of Herod the Great in Jericho.

ter of Simon, a well-known priest in Jerusalem (she will be referred to as Mariamne II). In 22 BC he sent his two sons of Mariamne I, Alexander and Aristobulus, to Rome for their education. Caesar was most cordial to them, and they stayed at the home of Asinius Pollio, who professed to be one of Caesar Augustus' most trusted friends.

It was at this time that Octavius (now named Augustus) gave Herod the territories of Trachonitis, Batanea, and Auranites. When Augustus came to Syria in 20 BC, he gave Herod the territory of Zenodorus and gave his brother Pheroras the territory of Perea. In gratitude to Augustus for his generosity, Herod built in Zenodorus' territory (near Panieon) a beautiful temple for him (*Antiq.* 15.10.1–3 §§342–63; *War* 1.20.4–21.3 §§398–406).

Around 17 or 16 BC Herod went to Rome to bring his sons home. They had completed their education, and upon returning home Aristobulus married Berenice, the daughter of Salome (Herod's sister), and Alexander married Glaphyra, the daughter of Archelaus, king of Cappadocia (*Antiq.* 16.1.2 §§6–11; *War* 1.23.1 §§445–46).

During this period Herod's rule was favorably accepted by the people. They were annoyed, however, by two things. First, he violated Jewish law by his introduction of the quinquennial games in honor of the caesar and second, he built theaters and race courses. He demanded a loyalty oath from his subjects, except for a privileged few. Also, he would not allow them to congregate freely for fear of a revolt. Despite these things he had good control of the people and twice favored them by lowering taxes (in 14 BC he reduced taxes by one-fourth, *Antiq.* 16.2.5 §§64–65).

The third period of Herod's rule was clearly marked by domestic troubles (14–4 BC). By now he had married 10 wives (*Antiq.* 17.1.3 §§19–22; *War* 1.28.4 §§562–63). His first wife, Doris, had only one son, Antipater (*Antiq.* 14.12.1 §§300). He repudiated Doris and Antipater when he married Mariamne I, allowing them to visit Jerusalem only during the festivals (*War* 1.22.1 §433). He married Mariamne I in 37 BC. She was the granddaughter of Hyrcanus and had five children, two daughters and three sons. The youngest son died while in Rome, and the remaining two sons were to play an important role in this part of Herod's reign. In late 24 BC he married his third wife, Mariamne II, to whom one child was born, Herod (Philip). Malthace, his fourth wife, was a Samaritan, and mother of two sons, Archelaus and Antipas. His fifth wife, Cleopatra of Jerusalem, was the mother of Philip the tetrarch. Of the remaining five wives only Pallas, Phaedra, and Elpsis are known by name, and none played a significant part in the events of this period (*Antiq.* 17.1.3 §§19–22; *War* 1.28.4 §§562–63).

Alexander and Aristobulus, the sons of Mariamne I, were his favorites. Immediately following their own marriages troubles began within the Herodian household. Salome, Herod's sister and mother of Berenice (wife of Aristobulus), hated these two sons, mainly because she wanted the position and favor they enjoyed for her own son. She spread rumors that the two young men had never forgiven Herod for their mother's murder and were seeking to avenge it. Because of this Herod decided to recall his exiled son, Antipater, to show Alexander and Aristobulus there was another heir to the throne. Antipater took full advantage of the situation and used every conceivable means to acquire the coveted throne. Slander of his half-brothers was one of his favorite methods. On two separate occasions during this period, Augustus tried to reconcile Herod and his sons. Alexander's father-in-law, the Cappadocian king, joined the effort and both times they met with temporary success. Finally, however, a man of bad character, Eurycles from Lacedaemon, took it upon himself to inflame the father against his two sons and vice versa (*Antiq.* 16.9.1–4 §§271–99). Soon other mischiefmakers joined Eurycles, and Herod's patience became exhausted. He put Alexander and Aristobulus in prison.

During this time Herod was also having po-

litical problems. Syllaeus, who ruled Arabia, was very hostile to Herod and irritated him by giving refuge to 40 rebels from Trachonitis. Also, he refused to repay a debt Arabia had contracted with Herod. Herod demanded that Syllaeus hand over the rebels and pay the debt. When Syllaeus refused, Herod, with the permission of the governor of Syria, invaded Arabia as a punitive measure, but with no intention of territorial gain. In reprisal Syllaeus went to Rome and told Augustus a distorted story about the whole incident. His report caused Augustus to suspect Herod and to let him know that their friendship had ended and that he would no longer be treated as an ally, but as a subject. Herod sent an embassy to Rome to clear up the matter, and when the first failed he sent a second under the leadership of Nicolas of Damascus (*Antiq.* 16.9.1–4 §§271–99). This time the mission was successful. In fact, when this embassy reached Augustus, they found the emperor in such a compliant mood that he not only changed his mind about the Arabian situation but also gave Herod permission to deal with Alexander and Aristobulus in any manner he desired. He did, however, specify that any trial should take place outside of Herod's territory at Berytus (modern Beirut) and that Roman officials should form part of the court and should investigate the charges made against the sons (*Antiq.* 15.10.5–11.1 §§320–360; *War* 1.27.1 §§534–37). Herod followed the advice of the emperor. His sons were found guilty and around 7 BC were executed by strangulation at Sebaste (Samaria) where Herod had married their mother Mariamne I 30 years earlier (*Antiq.* 16.11.2–8 §§361–404; *War* 1.27.2–6 §§538–51).

Antipater was now the sole heir, and in his impatience to gain the throne he attempted to poison Herod. This plot failed when Pheroras, Herod's brother, drank the poison by mistake. Herod put Antipater in prison and reported the matter to the emperor (*c.* 5 BC).

At this time Herod because very ill with an incurable disease. He drew up a new will which bypassed his oldest sons Archelaus and Philip because Antipater had poisoned his mind against them. He chose his youngest son, Antipas, as his sole successor (*Antiq.* 17.2.4–6.1 §§32–146; *War* 1.29.1–32.7 §§567–646).

Just before his death the wisemen arrived in Judea searching for the newborn king of the Jews. Herod instructed them to report to him the whereabouts of this child as soon as they found him. Being warned in a dream they did not do so, but rather returned to their homes by another route. God warned Joseph (husband of the mother of Jesus) to flee to Egypt because of Herod's intention to kill Jesus. Joseph took his family and left Bethlehem. Shortly after, Herod killed all the male children in Bethlehem who were two years old and under.

Herod's disease grew increasingly worse. Permission had come from Rome to execute Antipater, which he promptly did. He again altered his will—making Archelaus king, Antipas tetrarch of Galilee and Perea, and Philip tetrarch of Gaulanitis, Trachonitis, Batanea, and Paneas.

On the fifth day after Antipater's execution Herod died at Jericho in the spring of 4 BC. The people acclaimed Archelaus as their king.

Herod reigned for about 33 or 34 years. Although his rule was characterized by violence, it was really not much different than the reigns of most of his contemporaries. Violence was the order of the times.

Herod's Wills. Herod had written six wills during the course of his life. The sixth will was actually a codicil of his fifth will. Since this final version had been written only five days before his death, it had not been ratified by the emperor. Therefore, although Archelaus took over the leadership at Herod's death he did not use the title king (*Antiq.* 17.8.4 §§202–3; *War* 2.1.1 §§2–3). After the Passover he and Antipas set out for Rome to dispute the last two wills, leaving Philip behind to govern. Archelaus wanted to convince Augustus that he should ratify the will made just before Herod died, because it represented his wish. On the other hand, Antipas sought to convince the emperor that Herod had not been of sound mind and body when he wrote the last will. While they were in Rome there was a revolt in Palestine, and a Jewish delegation arrived in Rome to ask autonomy for the nation and for union with the province of Syria. After much debate Augustus devised a compromise. He made Archelaus ethnarch (meaning "ruler of a nation") over Idumaea, Judea, and Samaria. He made Antipas tetrarch (meaning "ruler of a

The Herodium, the magnificent fortress and palace of Herod the Great, where, at his own request, he was buried (Josephus, *War* 1.33.9), though his tomb has not yet been found.

quarter") of Galilee and Perea and Philip tetrarch over Gaulanitis, Trachonitis, Batanea, and Paneas (*Antiq.* 17.11.4 §§317–20; *War* 2.6.3 §§93–100). Thus, Antipas, while losing his bid to be king, did prevent Archelaus from ruling the entire nation.

Archelaus (4 BC–AD 6). Archelaus was the son of Herod the Great and Malthace (a Samaritan) and was born around 22 BC. Upon his return to Judea, Archelaus was faced with a multitude of problems. Before going to Rome he had killed 3000 people in putting down a revolution led by people avenging the blood of those killed by his father, Herod (*Antiq.* 17.8.4–9.3 §§200–218; *War* 2.1.1–3 §§1–13). Thus his rule got off to a bad start. While he was en route to Rome another revolt broke out at Pentecost in 4 BC, which lasted about two and a half months and during which the temple porticoes were burned and the treasury was pillaged by the Romans. This unrest spread to the countryside of Judea and to Galilee and Perea (*Antiq.* 17.10.2–5 §§254–72; *War* 2.3.1–4.1 §§40–56).

Upon his return, Archelaus treated both the Jews and Samaritans very brutally (*War* 2.7.3 §111), a fact borne out by the Gospels. When Joseph returned from his flight to Egypt and learned that Archelaus was ruling Judea, he was afraid to go there and was warned against it by God; he took the infant Jesus to Galilee instead (Mt 2:22).

Two incidents followed that led finally to the loss of Archelaus' power. First, he removed the high priest Joazar, stating that he had sided with the insurgents. He replaced him with Eleazar, brother of Joazar and later replaced Eleazar with Jesus, son of See (*Antiq.* 13.13.1 §§339–41). Next, he divorced Mariamne and married Glaphyra, daughter of King Archelaus of Cappadocia. She was the former wife of Alexander, Herod's son and Archelaus' half-brother. This was a transgression of ancestoral law (*Antiq.* 17.13.1, 4–5 §§341, 350–53; *War* 2.7.4 §§114–16). Either or both of these incidents was enough to cause the unrest that erupted, and Archelaus was brutal in dealing with opposition.

His tyranny finally caused the Jews and Samaritans to send a delegation to Rome and complain formally to Augustus. The fact that such bitter enemies as the Jews and Samaritans could cooperate in this matter indicates the serious nature of the complaint. Antipas and Philip also went to Rome to complain about him. Presumably they resented his neglect as their Roman representative for Palestine. Thus in AD 6 Archelaus was deposed and exiled to Vienna in Gaul (modern Vienne on the Rhône, south of Lyons). Antipas and Philip were allowed to continue their respective rules, and Archelaus' territories were reduced to a province ruled by prefects or procurators (*Antiq.* 17.13.1–5 §§342–55; *War* 2.7.3–8.1 §§111–18; Strabo 16.2.46: Dio Cassius 55.27.6).

Antipas (4 BC–AD 39). Antipas was the younger brother of Archelaus, born around 20 BC. Of all the Herodians, he is mentioned most in the NT because he ruled over Galilee and Perea, where both Christ and John the Baptist concentrated their ministries.

Like his brother Archelaus, Antipas returned from Rome to find his domain in the turmoil of the rebellion begun at Pentecost in 4 BC. He immediately set out to restore order and rebuild what had been destroyed. Following the example of his father, Herod the Great, Antipas founded cities. Sephoris was his first project; it was the largest city in Galilee and his capital city until he built Tiberias. Since Nazareth was only four miles S, SW of Sephoris it is quite possible that Joseph, Mary's husband, was employed as a carpenter (Mt 13:55; Mk 6:3) to help rebuild that city. Antipas' next project was probably Livias (or Julias) in Perea, built in honor of Livia, Augustus' wife. It was completed around AD 13.

Of the 12 cities built by the Herodian family, Tiberias is the most important. It was the first city in Jewish history to be founded with the municipal framework of a Greek *polis*. It was built in honor of the reigning emperor Tiberius. Due to the fact that a cemetery was destroyed in the process of building, Tiberias was considered unclean by the Jews. Antipas offered free houses and lands and tax exemptions for the first few years to anyone who would move into the city. He completed the city in AD 23 and made it his capital.

As was mentioned above, early in Antipas' rule he and his brother Philip helped to bring about the downfall of their brother, Archelaus. At this time Antipas received the dynastic title Herod (cf. *Antiq.* 18.2.1 §§26–27; *War* 2.9.1 §167). This was of great significance to his subjects and in the political and social circles of the Roman world.

In the Christian world the incident for which Antipas is most remembered is his beheading of John the Baptist (Mt 14:3–12; Mk 6:17–29; Lk 3:19–20; *Antiq.* 18.5.2 §§116–19).

There was a tangle of family events leading up to the death of John the Baptist. Antipas had married the daughter of Aretas IV, whose name is unknown. Aretas IV was the Nabatean king, and Augustus may have encouraged this marriage since he favored intermarriages between various rulers to promote peace in his empire.

Around AD 29 Antipas took a trip to Rome and on the way paid a visit to his half-brother Herod Philip, who must have lived in a coastal city in Palestine. Antipas fell in love with Herodias, Philip's wife, who was also Antipas' niece. The idea of becoming the wife of a tetrarch appealed to her and she agreed to marry him when he returned from Rome if he would oust Aretas' daughter (*Antiq.* 18.5.1 §§ 109–110). Antipas agreed to the plan, and when Aretas' daughter heard of it she fled to her father. This was a breach of political alliance as well as a personal insult which led to retaliation by Aretas.

The marriage of Antipas and Herodias was in violation of the Mosaic law which forbade marriage to a brother's wife (Lv 18:16; 20:21) except in order to raise children for a deceased childless brother by a levirate marriage (Dt 25:5; Mk 12:19). In this case, Philip not only had a child, Salome, but he was still alive. This is the situation which John the Baptist spoke so boldly against, and Antipas threw him in prison. Herodias' hatred of John the Baptist was too great merely to settle for his incarceration. At an appropriate time, possibly Antipas' birthday, she planned a banquet at Machaerus in Perea. Her daughter, Salome, danced for the king and in an impulsive moment Antipas promised her under oath that he would give her anything, up to half of his kingdom. Following her mother's advice she asked for John the Baptist's head on a platter. Immediately Antipas was sorry for his rash promise, but in order to save face in the presence of his underlords he granted the request. Thus, John's ministry ended around AD 31 or 32.

The identity of Herodias' first husband, Philip, is considered a problem by some scholars, since there seems to be a contradiction between the Scriptures and Josephus in the matter. In Matthew 14:3 and Mark 6:17 he is referred to as Philip, whereas Josephus refers to him as Herod, son of Herod the Great and Mariamne II (*Antiq.* 18.5.1 §109). Many scholars conclude on these ground that the scriptural account is incorrect. They think that Mark and Matthew confused this Herod with Philip the tetrarch, who later married Herodias' daughter, Salome.

Such a solution would mean that the Gospels contain three historical errors: (1) confusing Herod with his half-brother Philip, (2) making Philip, the tetrarch, husband of Herodias instead of husband of her daughter, and (3) making Salome the daughter of Philip the tetrarch, who according to Josephus had no children. However, the Christian community had some very reliable witnesses such as Joanna, wife of Chuza, Antipas' financial minister (Lk 8:3), and Manaen a close friend of Antipas (Acts 13:1), and it seems most unlikely that the Gospel writers would make such a historical blunder.

There are also other reasons why the Gospel account, though seeming to be contradictory, is accurate. First, the Gospels mention a daughter of Herodias before her marriage to Antipas (Mt 14:6,8–11; Mk 6:22,24–26,28). This is in accord with Josephus' reference to Salome (*Antiq.* 18.5.4 §136).

Second, there is no validity to the objection that Herod the Great would not have two sons with the name Philip. Many of his children had different mothers and their names were duplicated. He had two sons named Antipas/Antipater and two sons named Herod.

Third, the double name of Herodias's first husband, Herod Philip, is not unusual. Most scholars would agree that the Herod of Acts 12:1,6,11,19,20,21 is the Agrippa of Josephus. Nor do they accuse Luke of confusing this Herod with Herod, king of Chalcis (AD 41–48). Furthermore, they never question that Archelaus is Herod Archelaus.

Fourth, the Gospel writers certainly would have used the title tetrarch if they were referring to Philip the tetrarch as being Herodias' former husband since in the very same pericope they had used this title in referring to Antipas (Mt 14:1; Mk 6:14,26).

Therefore, the Philip in the Gospels and the Herod in Josephus is one and the same person.

There are three specific times when Antipas and Jesus are mentioned together in the Gospels.

Early in Jesus' ministry Antipas heard of him and commented, perhaps with irony, that Jesus was John the Baptist resurrected (Mt 14:1,2; Mk 6:14–16; Lk 9:7–9). It was obvious to Antipas that Jesus' ministry was even more remarkable than John's, but he was reluctant to use force to bring about the meeting for fear of once more arousing the people against him. Eventually, Jesus withdrew from Antipas' territories without the two meeting.

Later, as Jesus became more popular Antipas saw a potential threat to his own power and threatened to kill Jesus. Thus it was that on Jesus' final trip to Jerusalem he was warned by some of the Pharisees that he should leave Antipas' territories for his own safety (Lk 13:31–33). Jesus sent as answer to "that fox" that he would continue his ministry of healing and casting out demons for a little longer, and when he had finished he would then go to Jerusalem to perish. The lion and fox were often contrasted in ancient literature. The Lion of Judah, Jesus Christ, was not going to be coerced by the crafty coward, Antipas.

The final encounter between the two occurred when Jesus was tried by Antipas in AD 33 (Lk 23:6–12). Since this event is mentioned only by Luke some scholars consider it legendary. It must be remembered, however, that

Luke's addressee was Theophilus, probably Roman officer, who would be especially interested in the reconciliation between Pilate and Antipas mentioned in this passage.

According to Luke's account, when Pilate could find no fault in Jesus, he sent him to Antipas (who was celebrating the Passover in Jerusalem). Herod thus freed himself from an awkward situation. A more subtle reason may have been to reconcile himself to Antipas. Their relationship had been rather strained since the Galilean massacre (Lk 13:1), and because Pilate brought votive shields into Jerusalem, arousing the anger of the Jews (Philo *Legatio ad Gaium* 299–304). When Jesus was brought before Antipas, the ruler only mocked him and sent him back to Pilate. The main political accomplishment of the incident was Antipas' and Pilate's reconciliation.

In AD 36 Aretas attacked and defeated Antipas' army. The Jews considered this a divine punishment for Antipas' execution of John the Baptist (*Antiq.* 18.5.1–2 §§116–19). At Tiberius' command, Vitellius, governor of Syria, was to help Antipas retaliate. However, before this could be accomplished Tiberius died and Vitellius withheld his aid until he received orders from the new emperor Caligula.

Upon his accession Caligula gave his friend Agrippa I, brother of Herodias, the much coveted title "king" along with Philip the tetrarch's land and the tetrarchy of Lysanias (*Antiq.* 18.6.10 §§225–39). Herodias' ambition motivated her to urge Antipas to go to Rome to seek the title of king for himself, and in AD 39 they both set out for the capital on this mission. At the same time Agrippa sent a freedman to Rome to make accusations against Antipas. Instead of gaining the title of king, Antipas was banished to Lugdunum Convenarum, now Saint-Bertrand de Comminges in France. Herodias was not included in the banishment but she chose to go with her husband. Agrippa acquired Antipas' territories (*Antiq.* 18.7.1–2 §§240–55; *War* 2.9.6 §§181–83).

Philip the Tetrarch (4 BC–AD 34). Philip the tetrarch was the son of Herod the Great and Cleopatra of Jerusalem and was born around 22/21 BC.

When Herod's will was resolved, Philip was made tetrarch over Gaulanitis, Auranitis, Batanea, Trachonitis, Paneas, all in the northern part of Herod the Great's domain (*Antiq.* 17.8. §189; 9.4 §319; 18.4.6 §106; 5.4 §136; *War* 1.33.8 §668; ii.6.3 §95; Lk 3:1). His subjects were mainly Syrian and Greek. Thus he was the first and only Herodian to have his image on his coins.

He built two cities (*Antiq.* 18.2.1 §28; *War* 2.9.1 §168). First, he rebuilt and enlarged Paneas and renamed it Caesarea Philippi

Here Peter made his confession of faith to Jesus and was given the revelation of the church (Mt 16:13–20; Mk 8:27–30). Next, he rebuilt and enlarged Bethsaida and renamed it Julias. Here Jesus healed the blind man (Mk 8:22–26), and in a nearby desert place he fed the 5000 (Lk 9:10–17).

Philip was not as politically ambitious as his brothers. His rule was marked by tranquility and the loyalty of his subjects (*Antiq.* 18.5.4 §137). When Philip died in AD 34, Tiberius annexed his territories to Syria. After Caligula became emperor in AD 37, he gave the territories to Agrippa I, brother of Herodias.

Agrippa I (AD 37–44). Agrippa I was the son of Aristobulus (son of Herod the Great and Mariamne I) and Berenice. He was born in 10 BC (*War* 1.28.1 §552; *Antiq.* 19.8.2 §350). He was the brother of Herodias.

Agrippa I might be considered the black sheep of the Herodian family. While at school in Rome he lived a wanton life, incurring many debts. When Tiberius' son Drusus was poisoned by Sejanus in AD 23, Agrippa lost favor with the court and retired to Maltha leaving angry creditors in Rome (*Antiq.* 18.6.1–2 §§143–47; 6.4 §165).

Eventually his sister Herodias and her husband Antipas took him into their home, but hostilities developed when Antipas humiliated Agrippa by reminding him of his poverty and dependency. Finally Agrippa returned to Rome, where he incurred new debts (*Antiq.* 18.6.2–3 §§148–60). He became a friend of Gaius Caligula and at one point stated that he wished Caligula were king rather than Tiberius. This was overheard and reported to Tiberius, who imprisoned him. He remained in prison until Tiberius' death six months later (*Antiq.* 18.6.4–10 §§161–236; *War* 2.9.5 §§178–80; Dio Cassius 59.8.2).

Upon Caligula's accession to the throne, he released Agrippa and gave him Philip the tetrarch's territories and the northern part of Lysanias' territory as well as the title of king (*Antiq.* 18.6.10 §237; *War* 2.9.6 §181). The title of king aroused the jealousy of his sister Herodias, and that eventually led to her husband, Antipas', downfall. At that time (AD 39) Agrippa acquired all Antipas' territories and property (*Antiq.* 18.7.1–2 §§240–56; *War* 2.9.6 §§181–83).

When Caligula died in AD 41, Agrippa curried the favor of the new emperor Claudius, whereupon Claudius added Judea and Samaria to Agrippa's territory. Agrippa had now acquired all the territory once ruled by his grandfather, Herod the Great (*Antiq.* 19.5.1 §§274–75; *War* 2.11.5 §§214–15).

Agrippa I is mentioned in the NT for his persecution of the early church in order to gain favor of the Jews (Acts 12:1–19). He killed James, the son of Zebedee, and imprisoned Peter. When Peter was released by an angel, Agrippa put the sentries to death.

Agrippa died in AD 44 in Caesarea. Accounts of this incident are recorded both by Josephus and the Scriptures. The incident occurred at Caesarea; he was wearing a sparkling silver robe, and when the people flattered him by calling him a god, sudden death came upon him.

He was survived by his daughters Bernice, Mariamne, and Drusilla, and by a son Agrippa who was 17 at the time (*Antiq.* 19.9.1 §§354–55; *War* 2.11.6 §§218–20). Because of Agrippa II's

Traditional site of the family tomb of the Herods in Jerusalem. Note the stone that could be rolled in front of the entrance.

youth, his father's territories were temporarily made a province.

Agrippa II (AD 50–100). Agrippa II was the son of Agrippa I and Cypros. In AD 50, six years after his father's death, Claudius made him king of Chalcis (*Antiq.* 20.5.2 §104; *War* 2.12.1 §223). In AD 53 he was given the tetrarchy of Philip, Abilene (or Abila), Trachonitis, and Acra (tetrarchy of Varus) in exchange for Chalcis (*Antiq.* 20.7.1 §138; *War* 2.12.8 §247) When Nero became emperor in AD 54 he gave Agrippa the Galilean cities of Tiberias and Tarichea and their surrounding land and the Perean cities of Julias (Betharamphtha) along with Abila and the surrounding land (*Antiq.* 20.8.4 §159; *War* 2.13.2 §252). In appreciation Agrippa enlarged his capital Caesarea Philippi and renamed it Neronius (*Antiq.* 20.9.4 §211).

Agrippa II was in control of the temple treasury and the vestments of the high priest and thus could appoint the high priest (*Antiq.* 20.5.2 §103; 9.4 §213; 9.7 §222). The Romans consulted him on religious matters, which is probably why Festus asked him to hear the apostle Paul at Caesarea (AD 59), where he was accompanied by his sister Bernice (Acts 25,26).

In May AD 66 the Palestinian revolution began (*War* 2.14.4 §284). When Agrippa's attempt to quell the revolt failed, he became a staunch ally of the Romans throughout the entire war (66–70). During this time Nero committed suicide, the new emperor Galba was murdered, and Vespasian became the emperor. After pledging his allegiance to the new emperor, Agrippa remained with Titus, Vespasian's son, who was in charge of the war (Tacitus *Hist.* 5.81). After the fall of Jerusalem (5 Aug 70), Agrippa was probably present to celebrate the destruction of his own people (*War* 7.1.2–3 §§5–40).

Following this, Vespasian added new territories to Agrippa's kingdom, though just which ones is not known. In AD 79 Vespasian died and Titus became emperor. Little is known of Agrippa's rule after this, except that he wrote to the historian Josephus praising him for *The Jewish War*, and he purchased a copy of it (Josephus, *Life* 65 §§361–67; *Apion* 1.9 §§47–52).

Although the Talmud implies that Agrippa II had two wives (Babylonian Talmud: Sukkah 27a), Josephus gives no indication that he had any wives or children. Rather, he was known for his incestuous relationship with his sister Bernice. He died around AD 100. His death marked the end of the Herodian dynasty.

HAROLD W. HOEHNER

See JUDAISM; HERODIANS.

Bibliography. E. Bevan, *Jerusalem Under the High Priests*; F.O. Busch, *The Five Herods*; F.W. Farrer, *The Herods*; M. Grant, *Herod the Great*; H.W. Hoehner, *Herod Antipas*; A.H.M. Jones, *The Herods of Judea*; J.S. Minkin, *Herod, King of the Jews*; S. Perowne, *The Life and Times of Herod the Great* and *The Later Herods*.

Herodians. Jewish party mentioned three times in the Gospels in connection with two incidents (one in Galilee and one in Jerusalem) and associated with the Pharisees in their opposition to Christ. In Mark 3:6, after the healing of the man with the withered hand, the Pharisees went out and took counsel with the Herodians, plotting to destroy Jesus. In Matthew 22:16 and Mark 12:13, the Pharisees and Herodians allied against Christ to entrap him with their question as to the lawfulness of paying taxes to Caesar. The Herodians are never mentioned in either Luke or John.

The real problem comes in Mark 8:15, where it speaks of the "leaven of Herod." Another reading is the "leaven of the Herodians." However, the parallel passage in Matthew 16:6 speaks of the "leaven of the Sadducees." Are the Sadducees and the Herodians the same?

Matthew tends to label the religious leaders as Jesus' opponents, whereas Mark emphasizes that Jesus' opponents were both religious and political. What then is the significance of Matthew's use of "the leaven of the Sadducees" in place of Mark's "leaven of Herod," or "the Herodians"? Some have speculated that the Herodians were a political party composed principally of Sadducees. Some have identified them with the Sadducees, and others with the Boethusians, whose name more often than not was used interchangeably with that of the Sadducees. The Boethusians and the Sadducees were indistinguishable theologically, but the Sadducees were loyal to the Hasmonean dynasty, whereas the Boethusians were attached to the Herodian house and consequently were called the Herodians. Thus the Herodians had political affiliations with the Herodian house and religious affiliations with the Sadducees. Along with the Sadducees, the Herodians were men of influence—the aristocrats of Palestine.

Nevertheless during Jesus' time the political differences between the Herodians and the Sadducees were not as distinct because of the marriage of the Herodian Herod Antipas to the Hasmonean Herodias. The Herodians and the Sadducees would have been on the same side politically against the Pharisees, the former being progovernment while the Pharisees were both anti-Hasmonean and anti Herodian. Congruent with this, Matthew 16:12 and Mark 8:15 represent the Pharisees and the Sadducees/Herodians as contrary parties opposing Jesus.

In summary, the Herodians were also known as the Boethusians. Theologically they were in agreement with the Sadducees, but politically they were more pro-Herodian than the Sadducees. While the Pharisees looked for a cataclysmic messianic kingdom to remove the present Herodian rule, the Herodians worked to keep Herod's dynasty in power.

HAROLD W. HOEHNER

See HEROD, HERODIAN FAMILY.

Herodias. Daughter of Aristobulus, the son of Herod the Great, and Bernice. Born between 9 and 7 BC, her older brother was Herod Agrippa I. In 6 BC, while still in her infancy, she was betrothed by her grandfather, Herod the Great, to his son by Mariamne II named Herod Philip. Herodias was the mother of Salome, born between AD 15 and 19.

Herodias and Herod Philip lived on the sea coast of Judea, possibly at Azotus or Caesarea. In AD 29 Herod Antipas visited Herodias' (his niece) residence on his way to Rome. They were attracted to each other and Herodias agreed to marry him provided he would divorce his present wife, the daughter of Aretas IV, the Arabian king of Petra. Herodias, being a Hasmonean, did not want to share the house with an Arab—longtime foes of the Hasmonean dynasty. When Aretas' daughter got word of this plot, she secretly escaped to her father; and Herodias and Antipas were married. This incident was the beginning of hostilities between Antipas and Aretas which eventually led to Aretas' war against and defeat of Antipas in AD 36.

John the Baptist openly denounced this marriage (Mt 14:3–12; Mk 6:17–29; Lk 3:19,20) because Jewish law forbade marriage with one's brother's wife (Lv 18:16; 20:21), except in order to raise children for a deceased childless brother by a levirate marriage (Dt 25:5; Mk 12:19). In this case the brother, Herod Philip, was still alive and had a child, Salome. The bold denunciation by John the Baptist led to Antipas' imprisoning him around AD 30 or 31. Herodias wanted more than this. She arranged, possibly at Herod Antipas's birthday, to have her daughter dance before him and his magistrates. In appreciation, Herod Antipas promised Salome up to half of his kingdom. At her mother's bidding, she asked for John the Baptist's head on a platter.

Herodias last appears in history involved in an intrigue between her brother, Agrippa I, who had been designated king by the emperor Caligula, and her husband Antipas, who had long wanted such a title. Antipas, at his wife's insistence, went to Rome to plead his case, but lost and was banished. Herodias, however, did remain faithful and followed him into exile, even though Caligula would not have punished her because she was Agrippa's sister.

HAROLD W. HOEHNER

See HEROD, HERODIAN FAMILY.

Herodion. Christian of Jewish ancestry to whom Paul sent greetings at the conclusion of his epistle to the Romans (16:11).

Heron. Long-necked wading bird, considered unclean under Jewish law (Lv 11:19; Dt 14:18).

See BIRDS.

Hesed. Part of the name Benhesed (1 Kgs 4:10 KJV).

See BENHESED.

Heshbon. Important Transjordanian city about 50 miles due east of Jerusalem. It had originally been Moabite, but was conquered by Sihon, the Amorite king, and became the capital of his kingdom (Nm 21:25–30). The city was captured when Israel advanced into Canaan, and this portion of Amorite territory was placed under Reubenite control (32:37; Jos 13:17). However, its position on the boundary between Reuben and Gad (Jos 13:26) resulted in its being occupied by the tribe of Gad. The Moabites soon contested Israel's claim to the territory, and in the period of the judges it changed hands at least once (Jgs 3:12; 1 Sm 12:9–11). Israel controlled Heshbon until around 853 BC, when it was occupied by Mesha, king of Moab. Subsequently it was mentioned in preexilic prophetic censures of the Moabites (cf. Is 15:4; 16:8,9; Jer 48:2,33,34). Jeremiah 49:3 seems to indicate that Heshbon was finally occupied by the neighboring Ammonites.

It was an important Nabataean city in the Greek period, and was conquered by the Jews in the campaigns of Alexander Janneus (103–76 BC). In the Roman period it was incorporated into the province of Syria. The site, Tell Hesban, consists of Roman ruins but has Ammonite pottery dating to the 7th century BC.

Heshmon. Town mentioned only in Joshua 15:24. It was located near Beth-pelet in southern Judah. The notion that the Hasmoneans originated there is unsubstantiated.

Heth. Progenitor of the Hittite people and a descendant of Canaan, in Ham's line (Gn 10:15; 1 Chr 1:13).

See HITTITES.

Hethlon. Site mentioned by Ezekiel (47:15; 48:1) describing part of the northern boundary of the restored kingdom of Israel. Its actual location is unknown.

Hexateuch. Name meaning "the sixfold book," given to a grouping of the first six books of the Bible. Biblical critics added Joshua to the Pentateuch, the fivefold book (Genesis through Deuteronomy), because the contents and style of Joshua connected it intimately with the literary elements of the Pentateuch; thus creating the Hexateuch.

Literary-critical theory divides the Hexateuch into four documents called J, E, D, and P. The portions identified as J and E use the divine names Jehovah (Lord) and Elohim (God), respectively. The D document contains the core of Deuteronomy, and P presents the priestly viewpoint. However, the use of divine names as a starting point for documentary analysis, and the use of vocabulary and literary style for identifying documents, is too subjective a procedure, and makes scientific examination virtually impossible.

Many critics date J, E, D, and P from the 9th to the 4th centuries BC; however, such a conclusion involves a defective evolutionary theory. It is based on the myth of Israel's isolation from surrounding cultures, and on the assumption that Israel's religion evolved from a "primitive" to a "higher" or more "complex" form. Archaeology, however, reveals both the strongly imitative and derivative character of Israel's culture, and the unique character of her religion.

Today form criticism sees the Hexateuch as a combination of reliable oral traditions; but the end result is a variation of the Documentary Hypothesis. Although the theory of a unilateral historical process upon which the critical theory was based has been discarded, the Documentary Hypothesis of a single set of literary sources, in their order of precedence, is still widely assumed by many scholars.

J.G.S.S. THOMSON

See DOCUMENTARY HYPOTHESIS; FORM CRITICISM.

Hezeki. KJV spelling of Hizki, Elpaal's son, in 1 Chronicles 8:17.

See HIZKI.

Hezekiah. 1. King of Judah from 715–686 BC. The account of Hezekiah's reign is in 2 Kings 18:1–20:21; 2 Chronicles 29:1–32:33; Isaiah 36:1–39:8.

Chronology. Hezekiah succeeded to Judah's throne at 25 and ruled for 29 years (2 Kgs 18:2; 2 Chr 29:1). His mother was Abi (2 Kgs 18:2; 2 Chr 29:1, Abijah, a longer form),

a daughter of Zechariah. The chronology of Hezekiah's reign is difficult to establish with certainty. The Bible says the Assyrian siege of Samaria, capital of the northern kingdom of Israel, began in the 4th year of his reign and that Samaria fell in the 6th year (2 Kgs 18:9,10), which would make his reign begin about 728 BC and end about 699. Assyrian king Sennacherib besieged the fortified Judean cities during Hezekiah's 14th year (2 Kgs 18:13), which would have been 714. Assyrian records, however, indicate that Sennacherib came to the Assyrian throne in 705 and that his Judean campaign took place in 701. The most generally accepted solution to the discrepancy is that Hezekiah came to the throne in 715, probably after a co-regency with his father Ahaz that began in 728. That solution harmonizes with the statement that Sennacherib's siege took place in the 14th year of Hezekiah's reign, or 701.

Hezekiah's Religious Reforms. Hezekiah came to the throne at a critical juncture in Judah's history. Sargon II had taken Samaria in 722 BC, and Judah was militarily weakened from wars and raids by surrounding nations during the reign of Ahaz. Perhaps motivated by warnings to the northern kingdom delivered by the prophets Amos and Hosea that punishment would come if Israel did not turn back to God, Hezekiah began his religious reforms soon after becoming king.

In the first month of his reign Hezekiah opened the temple doors and repaired them. He brought the Levites together and ordered them to "sanctify" themselves and the temple and to reinstate the religious ceremonies that had long been neglected. Hezekiah brought sacrifices, and the priestly temple service was restored (2 Chr 29).

Hezekiah then sent invitations throughout Judah and Israel for the Passover celebration in Jerusalem (held a month later than the prescribed time because the priests and people could not be ready earlier). It was hoped that religious unification would be a prelude to political reunification of the northern kingdom of Israel and the southern kingdom of Judah. However, most of the northern tribes mocked the Judean messengers who brought the invitations, and only a few persons from the tribes of Asher, Manasseh, and Zebulun went to Jerusalem for the celebration (2 Chr 30).

After the Passover observance the worshipers set about destroying the high places and altars. They broke the pillars and cut down the Asherim throughout Judah, Benjamin, and also went into Ephraim and Manasseh (2 Chr 31:1). Hezekiah even smashed the bronze serpent that Moses had made (Nm 21:6–9) for it had become an object of worship and was iden tified with a serpent deity, Nehushtan (2 Kgs 18:4). Because of his sweeping reforms later generations said of Hezekiah: "there was none like him among all the kings of Judah after him, nor among those who were before him" (v 5).

The Assyrian Threat. Hezekiah knew that Assyria's growing international dominance was a serious threat to his kingdom, but following his father Ahaz's policy of submission, Hezekiah did not at first attempt any resistance.

The inscriptions of the Assyrian king Sargon II record his victorious campaign in 711 BC against a revolt by Aziru king of Ashdod, who requested help from Egypt and Judah. Perhaps a prophecy received by Isaiah warned Hezekiah not to interfere with the Ashdod siege (Is 20:1–6), and so no punitive action was taken against Judah by Assyria. Sargon died in 705, and his son Sennacherib came to the throne. This triggered widespread rebellion throughout the Assyrian provinces. Hezekiah withheld tribute from the new Assyrian ruler and, taking advantage of the confused situation, made raids against the Philistines (2 Kgs 18:8). After subduing rebellious elements in the East, Sennacherib began his campaign against the "land of Hatti" (the Assyrian name for the western countries) in 701 BC. In preparation Hezekiah repaired Jerusalem's city wall, raised towers on it, built another wall outside it, and strengthened the Millo in the City of David. He also stockpiled abundant quantities of weapons and shields (2 Chr 32:5). Knowing the necessity of an adequate water supply for a city under siege, Hezekiah had a 1777-foot tunnel cut through solid rock from the spring of Gihon to the Siloam pool to bring water into the city, and to prevent the Assyrians access to the spring water outside the city (2 Kgs 20:20; 2 Chr 32:3,4). The Siloam inscription, carved inside the tunnel itself, records the completion of that remarkable conduit, and is one of the oldest preserved examples of the Hebrew language.

Sennacherib invaded Palestine and after an extensive campaign put down the rebellion there. That campaign is well documented in Assyrian records, including a description of his siege on Jerusalem in 701, and is supplemented by the biblical account (2 Kgs 18:13–19:37; 2 Chr 32:1–22; Is 36,37). Sidon, the cities of Phoenicia, and the immediate neighbors of Judah, including Byblos, Arnon, Moab, Edom, and Ashdod submitted to the Assyrians. Resistant Philistine cities were also taken. Sennacherib laid siege against Ekron, whose king Padi (a loyal subject of Sennacherib) had been taken prisoner by his own subjects and turned over in chains to Hezekiah. A large Egyptian and Ethiopian army failed to relieve the Ekronites who

The tunnel leading to the pool of Siloam.

were defeated by the Assyrians in the vicinity of Eltekah. Ekron was captured, and Padi was recalled to his throne by Sennacherib.

Sennacherib then turned his attention to the fortified cities of Judah and took them one by one (2 Kgs 18:13). Assyrian records claim that he captured 46 walled cities and countless villages, including Lachish and Debi, southeast of Jerusalem, 200,150 people, homes, cattle, and flocks without number. While Lachish was still under siege, Hezekiah saw that it was hopeless to resist and sent word to Sennacherib offering to surrender and pay whatever tribute he would impose. The Assyrian ruler demanded an enormous tribute of 300 talents of silver (800 talents according to Assyrian records, either an exaggerated figure or computed by a different standard) and 30 talents of gold. In order to pay that tribute Hezekiah took all the silver in the temple and the royal treasuries, and stripped the gold from the temple doors and doorposts (2 Kgs 18:14–16). This treasure was sent to Sennacherib along with other gifts that, according to the Assyrian account, included some of Hezekiah's own daughters as concubines.

The account in 2 Kings 18:17–19:37 raises the question of whether there was another invasion of Judah at a later date, or whether this passage gives additional details about the invasion of 701. Although Hezekiah had already submitted and paid tribute, these verses describe further Assyrian demands. Those who believe it was a single invasion suggest that this is an account of the Assyrian deputation sent by Sennacherib to demand Jerusalem's surrender while Lachish was still under siege. The deputation included Tartan, Rabsaris, and Rabshakeh (titles of court officials rather than personal names). They warned the citizens that their God was no more able to save them than the gods of other cities defeated by the Assyrians. In distress Hezekiah sent word to the prophet Isaiah who assured the king that Sennacherib would hear a rumor and return to his own land and there die by the sword (19:1–7). Shortly afterward Sennacherib received word of Babylon's revolt in his eastern provinces, so he departed at once without taking Jerusalem. Assyrian records do not claim that Jerusalem was taken but only say that Hezekiah was "shut up in Jerusalem like a bird in a cage." Judah's surrounding neighbors celebrated their deliverance and brought gifts of gratitude to Hezekiah (2 Chr 32:23).

According to the second invasion theory, after repeated rebellions Babylon was defeated by Sennacherib in 689 BC. Then the Assyrian king heard that Tirhakah, king of Ethiopia, was advancing against him, so he sent another threatening message to Hezekiah probably to warn him against making an alliance with Tirhakah. Hezekiah took the matter before the Lord and received word from Isaiah that the Assyrian king would return the same way he came and that Jerusalem would be untouched. Soon afterward in a miraculous intervention by God 185,000 Assyrian troops were killed, and the Assyrian monarch abandoned his plans to conquer Hezekiah. That embarrassing calamity understandably is not mentioned by the Assyrian records. In 681 Sennacherib was killed by two of his sons as Isaiah had predicted (2 Kgs 19:7,37).

Sometime prior to 701 Hezekiah became seriously ill, and Isaiah told him to prepare for death. The king earnestly prayed for an extension of life, and God promised him 15 more years as well as deliverance from the Assyrians. Hezekiah asked Isaiah for a sign that he would be healed, and a shadow cast by the sun moved backward 10 steps contrary to its normal direction (2 Kgs 20:1–11).

Sometime after his recovery Hezekiah received a delegation with presents from Merodach-baladan of Babylon, ostensibly to congratulate Hezekiah on his return to health. The real object of the visit was probably to enlist Hezekiah as an ally in a conspiracy being formed against Assyria. The king showed the Babylonian envoys all the gold, silver, and other valuables he possessed. This act brought a warning from Isaiah that the day would come when all those treasures would be carried away to Babylon (2 Kgs 20:12–19).

Hezekiah lived the remainder of his life in peace and prosperity. It may have been during this time that he encouraged literary efforts in Judah, which included copying some of Solomon's proverbs (Prv 25–29). Upon his death in 686 he was succeeded by his son Manasseh, who probably had become co-regent 10 years earlier. F. B. Huey, Jr.

See ISRAEL, HISTORY OF; CHRONOLOGY, OLD TESTAMENT; KING, KINGSHIP.

2. KJV form of Hizkiah, Neuriah's son, in 1 Chronicles 3:23.

See HIZKIAH #1.

3. Head of a family of exiles (the sons of Ater), 98 of whose descendants returned from the Babylonian exile with Zerubbabel (Ezr 2:16; Neh 7:21; 10:17, KJV Hizkijah).

4. Ancestor of the prophet Zephaniah, possibly King Hezekiah himself (Zep 1:1, KJV Hizkiah).

Hezekiah's Tunnel. *See* SILOAM, POOL OF.

Hezion. Tabrimmon's father and the grandfather of Ben-hadad, king of Syria. Ben-hadad formed an alliance with King Asa of Judah (910–869 BC) and opposed Israel's king Baasha (908–886 BC; 1 Kgs 15:18).

Hezir. 1. Levite and head of the 17th of 24 divisions of priests for sanctuary service formed during David's reign (1 Chr 24:15).

2. Israelite leader who set his seal on Ezra's covenant during the postexilic era (Neh 10:20).

Hezro, Hezrai. One of David's mighty warriors (2 Sm 23:35, KJV Hezrai; 1 Chr 11:37), a Carmelite by birth.

Hezron (Place). Town on Judah's border (Jos 15:3). In Numbers 34:4 it probably forms part of the name Hazar-addar.

Hezron (Person). 1. Reuben's son (Gn 46:9; Ex 6:14; 1 Chr 5:3) and founder of the Hezronite family in Reuben's tribe (Nm 26:6).

2. Perez's son (Gn 46:12; Ru 4:18,19; 1 Chr 2:5–25; 4:1), founder of the Hezronite family in Judah's tribe (Nm 26:21), and an ancestor of Jesus Christ (Mt 1:3; Lk 3:33; KJV Esrom).

See GENEALOGY OF JESUS CHRIST.

Hiddai. Warrior among David's mighty men (2 Sm 23:30); alternately called Hurai in 1 Chronicles 11:32.

Hiddekel. Hebrew name for the Tigris River (Gn 2:14; Dn 10:4).

See TIGRIS RIVER.

Hierapolis.

Hiel. Bethelite in the days of King Ahab who fulfilled Joshua's curse upon the city of Jericho (Jos 6:26; 1 Kgs 16:34). Joshua had said centuries before that anyone attempting to rebuild the city would suffer the loss of his oldest and youngest sons. It is unclear whether or not Hiel's sons died a natural death or were killed in a punitive ritual.

Hierapolis. City of southwest Phrygia, strategically located between Colossae to the east and Laodicea to the south. The founding of the city is credited to Eumenes II of Pergamum (197–160 BC). Hierapolis, because of its mineral springs and deep cave known as Plutonium, came to be a cultic center for the worship of Phrygian gods. Lethal vapors issued from the cave, which was thought to be an entrance to the underworld. Residents believed that a priest was seated deep inside the cave and that on certain occasions prophecies would be uttered for those seeking them. The mineral baths attracted visitors, and gradually the city developed into a leading commercial center. As Roman rule enveloped the city, Hierapolis became part of the province of Asia.

Under Paul's influence, Christianity took hold there during his stay in Ephesus. Paul mentions Hierapolis in connection with the believer Epaphras, who worked diligently for the inhabitants as well as those in Laodicea and Colossae (Col 4:13). Even though several early Christians were martyred there, the church continued to grow. In the 4th century, Christians closed off the Plutonium with stones.

Hieroglyphics. *See* WRITING.

Higgaion. Musical notation in text of Psalm 9:16, presumably cueing the instrumental accompaniment to play softly, with a subdued sound.

See MUSIC AND MUSICAL INSTRUMENTS.

Higher Criticism. *See* BIBLICAL CRITICISM, NEW TESTAMENT; BIBLICAL CRITICISM, OLD TESTAMENT.

High Place. Phrase commonly translated from the Hebrew *bāmāh* (pl., *bōmah*) which apparently derived from a word originally meaning "the back or ridge of an animal." Thus it came to refer to a height or hill or a stone burial cairn. Usually it was an elevated worship center, such as the ones referred to in Numbers 33:52; 1 Samuel 9:13,14; 2 Kings 12:3; 2 Chronicles 21:11 and Ezekiel 36:1,2. But sometimes (as in 2 Kgs 23:8) it was a *bāmāh* of the gate, a sanctuary with no special reference to height, located at the city gate as in Dan and Beersheba. It might even have been placed in a declivity (Jer 7:31).

That a *bāmāh* might simply be a burial place with commemorative stela or memorial stones is clear from such a passage as Ezekiel 43:7b. An illustration of such a *bāmāh* is the so-called Gezer high place. This Bronze Age center with its 10 huge pillars is now interpreted as a mortuary shrine instead of a sanctuary in the strict sense of the term.

A second word translated "high place" is *rāmāh* (elevation), from the Hebrew meaning "to be high." Ezekiel used this term to refer to illicit worship centers (16:24,25,31,39) which evidently had no necessary connection with height.

One of the best-known and best-preserved of all high places in the vicinity of Palestine is the great high place at Petra, discovered by George L. Robinson in 1900. Located on a ridge west of the Khazneh, or treasury, it consists of a large rectangular court and adjacent altars. The court is about 47 feet long and 21 feet wide and is cut into the rock platform to a depth of 18 inches. West of the court stand a square and a round altar, each hewn from the solid rock. South of the court is a pool measur-

The snake monument, an altar at Petra.

ing about 8 1/2 by 9 1/2 feet and cut 4 feet into the rock. South of the pool stand two sacred obelisks or pillars, also cut out of the solid rock. This whole complex is reached from a lower terrace by two flights of stairs. At this center the ancient Nabataean inhabitants of Petra evidently engaged in feasts and sacrifices to honor their gods. Though the worship center in its present form does not date before the 1st century BC, it preserves a very ancient tradition of Transjordan and illustrates the pagan and Israelite high places of OT times.

Excavations begun at Dan in 1966 have uncovered what is thought to have been the *bāmāh* constructed by Jeroboam I when he introduced calf worship to Israel after the rupture of the kingdom (1 Kgs 12:28–33). This open-air platform passed through two stages of construction during the period of the divided monarchy. The lower stage, apparently dating to the reign of Jeroboam I in the 10th century BC, was about 20 by 61 feet in size; the upper, of Ahab's day in the following century, measured 60 by 62 feet, had walls of limestone 5 to 7 feet thick, and was approached by a monumental flight of steps 27 feet wide. In addition, at the gate was a construction which some have interpreted as the "*bāmāh* of the gate" (2 Kgs 23:8). Excavations at Tell Beersheba (1969–75) uncovered in that gate area a *bāmāh* with a round incense altar.

The pagan high place was usually locate on a physical height, where one could fee closer to the god. Its first essential was an al tar, which might be a heap of earth, unhew stones, or a unit cut out of the solid rock. Sec ond, there was a stone pillar (Dt 12:3) or obe lisk (*maṣṣebah*) representing the male deit and having phallic associations; third, a tre or pole (*asherāh*) representing the female deit (a fertility goddess); and fourth, a laver fo ceremonial washings. A sanctuary with an im age of the deity also required a building c some sort to protect it (2 Kgs 17:29).

At these pagan high places sacrifices of ani mals and sometimes of human beings too place, and religious prostitution or homosex ual acts were common. It is natural that suc practices should develop in a context of sympa thetic magic, where promiscuity and breedin among human beings was supposed to influ ence animals and crops.

The Hebrews had legitimate high places be tween the time of the destruction of the taber nacle at Shiloh and construction of the tem ple, though there was little similarity to paga accouterments or practices, apart from th presence of an altar and the offering of sacri fices. At one high place the people ate a sacrifi cial meal before Samuel anointed Saul kin (1 Sm 9:12–10:1). The tabernacle was locate at the high place of Gibeon during the reign c David (1 Chr 16:39; 21:29). Solomon offered sac rifices at several high places (1 Kgs 3:2,3), an at the high place of Gibeon he met God an was granted the gift of wisdom for his adminis tration (vv 4–15). Once Solomon's temple wa completed, high places were eliminated an were off-limits for the Hebrews.

When the Hebrews entered Canaan, they en countered pagan peoples who had long wor shiped at high places. God commanded the Is raelites to destroy those sanctuaries (Nm 33:52) to avoid contamination by them, bu the warning went largely unheeded. At th height of the Hebrew kingdom, after Solomo had completed the temple, he built hig places for the god Chemosh of Moab, Molec of Ammon, and other gods of his pagan wives For this sin God determined to split the He brew kingdom (1 Kgs 11:7–11).

After the division of the kingdom Jeroboan established high places at Dan and Bethe and Ahab and others proliferated their con struction. Judgment was prophesied (1 Kg 13:2,3; 2 Kgs 17:7–18), and ultimately the king dom of Israel went into captivity to Assyria fo her idolatry.

Rehoboam, the first king of the souther kingdom, spread high places all over his do main (1 Kgs 14:23,24). Though King As launched a revival of true religion, he did no remove the high places (15:12–14). Jehoshaphat also initiated revival, but again the high places remained (22:43). On the other hand, his son Jehoram and his wife, Athaliah, encouraged their construction (2 Chr 21:11). Joash during his revival did not eliminate the high places (2 Kgs 12:3), nor did the similar efforts of the good king Uzziah (15:3,4). Ahaz made no pretense of faithfulness to God, and actively encouraged the idolatry of the pagan sanctuaries (2 Kgs 16:3,4). Finally, Hezekiah launched a campaign against the high places (2 Chr 31:1); but his policies were reversed during the reign of his wicked son Manasseh (2 Kgs 21:2–9). Josiah led the last Judean revival and again attacked the high places (23:5,8).

The prophets roundly condemned these centers of idolatry: Isaiah (15:2; 16:12); Jeremiah (48:35); Ezekiel (6:3); Hosea (10:8); and Amos (7:9).

HOWARD F. VOS

See CANAANITE DEITIES AND RELIGION; GROVE; IDOLS, IDOLATRY; GODS, GODDESSES.

High Priest. *See* PRIESTS AND LEVITES.

Highway, King's. *See* KING'S HIGHWAY.

Hilen. Alternate name for Holon, a city assigned to Levites, in 1 Chronicles 6:58.

See HOLON #1.

Hilkiah. 1. Father of Eliakim, an overseer in King Hezekiah's household (2 Kgs 18:18,26; Is 22:20; 36:3,22).

2. High priest and Shallum's son in the reign of King Josiah who, during the repair of the temple, found the Book of the Law (2 Kgs 22:3–14; 1 Chr 6:13; 9:11; 2 Chr 34:14–22). According to Ezra 7:1 (cf. 1 Esd 8:1), he was also an ancestor of Ezra. He is an important figure in the events surrounding Josiah's religious reform, not only because he found the Book of the Law, but also led the king's messengers to consult Huldah the prophetess regarding God's Word (2 Kgs 22:14) and later presided over the purification of the temple (23:4).

3. Merarite Levite, the son of Amzi and Amaziah's father (1 Chr 6:45).

4. Merarite Levite and Hosah's son, who was appointed as a gatekeeper in the temple by David (1 Chr 26:11).

5. Companion of Ezra at the public reading of the Law (Neh 8:4). Scholars disagree as to whether he was a layman or a priest.

6. Priestly leader among the returned exiles (Neh 12:7,21).

7. Anathoth priest who was the father of Jeremiah (Jer 1:1).

8. Father of Gemariah whom King Zedekiah sent to Babylon with a letter of assurance from Jeremiah (Jer 29:3).

Hillel. 1. Father of Abdon, one of the judges (Jgs 12:13,15).

2. Jewish teacher and scholar (c. 60 BC–AD 20) who helped to develop the oral law and may have founded rabbinic Judaism. Hillel was called "the Elder," a title which indicates a person holding a position of honor, generally given to those who stood at the head of the community. Born in Babylonia, he moved to Palestine for more advanced studies under two outstanding scholars, Shemaiah and Abtalyon. He first gained recognition when the sons of Bathyra, the chief interpreters of the Law at the time, could not decide on an answer to an important legal problem, namely, whether or not the offering of the paschal lamb overrode the sabbath prohibitions. Having heard that there was a man living in Jerusalem who had studied under Shemaiah and Abtalyon, they sent for Hillel and told him the problem. Hillel's answer was that the paschal offering took precedence over the sabbath, and he argued his point so successfully that his ruling was accepted. He was then appointed to replace the sons of Bathyra. It has been argued, however, that Hillel's appointment can hardly be attributed solely to this one incident.

Hillel was one of the first persons to apply advanced principles of interpretation in determining practical law and action. Thus he is especially important for the development of the Talmud and the oral law. These rules provided the basis for later rabbinic interpretation.

There are many stories describing Hillel's character, picturing him as a man of great humility and extreme patience, pursuing peace even at the expense of truth. He is usually contrasted with his colleague Shammai, who is portrayed as impatient and ill-tempered. The most famous tale tells of a heathen who came to Shammai to be converted on the condition that he teach him the entire Law while he stood on one foot. Shammai snubbed him, and so the heathen went to Hillel. Hillel replied, "What is hateful to you do not do to your neighbor; this is the entire Law, all the rest is commentary. Now go and learn it." Hillel thus became a model for Jews throughout history.

See TALMUD; JUDAISM; SHAMMAI.

Hin. Liquid measure equal to one-sixth of a bath or about one gallon.

See WEIGHTS AND MEASURES.

Hind. Adult female red deer.

See ANIMALS (DEER).

The Valley of Hinnom.

Hinnom, Valley of. Deep, narrow ravine running south of Jerusalem which marked the boundary between Judah and Benjamin's territories.

See GEHENNA.

Hippopotamus. *See* ANIMALS (BEHEMOTH).

Hippos. One of the cities of the Decapolis (a loose federation of 10 Greek cities) established in Palestine after the death of Alexander the Great (323 BC; also called Susitha); not mentioned in the Bible. Its location is in doubt, but most likely it was eight miles north of Gadara and four miles east of the Sea of Galilee near the road to Damascus. Its position was of strategic military importance in the defense of Jerusalem, while its location was also ideal for trading, from which it exported not only its merchandise but also Greek culture.

See DECAPOLIS.

Hirah. Adullamite and friend of Judah to whose house Judah went after he and his brothers sold Joseph (Gn 38:1). He accompanied Judah to the sheepshearing after Judah's wife died (v 12), and served as the messenger to carry a kid from Judah to Tamar (v 20).

Hiram. 1. King of Tyre during the time of David and Solomon. After David had conquered Jerusalem and moved his capital there, Hiram sent cedar wood, masons, and carpenters to build David's palace (2 Sm 5:11; 1 Chr 14:1). Hiram remained David's friend throughout his life (1 Kgs 5:10), and after David's death he sought to continue that friendship with Solomon. When Solomon was ready to build the temple, Hiram provided wood from the forests of Lebanon, gold, and skilled craftsmen to help build and furnish the temple; and Solomon in return gave Hiram wheat and oil for his household. Moreover, Solomon gave Hiram 20 cities in Galilee, although the Scripture indicates that Hiram was not pleased with them (1 Kgs 5:1–11; 9:10–14).

Although the Israelites were not a maritime people, Solomon did maintain a fleet of ships at Ezion-geber (1 Kgs 9:26–28). Hiram gave his assistance to Solomon by supplying sailors and perhaps ships to make Solomon's fleet operable. The Phoenicians were noted sailors, who sailed the Mediterranean Sea as far west as Tarshish in Spain, and this aid was no doubt quite beneficial.

Josephus says that Hiram was the son of Abibal, that he reigned in Tyre for 34 years, and that he died at the age of 53. Phoenician historians record that Solomon married the daughter of Hiram.

2. Craftsman from Tyre who worked on Solomon's temple. He was said to be the son of a man of Tyre and a woman from the tribe of Naphtali (1 Kgs 7:13,14), although 2 Chronicles 2:14 says that his mother was from Dan's tribe. He was responsible for the creation of various furnishings in the temple: two brass pillars, the capitals that adorned the pillars, the molten sea and the 12 oxen on which it stood, the 10 lavers with their bases, the shovels, and basins.

His name is also spelled Huram in 2 Chronicles 4:11. He is called Huram-abi (abi meaning "master") in 2 Chronicles 2:13 and 4:16.

Hittites. Biblical people who figure largely in the promises of a land for the descendants of Abram and the children of Israel. Once unknown to secular history and thought to be a mythical people by some critics of Bible history, the Hittites have been recovered by the efforts of archaeologists and historians and now are known to have had an empire centered in Asia Minor. They were of sufficient military strength to challenge the armies of Egypt under the vainglorious Ramses II and fought him to a standstill at Kadesh on the Orontes.

For the most part, the biblical references do not suggest that the Hittites were more than a minor group, but the association of Hittite kings and Egypt with Solomon's trade in horses and their involvement in the conflicts of Syria and Israel in the divided monarchy indicate that the Hittites were a people of great consequence.

The Term "Hittite." Specialists give three meanings to the term Hittite: (1) the aboriginal inhabitants of Anatolia, whom the specialists prefer to call Hattian; (2) the Indo-European people who are generally known as the Hittites; (3) the small city-states in northern Syria that preserved certain elements of the Hittite culture and are often called Neo-Hittite. These kingdoms flourished in the 1st millennium BC but had been subservient to the Hittites of Asia Minor during the empire period (c. 1400–1190 BC).

Their neighbors of the 1st millennium BC, such as the Assyrians and the Hebrews, used the term "Hittite" to refer to the earlier empire as well as to the later Syrian city-states, without regard to linguistic or ethnic background.

Geography. The Hittite Empire had its center in Anatolia (Asia Minor, modern Turkey), with its capital at Hattusas (modern Boghazköy) at the bend of the Halys River (present Kizil Irmak). The empire at times extended over a much larger area without definite boundaries since it included city-states that were dependencies of the Anatolian kingdom, related to it by treaties but otherwise not a part of it. Because of their presence in Palestine-Syria, the Hittites made their influence felt in Egypt and are well known from the art and inscriptions of that country. The presence of Hittites in Palestine is widely attested in the Bible, and the power of the Hittites in Palestinian cities like Hebron is indicated in patriarchal times.

History. The Hattians were one of several groups of peoples, thought to be neither Semitic nor Indo-European, who occupied the Anatolian plateau in the 3rd millennium BC. In the late part of this millennium Indo-Europeans overran the area and assumed political power.

History in the true sense, that is, based on written records, begins in Anatolia around 1900 BC with the arrival of Assyrian traders. These merchants established themselves in various cities and corresponded with their homeland using cuneiform tablets. Numbers of these records have been found, principally at Kültepe (ancient Kanesh) near Kayseri. These mention the struggle among Hittite principalities for supremacy in Anatolia and refer to a King Anittas, who is known from Hittite sources of later date.

The Old Kingdom (c. 1740–1400 BC). Hittite kings traced their lineage to one Labarnas, from whose reign no records have survived, although later inscriptions tell of his activities. His successor, Hattusilis I (*c.* 1650–1620 BC), left the text of a speech which is the main source of knowledge of the political situation in this early period. It was during his reign that Hattusas (modern Boghazköy) became the administrative capital of the empire.

Mursilis I (*c.* 1620–1590 BC) even succeeded in taking the famous city of Babylon in about 1600 BC, but he was assassinated and the empire fell into disarray. In the East the Hurrians took over and Hittites also lost power in the south. The balance of the Old Kingdom period was marked by instability and internal friction.

Some alleviation of these conditions was brought about by a usurper, Telepinus, who seized the throne around 1525 BC and managed to do away with his rivals. He issued an edict concerning the succession, prefaced by an abbreviated survey of Hittite history and accompanied by rules regulating the conduct of the king and nobility.

Although the remainder of the period is obscure, the famous law code, one of the most important texts found at Boghazköy, dates from this time.

The Empire (c. 1400–1190 BC). During the 15th century BC the dominance of the Hurrians was broken by the campaigns of the Egyptian king Thutmose III, but another Hurrian kingdom, Mitanni, soon became prominent in western Asia. Mitanni presented a threat to the Hittites, but with the arrival of an ambitious and energetic monarch, Suppiluliuma I (*c.* 1380–1340 BC), there came a resurgence of Hittite vitality and the strength of the empire. This was the time of the writing of the Amarna Letters, with their testimony of the confused situation in Palestine-Syria.

Suppiluliuma carried out a brilliant military expedition against Mitanni and then by combining force with diplomatic genius, forged for himself a buffer zone of vassal city-states, which were bound to him by treaties, copies of which were found in the Hittite archives.

During the first half of the 14th century, the languor of Amenhotep III and the religious preoccupation of Akhenaten had allowed the Asiatic empire of Egypt to dwindle away into a memory. But with the beginning of the 19th dynasty, the Egyptians became concerned about regaining what was lost. The contest for Palestine-Syria reached its climax with the famous battle at Kadesh on the Orontes, where the initial advantage was won by Hittite chariots. Ramses II celebrated the battle as a victory, although he barely escaped with his life. The Hittite king, Muwatallis, also claimed a triumph, but in political terms the battle was inconclusive. The next Hittite king after him, Hattusilis III, signed a treaty with Ramses II in the 21st year of the reign of the Egyptian king; the pact was confirmed by the marriage of the daughter of Hattusilis to Ramses II.

Around the middle of the 13th century BC the Hittites were threatened from the west by the *Ahhiyawa,* possibly to be associated with the Achaeans and the Sea Peoples. It was a wave of the Sea Peoples that brought the Hittite Empire to an end around 1190 BC and surged along the eastern Mediterranean coast until it was finally stopped in the Nile Delta by Ramses III.

The Neo-Hittite Kingdoms (c. 1190–700 BC). In northern Syria, independent city-states continued to be ruled by kings who bore Hittite names and erected monuments inscribed with Hittite hieroglyphs. The Assyrians continued to refer to the area as the Land of Hatti, and the OT speaks of these rulers of principalities as "Kings of the Hittites." These little kingdoms were soon placed under Assyrian tribute and became Assyrian provinces in the reigns of Shalmaneser V and Sargon II, the rulers who also put an end to the northern kingdom of Israel by conquering Samaria in 721 BC.

Languages and Literature. In the texts found at Boghazköy, eight different languages were employed. Of these, only two, Hittite and Akkadian, were used for official royal records. Akkadian was the lingua franca of the empire and was also the main language of the Amarna Tablets. Hurrian is the only other language in which complete texts were written. The other languages occur mostly in short passages in Hittite religious documents, and one is identified only by some technical terms. These eight languages are:

(1) Hittite, also called Nesite, was recognized by B. Hrozný as having affinities with Indo-European. This proposal met with skepticism among scholars for a while, but has been proved beyond question. (2) Hattic (Hattian), the language of the aboriginal people of Anatolia, is used for speeches of the priests in the performance of the cultic ritual relating to the Hittite pantheon. (3) Luwian is another Indo-European language, closely related to Hittite. (4) Palaic, a little known language, is also Indo-European. (5) Hurrian appears in many ritual texts. Fragments of a Hurrian translation of the Epic of Gilgamesh were found. One of the Amarna Tablets, written by Tushratta, king of Mitanni, to Amenhotep III, was in Hurrian. Also represented are (6) the Aryan language of the Mitanni rulers, (7) Akkadian, and (8) Sumerian. In addition to the cuneiform script, the Hittites used hieroglyphs, which have been found inscribed on stone and lead.

The Hittite archives contained texts of official documents, such as treaties, laws, instructions, annals of the kings, letters, and other historical records. There was much religious literature, including myths, legends, epics, incantations, rituals, omens, prayers, and descriptions of festivals and their celebration.

The People. The diversity of language characteristic of Hittite civilization is paralleled by the great mixture of ethnic backgrounds, particularly over the geographic range covered by the empire. The physical appearance of the Hittites is known from their own reliefs and from representation on Egyptian monuments. Their own depictions show the Hittites with unattractive faces, heavy coats, tall pointed caps, and shoes with turned-up toes.

Religion. The Hittites had a pantheon of deities, known by name from the inscriptions and by appearance from the reliefs. Gods may be identified by a weapon or tool carried in the right hand, a symbol in the left hand, wings or similar appurtenances, or the sacred animal on which a divinity may stand.

A principal god was the weather god, whose sacred animal was the bull. Out of the multiplicity of local cults there arose an official pantheon, headed by the sun goddess, Arinna, who was the supreme deity of the state and of the king. The treaties of the Hittites typically have a long list of divinities who served as witnesses to the treaty and oath.

Hittites and the Bible. The name "Hittite(s)" occurs nearly 50 times in the OT but does not appear in the NT. If one includes the occurrences of the name of Heth, the father of the Hittites, there are more than 60 citations in the Bible. Most have to do with the presence of Hittites in Canaan. Their progenitor and eponym, Heth, is listed second among the sons of Canaan in the table of nations (Gn 10:15; cf. 1 Chr 1:13). Most of the references to the "sons of Heth" appear in the narrative of the purchase of the cave of Machpelah by Abraham (Gn 23).

The OT references to Hittites include Genesis 26:34; 27:46 (Hittite women); 49:29–32; 50:13 (Ephron); Exodus 33:2; Numbers 13:29; Deuteronomy 7:1; 20:17 (their destruction); Joshua 11:3; 12:8 (occupants of Canaan); 1 Samuel 26:6; 2 Samuel 11,12 (warriors under David); 1 Kings 9:20; 10:29 (laborers or traders under Solomon); 11:1 (wife of Solomon); Ezra 9:1 (foreigners); Ezekiel 16:3,45 (Jerusalem's ancestors).

CARL E. DEVRIES

Bibliography. F.F. Bruce, *The Hittites and the OT*; C.W. Ceram, *The Secret of the Hittites*; O.R. Gurney, *The Hittites*; S. Moscati, *The Face of the Ancient Orient*; A.H. Sayce, *The Hittites*; C.L. Woolley, *A Forgotten Kingdom*.

Hivites. Name of a pre-Israelite group living in Canaan. Though not yet demonstrated archaeologically or from secular history as a people, they were regarded as emerging from a son of Canaan (Gn 10:17) and as inhabiting areas of the Lebanon mountains (Jgs 3:3) and Hermon (Jos 11:3). They are referred to frequently as a group dispossessed by Israel (Jos 12:8; 24:11; 1 Kgs 9:20) but who managed to survive into the kingdom period (2 Sm 24:7) and lived at that time near Tyre as well as in other possible areas. Some scholars think that an error in copying, involving the changing of the letters *r* (resh) to *w* (waw) was responsible for the origin of the name Hivite from Horite.

The traditional site of the Cave of Machpelah in Hebron.

Others have suggested a scribal confusion of names, since Zibeon is called a Hivite in Genesis 36:2 and a Horite in verses 20 and 29. In several cases the Septuagint gives "Horite" in place of Masoretic text "Hivite" (Gn 34:2; Jos 9:7). Other passages in the Septuagint read "Hittite" rather than "Hivite" (Jos 11:3; Jgs 3:3).

The overlapping or equivalence of Hivite and Horite in Genesis 36 probably indicates some relationship between the two peoples (cf. Ishmaelites and Midianites in Gn 37:28, 36). Perhaps both Horites and Hivites are related to the Hurrians, who are well attested archaeologically.

The fact that there are some 25 occurrences of the name Hivite(s) in the OT, nearly one-third of which come in Joshua, makes it probable that they were a distinct people. Aside from Hivites in Palestine, they also appeared in Edomite territory (Gn 36:2). OT references to Hivites include Hamor (Gn 34:2), the men of Gibeon (Jos 9:7), the northern Hivites (Jgs 3:3–8), and those who lived near Tyre (2 Sm 24:7).

During the reign of Solomon the Hivites and other foreign inhabitants of the land were made slaves; that is, they were put under forced labor (1 Kgs 9:20,21; 2 Chr 8:7). The Hivites are not mentioned again in the Bible, and their fate is unknown.

Hizki. Elpaal's son from Benjamin's tribe (1 Chr 8:17, KJV Hezeki).

Hizkiah. 1. Neariah's son and a descendant of David through Rehoboam's line (1 Chr 3:23, KJV Hezekiah). He is perhaps identifiable with the Hezekiah in Ezra 2:16 and Nehemiah 7:21.

See HEZEKIAH #3.

2. KJV spelling of Hezekiah, Zephaniah's forefather, in Zephaniah 1:1.

See HEZEKIAH #4.

Hizkijah. KJV form of Hezekiah, Ater's descendant, in Nehemiah 10:17.

See HEZEKIAH #3.

Hobab. Name associated with Moses' father-in-law (Nm 10:29; Jgs 4:11), who was a priest of Midian (Ex 18:1) and ancestor of the Kenites (Jgs 4:11). He is usually called Jethro (Ex 3:1; 4:18; 18:1–12), but also Reuel (2:18) with its variant Raguel (Nm 10:29 KJV; RSV Reuel).

The confusion surrounding the name Hobab has never been satisfactorily resolved. Judges 4:11 seems to identify Hobab with Jethro; there is some manuscript evidence for adding "Hobab" to "the Kenite, Moses' father-in-law" in Judges 1:16, and to the mention of Reuel in Exodus 2:18. But Hobab could be Jethro's son, on one reading of Numbers 10:29a: "Hobab the son of Reuel the Midianite, Moses' father-in-law." In this passage Moses requests that Hobab accompany Israel as guide and advisor in the wilderness.

See JETHRO.

Hobah. Town to which Abraham pursued the armies under Chedorlaomer (Gn 14:15). Its location is uncertain but various suggestions have been made. Some equate it with the Hobah about 50 miles northwest of Damascus; others, with the territory called Ube in the Amarna letters; and still others, with Tell el-Salihite, 10 miles east of Damascus.

Hobaiah. Alternate spelling of Habaiah in Nehemiah 7:63.

See HABAIAH.

Hod. Zophah's son from Asher's tribe (1 Chr 7:37).

Hodaiah. KJV spelling of Hodaviah, David's descendant, in 1 Chronicles 3:24.

See HODAVIAH #1.

Hodaviah. 1. Postexilic descendant of David (1 Chr 3:24, KJV Hodaiah).

2. Chieftain of Manasseh's half-tribe east of the Jordan (1 Chr 5:24).

3. Hassenuah's son and the father of Meshullam from Benjamin's tribe (1 Chr 9:7).

4. Progenitor of a family of Levites that returned with the exiles from Babylon (Ezr 2:40); alternately called Judah in Ezra 3:9 and Hodevah in Nehemiah 7:43.

Hodesh. Name given to Shaharaim's wife from Benjamin's tribe in 1 Chronicles 8:9 (a textually corrupt passage).

Hodevah. Alternate spelling of Hodaviah in Nehemiah 7:43.

See HODAVIAH #4.

Hodiah, Hodijah. 1. Either (a) the wife of a man of Judah mentioned in 1 Chronicles 4:19 (KJV) or (b) the man of Judah himself (RSV).

2. Three of the men who signed the covenant of Ezra (Neh 10:10,13,18) bear this name; two of them are perhaps among those who interpreted the covenant to the people at Ezra's public reading of the Law (Neh 8:7, KJV Hodijah) and stood upon the stairs of the Levites during the service of covenant renewal (Neh 9:5, KJV Hodijah).

Hoglah. One of Zelophehad's five daughters (Nm 26:33; 27:1; Jos 17:3). Zelophehad, who was of Manasseh's tribe, had no sons, so that his inheritance passed to his daughters. They married within their own tribe according to God's command, so that their land "remained in the tribe of the family of their father" (Nm 36:12).

See BETH-HOGLAH, BETH-HOGLA.

Hoham. Amorite king of Hebron, confederate with four other kings in reprisals against Gibeon for making peace with Joshua (Jos 10:3). They were defeated and put to death at the cave of Makkedah (Jos 10:16–27).

Holiness. Chief attribute of God and a quality to be developed in his people. "Holiness" and the adjective "holy" occur more than 900 times in the Bible. The primary OT word for holiness means "to cut" or "to separate." Fundamentally, holiness is a cutting off or separation from what is unclean, and consecration to what is pure.

In the OT, holiness as applied to God signifies his transcendence over the creation and the moral perfection of his character. God is holy in that he is utterly distinct from his creation and exercises sovereign majesty and power over it. His holiness is especially prominent in the Psalms (47:8) and the prophets (Ez 39:7), where "holiness" emerges as a synonym for Israel's God. Thus Scripture ascribes to God the titles "Holy" (Is 57:15), "Holy One" (Jb 6:10; Is 43:15), and "Holy One of Israel" (Ps 89:18; Is 60:14; Jer 50:29).

In the OT God's holiness denotes that the Lord is separate from all that is evil and defiled (cf. Jb 34:10). His holy character is the standard of absolute moral perfection (Is 5:16). God's holiness—his transcendent majesty and the purity of his character—are skillfully balanced in Psalm 99. Verses 1 through 3 portray God's distance from the finite and earthbound, whereas verses 4 and 5 emphasize his separation from sin and evil.

In the OT God demanded holiness in the lives of his people. Through Moses, God said to the congregation of Israel, "You shall be holy; for I the Lord your God am holy" (Lv 19:2). The holiness enjoined by the OT was twofold: (1) external, or ceremonial; and (2) internal, or moral and spiritual. OT ceremonial holiness, prescribed in the Pentateuch (the first five books of the OT), included ritual consecration to God's service. Thus priests and Levites were sanctified by a complex process of ritual consecration (Ex 29), as were the Hebrew Nazirites, which means "separated ones" (Nm 6:1–21). Prophets like Elisha (2 Kgs 4:9) and Jeremiah (Jer 1:5) were also sanctified for a special prophetic ministry in Israel.

But the OT also draws attention to the inner, moral, and spiritual aspects of holiness. Men and women, created in the image of God, are called to cultivate the holiness of God's own character in their lives (Lv 19:2; Nm 15:40). Psalm 15, for example, deals with God's ethical requirements. To the question, "Who shall dwell on thy holy hill?" the Lord responds. "He who walks blamelessly, and does what is right, and speaks truth from his heart" (v 1,2). In a similar vein, Isaiah represents God's ransomed community as "the holy people, the redeemed of the Lord" (Is 62:12).

In the NT the ceremonial holiness prominent in the Pentateuch recedes to the background. Whereas much of Judaism in Jesus' time sought a ceremonial holiness by works (Mk 7:1–13), the NT stresses the ethical rather than the formal dimension of holiness. With the coming of the Holy Spirit, the early church perceived that holiness of life was a profound internal reality that should govern an individual's thoughts and attitudes in relation to persons and objects in the external world.

The NT Greek equivalent of the common Hebrew word for holiness signifies an inner state of freedom from moral fault and a relative harmony with the moral perfection of God. The word "godlikeness" or "godliness" captures the sense of the primary Greek word for holiness. Another Greek word approximates the dominant OT concept of holiness as external separation from the profane and dedication to the service of the Lord.

Because the NT writers assumed the OT portrait of deity, holiness is ascribed to God in relatively few apostolic texts. Jesus affirmed the ethical nature of God when he enjoined his disciples to pray that the Father's name might be esteemed for what it is: "Hallowed be thy name" (Mt 6:9). In the Book of Revelation the Father's moral perfection is extolled with the threefold ascription of holiness borrowed from Isaiah: "Holy, holy, holy, is the Lord God Almighty, who was and is and is to come" (4:8; cf. Is 6:13). Luke, however, contemplated God's holiness in terms of the dominant OT concept of his transcendence and majesty (1:49).

Similarly the holiness of Jesus Christ is asserted in the NT. Luke (1:35; 4:34), Peter (Acts 3:14; 4:27,30), the writer of Hebrews (7:26), and John (Rv 3:7) ascribe holiness to both the Father and the Son.

Since the Spirit comes from God, discloses his holy character, and is the instrument of God's holy purposes in the world, he also is absolutely holy (Mt 1:18; 3:16; 28:19; Lk 1:15; 4:14). The common title, "Holy Spirit," underscores the ethical perfection of the third person of the Godhead (Jn 3:5–8; 14:16,17,26).

In the NT holiness also characterizes Christ's church. The apostle Paul taught that Christ loved the church and died for it "that he might sanctify her, having cleansed her by the washing of water with the word" (Eph 5:26). The Greek forms of the verbs "sanctify" and "cleanse" suggest that Paul had in mind the "once for all" (1 Pt 3:18) imputation of Christ's righteousness to the church on the basis of his death and resurrection (cf. 1 Cor 6:11). Peter addressed the church as a holy people in language borrowed from the OT. Separated from the unbelieving nations and consecrated to the Lord, the church is "a holy nation" (1 Pt 2:9; cf. Ex 19:6).

But the NT more often discusses holiness in relation to individual Christians. Believers in Christ are frequently designated as "saints," literally meaning "holy ones," since through faith God justifies sinners, pronouncing them "holy" in his sight. A justified sinner is by no means morally perfect, but God does declare believers to be guiltless before the bar of his justice. Thus, although Christians at Corinth, for example, were plagued with numerous sins, Paul could address his erring friends as those who were "sanctified in Christ Jesus, called to be saints" (1 Cor 1:2). Despite their problems the Corinthian believers were "holy ones" in Christ.

The NT, however, places great stress upon the reality of practical holiness in the Christian's daily experience. The God who freely declares a person righteous through faith in Christ commands that the believer progress in holiness of life. In God's plan, a growth in holiness should accompany believing.

Paul urged Christians at Rome to "yield your members to righteousness for sanctification" (Rom 6:19). The Book of Hebrews urges believers to strive for "the holiness without which no one will see the Lord" (12:14). A goal of the Christian life, therefore, is conformity to the moral image of God. In this sense Paul enjoins believers at Ephesus to "put on the new nature, created after the likeness of God in true righteousness and holiness" (Eph 4:24). God graciously provides the spiritual resources to enable Christians to be "partakers of the divine nature" (2 Pt 1:4).

BRUCE A. DEMAREST

See GOD, BEING AND ATTRIBUTES OF.

Bibliography. O.R. Jones, *The Concept of Holiness*; S. Neill, *Christian Holiness*; R. Otto, *The Idea of the Holy*; J.C. Ryle, *Holiness*; S. Taylor, *Holy Living*; A.W. Tozer, *The Knowledge of the Holy*.

Holiness Code. Group of laws supposedly edited into the P (Priestly) source, comprising chapters 17–26 of Leviticus (referred to as the H document). It was either added by the authors of P or by an editor influenced by P. Liberal scholars date the work from the postexilic period in the time of Ezra (570 BC).

See DOCUMENTARY HYPOTHESIS.

Holiness of God. *See* GOD, BEING AND ATTRIBUTES OF; HOLINESS.

Holm Tree. Tree mentioned in Isaiah 44:14 whose wood was used for fuel and idol construction; its identity is uncertain.

See PLANTS.

Holon. 1. Town in the uplands of Judah's inheritance (Jos 15:51) given to the Levites (21:15). In 1 Chronicles 6:58, the town is called Hilen. Holon may be Khirbet 'Alin, northwest of Hebron.

See LEVITICAL CITIES.

2. City near Heshbon located in the plain of Moab (Jer 48:21). Its exact location is unknown.

Holy Ghost. *See* HOLY SPIRIT.

Holy of Holies. *See* TABERNACLE, TEMPLE.

Holy One of Israel. *See* GOD, NAMES OF.

Holy Place. *See* TABERNACLE, TEMPLE.

Holy Spirit. Third person of the Trinity. The word "spirit" (Hebrew *ruah*, Greek *pneuma*) is the word used from ancient times to describe and explain the experience of divine power working in, upon, and around men, and understood by them as the power of God.

Old Testament. There are three basic meanings evident in the use of spirit from the earliest Hebrew writings.

Period of the Judges. (1) Wind of God. It was a wind from God which caused the waters of the flood to subside (Gn 8:1), and which blew locusts over Egypt (Ex 10:13) and quails over the camp of Israel. The blast of his nostrils separated the waters of the Red Sea at the exodus (14:21).

(2) Breath of life. The breath of God constituted man as a living being (Gn 2:7). It is one of the earliest perceptions of Hebrew faith that man lives only because of the stirring of the divine breath or spirit within him (6:3; Jb 33:4; 34:14,15; Ps 104:29,30). Later a clearer distinction was drawn between divine Spirit and human spirit, and between spirit and soul, but at the earliest stage these were all more or less synonymous manifestations of the same divine power, the source of all life, animal as well as human (Gn 7:15,22; see Eccl 3:19,21).

(3) Spirit of ecstasy. There were occasions when this divine power seemed to overtake and possess an individual fully, so that his or her words or actions far transcended those of normal behavior. Such a person was clearly marked as an agent of God's purpose and given respect. This was apparently how leaders were recognized in the premonarchy period—Othniel (Jgs 3:10), Gideon (6:34), Jephthah (11:29), and the first king, Saul (1 Sm 11:6), as well. So too the earliest prophets were those whose inspiration came in ecstasy (19:20,23,24).

Such an understanding of divine appointment naturally posed some serious questions: Is ecstasy the *only* divine authentication, and is *all* ecstasy to be equally so regarded? There are some indications in the OT that these became relevant questions during the period of Israel's nationhood prior to the exile in Babylon.

Period of Monarchy. During the transition from the charismatic leadership of the judges to the institution of a hereditary monarchy, the issue was raised whether an anointing with the power of God was the qualification for kingship or part of the coronation ceremony itself. The issue was more lively in the northern kingdom of Israel, where hereditary monarchy did not long survive. Jehu's claim to the throne rested on his anointing by Elijah at divine command. In the southern kingdom the model ruler was David whose own claim to the throne rested on the charismatic anointing by Samuel (1 Sm 16:13; Ps 89:20,21).

The question of qualification for office and divine anointing arose in even sharper form in the preexilic period. Who should be regarded as authoritative speakers for God—the priests and cultic prophets, or the independent prophets? Did the authoritative Word of the Lord come from the priest or prophet who spoke by virtue of his place within the official cult or sanctuary, or from the prophet who spoke with the sole authority of compelling inspiration? Even with hindsight we cannot decide unequivocally for the latter alternative. While Isaiah and Jeremiah attack the corruptness of the official spokesmen of their day (Is 28:7; Jer 6:13; 23:11), it is quite likely that some of the canonical prophets, including Habakkuk and Zechariah, belonged to the cult. (Recent scholarship has concluded that at least some of the psalms began as prophetic utterances within the worship at the sanctuary.) On the other hand, where cult and charisma clash it is almost always the charismatic prophet whose utterances have been enshrined as the authoritative Word of the Lord. The two most famous incidents are the encounter between Micaiah and the 400 prophets of King Ahab (1 Kgs 22:5–28) and the confrontation between Amos and Amaziah, priest of Bethel (Am 7:10–17).

In the earlier stages of Hebrew thought ecstatic experience was seen as the direct effect of divine power. This was true even when the ecstasy was recognized as evil in character, as in the case of Saul's seizure by the Spirit (1 Sm 16:14–16). A spirit from God could be for evil as well as for good (see Jgs 9:23; 1 Kgs 22:19–23).

From the major prophets onward, however, talk about the Spirit becomes much more cautious. For Isaiah, spirit was that which characterized God and distinguished him and his actions from human affairs (Is 31:3). Later the adjective "holy" appeared as that which distinguished the Spirit of God from any other spirit, human or divine (Ps 51:11; Is 63:10,11).

The problem of false prophecy emphasized the danger of assuming that every message delivered in ecstasy was the Word of the Lord. Thus tests of prophecy evaluated the content of the message delivered or the character of the prophet's life, not the degree or quality of inspiration (see Dt 13:1–5; 18:22; Is 44:7,8; Jer

23:14; Mi 3:5). This sense of a need to discriminate between true and false inspiration and to distinguish the Word of God from the merely ecstatic oracle may help to explain the otherwise puzzling reluctance of the major 8th- and 7th-century BC prophets to attribute their inspiration to the Spirit (Mi 3:8 may be the only exception). Perhaps, as Hosea 9:7 may suggest, the Spirit had become too much identified with the madness of ecstasy, and a period of silence was necessary to separate the Word from the grosser manifestations which earlier had been regarded as its clearest expression.

The questions posed by the earliest understanding of the Spirit and agonized over by the great prophets are questions which remain: How is one to recognize the experience of the Spirit to be such? How can one distinguish true inspiration from false? How can a proper balance and healthy tension be maintained between the Spirit and the institutional forms of religion, between charisma and cult?

Exilic and Postexilic Periods. In exilic and postexilic literature the role of the Spirit is narrowed to two major functions.

(1) The prophetic Spirit. The later prophets again spoke of the Spirit in explicit terms as the inspirer of prophecy (see Ez 3:1–4,22–24; Hg 2:5; Zec 4:6). As they looked back to the preexilic period, these prophets freely attributed the inspiration of "the former prophets" to the Spirit as well (Zec 7:12).

This tendency to exalt the Spirit's role as the inspirer of prophecy became steadily stronger in the period between the OT and NT until in rabbinic Judaism the Spirit was almost exclusively the inspirer of the prophetic writings now regarded as Scripture.

(2) The eschatological Spirit. The other understanding of the Spirit's role during exilic and postexilic times was as the power of God that would characterize the age to come. That eschatological hope of divine power effecting a final cleansing and a renewed creation is rooted principally in Isaiah's prophecies (Is 4:4; 32:15; 44:3,4), where the hope of one anointed by the Spirit as the agent of final salvation comes to clearest expression (Is 11:2, 42:1; 61:1). Elsewhere the same longing is expressed for that time when the Spirit would be freely dispensed to all Israel (Ez 39:29; Jl 2:28,29; Zec 12:10), for that new creation and new covenant when relationship with God would be much more vital and immediate (Jer 31:31,34; Ez 36:26,27).

In the period prior to Jesus, the understanding of the Spirit as the Spirit of prophecy and as the Spirit of the age to come had developed into the widespread dogma that the Spirit was no longer to be experienced in the present. The Spirit had been known in the past as the inspirer of prophetic writings, but after Haggai, Zechariah, and Malachi the Spirit had been withdrawn (1 Mc 4:44–46; 9:27; 2 Bar 85:1–3; see also Ps 74:9; Zec 13:2–6). The Spirit would be known again in the age of the Messiah, but in the interim the Spirit was absent from Israel. Even the great Hillel, (learned Jewish leader and teacher, 60? BC–AD 20?) a near contemporary of Jesus, had not received the Spirit, though if anyone was worthy of the Spirit it was he. There is a tradition that at a meeting of Hillel and other wise men, a voice from heaven said, "Among those here present is one who would have deserved the Holy Spirit to rest upon him, if his time had been worthy of it." The wise men all looked at Hillel.

The consequence of this accepted dearth of the Spirit was that the Spirit in effect became subordinated to the Law. The Spirit was the inspirer of the Law, but since the Spirit could no longer be experienced directly, the Law became the sole voice of the Spirit. It was this increasing dominance of the Law and its authoritative interpreters that provided the background for the mission of Jesus and the initial spread of Christianity.

New Testament. If we are to understand rightly the NT's teaching on the Spirit we must recognize both its continuity and discontinuity with the OT. At many points NT usage cannot be fully understood except against the background of OT concepts or passages. For example, the ambiguity of John 3:8 ("wind," "Spirit"), 2 Thessalonians 2:8 ("breath"), and Revelation 11:11 ("breath of life") takes us back to the basic Hebrew meanings of "spirit," outlined at the beginning. Acts 8:39 and Revelation 17:3; 21:10 reflect the same conception of the Spirit that we find in 1 Kings 18:12; 2 Kings 2:16; and Ezekiel 3:14; and the NT writers generally share the rabbinic view that Scripture has the authority of the Spirit behind it (see Mk 12:36; Acts 28:25; Heb 3:7; 2 Pt 1:21). The principal continuity however is that of fulfillment of what the OT writers looked forward to in hope. At the same time Christianity is not simply fulfilled Judaism. In the central significance of Jesus and in the new definition of the Spirit which follows from the life and work of Jesus, we have an element of discontinuity that marks off the new faith as something distinct.

The Spirit of the New Age. The most striking feature of Jesus' ministry and of the message of the earliest Christians was their conviction and proclamation that the blessings of the new age were already present, that the eschatological Spirit had already been poured out. With the exception of the Essenes at Qumran, no other group or individual within the

The caves at Qumran, where the Essenes also proclaimed a new age.

Jewish religion of that time had dared to make such a bold claim. The prophets and the rabbis looked for a messianic age yet to come and the apocalyptic writers warned of its imminent arrival, but none thought of it as already present. Even John the Baptist spoke only of one about to come and of the Spirit's operation in the imminent future (Mk 1:8). But for Jesus and first-century Christians, the longed for hope was a living reality, and the claim carried with it the exciting sense of being in "the last days." Without some recognition of that eschatological dimension of the Christians' faith and life, we cannot understand this teaching on and experience of the Spirit.

Jesus clearly thought of his teachings and healings as fulfillment of the prophetic hope (Mt 12:41,42; 13:16,17; Lk 17:20,21). In particular, he saw himself as the One anointed by the Spirit as the agent of eschatological salvation (Mt 5:3–6; 11:5; Lk 4:17–19). So too Jesus understood his exorcisms as the effect of the eschatological power (Spirit) of God and as manifestations of the endtime rule (kingdom) of God (Mt 12:27,28; Mk 3:22–26). The Gospel writers, especially Luke, emphasize the eschatological character of Jesus' life and ministry by stressing the role of the Spirit in his birth (Mt 1:18; Lk 1:35,41,67; 2:25–27), his baptism (Mk 1:9,10; Acts 10:38), and his ministry (Mt 4:1; 12:18; Mk 1:12; Lk 4:1,14; 10:21; Jn 3:34).

Christianity proper began with the outpouring of the Spirit at Pentecost "in the last days," the overwhelming experience of vision and inspired utterance being taken as proof positive that the new age prophesied by Joel had now arrived (Acts 2:2–4,17,18). Similarly in Hebrews the gift of the Spirit is spoken of as "the powers of the age to come" (6:4,5). More striking still is Paul's understanding of the Spirit as the guarantee of God's complete salvation (2 Cor 1:22; 5:5; Eph 1:13,14), as the "first-fruits" of God's final harvest of men (Rom 8:23), and as the first installment of the believer's inheritance of God's kingdom (8:15–17; 1 Cor 6:9–11; 15:42–50; Gal 4:6,7; 5:16–18,21–23; Eph 1:13,14). The Spirit is here again thought of as the power of the age to come, as that power—which will characterize God's rule at the end of time—already shaping and transforming the lives of believers.

For Paul this means also that the gift of the Spirit is but the beginning of a lifelong process that will not end until the believer's whole person is brought under the Spirit's direction (Rom 8:11,23; 1 Cor 15:44–49; 2 Cor 3:18; 5:1–5). It also means that the present experience of faith is one of lifelong tension between what God has already begun to bring about in the believer's life and what has not yet been brought under God's grace (Phil 1:6), between Spirit and flesh, between life and death (Rom 8:10,12,13; Gal 5:16,17; 6:8). It is this eschatological tension between life "in the Spirit" and life "in the flesh" (see Gal 2:20) that comes to poignant expression in Romans 7:24 and 2 Corinthians 5:2–4.

The Spirit of New Life. Since the Spirit is the mark of the new age, it is not surprising that the NT writers as a whole understood the gift of the Spirit to be that which brings an individual into the new age. John the Baptist described the way the coming One would baptize with the Holy Spirit and with fire (Mt 3:11). According to Acts 1:5 and 11:16, this imagery was taken up by Jesus and the promise seen as fulfilled at Pentecost—the outpouring of the Spirit here being understood as the risen Christ's action in drawing his disciples into the new age, in initiating them into "the last days" (Acts 2:17,33).

It seems to be one of Luke's aims in Acts to highlight the central importance of the gift of the Spirit in conversion-initiation, as that decisive "gift of the Holy Spirit" that makes one a Christian (2:38,39). People could have been followers of Jesus on earth, but it was only with the gift of the Spirit at Pentecost that they could be said to have "believed in [i.e., committed themselves to] the Lord Jesus Christ" (11:16,17). Even belief of the gospel message in baptism could fall short of full commitment to and acceptance of Christ of which the Spirit was the decisive evidence (8:12–17).

When the Spirit's presence was manifested in and upon a life, that was recognized by Peter as proof enough that God had accepted that man even though he had not yet made any formal profession of faith or been baptized (Acts 10:44–48; 11:15–18; 15:7–9). So too Apollos, already "aglow with the Spirit" (18:25; cf. Rom 12:11), even though his knowledge of "the way of God" was slightly defective (Acts 18:24–26), apparently was not required to supplement his "baptism of John" with Christian baptism. However, the 12 so-called disciples at Ephesus proved by their very ignorance of the Spirit that they were not yet disciples of the Lord Jesus (19:1–6). Luke represents Paul as asking these 12 men, "Did you receive the Holy Spirit when you believed?" (19:2).

This is entirely of a piece with Paul's own emphasis in his letters. The step of faith and reception of the Spirit go together, two sides of the one coin: to receive the Spirit is to begin the Christian life (Gal 3:2,3); righteousness through faith and the promise of the Spirit are equivalently regarded as "the blessing of Abraham" (vv 1–14); to be baptized in the Spirit is to become a member of the body of Christ (1 Cor 12:13); if anyone does not "have the Spirit of Christ" that person does not belong to Christ, is not a Christian (Rom 8:9); only reception of the Spirit makes it possible for us to be sons of God, to call on God as Father (vv 14–17; Gal 4:6,7); the divine seal establishing the bond between God and the believer is now the Spirit himself, not circumcision (and not baptism) (2 Cor 1:22; Eph 1:13,14). The Spirit so characterizes the new age and the life of the new age that only the gift of the Spirit can bring a person into the new age to experience the life of the new age. For the Spirit is distinctively and peculiarly the lifegiver; the Spirit indeed *is* the life of the new age (Rom 8:2,6,10; 1 Cor 15:45; 2 Cor 3:6; Gal 5:25).

In just the same way in the Johannine writings, the Spirit is characteristically the life-giving Spirit (Jn 6:63), the power from above, the seed of divine life that brings about the new birth (3:3–8; 1 Jn 3:9), a river of living water that brings life when one believes in Christ (Jn 7:37–39; so also 4:10,14). Or again, reception of the Spirit in 20:22 is depicted as a new creation analogous to Genesis 2:7. Consequently in 1 John 3:24 and 4:13 possession and experience of the Spirit count as one of the "tests of life" listed in that letter.

The Spirit of the New Covenant. The life that begins with the Spirit depends on the Spirit for its continuance (Gal 3:3). As Christ fulfilled his mission in the power of the Spirit (Heb 9:14), so the person "in Christ" can only live life as a Christian out of the same Spirit. Jesus had promised the inspiration of the Spirit in times of trial (Mk 13:11), and the first Christians found this to be fulfilled in their own experience (Acts 4:8,31; 6:10; 13:9). But they also experienced the Spirit in a much more regular way as the one who directed their mission (1:8; 8:29,39; 10:19; 11:12; 13:2,4; 15:28; 17:16,17; 19:21; 1 Pt 1:12; also Jn 16:8–11; 20:21–23), and as a strengthening power (Acts 9:31; 1 Pt 4:14; Jn 14–16).

Paul in particular is quite clear that this living out of the resources and direction of the Spirit is what distinguishes Christianity from the Judaism of his day. There is a practice of religion which is "according to the letter, the written code" (Rom 2:28,29; 7:6; 2 Cor 3:6; Gal 4:9,10; Col 2:20–23), just as there is a quality of living which is "according to the flesh," on the level of one's appetites and selfish desires (Rom 8:4–6,12,13; Gal 5:13). But the Christian is one who "walks by the Spirit," is "led by the Spirit," "orders his life by the Spirit" (Rom 7:6; 8:4–6,14; Gal 5:1,16,18,25). The Spirit within is precisely the fulfillment of the prophetic hope of a new covenant, for a circumcision of the heart giving an immediate and direct knowledge of God's will and a spontaneity of worship that leaves all "rule-book religion" far behind (Rom 2:28,29; 7:6; 12:2; 2 Cor 3:3—alluding to Jer 31:31–34; Eph 2:18; 6:18; Phil 3:3; cf. 1 Jn 2:27; Jude 20).

Manifestations of the Spirit. It will be clear from what has already been said that when the first Christians, like the ancient Hebrews, spoke of the Spirit they were thinking of experiences of divine power. As in the OT so in the NT, "Spirit" is the word used to explain the experience of new life and vitality (see above), of liberation from legalism (e.g., Rom 8:2; 2 Cor 3:17), of spiritual refreshing and renewal (cf. e.g., Is 32:15; Ez 39:29 with Jn 7:37–39; Rom 5:5; 1 Cor 12:13; Ti 3:5,6). It is important to realize how wide a range of experiences were attributed to the Spirit—ecstatic experiences (Acts 2:2–4; 10:44–46; 19:6; cf. 10:10; 22:17—"in ecstasy"; 2 Cor 12:1–4; Rv 1:10; 4:2), emotional experiences (e.g., love—Rom 5:5; joy—Acts 13:52; 1 Thes 1:6; see also Gal 5:22; Phil 2:1,2), experiences of illumination (2 Cor 3:14–17; Eph 1:17,18; Heb 6:4; 1 Jn 2:20), experiences issuing in moral transformation (1 Cor 6:9–11). Likewise when Paul speaks of spiritual gifts, charismata (acts or words that bring divine grace to concrete expression), he evidently has a wide range of actual events in mind-inspired speech (1 Cor 12:8,10; see also 2:4,5; 1 Thes 1:5), miracles and healings (1 Cor 12:9; Gal 3:5; cf. Heb 2:4), acts of service and help, of counsel and administration, of aid and mercy (Rom 12:7,8; 1 Cor 12:28).

In talking thus of the Spirit in terms of experience, we should not overemphasize particular experiences or manifestations, as though earliest Christianity consisted of a sequence of mountaintop experiences or spiritual highs. There clearly were such experiences, indeed a wide range of experiences, but no one experience is singled out to be sought by all (except prophecy), there is no distinctively second (or third) experience of the Spirit in the NT, and Paul if anything warns against overvaluing particular manifestations of the Spirit (1 Cor 14:6–19; 2 Cor 12:1–10; cf. Mk 8:11–13). Where particular experiences are valued it is as manifestations of a more sustained experience, particular expressions of an underlying relationship (cf. Acts 6:3,5; 11:24—"full of the Spirit"; Eph 5:18). What we are in touch with here is the vigor of the experiential dimension of earliest Christianity. If the Spirit is the breath of the new life in Christ (cf. Ez 37:9,10,14; Jn 20:22; 1 Cor 15:45), then presumably the analogy extends further, and the experience of the Spirit is like the experience of breathing: one is not conscious of it all the time, but if one is not conscious of it, at least sometimes, something is wrong.

The Fellowship of the Spirit. It was out of this shared experience of the Spirit that the earliest Christian community grew and developed—for this is what "the fellowship (*koinōnia*) of the Spirit" properly means, common participation in the same Spirit (Phil 2:1; cf. Acts 2:42; 1 Cor 1:4–9). As it was the gift of the Spirit that brought those in Samaria, Caesarea, and elsewhere effectively into the community of the Spirit (Acts 8,10), so it was the experience of the one Spirit that provided the unifying bond in the churches of Paul's mission (1 Cor 12:13; Eph 4:3,4; Phil 2:1). Here we see the real importance of the divine manifestations of the Spirit for Paul: it is out of the diversity of these particular manifestations that the unity of the church emerges, that the body of Christ grows in unity (Rom 12:4–8; 1 Cor 12:12–27; Eph 4:4–16). It is as specific expressions of the divine life which all share that Paul thinks of the charismata. And it is only as they benefit and build up that common life and worship that Paul values them (1 Cor 12:7). This is why he ranks prophecy so highly (cf. Acts 2:17,18), because unlike glossolalia it ministers to the whole person (mind as well as spirit) and, more important, to the whole community (1 Cor 14). For the same reason he is cautious about accepting all claims to charismata—the experience of inspiration is not self-authenticating—and urges that every such claim be submitted to the judgment of the community. What does not find an echo among those who have the Spirit and does not build up the community of the Spirit is unlikely to be a gift of the Spirit (1 Cor 2:12–15; 14:29; 1 Thes 5:19–22; cf. Mt 7:15–23).

In this way Paul provides a resolution to the OT problem of whether authority lies in the individual utterance of the charismatic prophet or in the official of the institutionalized cult. For the antithesis of individual charismatic over against official spokesman has been transcended. All, not just one or two specially anointed individuals, have the Spirit; and all, not just a particular prophet, may be used by the Spirit as ministers of grace (Rom 8:9; 1 Cor 2:12; 12:7,11). This means that authority lies not in an either-or of charisma or office, but rather in the correlation and interaction of charisma and community, in the individual charisma (word or act) as tested and approved by the community as a whole.

The Spirit of Christ. The most important development and element in earliest Christian understanding of the Spirit is that the Spirit is now seen to be the Spirit of Jesus (Acts 16:7; Rom 8:9; Gal 4:6; Phil 1:19; 1 Pt 1:11; see also Jn 7:38; 15:26; 16:7; 19:30; Rv 3:1; 5:6). It is this more precise definition of the Spirit that provides the Christian answer to the other OT problem: how to recognize the experience of the Spirit to be such. The answer is partly that the Spirit is to be identified as the Spirit which bears witness to Jesus (Jn 15:26; 16:13,14; Acts 5:32; 1 Cor 12:3; 1 Jn 4:2; 5:7,8; Rv 19:10), but also and more profoundly, as the Spirit which inspired and empowered Jesus himself. Thus the Spirit is to be recognized as the Spirit of sonship—that is, as the one who inspires the same prayer and brings about the relation with God as Father that Jesus enjoyed (Rom 8:15–17—"fellow heirs"; Gal 4:6,7). The Spirit is to be recognized as the power of God that transforms the individual into the image of God, that makes the believer like Christ (2 Cor 3:18; cf. Rom 8:29; 1 Cor 13; 15:44–49; Phil 3:21; Col 3:10; 1 Jn 3:2). In particular, this means that experience of the Spirit of Jesus is experience of Christ the crucified as well as of Christ the Exalted One, experience not just of resurrection power but also of sharing his sufferings and death (Rom 8:17; 2 Cor 4:7–12,16–18; Gal 2:20; Phil 3:10,11). The mark of the Spirit of Christ is not so much experiences of divine power that leave behind or transform physical weakness, but rather the experience of power *in* weakness, of life through death (2 Cor 12:9,10).

The link between the Spirit and the exalted Jesus is even closer for the believer. The Spirit in a real sense is Jesus' mode of existence now (Rom 1:4; 1 Cor 15:45; 1 Tm 3:16; 1 Pt 3:18). To experience the Spirit is to experience Jesus (Jn 14:16–28; Rom 8:9,10; 1 Cor 6:17; 12:4–6; Eph 3:16,17; Rv 2,3). One cannot know Jesus apart from the Spirit or other than through the Spirit. One cannot experience the Spirit other than as that of power which bears the character of Christ and impresses that character on those who submit to it. Any other spiritual experience is to be discounted by the Christian, entirely disregarded and avoided.

JAMES D.G. DUNN

Bibliography. C.K. Barrett, *The Holy Spirit and the Gospel Tradition*; F.D. Bruner, *A Theology of the Holy Spirit*; M.

Green, *I Believe in the Holy Spirit;* G.S. Hendry, *The Holy Spirit in Christian Theology;* R.B. Hoyle, *The Holy Spirit in St. Paul;* M. Inch, *Saga of the Spirit;* C.D.F. Moule, *The Holy Spirit;* H.W. Robinson, *The Christian Experience of the Holy Spirit;* E. Schweizer, *The Holy Spirit;* H.B. Swete, *The Holy Spirit in the NT.*

Holy War. *See* War, Holy.

Homam. Alternate spelling of Heman, Lotan's son, in 1 Chronicles 1:39.

See Heman #1.

Homer. Dry measure of capacity estimated to be anywhere from four to six and one-half bushels.

See Weights and Measures.

Homes and Dwellings. Places of abode for people of Bible times.

The Earliest Houses. Precisely how long ago humans appeared in Palestine is not known. Before 10,000 BC people who were hunters, fishermen, and collectors of edible fruits and roots lived in caves and in temporary shelters. In the Wadi el Mughara near Mt Carmel, Professor Dorothy Garrod excavated caves between 1929 and 1934 which provided overlapping sequences of deposits left by man from the Palaeolithic Age (*c.* 25000–10000 BC) to the Mesolithic Age (*c.* 10000–7500 BC). These caves were the dwelling places of Old Stone Age man in the area. At the close of this period people became keepers of goats, sheep, and cattle and learned to cultivate grain crops. The Neolithic or New Stone Age (*c.* 7500–4000 BC) had come. One of the most significant sites of this period in Palestine was Jericho, which developed into a township some 10 acres in area with a massive town wall and a remarkable watchtower. The people moved from the caves and began constructing houses, which were probably a variation of the primitive shelters of the earlier hunters, round or curvilinear in plan. Their lower walls inclined inward, suggesting that they had domed roofs of some kind, probably made of wattling or brushwood plastered over with clay or mud. Each house had a projecting porch in which a number of steps or perhaps a sloping ramp led from the slightly sunken floor to a higher outside street level. The walls were made with hand-moulded plano-convex bricks with a flat base and a curved top. Sometimes wooden posts and wattling were incorporated in the walls. The houses had only one room, a single doorway, and probably no window. While most of the houses were roughly circular, a few were polygonal, square, or rectangular. At Beidha in southern Jordan a special house had

four rooms around a central court, although the houses at Beidha generally resembled those of the prepottery Neolithic A phase in Jericho (*c.* 7000 BC).

The houses of the prepottery Neolithic B phase in Jericho showed considerable development. The rooms were larger with wide doorways, and were flanked by timber posts. The plan was rectangular with slightly rounded corners, and the walls were straight and solid and built of hand-molded bricks somewhat different from earlier bricks made in molds. The floors were covered with a hard lime-plaster, often reddish or cream-colored, carried up the walls a little. The main rooms were flanked by smaller rooms, probably used for storage. Rain water was kept in plastered vats built against the walls. These houses were built round a courtyard where cooking was done, to judge from the thick charcoal layers on many floors. The only utensils were white limestone bowls, although skins and perhaps some wooden vessels were no doubt used.

With the discovery of pottery further changes appeared. The pottery Neolithic A people dwelt in pits dug in the mound, but their successors, the pottery Neolithic B people, began to build freestanding houses rectangular in shape with stone foundations and a superstructure of mud-bricks.

Houses of the Chalcolithic Age (c. 4000–3150 BC). The succeeding Chalcolithic Age saw some interesting variations in dwellings. In southern Palestine in the general area of Beersheba there was a good deal of subterranean dwelling and some quite remarkable artificial cave dwellings were dug into compacted, unstratified sediment (loess) at Abu Matar. These were entered either by horizontal passages or from the edge of the mound or by vertical shafts into which hand- and footholds were cut. They were on the average about 14 feet by 10 feet and were connected by galleries in groups of 5 to 7 chambers. Along the walls of the rooms were pits, some lined with plaster for water storage. Silos for storing grain were sunk in the rooms or in the connecting galleries. Fireplaces may have been on the surface of the mound. Eventually this community moved above ground and built rectilinear houses with walls set on stone foundations.

Along the coastal areas north of modern Tel Aviv there may have been another type of house. At Hedera near Caesarea, and at some other sites in the same general area, ossuaries (bone boxes) in the shape of a single-roomed house with a door at one end and a gabled roof were found. Some of the ossuaries had four feet, suggesting houses built on stilts. Some scholars have asked whether these models may not point to yet another type of house during the Chalcolithic period.

The most remarkable collection of houses from this period comes from Teleilat Ghassul, just north of the Dead Sea and three miles east of the Jordan River. A whole community of houses was closely grouped together here, each roughly rectangular or square in shape. The foundations were of stone and the walls of hand-molded bricks. Some of the walls still preserved fragments of plaster on which representations of animals, birds, and human beings were depicted in bright colors. Apparently cooking, grinding of grain, and other household chores were done in an open area near the house where paved threshingfloors, storage pits, basalt querns (millstones), open fireplaces, and ovens with sunken combustion chambers were discovered.

Early Bronze Age Houses (c. 3150–2200 BC).

The pattern established during the Chalcolithic period continued on into the Early Bronze Age. The houses of this age can be studied at a number of important sites. In general, two-roomed dwellings were more common, although the one-roomed house continued. The general shape was square or rectangular. At Tell el Far'ah (biblical Tirzah), one house measured 16 feet on each side and had walls two feet thick made of closely fitting field stones with mud-bricks above the lower walls. A stone bench 14 inches high stood against the interior walls. Pottery found in the house pointed to a date about 2600 BC. Other smaller one-roomed houses stood adjacent. The site of Arad in southern Palestine east of Beersheba produced a large area of domestic occupation and many houses of the period (c. 2850–2650 BC) were brought to light. These consisted largely of one broad room with an additional room (kitchen or storeroom) and a courtyard attached. The size of the room ranges from about 8 by 5.5 to 4.6 to 3.6 yards with the larger size more frequent. Lime plaster covered the floors and was carried up the walls. The door was always in the long wall with a few steps leading down into the room to a floor which was lower than street level. To the left of the entrance was a door socket. Low benches adjoined most of the walls and a stone base for a wooden post to support the roof was normally present. The roof was probably flat to judge from a small pottery model of a house. Large quantities of broken pottery, mortars, and grinding querns found in almost every room indicate the kind of household implement in use. Large amounts of charred grain in receptacles give a good idea of the crops that were cultivated.

At Jericho, too, there is good evidence of Early Bronze Age houses. A succession of sol-

A mud-brick house with thatch roof from Jericho.

idly built and spacious structures point to a period of full urban development. In one house a wall standing to a height of more than 15 feet may indicate that some houses were two-storied. The normal house, however, was the two-roomed dwelling. This style continued in use till the end of the Early Bronze Age. Changes came in the Middle Bronze Age which followed a period of severe depopulation at the end of the 3rd millennium (c. 2200–2000 BC). Towns such as Jericho, Beth-shan, Ai, Tirzah, and Megiddo provide evidence of this depopulation.

Middle Bronze Age Houses (c. 2000–1550 BC).

With the Middle Bronze Age we move into the period of the biblical patriarchs. Israel's early ancestors lived mostly in tents or temporary dwellings, but the Canaanites of the Middle Bronze Age into whose land they came lived in substantial houses of several rooms built around a courtyard.

The simplest form of this new type of house had a courtyard with one single room on one side, generally on the west of the courtyard, to avoid having the prevailing westerly winds blow smoke into the room. Silos for storing grain were normally in the room rather than in the courtyard. Good examples of such one-roomed houses were found at Tell Nagila northwest of Beersheba dating to about 1700 BC. Three such houses had a room 10 by 7 feet and a courtyard 10 by 16 feet, and partitions sometimes divided the room. The walls were made of rough stone and mud bricks covered by mud plaster, and were hardly thick enough to carry a second story. Houses were set close together to take advantage of a common back wall with entrances to the court on roughly parallel streets. Each house contained a stone and clay bench along the walls.

Sometimes several rooms were built off one side of the courtyard. The grandest of these yet found comes from Tell Beit Mirsim dating from about 1600 BC, probably the house of a local governor or patrician. There were no less than six rooms on the western side of the courtyard, which was some 35 by 19 feet in size. The roofed living space including both the ground and second floors was about 1500 square feet; a second floor is assumed from the thickness of the walls all around. The ground floor may have been partly functional with two stable rooms and two storage areas. Other less imposing variants of the courtyard house with rooms on one side only come from this same tell in Stratum E (c. 1700 BC).

The second type of house in the Middle Bronze Age had a roofed hall with rooms on one or two sides. A good example of such a house with rooms on one side comes from Tell Beit Mirsim dating from about 1800 BC. The large roofed rectangular hall contained three large flat stones set along the long axis to serve as foundations for the wooden roof supports. Rafters of wood and a roof of reeds covered with mud were found in the debris. Each of the three rooms on the west was entered from the hall. The stone foundations and mud brick walls were substantial enough to support a second story which could be reached by an exterior wooden staircase or ladder. The floor of earth, ashes, and straw was carefully smoothed over.

A third type of house consisted of an open courtyard with rooms on two adjacent sides of the court. A good example comes from Tell Beit Mirsim built on the ruins of the house with the roofed hall. The roofed hall became the court. A house at Tell Taanach from the Middle Bronze IIB period (c. 1700 BC) was of very strong construction with walls over three feet thick laid in mortar. The courtyard contained a cistern, and an oven was found in a room on the east side of the house. The ground floors were plastered and covered some 2300 square feet. An interior staircase led to a second story.

In some houses rooms were placed at opposite sides of the courtyard. Good examples come from Beth Shemesh (Tell er-Rumeilah) and Megiddo. At Beth Shemesh the city wall formed the south wall of the house, and rooms lay east and west of the courtyard. Entrance was from the street into one of the rooms. The other rooms were entered by crossing the courtyard. The outer walls were over three feet thick and interior walls a foot and a half. Mud and lime plaster coated the walls.

At Megiddo, too, houses were built against the north city wall. In level XII (c. 1700–1750 BC) three well-preserved houses of this kind have been found. The houses were separated by walls at right angles to the city wall. Entrance to each house was through one door onto the street, and through a room and into a courtyard paved with small stones and pebbles. The courtyards housed the ovens, and one house had a cistern.

A fourth type of Middle Bronze Age house had rooms on 3 sides of the courtyard. These rooms varied greatly in size and use. A good example dating to about 1600 BC comes from Megiddo, level IX. The house was 42 by 39 feet in size and contained 9 rooms of varying sizes. The courtyard was plastered with lime and had a large oven in the center. A second oven was found in an eastern room. Each room had a door to the courtyard. This house, like other Middle Bronze houses, had burials under the floors (cf. 1 Sm 25:11; 1 Kgs 2:34 for biblical references in the Iron Age).

The wide variety of Palestinian houses during the Middle Bronze Age points to a level of prosperity much higher than that of the Early Bronze Age. Both houses and tombs yielded quantities of graceful and well-made household utensils.

Late Bronze Age Houses (c. 1550–1200 BC). Information is limited for this period, due partly to the accidents of excavation and partly to the severe destruction at the close of the age of many sites at the hands of Israelites, Sea Peoples, Egyptians, and others. At Tell Beit Mirsim one earlier house was rebuilt on the same plan, probably by an Israelite, but it lacked the finesse of earlier buildings. The courtyard type house continued in general use. One residence at Beth-shemesh was some 49 by 39 feet in size, but its three-feet-thick walls were very rough. A stone staircase inside the courtyard suggests an upper story. At Megiddo around 1400 BC one house had rooms around four sides of the courtyard. Jericho, which was rich in Middle Bronze Age houses, did not produce Late Bronze Age houses because of serious erosion.

Israelite Houses of the Iron Age (c. 1200–600 BC). Many examples of domestic buildings come from this period. The Israelite structures were at first rather crude but the quality improved. Thus at Tell Qasile in the 12th century there were poor homes with a courtyard and a single room on one side. At contemporary Beth-shemesh one larger house had a foundation of large uncut stones, a courtyard some 34 by 20 feet, and 3 rooms on one side 11 by 10½ feet. There was rough stone paving in the court and in two of the rooms. At Hazor, Yigael Yadin discovered a house with a courtyard and rooms on one side dating to about 900 BC. Half of the courtyard was covered, the roof being supported on stone pillars. These stone pillars are very characteristic of the Iron Age houses in Palestine and have been found in sites all over the country.

The Late Bronze and Middle Bronze Age pattern with a courtyard and rooms on two adjoining sides was common in the Iron Age. A good example comes from Megiddo, level V from around 1050 BC. The house had two parts, each of which was entered from the street along a corridor which opened into three rooms. The courtyard was at the end of the corridor and a stairway off the courtyard led up to a second story. The floors were paved with lime plaster, and the range of high quality pottery found there suggests the home of a man of influence. Beyond this large structure lay many small structures in which querns, grinders, stone bowls, and ovens were found.

The most common type of house in the days of the kings of Judah and Israel was one in which rooms were built on three sides of a courtyard. Good examples of this type of house have been found at Tell Qasile (near Tel Aviv), Megiddo, Tell en Nasbeh (perhaps biblical Mizpah), Tell es Sa'idiyeh (across the Jordan River midway between Galilee and the Dead Sea), Tirzah, Hazor, and Shechem. This type of house has sometimes been called the "four-room house." A long room was built across the short axis of the courtyard, and two other rooms, one on each side of the court, were constructed on the long axis. The courtyard was divided into three by two rows of pillars which extended down the long axis of the court. These pillars supported the roof and gave support for walls, either half height or full height. Entrance to the house was from the street into the courtyard where ovens and silos were normally placed, although this varied. Such a framework could be expanded by adding a row of rooms outside the existing rooms on the long axis of the court. There were many ways to divide long rooms into smaller ones. In some cases where the walls were strong enough a second story was added. An excellent example of a four-roomed house which was later enlarged was found at Shechem and dated to the period around 748–724 BC. The courtyard contained a storage bin, a large open hearth, a quern, stone grinders, and the bases of pottery jars resting in stone pedestals. In the rooms that had been added there was a device for catching water from the roof and delivering it to an underground water system. A large silo in one room was connected to a kitchen.

Other houses of the same general plan belonging to the 8th century BC were found at Hazor. These usually had rooms on both sides of the courtyard and opening onto it. Stone pillars were set in a row to one side of the court and seem to have supported a roof. The courtyards housed an oven and storage jars. Some dwellings in Hazor had only one or two rooms.

There is evidence that larger Iron Age houses served as industrial or commercial buildings. Certain houses at Tell Beit Mirsim contained dye vats and loom weights. In other places the large number of querns suggests a wheat-grinding industry. There is evidence also of wine vats, of potters' equipment, and of shops. Some houses had rooms set apart for religious purposes and contained incense stands, figurines, small altars, and the like.

The excavations of Kathleen Kenyon at Jerusalem brought to light houses from the last days of Judah. They were rather small and irregularly planned, but of the same general design as those in the hill country sites of Judah—a courtyard divided by a row of stone pillars which supported the roof.

The contrast between big houses and small houses in some towns probably indicates the social inequality referred to in the prophets. In the 10th and 9th centuries BC there was a fairly uniform picture of many small houses and a few large ones. By the 8th century BC at a town like Tirzah there were 3 or 4 large houses and a great many flimsy structures.

Babylonian, Persian, and Hellenistic Houses. After the fall of Jerusalem to Nebuchadnezzar in 586 BC, Palestine was under the rule of Babylonians (586–539 BC), Persians (539–332 BC), and Greeks (332–37 BC). Archaeological evidence is at present somewhat limited for the Babylonian and Persian periods partly because of the extensive destruction caused by the Babylonians and partly because many Persian remains were destroyed by intensive Hellenistic and Roman constructions built over them. There are biblical references to the houses of the people in this period (Neh 7:3,4; Hg 1:4,9; Zec 13:6; 14:2). In a number of sites, for example, Lachish, Megadim, and Mevorakh, the Persian period is represented by a large palacelike structure, probably an administrative building on the top of a mound. The domestic areas of these towns lay off the tell. It is clear that already in the Persian period the towns began to be laid out in the rectangular Hellenistic pattern with houses set along parallel streets. One of the best examples of a Hellenistic town is Mareshah (Marisa). Two types of building were found in the city—the large structure with rooms surrounding an enclosed courtyard, and the small houses comprised of rooms not arranged in any clear plan. Several houses contained hearths, basins, shelves, and steps leading either to a roof or a cellar. One house contained a granary. The architecture was a blend of Hellenistic and Eastern elements. The city had a drainage system to which the private houses were connected.

Detail of the house of Neptune and Amphitrite (his wife) on a wall mural from Roman times.

Houses in NT Times. There are references in the NT to houses, roofs, doors, foundations, an upper room, and lamps. One of Jesus' parables refers to good and bad foundations (Mt 7:25). In one incident friends took a paralyzed man up to the roof which they took apart to lower him into the room where Jesus was (Mk 2:4). Jesus referred to proclamations made from the housetops (Mt 10:27; Lk 12:3), and Peter went up on the roof to pray (Acts 10:9). Houses were swept to find lost objects (Lk 15:8) and illuminated by lamps (Mt 5:15). There are several references to houses of specific individuals (Mk 8:3; Lk 10:5; 16:4; 19:9; Jn 11:20; Acts 4:34; 9:11; 10:32). Some houses had upper rooms on the roof reached by an outside staircase. The Passover meal was prepared in such a large upstairs room (Mk 14:12–15). The disciples lodged in a similar room after the death and resurrection of Jesus (Acts 1:13). Perhaps the reference to robbers breaking in was to one of these larger, better-class houses (Mt 6:19; Mk 3:27; Lk 12:39). In such houses there were sometimes servants (Acts 10:7) and some had a guest room (Mk 14:14). We conclude from the NT data that there was a variety in the size and elegance of the houses of Jesus' day. A typical street in Judea or Galilee would have houses ranging from the small house (25 to 30 feet square) to the mansion of the upper classes, which could be two or more stories high embellished by rows of pillars and architectural adornment.

For the precise character of these houses we have to turn to archaeological and literary evidence. The writings of the rabbis and Josephus fill in many details. Excavation in sites of the early Roman (Herodian) period (37 BC– AD 70) have provided more tangible evidence. A rich source of information is the excavation in the old Jewish quarter in Jerusalem. One large house of some 209 square yards in size had a central courtyard where three cooking ovens and a water cistern were found. Large niches set in some of the walls contained broken pottery and must have been cupboards. Traces of mosaic floors and plastered walls gave an idea of the beauty of this house. There were several rooms off the courtyard, perhaps as many as 10. The remains of other fine houses of the late second temple period have been found further west, notably in the area of

A room in a house (the Burnt House on Mt Zion) from the Roman period.

the Armenian cemetery on Mt Zion, in which beautiful frescoes were preserved exhibiting a unique representation of birds. Other houses have yielded mosaic pavements with purely geometric patterns, thus adhering to the injunction against depicting animal forms.

The wealthy house of NT times bore some resemblance to the Roman house with its courtyard (atrium) and rooms leading off from it, of the type preserved at Pompeii. There was a military occupation of Palestine from 63 BC onward and Roman governors and officials tended to build houses in their own style. The local Jewish population, however, adhered more to patterns which had been in use over many centuries.

JOHN A. THOMPSON

See ARCHITECTURE.

Honey. Sweet syrup produced by bees (Jgs 14:8), either wild (1 Sm 14:25,26) or domesticated (apparently so in 2 Chr 31:5). Sometimes, however, it may refer to thick grape syrup (as in Arabic) or date syrup (as described by Josephus). Honey was considered one of life's necessities (Ecclus 39:26); one must not, however, eat too much (Prv 25:16, 27). It was part of the diet of John the Baptist (Mk 1:6) and of Immanuel (Is 7:15). Its exclusion, along with leaven, from grain offerings (Lv 2:11) is undoubtedly because it is susceptible to ferment. Obviously sweet (Jgs 14:18), it became a familiar metaphor (Ps 19:10; Rv 10:9,10).

See FOOD AND FOOD PREPARATION.

Hoopoe. Any of a number of Old World singing birds; considered unclean (Lv 11:19; Dt 14:18).

See BIRDS.

Hope. An expectation or belief in the fulfillment of something desired. Present hurts and uncertainty over what the future holds create the constant need for hope. Worldwide poverty, hunger, disease, and human potential to generate terror and destruction create a longing for something better. Historically people have looked to the future with a mixture of longing and fear. Many have concluded that there is no reasonable basis for hope and therefore to hope is to live with an illusion. Scripture relates being without hope to being in the world without God: "remember that you were at that time separated from Christ, alienated from the commonwealth of Israel, and strangers to the covenants of promise, having no hope and without God in the world" (Eph 2:12).

The modern world has sought hope in human effort and a belief in the inevitability of progress that assumed everything would naturally get better and better. The threat and reality of war in the 20th century challenged that optimism and left growing despair in its wake. Though many still find little reason to hope, others have returned to a humanistic basis for hope. It is held that because people are the source of the world's problems they can also be the solution. This position can be called into question on the basis of present and historical evidence to the contrary.

Christianity has often been considered in discussions concerning hope. Unfortunately Christianity has not always received "good press" in this regard. In the early centuries of church history stress on the disparity between this world and the next seemed to create an attitude of escapism, futility, or indifference toward the problems and pains of human existence. In the 19th century Prussian philosopher Frederick Nietzsche (1844–1900) claimed that Christianity made people cowards because it taught that whatever happened was God's will, thus discouraging efforts to change the world. Karl Marx (1818–83) said that Christianity or religion was the "opiate of the people." For Marx religion kept people from rising against those who oppressed them.

The tendency for Christianity to be viewed as otherworldly was opposed by Jürgen Moltmann in what has been called "the theology of hope." That theology was the product of the pessimism and despair of post–World War II Europe. Moltmann's theology of hope says that the future is the basis for changing the present, and that Christian service should be an attempt to make otherworldly hopes a present reality. The resurrection is said to bring hope amid present suffering by becoming the catalyst for human effort to overcome that suffering.

Certain ideas suggested by proponents of this theology, for changing present political, social, and economic problems are thought by some to imply a use of violence and revolution which seems incongruous with the gospel of peace. Other objections point to that theology's potential for altogether denying the hope of God's future intervention in world affairs. Trust in human effort to change the future could lead to a humanistic notion that the resurrection is merely a hopeful symbol that will spur people into action, and not necessarily a reality of God's historical action in the world through Jesus Christ. Another concern is that the discussion of hope for this world by a transformation of political and social structures could neglect the need for personal transformation of people's lives through conversion and repentance. While critical questions have een raised about the theology of hope, on the positive side that theology has led to examination or reexamination of the biblical doctrine of hope.

The patriarch Abraham is a model of faith and hope. In spite of the realities that surrounded him, "no distrust made him waver concerning the promise of God, but he grew strong in his faith as he gave glory to God" (Rom 4:20,21). Christian faith and hope, like Abraham's, are based on the faithfulness of God. As the apostle Paul wrote of his struggles, "Why, we felt that we had received the sentence of death; but that was to make us rely not on ourselves but on God who raises the dead; he delivered us from so deadly a peril, and he will deliver us; on him we have set our hope and he will deliver us again" (2 Cor 1:9,10). Hope is, therefore, not irrational, but rather is based upon God, who has proven himself faithful.

Biblical hope is hope in what God will do in the future. At the heart of Christian hope is the resurrection of Jesus. Paul discussed the nature, certainty, and importance of the resurrection (1 Cor 15:12–28). That Paul is certain that Christian hope points to the future can be seen by his statement, "If for this life only we have hoped in Christ, we are of all men most to be pitied" (1 Cor 15:19). The significance of Christ's resurrection is not only that it points to his victory over death, but also extends that victory to those who are his: "But each in his own order: Christ the first fruits, then at his coming those who belong to Christ" (1 Cor 15:23). The apostle Peter said, "Blessed be the God and Father of our Lord Jesus Christ! By his great mercy we have been born anew to a living hope through the resurrection of Jesus Christ from the dead, and to an inheritance which is imperishable, undefiled, and unfading, kept in heaven for you" (1 Pt 1:3,4a). In that passage, Peter attributes living hope to the resurrection of Christ and points to God's future blessing upon those who belong to Christ. That future hope empowers the Christian to live without despair through the struggle and suffering of the present (cf. Rom 8:18; 2 Cor 4:16–18).

Does Christian hope lead one simply to wait for the future, or does that hope stimulate one to help allay the present hurts of humanity? In a number of NT passages hope is mentioned in contexts dealing with ministry to others. Hope is related to faith and love thus denying that hope can be selfish. Christian hope, far from leading to social unconcern, makes meaningful ministry in the world possible. Many humanistic efforts to transform society fail because of an inability to transform people's values so that they are able to live at peace and share what they have with others. In the context of the social implications of the Christian life, Paul brings together certain important categories. Showing the relevance of hope to ministry he wrote, "Rejoice in your hope, be patient in tribulation, be constant in prayer" (Rom 12:12). Paul said that the coming salvation should lead Christians to live differently, to live in accord with what they know of the future: "let us conduct ourselves becomingly as in the day" (13:13). The context brings together the future hope and present ministry, a combination made possible for those with transformed minds (12:1,2).

That transformation is made possible in part by Christian hope. Before people are willing to share with others, thus bringing relief to contemporary hurts, they need to overcome their selfish and self-justifying nature. When men and women hope only in their own abilities or possessions, they really are not free to give of their resources to others. When believers are justified by God's grace and receive his certain hope, they are free to share with others. Jesus hints at this: "Fear not, little flock, for it is your Father's good pleasure to give you the kingdom. Sell your possessions" (Lk 12:32,33a). "Therefore I tell you, do not be anxious about your life, what you shall eat or what you shall drink, nor about your body, what you shall put on" (Mt 6:25). Paul stated: "As for the rich in this world, charge them not to be haughty, nor to set their hopes on uncertain riches but on God who richly furnishes us with everything to enjoy. They are to do good, to be rich in good deeds, liberal and generous" (1 Tm 6:17,18). So, Christian hope not only grants certainty about the future, but by giving Christians that certainty enables them to give freely to the needs of others. To those who want to justify themselves or make their own future secure through selfish accumulation of riches, Christian hope offers fulfillment that they could not achieve on their own.

Christian hope is securely based upon the words and actions of God. The promises of God have proven to be dependable. The resurrection of Jesus becomes the ultimate basis for hope. Since God has already overcome death through Christ, the Christian can live with confidence in the present. No matter how dark the present age seems, the Christian has seen the light to come. People need to hope, and hope placed in the personal promise of God is secure. This secure hope is full of social significance, however, freeing one from bondage to materialism and its natural selfishness. Christian hope offers security for the future and loving involvement in sharing for the present.

PAUL K. MCALISTER

Bibliography. R.J. Banks (ed), *Reconciliation and Hope;* E. Brunner, *Eternal Hope;* G.B. Caird et al., *The Christian Hope;* F. Herzog (ed), *The Future of Hope;* P.S. Minear, *Christian Hope and the Second Coming;* C.F.D. Moule, *The Meaning of Hope;* S. Travis, *The Jesus Hope.*

Hophni. Brother of Phinehas, with whom he served as a priest at Shiloh (1 Sm 1:3). He was an evil man who flouted the sacrificial rituals (2:13–17) and behaved immorally (2:22). Condemned by God, Hophni died during a Philistine attack on Shiloh and its sanctuary (4:11).

Hophra. Son of Psammis, ruler over Egypt from 589–570 BC during the 26th dynasty, called Pharaoh Hophra in Jeremiah 44:30. He is also referred to as Apries (Herodotus II.161; Diodorus 1.69) or Onophra (Manetha; Septuagint Jer 44:30). Although he is alluded to several times during the divided kingdom period (Jer 43:8–13; Ez 29:1–3; 31:1–18), he is mentioned by name only in Jeremiah 44:30.

He came to power after the death of his father, and in 589 BC marched into Judah against Nebuchadnezzar and the Babylonians in order to assist Zedekiah. Apparently he retreated before superior forces, and Jerusalem was overthrown (Jer 37:5). Both Jeremiah (43:9–13; 46:13–26) and Ezekiel (Ez 29,30) foretold his defeat. This occurred in 566 BC, at the hands of Amasis, who had usurped the throne of Egypt in 569 BC. Hophra was killed as prophesied (Jer 44:30).

Hopping Locust. Type of locust (KJV cankerworm) mentioned in Joel 1:4.

See ANIMALS (LOCUST).

Hor, Mount. 1. Mountain located at the border of the land of Edom (Nm 20:23; 33:37). Mt Hor was the first place to which the Israelites came (20:22) after wandering nearly 40 years (Dt 2:14) because of their lack of faith in God's ability to lead them triumphantly into Canaan (Nm 14:33,34), a land that none of them (except Joshua and Caleb) would be allowed to enter (14:30). Moses' brother Aaron would not be permitted to enter Canaan because he had refused to carry out the Lord's instructions at Meribah (20:7–13,24). Stripped of his priestly garments, which were then put on his son Eleazar, Aaron died on the top of Mt Hor (20:25–29) at the age of 123, on the 1st day of the 5th month of the 40th year after the exodus of the people of Israel from Egypt (33:38,39). A similar punishment was later meted out to Moses, whose death on Mt Nebo is compared to Aaron's death on Mt Hor (Dt 32:49–51). According to Deuteronomy 10:6 (which is part of a long parenthetical note), Aaron died and was buried at Moserah (probably the Moseroth of Nm 33:30,31), a place that must have been very close to (or perhaps a part of) Mt Hor.

The location of Mt Hor remains uncertain. The traditional site, Jebel Nebi Harun (which means "the mountain of the prophet Aaron" is almost 4800 feet high and is the tallest mountain in Edom. The Muslims claim that a small building on its summit is the tomb of Aaron. But Jebel Nebi Harun is located near Petra—in the middle of Edom—and too far east of Kadesh. A more likely location is Jebel Madeira, situated on the northwest border of Edom about 15 miles northeast of Kadesh. In any event, the Hebrew word *hōr* probably means "mountain" (as in Gn 49:26), so that "Mt Hor" perhaps means simply "mountain of mountains" or "high mountain" rather than being a proper name.

2. Another mountain located in the far north (Nm 34:7,8). Generally identified as either Mt Hermon or Jebel Akkar, it too was perhaps simply an unusually high mountain.

RONALD F. YOUNGBLOOD

Horam. King of Gezer, who, while coming to the aid of Lachish, was defeated and killed by Joshua (Jos 10:33).

Horeb, Mount. Alternate name for Mt Sinai.

See SINAI, SINA.

Horem. Town set up for defense purposes in the uplands of Naphtali's territory (Jos 19:38). Its exact site is unknown, though undoubtedly in northern Galilee.

Horesh. Hebrew word translated as a place-name in 1 Samuel 23:15–19 (part of the wilderness of Ziph). David hid from Saul there and met secretly with Jonathan. The word is translated simply as "wooded hills" (KJV in the forests) in 2 Chronicles 27:4. Authorities differ on whether the place-name in 1 Samuel is warranted.

Hor-haggidgad, Hor-hagidgad. Camping place of the Israelites during their wilderness wanderings (Nm 33:32,33; KJV Hor-hagidgad). It may be the Gudgodah of Deuteronomy 10:7, and has been identified with Wadi Ghadaghed.

See WILDERNESS WANDERINGS.

Hori. 1. Lotan's first son. Lotan was the founder of a Horite subclan in Edom (Gn 36:22; 1 Chr 1:39).

2. Shaphat's father and a member of Simeon's tribe. Shaphat was one of the 12 spies (Nm 13:5).

The entrance to Siq, the mile-long passage (through cliffs 300 feet high) to Petra, in the area where tradition says the Horites lived.

Horite, Horim. Cave dwellers of Mt Seir, according to tradition. These pre-Edomites were called the children of Seir (Gn 36:20). In the Bible they were defeated by Chedorlaomer and his allies (14:6). They were governed by chieftains (36:29,30), and eventually destroyed by the descendants of Esau (2:12,22).

The popular and biblical etymology of "Horite" has been disputed since the discovery of the Hurrians (Khurians) as ethnic predecessors of many Near Eastern tribes. The Hurrians were a non-Semitic people from the mountains. About the 2nd millennium BC they migrated into north and northeast Mesopotamia, and later moved into the regions of Syria and Palestine. Since the Hurrian language was prevalent in the west Jordan area and since phonetically "Horite" is the OT Hebrew equivalent of the extrabiblical "Hurrian," several scholars and translators have substituted "Hurrian" for "Horite." Many have equated the Hivites, who were part of the Hurrian language and cultural group, with the Horites. These critics assumed an early textual corruption of the r(esh) in Horite to w(aw) in Hivite. A certain Zibeon is called a Horite in Genesis 36:20–30, whereas in verse 2 the man is called a Hivite. The Septuagint of Joshua 9:7 and Genesis 34:2 reads "Horite" instead of "Hi-

vite" as in the Masoretic text. Some manuscripts of the Septuagint read "Hittite" for the Masoretic text's "Hivite" (Jos 11:3; Jgs 3:3). In Genesis 36:2, the Hebrew erroneously reads "Hivite" for "Horite." It appears that the OT references do not fit the Hurrians, nor do the personal names of the Horites correspond to Hurrian examples (Gn 36:20–30). They seem instead to be Semitic. The Horites were from Transjordan, and were the predecessors of the Edomites (14:6). Later references to Horites may be to western Horites, who were perhaps Hurrians (Is 17:9) and non-Semitic, but quite distinct from the predecessors of the Edomites, the eastern Horites. The Hebrew of Genesis 34:2 and Joshua 9:7 may be from a different family of manuscripts than those used by the Septuagint translators, preserving its own ethnic traditions. It seems best to think of both Hivites and Horites as ethnic groups connected with the Hurrians by language and culture.

See HURRIANS; HIVITES.

Hormah. Town near Beersheba in the Negeb and on the border of the tribes of Judah and Simeon. Originally a Canaanite settlement, it became Judah's according to Joshua 15:30 and then Simeon's according to 19:4. Judah had dominated it again by the time of the early monarchy (1 Sm 30:30). The change of the Canaanite name Zephath to Hormah when the Hebrews first conquered it is noted in Judges 1:17. Hormah took David's side during his running feud with King Saul (1 Sm 30:30), and David rewarded the town by sending it some of the spoils of war from his conquest of Ziklag. Joshua 15:30 describes it as being in the south near Chesil and Ziklag, but its precise location remains unknown. From the reference in Numbers 14:45, it could well be south of Kadesh-barnea, where the Israelites spent much of the wilderness period. Other suggested locations of Hormah include Tell el-Milh, 7 miles east of Beersheba, and Tell esh-Sheri'ah, about 12 miles northwest of Beersheba.

Horn. 1. Musical instrument frequently made from a ram's horn.

See MUSIC AND MUSICAL INSTRUMENTS (HATZOTZROT).

2. Figuratively, a symbol of power (1 Kgs 22:11) expressing dominance over the weak (Ez 34:21), forces of destruction (Zec 1:18–21), and deliverance from oppression (1 Kgs 22:11; 2 Chr 18:10). Thus the horn has two aspects, to succour and to denote force (2 Sm 22:3; Ps 18:2). The succession of horns could mean the continuation of the kingly line (Ps 132:17). Psalm 75:10 declares that the horns of the

wicked shall be cut off but those of the righteous exalted. The symbolic imagery in Daniel and Revelation reinforces the use of the horn to represent power and authority (Dn 7,8; Rv 13,17). The ram's horn, goat's horn, and horn of a wild ox were used as containers for liquid. They were also ceremonial receptacles for oil (1 Sm 16:1,13; 1 Kgs 1:39). Cows' horns were forbidden for any religious or ceremonial use.

Four horn-shaped projections jutted forth from the four corners of the tabernacle and temple altars (Ex 27:2; 30:2,3). These altar horns were coated with sacrificial blood, and denoted an area of sanctuary (Ex 29:12; Lv 4:7,18). Altar horns are seen in the example found at Megiddo.

Hornet.   Large wasp.

See ANIMALS (WASP).

Horonaim.   Moabite settlement of uncertain location, listed in prophetic oracles against Moab (Is 15:5; Jer 48:3,5,34). It fell to Alexander Janneus, but the Hasmonean rule was subsequently returned to King Aretas by John Hyrcanus (Josephus, *Antiq.* 13.15.4; 14.1.4).

Horonite.   Reference to either the residence or birthplace of Sanballat who opposed Nehemiah's restoration program (Neh 2:10,19; 13:28). The name probably derives from the two cities of Upper and Lower Beth-horon.

Horse.   See ANIMALS.

Horse Gate.   Gate near the palace in Jerusalem (Jer 31:40), in the southeast part of the city wall. Here Queen Athaliah was put to death (2 Kgs 11:16; 2 Chr 23:15). The gate was restored under Nehemiah (Neh 3:28).

See JERUSALEM.

Horus.   See EGYPT, EGYPTIANS.

Hosah (Person).   Merarite Levite who guarded the gate of the tent where the sacred ark was kept (1 Chr 16:38) when David brought it to Jerusalem. His gatekeeping responsibilities were shared by his sons (1 Chr 26:10–16).

Hosah (Place).   City south of Tyre on Asher's border (Jos 19:29). Its exact location is unknown.

Hosanna.   Hebrew expression meaning "Save us, we beseech thee," taken from Psalm 118:25. The crowd welcomed Jesus to Jerusalem with the cry of "Hosanna" (Mt 21:9; Mk 11:9,10; Jn 12:13).

Psalm 118 is a declaration of confidence in the Lord's salvation, made in a time of need. The psalm as a whole was part of a longer hymn (the Hallel) which was sung on great occasions. Verse 25 in particular was used in the Jewish feast of tabernacles. At the point in the worship when this verse was read, the people would wave branches of myrtle, willow, and palm. Branches may have been waved at other times also as a general expression of jubilation. This happens in 2 Maccabees 10:6,7, at a ceremony for the rededication of the temple after it had been defiled. But because the people who welcomed Jesus not only waved branches but also sang "Hosanna," and "blessed be he who enters in the name of the Lord" (Ps 118:26) it appears they had the feast of tabernacles in mind.

This means the crowd was greeting Jesus as Messiah. Already before Jesus' time the phrase "blessed is he who comes in the name of the Lord" was taken to refer to the Messiah. And it is possible that the word "Hosanna" by itself had messianic significance. Other expressions in the report of Jesus' entry into Jerusalem support this. In Matthew 21:9 Jesus is called the "Son of David"; in Mark 11:9 there is reference to "the coming kingdom of our father David"; in John 12:13, Jesus is called "the King of Israel." All of these have messianic overtones.

We need not suppose that in shouting "Hosanna" the people had a political deliverance in mind. They probably did not know in what way Jesus would be a deliverer. The most one can say is they believed Jesus was One sent by God for their salvation. Had there not been something in their response to him which Jesus could recognize as proper worship, he would hardly have accepted their praise. It would only appear later, in his cross and resurrection, what his messiahship really meant.

J. GORDON McCONVILLE

See MESSIAH; HALLEL; HALLELUJAH.

Hosea (Person).   Prophet of ancient Israel whose sphere of activity was the northern kingdom. Little is known of him outside of the prophetic book that bears his name. His prophetic ministry is best placed in the third quarter of the 8th century BC. His name means "help" or "helper," and is based on the Hebrew word for salvation.

The evidence for placing Hosea in the northern kingdom is basically internal. The book is concerned mainly with the northern tribes whom he frequently identifies as "Ephraim," a common appellation for the northern kingdom and the dialect of Hebrew in which the book was written seems to be of a northern cast.

The circumstances surrounding the marriage of Hosea form the catalyst for his prophetic message. He was commanded by God to marry Gomer, who apparently was a harlot; his marriage provided an analogy with Israel who was guilty of spiritual adultery.

Scholars differ as to the interpretation of this controversial account but there is little reason for doubting that it was a literal event. The act of sacrifice involved in Hosea's obedience to God forms a marvelous picture of God's sacrificial love for man.

THOMAS E. MCCOMISKEY

See HOSEA, BOOK OF; PROPHET, PROPHETESS.

Hosea, Book of.

First of the 12 minor prophets in the traditional arrangement of the OT books. It was written in the last part of the 8th century BC. Hosea's prophecies were proclaimed to the northern kingdom of Israel in the final years of its existence. Hosea was the only prophet to reside in the northern kingdom and also to preach there. God commissioned Hosea to reveal the widespread apostasy and corruption in the northern kingdom and to exhort his fellow countrymen to repent and return to God. Hosea had the unique privilege of illustrating by his own family life the steadfast covenant love which God had for Israel.

Author. Hosea's ministry extended over a period of at least 34 years (c. 756–722 BC), and he appears as a knowledgeable individual whether he was a peasant or a member of the wealthier class in Israel.

Hosea's marriage to the prostitute Gomer may have been controversial in his own day, and it has certainly caused a great deal of controversy ever since among Bible students and commentators. It seems best to recognize that Gomer was a publicly known harlot whom Hosea was commanded to marry for the purpose of illustrating Israel's apostasy and God's steadfast covenant love.

Authenticity. The authenticity and unity of Hosea is not seriously questioned, even by higher criticism. Two areas of controversy are: (1) passages that refer to Judah (e.g., 1:1,7,11; 4:15; 5:5,10–14; 6:4,11; 8:14; 11:12; 12:2) and (2) those sections that refer to future blessing or national deliverance (e.g., 11:8–11; 14:2–9).

Hosea's references to Judah, however, could be expected from a man of God chagrined by the separation of Israel from the legitimate Davidic line. The northern kingdom with its ungodly kings was on the verge of judgment from God. Hosea evidently had received divine revelation concerning his dealings with Judah as well as Israel.

The references to the future blessings and deliverance of Israel do not neutralize the condemnation of the sins of Israel, any more than Hosea's constant love for and reconciliation with adulterous Gomer neutralizes her sin. Restoration and forgiveness need not ignore guilt.

Historical and Archaeological Background. Hosea lived during the prosperous days of the northern kingdom of Israel under Jeroboam II (793–753 BC). He also saw its defeat and the deportation of its people after the invasion by the Assyrians (722 BC).

In Hosea 1:1 the following kings are named: from the southern kingdom of Judah—Uzziah, Jotham, Ahaz, and Hezekiah; and from the northern kingdom of Israel—Joash and Jeroboam. Uzziah was a contemporary of both Joash and Jeroboam. Ahaz was king of Judah when Israel was taken captive by Assyria. Hezekiah seems to have been a co-regent with Ahaz at the time of the Assyrian captivity.

Jeroboam II reigned over Israel for 41 years (2 Kgs 14:23) and followed the evil example of his father Nebat (v 24).

Though Israel was prosperous and successful during Jeroboam's reign, the corruption in the government and the degeneracy in the spiritual lives of the people set the stage for more tumultuous times in the days of subsequent kings.

The deterioration of economy and morals in the reign of Jeroboam II paved the way for the fall of Israel. The rich landowners (including the king) oppressed the peasants and caused the lower class landowners to migrate from the farms to the cities. The social repercussions were soon to engulf Israel in a wave of corruption. Anarchy was a product of those times (Hos 4:1,2; 7:1,7; 8:3,4; 9:15).

Date. Hosea's prophetic ministry commenced with the reign of Jeroboam II (793–753 BC) and extended into that of Hezekiah of Judah (715–686 BC).

Several factors indicate that Hosea continued prophesying under Hoshea of Israel (732–722 BC): (1) "Shalman" (Hos 10:14) may be Shalmaneser of Assyria who invaded Israel early in the reign of Hoshea (2 Kgs 17:3). (2) "Jareb" (Hos 5:13; 10:6, both KJV) may be Sargon II (722–705 BC). (3) Predictions of the Assyrian invasion appear to refer to an imminent event (10:5,6; 13:15,16). (4) Mention of Egypt and Israel's dependence on that nation seem to fit the reign of Hoshea (7:11; 11:11). These factors confirm that the compilation of Hosea's messages may have taken place very near to the time of Israel's fall (722 BC).

Origin and Destination. Hosea prophesied while residing in Israel. He refers to the king in Samaria as "our king" (Hos 7:5). His descriptions of Israel evidence a degree of familiarity with the geography of the northern kingdom. Gilead is mentioned by Hosea as though he knew that area from personal observation (6:8; 12:11). Hosea was probably the only prophet to the northern kingdom who actually lived there throughout his ministry.

Purpose. Hosea proclaimed to Israel the need to repent and return to God. He presented the God of Israel as a patient and loving God who remained faithful to his covenant promises. This emphasis is characteristic of Hosea (cf. 2:19).

"Loving-kindness" is the word which best represents the covenant faithfulness and love of Jehovah, and Hosea's family life was a living illustration of that loving-kindness.

Outline and Content. The major divisions and topics of the Book of Hosea may be outlined as follows:

Introduction (1:1)
I. The Word of the Lord to Hosea (1:2–3:5)
   A. The Lord's command to marry Gomer and to have children (1:2–2:1)
     1. Gomer's children and Israel's rejection (1:2–9)
     2. God's children and Israel's restoration (1:10–2:1)
   B. The Lord's contention with Israel illustrated by Gomer's adultery (2:2–23)
   C. The Lord's command to remarry Gomer (3:1–5)
     1. The illustration (3:1–3)
     2. The application (3:4,5)
II. The Word of the Lord to Israel (4:1–14:9)
   A. Israel's apostasy (4:1–7:16)
     1. God's case against Israel (4:1–5:7)
     2. God's caution to Israel (5:8–14)
     3. God's call for repentance (5:15–6:3)
     4. God's concern for Israel (6:4–11)
     5. God's conclusion concerning Israel (7:1–16)
   B. Israel's punishment (8:1–10:15)
     1. Israel's reaping of judgment (8:1–14)
     2. Israel's return to exile (9:1–17)
     3. Israel's recompense (10:1–15)
   C. Israel's restoration (11:1–14:9)
     1. The Father's steadfast love (11:1–12)
     2. The Father's steadfast judgment (12:1–13:16)
     3. The Father's steadfast invitation (14:1–9)

The first three chapters of Hosea are concerned with the example of Hosea's life, stressing Hosea's faithfulness and love for his unfaithful wife.

God commanded Hosea to marry the harlot Gomer and to have children by her (1:2–3:5). This command has caused difficulties for some commentators, since priests and prophets in Is-

rael simply did not marry prostitutes. Medieval Jewish writers, therefore, regarded the material as symbolic but unhistorical. Some later scholars drew a distinction between chapters 1 and 3, regarding the latter as an intimate description by Hosea of his marriage; the first chapter was held to contain rather general recollections of his early days as a prophet. Other commentators regarded both chapters as literal fact, while certain scholars thought that chapter 1 was historical whereas chapter 3 represented an allegorical interpretation of the marriage by Hosea himself. Needless to say the premarital sexual activities of Gomer have also been discussed widely. Two views predominate. (1) Gomer was a faithful wife to Hosea in their early years of marriage. "A wife of whoredoms," which is not the common term for "prostitute," has reference to her sinful and wayward nature that God later caused to be exposed as an illustration of Israel's idolatry. (2) Gomer was a publicly known harlot whom Hosea was commanded to marry in order to illustrate Israel's idolatry and God's faithful and steadfast love. This latter view seems to have the greatest appeal to evangelical scholars, and is the simplest interpretation within a literal, grammatical, and historical framework of Bible interpretation.

Some scholars have interpreted the woman beloved of her paramour (3:1) as perhaps someone other than Gomer, but since the latter represents wayward Israel, and no other nation is mentioned, there can be little doubt that Gomer is intended. Why it was necessary for her to be ransomed by Hosea is not evident, nor is it known why part of the price was paid in grain and the remainder in money. Perhaps the entire transaction was meant to symbolize God's deliverance of Israel from future exile although as far as is known, the 10 northern tribes did not return from exile in Assyria. Such an interpretation could hardly apply to Judah, since Hosea's message was not directed at the southern kingdom, although Judah did receive a warning (6:11).

God's intention in this command to Hosea is revealed in 1:2b. Hosea's marriage was to illustrate Israel's relationship to Jehovah "for the land commits great harlotry by forsaking the Lord."

The children born to Hosea and Gomer were given symbolic names. The first child was a son named Jezreel (1:4a), signifying God's judgment on the house of Jehu for Jehu's slaughter of the house of Ahab in the valley of Jezreel (2 Kgs 10:1–11,30; 15:8–12).

Lo-ruhamah was the second child (Hos 1:6a), whose name meant "not compassioned or pitied." The judgment of Israel was thus symbolized. The spiritual corruption of the northern kingdom had run its course, and it would be defeated and taken away into captivity (1:6b).

Lo-ammi was the third child, a second son, whose name meant "not my people" (1:8,9). This rejection of Israel as God's covenanted people was to be temporary (1:10–2:1). God's covenant promises to Abraham (cf. 1:10; Gn 22:17) and to Moses (Ex 19:1–7) would be fulfilled in spite of the disobedience of any particular generation.

Hosea's declaration of divorce from Gomer for her adultery depicted Jehovah's divorce from Israel for her adultery (Hos 2:2; cf. Jer 3:1–4:2). The children are the individual members of the nation of Israel in Hosea's day (Hos 2:2–5).

Not satisfied with her relationship to her husband, Gomer sought other lovers. Israel pursued the same elusive satisfaction in her flirtation and adultery with heathen deities. The good which their merciful God had bestowed upon them they attributed to pagan gods (2:8,12). Repentant Israelites would return to their first love after discovering that there was no lasting satisfaction in their season of sin (v 7).

The illustration of restoration in chapter 3 highlights a concise summary of Israel's history. Israel's bondage to sin and Satan (cf. Heb 2:14,15) is symbolized by the price paid by Hosea for Gomer (Hos 3:2). The price was that of a female slave since Gomer had become the slave of her adultery (cf. Ex 21:32). The days of Gomer's isolation, like the days of Israel's exile, were established for cleansing (Hos 3:3; cf. Dt 21:13; 30:2).

After the exile period ("afterward") and "in the latter days" Israel will return to her husband to enjoy the blessings of the renewed relationship. In a messianic reference, David will be resurrected to lead Israel to the Lord (Hos 3:5).

The last major section of Hosea deals in detail with what has already been illustrated and briefly explained in chapters 1–3. Israel's apostasy (4:1–7:16), punishment (8:1–10:15), and restoration (11:1–14:9) are prophesied by Hosea.

Israel was totally given over to ungodly activities and had separated itself from God (4:1,2; cf. Ex 20:1–17). The people had rejected the Word of God through their own indifference and the deception of the priests (Hos 4:6–); cf. Is 5:13; Am 8:11,12; Zep 1:6). Israel followed the example of corrupt spiritual leaders in the same way her kings followed the corrupt leadership of their predecessors (4:9). In place of God's Word, Israel turned to idolatry and divination for guidance (vv 12,13). Finally, Israel lost its priestly character (v 6; cf. Ex 19:6), because the priests were chiefly responsible for national apostasy (Hos 5:1).

Upon revealing his case against the northern kingdom, God then issues a caution (5:8–14). The trumpet will be raised in the hills of Benjamin (v 8), the buffer zone between Israel and Judah. The alarm in that region will indicate that Israel is being overrun and Judah is endangered (vv 9–12). The northern kingdom had depended upon the commandment of man, not God (v 11). Israel had turned to Assyria for aid but received treachery and defeat at their hands (v 13). In this prophecy of the fall of Israel to the Assyrians (722 BC), Hosea depicts God as the ultimate instrument of chastisement (v 14).

God's call for repentance was fast upon the heels of the revelation of chastisement (5:15–6:3). (The division of chapters at this point is unfortunate. Hos 6:1–3 belongs with 5:15.) The exhortation to return to Jehovah could have been Hosea's own heart response to the revelation he had received. However, it is best to take 6:1–3 as the words employed by the future returning remnant. Assyria did not offer healing, nor would any other nation, but God will heal Israel spiritually, politically, and physically (6:1; cf. Ex 15:26; Dt 32:39; Is 53:5; Ez 37:1–14; Mal 4:2).

After the call to repentance, God returns to his concern for Israel (Hos 6:4–11; cf. 4:15). Israel has turned from its Creator and has disobeyed his Word (6:7). Gilead is but one example of the murderous character of Israel (v 8). Even the priests are known for their violence (v 9; cf. 1 Sm 2:12–17; Jer 5:31). The sin of Israel is "horrible" (Hos 6:10).

Chapter 7 presents God's conclusion concerning Israel (vv 1–16). Every attempt of God to bring Israel to repentance only reveals more fully the extent of their sin (v 1). They believe they can sin without God taking account (v 2; cf. Ps 90:8; Mt 12:36,37). Their civil leaders rejoice that the people are as wicked as the king and the princes (Hos 7:3). All Israel is characterized by habitual adultery (v 4). Israel has not separated itself from the heathen (v 8; cf. Ex 34:12–16; 2 Cor 6:14–7:1). Like "a cake not turned," Israel is not well balanced spiritually or politically but has one side done to a turn and the other side raw.

In the area of foreign affairs, Israel has flitted about from Egypt to Assyria and back again "like a silly dove" without understanding (Hos 7:11). They have not sought the Lord's counsel in their time of need, but have depended upon worldly powers. The lack of faith in Jehovah and the lack of separation from sin will bring chastisement from God (v 12; cf. 1 Cor 11:32; Heb 12:5–15).

Chapter 8 deals with Israel's reaping of

judgment (cf. v 7). An alarm is sounded to warn the people of the approach of the Assyrians (v 1; cf. Ez 17:2–21). They would come against Israel ("the house of the Lord," Hos 8:1) because of their transgression of the Sinai covenant (cf. Dt 27:9–29:29) and disobedience to the Law of Moses. Crying falsely to God for deliverance from his rod of punishment (cf. Is 10:5), Israel will receive no answer and Assyria will continue to pursue the 10 tribes (Hos 8:2,3). Other reasons for God's judgment include setting up kings without God's direction (v 4a) and idolatry (vv 4b–6). Israel's sacrifices are unacceptable because of the nation's disobedience (v 13; cf. 1 Sm 15:22; Is 1:11–15). Thus they will go into exile just like the earlier exile in Egypt (Hos 8:13).

The theme of exile is continued in chapter 9 of Hosea. There is no joy for Israel (v 1). The produce of the land will not sustain her because she will no longer dwell in the land (vv 2,3). Some Israelites will flee to Egypt in exile while others will be taken captive to Assyria. All the sacrifices will cease and the sacrificial wines and meats will be drunk and eaten to satisfy their own desires (vv 4,5). Those Israelites who flee to Egypt will be slain by the Egyptians (v 6).

The recompense of Israel's evil is further described in chapter 10. Israel is like a luxuriant vine (v 1), but its bounty is misappropriated, being poured out as sacrifice on heathen altars. They are guilty before God, and he is about to destroy their altars and take away their king (vv 2,3).

Gibeah is mentioned again (cf. 9:9), reminding Israel that apostasy is not only infectious, it is also indelible (10:9). The "two furrows" may refer to the two calf idols in Bethel and Dan which brought chastisement from God (v 10). The punishment will be a sentence of hard labor under a heavy yoke and with the added burden of the Assyrian rider (v 11).

Chapters 11 through 14 close the prophecies of Hosea with a message concerning the restoration of Israel at a future time (11:1–14:9). The steadfast love of the Father is first given as the ground of future restoration (11:1–12). Israel, as a nation, had been called out of Egypt as a son of Jehovah (v 1; cf. Ex 4:22,23).

Yet Israel did not return the Father's love, but sought heathen alliances (11:5) that would only bring judgment upon them (vv 5–7). The words of Jehovah reveal his irreversible judgment in his absolute holiness and righteousness (12:1–13:16). The sins of Israel can only be responded to with just recompense (12:1,2). The responsibility for the destruction of the northern kingdom rests upon Israel herself. In spite of Israel's sin, God can yet be her help (13:9).

Israel should have repented quickly but she did not (13:13). Yet the mercy of Jehovah would ultimately bring about the death of death itself so that Israel might live—spiritually, politically, and, perhaps, physically (v 14; cf. Ez 37:1–14; Dn 12:1,2,13).

The last chapter of Hosea sets forth the Father's loving invitation for Israel to repent and return to him (14:1–9) in confession, prayer,

Portion of a relief showing Assyrian captives.

and praise (v 2). "Calves of our lips" (v 2 KJV) refers to the thank-offering that normally consisted of young bullocks (Ex 24:5; Lv 7:11–13; cf. Pss 51:17–19; 69:30,31; Heb 13:15,16). Part of Israel's confession will involve recognizing that there is no salvation in either Assyria (political alliance) or idols (Hos 14:3).

God repeatedly promises blessing to Israel in their restoration (note "I will," 14:4,5). Jehovah will heal Israel spiritually, love them freely, prosper them completely, and protect them fully (vv 4–7). Israel will be as the lily, durable as the cedar, and fruitful as the olive tree.

Teaching. The primary emphasis of Hosea is summarized in the last verse (14:9). The wise will live godly, and the foolish will live ungodly lives. The godly will have restoration, victory over death (13:14), and blessing (14:4–7).

Idolatry is essentially anything that usurps the sole place of God in the human heart. Israel had substituted heathen deities (4:12–19), national pride (5:5), religious ceremony (6:6), political expediency (7:3), political alliances (7:11), civil government (8:4), building projects (8:14), selfish affluence (10:1), and idolatry (13:2) for Jehovah's counsel, aid, blessing, and salvation. Only in God could they find true blessing and security (13:4,9; 14:4–7).

Hosea's prophecies bring out the seriousness of sin and the terrible nature of divine judgment (1:4; 4:1–5; 5:2,4,9; 6:9,10; 7:13,16; 8:7; 9:11–17; 10:4,8,15). They also emphasize the mercy and the love of God (1:7; 2:19–23; 11:4,8,9; 14:4–7).

Apostasy is presented by Hosea as infectious. The cycle of apostasy may begin with the spiritual leaders or with the people and spread from one to the other (4:9). Apostasy is punished according to the degree of responsibility (v 14; 5:1; 13:9).

See HOSEA (PERSON); ISRAEL, HISTORY OF; PROPHECY; PROPHET, PROPHETESS.

Bibliography. C.F. Keil, *Biblical Commentary on the OT: The Twelve Minor Prophets,* vol 1; G.A.F. Knight, *Hosea;* J.L. Mays, *Hosea;* M. Scott, *The Message of Hosea;* G.A. Smith, *The Book of the Twelve Prophets,* vol 1; N.H. Snaith, *Amos, Hosea, and Micah;* C. von Orelli, *The Twelve Minor Prophets;* H.W. Wolff, *Hosea.*

Hoshaiah. 1. Prince of Judah who led a contingent of princes in procession at the dedication of the walls of Jerusalem after they were rebuilt (Neh 12:32).

2. Father of Azariah (Jer 42:1; 43:2). Azariah was a leader of the people of Judah after the fall of Jerusalem.

Hoshama. Jeconiah's descendant (1 Chr 3:18).

Hoshea. 1. Original name of Joshua, the son of Nun and Moses' successor, before his name was changed by Moses (Nm 13:8,16).

See JOSHUA (PERSON) #1.

2. Son of Elah and the last of the 19 kings of the northern kingdom of Israel (2 Kgs 17:1–6). He reigned for 9 years (732–723 BC) before being taken captive by the Assyrians. In the latter years of the northern kingdom, Assyria, ruled by Tiglath-pileser III (745–727 BC), had gained control of most of the Middle East and had reduced the scope of the northern kingdom to Ephraim, Issachar, and the half of Manasseh west of the Jordan.

Earlier, the northern kingdom, under Pekah (752–732 BC), entered an alliance with Rezin of Damascus (Syria) and attempted to coerce King Ahaz of Judah (735–715 BC) to join them in action against Tiglath-pileser (2 Kgs 16:5; Is 7:1–6). Assyria came to Judah's aid, and at this point Hoshea was one of a group of conspirators who assassinated Pekah (2 Kgs 15:30). Tiglath-pileser rewarded Hoshea by making him king over the remnant of the northern kingdom. Hoshea ruled only as a vassal of Assyria and paid heavy tribute, remaining loyal to Assyria until the death of Tiglath-pileser in 727 BC. When Shalmaneser V succeeded to the throne of Assyria, Hoshea withheld tribute and attempted to assert independence. He entered into negotiations with So, king of Egypt (2 Kgs 17:4), and found a favorable response, because Egypt would be in a precarious position if Assyria were to control Palestine. Therefore, Egypt was quite willing to support Hoshea in his resistance to Assyria in the hope that Samaria would remain a buffer between Egypt and Assyria. Soon, Shalmaneser directed his army against Samaria (724 BC), and Hoshea discovered that the alliance with Egypt was of little value. He attempted to avert disaster by resuming the tribute payments (2 Kgs 17:3), but Shalmaneser did not trust his loyalty and marched against Samaria. In a short time Hoshea was taken prisoner, and Assyria apparently besieged Samaria for three years. The city fell in 722 BC, and Sargon II, who had succeeded Shalmaneser about 726 BC, deported many Israelites to various places in Assyria, thus ending the northern kingdom.

See ISRAEL, HISTORY OF.

3. Son of Azaziah and one of King David's officers set over the Ephraimites (1 Chr 27:20).

4. One who set his seal on Ezra's covenant (Neh 10:23).

5. Eighth-century prophet of Israel best known as Hosea.

See HOSEA (PERSON); HOSEA, BOOK OF.

R.K. HARRISON

Hospitality. Biblical concept often used with the terms "guest," "stranger," and "sojourner." It is useful to limit the meaning of "hospitality" to benevolence done to those outside one's normal circle of friends, as is implied in the literal meaning of the Greek word ("love of strangers"). Although the concept is thoroughly endorsed in the Bible, it is clearly found in nonbiblical cultures as well, especially the nomadic, where definite obligations to provide food, shelter, and protection are recognized.

The normal exercise of hospitality in the OT can be seen in the examples of Abraham and the three visitors (Gn 18:2–8,16), Laban's reception of Abraham's servant (24:15–61), and Manoah's treatment of the angel (Jgs 13:15), but there are also cases in which the host felt compelled to take extreme steps to protect his guest, even to the harm of his own family (Gn 19:1–8; Jgs 19:14–25). The hospitality of the Shunammite family is also noteworthy, although Elisha was no stranger to them (2 Kgs 4:10).

In the NT Jesus relies on the general practice of hospitality in sending out the disciples (Lk 10:7) and in his own travels. As the gospel was spread by traveling missionaries, Christians were commended for entertaining them in their homes (Heb 13:2; 1 Pt 4:9; 3 Jn 5–8). Church leaders must not exempt themselves from this ministry (1 Tm 3:2; Ti 1:8); to do so is grounds for judgment (Mt 25:43).

DAVID K. HUTTAR

See FOREIGNER.

Host, Host of Heaven. Hebrew expressions found frequently in the OT and literally meaning "army" and "army of the skies." Host is basically a military term, occurring nearly 500 times in the OT, and can mean "army" (2 Kgs 18:17), "angels," "heavenly bodies," or "creation."

The phrase "host of heaven" has various applications in the Bible. Ancient writers sometimes referred symbolically to the sun, moon, and stars as an army (Dt 4:19; Jgs 5:20). In the astrological cults of antiquity it was believed that celestial bodies were animated by spirits and thus constituted a living army that controlled heavenly destiny. The worship of the host of heaven was one of the earliest forms of idolatry, and was common among the Israelites in their times of regression from serving God (Jer 19:13; Acts 7:42). Although warned against such pagan beliefs (Dt 4:19; 17:3), the Israelites fell into the practice of worshiping heavenly bodies, particularly during the Assyrian and Babylonian periods (2 Kgs 17:16; 21:3,5; 2 Chr 33:3,5; Jer 8:2; Zep 1:5). The correc-

tive of this pagan practice was Israel's belief in the Lord as the Creator of heaven and earth, the one who marshalled the heavenly bodies at his command and ordained them to perform a special function (Gn 1:14–19; 2:1; Neh 9:6; Pss 33:6; 103:21; 148:2; Is 40:26; 45:12).

God is frequently called "the Lord God of hosts," that is, of the celestial armies (Jer 5:14; 38:17; 44:7; Hos 12:5). The heavenly host includes angels or messengers who are associated with the Lord's work in heaven and on earth. God presides over a heavenly council composed of angels or "sons of God" (Gn 1:26; 1 Kgs 22:19; Jb 1,2; Ps 82; Is 6) whose messengers are sent from the Lord's council to accomplish his purpose (Gn 28:12–15; Lk 2:13).

Though the hosts are sometimes understood as the stars or angels, the tribes of Israel are also called "the hosts of the Lord" (Ex 12:41). The "host of heaven" referred to in Daniel 8:10,11, appears to be figurative language referring to Israel, "the holy people" (cf. v 24 KJV) and God, the King of Israel is called "the Prince of the host."

The Greek words translated "host" occur only twice in the NT (Lk 2:13; Acts 7:42). "Lord of hosts" is used by Paul and James (Rom 9:29; Jas 5:4) as a title for the Lord. The term expresses God's sovereign might and majesty in history, but the precise identification of the "hosts" that stand at his command is uncertain. The name "Lord of hosts" in the literature of the prophets does not identify the hosts with Israel's armies. The prophets do not relinquish the idea of God's action on behalf of Israel in the military sphere, but they often indicate that God would even turn military forces against his people in judgment for their sins. The epithet "Lord of hosts" sums up the Israelite faith that God alone is Lord in heaven and on earth.

WILLIAM B. TOLAR

Hosts, Lord of. OT name for God found mostly in the prophets. The hosts are the heavenly powers and angels that act at the Lord's command.

See GOD, NAMES OF.

Hotham. 1. Variant form of Helem in Chronicles 7:32.

See HELEM #1.

2. Shama and Jeiel's father. Shama and Jeiel were two of David's mighty men (1 Ch 11:44; KJV Hothan).

Hothan. KJV spelling of Hotham in 1 Chronicles 11:44.

See HOTHAM #2.

Hothir. Levite and the head of the 21st of 24 divisions of priests for sanctuary service, formed during David's reign (1 Chr 25:4,28).

Hour. *See* DAY.

House. *See* HOMES AND DWELLINGS.

Household. Persons who live in the same place and compose a family or extended family. In biblical times a household included father, mother(s), children, grandparents, servants, concubines, and sojourners. Jacob's household included 66 people, not counting the wives of his sons (Gn 46:26). Households were seen as corporately responsible for the honor of the family (2 Sm 3:27 gives an example of revenge by a household). Male members of the entire household were circumcised as a sign of the covenant (Gn 17:23). In the NT some entire households were baptized (Acts 11:14).

See FAMILY LIFE AND RELATIONS.

House of God. Common phrase used in the ancient Near Eastern world for a structure used to accommodate a deity or his servants. It referred in the OT to the tabernacle (Dt 23:18; 1 Kgs 8:11–20); the Solomonic temple (1 Kgs 12:27; Jer 20:1), to national shrines, or to pagan temples (Jgs 9:4; 2 Kgs 10:21).

In NT times the OT custom of referring to the temple as the "House of God" was still employed (Mt 12:4; Mk 2:26; 11:17; Lk 6:4; Jn 2:16,17), but with some significant changes. No longer was the personal name of God used in reference to the temple, as in the OT (Ex 23:19; Dt 23:18; 1 Sm 3:15), for it had become so sacred to the Jews that it was against the rabbinic law to publicly speak the personal name of God. The phrase "House of God" referred only to the temple in Jerusalem. After Christ's ascension, the church viewed itself as the house of God (1 Cor 3:9; Heb 3:6; 1 Pt 2:5; 4:17). God no longer dwelt in buildings made by human hands, but in the lives of those who confess Jesus as Lord.

See TABERNACLE, TEMPLE.

House of the Archives. *See* ARCHIVES, HOUSE OF THE.

House of the Forest of Lebanon. Exotic name for Solomon's palace in Jerusalem, adjacent to the temple, given this designation because of the amount of Lebanese cedar used in its construction. The structure was about 150 long, 75 feet wide, and 30 feet high. Three hundred gold shields were made to decorate it, and all the vessels of the house were made of

A cedar of Lebanon, the type of tree used to build the House of the Forest of Lebanon (1 Kgs 7:2).

gold. A large ivory throne overlaid with gold was constructed and placed within the palace (1 Kgs 7:2–5; 2 Chr 9:16–20). Besides providing housing and a formal palace for Solomon, it was also used to store arms (Is 22:8).

Hozai. Author of annals describing the life of Manasseh king of Judah, and included in the "Chronicles of the Kings of Israel" (2 Chr 33:18,19). The Septuagint renders Hozai as "seers," which is preferred by many commentators and the RSV.

Hukkok. Town on Naphtali and Zebulun's boundary, listed next to Aznoth-tabor (Jos 19:34). It has been identified with Yaquaq, northwest of Gennesaret.

Hukok. Alternate form of the Asherite town Helkath in 1 Chronicles 6:75.

See HELKATH.

Hul. Son of Aram and grandson of Shem (Gn 10:23; 1 Chr 1:17).

Huldah. Prophetess living in Jerusalem; a contemporary of the prophets Jeremiah and Zephaniah. Huldah is introduced as the wife of Shallum, the wardrobe keeper in King Josiah's court (2 Kgs 22:14; 2 Chr 34:22). Josiah sent his officers to ask Huldah's counsel concerning the book of the Mosiac law which had been found during the temple repair. She prophesied that disaster would strike the nation (2 Kgs 22:16), but that Josiah would be spared because he was penitent, humbling himself before the Lord (vv 18,19). She declared he would be buried in peace (v 20). Although Josiah later died in battle, he was properly entombed (23:30), avoiding the indignity of becoming prey for carrion-feeders. It was after receiving Huldah's advice that Josiah carried out his religious reform (2 Chr 35:1–25).

Humtah. Settlement in the Judean uplands near Hebron according to Joshua 15:54. No satisfactory site has yet been suggested for this place.

Hunchback. See DEFORMITY.

Hundred, Tower of the. Tower at the northernmost part of the Jerusalem wall (near where the wall crosses over the Tyropoean Valley). It stood west of the Sheep Gate near the Tower of Hananel (Neh 3:1; 12:39; KJV tower of Meah).

See JERUSALEM.

Hundred-weight. Measure equal to about 100 pounds mentioned only in Revelation 16:21.

See WEIGHTS AND MEASURES.

Hunting. Practice of tracking and pursuing animals for food, animal products, or sport, a practice as old as man. In Bible times hunting was practiced all over the biblical world. Genesis 10:9 refers to a certain Nimrod who was "a mighty hunter before the Lord" long before the patriarchs. In earliest human history hunting was an essential means of obtaining food, clothing, and tools, and even when civilization developed hunting provided supplementation for an agricultural diet.

In lands surrounding Israel hunting is well represented in paintings and bas-reliefs. In ancient Egypt hunting became a sport, and Egyptians hunted for game and birds often with the help of dogs and cats. Wild game was driven by dogs or humans into enclosures or toward pits and traps. Similarly in Mesopotamia hunting was widely practiced as is evident from many bas-reliefs depicting stags and deer caught in nets. In Assyria wild animals like lions were commonly hunted. The bas-reliefs of Nineveh provide many fine pictures of the hunter's art.

Palestine was a land where hunting was practiced very early. This is clear from the bones of hunted animals found in the excavation of early sites. Certainly by the Middle Bronze Age (c. 1800–1500 BC), which approximates the patriarchal age, hunting was widely practiced. The reference to Esau as a skillful hunter (Gn 25:27) would be typical of a time when both agricultural and hunting pursuits were followed. The Egyptian Tale of Sinuhe from the 20th century BC mentions hunting with hounds.

The Bible text gives a number of glimpses into the kinds of birds and animals that were hunted. Lists of animals that are "clean" are provided in Deuteronomy 14:4–6. An interesting variety of animals was available to the people of Israel; many were domestic, but there was a variety of wild animals to test the ingenuity of the hunter: the goat, the hare, the gazelle, the roebuck (cf. 1 Kgs 4:23), the wild goat, the ibex, the antelope, and the mountain sheep. In every case the blood of the animal had to be poured out. There was a proverb current in Israel about a slothful man who caught no prey (Prv 12:27).

Some passages in the OT record the killing of animals in self-protection (Jgs 14:6; 1 Sm 17:34–37; 2 Sm 23:20). Shepherds normally carried a club and a sling to protect their flocks from marauding beasts (1 Sm 17:40; Ps 23:4).

A variety of birds was hunted, for example, the partridge referred to in 1 Samuel 26:20 (Dt 14:11–18).

There are references also to some of the devices used in hunting: bows and arrows (Gn 27:3), clubs (Jb 41:29), sling-stones (1 Sm 17:40), nets (Jb 19:6), fowlers' snares (Ps 91:3), camouflaged pits (Pss 7:15; 35:7; Prv 22:14; 26:27; Is 24:17,18). Two kinds of bird traps are mentioned in the Bible (Jos 23:13 and Is 8:14). One of these seems to have been an automatic device (Am 3:5) that would spring up from the ground when an animal touched it (cf. Ps 69:22; Hos 9:8) or when the fowler pulled a cord (Ps 140:5; Jer 5:26). The many references to the fowler with his nets and snares are reminders that Palestine lies on one of the main flight routes of certain migratory birds (cf. Ex 16:13; Nm 11:31–34). Some of the common hunting expressions came to be used figuratively (Jb 18:10; Jer 5:26).

The method of driving animals into a trap seems to be referred to in Jeremiah 16:16 and Ezekiel 19:8.

Evidently hunting was practiced in NT times to judge from pictures in Matthew 22:15 Luke 11:54; and Romans 11:9. The writings of the Jewish rabbis in the early Christian era provide further evidence of hunting in the immediate postbiblical period.

JOHN A. THOMPSON

Hupham, Huphamite. Benjamite and the founder of the Huphamite family (Nm 26:39).

he is perhaps identifiable with Huppim (Gn 46:21; 1 Chr 7:12,15) and Huram (1 Chr 8:5).

See HUPPIM.

Huppah. One of the chief men appointed in charge of the 13th division of priests in the time of David and Solomon (1 Chr 24:13).

Huppim. Perhaps the son of Ir (Iri) and a descendant of Benjamin through Bela's line (Gn 46:21); 1 Chr 7:12,15). Huppim is probably an alternate spelling of Hupham, the father of the Huphamite family from Benjamin's tribe (Nm 26:39). His precise lineage is difficult to determine.

Hur. 1. First mention in the account of Israel's battle with the Amalekites at Rephidim, he aided Aaron in supporting Moses' hands until the Amalekites were defeated (Ex 17:8–13). He is mentioned again as assisting Aaron in overseeing Israel while Moses was on Mt Sinai (24:14). According to Josephus, Hur was the husband of Miriam, the sister of Moses (Josephus, *Antiq.* 3.2.4).

2. Fourth of the five kings of Midian who was killed with Balaam by the Israelites under Moses (Nm 31:8). He is also referred to as one of the "princes of Median" and "Sihon" (Jos 13:21).

3. Father of one of the 12 officers whom Solomon appointed to provide food for the king's household (1 Kgs 4:8, KJV; RSV Benhur).

4. Son of Caleb and Ephrath and the grandfather of Bezaleel (1 Chr 2:19,20). Although some interpreters regard the Hur discussed in #1 as the grandfather of Bezaleel, others think that the Hur who assisted Moses and the Hur who was Bezaleel's grandfather were different men.

5. Father (or perhaps family name) of Rephaiah, a postexilic leader who assisted Nehemiah in rebuilding the Jerusalem wall (Neh 3:9).

Hurai. Alternate form of Hiddai in 1 Chronicles 11:32.

See HIDDAI.

Huram. 1. Bela's son from Benjamin's tribe (1 Chr 8:5); perhaps the same person as Hupham (Nm 26:39).

2. Alternate spelling of Hiram, the Phoenician king of Tyre who was an ally of David and Solomon, and who supplied materials for the building of the temple (2 Chr 2:3,11,12; 8:2,18; 9:10,21).

See HIRAM #1.

3. Alternate spelling of Hiram, a craftsman

from Tyre who worked on Solomon's temple (2 Chr 4:11).

See HIRAM #2.

Huram-abi. Alternate name for Hiram, Solomon's temple architect, in 2 Chronicles 2:13 and 4:16.

See HIRAM #2.

Huri. Abihail's father from Gad's tribe who inhabited Gilead in Bashan (1 Chr 5:14).

Hurrians. People (also called Mitannians) who spoke a language different from Semitic and Indo-European, and yet played a significant cultural role in the Near East during the 2nd millennium BC, particularly in transmitting the culture of Sumer and Babylon to western Asia and to the Hittites.

The presence of Hurrians in an area can be inferred from the presence of Hurrian texts, the presence of people with Hurrian names (or Indo-Iranian as explained below), and from statements in other ancient literature, including the OT.

At the beginning of the 2nd millennium, and even somewhat before, Hurrians are found in the northernmost parts of Mesopotamia, having come there presumably from still farther north. They are found in the 18th century BC at Mari and Alalakh, and in the 15th and 14th centuries BC at Nuzi, Ugarit, Alalakh, a few cities in Palestine, and especially in their political center of Mitanni. During this latter period their rulers were actually an aristocracy of Indo-Iranian extraction, who often retained their Indo-Iranian names, but who in other respects had adopted Hurrian language, religion, and general culture, and so were for all practical purposes Hurrians.

The main question concerning Hurrian presence is the extent to which they were influential in Palestine, and here the evidence is not clear. The Amarna Letters, written by the Mitannian/Hurrian kings and by petty kings of Palestine to the Egyptian pharaohs during the 14th century, refer to a few Palestinian kings with Hurrian (some Indo-Iranian) names such as Abdikhepa of Jerusalem. However, the letters, written in Akkadian by the scribes of these Palestinian kings, betray a local Canaanite rather than Hurrian speech. On the other hand, the Egyptians referred to Palestine as the land of the Hurrians, and indeed one pharaoh claimed to have captured 36,000 Hurrians there, but this could mean inhabitants of Palestine rather than ethnic Hurrians. In view of the evidence of the Amarna Letters, it is likely that Palestine was only nominally Hurrian.

Furthermore, the extent to which Hurrians

are referred to by ethnic terms in the OT is likewise problematic. Some scholars believe that the Hurrians are the biblical Horites (Gn 14:6; 36:20–30; Dt 2:12,22). Linguistically this is possible, but the Horites are always located at Mt Seir, whereas the Hurrians are at Jerusalem, Taanach, Megiddo, Acco, Achshaph, Shechem, and possibly Hebron, but not likely at Mt Seir. In addition, the names of the Horites in Genesis 36 appear Semitic rather than Hurrian. Finally, if the Horites of Mt Seir are contemporary with Esau, who married the daughter of a Horite chief, this would be too early for patriarchal contacts with Hurrian penetration in the south, if the early date of the patriarchs is sustained by the newly discovered Ebla tablets.

A second theory identifies the Hivites as Hurrians, the linguistic differences between the two names usually being explained as due to confusion of similar-looking Hebrew consonants by the later scribes. In support of the Hivite identification of Hurrians it is pointed out that in two passages (Gn 34:2; Jos 9:7) the Septuagint (Greek translation) understands Hivites to be Hurrians, while in Genesis 36:2, 29 Zibeon is called both Hivite and Horite, the latter identified as Hurrian. However, the former argument places too much weight on the Septuagint, which may simply be mistaken, and the latter argument amounts again to the claim that the Mt Seir Horites were Hurrians.

A third theory sees the Hittites of Genesis 23 as Hurrians. While it is true that the term "Hittite" is often broad and may include ethnic Hurrians, this theory faces the same chronological difficulties as the first. On the other hand, it may well be that the *later* Hittite, Uriah, and Arauna the Jebusite were Hurrians, the name "Arauna" often being interpreted as clearly Hurrian.

The above theories all assume that a people will be referred to by a distinctive ethnic term. Alternatively, one might admit a Hurrian presence in Palestine and see them referred to (along with other peoples) under broad terms such as "Canaanite."

DAVID K. HUTTAR

See HITTITES; HIVITES; HORITE, HORIM.

Husband. *See* FAMILY LIFE AND RELATIONS.

Husbandman, Husbandry. Occupation and practice of farming and animal production; KJV rendering of farmer, tenant farmer, plowman, tiller, and vinedresser.

See AGRICULTURE; TRADES AND OCCUPATIONS (FARMER).

Hushah, Hushathites. Ezer's son (1 Chr 4:4) or perhaps a town which Ezer founded. The warriors Sibbecai (2 Sm 21:18; 1 Chr 11:29; 20:4; 27:11) and Mebunnai (2 Sm 23:27) were described as Hushathites; whether designating genealogical ancestry or geographical locality (or perhaps both) is uncertain.

Hushai. Friend and adviser who remained faithful to David when his other adviser, Ahithophel, defected to join the rebelling Absalom. According to David's instructions, Hushai pretended loyalty to Absalom and slipped information to David regarding Absalom's plans. Ahithophel urged Absalom to attack the fleeing David before he had a chance to strengthen his forces, but Absalom followed Hushai's advice, which gave David time to escape over the Jordan and ultimately to defeat Absalom's party. When his counsel was not followed, Ahithophel hanged himself, probably anticipating the disastrous outcome (2 Sm 15:32–37; 16:15–17:23). Hushai belonged to the Archite family from Ataroth, a town on Ephraim and Benjamin's border (Jos 16:2,7).

Husham. Temanite who succeeded Jobab as king of Edom (Gn 36:34,35; 1 Chr 1:45,46).

Hushim. 1. Dan's son (Gn 46:23), alternately called Shuham in Numbers 26:42 where he is mentioned as the founder of the Shuhamite family.

2. Benjamite descendants of Aher (1 Chr 7:12).

3. Benjamite and one of Shaharaim's two wives (1 Chr 8:8,11).

Huz. KJV rendering of Uz, Nahor's son, in Genesis 22:21.

See UZ (PERSON) #2.

Huzzab. Obscure Hebrew word found only in Nahum 2:7 (KJV). Scholars are uncertain whether the word is a verb meaning "it is decreed," a noun personifying Nineveh, or a reference to an Assyrian queen. The problem is perhaps due to textual error, but thus far neither textual scholarship nor archaeology has been able to resolve the question.

Hyacinth. Plant indigenous to the Holy Land yielding blue fragrant flowers.

See PLANTS.

Hyena. *See* ANIMALS.

Hyksos. Term used by Egyptian historian Manetho (c. 280 BC) to designate the foreign rulers of the 15th and 16th dynasties in Egypt

(1730?–1570? BC). Once called the shepherd kings, that expression is now thought to have come from a misrendering of an Egyptian text.

The Hyksos were Semites, probably entering Egypt from Syria and Palestine, though their exact origin is unknown. They gradually infiltrated Egypt during the 18th century BC, and it is possible that some intermarriage took place. This infiltration was aided by a weakening of Egyptian power as a result of internal dynastic rivalries. Some of the Hyksos may have held Egyptian administrative posts before the actual Hyksos takeover, which was probably more of a swift political maneuver than a great military conquest.

The Hyksos capital was probably established at Qantir in the delta region of northeastern Egypt. From there they could maintain ties with their cultural base in Palestine and Syria. Qantir was close to Goshen, the Egyptian territory inhabited by the Israelites during their sojourn in Egypt.

The Hyksos introduced the war chariot into Egypt, a military device later used to drive the Hyksos aliens out of Egypt. Horse and chariot warfare became the norm in the following centuries. The Hyksos presence also forced the Egyptians to acknowledge the surrounding Middle Eastern world. Previously Egyptians generally had viewed other peoples as barbarians and themselves as the cultural center of the world. When the Hyksos were evicted by Ahmose in 1570(?)BC, Egypt embarked on a course of conquests initiating its empire period (16th–12th centuries BC). No monuments from the Hyksos era have been found, and whatever monuments did exist were probably destroyed when Egyptian rule was reestablished.

The relation of the Hyksos to Israel's history is debated and depends on a correct interpretation of Exodus 1:8: "Now there arose a new king over Egypt, who did not know Joseph." If Joseph died just before 1800 BC, and the Hyksos takeover in Egypt was about 1730 BC, then the "new king" was a Hyksos ruler who did not know of Joseph, or perhaps had no reason to respect Joseph's descendants even if he had known Joseph. The new rigor of servitude described in Exodus 1:9–14 would, according to that interpretation, have been introduced by the Hyksos. If so, it may be that the Hyksos were fewer in number than the Hebrews and feared some kind of uprising (Ex 1:9), or the Hyksos may have feared an alliance between the Hebrews and the Egyptians, which also might have led to the Hyksos being deposed (v 10). In this view, the pharaoh who ordered the Hebrew midwives to kill newborn Hebrew boys (v 15) ruled Egypt after the Hyksos had been overthrown. Thus there would be a gap of at least 150 years between verses 14 and 15.

The other interpretation places Joseph's arrival in Egypt sometime during the Hyksos rule, not prior to it. Here it is assumed that a Semitic people such as the Hyksos would not be averse to having another Semite in their government, nor would they oppose the settlement of Jacob's family in Egypt. Further, the location of Jacob's family and descendants in Goshen fits with the known fact that the Hyksos had their center of control in that region. This view might also explain why Egyptian records do not mention Joseph—his name

The ruins of a fortress-temple built by the Hyksos at Shechem.

would have been offensive to later Egyptian national feeling, and therefore removed from any records. If this line of reasoning were accepted, then the king "who did not know Joseph" came to the throne after the Hyksos had been overthrown. With the Hyksos eliminated by the revived Egyptian dynasty, it follows that the Hebrews, another Semitic group, would be brought into subjection also.

In either case, it is clear that the Hyksos and the Hebrews were not in agreement on religious matters. The Hyksos worshiped the Canaanite gods, especially Baal, in their own lands and combined that worship with Egyptian sun-god worship when they ruled in Egypt.

WILLIAM TRAVIS

Hymenaeus. Believer, probably of Ephesus, cited by Paul as one who "rejected conscience" (1 Tm 1:19,20) and "swerved from the truth" (2 Tm 2:17). In the first instance, Hymenaeus (mentioned with Alexander) is viewed as having rejected correct beliefs and made a shipwreck of his faith. The seriousness of his offense is evident, as Paul sternly exhorts Timothy to deliver him over to Satan. The meaning of this phrase is uncertain, although it might have involved physical affliction as well as severance from the body of other Christians. The harsh action was meant to bring about, not ultimate destruction, but eventual and lasting benefit to Hymenaeus so he might as a result learn not to blaspheme (cf. 1 Cor 5:5). Apparently, this censure was not successful. In 2 Timothy 2:17,18, Hymenaneus appears as one who is "upsetting the faith." He (along with Philetus) was teaching that the resurrection had already taken place. Most probably, he was teaching that the resurrection takes place at the time of spiritual rebirth and baptism, based on a faulty interpretation of Romans 6:1–11 and Colossians 3:1. This teaching is probably a rejection of Gnosticism, which maintains that matter is evil and that real salvation is liberation from the body. Hymenaeus thus sought to teach a spiritualized resurrection taking place as the soul awakens from sin.

JAMES D. PRICE

Hymn, Hymnody. See MUSIC AND MUSICAL INSTRUMENTS.

Hyssop. Syrian or Egyptian marjoram plant (Ex 12:22; Lv 14:4).

See PLANTS.

Ii

Ibex. Species of wild goat, declared clean in the Law (Dt 14:5).

See ANIMALS (GOAT).

Ibhar. Son born to David during his reign in Jerusalem (2 Sm 5:15; 1 Chr 3:6; 14:5).

Ibis. Wading bird with a long, slender bill, declared unclean in Leviticus 11:17.

See BIRDS.

Ibleam. City in Manasseh's territory (Jos 17:11; Jgs 1:27; 2 Kgs 9:27), perhaps identifiable with Bileam, a levitical city west of the Jordan River between Samaria and Jezreel (1 Chr 6:70).

See LEVITICAL CITIES.

Ibneiah. Jeroham's son from Benjamin's tribe (1 Chr 9:8).

Ibnijah. Forefather of Meshullam from Benjamin's tribe (1 Chr 9:8).

Ibri. Merarite Levite and Jaaziah's son, who lived during David's time (1 Chr 24:27).

Ibsam. Tola's son from Issachar's tribe (1 Chr 7:2, KJV Jibsam).

Ibzan. Judge who ruled over Israel or part of it for 7 years (Jgs 12:8–10). Ibzan was a native of Bethlehem, probably of Zebulun, and was buried in his place of birth. Jewish tradition identified Ibzan with Boaz and consequently understood his native city to be Bethlehem in Judah. Ibzan had 30 sons and 30 daughters and was a man of wealth and high social standing.

See JUDGES, BOOK OF.

Ichabod. Name given to Phineas' son (Eli's grandson) to commemorate the glory that had departed from Israel, after the ark of God was taken by the Philistines (1 Sm 4:19–22; 14:3).

Phineas was killed in the battle of Aphek, at the same time the Philistines had captured the ark. When Phineas' wife heard of the tragedy, she went immediately into labor, and when the child was born she named him Ichabod (meaning "no glory") to sum up her despair.

Iconium. City in the southwest part of central Asia Minor located about 95 miles from the Mediterranean coast. It is known today as Konya, a Turkish city, and capital of the province bearing the same name.

Iconium was an agricultural center famous for its wheat fields and apricot and plum orchards. Its ideal location and climate helped establish its place as a major link in the trade routes between Syria, Ephesus, and Rome.

Little is known about the origin of the city. Its beginnings may be traced to a group of immigrant tribes from northern Greece—the Phrygians. Xenophon, a Greek historian (c. 428–354 BC), mentions it as a Phrygian city visited by Cyrus. Since the Phrygian language was spoken in Iconium, it is likely that the inhabitants considered themselves of this extraction. Although the name "Iconium" was originally Phrygian, a myth was later created to infuse it with Greek meaning. According to this legend, a great flood destroys mankind. Life is restored when Prometheus and Athena breathe life into human images made from mud left by the subsiding waters. The Greek word for "image" is *eikon* from which, so the legend goes, comes the name "Iconium."

In the 3rd century BC, Iconium was governed by the Seleucid kings of Syria. As disciples of Greek culture, the Seleucids soon turned Iconium into a Hellenistic city. The Greek language was spoken and the people were ruled by two magistrates appointed annually. Despite later domination by the Gauls and Pontic kings (c. 165–63 BC), Iconium retained its Hellenistic character until NT times. In 36 BC Mark Anthony gave the city to Antymas. Upon his death in 25 BC, Iconium joined the neighboring cities of Lystra, Derbe, and Pisidian Antioch as a part of the province of Galatia and so became incorporated into the Roman Empire.

The apostle Paul visited Iconium on his first missionary journey. Having been forced to leave Pisidian Antioch (Acts 13:51), Paul came to the synagogue in Iconium. His preaching initially won the approval of both the Jews and Greeks, but unbelieving Jews soon incited a riot against him (14:1–7). Paul fled to Lystra but was followed by the Iconian Jews who stoned him and left him for dead (v 19; cf. 2 Tm 3:11). Cared for by friends, Paul was able to join Barnabas in Derbe, where they made disciples who later returned to Iconium to strengthen the Christians there (Acts 14:20–23). During the second missionary journey, Timothy was recommended to Paul and Silas by the Christians at Iconium (16:1,2). The city served as the setting for the apocryphal Acts of Paul and Thecla—an indication that the impact of Christianity was still provoking opposition in this city as late as the 2nd century.

Idalah. Town assigned to Zebulun's tribe for an inheritance (Jos 19:15). It is generally identified with Khirbet el-Hawarah, northwest of Nazareth.

Idbash. One of Etam's three sons from Judah's tribe (1 Chr 4:3).

Iddo. 1. Father of Ahinadab, Solomon's official at Mahanaim, who administered the royal household (1 Kgs 4:14).

2. Gershonite Levite, descendant of Joah and forefather of Zerah (1 Chr 6:21); perhaps alternately called Adaiah in verse 41.

See ADAIAH #2.

3. Zechariah's son and the chief officer of Manasseh's half tribe in Gilead during David's reign (1 Chr 27:21).

4. Prophet and seer who chronicled the events of Solomon's reign in a book of visions concerning Jeroboam, Nebat's son (2 Chr 9:29), recorded Rehoboam's acts in the genealogies (12:15), and wrote a story of Abijah's life (13:22).

5. Grandfather of Zechariah the prophet (Zec 1:1,7). Iddo, presumably, was a well-known priest who returned to Jerusalem from exile in 538 BC, and whose household was headed by Zechariah during Joiakim's reign

as high priest during the postexilic era. According to Ezra 5:1 and 6:14, Zechariah and not Berechiah his father, was considered Iddo's successor.

See ZECHARIAH (PERSON) #20.

6. Leading man at Casiphia in Babylonia to whom Ezra sent a delegation of men requesting priests and temple servants to join Ezra's caravan returning to Palestine for service in the Jerusalem temple (Ezr 8:17).

Idols, Idolatry. Man-made images or representations worshiped as deities; any natural or manufactured objects worshiped as deity; anything receiving worship other than the one true God. Idolatry is the spiritual worship of an idol. Many idolaters literally serve idols: in ancient Egypt statues of gods were regularly and ritually clothed and fed. Some concept of the worship of a false god Baal is given in the account of the contest on Mt Carmel; the priests of Baal cried aloud, they "limped" around the altar, they cut themselves with swords and lances (1 Kgs 18:26–29). Baal worship was at times widely followed by Israel during the period of the monarchy.

The pre-Abrahamic progenitors of the Israelites were worshipers of idols in Mesopotamia (Jos 24:2). Archaeological excavations in that area have revealed the images of numerous deities and Mesopotamian religious literature reveals the gross polytheism out of which Abraham came.

The tendency of the Israelites toward idolatry was in part the expression of the universal human longing for a god one can see and know through the physical senses. It is in partial fulfillment of this desire that God sent his Son in the flesh (cf. Jn 1:18; 2 Cor 4:6). Rebellion against God also led to idol worship (Rom 1:18–23).

Most of the idolatry of the Israelites was borrowed from their neighbors. During the more than 400 years that the descendants of Jacob spent in Egypt, they were exposed to polytheistic idolatry, which influenced their religious mindset. At Sinai, while Moses was receiving the Ten Commandments from the Lord, the people were demanding that Aaron make gods for them (Ex 32:1–6). He fashioned a golden calf, following an Egyptian form, for the whole bovine family was worshiped in Egypt—the Apis bull, the Hathor cow, and the Mnevis calf.

It was after his stay in Egypt (1 Kgs 11:40) that Jeroboam became king of Israel and set up golden calves, one at Bethel and one at Dan (12:26–33), an action that earned him the label, "Jeroboam, the son of Nebat, who made Israel to sin."

Already in patriarchal times there are references to the teraphim, or household gods. Examples of these idols have been found at Ur of the Chaldees, Nuzi, and other sites, and are referred to in the cuneiform tablets. The teraphim which Rachel stole from Laban could be hidden in her camel's saddlebag (Gn 31:34). It seems, however, that in the time of David such idols were larger, for when Saul's men came to kill David, Michal, David's wife and the daughter of Saul, helped David to escape and then took such an image and placed it in a bed to make the men think that David was sick (1 Sm 19:11–17).

The prohibition of idolatry is explicitly stated in the second commandment (Ex 20:4,5; Dt 5:8,9): "You shall not make for yourself a graven image, or any likeness of anything that is in heaven above, or that is in the earth beneath, or that is in the water under the earth; you shall not bow down to them or serve them" (cf. Ex 34:17; Lv 19:4; 26:1; Dt 4:15–19; 27:1–5). This commandment is an extension or auxiliary of the first, for it seeks to preserve God's uniqueness and to protect his glory. The definition of idolatry was broadened during the time of Samuel, who confronted King Saul with the charge that "stubbornness is as iniquity and idolatry" (lit. "teraphim"; 1 Sm 15:23). In the NT the concept of idolatry was extended even more; covetousness is equated with idolatry (Gal 5:20; Col 3:5).

Previous to the conquest of Canaan, the Lord kept warning Israel against marrying members of the native populace, which he had ordered Israel to annihilate. This measure was intended to prevent the weakening of moral life in Israel (Ex 34:16; Dt 7:3,4). This principle is again expanded in the NT (cf. 1 Cor 15:33; 2 Cor 6:14). The history of Israel demonstrated the practicality of the prohibition against such marriages, for they inevitably led to apostasy. Perhaps the saddest example is Solomon (1 Kgs 11:1–8). "When Solomon was old his wives turned away his heart after other gods; and his heart was not wholly true to the Lord his God" (v 4).

In the time of the judges there was an infamous case of idol worship (Jgs 17:1–18:31). The mother of an Ephraimite named Micah took 200 pieces of silver and had a silversmith make them into a graven image for her son. He also had a shrine, an ephod, and teraphim. He hired a wandering Levite to be his priest, but men from the tribe of Dan came along and took the Levite, the image, and all the accouterments and set up this idol at Dan and used it as an object of their worship (18:30,31).

In Scripture the kings of Israel are evaluated on the basis of what they did with respect to the "high places" and idols. Asa removed all the idols his fathers had made (1 Kgs 15:12)

and would not let his mother be queen because she had "an abominable image made for Asherah"; he cut down and burned the image (v 13). The Israelite king Ahab, however, followed after idols (21:26; cf. 16:30–33).

Hezekiah destroyed the high places, broke down the pillars, and cut down the Asherah (2 Kgs 18:4; 2 Chr 31:1). He also put an end to a strange cult that illustrates the insidious nature of idolatry. The bronze serpent which Moses lifted up on a pole to save the Israelites from death by snakebite (Nm 21:9; cf. Jn 3:14) had been preserved until the time of Hezekiah. It had been given the name Nuhushtan, and people venerated it and burned incense to it, so Hezekiah destroyed it (2 Kgs 18:4) because what had been an instrument for good had become a thing of evil.

The prophet Isaiah described the making of an idol in human form (Is 40:19,20; 44:9–17). Images were cast in a mold using molten metal (40:19; 44:10). Statues were forged by smiths (44:12), carved from wood (vv 13–17), and overlaid with precious metal (40:19). Small clay images and plaques were also molded and fired in a kiln, and statues were sculptured from stone.

The psalmist spoke out against idols and images (96:5; 97:7; 106:34–39) and the helplessness of idols is described in Psalms 115:4–8 and 135:15–17.

The northern and southern kingdoms of Israel went into captivity because they forsook

A lararium (altar for household gods) in an ancient Roman home at Pompeii.

God and served idols. The Jews were well aware that idolatry had brought them into captivity, and during their time in Babylon they developed an abhorrence to idols which has characterized Judaism to this very day.

CARL E. DeVRIES

See GROVE; HIGH PLACE; GODS, GODDESSES; CANAANITE DEITIES AND RELIGION; SIN.

Idumaea, Idumeans. Term derived from the Greek form of Edom ("red"). The change from Edomite to Idumean resulted from the conquests of Alexander the Great, which made Greek the common language of the area. The name was applied to the former country of the Edomites and to the portion of south Judah occupied by the descendants of Esau after the Jews had been deported to Babylon following the conquest by Nebuchadnezzar in 586 BC. The country known as Idumaea in the intertestamental period, had its northern boundary at Bet-sur (Beth-zur), a few miles north of Hebron, and included some of the shephelah (low country) extending down into the former Philistine country (1 Mc 4:15,22,61; 5:65).

The inhabitants of Idumaea were the descendants of Esau, known as Edomites, then as Nabataeans, and finally as Idumeans. The ancestors of the Idumeans trace their lineage to the elder brother of Jacob, Esau, who was cheated out of his birthright (Gn 27:1–45). This led to conflict between the children of Israel and the descendants of Esau throughout the entire biblical period.

It is not surprising, therefore, that the Edomites rejoiced when the Babylonians conquered Israel. The Edomites then occupied the territory vacated by the Israelites following the subjugation of the kingdom by the Babylonians after 586 BC.

About 300 BC Arabian tribes invaded and took the Edomite capital, forcing the remaining Edomites into the area south of Judah, which then became known as Idumaea. These invaders, known as Nabataeans, made Sela or Petra the center of their caravan trade both from east and west and north to south. These desert tradesmen, influenced now by Greek ideas, fashioned the bowllike "crater" at Petra into a fantastic city with a concentration of rock-hewn temples, tombs, and buildings made from the colorful red sandstone of the area. In addition to creating the world's most unique city, the Nabataeans were excellent traders and farmers. As Josephus says, they were not warlike but skilled in commerce, art, and agriculture. The Nabataeans created the strategic desert stronghold of Avedat, which, with Petra, commanded the caravan routes. The Nabataeans flourished from about 100 BC

to AD 100, when the Romans gradually caused their demise by changing the caravan routes from south of the Dead Sea to the area around Damascus and Palmyra.

The religion of the Idumeans is virtually unknown. It is quite likely that the Nabataean deities were those they acquired from the Edomites. These included the god Dushara, symbolized by an obelisk, the storm god Hadad, adopted from Syrian neighbors, and Atargatis, the fertility goddess equivalent to the Greek Artemis. If these were the gods of the Edomites, the OT writers are surprisingly silent about them, whereas they were quite articulate about the gods of other neighbors (cf. 2 Chr 25:14).

During the intertestamental period the returning Jews had border scrimmages with the Idumeans. Hebron was captured by Judas Maccabeus (1 Mc 5:65). John Hyrcanus compelled the Idumeans to become Jews and submit to circumcision. The governor of Idumaea, Antipater, who had been made procurator of Judea by Julius Caesar, was an Idumean. Antipater assigned his son Herod as governor of Galilee. This paved the way for Herod to become king of Judea, under the title of Herod the Great. With the conquest of Judea by the Romans, first in AD 70, and later in AD 135, Idumaea disappears from history. Only in recent years have archaeologists begun to uncover some of the secrets of the Idumeans and of the Nabataeans, their conquerors.

See EDOM, EDOMITES; JUDAISM.

Iezer, Iezerites. Contractions of Abiezer and Abiezrite, the names of Gilead's son and that son's descendants (Nm 26:30).

See ABIEZER #1.

Igal. 1. Joseph's son from Issachar's tribe and one of the 12 spies sent by Moses to search out Canaan (Nm 13:7).

2. Nathan's son and one of David's mighty men (2 Sm 23:36). In 1 Chronicles 11:38 he is called Joel, Nathan's brother (in Hebrew, only one letter different from Igal).

3. Shemaiah's son and a descendant of King David through King Jehoiachin (1 Chr 3:22, KJV Igeal).

Igdaliah. Hanan's father. Hanan's sons had a room adjacent to the temple during Josiah's reign (Jer 35:4).

Igeal. KJV spelling of Igal, Shemaiah's son, in 1 Chronicles 3:22.

See IGAL #3.

im. 1. KJV rendering of Iyim, a shortened form of Iye-abarim, in Numbers 33:45.

See IYE-ABARIM, IYIM.

2. Town near Edom in the southern portion of the land assigned to Judah's tribe for an inheritance (Jos 15:29). Its exact location is unknown.

je-abarim. KJV spelling of Iye-abarim, one of Israel's stopping places in the wilderness, in Numbers 21:11 and 33:44.

See IYE-ABARIM, IYIM.

jon. Town assigned to Naphtali's tribe in the extreme north of Palestine. Some identify it with Tell ed-Dibbon between the Litani River and Mt Hermon, but this is disputed. Ijon was one of the towns taken by Ben-hadad of Damascus during Baasha's reign (c. 900 BC; 1 Kgs 15:20; 2 Chr 16:4). Tiglath-pileser III of Assyria captured the town and deported its people during Pekah's reign (c. 733 BC; 2 Kgs 15:29).

kkesh. Man from Tekoa whose son Ira was one of David's mighty men (2 Sm 23:26; 1 Chr 11:28), and head of a division of 24,000 men during the 6th month of the year (1 Chr 27:9).

lai. Alternate name for Zalmon, a renowned warrior, in 1 Chronicles 11:29.

See ZALMON (PERSON).

llness. See DISEASE; MEDICINE AND MEDICAL PRACTICE.

llyricum. Roman province northwest of Macedonia. Although its borders were at times uncertain, during the height of the Roman Empire (c. AD 117) Illyricum was bounded by the Adriatic Sea on the west and by the provinces of Pannonia on the north, Upper Moesia on the east, and Macedonia on the south. Today Yugoslavia and Albania occupy that territory.

Throughout the 4th century BC the people of Illyricum warred with the Macedonians, until the Macedonian ruler Philip II defeated them in 359 BC. During the 3rd century BC their acts of piracy against Greek and Roman ships led to a war with Rome that continued on and off for 60 years (229–168 BC). After a series of revolts and sporadic Roman rule, Illyricum was officially made a part of the empire in 11 BC. It took another 20 years for the people to be fully integrated into Roman culture.

In 229 BC the Roman historian Polybius stated that "the Illyrians were not the enemies of this people or that, but were the common enemies of all." Later Strabo, a 1st-century

Greek geographer, was still describing the people of Illyricum as savage and rapacious.

The sole NT reference to Illyricum is found in the apostle Paul's statement that he had preached the gospel "from Jerusalem and as far round as Illyricum" (Rom 15:19). Although Acts does not document a ministry in that region, Paul may have visited Illyricum during his visit to Macedonia and Achaia just before returning to Jerusalem (Acts 20:1,2). Paul expressed a desire to continue his ministry in Spain, a totally Latin environment (Rom 15:28); in Illyricum he would have had his first experience in a culture that was more Latin than Greek.

Image of God. Likeness to God, the most basic affirmation to be made concerning the nature of man from a Christian perspective. Man is unique among the creatures in that he is like God and therefore able to have communion and fellowship with God.

Genesis 1:26,27 teaches that God determined to create man in his own "image" and "likeness" with dominion over the animal creation. The two terms used in the creation account and found also in the NT convey closely related shades of meaning, but the difference between them is no longer thought to be theologically significant.

Because Genesis 2:7 states unambiguously that *man* became a living creature, the Bible does not countenance the view that a previously living creature developed into man, nor the view that the image of God evolved from a lower form of life. The moment man became a living creature, he was the image of God. Both male and female share this likeness to God (Gn 1:27).

Other passages that speak of man's creation in the image of God are Genesis 5:1; 9:6; 1 Corinthians 11:7; and James 3:9. Ephesians 4:24 and Colossians 3:10 refer to man's redemptive re-creation, but the passages are generally regarded as directly relevant for an understanding of man's original likeness to God. Although explicit references to man as the image of God are comparatively infrequent in the Bible, the truth itself underlies the whole relation between God and man and is therefore the presupposition of the entire biblical account.

The affirmation of man as the image of God in Genesis 1 is not made of any of the other living creatures. The animals, the fish, and the birds do not share this privilege. It is disputed whether the angels are in the image of God, but certain theologians so view them because they find the image to reside in moral righteousness. However, there is no explicit biblical statement to this effect.

By virtue of his creation from the dust of the ground, humankind has an obvious kinship with the earth. It is not strange, therefore, that the body, both in its constitution and functions, shows similarities with other earthly creatures. But man is unique in every aspect of his existence; for not some part of man or some faculty of man, but man as such, man in his integrity, is the image of God. The biblical concept is not that the image is *in* man, but that man *is* the image of God.

The problem is to understand how human bodily existence is to be included as an aspect of the image of God in view of the biblical teaching on the spirituality and incorporeality of God (Jn 4:24).

Some argue that man was made in the image of the incarnate Christ, or the Christ who would in time become incarnate. However, the need for the incarnation arises only after the fall into sin and with a view to the mediatorial office. Therefore in becoming flesh, Christ is said to have been made in the likeness of men (Phil 2:7; Heb 2:16,17), and not the other way round.

Another perspective is afforded by further reflection on the nature of man. Consideration of the image of God usually proceeds on the premise of a distinction between the material aspect (body) and immaterial aspect (spirit) of man's constitution; recent discussions have focused on the unity and integrity of man. Thus it is man as a physical-spiritual unity who is in the image of God as Spirit. This explains why the same words can be used both of God and man. God sees and hears as men do, but men do so in a way appropriate to their constitution as physical-spiritual creatures (with ears and mouth) and God in a way appropriate to his nature as spiritual and uncreated.

However, as man's kinship with the earth is most clearly visible in his body, so the image of God is best seen when man is viewed from the perspective of his spirituality. Theologians have sought at this point to enumerate those aspects of man's spirituality that define his humanity and set him apart from the animal creation. The image of God is then found to reside in some attribute or combination of attributes, such as rationality, will, freedom, responsibility, or the like. Contemporary theologians prefer not to enumerate attributes, and the Bible does not set forth the image of God in this way. Nevertheless, it is the personality of man which separates him from the animals, and is a reflection of the personality of God. The animals have their existence *from* God, but man has his being *in* God, and is his offspring (Acts 17:28,29).

Another major aspect of the doctrine of im-

age of God is developed from Ephesians 4: and Colossians 3:10. These verses describe redemption in terms of re-creation in the like ness of God, in righteousness, holiness of t truth, and true knowledge. The argument that what holds so prominent a place in t new creation must also have held a corr spondingly prominent place in the original cr ation. Without moral integrity, man wou have been created a sinner, or at best, mora neutral; but he is represented in the Bible upright from the beginning.

How the humanity or personality of ma on the one hand, and the righteousness man, on the other, are to be understood relation to the image of God is a matter disagreement among the major confession groupings.

In Roman Catholic theology, man is the i age of God by virtue of his humanity as a r tional and free person. His original righteou ness does not belong to the image but thought of as a supernatural gift, added in der to assist the soul in keeping the lower d sires of the flesh in control. Lutherans take t opposite position—the image resides excl sively in man's moral excellence and not in h nature as man. Their appeal is principally Ephesians 4:24 and Colossians 3:10. Reform theologians locate the image in both the pe sonality and the holiness of man, and ther fore distinguish between image in the broad sense, or personality, and in the narrow sense, righteousness. These are not two diffe ent images, but a single one in which t broader sense is inclusive of the narrower.

The classic Socinian and Remonstrant A minian theologians (17th century) presented quite different conception, arguing that the i age resides exclusively in the dominion wi which man was invested at his creation. Gen sis 1:26, the basic proof text for the image God, was thought to define the nature of t image. This view, however, is difficult to re oncile with Genesis 9:6; Ephesians 4:24; a Colossians 3:10, and the breadth of the conce tion suggested by biblical language. Most the logians would therefore include dominion an aspect of the image, or as a consequen arising from man's constitution as the ima of God.

Basic confessional differences are also flected in the way the fall into sin is seen affect the image. In Roman Catholic thoug the fall involves the loss of the superadded g of original righteousness but leaves the ima unimpaired. If the image were totally co rupted there would no longer be left a man redeem. On the other side, the Lutherans w find the image exclusively in man's moral i tegrity see the image as wholly destroyed the fall. Re-creation of the image in knowledge, righteousness, and holiness presupposes its previous total loss.

Using the distinction between image in the broader and narrower senses, the Reformed hold that with respect to moral integrity, the image of God is totally destroyed. In the broader sense, however, the image of God is corrupted and barely visible, but it is not destroyed. Passages like Genesis 9:6; 1 Corinthians 11:7; and James 3:9 refer to man even after the fall as the image of God.

The Reformed argue that the doctrine of total depravity does not require the total destruction of the image of God. Depravity is a moral condition affecting man in every part of his constitution, but only as a responsible person is man a sinner. The fact that man, precisely as the image of God, is a sinner, only serves to compound his guilt. Even in perdition where all grace is absent, man is still a person, and his personality is an indispensible condition of his suffering.

Just as the fall into sin was not without its effect on the image of God, so also redemption from sin affects man as the image of God. Ephesians and Colossians speak of renewal in the image of God the Creator, but other texts become even more specific in view of the mediatorial office of Christ.

Jesus Christ is preeminently the image of God (2 Cor 4:4; Col 1:15; Heb 1:3). Frequently this is understood exclusively as a reference to the deity of Christ. To see Christ is to see the Father (Jn 14:9). However, in the passages cited, it is the incarnate Mediator, the last Adam who is at least all that God intended the first Adam to be. Incarnation means that Jesus is truly man, and because he is truly man, he is truly the image of God.

As the last Adam and the Mediator of the New Covenant, Jesus brings his people into conformity with his own image, the image of the Son of God (Rom 8:29). He who became like his brethren, in the likeness of sinful flesh, destroys sin in order that his brethren might reflect his own glory. They are changed into the same image from glory to glory by the Spirit of the Lord (2 Cor 3:18). The believer is to "put on Christ" (Gal 3:27; Rom 13:14; cf. Eph 4:24; Col 3:10, putting on the new man in the image of God), an action also described as the formation of Christ in man (Gal 4:19).

Conformity to the image of Jesus Christ is achieved through the process of sanctification which is ultimately completed at the resurrection. Only then is the body changed until it is fashioned like unto the glorious body of Christ (Phil 3:21). Restoration in the image of Christ carries man beyond creation in the image of God, for the image of the earthly is then exchanged for the image of the heavenly (1 Cor 15:49).

Modern theologians view these classic confessional conceptions as too static. Their criticism is similar to that made of the historic doctrine of the Bible as the Word of God. Just as revelation is no longer thought of as given and present in history, but rather as occurring or taking place, so the image of God does not exist as a given entity, nor can it be possessed. The image of God is located in the continuing relation sustained between God and man.

Karl Barth (1886–1968) is a good example of this view. Barth took his cue from the fact that man is created male and female (Gn 1:26,27) and argued that the image is found in the relationship that is sustained between them, comparable to the relationship sustained among the persons of the Trinity. Between man and God there is not an analogy of being but an analogy of relation.

The full significance of this view emerges only with the further observation that the male-female relation is specifically the relation between Christ and his church, and that Jesus is the image of God. As Christ and the church have their existence only in relation to one another, so man, since he is the image of God, has his existence only in relation to God, that is, in Jesus Christ. All men are men only in Christ, and their redemption, therefore, is given with their creation.

Although the view of Barth contains fatal liabilities from the perspective of historic Christianity, the introduction of the concept of relationship is suggestive for a deepened understanding of the traditional view. The place given to moral integrity in the image of God shows that the historic conception was not purely static. At the same time, the image could not be described in purely functional terms since man himself, and not a relation, is the image of God.

When Adam surveyed the animals, he found no helper suitable for himself (Gn 2:18–23) and so God made a helper for him, bone of his bone and flesh of his flesh. The suitable and helpful partner was one like himself. This created relation underlies the heightened communion of the marriage covenant.

This account in Genesis 2 is analogous to what took place on a grander scale in Genesis 1. On the sixth day God surveyed his creation and it was good; but there was no one like him, suitable to be his helper. God made man (male and female) in his own image to be glorified in him, as woman is both the likeness and glory of man (1 Cor 11:7). The likeness between male and female, which underlies the marriage covenant, is analogous to the likeness between man and God, which underlies their covenant relation of union and communion. As man is God's helper, his vicegerent, exercising dominion in the earth, so the wife exercises rule in her sphere of authority in subjection to her husband (Prv 31:10–31; Eph 5:22,33). The relation of God to Israel and of Christ to his church is sometimes set forth as a marriage in the Bible.

The infrequent explicit reference to the image of God in Scripture is explained by the fact that man is made in the image of God for the sake of covenant relation with God, and therefore the concept of image is taken up immediately into the covenant relation which is fully expounded in both the OT and NT.

The revelation concerning the image of God in Genesis 1 does not serve as a springboard for an analysis of the structure of man in independence from revelation as sometimes happened in the traditional formulations. Rather, it leads directly to the covenant, and therefore to the biblical understanding of the point of contact for the persuasive proclamation of the gospel. Men are to be addressed as the image-bearers of God. They are not addressed as rational animals, but as sinners apostate from the covenant of creation. They are now invited to return to the Father by the blood of the New Covenant in Jesus. Their redemption involves conformity to the image of Christ and therefore the restoration of the image of God. They have communion with God through union with Christ.

NORMAN SHEPHERD

See MAN, DOCTRINE OF; WOMAN, DOCTRINE OF.

Bibliography. G.C. Berkouwer, *Man: The Image of God;* D. Cairns, *The Image of God in Man;* G.A. Clark, *A Christian View of Men and Things;* J.G. Machen, *The Christian View of Man;* J.A. Motyer, *The Image of God, Law and Liberty in Biblical Ethics;* J. Orr, *God's Image in Man;* H.W. Robinson, *The Christian Doctrine of Man.*

Imlah, Imla. Father of Michaiah, a prophet during King Ahab's reign, whom the king despised for speaking the truth (1 Kgs 22:8,9; 2 Chr 18:8, KJV Imlah).

Immanuel. Hebrew masculine name which means "God with us." It appears only twice in the OT (Is 7:14; 8:8) and once in the NT (Mt 1:23), where it is transliterated "Emmanuel." In the OT the name was given to a child born in the time of Ahaz as a sign to the king that Judah would receive relief from attacks by Israel and Syria. The name symbolized the fact that God would demonstrate his presence with his people in this deliverance.

The larger application, on which there is general agreement, is that this is a prophecy of the birth of the incarnate God, Jesus the Messiah, as shown in Matthew.

The concept of the special presence of God goes back to the Garden of Eden, where God conversed with Adam in the cool of the day. There was, however, a difference of viewpoint for most of the pre-Isaiah expressions are seen from the perspective of God. It was God's assurance, "I am with you," not man's recognition that "God is with us." God manifested his presence in many ways: by the pillar of cloud and of fire (Ex 13:21,22), and by the symbolism of the tabernacle and the temple, especially the Holy of Holies and the ark of the covenant. But most of this was remote, impersonal, or inaccessible, and when the glory of the Lord was seen in those buildings it produced such a sense of overwhelming awe that the normal ministration could not be conducted (Ex 40:34–38; 2 Chr 5:13,14; 7:1–3). God assured Israel of his presence when they confronted battle (Dt 20:1; 31:6; Jos 1:9) and promised to be with them when they were fearful and weak (Is 41:10) and when they were facing great trial (43:2). In Isaiah 7:14 the emphasis changes from "I with you" to "He with us."

In focusing on the birth of Immanuel Jesus there has been some neglect of the historical fulfillment that occurred in the time of Ahaz. Ahaz was the son of a good king, Jotham (2 Chr 27:2), and the grandson of another godly ruler, Uzziah (2 Chr 26:4), but his reign was marked by apostasy and idolatry. He made "molten images" for the baals, offered incense in the Hinnom Valley, and even burned his sons as an offering (2 Chr 28:2–4). Because of this the Lord gave him into the hand of Rezin, king of Syria, and of Pekah, king of Israel. The Edomites also invaded Judah and the Philistines attacked the Shephelah and the Negev and took several cities (2 Chr 28:17,18).

Ahaz appealed to Tiglath-pileser III of Assyria (745–727 BC) for help against Israel and Syria. Tiglath-pileser accepted tribute from Ahaz, but attacked him instead of helping him (2 Chr 28:21,22). When he went to Damascus to meet the Assyrian king, Ahaz saw an altar, upon which he made offerings to the gods of Syria (2 Chr 28:23). He had a replica of this made and placed in the temple of Jerusalem (2 Kgs 16:10–12). The prophet Isaiah was directed to accost Ahaz at the end of the conduit of the upper pool. God's message to the king was to "take heart," for the attacking kings would fall (Is 7:7–9). Isaiah directed Ahaz to ask the Lord for a sign of this, but the king demurred, having a sudden attack of piety (v 12).

Upon this refusal the Lord gave to Ahaz a sign: a young woman would conceive and bear a son and call his name Immanuel (Is 7:14). That son would eat curds and wild honey and before he could distinguish good from evil the

A magical figure from Assyria, the country that would devastate Judah before Immanuel was old enough to distinguish good from evil. The figure is a detail from a palace relief of Ashurnasirpal II.

two kings would be removed and the king of Assyria would devastate their lands. The people would be taken away captive, so that the land would lie desolate and uncultivated. A man would have a cow to provide milk for curds and wild honey would be gathered from the tangle of brush in the untended land.

The identity of this woman and child in Isaiah's time is uncertain. It has been proposed that the woman was Abijah, the wife of Ahaz, and that their son, Hezekiah, was this Immanuel. This is not demonstrable and it seems inappropriate that a man like Ahaz should be the father of Immanuel.

It has also been suggested that the wife of Isaiah was the mother of Immanuel. Isaiah 7:14 tells of the prospective birth of Immanuel; 8:3 tells of the conception and birth of Isaiah's son, whose name, Maher-shalal-hashbaz ("the spoil speeds, the prey hastes") is related to the prediction of the fall of Judah's enemies, for before the child would learn to talk the lands of Syria and Israel would be taken by the king of Assyria (v 4).

Isaiah's statement that he and his children were "signs and portents in Israel from the Lord" (v 18) enhances the view that it was his son who was also named Immanuel.

The Lord then directed a message to Immanuel (Is 8:8–10). Because the people had refused the gracious invitation of the Lord, the Assyrians would scourge and fill the land of Immanuel. The plotting and plans of the people would come to nothing, for "God is with us" (*'immanu 'el*). This is a play on words, using the name Immanuel to express the truth of the Lord's presence.

Although there may be varying perceptions as to the OT application, the ultimate meaning of the passage is clear. The rock of offense and the stone of stumbling (Is 8:14,15) could be none other than Immanuel Jesus, God Incarnate (Mt 1:23; Rom 9:32,33; 1 Pt 2:8,9).

In the fulness of time God sent forth his son; more than 700 years after Ahaz, Jesus was born and here all ambiguities fade away. His mother was a virgin from Nazareth named Mary (Miriam), betrothed to a solid citizen named Joseph. Matthew 1:23 cites Isaiah 7:14 as being fulfilled in the birth of Jesus. The Scripture is very explicit in stating that Mary had no sexual contact with her husband prior to the birth of Jesus (Mt 1:25). The same precision is seen in the Gospel of Luke. When the announcement of this child's conception was made to Mary, she asked, "How shall this be, since I have no husband?" (Lk 1:34; cf. NIV). The angelic messenger explained that this conception would be brought about by the coming of the Holy Spirit upon her and by the overshadowing power of the Most High (Lk 1:35). For this reason the child would be not only Jesus and Immanuel but he would be called Holy, the Son of God, God manifest in the flesh (Jn 1:18); the child would be unique, being both God and man.

There were great distinctions between the Immanuel of Isaiah's day and Immanuel the son of Mary. The first was a type; the other, the antitype; the first was the shadow, the other the Reality. The one symbolized deliverance from foreign oppression, the second was the Deliverer from the oppressor. The first represented God's presence for but a few years; the second Immanuel is the son who abides for ever.

The concept of "God with us" was often reiterated by Jesus. He told his disciples that where two or three gathered in his name he would be present (Mt 18:20). Before his ascension, he assured them that he would be with them until the end of the age (28:20).

He spoke also of the promise of the Holy Spirit, who "dwells with you, and will be in you" (Jn 14:17), who will abide with them forever (v 16). The "God with us" indwelling is spoken of in Colossians 1:27, "Christ in you, the hope of glory." In the consummation of all things, as shown to the apostle John, the Lord said: "Behold, the dwelling of God is with men. He will dwell with them, and they shall be his people, and God himself will be with them" (Rv 21:3).

There is a corollary to the principles of "God with us" and "I with you"; like the third side of an equilateral triangle the Lord asserts the assurance, "you (they) with Me (Him)." Jesus chose his disciples that they might be with him (Mk 3:14). When he foretold his departure he told them he was going to prepare a place for them so that they could be where he is (Jn 14:3). In another place the eternal summation is given: "So we shall always be with the Lord" (1 Thes 4:17).   CARL E. DeVRIES

See MESSIAH; GOD, NAMES OF.

Immer (Person). Priest in the time of David. He became the ancestral head of a house of priests: Pashhur, the priest who had Jeremiah arrested and placed in stocks, was a descendant of Immer (Jer 20:1). There were 1052 priests of the sub-clan of Immer who returned from the exile (1 Chr 9:12; Ezr 2:37; Neh 7:40); 128 priests under Amashsai (a descendant of Immer) helped rebuild the temple (Neh 11:13).

Immer (Place). Place in Babylon. The Jews who returned from Immer had lost the record of their ancestry and could not prove their Jewish lineage (Ezr 2:59; Neh 7:61). Its site is unknown.

Imna. Heler's son from Asher's tribe (1 Chr 7:35).

Imnah. 1. Asher's son (Gn 46:17; KJV Jimnah; 1 Chr 7:30) and founder of the Imnite family (Nm 26:44; KJV Jimna, Jimnites).

2. Levite and Kore's father. Kore was a temple assistant during King Hezekiah's reign (2 Chr 31:14).

Imnite. Descendant of Imnah from Asher's tribe (Nm 26:44).

See IMNAH #1.

Impalement. Driving of a pointed stake into a human body. It was apparently practiced in ancient Egypt, Assyria, Babylonia, Persia, and possibly also in Israel. There are, however, many problems in understanding the exact nature of impalement and what it means in individual OT passages.

It is not always clear from documents written in Greek whether impalement or crucifixion is being described since the same Greek word could refer to either procedure. (In crucifixion the body is fastened to a stake rather than being punctured by it.)

Nor is it always clear whether the impalement is done to a living body or to a corpse. Probably both types of impalement were employed, the former as a method of execution, the latter as a means of exposing the corpse to the elements, beasts, and general disgrace.

Furthermore, it is not clear to what extent "hanging" in the OT refers to impalement. Perhaps the fact that it is typically used with the preposition "on" (rather than "from") indicates that impalement of some kind is intended.

Some light is shed on the nature of impalement through Mesopotamian sources, where it was apparently a means of execution, in one case for a woman who has caused her husband's death because of another man (Code of Hammurabi, 153), in another for a woman performing an abortion on herself

(Middle Assyrian Laws, 53). The latter law makes it clear that the woman should be impaled whether or not she lived through the abortion. The claim of Assyrian kings to have hung captives of war on stakes correlates with the portrayal in Assyrian art of battle scenes where impaled bodies can be seen. The stake could be pushed up into the chest, with the body resting face down, or between the legs, with the body upright.

Darius' provision that violators of his decree should be "struck upon a stake" probably refers to impalement (Ezr 6:11). If the expression "hang on a tree (stake)" (Gn 40:19; Dt 21:22; Jos 8:29; 10:26; Est 2:23; as distinct from the expression describing Ahithophel's death in 2 Sm 17:23) refers to impalement, at least sometimes it is clear that it is a corpse being impaled (Jos 10:26). This interpretation also applies to Deuteronomy 21:22, in which the victim is first put to death and then "hung." The point of similarity to the crucifixion of Christ (Gal 3:13) is the disgrace involved and not the precise form of treatment. Other possible examples of impalement are found in 2 Samuel 4:12 and 21:6–13.

DAVID K. HUTTAR

See CRIMINAL LAW AND PUNISHMENT.

Imprecatory Psalms. Psalms which contain curses (imprecations, maledictions) against enemies. These elements do not make up an entire psalm, but verses of this nature appear in more than a dozen (5,17,28,35,40,55,59,70,71,79, 80,94,129,137,139,140). A number of other psalms express the same ideas as future or accomplished acts of the Lord. Usually these expressions are couched in the form of a prayer or a wish. They voice the desire that evil may come upon an enemy as judgment or retribution.

To the casual reader such statements may appear to be at variance with much of the rest of Scripture, especially with the teaching of Jesus. The clear injunction of Leviticus 19:17, 18 states: "You shall not hate your brother in your heart, but you shall reason with your neighbor, lest you bear sin because of him. You shall not take vengeance or bear any grudge against the sons of your own people, but you shall love your neighbor as yourself; I am the Lord." Jesus expanded the concept of neighbor to include even the despised Samaritan (Lk 10:29–37). In the Sermon on the Mount, Jesus declared, "Love your enemies and pray for those who persecute you" (Mt 5:44; cf. vv 38–48). This is in harmony with the teaching of the OT, which instructs one to feed a hungry enemy and give water to a thirsty one (Prv 25:21,22; cf. Rom 12:20).

In posing a difficult biblical question to the Jews, Jesus remarked parenthetically, "scripture cannot be broken" (Jn 10:35). The Bible does not contradict itself; the NT cannot be placed against the OT, neither can the psalms be in opposition to the Gospels. When the Lord declares in the OT, "Vengeance is mine, and recompense" (Dt 32:35), the statement is twice echoed in the NT (Rom 12:19; Heb 10:30).

We must be careful not to make ourselves judges of the Word of God, or to exalt ourselves to think that we are more fair or more just than God. Abraham wondered at the prospective destruction of the cities of the plain, but the question that he asked, "Shall not the Judge of all the earth do right?" was rhetorical, for he realized that he was not more just than God. The Lord prefaces his judgments with admonitions and warnings, but there comes a time when he says, "Enough." One who apologizes for God because God made hell for the eternal punishment for the unbeliever understands neither the enormity of sin nor the justice of God. Unbalanced emphasis on the love of God has been at the expense of his holiness.

Psalm 109 is often singled out, for it has the greatest imprecatory content, and its statements are stronger than other psalms of this character. Some have suggested that the maledictions of this psalm are unworthy of Scripture and are expressions of wicked human emotions that should not be included in the Bible. However, these curses cannot be explained away on the basis that they are quotations of human authors; they must be taken as the Word of God.

Historically this psalm has been regarded as both prophetic and messianic. It was the view of Chrysostom, Jerome, Augustine, and others. This was also the interpretation of Horne, who in his commentary translates the imperfect tenses of this psalm as futures, not the subjunctives of our English versions. He took his cue for this prophetic interpretation from Peter's quotation of verse 8 upon the occasion of choosing a successor for Judas (Acts 1:20). The psalm can then seem to fit the experiences of the life and passion of Jesus, which changes its tenor completely and in large measure removes it from being imprecatory and makes it predictive.

Another passage which has been abhorrent to many occurs in Psalm 137:8,9, which speaks of the happiness of those who dash Babylonian children on a rock. Horne took this as predictive of what took place when the armies of the Medes and Persians conquered the city of Babylon in 539 BC.

If one predicates that the expressions in the psalms are curses or desires for retribution, they are not out of keeping with the rest of Scripture. The prayer of Jeremiah for vengeance on his persecutors (Jer 11:20) received direct affirmative response from the Lord (vv 21–23). The plea of the righteous for justice and vindication will be answered speedily (Lk 18:1–8). In Revelation those who had been slain for the Word of God and for their testimony cry out, "How long before thou wilt judge and avenge our blood?" (6:10) and they were heard. David, to whom Psalm 109 is attributed, was given victory and vengeance over his enemies and he realized that those who were his enemies were also the enemies of God.

The argument that the imprecations are based on God's justice and not on personal vengeance is not completely accurate. In Psalm 41:10 after complaining against his enemies and his betrayer, the psalmist prays, "Raise me up, that I may requite them!" Also in Psalm 118:10–12 the writer three times states that he is surrounded by enemies but "in the name of the Lord I cut them off!" The personal involvement of David is also stated in Psalm 144: "Blessed be the Lord, my rock, who trains my hands for war; and my fingers for battle (v 1; cf. 2 Sm 22:35–43; Ps 18:34,37–42).

Evidently the enemies against whom the psalmists prayed had reached the place of judgment, and the imprecations of the writers coincided with the judgment of God.

CARL E. DEVRIES

See PSALMS, BOOK OF; JUDGMENT; WRATH OF GOD.

Imputation. Charging to an account, used in the Bible with legal reference to sin and salvation being recorded by God. The biblical teaching on imputation represents one of the principal doctrines of the Christian faith. Although the noun form is not found in Scripture, the verb "to impute" occurs frequently in the OT and NT. The basic meaning of the biblical word "impute" is, "to set down in a record or a ledger." In relation to the doctrine of salvation the word is consistently used in a legal sense. Philemon 18, which affirms that the apostle Paul assumed the debt of Onesimus, aptly illustrates the predominant theological usage of the word: "if he . . . owes you anything, charge that to my account."

Hence when Scripture speaks of the imputation of good or evil, it in no wise suggests that any change of moral character is involved. Scripture does affirm that, from God's perspective, righteousness or sin is charged to an individual's account. In the broadest sense, Scripture teaches that God participates in the process of imputing (Ps 32:2) as do people (1 Sm 22:15). Good deeds were commonly imputed for reward (Ps 106:30,31), and evil deeds were imputed for punishment (Lv 17:3,4).

The Bible sets forth the theological concept of imputation in three distinct yet related ways. First, Scripture affirms the imputation of Adam's original sin to the entire human race. In the sovereign plan of God, the first man's initial act of disobedience was set to the account of every member of the human family. Every person thus participates in the guilt and penalty of that original sin. Second, the sin and guilt of the human race was imputed to Christ, so that although the Savior was not a sinner, he nevertheless bore the penalty arising from sin. Finally, the Bible teaches that, as a result of his atoning work, Christ's righteousness is set to the believer's account. Although not yet perfectly holy or morally righteous, believers nevertheless are justified before the Law of God, and they are "clothed" with the imputed righteousness of Christ.

Imputation and Original Sin. The biblical doctrine of sin necessarily leads to the problem of the imputation of Adam's sin to his posterity. Genesis 3:1–13 describes the entrance of sin into the world, and verses 16–19 detail God's punishment of Adam and Eve for their disobedience. Although the perspective here is limited to sin's consequences for Adam and Eve, human experience shows that their sin ages ago has affected the entire race. In Romans 5, Paul the apostle affirmed that just as Adam's act of disobedience brought spiritual ruin for humankind, so Christ's obedient submission to death on the cross brought righteousness and eternal life. When Paul wrote that sin came into the world through one man and death through sin, and so death spread to all men because all men sinned (Rom 5:12), he was not teaching simply that all people sin and die. Rather, he emphasized that the guilt and penalty of Adam's sin was directly imputed to his descendants, so that all succumb to death. Paul reiterates that truth in various phrases: "if many died through one man's trespass"; "as one man's trespass led to condemnation for all"; and "by one man's disobedience many were made sinners" (Rom 5:15,18,19). The apostle's declaration in 1 Corinthians 15:22 that "in Adam all die" further highlights the biblical teaching that Adam's original act of disobedience has been charged to the whole human family.

The question remains as to how the human race participated in Adam's transgression. Although the Bible does not explicitly address that issue, two theories exist that draw together various strands of biblical teaching. (1) As the head and representative of the human race, Adam acted on behalf of all humanity (the "federal" theory). (2) The entire race, body and soul, was genetically present in Adam (the "realist" or "seminal" theory). The latter theory draws support from Hebrews 7:9,10, which states that Abraham's descendant Levi paid tithes to King Melchizedek in the sense that Levi was in Abraham's loins when the patriarch centuries earlier presented tithes to the king.

Imputation and Sacrifice. In terms of the judicial reckoning of humanity's sin to Christ, the Bible does not specifically use the word "impute." Nevertheless, the fundamental idea is plainly present. The imputation of sin to Christ was typified in the OT sacrificial system, where the sins of the offerer were symbolically transferred to the animal victim. The ritual of the scapegoat on the Day of Atonement (Lv 16:20–22) graphically symbolized the transfer of human sin and guilt to a divine substitute. When the high priest placed his hands on the head of the goat and confessed the sins of the people, he in effect shifted the sins of the people onto the animal. "The goat shall bear all their iniquities upon him to a solitary land" (v 22).

Isaiah 53 is replete with sacrificial imagery, affirming emphatically that the guilt of human sin was reckoned to the Servant of the Lord. "Surely he has borne our griefs and carried our sorrows"; "the Lord has laid on him the iniquity of us all"; and "he bore the sins of many" (vv 4,6,12).

The apostle Paul developed at length the theme that Christ on the cross bore the punishment due to believers' sins. Thus he wrote that God "made him to be sin who knew no sin" (2 Cor 5:21; cf. Heb 9:28). Similarly he depicted Christ as bearing the curse of the Mosaic law (Gal 3:13). Finally, reflecting on Isaiah 53, the apostle Peter affirmed that Christ "himself bore our sins in his body on the tree" (1 Pt 2:24). The idea that the guilt of the entire world was charged to the account of the sinless Savior largely explains Christ's impassioned cry on the cross, "My God, my God, why hast thou forsaken me?" (Mt 27:46).

Imputed Righteousness. The imputation motif is also employed, in the sense of Christ's righteousness being credited to believers. An incident in the life of the patriarch Abraham illustrates the imputation of righteousness on the basis of faith. After God had promised material and spiritual blessing to Abraham, Genesis 15:6 states that he "believed the Lord; and he [God] reckoned it to him as righteousness." The Bible teaches that no person naturally possesses the standard of righteousness demanded by God (Ps 130:3; Is 64:6; Rom 3:10). Yet, in his gracious plan of salvation, God himself supplies the righteousness to satisfy his holy character (Is 45:24; 54:17; Hos 10:12). That is, as a person accepts by faith the work of Christ in satisfying the demands of God's Law, God imputes or reckons Christ's righteousness to the believer. The imputation of divine righteousness to the believer constitutes a major theme of Paul's letter to the Romans (3:21–5:21). Thus the apostle speaks of the blessedness of a person "to whom God reckons righteousness apart from works" (4:6). Moreover, the imputation of Christ's righteousness results in justification before God's law court (5:18). The merits of Christ's death imputed to the sinner are the basis for acquittal by the holy God. The apostle triumphantly affirmed that through his sacrifice, Christ is "made our wisdom, our righteousness and sanctification and redemption" (1 Cor 1:30). The same thought occupied Paul's mind when he prayed that he would "be found in him, not having a righteousness of my own, based on the law, but that which is through faith in Christ, the righteousness from God that depends on faith" (Phil 3:9). The phrase "the righteousness of God" occurs nine times in Paul's writings. The apostle was gripped by the profound reality that God imputes objective righteousness through faith in Christ's atoning work.

Thus the Bible teaches that the ruinous effects of the imputation of Adam's sin are effectively reversed for those who believe in Christ. The imputation of human sin to Christ makes possible the imputation of his righteousness to believers. By God's judicial act of accounting righteousness to the unworthy, strangers and aliens share with Abraham the privileged status of "friend of God" (Jas 2:23).

BRUCE A. DEMAREST

See SIN; ADAM (PERSON); CHRISTOLOGY; FALL OF MAN.

Imrah. Zophah's son, a chief of Asher's tribe (1 Chr 7:36).

Imri. 1. Ancestor of Uthai, one of the postexilic Jews of Judah's tribe (1 Chr 9:4). In the genealogy of Nehemiah 11:4, he is apparently called Amariah.

2. Father of Zaccur, a rebuilder of the Jerusalem wall (Neh 3:2).

Incantation. Chant used in magic.

See MAGIC.

Incarnation. Literally, "in flesh"; theologically, the doctrine that in Jesus of Nazareth God took on human flesh and became the divine God-man. Historically, the doctrine of incarnation was central in the christological debates of patristic times and has recently come to the fore again in academic circles.

Biblically, it expresses the mystery of Jesus' identity.

New Testament Evidence. *The Synoptic Gospels.* The Gospel of Mark has no account of the incarnation and stresses Jesus' messiahship more than his deity. As a result, some believe that it represents an earlier stage in the development of the church's theology, before the doctrine of the incarnation had evolved. That is doubtful for two reasons: incarnation passages like the Philippians hymn (2:6–11) probably antedate Mark's Gospel; and Mark has a well-developed theology of the two natures of Christ. Although he stresses Jesus' humanity, Mark accents it with an emphasis on divinity. Jesus was called the "beloved Son" by a heavenly voice at his baptism and transfiguration (1:11; 9:7); demons called him divine (3:11; 5:7), as did a Roman centurion (15:39). Jesus' "Abba" prayers (14:36) indicate his sense of divine identity, and at his trial he was charged with claiming the title, "Son of the Blessed" (vv 61,62). Thus, though the incarnation is nowhere explicitly stated in Mark, it is implicitly affirmed.

Matthew and Luke are openly incarnational. The birth narratives, of course, stress the event itself, with Matthew emphasizing Jesus' royal messiahship and Luke, the divine witness of the Holy Spirit. Matthew's Gospel is Christ-centered; Luke concentrates on Christ as Savior, or, more precisely, on salvation-history. Although Matthew presents Jesus' humanity, he emphasizes his lordship (23:6–10) and divine sonship. The incarnation thus becomes the means whereby the divine becomes human in a universal sense (1:23; 18:20; 24:14; 28:18–20). Luke shows the greatest interest of the three in Jesus' earthly life. Nevertheless, his Gospel does not stress the human side of Jesus as much as Mark's. Luke portrays Jesus primarily as the divine Savior within history (2:11; 4:16–30). He combines Jesus' messianic office and divine nature, showing that the in-

carnate Son of God suffered and was exalted in order to bring humankind to God.

John's Writings. The apostle John's doctrine of incarnation is more explicit than any of the others, teaching not only Jesus' God-man status but also his preexistent "glory" (Jn 1:1–18). Central in this presentation is the oneness between Jesus and God the Father (10:29, 30; 14:8–11; 1 Jn 2:23). The "I Am" (a major title for Jesus, taken from the OT title for the one true God and probably signifying God's personal name "Yahweh") came to reveal God to his people (Jn 1:4,5,14,18). Yet John also has the most balanced presentation of the incarnation. The divine Logos or Word (7:1–18) is the exemplar of perfect humanity (4:7,31; 11:35) who "became flesh" (1:14) to enlighten people (vv 5,9) and generate in them "eternal life" (3:14–18; 1 Jn 1:1–3; 4:9).

Acts. Many argue that the Book of Acts does not exhibit an incarnational Christology but rather is adoptionist, portraying Jesus as God's appointed or anointed one with no hint of divine overtones (see e.g., 2:22; 10:38). But such OT titles as "Holy and Righteous One" (3:13,14; 7:52), "Author of life" (3:15), and especially "Lord" (2:36; 16:31; 20:24) have a definite exalted sense. In Peter's Pentecost sermon Jesus is the Lord who has poured out the Spirit (2:33–36,39). Other passages continue the same theme of the glorious resurrected Christ, showing the Christology of Acts as one of exaltation rather than adoptionism.

Paul's Letters. The apostle Paul presented the incarnation as Jesus' path to suffering and redemption. In Galatians 4:4,5 the incarnation ("born of woman") came "in the fullness of time" or at the apex of salvation-history, to "redeem those who were under the law." In the Philippians hymn (2:6–11), the incarnation is seen in terms of preexistence ("though he was in the form of God"), humiliation ("emptied . . . humbled"), and obedience ("became obedient to the point of death" NASB). The goal of the incarnation was the cross ("even death on the cross"), and its result was Christ's exaltation. The hymn is perhaps the supreme theological statement on the incarnation in the NT. Jesus' human life was an "emptying," a refusal to seize the prerogatives of his deity ("did not consider equality with God a thing to be grasped").

Paul described Christ as a second Adam (Rom 5:12–19; 1 Cor 15:45–47), who brought humanity a new possibility to attain what Adam had forsaken. Through assuming the form of a man, Christ became the redeemer who reconciles people to God (Rom 3:25; 2 Cor 5:19; 1 Tm 1:15). Paul's greatest stress, however, was that the exalted Christ provides newness of life (Rom 6:4–6; 2 Cor 3:17,18; Col 3:1–

The Church of the Nativity in Bethlehem, the town where Jesus was born.

4). A hymn in the Letter to the Colossians (1:15–20) employs ideas from Jewish wisdom speculation, and possibly Greek themes, to show Christ as the "firstborn" and the "fullness of God." The one who always existed as God, through his sacrificial death, became the exalted Lord and brought humankind to God (see also the "flesh-spirit" theme in Rom 1:3,4; 1 Tm 3:16).

Hebrews. The Letter to the Hebrews is strongly incarnational. The opening hymn (1:2b–4) accents Christ's exalted status as "the very stamp" of God's image, aligning it with his work of redemption ("purification for sins"). Christ is superior to the angels (1:4–9), yet he became a man in order to suffer for human salvation (2:9; 5:7–9). Once more the incarnation is aligned with sinful humankind's need for a Savior. The purpose of Hebrews is to show Christ's incomparable superiority to the OT's sacrifices, and at the same time to stress his salvific work. His real temptation (2:18; 4:15) combined with his sinlessness (4:15; 5:9; 7:26) is the human remedy for human sin. The incarnation was Christ's path to final, once-for-all atonement and victory over sin (7:28; 9:26).

Historical Development. The first group to challenge the traditional doctrine of the incarnation was the Gnostics, who in the 2nd century denied that Jesus was truly human. Their Greek belief that the physical creation was evil led them to deny the incarnation. They believed Christ to be a quasi-spiritual being who merely appeared human. The theologian Marcion (d. *c.* 160), trained by Gnostic teachers, also accepted a docetic interpretation of Christ (his humanity was only apparent). Marcion taught his doctrine as an antidote to the OT or Jewish-oriented Christianity in his day. After his excommunication in AD 144, Marcion founded his own church, and his views were widely disseminated in the next two centuries. Partly in reaction to Marcion's christological heresy, the orthodox churches unified their doctrine.

The next challenge to the orthodox view came through the Arian, Apollinarian, and Nestorian controversies in the 3rd and 4th centuries. Arianism held that the incarnation was total, so that Christ the "Logos" was no longer fully God. At the same time he was not fully human, so Christ was someone between two natures. The Council of Nicaea (AD 325) affirmed that Jesus was indeed both God and man. A further question soon arose, however, as to the relation between his two natures. Apollinarius (310?–390?) taught that only the body of Jesus was human; his soul was absorbed completely into the divine Logos. Nestorius (after 381–451) taught that the two

natures must always remain distinct in the person of Christ; they functioned together but were separate in his being. The Council of Chalcedon (AD 451) affirmed the unity of the two natures in Jesus. Many opponents of Chalcedon arose, called Monophysites, who believed in one divine nature in Jesus, who was only in a sense human. That movement caused serious political and religious divisions, and the Council of Constantinople (680–681) reaffirmed Chalcedon and established the orthodox incarnation theology.

In the 8th century, Spain and France were centers of the "adoptionist" controversy. Adoptionism taught that at birth Jesus was human, but at his baptism he underwent a "second birth" and was "adopted" as Son of God. It was condemned in a series of synods and never gained many adherents until modern times. During the scholastic age Peter Lombard (1095?–1160) advocated what became known as "nihilism." The incarnation supposedly caused no fundamental change in Jesus' deity, but his human nature was both insubstantial and unessential. That view likewise was condemned by Pope Alexander III (1159–81). Another debate at that time centered on the relationship between the fall and the incarnation. Thomas Aquinas (1224–74) concluded that there was a cause-effect connection; the incarnation was necessitated by sin rather than predestined apart from the fall.

The Roman Catholic Church and the Protestant reformers follow basically the same orthodox teaching about the incarnation. The conflict in the Reformation centered more on soteriology (doctrine of salvation). Several aberrant antitrinitarian movements took advantage of the breakdown in ecclesiastical authority, however. Michael Servetus (1511–53) taught a pantheistic view of the incarnation, focused on the divine Spirit becoming manifest in the human form of Jesus. Thus the Logos is not a distinct person in the Godhead, nor is it fundamentally different from a "divine spark" in every person. At the same time Laelius Socinus (1525–62) and his nephew, Faustus Socinus (1539–1604), taught a unitarian system. The incarnation was not a transferral of the divine essence, but a communication of divine authority and revelation. Christ thus did not die as an atonement, but as a moral example. Both Servetus and Socinianism were condemned by Catholics and Protestants alike.

In the 17th and 18th centuries "kenoticism" (from Greek for "empty") taught that in the incarnation the Logos totally "emptied himself" (Phil 2:7) of the divine attributes. That doctrine was the final step of a dialogue from the scholastic period, about the exact communication between Jesus' two natures. Was his human nature omnipotent? If not, how did the man Jesus exercise the divine attributes? The kenotic school believed that Jesus was fully human and that his divine nature was quiescent until after the ascension. His miraculous powers were external, given by the Spirit. Against that view the majority of theologians argued that Jesus was at all times both God and man, and that in Philippians 2:6–8 Jesus did not lay aside the attributes of deity (he still exhibited the "form of God") but rather the majesty associated with deity.

The 19th and 20th centuries have given rise to a view that the incarnation was a "myth," a pictorial way of describing how God spoke through Jesus. The virgin birth was not historical, nor did any of the supernatural events of the Gospels ever take place. Rather, the stories in the Gospels were concoctions of the later church, efforts to portray Jesus' impact on the movement. The Gospels, however, have too strong a flavor of accurate history for such a view to prevail (see Lk 1:1–5; Jn 19:35; 21:24).

Application. Recent incarnational theology has sometimes had difficulty balancing its understanding of Christ's humanity and deity. Some theologians have given too much emphasis to his manhood, with the result that his atoning work is neglected. He then becomes an example of God's gracious dealing with humanity. Such theological imbalance appears in those who have reacted too strongly to the "demythologizing" movement, stressing the Jesus of history to the extent that he has become little more than an object of rational thought.

On the other hand, some modern theology focuses only on Christ's divinity. The Bultmannian (after Rudolf Bultmann) school has separated the "Christ of faith" from the "Jesus of history," making him a hero in the Greek style. Some evangelicals make a similar error by removing Jesus' teachings from the real world of history and placing them in a subjective realm of religious experience. Jesus thus becomes a vague object of religious devotion having no contact with the real world.

Another group has interpreted the biblical image of the church as the "body of Christ" to mean that the church somehow continues the incarnation on earth. The NT does not teach that idea, however; it is based on a metaphor rather than on explicit biblical doctrine. Moreover, such an application of the theme can mislead the church to assume more divine authority for itself than it actually possesses.

Conclusion. The NT teaching on the incarnation balances the humanity and divinity of Christ. Those two facts must harmonize in any theological system, for both are absolutely nec-

essary parts of God's redemptive plan. In the incarnation, Jesus became a perfect human being. As God in human flesh, he suffered the divine penalty for sin as an innocent substitute. Being both God and a man, Jesus simultaneously revealed God's will for human life and reconciled sinful people to God through his own perfect life and death. Because of the incarnation, therefore, those who believe in Christ have peace with God and new life from God.

GRANT R. OSBORNE

See CHRISTOLOGY; JESUS CHRIST, LIFE AND TEACHING OF; VIRGIN BIRTH OF JESUS; GENEALOGY OF JESUS CHRIST.

Bibliography. N. Anderson, *The Mystery of the Incarnation;* D.M. Baillie, *God Was in Christ;* H.E. Brunner, *The Mediator;* O. Cullmann, *The Christology of the NT;* J. Murray, *Collected Writings,* vol 2; R.L. Ottley, *The Doctrine of the Incarnation,* 2 vols; K. Rahner, *Theological Investigations,* vol 1; B.B. Warfield, *The Person and Work of Christ.*

Incense. Perfume or sacrifice which sends up fragrant smoke to God in order to please him.

Perfumes. People of every age have loved fragrant odors. In ancient times, sacrifices included sweet smells to make the deity happy. The aroma was a crucial factor in whether the god would accept the offering. Therefore, aromatic plants and exotic perfumes were precious for both secular and religious purposes.

Spices and precious oils were valued along with silver and gold. The Queen of Sheba brought perfumes to Solomon as a gift (1 Kgs 10:2). Incense was kept in the royal treasury (2 Kgs 20:13). The price of spices and oils was extremely inflated because of the difficult work of extracting the juices, transportation costs to import them from faraway places, and high profits for the merchants who sold the perfumes.

Consequently, lovers sometimes compared their betrothed to "myrrh," a "mountain of myrrh" and a "hill of frankincense" (Sg 1:13; 4:6). The fragrance of incense set the right mood (Sg 1:12). Every perfume known to a merchant burned beside the "couch of Solomon" (Sg 3:6). A bridegroom delighted in the perfumes of his beloved. She was literally a "garden" of incense (Sg 4:10–14). Even a prostitute burned incense beside her bed (Ez 23:41). No wonder wise men said that "fragrant oil" makes the heart glad and the "sweetness of friendship" comforts the soul (Prv 27:9).

Types of Incense. Frankincense is mentioned most often in the Bible. It was imported from India, Somaliland, and Arabia Felix. Myrrh also came from Arabia Felix. Cinnamon was another important fragrance from

Ceylon and China. Nard was a popular perfume from Nepal and the Himalayas. Galbanum, tragacanth, and laudanum all were grown in the mountains of Asia Minor. Galbanum was the most popular of these three for it was also found in Turkestan, Persia, Syria, and Crete.

Several kinds of incense were grown in Israel. Henna, saffron, and balsam came from native aromatic plants. In postexilic times other plants were introduced to Palestine and cultivated there: the rose, narcissus, and jasmine. Onycha seems to have been produced from the local fauna, and musk (muskin) may have been extracted from a gland of the musk deer.

Incense itself came in many forms. It might be used as granules placed in a bag hung around the neck (Sg 1:13). In the main, however, perfumes were in a liquid form, dissolved in olive oil. A good example of this is the "holy anointing oil" (Ex 30:31). Such oils were used to anoint the priests and kings of Israel. Only holy priests were allowed to prepare and administer them. Raw perfumes were beaten into a fine consistency and seasoned with salt to make them holy. Stacte, onycha, galbanum, and pure frankincense were mixed in equal proportions, all according to the art of the perfumer (Ex 30:22–37). The perfumes for the sanctuary were donated as gifts (Nm 7:14–86; Jer 17:26; 41:5) and kept in the temple (Neh 13:5,9). Josephus described the incense of his day as a much more complicated compound. He listed 13 ingredients in the best incense of the Herodian era.

Incense Offering. Archaeology has demonstrated that incense offerings were common throughout the ancient Near East from the earliest times of organized worship. Egyptian paintings and reliefs from the New Kingdom occasionally show a man holding a censer of burning incense. Incense seems to have been used as well in the rituals of Assyria, Babylonia, and Arabia. Canaanite altars found at Megiddo and Tell Beit Mirsim have horned limestone altars (10th century BC) which may have been designed to hold a bowl of incense. Hence, it is safe to assume that incense offerings also played some part in the worship of Israel from the beginning.

Incense offerings seem to have served a multitude of purposes. They may have been used to drive away evil spirits and thereby sanctify all the utensils of the place of worship (Ex 30:26–29). Undoubtedly the sweet smell of incense provided an antidote to the putrid odor of the animal sacrifices. Therefore, if God was to receive a sweet savor and thereby be pleased with an offering, incense was necessary to compensate for the smell of the sacrifices. However, spices were never added to the flesh of the animals or birds.

In some instances, incense itself became a sacrifice. As a supplement to other sacrifices, frankincense alone was burned. To alleviate a plague, Aaron performed a ritual of incense (Nm 16:16,17). Finally, on the Day of Atonement, the high priest carried burning incense and hot coals on a pan (censer) into the Holy of Holies (Lv 16:12,13). The burning incense was thought to protect the life of the high priest, perhaps because the smoke kept him from seeing the full glory of God.

Frankincense was added to grain, or offerings on the altar of burnt offering (Lv 2:1,2, 15,16; 6:15). It also accompanied the bread of the Presence (24:7) in two dishes. The bronze serpent destroyed by Hezekiah in his reform may have been a profane vessel for incense burning (2 Kgs 18:4).

Except on the Day of Atonement, the incense was offered on a special altar, the *qetoret sammim* (Lv 4:7), where it burned morning and evening and came to be called "perpetual incense" (Ex 30:7,8). Probably the altar of gold in Solomon's temple (1 Kgs 6:20,22) was the incense altar.

Offering incense required the utmost care, and unqualified persons who offered it were condemned (Lv 10:1,2; Nm 16:6–50). Uzziah the king of Judah became a leper because he dared to offer incense (2 Chr 26:16–21). The burning of incense at "high places" is often criticized (e.g., 1 Kgs 22:43) either because the sanctuaries were idolatrous or because their priests did not take proper care as did the priesthood in Jerusalem. Prophets who criticized the offering of incense (Is 1:13; 66:3; Jer 6:20) did so to condemn a formalism that was void of devotion to the God of Israel.

Meaning of Incense. Since incense was such a precious commodity, incense was a fitting offering to God (Mal 1:11). Incense offerings also provided tangible sense of God's holiness in which the people could experience atonement for sin (Nm 16:46,47). The smoke rising to the sky symbolized the prayers of the people (Ps 141:2; Lk 1:10; Rv 5:8; 8:3,4). At the same time the smoke in the temple symbolized the presence of God as it had been portrayed by the cloud in the wilderness (Ex 19:18; 33:9,10; Nm 11:25). Together with the rising sun the smoke provided a powerful symbol for the glory of the Lord (Is 6:1–7).

The significance of incense is further enhanced by NT allusions. The Christian's testimony about Christ is paralleled with the offering of incense (2 Cor 2:14,15). The sweet smell of the gospel is contrasted with the smell of death which leads to death. Likewise, money from the Philippian Christians came to Paul in the spirit of an incense sacrifice (Phil 4:18), a costly expression of love and devotion. Finally, incense seems to sanctify and accompany the prayers of the saints into the presence of God (Rv 5:8; 8:3,4). None of the NT references call upon the Christian to offer incense, but rather to learn the devotion and dedication to holiness signified by the burning of this precious substance.

J. GORDON HARRIS

See PLANTS (FRANKINCENSE); TABERNACLE, TEMPLE.

Incest. Sexual relations between close relatives.

Prohibitions against incest are prominent in Leviticus 18. Leviticus 20 also addresses the matter and attaches the death penalty to some forms of incest named. The assignment of severe penalty and the judgments of dishonor and perversion clearly mark incest as a grave offense.

Actual cases in the Bible show incest to be a fruit of a flawed character. Lot's daughters sleep with their drunken father and both become pregnant (Gn 19:30–38). And, in 2 Samuel 13:1–22, the deceitful Amnon shows no shame in forcing himself upon his sister Tamar. Paul's strong rebuke in 1 Corinthians 5:1–5 demonstrates that neither the act nor its wickedness is limited to OT times.

Blood relationship, or consanguinity, is one ground for declaring sexual contact unlawful. This applies, for example, to brothers and sisters, parents and children, grandparents and grandchildren, and some aunts, uncles, nieces, and nephews.

The relationships denounced in Leviticus 18 are not, however, all based upon blood kinship. A number of them are matters of kinship through marriage, matters of affinity. In this connection, sexual relations with in-laws and certain aunts and uncles are declared incestuous. It should be noted that the in-law rule could be relaxed in ancient Israel when a widowed sister-in-law was left without a son (Dt 25:5–10).

While there are good genetic reasons to shun incest among blood relations, the fundamental problem with incest is that it strikes at the soundness of the family. And since the family is central to God's purposes and work on earth, his judgment on this practice is fierce. Families simply cannot survive carnal intrigue among their members.

MARK T. COPPENGER

India. Eastern land of uncertain geographical boundaries in Bible times. The only specific reference to the land of India in the Bible occurs in Esther 1:1 and 8:9, where the bound-

aries of the empire of Ahasuerus are said to have stretched Hoddu to Kush. The term "Hoddu" seems to have derived from an Old Persian word *Hindush*, which was itself related to a Sanskrit word *Sindhu* meaning "stream," that is, the Indus River. Inscriptions from Persia indicate that India was a province of the Achaemenid Empire (559–330 BC) and thus support the biblical statements. Even the Greek historian Herodotus in the 5th century BC seems to have been poorly informed about India (*Persian Wars*, 3.94–106; 4.40,44). There are some Hebrew legends and traditions that there were Jews in India in the days of King Solomon. Some interpreters have suggested that the river Pishon in Genesis 2:11 in the land of Havilah may refer to India. Others have proposed that goods brought from Ophir, such as sandalwood (almug trees, 1 Kgs 10:11; 2 Chr 2:8), ivory, and apes, were Indian in origin. Also, some of the items carried by the merchants of Tyre, such as ivory tusks and ebony (Ez 27:15), may have originated in India.

There are no references to India in the NT but there are a number of general references to the land in intertestamental literature and in the later Jewish writings (e.g., the Targums on Esther, the Midrashim, and the Talmud). It was only after the days of Alexander the Great (d. 323 BC) that the literary world of Palestine and Europe begin to record information about India. From 1 Maccabees 6:37, it would appear that Seleucid armies used war elephants (possibly Indian), mounted by Indian drivers in the 2nd century BC, and the reference in 8:8 indicates that the Romans compelled Antiochus III (223–187 BC) to surrender. India is of uncertain value because of textual problems. There is no other evidence that the Seleucid domains stretched as far as India. It is known, however, that the Romans had considerable trading activity in India via Egypt and the Red Sea, and this makes the lack of references in the NT strange. As the Christian centuries passed, references do appear in both Jewish and early Christian literature, and it is certain that early in the Christian era settlements of Jews and monophysite Christians were found in India. According to legend it was the apostle Thomas who took the gospel to India and founded the Mar Thoma Church.

JOHN A. THOMPSON

Industry and Commerce. Economic activity of a people or a state. Information about industry and commerce in Bible times comes from several sources. Within the range of about 2000 BC to AD 100 there is a variety of data regarding industry and commerce of the period. The Bible itself contains significant material, and there are other records from

Egypt, Assyria, Babylonia, Persia, and from Greek and Latin sources. Alongside the written material is the archaeological evidence of commercial activity in the form of documents, seals, weights, inscribed vessels, coins, and the like. Some paintings and bas-reliefs from Egypt, Assyria, Persia, and other lands that traded with Palestine provide vivid pictorial data. Some of these sources also provide information about industry, and excavations have brought to light a variety of industrial installations, such as potters' kilns, dye vats, large wine cellars, olive-presses, and smelting plants. The presence of numbers of loom weights points to weaving. Molds in the shape of metal tools or weapons suggest a foundry. Storehouses point to distribution centers. Collections of ivory pieces and hoards of metal items or of coins suggest commercial activity of some kind.

Long before the patriarchal age (c. 1900 BC–1700 BC) people in the ancient Middle East had developed commercial and industrial activities to a considerable extent. Thus one of the best-preserved pottery kilns found in Palestine at Tell el Far'ah belongs to the Early Bronze Age, perhaps as early as 2800 BC. The presence of large quantities of pottery in tombs and of broken potsherds in the remains of towns indicates the activities of potters, and the use of both mud bricks and baked bricks in earlier periods points to brickmakers. Indeed items made by human hands provide evidence of some kind of industrial activity in every age. Further, the discovery of obsidian blades in Palestine in the Early Bronze Age suggests

One type of olive press.

trade with some distant area like Anatolia, and at a shorter range, the presence of cowrie shells in Jericho or copper ore at Tell Abu Matar (near Beersheba) is evidence of trade between Jericho and the coast, and between Beersheba and the region of copper deposits near the Gulf of Aqaba to the south.

Commerce and Industry in the Patriarchal Age. The patriarchal stories provide some evidence of commercial activity between Palestine and Egypt. The Ishmaelite caravans carried gum, balm, and myrrh to Egypt (Gn 37:25–28). Later the sons of Jacob bought grain in Egypt in a time of famine (42–47). The movement of Abraham to and fro in the land probably involved the purchase of goods. In particular, the story of the purchase of the field of Ephron in Machpelah near Hebron (ch 23) provides significant evidence of what was evidently a normal act of land transfer. There is a reference to trading and the purchase of land in Shechem in the days of Jacob (ch 34). Some of these practices, as well as numerous other commercial procedures, are known from tablet records from several sites in western Asia during the 2nd millennium BC. There is a good deal of evidence of caravan trade in these lands during the same period. An important tomb painting from Beni Hasan in Egypt depicts a typical caravan group from Transjordan in about 1900 BC. In archaeological terms the early part of the 2nd millennium was the Middle Bronze Age. Excavation of cities like Jericho and the associated cemeteries have yielded significant pottery finds, which must have come from potters' shops. The remains of tables, stools, and beds suggest woodworkers. Bronze weapons and ornaments point to workers in metal, and small boxes with bone inlay suggest the activities of craftsmen. The narrow streets in Jericho were lined with houses, in which the ground floor rooms seem to have been shops and stores, to judge from the jars full of grain carbonized in the fire that destroyed the town. The upper story rooms and their contents collapsed in the fire. Numerous loom-weights suggest that weaving was carried out, and in some houses there were many saddle querns and rubbing stones suggesting a kind of corn-milling activity, and large grain jars were found in some of these houses.

The Early Israelite Period. The emergence of the Israelites as a recognizable group in Palestine dates from the 13th century BC. The premonarchy period is represented in the Bible by the books of Joshua, Judges, and 1 and 2 Samuel, and by the Late Bronze Age and Iron I ages in archaeological terms.

In this period the Philistines played a prominent part. Apparently their techniques of metalworking were more advanced than those of the Israelites, who had to call on their aid in sharpening tools. "There was no smith to be found throughout all the land of Israel; for the Philistines said, 'Lest the Hebrews make themselves swords or spears'" (1 Sm 13:19–21). Excavations at the Philistine town of Tell Qasile on the outskirts of Tel Aviv have produced small furnaces for working metal, and it is presumed that there were others elsewhere. Yet Israel must have had metalworkers, for the people manufactured their own weapons most of the time. Certainly by Solomon's time Israelite craftsmen were able to manufacture vessels for the temple, albeit with some help from Phoenician workers (1 Kgs 7:13–50). At least some casting was done in the Jordan Valley in the clay ground between Succoth and Zarethan (1 Kgs 7:46).

The period of the judges marked the end of the Late Bronze Age when Palestine was enriched by the import of large quantities of beautiful painted pottery—much of it of unusual shape—from Cyprus and the Aegean area, bearing witness to commerce and trade between Palestine and these lands.

One important group of craftsmen in early Israel were the stonemasons. Finely dressed masonry became a feature of the days of the kings (Iron II), but the beginnings of this industry were already in evidence in the premonarchy period. Excavations also attest the activities of weavers because of the numerous loom-weights, although in many cases weaving may have been a home industry. Evidence of trade with Egypt comes from a wall painting in Thebes, dating to the days of Amenhotep III (c. 1403–1364), which depicts a ship bearing large jars, probably filled with grain or oil, and characteristic of the large Late Bronze jars of Palestine.

Israel in the Days of the Kings. There is a good deal of evidence in biblical and nonbiblical records and in archaeological discoveries of industrial and commercial activity in Israel during this period. One of the results of war was the opening of markets in the defeated lands. Thus Ben-hadad of Damascus had to accept Israelite workers into the bazaars of Damascus, but in a similar way Ben-hadad's father had opened up bazaars in Samaria when he overwhelmed Israel (1 Kgs 20:34). It is clear from the booty removed from Israel by a succession of invaders that the people had a special liking for manufactured goods (2 Kgs 16:17; 24:13; 25:13–17). Confirmation of this comes from Assyrian records. Thus Sennacherib (c. 705–681 BC) claims to have removed from Jerusalem not merely gold, silver, and precious stones, but couches, chairs inlaid with ivory, and other treasures. At least some of these items were manufactured by local artisans.

There are some interesting references to commercial activities in the prophets. In Amos 8:5,6 the grain merchants are castigated for their burning desire to see the sabbath pass so they can go about their grain-selling, making the ephah small and the shekel great and dealing deceitfully with false balances. Specially prepared ephahs (a measure) and shekels (a weight) enabled them to profit by selling a little less than an ephah for a little more than a shekel of silver. Their balances were false, and they sold the refuse of the wheat to the poor (v 6). Isaiah refers to the land-grabbers (Is 5:8), that is, dealers in real estate. Jeremiah has references to potters (Jer 18,19) and to those who offered linen for sale (13:1,2), and gives a detailed account of procedures for the transfer of land from one owner to another (32:9–12). We have a glimpse into sea trade in Jonah 1, and a much more comprehensive picture of international trade in Ezekiel 27, which describes the wide range of commodities brought from afar by Phoenician ships and sold in local markets. No doubt many of these items found their way into the hands of Israelite traders. There are also references to baskets of fruit, indicating that orchards and vineyards played an important role in Israel's life (Jer 24; Am 8:1,2).

The building industry is well represented in the OT, most prominently in the building of Solomon's temple and palaces (1 Kgs 6,7). There are accounts of building fortified posts and cities (15:21,22; 16:24; 2 Chr 26:9,10), the repair of walls and buildings (2 Kgs 22:3–7; 2 Chr 34:9–13; Neh 3:1–32), and the construction of fine houses for the upper classes (Am 3:15; 5:11). One interesting detail is the use of a plumb line in building (7:7,8), giving a clue to some of the techniques used.

A suggestive picture of the number of craftsmen in Judah comes from the list of captives taken to Babylon by Nebuchadnezzar—"craftsmen and smiths, one thousand" (2 Kgs 24:14,16).

Excavations have brought to light helpful material for reconstructing a picture of industry and commerce in the Iron Age. The site of Tell Beit Mirsim just south of Bethlehem produced a wide range of pottery types. Several inscribed potsherds bear traces of the letters *bt l-mlk*, "the royal bath," a "bath" being a volume measure. Similar measures have been found in other sites, and there are now enough for reconstruction of a complete vessel with a volume of about five gallons (cf. 1 Kgs 7:26; 2 Chr 2:10; Is 5:10; Ez 45:10). A number of weights were discovered at the same site that bore no inscription.

Of particular interest industrially are several dye vats uncovered at Tell Beit Mirsim.

These were parts of round stone vats some 27 to 35 inches in height and diameter, with a roughly spherical basin some 12 to 18 inches in diameter, having a mouth ½ to ⅓ as wide. Around the rim of the vats a circular groove was chiselled to catch the dye as it was stirred, allowing it to run back into the vat through a connecting hole. These dye vats were found in various areas of the town. Each plant was located in the vicinity of a cistern, since water was necessary for dyeing. Since so much has been found when only part of the site has been excavated we may conjecture that this was a center for dyeing. Contemporary evidence of the dye industry also comes from other Palestinian sites: Beth-shemesh, Bethel, and Tell en-Nasbeh.

At Tell Beit Mirsim there were also olive presses. Two shallow vats of masonry were uncovered, one about 55 by 31 inches and the other 62 by 31 inches set 78 inches from the wall of the room in which they stood. Many large perforated stones found in the area seem to have formed elements in the crushing device. A wooden pole inserted through the holes in the wall could be moved around in the vat from its fulcrum point, which was a niche in the wall of the room some 19½ inches above the floor level of the vat. The device is very similar to simple olive presses that have been in use for many centuries.

The production of wine on a large scale for local use as well as for export seems to have been a well-developed industry. A fine example of a typical winery was excavated by J.B. Pritchard at ancient Gibeon. This town was a center for the production and export of wine in the 8th and 7th centuries BC. In the course of excavations in 1959–1960 63 rock-cut cellars were found where wine could be stored at a constant temperature of 18°C. The cellars are bottle-shaped and average about 9 feet in depth and 6½ feet in diameter at the bottom. The tops average 26 inches in diameter. In the same area wine presses were found carved from rock with channels for leading the grape juice into the fermentation tanks and settling basins. The jars in which the wine was stored had a capacity of 9 to 10 gallons so that the 63 cellars could have provided space for 25,000 gallons of wine. Smaller jars used for distribution of the wine carried proper names stamped on their handles. Among these the place-name "Gibeon" was very common, providing an example of an archaeological site that carries its original name. Jar-stoppers and a funnel for filling jars were also found.

There are some excellent examples of storehouses where grain and wine were collected for distribution. The ancient site of Tell Sheba (near modern Beersheba) had three such warehouses situated to the right of the city gate. Each room had three sections, the two outer ones for storage and a central one for beasts of burden. A large collection of storage jars of various shapes and sizes was discovered in the rooms. The city of Megiddo had many more of these storerooms than Beersheba. In addition Megiddo had a large storage silo some 37 feet in diameter at the top, 23 feet in diameter at the bottom, and 23 feet deep. Its capacity was some 12,800 bushels. At the sides were two winding stairways leading down. Chaff and grain were found in the chinks between the rubble stones of the unplastered walls. It is not certain, however, whether this was a commercial activity or some tax collecting arrangement.

Excavation has also provided information about the activities of the stonemasons. An ancient quarry apparently was outside the city walls of Jerusalem in the general area of the modern Church of the Holy Sepulchre, which was filled with debris in Roman times. It was last used in the 7th century BC and contained good evidence of the way blocks of stone were cut by the masons. There are numerous examples of walls of ancient buildings executed in well-cut masonry, but none so striking as the walls of the palace of Omri and Ahab and the city wall at Samaria. Stonemasons must have been in constant demand in ancient Palestine, and some at least did beautiful work.

Palestine During the Postexilic and Hellenistic Periods. With the fall of Jerusalem in 586 BC there was no independent Israelite state since both Israel and Judah had now ceased to exist. The land and the remaining people fell under the control, first of the Babylonians, then of the Persians, and then of the Hellenistic successors of Alexander the Great. There are glimpses of industrial and commercial activity during these years (586–63 BC).

The Book of Haggai refers to the building of paneled houses (Hg 1:4) and to the determination to rebuild the temple. This was completed in March 515 BC (Ezr 6:14,15), but no trace of this temple has been found by archaeologists. Some years later Nehemiah undertook the rebuilding of the wall of Jerusalem. This was done by the cooperative efforts of the citizens among whom groups like goldsmiths, perfumers, and merchants are mentioned (Neh 3). The wall of Nehemiah has been brought to light in recent years. It was built of undressed stones, a far cry from the beautiful masonry of Samaria from the days of the kings of Israel. The wall was, however, solidly built and was some 9 feet thick, but its finish was rough—as might be expected from the motley group that erected it so rapidly.

The people in Judah took a long time to

recover from the severe destructions of Nebuchadnezzar, so that the Persian period was not distinguished by great achievements. Yet there were the ever-present potters to produce wares of a distinctive type. Tombs from the Persian period have produced not only pottery but some fine artistic pieces including silver bowls and dippers, one of which had a handle in the shape of an undraped maiden. Imported red and black figure-ware from Greece attests trade activity with the Aegean region, and Palestinian mints began to turn out coinage following Greek models.

The Hellenistic age in Palestine introduced changes in many areas of life. Local potters were influenced by Hellenistic models in many of their jars, jugs, bowls, lamps, and the like. More finely prepared clays were used and the vessels were fired to a higher temperature. The walls of many of the vessels were thinner, more delicate, and brittle.

Architecture became increasingly Hellenized. Towns like Marisa, Lachish, Bethzun, Samaria, Shechem, Gezer, and others have yielded a good range of materials that enable us to study the work of the artisans, potters, jewelers, and builders. The presence of foreign troops in the land brought trade and commerce. Imported wine stored in large Rhodian jars was evidently preferred to the native product. The land passed under control of the Romans when Pompey entered Palestine in 63 BC.

Industry and Commerce in New Testament Times. It was 37 BC before the Romans appointed Herod as king of the whole area of Palestine. He and his family ruled parts of the country until near the end of the 1st century, although in the area of Judea, Archelaus (4 BC–AD 6) proved incompetent and was replaced by a Roman procurator. Thereafter, till the time of the great Jewish revolt in AD 66–70, a line of procurators ruled Judea from Caesarea. The period 37 BC to AD 70 is referred to archaeologically as the Roman I, or Herodian, period, which is the period of Jesus and the early Christian church. We know a good deal about many aspects of industry and commerce in the Roman world, and both the literature of the times and the excavated remains bear eloquent testimony to these activities both in Palestine and throughout the Roman world.

The NT makes reference to merchants (Mt 13:45; 25:16; Rv 18:3,11,15,23), dealers in purple (Acts 16:14), "money changers" in the temple (Mt 21:12; Mk 11:15), to various coins used in commercial transactions or in the payment of temple taxes, the Jewish coin (the lepton or "widow's mite," Mk 12:42; Lk 21:2). There are also references to Greek coins like the drachma (Lk 15:8), the di-drachma (Mt 17:24), the stater or tetra-drachma (Mt 17:27), Roman coins like the quadrans (Mt 5:26), the as (Mt 10:29; Lk 12:6), and the denarius (Lk 10:35). The "exchangers" of Matthew 25:27 were the regular bankers of the day. A specialized group of these operated in the temple precincts to change money into the acceptable coinage for the temple. Contemporary Roman documents indicate major trading activities by land and sea, although there was a dearth of good harbors in Palestine. For this reason an artificial harbor was built at Caesarea. Clearly goods were imported into Palestine to judge from foreign pottery vessels which once contained wine and other commodities.

We have a growing volume of evidence of the activities of the builders. King Herod embarked on ambitious building programs up and down the land. Among his achievements was the building of a new temple in Jerusalem. This was erected on a vast platform some 500 yards by 325 yards, made of huge stones, the largest yet found being 16½ feet long by 13 feet wide. Each of these had a distinctive bevel cut round the outer edge so that the face of the stone stood out from its border. Recent excavations have shown that at the time of Herod a bridge (Wilson's Arch) led across the Tyropean Valley to the western hill where many fine houses and other buildings lay. A second arch (Robinson's Arch) farther south led to a stairway and down to the street level. An impressive roadway skirted the walls and on the south side of the temple mount fine stairways led up from a plaza to entrances to the temple precinct. Remarkable engineering is displayed in these structures, and it is typical of similar workmanship in other areas of Palestine.

There are many evidences of beautiful artistic work in floor mosaics and wall-paintings in Jerusalem, on top of the Masada fortress overlooking the Dead Sea, and elsewhere.

In the general area of household furnishings excavations have brought to light small stone tables and other stone vessels, a wide

The remains of Robinson's Arch, the gate near the southwest corner of the temple platform.

range of pottery, items in iron, bronze, and bone, stone weights, and coins. Indeed bone-working was a well-developed craft, the material being used for delicate utensils and ornaments such as needles, pins, spoons, handles, awls, spatulas, buttons, and the like.

Important features of Jerusalem were the water installations, cisterns, reservoirs, ritual baths, steam baths, sewers, and water conduits.

Beautiful workmanship went into burial places, many of which contained handsome carved ossuaries.

Presumably there were also many industrial plants for wine-making, dyeing, olive pressing, weaving, the manufacture of coins, and for the production of tools and weapons. Examples of such plants have been found from this period in various sites in Palestine.

JOHN A. THOMPSON

See TRADES AND OCCUPATIONS; CLOTH, CLOTH MANUFACTURING; MONEY AND BANKING.

Bibliography. A. Edersheim, *Sketches of Jewish Social Life in the Days of Christ*, pp 182–212; R.J. Forbes, *Metallurgy in Antiquity*; H. Hodges, *Technology in the Ancient World*; M. Rostovtzeff, *The Social and Economic History of the Roman Empire*; A. van Deursen, *Illustrated Dictionary of Bible Manners and Customs*.

Infirmity. *See* DISEASE; MEDICINE AND MEDICAL PRACTICE.

Ingathering, Feast of. One of the three great festivals of Israel, also called the Feast of Booths, or tabernacles, which celebrated the completion of the agricultural year (Lv 23:39–43).

See FEASTS AND FESTIVALS OF ISRAEL.

Inheritance. Legacy or bequest. Inheritance plays an unusually significant role in the Scriptures when it is used to convey theological truths. As we might expect, however, these theological applications reflect legal customs in force during OT and NT times.

Legal and Historical. *The Patriarchs.* We learn something of early 2nd-millennium BC practices from the patriarchal stories in Genesis. For example, the narrative indicates that the firstborn could normally expect to receive the birthright, yet exceptions abound. Ishmael (Gn 17:15–21), Esau (25:23), and Reuben (49:3, 4) did not receive the birthright. Another item of special interest is Abraham's suggestion that, in the absence of a son, his servant Eliezer might be regarded as the heir (15:2–5); scholars have found confirmation of this practice in Hurrian legal documents of the 2nd millennium.

The Hebrew Nation. According to Deuteronomy 21:15–17, Hebrew firstborns were legally entitled to a double portion of the inheritance. Israelite law also made provision for widows through the practice of levirate marriage (Dt 15:5; see Gn 38:8; Ru 4:5).

According to Numbers 27:1–11, the daughters of Zelophehad argued that they should receive the inheritance since their father had died without sons. Consequently, God decreed that if a man died without sons, the inheritance should be transferred to his daughter; if he had no daughter, to his brothers; if he had no brothers, to his nearest relatives. This particular incident also illustrates the importance of preserving tribal possessions: the daughters of Zelophehad were not allowed to marry outside the tribe of Manasseh, for this would mean transferral of the property to another tribe (Nm 36).

How highly the Israelites valued their family's inherited possessions may be gathered from Leviticus 25:25–28. If an individual sold his land for financial reasons, provision must be made for a relative to redeem it; if he had no near relative, he could still purchase it back at a later time, and even if he could not afford to do so, the land automatically reverted to him in the year of jubilee, when all debts were canceled (note also Lv 27:14–25).

The New Testament. Apart from the reference to levirate marriage in Matthew 22:23–33 (Mk 12:18–27; Lk 20:27–40), the NT has little to say about principles of property transferral during Roman times.

In the parable of the lost (prodigal) son, the younger son in the family requested his share of the inheritance (Lk 15:12). One should also note that the elder son, who with false piety looked down on his brother's behavior, had not protested when his brother asked for the inheritance; on the contrary, the elder brother too, without complaining, received his share—presumably a double portion.

In another significant passage (Gal 4:1,2) Paul, seeking to illustrate a theological point, refers to secular practices. An heir, he tells us, is subject to guardians and managers during his childhood, up to the time of his father's disposition. The point Paul wants to establish is clear enough, but the illustration does not comport with Roman law and unfortunately scholars have been unable to identify the precise social custom in view. It may be that Paul is making reference, in general rather than strict legal terms, to some practice with which he and the Galatians were familiar.

Theological. *Canaan as Israel's Inheritance.* The conviction that God gave Palestine to the Israelites for their inheritance serves as a bridge between the historical and the theological data. The historical element lies in the obvious fact that the Promised Land, a physical entity, was certainly occupied by the Hebrews and distributed among their tribes. Theologically, however, the Scriptures speak of this occupation as a divine gift; in effect, even the method of distribution was based on the concept that the land belongs to God (Lv 25:23; see Ex 15:17; Jos 22:27; Ez 38:16; Jl 1:6).

The theme goes back to Genesis 12:1–3. God, in choosing Abraham, instructed him to move to a new country and promised to make him a great and blessed nation (Heb 11:8). The significance of the land in this Abrahamic promise is made more explicit later, when we are told that God covenanted to give Canaan to Abraham's descendants after four centuries of Egyptian bondage (Gn 15:12–21; see Acts 7:5).

Since Canaan was occupied by wicked inhabitants, the land was to be taken by force; to inherit the land therefore really means *to take possession* of it; Israel must trust God, whose land it is, to give them the victory (Jos 1:1–9; 21:43–45; Jgs 7:2; Ps 44:1–3; Acts 13:19). Once they conquered the land, it was apportioned among the tribes according to their size (following the instructions in Nm 26:52–54). God further commanded the people to divide the land by lot (vv 55,56). Thus from the initial promise to Abraham to the actual apportionment of the land and even with reference to the future (Is 60:21; Ez 45:1–8; 47:13–48:29), the people were made fully aware that their inheritance lay in the hands of a sovereign Lord.

The Believer's Inheritance. In the OT we find the concept of inheritance transferred from the purely physical to the spiritual. The tribe of Levi, which constituted the priestly clan, received no inheritance, because "the Lord is their inheritance" (Dt 18:1,2; see Nm 18:8–24). The Levites, in other words, received no land apportionment, but in their service of God they could begin to enjoy the fuller blessings to which the land inheritance pointed.

That this truth could not be artificially restricted to the Levites is hinted at in Exodus 19:6, where the whole nation is called "a kingdom of priests" (see 1 Pt 2:9). Psalm 16 makes it clear that no one understood more clearly than David what those words entailed. Even though he be deprived of Israel's physical inheritance, he has received by lot a more beautiful heritage, the Lord himself, in whose presence he finds full joy and everlasting pleasures (vv 5,6,11; see Pss 73:25,26; 142:5; Is 58:14; Lam 3:24).

In later Judaism, during and after the intertestamental period, the figure was extended considerably. For example, the rabbis began to speak of the Law as the inheritance of the faithful. Further, they might give the idea a

negative turn, as when the wicked are said to inherit hell (cf. Jb 27:13). Neither of these figures is found in the NT.

We also read in Jewish literature statements about inheriting the age to come, the kingdom, eternal life; these ideas occur frequently in the NT (Mt 19:29; 25:34; Lk 10:25; 18:18; 1 Cor 6:9,10; 15:50; Gal 5:21; Eph 5:5; Ti 3:7; Jas 2:5; 1 Pt 3:7–9). Such an inheritance, however, belongs only to those who are sanctified by God's Word (Acts 20:32; 26:18; Col 1:12; note also Jn 17:17; Col 3:23,24). These future blessings do not exclude the physical (Mt 5:5; note Ps 37:11,29; Is 60:21; Rom 4:13; 2 Pt 3:13), but they certainly exclude human frailty, for God's inheritance is imperishable (1 Cor 15:50; 1 Pt 1:4). In short, our heritage is nothing less than full salvation (Heb 1:14; 11:7), which God carefully guards for us in heaven (1 Pt 1:4).

Doubtless, the most significant feature in the NT is its emphasis that, as a result of the work of Christ, his people begin even *now* to receive the promised inheritance. The Gospel of John frequently stresses the present reality of eternal life, as does the Letter to the Hebrews (cf. 6:12–17 with 9:15 and 11:13,39,40).

Paul treats this whole question thoroughly in Galatians 3:7–4:7. In response to the Judaizers, who claim that the Abrahamic inheritance is restricted to those who become Jews through circumcision, Paul argues vigorously that Abraham's true children are those who believe, whether Jew or Gentile (3:7; see Acts 26:16–18; Eph 3:6). They become heirs of God's promise for they receive the Spirit (Gal 3:14). The principle of inheritance is promise, not the Law (v 18). Those who believe are brought into union with Christ (vv 27–29); but then they are not merely Abraham's children but God's (v 26), for Christ is the Son of God and God has determined to send the Spirit of his Son to believers so that they too may call God *Father* (4:4–7; v 2 emphasizes the sovereign disposition of the Father; see also Rom 8:15,16).

Indeed, Christ himself as the Son is the true heir (Mt 21:38; Mk 12:7; Lk 20:14); he has inherited a name above every name (Phil 2:9; Heb 1:4) and has been appointed heir of all things (Heb 1:2; see Ps 2:7,8; Mt 28:18). But by his grace all who become his through faith are counted joint heirs with him (Rom 8:17).

God's Inheritance. With a bold shift in the metaphor, the Scriptures speak of believers as God's inheritance. In the beautiful "Song of Moses" the author speaks of God as the Israelites' Father (Dt 32:6), who has taken special interest in their inheritance (v 8). Then we are told why God cares: "For the Lord's portion is his people, Jacob his allotted inheritance" (v 9 NIV). This theme becomes very prominent throughout the OT (e.g., Dt 9:26–29; 1 Kgs

8:51,53; Pss 28:9; 33:12; 74:2; Is 19:25; Jer 10:16; Zec 2:12). Elsewhere Israel is spoken of as God's special possession (e.g., Ex 19:5; Dt 7:6).

In Ephesians 1:14 "the redemption of the possession" refers to the final salvation of believers, who are God's treasure. Further, "we have obtained an inheritance" (v 11) may well be translated, "we have been made an inheritance," that is, been "chosen as God's portion," a view supported by verse 18. No more fundamental idea than this can be found in Scripture, and its essence is expressed by the words of the One who sits on the throne: "He who conquers shall have this heritage, and I will be his God and he shall be my son" (Rv 21:7; see v 3; Lv 26:11,12; 2 Sm 7:14).

Moises Silva

See Heir; Birthright; Firstborn; Adoption.

Bibliography. G. Dalman, *The Words of Jesus;* W.D. Davis, *The Gospel and the Land;* R. de Vaux, *Ancient Israel,* pp 53–55; J.D. Hester, *St. Paul's Concept of Inheritance;* E. Neufeld, *Ancient Hebrew Marriage Laws,* pp 259–65; J. Pedersen, *Israel, Its Life and Culture,* pp 89–96.

Iniquity. *See* Sin.

Ink, Inkhorn. *See* Writing and Books.

Inn. Place of lodging for travelers.

In the OT, the word "inn" occurs three times (KJV): twice in reference to overnight rests of Joseph's brothers during their journeys between Egypt and Canaan (Gn 42:27; 43:21), and once in a similar situation when Moses was returning to Egypt from Midian to lead the children of Israel (Ex 4:24).

The RSV translates each of these instances as "lodging place" because in the time of the patriarchs and Moses the Near East had nothing to correspond to the inn as a public place with accommodations for hire to travelers. In a settled country a traveler could ordinarily expect hospitality from the inhabitants. Throughout the Near East hospitality was viewed as a serious social responsibility (e.g., Gn 19:1–3; Jgs 19:15–21). In deserted areas travelers would provide for their own shelter (e.g., Gn 28:11) and sustenance (e.g., Jos 9:11–13).

The beginning of real inns in Palestine is obscure. It has been argued that they had a foreign origin, since the rabbinic words for "inn" are borrowed from Greek and Latin. References to Rahab as innkeeper in the Targum and in Josephus (*Antiq.* 5.1.12) may be anachronistic, and they provide no reliable witness to the existence of inns during the time of Joshua, though there are parallels in the Near East of women keeping an establishment providing both lodging and sexual activity for travelers. Certainly there is evidence for Greek inns as early as the 5th century BC, and they became

common in the Hellenized Mediterranean. They were typically uncomfortable and dangerous—a common haunt of thieves, prostitutes, and vermin.

Such an "inn" with an "innkeeper" (KJV "host") sheltered the victim of robbers whom the good Samaritan befriended (Lk 10:34,35). This inn was probably much like the khan or caravansary which has been common along the trade and pilgrimage routes of Syria since ancient times. It was built in the form of a square enclosing an open court where water and shelter were available, but the traveler typically supplied his own food and sometimes his own bedding. The good Samaritan clearly expected the host to provide full care for the wounded man; it is difficult to tell whether this was customary, or simply an accommodation to the emergency. The inn of Jesus' story has long been identified with the Khan Hathrur, halfway between Jerusalem and Jericho, though the present structure is probably only one of many built in the same place.

This inn of the good Samaritan is unique in Scripture as an instance of the inn as we know it. Two other well-known passages in the NT allude, not to a real inn, but to other social customs and arrangements. First, brethren from the church at Rome met the prisoner Paul at Three Taverns, a stopping place 33 miles from Rome at the intersection of the Appian Way with the road from Antium (Acts 28:15). Second, there is the "inn" from which Joseph and Mary were excluded (Lk 2:7), elsewhere translated "guestchamber" (KJV) and "guest room" (RSV Mk 14:14; Lk 22:11). The Jews of Jerusalem took pride in having enough such guestrooms to accommodate the huge influx of pilgrims keeping Passover in the city (cf. Acts 2:6–11 on the crowd at Pentecost); evidently Joseph and Mary expected such accommodation in Bethlehem for the census, but found their place already taken.

John W. Sider

See Travel and Transportation.

Inner Man. This Pauline phrase resembles the "hidden man" of 1 Peter 3:4 (cf. Rom 2:29), where outward appearance is contrasted with inward reality. It assumes the current Jewish conception of man as a unitary being having both observable and invisible aspects, a physical body including a "psychological" heart. Paul says his members submit to sin's rule even while his "inmost self" (RSV "inner man") delights in divine law (Rom 7:22). In 8:1–13, he speaks of "setting the mind on things of the flesh . . . and things of the spirit," describing this same conflict between the inner and outer man.

Inscriptions

This inner core of personality is already the locus where the Spirit's strength is instilled and where Christ dwells in the Christian. So another contrast is between the mortal and already decaying outward man, weakened by age and by sharing the dying of Christ, and the daily renewed inner man, as the life of the risen Jesus is manifested in mortal flesh (2 Cor 4:10–16). Taken with Romans 8:11, this may possibly echo a speculation of intertestamental Judaism, that a spiritual counterpart to the present body is already being prepared by the quickening of divine life in the devout inner man.

See MAN, DOCTRINE OF.

Inscriptions. Term used to refer to writing in the ancient world which was done on a material of a permanent nature, such as stone or clay, rather than on ordinary and impermanent substances, such as papyri or parchment. There are occasional references to inscriptions in the Bible, for example, the Ten Commandments were inscribed on stone (Ex 31:18) and given to Moses, and later written by Joshua on stone and set up at Shechem (Jos 8:32). In the excavations at Shechem, G.E. Wright found a large stone prepared to receive an inscription which he dated to the time of Joshua on stratigraphic grounds. It may still be seen at the site. A message from the hand of God to the Babylonian king Belshazzar was inscribed on the walls of his palace (Dn 5:24). Paul observed an altar with this inscription: "To an unknown god" in the marketplace of Athens (Acts 17:23). The Book of Revelation speaks of the names of the 12 tribes of the sons of Israel being inscribed on the gates of the heavenly city (21:12).

Inscriptions in the ancient world can be found in almost any language and from any period of history: Egyptian, Babylonian, Persian, Greek, Latin, Hebrew, Aramaic, Nabataean, Moabite, and so on. It was once popular to argue that Moses could not have written the Pentateuch because writing had not been invented that early. Inscriptions found at the turquoise mines of Serabit el-Khadim dating to the 15th century BC have disproven this allegation. In addition it might be noted that clay tablets found at Ras Shamra by Claude Schaeffer and dated to about 1400 BC demonstrate a considerable period of literary activity, as do the newly discovered tablets at Ebla from approximately a thousand years earlier.

Inscriptions may be found in almost any position or place, but the most common locations are in the floors of synagogues, church buildings, and mosques; the pavements of forums; the walls of public buildings; dedica-

Four tablets from Ebla.

tory stones and statues; stelae and monumental plaques; tombs and sarcophagi; and Roman milestones. An exhaustive list is impossible, but a few representative samples will illustrate the various kinds of extant inscriptional material.

Monumental Inscriptions. The Egyptian pharaoh Merneptah commemorated his victory over the Sea Peoples in the 13th century BC by inscribing a black granite stele with a record of his victory. It contains the earliest known reference to Israel outside the land of Palestine: "Israel lies desolate."

The Israelite king Omri (1 Kgs 16:16–30) is referred to in a text carved in the Moabite language on a stone dating near the end of the reign of the Moabite king Mesha, about 830 BC. It was found at Diban (OT Dibon) in 1868 and contains a record of the successful rebellion of the king against Israelite oppression.

Another monumental inscription was found in Persia carved into the steep slope of Mt Behistun. It is a trilingual (Old Persian, Elamite, Akkadian) record of the exploits of Darius I, providing the key to unlocking the mystery of the cuneiform script in which several of these ancient languages were written.

The Assyrian king Shalmeneser III left a record of his first 6 campaigns of conquest inscribed on a monolith found in 1861 at Kurkh on the Tigris. The stone is carved front and back in cuneiform that is written over a bas-relief of the king. This same king left a black stone obelisk, 6½ feet high, depicting his triumphs over several other kings, among whom is Jehu, king of Israel, depicted in the second panel from the top, prostrating himself before

The Merneptah Stele contains the first known mention of Israel in Egyptian records.

ing the years from 626 BC to the fall of Babylon to Cyrus in 539. One of these, the Babylonian Chronicle, provides an exact date of March 16, 597 BC for the fall of Jerusalem to the Babylonian king Nebuchadnezzar (cf. 2 Kgs 24:10–17).

Babylon itself fell to Cyrus the Mede, king of Persia in 539. The event is not only referred to in the Bible (Ezr 1:1–3) but is also described in a clay barrel-shaped cylinder nine inches in length, written in cuneiform script, during the reign of Cyrus. It refers to his policy which allowed captive nations to rebuild their cities and temples. This provides an explanation of his encouragement and financial help to the Jews in returning to Jerusalem to rebuild the temple of Solomon that Nebuchadnezzar had destroyed (Ezr 1:2–4).

Egyptian pharaohs were fond of publishing records of their exploits in hieroglyphic script on the walls of temples and tombs. These were usually incised into the stone and then painted. One of the most interesting is Shishak's description of his invasion of the land of Israel incised on the southern wall of a court of the temple of Amon at Karnak. The inclusion of Megiddo among the more than 75 cities whose names can still be read, adds historical interest to the biblical account of Shishak's invasion and conquest of Megiddo (1 Kgs 14:25,26; 2 Chr 12:2–10) as well as archaeological confirmation of a destruction and burning of the city at this time.

Myths, Epics, and Legends. Scores of texts exist containing legendary material from the Egyptians, Sumerians, Akkadians, Hittites, and Canaanites. They are conveniently collected in J.B. Pritchard's *Ancient Near Eastern Texts.* Among the most interesting and biblically relevant is the Gilgamesh Epic, an Assyrian account of the great flood recorded also in Genesis 6–9. The story is written on the 11th of 12 clay tablets in Akkadian and recounts the experiences of Utnapishtim (the counterpart to the biblical Noah) during a great flood. There are many interesting parallels to the Genesis account, along with some significant differences. The Gilgamesh Epic is also known from other versions older than 1000 BC, among which are the Babylonian, Sumerian, Hittite, and Hurrian accounts. The original composition of the Akkadian account, which is the fullest and best known, is placed by Pritchard somewhere at the turn of the 2nd millennium BC. The text we possess was found in the library of Ashurbanipal at Nineveh.

Official Announcements. When an ancient monarch or public official wanted to publish an announcement with some degree of permanency, it would be carved in stone or set in mosaic. An inscription on a marble slab

the Assyrian monarch. This is the earliest picture available of an Israelite and the only known representation of an Israelite king by a contemporary. The inscription above the picture reads, "The tribute of Jehu, son of Omri. . . ." It dates to the mid-9th century BC.

Historical Records. Frequently in the region of Mesopotamia, ancient kings recorded important events or proclamations in stone or clay. A notable example is the clay prism containing the final edition of Sennacherib's Annals dated to 691 BC. It is hexagonal, 15 inches high and 6 inches wide, and written on all sides in cuneiform script. The inscription speaks of "Hezekiah the Jew (king of Judah), who did not submit to my yoke . . . Himself, like a caged bird, I shut up in Jerusalem, his royal city . . ." (cf. 2 Kgs 18; Is 36–39).

Even though no annals comparable to those produced by the Assyrian kings have survived among the Babylonians, we do have some chronicles written on clay tablets cover-

dating to the reign of Claudius (AD 41–54) was found in 1878, originating in the city of Nazareth. It contains a warning against grave robbing or any other desecration of cemeteries. The penalty for such violation was declared to be death. The stone probably reflects some of the troubles Claudius had in Rome over the person of Christ (Suetonius, *Claudius* 25) which led to the expulsion of Jews from the capital city (Acts 18). At issue must have been the resurrection of Christ as proclaimed in Rome.

Announcements were placed even in temples. Josephus referred to a small wall surrounding the Jewish temple in Jerusalem that contained slabs of stone at regular intervals giving warning in Greek and Latin to Gentiles entering the temple (*War* 5.193–34; 6.125–26; *Antiq.* 15.417). Two fragmentary examples have been found. One discovered by Clermont-Ganneau in 1871 reads: "No foreigner is to enter within the balustrade and embankment around the sanctuary. Whoever is caught will have himself to blame for his death which follows." The Romans allowed the Jews to put anyone to death, even a Roman, who went beyond this barrier (*War* 6.126).

An important inscription was found at the beginning of this century in Delphi, Greece, which was commissioned by the emperor Claudius. It was written in Greek and mentions Gallio as proconsul with a date that can be established as AD 51–52 for his term of office. This Gallio is the proconsul before whom Paul was brought by the Jews of Corinth (Acts 18:12–17). It is therefore extremely important for establishing the date of Paul's 18-month stay in Corinth, and an important pivotal date for Pauline chronology in general. The inscription is an imperial announcement to the citizens of Delphi regarding the need for increasing the population of the city with eminent people.

The name Pontius Pilate has appeared in a Latin inscription carved into a stone found in the Roman theater at Caesarea Maritima on the coast of Israel. It refers to him, in partially mutilated words, as Prefect and contains the name Tiberium, which designates a structure built in honor of the emperor Tiberius.

Dedications. Inscriptions were commonly placed on walls or floors of buildings or attached to some other structure dedicating the completed edifice. An inscription was cut into the wall of a long tunnel built by the Jewish king Hezekiah in Jerusalem when the tunnel was finished (2 Kgs 20:20). It is in Hebrew and is now in the Istanbul museum. One of the oldest inscriptions we have in that language, it describes the construction of the Siloam tunnel.

The Pilate inscription found carved into a stone in the Roman theater at Caesarea.

In the city of Corinth in Greece there is a dedicatory inscription cut into the pavement of a plaza on the north side of the large theater. The abbreviated Latin inscription read: *Erastus pro aedilitate sua pecunia stravit* ("Erastus, in return for his aedileship, laid the pavement at his own expense"). The bronze has long since been removed from the letters deeply cut into the gray Acrocorinthian limestone. This is probably the same "Erastus, the city treasurer" mentioned by Paul in Romans 16:23. A similar inscription from the Corinthian Agora of Paul's day reads: "Gnaeus Babbius Philinus, aedile and pontifex, had this monument erected at his own expense, and he approved it in his official capacity as duovir."

A monumental dedicatory inscription in Greek was found in Jerusalem during excavations in 1913–14, which once stood on the wall of a 1st-century AD synagogue on Mt Ophel. It refers to a Theodotus, the son of a ruler of the synagogue named Vettenos, who built the synagogue. Since the name Vettenos is Roman, it may be that a Jewish slave who had been freed and given the Roman name of his master is referred to. If so, this inscription may have hung on the "synagogue of the Freedmen" in Jerusalem (Acts 6:9).

The British Museum contains a portion of a broken arch that stood over an entrance into the Greek city of Thessalonica from the 1st century AD until 1867, when it was torn down to provide stone for the repair of the vast city wall. The inscription begins: "In the time of the politarchs. . . ." This is a rare word referring to Roman officials and is used in the Book of Acts (17:6) in reference to city authorities of Thessalonica. Jack Finegan states that "it is otherwise unknown in extant Greek literature." Another occurrence of the word has been found on a stone pillar in the congested backyard of a museum in Thessalonica.

Correspondence. In the 2nd millennium before Christ, it was common practice to write correspondence on small clay tablets. More than a half million have been found in Mari, Nuzi, Nineveh, Ebla, and elsewhere. Interesting examples of such correspondence may be found in a great number of clay tablets found at Tell el-Amarna in upper Egypt. They were written in the Babylonian language using the cuneiform script during the time when Akhenaton was captivated with his reformation of Egyptian art and religion at his new capital Tell el-Amarna (Akhetaten) and Palestine and Syria were left to the mercy of marauders called Habiru in the documents. Many of these are written from cities in Canaan under attack and ask for help from the pharaoh, whose vassals they are at this time (late 14th century BC). Some find in these Habiru a reference to the ancient Hebrews who invaded the land under the direction of Joshua.

Sometimes correspondence was written in ink on broken pieces of ceramic pottery (potsherds) called ostraca. In 1935, 18 of these were found in the excavations at Lachish in southern Israel. They are written in Hebrew and provide examples of the kind of script used by the Judeans in the time of Jeremiah. The language is essentially identical with the Hebrew of the OT. The letters were sent by Hosha-'yahu, an officer in charge of a nearby town, to Ya'osh, the military governor of Lachish, during the invasion of Judea by the Babylonians, which ended in the destruction of the temple in Jerusalem in 586 BC.

Eleven such potsherds were found in Masada, on the western shore of the Dead Sea in excavations conducted by Yigael Yadin from 1963 to 1965. Masada was destroyed by the Roman army under the command of Flavius Silva in AD 73. Nine hundred and sixty men, women, and children committed suicide rather than surrender to the Romans. Ten men were chosen to cut the throats of those who remained. They drew lots for the heartbreaking task, according to Josephus (*War* 7.395), and Professor Yadin thinks the ostraca he found were the ones used in the drawing. One of them contained the name of Ben Yair, who was probably Eleazer ben Yair, the commander of the fortress.

Milestones. The Romans erected milestones at intervals along important roads throughout the empire. A number of these have been found in the Middle East. They are usually cylindrical stones, around six feet high, bearing the following information in Latin (and sometimes in Greek): (1) the distance—probably from the chief city of each province, or in some cases from important military posts; (2) the places between which the road extended;

A Roman milestone near the valley of Elah, where David encountered Goliath.

(3) the name of the road builder and of the emperor to whose honor the road was being built. Augustus Caesar may have been the first to erect milestones to a significant degree, although there is some evidence that some may have existed earlier. They apparently were not erected as a matter of course in Israel before Hadrian, although Vespasian temporarily erected them on some routes used by his army during the conquest of the country.

Tombs and Sarcophagi. As might be expected, one of the most likely places to find inscriptions is on objects and structures connected with human burials. Ancient Egyptians covered the walls of their tombs with inscriptions painted onto the walls and ceilings of their burial vaults as well as on their sarcophagi. These were done in hieroglyphics, the sacred language of the Egyptians, and usually contained petitions to the deities or records of all the possessions the deceased wanted to accompany them into the next world. Without this, there could be no immortality, a privilege which of necessity belonged to those who could afford it.

On Mt Scopus an ossuary was found with the inscription, "Hanania son of Jonathan the Nazirite" and another containing the bones of his wife with the inscription, "Salome wife of Hanania son of the Nazirite." At Givat Hamivtar in northeastern Jerusalem four caves of tombs were found with many ossuaries, about half of them containing inscriptions on their sides. One of them reads, "Simon the Temple builder." The inscription is in Aramaic and leads us to think that the person named had taken part in the construction of the Jerusalem temple.

Another ossuary connected with the temple is in the British Museum. It contains an inscription in Greek that reads: "Bones of the family of Nicanor the Alexandrian, who made the doors." This refers to a wealthy Jewish family of Alexandria who gave two huge brass or bronze doors, called the Nicanor Gate, to the temple of Herod.

A huge necropolis from the Roman period was found on the Mt of Olives near the Dominus Flevit Church in the early 1950s. It is the largest discovery of its kind in Jerusalem, including about 20 caves of the arcosolium type and 38 tombs of the pit type. They date from the 3rd and 4th centuries AD. The tombs contained 122 ossuaries with 43 inscriptions in Aramaic, Hebrew, and Greek. Common names appearing on these ossuaries include Jeshua (Jesus), Maria (Mary), Martha, Salome, and Simeon.

From 1967–74 additional tombs were discovered, including the one referred to above containing the tomb of Simon the Temple builder at Givat Hamivtar. One of the ossuaries contains a fascinating inscription in Paleo-Hebrew script for which no parallel has as yet been found. It reads: "I, Abba, son of the priest Eleaz(ar), son of Aaron the high (priest), I Abba, the oppressed and the persecuted, who was born in Jerusalem and went into exile into Babylonia and brought (back to Jerusalem) Mattathi(ah)."

In the mid-1970s, a Jewish cemetery more than 7 miles long was found, spanning 7 hills west of Jericho. Approximately 120 tomb caves were excavated and surveyed. They covered a period of 150 years, ending in the destruction of Jericho in AD 68 by the Romans. One cave alone had 32 different inscriptions on the ossuaries, 17 in Greek and 15 in Aramaic. One of them is of considerable interest because it contains the name of "Theodotus, a freedman of Queen Agrippina—ossuary." There is a possibility that this might be the same Theodotus referred to in the synagogue inscription found in Jerusalem. If so, the Hebrew family name was Goliath, the family to which the entire burial cave belonged.

Mosaic Floor Decorations. In the Roman and Byzantine periods it was popular to decorate the floors of basilicas, baths, synagogues, churches, and other public buildings with elaborate tessalation containing mosaic inscriptions and artwork. Excavation in 1972 dis-

closed a building in Caesarea Maritima with mosaic inscriptions in six floors throughout the structure. Two of them are the Greek text of Romans 13:3 set in a circular border. Another is a blessing on the one who enters and exits the room: "May the Lord bless your entry and your exit." Two of them invoke the aid of Christ for people associated with the function and construction of the building. These were a part of a building which was destroyed in the 7th century AD.

The floors of the synagogues at Tiberias-hamath, Beth Shan, Beth Alpha, Eshtemoa, Susiya, Hamath-gader, En Gedi, and others in Israel have inscriptions in Greek and Aramaic that usually refer to benefactors of the synagogue. A synagogue floor has been found in Naro, Tunisia, which contains a Latin inscription. In the Tiberias synagogue, Hebrew was used only for defining the astronomical symbols that appear in the zodiac. Aramaic was used primarily for halakha (religious rule or law) and Greek was principally used in honoring donors.

One of the best-known mosaic floor inscriptions in churches comes from Madaba, Jordan, where the oldest known map of Israel and Jordan was set into the floor in the 6th century AD. The place-names of cities, geographical features, and passages of Scripture are given in Greek. Church floors typically contain dated or undated dedications, blessings, and Scripture quotations that appear in Aramaic, Coptic, Syriac, Latin, and Greek. Symbolism often accompanies the inscriptions, but in AD 427 an edict was issued forbidding the use of crosses and other religious symbols on pavements so that they might not be stepped on. It is not clear how widespread this prohibition was.

JOHN R. MCRAY

See ARCHAEOLOGY; EBLA; AMARNA TABLETS; FLOOD MYTHS; MARI; NUZI; POTTERY; SILOAM, POOL OF; UGARIT; ARCHAEOLOGY AND THE BIBLE; SEAL; ALPHABET; CREATION MYTHS.

Bibliography. M. Avi-Yonah, *Encyclopedia of Archaeological Excavations in the Holy Land* (see esp. vol 2 on tombs in Jerusalem); R.D. Barnett, *Illustrations of OT History*; A Deissmann, *Light from the Ancient East* (4th ed); H.P.V Nunn, *Christian Inscriptions*; J.B. Pritchard, *The Ancien Near East in Pictures Relating to the OT* and *Ancient Near Eastern Texts Relating to the OT*; D.W. Thomas, *Document. from OT Times.*

Insect. Small invertebrates generally characterized by a segmented body (head, thorax abdomen) and three pairs of legs.

See ANIMALS (ANT; BEE; CRICKET; FLEA; FLY; GNAT GRASSHOPPER; LOCUST; MOTH; WASP).

Inspiration of the Bible. *See* BIBLE, INSPIRATION OF THE.

Installation Offering. *See* OFFERINGS AND SACRIFICES.

Instructor. *See* TRADES AND OCCUPATIONS (TEACHER).

Instruments, Musical. *See* MUSIC AND MUSICAL INSTRUMENTS.

Intercession. *See* PRAYER.

Interest. *See* MONEY AND BANKING.

Intermediate State. State of the human person after death and before resurrection. Such teaching is more developed in the NT than in the OT though it is a mistake to think that reference to it is totally absent in the OT (Jb 19:25). According to Christ the intermediate state is deducible from such texts as Exodus 3:6 (Mt 22:32). Even in the NT an account of the intermediate state is not given explicitly but may be inferred from teaching about the physical death and resurrection of all people, but especially of believers. This is taught by Christ himself (Mt 22:30–32) and by the apostles, particularly Paul (1 Cor 15). In addition the biblical teaching that the human being is a unity of soul and body and not simply a soul that happens to be embodied (Gn 2:7) has implications for a person's state after death. From such data two conclusions regarding the intermediate state may be drawn. The first is that physical death is not the total cessation of the life of the individual but that the person lives on, not merely in the memories of those who survive, but as a distinct personality, and in the case of believers with awareness of the loving presence of God (Phil 1:23). The second conclusion is that such an existence is not a fully human existence but is incomplete or anomalous, since being embodied is essential for an individual to be in God's image. The individual, surviving death, awaits the resurrection of the body when, in the case of a person "in Christ," he will experience complete redemption, a state of complete emancipation from sin in the presence of Christ (1 Cor 15:50–58). The biblical data regarding the character of the intermediate state of those who are outside Christ is less clear, including as it does the difficult reference to Christ's preaching to the "imprisoned" (1 Pt 3:19,20).

Scripture is restrained in its portrayal of what life in the intermediate state is like. Paul says of himself that after his death he will be "with Christ which is far better" but he gives no details. Nor is it wise to look for such details in such biblical incidents as that of Saul and the witch at Endor (1 Sm 28:7), which is subject to a number of different interpretations. Even Christ's parable of the rich man and Lazarus (Lk 16:19–31), because of its obviously symbolic character (v 22) and its avowed purpose of teaching about the importance of the present life for a person's eternal destiny, must be treated with caution. Perhaps the most that can be said is that the dead in Christ are "immediately with God" and that they rest in his loving presence until the resurrection, while the unsaved are in a comfortless condition awaiting their resurrection to judgment (Jn 5:29).

Discussion of the intermediate state in the history of Christian thought has focused upon three separate aspects that may help to clarify the biblical data further. First, under the influence of Greek philosophical ideas there has been a recurring Platonic influence in Christian theology in which the Pauline contrast between the flesh and the spirit has been misinterpreted, and the soul has been emphasized at the expense of the body with the result that the prospective resurrection of the dead and its eschatological setting has either been played down or eliminated altogether because of its allegedly physical (and therefore unspiritual) aspect. The doctrine of the immortality of the disembodied soul is sometimes substituted for the idea of an intermediate state prior to resurrection, but without any warrant from Scripture. In modern theology a tendency to discount the historical has tended to displace the earlier discounting of the physical, but with much the same effect, at best a spiritualizing of postmortem existence, at worst a denial of any such existence. But it is clear from Scripture that the intermediate state is a state between two phases of embodiment, the present state of physical embodiment and that of "spiritual embodiment" (1 Cor 15:44) which is to occur at Christ's second coming (1 Cor 15:23).

Second, during the Reformation a controversy arose between John Calvin and some of the Anabaptists over "soul sleep." Calvin vehemently maintained that the intermediate state is one of conscious awareness of God's presence, something his opponents denied. For Calvin such a denial was equivalent to holding that the soul is annihilated at death and to denying that Christ exercises rule over the dead before they are resurrected. Calvin's view is supported by Paul's affirmation that nothing separates the believer from the love of God (Rom 8:35,39). The biblical teaching that on death the believer "sleeps" (1 Thes 4:14) is interpreted to mean that the dead no longer communicate with the living on earth and no longer engage in labor, but are in repose. To "fall asleep in Jesus" is thus to enjoy the presence of Jesus in a disembodied state, the nearest analogy of which in present experience may be found in dreaming when the awareness of the dreamer does not depend upon the functioning of any of the bodily senses.

A third focus for Christian thought has been on whether or not a person's eternal state is fixed at the time of death, or whether repentance and spiritual growth and purgation are possible or inevitable after death. It is the teaching of the Roman Catholic Church that death is followed by purgatory for all who are imperfect. In purgatory the soul is freed from the remnants of sin, and the period of purgation may be lessened by the gifts, prayers, and masses of those who survive the deceased. Such a view is rejected by most Protestants as being inconsistent with the biblical teaching on the complete and finished work of Christ (Heb 9:28), on the impossibility of one human being meriting or otherwise gaining grace for another (Lk 17:10), and on the biblical teaching that the eternal state of the soul is determined by its condition at death (Heb 9:27).

PAUL HELM

See PARADISE; HELL; SHEOL; DEAD, ABODE OF THE; HEAVEN; HADES.

Interpretation of the Bible. *See* BIBLE, INTERPRETATION OF THE.

Interpreter. *See* TRADES AND OCCUPATIONS.

Intertestamental Period, The. Portion of time extending from the close of OT history to the beginning of NT history; also known as the silent years.

See JUDAISM.

Iob. Alternate name for Jashub, Issachar's son, in Genesis 46:13.

See JASHUB #1.

Iphdeiah, Iphedeiah. Shashak's son from Benjamin's tribe (1 Chr 8:25, KJV Iphedeiah).

Iphtah. City in the Shephelah assigned to Judah's tribe for an inheritance, listed between Ashan and Ashnah (Jos 15:43, KJV Jiphtah). Its location is unknown.

Iphtahel. Valley on Asher and Zebulun's border (Jos 19:14,27, KJV Jiphthah-el), possibly the modern Sahl el-Battof.

Ir. Benjamite father of Shuppim and Huppim (1 Chr 7:12), perhaps identical with Iri (1 Chr 7:7).

Ira. 1. David's priest or chief official in service at the time of Sheba's revolt (2 Sm 20:26).

2. Warrior among David's mighty men, known as "the thirty" (2 Sm 23:26). He was the son of Ikkesh of Tekoa (1 Chr 11:28; 27:9) and became commander of David's militia.

3. Warrior among David's mighty men, "the thirty," identified as an Ithrite (2 Sm 23:38; 1 Chr 11:40).

Irad. Enoch's son, a member of Cain's line (Gn 4:18).

Iram. Chieftain in Edom (Gn 36:43; 1 Chr 1:54).

Iri. Bela's son from Benjamin's tribe (1 Chr 7:7).

Irijah. Benjamite guard who apprehended Jeremiah as he left Jerusalem to claim his inheritance and charged him before the princes with deserting to the Chaldeans; as a consequence, Jeremiah was beaten and imprisoned (Jer 37:13,14).

Irnahash. Town founded by Tehinnah, Eshton's son from Judah's tribe (1 Chr 4:12). Its location is unknown.

Iron. Malleable, metallic element.

See MINERALS, METALS, AND PRECIOUS STONES.

Iron (City). KJV form of Yiron, a city in Naphtali's territory (Jos 19:38).

See YIRON.

Ironsmith. *See* TRADES AND OCCUPATIONS.

Irpeel. City of inheritance allotted to Benjamin's tribe (Jos 18:27), perhaps situated in the hill country several miles northeast of Jerusalem, near Gibeon.

Irrigation. Watering by artificial means.

See AGRICULTURE.

Ir-shemesh. City allotted to Dan's tribe for an inheritance (Jos 19:41), probably identical with Beth-shemesh.

Iru. Caleb's son from Judah's tribe (1 Chr 4:15).

Isaac. Son of Abraham and Sarah, father of Jacob and Esau, one of the patriarchs of Israel.

The name "Isaac" has an interesting etymology. It is the Anglicized form of the Hebrew *yiṣḥāq*, in Greek *Isaak*. If taken as an imperfect form, it means "he laughs"; as a perfect form it means "he laughed." Scholars have debated this problem and also the absence of an antecedent subject. If "God" is implied, the name could indicate divine amusement at an aged couple ridiculing the prospect of having a child (Gn 17:17; 18:12) and then suddenly becoming parents, as God had promised. On the analogy of Genesis 21:6, the implied subject could be "all who hear." However, it is doubtful that this interpretation would be given to Isaac's name during his lifetime, since it is not apparent from the narratives. W.F. Albright, arguing from the fact that Egyptian and West Semitic sentence-names comprised utterances of a parent or some other authoritative person when a child was born, suggests that *yiṣḥāq* was short for *Yiṣḥāq-el*, "may El [i.e., God] smile on you." This seems improbable, however, because the first occurrence of the name comes from God himself (17:19), where it stands independent of any subject. Thus it is probably best to render *yiṣḥāq* as "he laughs, he laughed."

Isaac's pedigree is also interesting, for Sarah was not only the wife of Abraham but also his half-sister (Gn 20:12), and this fact alone may have interfered with conception in their earlier years. Because of this relationship, Isaac belonged to both sides of Terah's family. According to prevailing custom, the son of the legal wife took precedence over the male offspring of concubines, so that Isaac had priority of inheritance over Ishmael. The gifts that Abraham subsequently gave to the sons of his concubines (25:6) were without prejudice to the inheritance of Isaac.

Following God's instructions (Gn 17:10–14), Isaac was circumcised on the eighth day as a member of the covenant community. The next ceremony came when he was old enough for weaning, probably around three years old. In eastern countries where this procedure is still observed, the child's transition from milk to solid protein and carbohydrates is normally celebrated in the context of a feast. During the celebration the mother chews a mouthful of solid food and then pushes it into the baby's mouth with her tongue. The infant is often so shocked by this treatment that it promptly expels the food, whereupon the mother repeats the process. For an observer the procedure can be hilarious, and Ishmael may have been laughing at such a spectacle when he incurred Sarah's wrath (21:8–10).

During the years of Isaac's adolescence, Abraham was living in Philistine territory (Gn 21:34). The supreme test of the father's faith and obedience came in this period. Having watched this son of God's promise grow up into a healthy young man, Abraham is asked by God to offer him as a sacrifice. Isaac was familiar with sacrificial rituals and helped

Dome of the Rock on Mount Moriah, where Abraham's faith was tested regarding the offering of his only son Isaac.

with the preparations, though probably not without some misgivings for he was also familiar with the patriarchal traditions that gave the head of the family power of life or death over everyone and everything in the family. If he voiced any protest as he lay bound on the sacrificial altar, it is not recorded. When Abraham's faith did not waver, God intervened at the crucial moment and provided another offering in the form of a ram. Because of his obedience, God promised Abraham great blessing, blessing in which Isaac also participated. It was this act of faith and obedience that Paul honored centuries later by calling Abraham the forefather of the Christian church (Rom 4:1).

After Sarah's death (Gn 23:1–20), Abraham set about securing a bride for Isaac, as it was the custom for parents to arrange marriages for their children. Rather than have Isaac marry a local pagan woman, Abraham sent his household steward to Nahor in Mesopotamia to seek a bride for his son from among his own relatives. In an account that emphasizes faith, perseverance, and divine blessing, Genesis 24 describes how the servant met Rebekah and betrothed her to Isaac even before he had met the rest of her family. Bethuel, her father, and Laban, her brother, assented to this arrangement, and she left with the family's blessing to take up her new responsibilities in Palestine as Isaac's wife.

When Abraham died at a ripe old age, Isaac and Ishmael buried him in the cave of Machpelah (Gn 25:8–9). Isaac was now patriarch of the family. He pleaded with God that his favorite wife Rebekah might bear children (v 21), and as a result she bore twin sons, Esau ("the hairy one") and Jacob ("supplanter"). Esau became a hunter and Isaac favored him, while Jacob was more of a settler and agriculturalist and was favored by his mother. Jacob was also crafty and took advantage of Esau's extreme hunger one day, bargaining with his older brother to exchange his birthright for some lentil stew. Possession of the birthright secured for Jacob a double portion of the inheritance (Dt 21:17).

When famine gripped the land, God instructed Isaac not to visit Egypt (Gn 26:2), but to stay in Palestine, where he would enjoy great prosperity. When the men of the area asked about Rebekah, Isaac became fearful and said she was his sister (v 7). When the deception was uncovered, Abimelech the king rebuked Isaac and forbade anyone to interfere with him. Isaac prospered so greatly that Abimelech finally asked him to relocate, so he moved to Beersheba where there was sufficient water for his flocks and his fortune increased.

Although Esau was Isaac's favorite son, he displeased his father by marrying two Hittite women. When Isaac felt that the end of his life was approaching, he wished to bless his firstborn in the traditional patriarchal manner (Gn 27). Rebekah overheard his instructions to Esau and she encouraged Jacob to deceive the blind old man by disguising himself as Esau and taking his brother's blessing. The deception succeeded, and Isaac gave Jacob the blessing of the firstborn. When Esau appeared to receive his blessing he was too late, and he was very bitter against Jacob because of what had happened. Rebekah sent Jacob away to her brother Laban in Mesopotamia, to escape Esau's anger and also to obtain a wife. Esau did receive a blessing from Isaac, but a lesser one. Two decades later a rich and prosperous Jacob returned with his family. He made peace with Esau before Isaac died and the brothers buried Isaac in Hebron (35:27).

Isaac is given less prominence in the patriarchal narratives than Abraham or Jacob, but his importance for covenantal faith was recognized in such NT passages as Acts 7:8; Romans 9:13; Galatians 4:21–31; and Hebrews 11:9–20.

R.K. HARRISON

See PATRIARCHS, PERIOD OF THE; ISRAEL, HISTORY OF.

Bibliography. K.A. Kitchen, *The Bible in Its World*; D.J. Wiseman and A.R. Millard (eds), *Patriarchal Narratives and Their Study*.

Isaiah (Person).

Eighth-century (BC) prophet during the reigns of the Judean kings Uzziah, Jotham, Ahaz, and Hezekiah; author of the biblical Book of Isaiah (called Esaias in KJV NT). Isaiah was the son of Amoz (Is 1:1) and may have been King Amaziah's brother. Growing up in Jerusalem, Isaiah received the best education the capital could supply. He was also deeply knowledgeable about people, and he became political and religious counselor of the nation. He had easy access to the monarchs and seems to have been the historiographer at the Judean court for several reigns (2 Chr 26:22; 32:32).

Isaiah's wife is referred to as a prophetess (Is 8:3) and they had at least two sons, Shearjashub (7:3) and Maher-shalal-hashbaz (8:3). Isaiah's customary attire was a prophet's clothing, that is, sandals and a garment of goat's hair or sackcloth around his loins. At one point during his ministry, the Lord commanded Isaiah to go barefoot for a period of three years, wearing only a loincloth (20:2–6). This must have seemed bizarre in a society that measured status by meticulous dress codes.

Isaiah worked to reform social and political wrongs. Even the highest members of society did not escape his censure. He berated soothsayers and denounced wealthy, influential people who ignored the responsibilities of their position. He exhorted the masses to be obedient rather than indifferent to God's covenant. He rebuked kings for their willfulness and lack of concern.

Isaiah's writings express a deep awareness of God's majesty and holiness. The prophet denounced not only Canaanite idolatry, but also the religious observances of his own people that were external ceremonies only and lacking in sincerity (1:10–17; 29:13). He preached impending judgment on the idolatrous Judeans, declaring that only a righteous remnant would be saved (6:13).

Isaiah foretold the coming of the Messiah, the "peaceful prince," and the ruler of God's kingdom (11:1–11). He also depicted this Messiah as a suffering, obedient servant (53:3–12). Isaiah was preeminent among the prophets for the variety and grandeur of his imagery. His imagination produced forceful, brilliant figures of speech.

Isaiah prophesied during the last three decades of the northern kingdom of Israel. Because he lived in Jerusalem, in Judah, he made little direct reference to Israel. However, when that kingdom fell, Judah lay open to conquest by Assyria. Isaiah advised King Ahaz to avoid foreign entanglements and depend on God to protect his people. Ignoring that advice, Ahaz made an alliance with Assyria.

It was Hezekiah, Ahaz's pious son, who sought to remove Judah from this dangerous situation. When the Assyrians under Sennacherib approached Jerusalem, Isaiah inspired Hezekiah and the Judeans to rely on the Lord for the city's defense, and "the angel of the Lord" destroyed Sennacherib's army (37:36–38), securing a short period of peace for Hezekiah and the Judeans.

Hebrew prophecy reached its pinnacle with Isaiah, who was greatly esteemed in both OT and NT times. One indication of that esteem is the collection of apocryphal literature associated with his name.

HAZEL W. PERKIN

See ISAIAH, BOOK OF; ISRAEL, HISTORY OF; PROPHECY; PROPHET, PROPHETESS.

Isaiah, Book of.

Author. The prophet Isaiah, whose name means "the Lord saves," lived and ministered in Jerusalem. Because of his repeated contact with the kings of Judah, some scholars believe that Isaiah was related to the royal family, but this is not certain. According to chapters 7 and 8, Isaiah was married and had at least two sons, Shear-jashub and Maher-shalal-hashbaz, whose symbolic names illustrated God's dealings with the nation as a whole. The "disciples" mentioned in 8:16 probably assisted Isaiah in his ministry and may have helped him record the book that bears his name.

When Isaiah saw the Lord in the famous temple vision described in chapter 6, he was willing to go wherever God sent him, even though he would face strong opposition (6:9, 10). King Ahaz proved to be particularly resistant to Isaiah's advice (7:4–17), and the people in general made fun of his preaching (5:19; 28:9,10). During the reign of the godly Hezekiah, however, Isaiah's ministry was much appreciated, and the king consulted him eagerly during times of crisis (37:1–7,21–35).

Isaiah is usually regarded as the greatest of the writing prophets. Some of the chapters in his book display an unparalleled literary beauty and make use of poetic devices and a rich variety of symbols. Chapters 40–66 contain many powerful passages that underscore the grandeur of the book. It is ironic, then, that many scholars attribute these chapters to a "second" or "third" Isaiah, unknown authors who wrote much later than Isaiah in connection with the Babylonian exile. Yet elsewhere in the OT, the names of all who wrote the prophetic books are preserved, and it would be most unusual for the Jews not to know who wrote such magnificent prophecy as chapters 40–66.

Date. Since many of the events recorded in chapters 1–39 took place during the ministry of Isaiah, most of these chapters were probably written by about 700 BC or shortly thereafter. The destruction of the Assyrian army in 701 BC represents the climax of the first half of the book, fulfilling the prophecy of 10:16,24–34 and 30:31–33. In 37:38 Isaiah refers to the death of King Sennacherib, which did not occur until 681 BC. This means that some of the earlier chapters, along with 40–66, were probably written later during Isaiah's retirement years. A gap of several decades could help account for the change in subject matter

that is found in the last half of the book. In these chapters Isaiah projects into the future as he addresses the Jews who would be in exile in Babylon about 550 BC.

Historical Background. Isaiah's public ministry occurred primarily from 740–700 BC, a period marked by the rapid expansion of the nation of Assyria. Under King Tiglath-pileser III (745–727 BC), the Assyrians moved to the west and south, and by 738 BC the Assyrian monarch was demanding tribute from Damascus and Israel. About 734 BC Rezin of Damascus and Pekah of Israel organized a coalition to rebel against Assyria, and they tried to enlist the support of King Ahaz of Judah. But Ahaz refused to join, and when the kings of Damascus and Israel invaded Judah (see 7:1), Ahaz appealed directly to Tiglath-pileser for help (cf. 2 Kgs 16:7–9). With little hesitation the Assyrians returned to capture Damascus and to turn the northern kingdom of Israel into an Assyrian province.

The puppet king Hoshea ruled over Israel from 732–723 BC but was imprisoned when he joined a revolt against Shalmaneser V, the new Assyrian king. Shalmaneser besieged the capital city of Samaria, which finally fell in 722 BC, spelling the end of the northern kingdom. Sargon succeeded Shalmaneser in 722 and had to quell a number of revolts. In 711 BC Sargon captured the Philistine city of Ashdod in a campaign that became the occasion of Isaiah's prophecy of 20:1–6.

Even more important was the widespread rebellion that broke out with the accession of Sennacherib in 705 BC. King Hezekiah of Judah withheld his normal tribute payment, and by 701 BC Sennacherib had invaded Palestine to punish the rebels. The details of this campaign are given in Isaiah 36,37 and tell how city after city was captured by the Assyrians before the invaders stood at the gates of Jerusalem and demanded total surrender. With almost no hope of survival, Hezekiah nevertheless was encouraged by Isaiah to trust in God, and in one night the angel of the Lord struck down 185,000 Assyrian soldiers, virtually wiping out Sennacherib's army (Is 37:36,37).

In an effort to befriend the enemies of Assyria, Hezekiah showed his treasures to envoys of the king of Babylon (39:1–4). Isaiah warned that some day the Babylonian armies would conquer Jerusalem and carry off those very treasures, along with the residents of the city (39:5–7). Not only did Isaiah predict the Babylonian captivity of 586–39 BC (cf. 6:11,12), but he also foretold that Israel would be released from Babylon (48:20). The Chaldean kingdom led by Nebuchadnezzar would be God's instrument of judgment upon Judah, but they too would suffer defeat. One of Isa-

A ship—with two banks of oars and two sets of rowers—from Nineveh, capital of the Assyrians, from whom Hezekiah withheld tribute.

iah's most remarkable prophecies was the naming of Cyrus, king of Persia, the ruler who would conquer the Babylonians in 539 BC and release Israel from exile (cf. 44:28; 45:1). Along with the Medes (cf. 13:17), Cyrus won several important victories before sending his troops against Babylon. Isaiah hailed him as one anointed by the Lord to bring deliverance for Israel (45:1–5).

Unity. Largely because of the references to the later kingdoms of Babylon and Persia, the unity of Isaiah has been called into question. Chapters 40–66 move abruptly into the exilic period of 550 BC, almost 150 years after Isaiah lived. Moreover, the Servant of the Lord plays a prominent role in these chapters and the messianic king fades into the background. Brilliant poetic passages are found in chapters 40, 53, 55, and 60, demonstrating remarkable depth and power.

Although these factors are sometimes cited as a sign of disunity, there are actually strong indications for unity in the book. For example, the historical interlude (chs 36–39) forms a hinge or bridge that links chapters 1–35 and 40–66. Chapters 36,37 complete the Assyrian section, and chapters 38,39 introduce the Babylonian material. Most of the linking chapters are written in prose, while the others are largely poetry. From the standpoint of verbal or stylistic unity, one can point to Isaiah's favorite title for God, "the Holy One of Israel." This title appears 12 times in chapters 1–39, and 14 times in chapters 40–66, but only 4 times in the rest of the OT. A study of the famous Servant Songs of 52:13–53:12 reveals several ties with earlier passages, especially in chapters 1–6. The servant who is smitten and wounded (53:4,5) receives the same punish-

ment as the beaten and injured nation of 1:5–6 (also cf. 52:13 with 2:12 and 6:1).

Theological Teaching. Isaiah is to the OT as the Book of Romans is to the NT, a book filled with rich theological truth. Like Romans, Isaiah unveils the sinfulness of God's rebellious people and his gracious provision of salvation. Because God is the Holy One of Israel (1:4; 6:3), he cannot ignore sin but must punish those who are guilty. Both Israel (5:30; 42:25) and the other nations (2:11,17,20) experience a time of judgment known as the day of the Lord. In anger God raises his hand against his people (cf. 5:25), but ultimately his wrath is poured out upon Babylon and the nations (cf. 13:3–5; 34:2).

With the fall of Assyria and Babylon, the day of the Lord becomes a day of joyous victory (10:27; 61:2). According to Isaiah 63:4 it is "the year of my redemption." Earlier, Israel had been redeemed from slavery in Egypt; now the return from the Babylonian captivity brings equal joy (52:9; 61:1). The ultimate redemption is to be accomplished through the death of Christ, and Isaiah 53 describes our Lord's suffering and death in graphic terms. His ministry as the Suffering Servant is also introduced in 49:4 and 50:6,7; 49:6 states that the servant will be "a light for the Gentiles." Looking ahead to the second coming, Isaiah predicts a messianic age of peace and righteousness. Nations will "beat their swords into plowshares" (2:4) and the "Prince of Peace" will rule forever (9:6,7).

Throughout the book God is pictured as the all-powerful Creator (48:13), the sovereign One "seated on a throne, high and exalted . . . the King, the Lord Almighty" (6:1,5). He controls the armies of the earth (13:4) and removes rulers as he wills (40:23,24). Before him "nations are like a drop in a bucket" (v 15), and compared with him all idols are worthless and without power (41:29; 44:6). This is the God who shows his fury to his foes and his love to his servants (66:14).

Content. *Messages of Judgment and Hope (chs 1–12).* In the opening chapter Isaiah characterizes Israel as a nation that has rebelled against God. Although the people regularly bring offerings to him, their worship is hypocritical, an attempt to mask their oppression of the poor and helpless. The Lord encourages the nation to repent of their sin or face the fires of judgment. After this introduction, Isaiah turns to describe the peace of the messianic age in 2:1–4. The day will come when all nations will obey God's Word and live at peace. "The mountain of the Lord"—Jerusalem—will be raised up "and all nations will stream to it" (vv 2,3). In the meantime, however, both Israel and the nations have exalted themselves against the Lord, and he will judge them in an awesome display of power. For Israel, God's judgment will bring great upheaval, including the loss of its leaders. Defiant and ruthless, the rulers will face either death or deportation. Chapter 3 ends by denouncing the pride and vanity of the women of Zion; they too will suffer disgrace. After Jerusalem is cleansed of its sin, the remnant will enjoy the rule of "the Branch of the Lord," who will protect and shield his people (4:2–6).

In 5:1–7 Isaiah presents a short song about Israel as God's vineyard. The Lord has done everything possible to insure a yield of good grapes, but the vineyard has produced nothing but bad fruit and must be destroyed. Isaiah then pronounces six words against Israel, and announces that the Assyrian army will invade the land. Against the backdrop of Israel's sin Isaiah (ch 6) gives an account of the vision through which he was called as a prophet. Overwhelmed by the holiness of God and by his own sinfulness, Isaiah thought he was ruined, but when he is assured that his sins are forgiven, he responds positively to God's call in spite of the stubbornness of the nation to which he is sent.

One of the most stubborn individuals in all of Israel is King Ahaz, and chapter 7 describes Isaiah's encounter with this godless ruler. When Ahaz is threatened by Damascus and the northern kingdom, he refuses to believe Isaiah's promise that God will protect him. This is occasion on which Isaiah gives Ahaz the sign of Immanuel (7:14). The "virgin" refers ultimately to Mary, but in the near fulfillment she is probably Isaiah's fiancée whom he marries (8:1–3) and who later gives birth to a boy named Maher-shalal-hashbaz and Imman-

uel (cf. 8:3,8). The birth of this child within a few years is a sign that God will be with Judah and will put an end to the threats of Damascus and Samaria. If Ahaz appeals for help to the king of Assyria, Isaiah warns him, Assyria's powerful armies will one day invade Judah also (cf. 7:17–25; 8:6–8). The destruction brought by Assyria will plunge Judah into a time of famine and distress (8:21,22).

Nevertheless, the gloom and darkness associated with the Assyrian invasion will not last indefinitely, and 9:1–5 speaks of a time of peace and joy. Verses 6,7 introduce a child who will become a righteous King and will rule forever. This "Prince of Peace" is the Messiah, the "Mighty God" whose kingdom is described in 2:2–4.

For the immediate future, however, both Israel and Judah will suffer the agony of war as punishment for their sins. God is angry with his people because they are proud and arrogant and their leaders disregard the pleas of the poor and needy. Civil war and foreign invasion will crush the hapless nation (9:8–10:4). But once Israel has been judged, God will turn his hand against Assyria, the instrument he has used to judge other nations. Because of her string of victories, Assyria is filled with pride and is eager for more triumph. Yet even at the moment when Jerusalem is about to succumb, God cuts down the Assyrian army like a cedar in Lebanon and spares his people (10:26–34).

After the joyous news of Assyria's defeat, Isaiah describes the restoration of Israel and the powerful rule of the Messiah (ch 11). Both Jews and Gentiles will be attracted to Jerusalem to enjoy an era of peace and justice. Like David, the Messiah will have the Spirit of God resting upon him as he judges the wicked and protects the needy. To conclude these opening messages, Isaiah offers two short songs of praise that reflect upon God's past deliverance and his promise of future blessing (12:1–6).

Oracles Against the Nations (chs 13–23). Although Babylon is not the major power of the day, Isaiah begins his announcements of judgment with two chapters about the destruction of Assyria's neighbor to the south. Babylon will eventually conquer Jerusalem (between 605 and 586 BC), but the Medes (13:17) along with the Persians will capture Babylon (539 BC). In spite of the glory to be achieved by future kings of Babylon, God will bring their pomp down to the grave (14:9–20). The chapter ends with short prophecies against Assyria and the Philistines.

One of Israel's oldest enemies was the nation of Moab, situated east of the Dead Sea. Even though it was a small country, Isaiah devotes two chapters to these descendants of

Lot. Chapter 15 describes the extensive mourning that will overwhelm their cities. After a brief interlude urging the Moabites to submit to Israel and to her God (16:1–5), Isaiah notes that pride will lead to Moab's downfall. Sounds of weeping fill the land as the vines and fields wither and are trampled.

In chapter 17 the fourth oracle is directed against Damascus and Ephraim (the northern kingdom of Israel), probably reflecting their alliance against Judah about 734 BC. Both nations will face ruin, and Ephraim is condemned for abandoning the Lord, her "Savior" and "Rock" (v 10).

In chapters 18 and 19 Isaiah turns to the south and addresses Ethiopia and Egypt, countries that had strong links from 715–633 BC, when an Ethiopian named Shabako became pharaoh in Egypt. But Egypt is plagued with disunity and suffers greatly at the hands of Assyrian kings. In spite of the supposed wisdom of her leaders, Egypt faces economic and political ruin (19:5–15). Yet the time is coming when the Egyptians will be restored and will worship the God of Israel. Along with Assyria and Israel, Egypt will be "a blessing on the earth" (v 24). Some interpreters feel that this is a prophecy of the salvation of Gentiles during the church age, but others relate this day to the peace of the millennial age (cf. 2:2–4; 11:6–9). For the immediate future, however, Isaiah announces that Assyria will take many Egyptians and Ethiopians into captivity (20:1–6).

A second oracle about Babylon (cf. 13:1–14:23) is contained in chapter 21. This time her attackers are identified as Elam and Media (v 2), and Isaiah is staggered as he considers the impact of Babylon's fall (vv 3,4). When Babylon collapses, the world will know that her gods were powerless (v 10; cf. Rv 14:8; 18:2).

Although it seems out of place among these oracles against the nations, chapter 22 condemns the city of Jerusalem. Like the nations, Jerusalem is full of "tumult and revelry" (v 2) and will soon experience the terrors of a siege. Since the people no longer rely on the Lord (v 11), he will hand them over to the enemy. Jerusalem's unfaithfulness is exemplified by Shebna, a high official guilty of pride and materialism whose position will be taken by the godly Eliakim (vv 15–23).

The last oracle (23:1–18) is directed against the city of Tyre, which resisted capture until Alexander the Great conquered the island fortress in 332 BC. When Tyre fell, the economy of the entire Mediterranean world was shaken, for her ships had carried the goods of the nations far and wide.

Final Judgment and Blessing (chs 24–27). This section functions as a grand finale to chapters 13–23 as it anticipates God's judgment upon the nations and the inauguration of the kingdom of God. A defiled earth must bear its punishment (24:5,6) and even the forces of Satan, "the powers in the heavens" (vv 21,22), face judgment.

In chapter 25 Isaiah rejoices over God's great triumph and looks ahead to a day when death will be swallowed up and tears will be wiped from all faces (v 8). Israel's longtime enemies, symbolized by Moab, will be laid low (vv 10–12), but Jerusalem will be a stronghold for the righteous (26:1–3). In 26:7–21 the nation prays that these promises will become a reality. Verses 20,21 indicate that the Lord will indeed respond, pouring out his wrath upon a sin-cursed earth and upon Satan himself (27:1). When that takes place, Israel will be a fruitful vineyard, a blessing to the whole world (vv 2–6; contrast 5:1–7). First, however, Israel will have to endure war and exile, and then the remnant will return to Jerusalem.

A Series of Woes (chs 28–33). Returning to his own historical period, Isaiah pronounces a series of woes upon both the northern and southern kingdoms, as well as one upon Assyria (ch 33). Chapter 28 begins with a description of the fading power of Samaria, the capital of the northern kingdom. Verses 7–10 portray the leaders of Judah in the same light; they have disregarded Isaiah's message and are out of touch with God. Judgment is on the way, and their false preparation (vv 15,18) will be of no avail. God will fight against Israel (vv 21,22), and even Jerusalem will be put under siege until God in his mercy intervenes (29:1–8). Because of their hypocritical worship, the people deserve to be punished, but in the future Israel will again acknowledge the Lord and be made physically and spiritually whole (vv 17–24).

Chapters 30 and 31 denounce Judah's proposed alliance with Egypt in the effort to thwart Assyria. God wants his people to trust him, not their unreliable neighbors to the south. The Lord promises to protect Jerusalem (30:18; 31:5) and defeat the invading Assyrian army (30:31–33; 31:8,9). None can stand before his mighty sword.

Continuing on this positive note, Isaiah goes on to emphasize the righteous rule of the messianic king in chapters 32 and 33. Zion will enjoy peace and security at last (32:2,17,18; 33:6), a great change from 8th-century BC Judah. In Isaiah's own time the women feel secure (32:9), but the Assyrian troops will devastate the crops and precipitate widespread mourning. However, the lamenting will soon end for the prophet pronounces woe upon Assyria in 33:1. After Isaiah prays for the destruction of Assyria (33:2–9), God promises to take action (vv 10–12). Gone will be the enemy soldiers and officials, for the Lord will save his people and bring them justice and security.

More Judgment and Blessing (chs 34,35). This section forms a climax to chapters 28–33. Once more, cataclysmic judgment precedes a time of blessing and restoration. In chapter 34 Isaiah depicts a judgment of cosmic dimensions as he moves to a consideration of the last days. Heaven and earth endure the wrath of God that is poured out upon the nations, and verse 4 provides the basis for John's description of the great tribulation in Revelation 6:13, 14. Edom—like Moab in 25:10–12—represents a world judged by the sword of the Lord in his day of vengeance.

Chapter 35, on the other hand, speaks of joy and restoration in a passage that pulsates with life. A blooming desert corresponds to the physical and spiritual healing that will characterize the messianic age when God will come to redeem his people. Both the return of the Israelites from the Babylonian captivity and the second coming of Christ fit this glorious scene.

Historical Interlude (chs 36–39). These chapters form the hinge that ties together the two halves of the book. Chapters 36 and 37 contain the fulfillment of Isaiah's prophecies about Assyria's collapse, and chapters 38 and 39 introduce the Babylonian captivity that forms the backdrop for chapters 40–66. In 701 BC King Sennacherib of Assyria demands the unconditional surrender of Jerusalem. He sends his field commander to address the people and try to gain their submission. With persuasive words, the commander tries to convince the city that surrender is the best policy. Amazingly the people do not panic, and King Hezekiah asks Isaiah to pray for the beleaguered city. The prophet does so and announces that the proud Assyrians will not triumph. Instead, they suffer a terrible disaster as the angel of the Lord strikes down 185,000 men.

Chapters 38 and 39 relate another crisis in Hezekiah's life when he becomes desperately ill. Miraculously, God heals him and Hezekiah praises the Lord for his gracious intervention. When the king of Babylon sends envoys to congratulate Hezekiah on his recovery, Hezekiah foolishly shows these messengers his royal treasures. Isaiah solemnly announces that someday the armies of Babylon will capture Jerusalem, plunder the land, and take away these treasures.

The Return from Babylon (chs 40–48). The Babylonian captivity eventually comes, but Isaiah promises that it will end. God, the incomparably powerful Creator, is far greater than any king, nation, or god, and he will bring his people back to Jerusalem. To accom-

plish this return from exile God raises up Cyrus the king of Persia (41:2,25). The Lord does not forget his people, and he encourages them to take heart and to rejoice.

In chapter 42 we are introduced to a person even more significant than Cyrus the Persian. Verses 1–7 describe the servant of the Lord, who will bring justice to the nations and will be "a light for the Gentiles" (v 6). This is the Messiah, and the redemption he will accomplish on Calvary (cf. ch 53) is greater than the release from Babylon. In light of the good news associated with the servant, Isaiah praises the Lord for punishing the wicked and rescuing his wayward people. Chapter 43 declares that nothing will stand in the way of Israel's return, and the Lord will remember their sins no more. In fact, he will pour out his Spirit on their descendants (44:3).

A God so great is far more powerful than any idol. In 44:6–20 Isaiah makes use of satire to show the worthlessness of manmade images. God alone has the power to create and to restore, and he will bring Cyrus on the scene to effect the release of the exiles and to begin the rebuilding of Jerusalem. Chapters 46 and 47 contrast the God of Israel and the idols of Babylon. When God raises up Cyrus, Babylon's idols will be unable to save their nation, and the "queen of kingdoms" (47:5) will collapse along with her sorcerers and astrologers. The final chapter in this section (48) restates God's purpose of gaining release of the Israelites from Babylon through his "chosen ally" (v 14), Cyrus of Persia.

Salvation Through the Servant of the Lord (chs 49–57). Chapters 49–53 contain the final three Servant Songs (cf. also 42:1–7), culminating in the death of the servant for the sins of the world (52:13–53:12). In the second Servant Song (49:1–7), Isaiah describes the call and ministry of the servant, noting that he will face strong opposition as he accomplishes salvation for Israel and the nations. The rest of chapter 49 (vv 8–26) deals primarily with the way God will bring Israel back from exile. Soon the land will be filled with a mighty

The Cylinder of Nebuchadnezzar II—which concerns the restoration of temples to a god and goddess—indicates the Babylonian idolatry about which Isaiah prophesied.

throng (vv 20,21), and the Gentiles will acknowledge Israel and her God (vv 22,23).

Although Israel has fully deserved the exile because of her sins (50:1–3), the suffering endured by the servant (vv 4–11) is wholly undeserved. The beating and mocking of verse 6 are prophetic of Christ's experience (cf. Mt 27:26, 30; Mk 15:19). In verses 10,11 the whole nation is challenged to trust in the Lord, as the servant did. There is, in fact, a believing remnant who obey the Lord (51:1–8), and the Lord promises that he will restore them to their homeland. Israel has drunk the cup of God's wrath (vv 17,22), but the good news of release from exile causes even the ruins of Jerusalem to burst into songs of joy (52:7–10).

Yet the best news of all is salvation from sin; the final Servant Song (52:13–53:12) tells how Christ wins freedom for those held in bondage to sin. In this brief passage we learn how Christ suffered rejection (53:3) and even disfigurement (52:14), but, "led like a lamb to the slaughter" (53:7), he carries our sins in his body as he dies in ignomy. The people think he is suffering for his own sins (v 4), but he is "pierced" and "crushed for our iniquities" (v 5). The first and last paragraphs of this section (52:13–15; 53:10–12) state that through his suffering the servant is highly exalted. What seemed like a terrible defeat is actually victory over death and Satan and brings salvation for many.

As a direct result of the servant's death, great joy comes to all people. In chapter 54 this joy is reflected in Jerusalem's new status as the Lord's wife. Her descendants will be numerous and eager to learn from the Lord (v 13). For the first time the term "servants of the Lord" appears (v 17), apparently including all believers, whether Jew or Gentile (cf. 65:8,9, 13–15). Joy and prosperity also characterize chapter 55, an invitation to a great spiritual banquet. All people are urged to turn to the Lord who keeps his promises to Israel. In 56:1–8, foreigners are invited to come to God's "holy mountain" in Jerusalem, for the temple will be "a house of prayer for all nations" (v 7; cf. Mt 21:13).

Believing Gentiles contrast sharply with unbelieving Jews, and in 56:9–57:13 Isaiah returns again to the theme of judgment. Israel suffers because her leaders are wicked and because the people are guilty of idolatry. Spiritual healing is available, but unless individuals repent they cannot be part of the remnant who will return from exile and enjoy peace in the Promised Land.

Ultimate Blessing and Final Judgment (chs 58–66). The last nine chapters of Isaiah emphasize redemption and glory, but the reality of judgment is also very much in evidence. In fact chapters 58 and 59 bemoan the sins of Israel. The people are hypocritical in their worship; they are selfish and fail to keep the sabbath. Lying, oppression, and murder separate the people from God. When Isaiah openly confesses these sins (59:12,13), the Lord suddenly takes action on behalf of his people. Like a mighty warrior he rescues the believing remnant from Babylon and brings them back to Jerusalem.

In chapter 60 the glory and wealth of Jerusalem reach new heights. Both the city and the sanctuary are adorned with splendor, matching the prosperity of Solomon's reign. Just as the nations treated Solomon with honor, so earth's leaders will assist and strengthen the returning exiles. While it is true that the Persian government did help the Jews repeatedly, the conditions described here will have their ultimate fulfillment during the millennium and in connection with the new Jerusalem (cf. Rv 21:23; 22:5). "The ancient ruins" will be rebuilt (61:4), and the Lord will fulfill the covenant made with Abraham and David (v 8; cf. Gn 12:1–3; Is 55:3). Jerusalem will be the city of the holy people, the redeemed of the Lord (62:12), and the Lord will take delight in her (v 4).

In order to accomplish salvation for his people, God will have to judge the ungodly first. The great trampling of the winepress (63:2,3) graphically portrays the judgment process and is linked with the day of the Lord (cf. 13:3; 34:2). Since God has promised to intervene on behalf of his people, Isaiah prays for the realization of that promise (63:7–64:12). He recalls God's faithfulness in the past and pleads that he will again have mercy upon his suffering people.

The answer to Isaiah's prayer is found in chapter 65. God does promise to give the holy land back to his servants, to those who worship him and obey him. But for that segment of the nation that continues in its obstinancy, God promises anguish and destruction. The ultimate joy of God's servants is contained in a description of "new heavens and a new earth" (vv 17–25). Peace, long life, and prosperity will be among the blessings enjoyed in an era that seems to combine features of the millennium and the eternal state (cf. 60:1–22).

In a fitting summary, chapter 66 ties together the themes of salvation and judgment. God will comfort Jerusalem and abundantly bless her, but sinners are the objects of his wrath. Those who honor him will endure forever, but those who rebel will suffer everlasting rejection.

HERBERT M. WOLF

See ISRAEL, HISTORY OF; ISAIAH (PERSON); MESSIAH; SERVANT OF THE LORD; VIRGIN BIRTH OF JESUS; PROPHECY; PROPHET, PROPHETESS.

Bibliography. J.A. Alexander, *Isaiah*, 2 vols; O.T. Allis, *The Unity of Isaiah*; H. Bultema, *Commentary on Isaiah*; W. Kelly, *An Exposition of the Book of Isaiah*; E.J. Kissane, *The Book of Isaiah*, 2 vols; G.A.F. Knight, *Isaiah 40–55* and *Isaiah 56–66*; J.N. Oswalt, *The Book of Isaiah*, chs 1–39; E.J. Young, *The Book of Isaiah*, 3 vols, and *Studies in Isaiah*.

Iscah. Haran's daughter and Milcah's sister (Gn 11:29).

Ishbah. Mered's son by Bithiah, the daughter of the pharaoh (1 Chr 4:17).

Ishbak. One of the sons of Abraham by Keturah (Gn 25:2; 1 Chr 1:32).

Ishbi-benob. Giant who nearly killed David. During one of his many battles with the Philistines, David grew faint and was nearly killed by Ishbi-benob. Abishai killed the giant, saving David's life (2 Sm 21:16). Some suggest that "Ishbi-benob" is not a proper name but means rather "they abode in Nob." Such a view, however, requires a reconstruction of verses 15,16, and Nob is an unlikely site from which David launched his attacks against the Philistines.

Ish-bosheth. Alternate name for Esh-baal, Saul's son and successor to Israel's throne (2 Sm 2–4).

See ESH-BAAL.

Ishhod. Hammolecheth's son from Manasseh's tribe (1 Chr 7:18, KJV Ishod).

Ishi. 1. Appaim's son, the father of Sheshan and a descendant of Judah through Jerahmeel's line (1 Chr 2:31).

2. Man from Judah's tribe whose descendants were Zoheth and Ben-zoheth (1 Chr 4:20).

3. Simeonite whose four sons led 500 men to Mt Seir where they destroyed the Amalekites and settled their own people (1 Chr 4:42).

4. One of the leaders of the half-tribe of Manasseh east of the Jordan (1 Chr 5:24).

5. Name of God, meaning "my husband," by which Israel will one day address him (Hos 2:16).

See GOD, NAMES OF.

Ishiah. KJV spelling of Isshiah, Izrahiah's son, in 1 Chronicles 7:3.

See ISSHIAH #1.

Ishijah. KJV spelling of Isshijah, Harim's son, in Ezra 10:31.

See ISSHIJAH.

Ishma. Etam's son from Judah's tribe (1 Chr 4:3).

Ishmael, Ishmaelites. 1. Abraham's first son, born of Hagar, Sarah's Egyptian handmaid, at the instigation of Sarah herself. God promised to make a great nation of the childless Abraham (Gn 12:2), assuring him that his son would be his heir (15:4). But when Sarah was past 75 years old and still barren, she invoked the custom whereby a childless wife gave her maid to her husband as concubine and laid claim to the offspring of their union.

When Hagar conceived, the reproach attendant on barrenness prompted the maid to behave contemptuously toward her mistress, and with Abraham's consent Sarah dealt harshly with her and she fled. An angel sent Hagar back to submit to her mistress and promised her a son to be named Ishmael. The boy was born near Hebron when Abraham was 86 years old (Gn 13:18; 16:16).

Abraham and Sarah received him as the son of God's promise, as attested by their surprise when the birth of Isaac was announced (17:17; 18:12), and by Abraham's subsequent wish that Ishmael should be accepted of God (17:18). At age 13 Ishmael participated in the institution of circumcision as a witness of God's covenant with Abraham (vv 9–14,22–27), and the Lord promised to "make him fruitful and multiply him exceedingly" as "the father of twelve princes, and . . . a great nation," though the covenant was to be established with Isaac (vv 20,21).

There is no evidence that Ishmael was out of favor until Isaac's weaning at about three years of age. When Sarah found Ishmael "playing" with her son Isaac—"playing" in this instance could mean mocking, fondling, or fraternizing—as an equal. She determined that the son of a slave-woman should not be heir with her son Isaac, and she demanded that Ishmael and Hagar be banished. Although vexed, Abraham received reassurance from the Lord and sent them away with some provisions. It was then clear to Abraham that Isaac, not Ishmael, was the son of God's promise.

Hagar survived in the wilderness with the guidance of an angel, and Ishmael became a hunter of wild animals. He settled in the wilderness of Paran and married an Egyptian woman (21:20,21). Little else is recorded of him, save that he lived to assist in the burial of Abraham (25:9,10), gave his daughter Mahalath in marriage (28:9), and died at the age of 137 (25:17). The names of his 12 sons and their settlements are recorded in Genesis 25:13–15. In subsequent history, a caravan of Ishmaelite traders (also called Midianites cf. 8:24) bought Joseph from his brothers and sold him in Egypt (Gn 37:25–28; 39:1; KJV Ishmaelites).

Though Isaac rather than Ishmael inherited the covenantal blessings, it is clear that the covenant was not the only means whereby divine favor could be bestowed. Abraham and Sarah overestimated the importance of Ishmael in God's plan by mistaking him for the heir of covenant promises, but they also underrated God's intentions for him by excluding him altogether from inheritance with Isaac.

In the NT, Paul alludes to Ishmael while urging the Galatians not to see the Law as a yoke (Gal 4:22). He states that those who trust the Law instead of putting their faith in God's promises do not inherit the kingdom, just as the son of the slave woman did not receive inheritance with the son of the free woman (v 30).

2. Son of Nethaniah, son of Elishama, of the royal family of Zedekiah (2 Kgs 25:25), incited by Baalis, king of the Ammonites, to assassinate Gedaliah, Judean governor of the puppet regime, which Nebuchadnezzar left behind at Mizpah at the time of the Babylonian exile. Gedaliah ignored advance warning of the plot and refused to allow Johanan to assassinate Ishmael first (Jer 40:14–16). While sharing a meal with Gedaliah, Ishmael and 10 companions set on him and killed him along with his retinue and the Babylonian troops attending. The next day he persuaded a group of 80 pilgrims passing from the north to the temple at Jerusalem to enter Mizpah, where he killed all but 10 who ransomed their lives with stores of food. Hiding all the bodies in a cistern, Ishmael took captive the rest of the population of Mizpah, including Jeremiah and women of the royal family, and set out to join the Ammonites. But Johanan, with an armed force, overtook Ishmael at Gibeon and rescued the captives, whereupon Ishmael fled to Ammonite territory (Jer 41).

3. Son of Azel, a Benjamite of the family of Saul (1 Chr 8:38; 9:44).

4. Father of Zebadiah, the "governor of the house of Judah in all the king's matters" under Jehoshaphat (2 Chr 19:11).

5. Son of Jehohanan, and one of the commanders who allied with Jehoiada the priest to enthrone the child Joash and thus end the reign of Athaliah (2 Chr 23:1).

6. Son of Pashhur, and one of the priests who put away foreign wives during Ezra's reforms (Ezr 10:22). HAZEL W. PERKIN

Ishmaiah. 1. Warrior from Benjamin's tribe who joined David at Ziklag in his struggle against King Saul. Ishmaiah was one of David's ambidextrous archers and slingers (1 Chr 12:4, KJV Ismaiah).

2. Obadiah's son, a chief officer in Zebulun's tribe in David's time (1 Chr 27:19).

Ishmeelite. Alternate KJV spelling for Ishmaelite (Gn 37:25–28; 39:1).

See ISHMAEL, ISHMAELITES.

Ishmerai. Elpaal's son and a chief in Benjamin's tribe (1 Chr 8:18).

Ishod. KJV spelling of Ishhod, Hammolecheth's son (1 Chr 7:18).

See ISHHOD.

Ishpah. Beriah's son from Benjamin's tribe (1 Chr 8:16, KJV Ispah).

Ishpan. Shashak's son and a chief of Benjamin's tribe (1 Chr 8:22).

Ishtar. Ancient fertility goddess.

See CANAANITE DEITIES AND RELIGION.

Ish-tob. KJV translation for "men of Tob" in 2 Samuel 10:6,8.

See TOB.

Ishuah. KJV spelling of Ishvah, Asher's son, in Genesis 46:17.

See ISHVAH.

Ishuai. KJV spelling of Ishvi, Asher's son, in 1 Chronicles 7:30.

See ISHVI #1.

Ishui. KJV spelling of Ishvi, Saul's son, in 1 Samuel 14:49.

See ISHVI #2.

Ishvah. Asher's son (Gn 46:17, KJV Ishuah; 1 Chr 7:30, KJV Isuah).

Ishvi. 1. Asher's third son (Gn 46:17, KJV Isui; Nm 26:44, KJV Jesui; 1 Chr 7:30, KJV Ishuai), and founder of the Ishvite family (Nm 26:44, KJV Jesuites).

2. One of King Saul's sons (1 Sm 14:49, KJV Ishui).

Ishvite. Descendant of Ishvi, Asher's son (Nm 26:44).

See ISHVI #1.

Ismachiah. Levite overseer of things dedicated at the temple during Hezekiah's reform (2 Chr 31:13).

Ismaiah. KJV spelling of Ishmaiah, a warrior from Benjamin's tribe who joined David at Ziklag in 1 Chronicles 12:4.

See ISHMAIAH #1.

Ispah. KJV spelling of Ishpah, Beriah's son, 1 Chronicles 8:16.

See ISHPAH.

Israel, History of. An account of God's sovereign purpose in calling a people out of paganism and establishing them as witnesses for the true faith among the nations, of God's sovereign power in protecting them from extinction, of his sovereign justice in dealing with their departure from his ways of holiness, of God's sovereign grace in forgiving their sins and restoring them to fellowship with himself by providing through them a Savior for the entire world.

Patriarchal Age. The story of Israel begins with Abraham, whom God called first at Ur, and perhaps later at Haran (Acts 7:2–4), to leave Mesopotamia and go into a land to which God would direct the way. In calling Abraham God made with him a covenant (Gn 12:1–3) that promised him a land, special divine favor ("I will bless those who bless you and the one who curses you I will curse" NASB), and the privilege of being a channel of blessing to the entire world ("In you all the families of the earth shall be blessed" NASB). In Genesis 12:14–18 God confirmed this unconditional covenant, promising Abraham this new land forever, along with innumerable descendants. Subsequently, in Genesis 15:1–21, God again confirmed the covenant but added the significant prediction that the guarantee of holding Canaan in perpetuity did not mean occupation of the land in every generation. God also spelled out the limits of the Promised Land (from the river of Egypt to the Euphrates, some 500 to 600 miles in extent). A final confirmation of the covenant to Abraham appears in Genesis 17:6–8. It guaranteed the land of Canaan to Abraham's posterity and added that kings (an anticipation of the Davidic dynasty) would arise in his line.

The covenant was confirmed to Abraham's son Isaac (Gn 26:3–5) and his grandson Jacob (ch 28).

This period is known as the patriarchal age in Hebrew history. The patriarchs were Abraham, Isaac, and Jacob. They were called patriarchs because they were fathers, not only to their immediate families, but also to the extended family of Hebrews, over which they exercised a fatherly control. They served as political, legal, and spiritual heads of their migratory community, looking after their interests and leading them in worship. Periodically they built altars on which they offered sacrifices. That the patriarchal community was very large can be seen from Genesis 14:14, which says that Abraham had 318 armed men

in his camp. If one assumes that most of the men were married and had one or more children each, the total extended family may have numbered in excess of 1000.

Additional developments in the life of Abraham and Jacob were particularly important for world history. Abraham, frustrated at not having an heir, accepted Sarah's suggestion, which was also the custom of the land, to obtain an heir by the slave girl Hagar. This he decided to do, and the son born was named Ishmael, progenitor of the Arabs. Thus Abraham is revered by Arabs and Muslims as he is by Jews and Christians. He is the father of the Jews through his son Isaac, child of promise. He holds a special place in Christianity as an example of justification by faith and as the ancestor of Christ, through whom all Christians obtain their salvation.

Jacob, a scheming scoundrel in his earlier years, wound up in exile in northern Mesopotamia for 20 years in the home of his Uncle Laban. There he married Leah and Rachel and fathered the sons who became the progenitors of the 12 tribes of Israel. On his return to Palestine he met God along the banks of the Jabbok River (Gn 32) and God changed his name to Israel ("prince with God").

The patriarchal period in Canaan lasted for 215 years. One estimate places Abraham's entry into Canaan about 2085 BC, when he was 75 years of age. Jacob and his sons migrated to Egypt to escape a severe famine in Canaan in about 1870 BC. During much of the patriarchal period Palestine experienced a decline in population and was occupied largely by nomadic or seminomadic tribes. It was relatively easy for the Hebrews to enter such a situation. After 1900 Palestine began to enjoy more settled conditions. Shortly after the Hebrews made the trek into Egypt.

Sojourn in Egypt. If Jacob and his sons entered Egypt about 1870 BC, it was the period of the Middle Kingdom. And by that time other migrants from Asia were coming in increasing numbers. The Hebrews settled in Goshen, in the eastern delta region, under the protecting care of Joseph, who held a position at the Egyptian court roughly equivalent to that of prime minister. As more and more Asiatic Hyksos came into Egypt, they began to take over the country—northern Egypt at least. During this same time the Hebrews became increasingly numerous. Some who hold to a different chronology believe the Hebrews were welcomed into Egypt during the days of Hyksos domination (after 1750 BC). At any rate, about 1580 BC native Egyptian princes regained control of the country and expelled many of the Asiatics.

In process of time there arose a king over

Egypt "who knew not Joseph" (Ex 1:8 KJV). Very possibly this meant that a native Egyptian dynasty had arisen in Egypt and they were apprehensive over the fact that the growing numbers and wealth of the Hebrews might jeopardize their own supremacy. Egyptian measures to subjugate the Hebrews and reduce their birth rate had a reverse effect (v 12). Finally, the Egyptians ordered the killing of all male Hebrew infants at birth. Among those who disobeyed were the parents of Moses, who set him afloat in a waterproof basket made of reeds. Found by a daughter of Pharaoh, he was brought up in the Egyptian court, was given a first-class education, and became a high official of the realm.

At the age of 40, Moses identified himself with his own people. He killed an Egyptian in defense of a fellow Hebrew, and immediately fled to the land of Midian in the northeastern part of the Sinai Peninsula. He married and lived there for 40 years, becoming thoroughly familiar with the geography and the ways of the wilderness through which he would later lead the Hebrews. The Egyptians continued to oppress the Hebrew people severely until they cried urgently to God for deliverance. In response, God confronted Moses in the famous burning bush experience and called on him to return to Egypt and lead the people back into the land of Canaan (Ex 3,4). He was to have the help of his brother Aaron.

The Exodus. Understandably the pharaoh of Egypt was reluctant to permit the Hebrews to leave permanently. The value of this great labor force was incalculable. But finally, after suffering a series of 10 plagues, lasting perhaps a year, the Egyptians were persuaded to let the Hebrews go (Ex 7–12).

The plagues had a theological as well as a practical purpose. They discredited the gods of Egypt and exalted the most high God of heaven (Ex 12:12). The plagues clearly discredited specific gods of Egypt (e.g., the Nile was worshiped as Hapi, plague 1; the frog, worshiped as Heqt, plague 2; the bull, worshiped as Ptah, plague 5; the sun, worshiped as Amon-Re, Aton, plague 9), and taken together they struck a direct blow at the Egyptian pantheon.

Just before the last plague, which was the night in which the death angel invaded the homes of the Egyptians, the Israelites made the Passover sacrifice according to divine instructions. This involved slaying a lamb for each household (unless the household was too small; in that event, households could combine). Anyone who was careless about applying the blood to the doorpost or who rejected this divine provision came under the judgment of God. After the death of the firstborn throughout the land, the Egyptians begged the Hebrews to leave. Their company numbered 600,000 men over 20 years of age, plus women and children, for a total of over 2,500,000. In addition they took their flocks and herds and personal belongings.

When they left is a matter of continuing debate. Traditionally a date of 1440 BC is given for the exodus (e.g., 1 Kgs 6:1, which places the exodus 480 years before the dedication of the temple in 966 BC) and 1400 BC for the conquest under Joshua, and there do not seem to be any compelling arguments for rejecting that position. But a great many prefer 1275 BC for a variety of reasons.

The early date of the exodus would place the later years of the wilderness wanderings and the subsequent conquest of Palestine during the reigns of Amenhotep III and IV (1412–1366), a time when the pharaohs allowed Egyptian control of Palestine to disintegrate.

The Sinai Peninsula, to which Moses fled after he killed the Egyptian.

When the Egyptians did reassert their power, about 1300, they restricted their movements largely to the coastal area, and thus did not come in contact with the Hebrews who were living in the hill country of Judea, Samaria, and Galilee.

Wilderness Wanderings. The wilderness wanderings were an important interlude in the history of Israel. During those years significant and basic institutions came into existence at God's command. At Sinai, Moses delivered to Israel the Law, the pattern of the tabernacle (which later became the model for the temple) and orders for its operation, as well as detailed instructions for the priesthood and sacrificial system of worship.

The period of the wanderings was truly a remarkable time. The presence of God was evidenced by a pillar of cloud that hovered over the people by day and a pillar of fire by night. God provided food in the form of manna, periodically provided water by miraculous means, and arranged that clothes did not wear out. In spite of all that, the people murmured and complained continually.

At Sinai, God gave the Law (Ex 19:2–24:18), and the people promptly made a commitment to keep it (24:3). Then God gave the pattern for the tabernacle and its furniture (chs 24–27,30,31,35–40) and established the priesthood (chs 28,29). While Moses was on the mountain receiving God's revelation, the people grew restless and clamored for gods they could see. Even Aaron was carried away with the idolatrous wave and supervised the casting of a golden calf and building an altar before it. The fact that they turned to Egyptian cattle worship so readily indicates that paganism must have made deep inroads among them while in captivity (chs 32–34). Moses' intercessory response to God's announcement that he would destroy Israel because of her idolatry led to a divine determination to execute judgment on only the worst offenders.

Subsequently God revealed the legal and priestly order (Lv 1:1–27:34). Among the divinely appointed institutions described or alluded to in Leviticus are several special days or feasts, including the sabbath, Passover, harvest or firstfruits, Pentecost or feast of weeks, feast of trumpets, day of atonement, feast of tabernacles, sabbatical year, and the year of jubilee.

After camping at Sinai for about a year, the Israelites got their orders to go forward. Miriam (Moses' sister) and Aaron rebelled against Moses' leadership and suffered divine punishment in consequence (Nm 12). When the people arrived at Kadesh-barnea, at the gate to southern Palestine, they were frightened by the majority report of their spies who had been reconnoitering in Canaan and decided that they should not advance into Canaan. They called for a new leader to bring them back to Egypt. God declared that the entire generation would wander in the wilderness until the adults had died. Only Joshua and Caleb (the two spies in favor of invading immediately) would enter the Promised Land. Near the end of the period of wandering, Moses also lost the privilege of entering the land by an act of disobedience (20:10–13).

The Conquest. The latter part of the Book of Numbers describes how Moses led the Israelites to victory over the peoples living east of the Jordan River. Reuben, Gad, and the half-tribe of Manasseh requested permission to settle there and reluctantly were allowed to do so on the condition they would join the rest of the Israelites in conquering Canaan before settling down. Prior to victories in Transjordan, a new census of adult males was taken, in order to determine the military capabilities of Israel and to provide a basis for equitable division of the land they were about to enter. The number of males above 20 years of age was 601,730 (Nm 26:51). The Book of Deuteronomy consists primarily of a series of speeches delivered by Moses in a covenant renewal ceremony on the plains of Moab just before his death, and the appointment of Joshua as leader.

Joshua lost no time in moving forward. Spies sent across the Jordan to Jericho to reconnoiter reported a situation quite different from what the Hebrews had experienced at Kadesh-barnea a generation earlier. Now the people of Canaan were terrified because they had heard of the numerical strength and victories of the Hebrews. Apparently the day after the spies returned, Joshua moved the people to the edge of the Jordan and prepared to cross over. The waters parted for them here as the Red Sea had parted earlier.

The narrative of conquest that appears in the Book of Joshua is not a detailed battle account. It describes a thrust into the middle of Palestine around Jericho and Ai, a southerly drive to defeat the Amorite league, and a northern campaign against Hazor and other towns. The history of Joshua is extremely telescoped, for his major military action must have required about 6 years. Joshua's friend Caleb was 79 when the conquest began and 85 after the last great battle with Jabin, king of Hazor (Jos 14:7,10).

When the war was over, major strongholds (e.g., Jerusalem) still remained in enemy hands, but the land west of the Jordan was allocated to the nine and one-half Hebrew tribes. The task of reducing enemy towns was left to the individual tribes in whose land they were located. The Joshua account was not so much a narrative of Israelite battle prowess as of God's faithfulness and intervention on behalf of his people. For example, at Jericho they did not attack but merely followed divine orders and watched the defenses collapse; at Gibeon hailstones killed more Amorites than Israelite soldiers did (Jos 10).

The Judges. Joshua died some 30 years after he had led the Hebrews into Canaan, and he was followed by a series of divinely appointed leaders who ruled, sometimes over the whole of Israel as a loose confederacy, and sometimes over one or more tribes. They were judges, civil functionaries, and military leaders, all at the same time. Their authority was not very strong; "every man did that which was right in his own eyes" (Jgs 17:6; 21:25).

The Book of Judges pictures a series of recurring cycles: apostasy from God, punishment in the form of oppression by neighboring tribes, cries to God for relief, release from bondage under the leadership of a judge, and a period of rest from oppression.

Establishment of the chronology of the judges is one of the thorniest problems of Scripture. Adding up all years of oppression and rest mentioned in the book gives a total of 410. The Book of Acts gives a total of 450 years from the days of Joshua to Samuel (Acts 13:20). The difference in Acts may be accounted for by the addition of the 40 years of Eli's ministry (1 Sm 4:18). Allowing 410 years for the period of the judges, about 30 for the conquest, and 40 for the wilderness wanderings, means 480 years from 1050 BC, the date for Saul's kingship, and would give a date of about 1530 for the exodus. This is about 100 years more than even the early date for the exodus. The most probable explanation is that there is some overlap in oppressions and judgeships. For instance, the activities of Jephthah were centered on the eastern frontier, those of Samson in the Philistine plain in the southwest, and those of Deborah and Barak in the north.

The United Monarchy. Because of the weakness of Israel resulting from political disunity and the ineptness and corruption of both Eli's and Samuel's sons, the people of Israel called for a king to rule over them. This demand was in reality a rejection of the divine plan of theocracy—the rule of God. God granted the Hebrews' wish but warned them of the disadvantages of monarchy (1 Sm 8:9–21). The concept of kingship was not new to Israel. It had been hinted at in Genesis 49:10 and Numbers 24:17, and Moses had made some very clear statements about it in Deuteronomy 17:14–20.

The first stage of Hebrew monarchy is commonly called the united monarchy because all Israel was ruled by a single king. This period lasted for 120 years—encompassing the 40-year reigns of Saul (Acts 13:21), David (2 Sm 5:5), and Solomon (1 Kgs 11:42).

The people asked for a king, and God granted them one, but not one like those of the surrounding nations. The Hebrew king was to be a man who followed God's dictates in his public and private life, who did not intrude into the affairs of the priesthood, and who did not fall into idolatry but exerted all his influence to keep the people faithful to God. If he failed in any of these respects, he ran the risk of being deposed by God, of having his line brought to an end, or even of having the people fall into captivity to a foreign power. All this must be kept in mind when evaluating the reigns of Saul, David, Solomon, and the kings of the divided monarchy.

Saul (c. 1020–1000 BC) began well. He won a great victory over the Ammonites at Jabesh-gilead and showed considerable wisdom in administrative matters. But after about two years he intruded into the priest's office to offer sacrifice, bringing the divine prediction that his kingdom would be taken from him. But he went on to enjoy great military victory, and was apparently an able ruler until about the middle of his reign.

After Saul's disobedience to God's command to destroy the Amalekites, the Lord repudiated Saul and instructed Samuel to anoint David privately as future king of Israel. David's rise to prominence was spurred by his victory over Goliath and the accompanying defeat of the Philistines. Saul later made David commander of the army, and the young man soon earned a reputation greater than that of the king himself. Saul, who had become increasingly mentally disturbed after his relationship with God was broken, began to make attempts on David's life, and for the last years of Saul's reign David lived as a fugitive. Meanwhile the Philistines got completely out of control and finally killed Saul and most of his sons in the great battle of Mt Gilboa, which gave the Philistines control over much of Palestine west of the Jordan.

Soon David became king in Judah with his capital in Hebron. A son of Saul, Ish-bosheth, established himself at Mahanaim, east of the Jordan. For seven years the two tiny kingdoms existed side by side. But after the Israelite king and his army commander were assassinated, David became ruler of a united Hebrew kingdom.

Not long after the beginning of his reign (1000–961) David completely defeated and subjugated the Philistines. Soon thereafter he captured Jerusalem, making it the capital of the united kingdom. During succeeding years David built up an empire (2 Sm 8,10; 1 Chr 18,19), conquering Moab, Edom, Damascus, Zobah and Hamath, and Ammon. So he controlled territory from the Gulf of Aqaba (branch of the Red Sea) and the Sinai in the south almost to the Euphrates in the north. Moreover, he established good relations, if not an alliance, with Tyre.

The establishment of David's empire was possible because of a power vacuum in the Middle East. The Egyptians, Myceneans, Hittites, and Assyrians were either decadent or removed from the stage of history. The Phoenicians, a peaceful commercial people, were also free to expand their trade, and they were happy to sell cedar to David for his palace and the temple.

Without doubt, David was Israel's greatest king. Jerusalem came to be known as the city of David. When the king wanted to build the temple as a house for God, God replied that his son should do it instead. But God would in a very real sense build David's house; he made a covenant with David, promising him that his house (dynasty, kingdom, throne) would be established forever (2 Sm 7). Christ, the infinite One who came from the line of David, alone was capable of fulfilling this divine promise (see Lk 1:31–33; Acts 2:29–36; 13:32–39; 15:14–17).

Like other oriental monarchs, David fell into the practice of keeping a harem. Scripture names eight wives and 21 children and refers to other wives and concubines. Such a situation opened the door to family rivalries and questions about succession to the throne. Two sons, Absalom and Adonijah, made a try for the throne; but both efforts were squelched and Solomon, son of David's favorite wife Bathsheba, became the next king.

Solomon (970–930 BC) was a man of peace and a builder of palaces, cities, fortifications, and the temple. He fortified cities all over his realm and outfitted cities for his chariot corps and cavalry units. With the help of the

Solomon's pillars near modern Eilat.

Phoenicians he built a seaport and kept a fleet at Ezion-geber, near modern Eilat on the Gulf of Aqaba. He greatly enlarged Jerusalem by enclosing the temple area to the north of David's city and the southwestern hill now known as Zion. His best-known project was the temple, which took 7 years to build. Just twice the size of the tabernacle, it was built on the same basic plan; it measured 90 feet long and 30 feet wide and had magnificent appointments. But he also constructed a palace complex that took 13 years to complete. This included an armory, a throne room, the king's private residence, and a house for the daughter of pharaoh.

Apparently much influenced by the spiritual testimony of David and desiring God's blessing on his rule, Solomon made a great sacrifice to God at Gibeon near the beginning of his reign. God met him there and offered to grant whatever he might request. Solomon replied, "Give thy servant therefore an understanding mind to govern thy people" (1 Kgs 3:9). His God-given wisdom is apparent in many administrative decisions and official policies and building plans.

Unfortunately, Solomon did not show such wisdom in maintaining a harem of 700 wives and 300 concubines or in excessive expenditures that left the state in serious financial straits. He even erected places of worship for his foreign wives, thus subsidizing their idolatries and incurring the wrath of God. In fact, foreign wives and their idolatry proved to be his downfall; before Solomon died, God informed him that for this reason he would divide the kingdom at his death and give most of it to someone other than Solomon's son. But for David's sake, God would keep Judah and Jerusalem in the hands of the Davidic line (1 Kgs 11:9–13).

The Divided Kingdom. After the death of Solomon the Near East was destined to become a very different place. Israel was no longer in a power vacuum. The Assyrian Empire rose in Mesopotamia, to be followed by the Neo-Babylonian and the Medo-Persian empires in turn. Egypt was temporarily powerful in the south, but it would later come under control of Assyria and Medo-Persia. These empires exerted great pressure on Israel and dominated one or both of the two Hebrew kingdoms.

When Solomon died, his son Rehoboam took the throne and was forced to deal with a rising tide of resentment over the high taxes and economic stagnation of Solomon's last years. When Rehoboam refused to give relief, all the northern tribes broke away and formed the northern kingdom, Israel, under the leadership of Jeroboam. The southern kingdom, Ju-

Kings and Prophets of the Divided Kingdom

Judah		Israel	
Prophets	**Kings**	**Kings**	**Prophets**
Shemaiah (1 Kgs 12:22–24; 2 Chr 11:2–4; 12:5–8,15) Iddo (2 Chr 9:29; 12:15)	Rehoboam	Jeroboam I	Ahijah (1 Kgs 11:29–39; 12:15; 14:1–18; 15:29; 2 Chr 9:29; 10:15) Anonymous "man of God" (1 Kgs 13:1–32)
Iddo (2 Chr 13:22) Azariah (2 Chr 15:1–7) Hanani (2 Chr 16:7–10)	Abijah (m) Asa	Nadab Baasha	Jehu (1 Kgs 16:1–4,7,12)
		Elah Zimri Tibni Omni Ahab	Elijah (1 Kgs 17–2 Kgs 2:12)
Jehu (2 Chr 19:1–3; 20:34) Jahaziel (2 Chr 20:14–17) Eliezer (2 Chr 20:37)	Jehoshaphat		Micaiah (1 Kgs 22:7–28) Anonymous "son of the prophets" (1 Kgs 20:35–42)
		Ahaziah	Elijah Elisha
		Jehoram [Joram]	Elisha (2 Kgs 2–8)
Elijah (2 Chr 21:12–15) Joel Zechariah (2 Chr 24:20–22)	Jehoram [Joram] Ahaziah Athaliah Jehoash [Joash]	Jehu	Elisha (2 Kgs 9,10)
		Jehoahaz Jehoash [Joash]	Elisha Elisha (2 Kgs 13:10–25)
Joel	Amaziah	Jeroboam II	Jonah (2 Kgs 14:25) Amos (1:1) Hosea (1:1)
Joel Zechariah (2 Chr 26:5) Isaiah (2:2; 6:1)	Uzziah [Azariah]	Zechariah Shallum Menahem Pekahiah	
Isaiah (1:1)/Micah (1:1)	Jotham	Pekah	Oded (2 Chr 28:9–15) Isaiah (7–9)
Isaiah (1:1,7)/Micah (1:1)	Ahaz		
Isaiah (1:1)/Micah (1:1)	Hezekiah Manasseh Amon	Hoshea	
Nahum/Habakkuk Huldah (2 Kgs 22:14–20) Zephaniah Jeremiah	Josiah		
Jeremiah Jeremiah Uriah (Jer 26:20–23) Jeremiah	Jehoahaz Jehoiakim		
Jeremiah	Jehoiachin Zedekiah		

dah, was left with only the territory of Judah and Benjamin. In each of the separate kingdoms there were 20 kings. While the north had several dynasties and the reigns of kings were generally short, in the south the dynasty of David continued to rule and the reigns were longer.

The Northern Kingdom. The northern kingdom lasted from the division in 931 BC until its conquest by Assyria in 722. Jeroboam, fearing that he would lose the loyalty of the people if they continued to go to Jerusalem to worship, set up a new religion of his own. Instituting calf worship, he built shrines at Dan in the north and Bethel in the south. This idolatry drew the condemnation of God and the prediction that Jeroboam's line would be wiped out. All his successors are said to have followed in his idolatrous steps. Israel found itself at war during much of its history—with Judah, Syria, or Assyria. Jeroboam established his capital first at Shechem and later at Tirzah.

Four other kings of the north require special comment: Omri, Ahab, Jehu, and Jeroboam II. Omri (885–874 BC) must have been an impressive ruler. Generations later Assyrians still spoke of Israel as the "land of Omri." After he had established himself on the throne, he located the permanent capital of the kingdom at Samaria and began the palace complex there. Early in his reign he was successful in conquering Moab, and later he reestablished the good relations with Tyre that existed in the days of David and Solomon. Apparently he established a full alliance and cemented it with the marriage of his son Ahab to Jezebel, a princess of Tyre.

Ahab (874–853 BC) was one of the most significant of Israel's kings. He and his wife Jezebel promoted the vile idolatry of Baal worship with its religious prostitution, arousing the powerful opposition of the prophet Elijah. Ahab was a formidable military man, defeating the Syrians in major campaigns and participating in a coalition that fought the Assyrians to a virtual standstill. He also built extensively at Samaria, Hazor, Megiddo, and other towns, as excavations show.

Jehu (841–814 BC) was God's agent for punishing the house of Omri and destroying Baal worship in Israel. He did eradicate Baal worship and liquidated literally scores of relatives and court officials of Ahab. But he was so ruthless that he killed off the people who knew how to run the government; subsequently it did not work well. Jehu also was forced to become a vassal to Assyria.

Jeroboam II ruled during most of the first half of the 8th century (793–753 BC) and brought the kingdom to its greatest extent and prosperity. He, with his contemporary Uzziah in the south, ruled most of the land David had once controlled. This was possible because the Assyrians were in a period of decline during most of the first half of the century.

Prophets who were active during the history of the northern kingdom include nonwriting prophets, Elijah and Elisha, and writing prophets, Jonah and Hosea.

The Southern Kingdom. The history of the southern kingdom of Judah was quite different from that of the northern kingdom. The temple was there and so were large numbers of Levites, many of whom came south after the division of the kingdom in protest against the idolatry of the north. In addition to this spiritual strength, there was greater political stability and unity, promoted by the fact that only two tribes—Judah and Benjamin—shared power, and all the kings were of the Davidic dynasty. Moreover, eight of the kings were good monarchs. There were also periodic religious revivals. God granted the southern

kingdom about 100 more years of existence than the north. But Judah too fell into idolatry and went into captivity for her sins.

Rehoboam, first king in the south, is especially remembered because he refused to listen to wise counsel about fiscal matters and perpetrated the division of the kingdom. He is also remembered for his religious policies. After a good beginning, he allowed apostasy to get out of control and brought the judgment of God in the form of an invasion in his fifth year (926 BC) by Shishak I of Egypt, resulting in extensive plunder and payment of tribute. Thereafter he launched an extensive program to fortify the realm. Shishak's invasion did have the effect of producing a partial and temporary spiritual reform, but the general trend of Rehoboam's reign was downward.

Conditions during the reign of his son, Abijam, were worse, but Asa (910–869 BC) initiated a religious reform that was effective for most of his reign. When threatened by the northern kingdom during his latter years, however, Asa turned to Syria for help instead of to God, and he seems to have defied the prophets of God to his dying day.

Asa's son Jehoshaphat (872–848 BC), was apparently influenced by his father's early religious devotion, and his reign was characterized by faithfulness, winning the favor of God. However, he seems to have made a full alliance with Ahab of Israel, which resulted in the marriage of his son Jehoram to Ahab's daughter Athaliah. This alliance involved Jehoshaphat in almost ruinous joint ventures with Ahab, and later with two of his sons when they became kings of Israel. It also opened the door for the introduction of Baal worship into Judah when Jehoram came to the throne in the southern kingdom. For his sin Jehoram (853–841) suffered internal revolt, invasion, and death from a horrible disease.

After his death, his last remaining son, Ahaziah, ruled less than a year, following the wicked ways of his father. When Ahaziah died in battle, the queen mother Athaliah decided to seize the throne for herself and to secure her power by killing off all those in line to the throne. But she missed Ahaziah's infant son Joash, who was kept hidden in the temple for six years.

When Joash was seven, Jehoida the high priest arranged his coronation and also for the execution of the murderous and idolatrous Athaliah. During his early years when Joash was influenced by good counsel, he did well. But after the middle of his reign (835–796 BC) he began to listen to the princes who wanted to restore idolatry, and conditions deteriorated.

Military reversals brought on economic decline and ultimately the king's assassination.

His son Amaziah (796–767 BC) started well with victory over Edom and faithfulness to God. But he too fell into idolatry and was totally defeated by the northern kingdom, being held prisoner there. At that point his son Uzziah took over (c. 792 BC) and began a long and generally successful reign. During the several decades that followed, Assyria was in decline, and Uzziah and his contemporary in the north, Jeroboam II, were able to expand Hebrew holdings so that between them they controlled most of the territory Solomon had ruled.

Uzziah (792–740 BC) was able to restore the power of Judah rather quickly after his father's defeat by Israel. Then he subjugated the Philistines in the southwest, the Ammonites across the Jordan, and strengthened his hold on the Edomites. All during his reign economic conditions improved. But at the height of his power Uzziah foolishly violated the high priest's prerogatives and offered sacrifice in the temple. For this he was smitten with leprosy; his son Jotham was co-regent during the years 750–735 BC, going on to rule alone for about five more years. Meanwhile, Assyrian power became resurgent.

By and large Jotham merely carried on the policies of Uzziah. But the administration of his son Ahaz (735–715 BC) was very much affected by the Assyrian threat. Israel and Syria wanted him to join in war against Assyria but he refused, being pro-Assyrian in sympathy. When Israel and Syria invaded Judah, King Ahaz sent tribute to Assyria and became her vassal in return for protection. This rash course of action was vainly opposed by Isaiah, who was prophet at court (c. 740–700 BC). Contemporaneously the prophet Micah ministered to the common people of Judah. The pro-Assyrian policy of Ahaz was accompanied by a renewed sympathy for idolatry, and this brought the judgment of God in the form of invasion by Edomites and Philistines and trouble with Assyria. In fact, during this period Assyria had annexed the northern kingdom (722 BC) and removed many of her people into captivity.

The next king of Judah, Hezekiah (715–686), was greatly sobered by the fall of Israel because of her sins, and he determined to launch a reform in his realm. He was anti-Assyrian too, but he did not dare to discontinue tribute payments and strike for independence until after Sennacherib came to the throne in Nineveh in 705 BC. At first Sennacherib was too preoccupied to attend to Judah, but finally in 701 he invaded. Despite tremendous initial success, he was stopped by a divinely sent plague before the walls of Jerusalem (Is 36–39). Isaiah stood by the king to reassure and sustain him during this emergency.

Hezekiah's son Manasseh (696–642 BC) ruled longer than any other king of Israel or Judah. Unfortunately he turned his back on his father's example and caused the people to fall into gross idolatry (2 Kgs 21:9). Carried away captive by the Assyrians late in his reign, he repented of his evil and God restored him to his throne; thereafter he led some reforms. But the land was too steeped in iniquity to be rescued. His son Amon (642–640) reverted to the idolatry he knew in his youth.

The situation was different with Josiah (640–609 BC), however. Throughout his reign he dedicated himself to reform. He sought to root out idolatry and to restore the temple and its worship. In 621 the Book of the Law was found during repair of the temple, and its demands—which had been forgotten—made a great impression on king and people alike. It is certain that Jeremiah and Zephaniah ministered during Josiah's reign, and probably Nahum and Habakkuk as well.

International conditions were now changing rapidly. Assyria was declining, and Nineveh fell to Babylon and the Medes in 612 BC. Three years later Pharaoh Neco of Egypt marched north to aid his Assyrian ally. When Josiah tried to stop him he was killed in battle.

From this point everything was downhill for Judah. None of the rest of the kings was devout, and political power and economic health rapidly declined. The people put one of Josiah's sons, Jehoahaz, on the throne. He lasted three months. Pharaoh Neco replaced him with Jehoiakim (609–598 BC), another son of Josiah. In 605 Nebuchadnezzar of Babylon defeated Neco, invaded Judah, and took tribute and hostages from Jehoiakim—including Daniel and his friends (Dn 1:1). Jehoiakim revolted in 600, but Nebuchadnezzar did not come to deal with him personally until 597 BC. He died before the Babylonians arrived; and his son Jehoiachin came to the throne to rule for only three months before the Babylonians carried him away into exile. Ezekiel was among the many captives taken on that occasion.

The Babylonians then put Zedekiah, youngest son of Josiah, on the throne. When he rebelled, Nebuchadnezzar laid siege to Jerusalem and took the city (587 BC), destroying it and the temple and carrying off large numbers of people. The judgment of God had finally fallen on the Jews for their idolatrous ways.

The Restoration. But in judgment God remembered mercy. This is evident in individ-

The Hill of Ophel, with a section of Nehemiah's wall (built in 444 BC) at the right.

ual lives, when faithful ones like Daniel, Esther, or Nehemiah rose to a position of importance in political life, or as numerous other persons became prosperous in the alien environment. It is evident on the community level as God moved to protect Hebrew enclaves scattered abroad and to restore an organized society in Palestine.

Among the exiles Judaism as a way of life separated from its own political system or cultic center and began to emerge. Jews finally turned their backs on idolatry. And without a temple, priesthood, king, or land, they turned to the divine Word as their rallying point and the foundation of their community. During this period they developed the synagogue as a place for fellowship, prayer, and Bible study.

God's restoration of an organized community to Palestine involved particularly the fortunes of his "anointed" Cyrus (Is 44:28; 45:1). Cyrus was a Persian prince who in 559 BC revolted against the dominant dynasty controlling the Medean Empire. After consolidating his hold on the throne, he proceeded to conquer Asia Minor and the Chaldean, or Neo-Babylonian Empire. As a humane man and a wise administrator, he permitted the captive peoples to return to their homes and rebuild their communities. Cyrus' decree to the Jews appears in Ezra 1 and dates probably to 538

BC. A total of almost 50,000 went back to Judah as a result of this edict (Ezr 2:64–65).

Under the stresses and strains of reestablishment, the people built their houses but got no farther than laying the foundation of a new temple. Finally the prophets Haggai and Zechariah stirred the people to build the house of God (Ezr 5:1). They began in the second year of Darius I the Great (521 BC; Hg 1:1; Zec 1:1) and completed the work in his sixth year (515; Ezr 6:15).

During the reign of Darius' son Xerxes (485–465), a plot was hatched to exterminate all the Jews in the Persian Empire, which at that time controlled the lands where Jews lived. Fortunately Xerxes (Ahasuerus in the Book of Esther) in his third year (483 BC; Est 1:3) went searching for a new queen and chose Esther, who managed to preserve her people.

Xerxes' son Artaxerxes I (464–424) also figured significantly in Jewish history. In his seventh year (458 BC; Ezr 7:7) a second contingent of Jews returned to Jerusalem under the leadership of Ezra. And in Xerxes' 20th year (445 BC; Neh 2:1), Nehemiah went to Jerusalem to supervise rebuilding the walls of the city. Malachi probably wrote his prophecy during the latter part of Artaxerxes' reign.

After the fall of Samaria and the captivity of Judah, the Hebrews remaining in the land intermarried with various pagan groups in the area. Their offspring became the Samaritans, a religious and racial admixture. These people had moved into the vacuum left by the destruction of Judah, and naturally they looked with disfavor on an intrusion of Babylonian Jews into an area they had come to call their own. They did all they could to frustrate the efforts of Nehemiah to rebuild the walls. It took all the courage, tact, energy, and persuasiveness Ezra and Nehemiah could muster to prevent the returning Jews from intermarrying with the racially mixed people of the land. Such intermarriage would have meant the ultimate absorption and destruction of the Jewish people.

A Samaritan temple was later built on Mt Gerizim (probably during the 4th century BC), and it became the center of the Samaritan worship. The hostility between Samaritans and Jews continued on into the NT period (Jn 4) and exists to the present.

The Intertestamental Period. Alexander the Great conquered the Persian Empire with lightning speed. When the people of Jerusalem threw open their gates in 332 BC and capitulated without a fight, Alexander treated them well. After his death in 323 BC, Palestine passed back and forth among his successors until Ptolemy I of Egypt managed to establish control in 301 BC. Thereafter the area remained in Egyptian hands until 198. The Ptolemies were tolerant and granted the Jews considerable autonomy, allowing them to develop their unique culture undisturbed as long as they paid their taxes and remained submissive. Many Jews settled in Alexandria and gradually forgot their Hebrew in the Hellenistic environment. As a result, a translation of the OT into Greek (the Septuagint) was produced there. While the Ptolemies did not force Hellenism on the Jews of either Alexandria or

Cartouche from the Rosetta Stone containing the word "ptolemy."

Palestine, many were influenced by Hellenistic ideas.

When Ptolemy V came to the throne as a minor in 203 BC, Antiochus III of Syria took advantage of the weakened Egypt and conquered Palestine (198). Apparently the Jews hoped to gain something from the change and welcomed the Syrians. But their hope was ill-founded. Antiochus III suffered disastrous defeat at the hands of Rome at Magnesia in 190 BC. Syria not only lost much territory but also was forced to pay a huge indemnity. Thereafter the Jews suffered under great financial burdens, along with all other peoples of the empire. The next Syrian king, Antiochus IV Epiphanes (175–164 BC), decided to launch an effort to achieve greater internal strength and unity within the empire by forcing, among other things, a greater acceptance of Greek culture and the cult of the divine ruler. Naturally this idolatrous requirement weighed heavily on the monotheistic Jews.

But this does not completely explain the Maccabean revolt against Syria. In 168 armed conflict broke out between Jewish factions in Jerusalem. Antiochus IV chose to interpret this as open rebellion and sent an army against the city. His forces demolished part of the city wall and many houses. After this Antiochus decided to suppress Judaism completely, and he dedicated the temple to Zeus and sacrificed swine on the altar. Circumcision, sabbath observance, and other religious festivals were no longer permitted, and public worship of heathen gods became compulsory.

Some Jews capitulated to Antiochus' orders or only resisted passively, but a few decided to resist openly. Chief among them were Mattathias and his five sons. After the early death of Mattathias, his son Judas Maccabeus led his forces to victory over the Syrians, regaining the right to restore Jewish worship. The rededication of the temple on December 25, 165 BC, inaugurated the festival of Hanukkah. Subsequently Jonathan and Simon (other sons of Mattathias) continued the struggle until independence was gained in 142; this was possible in large part because they saw how to take advantage of the increasing weakness of Syrian rulers and the competition for the royal office.

Simon ruled the Jewish state until his assassination in 135 BC when his son John Hyrcanus (135–104) took over. John Hyrcanus fought successfully in the east, north, and south, gaining land in Transjordan, capturing Shechem and the Samaritan temple on Mt Gerizim, and subjugating the Idumeans in the south and forcing them to adopt Judaism. His son Aristobulus ruled for only about a year (104–103), but he added a portion of Galilee to the kingdom.

When he died, his widow married his brother Alexander Jannaeus (103–76 BC). Jannaeus carried on almost incessant military action during his reign, and by the time of his death had almost recovered the kingdom of Solomon.

When Jannaeus died, Alexandra, widow of two kings, took the throne (76–69 BC) and her eldest son Hyrcanus II became high priest. Her reign was peaceful and prosperous; but when she died, her sons fell to squabbling. Their appeals to Pompey, who was campaigning in the eastern Mediterranean area, were responsible for Roman interference in the region and their conquest of Palestine in 63 BC.

The Roman Period. After the Romans took over Palestine, Hyrcanus II was confirmed as high priest and was appointed as ethnarch, or political ruler (63–40 BC). Antipater, father of Herod the Great, was the real power behind the throne, and during many of those years Hyrcanus was virtually unable to function because of the confusion of the Roman civil wars. Antipater was loyal to Rome and saw that Roman policies were carried out, and he won Julius Caesar's favor toward Jews of both Palestine and in the dispersion.

With the support of Mark Antony, Herod managed to get himself appointed king of the Jews by the Roman senate in 40 BC. But Parthian invasion of Syria and Jewish hatred for the Romans made it possible for Antigonus II to rule for three years (40–37). Finally Herod ascended his throne in 37 and ruled until 4 BC. As an allied king, Herod proved to be an excellent ruler from the Roman point of view and earned the title of "Great." He brought some order to regions east of the Jordan and made possible organization of the Roman province of Arabia. He also furthered the cultural plans of Augustus for development of a Greco-Roman civilization throughout the whole empire.

Herod admired Greek culture and contributed to building projects in Rhodes, Antioch, Damascus, Athens, and elsewhere outside Palestine. Within Palestine he rebuilt Samaria and named it Sebaste in honor of Augustus (*Sebastos* is the Greek for "Augustus") and also constructed the great port of Caesarea. Probably about as large as Manhattan Island, it became the capital of Roman Palestine. Among his many other building projects, the temple in Jerusalem was the most famous. Begun in 20 BC, it was not completed until just a few years before its destruction in AD 70.

The material splendor of Herod's reign did not win him the affection or support of the Jews, however. Nor did he achieve peace and harmony in his family, among whom there were periodic eruptions of treason, unfaithfulness, and murder. He worried about any

threat to his rule and cracked down hard to destroy such threats, as is evident from his slaughter of the infants in Bethlehem after the birth of Christ.

Ultimately Herod controlled Idumaea, Judea, Samaria, Galilee, Perea, and the area northeast of the Sea of Galilee. By his last will, his son Archelaus was to rule Idumaea, Judea, and Galilee; Antipas, Galilee and Perea; and Philip, the region northeast of the Sea of Galilee. Archelaus was deposed in AD 6, and his territory became a Roman province (AD 6–41) to be ruled by direct appointees of Rome. The best-known of these was Pontius Pilate (AD 26–36), who ordered the crucifixion of Jesus. Antipas was more successful and built a new capital at Tiberias, but he ran afoul of the emperor's good pleasure in AD 37 and was deposed. Philip was the most effective of the three and ruled until his death in AD 34. Philip's lands were given to Herod Agrippa I in AD 37; the holdings of Antipas were added later in the same year and in 41 Agrippa also received Samaria, Judea, and Idumaea.

Herod Agrippa I (AD 37–44) was the heir of the Maccabees (through his grandmother Mariamne, first wife of Herod the Great) and for this reason had the support of patriotic Jews and of the Pharisees for his observance of divine ordinances. But when he built a new north wall for Jerusalem and dabbled in foreign affairs, he aroused the suspicions of the Romans, and when he died in AD 44 they turned his kingdom into a Roman province.

As is clear from the Gospels, several sects had arisen in Palestine by Roman times and were active during the 1st century. The Zealots opposed Roman rule and advocated armed rebellion. Herodians supported the Herodian family and Roman power. The Pharisees were fanatically devoted to the Law and were supernaturalists in theological orientation. They were somewhat content to support Rome if given religious freedom, and they dominated the synagogues of the land. The Sadducees were antisupernaturalists, tended to collaborate with the ruling regime, and were dominant in the temple. Generally speaking, the literature of the intertestamental period and the popular mentality of the time tended to view the Messiah as a political deliverer who would free his people from foreign domination and set up a new independent kingdom.

Roman prefects ruled Palestine (AD 44–66). They had a knack for offending the religious scruples of the Jews and alienating them in other ways. With Felix (AD 51–60) began a constant tension between Jews and Romans which led to the first Jewish war (AD 66–70). While Paul was imprisoned in Caesarea (Acts 23:23–24:27) about 58–60, riots broke out there between Jews and Gentiles. Festus (AD 60–62; Acts 25) was an able administrator, but the situation was almost out of hand. After he died in office, there was virtual anarchy until his successor Albinus arrived (62–64). Totally incompetent and dishonest, Albinus was recalled in 64 and replaced by Florus (64–66). Florus was even worse, resorting to open robbery and bribery until there was no safety or justice in the land. Finally the Jews could take no more.

The spark that ignited the fires of rebellion was an anti-Semitic act by the Hellenistic population of Caesarea in AD 66. Soon riots spread to numerous cities, and Roman garrisons were massacred in several places. But unfortunately the Jews were not united, and in Jerusalem armed bands of Jews fought with each other for mastery. Vespasian was chosen to command the Roman army of some 60,000 to deal with the insurrection. He had subjugated most of Palestine by the time he was elevated to the imperial chair in AD 69 (after the death of Nero), and he left his son Titus in charge of completing operations. In August of AD 70 the walls of Jerusalem were breached, many of the people butchered, and the city and the temple leveled. Masada held out until AD 73. Palestine had been flattened by Roman might. Loss of life and property had been incalculable and indescribable.

Twice more the Jews were destined to fight disastrously against the Romans. Under Trajan's rule a rebellion of Jews broke out in Cyrenaica in AD 115 and spread rapidly to Cyprus, Egypt, Palestine, and Mesopotamia. In the beginning it was an outgrowth of agitation between the Jews and their Hellenistic neighbors, but it developed into a challenge to Roman authority. This was particularly true after the successes of Parthia on Rome's eastern frontier when there seemed to be some hope of success in throwing off the Roman yoke. Wherever Jews got the upper hand they perpetrated massacres, and the non-Semitic population retaliated in kind. Trajan ruthlessly suppressed the rebels and restored order everywhere except in Egypt; his successor Hadrian was left to accomplish that.

But Hadrian faced a new rebellion of his own, brought on by his law forbidding circumcision (which he considered to be inhumane) and his decision in AD 130 to rebuild Jerusalem as Aelia Capitolina and erect a temple to Jupiter on the site of the temple to Yahweh. The latter would not only profane the temple site but also would preclude any rebuilding of the Jewish temple.

Leader of the rebellion was Simeon, Prince of Israel, called Bar Kochba ("Son of the Star"). Both sides fought with such great feroc-

The monumental arch of Hadrian in Athens.

ity for over three years (AD 132–135) that the population of Judea was virtually exterminated. Jerusalem was rebuilt as a Roman colony, and Jews were forbidden to enter on pain of death. Even as late as the fourth century they were permitted to enter only once a year, on the anniversary of the destruction of the temple by Nebuchadnezzar. After the Bar Kochba revolt, Judaism retreated increasingly within the citadel of the written and oral law, thus separating itself from the Gentiles.

HOWARD F. VOS

See PATRIARCHS, PERIOD OF THE; EXODUS, THE; WILDERNESS WANDERINGS; CONQUEST AND ALLOTMENT OF THE LAND; SAUL #1; DAVID; SOLOMON; EXILE; CHRONOLOGY, OLD TESTAMENT; MOSES; ABRAHAM; ISRAEL, RELIGION OF; POSTEXILIC PERIOD, THE; JUDAISM; JEW; FIRST JEWISH REVOLT; TALMUD.

Bibliography. J. Bright, *A History of Israel*; F.F. Bruce, *Israel and the Nations*; R. de Vaux, *Early History of Israel*; M. Noth, *The History of Israel*; W.O.E. Oesterley and T.H. Robinson, *A History of Israel*, 2 vols; A.T. Olmstead, *History of Palestine and Syria to the Macedonian Conquest*; H.W. Robinson, *The History of Israel*; L.J. Wood, *Israel's United Monarchy*.

Israel, Religion of. Jewish conduct as related to God. It concerns the outward acts or forms by which men recognize and serve their deity. The term comes from the Latin *religio*, which originally referred to reverence for the gods, or the fear of the gods, rather than to a system of religious belief based upon revealed truth. It must be realized that the religion of Israel can and must be distinguished from the biblical theology of the OT. The latter portrays objectively the truths that God revealed prior to NT times, while Israel's religion, though based on these truths, is more subjective and portrays the feelings and acts of the ancient Hebrews in relation to their God. Israel's religion was based upon the Sinai covenant, with its advanced moral and spiritual ideals. Only in times of apostasy and outright Baal worship did her religious practices degenerate and become subject to condemnation.

Bases for Conduct. The religion of truly pious Israelites was based upon heart-feelings of commitment to their Lord. Some of the less godly Hebrews doubtless exercised faith in Jehovah's redeeming covenant without yielding their lives fully to him. But this was not true to the ideals of biblical religion.

Submission. The experience of the patriarch Jacob at Peniel (Gn 32) constitutes the most outstanding OT example of the submission that is basic to genuinely religious conduct. Twenty years before this event, Jacob is known to have been a believer; for God had renewed the patriarchal covenant with him and promised, "Behold, I am with you" (28:15). Yet in Jacob's dealings with Laban during the years that followed, his conduct continued to be marked by grasping and deceit— that is, until he was met by "a man" (the Angel of the Lord), who wrestled with him all night (32:24). Finally the angel touched his thigh and dislocated it (v 25); but Jacob, meanwhile, is said to have "prevailed with God" (v 28), which is the meaning of the name *Israel* that he then received. Scripture later explains that this wrestling was an external sign of the patriarch's inner struggle in prayer (Hos 12:4). The total picture would then be this: when a believer earnestly seeks God and yields up his life, "broken" in true submission to him, at this point he enters into the religious experience with which God would confront each of his people (Ps 51:17).

Consecration. The surrendered life, which distinguishes the religion of Israel, was one of activity and purpose. Devotion to the duty at hand is the theme of the words of Nehemiah, at the close of OT history: "I am doing a great work and I cannot come down. Why should the work stop while I leave it and come down to you?" (Neh 6:3). This attitude of consecration is brought into focus by two aspects of another experience in the life of the patriarch who provides us with the very name Israel. Both arise out of Jacob's vision at Bethel, in which he dreamed of a ladder that reached from his resting place up into

heaven itself (Gn 28:12), meaning that God was with him (v 15).

The first aspect of Jacob's experience concerns the form of his response to God, for he "made a vow" (v 20), a voluntary obligation undertaken toward God, generally because of blessings already received or hoped for. Vows may be either of abstinence or of devotion. The former serve as exhibitions of holiness, which means the believer's separation (Lv 20:26), both *from* what is profane, and *to* the One who is ultimately "separate," that is, the holy God. As long as the sons of Israel remained in control of their historical situation as an independent nation in their own "holy land," their obligation consisted in removing from their midst all religious falsehood, whether Canaanite (Dt 7:2) or from their own people (Dt 17:5). But at the close of the 8th century BC, when over 200,000 Hebrews were taken captive to live as a subject minority in the Assyria of Sennacherib (Is 36:1), Isaiah warned them to maintain religious separation (52:11; cf. Jer 50:8; 57:6). The other type of vow is that of positive devotion, whether of a person (cf. 1 Sm 1:11) or of property (Lv 27:9,16).

The second aspect of Jacob's response to God's blessing involves the actual content of his vow when he set up the stone at Bethel. It concerned tithing: "Of all that thou givest me I will give the tenth to thee" (Gn 28:22). Religion demands practical commitment to God. As expressed in Leviticus, "All the tithe of the land, whether of the seed of the land or of the fruit of the tree, is the Lord's; it is holy to the Lord" (27:30). And this obligation is not limited to the period of the Sinaitic Law; it was paid by Jacob's grandfather Abraham, years before (14:20) and is cited with approval in the NT (Heb 7:6–8); and God's people are encouraged to "prove" God by bringing all tithes to him and to see if he will not pour out numberless blessings (Mal 3:10). Behind this tithing practice, moreover, lies the threefold religious principle of consecrated stewardship: (1) All things come from God (1 Chr 29:14). (2) We are but temporary stewards, or managers, of what God commits to us (Ps 24:1), so that when we yield up everything to God we are but performing our expected service (see also Lk 17:10; Rom 6:12; 12:1). (3) God in his grace invokes only the principle of the "firstfruits": he accepts a token offering (cf. Ex 23:19; Dt 18:4).

Conduct of Life. The faith of the Israelites expressed itself in conduct. It was demonstrated by lives of obedience (Ex 19:5), both ceremonial and moral. Submission and consecration to God must be reflected in Godlike conduct toward those who are around us (Jas 2:17; 1 Jn 4:20). Faith must indeed come first:

if "the fear of God is not in this place" (Gn 20:11 KJV), then moral conduct may not be expected; but faith cannot exist without accompanying morality: we fear God by keeping from sin (Ex 20:20; cf. Jb 1:1; 28:28). As David said, "Trust in the Lord, *and* do good" (Ps 37:3).

Patriarchal Ethics. Though Scripture reveals no specific code of ethics prior to Israel's receiving the Mosaic law on Mt Sinai, the necessity for moral obedience had been clear from the first. Adam's status under the original "covenant of works" (Hos 6:7, ASV, NASB) had depended upon his obedience (Gn 2:17); and still under the gracious testament of Genesis 3:15, his son Cain was cautioned, "If you do well, will you not be accepted? And if you do not do well . . ." (4:7). Particular obligations included respecting human life (9:6) and avoiding such sins as Noah's drunkenness (9:21) and Ham's and Canaan's lack of sexual modesty (9:22; contrast v 23).

These last instances point up the way Genesis inculcates its principles of conduct through the moral example of the Hebrew patriarchs. Abraham exemplifies generosity (13:8,9), loyalty (14:12–14, toward Lot; cf. 18:22–32), and justice (14:24, toward his allies, even while refusing booty himself, v 23). Scripture refuses to gloss over Abraham's sins of cowardice and lying (12:11–13; 20:11–13), but by so doing it underscores its moral ideal, "Walk before me, and be blameless" (17:1). The supreme example of Abraham's obedience appeared in his willingness to sacrifice his beloved son Isaac (22:2,3; cf. Jas 2:21). In the following generation, his grandson's self-centered early life illustrates the meaning of the name Jacob, "He grasps at the heel" (cf. Gn 25:26,30–34; 27:19, 20; 31:1), though his subsequent progress into Israel has been noted above. Abraham's great-grandson Joseph then stands as an example of steadfastness, resisting the temptation to adultery as a sin against God (39:9), and loving his undeserving brothers (50:21).

Mosaic Ethics. In response to their adoption by God as his chosen people (Ex 19:5), the Israelites at Sinai promised, "All that the Lord has spoken we will do" (v 8). Moses then proceeded to reveal to them the Torah, a term often rendered as "Law," but really having the broader sense of "instruction."

Some of the particular applications of the Sinaitic Law are, of course, limited to the immediate situations in which the Israelites then lived, such as the granting of a double portion of inheritances to the firstborn (Dt 21:17), proportionate to the elder's added responsibilities in a patriarchal society; or the requirements of installing railings around roofs (22:8), for safety in lands where these surfaces can be

used for working, sleeping, and living. Yet behind such special social or national needs lie fundamental mortal principles, the most basic of which is "You shall love your neighbor as yourself" (Lv 19:18).

The Law of Moses occupies about half the Pentateuch and may be organized into four major codes. The Decalogue (Ex 20:2–17), which means "ten words" or commandments (34:28), was spoken by God on Mt Sinai at the time of Israel's adoption as his special nation. It was then written down by his own hand on two tablets of stone (31:18; 34:1,28) as the fundamental moral law for his people. The Book of the Covenant (20:22–23:33; cf. 24:7) was then spoken by God but recorded by Moses. Its purpose was to provide Israel with concrete applications of the Decalogue so they could accept it officially (24:3,7; see, e.g., how 21:16 applies the commandment against killing to kidnaping). God revealed the priestly codes (most of Lv—except for the narratives in chs 8–10 and 24:10–23—plus similar laws in Nm 5,6,9,10,15, 18,19) immediately after the construction of the tabernacle. These were for the professional guidance of the priests, who were to minister in it. By contrast, the Deuteronomic codes (primarily Dt 1–30, to which may be prefixed Nm 28–30), were revealed in a more popular style through the speeches of Moses some 40 years later. Israel was then about to enter the Promised Land of Canaan, 1406 BC; the aim of this "second law" was to arouse Israel to faithfulness during its settlement; its keynote was "You shall love the Lord your God with all your heart" (Dt 6:5). For practical purposes, all the moral Torah may be organized under the last six commandments of the Decalogue (cf. Mk 10:19), because these summarize the social aspects of Israel's religion, showing how the people were to act toward their fellows.

The fifth commandment, "Honor your father and your mother" (Ex 20:12), establishes the family as God's primary social unit on earth. Respect for authority is a religious duty (Lv 19:32), just like keeping God's sabbath (v 31; cf. the serious penalties described in Ex 21:15,17; Dt 21:20,21). Parents too are to cherish their children as gifts of God (Ps 127:3; cf. Ex 13:15, against child sacrifice) and to bring them up in the nurture and admonition of the Lord (Ex 12:26–28; Dt 6:7).

The seventh commandment, "You shall not commit adultery" (Ex 20:14), teaches sexual purity. Here the strict standards of Israel's conduct show a marked contrast to the laxness of their pagan neighbors or, for that matter, to much of modern thought. Adultery was punishable by death (Lv 20:10; Dt 22:21); and fornication (premarital sex) was equally serious, though with a lesser penalty (Lv 19:20; Hos

4:14). The man who raped a virgin was obliged to marry her (Ex 22:16; Dt 22:29). The very desire for another man's wife was wrong (see the 10th commandment). Because of the hardness of men's hearts, (Mt 19:8), God later reduced the death penalty for marital infidelity, permitting the "innocent" party to divorce the "shameful" one (Dt 24:1 NEB; Mt 5:32), though he hates divorce (Mal 2:16). Since immodesty leads to sin (cf. 2 Sm 11:2), the OT insists on proper bodily covering (Ex 20:26). Canaanite "sacred" prostitutes and homosexuals, called "dogs" (Dt 23:18), were banned, together with all other kinds of sexual perversion (Ex 22:19); and, to avoid even the suspicion of sodomy, both men and women were forbidden to wear clothes of the other sex (Dt 22:5).

The eighth commandment, "You shall not steal" (Ex 20:15), insures property rights. Ultimately, all property belongs to God: "The land is mine, for you are strangers and sojourners with me" (Lv 25:23). Yet once God chooses to delegate property to a certain person, no one else is to take it. The land of Canaan was assigned to the families of Israel by permanent tenure; it "shall not be sold in perpetuity" (v 23). If through pressure of circumstances one was forced to give up some property, it could be "redeemed" at any time (v 25); and in any event it reverted to him automatically at the year of jubilee. By way of contrast, property rights could be, and were, disregarded by the surrounding pagans, particularly rulers (cf. 1 Kgs 21:7, on Naboth's vineyard), whose conduct was not subject to Israel's religious standards. The OT condemns all forms of fraud, such as withholding wages (Lv 19:13) or exacting usury (25:36).

The ninth commandment, "You shall not bear false witness against your neighbor" (Ex 20:16), concerns truth. In specific court trials, the responsibility of witnesses is brought out by their having to participate in executing the death penalty (Dt 17:7); and in case of false testimony the witness suffered the same penalty that his words would have caused (19:19).

The tenth commandment, "You shall not covet" (Ex 20:17), turns from one's overt conduct to the underlying attitude of heart. Negatively, "You shall not take vengeance or bear any grudge against the sons of your people"; and, positively, "You shall love your neighbor as yourself." Why? Because, "I am the Lord" (Lv 19:18). Religious conduct thus reflects the goodness of God, and it goes beyond the letter of the law to sincere humanitarianism.

After Israel's entrance into Canaan, they lapsed badly from the standards of Moses (cf. Jgs 17–19, violating every one of the commandments). Yet when led by dedicated prophets, judges, priests, and kings, their religion re-

vived. Note the ethical stress in many of David's psalms: for example, "Depart from evil, and do good. . . . The eyes of the Lord are toward the righteous" (Ps 34:14,15).

Solomonic Ethics. The ethical side of the religious practice of Israel reaches another height of expression in the writings of Solomon (970–930 BC). Next to the Pentateuch, the Bible's lengthiest block of moral teaching appears in the Book of Proverbs. These pointed statements of Hebrew wisdom may be organized under categories of personal, economic, and social ethics, and they cover in detail the principles laid down in the Decalogue.

Personal religious life commences with God: "The fear of the Lord is the beginning of knowledge" (Prv 1:7). The pious Israelite restrains pride (11:2; 16:18) and exhibits composure (14:30), deliberation (29:20,22), and a willingness to leave vengeance in the hands of God (20:22; 24:29). Yet he also works hard (6:6–11, cf. 10:4,5; 14:4).

On the sanctity of life, Solomon demands for every person the standing to which each one is entitled (17:26; 18:5). Yet punishment, whether the "blows that wound" or stripes, is recommended to "cleanse away evil" (20:30). Correspondingly, it is necessary to guard against overevaluating one's own insights (16:2,25). The proverbs also stress moral purity. The prostitute and adulteress must be shunned (chs 5,6:24–35,7) because of their shame and also because of the other sins to which they may lead (13:18; 28:3). Temperance in all things is taught, whether in respect to gluttony (23:20; 28:7) or drunkenness (20:1; 23:31, 31:4,5, cf. vv 6,7). Israel's wisest king encourages a glad heart (15:13,15,30) and bodily comfort (27:9), but never to excess (25:16,27).

Proverbs condemns theft (29:24), dishonesty (11:1; 21:6), and bribery (15:27; 17:23). Solomon further insists on truth: "Lying lips are an abomination to the Lord" (12:22), as is any kind of hypocrisy (26:23,24). The wise are to impart needed truths (10:21,31,32) and reproofs (24:24,25), but an uncontrolled tongue brings disaster both to others (11:9) and to its owner (12:13). Everyone must speak with care (15:28) and with kindness (v 26) and be willing to accept the truth about oneself (10:8,17). Concern for others underlies many of the precepts taught in Proverbs, from generosity (11:24; 19:6) to peacemaking (12:20) to simply keeping up on one's correspondence (25:25). Status means nothing to God (22:2); so those who are his must honor the defenseless widow (15:25; 23:10), aid the poor (14:21,31), be kind to animals (12:10), and love even their enemies (25:21) from the heart (24:17).

The religion of Israel moves beyond personal ethics into the world of economics and business. The private ownership of property is encouraged: "The diligent man will get precious wealth" (12:27; cf. 13:8; 14:20). Property gains power (22:7), friends (19:4), protection (10:15; 21:14), and outweighs social position (12:9). Yet wealth obtained at the cost of righteousness is worthless (15:16; 16:8), and moderate substance is viewed as the ideal (30:8,9). "In all toil there is profit" (14:23; cf. 13:4); and, while wealth stems basically from God (3:10; 10:22; 22:4), property is to be gained through wisdom (24:3), discipline (13:18), and hard work (10:4; 13:4), whether by labor in the field (12:11) or with the flock (27:23–27). Possessions may be acquired through inheritance (19:14), but not by deceit (20:17; 21:6), false weights (20:10), shifted landmarks (22:28), or oppression (23:10,11; cf. 28:8) for no such wealth can last (13:11; 28:22). Borrowing is discouraged (22:7).

One's use of his property is to be directed by religion: "Honor the Lord with your substance and with the first fruits of all your produce" (3:9). This includes the support of worship through such regular offerings as the "firstfruits" (cf. 7:14) and the exercise of charity (3:28; 21:3). Believers are further expected to make provision for their own families (19:14, cf. 1 Tm 5:8) and for their personal needs (30:24,25). Wealth is not to be squandered (28:3); suretyship is to be avoided (6:1–5; 22:26). Yet, possessions are not everything: both peace and piety are preferable to wealth (15:16; 17:1), and "a good name is to be chosen rather than great riches" (22:1). Those who center their lives on their possessions (11:28) must ultimately fail (v 4).

The religion of Proverbs reaches also into the various circles of social life. The center of society is the family. A successful, happy marriage is one of God's greatest gifts (Prv 18:22; 19:14). It is to be founded on love (5:15–19). The husband must be able to support his wife (24:27), and she is to devote herself to her husband and to her household (12:4; 31:10–31; contrast the warnings given in 14:1; 19:13; 21:9). Children bring glory to a family (17:6; cf. 10:1; 15:20) and are to be trained in the fear of the Lord (14:26). "Spare the rod, and spoil the child" is a familiar adage (22:15; 23:13; cf. 29:15); but the equally well-known verse, "Train up a child in the way he should go . . ." (22:6) is perhaps more accurately rendered, "Train up a child according to his way [i.e., by methods that are adapted to his own special interests and capacities], and [then] even when he is old he will not depart from it." Children too are responsible before God (20:11). They must respect and obey their parents (6:20; 19:26; 20:20), even in later life (23:22), and heed their parents' instruction (1:8; 4:1).

Advancing into wider circles of society, Solomon commends the faithfulness of the "wise servant" (17:2; cf. 29:19). Masters, correspondingly, are to treat their servants well without overindulging them (29:21). Friendship is valuable (17:17); for "There is a friend who sticks closer than a brother" (18:24; cf. 27:10). Yet too many friends (18:24 NASB), or the wrong kinds of friends (fools, 13:20; angry men, 26:21, or tale-bearers, 26:20) can bring disaster.

On the broadest level, "righteousness exalts a nation" (14:34; cf. 28:2). Rulers are to be efficient (25:2), maintain justice (16:10; 29:12), and enforce due penalties (20:26), while at the same time showing mercy (v 28). Citizens must reverence the government (24:21; cf. 16:14; 20:22), even while seeking its reformation, insofar as they are able (Prv 25:5).

Two additional writings by Solomon make specialized contributions to our appreciation of the religious practices of Israel. The Song of Solomon appeared early in the king's career (cf. Sg 3:11), before his polygamous household had led him into apostasy (1 Kgs 11:11). It consists of a lyric portrayal of God-given love between a man and a woman: "For love is strong as death . . . the very flame of the Lord. Many waters cannot quench love" (8:6,7 NASB). The Song underscores God's standards of purity and chastity (4:12; 8:9); and in it Solomon seems honestly to describe the Shulamite heroine's rejection, both of himself and of his flagrant polygamy (cf. 1:12,13; 8:11,12). The refrain sets the tone of the book: "I adjure you, O daughters of Jerusalem, . . . that you stir not up nor awake love until it please" (2:7; 3:5; etc.).

Ecclesiastes, on the other hand, reflects the thought of a sadder but wiser Solomon near the close of a blighted career (cf. 12:1). Its primary goal is to demonstrate the futility of life apart from God (1:2; 12:8), yet it emphasizes a number of positive religious values as well. The righteous are to do good and to rejoice in the days that God allocates to them (3:12). These "good" things include: wisdom (2:13; 7:11; 10:10), contentment (4:5,6; 5:12), gracious speech (10:12), love to one's wife (9:9), obedience to the king (8:2–4), charity (11:2), cooperative enterprise (4:9–12), and that characteristic of so many of Solomon's wise proverbs, efficiency and industriousness (9:10; 10:18). This present world is filled with frustrations and evils but, while waiting for the day when the Lord will bring all things into judgment (11:9; 12:13,14), each religious Israelite "should eat and drink, and find enjoyment in his toil" (2:24; cf. 5:18; 7:14; etc.).

Prophetic Ethics. At Solomon's death in 930 BC none of the OT's prophetic books had yet been written. Israel's pattern of religion, however, had been set by the Mosaic and Solomonic writings. The main task of the prophets was to proclaim, apply, and defend God's Law as it had already been revealed (Isa 8:20; Hos 8:1; Mal 4:4). Unhappily, the people seemed quite willing to observe the Mosaic ceremonial laws (Am 4:4,5) while disregarding the Lord's moral requirements of justice, mercy, and humility before God (Mi 6:8). The prophets constantly called for deliverance for the oppressed (Is 1:17, cf. Dt 14:29) and consideration, even for enemy prisoners (2 Chr 28:9–11, cf. Prv 25:21). They condemned creditors who refused to return garments taken as pledges from the poor (Am 2:8; cf. Ex 22:26) and the wealthy who debauched themselves in drink (Is 5:11; cf. Prv 23:31).

The Book of Esther presents a vivid picture of the corruption of the Persian court of Xerxes (485–465) (1:10–12; 2:14; 3:11). The setting is after the fall of the Hebrew kingdoms and against a pagan background. Esther's standards of devotion and self-sacrifice stand out all the more clearly (cf. 4:16, 7:3). Nehemiah provides another example of selfless effort in his reconstruction of Jerusalem in 444 (Neh 5:7–16). Both Ezra and Nehemiah, together with the prophet Malachi, faced the problem of mixed marriages in postexilic Israel (Ezr 9:1,2; Neh 13:23–28; Mal 2:11), and they extended the Mosaic prohibition against marriage alliance with the Canaanites (Ex 34:16) to include any with those who were not of the Jewish faith (Neh 13:27).

Ritual Conduct. OT Israel was able to share in God's redemption through the means of symbolic worship (Ex 20:24). The person who failed to keep the moral law (Dt 5:29) could gain forgiveness and restoration through ritual observance (cf. Lv 6:2–7). It was by way of ceremonies that God in his grace was pleased to mediate his righteousness to those who trusted in him (Dt 6:25). The standards for Israel's ritual conduct were fixed by the Law of Moses and continued thereafter with little change or modification.

It must be understood that Israel's rituals possessed no intrinsic or mechanical value in themselves, despite what some legalistic Hebrews might have thought (1 Sm 4:3; Mi 3:11). Worship without faith was useless. Confession of sin had to precede the offerings (Lv 5:5), and no sacrifice was sufficient for "high-handed" or deliberate sin (Nm 15:30). The sacrifice of the wicked was, in fact, an abomination to God (Prv 15:8; 21:27). In the original Law of Moses, therefore, moral and ceremonial legislation are mingled almost without distinction. Only in the days of King Jehoshaphat (872–848 BC), does the first division appear between secular judges "in all the king's matters" and

priests in "all matters of the Lord" (2 Chr 19:11). The prophets in particular criticized hypocrites who observed the ceremonies but disregarded the moral law. The prophets who were used by God to emphasize that "to obey is better than sacrifice" (1 Sm 15:22; cf. Is 1:11–15; Am 5:21–24).

Sacred Places. The religion of Israel designated certain geographical localities and certain physical conditions as proper to the worship of the holy ("separated") God. As sanctuaries, the early patriarchs reverenced particular places where God had appeared to them (cf. Gn 12:7; 28:18), but without any special buildings. The earliest ritual law had a similar nonspecific character (Ex 20:24). It should be noted, however, that even while adapting itself to Israel's journeys through the wilderness, the Law did *not* authorize worship in more than one place at one time (cf. Lv 17:5); and the specification of a single centrally located place of worship only came 40 years later, when Israel was about to take up permanent residence in the Promised Land (Dt 12:5,11–14).

Immediately after God's adoption of Israel as his chosen people (Ex 19:5) and following their formal ratification of the older testament, at Mt Sinai (ch 24), God revealed to Moses the pattern for the tabernacle (chs 25–31). It was a movable sanctuary, designed to replace the provisional tent where God first met with his people (33:7–10). Its purpose was defined by God himself, "I will dwell among the people of Israel, and will be their God" (29:45). The tabernacle thus had sacramental value: it was the visible sign and seal of the Lord's testamentary promise to be present as Israel's God. This accounts for such names of the tabernacle as "the dwelling" (25:9, lit.), because his glory-cloud known later by the term "Shekinah," dwelt there, visibly resting over the holy ark in its inner room (Lv 16:2); "the tent of meeting" (Ex 29:42 NASB), where God met with his representatives; or "the house of the Lord" (34:26). Yet simultaneously the tabernacle depicted God's separateness from his people. This was shown by its very design. In the center of a curtained-off court, the building consisted of a two-roomed, windowless oblong, made of portable vertical frames covered with four layers of coverings. There, isolated within the inner chamber, in "the holy of holies" (meaning "the most holy, or most-separated, place"), God dwelt "in thick darkness" (1 Kgs 8:12).

In its teaching of "God's presence" as a type of heaven (Ps 11:4; Heb 9:24), the whole design of the tabernacle had meaning. Moses was repeatedly cautioned that it must conform in every respect to the pattern which had been shown him on Mt Sinai (Ex 25:9,40; Heb 8:5). Thus the first object within the court gate was the altar—for God can be approached only by way of sacrifice, a type of Christ's atoning death (Heb 8:2–3, 9:12)—and the second, was the laver (Ex 30:21), which depicts the necessity for purity, for the washing of regeneration and sanctification in Christ (Ti 3:5; Heb 9:10). Inside the first curtained room, called the holy place, stood the table with the "show bread," (bread of the Presence) which symbolized the reestablished harmony and fellowship of God's people with their heavenly Lord (Lv 24:8; cf. Ex 24:11), the candlestick or lampstand, indicating the Spirit-given light and truth that radiates from believers (Zec 4:2–6; Mt 5:14), and the altar of incense, suggesting communion with God through prayer (Ps 141:2; Lk 1:10; Rv 8:4). A veil divided the two chambers of the sanctuary to signify "that the way into the sanctuary is not yet opened as long as the outer tent is still standing" (Heb 9:8), that is, until Jesus the messianic High Priest should come and rend it at his death (Mt 27:51). Israel's religion permitted no representation of God himself; as the fourth commandment made clear: "You shall not make for yourself a graven image" (Ex 20:4). The ark served only as the throne of God's presence. There was no image of God (Ex 40:34).

Joshua carried the tabernacle into Canaan, where it was first set up at Gilgal on the west bank of the Jordan (Jos 9:6; 10:43). It was later settled more centrally at Shiloh (18:1), where it remained for some 300 years. By the time of Eli, a permanent "house of the Lord" had been built at Shiloh (1 Sm 1:7,24). This building was destroyed by the invading Philistines (4:10,11; Ps 78:60; Jer 7:12). The tabernacle was eventually located at Gibeon (1 Chr 16:39). Meanwhile, the absence of a central sanctuary explains Samuel's conducting of sacrifices at the major points in his circuit (1 Sm 7:9; 9:13); and it explicitly justifies the localized worship of the Lord at various "high places," prior to Solomon's completion of the temple (1 Kgs 3:2). It was King David who first conducted the ark to a tent shrine on Mt Zion in Jerusalem, after capturing the city and designating it his capital (2 Sm 5:7; 6:17; cf. Ps 24). God later revealed to David that Jerusalem was the place he had chosen out of all Israel in which to place his name (his personal presence; 1 Chr 21:18–28; cf. Dt 12:5). The king then devoted his last years to making preparations for a magnificent temple. In 959 BC his son Solomon completed it on Mt Moriah, just north of Jerusalem's city limits (2 Chr 3:1; 1 Kgs 6:38). The plans revealed to David (1 Chr 28:12,19) called for a structure of stone and carved cedar, overlaid with gold, on the same basic

plan as the tabernacle, but with double length and breadth, triple height, and certain other elaborations. Moses' ancient tent was brought up from Gibeon and housed inside the new sanctuary (1 Kgs 8:4). In times of apostasy Israel might revert to paganized high places for worship; but Jerusalem was henceforth "the city of God" (Pss 46:5; 48:3).

Israel's code for religious conduct specified the places that were holy, where God was to be sought. The code also specified certain places, objects, and situations that were to be avoided by God's people as unclean. Early in Genesis particular animals had been designated as unclean (7:2), and it was forbidden to eat blood (9:4). Moses developed the categories of cleanness with their corresponding concepts. Hygienic reasons must have accounted, at least in part, for the uncleanness of leprosy (Lv 13,14). Closely related are regulations designed to prevent bodily injury (19:28). Iron may have been forbidden in preparing the materials used in Israel's sanctuaries (Ex 20:25; 1 Kgs 8:7) because of its association with instruments of war; and leaven, because of physical decay and corruption. A natural loathsomeness probably contributed to the ban against eating certain creeping animals, birds of prey, insects, and worms (Lv 11:20,41). There is an ethical factor in the prohibited degrees of marriage between close relatives (Lv 18:6) and in the separation of women from normal responsibilities after childbirth (12:2). This rule may involve a humanitarian explanation as well.

Less obvious, however, are Israel's regulations that emphasize the separation involved in holiness. The prohibitions against wearing garments of mixed materials or of planting mixed seeds (Lev 19:19) seem to be based on the principle of separation. Israel's religious practices also included numerous reminders of the present depravity of man's natural life. Sexual relations, though not wrong in themselves, nevertheless kept one from what is holy (1 Sm 21:4), as did anything connected with birth (Lv 12:1–8; 15:2,3), death (Ex 22:31; Nm 19:11), idolatry (Ex 23:13), and even foreign lands (Am 7:17). Finally, certain meat was prohibited because it was reserved for sacrifice to the Lord (Lv 7:25); clothes had to be washed each day as a part of Israel's "sanctifying" at their adoption by God at Sinai (Ex 19:10). Many prohibitions may have involved more than one reason. Cutting oneself, for example (Lv 19:28; Dt 14:1), was harmful to the body but also had pagan connotations (1 Kgs 18:28). But cutting one's beard (Lv 19:27) seems to have been prohibited on purely antipagan grounds.

The exilic prophets stressed cleanness particularly (Ez 4:16; cf. 20:12,21) after Israel had been forcibly deprived of many of their other means of religious expression. Daniel's well-known refusal to be defiled with the Babylonian king's dainties (Dn 1:8) is still reflected in the Jewish "kosher" laws.

Ceremonial Actions. The sacred places of Israel furnished the stage for most of the nation's religious activities. Prayer and Scripture reading constituted major exceptions, since both of these acts could be performed by private individuals either in family groups (Dt 6:7-9) or, from exilic days onward, in what became local synagogues (Ps 74:8). The OT contains, in fact, only one set prayer, for use at the temple during Pentecost (Dt 26:5-10). But for Israel's services of song and of praise, and for the most central element in the nation's worship, sacrifice, the OT specified a professionally trained priesthood to perform its ceremonies. God's worship was a serious matter (cf. Nm 4:15; 1 Sm 6:7). The third commandment, "You shall not take the name of the Lord your God in vain" (Ex 20:7), had as its immediate reference a prohibition against invoking God's name in false or careless oaths; but it also warns against any irreverence (Dt 28:58). The priests were ministers, chosen by God, to officiate at the altar in his sanctuary (Dt 18:5; Heb 5:4) and to intercede for the people (Jl 2:17). Other functions included setting an example of faithfulness in personal living (Dt 33:9), "enquiring" for the Lord's guidance via divine oracles (Jgs 20:27,28), and teaching the Law to God's people (Lv 10:11; Mi 3:11; Mal 2:7). In patriarchal days a man might perform priestly sacrifice for himself (Gn 4:3) or for his household (12:8; Jb 1:5). But at Sinai the Lord restricted Israel's priesthood to the descendants of Aaron, brother of Moses, of the tribe of Levi (Ex 28:1; 40:12-15; Nm 16:17; 17:8). Aaron wore the names of the 12 tribes inscribed on his vestments (Ex 28:12,21,29); he literally "brought them before God" as he entered the sanctuary to accomplish reconciliation (v 38).

The Aaronic priests were assisted by their fellow tribesmen, the other Levites (Nm 8:13; cf. Ex 32:26, Dt 33:9). During the wilderness wanderings the levitical clans had specific functions in transporting the tabernacle and its furniture (Nm 1:50). At the conquest of Canaan, these same Levites received no tribal territory (Nm 18:23; cf. Gn 34:30; 49:7) but were allocated 48 towns, including the 6 cities of refuge (Nm 35:6). They were assigned Israel's tithes and offerings, so that they could be free to serve God (18:21,24-26), though in the dark days of the judges these provisions were not well enforced (cf. Jgs 17:7; 19:1). Under David, however, both the priests and the Levites were carefully organized into 24 "courses" each (1 Chr 23-24) to permit monthly rotations in

service. The king restructured the duties of the 38,000 Levites in service at this time to accommodate the newly established worship in the temple, with its chief musicians and groups of singers, and also to meet his own imperial needs for judicial and administrative officials (chs 25-27). The priestly courses were reinstituted after the exile (Neh 12:1-7) and were continued in NT times (Lk 1:5).

In the religion of Israel, the ceremonial functioning of the priesthood was concentrated upon animal sacrifice. Four explanations have been given for this practice: (1) The crudest concept is that sacrifice was intended as a meal to nourish hungry deities. But while the pagans surrounding Israel doubtless thought this, and while food terminology is sometimes incorporated into the OT's description of sacrifices (Lv 3:11,16), the idea that the true God needed to eat is categorically denied (Ps 50:9-13; Is 40:16). (2) Equally objectionable is the theory of physical communion, that by the sacrificial rituals worshipers could enter into covenants of blood brotherhood with their deity or even eat its flesh. But, again, while it is true that communion fellowship with God resulted from the OT rituals (Ex 24:11), its teachings on the spiritual nature of God forbade any such view of the sacrifices in themselves. (3) Of greater validity is the view that treats the OT sacrifices as gifts. A subdivision within the peace offerings consisted of Israel's thank offerings (Lv 7:12-15); certain of their acts of worship did involve sincere gifts of gratitude to God (cf. 1 Sm 1:24-27). But this theory fails to account for the emphasis upon blood in the rituals and for the OT's repeated stress upon the estrangement that exists between God and men, which requires the blood in the first place, representing the life of guilty humans before God. (4) The most adequate explanation for the sacrifices of Israel is atonement, the aim of which is to avert evil, especially punishment. All of Israel's sacrifices fall into one of two classes: guilt offerings to propitiate an offended God, and sweet-savor offerings, a phrase which means literally, an odor that placates (cf. Gn 8:21). Offerings were presented so that God would not deal with men "after their folly" (Jb 42:8; cf. 1:5).

In the Law given at Sinai, the atoning character of sacrifice becomes apparent in each of the five stages of the sacrificial ritual: (1) Choosing the offering: neither the animal nor the other materials involved could contain defects (Lv 22:21). (2) Presenting the offering: each offerer then laid his hands on the head of the victim (1:4), appointing it as a proxy for himself and transferring to it his sins (cf. Nm

8:18,19; 27:18–21). (3) Slaying the offering: by its death (Lv 1:5) the sacrifice suffered the penalty of the sins that had been laid upon it (Nm 6:11; cf. Lv 19:20,21). The symbol of surrendered life lay in the blood, "given for you upon the altar to make atonement for your souls" (Lv 17:11). (4) Committing the offering to God, by sprinkling and burning on the altar (1:6–9). (5) Demonstrating the restored fellowship with God by sprinkling the remainder of the blood on the now forgiven people (Ex 24:6–8); or in some of the guilt offerings, by removing the sin-laden victim's body outside the camp for burning (Lv 4:12,21), or most frequently, by using part of the sacrifice for a meal of fellowship in the presence of the Lord (Ex 24:11).

If sacrifice was Israel's chief ritual act for the maintenance of her relationship with God, then the ceremony for its initiation was circumcision. The revelation of this rite occurred historically in connection with God's choice of Abraham. God commanded circumcision to set Abraham's family apart (vv 11–13) and dramatically equated it with redemption itself. "This is my covenant" (v 10). To neglect the rite was most serious (Ex 4:24–26; cf. Ez 44:7). The man who refused it was cut off from inheritance among the people of God (Gn 17:14); he had, indeed, never joined them. As uncircumcision symbolized the unfitness of an unreformed life (Ex 6:12), and as uncircumcised hearts indicated those that were covered with their natural wickedness (Jer 4:4), so circumcision denoted the removal of one's sin (Dt 10:16). It symbolized regeneration (Lv 26:41) for those whom God had adopted as his own (Gn 17:7).

Circumcision was performed on the male infant's 8th day (Gn 17:12). It taught both mankind's need for redemption at the very outset of life (Ps 51:5) and also conveyed assurance about the incorporation of a believer's children into the grace of God's testament (Gn 17:7).

Holy Seasons. Israel's ceremonial actions at her sacred places were performed at stated times. The all-inclusive term which is rendered "feasts" (Lv 23:2) means literally appointed times (NASB), which emphasizes their divine revelation and appointment. The feasts of the Jews did not arise from the human observation of natural phenomena, such as the seven-day phases of the moon, or the annual agricultural cycle in Canaan—though God did incorporate certain agricultural elements in his calendar.

The institution of the sabbath dates back to creation itself (Gn 2:1–3); and it was observed by Israel prior to arriving at Sinai and receiving the Law (Ex 16:23–26). It became incorporated into the Decalogue as the 4th

commandment, "Remember the Sabbath day, to keep it holy" (Ex 20:8). At Sinai, the Lord also ordained seven special convocation sabbaths, these were days of rest and of special sacrifices that occurred during the five annual feasts which God revealed in the Mosaic Law; namely, Passover, Pentecost, trumpets, the day of atonement, and tabernacles. The first and last had two such convocation sabbaths assigned to them (Lv 23:7,8,35,36). On the first day in each of Israel's lunar months, that is, on the new moon, God prescribed another time of rest and offering, plus a memorial blowing of trumpets (Nm 10:10; cf. Ps 81:3). A final extension of the sabbath concept appeared in the sabbatical (7th) year, or "year of release" (from debts, Lv 25:4; Dt 15:1–15), and in the year of jubilee (after seven sabbatic years, meaning the 50th), with its return of all land to the original owner (Lv 25:8–34).

Out of the five annual Mosaic celebrations, three of them—Passover, Pentecost, and tabernacles—are called by a special name which means "pilgrimage feast" (Lv 23:4). These were times at which every adult male among God's people was expected to appear before the Lord at the central sanctuary (Ex 23:14–17; cf. 1 Kgs 9:25). The two other annual holy days came in the seventh month (Sept/Oct) preceding the pilgrimage feast of tabernacles: namely, the feast of trumpets, on the first day of the month, introducing the climactic fall season of harvest (Lv 23:24), and the day of atonement, Yom Kippur, on the 10th, when forgiveness and restoration to divine favor were achieved for the entire nation (Lv 16). The atonement was achieved by means of the ceremonies of the scapegoat, and by the high priest's entering for the only time in the year the sanctuary's most holy place. Yom Kippur was a day of national repentance and of sincere humiliation before God (Lv 16:29, 31; cf. Prv 28:13). The phrase, to "afflict your souls," was later interpreted to mean fasting (Is 58:3; cf. Acts 27:9, "the fast"); but it does not necessarily carry a connotation. Fasting as an observance is never prescribed in the OT.

In exilic times the people began to observe four dates that were connected with Jerusalem's fall to Babylon, as annual fasts (Zec 7:3,5; 8:19; cf. 2 Kgs 25:1–3,8,9,25). But when Zechariah was asked whether these should continue to be observed once the postexilic restoration and temple rebuilding had been accomplished, he predicted that if the people would but turn to God in genuine repentance, these four days would be turned into joyful feasts (Zec 8:15–19). However, the fasts continued. The only other post-Mosaic addition to Israel's religious calendar was the postexilic

feast of Purim. It was a time of joy over the national deliverance of the Jews from their persecution at the hands of Haman in Persia (Est 9:20–28).
J. BARTON PAYNE

See OFFERINGS AND SACRIFICES; PROPHET, PROPHETESS; PROPHECY; LAW, BIBLICAL CONCEPT OF; TABERNACLE, TEMPLE; PRIESTS AND LEVITES; FEASTS AND FESTIVALS OF ISRAEL; JEW; CIRCUMCISION.

Bibliography. W.F. Albright, *Archaeology and the Religion of Israel*; G.A. Barton, *The Religion of Ancient Israel*; R. de Vaux, *Ancient Israel*; G. Fohrer, *History of Israelite Religion*; J.H. Raven, *The History of the Religion of Israel*; H.W. Robinson, *The Religious Ideas of the OT*; H.H. Rowley, *The Faith of Israel*; N.A. Snaith, *The Distinctive Ideas of the OT*; G. Vos, *Biblical Theology.*

Israelite. Descendant of the 12 sons of Israel (the name God gave to Jacob, Gn 32:28). As the sons of Abraham they are distinguished from the Ishmaelites (descended from Abraham by Hagar his concubine), and as sons of Isaac from the Edomites (descendants of Esau), by having Jacob as their ancestor. They lived in Egypt from the time of Joseph until the exodus, when God led them into Canaan to fulfill his promise to Abraham (Gn 17:8).

God led the Israelites out of Egypt, through the wilderness, and into the land of Canaan that he had promised them. They were ruled by judges, kings, and conquered by other countries. In 722 BC, the northern kingdom was conquered by Assyria and became incorporated into that empire. After this time, "Israel" refers to members of the southern tribes, Judah and Benjamin. An "Israelite" then was one who, religiously as well as politically, belonged to the remnant of the covenant nation of Israel.

See ISRAEL, HISTORY OF; JUDAISM; ISRAEL, RELIGION OF; JEW.

Isis. *See* EGYPT, EGYPTIANS.

Issachar (Person). 1. Jacob's 9th son, the 5th by his wife Leah (Gn 30:17,18); his name perhaps means "reward" (v 18). Jacob, in his final message to his 12 sons, says, "Issachar is a strong donkey, lying down between the sheep folds" (49:14 NASB) and the picture suggested is a loaded donkey who refuses to move his burden, a lazy man who is unwilling to do his share of the work. Little is known about Issachar except what he did along with the other sons of Israel. He had 4 sons (46:13), who headed clans in the tribe (1 Chr 7:1–5). His family went with Jacob to Egypt, where they died (although Issachar was subsequently moved to Shechem with the other 12 patriarchs—Acts 7:16).

The descendants of Issachar numbered 54,400 at the 1st census (Nm 1:29), increased to 64,400 at the 2nd (26:25), and to 87,000 during David's reign (1 Chr 7:5). Issachar was the main tribe involved in the fighting led by Deborah, herself a member of the tribe (Jgs 5:15). During the time of David, there were "of Issachar men who had understanding of the times, to know what Israel ought to do, two hundred chiefs, and all their kinsmen under their command" (1 Chr 12:32). These men supported David as king to replace Saul.

Issachar was assigned the fourth lot of land after the ark was taken to Shiloh (Jos 19:17). This included the cities of Jezreel, Shunem, and Engannim, and it lay between the mountains of Gilboa and Tabor. Their allotment was bordered on the south and west by the tribe of Manasseh, on the north by Zebulun, and on the east by the River Jordan. This territory was largely a fertile plain, but was often threatened by the Canaanites nearby as well as by foreign invaders.

See ISSACHAR, TRIBE OF.

2. Obed-edom's son, who was a Levite gatekeeper during David's reign (1 Chr 26:5).

Issachar, Tribe of. Tribal inheritance of Issachar. The territory is defined in Joshua 19:17–23; detailed boundary descriptions are not included. On the east "its boundary ends at the Jordan" (v 22). The area can be located by the list of towns encompassed by the inheritance of which Jezreel, Chesulloth, Shunem, Anaharath, Kishion, Remeth, and Engannim have identifications of varying degrees of certainty. Jezreel and Engannim are in the southeast corner of the Valley of Jezreel; Chesulloth is just west of Mt Tabor and Shunem is at the foot of the Hill of Moreh. The northern border can be deduced from the southern boundary of Naphtali (Jos 19:33,34). All three areas, that of Issachar, Naphtali, and Zebulun, met at Mt Tabor (v 22). On the south side, there were some major towns not conquered in Joshua's time (Jgs 1:27) that were taken from Issachar and given to Manasseh (Jos 17:11); these included important centers such as Beth-shan, Ibleam, and Taanach.

In the same territory, there were disturbances among the local tribes (recorded on a stele of Seti I at Beth-shan); the area is called "Mt Yarunta," after Yarmuth (Jos 21:29 Jarmuth = Remeth). Issachar was located on the rich plateau stretching east of Tabor and the Hill of Moreh and north of the Beth-shan Valley; its soil is of heavy volcanic content.

ANSON F. RAINEY

See ISSACHAR (PERSON) #1.

Isshiah. 1. Izrahiah's son from Issachar's tribe (1 Chr 7:3, KJV Ishiah).

2. Warrior from Benjamin's tribe who

Beth-shan stele of Seti I (1313 BC).

joined David in his struggle against King Saul. Isshiah was one of David's ambidextrous archers and slingers (1 Chr 12:6, KJV Jesiah).

3. Uzziel's son from Levi's tribe (1 Chr 23:20, KJV Jesiah; 24:25).

4. Rehabiah's son from Levi's tribe and a descendant of Moses (1 Chr 24:21).

Isshijah. Harim's son, who obeyed Ezra's exhortation to divorce his pagan wife after the exile (Ezr 10:31, KJV Ishijah).

Issue of Blood. KJV rendering of "hemorrhage" in Matthew 9:20 and Mark 5:29 (fountain of blood).

See HEMORRHAGE.

Isuah. KJV spelling of Ishvah, Asher's son, in 1 Chronicles 7:30.

See ISHVAH.

Isui. KJV rendering of Ishvi, Asher's son, in Genesis 46:17.

See ISHVI #1.

Italian Cohort, Italian Band. Roman military unit to which the centurion Cornelius belonged. The single biblical reference is in Acts 10:1.

The Roman army included auxiliary cohorts or regiments, most of which seem to have comprised provincial subjects apart from Jews (who were exempted). Such units were sometimes referred to by distinctive names like "Italian" or "Augustan" (Imperial) (Acts 27:1). The Italian Band was evidently composed mainly of those who not only were Roman citizens but had been born in Rome. The bands were divided into 10 centuries of 100 men, each commanded by a centurion (in this instance, Cornelius).

Inscriptions indicate that such an Italian regiment had indeed been stationed in Syria during AD 69–157. This does not rule out an earlier presence in the province; military records are simply not available.

Italy. Boot-shaped peninsula located between the Tyrrhenian and the Adriatic seas. Uplands and two major mountain ranges—the Alps, which form a northern boundary, and the Appennines, which form the backbone of the peninsula—occupy 77 percent of the land. The plains, which are limited to the Po River Valley, cover the remaining 23 percent.

The earliest history of the region is found in the artifacts of the Abbevillian and Neanderthal cultures discovered in many areas, including the site at Rome. With the advent of agriculture (6000 BC), the population increased rapidly. By 3000 BC, large groups of farmers had located in southern Italy along the Mediterranean coast and in northern Italy along the Po Valley. During the 3rd millennium BC, a major culture developed in the central part of the peninsula, influenced by Minoan and Mycenaean civilizations and characterized by agriculture, animal husbandry, and bronze-working.

During the 2nd millennium BC, an invasion of Indo-European tribes reshaped the culture of the peninsula. Each area came to be known by the name of the tribe that inhabited it. Among the most important of these tribes were the Latins, who settled in the valley of the Tiber River—an area which came to be known as Latium. According to the historian, Antiochus of Syracuse (5th century BC), it was also during this time (1300 BC) that King Italos ruled the southwest part of the peninsula. This region came to take his name which, over the next millennium, was extended northward until, in the time of Augustus (27 BC–AD 14), the entire peninsula was called "Italy."

Toward the end of the 8th century BC, the Etruscans, immigrants from Asia Minor, invaded the peninsula and organized the less-civilized Italic tribes into Etruscan dominated city-states. The result was complete political chaos. Wars with Greek colonies, wars to throw off Etruscan domination, and wars between city-states dominated the next 5 centuries. The city-state that benefited the most from this unrest was Rome. By 220 BC, Rome had conquered the entire peninsula and had united all Italy south of the Po Valley under one rule. After a great revolt (90–88 BC), Italians throughout the peninsula obtained the rights of Roman citizenship and in 49 BC Julius Caesar extended these rights to the inhabitants of the Po Valley. Thus, by NT times, Italy had essentially come to have its present form.

"Italy" appears three times in the NT. Paul has the opportunity to meet Priscilla and Aquila, recently come from Italy because Claudius had expelled the Jews from Rome (Acts 18:2). Italy is mentioned as Paul's destination following his appeal to Caesar (27:1,6). The writer of Hebrews sends greetings to his readers from "those who come from Italy" (Heb 13:24).

See Rome, City of; Caesars, The.

Itching Disease.
Skin disease referred to five times in Scripture. In Leviticus 13 strict regulations are given with regards to a variety of skin conditions. Using these guidelines, the priest was able to declare whether a person was clean or unclean. While an exact diagnosis cannot be made based on the description of the skin diseases in the Bible, the key concept is that of isolating a person with spreading, running sores from the general community.

No man could become a priest who had "scurvy, or scabbed" skin lesions (Lv 21:20 KJV). "Scurvy" here means a wet or draining sore, while "scabbed" refers to a dry skin lesion.

The Israelites were warned that breaking God's laws would result in suffering a variety of skin diseases, including "the botch [boils] of Egypt," "emerods" (tumors), "scurvy," and "the itch" which could not be cured (Dt 28:27). The itching disease here may be a chronic irritating skin disease like scabies. Job also suffered from an itching disease and used a potsherd to scratch himself (Jb 2:8).

See Medicine and Medical Practice; Disease.

Ithai.
Alternate spelling of Ittai, a Benjamite warrior, in 1 Chronicles 11:31.

See Ittai #2.

Ithamar.
Aaron's fourth and youngest son, who served as a priest to the tribes of Israel during the wilderness period (Ex 6:23; Nm 3:2,4; 26:60; 1 Chr 6:3; 24:2). After the death of two of his brothers, he was given the special duty of overseeing the moving of the tabernacle (Nm 4:28,33; 7:8). During David's reign, the descendants of Ithamar and Eleazar were organized as the formal temple priesthood (1 Chr 24:3–6). Later, some of his descendants returned with Ezra from Babylon (Ezr 8:2).

Ithiel.
1. Ancestor of Sallu, a Benjamite who lived in Jerusalem after the Babylonian exile (Neh 11:7).

2. One of two persons to whom Agur spoke his proverbs (Prv 30:1).

Ithlah.
City given to Dan's tribe for an inheritance, after the initial conquest of Palestine by Joshua (Jos 19:42; KJV Jethlah). Its location is unknown, possibly near the city of Aijalon.

Ithmah.
Warrior of Moabite origin who joined David's company at Ziklag (1 Chr 11:46).

Ithnan.
Town in southern Judah (Jos 15:23). Its location is unknown.

Ithra.
Father of Amasa by Abigal, Zeruiah's sister (2 Sm 17:25). He is called Jether in 1 Kings 2:5,32 and 1 Chronicles 2:17.

Ithran.
1. Dishon's son, who was a Horite chief (Gn 36:26; 1 Chr 1:41).

2. One of Zobhah's sons (1 Chr 7:37). He is probably the same Jether mentioned in 1 Chronicles 7:38.

Ithream.
David's sixth son, borne by his wife Eglah at Hebron (2 Sm 3:5; 1 Chr 3:3).

Ithrite.
Family or clan that lived at Kiriath-jearim (1 Chr 2:53). Ira and Gareb, two of David's mighty men, were Ithrites (2 Sm 23:38; 1 Chr 11:40).

Ittah-kazin.
KJV form of the town Eth-kazin in Joshua 19:13.

See Eth-Kazin.

Ittai.
1. Philistine from Gath who, with 600 men from Gath, remained loyal to David and accompanied him on his flight from Absalom (2 Sm 15:18–22). Ittai commanded a third of David's army in the battle against Absalom's forces (2 Sm 18:2,5).

2. Warrior among David's mighty men (2 Sm 23:29; 1 Chr 11:31, Ithai).

Ituraea. Small province mentioned with Trachonitis as forming the tetrarchy of Philip, brother of Herod the Great, during the reign of Tiberius Caesar (Lk 3:1). A reasonable assumption places Ituraea northeast of the Sea of Galilee and south of Mt Hermon, but its location and boundaries have been much disputed. The name almost certainly comes from Jetur, a son of Ishmael (Gn 25:15), whose descendants were among those conquered by the Israelites east of the Jordan (1 Chr 5:19,20). Thereafter the Ituraeans virtually drop from sight until Josephus records another defeat inflicted on them by Aristobulus in 105–104 BC, at which time many of them were faced with a choice between circumcision and exile.

There are frequent mentions by classical writers of Ituraeans, sometimes described as Syrians or Arabians—skilled bowmen with the predatory tendencies often associated with groups unable or unwilling to settle for long in any one area. In view of this it is not surprising that we know more about Ituraeans than we do about Ituraea.

Strabo speaks of them as inhabitants of a mountainous country; Dio Cassius a little later tells us that they had a king. Any attempt to understand their history is complicated by divisions in the Roman Empire which affected them, but by the end of the 1st century AD many Ituraeans were to be found under the provincial rule of Syria.

It is easier, then, to discuss the people, for attempts to identify the place raise thorny problems. Some scholars, indeed, hold that Luke could not have used the noun "Ituraea," for this was a form unknown till three centuries later, and that the adjectival form better fits the case. This prompts another question: Was this Ituraean territory within Philip's tetrarchy? Could Luke have made a slip and anticipated a later regional regrouping? Josephus at one point lists the constituent parts of Philip's tetrarchy without including Ituraea.

Three facts are clear: (1) there is a certain flexibility and overlapping in descriptions of territorial demarcation; (2) the data we have is insufficient for exact conclusions about Ituraea; (3) the evidence is clear from other parts of Scripture that Luke is a careful and reliable writer.

Ivah. KJV spelling of Ivvah.

See IVVAH.

Ivory. Opaque dentine substance, often mentioned along with precious metals and gems in the Bible and ancient Near Eastern writings. As such, ivory was used for combs, small boxes, jars, and other cosmetic articles, for figurines and amulets, for games, and for the adornment of articles of furniture, buildings, and perhaps even ships (Ez 27:6). It is frequently mentioned in Egyptian and Assyrian annals of conquest as part of the spoils of war. Some excellent examples of work with ivory can be found in the famed collection of Tutankhamen.

In the Bible ivory is spoken of as the adornment of Solomon's throne (1 Kgs 10:18; 2 Chr 9:17) and of beds in the time of Amos (6:4). Both references are probably to ivory inlay. The ivory palaces of 1 Kings 22:39; Psalm 45:8; and Amos 3:15, however, may refer to forms of decoration other than inlay. Whether Ezekiel 27:6 actually implies that ships were decorated with ivory is debatable, since that passage forms part of the whole picture of Tyre as an extravagant ship. The articles of ivory that earth's merchants can no longer sell to Babylon (Rv 18:12) include smaller objects of the kind found at various archaeological sites (Megiddo, Samaria, Nimrud).

Originally ivory was available in northern Syria, where Assyrian monarchs hunted elephants. By Solomon's time, however, it was important (1 Kgs 10:22; 2 Chr 9:21), probably from the east (India) or south (Africa), while Tarshish may represent the seagoing capability of the ships rather than the source of the ivory. Tyre received its ivory from the "coastlands" (Ez 27:15).

See FASHION AND DRESS; FURNITURE; INDUSTRY AND COMMERCE.

Ivvah. City that had already fallen along with others to the Assyrians (2 Kgs 18:34, 19:13; Is 37:13; KJV Ivah). Sennacherib's representative mocked Hezekiah's belief that God would save Jerusalem. Ivvah was probably in Syria, but its exact location is unknown.

See AVVA.

Iye-abarim, Iyim. Israelite camping place on the southeast border of Moab during the wilderness wanderings (Nm 33:44; KJV Ijeabarim). Its exact site is unknown. In verse 45 the town is called Iyim (KJV Iim), which is a shortened form of Iye-abarim.

See WILDERNESS WANDERINGS.

Izehar, Izeharites. KJV spelling of Izhar, Kohath's son, and his descendants (Nm 3:19,27).

See IZHAR #1.

Izhar. 1. One of Kohath's sons from Levi's tribe (Ex 6:18,21; Nm 3:19; KJV Izehar; 16:1; 1 Chr 6:2,18,38; 23:12,18), and father of the Izharite family (Nm 3:27; KJV Izeharites; 1 Chr

24:22; 26:23,29); alternately called Amminadab in 1 Chronicles 6:22. One of Izhar's sons was Korah who led the rebellion against Moses and Aaron (Nm 16:1–11).

2. Helah's son from Judah's tribe (1 Chr 4:7, KJV Jezoar).

Izharite. Descendant of Izhar from Levi's tribe (Nm 3:27; 1 Chr 26:23,29).

See Izhar #1.

Izliah. Elpaal's son from Benjamin's tribe (1 Chr 8:18, KJV Jezliah).

Izrahiah. Uzzi's son and a leading member of Issachar's tribe (1 Chr 7:3).

Izrahite. Designation given to Shamhuth, one of David's 12 monthly captains, meaning a man of a family or town called Izra (1 Chr 27:8). The word "Izrahite" is perhaps a corruption of "Zerahite," a descendant of Zerah of Judah (1 Chr 27:11).

Izri. Temple musician and head of the 4th of the 24 divisions of priests for service in the sanctuary (1 Chr 25:11). He is called Zeri in verse 3.

Izziah. Parosh's son, who was encouraged by Ezra to divorce the foreign woman he married during the postexilic period (Ezr 10:25, KJV Jeziah).